MATHEWS'

CHINESE - ENGLISH DICTIONARY

(A Chinese-English Dictionary Compiled for the China Inland Mission by R. H. Mathews, Shanghai: China Inland Mission and Presbyterian Mission Press, 1931)

REVISED

AMERICAN EDITION

HARVARD UNIVERSITY PRESS

CAMBRIDGE, MASSACHUSETTS

TABLE OF CONTENTS

Eleventh Printing, 1969

SBN 674-12350-6

Printed in the United States of America

FOREWORD TO THE AMERICAN EDITION

With books no longer coming from the Far East, the need for Chinese dictionaries in this country has grown from chronic to acute. To answer the immediate demands of American students, the Harvard-Yenching Institute has undertaken to revise and reprint two practical dictionaries, (1) C. H. Fenn's *Pocket Dictionary*, which appeared in November, 1942, and (2) the present *Chinese-English Dictionary* by R. H. Mathews, both photolithographic reproductions.

Within the necessary limitations of a photographic edition, and as far as interstices of the original edition allow, errors have been corrected, pronunciations and definitions revised, and new entries inserted, — in all amounting to some 15,000 items. A whole Introduction on Pronunciation has been added, and a list of the syllabic headings is included for quick reference, since the original order of syllables is not strictly alphabetic. An additional feature of the new edition is that all cases of the neutral, *i.e.*, unstressed, tone are indicated. There has been a reduction in size from 8 x 11 to 7 x 10 inches to make the volume handier without at the same time sacrificing legibility.

Mr. M. Y. Wang is responsible for the mechanical details of preparing the book for reproduction, Dr. Y. R. Chao has written the Introduction and has checked the pronunciation of all the entries, and both have taken part in the revisions.

Cambridge, Massachusetts
March, 1943

NOTE ADDED TO THE SECOND PRINTING

The English Index to this Dictionary, which was published as a companion volume, has been revised to agree with the present form of the Dictionary and continues to be published separately. In conjunction with this work the Index can serve as an English-Chinese Dictionary.

August, 1944

PREFACE TO THE FIRST EDITION

Baller's Analytical Chinese-English Dictionary, now out of print, was first published in 1900. It has served a useful purpose and many students of Chinese acknowledge their indebtedness to it, but the rapid changes which have taken place in China, with the influx of modern inventions and the advance of scientific knowledge, have brought in a wealth of new ideas, necessitating a corresponding number of new expressions. These things have made the old dictionary out of date, and mere revision would have been inadequate. Therefore instead of revising the old book, a new dictionary has been compiled, keeping in view the object of the original work: "to supply the demand for a dictionary at once portable and inexpensive and at the same time sufficiently large to meet the wants of an ordinary student."

The number of Chinese characters included in the book has been increased to 7,785, not including different forms of the same character. This selection of characters should meet the needs of the average student, as most of the characters which have been added were not found in the founts of the Press and had to be specially engraved. The use of the characters has been illustrated by a greatly increased number of examples. In Baller's Dictionary there were about 40,000, while the present book gives over 104,000 illustrations drawn from the classics, general literature, magazines, newspapers, advertisements, legal documents, and many other sources. As far as possible, every use of a character has been illustrated by examples. Some of these expressions may have passed out of current use, but their inclusion in a dictionary is warranted by the fact that they occur in the literature of the period.

A departure has been made from the practice of beginning all phrases and sentences used in illustration with the character under which they appear. It is obvious that many characters, such for example as the final particles, could not be illustrated by this method. A better idea of the use of a character can be gained when sentences are also given in which it appears elsewhere than at the beginning of the phrase used. Some of the sentences have been duplicated, but this is no disadvantage if it affords any assistance to a better knowledge of the use of a character. From time to time examples were found after the earlier part of the book was in the press, necessitating their insertion under one of the other characters in the phrase. In a "rush job" such things are unavoidable, the urgent demand for the publication of the dictionary making it compulsory to go to press long before the compilation was completed.

In preparing this dictionary the question of keeping it down to as small a compass as possible had to be constantly borne in mind. Considerations of space, in view of the demand for a largely increased number of illustrative examples, made it advisable to omit details regarding the construction of Chinese characters. This also led to the omission of the Analytical References, inquiry showing that comparatively little use had been made of them. The etymology of Chinese characters is now being given scientific study, and special books dealing with the subject have been published. Those who desire to study the combinations of Radical and Phonetic will find Soothill's *Pocket Dictionary* invaluable.

The characters have been arranged in groups according to the classification of the Chinese Alphabet, usually known as the Chinese Phonetic Script, 注音字母, as used in the *Phonetic Dictionary of the Chinese National Language.* (國語正音字典. Commercial Press, Ltd., Shanghai.[1])

The sounds are given both in the Chinese Alphabet and in Romanized spelling. The system of Romanization followed is the slightly modified adaptation of Wade's *Syllabary* used in the *National Language Dictionary* and other useful publications of the Commercial Press. This is, at present, the most widely recognized system being used by the foreign press, the Chinese Post Office,

[1 Obsolete since 1932.]

and others. The Chinese government has given this question of Romanized spelling some consideration, and a society to investigate the matter has recently been formed, but the system evolved by the government is still in a more or less tentative form and has not come into general use. The object of that system is to give, as far as is possible, a rendering in Roman letters which will obviate the use of figures or other marks to indicate the different tones, so that a reader would be able to give a fairly accurate rendering of the Chinese sounds without a knowledge of the characters. In the meantime we have used the system which is well known and which has proved its usefulness. Where Wade's system differs from that used in the old dictionary, the latter is given in smaller type and is placed in brackets.

The Phonetic system being one of combining initials and finals, the Romanized combinations *hs*, *sh*, *ts*, or *tz*, are regarded as initials and follow the groups under *h*, *s*, and *t*, respectively, e.g., *huo*, *hsi; szŭ, sha; t'ung, tsa*, etc.

The tones are indicated by a figure at the right-hand top corner of the characters.

1	representing the	上平聲
2	representing the	下平聲
3	representing the	上　聲
4	representing the	去　聲
5	representing the	入　聲

The characters under the Fifth Tone or 入聲 will be found in a separate group immediately following the group in the other tones. The characters in this group are also marked with the alternative tone heard in Peking and other places where the Fifth Tone is not used.

Instead of giving a wealth of information in the definition at the head of the illustrative examples. often bewildering the student with apparently unrelated meanings, the definitions of the characters, where possible or necessary, have been divided into separate groups, beginning with the meanings most commonly given to the characters and going on to those under other sounds or tones, or to those more obscure definitions only found in the classics or ancient books. These groups are indicated by alphabetical reference marks in brackets, the initial group having no particular reference, while each subsequent group is marked (a) (b) (c), etc. Each of these definitions is copiously illustrated by examples, which for facility of reference have been arranged according to the sequence of the radical of the second character in the sentence or phrase. This arrangement saves considerable time when searching for any particular phrase in a long list of examples. Moreover, if one does not find that particular phrase in its place in the list according to the radical of its second character there is no need to waste any more time in looking up and down the column for it. The phrases that begin with the character under which they are placed are first dealt with, those beginning with other characters follow in the order of the radicals of their initial characters. These illustrative examples have been numbered by placing a small figure to the left of the column, thus enabling a person to turn at once to any sentence to which he may be referred from another part of the book. The number of these cross-references would have been greater but for the fact that the urgency of the demand made it compulsory to go to press before the compilation of the manuscript was completed.

The numbering of the illustrative examples has been used in compiling an English Index, which is bound separately for convenience of reference. In this Index an attempt has been made to give students the means whereby they may enlarge their vocabularies and also acquire a more extensive knowledge of what is in the dictionary. It also takes the place, to some extent, of an English-Chinese dictionary, though of course it must be remembered that this Index is based on a Chinese-English Dictionary which has been prepared primarily as an assistance in translating Chinese into English. Such a dictionary naturally omits many of the common phrases of everyday life as being too well known to need any assistance in translation into English, but in spite of this limitation the Index covers a wide field and should prove invaluable to students of the language.

A new method has been used in compiling the Radical Index. Much time is often wasted in searching up and down the columns of these indexes and any arrangement which tends to obviate this should be welcomed. The characters have been arranged in the usual way under their respective radicals and grouped according to the number of strokes in the phonetic or primitive, i.e., that part of a character which is not the radical, but instead of placing these characters in the usual haphazard way, they have been carefully arranged according to the sequence of the radicals of their phonetics. These radicals, though sometimes obscure, are usually obvious. A glance at the Radical Index will show what is meant, and practical experience in the use of this Index during the compilation of the dictionary has proved its value. If a character is not found where it should be according to the radical of its phonetic, it is not in the dictionary, and there is no need to waste time in looking up and down a long list for it.

Attention is specially directed to the Table of Errata at the end of the dictionary. It is regrettable that so many mistakes were missed by the proofreaders. A dictionary should be free from such typographical errors, and every effort has been made to find them. The whole book has been carefully read with a view to eliminate these errors by noting them in the Errata. Students are very earnestly advised to go through the dictionary and make the necessary corrections for themselves. Such mistakes prove the truth of the saying of Confucius: "Desire to have things done quickly prevents their being done thoroughly." 欲 速 則 不 達.

The suggestions and requests which were received have been rather bewildering. "Many m.... characters must be added, as well as many more illustrative examples, but the book should be very much smaller than the old one, and also very much lighter." It reminds us of the old lady who is said to have asked the Bible Society if they could supply her with a pocket edition of the Scriptures in large type. The question was frequently asked, "Are you including all the new terms?" People seem to have an idea that there is a nice treasure-house somewhere in which all these terms are arranged ready for the use of a poor compiler. Alas, there is no such place. These terms have to be hunted for through hundreds of pages of the newspapers, magazines, and other literature. He would be a bold man indeed who would assert that he had ascertained all the new terms. In fact, many of these expressions which are called new by those who meet them for the first time are hoary with age. However, every effort has been made to introduce the latest expressions, and the inclusion of terms relating to motors, electricity, aviation, wireless, and similar things has brought the book up to date.

Only such scientific terms as are commonly met with have been included. The lists are by no means complete, the intention being merely to give illustrations of the way in which characters are combined to express such ideas. Those who desire fuller information are referred to text-books or special dictionaries of scientific terms.

The rapid changes in official circles have made many of the official titles and designations obsolete, as far as being usable in current speech is concerned, but this is inevitable, changes coming so rapidly that before a thing is in print, a new set of titles has been evolved. It is quite true, as one has said, that a dictionary is the graveyard of a language. Everything political is at present in a state of flux and these titles are simply translated without any authoritative statement as to their currency in speech.

The book is now sent forth in the hope that it will contribute something to lighten the task of learning this great language and that by its use students will become more proficient in translating and speaking Chinese.

R. H. MATHEWS.

China Inland Mission, Shanghai,
April 1931.

INTRODUCTION ON PRONUNCIATION

1. Romanization and Standards of Pronunciation. — Three systems of pronunciation are represented in this dictionary. Take for example the syllabic heading on p. 431, col. 2. The form HSÜAN represents the Peiping pronunciation in the Wade system. The form SÜAN, as well as the three National Phonetic Letters in parentheses to the right, represents the standard National Pronunciation as embodied in the official book *Kuo-yin Tzŭ-tien* (國音字典), Shanghai, 1920. Finally, the form **Hsüen** in parentheses represents another system of pronunciation. in some respects similar to, but not identical with, the National Pronunciation of 1920 in the romanization used by the China Inland Mission. Of these forms, the second became obsolete only one year after the first publication of this dictionary, when a new standard of National Pronunciation was adopted. The official dictionary now in force, which has superseded *Kuo-yin Tzŭ-tien*, is *Gwoin Charngyonq Tzyhhuey* (國音常用字彙), Shanghai, 1932, of which a more accessible form is found in an appendix to the dictionary *Tz'ŭ-hai* (辭海), Shanghai, 1937. Besides giving the pronunciation in the National Phonetic Letters, the *Gwoin Charngyonq Tzyhhuey*, as the romanized title indicates, also employs a new system of romanization called Gwoyeu Romatzyh or National Romanization, of which the most easily available forms in this country are *The Chinese Sentence Series* and *The New Official Chinese Latin Script Gwoyeu Romatzyh*, both by W. Simon, London, 1942. Since the system corresponds, syllable by syllable, to the Wade system, and represents much the same dialect, we need not introduce it in the body of this dictionary.

While the old National Pronunciation was an eclectic system, closely resembling that of the original 1874 edition of S. W. Williams' *Syllabic Dictionary*, the new standard is practically a straightforward adoption of the pronunciation of Peiping. There are some unimportant differences of detail such as the treating of both *cho* and *shuo* as containing the final *-uo* (see note *a*, Section 6 below) and the assigning to the second tone of more cases of words from ancient *b'*, *d'*, *g'*, *z*, etc. ending in *-p*, *-t*, *-k*[1] than is actually common in Peiping, e.g. *chi*[2] 寂 instead of the more current *chi*[4]<*dz'iek*. But on the whole the present National Pronunciation is simply the pronunciation of the Peiping dialect.

2. Modifications in the Wade System. — In the preface to the first edition, reference was made to the use of a "slightly modified adaptation of Wade's *Syllabary*," i.e., modified to agree with the National Pronunciation of 1920. Now that the standard has come back to the pronunciation of Peiping, we can almost use the unmodified Wade's *Syllabary* or the more widely used Wade-Giles system, as found in H. A. Giles' *Chinese-English Dictionary*. However, a few points of simplification of the Wade-Giles system to agree with the dialect of Peiping should be noted. The four forms *chio*, *ch'io*, *hsio*, and *yo* in Giles' *Dictionary* are obsolete and have been combined with *chüeh*, *ch'üeh*, *hsüeh*, and *yüeh* respectively in this revised edition. The assignment of some characters to the syllable *i* and others to *yi* has no phonetic or etymological basis whatever and both have been put under the syllable *i* in this dictionary since the first edition. For the finals *o* and *ê*, the present edition follows Giles. In Chauncey Goodrich's *Pocket Dictionary*, the syllables *ko*, *k'o*, *ho*, and *o* of Wade-Giles are given as *kê*, *k'ê*, *hê*, and *ê*. While this is phonetically more accurate, it is phonemically not necessary, as one can understand that *o* is always unrounded in such positions, contrasting with the rounded *o* in *kuo*, *k'uo*, *huo*, and *wo*. In any case, we can follow the Wade-Giles usage without incurring ambiguity. (Cf. note *c*, Section 6 below.)

3. Order of Entries. — Owing to the complexity of the triple standard of pronunciation recorded in this dictionary, some syllables which are identical according to the new standard and consequently also identical in the Wade system are divided among several headings and often

---

[1] In Chinese idiom, this law or tendency is described as 全濁上聲變陽平 'the entering tone of voiced stops and fricatives becomes the second tone.'

widely separated in the book. Thus the syllable *chieh* (according to the present standard) is found on p. 83, col. II as CHIAI (街); on p. 103, col. II as CHIEH or TSIEH (嗟); on p. 104, col. II as CHIEH (莢); and on p. 107, col. I as CHIEH or TSIEH (浹). It is obviously out of the question in this reproduced edition to reshuffle the entries. Besides, when the *chieh*'s and *tsieh*'s are in separate groups, it may be of convenience if one has occasion to refer to the French systems of romanization, since the latter maintain such etymological distinctions. We have therefore left all the headings as they are and have made cross references to other groups with the same pronunciation if they are not contiguous. It must be understood, however, that only the very first romanization in each heading is the Wade romanization and represents the present pronunciation. Changes in the headings have been made only to conform to this rule, as for example the original heading "CHIAI," p. 103, col. II, which has been changed to read "CHIEH. CHIAI." The second heading *chiai* represents the old National Pronunciation as given also in National Phonetic Letters in parentheses.

The words "Read" and "Pronounce" are used synonymously, the latter being used only in revised items. When an additional pronunciation is given (indicated by the abbreviation "Pron." and put after the definitions of a single character), this pronunciation is to supersede that of the syllabic heading under which the character occurs. For example, the character No. 5933 under SHUN was marked "Also read *ch'un*[2]." Since *ch'un*[2] is the only pronunciation current now, it is changed to read "Pron. *ch'un*[2]," from which the reader is expected to disregard the main heading SHUN. As a cross reference, the character is added on p. 212, col. III as No. 1497½, and its definition is referred to No. 5933.

4. Levels of Pronunciation. — All languages or dialects have different levels or styles of pronunciation, and even if we take as standard the speech of the average educated person born in Peiping, as has been done in the case of the new National Pronunciation, there are still variations of pronunciation according to mood, speed, and context. Since the point of view of the user of this dictionary is more likely to be that of the reader of a text in characters rather than that of a listener to spoken words or of a student of linguistics, we have to take the character as the unit and treat *liao*[3] and the neutral-toned ·*lê*, for instance, as two pronunciations of the same character 了 , even though *liao*[3] and ·*lê* play very different parts in the language and may not even be etymologically the same word. The majority of variations of pronunciation for the same character belong to one of the following categories:

(1) Two or more pronunciations for the same character which are paralleled in other dialects. Thus 長 *ch'ang*[2] "long"; *chang*[3] "to grow," "elder"; or 乾 *ch'ien*[2] "the male or positive principle"; *kan*[1] "dry." Most of these variations have had a long history and can sometimes be traced to the time of the classics.

(2) Words with the entering tone in Ancient Chinese which ended in -*k* often have a literary and a colloquial pronunciation. They occur with the following finals:

Literary	-ê			-o			-u		-üeh
Colloquial	-ai	-ei		-ai	-ao	-ei		-iu	-ou	-iao
Example	色	賊		百	落	北		六	軸	角

The choice of such alternate forms depends sometimes upon the individual speaker, the mood, or the occasion, but especially upon the compound or phrase in which the syllable occurs. When position in a compound or phrase is the determining factor, the pronunciation is marked separately by respelling or by a cross sign against each entry, as for instance under No. 4122 落 *lo*[4] and *lao*[4] or No. 5445 色 *sê*[4] and *shai*[3].

(3) "Empty" words or particles have a strong, or reading, pronunciation and a weak, or spoken, pronunciation. The most important cases are as follows:

Character	着 or 著	了	麼	呢	的	子
Strong form	*cho*[1,2], *chao*[2]	*liao*[3]	*mo*[1,2]	*ni*[1,2]	*ti*[4,5]	*tzŭ*[3]
Weak form	·*chê*, ·*chih*	·*lê*	·*mê*	·*nê*	·*tê*	·*tzŭ*

In the body of the dictionary, a dot before one of these characters indicates not only that the syllable is unstressed (see Section 8 below on the neutral tone), but that the weak form of pronunciation is to be used. In the few cases where the full vowel of the strong form has to go with the neutral tone, it is explicitly so marked, as No. 5064.9 碰·着 *p'êng*[4]·*chao*, with the strong form, "to knock against," "to meet," as distinguished from 碰·着 *p'êng*[4]·*chih*, with the weak form, "to be in contact."

5. Initials and Finals. — The most convenient way of analyzing a Chinese syllable is to divide it into (1) an initial, or the beginning sound, (2) a final, or the rest of the syllable, and (3) a tone, which may be regarded as a quality of the whole syllable. Thus, in the syllable *nuan*[3] "warm," *n*- is the initial, -*uan* the final, and the figure 3 indicates that it has the third tone, or a low falling-rising circumflex tone. The initials and finals of Peiping as given in the Wade system, the Inland Mission system (as far as it corresponds to the Peiping dialect), the International Phonetic Alphabet, and the National Phonetic Alphabet are exhibited in Tables I and II.

TABLE I. INITIALS.

Articulatory group	Wade				Inland Miss.				I.P.A.				Nat. Phon.			
Labials	*p*	*p'*	*m*	*f*	*p*	*p'*	*m*	*f*	ḅ	p'	m	f	ㄅ	ㄆ	ㄇ	ㄈ (万)[1]
Dental stops and liquids	*t*	*t'*	*n*	*l*	*t*	*t'*	*n*	*l*	ḍ	t'	n	l	ㄉ	ㄊ	ㄋ	ㄌ
Dental sibilants	{*ts* *ts'* *s* / *tz*[2] *tz'* *ss* or *sz*}				*ts* *ts'* *s*				dẓ	ts'	s		ㄗ	ㄘ	ㄙ	
Retroflexes	*ch*[3]	*ch'*	*sh*	*j*	*ch*	*ch'*	*sh*	*r*	dʐ	tʂ'	ʂ	ʐ	ㄓ	ㄔ	ㄕ	ㄖ
Palatals	*ch*[3]	*ch'*		*hs*	*ch*	*ch'*		*hs*	dʑ	tɕ		ɕ	ㄐ	ㄑ	(广)[1]	ㄒ
Gutturals	*k*	*k'*		*h*	*k*	*k'*		*h*	g̊	k'		x	ㄍ	ㄎ	(兀)[1]	ㄏ

Note 1. The initials 万, 兀, and 广 in the old National Pronunciation, representing [v] [ŋ], and [ɲ] respectively, are abolished in the new standard. They are now replaced by *w*-, zero, and *n*- respectively.

Note 2. In the Wade system the variant forms *tz, tz'* and *ss* (or *sz*) are used only before the final -*ŭ* as a reminder of the buzzing quality of the final. Their sounds as initials here are identical with those represented by *ts, ts'*, and *s*.

Note 3. No ambiguity results from the use of *ch* and *ch'* for two different pairs of sounds, as the retroflex initials never precede the palatal vowels -*i*- and -*ŭ*-, while the palatal initials always precede the palatal vowels. Note that the -*ih* in the Wade system in Table II is a retroflex vowel and is to be regarded as a digraph which has nothing to do with *i*. The *ch* in *chih* and the *ch'* in *ch'ih* have therefore the retroflex values.

Note 4. On the use of the initials *y*- and *w*-, see the second table of finals for the Wade system in Table II.

TABLE II. FINALS.

Wade: with initials

-ŭ, -ih	-a	-o	-ê	(eh)	-ai	-ei	-ao	-ou	-an	-ên	-ang	-êng	(rh)
-ŭ, -ih	-a	-o	-ê		-ai	-ei	-ao	-ou	-an	-ên	-ang	-êng	———
-i	-ia			-ieh			-iao	-iu	-ien	-in	-iang	-ing	
-u	-ua	-uo			-uai	-uei, -ui			-uan	-un	-uang	-ung	
-ü				-üeh					-üan	-ün		-iung	

Wade: without initials

—	a	o	—	(eh)	ai	ei	ao	ou	an	ên	ang	êng	êrh
—	a	o	—		ai	ei	ao	ou	an	ên	ang	êng	êrh
ı	ya			yeh	yai		yao	yu	yen	yin	yang	ying	
wu	wa	wo			wai	wei			wan	wên	wang	wêng	
yü				yüeh					yüan	yün		yung	

Inland Mission

i	a	o	e	æ	ai	ei	ao	eo	an	en	ang	eng	rï
i	a	o	e	æ	ai	ei	ao	eo	an	en	ang	eng	rï
i	ia	ioh		ie	iai		iao	iu	ien	in	iang	ing	
u	ua	uo		ueh	uai	uei, ui			uan	uen	uang	ong	
ü				üe					üen	üin		iong	

I.P.A.

ʐ, ɻ	ɑ	ɔᴧ	ɤᴧ	ɛ	ai	ei	ɑu	ou	an	ən	ɑŋ	ʌŋ	ɝᴵ
ʐ, ɻ	ɑ	ɔᴧ	ɤᴧ	ɛ	ai	ei	ɑu	ou	an	ən	ɑŋ	ʌŋ	ɝᴵ
i	iɑ			iɛ	iai		iɑu	iᵒu	iɛn	in	iɑŋ	iŋ	
u	uɑ	uɔᴧ			uai	uᵉi			uan	uᵊn	uɑŋ	uʌŋ, -ʊŋ		
y				yɛ					yan	yⁱn		yʊŋ	

National Phonetic

ㄧ	ㄚ	ㄛ	ㄜ	ㄝ	ㄞ	ㄟ	ㄠ	ㄡ	ㄢ	ㄣ	ㄤ	ㄥ	ㄦ
ㄧ	ㄧㄚ			ㄧㄝ	ㄧㄞ		ㄧㄠ	ㄧㄡ	ㄧㄢ	ㄧㄣ	ㄧㄤ	ㄧㄥ	
ㄨ	ㄨㄚ	ㄨㄛ			ㄨㄞ	ㄨㄟ			ㄨㄢ	ㄨㄣ	ㄨㄤ	ㄨㄥ	
ㄩ				ㄩㄝ					ㄩㄢ	ㄩㄣ		ㄩㄥ	

Examples with initials

思詩	八	波	得	(eh)	該	杯	高	溝	千	根	岡	庚	一
思詩	八	波	得		該	杯	高	溝	千	根	岡	庚	一
基	加			街			交	鳩	肩	今	江	經	
孤	瓜	鍋			乖	歸,灰			官	棍	光	工	
居				厥					捐	君		局	

Examples without initials (see notes e, h, and j in Section 6 below)

—	啊	呃	—	(eh)	哀	—	奧	歐	安	恩	盎	鞥	兒
—	啊	呃	—		哀	—	奧	歐	安	恩	盎	鞥	兒
衣	鴉			噎	崖		要	幽	烟	音	央	英	
烏	蛙	窩			歪	威			彎	溫	王	翁	
迂				月					冤	氳		雍	

In the Wade system, all syllables with finals beginning with *i*, *u*, or *ü* must be written with *y*, *w*, or *yü* if there is no other consonantal initial, as for instance *wang*, but *huang*; and *yen*, but *chien*. The only exception is that the complete syllable *i* itself is written simply as *i*. The Inland Mission system does not use *y* or *w* at all.

Final *h* in *-ih*, *-eh* and the syllable *êrh* in the Wade system is to be considered as part of the whole notation, having no independent meaning of its own. In the Inland Mission system, however, a final *h* marks the entering tone. Thus the *shih* in Wade may be in any tone, being equivalent to Inland Mission *shĭ*, while *shih* in the latter system means *shih* or *shĭ* in the entering tone. In the National Phonetic Alphabet, these finals are not written; the signs for the initials *ch*, *ch'*, *sh*, *j*, *ts*, *ts'*, *s*, namely 出 , 彳 , 尸 , 囗 , 卩 , 亐 , 厶 , when not followed by any final, stand for complete syllables.

6. Syllabic Types. — Not every initial combines freely with every final. For example, the initials *k*, *k'*, and *h* never combine with finals beginning with *-i-* or *-ü-*. Table III gives a complete picture of the types of syllables which actually occur in the Peiping dialect. Unless otherwise marked, each character in the table has the first initial of the group and is in the first tone. For example, 八 is pa^1. But 拜^4 is pai^4, while 林^{l2} is lin^2.

TABLE III. SYLLABIC TYPES.

Final / Medial / Initial

Medial: —

Initial	ŭ, ih	a	o	ê, eh	ai	ei	ao	ou	an	ên	ang	êng	êrh
p p' m f		八	波		拜^4	杯	包	剖$^{p'3}$	班	奔	邦	崩	
t t' n l		搭	多	得^2	獃^4	內^{n4}	刀	兜	單	嫩^{n4}	當	登	
ts ts' s	茲	咂	作^4	則^2	災	賊^2	糟	鄒	簪	怎^3	臧	曾	
ch ch' sh j	知	渣	桌[a]	遮	齋	這^4[b]	招	周	占	眞	張	爭	
k k' h ○	○	嘎	哥[c]		該	給^3	高	溝	干	根	剛	更	兒$^{○2}$

Medial: -i-

Initial	i	ia		ieh	iai		iao	iu	ien	in	iang	ing	
p p' m	逼	□[d]		鱉			標	謬^{m4}	邊	賓		兵	
t t' n l	低	倆^{l3}		爹			刁	丟	顚	林^{l2}	娘^{n2}	丁	
ch ch' hs y[e]	基	家		街	崖^{y2}		焦	鳩	尖	今	江	精	

Medial: -u-

Initial	u	ua	uo		uai	u(e)i[f]			uan	un	uang	ung	
p p' m f	逋												
t t' n l	都					堆[g]			端	敦		東	
ts ts' s	租					堆			鑽	肫		宗	
ch ch' sh j	朱	抓	說^{sh}[a]		拽^4	追			專	諄	莊	中	
k k' h w[h]	孤	瓜	鍋		乖	歸			官	滾^3	光	工	

Medial: -ü-

Initial	ü			üeh					üan	ün		iung[i]	
n l	女^{n3}			虐^{n4}					攣^{l2}	淋^{l2}			
ch ch' hs y[j]	居			絕^2					捐	君		局	

Note (a). A peculiar feature of the Wade system is that *cho, ch'o, jo* and *shuo* form a series. In actual pronunciation, there is a trace of the semi-vowel *-u-* in all these syllables The National Phonetic spelling writes the semi-vowel in for all cases, the Inland Mission system omits it in all cases. We shall observe the contrast between *cho, ch'o,* and *jo* on the one hand and *shuo* on the other as a purely graphic convention of the Wade system.

Note (b). 這 is often pronounced *chei⁴ < chê⁴-i¹* 'this one,' though no longer limited to reference to one individual in present usage.

Note (c). The actual pronunciation of the syllables spelt *ko, k'o, ho, o* is *kê, k'ê, hê, ê,* that is, with an unrounded mid-back vowel. (Cf. Section 2 above.)

Note (d). *P'ia¹* is an onomatopoetic word without a character, representing the sound of a slap or a splash.

Note (e). When the initial is *y-,* the syllables are written thus: *i, ya, yeh, yai, yao, yu, yen, yin, yang, ying.* (See Table II.)

Note (f). This final is written *-ui* after the *t*-group, the *ts*-group, and the *ch*-group of initials and after the initial *h-* of the *k*-group, but written *-uei* after the initials *k-* and *k'-*. In actual pronunciation. the prominence of the *-e-* element is even more influenced by the tone than by the kind of initials which precede it. In general, the third and fourth tones are associated with the more open value of the final, while the first two tones are associated with the more close value. The same is true of the final *-iu* for which the actual pronunciation in the third and fourth tones is actually *-iou*. It should be noted however that even in the first two tones, *-ui* (灰) never rimes with *-i* (雞) and *-iu* (流) never rimes with *-u* (胡), which shows that some trace of a mid vowel between the *i* and the *u*, in whichever order, is never completely absent. The same is true, though to a lesser extent, of the final *-un*.

Note (g). Of the *t*-series of initials, only *t-* and *t'-* combine with *-ui*. The initials *n-* and *l-* combine with *-ei* but not with *-ui*.

Note (h). When the initial is *w-,* the syllables are written thus: *wu, wa, wo, wai, wei* (not *wui*), *wan, wên* (not *wun*), *wang, wêng* (not *wung*). (See Table II.)

Note (i). There is usually a slight rounding in the semi-vowel, but it is written *-i-* in the Wade system.

Note (j). When the initial is a (rounded) *y-,* the syllables are written thus: *yü, yüeh, yüan, yün, yung.* (See Table II.)

7. Tones. — A Chinese syllable, as we saw, consists of not only an initial and a final, but also a tone, or the time-pitch function during the whole voiced part of the syllable. Thus, *lang²,* with a high rising tone, 'wolf,' and *lang⁴,* with a falling tone, 'wave,' are as different from each other to the Chinese speaker as *long* and *wrong* or as *long* and *lung* are to an English-speaking person. The unsophisticated Chinese speaker, whose writing consists of characters for whole syllables, certainly does not find the conception of consonant and vowel any less elusive and intangible than the conception of tone. The task of the foreign student of Chinese, on the other hand, should be to realize that the constituent of tone is just as essential as those of consonant and vowel in forming Chinese words.

The dialect of Peiping has four tones in stressed syllables, the pronunciation of an isolated character being always considered as stressed. If the average range of speaking pitch is divided into four equal intervals marked by five points: 1 low, 2 half-low, 3 middle, 4 half-high, and 5 high, all tones can be sufficiently identified by naming its starting and ending pitch, and, in the case of circumflex tones, the turning point. The four tones of the Peiping dialect, together with their traditional names, can then be described as follows:

No.	Chinese Name	English Name	Description	Pitch
1	陰平(聲) *yin¹-p'ing² (shêng¹)*	Upper Even (Tone)	High level	55:
2	陽平(聲) *yang²-p'ing² (shêng¹)*	Lower Even (Tone)	High rising	35:
3	上聲 *shang³-shêng¹*	Rising Tone	Low rising	214:
4	去聲 *ch'ü⁴-shêng¹*	Falling, or Going, Tone	High falling to low	51:

Both the absolute pitch and the relative pitch, or range, of the tones depend upon the sex, the individual voice, and the mood of the speaker. The average interval for each step is between a whole tone and a tone and a half, so that the total range is somewhere between an augmented fifth and an octave. It goes without saying that in Chinese, as in any non-tonal language, the pitch of the speaking voice glides portamento fashion instead of jumping from one pitch to another discontinuously. Thus, no resemblance to the Chinese tones could be got by playing any sequence of notes on a keyed instrument. It should be noted that the usual figures for tones refer to the classes, as indicated in the first column of the preceding table, and have nothing to do with the five levels of pitch.

In the old National Pronunciation of 1920, as well as in the Inland Mission system, both of which take features of Central dialects into consideration, a fifth tone ju^4-$shêng^1$ 入聲 or 'entering tone' is recognized. Words in this tone are derived from those ending in -p, -t, and -k in Ancient Chinese, and are now pronounced with a short vowel, ending in a glottal stop when it is at the end of a phrase, as in Nanking, or simply form a separate tone class without being either short or ending in a glottal stop. as in Changsha.

In this dictionary, words in the fifth tone are grouped separately after those in the other tones. They are marked by the figure 5 and the Inland Mission system of romanization has a final -h to mark this tone. For example, in the form *Chih* in parentheses at the head of No. 988, p. 173, col. I the -h indicates that all characters in this group from No. 988 to No. 1013 belong to the entering tone class. As noted above, it has nothing to do with the last -h in the syllable *chih* of the Wade system, in which -ih is simply the conventional digraph to represent the r-like retroflex vowel, which is written i in the Inland Mission system.

Since the entering tone does not exist in the Peiping dialect, which is the present standard, practically all characters marked with a figure 5 are also marked with one of the first four figures according to the present Peiping pronunciation, as for example No. 267, p. 32, col. II 折$^{2\cdot5}$. The only exceptions are a small number of rare characters, or rare alternate pronunciations of common characters, for which there is no usage to follow in either reading or speaking in Peiping. A native scholar on being asked about any of these cases would probably turn to a dictionary, and finding that the *fan-ch'ieh* form of spelling had the entering tone, would give a fourth tone, or some other tone by whatever analogy might suggest itself to him at the moment, so that such "modern" pronunciations would be highly artificial and would represent no fact concerning the dialect or the usage of literary reading. Such cases have therefore been left as 5's without being marked with an additional Peiping tone-mark.

7. Tone-Sandhi. — In most Chinese dialects, the tones of syllables spoken in succession are different from those of the same syllables when spoken in isolation. This difference is called tone-sandhi. The tone-sandhi in Peiping is one of the simplest among the dialects. The rules are as follows:

(1) A third tone followed by any tone except another third tone is pronounced without its final rising pitch. This is sometimes called the half-third tone. Examples are:

3+1	好天	hao³ t'ien¹	'good weather'
3+2	好人	hao³ jên²	'good man'
3+4	好話	hao³ hua⁴	'good words'
3+neutral	好罷	hao³ ·pa	'good! all right!'

In each case, the tone of *hao³*, which has the pitch pattern of '214' when spoken alone or at the end of a phrase, now has the pitch pattern of '21,' in other words, it stays low without any rise.

(2) A third tone followed by another third tone changes into the second tone, as:

3+3 → 2+3	好酒	hao<u>³</u> chiu³	'good wine'

where <u>3</u> marks the third-tone syllable pronounced in the second tone when followed by another third tone.

Once understood to be automatic, neither of these changes need be marked in the body of the dictionary. There is however one exception. When the second syllable in the third tone has the unstressed or neutral tone, to be explained below, the case comes under (2) or (1) according to whether the speaker treats it as a third-tone syllable or not. If it is treated as quite unstressed and quite neutral, then only the neutral-tone mark '·' is used. Thus the compound 椅·子 *i*[3]·*tzŭ* has a half-third tone, followed by a half-high neutral tone. If however the second syllable is still treated as a third tone, the first syllable changes into the second even though the second syllable is actually pronounced unstressed, as for example in No. 2605.41 小·姐 *hsiao*[2]·*chieh*, where the underscored '3' stands for the second tone which comes from an original third.

8. The Neutral Tone. — From the standpoint of single characters, practically every character pronounced alone has one of the four regular tones. But in compounds and connected speech, a syllable is often unstressed and loses its characteristic tone, and its pitch is determined, not by its original tone, but by its tonal environment, chiefly by the tone of the preceding syllable. An unstressed syllable is said to be atonic and its tone may be called the neutral tone.

The notation for the neutral tone is a dot or a circle before the character (or the romanization for the syllable) according as the neutral tone is compulsory or optional. When the presence or absence of the neutral tone makes a difference in the meaning, then the dotted and undotted entries are written separately before their respective meanings, as for example in No. 996-A.1 執事 'to arrange'; 'deacons'; but 執·事 'official insignia.' Again, in No. 6180.6, 心疼 'pained at heart'; but 心·疼 'to love,' etc.

The pitch of the neutral tone is as follows:

Half-low	after tone 1	高·的	*kao*[1]·*tê*	'high ones'
Half-low (or half-high in more lively speech)	after tone 2	長·的	*ch'ang*[2]·*tê*	'long ones'
Half-high	after tone 3	短·的	*tuan*[3]·*tê*	'short ones'
Low	after tone 4	大·的	*ta*[4]·*tê*	'big ones'

In the relatively infrequent case when the neutral tone begins a phrase, its pitch is usually half-low.

While the preceding paragraphs give all the necessary practical information as to *how* the neutral tone is pronounced, it is a much more complicated problem to know *when* the neutral tone is used. On the whole, neutral tones may be divided into grammatical cases and lexical cases, though they often shade into each other. Particles, interjections, pronouns after verbs, and other "empty words" which do not carry important concrete meanings in a sentence have the neutral tone. Except for particles, these are mostly optional cases of the neutral tone (those which are marked with circles). What is most important in this dictionary is the recording of thousands of compounds containing the neutral tone as individual lexical facts, just as facts of the stress-accent in English have to be recorded individually in dictionaries and cannot be covered by rules. From the point of view of grammatical analysis, it is possible to account for a large proportion of neutral-tone syllables by recognizing them as suffixes, as ·子 --*tzŭ* (noun suffix), ·見 --*chien* (suffix for successful perception), ·處 --*ch'u* (suffix for respect or quality), ·來 --*lai* (suffix for motion or change towards the speaker, like German *her*-), etc., etc. But from the point of view of the user of the dictionary, who is confronted with a text in characters, he may not be able to decide whether a given character is a suffix or a full word, since frequently the same character is used in both ways. Hence the necessity of marking these suffixes with the neutral-tone sign in each case. For example, 老子[3] the philosopher Lao-tzŭ, but 老·子 popular term for 'father,' 'the old man.'

When the full tone and the neutral tone are associated with different pronunciations, the tone sign or dot is to imply that the pronunciation is the one which is associated with it. For example, since 了 has two pronunciations *liao*[3] and ·*lê*, writing 了[3] or ·了 will be sufficient notation to indicate which pronunciation is to be used. (In a similar way, the '2' in 長[2] implies that it is *ch'ang*[2] and the '3' in 長[3] implies that it is *chang*[3].)

The majority of occurrences of the neutral tone are the purely lexical cases, which have to be recorded as individual facts. It may be said that, on the whole, literary expressions, new terms, and technical terms do not contain the neutral tone, as 失 敬; 僞 裝; 電 子³. There remain then the colloquial compounds of old standing, of which some contain the neutral tone and some do not. It is among compounds of this type that it is most essential to distinguish those which contain the neutral tone from those which do not. Sometimes, the presence of the neutral tone serves as an indication as to which one of several synonymous compounds is the most commonly used or has the oldest standing. For example, in No. 2434.21 喜·歡 has at least 1,000 times the frequency of 喜 悅, though the latter is by no means obsolete. Similarly, in No. 3697.97, 工·錢 is the usual term for 'wages,' for which 工銀, 工值, and 工價 under the same heading are much less frequent synonyms.

In very formal reading of a literary text, there is no neutral tone, every syllable receiving its full etymological tone. For this reason, we shall simplify the marking of the neutral tone by adopting the following conventions: (1) The literary particles like 之, 乎, 矣, 也, etc. are never marked with a dot, it being understood that in actual reading one can give it the neutral tone according to the rhythm and mood. (2) All syllables marked with a dot are in the neutral tone in normal speech, but when read formally or read for dictation, they may all acquire full tones. The meaning of the dot as indicating "compulsory" neutral tone is that it is compulsory only in normal (deliberate) speech, and not in formalized reading.

Due to alternation of rhythm, three-syllable combinations in which there is no neutral tone usually have their second syllable slightly less prominent than the other two, and four-syllable combinations containing no neutral tone have their second and third syllables slightly less stressed. Once understood, such modifications are not marked in the dictionary.

9. The Retroflex Vowels. — An extreme case of the neutral tone is the diminutive suffix derived from 兒 *êrh*² 'child.' It is so weakened as to become either a consonantal ending -*r* added after the syllable or a simultaneous retroflexing modification of the preceding vowel. In either case, there is no addition of an extra syllable, though in a character text it is written with 兒 as a separate character. The pronunciation of this ending varies after various types of finals. After high vowels, except the complete final -*u*, i.e., after -*ŭ*, -*ih*, -*i*, and -*ü*, and after -*eh*, it becomes -*êr*. (In all cases, the vowel in the third and fourth tones is more open, approaching -*ar*.) Examples are 子兒³ *tsêr*³, 枝兒 *chêr*¹, 梨兒 *liêr*², 魚兒 *yüêr*², from *tzŭ*³, *chih*¹, *li*², *yü*². After -*u*, -*a*, -*o*, -*ê*, -*ao*, -*ou*, there is no change in the final except the addition of an ending -*r* or simultaneous retroflexion in the articulation of the preceding vowel. After finals ending in -*i* or in -*n*, the -*i* and -*n* are dropped entirely (with -*ien* becoming -*iar* instead of -*iêr* or *ier*), as 塊 *k'uai*⁴, 一 塊 兒 *i*²-*k'uar*⁴; 今 *chin*¹, 今兒 *chiêr*¹; 點 *tien*³, 一點兒 *i*⁴-*tiar*³. After finals ending in -*ng*, the whole vowel becomes simultaneously nasalized and retroflexed. For example, while the character 繩 is pronounced *shêng*², with three sounds *sh-ê-ng*, the compound 繩兒 is pronounced *shêng'r*², with only two sounds, the simple consonant *sh*, and the nasalized retroflex vowel written here as *êng'r* or [ə̃ɻ] in phonetic notation.

Besides representing the non-syllabic diminutive suffix, the character 兒 also represents the stressed form *êrh*² and the unstressed form ·*êrh*, both being syllabic and meaning 'child,' as 兒女 *êrh*²-*nü*³ 'sons and daughters'; 女·兒 *nü*³·*êrh* 'daughter.' To simplify our notation, these two types are marked as above, while the non-syllabic suffix 兒 or -*r* is left unmarked, as it is by far the most frequent in this dictionary. Compounds ending in an unmarked 兒 should therefore be pronounced according to the description given in the preceding paragraph.

For reasons of space, addition of the non-syllabic 兒 introduced in the new edition is often indicated by the insertion at the lower right-hand corner of the preceding character the National Phonetic letter 儿, as in No. 4303.15 麻花 儿.

LIST OF SYLLABIC HEADINGS

Owing to the numerous revisions of pronunciation, the original order of entries, which was not strictly alphabetic to start with, departs still further from alphabetic order. The following table will serve to help locate the syllables as well as exhibit a bird's-eye view of all the syllables. Letters in italics represent headings which are out of the alphabetic order; those in brackets are headings which were omitted in the dictionary but which should have been included according to the original system.

XIX

Syllable	Example	Page	Syllable	Example	Page	Syllable	Example	Page
Shuo	勺	821	To	奪	934	Tsu	祖	1002
Shou	收	821	T'o	它	934	Tsu	足	1004
Shu	殊	826	T'o	妥	936	Ts'u	粗	1006
Shu	菽	833	T'o	托	936	Ts'u	促	1007
Shua	耍	836	T'o	脫	937	Tsuan	攢	1007
Shuai	甩	836	Tou	兜	938	Ts'uan	竄	1009
Shuan	拴	837	T'ou	偷	941	Tsui	嘴	1009
Shuang	雙	837	*Tu*	杜	944	Ts'ui	崔	1011
Shui	水	839	*Tu*	督	944	Tsun	尊	1013
Shun	吮	842	*T'u*	塗	949	Ts'un	存	1014
Shuo	說	844	*T'u*	禿	953	Tsung	宗	1016
Ta	大	846	*Tuan*	端	953	Ts'ung	怱	1019
Ta	答	851	*T'uan*	團	955	Tzŭ	咨	1021
T'a	他	853	*Tui*	堆	956	Tz'ŭ	慈	1030
T'a	踏	854	*T'ui*	推	958	Wa	哇	1035
Tai	歹	855	*Tun*	敦	960	Wa	挖	1036
T'ai	台	859	*T'un*	吞	962	Wai	外	1036
Tan	丹	863	*Tung*	冬	963	Wan	丸	1038
T'an	探	868	*T'ung*	同	966	Wang	亡	1042
Tang	當	873	Tsa	雜	972	Wei	威	1047
T'ang	湯	876	Ts'a	擦	973	Wên	溫	1057
Tao	刀	879	Tsai	哉	973	Wêng	翁	1062
T'ao	叨	885	Ts'ai	猜	976	Wo	我	1063
Tê	得	888	Tsan	喒	979	Wo	喔	1063
T'ê	特	890	Ts'an	參	980	Wu	巫	1063
Têng	登	892	Tsang	臧	983	Wu	勿	1078
T'êng	疼	894	Ts'ang	倉	984	Ya	牙	1078
Ti	低	895	Tsao	糟	985	Ya	壓	1080
Ti	的	900	Ts'ao	操	988	Yai	崖	1082
T'i	提	902	Tsê	窄	990	Yang	央	1082
T'i	剔	907	Ts'ê	册	991	Yao	姚	1088
Tiao	刁	907	Tsên	怎	993	Yeh	耶	1093
T'iao	挑	909	Ts'ên	參	993	Yeh	葉	1095
Tieh	爹	912	Tsêng	增	993	Yen	焉	1096
[Tieh]	跌	912	Ts'êng	層	994	Yin	因	1108
T'ieh	帖	914	Tso	左	994	Ying	嬰	1117
Tien	滇	915	Tso	坐	995	*Yüeh*	約	1122
T'ien	天	920	Tso	作	996	Yu	幽	1124
Ting	丁	926	Tso	鑿	998	Yung	雍	1133
T'ing	汀	929	Ts'o	嵯	998	Yü	于	1138
Tiu	丟	932	Ts'o	挫	999	Yü	欲	1150
To	多	932	Ts'o	撮	1000	*Yüeh*	曰	1152
To	朶	933	Tsou	走	1000	*Yüan*	元	1154
To	鐸	934	Ts'ou	湊	1002	Yün	云	1160

THE STRUCTURE OF CHINESE CHARACTERS.*

Their Structure, how to find their Radicals, and how to find them in a Dictionary.

———————

1. A Chinese character, which is not itself a Radical, consists of two parts: the Radical and the Phonetic, or when it does not give the sound of the character, the Primitive. The Radical is one from the list of 214 Radicals, the Phonetic is the other half of the character, and strange to say, the Chinese language contains no name for it. It is sometimes itself another Radical, as in 近 記 理 罵, but more frequently a compound character formed of another Radical and Phonetic, as in 語 造 羅.

Speaking very generally, for the rule is frequently broken, it would seem as if Chinese characters were constructed on the following principle:—The Radical should give a clue to the meaning of a character, the Phonetic a clue to its sound. Thus 油 *yu*, oil, comes from 由 *yu* as phonetic, and the *water* radical indicating a liquid; 神 *shen*, god or spirit, from 申 *shen*, as phonetic, and the *omen* radical; 駕 *chia*, to ride, from 加 *chia*, as phonetic, and the *horse* radical; 議 *i*, to discuss, from 義 *i*, as phonetic, and the *words* radical.

The beginner will often find a new character to be an old radical with a new phonetic, or sometimes merely a new combination of a familiar radical with a familiar phonetic.

2. A good deal of difficulty will be found at first, in knowing under what radical to look for any particular character, and unfortunately some of the commonest characters are the hardest to find. However, no one need be discouraged, for a few months' steady practice will work wonders in removing the difficulties.

The radical may occupy any part of the character. It may be at the top, as 竹 in 管; or at the bottom, as 皿 in 盥; on the left, as 糸 in 給; on the right, as 阝 in 都; surrounding it, as 囗 in 固; or in the middle of it, as 口 in 周; partially surrounding it, as 疒 in 痕, or 辵 in 退, or 門 in 間; or the radical may be split in two, enclosing the phonetic, as 行 in 衝, or 衣 in 裏, or 二 in 五. Sometimes it is mixed up in a general sort of way with the phonetic, as 冂 in 再, or 大 in 奉, or 禾 in 穀, or 口 in 嘗.

3. *a.* Consider whether the character is a radical itself. Thus 音 香 高 辛 至 面 行 黑 麻 走 玉 色 are themselves radicals.

b. If the character is not a radical, the first step is to break it into two parts. In two cases out of three there will be one part on the right hand and another on the left; in which case it is easy to break the character up. Thus:一 初 就 物 創 的 沒 樣 暗 卻 認 叫 他 作. Or the division may be horizontal, one half being above, the other beneath, and in this case the division is not quite so simple; as, 界 意 告 督 覆 答 萬 負 罪 要 靈 拏. Or one half may enclose the other on two or more sides, as 有 道 同 在 造 反 底 問 因. There are in addition other forms which are harder to divide.

c. If one of the two parts is a radical and the other is not, obviously we must look for it under that part which is a radical; as for instance, 的 釘 福 雖 忽 花, which come from 白 金 示 隹 心 艹, respectively, the other halves not being radicals.

d. Where both halves of a character are radicals, the following rules must be applied:—

1. Where the character consists of a right-hand and a left-hand half, THE LEFT-HAND HALF is usually the radical; as, for instance, 信 加 塊 如 律 性 拉 明 根. Each of these examples consists of two radicals; but the one on the LEFT HAND is that under which one must look for it.

['Called 右文 'the right-hand side character.' Popularly a.c. 偏旁, a term also applied to the radical.]

Exceptions:—The radicals 刀 力 文 斤 殳 彡 欠 阝 (163) [阝 170 is regular] 隹 鳥, are generally found on the right side of the character, but in these cases the left side is seldom a radical.

The rule that the LEFT-HAND portion of the character is the radical also holds in cases where the radical extends to two or more sides of the character. For instance:— 庫 尼 建 房 虎 赴 連 間.

2. Where the character consists of an upper and lower half, both being radicals, the LOWER HALF is usually the radical. As, for instance: 思 昏 果 泉 兄 多 分 妾.

Exceptions:—The following radicals are placed at the top of the character:— 艹 竹 [two very large groups] 亠 宀 穴 皿 雨 爪.

These rules will dispose of nineteen-twentieths of the characters in Chinese; though, alas! many exceptions will be found to them, such as 相 from 目 instead of 木; 妝 from 女 instead of 爿; 取 from 又 instead of 耳; 和 from 口 instead of 禾; but it will often be found that the meaning gives a reason why the rule was broken.

A balance remains of eccentric characters for which no rules can be made. For example 賸 from 貝; 歸 from 止; 與 from 臼; 聚 from 耳; 望 from 月; 直 from 目; and many others, for which see Lists of Difficult Characters in dictionaries.

A Mandarin Primer. F. W. BALLER.

ABBREVIATIONS AND SIGNS

Abbreviation or Sign	Stand for	Example in
A.c.	Also called	26-A.2
A.p.	Also pronounced	2261-A.5
A.w.	Also written	383.9
Inter.	Interchanged with	817-A
N.A.	Numerary Adjunct or classifier of nouns	967
u.f.	used for	538-C
=	equal to—indicates that the term on the right-hand side is more commonly used	199.1
≡	identical with—indicates that the form of the character on the right-hand side is more commonly used	261.6
儿	non-syllabic suffix -*r*	1154.9
·	indicates that the following syllable must be in the neutral tone	9.29
°	indicates that the following syllable may be in the neutral tone	560.1
↑	added entry would be further back if radical order of arrangement were followed	1850.76
↓	added entry would be further down if radical order of arrangement were followed	3946.7
↘ ↗ ↘ ↗	English tone signs for the following syllable, used in translating certain grammatical particles	7300-A.13

REFERENCES

The first group of examples under each character has no particular indication for references. Subsequent groups are lettered (*a*), (*b*), etc.

B.5 . . . . Group (*b*), example 5.

See above — 76 . . . . See No. 76 in the first group of examples.

See below A.25 . . . . See below, example 25 in group (*a*).

See No. 3285-B.1 . . . . See character 3285, group (*b*), example 1.

No. 4876-8 or 4876.8 . . . . Character 4876, example 8.

A
CHINESE-ENGLISH
DICTIONARY

A.   (Υ)

阿 [4] Initial particle. Prefix to names of people.
1

阿 伯 husband's elder brother.
阿 兄 my elder brother.
阿 公 my grandfather; husband's father.
阿 哥 an elder brother; son of emperor under Manchus.
[5] 阿 妹 my younger sister.
阿 姐 my elder sister.
阿 娘 a mother.
阿 姨 mother's sister; wife's sisters; father's concubine.
阿 婆 husband's mother; term of respect for old woman.
[10] 阿 媽 a nurse; serving woman.
阿 嬌 child name of beautiful wife of *Wu-ti* of Han dynasty. A beautiful woman.
阿 膠 a medicine, a glue made from the skin of black asses and water from 阿井 in 山東.
阿 誰 Who?
阿 香 a fairy who assists the god of thunder.
[15] 阿 魏 asafoetida.

(a) To groan.

阿 侑 to groan.
阿 嗽 an exclamation of astonishment.
阿 嚏 the sound of a sneeze.
阿 阿 to sigh.

(b) Used for the sounds a, ah, in foreign words.

阿 剌 伯 Arabia.
阿 吽 *Ahong*, a Mohammedan mullah.
阿 富 汗 Afghanistan.
阿 尼 林 aniline.
[5] 阿 根 廷 Argentine.

阿 羅 漢 *Arhat* or *Lohan*, one of 500 disciples of Buddha.=羅°漢.
阿 脩 羅 *Asuras*, giant demons of Buddhism.
阿 難 *Ananda*, cousin of Gautama Buddha.
阿 鼻 地 獄 the lowest hell of Buddhism, from which there is no escape.

(c) Read o[1] **(ㄜ) A river bank.**

阿 丘 a slope or bank.
河 水 之 阿 on the bank of the river.

(d) To assent to; to flatter.

阿 媚 奉 承 to flatter and toady.
阿 比 [4] servile following of another.
阿 私 partiality.
阿 諛 to flatter; to toady.
阿 附 a sycophant manner; to assent to.
汙 不 至 阿 其 所 好 low, but not descending to flatter their favourite.

(e) Name prefix.

阿 斗 son of *Liu Pei;* used for a stupid.

(f) Pillars, beams. To lean towards.

阿 房 宮 famous palace built by *Ch'in Shih Huang*—the first emperor. 212 B.C.
阿 衡 pillar of state. Title of 伊 尹 a minister of 成 湯. 1766 B.C.
四 阿 重 [2] 屋 a hall with four pillars.—

(g) Used for transliterating.

阿 芙 蓉 opium. = 鴉°片 (烟).
阿 彌 陀 佛 Amida Buddha; this name is often used as an ex-

clamation, see under 佛 No. 1982-49.

啊 [1] A final particle.
2

AI.   (ㄞ)

哀 [1] To sympathize with. To pity. To wail. Alas!
3

哀 傷 sad; distressing.
哀 告 to importune; to make a piteous report.
哀 哀 痛 哭 bitter weeping and grief.
哀 哀 上 告 with deep grief is the petition presented.
[5] 哀 哉 Alas!
哀 哭 or 哀 泣 to cry and weep.
哀 啟 obituary notice sent with report of death.
哀 號 to wail with grief, making considerable noise
哀 鳴 to weep and wail.
[10] 哀 子 a child whose mother is dead.
哀 悼 to grieve; to mourn.
哀 情 sadness; grief.
哀 慟 mournful; grieving.
哀 慘 pitiful and distressing.
[15] 哀 懇 to implore; to entreat.
哀 憐 or 哀 惜 to pity; to sympathize with.
哀 歎 to sigh and moan.
哀 毀 骨 立 emaciated with grief.
哀 樂 grief and joy.
[20] 哀 樂 佚 時 grief or joy, when not in accord with circumstances (brings calamity).
哀 樂 相 生 grief and joy each produce the other.
哀 樂 樂 哀 grief and joy both out of place.

哀 求 to entreat.
哀 求 天 父 We implore Thee, Heavenly Father.
²⁵哀 矜 to extend sympathy to.
哀 矜 無 辜 royal pardon for those wrongly imprisoned.
哀 絲 豪 竹 the moving effect of sad music.
哀 而 不 傷 mournful, but not distressing.
哀 而 喪 重 民 數 he grieved for mourners and respected the census.
³⁰哀 衣 or 哀 麻 mourning garments.
哀 觀 主 義 pessimism; see under 悲 No. 4992—22, or under 厭 No. 7387—2ff.
哀 詞 or 哀 辭 elegies written on the death of a friend.
哀 詔 announcement of the death of an emperor.
哀 輓 funeral scrolls sent by friends on the occasion of a death.
⁵⁵哀 鴻 homeless—distressed population suffering from famine or other disaster.

唉¹ An interjection; exclamation of disgust or regret.
4　Also read ai³.
唉 可 憐 How sad!
唉 歎 to sigh.

埃¹ Fine dust; dirt.
Also read ai².
5
埃 及 Egypt.
埃 垢 dust; dirt.
塵 埃 dust, the defilements of the world. (Budd.).

挨¹ Near, next to. Close to.
6
挨 到 to come to in sequence.
挨 晚 or 傍 (pang¹) 晚 towards evening.
挨 次 in order.
挨 查 to examine consecutively.
⁵挨 着 side by side; in succession.
挨 肩 following closely; shoulder to shoulder.
挨 肩 弟 兄 brothers nearly the same age.
挨 肩 擦 臂 crowded together.

挨 門 挨 戶 to go from door to door.
(a) To lean to.
挨 靠 to rely on.
挨 背 back to back.
(b) To delay.
挨 了 一 年 I have waited for a year.
挨 延 to procrastinate.
(c) Read ai². To be beaten, to suffer. A.w. 捱.
挨 打 to be beaten.
挨 打 受 氣 to suffer beating and insult.
挨 餓 受 凍 to suffer cold and hunger.

欸¹ An interjection, used with 唉 No. 4. Read ai³. Sound of oars.
7
欸 乃 (ai³) the creaking or swishing sound of oars or sweeps in rowing.

矮³ Of short stature. Low in height.
8
矮 子 or 矮 人 a dwarf or man of short stature.
矮 子 看 戲 a dwarf at a theatre—he praises without adequate knowledge.
矮 小 undersized.
矮 屋 a low house.
矮 樹 a dwarf tree.
矮 櫈 子 a low stool.
矮 胖 子 a short, stout man.
身 量 矮 of short stature.

愛⁴ To love, to be fond of, to like. Love, affection.
9
愛 之 而 弗 仁 he is kind (to inferior creatures) but not loving.
愛 之 能 勿 勞 乎 can (a father) love and not train (his child)?
愛 人 人 愛 those who love are loved.
愛 人 以 德 to love others with a due regard to what is right.
⁵愛 人 如 己 to love one's neighbour as oneself.
愛 人 利 物 之 謂 仁 affection to man and kindness to creatures is called 仁.

愛 他 主 義 altruism.
愛 力 chemical affinity.
愛 卿 my dear.
¹⁰愛 同 胞 love of compatriots.
愛 國 patriotism.
愛 國 心 a patriotic spirit.
愛 國 捐 patriotic contributions.
愛 國 利 民 patriotism and love of the masses.
¹⁵愛 國 如 命 to love one's country as one's life.
愛 國 志 士 ardent patriots.
愛 好 to have a fancy for; to like.
愛 媚 to caress.
愛 屋 及 烏 when one loves another the affection extends even to the crows on the roof.
²⁰愛 己 主 義 selfishness; egoism.
愛 心 affection; love.
愛 恤 to shew sympathy.
愛 悅 to care for.
愛 惜 to love in compassion; to spare, to pity. See below. A. 2—4.
²⁵愛 情 affection; love.
愛 慕 to have ardent desires for.
愛 戀 不 捨 inseparable attachment. See below. A. 5.
愛 戴 to love with special respect.
愛 戴 高 帽 子 to love to wear a high hat—fond of flattery, must be puffed up.
³⁰愛 才 to appreciate talent and ability.
愛 抬 槓 fond of quibbling or arguing over anything, whether right or wrong.
愛 撫 to love and cherish.
愛 敬 to love with reverence.
愛 服 cheerful acquiescence.
³⁵愛 欲 其 周 wishes to have his love displayed everywhere.
愛 民 如 子 to love the people as his children.
愛 無 差 等 love without difference of degree.
愛 爲 憎 始 love is the beginning of hatred.
愛 物 kind to living creatures; careful of things.
⁴⁰愛 病 prone to illness.
愛 種 love of kindred or race.
愛 網 passionate love—like falling into a net.
愛 繼 to choose some loved person as an heir.
愛 羣 love for all.
⁴⁵愛 育 to love and cherish.

愛莫能助 to love but have no ability to render assistance.
愛顧 to love and think of.
愛體 to care for the body.
可愛 lovable.
50 兼愛 to love all equally.
溺愛 devoted to; fond, doting.
親愛 dearly beloved; to cherish—as parents.

(a) To covet; to grudge; to be sparing of.

愛小便宜 *p'ien² i* love of trifling advantages; keen on petty profits.
愛·惜·光·陰 careful of time; "redeeming the time."
愛·惜·性·命 to cling tenaciously to life.
愛·惜·皮肉 self-indulgent; afraid of hardship.
愛戀 to hanker after; to lust for.
愛日 careful of his days—a devoted son fears that the days for serving his parents are few, therefore he is careful of them.
愛財 covetous.
愛酒 fond of intoxicants.

(b) Complimentary term for a daughter.

令愛 your daughter.

(c) Used for transliterating.

愛克司光 X-rays.

噯 1.3. A tone of disapproval. Warm, genial atmosphere.
10

噯呀 an exclamation of surprise.

嬡 4 Complimentary term for a daughter.
11

令嬡 your daughter.

曖 4 The sun obscured by clouds. Obscure.
12

曖昧 dark.
曖曖 dark and obscured.

靉 4 A cloudy sky. Cloudy. Obscure.
13

靉靉 cloudy and dull; luxuriant growth.
靉靆 cloudy. Spectacles.

饐 4 Cooked food which has turned sour. Mouldy.
14

藹 3 Luxuriant vegetation; shady growth of trees.
15 Friendly; beautiful.

藹然可親 friendly; lovable.
藹藹 numerous; appearance of the moon when slightly obscured.
藹彩 fresh, new appearance.

靄 4 Cloudy sky, not necessarily dull.
16

靄氣 fair clouds; a beautiful sky.

閡 4 To shut others out. Obstructed. Also read *hê*⁵.
17

阻閡 prevented.

隘 4 A pass, a defile. Narrow, confined.
18 Also read *yai*⁴.

隘口 entrance to a pass.
隘害 dangerous and important.
隘巷 a narrow lane.
隘憊 disheartened on account of poverty.
隘險 dangerous and important, as a strategic post.
險隘 a dangerous pass.

AI. (NGAI.)　(ㄫㄞ)

艾 4 Mugwort, artemisia or any plant which produces moxa
19 punk. General name for plants like mint.

艾把 mugwort, steamed and used as a pain-killer.
艾旗招福 the mugwort flag brings luck—phrase used on 5th of the 5th lunar month.
艾灸 to cauterize with moxa.
艾炷 moxa torch for cauterization.
艾符 artemisia charm hung at the door on 5th of the 5th lunar month.
艾絨 moxa punk used for cauterization, also mixed with castor oil to make ink for red stamps.
艾蒿 common artemisia.

(a) Fifty years of age, when the hair is grey like moxa.

艾壯 fifty years of age and upwards.
艾服 fifty years of age.
艾老 fifty years of age and upwards.
艾者 between fifty and sixty years of age.

(b) Beautiful.

少艾 young and beautiful.
知好色則慕少艾 when a man becomes conscious of the attractions of beauty; his desire is towards young and beautiful women.

(c) To stutter.

艾艾 to stutter, from a man named 鄧艾 who stuttered when telling a ruler his name.

(d) To quieten; to finish.

夜未艾 the night is not yet ended.
憂未艾也 the anxiety is not quietened.

(e) To protect; to nurture.

保艾爾後 I will protect and nurture your posterity.

(f) To recompense.

艾人必豐 the recompense will be abundant.

(g) Pale green like the plant.

艾謂青而微白 *Ngai* is a pale green.

(h) Read *i*⁴. To correct; to order; to cultivate.

艾蕭 orderly and grave.
天下艾安 the empire is well ordered.
有私淑艾者 there are those who cultivate themselves in private.

哎 1 Interjection of surprise or regret.
20

哎呀 Alas! Hullo!

餲 4 Tainted food.
21

餲壞 to spoil (food) by keeping.

駾[3] Foolish. Stupid. To trot as a horse.

22

童駾無識 young and ignorantly stupid.

碍
㝵
礙[4]

To obstruct, to hinder, to stop progress. To injure, to offend. To concern. Hindrance, restraint.

23

碍不着 it does not interfere with....

碍口 to hesitate about telling.

碍手 or 碍事 to obstruct; to be in the way.

碍石 a stumbling block.

[5]碍眼 to see what one would wish not to see.

碍道 to obstruct the way.

不碍事 unimportant; "it doesn't matter."

妨碍 impediment; hindrance.

有碍於情 it hinders friendly feelings.

↑碍難 it is impossible for this office to . . .

皚[2]

24

Whiteness.

皚皚 pure and white as snow.

皚皚依庭 (the frost) was white on the hall.

積雪皚皚 the whiteness of driven snow.

捱[2]

25

To put off; to procrastinate. u.f. 挨 No. 6.

捱一會 delay a moment.

捱到晚間 until the evening.

延捱 delay; procrastination.

(a) To suffer, to endure.

捱·了打 to be beaten.

捱·不住 cannot endure it; more than can be borne.

捱世界 to suffer the hard usage of the world.

捱死 in danger of death.

捱苦 to endure hardship.

AN.　　(ㄢ)

安[1] Quiet, still. Peace, tranquillity.

26

安不忘危 in peace remember the possibilities of danger.

安不忘戰 in peace consider the possibilities of war.

安享太平 to enjoy times of peace.

安全 safe; in security; security.

[5]安全燈 a Davy lamp. safety zone.

安全瓣 safety valve. 安全界 (or 區)

安其危而利其菑 they rest peacefully in their dangers, and look upon calamities as matters of profit.

安危 peace and danger.

安善 in peace.

[10]安好 well, in peace.

安宅 a peaceful habitation (from 仁人之安宅) benevolence is the quiet habitation of man.

安寧 in repose. 安·徽 Anhwei.

安·息 to rest.

安·息日 the Sabbath.

[15]安·息年 the Sabbatic year.

安·息香 gum benzoin.

安泰 tranquil, peaceful.

安枕無憂 to sleep without anxiety.

安然無事 all quiet; "all's well."

[20]安然無懼 tranquil and fearless.

安眠 or 安睡 peaceful sleep.

安眠藥 anodynes; hypnotics.

↓安·靜 quiet, absence of noise.

安·靖 tranquil; peace after trouble or disaster.

↓[25]安·靜不動 at rest.

安禪 to sit absorbed in meditation—as a Buddhist.

安舒·的日·子 "days of refreshing." See below. A. 20.

安謐 quiet, in repose.

安車 a small one-horse chariot in which the occupant sat—given to honour aged statesmen.

[30]安輿 to take charge of aged parents.

安默 to reflect; to consider.

(a) Contented, at ease. To rest in.

安俗樂業 contented with one's lot.

安分守己 to mind one's own business. A.c. 安分[4].

安分[4]養福 contentment develops happiness.

安命 to accept one's lot; contented.

[5]安土 to dwell contentedly on one's native soil; to be contented anywhere.

安坐靜觀 to sit quietly looking on.

安坐而食 to sponge on another.

安堵 to dwell in contentment and undisturbed security.

安家 funds alloted to support the home; to marry.

[10]安居 to dwell in peace.

安居樂業 to live in peace and be content with one's occupation.

安康 hearty; vigorous.

安於所遇 content in any circumstances.

安樂 joyful; at ease; content.

[15]安樂公 a man of pleasure.

安樂棄予 now you are in easy circumstances, you cast me off.

安歇 to rest; to lodge at; to sleep.

安步當車 to walk quietly is as good as riding in a carriage—poor but contented.

安肆 careless, because at ease.

[20]安舒 contented; comfortable. See above.—27.

安賤固窮 humble, yet enduring poverty with firmness and content.

安·逸 or 安佚 indolent; slothful.

安適 to feel at home; comfortable.

安閑 leisure; idleness.

(b) To pacify; to soothe; to settle.

安人 to pacify the people; title of wives of former sixth grade officials.

安心 to compose the mind. See below. C.

安慰 to comfort.

安扶 to support and protect.

[5]安撫 or 撫慰 to soothe; to pacify.

安民 to quiet the people; to forbid looting and violence.

安瀾 to quiet the waves—river rising without bursting its banks, i.e., the country is at peace.

安社稷 to tranquilize the state.

安神 to calm the spirits; to dedicate an idol.

[10]安胎符 anti-abortion charms.

安邊 to settle frontier troubles.

安 體 定 神 to calm oneself in a crisis.

(c) **Intentionally.**

安 心 with intent. *See above.* B. 2.

安 心 害 人 intentionally injuring others.

(d) **To place; to fix on; to arrange.**

安 上 to fix on something that has become loose, as a hammer-head.

安 不 上 it cannot be fixed on properly; irrelevant.

安 主 文 pacificatory ode to tablet of deceased.

安 妥 or 安 穩 firm; solid; secure; stable.

⁵安 定 to decide; to settle.

安 帖 settled; satisfactory.

安 席 to arrange positions (of guests) at table.

安 抵 to arrive safely.

安 排 to appoint, to arrange.

¹⁰安 插 to get a situation for a person.

安 營 to pitch a camp.

安 立 to establish; to set up.

安 置 or 安 放 to put in its place; to lay down; to arrange.

安 葬 to inter.

¹⁵安 處 to settle in a place.

安 設 to arrange; to set out; to place.

安 設 權 the right of placing pipes, telephone wires, etc., across a neighbouring property when it is essential to making connections, or when it would entail heavy expense if crossing was avoided.

安 身 to hide; to stay in; to settle.

安 頓 to prepare—as a guest room; to arrange; to keep quiet.

(e) **An interrogative, how? where?**

安 取 禮 .... Why do you not show propriety?

安 在 Where?

　你 的 上 帝 安 在 Where is now your God?

安 從 授 之 From whom did you learn?

⁵安 得 How can it be?

安 所 往 乎 Where can I go?

安 敢 How dare you?

安 有 How can there be?

安 知 How can you know?

¹⁰安 能 How can it be?

安 處 Where?

安 處 先 生 one who is anywhere, who does not exist. Mr. Nobody.

(f) **Naturally, without effort.**

安 安 naturally; with ease; poised.

安 行 without constraint; slow in action.

或 安 而 行 之 some practice (their obligations) with a natural ease.

(g) **Used to represent foreign sounds.**

安 南 Annam.

安 培 amperes.

安 士 ounce.

安 琪 兒 angel.

安 立 甘 Anglican.

按⁴ **To place the hand on; to press down. Introductory word to an editorial note.**
27

按 下 to press down; not to mention

按 紐 to grasp the sword.

按 手 to press down with the hand.

⁵按 捺 massage; to press down firmly.

按 板 to press the keys—to tune.

按 摩 massage.

按 脈 to feel the pulse.

(a) **To stop; to repress.**

按 住 to repress.

按 抑 restraint.

按 止 to cause to stop.

按 轡 to rein in a horse.

↑按 兵 不 動 to keep troops entrenched.

(b) **To examine.**

按 問 to examine and judge a case.

按 察 to examine.

按 察 司 former title of a Provincial Judge.

按 治 to judge and punish according to law.

按 院 former name for Provincial Court.

(c) **According to; as.**

按 例 or 按 法 according to law.

按 值 *ad valorem*.

按 圖 索 驥 to select a horse according to a picture - very stupid; bigoted.

[this appearance.

按 外 貌 取 人 to judge a person by

⁵按 戶 派 丁 to levy troops according to the number in each house.

按 數 or 按 額 according to number; proportionately.

按 時 候 according to the season; at stated periods.

按 月 支 取 to advance (money) monthly.

按 月 輪 流 in monthly rotation.

¹⁰按 期 according to the stated periods.

按 本 分 mind one's own business.

按 法 嚴 懲 deal with it according to the rigour of the law.

按 畝 抽 捐 to levy taxes according to the acreage.

按 碼 索 字 reckon the characters according to the figures—in telegrams.

¹⁵按 著 or 按 照 as; according to.

按 著 理 according to reason.

按 部 就 班 orderly; well-behaved; careful to follow the prescribed way.

按 頭 製 帽 fit the hat to the head—be guided by circumstances.

按 點 reckon up one by one.

案⁴ **A table. A bench or bar before a judge.**
28

案 子 a table. *See below.* A. 6.

案 板 a chopping board.

案 頭 on the table. [or surprise.

拍 案 to strike the table in anger

書 案 a study table.

香 案 an altar for incense.

(a) **A case at law. Legal records.**

案 事 to examine into the facts.

案 件 or 公 案 a case; a trial.

案 件 未 清 there are cases not yet settled.

案 例 law cases.

⁵案 因 the case is owing to....

案 子 a case at law. *See above.*—1.

案 尚 未 決 the case is *sub-judice*.

案 情 抄 錄 copy of the records of a case; the minutes.

案 情 相 似 a similar case.

¹⁰案 房 record office.

案 據 legal precedents; records of cases.

案 查 the records show that....

案 歸 公 斷 case referred to the public for decision.

案 照 it is on record that....
[15] 案 牘 or 案 卷 records of cases.
案 牘 通 明 here all cases are thoroughly understood.
案 由 or 案 情 details of a case.
案 結 the conclusion of a case.
案 首 first on the list of students.
[20] 案 驗 to investigate a case.
不 到 案 non-appearance.
傳 案 summon to appear at court.
刑 名 案 件 criminal case.
反 案 to reverse a decision.
[25] 命 案 manslaughter or murder case.
和 案 amicable settlement of a case.
在 案 has been brought before the court.
定 案 a decision; a judgement.
慘 案 a tragic case.   case.
[30] 懸 案 to remand a case; a pending
本 案 the case before the court.
清 案 牘 to clear off pending or neglected business.
立 案 to register; to institute proceedings. 檔 案 files; archives.
翻 案 to reopen a case.
陳 案 old cases.

(b) Used like 按 No. 27. To place the hand on; to repress.

案 摩 to massage.
案 撫 戌 國 to pacify the frontier tribes.

鞍 [1] A saddle.
29
鞍 前 馬 後 officious.
鞍 心 子 the seat of a saddle.
鞍 橋 a saddle—the shape of a saddle is like a bridge, therefore it has this name.
鞍 韂 or 鞴 saddle and flaps.
備 鞍 子 to saddle a horse.

俺 [3] Personal pronoun. I, used in Shantung.
30
俺·們 we.
俺·的 mine.

唵 [3] A sound used by Buddhists for transliterating foreign sounds. To eat food with the hand.
31
唵 嘛 呢 叭 𠺀 吽 Om-mani-pad-me-hum. Invocation largely

used in Tibet as a means of averting evil. Variously interpreted—"O jewel in the lotus," is the most quoted, but it is also explained as an invocation to Mani.

腌 [3] Closed eyes.
32

菴 } [1] A hut. A small Buddhist
庵 } temple, nunnery or monastery.
33
菴 堂 a convent; a Buddhist shrine.
菴 廬 soldiers' huts.
菴 觀 寺 院 Buddhist nunneries and monasteries and Taoist monasteries.
入 菴 to become a nun.
山 菴 a summer retreat.

鵪 [1] See below.
34
鵪·鶉 The quail.

揞 [3] To cover with the hand; to hide. To suppress. To extinguish. To press on.
35
揞 滅 to extinguish.
揞 脈 to feel the pulse.

暗 [4] Dark; cloudy; obscure.
36
暗 世 the dark ages. =黑 暗 時 代
暗 室 a dark room.
暗 昧 obscure.
暗 澹 dull, not fresh in appearance.
暗 箱 a camera.
暗 虛 eclipse of the moon. =月 蝕

(a) Hidden.
暗 中 摸 索 to grope in the dark. See below. B. 1, 2.
暗 合 unintentional agreement.
暗 寓 to insinuate.
暗 想 to meditate; to reflect.
[5] 暗 流 subterranean flow.
暗 溝 underground or covered drain.
暗 火 hidden fire, smouldering.
暗 礁 hidden rocks; used fig.

暗 示 a suggestion; a hint.
[10] 暗 笑 to laugh in the sleeve.
暗 藏 to conceal.
暗 說 to hint.
暗 輪 propeller of a steamer.
暗 輪 汽 船 screw steamer.
[15] 雙 暗 輪 twin propellers.

(b) Secret.
暗 中 in secret. See above. A. 1.
暗 中 運 動 secret agitation.
暗 號 secret mark or sign; password.
暗 地 in secret; behind the back.
[5] 暗 害 人 命 to injure another secretly.
暗 探 detectives.
暗 暗 的 secretly.
暗 殺 assassination.
暗 潮 secret disaffection; covert unrest.
[10] 暗 碼 code.
暗 碼 電 報 code telegram.
暗 算 to plot in secret.
暗 箭 secret arrow—covert attack.
暗 箭 難 防 a covert attack is hard to avoid.
[15] 暗 記 secret marks; to memorize.
暗 訪 民 情 secret inquiries into the condition of the masses.
暗 射 地 圖 map with numbers for names of places; outline map.

諳 [1] Versed in; fully acquainted with.
37
諳 曉 to have a good knowledge of.
諳 究 well acquainted with.
諳 練 or 諳 習 or 諳 識 or 諳 達 skilled in; accustomed to.

闇 [4] To shut the door; to withdraw Dark; eclipse. Evening.
38
闇 同 or 闇 合 accordance with the ideas of another without previous consultation.
闇 弱 ignorant and irresolute.
闇 昏 時 night; evening.
闇 淺 obscure and superficial—of literature.
[5] 闇 漠 gloomy; dark.
闇 然 而 日 章 concealed, yet daily becoming more illustrious.
闇 蔽 dull and stupid.
闇 行 to go about in the dark; the behaviour in private.

閉 門 謝 客 to close the door and refuse visitors.

暗 [3] Very dark and black. Intense black.
39   Also read yen[3].

AN. (NGAN.)   (ㄢ)

岸 [4] Shore; bank; beach; coast.
40

岸 上 on the bank.
岸 畔 a bund; path by a river.
岸 陡 the bank is steep.
上 岸 to go ashore.
下 岸 to embark.
彼 岸 "that shore."—the next world.

(a) The end of a journey.

回 頭 是 岸 the shore is just behind you—repent, and reformation is easy.
道 岸 the end of the way—the shore of wisdom.

(b) A high forehead.

岸 巾 or 岸 幘 with forehead bare and kerchief over the head—in undress.

(c) Valorous or eminent.

岸 忽 proud; supercilious.
岸 然 loftily.
魁 岸 a hero; a valiant man.

(d) A lock-up.

宜 岸 宜 獄 either the lock-up or the gaol.

ANG.   (ㄤ)

航 [1] See below.
41   Also read ang[3], k'ang[4].

骯 髒 dirty; filthy. Fat; stiff.

盎 [4] A basin or dish. Sleek; well-favoured. Abundant.
42   A musical instrument.

盎 斯 "ounce."
盎 然 abundant.
盎 盂 a bowl.
盎 盎 abundant.

胦 [1]
43   The navel.

ANG. (NGANG.) (ㄤ)

卬 卬 [2] High. To raise. Used for the pronoun *I*. Inter. 昂 No. 45.
44

卬 卬 dignified appearance.
卬 自 myself.
卬 貴 high, or rising in price.

昂 [2.1] To rise; to raise prices. Lofty. Bold. Pompous.
45

昂 昂 movement of a horse; clear, bright—as a gem.
昂 昂 氣 象 a pompous bearing.
昂 然 dignified; exalted.
昂 然 無 懼 dignified and fearless.
[5] 昂 聳 lofty.
昂 藏 dignified.
昂 貴 rising in price.
昂 頭 to lift up the head.

AO.   (ㄠ)

奧 [4] Mysterious; obscure.
46

奧 區 the interior—of the land.
奧 妙 mysterious; marvellous; a mystery.
奧 意 a subtle meaning.
奧 旨 an obscure purpose.
[5] 奧 秘 subtle; hidden; mystery.
奧 義 a hidden meaning.
奧 衍 involved, subtle and profound—as literature.
深 奧 obscure and difficult to understand.

(a) Used for transliterating.

奧 地 利 Austria.

(b) The south-west corner of the house where the household gods used to be placed. The place of honour in the house.

奧 主 a popular leader, one who occupies a place of honour.
祭 奧 to worship the household gods.
與 其 媚 於 奧 rather than pay court to the south-west corner. *See* No. 7615-11.

懊 [4]
47   To regret. Angry; vexed.

懊 喪 disappointed; dissatisfied.
懊 恨 to hate.
懊 悔 to regret; to reproach oneself.
懊 悶 distressed; regretful.
懊 惱 angry; vexed.
懊 憹 to regret.
懊 淘 sorrowful; melancholy.

澳 [4] A bay. A bank. A dock.
48

澳 洲 or 澳 大 利 亞 Australia.
澳 甲 or 澳 長 headman of a fishing station.
澳 門 Macao.

襖 [3] A coat; a jacket; a robe.
49

隩 [4] A headland; a cove. Warm. Site for building.
50

隩 隈 headlands and bays.
四 隩 旣 宅 everywhere there was land made available for dwellings.

媼 [3] An old woman. Also read wên[3].
51

媼 婆 female examiner of corpses.
媼 娘 an old maid.
媼 神 the Goddess of Earth.

鏖 [1] Desperate fighting.
52

鏖 兵 to fight; to slaughter.
鏖 戰 a bloody battle.
鏖 糟 a fight to the death; obstinate; unclean.
鏖 騙 to deceive; to impose on.

AO. (NGAO.)   (ㄠ)

鏊 [4] Haughty. Vigorous.
53

鏊 盪 舟 Ngao could propel a boat on dry land.

敖 [2] To ramble. Proud. Tall.
Inter. next.
54

敖 敖 very tall.
敖 遊 or 遨 遊 to travel.

傲 [4] Proud; haughty; overbearing.
55

傲 佯 (*chiang*[4]) wilful; obstinate.
傲 口 difficult to pronounce.
傲 容 a haughty bearing.
傲 岸 overbearing; proud and unfriendly.
[5]傲 很 亂 德 a scornful bearing injures a man's excellencies.
傲 慢 rude; insolent; disrespectful.
傲 暴 tyrannical.
傲 氣 a proud temper.
傲 視 to regard with contempt.
[10]傲 縱 regardless of the advice or opinions of others.
傲 霜 枝 branches that have withstood the frost.
傲 骨 self-respecting; independent.

嗷 [2] A loud clamour. Hum of many voices.
56

嗷 嗷 a sound of wailing.
嗷 嘈 clamour; hubbub.
嘈 嗷 noise of instruments.

廒 [2] A granary.
57

倉 廒 a granary.

摋 擊 [4] To rattle; to shake. To smite.
58

摋 殺 to smite to death.
摋 簽 to shake up the divining slips.
撒 骰 ·子 to shake dice.

熬 [2] To boil; to decoct; to simmer.
59

熬 波 出 素 to boil sea water and extract white salt.
熬 煉 to boil and smelt—to discipline.
熬 粥 or � 熬 or 煮 熬 to boil congee.

熬 膏 to prepare opium for smoking—to simmer to a paste.
熬 藥 to decoct medicine. *ao*[1] or *ao*[2] in preceding 3 examples

(a) To keep awake through the night.

熬 夜 or 打 熬 or 夙 夜 to work at night; to watch by a sick bed.
熬 眼 皮 ·子 to be awake all night.

(b) To endure; to worry.

熬 不 過 刑 罰 unable to endure torture.
熬 煎 to harass; to worry.

獒 [2] A large fierce dog over four feet high.
60

螯 [2] Nippers of crabs and similar creatures.
61

謷 [2] Slander; calumniation. Appearance of greatness. Sound of weeping.
62

謷 乎 大 哉 How great!
謷 謷 sound of many weeping; reckless talk; slander.
謷 醜 to calumniate.

遨 [2] To ramble; to travel for pleasure.
63

遨 嬉 a pleasure excursion.
遨 遊 to roam.

鏊 [2.4.] A flat, iron cooking-plate for cakes.
64

鏊 ·子 an iron cooking-plate.

驁 [2] A vicious horse. Stubborn.
65

驁 放 uncontrolled and reckless.
驁 蹇 stubborn and undisciplined.

鰲 鼇 [2] A huge sea-turtle, said to support the earth.
66

鰲 峯 or 鰲 掖 or 鰲 禁 ancient names for the *Hanlin* Academy.
鰲 戴 expression of gratitude—I bear a weight (of favours) like the *ngao*.
鰲 抃 clapping and dancing with delight.

鰲 足 legs of a huge turtle used as supports for the earth.
鰲 魚 a species of scorpœna.
獨 占 鰲 頭 first in the final Hanlin examinations.

翱 [2] To soar like a bird.
67

翱 翔 to wheel in the air; to soar; to roam.

CHA. (ㄓㄚ)

喳 [1] To give assent to; to respond.
68

喳 喳 Yes, that is so.
喳 喳 ·的 亂 叫 twittering to each other—sparrows.

渣 [1] Sediment; refuse; dregs.
69

渣 ·子 any refuse.
渣 滓 leavings; refuse; siftings.
荳 渣 refuse from beans after making curd.

踃 [1] To tread on; to walk through.
70

踃 坭 to tramp through mud.
踃 雨 to walk through rain.

攎 揸 [1] A handful. To pick up with the fingers. To seize. A span. ≡ 1417 抓.
71

攎 得 穩 held fast.
攎 爛 to crush to pieces.
攎 緊 hold it tightly.

樝 [1] A sour red fruit of the size of a cherry; a species of hawthorn. See No. 106.
72

山 ·樝 糕 a jelly made from haws.

齇 [1] Pimples; blotches. Rosacae.
73

酒 齇 "grog blossoms."

奓 [1] To open out; to stretch open. To brag.
74

奓 戶 to open a door.

豝 腿 to straddle the legs.
豝 言 to boast; to draw the long bow.
豝 闊 widely extended.

吒
咤 [4] To shout with anger. To upbraid. To pity.
75

吒 叱 angry shouts.

挓 [4] To open out; to expand.
76

挓 挱 to expand—as flowers.

髽 [1] To dress the hair. Also read *chua*[1].
77

髽 髻 ancient style of hairdressing for mourning, binding a net of hemp in with the hair.
婦 人 髽 於 室 the wife · loosely netted her hair and sat in her room.

唶 [4] A sigh; a groan. Loud laughter.
78

唶 唶 cries of birds.

禚 [1] Imperial sacrifice of thanksgiving to the earth for crops, offered at the end of the year. The name varied in different dynasties.
79

乍 [4] At first; for the first time.
80

乍 來 to arrive for the first time.
乍 見 or 乍 會 to meet for the first time.
乍 聞 to hear for the first time.

(a) Suddenly; unexpectedly; abruptly; inadvertently.

乍 到 to arrive unexpectedly.
乍 可 rather than.
乍 富 sudden wealth.
乍 晴 to clear up suddenly—of the weather.
乍 涼 乍 熱 now cold, now hot—of the weather.
乍 然 abruptly.
乍 猛 的 or 猛 乍 的 suddenly.
乍 進 to enter suddenly.

瘂 [4] Scrofulous swellings and sores.
81

瘂 腮 running sores on the cheeks; the mumps.

詐 [4] To deceive; artful; false.
82

詐 作 不 知 pretended ignorance.
詐 偽 false; counterfeit.
詐 冒 to counterfeit.
詐 善 hypocrisy.
[5] 詐 巧 cunning tricks of deceit.
詐 故 clever stratagem.
詐 敗 to feign defeat.
詐 晴 temporarily fine after long rain.
詐 欺 取 財 to defraud by a swindle; to blackmail.
[10] 詐 狂 to feign madness.
詐 病 or 詐 疾 malingering.
詐 老 實 feigned simplicity.
詐 言 or 詐 語 falsehoods.
詐 淡 falsehood; deceitful tricks.
[15] 詐 謀 an artful scheme.

醡
榨 [4] A press for extracting oil, sugar or spirits. To squeeze; to express.
83

醡 房 a house or shed where there is an oil or similar press.

鮓 [5] A condiment made from minced fish salted. Preserved fish.
84

鮓 魚 a species of jellyfish, crabs and shrimps follow it.

CHA. (ㄔㄚ)
(Chah)

劄 [2.5.] To prick. A document; a contract. Subordinates. Stationed at. Inter. 札 No. 87.
85

劄 單 a contract for goods.
劄 文 or 紙 劄 or 劄 子 instructions from a superior officer.
劄 知 to communicate with a subordinate.
劄 記 to record in detail.
[5] 劄 詢 to write inquiring.
劄 請 to request that.
劄 貨 to buy goods to arrive.

劄 開 instructions stating that....

扎 [1.5.] To pull up—as weeds. To pierce. Inter. 劄 No. 85.
86

扎 傷 to stab.
扎 入 to stick into.
扎 根 to take root.
扎 營 or 扎 寨 to make a stockade; to camp.
[5] 扎 猪 to stick a pig.
扎 破 to pierce.
扎 透 to pierce through.
扎 鍼 acupuncture.

(a) To cut out.

扎 花 to make artificial flowers.
紙 扎 paper images, etc., burnt at funerals.

(b) To bind; to fasten.

扎 實 strong; robust; solid.
扎 撐 to make a vigorous effort.
扎 緊 to bind tightly.
扎 裹 to repair; to bind up.

札 [2.5.] A thin wooden tablet, anciently used for writing letters. A letter. A document sent from a superior. Inter. 劄 No. 85.
87

札 委 orders to undertake a particular work.
札 文 a despatch from a superior.
札 行 to send orders to.
札 記 to record in detail.
信 札 letters.
寶 札 your esteemed letter.
簡 札 writing tablets; blocks for printing.
華 札 your valued favour.

(a) To die young. Plates or layers of armour.

民 不 夭 札 the people do not die untimely.
徹 七 札 焉 pierced the seven layers of his armour.

蚻 [2.5.] Small species of cicada.
88

炸
煠
灼 [2.5.] To fry in fat or oil. To scald.
89

炸 熟 to fry well.
炸 糕 fried cakes.
炸 肉 丸 to fry meat balls.
炸 麻 花 to fry sweet twisted pastry-strips.

(a) Read *cha⁴*. To explode; to burst.
炸 彈 bombs.
炸 擊 to bomb; explosion.
炸 炮 a mortar; bombs.
炸 藥 high explosives.
炸 裂 to explode; to split.
炸 裂 性 explosive nature.
炸 雷 a clap of thunder.

劏 2.5.
鍘 A hinged shear or long knife for cutting fodder, sheet-iron, etc. To cut up.
90
劏 刀 the long knife as above.
劏 草 to cut straw into chaff.

鍘 1.5. A lever-knife for cutting chaff, etc.
91

眨 3.5. To wink.
92
眨* 眼 or 眨 目 to wink.
眨 眼 會 意 to intimate a wish by a wink.
眨* 眼 兒 的 工 夫 in the twinkling of an eye.

柵 2.5. A palisade; a railing of posts; window-bars; movable upright posts that serve as doors.
93
柵 夫 the keeper of the street gate.
柵 欄 or 柵 欞 or 柵 閘 gates that divide the streets into sections.
大 柵 欄 names of two streets in §

閘 2.5. A flood-gate; a water-gate; a lock in a canal. A barrier.
94
閘 卡 or 關 閘 a Customs barrier; a pass.
閘 口 entrance to a lock.
閘 欄 street gates, dividing a city into wards.
閘 水 to shut off the water by a lock.
閘 河 a name for the Grand Canal.
閘 門 or 閘 板 a lock-gate.

牐 4.5. Sluice gate. To block a door with a board. Inter. with preceding. The 'proper' character for 94.
95
牐 版 shutters of a shop.
下 牐 to let down the sluice.

CH'A. (ㄔㄚˊ)

叉 1 To cross the arms; to interlace the fingers; to fold the hands when bowing. A prong; a fork.
96
叉 形 forked.
叉 手 to interlace the fingers.
叉 灰 lime; mortar.
叉 牙 forked, as branches.
叉 竿 a pronged stick.

扠 1 To pick up with pincers or fork. To drive out.
97
扠 上 去 hang it up—on a nail.
扠 出 去 turn him out.
扠 腰 arms akimbo.

杈 1 Fork of a tree. A pitchfork.
98
杈 子 a *chevaux-de-frise*.
杈 枒 forked branches.
杈 雞 的 a fowl stealer.

汊 4 A branching stream.
99
汊 港 branching creeks.

衩 4 The open seam of a garment which allows freedom of movement.
100
衩 衣 single breasted garments.
衩 褲 half-length leggings drawn over the trousers.

茶 2 The tea plant. An infusion of tea leaves or any other infusion.
101
茶 具 a tea-service.
茶 几 a small side table; a teapoy.
茶 博 士 keeper of a teashop.
茶 壺 a teapot.
⁵茶 壺 桶 wadded case for keeping tea hot.
茶 客 tea dealer; one who comes to buy the new teas.

茶 市 tea-market.
茶 師 a tea-taster.
茶 引 special permit to tea merchants in Sung dynasty.
¹⁰茶 戶 a tea merchant.
茶 房 a tea attendant in restaurants or on steamers, etc.; waiter.
茶 晶 variety of quartz having the clear colour of strong green tea.
茶 會 a tea meeting.
茶 末 or 碎 茶 tea dust; refuse tea.
¹⁵茶 杯 or 茶 缸 or 茶 盅 tea cups.
茶 業 the tea trade.
茶 槍 茶 旗 tea buds with tiny leaves.
茶 法 law regarding taxes on tea.
茶 油 oil expressed from the seeds of 茶 梅 a species of camellia.
²⁰茶 焙 bamboo tray used in firing tea.
茶 盤 a tea tray. 茶 碗 tea cup.
茶 碟 saucers.
茶 禮 betrothal presents; to receive which may be called 受 茶.
茶 箱 tea chests.
²⁵茶 經 book written in T'ang dynasty describing the origin and preparation of tea.
茶 腳 the dregs of the teapot.
茶 舖 or 茶 店 tea-dealers' shops.
茶 船 = 茶 托 saucers for teacups.
茶 花 the camellia.
³⁰茶 葉 tea leaves.
茶 褐 色 a greenish brown, rather dark shade.
茶 話 會 a reception; tea-party.
茶 課 tax on tea.
茶 質 theine.
³⁵茶 鈐 a bent-iron apparatus used in firing tea.
茶 錢 gratuities given to servants who bring presents; any gratuity.
茶 青 色 a greenish brown.
茶 食 or 茶 果 cakes for eating with tea.
茶 食 店 a confectioner.
⁴⁰茶 飯 tea and rice—food.
茶 餅 or 茶 磚 brick tea.
茶 館 or 茶 居 or 茶 坊 tea-shops for sale of tea and hot-water.
茶 點 lunch; a light meal.
上 茶 the finest tea.
⁴⁵山 茶 wild tea.
武 彝 茶 Bohea tea, from name of place.

---

* 眨 巴 may also be used.
§ Peiping, pron. *ta⁴-cha⁴·lar* and *ta⁴·sha-lar⁴*.

搽 茶 to pick tea.
毛 茶 unfired green tea.
⁵⁰淡 茶 weak tea.
濃 茶 strong tea.
煎 茶 or 烹 茶 to boil tea, or water for tea.
紅 茶 black tea.

搽² To rub on; to smear.
102

搽 瘡 to anoint sores.
搽 粉 to paint the face.
搽 脂 抹 粉 to powder and paint.
搽 藥 to spread a plaster.

查² To seek out; to search into. Used at the beginning of a statement indicating— it would appear . . . , it seems that . . . ; I find that . . . ;
103

查·不 出 來 unable to find out.
查·出 to find out; to make a discovery.
查 傳 to summon to appear.
查 哨 a patrol.
⁵查 問 or 查 訊 make official inquiries.
查 字 典 to search the dictionary.
查 察 make official inquiries.
查 對 無 訛 audited and found correct.
查 帳 to audit accounts.
¹⁰查 帳 員 an auditor.
查 庫 inspection of the treasury.
查 抄 confiscation of an official's property for embezzlement or misuse of funds.
查 拿 to search for and arrest.
查 探 to find out by inquiries.
¹⁵查 收 to examine and receive.
查 明 to examine; to search into.
查 核 to investigate.
查 案 to investigate a case at law.
查 清 to clear up by an investigation.
²⁰查 照 to take official notice.
查 照 轉 知 note this and make it known in turn.
查 看 to look into a matter.
查 禁 to prohibit.
查 稟 to examine and report.
²⁵查 究 to hold an inquiry.
查 經 班 a class for Bible study.
查 考 to search out; to investigate.
查 考 憲 政 investigation of constitutional governments.

查 街 to patrol the streets.
³⁰查 議 to make a decision.
查 辦 examine into and deal with accordingly.
查 銷 to cancel.
查 驗 to verify; to search into.
查 點 to check a list or goods.

(a) A raft. = 106.

巨 查 the immense raft of *Yü* the Great.

齹² To break off. Read *ch'a*⁴. A potsherd, a flaw.
104

瓦 齹·子 piece of broken tile or pottery.

差¹⋅⁴ To err; to mistake. To differ. Error; discrepancy; unlike.
105

差⁴一 點ₙ it differs a little; very slight difference.
差¹一 著¹全 局 輸 one false move loses the whole game.
差⁴不 多ₙ or 差¹不 離 or 差¹不 許 多 or 差⁴不 遠 not very different; almost the same; not far out; near enough.
差¹之 毫 厘,失 之 千 里 the slightest divergence leads far astray.
⁵差¹債 or 差¹錢 to owe money.
差¹分 an even series of numbers.
差⁴多 a great difference.
差¹得 遠 very different; quite unlike.
差¹式 to make an error.
¹⁰差¹異 strange; different.
差¹級 數 arithmetical progression.
差¹錯 or 差¹忒 an error; a blunder; deviation.
差⁴錯 脚 to make a false step; to err.
差¹點 point of difference.
¹⁵日 差¹ diurnal variation. (*astron*.).
年 差¹ annual variation.
週 期 變 差¹ periodic variation.

(a) Read *ch'ai*¹. To send; to depute on official business. Servant of an official.

差·事 special official business.
差·來·的 sent; the one sent.
差·使 a commissioner; official employment.

差 傳 to send a summons.
⁵差 委 or 差 派 to depute.
差 官 officer sent on special business.
差·役 or 差·人 an official messenger; a runner.
差 徭 government service.
差 拘 to send and arrest.
¹⁰差 會 foreign mission board; a mission.
差 送 to send under escort.
差 遣 to send; to commission.
差 頭 head of *yamen* runners.
當 差 on duty in government offices; servant.

(b) Read *tz'ŭ*¹. Uneven; irregular. To go wrong. *See* 6685 G.

差 別 or 差 池 a distinction; different from.
差 等 peculiarities.

槎² A raft. To hew. To fell
楂 trees.
2nd form u.f. 檟 No. 72.
106

槎 枒 wood cut slantingly.
楂 楂 twittering of birds.
乘 槎 to go by raft.

侘⁴ To boast; irresolute.
107

侘 傺 disappointed; to fail in attaining one's purpose.

詫⁴ To wonder at; to brag.
108

詫·異 to be surprised at; amazed.

岔⁴ The point where roads fork. To diverge. To go astray.
109

岔 道 or 岔 路 a fork in the road; a diverging path.
打 岔 to interrupt.

CH'A.　　(彳丫)
(Ch'ah)

刹⁴⋅⁵ Buddhist monastery. A shrine.
110

刹 竿 a staff for banners before a temple.
刹 那 the minutest fraction of time, from Sanskrit *kshana*.

實 刹 your precious monastery—conventional phrase addressed to priests.

察譽 2.5.
111 To examine into judicially. To find out.

察 出 to ascertain.
察 合 to examine and find correct.
察 問 to inquire into.
察 奪 to try a case and give a decision.
¹察 察 爲 明 harsh investigation, paying attention only to vexatious trifles.
察 度 (to⁴) to consider; to give heed to.
察 找 to search for.
察 收 examine and receipt.
察 明 to ascertain clearly.
¹⁰察 核 to examine into and decide.
察 案 to investigate a case.
察 照 to take notice of. =103.20.

察 理 investigate the principle involved.
察 看 or 察 考 or 監 察 to look into.
¹⁵察 究 to investigate.
察 視 to investigate; to give consideration to.
察 言 觀 色 examine a man's words and observe his countenance—to measure his attention.
察 議 to weigh the pros and cons and arrange accordingly.
察 辨 to act after investigation.
²⁰密 察 private examination.
苛 察 severe, minute investigation.
警 察 policeman.

畬 2.5.
112 To separate the grain from the husk.

插 1.5.
113 To insert; to stick into.

插 入 to insert; to interpolate.
插 句 a parenthesis.
插 天 sticking into the sky—of high peaks.
插 屏 screens in front of doors which open on the public path.
⁵插 旗 to stick in flags; to plant a banner.

插 架 bookshelves.
插 柳 成 陰 to plant a willow slip hoping to enjoy the shade of the tree—working with far-seeing objects rather than for the present.
插 水 to wade.
插 消 a door bolt; also used for electric plug-in switch.
¹⁰插 燭 to stick in a candle—Chinese candles are stuck on to a spike in the candlestick.
插 班 to classify a pupil from another school according to his grade. An intermediate class.
插 畫 to insert maps, etc., into a book.
插 秧 or 栽 秧 to transplant young rice plants.
插 翅 to stick in wings—ambitious.
¹⁵插 花 to pay land taxes, which are due in one county, at the office of another county.
插 草 標 to put up a wisp of straw indicating that an article is for sale.
插 足 a position; a place.
插 路 燭 bamboo slips burnt by the roadside to attract demons.
插 關 to push the door bar home; the door bar.
²⁰插 電 開 關 electric plug-in switch.

(a) To interfere. To meddle.

插 手 or 插 身 to meddle officiously, to want a share in.
插 言 or 插 嘴 or 插 話 or 插 舌 to interrupt; to put in a word.
插 贓 to leave stolen articles secretly with another and accuse him of the theft.

鍤 2.5.
114 A spade. An iron bar for making holes.

CHAI. (坐历)

齋齋 1
115 To abstain from meat, wine, etc. To fast. Fasting; penance.

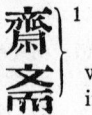

齋 僧 to feed Buddhist priests.
齋 壇 altar of fasting in Taoist halls.

齋 工 lay vegetarians in temples.
齋 戒 to abstain from meat and certain other things as a religious ordinance.
⁵齋 期 fast days.
齋 祈 or 齋 禱 to fast and pray.
齋 醮 Buddhist and Taoist sacrifices—fasting and prayers to avert calamity.
齋 飯 vegetarianism as a religious rite.
九 皇 齋 to fast on the first 9 days of the 9th lunar month, or for the whole month.
¹⁰化 齋 to beg for food, as Buddhist priests.
城 隍 齋 to fast on 1st and 15th of the month.
守 齋 to fast.
打 齋 to perform ritual to deliver souls in purgatory.
日 落 齋 daily fast till sunset.
¹⁵月 落 齋 to fast on the last day of the lunar month.
眞 武 齋 to fast on the 1st day of 1st, 3rd, 5th, 7th, and 9th, months.
竈 王 齋 to fast on the 1st, 15th, and 24th, of each month.
觀 音 齋 to fast on the 2nd, 6th, and 9th, of each month.
長 齋 perpetual abstinence from meat, wine, garlic, etc, or abstinence for three years.=長素
²⁰開 齋 to cease from observance of fasting as a rite.
食 齋 vegetarianism as a religious ordinance. = 喫素

(a) Refined; to purify. Pure.

齋 心 to purify the heart.
齋 慄 reverential awe.
齋 戒 沐 浴 to control the thoughts, fast and pray.
齋 莊 modest; reverent.

(b) A study; a library.

齋 夫 attendants in a library.
齋 居 to live in retirement or ease after a life of care.
齋 屋 a study; formerly a place of retirement for fasting.
聊 齋 a famous collection of weird stories by 蒲 松 齡.
齋 舍 a study or library.
書 齋 a study.
間 齋 a private room.

寨砦 [4]
116
A stockade; a military outpost. A walled village. A pen for stock.

寨·子 or 寨柵 a stronghold; a stockade.
山寨 hill fortress or refuge.
水寨 palisade of boats.

瘵 [4]
117
A wasting disease.

瘵愈 convalescent.
瘵瘵 consumption; wasting.
無自瘵焉 do not bring difficulties upon yourself.

債 [4]
118
A debt. To be in debt.

債主 or 債家 a creditor.
債人 a debtor.
債券 debentures or bonds.
債·務 debt; obligation.
[5]債務人 debtor.
債國 a debtor nation.
債多不愁 when debts are many one does not worry over them.
債息日重 debt and interest daily increasing.
債權 rights of creditor; right of claim.
[10]債權人 creditor.
債權人會議 meeting of creditors.
債權擔保 security for debt.
債權行爲 act of obligation. (legal).
債權證書 acknowledgement of debt.
[15]債票 debentures, etc.
債累 involved in debt.
免債 to cancel a debt.
公債票 government bonds.
公債證券 government securities.
[20]國債 national debts.
外債 loans from foreign powers.
放債 to lend money on usury.
討債 to dun for debts.
負債 to carry heavy debts.
[25]還債 to settle a debt by payment.

CH'AI.　(ㄔㄞ)

釵 [1]
119
A hairpin—women.

釵環 hairpins and ear-rings—ornaments.
釵簪 women's hair ornaments.
釵裙 hairpins and skirts—women.
釵釧 hairpins and bangles—ornaments.

儕 [2]
120
A class; a company. Sign of plural.

儕偶 companions; associates.
同儕 the same set.
我儕 or 吾儕 we, our class or set.

柴 [2]
121
Brushwood, faggots, fuel.

柴·火 or 柴薪 fuel.
柴米夫·妻 married to get necessities.
柴米油鹽 firewood, rice, oil, and salt—necessities of life.
柴荆 a humble abode.
[5]柴行 or 柴院·子 a reed yard; fuel-merchant's office. -hang[2]
柴車 an unornamented carriage; a fuel cart.
柴門 my cottage; my humble abode.
劈柴 split firewood—in short lengths.
火柴 matches.
柴毁 or 柴瘦 thin and worn, like a bundle of sticks.

(a) To make a burnt offering.

柴壇 altar for offering burnt sacrifice to Heaven.
柴望 burnt offering to heaven (柴) and offering to the hills and streams. (望).

豺犲 [2]
122
Ravenous beast, akin to the jackal; the wolf. Wicked; wolfish; cruel.

豺狗 a jackal.
豺狼 a wolf; fierce disposition.
豺狼當道 a wolf stops the road —said of evil men usurping authority.

瘥 [4]
123
To recover from any disease. Read ts'o[2]. An epidemic; epidemic disease.

瘥愈 convalescent.

蠆 [4]
124
An insect like a scorpion. Larva of the dragon fly.

蠆尾 said of Tsǔ-ch'an, whose father died on the road, leaving his son as a scorpion's tail to sting.

CHAN.　(ㄓㄢ)

占 [1]
125
To divine by casting lots. To observe signs; to foretell. Inter. 佔 No. 126.

占不應 [4] unfulfilled forecast.
占人 a prognosticator.
占候 to foretell the weather.
占候吉凶 to prophecy good or evil from meteorological phenomena.
[5]占兆 to observe omens.
占卜 or 占算 to divine; to cast lots.
占卦 to divine by means of the diagrams.
占口卦 to divine by what one first hears from a given person.
占坼 to divine from cracks in burnt tortoise-shell.
[10]占城 South Annam.
占夢 interpretation of dreams.
占年 to prognosticate for the coming year.
占應 or 占驗 a fulfilled divination.
占星家 astrologers. -術 -logy
[15]占燈花 telling fortunes from the wick of a lamp or candle.
占筮 witchcraft; sorcery.
占術 prognosticator's arts.
占象 astrology.
占風鐸 in ancient times pieces of jade were hung in bamboo groves outside the palace so that the breezes caused them to tinkle.

「≡佔

(a) Read chan[4]. To usurp; to seize.

占優勢 to hold a position of advantage.
占先 to assume precedence.
占奪 to appropriate lands, etc., belonging to others.
占有 "possession" (legal).
占有權 rights of possession.
占有物 property; possessions.
占有收回之訴 action for recovery of possession.
占領 to seize territory; "occupation."

佔⁴ To usurp; to take by force. Inter. preceding.
126

佔 上 風 to take the wind; to get the advantage of.

佔 人 妻 女 to s e i z e another's wife and daughters.

佔 便 (p'ien²)·宜 to peculate; to take advantage.

佔 先 to presume; to take front place.

⁵佔 地 步 to encroach; to occupy a position of advantage.

佔 多 to take more than a share.

佔 奪 to appropriate; to seize.

佔 據 to occupy forcibly; take possession.

佔 用 or 侵 佔 to encroach upon.

¹⁰佔 畢 to read carelessly, humming over the sounds and not seeking the meaning.

佔 踞 or 霸 佔 to occupy by force.

沾¹ To moisten, Inter. 霑 No. No. 132.
127

沾·染 steeped in; saturated with.

沾 泥 muddy—as shoes, etc.

沾 泥 絮 the willow catkins fall into the mud (no longer blown by the winds)—the mind at rest after cares.

沾 洽 steeped in; moistened by copious rains; full of; well learned.

⁵沾 潤 or 沾 漬 steeped in; imbued with.

沾 漑 時 雨 moistened with seasonable rains—also used of receiving kindness, etc.

沾 濡 or 沾 溺 to dip; to soak; to immerse.

沾 濕 damp; wet—garments, etc.

沾 透 saturated.

¹⁰沾 雨 moistened by rains.

(a) To receive benefits; to be a recipient of.

沾 光 to get an advantage; "by your leave."

沾 恩 to receive favours; under obligations.

沾 感 deeply indebted to; full of gratitude.

(b) To be infected by.

沾 塵 defiled; stained by dirt.

沾 寒 to take cold from damp, etc.

沾 染 世 俗 corrupted by the world.

沾 染 世 情 corrupted by the evil of the times.

沾 染 習·氣 corrupted by the prevailing customs.

沾 病 to take a disease.

沾 花 惹 草 enticing and seductive.

(c) Read t'ieh⁵. Self-satisfied. Harum-scarum.

沾 沾 自 喜 self-indulgent; frivolous.

(d) Read t'ien². River in S. E. Shansi.

站·⁴ To stand up; to stop.
128

站·不 住 or 站 立 不 住 unable to stand; unstable; untenable.

站 住 Stop! Stand still.

站 崗 to stand sentry; on duty as policemen on their beat.

站 班 to stand on duty; to line up.

⁵站 穩 to stand firmly.

站 立 or 站 起·來 to stand up; to erect.

站 籠 a cage in which a prisoner was confined till his death; the head was thrust through a hole in the top, and barely any support was provided for the body. A cruel punishment.

站·進·來 to stand inside.

站·開 stand aside; "move on."

（≡佔）

(a) To occupy; to take up room.

站 地 方 to take up room.

站 房·子 to occupy a house.

站 房 間 to occupy a room.

站 獨 房 to keep sole occupancy of a room in an inn.

白 站 地 土 to cumber the ground.

(b) A stage of a journey.

站 口 or 站 頭 a stopping place; end of a day's journey.

站 長 railway station-master.

車 站 railway station.

粘¹ To paste up; to attach to; to stick up. Also read nien².
129

粘·住 to adhere firmly.

粘 單 an enclosure in an official despatch.

粘·補 to paste a piece of paper over a wrongly written character.

粘 貼 to paste up; to post.

粘 送 to forward an enclosure.

粘 連 or 粘 附 to append; supplementary; annexed.

覘 1.4. To spy; to keep at. To take a sly glance at. Also read ch'an⁴.
130

覘 候 to look out for.

覘 其 醉 醒 see if he is sober.

覘 者 spies.

詀¹ Garrulous. Read ch'ê⁵. To whisper. To joke.
131

詀 詀 joking and chaffing.

詀 諵 to chatter; to whisper in the ear.

霑¹ To wet, to moisten. Inter. 沾 No. 127. ＝沾
132

霑·了 汚 穢 defiled; polluted.

霑·染 steeped in; saturated.

霑 泥 bespattered with mud.

霑 潤 or 霑 渥 soaked with.

⁵霑 濕 wet through; soaked.

霑 肌 wet to the skin.

霑 衣 soaked through the clothing.

霑 醉 helplessly drunk.

(a) To bestow favours; see under 沾 No. 127—A.

霑 恩 to be indebted to.

旃¹ A silken banner hanging from a staff bent over at the top. u.f. 氈, Felt. Used as a particle like 之 and 焉.
133

旃 帳 felt tents.

旃 檀 a deep-red hard wood, also written 栴檀, it is an imitation of the Sanskrit word, Chandana. Sandalwood.

旃 表 signal flag.

旜¹ A silken banner without ornament, used to herald princes in ancient times. Similar to the preceding.
134

氊 氈 毡 1
Felt; coarse fabrics used for rugs, carpets, wrappers, etc.
135

氈·子 a rug; felt.
氈 帽·子 felt caps.
氈 襪·子 felt socks.

顫[4] The head awry. Shivering, shaking, unsteady.
136 More commonly: ch'an[4]

顫 動 trembling; shaking, shivering.
顫 怒 shaking with anger.
顫 聲 an unsteady shaking voice, either from fear or cold.

饘 }
餰 } [1] Well-boiled congee or gruel. Thick, rich.
137

饘 粥 thick porridge; congee.

鸇 [1] A sparrow-hawk, very swift in flight.
138

展 [3] To open; to unroll.
139

展 卷[4] to open the roll; to open a book.
展 拜 to kotow.
展 放 to blossom out; to open.
展 看 to open up and look into.
[5]展 眉 to look pleasant.
展 笑 to break into smiles, or laughter.
展 翅 or 振翅 to spread the wings.
展 覽會 an exhibition.
展 誦 to open and read.
[10]展·開 to open out.
展·開 地·步 to spread the legs to be getting on.
↑ 展 望 outlook.
(a) To spread out; to extend.

展 佈 to spread.
展 修 鐵 路 extended railway construction.
展 假 to extend leave of absence.
展 技 to the extent of his ability.
[5]展 發 to exhibit.
展 眼 之 間 in the opening of an eye.
展 緩 to procrastinate.
展 舒 to expand; to make oneself comfortable.
展 轉 to turn it over in the mind.
[10]展 限 or 展期 to extend a time limit.

捵 [3] To wipe tears. To bind.
140

捵·布 a duster; a cloth for wiping a wet table, etc.

輾 [3] To turn half over; to roll over on the side.
141

輾 轉 to revolve; back and forth; over and over.
輾 轉 反 側 to toss to and fro— as when sleepless.
輾 轉 難 忘 constantly thinking of; unable to forget.

(a) Read nien[3]. To roll; to crush by rolling. ≡ 4719.

輾·了 他·的 頭 take off his head by passing the wheel over it.

斬 [3] To behead; to cut in two.
142

斬 伐 to subjugate, as rebels; to prune.
斬 傷 wounded by cutting.
斬 刈 to mow down.
斬 妖 to exercise evil influences.
[5]斬 新 brand-new. Also with 158, second form.
斬 斷 to cut off communications.
斬 決 execution by beheading.
斬 盡 to exterminate.
斬 罪 a capital offence.
[10]斬 衰 the heaviest mourning, of coarsest sackcloth with fringes, i.e., unhemmed; this is the garb worn for parents and husband, nominally for three years, actually for twenty-seven months. (chan[3]-ts'ui[1])
斬·開 to cut open.
斬 首 or 斬 頭[2]to behead.
斬 齊 perfectly uniform.
立 斬 summary execution by local authorities.

綻 [4] A seam which has come unsewn. To split. Rent.
143

綻·了 縫 the seam has come unsewn.
綻 線 frayed; to become unsewn.
綻 裂 ripped; split; unsewn.
打 綻 to caulk seams.
花 綻 the petals of a flower.

(a) A hint.

綻 露 to reveal a matter.
破·綻 a hint; also a rent or tear.

綻 [4] A seam which has come unsewn. Inter. preceding.
144

補 綻 to repair a rent.

蘸 [4] To dip into.
145

蘸·了 醋 to dip in vinegar.
蘸 濕 to soak in.
蘸 筆 to dip a brush in ink.

湛 [4] Deep, clear—as water.
146

湛 思 profound thought; brooding over.
湛 湛 deep; weighty. See below. A. 2.
湛 湛 江 水 兮 How deep is the river!
湛 碧 deep, clear water—from the jade-like colour.
湛 靜 profound quiet.

(a) To steep; to receive favour.

湛 恩 imbued with favours; under heavy obligations.
湛 湛 heavy dew—many favours received.
湛 露 heavy dew—under heavy obligation.

(b) Fresh.

湛 新 brand new; fresh.

戰 [4] To fight; to war. To contest.
147

戰 事 war.
戰 例 laws of war.
戰 具 weapons of war.
戰 利 品 prize of war; booty.
[5]戰 功 meritorious military service.
戰 務 things connected with warfare.
戰 勝 to fight to a victory.

戰 區 war-zone.
戰 史 history of a war.
[10]戰 國 belligerent n a t i o n s; the period of "Warring States" B.C. 403-221.

戰團 belligerents.

戰地 or 戰場 a battlefield.

戰壕 fighting-trenches.

戰壘 a fort; a defence.

¹⁵戰士 a warrior.

戰守 military operations.

戰局 a state of war.

戰役 war; active service.

戰征 a warlike expedition; to go to war against.

²⁰戰敗 defeat.

戰時佔領 occupation of territory during the time of war.

戰時公法 laws during period of war.

戰時國際法 international laws relating to war.

戰時徵發 war levies.

²⁵戰時禁制品 contraband of war.

戰時禁制海運 interdict of transportation during war.

戰時編制 war levies.

戰死 to die in battle.

戰法 or 戰術 military tactics.

³⁰戰爭 war; to wrangle.

戰爭行為 a hostile act. (legal).

戰略 or 戰策 military strategy. See No. 4075. A.1.ff.

戰線 (or 綫) the "front;" war-zone.

戰艦 or 戰船 warships.

³⁵戰艦政策 naval policy.

戰衣 military uniform.

↓作戰計畫 plan of campaign.

戰陣 in battle array.

戰鬥 to war; to wrangle and fight.

⁴⁰戰鬥力 fighting strength.

戰鬥員 combatant.

交戰 or 開戰 to engage in battle.

交戰區域 war-zone.

交戰國 belligerent nations.

⁴⁵停戰 a truce; cessation of battle.

免戰旗 flag of truce.

宣戰 to declare war.

挑戰 to challenge to a fight; to provoke strife.

死戰 a fight to a finish.

⁵⁰百戰百勝 invincible; "ever victorious."

血戰 a bloody battle.

非戰鬥員 non-combatants.

(a) To tremble; frightened.

戰慄 awestruck.

戰懼 scared; terrified.

戰戰兢兢的 trembling with fear.

戰色 of fearful countenance.

刁戰 to shiver.

棧⁴ A storehouse; a warehouse; a shop.
148

棧司 godown keeper.

棧單 receipt for goods in storage.

棧房 a warehouse; a godown.

棧租 storage charges.

貯棧 to put into storehouse or godown.

(a) A way made along a cliff.

棧道 planks laid across a dangerous, precipitous point. A covered way along a precipice.

(b) A hotel or inn.

客棧 a hotel.

(c) A hearse. A cart or barrow.

棧車 ancient form of vehicle made of wood and bamboo.

賓奠幣于棧 the visitors offered silks at the hearse.

(d) Read chien³. A shed or stable.

戀棧 loth to leave a place—as a horse its stable.

羊棧 a sheep pen.

馬棧 a stable.

盞³ A shallow cup for oil. A wine-cup. N. A. for lamps, etc.
149

盞子 the oil-cup of a Chinese lamp.

一盞燈 one lamp.

詹¹ To oversee; to direct. Verbose. Excellent. To reach. Sufficient.
150

詹事府 Imperial superintendent of instruction, charged with the studies of the heir-apparent.

瞻¹ To look up to, to reverence. To regard with respect.
151 Distinguish 1664.

瞻仰 to look up to with reverence.

瞻依 to look up to with trust.

瞻前顧後 circumspect.

瞻對 an audience with the emperor.

瞻彼淇澳 look at the winding course of the Ch'i.

瞻徇 to hold back from fear of giving offence; unduly lenient.

瞻望 to long for; to gaze at.

瞻視 or 瞻顧 to regard; to look up to.

譫¹ Talkative. Incoherent talk.
152

譫語 delirium; incoherent talk.

CH'AN.   (ㄔㄢ)

闡⁵ To open; to explain. Also read shan¹.
153

闡幽 to explain what is obscure.

闡拜天下 to enlarge the boundaries of empire.

闡明 or 闡達 to explain.

闡註 explanatory notes.

囅¹ To burst into laughter.
154

囅然而笑 to burst into loud laughter.

毚² A cunning hare. Cunning, artful.
155

毚兔 a crafty hare or rabbit.

毚欲 ardent longings.

儳³ Obstinate; stupid.
156

儳頭馬 a jibbing horse; a poor nag.

(a) Read ts'an¹. Irregular.

儳互 irregular; improper.

² Gluttonous; greedy.
157

嚵涎 mouth watering.

嚵獠 term of abuse for a glutton.

嚵燕 or 嚵嘴人 a glutton.

² A cliff. A precipitious peak. Second form also used in 142.5.
158

巉巖 precipitous slopes.

攙[1] To sustain; to support; to raise.
159

攙 扶 to uphold; to support—as a cripple.
攙 起 to assist a person to rise; to raise up.
攙 親 female relatives of the bridegroom who meet the bride and support her to the hall.
力 攙 顚 危 to support the feeble and the tottering.

(a) To mix, to blend. To supply.

攙 假 to adulterate.
攙 合 to blend; to mix.
攙 和 to blend flavours; to mix—also used in a social sense.
攙 和 差 吃 eat them mixed together.
⁵攙 嘴 to interrupt another when speaking.
攙 對 to add to; mix together.
攙 槍 a comet; a rebel leader—see No. 160.
攙 罅 to fill a crack.
攙 越 to interfere with; mixed up.
攙 雜 不 純 impure; diluted.

欃[1] A tree called 欃 檀, which grew near the grave of Confucius.
160

欃 槍 星 or 天 欃 a comet; the first is also used for a rebel leader.

讒[2] To slander; to misrepresent.
161

讒 人 a traducer; to slander.
讒 口 交 加 he is vilified everywhere.
讒 害 to injure by misrepresentation.
讒 毁 or 讒 謗 to vilify.
⁵讒 言 slander; defamation.
讒 言 惹 禍 calumny brings trouble.
讒 諂 to flatter.
讒 諂 面 諛 flattery.

鑱[2.4.] A chisel. To engrave.
162

鑱 頭 or 犁 頭 a coulter.
鑱 斧 mattock or hoe for weeding.

産[3] To bear offspring.
163

産 婦 a lying-in woman.
産 婆 or 穩 婆 a midwife.
産 後 熱 puerperal fever.
産 後 風 puerperal eclampsia.
⁵産 房 lying-in room.
産 期 time of child-birth.
産 生 or 生 産 to beget; to produce.
産 痛 birth pangs.
産 科 obstetrics.
¹⁰産 門 or 産 戶 the vagina.
産 難 to die in child-birth.
小 産 premature birth.
補 産 to nourish a woman after confinement.
難²産 difficult labour.

(a) Productions of a country. A native.

産 出 the output; productions.
産 品 products.
産 業 主 人 a producer.
産 業 國 有 state ownership of industries.
⁵産 物 productions.
産 額 rate of production; output.
土 産 local products.
水 産 marine products; fish, etc.
陳 良 楚 産 也 Ch'ên liang is a native of Ch'u.

(b) Livelihood.

制 民 之 産 to regulate the livelihood of the masses.
恒 産 a constant livelihood.
無 恒 産 因 無 恒 心 if the masses have no certain livelihood, they will be inconstant.

(c) Possessions; estate.

産 業 possessions; property.
産 業 稅 property tax.
産 業 革 命 主 義 syndicalism.
不 動 産 real estate.
⁵公 産 public property.
動 産 personal effects.
家 産 family possessions.
家 産 分 散 insolvent; bankrupt.
破 産 insolvent; bankruptcy.
¹⁰破 産 人 an insolvent; a bankrupt.
破 産 債 權 人 creditors of a bankrupt estate.
破 産 管 財 人 administrator of insolvent estate.
破 産 財 團 bankrupt estate.

私 産 private property.
¹⁵財 産 estate; property.
遺 産 or 嗣 産 inherited property.

剷
剗[3] To level off; to trim; to pare down.
u.f. 鏟 No. 165.
164

剷 刀 to shave the edge of a tool to sharpen it.
剷 削 to plane; to smooth off.
剷 地 to level a plot of land.

(a) To cut.

剷 傷 to wound.
剷·子 a large kitchen-knife.

(b) To root up.

剷·去 階·級 to obliterate classdistinction.
剷 草 破 根 extirpate root and branch.
剷 除 鴉 片 root up the opium.

鏟
鍘[3] A shovel, a spade. To cut; to pare.
165

鏟·子 or 鍋 鏟·子 a spade-shaped instrument used as a slice in Chinese kitchens.
鏟 幣 ancient coinage, shaped like a spade.

幨[1] The curtain of a carriage. A screen to an entrance.
166

襜[1] An apron or flap; covering for the knees; the skirt of a robe.
167

襜 如 也 his skirts were evenly adjusted.
襜 蔽 a screen; a covering.
襜 襦 or 前 襜 an apron.
襜 褕 a short cloak.
襜 襜 flapping, as of curtains; too fully dressed.

韂
鞊[1] A saddle-flap. Trappings.
168

孱[2] Embarrassed. Unfit for. Enfeebled.
169

孱劣不堪任事 inadequate for the management of affairs.
孱商 a poor trader.
孱弱 enervated; enfeebled.

傊[2] To revile; to abuse. Also read *ch'uan*[1].
170

傊懇 to revile.

(a) Read *chan*[3]. To display.

傊功 to display his meritorious actions.

潺[2] Water flowing.
171

潺涎 to drivel.
潺溪 a current; flowing tears.
吐潺 to spit.

羴[3.4.] Sheep crowding; confusion.
172

羴雜 in disorder, as records, etc; confused.

驏[3] A bare-backed horse.
173

驏騎馬 to ride a horse bare-backed.

諂[3] To flatter; to fawn upon; to curry favour.
174 Distinguish 諂 No. 239.

諂人 a flatterer.
諂媚 or 諂佞 or 諂笑 to flatter; to toady.
諂屈 to cringe.
諂笑病於夏畦 those who laugh with flattery, labour harder than those who toil in the summer fields.
諂耳 to tickle the ear, as sensuous music.
諂言 fair speech; flattery.
諂諛取容 flattery with a view to favours.
諂道佞佛 to flatter the gods.

鏟[3] To pull out; to stretch.
175

鏟住 stretch it tight.
鏟長了 stretched to its full length.
鏟麵 to work or pull at dough.

蔵[3] To prepare. To complete. To command. To release.
176

蔵事 to finish the matter.
蔵備 to prepare.
蔵兵 to muster the army.

廛[2] Ground allotted to a retainer. A shop; a market-place.
177

廛市 a bazaar; a market-place.
廛肆 market and shops.

(a) To levy a ground-rent.

廛以抑之少則不必廛 a ground-rent was levied in order to keep down their numbers, when they were few it was not needed.
廛無夫里之布 do not inflict the fines, *fu-pu* and *li-pu* on the dwellers in the market houses.
廛而不征 to levy a ground-rent on traders' houses, but not to tax their goods.

纏[2] To bind up; to wrap up; to bandage.
178

纏上 or 纏住 to wind round.
纏回 or 纏頭 turbaned Mohammedans. *See below.*—16.
纏手 to tie the hands; to impede; to hinder.
纏束 to bind together; to entangle.
[5]纏緊 tightly bound.
纏絲 inextricable; bound up with.
纏縣交結 closely connected; intimate.
纏繞 to bind round; entangled.
纏繞莖 climbing plants.
[10]纏聲 dying sounds of music.
纏脚 or 纏足 to bind the feet.
纏腰 to bind the waist with a girdle.
纏臂金 an armlet or bracelet.
纏袋 a waist-bag.
[15]纏裹 to entwine; to bind; to bandage.
纏頭 a turban; to bind the head; hire of a harlot. *See above.*—2.

(a) To implicate; to involve.

纏擾 to annoy.
纏磨 to bother a person; to tease.
纏累 to involve in trouble, etc.
纏身 implicated; bound by ties; not free.
延纏 delayed; hindered by circumstances.
難纏 hard to get rid of—as an importunate pleader.

躔[2] The orbit of a celestial body.
179

躔度 the course of the stars; the zodiac.
躔次 or 躔舍 the orbit of the planets.

(a) To follow a precedent.

躔迹 or 躔踐 to follow a precedent; to tread in the old paths.

懺[4] To regret; to repent. Buddhist and Taoist ritual.
180

懺悔 to confess sin.
懺悔所 a confessional.
懺悔自新 to reform and become renewed.
懺法 Buddhist ritual.
懺除罪障 repent and remove the hindrance of sin.

讖[4] To verify; to fulfil. A prophecy; a hint. An omen. Inter. preceding—to regret.
181

讖步 prognostication.
讖緯 the verification of a prophecy; or its interpretation.
讖緯術數 divinations and magical calculations.
讖記 the diagram or record of a prophecy.
讖語 a prophecy; a hint.
讖願 to fulfil a vow.
See also 136.

CHANG. (ㄓㄤ)

章[1] A chapter, a section or paragraph. Stanza of an ode.
182

章句 sections and paragraphs; chapters and sections.
章句法 syntax.

書章 chapters.
第三章 the third chapter.
首章 the first stanza.

(a) An essay. A document. An elegant literary composition.

章法 literary style.
作文章 to write essays.
數章 several documents or papers.
文·章 an essay, an article, a paper.

(b) To complete—as an essay.

不成章不達 (the student) does not advance, except by completing one lesson after another.
成章 to complete—as an essay or any work; to attain to excellence.
落筆成章 extemporaneous composition.

(c) Memorial to the throne.

奏章 to memorialize the throne; to pray for the sick or afflicted.

(d) Statutes; regulations; rules.

章京 secretaries attached to the grand council under the Manchu dynasty.
章制 regime.
章服 ceremonial dress.
章歲 the metonic cycle of nineteen years.
章甫 an ancient ceremonial cap.
章·程 regulations; policy; by-laws; constitution of a society.
章·程草稿 draft regulations.
舊章 the ancient statutes.
草章 draft rules.

(e) Variegated; beautiful; ornament.

章身 clothing.
章草 a form of rapid writing; "ts'ao."
章魚 the cuttle-fish.
五服五章 the five styles of ancient dress with the five appropriate ornaments.
出言有章 his speech was elegant in style.
采章 variegated.

(f) To display; to be displayed. Inter. 彰 No. 185.

章章 manifest; quite apparent.
章臺柳 harlots, from a poem about a courtesan; a brothel.

物品咸章 all things were manifested in their beauty—at the creation.

(g) A seal; a badge. A medal.

章綬 ribbon belonging to a medal, etc.
勳章 a decoration; a medal.
圖·章 a seal.
徽章 a badge; a medal; insignia; token.
袖章 badge of rank on sleeves.

(h) N.A. for trees; documents, etc.

三章書 three chapters.
六章大樹 six great trees.

偉[1] Terror-stricken. Inter. 憧 No. 186.
183

偉惶 scared; distracted; see No. 186.

嶂[4] A cliff. A range of peaks.
184

彰[1] To manifest, to display. To make known to. Ornamental; beautiful. Inter. 章 No. 182.
185

彰信兆民 to give evidence of sincerity to all people.
彰其德威 to display his virtue and dignity.
彰善 to show goodness.
彰善癉惡 to praise the good and punish the wicked—to encourage the people.
[5]彰彰 well known; evident.
彰癉 to distinguish between good and evil. See above.—4.
彰明 to exhibit clearly; to manifest.
彰顯 manifested; evident; to show forth.
以彰有德 to give distinction to the virtuous.

憧[1] Terrified, alarmed. Inter. 偉 No. 183.
186

憧惶 scared out of one's wits—there are many pairs of characters used in this way, with similar sounds and meaning.

樟[1] The camphor-laurel.
187

樟木 camphor-wood.
樟·腦 or 潮·腦 camphor.
樟·腦油 oil of camphor.
樟·腦精 essence of camphor.

漳[1] Large tributary of the River Wei in N. E. Honan and S. Chihli.
188

漳絨 superior class of silk named from Chang Chow in Fukien.
漳緞 a high-class figured satin.

獐[1]
麞[The roebuck; the hornless river-deer.
189

獐·子 the roebuck; the river-deer.
獐麖 the musk-deer.

璋[1] Ancient stone ornament used in state ceremonies. A jade plaything.
190

弄璋 to play with a sceptre—a son is born.

瘴[4] Malaria; miasma; pestilential vapours.
191

瘴·氣 malaria.
瘴癘 an epidemic arising from malaria; a plague.

瞕[4] Cataract in the eye.
192

瞕翳 or 瞕瞖 a cataract.

鄣[1] Name of ancient city in N. Kiangsu, near Shantung.
193

鄣郡 a province under the Ch'in Dynasty (秦), comprising most of S. Anhwei and the adjoining regions in Chekiang and Kiangsu.

(a) Read chang[4]. u.f. 障 No. 194.

障[4] To separate; to screen. A screen. A veil.
194

障扇 or 掌扇 a wooden fan carried in processions.

障 日 山 high mountains which screen off the sun.

障 泥 a protection against mud or dirt which was attached to the saddle-flaps.

障 紗 a veil.

障 翳 or 障 蔽 to screen off.

板 障 a wooden screen or partition.

遮 障 to screen off.

錦 障 a brocaded screen.

(a) A barricade; defence. A dike; a dam.

障 塞 to barricade.

障 害 hindrances; difficulties.

障 拒 to impede; to cut off communications.

障 礙 obstacle; barrier; hindrance; a set-back.

⁵障 礙 性 obstructiveness.

障 礙 物 a barrier; something that hinders.

障 衛 an entrenched camp.

障 閉 to close against ingress.

保◦障 a sure defence; used of faithful ministers of state.

¹⁰境 障 frontier defences.

築 障 to throw up earthworks for defence.

張¹
195
To draw a bow.

張 弓 or 張 絃 to draw a bow.

張 弛 tension and relaxation.

一 張 一 弛 now stretched, now relaxed—fast and loose.

(a) To stretch, to string.

張 力 tensile strength.

緊 張 tense; tightly stretched.

解 而 更 張 之 relax and re-stretch—the strings of the instruments.

(b) To set forth; to snare.

張 放 to set out; to arrange.

張 法 a plan; an arrangement.

張 綱 to spread a net.

張◦羅 to set a snare for a bird—to assist; to collect funds; to serve guests, etc.

張 羅 故 陷 to set a snare for the unwary.

張 羅 者 必 張 于 有 鳥 之 際 the snare must be set where there are birds.

張 設 to set out—as a feast.

(c) To open out; to extend.

張 傘 to open an umbrella.

張 口 or 張 嘴 to open the mouth.

張 口 結 舌 agape with astonishment.

張 幕 to pitch a tent.

⁵張 手 open-handed.

張 望 to look around; to gaze.

張◦開 to open wide.

伸 張 or 膨 張 to expand.

擴 張 expansion.

¹⁰擴 張◦的 expansive.

金 屬 因 熱 而 膨 張 metals expand with heat.

開 張 to open a business; to re-open after New Year; to sell.

開 張 大 吉 on re-opening may there be great good luck.

(d) To make a display. To publish, to proclaim.

張 掛 to hang up; to post notices, etc.

張 揚 to publish abroad; to make widely known.

張 燈 結 彩 to decorate with lanterns and coloured hangings.

張 皇 to display an array of troops.

⁵張 貼 to post up notices.

主◦張 to propose; to manage; to advocate; to support; to insist on; to be in favour of; to bring forward a proposition.

沒 有 主◦張 I have no plans; can do nothing.

鋪 張 華 麗 to make a great display; to decorate the home.

(e) To boast, arrogant.

張 大 boastful; arrogant demeanour.

張 大 之 詞 boastful words.

張 大 其 詞 to exaggerate.

張 威 display of power to overawe others.

⁵張 致 to pose.

張 狂 insolent; overbearing.

乖 張 unreasonable; perverse.

誇 張 boastful; "to draw the long bow."

(f) To draw up—as documents.

張 本 notes for future reference.

具 張 to draw up a document.

(g) Panic. fear.

張 惶 panic, confusion. *See* No. 186.

張 惶 失 措 scared out of one's wits.

張 惶 敗 露 to fail for lack of resolution.

慌◦張 confused; panic-stricken.

(h) A surname.

張 三 李 四 third son of *Chang* and fourth son of *Li*—this one and that one; either one or the other; anybody.

張 仙 a god who protects children.

張 仙 送 子 *Ch'ang Hsien* bestows children.

張 冠 李 戴 *Chang's* hat is worn by *Li*—on the wrong man.

張 天 師 Taoist pope who lives at 上 清 in Kiangsi.

張 家 口 Kalgan.

(i) N.A. for things that have large areas or surfaces, as tables, beds, paper, notices, etc.

一 張 棹◦子 a table.

三 張 廣 告 three advertising sheets.

兩 張 紙 two sheets of paper.

紙 張 paper.

(j) Read *chang⁴*.

Inter. 服 No. 198. To swell.

漲⁴
196
To rise as water; to inundate. Also *chang³* in nos. 4, 7, 8, A 1, 2, ≡213 A.

漲 出◦來 to overflow.

漲 海 Gulf of Tonquin.

漲 溢 or 漲 滿 filled to overflowing.

漲 潮 flood-tide.

⁵漲 灘 a place left dry by receding water.

漲 發 to rise—as the tide; to increase.

水 漲 the water is rising.

河 水 漲 起 the river is rising.

(a) To rise in price.

漲 價 to rise in price; at a premium.

價◦錢 必 漲 the prices will surely rise.

(b) To expand.

漲 破◦了 burst through expansion of fluid.

流 體 漲 力 power of expansion in fluids.

帳⁴ A tent.
197

帳下 a soldier—i.e., one who dwells in a tent.
帳幕 or 帳幄 tents; a tabernacle.
帳棚 a tent.
帳篷 tents for soldiers; mat-sheds.
帳落 halting-places of nomads.
營帳 a camp.

(a) A curtain or screen.

帳·子 curtains; mosquito-nets.
帳幔 bed-curtains.
帳簾 screen or curtain hung at a door.
帳紗 gauze for curtains.
⁵帳鈎 curtain-hooks.
帳頂 the roof of bed-curtains.
帳額 the ornamental front of bed-curtains.
帳鬚 fringes for curtains.
圍帳 curtains to screen off a place or alcove.
¹⁰布帳 an awning or screen.
錦帳 embroidered curtains.
銷金帳 gold embroidered curtains.

(b) Scrolls.

喜帳 congratulatory scrolls sent to a wedding.
壽帳 birthday-scrolls.
祭帳 scrolls sent to funerals.

(c) To spread out.

帳飲 to give a farewell banquet.
設祖帳 to spread a farewell feast.

(d) Accounts. Inter. 賬 No. 199, the modern, but not strictly correct form.

帳·房 cashier's department; office.
帳·目 details of accounts.
帳簿 accounts; account books.
了帳 an end of the matter.
⁵來往帳·目 current accounts.
倒帳 to sell out a business; bad debts.
會 (k'uai⁴)·計帳 account books.
消帳 to balance accounts.
結帳 to close accounts.
¹⁰記帳 to charge to an account; to keep accounts.
記載帳·目 account rendered.
顛倒帳·目 to falsify accounts.

脹 痕 ⁴ A swelled belly; drop-sical. To swell. Inflated.
198

脹氣 flatulence.
脹滿 swelled out with dropsy; fully inflated.
脹率 (lü⁴,⁵.) degree of expansion of bodies under heat.
水脹 dropsy.
膨脹 to expand.

賬 ⁴ An account; a bill. To reckon.
199

賬主 creditor. =118.1.
賬單 or 賬·目單 a bill; an invoice; memo of account.
賬尾 balance of an account.
賬檯 a counter in a shop.
⁵賬·目 accounts.
賬簿 or 賬部 account books.
賬頭 the head or beginning of an account.
賬項 items; entries in accounts.
上賬 to enter to an account.
¹⁰付賬 to pay an account.
倒³賬 See 197 D 6.
賬。房 counting-house; office.
拉賬 to run into debt.
放賬 to give credit; to pay interest.
¹⁵流水賬 a running or current account.
清賬 to settle an account.
管賬 a book-keeper.
算他·的賬 to reckon with a man; to dismiss an employee; to pay a man out.
花賬 false accounts, either in prices, quantity or quality of goods.
²⁰計賬 or 算賬 to collect debts.
討賬 or 要賬 to collect debts.
雜賬 sundries.
賴賬 refusal to acknowledge an account.

丈 ⁴ A measure of ten feet, *Chinese*; fixed at 141 inches for tariff purposes; the length varies greatly in the interior.
200

丈勘 to survey land.
丈尺 measurement.
丈尺有數 the measurement can be ascertained.

丈量² to measure—land, etc.
一丈長 ten feet long, *Chinese*.
有丈量² the measurement is known.

(a) A senior; elder; husband. One to be respected.

丈·人 a wife's father; elders.
丈·夫 a man of spirit; a reliable man; a husband; my husband.
丈·夫氣 pluck; manliness.
丈·母 or 丈·母娘 wife's mother.
國丈 emperor's father-in-law.
大丈·夫 a man of force; a hero; a great man.
岳丈 wife's father.
方·丈 abbot of Buddhist monastery; isle of bliss.
老丈 an old gentleman.

仗 ⁴ Weapons of war. To fight.
201

內仗 palace guard under T'ang dynasty.
兵仗 weapons of warfare.
勝仗 a victory.
打仗 to fight a battle.
接仗 to join battle.
操仗 to drill for war.
敗仗 a defeat.

(a) Read *chang⁴*. To rely on; to trust.

仗劍 to grasp the sword; to trust to force.
仗勢欺人 to insult others with impunity because one has powerful friends, or influence with authorities.
仗恃 to trust to power or influence.
仗氣 to get angry.
⁵仗·着嘴 to trust to eloquent powers of persuasion.
仗·着本事 relying on one's ability.
仗·着甚²麼 what do you rely on?
仗義 stirred to action by righteousness; devoted to duty.
仗義執言 relied on words of righteousness.
¹⁰仗義踈財 devoted to public duty and given to charitable undertakings.
仗腰 to back up another.
仗著 depending on.
仗賴 or 賴仗 or 倚仗 to trust to.

杖[4]　A staff.
202

杖 國 70 years of age—one permitted to use a staff in the capital.

杖 家 50 years of age—one permitted to use a staff at home.

杖 朝 80 years of age—one permitted to use a staff at court.

杖 期 a period of mourning. Cf.

[5]杖 策 a whip.　⌊526 C 6

杖 者 the elders—those who carried the staff.

杖 行 to walk with a staff.

杖 鄉 60 years of age—one permitted to use a staff in his village.

杖 頭 the head of a staff.

[10]杖 頭 錢 wine-money—from one who carried money on the top of his staff.

執 杖 to carry the mourning staff at a parent's funeral.

拐 杖 a staff.

錫 杖 Buddhist abbot's staff of metal—supposed to have power to release souls from purgatory.

(a) To beat. Heavy bamboo used for beating criminals.

杖 三 十 thirty heavy blows.

杖 刑 punishment with heavy bamboo.

杖 打 heavy beating.

杖 枷 heavy beating and wearing the cangue.

杖 責 heavy flogging.

(b) Read *chang*[4]. Inter. 仗 No. 201.

杖 仁 者 霸 杖 義 者 強 he who relies on benevolence will rule, and he who relies on righteousness will be powerful.

杖 信 to trust to; to rely on.

杖 信 以 待 晉 rely on perfect sincerity in dealing with Chin.

杖 莫 如 信 there is nothing like sincerity to trust to.

掌[3]　The palm of the hand; the sole of the foot. A paw.
203

掌 上 珠 a pearl in the palm—a loved son or daughter.

掌 嘴 to slap the face; to beat on

the mouth—punishment meted out to lying female witnesses.

掌 紋 相[+] 術 palmistry.

掌 骨 the metacarpal and metatarsal bones.

[5]仙 人 掌 hands of a genii; leaves of a form of cactus; the prickly pear.

秇 掌 to fold the hands as in prayer.

手 掌 the palm of the hand.

打 一 巴 掌 to slap with the palm.

拍 掌 or 鼓 掌 to clap the hands.

[10]指 掌 to point to the palm—easily done.

易 如 反 掌 as easy as turning the hand.

熊 掌 bear's paws, esteemed a great delicacy.

釘[+] 馬 掌 to shoe a horse.

(a) To manage, to control; to superintend.

掌 事 to manage an affair.

掌 作·的 head workmen.

掌 刑·的 sheriff; lictors who administer punishment.

掌 印 to keep the seal.

[5]掌 家 head of the family.

掌 握 to have in the grasp; under control.

掌 故 historical records.

掌 教 to superintend education.

掌 櫃·的 a manager; a shopkeeper; a superintendent; respectful form of address.

[10]掌 權 to exercise authority.

掌 班 manager of a troupe of actors.

掌 理 會 務 to manage the affairs of a society.

掌 秤 to weigh; to superintend weighing.

掌 管 or 掌 理 to direct; to control.

[15]掌 簿 官 the recording angel in the Chinese Hades.

掌 與 女 乘 to undertake the sole management of your chariot.

掌 船·的 a boatman; master of a boat.

掌 舵·的 a steersman.

仉[3]　Surname of the mother of Mencius.
204

孟 母 仉 氏 Mother of Mencius.

鞘[3]　The piece of leather used for soles on Chinese shoes.
205　A patch.

鞘·子 a patch for shoes.

CH'ANG.　(ㄔㄤ)

昌[1]　The light of the sun. Glorious, prosperous. Good.
206　To make prosperous.

昌 光 auspicious influences.

昌 則 繁 茂 flourishing and glorious.

昌 大 to increase in greatness.

昌 明 glorious; shining.　,

[5]昌 盛 prosperous; abundant.

昌 盡 必 殃 when good fortune reaches its limit, evil fortune follows.

昌 言 good words—straight talk.

昌 辭 brilliant writings.

吉 昌 lucky.

百 昌 all created things.

倡[4]　A guide, a leader; an example. To lead. To introduce. To seduce.
207

倡 一 陣 to lead a troop.

倡 亂 ringleader in disturbances; to lead a riot.

倡 始 to originate.

倡 導 to lead; to advocate; to mislead.

[5]倡 率 to lead; a leader.

倡 義 inaugurate.

倡 言 to speak first.

倡 … 說 the suggestion....; the proposal to....

倡 議 to make a motion; to advocate; to espouse a cause.

民 倡 leaders of the people.

(a) Inter. 唱 No. 208. To lead singing.

倡 隨 to lead and follow as husband and wife.

一 倡 百 和[+] one leads and all follow.

(b) Read *ch'ang*[1]. Inter. 娼 No. 209. To sing.

倡 優 actors and singing-girls.

倡 家 女 a singing-girl.

(c) Read *ch'ang*[1]. Inter. 猖 No. 210. Wild.

倡 狂 mad, violent; insubordinate.

唱 4
誯
䛠
208

To sing.

唱 二 簧 a slow style of theatrical singing.
唱·不 上 來 unable to sing it.
唱·不 入 調 to sing out of tune.
唱 和 to sing a duet.
⁵唱 戲 to act ('sing') plays.
唱 曲 to sing theatrical songs.
唱 本 a song-book; "book of words."
唱 梆·子 theatrical singing in a NW style.
唱 歌 or 歌 唱 to sing songs.
¹⁰唱 法 style of singing.
唱 片 phonograph-records.
唱 詩 to sing; to sing hymns.
唱 謳 謳·的 to hum; to sing in a low voice.
清 唱 to sing quietly; amateur singing.

(a) To call out.

唱 名 to call names; to muster.
唱 喏 to bow. = 6780.64.
唱 好 to applaud.
唱 禮 to act as master of cere-monies.
唱 開 侍 從 he shouted to the re-tainers to retire. -tsung⁴
唱 飯 to invite a departed spirit to come and eat.
鳴 鑼 唱 道 to beat the gong and shout to clear the way—when the mandarin went out.

娼 1
209

A singing-girl; a prostitute.

娼 優 隸 卒 prostitutes, a c t o r s and lictors—reckoned as out-side the pale of society.
娼 妓 or 娼 婦 or 娼 女 prosti-tutes.
娼 家 a brothel-keeper.
娼 門 descended from a prostitute.
土 娼 local prostitutes.

猖 1
210

A herd of animals fleeing. Mad.

猖 狂 or 猖 獗 mad; insubordin-ate; seditious; violent.
猖 狂 自 恣 wild; licentious.

猖 魔 神 possessed b y demons; raving mad.

菖 1
211

The sweet flag.

菖 蒲 the calamus. Its leaves are hung on the door lintels on the 5th of the 5th lunar month, to avert evil influences.

閶 1
212

The gate of heaven. Palace gates of the emperor. The west wind.

閶 闔 the gate of heaven.

長 2
213

Long, of space or time. Profitable. Excelling. Radical 168.

長·久 a long time; permanent.
長 吁 or 長 嘆 deep groans or sighs.
長 君 之 惡 to perpetuate t h e wickedness of the prince. chang³·
長 命 long-lived.
⁵長 命 富 貴 long-life, wealth and honour—a felicitous wish.
長 命 百 歲 long-life to you; may you live to be a hundred years of age.
長 號 wailing with a loud noise.
長 嘯 to whistle.
長 圍 to surround an army.
¹⁰長 城 the "Great Wall of China," about 1800 miles in length—used fig., of anything trust-worthy.
長 壽 a good old age.
長 壽 麵 vermicelli eaten on birth-days—there is a play on the words 長 麵, similar in sound to 長 綿, long-drawn-out or continuous.
長 夏 the long evenings of sum-mer.
長 夜 the long night—death.
¹⁵長 夜 室 the house of long night—the grave.
長 夜 飲 an all night carousal.
長 天 the whole day; a long day.
長 太 息 a great sigh.
長 存 long-life; enduring.
²⁰長 寬 length and breadth—area.
長 工 regular employment; used in some places of a man who is engaged to take charge of a farm.
長 年 學 期 full year's course.

「in the W.
長 庚 the planet Venus when seen
長 府 the "Long Treasury"—in the state of Lu.
²⁵長 度 length.
長 征 a long journey—death.
長 戚 戚 constantly in distress.
長 方 形 rectangular.
長 於 風 喻 good at instructing by illustrations.
³⁰長 日 the winter solstice, because the days begin to lengthen from that day; daytime in summer.
長 星 a comet. 長 春 Ch'angch'un.
長 時 工 作 long hours of labour.
長 林 豐 草 d e n s e forests and luxurious vegetation.
長 歸 return after long absence—death is like returning home.
³⁵長 毛 or 長 毛 賊 the long-haired rebels; the Taipings.
長 江 the long river—the Yangtze.
長 江 天 塹 the Yangtze is a na-tural boundary between north and south. 長 沙 Changsha.
長 河 or 長 漢 the Milky Way.
長 班 regular attendants.
⁴⁰長 生 long life; immortality; a coffin.
長 生 庫 the pawnshop.
長 生 果 the ground-nut or peanut.
長 生 樹 evergreen trees.
長 生 術 formula for the elixir of life.
⁴⁵長 生 不 老 long life without old age—the immortality of Tao-ism.
長 眠 the long sleep—death.
長 短 long and short; excellencies and defects; pros and cons; gossip.
長 石 feldspar.
長 策 a horsewhip; good tactics.
⁵⁰長 篇 累 牘 a ponderous thesis.
長 箋 prolix and laborious ex-pository notes.
長 編 one who gathers material from various sources and ar-ranges it into historical sequence; the material so gathered.
長 耳 公 the donkey.
長 腰 long-waisted; r i c e—r i c e cakes eaten in Soochow on the 2nd of the 2nd month.
⁵⁵長 臥 不 覺 long reclining in un-consciousness—death.
長 舌 loquacious; a long-tongued woman.
長·處 advantages; excellencies.
長·蟲 a long reptile—a snake.
↑長 至 either winter solstice (6603.15) or summer solstice (2521.18).

長 蛇 a long serpent—unrighteous man.

60 長 衣 long garments.

長 袖 善 舞 with long sleeves for posing it is easy to dance—fig., with something to assist, things are easily done.

長 跳 the broad jump. = 6287.36

長 跪 to prostrate oneself with reverence. 長 途 long-distance.

長 逝 the long journey from which there is no return—death.

65 長 遠 far-distant; long-standing.

長 鎗 rice.

長 鋏 a sword.

長 隨 regular attendants.

長 頸 烏 喙 long neck and black beak—i.e., a stingy, mean man.

70 長 風 破 浪 strong winds break the waves.

長 齋 to fast from meat, etc., for a whole year or for a longer period.

長 齡 old age.

↑ 長 崎 Nagasaki.

(a) Read *chang³*. To grow, to increase. To excel. Old, senior. To show respect for age.

長 一 歲 a year older.

長 上 elders; seniors.

長 人 聰 明 to make one grow wiser.

長 兄 sir; my elder brother.

5 長 公 主 ancient title for sisters of a prince.

長 勁 to grow in strength. ⌈thick.

長 厚 excellent; generous; to grow

長 君 your elder brother.

長 大 ·了 full grown; attained to manhood.

10 長 子³ eldest son. ⌈double surname.

長 孫 eldest son of eldest son; a

長 官 senior official.

長 幼 有 序 precedence should be maintained between seniors and juniors.

長 庶 eldest son of a concubine.

15 長 成 to grow to manhood; fully grown; to grow into.

長 成 ·的 an adult.

長 房 eldest son, or his apartments. ⌈corruption of 139 A 10

長 期 to extend the time limit;

長 殤 to die between the ages of 15 to 19 years.

20 長 毛 to mildew.

長 癩 to contract leprosy; mangy.

長 老 an elder.

長 老 會 Presbyterian Church.

長 者 seniors, honourable men.

25 長 而 無 述 to win no name when grown up.

長 苗 吐 穗 to germinate and put forth ears.

長 蟲 to breed worms.

長 見 識 to grow in experience.

長 ·起 ·來 to grow up.

30 長 輩 seniors; those of a generation above the speaker.

長 ·進 advancement; progress.

長 銹 to rust.

長 長 (*chang³*) to treat elders as they should be treated.

長 長 (*ch'ang²*) to grow long.

35 予 助 苗 長 矣 I have been helping the grain to grow.

(b) Read *chang⁴*. Remainder; Surplus.

長 一 身 有 半 half as long again as his body.

長 物 surplus; things left over.

倀¹
214

Rash. Wildly.

倀 倀 bewildered, aimless wandering.

倀 鬼 ghost of one eaten by a tiger, it urges the beast to devour others. Used fig., one who assists others to cruelty or oppressive acts.

悵⁴
215

Disappointed. Dissatisfied.

悵 快 disappointed; lowspirited.

悵 惘 depressed; disappointed.

悵 悵 然 provoking; annoying.

爲 悵 am sorry that . . . (*epistol.*)

萇²
216

A kind of fruit called Carambola, known as the 楊 桃 at Canton.

萇 楚 the above.

鋹³
217

Sharp. A keen edge; sharp point.

場 塲
218

3,2 An area of level ground; an open space. A threshing-floor. Arena for drill, etc. A place. N. A. of affairs, etc.

場 中 in the arena.

場 商 merchant who buys salt at the pans.

場 屋 place of examinations in former days; a theatre.

場 所 a place; location.

5 場 期 date of execution.

場 院 courtyard; threshing-floor.

場 面 a stage; in public; respectability.

一 場 夢 life—but a dream.

禾 場 place for spreading grain to dry, either of beaten earth or concrete.

10 在 場 on the spot; in the act.

大 場 former name of the examination for the higher degrees.

官 場 official circles; official life.

小 場 former name of the examination for the lowest degrees.

屋 場 site for a house.

15 戰 場 field of battle.

文 場 examination halls.

是 非 場 a place where there is much backbiting or gossip; a place where a man can never please or do anything right.

法 場 execution ground.

通 場 uniformly.

20 道 場 priestly ceremonies for delivering souls from purgatory.

暢⁴
219

Joyful; pleasant.

暢 叙 a pleasant conversation.

暢 ·快 pleased; happy.

暢 懷 gratified; happy.

暢 暢 joyful; happy.

5 暢 月 the 11th month.

暢 聆 to hear with joy.

暢 遂 things going on as one would wish. *See below*. B. 7.

暢 適 (to read) what gives pleasure and is agreeable, (not the whole of a book.)

暢 飲 to drink strong liquor with gusto.

爲 暢 it was a pleasure that . . .

(a) Clear. ⌊(*epist.*)

暢 達 clear; perspicuous style; cheerful.

通 暢 perspicuous style of writing.

(b) Long; expanding; luxuriant.

暢 充 to permeate; to pervade.

暢 旺 flourishing; prosperous.

暢 流 freely flowing.

暢滯 expansion and contraction—as of business.

⁵暢膽 bold; forward; daring.

暢茂 or 暢鬱 luxuriant growth.

暢遂 vegetation allowed to grow wild. *See above.*—7.

暢銷 to extend sales; a wide market.

不能暢銷 will not have a wide market.

腸² **The bowels. The affections; the feelings.**
220

腸·子 the bowels; the inner man.

腸斷 heart broken.

腸液 digestive juices.

腸痔 internal piles.

⁵腸窒扶斯 typhoid fever. (*Jap.*)

腸腺 intestinal glands.

大腸 lower intestine.

好心·腸 "bowels of mercies;" kindly.

小腸 small intestine.

直腸 rectum.

羊腸 sheep's intestines—winding, as a path.

↑腸加答兒 bowel catarrh.

常² **Constantly, frequently, usually, habitually. Regular.**
221 **Common. A rule, a principle.**

常不常 constantly; regularly; continually.

常·久 a long time; enduring. = 213.1

常事 ordinary matters; routine.

常人 an ordinary man.

⁵常令 a general rule; standing orders.

常任 or 常務委員會 a standing committee.

常作 to do constantly.

常住 a Buddhist priest who does not travel; to stay for a long time in a place.

常例 regular order; usual procedure.

¹⁰常俸 regular salary.

常倫 ordinary person.

常備軍 regular or standing army.

常價 current rates.

常則 common standard or rule.

¹⁵常勝軍 "ever victorious army."

常參 to call on a superior officer at stated periods.

常品 ordinary quality.

常在 concubines of third imperial rank under Manchus.

常川 uninterruptedly flowing.

²⁰常工 long term employees; in some places, it means a man engaged to superintend farm work. = 213.21

常常 or 常時 or 常日 uniformly; constantly; always; continually; often, frequently.

常年 in ordinary years; regular.

常年大會 annual meeting.

常年稅 regular taxes.

²⁵常度 ordinary manner or appearance; general attitude towards.

常式 regular style or pattern; common laws.

常心 a constant mind.

常忍久耐 always patient.

常性 continuance; perseverance.

³⁰常態 normal attitude towards.

常智 common sense.

常會 ordinary meeting of . . . .; to meet constantly.

常有 of frequent occurrence.

常服 ordinary dress.

³⁵常格 ordinary rules.

常業 ordinary business or employment; one's regular business.

常法 the laws of the land.

常用 common use; general usage.

常禮服 informal dress suit.

⁴⁰常禮帽 a derby or bowler hat.

常稅 native customs dues, as contrasted with those of the maritime customs.

常經 or 經常 constant; unchanging—as principles. Cf. 1123

↓常青樹 evergreen trees. ⌊E 1, 2

常羊 neither advancing nor retreating; neither prosperous nor decadent; easy-going.

⁴⁵常羞 regular diet.

常苦不給 constant hard work yet unable to keep up with—his duties as president.

常行 commonly; ordinarily.

常衡 avoirdupois.

常見 constantly seeing; accustomed sight.

⁵⁰常規 common practice; the regular custom.

常談 common talk.

常識 common sense; general knowledge which all should have.

常識科 general knowledge course.

常軌 or 常道 the ordinary course of events.

⁵⁵常關 the native customs, as contrasted with the maritime customs.

常隨 regular attendant or servant.

常飯 everyday food.

不可常 not for long.

五常 the five constant virtues—仁, 義, 禮, 智, 信.

⁶⁰如常 or 照常 as usual; according to precedent.

平常 ordinary.

無常 inconstant; irregular; Buddhist term for death.

無常鬼 supposed to be the spirit of a living man sent to arrest evil spirits and bring them to Hades.

非常 extraordinary; unusual, very.

嫦² *See below.*
222

嫦娥 Name of a lady who stole the elixir of immortality and fled with it to the moon, where she was changed into a frog. Originally called Heng²(2106 A)-o², changed to present form because of taboo of name of Wu Ti of Han.

徜² *See below.*
223

徜徉 unsteady; going to and fro.

蹡³ **To sit cross-legged like a Buddhist priest.**
224

敞³ **Open, spacious. To display.**
225

敞亮 ventilated and well lighted; cheerful.

敞心 to reveal the feelings; cheerful.

敞懷 cheerful and happy; without anxiety.

敞開門 open the door wide.

寬·敞 spacious; *see below.*

(a) High land; plateau.

寬·敞 broad spacious place.

險敞 a dangerous place.

高敞 a high level spot.

廠
廠 **A shed. A yard. A workshop or factory; a depot.**
226

廠·子 a yard; open space for working.

廠 面 surface; appearance; view.

篷 廠 a mat-shed.

製·造 廠 factory; workshop.

關 廠 customs' shed.

227

Alarmed; agitated.

惝 悦 agitated; flurried.

惝 恍 無 定 in a state of agitation and uncertainty.

228

3 Down or feathers from the crane or a similar bird, used for trimmings.

鶴 氅 swan's down; a cloak trimmed with crane's-down worn by *Chukoh Liang.*

嘗

229

2 To taste, to prove, to experience.

嘗·一·嘗 have a taste.

嘗 了 死 味 to taste death.

嘗 味 to taste.

嘗 巧 to test the skill of another.

5 嘗 新 to taste new season's products after offering in sacrifice.

嘗 業 habitual employment.

嘗 炷 to try the cautery,—of a filial son who had tasted the medicine prepared for his mother, and now desired to try the cautery, but was forbidden.

嘗 膽 to taste gall, from the next phrase; signifies lasting hatred and desire for revenge.

飲 食 嘗 膽 to taste gall in everything—Used of the prince of *Yüeh, Kou ch'ien,* who tasted gall in everything which he ate or drank, he also kept some by him to look at, in order to nurse his grievance against the state of *Wu,* by which he was defeated.

10 嘗 試 to make an attempt; to have a try.

嘗 過 味 道 to taste; to experience.

嘗 食 to taste food before royalty partook.

(a) Indication of past tense. Has, have.

嘗 聞 or 嘗 思 I have heard it said; it appears to me.

嘗 讀 他 論² he had read another copy of the *Analects.*

何 嘗 interrogative phrase, implying a negative answer.

何 嘗 不 是 how can it be otherwise?

時 嘗 病 always ill; often ill.

未 嘗 not yet; not tried it; have not experienced it.

未 嘗 不 by no means not.

未 嘗 不 可 there is no reason at all why it should not be.

未 嘗 不 在 I was always present.

(b) Autumnal offering of first fruits to ancestors.

禴 禘 嘗 烝 spring, summer, autumn and winter sacrifices—according to the *Book of Rites* —it was changed in later years.

償

230

2 To repay, make restitution; to indemnify. To fulfil.

償 却 to pay off a debt.

償 命 or 抵 命 to forfeit life; life for life.

償 清 國 債 to liquidate the national debt.

償 還 to restore.

5 償 還 覆 書 to send a reply.

償 金 indemnity.

償 錢 or 償 債 to pay debts.

償 願 the desire of the heart is attained.

賠 償 to recompense.

昶

231

3 A long day. Bright. Extended. Clear. inter. 暢 No. 219.

鬯

232

4 Sacrificial spirits made by fermenting millet and fragrant herbs. Radical 192.

鬯 茂 luxuriant growth.

鬯 酒 mixed wine.

鬯 叙 fragrant banquet.

CHAO.　　(坐幺)

朝

233

1 The dawn. Morning. Early.

No. 1 below now used in the same sense as No. 3.

朝 三 暮 四 3 in the morning and

4 in the evening—of one who promised his monkeys 3 chestnuts in the morning and 4 in the evening. They objected, so he offered 3 in the evening and 4 in the morning, which they agreed to—used to illustrate :— to swindle by a clever trick.

朝 不 保 夕 the morning cannot guarantee the evening—in imminent danger of death.

朝 令 暮 改 the orders of the morning countermanded a t night—inconstant policy.

朝 來 暮 往 they come in the morning and go in the evening —frequent and long visits.

5 朝 夕 or 朝 晚 or 朝 暮 morning and evening; early and late.

朝 日 or 朝 天 every day; daily.

朝 旭 brightness of dawn.

朝 暮 人 one in imminent danger of death.

朝 暾 dawning sunlight.

10 朝 會 morning session for moral instruction in schools; takes the place of "chapel."

朝 朝 去 they go every day.

朝 槿 the hibiscus — things that fade rapidly.

朝 氣 the stimulating air of the dawn—the vigor of youth.

朝 生 暮 死 we are born in the morning and pass away at night —the brevity of life.

15 朝 發 make an early start.

朝 發 夕 至 start early and arrive by evening—of good communications.

朝 秦 暮 楚 now *Ch'in,* now *Ch'u;* fickle and inconstant; used of prostitutes.

朝 聞 道 夕 死 可 矣 if a man hears the right Way in the morning, he can die at eventide without regret.

朝 菌 mushroom growth; springs in the morning and withers before evening.

20 朝 露 "early dew of morning;" evanescent.

朝 饔 夕 飱 breakfast in the morning and supper at night— of one who thinks only of his meals.

朝 鮮 Korea. Now usu. pron. *ch'ao²*

一 朝 suddenly.

明 朝 tomorrow morning.

連 朝 successive days.

(a) Read *ch'ao²* **The court; a dynasty.**

朝代 a dynasty.

朝儀 ancient court etiquette.

朝奉 a wealthy man; proprietor or manager of a shop.

朝廷 a dynasty; the hall of audience; the emperor.

⁵朝房 ante-chambers to the throne room.

朝服 or 朝衣 court-dress.

朝版 tablet or insignia of office held before the breast at court.

朝版餅 oblong cakes.

朝珠 necklace worn by officials.

¹⁰朝章 court regulations.

朝考 examination for admission to the Imperial Academy.

朝請 (*ch'ing⁴*) Spring and Autumn courts of the Han dyn. 朝 was the spring court, and 請 was the autumn court.

朝貴 men of influence at court.

朝隱 officials whose heart is not in their work.

(b) To visit—a father, elder, or superior.

朝山 to go to distant mountains to burn incense in the temples.

朝宗 rivers returning to the sea.

朝見 or 朝覲 or 朝天 or 上朝 to have audience with the emperor; to go to court.

(c) To face; fronting; towards.

朝上 or 朝天 looking upwards; face uppermost.

朝前坐 move forward a little.

朝日 facing the sun.

朝陽 facing the sun; the eastern slope of a hill.

坐東朝西 situate on the east and facing the west.

召⁴ **To call, to summon. To cite, to give notice.**
234

召他來 call him here.

召募 to enlist soldiers.

召回 to recall.

召忽死之 Shao-huh died with him.

⁵召租 "to let." =235.14.

召耕 to get a tenant for a farm.

召見 or 召對 or 宣召 to summon to court.

召請 to invite.

召辟 summons to court.

¹⁰召選 to call and select.

召集 to convene; to summon a council; to call to arms.

召集國會 to summon parliament.

召齊了 all summoned.

招¹ **To beckon; to call, To give notice. To proclaim.**
235

招來 to call; to beckon to.

招剌 to select.

招匪成軍 proclaim pardon for brigands or rebels and make an army of them.

招呼 to call; to give notice; to hail. *See below.* C. 2.

⁵招商局 China Merchants Steamship Company.

招安 to proclaim amnesty for rebels.

招安軍 pardoned brigands received into the army.

招尋 to advertise for things lost.

招工 to advertise for labourers.

¹⁰招引 to introduce—as new members.

招手 or 手招 to beckon with the hand.

招生 to advertise for pupils.

招登 to solicit advertisements.

招租 "to let."

¹⁵招考 entrance examinations.

招聚了 to assemble.

招親 a marriage where the husband enters the wife's family.

招邀 or 招要 invitation; to call.

招集 to gather together; to convene.

²⁰招集公司 to float a public company.

招魂 or 引魂 to call home the soul of one who dies abroad; to prepare clothing and funeral arrangements and bury an empty coffin with all the rites, for such as die away from home; to call back the soul of one dangerously ill.

招魂論 spiritism.

(a) To levy; to raise.

招兵 to recruit; to raise troops.

招兵買馬 to raise an army; to prepare for making an insurrection.

招募 to enlist; to summon troops.

招股 to call for capital; to invite shareholders.

招鄉民 to raise a militia.

(b) To confess.

招冊 record of criminal confessions.

招解 to send a copy of confession of a capital crime to the capital for judgement.

招認 or 招承 or 招罪 to own one's faults; to confess.

招認口供 to confess to a charge; to plead guilty.

招賠 to confess and apologize.

(c) To welcome; to receive.

招世 one welcomed by the world.

招呼 to welcome and care for; to attend to. *See above.*—4.

招待 to receive visitors, etc.

招待員 stewards or ushers; those appointed to receive visitors.

招待所 reception room.

招提 Buddhist monastery; dormitory for monks.

(d) A notice; a signboard.

招帖 handbills; notices.

招牌 shop-sign; a signboard.

(e) To cause; to effect; to incite.

招咎 to endure calamity.

招徠 to induce customers to purchase.

招徠運動 to encourage business; to boost trade.

招怨 to incite animosity.

⁵招恐樹敵 to arouse apprehension and incite animosity.

招惹 to provoke.

招搖 to shake; to cause disturbances; to swagger.

招搖市過 swaggering through the street.

招搖撞騙 to use the name or authority of another falsely; to use one's own name, etc., to swindle others.

¹⁰招損 to invite injury; to bring trouble upon.

招撫 to pacify.

招撫使 High Commissioner for Pacification.

招架 to resist; to ward off.

招權 abuse of power.

¹⁵招權納賄 abuse of power and bribery.

招 災 or 招 非 to bring evil on oneself.

招 財 童 子³ the lad who brings wealth.

招 蹶 之 機 the means by which paralysis or wasting is caused.

招 風 to catch the wind—when something grows so as to impede another.

招 風 耳 projecting ears.

(f) A target; a bull's-eye.

共 射 其 一 招 they all aimed at the same target.

(g) To tie the legs.

既 入 其 苙 又 從 而 招 之 after they have got it (the pig) into the pen, they proceed to tie its legs.

昭¹ **The brightness of the sun. Bright. Luminous. To**
236 **show, to display.**

昭 事 上 帝 to serve God openly.

昭 信 中 外 inspire confidence both in China and abroad.

昭 前 to make the former things luminous.

昭 回 glorious and bright.

⁵昭 彰 luminously displayed.

昭 明 or 昭 著 bright; clear; evident.

昭 昭 clear; patent to all.

昭 然 intelligently.

昭 示 clear explanation.

¹⁰昭 穆 the two rows of spirit tablets as arranged in the ancestral temple. 昭 on the left hand are the even numbers, 穆 on the right hand are the odd.

昭 耀 glorious; bright.

昭 蘇 to awaken; to arouse from hibernation.

昭 陽 bright and shining.

昭 陽 宮 palace of the empress.

¹⁵昭 雪 satisfactory settlement of a grievance; innocence clearly manifested.

昭 顯 famous; renowned; illustrious.

以 昭 畫 一 to obtain uniformity.

沼³ **A fishpond; a pool of irregular shape.**
237

沼 氣 fire-damp; marsh-gas.

照 ⎱⁴
焰 ⎰
238
     To illumine. To reflect.

照 亮 to throw light upon.

照 個 燈 來 show a light here.

照 壁 a wall opposite an entrance —as to *yamens,* etc.

照 址 everywhere.

⁵照 射 to reflect light; to illuminate.

照 對 to reflect.

照 度 degree of illumination.

照 日 葵 the sunflower. = 2549.20

照 明 to make manifest.

¹⁰照 映 to throw light upon.

照 曜 or 照 耀 to enlighten; bright light.

照 水 reflection from water.

照 海 燈 or 探 海 燈 a searchlight.

照 火 light of fireflies.

¹⁵照 煦 genial warmth of sunshine.

照 相 (*hsiang¹*) to take photographs.

照 相 器 a camera.

照 相 彫 刻 photo-engraving.

照 相 or 照 片 or 相 片 photographic prints.

²⁵照 相 版 photogravure; process block.

照 相 發 音 機 photo-phone.

照 相 石 版 photo-litho.

照 相 舘 photographic studio.

照 相 術 photography.

²⁵照 相 鏡 photographic lens; camera.

照 相 鑄 版 photo-process block.

照 耀 映 奪 dazzling lights.

照 臨 下 土 to illuminate the earth,—like the sun and moon.

照 臨 四 方 to spread illumination on all sides.

³⁰照 臨 敝 邑 deign to visit my humble place.

照 鏡·子 or 照 臉 to reflect one's face in a mirror.

反 照 reflected light.

夕 照 evening glow.

小 照 portrait.

³⁵心 照 to understand one another thoroughly.

手 照 a hand lamp.

正 照 to shine directly on or into.

(a) To look after.

照 地 to inspect land with a view to purchase.

照·應 or 照·料 to look after; to care for.

照 看 (*k'an¹*) to look after.

照 管 to control; to care for.

照·顧 to pay attention to; to buy of; to patronize.

台 照 for your honourable inspection—conventional phrase in letters.

(b) A permit, a pass. A document.

照 得 Be it known; Whereas; Referring to—opening phrase in proclamations.

照 復 to reply.

照 抄 or 照 錄 to make a copy of.

照 收 duly received.

⁵照 文 議 復 reply after due consideration.

照·會 a communication between foreign and local officials of equal standing; to inform officially

照 請 to write and request that.

照 送 to forward in a despatch.

執 照 a certificate, a pass; a license.

¹⁰存 照 to retain evidence—as a counterfoil or receipt.

護 照 a passport.

(c) According to, as, seeing that.

照 價 according to the price fixed.

照 准 permitted.

照 則 according to the tariff.

照 原 價 at cost price.

⁵照 實 in accordance with facts.

照 尺 scale sight on surveying instruments, etc.

照 常 as usual.

照 常 規 according to the regular custom.

照 式 according to pattern; to imitate.

¹⁰照 律 according to the statutes.

照 數 according to the number.

照 斷 abide by the decision.

照 案 according to precedent.

照 樣 作 follow the pattern; imitate the example.

¹⁵照 章 according to regulations.

照 章 納 稅 to pay taxes according to regulations.

照 算 reckon accordingly; according to the number.

照 約 保 護 grant protection according to treaty.

照·著 according to.

[20]照舊 as before; according to precedent, still.
照行 act accordingly.
照辦 act in accordance with.

詔 [4] **To proclaim. as a king. To appeal to. To encourage. Imperial mandate.**
239

詔告 to proclaim—as emperor.
詔命 or 王詔 or 皇詔 or 敕詔 or 鳳詔 or 詔書 an imperial mandate.
詔對 verbal commands issued by emperor.
詔導 to give orders or directions.
詔旨 imperial rescript.
恩詔 gracious proclamation.
降詔 to publish a proclamation.

爪 [3] **叉 爫 Claws of birds or animals. Feet. To scratch, to claw. To grasp. Attendants. Radical 87. Distinguish 叉 No. 96.**
240

爪印 a scar.
爪哇 Java. Also pron. *chua*[3] *wa*[1].
爪子 claw or talons. Pron. *chua*[3] *tzŭ*.
爪牙 or 爪翼 or 爪士 agents; attendants; servants. Lit., talons and teeth.
爪爛 or 爪破 to tear in pieces; to scratch raw. Pron. *chua*[1] =1417

筄 [4] **A bamboo skimmer. A ladle.**
241

筄籬 a wire ladle or skimmer.

找 [3] **To seek, to look for. To find. Distinguish. 我 No. 4778.**
242

找不着[2] or 找不到 unable to find.
找事 to look for employment; to make a disturbance.
找到了 or 找着了 found.
找尋 to seek for; to search.
找徧了 searched everywhere.
找杈[2]兒 or 找錯兒 or 找錯縫 to seek for faults; to criticize.
找門路 to seek employment, or an opening.

(a) **To pay a balance; to exchange.**

找他三百個錢 a balance due to him of 300 cash.

找價 to make up the price.
找出來 he has changed it—as a note.
找多少 how much do I owe?
[5]找換 to exchange money.
找票子 to change a bank-note.
找數尾 to pay the balance of an account.
找補 to supply the deficiency.
找足其數 make up the full number.
[10]找還 to repay.
找頭 the balance; the change.

(b) Read *hua*[2] u.f. 划 No. 2213. **To scull.**

櫂 [4] **An oar, a scull. To row.**
243

櫂槳 to pull an oar.
櫂歌 to chant a boat song.
櫂船 to row a boat.

趙 [4] **To hasten to; to visit.**
244

趙久 a considerable time.
趙趙 to hasten to.

(a) **Ancient feudal state. A surname.**

趙女 a woman of *Chao*—i.e., a beautiful girl, that state being famous for beauties.
趙氏之中牟宰 ruler of *Chung-mou* which belonged to the *Chao* family.
趙璧 a precious gem belonging to the state of *Chao*.
奉趙 to return it to *Chao*—to return a borrowed article.

肇 [4] **肇 To commence; to found; to devise. At first. To originate. To strike.**
245

肇亂 to stir up trouble and disorder.
肇事 to stir up trouble.
肇域 the boundary of a grave.
肇基王迹 laid the foundations of the royal fortune.
[5]肇巖 early spring.
肇端 the original plan.
肇緒 the beginning.

肇自漢魏 it first originated in the *Han* and *Wei* dynasties.
肇興 to initiate.
肇訟 to institute proceedings.
肇造 the earliest establishment of.

罩 [4] **笡 A cover, a shade. A basket used to catch fish.**
246

罩子 or 燈罩 a lamp shade or lamp glass.
罩棺 a pall.
罩着 covered, covering.
罩衣 a cloak or hood.
罩魚 to entrap fish in a basket.

兆 [4] **兆 A sign, an omen. A million.**
247

兆民 or 兆庶 the people; the masses.
兆邊 the north of China.
兆頭 an omen.
凶兆 evil omen; a portent.
吉兆 lucky omen.
預兆 signs of the times.

CH'AO.   (业)

啁 [1] **Twittering of birds.**
248

啁哳 twittering of birds.
啁啾 wailing.
啁噍 shrill cry of birds.

嘲 [2] **To ridicule, to jeer. To abuse. Also pron. *chao*[1].**
249

嘲哂 to sneer.
嘲嗤 to ridicule; to jeer.
嘲笑 to jeer at.
嘲詈 or 嘲罵 to abuse; to ridicule.
嘲詆 to make fun of.
嘲詬 to insult with anger.
嘲謗 to ridicule.

潮 [2] **The tide.**
250

潮信 fixed times of the tides.
潮水 the tide.

潮 (continued)

潮 水 滿·了 or 潮 平 high tide.
潮 汐 morning and evening tides.
[5]潮 流 current or flow of the tide—the tide of public opinion; carried as a tide by the masses.
潮 退 the tide is falling.
潮 長 (*chang*3) the tide is rising.
乘 潮 take advantage of the tide.
大 潮 spring tides.
[10]小 潮 neap tides.
思 潮 trend of popular opinions.
新 思 潮 new trends of thought.
滿 潮 乾 潮 high and low tides respectively.
順 潮 with the tide.
逆 潮 against the tide.

(a) Damp, moist, wet. Name of places.

潮 壞 damaged by damp.
潮 氣 damp; moisture; indecent.
潮 濕 damp; wet.
潮·腦 used in the north for camphor, from the name of a place.
潮 蒸 damp and heated—as grain.
潮 解 deliquescence.
潮 解 性 deliquescent.

超 [1]
[251]
To leap over. To stride.

[-*shêng*4]

超 乘 to spring into a carriage.
超 升 to promote over others; to rise rapidly in official life.
超 忽 far away.
超 距 to leap over.
超 遙 distant.
超 遷 rapid promotion of officials by missing grades or ranks.

(a) To go before. To excel. Superior to.

超 乎 萬 物 pre-eminent in all things.
超 倫 above the rank and file.
超 卓 very clever; pre-eminent.
超 格 above the average.
[5]超 然 transcendent; disappointed.
超 然·的 supernatural.
超 異 羣 生 he far excelled, in every way, all other men.
超 等 first rank in list of honours.
超 絕 surpassing all others; incomparable.
[10]超 絕 玄 著 transcendent and abstruse.
超 絕 羣 倫 pre-eminent; incomparably above everything.

超 群 or 超 常 or 超 凡 above the average; unusual; uncommon.
超 脫 to rise above the common things of life; transcendent.
超 自 然 supernatural.
[15]超 越 excelling; surpassing.
超 越 哲 學 transcendental philosophy.
超 越 論 transcendentalism.
超 軼 to surpass; to go beyond.
超 軼 逸 塵 far above all others.
超 逸 excelling; surpassing.

(a) To release; to save.

超 拔 to save; to rescue.
超 渡 or 超 幽 to release souls from suffering; to raise from a state of suffering in the next world.
超 生 to save from death.

鼂 [2]
[252]
A marine animal, said to sing by night and to go into the sea by day. u.f. 朝 No. 233.

巢 [2.1]
[253]
A nest in a tree. A haunt, a den. Name of an ancient state.

巢 居 to dwell.
巢 穴 a den; a haunt.
巢 窩 nest in a tree.
巢 覆 鳥 飛 destroy the nest and the birds fly.
賊 巢 a robber's den.

吵 [3]
[254]
To quarrel. To dispute, to make a noise. A row, an uproar.

吵 吵 noisy quarrelling.
吵 嘴 to wrangle or quarrel.
吵 嚷 angry disputation.
吵 鬧 to make a disturbance or quarrel.

抄 [1]
[255]
To seize; to confiscate.

抄 家 or 抄 沒 or 抄 占 to confiscate the property of a person.
抄 家 滅 門 to confiscate the property and ruin the family.
抄 拏 to seize.
抄 掠 to rob; to plunder.
抄 搶 to loot; to plunder.

抄 沒 家 業 to confiscate all the property. (*ch'ao*1-*mo*4-)
抄 襲 to make a surprise attack; to plagiarize.

(a) Near, as a short cut.

抄 近 走 take a short cut.

(b) To copy out. A document, a voucher.

抄 呈 to send a copy to a superior.
抄 單 copy of a paper.
抄 奉 .....have received......of which the following is an exact copy.
抄 批 to copy a decision of court.
[5]抄 掇 to copy and arrange in order.
抄 摺 copy of a memorial.
抄 本 MSS. of a book; copy-book.
抄 案 to take down the evidence.
抄 發 to send a copy to a subordinate.
[10]抄 白 to make a copy.
抄 示 to send a copy for information.
抄 稿 to make a fair copy of.
抄 給 to give a copy to.
抄 胥 man employed in copying official documents.
[15]抄 送 to send a copy of . . . .
抄 錄 or 抄 寫 or 抄 繕 to transcribe documents.
抄 錄 號 碼 took the number of—as of an offending motor car.
抄 附 a copy is appended.
抄 電 a copy is submitted for inspection.

(c) Wholesale.

抄 莊 a wholesale house.

(d) To beg.

抄 化 to solicit subscriptions, as a Buddhist priest.

炒 [3]
[256]
To roast in a pan. To fry. Inter. 吵 No. 254.

炒 米 roast rice.
炒 茶 to fire tea.
炒 鍋 a frying pan.
炒 鬧 to wrangle.
乾 炒 dry frying.

訬 [1]
[257]
Clamour, uproar, annoyance, etc. Inter. 吵 No. 254. Graceful. Cunning, high.

誂 婧 slender waisted; graceful.
誂 擾 to annoy.
誂 輕 annoying.

鈔[4] A money order. Paper
258 money. Tonnage dues.
Read *ch'ao*[1] A document, a
voucher, a receipt. Inter.
抄 No. 255.

鈔 票 government money orders;
bank-notes.
鈔 錢 paper money; cash notes.
鈔 關 office for stamping duty
receipts on goods.
鈔 項 or 鈔 課 or 鈔 銀 or 船 鈔
tonnage dues.
關 鈔 customs revenue.

CHE. (ㄓㄜ)
(Chae)

嘛[1] To screen. Loquacious.
259

遮[1] To cover, to protect, to
260 screen, to shade. An umbrella.

遮·不 了[3] it will not cover it, it
cannot be hid.
遮 庇 to protect.
遮 扦 to guard; to protect.
遮 掩 or 遮 瞞 or 遮 盖 to hide
from view; to cover over; to
hush up.
[5]遮 放 title of tribal chief in Yunnan.
遮 羞 or 遮 醜 to hide one's
shame; to evade.
遮 羞 錢 blackmail; money given
to cover shame.
遮 蔽 to hide; to conceal; to cover.
遮 蔭 to shade or shelter.
[10]遮 護 to shelter and protect.
遮 覆 to cover; to conceal.
遮 隱 to screen; to hide.
遮 陽 a shade from the sun; an
awning.
遮 飾 to disguise; to gloss over;
to put in a false light.

(a) To intercept; to check.

遮 抑 to check; to restrain.
遮 擋 to impede; to obstruct; to
hinder.
遮 攔 to fence off; to protect by
an enclosure.

遮 止 to impede; to stop.
[5]遮 絕 or 遮 斷 to cut off; to
sever.
遮 路 to block the way; to cut off
communications.
遮 道 借 寇 to oppose the re-
moval of a popular official.

(b) u.f. 這 No. 265. This, etc.

遮 回 on this occasion.
遮 莫 if; supposing.

蔗
蔗[4]
261 The sugar cane.

蔗 境 the region of sweetness—
the region of bliss, from *Ku
K'ai-chï* who began to eat
sugar-cane from the leafy, thin
end, and "gradually entered the
regions of bliss," i.e., the sweet
end. *See* No. 878—1.
蔗 杖 sugar-cane used as a walking stick.
蔗 渣 refuse cane after sugar is
expressed.
蔗 糖 cane sugar.
蔗 酒 spirits or alcoholic liquor
made from the juice of sugar-
cane.
蔗 霜 or 糖 霜 white sugar.
蔗 餳 white sugar.
榨 蔗 to press cane in order to
extract the juice.
甘·蔗 the sugar cane.

鷓[4]
262 The common partridge.

鷓 鴣 a partridge, from its cry.

者[3] A pronoun—this, that, it,
263 which, what, he who, those
who, etc. A particle imparting adjectival or adverbial
shades of meaning to words
to which it is joined.

者 者 to assent.
者 番 on this occasion—here it is
used as 這·
使 者 a messenger.
再 者 furthermore; "P.S."

或 者 perhaps.
能 者 those with ability.
茲 啟 者 now to begin—intro-
ductory phrase in letters.

赭[3]
264 A reddish brown.

赭 石 haematite iron ore, used as
paint.
赭 衣 a dress formerly worn by
criminals to execution or
banishment.
赭 衣 塞 塗 the number of
banished criminals blocked the
road.
赭 面 to dye the face red—said to
be a former custom among the
Tibetans.
赭 黃 yellow ochre.

這
这[4]
过
265 This; the; here.
[x]A.p. *chei*[4].

[x]這·一 向 this long while.
[x]這·些 these.
[x]這·件 事·情 this affair; this matter.
[x]這·個 this; this one.
[5]這 兒·的 人 the people of this
place.
[x]這 兩·個 字 是 通·的 these two
characters are used inter-
changeably.
這 兒 or 這 裡 here; over here.
這·就 at once; immediately.
這·時·候 now; at this time.
[10]這·會 兒 or 這 早 晚 just now;
at this time.
這·樣 so; in this way.
[x]這·班 人 this class of man.
這·種 this kind.
這·等 such; this kind.
[15]這·纔·是 that's just the thing.
這·般 like this.
這 還 了·得 can such a thing as
this be permitted? (*-hai*[2]*-liao*[3]*-*)
[x]這·邊 on this side; over here; in
these parts.
這·麼 so; thus; this is the way.
這·麼 下 雨 不 止 such incessant
rains.

柘[4] Thorny tree about fifteen
266 feet high, the leaves are used
for feeding silkworms before
the mulberry leaves are
ready or when they are
scarce. Bark produces a
yellow dye.

柘 漿 sugar-cane juice.

柘 橋 a tree of this species grown like a bridge.

柘 火 in ancient times this wood was used to produce fire by boring.

柘 硯 inkslabs from a place in Shantung.

柘 絲 silk from worms fed on these leaves.

柘 蠶 silkworms fed on these leaves.

柘 袍 garment dyed yellow with this dye.

柘 黃 dye from the bark of this tree.

CHÊ. (ㄓㄜ)
(Cheh)

折 **2.5. To take off, to diminish. to reduce, to deduct.**
267

折 交 to pay proportionately.

折 價 to abate the price.

折 兌 to discount; to exchange—as money into various currencies. *See below.* F. 1.

折 半 reduced by one half.

⁵折 墮 reduced to extremities.

折° 扣 or 扣 折 to discount.

折 抽 to levy taxes in proportion.

折 收 to receive a certain percentage.

折 減 to discount.

¹⁰折 罪 to diminish guilt by a counterbalance of merit.

折 責 lenient—by deducting a percentage of the punishment.

折·頭 percentage; discount.

七 折 30% discount, i.e., 7 out of 10, the amount left after deduction is called 折 .

八 五 折 15% discount.

(a) To snap; to break off.

折 中 broken in the middle; to strike an average. *See below.* C. 1.

折 傷 to wound.

折 兆 defeated; routed.

折 光 refracted light.

⁵折 券 to destroy a deed without asking for money.

折 右 to break the right arm—to fail in accomplishing one's purposes.

折 回 to return when only halfway—fruitless efforts.

折 射 refracted rays.

折 斷 snapped; broken off.

¹⁰折 於 外 defeated elsewhere.

折 木 蜚 屋 to break trees and fly over houses—the wind can be resisted by the small but it overcomes the large.

折 本 to fail in business.(*shê²-pên³*)

折 枝 to snap a twig—something easily done.

折 柳 to break a willow twig—to part from a friend, a parting present—from a story of one who broke off a twig of willow and gave it to his friend on parting from him at a bridge near Sianfu.

¹⁵折 桂 to pluck the cassia—to graduate in the old-style examinations, it was primarily used of successful candidates for Hanlin honours.

折 稿 振 落 to snap a dry twig and shake down falling leaves —very easily done.

折 死 or 折 殺 to cause death by having too much honour and thus using up the allotted share of happiness too soon.

折 毀 to break down; to destroy.

折 福 to break off the allotment of good fortune which one has, by having too much happiness.

²⁰折 脇 摺 齒 to break the ribs and teeth.

折 花 to pluck flowers.

折 衝 to break through the enemies' lines.

折 衝 尊 俎 to subdue the enemy at a feast—by diplomacy.

折 角 the angle of refraction.

²⁵折 鋒 衝 陣 breaking of spears and clash of troops—warfare.

折 骨 broken bones—weary.

短 折 cut off prematurely; to die young.

(b) To bend; to humble; to bow down.

折 挫 to try—as by adversity; to chasten; to polish.

折 服 to bring into submission.

折 磨 trials and afflictions; ill treatment.

折 節 to bend the joints—to humble oneself; to make a sudden change of attitude towards . . .

⁵折 節 下 交 humble to acquaintances.

折 節 下 賢 humble oneself before the gods.

折 節 謹 厚 to strive to be respectful and sincere.

折 腰 to bow.

折 辱 to humiliate.

曲 折 to bend; bent around.

(c) To decide a cause.

折 中 to decide equitably. *See above.* A. 1.

折 獄 to decide a lawsuit.

折 衷 to weigh opinions; to discriminate; to compromise.

折 衷 主 義 or 折 衷 說 eclecticism.

⁵折 衷·的 eclectic.

折 衷 家 eclectics.

折 衷 學 派 eclecticism.

折 衷 至 當 impartial decision.

折 證 an umpire or referee.

折 辨 to argue.

(d) To give an equivalent for; to set off against.

折 乾 a sum of money in lieu of presents.

折 徵 or 折 色 to send silver in lieu of tribute grain.

折 抵 to set off against.

折 漕 to exchange tribute for silver to send to the capital.

⁵折 還 to compromise with creditors.

折 餉 or 折 席 money equivalent for rations.

(e) To fold.

折 兒 a fold.

折 簡 or 折 柬 to send a card; to cut paper for letters.

折 紙 to fold paper.

折 角 to turn down a corner; to make "dog's ears."

(f) To sell or barter.

折 兌 sell or barter. *See above.* —3.

折 變 to sell a property for debt.

折 賣 to sell up.

折 閱 to sell at a loss; to fail.

(g) To calculate a proportion.

折 合 to calculate; to convert, as *taels* into dollars.

折 成 庫 平 convert into *Kuping taels.*

折 銀 to calculate the amount in silver.

(h) A mound for sacrifice to Earth.

泰 折 the Great Mound.

哲惢}
268
2.5.

Wise. To know intuitively.

哲 人 wise men.
哲 匠 clever artisan; a virtuous and wise man.
哲 嗣 Your son!
哲 夫 成 城 哲 婦 傾 城 the wisdom of a man can build a city, but the wisdom of a woman can overthrow it.
5哲 學 philosophy.
哲 學 史 history of philosophy.
哲 學 家 philosophers.
哲 母 a wise mother; wise and compassionate.
哲 王 wise kings.
10哲 理 philosophy.
哲 艾 a wise old man.
明 哲 shrewd; wise.
聖 哲 wisdom of the sages, not obtained by teaching.

浙
269
4.5. A river in Chekiang. The province of Chekiang.

蜇蜥}
270
4.5.

The jelly-fish. Stings of insects, etc. To sting.

蜇 吻 裂 鼻 to sting the lips and have chaps on the nose.
蜇 皮 or 海 蜇 dried skins of jelly-fish, used as food.

摺
271
2.5. To fold, to double together. To bend. A state paper.

摺 刀 a pocket or folding knife.
摺 奏 a memorial.
摺 子 a small folded paper; a memorial to the throne; pass book.
摺 尺 a folding rule.
5摺 差 a courier.
摺 扇 a folding fan.
摺 畧 a digest; a precis.

摺 疊 to fold up—as clothing, etc.
摺 稿 draft of a memorial.
10摺 紙 to fold paper.
摺 縐 a wrinkle or crease.
摺 腰 to bend the body.
摺 角 to turn down a corner; to make "dog's ears."
摺 開 to submit documents to a superior.

(a) Read $la^{5.2}$. To pull, to break.

摺 拉 to break.

懾
272
2

Afraid; faint-hearted.

懾 慴 fearful; not courageous.

(a) Read $sh\hat{e}^{4.5}$. To coerce, to subdue.

懾 服 人 心 to awe men into submission.

襵
273
3

A pleat in a skirt.

百 襵 裙 a many pleated skirt.

TSÊ. CHÊ. (坔)

(Tseh or Chai)

賾
274
4.5. Occult; abstruse; mysterious.

探 賾 to search out mysteries.

宅
275
2.5. A private dwelling; a neighbourhood.
Usually pron. $chai^2$.

宅 上 at your home.
宅 不 宅 者 a house that is not put to its proper use as a house.
宅 兆 auspicious day for a funeral.
宅 券 deed of rental or mortgage.
5宅 子 or 住 宅 a residence.
宅 憂 death of the head of the house.
宅 眷 the ladies of the house.
宅 經 geomantic treatise on choosing sites for graves.
宅 舍 a dwelling; a cottage.
10宅 門 the innermost gate or door.
宅 院 or 宅 園 a court-yard.
內 宅 women's apartments.
私 宅 private residence or apartments.

陰 宅 the dark dwelling—the grave.

(a) To settle; to rest in, to dwell.

宅 于 天 命 to rest in the appointment of Heaven.
宅 心 to settle the mind.
宅 是 鎬 京 he settled on *Hao-ching* as the capital.

擇
276
2.5. To select, to choose, to pick out.

擇 不 處 仁 to choose a neighbourhood for residence where virtuous manners do not prevail.
擇 主 而 歸 to select a leader and follow him with allegiance.
擇 交 to choose one's companions.
擇 吉 to select a lucky day.
5擇 地 to select a spot or a plot of land.
擇 尤 to choose the best.
擇 日 to choose lucky days.
擇 期 to choose a good time.
擇 木 from 良 禽 擇 木 而 棲 good birds select the trees on which they roost—one selects the leader which he would follow.
10擇 要 a selection of important points.
擇 親 or 擇 婿 to choose a son-in-law.
擇 選 to make a selection.
擇 音 (equiv. 陰) from 鹿 死 不 擇 音 a stricken deer has no time to choose his retreat.—when a man is hard pressed he cannot be particular about whom he follows.
擇 食 to pick and choose one's food.

澤
277
2.5.

A marsh. Damp.

澤 地 marshy place; a bog. [bank.
澤 國 the watery land; inundated
澤 宮 the damp palace—the place from whence the rain comes.
澤 梁 無 禁 there were no prohibitions regarding the weirs and the pools.
澤 瀉 the water plantain.
川 澤 streams and marshes.

(a) To fertilize; to anoint; to benefit; to enrich. Favour or kindness.

澤 人 to benefit man.

澤 及 枯 骨 kindness extending to dry bones—to bury stray bones.

澤 民 to benefit the people.

澤 流 於 後 世 his goodness extended to later generations.

5共 飯 不 澤 手 do not rub the hands when eating—to cleanse them, it should be done beforehand.

手 澤 猶 存 a relic of his work still remains.

潤 澤 to fertilize; to enrich; to moisten.

雨 澤 moistened by the rains.

香 澤 anointed with fragrant oils.

(b) Glossy, smooth, slippery.

光 澤 glossy; shining.

滑 澤 smooth; slippery.

肥 澤 greasy; fat.

(c) Read toh⁵ Name of a place.

摘 4.5. To pluck, to pick. To make extracts from. A.p. chai¹.
278

摘¹下·去 take it off—as a saddle, etc.

摘¹帽·子 to take off the hat.

摘 東 補 西 to pluck from one end to repair the other.

摘⁴根 to pull up the roots—to eradicate a bad habit.

⁵摘¹盔 卸 甲 to throw off the armour.

摘 菓·子 to pluck fruit.

摘 茶 to pick tea.

摘 要 to make an epitome.

摘 錄 to make extracts from a document.

摘¹鞍·子 to take the saddle off a horse.

(a) To deprive of.

摘¹⁴印 to take away the seal and degrade an official.

摘⁴脫 to separate from; to get away from.

摘⁴釋 to release.

摘 除 to deduct from.

摘 頂 to take away an official's button; to degrade him.

(b) To point out.

指 摘⁴ to point out faults.

(c) Read t'ih⁴.⁵. To reveal secrets.

摘 伏 to reveal a secret.

摘 姦 發 伏 to reveal the secret faults or evil of another.

謫
謫 2.5.
To blame, to find fault. To disgrace an official. Distinguish 讁 No. 5674.
279   tsê⁴.

謫 仙 banished from heaven to earth—said in praise of another.

謫 咎 to find fault.

謫 奸 to reprove evil.

謫 戍 banished to the frontiers.

謫 罰 to fine.

謫 降 degraded in office.

CH'Ê   (扯)
(Ch'æ)

車¹ A cart, a barrow, a carriage or chariot. Radical 159.
280 Also read chü³.

車 前 草 the plantain.

車 匠 a wheelwright.

車 圍 covering on a cart-top.

車 執 照 license for vehicles.

⁵車 塵 the dust of traffic.

車·夫 or 車 戶 or 趕 車 的 carters.

車·子 or 小 車 a wheelbarrow.

車 宮 a camping place protected by a ring of chariots.

車 捐 vehicle license fee.

¹⁰車 書 uniformity; from:— 車 同 軌, 書 同 文, 行 同 倫, all carriage wheels are of one size, all writing is with the same characters, and in conduct there are the same rules.

車 棚 awning in front of a cart, covering the horse or mule in the shafts.

車 殆 馬 煩 the weariness of travel.

車 水 馬 龍 carts and horses like a stream—very numerous.

車 狀 or 車 架 a lathe.

¹⁵車 票 railway ticket.

車 站 railway station.

車 箱·子 the inside of a cart.

車·脚 or 車 價 or 車·錢 cart hire.

車 行 place where carters assemble, from which they may be hired; carter's guild. -hang²

²⁰車 裂 or 車 磔 ancient punishment of being torn asunder between two chariots.

車 輛 or 車 皮 carts.

車 載 斗 量 from the 三 國, as for men like myself, there are cartloads and bushels full—very numerous.

車 輪 or 車 輗 輖 cart wheels.

車 輻 spokes of a wheel; imperial insignia shaped like spokes, painted red and having a white shaft.

²⁵車 轅 the shafts of a vehicle.

車 轍 cart ruts.

車 轍 鮒 魚 a perch in a dry rut—in desperate straits.

車 送 to send by cart or barrow.

車 門 large entrance by which carts may enter.

³⁰車 颺 to winnow.

車 馬 費 incidental expenses.

車 馬 臨 門 carriages and horses at the door—a rich man.

車 駕 title by which the emperor was spoken of.

下 車 to alight from a cart; to take up an official post.

³⁵專 車 special train or car.

搨 車 large hand truck for sacks, etc.

(東)洋 車 a ricksha; also 黃 包 車 for a public ricksha, or 包 車 for a private vehicle.

汽 車 automobile.

滑 車 a pulley.

⁴⁰火 車 railway train.

牙 車 the jawbone.

脚 踏 車 a bicycle.

貨 車 a goods train.

轎 車 a covered passenger cart.

⁴⁵電 車 electric tramcar.

飯 車 dining or restaurant car.

馬 車 a horse carriage.

(a) Apparatus for lifting water.

車 水 to lift water by means of this apparatus.

水 車 an apparatus for lifting water, an endless chain with paddles which enter the water, and fitting in a trough, push the water up.

筒 車 skeleton bamboo wheels, often 20 to 30 feet high, pipes of bamboo are fitted to the rim, and being turned by the current they lift the water into troughs on to the higher level, from

whence it flows by bamboo pipes to the fields.

龍 骨 車 a water lift with flexible joints which pass over a cogged wheel, and along a trough which they fit closely, the wheel is turned by human or by animal power.

(a')

(b) Read *chü*. A chariot in chess. The rook.

捨
扯 } 3

To drag, to haul. To prevaricate.

281

扯 上 扯 下 to haul up or down.
扯 · 住 to haul tight.
扯 手 to pull by hand; reins; to walk hand in hand.
扯 拉 to pull or drag. *See below.*—12.
⁵扯 旗 or 扯 挂 to haul up a flag.
扯 毀 to pull down; to destroy.
扯 淡 insipid.
扯 疲 careless; slovenly.
扯 篷 拉 縴 to hoist the sail and haul on the towline—to lend a hand.
¹⁰扯 脫 to pull off.
扯 舌 頭 to make mischief.
扯 謊 or 扯 拉 to lie. *See above.*—4.
扯 · 起 · 來 haul it up.
扯 · 起 · 大 旗 hoisted a large flag.
¹⁵扯 鈴 a humming top—diabolo.
扯 · 開 to pull apart.
扯 頭 髮 to tear the hair.

(a) To tear; to tear down.

扯 · 不 動 cannot be torn—as cloth, etc.
扯 壞 · 了 torn apart; spoilt by pulling—as a sash or tie.
扯 平 to strike the average.
扯 破 or 扯 碎 to tear in pieces.
⁵扯 簿 a tear-off notebook.
扯 裂 to tear asunder; to rend.
扯 絮 to pull cotton wool—to snow.
扯 麵 dough pulled into strips for noodles, instead of being cut.
招 貼 卽 扯 bills posted here will be torn down immediately.

(b) To buy cloth, etc.

扯 兩 尺 布 buy two feet of [cloth.
(a') To work with a rotating tool.
車 玉 to polish jade. 車 牀 a lathe.

CH'Ê.　(ㄔㄜ)
(Ch'eh)

掣 4.5. To choose. To hinder. To pull. Also read *ch'ih*.
282

掣 掣 的 throbbing.
掣 籤 or 掣 簽 to draw lots.
掣 肘 to impede the elbow—said of anything that impedes free action.
掣 電 speedily; like lightning.

屮 4.5. Plants sprouting. Radical 45.
283

軷
輆 } 4.5. The sides of a chariot where the arms were carried. Unceremoniously, abruptly, at once.
284

軷 以 易 之 unceremoniously gave his place to another.
軷 敢 I must forthwith presume—an apologetic phrase.
軷 然 hastily; suddenly.
軷 行 abruptly; hastily.

徹 4.5. Penetrating, discerning. Intelligible. To penetrate. Inter. 撤 No. 286.
285

徹 七 札 焉 penetrated the seven layers of his armour.
徹 上 徹 下 penetrating above and below.
徹 侯 feudal nobles under the Han dynasty.
徹 夜 from sunset to dawn.
⁵徹 天 reaching to heaven—of high peaks.
徹 始 徹 終 to understand thoroughly from beginning to end.
徹 底 to get to the bottom of.
徹 底 澄 清 to sift to the very bottom; to reform or purge thoroughly.
通 徹 to penetrate; fully comprehend.
¹⁰徹 頭 徹 尾 from beginning to end.
透 · 徹 thorough; penetrated.
徹 骨 penetrating to the bone—as a keen wind.
不 徹 not penetrated.
不 透 · 徹 superficial; not penetrated; not thorough.

(a) To remove, to strip off, to destroy. Inter. No. 286.

徹 · 去 to remove.
徹 我 牆 屋 he has destroyed our homes.
徹 饌 to remove the sacrificial dishes.
徹 供 to remove sacrificial food.

(b) To cultivate on the share system. Tithes.

徹 法 the tithing system.
徹 田 爲 糧 he allotted the revenue from the land.
何 其 徹 乎 How could I do with that system of tithing?
盍 徹 乎 Why not tithe the people?

撤 4.5. To remove. Inter. last. No. 285.
286

撤 任 to remove from office.
撤 出 to take away; to take off.
撤 · 去 to carry off; to remove.
撤 席 to end a feast.
⁵撤 平 to raze.
撤 消 to eliminate.
撤 災 to remove calamities.
撤 棘 ancient name for examination hall in the provinces—lit. to remove the thorn hedge, i.e., to close the examinations by opening the halls.
撤 簾 to remove the screen, behind which the empress heard government matters, on the young ruler coming of age and ascending the throne.
撤 銷 to cancel.
撤 · 開 to peel off a wrapper; to reject; to remove.

(a) To degrade, to cashier. To recall, as troops.

撤 兵 or 撤 戍 to withdraw troops.
撤 · 回 to withdraw or cancel, as a license; to recall; to turn back; to send back.
撤 委 to relieve an officer of his post.
撤 參 to remove from office and impeach.
撤 懲 to cashier; to degrade an officer.
撤 退 to resign; to dismiss; to withdraw.

澈 4.5. Clear water. To search thoroughly. Inter. 徹 No. 285.
287

澈底根究 to sift a matter to the bottom.
澈查 to make a thorough investigation.
澄澈 clear; sincere in heart.
澈白 pure white.

轍 4.5. The track of a wheel. A precedent.
288

轍亂旗靡 chariots in disorder and banners drooping—utterly routed.
轍迹 ruts; wheel tracks.
轍鮒 a fish in a dry rut—at the last gasp.
依轍行 follow in the old groove.
古轍 old ruts—precedents.
常轍 beaten tracks; ordinary ways.
蹈前轍 to return to his former ways.
蹈覆轍 to follow the tracks of an overthrown chariot — to repeat a disastrous blunder.

CH'Ê. (彳さ)
(Ts'eh or Ch'ai)

坼 4.5. To crack; to tear. To chap. To burst. ts'ê⁴.
289

不坼不副 no bursting nor rending—in parturition.
手坼裂 chapped hands.
龜坼 crackled like the shell of a tortoise—of chapped hands.

拆 1.5. To break open; to rip open; to split. Usually pron. ch'ai¹
290

拆信 or 拆書 to open a letter.
拆字 to dissect characters and re-combine them for fortune telling.
拆封 to break a seal.
拆息 interest in native banks.
⁵拆散 to disperse; to part.
拆散鴛鴦 parting of husband and wife.
拆股 to dissolve partnership.
拆衣·裳 to unpick garments.
拆·開 to tear open—as a wrapper or envelope.
分拆 to livide.

(a) To dismantle, to demolish, to destroy.

拆壞 to destroy utterly.
拆壞城池 to raze a city.
拆平 to raze; to demolish.
拆房屋 to pull down a building.
拆毀 to demolish; to pull down—as buildings.

(b) To take away.

拆艙 to remove the divisions of a Chinese boat.
拆配 to take from one to give to another.

CHÊN. (出)
(See also 346)

榛亲 ¹ The hazel nut or filbert tree. A thorny tree.
291

榛仁 the kernel of the hazel nut.
榛·子 the hazel-nut or filbert.
榛栗 small round nut with flavour like the chestnut.
榛梗 thorns—also used fig.
榛榛 or 榛莽 overgrown with thorns and brushwood.
榛蕪 overgrown; neglected growth.

溱 ¹ One of the sources of the River Hwai in Honan.
292

溱溱 abundant—as a crop.

臻 ¹ The utmost; the highest. To reach to. To collect. Many.
293

澤臻四表 his favours reached everywhere.
百福駢臻 May every blessing rest here!

蓁 ¹ Abundant. Luxuriant, as foliage. To wear on the head.
294

蓁莽 luxuriant growth.
蓁蓁 luxuriant vegetation; clustering together.

甄 ¹ To mould; to model, as in clay. To influence. To distinguish. To examine.
295

甄別人才 to discern men of talents.
甄陶 a potter—also used fig.
甄陶萬類 to mould and fashion all things.

蕀 ¹ A bright blue orchid, grows in S. China.
296

真眞 ¹ True, real, unfeigned, genuine. Thoroughly.
297

真信 trustworthy; reliable.
真假 the true and the false.
真像 the real image (optics.)
真·切 plain; clear; vivid.
⁵真吾 the true ego.
真因 the true origin; real cause.
真·實 genuine; real; sincere.
真心 true-hearted; sincere.
真情 the facts of the case.
¹⁰真材 real talent; good material.
真果 or 果真 in reality.
真正 real; genuine.
真理 truth; orthodox principles.
真珠貝 pearl shell.
¹⁵真皮 the dermis.
真相 exact image; real facts.
真·確 really; authentic; truly.
真神 The True God, used for God.
真空 a vacuum. See No. 3722-57ff.
²⁰真義 the true interpretation.
真肋骨 the true ribs.
真誠 real; sincere; true.
真話 the truth.
真詮 the true interpretation.
²⁵真道 the true doctrine; the right way or path.
失真 a forgery; see below. C. 1.
認真 to take seriously.
認真辦理 do the thing thoroughly or conscientiously.

(a) Used by Buddhists and Taoists somewhat as orthodox Confucianists use 誠. Spiritual, divine —as one's nature; ethereal; immortal.

真丹 Buddhist name for China.
真人 the spiritual man—one who has attained the Way, 道, and is no longer ruled by what he sees, hears or feels.

眞 元 the true nature of man—according to the orthodox school, it is good.

眞 君 honourable term for one who has attained a higher degree of purity than the 眞 人, and has become an immortal, 神·仙·

⁵眞 如 real, eternal and unchangeable truth. A Buddhist term defined as real, substantial and unchanging.

眞 宰 the first cause; used by Mohammedans for God. *See phrase below, from Chwangtsz. Last phrase of this group.*

眞 知 real or pure knowledge.

眞 靈 real or pure intelligence.

全 眞 to perfect the purity of the nature—to become an "immortal."

¹⁰天 眞 the natural goodness of a man—"the divine spark," natural endowments.

若 有 眞 宰 而 特 不 得 其 朕 there may be a God, but we cannot get any clue to his existence

(b) Substantial appointment to office, as opposed to a temporary post.

眞 除 substantial appointment to office.

卽 眞 to take up a definite appointment.

(c) A portrait.

失 眞 not at all like this. *See above—26.*

寫 眞 or 傳 眞 to paint a portrait —the first is used by Japanese for photographic likenesses.

得 其 眞 a lifelike portrait.

逼 眞 it strives with the original for likeness.

縝 ³
298
Close-woven. To tie.

縝 密 careful work, fine and close.

縝 紛 numerous; closely set.

(a) Black and thick, as hair, etc.

縝 黑 intense black.

鎭 ⁴
299
To press down; to guard; to repress.

鎭 亂 to put down disorder.

鎭 壓 to repress; to reduce to order.

鎭 守 to guard; to keep watch.

鎭·定 to soothe; to calm; to settle down.

⁵鎭 心 to quiet the mind.

鎭 懾 to subdue lawlessness.

鎭 撫 to pacify.

鎭 日 the whole day.

鎭 服 to reduce to submission.

¹⁰鎭 痛 劑 anodynes.

鎭 紙 brass frame to flatten paper when writing.

鎭 驚 to allay fears.

(a) To ward off evil influences.

鎭 宅 to rid a dwelling of evil spirits.

鎭 星 the planet Saturn.

鎭 物 spells; magic formulae; to drive off evil influences.

(b) A mart; a trading centre.

鎭·市 or 鎭 店 market town; a trading centre of over 50,000 inhabitants.

鎭·江 Chinkiang, a port on the Yangtze.

鎭 鄉 towns and villages.

(c) A regiment or brigade.

鎭 守 使 Defence Commissioner.

鎭 標 brigades under a 鎭 臺.

鎭 將 high rank military officers under the old system.

鎭 臺 Brigade-general under the old system.

 ³
300.
Bushy, black hair.

鬒 髮 如 雲 不 屑 髢 black hair like massed clouds and no false hair among it.

珍 ¹
301
Precious, rare—as gems. To prize.

珍 奇 or 珍 異 rare things.

珍 寶 or 珍 品 precious things.

珍 怪 strange, curious things.

珍 愛 or 珍 惜 to prize.

⁵珍 玩 or 珍 賞 costly toys or presents.

珍 珠 pearls.

珍 瑞 an auspicious token.

珍 祕 very valuable article, such as is rarely placed on exhibition.

珍 禽 奇 獸 rare birds and beasts.

珍·貴 valuable; costly; very precious.

珍 重 to take care of—phrase used in letters. —"take care of yourself."

(a) Delicate flavours.

珍 味 rare dainties.

珍 饈 美 味 delicacies, dainties.

畛 ³
302
Raised paths between fields. A border, a boundary. To come before the gods. To terminate, as life.

畛 域 a frontier or boundary.

畛 域 胥 化 the separating barriers all done away with.

不 分 畛 域 make no distinctions —free and easy.

疹
胗 ³
303
Pustules of any kind, a rash or eruption. Measles; various kinds of fever.

疹·子 measles; a rash; scarlet fever.

出 疹·子 to have measles; to get an eruption.

瘟 疹 scarlet fever.

紾 ³
304
To twist a cord round. Crooked. Obstinate.

紾 戾 crabbed; mulish.

紾 臂 from 紾 兄 之 臂 而 奪 之 食 to twist a brother's arm and snatch his food.—to twist the arm.

袗 ⁴
305
Plain, dark clothes. Unlined garment. Hem of a garment.

袗 絺 綌 unlined garment of linen or grass-cloth.

袗 衣 embroidered garments.

診 [3] To examine, as for disease. To give medical treatment.
306

診夢 to interpret a dream.
診所 dispensary; doctor's rooms.
診斷 or 診明 to diagnose.
診斷學 diagnostics.
診治 to heal.
診脈 or 診切 to feel the pulse.
診視 or 診候 to examine patients.
↑ 診察所 a physician's office.

軫 [3] Distressed, sorrowful.
307

軫念 kindly thoughts.
軫恤 pity; compassion.
軫悼 very sorrowful; utterly distressed.
軫慕 ardent thoughts; deep remembrance.
軫懷 compassion.
紆軫 discontented.

(a) To turn, to revolve. A carriage. Crossboard in a carriage, for which 枕 is also used.

軫轉 to roll.
輿軫 carriages.

(b) The pegs of a lute.

轉軫 to tune a lute.

(c) Numerous.

士卒殷軫 the soldiers were very numerous.
殷殷軫軫 flourishing, numerous.

枕 [3] A pillow. To use as a pillow. A stake to tether cattle.
308

枕上死 to die in bed—peacefully.
枕伴 a bed-fellow.
枕冷衾寒 pillow and bed cold—lonely, bereaved.
枕塊 pillowed on a clod—mourning for parents.
[5]枕巾 a pillow slip.
枕席 or 枕衾 pillow and mat—bedding.
枕席難安 not at rest, even in bed.
枕席未安 the throne not yet firmly established.
枕戈待旦 sleeping with weapons for a pillow, waiting for dawn—prepared for emergencies.
[10]枕戎 to use the weapons as a pillow—well prepared.
枕˳木 wooden sleepers or railway ties.
枕箱 box which is used as a pillow.
枕˳着 in bed; to recline the head on a pillow.
枕藉 mutual aid; lying about on each other, as the slain and wounded after a battle; close together.
[15]枕袋 or 枕套 a pillow-case.
枕邊 in bed; by the bedside.
枕˳頭 a pillow.
枕骨 the occiput.
門枕 a door-sill.

鴆 [4] A bird like the secretary **酖** falcon. Venomous; deadly. To poison.
309

鴆毒 destructive; poisonous.
鴆酒 poisoned wine.
飲鴆卒 drank poison and died.

(a) Read *tan*[1] Addicted to.

酖嗜 greedy.
酖酒色 lust for women and wine.

箴 [1] A probe; a needle. To pierce. To warn, to exhort.
310 Style of writing. Inter. next.

箴以自驚 warned himself by admonitions.
箴疵 to criticise others.
箴砭 or 石箴 stone probes.
箴言 or 箴規 warning words; admonitions.
箴諫 wise rebuke.
箴銘 warnings or admonitions carved on stone.

鍼 [1] A needle, a pin, a probe. **針** A sting. A stitch.
311

針尖 or 針頭 or 針杪 point of a needle.
針氈 a mat full of needles or pins—an uncomfortable situation.
針法 or 針科 practice of acupuncture.
針炙 acupuncture and cauterization.
[5]針皮削鐵 to scrape iron from the skin of a needle—mean; parsimonious.
針眼 or 針鼻 eye of a needle.
針砭 acupuncture—hence, words that hurt but do good.
針神 a clever needle-woman.
針˳綫 needle and thread—needlework; used fig.—clue to a matter; to mend a matter.
[10]針˳綫活 needlework; to make a living by sewing.
針˳脚 stitches.
針芥 needle and a tiny particle—the magnet attracts the needle, amber attracts tiny particles of matter; so the two characters are used for dispositions which attract each other.
針路 the compass course.
針鋒 or 針芒 the point of a needle—minute.
針頭綫腦 odds and ends of sewing.
針黹 fine needlework; embroidery..

娠 [4] Pregnant. **媷**
312

娠動 incipient labour; quickening.
娠喜 pregnant.
娠婦 a pregnant woman.
落娠 abortion.

振 [4] To shake. To move. To excite to action. To flap, as wings. Inter. 震 No. 315.
313

振˳作 to stir up; to urge.
振˳作有為 he has ability.
振刷 to rouse; to incite to action.
振˳動 to move; to shake; to set out to accomplish; vibrations.
[5]振˳動聲帶 the vibrations of the vocal chords.
振女 a young maiden.
振子 a lad. A pendulum. (*Jap.*)
振怖 to alarm.
振書 to flap a book to knock off the dust.
[10]振筆 rapid writing.
振翮 or 振翼 to spread the wings.

振 衣 to shake the clothing.
振 覺 to awaken.
振 鈴 to press a bell—as to call to order.
[15]威 振 四 海 he inspires awe everywhere.
手 振 to jar the hand.

(a) To relieve; to save. u.f., 賑 No. 314.
振 救 to save from danger.
振 拔 to save; to raise up.
振 捐 relief contributions.
振 興 to bring about prosperity.
振 興 實 業 to advance an industry; to cause to become prosperous.
振 乏 絕 to relieve the extremely distressed.

(b) To restore order. To recall.
振 旅 orderly return of victorious troops.

(c) To receive. To contain.
振 河 海 而 不 洩 it contains the rivers and seas, and they do not leak away.

(d) From; a preposition.
振 古 如 茲 from of old it was like this.

(e) Read chen[1] Numerous; noble.
振 振 公 子 noble sons.
子 孫 振 振 noble posterity.

(f) Read chen[4] In swarms; in flocks. u.f. 袗 No. 305.
振 絺 綌 single garments of linen.
振 鷺 于 飛 like flocks of egrets on the wing.

賑 [4] Liberal. To relieve, to aid the distressed. u.f., 振 No.
314   313.
賑 恤 to relieve and show mercy.
賑 捐 局 relief bureau.
賑 撫 貧 民 relief measures; to relieve the poor.
賑 撫 獎 章 decoration or reward for doing relief work.
[5]賑 欵 relief funds.
賑 濟 or 振 捐 to subscribe towards relief funds.
賑 災 to relieve famine or other distress.
賑 田 fields, the produce of which is devoted to charity.

賑 護 to relieve and protect.
[10]賑 贍 gifts in kind for relief purposes.
賑 饑 to feed the hungry.

震 [4] To shake; to excite. To terrify.
315

震 動 or 震 搖 to move; to excite; to tremble; to vibrate.
震 嚇 or 震 駭 to startle; to frighten.
震 壓 to repress.
震 威 awestricken.
[5]震 怒 great anger; a towering rage.
震 悼 the shock of grief.
震 悸 alarm; fear.
震 懾 or 震 服 to overawe.
震 懼 or 震 慄 fear and trembling.
[10]震 懾 to stand in awe of.
震 手 to jar the hand.
震 折 broken by concussion.
震 撼 to shake; to move; to stimulate.
震 旦 Buddhist term for China.
[15]震 耳 ear-splitting.
震 裂 ruin caused by earthquake.
震 雷 noise of thunder.
震 響 noise of concussion.
震 驚 terrified by shock.
[20]名 震 四 方 his name was heard on all sides.
震 死 了 killed by shock.
雷 震 struck by lightning (thunder).
↑地 震 earthquake.
(a) To quicken. The 4th of the diagrams.
腹 震 quickening.
載 震 to become pregnant.

朕 [4] I, We. The emperor. Formerly a general pronoun,
316   later appropriated to imperial use only. Mine.

安 朕 We are well—reply written on cards of inquiry sent to court by high officials.
朕 德 Our virtue.
朕 知 We know.
朕 躬 Our royal self.

(a) Subtle; incipient.
朕 兆 the subtle and mysterious; incipient.

眹 [3] Pupil of the eye. Inter.
317   last—Subtle; foreboding.

兆 眹 the incipience of good and evil before it is acted upon.

揕 [4] To stab. To strike. Noise of falling timber.
318

揕 其 匈 he stabbed him in the breast.

斟 [1] To deliberate; to arrange.
319

斟 妥 了 it is all settled.
斟 酌 or 斟 議 to consult; to consider.
細 斟 careful consideration.

(a) To pour out.
斟 滿 Fill up!
斟 茶 to pour tea.
斟 酒 to pour wine.

椹 [1] A chopping block. Target. Mulberry trees. Read shen[4]
320   Mulberry fruit.

砧 [1] A block on which clothes are beaten when being washed. An anvil. A heavy
碪   stone used by athletes.
321

砧 板 a chopping board as used by butchers.
砧 杵 a stone on which clothes are beaten and the club by which it is done.   [incus.
砧 骨 a small bone in the ear, the
鐵 砧 an anvil.

陣 [4] A file of soldiers. An army. To place in battle
陣   array. A battle. Distinguish 陳 No. 339.
322

陣 上 in the battle.
陣 亡 to die in battle.
陣 傷 wounded in battle.
陣 兵 to quarter troops.
[5]陣 勢 position of troops; disposition of forces.
陣 圖 plan of battle.
陣 法 tactics; plan of campaign.
上 陣 to go into battle.

八 陣 圖 the eight tactical dispositions of troops, according to *Chu-koh Liang*.

[10] 布 陣 to set out; to arrange.

排 陣 a draw up in battle array.

敗 陣 a defeat.

(a) A time; an occasion. N.A. of these things.

一 陣·一 陣 now and again; at intervals; repeated.

一 陣 煙 a puff of smoke.

一 陣 雨 a shower of rain.

走 一 陣 to take a turn together.

譖 [4]

Slander.

323

譖 言 slanders.

誣 譖 to slander.

CH'ÊN.   (彳)

綝 [1] To stop. Adjusted, in order.

324

嗔 [1] To be angry; to scold.

325

嗔 喝 angry shouts to stop.

嗔 嫌 anger and resentment.

嗔 怪 to rebuke.

嗔 訴 angry railing.

鷄 以 嗔 睨 the cock makes angry sidelong glances.

瞋 [1] To glare at with anger or scorn.

326

瞋 怒 to glare at in anger.

瞋 目 angry look; a scornful stare.

瞋 視 an angry stare.

臣 [2] A statesman. A subject. Formerly used by civil officials for "I". Radical 131.

327

臣 一 主 二 the minister is only one, but he can serve more than one ruler.

臣 下 "I," used by statesmen of themselves when addressing the throne.

臣 僕 servants and slaves.

臣 妾 my concubine; slaves and concubines.

[5] 臣·子 government officers; ministers of state.

臣 宦 or 臣 僚 officers of state.

臣 宰 a minister of state.

臣 工 all statesmen and officers.

臣 庶 or 臣 民 subjects.

[10] 臣 道 duties of a statesman.

不 臣 之 心 a disloyal heart.

人 臣 a subject.

君 臣 the first of the five relationships of men—

姦 臣 a traitor.

[15] 忠。臣 a loyal minister.

直 臣 an upright minister.

羣 臣 the crowd of courtiers; the whole of the court officials.

(a) To be subject to.

臣 服 to become subject to.

臣 者 人 道 也 to serve is the way of man.

臣 附 于 大 邑 周 they submitted to him at the great city of Chou.

臣 順 to submit; to own allegiance.

稱 臣 to become a subject.

塵 [2] Dust; dirt.

328

塵 俗 commonplace. *See below*. A. 2.

塵 土 or 塵 灰 or 塵 沙 dust.

塵 垢 dirt; pollution.

塵 埃 or 塵 塗 dust; dirt; the world. *See below*. A. 5.

[5] 塵 壤 earth; soil.

塵 尾 dust whisk of horsehair or a yak's tail.

塵 污 to defile.

塵 牘 dusty archives; musty accumulation of papers.

塵 羹 塗 飯 dusty broth and dirty rice—said of something which has fallen and is not worth picking up.

[10] 承 塵 a ceiling.

洗 塵 to wash off the dust—a welcome feast to a returning traveller.

(a) This world. Vice, sensual pleasure.

塵 世 or 塵 寰 this mortal life.

塵 俗 Buddhist term for human life.

塵 凡 creatures of dust—mortal life.

塵 嚣 an evil place; "Vanity Fair."

塵 壤 this world; this life.

塵 心 or 塵 念 carnal thoughts.

塵 軀 our mortal frame.

心 塵 the dust of the heart; evil desires.

紅 塵 red dust—this life of care.

絕 塵 to retire from the pursuits of this life—a monk, an ascetic.

岑 [2] A mountain peak. Isolated. A surname.

329 Pron. ts'ên.[2]

岑 寂 isolated and lonely—as a mountain top.

岑 樓 the pointed gable of a high building.

岑 蔚 in the dense places on the high peaks.

岑 蔚 isolated peaks and luxuriant growth.

湗 [2] River in Shensi. Mountain torrents. Pron.. ts'ên.[2]

330

湗 湗 淚 下 her tears flowed fast.

忱 [2] Sincere; trustworthy.

331

丹 忱 pure and sincere.

難 忱 not reliable.

沈 [2] To sink; to perish.

沉

332

沈·下 臉·來 his countenance fell.

沈 伏 a weak pulse; to fail of one's purpose.

沈 失 to sink; to be lost.

沈 底 sunk to the bottom.

[5] 沈 案 to quash a case by neglecting to hear it.

沈 水 to sink in water.

沈 沒 or 沈 沬 perished; sunk.

沈 浮 bobbing on the water; the ups and downs of fortune; uncertain.

沈 浸 to steep in water.

[10] 沈 淪 to perish.

沈 溺 drowned; infatuated.

沈 澱 precipitate.

沈 牛 water-buffaloes.

沈 落 to sink down.

[15] 沈 西 to sink in the west—sunset.

沈 迷 不 醒 deeply infatuated in vice.

(a) Heavy; very.

沈 冤 a deep grievance; wrongs that cannot be redressed.

沈 吟 in deep thought; hesitating; to chant in a low voice.

沈 心 or 沈 思 to contemplate; to ponder.

沈 晦 very obscure.

⁵沈 沈 very deep; very heavy.

沈 滯 a stoppage; long without a promotion.

沈 痼 chronic disease.

沈 痛 extremely painful.

沈 睡 or 沈 眠 deep and heavy slumber.

¹⁰沈 篤 serious, as a disease, etc.

沈 著 unmoved; impassive.

沈 酗 or 沈 醉 dead drunk.

沈 重 heavy; serious; grave.

沈 陰 heavy wet weather.

¹⁵沈 靜 very quiet; well-behaved.

沈 飲 a carousal.

沈 香 garu-wood; lign aloes.

沈 鬱 very miserable and despondent.

(b) Read *shen³*. **A surname.** Only first form of char. used.

霃 ²
333
Long continued rains.

磣 ³
334
Sand, grit.

牙 磣 grit in the food—indecent.

紖 ³
335
A rope for leading cattle.

辰 ²
336
Division of time, 7 to 9 a.m. Early morning. Radical 161. One of the twelve "branches," 地 支.

辰 光 the time of day.

辰 告 timely warning.

辰 時 from 7 to 9 a.m.

辰 月 the third lunar-month.

辰 牡 male beasts in season.

辰 砂 cinnabar, found at 辰 州 in Hunan.

宸 ²
337
Imperial apartments, imperial.

宸 垣 the imperial city.

宸 宮 the private part of the palace.

宸 翰 the imperial signature.

宸 衷 imperial opinions.

晨 ²
338
Daybreak; morning.

晨 光 daybreak; daylight.

晨 早 early dawn.

晨 星 the morning star.

晨 昏 顛 倒 to turn night into day.

晨 門 a gate-keeper.

晨 露 early dew.

晨 風 morning breeze.

陳 ²
339
To arrange; to spread out.

陳 列 or 布 陳 to arrange; to set out in detail.

陳 列 品 exhibits; curios.

陳 列 所 museum; exhibition; showroom.

陳 力 就 列 he puts forth effort and takes his position—as an officer.

⁵陳 卦 to prognosticate.

陳 尸 to expose the bodies of criminals.

陳 行 to marshal the ranks.(-*hang²*)

陳 設 to set out; to arrange.

陳 饌 to arrange the dishes of food.

(a) To make a statement. To make a plea.

陳 告 to state; to set forth a cause.

陳 對 to reply in detail.

陳 情 表 plaint made to the emperor.

陳 義 to explain the meaning.

⁵陳 請 to petition.

陳 請 權 right of petition.

陳 訴 pleadings.

陳 詞 a statement; an accusation.

陳 說 to explain; to state a case.

陳 述 to state a case; to explain.

陳 述 意 見 statement of one's views.

(b) A long time. Stale, as eggs, fruit, etc.

陳 久 old, a long time.

陳 案 long standing lawsuits.

陳 皮 dried orange peel.

陳 粟 or 陳 米 or 陳 糧 old, stale grain.

陳 腐 spoiled by keeping; old-fashioned.

陳 舊 stale; old-fashioned.

陳 迹 things that are past leave traces.

(c) Seasoned, as wine.

陳 紹 seasoned Shaohsing wine.

陳 酒 old wine.

陳 醋 the best vinegar.

(d) To expose.

欲 諫 不 欲 陳 desired to remonstrate with the prince but not to expose his faults.

(e) A path to the house.

胡 逝 我 陳 Why did he visit me?

(f) Ancient state in what is now central Honan.

在 陳 to be in difficulties or straits, from the next.

在 陳 絕 糧 (Confucius) was without food in Ch'en.

(g) Read *chen⁴* **A battle. N.A. inter.** 陣 **No. 322, which see.**

陳 斃 slain in battle.

陳 石 plinth of stone.

蔯 ²
340
A variety of artemisia.

茵 蔯 variety of artemisia.

櫬 ⁴
341
A coffin, especially the inner one. Name of a tree.

櫬 梧 a tree something like the *T'ung,* 桐.

棺 櫬 a coffin.

襯 ⁴
儭
342
To assist; to give alms.

襯 僧 to give money to Buddhist priests.

襯 施 供 具 to provide all necessaries for priests.

郣 襯 to assist; to strengthen.

(a) **To annotate; to ornament.**

襯 紙 a fly-leaf; extra page inserted between the pages of a book.

襯 色 to add colour to; to adorn the person.

添 襯 to add a colour.

陪。襯 to bring forward an illustration.

(b) **Underclothing; to line garments.**

襯 巾 handkerchief carried at the girdle. |eign style shirt.

襯 衫 unlined inner garment; for-

襯 袋 fob pockets in the girdle.

襯 裙 petticoat; underskirt.

疢 [4] A fever characterized by sores.
343

疢 如 疾 首 makes me feverish with something like a headache.

恒 存 乎 疢 疾 will be found to have been in sickness or trouble.

齓 [4] Period when the milk teeth are shed—the young.
344

趁 [4] To take advantage of; to
趂 avail oneself of. To follow; to go.
345

趁 便 to take advantage of the opportunity.

趁 勢 to take advantage of power or position to get a thing done.

趁 早 to take advantage of at once; to start early.

趁 時。候 to make use of the times; to take advantage of the chance.

[5]趁 時 風 to avail oneself of the opportunity of the moment.

趁 機 會 take advantage of the opportunity.

趁 空 avail oneself of leisure.

趁。著 to avail oneself of.

趁 行 (hang[2]) to sell at a lower price than is current with a view to monopolising the sales.

趁 願 just as I wished; to avail oneself of the willingness of another.

趁 風 揚 帆 hoist the sail when the wind blows.

CHÊN (坐)

貞 [1] To inquire by divination.
Lucky. The lower half of
346 the diagrams of the *Book of Changes.*

休 貞 auspicious; lucky site for a grave.

(a) **Upright; correct.**

貞 人 a virtuous, upright man.

貞 固 to know the right and inflexibly hold to it.

貞 固 足 以 幹 事 he who holds tenaciously to what he knows to be right is well able to transact important matters.

貞 幹 post and frame for building walls; important post in erecting a structure—an indispensible minister of state. *See* No. 349. *Also below.—*10.

[5]貞 忠 loyal; incorruptible.

貞 操 pure, moral rectitude.

貞 而 不 諒 really and not casually sincere.

貞 臣 a loyal and upright minister.

貞 諒 trustworthy and faithful.

[10]以 仲 尼 爲 貞 幹 *Chung-ni* (Confucius) was a pillar of state.

萬 邦 以 貞 the whole empire will be upright—if the emperor is a great and good man.

(b) **Pure, virtuous, chaste.**

貞 女 a virgin; virtuous woman.

貞 明 pure and bright as the rays of the sun and moon.

貞 木 a hard wood.

貞 潔 or 貞 淑 chaste and undefiled—virgin purity.

[5]貞 烈 to maintain chastity even unto death.

貞 石 pure white hard stone—used of grave stones.

貞 節 pure, undefiled—used of a widow who refuses to re-marry.

貞 節 坊 arches erected in honour of such widows.

貞 靜 virtuous and quiet; modest.

守 貞 to maintain chastity—of a girl whose betrothed dies and who remains unmarried.

(c) **Used for "four" as it is the fourth character in the** *Book of Changes.*

元 亨 利 貞 one, two, three, four. The four seasonable effects of Heaven.

偵 [4] A spy, a scout. To spy.
347

↓偵 探 小 說 detective story.

偵 伺 or 偵 探 a spy; detective.

偵 察 detectives.

偵 拏 or 偵 獲 to seize a person unawares.

偵 查 secret inquiries.

偵 知 ascertained by spying.

偵 緝 to examine and arrest.

偵 訪 to inquire into.

偵 騎 mounted spies.

↑偵 察 機 a reconnaissance plane.

幀 [1] A picture; one of a pair, as of scrolls, etc. N.A.
348

贈 畫 一 幀 he presented a picture to him.

楨 [1] An evergreen shrub common in N. China. A post.
349

楨 幹 post and boards for raising adobie walls; a support—used of men of ability. *See* No. 346. A4.

邦 之 楨 a pillar of state.

禎 [1] Lucky; auspicious.
350

禎 祥 a lucky omen.

CHÊNG (坐)

正 [4] Upright; true.
351

正 人 upright person; a true man.

正 分 a proper fraction.

正 因 the true cause.

正 大 光 明 upright and pure in mind.

[5]正 方 a rectangle.

正 氣 uprighteousness.

正 直 straightforward; upright in conduct.

正 直 無 私 upright, without partiality; perfectly fair and just.

正 立 to stand upright.

正 角 a right angle.

(a) Orthodox, correct, regular. Authorized.

正 則 a standard. *See below.* D. 1.

正 命 to fulfil the allotted span.

正 宗 orthodox teaching.

正 幣 currency; coinage.

[5]正 教⁺ the orthodox religion, specially used by Mohammedans.

正 書 orthodox style of Chinese writing.

正 果 the proper consequence of a regulated life here — future bliss.

正 格 proper; fitting.

正 欵 the authorized amount.

[10]正 法 capital punishment.

正 理 truth; orthodox principles.

正 用 lawful; proper use.

正 稅 the regular amount of duty; 5%.

正 統 orthodox; the rightful ruler or head of a state.

[15]正 統 派 the orthodox party.

正。經 respectable; serious.

正。經。事 lawful business: reputable matters; serious affairs.

正。義 orthodox interpretation of the classics; orthodox principles.

正 色 the standard colours; sedate; serious countenance.

[20]正 表 決 an affirmative vote.

正 覺 perfect intelligence.(*Budd.*).

正 貨 or 正 金 hard cash or currency, as opposed to notes.

正。路 or 正。道 or 正。途 the correct or orthodox path; the correct thing.

正 軌 the correct way or path.

[25]正 選 to vote "aye."

正 項 legitimate items of taxation.

正 額 a regular, stated amount.

正 顏 属 色 sedate and grave.

(b) Exact. Straight. Formal.

正 中¹ exactly in the middle.

正 中⁺ to hit the bull's eye.

正 合 時 at the right moment.

正 對 exactly right; the very thing.

正。式 formal; normal; final—not provisional.

[5]正。式 修 改 revision (of treaties) in due form.

正。式 公 文 a formal despatch.

正。式 委 任 a formal appointment.

正。式 宣 戰 formal declaration of war.

正。式 提 議 a formal motion.

[10]正。式 政 府 regularly constituted government.

正。式 演 說 formal speech.

正。式 發 布 formal promulgation.

正。式 答。復 formal reply.

正。式 解 決 a formal decision.

[15]正。式 談 判 formal discussion.

正。式 辭 職 formal resignation.

正。式 開 出 authorized edition.

正 數 an exact amount, without fractions.

正 東 due east.

[20]正 比 例 direct proportion.

正 當⁺ seemly; as it should be.

正 當⁺ 事 業 legitimate interests.

正 當⁺ 手 續 legitimate procedure.

正 當⁺ 營 業 legitimate business.

[25]正 當 理 由 a just cause.

正 當 的 權 利 legitimate privileges.

正 當⁺ 行 為 correct behaviour.

正 當⁺ 要 求 formal demand; fair claim.

正 當⁺ 防 衞 legal self-defence.

[30]正 確 exact.

正 言 a straight talk; straightforward speech.

↑正 當 ¹the exact thing to do is...

(c) Just; at the time of; during.

正 值 at that time; it just happened that.

正 午 or 正 晝 noon.

正。在 or 正。要 just as; during; on the point of.

正。在 裝 置 just in the course of construction.

[5]正。在。要 問 I was just about to ask.

正。在 進 行 during the advance; during the process.

正。在 面 前 directly in front of.

正 如 alike; similar to.

正 好 just right.

[10]正 對 面 just opposite.

正 科 年 the year in which the examinations took place—alternate third years.

正 適 answers exactly to the requirements.

花 正 開 the flowers are just in full bloom.

(d) To adjust; to regulate; to correct.

正 則 to adjust the standards. *See above.* A. 1.

正 名 to define the correct terms.

正 己 to rectify oneself.

正 心 to regulate the heart.

[5]正 是 四 國 he makes all the people upright.

正 襟 to adjust the dress; to pay respect to.

正 誤 to correct typographical errors.

正 誼 to conform to requirements.

正 顏 色 to regulate the countenance.

撥 正 to put a thing straight; to adjust.

(e) Principal as opposed to secondary. Chief.

正 位 principal seat.

正 兵 regular soldier, not a recruit.

正 副 or 正 從⁺ principal and subordinate or secondary.

正 印 prefects and magistrates under the Manchus.

[5]正 品 the full rank as opposed to "sub." or "vice."

正 堂 the main hall; prefects and magistrates.

正 室 or 正 房 or 正 妻 the lawful wife.

正 客 principal guest.

正 席 principal seat at a feast.

[10]正 廳 the main body or floor of an auditorium.

正 支 the eldest son of an eldest son.

正 犯 從 犯 principal and accessory to a crime.

正 獻 principal at a sacrifice.

正 目 a sergeant.

[15]正 身 in person, not by proxy.

正 門 the main entrance.

正 領 事 a consul.

令 正 Your wife!

會 正 chairman of an association, etc.

(f) Original.

正 文 original text.

正 本 original copy of a book kept in reserve by librarians; authentic writing.

(g) The right side of a thing.

正。面 反。面 right and wrong side respectively; the obverse and reverse; positive and negative of a question.

(h) Read *cheng*[1] **The first month of the year.**

正建寅爲人統 *Yin,* the cyclical character for the "beginning of man" was set up as the character for the first month.

正·月 the first month of the year.

正·月建寅 the first month is related to the cyclical character *Yin.*

新正 the new year.

來正 first month of the next year.

開正 to open the seals; to resume business after the new year.

(i) **The centre of a target.**

正鵠 a target.

射不中正 did not hit the centre.

(j) Read *cheng*[3] **Whole, entire, without fractions. Added to numeral expressions to prevent unauthorized additions. Inter. 356.**

正個·的 a whole one; unbroken.

正天·家 the whole day long.

式佰圓正 Dollars Two hundred only.

征[1] **To reduce to submission; to attack.**
352

征人 warriors.

征伐 to attack by declaring war; punitive military expedition.

征勦 or 征誅 to exterminate rebels.

征取 to take captive.

[5]征戰 to fight a battle.

征·服 to compel submission by force.

征派夫役 or 發派夫役 to send soldiers on an expedition.

征者上伐下也 correction is when the superior authority punishes subjects by force of arms.

征討 to subjugate; to quell, as an insurrection.

[10]南面而征 when—*T'ang*—was engaged in the south.

敵國不相征 hostile states do not correct each other.

湯一征 as soon as T'ang began to execute justice.

王往而征之 Your majesty went to punish them.

(a) **To levy taxes; to raise troops.**

征兵 to raise an army.

征收 to collect taxes.

征斂無藝 no limit to taxation.

征權 to farm the taxes.

[5]征稅 to levy taxes.

征糧 to collect the general land tax.

征納 to levy a tax or duty.

征繕 to get munitions, etc., ready for war.

關譏而不征 if, at his frontier passes, there is inspection of persons, but no taxes or duties.

(b) **To go; to pass time.**

征夫 a soldier or other person who is away on a long journey.

征帆 a boat on a long journey.

征雁 migratory geese.

征馬 a traveller's horse.

客赴長征 the travellers went forward on their long journey.

宵征 to travel by night.

長征 a trek, an expedition.

症[4]   **Disease; ailments.**
353

症候 or 病症 malady; disease; ailment; symptoms.

內症外症 internal and external complaints.

急症 acute diseases.

順症 a curable disease.

鉦[1]   **A gong used to sound a halt for troops. A priest's gong.**
354

鉦以退之 the gong sounded the retreat.

鉦鼓 the gong to sound a retreat and the drum to advance.

政[4] **To rule. Government; administration. Laws.**
355

政·事 or 政·務 politics; government affairs.

政事堂 council of state presided over by the premier.

政人 government officials.

政化 to influence men by government.

[5]政令 official orders.

政令愈疲 greater slackness in government discipline.

政況 political conditions.

政務廳 administration department.

政務會議 meeting of the administration to discuss policy.

[10]政合國 confederated states.

政團 political party.

政客 politician, one who lives at the game.

政局 the political situation.

政府 the government; the administration; constituted form of government.

[15]政府同意 agreed to by the government.

政府提案 government proposals; government bills.

政府擔任 government responsibility.

政府機關 government organ.

政府限制 government restrictions.

[20]政府黨 the government party.

政敵 political opponent.

政敎 official exhortations to keep order.

政敎分離 separation of church and state.

政會 a political association.

[25]政權 or 政柄 political power.

政·治 politics.

政·治哲學 political philosophy.

政·治器械 political instruments.

政·治團體 the body politic; political organization.

[30]政·治地理 political geography.

政·治學 political science.

政·治家 politicians; statesmen.

政·治工作 special office which controls propaganda and such things.

政·治平等 political equality.

[35]政·治活動 political activities.

政·治犯 political offenders.

政·治的 political.

政·治科 department of politics.

政·治組織 political organization.

[40]政·治經驗 experience in administration.

政·治經濟學 political economy.

政·治關係 political consequences.

政法分權 separation of legislative and executive.

政潮 political unrest; tide of political affairs.

[45]政界 government circles; the realm of politics.

政界現像 the present aspect of politics.

政 社 political associations.
政。策 or 政 略 statesmanship; administrative policy.
政 綱 platform; government programme.
50 政 綱 不 振 inefficient policy; government with a weak platform.
政 績 achievements of the government.
政 聲 reputation of the administration.
政 見 policy of the administration; political opinion.
政 要 important planks in the government platform.
55 政 訓 部 bureau for instruction in party principles.
政 變 overthrow of the administration; coup d'etat.
政 象 political aspect of affairs.
政 費 expense of administration.
政 體 system of government.
60 君 主 政 體 monarchy.
民 主 政 體 democracy.
專 制 or 獨 裁 政 體 autocracy.
共 和 政 體 republican form of gov't.
立 憲 政 體 constitutional government.
政 黨 內 閣 party cabinet.
七 政 the sun, moon and five planets.
65 家 政 domestic regulations.
從 政 in government service.
民 政 civil government.
無 政 府 anarchy.
行 政 administration; executive; *also see under* 行 No. 2754.
70 行 政 科 administrative section.
行 政 費 expenses of administration.
內 務 行 政 費 administration expenses for the interior.
實 業 行 政 費 administrative expenses for industries.
教 育 行 政 費 administrative expenses of education.
財 政 行 政 費 administrative expenses of the finance department.
軍 政 military government.

整 [3] **To set in order; to put**
356 **right; to repair; to adjust; to marshal.**

整 作 to put right.
整 備 to make ready.
整 列 to set out in order.

整 合 consistency.
5 整 壞 to spoil in trying to repair.
整 好 to put tidy; to straighten up.
整 容 to tidy the appearance, as by shaving and dressing the hair.
整 整 齊 齊 regular; in good order; tidy.
整 束 衣 冠 to adjust the wearing apparel.
10 整 治 to repair and set in order.
整 潔 clean; in good order and condition.
整 理 to adjust; put in order.
整 理 土 地 regulate the land administration.
整 理 規 模 to reform manners and customs.
15 整 理 金 融 to regulate the financial conditions.
整 翻 to make as before.
整 衣 to adjust the dress.
整 表 to repair or regulate a watch.
整 隊 to marshal troops.
20 整。頓 to arrange; to rehabilitate; to reconstruct; amend, etc.
整 頓 吏 治 reform local administration.
整 頓 幣 制 to readjust the currency.
整。頓 林 業 to reorganize industries.
整 飭 to rule and order.
25 整 飭 戎 行 to preserve order in the army.
整。齊 in good order.
整。齊 畫 一 adjusted to uniformity—as weights and measures.
整。齊 花 flowers with petals arranged regularly, as the plum, almond, etc.

Nos. 5, 6, and 16 are Cantonese.

(a) **The whole. After numbers it is equivalent to "only."** *See* 351 J.

整 個 complete; whole; completely.
整 個 的 人 a complete man.
整 塊 whole, not crushed or broken.
整 夜 the whole night.
5 整 天。家 or 整 天。的 the whole day.
整 年 the whole year.
整 數 a whole number.
整 整 三 日 three whole days.
玖 佰 兩 整 Tls. 900.00 only.

證 証 [4] **Evidence, proof. To give**
357 **evidence. To testify.**

證。人 or 干 證 a witness.
證。候 symptoms of disease; symptoms.
證 劵 bonds; scrip; bills, etc.
證 劵 交。易 所 The Stock Exchange.
5 證 實 to bear testimony to the truth of; confirm.
證 左 a witness.
證。據 documentary proofs.
證 明 to certify, to prove.
證 明 書 voucher; certificate.
10 證 書 certificate; credentials; diploma.
證 物 exhibits in a suit, used as evidence.
證 章 a badge.
證 結 evidence; testimony.
證 見 to testify to what one has seen.
15 證 言 evidence; testimony.
證 驗 to bear witness; to verify.
作 見。證 to bear testimony as an eyewitness.
明 證 examples; illustrations of.

徵 [1] **To prove; evidence; verification. Fulfilment. Distinguish 微 No. 7061, and 徽 No. 2354.**
358

徵 信 錄 to show a statement of receipts and expenditure in any public transactions.
徵 候 symptoms of disease.
徵 據 proof; evidence.
徵 驗 verified; fulfilled; the result is according to expectation.
5 吾 能 徵 之 矣 I can adduce them in support of my words.
宋 不 足 徵 也 Sung cannot sufficiently attest my words.
明 徵 clear proof.
有 徵 there is proof.
無 徵 之 言 unfounded statements.

(a) **To levy; to collect, as taxes or materials.**

徵 收 to levy and collect, as taxes.
徵 收 官 吏 tax collectors.
徵 收 費 the expenses of collection.
徵 收 賦 稅 to levy taxes or duties.

徵 收 額 the rate of a levy.
徵 斂 to gather taxes.
徵 發 to levy, as taxes or duties on property, etc.
徵 稅 to levy taxes.
徵 集 to gather together; to collect material.
徵 集 物 品 to collect materials.

(b) To levy or raise troops.

徵 兵 to enlist under conscription.
徵 兵 制 度 conscription.
徵 調 to transfer troops from one place to another; to conscript men.

(c) To seek for; to inquire after; to ask for; to solicit.

徵 文 articles in a paper or magazine not by members of the staff, but specially paid for.
徵 求 to petition; to solicit.
徵 求 意·見 to seek the opinions of.
徵 求 會 員 to convass for members.
徵 答 to ask a question and beg for a reply.
徵 詩 to ask another for a poem.
徵 逐 to wear out a friend by incessant and long visits.

(d) To complete, as marriage arrangements.

納 徵 the sending of betrothal presents to complete the arrangements for a wedding.

(e) To summon.

徵 召 a call to assist the government.
徵 士 or 徵 君 a scholar summoned to the court.
徵 引 to ennoble; to dignify.

(f) Read chih³ (chi̇̈) **One of the five musical notes, regarded as corresponding to fire , the note** sol.

瘾 ¹ Obstruction of the bowels.
359

瘕 痕 痞 塊 hard obstructions in the bowels.
瘕 結 obstructions or knots in the bowels, from which it gets the meaning of an obstinate disposition.

拯 ³ To save; to lift up.
360

拯 恤 to relieve and pity the distressed.
拯 救 to save from danger.
拯 濟 to relieve; to help.
拯 溺 鍾 石 救 火 投 薪 in saving the drowning to let down a stone, or in helping at a fire to throw on faggots—worse than useless.
拯 災 郵 患 to save and help those in distress or famine.

烝 ¹ Steam. To steam, to cook by steaming. To distil.
361. Inter. next.

烝 暑 damp heat.
烝 熟 to steam thoroughly.
烝 籠 a steamer for rice, etc.
烝 飯 to steam rice.
烝 饅·頭 to steam bread.

(a) Capable, as a ruler. To act in a princely manner.

文 王 烝 哉 Capable was Wen Wang as a ruler!

(b) To advance. To present to.

烝 烝 乂 gradually lead to government.
烝 畀 to present to.
烝 進 to offer, as presents.

(c) Incest, usually with those of an older generation.

烝 于 夷 姜 he committed incest with I Chiang.

(d) The winter sacrifice.

烝 祭 歲 the winter sacrifice.
烝 禋 a solemn sacrifice.
祠 禴 嘗 烝 spring, summer, autumn and winter sacrifices.

(e) Many, flourishing. Vigorous. Liberal. All.

烝 烝 皇 皇 generous and great.
烝 民 乃 粒 all the people had grain.
天 生 烝 民 Heaven produced the people.

(f) An expletive.

烝 然 an expletive.

蒸 ¹ Twigs of hemp used for fuel. To rise, as steam.
362. Steam. All. Inter. last.

蒸 庶 the masses.
蒸 暑 damp heat.
蒸 民 mankind.
蒸 氣 steam, vapour.
蒸 氣 浴 a vapour bath.
蒸 源 fierce heat.
蒸 發 evaporation.
蒸 發 皿 evaporating dish.
蒸 蒸 rising, ascending, as vapour.
蒸 蒸 日 上 之 勢 a growing improvement of conditions.
蒸 餅 steamed bread or cakes.
蒸 餾 to produce steam; to distil.
蒸 餾 水 distilled water.
蒸 騰 steam ascending.
蒸 騰 作 用 transpiration, as of leaves, etc.
蒸 鬱 vapour arising.

鄭 ⁴ A feudal state under the Chou Dynasty, B.C. 774-500. occupying the district of the present K'ai-feng in Honan.
363

鄭 聲 the lewd songs of Cheng.
鄭 重 earnest; important; to value.

嵊 ⁴ District in Shaohsing, Chekiang.
364 Pron. shêng⁴.

爭 ¹
争 To wrangle; to contend; to strive.
365

爭 光 to dazzle; brilliant.
爭 先 to contend for first place.
爭 勝 to press forward; to strive for mastery.
爭 功 to strive to excel.
爭 友 a faithful friend, who will admonish.
爭 口 o·爭 吵 or 爭 嘴 to quarrel.
爭 名 to strive for fame.
爭 名 奪 利 to struggle for fame and wealth.
爭 地 dispute over land.
爭 執 or 爭 拗 obstinate; stubborn; to disagree.
爭 奈 nevertheless; howbeit.
爭 如 not equal to.
爭 存 struggle for existence.
爭 家 產 dispute over family inheritance.

15爭 奪 to seize.

爭 強 較 力 to contend for mastery.

爭 強 賭 勝 seeking to outdo the other.

爭 戰 to fight.

爭 持 to struggle; to disagree.

20爭 權 to struggle for power.

爭 毆 to fight; to cause a disturbance.

爭 民 施 奪 to quarrel with the people and teach them to plunder.

爭 氣 to put forth effort; to squabble; determination.

爭 端 strife; cause of debate.

25爭 能 to strive for mastery. [-hang²-

爭 行 奪 市 trade competition.

爭 訟 to go to law.

爭∘論 to wrangle; to dispute; recrimination.

爭 論 不 定 unable to agree.

30爭 議 disputation.

爭 辨 to discuss; to wrangle.

爭 長 論 短 wrangling about anything.   [-hsien²-

爭 閒 氣 squabbles over trifles.

爭 雄 to strive for supremacy.

35爭 風 a quarrel from jealousy.

爭 鬪 or 爭 鬧 or 爭 競 to make a disturbance; to quarrel; to wrangle.

爭 點 the point in dispute; "bone of contention."

好 爭 quarrelsome; pugnacious.

相 爭 at variance with each other.

紙 上 爭 論 a paper warfare.

崝¹
366
To excel. Conspicuous.

崝 嶸 dignified; high; lofty.

猙¹
367
A mythical creature having one horn and several tails.

猙 獰 hideous; repulsive.

睜¹
368
To open the eyes.

睜 眼 to open the eyes.

睜∘着 一 隻 眼 to open one eye; to watch.

睜∘開 眼 睛 to open one's eyes.

箏¹
369
A kind of harpsichord. A kite.

箏 箏 a whistling sound.

風∘箏 a kite, from the aeolian harps sometimes attached to the string.

諍¹
370
To expostulate with.

諫 諍 to caution; to expostulate.

議 諍 to debate.

錚¹
371
A small gong. The clang of metals.

錚 錚 有 聲 jingling sounds.

鐵 中 錚 錚 one who is above the rank and file in ability and wisdom.

CH'ÊNG.   (ㄔㄥ)
(Ch'eng)

呈²
372
To present to a superior. A petition. An accusation.

呈 上 to file; to hand in.

呈 交 to deliver to; to pay in.

呈 保 to hand over a guarantee.

呈 具 to draw up a statement and hand it in.

5呈 准 to apply for and receive permission.

呈 出 to produce when called upon.

呈 告 to present an accusation.

呈 叩 to implore.

呈 報 to present a report.

10呈∘子 a charge; an accusation written on a special form provided for that purpose.

呈 存 to hand over for safe custody.

呈 官 to hand over to official authority.

呈 控 to accuse; to make a charge against.

呈 政 or 呈 正 to submit a manuscript to a friend for criticism.

15呈 明 to state clearly.

呈 期 days on which charges may be filed.

呈 核 to submit for reference.

呈 照 to submit documents, etc., for inspection.

呈 稱 to state (to a superior).

20呈 荷 to solicit for and receive.

呈 覽 or 呈 電 for your honour's inspection.

呈 訟 to institute legal proceedings.

呈 訴 to submit a statement.

呈 請 a petition; to apply for, as an appointment or position.

25呈 遞 to present; to transmit.

呈 閱 to hand in for inspection.

呈 驗 or 呈 關 to hand in to the customs for examination or inspection.

提 呈∘子 to hand in a charge.

進 呈 to make a petition.

(a) To reveal, to disclose, to manifest.

呈 現 or 呈 露 (lou⁴) manifested; disclosed.

呈 瑞 or 呈 祥 signs of prosperity.

埕²
373
Large earthen jar without handles, shaped like a pear.

油 埕 a large oil jar.

惺³
374
Obscure.

憛 惺 obscure.

程²
375
A journey; a road; a career.

程 儀 a parting present; travelling expenses.

程 途 or 路∘程 a road; a journey; a stage; a career.

程 限 stages of a work.

兼 程 forced marches.

前 程 the path ahead; one's career or prospects.

好 前 程 a good future before him.

起 程 to start on a journey.

(a) A pattern. Regulations. Standard. A job.

程 序 sequence; order; process, method.

程∘度 standard, grade, degree, required qualifications or attainments.

程 式 pattern; formula or forms.
程 系 order or symmetry.
⁵程 級 grade; stage.
工 程 engineering.
法 程 laws.
章 程 regulations; rules; by-laws.
課 程 curriculum.
工 程 師 an engineer.

(b) Percentage. Formerly a measure of one hundredth of a Chinese inch. "Touch", or the percentage of pure metal in an alloy.

程 數 percentage; quality or "touch" of silver.
一 程 one tenth. Usually written
八 程 80%. } with 379 B.
十 髮 爲 程 ten *hairs* are equal to one *ch'eng*.
十 程 爲 分 ten *ch'eng* are equal to one *fen* or one tenth of an inch.

(c) A surname.

程 朱 學 the *Sung* Dynasty exposition of the classics, the 宋 儒, from the names of 程 顥, 程 頤, 朱 熹.
程 門 立 雪 two men of the *Sung* Dynasty sought *Ch'êng I*, the great scholar, and were kept waiting in the snow at his door—hence the phrase is used to indicate sincere desire for learning.

裎² To take off the clothes and expose the body. To carry in the girdle.
376

裎 衣 under-garments.
裸 裎 half-naked.

逞³ To presume on. Presumptuous. To act in an outrageous manner.
377

逞 使 to presume on; to rely on.
逞 傲 pride and presumption.
逞 兇 to be abusive; to act violently or with murderous intent.
逞 勇 heroic; brave.
⁵逞 功 能 overmuch self-confidence.
逞 威 勢 to presume on power to intimidate others.
逞 強 to be violent; to intimidate; to make vigorous efforts.
逞 志 to get one's own way.

逞 志 棄 信 to break faith in order to get his will accomplished.
¹⁰逞 惡 行 刼 to rob and pillage.
逞 憾 to get one's will in revenge for an old grievance.
逞 暴 to oppress and intimidate.
逞 能 or 自 逞 boastful.
逞 蠻 to behave in an outrageous manner.

(a) To relax; to please oneself.

逞 心 to relax; to please oneself.
逞 欲 he acts in his own interests.
逞 顏 色 to relax the countenance.
不 逞 careless; reckless.

(b) To forecast.

不 可 億 逞 not possible to forecast the results.

酲² Drunk and stupid. To get sober.
378

解 酲 to get over a drinking bout.

成² To complete; to perfect; to succeed. To become finished.
379

成 丁 to become of full age.
成 了 器 to be fit for something.
成 了 客 to act as a visitor; to be reserved; to feign ignorance.
成 事 a thing that is passed; to accomplish anything.
⁵成 事 不 說 it is useless to speak of things that are past or finished.
成 事 在 天 *See* 4578.2

成 人 to become a man; to act as a full grown man; to succeed in life; an adult.
成 人 之 美 to assist others in a good object.
成 仇 to become an enemy; to establish a feud.
¹⁰成 仁 取 義 to die to preserve their virtue intact.
成 位 to establish one's position.
成 佛 to become a Buddha.
成 例 a precedent.
成 俗 to reform manners and customs.
¹⁵成 全 to help finish.
成 分 elements; constituents; ingredients.

成 功 finished; successful; the harvest.
成 勢 to gain the ascendency.
成 名 to make a name for oneself; to obtain a degree.
²⁰成 吉 思 汗 Genghiz-khan. The Mongol founder of the *Yuan* dynasty.
成 品 ready-made goods.
成 單 or 定 單 order for goods.
成 均 ancient name for a state college.
成 城 to build a rampart; soldiers standing firm.
²⁵成 始 成 終 well done from beginning to end.
成 子 a period.
成 家 to marry; to get on in life; to establish a family.
成 家 立 業 to establish a competency.
成 就 to bring to a successful issue; to fulfil; accomplishment.
³⁰成 工 to complete a piece of work; completed. [all the time.
成 年 to come of age; mature;
成 式 a precedent.
成 形 to take shape.
成 德 達 財 to perfect virtue and assist development.
³⁵成 心 to gratify the desires; to obtain one's wish; to make up the mind; foregone conclusions; similar to 成 見.
成 心 作 to act purposely.
成 擒 to apprehend.
成 效 effect.
成 敗 success or failure.
⁴⁰成 文 a set phrase; to compose.
成 文 憲 法 written constitution of a nation.
成 會 額 數 a quorum. = 1762.21
成 服 to put on mourning garments.
成 本 cost in business; to make into a volume.
⁴⁵成 案 a legal precedent; filed.
成 樣 子 to look well.
成 歡 sexual intercourse.
成 殮 to complete the funeral rites.
成 法 an established law.
⁵⁰成 湯 Prince *T'ang*, who overthrew the tyrant *Chieh* 桀 of *Hsia*, and established the *Shang* Dynasty, B.C. 1766.
成 熟 ripe; mature; ripened experience.
成 爲 一 體 to become one; united in one body.

成 物 ready-made things; to make things; to perfect things.

成 甚².麼 "What is that supposed to be?"— derogatory.

⁵⁵成 病 to fall ill.

成 禮 to conform to etiquette; to complete the ceremonies of marriage.

成 空 gone into space; made void.

成 窰 china ware of the period of 成 化 of the *Ming* Dynasty.— very valuable.

成 立 success in life; accomplished; established; effective, as a proposal that has been carried, or a motion that has been passed.

⁶⁰成 立 日 "Founder's Day."

成 章 to bring to a successful issue; a complete affair.

成 童 a youth;—according to some, one over eight years of age, another authority gives, over fifteen.

成 竹 the artist must have the complete image of the bamboo in his mind before he can put it on paper, hence the phrase is used to indicate—having the mind made up; to come to decision.

成 約 to make an agreement.

⁶⁵成 績 achievement; results; grade; marks gained; average marks.

成 羣 to form into groups.

成 聖 to sanctify.

成 蟲 the imago or perfect insect after passing all its metamorphoses.

成 衣 店 a ready-made clothes shop.

⁷⁰成 見 prejudice; a mind made up.

成 規 to become a regular rule or custom.

成 親 or 成 婚 to marry.

成 語 set phrases.

成 誦 to memorize; to repeat from memory.

⁷⁵成 議 to come to an agreement.

成 造 to construct.

成 道 to attain to spiritual perfection.

成 釁 quarrel; to have a feud.

現 成·的 ready-made

(a) The whole; perfect.

成 帙 whole volumes.

成 數 whole numbers.

成 日 or 成 天·家 the whole day.

成 疋 a whole piece—of cloth, etc.

成 百 the full hundred.

(b) One tenth; tenths. Ten square li.

成°色 the percentage of pure metal in alloy—"touch."

一 成 七 17%.

七 成 70%.

方 十 里 爲 成 10 square *li* is equal to one *ch'eng*.

有 田 一 成 10 square *li* of fields.

(c) Plump; fat.

犧 牲 不 成 if the sacrificial beasts were not plump.

城²　A city; the walls of a city.
380

城°上 on the city walls.

城°上 不 呼 do not shout when on the wall of a city—for fear of giving alarm.

城 下 之 盟 to make peace under the walls of the city— under the pressure of a strong enemy.

城 北 徐 公 an Adonis of past days in the state of *Ch'i*—now used of any handsome young man.

⁵城 坡 the mound inside the city wall.

城 某 or 城 根 or 城 脚 the base of the city wall.

城 堞 or 城 堞·子 battlements of a wall.

城 守 the city garrison; the Commandant.

城 市 towns and markets.

¹⁰城 市 生·活 city life.

城 府 the city and its *yamen*— deep seated thoughts, that are not easily got at.

城 廂 city and suburbs.

城 樓 the tower over a city gate.

城 池 or 城 濠 the moat of a city.

¹⁵城 牆 or 城 垣 the wall of a city.

城 狐 社 鼠 foxes in the city walls and rats on the altars— the injury that they can do is small. It is also explained as petty fellows who rely on officials and underlings to browbeat others.

城 裏 關 外 within the city and outside its environs.

城 邑 cities; towns; a *hsien* district.

城 郭 city and suburbs.

²⁰城 門 a city gate.

城 門 口 at the gate of the city.

城·隍 the dry city moat; the god of the city; the Pluto of the Chinese.

城 隍 廟 the city temple.

城 隅 a corner of the city wall.

²⁵城 陷 the city has fallen to the rebels.

城 頭 the top of the city wall.

困 城 to surround a city; to lay a siege.

土 城 a mud wall or rampart.

萬 里 長 城 10,000 *li* wall, the Great Wall of China.

³⁰紫 禁 城 the Imperial Palace and grounds at Peking.

金 城 湯 池 metal walls and hot water moat—impregnable city.

閉 城 to close the gates against the enemy.

誠²　Sincere, true, honest. To make sincere. Certainly;
381　honestly.

誠 中 形 外 what truly is within will be manifested without.

誠 之 之 目 the details of the attainment of sincerity.

誠 之 者 the attainment of sincerity.

誠 信 to trust; to shew good faith.

⁵誠 壹 single-hearted.

誠·實 sincere; guileless.

誠 屬 it was certainly a....

誠 心 true-hearted.

誠 心 在 乎 人 sincerity rests with man himself.

¹⁰誠 怕 it is to be feared that....

誠 意 unfeigned; with sincerity.

誠 摰 earnest purpose.

誠 敬 sincere regard; reverence.

誠 有 there really is....

¹⁵誠 有 百 姓 者 there really was a semblance of what the people— ridiculed.

誠 欲 truly desire to....

誠 然 really; undoubtedly.

誠 禱 to pray with sincerity—said of one in the *Sung* Dynasty who prayed for rain, and in two days it came.

誠 者 天 之 道 也 sincerity is the way of Heaven.

²⁰誠 能 if only they would.

誠 訓 true interpretation.

誠 身 有 道 there is a way to attain personal sincerity.

秤 [4] A steelyard. A weighing machine. u.f. next.
382

秤 到 準 weighed accurately.
秤 平 斗 滿 even balance and full measures—fair dealing.
秤 星 the brass marks on a steelyard.
秤 杆 [3] the beam of a steelyard.
秤 鈎·子 the hook at the end of a steelyard.
秤 鉈 or 秤 錘 the weight used with a steelyard.
秤 薪 而 爨 to weigh the firing before lighting the fire to cook —extreme stinginess.

稱 稱 偁 [1]
383. To praise.

稱 于 世 all praised him.
稱 人 to praise others.
稱 人 之 善 he commended their goodness.
稱 便 to commend a thing.
[5]稱 嘆 or 稱 賞 to extol or admire.
稱 觴 to drink the health of.
稱 許 to commend and allow.
稱 謝 to thank; to praise.
稱·讚 or 稱 頌 or 稱 揚 to praise; to commend. A.w. 稱 贊.

(a) To style; to declare; to call.

稱 人 之 惡 to publish abroad the wickedness of others.
稱·呼 or 稱 謂 or 稱 爲 to designate; to call.
稱 臣 to declare oneself a vassal.
稱 說 or 稱 言 to call; to state.
[5]稱 述 to state in detail.
報 稱 to report.
通 稱 are all called....

(b) To weigh. To estimate.

稱·一·稱 to weigh.
稱 算 to estimate; to calculate.
稱 貨 to weigh merchandise.
稱 進 and 稱 出 to weigh in and weigh out.
稱 量 or 稱 度 (to[4]) to estimate;
不 彀 稱 [4] not full weight.

(c) To feign.

稱 病 malingering.

(d) To raise. To take up. To proceed to, to go the length of.

稱 兵 to take up arms.
稱 制 the empress coming to court or taking the throne.
稱 引 to adduce.
稱 爾 戈 to take up arms against.

(e) Read *ch'eng*[4]. A steelyard. Inter. last.

稱 物 平 施 to give a fair weight.
壓 稱 to add a little for tare in weighing goods.

(f) Suitable; agreeable; corresponding to. Usu. pron. *ch'ên*[4].

稱 人 意 in accord with the desires of others.
稱 其 位 equal to the position.
稱 心 or 稱 意 in accord with one's wishes.
稱 旨 in accord with the royal command.
[5]稱 職 able to fulfil the responsibility of.
稱 願 agreeable to one's wishes.
稱 體 裁 衣 cut the garments to fit the figure—each agrees with the other.
不 相 稱 not in accordance with.
不 稱 其 職 not up to the requirements of the post.

(g) To raise; to proceed to.

稱 貸 to borrow.
稱 貸 而 益 之 to borrow in order to increase their earnings.

懲 征 [2]
384 To correct; to punish. To warn. To take warning. Punishment.

懲 一 警 百 punish one in order to warn many.
懲 前 毖 後 to warn a man first in order that he may afterwards exert himself to goodness.
懲 創 人 之 逸 志 to keep in order one's easy-going resolutions.
懲 役 punishment with hard labour.
[5]懲 忿 to restrain one's anger.
懲 惡 to punish and reprimand evil doers.
懲 戒 correction; discipline.

懲 戒 案 a case of discipline.
懲 戒 處 [3] 分 [4] punishment of officials.
[10]懲 戒 委 員 會 Board of Punishment dealing with officials.
懲 治 to punish.
懲 羹 吹 韲 a man who was scalded by hot broth afterwards blows on cold vegetables. —over cautious.
懲 罰 to reprimand and fine.
懲 警 to caution; to warn.
懲 責 to reprimand.
懲 辦 to deal with severely.

承 [2] To aid. A deputy; an assistant. Used chiefly in official titles.
385

丞 相 (*hsiang*[4]) ancient term for a secretary of state; a prime minister.
文 丞 the civil deputy, name of one of the pair of door-gods written on doors.
縣 丞 assistant *hsien* or district magistrate.
郡 丞 sub-prefect.

承 [2] To receive; to inherit.
386

承 下 塵 to take the dust—to be in the rear of a battle.
承 享 to receive and enjoy the use of.
承 先 to carry on ancestral traditions. See 光 No. 3583—8.
承 函 to receive a letter; I have received your favour.
[5]承 受 to receive; to inherit.
承 囑 to receive injunctions.
承 奉 to receive commands.
承 恩 or 承 寵 to receive grace or favour.
承 情 or 承 惠 to receive kindness. "Much obliged."
[10]承 接 to receive and carry on. *See below*. C.4.
承 敎 to receive instructions.
承 業 an inheritance.
承 派 to receive an appointment to go anywhere.
承 發 to receive a despatch and forward it.
[15]承 發 吏 receiving and despatching clerk in a *yamen*.
承 示 to receive an intimation.

承 祧 an heir.
承 祖 inherited.
承 繼 to adopt; to take an heir.
[20] 承 繼 人 an heir.
承 繼 權 right of inheritance.
承 襲 to inherit, as a title.
承 霤 spouting to take rain water.

(a) To hold, to contain. To support.

承·不 起 來 unable to support it.
承 塵 a ceiling—that which keeps the dust from falling.
承 載 to contain, as in a receptacle.
石 承 a base or plinth of stone.

(b) To contract for; to undertake.

承·不 起 unequal to the task or the responsibility.
承 乏 term of self-depreciation used by officials when taking office—officials are scarce, 乏, so I accept the post until a suitable man arrives.
承 交 to take over.
承 任 to fill an office or post.
[5] 承 允 to agree to.
承 充 to be put in charge of an office or of some duty.
承 典 to take a mortgage.
承 審 to officiate in a court.
承 審 公 堂 The Supreme Court.
[10] 承 審 官 a judge.
承 工 to undertake a piece of work.
承 差 servant in a yamen.
承 應 to undertake the responsibility of an office.
承 批 to take a lease of.
[15] 承 攬 to take the responsibility for.
承 當 to make oneself responsible for; to undertake for and abide by the consequences.
承 租 to rent.
承 約 to enter into a contract or agreement.
承 諾 acceptance; to consent.
[20] 承 買 to contract for the purchase of goods.
承 辦 to undertake; to manage.
承 重 the chief mourner.

(c) To continue; to carry on, as a theme.

承 上 文 continuing from the above.

承 平 之 世 times of peace.
承 承 continued for generations.
承 按 to continue; to succeed to.
承 父 業 to carry on the father's business or profession, etc.
承 繼 to continue what has gone before.
承 首 句 to enlarge the theme of the first paragraph.

(d) To confess; to acknowledge.

承 問 thank you for inquiring—conventional phrase in reply to inquiries as to health, etc.
承 情 "Much obliged." See above.—9.
承 招 to confess to a crime.
承 蒙 "I am obliged." "Much indebted."
承·認 to confess; to acknowledge; to recognise, as one government by another.

(e) To please; to flatter. To meet.

承 歡 to give delight to parents.
承 顏 接 辭 to meet and have a talk.
承 風 to follow the custom; to watch which way the wind blows.
奉·承 to toady to; to flatter.

塍 塖 墭 [2]　　A raised path between fields which acts as a dyke.
387

橙 [2]　The common or coolie orange. Pron. ch'ên[2].
388

橙 皮 dried orange peel. Usually ⌠wr. 陳 皮.
橙 膏 marmalade.
橙 糖 orange sweetmeats.
橙·子 an orange.

澄 [2]　Clear; pure.
389

澄 其 思 慮 quieten your anxieties.
澄 心 to make the heart pure and quiet.

(a) Read teng[1]. To settle and clear water.

澄 江 a clear river.
澄 波 limpid waves.

澄 清 transparent; clear; to clarify; see next.
澄 清 天 下 to bring about peace in the country.

掙 [1]　**To pierce; to stab.**
390

掙 扎 to pierce; to stab.
掙 牙 to stick in the teeth; to get something between the teeth.

(a) Read cheng[1] or tseng[4]. To make an effort; to get free from.

掙 壞·了 torn apart; wrenched out.
掙 脫 to get free from.
掙 開 to break away—as a horse from a halter.
扎 掙 to make an effort, as to rise or to get free.

(b) To earn.

掙·來 or 掙·得 to earn a living.
掙 子 a son who does something to help keep the family.
掙 家 立 業 to earn money and establish a competency.
掙 錢 to earn money.

撐 撑 [1]　**To prop up; to stretch out.**
391

撐·得 住 able to support it; or to succeed.
撐 持 to prop up; to support.
撐·起·來 to prop up, or prop open.
支 撐 to bear a weight; to support.

(a) To punt.

撐 搖 to work the sweeps of a large boat.
撐 渡 to punt a boat across a ferry —to intrigue.
撐 船 to pole a boat.

橕 [1]　**A prop; a shore. Inter. last.**
392

橕·子 a prop; a strut.
橕 柱 a truss to support a beam.
橕·開 窗·戶 to prop a window open.

饎[1] To eat much; to distend by eating.
393

饎餲 to gorge.

蟶[1] Mussels; a bivalve, the razor sheath.
394

蟶乾 dried mussels.
蟶田 fields on the seashore where these are cultivated, in Fukien and elsewhere.
↑ 蟶子 the razor clam.

騁[3] To gallop a horse. To hasten on.
395

騁懷 elated; hilarious; reckless.
騁望 to gaze into the distance.
騁步 to gallop.
騁目 to gaze around.
騁能 to show off one's talents.
騁詞 an animated style; forcible writing.
騁足 to run as fast as possible.

根[2] A prop, a stay. Doorposts.
396

根撥 to push aside with the hand.
根柱 a pillar; a doorpost.
根觸 to stir up; to touch.
根闑之間 the middle of the door, between the pillars.

赬[1] Deep red. To blush. To dye red.
397

赬尾 certain fish are said to turn red in their tails when in fear.
赬霞 a rosy sunset.
赬顏 a blushing face.

乘[2] To avail of. To ascend. To ride. Cf. 345.
398

乘使 take advantage of the chance; at your convenience.
乘勢 seize the right moment.
乘夜 get it done under the cover of darkness.
乘客 to take a passage on a boat.
[5]乘快 to take advantage and act while in the mood, as when elated.

乘時 or 乘機 improve the occasion.
乘時趨利 an opportunist—ready to use every opportunity for profit.
乘桴浮于海 I will get a raft and float on the sea.
乘殷之輅 to ride in the carriage of Yin.
[10]乘涼 to cool oneself in the shade or in the breeze.
乘潮 to take advantage of the tide, used both lit. and fig.
乘田 office held by Confucius—in charge of the government fields.
乘空 take advantage of the deficiency.
乘空若飛 they ascended the trees as if they flew.
[15]乘船 to take a passage on a boat.
乘著雲 to go up in a cloud.
乘車 to take a cart ride.
乘隙 take advantage of a crack—used in many ways.
乘風 avail oneself of the wind.
[20]乘風破浪 to ride the wind and break the waves—to have high ambitions; to be well under way
乘馬 to ride a horse.
乘駕 to mount a carriage or chariot.
乘龍 to ride the dragon—the son-in-law of high rank.

(a) To multiply.

↓乘號 sign of multiplication. x.
乘法 multiplication.
乘除 multiplication and division—increase and decrease.
用四乘之 multiply by four.

(b) Read ch'êng[4] A team of four horses. A set of four arrows.

乘馬 team of four horses.
發乘矢而後反 he shot four arrows and returned.

(c) N.A. of vehicles, etc.

一乘車 one cart or carriage.
一乘轎子 a sedan chair.
千乘之國 territory of a thousand chariots—that of a duke.

(d) Annals; records, etc.

史乘 historical records.
晋之乘 the annals of Chin.

(e) Buddhist teaching—a conveyance to bring the truth to men and help them.

三乘 the three conveyances—that of the Bôdhisatva, 菩薩乘 those who refrain from Nirvana to do good to man; that of Pratyeka 辟支乘 or a Buddha; and that of those who heard Buddha, 聲聞乘 i.e., his personal disciples.
大乘 the great conveyance or Mahâyâna. Buddhism as taught in China
小乘 the lesser conveyance—Hinâyâna.

CHI.   (ㄐ)

基[1] A foundation, A base. Property.
399

基圍 a dyke or embankment.
基址 the foundation of a wall.
基數 the numbers from one to nine, as the basis of all calculations.
基本 foundation; root; stock.
[5]基本實業 basic industries.
基本數例 the fundamental rules of calculation, i.e., addition, subtraction, multiplication, and division.
基本種 a fundamental species.
基本金 subscribed capital; reserve fund; endowment fund.
基根 a foundation.
[10]基業 property; inheritance; family estate.
基督 Christ.
基督化 Christianized.
基督徒 Christians.
基督教界 Christendom.
[15]基督節誕 Christmas.
基礎 base; foundation.
基礎的 basic; fundamental.
基礎的價值 fundamental values.
基線 the base, (maths.)
[20]基點 a base.
登基 to ascend the throne.
立基 to lay the foundation of an enterprise.
開基 to begin an undertaking.

嘰[1] Transliteration particle.
400

碁碁】¹ A full year. An anniver-
祺】 sary. Inter. 期 No. 526.

401

碁 之 喪 in mourning for one year.

碁 功 near relatives, those for whom a full year of mourning is worn.

碁 月 during twelve months.

碁 月 而 已 可 也 in the course of twelve months I should have done something considerable.

碁 服 garments for the period of one year of mourning.

箕 ¹ A winnowing basket. A basket for dust. A sieve.

402

〔箕 帚 dustpan and broom—de-preciatory term for a wife.

箕 帚 妾 self-depreciatory term used by a wife—I am your servant.

箕 斂 to rake in; to squeeze by illicit taxation.

箕 裘 世 業 "to carry on the father's trade," from 紹 箕 裘 a passage in the Book of Rites; The son of a good founder is sure to learn how to make a fur robe, and the son of a good maker of bows is sure to learn how to make a sieve; 箕 裘 thus has this meaning.

簸·箕 a winnower; a dustpan.

(a) To spread out fanwise. A constellation. Marks on the fin-ger-tips.

箕 伯 the god of wind.

箕 坐 to sit on the ground with the legs spread out fanwise, like the constellation.

箕 好 (hao⁴) 風，畢 好 雨 Sagit-tarius loves wind, and Taurus loves rain.—different people have different preferences.

箕 尾 Sagittarius and Scorpio.

箕 張 to advance troops with two wings spread out fanwise.

箕 斗 the "sieve" and the "dipper," lines on the finger-tips named from these constellations; spiral whorls are called 斗, and the non-spiral are called, 箕.

(b) Name of a mountain in what is now Honanfu district. An an-cient state.

箕 踞 而 坐 to squat with out-spread legs.

於 箕 山 之 陰 to the north of Mt. Chi.

其 ¹ Kind of grasses.

403

其 草 kind of aquatic grass woven into quivers and similar things.

(a) Read ch'i² The stalks of pulse. The tendrils of vines.

其 蕨 an edible fern.

几 ¹³ A bench, a small table. Radical 16. Distinguish 凡 No. 1771. Vulg. for 409 D.

404

几 案 a large long table.

↓炕 几 a small table with short legs for use on a brick-bed or divan.

文 几 a study table—a student.

條 几 a long narrow table.

茶 几 a teapoy; small square table for teacups, etc.

(a) Quiet, self-composed.

几 几 self-composed.

安 几 quiet and calm.

肌 ¹ The muscles or flesh. Meat on the bones.

405   [428.

肌·巴 the virile member. A.w. with

肌 膚 muscle; flesh.

肌 膚 之 會 the union of the dif-ferent parts of the body.

肌 體 or 肌 骨 the body.

浸 肌 drenched to the skin.

玉 肌 fine flesh—of a beautiful girl.

乩 ¹ To divine by means of a willow stick writing upon sand.

406

乩 仙 to consult a god or spirit.

乩 壇 a divining altar prepared with sand for writing.

扶 乩 to write on sand as a means of divination, the stick being supported by two blindfolded persons.

言 乩 to burn a question paper for the spirits to answer in this way.

筓 ¹ A hairpin on which the hair is bound at the back of the head. Fifteen years of age.

407

筓 卅 or 筓 年 marriageable age.

筓 禮 the ceremony of binding up the hair of a girl at fifteen.

筓 齓 a young girl.

姬 ¹ The family name of Hwangti.

408

姬 水 River Chi where Hwangti was born.

母 姬 a step-mother.

(a) Read i¹ A handsome girl. Imperial concubine.

姬 侍 concubines.

姬 姜 a beautiful concubine.

名 姬 a famous singing girl.

幾 ¹ Almost, nearly. About, somewhat. Rather, approxi-mate. Inter. next.

409

幾 不 欲 生 almost did not wish to live.

幾 乎 nearly; almost; within a trifle of.

幾 以 今 日 中 國 it almost seems that in the China of today.

幾 及 to come near to; to equal.

⁵幾 希 few, rare; a part.

幾 於 at the point of; almost.

幾 於 聖 人 nearly like the Sage.

幾 致 almost; until; not quite up to.

幾 致 刑 措 until punishments were almost put aside.

¹⁰幾 致 成 災 almost amounting to a calamity.

幾 非 任 我 will it not probably become mine?

事 父 母 幾 諫 in serving parents one should gently remonstrate with them—lit., almost remon-strate.

庶 幾 almost; nearly.

月 幾 望 the moon is almost at the full.

(a) Subtle, recondite. Hidden, as the springs of action.

幾 兆 an omen.

幾 微 an omen; a presage; subtle; incipient.

(b) Used to transliterate foreign sounds.

幾 尼 guinea.
幾 那 樹 the Cinchona tree.
幾 那 霜 quinine sulphate.
See 1057 C.

(c) Used for 期 No. 526. To expect, to be expected from.

不 幾 乎 一 言 may there not be expected from this one sentence?

言 不 可 以 若 是 其 幾 乎 such an effect connot be expected from one sentence.

(d) Read *chi*[3] How much? How many?

幾·個 or 幾 何 or 幾 多 how many? how much? *See below.* F. 1.

幾 分 what percentage?
幾·十 how many tens (less than a hundred implied)?
幾 回 or 幾 次 how many times?
[5]幾 度 how often? in what degree? what is the degree?—as of heat.
幾·時 or 幾 早 when? for how long?
幾·時 去 when will you be going?
幾 曾 interrogative—implying negative answer, similar to 何 嘗.
幾 更 天 in what watch of the night? what is the hour of night?
[10]幾 樣 how many kinds, as of dishes, etc.
幾 欵 how many items?
幾 歲 How old are you—my child?
幾 里 路 or 幾 里 地 How far is it?
幾 重 how heavy is it?
幾 點 鐘 what is the hour? what is the time?
第 幾 which one, or what is the number in a sequence?
↑ 十 幾 how many more than 10?

(e) A few. Some. Several.

幾·十 several tens; less than 100.
有 幾·個 there are a few.
未 幾 after a little time.
沒 有 幾 多 there are not many.
無 幾 not for very long.
無 幾 時 unexpectedly; very soon.
↑ 十 幾 a number between 10 and 20.

(f) Used for transliterating.

幾 何 geometry; used as a prefix to words about geometry.

幾 何 公 理 an axiom of geometry.
幾 何 學 the science of geometry.
幾 何 畫 or 用 器 畫 geometrical or mechanical drawing.
幾 何 的 geometrical, as contrasted with arithmetical, 算 術 的.
幾 何 級 數 or 等 比 級 數 geometrical progression.
平 面 幾 何 學 plane geometry.
立 體 幾 何 學 solid geometry.

曦 [1] Used for transliterating. A kind of cloth.
410

嗶 嘰 beiges.

機
机 [1] Changes, motions. The origin of; the moving power of—as of the universe.
411

機 先 when a political matter is in train, but has not yet become an accomplished fact.
機 緘 the springs of action; changes of the future.
機 能 function; strategic power.
感 覺 的 機 能 the function of the sensations.
理 性 的 機 能 the function of the reason.
天 機 nature; the secret springs of divine working; the bent of a man.
心 機 powers of the mind; devices of the heart.
洩 漏 天 機 to divulge the divine secrets by foretelling the future.
神 機 Nature.

(a) A machine, a loom. Mechanism. A catch or trigger.

機 匠 a mechanic; a weaver.
機·器 machinery.
機·器 工 作 mechanical work; machine made.
機·器 梯 a lift or elevator.= 654.23
[5]機·器 轉 運 mechanical transport.
機 女 or 機 婦 a female weaver.
機·子 a loom; a catch or trigger.
機 巧 ingenious; skilful. *See below.* C. 6.
機 師 an engineer.
[10]機 括 mechanical contrivance; the mechanism of; a trigger or catch.

機 杼 shuttle of a loom; the construction of an essay.
機 械 a mechanical contrivance; a tool; inplements; clever or skilful mechanism—used fig.
機 械 力 mechanical power.
機 械 圖 學 mechanical drawing.
[15]機 械 學 or 重 學 mechanics.
機 械 工 學 mechanical engineering.
機 械 師 a mechanic; mechanician.
機 械 性 of a mechanical nature—used of all sorts of things.
機 械·的 mechanical; mechanically.
[20]機 械·的 運 動 mechanical movements.
機 械·般·的 mechanical, as uninteresting labour, poor art or music.
機 械 論 mechanicalism—the mechanical theory of the universe which rules out a creator.
機 械 體 a machine.
機 構 mechanical structure; mechanism.
[25]機 檻 a snare.
機 鈕 a trigger.
機·關 a trick; an organ or instrument; organization; motive power.
機 關 報 a party organ.
機 關 槍 a machine gun.
[30]機 關 礮 a quickfiring gun.
機 關 車 a locomotive.
機 關 部 organ; bureau.
機 關 雜 誌 party magazine.
機 體 organism.
[35]機 體 之 組 織 organic arrangement.
機 齒 cogs.
有 機 化 學 organic chemistry.
有 機 感 覺 organic sensation.
有 機 物 organism.
有 機·的 organic as opposed to inorganic.
有 機 體 organism.

(b) Opportune. To seize an opportunity.

機 勢 opportunity.
機·會 an opportunity. *See below.* B. 5—8.
機 變 opportunism; versatility; astuteness.
機 變 百 出 full of clever tricks; ready to suit the occasion.
↑ 機 會 均 等 the principle of equal opportunity for all.

丨=345,6,

⁵乘 機·會 seize the opportunity.

利·用 機·會 avail oneself of and make the most of an opportunity.

千 載 一 遇 之 機·會 a golden opportunity.

失 機·會 to miss the opportunity.

時 機 opportunity.

臨 機 應⁴變 主 義 opportunism.

見 機 而 作 do a thing at the opportune moment.

(c) Secret. Occult. Cunning.

機 事 cunning dealings; important matters which are kept secret.

機 務 important matters; affairs of state.

機 宜 a policy; a line of action.

機 密 secret; confidential; hidden.

⁵機 密 信 confidential letter.

機 巧 skilful; cunning. *See above.* A. 8.

機 心 cunning.

機 智 tactfulness; words that hit the mark.

機 要 局 private office of state for the preparation and promulgation of mandates and such documents.

機 要 祕 書 confidential secretary.

機·警 sharp, quick-witted and cunning; alert.

機 鋒 astute; clever.

畿² The royal domains set apart in ancient times for 412 the emperor.

畿 輔 通 誌 the Imperial Records of Chihli Province.

畿 輔 重 地 the court and its surroundings are private.

皇 畿 the imperial domains.

璣¹ A pearl that is not quite globular; the gear of an as-413 tronomical instrument. See No. 2896—4.

璣 組 pearls strung as tassels or fringe for a girdle.

璣 鏡 a pearly mirror.

滿 腹 珠 璣 his belly is full of pearls—he has a well-stored mind.

磯¹ A jetty. An obstruction that causes an eddy; an eddy. 414

磯 頭 a breakwater; a jetty.

不 可 磯 do not obstruct them.

蟣¹ A louse; aphis; a nit. 415

蟣 蝨 lice.

譏¹ To ridicule; to make fun 416 of. Satire. To inspect.

譏 笑 or 譏 刺 or 譏 誚 to laugh at; to deride; to jeer at.

譏 評 to censure; to detract from.

譏 諷 to satirize.

(a) To inspect; to examine.

譏 呵 to examine.

譏 察 to inspect; an inspector who watched for spies, etc., at court.

饑 飢¹ Hunger; dearth, scarcity, famine. 417

饑 名 渴 勢 to hunger for fame and thirst for power—in an evil sense.

饑 寒 hunger and cold.

饑 歉 famine.

饑 死 death from starvation.

⁵饑 民 starving masses.

饑 渴 hunger and thirst—want.

饑 渴 之 際 between hunger and thirst—at the last gasp.

饑 溺 starving and drowning—the sufferings of the masses.

饑 者 易 爲 食 hungry men are not particular about what food they eat.

¹⁰饑 腸 flatulent rumblings of hunger.

饑·荒 famine.

饑 餓 hungry; starving.

饑 驅 under pressure of starvation.

饑 鷹 a hungry vulture—one who is brave but cannot satisfy his desires.

拉 饑·荒 to go into debt; to make trouble and quarrel.

肚 饑 hungry.

剞³ A curved wood graver. 418

剞 劂 氏 the wood engraving trade.

寄⁴ To lodge at. 419

寄 客 a sojourner; a visitor.

寄 宿 to pass the night.

寄 宿 生 boarding pupils.

寄 宿 舍 dormitories.

⁵寄 居 or 寄 寓 or 寄 身 to stop at a place; to lodge.

寄 生 parasitic.

寄 生 動·物 parasitic animals.

寄 生 植·物 parasitic plants generally.

寄 生 草 parasitic plants, as mistletoe, etc.

¹⁰寄 生 蟲 parasitic insects.

寄 碇 temporary anchorage for a boat.

寄 迹 a temporary standing.

(a) To send. To deposit. To entrust to. To deliver to.

寄 交 to send, as by post, etc.

寄 人 籬 下 to sponge on another.

寄·來 to receive from.

寄 信 to send a letter.

⁵寄 命 to entrust a commission to another; to entrust one's life to another.

寄 售 to sell on consignment.

寄 存 deposits; to deposit.

寄 怨 to take advantage of power to vent private spite.

寄 情 or 寄 懷 to express one's feelings by a gift, etc.

¹⁰寄 意 to convey wishes.

寄 百 里 之 命 to be entrusted with the affairs of a state of 100 *li*.

寄 聲 to ask another to make inquiries.

寄 託 to commission; to deposit; to entrust with.

寄 語 to send a verbal message.

¹⁵寄 貨 goods on consignment; to despatch goods.

寄 賣 to put on sale.

寄 送 to send; to forward.

寄 銷 to sell abroad or at another port.

寄 附 or 寄 放 to deposit with another.

寄 食 to sponge on another; to eat at another's expense.

敊[1] To pick up things with chopsticks or pincers.

420 Crooked. Distinguish 敊 No. 516.

敊 得 來 喫 pick up a little and eat it.

奊 敊 不 齊 irregular; uneven.

掎[3] To drag; to drag aside. To drag one foot.

421

掎 角 to separate into two wings to meet the foe; the wing of an army.

伐 木 掎 矣 he cut down the tree and dragged it aside.

畸[1] Surplus; odds and ends; fractional remainders.

422

畸 人 an odd person; a solitary man; an extraordinary person.

畸 人 者, 畸 於 人 而 侔 於 天 an extraordinary to other men but is ordinary to God.

畸 形 deformities of person, as when an organ or limb is abnormally developed.

畸 重 畸 輕 prejudiced, favouring either one side or other.

畸 零 bits; refuse; odds and ends; solitary.

(a) Odd pieces of land that would not fit into the *square* system of dividing the land.

畸 田 such odd pieces of land.

畸 籍 register of a wandering class of persons.

觭[1] One horn turned up and one turned down. Not a pair, odd. u.f. 奇 Odd. No. 514.

423

觭 偶 odd and even.

觭 角 irregular; uneven; triangular.

觭 輪 無 反 not a single chariot wheel returned.

羇[1] An inn. To lodge.

424

羇 客 the guest at an inn.

羇 愁 the discomforts of travel.

羇 旅 a wayfarer.

羈[1]
羇   A halter; to restrain.

425

羈 勒 fastened; tied.

羈 所 or 外 羈 a lock-up attached to a *yamen*.

羈 押 or 羈 禁 to keep in custody.

羈 束 to restrain or control.

[5]羈 留 or 羈 住 or 羈 候 to detain.

羈 絆 fettered; to tie.

羈 縻 halter and bridle—to curb.

羈 縻 to restrain; to control.

羈 繫 to tie up in restraint.

羈 貫 knots or tufts of hair on the heads of young girls and boys respectively.

嵇[1] A mountain in Honan, 修 武 縣.

426

嵇 康 a famous man of the Wei Dynasty who lived in that region.

稽[1] To examine into.

427

稽 察 a judicial investigation.

稽 征 to examine goods and collect duty.

稽 查 to muster; to examine; to investigate.

稽 考 or 稽 核 to investigate; to examine.

無 稽 之 談 unfounded statements.

(a) To search for; to hunt up—as quotations.

稽 古 to search out the ancient ways.

稽 古 閣 ancient libraries, from the time of the *Sung* Dynasty.

稽 覽 故 志 to search the ancient records.

(b) To delay; to hinder.

稽 固 to keep waiting.

稽 時 日 to procrastinate.

稽 淹 to protract.

稽 留 to detain.

稽 留 熱 prolonged fevers, as typhoid, etc.

稽 程 delay in presenting a memorial.

稽 遲 or 稽 延 or 稽 時 to hinder; to deter; to delay.

久 稽 to delay for a long time.

(c) To recriminate. To discuss. To compare. To reach to.

反 唇 而 相 稽 mutual recriminations.

大 浸 稽 天 (though) the waters rose to the heavens.

(d) Read *ch'i*[3] To bow to the ground.

稽 首 or 稽 顙 to knock the head; to kotow.

雞[1]
鷄   Chickens; fowls generally.

428

雞 冠 cock's comb; a plant with a similar name.

雞 口 牛 後 fowl's beak and ox buttocks—used to express—better to lead in a small position, than take a back seat under a greater leader.

雞 叫 or 雞 鳴 cock-crow.

雞 司 辰 the cock heralds the dawn.

[5]雞 鳴 狗 吠 fowls crowing and dogs barking—a populous village.

雞 姦 sodomy.

雞·子 fowls; young chickens; 雞 子(兒) hens' eggs.

雞 毛 fowls' feathers.

雞 毛 報 urgent notice to which a feather was attached as a reminder.

[10]雞 毛 官 ancient name for official couriers.

雞 犬 不 留 not a fowl nor a dog left—of utter extermination.

雞 犬 不 驚 not a cock crowed nor a dog barked—peaceful security.

雞 皮 鶴 髮 fowl-like skin and crane-like hair—very aged.

雞 盲 night-blindness; nyctalopia.

[15]雞·眼 corns.

雞 籠 or 雞 窩 basket for fowls.

雞 肋 chicken's ribs, i.e., something with little interest, yet, one is loth to part with it; also signifies weakness.

雞 蛋 or 雞 子(兒) hens' eggs.

雞 蛋 糕 sponge cakes.

20 雞 骨 chicken's bones—very emaciated.

雞 黍 fowl and millet—to welcome a friend, from the story of one who promised his friend this dish, and on the day appointed had it ready, although the friend had not yet arrived.

公 雞 or 雄 雞 the cock.

犏 雞 or 閹 雞 a capon.

火 雞 a turkey.

25 烏 雞 or 烏 骨 雞 a black-boned fowl, highly esteemed.

田 雞 or 水 雞 small frogs.

竹 雞 the partridge.

野 雞 the pheasant.

雌 雞 or 母 雞 a hen.

己 3 Self; personal; private. Radical 49. The sixth
429 "stem." Distinguish 巳 No. 2930. and 已 No. 5590.

己 何 與 焉 what has it to do with oneself?

己 所 不 欲 勿 施 於 人 do not do to others that which you do not wish to be done to yourself.

己 獨 he only; single.

己 肆 物 忤 if you are reckless, others will be insulting.

5 己 親 one's own relatives.

己 身 one's own person.

己 饑 己 溺 of a man who feels that he is responsible for the hungry and the drowning around him.

他 自 己 he, himself.

克 己 to put away self; to overcome self.

10 我 自 己 I, myself.

捨 己 self-denial; to yield one's desires.

知 己 an intimate friend.

私 己 to take for private use.

Read *ch'i³* A surname.

紀 3 A record; annals. To record.
430 Partly inter. 431

紀 事 to make a memorandum.

紀 功 recorded as worthy of merit.

紀 序 series; order or sequence.

紀 律 written laws; army discipline.

---

5 紀 念 to remember or commemorate.

紀 念 品 mementoes; keepsakes.

紀 念 日 commemoration day; memorial day; anniversary.

紀 念 會 memorial service; commemorative gathering.

紀 念 碑 a memorial stone or monument.

10 紀 綱 abstract of laws; servants of another.

紀 行 travel notes.

紀 述 to record; to relate.

紀 錄 to place on record; honourably recorded.

帝 紀 the imperial records; brief records of each reign of a dynasty.

(a) A century. A year. Period of twelve years.

紀 元 the beginning of a reign, or of an era.

紀 元 前 now understood as B.C.

紀 元 後 now understood as A.D.

紀 年 a dynasty; a reign.

5 世 紀 a century.

增 壽 一 紀 added twelve years to his life.

年 紀 a person's age.

既 歷 三 紀 I have been at my post for 36 years.

明 紀 the *Ming* Dynasty.

(b) To sort silk threads. A skein of forty threads. To regulate. Regulations.

五 紀 the five regulators of time—years, moon or months, days, planets, and the calendar calculations.

五 事 爲 天 之 經 紀 也 these five regulators are the principles or order of Heaven.

綱 紀 四 方 to regulate the four quarters of the kingdom, as one sorts ravelled skeins.

(c) Ancient feudal state, its territory was to the south of the present 壽 光 縣 in Shantung.

記 4 To record; to remember. A sign; a mark. Inter. last.
431

記 下 make a note of it.

記 不 得 unable to remember.

記 不 清 have no clear recollection.

記 不 過 來 cannot remember very many, or very much.

5 記 事 make a memorandum.

記 仇 or 記 恨 to bear a grudge; to cherish hatred.

記 住 Remember! Do not forget!

記 傳 historical records.

記 功 to record merit.

10 記 名 make a list of names; to register; to record merit.

記 問 之 學 learning got by rote; superficial scholarship.

記 在 下 面 "as follows."

記 在 書 上 recorded; on record.

記 室 a secretary. (*old.*)

15 記 帳 to charge to an account.

記 得 to remember.

記 念 to keep in mind.

記 念 日 commemoration day, *see under* 紀 *above. illus.* 7.

記 性 the memory.

20 記 憶 to remember; memory.

記 持 retention; conservation of memory.

記 罣 to bear in mind; to be anxious about.

記 者 a reporter; we—"the editorial we."

記 號 a sign; trade-mark; a mark.

25 記 言 record of a conversation.

記 誦 to repeat from memory.

記 載 to record; recorded.

記 述 的 descriptive, as literature.

記 過 to record demerits.

30 記 錯 to remember wrongly.

記 錄 to make a record of; minutes of meetings; athletic record.

忌 4 Superstitious fear. Superstition. To avoid, to shun.
432

忌 口 to fast; to diet.

忌 憚 to dread; to fear.; to scruple.

忌 日 or 忌 辰 days to be avoided—anniversary of the death of the emperor or empress of the reigning dynasty; no official business could be transacted on these days. The anniversary of the death of a friend or relative.

忌 月 the month after the death of a parent; the ninth month.

5 忌 諱 to shun the use of sacred names; to avoid things taboo; superstitious avoidance of things.

忌 避 to evade; to fight shy of; to shun.

忌 食 to fast ; to diet.

心 多 忌·諱 a mind full of superstitions.

戒 忌 to break off—as opium, etc.

[10]拜 忌 to observe the anniversary of a death.

無 忌 reckless ; rude ; mannerless.

百 無 禁 忌 no restrictions here; nothing to avoid or to fear.

(a) To be envious of; to hate.

忌 克 envy and malice.

忌 剋 envious and suspicious.

忌·妒 to be jealous of. =493.1.

忌 恨 or 忌 心 to be jealous or envious of.

(b) A final particle.

叔 善 射 忌 Shu is a skilful shot.

媳 [4]
433
To envy; to be angry with.

媳 妒 jealousy ; envy.

跽 [4]
434
To kneel for a long time. To go down on hands and knees. Awe-struck.

敬 跽 to regard with awe.

季 [4]
435
Tender and young. Last of a series. The youngest brother.

季 世 closing years of a dynasty.

季 冬 or 季 夏 the last month of winter and summer respectively.

季 女 the youngest daughter.

季 子 the youngest son.

[5]季 常 癖 hen-pecked—from the story of a man named 陳 季 常 who feared his jealous wife.

季 指 the little finger.

季 明 or 明 季 the period at the close of the *Ming* Dynasty.

季 春 or 季 秋 the last month of spring and autumn respectively.

季 月 the last month of the season in the lunar calendar, i.e. 3rd, 6th, 9th, and 12th months.

[10]季 母 an aunt, wife of father's youngest brother.

季 漢 or 蜀 漢 the Minor *Han* Dynasty.

季 父 youngest brother of one's father.

季 細 small ; junior.

季 絹 the finest gauze.

(a) The seasons. A quarter of the year. A crop. A half-year's rent of land.

季 候 風 the Monsoons.

下 季 the second half of the year; the second crop.

春 季 spring; the spring quarter, other seasons are similarly named.

每 季 quarterly.

悸 [4]
436
Perturbed.

悸 動 to throb; palpitating from nervous agitation.

悸 慄 trembling with fear.

心 悸 palpitation of the heart.

瘈 [4]
437
Nervous starting during sleep.

伎 [4]
438
Talent; ability; cleverness. Inter. 技 No. 442. q.v.

伎 倆 astute; cunning; cleverness.

伎 巧 ingenious; clever.

伎 能 skill; ability.

伎 藝 mechanical arts.

妓 [4]
439
A singing girl. A prostitute.

妓 女 or 妓 家 prostitutes.

妓 館 or 妓 院 a brothel.

庋 [3]
440
A cupboard or pantry. To store. Also read *kuei*[3].

庋 置 to put into a cupboard.

庋 閣 a press for storing valuables.

庋 食 物 to put away the food.

忮 [4]
441
Stubborn; perverse; aggressive.

忮 懫 violent and agressive.

技 [4]
442
Skill, ingenuity; talent, ability.

技 勇 military talent.

技 士 or 技 正 technical experts attached to the various boards of the government, all except the bureau of foreign affairs.

技 巧 ingenious; clever; expert.

技 師 technical expert, as a mining engineer, etc.

[5]技 擊 boxing; pugilism.

技 異 very clever; wonderful.

技 癢 anxious to display one's talents.

技 能 dexterity; skill; talent; technique.

技 藝 mechanical arts; the skill of an expert.

技·術 art; skill; expertness; sleight of hand.

冀 [4]
443
To hope; to desire.

冀 及 之 hoped to reach it.

冀 望 or 希 冀 to long for; to hope.

冀 幸 to wish another good luck.

(a) One of the nine divisions of ancient China.

冀 州 a division of China as above, embracing Chihli, Shansi, part of Honan and part of Manchuria.

驥 [4]
444
A thorough-bred horse.

驥 不 稱 其 力 稱 其 德 也 you do not praise a thorough-bred horse for its strength alone, but for its good qualities.

驥 尾 to follow a great man in order to get on in the world, as a fly on the tail of a horse.

驥 足 hoofs of a thorough-bred, used of a man capable of sustaining heavy responsibility.

蠅 附 驥 尾 a fly on the tail of a famous steed—*see above*. 2.

迣 [4]
445
To leap over. Read *li*[4] (*lih*[4]) To intercept.

洎 [4]
446
To reach to. And; when. Distinguish 泪 No. 4243.

洎 乎 and then; and when it reached to.

洎 見 and when he made his appearance.

於 斯 皆 洎 and then they all came to offer congratulations.

(a) Name of a river, Broth of meat. Meat juice.

去其肉而以其泊饋 he took out the meat and presented the broth.

薊 [4] 447　A general name for thistles.

罽 [4] 448　A kind of fishing net. A kind of square mat made of hair.

罽賓 ancient name for Cashmere.

覬 [4] 449　To covet; to long for.

覬望 ardent longings.
覬覦 to wish for ardently.
覬幸 to hope for a lucky hit.

彐 [4] 450　A pig's head. Radical 58.

髻 **鬐** } [4] 451　Dressed hair of a Chinese woman.

髻雲 curls of hair bound round.
丫角髻 the two tufts on the head of a young child, like two little horns.
梳髻 to comb and dress the hair.
禿髻 hair dressed without ornaments.
肉髻 wen or protuberance on the head of a Buddha.
螺髻 twisted and turned like dressed hair.

繼 [4] 452　To connect; to continue; to follow. To adopt.

繼世 for many generations.
繼位 to succeed to the throne.
繼則 and then . . . . ; or next.
繼善 benevolence.
[5]繼嗣 to adopt the son of a near relative, or of a brother.
繼嗣不定 the succession was not yet fixed.
繼室 a second wife.

繼序 succeeding in order.
繼往開來 to carry on past traditions and open up a way for those who follow.
[10]繼志 to carry out the wishes of the deceased. 「=386.19.
繼承 to inherit; to succeed to.
繼承人 an heir.
繼承權 right of succession, or of inheritance.
繼承法 the law of inheritance.
[15]繼業 to carry on the family estate; to continue the family profession.
繼武 in step, used of following the steps of a great predecessor.
繼母 a step-mother.
繼父 a step-father.
繼絕世 to restore families whose line of succession is broken.
[20]繼。續 to connect; to carry on; to re-marry; to continue to.
繼。續有效 continuous effects or results.
繼。續進行 to follow up a line of action; to continue an advance.
繼繼 continuous; unbroken.
繼而有師命 after this, orders were given for the massing of troops.
[25]繼聘 to arrange a second marriage for a man.
繼襲 hereditary rank.
繼配 to re-marry.
繼電器 a relay instrument for telegraphy or telephony.
繼體 to inherit by birth, as the son of a ruler.
過。繼 to adopt; to give a child for adoption by a near relative.

既 [4] 453　Since; when.

既來之則安之 since you have come, take your ease.
既已 since there has been already.
既昏便息 when evening comes, rest.
既是 since it is so; seeing that.
既然 whereas; this being the case.
既然如此 or 既是這樣 since it is so; this being the case.
既經 since already.

(a) Already. To finish.

既久 already; for a long time.
既往 the past; what is gone or done; the former standing or condition.
既往不咎 let bygones be bygones.
既得權 effective authority.
[5]既成 when it was completed.
既明且哲 he understands and is prudent.
既月 or 月既 the end of the lunar month.
既望 the 16th of a lunar month, i.e. the full moon 望 is passed.
既生明 the 4th of a lunar month. The 3rd is the day when the moon is first visible, so the expression means the day after the moon is first visible.
[10]既生魄 the 17th of a lunar month. The 16th is called 哉生魄 i.e. the beginning of the umbra, hence the 17th is the day after that beginning 既生.
既畢 on the expiration of . . . .
既稟稱 (*ch'eng*[4]) 事 let their rations be proportionate to the work done.
既而 finally; in the end.

墍 [4] 454　To plaster a wall.

塗墍 to plaster a wall; to fill up cracks.

(a) To collect or gather.

頃筐墍之 I have gathered them in my shallow basket.

(b) To rest; a rest.

一墍之安 a spell for rest.
民之攸墍 "be a centre of rest for your people."

暨 [4] 455　To reach to; the end.

暨今 up till the present.
大德無暨 your limitless virtue.
靡暨 without limit.
餘不盡暨 the rest cannot be finished—closing phrase in correspondence.

(a) To give.

暨 候 .... Please give my regards to ....

(b) And. With. Used in letters or despatches to connect names.

暨 久 相 交 associated with for a long time.

暨 及 and; together with.

(c) The sun peeping out. Resolute.

戎 容 暨 暨 his countenance was resolute and daring.

計 [4] A plan, a device, a stratagem. To plan, to calculate, 456 to reckon.

計 偕 a 2nd degree man going up for the degree of 進 士·

計 功 受 賞 to be rewarded according to deserts.

計 學 economics. now 1123 B 7.

計 明 to reckon up.

[5]計 最 to note the standing of all officials.

計 略 strategy.

計·畫 a plan, estimate; calculation; to plan, etc.

計 窮 resources and plans exhausted.

計·策 a device; a plan.

[10]計·算 or 計·核 to calculate.

計 算 器 a calculating machine.

計 算 尺 a slide rule.

計 薄 or 計 籍 an account book.

計 粘 appended, as to a despatch.

[15]計 綱 plan to implicate others so that they are caught as in a net.

計 臣 ancient name for a state counsellor.

計 謀 a scheme; a plan; a plot.

計 議 to debate; to consult with.

計·較 to discuss minutely; to find fault with; to go into a matter; to take note of.

[20]計 送 forwarded herewith.

計 過 to think on one's faults.

計 部 ancient name for the board of punishments.

計 量 to measure.

計 量 ... 表 a meter—any word may be inserted.

[25]計 量 電 表 meter for electricity.

計 開 as follows; namely.

計 附 appended.

計 點 or 計 數 to count.

中 (chung[4]) 計 to fall into a trap.

[30]共 計 the total comes to ....

妙 計 an excellent plan; a clever device or strategem.

心 計 mental calculations.

暗 計 a dark plot.

生·計 livelihood.

詭 計 crafty plans or plots; tricks.

CHI. (TSI.)　(ㄗ)

劑 [4] To trim; to adjust. A dose. To compound medi-457 cines.

一 劑 藥 a dose of medicine.

藥 劑 medicines.

調[2]劑 to adjust; to level up; to make up a deficiency.

擠 [3]　To crowd; to push 458　against. To squeeze.

擠。上 前·去 striving to get first.

擠·不 動 wedged tight in a crowd.

擠 佔 to push into a crowd.

擠 奶 to milk an animal.

[5]擠 手 to squeeze the hands—in straits.

擠 抑 to keep another down.

擠 水 to pump or force water up.

擠 滿 a full house.

擠 眼 to wink the eyes.

[10]擠 進 to force a passage through.

擠 開 to press one's way into a crowd.

擠 陷 to cherish malice in order to injure another.

擠 靠 to crowd against.

(a) Read ch'i[2] To arrange.

擠 排 人 短 處 to detail the shortcomings of others.

濟 [4]　To aid; to relieve.
459

濟 世 to benefit the age.

濟 世 主 義 philanthropy.

濟 人 to save men.

濟 困 to relieve the suffering and distressed.

[5]濟 困 扶 危 help the distressed and succour those in peril.

濟 急 to relieve one in need.

濟 惡 to assist an evil cause.

濟 弱 扶 傾 to help the weak and raise the fallen.

濟 民 to save the distressed masses.

[10]濟 涸 to help one who is in desperate need.

濟 火 以 油 to pour oil on flames —to make matters worse.

濟 燃 眉 之 急 to save from danger so near that it burns the eyebrows—to save from imminent danger, from a desperate emergency.

濟 私 to serve one's own ends.

濟 良 所 "Door of Hope"—refuge for unfortunate girls.

[15]濟 財 to give relief in cash.

濟 食 to give relief in kind.

不 濟 於 事 no help in the matter; irrelevant.

救·濟 to rescue or save.

(a) To cross a stream.

濟 川 to cross a stream—to meet a grave national crisis.

濟 度 to carry across—the seas of sorrow.　(Budd.)

濟 涉 to cross a ford.

(b) To complete. To be up to standard.

濟 事 a complete matter.

濟 美 to complete a good work.

不 濟·的 貨 not up to standard; inferior.

(c) Read chi[3] Numerous. Fine appearance.

濟 南 府 Tsinanfu, capital of Shantung.

濟 濟 多 士 the numerous array of officers.

濟 濟 蹌 蹌 with correct deportment.

四 驪 濟 濟 the fine handsome black steeds.

薺 [4]　The shepherd's purse.
460

薺 菜 various varieties of greens for vegetables.

躋
隮 [1]

　To go up; to increase.
461

躋 升 to be promoted.

躋 堂 稱 觥 go up the hall (of the prince) and raise the horn cup.

躋攀 to clamber up.
日躋 daily increase or advance.
氣躋 the mist is rising.

(a) Steep. Ruin.

道阻且躋 the Way is difficult and steep.
顚躋 ruined.

霽⁴ The sky clearing up.
462

霽威 the severity a little abated.
霽月 an unclouded moon.
霽紅 a fine red colour on porcelain, etc.
霽色 blue sky; azure.
晴霽 a clear sky.
雨霽 the rain has cleared up.

齏¹ A kind of leek. To mix, to blend. To salt. Pounded.
463

齏齏 everything very wet; saturated.
齏鹽 vegetable diet.
和齏 to mix, as seasonings.

齎
賫 To take in both hands and offer to.
464

齎呈 to present to a superior; to send.
齎志 to cherish unfulfilled ambitions.
齎恨 to cherish hatred and malice.
捧齎 to offer to.

(a) To send, as a present or a letter.

齎出 to pay.
齎奏官 government couriers.
齎至 send this to . . . .
齎裝 to pack the baggage.
齎解 to deliver to, as a letter.
齎賜 to bestow on.
齎赴 to forward to.
齎送 to forward to an equal or a superior.
親齎 hand to in person.

祭⁴ To sacrifice.
465

祭主 the one who offers the sacrifice.

祭儀 money presents for use in sacrifices.
祭司 a priest; one who superintends the sacrifices.
祭司長 the Jewish High Priest.
⁵祭告 in times of national crisis the emperor ordered sacrifices to announce the fact to the gods.
祭品 sacrificial articles or offerings.
祭地 annual sacrifice to the earth.
祭壇 an altar for sacrifice.
祭天 sacrifice to Heaven at the winter solstice.
¹⁰祭奠 sacrifices and libations; to offer sacrifices.
祭如在祭神如神在 he sacrificed (to his ancestors) as if they were present, and to the gods as if they were present.
祭幽 sacrifice to the shades.
祭掃 sacrifice and renovation of the tombs, done at *Tsing-ming* 清明.
祭文 funeral odes or addresses burnt at the grave.
¹⁵祭於公不宿肉 the flesh he received when at the prince's sacrifice, he would not keep overnight.
祭旗 sacrifice to the flag.
祭服 sacrificial robes.
祭物 an offering for sacrifice.
祭田 fields set apart, the produce of which is to maintain the annual sacrifices to the ancestors.
²⁰祭祀 to sacrifice; a sacrifice.
祭禮 sacrifice to ancestors.
祭竈 sacrifice to the Kitchen god on the 23rd of the 12th lunar month.
祭聖 to sacrifice to the Sage.
祭肉 meat that has been offered in sacrifice.
²⁵祭軸 a eulogistic scroll hung near the coffin at a funeral.
燔祭 the Burnt Offering.

穄⁴ A variety of panicled millet. A small coarse grain resembling sorghum.
466

際⁴ A border, a boundary. A limit.
467

際畔 a boundary.
男女之際 the boundary between the sexes.

天地之際 between heaven and earth.
死生之際 between life and death.
無際 limitless; endless.

(a) A time or occasion. While, at the time when.

際可 to meet with due ceremony.
際昌 a favourable time.
際會 meeting; intercourse.
際遇 a juncture; a crisis.
不際之際 an unfavourable juncture.
國際 international—used as a prefix, *see under* 國 No. 3738.
實際 the facts of the matter, *see under* 實 No. 5821.

CHI. (ㄐ)
(Chih)

及²·⁵· To extend; to reach to; to come up to.
468

及其知之一也 if they attain knowledge it comes to the same thing.
及冠 to come of age; manhood—lit. reached capping—formerly boys were ceremoniously capped on reaching the age of eighteen.
及早起來 rise up early.
及格 up to the mark; up to standard or grade; to pass in an examination.
⁵及歲 to come of age.
及筓 a girl who has reached the age of fifteen—lit. reached the hairpin,—marriageable.
及第 to graduate at any of the three examinations for 舉人, 進士, 翰林.
及肩 to come up to the shoulder.
及門 pupils; disciples—lit. those at the door.
¹⁰及階子曰階也 when they reached the steps the Sage said (to the blind music master), "There are the steps."
不及 not adequate for; unequal to.
來不及 will be too late; cannot overtake it, i.e., cannot do it.
愚者不及也 the stupid do not come up to it—the *Tao.*

(a) When, as long as, or, such as, and.

及 云 he continued, saying . . . .
及 其 but as to its . . . .; but when regarded in its . . . .
及 到 by the time; as soon as.
及 於 in reference to.
⁵及 時 seasonable.
及 此 in regard to this.
及 耳 a gill—from the Eng. sound.
及 至 until; up to a certain point; when.
及 茲 now.
及 長 when he grew up; when he came of age.

仮 2.5. Empty; unreal.
469
仮 仮 unreal; disappointing.

圾 2.5. Shaking.
470
天 動 地 圾 heaven and earth trembling.
殆 哉 圾 乎 How perilous! How shaken!

(a) Also read hsi⁵ (si) See 垃 No. 3755.

岌 4.5. A lofty peak. Hazardous.
471
岌 岌 可 危 in imminent peril.

汲 1.5. To draw water from a well.
472
汲 古 to draw inspiration from the ancient writings like water from a well.
汲 引 to draw out,—primarily water, but now used of drawing out a man's talents. See also below. A. 1.
汲 水 or 汲 井 to draw water.
汲 水 機 a chain pump.
汲 綆 a well-rope.
汲 路 or 汲 道 the path to the well, or to water.
汲 酒 to draw out wine.

(a) To imitate; to imbibe.

汲 引 高 風 to imitate the high attainments of another.
汲 汲 anxious, unwearied effort.

笈 2.5. A book-box or satchel.
473
負 笈 從 師 he shouldered his box of books and followed his teacher.

級 2.5. Threads arranged in order. A degree. A mark of merit. A step.
474
級 數 mathematical progressions.
級 階 steps; stairs.
一 級 一 級 a step at a time.
品 級 grades in rank.
等°級 a class; a grade.
階°級 official grades; class; caste. *See under* 階 No. 625.

(a) A decapitated head.

斬 首 十 五 級 there were fifteen heads of decapitated men.
首 級 head of a decapitated criminal.

芨 1.5. Name of a plant, it has mucilaginous roots which are used for various purposes; in medicine and mixing vermilion ink for seals, etc.
475

吉 2.5. Lucky; happy; auspicious.
476
吉 事 happy affairs—weddings.
吉 人 a good man, i.e., prosperous or fortunate, therefore good.
吉 人 天 相 Heaven protects the good, as above. Used to comfort the sick or those in trouble.
吉 便 at your convenience; when there is a favourable opportunity; "kindness of..."
⁵吉 信 or 吉 函 a family letter.
吉°兆 lucky.
吉°利 lucky; auspicious.
吉 慶 有 餘 May there be an overplus of joy.
吉 日 a lucky day.
¹⁰吉 星 a lucky star.
吉 星 高 照 May a lucky star shine upon you!
吉 月 or 初 吉 the first of the month.
吉 服 clothes for festive occasions.
吉 期 the "happy occasion"—a wedding day.
¹⁵吉 祥 good fortune.

吉 祥 如 意 May your good fortune be according to your wish!
吉 言 good wishes.
吉 語 good news.

姞 2.5. A concubine of the Yellow Emperor, *Huang-ti.*
477

敨 1.5. To respect. To beat.
478

激 1.5. To rouse; to intimidate.
479
激 切 roused to make an effort.
激 刺 to aggravate; to inflame; to move; to stir.
激 力 influence.
激 動 an impulse; to stimulate.
⁵激 勵 or 激 勸 to encourage; to stimulate.
激 勵 裁 抑 stimulation and repression.
激 射 to shoot an arrow.
激 忿 or 激 惱 popular indignation.
激 怒 very angry.
¹⁰激 情 to arouse the emotions.
激 惹 to provoke.
激 成 擾 亂 to incite to rebellion.
激 戰 to provoke to war; a challenge.
激 揚 to encourage; to arouse to the display of; crescendo and diminuendo.
¹⁵激 於 義 而 死 焉 者 (these five men) were those who, urged by a public spirit, died.
激 昂 to stimulate to a high degree of excitement.
激 烈 violent; with violence; radical.
激 烈 手 段 violent methods.
激 烈 派 The Radical Party.
²⁰激 生 to cause; to bring about.
激 病 sick with fretting or anxiety.
激 發 to arouse; to give an impulse to.
激 而 進 之 to stimulate him to advance.
激 越 swelling music with clear and shrill tones.
²⁵激 賞 to move to admiration.
感°激 grateful.
過°激 論 Radicalism.

a) Water flowing over. To over-flow.

激 反 to force water to flow back.
激 流 turbulent flow of water.
激 滾 boiling over—also used fig.
激 濁 揚 清 to remove evil-doers and promote the pure.
激 筒 a hose-pipe.

急 2.5. Anxious; hurried; urgent; hasty.
480

急 促 hurried; hasty.
急 公 zeal for public welfare.
急 公 好⁴義 zealous for the public interests.
急·出 病·來 he worried himself into illness.
急 切 keen; urgent.
急 務 important, urgent business.
急 客 an unexpected visitor.
急 忙 hurried; without delay.
急 性 a hasty disposition; acute, as a disease.
急 慌 or 急 燥 irritable; irritated; anxious.
急 救 法 first-aid methods; ambulance work.
急·於 anxious to . . . .; pressing for . . . .
急 於 本 而 緩 於 其 末 eager about the principal but remiss about the subordinate.
急 智 nimble-minded.
急 景 time passing rapidly.
急 機 quick-witted.
急 步 hasty steps.
急·死 worried to death; very much concerned about a thing.
急·殺 same as above.
急 湍 rapidly flowing stream.
急 熱 warmly attached to.
急 症 an acute disease.
急 疾 hurried; urgent.
急 痛 in great pain; acute suffering.
急 行 to hasten; to hurry to.
急 言 hasty speech.
急 變 an emergency; a crisis.
急 賑 to relieve distress.
急 賑 會 Relief Society.
急 迫 urgent; forced.
急 速 swiftly; urgently.
急 進 rapid advance.
急 進 黨 Radical Party.
急 遽 無 序 hasty disorder.
急 難 in difficulties; in straits.

急 雨 driving rains.
急 電 urgent telegram.
急 需 or 急 用 wanted soon; urgently necessary; to require for use.
急 驚 severe convulsions.

擊 1.5. To strike. To rout. Distinguish 繫 No. 2458.
481

擊 倒³ to strike to the ground.
擊 傷 injured by a blow or a shot.
擊 刺 to pierce with a sword; to stab.
擊 劍 to strike with a sword; to fence with swords.
⁵擊 冤 to strike the drum outside a magistrate's door in order to bring a grievance under his notice. *See below*. 22.
擊 打 to beat; to strike.
擊 掌 to strike with the hands; to clap the hands.
擊 攻 to attack the enemy.
擊 敗 to rout the enemy.
¹⁰擊 柝 to beat the watches.
擊 楫 to strike the oar—in an oath, from the story of one who struck his oar in crossing the river—may I be struck like this, etc.
擊 殺 to kill by a blow.
擊 沉 to sink with a shell, etc.
擊 甕 浮 球 to break the water jar and (drop stones in the well) to bring the ball up—used for presence of mind. One boy broke the jar to rescue his playmate who had fallen into it, thus saving his life; the other dropped stones into the well to bring his ball up.
¹⁵擊 目 to strike the eye.
擊 碎 to knock to pieces.
擊 磬 於 衛 he was striking the musical stones of Wei.
擊 節 to beat time; to applaud by beating the table.
擊 裂 to beat and tear.
²⁰擊 賞 to applaud.
擊 鼓 to strike a drum.
擊 鼓 鳴 冤 to strike the drum at the magistrate's door, only done under urgent necessity, when there is a grievance to be dealt with. *See above*. 5.
目 擊 eye-witness.

給 3.5. To give to; to provide. To grant; to issue. Also read *kei³*. c *chi³*, k *kei³*.
482

c 給 事 中 supervising censors of former days.
k 給 人 領 to grant to a person.
k 給·他 說 tell him; speak to him.
k 給 付 to hand over; to pay.
k⁵給 假 to grant leave of absence.
c 給 俸 or 給 金 wages; salary.
k 給·我 買 buy it for me.
c 給 扎 to give written instructions.
ck給 照 to grant a pass or certificate.
¹⁰給 發 to issue; to grant.
c 給 發 免 罪 to issue an exemption certificate.
c 給 發 免 票 to issue a free pass.
c 給 發 護 照 to grant a passport.
ck給 與 to give to.
k¹⁵給 足 ample; sufficient; comfortable. ↓c 給 養 provisions.
ck給 還 to hand back; to refund.
k 交·給 to hand over to.
c 供·給 to supply with food, etc.
c 日 給 daily needs.

(a) By,—indication of the passive.

k 給 小 小·的 利 害 絆 住 hampered by petty considerations of profit and loss.
k 給 政 事 鬧 hampered by official business.
k 長 衫 給 車 門 軋 牢·了 his long gown was caught in the door of the car. (*S. mand.*)

(b) Read *chieh²·⁵*. Glib-tongued.

禦 人 以 口 給 they who encounter men with smartness of speech.

亟 2.5. Haste; speed. Prompt, urgent. A crisis. (more polite than 480)
483

亟 切 pressing; important.
亟 加 with the utmost . . . .
亟 得 it is most necessary.
亟 意 most anxious to.
⁵亟 應¹ it is urgently necessary.
亟 欲 most ardently desirous.
亟 行 hastily.
亟 速 very urgent; hastily; as speedily as possible.
事 亟 a crisis.

(a) Read *ch'i⁴* Frequently.

亟 失 時 constantly let slip the right moment.

亟 稱 constant praising.
亟 問 frequently inquired.
亟 餽 鼎 肉 he sent him frequent presents of cooked meats.

極 ²·⁵· The ridgepole of a house. The utmost point. Very, extremely. To reach the end of. To push to extremities. The Poles.
484

極 光 The Aurora.
極 光 射 角 angle of polarization
極 光 鏡 polariscope.
極·其 very; exceedingly; extremely.
⁵極 其 浩 大 extremely great.
極 力 with the utmost effort.
極 品 highest rank: best quality.
極 圈 Arctic and Antarctic Circles.
極 多 very numerous.
¹⁰極 好 extremely good; the very best.
極 竟 one's parents.
極 峰 the peak—formerly used of high provincial officers, later used of the President.
極 度 the limit; the record.
極 性 polarity.
¹⁵極 星 Polar star.
極 是 just so; quite right.
極 東 or 遠 東 The Far East.
極 樂 世 界 The Paradise of Buddhists.
極 目 as far as the eye can see.
²⁰極 端 the extremity; to the last degree; used of any extreme action.
極 端·的 反 抗 extreme opposition.
極 端·的 民 權 absolute democracy.
極 著 most illustrious. (-chu⁴)
極 處 the uttermost; the extreme, the limit.
²⁵極 行⁴the highest standard of conduct.
極 表 同 情 cordial manifestation of sympathy.
極 量 full measure; maximum dose.
極 點 the apex; the climax; combines to form a strong superlative.
四 極 the cardinal points.
太 極 the Absolute of Chinese cosmogony.
平 極 polarization. (electric.)

民 極 an example or guide for the people.
無 極 the Limitless; endless.

殛 ²·⁵· To put to death. To imprison for life.
485

神 明 殛 之 May the gods strike me dead if . . . . !

棘 ²·⁵· The jujube tree. Thorny brambles. Troublesome; perilous. With earnestness. Prompt.
486

棘 人 term of depreciation, used in mourning notices of a son who desires to observe all the rites.
棘 闈 or 急 牆 the provincial examination hall.
棘 手 a "thorny" affair; to get pricked in the hand.
棘 楚 thorns.

戟 ³·⁵· A lance with two points. A halberd with a crescent-shaped blade.
487

戟 喉 an irritant to the throat.
戟 手 to point the fingers of both hands at a person in scorn or anger.
戟 手 詈 人 to point at and revile.
戟 盾 halberds and shields—weapons.

屐 ⁴·⁵· A patten, a wooden shoe.
屐
488

屐 痕 the impressions of pattens.
屐 聲 the clatter of pattens.
屐 齒 the teeth of pattens.
春 苔 雙 屐 痕 the impression of pattens on the spring moss.
泥 屐·子 pattens.

CHI. TSI.　(ㄐ)
(Chih. Tsih)

脊 ³·⁵· The spine; a ridge.
489

脊 柱 the spinal column.
脊 椎 動 物 or 有 脊 動 物 the vertebrates

脊 椎 骨 the vertebrae.
脊 樑 the ridge pole or beams.
⁵脊 背 or 脊 樑 背 the back.
脊 髓 the marrow.
屋 脊 the ridge of a house.
山 脊 a ridge of mountains or hills.
脊·樑 (niang) the back.

瘠 ²·⁵· Lean, barren.
490

瘠 土 barren soil.
瘠 瘦 lean; thin.
瘠 薄 sterile; unproductive.
瘠 馬 a lean horse.

鶺 ²·⁵· The pied wagtail.
491

鶺 鴒 the pied wagtail.
鶺 鴒 在 原 兄 弟 急 難 th[e] wagtails on the moor (ar[e] affectionate) the brothers i[n] trouble (look at each other lik[e] the birds.)

疾 ²·⁵· Sickness; illness; disease.
492

疾 疫 epidemics—as plague, etc.
疾 病 serious ailments; disease.
疾 苦 suffering under oppressiv[e] government.
疾 首 headache; worry.
疾 首 痛 心 headache and hear[t] ache—anxiety; hate.
疾 首 蹙 頞 knit the brows wi[th] headache.

(a) Urgency; haste.

疾 忙 quick; irritable; flurried.
疾 戰 a desperate battle.
疾 言 hasty words.
疾 言 遽 色 hasty speech an[d] agitated countenance—nervou[s] agitation.
⁵疾 走 rapid marching or runnin[g]
疾 趨 to go quickly.
疾 足 先 登 the hasty foot ge[ts] there first.
疾 速 in haste; quickly.
疾 雷 a sudden clap of thunder; crashing peal.
¹⁰疾 雷 不 及 掩 耳 when the cla[p] of thunder comes there is n[o] time to cover the ears—whe[n] a sudden emergency arises i[t] is too late to make preparation[s]

疾風知勁草 the strong wind reveals the strength of the grass—in time of disorder, the loyal and the disloyal are revealed.

疾馬 to gallop; to go quickly.

b) **To hate. To be hated. Angrily.**

疾之已甚 to dislike him bitterly.

疾固 to hate obstinacy.

疾夫舍曰欲之 to hate declining to say, "I want it."

疾惡 to hate evil.

疾惡若仇 to hate evil-doers as if they were personal enemies.

疾日 unlucky days—those on which the cyclical characters are 子 or 卯, these being the days on which Chou 紂, and Chieh 桀, the notorious tyrants were killed.

疾視 black looks; angry glare.

嫉 4.5.
493 Envy; jealousy. To hate.

嫉·妒 to be jealous; to envy.

嫉忌 to avoid; jealous hatred.

嫉恨 to hate from jealous motives.

嫉視 jealous looks.

嫉賢 envious of the good.

蒺 2.5.
494 Furze; gorse.

蒺藜 thorns; seeds used for medicine.

卽 2.5.
495 Immediately; now. Then; accordingly. Indicates supposition or sequence.

卽位 to ascend the throne.

卽刻 or 卽今 or 立卽 at once.

卽去卽來 go and return at once.

卽可 may then.

⁵卽始而見終 to know the end by the beginning.

卽將滿期 about to expire, as a term, etc.

卽席 on the spot; at once; at the same time.

卽日 on the same day.

卽時 or 卽輕 or 卽便 at this time; forthwith.

¹⁰卽此 just this; thus.

卽決的 summary, as in legal proceedings.

卽炤 the light of fireflies.

卽行 immediately.

卽速 quickly; in haste.

¹⁵卽選 or 卽用 or 卽補 about to be appointed—as an official.

飛卽 as speedily as possible.

(a) **Even if; if; even.**

卽如 or 卽使 for example; supposing; if; should it be so.

卽或 or else; supposing that.

卽或不然 even if it were not so—implies that it certainly is so.

卽是 namely; even; what if.

卽曰 if it is said …

卽非 even though it is not; then it is not.

(b) **To go to; to approach.**

卽世 to depart this life.

卽吉 to leave off mourning garments.

卽戎 to go to war.

唧 1.5.
496 Chirping of insects. The noise of a crowd.

唧·咕 to grumble and mutter.

唧唧 hum of cicadas; a sighing sound.

唧唧呱呱 hubbub; gabble of tongues.

唧噥唧噥 low hum as of talking.

唧溜 quick-witted.

唧筒 a pump.

蝍 2.5.
497 A centipede.

蝍蛆 the centipede. = 7203,1.

蝍蠋 the looper caterpillar, also called 尺蠖.

鯽 4.5.
498 The bastard carp.

鯽魚 a bream.

金鯽 the gold-fish.

勣 1.5.
499 Merit; conduct that deserves reward. Inter. 績 No. **501.**

積 1.5.
500 To amass; to store up.

積久 over a long period.

積儧 to hoard; to save.

積儲 to make savings.

積冰 The Arctic Regions.

⁵積分 total marks; integral calculus.

積勞成病 overwork causes illness.

積善之家 a virtuous family.

積地 reclaimed land.

積壓案牘 accumulation of documents and law cases—after a negligent magistrate has left.

¹⁰積存 to lay up.

積少成多 economy in trifles ensures abundance.

積年 for many years; year after year.

積德 to accumulate virtue.

積德累功 to accumulate merit by good works, etc.

¹⁵積怨 accumulated malice and hatred.

積慣 habituated; accustomed to.

積書 to collect books.

積案 lawsuits which have been pending for a long time.

積極 positive as opposed to negative.

²⁰積極抵抗 active resistance or opposition.

積極效果 positive results.

積極方面 positive tendency.

積極進行 positive advance.

積毀銷骨 much reviling and slander wears the bones—i.e., when everybody speaks against a person, it makes him tired of life.

²⁵積漸 gradually; little by little.

積玉堆金 to pile up gold and gems.

積痾 chronic disease.

積祖 inherited; handed down.

積福 to accumulate happiness by merit.

³⁰積穀 to purchase grain with public funds and store it against famine.

積穀倉 a granary.

積習 long standing practice; an old habit.

積羽沉舟羣輕折軸 feathers when accumulated will sink a boat, many light persons will break the axle of a carriage

—used fig. the power of insignificant people is to be feared when it is in the mass.

積聚 to accumulate; to gather together.

積蓄 to accumulate; savings.

↑ 積累 to accumulate.

積貯 to store up.

積財 to store up riches.

積雪 accumulated snow.

積非勝是 the accumulation of wrongs outnumbers the rights.

(a) Read *tzŭ⁴* (*tsĭ*) To pile up grain.

積累之漸 the slowness of accumulation.

績 1.5. **To spin thread, to twist, to join threads.**
501

績女 a woman who spins thread.

績紡 to spin; to wind.

績續 to connect; to join threads.

績麻 to twist threads.

(b) **To complete.**

績成 to complete.

績效 results; effects.

(c) **Merit; meritorious acts. An affair.**

績事 an affair.

績功 good deeds.

績用 utility.

成績 accomplishment; school 「marks.

蹟跡迹 4.5.

Traces, footsteps. Effects. To follow up; to search out.
502

蹟捕 to follow up and arrest.

蹟盜 to search out robbers.

蹟象 traces, scars; real existences.

功蹟 insignia; heroism.

⁵實蹟 clear proof.

形蹟 traces; movements.

心蹟 one's inner feelings; sentiments.

痕蹟 scar of a wound; tracks; traces.

發蹟 to make tracks; to come out and be known; one's means of livelihood.

¹⁰神蹟 or 異蹟 miracles; supernatural evidence.

蹤蹟 tracks; traces; footprints.

遺蹟 works of one that is dead.

陳蹟 examples; tracks that are well trod.

輯 4.5. **To connect and arrange. To compile; to edit.**
503

輯斂 to gather.

↓編·輯 to edit; editor.

輯要 to bring together the important items—as an epitome of a book; summary.

輯錄 to compile records.

(a) **To harmonize; united.**

輯和 to make peace.

輯睦 friendliness.

輯輯 friendly harmony.

修輯 to work for peace and harmony.

寧輯 peaceful.

稷 2.5.

Panicled millet.
504

稷·子 or 黍稷 varieties of millet.

后稷 Minister of Agriculture under Shun (Shuen) later worshipped as god of agriculture.

社稷 gods of the land of grain.

(a) **Quick.**

旣齊旣稷 "you have been both exact and expeditious."

(b) **Declining.**

日下稷 as the sun declined.

寂宋 2.5.

Still, silent. Solitary.
505

寂寂 quiet; contemplative vacancy.

寂寂無聊 lonely, with none to support and help.

寂寥 vacant; desolate.

寂歷 or 寂寞 or 寂如 alone; retired; solitary.

寂然不動 sitting still; at rest.

寂靜 silent; quiet.

戢 4.5. **To put away weapons. To fold up. To collect oneself.**
506

戢兵 to cease hostilities.

戢影 to secrete oneself.

戢斂 to gather in.

戢暴鋤強 violence subdued and cruelty done away with.

戢用光 to gather the people together and bring glory to the country.

戢翼 to fold the wings.

籍 2.5. **A record of population. A list. A register. To be registered as a native of.**
507

籍甚 his reputation is well known.

籍田 fields belonging to the state, ploughed by the emperor in person.

籍記 to register.

↓民籍 or 戶籍 census; a register of the population.

籍隸 to belong to a place.

入籍 or 入國籍 to become a naturalized citizen.

↑籍貫 or 原籍 one's native place.

回籍 to return to one's native place.

(a) **To confiscate.**

籍其財產 his property was confiscated.

籍斂 illegal taxation or extortion.

籍沒 to confiscate; to make a list of the property and confiscate it.

放縱狼籍 he was uncontrolled and violent.

集人 2.5. **To assemble. To gather together.**
508

集合 collective; to assemble, as troops, etc.

集合主義 collectivism.

集合力 collective strength.

集合名詞 collective nouns.

⁵集合契約 collective or group agreement or contract.

集合意識 symposium; collection of ideas.

集合體 a collective body.

集大成 a complete musical performance; to gather many proposals and formulate a theory from them.

集少成多 "many a little makes a mickle."

↑集中 to concentrate.

↑集中營 concentration camp.

[10]集 成 to gather and form into.
集 成 一 類 gathered under one category.
集 思 to get opinions from different sources; to make use of the opinions of others.
集 於 一 身 centred in one person.
集 會 to assemble; to convene.
[15]集 會 自 由 right to assemble public meetings.
集 權 the centralization of authority. 集 團 bloc.
集 產 主 義 collectivism.
集 矢 collected darts—used of a person who is the object of much criticism.
　親 身 集 矢 received many darts in his own person.
[20]集 綴 to gather together.
集 聚 to gather; to collect; a collection.
集 聚 的 collective.
集 股 to accumulate from shares.
集 腋 成 裘 gathering the little bits of fur from under the forelegs of animals to make a robe—do not despise small things.
[25]集 菀 集 枯 some gather on the flowers, I roost on the branches—the lot of men is not equal—fate is not the same.
集 議 to meet and discuss.
齊 集 a full assembly.

(a) To compile, to edit. Collections of writings, belles-lettres.
集 句 to piece together phrases from quotations into poems.
集 部 collections of literature—poems, odes, essays, etc., anthology.
一 集 a collection of essays; a section of such a collection.
修 集 to edit a book or a series of books.
文 集 類 編 collection of writings.

(b) A market.
集 市 a market.
趕 集 to go to market; to go to a country fair.

CH'I　　(ㄑㄧ)

嵠[1] A valley with a stream in it. A gorge.
509

↑ 集 體 collective; collectively.

山 嵠 之 險 dangers of the passes.
深 嵠 a deep gorge.

溪[1] A rivulet, a stream. A creek.
510

溪 水 a freshet; a stream.
深 溪 a deep ravine.
溪 船 boats used on rapids.
屯 溪 T'unch'i (Twankay), a large market town in the Hweichow district of South Anhwei, famous for its tea trade.

谿[1] A valley; a deep gorge. Similar to and inter. 嵠 No. 509.
511

谿 刻 mean and petty.
谿 壑 "extremely avaricious," the mountain gorge can be filled, but not the covetous heart. 509–11 also pron. hsi[1].

耆[2] A man of sixty, some give it as seventy. Old. Seniors.
512

耆 儒 an aged scholar.
耆 宿 a venerable scholar.
耆 老 or 耆 壽 old people; seniors.
耆 艾 aged and wise; an old experienced man.

(a) Read chih[3] (chī[3]) To cause; to adjust. Desirous of.
耆 定 to bring into effect.
耆 昧 to hoodwink people.
節 耆 欲 to curb the desires.

鬐[2] A horse's mane. Dorsal fins.
513

奇
竒 [2] Strange, wonderful, rare.
514

奇 事 a wonderful affair; something strange.
奇 人 an eccentric.
奇 儁 an eminent person.
奇 兵 佯 敗 place troops in ambush and feign defeat.
[5]奇 功 distinguished meritorious service.
奇 男 子[3] a remarkable (manly) man.

奇 士 an adept.
奇 妙 rare; mystic; strange.
奇 巧 clever; ingenious.
[10]奇 怪 strange; rare.
奇 怨 deep desire for revenge.
奇 想 a rare thought.
奇 技 clever contrivance.
奇 方 unfailing prescription.
[15]奇 書 a rare book.
奇 橫[4] obstinately perverse.
奇 特 unique; specially fine.
奇 珍 or 珍 奇 rarities; curios.
奇 異 unusual; extraordinary.
[20]奇 緣 singular destiny—said of two who have been brought together in a strange way.
奇 花 rare flowers.
奇 行 strange behaviour.
奇 觀 a strange, wonderful sight.
奇 計 clever strategy or plans.
[25]奇 談 strange talk; unusual story.
奇 貨 可 居 rare commodities may be kept for a better price—to corner the market.
奇 蹟 signs; wonders; miracles.
奇 遇 strange adventure.
奇 逢 wonderful opportunity.
奇 運 strange fate.
奇 邪 weird; uncanny things.
居 奇 to corner the market.

(a) Read chi[1] Odd; single. The surplus.

奇 偶 odd and even.
奇 數 odd numbers.
奇 日 the odd days of the month.
奇 羨 an overplus.
奇 零 the remainder.

崎[1] A path over mountains. Rugged. Steep.
515

崎 嶇 a rough road. Anxious.

攲[1] Leaning, not standing solidly on its base. Distinguish 攲 No. 420.
516

攲 器 易 覆 a leaning vessel is easily upset.

琦[1,2] A valuable stone. A curio, a rarity.
517

琦 瑋 valuable, as a gem.
琦 行 a rare disposition.
琦 賂 or 琦 貨 a valuable or unusual article.

綺 [3] A kind of open-work varie-gated thin silk. Also read *i*[3], esp. in transliterations.
518

綺 縠 fine silk garments; elegant apparel.

綺 羅 open silk used for summer dresses.

(a) Beautiful; pretty.

綺 年 young; youthful.

綺 想 or 綺 思 beautiful thoughts —lit. embroidered.

綺 襦 紈 袴 young fops of good family—lit. embroidered jacket and white silk trousers.

綺 語 fine phrases; literary elegance.

綺 靡 extravagant and gay.

綺 麗 beautiful and pretty.

踦 [1] One-legged. Crippled, halt. A defect.
519

踦 匾 hidden away.

踦 足 lame, halting.

踦 跂 limping along.

(a) Odd, not even. Alone.

相 與 踦 閭 而 語 they spoke to each other through the half-opened door.

(b) Read *chi*[1] The shin bone. Read *i*.[3] u.f. 倚 No. 2953.

錡 [3] Pot or pan with feet. Also read *i*[3].
520

維 錡 及 釜 in the pots and cauldrons.

(a) A stand for bows.

設 在 蘭 錡 put them on the stands for the spears and the bows respectively.

(b) Read *ch'i*[2] A chisel.

又 缺 我 錡 we spoilt our chisels.

騎 [2] To mount; to stride; to ride an animal.
521

騎·上 to mount.

騎 兵 or 騎 軍 cavalry.

騎 吹 ancient military songs.

騎 牆 派 Independent Party—fence sitters.

[5]騎 箕 or 騎 箕 尾 to straddle the constellations of Sagittarius and Scorpio.—to die.

騎 縫 印 stamped partly on each of two sheets, as two copies of a deed or contract, for security against alterations.

騎 置 mounted courier.

騎 藉 選 舉 plural voting.

騎 虎 之 勢 awkward predicament.

[10]騎 虎 難 下 unable to get down from the tiger's back—to get into a position from which there is no retiring.

騎 驢 覓 驢 to ride a donkey in order to look for it—to forget one's original intention and go off on side issues; also—to use a position as a stepping stone.

騎 鶴 上 揚 州 to ride a crane to *Yangchow*—foolish, impossible ambitions.

善 騎 a good rider.

飛 騎 light horse. Also pron. *-chi*[4].

岐 [2] A path over mountains. Precipitous. The home of the ancestors of the *Chou* Dynasty in S. W. Shensi. u.f. next.
522

岐 出 discrepant.

岐 嶷 outstanding; a mountain peak.

岐 語 divergent views of one affair.

岐 黃 篇 famous medical treatise by 岐 白, and Hwang ti 黃 帝.

歧 [2] Forked. Divergent. u.f. last.
523

歧 字 synonyms.

歧 念 conflicting thoughts.

歧 意 different interpretations; varying opinions.

歧 歧 with speed, as running.

歧 異 conflicting; discrepancies.

歧 誤 mistakes.

歧 路 a fork in the road; a "crooked way."

歧 路 亡 羊 a lost sheep—used by *Lieh tzu* of the difficulty of finding the way, 道.

跂 [2] A foot with six toes. Insects crawling.
524

跂 行 to creep.

跂 行 喙 息 to crawl and suck—i.e., caterpillars and insects.

跂 跂 to crawl like a caterpillar.

(a) Read *ch'i*[3,4]. To stand on tiptoe. id. 企 No. 545.

跂 想 on the lookout; anxiously expecting.

跂 望 on the tiptoe of expectation.

跂 訾 unconventional and boastful.

跂 足 以 待 to stand on tiptoe waiting.

跂 踵 而 望 to stand on tiptoe, on the lookout for; earnest expectation.

其 [2] His, her, its, their. This, that. A demonstrative and possessive pronoun.
525

其 上 above; on the top of it.

其 中 or 其 間 among; in the midst.

其 他 the others; the rest. Also -*t*

其 他 可 能 other possibilities. Also -*t'o*[1].

[5]其 便 一 也 its convenience is the same.

其 儀 不 忒 in his deportment there was nothing wrong.

其 內 or 其 裏 inside; within.

其 命 維 新 the (Heavenly) ordinance was new.

其 鳴 也 哀 its cry was mournful

[10]其 外 outside; without; beyond these.

其 奈 我 何 what harm can he do to me?

其 如 命 何 what can he do against the decrees of Heaven

其 始 播 百 穀 it is nearly time to begin sowing the various grains.

其 子 his son.

[15]其 冤 得 大 白 his reputation was cleared.

其 幾 何 離 "this separation but for a time." *Giles*.

其 後 after this; hereafter.

其 所 令 反 其 所 好 (*hao*[1]) their commands were contrary to their desires.

其 所 取 材 the subjects or material from which they choose.

[20]其 所 有 what they have.

其 揆 一 也 their principles are identical.

其 文 則 史 its style was historical.
其 斯 this.
其 斯 之 謂 與 is not that the meaning of this?
其 時 at that time.
其 有 所 試 矣 he has what will bear examination.
其 次 the next in order; the second.
其 次 致 曲 the next (to the Sage) applies himself to the developments (of goodness in himself.)
其 民 必 攜 his people will come over to you.
其 爲 說 也 their interpretation or statements.
其 目 之 大 者 those he regarded as important.
其 目 在 下 the details are as follows.
其 終 也 巳 he will always remain thus.
其 蔽 也 絞 that which leads to this is incivility.
其 誰 who?
其 賈 不 貲 priceless.
其 顙 有 泚 perspiration broke out on his forehead.
其 餘 the residue; the surplus, the rest.
其 麗 不 億 their number is not hundreds of thousands only.
其 默 足 以 容 his silence is enough to cause forbearance (toward himself.)

(a) Emphatic, imperative, demonstrative, interrogative, and optative particle.

其 何 以 堪 How can it be borne?
其 何 能 淑 載 胥 及 溺 How can you make the country good? You and it will be destroyed together.
其 君 也 哉 May he prove to be a prince indeed?
其 實 really; in fact; as a matter of fact.
其 難 其 慎 How difficult! How cautious!
其 雨 其 雨 Oh for rain! Oh for rain!

(b) If, as if.

其 如 as if; just as if.

(c) Read *chi*[1]. Final particle. Interrogative.

夜 如 何 其 What of the night?

期[2] A period, a date, a limit of time. A fixed date, a month. Also read *ch'i*[1].
526

期 促 the date has almost expired.
期 候 time.
期 日 a date fixed.
期 會 appointment to meet.
[5]期 滿 at the expiration of the set time.
期 畢 in the end; finally.
期 票 promissory note.
期 約 previous engagement; an appointment for a certain time.
期 間 within a specified time; the duration of.
[10]期 限 time limit.
到 期 to reach the appointed date.
定 期 to set a date.
後 會 有 期 we shall meet again.
日 期 the date already fixed.
[15]無 定 期 no date is fixed.
約 期 to agree upon a date.
限 期 to fix a time limit.
過 期 to exceed the time limit.

(a) To expect. To meet, to wait for.

期 合 五 族 to hope for a unity of the five races.
期 有 得 耳 what they have you get.
期 望 to hope, to look forward to.
期 當 to hope for what is suitable.
期 許 to hope that it will be allowed.
以 公 利 爲 期 with hopeful regard to public interests.
以 期 in the hope that.
可 期 reason to hope.

(b) One hundred years.

期 頤 a centenarian.

(c) Read *chi*[1]. A full year. Inter. 朞 No. 401.

期 功 near relatives—i.e., those for whom one year of mourning is worn.
期 耆 an elder for whom one year of mourning is worn.
期 巳 久 矣 one year is enough.
期 月 a whole month, or one year.

期 月 而 巳 可 也 in twelve months something would be performed.
期 服 a year of mourning.
期 而 小 祥 at the end of the year of mourning—there may be a little relaxation.

(d) To stammer.

期 期 艾 艾 to stammer, see No. 19. C.

棋 碁 基[2] The game of chess, draughts and other similar games.
527

棋 子 pieces in chess or draughts.
棋 子 塊 cubes.
棋 局 board set out for chess; a move in the game. To portion out the chessmen.
棋 布 spread out here and there like men on a board.
[5]棋 盤 a chess board.
棋 譜 a manual on chess.
下 棋 to play chess.
圍 棋 another game played on 324 squares, the players endeavour to surround the opposing pieces, — the game of *go*.
敲 棋 to tap a chess-man in thought—pondering.
象 棋 Chinese chess, it has some similarities to the western game.

(a) Read *chi*[1]. A foundation.

萬 物 根 棋 the foundation of all things.

欺[1] To cheat, to impose on, to take advantage of. To oppress.
528

欺 他 白 生 took a mean advantage of his unsophistication.
欺 侮 or 欺 弄 to insult; to ridicule.
欺 凌 to treat badly; to insult.
欺 哄 to swindle.
欺 善 to injure and oppress the good; to bully the good-natured.
欺 壓 to oppress.
欺 害 to injure by cheating.
欺 炫 to confuse another in order to cheat him.

欺生 to take advantage of strangers or of ignorance.

欺瞞 to defraud; to hoodwink.

欺誣 to impose on and falsely accuse.

欺詒 to impose on; to make a fool of.

欺·負 to humbug; to take advantage of.

欺隱 to conceal with fraudulent intent; to mislead by concealing facts.

淇 [529] [2] A tributary of the River Wei in N. E. Honan.

琪 [530] [2] A valuable stone or gem of a white colour.

琪玗 a fairy gem.

琪花瑤草 the flowers and plants of fairyland.

祺 [531] [2] Fortunate; lucky.

祺安 peace and happiness.

祺然 peaceful, without anxiety.

祺祜 blessings and prosperity.

祺祥 lucky; of good omen.

近祺不—— May plenteous happiness soon be yours!

綦 [532] [2] Dark grey. Variegated. Superlative.

綦嚴 very severe; very stringent, as discipline.

綦綺 variegated embroidery or woven work.

騏 [533] [2] A piebald horse. Spotted.

騏驥 one of the eight horses of *Mu Wang*, it could do 1,000 *li* in a day.

有駅有騏 there were bay and piebald horses.

麒 [534] [2] A fabulous, auspicious animal. The male is 麒, and the female is 麟. It has the body of a deer, tail of an ox, hoofs of a horse, one fleshy horn, and the hair

on its back is all varied colours, while on the belly it is yellow. It does not tread on the grass, nor eat anything living. Japanese use the term for the giraffe.

麒麟過山 the unicorn passes over the mountains scattering fire.

旗旂 [535] [2] A flag, a banner. Division of the Manchu army.

旗°下 or 旗°人 a Bannerman, either a Manchu, Mongol or registered Chinese.

旗號 a signal flag; a distinguishing flag.

旗·子 a flag.

旗幟 or 旗志 flags or pennons bearing an inscription.

[5] 旗旛 flags and pennons.

旗·杆 a flag-staff.

旗·杆斗 box-shaped ornament on a Chinese flag-staff.

旗槍 fine tea leaves, the leaf is called the "flag" and the stem the "spear," when the buds have only just burst into one tiny leaf.

旗章 a distinguishing flag.

[10] 旗粧 Manchu style of women's dress.

旗禮 Manchu etiquette.

旗纛 standards; banners.

旗艦 flag-ship.

旗語 flag-signals.

旗鼓對壘 joined in battle; in opposition.

憩愒 [536] [4] To rest.

憩息 to rest; to stop.

暫憩 rest awhile.

祁 [537] [2] Abundant. Large. Numerous. Leisurely, at ease.

祁寒 depth of winter.

祁祁 at ease; leisurely.

祁祁如雲 very numerous; in clouds.

祇 [538] [2] The spirit of the earth. Distinguish 祇 No. 952.

祇仰 to look up to with respect.

上下神祇 spirits of heaven and earth.

地祇 earth as a god.

(a) Rest.

俾我祇也 it would give me rest.

(b) Great.

无祇悔 no great regrets.

(c) Read *chih*[1] (*chi*[1]) u.f. 只 Only, but.

圻 [539] [2] A boundary, a border. Inter. 畿 No. 412. Imperial domains.

圻堮 to carve in relief; a sceptre carved in relief.

祈 [540] [2] To pray, to beseech, to request.

祈報 the spring sacrifice of petition and the autumn sacrifice of thanksgiving respectively.

祈年 to pray for a prosperous harvest.

祈文 a prayer burnt before the gods.

祈望 to hope; to expect that.

[5] 祈求 or 祈懇 to entreat.

祈爲 it is hoped that....

祈祈甘雨 gentle rain.

祈禱 to beseech; to pray; prayer.

祈禱會 prayer meeting.

[10] 祈請 to request.

祈賜 I pray you to grant.

祈賽 sacrifice of thanksgiving for blessing and prayer for the future.

蘄 [541] [2] To seek for; to beg.

蘄至其人 to endeavour to equal another.

蘄進歐美之強 to strive to develop power like Europe and America.

(a) Name of a place in Hupeh.

蘄 竹 variety of bamboo found at 蘄 春 縣 in Hupeh.
蘄 蛇 a pale mottled venomous snake found in Hupeh.

啟 啓 ³ 542
To explain; to inform; to state. To begin.

啟 予 足 啟 予 手 uncover my hands and my feet.
啟 事 a notice; to announce.
啟 初 at first.
啟 口 or 啟 齒 to talk; to broach a subject.
⁵啟 土 to develop new territory.
啟 奏 to send in a memorial.
啟 封 to break the seals—as on a door or a letter.
啟 迪 後 人 to hand down the teaching to posterity.
啟 戶 to open the door. [seen in the E.
¹⁰啟 明 daybreak; the planet Venus when
啟 發 to open up men's intelligence.
啟 知 to inform.
啟 示 to reveal; to unveil.
啟 程 or 啟 足 to start on a journey.
¹⁵啟 窗 以 覘 on opening the window and looking in. | = 3701.93
啟 羅 克 蘭 母 Kilogrammes.
啟 者 or 敬 啟 者 to begin—opening phrase in correspondence.
啟 蒙 to instruct the young.
啟 處 to rest.
啟 蟄 不 殺 he would not kill insects arousing from their torpidity.
²⁰啟 行 to start from.
啟 閉 to open and shut—the beginning and ending of a thing, as of spring and summer, autumn and winter.
啟 顏 to smile.
附 啟 a postscript.

綮 ³ 543
An embroidered banner. Sheath for a lancehead.

綮 幟 遙 臨 "The banners are approaching from afar."

(a) Read ch'ing³ Articulation of the joints.

肯 (k'ai³) 綮 point of articulation.
理 深 入 肯 綮 his truths are deep and enter the joints.

豈 ³ 544
An interrogative particle which implies a dissenting answer. How?

豈 不 是 Is it not so?
豈 不 知 Do you not know?
豈 不 說 Did he not say?
豈 其 然 乎 Can this be so?
⁵豈 可 How can it be?
豈 可 如 此 How can this be?
豈 奈 How can it be borne?
豈 敢 How dare I? a self-depreciatory term.
豈 是 這 樣 Can it be so?
¹⁰豈 有 此 理 There is no such rule! There is no such principle!
豈 無 他 人 Are there no others?
豈 能 How can he do it?
豈 非 如 此 How can it be otherwise?

(a) Read k'ai³ Delighted. Inter. 凱 No. 3205.

豈 弟 complacent and easy.
豈 樂 飲 酒 having a merry time.

企 ³·⁴ 545
To stand on tiptoe and look for; hence it means anxious. Erect.

企 不 穩 it is not steady.
企 仰 to look up to for help.
企 候 回 音 I stand anxiously awaiting a reply—phrase at close of letters.
企 倦 tired from long standing.
⁵企 及 to expect to attain.
企 及 尊 府 I have called at your house.
企 慕 to look for; expectant; to be desirous of.
企 望 to expect with eagerness; to look for with anxiety.
企 業 any business enterprise.
¹⁰企 立 to stand erect.
企 踵 on the tiptoe of expectancy.
企 高 to stand high up.

屺 ³ 546
A hill with trees or grass—some give the opposite meaning. See 陟 No. 1004.

杞 ³ 547
A medlar tree. A species of willow.

杞 柳 a kind of willow.
杞 梓 fine wood suitable for carving.

(a) A small feudal state.

杞 不 足 徵 也 Ch'i cannot sufficiently attest my words.
杞 國 a small feudal state.
杞 憂 the fear of the man of Ch'i—baseless anxiety, see next phrase.
杞 人 憂 天 the man of Ch'i feared that the sky was about to fall—used to express baseless anxiety; pessimistic fears, etc.

起 ³ 548
To rise; to raise.

起 予 者 商 也 It is Shang who can bring out my meaning.
起 事 to raise a revolt; uprising; to cause trouble.
起 伏 rampant and couchant, as in heraldry; now rising, now falling, as the changes of circumstances.
起 來 to rise; to get up; a complement of many verbs.
⁵起 兵 to raise troops; to go to war.
起 誓 to take an oath.
起 家 to raise the fortunes of the family; one's status in society.
起 居 rising and resting—one's usual behaviour; at all times.
起 居 萬 福 May you enjoy every blessing in your daily life—complimentary phrase in letters.
¹⁰起 布 衣 to come from the masses.
起 念 to think of.
起 意 to conceive the idea of a thing.
起 敬 to show respect.
起 早 to rise early.
¹⁵起 案 to produce, as evidence.
起 死 to raise the dead.
起 牀 to get out of bed.
起 用 to raise or reinstate one who has been rejected or degraded.
起 發 to raise one's fortunes; to get on; to become wealthy.

[20]起眼 worthy of notice.

起碼幾個錢 What is your lowest price?

起立 to stand erect, as a sign of respect, etc.

起立表決 a rising vote.

起義 to raise a righteous revolt.

[25]起興 (hsing[4]) the risings of (sexual) desire.

起舞 to jump for joy.

起色 to rise in value; improve in quality.

起。見 the object; the motive; the reason or purpose.

起贓 or 領贓 or 起賊 to recover property that has been stolen.

[30]起身 to rise.

起重機 a crane or derrick.

起錨 or 絞錨 to weigh anchor

(a) To start; to begin.

起初 or 起頭 or 起首 or 起先 or 起根 in the beginning; at the commencement; at first.

起名 to name; to give a name.

起息 to bear interest.

起承轉合 the introduction, the elucidation of the theme, changing round to another viewpoint, and the summing up— the four steps in composition of essays for old examination system.

[5]起數 to calculate fortunes.

起更 (keng[1]) to set the watch.

起租 first day of receiving rent from a property.

起稿 or 起草 to prepare a draft; to make a rough copy or outline sketch.

起端 the origin or beginning.

[10]起至 to start and to arrive—as far as.

起行 or 起程 to prepare and start on a journey.

起訴 to institute legal proceedings; to sue.

起訴權 right of procedure.

起課 to divine.

[15]起身 to set off on a journey.

起釁 to begin a feud.

起點 starting point.

一起 all together.

(b) To discharge, as cargo.

起單 or 起貨單 permit to land goods.

起貨 to land cargo; to take delivery of goods.

器
罍 }[4] A vessel, a utensil, a dish. Implements. Organ in the body.
549

器具 or 器械 vessels; tools; utensils.

君子[3]不器 the man of complete virtue is not a utensil having but one use.

器官 the organs of sense.

器材 materials for making articles.

[5]器械。的 mechanical, as labour, etc.

器械。的動作 mechanical movements.

器物 implements.

器用 utensils; capable; useful.

器皿 vessels; plates; dishes, etc.

(a) Capacity; ability.

器之 measures them; takes the measure of their capacity, etc.

器使 to measure the capacity of a man and use him accordingly.

器宇 a man's deportment.

器小 small capacity; little-minded.

[5]器局不大。方 small-minded; acting in a pettyfogging manner.

器識 versatile—with wide experience.

器。重 to regard with reverence.

所器。重 …. it was appreciated.

器。量 natural capacity.

棄
[4] To reject; to cast aside; to discard; to abandon. Distinguish 葉 No. 7319.
550

棄世 to renounce the world, as a recluse; to die.

棄之如遺 he passed him by; he rejected him.

棄井 to abandon a deep well before the water is reached—the former labour is wasted.

棄信 breach of faith.

[5]棄却 to reject; to cast aside.

棄嫌 to disdain.

棄婦 or 棄妻 a divorced wife.

棄官 to give up office; to abandon official life.

棄市 public execution.

[10]棄廢 to throw away as useless.

棄捐 to neglect and not use.

棄捨 or 棄掉 to throw away; to abandon.

棄暗就光 to forsake darkness and come to the light.

棄業 to discard one's profession.

[15]棄權 to forego rights or privileges; to abstain from voting.

棄法受賂 to abandon justice and receive bribes.

棄物 waste; refuse.

棄甲曳兵 they cast aside their coats of mail and dragged their weapons behind them.

棄疑 to get rid of doubts and suspicions.

[20]棄絕 to annul; to renounce.

棄羣臣 death of a prince.

棄留 to cast away; to throw aside; to neglect.

棄職守 to abandon one's post.

棄背 death of a person; cast aside and neglected.

[25]棄舊換新 to reject the old for the new.

棄言 unable to carry out a promise; useless talk.

棄逐 to expel.

棄邪歸正 to cast away the heterodox and return to orthodox beliefs. = 3196.76

棄除天命 disobedient to the commands of heaven.

[30]棄養 death of parents.

自棄 to injure one's own interests; to throw oneself away; to become dissolute.

契
[4] Lines on bamboo or wood used as records prior to the invention of writing. To notch. A contract, an agreement; a bond.
551

契丹 Kitan Tartars who ruled China in part, A.D. 907—1115. The word Cathay is a corruption of this.

契厚 close and enduring friendship; friendly.

契合 united—as halves of a tally.

契尾 a stamped document pasted to title deeds showing that the tax has been paid.

[5]契據 deeds and similar documents.

契 約 or 契 紙 or 契 書 or 契 卷 a written contract or agreement.

契 舟 求 劍 a man of Ts'u whose sword fell into the water from a boat, notched the place on the side of the moving boat from whence it fell, in order to find it—obstinately foolish.

白 契 white deed—unstamped deeds, substitutes for the originals.

紅 契 red deed, i.e., one that has been officially stamped with the red seal.

(a) To adopt. To dedicate to. Mournful.

契 友 sworn friends.

契 子 or 契 女 adopted child, sometimes those dedicated to the gods—an adoption not always genuine.

契 父 an adopted father.

契 神 dedicated to the gods by vows.

拜 契 to swear friendship.

(b) A divining instrument.

契 龜 to divine by means of burnt tortoise shell; the instrument by means of which this is done.

(c) Read *ch'ieh*[1] To be separated from. To cut.

契 闊 to be separated from one another.

(b) Read *hsieh*[4,5] One of the ministers of the Emperor *Shun.*

气 [4]
552
Breath. Radical 84.

汽 [4]
553
Steam, vapour. Inter. next.

汽 機 engines.
汽 水 aerated waters.
汽 笛 steam whistle.
汽 筒 steam cylinder.
[5] 汽 管 steam pipes.
汽 船 or 火 輪 船 steamer; steamship. = 4254.14.
汽 車 motor car, automobile; also used of steam locomotive in writings.
汽 鍋 boiler of an engine.

汽 雷 or 汽 彈 aerial torpedoes.

氣 / 炁 [4]
554
Breath, air, steam, gas. Weather. The second form is used in Taoist charms.

氣 化 vaporization.

氣 化 推 遷 successive changes caused by vaporization.

氣 促 dyspnoea; breathless.

氣°候 a solar term, of which there are 24 in the year called 節 氣; 5 days constituted a 候, and 3 候 constituted a 節 Now used for climate.

[5] 氣°候 學 climatology.

氣°候 帶 climatic zones.

氣 囊 air-cell or sac in birds.

氣 圈 the atmosphere as encircling the earth.

氣 壓 atmospheric pressure.

[10] 氣 壓 計 or 風 雨 表 a barometer.

氣 孔 breathing holes in insects; transpiration pores in vegetation.

氣 室 an air chamber.

氣 弇 or 氣 瓣 air-valves; steam valves.

氣°息 panting for want of breath; the breath of life; fusty.

[15] 氣 息 奄 奄 gasping for breath.

氣 息 掇 掇 the gasping of asthma.

氣 急 or 喘 息 asthma.

氣 枕 air-cushion.

氣 根 aerial roots.

[20] 氣 槍 air-gun.

氣 水 aerated waters.

氣 油 gasoline; motor spirit.

氣 溫 temperature of the atmosphere.

氣 燈 浮 標 gasbuoys.

[25] 氣 球 a balloon.

氣 笛 a steam whistle.

氣 筒 a steam cylinder.

氣 管 steam pipes; bronchial tubes; windpipe.

氣 管 支 steam pipes.

[30] 氣 節 or 節°氣 the 24 solar periods of the year. *See below.* A. 21.

氣 籠 a bamboo cylinder about a foot in diameter and over ten feet long, placed upright as a ventilator in a stack of grain in a granary.

氣 絕 or 氣 盡 exhausted; dead.

氣 脬 air-bladders.

氣 胞 air-cells.

[35] 氣 象 weather; circumstances; manner, etc., *see below.* A. 25.

氣 象 報 告 meteorological reports.

氣 象 學 meteorology.

氣 象 臺 an observatory.

氣 象 預 報 meteorological forecasts.

[40] 氣 表 steam-gauge.

氣 蓬 蓬 的 steaming hot.

氣 體 gases.

氣 體 之 充 也 *Ch'i* is that which pervades the whole body. *Legge* translates it "passion nature."

氣 體 機 關 or 氣 體 引 擎 gas-engine.

[45] 氣 閉 an impediment in breathing.

氣 道 airways.

一 氣 with one breath; at one effort.

二 氣 The Dual Powers. *Yin* 陰 and *Yang* 陽; positive and negative principles in nature.

地 氣 climate.

[50] 屏 氣 to hold the breath. (*ping*[3]-)

欷 氣 to sigh.

淡 氣 nitrogen.

煤 氣 coal gas; *see under* 煤 No. 4398—8ff.

空 氣 the air.

[55] 輕 氣 hydrogen.

鍊 氣 Taoist breathing exercises.

飲 氣 silent grief.

養 氣 oxygen.

(a) Manner. Demeanour. Temper. Force. Life-giving principle.

氣·不 忿 cannot restrain one's anger.

氣 使 to give orders in a haughty manner by expression of the countenance and not in words.

氣 傑 旺 strong; a vigorous constitution.

氣 冲 牛 斗 his anger mounted to the stars. 牛 and 斗 are the abbreviated names of two constellations.

[5] 氣·力 or 力·氣 strength.

氣·味 smell; flavour.

氣 度 ambitious; spirited.

氣 忿 anger.

氣 恨 or 氣 惱 hate; anger.

[10] 氣 性 disposition; temper; carriage.

氣˳數 destiny; fate.
氣 格 bearing of a person.
氣 概 bearing; manner.
氣˳死 人 enough to vex a man to death.
¹⁵氣 沮 weak constitution.
氣 滯 stoppage in the fluids; nervous system out of order; bilious.
氣 焰 flame; brilliance.
氣 無 不 和 the influences will be harmonious.
氣 盈 self-satisfied.
²⁰氣 稟 or 稟 性 natural endowment or disposition.
氣 節 moral courage; resolute determination; proud and strong. *See above.*—30.
氣 結 melancholy; with a sad air.
氣 習 habit; custom.
氣˳色 colour; appearance.
²⁵氣 象 manner; bearing; style; air; expression of the countenance. *See above for other meanings.*—35.
氣 貌 manner or bearing.
氣 質 disposition; temperament; physique.
氣 運 or 運˳氣 fate; luck.
氣˳量 natural capacity.

³⁰氣 韻 atmosphere, as of a picture; elegance; tone; refinement in art or literature.
氣 類 men of similar nature, or similar tastes.
氣 骨 "breeding." Hereditary instincts.
氣 高 arrogant and proud.
元 氣 inherited constitution.
³⁵出 氣 to vent the spleen; to be revenged upon; to aspirate, as Chinese sounds.
寃 氣 revengeful.
志 氣 energy; vigour.
文˳氣 with a literary air; polished; scholarly.
怒 氣 冲 天 his anger mounted to the skies, variant of 氣 冲 牛 斗˳
⁴⁰生 氣 to get angry.
筆 氣 special characteristics of a handwriting.
習˳氣 customs; habits.
語 氣 the purport of a message, etc.
風˳氣 pervading influences—moral or physical.
↑俗˳氣 vulgar, commonplace.

CH'I. TS'I. (ㄑㄧ)

妻 ¹
555
A legal wife.

妻 女 wives and daughters.
妻 子 wife and children. 妻˳子 a wife.
妻 孥 wife and children.
妻 室 or 妻 房 a legal wife.
⁵妻 小 or 家 小 a wife; a family.
妻 弟 brother of a wife.
妻 黨 relatives of a wife.
令 妻 your good wife!
客 妻 a prostitute.
賢 妻 my good wife; a good wife.

(a) Read *ch'i⁴* To give in marriage.

不 得 妻 也 he could not give his daughter for him to marry.
以 其 子 妻 之 he gave his daughter to him to wife.
帝 之 妻 舜 the emperor giving his daughters as wives to Shun.

凄
凄
556
¹
Intense cold, freezing. Afflicted; in misery.

凄 其 以 風 cold from a biting wind.
凄 涼 or 凄 冷 cold; lonely; mournful.
凄 凄 luxuriant, as vegetation; movement of clouds.
凄 滄 extreme cold.
凄 切 bitter suffering.
凄 楚 甚 in urgent necessity.
凄 淚 very bitterly cold.
凄 風 a bitter wind.

悽
557
¹ Grieved; suffering. Indignant.

悽 涼 sad and lonely, "out in the cold."
悽 婉 sad and complaisant; submissive.
悽 慘 sorrowful; anxious; melancholy.
悽 惶 anxious.
悽 愴 sorrowing; sick at heart; disappointed.
悽 悽 in great pain.
悽 戚 sad and anxious.

萋
558
¹ Luxuriant foliage. Courtly manner.

萋 且 敬 stately and respectful.
萋 萋 luxuriant; massing of clouds.

砌
559
⁴ A stone step. To raise in layers, as a wall.

砌 告 or 砌 控 to make false charges.
砌 牆 to build a wall.
砌 石 路 to pave a road with stone slabs.
砌 詞 揑 控 to heap up false charges.

齊
齊
560
² Even, regular, uniform. All alike. To arrange. In classics inter. 齋 No. 115. *See below.* B. Radical 210.

齊˳備 prepared; all in readiness.
齊˳全 perfect.
齊 其 思 慮 之 不 齊 者 to arrange those of his thoughts which were disordered.
齊 和 blended.
⁵齊 家 to rule the family.
齊 年 the same age.
齊 心 of one mind.
齊 心 努 力 to put forth a united effort.
齊 整 all put in order; well arranged.
¹⁰齊 民 the masses.
齊 畢 all finished.
齊 盛 regular; correct; exact.
齊 盟 to make an alliance; enter into an agreement.
齊 眉 married couple.
¹⁵齊 肅 regularly; in order; *see also below, read chai¹* B.6.
齊 行 (*hang²*) a trade combine.
齊 行 罷 工 a strike of the whole trade.
齊 集 all assembled.
齊 驅 to advance together; equal in ability and strength.
²⁰齊 體 equality.

(a) Ancient feudal state which occupied N. E. Shantung and part of Chihli.

齊 人 a man of *Ch'i* who begged meat from sacrifices, pretend-

ing to his wife that he had great friends, she found him out—the phrase is used for a beggar.

齊°國 ancient feudal state as above. It lasted for 857 years, from B.C. 1122—265. It was a powerful state.

齊國其庶幾乎 the kingdom of *Ch'i* be near to (good government).

齊女 wife of a prince of *Ch'i*, who was said to have changed in a cicada—u.f. a cicada.

齊東野語 name of a book; talk that is unfounded.

齊論 Confucian *Analects* compiled by scholars of *Ch'i*. The standard version is that of *Lu.*

齊魯 the states of *Ch'i* and *Lu.* i.e., things similar, as these states were in literary fame. N. of missionary college in Tsinan.

(b) u.f. 齋 *chai.* No. 115. To fast; to respect, etc.

齊主於敬 the chief point in fasting is reverence.

齊宿 to pass the night in fasting.

齊戒 to fast.

齊戒沐浴 to regulate the thoughts, fast and bathe.

齊明盛服 to fast and be purified and to put on the finest clothing.

齊肅 grave and sedate.

(c) Read *tzŭ*[1]. (*tsï*[1].) The lower edge of a mourning garment.

齊倍要 (= 腰) equal to twice the waist.

齊疏 a garment of coarse material felled in the lower seam.

齊衰者 a person in mourning.—wearing the second degree of mourning; it was of coarse hempen fabric with hemmed borders. Worn for one year by a man for his grandparents, uncle or uncle's wife, brother, unmarried sister, or son. By a wife for her parents and grandparents. Also for five months for great-grandparents, and three months for their parents, i.e., great-great-grandparents. -*ts'ui*[1]. Cf. 5908 A.

臍[2] The navel; the point where the grain joins on to the ear.
561

臍帶 the umbilical cord.
肚臍 the navel.

蠐[2] A large maggot.
562

蠐螬蟲 maggots.

泣[4] To weep silent tears.
563

泣叩 I implore you with tears.
泣哭 to weep.
泣念 to weep as one remembers.
泣數行下 tears coursed down her cheeks. (-*hang*[2]-)
[5]泣罪 to commiserate a criminal as *Yü* the Great did, descending from his carriage to do so.
泣血 to weep blood—used of mourning for parents.
泣血稽顙 weeping blood and knocking the head—bitter mourning. Cf. 427 D.
泣血三年 to mourn for parents for three years.
泣訴 to tell a woeful tale.
泣鬼神 enough to make the spirits weep—used of moving literature.

乞[3,4] To beg for alms; to entreat.
564

乞丐 or 乞子[3] or 乞兒[2] a beggar.
乞休 to resign.
乞企 to implore.
乞命 to beg for life.
[5]乞士 a mendicant priest.
乞巧 to test for skill on the 7th of the 7th month. There are many varying customs in this connection.
乞憐 to beg for pity and charity.
乞討 or 乞求 to beg for; to entreat.
乞諸其鄰而與之 begged it from his neighbours and gave it to him—as if it was from himself.
[10]乞身 or 乞假 (*chia*[4]) to ask for leave of absence.
乞靈 to trust in the strength of another.

乞頭 to take a percentage from a gambling party.
乞食 to beg for food.

仡[4] Strong; valiant.
565

仡仡 strong; valiant; dashing.
仡然 suddenly.

屹[4] A mountain peak.
566

屹峯 grand and imposing.

訖[4] To stop, to finish. To settle, as an account. Completed. Until; to reach to.
567

訖今 until the present; up to date.
付訖 settled the account.
收訖 received in full.
清訖 cleared; settled up.

迄[4] To reach to; up to; till. To extend; finally.
568

迄今 or 迄於今 even till now; up to this day.
迄無成功 has not yet accomplished it.
迄竟 after all; to the last.

CH'I.　　TS'I.　(ㄑㄧ)
(Ch'ih, Ts'ih)

踖[4.5.] To step. To walk reverently.
569

執爨踖踖 they gravely attended to the furnace.
踖踖 ashamed; alert.
踖跦 uneasy steps.

咠[4.5.] To whisper. To blame. To slander.
570

咠咠幡幡 whispering slanders.

緝[4.5.] To twist a cord. To join; to continue. To follow up. To arrest; to catch.
571

緝獲 or 緝捕 or 緝拿 to seize; to catch, as a thief.
緝私 to seize smugglers.

緝 穆 at peace with.
緝 究 to bring to justice.
緝 着 he has been caught.
緝 辦 to search for and deal with.
於 緝 熙 with bright countenance.

(a) Read *ch'i*[1.5]. **To fell a seam.**

緝 之 to fell the lower seam of a mourning garment.
緝 邊 to fell a seam; to hem a garment.

葺 [4.5.]
572　To repair.

葺 成 to complete the rebuilding.
葺 牆 to build a wall.
葺 理 舊 址 to repair the old foundations.
葺 絫 overlapping, as scales or tiles.
葺 補 to rebuild, as a wall.
葺 覆 to cover or roof in.

磧 [2.5.]
573　Rocks awash at low tide.

髤 [1.5.]
574　To lacquer. To varnish. To stick on.

戚 [1,4.5.]
575　Related to; relatives.

戚 串 related by marriage.
戚 屬 or 親 戚 relatives by marriage, of a different surname.
戚 戚 兄 弟 affectionate brothers.
戚 末 your junior relative—complimentary phrase in letters.
戚 里 place where relative of the emperor by marriage dwelt.
姻 戚 related by marriage.

(a) To pity; to distress. Mournful.

戚 戚 焉 moved by compassion.
哀 戚 mourning; distressed.
喪 與 其 易 也 甯 戚 in ceremonies of mourning, it is better that there be deep sorrow, rather than a minute observance of details.
小 人 長 戚 戚 the petty man is always miserable.
愛 戚 sorrows.

苫 塊 之 戚 the sorrow of the mat and the clod—mourning for parents.

(b) A battleaxe.

干 戈 戚 揚 with shield, spear, and the battleaxes.

(c) A hunchback.

得 此 戚 施 she got this hunchback for a husband.

(d) Read *ch'ü*[2] **To urge.**

戚 速 to hasten on; to speed.

墄 [1.5.]
576　The steps of a stairway.

階 墄 steps.

慼 慽 [1.5.]
577　Grief; sorrow. Pained. Also read *ts'u*[5] Ashamed.

漆 桼 榛 [1.5.]
578　The varnish tree. Paint. Lacquer, varnish. To paint or varnish. Black, sticky.

漆 器 lacquer ware.
漆 宅 the varnished, black home—a coffin.
漆 工 a painter.
漆 樹 the varnish tree.
漆 畫 to make pictures with lacquer.
漆 色 a deep, intense black.
漆 食 人 or 漆 咬 人 poisoned with lacquer; a skin disease from the contact with or smell of lacquer.
漆 黑 *ch'ü*[4] *hei*[1] pitch black; dark.

(a) Read *ch'ich*[1.5]. Dignified, ease.

濟 濟 漆 漆 dignified and quiet.

七 柒 [1.5.]
579　The number seven.

七 七 or 理 七 or 做 七 49 days—the period during which the ceremonies connected with the funeral and sacrifices are observed.

七 世 孫 the seventh descendant.
七 件 事 seven indispensible things; firing, rice, oil, salt, soy, vinegar and tea.
七 出 seven reasons for divorcing a wife.—no son, adultery, disobedience to husband's parents, bitter tongue, stealing, envy, and any evil disease.
[5]七 十 seventy.
七 十 子 the seventy disciples of Confucius.
七 十 二 行 (*hang*[4]) all trades—72 is used to express all, there are various reasons given, probably it is from the next phrase.
七 十 二 候 72 periods of five days, every period had its name which gave an indication of the season, three of these periods made one 節, and the total made one year, See under 氣 No. 554. illus. 4.
七 嘴 八 舌 confused talk; conflicting opinions.
[10]七 寶 Seven precious things, the Golden Disc. 金 輪, White Elephants 白 象, Lovely Women 玉 女, Horses 馬, Pearls 珠, Ministers to control the armies 主 兵 臣, Divine officers to guard the treasury 主 藏 神. There are other classifications, seven varieties of gems, etc.
七 巧 the 7th evening of the 7th month, when women competed in threading needles and other things. The constellations of the Cow-herd and the Spinning Damsel are supposed to meet on this evening. There are many poetical allusions found in the books. Cf. 4737. 41 & 989.
七 巧 板 the seven pieced puzzle or tangram. The pieces are cut from a square and may be formed into innumerable shapes and designs.
七 律 verse of eight lines with seven characters to a line.
七 情 seven passions—joy 喜, anger 怒, sorrow 哀, fear 懼, love 愛, hate 惡, and lust 欲.
[15]七 手 八 脚 seven hands and eight feet—great hurry and bustle.

七 政 the seven rulers of the times and seasons—the sun, moon, and five planets.

七 日 來 復 the returning seventh day.

七 星 the seven stars of the dipper, part of the constellation of Ursa Major.

七 曜 the seven luminaries as above, used by some for the days of the week.

[20]七 次 seven times.

七 略 the seven military stratagems; the seven epitomes of literature, as compiled by *Liu-yin* in *Han* Dynasty B.C. 7. Classics. Arts. Philosophy. Poetry. Divination and Numerics. Medicine and Surgery.

七 竅 the seven apertures in the human head, eyes, ears, nose and mouth.

七 絕 a verse of four lines with seven characters to a line.

七 緯 sun, moon and five planets.

[25]七 聲 the seven methods of producing speech—labial, glossal, dental, etc. Also the seven notes of the scale, as below.

七 色 the spectrum.

七 色 板 Newton's rings.

七 言 八 語 gossip; all sorts of opinions.

七 零 八 落 in scattered confusion.

[30]七 音 or 七 始 the seven notes of the scale, five main notes and two modified notes.

七 顛 八 倒 at sixes and sevens; topsyturvy.

七 魄 the seven inferior souls of Taoism.

CHIA.　　(ㄐㄚ)

加[1]　To add to; to increase.
580

加 一 等 double it; add one degree.

加 之 moreover; in addition to.

加 乎 人 上 excellency; above the average.

加 以 .... besides; in addition to.

[5]加 以 師 旅 in addition to this there are invading armies.

加 倍 to add to; to add one degree; to double.

加 入 to join; to enter.

加 入 戰 局 to enter the war.

加 刑 to punish in order to elicit evidence.

[10]加 利 to add profit.

加 功 the finish on goods; to give the *coup de grâce* to an injured man.

加 勉 strenuous.

加 印 to stamp or seal.

加 印 郵 票 to surcharge postage stamps, surcharged stamps.

[15]加 號 sign of addition—plus.

加 增 or 加 添 to augment; increase.

加 多 increased more and more.

加 害 to add injury to.

加 害 行 為 a dangerous act; a risky act. (*legal*.).

[20]加 工 extra work.

加 工 業 finishing work.

加 息 五 釐 add interest at .05% per month.—6% *per annum*.

加 意 to give special attention to.

加 意 提 防 watch him with special caution.

[25]加 意 養 護 give special attention to nourishment and protection.

加 我 數 年 五 十 以 學 易 if I had a few more years to finish the study of the *Book of Changes*!

加 戳 to seal.

加 敬 added respect.

加 水 to charge a discount on coin because of the difference in value of silver.

[30]加 減 increase and decrease—fluctuation.

加 減 乘 除 the four operations of arithmetic.

加 益 to add advantages; more advantageous.

加 稅 or 加 科 extra tax or duty.

加 算 器 adding machine.

[25]加 罪 於 他 put the blame on him.

加 衣 put on more clothing.

加 詳 with added attention to detail.

加 護 take special care of yourself.

加 車 a special train.

[40]加 速 力 acceleration.

加 速 度 rate of acceleration.

加 進 to increase.

加 重 to add weight.

(a) To grant; to raise to; to appoint.

加 冕 coronation.

加 冠 to invest with the cap—to come of age.

加 獎 to award praise.

加 官 to be promoted.

[5]加 官 進 爵 May you be raised to the peerage!

加 恩 to show favour.

加 級 to receive honourable mention.

加 虛 職 to confer an honorary title, or a nominal office.

加 諸 上 位 raised to the most exalted situation.

加 銜 nominal rank.

(b) Used in transliteration.

加 倫 gallon.

加 拿 大 Canada.

加 斯 gas.

加 路 里 caloric.

加 辣 carat. A.c. 開,卡 辣 特.

加 里 potash.

伽[1]　Used by Buddhists to transliterate the Sanskrit sounds *ga*, and *ka*. Also read *ch'ieh*.
581

伽 南 香 incense made from fragrant wood from Kwangtung.

伽 藍 or 僧 伽 藍 guardian demons of a Buddhist temple; a monastery or nunnery.

伽 藍 佛 a name for Buddha.

咖[1]　Used in transliterating. Also read *k'a*[1].
582

咖 啡 coffee.

咖 喇 curry.

架[4]　A frame, a stand, a rack. Framework or scaffold. To lay on a frame; to put up; to support. Distinguish 伽 next.
檫
583

架 不 住 cannot sustain the weight.—used both lit., and fig.

架 名 to use the name of another for one's own purposes.

架·子 a frame; a stand or scaffold.

架 子 大 putting on airs of greatness.

[5]架 子 桃 the Oleander.

架 弄 to swagger; to put on airs.

架 式 an affected style; assumed manner.

架 捏 to trump up charges.

架 橋 to make a bridge—to escape from any difficulty.

[10] 架 物 to prop up things.

架 花 to support flowers.

架·起 to prop up, as on a stand or on trestles.

架·起 腿·來 to prop up the feet so as to rest the legs.

十 字 架 frame like the character for ten; used for a cross, especially The Cross.

[15] 圖 架 picture frames.

屋 架 framework of a house.

帽 架 hat-stand.

打 架 a fight.

托 架 a wall bracket.

[20] 招 架 to oppose; to ward off.

擺 架·子 to swagger.

搭 架 to raise a scaffold.

書 架 book shelves.

筆 架 rack for pens.

[25] 花 架 stand for flower-pots; or a trellis for flowers.

衣 架 frame for hanging garments.

鷹 架 a scaffolding.

(a) N. A. for framed things.

一 架 畫 a picture.

一 架 算 盤 an abacus.

枷 [1] A flail. Wooden collar formerly worn by prisoners
584 —the cangue.

枷 號 the sentence written on the cangue.

枷 打 or 枷 責 to put in the cangue and administer a beating.

枷 示 the cangue as a warning.

枷 鎖 to carry the cangue and wear a lock.

痂 [1]
585 A scab over a sore.

痂 結 to form a scab.

笳 [1] Whistle made of reed
586 without holes for fingering.

笳 笛 a reed leaf whistle.

胡 笳 a name for the above.

耞 [1]
587 A flail.

打 耞 to thresh grain.

連 耞 a flail.

袈 [1]
588 A coarse kind of camlet.

袈 裟 the dress worn by Buddhist priests.

袈 裟 布 muslins.

跏 [1]
589 To sit cross-legged.

跏 趺 坐 to sit cross-legged like the Buddhists. do when in meditation—as we would say, in tailor fashion.

迦 [1] Used in transliterating the
590 Sanscrit sound *ka*.

迦 陵 a bird with a note of marvellous sweetness, but unequal to the voice of Buddha.

駕 [4] To ride; to go in a vessel.
591 A carriage. To yoke, hence the meaning, to control.

駕 上 to harness up.

駕 塵 dust raised by vehicles.

駕 士 outriders before the imperial chariot.

駕 崩 the death of the emperor.

[5] 駕 御 to drive a horse—to control; to subject; to lord it over.

駕 浪 to mount the waves.

駕 衣 uniform worn by musicians at a wedding.

駕 輀 to carry out the coffin.

駕 幸 imperial visits.

[10] 駕 長 head boatman.

駕 霧 to mount on the mists—to become an immortal.

駕 馬 or 駕 車 to harness horses to the vehicle.

駕 馭 to subject; to make use of.

駕 駛 to travel by boat; to drive a car.

[15] 駕 駛 民 權 to advance the rights of the people with rapidity.

御 駕 to start on a journey.

擋 駕 stop the carriage—polite refusal to receive a visitor—"not at home."

行 駕 to start on a journey.

返 駕 to return home.

(a) **Polite form of address.**

駕 台 or 台 駕 your excellency; yourself.

駕 臨 敝 處 will you deign to approach my humble abode—kindly give me a call.

法 駕 complimentary address to Buddhist priests—the vehicle of the Buddhist rule.

嘉 [1] Good, excellent, fine. To
592 commend, to admire. To marry a wife.

嘉 乃 丕 績 admirable are your great achievements.

嘉 偶 an excellent match.

嘉 名 "good name."

嘉 禾 章 *Excellent crop.* A decoration having nine classes.

[5] 嘉 善 to commend the good.

嘉 獎 to encourage.

嘉 尚 high commendation.

嘉 平 月 the twelfth lunar month.

嘉 意 your idea; an excellent thought.

[10] 嘉 慶 子 plums. = 3852.3

嘉 樂 君 子 our admirable prince.

嘉 歲 a prosperous year.

嘉 瑞 auspicious omens.

嘉 祥 章 *Auspicious omen,* A decoration awarded to those who contribute largely to education.

[15] 嘉 禮 a wedding.

嘉 納 to accept; to assent to, as a rebuke.

嘉 羞 delicacies.

嘉 言 good words.

嘉 許 complimentary.

[20] 嘉 謀 splendid plan.

嘉 貺 fine presents.

嘉 賓 honoured guests.

嘉 釀 excellent wine.

嘉 量 good measure—an ancient measure.

[25] 嘉 魚 a species of barbel used for presents.

可 嘉 worthy of praise; commendable.

佳 [1] Beautiful; good. Auspi-
593 cious. Excellent. Distinguish 佳 No. 1466.

佳 人 a beautiful woman.

佳 作 elegant literary composition.

佳 兵 sharp weapons; skilful in use of troops.

佳 味 delicate flavours.

[5]佳 士 man of good disposition.

佳 城 the graveyard; the cemetery.

佳 壻 a good son-in-law.

佳 境 the region of delights.

佳 妙 clever; excellent.

[10]佳 子弟 good posterity.

佳 期 the happy day—wedding day.

佳 木 valuable wood.

佳 禮 marriage.

佳 章 elegant compositions.

[15]佳 節 a festival.

佳 美 handsome; beautiful.

佳 肴 delicacies.

佳 製 good workmanship.

佳 話 a beautiful story.

[20]佳 雅 elegant and tasteful.

佳 音 good news; a good voice.

家 [1] A house; a family; a home. Relatives.
594

家 世 the state or condition of the family.

家 丁 a servant.

家 主 or 家 長 or 東 家 the head of the family; master of the house; captain of a boat.

家 主 婆 mistress of the house.

[5]家 主 翁 head of the family.

家 事 domestic affairs; family matters; house work.

家 事 經 濟 domestic economy.

家 人 the family; one of the family; a domestic.

家 信 or 家 書 or 家 問 a letter from home.

[10]家 傳 the family history or records.

家 傳 物 an heirloom.

家 僮 young hired male servants.

家 僕 servants.

家 內 at home; in the home; a wife or a woman.

[15]家 具 furniture, etc.

家 務 domestic affairs; private matters; housework.

家 去 to return home.

家 口 members of a family; a wife.

家 喻 戶 曉 everybody knows about it.

[20]家 堂 or 家 祠 or 家 廟 ancestral temples or shrines.

家 子 or 家 屬 or 家 庭 a family; a dwelling; a household.

家 學 or 家 塾 family school where only relatives are taught.

家 宅 family dwelling place.

家 宅 稅 house tax.

[25]家 室 husband and wife as makers of a home; a home.

家 宴 a family feast.

家 宰 a steward.

家 小 or 家 下 my wife.

家 常 common; usual; ordinary.

[30]家 常 便 飯 ordinary plain food, such as one gets at home.

家 常 話 informal talk, without ceremony.

家 常 里 短 local gossip. = 79.

家 庭 工 業 domestic industries.

家 庭 敎 育 parental instruction.

[35]家 庭 生 活 family life.

家 庭 的 domestic.

家 庭 禮 拜 family prayers.

家 庭 經 濟 domestic economy.

家 庭 革 命 reformation of family relationships.

[40]家 慶 parents' birthdays; family celebrations.

家 政 household government.

家 政 學 study of family government; home economics.

家 敗 人 亡 ruin of the family.

家 族 the same clan; the family clan.

[45]家 機 布 home-spun.

家 法 domestic regulations; law of the home.

家 烈 merit of the ancestors.

家 無 常 禮 do not stand on ceremony in the home.

家 犬 a watch-dog.

[50]家 產 or 家 業 family possessions.

家 用 family expenditure.

家 用 雜 物 household stuff; miscellaneous articles for the home.

家 畜 domestic animals.

家 當 property; substance; fortune.

[55]家 眷 a wife; a family.

家 衆 servants.

家 神 household gods.

家 祉 genealogy; family happiness.

家 祭 sacrifice to ancestors.

[60]家 禽 fowls, poultry.

家 私 private property or means.

家 累 care of a family where there is "little to earn and many to keep."

家 給 人 足 wealthy homes and contented people—a district where there are no poor.

家 聲 the family reputation.

[65]家 裡 人 women; a wife.

家 計 family livelihood.

家 訓 or 家 誡 family instruction; domestic training.

家 諱 family taboos; things to be avoided.

家 譜 or 譜 系 or 家 乘 family register and records.

[70]家 財 patrimony.

家 貧 poverty.

家 資 family property or wealth.

家 道 state of the family finances; status of the family.

家 道 復 興 revival of the family fortunes.

[75]家 鄉 or 家 邦 or 家 山 one's native place.

家 醜 the disgrace of the family; "the skeleton in the cupboard."

家 醜 不 可 外 揚 domestic shame should not be published; "do not wash dirty linen in public."

家 長 權 parental authority.

家 長 里 短 gossip of the neighbourhood.

[80]家 門 the clan; the family standing.

家 雀 兒 the house sparrow.

家 風 the family standing or reputation.

世 家 an ancient and honourable family.

出 家 to become a Buddhist priest or nun.

[85]合 家 the whole family.

國 家 a state; a nation.

大 家 a great family; everybody; all.

寃 家 an enemy.

思 家 home sickness.

[90]成 家 to succeed; to marry.

本 家 of the same surname.

齊 家 to regulate the family.

(a) **Used as a prefix—My, said of** one elder than oneself.

家 兄 my elder brother.

家 叔 my uncle.

家 嚴 or 家 父 or 家 君 my father.

家 慈 or 家 母 my mother.

家 祖 my ancestors.

(b) **Used as a suffix to indicate the agent. It indicates a specialist in any branch; a class or school. Equivalent to:—***ist,—ian*, **etc.**

The examples are given alphabetically.

運動家 athletes.
化學分析家 analysts.
解剖家 anatomists.
博古家 archaeologists.
5算術家 arithmeticians.
美術家 artists.
占星家 astrologers.
天文家 astronomers.
生物學家 biologists.
10資本家 capitalists.
化學家 chemists.
經學家 classicist.
鑒識家 connoisseur.
評論家 critic.
15外交家 diplomatist.
熱心家 enthusiasts.
實驗家 experimentalists.
鑑定家 experts.
探險家 explorers.
20財政家 financiers.
地理家 geographers.
幾何學家 geometrician.
文法家 grammarian.
史學家 historian.
25園藝家 horticulturist.
法學家 legalist.
語言學家 linguists.
算學家 mathematician.
冶金家 metallurgist.
30軍事家 militarist.
音樂家 musician.
小說家 novelist.
光學家 optician.
樂天家 or 樂觀家 optimist.
35演說家 orator.
組織家 organizer.
病理家 pathologist.
厭世家 pessimists.
製藥家 pharmacist.
40哲學家 philosopher.
慈善家 philanthropist.
生理學家 physiologist.
詩家 poet.
政治家 statesman.
45革命家 revolutionary.
科學家 scientist.
專門家 specialist.
統計家 statistician.
軍略家 strategist.
50敎育家 teachers; educationalists.
文學家 writers; literati.
法家 writers on Buddhism.
儒家 writers on Confucianism.
雜家 writers on miscellaneous subjects.
55兵家 writers on military tactics.

道家 writers on Taoism.
動物學家 zoologist.

傢 [1]
595
Furniture; tools.

傢·具 or 傢·伙 or 傢器 or 傢什 tools; utensils; furniture; commodities, etc.

嫁 [4]
596
To marry a husband. To give a daughter in marriage. To implicate.

嫁夫 or 出嫁 or 嫁人 to marry a husband.
嫁奩 or 嫁·妝 or 嫁資 a bride's dowry; her trousseau.
嫁女 to give a daughter in marriage.
嫁娶 marriage, in a general sense.
5嫁怨 to cherish a grievance; to feel resentment.
嫁母 title given by a son to his mother when she marries a second time.
嫁禍於人 to bring evil upon another in malice.
嫁粧鋪 shop where marriage outfits are sold or hired.
嫁雞隨雞，嫁狗隨狗 a woman follows her husband no matter what his lot.
10女大當嫁 when a girl is of age she should marry.
改嫁 to marry a second husband.
爲人作嫁 to do work for another's advantage.
送嫁 to escort a bride.

稼 [4]
597
To sow grain. Sheaves of grain. Agricultural work.

稼穡 farming, sowing and reaping.
稼穡艱難 the toils of a farmer's life.
莊稼 crops; growing grain.

叚 [3]
598
False. Also read *hsia*.[3] used as a surname.

假 [3]
599
False, unreal; to pretend.

假仁假義 pretended kindness and goodness.

假僞 false; make-believe.
假住 to reside temporarily.
5假借 one of the six classes of characters—used only for their sounds, as 令 or 汝.
假允 pretended compliance.
假充 to pretend to be.
假公濟私 working for one's own ends.
假冒 to counterfeit; pretence.
10假冒姓名 to disguise the identity; to falsely use another's name.
假冒爲善 hypocritical.
假冒罪 forgery.
假友 a false friend.
假名 a false name; Japanese *kana*.
15假報 a false report.
假子 a stepson.
假寐 to lie down dressed; to have a nap or doze.
假局 trap for the unwary; confidence trick.
假山 artificial rockeries in a garden.
20假情 pretence of affection.
假意 with false intent.
假慈悲 pretended sympathy and grief.
假扣押 provisional seizure.
假捏 to trump up.
25假撇清 to pretend that one has nothing to do with the matter.
假淚 pretended sorrow.(Shanghai).
假爲熱心 hypocritical zeal.
假粧 or 假裝 or 假作 feigned; to put on an appearance; to pretend; to simulate.
假計 a scheme; a sly ruse.
30假托 hypocritical; simulated.
假話 lies.
假象牙 celluloid.
假造 to forge; to invent a tale.
假釋 or 假出獄 liberated on probation; ticket of leave.
35假面 a mask.
假面具 to wear a mask—fig., to pretend to favour another.
假髮 a wig; false hair.
假髻 a wig for a woman.

(a) To borrow. Supposing. If. To avail of.

假之以年 if he had lived longer.
假借 to borrow; to use metaphors; a class of written char-

acters used only for their sounds.

假 定 supposition; hypothesis; to assume; presumptive.
假 定 理 a working hypothesis.
[5]假 定·的 hypothetical.
假 手 to use as a tool; to put a job into the hands of another; to commission.
假 手 於 人 to put into the hands of another; to entrust to the care of another.
假 比 as; for example.
假 然 granting that.
[10]假 若 or 假 使 or 假 如 if; supposing; granted that.
假 設 or 假 令 if; supposing it to be; hypothesis.
假 設 之 言 耳 merely an illustration; a supposition.
假 道 or 假 塗 to "borrow" a passage through the territory of another.
假 道 於 虞 borrowed a passage through Yü.
狐 假 虎 威 the fox borrowed the awe of the tiger.

(b) To bestow; to grant.
天 不 假 年 Heaven did not grant him a longer life.
天 假 之 緣 Heaven-sent coincidence.
天 假 其 便 his chance came from Heaven.

(c) Great.
假 哉 天 命 Great are the decrees of Heaven!

(d) Read chia.[4] Leave of absence.
假 滿 leave expired.
休 假 leisure.
告 假 to ask leave of absence.
寬 假 to extend leave.
暑 假 summer vacation.
年 假 new-year vacation.
放 假 to grant holidays.
病 假 sick-leave.

(e) Read ko.[1] or kê.[1] u.f. 格 No. 3309. To draw near to.
王 假 有 廟 the king drew near to the temple.

(f) u.f. 嘉 No. 592. Excellent.
假 樂 君 子 Our admirable prince!

瘕 [1] Asthma. Disease of the bowels.
600
瘕 喘 gasping or panting.

葭 [1] A bulrush or reed. A flute. Matrimonial alliance.
601
葭 月 the eleventh month.
葭 灰 飛 or 葭 管 飛 灰 the ash of the reed is flying—winter is at hand.
葭 笛 a reed or flute.
葭 莩 membrane of a reed stem.
葭 莩 之 親 relatives of another surname.
葭 葦 rushes; reeds.

斝 [3] A small cup of stone with ears, used in ancient times for libations.
602

價 [4] Price; value.
603
價 廉 or 價 賤 cheap.
價 廉 物 美 low prices and fine wares.
價 昂 or 高 價 high prices.
價 格 standard of value.
[5]價 漲 rising price.
價·目 單 price list.
價 銀 or 價 值 or 價 目 or 價 本 price in silver; price; market value.
價·錢 price; the price of.
估 價 to estimate the price; to value.
[10]半 價 half-price.
半 價 出 售 selling at half-price.
存 價 reserve price.
定 價 the list price; published price; fixed price.
實 價 the real price.
[15]市 價 the market price.
平 價 a fair price.
折 價 出 售 selling at less than cost.
批 發 價 目 wholesale prices.
時 價 current prices.
[20]標 面 價 目 face value.
標 明 價 目 the marked price.
正 價 the net price.
減 價 at reduced prices.
無 二 價 our prices are uniform.

[25]無 價 值 valueless.
無 價 寶 priceless.
虛 價 nominal price.
講 價 to haggle over prices.
買 價 賣 價 purchasing and selling prices respectively.
[30]還 價 to make an offer.
重 價 a high price.
重 價 買 來·的 bought at great cost.
開 價 to make a quotation.
零 售 價 目 retail prices.

檟 榎 [3] A small evergreen shrub, a bitter infusion is made from the leaves. Former name for the tea plant.
604

CHIA.　　(ㄐㄚ)
(Chiah)

恝 [1.5.] An indifferent manner; heartless.
605
恝 然 indifferent; unconcerned; careless.
恝 置 thoughtless; careless.

袷 裌 [2.5.] A lined garment without wadding. Read chieh.[1.5.] A kind of collar.
606
裌 衣 服 lined garments.
裌 衫 a lined dress.

鉿 [1.5.] Sound of creaking.
607

戛 [2.5.] A lance. To tap lightly. Read ka[5] in transliterations.
608
戛 擊 鳴 球 to tap the sounding stone.

(a) Propriety. Standing alone.
戛 戛 standing alone; prominent.
戛 戛 乎 其 難 哉 How difficult when there is lack of co-ordination!
戛 禮 propriety; usages.

嘎 [1.5.] The chirping of birds. Loud laughter. Read ka.[5] in transliterations.
609
嘎 嘎·的 笑 a loud, hearty laugh.

甲 3.5. Armour. Scaly. Finger-nails.
610

甲 兵 or 兵 甲 military equipments.
甲 士 armoured soldiers.
甲 帳 soldier's tent.
甲 板 the deck of a ship.
5甲 殼 類 *crustacea*.
甲 狀 軟 骨 the cartilage of the windpipe.
甲 冑 armour.
甲 蟲 reptiles.
甲 魚 the tortoise or turtle.
10懷 六 甲 to be with child.
指·甲 finger-nails.
爪 甲 claws.
鐵 甲 船 an iron-clad ship.
響 甲 pieces of jingling metal worn by actors, or carried by pedlars suspended from their poles.
魚 麟 甲 armour like the scales of a fish.

(a) A tithing.

甲 長 or 甲 頭 head of a tithing.
保 甲 a tithing.

(b) First; chief. The first of the *Ten Stems,* 天 干.

甲 乙 丙 the first three of the *stems,* used as ordinal numbers, or to indicate, this one and that one, etc.—as we use a.b.c., etc.
甲 仆 乙 起 this one falls, that one rises.
甲 午 之 役 The war of the year *Chia-wu.,* i.e., The Sino-Japanese war of 1894.
甲 地 乙 地 in one place.....in another......
5甲 夜 the first watch of the night.
甲 子 first of each group 天 干, and 地 支 , which combine in turn to form a cycle of sixty, used primarily for chronological purposes.
甲 族 a noble family.
甲 榜 or 甲 科 first on the list for the third degree 進士. A third degree graduate.
甲 第 a mansion.
10甲 部 Chinese Classics, in library classifications.
甲 館 a library.
三 鼎 甲 three first on list of *Hanlin* graduates.

科 甲 出 身 to have begun one's career as a second or third degree graduate.
花 甲 the cycle of sixty years; old age.

夾 1.5. To press, to squeeze. Near to. To insert between. Inter. 挾 No. 2632. and 梜 No. 612.
611

夾 不 停 的 not wedged firmly.
夾 攻 to attack from both sides.
夾 尾 to put the tail between the legs.
夾 打 to torture.
5夾 持 supported on both sides.
夾 板 wedges; boards for supporting or pressing the sides of anything, or for torturing.
夾 板 船 a foreign sailing ship.
夾 棍 torture instruments for squeezing in order to elicit evidence.
夾 榜 board for inscriptions over a door.
10夾 流 meeting of two currents.
夾 當 difficulties.
夾 緊 pressed or wedged tightly.
夾 肉 麵 包 sandwiches.
夾 輔 to support; assistants; aides-de-camp.
15夾 道 a path between two rows of trees ; a lane.
夾 道 楡 柳 the road was lined with willows and elms.
夾 道 種 樹 to plant trees by the sides of the road.
夾 鉗 pincers; pliers.
夾 領 小 袖 tight collar and small sleeves.
20夾 鼻 眼 鏡 *pince-nez* spectacles.
信 夾 case for holding letters; a letter clip.
書 夾 boards for holding a number of Chinese books together.
畫 夾 boards for keeping pictures in order.
紙 夾 a paper clip.

(a) To pick up with pincers or with chopsticks.

夾·不 住 cannot grip it properly.
夾·起·來 pick it up, as with chopsticks.
鉗 夾 pick it up with pincers, also used fig.

(b) Lined, as a garment; double. =606.
夾² 衣 lined garments.
夾² 衫 lined inner garment.
夾² 襖 lined jacket.

(c) To carry secretly.

夾 帶 to carry in the girdle; to smuggle notes into the examination hall.
夾 帶 影 射 suspicions of smuggling.
夾 袋 人 才 to have men of talent in his bag—of a ruler who kept a notebook in his bag in which he recorded characteristics of his visitors so as to classify them.
夾 雜 mixed up.
衣 夾 a portmanteau for clothing.
針 線 夾 a needle case; or case for needlework, or needles and threads.

梜 1.5. Pieces of wood hinged at the ends. Chopsticks.
612

梜 提 a name for chopsticks.
梜 棍 instrument for squeezing the ankles.

郟 1.5. A district in Honan.
613

郟 室 or 夾 室 the rooms on each side of the entrance to ancestral temples.
郟 鄏 Place, in the north of the present Hupeh, where *Ch'eng Wang* established the *Chou Dynasty.*

頰 2.5. The jaw; the cheeks.
614

頰 上 添 毫 to add hair to the jaws on a picture: used of wonderful literary skill.
頰 嗉 jaw pouches in monkeys, etc.
頰 車 or 頰 骨 the jaw-bone.
頰 輔 sides of the mouth.
頰 鬢 the whiskers.
掌 頰 to smack the face.
腮 頰 the jaws; cheeks.

CH'IA. (ㄑㄧㄚ)

髂[4]
615   The pelvis.

卡[3] A guard-house at a pass.
A customs barrier. Also
616   read k'a[3].

卡 倫 Mongolian watch-towers in important passes.
卡 口 or 卡 路 a guard-house.
卡 子 customs barrier.
卡 守 frontier stations.
卡 房 quarters for the guard.
卡 着 了 stopped; barred.

(a) Read k'a[3]. To cough. Also for foreign sounds.

卡 不 出 來 cannot cough it up.
卡 片 a visiting card, card, from the sound.
卡 路 里 Calories.

CH'IA. (ㄑㄧㄚ)
(Ch'iah)

恰[4..5] Luckily; opportunely.
617   Ingenious.

恰 似 just so; very like.
恰 値 just then; happily; at that time.
恰 到 好 處 just right.
恰 對 exactly agreeing.
[5]恰 巧 fortunately; suitably; just the thing; at the moment.
恰 恰 的 luckily; at the opportune moment.
恰 當 or 恰 好 in the nick of time; just right, etc.
恰 纔 just now.
恰 遇 opportune meeting; in the nick of time.

掐[1.5.] To pinch; to nip; to dig
618   the nails into. Distinguish
掐 No. 6143.

掐 不 齊 unevenly fitted.
掐 住 了 clamped firmly.
掐 喉 嚨 to seize by the throat.
掐 尖 子 to share illicit gains.
掐 指 頭 算 to reckon on the fingers.
掐 斷 to pull to pieces.
掐 死 了 choked to death.

掐 破 了 to pinch till the blood comes.
掐 籌 to count tallies.
掐 花 to break off a flower.
掐 鼻 to pinch a man's nose.

CHIEH. (ㄐㄧㄞ)
(Kiai or Chieh)

街[1] A street; a thoroughfare;
619   a small market-place.

街 上 in the street.
街 坊 neighbours; a neighbourhood.
街 市 streets and markets.
街 市 小 民 the masses.
[5]街 正 or 街 頭 the headman of a street.
街 肆 shops.
街 衢 or 街 路 highways.
街 言 巷 語 or 街 談 巷 議 common talk.
街 道 thoroughfares.
[10]街 門 the front door.
街 閘 barriers or gates dividing the streets.
上 街 to go on the street; to go to market.
掃 街 夫 or 滑 道 夫 a scavenger.
查 街 street patrols.
[15]橫 街 a cross street.
游 街 to go for a stroll; to be paraded, as a criminal
花 街 brothels.

皆[1] All, every, entirely.
620

皆 其 選 也 are all of his choice; are all choice.
皆 切 問 both are apposite questions.
皆 可 either of them will suit; any of them will do.
皆 同 一 樣 we are all the same.
[5]皆 因 only because of....; it is all owing to.....;—summing up all that has preceded.
皆 屬 all belong to....; the above ....are all....;
皆 得 may all . . .
皆 是 the above....are all called ....;
皆 然 all like this.
[10]皆 與 物 共 者 all had reference to outside things.

人 人 皆 知 everybody knows it.
具 皆 一 樣 all are alike.
四 海 之 內 皆 兄 弟 也 all within the four seas are brethren.
是 非 之 心 人 皆 有 之 a consciousness of right and wrong is common to all.

偕[1] To accompany; to take
621   with one, as a son with his
father. Together. Also read hsieh[2].

偕 同 to go together.
偕 老 to grow old together as man and wife.
偕 老 同 穴 name of a variety of sponge which grows in Japanese and Philippine waters; it is tubular, and shrimps, etc., enter when they are small and cannot get out when grown,—hence the name.
偕 行 to walk together.
同 偕 到 老 May you grow old together!
和 偕[2] harmonious; in agreement; in tune. ≡ 2546.11

(a) Robust.

偕 偕 士 子[3] a strong, robust officer.

喈[1]
622   Music; melody.

鳥 鳴 喈 喈 How sweetly the birds warble!

楷 Usually read k'ai[3].
623 [3] A straight, graceful and durable tree which grew at the grave of Confucius. A model or pattern. A style of writing.

楷 書 the regular style of writing Chinese.
楷 模 a pattern or model.
端 楷 formal and precise style of writing.

稭[1]
秸
624   The stalks of corn or hemp, etc. To weave hassocks.

稭 料 millet stalks, etc., mixed with willow twigs and mud, used for strengthening dikes.

秫稭 stalks of millet.
麥稭 wheat straw.

階
堦¹ Stairs; a flight of steps; a degree, a class, a rank or step.
625

階上 at the top of the steps; high in office.
階之級 one step of a stairway.
階前萬里 although it is far, it seems near.
階度 the number of steps.
⁵階梯 steps; stairs; procedure.
階沿上 on the side of the steps.
階·級 or 階次 an official grade; classes, steps, caste.
階·級制度 class system.
階·級削平 levelling of classes.
¹⁰階·級戰爭 class war.
階·級政治 class government.
階·級權利 class privilege.
階·級爭鬥 class struggle.
階·級的 graded; divided into classes.
¹⁵階·級自覺 class consciousness.
階·級鏟除 extinction of class distinctions.
　　工人階·級 or 勞動階·級 the working class.
　　知識階·級 intelligentsia.
　　社會階·級 caste; social distinctions.
²⁰　資本階·級 capitalist class.
階除 the steps to a porch or door.
階齒 steps of a stairway.
亂階 the steps by which the disordered conditions came about.
升階 promotion in rank.
天之不可階之升也 the heavens cannot be ascended as by the steps of a stair.

解
觧³ To loosen; to untie; to release. To get rid of.
626

解·不開 cannot loosen or untie it; cannot settle it, as a dispute.
解任 to retire from office.
解倒懸 to relieve one hanging upside down, i.e., in great straits.
解免 to avert.
⁵解剖 to cut open; to dissect. See below. A. 3.

解剖學 anatomy.
解剖術 anatomical methods of procedure.
解勸 to exhort; to persuade.
解危 to deliver from peril.
¹⁰解厄 to relieve distress.
解嚴 to relax military law after riots are settled. See below.— 68.
解囊 to loose the purse strings; to pay.
解圍 to raise a siege; to break through a cordon.
解小便 to urinate.
¹⁵解履 to take off the shoes, as in reverence.
解巾 to undo the garments of civil life and become an official.
解帶 to unloose the girdle.
解怨 to make up a quarrel; to forgive an injury.
解急 to disentangle a complication; to relieve urgent necessity.
²⁰解息 or 解和 to make up a quarrel.
解悶 to dispel sadness or melancholy.
解手 to depart from; to urinate.
解放 to release; to emancipate.
解救 to succour; to relieve.
²⁵解散 to scatter; to loosen; to dissolve, as parliament; to disperse.
解散國會 to dissolve parliament.
解散軍隊 to disband the army.
解暑湯 a cooling drink.
解析 to analyse.
³⁰解析幾何 analytical geometry.
解裝 to undo the baggage—to take a rest.
解構 to set at variance; annoying interference.
解毒 to nullify the effects of poison.
³⁵解毒劑 antidotes.
解毒藥 disinfectants.
解決 to solve; to decide.
解決政體 to decide the form of government.
解決辦法 decide the mode of procedure.
解渴 to allay thirst.
⁴⁰解滅 dissolution of the body.
解熱劑 febrifuge.
解疼 to alleviate pain.
解約 to annul an agreement.

解紛 to disentangle; to rectify disorderly conditions.
⁴⁵解紛免戰條約 arbitration treaty.
解紐 to undo buttons—to solve problems.
解素 to release from vegetarian vows.
解組 to undo the string of the seal—to resign office.
解綱 to release the nets, so as not to kill all the prey taken in hunting.
⁵⁰解維 to loose the painter.
解職 to resign office; to dismiss.
解脫 to free; to let go.
解舍 to let go; to release.
解衣 to loosen and put off the clothing.
⁵⁵解衣包火 to "take fire into the bosom," useless and harmful.
解鈴繫鈴 let him who tied the bell (on the tiger) loosen it.
解·開 to unloose; to untie; to expound; to solve difficulty; to settle disputes.
解除 to expel, as evil; to neutralize, as poison; to eliminate; to dissolve.
解除契約 to rescind an agreement.
⁶⁰解除條·件 conditional rescinding.
解除權 the right to rescind an agreement.
解除武裝 to disarm troops.
解除軍備 disarmament. See 裁 No. 6664.
解除陰鬱 to relieve the gloom.
⁶⁵解難 (nan⁴) to succour, as in extremity; to relieve one in distress.
解離 to separate; disassociation.
解鞋帶 to loosen the shoe strings.
解頤 or 解嚴 to relax the features; to smile. See above—11.
解體 double-minded; divided in heart.
⁷⁰分解 to dissolve.
鹿角解 the deer sheds its horns.

(a) **To explain; to expound.**

解事 to have a clear apprehension of.
解人 a man of intelligence.
解剖 to explain; to analyze. See above.—5.
解夢 to interpret a dream.

[5]解 悟 to understand.

解 惑 to elucidate doubts; to allay suspicions.

解 故 or 解 詁 to give a modern version of old writings.

解 明 to throw light upon; to explain clearly.

解 法 meaning; explanation.

[10]解 經 to expound the scriptures or the classics.

解 義 explanation.

解 罪 to explain an error; to beg pardon.

解·說 to explain.

解·釋 to explain; to relieve the feelings.

[15]解·釋 疑 難 to decipher; to elucidate.

解 錯·了 wrongly explained.

不 能 了[3]解 cannot understand it; cannot give any explanation.

不 解 自 明 the meaning is apparent.

易 解 easily understood.

[20]見 解 an opinion.

註 解 commentary; explanatory notes.

誤 解 misapprehend; misunderstand.

詳 細 註 解 a detailed commentary; full notes.

講 解 explanation; exposition.

[25]難 解 unintelligible; difficult to elucidate.

雙 方 了[3]解 both parties come to mutual understanding.

(b) Read *chieh*[4]. **To forward; to send; to hand over to.**

解 交 to forward and hand over to.

解·元 first on the list for the second degree.

解 勘 to send prisoners charged with grave offences to higher officials for re-trial, (*old*).

解 回 to send back.

[5]解 報 to forward with a report.

解 審 to commit for trial.

解 差 escort in charge of a prisoner.

解 案 to remit a case to a higher court.

解 犯 to deliver over a prisoner.

[10]解 發 to forward, as goods.

解 省 to send to the provincial capital, as prisoners.

解 辦 to send to be dealt with.

解 送 to forward, as a prisoner; to deliver or escort a prisoner.

解 餉 to forward 'duties to the capital.

押 解 to forward in custody.

(c) Read *hsieh*[4]. **Inter.** 懈 **No.** 2539. 邂 **No. 2543.** 獬 **No. 2541.** Also surname.

解 后 to meet unexpectedly.

不 解 于 位 not remiss in his duties.

戒[4] **To warn, to caution, To guard against. Warnings, precautions; precepts.**
627

戒 之 Beware, take care!

戒 之 在 得 be watchful against a grasping spirit.

戒 之 戒 之 出 乎 爾 者 反 乎 爾 者 也 Beware, beware, what proceeds from you will return to you!

戒 備 to take precautions.

[5]戒 刀 the knife of a Buddhist priest, not to shed blood.

戒 哉 Take care!

戒 嚴 to proclaim martial law.

戒 嚴 令 martial law.

戒 嚴 區 域 area under martial law.

[10]戒 壇 place of initiation for Buddhist priests.

戒 尺 a ferule; a ruler.

戒 律 the discipline. (*Budd.*).

戒 心 wary, cautious from; 一 予 有 戒 心 I took measures for my safety.

戒·指 a ring.

[15]戒 止 to desist; to warn.

戒 牒 priest's or nun's certificate; to take priestly vows. (*Buddhist*).

戒 飭 to restrain; to charge or warn.

以 戒 將 來 as a warning for the future.

切 戒 be most careful.

[20]勸 戒 to warn; to caution; to admonish.

十 戒 ten Buddhist precepts.

受 戒 to take priestly vows.

防 戒 to warn against; to strive against.

警 戒 precaution.

(a) **To abstain from; to avoid.**

戒 口 to fast; to be careful of the diet.

戒 忌 to beware of; to avoid.

戒 斷 癮 the craving is quite broken off.

戒 條 rules to be observed in fasting and abstaining from food.

[5]戒 殺 to avoid killing animals, etc.

戒 烟 to break off opium.

戒 烟 方 a prescription for breaking off opium.

戒 絕 to abstain from; to forbear.

戒 色 or 戒 淫 to avoid fornication.

[10]戒 葷 to take vegetarian vows.

戒 行 austerity; asceticism.

戒 賭 to break off gambling.

戒 酒 to take the total abstinence pledge.

戒 食 to diet; to fast.

節 戒 temperance.

誡[4] **A precept, a commandment. To warn. To prohibit. Distinguish** 誠 **No. 381.**
628

誡 命 a commandment.

十 條 誡 The Ten Commandments

大 誡 an important injunction.

教 誡 to instruct with warning.

禁 誡 prohibitory ordinances.

規 誡 rules of conduct.

介[4] **Small, insignificant, trifling. u.f.** 芥 **No. 634.**
629

介 次 a small place or market.

一 介 不 以 取 not a single straw would he have taken.

一 介 武 夫 a mere soldier.

纖 介 trifling; petty.

(a) **Armour, mail. Scales.**

介 夫 mailed soldier.

介 族 or 介 類 or 介 蟲 *crustacca*.

介 殼 shells.

介 者 不 拜 a man in arms does not bow.

介 冑 armour.

介 類 學 or 貝 類 學 conchology.

介 馬 armour-clad horse.

鱗 介 類 scaly and shelly tribes, fish, shrimps, turtles, etc.

(b) **Determined, resolute. Alone.**

介 介 or 耿 介 earnest; resolute.

介 士 a determined, unbending man.

介 性 a resolute disposition.

介 然 suddenly; alone; bigoted.

[5] 介 然 用 之 to make sudden use of.

介 特 alone; without support, as widows or widowers.

介 立 to stand alone.

不 以 三 公 易 其 介 (*Liu Hsia-hui*) would not have changed his firm purpose for the three highest offices of state.

節 介 of inflexible purpose.

(c) A servant, one brought by a visitor in ancient times.

大 夫 有 上 介 the great officers had their messengers.

小 介 a young servant lad.

貴 介 Your servant!

(d) To lie between. To border on.

介 在 兩 難 between two difficulties.

介 媒 an intermediary.

介 字 a preposition.

介 居 between two difficulties, in the middle.

[5] 介 成 intermediate. (*Chem.*).

介 於 兩 可 between two alternatives.

介 母 a medial in phonetics.

介 現 to interpose.

介 紹 or 紹 介 an intermediary; to introduce, as a speaker; to recommend, as a doctor or teacher, etc.

[10] 介 紹 人 an introducer; a middle-man or go-between.

介 紹 信 or 介 紹 書 a letter of introduction.

介 紹 新 文 化 to introduce the new culture.

介 紹 機 關 intermediary organ.

(e) Great. To regard as important. To aid; to increase.

介 壽 May you have long life!

介 弟 Your younger brother.

介 意 or 介 懷 to pay heed to.

不 介 意 pay no heed to it.

[5] 不 足 介 意 not worth considering.

以 介 景 福 in order to increase his happiness.

求 介 to seek assistance.

价 [4] A servant. A middle-man. Good. Great.
630

价 人 維 藩 a good man is a fence—a protection to his state.

诏 价 to introduce.

玠 [4] A small jade tablet, used by officials at court to indicate their respective ranks.
631

界 [4] A boundary, a limit.
632

界 上 at the frontier.

界 劃 delimitation; to mark out.

界 務 交 涉 boundary questions.

界 址 the border or boundary line.

[5] 界 石 a boundary stone.

界 稻 rice planted one autumn and reaped in the next spring.

界 約 a frontier agreement.

界 說 a definition; an explanation; a solution.

界·限 or 界 綫 a boundary line; a limit; restricted.

[10] 界 限 之 區 別 line of demarcation.

交 界 to border on; adjoining.

分 界 delimitation.

境 界 frontiers.

權 界 limited power.

(a) The world; a suffix expressing class, or world.

世·界 the world; an age. *See* 世 No. 5790.

動 物 界 the animal kingdom.

商 界 the commercial world.

基 督 教 界 the Christian world.

[5] 報 界 the press.

外 界 the external world.

外 交 界 diplomatic circles.

女 界 or 坤 界 woman's world.

娛 樂 界 the gay world.

[10] 學 界 the student world; educational circles.

官 界 officialdom.

意 界 or 精 神 界 the inner world of thought; mental faculties.

政 界 official circles.

教 界 the church, as contrasted with other groups in society.

[15] 教 育 界 educational circles.

文 學 界 the world of letters.

植 物 界 the vegetable kingdom.

法 界 legal circles.

眼 界 field of vision.

---

[20] 礦 務 界 mineral kingdom.

科 學 界 the scientific world.

空 界 space.

紳 界 the gentry.

美 術 界 the world of art.

[25] 軍 界 military circles.

農 界 the farming class.

(b) To rule a line.

界 尺 a ruler.

界 方 a square.

界 紙 ruled paper.

疥 [4] The itch. To itch.
633

疥 瘡 sores from itch.

疥 癩 a scabby itching skin disease.

疥 癬 ringworm and similar skin diseases.

疥 癬 蟲 the acarus.

長·了 疥 to get the itch.

芥 [4] The mustard plant. Small. Petty.
634

芥 子 a mustard seed—very small, trifling.

芥 子 泥 a mustard plaster.

芥·末 or 芥 麵 or 芥 粉 ground mustard.

芥 舟 a mustard seed as a boat (in a cup of water)—unimportant; from a phrase in *Chuang tzŭ*.

芥 草 a mustard stalk—contemptible; worthless.

芥 菜 the mustard plant.

芥 蒂 unimportant; a trifling cause of enmity.

芥 藍 菜 coarse greens.

蚧 [4] A red spotted lizard, called 蛤 蚧 used as medicine.
635

屆 屆 [4] To arrive at, in time or place; a limit; the set time. A term.
636

屆 期 or 屆 時 punctual; at the appointed time.

屆 滿 at the expiration of the term.

天 屆 the horizon.

本 屆 之 祝 典 the celebration arranged for this year.

靡 屆 靡 完 without limit or end.

CHIANG. (ㄐㄤ)

姜[1] The surname of *Shen nung*, 神農, the reputed
637 founder of agriculture. Distinguish 羗 No. 666.

姜太公 or 姜子牙 a sage of the time of *Wen wang*, many tales are told of his exploits.

姜太公釣魚、願者上鈎 when *Chiang T'ai kung* went fishing (without a barbed hook) the fish that were willing were caught—used of volunteers to help a worthy man.

江[1] A large river. The River, i.e., The Yangtze.
638

江北 North of the Yangtze in Kiangsu or Anhwei.

江南 the provinces of Kiangsu and Anhwei.

江口 the mouth of a river, an estuary.

江右 Kiangsi.

5 江寧 Nanking.

江山 rivers and hills—the country; the land; the state; scenery.

江山如畫 the scenery was like a picture.

江左 or 江東 Kiangsu.

江干 bank of a river.

10 江干送別 to say farewell on the river bank.

江心 the middle of a river.

江心補漏 to mend a leak in midstream—too late.

江水暴漲 river waters suddenly rising.

江河 rivers and streams.

15 江河日下 the rivers daily decrease their flow, i.e., going from bad to worse; gradual declension or decadence. Used in several ways.

江河行地 the rivers flow across the land—unchangeable.

江海 the waters of a country.

江海關 Shanghai Customs.

江浙 Kiangsu and Chekiang.

20 江淮 The Yangtze and the Huai Rivers. Kiangsu and Anhwei.

江湖 rivers and lakes; to travel, i.e., to see the rivers and lakes.

江湖人 a traveller; an adventurer; one who lives by his wits.

江湖奸漢 an adventurer; a boaster.

江湖客 itinerant traders.

25 江湖派 or 老江湖 tramps; experienced travellers; old scamps.

江照 special passports for steamers on the Yangtze.

江猪 or 江豚 the Yangtze porpoise.

江畔 the bank of a river.

江蘇 Kiangsu. 江西 Kiangsi.

30 江表 south of the Yangtze.

九江 Kiukiang, a port on the Yangtze.

兩江 Provinces of Kiangsu, Anhwei and Kiangsi, formerly under one viceroy.

渡江 to cross a river.

長江 or 大江 The Yangtze River.

僵[1] To lie down. Stiff in death. Inter. next.
639

僵人 a corpse.

僵仆 to fall; fallen; prostrate.

僵立 to stand upright without movement.

僵臥 to lie down at full length.

官僵 a curse—May you be stiffened!

手凍僵了 hands stiff with cold.

殭[1] Numbed, stiff. Dead.
640

殭尸 a corpse; vampire.

殭性 immovable; obstinate; without feeling.

殭臉子 an impassive countenance.

殭蠶 stiffened silkworms, as they are just before spinning.

繮[1] A bridle; reins.
韁
641

韁皮繩 or 韁繩 the reins.

收韁 to draw the rein.

馬韁 a bridle.

鬆韁 to give a horse his head.

薑[1]
䕬
姜
642
Ginger.—Applied to other aromatic plants.

薑末 or 薑粉 ground ginger.

薑桂 ginger and cassia; used as below.

薑桂之性愈老愈辣 a nature like ginger and cassia, the older it gets the more its pungency increases—used of those having such dispositions.

薑水 ginger tea.

薑酒 ginger wine, a feast given at the birth of a child.

薑黃 turmeric, a dye stuff.

生薑 green ginger.

糖薑 preserved ginger.

老薑 old dried ginger.

疆[1]
畺
643
A boundary, a border, a frontier.

疆吏 governor or viceroy under the Manchu dynasty. Officer in charge of the frontier in ancient times.

疆場 a field of battle; the territory within the frontiers; borders of fields. From 疆埸 (t[4]) of which this

疆徼 the frontiers. ⌊is a corruption.

疆理 to delineate the frontiers.

疆界 or 疆域 or 疆宇 or 疆土 a limit; the border; the frontier.

新疆 the new province. Sinkiang.

無疆 boundless; limitless.

(a) To act vigorously; to force.

疆而後可 it was agreed to after pressing. (*ch'iang*[3] -)

耩[3] To plough. To sow.
644

耩地 to plough.

講[3] To preach, to expound. To argue, to discuss. To
645 speak.

講不來 unable to explain, not able to preach.

講 人。情 to speak for another.
講 古 to tell old tales.
講 和 to discuss the settlement of a dispute.
⁵講 堂 lecture hall in a school, etc.
講 堂 訓 話 earnest address by the principal of a school.
講 師 lectureship in a college.
講 座 a "chair," professorship.
講 得 去 it bears that meaning.
¹⁰講 情 to intercede; to conciliate; to make an appeal.
講 授 to teach.
講 旅 to drill, etc.
講 明 to explain a matter clearly.
講 明。白 fully explained; clearly stated.
¹⁵講 書 to preach; to expound.
講 書 堂 preaching hall.
講 東 講 西 irrelevant talk.
講 武 to teach military arts, etc.
講 理 to discuss the pros and cons; to appeal to reason.
²⁰講。究 particular about; admirable; refined. *See below.* 八. 3.
不 講。究 not at all particular.
喫。得 講。究 particular about the food.
講 筵 the teacher's seat—complimentary phrase in letters—at your learned feet.
講 經 說 法 to expound Buddhism.
²⁵講 義 a commentary; exposition; lecture to students.
講 習 討 論 accustomed to explain what invites discussion.
講 茶 to meet in a tea shop to discuss a matter; both sides bringing their friends, it often ends a fight or ends in a fight.
講 解 to explain; to give the sense.
講 話 to talk.
³⁰講 說 to explain; to expound.
講 談 to have a chat.
講 論 to discuss; to expound.
講 道 or 講 道。理 to preach.
講 面。子 superficial; particular about appearances; give others face.
³⁵沒 有 講 inexplicable; has no meaning.
演 講 an oration; a speech or lecture. A.c. 講演.

(a) To investigate; to analyse.

講 學 a group of scholars who meet to investigate philosophy. etc., as the *Sung* Dynasty school of *Chu* 朱, and Ch'eng 程.

講 求 to investigate; to search; to endeavour to do.
講 究 to investigate; to analyse. *See above.*—20.
講 習 or 講 貫 to investigate knowledge and teach it to each other, carrying it into practice.
講 藝 to investigate the arts and sciences.

(b) To bargain.

講 價 to haggle over prices.
講 定 settled—as prices.
講 妥。了 settled; agreed upon.

腁 ³
646
Callous skin on the feet.

腁。子 callosities.

繦 ³
褓
647
Cloth in which children are carried on the back. Also pron. *ch'iang³*.

褓 屬 closely connected.
褓 屬 不 絕 flowing continuously.
褓 褓 the cloth in which a child is wrapped—infancy.
褓 負 to carry a child strapped on the back.
褓 負 其 子³ 而 至 矣 to come with their children strapped on their backs.

鏹 ³
648
Money; coin. A string of a thousand cash. Also pron. *ch'iang³*.

冥 鏹 paper money burnt at deaths.

倔 ⁴
649
Unsubmissive; obstreperous.

倔 嘴 stubborn speech.
倔 孩。子 a stubborn, unruly child.
倔 漢 obstinately stupid man.

悻 ⁴
650
To hate, wilful.

傲 悻 wilful; stubborn; disobedient.

洚 ⁴
651
A flood.

洚 水 警 余 the floods frightened me.
洚 洞 reckless; overflowing.
洚 洞 之 世 a dissolute age.

絳 ⁴
652
A deep red colour.

絳 工 a dyer.
絳 汗 sweat of the colour of blood.
絳 紫 or 絳。色 purple or deep crimson.
絳 紗 帳 a red silk curtain behind which *Ma yung* of the Han Dynasty taught.—a teacher's seat.

¹
653
A small kidney bean.

豇 豆 kidney beans.

降 ⁴
夆
654
To descend; to come down from heaven. To send down.

降。下。來 to descend; to have sent down to one.
降 乩 the spirits come down in response to the divination.
降 凡 to come into the world, as in an incarnation of the divine.
降 心 condescending.
⁵降 心 相 從 to meet half-way.
降 殺 (*shai*⁴) 以 兩 而 已 merely reduce by two as you descend.
降 爾 遐 福 May extensive blessings descend upon you!
降 生 or 降 世 incarnation; to be born into the world.
降 祉 to bestow blessings upon men.
¹⁰降 神 the spirits have come down to enjoy the sacrifice.
降 祥 or 降 瑞 to send down good fortune.
降 福 to bless; to send down blessings.
降 禍 or 降 咎 to send down calamity.

降 罰 to punish from heaven.
[15] 降 臨 to come down; to condescend to visit. "Advent."
降 落 to descend; to fall from; to alight. 降 落 傘 a parachute.
降 階 相 迎 to go down the steps to meet a guest.
降 雨 to send down rain.
降 香 laka-wood, an incense.
[20] 下 降 to descend.
何 勞 下 降 complimentary phrase —What trouble you have taken to come and visit me!
升 降 ups and downs; fluctuations.
升 降 機 an elevator, a lift.
(a) **To degrade; to fall.**
降 三 級 reduce three degrees of rank.
降 級 留 任 to degrade but keep in office.
降 調 to degrade and transfer to another post.
降 革 to degrade and deprive of rank.

(b) Read *hsiang*[2]. **To submit to; to return to allegiance. To bring to terms.**
降 伏 to surrender; to submit to.
降 兵 or 降 卒 troops that have returned to their allegiance.
降 旗 flag of surrender.
降 敵 or 降 過 去 to go over to the enemy.
[5] 降 服 to surrender; to yield; to return to allegiance.
降 表 conditions of surrender.
降 附 to return to allegiance.
降 魔 to exorcise demons.
降 魔 杵 a club for quelling demons.
[10] 降 龍 伏 虎 to cause the dragon to submit and to humble the tiger—said of a famous doctor.
投 降 to surrender; to go over to or to come over from the enemy.
歸 降 to return to allegiance.

CHIANG TSIANG. (ㄗㄤ)

糨 糊[4]

Starch; paste. To starch.

655

糨 子 or 糨 糊 or 漿 糨 paste.

糨 粉 or 糨 衣 粉 子 starch.
打 糨 子 to make paste or starch.

將 收[1]

To take, to hold. Used similarly to 把 in colloquial, 4829 A.

656

將 他 治 好 he healed him.
將 信 就 疑 halting between doubt and belief—indecision.
將 刀 切 肉 take a knife and cut the meat.
將 功 折 罪 to atone for mistakes by meritorious service.
[5] 將 勤 補 拙 make up for lack of skill by industry.
將 心 比 心 compare your feelings with his; to have sympathy.
將 有 餘 補 不 足 take the surplus here to make up the deficiency there.
將 機 就 機 to meet one scheme with another.
將 蝦 釣 鼈 to use shrimps to catch turtles.
將 軍 to seize the enemy, "Check" in chess; great, large, eminent.
將 錯 就 錯 meet one error with another—to make the best of a bad job.

(a) **Indicates the future; about to.**
將 下 雨 about to rain.
將 以 復 進 he wants to bring them in again.
將 來 in the future; by and by.
將 到 nearing; close to.
[5] 將 去 about to go; as he was going.
將 奚 先 what is the first thing to be done?
將 如 之 何 What shall we do about it?
將 將 的 just about; just the thing; just as.
將 就 to make the best of a thing; to overlook.
[10] 將 彀 just sufficient.
將 撤 when the things were being removed.
將 息 to rest.
將 晚 towards evening.
將 次 about to....
[15] 將 次 成 功 almost completed; about to be accomplished.
將 無 同 just about; a little different.

將 聖 almost a sage.
將 要 死 about to die; at the point of death.
將 近 almost; close to; about to be.
不 知 老 之 將 至 he is not aware that old age is creeping upon him.

(b) **To nourish; to care for; to protect.**
將 愛 to protect and care for.
將 父 母 to care for parents.
將 養 to nourish and bring up.

(c) **To act; to do; to ask.**
將 事 不 敬 he discharged his duties without respect.
將 伯 to ask for assistance.
將 順 to have no plans and to follow those of another.

(d) **To escort; to convey; to progress.**
將 命 to convey messages from visitor to host.
日 就 月 將 days and months advancing—gradual progress; time is gradually passing.
百 輛 將 之 one hundred chariots escorted her.

(e) **To lead.**
將 兵 to lead troops.
將 十 萬 騎 he led one hundred thousand mounted troops.
將 領 to lead.

(f) **By the side of.**
在 渭 之 將 by the side of the River Wei.

(g) **Strong; large.**
亦 孔 之 將 is also very great.

(h) Read *chiang*[4] or *tsiang*[4]. **A general; a leader. The thumb or great toe.**
將 令 general orders.
將 佐 former high rank military officers.
將 士 leaders and petty officers.
將 官 military officers.
[5] 將 帥 a commander.
將 弁 or 將 吏 military officers.
將 指 the thumb or great toe.
將 校 high military officers.
將 校 弁 兵 officers and privates.

[10]將 略 military tactics.

將 相 generals and ministers of state.

將 相 器 a man of great talent, able to bear responsibility.

將 軍 a general.

將 軍 府 headquarters of field-marshals in the capital; army council.

[15]將 種 or 將 家 子 sons and grandsons of great leaders.

將 門 family of a commander-in-chief.

將 門 有 將 in the home of a commander there are more commanders—like produces like.

海 軍 上 將 an admiral.

海 軍 中 將 a vice-admiral.

[20]海 軍 少 將 rear-admiral.

陸 軍 上 將 a field-marshal.

陸 軍 中 將 a lieutenant-general.

陸 軍 少 將 major-general; brigadier-general.

(i) Read *ch'iang[1]* or *ts'iang[1]*. **To beg; to ask. Imposing. Tinkling sounds.**

將 子 無 怒 I beg you not to be angry.

佩 玉 將 將 the tinkling of the gems pendant from her girdle.

應 門 將 將 How imposing was the gate of the court!

鼓 鐘 將 將 the clanging of the bell as it was struck.

獎 [3] **To exhort; to encourage. To commend. A prize or reward.**
657

獎 券 lottery ticket.

獎 勤 to encourage industry.

獎 勵 or 獎 勸 to encourage by rewards.

獎 勵 三 軍 to stimulate the ardour of the army by rewards.

[5]獎 勵 生 育 maternity bonus.

獎 勵 金 bounties; prizes.

獎 敘 to confer honours upon.

獎 品 prizes or rewards.

獎 拔 to advance or promote a man.

[10]獎 牌 a medal for reward.

獎 章 a decoration.

獎 譽 or 誇 獎 to praise.

獎 資 money prize or bounty.

獎 賞 to commend and award; a prize.

---

[15]獎 金 獎 銀 bounties in money.

獎 飾 to praise or commend.

得 獎 賞 to get a reward.

稱 獎 to admire; to commend.

請 獎 to ask for a reward to be granted.

過 獎 undue praise.

獎 金 or 獎 學 金 scholarship, fellowship.

槳 艣 [3]　An oar.
658

盪 槳 or 搖 槳 or 打 槳 to row a boat.

漿 [1] **Any thick fluid. Broth. Pus.**
659

漿 子 starch paste. ≡ 655.1

漿 水 mixed starch.

漿 洗 衣 服 to starch garments.

漿 粉 starch powder.

漿 糊 starch or paste.

蔣 [1] **A species of aquatic grass, the centre of the stalks is eaten under various names,**
660 菱 笋, 菱 瓜. *see* 菱 No. 710.

蔣 茅 stubble.

醬 [4] **Bean sauce; ketchup; salted preparations.**
661

醬 坊 or 醬 園 shop for sale of stores and condiments.

醬 油 bean sauce; soy.

醬 色 a dark, reddish brown.

醬 菜 pickled vegetables.

醬 薑 pickled ginger.

醬 豆 腐 pickled bean-curd.

打 爲 肉 醬 "beaten into a jelly."

果 醬 jams; preserves.

匠 [4] **A workman; a mechanic.**
662

匠 人 an artisan.

匠 役 forced government labourers.

匠 心 inventive mind.

匠 頭 a foreman; journeyman.

木 匠 and 泥 水 匠 or 瓦 匠 carpenters and bricklayers; used in this way for all trades.

CH'IANG.　(ㄑㄧㄤ)

腔 [1] **Sound of coughing. Phlegm in the throat.**
663

骻 **The skeleton of a sheep.**
664

腔 䏐 [1] **The breast, i.e., a hollow place in the body.**
665

腔 子 大 with hollow pretensions; bumptious.

腔 腸 動 物 polyps, as corals, etc. Jellyfish.

拿 腔 作 勢 to bluff.

滿 腔 熱 血 full of zeal; warm-hearted.

滿 腔 怨 氣 full of grievances on account of wrongs.

裝 腔 to put on airs; to assume an appearance.

裝 面 腔 to do eyeservice; to slight things.

(a) A tune. A brogue.

腔 調 a tune; tone of voice; accent.

土 腔 local patois.

改 腔 to change one's tune—to put another face on it.

高 腔 treble notes; higher notes.

羌 羗 [1] **Tribes in West China. Strong. Educated. Obstinate. A particle.**
666

羗 內 恕 己 condoning their own faults.

羌 帖 Russian Dollar notes.

羌 戎 or 羌 人 or 羌 胡 or 羌 戶 tribes in West China. The name goes back to the earliest records of Chinese history.

(a) Read *hsiang[1]*. **Helpless and alone.**

羗 量 helpless, as fledglings.

蜣 [1] **The dung beetle.**
667

蜣 蜋 the dung beetle, scarabaeus. called 運 屎 蟲 the scavenger beetle.

強强彊) ² Strong, violent. Energetic.
668

強 佔 forcible seizure. *See below.* B. 2.

強 制 coercion; compulsion.

強 制 手 段 compulsory means.

強 制 力 controlling force.

⁵強 制 執 行 compulsory action.

強 制 權 powers of compulsion or of coercion.

強 制·的 compulsory.

強 制 處 分 compulsory measure. (*legal.*)

強 制 解·釋 forced interpretation.

¹⁰強 力 force; physical force.

強 哉 矯 How strong is his energy!

強·壯 or 強 健 hale; vigorous.

強 壯 劑 tonics.

強 宗 a powerful family.

¹⁵強 幹 competent; masterful; powerful.

強 度 intensity.

強 弱 the strong and the weak.

強 志 determination.

強 性 a violent disposition.

²⁰強 悍 overbearing; masterful.

強 情 pretence of feeling; obstinate insistence on something contrary to facts.

強 戰 a fierce battle.

強 暴 fierce; overbearing; ruthless.

強 暴 不 順 fierce and unyielding.

²⁵強 梁 domineering; overbearing.

強 梁 霸 道 violent; overbearing.

強 梗 tyrannical; masterful.

強 橫 tyrannical; domineering.

強 橫 世·界 period of anarchy.

³⁰強 橫 手·段 forceful, unlawful methods.

強 權 brute force.

強 權 壓 制 oppressive methods; tyrannical oppression.

強 死 violent death.

強 水 corrosive acids.

³⁵硝 強 水 nitric acid.

強 熱 a very high degree of heat.

強 狠 vigorous.

強 猛 fierce and violent.

強 盛 powerful and flourishing, as a nation.

⁴⁰強·盜 or 強 寇 robbers.

強 硬 violently aggressive; unyielding.

強 硬 態 度 aggressive behaviour; harsh procedure.

強 硬 手·段 violent aggressive methods.

強 聒 tiresome talk.

⁴⁵強 舌 sharp-tongued.

強 詞 forced explanations.

強 諫 a strong rebuke.

強 買 forcible purchase.

強 賣 compulsory sale.

⁵⁰強³迫 forcible; compulsory.

強³迫 兵 役 a conscript.

強³迫 手·段 drastic measures.

強³迫 承 認 compulsory recognition.

強 迫 敎·育 compulsory education.

⁵⁵強 韌 a weak but obstinate disposition.

強 項 intractable; stiff-necked.

倔 強 perverse; headstrong.

列 強 "the Powers."

剛 強 wilful; perverse; stubborn.

⁶⁰富 強 rich and powerful, as a nation.

恃 強 to rely on force; to trust to violent methods.

持 強 violent; presumptuous.

爭 強 to struggle for mastery.

自 強 to make an effort.

(a) **Better.**

強·些 better.

強 半 the greater part; the majority.

強 如 or 強 似 better than.

強 處 superiority; points of superiority.

⁵不 以 爲 強 I do not consider it any better.

不 見 強 it does not seem to get any better, as an illness, etc.

比 他 強 better than he.

比 昨 天 強 better than it was yesterday.

賞 賜 百 千 強 bestowed on him more than 100,000.

(b) **Read** *ch'iang³.* **(the verb) To force; to compel. To insist.**

強 乞 to beg with threatening.

強 佔 to usurp. *See above.*—1.

強 借 to insist with violence; to beg with threats.

強 勝 to get the better of by violence.

⁵強 取 to take by force.

強 咽 to cram down the throat.

強 嘴 to deny evident truths, to bandy words.

強 壓 to bear down on; to oppress.

強⁸姦 to rape.

¹⁰強 志 to strengthen his will.

強 忍 forced to bear it.

強 扭 to wrench.

強 搶 or 強 刼 to rob with violence.

¹⁵強 求 to make forcible demands.

強 留 to detain with force.

強 立 to enforce, as rules.

強 行 to enforce; to enforce oneself.

強 要 to insist on something not right; or not due to one.

²⁰強 記 to make a strenuous effort to remember.

強 辯 to argue with obstinacy.

強 逼 to compel.

勉 強 forced. *See* 4495.7

壃⁴ A prop, a support.
669

𡫗⁴ A snare.
670

CH'IANG TS'IANG.   (ㄊㄧㄤ)

鏘¹ Tinkling of pendants and small bells.
671

鏘 鏘 tinkling.

鏗 鏘 clinking and clanging.

爿¹ A bed, a couch. Radical 90. Distinguish 片 No. 5256.
672 Half of a tree trunk. Also read *p'an⁴,* or *hsiang².*

戕¹'² A spear. To kill; to maltreat.
673

戕 傷 to wound; to injure.

戕 官 to slay rulers.

戕 官 生 民 to destroy the populace.

戕 暴 cruel; ruthless.

戕 物 to destroy living creatures.

戕 賊 to plunder; to force; to do violence to.

自 戕 suicide.

墻 牆 廧 [2]
674
A wall.

墻 內 事 domestic affairs.
墻 垣 walls.
墻 垛·子 battlements.
墻 壁 partitions; light walls.
[5]墻 宇 buildings.
墻 外 漢 derisive term for one who has merely picked up his learning, not having acquired it in the schools.
墻 脚 the foot of a wall.
墻 衣 moss on a wall.
墻 面 with the face to a wall—to see nothing, said of a man without culture.
[10]墻 頭 the top of a wall.
圍 墻 a surrounding wall.
女 墻 battlements of a wall; parapets.
山 墻 the gable wall of a building; also called 人字墻 or 金字墻.
照 墻 a screen wall.
[15]泥 墻 an adobe or mud wall.
砌 墻 to build a brick or a stone wall.
築 墻 to build a mud wall.
粉 墻 to plaster a wall.

嬙 [2]
675
Ancient term for female court officials.

嬪 嬙 ladies of the bed-chamber.

檣 艢 [2]
676
A mast; a yard-arm or boom.

桅 檣 a boom.

薔 [2]
677
A red rose.

薔·薇 a red rose.
薔 薇 戰 爭 "Wars of the Roses."
薔 薇 露 rose-water.

Read *se*[4·5]. **Water-pepper; smartweed.**

嗆 [4]
678
To peck. To cough.

嗆·了 嗓·子 violent coughing from irritation in the throat.
塵 土 嗆 人 the dust irritates the throat.

搶 [3] To take openly and by force.
679 To snatch. To ravish, to rob. To wrestle for.

搶 先 to struggle for precedence.
搶 出 來 to carry off with violence.
搶 刼 or 搶 掠 or 搶 奪 to plunder; to seize upon; to rob; to take by force.
搶 嘴 assertive; argumentative.
搶 白 to denounce to the face; to snatch away.
搶 親 to carry off a woman and marry her by force.

(a) Read *ch'iang*[1] or *ts'iang*[4]. Adverse, as winds.

搶 風 駛 行 to tack.
側 搶 to tack.
掉 搶 to make way against the wind, of boats.

(b) Read *ch'uang*[1]. To oppose; to rush against; to ruffle.

搶·起·來 to ruffle; to rub the wrong way.
以 角 搶 地 to strike the ground with the horns.
以 頭 搶 地 to strike the head on the ground in anger.
呼 搶 from 呼 天 搶 地 to call on Heaven and strike the head on the ground in grief.
飛 搶 楡 枋 I fly up into the elms and the *fang* trees.

槍 [1] A spear or lance. A gun.
680 Inter. 鎗 No. 683.

槍 刀 劍 戟 weapons of war.
槍 尖 the point of a spear.
槍 手 or 槍 替 a substitute who enters the examination instead of the candidate.
槍 法 spear drill; art of using weapons.
槍 斃 to execute by shooting.
槍 笆 or 槍 籬 a bamboo fence.
槍 頭 head of a spear.
投 槍 a javelin; javelin throw.

(a) Read *ch'eng*[2]. A comet.

槐 槍 星 a comet.

瑲 [1]
681
Tinkling of pendant gems.

瑲 瑲 tinkling, as of bells, etc.

蹌 蹡 [1]
682
To walk rapidly.

蹌 蹌 濟 濟 bustling about.

鎗 [1] A gun or pistol. Spears.
683 An opium pipe. Inter. 槍 No. 680.

鎗 匠 gunsmith.
鎗 子 shot; bullets; cartridges.
鎗 托 the stock of a gun.
鎗 斃 to execute by shooting.
[5]鎗 架·子 rack for guns.
鎗 機 trigger or lock of a gun.
鎗 矛 spears and javelins.
鎗 碼 or 鎗 彈 cartridges or bullets.
鎗 礮 small arms and artillery.
[10]鎗 礮 局 an arsenal.
鎗 筒 or 鎗 身 barrel of a gun.
鎗 藥 gunpowder.
鎗 靶 a target.
鎗 頭 刀 a bayonet. = 6985.5.
[15]手 鎗 pistol or revolver.
機 關 鎗 machine gun.
毛 瑟 鎗 mauser pistol.
雙 口 鎗 or 雙 筒 鎗 double-barrelled gun.
馬 鎗 a carbine.
鳥 鎗 fowling piece; shot-gun.
↑鎗 林 彈 雨 amidst gunfires.

CHIAO. (ㄐㄠ)

傲 [3·4]
684
To do. Intent on.

傲 倖 lucky; by chance; beyond the expectations.

噭 [1]
685
To wail; to call. To neigh.

噭 哭 to sob and wail.

徼 **3,4 To go around. The frontiers or boundaries.**
686

徼 妙 mysterious; occult.
徼 外 beyond the frontiers.
徼 循 to go on a circuit.
徼 藤 Wistaria.
徼 遊 禁 盜 to go on circuit to suppress brigandage.
邊 徼 the frontiers.

(a) A narrow road.

徼 道 a narrow road.
徼 道 綺 錯 the narrow paths cross and recross.

(b) Read *chiao*[1]**, inter. 徼 No. 684. To desire; to pry into. To pray for blessings. Lucky.**

徼 冀 a lucky chance.
徼 名 seek for fame.
徼³ 倖 happily; luckily; to seek for lucky occurrences.
徼³ 倖 萬 一 one lucky chance in ten thousand.
徼 福 to seek for happiness, as by prayer.
惡 徼 以 爲 知 者 I hate those who pry into matters and ascribe their knowledge to their wisdom.

(c) Read *yao*[1]**. To intercept.**

徼 麋 鹿 之 野 獸 the wild beasts which intercepted the deer.

皦 **3 White; dazzling.**
687

皦 日 the bright sun.
皦 皦 sparkling; twinkling.

繳 **3 To wind round. To bind. to involve.**
688

繳 線 to wind thread.
繳 繞 to wind round; to involve.

(a) To hand over; to deliver to; to surrender.

繳 價 to pay the price.
繳 出 to pay up.
繳 卷 to hand in an essay.
繳 呈 to hand in to a superior.
繳⁵ 回 to hand back; to deliver up.
繳 存 to deposit.
繳 庫 to pay into the treasury.

繳 案 to pay into court; to hand over a document.
繳 械 to hand over weapons.
¹⁰繳 稟 to give in a petition.
繳 納 to pay over, as taxes.
繳 股 to redeem, as debentures or bonds.
繳 解 to forward.
繳 贓 to deliver up stolen property.
¹⁵繳 還 to return; to repay.
繳 銷 to hand in for cancellation.
繳 驗 to submit for examination.
完 繳 to pay in full.

(b) Read *choh*[5]**. A string fastened to an arrow to draw it back after shooting.**

思 援 弓 繳 而 射 之 wishes to bend his bow, adjust the string to the arrow and shoot it.
矰 繳 to fasten a string to an arrow or a dart.

鐭 **3 To cut with shears.**
689

鐭 剪 to cut out.
鐭 開 to cut it into two pieces.

嬌 **1 Beautiful; graceful.**
690

嬌 妻 a charming wife.
嬌 姿 sprightly; elegant.
嬌 娃 a beautiful concubine.
嬌 娜 lovely.
⁵嬌 媚 handsome; beautiful.
嬌 嫩 seductive; fascinating; delicate colours.
嬌 嫩 細 膩 tender, delicate and glossy.
嬌 客 a son-in-law.
嬌 小 modest; refined.
¹⁰嬌 態 lady-like; genteel; attractive.
嬌 柔 soft and delicate; seductive; frail.
嬌 童 beautiful boys.
嬌 美 beautiful and graceful.
嬌 羞 bashful, modest and retiring.
¹⁵嬌 聲 a kind, winning voice; seductive tones; a shrill voice.
嬌 艷 vivid; bright; gay.
嬌 貴 dainty; highborn.
嬌 麗 lovely; beautiful.
妖 嬌 delicate and frail; seductive; fascinating.

(a) To bring up delicately. Indulged; petted.

嬌 兒 a pet; a spoilt child.
嬌 惰 delicately nurtured; effeminate and lazy.
嬌 生 to spoil a child.
嬌 癡 young; ignorant and foolish.
⁵嬌 養 to spoil a child by fondness.
嬌 養 慣 ·了 accustomed to soft and delicate ways; brought up delicately; spoilt.
↑嬌·慣 spoiled.

撟 **3 To bend or twist. Inter. next.**
691

撟 枉 過 正 to overbend the crooked in trying to make it straight the cure is worse than the disease, used of overstrictness, phonetic overcorrection, etc.
撟 正 to bend straight.
撟 然 straight and stiff; unbending.

(a) To dissemble; to feign.

撟 制 a false mandate.
撟 虔 dissemblers and oppressors.

(b) Read *chiao*[4]**. To lift up. To raise, as the hand.**

撟 捷 alert and nimble.
撟 舌 to stiffen and raise the tongue so that one cannot speak.
舌 撟 然 the tongue stiff with fright or astonishment so that speech is impossible—struck dumb.

矯 **3 To dissemble.**
692

矯 制 to feign orders from the authorities.
矯 命 to feign orders.
矯 廉 pretences to virtue or modesty; over-scrupulous.
矯 託 pretence to knowledge.
矯 詔 紛 出 many false mandates were being issued.
矯 誣 to dissemble; to deceive.
矯 情 affectation.

(a) To usurp; to force. Martial; strong.

矯 健 strong and active; brave.
矯 矯 虎 臣 his bold tigerish leaders.

矯 強 to force; to constrain; un-reasonable.

矯 揉 to subdue; to put straight.

(b) To bend straight; to reform. To raise. Inter. last.

矯 世 to reform the age.

矯 枉 過 正 to be overstrict, bending what is crooked in the endeavour to make it straight.

矯 正 to regulate; to rectify; to straighten the crooked.

矯 當 時 之 弊 to reform the evils of the times.

矯 首 to raise the head.

轎 [4]
693　A sedan-chair.

轎 夫 or 擡 轎 的 chair bearers.

轎 子 or 一 頂 轎 子 or 一 乘 轎 子 a sedan-chair.

轎 担 the short pole used when there are four chair bearers.

轎 杠 or 轎 桿 sedan-chair poles.

[5]轎 櫃 the space under the seat of a sedan-chair.

轎 簾 子 a curtain to hang before a chair as a screen.

轎 衣 子 the cloth covering of a chair.

轎 車 a covered passenger cart; a sedan car.

亮 轎 an open sedan chair.

[10]坐 轎 to ride in a sedan chair.

抬 轎 to carry a sedan-chair.

竹 轎 a bamboo chair.

花 轎 the gayly gilded red sedan-chair of a bride.

起 轎 or 遷 轎 to tilt a sedan-chair so that the passenger can step over the poles.

[15]騾 轎 a mule litter.

驕 [1]
694　A high spirited horse. Proud; arrogant; boastful.

驕 人 a flatterer for his own ends.

驕 傲 or 驕 誇 or 驕 矜 proud; over-bearing; haughty.

驕 兒 [2] or 驕 子 a favourite; a beloved son.

驕 兵 overbearing soldiers.

[5]驕 奢 proud and extravagant.

驕 奢 淫 佚 pride, luxury, profligacy, and idleness.

驕 態 a haughty manner; a proud bearing.

驕 慢 proudly contemptuous.

驕 戰 fierce conflict; skilful at fighting.

[10]驕 橫 presumptuous; overbearing.

驕 樂 extravagant pleasures.

驕 泰 proudly self-confident.

驕 狎 to treat with haughty disrespect.

驕 盈 proud and discontented.

[15]驕 縱 overbearing; disregardful of advice.

驕 肆 rude; violent.

驕 色 a haughty manner or look.

驕 蹇 scornful.

驕 陽 the summer sun.

[20]驕 驕 flourishing.

泰 而 不 驕 great but not proud, said of an emperor.

↑驕 傲 arrogant, conceited.

(a) Read *hsiao*[1]**. A short-nosed hunting dog.** *See* 獟 **No. 2642. B.**

僥 [3]
695　To be lucky. A chance. Inter. 684, 686.

僥 倖 luck; chance.

(a) Read *yao*[2] **Pigmies. False.**

僬 僥 a race of pigmies said to be three feet in height.

澆 [1]
696　To cleanse with water. To pour over.

澆 奠 to pour out a libation.

澆 灌 to pour upon.

澆 燭 to dip candles.

澆 花 to water flowers.

澆 裹 daily expenses; food and clothing respectively.

(a) Bad; demoralized.

澆 季 a degenerate age.

澆 浮 or 澆 漓 spoilt; demoralized.

澆 薄 bad, as customs; ungrateful.

澆 風 bad customs; evil reputation.

膠 [1]
697　Glue; gum; sticky.

膠 囊 gelatine capsules.

膠 捲 roll film.

膠 水 size.

膠 漆 glue and varnish. *See below.* A. 5, 11.

[5]膠 版 a manifolding apparatus, a tray containing a gelatinous composition.

膠 皮 indiarubber. *See under* 橡 皮 No. 2570.

膠 皮 車 a ricksha, used in North China.

膠 衣 藥 丸 gelatine coated pills.

膠 質 glue; gum; gelatinous substances.

[10]膠 鍊 boiled glue.

膠 黏 sticky—glue.

皮 膠 common glue.

魚 膠 fish glue.

(a) To adhere to; obstinate.

膠 固 firm; pigheaded.

膠 執 成 見 bigoted and prejudiced.

膠 戾 perverse; crooked ways.

膠 柱 鼓 瑟 to glue the stops and then try to play the lute—perverse and stupid.

[5]膠 漆 相 投 sticking together as if with glue and varnish—inseparable affection.

膠 結 closely joined together.

膠 續 to marry a second wife.

膠 葛 complications arising from a dispute.

膠 譎 guileful; untrustworthy.

[10]膠 連 banded together for no good.

如 膠 似 漆 as glue and varnish—close and inseparable friendship.

(b) Confused.

膠 膠 擾 擾 in utter confusion and turmoil.

鷄 鳴 膠 膠 the cocks are crowing in confusion.

膠 [1]
698　Confused; muddled. Also pron. *chiu*[1]

膠 轕 confused and disorderly; far distant.

攪 [3]
699　To stir up. To disturb. To annoy or give trouble.

攪 亂 to stir up a row.

攪 動 to disturb; to arouse.

攪 勻 to mix evenly.

攪 和 to mix; to stir. (*-huo*)

[5]攪 咬 to make mischief; to stir up illwill.

攪 拌 to stir or mix.

擾擾 to give trouble; to put to inconvenience; to make a disturbance.

擾星 a bad character.

擾混 to cause confusion.

[10]打擾 I have put you to much inconvenience—said to host on leaving, more frequently 打擾.

叫 [4]
叫！
700

To call; to summon.

叫不應 to call but get no response.

叫他來 call him here.

叫住 Stop!

叫做 called; spoken of as.

[5]叫倒好 to cry down a speaker or an actor.

叫化子 beggars.

叫哥哥 a large green cricket that chirps in the summer; children keep them in cages.

叫喚 or 叫呼 to call out.

叫喊 to yell; to shout.

[10]叫喊一聲 to give a shout.

叫號 to yell; to shout out.

叫救命 to cry for help.

叫甚麼 What is this called?

叫賊 Thieves; stop thief!

[15]叫賣 to cry goods for sale.

叫醒了 to awaken by a call.

叫門 or 打門 to call for a door to be opened; to knock at a door.

叫魂 to call back the spirit of a dead or dying child.

不相叫 not on speaking terms.

(a) To hire; to engage.

叫汽車來 call a car.

叫船 to hire a boat.

叫車(子)來 to engage a cart or barrow.

叫驢 a donkey for hire.

(b) To cause; to permit.

叫眾人散去 caused the crowd to scatter.

叫賊搶了 taken by thieves.

叫風吹了 blown about by the wind.

不叫他去 do not permit him to go.

不願意叫他餓 not willing that he should suffer hunger.

書叫誰拿去 by whom was the book taken?

(c) The cries of some birds and certain animals.

羊叫喚 the sheep or goats are bleating.

鴉鵲叫叫 the chattering of magpies.

雞叫 cockcrow.

疛 [3] Griping colic. Read chiu[1]. A swelling.
701

疛瘤 a swelling.

交 [1] To commit to; to hand to; to deliver; to pay.
702

交付 or 交與 or 交託 to hand over to; to entrust to; delivery.

交付審查 to hand over for investigation.

交付懲戒 delivered up to punishment.

交代清楚 everything handed over.

[5]交來 to be delivered over to.

交價 to pay the price of goods.

交兌 to pay.

交出 to render up.

交出贓品 to deliver up stolen property.

[10]交到 to deliver to.

交割 or 交代 to hand over to a successor.

交印 to hand over the seals of office.

交帶 to hand over to the custody of.

交手 to hand to .... personally.

[15]交捕 to hand over to the police.

交收 to make over to.

交案 to bring to the court.

交清 all handed over; everything delivered properly; nothing retained.

交盤 to hand over the whole business, etc., to another.

[20]交納 to pay duty.

交給 to give to; to allow; to hand to.

交解 to send to; to forward.

交課 to pay taxes.

交貨 to deliver goods.

[25]交貨付清 or 現銀交貨 cash on delivery.

交貨簿 a delivery book for goods.

交賬 to render accounts.

交足 paid in full.

交還 or 交回 to hand back; to restore.

[30]定期交付 delivery on term.

現場交付 delivery on the spot.

船側交付 delivery at the ship's side.

車站交付 delivery at the railway station.

(a) To exchange; to barter; to bargain.

交杯 or 合杯 to drink the nuptial cup.

交妥 to complete a transaction.

交婚 intermarriage.

交換 to exchange; mutual exchange.

[5]交換俘虜 exchange of prisoners.

交換利益 exchange of benefits.

交換國書 exchange of credentials.

交換意見 exchange of views.

交換條件 give and take conditions.

[10]交換條約 exchange of treaties.

交易 trade; business transactions; interchange.

交易所 the Exchange.

交替 to interchange; to substitute.

交盃盞 the nuptial cup.

[15]交質 exchange of hostages.

交鈔 paper notes used in *Yüan* and *Ming* dynasties.

成交 to close a bargain.

(b) To communicate.

交通 to communicate.

交通壕壘 communication trenches. Usually with 147.13.

交通斷絕 communications cut off.

交通機關 communications; organ of communications, as railways, roads, etc.

[5]交通次長 Assistant Minister of Communications.

交通部長 Minister of Communications.

交通部 Ministry of Communications.

交通銀行 Bank of Communications.

(c) To have intercourse with; intimacy; friendship.

交友 to make friends with.
交口 to wrangle.
交合 to blend with; to have intercourse with.
交好 intimate with; on good terms with.
[5]交媾 or 交嬸 sexual intercourse.
交孚 mutual trust, as in trading.
交往 association with; to have dealings with.
交情 friendship.
交感神經 the sympathetic nerve.
[10]交拜 to salute; to bow.
交接 to receive; to entertain.
交有王稱之名 in their intercourse both could be styled "king."
交淺 slight acquaintance.
交涉 intercourse; negotiations; mutual relations, as between two nations.
[15]交涉使 diplomatic commissioner.
交涉員 Provincial Commissioner for Foreign Affairs.
交涉專使 special diplomatic envoy.
交涉署 Bureau for Foreign Affairs.
交睫 to sleep.
[20]交納外賓 to entertain foreign guests.
交結 to have friendly intercourse with; to intertwine.
交耳 to whisper; confidential talk.
交臂 close together; meeting together.
交言 to have a talk.
[25]交談 to have an interview with.
交謫 recriminations.
交遊 to go with friends; social intercourse.
交遊甚廣 having friends in every place.
交關 relations or transactions between.
[30]交際 social intercourse; international amenities.
交際公開 unrestricted friendly intercourse.
交際官 envoy conveying special messages such as congratulations or condolence.
交頭接耳 intimate; whispering; confabulation.
[35]好交 easy to get on with.
心交 warm friendship.

絕交 to sever relations; break off intercourse.
親交 close friendship.
邦交 diplomatic relations.

(d) To join. To intertwine; to interlace. Adjoining; to engage, as in battle.

交互 to unite.
交交 flying to and fro.
交冬後 just after winter begins.
交切 to intersect.
[5]交加 to mix with; to pile up; to interlace; intertwining.
　雨雪交加 mingled rain and snow.
交加環洞 or 交乂拱 interlacing arches.
交午 crossed; noon.
交乂點 point of intersection.
交尾 copulation of birds.
[10]交戰 to join battle.
交戰區域 war zone.
交戰國 belligerent nations.
交戰團 belligerents.
交椅 armchair.
[15]交流 alternating current.
交爭 to strive or struggle.
交界 the frontier; adjoining.
交腳 to cross the legs.
交角 angle of intersection.
[20]交辰時 about 7 a.m.
交迸 clash, as of opinion.
交鋒 to cross spears or swords—to engage in battle.
交錯 interlocking; interchanging.
交鎖 interlocked.
[25]交雜 interlaced and intertwining, as tangled growths.
交點 point of intersection.
交齒 interlocked; dovetailed.
悲喜交集 mingled feelings.

佼 [3] **Handsome.**
703
佼人 a beauty.
佼佼 beautiful; out of the common; flying about of birds.
佼好 delightful.
佼童 a beautiful boy.

Read *chiao*[1]. **Artful; false.**

姣姟 [3] **Handsome; pretty. Cunning.**
704

姣態 attractive; coquettish.
姣生慣養 corrupt. of 690 A6.
姣童 a pretty boy.
姣美 or 姣俏 beautiful; seductive.

挍 [4] **To compare; to criticise; to oppose. Inter.,** 校 **next,**
705 **and** 較 **No. 713.**
挍講是非 to criticise.
讐挍 to compare documents.

校 [4] **To compare; to collate; to revise.**
706
校勘 to collate and compare.
校勘學 textual criticism.
校定 or 校正 to revise; to correct, as a proof.
校對 to correct proofs.
[5]校對人 proof reader.
校對無訛 examined and found correct. O.K.
校書 to collate books; a high grade of courtesan.
校綴 to collate scattered items and documents into a book.
校課 to correct errors.
[10]校讐 to compare documents.
校閱 to examine, as a proof.
考校 carefully compare.
計校 to audit accounts, etc.

(a) To enter into altercation.

犯而不校 though opposed he entered into no altercation.

(b) Read *hsiao*[4]. **A school. An enclosure for horses.**

校人 keeper of the fishponds or of the horses.
校友 alumni.
校友會 alumni association.
校址 college grounds. [school grounds.]
[5]校董 directors of a school of a
校董會 board of directors or trustees
校規 school rules or regulations.
校醫 resident medical officer of a school.
校長 [3] principal of a school or college; officer in charge of tombs.
[10]學校 a school.
鄉校 a village school.

(c) Military or naval title.

上校 colonel.
中校 lieutenant-colonel.
少校 major.

狡 3

707

Crafty; clever.

狡 供 to prevaricate.

狡 兔 三 窟 a wily rabbit has several exits to its burrow—crafty foresight.

狡 強 violent and crafty.

狡 徒 a fraud or sharper.

⁵狡 憒 perverse; stubborn.

狡 戾 brutal; perverse; uncontrolled.

狡 擺 to prevail on by mis-representation.

狡 棍 a fraudulent scoundrel.

狡 焉 思 略 artful schemes to enlarge one's territory.

¹⁰狡 為 or 狡 詐 cunning; deceitful.

狡 童 a handsome boy.

狡 脫 to evade; to palter.

狡 計 a wily plan.

狡 謀 artful devices; to conspire.

¹⁵狡 誘 evasion; fraudulent delays.

狡 譎 fraudulent; crafty.

狡 賴 to prevaricate; to shuffle.

狡 避 to lie in order to evade punishment.

狡 飾 fabricated; pretences.

²⁰狡 點 cunning; subtle, crafty.

皎 3

708

The bright, white moon; a pure glistening white. Splendid.

皎 之 行 聞 於 人 his brilliant actions were known by others.

皎 日 bright sunshine.

皎 潔 clean; unsullied.

皎 白 brilliantly white.

皎 皎 glistening white.

絞 3

709

To bind; to twist; to wrap; to strangle.

絞 力 torsion.

絞 死 or 絞 犯 to strangle a criminal.

絞 紗 to spin thread.

絞 緊 bind it tightly.

⁵絞 縊 to strangle; death by hanging or by strangling.

絞 纆 to twist ropes.

絞 罪 punishment by strangling.

絞 腸 痧 griping pains as of cholera or colic.

絞 頭 布 turbans.

¹⁰三 絞 繩 a "three-fold cord."

(a) A windlass; to turn, as a crank.

絞 椿 a windlass used to hoist boats in the Grand Canal. The stake at which a criminal was strangled.

絞 盤 or 絞 車 a windlass, winch or capstan.

絞 起 to wind up.

(b) Unceremonious; blunt; rudeness; disrespect.

絞 刺 人 非 to expose the faults of others.

直 而 無 禮 則 絞 straightforwardness without propriety is rudeness.

直 絞 bluntness; rudeness.

菱 1

710

An aquatic grass, the stalks of which are eaten as a vegetable. See 蔣 No. 660.

菱 笋 or 菱 白 or 菱 瓜 name for the above in different places.

菱 米 the seeds of the above.

菱 耳 菜 a water-cress.

蛟 1

711

A scaly dragon.

蛟 水 floods caused by this dragon.

蛟 篆 wriggly-shaped characters on bells, tripods, etc.

蛟 蚪 crouching; curled up.

蛟 蜻 蛉 the insect of which the larvae is called the ant-lion.

⁵蛟 龍 the flood-dragon—supposed to be the cause of landslides.

蛟 龍 得 水 the flood-dragon gets to water—i.e., a bold man gets an opportunity for showing his prowess; used for getting a good opportunity.

蛟 龍 得 雲 雨 similar to the last phrase.

蹻 1.4.

712

The bones of the leg; to wrestle.

較 3,4

713

To compare. To test. Than; more than.

較 之 compared with ....

較 兑 to tally; to agree.

較 勘 to compare; to collate.

較 場 a parade ground; a field for reviews.

⁵較 多 較 少 comparatively more or comparatively less than.

較 對 to compare things to ascertain whether they agree.

較 早 earlier; sooner.

較 易 為 力 will be rendered somewhat easier.

較 比 or 較 量 to compare; compared with; to test.

¹⁰較 準 to equalize; to adjust to standard.

較 炳 to make clear and bright.

較 繁 perplexing; troublesome.

較 著 to illumine a topic.

較 轉 equivocating.

¹⁵較 重 comparatively heavier.

大 較 generally; on the average.

比 較 to compare.

比 較 口 供 to compare evidence.

相 較 mutual comparison; in comparison with.

(a) Read *chüeh²*, *chioh⁵* To wrestle. A state carriage.

較 力 to wrestle.

較 力 爭 勝 to wrestle; to struggle for mastery.

魯 人 獵 較 the people of *Lu* struggled for the game taken in hunting.

郊 1

714

Waste land. Open spaces beyond a city. Frontiers.

郊 圻 space within a city.

郊 坰 in the wilds.

郊 外 in the wilds; lands not yet reached by civilization.

郊 畋 to hunt in the uncultivated outskirts.

郊 迎 to go to the outer suburbs to meet a visitor—as a mark of respect.

郊 遂 within and without a city.

(a) Sacrifices. Altars.

郊 壇 sacrificial altar to Heaven and Earth.

郊 天 an imperial sacrifice to Heaven.

郊 廟 a temple for sacrifices to Heaven.

郊 祀 state sacrifice and worship.

郊 社 之 禮 所 以 事 上 帝 也 the ceremonial of the sacrifice

to Heaven and Earth is the worship of *Shang ti*.

鉸³ Pivots on which a door turns. A hinge.
715

鉸釘 the pin of a hinge.
鉸鏈 hinges.
鉸鏈關節 a hinge joint.
鎖鉸 bolt of a lock.

(a) To shear. To cut out.

鉸刀 or 鉸剪 scissors; shears.
鉸刀·子 slender knife used by barbers.
鉸紙花 to cut out paper flowers.
鉸衣服 to cut out garments.

餃³ A meat dumpling.
716

餃·子 or 餃餌 a boiled dumpling made of dough and containing meat, etc.

鮫¹ The shark, now called 鯊.
717

鮫人 a mermaid of the southern seas, she lives and spins under water, her tears are pearls.
鮫函 coats of mail made from shagreen.
鮫綃 a kind of fibrous material from the sea, often associated with the above.
鮫鮒 a fabulous sea monster.

**窖
窌⁴ A cellar; a pit; a vault.**
718

窖冰 to store ice.
窖密 profound; deep, as the heart.
窖藏 stored in a cellar.
地窖 a cellar.

教¹ To teach; to instruct. As *chiao¹* coll., *chiao⁴* litt.
719

教⁴不能 to teach the incompetent.
教⁴化 to civilize; to influence by teaching. *See below.* B.4.

教⁴學 to teach school.
教⁴導 to educate; to guide into truth.
⁵教⁴授 to teach. *See below.* B. 8-11.
教¹書 to teach.
教¹法 teaching methods.
教⁴生 pupil teacher.
教⁴給 to teach or instruct.
¹⁰教⁴練 to train; to exercise; to drill.
教⁴訓 or 教誨 to teach; to educate. *See below.* B.52.
教¹話 to teach languages.
教⁴誘 to deceive; to seduce; to mislead.
教⁴誡 to warn; to admonish.
¹⁵教⁴養 to educate and bring up.
請·教⁴ Please instruct me! Give me your opinion!

(a) To cause; to allow; to command. *chiao¹·⁴* litt., *chiao⁴* coll.

教令 to command.
教唆 to instigate.
教唆犯罪 to instigate to crime.

(b) Read *chiao⁴*. **As a noun, though the distinction is not strictly observed. Education; teaching.**

教¹人作人 train them to be men.
教·務 school affairs or business. *See below.* C. 2.
教·務長 dean of a school or college.
教化 culture. *See above.*—2.
⁵教·員 a teacher.
教員會 faculty of a college.
教室 class-room.
教·授 a teacher; a professor. *See above.*—5.
教·授學 or 教·育學 pedagogy.
¹⁰教·授案 manual for teachers.
教·授法 methods of teaching.
教本 or 教·科書 text books.
教案 teacher's preparation for lessons. *See below.* C.13.
教無所施 no means of imparting instruction.
¹⁵教·育 education; cultural training.
教·育上·的 educational.
教·育事務 educational matters.
教·育司長 Secretary of the Ministry of Education.
教·育哲學 philosophy of education.
²⁰教·育問題 educational problems
教·育基金 endowment for educational purposes.

教·育學 pedagogy.
教·育家 educationalists.
教·育局 Local Board of Education.
²⁵教·育廳 Provincial Department of Education. *See* 6403.15
教·育會 a board of education.
教·育界 the educational world.
教·育的 educational.
教·育科 educational matters.
³⁰教·育部長 Minister of Education.
教·育行政 Educational Executive or Administration.
教·育資格 qualifications for teaching.
教·育部 Ministry of Education.
教·育雜誌 "Educational Review."
³⁵世俗教·育 secular education.
中等教·育 secondary education.
公民教·育 training in citizenship.
初等教·育 primary education.
古典教·育 classical education.
⁴⁰基本教·育 fundamental education.
專門教·育 or 特殊教·育 special training.
工藝教·育 or 實業教·育 technical education.
平民教·育 or 通俗教·育 education for the masses.
強迫教·育 compulsory education.
⁴⁵文學教·育 literary education; arts.
普通教·育 general education.
生計教·育 vocational education. *See* 990.23 livelihood.
科學教·育 scientific education.
高等教·育 or 大學教·育 higher education.
⁵⁰高等普通教·育 liberal education.
教言 Your advice, etc.,—conventional reply to good advice in letters.*
教·訓 teaching; instruction. *See above.*—11.
教鞭 a pointer.

* your words (in a previous conversation).

教 傷 亡 素 under your instructions we forget our previous relations (with *Lu*).

[35]教 館 a school-house.

來 領 教 I have called to receive your instructions—conventional phrase.

沒 [2]領 教 I have not learned (your name)—polite reply when asked one's surname.

(c) A sect. Religions. Doctrines. *chiao*[4].

教 主 Founder of a religion; leader of a sect.

教.務 church matters; *See above.* B. 2.

教 友 church members.

[5]教 堂 a church or chapel.

教 外 the *world*, outside the church.

教 師 or 教.士 evangelist; teacher of religion. Protestant missionary. 教師 also = B 5.

教 政 分 離 separation of church and state.

教.會 The Church.

教 會 問 答 Church catechism.

[10]凱 旋 教 會 the *Church triumphant*.

戰 鬥 教 會 the *Church militant*.

改 革 教 會 the *reformed Church*.

教 案 lawsuits between church members and the people. *See above.* B. 13.

教 案 蠭 起 church lawsuits arose like hornets.

[15]教 權 authority of the church.

教 民 church members, used by Roman Catholics.

教 派 a sect.

教 派 心 sectarianism.

教 派 的 sectarian.

[20]教 父 the *Fathers*.

教 王 or 教 皇 or 教 化 皇 The Pope.

教 禮 the ordinances of the church.

教 規 church rules.

教 門 a sect; school of philosophy; disciples. Mohammedans.

[25]三 教 the three religions of China. Confucianism, Buddhism, and Taoism. *See* 儒 No. 3145—12.

主 教 a bishop.

信 教 to believe a doctrine.

傳 教 to preach; to promulgate a religion.

入 教 to enter the church.

[30]出 教 to excommunicate.

奉 教 to become a convert.

背 教 apostatize.

(d) Various religions arranged alphabetically to illustrate use as a suffix. *chiao*[4].

婆 羅 門 教 Brahmanism.

佛 教 or 釋 教 Buddhism.

基.督 教 or 耶 教 Christianity

救 世 教 Christianity—the religion of salvation.

[5]儒 教 or 大 教 Confucianism.

國 立 教 會 or 公 認 教 Established Church.

希.臘 教 Greek Church.

印.度 教 Hinduism.

猶 太 教 Judaism.

[10]喇.嘛 教 Lamaism.

回.回 教 or 清 眞 教 Mohammedanism.

黃 教 Mongolian Lamaism.

白 然 教 Natural Religion.

異 教 or 邪 教 or 偶 像 教 Paganism.

[15]多 神 教 Polytheism.

宗 教 Religion. *See* 宗 No. 6896.

天 啟 教 Revealed Religion.

天 主 教 Roman Catholicism.

神 道 教 Shintoism.

[20]道 教 Taoism.

宇 宙 神 教 Universalism.

祅 教 or 拜 火 教 Zoroastrianism.

酵[4]

720

Leaven; yeast.

酵 母 yeast; leaven.

酵 餅 yeast cakes.

發 酵 to ferment; to rise as dough.

麵 酵 yeast.

CHIAO.   TSIAO. (ㄐㄠ)

焦[1]

721

Scorched or burned.

焦 乾 extremely dry.

焦 尾 琴 or 焦 桐 a lute made from a charred log pulled from the fire for the purpose because it gave out a musical note as it burned.

焦 月 the sixth month.

焦 枯 withered by the heat.

[5]焦 渴 parching thirst.

焦 灼 badly burnt; worried.

焦 炭 coke.

焦 熱 burning hot.

焦 燥 parched; hot.

[10]焦 脆 crisp.

焦 雷 a clap of thunder.

焦 面 focal plane.

焦 頭 爛 額 to be severely burned in assisting to extinguish a fire —used of one who has worked under great hardship.

焦 黃 sallow; bright yellow.

[15]焦 黑 or 曬 焦.了 sunburnt; burnt black.

焦 點 focus.

焦 點.的 focal.

焦 點 距 離 focal distance.

定 焦 點 or 合 焦 點 to focus

[20]實 焦 點 real or true focus.

未 合 焦 點 out of focus.

準 焦 to focalize.

炒 焦 to burn or scorch, as in cooking.

燒 焦 burned or scorched. [Icy.

↑ 焦 土 政 策 'scorched earth' po-

(a) Vexed; anxious.

焦 勞 weary and worn.

焦 急 vexed; grieved.

焦 思 or 焦 慮 worried; anxiety.

焦 悶 or 焦 愁 or 焦 心 sad at heart; distressed; melancholy.

焦 酸 very sour.

僬[1]

722

Clever; alert in mind. Pigmies.

僬 僥 pigmies.

僬 僥 國 人 長 一 尺 五 寸 there is the land of pigmies where men grow to 1 ft. 5 in., in height.

以 己 之 僬 僬 those who think themselves clever.

(a) Read *chiao*[4]. Hasty.

僬 人 僬 僬 the ordinary man goes hurriedly without any regard for appearances.

噍[4]

723

To chew, to munch.

噍 食 to eat.

襄 城 無 噍 類 nothing that chewed was left in Hsiang ch'eng—i.e., an utter extermination.

(a) Read *chiao*[1] or *tsiao*[1]. Distressed.

嘦 殺 (*shai*[4]) less.

其 聲 嘦 以 殺 (under the influence of grief) his voice became distressed and broken.

(b) Read *ch'iu*[1]. To twitter.

啁 嘦 the twittering of swallows.

燋 [4] To burn moxa. To cauterize; to char or scorch.
724

燋 夭 to die young.
燋 心 distress of heart.
燋 木 to char wood.
燋 爛 cooked to rags; well done.
燋 萎 夭 折 like burnt and withered grass, it is soon cut off.
燋 鑠 furnace heat to smelt metals.

礁 [1] Half-tide rocks. Stones in a river.
725

礁 淺 aground on the rocks.
礁 石 a rock; shoals.
觸 礁 to strike on a rock.

蕉 [1] The plantain or banana.
726

蕉 子 or 芭 蕉 banana tree.
蕉 布 or 蕉 葛 a linen made in Kwangtung, from the fibres of the plantain.
蕉 扇 palm-leaf fans.
蕉 萃 grieved and distressed.
蕉 薪 fuel.
香 蕉 bananas.

醮 [4] To sacrifice and pour libations to the dead. Idolatrous thanksgiving service.
727

醮 壇 idolatrous prayers for the sick, or to avert calamity.
醮 席 a wedding feast.
醮 金 fees for such idolatrous sacrifices as above.
再 醮 to re-marry, of a widow.
打 醮 to celebrate the feast of "All Souls."
設 醮 altar for celebrating a sacrifice on behalf of souls in purgatory.

(a) Exhausted. Finished.

水 醮 the water dried up.

鷦 [1] Small bird like the tit or wren.
728

鷦 鵬 the phœnix.
鷦 鷯 or 巧 婦 鳥 the tailor bird.

椒 [1] Pepper; various spices.
729

椒 丘 a mound sloping away on all sides.
椒 房 private apartments of the empress.
椒 月 the twelfth month.
椒 末 or 椒 麵 or 椒 粉 ground pepper.
椒 酒 pepper wine, an ancient offering at new year.
胡 椒 black pepper.
花 椒 a wild pepper with a numbing taste.
辣 椒 cayenne pepper.

愀 [1] Mournful; narrow. u.f. 湫 No. 1230.
730

愀 狹 narrow and confined.
愀 鄙 a poor and bare room.

剿 / 勦 [3] To attack; to destroy. To plagiarize. Distinguish 勦 next.
731

剿 共 清 匪 to extirpate communists and bandits.
剿 匪 or 剿 賊 to destroy rebels or robbers.
剿 捕 净 盡 to make an utter extermination.
剿 絕 or 剿 滅 to exterminate.
剿 襲 or 剿 說 to plagiarize.

勦 [3] To trouble; to annoy; nimble. Distinguish 剿 preceding.
732

勦 勞 to weary.
勦 勦 其 民 oppress the masses.

皭 [4] Pure white; clean.
733

皭 然 不 滓 pure, with no blemish.

釂 [2] To drain a goblet.
734

CH'IAO. (ㄑㄠ)

敲 [1] A club, a baton. To pound; to strike; to tap; to rap on.
735

敲 冰 煮 茗 breaking the ice to get water for tea; when a guest comes in winter.
敲 敲 打 打 to rap continually.
敲 打 to beat; to hammer at.
敲 木 魚 to beat the wooden fish, as is done through the night in temples.
[5]敲 枰 to tap a chess man when considering a move, thus used for a move in chess.
敲 梆 or 敲 更 to beat the hours of the night watches.
敲 樂 to beat time.
敲 死 他 beat him to death!
敲 碎 to smash to pieces.
[10]敲 經 念 佛 beating time and chanting prayers to Buddha.
敲 背 to massage; to beat the back.
敲 詐 to extort or blackmail.
敲 詩 to beat a tattoo on the table when meditating on the composition of verse.
敲 鐘 to strike a bell; to toll.
[15]敲 鑼 to beat the gong; a signal to cease hostilities.
敲 門 to knock at a door or gate.
敲 門 磚 the brickbat that knocked at the door and caused it to open—used of a man who neglects his studies after getting his degree—as a man throws away the brick after the door is opened.
敲 鼓 to beat a drum.
推 敲 to weigh; to consider, as in chess or composition.
↑ 敲 竹 槓 to work a 'racket' on.

撬 [1] To prise up or open. To force with a lever.
736

撬 不 動 it cannot be prised.
撬 不 開 it cannot be opened by prising.
撬 孔 to make a hole, as with a spike.
撬 棍 a crowbar.
撬 破 了 broken in opening.
撬 起 來 to prise up; to lever.
撬 開 門 to prise a door open.

橇 [2] **A sledge for mud or snow.**
737

磽 ⎫
墝 ⎭ [1] **Stony soil.**
738

磽埆 stony soil.
磽瘠 or 磽薄 barren ground.

翹 [2] **The long tail feathers which curl up. To elevate. To raise the head. Warped.**
739

翹人之過 to expose the faults of another.
翹企 anxiously looking for—lit., on tiptoe.
翹出衆人 above the average; pre-eminent.
翹[4]尾 to cock the tail.
5 翹彥 a man of talents.
翹思慕遠人 longing desires for one far away.
翹望 or 翹盼 to look for with hope.
翹曲 to warp; warped.
翹楚 pre-eminent ability or virtue in either man or woman, from the next.
10 翹翹錯薪言刈其楚 among the many bundles of firewood one sticks up prominently;—all women are pure and virtuous, but I will excel them.
翹瞻 to hope for; to look up to.
翹竦 standing high and erect.
翹翹 high; dangerous; distant.
翹脚 or 高翹[1] or 翹趫 stilts.
15 翹足 to stand on tiptoe.
翹關 to lift a heavy stone weight as a test of strength.
翹首 to raise the head.

(a) **Women's head ornaments.**

珊瑚翹 a coral head ornament.
(b) Read *chiao*[4] *Coll.* To be turned up.

𪒠 [1] **Hemp black from mildew.**
740

黑𪒠·子 black spots on the face; moles.

瞧 [2] **To look at; to glance at; to see.**
741

瞧·一·瞧 to have a look at it.
瞧·不上 or 瞧·不起 to hold cheap; to sneer at.
瞧·不見 I cannot see it.
瞧病 to see a patient; to consult a doctor.
瞧·瞧 to have a look at.
瞧破·了 to see through; to detect.
瞧·見·麽 do you see it?

丂 [3] **Breath or air seeking exit. Also read** *k'ao*[4]. **National Phonetic letter for** *k'*.
742

巧 [3] **Clever; ingenious; skilful; artful.**
743

巧奪天工 skilful handiwork rivalling nature.
巧妙 ingenious.
巧妙手·段 a clever stroke; a good move.
巧婦鳥 the tailor bird.
5 巧思 ingenious idea.
巧手 or 巧匠 a skilled workman.
巧捷 clever; witty.
巧日 7th day of the 7th lunar month; when women compete for skill in needlecraft.
巧月 7th month.
10 巧機 an ingenious piece of mechanism.
巧發奇中[4] skilful foretelling.
巧笑倩兮 the dimples of her artful smile.
巧舌 a plausible tongue.
巧言 artful words.
15 巧言令色鮮矣仁 fine words and an insinuating countenance are seldom associated with virtue.
巧計 a capital plan
巧詐 clever swindles.
巧詐求遷 to seek preferment by scheming.
巧詆 slander.
20 巧語花言 flowery speeches.
巧譬善導 skilful in illustrating profound truths.
巧辯 plausible argument.
巧避 artful evasion; to dodge.
乞巧 to seek for skill in needlework on 7th of the 7th month as above.—8.
淫巧 specious.

(a) **Opportunely; lucky.**

巧·了 luckily; possibly.
巧合 to meet by chance.
巧·得很 very fortunately.
巧極·了 just the very thing; just the right moment.
巧機·會 a splendid chance.
恰巧 or 湊巧 opportunely.
不巧 unfortunately.

喬 [2] **High, stately; proud. Inter. 橋 No. 747.**
744

喬嶽 lofty mountains.
喬志 insolence; arrogance.
喬木 tall, stately trees.
喬松 a lofty pine tree—longevity.
喬梓 straight upright trees and lowly bending ones—father and sons.
喬而野 proud and rude.
喬遷 to remove from a dwelling place, from the next.
出自幽谷遷於喬木 as a bird flies from the dark valleys into the lofty trees.
喬遷之喜 congratulations on entering a new house.

(a) **To disguise.**

喬妝 to disguise as a man or a woman.

(b) **Crooked. Hook on a spear.**

喬詰 discontented.
如羽喬 branches all twisted like the tail feathers of a bird.
矛喬 a hook for a tassel on a spear.

僑 [2] **An inn; to sojourn.**
745

僑商 or 華僑 Chinese overseas.
僑居却是家 the place of one's sojourn is home.
僑工事務所 Bureau of Labour Emigration.
僑民 emigrants.
僑胞 fellow countrymen overseas.
(a) **High. Inter., 喬 preceding.**

僑木與天參 tall trees reaching to the skies.

嶠 [4] **Ridge or highest peak of a mountain. Mountain track.**
746

嶠嶼 mountain peak arising from the sea.

橋 [2] 747   A bridge.

橋 墩 buttress of a bridge.
橋 梁 bridges; timbers or ties of a bridge.
橋 欄·杆 railing of a bridge.
橋 津 sides of a bridge.
[5] 橋 空 or 橋 洞 arches of a bridge.
修 橋 補 路 to repair bridges and make roads—works of merit.
吊 橋 or 懸 橋 a suspension bridge.
建 橋 to build bridges.
弔 橋 a drawbridge.
[10] 板 橋 a wooden bridge.
架 橋 a temporary bridge as thrown across by military exigencies.
浮 橋 floating or pontoon bridge.
石 橋 木 橋 stone and wooden bridges.
過 橋 丟 拐 to drop the staff after crossing the bridge—to neglect a benefactor.
[15] 過 橋 拆 橋 to remove the plank after crossing—to leave others in the lurch.
過 橋 挪 板, 落 井 下 石 to remove the planks after crossing a bridge, and drop stones on the head of one who has fallen into a well—to add injury to others in straits.
門 橋 a door lintel.
飛 橋 the rainbow.

(a) High. Inter. 喬 No. 744.

橋 梓 father and son. See No. 744.
山 有 橋 松 there are tall straight pines in the hills.

蕎 蕎 [2] 748   Buckwheat.

蕎·麥 buckwheat. ch'iao[2]·mai
蕎·麥 麵 buckwheat flour.

趫 [2] 749   Nimble; active. Good at climbing trees. To walk on stilts.

趫 戲 to walk on stilts.
趫 才 nimble; frivolous youth.

趫 趫 with rapid steps.
趫 足 to stand on tiptoe—it cannot be done for long, hence the phrase means—a very brief period.
亡 可 趫 足 待 也 unable to wait even for a brief period.
趫 蹻 active walker; nimble person.
輕·趫 or 趫 捷 nimble, active.

蹻 蹺 [1] 750   To raise the feet, as when sitting; to cross the legs.

蹻 勇 strong; active.
蹻 然 不 固 floating; unsettled.
蹻 脚 to cross the legs; the stroke to the right in writing, as in 戈.
蹻 脚 成 the cocked leg ch'eng character, i.e., the character written with the 乀 stroke as above.
[5] 蹻·起 脚·來 to stand on tiptoe; to cock the legs.
蹻 足 on tiptoe, hence used for a very brief period, see above No. 749—4.
蹻 蹻 martial bearing; strong.

(a) Read chioh[5]. Sandals. To go rapidly.

蹻 履 to step out boldly.
履 蹻 to wear sandals.

竅 [4] 751   A hole; a cavity. The mind. Intelligence.

竅 眼 intelligence; an open mind; a hole; an aperture.
竅 穴 an aperture; a hole.
七 竅 the seven apertures of the head, pertaining to the senses, eyes, nostrils, ears and mouth. The seven holes of the heart as media of intelligence.
中 竅 to hit the mark.
[5] 心 竅 intelligence. See below.—9.
懂 竅 to understand the knack of a thing.
有 竅 there is a trick or knack in it.
靈 竅 smart; clever.
開 心 竅 to give instruction; to open the mind.

CH'IAO. TS'IAO. (ㄘㄠ)

帗 [1] 752   Ancient mourning turban worn by women. To hem.

帗 邊 to hem a border.

愀 [3] 753   To blush.

愀 慘 sorrowful; melancholy.
孔 子 愀 然 作 色 Confucius changed colour.

㷕 [3] 754   To colour by smoke.

㷕 火 腿 to smoke a ham.
㷕 蚊·子 to smoke out mosquitoes.
㷕 黑 smoked black.

鍫 [1] 755   A shovel, a spade. To dig out.

鍫 塘 to dig a fish-pond.
鍫 泥 to dig the ground.
鍫 鍤 a spade.

憔 顇 [2] 756   Grieved; distressed; melancholy.

憔 悴 haggard from grief, or anxiety.
憔 悴 於 虐 政 suffering distress under tyrannical government.
憔 慮 distressing anxiety.

樵 [2] 757   Fuel. To burn; To gather fuel. A look-out.

樵 叟 an old wood-cutter.
樵 夫 or 樵 子 [3] wood-cutters.
樵 女 a female fuel gatherer.
樵 徑 a mountain path.
樵 斧 an axe.
樵 歌 or 樵 唱 wood-cutters' songs.
樵 薪 or 採 樵 to gather fuel.
樵 蘇 gathering sticks and grass for fuel.
樵 隱 a recluse who gathers fuel.

譙[4] To scold; to ridicule; to blame. Inter. 誚 No. 762.
758

譙 呵 scolding.
譙 讓 scolding.
譙 責 to scold; to blame.

(a) Read *ch'iao*[2] or *ts'iao*[2]. A look-out. A drum tower.

譙 樓 or 譙 門 a drum tower; look-out over the city gate.
譙 車 a high turret set on wheels for the use of archers.

俏[4] Like, similar.
759

俏 生 lifelike.
迷 生 於 俏 confusion arises from similarity.

(a) Handsome; beautiful.

俏 佳 人 a beautiful woman.
俏 步 walking with affected nicety.
俏 步 徐 行 a mincing gait.
俏 爭 pretty; elegant.
[5]俏 然 good looking; elegant.
俏·皮 pretty; winsome; smart.
俏·皮 皮·的 well proportioned; handsome.
俏 精 refined.
俏 貨 expensive goods.
[10]不 俏 not expensive.
賣 俏 to show off one's beauty.

峭[4]
陗 A steep hill. Precipitous.
760

峭 壁 a precipice.
峭 峻 steep and precipitous.
峭 嵯 precipitous cliffs.

(a) Harsh, severe, strict. Vigorous.

峭 乎 其 言 How severe are his words!
峭 亥 之 智 harsh and cruel practices.
峭 屬 harsh, sharp speech.
峭 寒 very severe cold.
[5]峭 急 eccentric and stern temper.
峭 拔 vigorous, as penmanship.
峭 法 harsh laws.
峭 直 stern and impatient.
峭 直 亥 深 very stern and impatient.

[10]峭 薄 mean; stingy; hard dealing.
峭 風 a biting wind.
精 峭 vigorous style of writing.

悄[3] Quiet; still; silent.
761

悄 悄 的 gently; softly.
悄 然 而 去 went very quietly.
悄 窺 stealthy looks.
悄 語 a whisper.
靜 悄 悄 的 quietly.

(a) Anxious; full of grief.

悄 切 bitter grief; with a voice full of grief.
憂 心 悄 悄 my heart is anxious and full of care.

誚[4] To blame; to scold; to ridicule.
762

誚 皮 人 to rail at; to humiliate.
誚 讓 to scold.
譏 誚 to ridicule; to satirize; to jeer.

CHIEH. TSIEH. (ㄐㄝ)

(Chie)

嗟[1] To sigh. An interjection of regret or sorrow.
763 Also pron. *chüeh*[1].

嗟 來 食 to pity a hungry man and invite him to take a meal without making any show of courtesy, in order to demean him.
嗟 呵 How lamentable!
嗟 呼 Alas!
嗟 嗟 heavy sighing.
[5]嗟 嘆 to sigh.
嗟 悼 to grieve and sigh.
嗟 憤 to sigh in vexation and anger.
嗟 懼 to be fearful.
嗟 我 婦 子 Alas! Our wives and families!
[10]嗟 嘆 詞 expression of grief or emotion.

(a) Read *chie*[4] or *tsie*[4]. To admire; to call.

嗟 稱 or 嗟 賞 to admire.
咄 嗟 at once; as soon as spoken.

咄 嗟 而 辦 no sooner was the order given than the thing was done.

褯[4] Children's garments. Read *hsi*[2.5]. A mat for wrapping garments. 褯·子 diaper.
764

借[4] To borrow. To lend. To avail of. To make a pretext of.
765

借 不 借 由 你 to lend or not rests with you.
借 債 之 抵 押 品 security for a loan.
借 債 還 債, 窟 隆 還 在 to incur debt in order to repay another debt, the hole still remains.
借 光 I am indebted to you, "allow me to pass." "By your leave."
[5]借 刀 殺 人 to borrow a knife to slay another—to involve another in the crime.
借 勢 to presume on power.
借 名 under pretext; under the name of.
借 問 "May I ask you?"
借 壽 to beg for life on behalf of a loved one dangerously ill, with the idea that one's life is shortened by so many years.
[10]借 外 債 to borrow foreign money.
借 字 or 借 畢 or 借 約 an IOU, a receipt for borrowed money.
借 宿 to beg a lodging.
借 意 or 借 喻 figuratively; metaphorically.
借 手 or 借 助 to lend a hand; to borrow assistance.
[15]借 據 receipts for loans.
借 本 to advance capital.
借 欵 a loan.
借 欵 合 同 loan agreement.
借 欵 大 綱 conditions of a loan.
[20]借 水 行 船 to borrow water to float the boat—to borrow capital.
借 用 to borrow.
借 端 開 釁 to make use of anything as a pretext for doing something else.
借 花 獻 佛 to borrow things from another to show respect to a guest—lit., borrow flowers to offer to Buddha.
借 貸 or 借 債 or 借 賬 to borrow.

²⁵借 賴 to rely on.
借·重 "May I beg of you?" To get someone to arrange a matter.
借 錢 to borrow money.
借 項 or 借 方 Dr. to, in bookkeeping, as 貸 項 or 貸 方 is Cr. by.

(a) If; supposing.
借 如 or 假 借 supposing; if.

姐 ³ An elder sister. Term of respect for a young lady.
766

姐·夫 or 姐 丈 an elder sister's husband.
姐·姐 an elder sister; young ladies.
姐·妹 sisters.
小·姐 a young lady; Miss.

藉 ⁴ To lean on; to avail oneself of; by means of. To help. Distinguish 籍 No. 507.
耤
767

藉 以 消 遣 made use of ....to pass the time.
藉 口 to make a pretext of.
藉 呈 beg you to take—this note for me.
藉 手 something to trust to.
⁵藉 故 推 辭 to make excuses under any pretext.
藉 有 resulted in.
藉 稱 to allege.
藉 端 to make excuses; to make a pretext.
藉 端 生 事 avail oneself of a pretext to stir up trouble.
¹⁰藉 端 敲 詐 to take advantage of the occasion to blackmail.
藉 神 庇 佑 relying upon the protection of the gods.
藉 詞 on the plea; to give as an excuse.
藉 資 to avail oneself of.
藉 重 to lean on the assistance of another.
¹⁵以 免 藉 口 to remove all pretexts.
助 者 藉 也 the aid system means mutual dependence.
憑 藉 to rely on; to trust to.

(a) A mat; rushes.
藉 用 白 茅 for mats use white rushes.

枕 藉 pillow and mat—close together, mutual assistance.

(b) Read *chi*²·⁵. In disorder; confusion.
口 語 藉 藉 confused jabbering.
狼 藉 in confusion, as the remains of a feast when the guests leave the table.

(c) To offer, as tribute; to tread on.
藉 恩 or 藉 福 M a n y thanks! Much obliged!
藉 田 fields cultivated for the emperor.
人 皆 藉 吾 弟 they all came to my residence.

CHIEH. (ㄐㄝ)
(under *chieh* also 619–636)

莢 ¹·⁵. Pods of leguminous plants. Seeds.
768

莢 果 leguminous seeds.
莢 物 pods.
莢 錢 small light coins used in *Han Dyn.*
榆 莢 or 榆·錢ㄦ seeds of the elm.
豆 莢 bean pods.

蛺 ²·⁵.
769 A butterfly.

蛺 蝶 a butterfly with yellow and red wings and black markings; the caterpillar is black.

鋏 ¹·⁵. A pair of pincers for use at a fire. A sword. Also
770 read *chia*⁵.

火 鋏 pincers to hold things in a fire.
長 鋏 歸 來 乎 Long sword! Let us go home.

刦 ²·⁵.
刧 To plunder; to rob openly.
771

刦 刦 eagerly; importunately.
刦 奪 or 打 刦 to plunder; to rob.
刦 掠 一 空 made a clean sweep.
刦 掠 敵 地 to invade e n e m y territory.

⁵刦 案 a case of robbery.
刦 灰 turned to ashes; perished.
刦 獄 to break open a gaol and liberate the prisoners.
刦 略 or 刦 制 oppression; coercion.
刦 盜 robbers; banditti.
¹⁰刦 色 to ravish; to rape.

(a) An era; a *kalpa*, a period of time beyond calculation. (*Budd.*).

刦 數 a fatal calamity.
刦 波 or 刦 波 簸 陀 a *kalpa*, of which there are three kinds.
浩 刦 a great calamity, from a misapprehension of the word, regarding it as meaning destructive. The steps of the palace.
萬 刦 莫 贖 countless a g e s—of pain—could not atone for it.
避 刦 to avoid an impending calamity, *see above.* A. 3.

潔 ²·⁵.
772 Clean; pure; clear.

潔 心 pure in heart.
潔 樽 to cleanse the cups—conventional phrase in invitations to feasts.
潔 淨 pure; clear; chaste.
潔 癖 so fond of cleanliness that it becomes an obsession.
潔 白 white and pure.
潔 盃 候 叙 I have cleansed my cups and await your conversation—conventional phrase in invitations.

桀 ²·⁵. A hen-roost. Cruel. The last ruler of the *Hsia*
773 Dynasty.

桀 犬 吠 堯 *Chieh's* dog barked at *Yao*—every one acts according to the nature of the one whom he serves.
桀 紂 *Chieh* and *Chou*, last rulers of the *Hsia* and *Shang* Dynasties respectively—used as typical of all that is fierce and cruel.
桀 驁 tyrannical and proud.
桀 黠 cruel and crafty.
桀 黠 者 流 the cruel and crafty class.
助 桀 爲 虐 helping *Chieh* to be tyrannical—adding evil to evil.

(a) A hero; brave. Inter., 傑 next. Luxuriant.

桀 桀 rank growth.
邦 之 桀 分 the hero of his country.

傑 杰 2.5.
774   A hero; heroic.

傑 作 masterpiece.
傑 出 eminent; outstanding.
傑 性 of heroic disposition.
豪·傑 brave man; a hero.

偈 775   2.5. Brave; martial. forceful. Hasty rush.

偈 偈 乎 forceful.
偈 偈 為 義 earnest in the performance of public duties.

(a) Read *chi*⁴. To versify or paraphrase in a chant; a hymn; a secret code. (Budd.).
偈 語 Buddhist hymns.

揭 776   1.5. To lift up; to lift off; to uncover; to raise; to pull open.

揭 印 to break open or remove seals.
揭 回 to remove; to take back.
揭 封 to tear off the strips of paper used as official seals.
揭 幕 禮 unveiling ceremony.
⁵揭 瓦 to take off tiles.
揭 蓋 紅 巾 to unveil the bride.
揭 竿 to raise a revolt.
揭 竿 起 亂 outbreak of rebellion.
揭 簾 to raise a screen blind.
¹⁰揭·起·來 to raise; to lift up.
揭·開 to open by lifting a cover or lid.

(a) To make known; to publish.

揭 參 to impeach.
揭 告 to prosecute.
揭 帖 or 揭 貼 placard, usually anonymous.
揭 揚 to publish abroad.
⁵揭 榜 or 揭 曉 to publish a list of successful candidates.
揭 短 to reveal the failings of another.
揭 示 to post proclamations.

揭 謬 to call attention to errors, as in a book, etc.
顛 沛 之 揭 when a tree falls the root is revealed.

(b) To borrow.

揭 借 to borrow money.
揭 單 or 揭 字 an IOU.
揭 項 borrowed capital.

(c) Growing rank.

葭 菼 揭 揭 rank growing sedges.

(d) Read *ch'i*⁴. To raise the skirts.

淺 則 揭 in shallow water I raise my skirts.

碣 777   2.5. A stone tablet. A peak.

碑 碣 commemorative pillars with inscriptions.

竭 778   2.5. To put forth effort to the utmost; to exhaust. Exhausted.

竭 到 to the utmost.
竭 力 to do the best.
竭 慮 the utmost anxiety.
竭 憊 utterly weary.
⁵竭 才 to exert the ability to the full.
竭 澤 而 漁 drain the pond and catch the fish—to ruin the source of supply, kill the goose that lays the golden egg.
竭 盡 exhausted; finished; with a full purpose.
竭 衷 with all my heart.
竭 誠 absolutely sincere.
¹⁰竭 蹶 to fall down.
竭 蹶 而 趨 to proceed with great haste.

羯 779   2.5. To castrate a ram. Deer's skin.

羯 古 a tribe of *Tartars* or *Hsiungnu* from the place in next phrase.
羯 室 ancient name for a place in Shansi.
羯 羊 a wether.
羯 鼓 a deer-skin drum.

拮 780   2.5. Occupied; labouring hard. To lay hold of. To pursue.

拮 据 hampered; perplexed; embarrassed, as for want of money.

桔 781   2.5. A well sweep.

桔·子 small mandarin orange.
桔 梗 a root from which is made a cough medicine.
桔 槔 a well sweep.

結 782   2.5. To contract; to give a bond for.

結 保 or 出 結 or 具 結 to give security; to enter into a bond.
結 實 信 據 a substantial guarantee.
結 拜 or 結 盟 to pledge in a sworn brotherhood.
結 訟 to go to law.
具 安 分 結 bound over to keep the peace.
具 甘 結 or 具 保 結 to give a bond.
取 結 to take a security.
甘 結 a bond.

(a) To tie knots. A knot. To connect or unite.

結 交 to form an acquaintance; to associate with.
結 交 須 勝 己 make friends with those superior to yourself.
結 仇 or 結 怨 to contract enmity; to arouse dislike.
結 絆 or 結 夥 to form companionships.
⁵結 合 to unite; to combine; to associate.
結 合 力 affinity. (*Chem.*).
結 喉 "Adam's apple."
結 契 to be on intimate terms with.
結 婚 證 書 certificate of marriage.
¹⁰結 婚 自 由 liberty to make one's own betrothal.
結 嫌 to contract a dislike for.
結·實 strong; tough; enduring. *See below.* C. 2.
結 廬 to build houses; to make booths.

結 念 to remember; to bear in mind.

[15]結 核 or 結 節 tubercles; nodules.

結 核 性·的 tubercular.

結 核 病 or 肺 結 核 or 肺 病 tuberculosis.

結 核 菌 tubercle bacillus.

結 構 or 結 撰 to construct; a structure; to compose, as literature.

[20]結 燥 constipation.

結 社 to form an association of two or more.

結 穴 the keynote of a phrase, the dominant idea; favourable site for a grave.

結 納 to associate with.

結 累 to entangle; to involve.

[25]結 綵 to festoon; festoons.

結 綱 to make a net.

結 締 tied together; united.

結 締 組 織 connective tissue.

結 縭 to tie the sash—to marry.

[30]結 繩 knotted cords—an ancient mode of reckoning and recording.

結 腸 the colon.

結 膜 the conjunctiva.

結 膜 炎 conjunctivitis.

結 舌 or 結 口 tongue-tied; stammering.

[35]結 草 from the next—to requite kindness.

結 草 神 from a legend of *Wei ko* 魏 顆 of 晋 who, at his father's request, married the father's favourite concubine rather than bury her with him. Later when fighting against *Ch'in* 秦, he was assisted by an old man who tied the grass into knots to prevent the enemy from running away, this old man afterwards revealed himself as the father of the girl.

結 草 衔 環 gratitude—from the above and another legend of *Yang pao* 楊 寶, who saved a bird which was injured, when the bird was able to fly he liberated it, and the same night a youth appeared to him and presented him with jade bracelets.

結 茅 to build a house.

結 親 or 結 婚 to marry. *See above.* A. 9-10.

[40]結 連 to band together; a confederacy.

結 髮 first wife; the wife to whom a man was betrothed in childhood.

結 黨 to form cliques; to make a conspiracy.

勾·結 to conspire.

單 結 a single knot.

[45]完 一 個 結 tie a knot.

巴·結 to toady to; to flatter.

帶 結 a knot of ribbon.

打 結 to tie knots.

死 結 a hard knot, one that will not slip.

[50]活 結 a slipknot, a running knot.

雙 結 a double knot.

(b) Cohesion; coagulation. To congeal.

結 冰 or 結 凍 to freeze.

結 冰·的 freezing.

結 凍 點 or 結 冰 點 freezing point.

結 力 or 凝 結 力 cohesion.

[5]結 晶 crystallization.

結 晶 體 crystals.

結 毒 an accumulation of virus, as in an abscess.

凝 結 to coagulate; to freeze; to congeal.

(c) To bear fruit; to form, as fruit; to finish.

結 句 the concluding sentence.

結[1] 實[2] or 結[1] 果·子 to bear fruit. *See above.* A. 12.

結 局 the outcome; the fruit of; the result; the issue.

結 意 to sum up.

[5]結·成 子[3] 粒 to form grains or seeds.

結 束 to wind up; to close.

結[2] 果 the finale; the outcome; result; effect; the final issue.

結 果 生 命 to put an end to life. *See below.* D. 2.

結 案 to wind up a lawsuit.

[10]結 痂 or 結 吧 to form a scab.

結 穗 to form into ears, as grain.

結 籠 to gather the threads of a narrative.

結 論 the conclusion.

了·結 or 完·結 to finish; completed.

收 結 to bring to a conclusion.

(d) To pay, as accounts.

結 冊 a balance sheet.

結[2] 果·了 他 "settled him;" "finished his account;" to kill off an enemy.

結 清 settled; all paid.

結 賬 to pay up an account.

月 結 monthly settlement.

節 結 quarterly settlements or statements of accounts.

草 草 了 結 careless winding up of a case.

詰 2.5. **To investigate. To keep in order or restrain. To punish.**
783

詰 口 供 to take depositions.

詰 屈 intractable; harsh, as sounds; abstruse; obscure.

詰 據 to take evidence.

詰 旦 or 詰 朝[1] tomorrow morning.

[5]詰 究 close scrutiny.

詰 罪 to examine culprits; to punish.

詰 訊 or 詰 問 or 盤 詰 to question; to examine.

詰 誅 暴 慢 to punish the rebellious.

詰 責 to disgrace; to hold up to reprobation.

[10]詰 邦 國 to reduce refractory states.

以 詰 四 方 so as to restrain the people on every side.

孑 4.5. **Alone; orphaned. Remainder.**
784

孑 影 孤 單 left solitary with one's shadow.

孑 然 一 身 solitary; lonely.

孑 焉 如 寄 a man without fixed abode.

孑 立 to stand alone.

[5]孑 身 alone; solitary.

孑 遺 the remainder, *see below.*—8.

不 可 以 孑 弦 求 五 音 you cannot get all the notes of music from a single string.

靡 有 孑 遺 not a solitary man was left.

(a) A halberd.

句 孑 a halberd.

(b) Conspicuous. Small.

孑 孑 干 旄 the staffs with the yak-tail tassels stand out prominently.

孑孒爲義 petty affairs.

孑孒 short and small—孑 is explained as a man who has lost his right arm, and 孒 as one who has lost the left arm; both are deficient, and the words are used for short, or for small, and from that referred to larvae, especially those of the mosquito.

小智孒義 small wisdom and petty patriotism.

踕 4.5. **To stumble; to fall back. To stammer.**
785

踕後 to stumble backwards.

訐 2.5. **To accuse; to charge with.**
786

告訐 to lay a charge against.
稟訐 to impeach.
面訐 a personal accusation.

(a) To pry into secrets.

訐揚 to gossip about a man's private affairs or about his faults.
訐直 to expose the faults of another under cover of being blunt.
惡訐以爲直也 I hate those who make known secrets and think that they are straightforward.

CHIEH TSIEH (ㄐㄝ)

浹 2.5. **Water penetrating; damp.**
787

浹日 ten days, from the cyclical character 甲 to that of 癸.
浹洽 on cordial terms with; friendly.
浹洽於中 or 浹於肌膚 to be thoroughly imbued with.
浹浹 damp; saturated.
浹辰 twelve days, from the cyclical character 子 to that of 亥.

婕 2.5. **Handsome.**
788

婕妤 a title conferred upon an accomplished imperial concubine of the *Han Dyn.*

捷 2.5. **Alert, nimble. Prompt. Clever, smart.**
789

捷徑 a short cut.
捷才 nimble wits.
捷捷 active; nimble; alert.
捷於影響 as quick in reply as an echo.
⁵捷發 rapid rise to prosperity.
捷給 smart repartee.
捷綱 rapid outlines.
捷足 light of foot; nimble.
捷足先登 the nimble man gets there first.
¹⁰捷速 rapidly.
敏捷 smart; quick-witted; nimble-minded; alert and active.
直捷 prompt; swift to act.

(a) To win a victory.

捷報 announcement of successes or victories.
報捷 to announce a victory.
連捷 successive victories.

(b) Used in transliterating.

捷克斯洛佛克 Czecho-Slovakia.

睫
睞 1.5. **Eyelashes.**
790

睫毛 eyelashes.
交睫 crossed eyelashes.
眉睫之間 between brow and lash—very near; urgent.
近在眉睫 pressing very close; urgent.
羣飛而集於蚊睫 (infinitesimally small midges) fly in swarms and gather on the eyelash of a mosquito.

箑 4.5. **A fan. Also read sha⁵.**
791

緁 2.5. **To join; to splice; to braid.**
792

緁續 to splice.

截 2.5. **To cut in two. To intercept; to obstruct.**
793

截一段去 cut off a piece.
截住 or 截止 or 截攔 to intercept; to cut off; to stop.
截住去路 or 截人歸路 to cut off the retreat.
截剿 to intercept the enemy.
⁵截奪 to carry by force to.
截拏 to arrest; to stop.
截敵 to cut off the enemy.
截斷 to divide; to sever.
截斷交通 to interrupt communications.
¹⁰截獲 to intercept.
截留 to detain; to retain goods or money for local use when it should have been forwarded on.
截留鹽稅 to withhold the salt revenue.
截紙 to cut paper.
截角 to cut off a corner, as of an envelope.
¹⁵截趾適履 to cut the toes to fit the shoes.
截路 communications cut off.
截還 to divert an officer on his way to one post, in order to fill another.
截金雕玉 cut gold and carved jade—a fine piece of writing.
截長補短 to cut off from the long to supply the deficiency of the short.
²⁰截開 to cut into strips or pieces.
截面 or 橫截面 a cross-section.
截髮剉薦 (a mother) cut off her hair and (sold it secretly to a neighbour) to procure dainties for her son's unexpected visitor, and straw for his horse.
截髮示信 she cut off her hair as a token of her faithfulness—to her husband, who in dying wished her to re-marry.
有截 to bring under restraint.
海外有截 his authority was recognised beyond the bounds of the empire.

(a) In the following.

截截 to quibble.
截截善辯 good at quibbling arguments.

巇 4.5.
794　Name of a hill; a high hill.

節 2.5.
795　A verse; a chapter; a section. A joint, a knot.
Details.

節 上 生 枝 branches springing from the joints—one complication arising from another.

節 文 details; externals; to adorn.

節 次 repeatedly; on several occasions.

節 略 an abridgement.

[5]節。目 sections; paragraphs.

節 節 難 difficulties at every joint —like a snake crawling through a bamboo tube.

節 節 高 growing higher every joint—gradually rising.

節 經 on several occasions.

七 節 車 a train with seven carriages or trucks.

[10]小 節 a trifle; unimportant.

有 關 節·的 jointed.

枝 節 branches and joints—complications and difficulties.

章 節 chapters and verses.

脫·了 節 put out of joint.

[15]關 節 or 結 節 joints.

(a) Moderation, economy. To economize.

節·制 limits to expenditure; under control; temperate; within bounds. *See below.* B. 1.

無 節 制 intemperate; uncontrolled; lavish.

節 度 economy; revenue; definite outlay. *See below.* C. 1.

節 用 or 儉 節 frugal; careful use of; within limits.

節 用 而 愛 人 economy in expenditure and love for the people.

節 省 economical.

節 衣 縮 食 economy in clothing and food.

節 飲 食 temperance in eating and drinking.

(b) Chastity, purity. To regulate, to restrain.

節 制 資 本 to regulate capital.

節 哀 to restrain grief; to receive consolation.

節 哀 順 變 restrain your grief and bow to the inevitable

changes—conventional phrase in condolences for death of parent.

節 婦 or 節 女 a chaste woman.

[5]節 孝 wifely fidelity and filial piety—used of a woman who does not marry when her betrothed dies.

節 孝 祠 shrines to the above.

節 慾 to curb the passions or desires.

節 操 [4] moral integrity; high moral principles; chaste.

節 烈 rigorously chaste, as a widow.

[10]節 義 chastity, purity—of a woman who does not marry, as above; or of a widow who does not re-marry.

節 齋 purification and fasting before sacrifice.

名 節 one's reputation.

失 節 to lose chastity by re-marrying or by marrying when her betrothed has died.

守 節 to remain single, as when a betrothed husband has died before the wedding is consummated; or to remain a widow.

[15]禮 節 formality; etiquette.

貞 節 chastity.

(c) Divisions of time. A term. A festival. A holiday. A birthday.

節 度 quarterly returns of revenue. *See above.* A. 3.

節 敬 a present to a teacher at stated periods.

節 期 or 節·氣 or 節 令 or 節 候 holiday times; festivals.

節·氣 the 24 periods of 15 days each which make a year, *see table in appendix.*

[5]節 禮 presents sent on a festival.

節 規 monies paid three times a year at the festivals.

中 秋 節 Mid-autumn Festival, 15th of 8th lunar month.

佳 節 a festival.

元 宵 節 Lantern Festival on the first full moon of the new year.

[10]八 節 the equinoxes, the solstices, and the first day of each season.

天 中 節 the Dragon-boat Festival on the 5th of the 5th lunar month.

季 節 a season.

季 節 風 or 季 合 風 the Monsoons.

收 賬 節 to collect the bills at the seasons.

[15]時 節 a season; a time; a juncture.

晚 節 the evening of life.

正 當[1]時 節 just in the height of the season.

端 午 節 or 端 陽 節 Dragon-boat Festival on the 5th of the 5th lunar month.

臨 大 節 in a great emergency; at a crisis.

[20]萬 壽 節 emperor's birthday.

過 節 to observe a festival.

(d) Rhythm.

節 奏 or 節 拍 rhythm or time of music.

節 樂 to keep time for music.

湊 節 to beat time.

大 禮 與 天 地 同 節 the rules of propriety have the same rhythm as heaven and earth.

應 節 to keep in time.

擊 節 to beat time.

(e) A tally or token; credentials.

節 旄 a tasselled staff sent with an imperial courier.

使 節 imperial messengers.

掌 節 to hold the token of authority.

旌 節 flag token for the road.

瑞 節 a jade token of rank, etc.

符 節 token of delegated authority.

(f) Lofty.

節 彼 南 山 lofty is that southern mountain.

(g) Capitals of pillars.

山 節 藻 梲 he had hills carved on the capitals and duckweed carved on the beams of the rafters.

櫛 2.5.
796　A comb. To comb the hair.

櫛 工 a hairdresser.

櫛 比 相 連 joined closely together like the teeth of a comb.

櫛 比 而 居 dwelling closely together like the teeth of a comb.

櫛 風 沐 雨 combed by the wind and bathed by the rain—hardships of travel.

巾 櫛 towel and comb—a concubine.

癤 2.5.

797 A small sore. A pimple.

癤·子 a boil; a rash.

大 癤·子 heat rash.

瘡 癤 a boil.

卪 2.5.

卩 A joint. A seal. Radical 26. Ancient form of 節 No. 795. National Phon.

798 letter for ts, written ㄗ.

楫 4.5.

艥

櫂 An oar or paddle. To row. Pron. chi².⁴

799

楫 師 boatman.

接 1.5. To receive; to welcome; to meet. To take with the

800 hand; to accept.

接 交 to accept a trust.

接 任 to take office; to take over a position.

接 准 to receive—from a superior or an equal.

接 印 to take over the seals of office.

⁵接 印 視 事 to take over the seals and attend to the business of the post.

接 取 to take; to receive.

接 奉 to receive—from a superior.

接 客 to welcome guests.

接 展 to receive and open a letter.

¹⁰接 待 to entertain.

接 待 室 reception room.

接 應 to be in reserve.

接 應 兵 reserve troops.

接 手 to take over, as duties; a receiver; an accomplice.

¹⁵接 據 to receive—from a subordinate.

接 收 or 接 受 to accept; to receive.

接 替 to take the place of.

接 班 to take a turn on duty.

接 生 婆 a midwife.

²⁰接 神 to welcome the gods.

接 管 to take charge of a situation; to take over the management of.

接 納 to receive; to accept.

接 聲 筒 ear-trumpet.

接 觸 to come in contact with; to strike against; to encounter; to be infected with.

²⁵接 見 to meet officially.

接 載 to receive for shipment.

接 辦 to take over the management of.

接·過·來 to receive; to take over.

接 運 to receive and forward.

³⁰接 閱 to receive and peruse.

接 防 to take over; to relieve, as troops, etc.

接 領 to take charge of.

接 頭 to meet and discuss.

接 風 to welcome back.

³⁵接 風 酒 a welcome feast to returning friend.

迎 接 to welcome.

(a) To join, to connect, to graft. To succeed to.

接·上 to join on.

接·上 帶 下 linked with what precedes and with what follows.

接·不 上 cannot be connected.

接 仗 or 接 戰 to join battle.

⁵接 伴 to make a comrade of.

接 力 賽 跑 relay race.

接 口 to join in a conversation.

接 合 to join; to link.

接 吻 to kiss.

¹⁰接 壤 adjoining boundary.

接 好 on good terms with.

接 尾 詞 or 接 尾 語 a suffix.

接 引 to guide; to lead astray.

接 木 to graft.

¹⁵接 武 measured tread; placing the foot almost in the print of that of another.

接 洽 to come to an agreement after negotiations; to meet together.

接 洽 事 件 a matter for negotiation.

接 淅 hasty preparation, from the next.

接 淅 而 行 he took up the washed rice and departed.

²⁰接°濟 to help; to supply; to reinstate.

接 濟 隊 reserve troops.

接 物 to be of help to others.

接 線 to make a telephone connection.

接 續 to spin thread.

²⁵接 續 or 接 連 to join on; to connect with.

接 續 詞 a conjunction.= 連 詞

接·着 唱 to join in chorus.

接 聯 to join two things together.

接·着 connectedly; to succeed to a position.

³⁰接 踵 而 至 they came on uninterruptedly; arriving successively.

接 近 near to; adjoining; to adjoin.

接 電 鈕 electric switch button.

接 骨 to unite a fractured bone.

榇 1.5.

801 To graft. Inter. preceding.

CH'IEH. (ㄑㄧㄝ)

(Ch'ie)

茄 ² The egg-plant or brinjal. The mandrake.

802

茄·子 or 牛 心 茄 the egg-plant.

CH'IEH.　TS'IEH. (ㄑㄧㄝ)

(Ch'ie or Ts'ie).

且 ³ Moreover; now; still; further.

803

且 住 Stop!

且 住 爲 佳 Won't you stop for a while?

且 別 temporary separation.

且 問 let me now ask.

⁵且 夫 or 且 今 now; for instance.

且 如 supposing that; thus; as.

且 慢 Gently! Not so fast!

且 或 or else.

且 然 granted that; it is also.

¹⁰且 爾 言 過 矣 and further, you speak wrongly.

且 說 to resume; let us now speak of; moreover; begins a new paragraph in narrative.

況 且 moreover; yet; furthermore.

姑 且 for a time; for a little while.

暫 且 for the time being.

¹⁵權 且 under the circumstances.

而 且 moreover.

苟 且 rude; remiss.

(a) Also, both. Indicates alternative or simultaneous action.

且 以 喜 樂, 且 以 永 日 both to give you pleasure and to prolong the day.

且 信 且 疑 between belief and doubt.

且 行 且 止 hesitating; faltering.

且 馳 且 射 as he galloped he shot his arrows.

富 且 貴 rich and also honourable.

(b) Read *chü*[4]. Dignified.

有 姜 有 且 reverent and dignified.

(c) Read *chü*[1]. A final particle; many and great. See No. 3601-1.

其 樂 只 且 his pleasure is great.

士 曰 旣 且 one said, "I have been."

曰 父 母 且 (Heaven) who art called our parent!

CH'IEH. (ㄑㄩㄝ)

匧 篋
804
4.5.
A trunk; a portfolio.

篋 笥 or 篋·子 a satchel; a portfolio.

篋 衍 a bamboo satchel.

愜
805
4.5. Satisfied; contented; cheerful.

愜 心 or 愜 意 satisfied and pleased.

愜 情 satisfied.

愜 洽 arranged satisfactorily.

爽 愜 elated; joyful.

慊
806
4.5. Happy; contented.

慊 於 己 to satisfy oneself.

自 慊 content; well-pleased.

(a) Read *ch'ien*[3]. Enraged; to hate; dissatisfied.

慊 慊 dissatisfied; displeased.

愒
807
3.5. To rest; to stop.

捿 愒 to sojourn.

汔 可 小 愒 it may be that they will get a little rest from their (oppressive) burdens.

(a) Read *k'ai*[4]. To desire.

愒 日 to desire long life.

愒 生 to love life.

挈
808
4.5. To raise. To assist.

挈 出 凡 塵 above the cares of the world.

提 挈 to recommend; to carry.

挈 缾 to raise or draw a bottle of water—of extremely limited experience or knowledge.

左 提 右 挈 mutual assistance.

(a) Read *ch'i*[4]. A convenant or deed. To cut. To record on a board. Inter. 契 No. 551.

挈 獄 訟 之 要 record the important criminal offences.

在 板 挈 也 to record it on a board.

書 挈 所 錄 what is recorded in the deed.

租 挈 deeds for rent of fields.

(b) An instrument for burning the tortoise shell in divining.

挈 龜 to scorch the tortoise shell.

(c) Exhausted; deficient.

鍥
809
4.5. A sickle. To cut; to oppress.

鍥 斷 to cut off, as communications.

鍥 朝 涉 之 脛 (*Chou hsin* 紂 辛) cut off the legs of those who were crossing the ford in the morning;—to please his concubine, who wished to know whether the bones of the young or those of the old contained marrow.

鍥 薄 to oppress; to treat badly.

刻 鍥 to carve; to engrave.

怯
810
2.5. To be afraid. Cowardly; nervous.

怯 場 scared; embarrassed.

怯 夫 a coward.

怯 志 weak of purpose; vacillating.

怯 恥 or 怯 羞 bashful; blushing.

⁵怯 懦 to manifest cowardice or fear; vacillating.

怯 症 pulmonary consumption; wasting disease.

怯 膽 or 膽 怯 cowardly; fearful.

怯 陣 afraid to go into battle.

怯 風 to fear draughts.

¹⁰畏 怯 timid; nervous; afraid.

瘦 怯 lean and nervous.

CH'IEH or TS'IEH. (ㄑㄩㄝ)

切
811
4.5. To slice; to mince.
Tone 1. "4" indicates optional tone.

切¹不 動 too tough to be cut or sliced.

切⁴中 or 切⁴當 or 親 切⁴ cutting into—to the purpose; apposite.

不 切⁴當 or 不 切⁴題 not to the point; inapposite.

切¹刀 a large kitchen knife.

⁵切¹分 (*fen*[4]) to divide into shares or parts.

切¹剮 to tear or rend.

切¹成 碎 片 cut into pieces.

切¹斷 to cut asunder.

切¹書 to cut a book.

¹⁰切¹片 to cut into slices.

切¹玉 如 切¹泥 it will slice jade like slicing mud—of a good sword.

切¹玉 斷 犀 it will slice jade and sever rhinoceros hide—said of a good sword.

切¹痛 severe, sharp pain.

切¹碎 to cut into small pieces. *See above.*—7.

¹⁵切¹磋 to cut and polish—to cultivate oneself.

切¹磋 得 體 to cut and polish until it was worthy—earnest remonstrance produced good results.

切¹線 a tangent.

切¹肉 minced meat; sliced meat; to buy cooked meat.

切 膚 之 痛 deep grief; sharp pain.

²⁰切 身 or 切 膚 something that must be borne personally, as grief, etc.

切 開 to cut apart; to sever or slice.

切 音 or 切 韻 pronunciation, from the 反 切 see below.—28.

切 骨 deep, bitter hatred that cuts to the bone.

切 麵 Noodles.

²⁵切 齒 to gnash the teeth.

切 齒 腐 心 gnashing the teeth in deep anger or hatred.

不 切 事 no practical value—"it cuts no ice."

反 切 system of spelling in Chinese dictionaries, two characters are given, the initial sound of one combining with the final of the other to give the sound and the tone. As 甫 晚 f(u w)an³ gives 反 fan³ The second character gives the tone and the final.

(a) To feel, to urge. Pressing; urgent. (a)–(d) Tone 4.

切 切 的 urgently.

切 切 偲 偲 怡 怡 如 也 earnest, pressing and pleased.

切 叩 I earnestly pray.

切 問 而 近 思 inquiring with earnestness and reflecting with self-application.

⁵切 囑 to charge or enjoin.

切 實 real; sincere; genuine.

切 實 辦 法 effective steps or methods.

切 峻 urgent and severe.

切 己 with personal consequences.

¹⁰切 底 根 究 sift it to the bottom.

切 心 urgently.

切 忌 prohibited.

切 愛 ardent affection.

切 於 學 者 之 身 adapted to the needs of the student.

¹⁵切 望 eager; earnest; keen.

切 直 之 言 straight talk.

切 結 a secure guarantee or bond.

切 脈 to feel the pulse.

²⁰切 要 very impo... ...re to remember; do n... ...ce.

切 諫 earnest remonstrance.

切 責 severe rebuke.

切 赴 "immediate," as a message or a letter.

切 速 urgent; immediate.

²⁵切 願 willing; most desirous.

(b) Intimate; related.

切 洽 on good terms; intimate.

切 近 close at hand; closely related.

親 切 closely related; intimate; also apposite, see above.—2.

關 切 concerned with; friendly with; having interest in; anxious about.

(c) All, entirely, the lot.

一 切 the whole lot; altogether.

一 切 所 有 all there is; all he has.

(d) Before a negative it adds emphasis.

切 勿 or 切 不 可 on no account; Don't!

確 切 不 疑 beyond all doubt; that is quite certain.

沏 1.5. **The noise of water rippling. Read ch'i¹·⁵. To infuse tea.**
812

沏 茶 to make tea.

竊
竊 4.5.
813 **To steal. Stealthy.**

竊 位 or 竊 命 to usurp authority; to assume authority.

竊 取 to take with stealth.

竊 號 to usurp imperial titles.

竊 柄 to usurp authority.

⁵竊 案 a case of theft.

竊 物 病 or 竊 盜 狂 kleptomania.

竊 窺 or 竊 視 to steal a glance.

竊 賊 or 竊 匪 or 竊 犯 a thief.

偷 竊 or 竊 盜 larceny; theft.

¹⁰失 竊 stolen.

小 竊 petty larceny.

行 竊 to steal.

(a) Term of depreciation used in petitions, etc.

竊 取 程 子 之 意 I have ventured to take the views of the philosopher Ch'eng.

竊 意 or 竊 思 or 竊 念 or 竊 查 My humble opinion is.

竊 有 請 I venture to ask.

竊 氏 I; as used by a woman.

⁵竊 民 We; I.

竊 比 I venture to compare.

竊 照 "I venture to inform you." —opening phrase of report from a subordinate.

竊 聞 I have heard....

竊 謂 I venture to say....

竊 身 I, myself; as used by a man.

妾 4.5. **A concubine. Conventional term used by women when speaking of themselves.**
814

妾 身 Your handmaiden; conventional term used by women.

侍 妾 female attendants.

立 妾 or 置 妾 to take a concubine.

處 妾 a virgin purchased as a concubine.

賤 妾 or 小 妾 my concubine.

喋 4.5. **Speaking evil. Gobbling sound made by ducks.**
815

喋 佞 slander.

喋 喋 slanders; specious talk.

喋 喋 noise made by ducks feeding.

CHIEN. (ㄐㄝ)

菅 1 **A coarse grass used for mats.**
816

草 菅 人 命 to regard human life as mere straw.

編 菅 a straw mat.

視 如 菅 草 to regard as straw—worthless.

姦 1 **Adultery, fornication, licentiousness. To debauch, to ravish.** Inter. 818.
817

姦 回 obscene; criminal.

姦 夫 an adulterer; a paramour.

姦 婦 an adulteress.

姦 婦 女 to rape; to ravish.

⁵姦 情 circumstances of adultery.

姦 拐 to seduce and carry off.

姦 淫 or 姦 汚 fornication; lewdness; to rape.

姦 生 illegitimate birth.

姦 邪 obscene; vile.

¹⁰強 姦 rape; forced intercourse.

情姦 or 順姦 illicit intercourse with the consent of the woman.
通姦 criminal intercourse.
雞姦 sodomy.

(a) Inter. 奸 next. Crafty, villainous; false; treacherous.

姦究 villains; scoundrels; traitors.
姦·細 a spy.
姦雄 an able scoundrel.

奸¹ Crafty, villainous, false, wicked, disloyal.
818

奸人 or 奸夫 an artful villain.
奸佞 or 奸巧 or 奸壞 or 奸骨 doublefaced; artful; deceptive.
奸刁 designing.
奸吏 corrupt underlings.
⁵奸商 dishonest traders.
奸惡 or 奸險 bad; malicious.
奸淫 treacherous; lecherous.
奸狠 brutal; cruel.
奸盜 villainy and robbery.
¹⁰奸·細 a spy.
奸臣 a traitor minister.
奸計 a crafty device.
奸詐 deceitful; fraudulent.
奸詭陷人 use crafty schemes in order to injure others.
¹⁵奸謀 to plot against; a treacherous plot.
奸賊 a scoundrel.
奸邪 corrupt; wicked.
奸雄 an able scoundrel; one who pretends to goodness.
奸頑 a cunning rogue.
²⁰奸黨 a cabal; a society for rebellion or other traitorous purposes.
作奸 to act the traitor.
漢奸 a traitorous Chinese, one who goes over to the other side.
衆奸 an evilly disposed mob.
盤奸緝盜 deal with smugglers and seize robbers.

开¹ Even, level. To raise in both hands.
开
819

开官氏 The wife of Confucius.

橐³
秆
820
A bunch; a handful.

豜¹
821
A pig of three years.

獻豜于公 they offered a pig to their ancestors.

趼³ Callous skin on hands or feet. Blisters.
822

胝趼 corns; callouses on hands or feet.
重趼 thick callosities.

(a) Read yen⁴. Cloven hoofs.

蹄趼 horny hoofs.

囝³ A child. This character has many readings according to locality, e.g., nŏ, or tsäi, or kiang.
823

肩¹ The top of the shoulder. To take a burden; to sustain. Competent to.
824

肩任 to bear a burden or take a responsibility.
肩巾 a scarf.
肩帶 a shoulder belt.
肩挑 to carry on the shoulder; porterage.
⁵肩挑生活 the life of a coolie.
肩摩 to rub shoulders; crowded.
肩章 epaulet.
肩胛骨 the shoulder blade.
肩臂 the arms.
¹⁰肩荷 or 肩負 to carry on the back; to be competent to.
肩負重任 sustaining great responsibilites.
肩輿 a sedan chair.
肩隨 walking just slightly behind another.
肩頭 or 肩膊 or 肩膀 the shoulder.
¹⁵一肩擔載 one undertakes the whole responsibility.
並肩 side by side; shoulder to shoulder.
並肩而行 to walk abreast.
仔肩 responsibility.

克肩其任 adequate to the office.
²⁰息肩 to rest; to retire from responsibility.
比肩 equal in height.
轉肩 to change the shoulder, as carriers do.

堅¹ Hard, durable, firm; strong, solid, robust.
825

堅乎磨而不磷 Is it really hard? Then you can rub it without making it thin.
堅凝 congealed; hardened; solidified.
堅厚 solid; substantial.
堅·固 firm; strong; stable.
⁵堅土 hard ground.
堅牢 strong; durable.
堅實 or 結實 solid; strong; durable.
堅果 nuts.
堅牆 a strong wall.
¹⁰堅硬 hard and solid.
堅緻 strong but finely finished.
堅韌 soft but tough, as fine leather.
中堅 the main body of an army; a strong centre; essential character.

(a) Determined; obstinate. To strengthen. To confirm, to maintain, to establish.

堅信 to confirm one's belief; to establish in faith.
堅信禮 the rite of confirmation.
堅勁 stiff-necked; firm; unyielding.
堅執 obstinate; pigheaded.
⁵堅執不肯 obstinate refusal.
堅如鐵石 as hard as iron and stone.
堅守 to guard securely.
堅定 fixed; decided; firm of purpose.
堅定不疑 to have the mind made up; fixed resolve; without doubts.
¹⁰堅定不移 immovable; stedfast; positively.
堅強 or 堅壯 unyielding.
堅強不⬛⬛ielding and firm resistan⬛⬛
堅心 determined purpose.
堅忍 firm endurance; to endure.
¹⁵堅意 confirmed in one's opinion.
堅意不移 determined to stand by one's opinions.

堅 拒 stolid, stubborn resistance.

堅 持 obstinate; firm; tenacious; to maintain or uphold.

堅 持 到 底 to hold on to the very end.

[20]堅 持 己 見·的 a self-opinionated man.

堅 持 己 論 to be self-opinionated.

堅 毅 resolute, with earnest determination.

堅 決 to be stedfastly steeled against.

堅 決·的 determined.

[25]堅 白 hard, (it cannot be worn) white, (it cannot be soiled) said of one whose determination is inflexible.

堅 確 certain; firm and solid.

堅 稱 positive assertion.

堅 立 to establish firmly.

堅 美 strong and beautiful.

[30]堅 苦 determined to s u c c e e d though suffering for it, as in study, etc.

堅 苦 自 厲 to endure hardness with fortitude.

堅 要 to insist on; to make a determined claim.

堅 貞 chaste; of inflexible virtue.

堅 靜 firm and sincere.

[35]自 堅 to steel oneself.

(b) Gives emphasis before negatives.

堅 不 吐 眞 obstinately refuses to speak truthfully.

堅 不 承 認 obstinately refuses to confess or acknowledge.

堅 不 認 案 strong denial of an accusation.

慳 [1] Stingy; economical. To spare. Also pron. *ch'ian*[1].
826

慳 儉 or 慳 省 close-fisted; sparing; frugal.

慳 力 to save the strength.

慳 客 unwilling to spend; stingy.

慳 囊 to tighten the purse strings.

[5]慳 煩 to save oneself the trouble.

慳 簡 to diminish expenses; to reduce outlay.

椷 [1] A casket; a box; a bowl. To allow. An envelope.
827

椷 粧 a dressing case.

减
減 [3] To lessen, to diminish, to decrease. 2nd form is not strictly correct.
828

減 俸 to reduce the salaries of officials.

減 價 reduced prices; to reduce the price.

減 刑 to mitigate punishment; to commute a sentence.

減 削 to abate; to reduce.

[5]減 牛 to reduce by one half.

減·去 to diminish.

減 號 sign of subtraction; minus.

減 少 to reduce; less.

減 折 to discount; to abate.

[10]減 政 主 義 a policy of retrenchment.

減 料 to reduce the amount.

減 法 subtraction.

減 痛 to alleviate pain.

減 省 to diminish; to retrench.

[15]減 省 費 用 to retrench the expenditure.

減 稅 to reduce the duty; a rebate on the duty.

減 筆 abbreviated form of writing.

減 罪 to extenuate a crime.

減 罪 之 情 extenuating circumstances.

[20]減 膳 to reduce the variety of food.

減 讓 to give in; to make an allowance.

減 輕 to extenuate; to mitigate.

減 輕 其 罪 to extenuate the crime.

減 輕·的 extenuating.

[25]減 量 to make a short allowance of food, etc.

原 情 減 罰 to m i t i g a t e the punishment on account of extenuating circumstances.

扣 減 期 票 to discount a bill.

節 減 or 裁 減 to retrench.

縮 減 to reduce; to retrench.

緘 [1] To bind; to close; to seal.
829

緘 口 無 言 to keep the mouth shut and say nothing.

緘 密 firmly sealed.

緘 封 to seal, as a letter.

緘 札 a letter.

緘 默 to keep silence.

吉 緘 a home letter.

書 緘 envelope.

玉 緘 Your esteemed favour!

兼 [1] To unite in one. To connect. And, also, together with, both, equally.
830

兼 人 之 量 to surpass others; with the energy of two men; to eat enough for two.

兼 全 both or all complete.

兼 利 compound interest.

兼 合 to blend; to mix.

[5]兼 司 or 兼 任 to take double duties.

兼 含 to contain more than one.

兼 味 variety of food.

兼 問 also asked.

兼 帶 at the same time; moreover.

[10]兼 幷 to monopolize; to annex.

兼 愛 love without distinction.

兼 日 day after day.

兼 旬 two decades; two periods of ten days.

兼 有 or 更 兼 or 兼 之 still there are more; further; there is yet another matter.

[15]兼 毫 pencils made with mixed sable or weasel and goat's hair.

兼 用 a double use of.

兼 衆 職 unites all offices.

兼 祧 to worship ancestors both in the direct and the indirect lines.

兼 程 or 兼 行 double stages; forced marches.

[20]兼 署 to take temporary charge of more than one office.

兼 聽 to hear both sides.

兼 詞 a phrase.

兼 辦 or 兼 管 or 兼 理 or 兼 轄 to fill more than one office.

兼 雜 to adulterate.

不 可 得 兼 if ᵀ cannot have both.

尲
尷 [1] To limp. Also read *kan*[1].
831

尷 尬 事 體 state of embarrassment and uncertainty. quandary.

縑 [1] Kind of silk woven with double threads and waterproof.
832

縑 素 white gauze silk for painting or writing on.

縑 緗 a variegated silk; fine writing.

縑 繒 flowered gauze.

縑 袋 運 水 the silk bags transported the water.

鶼[1] A fabulous bird with one eye and one wing, a pair must unite in order to fly.
833

鶼 鰈 a one-winged bird and a one-eyed fish—a husband and wife.

鶼 鶼 a pair—man and wife.

艱[1] Difficult, hard. Distressing.
834

艱 危 or 艱 險 difficult and dangerous.

艱 深 abstruse writings.

艱 煩 troublesome.

艱 窮 desperately poor.

[5]艱 虞 distressed and sorrowful.

艱 貞 to maintain rectitude with difficulty.

艱 辛 or 艱 苦 grievous; distressing.

艱 鉅 difficult; weighty.

艱 阻 serious obstruction.

[10]艱 難 trouble; distress.

生 意 艱 難 it is hard to make a living.

艱 食 hard-earned food.

外 艱 or 內 艱 mourning for father and mother respectively.

莫 知 我 艱 "nobody knows the trouble I bear."

間[1] Among, in, on, while. The space between. Distinguish 閒 No. 2672. This was the original form and is still found used in this sense.
835

間 不 容 髮 not a hair's breadth between them.

間 關 creaking sound of carts—the cares and toils of travel.

中 間 in the middle of; the centre; between.

中 間 人 a middleman or go-between.

[5]其 間 in the midst; in the matter.

夜 間 during the night.

少 間 in a little while.

居 間 intervention; mediation.

忽 然 間 suddenly.

[10]曰 間 during the day.

百 年 之 間 in the course of a hundred years.

置 之 案 間 laid on the table.

陽 間 during this life; in the upper world.

(a) A division of a house. N.A. of houses, rooms.

間 架 the framework of a house; size of a building.

間 架 稅 taxes assessed according to the number of *chien*.

間 量 the measurement of the rooms of a house.

一 間 屋·子 a room.

(b) Read *chien*[4]. To put a space between. To divide. To separate. Intermittent.

間 之 以 .. separating them by ..

間 入 to go into a place in disguise.

間 兩 天 every third day.

間 壁·的 next-door neighbours.

[5]間 或 有 之 there may be some among them; occasionally there are; it may be; it sometimes is.

間 接 indirect—opposite of 直 接·

間 接 匯 兌 indirect exchange.

間 接 匯 票 indirect bills.

間 接 占 有 indirect possession, as when A. mortgages to B., and B. re-mortgages to C. C. has direct possession, the others both have indirect possession. (*legal*).

[10]間 接 射 擊 indirect fire.

間 接 從 犯 indirect accessory. (*legal*).

間 接 手 段 indirect methods of procedure.

間 接 機 關 indirect organ.

間 接 正 犯 indirect guilt. (*legal*).

[15]間 接 目 的 語 indirect object. (*gramm.*).

間 接 稅 indirect taxation.

間 接 義 務 indirect obligation. (*legal*).

間 接 證 據 indirect evidence.

間 接 造 意 indirect instigation. (*legal*).

[20]間 接 選 舉 indirect election.

間 有 every now and then.

間 歇 intermittent.

間 歇 性 of an intermittent nature.

間 歇 泉 an intermittent spring, a geyser.

[25]間 歇 熱 intermittent fever.

間 然 suddenly.

間 疏·的 separated; apart.

間 知 or 間 接·的 知 識 indirect knowledge.

間 色 不 正 intermediate colours.

[30]間 諜 a spy.

間 道 a by-path.

間 遠 far apart.

間 間 separated from.

間 隔 to set apart; a partition; to intermit; intervals.

[35]乘 間 to seize the opportunity.

得 間 矣 I have got an opportunity.

無 間 no interval; incessantly.

無 間 可 乘 no chance to take hold of; no crevice to get in by.

相 間 alternately.

紅 白 相 間 red and white intermingled.

(c) To part friends.

間 人 to separate people.

間 隙 a crack; a grudge; to set at variance.

反 間 計 the trick of carrying tales to both sides so as to separate them and get a victory.

離 間 的·話 talk that causes separation between friends.

離 間 骨 肉 to cause separation between relatives.

(d) To find a flaw or defect in. To blame.

人 不 間 於 其 父 母 之 言 others say nothing of him different from the report of his parents.

禹 吾 無 間 然 矣 I cannot find a flaw in the character of *Yü*.

澗 磵[4] A mountain torrent.
836

跳 山 澗 to leap into a mountain torrent—to fulfil a vow for the health of parents, etc.

簡[3] A slip of bamboo for making notes. Documents.
837

簡 書 memorandum tablets.

簡 札 or 簡 策 an official document.

簡 牒 a note; a memorandum.

簡 素 bamboo slips and silk, used before the invention of paper as writing material, now used to indicate stationery.

簡 編 volumes.

牙 簡 an ivory tablet.

(a) To abridge. Simple; terse.

簡·便 simple; handy; convenient; a short cut; unceremonious.

簡·單 simple, as opposed to complex, 複 雜.

簡 單 分 數 a simple fraction.

簡 單 化 simplification.

⁵簡 單 生 活 the simple life.

↓ 腦 筋 簡 單 simple-minded.

簡 字 a form of phonetic writing.

簡 括 summarily; in brief.

簡 捷 short; to the point; expeditious.

¹⁰簡 明 simple, yet terse.

簡 易 to simplify; simple and easy; abridged.

簡 易 科 "short course," easy method of study.

簡 略 a synopsis; an abridgement.

簡 直 concise; direct; simply.

¹⁵簡 直 陳 說 plain spoken; to the point; to come to the point.

簡 短 brief; short.

簡 章 abridged regulations.

簡 篇 to arrange material for a book.

簡 約 brief; terse; concise; abridged.

²⁰簡 縴 to have simple desires.

簡 缺 a quiet post in a simple town.

簡 而 言 之 to sum up; in a few words.

簡 薄 poor; insignificant; not of much value.

簡 要 a sketch; a compendium.

簡 體 字 abbreviated characters.

(b) To choose. To examine. To appoint.

簡 任 Presidential appointment—a selection by the president of suitable men for offices such as vice-presidents of boards, etc.

簡 任 官 officer under such appointment.

簡 任 職 office under the president as above.

簡 命 or 簡 授 to appoint.

---

⁵簡 在 帝 心 the examination of these things rests with the heart of the ruler.

簡 拔 to select men from the masses and promote them to office.

簡 放 to appoint to.

簡 旨 specially appointed by the emperor.

簡 派 委 員 to choose and appoint a deputy.

¹⁰簡 畀 to select and appoint.

簡 稽 to muster and review troops.

簡 練 to select and make a thorough study of.

簡 辰 to choose a day.

簡 閱 to examine, as essays; to review, as troops.

¹⁵特 簡 special selection or special appointment.

記 名 簡 用 to record a name for promotion.

(c) Hasty, rude. To treat rudely. Lax and careless.

簡 忽 rude, impolite.

簡 忽 于 事 careless in transaction of business, etc.

簡 慢 or 簡 褻 to treat impolitely.

狂 簡 ambitious and hasty.

(d) Unruffled. Abundant. Full.

簡 簡 full toned; easy going; abundant.

簡 默 retiring; silent.

臨 下 以 簡 easy in small matters with regard to government of the people.

覸² 838 **To spy. To mix.**

監¹ 839 **To inspect; to oversee.**

監 事 員 invigilator.

監 事 會 Board of Comptrollers.

監 候 ancient law which provided that capital punishment should be delayed.

監 國 resident in a subdued state; heir to a throne.

⁵監 學 a school superintendent; to superintend school matters, or educational matters.

監 守 to guard; to be careful of.

監 守 自 盜 embezzlement.

監·察 to inspect; to examine.

監·察 人 examiners; inspectors.

¹⁰監·察 員 an inspector.

監 工 or 監 造 to oversee workmen; to superintend work.

監 廠 overseer of a factory, etc.

監 查 員 auditor; liquidator.

監 理 or 監 視 or 監 管 to oversee; to superintend.

¹⁵監 理 收 支 to superintend receipts and payments.

監 盤 an officer deputed to examine accounts, etc., when one official is handing over to another.

監·督 an overseer; head of a school of higher grade than higher primary; to supervise; also used for a bishop.

監·督 會 Episcopal Church.

監·督 辦 公 處 inspector's offices.

²⁰監 考 to examine; to inspect; to invigilate.

監 考 員 invigilator.

監 臨 to superintend the examinations—under the old system.

監 護 guardianship.

監 護 人 a guardian or trustee for minors.

²⁵監 院 president of a college.

總 監 inspector-general.

(a) A gaol.

監 牢 or 監 獄 a prison; a gaol.

監 押 to keep in custody.

監 斃 to die in prison.

監 犯 a prisoner; a gaolbird.

⁵監 獄 司 gaol department of ministry of justice.

監 獄 官 吏 prison officials.

監 獄 法 prison law.

監 禁 to immure; to imprison.

司 獄 監 a gaoler.

¹⁰坐 監 to be in prison.

收 監 to be put in prison.

走 監 犯 an escaped prisoner.

(b) Read chien⁴. To revise; to look into. Inter., 鑑 No. 841.

監 察 御 史 the censorate under the Manchu dynasty.

監 本 books issued by the imperial academy.

入 監 to enter the imperial academy.

國 子³ 監 the Imperial Academy of past dynasty.

太·監 a eunuch.

天 監 在 下 Heaven (God) looked down on the world below.

欽天監 Board of Astronomy under the former regime.

艦 [4]
840
In ancient times, a warship with wooden walls wherein the men were sheltered; now used for war-vessels in general.

艦長 naval commander.
艦隊 naval squadron.
艦隊司令官 captain of a squadron.
分遣艦隊 detached squadron.
[5] 常備艦隊 standing naval squadron; regular fleet.
義勇艦隊 naval volunteers.
遊擊艦隊 flying squadron.
巡洋艦 cruisers.
戰艦 a man-of-war.
[10] 旗艦 a flagship.
↑ 主力艦 capital ship; battleship.
↓ 航空母艦 aircraft carrier.
海防艦 coast-defence boat.
無畏艦 dreadnoughts.
礟艦 a gun-boat.
[15] 補助巡洋艦 auxiliary cruiser.
裝甲巡洋艦 armoured cruiser.
軍艦 a war-vessel.
驅逐艦 destroyer.

鑑｜
鑒｜
841
[4] A mirror of metal. To examine. To scrutinize; to criticise. An example or precept.

鑑之照物 the reflection of objects by a mirror.
鑑定 expert evidence. (legal).
鑑定人 or 鑑定家 experts.
鑑定書 expert evidence in writing.
[5] 鑑察 to inspect; to examine.
鑑戒 a warning example; to take warning from an occurence.
鑑核 to consider; to look into.
鑑觀 to look at; to examine.
鑑賞 enjoyment of—a piece of writing, a picture, etc.
[10] 冰鑑 reflected from ice as a mirror.
前車之鑑 (take) warning from the preceding cart, (if it overturns, be careful)—used fig.
台鑑 "For your inspection." opening phrase in letters.
明鑑 clear mirror—i.e., clearness of apprehension.

通鑑 Comprehensive Mirror. Name of a history by 司馬光 in 294 volumes, completed in A.D. 1084.
[15] 綱鑑 or 通鑑綱目 an abridged adaptation of the above by Chu hsi, 朱熹.
風鑑 physiognomy.

謇 [3]
842
To speak out boldly; to beg, to entreat.

謇而無憚 importunate.
謇諤 faithful, outspoken, as an advisor.
謇謇 or 蹇蹇 in difficulties.
謇謇爲忠 plain speaking brings trouble.
謇謇直言 honest speech; outspoken.
外似謇正 outwardly he is upright.

蹇 [3]
843
Lame; feeble.

蹇寒 stopped; hindered.
蹇跛 or 跛蹇 crippled; lame, feeble; unfit for service.

(a) Difficulties. Trouble. Dangerous.

蹇蹇 in straits; in trouble from dangers ahead.
蹇運 an evil destiny.
命蹇 my destiny is against me.

(b) Lofty; proud.

偃蹇 arrogant; proud; numerous; irresolute; disappointed.
彼皆偃蹇 they are all proud and arrogant.
瑤臺之偃蹇 the height of the jade terrace.

(c) To pull up; to pick up.

蹇裳躍步 picked up his skirts and went forward.
毋蹇華 do not pull the flowers.

(d) A surname.

蹇修 Minister, under FuHsi, who was responsible for marriages.
代作蹇修 to act as a go-between in a marriage arrangement—from the above.

繭 [3]
844
The cocoon of the silkworm; also cocoons of other moths.

繭栗 the small, cocoon-like, chestnut shape of the budding horns of a calf, such as was used for sacrifices; by analogy, the buds of flowers.
繭絲 a silken thread; to extort illegally, winding out the money like the threads from a cocoon.
繭綢 undyed, coarse, durable pongee made from wild silk.
繭蟲 pupae.
繭衣 the rough outside of a cocoon.
結繭 to spin a cocoon.
蠶繭 silkworm cocoons.

(a) Blistered and rough skin on the feet like the outside of cocoons.

手足重繭 hands and feet swollen and blistered.
重繭 calloused skin on the feet.
↑老繭 callus.

(b) Low tones.

繭繭 low, mournful tones.

柬 [3]
845
To condense; to select; to abridge. A visiting card.

柬帖 or 紅柬 the red visiting card formerly used.
柬書 note on a visiting card.
庚柬 or 媒柬 betrothal card giving the eight characters of the cycle, showing the year, month, day and hour of birth.
禮柬 a card sent with presents.

揀 [3]
846
To choose; to select; to pick up.

揀剩 the remainder after sorting.
揀好的 select the best; pick out a good one.
揀拾 to pick up.
揀擇 to choose; to pick out.
[5] 揀查 to pick out for examination.
揀柴 to gather firing.
揀淨 to sort; selected.
揀派 to select and send as an official.
揀貨 to sort merchandise.
[10] 揀起來 to pick out or pick up.

揀 選 to select; to elect; to choose for office.
挑 揀 to select; to pick out.

諫 847 **[4] To admonish, to remonstrate, to plead with; to reprove.**

諫 勸 or 諫 止 to urge one to desist from evil.
諫 官 or 諫 臣 or 給 諫 imperial counsellors; censors.
諫 菓 the olive.
諫 言 reproofs; admonitions.
[5]諫 諍 to reprove and warn; to oppose arbitrary dealings.
幾[1] 諫 almost a rebuke; gentle remonstrance, as from a child to parents.
忠 諫 a faithful rebuke.
苦 諫 bitter remonstrance.

儉 848 **[3,4] Temperate; frugal, economical.**

儉 則 固 parsimony leads to meanness.
儉 德 self-restraint.
儉 於 百 里 not more than 100 *li*.
儉·樸 careful; thrifty; not extravagant.
[5]儉 用 or 節 儉 or 省 儉 careful and thrifty.
儉 約 度 日 to live economically.
儉 腹 limited experience.
儉 薄 or 儉 吝 stingy; mean.
儉 要 得 其 所 economy must be observed, but only in its right place—there are occasions when it is wrong to economize.

劍
劒 849 **[4] A double-edged sword.**

劍 俠 a bravo or knight-errant.
劍 氣 珠 光 the vigour of a sword and the brightness of a pearl—of talents.
劍 術 sword-play.
劍 鋒 the point of a sword, or a sword and spear.
[5]劍 鞘 or 劍 殼 a scabbard.
一 把 劍 a sword.
伏 劍 to fall on the sword—suicide.

仙 劍 a magic sword that kills when it is commanded to do so.
寶 劍 a magic sword; a sword.
[10]撫 劍 to grasp the sword.
舞 劍 dancing with sword-play.
雙 劍 a pair of swords—a dilemma.

撿 850 **[3] To restrict; to bind. Inter. next.**

撿 束 to restrain; to bind.

(a) To check; to tally. To examine. cp., 檢 next.

撿 察 to examine; to inspect.
撿 察 官 or 撿 事 public procurator. ≡ 851 A5.
撿 驗 屍 首 to view the body; post-mortem.
撿 點 to search; to tally; to oversee. ≡ 851.7.
撿 點 人 數 make a muster of the men.

(b) To pick up; to gather.

撿 場·的 gleaners, etc.
撿 柴 to gather firing.
撿 窮·的 to pick up scraps, etc., on dust-heaps; rag-pickers.
撿 起·來 pick it up.

(c) To collate; to revise.

撿 書 to revise a book.
撿 校 to collate; to revise.
撿 齊 to collate and put in order, as sections of a book for binding, etc.

檢 851 **[3] A label on a book. An envelope. To arrange; to collate; Inter., last. To sort; to gather.**

檢·出 箱·子 to turn out and arrange boxes.
檢 字 collected characters—characters arranged under the number of strokes, as a guide to a dictionary, when the radical is not known.
檢 封 to label; to seal, as an envelope.
[5]檢 柴 to gather fuel.
檢 讎 to compare and collate documents, etc.
檢 點 to sort; to check; to count over.

檢 齊 to collect; to collate pages, etc., of a book ready for binding.

(a) To examine; to search.

檢 事 public procurator.
檢 出 to discover; to ferret out. *See above.*—1.
檢 定 to authorize; to weigh; official sanction.
檢 察 to inspect.
[5]檢 察 官 public procurator.
檢 察 廳 criminal court.
檢 察 長 chief public prosecutor.
檢 審 to have a clear investigation.
檢 括 looting and taking all there is by soldiers.
[10]檢 按 to examine into.
檢 搜 證 據 to get proof or evidence.
檢 書 to examine a book or documents.
檢 查 to examine the records; to censor; to investigate.
檢 查 人 an inspector.
[15]檢 查 使 inspecting commissioner.
檢 查 員 an official inspector.
檢 查 權 right of inspection.
檢 查 院 bureau of investigation.
檢 核 or 檢 校 to search into; to examine.
[20]檢 正 to examine, revise and correct.
檢 比 to examine into; to compare.
檢 疫 禁 quarantine restrictions.
檢 票 warrant for examining.
檢 禁 船 隻 an infected ship in quarantine.
[25]檢 究 to investigate.
檢 考 to examine.
檢 視 censorship; to censor.
檢 視 郵 件 censorship of the mails.
檢 證 to sift the evidence.
[30]檢 閱 to oversee; to review; to censor.
檢 革 to investigate and degrade or dismiss.
檢 驗 to hold an inquest; to examine, as a coroner; to inspect.
檢 驗 吏 a coroner.

(b) To restrict; to regulate.

檢 其 身 examine into his action.
檢 制 to restrict and restrain.
檢 押 to be restrained in movements.

檢束 to be attentive to one's conduct.

[5]檢格 restrained in conduct.
檢禁 to investigate and prohibit.
檢盜制賊 to search out and deal with robbers.
檢裁 self-restrained.
檢責 to blame oneself; to criticize oneself.
檢遏 to investigate and suppress.

(c) A rule, model or pattern.

檢式 an example.

鹼 鹻 [3] Impure carbonate of sodium or natron.
852

鹼地 or 鹼土 alkaline soil.
鹼水 lye.
鹼沙 soda in powder.
鹼質 or 鹼類 alkalies.
鹼質性·的or 鹼性·的 alkaline.
植物鹼質 vegetable alkaloids.

建 [4] To establish; to erect; to found.
853

建修 to construct; to build.
建功 to do a meritorious deed.
建功立業 to found an empire or a dynasty.
建國 to found a nation or a kingdom.
[5]建國大綱 Outline of Principles for the Establishment of the Nation, Title of a book by Dr. Sun Yat-sen.
建國方略 Scheme for the Establishment of the Nation. Title of a book by Dr. Sun Yat-sen.
建康 later name for Nanking, changed from 建業 during the Eastern Chin Dynasty. See next phrase.
建業 ancient name for Nanking, given, when it was founded as his capital, by Sun Ch'üan, 孫權 About A.D. 212.
建白 to make a statement of one's views on public matters; to give advice on such.
[10]建立 or 建樹 to erect; to establish; to found.
建立功勳 to do something praiseworthy; to establish a reputation for bravery.

建立名·聲 to establish a reputation.
建築 to build; to erect; to construct.
建築借欵 building loan.
[15]建築學 architecture.
建築師 an architect.
建築物 structures; buildings.
建築經費 building or construction expenses.
建築艦港 construction of docks for naval vessels.
[20]建築鐵路 railway construction.
建蓋 to build.
建設 to establish; to organize; to institute.
建設主義 contructive spirit.
建設之骨骼 the framework of reconstruction.
[25]建設委員會 Bureau of Reconstruction.
建議 to advise; to make a proposal for consideration.
建議案 to introduce a bill, etc., to make a proposal or motion.
建造 to build; building; architecture.
建造房屋 to build houses.
[30]建都 to found a capital.
再建 to re-construct.

(a) Used as an abbreviation for the province of Fukien 福建.

建煙 Fukien tobacco.
建窰 a smooth white china from Fukien.
建箔 tinfoil paper from Fukien.
建蓮 lotus seeds from Fukien.
建邦 Fukien Merchants Guild.

(b) The relation of the cyclical character to the months.

建丑 and 建子 the months with the characters ch'ou and tzŭ were set up as the first month of the year by the Shang and the Chou Dynasties respectively.
建寅之月爲歲首 The Hsia dynasty set up the Yin month as the first month of the year.

健 [4] Strong, robust, vigorous. To strengthen, to invigorate.
854

健僕 strong, sturdy retainers.
健兒 heroes; athletes.
健全 strong, robust; good health.
健卒 able-bodied soldiers.

[5]健壯 hearty, in good health.
健婦人 a sturdy woman.
健康 health and strength.
健康壯態 a healthy condition.
健康·的 or 健全·的 healthy.
[10]健康診斷 to diagnose the health.
健康證明書 a bill of health.
健捷 strong and active.
健筆 style of vigorous penmanship.
健羨 strong lusts; ardent desires.
[15]強健 strong; robust; vigorous.
硬健 strong and muscular.
精健 in robust health.

(a) Constant, regular, persevering.

健動 uniform operation of natural laws.
健啖 fond of eating.
健忘 forgetful; oblivion.
健步 active walking; unflinching.
[5]健燒 slow-burning.
健穿 lasting wear.
健訟 fond of litigation.
健談 ceaseless talk.
天行健 the movements of the heavenly bodies are constant and regular.

揵 [2] To carry on the shoulder. To raise. To shut. To block up. To fix boundaries.
855

揵之江 bounded by the river.

楗 [4] Bar of a gate or door. Bolt of a lock. Inter. 鍵 No. 859.
856

關楗 the catch of a lock; key to a situation; crux of a matter; the pivot; central part. ≡859.5

毽 [4] A shuttle-cock kicked from one player to another.
857

踢毽·子 to kick the shuttle-cock.

犍 [4] A bullock; a fabulous monster.
858

犍椎 bell, wooden fish, etc., used in a temple.
犍陀羅 musicians in attendance on Buddha.

鍵[4] The bolt of a Chinese lock. A door-bolt. Piano-key.
859

鍵子 a bolt lock.
鍵閉 to lock up.
時局關鍵 key to the situation.
管鍵 catch of a lock.
關鍵 catch of a lock—the key, to a situation or a book, etc.

見[4] To see, to perceive, to observe. Radical 147.
860

見不着[2] I cannot see it; I do not see it.
見世面 experienced; to have seen the world.
見事生風 to arouse trouble with very little cause.
見信 to believe — to have faith in.
[5] 見個高低 see who is master; see who is the best man.
見利 profitable; beneficial.
見危受命 to give up life when in sight of danger.
見菁如不及 to see good (and pursue it) as if it could not be reached.
見外 to treat as an outsider.
[10] 見天 every day.
見天來 come every day.
見天日 to see daylight; to get light on a problem.
見遍天日 to have seen the light of day—to have experience.
見影怖兒 to see a shadow and fear ghosts.
[15] 不見影 no trace of .... can be seen.
見得 evident; it may be seen.
何以見得 Why do you think so? 不見得 unlikely.
見新 it looks like new; as good as new; renovate.
見景生情 see the conditions and act accordingly; adapt yourself to circumstances.
[20] 見機而作 to act as the occasion serves.
見疑 suspicious; doubtful.
見票卽付 payable at sight.
見笑 laughable; it will make you smile.
見習 seen and practiced—practical experience.
[25] 見習生制 pupil-teacher system.

見義不爲無勇也 to see an opportunity for doing right and fail to do it, is cowardice.
見聞 seen and heard—experience; to have some knowledge of.
見色不亂 to see a beautiful woman without lust.
見解 view; opinion. *See below.* B. 23.
[30] 見證 witness; evidence; testimony.
見識 experience; knowledge; sense.
見識廣 of wide experience.
見財起意 to see wealth and arouse desires to get it—by robbery or murder.
見賢思齊 when good men are seen one wishes to be like them.
[35] 見透 to see through.
見過 I have seen it; met him.
見遠 or 遠見 far-seeing; foresight.
有遠見 to have foresight.
見食垂涎 seeing food causes the mouth to water.
[40] 見鬼 to see devils or bogies.
一見 as soon as seen.
不見 not seen; not quite clear.
偏見 prejudice; one-sided views.
初見 seen for the first time.
[45] 定見 with decided views.
少見多怪 things rarely seen are regarded as strange.
意見 opinions.
成見 prejudice; pre-conceived views.
我見 my opinion.
[50] 易見 easily seen; conspicuous; easily comprehended.
明見 or 高見 Your enlightened opinion.
淺見 shallow views or opinions.
無定見 irresolute; undecided; between two opinions.
看不見 invisible; cannot see it.
[55] 看見 to see.
瞥見 a glimpse of.
管見 a view through a tube—narrow outlook.
罕見 rarely seen.

(a) To interview. To visit or call on. To meet.

見不得人 ashamed to meet others; unpresentable.
見官 to meet an official.
見禮 rules of etiquette; to be polite.

見面 to have an interview with.
[5] 偶見 to happen to see; accidental meeting.
朝見 audience with a ruler.
相見 to meet; to interview.
謁見 to call on a superior.

(b) Used to indicate the passive.

見做 tedious work.
見傷 to be wounded.
見問 to be inquired of.
見好 to be better.
[5] 見小 to be mean or niggardly.
見強 to be better; to see an improvement in a sick man.
見怪 to take offence.
不要見怪 do not be offended.
見惠 to be the recipient of a gift or a favour.
[10] 見效 it is efficacious, as medicine.
見方 to be made square; square.
見棄 to be rejected.
見棄於人 "despised and rejected of men."
見殺 to be murdered.
[15] 見用 to be used or employed.
見短 to be treated lightly.
見稱 has been called.
見穿 will stand wear.
見絕 to be exterminated or cut off.
[20] 見羞 to feel ashamed.
見老 growing old.
見背 to lose one's parents.
見解 to be experienced; to be wise. *See above.—29.*
見說 it is reported; it is said.
[25] 見諒 to be excused.
見輕 he seems a little better, of a sick man.
見黜 to be degraded.
不見佳 it does not seem to be any good.
當見還 it should be returned.

(c) Read *hsien*[4]. To manifest; to appear; to introduce. Inter. 2864.

見錢 ready money.
見齒 to smile.
其見在者 those that remain.
良心發見 his conscience was aroused.
莫見乎隱 there is nothing more manifest than that which is hidden.

梘 3 A bamboo tube to carry water. A wooden peg.
861

梘·子 or 水 梘 a water spout; a pipe to carry off water.

件 4 An article; to divide. N.A. for various things.
862

件 件 everything; every article.
件 件 都 能 well versed in many trades.
件 色 description of packages.
一 件 事 a matter.
一 件 衣 裳 a garment.
有 條·件 conditional.
條·件 conditions, as in a contract, etc., an article.
物 件 things; articles.

CHIEN TSIEN. (ㄐㄧㄢ)

鐫
鋟
鑴
863

To engrave or carve, as a block for printing.

鐫 刻 to engrave—as a printing block.
鐫 石 to cut in stone.
鐫 鑿 to chisel out.

(a) To censure; to degrade.

鐫 汰 to get rid of unemployed officials.
鐫 級 to degrade to a lower rank.
鐫 罰 to deprive of rank as a punishment.
鐫 說 or 鐫 喩 earnest exhortation.
鐫 黜 to degrade an official.
以 仁 惠 鐫 喩 earnestly exhorted him with love and kindness.

殲 1 To destroy; to kill.
864

殲 除 or 殲 滅 to exterminate.

尖 1 Tapering; pointed. Acute, sharp. A sharp point.
865

尖 刀 sharp-pointed knife.

尖 利 clever; sharp.
尖 刻 sharp dealing.
尖 圓 conical.
尖 寒 a shudder.
尖 尖 tapering; pointed.
尖 指 頭 slender fingers—"a light fingered gentleman."
尖 石 a pinnacle of rock.
尖 頭 a sharp point.
筆 尖 point of a pencil.

(a) To have a slight lunch.

打 尖 to lunch by the way.

(b) a male crab.

尖 團 蟹 male and female crabs, crabs in general.

戔 1 Small, narrow. Prejudiced. Also read ts'an 2, inter., 殘
866 No. 6689.

戔 狹 straitened.

箋
牋
867

A memorandum tablet. Slip of paper. Fancy note-paper. A note, a document. Comments.

箋 扇 ornamental fan.
箋 札 a letter.
箋 疏 comments; notes of explanation; running commentary.
箋 注 comment on ancient books.
箋 紙 fancy note-paper.
蠟 箋 glazed note-paper; waxed paper.

賤 4 Mean, low, worthless; cheap. To hold lightly.
868

賤 丈 夫 lowbred, a greedy man.
賤 事 my humble business or affairs.
賤 人 or 賤 坯 a good-for-nothing.
賤 價 cheap.
賤 儒 a pretender to scholarship; a charlatan.
賤 內 or 賤 房 my wife—conventional phrase.
賤 姓 my surname is . . . .
賤 妾 a term formerly used by wives to their husbands in speaking of themselves.
賤 子 I, myself. (obs.)
賤 息 or·賤 賊 my son.

賤 格 my talents are poor.
賤 業 a low-down business.
賤 物 cheap; common goods.
賤 相 a bad countenance; a thief's face.
賤 行 base conduct; evil ways.
賤 視 to regard lightly; to treat with contempt.
賤 貨 to despise riches.
賤 賣 cheap sale.
賤 軀 my body.
賤 骨 頭 low scamp; a loafer.
下·賤 low, as used in "lower classes."
作 賤 to demean oneself.
卑 賤 humble; poor; "low birth."
微 賤 of humble extraction.
貧 賤 poor and humble.
貧 賤 生·活 the life of the poor.
貴 賤 high and low—as rank in society; nobles and commons.
輕 賤 to undervalue; to despise; to depreciate.

濺 4 To splash.
869

濺·了 一 身 水 the water splashed all over me.
濺 泥 to be splashed with mud.

(a) Read chien or tsien 1. Rushing water.

濺 濺 rushing water.

踐 4 To tread upon; to trample.
870

踐 履 to trample down, as by cattle; to fulfil a promise; to follow.
踐 殘 to spoil; to smash by trampling.
踐 踏 to trample; to tread down.
作 踐 to tread down, as in oppression; to put under the heel; to injure.

(a) To walk; to follow.

踐 人 之 約 to keep an appointment.
踐 其 位 to occupy the throne.
踐 冰 之 慮 the anxiety of walking on ice—apprehension.
踐 年 四 百 二 十 有 六 (the Han Dynasty) has lasted for 426 years.

[5]踐 形 to fulfil the good intentions.
踐 極 to ascend the throne.
踐 約 to keep an appointment or an agreement.
踐 言 to fulfil a promise.
踐 迹 precedent; to tread in the steps of others.
[10]踐 阼 to offer sacrifice while standing on the eastern steps of the imperial ancestral temple, on the occasion of ascending the throne.

(b) To arrange in rows.

籩 豆 有 踐 the vessels were arranged in rows.

餞[4]
871
To entertain a departing friend. A parting present of food or money.

餞 別 to bid farewell.
餞 禮 presents of food to a parting friend.
餞 行 to entertain one who is about to take a journey.
餞 酌 or 飲 餞 to drink a parting cup.

(a) Sweetmeats; preserves.

餞 菓 preserved fruits.
蜜 餞 sweetmeats.

薦[4]
872
To introduce; to recommend. To offer, to present. Inter. 荐 No. 928.

薦 主 a patron.
薦 任 to recommend for an appointment.
薦 引 to introduce; to bring forward.
薦 拔 to raise to dignity.
[5]薦 書 or 薦 函 a letter of recommendation.
薦 派 to nominate; to appoint.
薦 紙 recommendations brought by those seeking employment.
薦 舉 or 舉。薦 to recommend; recommendations for employment or promotion.
薦 賢 to recommend good men.
[10]推 薦 to recommend.
自 薦 self-recommendation.

(a) A sacrifice in which no animal was offered. To worship, to sacrifice.

薦 新 seasonable offerings to ancestors.

薦 祖 to worship ancestors.
薦 羞 sacrifices of food, before offering they were called 薦, and afterwards were known as 羞.
薦 菜 to help guests to dishes.
[5]薦 饌 to set food before a guest.
祖 薦 or 祖 餞 farewell entertainment to a friend—i.e., an offering to 祖 神 the god of the road.

(b) Fodder for animals. Grass. A sleeping mat; matting.

薦 居 a nomadic life.
白 茅 以 薦 white grass for mats.
草 薦 coarse matting.
食 薦 to eat grass.

(c) The sacrum.

薦 骨 the sacrum.

(d) Read ch'ien or ts'ien[4]. Inter. 荐 No. 928. Repeatedly.

薦 饑 repeated famines.
饑 饉 薦 臻 famines repeatedly occur.

韉[1]
873
A saddle cloth.

煎[1]
874
To fry in fat or in oil.

煎 炒 to fry.
煎 炙 to broil or grill.
煎 熟 to fry until it is well done.
煎 膏 to render down fat or lard.
[5]煎 餅 a very thin large pancake.
煎 魚 to fry fish.
油 煎 to fry in oil.
熬 煎 or 煎 熬 to fry in plenty of fat—long continued trouble or suffering.

(a) To decoct; to simmer.

煎 乾 boiled dry.
煎 湯 to warm broth or medicines.
煎 湯 熬 藥 to simmer decoctions of drugs.
煎 茶 to boil brick tea, to boil water for tea.
煎 藥 to make a decoction of medicines.

(b) Distressed; harassed.

煎 心 anxious, worried

煎 督 harassing oversight—harsh like being fried in oil.
急 煎 煎 very much harassed.

(c) Read chien[4] or tsien.[4] To crystallize fruit by dipping it in boiling sugar. Cf. 871 A.

蜜 煎 菓·子 candied fruit.

箭[4]
875
An arrow. The stem of a plant.

箭 如 雨 下 the arrows flew like rain.

箭 搭·上 弓 the arrow is fitted to the string—everything is in readiness.

箭 書 message sent by arrows.
[5]箭 猪 the porcupine.
箭 竹 small bamboo whose joints are three feet apart, used for arrows.
箭 竿·子 stem of an arrow.
箭 笋 small bamboo shoots.
箭 翎·子 feather of an arrow.
[10]箭 袋 a quiver.
箭 鏃 iron or metal barbs for arrows.
箭 靶 or 箭 垛 a target for archery.
箭 風 a sharp, biting, harmful wind.
一 箭 之 地 a bowshot.
[15]一 箭 雙 鵰 one arrow shot two eagles.
射 箭 to discharge an arrow.
弓 箭 bows and arrows.
懷 怨 暗 箭 to cherish a grievance and injure another secretly.
暗 箭 傷 人 a secret arrow injures a man—of slander and such things.
[20]暗 箭 難 防 it is not easy to avoid a secret arrow—similar to the last.
步 箭 archers on foot.
火 箭 fiery arrows; rockets.
馬 箭 mounted archers.

翦 剪 [3]
876
Scissors; to cut with scissors. To trim or clip.

翦 伐 to prune or cut trees.
翦。刀 or 翦·子 a pair of scissors.
翦 割 to cut off territory.

劋。去 cut it off.

[5] 劋 地 求 和 to cede territory and sue for peace.

劋 徑 highway robbers.

劋 柳 or 劋 絡 to cut a purse or a pocket.

劋 樣 to cut out, as a design.

劋 燭 花 to snuff a candle.

[10] 劋 絨 velvets.

劋 草 to mow grass. *See below.* B. 3.

劋。開 or 裁 劋 to cut out.

劋 髮 to cut the hair.

燭 劋 candle snuffers.

鉸 劋 shears.

(a) Eloquent.

劋 劋 eloquent; clever at disputation.

(b) To exterminate.

劋 定 to suppress, as robbers, etc.

劋 屠 to slaughter; to wipe out.

劋 草 除 根 to exterminate utterly, either refers to massacre or to evil habits.

劋 除 or 劋 滅 to exterminate.

譾 [3] Stupid. Shallow.
877

譾 劣 feeble; incompetent.

譾 陋 stupid; limited shallow experience.

漸 [4] Gradually, by degrees. To flow.
878

漸 入 佳 境 gradually enter the blissful regions—circumstances gradually improving. *See* No. 261-1.

漸 化 相 安 gradually became civilized and at peace with each other.

漸 形 明 顯 gradually becoming manifest.

漸 或 occasionally; rarely.

[5] 漸 次 one after the other; in order.

漸 次 後 退 retreated in succession; gradually retreated.

漸 消 to melt gradually.

漸 深 slowly deepening.

漸 減 gradually diminished.

[10] 漸 漸 的 gradually; little by little.

漸 漬 而 不 驟 to collect slowly, without haste.

漸 異 其 範 圍 gradually changes its sphere.

漸 磨 而 進 to make great advance by steady exertion.

漸 積 to accumulate gradually.

[15] 漸 至 負 債 gradually got into heavy debt.

漸 趨 極 端 gradually go to the extreme.

漸 進 gradual advance or progress.

漸 進 主 義 Liberalism, as opposed to Radicalism. 急 進 主 義.

(a) Read *chien[1]* **or** *tsien[1]*. **To soak. To reach.**

漸 仁 廲 義 imbued with love and public duty.

漸 染 to moisten with.

漸 民 以 仁 to imbue the people with virtue.

漸 潤 moistened with; soaking in.

漸 廲 to influence and transform.

僭 [4] To assume, to usurp. To go to excess.
879

僭 位 to usurp the throne.

僭 僭 I am overstepping my right place—depreciatory phrase on taking the place of honour.

僭 分 (*fen[4]*) to usurp the rights or the functions of others.

僭 國 號 to usurp the title of a country.

[5] 僭 妄 blasphemy; presumption.

僭 稱 to arrogate to oneself title or rank.

僭 竊 to assume functions unlawfully.

僭 越 to overstep; to exceed.

洊 [4] Flowing water. Incorrectly used for 荐 No. 928.
880

洊 瀝 continuous dripping.

洊 饑 successive famines.

CH'IEN. (ㄑㄧㄢ)

牽 [1] To pull, to haul, to drag.
881

牽 引 or 牽 曳 to drag; to draw.

牽 挽 to pull a person along.

牽 牛 to lead an ox; the star of the Herdboy, usually given as in the constellation of Aquila.

牽 牛 花 *Ipomoea.*

[5] 牽 絲 to stretch silk threads.

牽 纜 to track a boat.

牽 藤 climbing plants.

牽 郎 the star of the Herdboy, *see above* 3. *and also below.* A. 18.

牽 馬 墜 鐙 to lead a horse and hold the stirrups—to serve another.

(a) To implicate; to drag into an affair; to connect.

牽 制 to embarrass; to involve in difficulties; to hamper; obstruction.

牽 合 connected; joined to.

牽 就 to approximate to.

牽 念 to think fondly of; to be attached to.

[5] 牽 扯 or 牽 累 to involve; to implicate.

牽 掛 to hold in suspense.

牽 製 dragged into an affair by others.

牽 染 to implicate; to imbue with.

牽。涉 to be dragged into an affair.

[10] 牽 混 to bring in irrelevant matters.

牽 強 [3] forced, as an interpretation, etc., unnatural.

牽 強 [3] 附 會 to give a forced interpretation; to strain the sense.

牽 纏 to detain.

牽 腸 to have very grave anxieties.

[15] 牽 腸 割 肚 to be in deep distress and anxiety.

牽 計 to strike an average.

牽 連 to implicate; to compromise; to involve in a crime, etc.

牽 郎 郎 拽 弟 弟 a children's game in which this phrase is called out—used as a wish that another might have a numerous progeny. 拽 pron. *chuai[4].*

縴 [4] A tow-rope. To pull. To lead. To bring together.
882

縴 夫 or 縴 戶 boat-trackers.

縴 手 a go-between.

縴 板 piece of wood at the end of a tracking line, it is placed across the chest of the tracker who leans on it as he walks.

縴 繩 a tracking line.

繹¹ 馬 to lead a horse.
拉 繹 to track; to act as a go-between.
拉 繹 扯 篷 to haul on the tow-rope and pull up the sails —to give a hand.

嗛¹ Pouch of a monkey. To peck. Deficient. Disturbed in mind.
883

嗛 嗛 之 德 deficient in virtue.
嗛 嗛 於 膳 珍 not satisfied with the provisions.
嗛 羊 a sheep with four horns.

歉 3.4. To eat without being satisfied. Deficient, timid.
884

歉 事 an awkward business.
歉 仄 regretting, fidgetty, as when not able to keep an engagement.
歉 仄 實 深 I am fully conscious of my shortcomings—depreciatory phrase in correspondence.
歉 收 a bad harvest.
歉 歲 a year of dearth.
歉 然 dissatisfied.
歉 餘 deficiency and surplus.
抱 歉 to regret; to deplore; to be ashamed.

謙¹ Retiring; humble; modest. Humility.
885

謙 光 retiring and modest, therefore illustrious.
謙 克 humble and self-controlled.
謙 卑 遜 順 humble and retiring.
謙 受 益 the humble receive benefit.
⁵謙 口 polite, courteous speech.
謙 和 pleasant; agreeable.
謙 巽 modest; diffident; humble.
謙 恕 humble and forgiving.
謙 恭 or 謙 敬 respectful; unassuming.
'謙 沖 or 謙 挹 modest and unassuming.
謙 讓 to yield; courtesy.
謙 讓 未 皇 self-depreciatory phrase—I am humble and in no hurry to assume dignities, i.e., my talents are not up to the standard.
謙 辭 modest speech without self-aggrandizement.

謙 遜　or 謙 卑 or 謙 退 humble; diffident; lowly; self-depreciating.
¹⁵謙 順 humbly compliant.
太 謙 over modest; too shy.
自 謙 to humble oneself.
↑謙·虛 humble, modest.

掔¹ Firm, substantial. To drag along. To lead. Inter. 牽 No. 881.
886

鈙
鵮¹ To peck, as birds.
887

鈙 破·了 pecked a hole in it.

懺¹ A label, a tag. To record, to make a note.
888 Should be under ch'ien: ts'ien. See 916½.

帖 懺·子 paste on a label.

愆¹ A fault, error, transgression.
889

愆 伏 unseasonable, as weather.
愆 尤 or 愆 爽 crime, transgression, error.
愆 序 out of sequence; out of season.
愆 忒 errors; faults.
⁵愆 戾 山 積 his crimes are like mountains.
愆 義 to miss the right way; to fail in right conduct.
愆 謬 exaggeration; overstatement.
愆 陽 伏 陰 the Yin and the Yang have got out of their due relations.
不 愆 不 忘 "neither forgetful nor erring."
罪 愆 transgressions; faults.

(a) To prolong; to pass beyond.

愆 期 passed the appointed time.
愆 滯 hampered; detained beyond the time.

搴¹ To seize. To gather, to pluck up.
890

搴 旗 to capture a flag.
搴 簾 to raise a bamboo screen.

褰¹ Under garments. To pick up the skirts.
891

褰 裳 涉 溱 to lift the skirts when crossing a brook.

騫¹ To be defective. To fail. To pluck up. To raise the head.
892

騫 汙 to lose the reputation.
騫 騰 to fly up.
騫 舉 to soar.

掮² To bear on the shoulders.
893

掮 客 to buy for another.
保 險 掮 客 insurance broker.
股 份 掮 客 or 股 票 掮 客 a stock-broker.

虔² To act with reverence. Devout, sincere.
894

虔 婆 a Buddhist nun; a witch.
虔 格 reverent.
虔 虔 devout and reverent.
虔 敬 or 虔 心 reverently; devoutly; devout.
⁵虔 潔 pure, without spot.
虔 禱 or 虔 告 or 虔 求 to pray devoutly.
虔 肅 reverent and grave demeanour.
虔 製 or 虔 修 to prepare with care, as prescriptions, etc.
虔 誠 sincere and devout.

(a) To take by force; to kill.

虔 劉 to slay and ravage.
矯 虔 to oppress.

鈐² A stamp, a seal.
895

鈐 印 to seal; to stamp.
鈐 盖 關 防 to affix a seal.
鈐 章 a seal.
鈐 記 a wooden seal used by petty officials.

(a) Latch of a door.

鈐 鍵 a door key; latch of a door.
鈐 鎖 a lock for a door.

黔 2 Black. Province of Kwei-chow.
896

黔 中 the region west and north-west of the River *Hsiang* in Hunan.
黔 雷 or 黔 嬴 a Taoist god.
黔 首 black-heads,—the people.
黔 驢 之 技 the resource of the Kweichow donkey—a kick; used of one whose plans are weak, or of one who cannot hide his stupidity and invites disgrace by taking a position for which he is not fitted.
黔 黎 black-haired people—the people.

拑 2 To nip, to grasp, as with forceps. Inter. 箝 and 鉗, 897 the two next entries.

拑 住 他 hold him tight.
拑 口 "to hold the tongue."
拑 釘·子 to pull out nails.

箝 2 Tweezers, pliers. To gag. Inter. 鉗 next.
898

箝 其 口 gagged him.
箝 制 to force submission.
箝 語 to stop free speech.
馬 箝 a bit.

鉗 2 Forceps, pincers, pliers; tongs. Manacles. A collar 899 put on prisoners.

鉗 制 to nip—to bring another to submission by force.
鉗 口 to gag.
鉗 口 不 言 shut the mouth tight-ly and not speak.
鉗·子 pincers; tweezers; tongs
鉗 惡 grasping.
手 鉗 manacles.
火 鉗 fire-tongs.
老 虎 鉗 carpenters' pincers; monkey wrench.

鉛 1
鈆
Lead. Also read *yüan*2.
900

鉛 刀 a leaden knife—blunt.
鉛 印 printed from lead types.
鉛 子 3 or 鉛 丸·子 bullets.
鉛 字 lead types.

5 鉛 槧 lead and tablets—ancient writing materials.
鉛 片 sheet lead; printers' leads.
鉛 筆 a lead pencil.
鉛 筆 畫 pencil drawings.
鉛 粉 or 鉛 華 white lead; ceruse.
10 鉛 素 pencil and silk—writing materials.
鉛 罐 lead canisters for tea.
鉛 鶩 or 鉛 刀 鶩 馬 a lead knife and an old horse—useless, poor talents.
鉛 黃 lead to write and yellow to blot out—proof correcting.

遣 3 To send, to banish, to chase away.
901

遣 使 a messenger; an envoy.
遣 刑 banishment in lieu of capital punishment.
遣 回 or 遣 還 to send back.
遣 奠 offerings made at a funeral.
5 遣 悶 to drive away melancholy.
遣 散 to disperse.
遣 晝 after continued rain when it clears at noon.
遣 發 to send on a message; to despatch.
遣 罪 or 遣 戍 exile for crimes.
10 遣 詞 to amend a text.
遣 謫 to banish.
遣 車 to send one's carriage to a funeral—to send condolences and a sum towards funeral expenses.
遣 送 出 洋 sent abroad, as students, etc.
遣 逐 to drive out; to expel.
消 遣 世 慮 to banish the cares of life.

繾 3.4.
Attached to; loving.
902

繾 綣 close affection; love; firmly attached.
繾 綣 難 忘 I can never forget our love.

譴 4
To reprimand, to scold.
903

譴 喘 to scold oneself out of breath.
譴 怒 to be angry with.
譴 罪 to blame.

嚴 譴 severe punishment.
譴 責 to reprimand; to blame.

欠 4 To owe money. Deficient. Radical 76.
904

欠 人·的 債 to be in debt to anyone.
欠 命 to owe a life. (*Budd.*).
欠 單 or 欠 契 or 欠 據 or 欠 帖 an IOU.
欠 戶 or 欠 主 a debtor.
5 欠 落 to owe.
欠 錢 or 欠 債 or 欠 賬 to owe money.
欠 錢 大 王 a princely debtor—deeply in debt. -*tai*4.*wang*
欠 項 or 欠 數 or 欠 欸 liabilities.
抵 欠 to give security for borrowed money.
10 拖 欠 a dragging debt; bad debts.
清 欠 out of debt.

(a) Deficiency. Short of. Lacking.

欠 功 lacking diligent application.
欠 妥 not satisfactory.
欠 撿 點 careless; wanting in method or decorum.
欠 爽 or 欠 安 out of sorts; indisposed—conventional phrase used to or of another.
5 欠 缺 deficient of; short in.
欠 至 誠 lacking perfect sincerity.
欠 莊 整 slovenly; untidy in dress.
欠 解 lacking in explanation.
欠 雨 crops lacking rain.
10 欠 身 or 欠 伸 to bow; to bend low.
呵 欠 or 打 欠 to yawn.

芡 4 Plant allied to the water-lily.
905

芡 實 seeds of the above, used when ground into meal, as a coarse food, also as medicine.

CH'IEN
TS'IEN. (ㄘㄧㄢ)

千 1
A thousand. Many.
906

千 之 to do it a thousand times.
千 人 所 指 what everyone points to.

千 刀 萬 剮 the punishment of hacking to pieces.

千 千 萬 萬 myriads.

[5] 千 古 ancient times; for ever;— used in mourning to express, gone for ever.

千 夫 長 head of a thousand soldiers; used for captain in translation of N.T., *rare*.

千 奇 百 怪 all sorts of strange things.

千 字 文 a book formerly used as a primer. It has 1,000 characters, not one of which is repeated; it is said to have been composed to order in a single night.

千 山 萬 水 distance, as of separation; sea and land; all lands.

[10] 千 年 如 昨 "a thousand years are like yesterday when it is past."

千 感 萬 謝 unbounded gratitude.

千 方 versatile.

千 方 百 計 all sorts of schemes; by one means or another.

千 枝 萬 葉 all the leaves and branches—multitudinous detail.

[15] 千 條 multitudinous.

千 歲 Your highness!

千 歲 之 日 至 the solstice of a thousand years ago.

千 片 石 or 千 層 紙 mica; talc.

千 百 年 more than a thousand years.

[20] 千 秋 a thousand years; a birthday.

千 篇 一 律 monotony.

千 繁 multitudinous details and troubles; a great embarrassment.

千 總 or 千 戎 former title for a lieutenant.

千 萬 large, indefinite number; a form of entreaty—by all means; before a negative it makes a very strong emphasis—on no account.

[25] 千 萬 年 countless ages.

千 變 萬 化 changeable; tricky.

千 軍 萬 馬 great host of mounted and foot soldiers.

千 載 一 遇 a rare occasion; a rare opportunity.

千 辛 萬 苦 multiplied hardships; severe toil.

[30] 千 里 鏡 a telescope.

千 里 香 *Daphne*.

千 里 馬 a fleet horse capable of 1,000 *li* a day.

千 金 Your daughter.

千 鈞 一 髮 30,000 *catties* hanging by a single hair—imminent peril.

[35] 千 頭 萬 緒 many ramifications; very complicated.

打 千 to go down on one knee in salute.

仟
907 | **A leader of a thousand. Inter. 千 above.**

仟 仟 dense growth as of trees; sombre, similar to 森 森 No. 5722.

芊
908 | **Exuberant and vigorous foliage.**

芊 眠 luxuriant growth of trees and grass; deep colour.

茂 芊 luxuriant growth.

(a) A green tint.

草 色 芊 芊 the grass is green like jade.

阡
909 | **A road leading north and south.**

阡 陌 public roads; highways in every direction; path between rice-fields.

(a) u.f. preceding, 芊. Luxuriant foliage.

阡 眠 luxuriant foliage.

阡 阡 flourishing growth of trees and plants.

揙扦
910 | **To stick in. To graft.**

揙 子 a rod ending in a spoon-bowl with a sharp point, used by tide-waiters in examining packages.

揙 子 手 or 揙 手 tide-waiters in Customs service.

揙 插 菓 木 to graft fruit trees.

揙 脚 a chiropodist.

遷迁
911 | **To remove. To shift.**

遷 于 喬 木 the birds flitted to the lofty trees.

遷 化 to change—Buddhist phrase for death, especially of a priest.

遷 喬 to remove one's residence, from first example above.

遷 善 to reform and do good.

[5] 遷 善 改 過 to reform evil ways and do good.

遷 國 or 遷 都 to move the seat of government to another city as capital.

遷 室 to remove the residence; to be exiled.

遷 客 name by which a banished official is called by the people of the place to which he goes.

遷 就 to make a compromise.

[10] 遷 居 to remove one's residence; to live as nomads.

遷 居 對 面 we have removed to the premises opposite.

遷 延 to procrastinate.

遷 怒 to transfer one's anger from one thing to another.

遷 情 to move the affections or the emotions.

[15] 遷 戍 to move troops to other quarters.

遷 改 to change.

遷 方 the west, the place to which all things go.

遷 染 changed by habits or customs.

遷 柩 to remove a coffin containing the remains of the dead.

[20] 遷 棺 to remove the coffin; to start the funeral procession.

遷 正 to regulate the calendar.

遷 百 姓 to deport the people.

遷 移 or 遷 徙 to remove; to change the lodgings.

遷 讁 to degrade and banish an official.

[25] 遷 費 removal expense—of graves.

遷 避 to "flit;" to clear out.

遷 閉 to close a shop and move to another place.

押 遷 to evict a tenant.

韆[1] A swing.
912

鞦·韆 a swing.
打 鞦·韆 to swing.

鐫[1] To engrave.
913

鐫 板 to engrave blocks for printing.

僉[1] All, the whole. Plural particle. u.f. next, and 簽
914　No. 917.

僉 不 允 all were unwilling.
僉 事 ancient office of senior assistant, or secretary to a board, revived in recent years under the republic, and again abolished.
僉 以 爲 是 all were agreed that it was right.
僉 壬 mean, despicable fellow.
僉 稟 a joint petition.
僉 稱 to make a unanimous statement.
僉 言 如 一 all were of one opinion.
僉 謀 plan decided by all.
僉 議 public opinion.

簽[1] Bamboo slips used for drawing lots.
915　Inter. 籤 No. 917.

簽 分 to appoint by lot.
簽 制 to select officials by lot.
抽 簽 to draw lots.
牙 簽 toothpicks.

(a) To sign; to endorse.

簽·不 到 字 has no authority to sign.
簽 印 duly stamped.
簽 字 or 簽 名 to endorse; to sign.
簽 押 to endorse or sign; to witness a signature.
簽 訂 signed.
簽 訂 合 同 a signed agreement.
簽 訂 條 約 a signed treaty.
簽 題 to subscribe for; the superscription, as of a letter.
冒 簽 人 名 to counterfeit a signature.

(b) A label.

簽·子 the address slip on a parcel or letter.
簽 書 to label books; the family register.
簽 箋 or 簽 條 a label.

(c) To send, as police.

簽 傳 to summon.
簽 差 to send police.
簽 派 to send police with a summons.

韱[1] Wild onions or leeks.
916

籤[1] A slip of bamboo. A lot for divination, etc. A warrant. A tally.
917
Inter. 簽 No. 915.

籤 捐 a lottery.
籤 掣 or 掣 籤 to select places for officials by lot.
籤 票 a warrant.
籤 筒 bamboo tube for lots.
籤 詩 the verses on temple tallies.
籤 語 the response of the lot.
籤 譜 a book on divination by the lot.
出 籤 to issue a warrant.
抽 籤 to draw lots.
插 籤 to stick tallies into packages to check the number delivered, as when loading or unloading ships, etc.
求 籤 to draw lots before the idols.
求 籤 問 卜 to divine by the lot.
火 籤 an urgent warrant.
竹 籤 bamboo tallies; bamboo slips on which oracular verses are written as responses from the idols.

潛[2]
潜
918
To hide away; to secrete oneself; to lie hid under water. Retired. Secretly.

潛 伏 concealed; lying close; latent.
潛 伏 期 latent period.
潛 伏·的 latent; potentially.
潛 伏 芽 latent buds.
潛 住 to live in retirement.
潛 修 to reform in retirement.
潛 入 to enter with secrecy.
潛 勢 力 latent force or energy.

潛 匿 to hide; to secrete oneself.
潛 居 to live in retirement.
潛 師 secret moving of troops.
潛 德 secret virtues.
潛 心 於 聖 人 to inquire deeply into the teachings of the sage.
潛 心 而 勉 學 to study with diligence and a quiet mind.
潛 意 識 or 半 意 識 subconsciousness.
潛 步 hidden steps—to walk carefully.
潛 水 服 or 潛 水 衣 diving dress.
潛 水 艇 or 潛 艇 submarine boats.
潛 滋 暗 長 (chang[3]) to grow in secret.
潛 熱 latent heat.
潛 玩 to enter into the spirit of a book.
潛 聽 to overhear.
潛 航 水 雷 艇 submarine torpedo-boat.
潛 能 latent force; potentiality.
潛 藏 in hiding; in retirement.
潛 藏 隱 伏 to lie hidden.
潛 行 水 中 to walk under water.
潛 蹤 secret movements.
潛 逃 to abscond.
潛 邸 residence of the heir-apparent in ancient times.
潛 雖 伏 矣 although (the fish) sinks and lies at the bed of the river.
潛 龍 無 用 a concealed dragon is of no use—talent is useless when hidden.

前[2] Formerly; before; in front of.
919

前 世 former generations; in a previous life.
前 世·紀 last century.
前 事 or 前 件 antecedent.
前 人 a predecessor; by the same writer, as when extracts are given.
前 仰 to bend forward.
前 來 come to hand—phrase in letters, despatches, etc.
前 功 previous services.
前 功 盡 棄 the former labour is all wasted.
前 半 日 the forenoon.
前 古 antiquity; past ages.
前 哲 ancient sages.
前 哨 an outpost.

前因 antecedent as opposed to consequent, 後果.
前夫 former husband of a widow who re-marries.
[15] 前天 or 前日 the day before yesterday.
前定 to prepare; beforehand.
前審 antecedent trial.
前已 already. 前年 year before last.
前廳 or 堂前 a lobby or main hall in a house.
[20] 前引 or 前導 to lead forward.
前後 before and after; about; first and last.
前後左右 before and behind, right and left—in every direction.
前後有旒 fringes before and behind.
前心 the breast.
[25] 前志 one's former desires or ambition.
前愆 or 前失 past errors.
前慮 forethought; premeditated.
前提 or 前題 logical premise.
前敵 or 前線 the "front," front line of battle.
前敵司令 commander-in-charge of the front lines.
前時 or 以前 formerly; past.
前晚 evening before last.
前景 foreground.
前月 the month before last; a month ago; some time past.
前朝 the previous dynasty.
前次 on a former occasion.
前欸 the aforesaid. (legal).
前母 name by which the son of a second wife speaks of his father's former wife.
前民 the ancients.
前清 the Manchu Dynasty. A.D. 1644—1911.
前清制度 the Manchu regime.
前清末造 the closing period of the Manchu dynasty.
前烈 ancient worthies; the achievements of past worthies.
前生 a former life. (Budd.).
前知 foreknowledge; prediction.
前程 official career or status.
前程萬里 he will have a great career.
前程難料 it is hard to predict his future career.
前經 already; before.
前緣 predestined lot.
前署 predecessor in office.
前者後者 former and latter.
前置詞 preposition.=介詞.

前胡 Angelica.
前膛鎗 muzzle-loading gun.
[55] 前行 to go forward to; to go before.
前規 an example from one who has gone before.
前言 former words; prophecy.
前赴 or 前往 to proceed to.
前車之鑑 take warning from the cart ahead. See 鑑 No. 841-11.
[60] 前輩 seniors; previous generation.
前述 one above mentioned; the aforesaid. [the person who was corresponding with you.
前途 the future, the road ahead;
前進 to progress; to advance.
前部 the front of; anterior; the fore part.
[65] 前鋒 or 前隊 the advance guard.
前門 the front door; south gate of Peking.
前防 the "front;" advance line of troops.
前防司令部 headquarters at the front.
前項 the aforesaid item.
[70] 前頭 on ahead; in front.
前驅 a fore-runner; advanced guard.
光前裕後 to glorify ancestors and enrich posterity.
向前 forward; on in front.
在前 in front; before.
[75] 日前 formerly; the other day.
目前 or 眼前 now; in the present; before the eyes.
瞻前顧後 to observe both before and behind; circumspection.
雨前 the young tea buds—Hyson tea.
面前 in front of the eyes; in one's presence.

淺 [3] Shallow, superficial. Easy to comprehend. Vulgar.
920
淺信 weak in faith.
淺學 superficial scholarship; easily learnt.
淺毛 short hair—of fur.
淺水 shallow water.
[5] 淺淺的 very shallow.
淺淺可說 he can say a little—of a child.
淺灘 a shoal.
淺牽 pretentious and superficial.
淺白言之 to speak simply.

[10] 淺知 superficial knowledge.
淺窄 narrow-minded; shallow.
淺而易見 simple and easily understood.
淺聞 shallow experience.
淺薄 shallow; superficial.
[15] 淺見 limited experience.
淺註 easy explanation.
淺謀 superficial plans.
淺近 shallow.
淺近之徒 a shallow, superficial person.
[20] 淺陋 mean; vile.
淺露 superficial ideas, not at all profound.
淺鮮 insignificant; slight.
不淺 serious; no light matter.
擱淺 to be aground, as a boat; grounded high and dry.
[25] 深淺 deep and shallow—depth; the difference between things.
甚淺 very simple and easy; very shallow.
眼淺 shallow outlook.

(a) Light, of colour.

淺色 a light shade of colour.
淺黃 light yellow.

錢个 [2] Money, copper coin, cash. Wealth.
921

錢串 cash strings.
錢債細故 the mere debt of money is a trifle.
錢債案 civil cases in law.
錢囊 a money bag, purse.
[5] 錢塘 the Ts'ien T'ang River in Chekiang.
錢局 a mint.
錢幣學 or 古錢學 numismatics.
錢幣革命 currency reform.
錢店 or 錢舖 or 錢莊 a money-changers; a bank.
[10] 錢愚 or 守錢奴 a miser.
錢文 money.
錢樹子 prostitutes.
錢櫃 a cash box.
錢神 fig., money is as powerful as a god.
[15] 錢票 or 票子 bank-notes.
錢穀 to pay taxes; accountant in charge of taxes.
錢簿 an account book.

錢·糧 taxes; revenue from taxes.
錢 紙 cash paper, burnt for the dead.
20 錢 荒 scarcity of money.
錢 行 cash exchange rate. (-hang²)
錢°財 riches; wealth; property.
錢 賦 exactions; levies.
付 現 錢 to pay ready money.
25 付 錢 to pay out.
十 文 錢 ten *cash*.
小 錢 small *cash*.
換 錢 to change into cash.
銅 錢 銀 錢 copper a n d silver money.

(a) One tenth of a Chinese ounce. A *mace*.

四 兩 五 錢 銀·子 ￥4.50. i.e., 4½ ozs., (*Ch.*) of silver.
買 二 錢·的 buy 1/5 of an ounce.

(b) Read *chien³*. Weeding implement like a spade.

錢 鏟 a small hoe or spade for weeding.

倩 4 The appearance of the dimple in smiling. Pretty. 922 Handsome, of a man.

倩 女 離 魂 death of a young girl —from the story of a girl named 倩 娘, whose soul fled with her lover and left her body behind.
巧 笑 倩 兮 the artful dimples of her smile.
美 倩 handsome.

(a) Read *ch'ing* or *ts'ing⁴*. Husband of a daughter.

妹 倩 younger sister's husband.
姪 倩 husband of a niece.

(b) To hire. To plagiarize.

倩 人 a plagiarist.
倩 茶 to borrow.
代 倩 instead of; on behalf of.
僱 倩 to engage, as workmen.

箐 4 To draw a bamboo bow or crossbow. Bamboo groves 923 in Yunnan or Kweichow. Read *ching¹* or *tsing¹*. Fish-traps or baskets. Creels.

靖 4 A pall to cover the hearse. 924

蒨 4 Luxuriant growth. u.f. 茜 No. 929. 925

蒨 蒨 fresh and clear; luxuriant.
蒨 蔚 vigorous growth.
茂 蒨 flourishing vegetation.

塹 | 2 Moat around a city. A
壍 | channel. 926

坑 塹 a moat outside a rampart.
天 塹 natural boundary or moat, as the Yangtze River between north and south.

槧 4 Memorandum tablets. Boards for cutting blocks 927 for printing.

槧 本 printing blocks.
簡 槧 writing tablets.

荐 4 To repeat; repeated; recurring. u.f. 薦 No. 872. To 928 introduce, etc. Pron. *chien⁴*.

荐 饑 recurring famines.

(a) Inter. 薦 No. 872. Grass.

荐 居 nomads.
戎 狄 荐 居 the nomad tribes of *Jung* and *Ti*.
荐 食 to nibble like a silkworm— to encroach upon territory.
荐 食 上 國 gradually encroaching on our territory.

茜 4 The plant from which madder is prepared, also 929 used as a medicine.

CHIH. (业)
(Chï)

卮 1 A measuring cup; a goblet with handles. 930

卮 匜 winecup and water-basins.
卮 言 all-embracing expressions, words which flow from the heart like water overflowing from a goblet.

梔 1 The *Gardenia*, a plant of which the seeds produce a 931 yellow dye.

梔·子 or 黃 梔 the nut which produces a yellow dye.

知 1 To know; to perceive; to be aware of. 932

知 一 不 難, 難 在 于 終 It is not difficult to know the "One," the difficulty is in full knowledge.
知 一 者 無 一 不 知 H e who knows the "One."—there is no one thing he may not know.
知 世 experience of the world.
知 之 弗 豫 to know that he is not fit.
5 知 之 次 也 the second class of knowledge.
知·事 a confidential clerk formerly employed in the office of a provincial judge. A magistrate.
知 交 intimate.
知 人 to know men.
知 人 善 任 to use a man according to his ability.
10 知 兵 skilled in military arts.
知 其 先 後 to know the sequence of things.
知 其 內 幕 to be "in the know."
知 名 a wide reputation.
知 名 士 a famous man.
15 知 命 50 years of age—from 五 十 而 知 天 命, at 50 years Confucius knew the decrees of Heaven.
知 善 不 為 to know the good and yet not do it.
知 子 莫 如 父 no one knows a son like his father.
知 客 to entertain visitors—of Buddhist priests.
知 州 a department magistrate under former regimes.
20 知 己 "know thyself." *See below* 23, 24, 26.
知 幾 to have a foreknowledge of
知 府 prefect under former regimes.
知 彼 知 己 to know both sides to know others and to know oneself.
知 彼 知 己 百 戰 百 勝 t know your own plans and hav acquaintance with those of th enemy means constant victory

²⁵知徒莫如師 no one knows a pupil like his teacher.

知心 or 知音 or 知己 an intimate friend; one who knows me.

知恥 or 知羞 a sense of shame.

知恥近乎勇 a feeling of shame is near to courage.

知恩必報 conscious of a kindness and acknowledging a duty to repay it.

³⁰知悉 to be perfectly acquainted with; informed of a matter.

知情 to acknowledge obligations to; to be cognisant of facts.

知情縱⁴容 to permit that which is known to be evil.

知感 to entertain a sense of gratitude.

知慮 prudent.

³⁵知所先務 know how to put first things first.

知政 to administer government.

知·會 or 知照 to communicate; to inform.

知縣 a district magistrate.

知者 a sage; one who knows. *See below.* A.

⁴⁰知⁴能 knowledge and ability.

知°覺 perception; to perceive.

知言 wisdom; far-sighted words.

知言知人 to know the force of words is to know men.

知·識 knowledge and experience; common sense. +933. 21

⁴⁵知·識技能 knowledge and skill.

知變 to compromise; to accomodate oneself to circumstances.

知趣 a sense of the fitness of things; tactful.

知足 to be satisfied; contented.

知足之足常足矣 the satisfaction of knowing satisfaction is constant satisfaction.

⁵⁰知遇 to receive hospitality.

知·道 or 知曉 to know; aware of; conversant with.

知道了 "Noted." Formula used by emperor at the end of memorials and state papers.

知過必改 or 知過改過 to know one's faults and correct them.

知錯 or 知非 to know one's faults; an acknowledgement of a fault.

⁵⁵知非難行維難 to know is not difficult, but practice is difficult.

一知半解 imperfect knowledge.

不令人知 secretly; stealthily.

不知不覺 unconsciously; involuntarily.

不知世·故 ignorant of the world.

⁶⁰不知人事 insensible; unconscious.

不知好歹 with no sense of right and wrong or of the fitness of things.

不知底·細 ignorant of minute details.

不患莫己知求爲可知也 I am not concerned that I am not known, I seek to be worthy to be known.

先知 foreknowledge; used for prophet in translation of Scripture.

⁶⁵故知 my old friend.

明知 with knowledge; purposely.

深知 to have full knowledge or information of.

無知·的 an ignoramus.

通知·他 let him know; inform him.

(a) Read *chih⁴*. Used in the classics for 智, the next. Wisdom; knowledge.

知之至 the perfection of knowledge.

知無不知¹ the wise embrace all knowledge.

知者不失人 the wise do not err in regard to men.

知者不惑 the wise are free from perplexities.

智⁴ Wisdom, knowledge. Cleverness, prudence.
933

智利 Chile.

智利硝 nitrates from Chile.

智力 intellectual power.

智力測驗 intelligence test.

⁵智勇 brave and wise.

智器 a man of great wisdom and talents.

智囊 a bag of wisdom—wide experience and full knowledge.

智圓行方 wide knowledge but limited practice.

智將 a general who is a clever strategist.

¹⁰智·慧 perfect wisdom; prudence.

智·慧文學 Wisdom Literature.

智·慧板 the tangram or seven piece puzzle.

智明 sagacity.

智禽 the wild goose.

¹⁵智育 culture; mental training.

智能 or 智巧 wisdom and ability; intelligence.

智能權 right of talents. (*legal*).

智調 talent; ability.

智謀 or 智畧 cleverness, strategy.

²⁰知·識 knowledge and experience.

智·識階·級 intelligentsia.

急智 presence of mind.

智慧測·量⁴ intelligence test.

智力商數 "I.Q."

蜘¹ The spider.
934

蜘·蛛 the spider.

蜘·蛛絲 filaments of a spider's web.

蜘·蛛網 a spider's web.

之¹ To arrive at; to go to.
935

之一邦 to arrive at another state.

之死靡它 to death no other— said of a widow who swore never to remarry, now used of a determination that does not fear death.

將之楚 having to go to Ts'u.

將何之 Where are you going?

小大由之 in things small and great we follow them—the ancient worthies.

心之所之 the inclination of the heart.

(a) Personal pronoun, he, she, it; this, that, these, etc. Often used as a possessive, like the colloquial, 的 No. 6213.

之外 besides this; in addition.

之子³ this person; a bride, from the next:—

之子³于歸 the bride goes to her home.

之後 after this; afterwards.

⁵之謂 is a way of calling.

以其兄之子妻⁴之 gave him his brother's daughter to wife.

以其道得之 obtain them in the proper way.

其之未能信 I cannot trust in this.

如之何 What about it?

¹⁰我未之見也 I have not seen it.

未 之 有 也 there never has been such.

求 之 與² does he ask for information?

然 之 agreed with him.

(b) Zigzag, winding.

之 字 路 a winding path.

之 江 the winding river, the *Ch'ien T'ang* River in Chekiang. The province of Chekiang.

(c) Used for 於 No. 7643. In regard to.

之 其 所 畏 敬 as regards those whom they reverence.

之 於 天 下 也 as regards the empire.

(d) Finally; final particle, not translatable.

之 乎 者 也, auxiliary particles, used to embellish the style—used of a pedantic style of writing.

尹 公 之 他 *Yin kung t'o*, the character 之 is used here for euphony.

庾 公 之 斯 *Yü kung szǔ*, the character 之 is merely euphonic.

總 之 finally; to sum up. Cf. (a).

芝 ¹ A fungus with purplish
936 stalk, it will keep for a long time, it indicates long life and prosperity. A fragrant iris. Inter. 芷 No. 943.

芝 儀 Your fragrant present.
芝 眉 expression of countenance.
芝 艾 the above plant and artemisia—honourable and lowly.
芝 草 or 瑞 芝 names of the above.
⁵芝 蔴 sesame.
芝 蔴 油 sesame oil.
芝 蘭 之 室 a beautiful mansion.
芝 蘭 氣 味 sweet fragrance of iris and epidendrum—friendship.
芝 顏 or 芝 宇 Your fortunate face.

支 ¹ A branch, descendants.
937 Radical 65.

支 使 to send; to employ; an officer under the *T'ang* dynasty.

支 吾 or 支 托 to prevaricate; to make excuses; to evade; carelessly; to put off.
支 子³ younger sons.
支 厰 a branch office.
⁵支 屬 relatives.
支 店 a branch store or shop; an agency.
支 會 branch society or church.
支 水 or 支 流 tributary or affluent.
支 派 a tribe; branch of a family.
¹⁰支 裔 descendants.
支 解 dismemberment, an ancient punishment.
支 解 遺 骸 dismemberment of the corpse.
支 路 or 支 線 a branch railway.
支 那 transliteration of *China*.
¹⁵支 部 a department.
支 配 to assort; to allot; allotment. *See below.* B. 9.
支 離 irrelevant; separated and solitary.
支 骸 the members of the body.
地 支 the twelve "branches of earth," which, combined with the ten "stems of heaven" make a series or cycle of sixty. *See appendix.*
²⁰宗 支 branches of the same clan.
本 支 root and branches; father and son.
橫 支 collateral branches.
近 支 near relatives.

(a) To pay; to advance, as money.

支 付 to pay; to advance.
支 付 匯 票 drafts payable.
支 借 to advance money.
支 出 to disburse.
⁵支 出 欵 disbursements.
支 出 虧 耗 losses incurred.
支 取 to pay out.
支 應 to meet a demand; to wait on.
支 撥 to pay money; to meet expenses.
¹⁰支 消 to expend; expenses; outlay.
支 用 or 支 發 to give out; to advance pay, etc.
支 票 a cheque.
支 票 簿 cheque book.
支 絀 needy; in want of ready cash.
¹⁵支 給 to give; to advance wages.
支 費 expenses; expenditure.
支 錢 to draw money.

停 支 to stop payment.
濫 支 to waste money.
²⁰透 支 or 浮 支 欵 an overdraft.
預 支 薪 金 to advance wages or salary.

(b) To support; to prop up; to manage; to withstand.

支·持 to hold up; to bear up; to stand firm; to direct; to put on one side; to make excuses; to withstand; to control; to manage.
支·持 不 住 unable to hold down; not able to support or to manage.
支 搭 to erect; to set up, as a tent.
支 撐 to prop up.
⁵支 撐 危 局 to support a perilous situation.
支 更 a watchman.
支 柱 to support.
支 綴 to prop up; to support.
支 配 to manage; to direct; to control; to hold authority over; to distribute. *See above.*—16.
¹⁰支 頤 to support the cheek with the hand.
支 點 a fulcrum.

枝 ¹ A branch; to branch off.
938

枝·子 a twig; a branch.
枝 幹 or 枝 柯 trunk and branches; the cyclic terms; a rod.
枝 條 a twig.
枝 梢 the tips of branches.
⁵枝 梧 to prevaricate; to resist.
枝 水 tributary or affluent.
枝 節 branches and knots—complications.
枝 葉 leaves and branches; nonessentials; offspring.
枝 蔓 branches and tendrils.
¹⁰枝 誤 wrong; erroneous.
枝 路 branch roads.
棲 枝 to roost; to rest on a branch.
四 枝 four branches; the limbs.

(a) To prop. A post or prop. N.A.

枝 撐 to prop up.
枝 樓 to maintain a position.
一 枝 兵 detachment of troops.
一 枝 花 a flower.

(b) Read *ch'i²*. An extra finger or toe.

枝 指 extra fingers or toes.
生 有 枝 指 born with extra fingers.

止 **³ To stop. To desist. Radical 77.**
939

止·住 to cease; to desist.
止 妒 to allay the jealousy of a woman.
止 怒 to cease from anger.
止 戈 爲 武 the characters 止 and 戈 make 武, so that to stop the use of weapons and avoid war is truly military.
⁵止 或 尼 之 a man may be stopped by others.
止 步 stand still; "No admittance!"
止 水 stagnant water.
止 渴 to alleviate thirst.
止 痛 藥 anodynes.
¹⁰止 痛 藥 anodynes.
止 癢 to allay irritation.
止 血 to staunch bleeding.
止 血 藥 styptics.
止 謗 to shut the mouth of slanderers.
¹⁵止 過 to cause evil conduct to cease by severe punishment.
止 酒 to abstain from intoxicants.
止 饑 to allay hunger.
止 點 stopping point.
不 止 not merely . . . .; not as little as you say.
²⁰中 止 to stop suddenly.
停 止 to cease; to stop.
禁 止 to prohibit; to forbid.
舉 止 or 容 止 risings and ceasings—conduct; behaviour; air; deportment.
阻 止 to prevent; to hinder.

(a) To rest in; to detain.

止 宿 to stop for the night.
止 息 to give over; to rest.
止 於 至 善 to rest in the highest excellence.
止 泊 to come to rest.
⁵止 留 to detain.
知 止 to know the point wherein to rest.

(b) Only; u.f. 只 No. 946.

止·得 the only thing possible is to . . . .
止·是 it is only . . . .

址 **³ A foundation. A boundary.**
940

住 址 a dwelling; a house.
四 址 the four boundaries.
地 址 an allotment of land.
故 址 old ruins.

沚 **³ An islet in a stream.**
941

在 水 中 沚 he is on the islet in the stream.

祉 **³ Happiness; blessedness.**
942

祉 福 joy; blessedness.
順 頌 日 祉 May happiness be your daily portion—complimentary close to letters.

芷 **³ A fragrant plant, variety of iris, the root is used as medicine.**
943

白 芷 the root of the above.

趾 **³ The toes. The foot, a hoof.**
944

趾 骨 the metatarsus.
舉 趾 to lift the feet—to begin work.
高 趾 "high-stepping."

阯 **³ The foundations of a wall. Inter. 址 No. 940.**
945

交 阯 Cochin-China.
基 阯 foundations.

只 **³ Only; but; yet; merely.**
946

只 不 過 simply . . . .
只 今 at present; just now.
只 可 如 此 there is no alternative.
只 因 but; inasmuch as; only; the only cause; for the simple reason.
⁵只 如 just as if . . . .
只 好 I can only . . . . ; the best thing is to . . . .

只 宜 or 只 可 this only will be right; this alone is correct.
只·得 the only alternative is.
只 怕 I suspect; I think; most probably; the only thing is to.
¹⁰只 恨 unfortunately.
只 恐 lest; fearful lest.
只 想 to let the mind dwell on.
只·是 but; still; however.
只 有 there is only.
¹⁵只 此 一 家 we have no other shops.
只 此 而 已 only this and nothing more.
只 死 而 已 death is the only alternative.只 當 regard it only as . .
只 當 the only suitable thing is . . .
只 管 just; merely; nothing more than; do not hesitate to.
²⁰只 管 說 say on!
只 能 can only; there is no alternative.
只 要 only want; it is only necessary; if only.
只 見 just observed; only saw; it came to pass that.
只 須 it is only necessary.

(a) Final particle, not translatable.

不 諒 人 只 Why do you misunderstand me?
母 也 天 只 O Mother! O Heaven!

咫 **³ Foot measure of the *Chow* dynasty, divided into eight inches.**
947

咫 尺 之 間 very close; almost; within a foot of.
咫 尺 天 顏 intimate adviser of the emperor.
咫 聞 so close that one can hear.

枳 **³ A hedge thorn; bramble. Hurtful. Variety of orange with very thick skin.**
948

枳 實 dried oranges as above.
枳 棘 thorns; prickles.
枳 殼 skin of the dried orange from this tree.
枳 落 a hedge.
枳 首 蛇 a two-headed snake.

(a) Read *chi³*. The *Hovenia Dulcis*.

枳 椇 the above.

肢股 [1] The limbs. Wings of birds. Legs of animals.
949

肢 解 or 支 解 dismemberment.
肢 骨 bones of the extremities.
肢 體 the members and trunk of the body.
四 肢 五 內 the members and organs of the body.

軹 [3] End of the axle projecting from the hub. Divergent. Final particle.
950

軹 首 蛇 two-headed snake.
岐 軹 cross roads.

治 [4] To heal, etc. This is the current pron. of 1021 (a), q.v.

砥 [3] Smooth. To polish.
951

砥 矢 as smooth as a whetstone and as straight as a dart—good roads or good words.

(a) Read *tĭ*[3]. A whetstone.

砥 属 之 資 the help of grinding and polishing—as given by friends who tell us our faults.
砥 柱 a rock in the Yellow River in Honan—unmoveable under great stresses.
砥 礪 smooth and coarse whetstones.

祇 [1] To respect. Distinguish 祇 No. 538.
952

祇 候 to wait with respect.
祇 敬 to venerate.
祇 謝 respectful thanks.
祇 載 見 瞽 叟 he reverently carried out his affairs and waited on *Ku sou*.
祇 領 or 祇 承 to receive with reverence.

(a) Read *chih*[3]. Only; but. u.f. 只 No. 946.

祇 可 however; can only.
祇 望 to expect.

祇 有 一 樣 there is only one kind.
祇 此 only this.

紙帋 [3] Papers; stationery. A document. N.A. for papers, documents, etc.
953

紙 上 空 談 mere paper talk—impracticable schemes.
紙 傘 or 紙 遮·子 a paper umbrella.
紙 壓 paper weight.
紙 夾 a paper clip.
[5] 紙 帛 or 紙 扎 or 紙 劄 paper houses, animals, etc., burned for the use of the dead.
紙 幣 paper money; notes.
紙 幣 本 位 paper money as a standard.
紙 張 or 紙 聯 stationery; scroll-paper, etc.
紙 張 筆 墨 stationery.
[10] 紙 撚 twisted paper used as string.
紙 扇 a paper fan.
紙 殼·子 or 紙 褙·子 pasteboard.
紙 煙 cigarettes.
紙 煤 spill of twisted paper used as a match. Usually 紙 煤·子
[15] 紙 版 paper shells for stereos.
紙 牌 playing cards.
紙 田 to work fields on paper—unpractical.
紙 筋 paper pulp mixed into plaster or mortar to bind it.
紙 背 the reverse or wrong side of a sheet of paper.
[20] 紙 草 the papyrus.
紙 錁 paper ingots burned for the dead.
紙 錢 paper money used in idolatry. 紙 老 虎 pretended ferocity.
紙 馬 paper printed with the image of an idol, burned before the altar.
紙 魚 or 蠹 魚 the silver-fish.
[25] 紙 鳶 or 鷂·子 a paper kite.
一 刀 紙 a quire of paper, it varies, but 100 sheets is the usual quantity.
包 皮 紙 packing paper.
吸 墨 紙 blotting paper.
字 紙 written or printed paper.
手 紙 toilet paper.
[30] 抄 圖 紙 tracing paper.
新 報 紙 newspapers.
格·子 紙 ruled paper.

磨 紙 glass-paper or sand-paper.
草 紙 coarse wrapping paper.
[35] 遞 紙 to hand in a document.
↑ 複 寫 紙 carbon-paper.

峙 [3] A peak. To pile up. To store.
954

峙 立 不 搖 firm and unmoved.
峙 積 to store; to hoard.
峙 糧 to collect provisions.

痔 [4] Piles.
955

痔 瘡 bleeding piles.
外 痔 內 痔 external and internal piles.

黹 [3] Embroidery. Radical 204.
956

鍼 黹 needlework.

旨 [3] An imperial decree. A purpose.
957

旨 意 will; decree.
奉 旨 by imperial orders.
璽 旨 the imperial will.
請 旨 to ask for a mandate; to seek the will of the gods.

(a) Purport; drift.

旨 趣 meaning; essential thought or sentiment, as of a poem.
同 旨 the same purport as . . . .
大 旨 the leading thought.
意 旨 the purport of.
本 旨 the purport or drift of a thing.

(b) Good, excellent. Beautiful.

旨 哉 How delicious !
旨 蓄 vegetables stored for winter.
旨 酒 excellent wine.
稱 旨 it accords with my taste.
美 旨 delicacies.

恉 [3] Purport; drift. *Similar to the last.*
958

指 [3] A finger; a toe.
959

指 不 勝 屈 more than can be counted on the fingers—very many.

指¹甲 finger or toe nails.
指¹甲套 sheaths for long nails.
指¹甲草 the balsam, used to dye the nails.
⁵指節 finger or toe joints.
指背相聯 harmony between the members—used fig.
指臂之助 mutual assistance—the assistance of arm and fingers. 指語法 dactylology.
指語 to speak on the fingers as the deafmutes do.
指²頭 the fingers or toes.
¹⁰指²頭印·子 finger-print. A.c. 指紋.
指²頭尖 tips of the fingers.
指²骨 bones of the fingers or toes.
中指 the middle finger.
二指 or 食指 the index finger.
¹⁵修指¹甲 to pare the nails.
四指厚 as thick as four fingers held sideways.
大指 or 拇指 the thumb or great-toe.
小指 the little finger.
屈指計算 to count by bending down the fingers.
²⁰彈指 to snap the fingers—quickly.
染指 "to have a finger in the pie."
無名指 the third or ring finger.
養指¹甲 to cultivate long nails.
指紋學 dactylography.
(a) To point; to direct; to indicate.
指事 a class of characters whose form indicates the meaning, as 上 'up' and 下 'down.'
指令 instructions from a higher official in reply to inquiries as to duties, etc.
指使 to employ; to direct; to point out.
指出 to point out; to call to notice.
⁵指南 a guide-book.
指南針 the compass.
指向 direction of; pointing towards.
指名 to mention by name.
指天誓日 to point to heaven and swear by the sun.
¹⁰指官 in the name of an official.
指定 or 指明 to define; to mark; to designate.
指實 to tell the truth.
指導 to guide; to conduct; to manage.
指導員 a guide; director.
¹⁵指引 to point out; to guide.
指手畫脚 to gesticulate.
指授 to give definite directions.

指控 to lay a charge; to accuse.
指揮 to command; to point to; to indicate; to lead; military leader; to guide.
²⁰指揮刀 an officer's sword.
指揮棒 conductor's baton.
指摘 to point out a fault; to reprove mildly.
指撥 to order transfer of troops.
指教 to teach; to instruct; instruction.
²⁵指數 index figures in algebra.
指斥 to reprove; to correct..
指日 point to the day—at an early date.
指日可清 it will very shortly be cleared up.
指日成功 it soon will be an accomplished fact.
³⁰指日而待 wait for a speedy fulfilment.
指日高陞 May you soon be promoted!
指望 to expect; to hope for.
指東劃西 to point to east and west—irrelevant.
指東擊西 to make a feint.
³⁵指桑罵槐 to point to the mulberry and revile the locust tree—to scold a person indirectly.
指畫 to delineate.
指示 to point out; to indicate, as a fault.
指禿說瞎 to point to the bald and speak of the blind—to talk at.
指薦 to recommend for a position, etc.
⁴⁰指認 to identify.
指證 to prove; to give evidence.
指質 to point out in evidence.
指趣 the essence; the scope of; the sentiment of.
指路標 a signpost; a finger post.
⁴⁵指路碑 roadside tablet for guidance.
指針 an index; hand of a clock or dial.
指陳 to expound a theme.
指鹿爲馬 to call a stag a horse—wilful misrepresentation. *Chao Kao* plotted to put the second son of *Ch'in Shih Huang* on the throne; in order to ascertain those of the courtiers who were loyal to him, he presented the prince with a stag and said that it was a horse; the prince asked the courtiers

what it was; some did not reply, others said, "It is a stag." *Chao* noted these, and later on did away with them.
指麾 flag signalling; to direct.
十手所指 what ten hands point to.

脂¹ **The fat of animals; lard; grease; ointment. Cosmetics; gums. Wealth.** 960
脂油 lard; fat.
脂澤 smooth and glossy, as if oiled.
脂粉 cosmetics; feminine beauty.
脂粉氣 feminine; womanlike ways.
⁵脂粉費 pin-money.
脂肪 fats, especially animal fats.
脂肪線 sebaceous glands.
脂膏 grease; wealth.
脂色 rouge.
¹⁰脂車 to grease cart wheels.
脂韋 oiled, soft leather—pliable, servile, subservient.
脂飾 to paint the face.
脂麻 linseed.
民脂 the fat, i.e., the wealth, of the people.

搘¹ **To prop up; the base of a stone tablet.** A.w. 支. 961
搘起來 to prop up a thing.
搘起窗戶 to prop open a window.
搘頤 to support the cheek with the hands.

夂⁴ **To follow. Radical 34.** 962

彘⁴ **Swine.** 963

疐⁴ **Hindered; embarrassed. Read** *ti*⁴. **The stem of a fruit.** 964

懥⁴ 懫 **Enraged; resentful. To hate. To desist.** 965
忿懥 to be angry.

躓[4] To stumble.
966

躓蹶 to stumble and fall.
躓頓 to stumble and stop.

隻[1] Single. One of a pair.
967 N.A.

隻字無誤 not a single character is wrong.
隻字片紙 one character on a slip of paper—a brief note.
隻手不能遮天 a single hand cannot hide the sky.
隻日 odd days of the month.
隻立 to stand alone. ⌊=單日
隻身 myself; alone.
一隻牛 an ox.
一隻眼 an eye.
一隻船 a boat.

雉[4] The ringed pheasant.
968

雉兔者 catchers of hares and pheasants.
雉媒 a decoy pheasant.
雉鷄 the Tartar pheasant.

(a) A crenellated wall.

雉堞 a parapet.
雉經 to hang oneself.

稺
稚|[4] Young grain. Tender;
穉| young; delicate; small.
969

稺子[3] or 稺童 a child; a lad; children.
稺氣 gentle; innocence of childhood.
稺齒 young.
幼稺 young and tender.
幼稺園 kindergarten.
幼稺時代 the age of youth.
老稺 old and young.

觶[4] Goblet of horn. A tankard.
970

志[4] Determination; will; purpose. Ambition; scope.
971

志之所至氣必至焉 where determination reaches, energy (to perform) follows.
志于學 the mind bent on study.
志願 ideals; ambitions; wishes.
志願兵 volunteers.
[5]志願書 a written agreement, as signed by a pupil; a signed pledge.
志・向 purpose; inclination; bent; intention; aspiration, ambition.
志固心之所之 the will, doubtless, is that which the mind follows.
志士 a determined man.
志壹則動氣 if the will acts alone it will move the passions.
[10]志大而略於事 great in resolves and careless in action.
志帥氣 matter is ruled by the mind.
志意 or 心志 purpose; will; determination.
志慮 to think or ponder.
志操 ambition; determination.
[15]志於彀 to draw a bow to the fullest extent.
志於此 bent on this.
志於道 the mind bent on what is right.
志・氣 will; ambition; inclination.
志・氣不墜 not to lose heart or be discouraged.
[20]志・氣昏惰 a dull, lazy disposition.
志節 determined purpose.
志行 purpose and action.
志量恢宏 liberal-minded: with large views.
志量高 lofty ideals; high aspirations or ambitions.
[25]不滿志 dissatisfied.
大志 great purpose; lofty ambitions.
得志 to realize one's ambitions.

適志作 to follow the inclinations.

(a) Annals; topography; statistics. Inter. 誌 No. 973.

志乘 (shǒng or ch'ǒng[4]) topography of a place.
志書 gazetteers.

志略 annals; records.
土風志 the topography of any district.

痣[4] Spots on the body; moles.
972

痣記 a distinguishing mark upon a person's body.
痣鬚 hairs growing from a mole.
面痣 dark spots on the face.

誌[4] To remember. To record.
973

誌哀 to express one's grief.
誌喜 to express one's joy—a congratulatory phrase.
誌念 to keep in mind.
誌悼 condolences.
誌銘 to carve an inscription on stone.

(a) Annals; an official gazetteer.

誌乘 (sheng or ch'ǒng[4]) the topography of a place.
誌書 or 誌文 archives.
墓誌 an epitaph.

滯[4] To obstruct, to hinder, to congeal, to stop. Stoppage,
974 stagnation.

滯下 ancient name for dysentery.
滯伏 unambitious, humble.
滯住 impeded; restrained.
滯固 obstinate; pigheaded.
[5]滯流 to impede the course of a river.
滯滯泥泥 pigheaded; obstinate.
滯獄 accumulation of lawsuits.
滯病 or 滯胃 constipation.
滯礙 or 滯隔 to obstruct; to prevent.
[10]滯積 accumulation of foodstuffs; overstocking of the markets.
滯累 to involve; to implicate.
滯貨 unsaleable goods.
滯運 to interfere with the prosperity of; hindrance to good luck.

值[2.5] To hold in the hand.
975

值事 to attend to an affair.
值事人 directors, managers.

(a)   To meet; to happen. A turn in course.

值 宿 night duty.
值 年 to take duty, office or responsibility for that year.
值 日 on duty for the day.
值 日 官 officer on duty for the day.
值 日 生 monitors.
值 班 to take a turn on duty.
值 禍 to meet with misfortune.
適 值 just at that time; it just happened.

(b) Price; value.

值·不·值 is it worth it?
值·得 worth; worth while.
值 百 抽 五 a duty of 5% *ad valorem*.
值 錢 valuable.
不 值 錢 valueless.
價。值 price; value.

置 寘 ⌉4
976   To dismiss; to put aside.

置 之 不 理 entirely disregard it.
置 之 度 外 leave it out of the calculations; ignore it utterly.
置 之 死 to sentence to capital punishment.
置 之 高 擱 to place on a high shelf—to pay no attention to it; to neglect a thing.
5置 若 罔 聞 to treat with indifference; to act as if one had not heard; to turn a deaf ear to.
置 諸 不 問 to treat with indifference; not to bother asking.
置 諸 不 議 to reject a proposal without discussion.
置 諸 腦 後 put it at the back of the brain—disregard it, forget it.
置 身 事 外 I'll keep out of it.
10廢 置 to remove from office; to do away with.

(a) To place, to arrange, to lay out. To establish.

置 喙 to push the beak in—to get in a word of interference.
置 家 to marry a wife; to set up a home.

置 立 to establish; to set up.
置 筋 to lay down the chopsticks.
5置 答 to reply.
置 諸 懷 to keep in mind; to cherish it in the heart.
置 身 無 地 no way of escape; no place in which to hide.
置 辦 to arrange; to prepare; to settle; to buy.
置 辯 to protest against; to bring forward in contradiction.
10置 辭 to arrange what to say.
置 郵 to establish postal services.
置 酒 to give a feast.
置 錐 to stick in a awl.
   無 置 錐 之 地 not even enough ground in which to stick an awl—very poor.
15置 開 to set up; to start a business.
位 置 a place; position; situated.
宣 德 年 置 established in the reign of *Hsüan tê*.
處。置 to settle; to decide; to place; to decide a man's case either by punishment or reward.

(b) To purchase; to buy.

置 業 or 置 產 to buy an estate.
置 用 to buy for use.
置 田 to buy fields.
置 衣·服 to purchase clothing.
置 買 to make purchases.

幟 幟 ⌉4
977   A pennon; a flag. To fasten.

拔 幟 to pull up the enemy's flag.
自 立 一 幟 to set up one's pennon.

熾 4
978   Blaze of fire. To burn. Splendid; illustrious. Also pron. *ch'ih*[4].

熾 昌 illustrious.
熾 炭 to burn charcoal.
熾 肆 to give rein to passion.
熾 起 to blaze up; lustful.
孔 熾 ablaze with rebellion.

(a) Numerous.

熾 殖 increasing in numbers.
熾 盛 numerous.
熾 茂 prosperous.

摯 4
979   To seize with the hand; to grasp. To advance. To break down. Inter. next, to present offerings.

摯 倒 to pull down.
摯 獻 to offer; to present.

贄 4
980   Gifts to superiors or friends. Offerings of ceremony.

贄 儀 ceremonial presents.
贄 敬 wedding presents; a gift to a teacher, etc.
贄 見 to visit with a present; bridal gifts.
贄 見 禮 a fee or a present to a teacher.

鷙 4
981   Birds of prey. A hawk. Violent. Bloodthirsty.

鷙 勇 courageous; bold as a hawk.
鷙 強 fierce, strong and bold.
鷙 忍 cruel and fierce as a bird of prey.
鷙 戾 vicious; as cruel as a hawk.
5鷙 猛 ardent; ruthless.
鷙 蟲 fierce birds and strange beasts.
鷙 鳥 a vulture.
鷙 鳥 不 羣 vultures do not go in flocks.

至 4
982   To reach; to arrive at. Very. The extreme. Greatest, best. Radical 133.

至 交 closely intimate friends.
至 人 the sage. One in whom moral virtue and learned accomplishments reach the highest point.
至 仁 full of love.
至 今 up to now.
5至 公 absolute justice.
至 公 堂 the great hall where the examinations were held.
至 剛 most inflexible attitude.
至 善 the highest excellence.
至 好 the best.
10至 寶 of the highest value; most precious.
至 尊 ancient title of emperors; used of idols—supreme.
至 德 the highest virtue.
至 心 most earnestly implore.

至 性 the natural disposition to love parents, etc.

[15] 至 意 the good intention.

[0] 至。於 as to; to come to; with regard to; in the case of; with reference to, etc.

至 竟 after all. = 到 底 cf. 6133. 17.

至 日 the solstices.

至 易 extremely easy.

[20] 至 材 greatest ability.

至 極 the very limit; to the utmost degree; the acme.

至 死 to the death.

至 死 不 變 changeless; constant till death.

至 理 axioms; self-evident truths.

[25] 至 當 most suitable.

至 禱 it is my earnest prayer—phrase used in correspondence, etc.

至 聖 most holy. The Sage.

至 聖 先 師 the most holy sage. Confucius.

至 聖 所 the Most Holy Place.

[30] 至 若 respecting; regarding.

至 行 exemplary conduct.

至 要 most important.

至 親 very near relatives; most intimate.

至 言 most reasonable speech.

[35] 至 誠 most sincere; perfect sincerity.

至 貴 most honourable; very expensive.

至 重 most weighty or most important.

至 關 緊 要 of the utmost importance.

無 所 不 至 there is no place to which it does not extend.

跮 [4]

983

Hasty walking.

跮 踱 to walk to and fro; to pass in and out.

軽 [4]

983a

A chariot low behind. See 軒 No. 2660. A.2.

致 [4]

984

To cause; to bring about; to occasion or to result in.

致 傷 to cause an injury.

致 其 身 to devote one's life to.

致 力 to devote one's strength.

致 勝 to gain a strategic victory.

[5] 致 命 to devote one's life to; fatal.

致 太 平 之 化 so as to bring about a peaceful transformation.

致 富 to get wealth.

致 干 禁 例 so as to offend against the law.

致 干 罰 究 so as to result in prosecution or fines.

[10] 致 思 to cause thoughts; suggestive.

致 折 the cause of the fracture.

致 死 to cause death; fatal.

致 爲 to bring about; to cause.

致 祥 to bring good luck.

[15] 致 精 perfect in details.

一 致 as one man; with united action.

以 致 so as to cause . . . .

大 致 in all probability;on the whole.

(a) To retire; to resign.

致 事 to resign from office.

致 仕 to retire from official life.

致 政 to resign from the government.

(b) To extend to; to apply to.

致 師 to challenge to fight.

致 敬 to show deep respect.

致 曲 to cultivate the shoots of virtue with thoroughness.

致 極 to carry out to the utmost.

[5] 致 樂 to take pleasure in.

致 爲 臣 to relinquish office.

致 物 to call demons or supernatural beings.

致 知 to apply knowledge to final causes; to extend knowledge to the utmost.

風 致 demeanour.

(c) To send; to convey to; to transmit.

致 候 to send greetings to.

致 告 to announce.

致 奠 to send a representative to offer sacrifice at a funeral.

致 意 to inform; to intimate; to send kind regards.

[5] 致 書 or 致 函 to send a despatch or a letter.

致 謝 to convey thanks.

致 賀 to convey congratulations.

致 辭 or 致 語 to send words of felicitation.

轉 致 to be forwarded to.

緻 [4]

985

To mend garments; to patch. Soft, delicate. Secret.

緻 密 fine and close; dense.

精 緻 fine; delicate.

細 緻 very finely worked.

制 [4]

986

To regulate, to govern; to restrain. Laws, regulations.

制 伏 to restrain; to rule.

制 克 to subdue.

制 動 機 a brake.

制 國 有 常 to govern a nation there are the constant virtues.

[5] 制 地 the court; the seat of government.

制 府 a viceroy's *yamen*.

制·度 regulations, rules; system; policy; to govern.

制 度 品 節 various rules of government.

制 性 to regulate the disposition.

[10] 制 慾 to restrain the passions.

制 慾 主 義 asceticism.

制 抑 to restrain; rules.

制 敵 to subdue the enemy.

制 書 imperial orders.   [uniform

[15] 制 服 to subject; to subdue: a

制 水 以 隄 防 to restrain rivers by dykes.

制 法 or 制 令 orders; laws.

制·臺 or 制 軍 title of a governor-or-general under the old regime.

制 裁 restraint.

[20] 制 裁 力 power to restrain; controlling forces.

制 遏 to prohibit; to suppress.

制 限 a limitation; bonds; a limit beyond which it is not permitted to go.

制 限 選 舉 elections in which there are limits of class, standing or property qualification.

品 制 court etiquette.

[25] 專 制 tyranny; oppressive rule.

抵 制 to boycott.

禁 制 to forbid; to prohibit.

節 制 bye-laws;to control.

自 制 self-restraint.

[30] 限。制 to limit.

(a) To determine, to decide. To fix. To make. To prepare.

制 中 in mourning.

制 作 to make; to do; to create.
制 定 to enact; to decide.
制 定 法 度 to determine the statutes.
⁵制 幣 national currency.
制 憲 to formulate a constitution.
制 服 a uniform; three years mourning.
制 錢 the fixed rate, as of land rent; small cash.
守 制 in mourning—used on cards.

製 4 To cut out garments and make them. To make; to 987　construct.

製 凍 機 a refrigerator.
製 紙 植 物 raw materials for making paper—wood-pulp.
製 造 or 製 作 to manufacture.
製 造 原 料 or 製 品 raw material.
⁵製 造 品 manufactures.
製 造 家 a manufacturer.
製 造 局 or 製 造 場 (or 廠) a factory.
製 鋼 廠 steel-works.
機 製 洋 貨 machine-made foreign goods.

(a) To compound, as drugs.

製 藥 to compound medicines.
製 藥 學 pharmacy.
製 藥 術 art of dispensing, etc.

(b) To compose literature.

御 製 a work produced by authority.

CHIH.　　　(虫)
(Chïh)

戠 1.5. A sword. Potter's clay. To gather.
988

織 1.5. To weave.
989

織 女 "The Spinning Damsel."—The star Vega in the constellation of Lyra.
織 工 weavers.
織 布 to weave cotton cloth.
織 布 娘 name of a cicada.
⁵織 布 廠 cotton mills.
織 得 精 緻 beautifully and finely woven.

織 機 a loom.
織 物 woven goods.
織 紋 to weave figured fabrics.
¹⁰織 紡 to spin; to reel.
織 綱 to spin a web.
織 花 to weave figures into silks, etc.
織 花 手 工 pattern weaving skill.
織 補 to darn.
¹⁵織 質 textiles.
織 造 formerly superintendent of imperial silk factory which supplied the court with silks.
織 餘 the ends of threads; thrums.
織 廠 to weave linen.
促 織 a cricket.

職 2.5. To govern, to oversee,
臘 to manage, to direct. Official duty, office. Used
990　for "I" in connection with official title.

職 事 official duty; to manage an affair.
職 任 in office; a post; duties of a post.
職 分 (fen⁴) a title; official rank; official duties.
職 務 business; function; profession; duty; vocation; sphere.
⁵職 司 official duties.
職 名 statement of official rank, etc.
職 員 an official; a functionary; the faculty. "I."
職 員 會 meeting of the faculty or of the staff.
職 守 to govern; to be on duty.
¹⁰職 官 officers.
職 工 workmen; employees.
職 工 學 校 industrial school.
職 役 duties of office.
職 志 policy; former designation of an officer in charge of the flag.
¹⁵職 掌 to control.
職 方 司 designation of a former office—one who had charge of statistics, maps, tribute, etc., the duties varied under different dynasties.
職 業 occupation; business; vocation.
職 業 上 vocational; vocationally.
職 業 之 禮 儀 professional etiquette.
²⁰職 業 倫 理 ethics of a profession.
職 業 學 校 vocational schools.

職 業 指 導 vocational guidance.
職 業 教 育 vocational education.
職 業 組 合 trades' unions.
²⁵職 權 duties of office; functions; rights of an office or of a profession.
職 蜂 bee-keeping.
職 貢 tribute.
職 責 the demands or responsibilities of office.
職 銜 a decoration; real and brevet rank respectively.
³⁰世 職 hereditary office.
受 職 to receive an office.
盡 職 to do one's duty to its fullest extent.
革 職 to deprive of office.

(a) Only; particularly. To determine. Numerous.

職 是 only.
職 此 之 故 for this particular reason.
職 此 而 已 is nothing but this.
職 職 numerous; flourishing; plentiful.

侄 2.5. Firm; unbending. Foolish.
991

侄 伦 not advancing; hindered.

姪 2.5. Nephew or niece. Child of a brother.
992

姪 女 a brother's daughter.
姪 婦 wife of a nephew.
姪 婿 husband of a niece.
姪 子 or 姪 兒 a nephew or a niece.
內 姪 child of wife's brother.

桎 4.5. Fetters; handcuffs. To fetter.
993

桎 梏 fetters and handcuffs.
桎 械 而 不 問 fetter him and ask him no questions.
桎 鐕 a linch-pin.

窒 4.5. To stop up, to obstruct.
994

窒 塞 to stop up.
窒 息 to suffocate; to smother.
窒 慾 to restrain the lusts.

窒 手 or 窒 脚 difficult; troublesome.
窒 礙 obstruction.
氣 窒 to hiccough.

蛭 4.5. 994a
The leech or 水 蛭.

郅 4.5. 995
To go up to. Flourishing. A superlative.

郅 治 a good government under which the people are prosperous.
郅 隆 very prosperous.

執 2.5. 996
To grasp; to hold; to seize. To retain.

執 一 而 不 通 to hold a single idea without intelligence.
執 中 to maintain a just medium; candid.
執 中 無 權 to hold the middle path without any adaptation to circumstances.
執 其 兩 端 to lay hold of the two extremes.
5 執 友 a friend or comrade.
執 定 成 見 bigoted; prejudiced.
執 巾 櫛 to hold the towel and comb—a wife or concubine.
執 意 or 執 己 見 to hold to one's own opinion.
執 手 同 行 to walk hand in hand.
10 執 拗 or 固 · 執 or 拘 執 obstinate; bigoted.
執 持 to hold in the hand.
執 據 to hold to an agreement; to license.
執 杖 staff-holders—chief mourners at parent's funeral.
執 柯 to hold the axehandle—a marriage go-between.
15 執 柯 伐 柯 to hold an axehandle while cutting another—the pattern is not far off; to use a go-between.
執 業 to engage in a profession.
執 照 a certificate; a warrant; a license.
執 牛 耳 to hold the bull's ear—in ratifying a covenant in ancient times, the strongest party held the ear of the sacrificial beast; used to express—to lead and manage everything.
執 票 人 bond-holder.

20 執 紼 to attend a funeral.
執 經 叩 問 taking the book and respectfully inquiring about the difficulties.
執 言 positive assertions.
執 贄 以 爲 禮 to take a present as a mark of courtesy.
執 轡 愈 恭 he grasped the reins and was still more respectful.
25 執 迷 不 悟 blindly superstitious; obstinate adherence to error.
執 鞭 to hold the whip—a driver; expression of deep esteem for another, from the next.
願 爲 之 執 鞭 I am willing to be your coachdriver—reckoned a very humble position.
偏 執 partial; biassed.
捕 執 to arrest; to seize.
30 父 執 father's friend.

(a) To manage, to direct or control. To attend to.

執 事 to manage; deacons; you.
執 · 事 official insignia. [Sir.
執 守 to maintain; to guard.
執 掌 or 執 理 to superintend.
執 政 executive of the government.
5 執 正 to maintain the right.
執 法 to set the law in motion; to uphold the law.
執 炊 to superintend cooking.
執 獄 to superintend a gaol.
執 行 to administrate; to carry into effect.
10 執 行 刑 罰 to carry out a sentence.
執 行 委 員 the deputy entrusted with the matter; administrative officer.
執 行 委 員 會 executive committee.
執 行 機 關 The Executive.
執 行 死 刑 to carry out an execution.
15 執 行 職 務 to put into execution; to administrate.
執 行 部 administrative board or department.
執 金 吾 eunuch keeper of the palace.

縶 2.5. 997
To tie up; to fetter. To connect.

縶 維 to shackle; to be hampered.
縶 縛 to bind.
縶 塞 to tie up a beast.

蟄 2.5. 998
To hibernate; to become torpid.

蟄 伏 to hibernate.
蟄 獸 hibernating animals like the bear.
蟄 蟲 torpid insects.
蟄 雷 the first spring thunders.
出 蟄 to arouse from hibernation.
驚 蟄 "Excited Insects." A solar period. March 5-20.

(a) To cluster; to swarm.

蟄 蟄 swarms, gathered together.

汁 1.5. 999
Juice, liquor, gravy.

汁 巾 a dinner napkin.
汁 液 juice, sap.
汁 漿 or 汁 · 子 or 水 汁 juice; gravy.

(a) Read hsieh5. u.f. 協 No. 2639. United.

汁 合 united.

炙 4.5. 1000
To broil. To toast before a fire. Intimate with; affected by.

炙 乾 to dry by heating. (-kan1)
炙 手 to warm the hands at the fire.
炙 手 可 熱 put your hand on him and feel the heat—said of Ts'ui hsüan of the T'ang dynasty, in reference to his zeal.
炙 瘡 to cauterize a sore.
炙 炒 to broil.
炙 草 dried liquorice.
炙 衣 服 to dry clothing at the fire.
焚 炙 to burn or roast.
薰 炙 to burn; to be injured by bad companions.
親 炙 very intimate with.

撎 拓 2.5. 1001
To take up; to collect; to improve. Also read choh.

撎 取 to plagiarize; to take a rubbing; to take; to seize.
撎 拾 遺 文 to restore corrupt texts by collation.

撫 本 a rubbing from a stone tablet.
撫 落 to fail in an undertaking.

蹠 2.5. To tread on; to pass to; to follow. The sole of the foot. u.f. 跖 next.
1002

跖 2.5. The sole of the foot. Inter. preceding 蹠.
1003

跖 狗 吠 堯 the dog of 盜 跖 barked at Yao—to help the evil and be envious of the good.
跖 足 下 to tread under foot.
跖 蹻 i.e., 盜 跖 and 莊 蹻 two notorious brigands of classical times.

陟 4.5. To ascend. To advance, to proceed, to promote.
1004

陟 岵 and 陟 屺 yearning for one's father and mother respectively, as when away from home on active service, etc.—*from the next two phrases.*
陟 彼 屺 兮, 瞻 望 母 兮 I ascend that bare hill and yearn for my mother.
陟 彼 岵 兮, 瞻 望 父 兮 I climb that wooded hill and look for my father.
陟 方 to ascend to heaven—death of an emperor.
陟 梯 to climb a ladder.
陟 罰 promote the meritorious and degrade the unworthy.
陟 臨 to ascend and look down upon.
陟 降 ascending and descending.

隲
騭 } 4.5. A stallion. To go up. To promote. To determine.
1005

陰 隲 secretly determined — the blessings which accrue to good works done in secret.

直
亘 } 2.5. Straight; upright. Perpendicular. Direct.
1006

直 勤·的 direct movement; or direct acting, as machinery.
直 北 due north. ＝ 正 北 .
直 問 a straight question.
直 垂 到 脚 hanging down to the feet.
5 直 徑 a straight path; the diameter.
直 情 徑 行 heedless actions; thoughtlessly rushing ahead.
直 接 direct; first-hand—cp. 間 接 No. 835.—B.6. indirect.
直 接 交 涉 direct relationships or negotiations.
直 接 交 易 direct transactions in business.
10 直 接 參 加 direct intervention.
直 接 販 賣 direct sales.
直 接 稅 direct taxation.
直 接 節 制 direct control.
直 接 行 動 direct action, as of syndicalism.
15 直 接 負 責 direct responsibility.
直 接 輸 入 direct imports.
直 接 輸 出 direct exports.
直 接 選 舉 direct elections.
直 接 關 係 direct relations.
20 直 接 體 驗 personal experience.
直 木 the keel of a boat.
直 根 the tap root.
直 正 exactly straight. *See below.* A.2.
直·的 straight.
25 直 立 to stand on end; to stand erect.
直 系 direct descendants, as from father to son, contrasted with 傍 系 No. 4927, collateral descent. The Chihli party.
直 線 a straight line.
直 腸 the rectum.
直 至 direct to...; right up to....
30 直 行 to go direct; to continue to.
直 行 列 車 direct train.
直 行 (*hang*[2]) vertical columns.
直 角 a right-angle.
直 解 or 直 講 colloquial rendering or commentary.
35 直 覺 說 theory of intuition.
專 靠 直 覺 only rely on intuition.
直 觀 or 直 覺 direct view; intuition.
直 觀 教 授 or 直 覺 教 授 the intuitive method of teaching.
直 譯 literal translation.
40 直 豎 to set upright.
直 轄 direct control.
直 道 the straight path; true.
直 量 direct measurements.

直 隸 州 a department formerly ruled directly by the provincial government.「now called Hopei.
45 直 隸 省 the province of Chihli.
一 直 走 go straight ahead.
伸 直 腿 to straighten the legs—to die.
垂 直 vertical; upright.
垂 直 線 perpendicular line.
50 曲 直 crooked and straight, both physically and morally.
筆 直 as straight as a pencil.

(a) Honest; straightforward; just.

直 性 straightforward; honest.
直 正 無 私 perfectly just and upright.
直 漢 a straightforward man.
直·爽 or 直 快 frank; honest.
5 直 筆 a straight pen—used of unprejudiced writings.
直 言 or 直 說 plain speaking; no beating about the bush.
直 言 不 隱 to speak without reservations.
直 言 相 告 gave him a straight talking to.
直 說 to speak out; "straight talk."
10 直 認 to own up to; to avow.
直 認 不 諱 open confession with no concealments.
直 閣 ancient title for a Prime Minister.
直 陳 make a plain statement of the case.
司 直 to maintain the right.
15 忠 直 upright and loyal.
骨 直 blunt and honest; stiff but faithful.

(b) Only; merely. Till.

直 不 百 步 耳 they merely did not run a hundred paces (but they did run).
直 到 今 till now; right until.
直 同 it is merely.....
直 是 it is, as a matter of fact.
匪 直 not only.

(c) Occurs u.f. 值 No. 975. Price, value.

直 錢 valuable.
充 炭 直 to make up the price of the charcoal.
給 直 to give the price.

植 2.5. Trees; plants.
1007

植·物 plants, etc.

植 物 園 botanical gardens.
植 物 學 botany.
植 物 學 家 botanists.
[5]植 物 標 本 a herbarium.
植 物 界 the vegetable kingdom.
植 物 細 胞 vegetable cells.
植 物 鹽 基 vegetable salts.
植 物 鹼 質 vegetable alkaloids.

(a) To plant; to set up.

植 樹 日 Arbor Day.
植 立 to set up; to plant erect.
培 植 to plant out and bank up— to assist.
栽 植 to plant out trees.

殖 2.5. **To fatten; to prosper. To become wealthy.**
1008

殖 利 to make profits.
殖 產 to flourish; to increase in prosperity.
殖 財 to grow wealthy.
殖 貨 to gain possessions.
蕃 殖 flourishing.

(a) To plant; to set up; to colonize.

殖 殖 even; smooth.
殖 民 colonists.
殖 民 地 a colony.
殖 民 策 colonization policy.
殖 穀 to sow grain.
生 殖 器 generative organs, *see under* 生 No. 5738—78 ff.
骨 殖 bones.

質
質 2.5.
貭　**Disposition.**
1009

質 ○地 or 地 質 natural disposition.
質 地 過 人 original talents that surpass those of others.
質 實 simple and sincere.
質 樸 simple and unadorned.
[5]質 直 upright disposition.
品 質 one's disposition; ingredients.
性 ·質 a man's disposition.
文 質 elegant and polished.
氣 質 a man's moral characteristics.
[10]體 質 physical constitution of men and things.

(a) Matter. Substance. Elements.

質 勝 而 野 if the material predominates, uncouthness is the result.
質 幹 substance; a trunk.
質 明 dawn.
質 量 mass. (*physics*).
質 點 a particle; a molecule.

(b) To call as a witness. To confront. To present oneself before.

質 問 to question; to ask; to cross-examine.
質 問 書 a questionnaire; a letter demanding an explanation of a matter.
質 對 to confront the prosecutor with accused; to check, to tally.
質 成 to settle differences by coming to terms.
[5]質 斷 to confront both parties and decide between them.
質 疑 to ask questions about that of which one is doubtful.
質 言 plain talk.
質 訊 to cross-examine when both parties are present.
質 諸 鬼 神 to call the spirits to witness.
[10]質 證 to give evidence.
備 質 to call as witnesses.

(c) Read *chih*[4]. A pledge. To pawn. An introductory present.

質 借 to assign as security.
質 子 a hostage, as a king's son.
質 庫 or 質 鋪 or 質 當 a licensed pawnshop.
質 押 to pledge.
[5]質 權 right of mortgage.
質 物 a pledge.
交 質 to exchange hostages.
信 質 an earnest.
典 質 to pawn; to mortgage.

帙
袠 4.5.　**A book-wrapper. A satchel or bag. N.A. for despatches, etc.**
1010

公 文 一 帙 one despatch.
書 帙 a book cover; portfolio.

秩 4.5. **Orderly; order, precedence, rank.**
1011

秩 ·序 order, series; programme; arrangement.
秩 ·序 不 紊 systematic; orderly.
秩 ·序 井 然 equally divided; orderly arrangement.
秩 ·序 大 亂 in great disorder.
[5]秩 敘 orderly.
秩 次 series; rank; order.
秩 秩 其 干 the graceful lines of the river banks.
左 右 秩 秩 to the right and left in a graceful, orderly manner.
秩 秩 大 猷 the great plans are all arranged with wisdom.
[10]秩 秩 德 音 "his virtuous fame spread far and wide."
品 秩 official rank.

擲 1.5. **To throw; to pitch, as a stone; to fling away.**
1012

擲 下 or 拋 擲 to throw down.
擲 中 to throw and hit the mark.
擲 交 to hand over to a subordinate.
擲 以 瓦 石 (a man was so ugly that the boys) threw stones and brickbats at him.
[5]擲 傷 wounded by thrown stones.
擲 去 thrown away.
擲 擊 to stone.
擲 果 a handsome man, *from the next*.
擲 果 盈 車 they threw enough fruit to fill his carriage— 潘 安 仁 of the *Chin* Dyn., (晉) was so handsome that people threw fruit into his carriage, hence the phrase:—As handsome as *P'an an*, 貌 似 潘 安.
[10]擲 棄 to discard; to throw away.
擲 災 to scatter cash at the crossroads on the 15th of the 1st month, to avert calamity.
擲 還 to return to the writer, as a memorial.
擲 骰 ·子 throwing dice.
擲 黃 金 於 虛 牝 to throw gold into the bottomless void.

躑 4.5. **Embarrassed; bewildered.**
1013

躑 躅 to stagger; irresolute; uncertain whether to advance or to retire.

踯 躅 花 name of a variety of Rhododendron which causes sheep to stagger, hence the name.

CH'IH. (4)
(Ch'ï)

郗 [1]
1014 City under the *Chou* Dyn. A surname. Also read *hsi*[1]. The articulation of the joints.

綌 [1]
1015 The fine fibres of hemp. Grasscloth or linen.

綌 綌 fine and coarse linen.
綌 葛 布 fine linen.

螭 [1]
1016 A dragon whose horns have not grown. Cruel.

螭 坳 or 螭 頭 carved dragons at the entrance to temples, palaces, etc.
螭 紐 dragon handles to cups.
螭 蟠 to crouch like a dragon.
螭 陛 the dragon steps—the throne; the emperor. Peking.
螭 騰 to mount like a dragon.
螭 魅 a hobgoblin that likes eating human beings.

魑 [1]
1017 A mountain elf.

魑 魅 a hobgoblin produced from the weird emanations of the trees and rocks on the hills.

蚩 [1]
1018 A worm. Ignorant; rude, rustic. To despise.

蚩 尤 name of a legendary rebel who was overcome by *Hwang ti*.
蚩 尤 旗 the banner of *Ch'ih yu* —a comet.
蚩 昏 蒙 眛 stupid, foolish, doltish.
蚩 民 the masses; the "common people."
蚩 眩 stupid, muddled, confused.

嗤 [1]
1019 To laugh at.

嗤 笑 to laugh at

嗤 詆 to scoff at; to revile.
嗤 鄙 to ridicule.
自 嗤 to laugh at oneself.

媸 [1]
1020 An ugly woman, opposite of 姸 No. 7340. Handsome.

媸 奴 an old crone.

治 [2]
1021 To cure; to heal. Distinguish 冶 No. 7313. *ch'ih*[2] is obs., now always read *chih*[4].

治 好·了 healed.
治 病 to practice medicine; to heal disease.
治 療 to cure diseases.

(a) To govern, to direct, to regulate, to put in order.

治 亂 to suppress a revolt.
治 任 to gather up their baggage.
治 兵 to lead troops.
治 具 to make ready the utensils for a feast.
[5]治 劇 to regulate anomalies in official life.
治 喪 to attend to the funeral rites.
治 國 to rule a kingdom.
治 宜 the benefits of good government.
治 家 to regulate the family.
[10]治 平 to govern so as to cause peaceful conditions.
治 心 to regulate the desires; to cleanse the heart.
治 掌 to manage; to govern.
治 服 to bring into subjection.
治 民 to govern the people.
[15]治 水 to regulate the rivers and watercourses by repairing the dykes, etc.
治 理 to rule; to administer; to manage.
治 生 to make a living; formerly used as a personal designation when addressing a magistrate.
治 產 to put the estate in order; to regulate a business.
治 由 regime.
[20]治 絲 to unravel silk threads.
治 經 to study the classics.
治 縣 to govern a county.
治 行 裝 to prepare baggage.
治 身 or 治 躬 to control the body.
[25]自 治 autonomy.

(b) To punish.

治 死 to put to death.
治 獄 to judge criminal cases.
治 罪 to punish crime.
治 辦 to deal judicially with a case.
處[3] 治 to punish severely.

(c) Read *chih*[4]. The result of (a). The place of government, etc; The peace under good government.

治 下 under the jurisdiction of— depreciatory term once used by the people in addressing officials.
治 世 a peaceful era.
治 功 meritorious services to the State.
治 命 dying requests that may be carried out.
[5]治 外 法 權 extraterritoriality—as granted to ministers, ambassadors, etc. *See under* 領 No. 4058—5.
治 安 public peace and order.
治 屬 the jurisdiction of.
治 體 the administration; the constitution.
縣 治 the place ruled by a magistrate—a *hsien* district.

答 [1]
1022 To beat with the bamboo. A light bamboo used for such purposes.

答 掠 to flog.
答 杖 to beat with bamboos; the light and heavy bamboo respectively.
答 臀 to beat a man on the buttocks.
答 責 to flog with a bamboo.
答 辱 to beat a man in order to shame him.

墀 [2]
1023 A porch; a courtyard.

楷 墀 the palace courtyard.
丹 墀 the long courtyard at the entrance of the main court of Confucian temples.

遟 [2]
1024 Slow, dilatory, late. To delay, tardy.

遟 一 日 a day later.

遲 來 不 及 if you come late, you will miss it.

遲 回 irresolute; hesitating.

遲 延 to delay.

⁵遲 悞 to loiter; to spoil a matter by delay.

遲 慢 or 遲 緩 or 遲 滯 remiss; late; behindhand; slow; dilatory.

遲 日 some days late.

遲 旦 or 遲 明 dawn.

天 徇 遲 明 just at the dawn.

¹⁰遲 留 to postpone.

遲 疑 in doubt; hesitating.

遲 疑 不 答 hesitation in making a reply.

遲 累 to impede.

遲 莫 or 遲 暮 late; evening; old age.

¹⁵遲 速 不 同 the difference between slowness and celerity.

遲 遲 slowly; easy-going.

遲 鈍 obtuse; incapable; slow to comprehend.

太 遲 too late.

拖 遲 to procrastinate.

²⁰棲 遲 to stay for a while.

甚 遲 very late.

(a) Read *chih*⁴. To wait; to look for.

懸 心 遲 仰 之 anxiously looking for him.

懸 遲 to look for; to expect.

癡 痴 1.2 Silly, foolish, doting, idiotic.
1025

癡 人 a foolish person.

癡 人 得 癡 福 the idiot has his own happiness—do not despise him.

癡 人 說 夢 to tell a dream to a fool — one who misunderstands what he hears; a fool's talk.

癡·子 a simpleton.

⁵癡 心 infatuated with.

癡 心 妄 想·的 人 one who cherishes foolish and exaggerated ideas.

癡 情 子 a debauchee; a sentimentalist.

癡 想 vain thoughts.

癡 漢 a stupid.

¹⁰癡 物 a fool.

癡 狂 mad after; extravagant behaviour.

癡 獃 or 癡 呆 or 癡 儍 or 癡 慇 stupid, foolish.

癡 病 idiocy.

癡 笑 ceaseless giggling.

¹⁵癡 纏 bound up with; fond of.

癡 迷 doting; besotted.

癡 頭 癡 腦 idiotic; crazy.

跦 ² Undecided; embarrassed.
1026

跦 踷 or 跦 躇 indecision; hesitating.

箎 篪 ² A bamboo flute with seven holes.
1027

褫 ³ To strip off, to deprive of. To undress.
1028

褫 奪 to snatch away.

褫 奪 公 權 to disfranchise.

褫 氈 thick felt for sleeping on.

褫 職 to cashier.

褫 脫 to strip off.

褫 革 頂 翎 to take away the button and feather—to cashier an officer under the Manchus.

褫 魄 to be discouraged; disheartened.

坻 ² An islet, a rock in a river. Read *chih*³ or *ti*³. An embankment; to stop.
1029

坻 伏 to stop and hide.

坻 伏 鬱 堙 protruding but halfconcealed by the mounds.

坡 坻 a slope, a dike.

蚳 ² Eggs or larvae of ants.
1030

蚳 醢 larvae in pickle.

鴟 ¹ An owl. u.f. 鳶. A kite.
1031

鴟 吻 ornament on palace roof as a protection against fire.

鴟 夷 a leather pouch.

鴟 峙 fierce oppressor that usurps the land of another and still regards him as a foe.

鴟 張 to act with violence and oppression.

⁵鴟 目 虎 吻 owl's eyes and tiger's lips—very fierce and cunning.

鴟 義 conduct like that of an owl, fierce and yet cunning.

鴟 視 avaricious.

鴟 顧 to look back without moving the head, like an owl.

鴟 鴞 or 怪 鴟 the barn-owl; unfilial.

池 ² A round pool of water, a pond. A cistern. A moat.
1032

池 中 物 things from a pond—of no account as a dragon, etc., used for the idea of inexperienced.

池 塘 the bank of a pond.

池·子 or 池 塘 a pool or pond.

池 心 the middle of a pond.

池 沼 ornamental ponds, round and square respectively.

池 魚 fish in a pond or a moat.

阤 ³ A hillside, a bank. The earth breaking away.
1033

馳 ² To go quickly, as a horse. To spread abroad..
1034

馳 口 妄 談 to talk wildly.

馳 名 wide-spread fame; celebrated.

馳 城 飛 塹 (this horse can) pass over the walls and fly over the moats.

馳 念 or 馳 結 constant remembrance of.

⁵馳 檄 an urgent despatch.

馳 湍 rapid flow of a river.

馳 赴 to go direct to.

馳 辯 or 馳 說 eloquence; cleverness in argument.

馳 迎 to hasten to welcome.

¹⁰馳 送 to send by mounted couriers; to send with despatch.

馳 道 the imperial highway.

馳 飛 to fly swiftly.

馳 馬 to race or gallop horses.

馳 馬 報 mounted courier.

¹⁵馳 騖 to gallop; to hunt.

馳 騖 紛 華 to give oneself to dissipation.

馳 驅 fast riding.

馳驛 to ride post; mounted couriers.

(a) To pass away.

年與時馳 the years of our life pass with the hours.

持² **To support.**
1035

持危扶顛 to uphold the tottering and support the falling.
扶持 to support; to hold up; to sustain; to stand by.
扶持到底 to sustain, to stand by to the end.
維持 to maintain; to support; to prop up; to stand by.

(a) To manage; to hold; to grasp. To restrain.

持不逮之資 having talent which is unapproachable.
持久力 endurance.
持兩端 double-minded.
持其志無暴其氣 hold the determination firmly and do not violate the passions.
⁵持呪 to keep magic charms or formulae as a protection.
持執 to hold; to grant.
持守 to keep hold of; to observe religiously.
持定 to hold fast to.
持家 to manage the affairs of the family.
¹⁰持帖 to take a card.
持平 to maintain a fair balance; strictly just.
持循 a fixed rule or guide; to obey.
持意 to maintain one's opinions.
持戒 to keep the Buddhist precepts.
¹⁵持戟 to grasp a spear; to hold weapons.
持掌 to take control.
持服 mourning for parents.
持正 upright conduct.
持法 to maintain the law; to vindicate authority.
²⁰持照 to have a pass.
持狹欲奢 his offering was poor, but his petition was extravagant.
持盈 to preserve that which has been gained, as a position, business, etc.

持盈保泰 to maintain an advantage.
持節使 messenger with imperial insignia as a token.
²⁵持索捕風 to take a rope and bind the wind—impossible.
持衡 to weigh up the ability of a man.
持論 to argue with.
持贈 to carry a present to.
持身 to restrain the passions.
³⁰持身涉世 to go through the world with due self-control.
持躬 to maintain dignity.
持重 staid and grave; to maintain dignity; scrupulously exact.
持驗 to produce evidence as proof.
持齋 to fast; vegetable diet.
³⁵執持 to grasp firmly.
堅持 to hold fast to.
把持 to boycott; to manage; to monopolise.
挾持 administrative ability.
相持不下 to disagree.
⁴⁰自持 to restrain oneself.

恥 ³ 耻 **Ashamed. Shame. To feel ashamed.**
1036

恥其言而過其行 sparing of his words and excelling in his actions.
恥心 a sense of shame.
恥笑 to laugh at; to ridicule.
恥躬之不逮也 afraid lest their actions should not equal their words.
恥辱 shame and disgrace; to feel disgraced.
不知恥 no sense of shame.
無恥之行 shameless conduct; indelicate behaviour.

齒 ³ **The upper incisors. Radical 211.**
1037

齒亡舌存 the teeth are gone but the tongue still remains—i.e., a paradox—the tough are lost, while the weak and soft endures.
齒冠 the crown of a tooth.
齒危 teeth about to fall out.
齒吻 teeth and lips.
⁵齒垢 tartar.
齒根 the roots or fangs of a tooth.

齒狀 dentation.
齒狀裝 toothed pattern in ornament.
齒牙 or 牙齒 the teeth.
¹⁰齒牙相震 teeth chattering.
齒牙餘論 to praise another.
齒科 dentistry.
齒粉 dentifrice.
齒腔 the pulp cavity of teeth.
¹⁵齒落 toothless.
齒質 dentine.
齒軌 a rack railway.
齒輪 a cog-wheel.
*齒音 dentals in phonetics.
²⁰齒頸 the neck of a tooth, the part between the crown and the root.
齒齦 the gums.
不好啟齒 such things are rather awkward to mention; it is not easy to open the mouth about such matters.
不足掛齒 not worth mentioning.
乳齒 the milk teeth.
²⁵切齒 to gnash the teeth.
啟齒 to open the mouth; to speak. See above,—22.
掛齒 to hang on the teeth, to speak about. See above,—23.
沒齒 no teeth—dead.
沒齒不忘 I shall never forget (you).
³⁰犬齒 canine teeth; pointed ornament used in borders; uneven and jagged. = 3113.11.
生齒 dentition.
臼齒 molars.
象齒 elephant's teeth.
輪齒 gear teeth or cogs.
³⁵鋸齒 teeth of a saw.
門齒 front teeth; incisors.
露齒 protruding teeth.

(a) Age, seniority. To classify.

齒冷 to scorn.
齒座 to seat people in order of seniority.
齒德 the virtues of age.
齒德俱尊 honourable both in age and virtue—complimentary phrase.
⁵齒次 or 齒列 in order of seniority.
齒長³ elder; senior.
齒類 to classify.
不以人齒 do not regard him as in the class of human beings—he is beyond the pale.
* dental sounds — actually limited to dental sibilants ts, dz, s, z, etc.

不 齒 to regard another as not on an equality with oneself.

侈 [3] Wasteful; extravagant. To exaggerate.
1038

侈 用 lavish expenditure.
侈 談 extravagant talk.
侈 論 exaggerations.
侈 麋 wasteful extravagance.
奢○侈 extravagance.

眵 [1] Eyes diseased and dim.
1039

傺 [4] To hinder; to detain.
1040

侘 傺 to be disappointed in attaining the ambitions.

啻 [4] Only, merely. To be different from. To stop at.
1041

不 啻 not only; not less than.
何 啻 why only . . . . ?
奚 啻 or 奚 翅 why stop at . . . . ?

翅
翄 [4] Wings. Fins.
1042

翅 排 in a row.
翅 果 winged seed vessels.
翅 膀 or 翅 翼 wings.
翅 膀 刷 刷 flapping wings.
振 翅 to flap the wings.
魚 翅 shark's fins, a delicacy.

(a) Merely, only. To stop. Inter. 啻 preceding.

奚 翅 色 重 why stop with merely saying that gratifying the lusts is more important?
奚 翅 食 重 why stop with saying that eating is more important?

豸
廌 [4] To discriminate. Reptiles without feet. To loosen. Radical 153. A fabulous beast. Also read chai[3], when used for the beast. This monster is said to discern good and evil men,
1043

the evil are gored by it; it was used as an emblem by censors.

CH'IH.　　(彳)
(Ch'ïh)

彳 4.5. A step with the left foot. Radical 60. National Phonetic letter for ch'.
1044

彳 亍 to step with the left and right feet respectively.

尺 3.5. A foot—10 Chinese inches or 14.1 English measure, 0.3581 metres. A foot rule. The note *sol* in the scale (pron. ch'ê[3]).
1045

尺 五 a foot and a half—very near.
去 天 尺 五 very near to heaven.
尺 兵 hardly any or no weapons.
尺 地 or 尺 土 a small plot of ground—insufficient.
[5]尺[2]·寸 feet and inches; length; dimensions; etiquette; small; few.
尺 寸 不 合 the measurement does not agree.
無 尺 寸[4] 之 膚 不 愛 焉 there is no part of his body that a man does not care for.
尺[3] 寸[4] 之 兵 practically no weapons.
尺 度 measurement.
[10]尺 書 or 尺 繛 or 尺 翰 or 尺 簡 a letter.
尺 澤 a small pond; the pulse in the arm.
尺 牘 a note; letters; a card; a letter-writer or guide to correspondence styles.
尺 璧 a foot of jade—great and precious.
尺 蠖 the looper caterpillar.
[15]尺 錦 a foot of brocade—a beautiful piece of writing, but short.
尺 鐵 a short weapon.
尺 頭 a piece of silk or satin for a present.
丁 字 尺 a tee square. 公 尺 meter.
[20]卷 尺 a tape measure.
垂 線 尺 plumb-rule.
平 行 尺 parallel ruler.
木 摺 尺 folding rule.

比 例 尺 or 縮 算 尺 a scale, as in drawing maps, etc.
[25]水 平 尺 or 酒 平 尺 a spirit level.
深 淺 尺 depth gauge.
計 算 尺 or 滑 尺 the slide rule.
量 天 尺 a sextant or quadrant.
↑市尺 See 5792.59.

叱 4.5. To hoot at; to abuse.
1046

叱 咤 to make loud threatening noises.
叱 喝 to shout or bawl.
叱 怪 to vent the astonishment.
叱 狗 to drive away a dog.
叱 罵 or 呼 叱 or 辱 罵 to scold and abuse, to rail at.

吃
喫 1.5. To eat; to drink (S. mand.)
1047

吃·不·下 去 I cannot get it down.
吃·不·來 I cannot eat it.
吃·不·得 uneatable.
吃·不·愁 not anxious about enough to eat.
[5]吃·不 起 I cannot afford to eat that.
吃 傷 injured by improper diet.
吃·兩 口 烟 to have a smoke.
吃 喝 to eat and drink—feasting.
吃 喝 嫖 賭 dissipation, fast living.
[10]吃 大 烟 to smoke opium.
吃 屎·的 狗 term of vile abuse— you contemptible cur.
吃 怕·了 to eat until one is afraid to eat more, or is tired of it.
吃 水 to drink. *See below.* A. 6.
吃 烟 to have a smoke.
[15]吃 用 needs.
吃 盡·了 all eaten.
吃 糧 to eat rations;—to be a soldier.
吃 紅 糧 to be an executioner.
吃 着 (-cho[1]) food and clothing;
[20]吃 茶 to drink tea. (-·chê) is eating.
吃 葷 to take a meat diet.
吃 薑 醋 to drink ginger vinegar —to give birth to a child.
吃·過飯·了嗎 have you eaten? address of salutation equivalent to our, "Good morning" or, "How do you do?"

吃 酒 to drink wine.
25 吃 醋 to drink vinegar—to be jealous.
吃 醋 娘·子 a jealous woman.
吃 閒²飯 to be a loafer or a sponge.
吃 食 food; provisions; to feed, used of pigs.
吃 飽 to eat to the full.
30 吃 飯 to take food.
吃 齋 to practice vegetarianism.
難 吃 nasty; unpalatable.

(a) **To suffer. To absorb, to use up. Draught of a ship.**

吃·不 住 unable to bear it; upset.
吃 力 requiring strength; difficult.
吃 勁 to have a grip; to get a leverage.
吃 啞·吧 虧 to suffer with no power to get redress; suffering, but unable to speak of it.
5 吃 多·少 水 What does this ship draw?
吃 水 draught of a ship. *See above.*—13.
吃 疼 to suffer pain.
吃 緊 hard pressed.
吃 苦 to suffer hardship.
10 吃 虧 to suffer loss; to get the worst of it; to be wronged; to come to grief; to have a nasty time.
吃 驚 to be frightened.

(b) **To stammer.**
(only the form 吃 is used thus.)
吃 吃 giggling laughter.
吃 舌 an impediment in the speech.
口 吃 to stammer.

赤 4.5. **Red, the colour of fire. The south. Radical 155.**
1048

赤 俄 Soviet Russia.
赤 俄 政 府 Soviet Government.
赤 兎 "Red Hare." The famous horse of 呂 布 in the period of the "Three Kingdoms."
赤 化 Sovietized.
5 赤 化 主 義 Sovietism. Communism.
赤 土 red earth. *See below.* A.3.
赤 墀 emperor's court or palace—the long court before the main hall in Confucian temples.
赤 小 豆 red lentils.
赤 帝 the god of fire—the south.

10 赤 帶 leucorrhoea.
赤 心 sincere, lit., red-hearted; compassionate.
赤 方 the south.
赤 日 the red sun—a very hot day.
赤 日 當 空 the hot sun overhead.
15 赤 材 or 赤 木 質 duramen.
赤 楊 the Alder.
赤 瑪 瑙 jacinth.
赤 痢 dysentery.
赤 種 the red race—Indians.
20 赤 米 coarse rice.
赤 糖 brown sugar.
赤 縣 神 州 ancient name for China.
赤 繩 繫 足 the red thread binds the feet—united in marriage by the match-makers.
赤 膽 red galled—i.e., brave.
25 赤 舌 燒 城 a red tongue burns a city—specious words.
赤 芍 the peony.
赤 蓋 the sun.
赤 虹 化 玉 the rainbow changes into gems.
赤 血 red blood.
30 赤 血 球 red corpuscles.
赤 衣 red garments formerly worn by criminals.
赤 衣 使 者 red-winged dragon-flies.
赤 衣 塞 路 the red coats, i.e., the criminals being deported, blocked the road, they were so numerous.
赤 誠 sincere.
35 赤 軍 "The Red Army."
赤 道 the equator.
赤 道 儀 equatorial instruments.
赤 道 流 the equatorial current.
赤 道·的 equatorial.
40 赤 金 deep coloured gold; copper. 足 赤 pure gold.
赤 頰 poetical name for the stork.
赤 黨 = 3709.51.

(a) **Naked; bare.**

赤 光 bare, naked.
赤 口 毒 舌 a bitter curse—unlucky words.
赤 土 bare land. *See above.*—6.
赤 子 an infant; the people.
5 赤 子 之 心 innocence; simplicity of childhood.
赤 手 bare-handed.
赤 手 空 拳 empty-handed.
赤 立 to stand naked—in great distress.
赤·着 身·子 stripped.

10 赤 老 ancient term of abuse for soldiers; used in Shanghai and district in reviling—demons.
赤 脚 bare-footed.
赤 裸 裸·的 一 絲 不 掛 absolutely naked, without a stitch of clothing.
赤 貧 absolutely poverty-stricken.
赤 貧 如 洗 as poor as if everything was washed clean—not anything left.
15 赤 身 or 赤 體 naked.
赤 身 露 體 stark naked.
赤 露 exposure of person.

(b) **To destroy—meaning derived either from the red of the blood shed, or from the bareness of the place afterwards.**

赤 族 to exterminate the clan.

飭 4 **To order or instruct, as from a superior to a subordinate. To make ready. Distinguish 飾 No. 5812.**
1049

飭 交 order the delivery of.
飭 傳 to summon.
飭 催 to urge.
飭 屬 遵 照 instruct subordinates to act in accordance with.
5 飭 差 to give orders to runners.
飭 拿 or 勒 捕 to order the arrest of.
飭 查 to order an examination to be made.
飭 正 an orderly.
飭 派 to despatch.
10 飭 知 to make orders known to subordinates.
飭 行 or 飭 令 orders.
飭 補 to appoint to fill a vacancy.
飭 身 to govern the body.
飭 辦 to give orders to take action.
15 飭 遵 orders issued for guidance.
嚴 飭 to give a charge to.
整 飭 to preserve order.
申 飭 commands; rebukes.
謹 飭 orders to be careful.

勒 敕 勅 4
1050

Imperial orders. Third form is also read lai[4].

勅 封 by imperial appointment.

勅旨 or 勅令 an imperial order.
勅書 or 誥勅 credentials; letters patent.
勅行 the emperor's mandate promulgated.
勅賜 bestowed by imperial orders.
勅贈 to bestow honours upon the deceased parents of an officer.
勅造 founded by imperial orders.

抶 ⁴
To beat; to flog.
1051

斥 庍 庍 ⁴
To upbraid, to scold.
1052

斥喝 to scold; to shout at.
斥罵 to revile; to curse.
斥責 to blame; to reprimand.
斥退 to shout and order his retirement; "get out of this."
斥革 to degrade; to remove from office.
斥駁 or 駁斥 to find fault with; to show another to be in the wrong.

(a) To dismiss, to drive away.

斥放 to dismiss.
斥逐 or 屏斥 to drive out, to send away. (*ping³-*)

(b) To enlarge, to extend.

斥地 to enlarge territory.
斥斥 extensive, vast.
斥賣 to sell.

(c) Salt lands.

斥鷃 a bird of the salt lands, something like a quail.
斥鹵 salt lands unfit for crops.

CHIN.   (ㄐㄧㄣ)

今 ¹
Now, at present.
1053

今不如古 (the attainments, etc.) of the present are not equal to those of the past.
今世 or 當世 this generation; this present life.

今也純儉 now, a silk hat is worn, this economises (in the making.)
今人 contemporaries.
⁵今古 ancient and modern.
今夜 tonight.
今女 (*ru³.*) 畫 now you draw a limit in front of yourself.
今後 or 自今以後 from now on.
今日 or 今·天 or 今朝¹ or 今兒 (個)today.
¹⁰今日病矣 I am tired today.
今時 at this time.
今歲 or 今·年 this year.
今生 "the life that now is."
無古不成今 without the past there could be no present.
至今 or 迄今 up till the present time.

妗 ⁴
Wife of mother's brother.
1054

妗娘 sister-in-law on the wife's side.
妗弟兄 husbands of a wife's sisters.

紟 ¹
A sash. To tie.
1055

紟耆 gentry and elders.

巾 ¹
A napkin, kerchief or towel. A cap. Radical 50.
1056

巾帕 a head-wrapper.
巾幗 womankind.
巾櫛 towel and comb—one who holds these in service, a concubine.
手·巾 a towel.
頭巾 a turban.

金 ¹
Gold; precious.
1057

金不換 not to be exchanged for gold—Chinese ink.
金丹 the pill of immortality.
金人 or 女眞 the *Nü chen* Tartars.
金冕 or 金冠 golden crowns.
⁵金剛 precious and hard—can injure but cannot be injured, thus

used for some of the Buddhist gods. A.w. 金罡 cf. 3266.
四大金剛 the four guardians of Buddhist temples.
金剛怒目 frightful and angry looks (so as to subdue the four demon kings.)—said of the eyes of the club-wielding *Indra.*
金剛杵 the diamond club—wielded by *Indra,* weighted at both ends, and is used to quell demons.
金剛石 the diamond.
¹⁰金剛經 The *Diamond Sutra.*
金剛鑽 diamond for a small drill; a drill for boring porcelain,· etc.; diamond.
金力 the power of gold.
金口 or 金言 Your excellent advice! *See below.* A.2.
金口玉言 Your precious words!
¹⁵金婚 golden wedding. (*foreign*).
金·子 or 黃金 gold.
金安 Your precious health! a conventional phrase.
金字 gold letters; the gable end of a house, from the shape of the top of this character; used to describe pyramidal forms.
金字塔 The Pyramids.
²⁰金字招·牌 golden-lettered signboard.
金屋 women's apartments.
金山 golden mountain.
新金山 Australia. ⌈cisco.
舊金山 California; San Fran-
²⁵金工 goldsmith's work; metal work.
金帛 gold and silk—wealth.
金帶 gold lace.
金幣 gold currency.
金庫 amount of government money held by the banks.
³⁰金·朝 The *Chin* Dynasty, established by the *Nü chen* Tartars.
金旨 the precious commands (of Buddha).
金星 the planet Venus.
金本位 a gold standard.
金條 gold bars.
³⁵金樞 or 金鏡 The Golden Pivot or Mirror—the moon.
金水 liquid gold for gilding.·
金汁 molten gold.
金沙 or 金粉 gold dust—the latter also means face powder.
金烏 The Golden Crow.—the sun.
⁴⁰金玉 gold and jade—precious.
金玉之言 Your valued advice!

金 玉 其 外 gilded, outward adornment only—false pretences.

金 珠 gold and pearls; golden beads.

金 甌 無 缺 the golden goblet is not broken—the integrity of the national territory is maintained.

⁴⁵金 碧 glittering and bright.

金 礦 gold mines.

金 科 玉 條 the laws—golden and precious.

金 箔 gold-foil; tinsel; gold-leaf.

金 絲 or 金 線 gold thread.

⁵⁰金 色 a golden colour.

金 花 誥 patents of nobility granted to women.

金 葉 gold-leaf.

金 蘭 之 交 intimate, close friendship; friends with one aim and ambition.

金 融 currency; the money market.

⁵⁵金 融 停 滯 stoppage of the money market.

金 融 急 廹 a financial crisis.

金 融 情·形 financial conditions.

金 融 機 關 financial organ.

金 融 滯 澀 tightness of the money market.

⁶⁰金 融 界 the financial world.

金 融 緊 廹 a financial crisis.
    A.c. 金 融 恐 慌.

金 衡 Troy weight.

金 言 a motto.

金 諾 a secure promise.

⁶⁵金 貨 gold coin.

金 貲 wealth; money; treasures.

金 身 Buddha's image.

金 針 菜 dried flowers of a lily-like species.

金 釵 golden hairpins—women.

⁷⁰金 銀 gold and silver; wealth.

金 銀 花 Honeysuckle.

金 錢 money.

金 錢 債 權 right to recover debts in gold. (legal).

金 錢 勢 力 the power of money.

⁷⁵金 錢 懲 罰 fines.

金 錢 補 償 indemnity. (legal).

金 錢 運·動 use of money in propaganda.

金 陵 Nanking—the golden tombs.

金 鷄 the Golden Pheasant.

⁸⁰金 額 exchange rate of gold.

金 額 主 義 limited compensation. (legal).

金 馬 門 Hanlin Academy.

金 魚 the goldfish.

金 鳳 花 Balsams.

⁸⁵金 黃 色 orange colour.

一 字 千 金 one character is worth much gold.

包 金 to overlay with gold.

千 金 Your daughter!

吞 金 to swallow gold—euphemism for suicide.

⁹⁰屑 金 spangled with gold.

裝 金 to gild woodwork, as picture frames, etc.

足 金 pure gold.

鍍 金 to gild.

飛 金 bits of gold leaf stuck on scrolls, etc.

(a) Metals generally.

金 匱 iron cupboard for books—careful and secret.

金 口 木 舌 metal mouth and wooden tongue—ancient bell.

金 城 metal walls—impregnable.

金 城 湯 池 metal walls and scalding moat—an impregnable city.

⁵金 屬 or 金 類 metals.

金 屬 板 metal plates for printing.

金 文 inscriptions on bronzes, etc.

金 木 水 火 土 metal, wood, water, fire and earth—the five elements of Chinese philosophy.

金 斗 pan of iron containing charcoal, used for smoothing clothing by tailors. Also written 火 斗; 熨·斗·

¹⁰金 石 metal and stone; bronzes and tablets; strong and durable; bells and musical stones—music. (ancient).

金 石 交 a firm friendship.

金 石 人 a daring, fearless man.

金 石 學 the study of bronze and *

金 石 爲 開 the utmost sincerity can influence even metal and stone.

¹⁵金 石 語 words of gold and precious stone—unfailing words.

金 聲 玉 振 the sound of the metallic instruments begins (the harmony of the orchestra), and the musical stone gives the signal to cease.

金 鐘 gong used in imperial levees.

金 鼓 gong and drum—one beaten for retreat and the other for advance.

五 金 the five metals—gold, silver, copper, tin and iron.

²⁰白 金 white metal, silver; now used for platinum.

赤 金 the red metal—copper or dark coloured gold.

青 金 the dark metal—lead.

黑 金 the black metal—iron.

(b) Weapons.

金 戈 weapons, arms.

金 瘡 wounds from edged weapons.

金 革 arms, weapons.

金 革 之 危 the dangers of warfare.

(c) Transliterating foreign words.

金 雞 納 Cinchona or quinine.

金 雞 納 霜 Sulphate of quinine.

筋¹ The tendons; sinews or muscles. Nerves or veins.
1058

筋 力 muscular strength.

筋 力 衰 弱 weary; strength failing.

筋 炎 neuritis.

筋 疲 力 盡 utterly exhausted.

⁵筋 癲 numbed.

筋 竹 篦 fine toothed comb.

筋 節 joints; the position of the pulse in the wrist; articulations; the arrangement of a composition; just right.

筋 纖 維 muscular fibre.

筋 肉 muscle.

¹⁰筋 肉 組 織 the muscular system.

筋 覺 muscular sensitivity; reflex action.

筋 頭 the core of a boil.

筋 骨 flesh and bone—relations.

筋 骨 疼 rheumatic pains.

¹⁵筋 骸 sinews and bones.

筋 骸 之 束 the binding together of the muscles and bones.

打 筋 斗 to turn head over heels.

抽 筋 convulsions; cramps. | (-kên¹-).

血 筋 blood vessels.

斤
斦 ¹ Sixteen ounces, Chinese scale. A catty, fixed at 1⅓ lb. avoirdupois for tariff purposes. Axes. Radical 69.
1059

斤 兩 or 斤 重 weight.

斤 半 one and a half catties.

斧 斤 axes.

(a) Read chin⁴. To pierce; penetrating.

斤 斤 其 明 How clear was their intelligence!

* stone inscriptions: the carving of seals.

斤 斤 自 守 guard it with great care.

斤 斤 較 量 carefully compare it.

劤 [4] Great strength.
1060

不 吃 劤 it does not grip; it lacks force or stability; it exerts no force.

使 劤 use force.

近 [4] Near to; recent. To approach.
1061

近 世 recent times; modern times; used as a prefix for modern.

近 世 史 modern history.

近 世 哲 學 modern philosophy.

近 事 or 近 聞 recent news. See below.—5, 36.

[5]近 事 男 女 lay Buddhists who do not enter the monastic life.

近·些 nearer.

近 今 語 詞 modern phrases.

近 代 modern; contemporary.

近 似 similar to; like; approximate.

[10]近 作 recent productions.

近 來 or 近 日 or 近 時 recently; lately.

近 便 near; convenient; handy.

近 傍 near to; in the vicinity.

近 光 near-sighted, used of spectacles.

[15]近 到 recently arrived.

近 前 to come forward; to approach towards.

近 因 the immediate cause.

近 地 or 近·處 the vicinity; close quarters; in the neighbourhood.

近 地 點 perigee.

[20]近 城 close to the city.

近 密 intimate; close; tight.

近 岸 near the shore.

近 幸 favourites at court.

近 憂 immediate cause for grief.

[25]近 支 blood relatives.

近 數 年 來 in recent years.

近 日 點 perihelion.

近 朱 者 赤 近 墨 者 黑 he who handles vermilion will be reddened, and he who touches ink will be blackened—used of the influence of companionship.

近 朱 近 墨 an abbreviation of the preceding.

---

[30]近 東 the "Near East."

近 歲 or 近 年 recent years.

近 海 near the sea; maritime.

近 狀 the present aspect of affairs.

近 理 reasonable.

[35]近 程 a near stage in travelling.

近 聞 I have recently heard. See above.—4.

近 臣 courtiers.

近·視 眼 near-sight; short-sighted.

近 視 鏡 spectacles for near sight.

[40]近 親 close relations.

近 親 密 友 near relatives and close friends.

近 道 nearly approximating to the truth; not far from the Way.

近 郊 a radius of 50 li outside a city.

近 鄰 near neighbours; a near village.

[45]近 體 modern style of writing.

近 體 詩 poems in modern style.

近 點 near point.

將 近 about; on the point of; thereabouts.

迫 近 imminent; impending.

[50]接 近 adjoining.

臨 近 approaching; imminent.

行 近 to approach near to.

親·近 intimate; near; familiar.

附 近 near; close by; neighbouring.

靳 [4] Ornamental trappings under the neck of a horse.
1062

靳 制 其 行 the martingale impedes his progress.

(a) Stingy. Firm.

靳 固 firm, unwilling to part with.

靳 惜 loth to part with.

錦 [3] Thin brocade; tapestry; embroidered work. Elegant, flowery.
1063

錦·上 添 花 to add flowers to embroidery—superfluous.

錦 帆 embroidered sails.

錦 幕 embroidered hangings.

錦 心 繡 口 elegant thoughts and flowery speech.

[5]錦 文 fine writing.

錦 標 championship.

錦 盒 gilded caskets.

錦 綢 figured pongee.

錦 緞 figured satin.

---

[10]錦 繡 elegant; ornamental; worked in gold or colours.

錦 衣 玉 食 luxurious living.

錦 衾 or 錦 被 embroidered coverlets.

錦 車 carriage hung with tapestry.

錦 還 to return home with honours.

緊 [3] To bind tightly. Tight, close. Near.
1064

緊 妥 secure; held fast.

緊 張 tightly stretched.

緊 握 grasped firmly; to clutch at.

緊 緊 閉 門 shut the door tightly.

[5]緊 跟·着 close behind.

緊 鄰 in the neighbourhood.

緊 隨 following closely.

緊 靠 close by; adhering to.

抽 緊 tightly drawn.

綁 緊 tie it tightly.

(a) Urgent. Important, prompt. Strict.

緊 密 secret.

緊 急 in great straits; at a crisis; urgent.

緊 急 之 際 a crisis.

緊 急 動 議 motion introduced during a time of crisis.

[5]緊 急 命·令 an urgent order; mandate dealing with a crisis.

緊 慢 haste.

緊 等 多 時 anxiously waiting for a considerable time.

↓要 緊 important; necessary.

緊 要 urgent.

緊 要 地 段 important strategic centres.

[10]緊 趁 diligent; full of energy.

趕 緊 make haste.

堇 [3] Yellow loam; clay. Season. Few.
1065

僅 [4] Exactly, hardly enough; scarcely; almost, barely.
1066

僅 僅 barely; scarcely; only.

僅 僅 敷 用 barely sufficient for use.

僅 僅 用·得 I can just make it do.

僅 到 just come.

[5]僅 可 nothing to spare; barely enough.

僅 幸 得 免 I luckily just escaped.
僅 殼 just enough to.....
僅 能 barely able to.
僅 足 日 給 just able to meet daily expenses.
僅 隔 一 牆 only separated by a wall.

堇 3 **To plaster over with mud. To bury.**
1067

堇 戶 to plaster up cracks.
行 有 死 人 尙 或 堇 之 there is a corpse by the road, someone will probably bury him.

廑
廑 3 **A hut. Careful.**
1068

廑 念 or 廑 系 thoughtful of; anxious about.
廑 注 very careful thought.
廑 窄 narrow; confined.
廑 能 勿 失 with care you will be able to avoid a slip.

墐 1.4. **To wipe; to cleanse.**
1069

槿 3 **A tree, the blossoms of which fade in a day. Transient; fleeting.**
1070

木 槿 the common hibiscus.

殣 4 **To die of hunger.**
1071

道 殣 相 望 the corpses of those who, perishing of hunger, lie upon the roads.

瑾 3 **The brilliancy of gems.**
1072

瑾 瑜 a beautiful gem.
瑾 瑜 匿 瑕 even a beautiful gem has a flaw, from the next.
瑾 瑜 之 美 有 瑕 匿 焉 even in the most beautiful gems there are flaws.
瑾 發 奇 光 the gem emits its wondrous rays—genius will show itself.

覲 4 **To have audience with the emperor; to visit a superior.**
1073 **To display.**

覲 親 to visit parents.
朝 覲 or 覲 見 an audience.

謹 3 **Respectful, attentive. Carefully; cautious, to heed, to be watchful.**
1074

謹 之 於 始 be careful of the beginnings of a matter.
謹 介 rigidly precise.
謹 具 carefully arranged, as a present.
謹 具 菲 儀 this trifling present is sent with all respect.
⁵謹 呈 to hand in with respect.
謹 守 to guard; to watch over.
謹 度 carefully obey the laws.
謹 恪 reverent; respectful.
謹 恭 humbly.
¹⁰謹°愼 to take heed; to guard against.
謹 戒 respectful admonitions.
謹 敕 careful; heedful.
謹 權 量 審 法 度 he was careful of the weights and measures, and examined into the laws.
謹 毛 而 失 貌 careful of trifles and losing the likeness—said of an artist.
¹⁵謹 稟 respectful petition.
謹 而 信 careful and truthful.
謹 記 reverent remembrance.
謹 身 careful and content.
謹 選 to select with care.
²⁰謹 重 careful and attentive.
謹 防 to guard against; to be heedful.
謹 防 盜 賊 guard against robbers.
謹 領 to receive with respect.
以 謹 無 良 in order to warn the wicked.
²⁵敬 謹 to venerate.

饉 4 **A dearth. No crops.**
1075

饑 饉 no grain or green vegetables —famine.

卺
盞 3 **The nuptial winecup, in which the bridal pair pledge each other.**
1076

合 卺 or 交 卺 to drink the nuptial cup.

禁 4 **To prohibit, to forbid. To warn. To restrain, to restrict. Restrictions, prohibitions.**
1077

禁·不 下 來 impossible to suppress.
禁 例 interdicts.
禁 制 or 禁 令 to interdict; to restrict.
禁 卒 or 禁 子³ a gaoler.
⁵禁 品 prohibited articles; contraband.
禁 品 表 a list of contraband articles.
禁 地 forbidden ground.
禁 城 or 禁 中 or 禁 宸 the Forbidden City—palace and ground of the emperor at Peking.
禁 夜 to prohibit walking at night.
¹⁰禁 宮 the imperial harem—the forbidden palace.
禁 封 to seal up.
禁 屠 or 斷 屠 to prohibit the slaughter of animals in times of drought, etc.
禁 忌 be heedful of what is taboo.
禁 忌 無 犯 do not violate the prohibitions, or offend against what is taboo.
¹⁵禁 慾 主 義 asceticism.
禁 押 to keep in prison.
禁 方 secret prescription or formula.
禁 條 prohibitions; restrictions.
禁 止 or 禁 戒 to forbid; to interdict; to prohibit.
²⁰禁 止 出 版 to suppress publication.
禁 止 吸 烟 "No Smoking." "Smoking prohibited."
禁 止 期 限 period of prohibition
禁 止 發 聲 to gag; to suppress.
禁 止 發 賣 prohibition of sales.
²⁵禁 止 稅 率 a prohibitive tariff.
禁 止 辭 a prohibitive phrase.
禁 火 or 禁 煙 to prohibit fires and smoke—on the festival of "cold food," at the time of *Ts'ing ming* 清 明
禁 烟 條 例 anti-opium regulations.
禁 約 prohibitory regulations.
³⁰禁 絕 to expel; to cut off; to exterminate.

禁 絕 鴉 片 entirely to get rid of opium.

禁 網 prohibitions extend all around like a net.

禁 舌 to keep silence; to hold the tongue.

禁 衛 軍 imperial bodyguard.

[35] 禁 貨 contraband.

禁 賭 gambling prohibited.

禁 轉 載 prohibition of transport.

禁 遏 to prevent.

禁 運 prohibition of transport.

[40] 禁 門 the forbidden door.

禁 閉 to obstruct; to close against.

禁 阻 to obstruct; to forbid a passage through.

禁 食 or 禁 口 to fast.

入 境 而 問 禁 when entering any territory make inquiries about its prohibitions.

[45] 嚴 禁 strict prohibitions.

囚 禁 to take prisoner.

條 禁 甚 嚴 the prohibitions are very stringent.

違 禁 to violate the prohibitions.

開 禁 to remove prohibitions.

(a) Read *chin*[1]. **To bear; to suffer; to endure.**

禁 不 住 cannot bear it.

禁 燒 slow-burning.

禁 穿 durable; lasting wear.

不 禁 cannot help it.

不 禁 用 not lasting; not very durable.

喜 不 自 禁 could not control his delight.

漌[4] **Cold; chilly.**
1078

打 冷 漌 to shudder.

噤[4] **Unable to speak, as from tetanus. Silent.**
1079

噤 口 痢 dysentery and difficulty in swallowing.

襟袊[1] **A garment of single thickness. Lapel of a garment. Collar of a robe formerly worn by the literati, therefore used for educated classes.**
1080

襟 兄 弟 or 連 襟 husbands of two sisters.

襟 山 帶 河 cloaked by the hills and girded by the river.

襟 帶 lapel and belt—a place of importance; strategic pass.

襟 要 or 襟 喉 important strategic post.

[5] 單 襟 a single covering.

大 襟 a large lapel, the overlap of a Chinese garment that buttons on the right shoulder.

對 襟 or 對 面 襟 garments that fasten down the front.

小 襟 or 裏 襟 the inner lapel or small fold from the right side, fastening in the centre at the neck.

青 襟 blue collars—a *hsiu ts'ai*, or first degree graduate of the old system.

(a) **The feelings. The bosom.**

襟 契 firm friends.

襟 度 the capacity of the mind.

襟 情 the emotions.

襟 懷 the feelings or emotions.

襟 抱 or 襟 素 the feelings.

襟 曲 the mind; the heart.

胸 襟 the mind; the bosom.

CHIN. TSIN. (ㄐㄧㄣ)

津[1] **A ford, a ferry, a stream. Tientsin.**
1081

津 人 ferryman.

津 口 a ferry.

津 吏 officer in charge of important post.

津 梁 bridges and fords—assistance; helps.

[5] 為 之 津 梁 to serve as a bridge or ford—as an assistance, to tide over.

津 浦 鐵 路 Tientsin—Pukow Railway.

津 涯 a shore.

津 筏 bamboo ferry; a way into an opening.

津 要 place of importance; strategic post.

[10] 津 門 Tientsin.

津 關 customs barriers at important places, as at ferries, etc.

問 津 to ask the way to the ford—to seek advice, etc.

天 津 a constellation in Cygni.

天 津 (--*ching*, or --*chin*) Tientsin.

迷 津 to miss the ford—to go astray; the place where one is easily led astray.

(a) **Saliva. To moisten. To overflow.**

津 津 to overflow.

津 津 有 味 mouth watering—intensely interesting, as a story or a book.

津 液 saliva.

津 潤 to moisten.

津 貼 to moisten—thus it stands for extra pay, squeeze, gratuity; assistance, such as is given to schoolboys to help them with their board, etc.; scholarships.

津 生 to promote the flow of saliva.

盡盡[4] **The utmost; entirely, all, wholly. To use up; to exhaust.**
1082

盡 人 事 to fulfil one's duty as a man.

盡 力 to put forth the utmost effort.

盡 各 each and every; all.

盡 命 to sacrifice the life.

[5] 盡 孝 to fulfil one's duty to parents.

盡 己 to do the utmost.

盡 心 to do the best that one can; to put all one's heart into it.

盡 心 竭 力 to put forth the utmost exertion.

盡 忠 entirely loyal; faithful unto death.

[10] 盡 忠 報 國 utterly loyal, motto tattooed on the back of *Yüeh Fei*, 岳 飛.

盡 性 with the whole nature.

盡 情 to do the best possible; to get to the bottom of a matter.

盡 情 欵 待 to treat with the utmost kindness.

盡 意 with all the mind.

[15] 盡 日 盡 夜 by day and by night; incessant.

盡 是 這 樣 all are like this.

盡 根 absolutely; unreservedly.

盡 法 with the utmost rigor of the law.

盡 淨 altogether.

[20] 盡 瘁 worn out.

盡 皆 or 盡 都 every one of them.
盡 節 to preserve chastity till the end of life.
盡 絕 exhausted.
盡 美 盡 善 most beautiful and most virtuous—perfect, excellent.
25盡 義 務 to fulfil obligations.
盡 職 to do one's duty to the utmost.
盡 行 entirely.
盡 述 to tell all the story.
盡 頭 the end of; the final outcome.
30命 盡 his lot is finished; his sands have run out.
用 盡 to use up; exhausted.
自 盡 suicide.

儘 3 To finish; to complete. All. The utmost; the extreme.
1083
儘 下 得 去 it can easily be put in.
儘 先 the very first.
儘 先 補 用 first on the list for promotion.
儘 可 以 行 it can easily be done.
5儘 彀 quite enough.
儘 教 他 allow him to....
儘 末 後 兒 the very last.
儘 東 on the extreme east.
儘 着 量 or 儘 着 力 to do the best; with all the strength.
10儘 自 to be absorbed in.
儘 自 不 來 he will not come.
儘 行 totally.
儘 讓 very obliging.

濜 4 A rapid river. Branch of the River Han. u.f. 津 No.
1084　1081.
濜 溳 rapidly flowing.

燼 4 Ashes, embers. Remnants of.
1085
化 爲 灰 燼 reduced to ashes.
燈 燼 snuff on a wick.

藎 4 Plant whose roots furnish a yellow dye. Faithful, loyal.
1086
藎 忠 loyal, patriotic.

贐 }
贐 } 4 Farewell presents.
1087
贐 儀 parting gifts.
餽 贐 parting gift of delicacies.

晉 }
晉 } 4 To increase, to flourish. To attach to. A drum. To advance.
1088
晉 封 to bestow posthumous honours.
晉 接 to receive, to welcome.
晉 爵 take another glass—said to a guest; to rise in rank.
晉 謁 to visit; to have a personal interview.

(a) A feudal state. Shansi.
晉 國 a feudal state under the Chow Dynasty, B.C. 737-420. The province of Shansi.
晉 朝 or 晉 紀 the Chin Dynasty, which was divided into Eastern and Western, and lasted from A.D. 265-317, and from A.D. 317-420, respectively; also called 兩 晉.
如 晉 如 齊 kindly feelings; closely allied in a matrimonial alliance, like these two powerful states.

搢 4 To stick into. To shake.
1089
搢 插 to stick into.
搢 笏 於 紳 to stick the official tablet into the girdle.
搢 紳 court officials, from the preceding.

(a) To strike.
搢 鐸 to strike the bell—to spread the reputation of a man.

縉 4 Red silk. To gird, as with a sash.
1090
縉 紳 red girdles—those officials whose names were in the published guide to officials.

進 4 To enter. To make progress, to advance. To urge
1091 forward.
進 一 步 之 接 洽 further steps towards re-adjustments.
進 不 能 已 矣 no limit to his advance.
進 京 to go to the capital.
進 來 Enter! Come in!
5進 修 to advance in culture, etc.
進 入 to enter.
進 兵 to advance troops to the attack.
進 兵 佔 領 to advance troops to occupy a place.
進 前 to come forward; to advance.
10進 勦 to attack and destroy(rebels).
進 化 progress, culture.
進 化 世 代 age of progress; period of evolution.
進 化 主 義 evolutionism.
進 化 論 or 進 化 說 theory of evolution.
15進 去 to go in.
進 取 to make progress; to advance in personal attainments.
狂 者 進 取 the ardent will advance and lay hold of truth.
進 口 to enter a port—imports.
進 口 准 單 or 進 口 護 照 import permit.
20進 口 商 importers.
進 口 淨 數 net imports.
進 口 稅 import duty.
進 口 總 數 gross imports.
進 口 貨 imported goods.
25進 口 貿 易 import trade.
進 城 to enter the city.
進 場 to enter the arena; to enter an examination as a candidate.
進 士 a 3rd degree graduate under the old system, reckoned as equivalent to doctor's degree by foreigners.
進 學 to enter upon studies—a 1st degree man, or hsiu ts'ai, under the old system.
30進 寸 退 尺 to advance an inch and lose a foot—losing ground.
進 戰 to advance on the enemy.
進 攻 to make an assault.
進 教 to enter the church; to become a member of the church.
進 於 道 to make progress in the right direction.

[35] 進歁 or 進項 income, revenue, receipts.

進歁財源 source of income.

進步 advance; progress; to take steps forward.

↓ 不進則退 if not advancing, then (it) will recede.

進。步極速 extraordinarily rapid advance.

[40] 進。步黨 The Progressive Party.

進發 to start; to send forth troops.

進益 advancement; progress.

進程 progress.

進行 advancing; progressing.

[45] 進行中 in progress; in operation.

進行力 progressive force.

進行手續 progressive methods.

進行無礙 advancing without hindrances.

進行的 progressive.

[50] 進行的發軔 a forward movement.

進行表 working schedule.

進行順利 progressive methods.

進退 in both directions; advancing and retiring.

進退兩難 or 進退維谷 in a dilemma, neither able to advance nor retreat.

[55] 進達 to be promoted.

進門 to enter a door; to become a disciple; to begin to learn; to enter a family, as by marriage.

進飲食 to take a meal.

前進 advance.

引進 to introduce.

(a) To offer, as tribute, etc.

進呈 to present to the emperor.

進獻 to offer up; to present.

進謁 or 進見 to present oneself to a superior.

進貢 or 朝貢 to send tribute.

[5] 進酒 to send in wine.

進香 to worship; to offer incense.

進鮮 to present seasonable fruits, delicacies, etc., to the emperor.

浸 [4] **To soak, to flood, to immerse.**
1092

浸·不透 not soaked through.

浸入 to steep; to dip.

浸化 to soften by soaking.

浸晝 broad daylight.

[5] 浸染 to imbue; to influence gradually.

浸死 drowned. = 淹·死

浸水 to drench; to soak in water.

浸淫 to soak in gradually; to absorb; insidious.

浸淫羣籍 dipped into very many books.

[10] 浸漬 saturated.

浸漸 gradually.

浸潤 to imbue with; to bias; to prejudice against.

浸潤之譖 insidious slander which gradually soaks into the mind.

浸濕 wet; drenched.

[15] 浸灌 to water by irrigation.

浸禮 the rite of immersion; baptism by immersion.

浸 [1] **Ancient name of a river in N. Kiangsu. A marsh.**
1093 **Gradually, increasingly.**

寖以成俗 gradually became a fixed custom.

寖備 gradually perfected.

寖劇 gradually worse—of sickness.

祲 [1] **A malign halo round the sun. To influence. Full.**
1094

祲氣 malaria; noxious exhalations.

妖祲 evil influences of demons.

CH'IN.　　(ㄑㄧㄣ)

欽 [1] **Respectful; to command respect. That which proceeds**
1095 **from the emperor; imperial.**

欽仰 to look up to.

欽佩 to respect; heartily to agree with.

欽召進京 called to the capital by the emperor.

欽命 by imperial command.

[5] 欽哉訓辭 respect this admonition.

欽天監 former title of the Board of Astronomy.

欽奉 respectfully received, as an imperial mandate, etc.

欽定 by imperial orders, as books, etc.

欽工 work done under imperial orders.

[10] 欽差 one sent to represent the ruler; ambassador; a high commissioner. (-ch'ai[1])

欽敬 to reverence; highly to esteem.

欽此 or 欽遵 "Respect this." concluding phrase to imperial edicts, etc.

欽派 commissioned by imperial authority.

欽賜 a gift from the throne; imperial favours.

[15] 欽遲 to esteem highly.

欽頒 to issue an imperial command.

欽點 marked off by the emperor as members of the *Hanlin* Academy.

鬼神欽 even demons respect it.

(a) To sound, as a bell. To hope for.

憂心欽欽 I anxiously hope to see you.

鼓鐘欽欽 the rhythmic sound of the bells as struck.

芹 [2] Celery.
1096

芹儀 a gift; my humble present.

芹意 my humble opinion.

芹曝 or 芹獻 depreciatory phrase when sending a present, from the next.

獻芹獻曝 I offer you parsley and the warmth of the sun.

[5] 芹筵 or 芹酌 feast given to a successful 1st degree graduate or *hsiu ts'ai*.

芹菜 Celery.

掇芹 to pluck cress—to become a 1st degree graduate under the old system.

水芹 Chinese celery, with circular cross-sections.

勤 [2] **Diligent, industrious, willing to toil. To encourage**
1097 **labour. To aid.**

勤·儉 diligent and frugal.

勤儉耐苦 frugal, industrious and long suffering.

勤公 earnest in assisting public welfare.

勤務 active service.

[5] 勤勞 or 勤力 industry; taking pains.

勤學 earnest in study.

勤家立業 making strenuous efforts to establish oneself in business, or in a profession, etc.

勤工 a diligent workman; to labour with diligence.

勤恪 diligent and painstaking; carefully attentive.

[10] 勤慎 to give care and diligence to business.

勤政 diligent in the administration of government.

勤止 to labour with diligence, from the next.

文王既勤止 *Wen Wang* laboured with diligence.

勤民 diligent in attending to the welfare of the masses.

[15] 勤求 to seek with diligence.

勤王 to assist the king—to come forward to assist the State in times of crisis.

勤·苦 laborious toil.

勲 [2]
1098

Diligent; zealous.

勲恪 carefully attentive.
愍勲 careful, diligent and attentive.

懃 [2]
1099

Brave, cautious, sad.

此而不報無以立懃於天下 If this goes unavenged, the virtue of bravery will not be vindicated.

禽 [2]
1100

Birds. Animals, generally. Distinguish 离 No. 3896.

禽圖 civil insignia, mostly birds. (*obsolete*).
禽學 ornithology.
禽犢之愛 mere animal affection.
禽獸昆蟲 birds, beasts, and reptiles.
禽獸行 beastly ways; incestuous.
仙禽 the "fairy bird,"—the crane.
委禽 to send bridal presents.
家禽 the cock; domestic poultry.

(a) u.f. 擒 No. 1102. To arrest, to capture.

服者不禽 "those who submit will not be put under restraint."

噙 [2]
1101

To hold in the mouth. To hold back.

擒捦 [4]
1102

To seize, to clutch. To arrest, to capture.

擒·住·他 Seize him!
擒拿 or 擒獲 or 擒捉 or 擒捕 to seize, to arrest.
擒斬 to capture and behead.
擒虎 to catch a tiger.
擒賊 or 擒王 in capturing rebels, first take the leader—pay heed to what is important.
生擒 to take alive.

琴 [2]
1103

The Chinese lute or guitar, in ancient times it had 5 strings, now it has 7.

琴堂 the courtroom of a *yamen*.
琴心 to use a lute to convey the thoughts or intentions.
琴操 the music of the lute.
琴瑟不調 the lutes are out of tune—discord between husband and wife.
[5] 琴瑟之樂 the pleasures of married life.
琴瑟之絃 matrimony.
琴瑟調和 the lutes are in harmony—felicity of husband and wife.
琴鳥 the lyre bird.
口琴 the harmonica or mouth organ.
[10] 四絃提琴 the violin.
彈琴 or 撫琴 to play the lute, also used for playing the piano, etc
手風琴 an accordion or concertina.
洋琴 a stringed instrument like a zither.
胡·琴 small violin-like instrument with two or four strings, the bow passes between the strings.
[15] 鋼琴 the piano.
風琴 an organ.

芩 [2]
1104

Plant of the salt marshes, the root is medicinal.

黃芩 tonic root of a yellow colour.

衾 [1.2]
1105

A coverlet or quilt.

衾裯 bed-clothes.
枕冷衾寒 the pillow and quilt are cold—alone, with no bedfellow.
被衾 coverlet or quilt.

撳搇 [4]
1106

To press down with the hand. To lean on. (*S. dial.*)

撳地泅水 to swim with a foot on the ground—to have assistance.
撳壓 press it down.
撳撳 press it.
撳桌 to lean on the table.
撳鈴 to press an electric bell push.

CH'IN. TS'IN. (ㄑㄧㄣ)

親 [1]
1107

Related, relatives. Parents. Near to.

親串 closely related by marriage.
親友 relatives and friends.
親屬會 a family gathering.
親弟·兄 blood-brothers.
[5] 親房近支 near relatives.
親故 relatives and acquaintances.
親族 or 親派 of the same clan.
親權 parental rights.
親·王 hereditary prince of first rank.
[10] 親疏 near and distant—of relatives.
親·眷 or 親·戚 or 親屬 or 親人 family connections; relatives by marriage.
親知 friends and relatives.
親等 degrees of relationship.
親舊 relatives and old friends.
[15] 親親·的 intimately related.
親誼 kindred.
親·近 near to; to approach to.
親門·的 nearly related by marriage.
親附 close to, near.
[20] 親鄰 relations and neighbours; near neighbours.
內親 relatives on the mother's, or on the wife's side.
姻親 relatives by marriage.
成親 to complete a marriage.

搶親 the custom of stealing a bride.

²⁵求親 to seek matrimonial alliance.

結親 to marry.

舉目無親 sheer stranger in a place—not a relative or a friend to be seen.

血肉之親 blood-relations.

³⁰遠親 remote relations.

雙親在堂 both parents are living.

(a) **Intimate. Affection. To love.**

親交 intimate friendship. *See below.* B.2.

親仁 to make friends of the good.

親切 having intimate connections; apposite; to the point.

親男色 sodomy.

⁵親善 to show friendliness.

親嘴 to kiss.

親娘 one's own mother.

親情 warm affection; intimacy.

親愛 to love; beloved.

¹⁰親愛主義 humanitarianism.

親慕 to long for; to desire.

親暱 familiar; intimate.

親炙 intimate with and influenced by.

親熱 or 親厚 or 親密 cordial, intimate; close; secret.

¹⁵親睦 to keep on good terms with.

皇天無親 High Heaven has no affection, (except where it is merited).

(b) **Self, in person. To attend to in person.**

親事 to attend to business in person; weddings, etc.

親交 to be handed over personally. *See above.* A.1.

親供 personal depositions.

親兵 personal bodyguard.

⁵親勘 personal inspection or inquiry.

親口 with one's own mouth.

親告 information laid in person.

親夫 one's own husband.

親如五利之第 he went in person to call on *Wu li* in his home.

¹⁰親展 to meet; to be opened in person—on envelopes.

親征 imperial expedition.

親接形面 have personal dealings with them.

親政 to rule in person, as when a prince comes of age.

親數存之 personally came many times to inquire after me.

¹⁵親於其身爲不善 to do evil in his own person.

親母 one's own mother.

親牽 to lead in person.

親生 of one's own begetting.

親目所睹 what was seen with one's own eyes.

²⁰親眼 or 親目 with one's own eyes.

親眼看見 or 親眼目睹 seen with one's own eyes.

親筆 written with one's own hand.

親細事 to attend personally to petty business.

親耕 to plough in person, as the emperor.

²⁵親膳 to wait on parents or superiors.

親臨 to pay a visit in person.

親自 or 親身 personally; one-self.

親身負責 personally responsible.

親迎 to go in person and receive the bride.

³⁰親隨 personal attendants.

(c) **Read** *ch'ing⁴* or *ch'in⁴*. **Relationship.**

親家 married relationships.

親家翁 or 親家母 titles of address used by the parents of married couple to each other.

侵¹ **To usurp; to encroach upon; to appropriate. To raid.**
1108

侵伐 to invade.

侵佔 to occupy or encroach upon the land of another.

侵佔罪 criminal appropriation. (*legal.*).

侵入 to encroach upon.

⁵侵入住宅罪 crime of encroaching upon domestic privacy. (*legal*).

侵凌 to intimidate; to insult.

侵削 to make gradual encroachment.

侵剝 to usurp; to encroach gradually.

侵吞肥己 or 侵吞入己 to misappropriate; embezzlement.

¹⁰侵奪 to seize by violence.

侵害 to usurp; to encroach upon; to infringe, as the rights or person of another.

侵害主權 to encroach on sovereign rights.

侵害權利 to encroach upon the privileges of another.

侵掠 aggressive; to seize.

¹⁵侵擾 to invade and make disturbances.

侵早 or 侵晨 early morning.

侵欺 or 侵陵 to take by fraud.

侵毀 to usurp and defame.

侵犯 trespass; to violate; to encroach; to usurp the rights of another.

²⁰侵犯職權 to encroach upon the duties or functions of another.

侵用 to appropriate to one's own use.

侵畧 to invade; to encroach upon.

侵累政策 an aggressive policy.

侵越 to trespass; to infringe.

²⁵侵越法權 to act arbitrarily; illegal actions.

侵近 to approach unawares.

侵蝕 erosion.

侵蝕性的 erosive.

海侵陸地 the sea is encroaching upon the land.

嗫呐⁴ } **Vomiting of animals. To use bad language.**
1109

嗫不出好話 he never utters a decent word.

狗嗫 the dog vomits.

胡嗫 railing; spitting out bad language.

寢³ **To sleep, to rest. A bed-chamber. An apartment.**
1110

寢不寧 uneasy sleep; restless.

寢具 bedding.

寢室 a dormitory.

寢寐 to go to bed; to sleep.

⁵寢息 to rest.

寢疾多年 bedridden for many years.

寢苦枕塊 to sleep on a mat with a clod for a pillow—mourning for parents.

寢處³ place to sleep; dwelling.

寢衣 night-dress; coverlet.
[10] 寢衰 decadent, as a government.
寢車 a sleeping car.
寢食不安 no rest either in sleeping or eating.
寢食違節 sleeping arrangements and food were without any regard for cleanliness.
就寢 to go to bed.
[15] 獨寢 to sleep alone.
廢寢 loss of sleep.

(a) **Inner apartments of ancestral temple.**

寢廟 inner apartments of a temple.
寢門 main door of inner apartments of a palace.
內寢 death chamber of a woman, in the palace.
正寢 death chamber of a man, in the palace.

(b) **To stop; to desist from.**

寢兵 to stop fighting.
難寢 difficult to stop it.

(c) **Ugly; odd appearance.**

寢陋 very ugly in appearance.
貌甚寢 a very ugly face.

駸 [1]

A fleet horse.

1111

駸駸其馬 the coursers galloped on.
駸駸然 swiftly.

秦 [2] **A fine variety of rice. Name of a State. Shensi.**

1112

秦人 strangers; the man from Ch'in.
秦人之弟 he is a brother of the man of Ch'in, i.e., from afar—it is none of my business.
秦权寶 or 秦瓊 the white-faced guardian image painted at the gate of yamens.
秦°國 the State of Ch'in, which existed from B.C. 897-221, as a feudal State, after which it overthrew the other States and set up the Ch'in Dynasty.
[5] 秦地 the territory of Ch'in. Shensi.
秦嶺 a range of mountains in South Shensi.

秦庭 to beg for assistance in desperate straits.—The army of Wu, 吳, entered Ch'u, 楚, and 申包胥 wept for seven days leaning against the wall of the hall of the prince of Ch'in, begging for help against Wu, after which Ch'in gave him troops to help against the enemy.
秦晉之交 or 結爲秦晉 to form a marriage alliance, these powerful States had such alliances, and thus the phrase has come to have the above meaning.
秦椒 capsicum or red-pepper, which came from Ch'in in the west.
[10] 秦檜 a statesman of the Sung Dynasty, through whom Yüeh Fei was executed, he is universally execrated for this—used for a traitor.
秦腔 the songs of Ch'in. Shensi style of chanting.
秦贅 to live in the wife's family—this custom began in Ch'in, see under 贅. No. 1472. A.1,2,3.
秦越 two ancient States, Ch'in occupied the district in and near Shensi, Yüeh held part of the present Chekiang and Fukien, these were so far apart that they had few dealings with each other; thus the phrase has that significance.
視如秦越 to regard them as Ch'in and Yüeh, those who had no dealings.
[15] 秦鏡高懸 the mirror of Ch'in (which revealed the inner man) is hung on high—used of those whose decisions are perspicacious.
又生一秦 to add another dreaded enemy.
大秦 by some referred to as the Roman Empire; others refer it to Syria. The Nestorian Tablet refers to 大秦景敎.

蟭 [2] **A small cicada with a square head.**

1113

蟭首蛾眉 cicada-like head, broad forehead and silkworm

moth markings for eyebrows—a beauty.

沁 [4] **An affluent of the Yellow River in Shensi. Also read**
1114 shen[4]. **To soak into, to penetrate.**

沁入 to soak into.
沁心 to penetrate to the heart.
日沁乎其中 daily soaking in it.

CHING.　　(ㄐㄧㄥ)

矜 [1] **To pity, to feel for. To have compassion on. Sym-**
1115 **pathetic.** Pron. chin[1].

矜不成人 he pitied those whose limbs were imperfect.
矜孤恤寡 to have compassion on the orphan and the widow.
矜恤 sympathy.
矜惜 to have pity on.
矜憐 to commiserate.
天矜于民 Heaven pitied the people.
居以凶矜 to be in a pitiable state.

(a) **To boast; to brag.**

矜肆 boastful; reckless.
矜誇 or 矜張 to brag; to boast.
矜貴 to boast of high birth.
自矜其能 to boast of one's own ability.
驕矜 proud and boastful.

(b) **To respect, to esteem. Dignified. Firm.**

矜也廉 their stern dignity showed itself in a grave reserve.
矜尙 or 矜言 to esteem; to admire.
矜式 to respect and copy.
矜而不爭 he is dignified but he does not dispute.
矜重 grave and dignified.

(c) **To attend to.**

矜其血氣 he disciplined his passions.
不矜細行 he did not attend to small matters.

荆 [1]

A thorn, a bramble.

1116

荆棘 thorns; thorny; annoying.
荆釵 a thorn hairpin—very poor.

手生荆棘 thorns spring up in the hand—a thorny affair.

拙荆 stupid and thorny—my wife, a conventional depreciation.

紫荆樹 the Judas tree.

負荆 to carry a thornstick (and ask for punishment)—to make an apology.

(a) The State of *Ch'u* 楚.

荆州 one of the 9 divisions of the land under *Yü* the Great, 大禹. It comprised the province of Hunan, most of Hupeh, and part of Kweichow.

荆楚 the State of *Ch'u*, which occupied the above territory and extended into Anhwei, Kiangsi, Kiangsu, and Honan. B.C. 740—330.

巠¹ Streams running underground. Flowing water.
1117

剄³ To cut the throat.
1118

勁⁴ Strong, unyielding, muscular. Also read *chin⁴*, used for 1060.
1119

勁勇 able-bodied soldiers.
勁弓 a stiff bow.
勁敵 well matched foes.
勁風 a strong breeze.
使勁 to put forth effort (v. 1060).
對勁 well matched. (-*chin⁴*.)

徑⁴ A by-way; a short cut.
俓 Diameter, direct, straight.
1120

徑三尺 three feet in diameter.
徑到 to go direct to a place.
徑啟者 I beg to inform you.
徑圓 circumference.
⁵徑寸珠 a pearl one inch in diameter.
徑庭 a narrow path and a wide hall—vastly different.
徑復 to reply direct, not through another.
徑情 straightforward.
徑行 straight, the direct way.
¹⁰徑路 the direct road.
半徑 the radius.

捷徑 the easy way.
曲徑 roundabout; circuitous.
直徑 or 對徑 diameter.
¹⁵行不由徑 avoid bypaths.
路徑 a track.

涇¹ Large river in Kansuh, flowing into the River *Wei* in Shensi. To flow straight through.
1121

涇涏 to flow straight through.
分涇渭 distinguish between the rivers *Ching* and *Wei*.—discriminate between pros and cons.

痙⁴ Convulsions; fits.
1122

痙攣 fits; convulsive contractions.

經¹ Classic books.
1123

經云 the classics say....; it is written in the books.....
經傳 (*chuan⁴*) Classics and commentary; the classics.
經典 allusions drawn from the classics.
經典之句 classical expressions.
⁵經卷 the classical records; the classics.
經史 classics and history.
經咒 prayers; invocations.
經學 classical learning.
經師 teacher of the classics.
¹⁰經幢 round or hexagonal pillars with Buddhist inscriptions.
經律 the Buddhist books of discipline.
經旨 the general purport of the classics.
經書 the Confucian classics.
經神 god of the classics—said of 鄭康成 because of his incomparable knowledge of the Confucian books.
¹⁵經神學海 the above and 何休, who was called "the sea of knowledge."
經禮 principal forms of etiquette.
經筵 place for the exposition of the classics by official interpreters.
經義 the interpretation of the classics.

經藝 or 經術 classical accomplishments; knowledge, skill.
²⁰經籍 classics; books generally.
經部 and 經史子集 the first is the title given to Classics in catalogues, the second is a general classification, Classics, History, Philosophy, and Belles-lettres.
經院哲學 scholasticism.
三字經 the *Trimetrical Classic*—the first primer under the old system.
九經 an earlier classification than the 五經, containing in addition to those given under that head, *The Rites of* Chou, 周禮, the *Book of Ritual*, 儀禮, the *Filial Piety Classic*, 孝經, and the *Analects*, 論語.
²⁵五經 the classics or canon of Confucius; the *Book of Changes*, 易經, the *Odes*, 詩經, the *Book of History*, 書經, the *Book of Rites*, 禮記, and the *Spring and Autumn Annals*, 春秋.
佛經 or 法經 The Buddhist Canon; the words of Buddha.
十三經 those given under 九經, and *Mencius*, 孟子³, *Dictionary of Terms*, 爾雅, and the *Commentaries of Kung-yang*, 公羊傳, and *Ku-liang*, 穀梁傳.
南華經 the works of *Chuang tzŭ*.
念經 to repeat prayers; to chant liturgies.
³⁰眞經 the Taoist classics of *Chwang tzŭ*, *Lieh tzŭ*, and others.
聖經 the sacred books. The Bible.
非經 uncanonical.

(a) To pass through; to pass by; to experience. Indicates past tense.

經年 one year.
經年累月 a long-drawn-out period.
經明 experienced, educated, intelligent.
經歷 to pass through; to experience; chief secretary in prefect's *yamen*.
⁵經由 to pass through.
經目 to pass before the eye.
經練 experienced; skilful.

經。過 to pass by; to undergo.
經。過一帶 passed through the district.
[10]經過之事 experiences.
經。驗 to verify; to have experienced; experience.
經驗心理學 empirical psychology.
經驗派 the empirical school.
經驗·的 empirical.
[15]經驗論 empirical theories.
經·驗豐富 rich in experience.
已·經 already; past.
曾經說·過 it has already been mentioned.

(b) To manage, to regulate, to transact.

經世 statesmen.
經世濟民 to develop the land and save the people.
經商 commission agent; to trade.
經手 to negotiate; to manage; an agent.
[5]經手費 agent's commission; expenses.
經承 head clerk in an office.
經濟 from 經世濟民 above—B.2.—a capacity to rule; modern use gives economics, finances, etc.
經濟信用 financial credit.
經濟價。值 economic value.
[10]經濟充裕 free from financial difficulties.
經濟利益 economic interests.
經濟原理 principles of economics.
經濟問題 economic questions.
經濟困難 financial difficulties; economic straitness.
[15]經濟學 economics.
經濟建設 economic reconstruction.
經濟思想 economic ideas.
經濟恢復 restoration of financial conditions.
經濟政策 financial or economic policy.
[20]經濟方法 economic methods.
經濟生·活 the economic conditions of the masses.
經濟界 the financial world.
經濟發展 economic development.
經濟科 department of economics.
[25]經濟競爭 financial struggle; economic warfare.

經濟策略 economic policies.
經濟結構 economic structure.
經濟絕交 to break off economic relations.
經濟討論所 bureau of economic information.
[30]經濟財源 economic resources.
經濟軍器 economic weapons.
經濟革命 financial or economic revolution.
經濟風浪 financial storms.
經營 business, occupation or trade; to carry on; to develop; to transact.
[35]經營交易 to transact business.
經營生·活 to make a living.
經理 to manage, to direct or to oversee; manager.
經理事務 to manage affairs.
經理人 manager; director.
[40]經管 to have control over.
經紀 to deal in; broker.
經紀人 a broker or agent.
經紀營業 broker's business.
經紀費 brokerage; commission for brokers.
[45]經。費 expenditure; outlay.
經邦 to govern the country.

(c) To plan, to arrange.

經之營之 planning and arranging it.
經始勿亟 when he measured and began, (he charged them) not to hurry.
經始靈臺 he planned and began his marvellous tower.
經界 the division of the land into fields.
[5]經綸 principles; morals; administration; to arrange; to classify.

(d) The warp of a fabric; things running lengthwise, as meridians, the main arteries, etc.

經圈 or 經度圈 the meridians of longitude.
經天緯地之才 ability fit to make the warp and woof of the universe.
經度·的 longitudinal.
經緯 the warp and the woof: longitude and latitude, etc., cross-wise.
[5]經緯儀 a theodolite.
經緯萬端 under all conditions.
經線 or 經度 degrees of longitude.

經線儀 a chronometer; also 度時表.
文經武緯 both civil and military ability.

(e) An invariable rule; a standard of conduct. Constant, recurring.

經常 what is regular and necessary; moral basis of society.
經常費 regular expenses; running or current expenses.
經星 the 28 constellations of the Chinese zodiac.
經期 or 經時 the menstrual period.
[5]經水 or 月經 the menses.
經閉 stoppage of the menses.
月經不調 irregular menstruation.
行經 menstruation.

(f) Read ching[1]. Suicide by hanging.

自經 or 經死 suicide by hanging.

脛[4]   **The shinbone. Also read hsing[4].**
1124

脛脛然 erect bearing.
脛骨 the shinbone.

逕[4]   **To pass by; to approach. Direct. Inter. 徑 No. 1120.**
1125

逕到 direct to.
逕啟者 I beg to inform you—opening phrase in correspondence.
逕庭 a narrow track and a wide hall—very unlike.
逕直 directly; directness.
[5]逕赴 to go direct towards.
逕運進口 imported direct.
半逕 the radius.
山逕 a mountain path.
曲逕 circuitous path.
[10]直逕 the diameter.

頸[3]   **The neck; the throat.**
1126

頸椎 vertebræ of the neck.
頸筋 sinews and muscles of the neck.
頸項 or 頸·子 the neck.

頸朡 a mane.
刎頸之交 a cut-throat friend-ship—i.e., to the death.

京[1] A metropolis; the capital.
1127

京兆 Peking, under the republic this term is used instead of *Shun tien fu.* Also a district of *Ch'ang an* (now Sianfu), under the *Han* dynasty.
京口 Chinkiang; i.e., the port of the Grand Canal on the Yang-tze.
京城 or 京都 or 京師 the capital.
京報 the *Peking Gazette.*
[5]京官 metropolitan officials.
京師大學堂 The Peking University under the Manchus, established towards the close of the dynasty, Dr. W. A. P. Martin was the principal.
京式 Peking fashions.
京畿道 the Peking circuit.
京腔 a northern style of speech; northern brogue.
[10]京華 the capital.
南京 Nanking.
東京 Tokio.

(a) A height; exalted; great.

景山與京 mountains and heights.
莫之與京 to have no equal.

(b) Ten millions. Also u.f. 原 No. 7725. A plain.

勍[2] Violent; strong.
1128

勍敵 a powerful enemy.

景[3] Prospects, a view; circum-stances.
1129

景況 or 景象 affairs in general; circumstances; prospects.
景仰 to look up to.
景國 environment; atmosphere.
景物 the view.
[5]景物最勝 most beautiful scenery.
景狀 or 光景 circumstances; state; conditions; prospects.
See under 光 No. 3583—34 ff.

景緻 a vista; a prospect; scenery.
景色 the beauty of the scenery; the vista.
景象 conditions; appearance; out-look; a picture or portrait.
[10]佳景 comfortable circumstances.
冬景 winter scenery.
好晚景 good evening outlook—the close of life.
山水景 landscape; scenery.
年景 prospects for the year.
[15]時景 present prospects.
無景 disreputable.
短景 a narrow outlook—man's life.
見景生情 adjust your feelings to the scenery—adapt yourself to circumstances; be guided by the conditions as they arise.
順景 in good circumstances.
[20]風景如畫 the landscape is like a picture.

(a) Bright; luminous. Beautiful.

景敎 the luminous religion—term used for Christianity on the Nestorian Tablet.
景敎碑 The Nestorian Tablet, dated A.D. 782, found during the *Ming* Dynasty, near Sianfu, Shensi.
景星 lucky stars.
景祚 auspicious; lucky.
[5]景福 great happiness.
景雲 bright coloured clouds, aus-picious omens.

(b) Read *ying*[3]. Shadows. u.f. 影 No. 7484.

日景 the shadows caused by the sun.
駐景 to cause the shadow to stand still—to stay the going down of the sun.

憬[3] To rouse; to awaken; to become conscious of right.
1130

憬覺 to perceive; to rouse the perceptions.

(a) Read *chiung*[3]. Distant.

璟[3] The lustre of gems.
1131.

兢[1] To fear, to dread. Caution. Apprehensive.
1132 Distinguish from the next.

兢兢 fearful; cautious.
兢兢業業 cautious and atten-tive.
兢懼 to dread.

競 / 誩[4] To quarrel; to wrangle.
1133

競勝 emulation.
競存 or 生存競爭 struggle for existence.
競尙 to strive to excel; to emu-late.
競張 to make an uproar.
[5]競技 athletics; sports.
競技委員 contest committee.
競技會 or 運動會 athletic sports-meeting.
競爭 to compete; to rival; to emulate.
競爭主義 a competitive spirit.
[10]競爭人 athlete.
競爭場 an arena.
競爭潮流 the current is setting towards a clash, or towards war.
競爭的 competitive.
競爭試驗 competitive examin-ations.
[15]競爭選舉 election contest.
競節 plain spoken.
競美 to emulate virtues.
競言 violent speech.
競賣 auction sale. (*Jap.*).
[20]競走 a foot-race.
競馬 or 賽馬 horse-racing.
爭競 to wrangle.

鶄[2] A small bird with black neck.
1134

竟[4] The end. Finally. After all. At last; To finish.
1135 Actually. Really. Only.

竟不肯 quite unwilling.
竟不知 I have no idea.
竟敢 actually to dare.
竟然不理 paid no heed to it.
[5]竟然如此 after all, it was like this.
竟管 have only to . . . .

竟 自 actually; notwithstanding; all the same.
竟 至 altogether; at most; in short.
歲 竟 the close of the year.
¹⁰畢 竟 finally; after all.
究 竟 after; in the end.
已 竟 already.

境 ³ A boundary; a frontier; a region. A state, a position.
1136 Circumstances.

境 地 frontier; territory; status.
境 界 state; condition; boundary.
境 社 the local temple.
越 境 to go out of one's province —to interfere.

鏡 ⁴ A mirror; a speculum.
1137

鏡·子 a mirror.
鏡 粧 dressing-case with a mirror.
鏡 臺 a large mirror stand.
鏡 花 水 月 flowers in a mirror the reflection of the moon in water—insubstantial.
⁵鏡 鑒 to be warned by the example, as if it was the reflection of oneself in a mirror.
鏡 頭 or 透 鏡 a camera lens. *See under* 透 No. 6493.
千 里 鏡 a telescope. =7043.46
照 鏡 to look in a mirror.
眼 鏡 spectacles.
¹⁰花 鏡 spectacles suited for the sight of the aged.
金 鏡 or 反 射 鏡 a metal speculum.
面 鏡 a mirror for the face.

敬 ⁴ To reverence; to respect; to honour. A present.
1138 Reverent attention to.

敬 事 而 信 carefully attend to business and be sincere.
敬 以 直 之 reverently rectify it.
敬 信 devout belief.
敬 候 to pay compliments.
⁵敬 呈 respectfully presented.
敬 告 respectful warning.
敬 啟 者 I have the honour to inform you—opening phrase in correspondence.
敬 天 to worship Heaven.
敬 奉 to worship; to receive with respect.
¹⁰敬 崇 to reverence.

敬 忠 以 勸 reverent and faithful (to rulers), and rejoicing to follow (virtue).
敬 惜 字 紙 respect written or printed paper.
敬 意 a mark of respect—a present.
　無 敬 意 or 不 成 敬 意 I have been lacking in respect to you—said to a departing guest.
¹⁵敬 愛 to reverence and love; to honour.
敬 慎 careful; watchful; respectful.
敬 慕 to desire; to respect.
敬 承 to receive with respect.
敬 拜 to worship with reverence.
²⁰敬 於 事 reverent in the discharge of duties.
敬 服 respectfully to acquiesce; to obey.
敬 求 or 敬 祈 to pray with reverence; to petition.
敬 畏 to venerate; to fear, as to fear God.
敬 神 to worship the gods.
²⁵敬 祝 to wish blessings to another.
敬 禮 to salute.
敬 老 to venerate the aged.
敬 而 將 之 以 玉 帛 respectfully to approach one by a present of gems and silk.
敬 虔 devoutness; piety.
³⁰敬 請 道 安 I respectfully wish you peace—closing phrase in correspondence.
敬 謝 with deepest thanksgiving.
敬 謹 reverently; respectfully.
敬 讓 to be deferential.
敬 身 to be careful of one's behaviour.
³⁵敬 送 sent or presented with respect.
敬 遵 respectful obedience.
敬 酒 to present a cup of wine.
敬·重 to respect; to hold in reverence.
敬 長 to reverence elders.
⁴⁰敬 陳 to make a respectful statement.
敬 順 父 母 respect and obey your parents.
敬 頌 I respectfully wish you . . . . closing phrase in correspondence. 敬 煩 "kindness of…"
敬 鬼 神 而 遠 之 respect the spirits but do not be too familiar with them.

可 敬 worthy of respect; admirable.
⁴⁵回 敬 I return the compliment— a conventional phrase.
失 敬 I have been lacking in respect—I apologize.
恭 敬 to revere; to be respectful.
恭 敬 不 如 從 命 respectful demeanour does not equal obedience.
禮 主 於 敬 the essential in propriety is respect.
⁵⁰節 敬 a present sent at festivals.
肅 敬 with awe and reverence.
舉 鎗 致 敬 to present arms.

警
儆 ³ To warn; to arouse; to caution; to admonish. To notify beforehand.
1139

警 世 to arouse the age—used on tracts.
警 佐 police court registrar.
警 備 vigilant, prepared for emergencies.
警 備 區 域 special area under military during riots or war.
⁵警 動 to startle into action; to alarm; to bother anyone.
警 務 police affairs.
警 務 長 chief of police.
警 勵 to excite; to stimulate.
警 句 a striking sentence, as in a poem or a book.
¹⁰警 告 or 告 警 to give the alarm; to warn of danger.
警 報 warning; an alarm.
警 士 or 巡 警 constable.
警 官 police officers.
警 眾 to warn the masses; to arouse the masses.
¹⁵警 察 the police.
　水 上 警 察 water police.
警 察 權 police jurisdiction.
警 察 法 police law.
警 察 總 監 commissioner of police.
²⁰警 察 署 or 警 察 局 police station.
警 察 署 長 chief of a police district.
警 察 行 政 police administration.
警 察 醫 員 police medical officer.
警 察 隊 the police force.
²⁵警 察 隊 長 captain in the police force.
警 廳 or 警 察 廳 police station.

警 心 alert.
警 悟 to warn a man; to arouse and caution.
警 惕 alarmed; scared.
30 警 戒 warning; caution; to warn or caution.
警 戒 下 次 caution against a second offence.
警 戒 線 danger line.
警 戒 色 warning colour, as red lights; protective colouring of insects.
警 敕 to threaten.
35 警 敏 sharp; intelligent.
警 教 to warn and teach; to admonish.
警 枕 a round pillow that roused the sleeper when he moved.
警 標 a beacon.
警 界 police jurisdiction.
40 警 省 or 警 醒 to awaken; to arouse to consciousness of.
警 監 police superintendent.
警 章 police regulations.
警 笛 police whistle.
警 策 a riding whip; a phrase which brightens a passage or throws light upon it, as a whip livens a sluggish horse.
45 警 絶 skilful; clean.
警 覺 to arouse from slumber; to stir.
警 角 or 號 角 a bugle or horn.
警 言 warning words; a prophecy.
警 蹕 herald to clear the roads when the emperor was on a tour.
50 警 醒 不 倦 to admonish without weariness.
警 鍊 striking and polished—of literature.
警 鐘 a tocsin; firebell.
警 長 police sergeant.
警 鼓 an alarm drum.
55 以 警 將 來 as a warning for the future.
告 警 to give the alarm.

驚 [1] **To alarm, to frighten, to startle. Alarmed, frightened.**
1140

驚 亂 in confusion through fright.
驚 亂 人 心 to disturb the mind.
驚 人 terrifying; shocking; dreadful.
驚 倒 to fall down from fright.
5 驚 動 to trouble; to disturb.
驚 天 動 地 it startles the universe.

驚 奇 astonished beyond belief.
驚 座 to cause astonishment to fellow guests.
驚 死 scared to death.
10 驚 心 動 魄 extraordinary power of influence over others.
驚 怯 startled and afraid.
驚 悸 alarmed; startled and agitated.
驚 愕 startled; surprised.
驚 慌 or 驚 訝 or 驚 駭 or 驚 懼 or 驚 嚇 or 驚 恐 alarmed; startled; terrified.
15 驚 擾 to scare and trouble.
驚 呆 frightened out of one's wits.
驚 湍 rapid flow of water.
驚 鴻 a startlingly beautiful woman.
驚 猜 to suspect.
20 驚 異 marvellous; frightful; astonishing.
驚 疑 to doubt with apprehension; to suspect.
驚 癇 or 驚 瘋 or 驚 風 spasms; convulsions.
驚 眼 to arouse desires.
驚 衆 or 驚 場 bashful; stage fright.
25 驚 蛇 入 草 like a startled snake entering the grass—used of elegant running handwriting.
驚 蟄 *Excited Insects.* A solar term. March 5th to 18th.
驚 視 to open the eyes with astonishment.
驚 避 to hide from fear.
驚 閨 a small hand drum used by pedlars of cottons, powder, etc., for women.
30 可 驚 wonderful; startling; admirable.
吃 了 一 驚 to get a fright; he gave a start.
大 驚 great fright; astonishment.

CHING or TSING (ㄐㄥ)

晶 [1] Crystal. Bright. clear.
1141

晶 化 or 結 晶 crystallization.
晶 化 的 or 結 晶 的 crystallized.
晶 晶 clear and bright.
晶 瑩 brilliant; shining; lustrous.
5 晶 系 classification of crystals.
晶 華 or 晶 簇 crystal groups.
晶 質 岩 crystalline rocks.
墨 晶 smoky quartz.

水 晶 quartz.
10 紅 晶 garnet.
紫 水 晶 amethyst.
茶 晶 cairngorms.

旌 [1] **A banner; standard of chieftain; to signal; to make manifest.**
1142

旌 使 to reward service.
旌 別 淑 慝 to mark the difference between good and evil.
旌 郵 posthumous reward for merit.
旌 德 to exemplify virtuous conduct.
5 旌 旗 banners and flags.
旌 節 a kind of ancient waymark.
旌 表 insignia or testimonials of merit conferred by the emperor on deceased persons, as chaste widows, or loyal officials.
旌 門 tablet awarded for public service.
請 旌 request that distinction be conferred on someone.

井 [3] **A well, a pit, the shaft of a mine.**
1143

井 井 有 條 arranged in regular order.
井 口 the mouth of a well.
井 地 a piece of land divided into nine portions like the "well" character, and cultivated by eight families. The produce of the central portion was claimed by the State.
井 有 仁 (＝人) 焉 there is a man in the well.
5 井 水 well water.
井 臼 well and mortar—drawing water and pounding rice, woman's work, the management of a household.
井 蛙 a frog in a well—limited outlook and experience.
井 邊 the side of a well.
井 里 a village.
10 井 鹽 salt from wells, as in Szech'uan.

穽 阱 [4] **A pitfall; a hole.**
1144

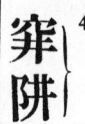

布 窪 自 陷 to dig a pit and fall into it oneself.
陷 窪 pitfalls.

婧 4
1145
Modest. Supple.

婧 婧 supple; lithe.

睛 1
1147
The pupil of the eye.

睛 珠 the crystalline lens.
定 睛 一 看 he fixed his eyes on him.
白 睛 the white of the eye.
藍 睛 blue eyes—demons, as Chinese depict them as having blue eyes.
5 黑 睛 the pupil of the eye.

靖 4
1148
To pacify; to make tranquil. Quiet, still.

靖 兵 to cease hostilities.
靖 國 to restore order.
靖 逆 to put down rebellion.
地 方 安·靖 the district is quiet.

精 1
1149
The essence of; the essential.

精 意 the essential idea or the spirit of a passage.
精 氣 the essential part; the essence.
精 氣 信 仰 animism.
精 油 essential oil.
5 精 粹 the essence of.
精 華 essential and ornamental; the sun and moon; the cream or choicest parts of—as of literature, etc.
精 要 the essential points.
精 選 to select with care.
酒 精 spirits of wine; alcohol.

(a) Unmixed; refined.

精 一 with unmixed motives; with one purpose.
精 忠 loyal; patriotic.
精 忠 服 務 patriotic service.
精 純 unmixed.
5 精 製 to refine.
精 製 品 articles of skilled manufacture.

精 采 brilliant; high lights.
精 金 pure, refined gold.
精 金 百 煉 gold refined a hundred times—purified by manifold trials.
10 精 銅 pure copper.

(b) Fine and delicate. Infinitesimal.

精 小 之 微 也 the minute is the subdivision of the small.
精 微 fine, delicate; minute. See below, C.6.
精 益 求 精 ever seeking refinement in what one does.
5 精 粗 fine and coarse—all sorts.
精 細 fine—as materials.
精 緻 beautifully fine and delicate.
精 美 elegant and refined.
精 肉 the finest part of the meat.

(c) Animal spirits. Spirit, the ethereal; subtle; ghosts.

精 力 energy; vigour; spirit.
精 壯 力 強 vigorous and strong.
精 奇 rare.
精 密 科 學 the exact sciences.
5 精 密 考 查 a careful survey; careful investigation.
精 微 abstract; subtle; abstruse.
精 微 之 奧 the subtleties of doctrine.
精 怪 spooks; bogeys; monsters.
精 深 abstruse and profound.
10 精 爽 lively and brisk in spirits; the spirit or soul; the ethereal part.
精 神 animal spirits; vitality; energy; the spiritual part of man that has an existence apart from the body; the spirit of; the mental faculty; as a prefix = psycho; morale.
精 神 上 的 解 放 emancipation of the spirit.
精 神 主 義 spiritualism.
精 神 作 用 mental actions; mentation.
15 精 神 倦 怠 strength and vitality broken down.
精 神 分 析 psycho-analysis.
精 神 動 力 mental activity.
精 神 喪 失 loss of vigor; mental weakness.
精 神 專 注 or 精 神 灌 注 to concentrate the whole energy upon.

20 精 神 工 作 mental achievement.
精 神 強 健 vigorous in mind; spirited.
精 神 恍 惚 mental disturbance.
精 神 態·度 spirit and attitude.
精 神 抖 擻 alert; faculties all ready for action.
25 精·神 敎·育 mental training; moral education.
精·神 活 潑 lively; full of animal spirits.
精 神 煥 發 in good spirits; elation.
精·神 物 理 學 psycho-physics.
精·神 現 象 mental phenomena.
30 精·神 生 活 mental life.
精·神 生 理 學 psycho-physiology.
精·神 界 the mental realm, the spiritual realm.
精·神 病 mental disease.
精·神 病 理 學 psycho-pathology.
35 精·神 療 法 psycho-therapy.
精·神 發 達 psycho-genesis.
精·神 的 mental; spiritual as opposed to physical.
精·神 研 究 psychical research.
精·神 科 學 mental science.
40 精·神 缺 陷 mentally defective.
精·神 能 力 psychic force.
精·神 衛 生 mental hygiene (in training of children).
精·神 論 spiritism.
精·神 貴 族 the nobility of mind —referring to poets, etc.
45 精·神 運·動 mental efforts.
精·神 錯 亂 mental disorder.
精·神 飽 滿 full of spirits and energy.
偉 大 精 神 great spirit—of our race.
抖·起 精·神 to brace oneself for an effort.
50 時 代 精 神 the spirit of the age.
沒·有 精·神 or 無 精·神 的 tired; listless; spiritless.
精 靈 ethereal; used for the soul or ethereal part of things. See below. D.15.
精 魂 spirits; pluck.
精 魅 bogeys; elves.

(d) Skill, clever, smart, versed in.

精 兵 picked troops.
精 利 ingenious.
精 勵·的 sedulous.
精 妙 ingenious; admirable.
5 精 工 clever workmanship.

精 巧 skilful; clever.
精·明 clever and smart.
精 明 强 幹 skilled and capable.
精 熟 thoroughly versed in.
[10]精 練 well drilled; trained troops.
精 通 well versed in.
精 進 skilfully acquired progress.
精 醫 skilful treatment of disease.
精 銳 picked trained soldiers.
[15]精 靈 smart, clever. *See above.*
C.52.
精 騎 picked cavalry.

(e) Very.

精 佳 very superior.
精 濕 soaking wet; very damp.
精 眞 very sincere indeed.
精 短 very short.
[5]精 薄 very thin.
精 誠 absolute sincerity.

(f) Secretions.

精 液 secretions; essence; semen.
精 絕 loss of vitality.
精 蟲 spermatozoa.
流 精 or 遺 精 involuntary emissions.

(g) A bird like a pheasant.

精 衛 a pheasant-like bird.
精 衛 啣 石 the *Ching wei* carrying stones in its beak—to fill the Eastern sea—used for labour in vain.

菁 [1]
Flower of the leek.
1150

菁 莪 luxuriant growth of artemisia—men who will encourage learning.
菁 華 splendour; showy.
蕪 菁 a vegetable, the rape turnip.

蜻 [1]
The dragon-fly. Pron. *ch'ing*[1]
1151

蜻·蜓 the dragon-fly.
蜻 蜓 點 水 like a dragon-fly sipping water—a delicate touch.

靚 [4]
To ornament, to paint the face.
1152

靚 粧 painted, as the face.
詐 靚 meretricious.

淨 }
淨 } [4]
Pure, clean. To cleanse.
To be constantly . . . -ing.
1153

净 几 a clean table for study.
净 口 to rinse the mouth before worship.
净 君 a broom.
净 土 the pure region—a grade of Buddhist priesthood.
[5]净 地 the pure place—a convent.
净 手 to wash one's hands of a thing.
净 掃 to sweep.
净 桶 a commode.
净 水 pure water.
[10]净 潔 clean.
净 界 or 净 域 the pure region—where the Buddhas live.
净 盡 perfectly clean; entirely.
净 福 pure happiness. (*Buddhist*).
净 空 a cloudless sky.
[15]净 身 chastity; celibacy of men; unembarrassed; destitute.
冷 净 alone; lonely.
洗 净 to purify; to cleanse.

(a) Net, as opposed to gross.

净 值 the net value.
净 價 the net cost or net price.
净 利 the net profit.
净 增 net increase.
[5]净 數 the net amount.
净 重 the net weight.
進 貨 净 價 net cost of goods coming in.

靜 [4]
Quiet, peaceful.
1154

靜 中 in silence.
靜 事 to cease all business.
靜 候 quietly waiting for.
靜 坐 to close the eyes and meditate. 靜 力 學 statics.
[5]靜 幽 silent and still.
靜 心 serenity; tranquility.
靜 思 meditation.
靜 息 to rest.
靜 悄 悄 的 quietly; stealthily.
[10]靜 時 the quiet hour.
靜 極 dead rest; absolute repose.
靜 止 at rest; no motion.
靜 聽 to listen quietly.
靜 脈 veins.
[15]靜 舍 the quiet home—Buddhist monastery.

靜 觀 contemplation.
靜 言 clever talk.
靜 閒 repose; quiet.
靜 電 static electricity.
[20]靜 鞭 whip cracked at intervals during the imperial worship to ensure silence.
靜 養 to rest and care for the health.
靜 默 無 聲 absolute quietness.
俱 靜 all quiet.
修 靜 to cultivate quietness.
[25]動 靜 movement and repose—action.
夜 靜 in the stillness of the night.
鎮 靜 immoveable; firm of purpose.

(a) Clean, modest, soft-voiced.

靜 女 a modest maiden.
貞 靜 chaste.
靜 嘉 clean and refined.

CH'ING.   (ㄑㄧㄥ)

卿 [1]
A noble; a high officer.
1155

卿 士 chief minister; premier.
卿 大 夫 assistant minister of a principality.
卿 子 [3] a young lord, son of an official.
卿 家 our ministry.
[5]卿 相 [+] a cabinet minister.
卿 貳 assistant minister.
六 卿 six chief ministers under the *Chow* Dynasty.
公 卿 大 夫 dukes, nobles and high officials.

(a) A term of respect.

卿 卿 term of endearment used to a wife.
先 卿 my late wife.
愛 卿 my dear.

(b) u.f. 慶 No. 1167. Good luck, etc.

卿 雲 for (慶 雲) propitious clouds.
卿 雲 歌 A former Chinese national anthem.
卿 雲 爛 兮, 糺 縵 縵 兮,
The auspicious clouds slowly roll in brilliance.

日 月 光 華, 旦 復 旦 兮, The glorious light of the sun and moon is renewed day by day.

輕[1] Light, as contrasted with heavy.
1156

輕 任 light duties.
輕 便 鐵 路 a light railway.
輕 兵 light infantry.
輕 刑 a light punishment.
[5]輕 吹 to blow lightly.
輕 噸 a light ton—2,000 lb.
輕 如 飛 燕 light as a swallow on the wing.
輕 妝 lightly clad.
輕 容 the lightest plain gauze.
[10]輕 寒 slight cold.
輕·巧 agile; light; handy.
輕 年 youth.
輕°快 light-hearted; in good spirits; cheerful.
輕 捷 light and fast.
[15]輕 敲 to tap lightly.
輕 氣 hydrogen. A.w. 氫氣.
輕 氣 球 a balloon.
輕 汗 a light perspiration.
輕 浮 light and floating. *See below.* A.8.
[20]輕 涼 cool and airy.
輕 症 benign disease.
輕 石 pumice stone; scoria.
輕 筆 light style of writing; an impressionist style.
輕 粉 calomel.
[25]輕 脫 light and fragile.
輕 舟 a lightly laden boat.
輕 薄 light and airy. *See below.* B.16.
輕 裘 light-weight furs.
輕 蹈 to tread lightly.
[30]輕 車 ancient chariot.
輕 車 熟 路 a light cart and a familiar road—easily done because accustomed to it.
輕 載 lightly laden.
輕 輕 的 lightly.
輕 重 light and heavy—weight. *See below.* A.15.
[35]輕 量 貨 物 light-weight goods, such as cotton.
輕 風 a light breeze.
輕 騎 light horse.
輕·鬆 light and free, relaxed; easy. 口 輕 not enough seasoning.
極 輕 extremely light; as light as possible. 輕 工 業 light industry

[40]精 輕 or 飄 輕 very light; gossamer. ↑輕 工 業 合 作 The Industrial Co-operative (movement).

(a) Frivolous; worthless; unimportant.

輕 佻 or 輕 窕 unstable; light; featherbrained.
輕 儇 frivolous; gay.
輕 其 去 就 regarded their coming and going as a light thing.
輕 弄 to twiddle; to trifle; to dally with.
[5]輕 微 slight; unimportant.
輕 弱 無 益 light and unprofitable.
輕 挑 or 輕 躁 flippant; lacking in seriousness.
輕 浮 untrustworthy; flippant. *See above,*—19.
輕·狂 frivolous and dissipated.
[10]輕 省 light; easy-going.
輕 脆 fickle and weak.
南 人 輕 脆, 終 無 能 爲 Southerners are fickle and weak and have no resources.
輕 言 heedless speech.
輕 賤 mean; of no value.
[15]無 所 輕 重 of no importance.
關 係 非 輕 the consequences are no light matter.

(b) To treat lightly. Disrespect; reckless; precipitate.

輕 侮 to insult; contemptuous.
輕 信 to take on trust; to believe without consideration.
輕 利 to despise gain or wealth.
輕 動 precipitate action.
[5]輕 忽 or 輕 牽 to make light of.
輕 慢 or 輕 棄 to treat with disrespect.
輕 於 任 事 to enter precipitately on any undertaking.
輕 於 挑 戰 to challenge others without due consideration.
輕·易 recklessly; to treat with unconcern; easy; lightly; hardly.
[10] 他 輕 易 不 來 he hardly ever comes.
輕 死 to despise death.
輕 玩 to scorn; to treat with contempt.
輕 生 to regard life lightly.
輕 看 or 輕 視 to esteem lightly.
[15]輕 舉 heedless; reckless; precipitate; to become an "immortal."

輕 薄 disrespectful; impudent; to slight; See above,—27.
輕 褻 contemptuous.
輕 辱 to treat with contempt.

擎[2] To lift up.
1157

擎 受 to receive with respect.
擎 天 柱 the pillar which bears the sky—a patriotic minister.
擎 拳 to elevate the folded hands in a salutation.
擎 起 to lift up; to raise.

鯨[2] A whale. Huge.
1158　Also pron. *ching*[1].

鯨 吞 to swallow all; to swindle another out of.
鯨 吞 地 方 to annex territory.
鯨 波 huge waves—as of rebellion.
鯨 蠟 ambergris.
[5]鯨 髮 whalebone.
鯨 鯢 giant fish; an oppressor; decapitation.

黥[2] To brand criminals on the face.
1159

黥 面 to brand faces.
黑 黥 to tattoo.

頃[3] An instant; a short time. A hundred *mou* 畝, about
1160　15.13 acres.

頃 刻 間 in an instant.
頃 接 來 函 I have just received your letter.
頃 聞 I have just heard.
頃 間 recently; of late; just now.
食 頃 during the space of a meal.

傾[1] To upset; to be overthrown. To collapse. To subvert. To
1161　fall flat.

傾 人 取 位 to overthrow a man and seize his post.
傾 倒 to fall flat.
傾 危 dangers.
傾 國 傾 城 overthrower of cities and states—female loveliness, from a poem by *Li yen nien* in praise of his sister, a concubine of *Han Wu ti.*

5 傾 國 將 軍 a general who is the cause of the overthrow of his country.

傾 圮 to collapse, as a building.

傾 家 to become bankrupt; to ruin a family.

傾 家 蕩 to waste the family fortune.

傾 掉 to overturn.

10 傾 敗 defeated; overthrown.

傾 滅 to overthrow and destroy.

傾 蓋 交 cordial friendship, from the next.

傾 蓋 而 語 he lowered the cover of the carriage and conversed (with his friend).

傾 者 覆 之 it overthrows the falling ones.

15 傾 覆 to turn over.

傾 覆 流 離 之 際 when matters are all topsy-turvy.

傾 跌 to fall; to stumble.

傾 跌 失 容 to stumble and show confusion.

傾 軋 to subvert another from envy or jealousy.

20 傾 陷 to subvert another and cause his downfall.

傾 頹 or 傾 塌 to be overthrown; to collapse.

↑ 傾 消 dumping (econ.)

(a) **To pour out.**

傾 吐 to pour out, as one's affections.

傾 囷 to empty the granaries.

傾 國 來 觀 the whole city poured out to see it.

傾 心 吐 膽 to make a clean breast of it; to pour out the heart.

5 傾 心 悅 服 to submit with a good grace.

傾 才 學 a trial of abilities.

傾 杯 to empty the glass; to turn the cup upside down to show that it is empty.

傾 溢 to run over.

傾 盆 to overturn a bowl.

10 傾 盆 大 雨 a heavy downpour of rain.

傾 筐 倒 篋 to empty the coffers.

(b) **To incline; to bend the head. To lean to.**

傾 側 leaning.

傾 倚 to lean to; to trust to.

傾 向 inclined towards; tendency.

傾 向 其 心 heart inclined to.....

---

5 有 漸 肥 之 傾 向 inclined to corpulence.

傾 心 以 守 法 incline our hearts to keep the law.

傾 斜 面 inclined plane.

傾 耳 to incline the ear.

傾 聽 to listen to; to bend the ear.

10 傾 角 or 傾 斜 inclination; (physics).

傾 身 營 救 put all his energy into saving them.

傾 頭 不 覺 金 烏 斜 he bowed his head and was not aware of the going down of the sun.

西 傾 to go down in the west—sunset.

(c) **To assay; to test. To smelt.**

傾 化 to smelt; to assay.

傾 銀 爐 crucible for silver.

傾 銷 to assay.

傾 鎔 to smelt.

傾 鎔 費 charge for melting silver.

蘔 ³ Fibrous plant of which cloth is made. Similar to the next.
1162

檾 蘔 Abutilon.

檾 ³ Grassy plant with fibres from which cloth is made.
1163

檾 蔴 Abutilon.

磬 ⁴ Musical stones; musical instrument made of stone, shaped like a carpenter's square, and hung from the apex.
1164

擊 磬 to strike the chimes—a felicitous wish. *See the next.*

編 磬 a chime of sixteen stones in two rows.

(a) **To gallop a horse.**

抑 磬 to give a horse the reins.

罄 ⁴ Exhausted, empty. Entirely; all, stern.
1165

罄 然 stern and self-possessed.

罄 盡 or 罄 淨 or 罄 竭 quite used up; all gone.

罄 竹 難 書 crimes so numerous that bamboo would be exhausted before they could all be record-

---

ed—now used for things too numerous to mention.

告 罄 used up, exhausted.

謦 ³ **To cough. To speak softly.**
1166

謦 欬 tone of voice—loud and soft.

謦 欬 不 他 逸 the lightest sound was not lost.

慶 ⁴ **Good luck; blessings. To congratulate. To reward.**
1167

慶 典 official rites of congratulation.

慶 喜 to rejoice in the success of another.

慶 壽 to congratulate on the occasion of a birthday.

慶 弔 congratulations and condolences.

5 慶 新 年 New-year congratulations.

慶 慰 consolation.

慶 會 or 慶 賀 會 congratulatory occasion or meeting; feast on such an occasion.

慶 祝 congratulatory wishes.

慶 祝 會 a celebration.

10 慶 與 merry; joyful.

慶 賀 to offer congratulations.

慶 賞 to enjoy; to reward.

慶 賞 元 宵 to enjoy the feast of lanterns on the first full moon of the year.

慶 賜 congratulations on being rewarded.

15 慶 鬧 boisterously jolly.

國 慶 national celebrations.

重 慶 Chungking.

餘 慶 overflowing happiness, that comes from virtuous conduct.

CH'ING. TS'ING. (ㄑㄥ)

青 ¹ **The colour of nature; green, blue, black. A drab neutral tint. Radical 174.**
1168

青 出 於 藍 而 勝 於 藍 green comes from blue, but it excels blue—used fig., in various ways, as when a pupil excels his master.

青 史 historians, from the use of green bamboo slips for records.

青 囊 geomancy, from the book of that name used by geomancers.

青 天 the blue sky—an honourable official.

⁵青 天 白 日 blue sky and bright sun—daylight. Chinese Nationalist flag.

青 天 霹 靂 a thunderclap from a blue sky—sudden and unexpected, a bolt from the blue.

青 女 a pure woman; name of a goddess.

青 娥 a young girl.

青 山 green hills.

¹⁰青 州 one of the 9 divisions of China under *Yü* the Great, it was situated in the eastern part of the present Shantung.

青 島 Ts'ingtao.

青 帘 sign of a wineshop.

青 年 or 青 春 youth; the verdant period of life.

青 年 會 Y.M.C.A.

¹⁵青 桐 the *Wu t'ung* tree, it has a beautiful green trunk.

青 梅 green plums.

青 楊 species of poplar.

青 樓 brothels.

青 海 Kokonor.

²⁰青 熒 or 青 燈 lamplight; brilliance of jade.

青 牛 black oxen.

青 狐 black fox.

青 玉 or 青 寶 石 the sapphire.

青 生 a 5th class graduate for the 1st degree, under the old system.

²⁵青 田 石 stone used for seals, from the district of that name in Chekiang.

青 白 a pale, bluish gray.

青 皮 green orange peel; scamps, rogues, low blackguards.

青 盲 amaurosis; having eyeballs but without sight; a form of colour-blindness.

青 眼 or 青 盼 or 青 顧 to give a sympathetic glance, so that the iris is visible, as 白 眼 is to turn the whites and look askance.

³⁰青 石 granite; also lapis-lazuli.

青 礬 or 皂 礬 sulphate of iron; copperas or green vitriol.

青 竹 green bamboos.

青 簡 green bamboo slips for records.

青 素 black and white.

³⁵青 紫 high officers of State in *Han* dynasty. The nobles used 紫 seals, and the nine ministers used 青 seals.

青 綠 lapis-lazuli.

青 翠 fresh and green; young foliage.

青 腫 "the blueness of a wound."

青 苔 moss; lichens.

⁴⁰青 苗 錢 法 a plan of *Wang an shih* 王 安 石, of *Sung* dynasty, whereby the government was to lend money at 12% interest per half year.

青 草 green grass.

青 莊 the heron.

青 菓 the Chinese olive.

青 萍 green duckweed—a famous sword.

⁴⁵青 蓮 居 士 pen name of *Li T'ai-po*, a poet of *T'ang* dynasty.

青 蚨 copper cash. *See* No. 1912—2.

青 蛙 green frogs.

青 蟲 the dragon-fly.

青 蠅 green flies—flatterers.

⁵⁰青 衣 black clothing — formerly worn by runners, police, etc.— a woman servant.

青 詞 Taoist charms used in offerings.

青 豆 green peas.

青 道 the succession of lunar phases.

青 金 lead or tin.

⁵⁵青 銅 bronze.

青 銅 世 代 the bronze age.

青 陽 ancient term for spring.

青 雲 the blue sky; the empyrean —official advancement.

青 雲 志 exalted ambitions; pure and lofty aims.

⁶⁰青 青 green and luxuriant.

青 馬 a grey horse.

青 鳥 the oriole; the bird messenger from fairyland, i.e., 西 王 母.

青 鳥 難 通 so far apart that even the bird messenger could not bring them news of each other.

青 鶴 the crane.

⁶⁵青 鷄 the edible frog.

青 魚 a carp-like savory fish.

青 黃 不 接 the green crops of this year will not be ripe before the yellow grain of last year is exhausted—used of bad years or a difficult time to tide over.

青 微 lichens; mould.

青 龍 green dragon—a river in Kiangsu—auspicious term in geomancy.

⁷⁰佛 青 purplish black.

玄 青 very black.

石 青 a dark green.

茶 青 yellowish green like an infusion of green tea.

凊 ⁴ To cool. Fresh, cool.
1169

凊 涼 cool; refreshing.

凊 暑 to allay the heat.

情 ² The affections, the feelings, desires.
1170

情 不 可 終 love never faileth.

情 不 自 禁 unable to restrain the emotions; no self-control.

情 交 love; affectionate relations.

情 人 or 情 郎 a lover; a sweetheart.

⁵情 何 以 堪 how can it be borne?

情 分 feelings; favour; affection; influence.

情 厚 warm-hearted; kindly.

情 同 手 足 brotherly love or affection.

情 同 膠 漆 united in affection as if with glue and varnish.

¹⁰情 同 金 石 fast bound in ties of affection.

情 婦 a kept mistress.

情 常 attachment; love.

情 弊 mean feelings; irregular ways. ↑ 情 場 realm of love.

情 急 under mental stress.

¹⁵情 思 sentiment; feelings.

情 性 temperament.

情 意 feelings; affections.

情 愛 affection; love.

情 感 emotion; sensibility.

²⁰情 感 衝 動 the rush of passions.

情 慾 or 情 欲 affections; lusts.

情 投 mutual affection.

情 投 意 合 perfectly suited to each other.

情 操 sentiments.

²⁵情 書 a love letter.

情 殷 warm regard for; devotion to.

情 深 deeply attached.

情 濃 strong affection.

情 物 a love token.

[30]情 絲 the ties of affection; silken ties.

情 緒 the course of love or friendship; affection; sensibilities; emotion.

情 緒 之 表 出 expression of emotion.

情 義 affection; kindness.

情 腸 sympathy; feelings.

[35]情 誼 favour; kindness.

情 調 feeling; affection. (-tiao[4])

情 趣 taste; relish; satisfaction.

情 長 lasting affection.

情·面 favour; partiality; out of respect to.

[40]情 面·的 sentimental; partial.

情°願 or 情 甘 or 情 允 willing.

七 情 the seven passions:—joy, anger, sorrow, fear, love, hatred, and desire 喜, 怒, 哀, 懼, 愛, 惡, 欲.

人 情 friendliness; a favour; sentiment; human nature.

以 目 送 情 to cast affectionate glances; to give a hint with the eyes.

[45]儌 情 illicit affection.

有 情 having affections; affectionate.

求 情 to ask a favour.

無 情 without human feelings.

留 情 to make allowance for.

[50]說 情 to plead for another.

(a) Circumstances; facts of a case.

情 況 證 據 circumstantial evidence.

情 偽 truth and falsehood—false.

情 勢 the circumstances of an affair; the trend of; the situation.

情 勢 變 遷 學 說 the doctrine of *rebus sic stantibus*.

[5]情 實 or 情 事 the facts of a case.

情 實 難 却 under the circumstances it is not easy to decline.

情·形 or 情 狀 condition, circumstances.

↓ 同 類 情·形 the same situation, the same circumstances.

情·形 已 變 the situation has changed; the circumstances have altered.

[10]情 景 the aspects of a matter.

情 理 reason; the whole aspect of a case.

情 理 之 外 unreasonable; beyond all consideration.

情 由 reasons; circumstances; origin of; statement of.

情 知 to know; to fathom.

[15]情 節 circumstances; the details of a matter.

情 節 相 同 details are similar; a parallel case.

不 知 情 no knowledge of details.

實 情 the real facts of.

晴[2]
Clear sky; fair weather.
1170a

晴 和 mild weather.

晴 天 or 晴 日 a fine day.

晴 爽 clear weather.

晴 雲 fair-weather clouds.

[5]天 晴·了 the weather has cleared.

雨 晴 the rain has cleared.

清[1]
Clear; pure; lucid.
1171

清 世 or 清 時 peaceful times.

清 公 pure and honourable.

清 冽 clear and cold, as water.

清 凉 or 清 冷 bracing; cold; refreshing.

[5]清·淨 secluded; pure.

清 史 History of the Manchu Dynasty.

清 和 clear.

清 和 月 the fourth month of the lunar calendar.

清 唱 or 清 曲 or 清 歌 amateur style of singing—quietly.

[10]清 曉 clear, as a voice.

清 士 an honest, pure man.

清 夜 in the stillness of the night.

清 夜 自 思 meditation in the night watches.

清 妍 a handsome woman.

[15]清 官 an honest, incorrupt official.

清 客 name for plums; one who lives in the home of a wealthy man; a retainer.

清 平 peace and brightness.

清 平 世°界 times of peace after the curse of militarism.

清 幽 secluded; pure and mysterious.

[20]清 廉 incorruptible; honest.

清 心 a pure heart; to purify the heart.

清 拔 refined style of writing.

清 操 or 清 徽 high principles or integrity.

清 教 徒 a Puritan.

[25]清 早 early morning; dawn.

清°明 *Clear and Bright*—a solar period at which the Chinese worship at the graves, roughly corresponds to our Easter time, about April 5th.

清 晨 dawn; break of day.

清°朝 the Manchu dynasty, A.D. 1644-1912. Early morning.

清 望 of a noble family; to be looked up to.

[30]清·楚 clear; lucid; settled.

清 標 the clear moon.

清 正 pure and upright.

清 氣 pure air.

清 水 clear water.

[35]清 水 貨 unadulterated goods.

清 油 clear oil, without sediment.

清 淡 poor; flat; thin.

清 湯 clear soup.

清 滅 business is dull; emaciated.

[40]清 潔 pure, unsullied.

清 澈 transparency.

清 濁 clear and muddy.

清 爽 lucid style; cheerful; in good spirits.

清 瘦 or 清 臞 emaciated.

[45]清 白 clear, intelligible, honourable rank, pure, of unsullied descent, one whose family had not engaged in occupations reckoned dishonourable.

世 家 清 白 a family of unsullied name.

清 白 良 民 a peaceful citizen.

清 真 used by Mohammedans for God.

清 真 教 or 回 回 教 Mohammedanism.

[50]清 真 寺 the Jewish synagogue, formerly at *Kaifengfu* in Honan.

清 秀 handsome.

清 細 clear and careful.

清 脆 clear and crisp, as sounds.

清 苦 poverty stricken.

[55]清 談 mere talk or argument.

清 識 clear explanation.

清 議 public opinion.

清 貧 extremely poor; poor but untarnished.

清 越 clear and shrill.

[60]清 蹕 or 清 道 to clear the way, as before officials on tour.

清 道 夫 a scavenger.

清 酒 or 清 酌 excellent wine.

清 醒 to sober up; clear-minded, alert.

清 門 a poor man.

65 清 閒 at leisure.

清 雅 or 清 俊 elegant; refined.

清 風 a clear breeze.

清 香 fragrant.

清 高 or 清 尚 pure and elevated —as lofty ideals.

70 清 齋 fasting; vegetarian food.

(a) Correct, accurate, to clear, as accounts.

清 償 compensation.

清 償 債 欵 refunding the loans.

清 單 statement of account.

清 理 人 liquidator.

5 清 理 債 務 to co-ordinate the debt.

清 算 to liquidate.

清 算 人 liquidator.

清 算 手 續 liquidation.

清 賬 to clear off an account.

請 3 To invite; to request; to desire; to engage. Please.
1172

請 上 坐 please take a higher seat.

請 乩 to invite the spirits to give a forecast—by the planchette.

請 事 斯 語 矣 I will try and carry out these words.

請 便 do not stand on ceremony; take your own time; do not let me trouble you.

5 請 假 to ask for leave of absence.

請 假 期 間 the period for which leave of absence is asked.

請 先 生 to engage a teacher or a doctor.

請 告 please tell me; to ask for information.

請 君 入 甕 kindly step into the jar—A man named *Chou hsing* was suspected of treason, the deputy who was asked to investigate the matter, asked him what was the best method to extort confessions from unwilling witnesses; he suggested the placing of a jar in hot coals and standing the prisoner in it; this was done, thereupon he was invited to step into the jar himself.

10 請 命 to request orders; to ask for sanction; to beg for a life.

請 問 or 請 敎 May I ask you? Will you kindly inform me?

請 嘗 試 之 I will endeavour to carry it out.

請 回 please return—conventional words when escorting guests.

請 坐 please be seated; take a seat.

15 請 夫 子 吃 Master, eat!

請 子 之 車 以 爲 之 椁 asked for the carriage of the sage in order to sell it and buy a shell for the coffin with the money.

請 安 to ask after; to pay respects to.

請 客 to invite guests; to give a party.

請 室 old term for a gaol.

20 請 宴 to give a feast.

請 帖 an invitation—taken by the guest and returned to the host.

請 所 與 asked to whom he should give them.

請 旨 to ask for instructions—from the throne.

請 期 to request that a date be fixed, as for a wedding.

25 請 求 to petition; to request; to claim; to demand.

請 求 保 護 claim for protection.

請 求 權 rights of claim. (*legal*).

該 方 可 請 求 對 方 that party or that State may request the opposite party or State.

請 煩 查 照 kindly take a note of it.

30 請 王 安 Hail, O king!

請 益 to ask for further information.

請 示 to ask for instruction.

請 纓 to tender an offer of service in the army.

請 罪 to confess; to beg pardon; to ask for punishment.

35 請 茶 please take some tea.

請 菜 please help yourself; please take a little meat, etc.

請 見 asked for an introduction.

請 託 or 請 寄 to ask on behalf of.

請 討 之 please punish him.

40 請 請 after you; please help yourself.

請 財 神 to hold for ransom.

請 酒 to invite to a feast.

請 醫 to call in a doctor.

請 閒 give me an opportunity to speak with you privately.

45 請 陪 客 please keep my guests company; to invite guests (to meet the guest of honor).

請 願 a petition.

請 願 事 件 the matter of a petition.

請 願 代 表 a delegate to accompany a petition.

請 願 委 員 會 committee dealing with petitions.

50 請 願 書 or 請 願 呈 文 a written petition.

請 願 權 right of petition.

堅 請 to implore.

申 請 to call to; to make application to.

邀 請 to invite.

鯖 1　Mackerel; mullet.
1173

鯖 魚 a fresh-water fish, two or three feet long, prettily marked.

鯖 鯆 a variety of the above.

(a) Read *ching*[1]. **To fry.**

CHÜEH. CHIO. (ㄐㄩㄝ)

(Chioh)

角 2.5. A horn. A corner. An angle. Radical 148.
1174 A. p. *chiao*[3].

角 冠 a Taoist's knot of hair.

角 妓 dancing girls; actresses.

角 尺 a protractor.

角 度 measurement of an angle.

5 角 聲 blast of a trumpet.

角 膜 the cornea.

角 色 an occupation or a class; the classification of actors.

角 落 corners of a room.

角 蒿 or 青 蒿 edible plant similar to 莢 No. 710.

10 角 門 a side door.

角 馬 the gnu; a horned horse, i.e., something out of the natural order.

角 鵠 the crested lark.

角 鷹 the horned falcon or hawk.

角 黍 or 糭 子 rice dumplings boiled in a bamboo leaf.

15 三 角 學 or 三 角 術 trigonometry.

三 角 形 a triangle.

三 角 的 triangular.

八 角 star-aniseed.

吹 角 to blow a horn.

20 地 角 a cape or headland.

拐 角 a corner; to turn a corner.

曲 角³ a crooked horn.
直 角²‧³ a right angle.
眼 角³ the corner of the eye.
²⁵總 角³ horn-like tufts in which the hair of young children is dressed; childhood.
解 角³ to shed the horns.
返 角²‧³ angle of reflection.
鈍 角²‧³ an obtuse angle.
銳 角²‧³ an acute angle.

(a) A tenth of a dollar.

角²‧子 a ten-cent piece. (S. dial.)

(b) To butt; to vie in contest.

角²力 to wrestle; to try the strength.
角²逐 to contend for; to strive for mastery.
角²鬥 to wrestle.
口 角² to wrangle; to quarrel; to dispute.

桷 2.5.
1175　　A rafter; a lath.

桷 板 lathing for a roof; shingles.

榷 1.5. **A footbridge. A toll levied at a bridge or a 1176　　ferry.**

榷 使 a name for Superintendent of Customs.
榷 茶 tea taxes.
榷 酤 to levy a toll on liquor.
榷 鹽 salt taxes.

脚
腳　2.5.
The foot; the leg or base. A. p. chiao³.
1177

脚²‧³下 at the feet; to learn; now.
脚³凳 a footstool.
脚³划船 boat propelled by the feet.
脚³前 in the presence of; before.
⁵脚³印‧子 footprints.
脚³婆 a foot-warmer; hot-water bottle. = 6101.9
脚³尖 the point of the foot.
脚³布 cloth for wrapping the feet before putting on the native socks.
脚³底‧下 幾 位 兄 弟 How many younger brothers have you?

¹⁰脚³心 or 脚²掌 the sole of the foot.
脚³手 or 跳³架 a scaffolding.
脚³指‧頭 or 脚³趾 the toes.
脚³板 the sole of the foot.(S. dial.)
脚³氣 Beri-beri.
¹⁵脚³爐 a foot-stove.
脚³瘋 gout.
脚³眼 ankles.　(S. dial.)
脚³程 journey on foot.
脚³肚 or 脚³囊 the calf of the leg.
²⁰脚³貨 inferior goods.
脚³跟 the heel.
脚³踏 實 地 plant the feet on solid ground—to get a footing.
脚³踏 機 or 脚³機 treadle-machines—words are added to indicate the nature of the machine.
脚³踏 車 a bicycle. = 自 行 車
²⁵脚³蹤 or 脚‧步 or 脚³跡 footprints; traces; evidences.
脚³車 treadles.
脚³闆 stocks to-squeeze the ankles.
脚³鐐 fetters.
脚³面 or 脚³背 the instep.
³⁰脚³驢 donkeys for hire by the roadside.
修 脚³ to cut corns; "chiropodist."
八 字 脚³ splay-footed.
墻 脚 base of a wall.
失 脚 to slip; to fall into error.
³⁵山 脚² foot of a mountain.
留 脚² to detain.
赤 脚 or 光 脚² bare-footed.

(a) Labourers; porters.

脚³價 or 脚‧錢 porterage; coolie hire; the second expression also means a gratuity to the messenger who brings a present.
脚³力 coolie hire; carriage.
脚³大 freight or carriage is high; influential.
脚³夫 or 脚‧子 a coolie.
⁵脚³行 Coolie Association, in some places also means a porter or coolie. (-hang²)
手‧脚 assistants. *See below.* B.3.
水 脚 freight by water.

(b) Cleverness.

脚²本 the libretto of a play.
脚²色 profession; occupation; life; antecedents; rank; actors.
弄 手‧脚 to do clever tricks; cunning.
脚²兒 characters in a play.

覺
覐　2.5.
To perceive; to be conscious of. A.p. chiao³.
1178

覺³世 to manifest to the world.
覺²丟 臉 a consciousness of shame or loss of face.
覺²劍 sword of consciousness.
覺²察 to keep an eye on; to understand.
⁵覺²希 奇 to regard as strange.
覺²得 to perceive; to be sensible of. = 覺²着
覺²得 痛 癢 to feel irritated.
覺²性 faculties; consciousness.
覺²悟 roused to a comprehension (of one's failings).
¹⁰覺²有 先 後 some are quick and some slow of perception.
覺²海 玄 門 the profundity and far-reaching value of the teaching of Buddha.
覺²王 Buddha.
覺²疼 to feel pain.
覺²羅 surname in Manchu of the imperial family.
¹⁵覺²非 to come to a knowledge of past wrongdoing.
不 知 不 覺² unconsciously; gradually; involuntarily.
失 覺² inattentive; unobservant.
發 覺² to reveal; to make known.
直 覺² intuition.
²⁰知‧覺² feeling; perception; consciousness.

(a) Read chiao⁴　　A nap.

睡 覺⁴ to sleep.

CHÜEH.　TSIO.　(ㄐㄩㄝ)

(Chioh)

爵　2.5. **A degree of nobility.
Rank.　Dignity.**
1179

爵 位 the rank of a noble.
爵 士 ennobled rank; jazz (*Mus.*)
爵 祿 nobility and emolument.
爵 祿 可 辭 rank and emolument may be refused.
⁵爵 章 badge of nobility conferred by the Republic on dukes and lords in Mongolia, Tibet, and in Mohammedan districts.

世爵 or 襲爵 hereditary nobility.
天爵人爵 divine nobility and that conferred by man.
錫爵 to bestow a title of nobility. *See below.* A.3.

(a) A cup or goblet with three feet and two ears.

爵杯 a wine-cup.
洗爵 to rinse a wine-cup.
錫爵 to hand a cup of wine. *See above,*—8.

(b) Small birds.

爲叢毆爵者鸇 the hawk aids the thickets by driving the birds into them.

嚼 2.5. Pron. *chiao²*.
　　 To chew; to ruminate.
1180

嚼·不動 or 嚼·不爛 cannot masticate it.
嚼環 or 嚼子 a bit.
嚼用 daily bread.
嚼舌 to slander.

CH'UEH. CH'IO. (ㄑㄩㄝ)
(Ch'ioh)

確 4.5. Solid, as a rock. Really; certainly; actual.
1181

確乎 assuredly; undoubtedly.
確事 a fact.
確信 or 確音 or 確耗 reliable information.
確信成功 sure of success; certainty.
⁵確切 utmost accuracy; definite.
確切解決 a definite settlement.
確受之損失 the actual injuries, damages or loss.
確否 Is it really so?
確定 certain.
¹⁰確定強硬政策 a strong and sure policy.
確實 true; certain; that is certain.
確情 the actual facts.
確據 reliable evidence; sure proof.
確查 carefully investigate.
¹⁵確然 certainly; without a doubt.
確當 correct and proper.
確真 really true.
確知 to know for a fact.
確認 to certify.
²⁰確認判決 final judgement.

確證 true testimony.
確辨 to distinguish with accuracy.
的確 actually; true; certain.

愨 4.5. Guileless; upright; ingenuous.
1182

謹愨 reserved; shy.

卻 4.5.
却 But, yet, still, etc. Distinguish 郤 No. 2474.
1183

卻不知 really did not know.
卻如 or 卻似 but it was like.
卻是 the fact is; nevertheless.
卻有一件 but there is a matter; another point is....; furthermore.
卻說 let us resume; to resume our story; now let us proceed.

(a) To reject, to decline, to withdraw.

卻意 disappointed.
卻步 to step back.
卻流 to flow backwards.
卻病 to drive away disease.
⁵卻立 to step behind.
卻縮 to shrink back.
卻老方 formula of perpetual youth; means of driving away old age.
卻走 or 卻行 or 卻退 to withdraw; to step backwards.
了³卻 finished with that. [invitation).
¹⁰勿見卻 do not reject (my gift,
忘卻 to forget it altogether.
推卻 to make excuses; to decline.

CH'ÜEH. TS'IO. (ㄑㄩㄝ)
(Ch'ioh)

鵲 4.5. The magpie, jackdaw, jay and similar birds.
1184

喜鵲 the Chinese magpie.(--*ch'iao*)
鳥鵲 crows and magpies.

雀 4.5.
　　 Small birds. Also pron.
1185 *ch'iao³*.
雀⁴屏 to select a son-in-law.
雀⁴巢 or 雀⁴窩 a bird's nest.

雀⁴梅 a small plum.
雀⁴爪 bird's claws.
⁵雀⁴斑 freckles.
雀⁴立 to hop like a sparrow.
雀⁴籠 a birdcage.
雀⁴羅 bird-net.
雀⁴舌 bird's tongue—the finest tea buds.
¹⁰雀⁴角 to quarrel; to go to law.
雀⁴躍 hopping like sparrows, for joy.
雀⁴釵 women's ornaments with the head shaped like a bird.
雀⁴鳥 small birds.
雀⁴鷹 the kite.
¹⁵雀⁴麥 or 野麥 or 油麥 oats.
孔雀⁴ the peacock. (or --*ch'iao*)
麻雀⁴ the sparrow. (or -*ch'iao'r³*)
黃雀⁴ the oriole.

CHIU. (ㄐㄧㄡ)

鬮 1
鬮 A lot, a ticket. To draw lots.
1186

鬮分 to divide by lot.
拈鬮 to draw lots.

摎 1 To strangle. To inquire into.
1187

摎天道其焉知 How can a man find the way of Heaven by searching?

(a) Read *nao²*. Confused.

生死相摎 life and death are inextricably mingled.

(b) Read *chiao¹*. To bind, to curl up.

摎結 rolled up.

久 3 Finally. A long time.
1188

久享 venerable; honourable.
久仰 or 久慕 I have long desired to know you—conventional phrase on being introduced.
久別 long separation.
久則徵 continuing long it evidences itself.
⁵久已 for a long time; long since.

久 常 lasting; enduring.
久 後 some time after; after all; by and by.
久 慣 habituated.
久 懸 long pending.
[10]久 用 to wear well; lasting.
久 留 to stay for a long time.
久 病 chronic disease.
久 矣 吾 不 復 夢 見 周 公 for a long time I have not again seen the Duke of *Chou* in my dreams.
久 經 has long ago been . . . -ed.
[15]久 而 久 之 in the course of time.
久 要 u.f., 舊 約 an old agreement.
久 要 (*iao*[1]) 不 忘 平 生 之 言 does not forget an old agreement, however far back it extends.
久 諫 成 仇 by constant reproof caused enmity.
久 遠 a long time—for ever.
[20]久 遠 綿 長 long drawn out; interminable.
久 違 I have not seen you for a long time—conventional phrase.
好 久 a long time.
由 來 久 矣 it has been so for a long time.
耐 久 to last; durable.
許 久 a considerable period.

灸 [4] To cauterize by burning moxa. Distinguish 炙 No. 1189 1000.

灸 災 to ward off noxious influences.
灸 瘡 to raise a blister by cauterization, as a counter-irritant.
艾 絨 灸 to cauterize with moxa.

疚 [4] Chronic disease. Sorrow. 1190

在 疚 still far from well; melancholy; in mourning.
災 疚 epidemic.

(a) Something out of order. Dissatisfaction.

疚 惡 wicked; evil.
心 疚 ashamed; dissatisfied with oneself.

柩 [4] A coffin with a corpse in it. 1191

柩 車 a hearse.
旅 柩 the coffins of those who die away from home.
送 柩 to escort a coffin to the grave.
運 柩 to transport a coffin.
靈 柩 a coffin with a corpse.

咎 [4] A fault, a defect, an error. To blame; to censure. 1192

咎 悔 repentance.
咎 戾 a fault; a crime.
咎 有 應 得 deserving reproof.
咎 罪 a crime; criminal.
[5]咎 責 to take to task.
引 咎 to take the blame on oneself.
改 咎 to reform.
既 往 不 咎 things that are past, it is needless to blame.
獲 咎 to do something wrong.
[10]畏 咎 to fear censure.

(a) Responsibility.

咎 無 可 辭 the responsibility cannot be avoided.
執 咎 to take responsibility.
孰 執 其 咎 who will take the responsibility?

(b) A calamity; inauspicious omen.

咎 徵 inauspicious prognostications.
休 咎 lucky or otherwise; propitious or otherwise.
天 降 之 咎 a Heaven-sent calamity.
災 咎 calamities; misfortunes.
萬 民 喜 樂 無 咎 殃 the multitudes rejoiced because there was no calamity.

救 [4] To save, to deliver, to rescue, to relieve, to aid. 1193

救 世 to save the world.
救 世 軍 The Salvation Army.
救 主 The Saviour.
救 兵 relief troops.
[5]救 出 來 to save from.
救 助 to aid, as with money, or in other ways.
救 助 償 金 salvage money.
救 助 貨 物 salvage of goods.
救 助 難 船 費 salvage money for ships.

[10]救 命 Save life! Help, help!
救 命 具 life-saving appliances.
救 命 火 箭 life-saving rocket.
救 命 的 life-saving.
救 命 綱 life-net.
[15]救 國 to save the State or the nation.
救 國 主 義 doctrine of national salvation.
救 國 團 patriotic group.
救 度 to save souls.
救 急 to help in extremity; to relieve urgent need.
[20]救 恩 the grace of salvation; saving grace.
救 患 to relieve sorrow or distress.
救 應 to respond.
救 拔 to uplift; to rescue.
救 援 to rescue; to raise a siege.
[25]救 日 救 月 or 護 日 to save the sun or the moon in the eclipses.
救 星 a star of salvation; a deliverer.
救 時 之 急 務 to save from the pressing needs of the times.
救 活 or 救 活 過 來 to save alive.
救 濟 to relieve distress either with money or with food.
[30]救 濟 方 法 relief methods.
救 濟 會 relief association; benevolent society.
救 火 or 救 息 火 to put out a fire.
救 火 機 fire-engine.
救 火 演 習 fire-drill.
[35]救 火 激 筒 fire-hose.
救 火 部 fire department.
救 火 隊 fire-brigade.
救 火 籠 頭 fire-hydrant.
救 災 to relieve or avert calamity, famine, flood, etc.
[40]救 災 會 famine-relief society.
救 生 to save life.
救 生 圈 or 救 難 浮 標 life-buoy.
救 生 局 life-boat office.
救 生 帶 life-belt.
[45]救 生 船 or 紅 船 lifeboats.
救 生 衣 life-jacket.
救 生 車 life-saving cradle of the rocket apparatus.
救 難 索 life-line.
救 苦 to rescue from sorrow and distress, a name for *Kwanyin*, the Goddess of Mercy.
[50]救 苦 經 ritual chanted by Taoists at funerals.
救 護 to save and protect; salvage.

救護章程 salvage regulations.
救護隊 ambulance corps.
救貨費用 or 救難費用 salvage expenses.
[55]救贖 to redeem; to effect redemption.
救難 to help out of distress.
救飢 to relieve hunger.
不可救藥 hopeless; incurable; nothing can be done.
拯救 to save; to rescue.
[60]搭救 to rescue.
無法可救 no way of relief or deliverance.

丩 [4]
1194
To join or connect.

糾 [1.3]
紏
1195
A confederacy. To collect.

糾刦 to band together for robbery.
糾合 to gather together.
糾散 to gather the scattered together.
糾會 a club, an association.
[5]糾衆 to collect a crowd.
糾約 to form unlawful associations.
糾紛 gathered together and scattered—disorder; confusion.
糾結 to band together.
糾結之事 tangled matters; involved and complicated affairs.
[10]糾纏 involved; tangled; perplexed. See below. C.1.
糾葛 complicated; mutually involved, as when there are cross accounts.
糾謀 to conspire; to plot.
糾邀 to be urged to join the unlawful associations.

(a) To investigate, to inform, to impeach, to correct.

糾參 or 糾劾 or 糾彈 to impeach; to reprimand.
糾察 disciplinary investigation.
糾察隊 inspectors, investigators.
糾戒 to correct and warn.
[5]糾正 or 糾繩 to correct errors; to expose shortcomings.
糾殛 to punish according to deserts.

糾禁 to investigate and prohibit.
糾奏 an impeachment.
糾虔 to respect.
[10]糾謬 to correct evil.
糾萬民 to investigate the conduct of the masses.

(b) Thin, loose.

糾糾 thin; loosely woven.
糾糾葛屨 thin shoes made of a fibre.

(c) A threefold cord.

糾纆 to bind with a cord; to twist a cord. See above.—10.

(d) Read chiao³. Profound, intense.

窈糾 intense longings.

赳 [3]
1196
To carry the head high. Valiant.

赳赳武夫 a gallant soldier.
果赳 decisive.

韭 [3]
韮
1197
Scallions, leeks, onions. Radical 179.

韭菜 leeks; scallions.

九 [3]
玖
1198
The number nine. The second form is used in accounts to prevent fraud.

九九 or 九歸 Chinese arithmetical tables; also the 9 periods of 9 days each, beginning from the day after the winter solstice, which constitute the limits of cold weather. (this refers to the first only).
九九合數 multiplication tables up to nine times nine. 九九表.
九九圖 cabalistic tables.
九代 or 九族 the nine generations, the present generation with the four above and four below it.
[5]九刑 the 9 punishments of former days—branding 墨, cutting off the nose 劓, cutting off the feet 刖, castration 宮, and death 大

辟;—these are also called the five punishments—to these are added banishment 流, fine in lieu of banishment or other punishment 贖, whipping 鞭, and flogging 朴.
九·十 ninety.
九千歲 9,000 years—1,000 years short of the imperial title of 萬歲.—a title given to Wei chung hsien the tyrannous eunuch of the Ming dynasty.— u.f., extreme flattery.
九品 the nine grades of rank in former regimes.
九地 the extreme depths of earth.
[10]九天 or 九霄 the highest heavens; the heaven of the Taoists.
九夷 the nine tribes or all the tribes of the "Eastern Barbarians."
九如 the nine similitudes—a felicitous wish, referring to a passage in the odes; "May you be as the mountains and the hills, as the greater and the lesser heights, as the streams which flow in all directions, having the constancy of the moon, like the rising sun, with the longevity of the southern mountain and the green luxuriance of the fir and the cypress."
九子母 a mother of nine sons.
九宮 the arrangements of colours according to the diagrams of the 八卦; the imperial palace.
[15]九州 the nine divisions of China under Yü the Great. Noted under their respective headings.

冀	No. 443.	兗	No. 7355.
豫	No. 7603.	青	No. 1168.
徐	No. 2841.	揚	No. 7259.
荊	No. 1116.	梁	No. 3951.
雍	No. 7554.		

九廻腸 deep anxiety from sorrow.
九成九有 most probably.
九折臂 break the arms nine times—then set up for a doctor, i.e., well experienced.
九日 or 重陽 the 9th of the 9th month, lunar calendar.
[20]九春九秋 ninety days of spring and of autumn respectively; the other seasons are similarly written.

九 死 一 生 imminent danger; a narrow escape.

九 江 the nine streams of China—the lists vary considerably; the nine affluents of the Yangtze River. Kiukiang, a port on the Yangtze below Hankow.

九 泉 or 九 原 or 九 京 the nine springs—the grave, Hades.

九 泉 之 下 the underworld; under the earth; Hades.

25 九 流 nine classes of literature or schools of philosophy—Confucian. Taoist, Divination, Law, Logic, Micius or *Motzŭ*, Politics, Miscellaneous and Agriculture. Also nine classes in society.

九 流 三 教 the nine classes and the three religions, Confucian, Taoist and Buddhist.

九 淵 "The Abyss."

九 牛 一 毛 one hair from nine oxen—the slightest particle.

九 竅 the orifices of the body.

30 九 章 the nine branches of mathematics, said to have been drawn up for *Huang ti, about* B.C. 2697 by *Li Shou*. 隸 首

九 連 環 nine links—a puzzle toy.

九 通 group of encyclopedias under three divisions, one dealing with manners, customs, costumes, etc., the others with matters biographical and geographical.

九 重 the nine divisions of the celestial sphere, i.e., the four cardinal points, the four intermediate points, and the centre. u.f., Heaven by Taoists.(*-ch'ung*²)

九 頭 鳥 nine-headed bird—an evil omen, still believed in in many places; also used for a slippery rogue.

36 九 鼎 the nine tripods of *Yü* the Great, 大 禹 :—said to have borne pictures of all the objects of nature; another version is that they were engraved with the maps and particulars of the nine divisions of the land.

九 龍 轎 a mountain chair.

(a) Read *chiu*¹. To collect.

九 合 諸 侯 to call the nobles together.

九 合 諸 侯 不 以 兵 車 he gathered the nobles together without the use of military power.

究 ¹,⁴ To examine into. To examine by torture.
1199

究 問 or 究 審 to examine; to try a case.
究 報 to investigate and report.
究 察 to investigate.
究 心 thoroughly.
5 究 情 to examine into the circumstances of.
究 抵 to inquire into and compel redress.
究 斷 to investigate and give a judgement.
究 治 to investigate and award punishment accordingly.
究 禁 to inquire into and prohibit.
10 究 結 to wind up a case.
究 處³ or 究 罰 or 究 懲 to bring to trial and punish.
究 詰 to question in court.
究 辦 to prosecute; to settle a case.
究 革 to investigate and dismiss.
15 究 鞫 to force a confession by investigation.
嚴 究 rigid investigation; strict inquiry into.
徹 底 根 究 sift a matter to the bottom.
深 究 to go deeply into a matter.
老 學 究 a scholastic pedant.
20 考 究 to inquire; to investigate.
窮 究 to make a thorough investigation.
講·究 particular about things; to sift out the good; fussy or careful about the appearance; well made or well finished.
追 究 to follow up a clue.
研·究 study, research.

(a) After all, in the end, finally.

究 之 finally; really.
究 乎 汙 下 to drop into meanness at the end.
究 竟 after all, in the end, finally.
究 竟 不 合 after all it is not suitable.
究 竟 如 何 after all, what was the outcome?
靡 屆 靡 究 limitless and endless.

(b) With hatred.

自 我 人 究 究 you treat us with much hatred.

鳩 ¹ The pigeon, the turtle dove.
1200

鳩 居 my humble abode—depreciatory phrase; to sponge on others; to occupy the nest of another.
鳩 形 鵠 面 very thin and emaciated.
鳩 拙 stupid as a dove which cannot make its own nest—a depreciatory phrase.
鳩 杖 staff presented to those over eighty years of age; it had a pigeon-like handle.
5 鳩 胸 pigeon-breasted.
班 鳩 the rock pigeon.
雎 鳩 the osprey.

(a) To collect; to assemble.

鳩 合 to gather together.
鳩 工 to gather workmen.
鳩 探 to collate; to compile.
鳩 斂 to gather the people in peace and collect the taxes.
5 鳩 民 to assemble the people peacefully.
鳩 率 to lead.
鳩 聚 to flock together.
鳩 車 a toy.
鳩 錢 修 路 to collect money for road repairs.

廄 廏 ⁴ A stable.
1201

廄 卒 a groom.
廄 圂 stall in a stable.
廄 號 a large stable.

臼 ⁴ A mortar; a bowl. Radical 134. Distinguish 白 No. 4975.
1202

臼·子 a mortar.
臼 杵 pestle and mortar.
臼 砲 a mortar for firing rockets, etc.
臼 磕 a mortar.
5 臼 齒 molars.
石 臼 stone mortar.
脫 臼 to dislocate a joint.

藥 臼 druggists' mortar.
門 臼 a socket in which the pivot of a door turns.

柏 ³
1203

The tallow tree.

柏 子 樹 or 柏 樹 the tallow tree.
柏 油 作 燈 燭 candles are made from the fat of the tallow tree.

舅 ³·⁴
1204

A maternal uncle.

舅 姑 a husband's parents.
舅 嫂 a wife's brother's wife.
舅 子 or 妻 舅 a wife's brothers.
舅 母 wife of mother's brother.
舅 父 or 母 舅 or 舅 爺 a mother's brothers.
舅 甥 cousins on the mother's side, child of the brother or sister of one's mother.
舅 舅 maternal uncle.

舊 旧 ⁴
1205

Old—of time, persons, places and things.

舊 事 重² 提 to bring up an old matter again. (-ch'ung²-)
舊 交 an old friendship.
舊 仇 or 舊 恨 an old grudge.
舊 例 usage.
⁵舊 俗 old customs.
舊 制 the former regime.
舊 員 one's former office.
舊 城 an ancient city.
舊 大 陸 The Old World, as contrasted with America, the new world.
¹⁰舊 套 monotonous; conventional.
舊 好 friendship, an old acquaintance.
舊 學 the old learning; classical.
舊 帳 outstanding accounts.
舊 年 last year; in former years.
¹⁵舊 式 old fashions.
舊 式 的 old fashioned.
舊 德 the virtues of a place.
舊 怨 an old grievance.
舊 惡 past faults or errors.
²⁰舊 教 The Roman Catholic religion.
舊 族 ancient family or clan.

舊 日 or 舊 時 formerly; in olden times.
舊 案 outstanding lawsuits.
舊 樣 old style.
²⁵舊 歡 a former lover.
舊 曆 the old calendar.
舊 派 the old school.
舊 涫 old evil practices.
舊 留 kept or detained for a long time.
³⁰舊 病 an old complaint.
舊 相 識 an old acquaintance.
舊 約 The Old Testament.
舊 老 an old man with a wide knowledge of affairs.
舊 衣 old clothes.
³⁵舊 規 established customs; precedent.
舊 觀 its former appearance or state.
舊 貫 former regime.
舊 貨 old goods.
舊 跡 ruins.
⁴⁰舊 邦 ancient kingdom.
舊 部 veteran troops.
舊 都 former capital.
舊 關 the Native Customs, before the opening of the Treaty Ports.
舊 雨 old friends.
⁴⁵依 舊 as before.
守 舊 的 conservative.
棄 舊 換 新 to reform; to reject the old and change into the new.
照 舊 according to the old method, etc.
↑舊 瓶 貯 新 酒 new wine in old bottles.

CHIU.　TSIU. (ㄇㄡ)

啾 ¹
1206

Wailing of a child.

啾 唧 murmurs; hum of insects.
啾 啾 sobbing and wailing of infants.

揫 ¹
1207

To gather up; to gather together.

揫 束 to bind, as a sheaf.
揫 斂 to gather up, as stalks of grain.

酒 ³
1208

Wine, spirits, fermented liquors. Distinguish 酒 No. 5624.

酒 不 解 眞 愁 liquor cannot dispel real sorrow.
酒 中 intoxicated; fuddled.
酒 仙 name for Li T'ai-po 李 太 白, the famous poet of the T'ang dynasty.
酒 令 wine drinking games conducted by an elected leader.
⁵酒 力 the strength of wine or spirits.
酒 囊 飯 袋 wine sack and rice bag—a term of abuse for a gluttonous man who is also useless and ignorant.
酒 困 a slave to drink though aware of its evils.
酒 池 肉 林 Chou Hsin 紂 辛 of the Shang dynasty is said to have made a lake of wine surrounded by trees upon which were hung various meats—obscene orgies took place there.
酒 坊 or 酒 局 or 酒 店 or 酒 樓 or 酒 館 a distillery; a wine-shop; a restaurant.
¹⁰酒 罈 子 a wine jar—a toper.
酒 失 things done under the influence of strong drink.
酒 客 a drinker.
酒 帘 or 酒 旗 or 酒 望 a wine-shop sign.
酒 席 or 酒 坐 or 酒 宴 a banquet.
¹⁵酒 後 失 儀 after drinking the sense of decorum is lost.
酒 悲 sorrow or regret after drinking—"the morning after."
酒 戒 to break off drinking liquor; to prohibit drinking wine, etc.
酒 數 行 after the cup had circulated a few times.
酒 暈 redness of face after drinking.
²⁰酒 材 materials from which liquor is made.
酒 正 or 酒 政 a butler or steward.
酒 狂 mad drunk; delirium tremens.
酒 病 or 酒 癖 dipsomania.
酒 瘋 脚 gout from drinking alcoholic liquors.
²⁵酒 盃 or 酒 鍾 or 酒 巵 wine cups.
酒 禁 prohibition of liquor.
酒 箴 temperance maxims.
酒 精 or 火 酒 spirits of wine.
酒 精 準 or 酒 平 尺 a spirit level.

30 酒精燈 spirit lamp.
酒罇 decanter.
酒肉朋·友 wine and meat friends—those who are friends while invitations last.
酒肴 wine and dainties.
酒興 (hsing[4]) elation caused by intoxicants.
35 酒色[4] wine and women—debauchery.
酒荒 constantly drinking.
酒菜單 menu; bill of fare.
酒醉 drunken.
酒醡 a wine-press.
40 酒醴 sweet spirits.
酒量 or 酒戶 a man's capacity for liquor.
酒錢 wine money; gratuities.
酒鎗 a vessel for warming wine.
酒飲 food; a feast.
45 酒餅 yeast-cakes.
酒骨 grains after brewing or distilling.
酒鬼 or 酒徒 a drunkard.
酒麴 or 酒母 distiller's grains or yeast.
酒龍 great capacity for liquor.

穋[4]
1209　To shrink.

穋一半 shrunk to half the size.
穋分 (fen[4])·兩 to lose in weight.
穋穋·了 shrivelled up.
穋短 shrunk; contracted in drying.
穋縮 shrunk, as in washing.

就[4]
Then, thereupon. In consequence. According to. At 1210 once; forthwith.

就中 thereby; to mediate between.
就便 thus it will be convenient.
就先 just now; only a little while ago.
就地取材 use local material—said of using men for officials.
5 就地正法 summary execution.
就地辦理 to settle a case on the spot.
就地鎗決 to be shot on the spot.
就如 for example, as if.
就手 convenient; at the same time; see next.
10 就手去做 go and do it at the

same time; do this while you are about it.
就日 the same day.
•就·是 is; that is; namely; even; even if; very well.
○就·是·了 that will do; that is all there is to it; expression of finality.
就此 then, at that time.
15 就算·咯 that's settled; that will do; that's enough.
就·著 take advantage of; avail of.
就·要去 you must go at once; I am going at once.

(a) To come or to go to. To complete. To follow.

就事 to take up duties.
就任 to go to an appointment; to take up office.
就來 he is coming; I am just coming.
就光來 to come to the light.
5 就勢 to seize an opportunity.
就寢 or 就枕 to go to bed.
就將 to progress; to advance.
就席 to sit at table.
就木 to go to the coffin—to die.
10 就正 to associate with men of virtue in order to rectify the conduct—from the next.
就有道而正焉 he consorts with men of principle and corrects himself.
就緒 to follow a clue; to be in good order.
就義 to die for a righteous cause.
就衰 to decline.
15 就近 to choose the near, as when appointing an official; to prefer the most convenient; to be near; at the first opportunity.
就逮 to submit to arrest.
就道 to start on a journey.
就醫 to seek medical advice.
就食 to seek a livelihood.
20 就養 to take parents to one's place of office in order to be able to care for them properly.
將·就 make the best of it; approximately.　[complishments.
成○就 to complete; to cause; ac-
所就三所去三 there were three cases in which they accepted office and three in which they refused it.
日就月將 daily progress, monthly advance.

僦[4]
1211　To hire, to rent.

僦僱 to hire workmen.
僦屋 to rent a dwelling.
僦載 to hire a boat, etc., for freight.

CH'IU.　(ㄑㄡ)

揪[1]
To clutch, to grasp with the hand. To pinch.
1212　Pron. chiu[1] ≡1207.

揪住 to seize fast.
揪心 anxious; grieved.
揪扭 to twist; to wrench.
揪束 to bind into a sheaf.
5 揪皮 to pinch and pull the skin—as a counter-irritant.
揪耳 to seize by the ears.
揪·着不撒手 hold tight and do not let go.
揪·着心繁兒去做 put your whole heart into it.
揪頭 to seize the head, as when in a rough-and-tumble fight.

丘 垊
1 A hillock or mound. The first form was read mou 某, out of respect for Confucius, as it was a part of 1213 his personal name.

丘墓 graves.
丘·子 a brick grave above ground, in which a coffin is housed, until it can be carried home.
丘起棺材 to heap earth over the coffin in making a mound.
丘里 a hamlet.
5 丘陵 mounds.
營丘 mound over a grave.

蚯[1]
1214　The common earthworm.

蚯蚓 the earthworm.

邱[1]
A place; a mound.
Inter. 丘 No. 1213.
1215

邱塋 a grave.
邱壇 an altar of earth.
邱壟 a high mound—something causing useless labour.
邱陵 a mound.

虬 蚪 [2] 1216

A young dragon. To wriggle, to curl.

虬 松 a twisted pine.
虬 蟠 curled up like a dragon.
虬 髯 curly whiskers.

求 [2] 1217

To implore, to beseech. To seek after. To beg, to pray.

求 之 不 得 fail to get the desired object.
求 乞 or 求 化 to beg.
求 仙 to seek to become an immortal.
求 代 to ask another to act as locum tenens, or as a substitute.
[5]求 借 to ask for a loan.
求 備 to aim at completeness.
求 允 to beg for permission.
求 全 to desire perfection.
求 全 之 毀 reproach even when seeking to be perfect.
[10]求 凰 to seek a wife.
求 勝 to seek to surpass.
求 友 to seek for a friendship.
求 名 求 利 to seek fame and riches.
求 告 to beg and pray.
[15]求 和 or 求 成 to sue for peace.
求 多 to seek for much.
求 子 to pray for a son.
求 學 to seek information; to study.
求 寵 to court favours.
[20]求 心 力 centripetal forces.
求 恩 to ask for mercy; to beg for favour.
求 情 to ask a favour; to seek another's good graces.
求 救 to pray for escape.
求 救 主 We beseech Thee, O Saviour!
[25]求 敎 to ask for advice.
求 未 達 to beseech with no success.
求 武 力 之 援 助 the appeal to arms.
求 爲 可 知 也 try to act so as to be worthy of a reputation.
求 牡 a pheasant calling its mate—woman seeking a husband.
[30]求 生 to sue for life.
求 療 to seek medical aid.
求 神 to pray to the gods.

求 福 免 禍 to seek happiness and avoid calamity.
求 籤 問 卜 to divine by the lot.
[35]求 美 術 雅 觀 seek for artistic refinement.
求 見 to seek for an interview.
求 親 or 求 婚 to seek a marriage alliance; to propose.
求 解 to beg for release from difficulties.
求 詳 to go carefully into details.
[40]求 諸 己 what he seeks is in himself.
求 諸 身 to inquire into one's own conduct.
求 謀 to suggest a plan.
求 財 to aim after wealth.
求 降 to ask for quarter; to indicate surrender. (-hsiang[2])
[45]求 雨 to pray for rain.
求 食 to beg for food.
求 饒 or 求 赦 or 求 宥 to seek pardon.
代 求 intercession.
切 求 to beg; to implore.
[50]力 求 to pray with earnestness.
懇 求 to implore with importunity or with tears.
有 求 必 應 every prayer will be answered.
苛 求 importunate pleading.

俅 [2] 1218

Ornamental cap.

俅 冠 to be capped—manhood.

屌 [2] 1219

The male organ.

毬 [2] 1220

A ball, a globe, a knob. Inter. next.

彩 毬 ball of silk or cloth for decorations.
抛 繡 毬 to toss the embroidered ball—to choose a husband, from an old story.
花 毬 bouquet of flowers.

球 [2] 1221

A round gem. A ball, a sphere. Inter. preceding.

球 場 tennis court; ground for various ball-games, football, etc.
球 形 spherical; globular.

球 拍 tennis or other racket.
球 莖 bulbs or corms.
[5]球 門 the goal in football, etc.
球 面 三 角 術 spherical trigonometry.
球 面 幾 何 學 spherical geometry.
球 面·的 spherical.
地 球 the earth as a sphere.
[10]天 球 the celestial sphere.
打 球 to play ball games.
棒 球 baseball. 籃 球 basket-ball.
網 球 lawn tennis.
踢 球 football; to kick a ball.
隊 球 volley-ball.

裘 [2] 1222

Fur garments.

裘 葛 furs and linen garments—summer and winter clothing—a year.
裘 裳 fur clothing.
克 紹 箕 裘 to carry on the family occupation or profession,—see 箕 No. 402-4.
狐 裘 fox-skin garment.
輕 裘 light furs, which were reckoned as valuable.

賕 [2] 1223

To seek in an underhanded way. To bribe.

賕 免 to purchase escape from punishment by bribes.
賕 謝 to give presents for favours received.
賕 賄 to bribe; to give presents.
受 賕 to receive bribes.

逑 [2] 1224

To collect. To pair, to match.

逑 偶 to match; betrothed:
逑 合 to pair; to save.
好 逑 "fortunate union;" a desirable match.

糗 [3] 1225

Parched wheat or rice. Broken grain.

糗 糧 cured dried grain.

餲 [3] 1226

Spoiled, broken viands.

CH'IU. TS'IU. (ㄑㄧㄡ)

秋 穐]¹

1227 The autumn, the fall of the year. A season, a time.

秋 事 harvest affairs.

秋 分 the autumnal equinox.

秋·千 a swing, *see* 鞦 No. 1231.

秋 去 春 來 autumn departs and spring returns—the lapse of time.

⁵秋 士 old and disappointed scholar.

秋·天 or 秋 季 autumn.

秋 官 or 秋 曹 officers of the Board of Punishments.

秋 審 the autumn assizes.

秋 後 autumn; ancient time for executions, after the assizes.

¹⁰秋 (後) 扇 a fan after autumn—no longer wanted, so discarded;—a deserted wife.

秋 思 restful thoughts of the autumn when the crops are all in.

秋 收 or 秋 成 autumn harvest.

秋 末 end of autumn.

秋 榜 the notice-board announcing the successful candidates at the autumn examinations.

¹⁵秋 毫 autumn down—very minute, the lightest particle.

秋 毫 無 害 without committing the lightest offence.

秋 氣 cool autumn weather.

秋 水 "Autumn Floods," a section of *Chuang tzǔ;* bright eyes; a sword-flash; bright and intelligent.

秋 汛 autumn floods.

²⁰秋 波 autumn ripples—bewitching eyes, clear and bright as autumn ripples.

秋 海 棠 the begonia.

秋 禊 old name for the 7th of the 7th month of the lunar calendar.

秋 禾 autum crops.

秋 節 or 中 秋 the *Mid-Autumn Festival,* 15th of the 8th month, lunar; it is a "quarter day" when rents are paid and debts collected, etc.

²⁵秋 羅 a thin gauzy silk with stripes.

秋 聲 the sounds of autumn—the rustle of leaves and the hum of insects.

秋 蟲 crickets which chirp on autumn nights.

秋 蟬 the autumn cicada which hums in the evenings.

秋 試 or 鄉 試 provincial examination for 2nd degree formerly held in the autumn.

³⁰秋 霜 autumn frosts—severity, sternness.

秋 風 過 耳 like an autumnal breeze passing the ear—of no importance, can be regarded with indifference.

今·年 有 秋 there is a good harvest this year.

危 急 之 秋 a critical time.

打 秋·風 to collect subscriptions; *see under* 抽 No. 1314—A.7.

³⁵蘭 秋 poetical name for the 1st month.

麥 秋 time of wheat harvest.

↑中 秋 *See* 1504.57.

俅]⁴

1228 To stare at.

佯 俅 不 睬 pretend not to notice anyone.

(a) Read *ch'iao⁴*. Disabled.

儍 俅 不 仁 paralysed.

楸]¹

1229 The catalpa.

楸 枰 chess-board made of catalpa wood.

湫]¹

1230 A pool, a pond. Branch of the Yellow River. Clear water.

龍 湫 a waterfall.

(a) Read *chiao* or *tsiao³*. Mournful and sad.

湫 狹 narrow and confined.

湫 鄙 bare and poor.

湫 風 a mournful wind.

鞦]¹

1231 Traces. A crupper.

鞦 轡 reins.

打 鞦 韆 to swing on a rope swing.

鰍 鰌]¹

1232 The loach.

泥·鰍 a small fish that lives in mud.

鶖]¹

1233 Long-legged bird like a crane.

禿 鶖 the bald crane or adjutant bird.

囚 ²

1234 A prisoner. To imprison. A criminal case. Distinguish 囚 No. 7407. Also read *hsiu²*.

囚 房 or 監 囚 a prison.

囚 服 prison-garb.

囚 犯 a prisoner; a convict.

囚 禁 a jailor; a turnkey; to imprison.

⁵囚 籠 a cage in which prisoners were transported from place to place.

囚 飯 prison-fare.

要 囚 important criminal cases.

酋 ²

1235 Liquor after fermentation. To finish. A chief or headman.

酋 矛 ancient weapons; a spear.

酋 長 chief of a tribe; a leader.

酋 長 世 代 the age of tribal chieftains.

酋 雄 warlike; valiant.

酋 領 a leader.

遒 ²

1236 To collect, to consolidate. Concentrated. Distinguish 遒 No. 4612.

遒 人 a marshal or herald.

遒 盡 drawing to a close.

百 祿 是 遒 all honours and riches were concentrated in him.

(a) Strong, unyielding.

遒 健 vigorous.

遒 勁 vigorous writing.

遒 逸 vigorous and original.

鷲 鳥]⁴

1237 A condor or vulture. Cruel, rapacious. Pron. *chiu⁴*.

鷲 山 (or 嶺) a mountain in India said to be like the head of a vulture; or that vultures were numerous on account of the corpses exposed. A resort of Buddha.

鷲 悍 rapacious; grasping.

CHIUNG.　　(ㄐㄩㄥ)

(Chiong)

冂
同
坰 [1]

1238

A desert, a border prairie. The 1st form is Radical 13.

冂 野 the plains of the borders.

扃 [1]

1239

A door bar placed outside a door. See 5674 A.

扃 門 to shut a door.

(a) Read *chiung*[3]. u.f. 熲 No. 1241. Hot, clear.

扃 扃 clear and lucid.

洞 [3]

1240

Vast. Distinguish 洞 No. 6609.

洞 洞 clear and deep.
洞 遠 distant; stretching far away.
洞 野 a wilderness.

炯
熲 [3]

1241

Hot; bright; clear. Severe.

熲 心 clear minded.
熲 戒 severe caution; clear warning.
熲 烺 clear, lucid—as an explanation.
法 之 熲 鑒 the clear mirror of the law.

絅
褧 [3]

1242

A garment of one colour with no lining. A dust coat.

衣 錦 尚 絅 惡 其 文 之 著 也 over her embroidered robe she put a plain single garment, intimating a dislike to display the elegance of the former.

迥 [3]

1243

Distant; different from; separated.

迥 不 相 同 quite different; utterly unlike.
迥 別 very dissimilar.
迥 拔 pre-eminent.
迥 然 不 同 quite different; not in the least alike.
[5] 迥 異 前 時 very different from former days.
迥 迥 distant.
迥 遠 very distant.
迥 隔 地 方 places widely apart.
迥 非 人 世 different from the mortal world.
迥 非 昔 比 so different that nothing of former times is comparable to it.

窘
駉 [3]

1244

Embarrassed, distressed. For compounds, see 1716.
[1] In good condition, as a horse.

駉 駉 horses in good condition.

CH'IUNG.　　(ㄑㄩㄥ)

(Ch'iong)

瓊 [2]

1245

A red stone. Excellent; beautiful.

瓊 姿 handsome and brave man.
瓊 州 *Kiungchow*—the island of Hainan.
瓊 枝 the red branch—coral.
瓊 枝 玉 葉 imperial descendants, sons and grandsons.
[5] 瓊 杯 a jade cup.
瓊 林 former imperial garden west of *K'aifengfu* in Honan, a place where new 2nd degree graduates were entertained.
瓊 林 宴 a feast, as above.
瓊 漿 nectar—wine.
瓊 玉 valuable variety of jade.
[10] 瓊 琚 beautiful precious stone—used as an adjective, valuable and beautiful.
瓊 瑤 beautiful; lustrous.

瓊 瑰 jasper.
瓊 筵 a banquet.
瓊 臺 a magnificent terrace.
[15] 瓊 花 a kind of hortensia which is said to confer immortality when eaten.

穹 [1,2]

1246

Arched. Lofty, vast. Eminent.

穹 冥 Heaven.
穹 廬 Mongolian felt tents with rounded tops.
穹 窿 eminent; lofty and arched.
穹 蒼 the azure canopy; the sky.
穹 谷 a deep valley.

窮
竆 [2]

1247

Exhausted; impoverished; poor.

窮 不 失 義 poor yet not losing his righteousness.
窮 人 a poor person.
窮 人 無 所 歸 (he felt like) a poor man who has nowhere to turn.
窮 儒 a poor scholar.
[5] 窮 兵 黷 武 warlike, militaristic.
窮 冬 the depth of winter.
窮 則 獨 善 if poor they attended to their own virtue in solitude.
窮 困 in need; without resources.
窮 天 death of parents.
[10] 窮 奢 極 慾 luxurious desires are fully indulged.
窮 奢 鬥 侈 extravagant competition in luxurious living.
窮 家 a poor family.
窮 寇 無 追 do not press a foe too far—do not be too exacting.
窮 迫 pressed by poverty; in straits through poverty.
[15] 窮 得 可 憐 pitiably poor.
窮 忙 the restless urge of poverty.
窮 愁 the distressing anxiety of poverty.
窮 措 大 a poverty-stricken scholar; a failure.
窮 日 之 力 travel with all their strength for a whole day.
[20] 窮 極 at the end of—resources, etc; extreme poverty.
窮 民 destitute people; the poor—formerly referred to widows, widowers and orphans.

窮 獨 solitary and lonely.

窮 當 益 堅 though poor one should cleave to principles.

窮 盡 utterly exhausted. *See below.*—40.

25窮 而 不 憫 when straitened by poverty he did not grieve.

窮 苦 or 窮 乏 very poor; in deep need.

窮 荒 年 a year of famine.

窮 途 no road ahead—straitened, in poor circumstances.

窮 通 failure and success.

30壽 夭 窮 通 longevity and premature death, success and failure—all conditions.

窮 達 failure and success.

窮 達 有 命 failure and success rest with the divine appointment.

窮 鄉 poor villages; a poor district.

窮 髮 之 地 utterly barren land—not even a hair on it.

35窮 鬼 a "poor devil."

窮 鳥 入 懷 an exhausted bird flew into the bosom—driven by poverty to seek relief.

窮 鼠 齧 貓 a rat at bay will bite the cat—do not press a foe too hard.

君 子³ 亦 有 窮 乎 Has the man of superior virtue to endure poverty in this way?

圖 窮 匕 見 when the map was unrolled to the end, a dagger was revealed—of a plot to assassinate *Ch'in Shih Huang* 秦 始 皇, the assassin evaded the prohibition regarding the bringing of weapons into the presence by hiding his dagger in a rolled-up map.—u.f. disclosures, or the discovery of a plot.

40無 窮 盡 infinite; inexhaustible.

其 味 無 窮 its flavour is inexhaustible.

變 化 無 窮 endless changes.

詞 窮 no word to utter.

無 窮 infinite, -ity. (*Math.*)

(a) **To investigate thoroughly; to sift out.**

窮 原 竟 委 analysing a matter.

窮 察 to sift a matter to the bottom.

窮 本 極 原 coming to the root of the matter; a thorough investigation.

窮 理 to probe a doctrine to the depths.

5窮 究 to make a thorough search into.

窮 追 to follow out to the end; to push to extremes.

睘² Gazing at in terror. Alone.
1248

睘 睘 lonely, helpless.

悙² Alone; helpless.
1249

悙 㷠 lonely and desolate person.

悙 悙 desolate and melancholy.

悙 獨 helpless and lonely.

煢² Alone; desolate; orphaned.
1250

煢 煢 在 疚 left desolate in his illness.

煢 煢 無 告 I have no friend to whom I can open my heart.

煢 獨 the friendless and childless.

邛² In distress. A mound.
1251

邛 杖 a staff made from bamboo grown at the old 邛 州 in 四 川; it is of great strength and has many knots. *See next.*

筇² A species of bamboo from Szechuan. It has many
1252 knots and is of great strength. A staff of this bamboo.

扶 筇 to lean on a staff.

蛬² The cricket. Anxious.
1253

蛬 吟 the chirping of crickets.

蛬 蛬 anxious; a fabulous creature of the northern plains, like a horse, *see* 駏 No. 1555.

飛 蛬 滿 野 the flying locusts fill the country.

CHO. (ㄓㄨㄛ)
(Choh)

斫²·⁵· To cut with a sword, to chop.
1254

斷¹·⁵· To cut in twain.
1255

斷 朝 涉 之 脛 (ChouHsin, 紂 辛) cut off the legs of those who were crossing the ford in the morning.

斷 筋 to hamstring.

灼²·⁵· Clear; luminous.
1256

灼 明 dazzling; clear.

灼 灼 gleaming, bright; flowers in gorgeous show.

灼 然 obvious.

灼 爍 brilliant; dazzling beauty.

灼 知 clear apprehension.

(a) **To burn; to cauterize.**

灼 爛 badly burnt.

灼 艾 to cauterize with moxa.

灼 龜 to burn tortoise-shell for divination.

酌²·⁵· To pour out liquor. A feast.
1257

酌 酒 to pour wine; to entertain guests.

便 酌 an informal dinner.

喜 酌 wedding festivities.

對 酌 to drink together; to toast.

5春 酌 new-year feast.

梅 酌 or 媒 酌 feast given by bridegroom in return.

薑 酌 feast given to celebrate birth of a child.

薄 酌 a simple repast—conventional phrase of depreciation.

(a) **To deliberate, to consult.**

酌 付 to pay out, to hand over.

酌 定 or 酌 奪 or 酌 度 or 酌 辦 to deliberate and come to a decision.

酌 情 準 理 to decide equitably; to make adjustments.

酌 復 to consider the matter and then reply.

⁵酌 損 or 酌 減 a proposal to diminish.

酌 擬 to make a proposal.

酌 改 to consult about alterations or changes.

酌 數 the stated sum; the authorized amount.

酌 用 to use after consideration.

¹⁰酌 看 to take into consideration and come to a decision.

酌 議 or 酌 參 or 酌 量 or 酌 核 to consult about; to deliberate.

酌 量 妥 當 satisfactorily settled.

酌 體 to treat with consideration; to meet the wishes of another.

斟 酌 to consult; to consider.

着 2.5. **To order; to call. Sign of the imperative. The proper form is** 著 **No. 1361, but by usage this form has taken its place when that character is read** *cho.*
1258

着 令 to order.
着·他 來 tell him to come.
着 各 界 注 意 calling all classes to give attention.

(a) To place or put; to cause, etc.

着 事 to work hard at; to get into trouble.
着¹ 人 to infect.
着 力 to exert strength.
着·實 in deed, in truth, in earnest; really.
⁵着 實 言 之 candidly speaking.
着 忙 to be in a hurry.
着¹ 急 impatient; anxious. (*chao¹-*)
着 意 to give attention to; to be careful.
着 手 to use energy; to start.
¹⁰着 氣 to get angry.
着 眼 to stare at.
着·落 to hold responsible for; settled; certainty; whereabouts. *See* No. 4122. B.6.A.p.*chao²·lao.*
全 無 着·落 cannot be found anywhere.
還 沒 着·落 not yet settled.
着 謹 diligent; industrious.

(b) A move in chess.

先 着 first move.
動 一 着 to make one move.
走 為 上 着 to move is the best move.

Pron.ˣ-*chao²* orˣ·*chê* or -ˣ*chih.*

(c) A participle. Auxiliary verb.

ˣ仰·着 頭 raising the head.
ˣ來·着 he has come; coming.
ˣ找 不 着² unable to find it. (-*chao²*)
找·着·了 found it. (--chao-)
⁵ˣ搆 不 着²cannot reach up to it.
ˣ擱·着 put it down.
ˣ用 不 着 no use for it; unnecessary.
ˣ睡 不 着 unable to sleep.
ˣ說·着 話 speaking.
ˣ¹⁰還 等·着 still waiting.
ˣ騎·着 驢 riding a donkey.

熗 2.5. **To set fire to; to catch fire.**
1259　Pron. *chao².* A.w. 着.

熗 旺 to burn fiercely.
一 點 就 熗 as soon as you light it, it burns—also used fig., of anger, etc.
火 熗·了 the fire has blazed up.

CHO. CHUO. (坐乚)

(Choh)

卓 1.5. **To establish. To surpass. Eminent; lofty, profound.**
1260

卓 午 noon.
卓 卓 stately.
卓 奪 to make a decision.
卓 殊 excelling.
⁵卓 然 stately, eminent; exceptional.
卓 然 而 立 to stand majestically.
卓 然 自 立 firmly established.
卓 爾 不 羣 standing alone; preeminent.
卓 異 meritorious; special excellence.
¹⁰卓 異 之 才 special gifts or talents.
卓 立 to stand alone.
卓 絕 一 時 prominent above all others of his time.
卓 著⁴ prominent; eminent; distinguished.
卓 裁 your wise, profound judgement.
¹⁵卓 見 high ideas; exalted views.
卓 詭 excelling all others in speech.
卓 識 lofty experience or outlook.
卓 越 surpassing.
卓 越 之 才 eminent ability.
²⁰卓 越 人 才 superior to all others.
卓 躒 (*loh⁴.*) extraordinary, as of talents. A.w. 卓 犖.

卓 錫 abode of monks, from the 錫 杖 or staff of the abbot.

倬 2.5.
1261　　**Manifest, clear.**

明 倬 luminous.

棹 }1.5.
桌 }　　**A table, a stand.**
1262

棹 單 tablecloth.
棹·子 a table.
棹 帷 a Chinese table-cover.
棹 椅 板·櫈 tables, chairs and stools.
⁵棹 燈 a table-lamp.
棹 腿 the leg of a table.
棹 面·子 the top of a table.
八 仙 棹 Chinese dinner-table for eight persons.
同 棹 to eat together.
¹⁰月·亮 棹 a round table.
獨 棹 to eat alone.

(a) Read *chao⁴.* **An oar.**

棹 謳 the song of the oars.

斱 }2.5.
劅 }　　**To cut to pieces; to hack. To chop or hew. To carve for ornaments.**
斲 }
1263

斲 削 to hew and trim.
斲 喪 to destroy or injure; to waste the vitality by dissipation.
斲 棺 to dig out a coffin from a tree.
斲 爛 to chop up small.
⁵斲 輪 老 手 "an old hand", experienced,–from *Chuang tzŭ.*
斲 雕 為 樸 to do away with ornamentation for unadorned simplicity.

擢 2.5.
1264　　**To pull out; to select.**

擢 德 to promote the virtuous.
擢 用 or 擢 取 to select for government employ.

擢 秀 talented; gifted with ability; luxuriant growth.

擢 髮 難 數 as countless as the hairs on the head.

拔 擢 人 才 promote talented men.

濯 2.5. To wash; to cleanse.
1265

濯 足 to wash the feet.

洗 濯 to wash; to cleanse.

誰 能 執 熱 逝 不 以 濯 Who can take up a heated substance without first wetting (his hand)?

(a) Grandly; bright.

濯 濯 glittering; sleek; brilliant.

啄 2.5. To peck, as a fowl. To preen the feathers. A quick stroke to the left in writing.
1266

啄 啄 sound of fowls pecking; or of tapping at a door.

啄 木 鳥 a woodpecker.

啄 殼 to break the shell, as a chicken.

啄 毛 to preen the plumage.

啄 食 to peck up food.

剝 啄 to rap at a door.

椓 2.5. To beat, to rap.
1267

椓 門 to knock at a gate or a door.

涿 1.5. To drip; to trickle. A river in Chihli.
1268

涿² 濕·了 衣 服 soaked through the clothing.

涿 鹿 capital of China under *Huangti* the *Yellow Emperor*.

瀧 涿 falling water.

琢 2.5. To cut or polish stones or jewels.
1269

琢 傘 well-finished umbrellas.

琢 句 to compose and polish phrases.

琢 工 a lapidary.

琢 玉 to polish gems.

琢 磨 to cut and polish—to improve one's virtue.

諑 2.5. To strike; to attack.
1270

濁 2.5. Muddy, turbid. Stupid, corrupt.
1271

濁 世 an evil age.

濁 其 源 fouled the source.

濁 到 very angry.

濁 口 foul-mouthed.

⁵濁 意 a muddy, foul thought.

濁 才 a fool.

濁 氣 a foul smell; evil odour.

濁 水 muddy water.

濁 流 the rabble—the great unwashed; a turbid stream.

¹⁰濁 淡 phlegm.

濁 物 a stupid; a lout.

濁 酒 or 濁 醪 unstrained wine.

濁 霧 thick fog.

白 濁 gonorrhea.

↑濁 音 voiced consonants.

鐲 2.5. Small bell, anciently used in the army. Bracelets, bangles.
1272

鐲·子 or 手 鐲 or 鐲 頭 a bracelet.

拙 2.5. Stupid—conventional depreciation applied to one's own person or belongings. Clumsy, unskilful.
1273

拙 作 or 拙 著⁴ my poor composition; my book.

拙 力 brute force.

拙 劣 very clumsy and inferior.

拙 口 笨 舌 of stammering speech.

⁵拙 嘴 stupid, blundering speaker; a dull fellow.

拙 子³ my son.

拙 工 unskilled labour.

拙 性 slow witted; dull of apprehension.

拙 昧 stupid and dull.

¹⁰拙 笨 stupid, clumsy.

拙 筆 my clumsy writing.

拙 算 a bad speculation.

拙 荆 my wife.

拙 計 a foolish plan.

拙 騃 stupid and foolish.

紬 2.5. Crimson silk. To stitch coarsely. An impediment. Deficiency. Now pron. *ch'u*¹·⁴.
1274

漸 紬 gradually diminished.

短 紬 or 發 紬 very short of money.

茁 2.5. Sprouts appearing above the ground. To increase, to sprout.
1275

捉 1.5. To seize, to apprehend. To grasp.
1276

捉·住 to lay hold of.

捉 刀 to seize a knife—to write for others.

捉 姦 to seize an adulterer.

捉 弄 to meddle.

⁵捉 拏 or 捉 獲 or 捕 捉 to seize; to arrest.

捉 搦 to apprehend.

捉 攫 to seize.

捉 月 to grasp at the moon—foolish ambition, etc.

捉 臂 to seize the arm.

¹⁰捉 襟 見 肘 to expose the elbow when fastening one's jacket—very poor; ragged clothing.

捉 賊 to apprehend thieves.

捉 鼠 to catch rats or mice.

啜 / 嗽 / 歠 4.5. To sip, to suck. Also pron. *ch'o*⁴·⁵.
1277

啜 茹 to live on vegetable diet.

啜 茗 to sip tea.

啜 面 to kiss.

(a) Read *ch'üeh*⁵. To sob.

啜 泣 to sob and weep.

惙 4.5. Mournful, uncertain. Also pron. *ch'o*⁴·⁵
1278

惙 怛 sad at heart.

憂 心 惙 惙 my heart is distressed and very sad.

梲 / 棁 2.4. Small pillars that support the roof, those which rest on the main beam. A joist. A club or cane.
1279

梲 杖 a club or staff.

山 節 藻 梲 hill-like ornamentation and representation of duckweed carved on the small pillars—extravagance.

輟 4.5. **To rest, to stop. To mend. Also pron.** *ch'o*⁴·⁵
1280

輟 工 to cease work.

輟 朝 to suspend business at Court on account of death.

輟 耕 to cease farm labours.

作 輟 working and ceasing—action.

餟
醊 } 2.5. **Wine poured in a libation. Also pron.** *ch'o*⁴·⁵
1281

奠 醊 to pour a libation.

CH'O. (辶)

(Ch'oh)

辵
辶 } 1.5. **Walking. Radical 162.**
1282

戳 1.5. **To seal, to stamp. A stamp.**
1283

戳 印 a seal, a stamp; to stamp.

戳 子 a stamp or seal.

戳 記 a wooden seal granted to petty officials.

戳 頭 機 to deceive; to trick.

(a) **To stab, to stick into.**

戳 傷 wounded by a stab.

戳 心 to rouse or stir.

戳 損 injured by piercing; damaged by piercing.

綽 4.5. **Spacious; ample. Liberal; generous. Kind, gentle.**
1284

綽 楔 sideposts of a door.

綽 裕 liberal.

綽 約 meek and modest.

綽 綽 然 有 餘 裕 acting freely without restraint.

⁵綽 號 or 混 名 a nickname:—*ch'ao.*

寬 綽 generous; liberal. Also pron.

踔 4.5. **To get ahead; to stride. To excel.**
1285

踔 絕 之 能 unusual ability.

踔 脚 to walk alone.

踔 遠 distant; to cover a distance.

CH'O. CH'UO. (辶)

(Ch'oh)

淖 1.5. **To soak, to steep in water. Now pron.** *cho*²·⁵
1286

齪 4.5. **To grate the teeth. Dirt.**
1287

齷 齪 dirty; peevish.

擉 1 **To pierce; to break through.** = 1283 A.
1288

擉 刄 a fishing prong.

擉 剌 to spear; to stab.

擉 火 to apply a light—as to a touch-hole.

擉 破 to poke a hole through; to burst.

擉 紗 to embroider.

(a) **To take a pinch, to pinch.**

擉 一 擉 take a pinch.

(b) **To strike. u.f.** 觸 No. 1416.

擉 手 to jar the hand.

擉 碰 to collide.

CHOU. (凷)

(Cheo)

州 1 **A region. A department or political division, anciently 2,500 families. Used for a state, as in U.S.A., or a county, as in England.**
1289

州 同 or 別 駕 first-class assistant Department Magistrate, now abolished.

州 官 放 火 a *Chou* Magistrate may commit arson—high officials may do what the people dare not attempt.

州 牧 Chief Magistrate of one of the nine *Chou* into which China was divided under *Yü* the Great.

州 里 a neighbourhood; a hamlet.

⁵州 閭 a hamlet.

五 黨 爲 州 5 *Tang*, (of 500 families), constitute one *Chou*, i.e., 2,500 families.

直 隷 州 an independent District Magistrate not under a prefecture, directly governed by provincial authorities. (abolished).

神 州 a name for China.

(a) **An islet, a sand bank in a river, for which the next is now used. Cf. 1290.**

水 中 可 居 曰 州 a place, surrounded by water, on which men can dwell is called a *chou*.

(b) **To assemble.**

羣 萃 而 州 處 to assemble and dwell together in one place.

洲 1 **An islet, an island.**
1290

洲 汀 or 沙 洲 a sand bank.

洲 沚 a small islet.

洲 田 alluvial fields.

在 河 之 洲 on the islets in the river.

(a) **A continent.**

亞 洲 Asia.

舟 1 **A boat, a vessel. Radical 137.**
1291

舟 人 or 舟 子 boatmen.

舟 山 Chusan Island, from its shape.

舟 師 master of a boat in ancient navy.

舟 楫 a boat and an oar—fig., one who comes to assist in a crisis of State.

⁵舟 次 on board a vessel.

舟 牧 captain of naval flotilla in ancient days.

舟 船 boats, sailing-vessels.

舟 車 之 苦 the fatigue of travel.

舟 載 cargo of a vessel.

¹⁰陸 地 行 舟 to sail a boat on dry land—to attempt the impossible or the ridiculous.

(a) To carry at the girdle.

何 以 舟 之 what did he wear at his girdle? Cf. 1293.

(b) A saucer. A stand for vessels, etc.

彝 皆 有 舟 the vessels for libations all had stands.

茶 舟 saucers for Chinese tea-cups.

俏 [1] To conceal; to cover. Inter. preceding.
1292

俏 張 or 譸 張 to deceive.

周 [1] To encircle. All round; everywhere. Inter. 週 No. 1295.
1293

周 匝 surrounded.
周 圍 encircled; all round.
周 折 deviation; curve; circuitous; complications.
周 旋 to treat friends cordially; to wait on; to walk circuitously.
[5] 周 旋 其 間 during his wanderings.
周 旋 中 禮 to act always in a proper manner.
周 浹 to encircle; to extend benefits all round.
周 流 to roam.
周 流 四 方 to make a circuit.
[10] 周 流 無 滯 to flow throughout without stopping.
周·章 to glance all around in fear; uneasy and hasty.
周 遊 to make a circuit.
周 遍 to extend on all sides.
周 遍 之 知 all-embracing knowledge.
[15] 周 防 to guard on every side.

(a) Complete; entire; the whole.

周 備 fully prepared.
周·全 perfect; all that could be desired.
周·到 or 周 致 completely; entirely; hospitable; liberal; adequate.
周 天 a whole day; a revolution of the sun.
[5] 周 晬 end of the first year of a child's life, when he is tested by allowing him to grasp whatever he fancies out of various articles; supposed to indicate his future career. See 試 No. 5798—3. Also called 抓 周 兒.

周 正 to complete or correct; well-proportioned.
周 歲 a full year of life from one birthday to another.
周 滿 completely full.
周 甲 a cycle of sixty years.
[10] 周 略 to consider.
周 知 to make known to all. See below. B.2.
周 給 all contributed.
周 詳 attend to minute details.
周 身 the whole body.

(b) Comprehensive, catholic.

周 於 利 者 one who has much laid by.
周 知 to have a general knowledge of. See above.—人.11.
周 而 不·比 catholic and not partisan.
周 至 comprehensive.

(c) To relieve; to assist.

周 急 to assist those who are in desperate straits.
周 急 不 繼 富 to relieve the poor and not add to the abundance of the wealthy.
周 恤 to have pity on.
周 濟 to relieve; to give charity; to assist.

(d) Near, as relatives.

雖 有 周 親 不 如 仁 人 although one has near relatives, they are not equal to a benevolent man.

(e) Dense, as dwelling. Secret.

周 密 secret; close together; hidden; complete; thorough; compact.
周 者 不 出 于 口 secrets are not to be mentioned.

(f) A place (in the present Shensi) from which the *Chou* Dynasty got its name. A surname.

周 公 The Duke of *Chou*, son of Wen wang 文 王 first ruler of the *Chou* Dynasty.
周 易 *The Book of Changes*, China's oldest book of philosophy.
周·朝 The *Chou* Dynasty, B.C. 1122—255.
周 禮 *The Book of Rites*.
周 行 or 周 道 a highway; "royal road;" lit., the road to *Chou*.

賙 [1] To bestow alms.
1294

賙 恤 charitable; generous.
賙 濟 or 賙 給 to give alms; to relieve distress.
賙 贍 to give alms.
禮 物 不 賙 the presents are not adequate.

週 [1] To revolve. A revolution. A year, a week. Inter. 周 No. 1293.
1295

週·到 completely; fully.
週 圍 to surround; the circumference.
週 報 or 週 刊 weekly publications.
週 年 a whole year.
[5] 週 年 旺 相 "May the whole year be prosperous."
週 年 紀 念 anniversary.
週 時 一 樣 ever the same.
週 期 a period.
週 期 律 periodic law. (*Chem.*).
[10] 週 期 表 periodic table.
週 期 彗 星 periodic comet.
週 流 不 息 to flow unceasingly— as the blood.
週 行 to circulate; to revolve.
週·轉 sufficient to meet all needs; continually in revolution.
[15] 週 遊 to walk around.
週 遭 all round.

胄 [4]
仙 Descendants; posterity. Distinguish 冑 No. 1297, 胃 No. 7075.
1296

胄 子 [3] eldest son.
貴 胄 nobleman.
胄 裔 descendants.

冑 [4] A helmet. Distinguish. 胄 No. 1296.
1297

甲 冑 armour and helmets.

宙 [4] Time—past, present and future.
1298

宇 宙 the universe.

帚]
篲]   A besom, a broom.
1299

帚 星 a broom star—a comet.

紂 [4] The crupper of a saddle. Traces.
1300

紂 桀 the names of two infamous tyrants, typical of all that is hateful.

紂 棍 a crupper used on pack-animals.

紂 辛 or 紂 王 the infamous ruler whose crimes caused the downfall of the *Shang* Dynasty, B.C. 1122.

肘 [3] The elbow, the forearm, the wrist.
1301

肘 之 to nudge.

肘·子 or 手 肘 the elbow.

肘 腋 相 交 the relation between armpit and elbow—near relatives, friendship.

交 肘 to fold the arms.

[5]扯 肘 to hinder.

捉 肘 to seize by the wrist.

掣 肘 to impede the elbow—hindrances.

晝 [4] Daytime; daylight. Distinguish 書 No. 5857, and 畫
1302 No. 2222.

晝 夜 day and night.

晝 夜 不 息 never ceasing, day nor night.

晝 寢 to sleep in the daytime.

晝 瞑 the daylight became dim.

[5]晝 爾 于 茅 宵 爾 索 綯 in the day go and gather the grass, at night make it into ropes.

不 分 晝 夜 no distinction between day and night.

倖 晝 作 夜 to turn the day into night—to do evil in the daylight.

白 晝 the day.

↑ 晝 間 in the daytime.

呪]
說] [4]   To curse, to swear an oath. Incantations.
1303

呪 詛 to imprecate; to rail at.

呪 語 curses; imprecations.

呪 逐 to ban; to drive from society.

呪 罵 to curse; to abuse.

[5]念 呪 to recite incantations.

賭 呪 to stake one's oath.

味 [4] To peck at. Beak of a bird.
1304

不 濡 其 味 it did not wet its beak.

鳥 味 a bird's beak.

(a) Read *chu*[1]. Talkative.

甃 [4] Brickwork of a well. To repair a well. To lay bricks.
1305

皺 [4] Wrinkles on the face. Creases in garments. Not level. Inter. next.
1306

皺 文 wrinkles, creases.

皺 眉 to frown.

皺 金 wrinkled gold leaf.

縐 [4] Wrinkled. To shrink. Crepe. Inter. preceding.
1307

縐·子 wrinkles, creases.

縐 布 crepe.

縐 紋 wrinkles or creases, folds.

縐 紗 crepe silk.

縮 縐 to shrink; to shrivel.

謅 [1] To jest, to chaff. To bawl. Pron. *tsou*[1].
1308

謅 讓 to bawl.

謅 鬧 to wrangle.

胡 謅 to talk wildly; humbug.

鄒 [1] Small State in what is now Shantung, the place where Mencius was born. Pron. *tsou*[1].
1309

鄒 魯 the States of *Chou* and *Lu* i.e., Confucius and Mencius.

騶 [1] To go. A fabulous beast. Pron. *tsou*[1].
1310

騶 卒 a servant.

騶 唱 the call of a mounted escort, as below.

騶 從 mounted escort of a nobleman.

騶 虞 a fabulous beast.

聚]
耶] [1] Birthplace of Confucius. A place which was near the site of the present 曲 阜 縣 in Shantung. Pron.
1311 *tsou*[1].

郰 人 the man of *Chou*—Confucius.

驟 [4] A fleet horse. Sudden and violent. Long continued.
1312 Pron. *tsou*[4].

驟 漲 a rapid rise.

驟 然 而 來 he came abruptly.

驟 行 at once.

驟 降 a rapid fall (of snow).

[5]驟 雨 violent storm of rain.

足 不 及 驟 no foot could equal its speed.

CH'OU.   (爰)
(Ch'eo)

怊 [2] To grieve. Sorrowful.
1313

怊 怊 sad and weary.

抽]
搦] [1]   To pull up or pull open. to draw out; to take out.
1314

抽·出 or 抽 取 to select from a lot.

抽 劍 to draw a sword.

抽·屜 a drawer.

抽 息 to sob.

[5]抽 拔 to rescue; to deliver.

抽 換 to take out of original packages and re-wrap.

抽 查 to take one out for inspection or examination.

抽 案 卷 to produce the papers of a case in court.

抽 櫃 a chest of drawers.

[10]抽 氣 to gasp.

抽 氣 機 an air-pump.

抽 水 機 pump for water.

抽 煙 or 吸 煙 to smoke a pipe.

抽 筋 spasms, cramps; to pull out the sinew; extortion.

[15]抽 籤 to draw lots.
抽 給 to give.
抽 絲 to reel silk.
抽 調 to withdraw; to detach from.
抽 象 abstract as opposed to concrete, 具 體.
[20]抽 象 名 詞 abstract nouns.
抽 象 名 辭 abstract expressions.
抽 象 文 字 abstract terms.
抽 象·的 觀 念 abstract ideas or
conceptions.
抽 身 to absent oneself; to get
away from.
[25]抽 身 跑 he got away.
抽 開 or 抽 空 to find time for
anything; to get away for a
time.
抽 除 to weed out.
不 能 抽 身 I cannot get away.

(a) To divide up; to levy.

抽 丁 a levy; conscription.
抽 剝 to flay by illegal taxation.
抽 收 to levy.
抽 水 or 抽 分 a percentage or
commission; to take a fee for
gambling from the gains.
[5]抽 發 to make a proportionate allotment.
抽 稅 or 抽 課 to levy taxes.
抽 豐 or 打 秋·風 to collect subscriptions, as by strangers who
collect money ostensibly to enable them to return home, etc.
抽 釐 金 to levy the *likin* tax.
抽 頭 魚 利 to take a percentage
from the winnings at gambling
(as the share of the 'house').

(b) To whip.

拏 鞭 抽 他 gave him a whipping.

紬[2] A thread, a clue. To investigate; to follow up.
1315 u.f. 綢 No. 1318.

紬 繹 to investigate.

惆[2] Vexed; disappointed.
1316

惆 悵 disappointed in obtaining
one's wishes.

稠[2] Growing closely like grain.
Crowded, dense. Thick, as
1317 soup, etc.

稠 人 廣 眾 a dense crowd.
稠 密 close together; crowded, as
houses or population.
稠 雲 cloudy.
書 策 稠 濁 the books and records
were very confused and disorderly.
人 烟 稠 密 densely populated.

(a) Read *t'iao*[2]. u.f. 調 No. 6298.
To regulate.

稠 適 well regulated, in order, as
a favourable season.

(b) Read *t'iao*[4]. To shake, to agitate.

綢[2] Thin silk. Silk goods.
Inter. 紬 No. 1315.
1318

綢·子 silks; silk goods.
綢 紗 silk gowns.
綢 絹 general name for silks.
綢 緞 silks and satins; silk goods.
[5]熟 綢 soft pongees.
生 綢 raw pongees.
紡 綢 reeled pongee.
綿 綢 silk and cotton mixture.

(a) Close and dense. Fine.
Inter. 稠 preceding.

綢 直 如 髮 thick and straight
like hair—of affectionate disposition.
綢 緻 closely woven; very fine.

(b) To bind.

綢 繆 from the next phrase—entanglements; close union, as
married life.
綢 繆 束 薪 the faggots are bound
round and round.
綢 繆 牖 戶 I bound (mulberry
roots) closely round my door
and window. (i.e., of its nest.)
—used of making preparations.

裯[2] A coverlet. Bed-curtain.
1319

裯 帳 a bed-curtain; a curtain.
裯 衽 single coverlet and a sleeping-mat.

(a) Read *tao*[1]. Short sleeves;
short undergarment.

酬
醻[2] To pledge with wine.
1320

酬 對 to respond to a pledge.
酬 酢 to pledge.
酬 酢 萬 變 之 主 the principle
which rules the various chang-
ings and interchangings.
應·酬 to entertain guests; to wait
on.

(a) To reward; to requite, to
repay.

酬 勞 or 酬 值 to reward services.
酬 和 or 酬 唱 exchange of writings or verses as presents.
酬 報 to requite; honorarium.
酬 客 to return an invitation.
[5]酬 恩 祭 The Thank-offering.
酬 愿 to make good a vow.
酬 應 exchange of presents between friends.
酬 神 to thank the gods.
酬 答 天 恩 thank-offering to
Heaven.
[10]酬 謝 to return thanks; a return
present.
酬 讌 a return feast.
酬 還 or 酬 債 to repay.
酬 金 a gratuity.
↑酬 志 to fulfil one's ambition.

儔[2] A party of four. A class or
kind. Comrades or friends.
1321 Inter. next.

儔 伴 friends, comrades.
儔 侶 a party of friends.
儔 匹 one of the same class or
group.
儔 類 a circle of friends; those of
one mind.
儔 黨 a clique.

(a) Who? *see under* 疇 *next*.

儔 爲 (*wei*[4]) 爲 之 Who will do
it for him?

疇[2] Arable land. Divisions.
1322

九 疇 The *Nine Divisions* of the
"Great Plan" of the *Book of
History.*
田 疇 rice fields and arable land.

(a) A class; companions. Hereditary. Inter. preceding.

疇 人 men of a class—as astronomers or mathematicians; those who carry on what has been handed down to them from other generations.

疇 日 or 疇 昔 formerly; of old.
疇 輩 十 餘 人 over ten men of the same generation.

(b) Who?

疇 咨 Who will inquire for.....?
予 將 疇 依 Who can I trust for this?

(c) Inter 酬 No. 1320. To requite.

疇 庸 to requite meritorious services.

籌 2 To calculate; to reckon; to devise.
1323

籌 借 to negotiate loans.
籌 備 to prepare for.
籌 備 中 in course of preparation; in hand.
籌 備 委 員 Committee of Arrangements.
5 籌 備 所 or 籌 備 處 Bureau of Preparation or of Arrangements.
籌 備 會 meeting for making arrangements.
籌 思 to ponder; to deliberate.
籌 措 to devise means.
籌 欵 to consider ways and means for raising funds.
10 籌 畫 or 籌 議 or 籌 辦 or 籌 商 to settle; to arrange; to deliberate.
籌 策 a scheme or plan.
籌 算 or 籌 計 to calculate; to reckon.
籌 維 再 四 to consider a matter from every standpoint.
籌 解 to arrange for remittance.
15 籌 謀 to plot; to scheme.
籌 貼 to provide funds for.
籌 邊 to plan for frontier defence.
籌 還 to devise means for repayment.
籌 防 to make provision against an emergency.
20 籌 餉 army estimates.
籌 餉 熱 zeal of the people in providing the army supplies.

(a) A tally, a counter, a ticket.

籌 矢 to pitch arrows into a vase —an ancient game described in the *Book of Rites*.
籌 碼 counters in a game.
執 籌 to hold a tally, as is done by porters when carrying a load to a ship, etc.
攢 籌 to take the tallies from porters as they bring in the loads.
5 派 籌 to issue tallies.
竹 籌 bamboo tallies used as above.

躊 2 Embarrassed.
1324
躊 佇 hesitating; irresolute; gratified.
躊 躇 irresolute; undecided.
躊 躇 滿 志 exceedingly gratified.

愁 2 Grieving; sad; melancholy; anxious.
1325

愁 人 vexing; annoying; a sad man.
愁 城 circumstances or place of grief and pain.
愁 容 mournful or anxious countenance.
愁 思 anxious thoughts.
5 愁 愁 anxiety.
愁 悶 sorrowing; grieved; melancholy.
愁 慘 mournful; grieved.
愁 盧 anxious sorrow.
愁 死 to die from grief or anxiety.
10 愁 煩 harassing anxiety.
愁 眉 brows knit in deep thought; gloomy countenance.
愁 緒 gloomy anxious thoughts.
愁 腸 anxious forbodings that twist and turn in the mind with no relief.
愁 腸 百 結 my bowels are tied in knots with anxiety.
15 愁 苦 grief; sadness; pain.
心 愁 愁 而 思 my mind is filled with anxious thoughts.

(a) Depressing; gloomy.

愁 雲 heavy clouds.
愁 霖 depressing, heavy rains.
愁 霧 overcast with dense fogs or mists.

瞅 3 To look at; to gaze.
1326

瞅 不 見 I cannot see it.
瞅 甚 麼 What are you gazing at?

醜 3 Ugly. Physical or moral deformity.
1327

醜 事 an ugly matter; a shameful business; disgraceful affair.
醜 地 poor, barren soil.
醜 婦 very ill-favoured woman.
醜 惡 repulsive.
5 醜 末 depreciatory term—deformed.
醜 行 disgraceful conduct.
醜 詆 to revile and curse.
醜 語 vile language.
醜 陋 or 貌 醜 or 醜 樣 ill-looking.
10 丟 醜 to disgrace oneself.
可 醜 disgraceful.
命 醜 having an evil destiny.
小 醜 a mean wretch; despicable fellow; a clown, cf. 1330.3.
希 醜 strangely hideous.
怕 醜 bashful.

(a) A crowd; one's own class.

醜 夷 a class or kind.
醜 虜 a crowd of captives.
醜 類 the class of vagabonds or rogues. *See below*. B.1.
醜 類 惡 物 low scamps and vagabonds.
羣 醜 the masses; crowds; flocks.

(b) To compare.

醜 類 to compare classes. *See above*. A.3.
比 物 醜 類 to compare various sorts and classes.

瘳 1 To be healed. To reform.
1328

瘳 愈 cured; healed.
厥 疾 弗 瘳 that disease is incurable.

(a) Injury.

於 己 何 瘳 what harm can it do?

搊 1 To pluck stringed instruments with the fingers.
1329

搊 彈 家 a teacher of the above.
搊 琵 琶 to pluck the strings of the guitar.

(a) To grasp in the hand; to roll tightly.

攓 衣 to grasp and hold up the skirts.

丑 3 The period from 1 to 3 a.m. 2nd character of the 1330 "branches" 地支.

丑 時 the period from 1 to 3 a.m.
丑 月 the twelfth month, lunar.
丑 脚 a low comedy actor in Chinese theatres; a clown.

臭 4 Stinking, offensive. Disreputable. Strong-smelling. 1331

臭 名 a foul reputation.
臭 味 of the same class,—from 君 之 臭 味 'you are both of one class.' A foul odour.
臭 氣 a bad smell; bad air.
臭 水 carbolic acid.
⁵臭 爛 rotten; putrid.
臭 皮 囊 the stinking skin-bag— the body.
臭 穢 rank; putrid; filthy.
臭 羶 frowsy smell as of sheep or goats.
臭 腐 rotten bean-curd.
¹⁰臭 腥 rancid; tainted food.
臭 舌 foul-mouthed.
臭·蟲 bed-bugs.

(a) Sweet-smelling. Also pron. hsiu⁴

以 臭 物 可 以 修 飾 she would use fragrant things for adornment.
其 臭 如 蘭 as fragrant as the epidendrum.

(b) Read hsiu⁴. To smell. u.f. 嗅 No. 2792.

三 臭 之 不 食 he smelt it thrice and would not eat it.
善 臭 a nice smell.

仇 2 An enemy, enmity, hatred. To hate. A rival. A match. 1332 Originally read ch'iu².

仇 人 an opponent.
仇 家 an enemy, a rival.
仇 恨 or 仇 氣 enmity; spite.
仇 鷹 revenge.
⁵仇 敵 an enemy, a rival.
仇 父 公 妻 the abolition of the family system.

仇 視 to look at with enmity; to regard as an enemy.
仇 隙 a breach; a quarrel; a feud.
宿 仇 hereditary feud; a blood feud.

(a) Read ch'iu². A surname.

讐 } 2 An enemy. To hate. A rival. Inter. preceding, which is now commonly 讎 } used. 1333

讐 當 to oppose; to withstand.
含 讐 to nurse a grievance.
報 讐 to revenge.

(a) To compare; to verify.

讐 校 to compare documents, etc.
讐 問 to question about difficulties.

(b) A mate or companion. A class or kind.

讎 匹 a pair; the same kind.
皆 讎 有 功 their achievements were all of a class.

(c) To reply. Inter. 酬 No. 1320. To requite; to pledge; also inter. 稠 No. 1317. Dense, etc.

讎 酢 to pledge in wine.
無 言 不 讎 there was no reply.

犫 2 The grunting of an ox. 1334

犫 牛 the grunting ox; the yak.

CHU. (坐)

3 A point, as of a flame. Radical 3. 1335

點 丶 to add the dot—on the ancestral tablet of a deceased parent—to the character 王 thus making it 主; this is thought to bring the parent into the tablet.

(a) Read tien³. A dot in writing.

主 3 A lord, a master, an owner. A ruler. To act as lord. 1336

主 事 manager of affairs in a

household an assistant in official offices.

主·人 a lord, a master, a host.
主 人 翁 one's host; a master; the
主 令 to order.　　　　[owner.
⁵主 任 principal; manager; one who is responsible; to take charge of; chairman.
主 任 幹 事 head of a society; chief executive officer.
主 位 or 主 詞 subject. (grammar).
主 使 to instigate, as crime, etc.
主 僕 or 主 奴 master and servant or slave.
¹⁰主 刑 principal punishment, as opposed to accessory or additional punishment—death, banishment or fine.
主 力 the main strength of an army. 主 力 艦 capital ship,
主 動 to move, a mover.[battleship.
主 動 力 action; motive power.
主 動 改 政·的 leading movers for reform.
¹⁵主 動·的 訴 訟 active proceeding in law.
主 動 者 a prime mover.
主 句 principal clause. (grammar).
主 名 chief offender in a group of criminals.
主 和 in favor of peace.
²⁰主 器 eldest son, chief in sacrificial rites.
主 因 principal cause.
主 國 the country in which an ambassador or minister resides.
主 坐 seat of the host.
主 婚 or 主 婚 人 one who arranges a wedding-match.
²⁵主 婦 mistress of a house.
主·子 or 主 公 or 主 上 a chief; a lord; the emperor.
主 宰 a controlling power. The Lord.
主 賓 host and guest—also used fig., as in literature and logic.
主 將 a chief general.
³⁰主 帥 a chief leader.
主 席 host at a dinner; a chairman. 主 席 團 presidium.
主 幣 standard coinage.
主·張 to manage; to advocate; to propose; to support; to insist on; to vote upon, to favour a proposal or motion.
主·張 召 集 會 議 insisted on a conference to discuss the matter.

55 主·張 資 本·的 社 會 supported the idea of a capitalistic society.

主·張 開 放 to advocate "the open-door."

這 兩·個 主·張 these two proposals.

主 從 各 犯 principal and accessory in a crime.

主 德 說 moralism.

40 主 情 說 sentimentalism or emotionalism.

主 意 plan; gist; the main idea.

主²意 decision; intention; resolution.

主 我 subjective self or ego.

主 我 論 egoism.

主·戶 a farmer on his own land.

45 主 指 essential point.

主 持 to take the direction of; to manage.

主 政 formerly a 2nd class assistant secretary of a board. An editor of a paper.

主 敎⁴ a bishop.

主 敬 to regard reverence as essential.

50 主 文 legal document giving the decision and the laws upon which it is based; formerly it was the title of an officer in charge of the examinations.

主 旗 national flag.

主 日 The Lord's Day. (Sunday.)

主 日 學 校 Sunday Schools.

主 格 subject. (grammar).

55 主 根 tap root.

主 權 or 統 治 權 sovereignty; sovereign rights.

主 權 國 a sovereign State.

侵 犯 主 權 violation of sovereignty.

土 地 主 權 territorial sovereignty.

60 政 治 上 主 權 political sovereignty.

主 母 mistress.

主 治 to govern; to control.

主 法 substantial law, as opposed to auxiliary. (legal).

主·物 principal thing in a suit. (legal).

65 主·物 同 合 identity of the subject.

主·物 存 在 existence of the subject.

主 犯 principal in a crime.

主 知 說 intellectualism.

主 祭 master of ceremonies at a funeral.

70 主 稅 the chief tax.

主 筆 editor, as of a newspaper.

主 管 to manage; general head or manager of.

主 簿 keeper of the records.

主 編 editor, head of compiling staff.

75 主 美 說 aestheticism.

主 義 theory; doctrine; used as a suffix similarly to—ism, etc. An alphabetical list is appended at the end of this group of illustrations, other examples may be found under the various characters.

主 義 務 principal obligation (legal).

主 考 the Grand Examiner who presided over the examinations for the 2nd degree.

主 股 original capital.

80 主 腦 the brain of a cause; leader; the leading principle.

主 臣 awestricken.

主 要 principal, important; chief; essential.

主 要 分⁴子³ essential part.

主 要 原 因 chief cause or reason.

85 主 要 原 素 principal element.

主 要 性·質 essential nature.

主 要 目 的 main object.

主 要 資 產 most important asset.

主 見 opinion; view of things.

90 主 觀 subjective, as opposed to objective 客 觀 No. 3324—23.

主 觀 主 義 subjective theory.

主 觀 分·析 subjective analysis.

主 觀 感 覺 subjective sensation.

主 觀·的 subjective.

95 主 觀·的 評 判 subjective criticism.

主 觀 觀 察 subjective observation.

主 觀 說 subjectivism.

共 同 主 觀 condominium.

主 角 the most important person; a leader; hero(ine) in a play.

100 主 計 official accountant.

海 軍 主 計 naval accountant.

主 謀 a scheme; a project; to head a conspiracy.

主 講 to lecture; a lecturer.

主 辭 subject, as opposed to predicate. (grammar).

105 主 醫 one who is responsible for getting medical aid when there is sickness.

主 題 topic; theme.

主·顧 a customer; a patron. (also pron. --hu)

主 體 host; theme. ⌐ 天·主 敎 Roman
公 主 a princess.   ⌐ Catholic religion.

110 君 主 sovereign; ruler; prince.

天 主 Lord of Heaven—title used with others for Indra by Buddhists. Chief of eight gods 神, mentioned in the history, 史 記; u.f. God by Roman Catholic Church, and by some others.

宗 主 founder of a religion.

家 主 head of a family.

業 主 landlord; estate owner; head of an industry.

115 神 主 ancestral tablet.

自 主 free; independent.

財 主 a wealthy man.

債 主 creditor.

(a) Alphabetic list of phrases showing the use of 主 義 as a suffix. See above—76.

侵 略 主 義 aggressive policy.

懷 疑 主 義 agnosticism.

利 他 主 義 altruism.

無 政 府 主 義 anarchism.

5 獸 慾 主 義 animalism.

排 外 主 義 anti-foreignism.

制 慾 主 義 asceticism.

無 神 主 義 atheism.

布 爾 札 維 主 義 Bolshevism.

10 排 貨 主 義 the boycott theory.

金 銀 通 貨 主 義 bullionism.

官 僚 政 治 主 義 bureaucratism.

資 本 主 義 capitalism.

古 典 主 義 classicism.

15 集 產 主 義 or 集 合 主 義 collectivism.

地 方 自 治 主 義 communalism.

共 產 主 義 communism.

競 爭 主 義 competitive spirit or policy.

孔 子³ 主 義 Confucianism.

20 會 衆 自 治 主 義 Congregationalism.

保 守 主 義 or 守 舊 主 義 conservatism.

立 憲 主 義 constitutionalism.

建 設 主 義 constructive policy.

慣 例 主 義 conventionalism.

25 世 界 主 義 cosmopolitanism.

割 據 地 方 主 義 de-centralization.

奸 雄 主 義 demagogy.

平 民 主 義 democracy. A.c. 民 治

專 制 主 義 despotism. │主 義·

30 破 壞 主 義 destructive policy.

經 濟 主 義 economic principles.

自 利 主 義 or 利 己 主 義 egoism.

經驗主義 empiricism.
精力主義 or 活動主義 energism.
[35] 平等主義 equality, both legal and social.
人種改良主義 eugenics.
排他主義 or 犯占主義 exclusivism.
閉關主義 exclusive policy.
極端主義 extremism.
[40] 命定主義 fatalism.
合從 (tsung[1]) 主義 or 聯盟主義 federalism; federationism.
女權主義 or 男女平等主義 feminism.
封建主義 or 封建制 feudalism.
形式主義 or 虛體主義 formalism.
[45] 根本的主義 fundamental principle.
未來主義 futurism.
政府全權主義 governmentalism.
幸福主義 hedonism.
人生主義 or 人類主義 humanism, or religion of humanity as opposed to divine religion.
[50] 人文主義 humanism—literary culture.
人道主義 or 汎愛主義 or 博愛主義 humanitarianism.
畫像破壞主義 or 迷信破壞主義 iconoclasm.
觀念主義 or 理想主義 idealism.
帝國主義 imperialism.
↑ 法西斯主義 Fascism.
[55] 印象主義 impressionism.
各教[4]會獨立主義 or 組合教[4]會主義 independency or congregationalism.
冷淡主義 or 局外主義 indifferentism.
個人主義 or 利己主義 individualism.
實業主義 industrialism.
[60] 團體主義 institutionalism.
機具主義 or 功利主義 instrumentalism.
叛亂主義 insurrectionism.
唯智主義 intellectualism.
國際主義 or 世界主義 internationalism.
[65] 直覺主義 intuitionism.
領土回復主義 irredentism.
武力主義 or 侵略主義 jingoism.

勞動組合主義 labour-unionism.
遵法主義 legalism.
[70] 正統主義 legitimism.
自由主義 or 進步主義 liberalism.
放肆主義 libertinism.
金額主義 limited compensation. (legal).
強硬主義 or 鐵血主義 mailed-fist policy.
[75] 馬克斯主義 Marxism.
實利主義 or 物質主義 or 崇實主義 materialism.
唯物主義 materialistic theories.
軍事主義 militarism.
金錢主義 money-grabbing spirit.
[80] 一夫一妻主義 monogamy.
壟斷主義 or 專賣主義 or 獨占主義 monopolization.
孟羅 or 門羅主義 Monroe Doctrine.
國家主義 or 民族主義 nationalism.
自然主義 or 寫實主義 naturalism, as in art, etc.
[85] 海洋優占主義 naval supremacy policy.
消極主義 negativism.
中立主義 neutralism.
虛無主義 nihilism.
唯名主義 nominalism.
[90] 客觀主義 objectivism.
蒙昧主義 obscurantism.
西洋主義 occidentalism.
秘密主義 occultism.
開放主義 open-door policy.
[95] 樂觀主義 or 樂天主義 optimism.
平和主義 pacificism or pacifism.
大亞西亞主義 Pan-Asiaticism.
寄食主義 parasitism.
自己主義 or 自黨主義 particularism.
[100] 和平主義 peaceful policy.
悲觀主義 or 厭世主義 pessimism.
政治上主義 political principles.
積極主義 positivism.
實用主義 pragmatism. (phil.).
[105] 干涉主義 pragmatism — dogmatic.
有主義的 principled.
主義建立的 principled.
進取主義 progressivism.

保商稅主義 protective tariff policy.
[110] 嚴格主義 puritanism.
靜寂主義 or 無為主義 quietism.
民族主義 nationalism.
急進主義 or 銳進主義 radicalism.
寫實主義 realism in art.
[115] 宗敎主義 religious principles.
共和主義 or 民主主義 republicanism.
革命主義 revolutionary policy.
浪漫主義 or 傳奇主義 romanticism.
三民主義 "Sanminism." Abbreviation of Dr. Sun Yat-sen's threefold theory of national essentials—race, livelihood, and power. 民族主義, 民生主義, 民權主義.
[120] 感覺主義 or 投時好之主義 sensationalism.
唯覺主義 or 肉慾主義 sensualism.
感情主義 or 激情主義 sentimentalism.
分離主義 separationism.
社會主義 or 均富主義 socialism.
[125] 象徵主義 symbolism.
大同主義 theory of the ideal State.
職業組合主義 trades-unionism.

(b) To indicate; to regard as chief.

主下雨 indicating rain.
主吉 or 主凶 indicating good and evil respectively.
主忠信 regard faithfulness and sincerity as first principles.

(c) To lodge at.

主司城貞子[3] he lodged with the city-master Chêng.
孔子[3]主我 if Confucius lodged with me.

住 [4]

To dwell, to stop, to cease.
1337

住下 or 住欻 to lodge at.
住了哭 to stop crying.
住口 to cease talking.
住址 address; dwelling-place.
[5] 住宅 or 住所 or 住處 a residence; a dwelling.

住 宅 稅 dwelling-house tax.
住 定 ·了 came to a stop.
住 家 to dwell: to live at.
住 宿 to rest; to stay for a time.
[10]住 居 or 居 住 to live; to dwell; to reside at.
住 所 residence; domicile; differs from 居 所 in that it conveys the idea of a more permanent residence.
住 手 to stay the hand; to cease operations.
住 扎 to camp.
住 持 the resident or head priest.
[15]住 步 Halt! Stop!
住 民 residents.
住 目 to fix the eyes on.

(a) Auxiliary verb indicating completed action or continuance.
住·不·住 are you going to stay?
住·不·住 cannot stop for long.
守·不·住 cannot keep it, as a post, a city, or chastity, etc.
忍·不·住 cannot endure it.
止·不·住 cannot stop it, as a flow of water or of blood.
[5]火 車 停·住 ·了 the train came to a standstill.
留·不·住 cannot detain him.
靠·不·住 unreliable.

拄 [3] A post; a prop. To oppose. *u.f.* 柱 *next.*
1338

拄 拐 or 拄 棍 or 拄 杖 a crutch or a staff; to lean on a staff.
拄 楣 a prop or stretcher for an awning.

柱 [4] A pillar, a post. To support.
1339

柱 子 a post or pillar.
柱 廳 hall supported by pillars.
柱 意 the leading thought.
柱 杖 staff given to aged Buddhist.
[5]柱 梁 pillars and beams—ministers of State.
柱 石 or 柱 墩 the base of a pillar; a plinth.
柱 石 之 臣 or 國 柱 a pillar of the State.
柱 脚 base or pedestal of a pillar.
柱 頂 石 the capital of a pillar.
[10]柱 頭 capital of a pillar.
柱 頭 斗 拱 the capitals and pillars of a house.

擎 天 柱 pillars of the State— loyal ministers.
支 柱 a bracket or corbel; a console.
墓 柱 pillars at the grave of a scholar.

注 [4] Water flowing.
1340

注 入 transfusion.
注 向 tending towards.
注 射 to inject: to syringe.
俯 注 to continue the present topic.
[5]大 雨 如 注 pouring with rain.
引 注 手 術 transfusion, as of blood.
流 注 to flow into, as a river.

(a) To comment on; notes. To make an entry. *u.f.* 註 No. 1343.

注 冊 to enter one's name; to register.
注 明 to explain by notes.
注 疏 commentaries on the classics.
注 筆 to compose; to write.
[5]注 解 or 注 釋 explanatory notes.
注 記 to record; to enter.

(b) To fix the mind on.

注 力 to put forth the strength.
注 存 to bear in mind.
注 念 to remember; to ponder.
注 意 give attention to; take notice; Look! Notice!
[5]注 意 力 power of observation.
注 意 點 point to be noted.
堪 注 意 worthy of attention.
注 目 to fix the gaze upon; to give attention to.
注 視 to stare at; to gaze.
[10]注·重 to emphasize.
注 重 點 point of emphasis.
注 音 mark with phonetic symbols.
注 音 字 母 National Phonetic Alphabet. Now called 注 音 符 號.
上 注 set the thoughts on things above.
[15]專 注 to give sole attention to.

(c) To stake.

注 以 黃 金 staked wagers in gold.
孤 注 to stake all on a venture.

炷 [3.4.] A candle wick. Stick of incense. To burn.
1341

炷 香 to burn incense.
燈 炷 wick of a lamp.

蛀 [4] Insects which eat books or clothes. To eat or bore.
1342

蛀 爛 spoiled by insects.
蛀 空 eaten into holes.
蛀 蟲 worm which eats into books.
蛀 齒 decayed teeth.
蟲 蛀·了 moth-eaten.

註 [4] To explain. Explanatory note; annotations.
1343

註 作 or 註 述 to write an essay on.
註 定 to explain; to define.
註 明 a clear explanation; to explain clearly in writing.
註 書 to make notes in books.
註·解 or 註·脚 explanatory notes.
註 釋 or 註 疏 to explain; explanations; notes; commentary.
補 註 additional notes.

(a) To sign; to record.

註 冊 to register; to keep a register. 註 冊 員 registrar.
註 冊 執 照 certificate of registration.
註 冊 費 registration fee.
註 失 to notify loss of a deed or contract, etc.
[5]註 生 註 死 to record the days of birth and of death.
註 記 to note particulars.
註 賬 charge to an account.
註 銷 to cancel; to write off.

駐 [4] To dwell temporarily; to halt.
1344

駐 使 minister or envoy.
駐 在 領 事 the resident consul.
駐 守 to occupy, as troops.
駐 屯 軍 army of occupation.
[5]駐 泊 to be anchored; to moor.
駐 節 to take up residence.
駐 紮 or 駐 劄 or 駐 扎 to be stationed at; to be appointed to.
駐 紮 影 響 the effects of occupation by troops.
駐 藏 大 臣 Resident Envoy in Tibet.
[10]駐 足 to lodge; to tarry; to maintain ground, as troops.

駐 蹕 places where the monarch halted when on circuit.
駐 車 to stop the carriage.
駐 防 城 a garrison city.
駐 顏 to preserve a youthful appearance.
駐 馬 to put up the horses.

麈 [3] A large stag; leader of the herd.
1345

麈 尾 a deer's tail; a chowry or whisk.
麈 論 to converse at ease.
麈 談 conversation.
拂 麈 而 談 to wave the chowry and converse.

朱 [1] Red; vermilion. Also read *shu*[1].
1346

朱 儒 a dwarf, *see next*, 侏.
朱 墨 red ink.
朱 提 (*shu*[2].) a mountain in Sze., which produces silver—used for silver.
朱 明 or 朱 夏 the summer.
[5]朱 朱 very red; to call fowls.
朱 樓 houses of the wealthy.
朱 熹 *Chu Hsi*, famous commentator and writer; his commentary was the standard exposition of the Confucian classics. A.D. 1130-1200.
朱 筆 the "vermilion pencil" used by the emperor in signing; any writing in red ink.
朱 紅 or 朱 色 scarlet; red.
[10]朱 紫 red and purple—nobles, because their seals were of these colours.
朱 衣 red clothing; attendant on the god of literature.
朱 軒 carriages of nobles in ancient times.
朱 輪 red wheels—used by nobles in ancient times.
朱 門 or 朱 戶 the gentry—ancient nobles had their doors painted red.
[15]朱 顏 to paint the face; to blush; a red face.
朱 顏 鶴 髮 red face and white hair—a hale old man.
朱 雀 the scarlet bird—a group of constellations in the south; a position in geomancy.

朱 魚 the goldfish.
共 結 朱 陳 to make a marriage contract.
(a) used in transliterating.
朱 古 力 chocolate.

侏 [1] A pigmy or dwarf.
1347

侏 儒 a dwarf.
侏 柱 short pillar in a roof truss.

株 [1] The trunk of a tree. N.A. of trees and similar things.
1348

株 塊 stump and clod—dull, stupid; valueless.
株 幹 trunk of a tree.
株 戮 to implicate in a crime and put to death.
株 林 a grove; a forest.
[5]株 枸 stump of a tree.
株 根 淨 盡 to extirpate root and branch.
株 連 to implicate—when the tree is felled the root is involved.

珠 [1] A pearl. A bead. The pupil of the eye.
1349

珠 串 or 串 珠 string of pearls or beads; references in the margin.
珠 圓 玉 潤 rounded and smoothed like pearls and jade—polished writing.
珠·子 pearls, beads.
珠 寶 pearls, gems and jewels.
[5]珠 母 or 眞 珠 母 the pearl oyster.
珠 汗 beads of perspiration.
珠 淚 tears like pearls.
珠 玉 precious and beautiful.
珠 算 reckoning by the abacus.
[10]珠 簾 a pearl-embroidered screen.
珠 翠 bridal head-dress; ornaments.
珠 聯 璧 合 collection of pearls and valuables—excellent composition.
珠 胎 pregnant.
珠 花 pearl head-ornaments.
[15]珠 蘭 *Chloranthus inconspicua*, a fragrant plant used for scenting tea.
珠 譚 your pearly words.
假 珠 artificial pearls.
念 珠 a rosary.
掌(上) 珠 a beloved child; now ref. more often to a daughter.

[20]有 眼 無 珠 having eyes but no pupils—ignorant.
珍 珠 or 眞 珠 real pearls.
眼 珠 the iris or pupil.
魚 目 混 珠 fishes' eyes are taken for pearls—spurious things that pass as real.

硃 [1] Vermilion. Imperial, because the emperor signed in red.
1350

硃 卷 essays of successful candidates which were copied out in red.
硃 批 the emperor's approval.
硃 砂 cinnabar.
硃 砂 桔 the red mandarin orange.
硃 筆 the imperial autograph.
硃 諭 imperial mandates.
銀 硃 vermilion.

蛛 螽 [1] The spider.
1351

蛛 絲 the threads of a spider's web.
蛛 蝥 poisonous.
蜘 蛛 網 a spider's web.

誅 [1] To punish; to put to death. To eradicate. Term of reproof.
1352

誅 其 過 to punish a crime.
誅 意 to judge one's intentions before acting.
誅 戮 to cut off; to execute.
誅 求 無 厭 inordinate desires; insatiable.
[5]誅 累 to involve in punishment.
誅 罰 to reduce to subjection; to punish.
誅 草 or 誅 茅 to weed.
誅 除 or 誅 滅 to exterminate—family, or rebels.
誅 降 戮 服 to massacre those who surrender.
[10]伏 誅 to be executed.
天 誅 a divine punishment.

邾 [1] A feudal state which existed B.C. 700-469. Now the district of 鄒 縣 in Shantung
1353

銖[1] Ancient silver coin. A weight equal to 100 grains of millet; the twenty-fourth part of a *tael*. Also read *shu*[2].

1354

銖 兩 very small; minute.

銖 積 寸 累 trifles when accumulated make much.

渚 陼 [3] An islet. A bank.

1355

寶 渚 ancient name for Ceylon.

煮 [3] To boil; to cook; to decoct.

1356

煮 字 a scholar who lives by writing.

煮 泉 to boil water until it bubbles.

煮 熟 boiled thoroughly; well done.

煮 爛 or 煮 老 boiled to shreds; to cook till tender.

煮 藥 to decoct medicines.

煮 豆 燃 箕 to make a fire of beanstalks for boiling beans.—one member of a family injuring another. From a verse by 曹 植 which he was ordered to compose in seven paces by his brother Ts'ao P'ei, the emperor. 一煮 豆 持 作 羹, 漉 豆 以 爲 汁, 箕 在 釜 底 燃, 豆 在 釜 中 泣.

煮 飯 or 煮 菜 to prepare a dinner; to cook food.

猪 豬 [1] A hog; a pig.

1357

猪 公 or 公 猪 a boar.
猪 子 a young pig.
猪 排 骨 pork ribs.
猪 毛 or 猪 鬃 hog's bristles.
[5]猪 母 or 母 猪 a sow.
猪 水 swill for pigs.
猪 油 or 猪 膏 lard.
猪 獾 the badger.
猪 籠 草 the pitcher-plant.
[9]猪 肉 pork.
猪 肝 色 liver-coloured.

猪 脚 凍·子 pig's-foot jelly.
猪 苓 a variety of "China Root."
猪 蠳 地 the pigs root up the ground.
[15]猪 行 a pig dealer's. (-hang[2])
猪 頭 三 牲 boar's head, carp and a cock—used in idolatry.
一 口 猪 one pig.
豪 猪 the porcupine.
野 猪 the wild boar. 「(Shanghai)
↑猪 頭 三 fool; victim of a trick.

潴 [1] A pool or small lake.

1358

潴 水 pools; ponds.

翥 翥 [1] To soar.

1359

鳳 翥 the phœnix soars—the bride is off.

箸 筯 [4] Chopsticks.

1360

箸·子 chopsticks. *Rare.*
加 一 雙 箸 add another pair of chopsticks,—when a guest arrives unexpectedly.
牙 箸 or 象 箸 ivory chopsticks.
竹 箸 bamboo chopsticks.

(a) Read *cho*[5]. *u.f.* next, or 着 No. 1258.

著 [4] To set forth, to manifest, to make known. To write, as a book. The original form of 着 No. 1258. Inter. 註 No. 1343.

1361

著·作 to write; to do literary work.
著 作 品 or 著 作 物 literary productions.
著 作 家 authors.
著 作 權 copyright. = 版 權.
[5]著 作 等 身 his writings made a pile as high as himself.
著 其 善 make a display of his goodness.
著 匪 notorious criminal.
著 名 famous; prominent; notorious.

著 小 書 to write pamphlets.
[10]著 明 to make clear.
著 書 to write a book.
著 論 to write essays.
著 述 or 標 著 to narrate; to write down.
顯 著 or 彰 著 to make known; to bring to light; to spread abroad.

(a) Read *cho*[1.5] Inter. 着 No. 1258. To put on, to wear. To put.

著[1] 手 to make an effort; to begin to work on.
著[1] 手 成 春 used of wonderful literary skill,—now applied to medical skill, "it brings back youth."
著[1] 履 to put on shoes.
著[1] 衣 to dress, put on garments.
著[1] 衣 鏡 large mirror for dressing.
著[1] 袈 裟 to take the priestly robes —to become a Buddhist priest.

(b) To belong to a place.

土 著 of native stock, long resident and not willing to move.
中 國 土 著 Chinese born.

(c) To blossom.

著 花 to put forth flowers.

諸 [1] All, every.

1362

諸 事 如 意 May everything be as you wish!
諸 事 承 情 I am greatly indebted to you.
諸 侯 the feudal princes.
諸 侯 未 踰 年 之 稱 the designation of a prince who has not yet reigned for a whole year.
[5]諸 公 or 諸 位 or 諸 君 Gentlemen! Sirs!
諸 凡 all of; every; the whole.
諸 史 historians.
諸 夏 many (States) and great—China, in feudal times.
不 如 諸 夏 之 亡 也 not like the States of our great land which are without (princes).
[10]諸 多 very many,〔and things like this.
諸 如 此 類 all are similar to this;

諸 子 百 家 all classes of philosophers, etc.

諸 父 uncles.

諸 生 a *hsiu ts'ai* or 1st degree graduate.

[15] 諸 般 all sorts.

諸 色 all classes.

諸 蔗 sugar-cane.

諸 說 various opinions.

錯 諸 枉 put aside all the crooked.

(a) Fusion of 之 於 ' it in '.

加 諸 我 也 .... to do that to me

君 子 求 諸 己 the superior man seeks it in himself.

如 示 諸 掌 like showing it in his palm.

如 示 諸 斯 like looking at this.

[5] 有 諸 己 he must have (the goodness) in himself.

遇 諸 塗 he met him on the way.

聞 諸 夫 子 I have heard it from you.

其 諸 異 乎 is it not different?

告 諸 往 而 知 來 者 I told him one point and he knew its proper sequence.

失 諸 正 鵠 misses the centre of the target.

譬 諸 草 木 compare it with the case of plants.

(b) Fusion of 之 歟 ' it ' + ' ? '.

一 言 而 喪 邦 有 諸 Is there a single sentence which can ruin a country?

子 曰 有 諸 Confucius said, "May such a thing be done?"

寇 至 盍 去 諸 the robbers are coming, why not leave this place?

櫧 [1] An evergreen oak; something similar to beancurd is 1363 made from the acorns.

宁 [4] Space between the throne and the retiring room behind 1364 it.

宁 立 之 處 the space between the throne and the retiring room of the prince.

伫
竚 } [4] To stand and wait; to hope for.
1365

伫 切 eagerly waiting.

伫 看 to gaze upwards.

伫 立 to stand still.

望 伫 hopefully waiting.

紵 [4] Sackcloth.
1366

絺 紵 fine and coarse hemp.

苧 [4] A hemp-producing plant like a nettle. *Bœhmeria* 1367 *nivea*.

苧 店 linen shop.

苧 根 hemp roots—ground with rice and used as food.

苧 蔴 the fibres from which grass-cloth or linen is made, commercially known as China Grass or Ramie fibre.

苧 蔴 裙 衫 linen garments.

貯 [3] To store up; to hoard.
1368

貯 備 to lay in; to prepare for; to have a reserve.

貯 備 金 or 預 備 金 reserve funds.

貯 墨 筆 or 自 來 墨 筆 fountain pen.

貯 粟 to store grain.

[5] 貯 庫 to store in the treasury.

貯 收 or 貯 存 or 貯 藏 to hoard; to store.

貯 棧 to warehouse.

貯 蓄 or 儲 蓄 to save; savings.

貯 金 累 玉 to accumulate wealth.

[10] 積 貯 to store grain against famine.

杼 [4] The shuttle of a loom. Thin, as the wheels of a cart 1369 which sink in the mud. Long-headed. Read *shu⁴*. A scrub oak.

杼 柚 其 空 the looms are empty —indicating extreme want.

斷 機 杼 cut the web from the loom—as the mother of Mencius

did, in grief at her son's inattention to study.

助 [4] To aid, to help, to assist. Also read *tsu⁴*.
1370

助 一 臂 之 力 to lend a hand.

助 不 給 to help where there is lack.

助 力 assistance.

助 動 詞 auxiliary verb.

[5] 助 忙 to give a hand when busy.

助 成 其 事 to help to finish a matter.

助 手 a helper; an assistant.

助 捐 to subscribe.

助 教 (員) assistant teacher.

[10] 助 款 auxiliary funds.

助 法 auxiliary laws.

助 理 to help; assistant.

助 紂 爲 虐 helping *Chou* to do evil—adding bad to worse.

助 言 a helping word.

[15] 助 語 詞 auxiliary particle; expletive.

助 賑 to relieve distress.

助 錢 or 助 銀 or 資 助 monetary assistance.

借 助 to lend assistance.

內 助 a wife.

[20] 協 助 co-operation.

樂 助 willing assistance.

相 助 mutual aid.

輔 助 assistance.

騜 [4] A horse with the near hind leg white.
1371

鑄 [4] To cast metals; to coin.
1372

鑄 人 to mould men.

鑄 像 to cast a molten image.

鑄 山 煮 海 to cast a mountain of brass into cash, and to boil the sea down for salt—to avoid the necessity for taxes and levies.

鑄 成 or 鑄 就 to cast.

[5] 鑄 模 to cast a model.

鑄 版 to cast a plate, as for printing.

鑄 礮 to cast cannon.

鑄 粗 to cast agricultural implements.

鑄 造 to make castings.

[10] 鑄 金 事 之 to cast an image and worship it.

鑄錢 or 鑄幣 to coin money.
鑄錯 to cast a "mistake" character—to make a great blunder.
鑄鐵 or 生鐵 cast iron.
鑄鐘 to cast a bell.
鑄鼎象物 nine tripods cast by *Yü* the Great, having representations of the products of the nine provinces of his time. *See* 九 No. 1198—35.
印鑄局 Bureau of Printing.

CHU. (ㄓㄨ)

(Chuh)

竹 / ⺮ 2.5. **The bamboo.**
1373

竹報 a family letter.
竹·子 the bamboo.
竹實 bamboo seeds.
竹布 glazed cotton cloth.
5竹杠 bamboo pole for carrying.
竹林 bamboo grove; an ancient club composed of seven convivial worthies.
竹皺 bamboo shavings for stuffing things.
竹竿 bamboo canes or poles.
竹笋 or 竹芽 bamboo shoots.
10竹筒 a bamboo tube.
竹節 joints of the bamboo.
竹簡 slips of bamboo for writing, before paper was invented.
竹籌·子 bamboo tallies for checking loads, etc.
竹紙 paper made from bamboo.
15竹絲 bamboo splints or threads.
竹膜 membrane of the bamboo.
竹茹 the silicious skin of the bamboo.
竹頭木屑 ends and odd pieces of bamboo and wood—not of much value, but they have their uses.
竹黃 or 竹青 medicine obtained from the bamboo—tabasheer.
20勢如破竹 the situation is like splitting bamboo — once a start is made, it is easy to split through; hence an increasingly easy and favorable situation.
成竹在胸 before an artist can draw a bamboo, he must have the image in his mind—used of preconceived ideas or foregone conclusions.

竺 2.5. **A kind of bamboo. India.**
1374

竺國 or 天竺國 or 西竺國 India.

筑 2.5. **The five-stringed lute.**
1375

築 2.5. **To beat down hard; to ram earth. To build.**
1376

築坭牆 to build a mud wall.
築城 to build a city wall.
築堤 to raise a dyke or embankment.
築壇 to build an altar of earth.
5築室 to build a house.
築壘 to raise earthworks for fortification.
築石磡 to build stone piers or bunding.
築碼頭 to construct a jetty.
修築 to repair walls, etc.
建築 *See* 856.13 ff.

妯 2.5. **Sisters-in-law; the wives of brothers.**
1377

妯·娌 sisters-in-law.

(a) **Read** *ch'ou*1. **Disquieted.**

軸 2.5. **An axletree. A pivot. Roller for maps or scrolls. N.A.**
1378

軸兒 a catch or bolt.
軸·子 or 車軸 an axletree.
軸頭 the projecting end of an axle-tree.
一軸畫 a picture scroll.
5傳力軸 shafting for machinery.
剪軸 pivot of scissors.
卷軸 roller for scrolls, etc.
當軸 the pivot of a thing—headman, manager.
螺輪軸 propeller-shaft.

柷 4.5. **Instrument of wood used in ancient times to start the orchestra.**
1379

祝 4.5. **To bless, to invoke, to pray to.**
1380

祝告 or 祝禱 to implore the gods; to pray.
祝嘏 to implore blessings.
祝壽 to offer birthday congratulations.
祝宗 to invoke the ancestors.
5祝敬 to offer respectful congratulations.
祝文 forms of invocation.
祝板 a tablet on which a prayer is written to be burnt before the gods.
祝福 to bless; to invoke a blessing.
祝融 the god of fire.
10祝詞 sacrificial odes; congratulatory wishes.
祝謝 to give thanks.
祝讚 to praise; to glorify.
祝賀 to tender congratulations.
祝鮀 the precentor (leader of the liturgy) *T'o*.

(a) **To bind; to cut off.**

祝髮文身 to cut off the hair and tattoo the body.
祝髮而裸 to cut off the hair and go naked—savages.
孔子曰天祝予 Confucius said, "Heaven is cutting me off."
素絲祝之 bound with cords of white silk.

(b) **Read** *chou*4. **To curse, to make an oath.**

侯作侯祝 "they go on cursing."
厥口詛祝 he invoked curses.

豖 2.5. **A shackled pig.**
1381

瘃 2.5. **Sores from cold.**
1382

凍瘃 chilblains.

逐 2.5. **To expel. To follow. To pursue. Distinguish 遂 No. 5530.**
1383

逐出 or 逐去 to cast out.
逐出公會 to excommunicate.

逐出本境 or 逐籍 to expatriate.

逐利 to follow the way of gain.

⁵逐勝 to take advantage of victory and drive out the foe.

逐勢 trend or tendency.

逐北 to pursue defeated troops.

逐客令 dismissal orders for visiting counsellors.

逐日千里 chasing the sun for a thousand *li*,—of a fleet horse.

¹⁰逐日追風 to chase the sun and drive the wind—fast travelling.

逐末 to follow the inferior—to trade, as agriculture was reckoned superior.

逐末者多 if the traders are too many.

逐殃 or 逐邪 to expel noxious influences which cause calamity.

逐疫 to drive out the demon of pestilence.

¹⁵逐罵 to drive out with curses.

逐臭之夫 a man whose smell was so bad that none would live with him was about to live by himself near the sea, when he found one who was pleased with the smell,—said of eccentricity.

逐走 to drive out (the wild beasts).

逐逐 eagerly; quickly.

逐除 to expel and remove; to do away with.

²⁰逐隊 to follow the rest.

逐鬼 to exorcise demons.

逐鹿 to chase the deer—to snatch at high position.

放逐 to cast off; to turn out.

(a) In order, in succession, one by one.

逐一逐二 or 逐個逐個 one by one; to arrange in order; in succession.

逐加 separately; individually.

逐層 successively.

逐日 day by day; every day.

⁵逐欵 item by item.

逐漸 gradually; little by little.

逐漸發達 gradual development of activities.

逐漸緊張 (relations) gradually became very strained.

逐漸而進 gradual advancement.

¹⁰逐細 in detail.

粥 ¹·⁵ Rice boiled to gruel. Congee. Also read *chou*¹.
1384

粥廠·子 a shed where congee is given away; a "soup kitchen."

燭 |
烛 | ²·⁵ A candle; to illumine.
1385

燭光 candlelight; candle-power.

燭剪 snuffers.

燭力 candle-power.

燭斗 or 燭臺 or 燭插 a candlestick.

⁵燭淚 guttering of a candle.

燭照無私 impartiality.

燭照計算 a clear estimation of.

燭籠 a lantern.

燭花 snuff of a candle.

¹⁰明燭 a clear understanding of.

爉燭 wax candles.

花燭 painted candles.

花燭之喜 the wedding night.

囑 |
嘱 | ³·⁵ To enjoin, to charge, to order.
1386

囑令 to order.

囑·咐 to charge.

囑書 the will—of a deceased parent.

囑爲 to direct that.

囑託 to order emphatically; to charge.

囑請 to request; to desire—between equals.

賄囑 to bribe.

矚 ³·⁵ To gaze at steadily.
1387

凝神遠矚 to gaze at in a fit of abstraction.

躅 |
躑 | ⁴·⁵ To walk slowly and cautiously; to limp.
1388

躑躅 to halt.

躅躅 prancing of an unmanageable horse.

CH'U.   (彳)

杵 ³ A pestle; a baton used to pound clothes in washing.
1389 To pound.

杵臼之交 a close friendship.

初 ¹ The beginning; the first.
1390

初一 the first of the month.

初一十五 new moon and full moon; 1st and 15th of lunar month.

初九 the 9th of the lunar month—this use of 初 is confined to the first decade.

初交 the beginnings of friendship or of relations with.

⁵初伏 first ten days of the hottest weather—there are three decades, the first beginning about the middle of July.

初來 the first visit; on first arrival.

初元 the accession of a new monarch.

初冬 the 10th lunar month.

初創 or 初立 newly established.

¹⁰初夏 the 4th month of the lunar year.

初婚 newly married.

初學 to commence studies.

初審 a first hearing.

初幾來 which day did you come? (which day of the first ten days of the month)?

¹⁵初度 when first born; old term for a birthday; for the first time.

初心 the first intention.

初政 the beginning of a reign.

初日初月 the rising sun and the new moon.

初旬 or 初間 the first ten days of the lunar month.

²⁰初時 or 起初 or 當初 in the beginning; at the first.

初更 the first watch of the night.

初會 at the first meeting.

初末 the beginning and the ending.

初次 on the first occasion; the first time.

²⁵初步 or 初階 the first step; introduction.

講和初步 peace preliminaries.

初步計畫 preliminary plans.

初 民 primitive man.
初 民 敎 育 primitive education.
30 初 無 there has never been ....; there has never been any question of.
初 版 first edition.
初 犯 first offence; first offender.
初 生 first-born.
初 發 市 the opening of a shop for the first time.
35 初 秋 the 7th month of the lunar year.
初 稿 first draft of a poem, etc.
初 等 primary.
初 等 小 學 primary schools.
初 等 敎·育 primary education.
40 初 級 the first grade.
初 級 中 學 junior middle school.
初 級 實 業 primary industries.
初 級 師 範 學 校 junior normal school.
初 見 the first meeting or interview.
45 初 試 first trial or experience.
初 讀 first reading of a bill.
初 選 preliminary election.
初 開 to open for the first time.
初 開 埠 newly opened port.
50 初 開 天 地 at the creation.
初 開 門 or 初 開 張 first opening of .....
人 之 初 men at their birth.
太 初 at the very beginning of things; "in the beginning."

除 ² **To remove; to do away with.**
1391

除 免 to avoid; to excuse; to dispense with.
除 名 or 除 籍 to disenroll.
除 害 安 良 suppress the evil and pacify the good.
除 弊 to get rid of abuses.
5 除 服 or 除 喪 to lay aside mourning.
除 根 to eradicate; to do away with entirely.
除 權 判 決 sentence of expulsion.
除 治 to rectify; to regulate.
除 滅 他 Away with him!
10 除 災 to save from calamity.
除 病 to get rid of a disease or of a bad habit.
除 罪 to get rid of sin; to remit sin.

除 習·氣 or 除 惡 習 to get rid of evil habits or customs.
除 蟲 菊 the pyrethrum from which insect powder is made.
15 除 道 to remove noxious influences from the road; to open a road.
除 邪 to remove noxious influences; to exorcise.
除 酵 節 The Feast of Unleavened Bread.
除 銷 to cancel.
廢 除 to abolish

(a) **To subtract; to divide; to deduct.**

除 三 斤 包 take off three *catties* tare.
除 了 皮 deducting the tare.
除 以 一 百 divide by one hundred.
除 支 deducting payments.
5 除 收 以 外 deducting what has already been received.
除 收 尙 欠 deducting what has been paid, there is still owing .....
除 數 divisor.
除 法 or 除 起 or 歸 除 division —in arithmetic.
除 皮 核 算 deduct the tare and calculate the net weight.
10 除 號 sign of division.
以 九 除 之 divide by nine.

(b) **Besides; except.**

除·了 with the exception of; deducting; to get rid of.
除 此 以 外 besides this; with the exception of.
除·非 with the exception; only if; unless.

(c) **To appoint a new official to office.**

除 官 to appoint to office.
除 拔 to select; to pull out.
除 拜 to appoint a new official.
除 授 to appoint to.
除 書 a letter of appointment.
除 臣 洗 馬 appointed me as equerry.

(d) **Portico steps; vestibule.**

前 除 the front steps.
庭 除 the outer porch.
階 除 the steps to a house.

(e) **To change. To pass away.** (also read *chu⁴*.)

除 夜 or 除 夕 or 除 日 new-year's eve.
俾 爾 單 厚 何 福 不 除 (*chu⁴*) To make you perfectly virtuous, what happiness does He withhold from you?
日 月 其 除 (*chu⁴*) the days and months pass away.

滁 ² River which joins the Yangtze near Nanking.
1392
滁·州 place in Anhwei near Nanking.

楚 ³ Name of a feudal State which existed from B.C. 740 —330, see under 荆. No. 1116. The province of Hupeh.
1393

楚 亡 楚 得 or 楚 弓 楚 得 the bow of *Ch'u* will be found by the man of *Ch'u*—narrow-minded.
楚 囚 對 泣 the captives from *Ch'u* wept with each other— from the *Tso Chuan*, when 鍾 儀 was made a captive by the State of *Chin* 晋. It is used to illustrate helplessness in desperate straits.
楚 服 full dress.
楚 材 晋 用 the talents of *Ch'u* used by *Chin*—used in speaking of using other nationals. ⌈11.
5 楚 歌 the songs of *Ch'u*. *See below*
楚 腰 slender waists—Duke *Chuang* of *Ch'u* was fond of slender women, thus the phrase has come to be used as indicated.
三 楚 the three divisions of the State of *Ch'u*, as *below*.
南 楚 part of modern Kiangsi and Anhwei.
東 楚 part of modern Kiangsu.
10 西 楚 part of modern Hupeh.
四 面 楚 歌 surrounded on all sides by foes—from the history; 項 羽 was hard pressed by the troops of *Han* 漢, at night he heard the men singing these songs, from which he thought that *Ch'u* was also taken. Used to illustrate pressure on all sides, desperate straits.

(a) Sharp, keen. Clear, distinct.

楚 楚 clear and distinct.
楚 痛 or 痛 楚 painful and distressing.
夏 楚 a rod for punishing school boys in former days.
清·楚 clear and distinct.
苦 楚 distress; suffering and pain.
鞭 楚 to flog.

憷 [4]
1394   Rough and rugged.

礎 [3]
1395   Plinth or base of a pillar.

礎 潤 而 雨 a damp plinth indicates rain.
基 礎 foundation.

楮 [3] The paper mulberry, from the bark of which paper is
1396 made.

楮 儀 money given by friends towards funeral expenses.
楮 幣 or 楮 劵 bank-notes.
楮 片 a slip of paper.
楮·先·生 paper.
楮 紙 paper made from the mulberry.
楮 錢 paper money burnt in idolatry.
特 修 寸 楮 I specially write this note to you.

褚 [3]
1397   A bag or satchel.

褚 幕 a pall, covering for a bier.

躇 [2]
1398   Undecided; irresolute.

躊·躇 hesitating. (--chu, -ch'u²)

儲 [2]
1399   To collect; to store.

儲 力 potential energy.
電 儲 力 potential, of electricity.
儲 君 or 東 儲 heir-apparent.
英 儲 the Prince of Wales.
⁵儲 收 to collect.

儲 積 accumulated; in store.
儲 積 糧 草 to store grain, etc.
儲 蓄 問 題 the problem of savings.
儲 蓄 所 conservatory.
¹⁰儲 蓄 會 savings society.
儲 蓄 正 軌 the straight path of saving.
儲 蓄 銀 行 Savings Bank.
儲 貨 stored, warehoused, or bonded goods.
儲 金 or 儲 蓄 savings.
¹⁵儲 金 簿 savings pass-book.
郵 政 儲 金 Post-office Savings (Bank).

廚
廚 [2]
厨
1400   A kitchen.

廚 下 in the kitchen.
廚 人 or 廚·子 or 廚·師·傅 a cook.
廚 刀 kitchen-knife.
廚 娘 female cook.
⁵廚 店 a restaurant.
廚 房 a kitchen.
廚 竈 kitchen-range.
幫 廚 cook's assistant.

(a) A press, a wardrobe, cupboard. A quiver.

廚 櫃·子 or 書 廚 a bookcase.
衣 廚 clothes-press.

幮 [2]   Screen to make a temporary kitchen.
1401

躕 [2]   Puzzled; undecided.
1402

躊·躕 uncertain; hesitating.
    (--chu, -ch'u²)

鋤
鉏 [2]
1403   A hoe. To hoe.

鋤 刨 to hoe and dig.
鋤 地 or 誅 鋤 to hoe the ground.
鋤 草 or 鋤 田 to weed.
鋤 鋙 難 入 unfitted for each other; unsuitable.
鋤·頭 a hoe.

耡 [2]
1404   To till. Inter. preceding.

耡 耘 to cultivate the land; to plough and harrow.
耡 耕 to till.

芻
蒭 [2]
   To cut grass; hay, fodder.
1405

芻 尼 a name for the magpie.
芻 牧 a shepherd.
芻 狗 a straw dog — something worthless, thrown away after its use in magic — to use a man, and when finished with him, to have no further dealings with him.
芻 糧 fodder.
⁵芻 草 weeds.
芻 蕘 者 grass and reed cutters.
芻 言 simple, plain talk; rustic speech.
芻 議 rustic opinion — a depreciatory phrase.
芻 豢 the flesh of animals which have fed on grass and grain respectively.
¹⁰芻 靈 a scarecrow; effigies burned with or on behalf of a dead man.

雛
鶵 [2]
   A chick, a fledgling. To rear a brood.
1406

雛 女 a slave-girl; a young girl.
雛 形 reduced model of anything.
雛·得 狠 very callow; unfledged.
雛 於 其 中 reared among them.
⁵雛 鳳 a young phœnix — said in praise of a child.
雛 鴿 a young pigeon.
雛 雞 a young chicken.

處
處 [3]
处
   To dwell, to abide in, to stay on, to be at rest in, to occupy. In this tone it has a verbal use.
1407

處 世 to be born; to be in the world.

處世學識 knowledge of the world.
處·不·來 cannot get on with a person.
處于同等地位 to stand on an equal footing.
5處兩難 between two difficulties.
處士 a scholar in retirement.
處夫婦 to be married.
處女 a young lady; a virgin.
處妾 a virgin.
10處子³ a young lady; a recluse scholar.
處宅 a dwelling, i.e., benevolence or love as man's dwelling. 仁人之安宅. See No. 26—11.
處己爲人 put himself in the place of others.
處常 to abide in peace and prosperity.
處心積慮 to brood over a matter for a long time.
15處約 to be in adversity; in straitened circumstances.
處變 to be in difficulties.
處貧賤 to live in poverty; in humble circumstances.
處長 long enduring; a long time.
相處 to dwell together.

(a) To decide; to judge; to punish; to settle or end.

處決 to sentence after trial; to execute.
處分⁴ to settle or adjust; to punish officials; to put into execution; disposition or arrangement.
處刑 or 處罰 to punish according to the law.
處斷 to decide; to settle.
5處暑 limit of heat—a solar period about August 23rd to September 7th.
處死 to punish with death—I'll be the death of you!
處舘 to reside in a family, as secretary or tutor.

(b) To manage, to adjust, to attend to, to place.

處事 to manage business; to administer.
處事精詳 to attend to business, giving minute attention to details.
處務細則 detailed rules for guidance of officials.
處守 to hold his post.

5處家 to manage a household.
處治 to govern; to control.
處理 to dispose; disposition.
處理法 method of disposition; arrangement.
處置 to manage; to place; to settle.
10處置·他 to settle it.
處置失當 badly managed.

(c) To have use for.

未有處也 I had no occasion or use for money.
無處而餽之 sending presents when a man has no use for them.

(d) Read ch'u¹. A place, an office, a department. A side or party. Condition, circumstances. In this tone it is a noun.

處所 a location or place.
處處 or 四處 or 各處 or 到處 everywhere.
好·處 an advantage; a good point, of a thing or of a person.
敝處 my poor locality or province.
5有去·處 has a home—a man who can be trusted to a certain extent,—he is not a vagrant, but one who can be found if necessary.
此處 this place.
無處不到 he goes everywhere.
疑處 doubts, suspicions.
短·處 shortcomings, demerits, failures.
10聚處 a meeting place; place of assembly.
長·處 merits; the good points or advantages of.
難·處 difficulties.
↑辦事處 office.

CH'U.　　(ㄔㄨ)

(Ch'uh)

丁 4.5. A step with the right foot, as 彳 is a step with the left foot.
1408
彳亍 left, right. To walk.

出 1.5. To come out, to go out; this verb is coloured by the word which it follows; an attempt has been made to group these meanings for study or reference.
1409

出·來 to come out; to appear; gives the force of the present to the preceding verb. A number of illustrations is given below.
倒·出·來 to pour.
刨·出·來 (p'ao²) to dig out.
剜·出·來 to gouge out; to scoop out.
5剔·出·來 to pick out the bones, as of meat.
吐·出·來 to vomit; to vent abusive language.
找·出·來 or 尋·出·來 to make a search for.
抱·出·來 to carry out in the arms.
拿·出·來 to bring out.
10揀·出·來 to choose or select.
摘·出·來 to pick out.
放·出·來 to release.
沸·出·來 or 滾·出·來 to boil over.
發·出·來 to issue forth.
15說·出·來 to utter; to speak.
走·出·來 to walk out.
跑·出·來 to run out.
迸·出·來 to jump out.
送·出·來 to escort.
20逐·出·來 to expel.
出入 to come and go.
出入自得 going out and in at will.
出兵 or 出征 to go forth to battle.
出動 movements, as of troops.
25出去 to go out. (also 拿·出·去, etc.)
出口 to export; to leave port.
出口商人 exporters.
出口稅 export duty.
出口貨 exports.
30出口貨單 or 出口紅單 port clearance.
出口貿易 export trade.
出城 to go out of the city.
出場 to come out from—as from an examination hall.
出境護照 special passport in wartime.
35出外 to go on a journey; to go abroad.
出嫁 or 出閣 to marry a husband.
出學 to leave school.
出家 or 出俗 to leave home life and become a devotee.
出山 to come out of retirement.
40出席 to be present at a meeting.
↓出征 to go on a military expedition.

出 席 演 說 to be present and address a meeting.
出 席 總 數 total number present.
出 恭 to retire in order to ease nature.
出 會 to go in procession.
45出 格 to leave the pattern; out of order; contrary to rule or routine.
出 霉 the end of the mildew season of early summer.
出 死 星 to let out evil influences by poking a hole in the roof.
出 殯 or 送 殯 to carry a coffin out to the grave; to escort a funeral.
出 洋 to go abroad; to emigrate.
50出 洋 輪 船 ocean-going steamer.
出 班 to go on duty; to take a turn on duty.
出 神 to be absent-minded; to concentrate upon anything.
出 缺 to vacate an office either for sickness or death, or because the time has expired.
出 舍 to go out from a family, as a son-in-law who has entered his wife's family and afterwards goes out from them, taking her with him.
55出 舍 於 郊 he went out and lived in a shed on the borders.
出 處 to go out from, and to take office: origin of a quotation.
出 行 to go on a journey.
出 路 a way of escape; an outlet.
出 軌 to leave the rails; to depart from routine; to follow wrong courses; derailment.
60出 遠 門 to go on a long journey to a distant place.
出 門 to travel; to go out from her mother's home to be married.
出 門 如 見 大 賓 when abroad treat others as if they were your important guests.
出 關 to go out of frontiers.
出 闈 to leave the hall, as officials leaving the examination hall.
65出 隊 to go to war; to march out in ranks.
出 險 to escape from danger.
出 離 to leave; to depart from.
出 風 頭 or 出 鋒 頭 to be satisfied with one's appearance; to be well dressed; to excel others in style, etc. to cut a figure.

(a) To put forth, to issue, to send forth.

出 具 甘 結 to enter into a bond.
出 主 意 to make a suggestion; to plan; to issue.
出 乎 to proceed from.
出 乎 情 理 之 外 utterly beyond all reason.
5出 乎 爾 者 反 乎 爾 者 what goes from you will return to you—as curses, etc.
出 事 to have some unfortunate happening.
出 令 to issue orders.
出 使 to be sent on a mission; an envoy.
出 使 大 臣 an ambassador.
10出 力 to put forth effort; to work hard.
出 告 示 to issue a proclamation.
出 天 花 or 出 痘 to have small-pox.
出 奏 to present a memorial.
出 妻 to divorce a wife.
15出 師 北 發 the military expedition to the north.
出 張 to expand.
出 教 to excommunicate; to leave a sect.
出 方 法 to plan; to devise means.
出 於 to proceed from.
20出 於 人 to emanate from men.
出 於 望 外 beyond all expectation.
出 於 無 奈 it cannot be helped.
出 於 自 然 it came about quite naturally.
出 榜 or 出 案 to issue the list of successful candidates.
25出 母 a divorced mother.
出 氣 to vent the spleen; to aspirate, as certain Chinese sounds.
出 汗 to perspire.
出 涕 to weep.
出 爾 反 爾 contradictory; inconsistent.
30出 版 to publish; to issue, as from a printer or an author.
出 版 品 or 出 版 物 publications.
出 版 家 publishers.
出 版 業 the publishing business.
出 版 法 laws relating to publishing.
35出 版 界 the publishing world.
出 版 自 由 liberty of the press.
出 犯 言 to insult; to be impertinent.

出 現 to issue. See below. D.6.
條 例 出 現 ...... laws were promulgated.
40出 疹 子 to have measles or scarlet fever and similar diseases.
出 發 to issue forth, as troops.
出 柑 or 出 醜 to incur disgrace.
出 示 to issue a notice; to give information.
出 票 to issue a warrant.
45出 結 to arrange and draw up a settlement.
出 聲 to speak.
出 自 to proceed from; to come from; to rest with.
出 芽 to put forth buds.
出 訴 to take legal proceedings.
50出 諭 to issue a mandate.
出 賞 格 to issue a notice of reward.
出 遊 to go on an excursion.
出 韻 it does not rhyme.
出 題 to set a theme.
55出 題 外 irrelevant; beside the mark.
出 首 to act as an informer.

(b) To produce; to beget.

出 世 to be born.
出 品 productions.
出 息 or 出 利 to bear interest; to make gain or profit; perquisites.
出 生 to be born.
5出 生 死 亡 births and deaths.
出 生 牽 or 出 生 額 or 人 口 出 產 牽 the birth-rate.
出 產 products; natural products.
出 產 保 險 birth-insurance.
出 產 能 力 power of production; productive capacity.
10出 貨 to bring forth goods; products of a factory. See below. C.10.
出 身 to begin life; to enter into public service.
出 身 微 賤 of humble origin.
出 鐵 to produce iron.

(c) To have on sale; to pay; to spend; to lend, etc.

出 借 to lend.
出 典 to mortgage.
出 名 定 宗 to lend one's name to settle a matter.
出 售 or 出 賣 to have on sale.
5出 東 to pay for others; to "treat", to "shout."

出 欵 to furnish money to finance a project.

出 租 or 出 賃 to rent or hire to.

出 納 receipts and expenditure.

出 納 科 cashier's department.

[10]出 貨 to bribe; to pay a fine in lieu of other punishment, *See above.* B.10.

出 資 contributions either in money or labour, credits, etc.

出 進 returns.

(d) To manifest; to appear.

出 庭 to appear in court.

出 悖 來 違 if you shew perverseness others will manifest disobedience.

出 沒 appearing and disappearing; fluctuating; came and went.

出 沒 無 常 inconstant; appearing at intervals.

出 沒·的 所 在 a basis of operations; a resort.

出 現 to manifest; to appear; to issue. *See above.* A.38.

(e) To surpass; beyond.

出 人 頭 地 beyond all others.

出 凡 out of the common.

出 名 famous; celebrated; notorious. *See above.* C.3.

出 衆 or 出 羣 or 出 類 above the average; extra special.

出 奇 marvellous; strange.

出 色 above the average.

出 頭 to come to the front; to take the lead; to bear responsibility.

出 類 拔 萃 far above the average; to stand out from one's fellows.

**黜 [1.5.]
1410　To degrade; to dismiss.**

黜 會 to excommunicate; to expel from a society.

黜 異 端 以 崇 正 學 expel pernicious heresies in order to honour the truth.

黜 辱 to expel with dishonour.

黜 陟 幽 明 to degrade the inefficient, and promote the intelligent.

黜 革 or 黜 退 to cashier; to dismiss.

**怵 [4.5.]
1411　To entice. Afraid, timorous.**

怵 惕 惻 隱 frightened and distressed.

怵 迫 之 徒 a person who is tempted or urged on.

**畜 [4.5.]
1412　Cattle, domestic animals.**

畜·生 a domestic animal; term of abuse, You brute!

畜 類 animals; brute beasts.

六 畜 the domestic animals, oxen, sheep or goats, horses, pigs, dogs and fowls.

家 畜 domestic animals.

(a) Read *hsü* [4.5.] To rear; to feed. To cultivate. Inter. 蓄 No. 2860.

畜 德 to cultivate virtue.

畜 牧 to rear domestic animals.

畜 牧 世 代 the pastoral age.

畜 產 to breed cattle, etc.

畜 衆 to care for the masses.

畜 養 to rear, to feed.

畜 馬 to breed horses.

(b) To accumulate, to store up.

畜 穀 to store grain.

畜 積 to gather together.

畜 聚 to store; to accumulate.

(c) To restrain.

畜 君 何 尤 Is it a fault to restrain one's prince?

**搐 [4.5.]
1413　To drag along; to shake. A spasm.**

抽 搐 spasms; cramp; convulsions.

**齣 [1.5.]
1414　A stanza, a couplet. N.A. for plays.**

一 齣 戲 a play.

**矗 [4.5.]
1415　Lofty, upright, straight. Luxuriant growth.**

矗 然 不 誣 upright, without deceit.

矗 立 雲 表 sticking up into the clouds.

崇 山 矗 矗 the ranges rising in lofty tiers.

直 矗 矗·的 very straight; perfectly erect.

**觸 [4.5.]
1416　To butt; to gore.**

觸 到 在 地 butted him so that he fell.

觸 山 之 力 immense strength.

觸 藩 to butt a hedge—like a ram, and become inextricably entangled—to get into inextricable difficulties through obstinate rashness.

觸 角 to butt. *See below.* A.23.

頂 觸 to butt.

(a) To run against; to offend or insult; to arouse or stimulate; to touch.

觸 動 to excite, to stimulate; to provoke.

觸 動 慾 火 to excite the passions.

觸 官 or 觸 覺 器 organs of touch.

觸 怒 to irritate; to exasperate.

[5]觸 悟 to move; to arouse.

觸 懷 to flash into the mind.

觸 戰 to rush into deadly conflict.

觸 搏 clashing together, as waves.

觸 擊 to strike, to clash.

[10]觸 機·會 to strike the opportunity.

觸 激 to strike against; to arouse; to stimulate.

觸 熱 oppressive summer-heat.

觸 犯 to offend; to affront; to wound the feelings.

觸 發 to arouse; to stimulate.

[15]觸 目 to strike the eye.

觸 目 傷 心 to see an object which brings a person to mind with sorrow.

觸 眼·的 conspicuous.

觸 礁 to strike a hidden rock.

觸 羅 to fall into the net.

[20]觸 脣 organ of touch in molluscs.

觸 處 like 到 處 or 隨 處 wherever one goes; everywhere.

觸 覺 touch; the sense of touch.

觸 角 or 觸 鬚 or 觸 覺 角 antennae or feelers.

觸 試 a feeler.

[25]觸 諫 rashly and offensively remonstrating with a superior.

觸諱 heedless mention of unwelcome truths:

觸起 to recollect suddenly.

觸類 引 伸 to show by analogy.

觸鼻 to smell.

30 觸齧 to gnaw.

感 觸 to feel; the sense of touch.

手 觸 to touch; to feel.

接 觸 to come into contact with.

相 觸 to clash against; to have contact with.

CHUA.　　(ㄓㄨㄚ)

抓 [1] To scratch. Also read *chao*[3].

1417

抓 癢 to scratch an itchy place.

抓 破 臉 to scratch the face so that it bleeds.

抓 頭 or 抓 首 to scratch the head, as when in preplexity.

(a) To clutch; to seize.

抓·住 to clutch; to seize; to pounce upon.

抓 取 to select; to choose.

抓 周 兒 to test a child on his first birthday. *See* No. 1293--A.5.

抓 尋 to search for.

抓 替·身 to seize a substitute—it is believed that the spirits of the drowned, or of those who have met a violent death will do this.

抓 空 an unsuccessful attempt.

抓 賊 to arrest a thief.

抓 鬮 to draw lots.

摳 [1] To beat; to strike.

1418

摳 門 to pound at a door.

摳 鼓 to beat the drum—especially the drum outside a magistrate's *yamen,* at the sound of which he was obliged to give heed to the suppliant.

CHUAI.　　(ㄓㄨㄞ)

拽 [4] To drag, to pull. Also read *i*[5]. Inter. 曳 No. 3008.

1419

拽 大 步 to swagger; to take a big stride.

拽 根 to drag out the roots; to extort a confession.

拉 拽 to drag and pull.

(a) Read *chuai*[1]. To fling, to throw.

拽 泥 to throw mud.

跩 [3] To waddle, to limp.

1420

跩·起·來 to walk with a swagger.

輠 [3] Pits in the road. "Pot-holes."

1421

輠 窩 to bump and jolt because of the holes in the road.

CH'UAI.　　(彳ㄨㄞ)

揣 [3] To estimate; to measure. To try; to feel for. To look into.

1422

揣 人 主 意 to measure the intentions of a man.

揣 度 or 揣 摩 to feel after; to turn over in the mind; to examine thoroughly.

揣 測 to fathom; to measure.

揣 練 to study and imitate—as a good author.

踹 [4] To stamp; to trample on; to destroy. The heel. Also read *ch'uan*[4]. To follow, to trade. Also read *ch'ai*[3], and inter. 跐 No. 6977.

1423

踹 一 脚 泥 stepped up to the ankles in mud.

踹·住·他 tread on it.

踹 實 to step firmly; a firm footing.

踹·死 trampled to death.

5 踹 空 to tread on nothing—disappointed.

踹 西·瓜 皮 to tread on a watermelon skin—to be deceived.

踹 足 而 怒 he stamped his foot in anger.

踹 輭 索 to walk the slack rope.

踹 高 脚 to walk on stilts.

臎 [2] Ugly and fat; too fat to move.

1424

臎 肉 very fat pork.

臎 豬 a fat pig.

膪 [4] Soft fat.

1425

下 膪 the pendent fat of a pig's belly.

摣 [1] To thump.

1426

摣 麵 to knead dough.

(a) To place in the bosom.

摣·在 懷·裏 to carry or to place in the bosom.

摣·着 一 本 書 take away a book in the bosom.

摣·起·來 to put into the bosom.

(b) Read *ch'i*[1]. To split in pieces.

喋 [4] To lap; to suck.

1427

喋 血 to suck blood.

CHUAN.　　(ㄓㄨㄢ)

專 [1] Only, specially. solely. Alone, unassisted. Distinguish 耑 No. 1950.

1428

專 一 devoted to one thing; specially; wholly.

專 主 specially devoted to.

專 人 a special messenger.

專 任 to shoulder entire responsibility.

5 專 件 special item or article.

專 使 special commissioner.

專 修 to take up one branch of study.

專 修 科 special curriculum.

專 信 a special note.

10 專 候 specially waiting for.

專 制 despotic., autocratic.

專 制 主 義 despotism; tyranny.

專 制 政 治 despotic government.
專 制 政 體 despotic form of government; absolute monarchy.
¹⁵專 制 流 毒 the evils of despotic government or autocracy.
專 制 精 神 the spirit of autocracy.
專 制 觀 念 the autocratic view.
專 攻 to apply oneself specially to; to specialize in.
專 利 monopoly; patent.
²⁰專 利 權 exclusive rights.
專 利 特 書 局 patent office.
專 利 特 書·的 or 專 賣 特 書·的 patent rights. *See below,*—82.
專 利 特 書 證 or 專 利 證 書 letters patent; patent rights.
專 務 to devote special attention to; special business.
²⁵專 務 求 名 he only seeks fame.
專 司 to accept responsibility for one duty only; special departments.
專 呈 I specially address this.
專 單 special permit.
專 好 問 難 experts at cavilling.
³⁰專 官 special officer for any purpose.
專 家 specialist.
專 寄 to forward by special messenger.
專 專·的 especially; purposely; having one occupation.
專 對 wise in council; a ready wit; a referee; specially towards.
³⁵專 屬·的 exclusive.
專 屬 權 exclusive or intransferable rights. (*legal*).
專 屬 管 轄 exclusive rights.
專 差 specially sent—as on a mission.
專 己 selfish.
⁴⁰專 席 而 坐 to sit alone, as when in mourning.
專 征 general in full command of an expedition; sole authority; to act without waiting for orders from higher authorities.
專 律 special laws.
專 心 solely; with one mind.
專 心 一 志 or 專 心 致 志 with fixed purpose; mental concentration.
⁴⁵專 意 with one purpose.
專 意 來 to come on purpose.
專 房 specially favoured concubine.
專 房 之 寵 favours granted to a favourite concubine.
專 才 specialized skill.

⁵⁰專 批 往 索 賊 special warrant to arrest the thieves.
專 指 with special reference to.
專 有 權 exclusive rights.
專 橫 to lay down the law.
專 權 exclusive rights; to grasp power.
⁵⁵專 欲 難 成 the purpose of a solitary individual is not easily accomplished.
專 此 佈 達 I write specially to inform you.
專 此 敬 祝 specially writing to respectfully wish you....
專 此 敬 覆 Yours respectfully in reply.
專 此 肅 佈 I write specially to inform you, with all due respect.
⁶⁰專 注 absorbed attention.
專 注 資 本 specialized capital.
專 淩 to write specially.
專 照 a special certificate.
專 用 for exclusive use.
⁶⁵專 科 special course of study.
專 科 敎 師 teacher of a special subject.
專 科 醫 生 medical specialist.
專 章 or 專 條 special regulations.
專 管 to deal specially with.
⁷⁰專 管 租 界 leased concessions.
專 精 務 本 to devote earnest attention to what is fundamental.
專 約 special treaty.
專 美 to gain a special favour.
專 臨 specially called on .....
⁷⁵專 號 special number.
專 行 (-*hang*²) special line.
專 誠 for the special purpose of . . -ing.
專 說 to make particular allusion to.
專 課 special course.
⁸⁰專 責 成 to assign as a special task.
專 賣 事 業 monopoly.
專 賣 權 sole rights of sale in certain goods; monopoly, as in salt, etc. *See above.*—22.
專 賣 特 許 all rights reserved.
專 賣 特 許 法 patent laws.
⁸⁵專 足 courier with important letter.
專 車 or 特 別 列 車 or 臨 時 列 車 special train. insistently.
專 門 special branch; technical;
專 門 人 才 specialized talents.
專 門 化 specialized.
⁹⁰專 門 學 校 technical schools; professional schools, for law, medicine, art, etc.

專 門 學 術 technical knowledge or skill.
專 門 家 specialists.
專 門 技 藝 technical skill.
專 門 敎·育 technical education.
⁹⁵專 門·的 technical; professional.
專 門 詞 or 專 門 名 詞 or 專 門 說 technical terms.
專 門 點 technicalities.
專 電 special telegram; exclusive telegrams.

(a) **To assume responsibility.**

自 專 or 擅 專 to act on one's own responsibility.

甎
磚 ¹
1429
A brick, a square tile, a slab. Brick tea.

甎 瓦 行 a dealer in bricks and tiles. (-*hang*²)
甎 窰 a brick-kiln.
甎 茶 or 茶 甎 brick-tea.
甎·頭 a brickbat, in the north; in the south, a brick.
甎·頭 瓦 片 brickbats and pieces of tiles.

縛 ⁴
1430
A bright white colour. To tie up. Distinguish 縛 No. 1901. Inter, 絹 No. 1635.

縛 行 囊 to tie up the baggage.

轉 ³
1431
Lit. *chuan*³ to turn. Coll. *chuan*³ to change direction; but *chuan*⁴ to turn around, to revolve; to cause to turn.

轉 世 or 轉 生 to come back to life; transmigration.
轉 丸 to roll a pill—very easy.
轉 乎 溝 壑 to turn over and die in the gutters and ditches.
轉 個 圈 to go in a circle; to make a circuit.
⁵轉 側 to turn half-round; to toss to and fro.
轉 兇 爲 吉 to change evil for good fortune.
轉 凡 爲 聖 to change from an ordinary person into a sage.
轉 化 inversion; mutation.
轉 動 to revolve.
¹⁰轉 向 to turn to; to change from one side to the other; confused.
轉 回 to turn round; inversion.
轉 回·來 returned; to turn back.

轉 圓 a circle; endless plans and devices.

轉 圜 a complete revolution; to bring about a complete change; rapid action.

[15] 轉 地 療 養 change of scene for convalescence.

轉 年 next year.

轉 廻 or 輪 廻 transmigration; metempsychosis.

轉 彎 抹 角 to turn a corner, also used fig.

轉 徙 migration.

[20] 轉 心 conversion.

轉 念 to change the mind.

轉 意 to change the mind.

轉 手 to turn the hand; empty-handed.

轉 折 changing.

[25] 轉 敗 爲 功 to change defeat into a victory.

轉 旋 to revolve; revolution.

轉 旗 to change one's flag; to go over to the other side.

轉 曲 winding; serpentine.

轉 更 to change the watch.

[30] 轉 機 a crisis; a turning-point.

轉 機 之 際 a critical juncture.

轉 歸 to pass the crisis, as in illness.

轉 求 to intercede for.

轉 注 one of the six groups of Chinese characters—characters which have more than one sound, the meaning of which also changes with the sound.

[35] 轉 法 輪 the turning of the wheel of law—to preach Buddhism.

轉 漏 between the drips of the clepsydra—the briefest space of time.

轉 症 the crisis in a disease.

轉 目 不 顧 to turn away the eyes from beholding.

轉 盼 to look in every direction.

[40] 轉 眼 to turn the eye.

轉 眼 成 空 in a twinkling it is gone—the vanity of life.

轉 相 仿 效 to change one's opinion and agree with another.

轉 相 效 尤 to get into bad ways through evil example.

轉 相 汲 引 to change one's ways and emulate a lofty example.

[45] 轉 瞬 or 轉 眼 間 or 轉 息 間 in the twinkling of an eye.

轉 票 to renew a pawn ticket.

轉 禍 爲 福 to turn calamity into blessing.

轉 翼 to turn the flank of an army.

轉 肘 pivot on which a door turns.

[50] 轉 臂 之 間 instantly, at once, while you can turn round.

轉 臉 to change countenance—to come well out of a crisis.

轉 致 to convey a hint; to send a message.

轉 補 to promote to office.

轉 語 辭 disjunctive particle.

[55] 轉 變 modifications.

轉 變 不 定 changeable; inconstant.

轉 貨 to negotiate a loan. *See below*. A.15.

轉 質 to re-pledge.

轉 身 to turn round; to turn the body.

[60] 轉 身 而 去 to turn away and go.

轉 輪 骨 ball and socket joint.

轉 輾 repeatedly.

轉 過 來 to turn round.

轉 開 to turn aside; turn away from.

[65] 轉 限 to extend a limit, as of time.

轉 面 to turn the face; to turn away; to change front.

轉 韻 change of rhyme.

轉 頭 to turn the head.

轉 風 change of wind—used also fig., of a sudden change of attitude.

[70] 反 轉 turn upside down.

回 轉 to turn back again.

旋 轉 to whirl; to revolve.

翻 轉 to overturn; to reverse; to upset, as a boat.

輾 轉 to roll over and over.

(a) To transfer; to transmit; to pass on. Pron. chuan[3].

轉 任 transfer of office.

轉 仲 to forward the communications of another to a superior.

轉 准 to pass on a communication received from a higher official.

轉 咨 or 轉 照 to forward a communication to an equal.

[5] 轉 報 to report information received.

轉 奏 to memorialize on behalf of.

轉 學 to transfer to another school.

轉 租 or 轉 賃 to sub-let.

轉 移 to communicate through . . . ; to communicate to equals on behalf of.

[10] 轉 稟 to petition by proxy.

轉 精 to transport tribute-grain.

轉 職 transference of office.

轉 諭 or 轉 札 to issue orders received.

轉 讓 於 人 negotiated to another person.

[15] 轉 貨 to transport goods. *See above.*—57.

轉 述 to report what has been said.

轉 送 or 轉 發 or 轉 交 to send on; to pass on; "care of."

轉 達 to transmit to; to communicate to another.

轉 運 to change the luck for better; to transport goods.

[20] 轉 運 公 司 transport company; parcels express.

轉 運 所 express office for parcels, etc.

轉 運 艦 or 轉 送 艦 transport ship. Now called 運 輸 艦.

轉 遞 to forward; to hand over.

轉 飭 to give orders according to instructions received.

(b) Read chuan[4]. A revolution.

轉 筋 spasms, convulsions.

日 輪 一 轉 one revolution of the sun.

囀[3]
1432
To warble like a bird.

聲 嬌 囀 a sweet voice.

顓[1]
1433
Good; sedate; simple; respectful.

顓 民 tne good people.

顓 蒙 dull, stupid, inexperienced.

顓 頊 a legendary ruler of China B.C. 2513-2435.

(a) u.f. 專. Only, alone.

顓 兵 秉 政 to grasp at military power and usurp the government.

顓 制 to usurp authority.

顓 房 a favourite concubine.

顓 門 special, expert.

顓 顓 alone, myself alone.

撰[4]
1434
To compose, to record, to edit, to write a book. Inter. next.

撰 制 to prepare a book for the press.

撰 文 to compose.
撰 次 to select and arrange—as for a book.
撰 述 to compile a narrative.
著 撰 to write a book.

(a) **To grasp, to take up. Object, aim.**

撰 杖 屨 to take up staff and sandals.
天 地 之 撰 the principles of Heaven and Earth.
異 乎 三 子³者 之 撰 my wishes are different from the cherished purposes of these three gentlemen.

(b) Read *hsüan, süan*³. Inter. 選 No. 2898. To select, etc.

譔⁴ **To exhort by precept. To discourse in praise of. In-**
1435 **ter. preceding, To compose, etc.**

譔 文 or 論 譔 eulogy—as of a worthy person.
手 譔 his own composition.

饌⁴
籑⌇ **To feed, to provide for. Delicacies, dainties.**
1436

饌 具 food-vessels.
殽 饌 dainties; delicacies.
盛 饌 a feast.
菜 饌 viands; vegetables and meats.
設 饌 to set out a dinner.

(a) Read *hsüan*⁴. **Ancient weight of six ounces (*taels*) of silver.**

賺⁴
聽⌇ **To earn, to make a profit.**
賺⌇
1437
[-*chao*²

賺·不·着 to make nothing of it.
賺 利 interest accruing.
賺·得 多 very profitable; great gains.
賺·得 作 to gain nothing but the trouble of the transaction.
賺 賬 profit account.

賺 辛·苦 to reap disappointment and sorrow.
賺 錢 to make money.
賺 食 to earn a livelihood.

(a) **To cheat.**

賺 人 or 賺 哄 to cheat.
賺 詐 to palm off.

篆⁴ **A form of Chinese writing commonly known as the *seal***
1438 **character, on account of its use for that purpose. A seal of office; to style or name.**

篆 刻 to engrave seal characters.
篆 文 the seal character; ornamental writing.
篆 章 a seal.
篆 額 heading in seal-character, on a stone, etc.
接 篆 to take over the seals of office.

CH'UAN.　(ㄔㄨㄢ)

川
巛¹ **Streams. To flow. To travel. The province of Szechwan. Radical 47.**
1439

川 土 opium from Szechwan.
川 資 or 盤·川 or 盤·纏 travelling expenses.
川 流 不 息 uninterrupted flow; continually going on.
川 澤 marshes.
川 綢 silks from Szechwan.
川 邊 the province west of Szechwan.
山 川 hills and streams—the country.
平 川 大 路 a level road.
百 川 會 於 海 all streams meet in the sea.

釧⁴ **An armlet, a bracelet.**
1440

釧 簪 or 釵 釧 women's ornaments.

舛³ **To oppose, contrary to. Radical 136.**
1441

舛 午 or 乖 舛 opposing; perverse; disobedient.

舛 謬 to deceive purposely.
舛 錯 or 舛 愕 error; erroneous; in disorder.
舛 雜 contradictory; confused.
舛 駁 contradictory.
前 後 之 舛 discrepancy.

穿¹ **To wear.**
1442

穿·上 衣·服 to put on clothing.
穿·不·上 unable to wear it.
穿 孝 to wear mourning.
穿 戴 to wear; apparel.
穿 紅 掛 綠 to be gaily dressed.
穿 衣 to wear clothing.
穿 鞋 to wear shoes.

(a) **To thread; to bore.**

穿 井 to dig a well.
穿 入 to enter; to have the run of.
穿 出 to go through; to penetrate.
穿 山 甲 scaly ant-eater; tricky.
⁵穿 心 to go through the heart of.
穿 往 to come and go; intimacy; to have relations with.
穿 房 使·喚 a domestic; a messenger.
穿 換 dealings; intercourse.
穿 楊 to shoot an arrow through a willow leaf—good marksmanship.
¹⁰穿 珠 to string beads or pearls.
穿 窬 to bore through, as a thief through a wall.
穿 耳 to pierce the ears.
穿 通 to penetrate, to go through.
穿 透 to penetrate.
¹⁵穿·過·去 to thread through.
穿 針 or 級 針 or 引 針 to thread a needle.
穿 鑿 to bore through.
穿 鑿 道 理 to bore through principles—to act contrary to all reason.
穿 鼻 to bore the nose, as of cattle.

喘³ **To pant; asthmatic breathing.**
1443

喘 吷 to cough; wheezy.
喘 喘 氣 to rest and take a breath.
喘 嗽 to cough.
喘·定·了 or 喘·息·了 the fit of asthma is over.
⁵喘 息 asthma.
喘 氣 to pant for want of breath.

喘 逆 hiccough; shortwindedness.
殘 喘 difficulties of breathing, as
in old age.
痠 喘 asthma.

遄[2] To hurry. To go to and fro.
1444

遄 往 or 遄 行 to go quickly.
遄 征 to hasten forward on a
punitive expedition.

串[4] To string together; to connect; to league. Cash strings.
1445

串 供 collusion between witnesses.
串 合 in connection; joined.
串 同 作 弊 leagued for evil purposes.
串 客 to play marionettes—used
of one who is a "passenger,"
one who does not take his fair
share of responsibility.
[5]串 戲 to act a part in a play.
串 炮 a string of fire-crackers.
串 珠 a string of pearls; reference
book; marginal references.
串 票 receipt for land-taxes.
串 計 or 串 謀 to swindle; to combine.
[10]串 貫 or 貫 串 to string, as beads,
etc.
串 通 to band together; to conspire.
串 通 詐 欺 associated for blackmail, etc.
串 錢 to string cash.
串 門 子 to visit; to gossip from
door to door.
[15]串 騙 or 串 吞 to swindle; to combine for such a purpose.
一 串 珍 珠 a string or rope of
pearls.

傳[2] To propagate; to preach. Distinguish 傳 No. 1948.
1446

傳 世 to make known to mankind.
See below. A.2.
傳 單 hand-bills; circulars; notices.
傳 宣 to herald; to proclaim.
傳 布 to propagate.
[5]傳 布 團 propagandists.
傳 教 to preach religion.
傳 旨 to promulgate imperial decrees.

傳 法 or 傳 燈 to preach Buddhism.
傳 福 音 to preach the gospel.
[10]傳 道 to preach; to propagate doctrines.
傳 遍 to preach everywhere.

(a) To hand down; to perpetuate.

傳 下 來 to hand down; to bequeath.
傳 代 or 傳 世 handed on from
age to age. *See above.*—1.
傳 位 to transmit the throne.
傳 名 to hand down one's name;
to publish the fame of another;
to make famous.
[5]傳 國 璽 the imperial seal.
傳 子 to transmit from father to
son, as a monarchy, etc.
傳 家 handed down in the family.
傳 家 寶 heirloom.
傳 真 or 傳 神 a life-like portrait.
[10]傳 種 to propagate species.
傳 統 traditions; traditional.
傳 衍 to hand down.
傳 衣 garments passed on to a
novice by Buddhist priest; to
hand down a craft.
傳 襲 的 模 式 traditional forms,
as of art, etc.
[15]可 傳 worthy of being perpetuated.
歷 代 相 傳 handed down from
generation to generation.
祖 傳 hereditary.
祕 傳 secretly handed down—as a
prescription.
遺 傳 heredity.

(b) To summon; to transmit verbally; to interpret.

傳 他 來 order him to come.
傳 令 to issue orders; to summon.
傳 命 to make known a mandate;
to report orders.
傳 供 an interpreter who acts between the magistrate and the
principals in a case.
[5]傳 信 to send word.
傳 信 鴿 a carrier pigeon.
傳 喚 to summon.
傳 奇 a story-book, a drama.
傳 審 to summon for trial.
[10]傳 情 to give a hint.
傳 戒 to summon novices for initiation into Buddhist priesthood.
傳 授 to teach; to deliver to.
傳 案 to summon to a hearing.
傳 知 to notify.

[15]傳 示 to give notice; to send word.
傳 票 a summons.
傳 言 to send verbal messages;
hearsay.
傳 話 to transmit an order or information.
傳 諭 to give instructions through
another.
[20]傳 證 to summon witnesses.
傳 達 to carry messages.
傳 遞 消 息 to pass on a message.
傳 集 人 等 summon all the parties to the case.

(c) To spread, as a rumour or a disease. To conduct, as heat or electricity.

傳 導 to conduct.
傳 導 體 conductors, as of heat
etc.
傳 播 謠 言 to spread rumours.
傳 散 to spread, as a disease, etc.
[5]傳 揚 to spread far and wide.
傳 染 infectious; to infect.
傳 染 病 infectious disease.
傳 流 to spread by telling.
傳 熱 to radiate heat.
[10]傳 聞 hearsay.
傳 聲 to conduct sound.
傳 說 to spread a rumour; to tell
to another; tradition.
傳 述 to spread by telling.
傳 開 to spread.

(d) To send.

傳 飯 to send dinners from a restaurant.

(e) Read *chuan*[4]. A record, a chronicle.

傳 注 commentaries.
列 傳 biographies.
古 傳 ancient records.
外 傳 unauthorized biographies.
家 傳 family records.

船[2] A boat, a canoe, a junk, ship.
1447

船 主 or 船 老 板 captain of
boat.
船 務 shipping business.
船 務 執 事 shipping clerk.
船 匠 or 造 船 師 boatbuilder.
[5]船 員 the crew of a vessel. (*legal*
船 夫 or 船 戶 sailors, boatmen,
crew.
船 家 the crew of a vessel.

船尾 or 船梢 the stern of a vessel.
船廠 a dockyard.
10船房 cabins on a ship.
船捐 boat tax.
船旁梯 gangway-ladder.
船東 owner of a boat.
船桅 a mast.
15船業主 shipowners.
船步 or 船埠 or 船渠 port of call.
船澳 or 船塢 a dock.
船照 ship's certificate of registration.
船牌 boat register or license.
20船票 passage tickets; shipping-orders.
船篷 sails, the mat-covering of small boats.
船籍港 port of registry.
船經紀 ship-broker.
船脚 freight.
25船舵 the rudder.
船舶保險憑單 insurance policy of a ship.
船舶註冊簿 shipping register.
船艙 the hold; cabins.
船行 a shipping-office, boat-agency.(-hang²)
30船課 native boat tonnage dues.
船費 or 船價 passage money.
船身 the hull of a vessel.
船鈔 tonnage dues; port charges.
船鈔執照 tonnage dues certificate.
35船長³ master of a ship.
船長³收貨憑單 ship's receipt for cargo, etc., received.
船隻 vessels; boats; shipping.
船隻牌照 or 船冊 a ship's papers.
船面 or 船板 the deck of a vessel. Also called 甲板.
40船頭 the prow of a boat.
船骨 the keel.
上船 to go on board. 「junk.
下船 to go on shore; to go on a
兵船 war vessels.
45夾板船 a sailing ship.
巡船 revenue cruisers.
雇船 to charter a boat.
拖船 towboats; a tug.
明輪船 a paddle-steamer.
50暗輪船 screw-steamer.
汽船 or 輪船 steamships.
浮橋船 pontoon bridge.
浮駁船 a pontoon.
花船 floating brothels.
55駁船 a lighter.

椽² A beam, rafters. Houses.
1448
椽·子 rafters.

篡⁴ To rebel against a sovereign; to usurp the throne.
1449
篡位 to usurp the throne.
篡弒 to rebel and murder the ruler.
篡漢稱帝 rebelled against the *Han* dynasty and proclaimed himself emperor.
篡逆 or 篡賊 to plot and rebel.

CHUANG.   (ㄓㄨㄤ)

庄¹ A cottage. A farm. A workshop. A store, a house.
1450 A place of business, a warehouse. A hamlet or village. Inter. 莊 No. 1454. which is the correct form.
庄口 a business firm.
庄·子 a village; a farmstead; a restaurant.
庄田 a farmstead.
庄稼 farming operations; growing crops.
庄稼漢 or 庄戶 farmers, peasants.
庄總 head of a village.
布庄 piece-goods merchants.

妝)
粧) ¹ To adorn oneself. To disguise, to pretend.
1451
妝修 to adorn; to dress up.
妝假 or 妝·出·來·的 to act a part; to pretend.
妝匣 lady's dressing-case.
妝奩 or 嫁妝 or 妝資 bride's trousseau; marriage portion.
5妝·扮 costume; to decorate; to dress.
妝模作樣 to pretend; to play a part.
妝次 or 妝臺 or 梳妝 your ladyship.
妝病 to malinger.
妝腔 to affect; falsetto voice.
10妝飾 to adorn, to ornament; to gloss, to pretend.
素妝 not painted; plainly dressed.

狀⁴ Form, appearance, shape.
1452
狀·況 circumstances; state of affairs.
狀仁之體 to sketch the appearance of virtue.
狀·元 or 狀頭 highest graduate of the *Hanlin* Academy.
狀·元紅 a rich red; *lichee* fruit; good wine.
5狀如 as if; like.
狀式 appearance.
狀態 bearing; mien.
狀貌 manner; style.
狀貌非常 unusually engaging; a captivating manner.
10不可名狀 cannot be described.
形狀 form or outline.
情狀 circumstances; aspects of a matter.
毫無善狀 I have no good features at all—a conventional phrase.
無狀 rude behaviour.
15體狀 the form or shape of.

(a) To state, to accuse. An accusation.
狀·子 or 狀詞 a written accusation or charge.
狀棍 a pettifogger; one who lives by getting up lawsuits.
狀紙 official form for filing a plaint.
具狀 to draw up a plaint.
告狀 to file a plaint.

壯⁴ Stout, strong, able-bodied, healthy. Fertile, flourishing.
1453
壯丁 an able-bodied man; an adult, subject to military service.
壯·他·的膽 to strengthen his courage.
壯勇 volunteers; irregular troops.
壯士 a strong soldier; a good fellow.
5壯大 lusty; strong.
壯年 manhood, in the prime of life.
壯志 or 壯心 firmness; resolution; determination.
壯旺 vigorous; flourishing.
壯盛 or 壯健 healthy; hearty.
10壯麗 grand and imposing, as a building.
少壯 strong young man.

莊[1] Sedate, serious, grave. Correct in conduct.
1454

莊 以 涖 之 to govern with dignity.
莊 嚴 grave and stern; of ornament—splendid, imposing.
莊 子[3] or 莊 周 *Chuangtsŭ*, a famous Taoist philosopher and writer who lived *circa* B.C. 300.
莊 容 grave and sober mien.
[5]莊 誠 grave and earnest.
莊 語 serious talk.
莊 重 or 莊 敬 serious and respectful; grave and reverent.
端 莊 proper and correct in deportment, etc.

(a) u.f. 妝 No. 1451. To adorn, to dress up.

莊 整 dressed in the height of fashion.
漢 莊 Chinese. dress.
色 莊 pretended; hypocritical.

(b) Correct form of 庄 No. 1450. A village or farm; place of business, etc.

莊 票 cash notes of a local bank.
莊·稼 growing crops.
坐 莊 branch establishment.·
票 莊 bank that deals in drafts and exchange bills only.
義 莊 a free cemetery.
錢 莊 an exchange shop, local bank.　「in *majong*.
↑ 做 莊 the first player in a game, as

裝[1] To fill up, to load or pack.
1455

裝·不 下 cannot hold any more.
裝·口·袋 to fill a sack or bag.
裝 房 a store-room.
裝 整 to put in order; to furnish.
[5]裝 滿 to fill full; packed full.
裝 箱 to pack a box.
裝 置 to instal.
裝 置 無 線 電 to instal wireless.
裝 置 電 話 to instal the telephone.
[10]裝 船 to load a ship or boat.
裝 船 下 貨 單 shipping-order.
裝 船 代 理 人 shipping-agent.
裝 船 費 shipping-expenses.
便 即 裝 船 ship by earliest opportunity.
[15]裝 貨 shipment.

裝 貨 准 單 shipping-permit.
裝 車 to load a cart.
裝 載 to load.
裝 運 to load and transport.
[20]裝 釘 to bind a book; binding.
裝 鎗 to load a gun.
裝 電 燈 to instal electric light.
裝 齊·了 all loaded.
行 裝 baggage.

(a) To pretend, to dress. Inter. 妝 No. 1451.

裝 作 to feign to be; to pretend.
裝 作 好 人 hypocrite. ＝偽 君 子
裝 佯 to feign ignorance.
裝 修 external woodwork; fittings.
[5]裝 傻 pretend to be a fool.
裝 像 to imitate cries of birds, etc.
裝 幌·子 to counterfeit a trademark or sign; to wear the badge of a calling.
裝·扮 to dress up; to disguise.
裝·扮 華 美 elegantly dressed.
[10]裝 束 to dress up; style of dress.
裝 模 作 樣 affectation; to assume airs.
裝 殮 to prepare a corpse for burial.
裝°潢 to dye paper; to deck or ornament.　　「鐵 甲 車
裝 甲 列 車 armoured train. A.c.
[15]裝 甲 汽 車 armoured car.
裝 甲 艦 armoured vessel.
裝 睡 pretending to be asleep.
裝 神 像 to dress up idols.
裝 胖 pretence to having wealth.
[20]裝 腔 to assume; specious; to sing in a falsetto voice.
裝 腔 作 勢 to pretend unwillingness; affected coyness.
裝 裱 to mount scrolls, maps, etc.
裝 門 面 pretentious.
裝 頭 a style; a sort; a pattern.
[25]裝 頭 賣 面 to put the best goods on top.
裝·飾 dressed up; got up; ornamented.
裝·飾 品 fittings; decorative fittings; ornaments.
裝 點 to dress up a statement; to falsify, as accounts.
西 裝 or 洋 裝 foreign style of dress.
[30]開 裝 ordinary, everyday dress.

撞[4] To knock against; to strike accidentally; to collide.
1456

撞 倒 to knock or push over; to upset.
撞 口 卦 to hear words of ill-omen.
撞 壞 damage in collision.
撞 沉 to sink a boat in collision.
[5]撞 石 stone breaking or crushing.
撞 破 to break by collision.
撞 碰 to come into collision with.
撞·着 or 相 撞 to meet; to run against another. (--*chao*)
撞·着 和·尚 to meet a priest—a bad omen. (--*chao*)
[10]撞·見 or 撞 遇 to meet unexpectedly.
撞 鐘 to strike the bell—a game played by boys, striking cash against a wall.
撞 門 to knock or push at a door.
撞 開 to burst open.
撞 額 to bump foreheads—face to face, confidential talk.
[15]撞 鬼 to meet a demon—to get a fright.

椿[1] A post. A stake or stick. A beacon or buoy. To strike.
1457 N.A. Distinguish 椿 No. 1494.

椿·子 a stake, a pile.
一 椿 事 an affair.
打 椿 to drive stakes or piles.
打 椿 機 pile-driver.
拔 椿 to pull up the stakes—to give it up as a bad job; to retire from the matter.
拴 牛 椿 stake or post to tether an ox to.

戇[4] Simple, stupid.
1458

戇 拙 simple.
愚 戇 idiotic.
詐 戇 to feign stupidity.

CH'UANG.　　(彳ㄨㄤ)

牀|床[2] A couch or bed. A board or framework on which things rest.
1459

牀·上 on a bed or a couch.
牀 席 the matting of a bed.
(牀)帳·子 bed-curtains.
牀 榻 a bed; a couch.
[5]牀 褥·子 a mattress.

牀 鋪 bed and bedding.
一 牀 被 one quilt or coverlet.
上 牀 下 牀 to get into or out of bed.
停 牀 a death-bed to which dying people are generally moved.
10 東 牀 a son-in-law.
欓 牀 a litter.
牙 牀 the jawbone.
籐 牀 a cane-bed.

淙² Noise of water. Also read tsung².
1460

淙 淙 the roaring of a river.
淙 琤 tinkling of gems.
雨 淙 淙 pattering of falling rain.

窗 牎 窻 ¹
A window, a shutter.
1461

窗 下 under the window—studying.
窗 友 or 同 窗 fellow-students.
窗 戶 a window.
窗 押 bar to close a window.
5 窗 搭 or 雨 搭 a projecting shade over a window to keep off rain or glare.
窗 框 window-frame.
窗 臺 or 窗 檻 window-sill.
窗 課 study.
天 窗 a skylight.
10 寒 窗 a cold window—a poor student.
氣 窗 a transom.
百 葉 窗 Venetian shutters.
紗 窗 gauze-covered windows.
紙 窗 paper windows.

創 鎗 ⁴
To create, to make. To invent. To begin.
1462

創 世 以 來 from the creation until the present.
創 世 記 The Book of Genesis.
創 事 業 or 創 業 to found a family, estate or business. See below.　　　［artistic work.
創 作 to create or originate; lit. or

5 創 作 之 才 talent for originality.
創 作 家 originators; creative writers.
創 作·的 or 創 造·的 creator; creative.
創 動 initiative.
創 化 creative evolution.
10 創 國 基 to found a dynasty.
創 基 to lay the foundation.
創 始 to begin; to initiate; at the beginning; originality.
　事 屬 創 始 the matter was in its initial stages.
創 始 才 originality.
15 創·得 狠 好 to get on well; thriving.
創 意 original thought.
創 業 垂 統 to found and hand down an inheritance.
創 獲 to discover.
創 立 or 創 開 to found; to begin; to inaugurate.
20 創 立 會 first general meeting of a limited-liability c o m p a n y. (legal).
創 藝 精 緻 a clever contrivance.
創 見 to see for the first time.
創 設 or 創 辦 to establish; to found; to inaugurate.
創 論 to propound a theory.
25 創 造 or 創 修 to create; to invent.
創 造 哲 學 creative philosophy.
創 造 天 地 creation of heaven and earth.
創 造 想 像 creative imagination.
創 造·的 思 想 creative thought.

(a) Read ch'uang¹. To wound. To cut. To punish.

創 劇 to be very ill.
創 口 a wound, a sore.
創 巨 痛 深 sorely wounded and in great pain—in deep distress.
創 痍 injury; used also fig., deep distress.
5 懲 創 to reprove; to punish.
身 被 七 十 創 he received seventy wounds.
金 創 wounded by edged weapons.

瘡 ¹
A sore, a boil, an ulcer.
1463

瘡 口 the opening of a sore.
瘡 疤 or 瘡 瘢 a scab or scar.
瘡 症 ulcers, boils or sores.
瘡 痍 sores, ulcers; also fig., calamity, distress; sorrow and pain.

5 瘡 痍 滿 目 the wounded meet the eye everywhere—distress and suffering are seen on every side.
牛 瘡 to have a boil.
瘡 瘭 a running sore.
瘡 瘤 a rash; a swelling.
割 瘡 to lance a boil.
10 對 口 瘡 dangerous carbuncle on the back of the neck.
惡 瘡 malignant boils.
漏 瘡 a fistula.

幢 ⁴ A curtain for a carriage, to screen from the sun.
1464
　　Read ch'uang². A pennant or streamer; streamers from the roof of a temple.

幢 幡 pendant streamers of silk hung before a shrine.
幢 牙 a pennant.
幢 節 proof of identity given to a messenger, a sort of tally in two pieces.
幢 隊 standard bearers of an army.

(a) Read t'ung². To screen.

幢 幢 flickering like lightning; waving like feathers.
焰 影 幢 幢 the flickering shadows of the flame.

闖 ³,⁴ To rush in suddenly. Rudely; suddenly.
1465

闖 下 山 崖 rush down the precipice.
闖 亮·的 or 闖 將·的 a thief who rushes in at daylight as soon as the door is opened.
闖 入 or 闖·進·來 to burst in.
闖 出 頭 to obtrude oneself.
闖 禍 to rush into calamity.
闖 轅 門 to force a way into a yamen.
闖 關 to evade the customs.

CHUI. (ㄔㄨㄟ)

隹 ¹ Short-tailed birds. Radical 172. Distinguish 佳 No. 593.
1466 Also read tsui¹. u.f. 崔 No. 6864. High and precipitous, (some give it as the blowing of the wind).

山林之畏佳 the forest nestles in the secluded nook of the hills—(畏 u.f. 偎) also explained as:—the mountain forest fears the gale.

錐[1] An awl, a sharp-pointed tool. The tip. To bore, to 1467 pierce. A trifle.

錐刀之末 the tip of an awl—a trifle.

錐刺股 piercing the thigh with an awl—to keep awake for study.

錐子 an awl.

錐孔 or 錐眼兒 to bore a hole.

[5]錐指 to point with an awl—a very small outlook.

錐捺底 to stitch shoe-soles.

錐處囊中 an awl in a bag—it will soon find its way out; fig., genius cannot be hid.

錐銛 pointed and sharp.

錐鑽不動 the awl will not pierce it.

[10]毛錐 an awl of hair—Chinese pencil.

無立錐之地 not even enough ground in which to stick an awl—desperately poor.

釘錐 a bradawl.

騅[1] A piebald horse.
1468

追[1] To follow, to pursue, to 1469 overtake. To escort, to go back.

追不到 unable to overtake.

追他回來 run and call him back.

追兵 soldiers in pursuit.

追到 or 追及 to catch up with.

[5]追及權 right of pursuit. (legal).

追回 to follow and bring back.

追奔逐北 to pursue a routed army.

追捕 or 追拿 to pursue and apprehend.

追歡 to pursue pleasure.

[10]追王 to carry back the designation of king.

追贓 to recover stolen booty.

追趕 to chase; to try and overtake.

追踪 to follow a trail or clue.

追蹤 to follow in the steps of those who have gone before.

[15]追遠 to follow ancestors, when long gone, with the proper sacrifices.

追陪 to follow in company.

追隨 to follow; to pursue.

追風逐電 to chase the wind and pursue the lightning—of speedy horses.

不可追 irrecoverable.

(a) To trace out, to follow to its source; to seek for.

追原 to seek out the cause.

追原禍首 to seek for the chief causes of a misfortune.

追問 to examine into a matter with thoroughness; to examine with severity.

追尋 to inquire into; to follow out and seek after.

[5]追情問事 to investigate the circumstances of a matter.

追本溯源 to investigate the origins; to go into a matter with thoroughness. [run after.

追求 to go into thoroughly; to

追求賕私 to seek for bribes.

追溯 to trace the origins of; to recall.

[10]追究 to search into; to investigate

追認 to ratify; ratification. (legal).

追認條約 ratification of a treaty.

追非 to lay blame elsewhere.

(b) To reflect upon; to look back upon; retrospective.

追傷 grieved by memories of a lost friend, past joy, etc.

追加 to add to afterwards; supplementary.

追加條件 additional clauses.

追加費 additional expenses.

[5]追加預算 additional or supplementary budget or estimates.

追封 to seek posthumous honours for.

追念 to reflect upon; to think over.

追思往日 to recall bygone days.

追悔 to feel remorse.

[10]追悔莫及 too late for regrets now.

追悼會 a memorial service.

追想 to reflect upon the past; retrospective musings.

追謚 to canonize.

(c) To press for payment; to extort, to annoy.

追債 or 追討 to dun for debt.

追奪擔保 eviction. (legal).

追比 to bring pressure to bear.

追索 to make forcible demands for payment.

追逼 to press; to annoy.

追還 or 追償 or 追出 to recover—as debts.

(d) Read tui[1]. To engrave.

追琢其章 to engrave ornaments

(e) Read t'ui[1]. Knob of a bell.

追蠡 the knob of the bell is nearly worn through (by handling).

縋[4] A cord. To let down.
1470

縋下來 let it down.

縋城 to let down over a city wall.

夜縋而出 he was let down at night and got out of (the city).

墜[4] To fall down; to sink.
1471

墜下 or 墜落 to fall down.

墜地 to fall down; to collapse. *

墜子 pendant eardrops; folk-songs

墜底 to sink to the bottom.

墜星 a meteor.

墜胎 a miscarriage; prolapsus.

墜跌 to topple over.

墜馬 to fall off a horse.

墜體 a falling body.

贅[4] To repeat; to connect. Tautology, repetition, iteration; irrelevant.
1472

贅瀆 to importune.

贅筆 or 贅及 or 贅叙 to add a postscript.

贅語 or 贅言 reiteration; verbose.

贅述 to make repeated reference to.

多贅 repetition to a tiresome extent.

*of Honan.

累·贅 vexing; troublesome; verbose.

(a) Useless; an excrescence; a parasite.

贅 壻 a son-in-law who lives in the family.
　入 贅 to enter the wife's family.
　招 贅 to have a daughter married to a husband who comes to live in her family.
贅 物 an excrescence.
贅 疣 or 贅 瘤 a wen, tumour, excrescence—fig., unimportant matters.

惴 4
1473
Mournful, sad.

惴 惴 其 慄 terrified; scared.
惴 慄 anxious and tremblingly afraid.
惴 懼 anxious, worried.

硾 4
1474
To press down. To weight.

千 斤 硾 heavy weight for pressing.
秤 硾 weight on a steel-yard.

綴 4·
1475
To baste together.

綴 衣 an imperial pavilion; keeper of the imperial wardrobe.
補 綴 to mend a garment.

(a) To connect; to continue.

綴 之 以 祀 connect them by sacrifices.
綴 宅 the body.
綴 文 to narrate, to make a narrative.
綴 旒 pendants on banners—fig., connected with, dependent on, a figure-head with no power.
爲 下 國 綴 旒 he was merely a dependent of the nobles; another version gives—the nobles of the states were dependent upon him.
綴 法 composition; putting characters together into sentences.
綴 綴 然 connected; intimate; friendly.

綴 輯 to collect together.
綴 錄 前 報 continued from the last number.
點 綴 to add detail—as to a picture; accessories; to adorn.
點 綴 結 搆 to lay out—as a park or gardens.

(b) To mix; variegated.

綴 純 variegated borders for the mats.

(c) Read cho⁴·⁵. To stop, to cause to cease.

禮 者 所 以 綴 淫 也 propriety is that which causes lewdness to cease.

CH'UI. (ꮯ)

吹
歈
1476
To blow; to breathe; to puff; to praise.

吹 一 口 氣 to breathe upon.
吹 乾 dried up by the wind; to blow a thing dry.
吹 倒 blown down.
吹 吹 打 打 clang of musical instruments—rejoicing.
⁵吹 哨·子 to whistle; whistling.
吹°嘘 to recommend; to say a good word for; to encourage by a word.
吹 壞 blown to tatters by the wind.
吹 獎 to flatter.
吹 張 肉 to blow water into-meat.
¹⁰吹 彈 wind and strings—musical instruments.
吹 彈 歌 舞 to make merry.
吹 手 muscians.
吹 打 to blow and to beat—music.
吹 散 scattered by wind.
¹⁵吹 毛 求 疵 to blow aside the fur to seek for faults—to go out of the way to discover weak points.
吹 氣 to blow a steam whistle; to blow off.
吹 水 to blow water into meat: to brag.
吹 滅 to extinguish; to blow out.
吹 火 to blow a fire.
²⁰吹 灰 very easy.
吹 灰 之 力 (as easy as) blowing dust away.

吹 熄 to blow out—a lamp or candle.
吹 燈 or 滅 燈 to blow out a lamp.吹 牛 吹 牛 皮 euphemism for *
吹 牛 角 to blow a horn—to boast.
²⁵吹 玻·璃 to blow glass.
吹 笙 to play the Chinese reed mouth-organ.
吹 笛 to play the flute.
吹 管 a blow-pipe.
吹 簫 to play the Chinese flageolet.
³⁰吹 脹 to inflate.
吹 葫·蘆 to blow a gourd—to brag; to vociferate.
吹 號 to blow a bugle or signal-horn.
吹 角 to blow a horn.
吹°起 to blow into the air; to raise by blowing; to stir up.
³⁵吹°開 to blow open—as a door.
吹 響 to sound by blowing.
過 事 吹 求 to take up old grievances.
風 吹 日 曬 exposed to the weather.
鼓 吹 to incite; to stir up to action. See below. A.2.

(a) Read ch'ui⁴. The wind; sound of music.

吹 唱 playing and singing.
鼓 吹 drums and pipes.—music. See above,—39.

炊 1
1477
To dress food. To steam. Inter. preceding.

炊 桂 to dress food by burning cassia-wood—firing very scarce.
炊 沙 作 飯 to cook sand for food —labour in vain.
炊 煮 cooking—boiling tea and making food.
炊 爨 to prepare food.
炊 飯 to steam rice.
先 炊 my late mother.

垂
埀
1478
To hang down; to let fall; to hand down.

垂·下·來 hanging down.
垂 低 to hang down.
垂 危 in imminent danger.
垂 垂 gradually.
⁵垂 戒 to hand down—as a warning.

* 吹 牛 尻 to boast.

垂 手 to hang the hands in respect.

垂 手 而 得 to drop the hands and get it—to acquire a thing easily.

垂 拱 而 天 下 治 they let fall their robes and the empire was governed.

垂 暮 towards evening—old age coming on.

[10]垂 楊 柳 weeping willow.

垂 法 an example handed down from the past.

垂 法 於 後 to set an example for posterity.

垂 涎 the mouth watering with desire.

垂 淚 to weep with tears.

[15]垂 烟 overhanging—as smoke, or a willow-branch, etc.

垂 示 to hand down for information of posterity.

垂 目 to cast the eyes down.

垂 直 perpendicular.

垂 直 線 a perpendicular line.

[20]垂 眉 falling eyebrows—approaching death.

垂 簾 聽 政 to let fall the screen and listen to politics—of an empress-dowager.

垂 系 to reach as far as . . . .

垂 絕 about to die.

垂 統 to carry on the imperial throne to the next generation.

[25]垂 線 perpendicular (noun).

垂 線·的 perpendicular (adj.).

垂 綸 to angle for fish.

垂 老 old age approaching.

垂 花 門 the second gate before entering the inner gates of a *yamen*.

[30]垂 語 to hand down information.

垂 釣 to fish with a hook and line.

垂 面 vertical plane.

垂 頭 to hang the head.

垂 頭 喪 氣 crestfallen.

[35]垂 髫 hanging tufts of hair—young children.

名 垂 後 世 to hand down a name to posterity.

家 纍 千 金 坐 不 垂 堂 one whose life is highly valued does not sit near the steps of the hall—where a tile might fall from the eaves and endanger his life.

(a) **To condescend; to be favour-able to.**

垂 告 to condescend to inform.

垂 念 to have gracious thoughts towards.

垂 情 or 垂 恩 to have pity; to feel for; condescension.

垂 憐 your kindly compassion.

[5]垂 照 to look down from heaven.

垂 聽 to deign to listen.

垂 訓 to condescend to instruct.

垂 詢 to make gracious inquiries.

垂 顧 or 垂 愛 to regard with kindness.

[10]垂 青 to cast a favourable glance upon.

天 垂 雨 露 Heaven sends down the rain and the dew.

捶 [3] **To beat; to thrash. Inter. 搥 No. 1483.**
1479

捶 扑 to beat a criminal.

捶 鉤 the bit of a bridle.

(a) Read *to*[3]. **Luxuriant growth.**

箠 [3] **To flog. A whip. Twigs of bamboo.**
1480

箠 策 a horse-whip.

箠 罵 to flog and curse.

笞 箠 to flog a criminal.

鞭 箠 to flog with a whip.

陲 [2] **A frontier; a boundary.**
1481

陲 命 despatches from the frontier.

邊 陲 the frontier.

錘 [2] **Ancient weight of 12 Chin-ese ounces. The weight on a steelyard.**
1482

秤 錘 the weight on a steelyard.

(a) Read *chui*[1]. **To hammer.**

錘 煉 to hammer—as wrought iron.

搥 [2] **To beat; to pound. To shampoo. To throw. Inter.**
1483 捶 No. 1479. **Also read** *chui*[1].

搥 打 一 頓 give him a pommel-ling.

搥 提 仁 義 to discard love and duty.

搥 楚 to give a severe beating.

搥 牀 大 怒 she thumped the bed in a great rage.

[5]搥 石 to cast stones.

搥 背 to massage the back — by pounding.

搥 胸 頓 足 to beat the breast and stamp—in anger.

搥 金 箔 to beat gold-leaf.

搥 鐘 to strike a bell.

[10]搥 魯 stupid.

搥 鼓 to beat a drum.

槌
椎 [2] **A mallet; a bludgeon. To strike. A rammer.**
1484

槌·子 a pestle.

槌 魯 stupid.

槌 鼓 to beat a drum.

打 椿 槌 a pile-driver.

研 槌 a rammer.

鼓 槌 a drumstick.

鎚 [2] **A hammer; a mallet; a club. To hammer; to pound.**
1485

鎚 鑿 to hammer and chisel.

CHUN.   (㞷)

(Chuen)

准 [3] **To grant, to permit, to allow, to authorize.**
1486 **Inter. 準 No. 1488.**

准 令 or 准 為 or 准 與 to allow.

准 以 十 日 to get permission for ten days.

准 信 to rely upon; a certain, de-finite promise. 准 假 [4] to grant lea

准 備 to prepare; completed.

[5]准 入 to admit.

准 單 a customs' permit.

夜 間 准 單 a night-permit.

特 發 准 單 special permit.

長 期 准 單 a standing permit.

[10]准 奏 his memorial is granted.

准 情 面 to show partiality or favour.

准 期 to set a day.

准 狀 to allow a plaint to be filed.

准 禱 告 to grant a prayer.

[15]准 行 or 准 許 to sanction; to permit.

不 准 not granted—when a plaint is summarily rejected.

允 准 to grant; to permit; to allow.
批 准 to allow a plaint to go through; to ratify.

(a) To acknowledge receipt of a communication.

准 文 to receive a despatch.
准 此 on receipt of the above—used between equals.

隼 / 鶽 [3]
1487

A hawk. Also read *shuen*[3].

隼 發 必 中 when the hawk swoops it always hits its mark.

準 [3]
1488

A water-level. To regulate; to adjust; to equalize. Exact; true. To weigh; to measure.

準·不·準 Is it accurate or not?—as a timepiece.
　較 準 表 to regulate a watch.
準 人 a magistrate.
準 備 to prepare; to get ready.
[5]準 備 書 狀 preparatory pleadings. (*legal*).
準 備 程 序 preparatory proceedings. (*legal*).
準 備 金 reserve fund.
準 則 or 準 規 a rule; a standard; a right way.
準 家 屬 legal member of a family.
[10]準 折 多 少 How much discount will you allow?
準 星 the sight of a gun.
準 時 刻 the proper time.
　時 刻 不 準 the time is not correct.
準 準·的 exactly; just the thing.
[15]準 率 (*lü*[4]) standard rate.
準 的 a standard or aim.
準 確 or 準 對 quite correct.
準 秤 adjusted scales.
準 程 a standard; the correct method.
[20]準 繩 a marking line; a rule of conduct; a plumb-line.
準 話 the truth.
描 準 to take aim.
標 準 a standard; basis of comparison; used as a prefix:—standard . . . .

(a) u.f. Quasi, in legal phraseology. Inter. 准 No. 1486.

準 佔 有 quasi-possession.
準 共 有 quasi-joint-possession.
準 契 約 quasi-contract.
準 犯 罪 quasi-offence.
準 禁 治 產 quasi-incompetent (person).

(b) Read *cho*[2.5]**. The nose.**

準 頭 the tip of the nose; accurate aim.
鼻 準 the end of the nose.
隆 準 a big nose.

肫 [1]
1489

Honest, sincere; earnest.

肫 篤 earnest perseverance.
肫 肫 其 仁 his benevolence was genuine.
肫 誠 trustworthy; earnest.

(a) The gizzard of a fowl.

(b) Read *shuen*[2]**. Meat dried for winter use. The cheek bones.**

諄 [1.4.]
1490

To reiterate; to impress upon; repeatedly.

諄 囑 to give specific injunctions.
諄 切 straitly; emphatically.
諄 憎 mutual hatred.
諄 懇 to beseech.
[5]諄 諄 repeatedly.
諄 諄 然 命 之 乎 did (Heaven) confer the appointment with repeated, specific injunctions?
諄 諄·的 求 雨 earnestly prayed for rain
誨 爾 諄 諄 I taught you with untiring diligence.

CH'UN.   (ㄔㄨㄣ)
See Nos. 5930-33.
(Ch'uen)

脣 / 唇 [2]
1491

The lips.

脣 乾 口 燥 lips dry and throat parched.
脣 亡 齒 寒 the lips being gone, the teeth are cold; used fig.,

when my outlying dependencies are taken, my central power is endangered.
脣 如 渥 丹 lips as if they had been smeared with vermilion.
↓脣 膏 lipstick. A.c. 口 紅.
[5]脣 紅 齒 白 rosy lips and pearly teeth—pretty.
脣 舌 lips and tongue—plausible speech, etc.
脣 齒 to compress the lips; intimately related, as lips and teeth.
脣 齒 之 邦 states that are mutually dependent.
脣 齒 相 依 mutually dependent.
[10]上 下 脣 upper and lower lips.
缺 脣 or 劙 脣·子 hare-lip.
點 脣 to use lipstick.

漘 [2]
1492

Marshes.

春 [1]
1493

Spring. Distinguish 舂 No. 1525.

春 假 spring vacation.
春 冰 thin ice—easily broken through, used of imminently dangerous places.
春 分 the vernal equinox.
春 困 the lassitude of spring.
[5]春·天 springtime.
春 夢 spring dreams—muddled ideas, visionary fancies.
春 忙 the busy days of spring.
春 景 spring landscape.
春 暉 the light of spring—parent's kindness.
[10]春 曉 a spring morning; early spring.
春 樹 暮 雲 spring trees and evening skies—from a poem by *Tu Fu* 杜 甫, on his friend *Li Po* 李 白. The reference is to their respective places of abode—the phrase is used to express longing for absent friends.
春 牛 a clay ox carried at the ceremony of welcoming the spring.
春 王 月 the first month of the lunar year.
春 社 spring festival in honour of the household-gods.
[15]春 祈 秋 報 to pray in the spring and offer thanks in the autumn—for crops.

春祭 spring sacrifices.

春秋 the only book attributed to Confucius—the *Spring and Autumn Annals* or the *Annals of the State of Lu* 魯 722—484. B.C. From this the term has been used for other annals, also for a year or an era.

春秋高 your years are many.

春秋鼎盛 the spring and autumn are in their prime—said of youth.

[20]春筍 or 春葱 in spring, bamboo shoots or onions are slender and delicate,—fig., lady's fingers.

春節 the new-year festival.

春聯 new-year mottoes written on scrolls of red paper and pasted on doors, etc.

春茶 spring tea—name of a class of tea-leaves.

春茗 spring tea—conventional phrase in invitations to new-year feasts.

[25]春華秋實 glorious flowers in spring and solid fruit in autumn—of a man whose talents in writing and whose disposition are above the average.

春蘭秋菊 spring epidendrum and autumn chrysanthemum—both excellent, but each in its season.

春蚓秋蛇 spring worms and autumn snakes—used of poor hand-writing.

春賽 spring idol-procession.

春酌 a new-year entertainment.

[30]春酒 wine made in spring and kept till winter.

春雨 or 春霖 spring rains.

春雨如膏 like the spring rains which have fertilised the soil—fig., your kindness is like, etc.

春露秋霜 spring dews and autumn frosts— favour and severity—also spring and autumn sacrifices.

春風 spring breezes—genial, as favours are. *See below*. B. 3. Also :—the spring breezes cause things to grow, thus the expression is used of culture and education of children, etc.

[35]新春 new-year.

立春 *Beginning of Spring*—a solar term, about February 6th to 20th.

迎春 the ceremony of welcoming spring;(the magistrate went out, performed certain rites, and the clay ox was broken up by the people;) it was held on the day before 立春.

迎春花 the yellow jessamine.

陽春 the tenth month of the lunar year.

(a) Wanton, lewd, lustful.

春工 or 春冊 or 春畫 or 春宮 obscene, lewd pictures.

春心 or 春意 or 春情 lewd thoughts, lustful desires.

春方 or 春藥 aphrodisiacs.

春期 puberty; mating season.

(b) Joyful, gay. Youthful.

春氣 ardour of youth; spring warmth.

春色 cheerful countenance; merry, as with wine.

春風 pleasant countenance or speech. *See above*,—34.

百病回春 able to bring back youth, no matter what the disease.

青春 youthful years.

椿 [1] A long-lived tree. A father. Distinguish 椿 No. 1457.
1494

椿堂 or 大椿 your father.

椿萱並茂 parents both well and flourishing.

臭·椿 *Ailantus*.

香·椿 *Cedrela odorata*.

香·椿(芽)buds of the last, used as a vegetable.

杶 [1] The wild varnish-tree. u.f. preceding.
1495

蠢 [3] Stupid, doltish. To wriggle.
1496

蠢動 wriggling like worms.
蠢·子 dolt!
蠢笨 or 蠢·才 or 蠢鈍 clumsy, awkward, foolish.

鶉 [2] The quail. Also read *shuen²*.
1497

鶉之奔奔 the rush of the quails to fight.

鶉衣百結 ragged clothes with many patches.

醇 [2] *See* 5933.
1497½ **CHUNG.** (ㄓㄨㄥ)
(Chong)

㣎
㣎 [1] Restless, agitated.
1498

征㣎 restless, nervous.

忪 [1] Agitated.
1499

終 [1] The end, finally. Death. The whole of. After all. Still, etc.
1500

終不悔改 never to be repented of.

終不可諼兮 we shall never forget him.

終久 after all; finally; in the end.

終其天年 reached the allotted span.

[5]終制 period of three years mourning for parents.

終南捷徑 taking advantage of seclusion to get preferment—a short cut.

終古 throughout antiquity; for a long time past.

終場 the final; the climax.

終夜 all night.

[10]終天抱恨 a lifelong sorrow—the death of parents.

終審 final trial.

終局 the outcome; the final; the end; conclusion; the result.

終須 absolutely necessary.

終必 in the end.

[15]終性難改 how hard it is to change the disposition!

終息 to expire.

終日 the whole day; every day.

終·是 in the end it was; although; still.

終期 expired term.

[20]終朝 the whole of the early morning.

終極 final.

終歸 in the end; finally.

終然不聽 he did not give the slightest heed.
終竟 finally; after all.
[25]終結 final summing up.
終譽 fame extending after death.
終身 or 終生 a lifetime; the end of life.
終身保險 insurance un er a life-policy.
終身大事 the great affair of a lifetime—marriage, of a woman.
[30]終非 by no means; is in no sense.
終食之間 during the space of a meal.
終養 to retire from office in order to care for parents.
終點 destination; terminus.
不知其終 ignorant of his final whereabouts. ⌊ful death.
[35]善終 a happy end; to die a peace-
壽終 to die in old age.
始終 beginning and ending—the whole course of an affair; to
年終 end of the year. ⌊the end.
從一而終 faithful to one husband to the last.
[40]臨終 near to the end—at death's door.
送終 to be present at the death-bed of ...

螽 [1] A long-headed green grasshopper.
1501

螽斯衍慶 May your children be as numerous as grasshoppers.
螽蟲 grasshoppers.

踵 [1] To stagger along; to fall.
1502

踵下水 to fall into water.

鐘 [1] A bell; a clock. Distinguish 鍾 No. 1514.
1503

鐘樓 a belfry; a clock tower.
鐘絃 a clock-spring.
鐘表 clocks and watches.
鐘表舖 watchmaker's shop.
[5]鐘頭 or 一點鐘 the hour; an hour.
　三個鐘頭 three hours.
　三點鐘 three o'clock.
鐘鳴漏盡 the bell ceases and the clepsydra has run out—old age.

鐘鼎文 ancient inscriptions on bronzes.
[10]坐鐘 a standing clock.
打木鐘 to strike a wooden bell—labour in vain.
木鐘 a wooden bell—useless, stupid.
自鳴鐘 a striking clock.
鬧鐘 alarm-clock.

中 [1] The middle. Among, within, in, between.
1504　　　　⌊day.
中上 or 中時 or 晌午(-huo) mid-
中世 or 中古 middle ages; mediæval.
中丞 earlier name for the governor of a province.
中人 or 中保 a middle-man; a go-between; mediator; a witness.
[5]中介物 or 媒介物 medium or vehicle.
中價 an average price.
中元 15th of the 1st month, lunar.
中古時代的 mediaeval.
中和 good, equable. Neutralize—(chem.).
[10]中堅 a strong centre, the main body of an army; essential.
中堅分子 an essential person.
中堂 a grand secretary of former days; a large picture or scroll for reception room.
中天 noon. ↑中士 sergeant.
中央 the centre; the heart of; the capital.
[15]中央上訴院 Central Court (Yüan) of Appeal.
中央制 central-government system.
中央命令 mandates of the central government.
中央政府 the central government.
中央政治委員會 Central Political Council.
[20]中央權限 limitation of the central authority.
中央的 central.
中央行政 the central administration.
中央觀象臺 central observatory.
中央銀行 The Central Bank.
[25]中央集權 centralization of authority.
中央點 central point; focus.
中學校 secondary school; middle school; high school.
↑中央研究院 Academia Sinica.

中宮 the empress.
中將 lieutenant-general; vice-admiral.
[30]中尉 lieutenant.
中平 fair; equable.
中年 middle age.
中庸 one of the "Four Books." "Doctrine of the Mean." Legge. "The Invariable Medium." Giles.
中心 fairminded; impartial; the centre.
[35]中心的 central; centrally.
中心點 the centre; the central point.
中性 neutral.
中性反應 neutral reaction. (chem.).
中懸 suspense.
[40]中才 mediocrity.
中指 or 將指 the middle finger.
中數 or 折中數 the average; an average.
中斷 interruption. (legal).
中旬 or 中浣 middle decade of a month.
[45]中校 lieutenant-colonel.
中樞 central point—the central administration.
神經中樞 nerve-centres.
中止 suspension; interruption. (legal).
中止判決 suspended judgement.
[50]中止訴訟 suspension or interruption of litigation.
中正 in the centre; upright.
中流 mediocre; average, of class, etc.
中流砥柱 the solitary rock in a turbulent stream—a loyal minister.
中嶽 the central one of the five sacred mountains—Mt. Sung in Honan.
[55]中產以下 the middle classes and below. ⌊bourgeoisie.
中產階級 the middle classes;
中秋 Mid-autumn festival. 15th of the 8th lunar month.
中立 neutrality.
中立國 neutral states.
[60]中立地 neutral territory.
中立地帶 or 中立區域 neutral zone.
↓中立法 law of neutrality.
中立性 neutral. (chem.).
中立感情 neutral feelings.
[65]中的 neutral.
中立政府 neutral government.
↑中央執行委員會 Central Executive Committee.

中立法權 neutral jurisdiction.
中立港 neutral ports.
中立線 neutral line.
[70]中立而不倚 to occupy a middle position without leaning to either side—neutral.
中立觀望 neutral onlooker.
中立黨 or 中立派 neutral party.
偏一中立 benevolent neutrality.
嚴守中立 strict neutrality.
[75]完全中立 complete neutrality.
宣告中立 to proclaim neutrality.
武裝中立 armed neutrality.
中端 the middle term. (*logic*).
中等 middle class; middling.
[80]中等人才 common, ordinary mediocre talents.
中等社會 the middle classes.
中綫 or 中線 the centre line.
中耳 the middle ear.
中膈 the diaphragm.
[85]中覺 midday siesta. (-*chiao*[4])
中證 or 中見 a witness.
中費 or 中用 brokerage; commission.
中軍 military secretary under a governor of a province in imperial days.
中輟 to give up halfway.
[90]中道 or 中途 halfway, incomplete, the middle path; the mean.
中道而歿 he died in the midst of his career.
中道而廢 to give up halfway; to be discouraged before accomplishing one's purpose.
中間[1] in the midst of; between; among.
中間[1]分配 internal distribution, as in bankruptcy.
[95]中間[1]判決 interlocutory judgement. (*legal*).
中飯 the midday meal.
中飽 to become rich in handling the affairs of others; to squeeze; to help oneself to pickings.
中饋 one who manages the home —a wife.
中點 central point; centre, mean point.
[100]個中人 an initiate.
內中 among them; in the midst.
失中 inclining too much to one side; to miss the happy medium.

適中 or 適之中庸 to strike the happy medium.

(a) China. Chinese.

中交兩行 The Bank of China and the Bank of Communications.
中俄談判 Sino-Russian negotiations.
中國 or 中華 or 中土 China. "The Middle Kingdom."
中國主權 China's sovereign rights.
[5]中國事務會社 The China Association.
中國化的 Chinafied; Sinicized. *See* No. 2211-51.
中原 or 中州 China; also Honan Province.
中國年報 The China Year Book.
中國文化 Chinese culture.
[10]中國海 The China Sea.
中國統治權 Sovereignty of China.
中國銀行 The Bank of China.
中國銀行團公會 Council of the China Consortium.
中外 or 中西 Chinese and foreigners; China and the Western Powers.
[15]中外互市 trade between China and foreign countries.
中外交涉 Chinese and foreign relations.
中外合股 Chinese and foreign shareholders.
中日交涉 Sino-Japanese relations.
中日的 Sino-Japanese.
[20]中日衝突 clash between China and Japan.
↑中日戰爭 Sino-Japanese War.
中英條約 Anglo-Chinese treaty.
中華民國 The Chinese Republic.
中華的 or 中國的 or 華 or 漢 Chinese.
[25]中華領土 Chinese territory.
中蘇 Sino-Russian.
中醫 Chinese doctor.

(b) Read *chung*[4]. **To hit the centre. To attain; to be affected by; to fancy; to fall into a trap.**

中不得 unattainable.

中了 a hit.
看中了 approved; taken a liking to.
中[1]吃的 good to eat.
[5]不中吃 unpalatable.
中寒 to catch a cold.
中[1]意 meets the wish; suitable; acceptable.
中慮 to agree with the wishes of others.
中暑 sunstroke.
[10]中槍 struck by a bullet.
中毒 accidentally poisoned.
中犧牲 suitable for sacrifice.
中狀元 to obtain the highest degree.
中[1]用 useful; in some parts it means a son.
[15]中用的 capable; useful; efficient.
不中[1]用 useless—used in some parts for a girl; hopeless; on the point of death.
中的[4] to hit the bull's eye.
言必有中 when he speaks he is sure to hit the mark.
中科甲 to obtain a literary degree under the old system.
[20]中肯 right; meets the exigency.
中舉 to obtain the 2nd degree under the old system.
中計 to make a lucky hit; to be deceived.
中進士 to obtain the 3rd degree under the old examination system.
中邪氣 to be possessed by evil spirits.
[25]中酒 to be intoxicated.
中風不語 paralytic stroke.
廢中權 in retirement they acted according to the exigencies of the times.

仲[4] **The second in order of birth. The younger of two.**
1505

仲冬 the second month of winter.
仲尼 the style of Confucius.
仲父 a father's younger brother.
仲秋 the eighth month of lunar calendar.
[5]仲裁 arbitration.
仲裁人 arbitrator.
仲裁決定之案 arbitration award.
仲裁條約 arbitration agreement.
仲裁裁判 arbitration tribunal.

忠¹ Loyal, faithful, devoted, honest, patriotic.
1506

忠 信 honest, faithful.
忠 勇 loyal.
忠.厚 honest; upright; worthy.
忠 告 faithful counsel.
⁵忠 告 而 善 道 之 loyally to reprove and skilfully to lead on.
忠 君 loyal to the sovereign.
忠 孝 loyal and filial.
忠 實 loyal and sincere.
忠 心 faithful.
¹⁰忠 心 耿 耿 most faithful and true; an unchanging regard.
忠 恕 magnanimous; the summary made by Confucius of his teaching—"true to the principles of our nature and the benevolent exercise of them to others" Legge.
忠 果 the olive.
忠 烈 true till death.
忠 焉 能 勿 誨 乎 can (a minister) be loyal and not try to instruct (his prince)?
¹⁵忠 直 straightforward.
忠 義 loyal.
忠 者 體 恕 者 用 loyalty is the principle, reciprocity the application.
忠 臣 a loyal statesman.
忠 良 honest and virtuous.
²⁰忠 蓋 a loyal officer.
忠 裔 children of patriots.
忠 言 逆 耳 sincere reproofs grate on the ear.
忠 誠 faithful and sincere.
忠 讜 faithful admonition.
忠 貞 loyal and chaste.

盅¹ A covered cup. A bowl.
1507

酒 盅 winecup.
金 盅 teacup with a cover.

衷 1.4. Inner garments. The inner man. The heart.
1508
Rectitude, right feelings; a sense of justice; sincerity; equity. To agree.

衷 懷 the mind; to bear in mind; to cherish.
衷 曲 the inner feelings.
衷 欵 or 衷 誠 sincere.
衷 甲 secret armour.

⁵衷 腸 or 衷 情 the feelings; the emotions.
衷 藏 the inner man.
衷 衣 inner garments.
上 帝 降 衷 于 下 民 God has given mankind a moral sense.
不 衷 insincere.[to strike a medium.
¹⁰折 衷 to conciliate; to discriminate;
折 衷 說 a compromise theory.

重⁴ Weighty, in the sense of important.
1509

重.任 or 重 位 weighty responsibility or office.
重 使 minister charged with matters of grave import.
重 價 a great price.
重 地 reserved, secluded place; not open to the general public.
⁵重 報 heavy reward.
重 大 great, heavy. weighty, important.
重 好 still better. (Cantonese)
重 客 important, honourable guest.
重 寄 important trust or commission.
¹⁰重 情 an important affair.
重 撿 束 close detention for military officers—no communication with outsiders was permitted, not even letters were allowed, and half the pay was stopped.
重 數 a large number.
重 文 important documents.
重 施 而 報 君 將 何 求 if you give (grain to Chin 晋) with liberality and he recompenses you, what more can you ask?
¹⁵重 案 important case.
重 用 to put into an important position.
重 聘 to engage at a heavy salary.
重 禁 閉 military punishment of close detention—hot water and salt were provided, no bedding, and 40% of the wages was docked.
重 科 a heavy crime.
²⁰重 稅 heavy taxes.
重 究 不 貸 to be severely dealt with.
重 筆 laboured style of writing.
重 累 heavy entanglements; burdens.
重 罪 aggravated offence.
²⁵重 臣 important official.
重 要 important.
↑重 商 主 義 mercantilism.

重 要 人 an important man.
重 要 問 題 grave question; weighty matter.
重 要 時 機 a critical juncture.
³⁰重 要 職 員 an important officer.
重 要 關 鍵 a vital point; very important matter.
重 視 to give attention to. See below. B. 6.
重 言 weighty words.
重 負 heavy burdens or responsibility.
³⁵重 身 pregnant.
重 遷 (people) unwilling to be moved from their native place.
重 酬 substantial recompense.
重 重.的 heavily; liberally.
重 鎭 a strategic post.
⁴⁰重 馬 a pregnant horse.
任 重 or 負 重 to bear heavy responsibility.

(a) Heavy, as opposed to light in weight.

重 力 or 地 心 引 力 gravity.
重 十 斤 it weighs ten cattics.
重 噸 the long ton of 2240 lb. as contrasted with the American ton of 2,000 lb.
重 學 mechanics. ＝ 力 學
⁵重 心 or 重 心 點 center of gravity.
↓重 點 load (in a lever).

重 擔 a heavy load, both lit. and fig.
重 星 the planet Jupiter.
重 率 (lü⁴) specific gravity.
¹⁰重.量 or 輕 重 weight.
重 量 單 位 表 table of weights and measures.
重 量 貨 物 heavy-weight goods.

(b) To secure respect for.

重 人 倫 to give weight to social relations.
重 以 to regard with attention.
重 信 義 to lay emphasis on faith and righteousness.
重 看 to regard with esteem; to favour.
⁵重 經 驗 to emphasize experience.
重 視 to regard with esteem. See above.—32.
重 農 to give importance to agriculture.
以 重 國 課 in order that the national taxes may be respected.
自 重 to have self-respect.

(c) Severe.

重 傷 severely wounded.
重 打 to beat with severity.

(d) Read *ch'ung²*. To repeat; again. A thickness, a layer.

重 九 or 重 陽 節 double nine—the 9th of the 9th month.
重 作 to repeat.
重 修 to repeat; to repair; to re-vise.
重 兵 reinforcements.
⁵重 出 to occur again.
重 刊 to issue a new edition.
重 加 or 重 複 re-duplicate.
重 午 5th of the 5th lunar month.
重 夫 a second husband.
¹⁰重 婚 bigamy.
重 孫 a great-grandson.
重 寫 re-write.
重 岡 repeated ridges.
重 底 having a false bottom.
¹⁵重 建 re-building; re-construction.
重 慶 parents and grandparents both living. Chungking, a city on the Yangtze River.
重 抄 to re-copy.
重 整 re-adjust.
重 新 anew; afresh.
²⁰重 新 作 renew, repeat, do it again.
重 新 分 配 re-dispose; re-distribute.
重 新 勉 勵 renew one's efforts.
重 新 組 織 re-organization.
重 新 裝 備 re-fit.
²⁵重 新 類 別 re-classify.
重 明 or 重 瞳 eye with double pupil.
重 泉 deep water—the grave, Hades.
重 洋 or 重 溟 the ocean.
重 淵 the "Abyss."
³⁰重 演 repeated performance.
重 煩 repeated; reiteration.
重 生 to be born again; regeneration.
重 疊 or 重 重 疊 疊 reiterated; duplicated; often; piled one on another.
重 算 re-count.
³⁵重 組 or 重 行 組 織 reorganize; re-constitute.
重 羅 麵 double-bolted flour.
重 興 文 學 revival of learning.
重 茵 several layers of carpet.
重 繭 callosities on the feet.
⁴⁰重 行 考 慮 re-consideration.
重·複 again and again.

重 複 話 or 重 說 repetition; re-iteration.
重 親 parents and grandparents.
重 言 repeated words, as for em-phasis—like 種 種 all sorts, or 重 重 疊 疊 above,—D. 33.
⁴⁵重 訂 renewed, as a treaty, etc.
重 託 re-commission.
重 譯 several stages of trans-lation, as when more than two languages are being used.
重 議 or 覆 議 reconsider.
重 選 re-election.
⁵⁰重 霄 the empyrean; heaven.

渱⁴ Milk of cows or mares, etc. Also read *t'ung³*.
1510

牛 馬 之 渱 milk of cows or mares.

(a) Sound of drums.

渱 然 擊 鼓 to beat a tattoo on the drums.

種³ Seed, grain. A kind or sort.
1511
　Also read ·*tsung* in 這 種.

種 切 in detail.
種 別 classes of seeds; to classify.
種°子 or 籽 種 seeds.
種 族 clan, race or tribe.
⁵種 族 心 理 學 ethnic psychology.
無 分 種 族 without distinc-tion of race.
種 核 kernel or centre.
種 樣 or 種 式 model or pattern.
種 皮 husk or shell.
¹⁰種 種 all sorts.
種 種 不 對 nothing is right.
種 種 手 段 all methods; by every means.
種 類 variety; type; species and genus.
傳 種 to propagate.
¹⁵播 種 or 布 種 to sow; to scatter seed.
痘 種 vaccine; lymph.
石 種·子 sterile seeds.
禍 種 seeds of misfortune or cala-mity.
遺 種 posterity.
²⁰雜 種 mixed seeds; halfbred; ille-gitimate—a term of abuse.
黃 種 The Yellow Race.

(a) Read *chung⁴*. To sow, to plant.

種 因 to sow causes—to do things that will entail consequences in later life or another life.
種 德 to cultivate virtue.
種 植 to set out trees; to plant.
種 牛 痘 or 種 痘 to vaccinate.
⁵種 瓜 得 瓜，種 豆 得 豆 plant melons and get melons, sow beans and get beans.—"whatso-ever a man soweth, that also shall he reap."
種 田 or 種 地 to cultivate the soil; to engage in agriculture.
種 福 to sow happiness—to leave prosperity to one's descendants.
種 禍 to sow the seeds of misfor-tune.
種 花 to cultivate flowers.
種 菜 to plant vegetables.
種 豆 to sow beans.

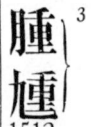

腫³
尰
To swell, a swelling.
1512

腫 傷 a bruise; contusion.
腫 疼 swollen and painful.
腫 脹 to swell.
腫 起 青 黑 swollen up black and blue.

踵³ The heel. To follow in the footsteps of. To reach.
1513

踵 事 增 華 to follow a precedent with greater flourish.
踵 決 肘 見 down at the heels and out at elbow—very poor and slovenly.
踵 至 to arrive afterwards.
踵 見 to call frequently.
⁵踵 貴 國 to visit your honourable country.
踵 趾 相 接 one after another.
踵 跡 to follow someone's steps or instructions.
踵 門 to visit; to go in person.
不 旋 踵 without turning the heel; at once; no return; no retreat.
¹⁰接 踵 following closely after.
接 踵 而 至 to come in rapid suc-cession.
曳 踵 to drag the feet.

鍾[1] An ancient measure equal to 4 斗. A cup, a goblet.
1514

鍾 杯 a cup.
蓋 鍾 or 茶 鍾 covered teacups.
酒 鍾 winecups.

(a) To bring together. To cherish, to love.

鍾 念 very affectionate remembrance or thoughts.
鍾 情 to fall in love with.
鍾 愛 to love faithfully and ardently.
鍾 靈 the auspiciousness of a site.
鍾 靈 毓 秀 all the talents bestowed upon one—a genius, one with supernatural talents.
鍾 馗 a hero of *T'ang* Dynasty deified as a protector against demons.
天 鍾 美 於 是 God has gathered many beauties into this spot.

冢[3] A mound, a peak.
1515

冢 中 枯 骨 term of reviling—dry bones from a tomb—you useless good-for-nothing.
冢 土 a mound, an altar of earth.
冢 碣 a boundary mark.
山 冢 the peaks of the mountains.

(a) Eminent; great.

冢 君 ancient term for a sovereign.
冢 嗣 or 冢 子[3] eldest son; heir-apparent.
冢 婦 wife of the heir-apparent.
冢 宰 a minister of state; the premier; the president of Board of Civil Office. (*obs.*).

塚[3] A cemetery; a tomb; a mound.
1516

塚 墓 or 墳 塚 a grave; a burying ground.
挖 塚 to rifle graves.
疑 塚 mounds made to look like graves and deceive the foe.
義 塚 public cemetery.
荒 塚 abandoned graves.
開 塚 to dig a grave.

眾 眾 衆[4]
1517

All; the whole of; a multitude. A crowd—three or more.

衆 人 or 衆 民 everyone; the multitude; the crowd; mankind.
衆 位 Gentlemen! The present company.
衆 全 entirely; all.
衆 口 or 衆 意 public opinion.
[5]衆 口 一 詞 or 衆 口 如 一 unanimous.
衆 口 鑠 金 public opinion will fuse metals.
衆 多 a great many.
衆 庶 the masses.
衆 志 專 一 unanimity of purpose.
[10]衆 志 成 城 unanimity of purpose is like a fenced city.
衆 怒 難 犯 專 欲 難 成 the anger of a crowd is difficult to oppose, and the desire of a single person is not easily accomplished.
衆 技 all the different talents.
衆 擎 易 舉 with united effort it is easily raised.
衆 楚 人 咻 之 many men of *Ch'u* were clamouring around him (while he was trying to learn
[15]衆 生 all living beings. [the dialect of
衆 皆 all, every. [*Ch'i*).
衆 盛 a great crowd; an abundance.
衆 目 所 見 what every eye saw.
衆 約 all the wards and neighbourhoods, at Canton.
[20]衆 類 general presentation of princes at court.
衆 論 or 衆 議 public opinion.
衆 論 不 同 之 極 致 the extremes of differing opinions.
衆 雨 copious rains.
公 衆 public.
[25]出 衆 emerged from the masses; uncommon. [Cf. 2520 C. 58.
衆 議 院 the lower house of a parliament.

CH'UNG.　　(ㄔㄨㄥ)

(Ch'ong)

虫[2] Worms, insects. Radical 142. Properly read *hui*[2], but
1518 now used for the next.

蟲[2] Worms, insects, reptiles. Inter. preceding.
1519

蟲 子[3] insects' eggs.
蟲 吟 hum of insects.
蟲·子 worms; insects. = 蟲
蟲 書 or 蟲 篆 spider-like form of written characters, as is found on ancient bronzes—used of literary men with skill in trifles.
蟲 樣 垂 the vermiform appendix.
[5]蟲 樣 垂 炎 appendicitis. *See* 闌
No. 3789. G. 1, pop. called 盲 腸
蟲 災 plague of locusts. [炎
蟲 白 蠟 white wax produced from insects that live on trees in W. China.
　水 蠟 蟲 the wax-insects as above.
蟲 積 worms in the bowels.
[10]蟲 聚 to swarm, as insects.
蟲 蟲 irritation caused by hot damp climates.
　薀 隆 蟲 蟲 the weather is extremely hot and muggy.
蟲 蟻 antlike—ability in trifling matters.
蟲 豸 insects and reptiles—term of abuse.
[15]蟲 霜 水 旱 locusts or insects, frosts, floods, and drought—the troubles of the farmer.
蟲 類 or 蟲 部 the class of insects or reptiles.
蟲 蝕 or 蟲 蛀·了 worm-eaten.
害 蟲 destructive insects.
微 生 蟲 or 微 生 物 microbes.
[20]生 蟲 to breed worms.

充[1]　To fill up; to satisfy.
1520

充 乎 內 而 發 乎 外 fill up the interior and the outward flow will follow.
充 任 to fill a position.
充 其 性 to give their nature its full development.
充 其 操 to carry out his principles. [at most.
[5]充 其 量 to fill up its measure,—
充 分 a full measure; sufficiently; complete; to its fullest extent.
充 分 的 efficient; ample; sufficient.
充 分 賠 償 compensation in full.
充 塞 full; filled.

10 仁 義 充 寒 imbued with the principles of humanity and righteousness.

充 實 abundant; filled quite full.

充 實·的 生 活 a full life; abundant life.

充 徒 banishment for seven years.

充 數 to complete the number.

15 充 滿 or 充 盈 full; to fill.

充 當 or 承 充 to fill an office.

充 耳 盈 聽 the ears are filled with melody.

充 補 to fill a vacancy.

充 裕 replete; abundant.

20 充 足 ample; well supplied; enough; sufficient for.

充 足 有 餘 more than sufficient.

充 足 理 由 sufficient cause; satisfactory reasons.

充 軍 to transport for ten years.

充 量 a full measure.

25 充 雜 adulterated; mixed.

盜 賊 充 斥 robbers were very numerous.

(a) To act in place of; to become; to pretend to be.

充 作 to act as; to serve as; to pretend to be.

充 公 to become public property; to confiscate.

充 兵 to enlist as a soldier.

充 名 冒 籍 to assume another's name and address.

5 充 好 to pretend to goodness or honesty.

充 役 or 充 吏 to act as a *yamen* runner.

不 能 充 二 役 cannot fill two positions; "cannot serve two masters."

充 正 經 人 to pretend to be a respectable man.

充 爲 to act as; to fill the post of.

銃 ⁴ A blunderbuss; a gingal.
1521 A mortar. A pistol or gun.

銃 手 or 銃 首 cannoniers; those who fired salutes from the petards in a *yamen*.

銃 炮 cannon; firearms.

水 銃 Chinese fire-engine.

忡 ¹ Uneasy; sad.
1522

忡 忺 uneasy.

憂 心 忡 忡 uneasy in heart; deeply grieved.

沖 ² To dash against. To
沖 clash with, in this sense
1523 Inter. 衝 No. 1532. To be rude to.

沖 動 to shake.

沖 卸 to pour over, like a cascade.

沖 塌 or 沖 倒·了 to burst through and break down, as dikes, etc.

沖 壞 to destroy by floods or rush of waters.

5 沖 撞 to treat rudely; to give offence.

沖 散 to break up a gathering.

沖 沖 bubbling sound of water; tinkling as of pendants.

　　鑿 冰 沖 沖 the sounds of breaking ice.

沖 煞 to provoke bad influences; malign—in geomancy.

10 沖 破 to defeat; ruined; to burst over, as a flood.

沖 積 土 alluvial soil.

沖 積·的 alluvial.

沖 鋒 to rush on the spears; to make a bold attack.

沖 開 to burst open.

日·子 相 沖 the days clash—the dates are not propitious.

(a) To pour out; to infuse.

沖 糨·子 or 打 糨·子 to make starch paste.

沖 茶 or 泡 茶 to infuse tea.

沖 開 水 to buy hot water.

(b) Empty; void.

沖 虛 empty; void.

(c) To soar to; to wander from.

沖 天 to rise to heaven; to soar to the skies.

沖 天 而 去 they soared to the skies and disappeared.

怒 氣 沖 天 his anger mounted to heaven.

沖 遠 to digress; to ramble on.

沖 霄 to rise towards the skies, as a glare, etc.

(d) Weak; young.

沖 人 a sovereign who is a minor; depreciatory term for I, used by emperor.

沖 年 or 沖 齡 young; a minor.

沖 弱 weak and young.

沖 童 a youth.

(e) Complaisant; agreeable; blending.

沖 凝 melted and congealed; blended together.

沖 和 on good terms.

沖 寂 quiet and peaceful.

沖 挹 unassuming and modest.

沖 襟 liberal; magnanimous.

沖 退 of a retiring disposition.

种 ¹
1524 　　Tender; delicate.

幼 种 young and delicate.

舂 ¹ To pound grain in order
1525 to remove the husk. To ram down. Distinguish 春 No. 1493.

舂 墻 to make mud or adobe walls.

舂 碓 a pestle.

舂 米 or 舂 糧 to hull rice.

舂 鋤 the white egret or paddy bird.

惷 ¹
1526 　　Simple; stupid.

惷 愚 an idiot.

惷 笨 dull; stupid.

椿 ¹ To pound; to ram; to run
1527 against.

椿 碗 盞 to smash the dishes.

椿 跌 倒 knocked down.

椿 門 甚 趄 to pound violently on the gate.

崇 ² To venerate; to reverence.
崇 Lofty, noble. Distinguish 祟
1528 No. 5539.

崇 安 May you be in peace !

崇 尙 or 崇 奉 or 崇 信 to regard as preëminent; to esteem.

崇 山 high mountain in Hunan.
崇 崖 a lofty precipice.
⁵崇 德 exalted virtue.
崇 德 辨 惑 to exalt virtue and discriminate doubtful things.
崇 拜 to worship.
崇 明 島 island in the mouth of the Yangtze River.
崇 朝 the early morning before breakfast. (-chao¹)
¹⁰崇 邱 a peak; a high hill.
崇 階 Your house!
崇 高 lofty; exalted.
敬 崇 to reverence; to respect.

憧¹
1529
Unsettled; irresolute.

憧 憧 往 來 wavering; irresolute.

(a) Read ch'uang¹. **Crazy.**

戆 憧 wild and crazy.

艟
舸}²
1530
A long, swift boat. Also read t'ung².

艨 艟 war junks.

捶⁴
1531
To push into; to poke out. A punch.

捶 不 通 unable to poke a way through.
捶 個 眼 punch a hole in it.
捶 床 or 鐵 捶·子 a punch.
捶 蜂 to stir a hornet's nest—to interfere in dangerous things.
捶 通 水 溝 to clear out a drain with a pole.
中 捶 a centre-punch.

衝¹
1532
To rush against. To insult.

衝 倒 to throw down, as by collision; to overthrow.
衝 冠 to raise the hat—by the hair standing on end—extreme anger.
衝 動 to irritate; to provoke.
衝 動 彈 力 reaction to stimulus.
⁵衝 撞 to treat with rudeness; to give offence.
衝 撞 馬 頭 to impede; to come into conflict with.

衝 擁 to break through a surrounding mob.
衝 擊 to rush at; to make an onset.
衝 散 to scatter; to rout.
¹⁰衝 決 to burst open, as a dyke.
衝 激 to burst through with force.
衝·突 a clash, as of opinions, etc.; to collide with.
衝 繁 疲 難 frequented, troublesome, wearisome, and difficult —four terms applied to official posts indicating their relative importance.
衝 車 a war chariot.
¹⁵衝 軼 to rush out.
衝 鋒 to have a desperate clash; to charge with bayonets; hand to hand fighting.
衝 陷 to rush boldly into attack when there is much danger.
衝 霄 or 衝 斗 (anger) mounted to the heavens.

(a) A thoroughfare.

衝 要 important place, as where roads meet; a key position.
衝 途 a public road.
中 衝 pulse in the middle finger.
水 衝 a canal or sluice.

𣂑⁴
1533
To enter abruptly. To nod.
[(-chao²-)

𣂑 睡 or 𣂑 着·了 nodding, sleepy.
𣂑 食 to drop in to a meal; to "sponge."

寵
䭫}³
1534
To esteem, to favour. Kindness, grace.

寵 之 四 方 made them remarkable through the whole land.
寵 妾 or 內 寵 favourite concubine.
寵 幸 favour; good graces.
寵 愛 to delight in; to love.
⁵寵 愛·的 favourite.
寵 異 to show special favour to.
寵 辱 不 驚 unmoved either by favour or disgrace.
寵 錫 or 寵 貺 a special favour.
寵 顧 favour.
¹⁰失 寵 to lose favour.
希 爲 寵 臨 I hope that you will favour me with a visit.

得 寵 to find favour; to win affection.
恩 寵 grace; kindness.
納 寵 to take a concubine.

CHÜ.　　　(ㄐㄩ)

居
凥}¹
1535
To dwell, to remain. To be in—of various states and conditions. To occupy, the course of one's life.

居 一 於 此 to agree to one of these conditions.
居 上 不 寬 to hold high office and show no generosity to others.
居 下 流 而 訕 上 to be in a low position of life and revile those above you.
居 世 to live in the world.
⁵居 中 to hold a middle position.
居 之 不 疑 to hold to a course without hesitation.
居 之 無 倦 to hold in the mind without weariness.
居 人 inhabitants.
居 人 下 to occupy a position below others.
¹⁰居 仁 由 義 to dwell in benevolence and act from righteous motives.
居 住 to reside at.
居 住 遷 徙 to remove the residence.
居 位 to hold office.
居 今 稽 古 to live in the present and cleave to the ideals of the past.
¹⁵居 停 to rest, as in an inn when travelling.
居 停 主 人 one's host; an employer.
居 其 所 而 衆 星 共 之 (the North Star) keeps its place and all the stars bow to it.
居 則 曰 不 吾 知 也 daily you are saying, "No one knows us."
居 喪 to be in mourning.
²⁰居 坐 to occupy a room.
居 士 a retired scholar; official out of office; a Buddhist devotee.
居 多 the greater part.
居 奇 goods kept back to raise the price,—from the next:
　其 奇 貨 可 居 也 rare commodities may be kept— for higher prices.

²⁵居孀 widowed; to remain a widow.

居 安 資 深 abiding in it calmly and firmly, he reposes a deep reliance on it—of earnestness in study.

居 官 in office; to hold a post.

官 居 極 品 to reach the highest rank.

居 室 to dwell together; husband and wife, from Mencius, *see next*.

³⁰ 男 女 居 室 人 之 大 倫 that male and female should dwell together, is the greatest of all human relations.

善 居 室 clever in domestic affairs.

居 家 to manage a family; to live at home.

居 家 人 等 the whole family.

居 常 usually; customary.

³⁵居 廬 to dwell in a booth—in mourning.

居 惡 (*wu*¹) 在, 仁 是 也 What should he rest in? In benevolence.

居 憂 to be in mourning.

居 所 prolonged temporary residence (*legal*), differs from 住 which indicates more permanency.

居 所 地 法 law of settlement. (*legal*).

⁴⁰居 攝 to act as regent.

居 敬 to be respectful.

居 於 位 sat in the seats (of the men).

居 易 以 俟 命 to remain quiet and await the orders of Providence.

居 月 in childbed.

⁴⁵居 次 daughter of a chief among the *Hsiung nu* 匈奴.

居 正 to live uprightly.

居 民 inhabitants; resident population.

居 然 reserved; to presume on; off-hand; contrary to expectations; easily; after all; simply; nothing else than.

他 居 然 敢 這·樣 will he presume to act in this manner?

⁵⁰居 然 生 子³ she brought forth her son without difficulty.

居 無 何 after a short time.

居 留 地 f o r e i g n settlements. (*Jap.*).

居 留 民 團 foreign community.

居 相 似 也 their positions are corresponding.

⁵⁵居 移 氣 . . . . 大 哉 居 one's position affects the air . . . . great is the influence of position!

居 積 to accumulate, especially wealth.

居 第 a residence.

居 簡 而 行 簡 to be easy with oneself, and to be lax in carrying out matters.

居 約 to be in straitened circumstances.

⁶⁰居 艱 難 in difficulties.

居 處 or 居 址 residence; dwelling place.

居 處 恭 執 事 敬 與 人 忠 to be reverent in demeanour in private, to be respectfully attentive in managing affairs, and to be loyal in intercourse with others.

居 身 personal habits; disposition.

居 錯 to dwell in peace.

⁶⁵居 長 eldest; chief.

居 間 to dwell in harmony; to be a mediator; to negotiate between.

居 間 人 a mediator; middleman.

居 間 態 度 a neutral position.

居 間 業 b r o k i n g business. (*legal*).

⁷⁰居 間 介 紹 to interpose.

居 間 調 和 to intervene and make peace.

居 首 位 to occupy the chief seats; to have pre-eminence.

居 高 to occupy a high position.

另 居 to live apart.

⁷⁵寄 居 to reside temporarily.

歇 居 to stay for a short time.

自 居 to consider oneself as.

起 居 rising and resting—action; circumstances; one's conditions.

閒 居 in retirement.

(a) Bent on; to put into practice.

居 心 the mind bent on; concentration of mental powers; to maintain a certain state of mind; attitude; motive.

居 心 不 良 bent on evil.

居 心 不 忍 intentionally done—for evil.

居 心 散 蕩 his mind is bent on dissipation.

(b) To sit.

居, 吾 語 女 sit down and I will tell you. (-*ju*³)

(c) Unkindly.

居 居 究 究 unkindly; unfriendly.

(d) Read *chi*¹. **A final and expletive particle.**

居 諸 final particles—the sun and moon, the passing of time, from 日 居 月 諸 照 臨 下 土 O sun, O moon, which shine on the earth below!

何 居 Why? Wherefore?

其 意 何 居 What is the meaning of it?

倨 ⁴ Haughty; bold; rude. Strong.
1536

倨 倨 or 居 居 dreamless sleep.

倨 傲 or 驕 倨 haughty; imperious.

倨 強 overbearing; imperious.

倨 牙 strong teeth, like those of a horse; a stubborn person.

(a) The long side of a carpenter's square. To measure, as angles.

倨 句 (*kou*⁴) the long and short sides of a square; an angle.

倨 曲 square.

据 ¹ A disabled hand—embarrassed, distressed, restricted. Handle of a spear. A position.
1537

据 難 開 口 unable to speak plainly, as from nervousness or fright.

予 手 拮 据 I tore (the grass for my nest) and placed it with my claws. *See* 780.1

(a) Read *chü*¹. **u.f.** 據 **No. 1563. To seize, etc.**

据 以 驕 傲 he is haughty and unsubmissive.

据 法 守 正 he acted in accordance with the law and maintained an upright character.

裾 ¹ The overlap of a robe. A robe or skirt.
1538

裾 裾 over-dressed; dressed up.

(a) Read *chü*⁴. u.f. 倨 No. 1536. Proud, etc.

矯裾 proud; stiff-necked.

禹爲人廉裾 *Yü* was an honourable but proud man.

踞⁴ To crouch; to squat. To occupy.
1539

踞坐 to occupy; to squat.

踞抗 to hold a city, as rebels.

踞處 a squatting place.

箕踞而坐 to sit with the legs spread out.

盤踞 to sit with the legs doubled under.

鋸⁴ A saw; To saw. Toothed.
1540

鋸價 or 鋸減價 cheapen the price a little.

鋸木頭 or 拉鋸 to saw wood.

鋸糠 or 鋸屑 or 鋸末·子 or 鋸麵 saw-dust.

鋸°開 to cut in two.

鋸頸 to cut the throat.

鋸齒 or 鋸牙 teeth of a saw.

鋸齒葉 serrated leaves.

刀鋸 to cut and maim—ancient punishments.

(a) Read *chü*¹. To mend crockery.

鋸·上 to bring together; to rivet.

鋸·不結實 it is not mended securely.

鋸碗 to mend crockery.

句⁴ A sentence; an expression; a phrase. Distinguish 勾
1541 No. 3409.

句句都懂 every sentence intelligible.

句句都有理 there is reason in all he says.

句段 clauses and sentences.

句法 syntax.

⁵句語 a sentence, a period.

句讀 (*tou*⁴) sentences and phrases.

分句讀 punctuate, or divide, into sentences and phrases.

一句話 a sentence; just a word.

三句鐘 three o'clock.

¹⁰不成句 ungrammatical; illogical.

引句 to quote a sentence.

成句 a complete sentence.

琢句 to polish up a literary effort.

造句 to compose sentences.

¹⁵逐句 sentence after sentence.

題句 to set a theme; to write a motto or headline, etc.

點句 to punctuate.

(a) Read *kou*¹. now written 勾, To bend, crooked.

句引 to inveigle.

句留 detained by business, etc.

句票 or 提票 warrant to arrest criminals.

句結 to implicate.

句通 in collusion.

(b) Read *kou*⁴. To stretch a bow. The short side of a carpenter's square.

句當 business; affairs; duties; functions.

句¹股形 a right triangle. ⌈triangle¹.

勾¹股 short and long legs of a right

拘¹ To grasp; to restrain; to seize. To adhere to, as an
1542 opinion.

拘囚 to detain in prison.

拘執 self-opinionated; obstinate.

拘守遺傳 holding fast to traditions.

拘役 detention in custody above one day and less than two months.

⁵拘忌 superstitious restraints.

無所拘忌 to be afraid of nothing, especially superstitions.

拘懦 narrow-minded,

拘挐 or 拘拿 or 拘追 to arrest; to seize.

拘捆 to seize and bind.

¹⁰拘攣 cramps; spasms.

拘文 adhering to the letter of the law, etc.

拘·束 to keep in order; to restrain; to feel restrained.

拘案 to arrest and bring into court.

拘泥 or 拘板 to be bigoted; to adhere to the letter of the law.

¹⁵拘泥不通 bigoted and obstinately impervious to reason.

拘泥小節 bigoted adherence to petty formalisms.

拘泥禮節 too closely adhering to formal rules.

拘泥於字義 to insist on a literal interpretation.

拘牽 obstinate.

²⁰拘留 to detain forcibly; detention awaiting trial.

在拘留中 in detention; under custody.

拘票 warrant for arrest.

拘禮 to stand on ceremony; formal.

不拘禮節 to neglect social formalities.

²⁵拘究 or 拘訊 to arrest and bring to trial.

拘管 or 拘押 or 拘禁 to keep in custody; to control.

拘繫 constrained; bound.

拘而不化 perversely unwilling to be convinced.

拘虛 narrow-minded.

³⁰拘謹 precise.

拘鬼·的 exorcists.

拘魂·的 those who profess to seize spirits.

不拘 no matter; irrespective of; any.

駒¹ A foal, a colt. Strong.
1543

駒光易逝 the bright rays soon fly—of the passing of time.

千里駒 a 1,000 *li* horse—a strong reliable man.

白駒 a white colt—a sunbeam.

白駒過隙 a sunbeam passing a crack—a comparison with the brevity of human life.

巨⁴ A carpenter's square. Chief, great, very. Numerous. Distinguish 臣 No. 327.
1544

巨億 a very great number; many millions.

巨勢 great power.

巨勝 black sesame or linseed.

巨室 a powerful family; a large house.

⁵巨室之所慕 he whom the great families affect.

巨工 a fine performance. standing.

巨指 or 巨擘 the thumb; out-

巨木 great trees.

巨波 great billows.

¹⁰巨浪湯湯 heavy seas rolling in.

巨海 the ocean.

巨盜 powerful insurgents.

巨 燭 a great candle—light in a dark place.

巨 猾 great evil; unscrupulousness.

15 巨 眼 great eyes.

巨 禍 a great calamity.

巨 端 a grave matter.

巨 紅 deep crimson.

巨 細 great and small—size.

20 巨 萬 myriads.

巨 鎮 great markets or trading centres.

拒 4 **To oppose, to ward off with the hand. To resist.**
1545

拒 人 之 權 right of refusal. (*legal*).

拒 住 to hold at bay.

拒 力 opposition; power of resistance.

拒 卻 to ward off.

5 拒 受 條 約 之 束 縛 refused to be bound by the treaty.

拒 外 貨 之 輸 入 oppose the importation of foreign goods.

拒 守 to guard.

拒 客 權 利 right of refusing hospitality (*legal*).

拒 性 repellent.

10 拒 扞 to resist; to ward off.

拒 捕 to resist arrest.

拒 敵 to keep the foe at bay.

拒 斥 to repel.

拒 斥·的 repellent.

15 拒 木 or 拒 馬 鎗 abattis.

拒 格 to resist an enemy and fight with bare hands.

拒 絕 to break off communications or intercourse; to refuse; refusal.

拒 絕 交 易 boycott.

拒 絕 同 意 refusal of consent.

20 拒 絕 症 negativism—a mental disorder.

拒 絕 證 書 protest. (*commerce*).

拒 絕 承 受 之 證 書 protest for non-acceptance.

拒 絕 支 付 之 證 書 protest for non-payment.

拒 諫 to reject good counsel.

25 拒 阻 to impede; to raise objections.

拒 霜 to resist the frost; the hibiscus.

拒 霸 to usurp and hold on to.

力 拒 strong resistance.

抗 拒 to oppose; to resist.

30 死 拒 resistance to the death.

柜 3 A tree of the willow family of which the bark produces an infusion like tea.
1546
　　　Read *chü*⁴. u.f. 櫃 A counter in a shop.

炬 4 A torch, made of twisted reeds.
1547

炬 枝 twigs used as a torch.

炬 蠟 or 蠟 燭 a candle.

寶 炬 painted candles used in festivals.

火 炬 or 火 把 a torch.

矩 3 A carpenter's square. A rule. A pattern. Usage, a custom.
1548

矩 尺 carpenter's square.

矩 形 rectangle.

不 踰 矩 not go beyond the pattern; not transgress.

中 矩 a right angle; pattern of correct conduct.

絜 矩 之 道 the principles by which conduct may be rectified.

規 矩 compasses and square.

規·矩 rule; true (carpentry); well-behaved.

(a) u.f. 炬 preceding. Torch.

法 矩 the light of Buddhism.

秬 3 Black millet.
1549

秬 黍 black millet.

秬 鬯 a sacrificial wine made from millet and fragrant herbs, and given as an imperial favour.

粔 4 Cakes made from rice flour twisted into rings.
1550

粔 籹 細 點 the finest kinds of cakes and pastry.

苣 4 Plants like endive, lettuce, chicory, etc. A small rush.
1551

苣 藤 sesame.

菊 苣 or 萵 苣 endive or lettuce.

萵 苣 筍 or 萵 筍 young stalks of a plant like lettuce cooked as a vegetable.

詎 4 How? Interjection of surprise.
1552

詎 于 此 乎 Has it come to this?

詎 可 待 How can we wait?

詎 否 or 詎 非 Is it so? Is it not; expecting an affirmative answer.

詎 意 or 詎 料 or 詎 知 Who would have thought it? Unexpectedly; exclamation of surprise.

距 4 To go to; to reach. The distance between; distant from.
1553

距 於 千 里 之 外 keep men at a distance of a thousand *li*.

距 四 海 I have been all over the country.

距 城 有 三 里 three *li* distant from the city.

距 水 面 above water-level.

距 躍 to leap over.

距 離 distance; distant from.

超 距 to leap over; to exceed.

(a) To resist; to oppose. Inter. 拒 No. 1545.

距 塞 to block up; to repudiate.

距 絕 to repudiate.

距 誼 行 oppose one-sided actions.

佔 距 to occupy territory, as by enemy force.

敢 距 大 邦 they dare to oppose this great realm.

違 距 to resist.

閉 距 to obstruct.

(b) A bird's spur; to strike downwards with spears, etc.

雞 距 a cock's spur.

(c) Great.

距 國 a very great kingdom.

距 戰 a great battle.

鉅 4 Great. Inter. 巨 No. 1544.
1554

鉅 公 the emperor; venerable sir.

鉅 子 great men.

鉅 累 injustice; great hardship.

積 小 致 鉅 collecting the small produces the great.

(a) u.f. 鋸 No. 1540. A saw, etc. Also, Hard, fierce, obdurate.

鉅 鐵 hard iron.

駏 [4] Offspring of a stallion and a she-mule.
1555

駏 蛩 i.e., 駏 驉 and 蛩 蛩 two fabulous creatures which are inseparable; they consort with the jerboa and carry it off when danger appears—used for inseparable attachment.

駏 驉 a wild animal like the mule.

具 [4] To prepare; to draw up; to write out.
1556

具 結 to write out a statement of the case.
具 保 狀 to give written bond for another.
具 備 or 具 辦 to make ready.
具 呈 to file a plea.
[5]具 報 to present a report.
具 奏 to draw up a memorial.
具 存 kept; filed.
具 帖 to write a card of invitation.
具 復 to reply to inquiries.
[10]具 控 or 具 狀 to file an accusation.
具 文 to prepare a document; a merely formal document; mere formality.
具 稟 to present a petition.
具 結 to enter into a bond.
具 繳 to prepare and hand over.
[15]具 訴 to draw up a defence; to make out a counter-charge.
具 詳 to prepare a report.
具 限 to enter into a bond with time limit.
具 陳 章 疏 to prepare and draw up memorials.
全 具 all prepared.
[20]名 內 具 my name is written inside—not on the envelope.
知 名 不 具 as you know my name I do not sign it.
謹 具 respectfully prepared.
開 具 清 摺 to make out a clear statement, etc.

(a) All, the whole. Inter. next,具.

具 以 告 to tell the whole truth.
具 在 all in existence.
具 慶 parents both living.

具 此 生 理 these are all natural principles.
[5]具 衆 理 to contain all principles.
具 瞻 (one whom) all look up to.
具 臣 ordinary ministers.
具 見 very evident.
具 領 received in full.
[10]具 體 the whole body; all the members of the body; the complete thing; concrete; practical.
具 體 名 詞 concrete nouns.
具 體 方 法 concrete or practical methods
具 體·的 concrete as opposed to abstract 抽 象.
具 體 而 微 they have all the members (of the Sage) but in small proportions.
[15]具 體 規 定 a concrete decision.
具 體 觀 念 concrete ideas or conceptions.
具 體 計 畫 practical plans.
具 體 辦 法 practical methods of managing.

(b) Implement; utensil; tool, etc.

刑 具 instruments of punishment.
器 具 tools; instruments, etc.
將 相 之 具 talents of a general or a statesman.
文 具 stationery.
農 具 agricultural implements.

(c) N.A. for bodies, etc.

屍 首 一 具 one corpse.

俱 [1] All, altogether; the whole; every. Inter. preceding.
1557

俱 備 all complete; made ready.
俱 全 all complete; all on hand.
俱 各 each; all.
俱 各 平 安 all were in peace.
[5]俱 因 all because of . . . . .
俱 在 both alive, as parents.
俱 已 the whole of.
俱 已 齊 備 everything is now ready.
俱 收 all duly received.
[10]俱 是 all are . . . .; in everything.
俱 是 如 此 they are all like this.
俱 有 all are . . . .; all have . . . . .
俱 樂 部 a club, guild, association. (Jap.).
俱 發 罪 concurrent offences. (legal).
[15]俱 盡 totally exhausted; finished.

俱 藍 ancient name for Ceylon. A.D. 1300.
俱 行 to accompany.
俱 都 all, every one; the whole of.
俱 都 滅 淨 utterly wiped out.

坥 [4] An embankment. Distinguish 埧 No. 4843.
1558

堤 埧 a dike.
築 埧 to build a dike.

颶 [4] A typhoon; a cyclone.
1559

颶 母 or 颶 風 蓋 clouds which indicate a typhoon.
颶 風 a typhoon; a cyclone.

懼 [4] To fear, to dread. Solicitude, carefulness.
懼
1560

懼 內 to fear one's wife.
懼 怕 or 恐 懼 or 畏 懼 to fear.
毫 無 懼 怕 fearing naught.
戰 懼 to tremble with fear.
赧 懼 shamefaced.

豦 [4] A wild boar. To fight.
1561

懅 [4] Bashful; ashamed.
1562

據 [4] To receive, as communications from a subordinate.
1563

據 此 on receipt of this. See below. A.10.
據 稟 已 悉 the petition has been received and contents noted.
茲 據 覆 稱 I have received a reply stating.

(a) To rely on, to lean on. Evidence; proof. According to; whereas.

據 云 according to what is said; it is said; in reference to.
據 來 函 云 according to your letter.

據 億 丈 之 城 relying on the 100,000 *chang* wall—the Great Wall.

據 地 to prostrate oneself.

5據 實 according to facts.

據 情 judging by the circumstances.

據 我 看 來 from my viewpoint; as I see the matter.

據 掌 致 諸 地 place both hands on the ground in making an obeisance.

據 案 坐 leaning on the table as he sat.

10據 此 on these grounds. *See above*.—1.

據 爲 to use it as .....

據 說 from what people say.

據 軾 to lean upon the front bar of the carriage.

印 據 stamped deeds.

15失 據 to lose the clue from fear or nervousness.

字○據 written evidence; a contract, etc.

實 據 substantial proof or evidence.

左 手 據 膝 with the left hand resting on the knee.

憑○據 proof; testimony; evidence.

20推 據 deed of renunciation.

根○據 or 依 據 to base on; to use as a support.

有 根○據 well-supported; well-founded.

無 實 據 no evidence against.

立 此 爲 據 this deed is now drawn up as evidence.

25契 據 written agreements or contracts.

證○據 testimony; proof.

轉 據 deed of transfer.

(b) To occupy; to take possession; to take in the hand.

據 以 爲 質 to seize as a hostage or a security.

據 守 to guard vigilantly; to maintain.

據 於 德 firmly lay hold of every right attachment.

據 爲 己 有 to appropriate; to take forcible possession.

5據 虛 捕 影 military strategy—to cause the foe to grasp the wind —to be deceived.

據 邑 背 叛 to seize lands and rebel.

據 邑 以 請 held possession of the city in order to secure his request.

佔○據 to occupy by force.

鐻[4] A padded drumstick. A musical instrument.
1564

肖 木 爲 鐻 to carve wood into a musical instrument.

(a) Read *ch'ü*[1]. Gold and silver dishes, etc.

遽[4] Hurried, agitated. Suddenly, with despatch.
1565

遽 人 a courier; a messenger.

遽 施 to act without consideration.

遽 然 or 遽 爾 or 卒 遽 suddenly, unexpectedly.

遽 見 to see suddenly.

遽 議 to make a hasty decision.

遽 責 to blame without giving the matter consideration.

醵[2.4] To contribute to a feast.
1566

醵 金 or 醵 資 contribution towards expenses.

舉[3] To raise; to elevate with the hands.
1567

舉 一 反 三 to raise one corner of a subject and expect the pupil to infer the other three— the method of Confucius,—as in the next:

舉 一 隅 不 以 三 隅 反 則 不 復 也 if I show a man one corner and he is not able to gather the other three from this, I do not show it to him again.

舉 兵 to take up arms.

舉 手 to raise the hand, as in a salute.

5舉 手 禮 the salute.

舉 手 表 決 to vote by raising the hand.

舉 目 to lift up the eyes.

舉○起○來 to raise up.

舉○起 杯○來 to lift the cup—to drink.

10舉 踵 to raise the heels—in expectation, on tiptoe.

舉 重 機 器 jack for raising weights.

舉 重 螺 絲 器 a screw-jack.

舉 錯 from 舉 直 錯 枉 introduce good officials and remove those who are bad.

舉 鎗 to shoulder arms.

15舉 鎗 致 敬 to present arms.

舉 首 to raise the head; to come to the front.

舉 鼎 to lift a cauldron—immense strength.

舉 鼎 絕 臏 to lift a great weight and wrench the sinews of the knee—to over-estimate the strength of ...

(a) To begin. To initiate, to move, to recommend, to bring forward.

舉 事 to begin a matter. [2601.5

舉 人 to recommend a man. *See*

舉 例 以 明 to introduce a parallel to illustrate a point.

舉 前 曳 踵 to stagger forward.

5舉 助 moved and seconded.

舉 動 or 行○動 beginning and stopping—deportment; conduct; behaviour.

舉○動 輕 率 rash, heedless behaviour.

舉 哀 to begin to weep; to mourn.

舉 善 to advance the good.

10舉 報 to notify.

舉 子 to bear children; literati candidates for the examinations.

舉 意 to move; to ask a question.

舉 措 to put into operation.

舉 族 去 to swarm, as bees.

15舉 棋 不 定 to make no certain move, as in chess—inconstant not persevering.

舉 止 beginning and ending—deportment, behaviour.

舉 止 大 方 rectitude of character.

舉 止 端○正 upright conduct.

舉 步 to lift the feet; to start.

20舉 火 to light a fire.

舉 端 to make a proposal.

舉 行 to put into operation; to convene; to gather together as at a sports-meeting, etc.

舉 行 祝 典 to celebrate.

舉 進○士 to go up for the third degree under the old system.

↑ 舉○薦 to recommend.

[25]舉 辦 to initiate; to deal with a case.

舉 辦 新 政 to initiate reform measures.

一 舉 兩 得 "to kill two birds with one stone."

一 舉 成 名 to become famous with one move.

美 舉 or 善 舉 worthy cause; a good deed.

義 舉 public-spirited act; a just deed.

(b) All, the whole.

舉 一 身 而 言 speaks in reference to the whole body.

舉 世 the whole world.

舉 世 不 忘 I shall never forget it.

舉 世 無 異 說 all ages agree in this statement.

[5]舉 世 風 從 the whole world began to follow him.

舉 凡 in all cases of; the whole of.

舉 國 the whole nation.

舉 家 the whole family.

欅 [3] 1568 A large tree with beautifully grained wood suitable for furniture, etc., a kind of elm. Giles explains it as a small tree resembling a willow.

苴 [3] 1569 Fibrous plant like hemp. Name of a State.

苴 國 a petty State in the southeast of what is now Shantung.

踽 偊 [3] 1570 To walk alone; self-reliant.

踽 踽 涼 涼 peculiar in action; reserved; self-reliant.

襃 襃 [4] 1571 Unceremonious, rustic. In want.

襃 人 子 [3] an indigent man.

襃 藪 a straw pad used when carrying burdens on the head.

家 襃 狹 a poor, humble home.

屨 [4] 1572 Sandals, straw shoes.

瓜 田 不 納 屨 do not fasten your sandals in a melon patch—avoid the appearance of evil.

CHÜ TSÜ. (ㄗㄩ)

咀 [3] 1573 To suck, to chew.

咀 嚼 to suck and chew.

咀 片 lozenges.

岨 砠 [1] 1574 Rocky; hilly; uneven. Pron. *ch'ü*[1].

岨 峿 hilly; uneven; irregular.

沮 [3] 1575 To stop.

沮 止 to end; to stop.

沮 之 以 兵 stop him with troops.

沮 格 to prevent.

(a) To spoil; to injure or ruin.

沮 人 是 非 to backbite.

沮 喪 downcast; low-spirited.

沮 壞 ruined.

沮 敗 defeated.

[5]沮 舍 a ruined home.

沮 色 spoiled; injured.

沮 衄 to defeat; to ruin.

沮 訾 or 沮 短 to slander.

沮 誹 to backbite.

[10]沮 顔 to tattoo the face.

沮 駭 to ruin another and put him in fear.

(b) Read *chü* or *tsü*[4]. Marshy.

沮 泄 to leak out.

沮 洳 marshy.

沮 洩 to leak out; to become known.

沮 澤 marshes.

(c) Read *chü* or *tsü*[1]. Name of some rivers in Shensi, etc. Surname.

沮 蒼 i.e., 沮 誦 and 蒼 頡 the reputed inventors of Chinese writing.

狙 [1] 1576 A monkey. To spy; to watch for.

狙 伏 to lie in ambush.

狙 伺 to lie in wait for.

狙 察 to examine minutely.

狙 猿 a monkey.

狙 詐 tricks.

狙 詐 之 兵 troops in ambush.

疽 [1] 1577 An ulcer, a cancer, carbuncle.

疽 爛 了 the abcess has suppurated.

乳 疽 mammary cancer.

苴 [1] 1578 Sackcloth. A rush. Coarse; rustic. Read *chü* or *tsü*[3] or *cha*[3]. The female plant of the nettle hemp.

苴 布 sackcloth; mourning apparel.

苴 杖 the chief mourner's staff.

苴 麻 the female plant of the common hemp.

趄 跙 [1] 1579 Weak, lame.

趄 坡·子 a slope or bank.

趄 傖·子 a country bumpkin.

趄 阻 to stumble along.

雎 [1] 1580 A kind of fish-hawk. The osprey.

雎 鳩 a waterfowl, emblematical of conjugal harmony.

關 雎 cry of the above; the opening words of the *Odes*.—marriage.

聚 [4] 1581 To assemble, to meet together. To collect. Also read *chi*[4].

聚 光 器 a condenser. (*optics*)

聚 合 to unite.

聚 居 to dwell together.

聚 散 meeting and parting.

[5]人 生 聚 散 無 常 the meetings and partings in human life are irregular.

聚 散 之 情 the emotions of meeting and parting.

聚 斂 to gather; to collect; to amass property.

聚 斂 而 附 益 之 collected the taxes for him and enlarged his wealth.

聚 會 or 聚 集 or 聚 同 to gather together; to assemble.

[10]聚 珍 版 old name for printing from movable types.

聚 衆 to assemble a crowd.

聚 精 會 神 concentration of attention and energy.

聚 落 or 鄉 聚 a village or hamlet.

聚 蚊 成 雷 a swarm of mosquitoes makes a noise like thunder—small, petty things can cause much disturbance if multiplied.

[15]聚 議 to meet for discussion.

聚 賭 to assemble for gambling.

聚 頭 扇 a folding fan.

聚 首 a re-union; gathering of friends.

聚 黨 gathering together of associates for conspiracy, etc.

[20]聚 齊·了 all present.

團 聚 a united gathering.

完 聚 re-union, especially of a family.

CHÜ.　　　(ㄐㄩ)
(Chüh)

鵙
缺 } 1.5.　　A shrike. Also read *chüeh*[2]

1582

缺 鳥 also 伯(or 博)勞 the butcher bird—this bird is said to eat its mother; therefore used for :—unfilial children.

南 蠻 缺 舌 之 人 "this shrike-tongued barbarian from the south," this man from the southern barbarians who chatters like a bird.

大鳥 2.5.　The tailor-bird; it is said to sing at the equinoxes, and is also called 工 雀 1583 the working bird, 女 匠 or 巧 婦 鳥 the clever-woman

bird. Dictionaries class it as an owl.

是鳥夬鳥 (*kuei*[1]) the goatsucker.

局 2.5.　**Position, circumstances. Style or fashion.**
1584

局 促 cramped, restrained, not at liberty to act freely. A confined place or quarters.

局 勢 style, fashion, etc., the situation or outlook. *See below.* A.2.

局 度 a man's capacity or ability.

局 式 style or fashion.

[5]局 於 藝 confined by (self-imposed) restraints.

局 量 presence or bearing.

局 量 堂 堂 grave and stately bearing; conscientious ways.

局 量 大·方 with a good presence and great abilities.

局 量 褊 淺 a mean person.

[10]局 部 痲 醉 local anæsthetic.

局 限 概 念 limited conceptions or outlook.

局 面 appearance, size, etc., of an establishment; correct; elegant; stylish; good form.

暫 時·的 局 面 temporary state of affairs.

新 奇·的 局 面 new and strange circumstances.

[15]世 局 the world situation.

大 局 the general condition of; the object of; the arrangements of; the public interests; general situation.

大 局 決 裂 the general situation is disastrous.

大 局 牽 動 the general situation is involved.

大 局 變 遷 the changing of the general situation; the changes in the government.

[20]政 局 the political conditions.

時 局 the present situation.

格 局 bearing, manner; appearance.

(a) A game of chess, etc., the other meanings of this character are derived from this.

局 內 局 外 players and bystanders; those concerned and those outside.

局 勢 the state of the game. *See above.*—2.

局 勢 已 成 the winning position is secured; the matter is arranged. .

局 外 中 立 neutral; unbiassed.

[5]局 外 中 立 國 neutral countries.

局 外 之 人 a bystander; one not concerned in the game.

局 外 之 例 laws of neutrality.

局 子 chess men.

局 家 keeper of a gambling den.

[10]局 戲 games of chance.

不 入 局 to keep out of the game.

不 成 局 incomplete.

串 局 collusion.

了[3]局 to finish the game.

[15]和 局 a drawn game.

棋 局 the arrangement of the pieces on the board.

當 局 those who are playing; the present authorities.

美 人 局 to entice into evil through a pretty face.

賭 局 gambling place.

騙 局 a cheating trick.

(b) An office, a shop; an association; a company; a board; used as suffix for bureau, etc.

局 務 departmental affairs.

局 部 departments, as in a college, etc.

局 長[3] head of a bureau.

偵 探 局 Bureau of Investigation.

[5]僑 工 事 務 局 Overseas Labour Bureau.

全 國 水 利 局 National Conservancy Bureau.

分 局 branch office or shop.

印 書 局 a printing office.

印 鑄 局 Bureau of Printing.

[10]商 標 局 Trademarks Bureau.

工 務 局 Bureau of Works.

工·部 局 Municipal Council, International Settlement, Shanghai.

徵 收 局 tax-collecting office.

戒 煙 局 opium refuge.

[15]昆 蟲 局 Entomological Bureau.

民 局 native post offices.

法 制 局 Bureau of Laws.

稽 勳 局 Bureau for Investigation of Merit.

管 理 局 District Head Office.

[20]統 計 局 Bureau of Statistics.

藥 局 dispensary.

衛 生 局 Health Bureau.

賑 濟 局 Relief Bureau.

轉 運 局 Transport Department.

[25]郵 政 局 Post Office.

銓 敍 局 Bureau of Civil Appointments.
錢 局 or 鑄 幣 局 a mint.
鎗 礮 局 arsenal.

(c) To stoop; to bend; to curl up; inter. 跼. No. 1586.

曲 局 twisted, as hair.
謂 天 蓋 高 不 敢 不 局 Heaven is high above me, I dare not but bow.

侷 2.5.　Narrow, cramped.
1585

侷 促 cramped; hampered.

跼 2.5.　Bent down, contracted, cramped.
1586

跼 促 不 安 uneasy, constrained.
跼 蹐 to hobble.

掬
匊 2.5.　To grasp with both hands. A double handful.
1587

掬 水 月 在 手 holding the water, which reflects the moon, in both hands, one seems to have the moon in the grasp.
掬 氣 包 腮 cheeks swelled with anger.
不 盈 一 掬 not enough for a handful.
笑 容 可 掬 the face beams with a broad smile.

毬 2.5.　A leather ball for kicking.
1588

菊 2.1.5　The China aster. The chrysanthemum.
1589

菊 月 the 9th lunar month.
菊 花 chrysanthemums.
菊 花 茶 infusion made from dried flowers of the chrysanthemum.
菊 花 酒 chrysanthemum wine.
萬 壽 菊 the African Marigold.
賞 菊 to enjoy the chrysanthemums.

鞠 2.5.　To nourish.
1590

鞠 于 祖 母 brought up by his grandmother.
鞠 育 to rear; to nurture.

(a) To inform.
鞠 旅 he addressed his troops.

(b) Much; full.
降 此 鞠 訩 (God) sent down all these numerous calamities.

(c) A ball.
鞠 丸 a ball.
善 蹴 鞠 good at kicking a ball.
騎 鞠 polo.

(d) A child.
鞠 子 a young lad.

(e) To bend in submission. To reduce to extremities. u.f. next, to investigate, etc.
鞠 躬 to bow.
鞠 躬 如 也 如 不 容 with his body bent as if there were not room for him to pass.
鞠 躬 盡 瘁 "Bowed down I exhaust my energy (in the public service)."
三 鞠 躬 the three formal bows of modern ceremonial in China.
自 鞠 自 苦 what you bring upon yourself you must bear.

鞫
諊 2.5.　To make a judicial investigation.
1591

鞫 審 or 訊 諊 to examine and judge a case.

(a) To reduce to extremities.
鞫 人 to beat people down.
鞫 哉 庶 正 the chiefs of departments are all exhausted.
鞫 窮 to reduce to extremities.

(b) The further shore of a river.
芮 鞫 之 卽 they went to the other side of the River Jui.

橘 2.5.　The orange.
1592

橘 子 an orange, a tangerine.
橘 瓣 the sections of an orange.
橘 白 or 橘 絡 the dried fibres of the orange.
橘 皮 or 橘 紅 dried orange-peel, used in medicine.
福 橘 oranges from Foochow.
金 橘 the cumquat.

劇 4.5.　To increase. More, very. Troublesome.
1593

劇 寇 powerful robbers.
劇 烈 very violent; intense.
劇 藥 very powerful drugs.
劇 賊 great robber.
劇 飲 great capacity for liquor.
日 劇 daily increasing, as sickness.
病 劇 a troublesome, distressing complaint.
苦 劇 unhappy, miserable.

(a) A comedy, a play; drama.
劇 場 the stage, a theatre.
劇 本 play-book; written drama.
戲 劇 drama.
劇 談 pleasant chat; to discuss a play.
一 劇 戲 a play.

CH'Ü.　(ㄑㄩ)

去 4　To go away. Past; gone. An auxiliary verb.
1594

去 不 去 are you going or not?
去 不 得 may not go; must not go.
去 世 or 過 世 or 辭 世 to die.
去 作 甚 麼 what is the use of going? why should you go?
⁵去 你 的 罷 mind your own business.
去 向 one's direction; where one is going.
去 喪 無 所 不 佩 when out of mourning he wore all his girdle ornaments.
去 國 to depart from one's own country.
去 後 subsequently.
¹⁰去 年 last year.
去 聲 the "departing tone", the "4th" tone in Chinese speech.
去 處 occasion; opportunity; a place.
投 一 個 去 處 安 身 must find a place to live in.

清淨去處 a clean place.

¹⁵去 路 way of escape; a way out of.

去 邪 歸 正 to depart from evil and return to the good.

挐·去 take it away.

相 去 不 遠 not very far apart.

進·去 to enter.

²⁰過·不 去 cannot cross it; it cannot be done.

過 去 the past; 過·去 past, to go by.

(a) Read *ch'ü*³. To remove, to get rid of. To do away with. To kill.

去 勢 castration.

去 官 to deprive of office.

去 惡 to do away with evil.

去 掉 to remove; to take away; to do away with.

去 留 to dismiss or to retain officials.

呿¹
1595

To yawn.

祛¹
1596

To disperse; to drive off.

祛 散 to disperse; to relieve.

祛 服 to abandon mourning.

祛 退 to exorcise.

祛 風 去 濕 to disperse wind and damp vapours.

胠¹
1597

To open. To rifle.

胠 篋 to open boxes; used for burglary.

(a) Flank of an animal.

右 胠 the right flank of an army.

阹¹
1598

A pen. To surround.

區¹
1599

A place, a district. N.A.

區 域 a region.

區 夏 China.

華 夏 之 區 the territory of the kingdom of *Chou*—or of China.

區 宇 the empire; all that is bounded by the frontiers.

⁵區 官 head of a police district.

區 處 a place to live in; a way out; a plan.

別 作 區 處 make some other plan.

自 有 區 處 there must be some way out of it.

區 裁 判 所 local or district court.

¹⁰大 區 the universe.

省 會 區 provincial capital.

賜 宅 一 區 presented him with a mansion.

選 舉 區 electoral district.

(a) To store.

區 藏 to hoard or store.

(b) To discriminate. To assign to.

區 以 別 矣 they are divided according to classes.

區·別 to discriminate between.

區 別 字 adjective. = 形 容 詞.

區 畫 to arrange or plan.

(c) Small, unimportant.

區 區 small, unimportant — self-depreciatory phrase for I.

區 區 之 地 a petty place.

區 區 之 心 my private feelings.

是 區 區 者 this is a mere trifle.

嶇¹
嶇¹
1600

A rugged, steep mountain.

崎 嶇 rugged mountain path.

軀¹
1601

The human body. Oneself.

軀 幹 the trunk of the human body.

軀 殼 the physical body as contrasted with the spirit and the mind.

軀 體 or 肉 軀 the body, the person.

捐 軀 to die for the State.

驅¹
歐¹
1602

To expel, to drive away, to urge on.

驅 令 to cause to go.

驅 使 to send; to urge on by force.

驅 兵 前 進 to advance troops to attack.

驅 制 to urge on; to drive—as horses.

⁵驅 口 prisoners of war kept as slaves. (*Mongol.*).

驅 暑 to drive away heat.

驅 神 or 驅 鬼 to drive away spirits.

驅 策 to urge men on, as a horse is urged by whip and spur.

驅 策 龍 蛇 to send away dragons and snakes on errand of vengeance.

¹⁰驅 而 之 善 he urges them and they move towards the good.

驅 而 納 諸 罟 to be driven and captured in a net.

驅 蟲 藥 anthelmintic.

驅 逐 艦 torpedo-boat destroyers.

驅 邪 to expel noxious influences.

¹⁵驅 除 or 驅 逐 or 驅·出 to get rid of, to drive out.

驅 馬 to spur a horse.

驅 馳 to run for others, to exert oneself.

先 驅 antecedent; forerunner; pioneer.

前 驅 the van of an army.

²⁰後 驅 the rear of an army.

驅 逐 機 pursuit plane.

驅 逐 艦 destroyer.

渠²
1603

A drain or gutter. The felloe of a wheel. Great; ample. A personal pronoun.

渠 帥 a leader.

渠 答 a spiked iron ball thrown down before cavalry.

渠 魁 the chief rebels.

劬²
1604

Labour, toil.

劬 劬 hard labour; laborious.

劬 勞 hard toilsome labour.

朐²
1605

Strips of meat cut from the flank and dried in the wind. To offer dried meat in sacrifice.

朐 肉 cutlets.

朐 脯 slices of dried meat.

鴝鵒 [2]

A species of mynah.

1606

鸜鵒 or 八哥 the mynah.

鶋 [2] A sea-bird with a white breast.

1607

瞿眗 [1,2]

The timid look of a bird. Nervous.

1608

瞿曇 u.f. Gautama—the name of Buddha.
瞿然 alarmed; drawing back.
瞿瞿 startled; awestricken.
瞿視 to gaze at in terror.

(a) A surname.

氍 [2] Fine woollen cloth. A mat used by the emperor in wor-

1609 shipping 上帝.

氍毹 the mat, as above.

癯 [2] Worn, wasted.

1610

形容甚癯 very thin and emaciated.

衢 [2] A point where two highways meet. A highway, a

1611 thoroughfare.

天衢 the imperial highway; the way of the birds; a constellation; the milky way.
昏衢 the dark road—life.
通衢 thoroughfare,
雲衢 the cloudy way—scholarly eminence.

璩 [2] An ear-ring. Inter. 鑢 No. 1564.

1612

蘧 [2] A plant which resembles wheat but has no edible

1613 grain.

蘧蔬 a fungus which grows on rotten plants and is eaten when fresh.

麱 [2] Young wheat; ears of wheat.

1614

CH'Ü   TS'Ü. (ㄑㄩ)

取 [3] To select, to take out from, to fetch, to take hold of, to

1615 obtain.

取·下·來 to take down.
取·不·上 to be unsuccessful, as in examinations, etc.
取事 to make arrangements.
取人 to choose men.
[5]取人以身 to attract others by one's character.
取供 to take depositions.
取保狀 to take security; bail.
取信 to inspire confidence; to bring a letter.
取值 the price demanded.
[10]取債 to collect a debt.
取償 to demand compensation or indemnity.
取其 with the object of ....; to consider as.
取其利便 because of its convenience.
取其殘而已矣 he merely destroyed those who were oppressors.
[15]取·出·來 to select from.
取利 to take interest; to get a profit from.
取勝 to get a victory.
取勢 to make use of circumstances.
取友必端 in choosing friends take only those of upright conduct.
[20]取名 to select a name; to seek fame.
取命關 crisis in the life of a child when there is fear of demons snatching its life.
取善輔仁 selecting the good and aiding the virtuous.
取回·來 to withdraw.
取外貌 to have regard to outward appearance.
[25]取攻勢 to take the offensive.
取巧 to devise ingenious methods; to take the easiest tasks.
取引 to exchange; to trade. (*Jap.*).
取得 to gain, to make profit.
取憂 to bring sorrow.

---

[30]取慾 to seek to gratify lusts.
取扱 to collect.
取捨權 right of acceptance or refusal; option.
取替 to exchange, as money.
取樂 to run after pleasure.
[35]取死 to choose death.
取決 to decide.
取決勝負 decide who is master.
取法 to take example from.
取消 to cancel, to rescind, to abrogate, to countermand.
[40]取消前約 to rescind an agreement or contract.
取消權 power to annul or countermand.
取火 to strike fire.
取燈 matches.
取禍 to court disaster or calamity.
[45]取笑 to ridicule; to make a butt of.
取結 to require a bond.
取締 to supervise or control; to repress. (*Jap.*).
取締人 inspector or supervisor.
取罪 to get into trouble; to fall into sin.
[50]取討 to demand.
取贖 to redeem a pledge.
取贏 to reap a profit.
取還 to take back.
取錢 to receive money.
[55]取鍼 to attract a needle, as a magnet.
取除 to deduct.
一無可取 good for nothing.
自取禍 to bring disaster on oneself.

(a) To take a wife, (rarely to take a husband), for which the next is now used.

娶 [3.4] To marry; to take a wife.

1616

娶妾 or 娶偏房 to take a concubine.
娶媳婦 to get married.
娶親 or 娶妻 to marry.
續娶 to marry again.

趣 [4] To advance quickly; to hasten to.

1617

趣之 hurried towards him.
趣走 to hurry.

(a) Bias, tendency.

趣 勢 tendency; trend.
趣 向 inclination, bias towards.
趣 操 不 同 tastes differ.
趣 於 with a view to ....;
意 趣 tendency towards.

(b) Interesting; amusing; pleasant.

趣 事 interesting matters.
趣·味 agreeable flavours; interest.
趣 女 人 a beautiful woman.
趣 話 a joke. 與 趣 interest.

(c) Read tsou[3]. To breed.

趣 馬 to breed horses; an equerry.

(d) Read ts'u[4.5]. To urge.

趣 裝 to pack the baggage.

趨 趍 [1]
1618
To run, to hasten.

趨 候 to wait on; to pay respects.
趨 出 to hasten out.
趨 利 to hasten after wealth.
趨 前 to press forward.
⁵趨 勢 trend; tendency.
　大 勢 所 趨 the trend of the age.
　自 然 趨 勢 a natural tendency.
趨 厮 a servant to one who is on a journey.
趨 向 to long for; direction; tendency.
¹⁰趨 吉 避 凶 to pursue good fortune and avoid that which brings calamity.
趨 奉 to flatter; to toady to.
趨 庭 to receive the teachings of one's father,–from the next:
　趨 而 過 庭 as I (the son of Confucius) hastened across the hall—I was asked a question by my father.
趨 承 to be subservient; to ascertain the desires of others.
¹⁵趨 承 附 和 to play the sycophant.
趨 拜 to go and pay respects to.
趨 敎 to hasten to an interview.
趨 時 to follow the trend of the times; to keep up to date; to be fashionable.
趨 步 to hasten; to run quickly.
²⁰趨 炎 附 熱 to hasten to the light and cling to the warmth—of

one who sponges on another, or uses the influence of another.

趨 異 variation. (biol.).
趨 異 性 variability.
　相 關 趨 異 correlated variation.
趨 義 to see right and hasten to follow it.
²⁵趨 舍 to hasten to one's abode; to be in a dilemma.
趨 謁 to pay a visit.
趨 走 to run; to go in haste.
趨 赴 逢 迎 to hasten to meet.
趨 趨 to hurry on.
³⁰趨 蹌 to run to and fro—waiting on others.
趨 道 to hasten towards the Way —of right conduct.
趨 避 to advance or withdraw according to the possibilities of advantage.
趨 領 to hasten to receive.
趨 風 to go like the wind.
³⁵亦 步 亦 趨 step for step, stride for stride—the following of a good example,—from
　步 亦 步 趨 亦 趨 (the meaning is as above) said of Yen hui 顏 回, the favourite disciple of Confucius.

(a) Read ts'u [1.5]. To urge.

趨 民 收 斂 urge the people to gather in the harvest.
趨 數 or 促 速 to urge to haste.
趨 織 or 促 織 the cricket—lit., to urge to the spinning, as the chirping of the cricket resembles the whirr of the wheel.

蛆 蠞 [1]
1619
Maggots.

蛆 蟲 maggots.
發 蛆 to breed maggots.

(a) Read tsü or chü[1]. A centipede.

蚰 蛆 the centipede.

虗見 覰 [4]
1620
To spy; to watch for.

覰 便 而 行 to watch for a good opportunity to act.

覰 機 會 to watch one's chance.
覤 覰 petty, narrow.

CH'Ü　　(ㄑㄩ)
(Ch'üh)

屈 [1.5]
1621
To crouch; to bend down. To submit to the dominion of; a grievance, wrong or injustice.

屈 人 one who has a grievance.
屈 伏 to submit under protest.
屈 伸 as 能 屈 能 伸 having elasticity; not hidebound; able to submit or to rise at will.
屈 伸 導 引 to extend and contract the limbs—a Taoist practice.
⁵屈 坐 please yield your seat—either to a guest of higher rank, or to take a higher seat.
屈 尊 condescension; to take a humbler rank than one's station demands; conventional apology to a visitor—I am humbling you.
屈 小 己 而 利 大 羣 to study the welfare of the community rather than the interests of a few.
屈 就 to condescend to.
屈 居 人 下 reluctantly to remain under the control of others.
¹⁰屈 己 to yield to circumstances.
屈 從 to force; to submit under protest.
屈 心 malicious intent; deceitful rascality.
屈 志 to curb the ambition.
屈 志 老 成 to keep on friendly terms.
¹⁵屈 情 ingratitude.
屈 打 成 招 to beat a man in order to extort a confession.
屈 折 bending; refraction.
　不 可 屈 折 cannot be bent— as hard brass.
屈 折 線 line of refraction.
²⁰屈 折 能 力 refractive power.
屈 折 角 angle of refraction.
屈 指 to bend the fingers; to count on the fingers.
　指 不 勝 屈 countless—lit., not enough fingers on which to count.
屈 斷 an unjust decision.
²⁵屈 於 慾 under the domination of the passions.

屈曲 to bend by force; crooked, winding.
屈服 to yield an unwilling assent to.
屈枉 wronged; oppressed.
屈枉好人 to wrongfully injure a good man.
30 屈‧死 an untimely death; done to death.
屈‧死鬼 spirit of one who has died through injustice.
屈殺 to kill wrongfully.
屈理 unreasonable; unfair; unjust.
屈竭 exhausted.
35 屈節 to cringe; to crouch before.
屈背 to bend the back.
屈膝 to bow the knee.
屈膝易屈心難 it is easier to bend the knee than the will.
屈臨 to visit—will you humble yourself to call?
40 屈致 to order; to command.
屈苦 unjust suffering.
屈蟠 overhanging and twisted—as branches.
屈蠖 to walk like the looper caterpillar—a man in difficulties.
尺蠖之屈以求伸 the looper bends that it may stretch out further on.
45 屈計 to reckon, from bending the fingers in counting.
屈身 to bend the body.
屈身忍耐 to suffer patiently.
屈身降世 he humbled himself and came into the world.
屈辱 to receive insults and be forced to submit to them.
50 甘受屈辱 willing to submit to humiliation.
屈量 to have drunk sparingly.
屈首 to bow the head.
不屈 unsubmissive.
受屈 wronged; to receive injury unjustly.
55 冤‧屈 grievance; wrong; injustice.
忠勇不屈 the loyal and the bold do not submit.
絲毫不屈 will not yield an inch.
(a) Read chüeh. u.f. 倔 Tough, surly.
屈彊 unsubmissive.
屈起 to distinguish oneself.

詘 1.5. To contract. To wrinkle. To crouch. To stammer.
1622

詘伸 u.f. 屈伸 contracting or expanding according to circumstances.
詘意於人 to yield to the ideas of others.
詘折 wrongs; complications.
詘詞 to hesitate in speech.
詘身以信道 bent himself in order to widen the sway of truth.
身詘何傷 what harm is done by bending the body?
道不可詘 do not bend the truth.

曲 1.5. Crooked, bent. Wrong, false.
1623

曲全, 委曲求全 accommodate oneself to circumstances in order to complete the object which one has in view.

曲士 a countryman.
曲尺 a carpenter's square.
5 曲徇 to heed things that should be ignored; to give illicit help.
曲從 to bend to circumstances.
曲徑 a crooked path; winding paths.—also used fig.
曲徑通幽 the winding path leads to quiet seclusion.
曲心‧的 deceitful.
10 曲意徇物 distorting one's own ideas to make them fit in with the wishes of others.
曲房 private or inner room.
曲折 ins and outs; complications.
曲折反覆 intricate; involved.
曲撓 unjust accusation; unfair blame.
15 曲枴 or 曲柄 a crank—of a machine, etc.
曲欄 a winding balustrade.
曲水 or 曲溪 or 曲澗 winding river or creek.
曲直 crooked and straight; rights and wrongs.
曲突徙薪 to bend the chimney and remove the fuel—to guard against danger.
20 曲筆 dishonest; unfair reports of cases sent in by officials, etc.
曲簿 bamboo frame made of doubled splints on which silkworms spin their cocoons; it is also called 蠶箔, see 箔 next.

曲線 a curve; curved lines—as of a graceful figure.
曲線板 instrument for drawing curves.　「the female beauty.
曲線美 curves of beauty, esp. of
25 磁曲線 magnetic curve.
曲辮‧子 stupid, a country bumpkin. (Shanghai)
曲肱而枕之 to use the bended arm as a pillow.
曲膝 to bend the knee.
曲蟮 the earthworm.
30 曲行 crooked ways.
曲解 to distort the sense of a passage, etc.
曲說 onesided statement.
曲論 a paradox.
曲射礮 a mortar.
35 曲面 curved surface.
曲頸瓿 a retort.
受委‧曲 to suffer wrongs.
彎曲 winding; crooked.
心曲 or 衷曲 the feelings; the mind.
40 理曲 perverted; distorted.
私曲 tricky, underhand.

(a) Songs, plays. Brogue. Pron. ch'ü³·⁵.
曲‧子 or 曲詞 songs.
曲目 a list of plays.
曲終奏雅 to sing better at the end of a play—a good ending to a matter.
曲調 song tunes.
5 曲譜 a music book.
曲高和⁺寡 high singers find few to sing in tune with them—expressing the difficulty of keeping up with those whose talents are high.
唱曲 to sing songs.
鄉曲 village, native place; local dialects.
↑戲曲 plays, drama.
(b) Shoots, small things.
曲學 minor studies.
曲禮 minutiæ of etiquette.
曲藝 small arts.
曲謹 careful about trifles.

箇 4.5. A bamboo frame on which silkworms spin their cocoons.
1624

蛐 1.5. The common earthworm, called the 蛐蟮; the cricket.
1625

麴
麯) 2.5.
    Leaven, barm, yeast.
    The "mother" of vinegar,
    etc.
1626

麴 丸 balls of leaven.
麴 生 liquor, wine.
麴 糵 yeast for fermenting liquor.
麴 錢 or 麴 引 錢 excise duty.
麴 院 brewery, distillery.
麴 黴 the yeast plant.
酒 麴 grains from the distillery.

闃 4.5. To live alone. Still,
    quiet. Distinguish 鬩 No.
1627   4699.

闃 其 無 人 there was no one in
    the house.
闃 寂 silent; solitary.
闃 然 deserted; lonely.

CHÜAN.   (ㄐㄩㄢ)
(Chüen)

娟 1 Beautiful; graceful;
    elegant.
1628

娟 好 靜 秀 beautiful, modest and
    refined.
娟 娟 swaying gracefully.
娟 娟 羣 松 the graceful swaying
    of the pines.
便 娟 graceful and easy.
月 娟 娟 the beauty of the moon-
    light.

悁 4 Angry, irritated.
    Anxious.
1629

悁 忿 anger; indignation.
悁 急 irritable; irascible.
悁 邑 distressing anxiety.
中 心 悁 悁 my heart is full of
    anxious thoughts.

捐 1 To contribute; to sub-
    scribe. Distinguish 捛 No.
1630   5548.

捐 冊 or 捐 簿 a subscription list.
捐 助 to subscribe, to endow.
捐 助 善 舉 to contribute to a
    worthy object.
捐 助 圖 書 館 to endow a
    library.

⁵捐 助 美 術 館 to endow or to
    make contributions towards an
    art gallery.
捐 助 行 爲 act of endowment.
    (legal).
捐 助 軍 餉 to contribute towards
    the army expenses.
捐 貲 or 捐 給 or 捐 銀 to con-
    tribute to.
捐 貲 與 學 褒 奬 decoration
    awarded to those who con-
    tribute towards any educational
    schemes, either schools, libra-
    ries, museums, etc.
¹⁰遺 囑 捐 貲 to bequeath; a
    · bequest.
捐 賑 or 捐 濟 to contribute to...
捐 錢 to subscribe to.
捐 項 or 捐 欵 collections, sub-
    scriptions.
捐 題 to give for the use of the
    State.
¹⁵倡 捐 to head a subscription list.
勸 捐 or 募 捐 to solicit subscrip-
    tions.
開 捐 to open a subscription list.

(a) To pay taxes. Special taxes.

捐 房 revenue office.
捐 票 likin receipt or pass.
捐 納 to pay taxes.
捐 輸 to subscribe to the govern-
    ment; to pay taxes.
房 捐 special tax on houses.
釐 捐 or 釐 金 the likin tax, see
    under 釐 No. 3883.
釐 捐 總 局 central office for the
    collection of likin.

(b) To reject, to renounce.

捐 命 or 捐 生 命 to throw away
    one's life.
捐 天 下 to renounce the throne.
捐 忘 cast away and forgotten.
捐 棄 to hazard; to cast away; to
    die.
⁵捐 瘠 to die of starvation.
捐 義 to renounce all regard for
    righteousness.
捐 軀 赴 義 to sacrifice one's life
    in the cause of duty.
捐 軀 隕 命 to sacrifice one's life.
捐 金 to reject (a pot of) gold.
¹⁰捐 階 to remove the ladder.
捐 館 to die—to leave all one has
    behind.

(c) To purchase office or rank.

捐 升 promotion by purchase.

捐 官 an official who has purchas-
    ed his post; to purchase office.
捐 班 those who have purchased
    their position.
捐 生 those who purchase gradu-
    ation degrees.
捐 職 or 捐 衙 to purchase official
    titles.
捐 花 樣 to purchase the right to
    the next vacancy.

涓 1 A brook.
1631

涓 埃 or 涓 毫 a drop or a grain;
    or a drop and a hair—nothing.
涓 水 the clear water of a brook.
涓 涓 不 壅 bubbling up without
    hindrance.
    泉 涓 涓 the bubbling of a
    spring.
涓 流 the flowing of a spring.
涓 滴 the smallest drop of water.

(a) Pure.

涓 人 an ascetic.
涓 潔 pure.
中 涓 a eunuch.

(b) To expel.

涓 惡 to expel evil influences.

(c) To select.

涓 吉 日 to choose a lucky day.

狷
獧) 4
    Cautious, timid.
1632

狷 介 timid, cautious.
狷 介 不 敢 行 也 timid and
    afraid to venture.
狷 者 有 所 不 爲 也 the cautious
    will keep themselves from doing
    (what is wrong).

睊 4 To look askance at. To
    dislike.
1633

睊 睊 胥 讒 maledictions are ut-
    tered by one to another with
    eyes askance.

稍 1
    Stalks of grain.
1634

絹[4] A thin, cheap silk; a kind of pongee.
1635

絹·子 thin silk; a silk handkerchief.
絹 布 cotton goods like lustring.
絹 燈 gauze lanterns.
絹 籮 silk sieve.
絹 紬 lustring; gauzy silk.
絹 邊 a silk border, as to scrolls.
畫 絹 thin glazed silk for painting on.
紗 絹 lustring.
↑手 絹 兒 handkerchief.

罥[2] To hang up; to bind, to entangle.
1636

罥 結 caught in a net.

蜎[1] Larvae of the mosquito. See 孑 孑 No. 784-B. 3. To move, to flinch, to be nimble. Inter. 娟 No. 1628.
1637

蜎 蜎 者 蠋 the green caterpillars were creeping about.

韏[1] A scabbard. Reins or traces.
1638

韏 韏 佩 璲 long pendant gems.

鵑[1] The cuckoo.
1639

杜 鵑 or 子[3]規 the little cuckoo.
杜 鵑 花 azaleas.

卷[4] A roll of paper; a book; an essay or document.
1640

卷 一 Vol., 1.
卷·子 examination papers when handed in.
卷 宗 or 案 卷 archives; the records of cases.
卷 帙 books.
[5]卷 紙 or 試 卷 examination papers.
卷 袋 a satchel.
卷 軸 roller for a map or scrolls.
交 卷 to hand in examination papers.
在 卷 in the archives.
[10]手 卷 scroll pictures.
書 卷 books.

珠 卷 an accepted essay.
落 卷 rejected essays.
開 卷 to open the book; to commence studies.
[15]黃 卷 yellow rolls—the classics.

(a) Read chüan[3]. **To roll up.** u.f. 捲 No. 1642.

卷 土 重 來 roll up the earth and return—to make a strong attempt to recover lost ground after a defeat.
卷 尺 a tape-measure.
卷 懷 to roll up and secrete.
　卷 而 懷 之 to 'roll up' one's principles and hide them in one's bosom.
卷 曲 to roll up.
卷 毛 curly hair, of animals.
卷 舌 to curl up the tongue—to keep silence.
卷 鬚 tendrils.

(b) Read ch'üan[2]. **To curl.**

卷 丹 the tiger-lily.
卷 髮 to curl hair.

(c) u.f. 拳 No. 1654. To grasp firmly.

卷 卷 to grasp.
不 勝 卷 卷 very carefully.

倦[4] Tired; weary.
1641

倦 勤 old and unwilling to exert himself.
倦 惰 or 倦 怠 lazy; remiss.
倦 極 dead tired.
倦 遊 weary of wandering and sight-seeing.
厭 倦 fatigue.
困 倦 very tired.

捲[3] To roll up; to gather; to grasp. Rolled up; curly.
1642

捲 上 to roll up.
捲 刃 to turn the edge of a knife or sword.
捲 地 皮 to roll up the land—used of covetous officials.
捲 堂 to refuse in a body to sit for examinations.
[5]捲 尺 a tape-measure or any rolled up measures.
捲 席 to roll up the mat—to travel.

捲 心 菜 Western cabbage.
捲 手 to double the fist.
捲 握 to grasp; to hold.
[10]捲 握 物 precious things, as jewels, etc.
捲 簾 to roll up a screen.
捲 舒 to roll and unroll.
捲 角 to turn down a corner; dog's-ears.
捲·起·來 to roll up.
[15]捲 髮 curly hair.
席 捲 to roll the mat; to travel.
席 捲 而 去 to clear up everything and go.
帶 捲 天 下 to absorb the empire like rolling up a mat.
風 捲 殘 雲 like the wind rolling away the scattered clouds.
[20]風 捲 雨 the wind blows the rain around.

睠[4] To look back with longing glances.
1643

睠 睠 不 捨 loving and unremitting care.

錈[3] To bend iron.
1644

柔 則 錈 剛 則 折 when soft, it will bend, when hard, it will snap — of forging steel and tempering it for swords.

餶[3] Thin wafers in which meat, etc. is rolled and eaten.
1645

春 餶兒 thin wafers as above, eaten at the new-year.
蛋 餶兒 thin dry wafer cakes.

希[4] A bag which will hold 3 斛. To turn down the sleeves in making a bow of ceremony.
1646

桊[1] Ring through the nose of an animal. To put a ring through the nose of a beast.
1647

眷[4] To regard. To look after. Family, relatives.
1648

眷 佑 to protect; to give special care to.

眷 屬 or 眷 口 or 家·眷 a family, a household; a wife.
眷 愛 to love with special affection.
眷 族 relatives of same clan.
[5]眷 注 to set the heart on.
眷 眷 不 忘 unalterable affection.
眷 顧 or 眷 戀 or 眷 念 to regard with tenderness; to give fond devotion to.
內 眷 female members of a family.
天 眷 世 人 God loves mankind.
[10]失 眷 to lose favour—as a concubine.
資 眷 Your wife.
親·眷 close relatives.

蜎 [1] The millipede or galley-worm, sometimes confounded with the glow-worm. Bright, clean, pure.
1649

蜎 其 大 德 made his great virtue illustrious.
蜎 滌 to cleanse.
蜎 潔 to cleanse; purified.
蜎 體 to cleanse the body.

(a) To remit, taxes, etc.
蜎 免 to remit taxes.
蜎 減 to remove or lighten; to diminish, as taxes, etc.
蜎 租 to remit land-taxes.
蜎 緩 temporary remission of taxes.
蜎 苛 to remove oppressive laws.
蜎 賦 to remit levies.
蜎 賬 to excuse from paying an account.
蜎 除 to alleviate oppressive government and forced labour, etc.

(b) To store up. To select. u.f. 涓 No. 1631.
蜎 吉 to select a lucky day.

CH'ÜAN.　　(ㄑㄩㄢ)
(Ch'üen)

犬 [3]
犭
1650

The dog. Radical 94.

犬 吠 to bark.
犬 子[3] or 小 犬 a puppy; conventional phrase for, "My son."

犬 守 夜 the dogs watch at night.
犬 戎 or 畎 夷 or 昆 夷 western tribes.
[5]犬 所 吠 也 the dogs would bark at it—something strange.
犬 效 depreciatory phrase—I have only imitated your dog in his faithfulness; used by a minister when praised for his loyalty.
犬 牙 相 錯 interlocked like dog's teeth—firmly secure.
犬 窩 dog-kennel.
犬 馬 之 勞 depreciatory phrase—I have merely rendered to you the services of a dog or of a horse.
[10]犬 馬 之 齒 七 十 六 I have merely the age of a dog or a horse—I am 76.
犬 馬 難 鬼 魅 易 it is easy (to picture) demons and elfs, but it is difficult (to draw) dogs and horses.
犬 類 or 犬 屬 of the dog tribe.

畎 [3]
甽
1651

Small drain between fields. To flow, to spread abroad.

畎 夷 a name for the tribes in West China.
畎 流 大 道 let the great principles be diffused.
畎 澮 ditches between fields.
畎 田 to divide fields by ditches.
畎 畝 fields drained by ditches.

劵 [4]
1652

A bond, a deed, a contract.

劵 契 or 劵 書 a deed, a bond.
劵 據 a certificate or voucher.
劵 約 a bond or contract.
債 劵 bonds or debentures.
[5]入 場 劵 admission ticket.
地 劵 written tiles placed in graves as proof of ownership.
契 劵 a deed or bond.
左 劵 or 左 契 the left half of a deed—held by a creditor.
執 左 劵 to hold the left half of the deed—to be certain of success.
[10]書 劵 books, documents, papers.
無 劵 可 憑 there is no written evidence.
證 劵 bonds, securities.

酒 劵 a ticket for a feast.
鐵 劵 an iron bond—irrevocable.
[15]預 約 劵 receipt for the subscription price, as of a book, etc.

弮 [1] A crossbow which discharged several bolts in succession. Also called 連 弩.
1653

拳 [2] The fist. To clasp.
1654

拳 匪 The Boxers.
拳 打 to strike with the fists.
拳 拳 to hold fast; earnestly giving attention.
拳 拳 服 膺 to clasp firmly to the breast.
[5]拳 敎·師 a pugilist; one who teaches pugilism; boxing teacher.
拳 曲 crooked; twisted.
拳 棒 boxing and fencing.
拳 法 the science of boxing.
拳 術 the boxing art; pugilism.
[10]拳·頭 the fist.
一 拳 致 命 killed with one blow of the fist.
交 拳 to exchange blows.
殷 拳 very thoughtful; attentive.
猜 拳 the game of mora, or guess-fingers, in which the number of fingers held up is guessed.
[15]空 拳 empty-handed.
賣 拳 to box for money.

圈 [1] A circle, a ring. To encircle, to punctuate. Used to mark striking passages.
1655

圈 住 to hem in.
圈 內 within a circle; a clique.
圈 套 a snare or noose; also used fig.
落 圈 套 fell into the snare.
[5]圈 椅 an arm-chair.
圈 禁 to imprison.
圈 聲 or 圈 破 to mark the tones at the corners of a character.
圈 閉 to shut in; to hem in.
圈 點 punctuation marks.
[10]尖 圈 triangular mark for emphasis, used by Chinese.
打 圈 to draw a circle.
迷 人 圈·子 deceitful snares of evil doings.

(a) Read chüan[1.4]. A pen or fold.
羊 圈 a sheep-fold.
圈 限 sphere of influence.

倦² Careful; mournful.
1656

倦倦 careful and attentive.

棬² A small wooden bowl.
1657

綣⁴ Bound in a league. A parasite.
1658

困綣 bound up.

蜷² To wriggle like a worm. Coiled like a snake.
1659

踡² The legs drawn up under one.
1660

踡着腿 drawing the legs up as when curled up in bed.
踡跼 huddled and crouching.

鬈² Fine growth of hair. Curly hair.
1661

勸
勸⁴ To exhort; to advise; to persuade; to encourage.
1662

勸·不動 or 勸·不開 unable to move a person by exhortation or advice.
勸世文 tracts; writings to reform the world.
勸人 to exhort others.
勸允 use persuasion to get consent.
⁵勸勉 or 勸勵 to encourage; to stimulate.
勸化 or 勸敎 or 勸導 to urge to reform.
勸告 advice; remonstration.
勸善 to exhort to reformation.
勸喩 to advise; a public admonition.
¹⁰勸懲 to exhort and warn.
勸慰 to console.
勸戒 to warn against a wrong course of action.
勸捐 to call upon people for subscriptions.

勸散 to induce quarrellers to separate.
¹⁵勸業場 or 勸工場 an industrial exposition where goods may be purchased.
勸業銀行 The Industrial Bank; a bank opened to encourage industry and agriculture.
勸相 to encourage and assist.
勸蠶 encourage (the women) to attend to the silkworms.
勸解 or 勸和 or 勸息 to exhort to peace; to make peace.
²⁰勸說 to advise; counsel.
勸諭 to advise; to persuade; to instruct.
勸誘 to counsel and lead.
勸諫 to remonstrate with a superior.
勸責 to reprove.
²⁵勸賀 or 勸進 to exhort a leader to take the throne.
勸農 to encourage agriculture.
勸酒 or 勸酬 to pledge in wine.
勸醒 to arouse.
勸駕 to urge (them) to accompany him.
³⁰相勸 mutual admonitions.

權² To weigh. The weight on a steelyard.
1663

權稱 to weigh on a scale.
權衡 the weight and the beam of the steelyard; to weigh; to consider.
權輕重 to weigh; to estimate; to consider.
權輿
　—the beginnings of things; to begin; to originate; to initiate.

平權 to balance; to adjust; equal rights (for men and women).

(a) Inherent rights. Authority, power, influence; used as a suffix to express this thought,—a list is given below for illustration.

權佞 powerful statesmen and glib-tongued ministers.
權·利 rights and privileges.
權利主義 the doctrine of privileges.
權利平等 equal rights and privileges.
⁵權利義務 privilege and duty.
權制 despotic rule.

權勢 or 權力 power and influence—generally used in a bad sense.
權右 one in high office who wields authority.
權幸 or 權寵 a favourite usurping authority.
¹⁰權戚 powerful relatives.
權枉 using the influence of one who is in authority for evil purposes.
權柄 or 權能 power; power and ability; authority.
權橫之家 powerful families who use their power for oppression.↑權威 authority.
權界 the world of power.
¹⁵權臣 powerful officials.
權藉 to rely on influence and power for oppressing others.
權衡執掌 the authority is in his hands.
權要 or 權軸 a position of power and influence.
權責 power and responsibility.
²⁰權門 or 權家 those who have power and influence.
權°限 prescribed rights; competency; limitation of authority.
權限爭議 contention as to the limits of authority.
權首 one who leads in giving strategic advice, etc.
上訴權 right of appeal.
²⁵三權鼎立 judicial, legislative, and executive powers stand like a tripod.
主張權利 to stand on one's rights.
主權 sovereign rights.
人權 rights as a man.
代理權 power of attorney.
³⁰個人自由權 individual liberty.
債權 rights of the creditor; credit.
全權 full power; full authority. See No. 1666-29.ff.
公權 civil rights.
兵權 military power.
³⁵剝權 to strip away the rights of.
取消權 right to rescind or abrogate.
占有權 rights of tenure.
國權 national sovereignty.
國家主權 right of sovereignty.
⁴⁰家長³權 rights of the head of a family.
平均地權 equalization of land ownership.

弄 權 to wield power or influence.
授 權 to empower.
操 權 to wield power; to assume authority.
[45] 政 權 political power—of the people, under which are included
選 舉 權 suffrage.
罷 免 權 the right of recall.
創 制 權 the initiative.
複 決 權 the referendum.
[50] 民 權 案 the *Bill of Rights*.
治 權 administrative authority—of the government, under which are included
司 法 權 judicial authority.
立 法 權 legislative authority.
行 政 權 executive authority.
[55] 攷 試 權 authority for conducting civil service tests.
監 察 權 rights of censorship.
治 外 法 權 extraterritoriality, as granted to ministers, envoys, etc. *See below,*—74.
海 權 naval power.
無 權 no authority; not in .... province.
[60] 無 限 之 權 unlimited authority or power.
版 權 copyright.
特 權 special rights or privilege.
獨 立 權 autonomy; rights of inpendence.
王 權 royal power.
[65] 生 命 權 right of life.
統 治 權 dominion; power of government over.
行 使 職 權 to exercise authority; to wield power.
親 權 rights of parents.
請 求 權 right of claim.
[70] 請 求 保 護 權 the right to claim protection.
議 決 權 right of decision.
質 權 right of the mortgagee.
通 行 權 right of way.
領 事 裁 判 權 extraterritoriality, as applied to nationals of other countries residing in the land. *See above,*—57.

(b) Exigency, circumstances. To act according to circumstances or expediency; opportunism; that which is irregular, and opposed to 經, that which is constant and normal—from this therefore comes the idea of temporary, etc. See 以 No. 2932. D. 3.

權 且 under the circumstances; for the time being.
權 且 之 計 a makeshift plan.
權 任 a substitute or deputy.
權 使 to use a man according to the exigencies of the position.
[5] 權 便 opportunism; to adapt oneself to the circumstances.
權 典 temporary enactment.
權 子³ 母 to get compound interest.
權 宜 temporarily obliged to do so.
權 宜 之 舉 a measure of expediency.
[10] 權 攝 an acting-appointment.
權 數 opportunism; expediency.
權 時 for the time being.
權 智 the wisdom of the opportunist.
權 濟 目 前 makeshift; temporary expedient.
[15] 權 爭 wrangle over expedients.
權 用 to make an exception to the rule.
權 知 temporarily in charge.
權 而 得 中 acted according to the exigencies of the case without deviating from the right.
權 術 the art of making allowances.
[20] 權 詐 intriguing; treacherous.
權 謀 or 權 略 intrigue; expedients.
權 變 versatile; adaptation to circumstances.
權 辦 to act under the pressure of circumstances; to adopt exceptional measures.
嫂 溺 援 之 以 手 者 權 也 to rescue a drowning sister-in-law by the hand is a peculiar exigency.
[25] 從 權 to act in an irregular manner because of the abnormal conditions.
通 權 達 變 versatile; able to adapt oneself to circumstances.

(c) Inter. next—The cheek-bones.

權 骨 the cheek-bones.

(d) Used like 爟 No. 3573a. To set fire to.

權 火 a beacon.
權 星 a star which is under the element of fire.

顴² The cheek-bones.
1664
顴 骨 高 聳 high cheek-bones—indicative of cruel character.

縓² Orange or reddish-yellow silk. Also read *yüan²*.
1665
縓 緣 a red collar.

CH'ÜAN　TS'ÜAN. (ㄘㄩㄢ)
(Ch'üen)

全
仝
1666

² Perfect, entire, the whole, all, complete. Absolute. To keep. Added as a suffix implies totality, "with all accessories," etc.

全 交 to preserve friendly relations.
全 人 a perfect man; the Sage.
全 備 complete; all ready.
全 牙 complete, as an outfit, etc.
[5] 全 副 精 神 with all the energies at one's disposal.
全 力 with all the strength.
全 史 a complete record.
全 國 the whole nation.
全 國 一 致 the whole nation as one.
[10] 全 國 之 公 敵 a national enemy; a foe to the whole nation.
全 國 戶 口 調 查 national census.
全 國 水 利 局 National Conservancy Bureau.
全 國 省 敎 育 會 聯 合 會 United Association of the Provincial Boards of Education.
全 國 菸 酒 事 務 署 National Tobacco and Wine Bureau.
[15] 全 國 黨 會 National Parties.
全 卷 照 錄 to copy all the documents in a case.
全 地 the whole land.
全 家 the entire family.
全 就 to complete.
[20] 全 局 the general position; the interests involved.
全 局 勝 利 wholly successful.
以 全 大 局 for the sake of the whole.
全 年 the whole year.
全 才 extensive abilities.
[25] 全 數 the whole amount; the total number.
↑ 全 文 complete text.

全 日 the whole day.

全 智 全 能 omniscient and almighty.

全 案 the complete records of a matter.

全 權 plenary powers.

[80] 全 權 代 表 fully accredited representative.

全 權 公 使 Minister Plenipotentiary.

全 民 政 治 government by all the people. 全 民 戰 爭 total war.

全 活 to save alive; the save the whole number.

全 然 entirely; completely.

[35] 全 然 自 由 entire freedom; perfect liberty.

全 無 absolutely nothing or none.

全 無 心 肝 without heart or liver; utterly without feeling, a hardened wretch.

全 生 to preserve life.

全 盤 the whole matter; entirely.

[40] 全 省 漁 業 provincial fishing-industry.

全 福 perfect happiness; both parents living.

全 能 almighty.

全 軍 the whole army; to preserve the army.

全 軍 覆 沒 the army was totally defeated.

[45] 全 都 all, altogether, every one.

全 部 the whole department or section.

全 部 內 容 total contents.

全 部 撤 退 the whole section withdrew.

全 量 sum total; full measure.

[50] 全 銜 the full title or style of an official, etc.

全 錄 a complete copy, to copy in full. 全 長 the whole length.

全 體 the whole body; the whole section, etc.

全 體 出 席 full attendance.

全 體 列 席 a full attendance.

[55] 全 體 反 對 unanimous opposition.

全 體 國 務 員 all the cabinet.

全 體 打 消 unanimous disagreement with the proposals.

全 體 贊 成 unanimous approval.

全 體 進 行 general advance of the whole.

[60] 以 全 和 好 to preserve the friendly relations.

大 全 complete, as the complete works of.

完 全 complete; perfect, whole.

↑ 全 無 根 據 utterly unfounded.

忠 孝 兩 全 both filial piety and loyalty complete.

才 貌 雙 全 having both beauty and talents in full measure.

佺 [2] 1667   An immortal.

牷 [2] 1668   Bullock all of one colour, perfect in all its parts and fit for sacrifice.

痊 [2] 1669   Healed, cured. To cure.

痊 愈 or 痊 可 to cure; healed.

告 痊 to report recovery.

筌 [1] 1670   A bamboo fish-trap.

得 魚 忘 筌 forget the trap when you have caught the fish—ingratitude.

荃 [1] 1671   A fragrant plant.

荃 照 or 荃 鑒 to inform your fragrant intelligence.—conventional phrase in correspondence.

詮 [1] 1672   To explain, to comment, to illustrate. To enforce.

詮 義 to explain the meaning.

詮 諭 Your instructions—used in letters.

詮 證 explanatory proof or evidence.

註 詮 commentary, notes.

銓 [1] 1673   To estimate the quantity or the quality. To select.

銓 叙 局 Bureau of Civil Appointments.

銓 叙 局 局 長 Chief of the Bureau of Civil Appointments.

銓 度 (*to* [4.5]) to estimate; to calculate; to weigh.

銓 才 small abilities.

銓 衡 to put in the balance; to weigh.

銓 選 to select for a post.

銓 部 or 銓 曹 the former Board of Civil Office.

銓 量 to judge of; to estimate.

銓 叙 部 Department of Civil Appointments.

泉 [2]
洤 1674   A fountain or spring.

泉 壤 the underworld or Hades.

泉 源 or 泉 水 a fountain or spring.

泉 石 mountain springs.

泉 石 膏 肓 a craze for travel (almost amounting to a disease)—especially among mountains and springs.

[5] 泉 眼 the opening of a spring.

泉 聲 苦 the sad murmur of a spring.

泉 脈 the 'pulse' or supplies of a spring.

泉 路 = 黃 泉 路 上 on the way to the yellow springs—dying.

九 泉 Hades—the nether regions.

[10] 歸 泉 to go to the grave—to die.

飛 泉 a cascade.

(a) Wealth.

泉 布 money, refers to its widespread use.

泉 幣 money.

泉 府 ancient term for officer of the treasury.

泉 貝 cowries, formerly used as money.

巏 [2] 1675   A fountain in the side of a hill.

悛 [1] 1676   To alter, to reform. Wilful.

悛 心 penitent.

悛 改 to reform or repent.

雋 [4]
隽 1677   Fat, fleshy. Surname.

肥 雋 fat.

(a) Read *chün* [4]. Strange. Brave.

雋 拔 outstanding excellence.

雋永 strange and lasting—of an interesting story or poetry.
雋聞 strange news.
雋茂 beautiful, excelling.
雋譽 good reputation.

CHÜEH.   (ㄐㄩㄝ)

歗 1.5. To hiccough. To dig out. To expand.
1678

瘚 2.5. To hiccough. The humours of the body.
1679

氣瘚 convulsions.

厥 2.5. A personal pronoun—he, she, it, its, his, hers, theirs, etc.
1680

厥初 and 厥終 the beginning and the ending of things.
厥德不回 his virtue was not turned aside.
厥明 to-morrow.
厥疾不瘳 that malady is incurable.
厥等 those persons.
厥角 to kotow.

劂 2.5. A gouge, a chisel for engraving.
1681

剞劂 a graver's tool.

劂 4.5. To urge; to compel.
1682

噘 1.5. Pouting.
1683

噘嘴 protruding lips.

撅 2.5. To stick up, as a tail. To break off; to strike.
1684

撅下來 to break off.

(a) Read kuei⁴. To lift the skirts.

不涉不撅 except when crossing a stream the skirts were not lifted.

橜 2.5. A post, a stake. An axle.
1685

橜子 a peg.
橜杙 a stake or post.

獗 2.5. Unruly, rude.
1686

猖獗 lawless, wild, fierce.

蕨 2.5. Bracken, called "turtle foot,"—the root is used for food.
1687

蕨粉 starch prepared from the roots of the above, used as food.

蟨 2.5. The Siberian jerboa.
1688

蟨鼠 the above.

趹 2.5. To step, to jump.
1689

蹶 2.5. To stumble, to slip, to fall.
1690

懼馬蹶失 I fear my horse may stumble.

(a) Read chüeh³·⁵. To kick, of animals.
尥蹶子 to kick back (of animals).

(b) Read kuei⁴. To excite, to move.
蹶蹶然 suddenly; sprightly.
子夏蹶然而起 Tzŭ Hsia rose up with a start.

鐝 2.5. A pick, a hoe.
1691

骹 2.5. The end of the backbone. Bones of the tail.
1692

倔 2.5. Crabbed, tough.
1693

倔強 to oppose; wilful; obstinate.
倔氣 or 倔喪 boorish, stubborn spirit.

崛 2.5. Eminent, towering, as a peak.
1694

崛起 to become eminent.
洪臺崛其獨出兮 a great tower standing alone.

掘 2.5. To dig, to excavate.
1695

掘井 to dig a well.
掘低 to lower; to reduce the height by digging.
掘地 to dig the earth.
掘坑 to dig a pit.
掘塚 to prepare a tomb.
掘軍 sappers.
掘開 to dig open.
↑ 掘藏 to dig at a hidden treasure
發掘 to excavate; excavation.

抉 2.5. To dig; to select or pluck out.
1696

抉剔 to pick out.
抉摘 to select the important items.
抉眼 to gouge out an eye.
抉首 to decapitate.

(a) To draw, as a bow.

抉弦 to stretch a bow.

決 2.5. To sentence, to decide. Decidedly. Before a negative adds strong emphasis.
1697

決不 on no account . . .
決不姑寬 no indulgence whatever will be shown.
決不寬貸 no leniency will be given.
決不爲難 there will be no difficulty at all in that.
決不肯從 not at all willing to follow.
決不能 on no account; it cannot possibly be done.
決不至於 it certainly will not come to . . . .
決不該信 should on no account be believed or trusted.

決不食言 I certainly will not go back on my words.

[10]決別 to bid farewell.

決定 to decide upon; certain; fixed.

決定書 document of settlement.

決心 decision.

決志 determined, unyielding purpose.

[15]決意 decision; determination; decisive vote; to determine.

決意主戰 to decide on war.

決戰 to fight a decisive battle.

決擇歌 counting-out rhymes, of children's games.

決斷 to make a decision.

↑決判 to make a decision, as a judge.

[20]決書 an ultimatum. = 6858.39.

決死隊 suicide squad.

決決乎 certainly; positively.

決沒人信 certainly no one will believe that.(-mei²-)

決然 certainly; decidedly.

[25]決然不受 on no account to endure it.

決無此事 there is no such thing; such a thing never happened.

決獄 to decide a case.

決疑 to elucidate doubts; to determine a doubtful problem.

決算 to balance accounts; final estimates.

[30]決算表 balance-sheet.

對除決算 to strike a balance.

決絕 to renounce utterly.

決裂 to break off relations with; completed; suddenly dissipated; certain to be destroyed; decided. *See below.* A.4.

決要 indispensable; I must have it.

[35]決計 decided; come to a decision.

決議 to decide by majority after a vote.

決議案 closing bill.

決議錄 register of decisions.

決賽 final heat of a race.

[40]決選 decisive vote; to decide by a second election.

決雌雄 to decide the mastery.

決非 different from; anything but ....

決鬪 a duel.

可決 to pass.

[45]否決 to negative.

解決爭端 to decide a dispute.

圓滿解決 satisfactorily settled.

(a) To burst open; to clear, as water-ways.

決口 a breach, as of a dike.

決水 to inundate.

決水罪 the crime of inundation. (*legal*).

決裂 to burst open, as dikes. *See above.*—33.

決諸東方則東流 open a passage for it to the east and it flows east.

決防 taking precaution against the bursting of dikes.

河決 the river bursts its banks.

(b) To cut off, to slay; to execute.

決其首 behead her.

大決 annual execution of criminals in former days, generally ten days before winter solstice.

引決自裁 to commit suicide.

立決 summary execution.

自決 suicide.

處決 to pass a capital sentence.

(c) To bite things through with the teeth.

而問無齒決 and ask about the injunction not to tear the meat with the teeth.

(d) An archer's thumb-ring.

決拾 ivory ring worn when pulling a string.

玦 2.5. A jade ring not quite complete, there being a small segment cut from it—used to indicate separation. Also used for the last—a thumb-ring worn by archers.
1698

指玦 thumb-ring.

佩玦 girdle-pendants.

觖 2.5. To long for; dissatisfied. To criticize.
1699

觖事 a defect.

觖望 impatiently longing for; disappointed.

摘觖 to criticize others.

訣 2.5. Parting or dying words. An art, a mystery or secret. Esoteric; occult.
1700

訣別 to part from.

訣法 the secrets of a craft.

訣疑 to remove doubts.

訣竅 the secret; the knack of a thing.

[5]訣詞 farewell words.

口訣 charms; magic formula.

妙訣 occult; the secret.

永訣 an eternal farewell.

留訣 last dying words.

[10]祕訣 secrets of an art, etc.

脈訣 the secrets of the pulse.

長生之訣 the secret of immortality.

開訣 to give the initial strokes—as to a painting, etc.

鈌 2.5. To pierce, to stab. To take.
1701

譎憰 2.5. Wily, time-serving. To feign, to act the hypocrite.
1702

譎而不正 disingenuous; crafty and not upright.

欺譎 to deceive.

詐譎 deceitful; artful.

詭譎 untrustworthy.

CHÜEH TSÜEH. (ㄘㄩㄝ)

絕 2.5. To cut short; to break off; to interrupt.
1703

絕了糧 starved out; without food.

絕交 to break off intercourse or friendship.

絕俗 to retire from the cares of the world; in word and deed far above the average.

絕口 never been said before; not to be mentioned.

[5]罵不絕口 cursing without ceasing.

絕命 death; to cut short the life.

絕命詞 last words before death.

絕聞 cut off from news.

絕四 he (Confucius) was free from four things, *as below*.

[10]毋意, 毋必, 毋固, 毋我. no foregone conclusions, no arbitrary predeterminations, no obstinacy, no egoism.

絕 地 inaccessible place, place of danger.

絕 域 distant lands.

絕 境 inaccessible places; place of retirement for a recluse.

絕 塵 flying faster than the dust—of the rapid progress in virtuous attainments of *Yen Hui* the favourite disciple of Confucius.

15 絕 壁 an inaccessible precipice.

絕 奶 to be weaned.

絕 山 to cross mountains.

絕 島 a desert island.

絕 後 or 絕 嗣 or 絕 戶 posterity cut off; without an heir.

20 絕 斷 to cease; to cut off.

絕 望 hope lost; in despair.

絕 流 to stop the flow of; to cross a stream.

絕 物 to cut off intercourse with the world. 物 u.f. 人

絕 目 as far as the eye can see.

25 絕 筆 to cease writing—by the death of the writer.

絕 種³ extinct.

絕 緣 器 an insulator.

絕 緣 抵 抗 resistance to insulation.

絕 緣 線 insulated wire.

30 絕 緣 體 or 隔 電 物 insulators, non-conductors.

絕 裂 to break off relations.

絕 賣 absolute sale.

絕 路 to cut off a retreat, or cut off communications; predicament.

絕 迹 to cease intercourse; a strange affair.

35 絕 長 補 短 to cut off the length to make up for the shortage.

絕 離 left at a great distance.

絕 電 質 insulating substances.

絕 食 to fast (to death).

自 絕 suicide.

(a) Decidedly; extremely; very. Used to strengthen a negative.

絕 不 or 絕 無 never, on no account, etc.

絕 不 相 干 no concern whatever (of others.)

絕 世 之 姿 a paragon of beauty.

絕 人 to excel; to surpass others.

5 絕 代 佳 人 the most beautiful woman ever seen.

絕 佳 very good; excellent.

絕 倫 to surpass; to excel.

絕 倒 in full agreement with; in convulsions of laughter; dizzy with pain.

絕 大 the greatest.

10 絕 好 incomparable.

絕 妙 or 絕 美 excellent.

絕 對 absolute; having a single possible antithesis.

絕 對 值 absolute magnitude. (*algeb.*).

絕 對 否 認 absolute refusal.

15 絕 對 單 位 absolute unit.

絕 對 壓 力 absolute pressure.

絕 對 所 有 權 absolute ownership.

絕 對 政 策 a positive policy.

絕 對 權 absolute right or authority.

20 絕 對 溫 度 absolute temperature.

絕 對 的 unconditional; absolute.

絕 對 的 實 在 absolute being.

絕 對 的 要 求 absolute demands.

絕 對 零 度 absolute zero.

25 絕 對 高 度 absolute height.

絕 才 extraordinary talents.

絕 技 extraordinary skill.

絕 景 beautiful, unsurpassed scenery.

絕 無 not in the least, never.

30 絕 無 僅 有 unique.

絕 無 好 處 with no possible advantage.

絕 端 標 準 absolute standard.

絕 等 outclassed; excellent.

絕 色 unsurpassed beauty.

35 絕 頂 the summit; tiptop.

絕 頂 聰 明 marvellous intelligence.

(b) A stanza of four lines.

絕 句 a stanza of four lines.

CHÜEH. CHÜOH or CHIO.   (ㄐㄩㄝ)

瞿 4.5.   To look right and left in alarm.
1704

瞿 瞿 scared, terrified.

瞿 視 to look hastily at.

瞿 踢 running here and there, seeking to escape.

攫 4.5.   To seize, as a bird of prey, or a wild beast.
1705

攫 取 to seize and carry off.

攫 捕 to grasp.

玃 1.5.   A large ape found in W. China.
1706

埆 2.5.   Stony soil.
1707

墝 埆 rough, stony and barren land.

CH'ÜEH.   (ㄑㄩㄝ)

缺 1.5.   A deficiency, a vacancy, an official post. Broken, defective.
1708

缺 去 to break off.

缺 吃 穿 lacking food and clothing.

缺 唇 or 缺 口 hare-lip.

缺 席 absence, as from roll-call.

5 缺 席 判 決 judgement by default; decision given in the absence of one party.

缺 憾 disappointment.

缺 效 unsuccessful.

缺 效 未 遂 犯 unsuccessful crime. (*legal*).

缺 望 disappointed, hopeless.

10 缺 本 short of capital.

缺 欠 or 缺 少 or 缺 乏 deficient; a lack, a need.

缺 殘 smashed; ruined.

缺 水 a deficiency of water.

缺 玷 a defect; a flaw.

15 缺 疑 points about which there is a doubt.

缺 筆 a stroke or more missing from a character in writing.

缺 着 手 short of capital.

缺 處 an open spot; an empty place.

缺 虧 a deficit or loss.

20 缺 角 a corner knocked off.

缺 陷 deficient; imperfect; defective.

缺 點 a shortcoming, a defect.

出 缺 there is a vacancy.

好 缺 a lucrative post.

25 崩 缺 given way; to break down.

月 有 盈 缺 the moon waxes and wanes.

欠 缺 deficiency, need.

破 缺 cracked.

空 缺 a vacancy.

30 繁 缺 a post where there is plenty of business.

補 缺 to fill up a vacancy.

舵[1] Stiffness of the joints.
1709

癱[2] Lame; paralysis of hands or feet.
1710

癱·子 a cripple.
癱 精 瞎 怪 deformed and maimed.
癱 腿·的 a cripple, a lame man.
癱 跤 lame.
胎·裏 癱 lame from birth.

関 4.5. To shut the door; to close; to rest.
1711

不 関 時 月 without ceasing.
服 関 to lay aside mourning.
樂 関 the music ceased.

闕 4.5. The look-out tower above a gate. An imperial city.
1712

闕 下 the emperor; Your Majesty.
闕 里 old home of Confucius.
闕 門 or 闕 庭 the imperial palace.
望 闕 行 禮 to make obeisances towards the capital.
金 闕 the golden gate—the palace.

(a) A hiatus, a deficiency; wanting; to omit; to be reserved.

闕 如 也 hesitating, showing reserve.
闕 文 a hiatus in the text.
闕 略 incomplete.
闕 翦 to destroy; to ruin.
⁵闕 遺 omissions.
多 聞 闕 疑 hear much, and put on one side the points of which you are in doubt.
尙 付 闕 如 regard it as a thing unknown.
月 闕 the waning of the moon.
盈 闕 waxing and waning.
¹⁰義 闕 the meaning has been lost.
衰 職 有 闕 in the case of any remissness on the part of the sovereign.

CH'ÜEH   CH'ÜOH. (ㄑㄩㄝ)

摧 4.5. To knock, to pick out. To ridicule.
1713

摧 瓜 子³ to pick out melon seeds from the pulp. (pron. k'o⁴)
摧 眼 to gouge out the eyes.
摧 腫 swollen, as from a blow.
商 摧 to consult about.

躩 1.5. To leap. To bend. Respectful steps before a superior. Pron. chüeh².
1714

躩 走 to walk with a long stride.
躩 跳 to leap; to leap across.
足 躩 如 也 his legs seemed to bend under him—of Confucius.
塞 裳 躩 步 he gathered up his skirts and strode across.

CHÜN. (ㄐㄩㄣ)

(Chüin)

君[1] A chief, a sovereign, a ruler. A gentleman.
1715

君 主 or 人 君 a monarch.
君 主 主 權 說 theory. of sovereignty. (legal).
君 主 主 義 monarchism.
君 主 制 the monarchic system.
⁵君 主 國 monarchy.
君 主 專 制 autocratic monarchy.
君 主 政 體 monarchical form of government.
君 主 獨 裁 sole authority for decision rests with the monarch.
君 主 立 憲 constitutional monarchy.
¹⁰君 取 於 吳 爲 同 姓 the prince married a princess of Wu of the same surname as himself.
君 召 使 擯 the prince called him and sent him to receive the visitors.
君 合 國 two or more States united under one monarch, but not necessarily under one government.
君 后 按 摩 the royal touch.
君 君 臣 臣 let the prince be a prince, and the statesmen be statesmen.
¹⁵君 嗣 the son of a monarch.
君 國 to rule a State.

君 士 坦 丁 Constantine.
君 天 下 to rule over the empire.
君 子³ the princely man—a gentleman, the wise man, a man of complete virtue, the beau-ideal of Confucianism.
²⁰君 子³ 不 可 小 知 而 可 大 受 the princely man may not be known by small matters, but can be entrusted with great affairs.
君 子³ 不 器 the princely man is not a utensil—merely an article with one use.
君 子³ 不 重 則 不 威 without self-respect a man will not be respected.
君 子³ 之 德 風 小 人 之 德 草 the virtue of the men who lead is like the wind, that of those who follow is like the grass.
君 子³ 可 逝 也 不 可 陷 the superior man can be made to save (the person who is drowning) but he cannot be entrapped (in the well).
²⁵君 子³ 恕 以 爲 必 歸 the superior men among us (judging the State of Ch'in 秦 by themselves) believe that Ch'in will pardon their prince (of Chin 晉) and set him at liberty.
君 子³ 愛 其 君 而 知 其 罪 the superior men (among us) love their prince (captive in Ch'in 秦) and recognize that he was in the wrong.
君 子³ 憂 道 不 憂 貧 the man of superior attainments is anxious lest he should not get the truth, he is not anxious lest poverty should overcome him.
君 子³ 無 戲 言 the man of superior virtue never jests.
君 子³ 疾 夫 舍 曰 欲 之 而 必 爲 之 辭 the refusing to say that you wish so-and-so, and the making of explanations to gloss your conduct—this is what the princely man dislikes.
³⁰君 子³ 謀 道 不 謀 食 the superior man seeks for the truth, not merely for a living.
君 權 sovereignty of the king.
君 民 sovereign and people.
君 民 共 主 limited monarchy, power divided between the king and the people.

君 無 見 焉 do not see him, Prince!

³⁵君 王 or 君 上 a ruler, a sovereign.

君 知 否 Do you know, sir?

君 臣 prince and minister.

君 臣 有 義 righteousness is the relation which should exist between the prince and his ministers.

君 長 (*chang³*) a chief.

⁴⁰先 君 my deceased father.

太 君 my mother, used on tombstones, etc.

太 上 老 君 Laotzŭ, the founder of Taoism.

夫 君 my husband.

少 君 your son.

⁴⁵府 君 my father, used on tombstones, etc.

昏 君 a blinded prince.

細 君 my wife.

義 動 君 子³ a man of complete virtue is moved to action by duty.

諸 君 Gentlemen. Sirs!

窘 ⁴ Distressed; afflicted.
1716   Pron. *chiung³*.

窘 口 無 言 he said nothing—being conscious of guilt.

窘 急 in the utmost need.

窘 窮 or 窘 困 miserably poor.

窘 辱 deeply insulted.

窘 迫 in straits; in distress; to molest.

菨 ¹ A water-grass; hippuris.
1717

菨 蓬 荣 beetroot.

郡 ⁴ A political division, the extent of which has varied
1718   in different times, from a province to a prefectural district. A Prefecture, a sub-Prefecture, an independent Department or county.

郡 主 daughter of an Imperial prince of the first degree.

郡 君 daughter of a prince of the Imperial house—from the *Sung* dynasty; formerly the wife of officials of the fourth rank.

郡 城 a prefectural city.

郡 宰 assistant sub-Prefect.

⁵郡 會 之 區 a large city.

郡 馬 son-in-law of an Imperial prince.

郡 首 or 郡 守 or 郡 候 a Prefect.

囷 ¹ A granary, a pen, a bin. Spiral. Distinguish 囷 No.
1719   3688.

輪 囷 spiral.

菌
蕈 ³
    The mushroom. Mould or mildew. Second form
1720   is also read *hsin⁴*.

菌 傘 the mushroom.

菌 性·的 fungoid.

菌 柄 mushroom stalk.

菌 種 mushroom spawn or spores.

⁵菌 絲 mushroom spores.

菌 薰 fragrant plants.

菌 褶 the appearance of the underside of a mushroom.

麇
麕 ¹
    General name for the hornless deer. A small
    deer—the muntjac.
1721   Read *chün²*. To collect, to band together.

麇 集 banded together; in league.

麇 脯 dried venison.

賊 匪 麇 聚 banding together of brigands, etc.

軍 ¹
    Military; an army.
1722

軍 事 military matters.

軍 事 公 債 loan for military purposes.

軍 事 封 鎖 military blockade.

軍 事 教 練 官 army training officer.

⁵軍 事 教 育 military knowledge.

軍 事 會 審 or 軍 事 裁 判 military court.

軍 事 會 議 army council.

軍 事 知 識 military experience.

軍 事 科 department of army affairs.

¹⁰軍 事 秘 密 military secrets.

軍 事 飛 行 家 military aviators.

軍 事 負 擔 a military charge. (*legal*).

軍 人 one of the army.

軍 人 資 格 qualifications for military service.

¹⁵軍 令 military orders.

軍 令 狀 under strict martial law.

軍 令 鎗 斃 executed under martial law.

軍 使 military commissioner—envoy.

軍 備 military preparations.

²⁰軍 備 器 械 reserves of munitions.

軍 備 費 military expenditure.

軍 兵 soldiers.

軍 翼 the flank of an army.

軍 制 military system.

²⁵軍 功 military honours.

軍 務 or 軍 情 military matters.

軍 務 交 通 army communications.

軍 務 司 Army Department in the War Office.

軍 勢·上 地 位 strategical position.

³⁰軍 區 military area.

軍 卒 soldiers.

軍 命 military commands.

軍 國 主 義 militarism.

軍 國 民 教 育 national military training.

³⁵軍 團 corps; army.

軍 官 officer in the army.

軍 官 學 校 school for cadets.

軍 容 the morale of troops.

軍 工 學 military engineering.

⁴⁰軍 帖 military despatch.

軍 師 行 伍 之 列 the marshalling of the ranks. (-*hang²*-)

軍 庫 military stores.

軍 役 active military service.

軍 律 military laws.

⁴⁵軍 威 military prestige.

軍 政 army administration.

軍 政 部 Ministry of War.

軍 政 部 長 Minister of War.

軍 政 府 military government.

軍 旅 之 事 military matters.

⁵⁰軍 服 uniform.

軍 械 or 軍 器 or 兵 械 weapons; military equipment.

軍 械 借 欵 loan to supply military equipment, arms, etc.

軍 械 司 bureau for the supply of arms.

軍 械 局 depot for arms, etc.

⁵⁵軍 械 製 造 廠 or 兵 工 廠 arsenal.

軍 樂 隊 military band.

軍 權 偏 重 military authority became paramount.

軍 情 military intelligence.

軍機處 Grand Council of State; Privy Council of the Emperor.
軍民 military and civil.
[60]軍民分治 separation of military and civil rule.
軍民府 military sub-Prefect with civil jurisdiction, formerly stationed at important places.
軍民長官 civil and military authorities.
軍法 military law.
軍法司 army law-court.
[65]軍法會議 a sitting of a military court.
軍法裁判 court-martial.
軍法課 the branch of law pertaining to military matters.
軍港 naval dock.
軍火 munitions of war.
[70]軍營 military camp.
軍犯 military offenders.
軍用 for military use.
軍用品 articles for use of the army.
軍用鈔票 paper-money issued for the use of troops.
[75]軍用鐵路 military railway.
軍用電信 field-telegraph for army use.
軍用電話 military telephone.
軍田 lands formerly set apart for soldiers or exiles.
軍界 the army world; the military; military circles. [military rites.
[80]軍禮 the last argument—war; military circles.
軍系 the army connections; army circles.
軍紀 military discipline.
軍署 military yamen.
軍艦 warship.
[85]軍艦特權 international privileges granted to warships.
軍籍 army register.
軍號 military call, trumpet or bugle, etc.
軍裝 military equipment.
軍規 military discipline.
[90]軍謨 military matters.
軍費 army expenses.
軍逃 deserters.
軍醫司 army medical bureau.
軍門 former title of Admiral or a provincial Commander-in-chief.
[95]軍閥 military exclusives; the military caste.
軍閥派 military party.
軍隊 a band of soldiers; the army.
軍需 military supplies.
軍長[3] commander of an army.

軍需品 army supplies.
[100]軍需局 or 軍需司 bureau for supply of army necessities.
軍需科 army-service department.
勒派軍需 compulsory contribution for military supplies.
軍雞 a fighting cock.
軍餉 rations, etc., for the army.
[105]軍騎 or 騎軍 mounted troops.
充軍 banishment for life with military service.
將軍 a general.
屯軍 to entrench troops.
招軍 to recruit.
[110]投軍 to enlist.
督軍 Tuchun. Military Governor.
監軍 Inspecting Commissioner for the army.

皸[1]　Chapped skin.
1723

手足皸裂 hands and feet chapped from cold.

均[1]　Equal, equally, fairly. All. A potter's wheel. To rule fairly, to adjust.
1724

均一 all equally.
均之 and similarly; in like manner.
均係 are all....
均分 or 均攤 to allot equally.
[5]有利均分 the profits, if any, to be equally divided.
均勢 balance of power.
均勻 or 均平 impartial; uniform; equal.
均可 either will do.
均富主義 another name for communism.
[10]均平無偏 balanced; regulated.
均悉 has been noted with care.
均應 all should....
均淨 complete; unspotted.
均爲 are all....; are each....
[15]均產黨 or 均富黨 Communist Party.
均當 all should....
均等 equality.
均背拉一算 to strike the average.
均見增多 have all experienced an increase.
[20]均重 equal weight; equipoise.
均須 all must....

均齊 regular; even.
均齊方正 all even and regular.

鈞[1]
鈞
1725

A weight of thirty catties. Distinguish 鈎 No. 6279.

千鈞一髮之際 a desperate crisis—hanging a heavy weight by a hair.
今日舉百鈞 today he says, "I can lift 3,000 catties."

(a) You, your.

鈞函 your favour.
鈞安 may you enjoy repose!
鈞諭 or 鈞命 your instructions.

(b) To harmonize, to balance.

鈞同其聲 he harmonized their voices.
鈞座 civil officials.
鈞裁 to make an equitable decision.

(c) A potter's wheel.

鈞陶 to mould—the talents of men.
大鈞 the Great Potter—God.
陶鈞萬品 (God) moulded all things into order.

CHÜN　　TSÜN. (ㄐㄩㄣ)

(Chüin)

儁[4]　Valiant, brave. Eminent. u.f. next.
1726

儁異 extraordinary; unrivalled; strange.

俊[4]　Superior, handsome, refined, eminent.
1727

俊人物 a refined-looking man.
俊俏 graceful, elegant.
俊傑在位 brave and sterling men are in office.
俊器 men of eminent ability.
[5]俊士 a refined person.
俊德 great virtue.
俊民 superior talented men.
俊爽 handsome and able.
俊美 or 俊雅 or 俊秀 refined and elegant.

¹⁰俊 邁 excelling in all grace and elegance.

峻⁴ Dangerous, lofty, steep. Inter. 駿 No. 1735.
1728

峻 命 不 易 the great decree is not easily (preserved.)
峻 宇 雕 牆 lofty buildings and carved walls—a wealthy style.
峻 嶺 a lofty range.
峻 拒 to make a stubborn resistance.
峻 絕 precipitous; dangerous.
峻 險 high and dangerous.

濬⁴ **浚** Deep, abstruse. To enlighten.
1729

浚 哲 文 明 both profound and clear-sighted.
子 浚 我 以 生 you take of mine to nourish yourself.
深 浚 very deep.

(a) To dig.

浚 井 to dig a well.
浚 湖 to dredge a lake.

畯⁴ A bailiff or landlord.
1730

田 畯 a bailiff.

竣⁴ To complete, to finish. Completed, done. Also read ch'ün¹.
1731

竣 事 or 完 竣 to complete.
告 竣 to announce the completion of a task or an undertaking.

踆² To cease. To fall back. To hop.
1732

踆 踆 hopping like a bird.
日 中 踆 烏 the three-legged crow in the sun.

(a) Read ts'un². To wrench or strain.

踆 了 腿 to wrench the leg.

逡¹ To feel abashed; to shrink from. A revolution of the moon. Pron. ch'ün¹.
1733

逡 次 to proceed in order.
逡 行 to shrink, to shirk.
逡 巡 退 縮 to shrink back.

餕⁴ The remains of a sacrifice or a meal. To eat up the remnants.
1734

餕 旣 盡 也 everything has been eaten.
餕 餘 scraps, leavings.
餕 餘 不 祭 leavings cannot be used for offerings.

駿⁴ A fine horse. Swift, fleet. Great, lofty. Inter. 峻 No. 1728.
1735

駿 命 不 易 the great appointment is hard—to carry out.
駿 極 于 天 they reach to the skies.
駿 發 其 私 to make clear his personal opinions.
駿 速 fleet.
⁵駿 馬 a noble horse.
駿 駿 very exalted; grand.
精 駿 excellent; fine, skilful workmanship.
追 風 駿 a horse that speeds like the wind.

CH'ÜN. (ㄑㄩㄣ)
(Ch'üin)

夋¹ To dawdle. The name of the father of the Emperor Yao.
1736

夋 夋 a mincing gait.

羣 **群**² A flock of sheep; a herd; a company; a multitude. All. A class. To move in agreement. Social; to be sociable.
1737

羣 下 courtiers—men and women.
羣 侶 friends.
羣 力 the force of numbers.
羣 化 social reform.
⁵羣 友 one's circle of friends.
羣 后 all the feudal princes.
羣 學 sociology. 社 會 學
羣 學 家 a student of sociology.
羣 小 a mob of bad men.

¹⁰羣 居 to dwell closely; a dense population.
羣 居 終 日 when a number of people are together for a whole day.
羣 島 archipelago.
羣 庶 or 羣 黎 the masses.
羣 心 or 羣 情 popular feelings.
¹⁵羣 才 the talented.
羣 有 all things.
羣 治 rule of the mob; democracy; communistic rule.
羣 生 mankind; the people.
羣 畜 flocks of domestic animals.
²⁰羣 疑 full of doubts.
羣 相 懷 疑 looked at with suspicion by the masses.
羣 衆 all people; mob.
羣 神 敎 polytheism.
羣 策 concensus of opinion.
²⁵羣 策 羣 力 united strength and wisdom.
羣 籍 all kinds of books.
↑羣 衆 運 動 mass movement.
羣 羊 a flock of sheep.
羣 而 不 黨 he mixes with others but he is not partisan.
³⁰羣 臣 all the officers.
羣 芳 or 羣 葩 all kinds of flowers.
羣 芳 譜 botanical treatise.
羣 花 masses of flowers; all kinds of flowers; many prostitutes.
羣 蜂 a swarm of bees or wasps.
³⁵羣 蟻 附 羶 myriad ants on the putrid carcase—the mob-spirit for selfish gains.
羣 言 anthology.
羣 譟 noise of a mob in tumult.
羣 議 popular discussion.
羣 起 反 對 popular opposition.
⁴⁰羣 起 而 攻 之 all rise and attack him (it).
羣 迷 the deceived masses.
羣 遊 to travel together.
羣 集 or 羣 聚 to swarm; to gather in great numbers.
羣 雄 all the heroes.
⁴⁵羣 鶴 a flock of storks—distinguished men.
羣 黨 clans; cliques; parties.
合 羣 gregarious.
同 羣 of the same class.
失 羣 to lose the company of.
⁵⁰狐 羣 狗 黨 foxes and dogs in league—a company of evildoers.
物 以 羣 分 things are distinguished according to their classes.

超羣 above the mass; talented, eminent.

離羣索居 to leave the mass of men and dwell alone.

裙幃 [2] The skirt of a lady's dress. A petticoat.
1738

裙·子 a skirt, a petticoat.

裙屐少年 young dandies or fops.

裙帶親 relatives by marriage.

裙釵 skirts and hairpins—women.

帷裙 an apron.

O. Ê.   (ㄜ)
(Eh)

厄戹 [4.5.] In difficulty; distressed. A ring.
1739

厄窮而不憫 poor but light-hearted.

危厄 in peril.

困厄 in straits, poor.

呝 [4.5.] To hiccough. To cackle.
1740

呝喔 cackling of hens; call of a pheasant.

呝逆 to hiccough.

軛 [4.5.] A yoke, a collar. To restrain.
1741

軛制 to restrain; to curb.

加之以衡軛 put the yoke upon —either lit., or fig.

額額 [2.5.] The forehead. A fixed number.
1742

額兵 a fixed number of soldiers.

額外 beyond the stated quantity; supernumerary.

額引 government salt.

額徵 a fixed tax.

[5]額手相慶 to salute each other by raising the hand to the brow.

以手加額 to salute.

額支 the regular expenditure for any certain period, as one year, etc.

額數 a fixed number.

額汗涔涔 perspiration dropping from the forehead.

[10]額滿 the number is filled up.

額然 suddenly.

額眞 a leader or chief among the Mongols.

顱角 the temples.

額面價格 face-value.

[15]額頂 the top of the head.

額頭 or 額顱 the forehead.

額骨 the frontal bone.

匾額 a tablet.

學額 a fixed number of scholars.

[20]寬額 a liberal allowance.

缺額 a vacancy.

ÊN.   (ㄣ)

恩 [1] Grace, favour; kindness, mercy. Distinguish 思 No. 5580.
1743

恩上加恩 grace added to grace; special favour.

恩主 or 恩人 a benefactor.

恩信相孚 bound by mutual ties, on the one side grace, and on the other loyalty.

恩公兩便 both mercy and justice satisfied.

[5]恩·典 or 恩·惠 or 恩澤 or 恩德 or 恩慈 grace, favour, kindness, bounty.

恩准 graciously to grant.

恩寵 favour; grace.

恩將仇報 to return evil for good.

恩情 graciousness; grace.

[10]恩愛 affection; love between the sexes.

恩愛夫妻 an affectionate couple.

恩物 kindergarten toys.

恩眷 or 恩寵 imperial favour.

恩禮 gracious courtesy.

[15]恩禮優加 special favours were conferred upon him.

恩科 or 恩試 special examinations.

恩綸 gracious words—from the throne.

恩義 bound by ties of mutual affection.

恩膏 anointing; unction; rich favours.

[20]恩臺 or 恩座 the mercy-seat.

恩舊 old acquaintances.

恩詔 gracious proclamation from the Emperor.

恩貢·生 degree granted to a *hsiuts'ai* at a special examination in honour of some event.

恩賞 graciously to reward.

[25]恩賜 gifts of grace.

恩赦 gracious pardon.

恩餉 bounty for troops.

受恩 or 承恩 to receive favours.

天恩 divine favour.

[30]忘恩負義 ingratitude.

感恩 grateful for kindness; much obliged.

施恩 to bestow favours; to shew kindness.

求恩 or 乞恩 to beg for a favour; to sue for grace.

謝恩 to acknowledge a favour.

[35]開恩 to show mercy; to give grace.

摁 [4] To press with the hand.
1743½

ÊRH.   (ㄦ)
(Rï)

耳 [3] The ear. That which is at the side. Radical 128.
1744

耳倦 weary of listening.

耳刮·子 the back of the ear; a box on the ear.

耳剽 to take what one has heard and put it forth as one's own.

耳力 the power of hearing.

[5]耳鳴 buzzing in the ears—it is only heard by oneself; thus by analogy it means "secret virtues"; it is also used in the sense of our "my ears are burning," somebody is talking about me.

耳垂 the lobe of the ear.

耳孔 aperture of the ear.

耳孫 or 仍孫 grandson of a great-great-grandson—one who only hears of his ancestor.

耳學 to learn by hearing only; otology.

[10]耳小骨 or 耳中骨 the small bones of the ear.

耳屎 or 耳垢 or 耳塞·子 or 耳蠟 the wax-secretions of the ear.

耳 屏 or 耳 門 the tragus or prominence at the aperture of the outer ear.

耳 屬 于 垣 there are ears connected with the wall—"walls have ears."

耳 巴·子 or 耳 瓜·子 the cheekbones; the side of the face.

15 打 耳 巴·子 to box the ears, to slap the side of the face.

耳 挖 ear-picks. 耳 挖·子

耳 掃 or 耳 刷 ear-brush.

耳 提 to stimulate the ear.

耳 提 面 命 earnestness in imparting instruction.

20 耳 旁 風 a mere rumour; a matter of no concern.

耳·朵 the ear. (·tou)

耳·朵 帽 or 耳 包 or 耳 套 ear-caps.

耳·朵 發 沉 the ears have become dull.

耳·朵 軟 soft-ears—credulous; in some places—hen-pecked.

25 耳·朵 長 long ears—to hear all that is said.

耳 根 the protuberance at the back of the ear.

耳 殼 or 耳 輪 the rim of the ear.

耳 氣 管 the eustachian tube.

耳 漏 or 耳 膿 otorrhea.

30 耳 濡 目 染 thoroughly imbued with what has been seen and heard—profound scholarship.

耳 熱 burning ears.

耳 熟 能 詳 what has been well-heard can be repeated in detail.

耳 狀·的 eared; ear-like projection on vases, pitchers, etc.

耳 珠 ear-lobe; ear-drops.

35 耳 環 or 耳 璫 ear-rings.

耳 界 within the range of the ear.

耳 痛 or 中 耳 炎 earache.

耳 白 於 面 名 滿 天 下 your ears are whiter than your face, you will be famous.

耳 目 ears and eyes; the senses.

40 耳 目 一 新 all made new, a new outlook.

耳 目 之 官 the Censors.

耳 目 之 官 不 思 the organs of hearing and seeing do not think.

耳 目 口 鼻 ears, eyes, mouth and nose.

耳 目 從 欲 following the desires of the ears and the eyes.

45 耳 科 diseases of the ear, as a department in medicine.

耳 科 醫 ear specialist.

耳 竅 the cavity of the ear.

耳 筒 an ear-trumpet.

耳 紅 面 赤 suffused with blushes.

50 耳 聞 to hear—as a report.

耳 聞 不 如 目 見 hearsay is not equal to observation.

耳 聰 目 明 observant; wide-awake.

耳 聲 deaf.

耳 腺 or 耳 下 腺 the parotid gland.

55 耳 下 腺 炎 mumps.

耳 號 ear-mark, as on sheep, etc.

耳 視 blindly following what is heard.

耳 視 目 聽 to hear with the eyes and see with the ears—said by Lieh tzŭ, of one who was able to do this after a study of the doctrines of Laotzŭ.

耳 語 to whisper.

60 耳 鑒 only known by hearsay, therefore not as sure as examination by the eye.

耳 門 鏡 otoscope.

耳 順 an obedient ear for the reception of truth—used to express 60 years of age, from 六 十 而 耳 順 (Confucius said) "At sixty my ear was an obedient organ for the reception of truth."

耳 食 credibility; readiness to believe anything that is heard.

耳 食 不 化 to hear readily without comprehending what is heard.

65 耳 食 之 徒 rumour-mongers.

耳 鼓 the ear-drum.

中 耳 the middle ear.

入 耳 to enter the ears; to hear.

內 耳 the inner ear.

70 傾 耳 to incline the ear.

害 耳·朵 底·子 ear-ache; disease of the ears. (·tou-)

掩 耳 to stop the ears.

掏 耳 to pick the ears.

洗 耳 靜 聽 to cleanse the ears and quietly listen—to listen with respect. 「advice).

75 逆 耳 offensive to the ear (of frank ↑ 心 耳 auricles.

(a) A handle; that which is at the side. A fungus. Projections.

耳·子 small ear-like projections; a fungus which grows on wood, etc., used as a flavouring; the pegs of a stringed instrument.

耳 房 a side-room.

耳 門 a side-door.

門 耳 a knocker on a door.

(b) Soft; pliant.

六 轡 耳 耳 the six reins were soft and pliable.

(c) Particle from fusion of 而 已 (Anc. Ch. ńiɐ + 'i: > 耳 'ńɐi:), giving the force of 'merely, only.'

人 病 不 求 耳 the evil is only that men will not seek it (truth).

前 言 戲 之 耳 what I have said was merely in sport.

女 (ru³) 得 人 焉 耳 乎 have you got good men there?

弗 思 耳 矣 it is simply a want of reflection.

弗 爲 耳 it is only that he will not do it.

盡 心 焉 耳 矣 I do exert my mind to the utmost—the three particles here give very great emphasis.

能 勿 喪 耳 they simply do not lose it.

佴⁴ A second, an assistant. Also read ni⁴.
1745

佴 次 an assistant.

刵⁴ To cut off the ears as a punishment.
1746

洱³ Affluent of the Yellow River in Honan.
1747

珥³ Ear-ornaments.
1748

衈⁴ The blood of a sacrificial fowl which was sprinkled or smeared on the doors and vessels, etc. Blood of other victims used in this manner.
1749

餌³ Cakes, meat dumplings. Read ni⁴. A bait.
1750

誘 餌 to entice.

食 餌 to take the bait.

二 弍 〕 [4] Two, the second; twice. To divide in two. Radical 7. The second form and the next are used in accounts, to prevent fraud. Double-minded.

1751

二 三 two or three; divided

二 三 子[3] two or three of you; my disciples —of Confucius.

二 五 眼·子 mean; soft, credulous.

二 人 or 二 親 parents.

[5] 二 人 同 心 two men of the same mind.

二 倍 double; twofold; duplicate.

二 儀 heaven and earth; the two primordial forms or symbols, the *Yin* and the *Yang* evolved by the 太 極 or ultimate principle of existence. They are symbolized by a continuous straight line —, and a broken line – – ; from these two the eight diagrams were constructed (八 卦). *See* No. 3514—5.

二 元 論 dualism.

二 八 佳 人 a beautiful young maiden of sixteen.

[10] 二 八 年 華 sixteen years of age, in the prime of youth.

二 其 心 to vacillate.

二 具 both.

二 分[1] the equinoxes.

二 則 or 二 來 in the second place; secondly.

[15] 二·十 twenty.

二·十 八 天 the 28 paradises.

二·十 八 宿 the 28 constellations or mansions of the Chinese zodiac. *See appendix.*

二·十 四 史 Chinese History, up to the Manchu dynasty.

二·十 四 孝 the 24 examples of filial piety.

[20] 二 天 a second Heaven—used to express gratitude to one who has saved another from death.

二 尖 瓣 bicuspid or mitral valves.

二 帝 Emperors *Yao* and *Shun*.

二 年 生 植 物 biennial plants.

二 府 a sub-Prefect.

[25] 二 心 double-minded; insincere.

二 把 手 a four-handled wheelbarrow; one who lends a hand to another; second fiddle player.

二 更 or 二 炮 the second watch of the night.

二·月 the second lunar month. February. 　　　　　　　[a day.

↑ 二·十 四 小 時 twenty-four hours;

二°次 or 二°回 the second time or occasion; twice. 二·回 next time.

[30] 二 比 both parties being mutually —a phrase used in deeds.

二 毛 a grey-haired man.

二 氣 the primary essences, *Yin* and *Yang,* evolved from 太 極 the ultimate principle of existence. *See above,*—7.

二·百 五 a simpleton, term of ridicule.

二 皇 *FuHsi* and *Shên Nung.*

[35] 二 等 邊 三 角 形 isosceles triangle.

二 至 the solstices.

二 色·的 bi-coloured.

二 角[3]·的 bicorn; crescentic.

二 說 相 反 the two statements are contradictory.

[40] 二 足 動 物 bipeds.

二 過 to repeat a fault.

二 重[2] 人 格 a dual personality.

二 重[2] 電 信 法 duplex telegraph-system.

二 院 制 system of legislation by two houses.

[45] 二 項 式 binomial. (*alg.*).

二 頭 肌 the biceps.

二 頭 齒 bicuspid teeth.

不 二 價 we have only one price; fixed prices.

不 二 色 fidelity to one woman.

貳 [4] Double. Changeable, double-minded.

1752 Inter. preceding for Two, used in accounts, etc., to prevent fraud. Used esp. in 1751. 41, 48, 49.

貳 宗 second son of a minister, in ancient times.

貳 室 the second palace of the emperor.

貳 臣 a statesman who has served two dynasties.

貳 言 having a double meaning.

[5] 勿 貳 do not have any doubts.

無 貳 爾 心 be not double-minded.

樲 [4] Acid variety of the jujube-plum.

1753

爾 尒 尔 [3] You, your. Dr. Hu Shih explains it as the possessive, or plural of address; a relative pronoun before 所; when used as singular, he says it is more distant and formal than 汝, No. 3142.

1754

爾 子[3] Your son.

爾 曹 or 爾 等 you all; you.

爾 衆 士 all you scholars.

爾 罪 your faults.

爾 鄰 里 your neighbours.

求 爾 何 如 *Ch'iu,* what are your wishes?

非 爾 所 及 you have not attained to that.

(a) So, like that, -like; sometimes used like 耳, merely, etc.

爾 爾 repeatedly, alike, many.

不 過 爾 爾 no better than that, so-so.

不 得 不 爾 no other alternative.

不 知 老 之 將 至 云 爾 does not perceive that old age is coming on.

[5] 乃 爾 thus, it is so, so.

云 爾 and so on; as you say.

僕 僕 爾 亟 拜 也 the trouble of making repeated obeisances.

率 爾 hastily; suddenly; rashly.

可 謂 云 爾 已 矣 it may *simply* be said of me.

[10] 君 子 胡 不 慥 慥 爾 "Is it not *just* an entire sincerity that marks the superior man?"

唯 謹 爾 but *precisely,* simply, merely.

嘑 爾 蹴 爾 (offer them) with an insulting voice, or trample upon them (before offering them).

故 爾 如 是 it happened like this.

莞 爾 smilingly.

(b) u.f. next. Near, etc.

道 在 爾 the Path is not far.

(c) For foreign postvocalic -*l* or -*r*.

威 爾 遜 Wilson.

達 爾 文 Darwin.

邇 迩 [3] Near, close, proximate.

1755

邇 來 hitherto; recently.

邇 言 shallow words.

邇 近 near, close at hand.

而 [2] And, and yet, also, but, nevertheless, like, as. Radical 126.

1756

而且 moreover; besides; in addition.

而乃 and then; withal.

而況 with still stronger reason; still more.

而今 or 此而今 now, at the present time.

⁵而今而後 from now onwards— here it is equivalent to 自, from.

而后 after that; then.

而已 that is all; nothing more— gives finality to the clause.

而已矣 there is nothing more to be said—this is more emphatic than 而已.

而益 still more; yet again.

¹⁰而立 to stand firm; used to express 30 years of age, from

三十而立 (Confucius said), "When I was thirty years of age I stood firm."

而竟 and yet; still.

人而無信 a man without sincerity.

富而可求 if the search for riches is sure to be successful ... here the 而 is equivalent to 若, if.

(a) You, your.

而康而色 you should calm your countenance.

而月斯征 your months are passing.

(b) Whiskers; bristles on the jaws. Inter. 髵 No. 1758, a more modern form.

其鱗之而 the bristles on the jaws.

輀² A hearse.
1757

靈輀反里 the remains were returned to his native place.

髵² Whiskers, bristles on the jaws of an animal. A more
1758 modern form of 而, when it has this meaning.

兒² A son, a child. Added to many nouns, pron. as non-syl
1759 labic -r. Distinguish 兒 No. 4368.

兒² 啼 to whimper.

兒² 夫 a husband.

兒² 女 sons and daughters.

兒² 媳 or 兒婦 a daughter-in-law.

⁵兒² 子 sons.

兒² 孫 children and grandchildren; posterity.

兒² 戲 a plaything; a trifling matter.

不是兒² 戲 it is no trifling matter.

當⁴兒² 戲 to regard as a mere trifle.

¹⁰兒² 時 when he or she was a child.

兒² 時之追憶 one's earliest recollections.

兒² 茶 catechu.

兒² 葵 the sunflower.

兒² 郎 a son, a young gentleman, a husband.

¹⁵兒² 馬 a stallion.

可兒² a charming person.

(a) Read ni^1. A surname. Inter. 倪 No. 4662.

晲²　Forced laughter.
1760

嚅晲 forced laughter.

(a) Read wa^2. The prattle of children.

晲 嘔 prattling of infants.

FA.　　　(ㄈㄚ)
(Fah)

乏　2.5. To be in want. Weary,
1761　exhausted.
　Distinguish 之 No. 935.

乏人照應 there is no one to take care of him.

乏倦 or 乏·了 tired; exhausted.

乏用 in straits; short of.

乏費用 short of funds—used in begging letters, etc.

⁵乏錢 short of money.

不乏人才 there is no lack of able men.

困乏 or 疲乏 worn out with fatigue.

空乏 destitute; no resources.

缺乏 deficiency; lack.

¹⁰走乏·了 tired with a long walk.

法　3.5. Statutes, laws, regula-
1762　tions. A rule. Legal stan-
　dard. Plan or method, etc.

法人 a legal person, an imaginary person for legal purposes in dealing with organizations, companies, etc.

法令 laws, orders, regulations, ordinances.

法令全書 digest of laws, regulations, etc.

法令機關 organ for the issue of laws, ordinances, etc.

⁵法令·的勢·力 the power of laws and ordinances.

法例 legal code.

法價 legal price; standard legal price.

法典 code of laws; statute, canon.

法制 legislation; legal system; rules, restrictions.

¹⁰法制局 bureau for drafting laws; legislative bureau.

法則 rule, pattern; provision of the law; means.

法吏 a gaoler.

法堂 law court in a *yamen*.

法場 place of execution.

¹⁵法子 a method or plan.

法學 the study of law.

法學士 Bachelor of Laws.

法學知識 legal knowledge.

法官 a judge, a justice.

²⁰法定 provided by law; legal.

法定人數 quorum; legal number.

法定代理 legal representation.

法定代理人 legal representative.

法定住址 legal domicile.

²⁵法定價格 legal standard of value.

法定公積金 legal public-loan fund.

法定利率 legal rate of interest.

法定利·息 legal interest.

法定勞役 legal service of labour.

³⁰法定團體 legal association or corporation, etc.

法定年齡 legal age.

法定數 legal number; quorum.

法定期限 legal time-limit.

法定果實 or 法定孳息 legal payment, as of mortgages, etc.

³⁵法定權利 legal rights.

法定清算 legal liquidation.

法定·的 legal.

法定繼承分⁴ legal portion of inheritance.

法定職業 legal occupation; lawful business.

40法定證·據 legal evidences.

法定貨幣 or 法幣 legal tender.

法定資·格 legal qualifications.

法定關·係 pertaining to legal matters.

法度 laws, plans, regulations, etc.

45法庭 court room; court of law.

法庭審判 decision of the court.

法庭規則 law-court regulations.

法式 legal forms; the shape of a thing; form.

法律 law; items of the law.

50法律·上 legal.

法律·上責任 legal liability.

法律制裁 legal restraint.

法律問題 a legal question.

法律學 jurisprudence.

55法律家 lawyer.

法律審查員 committee for examining into the laws.

法律所制定 legal sanctions.

法律案 a law-case.

法律派 legal party.

60法律科 department of law, in a college.

法律範圍 the sphere of the law.

法律行·爲 a legal action.

法律解釋案 bill for explaining the statutes.

法律關·係 having relations with the law.

65法律顧問 legal advisors.

法意 the spirit of the law.

法政學校 college of law and politics.

法數 divisor or multiplier, compare 實數, dividend or multiplicand.

法書 praise of the writings of another.

70法案 a law-case.

法櫃 The Ark of the Law.

法權 jurisdiction.

法治國 a constitutional State.

法理 legal principles; theory of law.

75法理學 jurisprudence.

法界 the legal world; legal circles.

法碼 legal weights; standard weights.

法科大學 college of law.

法禁 restrictions; prohibitions.

80法系 legal system, or code.

中國法系 Chinese Legal System.

羅馬法系 Roman Legal System.

法約 a legal agreement or contract.

法綱 the meshes of the law.

85　投入法綱 to fall into the meshes of the law.

法螺 a conch shell, used as a horn by the armies of ancient days, now used by priests—to blow one's own horn.

法規 law, legal privilege or right; usages, etc.

法言 devices and schemes.

法語之言能無從乎 does one refuse to agree to words of admonition?

90法貨 legal tender.

法部 Board of Justice.

法醫學 medical jurisprudence.

法院 Yüan or law-courts.

最高法院 Supreme Court.

95法院編制法 law of procedure in the courts.

不法之行·爲 an illegal act.

以身試法 to defy the law.

合法 legitimate.

守法 to observe the law.

100屈法 perversion of the law.

方法 procedure; method; process.

無法 without resources; lawless.

犯法 to break the law.

立法 to legislate. See under 立 No. 3921. A.39ff.

105行法 to enforce the laws.

設法 to provide means.

辦法 process; method of procedure.

(a) Used as a suffix to express law; pattern; method, etc.

人爲法 artificial law.

公法 public and criminal law.

分·析法 analytical methods.

刑法 criminal law.

5刑事訴訟法 code of criminal procedure.

商法 commercial law.

問題法 questionnaire method.

國法 the national laws.

國籍法 law of nationality.

10國際公法 international public law.

國際私法 international private law.

平時國際公法 international public law in times of peace.

戰時國際公法 international law during war.

天法 the laws of Heaven.

15契合法 law of contracts.

對話法 Socratic methods.

憲法 constitutional law.

成文法 statute-law—of England.

不文法 unwritten law.

20投票法 suffrage law.

普通立法 ordinary process of legislation.

會計法 (會 read ku'ai⁴) accountancy law.

歸納法 inductive methods.

民法 civil law.

25民事訴訟法 civil procedure.

海船法 maritime law.

演繹法 deductive methods.

特別法 special laws or methods.

登記法 registration law.

30監獄法 prison law.

破產法 bankruptcy law.

研究之方法 methods of study or research.

票據法 laws relating to vouchers, documents, cheques, etc.

禮法 etiquette.

35綜合法 synthetic methods.

繼受法 law of transfer.

繼承法 law of inheritance.

老式的方法 old fashioned methods.

習慣法 or 普通法 common law.

40自然之法則 natural laws.

萬國公法 international law.

行政法 administrative law.

複合法 method of composing.

複選法 law of re-election.

45親族法 family law.

觀察法 method of observation.

訴訟法 law of legal procedure.

議院法 law of the house.

警察法 police law.

50軍法 military law.

遺傳法 law of heredity.

運動之法則 laws of motion.

選舉法 election law.

非訴事件手續法 law of civil process.

(b) To act as an example. An example.

法帖 to set a copy; copy ior pupils to write from.

法傚 to exemplify; to imitate or follow.

(c) The doctrines or law of Buddha, from the Sanskrit, *dharma.* Pron. *fa*³,⁴

法力 power of the Buddhist doctrine.

法 侶 Buddhist priest; clergy.

法 化 transformed by Buddhist teaching; brought under Buddhism.

法 名 or 法 號 name in religion of a Buddhist priest.

5 法 家 writers on Buddhism.

法 寶 the Sutras.

法 師 honorific style of a Buddhist priest or a Taoist exorcist; a teaching-priest.

法 座 a throne; Buddha's hall of exposition.

法 徒 Buddhist priests or disciples.

10 法 敎 Buddhism.

法 施 to teach the mysteries of Buddhism.

法 旨 Buddhist precept.

法 會 Buddhist or Taoist fasts or festivals.

法 水 holy water; to cleanse with the Buddhist teachings.

15 法 海 of the wideness of the principles of Buddha.

法 王 Buddha.

法 相 Buddhist incarnation.

法 術 the black art.

法 象 Buddhist phenomena.

20 法 身 spiritual or ethereal body—image of Buddha.

法 輪 the wheel of the law; emblem of Buddha; praying-machine.

法 道 the way of Buddha; to exemplify the teachings of Buddha.

法 門 Buddhists.

得 法 to realize Buddhism as truth.

25 符 法 exorcist charms or spells.

說 法 to expound the teachings of Buddhism.

(d) Used in transliterating.
Pron. *fa⁴*.

法 倫 表 Fahrenheit's thermometer. ＝華 氏 表.

法 國 or 法 蘭 西 France.

法 文 French language.

法 藍 enamel ware; *cloisonné*.
See next character.

法 蘭 絨 flannel.

棉 法 絨 flannelette.

法 郎 the *franc*.

↑ 法 西 斯 主 義 Fascism.

琺 4.5. **Enamel ware.** *Cloisonné*
1763 **ware.**

琺 瑯 品 enamel ware.

砝 4.5.   Standard weights.
1764

砝 碼 weights of a scale.

(a) Read *chieh⁵.* Stiff; unyielding.

伐 1,2.5 **To reduce a dependency**
1765 **to order; to chastise rebels —used of a regularly organized attack. Distinguish 代 No. 5996.**

伐 國 to subject a country.

伐 罪 to punish an offence.

伐 鼓 to beat a drum.

(a) To cut down; to fell.

伐 冰 to cut ice for storing.

伐 木 or 伐 樹 to fell trees.

伐 柯 to cut a handle for an axe.

(b) To act as a go-between.

作 伐 to act as a go-between,–from

伐 柯 如 何 匪 斧 不 克，
娶 妻 如 何 匪 媒 不 得.
  How is an axe handle hewn?
  Without an axe it is not possible.
  How do you get a wife?
  Without a go-between it cannot be done.

(c) To make a show of.

伐 善 to boast of one's goodness.

自 伐 boastful.

筏 2.5.
栰
1766   A bamboo raft.

筏 子 a raft.

筏 渡 a ferry-boat.

排 筏 bamboo rafts with the ends turned up.

寶 筏 precious raft—the teachings of Buddha which ferry believers across to bliss.

閥 2.5. **The left-hand entrance**
1767 **in a triple gate. Classification according to rank.**

閥 閱 rank and length of service.

閥 閱 之 家 powerful and distinguished families.

宗 閥 the family.

軍 閥 之 橫 行 the wicked conduct of the militarists.

發 1.5. **To issue, to put or to**
1768 **send forth. To rise. To manifest. To issue stores.**

發 丁 to have many descendants.

發 了 財 to have acquired wealth.

發 亮 bright and burnished.

發 令 to give the order.

5 發 作 to become; to develop into; to break out, as illness, temper.

發 信 to send a letter.

發 信 機 addressograph.

發 僵 or 發 硬 to grow stiff; to be obstinate.

發 光 to emit light; to shine forth.

10 發 光 體 light-bearing bodies; luminaries.

發 兌 to sell by retail; on sale.

發 兵 to despatch troops.

發 冷 to shiver, as with malaria.

發 凡 an introduction.

15 發 出 or 發 給 to send forth; to issue.

出 發 to issue forth, as troops.

發 出 來 to proceed from.

忽 然 發 出 to burst out; to break forth suddenly.

發 刊 to issue a new publication.

20 發 刊 詞 a foreword.

發 動 the beginnings of a thing; motion; active, as opposed to passive, 受 動.

發 動 力 initiative power; power of initiative.

發 動 所 由 the source of action.

發 命 to issue an order.

25 發 咒 起 誓 to swear, to take an oath.

發 問 to question.

發 喪 to escort a funeral to the grave.

發 單 to issue a permit; invoice.

發 單 起 貨 to issue a permit to land goods.

30 發 噱 to make a joke.

發 回 or 發 還 to return; to send back.

發 塚 to open graves.

發 奮 to be energetic; to devote strength to.

發 奮 爲 雄 exerted themselves and displayed heroism.

35 發 姦 摘 伏 to bring hidden treason and crime to light.

發摘 to reveal the hidden crimes of another; to explain difficulties or resolve doubts.

發客 for customers; "we sell retail."

發富 to become wealthy.

發審 to send up for examination.

40 發展 development; expansion; to extend.

發展主義 policy of expansion or of development.

發展之可能性 potentialities for development.

發展力 power of expansion.

發展政策 policy of expansion.

45 發展說 theory of development or expansion.

發己自盡 to do the utmost one can.

發市 to get customers; to begin business.

發布 promulgation; a bulletin.

發帖 to issue invitations.

50 發幹生條 to develop, root and branch.

發引 a funeral.

↓ 發狠 to get angry; to become wrath; to make a great effort.

發怯 to give way to fear.

發怒 or 發腦 or 發火 or 發氣 to manifest an angry spirit.

55 發急 to get excited or worried.

發怨言 to murmur.

發息 to pay a dividend.

發情期 or 發身 puberty.

發慈悲 to show pity.

60 發慌 or 發忙 agitated; to lose presence of mind.

發憤忘食 he studied with such eagerness that he forgot his food.

發威 to stand on one's dignity.

發抄 to make public.

發批 to lease; to issue a reply—to an inferior.

65 發揚 to bring to light.

發揚國光 to extend the glory of the nation. ⌈develope.

發揮 to manifest; to elucidate; to

發放 to discharge—a prisoner; to distribute.

發散 to scatter; to disperse.

70 發散透鏡 a diverging lens.

發明 to dawn; to explain; to make clear; to invent, to devise what was never made before. See below 96.

新發明 new discoveries, as of science; new inventions.

發明家 inventor.

發旺 to prosper; to brighten up—as a fire.

75 發昏 to faint; to turn giddy.

發暈 to turn giddy.

發條 a watch or clock-spring, or any similar spring.

發案 to take the initiative.

發榮滋長 to flourish and grow.

80 發橫財 to become wealthy by illegal and dishonest methods.

發毛 or 發霉 to grow mildewed.

發氣滿容 his whole countenance was moved.

發泄 to leak out; to divulge.

發洪 sudden rise of a mountain torrent.

85 發洩 to exude; to give vent to.

發源地 place of origin; source.

發漲 to increase—as a body.

發潮 to get mouldy; to get damp.

發火溫度 flash-point; temperature at which anything will ignite.

90 發炎 to become inflamed.

發煩 to be annoyed; to be bothered.

發熱心 to be zealous.

發燒 or 發熱 to have a fever.

發狂 to go crazy; to become demented.

95 發默 to act the fool; to be silly.

發現 to manifest, to appear; to disclose; to discover, as new territory, new truths, etc. See 71.

發生 to stir, to set in, as a season; to send forth shoots; to arise, to produce.

發生問題 give rise to questions.

發生學 embryology.

100 發生機 nascency.

發生的 nascent.

發生衝突 to cause a clash; to arouse opposition.

發病 to fall ill.

發疹 to have an infectious disease, such as measles, scarlet fever, etc.

103 發疹窒扶斯 typhus fever. (Jap.).

發瘧疾 to have an attack of malaria.

發瘋 to have a fit; to go mad.

發白 to turn white.

發皇 to flourish.

110 發票 a ticket issued with goods sold, a price-ticket; invoice; to issue a warrant.

發福 to be in good health and condition; to become fat.

發科甲 to graduate under the old system of examinations.

發端 to begin; the commencement.

發笑 to laugh.

115 發笨 to be numbed or palsied.

發紅 to turn red; to blush.

發而皆中 (chung⁴) 節 (the feelings) manifested aright.

發聲 vocalization.

發育 to grow up.

120 發背 to get a malignant tumour on the back.

發脾·氣 to fly into a temper.

發脹 swollen.

發花 to grow dim—as eyesight.

發芽 to bud. ↓ 發薪 to pay salary.

125 發苗 to send forth shoots; to sprout.

發萌 to sprout.

發葉 to put forth leaves.

發落 to dispose; to appoint.

發蒙 to enlighten; to instruct the young.

130 發蒙啟滯 to enlighten the young and open the minds of the dull.

發蒙振落 to remove the covering, as of a table, etc., or to shake down, as leaves; both easily done,—used to express things easily accomplished—as defeating an army, etc.

發血管 arteries. = 動脈.

發行 (hang²) to sell wholesale.

發行 to issue; publication.

135 發行人 publisher.

發行匯票 to issue a draft.

發行所 office of publication.

發行紙幣 to issue paper-money.

發表 to make known; publication.

140 發表意見 to pass an opinion.

發覆 to reveal the true purpose, thought or intent behind the false appearance.

發見 to discover, a discovery.

發覺 to come to light.

發覺書 an exposing document.

145 發解 to send on; to forward.

發言 or 發語 to speak, to call out, speech.

發言之自由 liberty of speech.

發言權 rights of free speech.

有發言權 to have the right to speak.

150 發語辭 an introductory particle.

發誓 or 發盟 or 矢盟 or 賭咒 to take an oath; to swear.

發議 to make a proposition.

發財 to prosper by becoming wealthy; a felicitous wish.

以財發身 to get on in life by means of wealth.

155 以身發財 to get wealth but at the expense of health or of life.

發賣 or 發售 to have on sale.

發起 to initiate; to promote; to start.

發起人 promoter; founder; proposer.

發·起·來 to manifest; to rise, etc.

160 發起革命 to promote a revolution.

發身 to reach puberty; to get on in life; to emerge from obscurity.

發射 to emanate.

發軔 the beginnings of a thing.

發迹 to start from.

165 發達 or 上達 or 發揚 to advance in office; to rise to distinction; to increase; to develop; to evolve; development.

發達女權 to extend women's rights.

不發達 not prosperous; to fail; to be badly managed.

發遣 or 發配 to send away; to banish.

發邊 to banish to the frontier.

170 發還存票 to issue a drawback.

發酒瘋 to be drunk and excited.

發配 to exile.

發酸 to ache, as a limb; to become sour, as dough, etc.

發酵 to ferment; yeast for dough, etc.

175 發鏢 to cast a javelin.

發難 the beginning of troubles.

發電 to send a telegram; to generate electricity.

發電力 electric power.

發電機 generator for electricity; a dynamo.

180 發音 to pronounce.

發音學 phonetics.

發音機關 organs of sound.

發願 to vow.

發顫 or 發抖 to tremble.

185 發麵 yeast.

發黏 to become sticky.

告發 to give information to the law.

朝發夕至 to start in the morning and arrive in the evening.

(a) N. A. for cartridges, etc.

子彈千餘發 over a thousand rounds of ammunition.

罰 2.5.　To punish, to fine. Punishment.
1769

罰令 to compel by way of punishment.

罰作 compulsory penal servitude.

罰俸 to deduct from the salary, as a fine.

罰偷 to punish idleness.

5 罰則 laws relating to punishments and fines.

罰歀 or 罰項 fines; to fine; money accruing from fines.

罰糧 or 罰米 to cut the rations, for punishment.

罰辦 to decide a case.

罰酒 to fine a person a drinking-forfeit—the loser has to drink.

10 罰金刑 fines; penalties.

罰錢 or 罰銀 to fine.

刑罰 corporal punishment.

受罰 to receive punishment.

懲罰 chastisement; correction by punishment.

責罰 to punish.

賞罰 rewards and punishments.

髮 3.5.　The hair on the human head.
1770

髮亂如麻 dishevelled hair.

髮冠 a cap of hair, the knot of the Taoists.

髮同漆黑 hair as black as lacquer.

髮如霜草 his hair was like the frost on the grass.

5 髮妻 a man's first wife, to whom he was betrothed as a child,—from

結髮爲夫妻恩愛兩不疑 made man and wife in their prime,—when the hair is first put up,—their love and affection cannot be doubted.

髮指 angry enough for the hair to rise.

令人髮指 enough to make a man's hair stand on end.

髮狀發條 hairspring of a watch.

10 髮白更黑 his hair changed from white to black.

髮短心長 his hair is sparse from age, but his heart is wise from experience.

髮積 paper-receptacle for combings, etc.

髮膚 hair and skin—the whole body.

髮落 to become bald.

15 髮赤 red hair—a child.

假髮 a wig, false hair.

削髮 to shave the whole head.

披髮佯狂 to dishevel the hair and feign madness.

束髮 to bind the hair in a knot on the top of the head.

20 毛髮竦然 the hair standing on end.

留髮 to let the hair grow, as girls do, or as a priest does when he returns to the laity.

素髮 white hair.

落髮 to become a priest.

頭髮 human hair.

25 鬢髮 the hair curled on the temples.

黃髮 yellow hair.—the hoary hair of the aged.

(a) One thousandth part of an inch.

十髮爲程，十程爲分，十分爲寸 10 hairs make 1 *ch'êng*, 10 *ch'êng* make 1 *fên*, 10 *fên* make 1 inch.

(b) u.f. vegetation, moss, hair-like substances.

髮晶 hair-like needle-crystals of quartz.

髮菜 edible hair-like seaweed.

石髮 or 苔髮 mosses.

窮髮之地 utterly barren soil.

FAN.　(ㄈㄢ)

凡 / 凡 2
1771

All; common; general. Every, whenever. Generally. Distinguish 几 No. 404.

凡事 all matters, everything.

凡事留餘地 leave a loophole in everything—do not press any man too hard.

凡例 directions to the reader; a chapter of introductory matter affixed to works of importance,

explaining the plan and style of the book, etc.

凡 信 他·的 all who believe in Him.

[5]凡 夫 one of the masses, an ordinary person.

凡 常 ordinary, common.

凡 幾 how many in all?

不 知 凡 幾 I do not know how many there are.

凡 有 wherever there is.

[10]凡 民 the masses.

凡 為 天 下 國 家 all who rule the empire.

凡 百 or 凡 物 all; every.

凡 禮 之 體 主 於 敬 all the embodiments of *li* are dominated by respect.

凡 童 an ordinary child.

[15]凡 要 all who would ....; the most important of the whole.

凡 遇 or 凡·是 whenever; every.

大 凡 in general; generally speaking.

諸 凡 all, every.

非 凡 uncommon; above the average.

(a) Mortal, secular, earthly.

凡 人 men, mankind; the laity, as contrasted with the Buddhist priesthood.

凡 囂 the turmoil of the world.

凡 塵 the cares of the world.

凡 心 worldly desires.

[5]凡 眼 or 凡 目 mortal eyesight.

凡 胎 of human birth.

凡 間 or 凡 世 the world.

凡 雲 earth-clouds.

凡 骨 the natural disposition, as contrasted with the 仙 骨, the frame of the immortals.

[10]下 凡 incarnation; to descend into the world.

思 凡 to long for the things of the world.

脫 凡 尸 to put off this mortal body.

凡 爾 賽 Versailles.　Cf. 7067 B 4.

帆 [2]
A sail. To sail.
1772

帆 布 canvas; sail-cloth.

帆 柱 a mast.

帆 檣 sails and masts.

帆 篷 a sail.

[5]帆 船 a sailing-vessel.

揚 帆 to set the sails.

汎 [4]
泛
To float; to drift. Careless; reckless.
Distinguish 汛 No. 2749.
1773

汎 亞 西 亞 主 義 Pan-Asianism.

汎 埽 to sweep all around a place.

汎 常 customary, ordinary.

汎 心 論 pan-psychism, theory that everything in the universe has a spirit.

[5]汎 意 論 or 萬 有 意 志 論 pan-thelism, the theory of Schopenhauer.

汎 愛 universal love; love overflowing to all.

汎 愛 主 義 philanthropism.

汎 愛 衆 而 親 仁 overflowing with love to all, and cultivating the friendship of the good.

汎 愛 萬 物 love overflowing to all things.

[10]汎 應 曲 當 various statements and answers.

汎 指 a vague reference; general allusion to.

汎 探 to select from all sources.

汎 揚 to spread widely.

汎 斯 拉 夫 主 義 Pan-Slavism.

[15]汎 汎 其 流 drifting with the current.

汎 汎·的 交 情 superficial acquaintance; casual acquaintance.

泛 泛 浮 浮 unsettled; unstable; flippant.

汎 沛 abundant; overflowing.

汎 沫 foam; bubbles; froth.

[20]汎 海 to sail on the sea.

汎 淫 excessive; overwhelming.

汎 溢 to overflow; to flow.

汎 漲 to overflow.

汎 漂 light; buoyant.

[25]汎 濫 to overflow; verbose.

汎 灑 to sprinkle freely.

汎 理 論 Hegelism—panlogism.

汎 神 敎 or 萬 有 神 敎 pantheism, all things being the manifestation of God.

汎 舟 sailing in a boat; to float a vessel.

[30]汎 視 regard lightly; to look upon as a matter of form.

汎 言 vague talk.

汎 言 之 spoke of it in general terms.

汎 訊 之 made extensive inquiries about it.

汎 說 to speak vaguely.

[35]汎 遊 to wander; to ramble, to travel.

汎 酒 or 流 觴 to float cups of wine on the stream—at a picnic —till they reached the guests.

普 泛 之 問 題 a vague question.

(a) Read *feng*[3]. To throw a rider.

泛 駕 之 馬 a horse that throws its rider.

(b) Read *fa*[2.5]. Sound of waves.

泛 淲 (*chieh*[5]) sound of breakers on a shore; also explained as a slight sound.

梵 [4]　**Brahma. Sanskrit or Pali. Pure and clean.**
1774

梵 刹 or 梵 宮 Buddhist monastery.

梵 咒 Buddhist prayers and charms.

梵 國 India.

梵 天 the heavenly mansions, the abode of Brahma.

[5]梵 夾 Buddhist books.

梵 學 Buddhism.

梵 宇 hall of idols in a monastery.

梵 志 Brahma.

梵 書 or 梵 字 Sanskrit writings.

[10]梵 淨 a famous mountain in Kweichow.

梵 王 or 梵 天 王 Brahma, the first person of the Brahminical Trinity.

樊 [2]
棥
A railing, a fence; an enclosed place.
1775

樊 籠 a cage.

樊 籬 a fence, a railing.

金 樊 a golden cage.

礬 [2]　**Metallic salts for dyeing or painting. Alum; to tan leather with lime and copperas.**
1776

礬 皮 店 a tannery.

礬 石 alum shale.

礬 紙 paper sized with alum.

白 礬 or 明 礬 alum.

皂 礬 or 青 礬 copperas, sulphate of iron.

氾 ⁴ Water overflowing. u.f., 況 No. 1773.
1777

氾 博 great, extensive.
氾 氾 unsettled; floating about.
氾 濫 an inundation; overflowing.
氾 論 to make a general discussion.

范 ³ Plants, grass.
1778

范 冠 ancient style of cap.

犯 ⁴ To transgress; to offend; to violate. To invade, to clash. To withstand.
1779

犯 上 to be impertinent to superiors; to rebel.
犯・不 上 or 犯・不 着 it won't pay; it is not worth while; inconsistent with dignity. (-chao²)
犯・了 事 to get into difficulties; for a matter to become known.
犯・了 脾 氣 to get into a rage.
⁵犯・了 舊 病 or 犯 病 to have a relapse.
犯 人 criminals; prisoners.
犯・他・的 病 to offend by exposing the failings of another.
犯 分 to go beyond one's duty; to go beyond one's station in life.
犯 土 to offend the god of the locality—as in building, or by getting ill.
¹⁰犯 地 or 侵 犯 to invade territory.
犯 境 to cross the frontier, to invade.
犯 夜 benighted; to prowl at night when it is forbidden.
犯 姦 to commit adultery.
犯 忌・諱 to offend prejudices or superstitions; to break a taboo.
¹⁵犯 思 量 to set people wondering.
犯 意 guilty intention.
犯 暴 行・爲 acts of rioting.
犯 案 to be arrested; to be convicted; to commit an offence.
犯 死 to risk the life.
²⁰犯 死 罪 to commit a capital offence.
犯 法 or 犯 例 to break the law.
犯 潮 to get damp.
犯 界 to break bounds.
犯 疑 to arouse suspicions.
²⁵ 叫 人 犯 疑 to cause suspicions to be aroused.

犯 禁 to break prohibitions.
犯 禁 品 contraband.
犯 科 to transgress the laws.
犯 罪 to commit sin; an offence.
³⁰犯 罪 之 主 體 subject of crime. (legal).
犯 罪 之 客 體 object of crime. (legal).
犯 罪 之 被 害 者 injured person in a crime. (legal).
犯 罪 人 culprit; sinner.
犯 罪 人 執 交 extradition.
³⁵犯 罪 地 the locality of a crime. (legal).
犯 罪 學 criminology.
犯 罪 庇 護 to shield criminals. (legal).
犯 罪 心 理 學 criminal psychology.
犯 罪 構 成 要 素 elements of a crime.
⁴⁰犯 罪 社 會 學 criminal sociology.
犯 罪 行・爲 a criminal act. (legal).
犯 而 不 校 to take no notice of offences against himself.
犯 聲 discord; out of harmony.
犯 規 or 犯・了 規・矩 to offend against a rule or custom.
⁴⁵犯 諱 to use names regarded as sacred and taboo, to use forms of characters which were forbidden for this reason.
犯 重 喪 the deceased has done some deed which will cause the death of another.
犯 順 to rebuke elders or superiors without any regard for their status; to act in a disorderly manner.
犯 顏 諫 爭 to rebuke with no regard to superior status; to withstand to the face.
犯 頭 七 the whole thing is spoiled.
⁵⁰囚 犯 a prisoner.
悞 犯 unintentional sin or offence.
夥 犯 accomplice.
相 犯 to clash; to violate.
觸 犯 intentional crime or offence.
⁵⁵首 犯 ringleader; principal in a crime or a rebellion.

範 ⁴ A law, a rule, a custom. A pattern.
1780

範 圍 sphere; jurisdiction.
範 圍 圈 sphere of influence.

勢 力 範 圍 sphere of influence,—see under 勢 No. 5799-11.
利 益 範 圍 sphere of interest.
⁵ 活 動 之 範 圍 sphere of activity.
範 常 a custom, a constant rule or law.
範 式 model or example.
範 我 馳 驅 I managed my driving according to the correct rules. 範 疇 category.
模 範 a mould, a pattern, an example.
¹⁰洪 範 The Great Plan, a section of the Book of History, 書 經.
雅 範 yourself.
風 範 stylish; graceful manner.

反 ³ To turn over. To retreat. To rebel, to turn back.
1781

反 不 如 初 it is now different from at first.
反 之 自 責 applied it to himself.
反 亂 rebellion; anarchy.
反 仄 turning over and over; uneasy; double-minded.
⁵反 作 用 reaction.
反 供 counter-evidence.
反 側 rebellious; unsettled, wavering; tossing from inability to sleep.
反 側 子 a man who is restless and uneasy from anxiety and rebellious plans.
反 光 reflection.
¹⁰反 光 鏡 or 反 射 鏡 reflecting mirror; reflector.
反 兵 mutinous troops.
反 共 (產) 運 動 movement against communism.
反 其 仁 to look within and examine his own goodness.
反 其 本 to return to the right way.
¹⁵反 切 or 反 音 the Chinese way of spelling—by joining the initial of one sound to the final of another. See No. 811—28.
反 助 a negative help.
反 動 reaction.
反 動 份 子 reactionary interests;
反 動 力 a reacting force; reaction.
²⁰反 動 性 having a reactionary nature.
反 動 派 reactionary party.
↓反 戈 to rebel.
↓反 攻 (to) counter-attack.

反 動·的 reactionary.

反·反 覆 覆·的 reiteration; over and over again.

反 叛 or 反 寇 or 反 賊 rebels; the seditious.

[25] 反 口 to retract, to deny one's words; to disown.

反 告 counter-charge.

反 命 returned with the message.

反 哺 to disgorge to feed the old birds—used of kindness to parents.

反 回 or 反 還 to revert to; to go back again.

[30] 反 坐 retribution.

反 站 a stand on which to place the cups when finished with them.

反 射 to reflect; reflection; deflection of light or sound-waves.

反 射 作·用 reflex action.

反 射 光 線 a reflected ray of light.

[35] 反 射 器 a reflector.

反 射 注 意 reflex attention.

反 射 波 deflected waves, of sound.

反 射 爐 reverberatory furnace.

反 射·的 reflex; reflection.

[40] 反 射 角 angle of reflection.

反 射 運·動 reflex action.

反 對 to oppose.

反 對 作·用 counter-action.

反 對 刺 戟 藥 counter-irritant.

[45] 反 對 勢·力 counter-influence.

反 對 命·令 countermands.

反 對 引 力 counter-attraction.

反 對 意·見 contrary opinion.

反 對 甚 力 strong opposition.

[50] 反 對 策 略 counter-move, counter-policy.

反 對 者 opposer.

反 對 色 contrasting colours.

反 對 說 opposite view; contrary theories.

反(對)革 命 counter-revolution.

[55] 反 對 黨 The Opposition.

反 己 or 自 反 reflection, self-examination.

反 己 自 修 self-examination and self-culture.

反 帝 運 動 agitation against imperialism.

反 覆 相 因 complementary.

[60] 反 性 to become unruly or violent.

反 悔 to repent; to recall a promise.

反 應 response; resentment; antagonism; counteraction. Reaction. (chem.).

反 應 時 間 reaction time; the time which it takes to respond to a stimulus.

[65] 反 應 量 re-acting weight.

中 性 反 應 neutral reaction. (chem.).

反 成 became; on the contrary it became; it was turned into.

反 手 or 反 掌 to turn the hand—very easily done.

反 抗 opposition; to oppose.

反 抗 侵 畧 to resist aggression.

[70] 反 抗 力 the force of the resistance, power of resistance.

反 搶 to sail back; to back water.

反 撞 力 reactionary force.

反 擊 counter-attack.

反 政 府 黨 the opposition party—to the government.

[75] 反 教 an apostate.

反 映 to foreshadow; reflection.

反 服 to wear the wrong mourning.

反 案 to reverse a sentence.

反 正 to return to rectitude; to turn right into wrong; also used as below.

[80] 反·正 老 雅 都 是 黑·的 after all, all crows are black.

反·正 要 去 right or wrong, you must certainly go.

反 正 表 決 a vote by show of hands for or against.

反 汗 to go back on one's word.

反 流 contrary to the current; a contrary current.

[85] 反 照 reflected light; the afternoon sun.

反 理 anomaly.

反 病 to have a relapse.

反 目 a quarrel between husband and wife; lit., to turn the eyes.

反 眼 to look askance at.

[90] 反 眼 不 相 識 to turn the eyes and pretend not to see.

反 省 introspection. (-hsing).

↑ 反·正 in any case, anyway.

反 磁 性 體 non-magnetic body.

反 老 還 童 to renew the youth.

[95] 反 背 to go back on one's word; to turn the back.

反 胃 噎 食 the stomach rejects food.

反 腔 to get the better of.

反 唇 to pout in disagreement.

反 臉 to change countenance; to look with disfavour on old friends, etc.

[100] 反 芻 to chew the cud.

反 葬 to return the body of one who has died away from home for burial.

反 衝 reaction; resistance.

反·覆 backward and forward; tautological; over again; now one thing, now another; to retract.

反 覆 不 定 unstable in mind.

[105] 反 覆 小 人 a man who is untrustworthy, who goes from one side to another.

反 觀 自 省 introspection. (-hsing

反 言 or 反 話 irony, sarcasm.

反 訴 cross-action; counter-claim (legal).

反 語 辭 a disjunctive particle.

[110] 反 論 negative argument; adverse discussion; irony.

反 證 contrary evidence.

反 貨 = 販 貨 to sell goods.

反 赤 to oppose the "Reds."

反 身 代 名 詞 reflexive pronouns—myself, etc.

[115] 反 身 動 詞 reflexive verbs.

反 躬 (or 心) 自 問 self-examination.

反 軍 閥 anti-military.

反 轉 to turn round; to turn over.

反 轉·的 reversible.

[120] 反 轉 面 皮 to change countenance.

反 逆 rebellion.

反·過·來 reverse it.

反 道 to go contrary to the correct Path.

反 選 or 反 表 決 negative vote.

[125] 反 間 (chien) 計 a device in which means are used to cause disagreement and alienation among those of the other side.

反·面 the opposite; the other side; to turn away from; to be cold towards.

反·面 正·面 wrong side and right side of anything.

反 面 無 情 said when two friends fall out and become enemies—when the face is turned away, there is no more affection.

反 面 解 決 contrary explanation; to explain by contraries.

[130] 反 響 an echo; opposing voices.

反 響·的 reverberating.

反 顧 to look back at.

無 所 反 顧 there are none who look back.

反 風 a contrary wind.
[135] 反 首 dishevelled hair.
反 駁 to overthrow by criticism; counterpleading.
反 骨 having a rebellious disposition; of one who cannot but rebel.
謀 反 to plot rebellion; treason.

(a) Contrary, but, instead of.

反 之 contrarily; on the other hand; vice-versa.
反 之 亦 然 vice-versa.
反 倒 on the contrary.
反 是 on the contrary.
[5] 反 求 諸 其 身 on the contrary he turns and seeks for the cause in himself.
反 爲 不 美 on the contrary it was not good.
反 着 說 on the contrary; to speak on the other side.
反 者 but; on the other hand.
相 反 contrary to; opposite.
[10] 相 反 之 性 質 contrary natures.
相 反 之 結 果 a contrary result.
全 然 相 反 quite the contrary.

坂[3] A hillside, a bank, a cliff, a slope. Inter. 阪 No. 1786.
1782 Usually pron. *pan*[3].

坡 坂 a bank, a slope.
大 坂 Osaka.

疢[4] To faint, to feel nausea.
1783

販[4]
貾　To traffic, to deal in, to carry about for sale.
1784

販 夫 or 販 客 or 販 仔 a pedlar.
販 婦 a female pedlar.
販 家 a dealer in women.
販 寶 翁 a dealer in precious gems, etc.
[5] 販 糧 to deal in grain.
販 莊 a warehouse; a large shop.
販 貨 to trade.
販 賣 人 口 to deal in human beings—especially children.
販 運 to trade.
[10] 販 馬 to trade in horses.
販 鹽 虜 one who traffics in smuggled salt.

拐 販 to kidnap and sell.

返[3] To return, to revert to. u.f. 反 No. 1781.
1785

返 之 於 天 to go back to heaven.
返 旋 to return to; to revert to.
返 棹 to back water.
返 程 a return journey.
返 魂 the return of the soul to the body after death.

阪[3] A bank, a slope or hillside.
1786 Now commonly pron. *pan*[3].

阪 田 hillside-terraces; fields banked up to retain water for rice growing.
大 阪 Osaka.

飯[4] Cooked rice; food; provisions.
1787

飯 後 after eating; after the meal.
飯 攤 子 an eating-stall.
飯 碗 a rice-bowl.
飯 碗 主 義 time-serving—working on the rice-bowl principle.
[5] 飯 碗 問 題 a question of the rice-bowl—c.p., our "bread and butter."
飯 袋 a food-bag—a glutton.
飯 量 appetite; capacity for eating.
飯 食 food.
飯 館 子 or 飯 舖 or 飯 店 an eating-house, a restaurant.
[10] 一 頓 飯 a meal.
夜 飯 supper. = 晚 飯.
早 飯 breakfast.
做 飯 to prepare food.
討 飯 to beg for food.

(a) Read *fan*[3]. To eat.

飯 疏 食 飲 水 eating coarse food and drinking water.
不 飯 俱 去 they all left before they had eaten.

繁[2] Many, troublesome. Inter. 煩 next.
1788

繁 冠 ancient style of cap worn by military officials.
繁 濆 very numerous.

繁 分 數 compound fraction.
繁 利 息 compound interest.
[5] 繁 劇 之 任 an official post where there is plenty of business and many complications.
繁 博 learned.
繁 多 many; overburdened.
繁 弱 name of a great bow, belonging to *Hsia Hou* 夏 后 or *Yü* the Great.
繁 影 鏡 a multiplying-glass.
[10] 繁 暑 very hot weather.
繁 朵 multiflorous.
繁 柯 many branches.
繁 條 multitudinous branches.
繁 榮 abundant and flourishing—as the growth of flowers, etc.
[15] 繁 殖 to multiply by generation; to propagate in abundance.
繁 比 例 compound ratio.
繁 法 嚴 刑 multifarious laws and stringent punishments.
繁 滋 heavy interest.
繁 湊 many gathered together.
[20] 繁 省 many and few.
繁 盛 prolific; abundant.
繁 祉 much happiness.
繁 禮 the complex multiplicity of ceremonial.
繁 稠 dense, as growth of trees, etc.
[25] 繁 簡 complex and simple.
繁 縈 tangled and involved; full of complications.
繁 細 vexatious.
繁 緒 or 繁 冗 harassed by many cares; burdened with overwork.
繁 縟 gay and variegated.
[30] 繁 缺 a busy official post.
繁 而 不 殺 (*shai*[4]) not concise.
繁 茂 luxuriant, as the growth of vegetation.
繁 華 gaiety, pomp; extravagant display; festive.
繁 華 一 夢 the glory was all a dream.
[35] 繁 華 世 界 this vain world—Vanity Fair.
繁 蔚 flourishing and abundant; numerous and elegant—of writings.
繁 蕪 numerous and disorderly—needing to be sorted or edited.
繁 複 complex; complicated.
繁 說 having plenty to say.
[40] 繁 費 expensive; extravagant.
繁 重 cumbrous; unwieldy.
繁 陰 abundant shade.

繁 雜 or 紛 繁 complex; intricate; multifarious; confused.

繁 難 or 繁 疲 a troublesome and busy post; difficult, bothersome.

45 繁 霜 heavy frosts.

繁 露 the coloured fringes of ceremonial caps.

繁 音 sounds of musical instruments.

事 繁 multiplicity of business.

(a) Read *p'an²*. Girth of a horse.

繁 纓 ornamental silk trapping on the girth of a horse.

煩 ²
1789   To trouble, to annoy.

煩 亂 in confusion; bothered.

禮 煩 則 亂 overmuch ceremony is confusing.

煩 交 I'll trouble you to deliver to —please hand this on, "favoured by."

煩 務 very busy, plenty to attend to.

5 煩 勞 or 敢 煩 or 多 煩·你 I give you much trouble—conventional phrase.

煩 喧 noisy.

煩 囂 the hubbub of a dusty, noisy place—cares of this world.

煩 帶 此 信 May I trouble you to take this letter?

煩 心 troublesome; vexatious.

10 煩 急 anxious and irritable from overmuch work, etc.

煩 悗 annoyed and vexed from disappointment.

煩 惑 vexed and troubled by doubts and suspicions.

煩 悶 grieved, melancholy.

煩 惱 vexed; vexation.

15 自 尋 煩 惱 to bring vexation upon oneself.

煩 想 confused thoughts.

煩 憂 low-spirited; depressed.

煩 慮 anxious; worrying.

煩 抱 or 煩 襟 a troubled bosom, troubled in heart.

20 煩 擾 to annoy; to disturb.

煩 擾 心 志 preying on the mind.

煩 攪 不 安 restless and uneasy.

煩 瀆 to bother; to importune; bothering.

煩 文 a prolix style of writing.

25 煩 毒 annoyed, and harbouring malicious intentions.

煩·氣 unhappy and troubled.

煩 治 vexatious treatment by officials.

煩 法 細 文 harassing laws and vexatious trifles.

煩 渴 thirsty; longing desire.

30 煩 溽 very damp, hot and muggy weather.

煩 烝 hot, muggy weather.

煩 熱 miserable with fever.

煩 瑣 or 煩 碎 troublesome; impertinent and vexing.

煩 瑣 哲 學 scholasticism.

35 煩 簡 many and few; diffuse and terse, etc.

煩 細 petty, troublesome details.

煩 絮 tautology; prolix.

煩 縈 implicated; bound by harassing entanglements.

煩 言 quarrelling o r wrangling; much talk.

40 煩 託 to request; to trouble one to do something.

煩 躁 perplexed; harassed.

煩 闐 a confusing, busy place, as a noisy market, etc.

煩 雜 confused; troublesome; multitudinous.

煩 難 in difficulty; in trouble and perplexity.

45 煩 難 問 題 a vexed question.

煩 駕 May I trouble you?

不 耐 煩 impatient; cannot bear the vexation.

怪 煩 very annoying.

敢 煩 May I trouble you?

番 ¹
1790   Foreign; barbarous. Aborigines, savages of Formosa.

番 人 or 老 番 or 番 鬼·子 foreigners.

番 地 districts where tribes dwell; strange barbarous countries.

番 役 policemen, constables.

番 戶 the tribes in West China which are enrolled among the population.

5 番 攤 "Fantan"—a form of gambling.

番 椒 or 辣 椒 capsicum.

番 紅 花 saffron.

番 茄 tomatoes. = 2460.46.

番 話 foreign talk.

10 番 銀 or 番 佛 Mexican dollars—because of the image on them.

熟 番 acculturized aboriginal tribes, those brought under Chinese rule.

生 番 "raw" or unacculturized aboriginal tribes.

(a) A turn, a time. To change. to repeat.

番 代 turns of military duty.

番 外 extra.

番 戍 to take turns on frontier-duty.

今 番 now, in the present.

幾 番 several times.

更 番 to change.

連 番 continuously.

(b) Read *po¹*. Warlike.

番 番 良 士 a courageous warrior.

土 番 (or 蕃) Tibet; tribes living on the west of China.

(c) Read *p'an¹*. A constellation; district in Kwangtung.

番 禺 縣 district of which the chief city is Canton.

墦 ²
1791   The grave.

墦 間 之 祭 worship at the tombs.

幡 ²
1792   A pennant, a banner, a streamer.

幡 幡 changeable; fluttering.

幡 然 forthwith; suddenly.

幡 縚 flapping or fluttering.

素 幡 white flag—for truce or surrender.

旛 ¹
1793   A streamer, a funeral flag. Inter. 幡 preceding.

招 魂 旛 banner used to call home the soul of one who has died away from home.

旗 旛 flags and pennons.

燔 ²
1794   To roast meat for sacrifice. To burn.

燔 書 the burning of the classics by *Ch'in Shih huang* 秦 始 皇.

燔 柴 an ancient form of burnt offering.

燔 炙 roasted or grilled.

燔 祭 The Burnt Offering.
燔 糧 穀 to burn the grain.

繙 ¹ To interpret; to translate.
1795

繙·不 出 來 unable to translate.
繙·出 來 to translate.
繙 書 to translate books.
繙 譯 to interpret or translate.
繙 譯 官 an official interpreter or translator.

(a) To flutter in the wind, as a pennon.

繽 繙 confusion of waving pennons.

翻 ¹ To upset, to overturn. To come back. To re-open, as
1796 a case at law.

翻 供 to retract testimony.
翻 來 覆 去 to go backwards and forwards; reiteration.
翻 觔 (ken) 斗 to turn a somersault.
翻 印 or 翻 版 to reprint; to infringe a copyright.
⁵翻 印 必 究 he who reprints this will be prosecuted. "All rights reserved."
翻 壓 overturned and crushed—as by a cart.
翻 書 to turn over the leaves of a book; to find a place in a book; to translate a book.
翻 案 to re-open a case at law.
翻 江 倒 海 to overturn the river and pour out the sea—to use every effort.
¹⁰翻 濤 rolling billows.
翻 生 to come back to life.
翻 眼 to turn the eyes—to play false; to back out of.
翻 砂 to make a mould, as for castings.
翻 箱 倒 篋 to overturn boxes and empty out the contents—burglary.
¹⁵翻 築 to open up and re-lay a road.
翻 胃 to turn the stomach.
翻 臉 to change colour; to get angry.
翻 臉 不 認 人 he was angry and would not recognise me(as a friend).
翻 船 to capsize a boat.

²⁰翻 覆 無 定 vacillating.
翻·譯 to interpret; to translate.
翻 身 to turn the body over.
翻 車 to overturn a cart; waterwheels; spring-nets for snaring birds.
翻 車 魚 the sunfish.
²⁵翻 轉 turned round; wrong side up.
翻·過·來 turn it over.
翻 閱 to refer to a place in a book; to turn over the leaves of a book.
翻 雲 覆 雨 as changeable as clouds and rain—human affections.
翻·騰 東·西 to turn things over and over; to throw into disorder.
³⁰翻·騰·起·來 to rise up, as waves.
打 翻 to upset, to overturn.

(a) To flutter about.

翻 泊 to soar and fly to and fro.
翻 飛 to flutter hither and thither.
飛 鳥 翻 翔 the birds soar and wheel about.

膰 ² Meats used in sacrifice.
1797

膰 肉 sacrificial meats.

蕃 ² Luxurious growth of vegetation. Numerous; to increase.
1798

蕃 庶 numerous, increasing—as progeny or population.
蕃 昌 numerous—of posterity.
蕃 滋 or 蕃 茂 flourishing, as a garden; to increase.
蕃 盛 abundant; full; luxuriant.
蕃 臺 to ramify—as plants.
蕃 衍 numerous; large and luxuriant.

(a) To breed.

蕃 生 to bear; to produce.
蕃 馬 to breed horses.

(b) Read po¹. u.f. 番 No. 1790.

西 蕃 Western tribes. Tibetans.
南 蕃 Szech'uan.

蹯 ² Paws of an animal.
1799

熊 蹯 bear's paws—an imperial delicacy.

藩 ¹ A hedge, a boundary, a frontier. To protect.
1800

藩 司 or 藩 臺 former title of a Provincial Treasurer.
藩 垣 a boundary wall.
藩 域 the frontier.
藩 屏 a screen—an officer who protects the frontier.
⁵藩 庫 Provincial treasury.
藩 籬 a bamboo fence; a barrier, a division, (fig.).
藩 維 a defence; an outlying dependency.
藩 蔽 to protect and screen.
藩 臣 officers near the throne.
¹⁰藩 邦 feudatory States.
藩 邸 court of a feudatory prince.
理 藩 院 (or 部) Department in charge of Tibetan and Mongolian affairs, changed into 蒙藏院.

FANG.　　(ㄈㄤ)

匚 ¹ A box, a basket. Radical 22. National Phonetic letter
1801 for f, written ㄈ.

方 ¹ Square. Radical 70.
1802

方 三 尺 three feet square.
方 丈 a square chang, 100 square feet, Chinese. Cf. 200 A 8.
方 倉 圓 廩 granaries, both round and square.
方 喙 鈎 爪 square muzzle and hooked claws—of beasts of prey.
⁵方 圓 (or 員) squares and circles; all round. See below. 18, 22, 44.
方 圓 有 異 there is a difference between square and round.
方 塊 square blocks; cubes.
方 塊 糖 or 塔 糖 loaf-sugar.
方 字 characters written on squares, used for teaching pupils.
¹⁰方 寸 a square inch; the heart, as it is supposed to be that size.
方 寸 不 亂 presence of mind.
方 寸 之 印 a square seal.

方 寸 無 主 confused in mind.
方 尖 塔 pyramid.
15 方 尖 碑 an obelisk.
方 尺 or 方 呎 a square foot—the second is used for the "standard foot."
方 平 plane quadrilateral surface.
方 底 圓 蓋 a square base and round cover—not in harmony, unsuited to each other.
方 式 square. *See below.* C. 6.
20 方 數 product obtained by multiplying a number into itself—a power.
方 指 數 index-figures in mathematics.
方 柄 圓 鑿 square head and round socket—cannot be fitted, used of impossibilities.
方 格 chequered. *See below.* C.7.
方 根 roots. (*math.*)
25 平 方 根 square root.
立 方 根 cube root.
方 棹 a square table.
方 步 a square pace.
方 田 plane mensuration.
30 方·的 square.
方 目 squares of a chess-board.
方 磚 square tiles for paving.
方 程 equations. (*math.*)
方 程 式 in the form of an equation.
35 二 次 方 程 式 quadratic equations.
通 同 方 程 式 simultaneous equations.
方 程 式 根 root of an equation.
方 穿 a square hole; to make a square hole.
方 竹 square bamboo, a rare variety.
40 方 罫 squares on a chess-board.
方 舟 The Ark. *See below.* F. 2.
方 袍 a square robe—Buddhist priest.
方 諸 a large toad; a vessel in which pure water was collected.
方 趾 圓 顱 square foot and round skull—man.
45 方 里 a square *li.*
方 陣 the military square.
空 方 陣 the hollow square.
方 面 square-faced. *See below.* B. 37.
方 面 大 耳 square face and large ears—handsome man.
50 方 頂 square-topped.
方 領 square collars—dress of a student in former days.

方 頰 square jaws.
方 額 or 方 顙 a square forehead.
一 方 a square, as
55   墨 一 方 one square of ink.
四 方 rectangular.
孔 方 a square hole—cash.
斜 方 a rhombus.
正 方 a square.
60 立 方 a cube.
長 方 a rectangle.

(a) Square—morally.

方 嚴 upright and stern.
方 廉 scrupulous and incorrupt.
方 慎 square-dealing and cautious.
方 檢 honourable, and possessing powers of self-restraint.
5 方 正 square and upright—a good moral character.
方 潔 honourable in actions and pure.
方 雅 正 直 square-dealing, courteous and upright.
大·方 courteous and upright; magnanimous; of good taste.
端 方 upright and correct in behaviour.
行 方 to act on the square.

(b) Direction, trend. Aspect of. A place, a region.

方 丘 or 方 澤 altar to Earth, a square mound where sacrifices were offered to Earth on the summer solstice.
方 伯 a governor; Provincial Treasurer.
方 位 location; aspect of; bearings.
  依 方 位 to go in the direction indicated.
5 方 俗 local customs.
方 內 or 海 內 within the bounds of China.
方 內 安 寧 the country is peaceful.
方·向 direction, tendency; phase.
方·向 不 對 the aspect of affairs is not right; the direction is wrong.
10 方 向 線 tendency; direction.
  一 個 方·向·的 動 力 single-acting.
  兩 個 方·向·的 動 力 double-acting.
方 名 a name well known in every direction.
方 土 local.

15 方 土 所 生 之 物 or 方 物 local products.
  不 可 方 物 not able to discriminate between them.
方 夏 China.
方 外 beyond the universe; transcendentalism, Buddhist teachings; abroad, out of bounds.
方 外 侶 Buddhist priest.
20   從 方 外 之 學 to follow the transcendental teachings—Buddhism.
  逍 遙 方 外 wandering in the transcendental regions of bliss.
方 家 great families.
方 岳 or 方 嶽 the four famous mountains.
方 志 topographical records of any place.
25 方 望 之 事 the sacrifices offered by the Emperor, at the outer suburbs, to the gods of the four regions.
方 祇 Earth—as a god.
方 良 spirit of the trees and rocks; also explained as of the lakes and hills.
方 行 天 下 to travel all over the empire.
方 裔 the frontiers.
30 方 言 patois; local dialects. An ancient book on dialects.
方 輿 the earth; geography.
  方 地 爲 輿 圓 天 爲 蓋 the square earth below to support, and the dome of heaven above to cover.
方 輿 圖 map on Mercator's projection.
方 鍼 phase; tendency; direction—where the needle points.
35 方 鎮 strong military ruler.
方 鎮 名 詞 a "*Fang Chen*" title,—from the above:—one who showed no restraint in his rule.
方 面 phase, aspect; sides (in a war). *See above* 48.
  他 方 面 another phase; other aspects of.
一 方 in the same direction.
40 上 方 a superior place; Buddhist monastery.
修 方 to change the aspect—as of a grave.
地·方 place; local authorities.
天 各 一 方 we are each in a different quarter—said of separated friends.

(c) A plan, method, device. A road.

方○便 convenient, from 隨方因便 that which is not strictly according to rule, but which is convenient. Used by Buddhists for good works, by means of which men are led into an appreciation of the deeper truths of the Buddhist philosophy; now used generally of things beneficial.

於人方○便 study the convenience of others.

行方○便 to do good works.

說方○便 to say a good word for.

⁵方客 a Taoist, one who follows the *Tao*.

方式 method. *See above.*—19.

方格 a copy-slip. *See above.*—23.

方法 procedure; method; device, etc.

各種方法 every means; all sorts of plans.

¹⁰方略 strategy; a mode of action; a scheme.

方術 a trick; a stratagem.

千方百計 all sorts of devices.

多方 in every way; by many means.

(d) Then, now, at. Actually; just then.

方且 about to; forthwith; then.

方今 the present time; now-a-days.

方可 then and only then may it...

方始 then and not till then....

⁵方知 thereupon he knew.

方纔 just now; a moment ago.

方長不折 what was just growing he would not break.

方顯 and then it became apparent.

(e) A prescription, a recipe.

方劑 a prescription.

方士 a necromancer; one versed in prescriptions; Taoist.

方·子 a prescription.

方脈 to feel the pulse and write a prescription.

⁵良方 a good prescription.

處方 or 藥方 a prescription for medicine.

開方·子 to write a prescription.

(f) To compare. Side by side.

方人 to compare the abilities of men.

方舟 or 方船 two boats proceeding side by side. *See above.*—41.

方軌 or 方駕 carriages proceeding side by side.

方轂 chariots side by side.

⁵方轅 with the shafts side by side.

方轡 bridle to bridle.

方駕齊驅 riding neither before nor behind.

(g) Used like 放 No. 1807. To relax, to disobey. To neglect.

方命 to decline to obey orders.

方命虐民 commands are disobeyed and the people oppressed.

方相 likeness of an ugly god with four eyes, used to expel evil influences from graves, etc.

方相⁴氏 exorcists who dressed in bear's skin, and carried on with wild antics in order to expel noxious influences from dwellings or graves.

(h) The centre or focus.

萬邦之方 the centre of all the States.

(i) To possess.

維鳩方之 the turtle-dove occupies the nest of the (*magpie*).

(j) Slips or tablets of wood.

方策 or 方冊 records of wood and bamboo.

(k) Used like 彷 No. 1805. Like.

方羊 undecided; irresolute.

方皇 agitated; irresolute.

坊 1803 ¹ A subdivision of a city; a neighbourhood; a ward.

坊社 altars to the local gods.

坊里 a street; a neighbourhood; a village or hamlet.

牌·坊 honorary arch or gateway.

(a) A workshop; a store.

作坊 a workshop.

僧坊 a monastery.

書坊 a bookshop.

妨 1804 ¹·⁴· To hinder, to oppose. Obstacle or difficulty. To interfere with.

妨事 to matter, consequence.

妨礙 to hinder; a hindrance.

妨害交通 interference with public communications. (*legal*).

妨害公務 injurious to public affairs. (*legal*).

⁵妨害公安 disturbing the public peace. (*legal*).

妨害商務 injurious to trade. (*legal*).

妨害國交 hindering friendly international relations.

妨害安全，信用，名譽，及秘·密罪, offences relating to personal safety, credit, reputation, and secrets. (*legal*).

妨害會議 to hinder a meeting.

¹⁰妨害水利 interference with irrigation. (*legal*).

妨害秩序 offence against public order. (*legal*).

妨害衛生 offence against public health. (*legal*).

妨害郵電 interference with posts and telegraphs. (*legal*).

妨訴 a declaration of damage.

¹⁵妨賢 to hinder good men from success.

不妨 it does not matter; no hindrance to it; it does no harm ...

彷髣 1805 ³ Like; resembling. u.f. 做 No. 1808.

彷·彿 like, similar to.

(a) Read *p'ang²*. Hesitating; unsettled.

彷徉 unsettled; doubtful.

彷徨 undecided; agitated.

房 1806 ² A house, a building. A room.

房契 title-deeds for houses.

房·子 in South China—a room; in North China—a house.

房客 a tenant.

房屋 or 房間 or 房宅 houses.

⁵房東 landlord.

房產地土 property.

房租 or 房錢 rent.

房簷 or 屋簷 the eaves.

房春 the ridge of the roof.

[10] 房金 house-allowance.

房院 dwellings.

房頂 the roof of a house.

上房 the best rooms, as of an inn.

下房 servants' quarters.

[15] 內房 women's apartments.

同房 or 行房 or 房事 sexual intercourse.

廂房 side-rooms; ante-chambers.

耳房 small end-rooms.

號房 ante-room where a visitor waits while his card is presented.

門房 porter's lodge.

(a) A wife or concubine.

房老 or 房長³ a concubine who has grown old in the family.

偏房 or 二房 or 房下 a concubine.

妻房 wives.

補妻房 to take a second wife.

專房 a favourite concubine.

正房 the legal wife.

賤房 My wife — conventional term.

(b) Branches of a family.

房族 or 房分⁴ those of the same branch of the family.

房累 relatives.

房親 agnates.

房長 head of a branch of the family.

長³房 the eldest (married) brother.

(c) Office or bureau in a _yamen_.

房官 or 房司 preliminary examiner of the essays under the old system.

房科 an office.

六房 the six offices into which the business of the _yamen_ is divided.

放 ⁴ **To loosen, to liberate; to let go.**

1807

放下 loosed; put it down.

放下屠刀 drop the butcher's knife — to reform; to repent and become a Buddhist.

放下簾子 let down the screen-blinds.

放了 loosed; liberated.

---

[5] 放人 or 自放 a retired official or scholar who studies his own convenience.

放任 indifference; inattention; to relegate.

放任主義 go-as-you-please policy — laissez-faire.

放債取利 to let out money on usury.

放光 to glisten; to shine.

[10] 放免 to release, as a suspect.

放冷箭 to draw a bow at a venture; to make sarcastic remarks.

放出去 or 放出來 to liberate; to release, as birds, etc.

放刀成佛 drop the knife and become a Buddha.

放利 to exact; to fleece.

[15] 放去 to release; to let go.

放哨 to do sentry.

放夜 to relax prohibitions about going out at night.

放大 to enlarge, as a photograph.

放大器 a pantograph.

[20] 放大鏡 magnifying-glass.

照片放大 to enlarge a photograph.

放學 to give the school children a holiday; to release from school.

放寬 to open wide; to loosen.

放射 _Radio.,_ as a prefix. To radiate.

[25] 放射動物 radiata — as corals, starfish, etc.

放射化學 radio-chemistry.

放射狀 or 放散 radiating.

放射療法 radio-therapy.

放射線照相 radio-graph.

[30] 放射能的 radio-active.

放屁 to break wind.

放屁胡說 Stuff and nonsense! What rot! (_abusive_).

放工 to release from work.

放差 to release from duty. Commissioner from the capital who was sent to superintend examinations under the old system. (-_ch'ai_¹)

[35] 放心 or 放懷 make the mind easy; to be free from anxiety.

放心不下 unable to be easy in mind about anything.

放手 hands off; let go.

放手不得 you dare not let go — as when one has a matter in hand which would be ruined if allowed to lapse.

放捨 to relinquish.

---

[40] 放於利而行多怨 he who acts with a view to his own profit will be much resented.

放春 the sprouting of vegetation in the spring.

放晴 to clear up — after rain, etc.

放暑假 summer vacation.

放棄 to abandon; to renounce; to discard.

[45] 放棄權利 to relinquish rights or privileges.

放棄計畫 to give up the attempt.

放棄責任 neglect of duty.

放歌 to sing with a loud voice; to lift up the voice in song.

放歘 to lend; to invest money.

[50] 放步 to walk with free steps.

放水燈 to light and release floating lanterns.

放汽 to blow off steam; to blow a steam-whistle.

放洋 to go to sea; to go abroad.

放火 to set on fire.

[55] 放火罪 arson. (_legal_).

放烽火 to fire a beacon.

放熱 radiation of heat.

放熱器 radiator.

放餕口 a ritual to release souls from torment.

[60] 放猪的 a swineherd.

放生 to liberate living creatures, birds, fish, etc., for merit.

放生池 a pond or section of a river set apart for that purpose.

放白鴿 a confidence-trick — to fly the white pigeon: — when a woman marries a man, and after a time runs away with his valuables; and other similar tricks.

放盤 to sell at a great reduction; to buy at increased prices.

[65] 放目四矚 to gaze in every direction.

放砲 or 開砲 to fire a cannon.

放禽 to release birds from the snares.

放空 to travel empty, as a cart.

放空鎗 to fire blank-cartridge.

[70] 放箭 to shoot an arrow.

放羊 to tend sheep or goats.

放膽 to grow bold; to pluck up courage.

放聲 to lift up the voice; to give free vent to the feelings.

放良 to free a slave-girl so that she may marry.

75 放 花 or 放 爆 竹 to let off fireworks or crackers.

放 虎 歸 山 to release a tiger that he might return to the hills—to lay by trouble for the future.

放 虎 自 衛 to release a tiger to protect oneself—to bring disaster on oneself when trying to avoid it from other sources.

放 號 礟 to fire a signal-gun; to fire a salute.

放 號 筒 to blow a steam-whistle.

80 放 血 to bleed.

放 行 or 放 回 or 放 開 to release; to open; to liberate.

放 行 單 a release-permit.

放 解 to liberate or release.

放 言 or 放 論 free speech or discussion; to speak one's mind.

85 放 賑 to give relief to distress.

放 賴 to demand satisfaction for a trumped-up offence.

放 賬 to give credit.

放 走 to let a prisoner escape; to release.

放 路 燈 to burn incense lamps on the road—on 15th of the 7th month.

90 放 量 to put forth great effort.

放 銜 垂 轡 to give the horse his head.

放 長 耳 朵 聽 聽 keep your ears open and hear all that is to be said.

放·開 嗓·子 to give voice; to sing lustily.

放·開 門 戶 the open-door, as a policy.

95 放 電 to discharge electricity.

放 風·箏 to fly a kite.

放 飲 to water cattle, etc.

放 鬆 to relax; to loosen.

放 龍 入 海 to release a dragon into the sea—to give a man an opportunity to show what he can do.

釋 放 or 解 放 to set at liberty.

解 放 to emancipate.

(a) To drive away; to banish.

放 殛 to banish and punish severely.

放 流 to deport, to banish.

放 逐 to drive away, to banish.

放 遠 to drive to a distance.

(b) To place in or on.

放·下 put it down; to deposit.

放·在 心·裏 bear it in mind.

放·在 這·裏 put it here.

放 桌·子 to set the table for food.

5 放 置 to place or arrange; to deposit.

存 放 to deposit.

安 放 to place; to fit in or on.

(c) To indulge; to give license.

放 刁 dogged and obstreperous.

放 恣 self-indulgence; debauchery.

放 曠 爲 非 dissolute and given to evil practices.

放 縱 to give the reins to; to allow to run wild.

5 放 肆 to be disorderly and rude.

放 蕩 profligate; going to excess; heedless, reckless.

放 誕 reckless both in conduct and in speech; disorderly behaviour and wild talk.

放 僻 邪 侈 recklessness and depravity.

放 飯 gluttony.

(d) To issue.

放 給 to issue; to pay out.

(e) Read *fang*³. u.f. next. To accord with, to reach to; having regard to; to imitate, etc.

放 乎 四 海 it reaches to the four seas.

放 古 to copy the rule of the ancients.

放 效 like, in imitation of.

做
仿 ³ To imitate. Like, resembling, according to.
1808

做 古 筆 意 to imitate the writings of the ancients; after the old masters.

做 圈 a brass circle or frame placed on writing paper to keep the surface smooth.

做 效 時 式 to follow the fashions.

做 本 or 字 本 a copy-book.

5 做 格 or 做 紙 a copy-slip to be traced over.

做 樣 to follow the pattern.

做 照 like, to imitate; as, according to.

做 造 make it like the pattern.

相 做 very like.

↑ 做 宋 style of printing, as: 仿宋.

肪 ³ Bright dawn. To appear, to manifest.
1809

肪 亮 dawn.

肪 亮 炮 the morning gun.

肪 於 何 時 when was it known?

枋 ¹ A tree which is used as timber for boats, etc.
1810

枋 榆 之 飛 short flights from tree to tree.

枋 木 laths, thin strips of wood.

枋·子 a support for roof-timbers, etc.

蘇 枋 木 sapan wood—the dried sap is used for red and yellow dyes.

(a) u.f., 舫 No. 1814. A boat, etc.

枋 篺 a raft.

(b) Read *ping*⁴. u.f. 柄 Authority.

枋 國 to wield authority.

肪 ³ Indistinct. u.f. 彷 No. 1805. Alike.
1811

肪 彿 resembling.

相 肪 much alike; resembling one another.

紡 ³ To reel, to twist, to spin.
1812

紡 毛 to make hair into thread.

紡 紗 織 布 to spin and weave.

紡 絲 to spin silk thread.

紡 綢 reeled pongee.

5 紡 綫 車 a spinning-wheel.

紡 線 or 紡 紗 or 紡 績 to reel thread.

紡 織 娘 the spinning-woman—name of a cicada whose buzzing resembles the sound of the wheel.

紡 花 to spin cotton.

肪 ² Animal fat.
1813

脂 肪 oils, fats.

舫 [3] A large boat. Two boats lashed together.
1814

畫 舫 a gaily-decorated pleasure-boat.
輕 舫 a skiff.

芳 [1] Fragrant; beautiful; pleasant; virtuous; excellent.
1815

芳 叢 a place of abundant flowers.
芳 名 a fragrant reputation.
芳 味 the bouquet of wine.
芳 塵 fragrant dust—the scent of flowers.
[5]芳 序 a favourable time.
芳 德 fragrant excellencies.
芳 意 amorous thoughts.
芳 旨 fragrance.
芳 朝 an auspicious hour.
[10]芳 札 your fragrant epistle.
芳 枝 a flowering branch.
芳 槿 the Hibiscus.
芳 歲 youth.
芳 氣 fragrance.
[15]芳 汗 似 蘭 湯 fragrant perspiration like the scent of the orchid.
芳 液 scent.
芳 節 the time of flowers.
芳 芬 fragrance.
芳 芷 or 芳 草 fragrant plants.
[20]芳 芽 buds; also tea.
芳 苞 flower buds.
芳 茗 fragrant tea.
芳 菲 beauty and fragrance of flowers.
芳 華 beautiful season, as spring.
[25]芳 訊 "your whereabouts"; the whereabouts of a girl.
芳 踪 the fragrant records—of the ancient worthies.
芳 辰 spring.
芳 郁 plentiful fragrance.
芳 醴 fragrant wine.
[30]芳 鈿 women's head ornaments of filagree.
芳 馥 fragrant.

訪 [3] To inquire about. To search out; To visit.
1816

訪 事 處 inquiry office.
訪 候 to pay a call.
訪 友 to call on friends; to inquire after the health of friends.
訪 古 to search for ancient relics, etc.

[5]訪 員 or 訪 事 a reporter on a newspaper.
訪 察 or 訪 問 to make inquiries.
訪 尋 to search for.
訪 慰 a visit of condolence.
訪 拿 to hunt for and arrest.
[10]訪 查 的 確 make inquiries into the facts; ascertain the facts.
訪 案 to make private investigation into a case at law.
訪 求 to inquire and search for.
訪 稿 report of news.
訪 聞 to seek information about; to learn after inquiry.
[15]訪 親 to inquire about relatives; to ascertain the connections, as of families with whom marriage is suggested.
訪 謁 or 訪 見 to visit.
訪 議 to deliberate; to inquire.
訪 賊 to search for thieves.
訪 質 to investigate.
[20]訪 道 to inquire into the Way.
拜 訪 to make a call.
相 訪 mutual inquiries.
詳 訪 to make careful inquiries.
過 訪 to call, a short visit.

防 [2] To guard. against; to protect from. An embankment.
1817

防 不 勝 防 impossible to guard against.
防 亂 guard against disorder.
防 備 to be ready for; to watch for; to guard against.
防 制 to keep under; to restrain.
[5]防 務 defence measures.
防 口 to suppress public opinion.
防 堵 to raise defence-works.
防 塞 to block up; to resist the encroachment of.
防 姦 邪 to avoid lewdness and crime.
[10]防 守 or 防 禦 or 防 護 or 防 衛 to protect, to guard.
防 寒 to prepare for the cold.
防 川 or 防 水 river conservancy.
防 民 之 口 甚 於 防 川 to stop the mouths of the people is more difficult than dealing with a river in flood.
防 後 to provide for the future.
[15]防 惡 to guard against evil.
防 患 未 然 to take precautions against calamity.
防 意 如 城 guard the thoughts of the heart as you would defend a city.
防 扞 to guard; defend.
防 拒 to resist; to oppose; to defend.
[20]防 排 embankments.
防 救 to defend and save.
防 止 to avert; to prevent.
防 毒 劑 antiseptics.
防 水 布 waterproof cloth.
[25]防 波 隄 breakwater.
防 海 to guard against the seas.
防 火 布 fireproof cloth; asbestos sheeting.
防 疫 所 or 檢 疫 所 quarantine station.
防 症 藥 prophylactics.
[30]防 盜 defence against robbers.
防 禦 權 right of defence.
防 禦 盟 約 defensive alliance.
防 禦 線 line of defence.
防 秋 to guard against (the raids of the barbarians) during the autumn.
[35]防 範 measures for defence.
防 老 to provide against old age.
防 腐 藥 preservatives.
防 臭 劑 disinfectants; deodorants.
防 荒 or 防 饑 to provide against famine—by storing grain.
[40]防 虞 to guard against mishap.
防 賊 to guard against thieves.
防 身 self-defence.
防 軍 or 防 兵 defence corps.
防 遏 羣 蠻 to repress the barbarians.
[45]防 避 to avoid.
防 邊 to guard the frontiers.
防 閑 to guard against; to train.
防 風 to prevent flatulency—a medicine.
防 風 雨 to make provision against the storms—to hide behind another's power.
[50]不 防 後 患 improvident.
提 防 to beware of.
謹 防 to guard against; to be careful.
邊 防 frontier-defence.
預 防 to take precautions against.

魴 [2] A bream.
1818

魴 魚 the bream.
魴 鱧 甫 甫 with many large bream and tench.

FEI.　　　　(ㄷ)

非¹ Wrong, bad. A negative; not, not to be, without. 1819 Radical 175.

非不 two negatives—very strong affirmative, "not un-".

非不説子³之道 it is not that I do not desire the doctrine of the Sage. (-yüeh⁴-)

非也 or 非然 not so; not right.

非人 a strange, uncanny thing; a bogy; a cripple or deformed person.

⁵非人不煖 (at 80) a man cannot be warm without a bed-mate.

非他不可 he is indispensable.

非但 or 非止 or 非獨 not only.

非其鬼而祭之諂也 it is flattery for a person to sacrifice to a spirit which does not belong to him.

非僻 profligate; abandoned.

¹⁰非凡 uncommon; out of the ordinary.

非凡器 no ordinary person; a man of unusual ability.

非分⁴ not included in one's duties.

非分⁴之事 not one's own affair.

非刑 unlawful punishments.

¹⁵非名數 abstract number.

非同 not the same as.

非同小可 not a small matter; in no ordinary degree.

非同業組合主義 non-union-ism.

非喫卽喝 if not eating then drinking.

²⁰非命 unnatural death; to act against the fixed decree.

非基督教 anti-Christianity.

非大卽小 either too large or too small.

非定命論 indeterminism.

非對話人 person at a distance. (legal).

²⁵非帝國主義 anti-imperialism.

非常 extraordinary; unusual; uncommon; very.

非常上告 special appeal to higher court. (legal).

非常刑事訴訟 extraordinary criminal action. (legal).

非常危險 unusually dangerous; very critical.

³⁰非常會議 extraordinary session.

非常秘密 unusually private or secret.

非常緊急 unusually urgent or important.

非常薄弱 exceptionally weak.

非常重大 exceptionally important.

³⁵非帷裳必殺 (shai⁴) 之 except in the curtain-like lower garment, (required for special occasions), he would reduce it in size.

非幾¹ a bad omen.

非徒無益 not only is there no advantage....

非心 an evil heart.

非認 non-recognition.

⁴⁰非意 not expected; not according to expectations.

非我之意 that is not my intention.

非我所能必 it is not in my power to decide it.

非戰員 non-combatant.

非戰鬭員 non-combatant officers, as surgeons, secretaries, etc.

⁴⁵非敢後 not that I dare to be last.

非斯人之徒與而誰與 if I may not associate with these people, with whom may I associate?

非族 of another clan or tribe.

非易 not easy.

非是 that is wrong; that is not so.

⁵⁰非時不食 to refrain from eating certain things except at the proper seasons; not to eat except at the times appointed by the Buddhist ritual.

非會員 non-member.

非望 or 非想 unhoped for; unexpected.

非次 out of sequence; unusual; out of the ordinary course.

非次之恩 special favours.

⁵⁵非正式 informal; irregular; unofficial.

非正式交涉 unofficial negotiation.

非正式方法 informal methods.

非此不行 it cannot be done without this; this is imperatively necessary.

非毀 or 非訾 destructive criticism; slander.

⁶⁰非池中物 not a mere creature of the ponds—of a man of great ability.
[Pact.

↑非戰公約 the Kellogg-Briand
（　264　）

非法行爲 an illegal act. (legal).

非爲 evil conduct.

非特予以維持 will not only be maintained....

非理 unreasonable.

⁶⁵非生物 inorganic matter.

非短 faults; shortcomings.

非禁止品 non-contraband.

非禮 indecent; improper; disreputable.

非禮勿視 do not look at what is improper.

⁷⁰非禮勿言非禮勿動 neither speak nor act without observing propriety.

非笑 to ridicule; to make a laughing stock of.

非義無生 apart from righteousness he cannot live.

非能願學 it is not that I have ability, but I am willing to learn.

非見聞所及 may not be reached by the senses.

⁷⁵非解 ambiguous; difficult to understand.

非計 an ill-considered plan.

非訟事件手續法 law of civil process. (legal).

非訟案件 non-contentious action. (legal).

非語 wrong language.

⁸⁰非賣品 not for sale.

非身之所能爲也 one cannot himself act in this matter.

非量直覺 intuition.

非金類 non-metallic.

非錢不行 nothing can be done (in this case) without money.

⁸⁵非離 unless; no way but; except.

非類 u.f. 匪類 rogues, bad characters.

非類 of a different class, as the gods differ from men.

非驢非馬 neither ass nor horse —to copy another and fail, losing one's own originality.

非體 not respectable; disgraceful.

⁹⁰並非 in no wise; by no means.

是非 right and wrong; pros and cons. See No. 5794-14ff.

是非塲 a situation where one cannot give satisfaction.

無非 or 莫非 really; it must be.

知非 from 知四十九年非 a man at 50 said that he knew he had spoiled 49 years of his life.

↑是·非 gossip, scandal.

(a) **To blame; to condemn. To disown.**

非 其 上 they condemned those over them.

非 我 to point out my faults.

非 聖 to blaspheme; to revile the teachings of the Sage.

非 訐 to impeach.

非 間 (*chien*[4]) to blame, to find fault with.

非 難 to criticize.

非 非 to oppose the wrong.

(b) **Used for foreign sounds.**

非 洲 Africa.

匪 [3] **Vagabonds, rebels. Used with the preceding.**
1820

匪 人 a bad man.

匪 巢 a rebel-stronghold.

匪 犯 one who has been convicted of highway-robbery, brigand-age, etc.

匪 類 or 匪 徒 a bad class; brig-ands, robbers, etc.

[5] 匪 首 brigand or rebel-leaders.

匪 黨 or 會 匪 members of secret societies, robber or rebel-leagues.

土 匪 local banditti.

奸 匪 rebels.

敎 匪 members of secret sects, ostensibly religious, but promot-ing sedition and such things.

(a) **Not, no. Inter. preceding.**

匪 夷 所 思 no ordinary person could think of it.

匪 懈 not indolent nor careless.

匪 特 not only.

匪 石 匪 席 firm and decided in character—not like a stone that can be rolled away or turned round, nor like a mat that can be rolled up.

匪 遙 not far off.

(b) **Variegated.**

匪 色 variegated.

啡 [1] **Used in transliterating.**
1821

咖 啡 coffee.

悱 [3] **To be desirous of speaking.**
1822

悱 憤 eager to speak but unable, seeking to understand but fail-ing to do so.

不 悱 不 發 I do not assist any-one who is not able to explain him-self.

口 悱 悱 mouth desirous of speak-ing but unable to do so.

扉 [1] **A door with only one leaf. A cottage.**
1823

斐 [3] **Streaks or veins. Grace-ful, elegant, adorned, polish-ed. Distinguish** 裴 No. 5018.
1824

斐 斐 有 光 elegant and polished —as a composition.

斐 然 成 章 they are accomplish-ed and complete.

斐 美 elegant, graceful, polished.

(a) **Used for foreign sounds.**

斐 律 賓 Philippine Islands.

框 棐 [3] **A species of yew found in North China.**
1825

框 几 a table made of yew.

框 子 the nuts of the above tree.

(a) **To strengthen, to assist.**

篤 棐 zealous in rendering assist-ance.

痱 [4] **Ulcers. Swollen feet. Inter.** 痲 No. 1846. **Prick-ly heat.**
1826

篚 [3] **Round or oval covered baskets with short legs.**
1827

女 受 以 篚 a woman should re-ceive things (from a man) in a basket.

緋 [1] **Dark red, Purple silk for 5th grade officials.**
1828

緋 衲 a deep-red robe or cassock.

兩 頰 緋 紅 both cheeks bright red.

翡 [3] **A cock kingfisher.**
1829

翡 翠 the kingfisher.

翡 翠 玉 chrysoprase; malachite.

腓 [2] **The calf of the legs.**
1830

腓 腸 the calf of the leg.

腓 骨 the fibula.

(a) **To decay, to change.**

百 卉 具 腓 all the plants decay.

(b) **To protect.**

小 人 所 腓 the protection of our men—the horses of the general.

牛 羊 腓 字 之 the sheep and cat-tle herded together and pro-tected him.

菲 [3] **A kind of radish—from this it gets the meaning of frugal, sparing, trifling or mean. Straw sandals.**
1831

菲 儀 or 菲 物 my poor gift; my trifling present.

菲 慼 or 菲 悵 sad, mournful.

菲 敬 with poor respects—written on a present.

菲 薄 poor, mean.

菲 飲 食 coarse food and simple drink.

(a) **Read** *fei*[1]. **Fragrant.**

菲 菲 very fragrant.

芳 菲 fragrant and luxurious growth.

蜚 [3] **Offensive insect produced in moist places. The cock-roach.**
1832

蜚 零 the ground-bee.

(a) **Read** *fei*[1]. **u.f.** 飛 No. 1850. **To fly, etc.**

蜚 流 之 言 evil flying-rumours.

蜚 芻 輓 粟 bring fodder and grain—to the battlefield.

蜚 英 騰 茂 or 蜚 聲 騰 實 both reputation and reality are good.

蜚 語 slander; rumours.

蜚 鴻 滿 野 the flying geese, i.e., the distressed populace, fill the wilds.

誹 [3] To backbite, to slander.
1833

誹 章 libellous writings.
誹 謗 to slander; to defame.
誹 謗 木 a board set on the side of the road on which people could record the errors of the administration.—an ancient practice.
誹 譽 to injure a reputation by slander.
怨 誹 malicious slander.

霏 [1] Driving sleet. Fall of snow.
1834

霏 微 如 雨 露 light sleet like very fine rain.
霏 微 light—of mists.
霏 霏 承 宇 used of clouds resting on the housetops.
雨 雪 霏 霏 the sleet is driving hard.

緋 [1] Aromatic, fragrant.
1835

緋 緋 or 芳 緋 fragrant.

騑 [1] Outer of four horses driven abreast—the inner pair was called 服. An extra horse fastened to the axle with a long trace.
1836

騑 騑 horses going on without stopping.

吠 [4] To bark, as a dog.
1837

吠 噬 to bark and bite.
吠 影 吠 聲 one dog barks at a shadow, and many bark at the sound—used of scandal.
吠 日 (in rainy places where the sun rarely shines,) the dogs bark at the sun—n.f. things rarely seen.

妃 [1] A wife. Imperial concubine of the third rank.
1838

妃 嬪 or 妃 子 concubines of the third and fourth rank respectively; ladies-in-waiting.

王 妃 wife of a prince of the blood.
貴 妃 imperial concubine of first or second rank.

肥 [2] Fat, plump. Fertile, rich.
1839

肥 地 or 肥 土 or 肥 沃 or 肥 饒 rich, fertile soil.
肥 壯 fat—as animals; rich, of soil; strong and sturdy.
肥 己 to enrich oneself—at the expense of others.
肥 強 strong and flourishing.
[5]肥 潤 smooth and glossy.
肥 澤 sleek.
肥 猪 a fat pig—used of a captive held for ransom by brigands.
　拉 肥 猪 to take a wealthy man captive. 　　　　　[delicacy.
肥 甘 fat and sweet—as pork; any
[10]肥 田 to fertilise the fields.
肥 畜 well-fed beasts.
肥 皂 or 胰 子 soap.
肥 皂 子 soap-berries.
肥 料 fertilizers.
[15]肥 絲 coarse, homespun thread.
肥 美 plump.
肥 肉 fat meat.
肥 胖 or 肥 大 corpulent.
肥 豚 豚 的 fat as a pig.
[20]肥 蠢 fat and stupid—useless, gross.
肥 遯 to live in retirement.
肥 醴 fat meat and rich wines.
肥 鮮 plump and fresh.
肥 頭 大 耳 large head and prominent ears—sign of a prosperous man. 　[thing ill-gotten.
[25]分 肥 to divide the spoils, or any-

淝 [2] Name of an affluent of the Poyang Lake.
1840

淝 水 small river in North Anhwei.
淝 澺 diverging streams from the same source.

朏 [3] The appearance of the moon when three days old. Also read pʻiʻ[4], or kʻu[5].
1841

朏 明 the light of the crescent moon; early dawn before it is light.

朏 朏 early dawn as the light begins to appear.
朏 魄 之 變 the phases of the moon.

(a) A fabulous animal like a wild-cat.

朏 朏 the creature as above, described as like a wild-cat, white in colour and tameable.

(b) Appearance of dust.

塵 埃 朏 朏 甚 高 the dust rose in clouds to great height.

柹 柿 [4] Slips of wood-shavings for writing on; to shave errors off such slips by planing. 2nd form is commonly used for 柿 (szŭ) No. 5793. The persimmon.
1842

肺 [4] The lungs.
1843

肺 家 or 肺 子 the lungs.
肺 尖 apex of the lungs.
肺 底 base of the lungs.
肺 循 環 pulmonary circulation.
[5]肺 泡 or 肺 脹 or 肺 氣 腫 alveolus of the lungs.
肺 炎 pneumonia.
肺 疫 pneumonic plague.
肺 病 or 肺 結 核 or 肺 癆 症 pulmonary consumption.
肺 癰 an abcess on the lungs.
[10]肺 石 reddish kind of jasper.
肺 肝 lungs and liver—the inmost feelings.
肺 腑 or 肺 附 the inner organs—secret, private.
肺 腑 話 confidential conversation.
肺 膜 the pleura.
[15]肺 臟 the inner organs.—also used of feelings, etc.
肺 葉 lobe of the lungs.
肺 魚 類 a class of fish having lungs.

(a) Read pei[4]. Luxuriant.

其 葉 肺 肺 the leaves are luxuriant.

市 [4] Shade of trees. Read fu[4.5]. Kneecaps worn with sacrificial dress.
1844

沸潰｝[4]
To bubble up; to gush; to boil.
1845

沸 末 bubbles on water.
沸 水 bubbling water.
沸 淫 to boil.
沸 溢 boiling over.
[5]沸 羹 hubbub of voices—lit., boiling broth.
沸 騰 bubbling and boiling—unrest.
沸 點 boiling-point.
沸 鼎 a bubbling cauldron.
水 沸 山 崩 bubbling water and tumbling hills—anarchy.

(a) Read *fu*[4,5]. The appearance of water issuing from a spring.

沸 沸 water gushing from a spring.
沸 泉 a geyser.

疿 [1] Pimples, eruptions on the skin.
1846

疿 子 or 熱 疿 prickly-heat.

費 [4] To waste, to expend. Expenditure.
1847

費 事 vexatious; fussy; troublesome.
白 費 事 to labour in vain.
費 力 or 費 勁 兒 to use effort; to put oneself to trouble.
費 力 不 討 好 to put forth energy and accomplish no good.
[5]費 唇 舌 to waste one's breath.
費 心 or 費 勞 I have put you to trouble—thank you.
費 心 機 it needs mental effort.
枉 費 心 機 a waste of energy and thought.
枉 費 心 力 all the mental care expended to no purpose.
[10]費 手 difficult to accomplish.
費 手 續 laborious; troublesome.
手 續 費 running-expenses; auxiliary expenses.
費 日 waste time.
日 費 daily expenses.
[15]費·用 or 費 項 expenses; fees.
費·用 支 配 control of expenditure—as of loans by the powers.
費 盡 all wasted; all spent.

費 盡 心 機 to expend much care and thought.
費 眼 or 費 目 力 to strain the eyes.
[20]費 神 mental fatigue.
費 神 感 感 Thank you for all your trouble.
費 解 difficult of explanation.
費 財 or 費 錢 to spend lavishly; expensive.
保 護 費 bounty.
[25]免 費 free of charge.
出 港 費 clearance fee from a port.
學 費 school expenses or fees.
常 費 ordinary everyday expenses.
常 用 經 費 current expenses.
[30]旅 費 or 盤 費 or 路 費 travelling expenses.
耗·費 waste; extravagance.
浩 費 heavy expenses.
浪 費 to squander.
營 業 費 trade expenses.
[35]破·費 You have spent too much! —conventional phrase.
碼 頭 費 wharfage.
花 費 expenditure.
虛 費 or 廢 費 unnecessary expenditure.
診 費 doctor's fees.
[40]車 馬 費 incidental expenses.
軍 費 military expenditure.
辦 事 經 費 running-expenses.
進 口 費 import expenses; entry expenses—of coming into a port.
過 費 I have put you to much expense—complimentary phrase to a host.
[45]雜 費 sundry expenses.
領 港 費 pilotage.
駁 船 費 lighterage.

(a) Extensive; far-reaching.

費 而 隱 is far-reaching and subtle.

(b) Read *pi*[4]. A district in Shantung.

廢 [4] To do away with; to abrogate. To waste; to destroy.
1848 To dispense with.

廢·了 wasted.
廢·了 他 destroy it; get rid of it, or of him.
廢 事 to lose one's labour; to neglect one's work.
廢 其 一 則 無 以 造 道 if you

do away with one of these, there is nothing wherewith to make the Path.
[5]廢·去 abandoned; cast aside.
廢 址 ruins.
廢 墜 to fall into ruins.
廢 惰 lazy; unthrifty.
廢 壞 ruined; to render useless.
[10]廢 學 to give up studies.
廢 學 若 斷 織 to be remiss in studies is like cutting the web from the loom—by the mother of Mencius.
廢 家 to bring the family to an end—as when an only son follows his mother into another family, or when he marries into another family.
廢 寢 忘 餐 to lose sleep and forget to eat—from anxiety.
廢 居 or 廢 著 to get rid of goods, or to store them for higher prices, respectively.
[15]廢 帝 or 廢 王 to depose an emperor or a king.
廢 弛 careless, lax; failing; obsolete; neglect.
國 政 廢 弛 the administration is going to pieces.
紀 律 廢 弛 discipline is very lax.
農 功 皆 廢 弛 agricultural labours are all neglected.
[20]廢 徹 不 遲 remove (the sacrificial vessels) without delay.
廢·掉 abrogated; discarded.
廢 時 失 業 to waste time and fail in business or profession, etc.
廢 曲 to abrogate the statutes; to be lax in the administration of the law.
廢 書 而 歎 lay aside the book and sigh—said by one who in reading Mencius came to the words:—King *Hui* asked, "Are you provided with counsels to profit my kingdom?"
[25]廢 棄 to discard; to abandon; to give up.
廢 棄 不 用 obsolete; of no more use; to discard as useless.
廢 業 to give up or abandon the ancestral calling or profession.
廢 止 or 廢 罷 to annul; to make of no effect.
廢 滅 to destroy.
[30]廢 用 to use recklessly.
現 在 廢 而 不 用 it is now obsolete.

廢 病 a wasting disease; debility; unfit for anything.

廢 督 裁 兵 abolish the *Tuchüns* (military governors) and disband the army.

廢 約 to abrogate the treaties; to annul an agreement or contract.

35 廢 約 同 盟 會 (Students) Association for the Abolition of the Treaties.

廢 約 運 動 movement for the abolition of the treaties.

廢 絕 to break off; to cease—as studies.

廢 缺 defective; abrogated.

廢 置 to discard and place on one side.

40 廢 職 to be remiss in official duties.

廢 退 to be dismissed from office.

廢 遠 deprive her of my care by going far away.

廢 錮 deprived of rights for life.

廢 長 立 幼 to set aside the elder and put the younger on the throne.

45 廢 除 to remove; to cast on one side; to abolish.

廢 除 舊 俗 to abolish old customs.

廢 黜 功 臣 to dismiss worthy statesmen who have deserved reward.

作 廢 to terminate; to nullify.

作 廢 的 obsolete.

(a) Waste, useless, deficient.

廢 人 cripples; the infirm or superannuated.

廢 兵 disabled soldier.

廢 字 or 廢 語 obsolete word.

廢 淤 waste.

5 廢 物 or 廢 料 waste material; a useless thing—the first is abusive.

廢 物 利 用 utilization of waste material.

廢 票 cancelled cheques.

廢 紙 waste paper.

視 爲 廢 紙 regard it as waste paper.

10 廢 紙 簍 waste-paper basket.

廢 話 verbiage; irrelevant talk.

廢 鐵 old iron; scrap iron.

將 廢 obsolescent.

殘 廢 decrepit; maimed; useless; disabled.

(b) To be out of office.

廢 止 (*chung⁴*) 權 in their retire-

ment they hit the mean of opportunism.

廢 官 or 廢 員 dismissed officials.

(c) To stop short.

半 途 而 廢 to stop when only halfway.

癈 ⁴ Incurable disease.
1849

癈 疾 maimed; disabled; incurably diseased.

飛 ¹ To fly; to go quickly. Quick. Radical 183.
1850

飛 下 來 to fly down.

飛 丹 a Taoist pill—it was white as snow, and when taken gave the body a peculiar feeling of lightness.

飛 兔 Flying Hare—a famous horse that could do 10,000 *li* in a day.

飛 刀 to fling a knife; to brandish knives as if they were flying.

5 飛 券 ancient form of draft or bill of exchange.

飛 劍 to brandish or throw a sword.

飛 去 flown; to fly away.

飛 報 handbills, posters; a fleet messenger.

飛 天 本 事 he has abilities which soar to heaven.

10 飛 奔 to hurry; to run swiftly.

飛 奴 a carrier-pigeon.

飛 客 flying-visitors—arrows.

飛 將 the flying leader—said of several ancient generals.

飛 彈 (time) flies like a bullet.

15 飛 快 as speedy as flying.

飛 揚 flying about, as dust; spreading, as a fire, rumours, etc.

飛 散 火 花 a shower of flying sparks.

飛 星 a meteor. = 流 星.

飛 昇 to ascend; to go to heaven.

20 飛 書 a hasty or urgent letter.

飛 書 募 健 he rapidly wrote a proclamation calling able-bodied men to enlist.

飛 札 or 飛 函 or 飛 翰 an urgent letter.

飛 梯 a flying ladder—ancient instrument for scaling city walls.

飛 梁 石 磴 a high stone-bridge and steps.

25 飛 梭 the flying shuttle—time.

飛 梭 連 雲 the covered plankways along the precipices reach to the clouds. See No. 148—A.1.

飛 樓 ancient instrument for a siege; a mirage.

飛 檄 urgent military despatch.

飛 機 airplane. 飛 機 場 airfield.

30 飛 機 廠 airdrome.

飛 機 站 or 飛 機 停 留 場 airport.

郵 務 飛 機 air-mail carrier.

飛 沖 to get one's will; complaisant.

35 飛 沖 空 中 to fly through the air.

飛 注 rapid pouring of water; a cataract.

飛 泉 a fountain.

飛 潛 走 植 birds, fish, animals and plants—flora and fauna.

飛 浪 突 雲 the mounting billows dashed against the clouds.

40 飛 淙 the rapid rush of a stream.

飛 湍 千 里 it rushes along for 1,000 *li*—of the River Yangtze.

飛 漲 a rapid rise—of a river or of prices.

飛 災 or 飛 禍 sudden calamity; unexpected disaster.

飛 狐 the flying fox.

45 飛 生 flying squirrels and other similar creatures.

飛 白 to write characters as if there was insufficient ink in the brush, leaving white spaces—a fancy style invented by *Ts'ai Yung*, A.D. 133—192.

飛 矢 雨 集 the arrows flew like rain.

飛 石 a ballista.

飛 砂 走 石 flying sand and pebbles—of a terrible storm.

50 飛 礫 flying pebbles.

飛 禽 走 獸 birds and beasts.

飛 空 to fly into space.

飛 筆 a rapid pen.

飛 簷 走 壁 to fly over the eaves and run along the dividing walls—expert thieves.

55 飛 索 a knotted rope used by the *Kitan* Tartars in attacking cities.

飛 翔 to soar—as birds.

飛 耳 an ear which can hear far-distant sounds.

飛 肉 birds.

飛·脚 fleet of foot.

60 飛 舟 a fast boat.

飛 艇 a flying-ship; a Zeppelin.

航 空 飛 艇 air-liner.

飛 艇 之 襲 擊 an air-raid＝空 襲

飛 花 flying flowers—snow.

65 飛 草 a rapid style of Chinese writing.

飛 落 to fly and settle—to locate.

飛 蓬 tangled and matted—used of dishevelled hair.

飛 蛾 赴 火 the flying moth approaches the flame.

飛 蝗 flying locusts.

70 飛 蟲 birds; also used of insects.

飛 蟻 flying ants.

飛 行 協 會 aero-club.

飛 行 場 airfield.

飛 行 家 aviators.

75 飛 (行) 機 airplane.

↑飛 行 堡 壘 Flying Fortress.

飛 行 法 aviation.

飛 行 船 an air-ship.

飛 行 郵 遞 air-mail＝航 空 郵 遞

80 飛 行 隊 or 航 空 隊 air-force.

飛 言 如 雨 words poured forth like rain—verbose.

飛 語 or 飛 文 or 飛 條 anonymous placards or handbills.

流 言 飛 文 evil rumours and anonymous placards.

飛 變 sudden change in conditions, etc.

85 飛 賊 flying rebels—here today and gone tomorrow.

飛 走 birds and beasts.

飛 跑 or 飛 馳 to run swiftly; to go at express speed.

飛 車 a balloon; ancient flying-machine.

飛 輪 the flying wheel—the sun.

90 飛 送 forward by express courier.

飛 逝 or 時 日 飛 逝 time flies.

飛 速 posthaste.

飛 錫 Buddhist mendicants, from the staff once carried by them.

飛 集 to gather in flocks—as birds.

95 飛 雁 the wild goose.

飛 雨 driving rains.

飛 雪 flying snowflakes.

飛 雲 flying clouds.

飛 雲 丹 a cosmetic prepared from mercury, used by women in ancient times.

100 飛 電 flying hailstones.

飛 霍 to fly swiftly.

飛 霞 粧 rosy-sunset adornment —— lightly rouged and then powdered.

飛 風 to go like the wind.

飛 颺 driven by the wind—as sleet, rain, dust, etc.

105 飛 飭 to send an urgent order.

飛 馴 chariot with four horses driven at great speed.

飛 騰 to fly upwards—of rapid advancement and promotion.

飛 魚 the flying fish.

飛 鳥 birds generally.

110 飛 鳥 使 fast mounted-courier.

飛 鳧 flying ducks—arrows, with red shafts and white feathers, having iron points; also u.f. light and swift boats.

飛 鴻 羽 翼 wings and feathers of the flying goose—of one who has got help from another, as a bird is helped in its flight by wings.

飛 鷹 走 狗 flying falcons and running dogs—field-sports.

飛 黃 Fei-huang—a famous horse.

115 飛 黃 騰 踏 (or 達) Fei-huang is prancing—used of the proud gratification of one who has made rapid advance towards success in his career.

飛 鼠 the flying squirrel; bats.

飛 龍 在 天 the dragon is in heaven—the emperor ascends the throne.

高 飛 to soar; to achieve success and advancement.

↑起 飛 to take off, as of planes.

(a) High and lofty, as buildings.

飛 宇 lofty buildings.

飛 棟 lofty beams of the roof.

飛 橋 very high bridge.

飛 檐 the turned-up corners of the eaves in Chinese buildings.

飛 閣 層 樓 high and imposing buildings.

FÊN.   (ㄈㄣ)

分 ¹ To divide; to share; to separate; to distinguish.

1851

分 上 下 distinguish high from low.

不 分 上 下 to make no distinction between high and low in rank; to disregard precedence.

分·不 出 cannot distinguish or discriminate.

分·不 出 勝 敗 unable to decide who was victor.

⁵分 人 以 財 to share one's wealth with others.

分·付 or 吩·咐 a command; to command.

分 任 to share responsibility.

分 作 十 分⁴ divide it into ten parts.

分 佈 to distribute over—as officers over a district.

10 分 保 part-security for a sum.

分 光 diffusion of light.

分 光 分·析 spectrum analysis.

分 光 器 or 分 光 鏡 spectroscope.

分 兵 to station troops.

15 分 兵 站 guard-stations.

分·出·去 divide up; to separate the estate and live apart.

分 列 to divide and arrange.

分°別 or 分 辨 to discriminate; to distinguish.

分°別 先 後 to distinguish between former and latter.

20 分°別 共 有 division of joint-ownership.

分°別 賞 罰 to reward or punish, respectively.

分 利 to sponge on another; a non-productive partner; a consumer.

分 剖 to make clear.

分 割 to divide up, as territory.

25 分 劑 a dose.

分 功 易 事 division of labour.

分 化 differentiation.

分 化 機 關 organs of differentiation—as the five senses.

分 區 投 票 voting according to districts.

30 分 半 divide into halves.

分 句 a clause in a sentence.

分 句 讀 (-tou⁴) to punctuate; to mark off into clauses.

分 合 analysis and synthesis.

分 咨 to communicate with various authorities.

35 分 售 處 retail sales-office.

分 多 分 少 (wrangle over) dividing shares.

分 夥 to dissolve partnership.

分 好 歹 differentiate between good and evil.

分 娩 child-birth.

40 分 妻 or 休 妻 to divorce a wife.

分 守 to have administrative control over several districts.

分 定 should be; fitting; allotted.

分 封 part of a principality—u.f. Tetrarch.

分 局 branch-office.

[45]分 居 to dwell apart.

分 崩 離 析 divisions and collapses, with separations—utter disorder, a kingdom divided against itself.

分 工 to divide work; division of labour.

分 府 a sub-Prefect.

分 度 規 or 分 角 器 a protractor.

[50]分 庭 亢 禮 to meet on equal terms without ceremony.

分 得 均 勻 divided equally.

分 微 尺 micrometer.

分 心 distracted; indecision; give a thought to.

分 憂 divide the sorrow—to condole.

[55]分 成 色 to test the quality of silver.

分 我 餘 光 divide your surplus light with me—a well-to-do woman and a poor woman were spinning together; the poor woman could not afford a candle and begged the other to share her surplus light with her —used when asking for a favour.

分 手 to separate; farewell.

分 捕 而 瘞 之 divide up the locality to catch (the locusts) and bury them.

分 掠 to divide the loot.

[60]分 撥 to detach; to divide responsibility; to hand over certain goods to another for sale.

分 支 branches; divides into branches.

分 散 to scatter; to disperse.

分 散 點 point of divergence.

分·數 fractions; percentage, as in examinations, etc.

[65] 品°行[4]分·數 conduct marks.

每 日 分·數 daily marks.

最 多 分·數 maximum marks.

分 文 不 取 not a cash will be taken; gratis.

分 曉 clearly understood.

[70]分 明 or 分 清 clearly; evident; to distinguish clearly.

不 見 分 明 not yet cleared up, as a difficult problem.

分 會 branch society or organization.

分 枝 下 來 to branch down.

分·析 analysis; to discriminate.

[75]分·析 上 analytical.

分·析 化 學 analytical chemistry.

分·析 心 理 學 analytical psychology.

精 神 分·析 psycho-analysis.

分·析 的 敎 授 analytical methods of teaching.

[80]分·析 的 方 法 analytical methods.

分 柑 同 味 half an orange tastes as sweet as the whole.

分 業 or 分 家 to divide an estate.

分 極 鏡 polariscope.

分 機 關 branch-agency establishments.

[85]分 權 to divide authority, as in the government.

分 次 by instalments.

分 次·序 to arrange in order.

分 歲 to see the old year out—an ancient feast.

分 母 denominator of a fraction.

[90]分 水 口 where two rivers join.

分 水 嶺 or 分 水 脊 watershed.

分 泌 secretions.

分 法 division. (math.) =除法.

分 治 separation of the executive and the administrative.

[95]分 流 division of a river into two arms.

分 派 to depute; to appoint.

分 潤 to share benefits; to profit by.

分 爨 to cook separately, as when brothers live together but run separate kitchens.

分 爭 to quarrel.

[100]分 爲 兩 歧 divided into two branches.

分 班 to divide into classes, as in schools.

分 甘 共 苦 to share the sweet and the bitter.

分 生 菌 or 分 裂 菌 bacteria.

分 產 to divide a property.

[105]分 界 to delimit.

分 疆 畫 界 delimitation of boundaries or frontiers.

分 發 to send in different directions.

分 破 鏡 divide the broken mirror —separation of husband and wife.

分 秘 書 under-secretary.

[110]分 科 大 學 university where the courses are divided into various schools.

分 租 to rent to joint tenants.

分 秧 to plant out young rice plants—early summer.

分 種 界 distribution of races.

分 立 a branch establishment.

[115]分 章 by-laws.

分 竄 scattering and fleeing into their retreats—as robbers, etc.

分 紅 to distribute a bonus or dividend.

分 給 to apportion.

分 署 branch-office.

[120]分 肉 甚 均 divide the meat fairly.

分 肥 to give a bonus; to divide the spoils.

分 號 a semi-colon; branch office.

分 裂 rent asunder; divided.

分 行 (hang[2]) branch-office or shop.

[125]分 袂 or 分 襟 to part; to separate--as friends.

分 解 to dissolve, to decompose, to resolve into component parts; analysis.

分·解 分·解 please explain it to me.

分 解 熱 heat at which a body is decomposed. (chem.).

分 計 departmental accounts.

[130]分 設 to establish in various places.

分 訴 to state in detail.

分 說 to explain.

不 由 分 說 no need for explanation; not allowed to explain.

分 謗 to share the slander, as when another is slandered by the same persons.

[135]分 辨 是 非 distinguish right and wrong; to argue a point.

分 贓 to share the booty; to receive illgotten gains in secret.

分 贓 制·度 the "spoils" system.

分 路 or 分 途 separate roads; branch roads; to go different ways.

分 蹄 cloven hoof; to divide the hoof.

[140]分 身 to get away; to be absent; to divide one's personality; to be in two places at once.

分 身 不 眼 unable to disengage oneself from duties, etc.

分 輕 重 to study values.

分 巡 天 下 to patrol the whole land.

分 送 to distribute.

145 分 送 程 功 duties will be divided.

分 道 to go by different routes; our paths divide.

分 還 to distribute—as type.

分 部 制 度 bureaucracy.

分 配 arrangement; distribution.

150 分 配 問 題 problem of distribution.

分 釵 破 鏡 separation of husband and wife.

分 銷 to retail.

分 錢 to distribute cash.

分 門 various grades or professions; schisms.

155 分 門 結 黨 schisms; to form cliques.

分 開 to divide; to separate.

分 不 開 cannot be separated; cannot be distinguished.

分 開 辯 論 debate the items separately.

分 際 near the frontier; on the border line; almost accomplished.

160 分 離 to separate; to divide.

分 頁 另 繕 prepare on separate sheets.

分 項 a dividend.

分 頭 探 索 separate from each other and search diligently.

分 頭 核 判 discuss each item separately.

165 分 額 to ration; allowance.

分 類 to classify; to sort.

分 類 法 methods of classification.

分 體 生 殖 reproduction by division.

分 高 低 ascertain who is on top; distinguish between high and low.

170 平 分 divide equally.

自 分 必 死 knowing that he should die.

(a) One tenth of an inch, and of things generally. One hundredth part of a *tael* or ounce.

分 毫 the least portion.

分 量 measure; capacity.

分 陰 the least space of time.

十 分 very; full measure; completely.

十 二 分 年 成 abundant harvest —a full supply for this year

and a proportion over for the next. 公 分 centimeter; gram.

無 分 寸 no measurements—used of a tactless person.

(b) Read *fên⁴*. Inter. 份 next. A part, a share. Function, duty, lot in life.

分 位 or 位 分 social standing; condition.

分 內 之 事 included in one's duties.

分 兩 weight.↓ 分 量 amount.

分 外 extra, beyond one's province.

⁵分 外 營 求 ambitious for what is beyond one's lot.

分 子 a share; a numerator; a molecule.

分 子 力 molecular force.

分 子 吸 力 molecular attraction.

分 子 量 molecular weight.

10 分 所 當 然 in accord with the fitness of things.

分 當 right; in duty bound.

名 分 fame; reputation.

天 分 高 having great natural ability.

安 分 to be contented with one's lot; law abiding.

15 情 分 obligations to friends, etc.

本 分 duty and general obligations.

瓜 分 partition; "slicing the melon."

緣 分 fate or lot, especially in marriage.

越 分 to overstep the mark.

20 身 分 one's standing in society.

非 分 improper; beyond measure.

份⁴ A part, a portion, a share, a dividend. The duties of a post; a lot; a position. Inter. preceding.
1852

份 子 a section, an element.

搗 亂 份 子 a disturbing element; one who is always causing trouble.

一 份 one lot; one copy, as when taking a magazine, etc.

月 份 牌 a calendar.

股 份 shares, as in a public company.

吩¹ To command. A command. Inter. 分 No. 1851.
1853

吩 咐 a command; to command.

忿⁴ Anger; indignation.
1854

忿 則 爭 爭 則 亂 anger causes wrangling, and wrangling breeds disorder.

忿 嫉 envious hatred.

忿 忿 不 平 indignant and disturbed, as when one sees an injustice.

忿 忿 不 消 implacable anger.

⁵忿 忮 angry and jealous.

忿 怒 wrath; fury; anger.

忿 思 難 in anger think of the trouble which follows it.

忿 怨 to harbour a grudge for wrongs done.

忿 悁 easily provoked to wrath.

10 忿 恨 bitter hate; to hate with bitterness.

忿 悶 angry and grieved.

忿 憤 anger.

忿 懟 resentment.

忿 懥 incensed; irritated; perturbed.

15 忿 火 hatred; fury.

忿 爭 wrangling.

忿 疾 or 忿 戾 cross; displeased.

忿 罵 extreme anger with cursing.

忿 言 angry words.

20 忿 躁 irascible.

忿 隙 bitter enmity.

家 人 未 見 其 有 忿 恚 the family have never seen him out of temper.

小 忿 petty resentment.

枌² A variety of elm with small seeds and white bark.
1855

氛¹ Vapour, miasma, poisonous exhalations.
1856

氛 垢 or 氛 埃 dirt, filth, dust.

氛 祲 dark portents; infelicitous omens.

氛 邪 evil influences.

妖 氛 evil portents.

海 氛 noxious sea-vapours— pirates.

賊 氛 seditious exhalations.

(a) Dense, abundant—as falling snow.

氛 氳 denseness of the atmosphere —as when laden with snow; heavy, as with perfume.

汾² The chief river of Shansi.
1857

汾 酒 wine distilled in *Fenchoufu.*
汾 陽 點 頭 the prince of *Fen yang* bowing to his numerous progeny.—may you have a numerous progeny.

粉³ Powder; meal, rice-flour. To powder; to plaster.
1858

粉 不 厭 白 powder is not disliked for being too white.
粉 侯 imperial son-in-law.
粉 堵 a whited wall.
粉 嫩 ruddy and blooming.
⁵粉 板 board on which schoolboys practiced writing; board used by fortune-tellers and others who live by their wits.
粉 油 distemper; whitewash.
粉 澤 adorned; beautified; made up; glossy.
粉 牆 or 粉 皮 牆 to whitewash a wall.
粉 瘤 a tumour.
¹⁰粉 白 黛 黑 white powder (for the face) and black pencil (for the eyebrows)—beautiful young women. A.w. 粉 白 黛 綠.
粉 碎 smashed to pieces; ground to powder.
粉 筆 chalk or crayon for writing.
粉 紅 delicate pale-pink, flesh-coloured.
粉 絲 or 粉 條 or 粉 皮 vermicelli made from bean-starch.
¹⁵粉 線 (or 綫) chalk-line used by tailors.
粉 線 盒 chalk-line and reel.
粉 衣 藥 丸 pearl-coated pills.
粉 袋 tailor's chalk-bag.
粉 面 to powder or paint the face; a delicate complexion.
²⁰粉 面 油 頭 to paint the face and anoint the head—to make up.
粉 頭 a prostitute.
粉 飾 to adorn; to gloss; to put on appearances.
粉 飾 太 平 false prosperity or peace.
粉 飾 彌 窮 to conceal faults.
²⁵粉 飾 邀 功 to seek fame by false pretences.
傅 粉 to powder; to rouge.
宮 粉 pink face-powder.
粉 鏡 盒 compact.

涼 粉 a kind of jelly made from agar-agar.
牙 粉 tooth-powder.
²⁰米 粉 rice-flour.
紅 粉 pink powder; red and white—women.
脂 粉 cosmetic; lip-stick.
麥 粉 or 麵 粉 wheat-flour.

紛¹ Confused; disorderly; mixed. Numerous.
1859

紛 亂 in confusion; disorderly; a hubbub.
紛 亂 無 主 puzzled and perplexed.
紛 囂 noisy tumult; uproar.
紛 岐 a misunderstanding; in disorder, diverging; side-issue.
⁵紛 拏 to brawl.
紛 更 to confuse; to change.
紛 沓 ceaseless continuity.
紛 至 沓 來 came in continuous crowds.
紛 然 雜 出 thing coming forth in confusion.
¹⁰紛 紜 to wrangle.
紛 紜 confused; numerous.
紛 紜 舛 錯 confused through many affairs.
紛 紅 駭 綠 the waving of red flowers and green leaves.
紛 紛 不 一 confused; all sorts.
¹⁵紛 紛 亂 亂 disorderly, in confusion.
紛 紛 四 散 dispersed in all directions.
紛 紛 多 事 distracted by numerous affairs.
紛 華 gaiety; bustle.
紛 雜 mixed; not sorted.
²⁰紛 馳 the mind preoccupied.
公 事 紛 繁 busy with official duties.

翁¹ To fly. Distinguish 翁 No. 7146.
1860

翁 翁 soaring about.

芬¹ Perfume, fragrance. Sweet-smelling. u.f. 紛 No. 1859.
1861

芬 烈 exceedingly fragrant.
芬 然 like a cloud of dust.
芬 芳 fragrant.
芬 芬 sweetly perfumed.
芬 菲 fragrance of flowers.

(a) Used in transliteration.

芬 蘭 Finland.

酚 積² Aromatic, perfumed.
1862

花 酚 香 sweet are the flowers.
香 酚 酚 strongly fragrant.

鼢³ A variety of mole.
1863

犂 鼢 the mole.

蒶¹ Kind of wood burnt for perfume.
1864

棼² Beams in the roof of a house. Confused, disordered.
1865 u.f. 紛 No. 1859.

棼 棼 confused, tangled.

焚² To burn; to set fire to.
1866

焚 修 to burn incense and regulate the conduct.
焚 券 to destroy the vouchers or bonds—as 馮 驩 did when sent by 孟 嘗 君 to collect his debts in a neighbouring State.
焚 化 to burn paper-money; to consume by burning.
焚 和 to destroy peace and harmony—as when men think only of themselves and of making gain, without any consideration for others.
⁵焚 如 burned down; destroyed by fire.
焚 掠 or 焚 劫 burning and looting.
焚 擲 burnt and thrown out.
焚 斃 burnt to death.
焚 書 坑 儒 burnt the books and buried the scholars alive—said of *Ch'in Shih-Huang.* 秦 始 皇 213 B.C.
¹⁰焚 棄 之 got rid of by burning.
焚 滅 詩 書 to destroy the books by fire.

焚 溺 drowning and burning—the suffering of the masses under evil men who pretend to govern, but use their position to get wealthy.

焚 灼 burning—as with anxiety, indignation, etc.

焚 燒 to destroy by fire; to set fire to.

[15]焚 燬 or 焚 拆 to burn down.

焚 研 to destroy ink-slab and pens—to write no more.

焚 紙 錢 to burn paper-money for the dead.

焚 膏 繼 晷 burning oil to prolong the day—burning the midnight-oil.

焚 舟 to burn the boats after crossing to the attack—"dare to die."

[20]焚 萊 to burn the grass.

焚 薙 to destroy by fire.

焚 頂 燒 指 to burn the scalp and fingers—to become a Buddhist priest or nun.

焚 香 to burn incense.

(a) Read *fên*⁴. To destroy, to overthrow.

焚 身 to die,—from the next:

象 有 齒 以 焚 其 身 the tusks of the elephant cause its death—of the danger of covetousness and bribes.

僨 [4]
1867
To ruin. Prostrate.

僨 事 to spoil an affair.

墳 [2] 坆
1868
A grave, a mound.

墳 地 or 墳 院 a cemetery.

墳 墓 or 墳 塋 or 墳 山 or 墳 圈 子 a grave, a place of burial.

墳 樹 trees planted by the graves.

墳 碑 tomb-stone.

拜 墳 to worship the graves of ancestors.

掃 墳 to sweep the tombs of ancestors, done at the 清 明 festival.

荒 墳 a neglected grave.

(a) An embankment or dike.

墳 衍 the embankments and the flats.

導 彼 汝 墳 along the dikes of the River *Ju*.

(b) Great.

墳 首 large heads.

墳 燭 a great candle.

三 墳 五 典 the records of the 三 皇 and the 五 帝, the most ancient Chinese records.

(c) Inter. 羵 No. 1871. A monstrosity—a sexless sheep or goat.

墳 羊 the above—the tutelary spirit, 土 之 怪, of a place; "clay sheep buried with the dead." *Giles.*

(d) Read *fên*⁴. Soil.

墳 壤 rich soil.

墳 墟 lumpy ground with black hard soil.

黑 墳 black soil.

(e) Read *pên*⁴. To heap up.

墳 起 a growing heap—of ashes, etc.

地 墳 it is becoming a mound.

幩 [2]
1869
Ornamental tassels on a bridle.

憤 [4]
1870
Zeal; ardour.

憤 力 to exert the strength.

憤 悱 eager to speak but unable to do so.

憤 發 zealous, earnest; impetuous.

憤 盈 great zeal and ardour.

[5]憤 興 to revive; to renew the ardour.

憤 言 eager speech.

發 憤 to shake oneself together; to put forth effort.

發 憤 忘 食 in eagerness to study to forget food.

(a) Very angry, exasperated.

憤 世 misanthropy.

憤 厥 choking with anger; to have a fit (from anger).

憤 嫉 bitter malice.

憤 心 angry intentions.

[5]憤 怒 full of anger and vexation.

憤 怨 filled with resentment.

憤 恨 angry.

憤 恨 不 平 implacable anger.

憤 懣 歎 息 to sigh or groan with anger or indignation at injustice.

[10]憤 悶 vexation.

憤 憤 uneasy from anger, etc.

憤 慨 or 憤 歎 to groan with anger or righteous indignation.

憤 激 moved, stirred with indignation.

憤 濤 angry billows.

氣 憤 angry.

羵 [2]
A sexless goat or sheep. Inter. 墳 No. 1868 in this sense.
1871

羵 羊 the above—tutelary spirit, 土 之 怪, of a place; "clay sheep buried with the dead." *Giles.*

蕡 [2]
1872
Luxurious, abundant.

蕡 子 hemp seeds.

蕡 實 bearing abundant fruit.

豮 [2]
1873
To geld a pig.

豮 豕 a gelded boar.

奮 [4]
1874
To rouse. Impetuous; determined.

奮 伐 to attack vigorously.

奮 信 to rouse oneself to energy.

奮 力 to put forth effort.

奮 勉 to incite.

[5]奮 勇 undaunted; rashly courageous.

奮 志 determined.

奮 志 不 懈 unwearied; fully determined.

奮 擊 strenuous attack—name of a band of "shock troops."

奮 武 martial.

[10]奮 激 aroused to effort; moved to enthusiasm.

奮 然 energetically.

奮 發 to burst forth; enthusiasm.

奮 發 有 爲 put forth every effort and it can be done.

奮 與 or 奮 氣 to rouse the energies.
[15]奮 與 會 revival meetings.
奮 討 strenuous demands.
奮 起 to rise up at a bound.
奮 迅 prompt; to put forth effort —as a horse.
奮 鬭 to make strenuous efforts; to advance in spite of difficulties and opposition.

(a) To spread the wings.

不 能 奮 飛 I cannot spread my wings and fly.

(b) To diffuse.

奮 至 德 之 光 to diffuse the lustre of great virtue.

糞 [4]
1875
Manure, dung, nightsoil.

糞 厠 or 糞 澗 a privy.
糞 土 or 糞 壤 or 糞 料 or 糞 肥 refuse, manure.
糞 土 之 牆 不 可 杇 也 a wall of filthy earth cannot be plastered.
　其 言 糞 土 也 his talk is valueless.
[5]糞 堆 a dunghill.
糞 夫 a nightman, scavenger.
糞 廠·子 a manure-yard.
糞 池 or 糞 坑 or 糞 窟 or 糞 窖·子 a cesspool.
糞 田 or 上 糞 to manure the fields.
[10]糞 箕 a manure-basket.
糞 草 refuse; sweepings.
糞 門 the anus.
糞 除 a dust-pan; to clean up.
絞 糞 汁 飲 之 he poured liquid manure down his throat —as an emetic.

FÊNG. 　　　(ㄈㄥ)

丰 [1]
1876
Plump; good-looking. Graceful, fine.

丰 儀 dignified appearance.
丰 姿 or 丰 神 slender and graceful in appearance.
丰 容 a beautiful face.
丰 格 an easy carriage; graceful.
[5]丰 茸 luxuriant growth.
丰 采 graceful; elegant; plump.

丰 雅 accomplished, refined.
丰 韻 a mellow voice.

夆 [1]
1877
To butt, as horned beasts.

峯 [1]
1878
The peak of a mountain. The hump of a camel.

峯 嶺 mountain ranges.
峯 巒 ridges and peaks.
孤 峯 a solitary peak.
高 峯 a lofty peak.
鼻 峯 the high bridge of a nose.

烽 [1]
1879
A conical brick-structure in which to light a beacon.

烽 烟 or 烽·火 a beacon fire.
燒 烽·火 fire the beacons.

蜂 [1] 逢 蠭
1880
Bees, hornets, wasps.

蜂 午 all gathered together in confusion.
蜂 媒 蝶 使 the bee and the butterfly as fertilizing agents.
蜂 巢 the honeycomb.
蜂 巢·的 honeycombed.
[5]蜂 扇 蟻 聚 moving about like bees and clustering like ants.
蜂 擁 而 上 pressed forward in swarms.
蜂 準 a high nose—said of Ch'in Shih huang.
蜂 王 the queen-bee.
蜂 目 豺 聲 wasp-like eyes and the howl of a jackal—very fierce.
[10]蜂 窩 or 蜂 房 or 蜂 衙 a beehive, a wasp's nest.
蜂 羣 a swarm of bees.
蜂 聚 to swarm—as bees.
蜂 聲 the hum of bees.
蜂 腰 wasp-like waist; error in versification, when the second and fourth sounds in a line are similar.
[15]蜂 蜜 honey.
蜂 蠆 sting of a bee or wasp.—a small affair.
蜂 蠆 有 毒 a bee-sting has poison —used of the harm done by

---

what 'seems to be very unimportant.
蜂 蠟 bees-wax.
蜂 起 to rise, as bees; to gather together; to swarm, as robbers.
[20]蜂 軼 to rise up in great numbers —as a swarm of bees, used of rebels, etc.
蜂 釀 蜜 bees make honey.
蜂 針 or 蜂 蠆 or 蜂 釘 the sting of bees or wasps.
蜂 集 or 蜂 至 to come in swarms.
蜂 駭 to rise like disturbed bees or hornets.
[25]蜂 鳥 the humming-bird.
蜂 黃 a yellow colour, as of a wasp's body.
土 蜂 the carpenter bee.
蜜。蜂 the honey bee.
養 蜂 房 an apiary.
[30]馬。蜂 a hornet.
黃 蜂 the wasp.

逢 [2]
1881
To meet with. To happen, to hit on. Whenever.

逢 世 時 以 變 易 to change with the times.
逢 人 之 怒 to encounter the anger of another.
逢 人 便 說 to tell everybody a person meets; to gossip.
逢 人 說 項 to tell everybody of a person's virtue.
[5]逢 凶 化 吉 evil turned to good fortune.
逢 危 to incur danger.
逢 原 clear, penetrating grasp of things, from :—
　則 取 之 左 右 逢 其 原 "he seizes the principles (之 ＝ 理) on either hand, meeting everywhere with them as a fountain (from which things flow)."
逢 吉 or 逢 喜 to meet with good fortune.
[10]逢 君 之 惡 to countenance a prince in doing evil.
逢 場 when there happens to be...
逢 場 作 戲 to take part in an activity (gambling, etc.) merely for fun without taking it seriously.
逢 山 開 路 opening up the road as you go—to use every effort.
逢 年 to have a good harvest.
[15]逢 掖 之 衣 the robes of the literati with their ample sleeves.

逢 春 to meet with spring—to have a run of good luck.

枯 木 逢 春 the d r i e d tree meets with the spring—getting a new chance.

逢 時 to succeed in life.

逢 時 過 節 at holiday times.

20逢 福 to meet good fortune.

逢·着 to meet.

逢 處 everywhere.

逢 迎 to receive a guest.

巧 於 逢 迎 artful in seeking to please.

25逢 遇 to meet.

一 朝 逢 遇 one morning they met.

時 逢 it is the time of ....; during.

每 逢 whenever; every occasion.

相 逢 to meet each other.

30 狹 路 相 逢 to meet in a narrow path—when it is not possible for one to avoid the other.

難 逢 hard to meet with.

(a) Read *p'êng²*. The roll of drums.

縫 2.4. To sew, to stitch, to mend.
1882

縫·上 幾 針 sewed it over several stitches.

縫 口 to stitch the mouth of a bag; to bribe; to mend a rent.

縫 合 to stitch up.

縫 密 行 (*hang²*) to sew with fine stitches.

5縫 新 to make new garments.

縫 皮 to stitch furs together.

縫 窮 婦 women who do odd jobs of mending on the streets.

縫 紉 to mend; to stitch together.

縫 紉 機(器)a sewing-machine.

10縫 紕 to bind the edges of garments, etc.

縫 組 於 旌 旗 sewed tassels on the banners.

縫 綴 to baste; to sew.

縫 綻 to mend garments; to stitch a seam that has come undone.

縫 線 sewing-thread.

15縫 補 to patch.

縫 衣 to make garments.

彌 縫 to rectify a mistake.

裁·縫 a tailor.

(a) Read *fêng⁴*. A joint, a seam, a crack. A stitch.

縫 界 the seams of a garment.

地 縫 cracks in the earth.

天 衣 無 縫 the heavenly garment has no seams—of anything that is connected without a break.

指 縫 the creases in the fingers.

5漏 縫 to let out a secret; to let slip.

糊 縫·子 to paste up cracks with strips of paper.

綻·了 縫 given way at the seams.

錯 縫·子 a person's faults.

鋒 1 A sharp point, the tip of a lance or bayonet.
1883

鋒 刃 weapons; "points a n d edges."

鋒 刃 交 加 their weapons crossed in battle.

鋒 利 incisive.

鋒 快 sharp, keen.

5鋒 毫 tip of a Chinese pencil.

鋒 鋩 or 鋒 鏑 the point.

交 鋒 to cross swords.　「前 鋒

先 鋒 the vanguard; pioneers. A.c.

爭 鋒 struggle for mastery.

10音 辭 鋒 起 no end of sharp words arose.

奉 4 To receive with both hands; to offer; to serve.
1884 Respectfully. To have the honour to ....

奉 上 to present a gift to a superior.

奉 事 to serve, to wait on.

奉 使 to be commissioned.

奉 候 to offer congratulations.

5奉 公 employed in public business.

奉 公 守 法 to be just and respect the laws.

奉 勸 to venture to exhort.

奉 命 to receive orders or commands from above; a divine commission.

奉 報 to have the honour to announce.

10奉·天 old name for 遼 寧.

奉·天 府 old name for 瀋 陽.

奉 天 承 運 entrusted by Heaven with the care of—the empire.

奉 安 imperial funeral.

奉 官 officially licensed or appointed.

15奉 差·遣 sent; commissioned.(-*ch'ai¹*-)

奉 復 to have the honour to reply.

奉 懇 respectfully beg.

奉·承 to attend to; to look after; to flatter; to pay court to.

奉 承 之 語 flattering words.

20奉 拜 to pay respects to.

奉 拜 爲 師 to acknowledge as one's master or teacher.

奉 敎 to enter the church; to receive instruction; to become a convert.

奉 旨 by imperial decree.

奉 申 to write a despatch to a superior.

25奉 朔 to obey the imperial commands.

奉 檄 守 禦 received a mandate to resist him and guard the district.

奉 此 upon receipt of this.

奉 求 to entreat.

奉 法⁴to profess Buddhism.

30奉 煩 May I trouble you?

奉 獻 to offer with reverence.

奉 留 I venture to detain.

奉 祖 爲 孝 filial respect.

奉 箕 帚 holding the broom and the dustpan—to be a wife.

35奉 給 to give with respect.

奉 職 to receive an appointment.

奉 行 or 奉 遵 to carry out orders.

奉 行 故 事 to follow old customs; to be formal.

奉 託 to commission with respect.

40奉 請 I have the honour to invite.

奉 諭 to receive commands.

奉 賀 to congratulate.

奉 送 to send a present.

↑奉 趨 to return a present.

45奉 達 or 奉 致 to have the honour to inform.

奉 還 to have the honour to return.

奉 陪 to bear another company.

奉 領 I have had the honour to receive.

奉 養 to support parents.

50供 奉 to wait upon.

侍 奉 晨 昏 to wait upon morning and night.

自 奉 personal expenditure. (u.f. 俸).

俸 4 Emolument; salary—usually from the State.
1885

俸 廉 or 養 廉 salary and allowance.

俸 滿 when the term of office is at an end.

俸 祿 or 俸 米 or 薪 俸 or 俸 脩 or 俸 銀 official salary, up till the *Han* dynasty, it was paid in grain.

俸 秩 emoluments and rank.

5 加 俸 increase of salary.

自 俸 personal expenditure.

唪[4]   **To recite, to intone or chant.**
1886

唪 經 to chant the liturgies—as the Buddhist priests.

唪 唪 very productive.

(a) Read *pêng*[3].   **To laugh aloud.**

封[1]   **To seal up; to blockade.**
1887

封 了 to seal up; sealed.

封 事 or 封 奏 or 封 章 to seal a despatch or memorials.

封 住 closed up; sealed.

封 傷 to close a wound.

5 封 印 to close up the official seals —as at new-year.

封 地 frozen ground.

封 套 an envelope.

封 存 to keep under bond.

封 密 securely sealed.

10 封 河 river closed by frost.

封 港 blockade. *See below*—15, 22, ff.

虛 聲 封 港 "paper" blockade.

封 皮ル or 封 條 strips of red paper pasted across parcels, letters, doors, etc., as seals.

封 禁 to seal up and prohibit access.

15 封 禁 海 口 a blockade. *See above*—11, *and below*—22, ff.

告 封 禁 to proclaim a blockade.

封 筒 bamboo tube used for an envelope.

封 緘 to seal a letter.

封 舖 to seal up a shop.

20 封 船 to impress a boat for government service.

封 蠟 sealing-wax.

封 鎖 to seal and lock up; to blockade. *See above*—11, 15.

破 封 鎖 to break a blockade.

衝 破 封 鎖 to run a blockade.

25 違 犯 封 鎖 violation of the blockade.

開 封 鎖 to raise a blockade.

封 門 to seal a door officially by pasting strips of paper across the opening.

封 門 大 吉 may there be great good luck as the door is sealed —New Year's motto pasted on doors.

封 閉 shut up; closed.

30 封 關 to close the customs, as for holidays; also used for bank-holidays.

封 面 title-page; front cover.

密 封 to seal up closely.

查 封 入 官 to confiscate.

查 封 家 產 to attach property by writ.

(a) **To appoint to office or to territory; a fief or principality. To bestow honours, to confer nobility; to canonize.**

封 內 山 川 the hills and rivers within the fief.

封 典 granting of hereditary rank.

封 君 nobles; title by which the father of one who is of high rank is spoken of.

封 國 to confer feudal rights.

5 封 建 to set up as a feudal prince.

封 建 制 度 feudalism.

封 殖 to appoint to office.

封 爵 to raise to the nobility.

封 神 to deify; to canonize.

10 封 祿 emoluments.

封 號 to designate.

封 誥 to raise the parents of an official to the nobility; patent of such nobility.

封 贈 titles of honour bestowed on wife, parents; or grandparents of an official.

(b) **A boundary or dike.**

封 域 or 封 疆 or 封 略 the borders or frontiers.

封 守 to guard the borders.

封 畛 or 封 界 the frontiers, the borders.

封 疆 之 官 keeper of the frontiers.

封 疆 大 臣 former designation of high provincial officials.

(c) **A mound. To heap up.**

封 土 to raise a mound.

封 垤 an anthill.

封 冢 to heap up a tumulus over a grave.

封 樹 to heap earth round a tree; the graves of the nobles.

封 祀 to sacrifice on a mound.

封 禪 to sacrifice on a mound, and on the level respectively.

(d) **N.A. A package, etc.**

一 封 信 one letter.

一 封 銀 子 a package of silver.

賞 封 to give a tip.

門 封 tip to a door-keeper.

犎[1]   **The zebu, or humped-ox.**
1888

葑[1]   **The rape-turnip, or 蕪 菁.**
1889

葑 菲 radishes and turnips—used of men and things that have only one point of value.

風[1]   **Wind, breath. Radical 182.**
1890

風 乾 to dry in the wind.

風 伯 or 風 神 or 風 師 the god of the winds. *See below*. A. 20.

風 信 direction of the wind.

風 信 器 (or 機) anemoscope.

5 花 傳 風 信 the flowers indicate the direction of the wind.

風 力 the force of the wind.

風 力 表 or 風 力 計 wind-gauge.

風 吹 的 blown by the wind.

風 吹 草 動 when the wind blows the grass bends—used of influence.

10 風 圈 lunar halo—a sign of wind.

風 土 climate. *See below*. A. 5.

風 土 誌 topography.

風 塵 winds and dust—the cares and confusion of travel; military disorders; the life of a harlot.

風 塵 表 物 one who rises above the rank and file.

15 風 媒 花 anemophilous flowers; those in which the wind carries the pollen and acts as a fertilizer.

風 帆 wind-sails.

風 帽 a hat like a cowl worn in winter when travelling.

風 從 虎 wind comes in with the tiger,—which represents the 陰 or negative principle of nature and is associated with wind.

風 快 or 風 行 with great speed.

↑[20]風 平 浪 靜 calm and unruffled sea.

風 扇 a punkah; electric fan.

風 捲 殘 雲 the wind blows the scattered clouds away—everything is cleared up.

風 日 晴 和 clear weather.

風 木 or 風 樹 not long able to care for parents,—from the lines :—

[25] 木 欲 靜 而 風 不 止, 子[3] 欲 養 而 親 不 待 The trees would be still but the wind ceases not; the son would care for his parents but they tarry not. *See* No. 3285.-B. 1.

風 栗 chestnuts.

風 毛 a fringe; the edge of a fur.

風 水 wind and water—the geomantic system of the Chinese, by means of which sites are determined for graves, houses and other buildings, which sites are said to have an influence on the people. In some places it means a grave.

風 水 先 生 professor of geomancy.

[30]風 水 好 a good locality (in the geomantic sense.)

風 水 學 geomantic studies.

風 水 轉 了 the luck has changed.

看 風 水 to examine the locality for sites; to practice geomancy.

風 波 or 風 浪 wind and waves—changes of men and affairs.

[35]風 流 雲 散 dispersed; scattered.

風 涼 cool and breezy—free and easy.

風 潮 wind and tide—unrest, agitation, the ferment of ideas in politics; the changes of the times.

風 潮 大 起 a sudden rush of new ideas; a great wave of opinion; upheaval of public opinion.

風 濕 damp; malarious; rheumatism.

[40]風 燈 a hurricane-lantern.

風 燭 草 霜 (like) the candle before the wind or the frost on the grass—soon gone, of old age.

風 爐 a small portable stove.

風 琴 an organ.

風 琴 鍵 keys of an organ.

[45]風 穴 cave of the winds—where the wind comes from.

風 笛 a whistle.

風 箏 a kite.

風 箱 a bellows for a forge, etc.

風 蓬 a sail.

[50]風 簷 寸 晷 (there was) no shelter from the wind, and (only) the shortest space of time by the dial—used of the examinations under the old system.

風 絃 æolian harp.

風 聲 鶴 唳, 草 木 皆 兵 scared by the sound of the wind and the cry of the cranes, fearing ambush in every tree and tuft of grass—of disordered, retreating troops.

風 色 the weather. *See below.* A. 25.

風 行 草 偃 when the wind blows the grass bends—of the influence of superiors. *See above* —9.

[55]風 調 雨 順 seasonable weather.

風 車 a winnowing-machine; wind-mill.

風 車 花 the passion-flower.

風 輪 whirligig; a windmill.

風 鐸 tinkling bells on pagodas.

[60]風 門 a touch-hole; an opening for ventilation; a draught hole.

風 門 制 器 regulator for the damper on a furnace, etc.

風 雨 wind and rain—the weather.

風 雨 表 a barometer.

風 雨 飄 搖 stormy weather—crises, times of stress.

[65] 冒 風 雨 to brave the weather.

風 雲 際 會 meeting of wind and clouds—of the familiarity of friendly intercourse.

風 霜 wind and frost—the hardships of travel; the changes of the years; very severe.

風 領 a hood or cowl.

風 馳 to outstrip the wind.

[70]風 鳥 bird of paradise.

一 陣 風 a gust of wind.

上 風 the wind which gives a man the advantage in sailing or shooting; advantageous position.

下 風 the wind which gives a disadvantage; a disadvantageous position.

傷 風 to catch a cold.

[75]凱 風 fancy name for the south wind.

和 風 pleasant breezes.

大 風 a gale, a typhoon.

寒 風 cold wind, the north wind.

橫 風 a side wind.

[80]涼 風 a cool breeze, the southwest wind.

狂 風 or 暴 風 a blustering gale.

秦 風 the west wind—a fancy name.

羊 角 風 a whirlwind.

耳 旁 風 a breeze passing the ear —of no consequence.

[85]谷 風 fancy name for the east wind.

賊 風 a draught.

輕 風 light breezes.

邪 風 a shifting breeze.

頂 風 or 逆 風 a head wind.

[90]順 風 favourable winds.

颮 風 to blow.

鬼 頭 風 a hot wind.

季 候 風 monsoon.

(a) Usage, habits, custom, influence. Manner and deportment, style, taste. Scenery. Inspiration.

風 人 a poet—one inspired.

風 俗 customs, usages, practices, public morals; observances.

風 光 scenes, manners and appearances or customs.

風 化 influence or example; customs; public morals; to reform by example.

[5]風 土 人 情 local manners and customs.

風 姿 娟 秀 her manner and air was refined and attractive.

風 度 or 風 采 appearance and bearing; deportment.

風 情 dissipation.

風 操[4] or 風 節 moral character; bearing or demeanour.

[10]風 景 a view; a prospect.

風 月 seductive arts of a woman; dissipation; gaiety; also elegant and poetical.

風 月 子[3] 弟 profligates; young men fond of dissipation.

好[4] 風 月 fond of a gay life.

風 格 style; air; manner; disposition.

¹⁵風｡氣 influence; appearance and bearing; style, manner and fashions.

風｡氣 未 開 unenlightened; old fashioned.

風｡流 gaiety, vice, dissipation; unconventionality; sex influence and attraction; deportment and manner; style, beauty.

風 流 少 年 a young dandy.

風 狂 profligates.

²⁰風 神 manner and deportment. *See above.*—2.

風 紀 discipline.

風 紀 嚴 肅 strict discipline of troops.

風 紀 敗 壞 demoralization.

風 致 temperament of a man.

²⁵風 色 a man's countenance; the motive of anything. *See above.* —53.

風 花 雪 月 said of a gay and lively place.

風 謠 folk-songs.

風 趣 or 風 味 flavour; the taste of a book, etc., delicacy.

顏 有 風 味 it has a relish.

³⁰風 雅 elegant, refined, graceful and cultured.

風 騷 bewitching; fascinating; seductive manner.

風 骨 talents and appearance, deportment and manner above the average.

刁 風 corrupt morals.

國 風 first book of the *Odes.*

³⁵失 風 to be beaten—as an army.

成 風 it has become a custom.

民 風 national characteristics.

文 風 a literary spirit.

淫 風 wanton; lewd custom.

⁴⁰男 風 sodomy.

節 烈 可 風 her chastity should be made a custom to be followed.

↑ 作 風 style; way of doing things.

(b) Fame, reputation, rumour.

風｡聲 reputation, fame; rumor.

風 言 or 風 語 idle rumours.

風 說 rumour.

聞 風 to get wind of; to hear about.

門 風 or 家 風 the reputation or standing of a family.

露 風 to allow a matter to leak out.

(c) u.f. 瘋 No. 1892. Insane.

風 漢 an insane person.

中⁴風 had a fit; an attack of paralysis; apoplexy.

(d) Read *fêng*¹. u.f. 諷 No. 1893. To abuse.

風 示 to make inquiries.

風 刺 to ridicule.

風 議 to satirize.

(e) Read *fêng*¹. To be on heat.

風 馬 牛 不 相 及 也 our horses and oxen in the breeding season will be unable to meet (our territories are so far apart);—used of those whose occupations are far apart, or of those who have no dealings with each other.

楓¹ The maple tree. Also used for the plane tree, the syca-
1891 more and the tallow-tree.

楓 宸 the palace, a name for Peking.

楓 樹 the maple, etc.

楓 葉 maple-leaves.

楓 香 gum of the liquidambar.

丹 楓 the maple, from the autumn tints of the leaves.

瘋¹ Paralysis. Leprosy. Insanity.
1892

瘋 人 院 a lunatic asylum.

瘋 傻 stupid.

瘋｡子 or 瘋 魔 a maniac.

瘋 氣 lunacy.

⁵瘋 狗 a mad dog.

瘋 病 or 瘋 癱 paralysis.

瘋 癲 or 瘋 狂 mad; deluded; insane.

瘋 話 gibberish.

瘋 院 a leper hospital.

¹⁰瘋 癘 leprosy.

發 瘋 to have leprosy; to become insane.

羊 痾 瘋 or 羊 角 瘋 epilepsy.

諷⁴ To chant.
1893

諷 味 to enjoy (a book); to relish.

諷 誦 to chant; to hum, to intone.

(a) To satirize; to ridicule.

諷 使 速 仕 to ridicule him into taking office quickly.

諷 刺 or 譏 諷 to ridicule.

諷 畫 to caricature.

諷 語 satire, ridicule.

諷 諫 to remonstrate with—as by satire.

鳳⁴ The male phœnix. An emblem of joy and happiness.
1894

鳳 不 離 闕 a phœnix does not leave its perch on the imperial gate—used to signify :—confine yourself to your own affairs.

鳳｡仙 花 the balsam.

鳳 占 consulting divination about giving a daughter in marriage.

鳳 冠 霞 帔 the garments of a bride.

⁵鳳 吹 fine music, the 笙 and such instruments.

鳳 鳴 朝 陽 the phœnix is facing the sun and singing—a good omen.

鳳 棲 梧 桐 the phœnix rests on the *Wu-tung* tree—a favourable omen. Used to express :—goodness will be rewarded.

鳳 毛 phœnix feathers—complimentary expression referring to another's son, or to his talents.

鳳 毛 濟 美 helping the beauty of the plumage of the phœnix—referring to the worthy son of a high officer.

¹⁰鳳 尾 竹 a variety of bamboo,—it grows about five feet high, and is feathery and graceful, like the tail of a phœnix.

鳳 尾 草 ferns.

鳳 尾 蕉 a graceful, feathery palm.

鳳 毛 麟 角 phœnix feathers and unicorn's horns—very rare things.

鳳 眼 the eye of the emperor.

¹⁵鳳 翹 or 鳳 頭 鞋 ornamental women's shoes of ancient times.

鳳 舉 to raise to high rank.

鳳 藻 as beautifully marked as the phœnix—said of the writings of another.

鳳 詔 imperial mandate.

鳳 雛 young phœnix—complimentary phrase referring to a fine young man.

²⁰鳳｡凰 the male and female phœnix; the phœnix.

鳳·凰于飛 conjugal felicity.
鳳·凰蛋 the egg of a phœnix—a filial son on whose support the parents rely.
吐鳳之才 used of great literary ability.
起鳳騰蛟 the soaring phœnix and the prancing dragon—in praise of one whose name for literature is becoming famous.
25 鳥中之鳳 a phœnix among birds—pre-eminent.

馮[2] A surname. Read *p'ing*[2]. **To cross a stream without a boat. To mount, to ascend. Only read *feng*[2] when used as a surname.**
1895

馮夷 the god of streams.
馮河 to cross a river without a boat.
馮陵於河 to walk on the water and cross a river *See* B. 2.

(a) A horse galloping.

馮馮 galloping like a fast horse.

(b) To insult. To rely on. u.f. 憑 No. 5310.

馮怒 very angry.
馮陵 to rely on power to insult another.

覂[3] **To throw a rider. See 泛 No. 1773-A.**
1896

覂駕之馬 an unmanageable horse.

豐[1] **Abundant, fruitful, luxuriant.**
1897

豐上銳下 broad forehead and narrow chin.
豐人 stout man; a full-grown man.
豐偉 tall and stout.
豐厚 plentiful; sumptuous.
5 豐收 a good harvest.
豐壤 fertile soil.
豐富 rich; wealthy; prosperous; rich in content.
豐寧 prosperity and peace.
豐年 a plentiful year.
10 豐悴 prosperity and failure.
豐樂 prosperous and happy.
豐歉 plenty and deficiency.
豐注 heavy rains.
豐熟 ripe; full-grown.
15 豐登 a prosperous harvest.
豐盛 or 豐盈 or 豐滿 abundance; prosperous.
食物豐盈 (or 裕) foodstuffs in abundance.
豐美 luxuriant and abundant.
豐肌 plump.
20 豐腴 or 豐潤 fertile.
豐芙 flourishing; luxuriant.
豐草 luxuriant growth.
豐華 excellent and abundant.
豐衍 plentiful.
25 豐衣 fine clothing.
豐豐阜阜 very abundant.
豐足 wealthy; well-to-do.
豐饒 productiveness.
面貌豐隆 a full, round, healthy countenance.

灃[1] **A stream in Shensi.**
1898

葑[1] **Young shoots of the rape-turnip. 蕪菁.**
1899

酆[1] **A district. A way of writing 豐 No. 1897.**
1900

酆都 a district in Szechwan, said to be near the entrance to the infernal regions.
酆都城 Hades.

佛[2.5] FO *See* 1982.
1900½

FU FO (ㄈㄛ) (Foh)

縛[2.5.] **To bind, to tie. Also pron. *fo*[4]. Distinguish 縛 No. 1430.**
1901

縛·上一道箍 bind it with a hoop.
縛·在車下 tie it under the cart.
縛帶 to tighten a girdle.
縛束 or 縛綁 or 捆縛 to bind.
縛緊 bind it tightly; tie it tightly.

FOU. (ㄈㄡ) (Feo)

否[3] **Not, if not, whether or not, on the contrary. To deny.**
1902

否則 if not, then. . . . ; otherwise; or else.
否定 not so; uncertain; a negation.
否定·的例 negative instances or examples.
否決 to veto, to vote in the negative.
5 否決之議案 a rejected proposal or bill.
否決權 the right to negative.
否認 to contest a case; to deny; to deny recognition of; to disapprove.
否認權 right of contest.
以定然否 in order to come to a decision–yes or no.
10 可否 may it be done?
可否能否·的問題 a question of whether you may or whether you can.
是否 is it so?
未知是否 uncertain whether it is or not.

(a) Read *p'i*[3]. One of the diagrams. Wicked, evil. Clogged, stopped.

否世 this evil world.
否塞 clogged; stopped.
晦盲否塞 dark and gloomy.
否婦 ignorant women.
↓臧否 good and evil.
否終即泰 when misfortune reaches its limit, then prosperity comes.
否運 or 命否 an evil tate; misfortune.

紑[2] **Bright, fresh appearance of garments.**
1903

絲衣其紑 his silk robes were fresh and bright.

罘[2] **A net to catch rabbits or hares. A screen.**
1904

罘罳 a wooden screen placed across a doorway, before which the minister would stop to think before going in to the presence of his prince; said to be 復思 think again.
芝罘 Chefoo. (-*fu*[2])

缶 } [3] **Pottery, earthenware. Radical 121.**
缻 }
1905

瓦缶 earthenware generally.

浮² To float; to drift. Light.
1906　Usually pron. *fu²*.

浮 于 to float above; to excel.
紂 罪 浮 于 桀 the crimes of *Chou* exceed those of *Chieh*.
浮 力 buoyance.
浮 動·的 floating.
⁵浮 喧 rising sound of voices carried on the air.
浮 囊 skin-bags used as floats.
浮 圖 or 浮 屠 a pagoda; used for Buddha, from the sound.
浮 在 眼 前 floating before the eyes.
浮 塵 or 浮 埃 floating dust.
¹⁰浮 塵°子 small insects injurious to growing rice.
浮 家 泛 宅 floating population living on boats.
浮 屍 盈 河 the river was filled with floating corpses.
浮 島 a floating island.
浮 影 floating shadows—visions.
¹⁵浮 揚 to float upwards; to soar; to fly up.
浮 月 the floating reflection of the moon—insubstantial.
浮 木 floating wood, as a raft.
浮 標 a buoy.
浮 橋 or 浮 梁 a pontoon-bridge.
²⁰浮 民 vagrants.
浮 氣 mirage.
浮 水 to float; to swim—(read *fu.⁴*).
浮 汎 floating about; superficial.
浮 沒 now appearing, now disappearing; inconstant, as a disappearing star.
²⁵浮 沉 or 浮 湛 floating and sinking, bobbing on the water; unsettled; ups and downs; going with the times.
與 世 浮 沉 to go with the current of the age; to have no decided opinions.
浮 沬 bubbles or froth on the surface.
浮 流 水 雷 a floating mine.
浮 海 to float across the sea.
³⁰浮 浪 floating waves—those who have no fixed place of abode.
浮 浪 罪 vagrancy. (*legal*).
浮 淺 shallow, superficial.
浮 涉 江 海 to cross the waters.
浮 游 在 世 drifting about the world.

³⁵浮 游 塵 埃 之 外 to roam beyond the regions of this dusty world—in bliss.
浮 漚 bubbles on the water; froth.
浮 漚 釘 bubble-headed nails used for heavy doors—i.e. nails with large round heads.
浮 煙 floating mists—as when clouds are low down on the mountains.
浮 現 floating visions.
⁴⁰浮 石 pumice stone.
浮 礮 臺 floating battery.
浮 空 floating in space.
浮 置 unstable; insecurely placed.
浮 肋 骨 floating ribs.
⁴⁵浮 胡 琴 a violin.
浮 芥 floating trifles, as light seed-vessels, etc.
飛 羽 浮 芥 floating down and fluff—trifles.
浮 花 flowers cast into a stream; ornaments carved or cast in relief.
浮 萍 duckweed—used of drifting without certain employment, etc.
⁵⁰浮 蟻 scum floating on wine.
浮 表 or 浮 量⁴表 a hygrometer.
浮 頭 flotsam.
浮 頭 浪³子 a thriftless man, one who does not settle to any regular employment.
浮 香 gum-olibanum.

(a) Volatile, fleeting, insubstantial, giddy, frivolous.

浮 世 the uncertainty of life; the changes of the times.
浮 僞 hypocritical; insincere.
浮 利 insubstantial benefit; uncertain gains.
浮 名 an empty name.
⁵浮 囂 inconstant; fickle and excitable.
浮 妄 fickle, false, inconstant.
浮 幻 之 景 floating visions; unreality.
浮 文 inflated style of literature.
浮 榮 empty honours.
¹⁰浮 狂 frivolous and eccentric.
浮 生 若 夢 life is like an empty dream.
浮 華 dissolute; gay; empty vanity; empty show.
浮 薄 fickle; unstable.
浮 言 random talk; rumours.
¹⁵浮 詞 unreliable, high-sounding talk.

浮 誇 pompous, high-flown but empty boasting.
浮 議 frivolous discussions.
浮 財 uncertain gains—not a fixed income.
浮 躁 light and fickle minded; unstable.
²⁰浮 面 皮 an insincere countenance.

(b) Excess; excessive.

浮 收 to take more money than is due.
浮 報 to return more than is actually due.
浮 浮 abundant; excessive.
江 漢 浮 浮 the rivers are rising to overflowing.
⁵　雨 雪 浮 浮 excessive rain and snow.
浮 額 more than the prescribed number or amount.
浮 餘 over and above; surplus.
事 浮 於 人 there are more things to be done than there are men to do them.

蜉² A large species of ant.
1907
蚍 蜉 large ants.

FU.　　　(ㄈㄨ)

夫¹ A sage, a distinguished person, a man. A husband.
1908　A labourer or artisan.

夫·人 ladies of high rank, formerly used of wives of highest officials; now a courtesy title in speaking of the wife of another; everybody—like 人 人.
如·夫·人 like a wife—a concubine.
太·夫·人 your mother.
竹 夫·人 a bamboo wife—leg-rest for use in summer when in bed. "Dutch wife."
⁵夫 君 or 夫 主 or 丈·夫 a husband.
夫 唱 婦 隨 domestic harmony.
夫 壻 my husband.
夫°妻 or 夫 婦 husband and wife.
夫 妻 反 目 lack of harmony between husband and wife.
¹⁰夫 妻 合 好 conjugal felicity.
夫 婦 之 倫 the conjugal relationship.

夫 婦 之 愚 ordinary people.

夫 婦 偕 老 growing old together as man and wife.

夫 婦 有 別 a distinction should exist between husband and wife.

¹⁵夫 子³ a sage, a master, a hero, title of respect for the great teachers of old. 夫·子 a coolie.

孔 夫 子³ Confucius.

夫·家 husband's home.

夫 役 servants or coolies sent with a message.

夫 頭 a head-coolie.

²⁰夫 黨 my husband's people.

丈·夫 a husband. 未 婚 夫 fiancé.

大 丈·夫 a man of heroic mould.

匹 夫 a common man, one of the masses.

大·夫 a great officer, high minister of state in ancient times; a doctor—(大 read tai⁴).

²⁵廚·夫 a cook.

挑·夫 a porter; bearer; coolie.

百 夫 長 a centurion.

車·夫 a carter or barrow-man.

轎·夫 sedan-chair bearers.

³⁰農·夫 farmers.

馬·夫 grooms.

(a) **Read** *fu²*. **An initial particle —now, therefore, moreover, forasmuch as, however, wherefore, if.** Cf. (b).

夫 人 豈 以 不 勝 爲 患 Why should a man grieve because of his lack of ability?

夫 仁 者 *now*, the man of perfect virtue....

夫 如 是 now that it is so ...

夫 旣 或 治 之 *now* there were officials to attend to this business.

⁵夫 微 之 顯 *such* are the manifestations of what is minute.

夫 孝 者 *now* filial piety....

夫 是 以 謂 之 *now* this may be called....

夫 然 that being so ...

夫 苟 好⁴ 善 if he loves the good.

¹⁰夫 豈 不 知 is it possible that he does not know that?

夫 道 若 大 路 然 *now* the way of truth is like a highway.

夫 達 也 者 *now* the man of distinction....

且 夫 moreover, the ...

今 夫 麰 麥 *now* there is barley.

今 夫 弈 之 數 *now* the art of chess-playing...

(b) **A demonstrative pronoun, "a term of definite indication."** 有 所 指 之 辭. **When joined to a noun it gives emphasis.**

夫 也 不 良 *that* man is not good.

夫 二 三 子³ 也 *it* belongs to you, O disciples.

夫 人 不 言 .... *that* man does not speak often....

告 夫 三 子³ 者 inform the chiefs of the three families of *it*.

⁵宜 與 夫 禮 若 不 相 似 然 this does not seem as if it were in accordance with *that* rule of propriety.

是 故 惡 夫 佞 者 it is on that account that I hate *your* glibtongued people.

賊 夫 人 之 子³ you are injuring *this* man's son.

(c) **An adversative particle.**

夫 何 遠 之 有 *but* how is it distant?

吾 王 之 好 獵 夫 何 使 我 至 於 此 極 也 our king loves his hunting, *but* why does he reduce us to this extremity?

(d) **A preposition like** 於.

專 意 夫 軍 謨 specially consider military matters.

(e) **Final particle like** 乎.

吾 已 矣 夫 it is all over with me!

吾 死 矣 夫 I am a dead man!

莫 我 知 也 夫 Alas there is no one that knows me!

必 子³ 之 言 夫 Your words, alas!

逝 者 如 斯 夫 It passes away just like this.

道 其 不 行 矣 夫 How untrodden is the Way!

(f) **A particle indicating consequence or result, similar to** 則.

內 省 不 疚 夫 何 憂 何 懼 when internal examination discovers nothing wrong, what *then* is there to be anxious about, or what is there to fear?

王 往 而 征 之 夫 誰 與 王 敵 your majesty will go and punish

them; *in such a case,* who will oppose your majesty?

(g) **As a pronoun.**

夫 召 我 者 而 豈 徒 哉 *He* has invited me; can there be no reason for it? Cf. (b).

扶² **To support; to prop up; to help.**
1909

扶 乩 or 扶 箕 or 扶 鸞 to write in sand with a stick supported by two blindfolded persons; it is usually practiced in temples; a form of planchette.

扶 伏 or 扶 服 to crawl on all fours.

扶 保 to protect.

扶 助 to succour; to aid; to second.

⁵扶 助 費 support given to the families of those who have spent their lives for the country, as soldiers, etc.

扶 危 to support those in distress, to aid.

扶 壁 buttresses.

扶 微 to rescue or succour the weak and feeble.

扶·我·下·去 help me down.

¹⁰扶·手 a support for the hand; a staff or a banister.

扶·手 板 a board on which to rest the hands, placed across a sedan-chair.

扶 持 or 扶 挾 to support; to sustain; to help; to steady.

扶 持 法 權 to maintain the authority of the law.

扶 挈 老 幼 to assist and support the aged and the young.

¹⁵扶 接 to meet.

扶 掖 to support by the armpits.

扶 揄 name of a sword.

扶 搖 the rising and falling of a great wind; a typhoon.

扶 搖 直 上 he is mounted on the wings of the typhoon,—of rapid success in one's career.

²⁰扶 搖 而 上 the roc soars away on the typhoon.

扶 搏 the pressure of a bird's feathers when flying high.

扶 擁 to crowd together.

扶 救 to rescue.

扶 木 the wood of the 扶 桑. *See below—27.*

²⁵扶 杖 to lean on a staff.

扶 枝 a crooked bough.

扶 桑 the extreme east; an old name for Japan; sunrise; the red hibiscus—a divine plant, not identified,—its leaves are described as similar to those of the mulberry, it grows to great height and is of immense circumference,—it is said to grow in pairs, one supporting the other, hence the name.

扶 植 to plant—used fig.

扶 柩 or 扶 靈 or 扶 櫬 to escort a coffin.

³⁰扶 殖 to assist to independence.

扶 災 to bear up under calamity.

扶 留 a climbing plant.

扶 疏 spreading; luxurious.

扶 病 到 山 (he went), ill as he was, to the mountain.

³⁵扶 窮 to relieve the poor.

扶 翼 to support and shelter.

扶 老 an old man's staff; to support the aged; name for the adjutant bird.

扶 老 攜 幼 supporting the aged and leading the children by the hand.

扶 老 繦 幼 supporting the aged and carrying the babies on their backs.

⁴⁰扶 臥 to assist to bed.

扶 著 to uphold.

扶 蘇 the mulberry.

扶 贊 to succour; to aid.

扶·起 to assist to rise; to help up.

⁴⁵扶 輿 to be successful in one's career.

扶 風 a tempest; also, bending to the breeze.

扶 養 support of the poor; to support and care for.

扶 養 權 利 者 the person who has the right to receive support. (*legal*).

扶 養 義 務 duty of support. (*legal*).

⁵⁰扶 養 義 務 者 a person who is bound to furnish support. (*legal*).

珷¹
1910
An inferior agate.

珷 石 inferior stones to jade; pebbles.

芙²
1911
The hibiscus.

芙 蓉 城 fairyland; the other world.

芙 蓉 面 a pretty face.

阿 芙 蓉 opium, from the sound.

芙 蕖 the lotus flower when fully open.

蚨²
1912
A kind of water-beetle,— see below; from which it has come to mean:—cash, then dollars and money generally.

花 蚨 dollars, rupees, etc.

青 蚨 a water beetle:—according to the books, if the blood of the mother is smeared on 81 copper cash, and the blood of the young one is also smeared on another 81 cash, these cash will always come together, no matter how they are circulated,—from the 搜 神 記.

趺²
1913
To sit cross-legged, as a Buddhist devotee.

趺 坐 to sit cross-legged, like a Buddhist priest.

(a) To bow.

趺 趺 然 bowing low.

鈇¹
1914
An axe.

鈇 質 or 鈇 鑕 (*chih*¹·⁵·) an instrument for chopping the body in two.

鈇 鉞 hatchets and battle-axes.

颶²
1915
A storm.

颶 風 a tempest or gale.

颶 飆 a gust of wind.

麩¹
1916
Bran; refuse.

麩·子 or 麩·皮 bran.

麩 料 horse-feed; chopped straw.

麩 炭 火 or 浮 炭 火 a slight fire of light charcoal, as in a hand-stove.

麩 金 gold-dust, as obtained from river beds.

付⁴
1917
To hand over, to transfer; to commit to; to give to, to pay.

付 丙 destroy by fire—phrase at the end of a letter.

付 之 to entrust to ....

付 之 拍 賣 put up for auction.

付 之 流 水 to entrust to the flowing streams—to be careless of a matter.

⁵付 信 or 付 書 to send a letter.

付 償 to repay; to recompense.

付 刊 or 付 梓 sent to the engraver; sent to be published.

付 到 paid over; delivered.

付 制 幣 payment in specie.

¹⁰付 寄 to send to.

付 工·錢 to pay wages.

付 款 保 證 銀 行 certifying bank.

付 款 員 paying teller.

付 款 日 pay-day.

¹⁵付 款 期 date of payment.

付 款 條 件 terms of payment.

付 款 處 place of payment.

付 清 pay in full; to clear off an account.

付 現 銀 to pay ready money.

²⁰付 現 錢 to pay in cash.

貨 到 付 現 cash on delivery.

付 畀 之 重 the greatest of Heaven's gifts.

付 管 to entrust to the care of.

付 約 a deed of transfer; to hand over a deed.

²⁵付·給·他 hand over to him.

付 與 to hand over to.

付 託 to charge; to commission.

付 訖 stamped; settled; advanced; paid—as a bill.

運 費 付 訖 carriage paid.

³⁰付 諸 一 笑 to laugh it off.

付 諸 罔 聞 to put a matter off as if one had not heard about it.

付 諸 東 流 to entrust to the eastward-flowing streams—to trust a matter to luck, to take no care about it.

付 銀 罫 bills payable.

付 銀 簿 Bills Payable—account-book.

³⁵不 付 non-payment.

交 付 to transfer—as to a successor.

代 付 to pay for another.

先 付 若 干 part-payment.

⁴⁰分 期 交 付 之 款 an instalment.

分 期 付 to pay by instalments.

卽 付 payable at sight.

天 付 instinct.

定 期 付 time-payment.

定 期 交 付 delivery on term.

⁴⁵支 付 to pay.

名 譽 支 付 payment for honour.

未 付 支 票 outstanding cheques.

止 付 to stop payment.

祈 付 please pay.

⁵⁰見 票 卽 付 bill at sight; demand draft; pay at sight.

費 先 付 charges prepaid

關 稅 已 付 duty paid.

關 稅 未 付 duty unpaid.

咐 ⁴ To order.
1918

吩·咐 to command.

囑·咐 to charge; to enjoin.

拊 ³ To pat; to slap; to tap; Inter. 撫 No. 1932.
1919

拊 其 背 patted him on the back.

拊 循 to soothe and comfort.

拊 心 to lay the hand on the heart.

拊 掌 to clap the hands.

拊 我 畜 我 you, my parents, patted me and fed me.

拊 琴 to play the organ, piano or harp, etc.

泭 ¹ A raft.
1920

泭 漚 bubbles on the water; froth.

祔 ⁴ To worship ancestors. To inter.
1921

祔 葬 to bury together.

祔 食 to sacrifice to all—as when a newly-deceased ancestor has his tablet added to the rest.

升 祔 太 廟 ascended to the great temple—has gone to be with his fathers.

符 ² To agree with; to tally. The two halves of a tally.
1922

符 信 evidence; proof of identity; credentials.

符 前 言 to fulfil a promise; to keep one's word.

符 合 to reconcile.

符 應 the mutual agreement between Heaven's appointment and human affairs.

⁵符 板 a tally; a check.

符 璽 Imperial seal or stamp.

符 節 a warrant or commission; credentials; a tally.

若 合 符 節 like fitting the two halves of a tally—in exact agreement.

符 號 a symbol; a sign.—as a punctuation mark.

¹⁰符 驗 counterfoil; to verify.

不 符 or 不 相 符 not in agreement; does not fit, as a tally.

字 跡 不 符 the writing does not agree. 音 符 notes. (music)

↑ 注 音 符 號 National Phon. Letters.

(a) A charm, amulet or spell.

符 咒 charms, spells, amulets.

符 命 an auspicious omen granted to a prince as a token of his appointment from Heaven.

符 拔 a hornless animal described as like the unicorn.

符 瑞 auspicious influences.

⁵符 籙 books on magic; an amulet.

符 袋 or 符 囊 small bag for carrying charms or amulets.

符 采 markings on jade.

符 頤 to happen according to the good wishes expressed.

保 生 符 a ring locked round the neck.

¹⁰催 命 符 death-warrant.

催 生 符 charm for hastening childbirth.

書 符 or 畫 符 to write or draw incantations, or spells.

桃 符 peachwood charms.

治 鬼 符 charm for controlling demons.

¹⁵護 符 or 辟 邪 符 a protective charm against demon influences.

靈 符 a charm that has proved efficacious.

驅 邪 符 the charm which drives away demon-influences.

跗 ² The instep.
1923

跗 注 gaiters and leggings.

跗 前 骨 the metatarsal bones.

(a) Calyx of a flower.

栗 跗 the burrs of a chestnut.

附 ⁴ Near to.
1924

附 耳 close to the ear; a small star which seems to be appended to a larger one.

附 耳 之 言 whispers.

附 語 a whispered conversation.

附 近 near to; neighbouring.

附 鄰 to border on; neighbouring.

(a) To adhere to; dependent on.

附 依 to depend on.

均 不 依 附 in no way subordinate.

附 勢 to adhere to the strongest side.

附 化 to become a citizen of another country, as when the barbarians became civilized by becoming Chinese subjects.

⁵附 和 (ho⁴) to play the sycophant; to agree with, regardless of facts.

附 庸 a petty, dependent State of feudal times, the chieftain of which had not the right of audience.

附 庸 蔚 爲 大 國 an obscure dependency becomes a great State—illustrates secondary things getting the first place.

第 三 國 際·的 附 庸 a petty dependency of the Third Internationale.

附 從 to accord with; to submit to; to obey; to become adherents of.

¹⁰附 籍 to enter another family by adoption, or by marrying a daughter and taking her surname.

附 著 adhering to. (-cho²)

附 著 力 adhesive strength; power of adhesion. (-cho²-)

附 賴 to depend on; to trust to.

附 順 to follow.

[15]附 驥 from 蠅附驥尾 a fly on the tail of a famous steed—used of one who climbs to position through the greatness of another.

歸 附 to return to allegiance—as rebels.

(b) To append; to enclose. An appendix. Accessory. See also C.

附◦上 or 附 送 to annex or forward as an enclosure—in a despatch (to equals or superiors)

附 交 to send the appended ....

附 件 an enclosure.

附 例 or 附 則 by-laws; supplementary rules.

[5]附 佩 to append to the girdle or to the dress.

附 印 to attach a seal.

附◦去 enclosed; forwarded herewith (to inferiors).

附 句 or 疊 句 the chorus of a hymn or song.

附 呈 to send enclosed.

[10]附 單 to enclose an account.

附 尾 to append.

附 屬 accessory; incidental; secondary; collateral.

附 屬 品 accessories; accretions.

經 學 附 屬 品 mere accessories of classical scholarship.

[15]附 屬 權 利 additional privileges.

附 屬 物 accessories.

附 屬 請 求 accessory claim. (legal).

附 帶 incidental; accessory.

附 帶 上 訴 incidental appeal (legal).

[20]附 帶 影 響 incidental effects of.

附 帶 民 事 訴 訟 incidental civil suit. (legal).

附 帶 犯 a person who is guilty of a second offence which transpires during the hearing of the first. (legal).

附 帶 請 求 incidental claims; accessory claims. (legal).

附 張 a supplement.

[25]附 戴 appendage to a hat or cap.

附 手 to join hands.

附 抄 to append a copy of.

附 擔 負 遺 贈 legacy with certain obligations.

附◦於 attached to.

[30]附◦於 其 末 to put oneself last.

政 府 代 表 隨 附 於 a government representative at-

tached to ....

附 有 "enclosed please find," "herewith."

附 有 條 件◦的 conditional.

附 條 件 with conditions.

[35]附 條 件 之 簽 署 qualified endorsement.

附 條 件 之 認 支 qualified acceptance—as of a draft, etc.

附 條 件 遺 贈 conditional legacy.

附 片 a postscript to a memorial.

附 登 to insert—as in a newspaper.

[40]附 繳 to send enclosed.

附 續 or 目 錄 or 附 編 to append; an appendix.

附 置 accessory.

附 股 to have shares in.

附 葬 to bury together.

[45]附 薦 to engage priests to perform a ritual for one's dead.

附 設 auxiliary.

附 證 書 documents attached.

附 議 to second.

附 貼 attached to.

[50]附 贅 useless appendage—a tumour.

附 贅 縣 疣 useless—from Chuang tzŭ—(they regarded life) as a wen, and death as cutting it off.

附 連 appended.

附 還 to return enclosed.

附 隨 事 物 accessories.

[55]附 隨◦的 or 附 從◦的 secondary; collateral.

附 麗 or 附 比 attached to; connected with.

附 點 音 符 dotted notes. (music).

(c) To add to; to increase.

附 加 to supplement.

附 加 刑 additional punishment.

附 加 稅 supplementary taxes.

附 卷 to place additional papers with the records of a case.

[5]附 搭 to add to, as an extra.

附◦會 to add to; to gloss; to force an interpretation; to adhere to.

附◦會 穿 鑿 forced and trivial moralizing; far-fetched.

何 必 附◦會 他 why cleave to such a fellow?

遂 附 會 爲 管 仲 所 作 this was, by later editors, said to be by KuanChung.

[10]附 生 a licentiate of the 1st degree under the old system of examinations; students accepted

beyond the prescribed number.

附 益 to increase; to add to; to better one's position.

(d) To be possessed by.

附 在 人 身 to possess a man's body,—as a demon.

附 鬼 or 鬼 附◦着 possessed by an evil spirit.

(e) Inter. 蒯 next. Aconite or wolf's-bane.

附 子[3] or 黑 附 子[3] seeds of aconite.

蒯[4] Aconite or wolf's-bane.
1925

蒯 子[3] or 黑 蒯 子[3] seeds of aconite.

駙[4] An extra horse harnessed by the side of the team.
1926

駙 馬 old name for an imperial son-in-law, afterwards known as 額 駙 under the Manchus.

鮒[4] A fish like a perch.
1927

鮒 行 to go in pairs, as perches are said to do.

鮒 魚 涸 轍 like a perch in a dry rut—in desperate straits.

府[3] A Prefecture; the officer governing it. A treasury; a palace; a store-house.
1928

府◦上 or 貴 府 polite terms for, "Your residence."

府◦上 好 否 "Is your family all well?"

府 丞 former Vice-Governor of 順 天 府.

府 史 clerk; secretary in charge of documents.

[5]府 君 my father or grandfather—when deceased.

府 城 a Prefectural city.

府 尊 or 太 府 His Honour the Prefect.

府 尹 Governor of the former Imperial Prefecture of 順 天 in which lies Peking.

府 庫 a treasury; a depot.

[10]府 案 首 the first on the lists at the former Prefectural examinations.

府 治 the Prefecture.

府 考 or 府 試 the former Prefectural examination of students.

佩 文 韻 府 *The Great Treasury* of Chinese literature, a thesaurus of quotations, etc.

六 府 the six treasuries—of nature, i.e., water, fire, metal, wood, earth and grain.

[15]天 府 the storehouse of God.—eternity.

王 府 a prince's palace.

知 府 a Prefect of a county or Department.

萬 物 一 府 all things are one.

首 府 the provincial Prefecture, that in which the provincial capital is situated.

俯
頫 [3] To bow down; to come down. To bend; to condescend. The second form is also read *t'iao*[4], to have audience as the feudal princes did; to bring tribute.

1929

俯 仰 to look up and down; to go with the times.

俯 仰 之 間 between looking down and up again—in the briefest space of time.

俯 仰 皆 寬 he treats everybody with kindness—those above and those below.

俯 仰 進 退 manner and deportment.

[5] 因 不 能 與 世 俯 仰 because he was not able to adapt himself to the exigencies of the times.

俯 伏 to prostrate; to make obeisance.

俯 傴 to bend the back;—reverence.

俯 允 kindly grant this—phrase in letters.

俯 准 graciously to authorize.

[10]俯 察 to look into.

俯 察 地 理 to examine the configuration of the land—as a geomancer.

俯 就 to adapt oneself to others; to adopt a plan; to make the best of.

俯 從 to give way to.

俯 念 to condescend to read; to remember graciously.

[15]俯 念 商 艱 to give gracious consideration to the difficulties of the merchants.

俯 思 to bow the head and reflect.

俯 拜 to do obeisance.

俯 拾 to stoop and pick it up—a thing easily done.

俯 窺 to look down from a height.

[20] 可 俯 而 窺 (the nest) could be seen on looking down.

俯 而 就 之 to reach by stooping.

俯 聽 to deign to hear.

俯 臨 to condescend to visit.

俯 視 to look down; to look from above.

[25]俯 角 the angle of depression.

俯 賜 咨 商 kindly write and consult with.

俯 賜 照 會 to favour with a despatch.

俯 身 傾 耳 to bend down and listen intently.

俯 順 to defer to.

[30]俯 顧 condescend to regard.

俯 首 to bow.

俯 首 就 範 to submit to authority with meekness.

俯 首 帖 耳 servile, submissive—as a dog.

俯 首 無 言 he bowed his head and kept silent.

[35]俯 首 鞠 躬 to make a low bow.

腐 [3] Rotten, corrupt, putrid, worthless.

1930

腐 乳 soured bean-curd.

腐 儒 a pedant.

腐 刑 castration as a punishment.

腐 刻 to etch; etching.

[5]腐 化 份 子 one who tries to injure the cause—of any society, etc; corrupt element.

腐 心 expresses utter weariness after effort.

腐 木 不 可 爲 柱 decayed wood cannot be used for pillars.

腐 氣 foolish; obstinate; pedantic.

腐 爛 or 腐 朽 putrid; spoilt.

[10]腐 肉 rotten flesh.

腐 草 爲 螢 decayed grass is transformed into fireflies.

腐 語 or 陳 腐 platitudes.

腐 敗 corrupt; decadent; old; worn out and obsolete.

腐 敗 狀 態 musty condition, as of goods, etc.

[15]腐 鼠 poor; mean and trashy.

荳 腐 bean-curd.

陳 腐 out of date; stale.

腑 [3]

1931   The bowels.

腑 臟 the bowels.

肺 腑 lungs and bowels—the secrets of the heart.

撫
捬 [3]   To cherish. To soothe. To rub, to clap.

1932

撫 世 to comfort the hearts of men.

撫 今 追 昔 to compare past and present.

撫 劍 to grasp a sword.

撫 劍 疾 視 to flourish a sword with angry looks.

[5]撫 勞 to reward.

撫 卹 to relieve; to show pity.

撫 卹 金 pension to war-survivors.

撫 和 to quieten disorders.

撫 存 to make kind enquiries after the health of another.

[10]撫 存 萬 姓 to care for all men.

撫 字 to nourish and tend—as a father his child.

撫 定 to pacify and settle the people.

撫 寧 四 海 brought about peaceful conditions within China.

撫 左 and 撫 右 the governor's left and right—troops or escort.

[15]撫 弄 to finger, to feel or handle.

撫 御 士 卒 to pacify and urge officers and men—to govern them.

撫 心 to lay the hand on the heart.

撫 慰 or 安 撫 to pacify; to soothe.

撫 抱 to fondle and embrace—as a mother her baby.

[20]撫 拍 to fondle; to dally with.

撫 接 to receive and welcome.

撫 掌 to clap the hands.

撫 摸 to stroke; to rub.

撫 政 策 a conciliatory policy.

[25]撫 教 萬 民 to care for and instruct the people.

撫 柔 萬 人 is tender towards all men.

撫 棺 to mourn by the side of a coffin.

撫 標 troops formerly under the control of the Governor.

撫 檻 to lean on the railing.

30 撫 琴 to strum the harp; to play the piano or organ, etc.

撫 番 to subjugate the barbarians.

撫 節 悲 歌 beating the time as he chanted a mournful strain.

撫 絲 竹 to perform on musical instruments.

撫 綏 萬 方 to pacify the people.

35 撫 膺 to bow to circumstances.

撫 臆 to lay the hand on the bosom.

撫 臺 or 巡 撫 or 撫 院 or 撫 軍 the governor of a province,—a former title.

撫 訓 to care for and instruct.

撫 躬 自 問 self-examination.

40 撫 軾 歎 兮 he leaned on the crossbar of the carriage and sighed.

撫 輯 to bring the people together in peace.

撫 鎮 to pacify.

撫 鞠 to rear; to bring up.

撫 養 or 撫 育 to rear; to foster; to nurture.

45 撫 養 人 才 to foster ability.

撫 馭 to bring under control.

父 [4] A father. An uncle; elderly relatives of the same surname. Radical 88.

1933

父 作 子 述 written by the father and transmitted by the son.

父 債 子 還 the son must pay his father's debts.

父 兄 father and elder brothers—seniors.

父 台 a polite form of address—"You, sir!"

5 父 命 呼 唯 而 不 諾 to respond without hesitation to the commands of a father.

父 嚴 母 慈 the father is severe, the mother is indulgent.

父 在 觀 其 志 父 沒 觀 其 行 while the father is alive, watch the bent of the son; when the father is dead, watch his actions.

父 執 a father's friends.

父 子 天 性 the natural bond between father and son.

10 父 慈 子 孝 a kind father makes a filial son.

父 族 the same generation of the clan as his father.

父 權 paternal rights.

父 母 father and mother.

父 母 唯 其 疾 之 憂 parents are anxious lest their children should be sick.

15 父 母 國 one's native land.

父 母 官 a popular term for a magistrate.

父 父 子 子 a father as a father, and a son as a son.

父 王 my Imperial father.

父 祖 名 播 四 海 the names of my father and grandfather are well known everywhere.

20 父 老 elders; fathers.

父 親 father.

父 詔 兄 勉 the father to summon, the elder brother to encourage — mutual encouragement.

父 道 the duties of a parent.

父 馬 a stallion.

25 父 黨 one's own clan.

事 父 母 to serve one's parents.

伯 父 叔 父 father's elder and younger brothers.

先 父 my late father.

嗣 父 an adopted father.

30 家 父 my father, in speaking of him.

是 父 是 子 like father, like son—such a good father must have a good son.

神 父 spiritual father—a Roman Catholic priest.

祖 父 grandfather on father's side.

繼 父 step-father.

35 養 身 父 母 foster-parents. 生 父

義 父 foster father, as contrasted w

(a) Read fu. Term of respect for old men. u.f. 甫 No. 1942.

漁 父 a old fisherman.

田 父 an old farmer.

斧 [3] An axe, a hatchet.

1934

斧 削 or 斧 政 to prune; to lop—depreciatory phrase when asking a friend to correct a composition.

斧 子 or 斧 頭 or 斧 斤 an axe.

斧 扆 a silken screen with axes figured on it, used behind the throne.

斧 木 rough-hewn logs.

5 斧 柯 or 斧 柄 an axe-handle.

斧 藻 ornament, elegance.

斧 質 (or 鑕 chih[1,5]) executioner's axe.

斧 鉞 battle-axes and halberds; the punishment of dismemberment.

斧 鑊 axe and cauldron—i.e., heavy punishment, beheading or boiling.

10 斧 鑿 痕 marks of the hatchet and chisel—flaws in a composition that shows traces of revising and polishing.

冰 斧 marriage go-betweens.

資 斧 travelling expenses.

釜 [4] A cauldron, a pot, a pan.

1935

釜 中 生 魚 a fish in a kettle—imminent danger—also to have a fish and not be able to cook it—extreme poverty.

釜 底 游 魂 a wandering soul in the bottom of a cauldron—in hell.

釜 甀 a boiler and an earthenware pan.

(a) Large grain-measure containing 6 斗 4 升.

釜 庾 two large measures for grain, the latter containing 16 斗.

孚 [2] To brood over eggs; Inter. 孵 No. 1938, from which the

1936 meaning of confidence is derived, as the time of hatching is sure. To trust in. To have confidence in. Sincere.

孚 乳 to sit on eggs.

孚 佑 to believe in and help another.

上 天 孚 佑 下 民 High Heaven has confidence in the people and assists them.

孚 信 to rely on; to trust.

孚 甲 the calyx of a flower.

交 孚 mutual confidence.

成 王 之 孚 he obtained the confidence due to a king.

俘 [2] A prisoner of war. To take prisoner.

1937

俘 兵 prisoners of war.

俘 囚 captives ; prisoners.
俘 掠 or 俘 虜 to take captive ; prisoners of war.
俘 獲 品 Looty of war—ammunition, etc.
俘 虜 交 換 exchange of prisoners.
俘 虜 taken captive by the enemy.
俘 虜 營 the place where prisoners of war are confined.
俘 馘 to cut off the left ear of captives.

孵 [1]
1938
Birds hatching from eggs. To sit on eggs. Insects and fish, etc., being produced from eggs or spawn.

孵 化 the emergence of fish from spawn, insects or birds from eggs, etc.

桴 [2]
1939
A raft.

桴 炭 floating charcoal ; anything light.
乘 桴 to float on a raft.

(a) A drumstick. Inter. 枹 No. 1962.
桴 鼓 影 響 the drum is beaten and the sound comes at once.

(b) Read fou[2]. The ridge pole in a roof.
桴 罳 wooden screen before a door.

莩 [2]
1940
The white pellicle lining the culms of a water-plant, from which the meaning of intimate, friendly, related, is derived.

莩 葭 the pellicle as above.
葭 莩 之 親 closely related.

(a) Read p'iao[3]. u.f. 殍 No. 5191. Starved to death.
野 有 餓 莩 in the fields there were people starved to death.

郛 [2]
1941
The parts outside a city. Suburbs ; territory.

郛 郭 city walls—to protect.

郛 郭 不 修 the walls were not in repair.
入 其 郛 entered their territory.

甫 [3]
1942
To begin.

甫 及 月 a month ago.
甫 初 a beginning ; at first.
甫 謂 first began to say ....
甫 識 to first become acquainted with.

(a) Just now ; recently.
甫 立 just established.
年 甫 十 歲 just ten years of age.

(b) Great, large, eminent.
甫 侯 palace-eunuchs.
甫 刑 the great punishment—castration.
倬 彼 甫 田 "bright are those extensive fields."
魴 鱮 甫 甫 full of large bream and tench.

(c) A "style" or name. Title of respect for father.
台 甫 Your honourable "style."—the special name used by friends.
尊 甫 Your father—in speaking to another.
尼 甫 Confucius.

(d) Read pu[3]. A garden.
甫 草 field-plants ; vegetables.

盙 簠 [1.3.]
1943
A basket, square outside and round inside, used to hold boiled grain in State worship.

盙 簠 不 飭 the sacrificial vessels in disorder—said of a careless, covetous official.
盙 簠 籩 豆 罍 爵 sacrificial vessels.

脯 [3]
1944
Dried meat.

脯 資 expenses for board.
脯 醢 minced meat—to make mincemeat of a foe, barbarous ancient custom.
脯 鮓 品 preserved meats.
脩 脯 strips of dried meat formerly given as payment to a teacher —hence the term is used for the salary of a teacher.
市 脯 dried meats from the markets.

輔 [3]
1945
Poles attached to a cart to keep it from upsetting.

乃 棄 爾 輔 if you discard the props—the cart will overturn.

(a) The upper jawbone of a man.
輔 牙 jaws and teeth—mutual reliance ; intimate connection.
輔 車 相 依 the mutual reliance of cheek and jawbone—when one is removed the other fails.
輔 頰 the jawbones.

(b) From the above definitions comes the meaning :—to help or support.
輔 世 長 民 to assist one's generation and head the people.
輔 仁 to establish one's virtue,- from :
以 友 輔 仁 establish virtue by means of friendships.
輔 佐 or 輔 助 or 輔 翼 to aid ; to succour.
[5]輔 佐 人 counsel—either a legal representative, guardian or husband. (legal).
輔 佐 物 pickles or condiments.
輔 保 or 輔 衞 to protect.
輔 保 禁 防 to protect and restrain.
輔 助 參 加 intervention, as by a third party.
[10]輔 助 參 加 人 one who intervenes—having no personal interest in the case. (legal).
輔 國 公 nobility in the imperial line of the Manchu dynasty.
輔 導 to assist and guide—as a diligent minister guides his prince.
輔 時 to make full use of the times —not neglecting the seasons.
輔 治 to assist in the government, as officer or minister.
[15]輔 湛 a star in Ursa Major.
輔 濟 大 業 helped him to complete the great undertaking.
輔 相 (hsiang[4]) to join and help —to co-operate.
輔 翊 to help ; an assistant, as wings are to a bird.

輔 笏 high officers of State; in geomancy, hills or knolls which surround or guard.

[20] 輔 行 to assist in carrying out; a colleague.

輔 護 to support and shelter.

輔 贊 彌 縫 assist to make up the deficiencies.

↑ 輔 音 consonant.

(c) Territory around the capital.

關 輔 or 畿 輔 the territory near the capital. *See* No. 412.

疆 域 相 輔 adjacent boundaries.

鬴 [3] u.f. 釜 No. 1935. A large grain-measure of 6 斗 4 升.
1946 A cauldron.

黼 [3] Embroidered garments used to indicate rank, axes were figured on them in black and white.
1947

黼 依 or 黼 扆 a screen used at audiences with the emperor, ornamented with figures of axes. *See* 斧 No. 1934—3.

黼 座 the imperial throne having the above as its background.

黼 繡 finely embroidered.

黼 黻 ancient sacrificial dresses embroidered with black and white stripes or axes.

黼 黻 文 章 elegant composition.

傅 [4] A teacher. To teach. Distinguish 傳 No. 1446.
1948

傅 訓 to teach, the instructions of a teacher.

太 傅 Grand Tutor of the Heir-Apparent under the Manchu dynasty.

師 傅 a teacher, instructor or master; a master; a master-workman; complimentary for Buddhist priest.

(a) To reach to. Near. Similar to 附 No. 1924.

傅 近 adjoining; near to.

(b) To gloss, to lay on colours. Similar to 附 No. 1924.

傅 別 a sort of deed or warrant; it had characters written on the back and could be divided along the centre of the writing; each party retained one half.

傅 以 土 堊 covered with dirt and whitewash.

傅 會 like 附 會 No. 1924-C.6. to yield to the opinion of the majority; to give a forced interpretation, etc.

傅 會 其 說 a forced interpretation of what was said.

[5] 以 善 傅 會 able to make a good show without substantial scholastic basis.

傅 油 to anoint.

傅 粉 施 朱 to powder and rouge.

傅 顏 色 or 傅 彩 to lay on colours.

(c) To assist or support, similar to 輔 No. 1945.

傅 佐 to assist; to render aid.

(d) To charge.

王 命 傅 御 the king charged the chief minister; another interpretation gives chief steward.

賻 [4] To contribute towards funeral expenses.
1949

賻 儀 or 賻 賚 presents for funeral expenses.

賻 贈 to give pecuniary assistance.

賻 祭 to contribute towards sacrificial expenses at a funeral.

敷 敷 敷 [1]
1950　　To state to, to announce.

敷 告 天 下 to proclaim to all in the empire.

敷 奏 to memorialize the throne.

敷 治 to set forth regulations for government.

敷 陳 其 事 to disclose; to set forth.

(a) To diffuse, to distribute, to make known.

敷 于 天 下 extend all over the empire.

敷 弘 五 教 he widely diffused the principles of the five relationships of humanity, i.e., between prince and minister, father and son, husband and wife, elder and younger brothers, and friends.

敷 揚 or 敷 宣 to diffuse teachings; to make widely known.

敷 放 or 敷 布 or 敷 施 to distribute, to make known; to circulate.

[5] 敷 政 優 優 his kindly rule was widely diffused.

敷 教 to diffuse doctrines.

敷 枝 wide-spreading branches of a tree.

敷 求 to extend one's researches.

敷 泛 verbose; diffuse.

[10] 敷 演 經 典 to extend the knowledge of the canonical books.

敷 衍 surplus words; negligence; to publish abroad; to draw inferences from; to make a display.

敷 衍 了 事 [3] negligently finish up a matter—without making due inquiry.

敷 衍 手 段 slovenly methods of doing business.

敷 言 surplus words or padding.

(b) To open, as a flower.

敷 榮 to blossom.

未 敷 not fully expanded, as an opening bud.

(c) To arrange.

敷 下 土 方 to divide the country into districts.

敷 設 to establish.

敷 設 權 construction-rights.

敷 設 鐵 路 to construct railways.

(d) To apply.

敷 傷 to dress an injury.

敷 傷 棉 花 cotton-wool dressing.

敷 藥 to apply external remedies.

敷 油 to rub in oil.

(e) Sufficient; ample; plenty.

敷 你 所 用 sufficient for your expenses.

敷 愉 or 敷 暢 cheerful; happy; satisfied.

敷 解 to remit in full.

敷 足 abundant; sufficient.

敷 餘 surplus, extra, having enough and more.

不 敷 insufficient.

入 不 敷 出 income will not meet expenditure.

副 [4] To aid; to second. An assistant:—opposite of 正 No.
1951　351—E.

副 主 the heir-apparent.
副 作·用 secondary effects.
副 使 an assistant commissioner; a subordinate rank among the tribes of the south-west frontier. The second in an embassy.
副 兵 recruit.
[5] 副 啟 a postscript.
副 官 assistant officials on the staff; adjutants; aides-de-camp.
副 室 a second wife.
副 成 分 accessory ingredients.
副 手 an assistant; a second in a duel or a fight.
[10] 副 會 (k'uai⁴)·計 assistant treasurer.
副 會 長³ vice-president.
副 本 a duplicate copy.
副 業 a side-line of business.
副 榜 or 副 舉 人 supplementary list for the second degree under the old system.
[15] 副 理 assistant manager.
副 產 品 or 副 生 物 by-products.
副 目 a corporal.
副 經 理 assistant manager.
副 總 統 or 副 座 the vice-president of a republic.
[20] 副 總 裁 assistant bank-manager.
副 署 or 副 書 counter-signature.
副 羽 accessory feathers.
副 腺 accessory glands.
副 詞 an adverb.
[25] 副 詞·的 adverbial.
副 議 長 vice-chairman.＝副 主 席.
副 貢 生 an accessory senior licentiate under the old system.
副 貳 to assist.
副 買·辦 assistant compradore.
[30] 副 都 統 a brigadier-general—obsolete.
副 領·事 Vice-Consul.
以 副 民 衆 之 熱 望 to meet the ardent desires of the people.
正 副 original and duplicate; primary and secondary; chief and vice or deputy, etc.

(a) N.A. of pairs or sets, etc.

副 笄 a set of head-ornaments for a woman.
一 副 眼 鏡 a pair of spectacles.

一 副 精 神 all the vigor or energy of a person.
一 副 骨 格 a set of human bones as produced at an inquest.

(b) Read *fu*[1.5]. To rend or tear.

不 坼 不 副 there was no bursting nor tearing—in parturition.

(c) Read *pi*[4]. Queen's head-dress.

副 褘 queen's head-dress and sacrificial robes.

富 [4] Wealth; wealthy. To enrich.
1952

富·不 了³ 他 it won't make him wealthy—do not bother about losing such a small sum.
富 之 to enrich; to benefit.
富 厚 rich and influential.
富 商 大 賈 wealthy traders.(-ku³)
[5] 富 國 強 兵 enrich the nation and increase its military power.
富 在 知 足 wealth lies in contentment.
富 士 山 Fujiyama.
富 強 rich and powerful.
富 庶 wealthy and numerous—population; rich—as in mineral wealth.
[10] 富 態 態·的 a well-to-do look; genteel.
富 戶 or 富 家 a wealthy family.
富 春 秋 in the prime of life.
富 有 well off; rich in.
富 殖 wealthy and powerful—of families that are feared.
[15] 富 歲 a plentiful year.
富 民 to make the people prosperous. 富 源 resources.
富 溢 overflowing with abundance.
富 潤 屋 德 潤 身 riches adorn the house, virtue adorns the person.
富 益 profitable; beneficial.
[20] 富 盛 flourishing, numerous, used of a clan.
富 給 well-to-do. (-chi³)
富 翁 a rich man. A.c. 富 家 翁.
富 而 可 求 if riches could be got by seeking....
富 而 好 禮 rich, yet fond of the rules of propriety.
[25] 富 而 無 驕 rich, yet not arrogant.
富 茂 abundant; flourishing.
富 裕 prosperous; in easy circumstances; plenty; extra.

富 貴 riches and honour.
富 貴 不 斷 頭 the swastika.
[30] 富 貴 如 浮 雲 riches and honour are like a floating cloud.
富 貴 在 天 riches and honour depend on the appointment of Heaven.
富 貴 神·仙 wealthy, honourable and immortal—said of a prosperous, contented man.
富 貴 花 the peony.
富 贍 rich and numerous—of a man's literary output.
[35] 富 足 or 富 厚 or 富 豪 wealthy.
富·餘 having abundance of wealth.
富 饒 having profusion; in great abundance.
富 逸 wealthy and contented; rich in thought—of writings.
富 骨 "wealthy bone"—born with the bump of acquisitiveness.
[40] 富 麗 splendid; luxurious.
學 富 者 a learned man; one rich in scholarship.
年 富 in the prime of life.
求 富 to seek wealth.
致 富 to become wealthy.
[45] 驟 富 to get wealth quickly.

(a) For foreign sounds.

富 呵 浪 furlong.

仆 [4] To fall prostrate. Sometimes read *p'u*[1.5].
1953

仆 倒 在 地 fallen to the ground; to fall prostrate.
仆 斃 to drop dead.

訃 [4] To announce the death of a parent.
1954

訃 告 obituary notice.
訃 音 or 訃 聞 or 訃 報 an announcement of death.

赴 [4] To go to; to attend.
1955

赴 任 or 上 任 to take up the duties of a post.
赴 保 to come forward as bail.
赴 前 敵 to go to the front.
赴 告 to go and inform.
[5] 赴 命 to obey a call.
赴 官 to go before the authorities.
赴 席 or 赴 宴 to go to a feast.

赴幽冥 to go to the dark regions —to die.

赴救 to go to the rescue of.

¹⁰赴敵 to rush forward to engage the foe.

赴會 to attend a meeting.

赴機 to take advantage of an opportunity.

赴海 to drown oneself.

赴湯蹈火 to go through fire and water for another.

¹⁵赴約 to go to an engagement.

赴蓬萊 to go to fairyland—to die.

赴討 to go on a punitive expedition.

赴試 or 赴考 to sit for an examination.

赴質 to come forward with evidence.

²⁰赴難 or 赴援 to go to the assistance of.

赴體 to be possessed by a demon.

(a) **To announce a death in the family.**

負 4 To bear, to sustain. To carry on the back; to trust to.
1956

負事繁多 burdened with many cares and duties.

負冰 early spring;— when fish swim under thawing ice.

負劍 to carry a sword on the back—to trust to the sword; to carry, as one carries a child.

負咎 to bear the consequences of an offence.

⁵負固不服 trusting in the defences, they will not submit.

負塗 daubed with mud—as a pig.

負姆 a nurse for an infant.

負姥 ancient term for a midwife.

負屈 to suffer a wrong.

¹⁰負嵎 took refuge in the mountains—said of a tiger.

負嵎死守 have the back to a hill and fight to the death.

負愧 or 負慚 to bear a load of shame; to have cause for shame.

負戴 to bear on the head; laborious service—such as a mother gives.

負戴山嶽 the earth—bears the mountains.

¹⁵負扆而朝諸侯 with his back

to the silken screen he gave audience to the feudal princes.

負持 to carry away.

負擔 to bear a burden; to sustain —as responsibility.

負擔全權責任 to bear full responsibility.

負擔力 responsibility; sustaining power.

²⁰負暄 to warm the back—to seek a sunny place in winter.

負書來學 carrying their books and coming to study.

負欠 or 負債 to carry a load of debt; liabilities.

負氣 to be in a bad temper; proud and peevish.

負版者 bearer of the census-boards.

²⁵負疚 utterly uneasy in heart—as bearing a guilty conscience.

負笈從師 to carry a satchel and leave home seeking scholarship.

負米百里之外 to carry rice for over a hundred *li*, to nourish his parents—said of *Tzŭ-lu*.

負累 to involve; to be involved.

負義務 being under obligations.

³⁰負芻 carrying grass for firing— fomenters of disorder,— from Mencius :—

昔沈猶有負芻之禍 formerly when *Shen Yu* was exposed to the outbreak of the grass-cutters.

負苦 to bear hardships; to toil.

負荷 (*ho*⁴) to bear a burden on the back—of care and responsibility.

負茲 (the Emperor) is not well —explained as lying on his bed and thus bearing the mat on his back.

³⁵負荊謝罪 bearing the rod and willingly taking the punishment—making a humble apology.

負薪 carrying firing—menial service; of small ability.

負薪之憂 or 采薪之憂 a form of excuse—I am not very well.

負薪救火 carrying firing to put out a fire—making bad worse.

負負無可言 so overcome with shame that speech is impossible.

⁴⁰負販如古 the small pedlars carried on as before.

負責 to be under obligations.

失敗不負責 not responsible for any failure.

負責任 to bear responsibility; to take the consequences.

不負責任 will not take any responsibility.

⁴⁵負郭田 fields near the capital.

負重 to bear a heavy burden.

負重致遠 carrying heavy burdens a great distance—having patient endurance like an ox.

如釋重負 as if released from a heavy burden.

負養 menial service.

⁵⁰強者負力 the violent rely upon their strength.

自負 self-confident.

自負其材 confident of his own ability.

(a) **To turn the back on—thus, ungrateful or defeated. To lose, to fail.**

負主 to turn against one's master.

負俗之累 to suffer for offending the popular prejudices.

負國 to turn on one's country.

負失 to lose, to fail.

⁵負德 to turn the back upon the good.

負心 or 負情 heartless; ungrateful.

負恩 or 負義 ungrateful for kindnesses.

負手 to cross the hands behind the back.

負棋 to lose a game of chess.

¹⁰負租 to fail with the rent.

負約 to break an agreement.

負背 to turn the back on—ungrateful.

負敗 defeated.

負違 to rebel.

¹⁵勝負 success and failure; victory and defeat.

辜負 ungrateful.

虧負他 did not deal fairly with him.

(b) **Negative. Minus.**

負像 a negative image. (*photo*.).

負名 negative term. (*logic*).

負指數 negative indices. (*alg*.).

負數 or 負項 negative quantity. (*alg*.).

⁵負極 or 消極 negative pole. (*elec*.).

負號 or 負數號 sign of the minus or negative.

負 角 negative angle. (*trig.*).
負 電 negative electricity.
負 電 流 negative current.
[10]正 負 plus and minus; positive and negative.

賦 [4] **To diffuse, to spread; to give, to bestow.**
1957

賦 予 to give.
賦 分 a man's allotment from Heaven, as of wealth or ability, etc.
賦 邺 to bestow pity on.
賦 布 to spread out.
[5]賦 性 or 賦 質 one's natural powers or talents.
賦 有 endowed with.
賦 畀 之 初 the moment of birth.
賦 畀 獨 厚 也 a specially liberal endowment was bestowed on man only.
賦 稟 a man's natural endowments.
[10]賦 與 to give.
天 賦 之 才 very gifted—having an endowment of ability from Heaven.

(a) **To levy; to exact.**

賦 役 or 賦 徭 taxes and levies of service; government service.
賦 斂 to exact levies.
賦 斂 之 臣 a collector of the revenue in ancient times.
賦 租 taxes.
[5]賦 稅 to pay taxes; taxes.
賦 納 to send taxes to the emperor.
賦 貢 to pay tribute.
賦 額 the fixed rate for taxes and levies.
重 賦 於 民 to impose heavy taxes on the people.

(b) **Irregular, metrical, rhyming composition. To narrate in verse.**

賦 事 陳 詞 to write one's ideas in verse.
賦 歸 or 賦 歸 去 來 to announce one's intention of returning home.
賦 草 or 賦 稿 a rough draft of verses—conventional term:— my poor verses.
賦 詩 to compose verse; poetry.
賦 閒 leisure for poetry—out of employment; out of office.

膚 [1] **The skin; the flesh.**
1958

膚 受 之 愬 the wound (or wrong) received in one's own flesh.
膚 如 凝 脂 her flesh was as white and smooth as congealed lard.
膚 汗 perspiration.
膚 肌 or 肌 膚 flesh and skin— the flesh on the human bones.
不 膚 撓 不 目 逃 he did not flinch from blows nor turn his eyes from thrusts—of valiant fighting.
皮 ·膚 the skin.
髮 膚 skin and hair—the body.

(a) **Skin-deep; superficial.**

膚 廓 extensive but superficial—of writings.
膚 文 superficial writing.
膚 淺 skin-deep; superficial—used of literature.

(b) **Great, admirable.**

膚 敏 admirable and alert.
以 奏 膚 公 (= 功) thus displaying great merit.

(c) **Pork; minced meat.**

膚 鮮 fresh pork.
麋 膚 hashed meat of the deer.

(d) **Ancient measure—a hand-breadth.**

膚 寸 the smallest measure.
膚 寸 之 地 無 得 者 they did not gain an inch of territory— thus displaying great merit.
膚 合 gathering together—of scattered clouds.

鳧 [2] **Various kinds of wild duck.**
1959

鳧 乙 a duck and a swallow—a misunderstanding:—s e e i n g a wild goose in the distance, some said that it was a duck, and some said that it was a martin.
鳧 尊 a wine-vessel in the shape of a duck—it was used in the *Han* dynasty; the symbol of the duck, which swims on the surface only, was intended as a warning against intemperance.

鳧 [4] 水 to swim. ≡ 1906.22.
鳧 脛 難 加 it is not easy to lengthen a duck's leg—it would pain the duck, and is best as it is.
[5]鳧 舟 duck-shaped boats.
鳧 藻 duckweed and ducks—contented and happy.
鳧 趨 to waddle; to hasten to.
鳧 趨 雀 躍 ducks waddling and sparrows hopping—to dance for joy.
鳧 鴨 a wild duck—a speedy messenger.
[10]鳧 鷖 在 涇 duck and widgeon are on the River *Ching*.
雙 鳧 a pair of ducks—shoes.

阜 阝 [4] **A mound. Abundant; fertile. The contracted form is written to the left of the character. Radical 170. Also read** *fou*[4].
1960

阜 成 兆 民 to improve the condition of the masses.
阜 繁 abundant.
阜 螽 grasshoppers.
阜 財 very wealthy.
物 阜 民 康 things in plenty and people in health—peace.
盛 阜 abundant.

涪 [2] **A river in Szechwan.**
1961

涪 漚 foam, bubbles on the water.

枹 [1] **A drumstick.**
1962

枹 鼓 to beat the drum.

Read *pao*[1]. Bushy. A tree,—the wood is used for firing and the bark for dye.

婦 [4] **A wife, a lady, a woman.**
1963

婦 ·人 a wife; a woman.
婦 ·人 之 仁 the goodness of a woman—is in small things.
婦 女 a woman; women.
婦 女 勞 動 界 women's labour-world.
[5]婦 女 參 政 權 female suffrage.

婦孺 women and children.
婦容 feminine deportment and appearance.
婦工 (or 功) women's work.
婦弟 wife's brother.
[10]婦從 or 婦順 wifely obedience.
婦德 female virtues.
信婦德也 faithfulness is the virtue of a woman.
婦父 wife's father.
婦業 the work of a woman.
[15]婦節 female virtue.
婦言 women's conversation.
婦·道·人·家 women-folk.
夫婦 husband and wife.
寡·婦 a widow.
[20]少婦 a young wife.
新婦 a bride.

FU. (ㄈㄨ)
(Fuh)

伏 2.5. To prostrate; to yield; to suffer. Humble.
1964

伏不敢起 prostrate from fear.
伏乞 or 伏祈 I humbly beg you.
伏侍 to serve; to wait on.
伏候 to wait with humility.
[5]伏几 to rest the head on the hands at a table.
伏劍 to fall on the sword—suicide.
伏地 to fall to the earth.
伏地僵臥 lying prostrate on the ground.
伏地待罪 lying prostrate waiting for punishment.
[10]伏屍百萬 numberless corpses lying on the ground.
伏屍滿野 corpses lie strewn over the wilderness.
伏思 or 伏念 to presume to think.
伏惟 I bow down and consider—phrase in ancient correspondence.
伏手 convenient for use.
[15]伏拜 prostrate oneself in reverence.
伏斧質 to prostrate oneself before the axe and block—acknowledgement of fault.
伏查 it is my humble opinion.
伏望 or 伏希 I humbly hope,—used in letters.
伏案 to bow at the table—to study and write.

[20]伏歷 to break a horse in.
伏氣 to be satisfied; appeased.
伏法受誅 to suffer the extreme penalty.
伏盆 a name for the epidendrum, as it lives for a long time in a pot.
伏眺盡山川 looking down, the view was all hills and streams.
[25]伏祈鑒察 I humbly pray that you will consider it.
伏罪 to own to guilt; to accept punishment.
伏義 Fu Hsi—legendary emperor, 2852-2738 B.C. He is said to have invented writing from the mystic diagrams supposed to have been seen on the back of a tortoise; he also taught the people to cook flesh, etc.
伏虎 a crouching tiger—Buddhist and Taoist term; a chamber-utensil.
伏行 to crawl on the belly.
[30]伏身 to conceal oneself; to throw oneself down.
伏願 my humble desire is.
伏魔大帝 Kuan Yü 關羽 was canonized under this title by Wan-li of the Ming dynasty A.D. 1594.
伏龍鳳雛 Crouching Dragon and Young Phœnix—Chu-ko Liang and P'ang T'ung. 諸葛亮, 龐統.
匍伏 to crouch in obeisance.

(a) To lie in ambush. To hide, to conceal, to suppress. Secret. Hidden.

伏下 to place in ambush.
伏出 half-concealed.
伏匿 to secrete oneself; to withdraw from notice.
伏戎于莽 armed robbers lurking in the thickets.
[5]伏流 subterranean flow.
伏甲 ambushed soldiers.
伏竄 to slink away into hiding places, as robbers, etc.
伏礁 submerged rocks.
伏莽 secreted in the thickets—bandits.
[10]伏藏 or 埋伏 in ambush.
伏道 a tunnel; underground passage.
潛伏 to slink away; to hide.
潛伏期 period of incubation of a contagious disease.

(b) To sit on eggs.

伏卵 or 伏窩 to brood over eggs.
伏雌 a sitting hen-bird.

(c) A decade of summer.

伏汛 summer rise of rivers.
伏臘 summer and winter months.
伏醬臘醋 summer sauce and winter vinegar.
伏天 the dog-days—from July 19th to August 18th approximately.
三伏 i.e., 初, 中, 末 the three decades of the hottest weather.
歇伏 to go away for the hottest part of the summer.

洑 2.5. An eddy, a race. To swim—as fishes. Used in place-names to indicate the spot as a stopping-place for boats.
1965

洑流 an eddy; undercurrent.

茯 2.5. The medicine known as China Root, a fungus-like substance found on the roots of fir-trees.
1966

茯苓糕 kind of cake made from the above.

袱 2.5. A square of cloth for wrapping bundles.
1967

包袱 a bundle wrapped in cloth.

犮/犮 2.5. To prick a dog to make him go.
1968

波 5 To open sluices. Also read fa[4.5].
1969

祓 4.5. To remove evil; to cleanse; to wash away.
1970

祓濯 to cleanse from filth.
祓除釁浴 to cleanse—for the removal of sins.
祓飾厥文 to do away with the old fancy style and—make a new style of literature; to repudiate the old and begin anew.

紱 2.5. A ribbon for a seal. A sash.
1971

朱 紱 red-sashes—the gentry.

袚 2.5. Greaves. Knee-pads. Buskins.
1972

袚 補 knee-pads.

鞴 2.5. A leather knee-pad used in ancient sacrificial dress. A strap for a seal. Ceremonial cap.
1973

黻 2.5. An ornamental texture of black and blue in stripes, used for the sacrificial robes of the emperor.
1974

黻 冕 apron and cap worn when offering sacrifice.
黻 袟 an ornamental skirt.
黻 衣 繡 裳 his embroidered sacrificial robe.

富 2.5. To fill. A roll of cloth.
1975

匍 2.5. To fall prostrate; to crawl on the hands and knees. Also read p'o 2.5.
1976

匍 匐 to crawl on hands and knees.
匍 匐 撫 柩 he fell on his knees and clasped the coffin.

幅 2.5. A strip of cloth; a breadth of material. A hem, a border.
1977

幅 員 the area of a country.
幅 員 益 廣 the area is widely extended.
幅 寛 the breadth of a flag.
邊 幅 boundary; externals; thus it comes to mean, etiquette, etc.
　修 飾 邊 幅 to adorn the exterior; to pay attention to mere externals.
　脫 邊 幅 lay aside formalities.

(a) N.A. for scrolls, maps and things having breadth.

一 幅 對·子 pair of scrolls.
四 條 幅 four scrolls or pictures.

(b) Read p'i 1.5. Bandages wrapped round the feet for shoes.

福 2.5. Happiness, good fortune, prosperity. Happy, blessed.
1978

福 人 a happy man; a lucky man.
福 分 happiness; the allotted measure of happiness which each man is said to have.
福 利 happiness and profit; welfare.
福 命 a happy destiny.
⁵福 善 to bless the good.
福 地 a lucky spot; one's native place; where the gods live.
福 安 may you be happy—felicitous wish at the close of a letter, to a p. of an elder generation.
福 將 a leader of troops when the enemy retreats without a battle.
福 庇 under the fortunate protection of.
¹⁰福 德 religious merit.
福 德 祠 temple or shrine of the T'u-ti or local god.
福 慧 blessedness and wisdom.
福 星 a lucky star—one who saves from suffering or poverty, a benevolent man.
福 澤 favour.
¹⁵福 無 雙 至 blessings never come in pairs.
福 田 to worship the Buddhist trinity 三 寶, to recompense the favour of prince or father, and to assist the poor, is like planting a field with happiness—there will be a reaping.
　樹 福 田 to plant the fields of happiness.
福 祉 happiness; blessedness.
↑福·氣 good luck.
福 神 beneficent deities.
²⁰福 祿 happiness and a prosperous career.
福 祿 壽 三 星 the three stars—happiness, emoluments, and longevity.
福 自 天 申 happiness comes from Heaven.
福 至 心 靈 when good fortune comes the mind is clear.
福 色 a very deep red.
²⁵福 薄 his allotment of happiness is poor.
福 躬 your happy or fortunate person—complimentary phrase

in letters to a superior rank or to elders.
福 酒 wine left after sacrifice.
福 音 the happy sound—the gospel.
五 福 the five blessings—longevity 壽, wealth 富, health 康 寗, virtue 攸 好 德, and to finish the allotted span 考 終 命.
³⁰享 福 to enjoy bliss.
有 福 happy; blest.
發 福 to grow fat.
↑福 音 堂 chapel; gospel hall.

(a) Fukien Province. u.f. Transliterating.

福 鹿 林 florin.
福·建 Fukien.
福 晋 Manchu word—an imperial princess.
福 爾 麥 令 formalin.

蝠 2.5. The bat; used as an emblem of happiness, from the sound.
1979

蝠 鼠 or 蝠 蝙 a bat; the first also means a flying-squirrel.
蝠 蛇 a scorpion—an evil person.
蝠 荳 broad beans.
五 蝠 pictorially used for 五 福, see No. 1978—29.

輻 2.5. The spokes of a wheel. The blade of a water-wheel.
1980

輻·子 or 車 輻·子 the spokes of a wheel.
輻 射 to radiate.
輻 射 熱 radiation of heat.
輻 射 點 point of radiation.
輻 輳 a place of concourse, like the spokes at the hub.
四 方 輻 輳 the centre of things —"the hub of the universe."

弗 2.5. A negative. Not.
1981

弗 克 inadequate for.
弗 如 not equal to.
弗 成 incomplete.
弗 措 insufficient.
弗 豫 not well, out of sorts.
弗 齒 or 不 齒 unworthy; not to be classed among decent men, cp., No. 1037.A.7,8.

(a) Transliterating sounds.

弗 安 volt-ampere.

弗 打 or 弗 volt.
弗 打 電 瓶 voltaic cell.

佛
偈 2.5.
Buddha, Buddhism.
Pron. *fo*²·⁵
1982

佛·事 or 做 佛·事 Buddhist ritual in connection with death.
佛 像 images of Buddha.
佛 刹 Buddhist monastery.
佛 力 the energy of Buddha.
⁵佛 口 蛇 心 good words but a wicked heart.
佛 國 India; the Buddhistic kingdoms.
佛 塔 pagodas.
佛 天 the heaven of Buddhism.
佛 徒 Buddhist disciples.
¹⁰佛 性 a nature like that of Buddha —kind and placid.
佛 手 a kind of citron, with scarcely any juice,–the end tapers into finger-like projections. u.f. 福 in pictorial representations.
佛 敎 or 佛 道 Buddhism.
佛 果 the fruits of becoming a Buddha.
佛 殿 Hall of Buddhas in a temple.
¹⁵佛 母 the mother of Buddha.
佛 法 the law of Buddha.
佛 法 僧 the 三 寶 of Buddhism:– Buddha, the Law and the priesthood.
佛 海 expresses the wideness of Buddha's teachings.
佛 生·日 the birthday of Buddha, 8th of the 4th month.
²⁰佛 眼 相 看 to regard with the eye of Buddha—with kindness.
佛 祖 or 佛 陀 or 佛·爺 or 佛 圖 Buddha, i.e., *Shakyamuni*. The 2nd and 4th are imitations of the sound.
佛 經 Buddhist classics.
佛 老 Buddha and Laotzŭ, founders of the two religions.
佛 舍 (or 沙) 利 bone of Buddha.
²⁵佛 訣 Buddhist precepts.
佛 門 or 佛 家 Buddhism.
佛 門 弟 子 disciples of Buddhism—monks and nuns.
佛 陀 Buddha. *Shakyamuni*.
佛 靑 ultramarine, the colour of Buddha's hair.
³⁰佛 骨 a bone of Buddha, the essentials of Buddhism.

佛 頭 Buddha's head; prominent hills; the large beads in a rosary.
佛 面 上 刮 金 scraping the gilt off the face of a Buddhist idol —shameless in exacting the last penny; mean.
佛 龕 niche for the figure of a god.
三 寶 佛 the three perfect Buddhas. *Shakyamuni, Amida Buddha,* and *Maitreya Buddha.*
³⁵如 來 佛 or 多 陀 伽 陀 *Tat'a-gata.* He who thus comes, he who comes from nowhere and goes nowhere—he who really comes.
　三 世 如 來 the Buddha of the three ages, past, present, and future.
心 堅 卽 是 佛 a determined mind makes a man a Buddha.
念 佛 to repeat the name of Buddha.
拜 佛 to worship Buddha.
⁴⁰活 佛 a living Buddha—powerful lamas who are supposed to be light-emanations or incarnations of Buddha,–they wield temporal power in Tibet; parents.
浴 佛 節 festival of the bathing of Buddha—8th of the 4th month.
燃 燈 佛 Buddha of the burning lamp. *Dipankara.*
臥 佛 the Recumbent Buddha.
自 心 是 佛 your mind is Buddha.
⁴⁵萬 家 生 佛 the living Buddha of all families—said in praise of a good and incorrupt official.
身 佛 無 別 Buddha is within you.
辟 支 佛 *Pratyeka* Buddha—h e who understands the twelve causes.
釋 迦 牟 尼 佛 *Shakyamuni,* the real founder of Buddhism.
阿 彌 陀 佛 *Amitabha Buddha*— the immeasurable. Used as an incantation, or an exclamation, something like "for God's sake," "goodness me," etc.

(a) **Transliterating sounds.**
Cf. 1762 D.
佛 郎 francs.
佛 郎 機 The Franks.
佛 蘭 絨 flannel.
番 佛 or 番 餅 Mexican dollars.

(b) Read *pi*¹·⁵. Great. To help, to support.
佛 時 仔 肩 assist me to bear the burden—of my position.
佛 肸 *Pi Hsi,* a rebellious military official of the time of Confucius.
(c) u.f. **1984.**

咈 2.5.   To oppose, contrary to.
1983
咈 其 耉 長 (*chang*³) to oppose the elders.

彿 2.5.   Like, similar to.
1984
彷·彿 similar to, as if. A.w. 仿·佛

怫 2.5.   Sorry, anxious.
1985
怫 而 不 釋 unable to quiet one's anxiety.
怫 鬱 disquieted, anxious.

(a) Read *fei*¹. Anger, annoyance.
怫 恚 angry.
怫 然 作 色 flushed with anger.

拂 2.5.   To shake off, to brush away.
1986
拂 塵 to brush off the dust.
拂 手 a duster.
拂 拭 to wipe off; to wipe clean.
拂 拂 gentle blowing of a light breeze.
⁵拂 曙 daybreak.
拂 淚 to wipe away tears.
拂 蠅 to brush away flies.
拂 衣 to shake the clothing.
拂 袖 to shake the sleeve—as a mark of disapproval.

(a) To expel, to oppose.
拂 人 性 to thwart people's wishes.
拂 意 contrary to one's inclination.
拂 慮 to drive away care.
拂 戾 or 拂 逆 perverse;   contrary.
拂 暑 to drive away heat.
拂 菻 a name which has been identified with Bethlehem, or Byzantium.
拂 與 情 in defiance of popular wishes.

(b) Read *pi*[4.5.]   To assist.

拂 士 wise counsellors.

紼 [2.5.]   **A rope for dragging a bier.**
1987

紼 縴 a cord, a rope.

執 紼 to hold the ropes of a hearse; to go to a funeral.

(a) Tangled silk.

紼 袍 a coarse silk outer robe.

艴 [2.5.]   **The countenance changing.**
1988

艴 然 不 悦 his countenance showed his displeasure.

(a) Read *pu*[2.5.]   Flushed.

色 艴 如 也 his face flushed.

茀 [2.5.]   **Luxuriant growth of vegetation that blocks the path.**
1989

道 茀 不 可 行 也 the path was overgrown and impossible for travel.

(a) To clear away.

茀 厥 豐 草 after clearing away the dense growth.

(b) A carriage-screen.

翟 茀 以 朝 with feather screens to her carriage she went to court.

(c) Head-ornaments.

婦 喪 其 茀 she lost her hair-ornaments.

(d) Happiness, vigor. u.f. 福 **No. 1978.**

茀 祿 happiness and emolument.

茀 茀 strong and vigorous.

(e) Read *po*[5.]   Angry.

氣 息 茀 然 used of the angry howl of a beast at bay.

髴 [2.5.]
1990
   Dishevelled hair.

复 [2.5.]
1991
    To go back, to retrace.

復 [4.5.]
1992
    To return; to repeat; to reply. Again, repeatedly. Alternative. To make good. u.f. next.

復 仇 or 復 讐 or 報 復 to take revenge.

   復 九 世 讐 revenge for an injury dating back for nine generations.

復 代 理 人 substitute of a representative. (*legal*).

復 任 to resume office; re-appointment.

[5]復 來 returned; to come again.

復 其 初 to restore one's original moral nature.

復 准 to send a reply authorizing.

復 出 口 or 復 運 to re-export.

復 出 爲 惡 on the contrary he waxes worse.

[10]復 到 to send back in reply.

復 原 or 復 元 restored to health.

   復 幾 分 原 partly restored.

復 又 to repeat; to do over again.

復 古 to revive old customs.

[15]復 古 時 代 period of reaction.

復 合 to re-unite.

復 命 to report on a commission.

復 和 reconciled.

復 啟 者 In reply to your letter, I beg to say ....

[20]復 回 to return.

復 土 to fill in a grave, etc.

復 姓 to take his original surname after having been adopted into another family.

復 思 think again.

復 我 諸 兄 I will go back to my brothers.

[25]復 戰 to renew the battle.

復 政 to resume the reins of government.

復 文 a despatch in reply.

復 新 anew; again.

復 旦 the dawning of light after darkness.

[30]復 是 其 言 again emphasized his words.

復 業 to take up their old occupations.

復 權 rehabilitation—of rights, etc.

復 活 or 復 生 resurrection; restored to life.

復 活 日 Easter Day.

[35]復 現 re-appearance.

復 示 instructions in reply—formal phrase in letters asking for an answer.

復 經 further ....

復 習 to revise a lesson.

復 職 to reinstate an official.

[40]復 興 revival; a return of prosperity.

復 興 會 revival meetings.

復 舊 如 初 returned to its original condition.

復 言 to keep a promise,–from :—

   言 可 復 也 what is spoken can be made good.

[45]復 許 to look forward again.

復 辟 or 復 歸 or 復 位 restoration of a monarchy.

復 逆 to act as messenger between the princes and the throne.

復 道 or 複 道 a covered way; a covered bridge.

復 還 or 復 轉 or 復 返 to repay; to return.

[50]復 除 to free from obligation to compulsory service.

復 陶 a garment of feathers to shield from rain or snow, worn in ancient times.

復 降 在 原 he descended again to the plains.

復 電 a reply telegram.

復 音 an answer.

[55]復 音 字 words having more than one sound.

不 復 no longer, no more. | (illness).

反 復 repeatedly; alternately, relapse

恢 復 to restore to former condition.

恢 復 帝 制 restoration of the monarchy, or of imperialism.

[60]照 復 reply to a despatch.

覆 [2.5.]
1993
   To reply to; to repeat. u.f. 復 preceding and 複 No. 1996.

覆 信 or 覆 書 a letter in reply.

覆 奏 to reply to a memorial.

覆 命 to report.

覆 審 to re-examine a case.

[5]覆 校 to revise a book.

覆 版 to reprint.

覆 白 to report on clearly; to make a further report.

覆 考 re-examination.

覆 言 to repeat in words.

[10]覆 試 preliminary examination formerly held before candidates sat for the 3rd degree.

覆 議 re-discussion.
覆 選 re-election.
覆 電 費 已 付 訖 reply-paid telegram.
查 覆 examine and report.

(a) To overturn; to defeat. On the contrary. Backwards and forwards.

覆 墜 to overturn.
覆 手 to turn the hand—very easily done.
覆 巢 無 完 卵 when the nest is overturned there are no whole eggs—if one section is defeated, the whole cannot hold its own; all alike involved.
覆 敗 utterly defeated.
[5]覆 水 難 收 spilt water cannot be gathered—no help for what is already done.
覆 沒 sunk, lost, routed.
　全 軍 覆 沒 the whole army utterly routed.
覆 滅 destroyed; destruction.
覆 盂 an inverted cup—firmly settled.
[10]覆 盆 overturned basin—to cover a man as with an inverted basin—used of injustice.
覆 盆 難 照 difficult to show light under an inverted basin—not easy to right unjust inflictions.
覆 車 之 戒 take the warning of the overturned cart ahead.
覆 軋 to press down.
覆 轍 an overturned cart — as a warning. *See above* A. 12.
[15]覆 餗 unequal to the office and muddling the business.
傾 覆 or 顛 覆 overthrown.
反 覆 backwards and forwards; alternating.

(b) Read *fou*[4]. To cover over; to sit, as a bird. To ambush.

覆 土 to cover with earth.
覆 幬 a canopy—heaven.
覆 庇 to shelter and protect.
覆 照 covered over by the sky and lit by the sun, moon and stars.
[5]覆 醬 to cover sauce-jars—a depreciatory phrase from 楊 雄 — My MS. is only fit for covering sauce-jars.
覆 蓋 to cover over.
覆 載 Heaven and Earth,–from :—

天 覆 地 載 covered by Heaven and supported by Earth.

腹 [4.5.] The belly; the stomach.
1994

腹 地 or 腹·裏 the interior.
腹 大 如 鼓 belly as big as a drum —well-fed and content.
腹 心 beloved, dear; intimate, sincere.
腹 心 之 靠 to depend on entirely.
[5]腹 心 交 a real, close friendship.
心 腹 之 言 reliable words.
心 腹 人 a trusted person.
心 腹 朋 友 a trustworthy friend.
腹 疾 diarrhoea.
[10]腹 痛 pain in the abdomen—bitter grief, from a vow made between *Ch'iao Hsüan* 橋 玄, and *Ts'ao Ts'ao,* 曹 操, that if after the death of either, the other did not sacrifice, he would suffer this pain.
腹 稿 the concept of a composition in the brain before committing it to paper.
腹 笥 to make a satchel of the belly—to memorize the books.
腹 筋 muscles and flesh of the abdomen.
腹 結 constipated.
[15]腹 肚 the belly.
腹 背 front and rear; intimate, near.
腹 脹 swelling of the belly; dropsy.
腹 膜 炎 peritonitis.
腹·裏 藏 刀 a dagger secreted in the belly—treacherous and plausible person.
[20]腹 語 ventriloquism.
腹 誹 hidden reviling—not spoken out.
剖 腹 明 心 to expose the innermost intentions; to make a clean breast of.
口 蜜 腹 劍 false at heart.
專 爲 口 腹 only having regard to the belly.
[25]捧 腹 to hold the sides with laughter.
果 腹 to fill the stomach.

(a) To bear in the arms.

出 入 腹 我 out and in you bore me in your arms.

(b) Solid, thick.

水 澤 腹 堅 the watery places congeal—at the beginning of winter.

蝮 [2.5.] A venomous snake.
1995

蝮 虺 a python.
蝮 蛇 the cobra or viper.

複 [4.5.] Double. To repeat. To reiterate.
1996

複 分 數 compound fractions.
複 利 compound interest.
複 句 compound sentence.
複 合 國 a complex State—like the U. S. A.
[5]複 合 概 念 complex concept.
複 合 法 method of composition.
複 合 物 a compound.
複 合 詞 complex word.
複 名 數 compound numbers.
[10]複 名 數 之一加, 減, 乘, 除, 一 法 addition, subtraction, multiplication, and division of compound numbers.
複 壁 double partition-walls—wherein men could be secreted.
複 姓 double surnames.
複 寫 器 or 複 寫 具 duplicating apparatus.
複 寫 紙 carbon-paper.
[15]複 式 敎 授 teaching more than one form.
複 念 complex idea.
複 意 having a purport which is more than the words indicate on the surface.
複 折 or 複 曲 折·的 zigzag.
複 本 位 制 bimetallic system.
[20]複 比 例 compound proportion.
複 眼 a compound eye, as of an insect.
複 穴 ancient mounds, heaped up for dwelling-places.
複 葉 compound leaf.
複 製 a revision, to remake.
[25]複 襟 a double lapel.
複 記 法 or 複 登 法 double-entry in book-keeping.
複 道 covered ways between buildings; a covered bridge.
複 選 舉 second election.
複 闕 doubled towers over gates, etc.

³⁰複 雜 complex, as contrasted with 簡 單, simple.

複 雜 事 件 a complex affair.

複 雜·的 感 情 mixed feelings.

複 音 a word with two sounds; *

重 (*ch'ung²*)·複 repeated.

* polyphonic music.

輹 2.5. Two pieces of wood which hold the axle firm on both sides, underneath a cart. Inter. 輻 No. 1980.
1997

馥 2.5.
1998　Fragrance.

馥 郁 fragrant and beautiful.

服
服 2.5.　Clothes; mourning garments. To wear, as clothing.
1999

服 中 生 子³ to have a child while in mourning for parents,—a punishable offence if occurring between 10 months after the death and the expiration of the full period of mourning.

服 內 or 有 服 within the five degrees of mourning, *as below* :—

斬 衰 No. 142—10, for husbands and parents, 27 months.

齊 衰 No. 560—C3. for grandparents, etc., 1 year.

大 功 No. 5943—41. for brothers, sisters, etc., 9 months.

小 功 No. 2605—29. for uncles, aunts, etc., 5 months.

總 麻 No. 5582—1. for distant relatives, 3 months.

服 內 納 妾 to take a concubine within the period of mourning —an offence.

服 具 articles for use.

⁵服 制 regulations c o n c e r n i n g mourning; rules relating to the style of dress, etc.

服 周 之 冕 to wear the ceremonial cap of *Chou*.

服 喪 服 to wear mourning.

服 官 to put on official dress—to take office.

服 式 styles of dress.

¹⁰服 滿 or 服 闋 expiry of the period of mourning.

服 育 or 復 育 pupa of the cicada.

服 膺 to wear on the breast—to prize.

服 舍 (服 ＝ 鵬 a small owl.) to mourn for the early decease of a literary man :—when this bird came with its mournful note to rest on a house, it was said to indicate a death, especially of the master.

服 色 colour of garments.

¹⁵服 衣 to put on clothes.

衣·服 clothing.

服 裝 dress; fashions in dress.

服 食 dress and food—necessities.

服 飾 personal adornment.

²⁰便 服 ordinary everyday dress.

凶 服 mourning.

吉 服 ordinary dress as contrasted with mourning.

國 服 national mourning.

報 服 three months mourning for a son.

²⁵朝²服 court-dress.

正 服 proper, legally-prescribed dress.

禮 服 dress-clothes.

全 禮 服 full-dress.

大 禮 服 a frock-coat.

³⁰　小 禮 服 informal dress.

素 服 white garments—mourning.

除 服 or 脫 服 or 釋 服 to go out of mourning.

(a) To serve, to submit. To be willing.

服·事 or 服·侍 to serve, to wait on.

服 人 to submit to another; to accept his teaching or guidance.

以 德 服 人 cause men to submit by virtue.

服 務 to serve; service.

⁵服 勞 to bear the burden of troublesome matters.

服 勞 奉 養 to toil for—parents.

服 役 to render service.

服 從 or 歸 服 to follow obediently; obedience; to accord with.

服 從 命·令 to obey orders.

¹⁰服 水°土 acclimatized.

不 服 水°土 unaccustomed to the climate.

服 法 to submit to the law.

服 理 to submit to reason.

服 田 to serve the fields—farmers.

¹⁵服 眾 心 to conciliate popular feeling.

服 禮 to apologize.

服 管 to yield to the control of.

服 罪 to accept punishment.

服 而 舍 之 if 晉 *Chin* acknowledge their fault, then 秦 *Ch'in* will forgive them.

²⁰不 服 to object, disagree, dislike, disobey, resist; it has many shades of meaning :—"I cannot stand it," etc.

不 服 判 斷 not satisfied with the decision.

不 服 手 the hand is awkward; unaccustomed to it.

不 服 教 ungovernable.

不 服 氣 unwilling to submit; to disagree; unwilling to take second place.

²⁵不 服 理 由 書 protest in writing with reasons.

不 服 輸 unwilling to acknowledge a fault, or a defeat.

佩·服 to admire, worship.

↓ 欽 服 to respect or reverence.

屈 服 to be humiliated and brought into subjection.

悅 服 to submit with a good grace.

(b) A dose of medicine. To swallow.

服 毒 to swallow poison.

服 藥 to take medicine.

一 服 藥 a dose of medicine.

喫·不 服 it disagrees with me.

(c) The two inner horses of a team —the outer pair was called 騑 No. 1836.

服 馬 the shaft-horses.

兩 服 上 裏 the inside pair are fine horses.

(d) To think of.

寤 寐 思 服 asleep or awake he thought of her.

(e) A quiver.

象 弭 魚 服 ivory-tipped bow and sealskin quiver.

葍 2.5.
2000　A turnip.

綍 2.5.　The ropes which are used to lift or carry coffins.
2001　Weighty, powerful.

執 綍 to hold the rope of the coffin.

踣 4.5. To stumble and fall prone. Stiff in death.
2002 Also read *po*².

踣 尸 a rigid corpse.

HA. (ㄏㄚ)

哈 1.5. Sound of laughter. Also read *ka*.
2003

哈 哈 大 笑 hearty laughter; a horse laugh.
哈³·巴 狗 Pekingese dog.

(a) Read *ka* in 哈 喇 for *kara*, i.e., black, and now used to denote Russian woollen cloth.

哈 密 Hamil or Khamil, a town in Sinkiang.
(b) *ha*³. Surname; for transliterations.
哈 佛 Harvard.

HAI. (ㄏㄞ)

亥 4 The last of the twelve branches 地支: 9—11 p.m.
2004 The north.

亥 初 between 9 and 10 p.m.
亥 市 markets held on days having this cyclical character.
亥 年 every twelfth year in the cycle, beginning with the twelfth.
亥 時 the period from 9 to 11 p.m.
亥 月 the 10th lunar month.
亥 豕 to confound *hai* and *shih*— used of typographical errors and similar things.

孩 2 A child, children; young of animals. N.B. 小孩兒 *hsiao³-har²* is
2005 a commoner form than 孩兒 in cases marked "x".

孩 乳 a babe in arms not yet weaned.
ˣ 孩·兒 or 孩·子 a child, a son.
ˣ 孩·兒·似·的 childish.
孩·兒 兵 boisterous play of children.
⁵孩·兒 參 a kind of ginseng especially valued,—it roughly resembles the human form; usually it is not genuine.
ˣ 孩·兒 撒 潑 to behave like a child when in a peevish fit.
孩 氣 未 除 his childishness still remains—although in years he is a man.

ˣ 孩·兒 氣 or 孩·子·脾·氣 childishness; playfulness.
孩·兒 茶 cutch; catechu.
¹⁰孩·兒 菊 a very pale pink chrysanthemum.
ˣ 孩·兒 見·識 the outlook of a child, inexperienced.
孩·兒 面 a child's complexion— variety of jade of this colour, very valuable.
孩 娃 or 耍 孩·兒 dolls.
孩 嬰 or 嬰 孩 infants.
¹⁵孩·子 淘 氣 mischievous behaviour of children.
孩·子 爹 the child's father—said by a woman of her husband when speaking about him.
孩 孺 a young child.
孩 幼 the young and tender.
孩 抱 a child in arms.
²⁰ 雖 在 孩 抱 although merely a child.
孩 提 之 童 young children; babies in arms.
孩 稚 children.
孩 虎 a young tiger.
孩 童 a lad.
²⁵無 殺 孩 蟲 do not kill the immature insects.

(a) Laughter of a child.

小 兒²知 孩 笑 a child knows how to laugh.

恑 4 Sorrowful, anxious.
2006

恑 病 to be very ill.
恑 眼 to suffer with one's eyes.

祴 4 A deity. To raise.
2007

頦 2 The chin. Also read *k'o*¹.
2008

頦 皮 fur on the neck of an animal.
頦 頷 or 頦 頰 or 頰 巴 頦 the chin.

駭 4 To terrify; startled. Also read *hsie* or *heh*.
2009

駭 形 to look scared.
駭 怕 to be frightened.

駭 慌 scared.
駭 愕 startling; amazing.
⁵駭 汗 break into perspiration from fear.
駭 浪 fearful waves.
駭 然 suddenly alarmed.
駭 異 strange; frightful; horrid.
駭 突 to run away in fright.
¹⁰駭 羞 abashed; ashamed.
駭 視 to stare in amazement.
駭 詫 to astonish.
可 駭 appalling; frightful.

骸 2 The bones of the legs, bones of the body. Dry
2010 bones. Also read *hsieh*².

骸 骨 a skeleton; human bones.
骸 骼 dry bones.
六 骸 the limbs, head and trunk.

(a) The form of the body.

形 骸 objective existence; the body itself.

䆪 3 A wine-jar.
2011

醢 3 Minced and hashed meat. Pickled meat. To mince.
2012

醢 蝦 pickled shrimps.
醢 醬 pickled condiments.
斬 爲 肉 醢 a curse—may you be made into mincemeat.
烹 醢 boiled alive—ancient punishment.

咍 1 The sound of laughter. Happy. Interjection of as-
2013 tonishment.

咍 臺 to snore.
歡 咍 pleased.

海 3 The sea. Maritime. Vast; large; extensive. Marshes.
2014 Used to describe an accumulation of things.

海 上 保 險 marine insurance.
海 上 法 maritime law.
海 上 貿 易 or 海 商 maritime commerce.
海 上 飛 機 sea-plane.
⁵海 不 揚 波 there was no rough sea—when the sages lived, in the golden age.
↓海 員 Seaman, sailor.

海 人 strangers, men from over-seas.

海 僑 overseas emigrants.

海 內 within the seas—China.

四 海 之 內 within the four seas—China; everywhere.

[10]海 南 Hainan.

海 參 sea-slugs.

海 口 a seaport; estuary; a big mouth; a boaster.

誇 海 口 to boast; to brag.

海 味 marine delicacies.

[15]海 嘯 noise of a submarine earth-quake with tidal wave and boil-ing up of the seas.

海 國 maritime countries.

海 圖 a sea-chart.

海 塘 a bund or sea-wall.

海 外 beyond the seas; a foreign land; anything very strange.

[20]海 外 電 費 rates for sending cablegrams.

海 子 a pond, a city moat; park in the imperial city in Peking.

海 宇 within the land—China.

海 客 sailor, seaman; sea traveller.

海 岔 straits, wider than 峽 See below.—27.

[25]海 岸 the coast, shore, beach.

海 岸 線 coast-line.

海 峽 straits, narrower than 岔 see above.—24.

海 峽 殖 民 地 The Straits Settle-ments.

海 島 an island.

[30]海 嶠 high, rocky coast.

海 市 蜃 樓 a mirage; strange, unreal appearance; imaginary.

海 師 a sailor.

海 帶 edible seaweed, kelp.

海 底 the bottom of the sea; secret.

[35]海 底 撈 針 to fish up a needle from the bottom of the sea—impossible task.

海 底 潛 水 艇 submarine boats.

海 底 無 線 電 信 submarine wireless messages.

海 底 電 線 submarine cables.

海 戰 naval warfare.

[40]海 扇 a scallop shell.

海 拔 height above sea-level.

海 捕 to arrest wherever found.

海 損 sea-damage.

海 損 貨 sea-damaged goods.

[45]海 星 or 海 燕 or 海 盤 車 the star-fish—the second also means sea-birds. See below,—91.

海 景 seascape.

海 松 a pine.

海 枯 石 爛 when the seas dry up and the rocks decay—an oath of unchanging fidelity.

海 棠 樹 or 海 棠 果ㄦ or 海 紅 the cherry-apple.

[50]海 權 sea-power.

制 海 權 command of the seas.

海 概 collectively; altogether.

海 氛 sea-mists—pirates.

海 水 不 可 斗 量 you cannot measure the sea with a bushel—do not estimate the abilities of a great man with a small mea-sure.

[55]海 水 浴 sea-bathing.

海 汊 tidal creeks.

海 洋 the ocean.

海 洋 州 Oceania.

海 浪 平 靜 the sea was calm.

[60]海 浪 𣷱 𣷱 the roaring of the waves.

海 流 sea-currents.

海 源 the fountains of the deep.

海 港 a harbour.

海 港 檢 疫 quarantine of a sea-port.

[65]海 潮 the sound of the tide—Buddhist priests chanting.

海 濤 billows.

海 灘 漲 出 之 地 land gradually left by the sea.

海 灣 a bay.

海 牛 the sea-cow or manatee.

[70]海 狗 or 海 豹 the seal; sea-leo-pard.

海 狸 the beaver.

海 猪 or 海 豚 the dolphin or porpoise.

海 獅 the sea-lion.

海 王 星 the planet Neptune.

[75]海 產 or 海 貨 marine products.

海 百 合 the sea-lily, crinoid.

海 碗 a very large bowl for food.

海 禁 大 開 open for trade, re-strictions removed.

海 程 sea travel.

[80]海 綿 or 海 絨 sponge.

海 線 電 報 cablegram.

海 罵 to abuse everybody.

海 股 a gulf.

海 腰 a strait.

[85]海 膽 or 海 猬 the sea-urchin.

海 船 之 共 質 joint-ownership of sea-going vessels. (legal).

海 船 衝 突 collision between sea-going vessels.

海 若 god of the seas.

海 菜 agar-agar, an edible seaweed.

[90]海 葵 sea-anemone.

海 燕 sea-birds—petrels; also the star-fish. See above,—45.

海 藻 or 海 草 or 海 蘊 names for different kinds of seaweed.

海 虎 or 海 獺 sea-otter.

海 蛇 sea-serpents; some varieties of jelly-fish.

[95]海 蜇 sea-blubber; jelly-fish.

海 螺 or 海 波 a conch-shell.

海 行 to travel the seas; in current use.

海 表 beyond the seas.

海 西 Syria.

[100]海 角 天 涯 far-off—the horizon.

海 說 or 海 外 奇 談 a sea-yarn; a tall story.

海 象 the walrus.

海 賊 or 海 盜 pirates.

海 巡 coast-patrols against smug-glers.

[105]海 運 to transport by sea; to send tribute grain by sea.

海 運 業 sea-carrying trade.

海 邊 or 海 濱 or 沿 海 the sea-side, the shore, the coast.

海 里 a nautical mile.

海 量 or 海 涵 broad measure like the sea—indulgent, liberal-minded, generous; large capa-city for liquor, etc.

[110]海 關 Custom House.

海 關 人 員 customs employees.

海 關 公 署 Custom House.

海 關 稅 則 customs tariff.

海 關 稅 務 司 Commissioner of Customs.

[115]海 關 監 督 Superintendent of Customs.

海 關 巡 船 customs cruiser.

海 關 進 欵 customs receipts.

海 防 coast-defence.

海 防 艦 coast-defence vessels.

[120]海 險 sea-risk.

海 難 perils of the sea.

海 難 救 助 salvage at sea.

海 青 wide-sleeved garments—Buddhist priests' robes.

海 面 sea-level.

[125]海 風 sea-breeze; monsoons.

海 馬 the hippocampus; also the walrus.

海 鮮 fresh fish; marine delica-cies.

海 鰾 蛸 dried inner substance of the cuttle-fish.

海 鰻 sea-eels.

[130]海 鰡 a large kind of whale.

海 鳥 sea-birds generally.

海 鷗 sea-gulls.

海 鷹 the sea-eagle; osprey.

海 龍。王 The Dragon King of the Sea—Chinese Neptune.

[135] 北 海 Lake Baikal.

南 海 the South Seas, or South China Sea.

四 海 the four seas—China, also everywhere, liberal, great, etc.

苦 海 the bitter sea—this life.

裏 海 Caspian Sea.

[110] 青 海 Kokonor.

海 蔘 威 Vladivostock. (-shên[1]-)

(a) Terms relating to the navy are grouped below.

海 軍 the Navy.

海 軍 制 naval regime.

海 軍 部 Ministry of the Navy; Admiralty.

海 軍 部 長 Minister of the Navy.

[5] 海 軍 司 令 處 Admiralty.

海 軍 總 司 令 Commander-in-chief of the Navy.

海 軍 上 將 Admiral.

海 軍 中 將 Vice-Admiral.

海 軍 少 將 Rear-Admiral.

[10] 海 軍 上 (中, 少) 校 Captain, junior Captain and Commander.

海 軍 上 (中, 少) 尉 Lieutenant, sub-Lieutenant and midshipman.

海 軍 參 贊 Naval Attaché of a legation.

海 軍 學 校 Naval college.

海 軍 根 據 地 Naval base.

[15] 海 軍 裁 判 所 Admiralty Court.

海 軍 陸 戰 隊 marines.

(b) Used in transliteration.

海 克 脫 克 蘭 姆 hectogramme.

海 克 脫 立 脫 爾 hectolitre.

海 克 脫 米 突 hectometre.

海 牙 和 平 會 The Hague Conference.

海 洛 因 heroin.

害 [4] **To injure; to destroy. Injury. To suffer, to take a disease.**
2015

害。不 着 unable to injure; of no consequence. (-chao[2])

害 人 利 己 to benefit oneself at the expense of others.

害 人 卽 害 己 you injure yourself in injuring others.

害 傷 or 戕 害 to wound.

[5] 害 命 to take life; to murder.

害 心 or 殺 心 a malicious heart.

害 怕 to fear.

害。死 人 or 殺 害 to kill a person.

害 甚[2]。麼 怕 what are you afraid of?

[10] 害 病 to take a disease.

害 羞 disgraced; shy; sensitive to shame; ashamed.

害 羣 or 害 乘 injurious to society; detrimental to public interests.

害 臊 greatly ashamed; very bashful.

害 自 己 to injure oneself.

[15] 害。處 injuries; damages; injurious features.

害 蟲 injurious insects.

害 課 injurious to the revenue.

害 馬 from 害 羣 之 馬 a horse that injures the mob—one who acts in a way detrimental to public welfare.

傷 害 to injure.

[20] 利。害 severe, injurious, dangerous. 利 害 advantage and disadvantage.

有 害 hurtful.

殘 害 to do severe injury.

爲 害 不 淺 it does no little damage.

自 害 to injure oneself; to ruin one's career, etc.

[25] 要 害 之 處 important strategic posts.

謀 害 to brew mischief.

(a) Read *ho[2]*. **What? Which? When?**

害 澣 害 否 which shall be washed and which not?

HAN. (ㄏㄢ)

厂 [4]
2016
A cliff. Radical 27.

含 [2] **To hold in the mouth. Inter.** 函 **No. 2049, and** 涵 **No.**
2017 **2050.**

含 囈 to talk in one's sleep.

含 殮 to prepare a corpse for burial,—it was once the custom to place a gem in the mouth.

含 沙。的 gritty.

含 沙 射 影 to hold sand in the mouth and spurt it at others—to do evil maliciously.

[5] 含 珠 to hold a pearl in the mouth after death.

含 笑 to hold a laugh in the mouth, i.e., to smile; opening of flowers.

含 笑 花 the magnolia.

含 筆 to hold a pencil-tip in the mouth.

含。胡 or 含。糊 or 含。混 muddled; speaking indistinctly; to do things in a muddling manner.

[10] 含。著 to hold in the mouth. A. p. *hên[2]*

含 血 噴 人 to hold blood in the mouth and spurt it at others—malicious words to injure another; to cherish malicious purposes.

含 辛 茹 苦 to drink the bitter cup.

含 飴 to eat sweets.

(a) To contain, to cherish, to embody; full.

含 垢 忍 辱 to bear insult and obloquy with patience.

含 冤 to cherish a grievance.

含 冤 負 屈 to suffer an unjust wrong.

含 弘 光 大 the vast and all-embracing bright canopy.

[5] 含 德 to maintain one's natural goodness.

含 忍 to be patient with.

含 怒 or 含 忿 to cherish anger.

含 恨 to cherish resentment.

含 悲 to feel compassion.

[10] 含 愁。的 gloomy, sad.

含 春 to look happy.

含 烟 to hold the mist—beautiful, as of trees showing through the mists.

含 羞 to blush; to be bashful.

含 羞 帶 愧 bashful; shamefaced.

[15] 含 蓄 要 義 contains much that is suggestive; significant.

含 記 to bear in mind.

包 含 to contain; enclosed in.

海 含 to forgive.

(b) To restrain.

含 容 巽 順 forbearing and mild.

含 情 to restrain the emotions.

含 淚 to restrain tears.

哈 [2] A sound. To put in the mouth.
2018

哺 哈 to feed a baby.

琀 [4] Gems or pearls formerly put into the mouth of a corpse. See 含 No. 2017—2.
2019

瓵 [2] A water-jar with ears for carrying it.
2020

瓵 空 a drain or spout.
水 瓵 a sluice.
溝 瓵·子 drain-pipes.

谽 [1] A mouth or opening.
2021

谽 谺 entrance to a cave or to a gorge.

頷 [4] The chin; the jaws.
2022

頷 下 珠 a pearl under the chin—of a dragon,—something difficult to get at.
頷 車 the lower jawbone.
頷 頤 to move the jaws.
下 頷 尖 a sharp chin.
燕 頷 swallow's beak—a sharp point.
頤 頷 the chin, the jaws.

(a) Read *ngan*[2]. To shake the head.

頷 首 to nod assent.

旱 [4] Dry weather; drought. Dry land as opposed to water.
2023

旱 乾 drought.
旱 釐 金 *likin* tax on merchandise carried overland.
旱 地 dry land; road-travel.
旱 歉 米 如 珠 in times of drought grains of rice are like pearls.
[5] 旱 海 desert in Kansu.
旱 潦 drought and floods.
旱 烟 tobacco smoked in an ordinary pipe, as contrasted with 水 烟 that smoked in the water-pipe.
旱 獺 the tarbagan or Russian marmot, the carrier of plague in Manchuria.

旱 祭 sacrificial offerings in time of drought.
[10] 旱 稻 rice grown on dry land.
旱 荒 or 旱 災 drought.
旱 蝗 drought and locusts—calamities.
旱 道 or 旱 路 overland travelling.
走 旱 路 to travel by road.
[15] 起 旱 to start on a road-journey.
旱 雷 thunder without rain.
旱 風 a blasting, dry wind.
旱 魃 or 旱 母 the drought-demon—a dwarf who is said to be naked, and to move with incredible speed; he has an eye in the top of his head.
旱 魃 爲 虐 the drought-demon is very cruel.
[20] 久 旱 a prolonged drought.
天 旱 dry weather.
歲 旱 a year of drought.
連 年 大 旱 successive years of drought.

悍 [4] Cruel; ruthless; violent; fierce.
2024

悍 勇 cruel and fearless.
悍 婦 a shrew.
悍 室 or 悍 妻 a shrewish wife.
悍 忌 jealous and vindictive.
[5] 悍 急 fierce and rash; hasty.
悍 戇 好 鬬 the cruel and stupidly obstinate are fond of quarreling.
悍 戾 fierce and ruthless.
悍 梗 overbearing, masterful.
悍 潑 unabashed; bold.
[10] 悍 然 不 顧 fearless and careless.
悍 銳 cruel, resolute fighters.
悍 鷙 untameable; savage.
兇 悍 fierce and cruel.
強 悍 imperious; tyrannical.

扞 [4] To ward off; to defend. To forbid. u.f. 扞 No. 2027
2025

扞 禦 to guard against.
扞 大 患 to ward off a great calamity.

銲
釬 [4] To solder. Greaves.
2026

銲·上·他 solder·it on.
銲 口 or 銲 住 to solder.
銲 錫 solder.
電 銲 electric welding.

扞 [4] To ward off; to guard. An obstacle, a hindrance. Also read *kan*. u.f. 捍 No. 2025.
2027

扞 堅 strongly guarded.
扞 拒 to withstand; to oppose.
扞 格 an obstacle; to impede.
扞 格 不 入 conflicting; obstructed; unable to enter. Used to show the difficulty of cancelling a permission once granted. etc.
扞 禁 to prohibit.
扞 藏 to screen; to protect.
扞 衛 to guard; to protect.
扞 關 to guard a pass.

汗 [4] Perspiration.
2028

汗 下 ashamed—a sense of shame causes one to perspire, thus the expression comes to be used for shamefacedness.
汗 出 洽 背 wet through with perspiration.
汗 垢 dirt; perspiring and dirty.
[5] 汗 斑 dark spots on the skin supposed to be caused by obstructed perspiration.
汗 毛 the fine hairs on the body; also written 寒 毛.
汗 注 汪·的 perspiring freely.
汗 津 津·的 very freely perspiring.
汗 流 滿 面 the face covered with sweat.
[10] 汗 浴 sweat-bath.
汗 液 perspiration.
汗 濕 了 wet through with perspiration.
汗 濕 子 a sweater; inner shirt.
汗 牛 充 棟 (so many as) to make the oxen (bearing them) perspire and to fill (the house) to the rafters,—of numerous books.
[15] 汗 眩 eyes obscured by perspiration.
汗 腺 sweat-glands.
汗 衫 a shirt; an under-garment.
汗 酒 another name for 燒 酒, distilled spirits.

汗青 or 汗簡 to write on bamboo tablets; from the use of fire to sweat out the sap.

20 汗顏 shame, bashfulness. *See above.*—1.

汗馬功勞 sweating-horse merit—achievements in war.

一身冷汗 broken out into a cold perspiration.

發汗藥 sudorifics.

盜汗 night-sweats.

(a) A wide expanse of—as water. u.f. 瀚 No. 2043.

汗汗 a vast expanse of water.

汗漫 floods, wide expanse of water; irregular.

汗漫遊 to travel; to wander about.

(b) Read *han²*. u.f. Khan.

可汗 a Khan or Mongol chief.

犴 4　A wild dog, not very large. Read *an⁴*. A lock-up.
犴
2029

犴獄 or 犴牢 a village lockup.

矸 4　A rock or cliff.
2030

矸白玉 marble.

丹矸 cinnabar.

罕 3　Rare, strange, scarce, few.
2031

罕有 of rare occurrence.

罕漫 confused; indistinct.

罕物 a curiosity.

罕見 seldom seen; seldom noticed.

罕規 a strange custom.

罕言 reticent.

罕譬而喻 few illustrations—yet the listeners clearly understood—used of a lucid speaker or teacher.

希罕 rare, and therefore strange; to treasure.

(a) A flag.

雲罕 an ornamental flag.

(b) A net or snare.

罕車 a chariot carrying a net; eight stars in the constellation of Hydra, arranged like a net.

邗 2　An ancient place in the state of Wu 吳.
2032

邗州 ancient name for Yangchow.

邗溝 ancient canal, now part of the Grand Canal.

閈 4　The gate of a walled village; a village.
2033

同閈 of the same village.

里閈 walled villages.

頇 1　A large face.
2034

頇額 high forehead; bald.

顢頇 dawdling, dilatory; vacillating.

鼾 4　To snore.
2035

鼾睡 heavy sleep with snoring.

鼾齁 or 鼻鼾 to snore.

邯 2　Capital of the State of *Chao,* 趙.
2036

邯鄲 a district in Chihli.

邯鄲夢覺 a man named 盧生 had a dream wherein he married a handsome wife, gained wealth and official honours, etc., and died at 80 years of age—when he awoke the millet which was being prepared for his supper was not yet cooked.

邯鄲學步 to study at *Hantan,* as certain men did who lost all they knew before—used of following others and losing one's originality.

酣 1　Intoxicated. Merry, as with drink.
2037

酣中客 those infatuated with the desire for riches and honour.

酣呼 or 酣叫 noisily shouting, as when drunk.

酣娛 merry, as with drink.

酣放 unrestrained and free—of writing.

⁵酣春 the brightness of spring.

酣暢 cheerful, delightful—as a view, or literary style.

酣樂 unrestrained pleasure.

酣歌 drunken singing.

酣縱 unlimited appetite for intoxicants.

¹⁰酣興 the exhilaration of liquor.

酣謔 drunken joking.

酣讌 a banquet.

酣賞 following the inclinations for enjoyment.

酣酣 merry and lively with liquor; a delightful view; luxuriance of flowers, etc.

¹⁵酣酺 a convivial gathering.

酣醉 drunk.

酣飫 to drink to the full.

酣飲 to carouse.

(a) Deep, as sleep.

酣睡 a deep slumber.

睡·得很酣 I have slept very heavily.

(b) Fearless.

酣戰 a bloody conflict.

酣鬪 a long fierce fight.

暵 3.4.　Hot, dry and parched.
2038

漢 4　Name of a dynasty. Belonging to China. The Milky Way. The Han River. Hankow.
2039

漢·人 the men of Han—Chinese.

漢仗 figure; person.

漢兵 Chinese troops.

漢口 Hankow—lit:—the mouth of the Han.

⁵漢奸 traitor to China—a spy for foreigners, etc.

漢妝 the Chinese style of female dress.

漢·子 (he-) man; a brave fellow.

漢學 the school of classical studies under the *Han* dynasty;—sinology. [school; sinologist.

8½漢學家 a scholar of the aforesaid

漢官威儀 the usages of the *Han* regime—now used for:—the old regime.

¹⁰漢室 the house of *Han*—the dynasty of that name.

漢 文 Chinese writing; the emperor of the *Han* dynasty whose style was *Wen ti;* the writings of that dynasty.

漢 文 參 贊 or 漢 務 參 贊 Chinese secretary to a legation.

漢 族 or 漢 重 the Chinese race.

漢 書 a history of the Former or Western *Han* dynasty in 120 vols.

[15] 漢。朝 the *Han* dynasty. It lasted from 206 B.C.—A.D. 220.

漢 氣 a bold spirit.

漢 江 The River Han.

漢 津 or 雲 漢 or 銀 漢 or 天 漢 The Milky Way.

漢 滿 Chinese and Manchu.

[20] 漢 白 玉 a sort of white marble.

漢 碑 records of the *Han* dynasty.

漢 禮 Chinese fashions and etiquette.

漢 璽 name given to 劉 臻, who was expert in the literature of that period.

漢 話 the Chinese spoken language.

[25] 漢 軍 descendants of natives of north China, who joined the Manchu invaders against the *Ming* dynasty.

好 漢 a brave man—sometimes used ironically.

妻 養 漢 a man who lives on his wife.

老 漢 an old man.

(a) Used in transliterating.

漢 堡 Hamburg.

漢 諾 威 Hanover.

熯[4] Freely burning. To roast; to dry.
2040

熯 焚 a great conflagration.

燥 萬 物 莫 熯 乎 火 nothing dries things like fire.

(a) Read *han*[3]. To respect.

我 孔 熯 矣 I have great respect for.

韓[2] A fence. Name of a star. A small feudal State. Old name for Korea.
2041

韓 弘 輿 疾 討 賊 *Han Hung,* though ill, took a chariot and went to punish the rebels.

韓 愈 or 韓 文 公 famous poet and philosopher of the *T'ang* dynasty, A.D. 768 —824.

韓 湘 子[3] one of the eight immortals of Taoism, reputed to be grandnephew of the above.

韓 非 子[3] a philosopher of 3rd century B.C.

三 韓 the Liaotung Peninsula—Korea.

翰[4] A pencil or pen.
2042

翰 扎 or 翰 書 a letter or document.

翰·林 *Hanlin,* the highest literary degree of the old system.

翰。林 院 the *Hanlin Academy;* the former College of Literature at Peking.

點 翰·林 to be nominated as a *Hanlin.*

[5] 翰 筆 a pencil.

翰 菀 a *Hanlin* graduate.

文 翰 a polished style of writing.

華 翰 your favour of ....

墨 翰 writing materials; pens and ink.

(a) Red feathers of the pheasant. To fly high.

翰 音 登 於 天 the sound of the cockcrow reaches to heaven—the first two characters are also used for a cock.

翰 飛 戾 天 it flies up to heaven.

(b) u.f. 幹 No. 3235. A support.

維 周 之 翰 the support of *Chou.*

(c) u.f. 2043. The Desert called Gobi.

翰 海 Gobi Desert. (*gobi* really means a desert, so that it is not strictly correct to say Gobi Desert, but it is used conventionally.)

瀚[4] The northern sea. The ocean.
2043

瀚 海 the Gobi Desert.

瀚 海 石 petrified wood from the desert.

曲 籍 繁 瀚 —the canons of Buddhism—are a trackless wilderness.

浩 瀚 the vast expanse of ocean.

鷳[4] A white pheasant.
2044

喊[3] To call; to halloo.
2045

喊·他 來 call him to come here.

喊 叩 to implore.   S. dial.

喊 告 or 喊 控 to call for redress; to accuse.

喊 叫 to shout, as in anger.

[5] 喊 呼 to shout.

喊 嚷·起·來 began to shout and create a disturbance.

喊 寃 to shout one's grievance along the streets until the magistrate takes action.

喊 拏 to call out to people to stop a man, as a thief.

喊 捉 賊 Stop thief!

[10] 喊 救 to cry for help.

喊 殺 連 天 the battle-cry reached the heavens.

喊 苦 bitter wailing.

憾[4] Vexation; remorse; regret. To be dissatisfied with. Hatred.
2046

憾 事 a matter for regret.

憾 怨 vexation; resentment.

憾 恚 resentment

憾 恨 deep resentment; extreme vexation.

[5] 憾 悔 deep regret.

抱 憾 to deplore.

抱 憾 終 身 a lifelong regret.

死 而 無 憾 to die without regret.

缺 憾 disappointed.

撼[4] To move, to shake.
2047

撼 動 or 撼 搖 to shake; to move.

撼 山 岳,泣 鬼 神 shakes the mountains and hills, and moves the spiritual beings to tears—of moving writings, etc.

撼 振 人 心 excites the minds of men.

撼 膝 to rock the knees.

[5] 撼 鈴 to shake a bell.

撼 頓 to shake and topple over.

風 撼 shaken by the wind.

↑ 動·撼 to move.

寒² 2048   Cold, wintry. Poor.

寒 不 可 支 unbearably cold.
寒 不 擇 衣 a cold man is not "choosy" about his clothing.
寒 乞 reduced to beggary.
寒 人 or 寒 賤 in humble circumstances.
⁵寒 假 winter vacation.
寒 來 暑 往 cold comes and heat goes—the alternations of the seasons; a year; ague.
寒 俊 or 寒 畯 or 寒 素 a scholar in poor circumstances.
寒 儒 or 寒 士 a poor scholar.
寒 具 ancient name for a kind of fried cake, a sort of doughnut; they could be kept, so were used for the cold food observance See—56.
¹⁰寒 冰 地 獄 or 阿 羅 羅 the frozen hell.
寒 冷 or 寒 凍 or 寒 涼 bitterly cold.
寒 涼 藥 cooling medicines.
寒 劑 freezing mixture.
寒﹒噤 the shivers.
¹⁵寒 天 cold days; a Japanese name for agar-agar, as it is made into jelly in cold weather.
寒 女 daughter of a poor man.
寒 客 the cold visitor—the *La mei* or *Chimonanthus fragrans.*
寒 家 a poor family.
寒 微 poor with no power or influence.
²⁰寒 帶 arctic circle; frigid zone.
寒 心 afraid; "the blood running cold."
寒 房 a humble dwelling.
寒 族 our poor clan.
寒 暑 cold and heat.
²⁵寒 暑 表 a thermometer.
寒 暄 的 套 話 or 叙 寒 溫 commonplaces of conversation about the weather.
寒 森 森﹒的 cold and dull.
寒﹒毛 the fine hair on the skin.
寒﹒氣 cold air; cold.
³⁰寒 沍 freezing.
寒 流 polar currents; a poor scholar.
寒 溫 or 寒 暄 cold and warm; adversity and success; the weather.
寒 灰 or 死 灰 cold ashes of a fire—poverty.

寒 烈 biting, severe cold.
³⁵寒 烟 cold mists arising from the rivers.
寒 燠 cold and heat—the climate.
寒 玉 the bamboo.
寒 瓜 = 西﹒瓜 the water-melon.
寒 生 a poor student.
⁴⁰寒 疾 a chill, a cold.
寒 臬 the mina or mynah.
寒 盟 to go back on an oath.
寒 突 無 晨 煙 the cold chimney sends forth no smoke in the early mornings—poverty-stricken.
寒 窓 誦 讀 studying at a cold window—the life of poor students.
⁴⁵寒 舍 or 寒 門 my poor home; my family.
寒 芒 cold rays, as light from the stars on a cold night.
寒 苦 poverty-stricken.
寒 蟬 the cicada—it is silent in cold weather, so the expression means a man who can keep his mouth closed.
寒 象 cold phenomena, as seen in northern regions.
⁵⁰寒 鄉 a poor district; the colder districts of the north.
寒﹒酸 or 寒﹒痠 or 寒﹒塵 the poverty-stricken circumstances of poor scholars. 寒﹒塵 ugly.
寒 雨 a bitterly cold rain.
寒 露 *Cold Dew*—a solar term from October 8 to 22; the 9th lunar month.
寒 顫 shivering with cold.
⁵⁵寒 風 the north wind.
寒 食 節 the day before *Ch'ing ming* 清 明, when only cold provisions are eaten.
寒 餕 or 寒 餓 cold and hungry.
傷 寒 typhoid.
嚴 寒 severe cold.
⁶⁰孤 寒 destitute and alone.
打 寒 戰 to shudder.
發 寒 病 malaria.

函 圅 凾 } ² 2049   To contain; to envelop. The 3rd form is not strictly correct.

函 丈 a space of ten (Chinese) square feet, for master and

pupil—hence:—a teacher, my teacher.
函 丈 之 下 at the feet of the teacher—I, who am your pupil.
函 之 如 海 enveloping it like the sea.
函 洞 or 涵 洞 a railway-tunnel.

(a) A letter.

函 件 or 信 函 or 書 函 a letter.
函 商 to consult by letter.
函 托 or 函 請 or 函 懇 to request by letter.
函 授 學 校 a correspondence-school.
⁵函 授 科 correspondence-course.
函 復 reply by letter.
函 稱 to state by letter; the despatch says....
函 索 卽 寄 will be forwarded immediately on request by letter.
函 致 or 函 達 or 函 知 or 函 布 to inform by letter.
¹⁰函 詢 to inquire by letter.
函 請 核 示 request for instructions by letter.
函 送 send with a note.
函 開 stating in a letter that ....
修 函 to write a letter.
¹⁵專 函 I write this specially.
手 函 autograph-letter.
華 函 or 吉 函 or 尊 函 your valued favour.

(b) Armour. u.f. 錏 No. 2051.

函 人 an armourer.
函 甲 armour.

(c) Magnanimous.

函 容 patiently; generous and forbearing.
函 忍 to be patient with.

(d) Read *hsien²*. A case or cover for books. A box.

劍 函 case for a sword.
鏡 函 case for a mirror.

涵² 2050   To submerge; to soak.

涵 泳 to swim about, as fishes.
涵 沉 submerged, sunk.
涵 洞 a sluice or weir; a railway-tunnel.
涵 淹 to lie hid at the bottom of the water.

涵 濡 imbued with.
涵 蓄 deep; abstruse.

(a) Lenient; magnanimous.

涵 容 to contain; liberal-minded.
涵 煦 to cherish and nourish.
涵 量 magnanimous.
涵 養 to keep one's temper; to cherish a virtue; kindly, patient; to nourish and care for.
包 涵 lenient.

(b) To hold in the mouth.

涵 咀 義 味 to masticate and relish the flavour.

鋗[2]
2051　Armour.

鋗 人 an armourer.
鋗 甲 armour.

歛[4] To desire; to ask for a thing playfully. Distinguish
2052　斂 No. 3999.

憨[1]
2053　Foolish, silly.
　　　Thick (of rods, etc.)

憨 厚 simple and honest.
憨 寢 deep, heavy slumber.
憨 態 a silly disposition.
憨 生 silly.
[5]憨 癡 idiotic, silly.
憨 笑 silly giggling.
憨 頑 childish.
憨 頭 郎 a crazy person.
憨 頭 憨 腦 stupid and dull.

閈[4]
　　　A threshold.
2054

門 閈 door-sill.

HANG. (ㄏㄤ)

吭[2.3.] The throat, usually of
2055　birds.

杭[2] A large barge. To cross
2056　a stream. Hangchow.

杭 綢 silks from Hangchow.

杭 州 Hangchow, the capital of Chekiang; accounted one of the most beautiful cities in China.

沆[3] Mist, fog. A vast expanse
2057　of fog.

沆 莽 a marshy waste.
沆 瀁 deep and vast—as a great lake.
沆 瀣 a smoky mist.
沆 碭 white mists.

笐[1] Bamboos placed across
2058　wooden frames on which grain may be stored in damp climates.

航[2] Two boats lashed together.
2059　To sail, to navigate.

航 務 大 監 Chief Inspector of Navigation.
航 業 shipping-business.
航 權 sea-power.
航 海 to navigate.
[5]航 海 信 號 navigating signals of steamers when meeting each other.
航 海 學 the art of navigation.
航 海 家 navigators.
航 海 日 誌 the log-book.
航 海 日 誌 板 the log-board.
[10]航 海 曆 or 航 海 通 書 Nautical Almanac.
航 海 自 由 freedom of the seas.
航 海 飛 船 a supermarine flying-ship.
航 海 駕 駛 navigation.
航 空 aviation.
[15]航 空 事 務 處 Board of Aviation.↓航 空 學 aeronautics.
航 空 事 業 aviation as a profession or a business.
航 空 學 校 school of aviation.
航 空 線 air-ways.
航 空 署 Air-service Department.
[20]航 空 術 art of aviation.　　　[郵
航 空 運 寄 air-mail service.＝航
航 船 a passenger-boat which plies between certain places at regular intervals; legal term for ships, other than those belonging to the government.
航 行 to navigate.
航 路 or 航 線 shipping-routes; trade-routes.
↑航 空 界 sphere of the air.

---

[25]航 路 圖 a sea-chart.
航 路 標 記 beacons, buoys, light-houses, etc.
↑航 空 母 艦 aircraft carrier.

頏[2]
2060　To fly down.

頡 頏 fluttering up and down of birds.

硿[1] Noise of stones rolling
　　　down. To ram the earth for
2061　foundations. A.w. 夯

硿 歌 song of workmen when driving piles, or digging foundations.
硿 磅 rumbling sound of rolling stones.
硿 號 signal given by leader to pile-drivers and those who dig foundations.
打 夯 to drive piles.

HAO. (ㄏㄠ)

好[3] Good, excellent; well; su-
2062　perior; right, etc.

好 不 好 will it do? Are you well? Is it good?
好 事 good deeds; works of charity. *See below* E. 1.
好 人 a good man; a "soft" character.
好 人 難 做 it is not easy to be a good man—there will always be those who criticise and are not satisfied with him.
[5]好 使 usable; quite suitable for use, as a pen, etc.
好 兆 a good omen.
好 吃 good to eat; palatable.
好 合 a good match in marriage.
好 哇 Are you well? How do you do?
[10]好 名 a good name. *See below* E. 5.
好 命 a favourable lot in life.
好 天 a fine day; good weather.
好 好 的 quite good; whole; deliberately; quietly.
好 妙 excellent; fine; clever!
[15]好 小 子 said in praise of a man's ability and skill, etc., generally with ironical hints that the ability is used rather wrongfully.

好 彩 氣 good fortune.
好·得 利·害 exceedingly good.
好·得 很 very good indeed.
好 心 不 得 好 報 goodheartedness often meets with no recompense.
[20] 好 心°腸 sympathetic; kindly disposed.
好 性·情 a kindly disposition.
好 意 or 好 心 a good idea; a friendly feeling.
好 手 an adept; clever workman; clever fellow.
好 手 脚 clever; sprightly; apt; good workmanship.
[25] 好 日·子 a lucky day.
好·是 好 it is well enough, but ...
好·是 好·就·是 太 貴 these are very nice, but really they are too dear.
好 景·況 a pleasant prospect; good circumstances
好 望 角 Cape of Good Hope.
[30] 好 極·了 exceedingly good. Fine! That's capital!
好°歹 good and bad; common sense; anyhow; right or wrong; come what may; interests; quality.
好°歹 不 知·道 not to know when one is well off; to take leave of one's senses.
好 歹 不 等 good and bad are not equal;—there are various qualities.
好 歹 給 我 一 點 體·面 right or wrong, you must give me a little face in the matter.
[35] 不 知 好 歹 not discriminating; "does not know when to get out of the wet."
好 死 a good death—natural, not violent.
好 消·息 good news.
好 漢·子 a manly fellow; a true man.
好 燒 it burns well—as fuel or a stove.
[40] 好 用 good for use; suitable.
好 看 or 受 看 good to look at; handsome—used also fig.
好 種 (chung[3]) good seed.
好 端 端·的 everything peaceful; all well; all as it should be.
好 結 果 good results.
[45] 好 缺 or 好 官 a lucrative post.
好 聽 pleasant to listen to; good to hear about.
好 脾·氣 a good temper.

好 色 good complexion; beautiful face. See below—E. 18.
好·處 advantage; benefit; profit; kindnesses; attention; merit.
[50] 好 話 a complimentary remark; persuasion.
好 說 you compliment me; very kind of you to say so.
好 貨 不 賤 fine goods are not cheap.
好 身 手 strong and masterful.
好 造·化 good fortune.
[55] 好 逑 a good match—"fortunate union."
好 道 the proper course; the right way.
好 音 good news.
好 風·俗 a good custom.
好 風·水 a good site, in accordance with rules of geomancy, as for a grave or a house, etc.
[60] 叫 好 to applaud.
買 好 to purchase praise by charity, etc.
討 好 ingratiating.

(a) An adverb—well, exceedingly, better, extremely. Superlative.

好 久 a long time.
好·了 finished; all right; ready; it is better now; he is well; that'll do, etc.
　　不 好·了 exclamation of dismay—when things get to a crisis.
好·了·沒·有 Is it finished or not? Is it any better? Have you finished?
[5] 好·些 or 好·一·些 a little better; improving.
好 些 (個) a great many.
好 似 or 好·像 or 好·比 very similar; as if; very much like.
好·像·是 as though it were ....; very much as if.
好 半 天 quite a long time.
[10] 好 哄 easily deceived; gullible.
好·在 fortunately ....; happily...
好 大 very large.
好 大 架·子 pompous and self-sufficient bearing.
好 多 very many. ＝許 多
[15] 好 幾 次 (or 回) a good few times; on many occasions.
好 打 a good thrashing.
好 晦·氣 what bad luck!
好 熱 extremely hot.
好·生 別 跌 倒 be careful lest you fall down.

[20] 好·生 奇 怪 what an exceedingly strange thing!
好 笑 laughable.
好 費 事 very troublesome; not at all easy. See below. B. 3.

(b) Indicates irony, generally followed by a negative.

好 不 疼 it doesn't hurt, O no, not at all! meaning that it hurts considerably.
好 不 爲 難 exceedingly difficult.
好 不 費 事 very troublesome indeed.
好 不 辛 苦 extremely distressing.
好 容·易 How easy! i.e., not at all easy.

(c) Causative.

好 去 拏·他 that one may apprehend him.
好 叫 so that; in order that.
好 回 話 that I may return an answer.

(d) On good terms with.

好 主 好 客 on good terms with each other.
好 聚 好 散 able to get on well together.
好 說 話 affable, easy to get on with. See below E. 21.
相 好 on friendly terms.

(e) Read hao[4]. To love; to be fond of; to be addicted to.

好 事 fond of meddling; mischief making; pettifogging; full of tricks. See above.—2.
好 交 friendly.
好 勝 love of pre-eminence.
好 吃 懶 做 gluttonous and lazy —good-for-nothing.
[5] 好 名 to love fame. See above.—10.
好 問 難 fond of heckling.
好 善 惡 惡 love the good and hate the evil.
好 嘴 fond of talk; loquacious.
好 奇 full of curiosity.
[10] 好 學 given to study.
好 強 love of pre-eminence.
好 施 散·的 philanthropic.
好 武 藝 addicted to military pursuits.
好 氣 touchy; spirited; easily offended.
[15] 好 淫 亂 or 好 嫖 given to debauchery.

好生之德 love for the welfare of living things; the virtue of loving to produce things, in creation.

好臣其所敎 fond of giving office to those whom they have taught.

好色 fond of women. *See above* —48.

好花錢 fond of spending money.

20 好行小慧 fond of doing things that demand a little cleverness.

好說話 fond of talking. *See above* D. 3.

好諛悅色 fond of flattery and beauty.

好謀而成者也 one who is fond of arranging his plans and then carrying them out.

好財 covetous.

25 好酒 given to wine.

好閒 lazy; lounging.

好閒遊 fond of strolling about.

好非人 fond of fault-finding.

好高 love to have the pre-eminence.

嗃 [1] Voice of anger. Also read *hsiao*[1]. Vast, spacious.
2063

嗃然 boundless.

號
号 [4]   A mark, a sign; a designation. A number. A name or style. A business house.
2064

號·上個記·號 to mark; to brand.

號主 head of a firm.

號令 a word of command; an order.

號召 to summon.

5 號叫 a shout of command.

號單 or 號照 a certificate, as of registry, etc.

號外 an extra-special number, as of a paper.

號家 a banker.

號房 the registry office of a *yamen;* station for sentries.

10 號數 a register number.

號旗 signal-flags.

號燈 signal-lamps; steamer-lights.

號碼 a number, as of a telephone; marks, etc.

號礮 signal-gun.

15 號稱 designation; is said to be.

號筒 a trumpet or bugle.

號簿 a register of names.

號脈 to feel the pulse.

號船 a registered vessel.

20 號衣 uniform.

號角 a trumpet or horn.

號記 or 記號 signals.

號軍 the attendants at the old system of examinations.

號頭 a brand, a sign, distinguishing mark; head-workman; bugler; a carter; a bugle.

25 別號 the style of a man, the name by which he is generally known.

口號 a saying; a watchword, a slogan.

吹號 to blow a horn or trumpet.

國號 name of a dynasty.

字·號 name of a business house.

30 專號 special number, as of a magazine.

年號 style of the reign, often changed with the years in earlier dynasties. ⌈commas.

引號 quotation marks; inverted

感歎符號 mark of exclamation.

掛號 to register.

35 暗號 a password, secret sign.

法號 style of a Buddhist priest.

疑問符號 mark of interrogation.

符號 punctuation signs; indications; marks. ⌈name.

綽號 or 混號 or 外號兒 nick-

40 記·號 a mark or something to remember by.

豎旗爲號 to hoist signal-flags.

銀號 a bank.

(a) Read *hao*[2]. To call out; to wail.

號呼 to shout.

號咷 or 號哭 to wail; bitter weeping.

號嗁 to scream, as a bird; to crow, as a cock.

號天 to call on Heaven for aid.

號泣于昊天 to invoke High Heaven with tears and cries.

耗
耗 [4]   To waste, to destroy, to diminish; hence it came to mean, a rat.
2065

耗乾·了 completely wasted; boiled dry.

耗人貨財 to squander the wealth of the nation.

耗去一寸 diminished by an inch —of water.

耗土 poor land.

5 耗·子 a rat.

耗得精光 to squander until all is gone.

耗損 to destroy; to waste.

耗散其眞 to undermine the constitution.

耗斁下土 wasting and ruining our country.

10 耗減 to diminish—as taxes and levies.

耗盡·了 all wasted—as an inheritance.

耗磨日 16th of the 1st lunar month.

耗磨日·子 to waste time.

耗竭 drained dry, said of ricefields.

15 耗米 extra allowance of tribute-rice to make up for wastage on the way.

耗羨 extra silver demanded by officials in charge of taxes, to make up the loss in melting.

耗·費 to squander; to waste; loss in value or weight.

耗銀·子 inferior silver.

傷耗 loss or damage.

20 加耗 to make up a deficiency.

視年之豐耗 according to the year, whether prosperous or poor.

鼠耗 loss by rats.

(a) News, etc.

耗息 or 音耗 news; rumours.

噩耗 evil tidings.

(b) Read *mao*[1]. Confused.

耗亂 numerous and confused.

(c) Read *mao*[2]. None; exhausted.

靡有孑遺耗矣 not a solitary man was left; utterly destroyed.

毫 [2]   The ten-thousandth part of an ounce 兩. An atom. The down on plants. An intensive, especially before negatives. Distinguish 豪 No. 5336.
2066

毫不容情 he will make no allowances.

毫不記 not taking into account.

毫不隱瞞 not the slightest concealment.

毫 末 minute particles; the least thing.

[5] 毫 末 事 petty trivialities.

毫 楮 Chinese brush and paper.

毫 毛 soft hairs on the body.

↑ 毫 子³ dime. (Cantonese)

毫 無 not the slightest.

[10] 毫 無 可 取 not a single good point.

毫 無 權 柄 not the least authority.

毫 無 相 干 no connections whatever.

毫 無 紀 律 without any discipline at all.

毫 素 pen and silk — w r i t i n g - materials.

[15] 毫 芒 the very least particle.

毫 釐 不 差 not the least error.

毫 釐 千 里 abbreviated from a phrase which means:—the least divergence in the beginning will lead many miles astray.

毫 釐 尺 or 奇 零 尺 vernier.

毫 釐 有 差 just the slightest error. (-ch'a¹)

[20] 毫 髮 之 多 very trifling.

濡 毫 to wet the tip of the pencil.

白 毫 茶 Pekoe tea, from the white down on the buds.

秋 毫 an autumn hair, or down on plants—the veriest trifle.

豪 ²
2067　Martial, brave. Gay.

豪 侈 wasteful extravagance and gaiety.

豪 俠 courageous brave; a redresser of wrongs; a knight-errant.

豪 傑 a hero.

豪 光 sudden flash; dazzling glory.

[5] 豪 制 oppressive and tyrannical.

豪 力 having power and influence.

豪 士 a man of outstanding talents.

豪 奪 forcible seizure.

豪 奴 bullying underlings.

[10] 豪 宗 or 豪 姓 a powerful clan.

豪 客 a robber.

豪 家 or 豪 門 powerful families.

豪 富 very wealthy.

豪 強 or 豪 右 violent; overbearing.

[15] 豪 怀 extravagance and luxury.

豪 恣 unrestrained dissipation.

豪 放 unrestrained; v i g o r o u s; virile.

豪 橫 tyrannical; overbearing.

豪 民 a martial, brave people.

[20] 豪 氣 pluck; bravery; heroism.

豪 猾 violent; lawless characters.

豪 臣 powerful ministers of State.

豪 興 exhilarated.

豪 舉 heroic plans or measures.

[25] 豪 華 luxurious; gay and extravagant.

豪 蕩 unbridled licence.

豪 邁 great, magnanimous; unrestrained.

豪 雄 heroic; virile.

豪 飲 deep drinking.

[30] 豪 馬 a splendid horse.

土 豪 local bullies.

白 浪 豪 壯 the white waves foaming in their strength.

(a) The porcupine.

豪 猪 a porcupine.

(b) u.f. 毫 preceding. Downy, etc.

豪 芥 or 豪 芒 hairs—minute and trifling.

豪 釐 the least trifle.

豪 端 the tip of a brush.

壕 ²
2068　2070　The ditch around a city wall; a moat. Inter. 濠 No. 2070.

壕 塹 架 吊 橋 let down the draw-bridge over the moat.

壕 溝 a ditch or trench.

城 壕 the moat around a city.

戰 壕 a trench in warfare.

漏 壕 to dig a trench.

防 空 壕 air raid shelter.

攭 ²
2069　To compare; to estimate.

攭 較 to make comparisons.

濠 ²
2070　A moat or trench. Inter. 壕 No. 2068.

濠 溝 a trench or ditch.

通 濠 to clear out a drain or ditch.

蠔 ²
2071　An oyster.

蠔 塘 an oyster-bed.

蠔 山 oyster-spat.

蠔 殼 oyster-shells.

蠔 油 oyster-sauce—a native preparation.

蠔 鼓 dried oysters.

昊 ⁴
2072　Clear summer sky. Vast; grand. The Power that rules in the heavens.

昊 天 the vast heavens; Imperial Heaven—it seems to be used both of the heavens in their expanse, and of Heaven as having a ruling personality.

昊 天 上 帝 The Sovereign on high in the vast heavens.

昊 天 罔 極 as vast as the boundless heavens—a parent's love.

昊 天 金 闕 the golden palace of the vast heavens.

悠 悠 昊 天，曰 父 母 且 "O vast and distant Heaven, who art called our parent"!

昊 慈 Heaven's compassion.

昊 昊 然 bright.

嗥 嗅 嚎 ²
2073　The roaring of wild beasts. To howl, to wail, to bawl.

嗥 啕 to wail, to bawl.

嗥 嗥 聲 a roaring or bawling.

暤 ⁴
2074　Bright, brilliant. Inter. next.

皞 皡 ⁴
2075　Bright; brilliant. Inter. preceding and 昊 No. 2072. The second form is correctly written as below.

皞 皞 如 也 contented; satisfied.

皞 皞 氣 象 a contented and prosperous condition.

太 皞 dynastic title of the legendary emperor *Fu Hsi* 伏 羲 about 2953 B.C.

少 皞 dynastic title of the legendary emperor *Chin T'ien* 金 天 about 2597 B.C.

晧 ⁴
2076　Bright; luminous; hoary. u.f. 皓 No. 2078.

浩 [4]
Great; grand.
2077

浩劫 a great disaster or calamity —strictly a vast period; the former meaning comes from a misapprehension of the word 劫.

浩博 extensive; wide-embracing.
浩壤 a large tract of land.
浩大 very great.
[5]浩歌 to lift up the voice in song.
浩歎 to heave a deep sigh.
浩浩滔天 —the waters—dashed against the sky.
浩浩蕩蕩 exceedingly great.
浩茫 vast expanse of water.
[10]浩渺 vast expanse of water extending into the distance.
浩然 overwhelming; on a large scale; without hesitation.
浩然之氣 the natural greatness of a soul; magnanimous. "passion-nature" *Legge*.
浩然而去 to leave quickly.
浩繁 or 浩漫 perplexing; numerous.
[15]浩飲 to drink deeply; carousal.

皓 顥 皝 } [4]
Luminous; bright. Hoary, white. The 3rd form is also read *hu* or *huang*.
2078

皓皓 shining; glittering; brilliant.
皓耀 dazzling brilliance.
皓首 a hoary head.
皓齒 gleaming teeth.
太皓 the firmament.

灝 [4]
Vast; boundless.
2079

灝溔 a boundless waste of waters.
灝灝 deep; obscure.

暤 暠 } [4]
Clear; pure; white.
2080

暤然白首 a venerable. hoary head.
暤身赤足 naked and barefooted.

蒿 [1]
Jungle; different kinds of plants according to the other characters joined with this.
2081

蒿·子 or 香蒿 artemisia — used for smoking out mosquitoes.
蒿目 blindly.
蒿草 jungle.
蒿里 a tomb.
青蒿 artemisia; southernwood.

嚆 [1]
Sound; noise.
2082

嚆矢 a whirring dart—discharged by bandits as a signal to begin the attack—thus used for the beginning of an affair.

鄗 [4]
The name of a place in the south-west of Hopei.
2083

鎬 [4]
A stove. Bright. The name of a place.
2084

鎬京 the capital when *Wu Wang* 武王 was in power.

薅 揫 茠 } [1]
To weed; to eradicate.
2085

薅亂絲膠 to unravel the sticky tangles of raw silk.
薅草 to weed.
薅頭髮 to pull out the hair—in a rage.

HO. HE. (ㄏㄜ)
(Heh)

紇 2.5.
Tassels; the end of a fringe. Also read *kol¹*.
2086

紇國 a tribe of the *Wigours* or *Ouigours*.
回紇其先匈奴也 the ancesters of the *Wigours* were called the *Hsiung nu*.

齕 2.5.
To gnaw. To peculate.
2087

齕吞 to swallow without mastication, as birds and certain animals.
齕噬 to nibble—as at a biscuit.

劾 2.5.
To examine into. To impeach.
2088

劾參 or 彈劾 to impeach.
劾問 preliminary inquiry.
劾奏 to accuse in a memorial to the throne.
劾實 to investigate the facts of a charge.
[5]劾按 to investigate a charge.
劾狀 an impeachment.
劾究 or 糾劾 to make an official investigation.
劾繫 to impeach and bind.

核 2.5.
A kernel; a walnut; a hard lump.
2089

核·子瘟 bubonic plague.
核果 nuts.
核·桃 walnuts.
核桃仁 the meat of a walnut
桃核 peach-stones. (-*hur*²)
生核 to have a hard lump on the body.

(a) To investigate; to consider the facts; to estimate.

核佶 to assess the value.
核准 to grant after due consideration.
核加 to add.
核奪 or 核定 or 核斷 to decide upon the merits of the case.
[5]核實 to verify.
核對 to audit; to compare.
核明辦理 make an investigation and deal with the matter.
核查 or 核明 or 察核 to investigate.
核發 to issue after due investigation.
[10]核示 to consider the matter and give instructions accordingly.
核算 or 核數 to calculate.
核與上年 compared with previous years.
核計 to examine an account; to find that the sum amounts to . . . . .
核議 to deliberate; to decide on.
[15]核辦 to act accordingly.

求 核 to seek for the motive behind an action.

黑 4.5. Black, dark, evil. Secret.
2090 Radical 203. Mostly pron. *hei*[1].

黑·下 night-time.
黑 乾 枯 瘦 sallow and emaciated.
黑 夜 night ; the dark night.
黑 夜 巳 深 the night is far spent.
5 黑 奴 Negro slaves.
黑 子³ a black spot ; a mole ; a tiny
piece—as of land, etc.
黑 家 走 to walk in the dark.
黑 幕 hidden works of darkness—
a black screen.
黑 影 a dark shadow.
10 黑 心 black-hearted ; villainous.
黑 暗 dark ; darkness ; secret ; the
rhinoceros.
黑 暗 世 界 a dark age—a
position in which there is no
justice or fairness.
黑 暗 地 獄 a dark hell—a
position in which there is no
ray of light, no way out, no
redress.
黑 暗 大 陸 The Dark Continent.
15 黑 暗 時 代 the dark ages.
黑 曜 石 obsidian.
黑 板 a blackboard.
黑 死 病 The Black Death.
黑 海 The Black Sea.
20 黑 潮 the Pacific Current.
黑 漆 漆·的 or 黑 碌 碌·的 in-
tense black.
黑 煤 or 烟 煤 black coal, soft
coal—anthracite is called 白 煤·
黑 牲·口 used by Mohammedans
for the pig, as they dislike using even the word for pig.
黑 甜 鄉 the dark and sweet land
—sleep ; compare "the land of
nod."
25 黑 白 不 分 does not distinguish
between black and white, good
and bad—stupid.
黑 眸 the pupil of the eye.
黑 種 the black races.
黑 稿 an outline ; a pencil sketch.
黑 股 冬 or 黑 股 影 dark and
murky.
30 黑 良 心 a darkened conscience—
utterly unprincipled.
黑 色 black colour.
黑 蒼 蒼·的 very black—as hair ;
swarthy.
黑 話 mysterious language.

黑 貨 or 黑 烟 or 黑 土 opium.
35 黑 道 日·子 an unlucky day.
黑 金 the black metal—iron.
黑 鉛 graphite.
黑 雲 密 佈 dark clouds over-
spreading—a gathering storm.
黑 靜 雷 波 Hertzian waves.
40 黑 魚 or 黑 鱧 the snake-fish.
黑 麵 dark flour.
黑 黴 lichens.
黑 龍 江 the Amur River (up to
its junction with the Songari.)
A province of Manchuria.
摸 黑 兒 to grope in the dark.

赫 4.5. Bright ; luminous.
2091 Glorious.

赫 光 bright, glorious.
赫 奕 glorious ; grand ; mighty.
赫 明 to burn brightly.
赫 耀 bright and glorious.
赫 顯 a brilliant manifestation.

(a) Awe-inspiring. To frighten ;
to be angry at.

赫 兮 咺 兮 How majestic, how
distinguished !
赫 大 great ; very awe-inspiring.
赫 怒 fearful anger.
赫 然 angered ; stiff, like a corpse.
5 赫 甚 very powerful—as a ruler.
赫 赫 awful ; fiery.
赫 赫 施 威 he displayed his great
majesty.
赫 赫 有 名 having a great reputation.

(b) Red.

赫 如 渥 赭 I am as red as if I
had been rouged.

嚇 4.5. To scare ; to intimidate.
2092 Also read *hsia*[4].

嚇·了 一 跳 gave him a great
fright. (*hsia*[4]-)
嚇 勢 to use power or influence
to intimidate.
嚇·唬 to intimidate ; to scare.(*hsia*[4]-)
嚇 嚇 sound of laughter.
5 嚇·掉·了 魂 scared out of his
wits. (*hsia*[4]-)
嚇 昏 afraid of the dark.(*hsia*[4]-)
嚇·死 greatly terrified ; scared to
death. (*hsia*[4]-)
嚇·殺 killed by fright ; used as a
superlative. (*hsia*[4]-)

嚇 禁 to deter.
10 嚇·着 scared ; terrified. (*hsia*[4]·*chao*)
嚇 詐 to extort ; to impose on by
threats. ⌠(*hsia*[4]-)
嚇 跑·了 to run away from fear.
嚇 醒·了 to awake with a start.
恐 嚇 to terrify. ⌊(*hsia*[4]-)
15 驚 嚇 to startle.

覈 2.5. To examine into with
2093 thoroughness.
Inter. 核 No. 2089.

覈 查 or 覈 問 or 考 覈 o1 審 覈
to inquire into ; to investigate ;
to ascertain by inquiries.
覈 驗 to verify.

HÊN. (ㄏㄣ)

很 ³ Angry. Quarrelsome. Dis-
2094 obedient. Cruel, fierce. Inter. 狠 No. 2097.

很·不 起 來 abortive anger ; inability to carry out threats.
很 口 unwilling to yield the last
word ; an experienced man in
managing affairs.
很 命 with all the force at command.
很·得 很 dreadfully overbearing.
5 很 心 harsh ; quarrelsome.
很 忤 perverse.
很 毒 an unforgiving spirit.
很 無 求 勝 in disputes do not
seek merely to overcome.
凶 很 very fierce.
10 發 很 to become angry.

(a) Very ; an intensive.

很 好 very good.
很 多 numerous.
很 小 very small.
很 是 quite so ; very true.
5 很 苦 in great distress ; poverty-
stricken.
很 見 長 進 shows a marked advance or improvement.
很 難 exceedingly difficult.

恨 ⁴ To hate ; to dislike.
2095

恨·不 了³ no means of giving effect
to hatred ; would I . . . !
恨 事 a disappointing matter.
恨 人 irritating ; one who is full of
hatred.

恨 入 骨 髓 the deepest hatred.
⁵恨 怒 animosity; resentment.
恨 怨 to abhor.
恨 恨 to cherish lasting hatred.
恨 惡 (u¹) to loathe; to abhor.
恨 極 very odious.
¹⁰恨 毒 malicious hatred.
恨 視 to glare with anger.
恨 鐵 不 成 鋼 vexed at the stupidity of a scholar.
仇 恨 or 怨 恨 to cherish a grudge against.
可 恨 hateful.
¹⁵懷 恨 to cherish malice.
舊 恨 an old grievance.
雪 恨 to wipe out a grievance.

(a) An expression of strong desire. To regret; remorse. Alas.

悔 恨 deep remorse.
恨·不·得 would that....! oh that ....!
恨 不 復 返 would certainly turn back.
恨 不 能 vexed at not being able to....; Alas! that I was unable to....!

狠 ² To pull; to drag; to stop.
2096

狠 搭 to turn out; to drag out.
狠 抑 to keep down; to restrain.

狠 ³ Fierce, angry. Inter. 很 No. 2094.
2097

狠 口 fierce in heart and cruel in action; unwilling to yield.
狠 巴 巴·的 very severe.
狠 心 cruel; savage.
狠 戾 vicious; cruel.
狠 毒 cruel; malicious.

(a) Inter. 很 No. 2094. Very, extremely.

狠 是 that is so; quite true.
狠 大 very large.
狠 狠 狠 in a dilemma; in a fix.

(b) Read wan² or yen². Sound of dogs snarling.

痕 ² A scar; marks or traces.
2098

痕 跡 a trace of, as a footstep; a seam, as in glass.
傷 痕 scars from wounds.
淚 痕 traces of tears.

HÊNG.　　(ㄏ)

亨 ¹ To pervade. To be successful. To pervade. To persevere.
2099 Distinguish 享 No. 2552.

亨 嘉 or 泰 亨 prosperous; successful.
亨 通 prosperous; flourishing.

(a) Read p'êng¹. To boil. u.f. 烹 No. 5052.

亨 熟 to boil till thoroughly cooked.

哼 ¹ Grunt of disapproval. To groan. To moan. Frightened.
2100 Distinguish 啍 No. 6588.

哼 哈 to hum and haw.
哼 咳 to moan.
哼 唧 唧 groaning and moaning.
哼·哼 嘆 氣 panting, out of breath.
哼 嗜 to grunt.
哼 嘻 二 將 the fierce-looking gods painted on doors, named Shu yü 荼 與 and Yü lü 鬱 壘.
哼 啊 哼 啊 to groan; the cry of carriers.
↑哼·哼 to hum; to groan.

脝 ¹ Fat, bloated.
2101

桁 ² The purlines of a roof. A wooden stopper. In some places used for a row, as of tiles or trees.
2102

桁 桷 purlines and rafters.
屋 桁 the beams of a house.
木 桁 塞 其 口 stopped the mouths of the vessels with wooden stoppers.

(a) Read hang². A wooden collar for punishment. A pontoonbridge.

桁 楊 the cangue.

(b) Read hang¹. A clothes-horse.

桁 上 無 懸 衣 there are no garments hanging on the clothes-horse.

珩 ² The top gem of the pendants from a girdle.
2103

衡 2· The yoke of an ox. Transverse. Horizontal; from east to west. A railing. Similar to 橫 No. 2106.
衕
2104

衡 宇 houses, buildings.
衡 從 crosswise and lengthwise; in both directions. (-tsung¹)
衡 從 其 畝 the acres are to be (ploughed) in both directions.
衡 門 or 衡 泌 the humble home of a man who has retired from public life:—from
衡 門 之 下 .... 泌 之 洋 洋 beneath my simple door... ..beside my flowing fountain...
衡 行 於 天 下 pursuing a disorderly course in the empire.
楅 衡 a stick across the horns of an ox to prevent his goring.

(a) To weigh; to adjust. The beam of a steelyard. Perplexed.

衡 平 a pair of scales.
衡 情 to judge of the circumstances of a case.
衡 文 to examine essays.
衡 於 慮 perplexed in thought.
⁵衡 石 or 衡 權 the beam and the weight of the steelyard.
衡 衡 to measure; to estimate.
衡 論 to discuss; to consider.
衡 量 to measure; to estimate.
衡 鑑 scales and mirror—to distinguish between right and wrong.
玉 衡 part of an astronomical instrument used in very ancient times.

(b) Authority, from the above meaning.

衡 命 a divine right to rule.
衡 軸 important place in the State —as an axle is to a cart.
台 衡 a Grand Secretary under imperial regimes.
抗 衡 to resist authority.
權 衡 weight and beam—authority.
權 衡 執 掌 the whole power in the hands of one.
爭 衡 to contend for mastery.

(c) A mountain in Hunan.

衡 山 mountain in Hunan, one of the five sacred mountains or 五 岳.

(d) Space between the eyebrows.

盰 衡 angrily glaring.

衡² A fragrant plant 杜 蘅 which grows in shady places on hillsides, described as having purple flowers which blossom in early winter; the root is medicinal.
2105

橫² Crosswise; horizontal. East to west. At right angles to; sideways. Opposite of 縱 from north to south.
2106

橫 七 豎 八 all at sixes and sevens.
橫 三 豎 四·的 this way and that way; every way.
橫 亙 to cross.
橫 住·了 to withstand; to stop; to parry.
⁵橫 倒 lying across.
橫 力 transverse strain.
橫 口 a transverse opening.
橫 向 the profile or side-view of a thing.
橫 徑 dimension across.
¹⁰橫 截 面 a cross-section; transverse section.
橫 披 horizontal scroll or picture.
橫 擺 or 打 橫 to lay crosswise.
橫 支 a collateral branch.
橫 斜 criss-cross.
¹⁵橫 木 a cross-beam; an axle, etc.
橫 桅 yard-arms.
橫 梁 cross-beams.
橫 槊 賦 詩 to compose while in the saddle—said of Ts'ao Ts'ao.
橫 水 渡 ferries.
²⁰橫 波 cross-seas.
橫 濱 Yokohama.
橫 生 or 橫 產 cross-presentation at birth.
橫 生 事 端 trouble arising on every hand.
美 貌 橫 生 beauties appeared on every side.
²⁵橫 痃 buboes.
橫 目 the horizontal eye—hidden allusion to the character for four 四.

橫 目 之 民 the horizontal-eyed—human beings.
橫 直 at right angles.
橫 眉 立 目 angry looks; surly appearance.
³⁰橫 摩 劍 a sharp sword.
橫 笛 a flute.
橫 筋 chopsticks placed across a bowl to indicate respect when finished before another.
橫 紋 木 cross-grained timber.
橫 紋 筋 or 隨 意 筋 voluntary muscular tissue.
³⁵橫 線 horizontal lines or stripes.
橫 膈 膜 the diaphragm.
橫 行 介 士 the crab—he who walks sideways.
橫 行 曲 腸 the transverse colon.
橫 衝 直 撞 colliding with (vehicles, etc.) in every direction.
⁴⁰橫 衝 直 撞 going first in one direction and then another; battered from pillar to post.
橫 豎 horizontal and perpendicular; in every direction.
⁴¹橫·豎 or 橫·是 in any case, anyway.
橫 豎 要 過 河 right or wrong I must cross this river—there is no alternative to it.
橫 路 a cross-road.
橫 軸 transverse axis (geom.).
⁴⁵橫 道 a horizontal line.
橫 量 (liang²) the breadth; to measure sidewise.
橫 門 a side-door.
橫 門 cross-bar of a door, etc.
橫 阻 當 路 obstructing the path.
⁵⁰橫 陳 to lounge about; to lie on a bed.
橫 骨 the share-bone; pubic bone.
橫 鼻 to turn up the nose.
縱 橫 length and breadth; both dimensions.

(a) Read hêng¹. Perverse, evil, unreasonable, overbearing; unexpected.

橫 丟 丟·的 or 橫 虎 虎·的 reckless; violent; fierce.
橫 事 things that go contrarily.
橫 征 暴 斂 to extort illegal taxes.
橫 手 買 to buy underhand.
⁵橫 抽 to levy blackmail.
橫 政 a lawless government.
橫 暴 perverse and irritable.
橫 死 an untimely death.
橫 死 私 埋 to bury a suicide secretly.

¹⁰橫 流 river flowing out of its accustomed channel.
橫 目 angry looks. See above.—27.
橫 禍 an unexpected calamity.
橫 行 to act on the cross; unreasonable conduct; outrageous behaviour; perversity.
橫 行 霸 道 to act contrary to reason; to act in an overbearing, tyrannous manner.
¹⁵橫 計 cross purpose.
橫 議 unreasonable discussions.
橫 財 a windfall; unexpected profit; underhand gains.
橫 逆 perverse; undutiful; peevish.
橫 遭 to meet sudden misfortune.
²⁰刁 橫 perverse; violent.
蠻 橫 savage and cruel.
豪 橫 arrogant; overbearing.

姮² See 嫦 No. 222.
2106a

恆 恒² Constant; regular; continually; persevering.
2107

恆 久 for a long time.
恆 勁 perseverance.
恆 多 參 差 constant discrepancies. (-ts'ên¹-tz'ŭ¹)
恆 姿 the usual appearance of anything.
⁵恆 山 the northern of the Five Sacred Mountains, 五 岳.
恆 常 permanent; enduring; constant.
恆 心 a constant mind; perseverance.
恆 念 constant thought or remembrance.
恆 忍 久 耐 long-suffering; forbearance.
¹⁰恆 性 a persevering disposition.
恆 情 general propensity.
恆 於 善 perseverance in doing good.
恆 春 lign aloes.
恆 星 fixed stars or permanent stars.
¹⁵恆 星 年 the sidereal year.
恆 星 時 sidereal time.
恆 河 or 恆 迦 the Ganges.
恆 河 沙 數 as numerous as the sands of the Ganges—innumerable.
恆 相 constantly . . . with each other.

20 恆 等 式 constant equation. (*math.*)

恆 言 a saying.

恆 足 always sufficient.

恆 醫 an ordinary doctor.

恆 風 prevailing winds, as the trade-winds.

25 非 恆 士 no ordinary person.

(a) Read *kêng¹*. The moon when nearly full.

如 月 之 恆 like the waxing moon.

訶 **4**
Angry. Reproof, scolding.
2108

HO.　　　(ㄏ)

何 **2** What? How? Why? Which?
2109

何 不 早 來 why did you not come earlier?

何 乃 why?

何 事 非 君 how can I serve one who is not my ruler? i.e., he becomes my ruler by my serving him.

何 況 how much more? how much less?

5 何 人 who?

何 以 wherefore? by what means? how shall I?

何 以 別 乎 what difference is there?

何 以 告 之 what did he tell them?

何 以 爲 用 what would you do?

10 何 以 自 解 how can you explain yourself?—when wrong has been done.

何 以 言 之 what is the explanation of this?

吾 何 以 識 其 不 才 how shall I know that they have no ability?

何 傷 what injury...? what harm will it....?

何 功 之 有 哉 what do you expect to accomplish?

15 何 可 勝 數 how can they be reckoned up?

何 哉 why, pray?

天 何 言 哉 does Heaven speak?

何 嘗 was it ever so?—it never happened.

何 因 why? for what reason?

20 何 在 where is?

何 堪 how can I?—I am unworthy to.

何 如 what better than? what say you? used as a correlative of 與 其 rather than . . .

何 妨 what's the hindrance? why not? what does it matter?

何 居 for what reason?

25 汝 意 何 居 what was your reason?

何 干 what concern? what has it to do with....?

何 往 where are you going?

何 得 擅 自 作 主 how dare I take it upon myself to decide?

何 必 what need? why?

30 何 必 如 此 why thus?

何 愁 why worry about it?

何 擇 焉 what choice between them?

何 故 why? for what reason?

何 敢 how dare I? how can I?

35 何 日 when? on what day?

何 時 at what time?

何 嘗 has it ever happened? implying a negative answer.

何 嘗 不 曉 得 didn't he know all along?

何 晏 why are you so late?

40 何 有 what difficulty is there?

何 有 何 無 there may, there may not—of no consequence.

何 有 於 我 哉 what is that to me?

何 期 how can I hope?

何 然 what is there right in....?

45 何 爲 how can it be? how is it that...?

何 爲 不 行 why do you not do it?

何 爲 其 然 why should he do so?

何 爲 是 栖 栖 者 與 why do you roost about like this?

何 獨 不 然 why should this be an exception to the rule?

50 何 用 不 臧 what evil does he do?

何 由 知 吾 可 也 how do you know that I am competent?

何 由 至 此 how did you get here?

何 益 what is the advantage? what is the good of...?

何 益 之 有 哉 of what value is it?

55 何 等 in what degree? how? how greatly? a superlative.

何 者 what is there which is...? whatever?

何 至 於 此 or 何 至 如 此 why need you have let things develop into such a state?

何 苦 or 何 苦 來 what need? why so much trouble to...?

60 何 處 at what place? wherever?

何 解 what is the reason? how do you explain it? what meaning?

何 言 why say...? what words are these?

何 許 人 where he was from. 許 is equiv. 所.

何 謝 之 有 what is there to thank me for?

65 何 足 how is it sufficient to...? why?

何 足 掛 齒 don't mention it.

亡 何 in no time; shortly. (*wú*)

其 如 予 何 what can he do to me?

幾 何 how many? geometry.

(a) Read *ho¹*. To carry; to bear. u.f. 荷 No. 2113.

何 戈 to carry arms.

何 天 之 休 he received the blessing of Heaven.

呵 **1** To expel the breath. Also read *k'o¹*.
2110

呵 凍 作 字 to breathe on the frozen tip (of a brush to warm it) for writing.

呵 叱 to scold with loud voice.

呵 喝 to shout and order anyone to desist.

呵 導 or 呵 引 or 喝 道 runners who shout "Clear the way" before a magistrate.

(a) Read *ha¹*. To laugh; to yawn.

呵 呵 大 笑 a fit of loud laughing.

呵 欠 or 打 呵 欠 to yawn.

河 **2** A stream; a river. The province of Honan. In classical books, when used alone without any definite river being specified, it generally refers to the Yellow River.
2111

河 下 in the river; on the river.

河 下 民 boating population.

河 伯 or 河 公 or 河 宗 or 河 靈 the god of a river.

河伯娶婦 the custom of throwing a young woman into the Yellow River as the bride of the god. It was broken by *Hsi-mên Pao* 西門豹 about 424 B.C. when he was magistrate in Honan, near the present *Chang-tehfu,* he threw the old woman, who acted as chief instigator of the superstition, into the river as the bride.

5 河伯從事 the runner of the river-god—the cuttle-fish.

河內 land on the east of the Yellow River as it flows between Shensi and Shansi.

河北 the province formerly known as Chihli,—Hopei.

河·南 the province of Honan.

河口 the mouth of a river.

10 河圖洛書 the plan of the Yellow River and the book of the River Lo—mystic diagrams said to have been supernaturally revealed.

河外 beyond the river.

河套 Ordos bend of the Yellow River.

河女之章 a young girl of 14, named *Ts'ao O* 曹娥 threw herself into the river to find the lost body of her father, who was drowned; afterwards both bodies were found together.

河山之險 the country in peril.*

15 河嶽 the Yellow River and the Five Sacred Mountains.

河工 river conservancy works.

河干 bank of a river.

河心 the bed of a river; the middle of a river.

河東 S. W. Shansi.

20 河東獅吼 the roar of the lioness from the east of the river—said of a virago in a temper.

河朔 north of the River—Yellow River.

河梁 bridges.

河決 bursting of the dikes.

河沿 or 河岸 by the riverside; the bank.

25 河沿上 on the river bank; by the riverside.

河洲 a habitable islet in a river.

河流迅急 said of the rapid flow of the Yellow River.

河海 rivers and seas.

慈如河海 the love of a parent is like the rivers

*Also, the strategic importance of rivers and mountains.

and seas, ever flowing and extensive.

30 河淺 the river is shallow.

河清 when the Yellow River is clear—a rare occurrence, therefore used for an indefinite time, cf., "a blue moon."

河清海晏 a peaceful era.

河清難俟 it is hard to wait till the river is clear—the time would be too long.

俟河之清 wait till the Yellow River runs clear water—wait indefinitely.

35 黃河千年一清 the Yellow River runs clear once in a thousand years.

河渠 rivers and creeks.

河源 the source of the river—i.e., the Yellow River.

河漢 or 天河 or 銀河 or 明河 the Heavenly River—i.e., the Milky Way.

河漢斯言 to take these as far-fetched words.

40 河漢無極 high-flown talk—as far off as the Milky Way.

不以為河漢 do not think it far-fetched.

河漏 a northern term for fine flour from buckwheat; also for vermicelli made by forcing dough through a vessel with fine holes.

河潤之 aided him—as a river fertilizes the fields.

河濱 the bank of a river; the side of a river.

45 河灘 a rapid.

河燈 river-lamps — paper lamps set floating to light wandering spirits on the 15th of the 7th month, lunar.

河目海口 large open eyes and large mouth.

河豚 the globe-fish, which is able to inflate itself; it is good eating but there is danger from poison in the liver and roe; sometimes this phrase is referred to the Yangtze porpoise. *See* 鯆 No. 6599.

河西 or 河右 west of the Yellow River—i.e., Shensi, Kansu, Mongolia, etc.

50 河路 a navigable river.

河身 the volume of the current in a river.

河道 the middle of a stream; the channel of a river.

河運 to send the tribute by river to the capital.

河開口 the river bursts its banks.

55 河閘 a lock; a water-gate.

河防 those in charge of the conservancy works on the Yellow River.

河隄 a dike.

河面 surface of a river.

河馬 a hippopotamus.

60 河魚腹疾 illustrating a bowel complaint—as the belly of a fish is the first to decay so this trouble began in the bowels.

河鼓 another name for the Herd-boy—a star in Aquilae. *See* 4737. 41 .

訶[1] To blame, to ridicule. Also read *k'o*[1].
2112

訶咄 to blame and scold.

訶子[3] or 訶黎草 (or 勒) an astringent nut used for toothache; the first also means a kind of stomacher.

訶求責備 to find fault for trifles.

訶藜棒 a heavy club about five feet in length, covered with iron at the end—an ancient military weapon.

訶詈童僕 to scold servants harshly.

訶詰 to reprimand and investigate.

訶譏 to ridicule.

訶責 to blame.

訶遣役卒 to browbeat and order about one's servants without reasonable excuse.

荷[2]   The lotus or water-lily.
2113

荷月 the sixth lunar month.

荷池 a lotus pond.

荷葉 a lotus leaf; butt of a door; hinges.

荷蓮 or 荷花 the lotus flower.

5 荷衣 lotus leaves.

荷錢 the very young lotus leaves.

荷露 the dew on a lotus leaf.

荷風 a pleasant breeze.

(a) Read *ho*[1]. To wear; to carry on the back, from which also

comes the idea of gratitude or responsibility.

荷² 包 an ornamental purse or pouch worn in ancient times.

荷 校 to wear the cangue.

荷 物 luggage—(*Jap.*).

荷 禮 vexatious trifles of etiquette.

⁵荷 荷 grunt of resentment or hatred.

荷 蒙 大 恩 I have received great kindness from you.

荷 蕢 carrying a basket.

荷 負 to carry; to be competent; to bear responsibility; adequate for.

荷 鎗 實 彈 carrying loaded rifles —ready for emergencies.

¹⁰感 荷 I am very grateful.

拜 荷 with kind regards, etc.

是 荷 closing phrase at the end of a request—I shall be obliged.

爲 盼 是 荷 I shall be grateful if you....as I hope you will.

覆 示 爲 荷 I shall be grateful for a reply.

(b) Transliterating foreign sounds.

荷⁴ 蘭 國 Holland.

荷⁴ 蘭 水 aerated waters.

禾² Growing grain; crops. Radical 115.
2114

禾 場 a threshing floor.

禾 捆 sheaves of grain.

禾 田 grain fields; arable land.

禾 稼 crops in general.

⁵禾 稭 wheat or other straw.

禾 穗 an ear of grain.

禾 米 unhulled rice; paddy.

禾 苗 growing rice.

禾 蟲 harvest grub.

¹⁰禾 黍 millet.

和味龢² Harmony; peace; conciliation; to be on good terms with; kindly; to harmonize; mild; to rehearse ensemble music.
2115

和 也 者 天 下 之 達 道 也 harmony is the universal path which they should all pursue.

和 事 人 or 和 事 老 a peacemaker.

和 光 one's personal but hidden virtue and wisdom.

和 合 to agree; harmonious union; name of gods which are worshipped at weddings.

⁵和 合 飯 a wedding breakfast.

和 善 affable.

和 喜 peaceful and happy.

和 奏 instruments playing in harmony.

和 好 or 和 美 on good terms; reconciled.

¹⁰和 姦 or 姦 情 adultery with consent.

和 局 a drawn game; amicable relations.

和 平 or 平 和 pleasant; good-natured; even-tempered; mild, as the weather; peace.

和 平 主 義 pacific policy; pacifism.

和 平 會 Peace Society.

¹⁵和 平 派 the Peace Party.

和 平 解 決 an amicable settlement.

和 平 辦 結 a peaceful settlement of any trouble.

和 息 to close—litigation or quarrels; agreement.

和 息 呈 詞 a statement of the amicable understanding arrived at.

²⁰和 愉 peaceful and pleasant.

和 (數) the sum of several numbers.

和 景 a beautiful prospect.

和 暢 very pleasant, as fine weather or cool breezes.

和 暖 mild weather; warm.

²⁵和 樂 friendly, happy feeling.

和·氣 agreeable; affable; friendly feeling; a peaceful disposition.

和 氣 生 財 harmony and goodwill produces wealth.

和 氣 致 祥 goodwill brings good luck.

和 洽 or 相 洽 intimate, as friends; mutual liking; agreeable to; congenial.

³⁰和 沖 complaisant.

和 煦 warm; mild.

和 爲 貴 a natural ease is to be prized.

和 盤 托 出 to make the whole thing known; not the slightest concealment.

和 睦 or 和 誼 peace; peaceful.

³⁵和 睦 鄉 里 peace with neighbours.

和 碩 a Manchu term for a prince.

和 約 a treaty. 和 絃 chord.

和 緩 輿 論 pacify public opinion.

和 美 harmony; peaceful; reconciled.

⁴⁰和 而 不 流 peaceful and yet not weak. 和 聲 學 harmony.

和 舒 quiet ease.

和 藹 dignified and courteous.

和 衷 accommodating; friendly.

和 衷 共 濟 by common consent.

⁴⁵和 解 conciliation; to come to an amicable understanding; compromise.

和 解 狀 a deed of compromise.

和 親 to make terms of peace by marrying into the opposing State, as was done in more than one instance in Chinese history.

和 諧 harmonious, as sound; agreeing in concert; conjugal harmony.

和 謙 agreeable and pleasant without arrogance.

⁵⁰和 謹 pleasant and respectful.

和 議 會 a meeting to discuss peace proposals.

和 豫 pleased, happy.

和 輯 in accord; to pacify and arrange.

和 集 to gather the people together in peace.

⁵⁵和 順 civil and obliging.

和 顏 悅 色 a pleasant countenance.

和 風 甘 雨 gentle breezes and sweet rains.

交 和 to come to terms.

太 和 universal peace.

⁶⁰求 和 to sue for peace.

發 而 皆 中 節 謂 之 和 when feelings have been stirred, and they act in their due degree there ensues what may be termed a state of harmony.

講 和 to treat for peace; to discuss peace proposals.

(a) To mix. Well flavoured. Pron. [huo⁴.

和 味 well flavoured.

和 泥 to mix mud for plaster.|dishes.

和 菜 mixed vegetables; table d'hôte.

酒 旣 和 旨 the wine was well blended and good.

和 麪 dough.

(b) Bells on the crossbar of a carriage.

和 鈴 央 央 the bells on the crossbar and those on the bridles tinkle merrily.

和 鸞 雝 雝 the merry tinkling of the carriage-bells.

(c) Transliterating foreign sounds.

和 上 Buddhist priests.

和 伽 那 one of the twelve divisions of the Buddhist scriptures.

和 南 to fold the hands in reverence or prayer like a Buddhist priest—used as a title by priests on cards, etc.

和·尙 Buddhist priest; explained as derived through the Turkish at Khoten, from the Sanskrit, —*Upadhyâya,* and meaning 親 敎 師 a self-taught teacher.

和 文 Japanese language and literature.

和 服 Japanese dress.

和 漢 Japanese and Chinese.

(d) The front of a coffin. Gate of a camp. An ancient reed instrument like the *sheng* 笙**, but smaller.**

和 頭 the front of a coffin.

(e) Read *ho²*, **but spoken** *han⁴, hai⁴.* **As a preposition— with, together with, and.**

和 他 一 樣 the same as he is.

和 別·人 with another.

和²衣 睡 to sleep with the clothes on.(*ho²*)

(f) Read *ho⁴.* **To respond to in singing; to keep in tune with; to agree with; to rhyme with. To blend flavours.**

和 勻 well blended.

和 歌 chorus.

和 韻 to rhyme.

一 唱 百 和 one leads and the rest follow in harmony.

鳴 鶴 在 陰 其 子³和 之 the crane cries in the shade and her young answer her.

隨 聲 附 和 to agree with what is said by another without due consideration.

賀⁴ **To send a present with congratulations. To congratulate.**

2116

賀 喜 or 道 賀 or 慶 賀 to congratulate.

賀 壽 birthday greetings.

賀 年 new-year's greetings.

賀 戟 to carry a spear.

⁵賀 禮 congratulatory presents.

賀 節 to wish the compliments of the season.

可 賀 可 賀 Congratulations!

奉 賀 to present a congratulatory gift.

恭 賀 with my respects—sent with a present.

HO.　(ㄏㄛ)
(Hoh)

合 2.5. **To shut; to enclose; to close.**
2117

合 住 to close—as an umbrella, etc.

合 十 or 合 掌 to clasp the hands —in prayer, as Buddhists do.

合 口 to close the mouth; to bring two openings together; labialized. *See below* A. 29.

合·子 a box, having a lid to shut or open, hence the name.

⁵合 抱 to encircle a tree with arms outstretched and measure the circumference.

合 拱 to measure by enclosing in the hands, as a branch, etc.

合 書 to close a book.

合 甲 strong, well-fitting armour that gave a man good protection.

合 目 or 合 眼 to close the eyes.

¹⁰合 門 to close the door.

合 閉 to close.

(a) To join, to pair, to agree, to total. In agreement with; side by side; joined.

合 一 to unite in one.

合 一 打·算 to reckon and compare two or more estimates; to estimate for the whole thing.

合 上 to fit a thing on; to unite.

合 中 to strike an average; to hit the medium.

⁵合·乎 理 reasonable, right.

合·乎 當 然 in accord with what is right and fitting.

合·乎 規·矩 in accordance with prescribed rule.

合 亟 照 送 it is incumbent on me to forward at once.

合 作 to join; co-operation.

¹⁰合 作 之 助 力 the aid of co-operation.

合 作 制 度 co-operative system.

合 作 殖 產 co-operative productions.

合 作·的 精·神 the spirit of co-operation.

合 作 社 co-operative society.

¹⁵當 局 之 合 作 co-operation of the authorities.

通 力 合 作 general effort for co-operation.

合 例 in accord with precedent.

合 倂 to amalgamate; to unite.

合 偶 to pair; wedlock.

²⁰合 共 or 共 合 the sum total.

合 券 to compare and verify accounts.

合 力 with united effort; co-operation.

合 力 而 行 co-operative effort.

合 力 管 理 co-operative control.

²⁵合 力 經 營 co-operative management.

相 協 合 力 to co-operate.

合 勢 advantageous.

合 巹 to drink the nuptial cup— marriage.

合 口 同 聲 with one voice. *See above illus.* 3.

³⁰合 同 an agreement, of which each party retains one copy.

合 同 尺²·寸 contract length.

借 欵 合 同 loan-agreement.

立 (or 打 or 訂) 合 同 to draw up an agreement.

買·賣 合 同 contract note.

³⁵長 期 合 同 long-term agreement.

合 團 to unite in one; to join into one group.

合·在 一 塊 put together in one place; to join; to unite.

合 夥 a partnership.

合 奏 to play together in harmony as an orchestra.

⁴⁰合 婚 and 成 婚 and 完 婚 denote successively the comparison of the horoscopes, the exchange of presents and the completion of the marriage.

合 宜 or 合 就 fitting; exactly suitable.

合 宜 主 義 conventionalism.

合 宜 之 至 extremely fitting.

合 宜 說 theory of fitness.

⁴⁵合 局 to enter into a partnership.

合 式 suitable; agreeable; fitting.

合 律 性 regularity.

合 從¹ or 縱 合 the union of feudal States to combat *Ch'in* 秦.

合 心 agreeing, of one mind.

⁵⁰合 意 agreeable; in accord with one's ideas.

合 成 to complete; to make.

合 我 心 意 in accordance with my views.

合 我 用 quite suitable for what I want.

合 戰 to join in battle.

⁵⁵戰 不 數 合 they had not fought many rounds.

合 於 .... in harmony with....; corresponding to....

合 時 宜 in accord with the times; to fit in with the times.

合 會 or 會 合 to assemble; to form a society.

合 朔 conjunction of sun and moon.

⁶⁰合 本 to unite capital and go into partnership.

合 格 up to the required standard; qualified.

合 歡 to meet for enjoyment; a tree like the acacia.

合 法 legal; in accordance with the law.

合 法 外 債 legitimate foreign obligations.

⁶⁵合 理 or 理 合 s e e m l y; fitting; right; in accord with what is right; rational.

合 璧 junction of two parts to make a whole; side by side, as original and translation.

合 當 suitable; it so happened.

合 盤 打·算 to estimate for the whole thing.

合 衆 to gather a crowd; to co-operate in a matter.

⁷⁰合 衆 國 a union of States, like the United States of America.

合 符 or 符 合 to tally with.

合 算 to reckon up; to add.

合 縫 to fit the seams together; to join a crack.

合 羣 union; to gather into a group.

⁷⁵合 羣 性 質 of a gregarious nature.

合 而 爲 一 to unite in one; united into one.

合 而 言 之 to speak of them collectively.

合 股 partnership; a company for business purposes.

合 葬 to bury husband and wife in one grave.

⁸⁰合 衣 睡 to sleep without undressing.

合 計 the total equals...; equivalent to—of sums in different denominations.

合 該 it was his destiny.

合 謀 to plot together.

合 資 公 司 co-partnership; limited partnership.

⁸⁵合 質 an amalgamation; a compound.

合 轍 in the same groove.

合 選 eligible for election.

合 配 to pair; to mate.

合 金 an alloy.

⁹⁰合 音 in tune; similar sounds.

合 頁 hinges.

一 合 a handful.

不 合 道·理 not in accord with right principles.

六 合 the four cardinal points, the zenith and the nadir; used for —the universe; the empire, etc.

⁹⁵吾 合 盡 矣 my destiny is finished and it is fitting that I should die.

妻 子 好 合 in loving harmony with wife and children.

天 作 之 合 a H e a v e n-m a d e match.

聯 合 to combine; to unite; to incorporate.

(b) The whole.

合 城 or 合 邑 the whole city.

合 家 the whole family.

合 府 (or 郡) the whole county.

合 族 the whole clan.

(c) Read *ko²·⁵.* **One tenth of a pint** 升

盒 2118 ²·⁵. **A small box with a lid; a casket; a preserve-tin, etc.**

盒·子 or 盒 兒 small boxes of different kinds.

盒·子 錢 box-money—gratuities to servants who bring presents.

盒 蓋 ²the lid of a box.

盍 盇 2119 ²·⁵. **Why not? Would it not be better to?**

盍‘何’不’也 *ho* means.' Why not?'

盍 去 諸 why not leave here?

盍 各 言 爾 志 why not each tell his wish?

盍 徹 乎 why not simply gather in the tithes?

盍 歸 乎 來 why should I not go and follow him?

盍 簪 surrounded by friends.

盍 返 其 本 矣 why not go back to the root of the matter?

嗑 2120 ²·⁵. **Loquacious. Sound of voices. u.f. 喝 No. 2123.**

嗑 嗑 the hum of conversation.

嗑 然 sound of laughter.

闔 2121 ²·⁵. **A leaf of a door. To close, to cover. Inter. 合 No. 2117.**

闔 廬 to close one's cottage—to retire from public life.

闔 門 or 闔 戶 to close the door; the whole household.

闔 閉 to close; to shut up.

(a) The whole, etc.

闔 宅 the entire family.

闔 家 the whole family.

闔 屬 all who belong to...

闔 朝 the whole court—civil and military.

闔 潭 均 吉 I hope that your whole family is well.

闔 郡 公 啓 the whole prefecture unites in this public notice.

曷 2122 ²·⁵. **Why? How? When? What? Where? To stop.**

曷 之 用 to decline to use.

曷 勝¹ 感 戴 how can I adequately express my gratitude?

曷 勝¹ 欣 躍 how can I express my delight?

曷 勝¹ 詫 異 how can I express my astonishment?

⁵曷 可 how is it possible to....?

曷 嘗 an interrogative p h r a s e needing an answer in the negative.

曷 故 what is the reason?

曷 月 in what month?

曷 至 哉 where is he?

¹⁰曷 興 乎 來 why should we not rise up—and do this thing?

曷 虐 朕 民 why does he harass our people?

喝 ¹·⁵·
2123   **To shout out.**

喝 令 to egg on; to incite; to shout an order.

喝 住 be quiet! Stop!

喝 喝 咧 咧 vociferous; uproarious.

喝 大 聲 to shout with loud voice.

⁵**喝 道** or **呵 導** to clear the road—as runners do.

喝 道 to shout at; shouting, he said....

喝 采 to applaud; to encore.

   滿 場 喝 采 the whole house applauded.

喝。開 to separate people who are quarrelling.

¹⁰**喝 阻** to check; to call on to stop.

呼 喝 to shout at.

(a) To drink.

喝 湯 to drink soup or gruel.

喝 茶 to drink tea.

喝 西 風 or **喝 風** to drink the wind—to work and get nothing for it; to have nothing to eat; vanity; to stand in a draught.

喝 足·了 to have drunk sufficiently.

喝 酒 to drink wine.

喝 醉·了 to be intoxicated.

喝 墨 水 to drink ink—to study; boys put their pens in their mouths and get very inky.

蝎 ¹·⁵· **A grub which bores into**
2124   **trees and destroys them. Used for 蠍 No. 2644, and read** *hsieh*¹·⁵·

蝎 盛 則 木 朽 when grubs multiply, the trees decay.

蝎 虎 another name for the gecko or **守 宮·**

蝎 蠹 grubs and larvæ of all kinds.

褐 ²·⁵· **Very coarse woollen**
2125   **stuff; serge.**

褐 夫 a poor person.

解 褐 to cast off rough clothing—to become an official.

(a) A dull, dark brown.

褐 炭 brown coal or lignite.

褐 色 dark, dull brown.

褐 鐵 礦 brown hæmatite.

鵰 ²·⁵· **A variety of the long-**
2126   **tailed pheasant, very fond of fighting and of great courage,—thus it is used as an emblem of courage.**

鵰 冠 a cap adorned with pheasant's feathers, formerly worn by the Imperial Bodyguard.

鵰 冠·子 actors who wear the above cap.

鵰 鵙 or **鵰 旦** a sort of nightingale which is said to sing for the dawn; also the name for a large bat 寒 號 蟲 with a wingspread of two feet.

鵰 鳴 不 鳴 the night-bird ceases to sing.

貉 ²·⁵· **Animal something like**
2127   **a fox, having a sharp head and pointed nose; it has thick fur, is nocturnal in habits and fond of sleep. The racoon dog. It has also been classed as a badger.**

貉 裘 badger-skin robes.

狐 貉 之 厚 以 居 when at home (Confucius) wore the thick furs of the fox and badger.

(a) Read *mo*⁴·⁵· A name for the wild tribes of the north.

貉 道 the principles of savages.

壑 ⁴·⁵· **The bed of a torrent; a**
2128   **gully. A pool. Also pron.** *huo*⁴·

大 壑 the ocean.

溝 壑 a ditch, a moat around a city.

谿 壑 a ravine or gully.

郝 ⁴·⁵· **Name of a place. A**
2129   **surname. Read** *shih*⁴·⁵· **To plough. Also pron.** *hao*³·

崔 ⁴·⁵· **A bird flying high. Read**
2130   *chio*⁴·⁵· **Ambition.**

崔 然 ambition; exaltation.

鶴 ²·⁵· **The crane—emblem of**
2131   **longevity. Also read** *hao*²·

鶴 神 the god of cranes.

鶴 立 雞 群 (he excels them all) as a crane among chickens.

鶴 算 同 長 may your life be as long as that of the crane!

鶴 脛 雖 長 斷 之 則 悲 a crane's leg may be long, but you cannot make it shorter without misery to the crane—everything is suited to its own purpose.

⁵**鶴 膝 瘋** disease of the knee-joints.

鶴 頂 the fleshy knob on the head of a crane, said to be poisonous.

鶴 骨 松 姿 lean and shrivelled.

鶴 髮 童 顏 a hoary head with a youthful face.

仙 鶴 the Manchurian c r a n e — paper images of it are burnt in the hope that the departed spirit will ride to heaven on them.(-*hao*²)

¹⁰**玄 鶴** a black or aged crane—a long time.

膲 ⁴·⁵·
2132   **Meat broth. To burn.**

乃 膲 其 目 to destroy the sight by fire.

涸 ²·⁵· **Dried up; exhausted. To**
2133   **dry up. Also read** *hao*,⁴ **or** *ku*⁴·

涸 其 船 cause their ships to be stranded.

涸 轍 之 魚 a fish in a dry rut—in extremities.

涸 鮒 stranded, at the last gasp.

乾 涸 parched; dried up.

嗃 ⁴·⁵·
2134   **To scold with severity.**

HOU.   (ㄡ)
(Heo)

侯 ² A marquis. Distinguish 候
2135   No. 2136.

侯 伯 marquis and earl; a noble.

侯 位 or **侯 爵** the rank of a marquis or count.

侯 度 the duties of a prince.
侯 服 the territory ruled over by a marquis.
侯·爺 a marquis.
侯 畿 the territory of the feudal princes, consisting of 500 sq. *li*, outside that of the State.
諸 侯 the feudal princes.

(a) A target for archery.

大 侯 旣 抗 the great target is set up.
射 侯 to shoot arrows at a target.
皮 侯 a target of leather used in ceremonial archery.

(b) Beautiful, excellent.

洵 直 且 侯 smooth and beautiful —of furs.

(c) A particle, similar to 維 No. 7067.

侯 作 侯 祝 they go on cursing.
侯 誰 在 矣 and who are there?

侯 4 To wait. To expect. Distinguish 侯 preceding.
2136

侯 于 周 服 were submissive to the House of *Chou*.
侯 人 an usher; to wait for another.
侯 敍 I await your conversation— a conventional phrase in invitations.
侯 命 to await commands.
5 侯 敎 I await your instructions.
侯 晤 to await an interview.
侯 示 to await a reply or instructions.
侯 結 to wait for the winding up of a trial.
侯 脈 to feel the pulse.
10 侯 補 or 侯 缺 waiting to fill a vacancy—used of expectant officials waiting for an appointment to office.
侯 訊 to await cross-examination.
侯 許 久 to wait for a long time.
侯 賬 to wait for the account—i.e., I'll pay for it; it's my treat.
我 侯 罷 I'll pay for all this.
15 侯 選 to await selection for official employment.
侯 駕 I await your chariot—conventional phrase used in invitations. Also 侯 光.

侯 驗 waiting for goods to pass the customs.
火 侯 the strength of a fire for cooking.
症·侯 symptoms of a disease.
20 等·侯 or 守 侯 to wait for.
過 午 不 侯 will not receive visitors after noon.

(a) To ask after; to greet.

侯·侯 to inquire after.
問·侯 to send greetings or inquire after.
恭 侯 to pay a ceremonial call.
致 侯 to send greetings.

(b) A period of five days.

七 十 二 侯 72 periods of 5 days which make up the year. *See* 七 No. 579—8.
氣·侯 or 節 侯 climate. *See* 氣 No. 554—4.

喉 2. The throat; the gullet.
2137

喉 嗓 the throat; the voice.
喉·嚨 the gullet; the windpipe.
喉 欖 or 結 喉 or 喉 結 Adam's apple.
喉 痧 or 假 皮 喉 症 or 白 喉 diphtheria.
5 喉 科 the throat, as a branch of surgical treatment or study.
喉 腫 症 a name for goitre.
鵝 喉 凸 goitre.
喉 舌 a mouthpiece—an assistant or interpreter.
令 人 喉 舌 to give people cause to talk.
10 斗 爲 天 喉 舌 the Dipper is the interpreter of Heaven.
王 之 喉 舌 the king's mouthpiece.
喉 衿 or 咽 喉 之 地 a throat— an important pass.
喉 鏡 laryngoscope.
喉 頭 space between the air-passage and the gullet.
15 咽 喉 or 軟 喉 the gullet.
好 喉 嚨 a good voice.
↑ 喉 音 glottals. (*phonet.*)

堠 4 Mounds for beacons.
2138

猴 2 The monkey.
2139

猴 三 兒 a monkey.
猴·子 or 獼 猴 a monkey; an ape.
猴·子 戲 games with monkeys; monkey-tricks.
猴 快 smart; nimble; clever.
5 猴 棗 a variety of persimmon; a kind of bezoar from monkeys.
猴 熊 a kind of bear.
猴ル精 clever; shrewd.
猴 頭 猴 腦 as ugly as a monkey.
要 猴·子 to show performing monkeys.
↑ 猴 兒 筋 small rubber bands.

瘊 2 Warts, pimples.
2140

篌 2 A musical instrument like a lute.
2141

糇
餱 2 Dry provisions.
2142

糇 糧 food taken on a journey.

後 4 Afterwards; behind. Descendants; posterity. The back of; to follow, to come after.
2143

後 乘 I'll see you mount—see you off.
後 事 after death.
置 後 事 to set one's house in order—for death.
後 人 or 後 嗣 successors; posterity; heirs.
5 後 代 or 後 世 after ages; posterity.
後·來 or 後 首 or 以 後 afterwards; later on; in the time to come.
後 來 居 上 those that came last occupy the higher posts.
後 倫 not equal to others.
後 備 軍 reserve forces.
10 後 其 效 之 所 得 puts success last. ↓ 後 效 after-effects.
後·半 天ル the afternoon.
後·半·夜 after midnight.
後 卒 afterwards; in the end.
後 圖 to plan for the future.
15 後 堂 the rear of a house; the breech of a gun.
後 場 the green-room of a theatre.

後 塵 the dust in the rear—to follow another.

後·天 or 後 日 or 後 兒 the day after tomorrow; the first is also the name of the arrangement of the eight diagrams 八 卦 by *Wen Wang,* 文 王; it is also used for the present, visible state of existence; that which is acquired by study and experience, as contrasted with 先 天 the natural endowment.

  大 後·天 the third day after today＝大 後 兒

[20]後 夫 a second husband.

後 妻 a second wife.

後 婚 or 後 婚 兒 a widow re-marrying.

後 學 I, your pupil.

後 宮 the seraglio or harem; used for the women of the palace.

[25]後 帶 岡 嶺 at the rear (of the town) is a range of hills.

後 年 the year after next.

後 庭 the women's part of the building.

後 心 the back.

後 患 disastrous aftermaths.

[30]後 悔 or 後 爷 to regret; to repent.

後 悔 無 及 too late for repentance.

後 應 a force in reserve.

後 房 a backroom; women's apartments.

後 方 the rear.

[35]後 昆 grandchildren; posterity.

後 期 late; the latter period.

後 會 有 期 we shall meet again.

後 果 consequence, the effect of 前 因 a cause.

後 殿 or 後 拒 the rear-guard.

[40]後 母 or 後 娘 or 後 媽 or 繼 母 a step-mother.

後 漢 朝 the *Later Han* Dynasty: A.D. 25—220.

後 生 after–born—a young man; descendants; used respectfully for "I" or "me". 後·生 youthful.

後 生 可 畏 the young students should be treated with respect.

後 知 those later-informed.

[45]後 矩 a pattern for later generations.

後 福 the happiness which comes in old age.

後 義 而 先 利 to put righteousness last and profit first.

後 補 to make up later; reserve.

後 膛 鎗 a breech-loading gun or rifle.

後 葉 after generations.

[50]後 街 a back street.

後 裔 or 後 繼 descendants.

後 距 the spurs of a bird.

後 路 the rear of an army; a back road.

後 輩 juniors; inferiors.

[55]後 進 國 backward nations.

後·邊 at the rear.

後 門 a back-door; the breech of a gun. [guard.

後 防 to guard the rear. 後 衞 rear-

後 隊 the rear-rank.

[60]後 難 the difficulties of the future.

後·面 or 後·頭 or 後 身 behind; the after part.

後·面 的 the latter. A.c. 後 者.

後 顧 茫 茫 the future outlook is uncertain.

後 顧 前 瞻 to look behind and before.

[65]先 後 before and behind; former and latter.

午 後 afternoon.

最 後 一 著 the final move; the finishing stroke. (-*cho¹*)

最 後 之 策 the last resort.

然 後 then; after that; consequently.

[70]背 後 the back; the rear; behind.

觀 其 後 see the development of.

飯 後 after the meal.

先 賞 而 後 罰 let rewards come first and punishments afterwards. [hostile action afterwards.

↑先 禮 而 後 兵 courtesy first and

后 [4] An empress. A king, a ruler.
2144

后 土 the God of the Earth; Earth personified as a god; a minister of *Huang Ti.*

后 妃 maids of honour.

后 稷 Minister of Agriculture under the Emperor *Shun* 舜; the God of Agriculture.

二 后 the two rulers, *Wen Wang* 文 王 and *Wu Wang* 武 王.

[5]君 后 the ruler.

天 后 goddess of sailors.

王 后 烝 哉 our royal prince was a sovereign indeed.

皇 后 the Empress.

皇 太 后 the Dowager-Empress.

[10]皇 皇 后 帝 "O Most Great and Sovereign God." *Legge.* "Al-

mighty God." *Giles.* Most Great and August Supreme. This is quoted from the *Analects*; in the parallel passage as recorded in the *Book of History* we read 上 天 神 后 "Divine Sovereign of the High Heavens."

(a) u.f. 後 preceding

知 止 而 后 有 定 the point where to rest being known, the object of pursuit is then determined.

逅 [4] To meet unexpectedly.
2145

郈 [4] Name of an ancient place in the State of *Lu.*
2146

厚 [4] Thick; substantial; generous.
2147

厚 交 close friendship.

厚 人 自 薄 謂 之 讓 liberal to others and mean towards oneself may be termed humility.

厚 利 large profits.

厚 勝 a great advantage.

[5]厚 味 savoury.

厚 密 very intimate.

厚·實 rich; well off.

厚 幸 great, good fortune.

厚 往 薄 來 to send back with liberal presents those who only brought small ones.

[10]厚 待 to treat kindly.

厚 德 liberality; generosity.

厚 恩 great kindness.

厚 惠 a liberal donation.

厚 情 kind feelings; friendly.

[15]厚 撫 境 外 之 人 be liberal and kind to strangers from other lands.

厚 望 earnestly hopes for.

厚 朴 a variety of magnolia, the bark of which is thick and is valued as a medicine, that from Szechwan specially so.

厚 此 薄 彼 to treat with partiality.

厚 澤 very great favours.

[20]厚 玻 璃 plate-glass.

厚 生 or 厚 民 之 生 to enrich the well-being of the masses.

厚眷 great kindness and grace bestowed.

厚祿 a good salary; rich emoluments.

厚福 great happiness.

[25]厚禮 liberal presents.

厚秩 rich emoluments.

厚紙 thick paper.

厚紙版 cardboard.

厚聘 liberal marriage portion.

[30]厚脣 thick lips.

厚臉 or 面皮厚 having no sense of shame—thick-skinned.

厚葬 an elaborate funeral.

厚薄 thick and thin; rich and poor; liberal and stingy; much and little.

厚謝 liberal recompense.

[35]厚貌深情 the appearance is generous and kindly, but the heart is unfathomable.

厚貺 liberal gifts.

厚費 lavish expenditure; to go to too great expense.

厚資 a large fortune.

厚賜 or 厚贈 to give with liberality.

[40]厚賞 liberal rewards or bounties.

厚載 said of the earth—it is substantial and can support things.

厚遇之 met him with very great kindness; treated him very well.

厚道 kind; considerate; generous.

厚遺之 made him a handsome present.

[45]厚酒 rich wines.

厚酬 or 厚報 to make a liberal recompense.

厚重 generous; dignified; fat and heavy, as a person.

厚重不遷 weighty and immovable.

厚顏 brazen-faced, no sense of shame. *See above* 31.

(a) Sincere, virtuous, genuine.

厚意 with sincere purpose.

厚敦 敦·的 sincere; honest and generous.

忠厚 loyal; trustworthy.

誠厚 sincere, honest.

(b) Secure.

孔之厚矣 perfectly secure.

吼 3.4. The roar of animals. Angry tones.
2148

吼叫 to roar.

吼怒 to roar in anger.

吼號 to cry with loud voice.

犼 3 A fierce Mongolian wolf. Dragon's head on roofs.
2149

齁 1 To snore.
2150

齁餲 to shudder.

齁齁 or 齁齁 to snore.

(a) Very.

齁腥氣 very rank or fishy.

齁臭的 very foul odours.

齁苦 very bitter.

齁酸 very sour indeed.

鱟 4 The king crab.
2151

鱟魚 the king crab.

For *HS-* see after *HUO.*

HU. (ㄏㄨ)

互 4 Mutually; together; each other. Distinguish 万 No.
2152 3344.

互働說 interactionism, as of the body and the mind.

互助 to render mutual assistance.

互婚 intermarriage.

互定 mutual decision.

[5]互尊主權 mutual respect for sovereign rights.

互市 commerce; interchange of trade.

互感 mutually influencing.

互惠主義 reciprocity.

互戰 to meet in conflict.

[10]互換 interchange, as of presents, etc.

互搭 mutual help.

互文 reciprocal phrases.

互易 exchange. (*legal*).

互物 tortoises, turtles, etc., things which fit or dovetail one into the other.

[15]互生嫌隙 to beget mutual disagreements.

互相 mutually; reciprocally.

互相交加 (or 交叉) interlocking; interlacing.

互相交合 to dovetail together.

互相作用 interaction; interplay.

[20]互相來往 constant intercourse.

互相依賴 interdependence.

互相保險 mutual insurance.

互相傳觀 passed around for inspection.

互相呈控 mutual accusation.

[25]互相寬容 forbearing one another.

互相愛 mutual love.

互相接合 or 互合 interlocking.

互相接觸 interacting; intermingling.

互相標榜 mutual admiration. 〔and eulogy.

[30]互相殘殺 (or 毀滅) internecine.

互相比例 in mutual proportion.

互相為肢體 members one of another.

互相組合 mutual association.

互相表裏 inter-relationship, as of physics and chemistry, one dealing with the outer aspects and the other explaining the inner functions and associations.

[35]互相貫通 to interpenetrate.

互相鈎結 interlocking.

互相關照 mutual collusion, as in a combine.

相互條約 reciprocal treaties.

相互訴訟 to interplead.

[40]相互關係 inter-relations; reciprocity.

互結 mutual guarantee.

互訟 litigation.

互訊 to make a joint examination.

互議 or 互商 to deliberate together; to discuss.

[45]互較 to confront—as witnesses.

互選 mutual selection. (*legal*).

互鄉 name of a region which had a bad repute.

前後互異 discrepancy between former and latter.

↑互不侵犯 mutual non-aggression.

沍 4 Frozen; congealed.
沍
2153

沍寒 freezing cold.

暴沍 frozen hard.

乎 1 Preposition—at, in, from, than. Distinguish 平 No.
2154 5303.

合乎此 it agrees with this.

吾一日長乎爾 I am a day older than you.

孝乎鬼神 observe filial piety towards the spirits of those who have departed.

異乎此 it differs from this.

[5]莫大乎是 nothing greater than this.

莫顯乎微 nothing is more manifest than what is minute.

(a) An interrogative particle.

予死於道路乎 shall I die by the roadside?

人而不如鳥乎 is it possible that a man is not equal to a bird?

仁遠乎哉 is virtue then, a thing remote? 哉 following 乎 indicates a negative answer.

君子者乎 is he really a superior man?

怨乎 did they repine?

(b) Exclamatory particle. Expletive.

使乎使乎 A messenger indeed!

如示諸掌乎 as easy as looking at his palm.

富哉言乎 Truly rich is his saying!

巍巍乎 How vast!

[5]已矣乎 Alas, it is all over!

幾乎 Almost; nearly.

蕩蕩乎 How majestic!

呼[1]
2155
To call out; to cry out.

呼使 to call for; to order.

呼來喝去 giving orders in an arrogant manner; inconsiderate; undecided.

呼召 to summon.

呼吼 to roar.

[5]呼叫 to call; to summon.

呼呼喝喝 calling and scolding—displeased.

呼問 to demand.

呼喚 to call to.

呼喊 to bawl.

[10]呼嘯 to scream like a tiger.

呼天喊地 to call upon Heaven and Earth.

呼冤 to cry out grievances.

呼幺喝六 to call the figures on the dice—often used for any disorderly shouting.

呼應[4] to respond to.

[15]呼拜 to take an oath of allegiance to.

呼救 to cry for help.

呼求 to beseech.

呼猫呼狗 (like) calling a cat or a dog.

呼痛 to cry out in pain.

[20]呼聲 a challenge.

呼號 (hao[2]) to weep; to wail.

呼門 to call out at a door.

呼籲 to cry out for aid.

呼風喚雨 to call for wind and rain.

[25]嗚呼 Alas!

(a) To exhale.

呼吸 to breathe.

呼吸作用 the respiratory functions.

呼吸器 the respiratory organs.

呼吸數 rate of respiration.

[5]呼吸系統 the respiratory system.

呼吸表 spirometer.

呼吸運動 respiratory movements.

呼呼睡了 in deep slumber with regular breathing.

呼打 to throb; to palpitate.

(b) To name.

呼作 named....

呼其小字 calling him by name.

稱呼 to address; to call.

(c) Transliterating foreign sounds.

呼畢勒罕 Mongolian term meaning to change into another form.

呼圖克圖 Hutuhktu—Mongolian term for those popularly known as incarnations of Buddhas, e.g., the Dalai Lama, and the Panchen Lama.

虖[1]
2156
The scream of a tiger. u.f. 乎 No. 2154.

嗚虖 Alas!

嘑[4]
2157
To menace; to howl at; to bawl.

嘑爾 an insulting tone of voice.

(a) Read hu[1]. To call. Similar to 呼 No. 2155.

嘑旦 to announce the dawn by shouting.

滹[1]
2158
The bank of a stream. Name of a river which flows into the River Pei above Tientsin.

謼[1]
2159
To shout. To mourn. To invoke. u.f. 呼 No. 2155.

虍[1]
2160
The tiger. Radical 141.

虎[3]
2161
The tiger—an emblem of bravery, cruelty, etc. Used in geomancy to indicate the Yin or negative principle of nature; it is associated with wind.

虎倀 it is reputed that one who has been killed by a tiger becomes his assistant, and helps him to get others—used to express:—assisting an evil man. See 倀 No. 214—2.

虎兕出於柙 if a tiger or a rhinoceros breaks from its cage.

虎添翼 adding wings to a tiger—making bad worse.

虎列拉 Cholera. (Jap.).

[5]虎口 a tiger's mouth; a magistrate's yamen; a dangerous place; space between the thumb and forefinger.

虎口取食 to seek food in a tiger's mouth—to engage in a hazardous occupation.

虎口餘生 saved from the mouth of a tiger—a wonderful escape.

虎叱 to scold with a roaring voice.

虎吻 tiger's mouth.

[10]虎圈 a tiger's pen.

虎士 a brave man; a hero.

虎子[3] the cub of a tiger.

虎將[4] a bold general or fighter.

虎尾春冰 (like) treading on the tail of a tiger, or (walking) on the ice in springtime—very precarious conditions; full of apprehension.

[15]虎形 ferocious appearance; stern.

虎威 warlike; stern; dreadful.

虎拜 interviews of ministers with the ruler.

虎撐 an iron ring filled with pieces of metal, used as a rattle by vendors of quack medicines.

虎政 a cruel, heartless government.

20 虎榜 board announcing successful military graduates, under the Manchu dynasty.

虎步 a tiger's advance—dreadful and terrible; menacing.

虎死雄心在 a tiger is terrible even in death.

虎殘 the remains of a tiger's meal.

虎爪 tiger's claws, prized as a talisman.

25 虎狼之國 fierce, covetous, unsatisfied nation.

虎狼之性 savage, wolfish disposition.

虎皮 tiger's skin—merely a bold exterior.

羊質虎皮 although clad in a tiger's skin, it is still a sheep—bold enough outwardly but afraid at heart.

虎穴龍潭 tiger's den and dragon's lair—a very dangerous place.

30 虎符 tally used in wartime.

虎而冠 a dressed-up tiger, used of a cruelly vindictive man.

虎背熊腰 stalwart men—backs like tigers and loins like bears.

虎臂 a tiger's shoulder; the right side of a grave; boulders in a rapid.

虎臣 officer in charge of the guards.

35 虎舅 another name for the cat.

虎視 to glare at with covetous desire,—from the next—

虎視眈眈 to glare at with fierceness

虎變 the bright stripes of a tiger's skin.

虎豹之鞟猶犬羊之鞟 the bare hide of a tiger or a leopard is just like the bare hide of a dog or a sheep.

40 虎賁百人 a hundred lifeguards.

虎起面孔 a fierce countenance.

虎踞 a crouching tiger—a strategic post.

虎頭捉蝨 to catch lice on the head of a tiger—a daring occupation.

虎頭牌 tiger-headed tablets (outside public offices — warning against disorder, etc.)

45 虎頭蛇尾 a brave beginning but a weak ending.

虎頭軍 troops with tiger-faced helmets (to frighten the foe.)

虎飽 the tiger is satisfied—of an official who has embezzled a large amount.

虎鬚 tiger's whiskers; lamp-pith.

拔虎鬚 to pull out a tiger's whiskers—very daring.

50 虎魄 or 琥珀 a name for amber.

虎鷙 like tigers and vultures—used of fierce troops.

白虎 the white tiger—the west, a geomantic term for subterranean currents and influences, etc., lime.

老虎 a tiger. (lao³-hu³ or lao³-hu)

迎虎于門 to go out to meet a tiger at the door—to meet trouble halfway.

55 雌虎 female tiger.

騎虎之勢 like riding on a tiger—in an awkward position.

騎虎難下 a variant of the above —once mounted it is hard to get off—start something that proves more than one can carry through without danger.

養虎 to breed trouble for the future.

飛虎隊 The Flying Tigers. (fliers)

琥 3 A signet of jade, shaped like a tiger. Amber.
2162

琥·珀 amber.

琥珀拾芥 amber attracts small particles.

琥珀珠 amber beads.

諕
唬 3 To intimidate. Also read hao². The second form is also read hsiao². See No. 2582. The scream of a tiger.
2163

諕·了一跳 made me jump.

諕然 timidly.

嚇諕 to roar in anger and intimidate another.

岵 4 A well-wooded hill. cf. 陟 No. 1004.
2164

陟岵 to long for one's father,—from the following:—

陟彼岵兮 I climb that wooded hill and think of my father.

怙 4 To rely on; to presume on.
2165

怙勢 to presume on power or influence.

怙富 to presume on wealth.

怙恃 those on whom one relies: i.e., parents,—from the following:—

無父何怙，無母何恃 without father on whom can I rely? Without mother who will sustain me?

怙恃其衆 he trusted in numbers.

怙惡不悛 obdurate and irreclaimable.

怙惡凌人 to intimidate and oppress others.

怙終不改 to the last he did not amend.

怙終賊刑 those who offended repeatedly were to be punished with death.

怙過 those who presume on evil.

祜 3 The favour or protection of Heaven; prosperity; blessing.
2166

受天之祜 receive the blessing of Heaven.

胡 2 Recklessly; foolishly; blindly; u.f. 糊 No. 2172.
2167

胡亂 irregular; confused; at random.

胡吵亂鬧 unreasonable altercation.

胡呺 or 亂呺 to rail; to talk obscenely; to talk humbug.

胡吹亂打 to play instruments all out of time and tune.

5 胡哨 to whistle or call one's confederates.

胡·哩嗎哩·的 offhand; recklessly. [fumble.

胡弄 to humbug; to deceive; to

胡思亂想 stupid thoughts; vain imaginings.

胡攪 to create a disturbance.

10 胡混 a loafer; a ne'er-do-well.

胡·盧 to laugh with the hand on the mouth.

胡 花 亂 用 reckless expenditure.

胡 行 careless; reckless.

胡 行 亂 走 to go on at any risk.

15 胡 言 亂 道 to talk folly; foolish talk.

胡 說 or 胡 講 or 胡 纏 to talk rubbish.

胡 說 霸 道 random talk; nonsense.

胡 謅 to extemporize wildly.

胡 鬧 reckless quarreling or action.

20 胡 鬧 八 開 reckless, incompetent —as one who is not in the trade trying to run a business.

胡 鬧 局 a fraud; a "sell", a cheat.

(a) Interrogative particle. How? When? Why?

胡 不 歸 why not return?

胡 爲 如 此 how is this so?

胡 爾 作 劇 why do you mock me?

君 子 胡 不 慥 慥 爾 Is it not entire sincerity which marks the superior man?

5 弗 慮 胡 獲 without careful thought how can you obtain anything?

此 胡 爲 者 what is the meaning of this?

(b) Interjection of admiration.

胡 然 而 天 也 she appears like a goddess.

胡 然 我 念 之 How I think of you!

(c) Long life.

胡 考 之 寧 the rest of old age.

胡 耇 an old man.

永 受 胡 福 to enjoy everlasting happiness.

(d) A dewlap. Whiskers.

胡 顏 the whiskers of an animal.

狼 跋 其 胡 the wolf treads on his dewlap—when it has grown large and impedes him.

(e) A name for foreigners, especially the Mongol and Tartar tribes, including Turks and others.

胡 人 Tartars. Mongols.

胡 同 or 衚 衕 a lane or side street, in the North. - 胡·同 in street names.

胡 地 Mongolia.

胡 孫 or 王 孫 the ape.

5 胡 寇 Tartar invaders.

胡 服 Mongol or Tartar dress.

胡·桃 the walnut.

胡 椒 black pepper.

胡 牀 a light chair something like a rocking-chair.

10 胡·琴 the small Chinese violin with two strings between which the bow is passed.

胡 瓜 the cucumber and similar vegetables.

胡 笳 a whistle made by rolling up the leaf of a reed, used by Tartars.

胡 粉 a cosmetic made from lead.

胡 荽 caraway seeds.

15 胡 葱 a variety of onion from Central Asia.

胡 虜 northern barbarians.

胡 (or 蝴) 蝶 a butterfly. A.p. *hu*[4].

胡 語 Tartar languages. *t'ieh*[3]

胡 越 Mongolia and *Yüeh,* one in the north and the other in the south—far apart.

20 胡 餅 or 燒·餅 a round baked cake of wheaten flour.

胡 馬 依 北 風 the Tartar horse likes the north wind—used of remembrance of home.

胡 騎 mounted Mongolians.

胡 麻 linseed or sesame.

東 胡 Eastern Tartars—Tunguses.

(f) A crescent-shaped blade; a trident.

胡 孑 a crescent-shaped halberd.

胡 戈 a trident.

(g) Sacrificial vessel to hold grain. u.f. 瑚 No. 2171.

胡 簋 vessel to hold grain.

湖 [2] A lake, a sheet of water. The provinces of Hupeh and
2168   Hunan.

湖 廣 or 兩 湖 the provinces of Hunan and Hupeh.

湖 海 lakes and seas.

湖 絲 raw silk from *Huchou.*

湖 邊 by the side of the lake.

5 湖·南 and 湖 北 the provinces of Hunan and Hupeh.

西 湖 the famous lake near Hangchow.

五 湖 the Five Lakes; those of modern classification are:—

鄱 陽 湖 Poyang Lake in Kiangsi.

靑 草 湖 Ts'ing-ts'ao Lake in Hunan.

10 丹 陽 湖 Tan-yang Lake in Kiangsu.

洞 庭 湖 Tung-t'ing Lake in Hunan.

太 湖 T'ai Lake in Kiangsu.

五 湖 四 海 the empire.

煳
燘 [2]   To burn food in cooking; singed; burnt.
2169

煳 底 burnt to the bottom of the pot.

煳 焦 singed, burnt; smoked.

猢 [2] A kind of monkey found in West China.
2170

瑚 [2] A vessel used to contain grain in the imperial sacri-
2171   fices.

瑚 璉 a sacrificial vessel studded with gems.

糊 [2] To paste. Paste. Inter 餬 No. 2177.
2172

糊 口 to make a living.

糊 漿 or 漿 糊 paste.

糊 牆 to paper a wall.

糊 窗 to paper a window.

5 糊 精 dextrine.

裱·糊 to paste, to mount, as maps, etc.

(a) Stupid, foolish, muddled.

糊 來·的 suddenly, in no time; rashly; heedlessly.

糊 倒 to make excuses; to put off.

糊 嗎·的 in no time.

糊·塗 or 糊 裏 糊 塗·的 muddled; stupidly, foolishly.

5 糊 弄 to be disorderly; to fool; to deceive.

糊 混 confused; blurred.

糊 說 亂 道 talking utter rubbish.

糢·糊 indistinct; blurred.

葫 [2] The bottle-gourd or calabash.
2173

葫 荽 caraway seed.
葫 蒜 garlic and leeks.
葫 蕛 flax.
葫·蘆 瓜 the bottle-gourd.

蝴 [2] The butterfly.
2174

蝴 蝶 the butterfly. A.p. *hu⁴-t'iêr³*
蝴 蝶 店 shops on each side, as of an arcade.
蝴 蝶 花 the iris or flag, fleur-de-lis.
蝴 蝶 鉸 broad hinges.

衚 [2] A side street or lane.
2175

衚 衕 a side-street.
死 衚 衕 a blind alley.

醐 [2] The oily scum which floats on boiling butter.
2176

醐 醍 oil of butter.

餬 [2] Congee; thick gruel. To seek or make a living.
2177

餬 一 家·的 口 to support the whole family.
餬 口 to make a living.
餬 口 四 方 to go in search of a livelihood.
餬 饘 thick gruel.

鬍 [2] The beard.
2178

鬍·子 the beard, or moustache.
鬍 梳 a comb for moustaches.
鬍 鬚 the beard.
吹 鬍·子 to blow the moustaches —to talk excitedly.
紅 鬍·子 the *Hunghutzŭ* or Manchurian bandits.

鶘 [2] The pelican.
2179

戶 [4] A door. An individual. A family; population. Radical 63.
2180

戶 丁 a conscript.
戶 冊 register of population.
戶 口 the population.
戶 口 調 查 a census.
[5]戶 喩 or 戶 曉 to make known to the people.
戶 帖 ancient name for a door-plate or 門 牌.
戶 庭 the entrance hall of a house.
戶 房 the revenue department in a *yamen*.
戶 扇 or 門 扇 the leaves of an inner door.
[10]戶 樞 不 蠹 a door-pivot does not get worm-eaten—it is always being moved—used to illustrate the blessing of hard work and stress.
戶 稅 the taxes paid by each household.
戶 籍 record of the population.
戶 者 a gate-keeper.
戶 部 the former Board of Revenue and Population.
[15]戶 限 a piece of wood across the lower half of a door to indicate the inner and outer rooms.
大 (門) 戶 a powerful family.
窓 戶 a window.

(a) Used as a suffix to indicate various classes of people.

店 戶 a shop-keeper.
船 戶 boatmen.
魚 戶 fishermen.

戽 洿 [4] To bale out water.
2181

戽 斗 a bucket fitted with a rope to each side for baling water.
戽 水 上 田 to bale water upon the fields—a method of irrigation.
戽 起 to bale out and float—a vessel.

扈 [4] A tail, thus used for a suite, a retinue.
2182

扈 從 retinue—of officials.

扈 蹕 the Imperial retinue.
扈 養 followers, grooms.
扈 駕 the Imperial escort.

(a) Broad.

扈 冶 full and long—of robes.
扈 扈 extensive.

(b) To restrain.

扈 民 無 淫 restrain the people from disorderly conduct.

滬 [4] To fish by stakes, or placing weirs in the tide-way.
2183 Shanghai.

滬 報 or 申 報 The Shanghai News.
滬 甯 鐵 路 Shanghai-Nanking Railway. A.c. 京 滬 鐵 路
滬 杭 甬 鐵 路 Shanghai, Hangchow and Ningpo Railway.
滬 江 or 滬 a name for Shanghai, derived from the 玄 滬 one of the branches of the *Huangp'u* River 黃 浦.
滬 關 The Shanghai Customs.

弧 [2] An arc or crescent; a bow.
2184

弧 三 角 a spherical triangle.
弧 光 electric arc.
弧 光 燈 an arc lamp.
弧 形 bow-shaped.
弧 行 進 路 arc of progression. (*astron.*).

狐 [2] A fox.
2185

狐 仙 or 狐 魅 a fairy fox.
狐 仙 爺 title under which the fox is worshipped.
狐 假 虎 威 the fox borrows the terror of the tiger—pretending to power, etc.
狐 埋 狐 搰 the fox buries and the fox digs it up.
[5]狐 媚 an enchantress; bewitching; seductive.
狐 尾 猴 bushy-tailed monkey.
狐 嵌 a fox-fur garment of one colour and one quality of skins.
狐 惑 or 狐 疑 suspicious; distrustful; doubt—the fox is said to be very suspicious.

狐 死 兎 泣 or 兎 死 狐 悲 when the fox dies the hare weeps, or, when the hare dies the fox is in distress—fellow-feelings.

[10]狐·狸 the fox.

狐·狸 精 or 妖 狐 an elf; a bewitching woman, supposed to be a fox in disguise.

狐·狸 精 纏·着 bewitched, as by a woman who is really a fox.

狐 羣 狗 黨 a set of rogues.

狐 臭 or 狐 騷   odour from the armpits.

[15]狐 裘 a fox-skin robe.

狐 裘 羔 袖 a fox-skin robe with lambskin sleeves—the greater part of the robe is made of valuable fur, only the sleeves being of the cheaper kind—used to illustrate one whose general character is good, his faults being minor ones.

瓠 [4]   A calabash or gourd. u.f. 葫 No. 2173.
2186

瓠 犀 the rows of seeds in a melon.

齒 如 瓠 犀 her teeth were even and regular like the seeds in a melon.

瓠 果 hard-skinned fruits like gourds, etc., *cucurbitacae*.

瓠 棚 frame for growing gourds.

[5]瓠 瓢 gourd used as a ladle or dipper.

瓠·瓠 the bottle-gourd.

瓠 (*huo*[1.5].) 落 large, yet useless—said of a big gourd which a man tried to use as a water-jar; it collapsed under the weight, and he then found it too big for a ladle.

(a) A pot, a wine-vessel, used like the next.

瓠 觶 wine-vessels.

壺 [2]   A pot; a jug; a vase. Distinguish 壼 No. 3687.
2187

壺 天 heaven in a pot—Taoist expression.

壺 蜂 a large bee with honey.

一 壺 茶 a pot of tea.

夜 壺 or 便 壺 a chamber-pot.

投 壺 the ancient game of pitch-pot, throwing arrows into the three necks of a vase placed for the purpose.

揚 壺 bring in the winepot (or teapot.)

茶 壺 a teapot.

(a) A gourd, similar to preceding.

壺·盧 a gourd.

滸 [3]   The bank of a river.
2188

水 滸 傳 name of a famous novel.

鄠 [4]   Name of a district in Shensi.
2189

護 [4]   To guard, to protect. To assist, to take the part of. To escort. To shelter.
2190

護 儲 戶 protect the thrifty.

護 兵 military guards.

護 前 to cover up a fault and be unwilling to acknowledge it.

護 助 or 救 護 to rescue; to save; to succour; to assist.

[5]護 喪 to manage funeral arrangements.

護 國 安 民 to guard the State and pacify the people.

護 國 軍 National Guard.

護 城 河 a city moat.

護 封 safely sealed—used on the back of envelopes.

[10]護 己 to look after oneself.

護 庇 to guard; to preserve; to shelter.

護 心 甲 or 護 胸 a breast-plate.

護 心 鏡 a metal mirror worn to protect from evil influences.

護 手 the hilt of a sword.

[15]護 持 to protect and assist.

護 日 護 月 to guard the sun and moon (during the eclipses.)

護·書 a portfolio; a case for papers when paying a visit.

護 梯 a staircase.

護 法 to defend or protect Buddhism; defender of the Buddhist faith.

[20]護 照 or 護 票 a passport.

填 發 護 照 to fill in and issue a passport.

護 理 to look after the interests of a post in the absence of the senior in charge; to act as a locum-tenens.

護 衆 philanthropic; to protect the welfare of the masses.

護 短 to screen one's faults; to condone.

[25]護 符 to use another as a screen behind which one can do wrong, or take shelter.

護 肩 a horse's collar.

護 膝 knee-caps for horses, etc.

護 艦 or 護 商 兵 船 naval convoy.

護 花 to protect the flowers—one who pities fallen women.

[30]護 衛 to protect; officer of the Imperial Guards; safeguards.

護 解 to send under escort.

護 身 披 a powerful protecter.

護 身 符 a charm to preserve the body from evil; one behind whom another takes shelter, or in whose power he trusts in order to do evil.

護 軍 or 護 隊 outposts; covering or supporting detachment.

[35]護 送 to escort; to convoy.

護 防 or 護 守 or 護 佑 to guard and protect.

護 領 Captain-General of the Guards.

護 頭 盔 a helmet.

護 駕 the Imperial Escort.

[40]護 髒 to protect from dirt; to keep clean.

看 護 or 看 護 婦 a nurse.

HU.   (ㄏㄨ)
(Huh)

囫 [2.5.]   Round; entire; the whole.
2191

囫 圇 or 渾 侖 complete; whole.

囫 圇 吞 下 swallowed it whole.

囫 圇 吞 棗 swallowed a date-whole—to do a thing without thought; to read without doing any thinking for oneself.

囫 圇 的 衣 服 a complete suit of clothes.

智 [1.5.]   Dawn. To see obscurely. Also read *mei*[4].
2192

笏 2193 4.5. A tablet, about three feet in length by about three inches wide, slightly tapering to the ends, made of various materials—that of the emperor was made of jade; that of a feudal prince of ivory; that of a great officer of mottled bamboo ornamented with beards of shark's skin; that of a smaller official of bamboo bordered with ivory. It was held before the breast at an audience, and was used as a writing tablet.

進象笏思書對命 the official writes on the *hu* what he wishes to say, then presents it to his sovereign, in reply to his commands.

執笏 to hold the tablet—to be a statesman.

忽 2194 1.5. Suddenly; unexpectedly. Distinguish 忽 No. 6915.

忽作忽止 in fits and starts; at intervals.

忽冷忽熱 now hot, now cold; sudden changes of temperature.

忽地 suddenly.

忽忽將暮 suddenly the twilight came upon them.

⁵忽恍 blurred; confused.

忽恍 suddenly startled; confused, blurred.

忽明忽滅 appearing and disappearing, as a flashing light.

忽有感觸 an idea suddenly occurred to him.

忽漫 unexpectedly; suddenly.

¹⁰忽然 or 忽然間 suddenly; in a moment; all at once.

忽發奇想 suddenly came forth with a strange notion.

忽諸 suddenly came to an end.

忽起忽落 sudden rise and fall.

忽遭危疾 suddenly became dangerously ill.

¹⁵忽邊 unawares; all at once; suddenly.

(a) To disregard; to be careless or indifferent; to despise.

忽傲 arrogantly indifferent.

忽其易 to be indifferent to what is easy.

忽心忘懷 absent-minded; careless; indifferent.

忽忽悠悠 careless; indifferent to the passing of time.

⁵忽畧 careless; forgetful of; to disregard; to neglect.

毋忽 do not disregard—these orders.

視之忽然 regarded it with indifference.

輕忽 careless; to slight; to treat with indifference.

(b) Minute, fine. One millionth part of a *tael*.

忽微 an extremely fine thread-like particle.

忽達 the fine point of grasses.

絲忽之間 in the briefest space—instantly.

惚 2195 3.5. Sad. A sound.

惚嗜 a whistle or call, as a signal between thieves, etc.

惚 2196 1.5. Obscure, indistinct.

恍惚 confused and dim; blurred.

搈 2197 1.5. To strike. To bale out; to clean up.

搈斗 a dust-pan; a dirt-basket.

搈水 to bale out water.

颮 2198 1.5. The sound of wind.

浵 2199 2 The dashing of waves.

斛 2200 2.5. A corn measure nominally holding ten pecks 斗, but generally holding about five.

斛手 a clever hand at giving bad measure.

斛行 professional measurers of grain.

槲 2201 2.5. A species of oak; the acorns are used for a black dye.

薢 2202 2.5. A small orchid-like plant; it bears white flowers; a dendrobium.

縠 2203 2.5. Fine silk gauze.

縠粟 a kind of gauze woven with corded thread, crossed and knotted, so as to resemble millet seeds.

觳 2204 2.5. An ancient measure; a goblet. Mean; frightened.

觳瘠 poor, emaciated, thin.

觳薄 lean; mean; poor.

觳觫 frightened; trembling.

(a) Read *hsüeh*[1·5] The foot, a hoof. Exhausted.

衣長及觳 the garments reached to the feet.

(b) Read *chüeh*[3·5] To wrestle; to contend with

強弱不觳力 the strong cannot wrestle with the weak—they are no match.

嘩 2205 4.5. To bawl. Also read *huo*[4·5]

嘩嗜 loud talking.

擭 2206 4.5. A trap, a pit, a snare. Also read *hua*[4]. Read *huo*[4·5] To seize with the hand.

穫 2207 4.5. To cut grain; to reap. Also read *huo*[4].

蠖 2208 4.5. The looper caterpillar. Also read *huo*[4].

尺蠖 the looper caterpillar—used of measuring a span with the fingers.

蝼 屈 to draw back like the looper, in order to get farther ahead; to humble oneself for a time with a view to higher position later on.

鑊 ^{4.5.} A boiler or cauldron; an iron pan. To boil. Also read *huo*[4].
2209

鑊 烹 之 刑 ancient punishment of boiling alive.

矆 ^{4.5.} Red earth used for lacquers, paints, etc. Also read *huo*[4].
2210

HUA. (ㄏㄚ)

化 ⁴ To smelt. To transform; to influence; to change. A suffix for—*ized*, etc,
2211

化·了 gone, melted, finished.
化 人 a magician.
化 作 沙 門 he took the form of a Buddhist priest.
化 俗 to change the customs of a place.
⁵化 凍 to thaw.
化 分 chemical decomposition; to resolve into its elements.
化 合 chemical affinity; to unite into one.
化 合 力 chemical affinity.
化 合 物 chemical compounds.
¹⁰化 命 a fate that cannot be resisted.
化·子 or 叫 化·子 a beggar.
化 外 barbarian; beyond the pale of civilization.
化 學 chemistry.
化 學·上·的 chemical or chemically.
¹⁵化 學 作·用 chemical action.
化 學 分·析 chemical analysis.
化 學 反 應 chemical reaction.
化 學 家 chemists.
工 業 化 學 家 technical chemists.
²⁰化 學 工 業 chemical industries.
化 學 式 chemical formula.
化 學 變 化 chemical changes.
有 幾 化 學 organic chemistry.
無 幾 化 學 inorganic chemistry.
²⁵ 物 理 化 學 physical chemistry; theoretical chemistry.
生 物 化 學 biological chemistry.
↑化 學 工 程 chemical engineering.

化 導 to transform by teaching.
化 工 the operations of nature in producing changes.
化 布 施 to take up subscriptions.
³⁰化 度 to transform the masses and save them—said of Buddha.
化 我 to treat one without propriety.
化 成 to reform completely; to melt into.
化 日 光 天 the sun lights up the skies—times of peace.
化 止 一 國 his influence extended to one State only.
³⁵化 民 to reform the people.
化 汽 evaporation.
化 生 birth by transformation—as insects; used in Buddhism for birth without parents.
化 石 fossils.
化 石 性 of the nature of fossils.
⁴⁰ 石 化 fossilization.
化 緣 or 募 化 to beg for alms—as Buddhist priests.
化 育 the transforming and sustaining force—of Heaven and Earth.
化 裝 品 cosmetics.
化 身 to burn the corpse of a priest; to change oneself into another shape, as the Buddhas are said to do.
⁴⁵化 錢 or 化 紙 or 化 元 寶 to burn paper or mock money for the dead.
化°開 to melt; to digest; to thaw.
化 不 開 will not melt, or digest.
化 除 畛 域 to sink all differences.
化 驗 chemical examination or investigation of.
⁵⁰化 鶴 become a crane—has died.
中 華 化·的 made Chinese in form and character.
基 督 化 Christianized.
文 化 civilization; culture.
歐 化 Europeanized.
⁵⁵氣 化 changes caused by the operations of *Yin* and *Yang*, 陰 陽.
造°化 creation; operations of nature.
風 化 changes for good in manners and customs.
↑分 化 to differentiate.

花 ¹ Flowers, blossoms. Substituted for 華 No. 2217, which was used in ancient times.
2212

花 乳 or 花 蕾 or 花 芽 flower-buds.
花 亭·子 a summer-house.
花 信 風 the spring breezes bringing the news of the flowers.
花 冠 corolla.
⁵花 凋 謝 the flowers have faded.
花 匠 a gardener.
花 卉 flowers; plants; the vegetable world.
花 卸 瓣 the flowers are falling off.
花 史 treatise on botany.
¹⁰花 品 a classification of flowers into ranks like officials.
花 圈 or 花 箍 garlands.
花 圈 弔 亡 funeral wreaths.
花 園 or 花 圃 flower-gardens.
花 塢 (or 壇) raised beds of flowers; rockeries.
¹⁵花 蜜 nectar of flowers.
花 序 inflorescence or the arrangement of blossoms in relation to each other.
花 廠·子 flower-shop.
花 心 the centre of a flower.
花 戶 florists. *See below*. C. 5.
²⁰花 房 greenhouse; conservatory.
花 托 floral receptacle. (*bot*.).
花 時 or 花 期 the flowering season.
花 朝 the birthday of flowers; the date has varied, but the 12th of the 2nd lunar month is generally accepted as correct.
花 朝 月 夕 the day of flowers and the evening of the moon—15th of the 8th lunar month—used to express delightful weather and beautiful prospects.
²⁵花 木 flowers and trees—vegetation.
花 朵 a cluster of flowers; a bud.
花 杖 or 花 欄 a trellis for flowers.
花 柱 a style. (*bot*.).
花 架·子 flower-pot stand.
³⁰花 木 瓜 flowering quince—handsome but of no practical value; used of a handsome but useless man.
花 梗 the peduncle. (*bot*.).
花 椒 a pungent wild pepper which grows in W. China. Also used of cayenne-pepper.
花 氣 or 花 香 fragrance of flowers.

花王 the king of flowers, the peony or 牡丹.

[35]花球 bouquet, ball of flowers.

花瓣 petals.

花瓶 flower-vase.

花生 or 落花生 the groundnut or peanut.

花畦 or 花池·子 beds of flowers.

[40]花當 the green stem of flowers.

花盆 a flower-pot.

花神 the goddess who cares for flowers—Flora. The very soul of the flowers, as, e.g., expressed in a painting.

花秧·子 young seedlings.

花粉 pollen. *See below* A.29.

[45]花粉囊 anthers. (*bot.*).

花絲 filaments, the part of the stamen that supports the anthers. (*bot.*).

花臘 (*hsi*[4,5].) dried petals.

花苞 calyx. (*bot.*).

花苑 flower-garden or park.

[50]花茵 to heap up fallen flowers for a cushion.

花草 flowers and grass—vegetation.

花草展覽會 a flower-show.

花菜 cauliflower. A.c. 菜花.

花蒂 a flower-staik.

[55]花蕊 or 花鬚 the pistils and stamens. (*bot.*).

花寅 or 蜚 寅 the gadfly.

花被 general name for the calyx and corolla. (*bot.*).

花見羞 when the flowers saw her they were put to shame—she was so beautiful.

花露 dew on the flowers; scents, essences of flowers.

[60]花魁 the first of flowers—the *Mei* 梅 or flowering plum; the lotus among water plants; sometimes used of the *Lan ts'ao* 蘭草 or epidendrum.

花魂 the soul of the flowers.

花鳥 name for pictures of flowers and birds.

天花 snow; flowers from heaven; smallpox.

惜花 to care for flowers with affection.

[65]賞花 to enjoy flowers.

↑ 出花, 出天花 to have smallpox.

(a) Used fig. for beauty, ornamental, figured, spotted, variegated, piebald, pertaining to wo-

men, figures of speech, etc. Also used for cotton.

花冠 an ornamental crown. *See above*—4.

花口 eloquent.

花塔 pagoda of several stories.

花·子 a beggar. 花子[3]ₙ flower seed.

[5]花容 or 花貌 fair; pretty features.

花崗岩 (or 石) granite.

花布 coloured cotton cloth; figured calicos.

花廳 reception room of a *yamen*, etc.

花旗 the stars and stripes.

[10]花旗國 The United States.

花旦 an actor who takes female parts.

花板 a ceiling. = 天花板.

花枝招展 the flowering branch attracts attention — describing the beauty of a woman.

花梨木 rosewood.

[15]花樣 a pattern; an expectant official.

花樣翻新 constantly appearing in new forms.

花氈·子 a flowered carpet.

花洋布 printed calicos.

花炮 fireworks.

[20]花燈 coloured lanterns.

花燭 painted candles used at weddings, etc.

花燭之夜 the wedding-night.

花燭夫妻 said of those who have been regularly married.

花牛 a piebald cow.

[25]花白 grey—as hair; white and black mixed.

花眉·子 the grey thrush. = 畫眉

花石 variegated marble.

花箋 fancy note-paper.

花粉 women's toilet-articles—thus ·used for women generally. *See above*—44.

[30]花粉銀 pin-money.

花紅 scarlet; small apples. *See below* B.10.

花紅色 variegated colours.

花綫 variegated thread.

花綢 flowered silks.

[35]花緞 brocades; flowered satins.

花羽紗 figured lustres.

花翎 peacock's plumes, once used as an official badge.

花臉 a beauty; painted faces—heroic characters in a play.

花色 varieties; kinds; descriptions of.

[40]花花搭搭 chequered.

花花綠綠 gay; many-coloured.

花街 a street festooned with flags and lanterns. *See below* B.15.

花衣 a uniform; flowered clothes.

花言巧語 figures of speech; exaggeration.

[45]花賬 a flowery bill—overcharged accounts.

花車 a carriage for festive occasions.

花轎 bridal sedan-chair, generally gay with red and gilding.

花邊 fancy borders in printing; laces; slang term for dollars, from the milled edges.

花酒 a fermented liquor made from flowers. *See below* B.18.

[50]花針 fine needle for embroidery.

花釵 women's hair-ornaments.

花鈿 ornamental head-dress of women.

花頭 flowered patterns; also used for trouble.

出花頭 brought trouble upon; caused him some difficulty.

[55]花顏 a beautiful face.

花鯶魚 the "mandarin" fish, a kind of perch. = 鯶·花魚

(b) Waste, expense. Dissipation, vice, etc.

花·不來 it will not pay; cannot afford it.

花·不起 cannot afford the expense.

花債 riotous waste.

花娘 or 花姐 prostitutes.

[5]花會 a form of gambling in which a certain number of names, etc., is taken, one of which is secretly placed in a receptacle, after which the gamblers make their selection; those whose money is on the one in the receptacle winning about thirty times their stake.

花林 or 花樓 brothels.

花柳 prostitutes.

花柳地·方 flowery willow lanes —places of dissipation.

花柳病 venereal diseases.

[10]花紅 a reward, a bonus, a dividend. *See above* A.31.

出花紅 to offer a reward for anything lost or stolen.

花船 a floating brothel.

花花世界 a dissolute age.
花花公子³ a profligate; a debauchee; a fop.
¹⁵花街柳巷 streets of ill-fame.
花費 or 花散 expenditure.
花°費人·家 to put others to expense.
花酒 to drink with singsong girls. See above—A. 49.
花錢 to spend money.
²⁰花騙 suffering the consequences of dissipation.
花骨頭 another name for dice.

(c) Confused; blurred; muddled; assorted.

花名 a nickname, an alias.
花名冊 a roll of names—so called from the assorted names on it.
花團錦簇 confusion and gay bustle.
花天酒地 gay bustle and debauchery.
⁵花戶 register of population or taxpayers—from the many various names on it.
花甲 the cycle of sixty years—sixty years of age.
花花絮絮 confused; muddled and ill-assorted.
眼發花 the sight growing dim.

(d) Seal; signature.

花字 a signature.
花押 a signature, generally composed of several characters blended into a composite character.
花押蓋章 signed and sealed.
花碼 figures, the abbreviated forms of figures.

(e) In imitation of sounds.

花郎花郎·的聲 the sound of running waters.

划² To pole or punt a boat; a bill-hook. A small open boat.
2213

划·子 a small open boat.
划艇 name of a boat used at Macao.

踝⁴ The ankle. Also read huai², kiai³.
2214

踝·子骨 the ankle bone. Pron.
踝跟 the heel.　⌊huai²,³
踝踝忙行 to hurry on alone.

話
語　⁴　Words, saying, talk. To speak. The second is an ancient form.
2215

話不投機半句多 half a sentence of uncongenial talk is too much.
話中有話 something hidden in the speech—more than is apparent.
話別 a farewell; to bid adieu.
話匣·子 a phonograph; a chatterbox.
⁵話多不甜 too much talk is distasteful.
話敗人 or 敗壞人 to malign another.
話柄 or 話杷 or 話靶 or 話欛 a topic for conversation; material for gossip.
話私 to talk about private affairs; to talk in private.
話箱 a chatter-box.
¹⁰開·了話箱(or 匣·子) to start a loquacious person talking.
話絮叨 or 話叨叨 prosy talk; repetitions.
話舊 to talk over old times.
話·裏有因 there was something more implied than what was said.
話°語 conversation; phraseology.
¹⁵話說 the story goes that—an initial phrase in novels.
話談 conversation.
話音 the tone of voice, its sound or intonation.
話頭 something to talk about; a subject; a term or expression.
俗話 or 白話 colloquial.
²⁰說白話 to tell lies.
土話 local patois. 官話 mandarin.
大話 big talk; braggadocio; threatening language.
瞎話 nonsense; lies.
笑·話 a joke; funny stories; to en laugh at. 廢話 nonsense.
²⁵閒話 idle talk; gossip.

(a) Good.

告之話言 give them good words.

著之話言 write good words.

華² One of the five celebrated mountains of China, in Shensi, called 華嶽 or 西華.
2216

華
葆　² Flowers. Flowery, variegated. Glory, splendour. Inter. 花 No. 2212. of which it was the original form.
2217

華侈 luxurious extravagance.
華光 the God of Fire.
華函 or 華翰 your esteemed favour.
華勝 an ornamental head-dress for women.
⁵華名 an honourable name.
華報 recompense in this life, as contrasted with that meted out in a future life 果報·
華妝 gaily dressed.
華婉 elegant and skilfully turned writings.
華容 handsome.
¹⁰華實 flowers and fruits—show and reality.
華居 your glorious abode—conventional phrase.
華屋山丘 a splendid mansion becomes a mound—used to indicate sudden prosperity and as sudden a collapse.
華年 the young.
華族 nobility. See below—A.10.
¹⁵華服 gay, bright-coloured clothing.
華榮 or 榮華 glory; splendour; grandeur.
華樸 gaudy and simple; ornamental and plain.
華池 the mouth.
華池豐屋 ornamental pond and splendid mansion.
²⁰華燈 coloured lanterns.
華燭 painted candles—the wedding-night.
華王 the 牡丹 or peony, called king of flowers.
華石 ornamental stone; pavement.
華美 or 華麗 or 華彩 gay; elegant; beautiful; variegated.
²⁵華耀 or 榮耀 glorious.
華胄 the descendants of a nobleman.
華胥 the place where FuHsi 伏羲 was born; the mother of Fu Hsi, according to some com-

mentators; the land visited by *Huangti* in his dreams—thus u.f. sleep, the land of dreams.

華 腴 food and clothing in abundance; nobility.

華 英 glorious; splendid.

[20]華 蓋 or 華 芝 a State umbrella; the covering of a bier.

華 蟲 an emblematic pheasant, embroidered on the upper robe of the Emperor; used for the pheasant.

華 表柱 ornamental pillars before a grave.

華 袞 the Emperor's raiment.

華 言 or 華 辭 specious talk; untruth.

[35]華 誕 a birthday; vanity.

華 貴 honourable.

華 贍 splendid and elegant — of literature.

華 近 an honourable post.

華 邊 a dollar, from the milled edge.

[40]華 萼 (or 葶) the calyx of a flower.

華 陀復生 *Hua T'o* has come back to life—he was a famous doctor of the 3rd century A.D. Used on complimentary scrolls, etc., given to doctors.

華 陽 巾 a Taoist cap.

華 首 or 華 顛 a hoary head.

華 驪 gay trappings on a horse.

(a) China. Chinese.

華 人 or 華 民 Chinese people.

華 僑 Chinese overseas.

華 僑 聯 合 會 League of Overseas Chinese.

華 商 Chinese merchants.

[5]華 夏 glorious and extensive—ancient name for China.

華 字 Chinese characters or ideographs.

華 宗 of Chinese stock.

華 工 Chinese labourers abroad.

華 文 Chinese language.

[10]華 族 the Chinese race. *See above* — 14.

華 洋 China and foreign lands; Chinese and foreign.

華 洋 義 賑 救 災 會 International Famine Relief Commission.

華 洋 貿 易 Sino-foreign trade.

華 界 Chinese district of Shanghai.

[15]華 美 Sino-American.

華 顧 問 Chinese advisors.

中 華 民 國 The Chinese Republic.

(b) Used for transliterating.

華 撝 林 vaseline.

華 氏 寒 暑 表 Fahrenheit thermometer.

華 盛 頓 Washington.

華 府 會 議 Washington Conference.

(c) Read hua⁴. A surname.

嘩 譁
2218

Clamour; noise, hubbub.

嘩 拳 to play at *mora* or guess-fingers.

嘩 然 a general hurrah.

嘩 笑 noisy laughter.

嘩 譟 wrangling.

嘩 釦 to shout.

(a) Read wa¹. To change.

嘩 湟 eggs not yet hatched.

樺 ².⁴.
2219

A kind of birch found in Manchuria.

樺 燭 a torch made by rolling birch bark around beeswax.

鏵 ²
2220

A spade or shovel.

驊 ¹
2221

A chestnut horse.

驊 騮 a famous steed, one of the eight belonging to *Mu Wang*. 穆 王.

畫 畫 ⁴
2222

A picture, a painting, a drawing; a mark, a line.

畫 一 uniform; congruous.

畫 一 式 樣 uniform pattern.

畫 一 辦 理 uniformity of treatment.

畫 一 組 織 uniform arrangement or organization.

[5]畫 中 人 (like) a person in a picture—beautiful.

畫 例 rules of art.

畫 供 to sign or make a finger-print on a deposition.

畫 像 or 畫 相 (*hsiang⁴*) to paint portraits.

畫 具 artist's materials.

[10]畫 圖 to draw a plan; to illustrate; a drawing or painting.

畫 圖 器 drawing instruments.

畫 堂 hall decorated with carvings, etc.

畫 學 an art school, during *Sung* Dynasty.

畫 工 or 畫 匠 painters or decorators.

[15]畫 布 canvas for paintings.

畫 師 or 畫 手 or 畫 人 artists.

畫 得 像 drawn accurately; life-like.

畫 戟 a halberd.

畫 所 a studio.

[20]畫 押 or 畫 號 to sign one's private mark or cypher.

畫 杖 a maulstick.

畫 架 an easel.

畫 格 style in paintings.

畫 梁 painted or decorated beams —wealthy families.

[25]畫 棟 雕 梁 painted rafters and carved beams.

畫 樣·子 to draw a plan.

畫 活·了 drawn to the life.

畫 畫 to paint pictures; to paint or draw.

畫 癖 love for pictures amounting to a craze.   ⌐eyebrows.

[30]畫 眉 the grey thrush; to paint the

畫 稿 to prepare a rough draft.

畫 符 or 書 符 to write or draw spells or incantations.

畫 舫 a gaily decorated pleasure-boat.

畫 花 to paint flowers.

[35]畫 花 押 to make one's mark; to draw or sign a device.

畫 虎 畫 皮 難 畫 骨 it is not so easy to paint the bones when making a picture of the tiger, as it is to depict his skin—it is difficult to know the heart.

畫 虎 類 狗 (or 犬) to make an attempt at a picture of a tiger and only achieve the likeness of a dog—attempting more than one has ability for.

畫 蛇 添 足 to draw a snake and add feet—superfluous.

畫 行 to write a sign of assent on a proclamation, etc., to give it authority.

40 畫諾 a sign of assent.
畫餅充饑 to draw cakes in order to satisfy hunger.
畫黛 to pencil the eyebrows.
畫龍點睛 to add eyeballs to the picture of a dragon—said of one or two illuminating sentences in a composition.
一張畫 a picture.
45 山水畫 landscapes.
插畫 illustrations or maps inserted in a book.
水彩畫 water-colour drawings.
油畫 oil-paintings.
漫畫 cartoons. A.c. 卡通.

(a) Also read *hua*². **To draw a horizontal line. To define boundaries; to plan; to delimit.**

畫分 to mark off.
畫地爲牢 to draw a circle on the ground for a prison, as was done in the "good old days."
畫地而受 may be retained by merely making a circle on the ground.
畫地自限 to limit oneself.
5 畫定界限 to delimit boundaries.
畫撥 to transfer, as troops, etc.
畫止 to stop short.
畫策 to lay plans; to make strategems.
畫綫 to draw a line.
10 畫野 to mark out boundaries of land, etc.
畫限 to limit.
一畫 a horizontal line or stroke in writing.
今女(*ju*³)畫 now you are setting a limit to yourself.
筆·畫 the strokes in a Chinese character.
↑ 比·畫 to gesticulate.

HUA. (ㄏㄚ)

(Huah)

劃 2.4.5 **To rive, to divide, to mark, to cut. Inter. preceding.**
2223

劃一不二 uniform—as prices.
劃一定價 prices on a uniform basis.
劃一升斗 uniform dry-measures.
劃一立法 uniform legislation.
5 以期各站劃一 in order to bring all to a uniform standard.
劃·了一下 to make a crease—as with the finger-nail.
劃傷 to wound; to deface.
劃定 to define or mark off—as boundaries.
劃抵 to transfer a debt to a third person.
10 劃損 to deface.
劃玻·璃 to cut glass.
劃界 to delimit boundaries.
劃破 to scratch; to cut open.
劃租 to rent part of a property.
15 劃荻 to sharpen a reed—to write with.
劃裂 or 綻裂 ripped; torn—as clothes.
劃補 to cut and patch a piece in—as in garments, or correcting a document.
劃·開 to cut open; to open out.

⿰巾畫 1.5. **The noise of tearing silk. To tear.**
2224

⿰巾畫嘴 cut his mouth.
⿰巾畫·的一聲 a ripping sound, as of tearing cloth or silk.

繣 4.5. **Obstinate; perverse.**
2225

繣瓦解而冰銷 the tiles are broken and the ice melted—it is all over, said of the utter defeat of an army.

搰 2.5. **To dig.**
2226

狐埋之而狐搰之 what the fox buries, the fox can dig up.

(a) **To mix; turbid.**

搰濁 make the water turbid.

(b) **To exert strength.**

搰搰然用力甚多 to make a strenuous effort and exert much force.

滑 2.5. **Smooth, polished, shining, slippery. Cunning, knavish, subtle.**
2227

滑串流口 glib speech.
滑·了一脚³ to slip.
滑倒³ to slip and fall.
滑·個觔·斗 to slip and turn a somersault.
5 滑利 or 賊滑 or 巧滑 keen, deceitful, tricky.
滑口 or 滑舌 flattering; plausible.
滑學 or 逃學 or 躲學 to play truant.
滑尺 a slide-rule. = 計算尺.
滑戶 a knave.
10 滑擦 to rub smooth; to scrape clean.
滑棍 a slippery customer; a rascal.
滑流 or 滑澤 smooth; slippery.
滑涽 uncertain; confused.
滑·溜 slippery; cunning.
15 滑潤 glossy; smooth.
滑澾澾 or 滑流流 slippery; muddy.
滑石 soapstone.
滑·稽 fawning, plausible; humorous, a wag, comical *See below* C—1.
滑稽文 burlesque; travesty.
20 滑稽畫 cartoons.
滑窗 a sash-window.
滑精 nocturnal emissions.
滑膩 glossy; greasy.
滑賊 or 滑頭 a knave; a slippery customer.
25 滑路 a slippery road.
滑蹶 or 滑跌 to slip; to stumble.
滑錫 slippery; smooth.
滑骨 sesamoid bone.
狡滑 cunning; slippery; knavish.
30 磨滑 grind it smooth.

(a) **A pulley. To turn or wrench.**

滑·子 a catch.
滑車 a pulley.

(b) **Used in transliterating.**

滑脫 Watt—electric unit. = 瓦脫.
滑鐵盧 Waterloo.

(c) **Read** *ku*³·⁵. **Confused.**

滑稽 a syphon—therefore used for a loquacious person. *See above, illus.* 18—20.

猾 2.5. **Artful, cunning, treacherous. A boneless animal which is said to get into tigers and devour them; u.f. preceding.**
2228

猾·的很 very slippery—rascal.
猾胥 unscrupulous clerks.
猾賊 a scamp; a glib rascal.

HUAI. (ㄏㄨㄞ)

淮² A large river which drains part of Honan and N. Anhwei.
2229
Distinguish 淮 No. 1486.

淮夷來求 we came seeking the tribes on the *Huai*.

淮雨 heavy rains, used in error for 淫.

淮鹽 salt from the *Huai* district.

槐² A large tree which grows in North China; it is a kind
2230 of locust, the flowers are used for yellow dye, the timber is useful. *Sophora japonica*.

槐月 the fourth lunar month.

槐檀 a tree, the wood of which was used to produce fire by friction.

洋槐 the ash-tree.

褱² / 裹 To carry in the bosom or the sleeve. To wrap, to conceal.
2231

壞⁴ Bad, spoilt, useless. Vicious. To ruin, to spoil.
2232

壞·了 spoiled; bad; dead.

壞事 wickedness; to ruin an affair.

壞·了·我·的·事 injured what I had in hand.

壞人 a bad man; to ruin a reputation.

⁵壞人名節 destroy the reputation of a man.

壞名 an evil reputation; to ruin a reputation.

壞地·方 a very bad place.

壞地褊小 the territory is small and narrow.

壞坯·子 abusive—you badly moulded, unburnt brick—a reflection on one's bringing-up.

¹⁰壞子³ or 壞品 a spoilt child.

壞宮室以為汙池 they destroyed dwellings to make ponds and lakes.

壞心·的 rascally.

壞意 evil intentions.

壞敗·了 ruined; spoilt; collapsed.

¹⁵壞木 a decaying tree.

壞東·西 bad things; a depraved person, (abusive).

壞根 fundamentally bad.

壞決垣牆 destroyed the walls.

壞法亂紀 breaking the laws and lax in discipline—causing disorder.

²⁰壞牆 ruined, broken-down walls.

壞病 to treat a disease and make it worse.

壞色衣 Buddhist-priest's garments.

壞船 a wreck.

壞良·心 a depraved conscience.

²⁵壞落 a bad end.

壞·處 evil; injury; bad features.

壞蛋 a bad egg, good-for-nothing, (abusive).

壞行⁴ an evil course; corrupt conduct.

壞話 slander.

³⁰壞透 utterly bad; bad through and through.

壞鈔 extravagant and wasteful.

壞骨²頭 said of an utterly unprincipled person.

嚇壞·了 badly scared.

學壞 corrupted by evil associations.

³⁵弄壞 to put a thing out of order; to spoil.

朽壞 decayed, rotten.

發壞 to get into bad ways.

肚·子壞·了 diarrhoea.

酒吃壞·了 injured through drinking intoxicants.

懷 / 怀² The bosom. To carry in the bosom. To cherish. To dwell on. To long for. To comfort.
2233

懷中 in the bosom.

懷人 to remember another.

懷兄懷弟 uterine brothers.

懷其寶而迷其邦可謂仁乎 can he be called humane who keeps his pearl in his bosom, while his country goes to ruin?

⁵懷刑 to carry punishment in the bosom—to have a wholesome fear of the law.

懷利 to think only of profit and gain.

懷古 to cherish thoughts of the past.

懷哉懷哉 perfect rest; sorrow all relieved.

懷土 to think of earthly things—comfort, ease, pleasure, etc.

¹⁰懷孕 or 懷胎 to be pregnant.

懷安 indolent; seeking ease and quiet.

懷居 to love ease.

懷德 to cherish virtue; to cherish kindness.

懷念 to think of; to long for.

¹⁵懷恨 or 懷仇 to cherish resentment; to bear ill-will.

懷想 to long for; to remember with fondness.

懷慚 to be shamefaced; to blush.

懷憂 to brood over sorrows.

懷懼 to be fearful; apprehensive.

²⁰懷抱 to nurse in the arms; to care for; to think of.

懷挾 to carry notes, cribs, etc., into an examination.

懷服 submissive.

懷望 to cherish hopes.

懷春 first thoughts of marriage in a young woman's heart.

²⁵懷柔 to treat (strangers) kindly in order to win their hearts.

懷瑾握瑜 carrying gems in his bosom and grasping valuables.—a man of scholarly virtue.

懷疑 to harbour doubts; to hesitate.

懷疑說 (or 論) scepticism.

懷福 to be fortunate; gathering happiness into one's embrace.

³⁰懷私 to have an eye to one's own interests.

懷舊 to think of old times and old friends.

懷·著 to harbour; to conceive (as a child).

懷諸侯 be kind to the visiting princes.

懷貳 double-minded.

³⁵懷邪 to cherish an evil heart.

懷頭 or 橫頭 an end-piece, the ends of a coffin.

懷鬼胎 to scheme to do evil; to hatch mischief.

不能去懷 cannot but think of it.

不足掛懷 not worth giving a thought to.

⁴⁰襄懷 all-embracing.

坐懷 to sit in the lap.

心懷 thoughts; the intents of the heart.

抱·在懷·裏 to hug to the bosom; to keep in mind.

放懷 to relax the mind and forget cares.

⁴⁵身懷利刃 he carried a sharp dagger in his bosom.

開懷暢飲 to have a jolly carousal and forget all cares.

儈 [4]
2234　A wide room.

儈儈 high and grand—as a large hall.

HUAN.　　(ㄏㄨㄢ)

幻 [4] Deception; sleight of hand; magic.
2235

幻世 the illusions of the world of sense.

幻人 a. conjurer, sleight-of-hand performer, a magician.

幻化 magical changes, death, metamorphoses.

幻境 dreamland.

[5]幻塵 the world of illusions. (*Buddh.*).

幻夢·的 visionary; illusory.

幻妖 magic; sleight of hand.

幻妄論 illusionism — the theory that all objective existence is an illusion.

幻影 shadowy; unreal; illusory.

[10]幻惑 illusions.

幻想 or 幻覺 illusions; hallucinations.

幻戲 conjuring.

幻燈 a magic-lantern.

幻術 magical arts.

[15]幻象 unreal images — as in a mirage, etc.

虛幻 illusory; unreal.

桓 [2] A tree having leaves like the willow and a white bark.
2236　Pillars or tablets before a grave. Posts to steady a coffin when lowering it.

桓公 Duke *Huan* of *Ch'i* 齊, died B.C. 643. The most celebrated among the five leading chieftains who held power in China during the 7th cent. B.C.

桓楹 supports for a coffin at a grave.

桓表 pillars erected before a grave.

(a) Martial.

桓撥 to wield power.

桓桓 martial.

睅 [3]
2237　Protuberant eyes.

睅目 goggle-eyes.

宦 [4]
俖 [4] A government servant; an official. Distinguish 官 No. 3552.
2238

宦囊不敷 his official perquisites are insufficient.

宦女 daughter of an official; women sold as concubines.

宦學 travelling to seek scholarship.

宦官 or 閹宦 or 宦寺 or 太監 eunuchs.

[5]宦家子弟 the scion of an official family.

宦情 desire for official life.

宦況 official life with its troubles.

宦牛 a bullock, a castrated ox.

宦者 a eunuch.

[10]宦者令 head of the eunuchs of the palace.

宦貲 official income.

宦途 official life with its ups and downs.

宦遊 travelling officials seeking office.

逭 [4] To escape from; to flee. To avoid.
2239

逭暑 to escape the heat—name of palaces used for this purpose in *T'ang* Dynasty.

逭逃 to run away.

患 [4] Calamity, evil. To suffer. To be troubled or grieved.
2240

患不均 troubled lest (the people) should not keep their proper position.

患不知人也 I am concerned that I do not know men.

不患人之不己知 I am not concerned that men do not know me.

患在几席之下 the trouble is close at hand.

[5]患孰恤之 who would pity such a State when it was in trouble?

患害 or 禍患 calamity.

患得患失 distressed in mind trying to get rich, and then troubled lest he lose it—a small-minded man.

患苦 distress and suffering—of the masses.

患難之交 friendships made during adversity.

後患 after regrets; evil consequences.

思患預防 to be prepared against calamity by forethought.

(a) To contract, as a disease.

患憂鬱病·的 hypochondriac.

患病 to be ill.

患瘋瘋·的 a leper.

㴠 [4]
2241　Indecipherable.

漫㴠單簡 (the characters had) disappeared and were indecipherable (except for) a few odd characters here and there.

緩 [3] Slow, tardy, leisurely; easily, gradually. To delay.
2242　To neglect. To retard.

緩一天 postpone it for a day.

緩不濟急 leisurely action will not help in desperate crises.

緩兵之計 the strategy of delaying the approach of the enemy —to gain by the delay.

緩刑 to reprieve.

[5]緩和 to moderate; to allay.

緩圖 to make plans with great deliberation.

緩徵 to remit taxes for a period, after famine, etc.

緩急 slow and fast; adverse and prosperous.

緩急相應 mutual help in emergency.

[10]緩慢 slow; tardy.

緩步當車 to walk slowly is as comfortable as riding in a carriage.

緩死 to reprieve a capital sentence.

緩決 to delay a capital sentence.

緩流 flowing slowly.

[15]緩無可緩 there cannot be any delay.

緩禍 to mitigate the calamity of another.

緩緩而行 leisurely; carefully walking.

緩行 to go very slowly.

緩衝國 a buffer State.

20 緩衝機 a buffer.

緩議 to defer a discussion.

緩辦 to delay taking action.

緩·過·來·了 he is reviving.

緩限 or 寬緩 to extend a time-limit.

25 緩頰 to exhort another with pleasant words to refrain from certain actions.

事不容緩 the matter admits of no delay.

怠緩 careless, negligent.

延緩 to delay.

舒緩 easy-going.

遲緩 dilatory, slow.

豢 4 To feed pigs and dogs with grain. To rear, to support.
2243

豢養 to rear; to support; to nourish.

浣 3
澣 To cleanse; to bathe. A period of ten days. Also read wan³.
2244

浣染 to wash and dye—garments.

浣沐 to bathe.

浣沐之資 the pay of the court officials during the T'ang dynasty. It was distributed every ten days, thus the character 浣 came to be used for a period of ten days.

上, 中, 下浣 the three decades of a month, respectively.

5 浣滌 to purify; to cleanse.

浣濯 to wash; to cleanse.

浣練 the inside of a pumpkin, 冬瓜.

浣衣 to wash clothes.

浣雪 to wipe out a charge and prove innocence.

皖 3 Bright, luminous. An ancient small State in Anhwei.
2245 The province of Anhwei. Pron. wan³.

皖南 and 皖北 the regions lying to the north and the south of the River Yangtze in Anhwei.

睆 3 Beautiful, brilliant, bright. To look around. Also read
2246 wan³.

睆睆然 looking at with attention.

莞 3 Marshy plants; sedge. To smile. Pron. wan³.
2247

莞爾而笑 well-pleased and smiling.

(a) Read kuan³. A district in Kwangtung.

奐 4 Excellent; gay; lively.
2248

奐奐新宮 How elegant is the new house!

奐衍 brilliant array.

美哉奐焉 How beautiful, how brilliant!

喚 4 To call, to summon, to invite.
2249

喚令 to summon, to call to.

喚他止住 tell him to stop.

喚嬌娘 a hand-drum with rattles, which sounds on being twirled round.

喚春 or 喚起 name of a bird which calls at dawn; it is described as small and black.

5 喚醒民衆 to arouse the masses.

喚醒迷途 to arouse those who are in the path of error or superstition.

使·喚 to employ as a servant.

名喚 called....

換 4 To exchange, to change. To remove, to substitute.
2250

換·上新·的 change it for a new one.

換·不回·來 cannot be restored.

換位 displacement. (logic).

換位法 transposition of subject and predicate—conversion. (logic).

5 換·句話·說 in other words.

換奶牙 to change the milk teeth for the permanent set.

換季 to change the official clothing, etc., in spring and autumn,

as was the custom under the dynasties.

換帖 to exchange cards, giving all the particulars of birth, etc., and thus become sworn brothers.

換救 to remedy.

10 換文 exchange of notes by diplomats.

換新 to renew; to change for new.

換易 exchange; to barter.

換替 by turns; alternately.

換氣 to ventilate.

15 換湯不換藥 change the liquid but not the drugs—said when changing goods and getting the same as before; a superficial reform.

換班 to relieve guard; to change a shift.

換班時間 a shift.

換發 to issue in exchange for.

換票 to change bank notes for coin.

20 換約 to exchange treaties.

換肩 to change shoulders as porters or chair-bearers do.

換船 to transship.

換衣·服 to change the clothing.

換親 exchange of cards with a view to making a marriage agreement.

25 換言之 in other words.

換貨 to barter, to exchange goods.

換轉 to transpose; to exchange.

換·過·來 change, as plates, etc., at table.

換錢 to change money.

30 換門道 to change one's profession.

換骨 a thorough change of character and disposition. (Taoist).

換骨奪胎 to reform the disposition and character and become an immortal; used also of writing poetry, to retain the ideas and spirit of the ancients, but changing the words.

包換 to agree to change—an article of purchase, if it is unsuitable.

對換 to exchange.

改換 to change, to alter.

煥 4 Elegant; coloured.
2251

煥爛 variegated; coloured.

渙 [4] To expand. Wide, scattered.

2252

渙 汗 an imperial edict.—as perspiration once produced cannot be recalled, so an edict cannot be revoked.

渙 渙 broad; swelling, as a river.

煥 [4] Flaming, brilliant; lustrous.

2253

煥 乎 其 有 文 章 in what elegant style it is!

煥 別 luminous, clearly distinguished.

煥 然 一 新 quite new.

煥 煥 awe-inspiring.

煥 目 agreeable to the eye.

明 煥 lustrous.

瘓 [4] Illness; numbness of the limbs.

2254

癱 瘓 病 palsy; paralysis.

圜 [2] To revolve, to encircle. To look alarmed. A circle.

2255

圜 土 wall of a prison.

圜 視 to look around in alarm.

圜 轉 to revolve round a centre.

轉 圜 a complete reversal.

(a) Read yüan[2]. A circle. u.f. 圓 No. 7722.

圜 法 ancient term for copper cash.

寰 [2] A wall round the imperial palace; a large domain.

2256

寰 內 within the imperial domain.

寰 區 the whole kingdom.

寰 宇 the world.

擐 [4] To put on.

2257

擐 甲 冑 to put on the armour.

(a) Read hsüan[1]. To strip.

擐 衣 出 其 臂 脛 to strip off the clothing and expose the limbs.

環 [2] A ring, a bracelet. To encircle.

2258

環 中 the middle of a ring—emptiness.

環 列 to place in a circle.

環 坐 to sit in a ring.

環 堵 a low encircling wall; to stand round like a wall.

[5]環 堵 之 室 a house within a low encircling wall—poverty.

環 境 environment.

環 墜 or 耳 環 ear-rings.

環 攻 to attack on all sides.

環 旋 to revolve.

[10]環 暈 lunar or solar halo.

環 海 China—similar to 海 內.

環 狀 軟 骨 the cricoid cartilage of the larynx.

環 珮 a lady's girdle with pendants.

環 球 throughout the world.

[15]環 繞 to encircle; to go round.

環 肥 燕 瘦 Yang kuei fei whose name was 玉 環, was plump, while the favourite of another emperor, (Ch'eng ti of Han dyn.), whose name was Chao fei yen 飛 燕, was thin and lithe—both beauties, yet each in her own way.

環 蟲 ringed worms, as the earthworm, etc., annelida.

環 衛 to surround and guard.

環 視 to look round.

[20]環 護 to compass about and deliver; to aid on all sides.

投 環 to hang oneself—to fall into a noose.

繯 [2] Fine silk. Also read hsüan[3]. To bind, to tie; a noose.

2259

繯 首 to strangle.

投 繯 to commit suicide by hanging.

轘 [2.4.] To tear asunder between chariots.

2260

還 还 [2] To restore, to repay; to recompense.

2261

還 價 to abate a price; to make a lower bid for an article.

還 原 to return to the original condition; to be restored to health.

還 口 to retort; to answer back.

還 席 to give a return-dinner.

[5]還 帶 to restore what one has lost.

還 手 to return a blow.

還 拜 to return a visit.

還 欠 or 還 賬 or 還 債 to pay up a debt.

還 清 all paid—as an account or a debt.

[10]還 甦·過·來 restored to consciousness; to come round.

還 神 to thank the gods.

還 翰 a return letter.

還 起·手·來 to start returning blows.

還 足 to restore in full.

[15]還 錢 to pay for goods which have been purchased.

還 雲 your return letter.

還 願 to fulfil a vow.

(a) To go or to come back.

還 俗 to return to the laity.

還 來 to come back.

還 內 to return to the room.

還 家 or 還 鄉 to return home.

[5]還 踵 in a turning of the heel—very quickly. A.p. hsüan[2].

還 陽 to return to life.

還 魂 the return of the soul to earth after death.

回 還 a return.

往 還 to go and return; to and fro.

(b) Also read hai[2], han[2]. Still, yet, also, even, at the same time. To continue, etc.

還 不 怕 Still they do not fear!

還 不 彀 Still not enough!

還 了³ 得 The idea of such a thing! Can it be? Can it be allowed?

還 在 it is still extant; he is still here; he is still alive.

[5]還 多 still plenty more.

還 好 passable; good enough, but ....; luckily.

還 帶·着 still; moreover; still leading....; still wearing....

還 早 still early; plenty of time.

還·是 這·樣 做 還·是 那·樣 做 Is it to be done in this way or in that way?

[10]還 有 there is still; further.

還有·沒·有,還有 Are there any more? Yes!

還欠多少 How much is still owing?

還沒吃飯 I have not yet had my dinner.

還沒·有 來 he has not come yet.

還罷了 very well; that will do—an expression of satisfaction. --·lê or *liao*³.

(c) Read *hsüan*². **To revolve.** u.f. 旋 No. 2894.

還歸 let us return home.

鐶鍰鋍 ²
2262
A metal ring. An ancient weight of over six taels.

鐶·子 a ring.
門 鐶 a ring on a door.

闤 ² **A wall round a market place; the gate leading to it.**
2263

鬟 ² **To dress the hair in a knot on the top of the head. A slave-girl.**
2264

上 鬟 to do up the hair.
丫 鬟 a slave-girl.

懽 ¹ Used for the next. Pleased, etc. Read *kuan*⁴. Grieved, desolate, alone. Also written 悁.
2265

懽懽悁悁 friendless and distressed in mind.

歡 ¹
2266
Pleased; joy, to be glad.

歡伯 the lord of pleasure—wine.
歡呀 to exclaim with pleasure.
歡呼 to cheer; to shout for joy; hurrah.
歡·喜 or 歡樂 or 歡笑 or 歡欣 or 歡暢 or 歡娛 pleased; delighted; to be merry; happy.
⁵歡 喜 不 盡 extremely pleased.
歡 喜 團 a ball of puffed rice rolled in sugar; round coal-briquettes.

歡天喜地 extravagant joy and rejoicing.
歡 奔 亂 跳·的 running and skipping for joy.
歡娛 joy and pleasure.
¹⁰歡 客 an honourable visitor; the day-lily.
歡 宴 a banquet.
歡 容 a happy face.
歡 心 樂 意 very glad.
歡 悚 pleased yet alarmed.
¹⁵歡 情 sensuality.
歡 故 an old friend.
歡 會 a pleasurable meeting: also an assignation with a woman.
歡 慼 pleasure and pain.
歡 愛 to love; to take delight in.
²⁰歡 聚 a gathering for pleasure, as a family re-union.
歡 諧 (or 謔) to make jokes.
歡 跑 to run fast; to frisk about.
歡 躍 happy and dancing for joy; very delighted.
歡 迎 to give a happy welcome to.
²⁵歡 迎 會 a welcome meeting.
歡 送 to send off with happiness.
歡 送 會 valedictory meetings.
歡 遊 to ramble with delight.
歡 門 a doorway gay with festoons.
³⁰歡 顏 a pleasant countenance.
兆 庶 歡 康 the masses were well and contented.

貛
貆 ¹
2267
The badger. 胡貛.

狗 貛 the jackal.
豬 貛 the badger.

讙 ¹ **To bawl; to stimulate by cheering words. Good news.**
2268

讙 呼 道 左 acclamations at the roadside.
讙 囂 acclamations; shoutings.
讙 悅 a cry of joy.
讙 鬧 clamour; hubbub.

驩 ¹ **A tractable horse; a horse frisking;** u.f. 歡 No. 2266.
2269 **Peaceable; happy.**

驩 兜 an unworthy minister of *Yao*, 堯.
驩 洽 a happy gathering.

驩 虞 之 民 a happy, peaceable people.
驩 迎 to welcome.
驩 附 to submit with a good grace.

HUANG.   (ㄏㄨㄤ)

宺 ¹
2270
A watery waste. To reach.

荒 ¹ **Wild, barren. Uncultivated, allowed to become uncultivated.**
2271

荒 原 a desert place.
荒 土 unopened land which has not been brought under cultivation.
荒 塚 an abandoned grave.
⁵荒 墟 waste; deserted; wild land.
荒 塲 a desert place; neglected lands.
荒 年 a year of drought.
荒 年 穀 grain in a year of dearth —a man of extraordinary worth.
荒 年 說 亂 話 in years of drought rumours are easily spread.
¹⁰荒 政 steps taken by the government to relieve famine. *See below.* A.9.
荒 旱 drought and famine.
荒 村 a deserted village.
荒 林 a deserted grove; faded trees.
荒 歉 or 饑 荒 dearth; deficiency.
¹⁵荒 民 famine sufferers.
荒 田 or 荒 地 uncultivated land; fields that have been allowed to lie fallow.
荒 蕪 or 荒 草 bush, jungle.
荒 谷 a lonely valley.
荒 邱 a mound.
²⁰荒 野 or 荒 郊 a wilderness; a desert.
荒 雞 啼 cock-crow at the first watch—out of time.
荒 饉 famine: dearth.

(a) Discarded; deserted; neglected. Reckless; to go to excess.

荒 亂 in disorder.
荒 于 嬉 neglected for pleasure.
荒 亡 wild (with excessive love of hunting) and lost (through wine).

荒·唐 exaggerated; incoherent; boastful; idle; frivolous.

5荒 宴 profligate; unlawful pleasures.

荒 廢 to fall into disuse; forgotten.

荒 怠 lazy; remiss.

荒 惑 besotted.

荒 政 profligate government. *See above*—10.

10荒 於 色 given to debauchery.

荒 棄 to set aside; to discard.

荒 涼 desolate.

荒 淫 profligate; dissipated.

荒 淫 之 樂 sensual joys; dissipation.

15荒 渺 incoherent; vague.

荒 渺 無 憑 fictitious.

荒 疎 obsolete; to be neglected; to grow careless.

荒 空 empty; deserted; ruined.

荒 謬 absurd; irrational.

荒 閒 deserted; unoccupied.

(b) Great, extensive. All. The bounds of.

荒 服 ancient name for the territory 2,000—2,500 *li* from the capital.

荒 服 戎 服 the various tribes of the frontier submitted.

荒 裔 on the frontiers.

荒 遐 very far-extending.

5荒 遠 very far-distant.

太 荒 the uttermost bounds of space.

天 荒 地 老 the extent of heaven and the age of earth.

幷 吞 八 荒 he swallowed up the whole country.

(c) A covering for a coffin.

黼 荒 covering for the top of a coffin.

(d) u.f. next. Flurried.

荒 忽 confused and agitated.

慌
2272
1 Flurried, nervous, hurried, timid.

慌 亂 in confusion; flustered.

慌 做 一 團 all excitement; trembling with nervous agitation.

慌·張 or 心 慌 confusion; bewilderment; trepidation.

慌 忙 or 慌 速 hurriedly.

5慌 慌 不 定 flurried; agitated; confused.

慌 手 忙 脚 all in a bustle of excitement.

慌 疎 agitated.

慌·裹 慌 張·的 in a fluster.

慌 醒 to wake up in a fright.

不 要 慌 don't get flustered.

(a) Read *huang*³. Inter. 恍 No. 2276. Obscure, dim.

慌·惚 obscure; blurred vision; indistinct; confused in mind.

謊
謊
2273
3 To make wild statements. To lie; to mis-state. Lies, falsehood.

謊(價)an overcharge; an exhorbitant price.

謊 詐 false; crafty; double-tongued.

謊 話 or 謊 言 falsehoods; lies.

謊 謬 untrue; fabulous.

5謊 騙 to cheat; to deceive by lies.

扯 謊 to lie.

說 謊 or 撒 謊 to tell lies.

肓
2274
1 The region between the heart and the diaphragm; the vitals.

病 入 膏 肓 the complaint has entered the vital region—it is hopeless.

衁
2275
1 Blood.

衁 池 the reservoir of blood supposed to be found in the body.

恍
恍
2276
3 Wild, mad. Flurried. Inter. 慌 No. 2272.

恍·惚 or 恍 恍 惚 惚 confused; dim; blurred and indistinct; dim vision.

恍 然 irresolute; unready.

恍 狂 delirious; raving.

恍 若 as if; rather like.

晃
2277
3 The full brightness of the sun; dazzling.

晃 曜 or 晃 耀 brilliant; dazzling.

晃 晃 shimmering brightness.

晃 朗 bright; dazzling.

晃 眼 dazzling to the eyes.

晃 蕩 dancing rays of light.

(a) Read *huang*⁴. To sway, shake.

幌
2278
3 A curtain.

幌 傘 a screen; a sunshade.

幌 帷 curtains.

(a) A shop-sign, indicating, by picture or symbol, the nature of the goods sold.

幌·子 shop-signs as above.

妝 幌·子 to make a pretence of ability; to put on airs; an imposter.

膏 藥 幌·子 diamond-shaped squares of wood having a black ball painted on a white ground, to represent plaster—used as druggist's sign.

錢 幌·子 a carved wooden string of cash—a money-changer's sign.

怳
2279
3.4. Clearness of mind. Doubtful; uncertain.

怳 怳 兒 suddenly; at times.

怳 懭 the mind unsettled.

怳 蕩 to jolt; to shake.

怳·裏 怳 蕩·的 shaking; rocking.

榥
2280
3 A screen.

熀
2281
3 The blaze of fire; dazzling. Inter. 晃 No. 2277.

熀 眼 睛 to dazzle the eyes.

旟
2282
3 A sign denoting a tavern formerly a banner or flag was used for this purpose. A shop-sign. Inter. 幌 No. 2278.

皇 ²
2283
Supreme; exalted. August. Imperial. The ruler, the sovereign. Also applied to deceased parents.

皇后 or 國后 an empress; a queen.
皇后娘·娘 the Empress.
皇城 the Imperial city.
皇天 High Heaven.
⁵皇天上帝 The Supreme Ruler of Heaven.
皇天不忒 High Heaven makes no mistakes.
皇天無私阿兮 "O Thou, High Heaven, who art without partiality."
皇天用訓厥道 "High Heaven approved of their ways."
皇太后 or 太后 the Empress-dowager.
¹⁰皇太子³ the heir-apparent.
皇妣 a deceased mother.
皇宮 the palace.
皇·帝 or 皇·上 or 天皇 or 聖皇 the Emperor.
皇恩 Imperial favour.
¹⁵皇曆 the Imperial Almanac.
皇清 the Manchu dynasty.
皇矣上帝, 臨下有赫, 監觀四方求民之莫 "Great is the Supreme! Looking down in majesty, surveying all regions, seeking the repose of the populace."
皇祖 Our Imperial Ancestor.
皇穹宇 the vast heavens.
²⁰皇考 a deceased father.
皇華 Imperial,—said of Imperial envoys.
皇親 relatives of the Emperor by marriage.
皇都 or 皇畿 or 皇州 Peking.
皇陵 or 皇寢 Imperial tombs.
²⁵皇魚 the sturgeon.
惟皇上帝降衷下民 The August Supreme has conferred upon the populace a moral sense —explained as 皇大也; 上帝, 天也, huang signifies great, and Shang Ti means Heaven.
有皇上帝伊誰云憎, "There is the August Supreme. Does He hate anyone?"
敢昭告于皇皇后帝 ···· and presume to announce to Thee, O Most Great and August Supreme. (Giles:—Almighty God.) In the Book of His-

tory, the same instance gives 上天神后 Divine Sovereign of High Heaven.

(a) Good, bright, superior, excellent.
皇皇者華 How brilliant are the flowers!
皇組 a sash to carry a sword.
於 (ㄨ) 皇來牟 How beautiful are the wheat and barley!
穆穆皇皇 How reverent! How magnificent!

(b) A ceremonial cap; ornamented with a feather-like pattern.
有虞氏皇而祭 the lord of Yü (Shun 舜) wore the huang cap when sacrificing.

(c) A screen.
皇邸 a screen behind the throne.
窒皇 screen-door leading to the inner apartments of the palace.
経皇 screen before a grave.

(d) Yellow horse with white spots.
皇駁其馬 yellow and red horses, spotted with white.
有騅有皇 there were black horses with white legs, and yellow and white spotted ones.

(e) An open hall or court.
列坐堂皇 sitting in the open court.
傳集堂皇 summoned them to gather in the open court.
堂·皇 grand in appearance.
(f) u.f. 鳳 No. 2285. The female phœnix.
鳳·皇 the phœnix.
皇一名黃鳥 the huang is also the Yellow Bird or Golden Oriole.

(g) u.f. 遑 No. 2294. Leisure, careless.
皇恤我後 What leisure have I to care for what comes after me?

(h) u.f. 惶 No. 2284, and 徨 No. 2287. Irresolute.
皇皇如也 disturbed; uncomfortable.

(i) A plant described as like wild oats.

(j) Still more.
皇自敬德 let yourself be still more respectful in manner.

偟 ²
2284
Agitated; alarmed.

仿偟 vacillating: irresolute.

(a) Similar to 遑 No. 2294. Leisure.
偟乎不偟 have they leisure or no?

凰 ²
2285
The female phœnix, see 皇 No. 2283—F. 鳳 No. 1894- 20ff.

求凰 to seek a wife.

喤 ²
2286
Sound of jingling bells, or of sobbing.

鐘鼓喤喤 sound of bells and drums.

徨 ²
2287
Doubtful; irresolute.

徊徊徨徨 irresolute; hesitating; going backwards and forwards.
徬徨無家 in doubt, not knowing where to go, not having a home.

惶 ²
2288
Fearful; agitated; nervous.

惶恐 or 恐惶 alarmed; to fear.
惶惑 in doubt; afraid to act.
惶惶 fearing; trembling.
惶擾 perturbed; excited.
惶遽 in haste and agitation.

湟 ²
2289
Name of rivers in Kwang-tung and Kansu.

煌 ²
2290
A great blaze; luminous; glittering, as the stars.

煌煌 resplendent.
明星煌煌 glittering as the stars.

煌 燃 flashing of lightning.

煌 煜 之 朝 顯 the bright light of the dawning sun appears.

篁[2] A clump of bamboos. A hard kind of bamboo with

2291 a white skin, the slender shoots are used for flutes.

篁 笋 bamboo shoots that are too old for eating.

幽 篁 a dense grove of bamboos.

艎[2] A fast-sailing boat.

2292

蝗[2] The locust.

2293

蝗 ○ 蟲 the locust.

遑[2] Leisure. To waste time in trifling; careless.

2294

遑 急 very much pressed and agitated.

遑 遑 disturbed and vacillating in mind.

不 遑 暇 食 no leisure even to eat.

莫 敢 或 遑 not daring to take my leisure.

隍
堭[2] A dry moat outside a city wall; a dry ditch.

2295

城 ○ 隍 the wall and the moat—the guardian deity of every city—the Pluto of the Chinese.

鰉
鱑[2] The sturgeon.

2296

黃[2] Yellow. It was the Imperial colour. Radical 201.

2297

黃 丹 yellow lead.

黃 冊 the register of population under the T'ang Dynasty.

黃 冠 a Taoist priest.

黃 包 車 a ricksha. (Shanghai).

[5]黃 卷 books :—in ancient times yellow-dyed paper was used for books, the dye being used to preserve them from insects.

黃 口 孺 子 a sucking child; an infant—term of abuse.

黃 吻 yellow bills—as young birds have yellow bills, this is used for the young.

黃 土 or 黃 泥 clay; loess.

黃 埔 Whampoa—the port of Canton.

[10]黃 堂 a name once given to prefects.

↓黃 色 新 聞 yellow journalism.

黃 壤 the grave.

黃 天 the name of Chang Chüeh 張 角, leader of the Yellow Turban Rebels at the close of the Eastern Han Dynasty.

黃 嫩 嫩 ○ 的 pale yellow—of flowers only.

[15]黃 宮 the top of the brain—(Taoist).

黃 寶 ○ 石 red cornelian; sardius.

黃 巾 cap of a Taoist priest; rebels which arose at the close of Eastern Han Dynasty.

黃 帝 the Yellow Emperor or Huangti. a legendary monarch—B.C. 2698.

黃 帶 ○ 子 a distinctive badge worn by imperial clansmen of the Manchus.

[20]黃 敎 Yellow Lamaism.

黃 斑 the yellow spot in the eye—point of acutest vision.

黃 旗 the yellow flag for quarantine.

黃 明 the day after Ch'ing ming, about April 6th.

黃 石 英 or 英 水 晶 false topaz.

[25]黃 禍 The Yellow Peril.

黃 童 a young lad.

黃 米 coarse rice.

黃 粱 夢 悟 see under 邯 No. 2036—2. Used to illustrate rapidity.

黃 綾 夾 板 yellow-silk boards in which imperial orders were forwarded.

[30]黃 綿 襖 the yellow wadded-coat—the sun in winter.

黃 綠 or 黃 六 yellow and green—the harvest of last year will not last till that of this year is ripe—used of things failing to come to a successful issue.

黃 羊 the yellow goat.

黃 老 abbrev. for Huangti and Laotzŭ, the reputed founders of Taoism—u.f. Taoism.

黃 耇 an old man.

[35]黃 胖 a clay image; an anænic complaint.

黃 腫 or 黃 疸 jaundice.

黃 臉 鴨 the teal.

黃 朧 朧 ○ 的 pale yellow.

黃 色 yellow.

[40]黃 芩 scutellaria.

黃 花 地 丁 the dandelion.

黃 花 女 a virgin.

黃 花 岡 place outside the north of Canton, where a number of revolutionaries lost their lives in an attempt to take the place at the beginning of the revolution of 1911.

黃 芽 菜 celery cabbage.

[45]黃 華 the chrysanthemum. = 菊 花

黃 落 fall of the leaves in autumn—the miscarriage of a matter; things not going successfully.

黃 薑 turmeric.

黃 蜂 wasps, hornets.

黃 昏 twilight; eventide.

[50]黃 梅 or 杏 ○ 子 the apricot.

黃 梅 雨 rain about the time of the summer solstice.

黃 楊 木 box-wood.

黃 檀 yellow sandalwood.

黃 水 瘡 eczema.

[55]黃 河 the Yellow River.

黃 河 清 (when)the Yellow River is clear—i.e., never—See 河 No. 2111-31.ff.

黃 油 yellow fat—butter.

黃 泉 or 九 泉 the grave; Hades.

黃 流 or 黃 嬌 wine.

[60]黃 海 the Yellow Sea.

黃 浦 the River Huangpu on which Shanghai is built.

黃 潤 a very finely-woven cloth.

黃 炎 used as abbrev. for Huangti and Yen ti or Shên Nung.

黃 熱 病 yellow fever.

[65]黃 燐 yellow phosphorus.

黃 牛 the common ox of China.

黃 犬 the earthworm; the mole-cricket.

黃 玉 the topaz or chrysolite.

黃 璧 璽 chrysolite.

[70]黃 瓜 or 王 ○ 瓜 the cucumber.

黃 生 生 ○ 的 yellow—as ripening grain.

黃 瘦 cadaverous; jaundiced.

黃 白 術 alchemy.

↓ 黃 皮 書 The Yellow Book.

黃 皮 the whampee or yellow-skin, a fruit from Kwangtung.

⁷⁵黃 目 a vessel used in ancient rites for libations; it was decorated with two eyes and gilded.

黃 祖 descendant of the Yellow Emperor.

黃 蜂 窩 (or 房) wasps' nest.

黃 蜂 螫 sting of a wasp; also used fig.

黃 蠟 beeswax.

⁸⁰黃 表 yellow joss-paper.

黃 褐 色 tawny.

黃 豆 soy beans.

黃 赭 石 yellow ochre.

黃 連 a bitter plant used for medicine.

⁸⁵黃 道 the ecliptic; a lucky day; good luck; conjunction of the sun and moon; a state of unconscious innocence. (Tao.).

黃 道 光 the zodiacal light.

黃 道 帶 the zodiac.

黃 道 帶 十 二 宿 the twelve divisions of the zodiac.

黃 道 日 子 a lucky day.

⁹⁰黃 金 gold.

黃 金 時 代 The Golden Age.

黃 金 海 岸 the Gold Coast.

黃 銅 brass.

黃 錢 紙 yellow paper burnt to represent money.

⁹⁵黃 鐘 one of the pitch-pipes of ancient music.

黃 門 the palace door; officers of the palace, afterwards eunuchs; used of those men who have no offspring.

黃 門 之 病 sorrow for the loss of a wife.

黃 門 官 eunuchs.

黃 門 監 chief of the eunuchs.

¹⁰⁰黃 悶 雞 chicken stewed in a closed vessel.

黃 青 玉 the yellow sapphire or oriental topaz.

黃 風 a dust-storm.

黃 香 resin.

黃 馬 褂 the Yellow Riding-Jacket—given by the emperor as a mark of special honour.

¹⁰⁵黃 髮 old age; hoary head.

黃 髮 垂 髫 old and young.

黃 魚 a kind of herring.

黃 鱔 the common eel.

黃 鵠 large bird like the crane.

¹¹⁰黃 鶴 樓 上 看 翻 船 to see a boat overturn while standing on the Yellow-Crane Tower—un-

able to render any assistance.

黃 鸝 or 黃 鳥 the golden oriole.

黃 鼠 狼 the weasel.

大 黃 rhubarb. (tai⁴·huang)

明 黃 orpiment.

¹¹⁵杏 黃 apricot-yellow.

炎 黃 flame-coloured.

牙 黃 ivory-yellow.

籐 黃 gamboge.

草 黃 straw-coloured.

蛋 黃 yolk of egg.

潢¹
2298   A lake or pond.

潢 池 a pool to conserve water.

天 潢 a cluster of stars near Auriga; an imperial generation.

銀 潢 the Milky Way.

(a) Read *huang²*.   Expanse of water.

潢 漾 the vast expanse of water.

(b) Read *huang.¹*   To dye paper.

裝 潢 to dye paper; to mount scrolls, etc., to ornament—used for outward show and adornment.

璜²
2299   Ancient ornament of jade, of a semi-circular shape; it was hung up as a tinkling pendant.

癀²
2300   Jaundice.

癀 病 jaundice.

磺²
2301   Brimstone, sulphur.

磺 坑 or 磺 孔 sulphur-springs.

硫 磺 or 硫 黃 sulphur.

簧²
2302   The metallic tongue in the tubes of the 笙 No. 5742.

簧 口 言 語 plausible talk.

簧 鼓 to spread reports; to make mischief.

笙 簧 a reed-organ.

(a) The catch or spring in a lock.

彈 簧 springs.

鎖 簧 catch of a lock.

蟥²
2303   A green beetle which makes a noise with its wings like a cicada. The horse-leech.

馬 蟥 or 馬 蜞 the horse-leech; often used for common leeches.

麴²
2304   Light yellow dust-like fungoid growth on wine, etc. Barley. Chaff or husks of wheat.

龥²
2305   Yolk of an egg.

HUI.   (ㄏㄨㄟ)
(Huei)

灰¹
2306   Ashes; dust; lime; mortar. From which comes:—grey, drab-coloured.

灰 了 心 or 心 灰 the heart is ashes—disheartened; no desire for; disillusioned.

灰 兜 a piece of cloth with a string at each corner, used to carry mortar.

灰 刼 or 刼 灰 the ashes left after a brigand raid—used to describe such raids.

灰 土 or 灰 塵 o⁻ 灰 泥 dust; dirt.

⁵灰 心 喪 膽 utterly disheartened.

灰 斗 子 a box for keeping a marking-line.

灰 汁 lye.

灰 滅 utterly destroyed—like ashes.

灰 燼 ashes.

¹⁰灰 牆 to plaster a wall.

灰 砌 的 laid with mortar, as contrasted with mud, often used for mortar.

灰 綫 a marking-line.

灰 色 grey; drab-coloured.

灰 蚱 蜢 a destructive grasshopper.

¹⁵灰 頭 土 臉 covered with dust and dirt.

灰 鶴 the crane.

灰 鼠 the squirrel.

成 灰 reduced to ashes.

死 灰 dead ashes—used by *Chuangtzŭ* to compare a state in which the mind ceases to function.

20 生 灰 quicklime.
石 灰 lime.

恢[1] Great; liberal. To magnify. Very. Also read *k'uei.*
2307

恢 偉 great.
恢 奇 great and extraordinary.
恢 廓 broad and extensive.
恢 弘 (or 宏) wide; extensive.
5 恢 張 to extend; to widen.
恢 恢 有 餘 plenty of room to move.
恢·復 to restore; to re-establish; to recover, as lost ground, etc.
恢·復 原 狀 to revert to type; to restore to its former condition.
恢·復 秩 序 to restore order by effort.
10 恢·復 青 春 renewal of youth.
恢 誕 empty boasting; big talk.
天 網 恢 恢 the net of Heaven is all-embracing.

詼[1] To ridicule; to make jokes. Also read *k'uei*[1].
2308

詼 俳 to ridicule.
詼 劇 to play with.
詼 嘲 to banter.
詼 笑 to make sport of.
詼 諧 to joke.

回 叵 囘[2]

To return to or from.
2309

回 不 脱 or 回 不 斷 no breaking off—as an engagement.
回 事 to give a reply concerning the business he was sent on.
回 任 to return to duty.
回·來 to return; by and by.
5 回·來 再 說 we shall talk of this by and by.
回·來·去 辦 settle that afterwards.
回·來·得 慢 a long time in returning.
來 回 there and back.
回 信 or 回 書 or 回 示 or 回 字 a written answer.
10 回 光 reflected light.
回 光 反 照 the reflected rays of the setting sun—the transient

reviving of the dying.
回 光 鏡 reflecting-mirror, as in a microscope.
回·到 to return to....
回·去 to go back.
15 回 向 to do good deeds in the hope that the merit will accrue to others. (*Budd.*)
回 味 returning flavour—as of an olive; the taste is not pleasant at first but it improves afterwards.
回 味 思·量[2] to profit by experience.
回 嘴 to retort; to give a back answer.
回 回 brilliant; dazzling. *See below. A.1.*
20 回 回 然 the sound of strumming on an instrument.
回 國 to return to one's country.
回 報 to bring back a report.
回 天 to propitiate a ruler; to restore the national prestige.
回 天 意 盡 人 力 propitiate Heaven and do your best.
25 回 奏 a memorial in reply.
回 家 to return home.
回 射 reflection.
回 帖 or 回 片·子 a card in acknowledgement.
回 席 a return dinner.
30 回 府 return to your home.
回 廊 passages or verandahs.
回 往 to go and come; to go back.
回 復 to return; to reply; to send an answer.
回 心 向 道 to turn the mind to the true path.
35 回 心 轉 意 to repent; to change one's views.
回 忌 to shun; to fear.
回 想 or 回 思 or 回 憶 to reflect; to recall; to consider.
回 憶 錄 memoirs.
回 手 to return a blow.
40 回 扣 commission on sales.
回 拜 to return a visit.
回 換 to return goods to be exchanged.
回 撓 bent; crooked; winding.
回 擊 return-fire; counter-attack.
45 回 文 a despatch in reply.
回 (廻) 文 詩 verse that can be read both ways; a palindrome.
回 (or 廻) 文 錦 a pattern of embroidery which returns on itself and is the same either way.

回 春 return of spring or of youth —cured.
回 歸 熱 relapsing fever. (*Jap.*).
50 北 回 歸 線 Tropic of Cancer.
南 回 歸 線 Tropic of Capricorn.
回 殘 what is left over; surplus.
回 毛 curly hair.
回 氣 to draw in the breath.
55 回 流 an eddy; a backwater.
回 煞 the return of the soul, which is said to take place several days after death.
回 當 to redeem a pawned article.
回 看 on looking back I see.
回 稟 a return answer to an inquiry from a superior.
60 回 祿 a fire; the God of Fire.
遭 回 祿 to have a fire.
回 禮 a return salute; a return present.
回 空 returning empty.
回 答 to reply.
65 回 籍 to return to one's native place.
回 紆 to bend back.
回 繚 winding, as a stream.
回 翔 to wheel around in the air.
回 老 家 gathered to his fathers; to return home.
70 回 聲 or 回 響 reverberations.
回 西 方 to return to the west—to die.
回 角 angle of reflection
回 話 to bring back word; to report.
回 請 to invite to a return feast.
75 回 護 to screen and give (improper) protection to.
回 蹕 the return of the emperor when on tour.
回 輪 or 退 輪 to reverse a steamer.
回 轉 to turn; to return.
回 轉 儀 gyroscope.
80 回 遹 crooked in heart; not upright.
回 避 to avoid visitors; to withdraw from public life.
回 邪 不 正 crooked, not upright in heart.
回 門 the first visit of a bride to her parents.
回 雪 the graceful attitudes of a dancer—like flakes of whirling snow.
85 回 音 a reply; an answer; an echo.
回 頭 to turn the head; to repent; to reform; later.

回 頭 是 岸 turn the head and there is the shore—repent and salvation is at hand.
回 頭 食 stale food.
浪 子³ 回 頭 the prodigal son's return.
⁹⁰回 顧 to look back; to regret.
回 風 a whirlwind.
回 首 to turn the head.
推 回 decline to receive.
換 回 to recall.
⁹⁵精 魂 回 移 her spirit is stirred to restlessness.
追 回 to recall; to bring back.

(a) Name of ancient Turkish tribes. Mohammedans.

回·回 敎 Mohammedanism.=囘 敎
回·子 a Mohammedan. A.c. 囘·囘.
回 疆 Turkestan.
回 紇 or 黑 回 the Ouigours or Wigours.
回 絨 fustian.

(b) A time, an occasion. A chapter in a novel

一 回 兒³ a period, a time.≡2345.C5.
上 一 回 on the former occasion.
三 回 五 次 time and again; repeatedly.↑囘 囘(兒) every time.
此 回 this occasion.
第 一 回 Chapter One.(of novels).

(c) Inter. 佪 No. 2311. Irresolute.

俯 仰 回 惶 every way I look I am filled with apprehension.

徊² **Undecided; irresolute.**
2310

徘 徊 backwards and forwards; irresolute.

佪² **Disordered; indistinct; doubtful; blurred.**
2311

洄² **A back-water; an eddy; a whirlpool.**
2312

洄 汩 the swirling of rushing waters.
洄 洑 a whirlpool; a race.
洄 洄 the appearance of flowing waters.
洄 瀾 or 洄 洘 the recoil of waves; an eddy; a back-water.

茴² **Fennel.**
2313

小 茴 香 sweet fennel.
大 茴 香 star-aniseed.

蛔
蛕² **The common intestinal worms, the tape-worm.**
蚘
2314

迴
廻² **To bend around and return. To revolve. Inter. 回 No. 2309.**
2315

迴 廊 a corridor or verandah.
迴 憶 to recall; to remember.
迴 抱 or 迴 合 to embrace; to reconcile.
迴 文 詩 a palindrome, verse which can be read forwards or backwards.
⁵迴 曲 bending; winding.
迴 流 水 an eddy, a back-water.
迴 環 to surround; to encircle.
迴 繞 surrounding; to enclose.
迴 迂 winding like a river.
¹⁰臨 事 迴 迂 slow and dilatory in a crisis.
迴 避 to avoid meeting; to withdraw from publicity; to shirk; to withdraw from the presence of a superior.
迴 鑾 the emperor's return to the capital.
迴 風 a whirlwind.

虺³ **A large and dangerous venomous snake. Also occurs used for a viper.**
2316

虺 虺 其 雷 the rumbling of thunder.
虺 蛇 a very large, poisonous snake.
土 虺 蛇 a viper.
虺 蝎 the lizard.
虺 蝎 之 性 fearful like a lizard, which always tries to escape; also explained as a poisonous, sneaking disposition.
虺 蜴 之 行 serpentine ways; ingratitude.

(a) Worn out; fatigued.

虺 隤 fatigued; diseased or weary.

豗¹ **Grunting of pigs. To clash, altercation.**
2317

揮¹ **To move; to shake; to wield. To direct.**
2318

揮 劍 to brandish a sword.
揮 手 to wave the hand; to direct.
揮 拳 to fight with fists.
揮 斥 to direct affairs in a lordly manner.
⁵揮 春 to write scrolls, mottoes, etc., for the new-year.
揮 棹 to ply the oars. (-chao⁴)
揮 毫 or 揮 寫 to flourish the pen —to write.
揮 絃 to thrum on a stringed instrument.
揮 羽 to wave a feather-fan.
¹⁰揮 軍 前 進 to wave a signal to the troops to advance.
揮 鞭 而 定 it can be done (without recourse to arms) by a wave of the whip.
揮 頭 to shake the head.

(a) To sprinkle; to scatter.

揮 散 to disperse.
揮 棄 to reject; to throw away.
揮 灑 to sprinkle; to spend freely —to write much, a scribbler.
揮 發 volatization.
⁵揮 發 性 of a volatile nature.
揮 發 油 naphtha, or other volatile oils.
揮 金 如 土 scatter money like dirt.
揮 霍 to waste; lavish in expenditure; anxious and nervous.

(b) To wipe away.

揮 汗 to wipe off perspiration.
揮 汗 如 雨 wiping off perspiration like rain—used of a great crowd.
揮 沐 捉 髮 in bathing he grasped his hair—to rush out and attend to business, said of Chou kung 周公.
揮 淚 or 揮 涕 to wipe away tears.

暉[1] Bright; radiant. Inter 輝 No. 2321. and 煇 No. 2323.
2319

暉 映 brilliant; dazzling.
暉 煜 brilliantly shining.
暉 目 a name for the secretary-falcon—as it is said to cry when fine weather is coming.
二 月 春 暉 暉 in the second month the spring is clear and bright.
[5]太 白 暉 芒 the bright rays of Venus—as the morning-star.
斜 暉 the slanting rays of the sun.

楎[1] A peg for hanging things on. A clothes-horse.
2320

輝[1] Bright; glorious. Inter 暉 No. 2319. and 煇 No. 2323.
2321

輝 光 or 輝 煌 brilliant; luminous; splendid.
輝 德 distinguished virtue.

(a) Read hsün[1]. To burn.

去 眼 輝 耳 destroyed her sight and hearing.

(b) Read hsüan[4]. A skinner at the ancient sacrifices.

(c) Read yün[4]. u.f. 暈 A halo.

翬[1] Variegated. To fly. A pheasant.
2322

煇[1] Brightness, glory, shining. Inter. 暉 No. 2319, and 輝 No. 2321.
2323

煇 然 very happy; to brighten up.
煇 耀 glorious; very bright.
交 煇 brightly shining; flashing.

廆[1] A room; the wall of a house. A man's name.
2324

麾[1] A signal flag; a standard. To signal to; to beckon.
2325

麾 下 beneath the banner—under the orders of.
麾 之 不 去 motioned to him, but he would not go.

麾 之 以 肱 motioned to him with his arm.
麾 之 使 去 he motioned him away.
[5]麾 手 to wave the hand.
麾 斥 來 使 he waved off the messenger.
麾 節 signals by flags in ancient battles.
麾 蓋 an umbrella or shade used as insignia in ancient times.
麾 軍 to lead an army.

卉[4] A general term for plants.
2326

卉 木 plants and trees.
百 卉 the vegetable kingdom.
花 卉 flowering plants.

毀[3] To ruin, to destroy, to break down. The form of this character as printed below is the strictly correct one.
2327

毀 人 自 益 to ruin another in order to secure advantage to oneself.
毀 傷 to injure the body; to wound.
毀 城 鑠 兵 destroyed the cities and melted the weapons.
毀°壞 to suffer injury; a loss.
[5]毀 失 to spoil, to destroy; to deface.
毀 家 紓 難 to spend one's fortune on behalf of the State,(in a crisis.)
毀 屋 to destroy dwellings; a ruined house.
毀 形 滅 性 emaciation and utter change of disposition through grief.
毀 慕 worn out with longing for the departed.
[10]毀 損 to spoil; to injure oneself through excessive grief.
毀 敗 or 毀 爛 to destroy; to ruin.
毀 棄 to destroy and cast away.
毀 棄 損 害 罪 the crime of spoiling or damaging the property, documents, etc., of another.
毀 沮 ruined; spoilt.
[15]毀 滅 to exterminate utterly.
毀 玷 flaws, faults, blemishes.

毀 瑕 flaws in a gem.
毀 疾 or 毀 病 illness caused through excessive grief.
毀 瘠 不 形 extreme emaciation and disfigurement through grief.
[20]毀 碎 smashed to fragments.
毀 義 to destroy righteous principles.
毀 薄 decadent. See below. A.4.
毀 裂 軒 冕 destroyed his official cap,—so that he could not receive visitors.
毀 面 to injure the face; to destroy her beauty,—a woman did this to avoid an undesirable engagement.
[25]毀 除 utterly to destroy.
毀 頓 wearied and worn with grief.
哀 毀 worn out with excessive grief.
拆 毀 to pull down—buildings, etc.

(a) To slander. Inter. 譭 No. 2329.

毀 惡 to vilify.
毀 短 to tell the shortcomings of another.
毀 罵 to revile.
毀 薄 to defame. See above—22.
[5]毀 訾 to slander.
毀 訛 to speak of the faults of another.
毀 謗 to defame.
毀 讒 misrepresentation; slander.
毀 辱 to disgrace; to bring shame on another.
不 拘 毀 譽 not prejudiced either by slander or flattery—in seeking men for office.

(b) To shed milk-teeth.

八 歲 毀 齒 at eight the milk-teeth are shed.

燬[3] To destroy by fire. A fire, a blaze.
2328

燬 失 destroyed by fire—as documents, etc.
燬 焚 or 燒 燬 burned; consumed by fire.

譭 諢[3] To slander; to defame. Inter. 毀 No. 2327.
2329

讒 謗 to backbite; to slander.
讒 譽 to curse and to bless.

賄[4] Riches, wealth. Bribes.
2330

賄 和 to give a bribe to hush up a charge.
賄 囑 or 送 賄 or 賄°賂 to bribe; to fee in a case.
賄 托 or 囑 托 to give a bribe in order to get a thing put through.
賄 買 to suborn.
[5]受 賄 to receive bribes.
行 賄 to bribe.

彗[4] A broom. Also read *sao*[4].
2331

彗 星 a comet.

嘒[4] A shrill sound. Twinkling. Small. A soft, melodious voice.
2332

嘒 嘒 管 聲 the harmonious concert of the flutes.
嘒 彼 小 星 tiny indeed are those small stars—said by a girl in speaking of herself and her friends.
鳴 蜩 嘒 嘒 buzz, buzz, the cicadas hum.
有 嘒 其 星 brightly the stars twinkle.
鸞 聲 嘒 嘒 the melodious tinkling of the bells on the bridles.

慧[4] Clever, intellectual, wise. Quick-witted.
2333

慧 劍 the sword of intelligence—which can cut worldly affections. (*Budd.*).
慧 力 the power of intelligence. (*Budd.*).
慧 心 a clever, alert mind.
慧 性 clever, smart.
[5]慧 日 初 長 the sun of wisdom is just rising—i.e., we begin to prosper when we become wise.
慧 明 or 聰 慧 or 敏 慧 sagacious; intelligent; wise.
慧 根 the root of intelligence. (*Budd.*).
慧 業 or 夙 慧 naturally intelligent.

慧 目 mental discernment; eyes that can see all realities,—like those of Buddha, seeing both past and future.
[10]慧 眼 mental perception; eyes that can see the realities of existence, unlike those of the flesh whose vision sees only phantoms and illusions. (*Budd.*).
慧 給 intelligent and eloquent.
慧 覺 self-intelligence which can render others intelligent. (*Budd.*).
慧 門 法 海 the depths of intelligence, and the wide sea of Buddha's system.
慧 黠 quick-witted.
小 慧 petty cleverness; skill, shrewdness.
秀 外 慧 中 beautiful and intelligent.

槥[1] A small coffin used for bringing home the bodies of soldiers. Also read *sui*[4].
2334

槥 櫝 a small coffin, as above.

悔[4] To repent. The name of the three upper lines of any of the diagrams formed from the 八卦. The old form of the next.
2335

悔[3] To repent, to regret. To reject, to turn from.
2336

悔 之 晚 矣 tardy repentance.
悔 之 無 益 repentance is of no use.
悔 前 非 or 悔 非 to repent of former misdeeds.
悔 吝 regret; vexed with oneself.
[5]悔 尤 occasions for regret and matters for blame.
悔 心 regret.
悔 恨 remorse; contrition; vexation.
悔 悟 to awake to a sense of wrongdoing and repent.
悔 懼 to be fearful of the consequences.
[10]悔 改 to repent, to reform.
悔 改 自 新 to repent and make a new start.
悔 禍 regret for former evil deeds which brought calamity.
悔 罪 改 過 to repent and reform.

悔 艾 無 訟 they repented and broke off the litigation.
[15]悔 謝 to regret and confess a fault.
悔 賴 to repudiate.
悔 過 or 悔 罪 or 悔 愆 to acknowledge errors; to repent of one's sins.
悔 過 遷 善 to reform.
後 悔 remorse.
[20]後 悔 遲·了 to repent when it is too late.
死 而 無 悔 to die without regrets.
痛 悔 bitter regrets; remorse.
自 悔 self-reproach.
赧 然 悔 恥 blushing with shame and regret.

晦[4] The last day of the moon. Obscure; dark. Night.
2337

晦 冥 dark; thick—of weather.
雷 電 晦 冥 thick darkness and thunder.
晦 匿 to retire into obscurity.
晦 夜 a dark night.
[5]晦 庵 the name of the house where *Chu Hsi* taught in Fukien, sometimes used for the philosopher himself.
晦 惑 besotted; to lead astray.
晦 明 night and morning.
人 有 不 識 晦 明 者 there are those among men who cannot distinguish light and darkness.
晦 昧 dark and gloomy.
[10]晦 暗 gloomy; dark.
晦 朔 the last day and the first day of the moon, respectively.
晦 蒙 dark; obscure; gloomy.
晦 藏 to go into retirement.
晦 顯 obscurity and manifestation; success and prosperity—ups and downs of a career.

(a) Unpropitious; unlucky.

晦·得 狠 very unlucky.
晦·氣 bad luck; unpropitious.
晦·氣 星 進 命 born under an unlucky star.

誨[4] To instruct; to admonish.
2338

誨 人 不 倦 to teach without weariness.

誨 化 諄 諄 constantly teaching and influencing me.

誨 女 (*ju³*) 知 之 乎 Shall I teach you what knowledge is?

誨 妹 如 嚴 師 she taught her younger sisters like a strict teacher.

[5]誨 授 to impart instruction.

誨 爾 諄 諄 or 叮 嚀 誨 之 constantly instructing you.

誨 示 instructions.

誨 育 門·生 he instructed and cared for his disciples.

誨 諭 teachings; instructions.

[10]冶 容 誨 淫 adorning the face (in a woman) induces men to wantonness.

慢 藏 誨 盜 carelessness in secreting valuables induces men to steal.

惠 [4] ·Favour, benefit. To confer kindness. To accord with. Kind, gracious.
2339

惠 函 or 惠 翰 or 惠 音 Your kind favour.

惠 和 to accord with.

惠 好 to show kindness.

惠 康 小 民 benevolent interest in the welfare of the masses.

[5]惠 心 kind-hearted.

惠 念 gracious thoughts.

惠 恤 耆 老 be kindly sympathetic towards the aged.

惠 愛 benevolence; kindness.

惠 我 良 多 he has been very kind to me.

[10]惠 致 a gracious gesture—of the government.

惠 渥 or 惠 潤 enriched with favours.

惠 澤 or 恩 惠 favour; grace.

惠 然 肯 來 you have honoured me by your visit.

惠 綏 to pacify the masses; kindly passed the strap to assist in mounting his carriage—thus:—to meet with a carriage.

[15]惠 而 不 費 kindness need not be expensive.

惠 聲 溢 于 遠 近 the fame of his kindly virtue spread far and wide.

惠 育 to care for with tenderness.

惠 臨 to honour with a visit.

惠 訓 不 倦 gracious and unwearied teaching.

[20]惠 語 gracious words.

惠 賜 禮 物 graciously sent him a present.

惠 貺 gracious bounties.

惠 連 love to a younger brother—from the name of a man 謝 惠 連, who lived during the *Sung* Dynasty.

惠 顧 your kind attentions.

[25]惠 風 a gentle breeze.

以 惠 政 得 民 won the people by kindly government.

受 惠 to receive kindness.

蒙 惠 to be indebted to the kindness of another.

(a) A kind of three-cornered halberd.

蕙 [4] A fragrant species of orchid, called 蕙 蘭; it grows in marshy places and produces eight or nine blossoms on one stalk.
2340

蟪 [4] A kind of cicada, the 蟪 蛄.
2341

蟪 蛄 不 知 春 秋 from *Chuang tzŭ*—the *hui ku* knows not both spring and autumn,—as it does not live to see both.

殨 [4] To open, as an ulcer or sore.
2342

通 身 殨 爛 the whole body broken out in sores.

潰 [4] A stream overflowing its banks. To rush, as a stream.
2343 Pron. *k'uei⁴*.

潰 亂 in disorder; seditious.

潰 出 to overflow.

潰 決 bursting of dikes or banks and overflowing of the stream—to break up, as a compact of friendship.

潰 漏 leaking of water.

潰 濩 the dashing of waves.

潰 爛 to burst, as the bursting of an abcess, or of a bag.

(a) Dispersed; scattered; destroyed.

潰 兵 scattered troops.

潰 圍 to burst through a cordon and escape.

潰 敗 or 潰 墜 defeated and dispersed.

潰 盟 to break an agreement.

[5]潰 腹 to burst asunder—fig., of the effects of unbridled lusts.

潰 茂 luxuriant growth of vegetation spreading in every direction.

軍 人 潰 散 the troops were dispersed.

↑潰 不 成 軍 dispersed in disorder.

靧 [4]
頮 　　To wash the face.
2344

靧 粱 water from millet, formerly used for washing the face.

靧 面 to wash the face.

會 [4] To meet; to assemble. To co-operate. A society; a
会 guild; an association. Distinguish 會 No. 6771.
2345

會 元 the first on the list of the examinations for *Chin shih* 進·士·

會 兵 to assemble troops.

會 務 affairs of a society; church-matters.

會 勘 joint-inspection.

[5]會 匪 banditti—members of secret societies banded for seditious purposes.

會 友 a member of a society, especially secret societies.

會 吏 deacon's orders.

會 同 to act in concert; joint-action.

會 咨 to make a joint-communication—to equals.

[10]會 員 a member of a society.

名 譽 會 員 honorary members.

普 通 會 員 regular members.

會 商 　　　to consult together.

會 堂 a meeting house; a synagogue.

[15]會 場 place of meeting.

會 奏 joint-memorial.

會 客 to meet a guest; to visit.

會 審 or 會 訊 joint-investigation.

會 審 公 廨 The Mixed Court. Shanghai.

↓會 晤 to meet; to interview.

20 會 師 to muster troops; to mobilize.

會 幕 The Tent of Meeting.

會 弔 gathering together for mourning.

會 景 a gay procession.

會 期 time appointed for a meeting.

25 會 末 the humblest member—depreciatory term used in letters, etc.

會 查 委 員 joint-committee of investigation.

會 正 president of a society.

會 獵 to meet for hunting—euphemism for going to war.

會 理 to manage conjointly.

30 會 盟 a covenant of peace in feudal times.

會 衆 a general meeting; to meet collectively.

會 督 used by some for a bishop.

會 章 regulations or rules of a society.

會 萃 to assemble.

35 會 葬 to attend a funeral.

會 要 or 會 典 Institutes of the Empire—a compilation of State regulations.

會 親 meeting of relatives.

會 試 the examination for the third degree or 進 士.

會 話 to converse, especially in a foreign language; conversation.

40 會 課 ancient name of a literary club; school-examinations.

會 議 a conference.

會 議 制 the conference-system.

會 議 地 點 place of conference.

會 議 結 果 results of a conference.

45 和 平 會 議 Peace Conference.

特 別 會 議 special meeting or conference.

經 常 會 議 ordinary general meeting.

會 貨 的 a commercial traveller.

會 費 dues of a society.

50 會 遇 to meet by chance.

會 過 一 面 to have met once—slight acquaintance.

會 郎 feast given by relatives of the bride to welcome the bridegroom.

會 鈔 to pay for; to advance money for.

會 銜 a document presented in the name of two or more officials.

55 會 長 president of a society; chairman.

↑ 會 議 錄 record of conferences; minutes.

---

man of a meeting; a man in priest's orders, Anglican.

會 陰 處 the perineum.

會 面 to meet face to face; to interview.

會 食 to assemble for a feast.

會 飯 to have a meal together.

60 會 飲 to assemble for a banquet.

會 館 a guildhall.

會 首 or 會 頭 or 會 主 the manager of a club; chairman, etc.

會 驗 or 會 同 驗 明 a joint-investigation.

會 黨 a faction or party.

65 會 齊 or 會 集 or 會 合 to assemble.

不 期 而 會 a chance meeting.

入 會 to enter a society.

全 體 大 會 a full meeting of the whole society.

再 會 we'll meet again. Goodbye.

70 出 會 to hold a procession.

午 後 宴 會 an afternoon-party.

宴 會 a social-gathering.

拜 會 to pay a visit.

散 會 to adjourn a meeting.

75 正 式 開 會 the meeting was formally opened.

照 會 a communication between officials; a "note."

省 會 Provincial capital.

股 東 常 會 general meeting of shareholders.

都 會 cities.

80 開 會 如 儀 the meeting was opened with the usual ceremonies.

(a) Used as a suffix to indicate a society, association, council, etc. A selected list is given below, in alphabetical order, to illustrate this.

同 學 會 Alumni Association.

同 鄉 會 Association of Fellow Provincials.

議 事 會 business-meeting.

商 會 Chamber of Commerce.

5 中 國 事 務 會 社 China Association.

教 會 the Church.

記 念 會 Commemoration.

教 育 會 Educational Society.

董 事 會 Executive Body.

10 博 覽 會 Exhibition.

職 員 會 Faculty or Staff Meeting.

義 賑 會 Famine Relief Commission.

工 統 會 General Labour Union.

勸 業 會 Industrial Exposition.

15 司 法 會 Legal Association.

文 會 Literary Society.

追 悼 會 Memorial Service.

國 會 National Assembly.

省 議 會 Provincial Assembly.

20 紅 十 字 會 Red-Cross Society.

職 工 會 Shop-assistants Union.

社 會 Society in general.

運 動 會 Sports Meeting.

學 聯 會 Student's Union.

三 合 會 or 天 地 會 Triad Society—a famous secret society in South China.

(b) To understand, acquired ability.

會 不 出 unable to make out—what you mean.

會 作 able to do it; competent.

會 其 意 旨 took the hint.

會 心 to understand; to be mentally alive.

5 會 意 to take a hint; a group of Chinese characters the construction of which suggests the meaning, e.g., 信 from 人 and 言, a man and his word, either a letter, or to trust.

會 悟 靈 明 very intelligent.

會 氣 to have an understanding with; collusion.

會 水 to know how to swim.

會 生 病 liable to cause disease.

10 會 通 thoroughly to understand.

天 不 會 晴 it will not clear up.

理 會 to give heed to.(lü³-)

(c) A little while; short space of time; occasion.

會 子 an interval; a time.

多 會 兒 at any time.

機 會 an opportunity.

立 功 之 會 opportunity to do meritorious service.

一 會 兒(i⁴-huêr³)a moment.

(d) Read k'uai⁴ or kuei⁴. To calculate.

會 計 to calculate; accounting.

會 計 (員) accountant,—as in an office.

會 計 帳 (or 簿) account-books.

會 計 師 accountant—a specialist in accountancy.

5 會 計 年 度 fiscal year.

會 計 法 accountancy.

會 計 處 accountant's department.

繪 [4] To draw, to sketch; to paint.
2346

繪 事 painting and drawing.
繪 事 後 素 the laying on of the colours comes after the preparation of the plain ground.
繪 像 to draw portraits.
繪 具 drawing materials.
[5] 繪 地 圖 to draw maps.
繪 畫 or 繪 塑 to draw and paint.

薈 [4] To flourish, as plants. A species of squills.
2347

薈 蔚 dense, tangled undergrowth —as in a forest.
薈 萃 gathered together.
薈 蔚 luxuriant growth of vegetation; gathering of clouds.
薈 蔚 densely wooded.

喙 [4] A beak, a bill, a snout. Distinguish 啄 No. 1266.
2348

擊 喙 to smack on the mouth.
無 從 置 喙 cannot find a place to stick his beak in—cannot interfere.

(a) To pant.

喙 息 to pant.
困 喙 panting from fatigue.
維 其 喙 矣 startled and panting. —they fled.

彙 [4] A class; a series. To classify.
2349

彙 報 to make a collective report.
彙 征 to promote the wise.
彙 核 to examine collectively.
彙 集 to collect.
彙 解 a collection of opinions, for expounding a book.
彙 訂 to arrange; to classify.
字 彙 a dictionary published under the *Ming* Dynasty, in which the radicals were revised and reduced to 214, and on which later dictionaries were based; a vocabulary.

瀎 [4] Vast, expansive. Read *huo*[4,5].
2350

穢 [4] Dirty, unclean, uncleanness. Also read *wei*[4].
2351

穢 亂 宮 中 foul debauchery in the palace.
穢 事 improper things; disgraceful affairs.
穢 史 a history that only related obscene affairs, and obscured things that were decent.
穢 名 an evil reputation.
[5] 穢 囊 the foul bag—the body. (*Budd.*).
穢 土 the corruptions of the world. (*Budd.*).
穢 德 彰 聞 his foulness was manifest on high—said of Chou 紂.
穢 播 千 秋 the shame extends for a thousand years.
穢 氣 冲 天 it smells to heaven.
[10] 穢 濁 evil, said of men of evil repute.
穢 臭 foul odours.
穢 言 vile talk; lewd speech.

(a) A growth of weeds.

蕉 穢 不 治 the weeds were not kept under control.

(b) Mean.

覺 我 形 穢 conscious that I was acting meanly.

翽 [4] Noise of bird's wings.
2352

匯 滙 [4] Waters converging to one spot; whirling waters.
2353

滙 集 to gather into one place; to collect.
匯 源 a fountain; a source.

(a) To advance money; to remit; a bank draft; a letter of credit.

匯 付 pay to....
匯 息 or 匯 費 the loss by exchange.
匯 撥 to give a draft on.
匯 欵 remittance; drafts.
匯 票 or 匯 單 a money-order; a draft; letter of credit; bill of exchange.

定 期 匯 票 bill for a term.
卽 付 匯 票 bill at sight.
匯 銀 行 or 匯 兌 局 a bank. (*hang*[2])

徽 [1] Honourable; excellent; beautiful.
2354

徽 墨 ink from Hweichow in Anhwei.
徽 猷 good services; high reputation.
徽 美 excellent; admirable.
徽 號 an honorary title. *See below*, C.1.
徽 言 good advice.
徽 音 an excellent reputation; sweet music.

(a) A three-fold cord.

徽 索 a strong rope.
係 用 徽 纆 bind with strong ropes.

(b) Stops on a lute.

以 玉 爲 徽 use jade for the stops.

(c) A pennant, a flag.

徽 號 the blazonry on a flag. *See above*—4.
徽 車 a chariot with a pennant.

(d) Inter. 褘 No. 7092. The sacrificial robes of a queen.

隳 [1] To destroy; to overthrow.
2355

隳 心 disheartened; discouraged.
隳 敗 or 隳 廢 ruined; destroyed; obsolete.
隳 棄 和 好 to break off friendly relations.
隳 突 insolently.

撝 [1] To wave. Inter. 麾 No. 2325.
2356

撝 戈 waved his spear.

(a) Unassuming.

撝 挹 unassuming; humble.
撝 謙 modest; humble.

諱 [4] To conceal. To shun; to avoid the use of, as certain personal names. Taboo.
2357

諱 名 不 諱 姓 avoid using the name, but not the surname, of another.

諱 法 rules for applying names to deceased persons.

諱 疾 而 忌 醫 to conceal the disease and avoid the doctor.

諱 言 forbidden talk; not to be mentioned.

忌·諱 taboo; prohibitions, as certain things which may not be said (on certain occasions) or done (on boats, etc.).

犯 諱 to use sacred names wrongfully; to break taboo=犯 忌 諱

避 諱 avoidance of the use of certain names, as the personal name of one in a superior station.

隱 諱 to conceal.

躗 [4]　To exaggerate.
2358

HUN. (ㄏㄨㄣ)
(Huen)

昏 昏 [1]　Dusk, dark,—thus coming to mean confused; stupid.
2359

昏 亂 confusion; muddled; stupid.

昏 亂 貪 墨 disorderly and covetous, grasping officials.

昏 倒 不 能 記 名·字 I am old and cannot remember names.

昏 君 a libertine; a despot.

[5]昏 夙 morning and evening.

昏 夜 or 定 昏 night.

昏 天 醉 地 intoxicated; fuddled with drink.

昏 天 黑 地 intense darkness.

昏 季 times of disorder and confusion.

[10]昏 定 晨 省 in the evening, settle and arrange the parents' bed; in the morning, inquire after their health.

昏 德 vicious conduct.

昏 忘 stupid; dull and forgetful.

昏 怠 dull and indolent.

昏 恣 disorderly, unbridled licentiousness.

[15]昏 憊 extremely weary.

昏 旦 含 吐 evening and morning, concealing and revealing:—i.e., at all times.

昏 昕 just before the light of dawn.

昏 明 dusk and dawn.

昏 昏 睡 熟 sleeping soundly.

[20]昏 昏 默 默 obscure; abstruse.

昏 昧 dark; unintelligible; obscure.

昏 暗 or 昏 黑 or 昏 暮 late; dark; dull.

昏 椓 a eunuch.

昏 沉 沉·的 dull; stupid; misty.

[25]昏 眊 very dim vision.

昏 眩 dizziness.

昏 瞶 dim of vision; the decrepitude of age; old age.

昏 竅 之 腦 筋 befogged brain.

昏 絕 於 地 fell insensible to the ground.

[30]昏 耄 the dullness of senility.

昏 腦 or 昏 頭 addle-pated; dull.

昏 花 indistinct vision; specks before the eyes.

昏 蒙 黑 暗 dark; confused; wandering in mind.

昏 蔽 dull; obscure.

[35]昏 行 to travel by night.

昏 謬 wrong; confused; incoherent.

昏 迷 unconscious; confused; delirious.

昏·過·去 or 發 昏 to swoon; to lose consciousness.

昏 邁 in the evening of life.

[40]昏 醉 muddled through drink.

昏 鈔 an indecipherable bank-note.

昏 鏡 a dull mirror.

昏 鐘 the evening-bell.

昏 闇 之 世 dark ages; times of unrest and disorder:

[45]昏 黃 or 黃 昏 twilight; the dull light of the obscured moon.

通 宵 之 昏 寐 a heavy slumber all through the night.

錯 昏 晝 confused night and day.

(a) u.f. the next. To marry

昏 姻 bride and bridegroom—marriage.

昏 禮 marriage rites.

婚 [1]　To marry a wife; a bridegroom.
2360

婚 姻 bride and bridegroom,—the

---

father of the bride is called 婚, and the groom's father is called 姻; now used for marriage generally.

婚 姻 之 道 marriage.

婚 姻 最 重 marriage is of the utmost importance.

婚 娶 to marry; matrimonial affairs.

[5]婚 嫁 to marry.

婚 家 the bridegroom's family.

婚 屬 marriage connections.

婚 書 marriage contract; the horoscopes of a betrothed couple.

婚 禮 rites of marriage.

[10]婚 筵 a wedding-feast.

婚 親 the wife's family.

婚 配 or 同 婚 or 結 婚 to contract a marriage.

婚 閥 to marry into a nobleman's family.

成 婚 to consummate a marriage.

[15]求 婚 to seek a marriage.

異 種 婚 姻 mixed marriages.

結 婚 證 書 certificate of marriage.

離 婚 divorce.

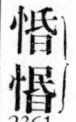

惽 惽 [1]　Confused; stupid, dull.
2361

惽 惽 disorderly; incoherent.

惽 悶 stupid; dull.

惽 耄 failure of mental faculties due to senile decay.

惽 迷 不 醒 incoherent; dull and stupid.

婚 [1]　To die by taking poison.
2362

睧 [1]　Dull vision.
2363

閽 [1]　A door-keeper. An entrance.
2364

閽 人 or 閽 吏 or 閽 侍 eunuchs, doorkeepers at the palace.

閽 闈 or 閽 寺 a gatekeeper.

魂 2 The soul, the spiritual part of man that ascends to heaven, as contrasted with 魄 No. 4988. The wits; the spiritual faculties.
2365

魂 不 守 舍 or 魂 不 在 身 scared out of one's wits.

魂 不 附 體 soul and body parted.

魂 交 intercourse of souls when the body is sleeping.

魂 升 於 天 魄 降 於 地 the rational soul ascends to heaven, the sentient or animal-soul descends to earth.

[5]魂 夢 a dream; a trance.

魂 迷 bewitched.

魂 遊 象 外 in a trance.

魂 靈 論 animism.

魂 飛 魄 散 frightened out of one's senses.

[10]魂 魂 萬 物 the vast variety of created things.

魂 魄 or 魂·靈 or 靈 魂 the soul.

魂 魄 不 愧 my soul will then be unashamed—said by one who hoped to achieve his revenge on another in order to wipe out a wrong done.

三 魂, i.e., 生 魂, 覺 魂, 靈 魂, see each below.—20, 23, 25.

勾 魂 to bewitch; to fascinate.

[15]反 魂 to return to life.

回 魂 the return of the soul to the ancestral tablet.

失 魂 to lose one's wits.

招 魂 to call back the souls of those who have died away from home.

斷 魂 to die. to swoon.

[20]生 魂 the life-principle.

神 魂 出 現 his spirit appeared.

神 魂 行 於 天 the rational soul or spirit moves about in the heavens.

覺 魂 the senses.

遊 魂 or 孤 魂 wandering ghosts—of those who have none to sacrifice for them.

[25]靈 魂 the soul or. spiritual part of man.

渾 2 A turbid torrent; dirty. Chaotic, confused. Blended.
2366 Inter. 混 No. 2371.

渾 不 似 it is dissimilar—said of a lute or guitar which was not as large as the pattern; later it

was used for the 琵·琶 or guitar, and corrupted to 渾 撥 四.

渾 人 a stupid; a lout.

渾 和 blended; confused; mixed.

渾 靄 primeval period.

[5]渾 大 miscellaneous and extensive —of knowledge.

渾 家 depreciatory term for one's wife.

渾 水 turbid water.

渾 沌 confusion; disorder; chaos.

渾 河 the Yung-ting River near Peking.

[10]渾 淆 mixed; confused.

渾 深 宜 鯉 deep and muddy water is good for carp.

渾 渾 如 泉 源 flowing on like a fountain.

渾 濁 turbid; foul; muddy.

渾 金 璞 玉 gold-ore and un-worked jade—of one who has not been spoiled.

[15]渾 鐵 iron-ore.

渾 雜 mixed; confused; blended.

渾 麗 confused.

(a) The whole of; complete; the mass.

渾 元 之 氣 the life-principle.

渾 化 a total transformation.

渾 厚 人 honest, lenient.

渾 圇 or 渾 成 complete; entire; whole.

[5]渾 圓 completely rounded-out.

渾 堅 thoroughly strong.

渾 天 the ancient theory that the earth is inside the heavens as a yoke is in an egg.

渾 天 儀 or 渾 天 球 armillary sphere.

渾 忘 entirely forgetful.

[10]渾 涵 all-embracing.

渾 淪 whole; in one lump.

渾 然 一 新 everything made new.

渾 然 天 理 in entire accord with the principles of Heaven.

渾 然 無 間 斷 perfect; faultless.

[15]渾 身 the whole body.

天 下 一 渾 the whole of the empire under one rule.

琿 2 A fine piece of jade; precious gem.
2367

葷 1 Meat diet; food such as garlic, etc., which is forbidden to vegetarians.
2368

葷 腥 flesh-food; meat and garlic.

葷 茶 a meat diet.

戒 葷 to abstain from these articles of diet.

破 葷 to break a vegetarian vow.

(a) Read hsiin[1]. Strong-smelling vegetables, garlic, onions, leeks, etc.

葷 辛 the vegetables, as above.

(b) Name of a tribe.

葷 粥 (or 育) the Huns, ancestors of the Hsiung-nu.

譚 4 Obscene jests; jokes.
2369

譚 名 a nickname.

譚 衣 harlequin garments in black and white with obscene inscriptions.

譚 言 jests; obscene jokes.

餫 2
餛   See below:
2370

餫 飩 fluffy stuffed dumplings.

混 3 A turbid torrent—thus coming to mean:—muddy; disorderly; mixed; confused.
2371

混 一 to unite in one.

混·不 下 去 cannot make it pay.

混·不 過 去 cannot make ends meet and pass the new-year.

混 世 界 society in disorder.

[5]混 世 蟲 a ne'er-do-well.

混 亂 in confusion.

混·了 一 年 muddled through another year.

混 交 人 種 mixed races.

混 來 to intrude; out of order.

[10]混 充 to palm off; to deceive.

混 入 教 會 to get into the church in an improper way—without qualifications of belief, etc.

混 冒 reckless.

混 到 頭 to come to the end of one's tether.

混 合 mixed; to combine; a confused mass.

[15]混 合 內 閣 a coalition cabinet.

混 合 性 質 of a composite nature.

混 合 説 or 混 合 主 義 syncretic theories.

混 名 or 混 號 or 綽 號 an alias, a nickname.

混 和 to jumble up; to mix together.

20混 嘴 to make a bare living.

混 堂 a bath-house where all bathe in the same water.

混 小·子 a young blackguard.

混 得 很 熟 able to bawl the tunes quite familiarly.

混 成 旅 a mixed brigade of about 10,000 troops, having infantry and mounted troops with artillery, etc.

25混 手·子 or 混 星·子 roughs; rowdies; loafers.

混 捏 or 混 控 to make false accusations.

混 撞 carelessly bumping into.

混 於 所 施 to confuse what has been given.

混 殺 confused.

30混 水 turbid water.

混 沌 or 混 混 沌 沌 confused; unintelligible; chaotic.

混 沌 氏 P'an-ku 盤 古.

混 沌 無 端 confused; in great disorder.

混 混 to gush out.

35混 濁 turbid; muddy; impure.

混 罵 to abuse and revile.

混 要 to be exhorbitant.

混 話 random statements; mischievous talk.

混 認 extorted confessions.

40混 說 foolish talk; to talk at random.

混 賴 to put the blame elsewhere.

混 賬 東·西 you.... ! you scoundrel ! (abusive).

混 跑 to run helter-skelter.

混 鬧 clamour; to brawl; to make an uproar.

45混 雜 mixed up.

男 女 混 雜 men and women mixed indiscriminately.

混 頭 the possibilities of a position or an office.

混 飯 吃 to make a bare living; to live from hand to mouth.

混 鬼 a vagabond ruffian.

50含 混 ambiguous.

焜 ³ 2372   Fire, flames. Pron. k'un¹.

焜 燿 blazing.

圂 ⁴ 2373   A pig-sty; a privy. Inter. 溷 No. 2375. Read huan⁴. u.f. 豢 No. 2243. Grain-fed animals.

君 子³ 不 食 圂 腴 a superior man does not eat the flesh of pigs and dogs.

惛 惽 ⁴ 2374   To dishonour; to disgrace; to distress. Grief; shame; to disobey.

惛 君 to dishonour the sovereign.

惛 命 to disobey orders.

惛 賓 to disgrace a guest, to take away his 'face.'

溷 3.4.   A privy. Confused; 2375   dirty; turbid.

溷 坑 a cesspool.

溷 濁 turbid, disordered.

溷 說 to use bad language.

HUNG.   (ㄏㄨㄥ)

(Hong)

吽 ¹ 2376   Used for last syllable of Om-mani-padme-hum. See 唵 No. 31.

宏 ² 2377   Wide; spacious, as a hall; vast; ample. u.f. 弘 No. 2380.

宏 圖 ambitious plans.

宏 廣 far-reaching; extensive.

宏 恩 abounding grace; great favour.

宏 才 great talents.

5宏 敞 spacious.

宏 業 an extensive business.

宏 發 prosperous, as a business.

宏 遠 long-standing; widely extended.

宏 願 a great ambition; a vow.

10宏 麗 spacious and beautiful—as a mansion.

(a) The echo of a spacious hall.

宏 亮 echoing.

紘 ² 2378   A cord which fastened under the chin to keep an official hat in place, the ends hanging down as tassels.

紘 纓 hat string and tassel.

(a) Vast, similar to 宏 No. 2377.

至 紘 以 大 very expansive and great.

閎 ² 2379   A gate or barrier across a lane. Wide, expansive. Waste.

閎 中 肆 外 store up learning within, to be ready for emergencies from without.

閎 廓 vast wastes; prairies.

閎 衍 numerous and elegant— writings.

閎 謀 extensive schemes.

九 閎 the gates of Heaven.

弘 ² 2380   To enlarge; to expand. Liberal; great; magnanimous.

弘 基 the great office—of a king.

弘 多 very numerous.

弘 大 very great.

器 量 弘 大 capacious.

5弘 獎 liberal bounties.

弘 宣 天 意 to extend the knowledge of the will of Heaven.

弘 播 to make widely known; to broadcast.

弘 教 extensive teachings.

弘 毅 liberal-mindedness and constant endurance.

10弘 深 large and capacious.

弘 茂 flourishing.

弘 誓 深 如 海 an oath as deep as the sea.

弘 遠 far-reaching.

弘 量 liberal; great capacity.

15人 能 弘 道 man can glorify the truth.

泓 ¹ 2381   A clear deep pool. A stream in Shensi.

泓 淳 (t'ing²) a deep pool.

泓 澄 deep, clear water.

清 泉 泓 泓 the deep, clear spring.

汞 ¹ 2382   Mercury, Also read hung².⁴.

汞 粉 or 水 銀 粉 calomel.
汞 膏 mercurial ointment.

紅 [2] Red—emblematic of good-luck, etc.
2383

紅 丹 red lead.
紅 ·了 臉 blushed.
紅 人 a man at the height of his career.
紅 光 the redness of the sky.
[5] 紅 八 仙 the hydrangea.
紅 利 or 官 利 bonus or dividend.
紅 十 字 the Red Cross.
紅 單 port clearance certificate.
紅 土 or 紅 灰 red ochre.
[10] 紅 塵 or 塵 世 or 凡 塵 the world with its cares. (Budd.).
紅 契 a stamped deed,—from the red stamp; an unstamped deed is called a 白 契.
紅 妝 女 or 紅 粉 佳 人 a girl dressed in red—red trousers being worn only by unmarried girls.
紅 娘 the lady-bird.
紅 寶 石 jacinth; sometimes used for other red gems, as rubies.
[15] 紅 帶 ·子 red girdle—distinctive badge worn by members of the collateral branches of the Imperial Clan. 紅 幫 a secret society.
紅 教 Mongolian Lamaism.
紅 日 the morning sun; a lucky day.
紅 旭 a rosy dawn.
紅 晶 rose quartz.
[20] 紅 暈 red flush, from anger or drink, etc.
紅 木 redwood.
紅 梅 the red-flowering plum.
紅 棗 red dates.
紅 樓 or 紅 閨 part of a mansion set apart for the residence of young ladies.
[25] 紅 毛 red hair—formerly referred to the Dutch,—used for foreigners generally.
紅 河 The Red River in Yunnan.
紅 海 The Red Sea.
紅 漲 ·了 臉 a blush overspread (her) face.
紅 潮 menstruation.
[30] 紅 炭 live charcoal.
紅 爪 草 red clover.
紅 片 a red visiting-card.
紅 玉 rubies.
紅 瑪 瑙 red agate; sardonyx.

[35] 紅 璧 璽 onyx.
紅 男 綠 女 gaily dressed men and women.
紅 疹 ·子 or 紅 熱 病 scarlet fever. = 2774.A.4.
紅 痢 or 血 痢 a bloody flux; dysentery.
紅 白 二 事 weddings and funerals.
[40] 紅 眼 or 紅 ·了 眼 red eyes—covetous; greedy; desirous of.
紅 睿 name of a cosmetic.
紅 礬 arsenic.
紅 種 The Red Races.
紅 福 earthly happiness.
[45] 紅 粉 pink powder—women.
紅 糖 brown sugar.
紅 絲 the red silken thread—marriage.
紅 絲 疔 a boil,—from the red line often seen on it.
紅 紫 不 以 爲 褻 服 Confucius would not wear red or purple for his ordinary dress.
[50] 紅 紫 色 reddish purple; mauve.
紅 羅 a name for the lichee.
紅 股 shares in a company which are given without a cash payment, as to the promoter, etc.
紅 臉 飯 food earned by hard labour; food that causes a blush.
紅 船 a life-boat on the Yangtze.
[55] 紅 色 red; vermilion.
紅 花 or 大 紅 花 the red hibiscus.
紅 花 or 藏 紅 花 saffron.
紅 花 or 紅 藍 花 the safflower.
紅 茶 black tea, from the red colour of the infusion.
[60] 紅 茄 the tomato.
紅 薯 sweet-potatoes.
紅 蘿 葡 carrots; radishes.
紅 血 輪 red corpuscles.
紅 衫 red dress of a bride.
[65] 紅 袖 red-sleeves—a term for women.
紅 貨 jewels such as the ruby, etc; red dyed-stuffs.
紅 赤 赤 ·的 very red indeed, as a rosy dawn.
紅 轎 red sedan-chair for a bride.
紅 銅 copper.
[70] 紅 鋪 鋪 ·的 very red, flushed face.
紅 錢 or 門 錢 red paper-slips with 福 cut in them, hung on doors at the new-year.
紅 鐵 礦 hematite.
紅 雨 red rain; the fall of peach-blossoms.
↑ 紅 軍 The Red Army. See 1048.35.

紅 靑 plum-colour.
[75] 紅 面 白 面 determined and resolute, easy-going and placid, respectively.
紅 頂 a red button, formerly worn at the top of an official hat to indicate rank.
紅 顏 ruddy: fair; pretty women.
紅 顏 薄 命 a pretty face that dies young.
紅 魚 the gurnard.
[80] 紅 鶴 the eastern ibis.
紅 鸞 a lucky star.
桃 紅 pink; peach-blossom colour.
狀 ·元 紅 a kind of wine; a kind of dice game.
紫 紅 crimson.
[85] 通 紅 quite red; red all over—as a flushed face.
銀 紅 or 朱 紅 vermilion.
鮮 紅 fresh bright red.

(a) Read kung[1]. u.f. 工 Work.

女 紅 women's work; needlework, etc.

虹 [2.1.] The rainbow. The iris. Used poetically for describing height. Also read chiang[4], kang[4], and kung[4].
2384

虹 吸 管 a syphon, from the shape.
虹 彩 rainbow-coloured; used as an abbreviation for the next.
虹 彩 膜 or 眼 簾 the iris.
虹 橋 as lofty as the rainbow.
虹 沴 (li[4]) foul air.
虹 蜺 the rainbow and the secondary reflection.
虹 霓 or 虹 蟒 or 虹 橋 or 長 虹 the rainbow.
出 ·了 虹 a rainbow appeared. kang[4]
副 虹 the secondary rainbow.

(a) Read hung[4]. Vast. Joined to. Similar to 鴻, No. 2386.

天 地 虹 洞 heaven and earth joined together.

(b) u.f. 訌 To weary.

彼 童 而 角 實 虹 小 子 [3] to look for horns on a young ram will only weary you, my son.

訌 [2] To make mischief; to slander; discord; revolution.
2385

訌 亂 rebellious; seditious.
訌 敗 utter defeat.

訌 阋 internal discord and external opposition.

螽 賊 內 訌 destructive insects that weary men—said of the rulers.

內 訌 internal strife.

鴻[2] Vast; profound. Similar to 洪 No. 2388.
2386

鴻 便 an occasion for sending a letter.

鴻 儀 your valued present; your high attainments.

鴻 儒 a man of wide scholarship.

鴻 博 之 士 a man of extensive learning.

[5]鴻 名 a famous name.

鴻 圖 or 鴻 猷 far-reaching plans.

鴻 啟 open this (in profound peace), used on envelopes.

鴻 均 之 世 times of peace and prosperity.

鴻 寶 Taoist emblems.

[10]鴻 恩 great grace; mercy.

鴻 慈 great mercy or kindness.

鴻 才 great talents.

鴻 業 the great undertaking—the duties of a ruler.

鴻 洞 vast; far-reaching; joined together.

[15] 風 鴻 洞 而 不 絕 the wind blew without cessation.

鴻 烈 illustrious.

鴻 生 men of extensive learning.

鴻 禧 vast felicity; may you have great joy.

鴻 筆 a great pen—a writer with extensive scholarship.

[20]鴻 範 a great plan or undertaking.

鴻 緒 carrying on a great engagement—that of a king.

鴻 荒 a vast waste—the chaos of primeval era.

鴻 蒙 (or 濛) defined as 自 然 元 氣 也 the vital principle in nature, before creation.

鴻 釐 great felicity.

[25]鴻 鐘 a great bell.

鴻 鵠 之 志 soaring ambitions.

(a) A wild swan; the wild goose.

鴻 漸 the high flight of the wild goose.

鴻 毛 swansdown—very light.

鴻 爪 traces of past events.

鴻 豹 the bustard.

[5]鴻 雁 or 賓 鴻 the wild goose.

鴻 雁 傳 書 the wild goose brings a letter.

鴻 鵠 the wild swan.

鴻 鶴 the stork.

哀 鴻 distressed population; refugees.

哄[4] Din, noise.
2387

哄 動 a rumpus. *See below* A.3.

哄 哄 a din; clamour.

哄 唆 to sow dissension.

哄 喝 to browbeat.

哄 堂 大 笑 the whole company bursting into laughter.

哄 鬧 to make an uproar.

(a) To beguile; to cheat. *hung*[3].

哄·他 來 dupe him into coming.

哄·出·去 coax him out.

哄 動 to prevail upon; to delude into. *See above*—1.

哄 孩·子 to coax a child.

哄 德·他·的 東·西 to get a man's things by a trick.

哄 誆 or 哄 騙 or 哄 弄 to cheat; to swindle; to take in.

哄 誘 to beguile.

洪[2] Very. Liberal. Vast. A flood.
2388

洪 亮 or 洪 大 high, clear—as a tone.

洪 儒 a great scholar.

洪 勳 or 洪 伐 great meritorious service.

洪 宣 化 流 a widespread moral reformation.

[5]洪 原 a great plain.

洪 圓 織 長 large and round, fine and long—describing an elephant's trunk.

洪 家 The Triad Society or 三 合 會 a secret society in South China.

洪 寧 great peace.

洪 志 ambitious.

[10]洪 恩 great favour.

洪 惠 great kindness.

洪 惟 作 威 having exercised great tyranny.

洪 才 great talents.

洪 族 a nobleman's family.

[15]洪 武 first era name of the Ming Dynasty.

洪 智 great sagacity.

洪 業 a great undertaking—the duties of a king.

洪 水 the Flood; a flood which took place during the reign of the Emperor *Yao*. B.C. 2357—2258. A cataclysm.

洪 水 芒 芒 the floods spread far and wide.

[20]洪 水 衝 没 washed away by a flood.

洪 河 a branch of the River *Huai*.

洪 津 a wide ferry.

洪 澩 a very heavy downpour.

洪 淵 而 有 謀 broad-minded with far-reaching plans.

[25]洪 溶 wide and deep—as the sea.

洪 潰 an inundation.

洪 潦 great floods.

洪 濤 rolling billows.

洪 福 vast happiness.

[30]洪 範 *The Great Plan*—title of one section of the *Book of History*.

洪 細 great and small.

洪 聲 遠 布 a great reputation spread far and wide.

洪 脈 an irregular pulse.

洪 腫 a great swelling.

[35]洪 茂 flourishing exceedingly.

洪 荒 the wilderness of chaos.

洪 規 遠 略 far-reaching schemes.

洪 輝 great glory.

洪 量 的 magnanimous.

[40]洪 鈞 the Great Potter—the Creator, defined as 天 Heaven. *See* 鈞 No. 1725 C.

洪 鐘 a large bell.

洪 飆 扇 海 a great gale swept the sea.

洪 飲 a carousal.

洪 鬱 dense and flourishing growth of vegetation.

[45]流 美 洪 模 left a splendid example for posterity.

烘 灶[1] To bake, to roast; to dry at a fire.
2389

烘 乾 to dry by the fire till thoroughly dried.

烘 屋·子 to warm the room.

烘 彎 warped by heat.

烘 托 to paint around an outline leaving the object in white, as in indicating white flowers, etc.

⁵烘 火 a flame; to dry.

烘·烘 手 to warm the hands at a fire.

烘 烤 or 烘 焙 to warm before a fire; to roast; to toast.

烘 爐 a portable stove.

烘 襯 an inference; a contrast; to shade (a drawing).

鬨 鬥 ⁴
2390 The din of battle; noise of fighting. To fight.

鬨 兵 之 日 the day of the battle.

鬨 囔 clamour and uproar.

鬨 戰 a battle; to fight.

鬨 鬥 to quarrel and fight; to brawl.

(a) Read *hung*[1]. To push aside; to shout in order to clear the way. A.w. 搰.

鬨·出·去 drive them out.

鬨·開 to cause to fall back—as a crowd.

鬨·開 狗 drive away the dog.

訇 ¹
2391 The sound of a crash.

訇 哮 the noise of a great wind.

訇 橙 noise of a drum.

訇 礚 the booming of surf.

訇 訇 a great rumbling.

訇 隱 the roar of billows.

黌 ²
2392 A school.

黌 宇 a college built in the *Han* dynasty, A.D. 126—145.

薨 ¹
2393 The death of a prince.

薨 逝 to die.

(a) Swarming; shouting; crashing.

薨 薨 whirring, as of locusts' wings.

轟 轟 ¹
2394 The rumbling of carts or of thunder. To explode; to blow up.

轟 勸·起·來 to make a great uproar.

轟 塌·了 fell in with a crash.

轟 擊 to crash; to bombard.

轟 擊 物 explosives.

⁵轟 毀 to destroy by explosion.

轟 然 boom!-as a cannon.

轟 發 to explode.

轟 石 to blast rocks.

轟 破 to blow to pieces.

¹⁰轟 行 天 下 to make a noise in the world.

轟 轟 roaring; deafening; imposing.

轟 轟 烈 烈 grand; imposing.

轟 醉 mad drunk.

轟 陷 blown to ruins—by explosion.

轟 雷 the crash of thunder.

轟 飲 a carousal.

轟 炸 to bomb. 轟 炸 機 a bomber.

HUO. (ㄏㄨㄛˇ)
(Ho.)

火 川 ³
2395 Fire, flame. Used also fig., for the fire of lust, anger, etc. Radical 86.

火 上 加 油 pouring oil on the fire—only making matters worse.

火 主 one whose house is burned.

火 事 a conflagration; a fire-disaster. (*Jap.*)

火 井 a natural-gas well.

⁵火 伏 a period of one day and one night in evaporating salt by heat.

火 伴 or 火 計 a comrade,—soldiers were divided into messes of ten, each mess of ten being a *huo*.

火 伯 cook for a soldiers' mess.

火 候 strength of a fire for cooking; the time it takes to cook anything.

火 冒 blazing up with anger, etc.

¹⁰火 刑 柱 the stake. [power, as of guns.

火 力 force of combustion; firing

火 化 transmuting by heat; cremation. *See below.*—92.

火 坑 the fiery pit—descriptive of extreme hardship, difficulty, etc.

火 堰 a fire-bridge in a furnace.

¹⁵火 塊 clinkers from a furnace.

火 夫 or 火 頭 a cook.

火 宅 a burning house—no place for rest.

火 宅 僧 a married Buddhist priest.

火 室 a fire-box, as of a locomotive.

²⁰火 家 those who burn corpses; attendants on one who is travelling.

火 居 道 士 a married Taoist priest.

火 山 a volcano.

火 山 口 volcanic crater.

火 山 岩 volcanic rocks.

²⁵火 引·子 kindling material to start a fire.

火 急 desperately urgent.

火 成 岩 igneous rocks.

火 把 or 火 炬 a torch.

火 攻 to attack with fire.

³⁰火 政 or 火 憲 regulations against fire, issued by the government.

火 教 the Parsee religion.

火 斗 smoothing-iron used by Chinese tailors.

火 旺 or 火 苗 旺 a bright fire; the blazing up of a fire.

火 星 sparks; the planet Mars.

³⁵火 暴 or 火 性 a fiery temperament.

火 曜 日 used by Japanese for Tuesday.

火 杖 or 火 夾 a poker.

火 柴 or 洋 火 matches.

火 棉 gun-cotton.

⁴⁰火 樑 木 to bend wood by heat.

火 樹 銀 花 fiery trees with silver flowers—descriptive of the brilliance of lanterns.

火 毒 virus causing inflammation.

火 毬 fire-balls used in attacking an enemy.

火·氣 heat; anger, etc.

⁴⁵火·氣 大 furious; bad tempered.

火 氣 球 fire-balloon.

火 泥 fire-clay.

火 油 or 洋 油 kerosene.

火 浣 布 a fireproof cloth, a kind of asbestos that could be cleansed by fire.

⁵⁰火 漆 sealing-wax.

火 災 a conflagration; fire-disaster.

火 災 保 險 or 火 險 fire-insurance.

火 烈 鳥 the flamingo.

火 餤 or 火 光 flames.

⁵⁵火 燒 to burn; to destroy by fire.

火·燒 a round wheaten cake baked with fire.

火 燒 眉·毛 fire singeing the eye-brows—a very imminent crisis.
火 燎 or 火 焚 blackened by fire.
火 燭 fire and lights.
火 爐 a stove; a censer.
⁶⁰火 牌 an urgent warrant.
火 牛 flaming reeds tied to the tails of oxen—device used in ancient warfare, cp. Samson and the foxes.
火 狐 the red fox.
火 田 burning the undergrowth to drive out the game for hunting.
火 發 暴 躁 describing, a testy, irritable disposition.
⁶⁵火 盆 a chafing-dish—a fire-pan.
火 石 flint.
火 石 粉 lime; chalk.
火 砲 a cannon.
火 硝 saltpetre.
⁷⁰火 磚 fire-bricks.
火 神 god of fire.
火 票 an urgent despatch.
火 祭 burnt offerings.
火 禁 ordinances regulating the use of fires; the cold-food festival. See 寒 No. 2048—56.
⁷⁵火 窰 a kiln.
火 箸 metal chopsticks used as tongs.
火 箭 a fiery dart; a rocket.
火 籤 an urgent warrant.
火 紅 red-hot.
⁸⁰火 紙 touch-paper.
火 綫 the line of fire, in battle, etc.
火 繩 or 火 絨 or 火 種 tinder.
火 着·了 the fire has kindled.
火 老 鼠 a fire-rat—one who steals from a place which is on fire.
⁸⁵火 耗 loss in melting; wastage—an allowance for which had to be made when paying taxes, etc., in silver.
火 腿 a ham.
火 船 fire-ships.
火 艙 galley on a boat.
火 色 strength of a fire for cooking, etc., colour of fire; a red face.
⁹⁰火 花 sparks; the electric spark; also used of moths flying at a flame.
火 苗 子 a tongue of flame; flames.
火 葬 cremation. See above—12.
火·藥 gunpowder.
火 藥 局 powder-magazine.

⁹⁵火 藥 罐 powder-flask.
火 險 the danger of fire; fire insurance, See above 52.
火 號 signalling by fire.
火 蟲 or 打 燈 蟲 a firefly.
火 車 a railway train.
¹⁰⁰火 車 站 railway station.
火 車 費 railway fare.
火 車 頭 a locomotive.
火 輪 the sun; a steamer, abbrev. for 火 輪 船. = 輪 船.
火 辣 辣 peppery—as a disposition.
¹⁰⁵火 速 quickly; at express speed.
火 過 了 the fire has gone out.
火 酒 spirits of wine; alcohol.
火 鈎 hooks for tearing down burning buildings.
火 鉗 fire-tongs.
¹¹⁰火 鎗 or 火 器 fire-arms.
火 鏡 a burning-glass.
火 鏟 fire-shovel.
火 雞 a turkey.
火 雲 red clouds of summer.
¹¹⁵火 頭 軍 mess-cook for soldiers.
火·食 provisions; stores; supplies; wages; allowance.
火·食 多 少 what does your food-bill run into?
火·食 車 a provision-cart.
火 飯 coarse food.
¹²⁰火 麻 hemp.
火 齊 food duly prepared.
火 齊 珠 red beads, like glass.
火 龍 a fiery dragon, once used as ornament on garments, etc.
一 火 a mess of ten soldiers.
¹²⁵報 火 警 鈴 fire-alarm.
失 火 to catch fire accidentally.
封 火 to bank the fire.
心 裏 冒 火 blazing with rage.
息 (or 滅) 火 to put out a fire.
¹³⁰慧 火 the fire of genius.
慾 火 the fire of lust.
放 火 arson; to set on fire.
救 火 to put out a fire. See under 救 No. 1193—32 ff.
文 火 武 火 a slow and a quick fire respectively.
¹³⁵無 名 火 passion; a fit of anger.
生 火 or 點 火 or 弄 火 or 舉 火 to light a fire; to strike a light.
發 火 to catch fire; to get into a rage; out of sorts; bilious.
虛 火 feverish.
軍·火 munitions of war.
¹⁴⁰避 火 梯 fire-escape.
野 (or 鬼) 火 will-o'-the-wisp.

伙 ³ Utensils; goods; furniture. Inter. preceding and following.
²³⁹⁶

伙 伴 a comrade.
伙·食 food, provisions.
伙·食 房 a pantry.
伙·食 籃·子 food-basket.
中 伙 lunch by the way.
傢·伙 tools; utensils; furniture; vulgarly used of a man, etc.

夥 ³ A band, a company; a partner, an assistant.
²³⁹⁷

夥 伴 partner in business.
夥 友 a comrade.
夥 居 to mess together.
夥 盜 or 夥 匪 banded-together as robbers.
⁵夥·計 to go into partnership; an assistant in a shop; a waiter.
夥 辦 to go shares.
夥 長 (chang³) or 大 夥 the chief officer of a ship.
夥 開 一 店 to go into partnership and open a shop.
夥 騙 to combine for fraudulent purposes.
¹⁰夥 黨 a cabal; a clique.
同 夥 accomplices.
小 夥·子 a young man.
搭 夥 to join as an assistant; to go into partnership; to band together for any purpose.
散 夥 to dissolve partnership.
大 夥 兒 everybody.
(a) Numerous.

夥 多 numerous.
夥 頣 alarmed at the number; to refuse an honour.

貨 ⁴ Goods, commodities, produce, cargo. Distinguish 貸
²³⁹⁸ No. 6000.

貨 主 the vendor.
貨 主 負 責 at owner's risk.
貨 價 運 費 在 內 cost and freight included.
貨 價 運 費 保 險 在 內 cost, freight and insurance; c.i.f.
⁵貨 利 profits.
貨 到 交 付 delivery on arrival.
貨 到 兌 欵 cash on delivery.
貨 單 an invoice; a manifest.
貨 單 內 之·重·量 weight according to the manifest.

[10]貨 布 an ancient coinage.

貨 帳 invoice.

貨 幣 coin.

貨 有 好 歹 goods are of different qualities.

貨 棧 a warehouse or godown.

[15]貨 樣 samples of goods.

貨 樣 室 sample-room.

貨 樣 片 sample-card.

貨 樣 類 samples—as in sample-post.

貨 殖 to increase in wealth.

[20]貨 物 articles of merchandise.

貨 物 陳 列 室 showroom.

貨 物 陳 列 架 showcase.

備 存 貨 物 goods in stock.

危 險 貨 物 dangerous goods.

[25] 扣 留 貨 物 detained goods.

海 損 貨 物 goods damaged by sea.

零 星 貨 物 unenumerated articles.

貨 眞 價 實 genuine goods and real prices—i.e., the prices are not nominal.

貨 船 a cargo-ship, a freighter.

[30]貨 艙 the hold of a vessel.

貨 色 description of goods.

貨 裝 直 達 輪 船 ship by direct steamer.

貨 財 goods and wealth; possessions.

貨 車 a goods-train.

[35]上 貨 or 起 貨 to unload goods.

下 貨 or 裝 貨 to load goods.

中 止 定 貨 suspend an order for goods.

低 貨 inferior goods.

停 止 定 貨 to stop an order.

[40]出 貨 to take delivery of goods.

取 銷 定 貨 to cancel an order.

囤 貨 to corner the market.

時 行 貨 articles in great demand.

發 客 貨 wholesale goods.

[45]門 市 貨 goods sold over the counter.

高 貨 first-grade goods.

(a) To bribe; a bribe.

貨 賄 to bribe.

禍 [4] Calamity; misfortune; judgements from heaven.

2399

禍 不 單 行 misfortune never comes singly.

禍 不 遠 矣 trouble is not far off.

禍 亂 之 災 the horrors of civil war.

禍 事 a serious difficulty.

[5]禍 人 one who brings calamity upon others.

禍 始 the beginnings of trouble.

禍 從 口 生 all calamities come by means of the mouth—either through carelessness in diet causing sickness, or through carelessness and maliciousness in speech.

禍 害 injury; damage.

禍 心 malice; malicious designs.

[10]禍 患 or 禍 難 or 禍 災 misfortune; calamity.

禍 梯 the ladder of misfortune—that by which misfortune or calamity comes upon one.

禍 根 or 禍 原 a root of evil; seeds of misfortune.

禍 水 one who will bring disaster —said of a woman.

禍 泉 fountain of misfortune—said of wine.

[15]禍 福 倚 伏 failure and success, fortune and misfortune are dependent upon each other.

禍 福 無 門 calamity and happiness never enter a door—except when invited.

禍 積 有 日 this trouble has been accumulating for a long time.

禍 胎 possibilities of calamity; undutiful sons.

禍 首 a ringleader; cause of trouble.

[20]自 取 其 禍 to bring disaster upon oneself.

避 禍 to run away from calamity.

HUO.   (ㄏㄛ)
(Hoh)

佸 [4.5.] To unite. To meet with; to co-operate. Also read

2400   k'uo[4.5.]

曷 其 有 佸 When will he return to me?

活 [2.5.] Living, lively, active. Moveable; moving; a live-

2401   lihood, an occupation.

活 不 了 cannot live.

活 世 養 人 to give life to the world and length of days to man—a doctor's advertisement.

活 了 alive; revived.

活 人 a living man.

[5]活 佛 living Buddhas, the incarnations of Mongolian and Tibetan Lamaism; one's parents.

活 便 versatile; accommodating.

活 到 老 學 不 了 even though a man lives to old age, he cannot finish his studies.

活 剝 生 呑 an expression of extreme hatred; mere plagiarism, having nothing original in one's compositions.

活 劇 a moving scene.

[10]活 動 handy; loose; moveable; active; flourishing.

活 動 主 義 energism.

活 動 之 範 圍 sphere of activity.

活 動 影 戲 cinema.

活 動 滑 車 loose pulley.

[15]活 動 的 餘 地 still room for activity.

活 動 目 標 moving target.

活 動 電 影 片 films for the cinema.

活 口 the evidence of the survivors; to be on speaking terms.

活 口 氣 indefinite statements; vagueness.

[20]活 口 米 grain for famine relief.

活 句 a living sentence—in poetry.

活 命 life; to maintain a livelihood.

活 圈 a swivel.

活 塞 a piston; a stopper.

[25]活 塞 桿 piston-rod.

活 塞 環 piston-rings.

活 存 a current account.

活 字 a verb; moveable types.

活 字 板 plate for printing, composed of moveable types.

[30]活 扣 兒 a slip-knot.

活 拿 or 活 捉 to take prisoner.

活 期 存 欵 current account.

活 本 ready-money capital.

活 東 a name for tadpoles.

[35]活 板 moveable types.

活 死 人 a person who is dead while he lives—a fool; an invalid.

活 水 living water; running streams.

活 活 的 naturally; without effort; simply; alive and well.

活 潑 living; lively; quick; bustling.

[40]活 潑 潑 地 extremely active and lively.

活 火 a living fire as contrasted with smouldering.

活 物 living creatures.
活 現 apparent; vivid; life-like; to manifest. [verb.
活 用 法 flexible use; use as a
45 活·的 alive; movable; living; versatile.
活·的 人 物 living personalities.
活 石 "living stones."
活 神 The Living God.
活 絡 話 ambiguous, slippery talk.
50 活 罪 punishment other than capital.
活 罨 or 活 頁 or 活 瓣 a valve.
活 畫 a vivid portrayal.
活 脫 a living, striking resemblance; life-like.
活 著·ᵃ skilful move in chess.
55 活 葉 本 a loose-leaf notebook.
活 襯 to repair old books, inserting white paper between the leaves and leaving a margin all round for protection.
活 血 to stimulate the circulation.
活·計 an employment; a plan for a living; women's work.
活 詞 a living language; verbs.
60 活 該 served you right!
活 路 a thoroughfare.
活 躍 紙 上 it leaps living on to the paper—of a vivid delineation.
活 門 a means of livelihood; a valve.
活 鱗 a live fish.
65 活 龍 活 現 to make the matter real; to carry conviction; genuine.
做 活 to work; to do needlework.
圓 活 accommodating; complete.
復 活 to revive; resurrection.
快·活 happy.
70 沒·得 過 活 nothing to live on.
生·活 life; living; livelihood.
針 線 活 or 做 活 needlework.

(a) Read kua².⁵. Sound of waters.

或 4.5. Perhaps, if, whether, or else, either. Doubtful, uncertain. Also read huch.
2402

或 入 焉 而 與 舊 俱 化 or else become mingled with the native products (grain, animals, etc.,) and lose their character.
或 可 perhaps may.
或 大 或 小 either large or small.
或 往 或 來 either coming or going; unsteady.

⁵或 得 if possible that it could be so.
或 早 或 晚 either early or late.
或 時 occasionally.
或 此 或 彼 either this or that.
或 然 it may be....
¹⁰或 相 倍 蓰 either twice, or five times as good.
或 者 or 或 是 perhaps; or else; or if; it may be that; very likely.
或 者 他 能 也 未 可 知 who knows but that he may perhaps be able to ...?
彼 或 不 允 perhaps he will refuse.
莫 之 或 欺 no one would impose upon him.
¹⁵間 或 有·之 at times there are; there may be some.

(a) Some, someone; something.
或 人 a certain person.
或 問 some one asked; if one asks.
或 曰 some one said; it has been said; if it be said; others say.
或 遠 或 近 或 去 或 不 去 some have kept remote (from courts) some have drawn near to them, some have left their offices, and some have not done so.
夫 既 或 治 之 now there were those to attend to these things.

(b) Occurs used for next 惑. To doubt.
無 或 乎 王 之 不 智 也 it is not to be wondered at that the king is not wise.

惑 4.5. To mislead; to delude; to doubt. Suspicions; doubt. Also read huch⁴.
2403

惑 世 to deceive mankind.
惑 亂 黔 首 deluding and causing disorder among the black-haired people. (Chinese).
惑 弄 to befool.
惑 心 to suspect.
⁵惑 志 suspicious; doubtful.
惑 於 婦 言 deceived by his wife's statements.
惑 星 a name for the planets.
惑 疾 ill through doubts and suspicions.
惑 衆 to delude the people; the deluded people.

¹⁰惑 術 humbugging methods.
疑 惑 doubts; suspicions; to doubt.
迷 惑 to delude; bewitched; led astray.

豁 1,4.5 Open, clear. Intelligent; to understand, liberal-minded.
2404

豁 嘴 hare-lipped. (ho¹-)
豁 如 也 open and clear.
豁 心 眼 to enlarge the understanding.
豁 拳 to play at mora or guess-fingers. (hua¹-)
⁵豁 濱 to flow freely.
豁 然 貫 通 suddenly to dawn upon one.
豁 蕩 broad-minded, not bigoted.
豁 達 intelligent; broad-minded; liberal.
豁 門 an open door.

(a) To remit; to forego.
豁 免 to remit—taxes; to forgive.
豁 免 錢 糧 to remit the taxes.

(b) A crashing sound.
豁 剌 一 聲 the sound of a crash. (hua¹-)

霍 4.5. Quickly; suddenly.
2405

霍 亂 cholera.
霍 然 病 已 suddenly the complaint was gone.
霍 然 雲 消 suddenly the clouds dispersed.
霍 閃 a flash of lightning.

(a) The south. To guard.
霍 山 the name formerly given to the Southern Sacred Mountain 南 嶽 or 衡 山 in Hunan. i.e., the Southern Guardian. From the Han dynasty, this name was given to a mountain west of 霍 山 縣 in Anhwei.

攉 4.5. To beckon. To urge.
2406

攉 弄 to make a fool of.
攉 手 to beckon with the hand.
攉 較 to compare.

癨 2407

4.5. Cholera.

癨 亂 症 cholera. *See* 霍 No. 2405—1.

藿 2408

4.5. A coarse vegetable; greens. Pulse, beans.

藿 蠋 a large green caterpillar that feeds on the leaves of the bean-plants.
藿 香 betony.
荳 藿 beans, pulse.

彠 2409

4.5. To measure; to calculate.

劐 2410

1.5. To split; to tear; to rip. Pron. *ho*[1.5]. ≡ 2404.

劐·上·命 to risk life.
劐 口·子 a gap, an opening.
劐 嘴 a hare-lip.
劐 地 to dig up the ground.
劐·子 a hare-lipped person.
劐·着 不 要 throw it away as useless.
劐·着 幹 do it at any risk.
劐 肚·子 to rip up the belly.

濩 2411

4.5. Water pouring down; the dashing of water. To boil.

(a) Read *hu*[4]. To diffuse.

聲 敎 布 濩 reputation and influence diffused in every direction.

獲 2412

4. To take in hunting; to seize; to catch. To obtain. Also read *huai*[2], *ho*[5].

獲·乎 上 to obtain the confidence of the king.
獲·住·了 arrested.
獲 利 to get gain; to make profit.
獲 勝 to get the victory.
[5]獲 得 to obtain; to come into possession.
獲 恩 to obtain grace; to find favour.
獲 戰 利 品 to get loot.
獲 戾 to sin; to offend.
獲 敎 to have the favour of an interview.

[10]獲 於 上 有 道 there is a way to obtain the confidence of the king.
獲 案 to bring before the court.
獲 榮 譽 to get fame and glory.
獲 犯 to arrest a criminal.
獲 石 田 to get possession of a field of stones—i.e., something useless.
[15]獲 福 to gain advantage; to get the benefit of.
獲 罪 於 天 to sin against Heaven.
獲 解 or 獲 送 to take into custody.
獲 賊 or 獲 盜 to arrest thieves or robbers.
獲 辦 to bring to justice.
[20]獲 醜 to seize a number of prisoners.
獲 麟 絕 筆 when (Confucius) had written of the capture of the *lin*, (female unicorn) he ceased to write—the words "the western hunters captured a *lin*," ending the *Spring and Autumn Annals,* the only work of Confucius.
如 獲 珍 寶 as delighted as if he had obtained a precious gem.

HSI. (ㄒ)

匸 2413

3. A box, to conceal. Radical 23.

兮 2414

2. A particle of pause used in poetry current in the Han and Tsin dynasties.

不 素 餐 兮 he will not eat the bread of idleness.
瑟 兮 僩 兮 赫 兮 喧 兮 How grave is he, and dignified! How majestic and distinguished!
終 不 可 諠 兮 He can never be forgotten!
美 目 盼 兮 How beautiful her eyes, so clearly defined!

盻 2415

4. To look at in anger. Distinguish 盼 No. 4906.

盻 恨 to look at with anger.
盻 視 to glare at.
盻 盻 然 to wear an angry look.

(a) Perplexed.

使 民 盻 盻 然 causes the people to wear looks of distress.

希 2416

1. Rare, strange, curious. Few. Distinguish 市 No. 5792. 布 No. 5364.

希 世 之 珍 a rare gem—used fig.
希 乎 almost; nearly.
希 壽 or 古 希 seventy years of age—from a poem which says that men of this age have been rare "from of old." *See* 稀 No. 2421. B. 9.
希 夷 a name for the plant of long life or 芝 No. 936. That which cannot be seen is called 希, and that which cannot be heard is called 夷, i.e., the infinitesimal.
希·奇 strange.
希 客 a rare visitor, one who has not been for a long time.
希·罕 uncommon; to value; to regard as strange.
希 有 之 事 something that is of rare occurrence.

(a) To moult; to lose hair—from the idea of few, or sparse.

希 毛 sparse hair on animals.
鳥 獸 希 革 moulting, of birds, and casting the coat, of animals.

(b) To hope for, to emulate, to strive after.

希 世 而 行 time-serving.
希·冀 to desire; to wish for.
希 圖 to scheme for.
希 圖 重 利 to scheme in the hope of great profit.
[5]希 寵 seeking to curry favour.
希 慕 to long for.
希 指 or 希 意 to fall in with the wishes of others.
希 望 to hope for.
希 爲 見 復 I hope for a reply.
[10]希 聖 to emulate the sage as he emulates Heaven 希 天.
希 請 to request.
希 風 striving for reputation.
伫 希 晒 納 I hope that you will kindly accept this with a smile.

(c) A superlative—very. Inter 稀 No. 2421.

希 冷 清 very lonely.

希 滑 **不 好** 走 very slippery, not at all easy to walk on.
希 矮 very dwarfed or low.
希 破·的 very ragged.
⁵希 碎·的 all in fragments; smashed to atoms.
希 窄 exceedingly narrow.
希 軟 soft and supple.
希 鈍 very dull.

(d) Used for transliterating.

希 伯 來 Hebrew.
希 利 尼 Hellenic—Greek.
希 臘 Greece; Greek. (Hellas)
希 臘 字 母 the Greek alphabet.
希 臘 敎 The Greek Church.

晞 ¹
2417　To whimper.

晞 ¹
2418　To dry in the sun.

晞 埠 dry earth.
晞 髮 to loosen the hair in order to allow it to dry.
白 露 未 晞 the dew is not yet dry.

(a) The dawn.

東 方 未 晞 it is not yet light in the east.

欷 ¹
2419　To sob.

欷 吁 sighing and sobbing.

睎 ¹
2420　To long for; to gaze at.

稀 ¹
2421　Open, loose—as textures. Inter 希 No. 2416.

稀 密 density; openness.
稀 布 thin cloth.
稀 稀·的 open, loose as textures.

(a) Thin, of liquids. Diluted.

稀 溜 溜·的 quite thin and liquid; flowing.
稀 爛 cooked till quite soft.
稀 硫 酸 dilute sulphuric acid.
稀 稠 consistency—of fluids.

⁵稀 薄 or 稀 稀·的 thin; watery.
稀 釋 to dilute.
稀 釋 度 dilution.
稀 飯 rice gruel.
稀 鹽 酸 dilute hydrochloric acid.

(b) Scattered, few, rare.

稀 少 few, scarce, rarely.
人 烟 稀 少 a scattered population.
稀 拉 拉·的 sparse—as a crop.
稀 疏 sparse; scattered.
稀 罕 or 稀 奇 rare, strange, curious, infrequent.
⁵稀 遠 世 路 he separated himself from the world.
稀 鬆 平 常 of little importance; commonplace.
古 稀 seventy years of age. See 希 No. 2416—3. lit:—from of old rarely seen; from the next:—
人 生 七 十 古 來 稀 from of old men of seventy years have rarely been seen.
月 明 星 稀 when the moon is bright the stars are few.

(c) A superlative—very. See 希 No. 2416.—C.

稀 破 tattered.
稀 賤 very poor.

豨 ¹
2422　Swine. Sound used in calling pigs.

豨 豨 noise of pigs grunting.

系 ⁴
2423　A connection, a link or succession; family connection; related. A duct.

系 出 皖 南 my ancestors came from the south of Anhwei.
系 數 coefficient.
系 累 無 窮 an interminable succession.
系 繫 to tie together.
⁵系 繼 to be connected.
世 系 genealogy traced back to ancestors.
懸 系 之 至 very deeply concerned.
直 系 direct descendants. See No. 1006—26.
相 系 connected, joined.
¹⁰譜 系 a genealogy.

(a) A system.

系 統 or 體 系 a system.
系 統 化·的 reduced to a system; systematized.
呼 吸 系 統 the respiratory system.
哲 學 體 系 a system of philosophy.
⁵太 陽 系 the solar system.
山 脈 系 a mountain system.
排 洩 統 系 excretory system.
有 統 系·的 systematic.
河 系 a river system.
¹⁰營 衛 統 系 circulatory system.
神 經 統 系 nervous system.
科 學 體 系 scientific system.
食 道 統 系 or 消 化 統 系 the digestive system.
骨 絡 系 統 (or 統 系) the bony system. 「math., etc.
國 文 系, 算 學 系…dept. of Chinese, ↑系 主 任 head of a (college) dept.

係 ⁴
2424　To belong to. Consequences. Inter. preceding and 繫 No. 2458.

係 友 friendly relationship.
係 屬 connected with; belonging to.
係 戀 very much in love with.
係 數 coefficient.
⁵係 累 bound-up with; to bind; a family.
係 親 related to.
係 踵 closely following one another.
係 風 捕 影 to bind the wind and grasp the shadows—to do the impossible.
關·係 consequences, relations to. *See under* 關 No. 3571—A.3ff.

(a) To be, is, are; it is that; this is.

係 爲 保 護 起 見 it is for the purpose of protection.
係 爲 減 發 軍 餉 it was because of the reduction in the pay of the troops.
委 係 一 人 there was only one man.
實 係 .... truly it is....
⁵本 係 as a matter of fact it is....
果 係 如 此 it is indeed like this.
此 事 係 彼 輩 所 爲 this was indeed done by the other man.
第 一 次 係 .... the first occasion was....

奚 ¹ Interrogative implying a
2425 doubt; why? how? that?
which?

奚 不 爲 政 why do you not take
office?

奚 似 to what degree?

奚 其 喪 how should he lose—his
State?

奚 其 爲 爲 政 why do you need
that—to be reckoned in the
government?

⁵奚 取 what has this to do with?

奚 可 以 與 我 友 how can he
become my friend?

奚 堪 how is it to be endured?

奚 如 what do you think about it?

奚 爲 後 我 why does he leave us
to the last?

¹⁰奚 自 from whom did you come?

奚 落 to make a fool of,—correctly written 謑 落.

亦 奚 以 爲 of what practical use
is it?

子 以 爲 奚 what do you think of
it, Sir?

子 將 奚 先 what do you consider
the first thing to be done?

(a) A servant, described as those
who have ability. Inter. next.

奚 仲 Director of Chariots under
Yü the Great, said to be the
first to use horses for drawing
a vehicle. About B.C. 2205.

奚 奴 a servant or slave.

奚 官 grooms; government-slaves;
eunuchs.

奚 童 a page; a young lad as a
servant.

奚 隸 male and female slaves.

(b) Name of a Tartar tribe which
sprang from the 東 胡; they were
defeated by the Hsiung-nu about
B.C. 200. During the T'ang
Dynasty they lived around the
present Jehol. Once known as
庫 莫 奚.

奚 兒 a Tartar.

奚 琴 a two-stringed violin which
originally came from the tribe
as above.

奚 軍 Tartar armies.

傒 ¹ A servant, inter. preceding.
2426 A man from the South of
the Yangtze. Kiangsi.

傒 語 ancient term for Kiangsi
speech.

俟 ¹ To wait for; to expect.
2427

俟 待 to wait.

俟 我 后 we have waited for our
prince.

(a) u.f. 蹊 No. 2429. A path over
the hills.

俟 徑 a narrow path; a short cut.

謑 ² Shame, disgrace.
2428

謑 落 to make fun of—often
wrongly written 奚 落.

謑 詬 shame, reviling.

蹊 ¹ A footpath; a track over
2429 a hill.

蹊 徑 a narrow path; a short cut.

蹊 蹺 古 怪 very extraordinary.

山 蹊 a mountain-path.

(a) To cross. To penetrate a
pathless wild.

蹊 人 之 田 to cross a man's
fields.

蹊 橋 to cross a bridge.

鼷 ¹ A mouse, described as
2430 about 2½ inches long, dark
grey on the back and lighter
beneath.

鼷 穴 a mouse-hole; a little hole.

鼷 鹿 the tragullus or mouse-deer.

鼷 鼠 a mouse.

羲 ¹ Breath, vapour. The name
2431 of an ancient emperor.

羲 和 two astronomers in the time
of Yao; the charioteer of the
sun.

羲 文 Fu-hsi and Wen-Wang.

羲 氏 or 伏 羲 Fu-hsi a legendary monarch.

羲 獻 abbrev. for Wang Hsi-chih
王 羲 之, and his son Wang
Hsien-chih 王 獻 之, two
famous calligraphists A.D. 321—

379. The former is said to
have invented the 楷 書 or
orthodox style of writing.

⁵羲 皇 上 人 the ancient worthies.

羲 經 a name for the Book of
Changes, because Fu-hsi was
said to have discovered the
diagrams 八 卦 on the back of
a tortoise.

羲 農 Fu-hsi and Shen-nung.

羲 黃 Fu-hsi and Huang-ti, the
Yellow Emperor.

曦 ¹ The light of day.
2432

曦 馭 the bright chariot—the sun.

曦 光 the brightness of the dawn.

犧 ¹ Victims for sacrifice, beasts
2433 of a uniform colour.

犧 牛 a bullock for an offering.

犧 牲 sacrificial victims.

犧 牲 一 身 to sacrifice self.

犧 牲 主 義 sacrificed his principles; principle of sacrifice.

⁵犧 牲 快 樂 sacrifice of pleasure—
to duty.

犧 牲 性 命 to give one's life to a
cause.

犧 牲 意 見 to yield one's opinion.

犧 牲 的 精 神 the spirit of sacrifice.

犧 牲 自 己 to sacrifice oneself.

犧 牲 財 產 or 犧 牲 資 財 sac-
rifice of money or property in
a cause.

喜 ³ Pleasure; joy; pleased
2434 with.

喜 不 自 禁 overjoyed.

喜 事 or 喜 慶 a wedding; an
occasion for joy.

喜 信 good news.

喜 兆 a joyful omen.

⁵喜 出 望 外 joy beyond all expectation.

喜 劇 a comedy.

喜 功 taking pleasure in meritorious deeds.

喜 吃 懶 作 lazy and good-for-
nothing.

喜 報 三 元 news of a triple first
in the old examinations—magpies calling, reckoned lucky.

10 喜 夢 a pleasant dream.

喜 好 (*hao*[4]) to delight in.

喜 子 or 喜 母 or 喜 蛛 a small blackish spider,-it has very long legs, and is reckoned a lucky omen. *See* 蟢 No. 2441.

喜 安 happiness and peace—wedding congratulations in letters, etc.

喜 怒 不 形 to display neither pleasure nor anger.

15 喜 怒 哀 樂 pleasure, anger, sorrow and joy—the passions.

喜 愛 to delight in.

喜 戴 高 帽 fond of praise.

喜 敬 present of money given at a wedding.

喜 新 厭 古 pleased with the new, loathing the old.

20 喜 樂 pleasure; joy.

喜·歡 or 喜 悅 pleased; glad of; fond of; pleased with.

喜 氣 or 喜 色 or 喜 容 a joyful expression on the face.

喜 氣 盈 門 may joy fill your habitation!

喜 病 sickness of pregnancy.

25 喜·的 沒 法 extravagantly pleased.

喜 神 the god of good luck.

喜 笑 顏 開 beaming with smiles.

喜 結 a happy union.

喜 聲 a sound of good omen.

30 喜 自 天 來 happiness comes from Heaven.

喜 詔 the edict announcing the accession of a new emperor.

喜 說 往 事 fond of dwelling on the past.

喜 躍·之 至 dancing for joy.

喜 轎 or 花 轎 a bridal sedan-chair.

35 喜 酒 a wedding feast.

喜 雨 timely rains.

喜 雪 timely snows.

喜·鵲 the magpie.　(--*ch'iao*)

喜·鵲 尾 magpies' tails—the turned-up ends of the ridge-pole on a Chinese house.

40 喜 麵 noodles, when eaten at a wedding feast.

報 喜 to bring good news; a good omen.

恭·喜 congratulations, as at new-year, etc.

新 喜 new-year congratulations.

道 喜 to congratulate.

(a) Used for transliterating.

喜 馬 拉 雅 The Himalayas.

儶[1] Cautious.
2435

嘻[1] An interjection of joy, surprise or grief.
2436

嘻 嘻 哈 哈 tittering; laughing aloud.

嘻 笑 to smile.

嬉[1] Handsome. An excursion, a picnic. To play, to amuse oneself. Amusement.
2437

嬉 戲 to giggle; to have some fun.

嬉 樂 amusements.

嬉 玩 or 嬉 耍 to play games with; to sport; pastimes.

嬉 皮 笑 臉 grinning; rollicksome.

嬉 笑 to make fun of.

嬉 翔 soared exultingly away.

遊 嬉 a picnic; an excursion.

憙[3] To be delighted with; to take delight in.
2438

熹[1] To heat, to roast, to toast. Hot; bright. Illustrious. Diversified.
2439

熹 微 the faint warmth of the morning.

未 熹 not yet bright.

禧[1] Blessings from the gods. To pray to the gods.
2440

禧 事 an auspicious occasion.

禧 年 A Happy New-Year.

禧 慶 auspicious.

賀 禧 congratulations.

蟢[3] A small long-bodied blackish spider,-it has very long legs, and makes its webs in gardens, etc.; these webs are described as being like the 八 卦.
2441

蟢·子 the spider, as above—See 喜 No. 2434—12.

壁 蟢 or 壁 錢 a small, flat-bodied spider, very dark brown in colour; its web is white and about the size of a cash.

畦[1] A field containing about fifty 畝 *mou*. A parcel of ground. A small plot in a garden, etc. Also read *ch'i*.
2442

畦·子 a small plot of land.

病 于 夏 畦 toil harder than the labourers in the summer-fields.

菜 畦 a vegetable-plot.

(a) Read *kuei*[1]. A low wall between fields.

町 畦 boundary between fields; also used fig., by *Chuang tzŭ* for moral bounds.

攜 }[1] To lead by the hand. To conduct to; to take with.
携 }
2443

攜 僕 personal attendants.

攜 同 to bring along with one.

攜 失 carried off and lost.

攜 帶 to bring along with one.

5 攜 手 to lead by the hand; hand in hand.

攜 手 同 行 went hand in hand together.

攜 手 排 立 holding hands and standing in a row.

攜 持 or 攜 起 to lift up and carry away.

攜 眷 to bring the family.

10 攜 筐 to carry a basket on the arm.

(a) To become disaffected; to leave.

攜 而 討 焉 無 衆 必 敗 if (the people of *Chin* 晉) come over in heart to (*Ch'in* 秦), then because their people are few, they would certainly be defeated.

攜 貳 disaffected in heart.

其 民 必 攜 the people (of *Chin* 晉) would become disaffected and come over to (*Ch'in* 秦).

蟕[1] Large turtles.
2444

蟕 龜 the loggerhead turtle.

綠 蟕 龜 the green turtle.

觿[1] An ivory bodkin worn at the girdle and used for undoing knots.
2445

艦 年 a youth before he was capped—as these youths wore this article in their girdles. *See below*—3.

艦 礪 an ivory spike and a whetstone.

童 子³ 佩 艦 there is a lad with a bodkin at his girdle.

(a) A large turtle. Inter. preceding.

鄾¹
2446　Name of towns in the State of *Chi* 紀, near the present 臨淄縣 and 東阿縣 in Shantung.

舊¹
2447　Revolution of a wheel. Read *kuei*¹. The little cuckoo, also called 杜鵑 or 子³ 舊 or 子³ 周.

Read *sui*³. Old name of a town in the present 西昌縣 in Szechwan.

醯¹
2448　Sour. Pickles, etc.

醯 臨 pickled mincemeat.
醯 醬 pickled condiments.
醯 醲 highly flavoured.
醯 雞 animalculæ in vinegar.

屣 躧 蹝
2449　Straw sandals or slippers that have no heel-backs.
3,4.

屣 履 to walk with the shoes trodden down at the heels.
猶 棄 敝 屣 也 like casting off an old sandal.

葰³
2450　To increase five-fold.

或 相 倍 葰 some twice, some five-fold.

熙 熙¹
2451　Bright, splendid. Intelligent. Prosperous.

熙 事 or 禧 事 auspicious event.
熙 光 glory; splendour.
熙 和 之 世 a prosperous and peaceful age.
熙 怡 expressing gratification on the face.
⁵熙 春 hyson tea.
熙 朝 our glorious dynasty.
熙 朝 人 瑞 glorious dynasty and fortunate people.
熙 洽 peaceful co-operation.
熙 熙 crowds.
¹⁰熙 熙 壤 壤 coming and going in crowds.
廣 哉 熙 熙 How vast!
衆 人 熙 熙 the people are enjoying themselves.
熙 笑 而 稱 曰 he said with a look of gratification....
熙 載 to put life into a cause.
¹⁵熙 隆 brilliant and glorious.
百 姓 熙 雍 the people are living in harmony.

戲 戲
2452　A play. To play; to sport; to jest.
4

戲 侮 or 戲 慢 to insult; to make game of.
戲 劇 plays, dramas.
戲 單·子 a play-bill.
戲 園 or 戲 場 or 戲 樓 a theatre.
⁵戲·子 an actor.
戲 幕 stage-curtain.
戲 弄 or 戲 謔 to make fun of; to dally with; to play jokes upon.
莫 戲 弄 我 do not play tricks on me!
戲 彩 to amuse one's parents—from a story of *Lao Lai-tzǔ* 老 萊 子³ who at 70 years of age dressed in variegated garments, and played all sorts of antics to amuse his aged parents.
¹⁰戲 戲 哈 哈·的 horse-play; a loud manner.
戲 房 the green-room.
戲 文 the words of a play.
戲 景 a spectacle; a gazing-stock.
戲 曲 drama, musical plays under the *Sung* dynasty.
¹⁵戲 曲 家 dramatists.
戲 本 a book of the play.
戲 殺 manslaughter through practical joking or rough horse-play.

戲 法 jugglery or sleight-of-hand.
戲 班 a troupe of actors.
²⁰戲 笑 to laugh at.
戲 箱 the boxes of clothing and properties belonging to a troupe.
戲 耍 to trifle; to play.
戲 臺 the stage.
戲 螞 蟻 a troupe of actors.
²⁵戲 衣 costumes for a play.
戲 言 pleasantry; joking.
戲 諕 to make jokes.
一 齣 戲 one act of a play; a play.
以 戲 其 友 to make sport of his friends.
³⁰兒 戲 child's-play.
渾 戲 licentious plays.
猴 戲 monkey-tricks.
逢 場 作 戲 act according to the circumstances; "playing the game.

(a) Read *hu*¹. An exclamation of regret.

於 (*u*¹.) 戲 Alas!

嵯¹
2453　A mountain-gorge; a ravine.

險 嵯 dangerous passes.

(a) A crack, a pretext for anything.

愾
2454　To sigh; to groan.
4

愾 我 寤 嘆 with a groan I awake and sigh!
愾 然 太 息 to heave a deep sigh.

(a) Read *k'ai*⁴. Anger.

愾 慣 hatred to an enemy.
敵 愾 hatred; hostility.

(b) Read *hsi*³,⁵. To reach to, similar to 迄 No. 568.

餼
2455　A sacrificial victim, explained as used of the living beast. Some dispute this.
4

餼 牽 a sacrificial beast,—ox, sheep, or pig that could be led.
餼 羊 a sheep presented at the new moon.

(a) To give a supply of grain for rations. Grain.

廩 餼 the grain allowance for salaried graduates.

咥 [4] A loud laugh. Read
tieh[2.5]. To gnaw, to bite.
2456

褉 [4] A ceremony of purification
held in the spring and au-
2457 tumn, with a view to avert
evils.

修褉 to remove evils.

繋 [4] To bind; to gird; to be
attached to. Also read *chi*[4].
2458

繋·上·去 tie it on. (*ch-*)

繋·上 帶·子 to put on a girdle. (*ch-*)

繋·於 一·髮 hanging by a hair—
very precarious.

繋 於 世 類 尚 bound by the
wishes of men.

[5]繋 泊 to moor a boat.

繋 獄 or 繋 囚 to imprison.

繋 累 to implicate.

繋 續 to join.

繋 聯 connected; consequences.

[10]繋 羈 to bind and bring under restraint, as an animal.

繋 腰 to gird the loins.

繋 辭 name of a section of the
Book of Changes, an explanation of the prognostics; an
appendix or commentary.

繋 鈴 解 鈴 let him who tied the
bell (on the neck of the tiger)
take it off again, used fig.

繋 馬 to tie up a horse.

(a) To remember.

繋 念 to be anxious about.

繋 戀 or 繋 懷 to dote on; to remember with affection.

(b) To draw; to let down.

繋·下·來 to let down.

繋 掛 to suspend.

贔 [4]
Gigantic strength.
2459

贔 屭 a river-god, figured as a
tortoise of gigantic size. *See*
No. 5168.

HSI. SI.   (厶)

西 [1] The west, western. European. u.f. Radical 146. See
2460 丙 No. 2524. Distinguish
酉 No. 7526, Radical 164.

西 京 Cochin-China, (in ancient
works); also the names of
various capitals under different
dynasties; it is used for Ch'ang-
an, Sianfu, Lohyang, Taiyüan,
etc; also Kyoto.

西 人 men from the west; used
for western peoples generally—
foreigners.

西 伯 Chief of the West—title of
the chief who was afterwards
canonized as *Wen Wang,* the
virtual founder of the *Chou*
Dynasty.

西 俗 western ways or customs.

[5]西 僑 westerners living in China.

西 南 south-west.

西 半 球 the Western Hemi-
sphere.

西 南 夷 name given under the
Han Dynasty to the present
region of Szechwan, Yunnan,
Kweichow, Burma, etc.

西 北 north-west.

[10]西 印·度 The West Indies.

西 口 the western passes; to the
west of the Great Wall.

西 國 western nations.

西 域 general name for the countries bordering on Western
China.

西 垂 the western frontier.

[15]西 夏 Tangut. A kingdom founded by the family of 拓 跋, it
held sway on the N.W. of
China.

西 大 陸 The Western Continent
—i.e., America.

西 天 the Western Paradise.
(*Budd.*).

西 字 臉 a large, broad face.

西 學 western learning.

[20]西 宮 highest Imperial concubines.

西 家 servants, employees.

西 賓 or 西 席 a private tutor,
from the room which he occupied.

西 嶽 the Western Sacred Mountain, i.e., 華 山 in Shensi.

西 式 western styles.

[25]西 式 便 帽 soft foreign-style cap.

西 戎 the western frontier-tribes.

西 成 completion of harvest.

西 施 or 西 子 a famous beauty
during 5th cent. B.C. A daughter of humble parents in Chekiang, she was taken and trained, and afterwards used to

debauch the prince of *Wu* and
cause his defeat.

西 曆 or 西 元 the western calendar, the Christian era.

[30]西 極 the farthest west—where
the sun sets.

西 法 European or American
methods.

西 洋 the western ocean—i.e.,
foreign countries.

西 洋 貨 western goods.

西 湖 the West Lake,—there are
several, the most famous is
outside Hangchow in Chekiang,
a very beautiful spot.

[35]西 王 母 a fabulous fairy princess
said to dwell in the *Kunlun*
Mountains, and to have troops
of fairies and genii under her
command.

西·瓜 the water-melon, which
originally came from the west
through the *Chin* Tartars, or
through the *Chitan* Tartars who
defeated the *Ouigurs.*

西 穀 米 or 西 米 sago.

西 羌 the *Ch'iang* tribes on the
western frontier.

西 苑 a park that was laid out to
the north of *Loyang* in Honan
by *Yang ti* 煬 帝, of the Sui
Dynasty. It was 200 *li* in
circuit and a place of licentious
revelry. Palace of the Mongols
near Peking.

[40]西 藏 or 西 番 (*po*[1]) Tibet.

西 裝 or 西 服 western dress.

西 語 foreign languages.

西 邊 the west side; in the west.

西 門 the west gate.

[45]西 門 豹 famous governor of Yeh
鄴, near the present *Changtefu*
in Honan. *See under* 河 No.
2111—4.

西 紅 柿 tomato.

(a) Used for transliterating.

西 伯 利 亞 Siberia.

西 原 借 欵 Nishihara loans.

西 班 牙 Spain.

西 貢 Saigon.

西 里 伯 Celebes.

㥽 [1]
Troubled, vexed.
2461

㥽 惶 vexed, grieved.

棲栖 2462
To roost, to perch, to settle. To stay. Also read ch'i[1].

棲宿 to rest for the night.

棲宿其上 (thousands of crows) roost on its (branches).

棲屑 to and fro, going and coming; back and forth.

棲息 to rest.

[5]棲止 to alight on; to stay at; to settle on.

棲棲 all bustle and excitement.

棲棲遑遑 uneasy; anxious.

棲泊 to come to anchor.

棲流所 refuge for vagrants.

[10]棲神之域 the grave—the resting place of the spirit—of his parents.

棲禽 roosting birds.

棲苴 floating water-weed.

棲身之所 a dwelling-place.

棲身無定 no fixed abode.

[15]棲遲 to sojourn.

棲陸 animals that rest on dry land.

棲革於其中爲的[4] placed leather in the centre as a target.

犀 2463
A bovine animal described as a buffalo having a single horn, (though it is also described as having two, or three horns.) Modern books use it for the rhinoceros.

犀圍 or 犀帶 girdles of rhinoceros hide worn in ancient times by officials.

犀照 a mind quick of apprehension—from a story of Wen Chiao 溫嶠 who lit a rhinoceros horn to enable him to see the uncanny creatures in a deep, dark river; he is said to have seen into the dark regions.

犀牛 or 犀兕 the rhinoceros.

犀甲 (or 函) armour of rhinoceros hide.

犀簟 mat of rhinoceros hide.

犀箸 hair ornaments decorated with this hide.

犀角 rhinoceros horn; the bone of the temples.

犀角偃月 beautifully curved temples.

(a) Well tempered; sharp.

犀兵 sharp weapons.

犀利 sharp-edged.

(b) Section of a melon.

齒如瓠犀 her teeth were even and regular like the seeds of a melon.

枲 2464
The male nettle-hemp.

枲布 linen.

枲耳 the burr-weed.

枲箸 quilted with hemp.

洗 2465
To wash; to bathe; to purify.

洗三 to wash a child on the third day after birth.

洗·不乾·淨 cannot be washed clean.

洗·不掉 or 洗·不下來 cannot be washed out—as a stain.

洗傷 to bathe an injury.

[5]洗兵 or 洗甲 to cleanse the weapons or armour—to cease hostilities.

洗刷 washed and brushed; to clear another's name.

洗刮 to wash and scrape clean—also used fig.

洗剝 to strip naked.

洗却 or 洗·掉 to wash clean.

[10]洗城 to massacre the entire population of a city.

洗塵 to wash away the dust—a feast to a returning friend.

洗冤 or 雪冤 or 解冤 to avenge a wrong.

洗心 to cleanse or reform the heart.

洗心革面 to make a thorough reformation of one's habits.

[15]洗恥 to wipe out a disgrace.

洗手 to wash the hands; to have nothing more to do with it.

洗手不幹 to wash one's hands of an affair; to reform one's ways.

洗拭 to wash and rub clean.

洗指盞 finger-bowls.

[20]洗房 a laundry.

洗沐 to bathe and wash the hair—ancient term for leave of absence.

洗浴 or 洗澡 or 洗身 to bathe.

洗淨·的版本 an expurgated edition. = 删本.

洗澡盆 or 浴盆 a bathing-tub.

[25]洗澡塘 a bath-house.

洗潔 or 洗滌 to cleanse; to purify or reform.

洗熨 to wash and iron smooth.

洗瓶 a washing-bottle. (Chem.).

洗盥 to cleanse from evil.

[30]洗石 an alkaline stone used as a lye.

洗禮 or 浸禮 the rite of baptism.

洗網 washing the nets.

洗耳 to cleanse the ear; to refrain from listening to worldly claims, etc., from the story of 許由, who washed his ears after Emperor Yao had offered to resign in his favour, lest he incur any defilement from worldly ambitions.

洗耳恭聽 to listen with reverent attention.

[35]洗脚 to wash the feet.

洗臉 or 洗面 to wash the face.

洗臉盆 or 面盆 a basin for washing the face.

洗藥 a lotion.

洗衣 to wash clothes.

[40]洗衣作 a laundry.

洗除淨盡 a thorough cleansing.

洗雪 to wipe out wrongs for another.

洗面架 a washstand.

(a) To polish and grind gems. etc.

洗瑕 to grind out a flaw.

(b) Read hsien[3]. To wash the feet. To clarify spirits.

太子洗馬 equerry to the heir-apparent.

自洗腆致用酒 then you may clarify and make strong your wine for use.

葸 2466
Afraid, bashful.

慎而無禮則葸 caution, without propriety, becomes timidity.

細 2467
Fine, minute. Delicate. Thin, small. Carefully; careful.

Distinguish 紬 No. 1315.

細事 or 細故 a trifling affair.

細 人 or 細 士 a petty-minded man; a *small* man.

細 作 a spy.

細 兒² a little child.

⁵細 切 to mince.

細 則 minute details; detailed regulations.

細 君 my wife.

細 問 (or 訪) make careful inquiries.

細 大 盡 力 in great and in minor matters put forth every effort.

¹⁰細 密 delicate and fine.

細 察 or 細 審 or 細 究 to examine minutely.

細 小 small, petty.

細 崽 a servant; *boy*.

細 工 fine workmanship.

¹⁵細 巧 fine and skilful, as opposed to rough and clumsy.

細 弱 slender and weak—of children; unmanly.

細 微 minute; small; subtle.

細 心 carefully.

細 心 揣 摸 ponder the matter carefully.

²⁰細 思 (or 想) give it careful thought.

細 推 物 理 carefully investigate the theories of matter.

細 數 make a careful count.

細 書 fine, delicate writing.

細 梗 or 細 莖 a slender stem.

²⁵細 柳 willowy; lithe and slender.

細 步 short steps.

細 民 the populace.

細 洋 紗 fine cambrics.

細 流 a little, trickling stream.

³⁰細 疵 a tiny flaw.

細 目 details.

細 眉 delicate eyebrows.

細 磁 器 fine chinaware.

細 窺 or 詳 察 to examine minutely into details.

³⁵細 細的 finely, particularly; accurately.

細 絲 fine silk—pure silver; the word *sycee* is derived from this term.

細 縷 very fine silk thread.

細 緻 fine; beautiful.

細 胞 a cell. (*biol.*).

⁴⁰細 胞 分 裂 cell-division. (*biol.*).

細 腰 蜂 a wasp that secretes caterpillars with its eggs as food for the young.

細 膩 very fine and smooth.

細 花 small flowers.

↑細 情 minute details.

細 苛 or 苛 細 petty, vexatious trifles.

⁴⁵細 若 塵 埃 as fine as dust.

細 菌 germs; bacteria.

細 菌 學 bacteriology.

細 葛 fine cloth.

細 行 small details of conduct; trifling faults of conduct.

⁵⁰細 視 carefully perused.

細 計 carefully thought-out plans.

細 說 petty talk; circumstantial detail.

細 談 to speak about with minute details.

細 講 to enter into detail.

⁵⁵細 路 a narrow path or track.

細 軟 fine and soft—i.e., jewels and clothing.

細 針 密 縷 fine needle and closely wrought threads—used of fine workmanship.

細 長 slender and long—used poetically of pine needles.

細 雨 fine rain.

⁶⁰細 驗 detailed examination of goods by customs.

細 高 姚 兒 a tall, thin man.

細 麻 布 fine linen.

徙³ To move one's abode; to shift. Distinguish 從 No.
2468 6919. 徒 No. 6536.

徙 任 to be transferred to another post.

徙 倚 indecision; hesitancy.

徙 善 to change for the better; to reform.

徙 宅 忘 妻 to change one's abode and forget one's wife—of extreme forgetfulness.

⁵徙 居 or 遷 徙 or 移 徙 to change one's residence.

徙 月 to encroach upon another month.

徙 義 to move towards virtue.

徙 貫 to change one's place of abode.

徙 邊 to banish to the frontier.

¹⁰徙 陽 an old name for Yachow in Szechwan.

璽³
爾 The Imperial signet; the great seal.
璽
2469

璽 書 an Imperial letter.

玉 璽 or 國 璽 the State seal.

胖 ⁴·⁵· Sounds of bells, buzzing, soughing of wind, etc.
2470

吸 ¹·⁵·
嗡 To draw in the breath; to inhale; to suck up. To attract.
2471

吸 一 口 氣 to take an inspiration.

吸 了 一 點 文 明 空 氣 he has taken in a whiff of *civilized air*—a mere smattering of culture.

吸 入 sucking.

吸 力 power of attraction; attraction.

⁵吸 去 魂 靈 to suck the soul out of a person.

吸 收 assimilation; suction.

吸 呼 respiration.

吸 墨 紙 blotting-paper.

吸 大 烟 to smoke opium.

¹⁰吸 蜜 鳥 honeysucker.

吸 引 attraction; to attract.

吸 引 力 attractive force; power of attraction.

吸 氣 器 aspirator.

吸 水 to suck up water, as fishes.

¹⁵吸 濕 性 hydroscopic.

吸 鐵 石 a loadstone.

吸 露 水 to drink dew—very poor.

吸 飲 to sip.

扱 ¹·⁵·
To receive; to collect.
2472

收 扱 to collect or gather.

(a) Read *ch'a*²·⁵·. To introduce.

扱 引 高 賢 introduce the wise and virtuous.

扱 袵 to tuck the skirts into the girdle.

(b) To bow to the ground.

扱 地 to bow to the ground.

扱 平 to sink in the west—sunset.

綌 ⁴·⁵· A coarse hempen fabric. Also read *ch'i*¹·⁵·.
2473

絺 綌 fine and coarse linen.

郤 郤 2474   4.5. Name of a city in the state of *Chin* 晉. To look up to. u.f. 隙 No. 2481. Distinguish 郤 No. 1183.

郤 地 adjacent countries.
與 臣 有 郤 he has a grudge against me.

翕 2475   4.5. To unite; to contract. To be in harmony.

翕 合 joined; reunited.
翕 如 也 all the parts sounding together.
翕 河 a river that does not overflow.
翕 然 closely; tightly.

(a) All.
翕 受 to receive all.

歙 2476   4.5. To shut; to contract. Inter. preceding.

歙 張 to collect and to scatter; to shut and to open.

(a) Read *she*[2.5]. The chief district of the old prefecture of Hweichow in South Anhwei.

潝 渻 2477   1.5. The noise of flowing water. To follow others.

潝 潝 訿 訿 a sycophantic manner.

爔 2478   1.5. To heat; to roast; to burn.

爔 死 suffocated.
爔 熟 之 肉 meat thoroughly roasted.

翕 2479   4.5. Peacefully; quietly.

翕 然 更 始 peacefully inaugurated a new regime.
翕 然 止 suddenly to stand still.
翕 茸 stupid; countrified.

(a) An ancient weapon, a kind of halberd.
閟 戟 spears and halberds.

(b) Read *t'a*[4]. The sound of a thing falling to the ground.
閟 然 投 鎌 於 地 flung the sickle on the ground with a clang.

虩 2480   4.5. Frightened; terrified.

震 來 虩 虩 scared of the thunder.

(a) A small spider, light in colour; it runs about on walls and trees and hunts flies; also called 蠅 虎 fly-tiger.

隙 㥚 2481   4.5. A crack, a fissure; from which comes the meaning:—an occasion for dislike; a grudge or quarrel. A pretext. Leisure. Inter. 郤 No. 2474. Also read *ch'i*[4.5].

隙 地 waste land.
乘 隙 to avail oneself of a pretext.
尋 隙 to seek a pretext for a quarrel.
求 隙 seeking faults; hypercritical.
蹈 隙 to take advantage of every opportunity.

鬩 2482   4.5. To quarrel. Contention; animosity; resentment; recriminations.

鬩 牆 civil strife, from 兄 弟 鬩 于 牆 brothers quarrelling in the house.
鬩 恨 hatred; resentment.
鬩 訟 family litigation.
鬩 釁 causes of strife.

覡 2483   4.5. A wizard. Also read *chi*[4.5].

覡 公 a wizard.
巫 覡 witches and wizards.

檄 2484   2.5. A summons to war, anciently written on boards 1 ft. 2 ins. long. To call to arms. Urgency.

檄 催 to give urgent orders.
檄 委 to commission for service.

檄 文 a despatch; official summons; proclamation of warning.
檄 行 to give orders to act.
檄 調 an order for immediate transfer to another post.

(a) A branchless tree.

HSI. SI.   (ㄙ)
(Hsih)

夕 2485   4.5. Evening, dusk. Radical 36.

夕 市 evening markets.
夕 惕 vigilant of (one's conduct) at night.
夕 月 the evening moon; ancient sacrifice offered by the ruler to the moon.
夕 照 the western glow.
[5]夕 郎 those whose duty it was to see that the gates of the palace were closed at night.
夕 陽 the afternoon; the evening of life; that side of a hill which receives the afternoon sun— the west; the setting sun.
旦 夕 or 朝 夕 morning and evening.
除 夕 the last night of the old year.

(a) Not properly oriented.
夕 室 a house which is not oriented.

汐 2486   4.5. Night tides.

潮 汐·之 水 tidal waters.
無 潮 汐·的 tideless.

窆 2487   4.5. The gloom of the grave; a tomb or grave; death.

窀 穸 a grave or tomb.

析 2488   1.5. To split wood. To discriminate; to explain; to distinguish. To divide, to separate. Distinguish 柝 No. 6462.

析 之 to separate them; to divide them up.

析 愿 禁 悍 to bring the good into prominence and restrain those who are evil.

析 木 a constellation between 箕 and 斗 in Sagittarius.

析 產 to divide property.

⁵析 疑 to resolve doubts ; to remove suspicions.

析 義 to elucidate the meaning ; to explain.

析 翳 the rainbow. *See* 虹 No. 2384.

析 而 二 之 divide them into two parts.

析 薪 to cut up firewood.

¹⁰分·析 字 句 to analyze a sentence.

解·析 幾 何 analytic geometry.

唽 1.5.
2489　　To twitter.

晰 1.5.
晢　　Clear, bright. To discriminate.
2490

晰 疑 to elucidate one's doubts.

明 晰 clear ; perspicuous.

(a) Dazzling white.

白 晰 晰 dazzling white.

淅 1.5. An affluent of the River *Han*. The soughing of
2491　　wind.

淅 振 條 風 the wind stirs the branches with a soughing sound.

朔 風 鳴 淅 淅 the northern wind is sighing.

淅 瀝 the pattering of sleet ; the soughing of wind.

淅 颯 sound of the gentle movements—as of a bird.

(a) To wash rice.

淅 米 to wash rice.

接 淅 而 去 he took the washed rice and went.

蜥 1.5. The lizard, the 蜥 蜴—
2492　　there are many other names of which 石 龍 子 is one of the commonest.
　　A.c. 2644.2.

昔 2.5. Formerly ; of old ; in the
2493　　beginning.

昔 年 in past years.　[A.c. 昔 賢

昔 彥 a scholar of former days.

昔 時 or 昔 日 in old times ; formerly.

昔 者 formerly.

昔 者 辭 以 病 yesterday you excused yourself on the ground of indisposition.

昔 談 the words of the ancients.

古 昔 of old.

(a) A long time.

昔 愁 long sorrow—at separation.

昔 然 for a long time.

(b) A night.

昔 昔 every night.

一 昔 之 期 for one night.

通 昔 the whole night.

惜 2.5. To regard, to love ; to
2494　　pity.

惜 乎 unfortunately.

惜 乎 夫 子³ 之 說 君 子³ 也 Alas ! Your words, Sir, are the words of a princely man.

惜 念 to feel for.

惜 愛 to have compassion upon.

惜 老 憐 貧 pity the aged and the poor.

可 惜 Alas ! How sad ! Pitiable !

(a) To be sparing of. To grudge. To take care of.

惜 光 陰 careful of one's time.

惜 客 parsimonious.

惜 墨 如 金 as careful of his ink as if it were gold—said of one who would not write too readily.

惜 字 紙 be careful of written paper—do not allow it to become defiled.

⁵惜 指 失 掌 to lose much in being careful of little—to care for the fingers and lose the hand.

惜 物 careful of ; not wasteful.

惜 福 to be sparing in using up one's quota of happiness, so as to conserve it.

惜 花 to be fond of flowers and care for them.

惜 身 careful of oneself.

¹⁰惜 錢 to be sparing in the use of money ; to save money.

惜 陰 to be very careful in the use of one's time.

愛·惜 to grudge ; loving care.

息 2.5. To rest ; to desist. To
2495　　put a stop to ; to appease.

息 事 to finish up a matter.

息 交 to break off intercourse with the world ; to go into seclusion.

息 停 to pause ; to rest.

息 偃 to lie down for a rest.

⁵息 兵 to cease hostilities.

息 干 戈 to declare a truce.

息 影 or 息 迹 to dwell in retirement.

息 心 to have no more anxiety about a matter ; to set the heart at rest.

息 心 靜 氣 to take matters quietly.

¹⁰息 念·頭 to give up the idea.

息 怒 to appease anger.

息 戰 to cease hostilities ; a truce.

息 宴 to take one's ease in retirement.

息 業 to go out of business.

¹⁵息 民 to pacify the people.

息 游 to take recreation.

息 滅 to quench a fire.

息 火 to put out a fire.

息 爭 罷 訟 to give up wrangling and litigation.

²⁰息 留 to rest for awhile ; to perch.

息 禍 to bring disasters to an end.

息 絕 to cease completely, as when a family is cut off without posterity.

息 緣 安 心 to cause all affinities to cease and bring the heart to rest. (*Budd.*).

息 肩 to rest the shoulders, as porters or chair-bearers do ; also used fig.

²⁵息 謗 to cause slanders to cease.

息 足 to rest the feet ; to halt for a little while.

歇 息 to rest.

睡 息 to sleep.

(a) Breath, vapour. To breathe ; to sigh. To blow.

息 喘 to pant.

息 息 相 同 exactly similar.

息 燈 to blow out a lamp.

息 燭 to blow out a candle.

息 脈 the pulse.

一 息 間 in a breath ; instantly.

太 息 a deep sigh.

屏 息 to hold the breath. (*ping*³-)

氣·息 breath ; vapour.

(b) That which is produced—as posterity, interest, etc. To grow.

息 債 loan on interest.

息 利 or 利 息 interest; profit.

息 壤 or 息 生 之 土 productive soil.

⁵息 女 my daughter.

息‧婦 a daughter-in-law. *See next*, No. 2496.

息 欵 interest on a deposit.

息 生 productive.

息 男 my son.

息 票 interest-coupons.

¹⁰息 耗 profit and loss. *See below* C.2.

息 銀 (or 錢) interest on money.

出 息 bearing interest; profitable.

抽 息 to exact interest.

股 息 dividends.

¹⁵行 息 to bear interest.〔good in life.

有 出‧息 (沒 出‧息) can (not) make

(c) News.

信‧息 or 消‧息 news; intelligence.

息 耗 news; intelligence. *See above* B.10.

(d) Used for transliterating. Name of ancient tribe.

息 慎 or 肅 慎 a Tungusic tribe which dates back in Chinese books to the 25th year of *Shun* 2230. B.C.

(e) u.f. 瘜 No. 2498. A polypus.

息 肉 a polypus.

媳 2.5. The wife of a son, grandson or nephew.
2496

媳‧婦 or 子 媳 or 兒 媳 a daughter-in-law.

新 媳‧婦 a bride.

童 養 媳‧婦 or 團 圓 媳‧婦 a girl brought up in the home of her fiancée, generally for reasons of poverty.

媳‧婦 (兒) wife.

熄 2.5. To extinguish a fire.
2497

熄 燈 to extinguish a lamp.

跡 熄 traces obliterated.

瘜 2.5. A polypus.
2498

瘜 肉 or 鼻 瘜 a nasal polypus.

習 2.5. The rapid, frequent motion of the wings in flying:—from which comes the idea of—to practise; to study; customs; practices.
2499

習 俗 to become a custom by practice—as a matter of course.

習 俗 使 然 by usage it has become a custom.

習 兵 familiar with weapons; to drill.

習 口‧音 to practise enunciation.

⁵習 壞 corrupted by bad habits or example.

習 字 to practise writing.

習 字 帖 a copy-book.

習 學 to study.

習 定 to cultivate stillness.

¹⁰習 尚 to learn to esteem another.

習 尚 勤 儉 habituated to industry and economy.

習‧慣 accustomed to; custom; habit.

習 慣 成 自 然 practice makes perfect; habit is second nature.

習 慣 法 customs having the force of law; consuetudinary law.

¹⁵習 慣 犯 habitual criminal.

普 通 習 慣 a general custom.

習 於 versed in....

習 於 容 止 practised in putting on airs.

習 於 威 儀 practised in dignity of demeanour.

²⁰習 染 corrupted by evil custom.

習 業 practice of a profession.

習‧氣 evil habit or custom; mannerisms.

成‧了 習‧氣 become a habit.

習 流 trained naval men.

²⁵習 熟 habituated to; versed in.

習 熟 常 規 to act according to general usage.

習 癖 a bad habit; vice acquired by practice.

習 練 to gain experience by practice.

習 而 不 察 to act without due investigation—because of familiarity with the subject.

³⁰習 聞 a common report.

習 與 性 成 use becomes second nature.

習 藝 所 industrial school or reformatory.

習 見 accustomed to seeing.

習 非 habituated to evil practices.

³⁵習 題 an exercise; a problem in a course of study.

習 非 成 是 through usage the erroneous becomes the correct, of use of words, etc.

時 習 to practise constantly.

溫 習 to review lessons.

陋 習 evil customs; bad habits.

(a) Gentle—as a breeze.

習 習 谷 風 gently blows the breeze from the east.

慴 2.5. To be terrified; fear. Also read *che*²·⁵. and *tieh*²·⁵.
2500

慴 伏 to submit from fear; overawed.

樶 2.5. A hard wood.
2501

席 2.5. A mat—thus:—a feast, an entertainment. Inter. next.
2502

席 不 暇 暖 does not sit long enough to warm the mat—said of a busy man.

席 卷 天 下 he rolled up the empire like a mat—conquered it.

席 單 a bill of fare.

席 地 而 坐 to sit on the bare ground.

⁵席 捲 rolled like a mat—all inclusive; bed and baggage.

席 捲 而 逃 absconded with everything.

席 珍 a delicacy for the table—said of a scholarly man.

席 稿 to make straw into mats.

席 豐 履 厚 the mat is rich and the shoes thick—of a rich inheritance or a good position.

¹⁰主 席 chairman.

割 席 to divide the mat—to break off a friendship.

坐 席 to take one's place at the table.

西 席 a private tutor.

設 席 to prepare a feast.

¹⁵赴 席 to go to a feast.

還 席 a return feast.

酒 席 a banquet.〔at a meeting.

出 (缺) 席 to be present (absent)

(a) To rely on.

席 勝 to rely on a victory to make further aggression.

席 寵 惟 舊 relied on the long-continued favours which they had received.

(b) A sail.

蓆 2.5.
2503

A mat. Inter. preceding.

蓆 包 mat-bags.
蓆·子 or 草 蓆 matting; mats.
織 蓆 to make mats.

(a) Easy fitting; flowing and ample.

緇 衣 之 蓆 兮 How easy the black robes sit on you!

褉 2.5.
2504

To turn up the sleeves of a wrapper or outer gar-ment worn over a fur.

褉 衣 a thin garment.
褉 裘 a garment or jacket worn over a fur, the sleeves of which were turned up to show the fur beneath.
裘 之 褉 也 見 美 也 the sleeves were turned back to display the beauty of the fur beneath.

(a) To expose the upper part of the body.

祖 褉 with bare arms.
祖 褉 裸 裎 naked; unclad.

(b) Read t'i⁴. A swaddling-cloth.

裁 衣 之 褉 wrapped up in a cloth —of a girl-baby.

錫 2.5.
2505

Tin; pewter.

錫·匠 a tinman
錫·器 pewter articles.
錫 杖 or 禪 杖 a Buddhist abbot's staff. See No. 202—13.
錫 箔 tinfoil.
錫·鑞 solder; pewter.
包 錫 or 盥 錫 to tin.
粉 錫 white-lead.
飛 錫 a mendicant priest—from the staff once carried by them.

(a) A gift; to confer; to grant.

錫 以 榮 譽 to confer honours.
錫 民 爵 位 to raise to the peer-age.
九 錫 nine marks of imperial fa-vour; symbols of authority be-stowed on minister, etc.,—i.e., chariot and horses, state robes,

musical instruments, right to have vermilion doors, right of audience, right to armed atten-dants, bows and arrows, battle-axes, and sacrificial wines.

永 錫 無 疆 a bestowal that is endless and illimitable.

悉 1.5.
2506

To comprehend; to know.

知 悉 to take notice of; acquainted with.

(a) All, fully, entirely, altogether, minutely.

悉 力 with all the strength at one's disposal.
悉 心 with the entire mind.
悉 數 the whole of.
悉 皆 all; altogether.
悉 索 敝 賦 we collect all the con-tributions due from us.

蟋 1.5.
2507

A cricket.

蟋 蟀 the cricket.

膝 1.5.
2508

The knee, the lap:—thus, children. To kneel.

膝 下 children, used in address to parents.
膝 前 before the knees—in one's presence.
膝 蓋 骨 or 膝 頭 骨 the knee-joint.
膝 蓋 the knee-cap.
⁵膝 行 to creep or crawl.
膝 頭² or 磕²膝 頭² the knee.
屈 膝 to bow the knee.
跪 膝 knee-pads.
雙 膝 跪°下 to drop on both knees.

舄 | 4.5.
舃 |
2509

A shoe; the sole of a shoe.

赤 舄 red slippers.

(a) Large; glorious.

舄 奕 乎 千 載 "gloriously to en-dure for a thousand years."

松 梲 有 舃 the projecting beams of pine were large.

(b) u.f. next. Salt marshes.

潟 4.5.
2510

Land that has become impregnated with salt from the tide.

隰 2.5.
2511

Low, marshy land.

隰 田 marshy fields; swampy land.
隰 草 a marsh-grass.

襲 2.5.
2512

The lining of garments. To line a garment. N.A. for clothing.

襲·個 裏·子 to put in a lining.
衣 一 襲 a suit of garments.

(a) To wear. To prepare for burial.

襲 事 the preparation of a body for burial.
襲 朝²服 to wear court-dress.

(b) To turn down the sleeves which have been turned up over a fur robe. See 褉 No. 2504.

服 之 襲 也 充 美 也 the turning down of the sleeves is to display the beauty of the garment.

(c) Double, doubled, to repeat.

襲 雜 mixed; confused.
卜 不 襲 吉 divination, when pro-pitious, may not be repeated.

(d) To inherit. Hereditary.

襲 封 to inherit a feudal title.
襲 恩 to receive favours.
襲 爵 hereditary rank.
襲 職 hereditary office.
襲 蔭 to inherit a title bestowed on a relative who has died in the service.
世 襲 hereditary.
承 襲 to inherit a title.

(e) To make a surprise attack. To invade.

襲 取 to steal in and carry off.
襲 國 to make a raid.
襲 奪 to attack and seize.

襲 彼 後 路 to take the enemy in the rear.

⁵襲 擊 to make a surprise raid; to pounce upon.

襲 殺 to make a slaughter during a raid.

襲 營 to surprise a camp.

襲 虛 to attack the enemy when he is unprepared.

侵 襲 a surprise attack; a raid.

空 襲 air raid.

(f) **To plagiarize; to appropriate.**

襲 以 爲 利 appropriated it for his own profit.

剿 襲 to crib.

抄 襲 to plagiarize.

(g) **To accord with; to unite or draw together.**

下 襲 水 土 (Confucius) conformed to his environment.

天 地 之 襲 精 爲 陰 陽 the union of the essence of heaven and earth produces *Yin* and *Yang*.

HSIA.   (ㄒㄚ)

谺¹ The mouth of a valley.
2513

谽 谺 the mouth of a gorge or of a cave.

暇⁴ Leisure; relaxation.
2514

暇 時 leisure.

暇 景 (or 日) days of leisure.

暇 晷 leisure hours.

暇 豫 leisure and ease, plenty of time on one's hands.

⁵暇 逸 to take things easy.

暇 透 indulgent ease.

偷 暇 to take a rest.

無 暇 to have no leisure; busy; fully occupied.

餘 暇 spare time after working-hours.

瑕² A flaw in a piece of jade. A blemish.
2515

瑕 不 揜 瑜 his defects do not obscure his virtues.

瑕 病 a defect; a flaw; a vice.

瑕 疵 a fault; a defect.

瑕 瑜 互 見 he has both good and bad qualities.

瑕 璺 cracks and spots.

瑕 裂 a rent; a split.

瑕 釁 faults; defects.

無 瑕 without a flaw.

(a) u.f. 遐 No. 2517. What? How?

不 瑕 有 害 what wrong could there be in this?

(b) u.f. 霞 No. 2518. Rosy clouds.

蝦¹ A shrimp, a prawn. Inter. 鰕 No. 2519.
2516

蝦 夷 Ainos, the inhabitants of the island of Yezo. Japan.

蝦 蛄 the locust-shrimp.

(a) Read *ha*². A frog.

蝦 蟆 a frog, a toad.   (— *ma*)

遐² Distant; far-reaching; enduring—thus:—advanced in years.
2517

遐 年 old age.

遐 福 long-enduring happiness.

遐 終 to make an end of; for ever.

遐 舉 going far away.

遐 荒 far-off wilds.

遐 邇 一 體 both near and distant are treated alike.

遐 邇 皆 知 everybody far and near knows it.

遐 齡 to grow old; old age.

(a) **To abandon, to cast off.**

遐 心 to have a purpose to cast another off.

遐 棄 to abandon.

(b) How? What?

遐 不 作 人 Did he not influence men?

遐 不 謂 矣 Why not say so?

霞² Rosy clouds.
2518

霞 光 rosy rays of light.

霞 映 sunlight; radiance.

早 霞 red sky in the morning.

晚 霞 a rosy sunset.

(a) u.f. preceding. Far-distant.

登 霞 to ascend to the distant places—to die. (*Taoist*.)

(b) Vapour, mist; obscurity.

霞 霧 天 a misty morning.

(c) A garment.

霞 帔 (or 珮) a kind of collar worn as ceremonial dress by women in ancient times.

鰕¹ A shrimp, a prawn. Inter. 蝦 No. 2516.
2519

鰕 仁 flesh of shrimps.

鰕 子 or 子 母 鰕 a shrimp.= 鰕

鰕 油 shrimp-oil.

鰕 皮 or 鰕 売 the shell of the shrimp.

鰕 米 dried shrimps.

鰕 醬 shrimp-sauce.

鰕 鬚 shrimps' feelers.

明 鰕 large yellow prawns.

江 鰕 large prawns.

龍 鰕 the crayfish; lobster.

鰕 子 shrimps' eggs.

下⁴ To descend, to fall.
2520

下 不 下 cannot get it down.

下 不 下 does it rain or not?

下 不 下 來 no getting it down; unable to come down, or to recede from a position.

下 不 來 臺 cannot come down; cannot bring things to a satisfactory conclusion.

下 不 來 馬 cannot get off the horse—difficult to get out of a predicament.

⁵下 不 去 cannot get down—expression of dissatisfaction, "I can't stand it."

下 世 to come into the world; also, to die.

下 來 come down; to come down; an auxiliary verb.

下 問 to seek instruction from those in an inferior station.

下 地 獄 to go to hell.

¹⁰下 坐 to retire from the table.

下 堂 to descend from the throne to the hall; to put away a wife.

下 場 to sit for an examination; to resign from an office; the close of a performance; the exit of a stage.

下 場 人 one out of the running; out of office; out of favour.

下 嫁 to marry beneath her.

15 下 學 to give up study. *See below A.6.*

下 山 to descend a mountain.

下 席 to mourn for parents—defined as "to sleep on the ground and dwell in a hut by the grave."

下 店 to go to an inn.

下·得·去 I can get down to it—it leaves me some face; passable; allowable.

20 臉·上 下·得·去 I have some face left in getting out of the matter.

下 拜 to make an obeisance.

下 梯 a ladder to come down by—i.e., a mediator between disputants who want some face to give in to each other.

下 樓 to come down stairs.

下 水 to go into the water; to go down stream; to be a sailor.

25 下 水 船 down-river boat or steamer.

下 江 down river—referring to the lower reaches of the Yangtze; Kiangsu and Anhwei provinces.

下 游 down river—the region near the mouth of the Yangtze.

下 牀 to get out of bed.

下 界 or 下 凡 to descend into this world, to become incarnated.

30 下 監 to go into prison. A.c. 下 獄.

下 臨 to visit.

下 船 to disembark; to embark (on a junk).

下 蘇 州 嗎 Are you going to Soochow?

下 處 or 下 落 a lodging; a place where one resides.

35 下 車 to descend from a cart; to take over a post for the first time.

下 里 to go home—to be buried; rustic.

下 野 to withdraw from public life; to resign office.

下 降 to descend into this world; to come down.

下 陰 府 to descend into Hades.

40 下 雨 to rain.

下 雪 to snow.

下 雹·子 to hail.

下 霧 foggy; a mist descends.

下 露 the dew falls.

45 下 馬 to arrive; to get off a horse.

(a) To take down, to take off, to put down. To lay—as eggs; to produce young; to deposit; to issue.

下 個 定 義 to propose a definition of a term.

下 保 to deposit a guarantee or security.

下 力 or 下 苦 to give diligence to; to give oneself to.

下 勁 to put some effort into it.

5 下 命 (or 令) to issue a command.

下 學 上 達 to study the lower things and advance to the higher.

下 定 to give a deposit on goods; to send betrothal presents.

下 棋 or 着 棋 to play chess.

下 毒 to give poison; to do secret injury.

10 下 注 to stake a wager. [the actor's profession.

下 海 to transport by sea; to enter

下 狗 to give birth to puppies.

下 筆 to put pen to paper.

下 筆 成 章 great facility in composition.

15 下 網 to cast the nets.

下 緊 to push; to have diligence.

下 聘 to send betrothal presents.

下 葬 to inter.

下 藥 to give a dose of medicine; to take medicine.

20 下 蛋 to lay eggs.

下 貨 to ship goods.

下 貨 單 shipping order.

下 載 to ship goods.

下 錨 to cast anchor.

25 下 飯 to help down the rice—i.e., vegetables and savouries.

下·點 工·夫 devote some time to it.

收·下 received.

坐·下 to sit down.

(b) To begin; to set to work.

下 剪 to cut out with scissors.

下 戰 書 to challenge to war.

下 手 to take the initiative; to set to work; to lay hold of. *See below C.70.*

下 鋸 to cut out roughly with a saw.

(c) Beneath, below, lower down—thus inferior in quality or status. Under, inside.

下 下 禮 拜 the week after next.

下 乘 worn-out horse—inferior

---

scholarship.

下 交 to associate with those of inferior status.

下·人 servants; attendants.

5 下·作 人 a low scamp.

下 元 15th of the 10th lunar month.

下 則 secondly; in the second place; lowest order of traders.

下 劑 a purgative.

下 劣 very inferior.

10 下·半·天 or 下 午 the afternoon.

下·半·夜 after midnight.

下 半 截 the lower half.

下 半 旗 half-mast flag.

下 半 章 the latter part of the chapter.

15 下 古 later antiquity.

下 品 inferior goods; lower grade.

下 土 (or 塵) the earth below.

下 地 lowlying land.

下 壓 力 downward pressure.

20 下 壽 60 years of age according to *Chuang tzŭ*; others say 80.

下 妻 a concubine.

下 屬 subordinates.

下 巴 or 下·巴 頦 the chin.

下 平 聲 the lower even-tone, often called the second tone.

25 下 弦 the last quarter of the moon.

下 情 the feelings of the masses.

下 愚 very stupid and dull.

下 意·識 subconsciousness.

下 戶 or 下 民 the proletariat.

30 下 找 多 少 how much is there still owing?

下 文 the context below.

下 方 the world of men below.

下 旬 or 下 浣 or 下 澣 the last decade of a lunar month.

下 晚 or 下 黑 evening; dusk.

35 下 月 next month.

下 服 castration.

下 榻 to lodge; to take a residence.

下·次 or 下·回 or 下·趟 the next time or occasion.

下 殤 premature death between the ages of 11—18.

40 下 氣 lowly and submissive.

下 氣 怡 色 mildly and pleasantly.

下·流 flowing downwards; the lowest class; depraved; near the mouth of a river.

下·流 社 會 lowest class of society.

下 濕 marshy; lowlying.

45 下 略 what follows (in the original) is omitted (in the quotation). [year.

下·半 年 the latter six months of a

下 任 next administration; to

---

leave an official position.

下 疳 chancres.

下 禮拜 next week.

下 等 inferior, second-rate—of both things and persons.

下 等 動‧物 the lowest types of animal life.

50 下 等 植‧物 the lowest types of vegetable life.

下 級 low grades.

下 者 爲 巢 in the low lands (which were inundated) they built nests to live in.

下 聯 second of a pair of scrolls.

下 聲 a low tone; low-pitched.

55 下 肢 the lower limbs.

下 膊 the forearm.

下 行 星 the inferior planets, Mercury and Venus.

下 議 院 the Lower House of a Parliament.

下‧賤 low, mean, vile.

60 下 身 or 下 體 the privates.

下 達 success on a low plane—mere material prosperity.

下‧邊 or 下‧頭 below, beneath, inferior, lower down, on the other hand, the left side.

下 風 the inferior wind; leeward.

下 餘 or 下 剩 surplus; remainder.

65 一 下 (ha⁴) 子 one time; one moment; one blow. (dial.)

兩 下 both parties.

四 下 on all sides.

天 下 under the sky—China as an empire.

底 下 underneath.

70 手 下 subordinates; under one's hand.

打‧下 victorious, beaten down—the foe.

燈 下 under the lamps—in the evening.

目 下 the present.

(d) Depreciatory phrase in addressing superiors and speaking of oneself.

下 國 our feudal States.

下 官 an official speaking of himself.

下 懷 my ambitions or ideas.

下 走 he who walks behind—myself.

帳 下 or 麾 下 under your tent or flag—junior officer speaking to a senior.

治 下 we who are ruled by you—addressing a magistrate.

舍 下 my home.

部 下 your subordinate.

夏 ⁴ Summer.
2521

夏 五 the fifth month.

夏 令 the summer season.

夏 令 學 校 summer school.

夏 令 會 a summer conference.

5 夏 坐 a summer retreat; a Buddhist term for a season of retirement during the summer.

夏‧天 or 夏 季 the summer.

夏 布 Chinese linen, often called by foreigners, grass-cloth.

夏 日 可 畏 summer days are to be dreaded—used fig., of despotism, etc.

夏 月 the summer months.

10 夏 枯 草 a labiate plant which dries up in the summer, used in medicine.

夏 爐 冬 扇 stoves in summer and fans in winter—out of season; of no use at that time.

夏 生 冬 死 ephemeral.

夏 畦 the summer fields.

夏 眠 summer sleep of crocodiles, etc.

15 夏 礿 a summer sacrifice to the imperial ancestors.

夏 節 the summer holiday, the 5th of the 5th lunar month.

夏 翟 the pheasant.

夏 至 the summer solstice.

夏 至 線 or 北 回 歸 線 Tropic of Cancer.

20 夏 葛 冬 裘 linens for the summer and furs for the winter.

夏 蟲 不 可 以 語 於 冰 you cannot talk to summer insects about the ice—used of limited experience.

夏 蠶 or 二 蠶 summer silkworms.

夏 衣 or 夏 服 summer dress.

夏 雨 the summer rains.

25 夏 雲 the summer clouds.

夏 食 冬 蟄 the life of insects which eat in summer and sleep in winter.

炎 夏 the heat of summer.

(a) Great, spacious. An ancient name for China. See under 華 No. 2217—A. 5.

夏 后 氏 Yü the Great, founder of the Hsia dynasty.

夏 國 or 大 夏 ancient name for Bactria.

夏 屋 a spacious house.

夏‧朝 The Hsia Dynasty. 2205—1766 B.C.

夏 海 the vast sea.

夏 禮 the ceremonial rites of the Hsia Dynasty.

(b) Read chia³. u.f. 榎 A tree—a stick.

夏 楚 a ferule or rod.

夏 楚 二 物 收 其 威 也 the cane and the thorns were there in order to secure in them a proper awe.

(c) 夏 威 夷 Hawaii.

廈 ⁴
厦 | A great house; a mansion. A room. Amoy.
2522

廈 廳 the main hall.

廈 門 Amoy.

便 廈 the side-rooms in a courtyard.

後 廈 a lean-to or verandah at the back of a house.

抱 廈 a verandah in front of a house. [office buildings

大 廈 used in names of modern

罅 ⁴
隙 | A crack in earthenware, a split; thus:—a grudge.
2523

罅 隙 a crack; a cause of offence; a grudge; a flaw; a defect.

孔 罅 a hole.

牆 罅 a hole in a wall.

裂 罅 a rent or crack.

 ⁴ A cover. Radical 146. Also read ya⁴. Often confused with 西 which is commonly regarded as the radical.
2524

HSIA. (丁ㄚ)
(Hsiah)

匣 ²·⁵
2525   A small box; a casket.

匣 劍 圍 燈 he encloses a sword and surrounds a lamp—of hidden talent.

匣·子 a case; a casket or coffer.

呷 4.5. **To swallow; to drink. Also read** *chia*[4.5].
2526

呷 一 口 酒 take a sip of wine.
吸 呷 breathless.

柙 2.5. **A pen for wild beasts; a cage for prisoners. A scabbard. Also read** *chia*[2.5].
2527

柙 而 藏 keep them in their scabbards.

狎 2.5. **To approach near; to be familiar with.**
2528

狎 優 to be on intimate terms with.
狎 愛 attachment; love.
狎 獸 a pet animal.
狎 習 intimate with; expert in.
狎 而 敬 之 intimate but respectful.
狎 近 intimate with.

(a) **Disrespectful; improper intimacy.**

狎 侮 or 輕 狎 to treat with disrespect because of familiarity.
狎 好 improper intimacy.
狎 妓 intimacy with prostitutes.
狎 客 a disrespectful, rude person; a boor.
⁵狎 弄 to dally with; to toy with.
狎 忽 to be familiar and contemptuous.
狎 暱 intimacy in an improper sense.
狎 暱 惡 少 to associate with evil youths.
狎 褻 indecent.
¹⁰狎 邪 profligate; lewd.
作 狎 邪 遊 to frequent houses of ill-fame.
玩 狎 to take liberties with a woman.

(b) **To change.**

狎 主 諸 侯 之 盟 they went back on the oath they made with the feudal chiefs.

洽 2.5. **To blend with; to be in harmony. Also read** *ch'iah*[4].
2529

洽 于 民 心 in harmony with popular feeling.
洽 可 very well done; all right.
洽 情 合 理 in accordance with the bearings of the case.
洽 比 其 鄰 on good terms with the neighbours.
⁵洽 然 harmoniously; equally.
洽 暢 affable; pleasant.
洽 當 proper; agreeable.
洽 驩 pleased; elated.
天 下 洽 和 the empire would be in harmony.

(a) **To penetrate; imbued with.**

洽 博 or 洽 聞 of wide experience and knowledge.
洽 於 天 下 penetrated through the empire.
洽 汗 wet through with perspiration.
洽 浹 imbued with; agreeing with.
⁵洽 濡 saturated with—of plants after rain.
洽 覽 wide experience.
仁 恩 洽 普 his love and grace penetrated to all.
仁 聲 洽 著 the fame of his goodness extended far and wide.
水 洽 juicy.
¹⁰道 洽 政 治 penetrating principles and effective administration of government.

(b) **Read** *ho*[2.5]. **A river in Shensi, now known as** 金 河.

在 洽 之 陽 on the south bank of the *Ho*.

祫 2.5. **A triennial sacrifice to ancestors.**
2530

峽 2.5. **Hills on each side of a chasm; a gorge; a strait.**
2531

峽 口 a mountain-pass; a defile.
巫 峽 a famous gorge in the Upper Yangtze.
水 峽 water flowing down a chasm.

狹 2.5. **Narrow. Narrow-minded.**
2532

狹 志 or 卑 狹 mean; sordid.
狹 斜 遊 or 狎 邪 遊 to frequent houses of ill-fame.

狹 窄 or 狹 小 narrow; confined.
肚 皮 狹 窄 a man whose *bowels* are contracted:—i.e., illiberal; parsimonious; narrow.
⁵狹 義 a restricted sense; specific.
狹 路 相 逢 they met in a narrow path—where they could not avoid each other.
狹 軌 鐵 路 a narrow-gauge railway.
狹 道 or 狹 徑 a narrow path.
狹 鄉 a congested locality, a term used during the *T'ang* dynasty, for a district where the land is not sufficient to support the population.
¹⁰狹 隘 narrow; contracted.
狹 韻 a rhyme for which there are only a few characters.

硤 2.5. **Ancient town near the present Ichang in Hupeh.**
2533

嗐 2.5. **An exclamation of surprise or regret.** Pron. *hai*[4].
2534

嗐 呀 Alack! Haiya!
嗐，可 惜·了 what a pity! How sad!

瞎 1.5. **Blind—thus:—heedless, rash; reckless. One eye closed.**
2535

瞎 一 眼 blind of one eye.
瞎 七 瞎 八 all in confusion.
瞎 充 inefficient blundering.
瞎·子 摸 魚 a blind man feeling for fish—blindman's buff.
⁵瞎 弄 to meddle with; to throw into disorder.
瞎 抓 blindly clutching—to do anything for a living.
瞎 攪 to make a muddle of.
瞎 漢 a rash, ignorant fellow.
瞎 眼 blind; sore eyes.
¹⁰瞎 眼·的 or 瞎·子 a blind man.
瞎 碰 to muddle through; to hit the right way by accident.
瞎 答 or 瞎 講 to talk nonsense.
瞎 話 reckless talk; a lie.
瞎 說 to talk recklessly; to lie.
¹⁵瞎 貓 拖 死 老 鼠 a blind cat dragging a dead rat,—an unexpected gain, a lucky chance.
瞎 賴 to put the blame on to another.

瞎 走 to go blindly on.
瞎 闖 to run against, like a blind man.
瞎 鬧 to create a disturbance.
[20]瞎 眼 瞎·子 a blind man whose eyes are open—sometimes said by one who cannot read.

轄
鎋 2.5. The linch-pin of a wheel; thus:—to govern or control. The noise of a barrow.
2536

轄 制 to govern.
轄 境 limits of jurisdiction.
轄 管 to manage; to control.
受 轄 to be under the control of.
投 轄 留 客 to detain a visitor by throwing his linch-pin into the well.
統 轄 to oversee; to direct affairs.

黠 2.5. Crafty; artful. Also read chieh[4.5].
2537

黠 智 wise, crafty.
黠 慧 clever, intelligent.
黠 鼠 crafty, like rats.

(a) Transliterating particle.

黠 戛 斯 ancient name for the Kirghiz:—lit. "red-yellow faces, in allusion to their red hair, white complexion and green eyes." *Giles.*

HSIAI or (ㄒㄞ) HSIEH. (Hsiai)

械 [4] Weapons, implements, fetters. Also read *chiai* or *chieh[4]*.
2538

械 杻 fetters; bonds.
械 用 implement for use.
械 繫 to fetter.
械 鬥·的 事 fighting with weapons.
器 械 machinery; vessels; implements. *See* 器 No. 549—5,6.
機 械 mechanism, etc. *See* 機 No. 411—A.12ff.
軍 械 weapons of war. *See* 軍 No. 1722—51ff.

懈 [4] Remiss; inattentive; idle.
2539

懈 忒 making errors through negligence.
懈 怠 or 鬆 懈 or 懈 弛 negligent; lax.
懈 惰 idle; shiftless.
不 懈 unremitting effort.

澥 [4] A creek. To become watery—as paste.
2540

獬 [4] A fabulous monster called 獬 豸, described as being like a unicorn; its habitat is the wilds, it can discriminate between right and wrong, and it destroys the wicked when it meets them. It is said to be fire-eating even to its own destruction. Formerly used as a badge by *taotais.* See 豸 No. 1043.
2541

蟹 [4] A crab.
2542

蟹 匡 the back of a crab.
蟹 厄 damage done to fields by crabs.
蟹 戶 crab-catchers.
蟹 斷 or 蟹 簾 to stretch a bamboo network across a stream to intercept the crabs.
[5]蟹 杯 crab-shell used as a wine-cup.
蟹 火 a light used when catching crabs.
蟹 眼 bubbles on water.
蟹 羹 crab-soup.
蟹 舍 huts used by those who catch crabs.
[10]蟹 螯 the pincers of a crab.
蟹 螺 high-land.
蟹 行 a sideways walk—used fig., for 橫 行 lawless conduct; browbeating ways, etc.
蟹 黃 crab-spawn.
毛 蟹 the hairy crab.
[15]膏 蟹 a red species of edible crab.
螃·蟹 crabs generally.

邂 [4] To meet unexpectedly.
2543

邂 逅 相 逢 to meet unexpectedly.

瀣 [4] Sea-mist; vapours.
2544

鞋
鞵 [2] Shoes; boots. Also read *hai[2].*
2545

鞋 刷·子 a shoe-brush.
鞋 匠 or 做 鞋·的 shoemaker.
鞋 帶 or 鞋 絆 shoe-laces.
鞋 底 sole of a shoe.
[5]鞋 底 魚 or 比 目 魚 the sole.
鞋 拔·子 a shoe-horn.
鞋 梁兒 the double seam on the toe of some Chinese shoes.
鞋 油 shoe-polish.
鞋 舖 or 鞋 店 a shop where boots and shoes are sold.
[10]鞋 金 or 鞋 錢 broker's commission.
鞋 幫·子 the uppers of a shoe.
提 鞋 to carry shoes.
穿 鞋 to put shoes on; to wear shoes.
脫 鞋 to take off the shoes.

諧
諧 [2] To harmonize; to accord with; to agree.
2546

諧 價 to discuss, and agree about, a price.
諧 協 to bring into agreement.
諧 和 to bring into harmony.
諧 婉 affable and complaisant.
[5]諧 暢 agreeable and pleasant.
諧 老 to grow old together—of a married couple. A.w. 偕老.
諧 比 partizan; forming a clique.
諧 緝 at peace; in agreement.
諧 聲 or 形 聲 one of the six groups of Chinese characters, in which the radical gives the idea of the meaning and the other part the sound.
[10]音 不 諧 out of tune.
和 諧 harmonious.
(a) To laugh at; to make a joke of.

諧 笑 or 詼 諧 to ridicule.
諧 謔 raillery; jesting.

HSIANG. (丅兀)

香[1] Fragrant. Radical 186.
2547

香 口 fragrant mouth—describing a woman's voice.
香 味 aromatic flavours.
香 品 superior quality.
香 囊 or 香 袋 perfume-sachets.
[5]香 圓 a variety of lemon.
香 塵 fragrant dust—falling petals.
香 奩 lady's dressing-case.
香 房 or 香 閣 or 香 閨 women's apartments.
香 木 fragrant wood.
[10]香 柏 the cypress.
香 楠 木 the fragrant *Nanmu* which grows in western China. *Machilus Nanmu.* Its wood is yellow and finely marked, valuable for cabinet work.
香 椿 *Cedrela odorata*, the young leaf shoots are eaten.
香 楓 the Liquidambar.
香 橙 the common sweet orange.
[15]香 檬 or 芒 果 the mango.
香 氣 or 香 味 fragrance.
香 水 scents.
香 油 fragrant or aromatic oils; sesamum oil.
香 油 蟲 or 馬 陸 (or 蚿) the millipede or galley-worm.
[20]香 港 Hongkong. lit., fragrant lagoon.
香 澤 fragrant oil for anointing the hair.
香 濃 spicy; highly flavoured.
香 煙 cigarettes.
香 牀 bed made of fragrant woods.
[25]香 牛 皮 Russia leather.
香 珠 a rosary of fragrant beads.
香 瓜 the musk-melon.
香 甜 agreeable to the taste.
香 祖 the progenitor of fragrance—applied to the *epidendrum* 蘭 花, because it flowers early in the spring.
[30]香 米 or 香 稻 scented rice.
香 粉 or 香 脂 cosmetics.
香 料 spices; perfumery.
香 膏 fragrant ointment.
香 艷 bewitching; fascinating.
[35]香 花 畦 beds of fragrant flowers.
香 草 or 香 蘭 草 or 香 水 蘭 *Eupatorium chinensis.*
香 茶 or 香 片 scented tea, flow-

ers being mixed with it for this purpose; it is generally of a lower grade.
香 荽 or 香 荾 coriander.
香 蕈 or 香 信 mushrooms.
[40]香 蕉 bananas.
香 蟻 wine.
香 貍 the civet.
香 雲 紗 a light silk for summer wear.
香 風 fragrant breezes.
[45]香 餌 a good bait for fishing.
香 魂 fragrant soul—that of a woman.
不 知 香 臭 does not know the difference between fragrance and stench,—senseless.
書 香 literary fragrance.
酒 香 the bouquet of wine.
↑香 草 vanilla.

(a) Incense.

香 壇 the altar of incense.
香 婆 a female devotee.
香 客 visitors to temples; pilgrims to shrines; devotees.
香 室 the hall of a Buddhist temple.
[5]香 市 incense-market—of the crowds of pilgrims assembling to burn incense.
香 會 idolatrous gathering.
香 案 or 香 几 an incense-table.
香 桶 incense-holders.
香 火 incense and paper money; servants in a temple; an oath, from the fact that incense was burned in taking the oaths; also from this sense, a husband and wife.
[10]香 火 兄 弟 girls who swore an oath of brotherhood.
香 火 因 緣 an oath of brotherhood.
香 火 重 誓 a solemn oath taken with burning incense.
何 獨 無 香 火 情 耶 How is it that you have forgotten your oath?
香 烟 冷 落 the smoke of incense has ceased—of a ruined temple.
[15]香 燭 incense and candles for idolatry.
香 燈 lamp burning before the tablet of a deceased person.
香 界 Buddhist temples.
香 色 a yellowish-brown colour.
香 資 incense - money — contributions to temples.

[20]香 錢 presents to priests.
香 鑪 a censer.

肛[1] A boat.
2548

肛 魚 the paper-nautilus.

向[4] Facing towards; to or from.
2549

向 上 (or 下) upwards or downwards respectively.
向 上 帝 求 to ask of God.
向 人 before others.
向 他 借 錢 borrow money of him.
[5]向 你 說 to speak to you.
向 使 if it is really.
向 先 走 or 向 前 去 to go first; to go on ahead.
向 內 (or 外) facing inwards or outwards respectively.
向 前 to press forward.
[10]向 前 來 to come to the front.
向 前 進 行 go straight ahead.
向 右 (or 左) to the right or the left respectively.
向 善 心 a heart inclined to goodness.
向 在 to live at.
[15]向 地 性 geotropism, the tendency of plants to grow towards the earth.
向 大 街 facing the main street.
向 學 inclined to study.
向 心 力 centripetal.
向 日 性 heliotropism, the tendency of plants to turn towards the sun.
[20]向 日 葵 the sunflower.
向 晚 toward evening.
向 榮 facing glory—i.e., successful, flourishing.
向 水 性 hydrotropism, the tendency of plants to seek water.
向 活 的 to give the living the benefit of the doubt. in a legal decision.
[25]向 理 or 向 論 to discuss with; to argue.
向 着 to side with; to face.
向 義 inclined to righteousness or loyalty.
向 背 front and rear; toward or away from.
向 至 on the coming date; when.
[30]向 西 facing west.

向 那³ 方 走 which way shall I go?

向 隅 facing the corner—when a guest is left out in the cold; when things are not fairly apportioned.

向 陽 facing the south or the sunny side.

向 風 facing the wind.

³⁵二 十 四 向 the 24 points of the compass.

定 向 a set course.

意 向 meaning or intention.

方°向 direction.

歸 向 inclined towards; to turn to.

⁴⁰水 流 之 向 the set of a current.

河 向 東 流 the river flows towards the east.

終 向 the final object or aim.

(a) Hitherto.

向 來 hitherto.

向 來 不 見 he had never seen it.

向 例 according to custom; precedent.

向 常 in the usual way.

向 年 in previous years.

向 日 on a former day; previously.

一 向 formerly, of late.

晌⁴ Noon, mid-day. Also read *shang³*.
2550

晌·午 or 晌 天 noon. (*shang³·huo*)

晌·午 錯·了 afternoon; noontide is past.

晌·午 飯 or 中 飯 or 午 飯 *wu³* midday meal.

下·半 晌 the afternoon.

半 晌 for some time.

早·半 晌 the forenoon.

片 晌 a little while.

(a) A land measure in Manchuria. It is equivalent to seven *mou* 畝; also defined as being a piece of land that can be sown in one day.

餉³ Rations or pay for troops. Revenue. Provision given to field-labourers as part of their wages.
2551

餉 單 a statement of expenses for rations, pay, etc., in the army; duty-receipt.

餉 平 a standard weight used for paying duty in silver.

餉 械 rations and munitions.

餉 源 sources of revenue; revenue.

⁵餉 給 to issue soldiers' rations.

餉 釐 revenue from *likin* barriers.

餉 需 rations and pay.

餉 鞘 hollow logs for carrying silver.

餉 項 or 餉 銀 soldiers' pay, collective and individual respectively.

¹⁰餉 饋 soldiers' rations.

兵 餉 pay and rations.

無 人 餉 之 "no man gave into him."

納 餉 to pay duty.

關 餉 to draw (a soldier's) pay.

(a) Presents of provisions.

餉 億 a present, the gift itself; also used for rations.

餉 客 to entertain a visitor to a meal.

餉 遺 to send a present.

餉 酬 to recompense.

享³ To receive. To enjoy. Distinguish 亨 No. 2099.
2552

享 利 to enjoy the profit from the labours of another.

享 受 to accept: to receive.

享 國 祚 to reign.

享 壽 or 享 年 to enjoy old age.

⁵享 多 儀 in making a present to a superior, the attitude of respect is the most important thing.

享 安 靜 to enjoy peace.

享 榮 華 to enjoy good fortune.

享 有 to enjoy; enjoyment.

享 有 特 權 (ambassadors) enjoy special privileges—i.e., extra-territoriality.

¹⁰享 用 to enjoy the use of.

享 福 to enjoy happiness.

享 過 福 to have seen better days.

(a) To present offerings in sacrifice. To accept a sacrificial offering.

享 于 祖 考 to sacrifice to ancestors.

享 侑 to offer sacrifice and have it accepted.

享 堂 the room where a corpse is laid out; the hall of sacrifice.

享 祭 to offer a sacrifice.

巷⁴ A lane, an alley. Also read *hang*⁴.
2553

巷 伯 a chief eunuch.

巷 口 entrance to a lane.

巷 哭 weeping of the dwellers in a lane.

巷·子 a lane; an alley.

⁵巷 戰 street-fighting.

巷 歌 singing in the lanes—ancient rites forbade this when there were funerals.

巷 祭 an offering at the head of a street when a funeral is leaving.

巷 議 街 談 street-rumours; village-gossip.

巷 遇 to meet in a lane.

¹⁰巷 陌 streets generally.

柳 巷 the willow-lane—a brothel.

衖⁴ A road through a village. A lane. Also read *lung*⁴.
2554

衖·堂·裏 拜 丈·母 bows to his mother-in-law in lane and hall—ostentatious politeness.

項⁴ The nape of the neck. Also read *hang*⁴.
2555

項 圈 a neck-ring.

項 巾 a scarf; a tippet.

項 帶 a necktie. ＝ 領 帶.

項 縮 to, as it were, draw in the neck—to be ashamed.

⁵項 背 相 望 to look in both directions.

項 領 a thick neck; an important strategic position.

強 項 stiff-necked.

頸 項 the neck.

(a) An item; a kind. Income; funds. A term, as in algebra. N.A. for items, etc.

一 項 一 項·的 item by item.

公 項 public funds.

初 項 first term. (algebra).

同 類 項 like terms. (algebra).

⁵外 項 external term. (algebra).

末 項 last term. (algebra).

欠 項 liabilities.

欵 項 funds; an amount.

用 項 expenditure.

¹⁰進·項 income.

進 項 稅 income tax. *See* 所 No. 5465-13.

鄉[1] The country, as contrasted
2556 with the town. A village;
a neighbourhood. Dis-
tinguish 卿 No. 1155. An-
ciently a district of 12,500
families; a district of not
more than 50,000 inhabit-
ants.

鄉·下 the country; one's native
place.

鄉·下土老 the ignorant country
people.

鄉井 one's native place.

鄉人儺 the villagers drove away
the demons of pestilence.

[5]鄉保 or 鄉老 village-elders.

鄉信 (or 書) a letter from home.

鄉俗 local customs.

鄉·先·生 a country-elder.

鄉先達 a man of one's locality
who has made a name for himself.

[10]鄉勇 village-braves.

鄉味 delicacies from one's native
place.

鄉君 ancient title given to women.

鄉國 one's native place.

鄉土 or 鄉土科 local geogra-
phy, productions and history,
etc., as a school subject.

[15]鄉士 the criminal officer in
charge of six *hsiang* districts.

鄉姪 depreciatory term used of
oneself in addressing seniors
from one's district.

鄉宦 country gentlemen.

鄉弟 depreciatory term used of
oneself in addressing those of
the same locality.

鄉愿 a hypocrite; an impostor.

[20]鄉愿德之賊也 you hyper-
honest village people are the
thieves of virtue.

鄉戶 local people; fellow villagers.

鄉曲 a poor village; my native
place.

鄉望 famous in his own district.

鄉末 I—depreciatory term used
in speaking of oneself to those
of the same place.

[25]鄉村學校 rural district-schools.

鄉村敎·育 rural education.

鄉村投遞 rural delivery.

鄉村生活 rural life.

鄉民 the people of the villages.

[30]鄉氣 or 鄉風 the customs of a
locality; the country air.

鄉衆 villagers; the whole village.

鄉科 or 鄉試 the former triennial examination for the second
degree of 舉人.

鄉約 a village-headman appointed
by the villagers.

鄉紳 country-gentry.

[35]鄉薦 old name for the former
second-degree graduates.

鄉親 fellow-countrymen; of the
same village.

鄉評 village-opinions.

鄉豪 village-bullies.

鄉談 or 鄉音 local patois.

[40]鄉貫 or 家鄉 one's native village.

鄉邑報章 provincial newspa-
pers.

鄉鄉 country neighbours.

鄉里 or 鄉村 country villages;
one's native place.

鄉長 village-elder.

[45]鄉黨 district-communities.

鄉黨州閭 neighbours.

(a) Read *hsiang*[4]. u.f., 向 No.
2549. Formerly; towards, etc.

鄉也 just now, a little while ago.

鄉化 to turn towards the right;
to reform.

鄉導 to show the way, to guide.

鄉背 front and rear; opposite,
contrary.

(b) Conditional particle.

鄉使不守法律 if the laws are
not strictly observed.

鼳[4] A little while, formerly.
2557 u.f., 向 No. 2549.

鼳役之三月 I lately employed
him for three months.

鼳者 recently; up till now.

蠁 3.4.
2558 Larvae; grubs.

蠁智 in great haste.

肸蠁 small flies rising in swarms
from damp ground—used to
illustrate a flourishing state of
things.

響[3]
响 Noise, sound, echo. To
make a noise.
2559

bright.

響亮 a crash; clear-sounding;

響卜 to divine from voices heard
on the last evening of the year.

響器 musical instruments.

響尾蛇 the rattlesnake.

[5]響快 prompt, as quick as an echo.

響應 an echo—speedily; to respond.

響箭 sounding-arrow, once used
by brigands as a signal.

響聲 a sound; an echo.

響音 noise; sound.

[10]響馬 mounted highwaymen.

饗[3] To offer in sacrifice or at
a feast. To enjoy a sacrifice
2560 —as the gods.

饗祭 or 饗供 to sacrifice.

饗糖 sugar-figures carried at weddings.

上饗 to offer a sacrifice.

尙饗 May this my offering be
acceptable to thee—final words
of a sacrificial ode.

神饗 offering to the gods.

嚮[4] Opposite; to incline towards. u.f., 向 No. 2549.
2561

嚮北 facing the north

嚮午 noon.

嚮往 to desire; to incline to.

嚮應 to turn towards; to look up
to.

嚮 (or 響) 搨 to make a tracing
of writings, etc., by holding
them up to the light.

嚮明 the hour of dawn.

嚮明而治 matters are best
regulated if an early start is
made.

嚮晦 the hour of sunset.

嚮晨 the approach of dawn.

嚮背 backwards and forwards
contraries.

(a) To guide, to approach.

嚮道 a guide.

嚮邇 to approach; to draw near
to.

(b) To indicate one's mind.

嚮 于 時 夏 (God) indicated His will to the sovereigns of *Hsia* through the signs of the times.

(c) u.f. preceding 饗, To offer a sacrifice.

上 帝 嘉 嚮 God approved of the offering.

(d) To encourage.

嚮 用 五 福 encourage the full use of the five blessings—longevity, riches, peacefulness and serenity, love of virtue, and a good end to crown the life.

(e) A conditional particle.

嚮 使 supposing.

HSIANG. SIANG. (ㄒㄧㄤ)

相 1 Mutual; reciprocal. Direction towards.
2562

相 下 in accord with.
  兩 不 相 下 two persons not getting on well together.
相 並 abreast; side by side.
相 互 mutual, reciprocal.
5 相 互 作 用 interaction; reciprocal action.
相 互 保 險 mutual insurance.
相 互 利 益 mutual advantage.
相 互 關·係 mutual relationships.
相 交 intercourse, dealings with; to associate with; friendship; to exchange; intersect.
10 相 交·之 禮 the ceremony of intercourse—the reception of church members.
相 似 or 相 若 alike; resembling.
相 似 號 sign of similarity: ∽ or ∾
相 輔 to help; to complement.
相 伴 a companion.
相 依 mutually dependent; interdependent.
15 相 信 mutual trust and confidence; to believe in.
相 做 alike.
相 候 to wait for; to be prepared to receive.
相 傳 tradition; orally reported; handed down.
相 克 mutually destructive.
20 相 切 in close contact; to be tangent.
相 別 to part.

相 制 to oppose; to withstand; interaction.
相 加 behaviour towards.
相 勸 to exhort; to warn.
25 相 參 to consult together.
相 反 contrary; opposed to each other; contradictory.
相 受 on good terms.
相 合 mutual affinity; to agree; to unite.
相 向 facing each other.
30 相 同 alike; the same; similar.
相 吞 吐 alternately rising and falling—as music on the breeze.
相 告 to inform.
相 和 to harmonize; to rhyme.
相 商 to talk a matter over.
35 相 囑 to enjoin.
相 因 complementary; relative cause.
相 因·的 relatively.
相 坐 to implicate another in a crime.
相 報 to requite; tit-for-tat.
40 相 好 on good terms; a lover; to live as man and wife without regular marriage.
相 安 in peace.
相 宜 fitting; what is right; convenient; suitable.
相 將 to go together.
相 尋 with the result that; in consequence.
45 相 對 corresponding; face to face; relative; to agree together; relation between one and another.
相 對 人 one's opponent. (*legal*).
相 對 律 law of relativity.
相 對 我 relative self.
相 對 權 relative rights (*legal*).
50 相 對·的 relatively; contrastingly.
相 對 直 立 stood erect, facing him.
相 對 論 theory of relativity.
相 對 速 率 relative velocity.
相 屬 in succession; one after the other.
55 相 左 at variance; to differ.
相 引 to lead each other.
相 強 to compel; to oblige to.
相 幫 or 相 助 or 相 援 mutual aid.
相 干 concern; interest.
60   不 相 干 not concerned with; no concern of.
相 形 之 下 mutual comparison.
相 形 見 絀 on comparison found to be very different.
相 彷 similar.

相 待 to treat one another.
65 相 得 suitable; fitting; adapted to each other.
相 忘 forgetfulness.
相 思 or 相 愛 mutual love; to be in love with.
相 思 子 red beans, seeds of *Abrus precatorius,* or love-seeds.
相 思 病 lovesickness.
70 異 地 相 思 though far apart, yet thinking of each other.
相 怨 mutual recriminations.
相 愜 agreement.
相 應 or 相 當 appropriate; in correspondence; suitable; proper; legal; as in duty bound; proportionate.
相 憶 mutual remembrances.
75 相 成 complementary.
相 手 opposite party; connected with. (*Jap.*).
相 手 方 party in a suit. (*Jap.*).
相 打 to fight together.
相 投 on good terms.
80 相 持 to wrangle; to quarrel.
相 持 不 下 both parties unwilling to yield.
相 抵 to counterbalance.
相 承 to agree with; inherited.
相 接 to receive; to join; contiguous; end to end.
85 相 撞 to collide; to strike against; to meet.
相 援 成 例 to create a precedent.
相 摩 mutual attraction, as of natural forces.
相 摩 則 燃 friction produces fire.
相 擊 之 聲 (thunder) is the sound of their clashing together.
90 相 擬 resembling each other.
相 紋 to meet together.
相 敬 mutual respect.
相 於 mutually; closely related.
相 會 to meet together.
95 相 會 之 處 the place of meeting.
相 月 the seventh month of lunar calendar.
相 欵 to entertain.
相 歷 consecutive periods.
相 比 to compare; close together.
100 相 求 to entreat; to beg.
相 沿 or 相 循 to comply with the views of another.
相 消 to cancel each other. (*math.*)
相 激 to provoke; to arouse.
相 激 之 光 (lightning) is the flash of their collision.

[105]相 照 in perfect sympathy.

相 煩 I will trouble you.

相 熟 intimately acquainted.

相 爭 相 傲 proud contention.

相 爭 相 競 contention and strife.

[110]相 犯 in opposition to; not in accord with; incongruous.

相 狎 相 優 because of familiarity to treat with disrespect.

相 牽 to follow one another; to lead away.

相 生 相 剋 reciprocally producing and destroying each other, as the five elements.

相 當 位 置 legal position.

[115]相 當 對 待 a proper attitude.

相 當 行·爲 a legal act.

相 盪 mutual reaction.

相 矛 盾 mutually contradictory. *See* 矛 No. 4570.

相 知 friends; acquaintances.

[120]相 斫 書 a name given to the *Tso Chuan* 左 傳 because it treats only of wars.

相 碍 to interfere with; a hindrance to.

相 稱 (*ch'ên*⁴) in symmetry; fitting each other.

相 符 in agreement; to tally.

相 等 equal; equivalent.

[125]相 約 came to a mutual understanding or agreement.

相 維 supporting each other.

相 續 to succeed to an inheritance. (*Jap.*).

相 續 權 right of inheritance. (*Jap.*).

相 繼 in succession.

[130]相 罵 mutual reviling and recriminations.

相 羊 (or 徉) backwards and forwards; irresolute.

相 習 intimate with; to comply with the views of another.

相 聚 to meet together; to assemble.

相 聯 or 相 連 joined.

[135]相 背 opposite; contrary.

相 能 to agree together without quarrelling.

相 與 to associate with.

相 與 竭 力 unitedly using every effort.　　unrelated, irrelevant.

相 蒙 mutually confused. 不 相 蒙

[140]相 薄 gathered together; mixed with.

相 處 to live together.

相 襯 to match—as garments.

相 見 to meet; to interview.

相 見 恨 晚 sorry that we have not met before.—a conventional phrase.

[145]相 親 相 敬 mutual affection with respect.

相 觀 而 善 the good influence (of pupils) observing each other.

相 託 to entrust to; to confide to the care of.

相 說 以 解 (the teacher and pupil) talk together and the matter is explained.

相 談 a conversation; to chat.

[150]相 識 to recognize; acquaintance.

相 贈 to make a present to.

相 距 distant from.

相 輳 相 赴 gathered towards each other, like spokes in a wheel; converging towards each other.

相 轄 mutual control.

[155]相 近 almost; near to.

相 迎 to welcome.

相 逢 or 相 遇 to meet, to visit; to become acquainted with.

相 連 connected; consecutive.

相 遂 agreeable to.

[160]相 遠 widely apart; very different.

相 適 suitable; fit; agreeable.

相 邀 to invite.

相 配 mates; partners.

相 錯 contused; mixed up.

[165]相 錯 如 繡 interlacing and confused like the pattern of embroidery—said of the boundaries of two States.

相 關 mutually affected by; having a sympathetic feeling between.

相 陪 attendant on; in company with.

相 隔 一 日 difference of one day.

相 隔 天 淵 as far apart as heaven is from the abyss.

[170]相 隨 following immediately after.

相 離 separated from; apart.

相 離 還 遠 while still a great way off.

相 非 mutual recrimination and reproach.

相 類 of the same species.

[175]相 顧 mutual care.

愛 惡 相 攻 love and hatred attack each other.

(*a*) Read *hsiang*⁴. **To look at; to see. To practice physiognomy. Form or symbol.**

相 人 to study a man's physiognomy and foretell his future.

相 攸 to select a suitable son-in-law.

相 印 法 foretelling events from the characters of a seal.

相 女 配 夫 to study one's daughter in selecting a husband for her.

[5]相 字 to dissect characters in fortune telling. *See* 拆 No. 290—2.

相 工 a student of physiognomy.

相 度 (*tŏ*⁵) 機 宜 consider the suitability of; consider a suitable plan.

相 方 to examine the aspects of a place for residence.

相 時 而 動 take action at a favourable time.

[10]相 機 行 事 act according to the circumstances.

相 法 rules of physiognomy.

相 者 physiognomist; leader of a blind man.　　　　monologue

相·聲 to mimic; mimicry; comic

相 術 physiognomy.

[15]相·貌 appearance; looks; countenance.

相·貌 堂 堂 to have a dignified appearance.

不 可 貌 相 do not judge by outward appearances.

相 風 銅 鳥 a weather-cock.

相 馬 to tell the good points of a horse.

[20]相 鼠 有 齒 look at that rat, it has teeth!

本 相 one's natural form.

法 相 a form assumed by magical powers.

無 相 without form—referring to God.

照 相 to take a photograph.

[25]看 相 to practice physiognomy; to consult a physiognomist.

(*b*) **To assist—thus:—a minister of State.**

相·公 a young gentleman; a catamite.

相 國 a premier; to assist in the administration; former title of a Grand-Secretary.

相 室 a sort of matron.

相 府 a statesman's residence.

[5]相 火 the secondary source of heat in the body—said to be situated in the lower part of the body; the heat of passion.

相 維 辟 公 the princes assist.

相 臣 a prime-minister.

相 門 the home or family of a statesman.

相 體 the deportment of a minister.

[10]吉 人 天 相 Heaven assists the good.

廂 [1] The side rooms. The suburbs of a city.
2563

廂 房 or 廂 屋 rooms on the east and west of the courtyard of a Chinese house.

城 廂 city and suburbs.

關 廂·子 house over a city gate.

包 廂 box seats in a theatre.

想 [3] To think; to consider, to call to mind.
2564

想·一·想 think it over.

想·不·來 or 想·不·起·來 I cannot recall it; I do not remember it.

想·不·開 cannot get it out of the mind.

想·來 想·去 turning it over and over in the mind.

[5]想 像 imagination; an idea.

想 像 作 用 the function of imagination.

想 像 力 power of imagination.

想 像·的 imaginary.

創 造·的 想 像 creative imagination.

[10] 再 生·的 想 像 reproductive imagination.

想 入 非 非 to allow the fancy to run wild.

想·到 to anticipate; to think of.

想·家 to think of home; homesick.

想·必·是 probably it is so.

[15]想·念 to think on; to call to mind.

想 念 之 間 while thinking of it.

想·思 to dote on. ≡ 2562.67.

想·思 病 love sickness. ≡ 2562.69.

想 死 long for death.

[20]想 法·子 to devise means; to plan.

想 當 然 I think it is so; most probably.

想 空 了 心 the mind is exhausted and has no further suggestions to make.

想·着 to be thinking.

想 見 to visualize.

[25]想 許 possibly there are; I think there may be.

想 起 來 to think of; to call to mind.

想 通 to think a matter through.

想 錯 略 you are mistaken; you have thought wrongly.

想·頭 a thought or expectation.

[30]回 想 to call to mind.

思 想 to think over; to reflect on.

推 想 to assume.

渴 想 longingly to think of.

狂 想 heated imagination; vain thoughts.

[35]設 想 to imagine or conceive; to form a conception.

(a) To hope. To expect. To plan.

想·不·到 unexpected.

想 望 to hope; to expect.

想 慕 to long for; to expect.

妄 想 extravagant hopes.

莫 想 do not expect it.

湘 [1] A large tributary of the Yangtze which flows through Hunan.
2565

湘 妃 竹 a speckled bamboo which grows in Hunan and Kwangsi—a legend is told that it became speckled by the tears which the wives of *Shun* 舜, shed over his grave.

(a) To boil, to cook.

于 以 湘 之 she boils it.

箱 [1] A box, a chest.
2566

箱 包 boxes and packages.

箱·子 a box, a case.

箱 屉·子 a box-tray.

箱 廚 a sideboard with cupboard and drawers.

箱 房 or 倉 箱 a granary.

箱 盖·子 the lid of a box.

箱 篋 or 箱 籠 cases; boxes.

車 箱 the body of a cart.

緗 [1] A light-yellow colour.
2567

緗 色 the colour of the budding mulberry leaves.

象 [4] An elephant; ivory.
2568

象 主 u.f. India, because of the number of elephants found there.

象 奴 or 象 公 an elephant driver.

象 弭 a bow, the tips of which were decorated with ivory.

象 牀 ivory bed.

[5]象 牙 elephants' tusks; ivory.

象 牙 器 ivory ware.

象 牙 海 岸 The Ivory Coast.

象 牙 球 ivory billiard-balls.

象 牙 質 dentine.

[10]象 皮 elephants' skin; india-rubber.

象 笏 ivory tablet for memoranda, etc. *See* No. 2193.

象 箸 ivory chopsticks.

象 簡 ivory tablets.

象 路 carriage decorated with ivory.

[15]象 闕 the ivory gate—the palace.

象 鼻 trunk of an elephant.

象 鼻 蟲 or 象 蟲 general name for a very large group of destructive beetles, with trunk-like proboscis.

象 齒 焚 身 the elephant is destroyed for the sake of its tusks. *See* 焚 No. 1866—A.2.

(a) To resemble; an image, a representation. Inter. next.

象 不 離 璞 the image or figure is just in the rough.

象 事 or 指 事 one of the six groups into which Chinese characters are divided, it indicates actions or states, as 上 above and 下 below.

象 人 an image of a man.

象 刑 wearing a special dress as a punishment in ancient times.

[5]象 外 transcendental.

象 形 one of the six groups into which Chinese characters are divided, it contains representations of objects as 日 the sun, and 月 the moon.

象 形 文 字 hieroglyphics.

象 徵 a symbol.

象 教 the religion of images—Buddhism.

[10]象 數 the inherent character of...

象 服 figured dresses worn as ceremonial dress by women in ancient times.

象 賢 to emulate the worthies who have gone before.

圖 象 or 畫 象 pictorial representations.

樂 象 the natural symbols of music.

[15]無 象 confused; chaotic.

影 象 an image. 印 象 impression.

(b) Stars, constellations. Omens, portents.

象 度 measurements of the movements of the heavenly bodies.

象 緯 sun, moon and five planets.

象 限 a quadrant.

象 限 儀 or 紀 限 儀 a quadrant instrument.

[5]象 限 電 位 計 quadrant electrometer.

天 象 the heavenly bodies, also their portents.

懸 象 the suspended bodies, i.e., the sun and moon.

星 象 appearance of the stars.

萬 象 all the manifestations of nature.

[10]顛 倒 之 象 a portent of revolution.

(c) Chinese chess. The elephant in chess, a piece which corresponds somewhat to the bishop, for which 相 is used of the black pieces.

象 棋 the game of chess.

(d) Acting, playing. Ancient music.

成 童 舞 象 lads act as the pantomimes.

(e) An official interpreter.

象 胥 傳 言 the interpreters conveyed his words.

南 方 曰 象 those who interpreted for the southern regions were called *siang*.

(f) The figures of the diagrams.

象 辭 the illustrations of the *Book of Changes*, said to have been made by *Chou Kung* or *Wên Wang*.

(g) A law or ordinance.

像 [4] Appearance; resemblance; like, similar. An image.
2569 Inter. preceding-A.

像 不 像 Is it like? Is there any resemblance?

不 像 not at all like; not fitting; not presentable.

像 他 like him.

像 似 similar to; like; resembling.

[5]像 形 hieroglyphics; resemblance.

像 教 the religion of images. Buddhism.

像 是 it seems.

像 模 像 樣 兒 的 elegant, well-arranged, etc.

像 樣 兒 respectable-looking.

[10]像 甚 麼 what sort of an arrangement do you call this? Lit:— what is this like?

像 生 life-like.

像 生 花 artificial flowers.

像 真 的 life-like; like the real thing.

像 貌 appearance; likeness.

[15]像 贊 title of a portrait.

倒 像 an inverted image.

正 像 an upright image.

照 像 to take a portrait or photograph.　　　[≡2684.11.

現 像 appearance; phenomenon.

[20]畫 像 to paint portraits.

神 像 an idol.

遺 像 portrait of a deceased person.

橡 [4] The chestnut-oak.
2570

橡 椀 子 the cupules of acorns—used as dye.

橡 椀 樹 the chestnut-oak.

橡 皮 india-rubber.

橡 皮 樹 the rubber tree—*ficus elastica* or *hevea*.

橡 粉 meal made from acorns.

襄 [1] To disrobe for agricultural toil; thus:—to remove; to
2571 put away.

牆 有 茨 不 可 襄 也 the tribulus grows on the wall but it cannot be removed—as the wall would suffer.

(a) To assist. To complete.

襄 事 to assist.

襄 助 to facilitate; to assist.

襄 同 to take part in.

襄 理 to assist in managing a matter.

不 克 襄 事 could not be carried out.

(b) To rise as a flood. High.

襄 岑 a high hill.

襄 陵 to overflow the hills, as when the water rises in the gorges.

(c) To yoke.

上 襄 fine horses, fit to be harnessed to a chariot.

(d) To change a position, etc.

終 日 七 襄 during the course of a day it changed its position seven times—of a star.

儴 [1]
2572　　To stroll; to ramble.

儴 徉 or 襄 羊 to wander; to saunter.

儴 儴 walking rapidly.

瓖 [1]
2573　　Ornaments.

瓖 珠 子 的 扁 簪 flat hair-pins embossed with pearls. Usually written with 2574.

鑲 [1] To inlay; to set jewels;
2574　　to let in.

鑲 嵌 to inlay; to emboss.

鑲 嵌 品 inlaid articles.

鑲 工 inlaid work.

鑲 筷 子 inlaid chopsticks.

[5]鑲 杯 鑲 盞 an inlaid wine-cup and saucer.

鑲 檯 an inlaid table.

鑲 牙 artificial teeth.

鑲 玻 璃 to glaze a window.

鑲 花 to inlay with flowers.

[10]鑲 金 inlaid with gold.

(a) To clamp on; to border; bordered.

鑲 上 to frame.

鑲 成 的 bordered.

鑲 旗 a bordered banner.

鑲 沿 a border; to border.

鑲 邊 a border; to border.

鑲 鞋 to bind the edges of shoes.

驤[1] To prance like a spirited horse. A horse with a white hind leg.
2575

騰驤 prancing.

庠[2] An asylum for old people. A country school in ancient times, the same place seemed to be used both as a school and an asylum for the aged.
2576

庠生 a graduate of the first degree or 秀·才·

祥[2] Happiness, good luck; a good omen. Also read *ch'iang*[2].
2577 It occurs used also for evil omens.

祥兆 a lucky omen.
祥刑 to use punishment to effect the reformation of the punished; to have no punishments to order when the time of the assizes came round.
祥瑞 lucky signs.
祥麟 the unicorn, whose appearance was a good omen.
不祥 unlucky.
凶祥 a·evil omen.
吉祥 lucky; a good omen.

(a) A sacrificial service for deceased parents.

小祥 the mourning service at the end of one year after death of parents.
大祥 the mourning service at the end of two years after the parents' death.

(b) u.f. 詳 No. 2579. Detailed.

翔[2] To soar; to hover over.
2578

翔泳歸仁 when goodness flourishes it reaches even to the birds and the fishes.
翔空 to wheel around in the air.
翔翔 grave and sedate.
翔而後集 it flies around and by and by it settles.
⁵翔貴 high-priced—goods.
翔陽 the sun.
翔集 to hover and then alight— used to illustrate reading many books and getting the essence of their teachings.

翔鸞 or 翔鳳 the soaring phœnix—rising talent.
回翔 to hover and wheel in the air.
¹⁰室中不翔 do not stick out the elbows like wings, when in a room.
羣鳥翔天 the birds wheel around in the air in flocks.
高翔 to soar high.

(a) To roam.

翔畋 to roam in the hunting fields.

(b) u.f. next. Detailed, etc.

翔實 accurate in details.

詳[2] In detail; particulars. To examine with care; to judge.
2579 Carefully. Also read *ch'iang*[2].

詳分 carefully to distinguish between them.
詳勉 carefully to press on.
詳問 to go into the details of a case.
詳夢 to interpret a dream.
⁵詳審 or 詳察 or 詳詰 to judge carefully; to go into the details.
詳審精密 to take the greatest care.
詳平 to give a fair decision.
詳悉 clearly; intelligibly.
詳愼 circumspectly.
¹⁰詳細 minute; special; detailed.
詳細講 to tell every particular.
詳練 to become practiced in.
詳訂 clearly to define.
詳記 to make a detailed record.
¹⁵詳詢 closely to investigate.
詳說 to discuss in detail.
詳辦 to deal with in detail.
詳述無遺 an accurate, detailed record or statement.
詳閲 carefully peruse.
²⁰未詳 not known; not clear.

(a) To report to a superior.

詳准 beg to acknowledge receipt of.
詳咨 to communicate in detail.
詳復 to report in reply; to give particulars.
詳文 an official report to a superior.
⁵詳明 report in detail.

詳知 to inform minutely; to bring to the notice of a superior.
詳祈 respectfully to request.
詳稟 or 詳稱 or 詳報 to report to a superior.
詳請 to report requesting....
¹⁰詳錄 to write a detailed report.
詳陳 to make a report.
詳革 to impeach and cause degradation.

(b) u.f. preceding. To roam, to soar.

敖詳 to ramble.

(c) u.f. 祥 No. 2577. Good, lucky.

不詳 unlucky; not good.

鯗}
鱶}[3] Dried salt fish.
2580

HSIAO. (ㄒㄧㄠ)

[1] To boil or fumigate.
2581

炰然 boastful swaggering.

(a) Read *hsiu*[1]. Minute. Excellent. Fortunate.

[1] The scream or roar of a tiger. To intimidate; to scare. See No. 2163.
2582

虓怒 very angry; to roar with anger.

爻[2] To intertwine; to change. Crosswise. Radical 89.
2583 Pron. *yao*[2].

爻亂 confusion; complications.
爻靜 the explanation of a diagram in the *Book of Changes* 易經
上爻 the highest line of a diagram as above.
六爻 the six lines of a diagram as above.
初爻 the lowest of the six lines of a diagram.

肴² Savoury food. Sacrificial meats. Inter. 餚 No. 2588.
2584　Pron. *yao*².

肴 蔌 meat and vegetables.
肴 覈 cooked food.
肴 饌 table delicacies.

嶢¹ Name of a mountain in Honan.　Pron. *yao*².
2585

嶢 山 or 嶢 陵 two mountains to the N.W. of Honan on the Shensi border.
嶢 函 之 固 a strong pass in Honan, the eastern boundary of the ancient State of *Ch'in* 秦.

殽² To eat, to use as food. Viands. Inter. next.
2586 Pron. *yao*².

殽 列 set out, as dishes on a table.
嘉 殽 delicacies.

(a) Mixed; confused.

殽 亂 in confusion.
殽 雜 mixed; miscellaneous.

淆² Mixed, muddy, confused. Inter. preceding.　Pron.
2587 *yao*².

淆 亂 confused, out of order.
淆 列 to set out in order; arranged.
淆 雜 miscellaneous; mixed.
混 淆 mixed up together.

(a) A tributary of the Yellow River in Shansi.

餚² Meats; rich food; a feast. Inter. 肴 No. 2584
2588

餚 核 meats and fruits—as arranged for an offering.
餚 饌 dressed meats; delicacies.
燒 餚 roast meats.
餚, 餚 肉 fresh salted pork. (*hsiao*²-)

梟¹ An owl, said to eat its mother; therefore used as a
2589 type of unfilial sons.

梟 獍 (*ching*⁴) the owl, said to eat its mother, and the muntjac-tiger, said to eat its father—used of unfilial children.
梟 鳥 owls generally.
梟 鴟 the eared owl.

(a) Brave and unscrupulous.

梟 將 a brave leader of troops.
梟 雄 wicked, fierce and brave.
梟 騎 a bold cavalryman.
私 梟 a smuggler.

(b) To expose the heads of criminals in a cage.

梟 示 or 梟 首 示 衆 the head of a decapitated person, exposed as a warning to others.

(c) Highest throw in dice.

枵¹ Hollow stump of a tree; thus:—empty, thin.
2590

枵 厚 thin and thick—thickness.
枵 耗 to waste.
枵 腹 an empty belly; hungry; ignorant.
枵 腹 從 公 to serve others without salary.
枵 薄 thin; flimsy.

鴞¹ An owl. A fabulous bird, which is said to eat its own
2591 mother, all but the head. See 梟 No. 2589.

鴞 炙 roast owl—extravagant expectations, "counting the chickens before they are hatched." from *Chuangtzŭ*:—
　見 彈 而 求 鴞 炙 to see the crossbow bolt and expect roast owl.
鴞 音 the note of the owl—of a fierce savage man.
鴞 首 a head that has been cut off as a punishment.
鴟 鴞 the eared owl.

膠¹ To boast.
2592

嘐 嘐 然 其 志 也 he boasted of his determination.
其 志 嘐 嘐 然 their aim led them to talk extravagantly.

(a) Read *chiao*¹. The crowing of a cock.

(b) Read *liao*² or *lao*¹. Verbose.

嘐 啁 verbose.

嘵¹ Querulous.
2593

嘵 嘵 辯 論 arguing for the sake of argument.

(a) A cry of alarm.

予 維 音 嘵 嘵 I cannot but cry out with rage and fear—when the storm is raging.
嘵 哮 a howl.

曉³ Dawn; light; thus:—to know, to understand. To
2594 make known. Perspicuous.

曉·不·得 cannot understand; do not know.(*S. dial.*) [(*S. dial.*)
曉·了 to understand; to know.
曉 事 efficient; clear-headed.
曉 人 to inform another; an intelligent man.
⁵曉·得 to know; to understand, to comprehend.
曉 悟 to awaken; to enlighten.
曉 日 or 曉 天 or 曉 旦 morning; dawn.
曉 日 上 朱 輪 the sun rises like a red ball.
曉 明 daybreak; to make known clearly.
¹⁰曉 星 the morning star.
曉 月 bright moonlight.
曉 烏 the crows calling at dawn.
曉 眠 early-morning sleep.
曉 習 well-informed—fully acquainted with the facts.
¹⁵曉 色 奪 明 月 the brightness of the dawn obscures the moon.
曉 行 夜 宿 to start early and stop late.
曉 角 the reveille.
曉 解 a clear explanation.
曉 諭 or 曉 示 or 曉 布 to proclaim.
²⁰曉 譬 to render perspicuous.
曉 達 perspicuous.
曉 鐘 the matin-bell—in a monastery.
曉 雞 a crowing cock.
曉 霞 rosy clouds of dawn.
²⁵曉 霧 morning mists.
曉 露 morning dew.
曉 領 to comprehend.
曉 風 early morning breezes.
初 曉 or 破 曉 daybreak.
³⁰報 曉 to announce the dawn—cockcrow.

天將曉 the day is dawning.
洞曉其事 fully understanding the matter.
通曉 known to all; make known to all.

曉[1] A good horse. Strong; brave; skilful.
2595

曉中 to pitch the arrow into the neck of a vase—an ancient game, u.f. to hit the mark.
曉將 a brave general.
曉騰 a spirited charger.

囂[1] Hubbub, clamour, din. Also read *ao*[2].
2596

囂塵 the world—bustle and dust.
囂雜 disorderly and clamorous.
囂謗 popular clamour against.
俗囂 this world, with its clamour and bustle.
浮囂 fickle, excitable.

(a) To treat with contempt.

囂凌 to treat harshly.
囂囂然 indifferent; self-satisfied.
囂薄 impoverished; without resources.

劾[4] To toil; to serve in the army. Inter. 效 No. 2599.B.
2597

劾力 effort; toil; exertion.
劾力贖罪 to retrieve the past by further exertions.
劾勞 to put oneself to trouble for another.
劾命 to devote the life to.
劾命疆埸 to devote the life to the defence of the empire.
劾用 to function; to offer for service.
報劾 to return a kindness; to recompense for efforts made on one's behalf.
投劾 to offer one's services.

(a) To imitate, inter. 效 No. 2599.

劾驗 efficacy; verification.
上行下劾 the masses will follow the example of their leader.

恔[4] Cheerful.
2598

於人心獨無恔乎 shall this alone give no satisfaction to the natural feelings of a man?

(a) Read *chiao*[3]. Sagacious.

效[4] To imitate. Like; similar to; Inter. 劾 No. 2597
2599

效彷 or 學效 to imitate; to emulate.
效尤 to imitate and exceed the pattern—in evil.
效法 to imitate; to follow an example.
效顰 to imitate (*Hsi Shih* 西施—a famous beauty. *See* No. 2460—28.) in knitting her brows—which she did to enhance her beauty—used of slavish imitation of another and failing to accomplish the result expected.

(a) Efficacious; to yield the expected result; to fulfil, to verify.

效力 efficacy. *See below* B.1.
知茶效力 to know the efficacy of a cup of tea.
效果 the result of any course of action.
效用 power in action; function. *See below* B.8.
[5]契約之效用 efficacy of a contract.
效績 meritorious achievement.
效祥 signs of prosperity.
效能 potentiality.
效驗 efficacy; fulfilment; effect; verification.
[10]功效 result; efficacy.
無效 inefficacious; no good result has accrued.
神效 divinely efficacious.
見效 it has proved efficacious—as a medicine, etc.
效率 (rate of) efficiency. (-*lü*[4.5])

(b) To put forth effort; to labour earnestly.

效力 to devote the life and strength to; toil, effort.
效勞 to oblige; to be of service; to serve in return for favours received.
效命 to devote the life to.
效忠 devoted loyalty.
[5]效情 to devote the affections to.

效愚 depreciatory phrase—I will devote my unworthy energies to it.
效死而民弗去 devote your life to them and the people will not leave you.
效用 devote the energies to; to offer for service. *See above* A.4.
效義 devote oneself to a righteous cause.
[10]效用漸減律 law of diminishing utility.
效順 loyal to.

(c) To present.

效馬效羊者右牽之 he who is presenting a horse or a sheep should lead it with his right hand.

傚[4] To follow; to imitate. Inter. preceding.
2600

傚傚 to imitate.

孝[4] To honour one's parents; filial.
2601

孝乎鬼神 to worship the spirits of ancestors.
孝友 filial piety and brotherly harmony.
孝子[3] a filial son. *See below* A.2.
孝孫有慶 filial descendants receive the blessings—from their ancestors when worshipped.
[5]孝廉 a 舉人 a second-degree graduate.
孝弟 filial piety and submission to elder brothers.
孝弟力田 model sons who were dutiful at home and industrious in the fields—had special privileges under the *Han* dynasty.
孝弟忠信 filial piety, brotherly subordination, loyalty, and sincerity.
孝心 a filial heart.
[10]孝思 to cherish loving memories of the grace received from one's parents.
孝感動天 filial piety can move Heaven—used of an extreme expression of filial devotion.
孝慈 filial piety and parental tenderness.
孝愛 love to parents,

孝·敬 filial and respectful; a present offered to superiors.

[15] 孝敬不到 to fail in filial duty.

孝·敬父母 to honour father and mother.

孝烏 (or 鳥) the filial bird, i.e., the crow, it being said to disgorge to feed its parents.

孝祀 a filial sacrifical offering.

孝·經 *The Canon of Filial Piety.*

[20] 孝義雙全 duty to parents and to the State both fulfilled.

孝行 filial devotion.

孝親 to honour one's parents.

孝道 the requirements of filial piety.

孝·順 to show filial piety; to do one's duty by one's parents.

[25] 孝養 to care for parents.

(a) Mourning.

孝堂 the hall of mourning, draped in white for funeral rites.

孝·子[3] a filial son in mourning.

孝服 (or 衣) mourning garments.

孝陵 the Ming Tombs at Nanking.

[5] 穿孝 to wear mourning.

脫孝 to put off mourning apparel.

謝孝 to visit friends with thanks after a funeral.

重孝 deep mourning.

哮 [1] **To pant; to roar. Inter. next.**
2602

哮嚇 to scare; to scream at.

哮瘕 or 哮喘 short of breath; asthma.

痟 [1] **Difficulty in breathing. Asthma.**
2603

痟癩 a hacking cough.

痟症 or 痟疾 asthma.

斅 [1] **To imitate; to teach. To arouse, to incite to effort.**
2604

斅愓 to arouse a person from apathy.

斅鷄鳴 to imitate a cock crowing.

(a) Read *chiao*[3]**. Clever; intelligent.**

HSIAO. SIAO. (ㄒㄧㄠ)

小 [3] **Small, insignificant, petty. Mean. A concubine.**
2605

小不忍則亂大謀 lack of forbearance in small matters upsets great plans.

小不言·的事 a mere trifle, nothing to fuss about.

小丑 the low comedy man; a clown.

小九九 Chinese multiplication table.

[5] 小事 a trivial matter.

小亞西亞 Asia Minor.

小人 a mean man, the opposite of the princely man 君子[3] in Chinese classics; the masses.

小人恥失其君 the mean man is ashamed because (Ch'in 秦) holds his prince in captivity.

小人感謂之不免 the mean man mourns, saying that it is inevitable—that Ch'in 秦 will slay his prince, judging Ch'in by himself.

[10] 小人懷土 the small man thinks of comforts.

小人懷惠 the small man thinks of the favours which he is to receive.

小人窮斯濫矣 the mean man in distress gives way to excess.

小使 servants.

小便 to make water.

[15] 小便 (*p'ien*[2])·宜 small profits; petty advantages.

小偷 a pilferer.

小偏 a concubine.

小傳 biographies.

小像 a small likeness—either painting, photograph or sculpture.

[20] 小兒[2]·子 the youngest son.

最小公倍數[4] lowest common multiple.

小其器 made little of his capacity.

小冊 pamphlets.

小刀會 The Small-Sword Society—a secret society very active in Shantung during the latter period of the Manchu dynasty. It was extremely anti-foreign.

[25] 小刼 a small *kalpa*, a period of 16,000,000 years; tribulation; calamity. (*Budd.*).

小利害信 striving for petty advantages injures confidence.

小別 to part for a short time.

小前提 minor premise.

小功 mourning worn for five months for uncles, aunts, first cousins once removed, mother's brother or sister, etc.

[30] 小半 the smaller half.

小取 getting gain by shady tricks.

小廝 a serving boy; a page; a son.

小口 young—of horses.

小可 a trifle. *See below* A.3.

[35] 小名 or 乳名 name given to a young child.

小品文 short essays, etc., trifles of literature.

小器 a small vessel; a small-minded person.

小夥·子 or 小漢·子 a youth; a young fellow.

小失 a trifling flaw; a peccadillo.

[40] 小奶·奶 or 小老·婆 or 小女·人 a concubine.

小姐 a young lady; "Miss."

小妻 a concubine.

小姑 husband's younger sister.

小娃·娃 a baby; small children.

[45] 小姨·子 younger sister of a wife.

小娘貨 frail, easily-broken articles.

小孔不補大孔叫苦 a stitch in time saves nine.

小學 unprofitable learning; minor studies; philology.

小學(校) primary schools.

[50] 小宗 the younger branches of a family.

小家·子氣 very mean-spirited—rather abusive.

小家庭 a separate home set up by a young couple.

小家數 a petty person; acting in a mean-spirited manner.

小家碧玉 a pretty girl from a humble home.

[55] 小寒 a solar period from about January 7—21.

小寫 small letters.

小尼·子 a slave-girl.

小工 a labourer; unskilled labour.

小工藝 small industries.

[60] 小巧玲瓏 delicate and fragile.

小己 individual.

小巷 a narrow lane.

小布 narrow cloth.

小帽 or 瓜皮帽 the small, round skull-cap of the Chinese.

[65] 小 年 the young.

小 年 夜 or 小 除 the day before the last day of the year.

小·底 or 小·的 a young person. *See below.* A. 12.

小 康 peaceful era—under the ancient kings.

小 康 之 家 one who has a fair competency.

[70] 小 引 a preface.

小·心 careful; take care.

小 心 小 膽 chicken-hearted; scared at trifles.

小 怨 petty resentments.

小 怨 傷 義 anger over trifles does harm to right feeling.

[75] 小 性 兒 narrow, petty-spirited disposition.

小 息 a short rest.

小 意·思 a mere trifle; nothing important; a slight token of regard.

小 意 智 petty tricks and dodges.

小 意·見 a narrow outlook.

[80] 小 戎 ancient war chariot.

小 成 small attainments.

小 戶 one who has a small capacity for liquor; a humble family.

小°戶·人°家 or 小 姓 families who are reckoned as low-caste; they have no standing in society, and are under certain obligations to other families; certain occupations are open to them only. There are many of these in S. Anhwei and Chekiang.

小 摸 手 a petty thief.

[85] 小 數[4] decimal fractions.

小 數[4] 點 a decimal point.

　循 環 小 數[4] recurring decimals.

　有 限 小 數[4] finite decimals.

　無 限 小 數[4] infinite decimals.

[90] 小 斂 the preparatory laying out of a corpse for burial.

小 方 脈 treatment of children's complaints.

小 旦 an actor who takes female parts.

小 星 concubines.

小 時 an hour.

[95] 小 時 了[3] 了[3] very intelligent when young.

小·時·候 in infancy; when I was young.

小 暑 a solar period, about July 7—21.

小 曲 ballads.

小 月 or 小 建 or 小 盡 a short month of 29 days in the lunar calendar, or 30 days in the solar.

[100] 小 有 to some extent.

小 本 經 營 business with a small capital.

小 板·子 the lighter bamboo for punishing offenders.

小 極 weariness; indisposition.

小 樓 an attic.

[105] 小·氣 petty-minded; mean-spirited.

小 洋 subsidiary silver coins, tencent and twenty-cent pieces.

小 流 a rivulet.

小 滿 a solar period, about May 21—June 4.

小 潮 neap tides.

[110] 小 火 輪 a steam-launch.

小 照 a photographic portrait.

小 爐 匠 a tinker.

小 狗 puppies.

小 生·意 a small way of business.

[115] 小 產 or 小 月·子 an abortion; premature birth.

小 看·了·他 despised him; underrated him.

小 碟 or 小 盤 the knee-cap.

小 秋 the beginning of autumn.

小 種 Souchong tea.

[120] 小 築 a small, but finely-built house.

小 節 minor matters of behaviour or deportment.

小 簡 a note.

小 米 yellow millet; canary-seed.

小 粉 starch.

[125] 小 綹 or 小 李 or 小 掠 pickpockets.

小 考 or 府 考 annual Prefectural examination under the old system, for the degree of 秀·才.

小 聰·明 sharp-witted but pettyminded.

小 聲 a low tone; a low voice.

小 腦 the cerebellum.

[130] 小 腹 or 小 肚 子 the lower abdomen.

小 腸 the small intestine.

小 腸 氣 or 疝 氣 hernia.

小 腿 calf of the leg.

小 至 the day before the winter solstice.

[135] 小 舅·子 younger brother of a wife.

小 艇 a small skiff.

小°菜 vegetables; dressings; salted pickles, etc.

小 行 星 the minor planets; asteroid.

小 衣 short trousers; hosiery.

[140] 小 衫 a shirt, under-vest.

小 註 a marginal note; a comment.

小 說 a novel.

小 語 to speak in a low tone.

小 調 local ballads; folk-songs.

[145] 小 豆 lentils.

小 販 small traders; hawkers.

小 賤 mean; inferior.

小 賣 retail.

小 車 a wheelbarrow.

[150] 小 轎 a two-bearer sedan-chair.

小 道 inferior studies and employments—referred to husbandry, divining, medicine, etc.

小 道 貨 stolen goods.

小 遺 or 小 解 to urinate.

小 郎 (or 叔) younger brother of husband.

[155] 小 部·分 the smaller part; a part.

小 酌 refreshment.

小 醜 the class of petty fellows; ne'er-do-wells.

小 針 hour-hand on a watch.

小 錢 or 私 錢 illicit cash, in the days when the cash-coins with a hole were used.

[160] 小 門·生 pupils of a pupil.

小 陀 a young Buddhist priest.

小 陽 春 the tenth lunar month.

小 雪 a solar period, about Nov. 22—Dec. 7.

小 頓 a pause, in composition.

[165] 小 題 大 做 to make great trouble out of a trifling matter.

小 食 light refreshment.

小 鷄 a young chicken.

小 麥 wheat.

小 麻 hemp.

[170] 小 點 點·的 extremely minute.

(a) Depreciatory term for 1st personal pronoun. I, my, our, etc.

小 兒[2] my son; I, your son.

小 印 a private seal.

小 可 I, in self depreciation, *See above*—34.

小 地·方 a small place—my home.

[5] 小 女 my daughter.

小 姪 I, your nephew.

小 子[3] young men, children; I; you, my son; 小·子 boy.

小 寓 my house.

小 店 my shop.

[10] 小 弟 your younger brother, I,

小 犬 little puppies—conventional expression, my sons.

小·的 I—used by those in inferior stations. *See above*—67.

小 老·兒 I—used by elderly men in addressing superiors.

妻 小 my wife.

肖 [4] To be like; to imitate. A likeness.
2606

肖 似 resembling, like.

肖 像 a likeness, either painted or carved.

肖 子 a filial son—i.e., one who is like—his father.

不 肖 unlike, used by a son in depreciation of himself, i.e., unfilial, degenerate.

不 肖 之 徒 worthless characters.

微 肖 a slight resemblance.

酷 肖 very similar.

(a) Read *hsiao*[1]. Scattered and lost.

達 於 知 者 肖 those who know are scattered and lost.

(b) Dwindling, deteriorated.

宵 [1] Night, dark.
2607

宵 中 through the night.

宵 分 or 宵 中 or 中 宵 midnight.

宵 小 or 宵 人 night-prowlers; evildoers.

宵 征 to travel by night.

[5]宵 旰·之 勞 the arduous life of the Emperor—*See below*—13.

宵 會 a night-meeting.

宵 民 the masses.

宵 燭 or 宵 行 a glow-worm.

宵 田 to hunt by night.

[10]宵 程 a night-stage.

宵 行 to travel by night. *See above*—8.

宵 衣 dark silk gowns, ancient ceremonial dress worn by women; to dress in the dark, or before daylight.

宵 衣 旰 食 to dress before dawn and wait until evening for food—the strenuous life of the Emperor.

宵 錦 abbreviation for wearing embroidered garments and walking at night—said of a man whose talents are not recognised.

[15]宵 類 robbers, those who prowl at night.

宵 魚 to stay awake at night—as fish.

元 宵 the first full moon of the lunar year. The Feast of Lanterns. 元·宵 dumplings eaten at such a feast.

太 宵 the long night—death.

深 宵 the dead of night.

[20]通 宵 all night.

(a) Small.

宵 雅 肆 三 practised the first three pieces of the Minor Odes.

消 [1] To melt, to thaw. To disperse, to dissipate. To cancel, to annul. Inter. 銷 No. 2611.
2607a

消 亡 or 消 喪 destroyed.

消·停 to rest for a while; to take a breather.

消 冰 to thaw ice.

消·化 to melt; to transform; to digest; to thaw.

[5]消 化 不 動 (or 不 了) indigestible.

消 化 作 用 the digestive function; the function of assimilation.

消·化 器 官 digestive organs.

消·化 時 刻 time for digestion.

消·化 液 digestive fluids.

[10]消·化 系 統 the digestive system.

消·化 經 具 digestive apparatus.

文 明 之 消 化 the assimilation of civilization.

消 受 to enjoy possession of.

消 售 to sell; for sale.

[15]消 夏 to go away for the summer.

消 夜 midnight supper.

消 弭 to pacify; to soothe.

消 彌 to bring to an end.

消 恨 to be appeased.

[20]消·息 to disperse and to add; ebb and flow; fluctuations; inspiration and expiration; the alternations of blessing and disaster; from which comes:—news, report, information.

消·息 靈 通 intercommunication of news; well-informed.

消 悶 to cheer up; to dissipate grief.

消 折 to dissipate—as property.

消 搖 to ramble about in aimless distraction. *See* 逍 No. 2610.

[25]消 散 to disperse; to get rid of—as by medicine; to thaw.

消 極 negative; minimum.

消 極 主 義 negative theories.

消 極 代 理 negative representation. (*legal*).

消 極 手 段 negative methods.

[30]消 極 條 件 negative conditions. (*legal*).

消 極·的 例 negative instance.

消 極·的 德 行 negative virtues.

消 極·的 態·度 a negative attitude.

消 極·的 抵 制 negative resistance; passive opposition.

[35]消 極 義·務 negative obligations, as not injuring a man's property or his good name. (*legal*).

消 極 行·為 a negative act. (*legal*).

消 極 證·據 negative evidence.

消 極 資·格 negative qualifications.

消 毒 disinfection; sterilize.

[40]消 毒 藥 disinfectants.

消 毒 棉 antiseptic cotton.

消 氣 to abate one's anger; to be reconciled. [-*mo*⁴·⁵]

消 沒 to destroy; to swallow up.

消 沮 閉 藏 to draw back and conceal—from a sense of shame..

[45]消 消 性 to calm the temper.

消 減 to diminish; to reduce.

消 渴 to allay thirst; diabetes.

消·滅 to destroy.

消 滅 時 效 negative prescription, the limitation of time during which action or claim can be raised. (*legal*.).

[50]消 滅 無 存 have ceased to exist.

消 滯 to aid digestion; to relieve repletion.

消 火 器 fire-extinguisher.

消 火 栓 fire-sprinkler.

消 災 to get rid of calamities.

[55]消 災 降 福 to disperse calamity and bring down blessings.

消 熱 to reduce a fever.

消 瘦 or 消 肉 wasted; thin.

消 盡 點 vanishing point.

消 石 or 硝 石 nitre.

[60]消 靡 to melt away; to ooze out—as courage; to use up—as energy.

消 罪 to cancel sin.

消°耗 or 消費 wasteful; to waste.

消•耗品 luxuries.

消 胂 to reduce a swelling.

[65]消 融 melted; dissolved.

消融其渣滓 to melt away the dregs of his nature.

消貨 to sell goods.

消費 to consume; expenditure; consumption of goods.

消費人 the consumer.

[70]消費物 articles that cause expenditure, as firing, rice, etc.

消費稅 excise duties.

消•路 market for goods; circulation or sales.

消退 to recede—as floods.

消遣品 something with which to pass the time.

[75]消釋 to melt away.

消長[3] waning and waxing.

消開 or 消°遣 to pass away the time.

消防隊 fire-brigade.

消除 to remove; to abrogate; to eliminate; to delete.

[80]消靡 consumption.

消食化痰 to relieve dyspepsia.

消魂 overwhelmed by beauty, love, etc.

不消說•了 that goes without saying.

取消 to cancel; to annul.

硝[1] Nitre; saltpetre. To tan.
2608

硝廠 a tannery.

硝強水 nitric acid.

硝瘠 sterile; barren and stony.

硝皮 to tan leather.

硝石 or 火硝 saltpetre.

硝磺 saltpetre; nitre.

硝行 (hang[2]) a tannery.

硝鹽 carbonate of soda.

綃[1] Raw silk; plain silk. Read shao[1]. To comb the hair.
2609 A spar. Inter. 梢 No. 5679.

逍[1] To ramble; to wander.
2610

逍遙 at leisure; to wander about.

逍遙•子 a bamboo sedan-chair.

逍遙自在 a state of blissful abstraction.

逍遙遊 transcendental bliss.

銷[1] To melt; to fuse. Cast iron. Inter 消 No. 2607a.
2611

銷化 to melt.

銷金 to wash with gold; to waste money.

銷鎔 to smelt.

(a) To sell.

銷售 to sell; to put into circulation.

銷•場 demand for goods; lit :—a place for selling goods.

銷賣 to sell; to dispose of.

銷•路 circulation, as of goods, or of a paper.

(b) To pass away; to annul; to cancel; to finish.

銷夏 (or 暑) to pass away the summer; to go away for the summer.

銷差 to report that instructions have been carried out. (-ch'ai[1])

銷案 to close a case.

銷歲月 to waste time.

[5]銷毀 to destroy; to ruin.

銷泯 to obliterate.

銷滅 to destroy; to render useless; to obliterate.

銷災 to avert calamity.

銷•耗 wear and tear; waste.

[10]銷號 to cancel an agreement or permit, etc.

銷除 to cancel. (legal.).

銷骨 wearing to the bones—said of slander. See 積 No. 500—24.

銷魂 ≡ 2607.82.

鉤銷 to cancel; to annul.

[15]開•銷 expenditure.

除銷 to get rid of; to clear off.

霄[1] Mist; clouds; the empyrean.
2612

霄元 heaven.

霄壤 heaven and earth.

霄峙 cloud-penetrating peak.

霄嶺 lofty ranges.

霄房 heaven.

霄漢 the Milky Way.

鞘[4] A scabbard; a sheath. Also read ch'iao[4].
2613

鞘•子 a scabbard.

銀鞘 hollowed logs for carrying silver.

(a) Read shao[1]. A whip-lash.

鞘鳴 the crack of a lash.

魈[1] An elf. An evil spirit of the hills.
2614

山魈 a mountain elf which does no end of mischief.

笑 / 哯 [4] To laugh; to smile. To laugh at; to ridicule.
2615

笑一笑 to give a laugh.

笑中刀 to 'smile and smile and be a villain.'

笑他 to laugh at him.

笑倒[3] convulsed with laughter.

[5]笑•出眼淚 to laugh until tears come.

笑口 smiles.

笑哈哈 hearty laughter.

笑嗤嗤 to laugh aloud.

笑嘻嘻 giggling; to titter.

[10]笑㗋 to laugh aloud.

笑容可掬 a face beaming with smiles.

笑引笑 laughter is contagious.

笑•得捧腹絕倒[3] to split the sides with laughter.

笑抃 to laugh and clap the hands.

[15]笑敖 to ridicule.

笑斷肚腸 splitting the sides with laughter.

笑林 the funny column of a paper.

笑柄 a laughing-stock.

笑樂 gay and cheerful.

[20]笑•死人 extremely laughable.

笑•死天下人 enough to make everybody die of laughter.

笑氣 laughing-gas; nitrous oxide.

笑疾 fits of laughter; hysterical laughter.

笑眯眯 laughing till one's eyes are dim.

[25]笑矣乎 name of a fungus that is said to cause uncontrollable laughter.

笑罵 invective.

笑罵由他 let him ridicule and revile me!

笑臉 or 笑面 or 笑容 a smiling face.

笑臉生花 beaming with smiles.

[30]笑視 to make fun of.

笑話 jokes.

笑話人 to ridicule another.

笑語 pleasantry.

笑談 amusing conversation.

[35]笑諾 to consent by a smile.

笑逐顏開 the countenance beaming with smiles.

笑道 said with a smile.

笑面虎 a smiling tiger—treacherous.

笑而相迎 met him with a smile.

[40]笑靨 the dimple which appears with a smile.

笑靨花 spiræa.

笑靨金 fancy name for the chrysanthemum.

笑頭 something to laugh at.

笑顏 a smiling face.

[45]冷笑 a cold smile.

取笑 to cause laughter; to make a laughing-stock of.

可笑 laughable.

天笑 the Aurora Borealis.

微笑 a slight smile.

[50]恥笑 to ridicule; to mock at.

暗笑 to laugh in the sleeve.

露齒而笑 grinning.

篠筱]3

A dwarf bamboo. Small. u.f. 小 No. 2605. in names, etc.

2616

翛]1 Straggling appearance of feathers.

2617

予尾翛翛 my tail is all broken.

(a) Read *yu*[3]. Hastiness.

翛然而往 he went away quite suddenly.

翛然終日 the day passed quickly.

(b) Read *shu*[2,5]. Rapid flight.

嘯歗]4

A whistling, hissing sound. To scream; to whistle.

2618

嘯傲 whistling and swaggering about.

嘯鳴 to roar.

嘯聚 to assemble by means of a whistle.

嘯葉 whistle made of a leaf.

虎嘯 the scream of a tiger.

長嘯歌吟 whistling and singing.

(a) Read *su*[4]. A moan.

簫箾]1 Pan-pipes,—these have varied through the ages; in ancient times some were made of 23 pipes, others of 16 pipes bound together. A flute of bamboo.

2619

簫管 the flute.

簫韶 ancient pan-pipes.

吹簫 to play the flute.

品簫 to tune pipes.

排簫 pan-pipes, a modern variety has 16 pipes, the shortest being in the centre, and the longest at each side.

(a) The tips of a bow.

右手執簫 (in presenting a bow to another) take the tip in the right hand.

蕭]1 A common variety of artemisia; southernwood.

2620

蕭晨 an autumn morning.

蕭斧 a billhook.

蕭艾 artemisia, very common plants—used of a man of humble attainments.

蕭荻 a species of artemisia.

蕭衰 old and failing.

(a) Soughing of wind. Mournful.

蕭寂 gloomy and desolate.

蕭爽 or 蕭然 quiet and restful to the heart.

蕭瑟 or 蕭條 or 蕭疏 lonely and desolate; bleak and chilly.

蕭索 or 蕭森 lonely, desolate and silent; ruinous and decaying.

蕭蕭 whistling of strong winds.

蕭蕭馬鳴 the neighing of the horses.

蕭颯 the soughing of the wind in trees.

蕭騷 lonely, cold and desolate.

(b) Annoying, troublesome.

蕭然煩事 troublesome and annoying.

(c) Reverent—explained as 肅 No. 5509.

蕭牆 defined as reverent and a screen, i.e., the screen before the court.

蕭牆之內 within his own screen, i.e., in his own court.

蕭牆之禍 troubles within the home.

(d) Name of the ruling family in the *Liang* dynasty.

蕭寺 or 蕭齋 Buddhist temples—the emperor *Wu ti* of the *Liang* dynasty 梁武帝, was a patron of Buddhism and had this character written on the temples which he endowed.

蠨]1 A small spider with long legs.

2621

瀟]1 Sound of beating rain and wind.

2622

風雨瀟瀟 the sound of the driving storm.

(a) Light, ethereal.

瀟灑 light-hearted, lifted above the sordid bustle of life; unconventional.

(b) River flowing through Hunan, a tributary of the *Hsiang*.

HSIEH. SIEH. (ㄒㄝ)

(Hsie)

些]1 A little, a few, some, slightly. Sign of the comparative. Rather, somewhat.

2623

些子 a little.

些子不妥當 not quite satisfactory.

些少 or 罘小 just a little; a trifle.

些微 very little; slightly; rather.

[5]些須 trifling; a little of.

一些 a little; some.

好些 better; 好些個 ; many.

快些 quicker.

有些不是 there are faults.

[10]這些 these.

(a) Read *so*¹. A final particle of regret, lament, etc.

何爲四方些 "Why wander about? Alas!"—of a restless, disembodied spirit. *Giles'* tr. of *Ch'u tz'ŭ: Chao hun.*

(b) u.f. 娑 No. 5455. for transliterating.

邏些 Lhasa, capital of Tibet. =3756.A.3.

斜² Slanting, inclined, oblique. Not upright. Also read *hsia²*
2624 when necessary for rhyming.

斜側 sideways; leaning.
斜傾 pouring over a slope—as a cascade.
斜坡 a slope; gradient.
斜對面 not directly opposite.
⁵斜平行體 parallelepiped.
斜度 obliquity; gradient.
斜度標 gradient-marks by the side of a railway.
斜截 oblique section.
斜插 stuck in crookedly.
¹⁰斜斜兒的 awry.
斜方形 rhombus.
長斜方形 rhomboid.
斜日斜月 the slanting rays of sun or moon.
斜橋 an oblique bridge.
¹⁵斜漢 the Milky Way.
斜眼 cross-eyes; squinting.
斜蠢 lofty but leaning.
斜稜 inclined; tilted.
斜窺 to take a sidelong glance at.
²⁰斜紋 transverse stripes.
斜紋布 twills; drills.
斜線 an oblique line.
斜着 slanting.
斜街 a side-street.
²⁵斜視 to look askance; sidelong glances.
斜角 an oblique angle.
斜豎 erected, but slanting.
斜射 oblique fire.
斜長 diagonal length.
³⁰斜陽 slanting beams of the sun.
斜雨 driving rains.
斜面 inclined plane.
斜風 a side wind.
斜高 measurement of height along a slope, as of a cone.
³⁵橫斜 slanting, not level.

(a) Read *ych*¹. A valley in Shensi.

邪² Heterodox; depraved; vicious; evil. To be deflected.
2625 Pertaining to magic or demonism. Harmful emanations, as miasma, etc.

邪不勝正 heresy cannot overthrow the truth—the upright need not fear the crooked.
邪世 a crooked generation; a corrupt age.
邪佞 treacherous and cunning.
邪僞 false; heterodox.
⁵邪僻 depraved; good-for-nothing.
邪味 an evil odour.
邪地·方 a haunted place; place of ill fame.
邪媚 treacherous flattery.
邪巧之言 specious talk.
¹⁰邪幅 buskins.
邪念 depraved thoughts.
邪惡 vicious; viciousness.
邪情 sensual passions.
邪意 depraved thoughts and intents.
¹⁵邪指 depraved tendencies; heterodox tendencies.
邪敎 or 邪道 heterodoxy; paganism; doctrines opposed to traditional teaching.
邪散 depraved; not upright.
邪曲 moral obliquity; depraved.
邪枉之道 crooked, depraved courses.
²⁰邪氣 evil aura; noxious influences; influences as of evil spirits; evil emanations; used in *Wu* 吳 dialects for:— very, extremely.
邪汚 moral depravity.
邪法 sorcery, unlawful tricks.
邪淫 lewdness; lustful.
邪物 uncanny things; ghosts.
²⁵邪病 epilepsy.
邪神 false gods.
邪祟 or 邪魅 evil spirits; demons.
邪萌 incipient depravity.
邪蕩 debauchery.
³⁰邪虐 depraved and tyrannical.
邪術 the black art; magic; sorcery.
邪計 or 邪謀 treacherous designs.
邪說 heterodox theories.
邪說暴行 corrupt speech and tyrannous actions.
³⁵邪謬 error; depravity.
邪路 or 邪途 evil ways.

邪辭 evil communications.
邪風 a changeable wind.
邪鬼 evil spirits; demons.
⁴⁰邪魔 the evil one; powers of darkness.
中·了邪 to be possessed by demons.
奸邪 treacherous; malicious.
心邪 an impure and treacherous heart.
避邪 to avoid noxious influences, often by moving to another place.

(a) Read *yeh²*. Interrogative particle, for which 耶 is now used.

其信然邪 Is it believable?
其夢邪 Is it a dream?
汝其知也邪 Do you indeed know this?
爲可邪 Should such things be?

(b) Similar to 揶 No. 7308. To point at in ridicule.

邪揄 to point the finger in ridicule.

(c) Read *yeh²*. Used to imitate sounds.

邪許 or 邪呼 sound of a crowd shouting; the sing-song of coolies.

(d) Read *yü²*. u.f. 餘 No. 7608. Surplus.

歸邪於終 the surplus days revert to the intercalary month.

(e) Read *hsü²*. To delay.

其虛其邪 "Is it a time for delay?"

(f) Read *sheh*¹. Auspicious appearance in the heavens.

卸⁴ To unload; to get rid of; thus:—to retire from office.
2626

卸事 to throw up an affair.
卸交 to consign goods to.
卸任 or 卸仕 to resign office.
卸妝 to take off one's ornaments.
⁵卸擔 to lay down a burden; to throw off responsibility.
卸煤 to deliver coal.

卸 牲·口 to unharness the animals.
卸 瓣 to shed the petals.
卸 禍 to get rid of trouble.
¹⁰卸 罪 擔 to throw off the burden of sin.
卸 肩 to rest the shoulders; to lay down responsibility, etc.
卸 落 to drop—as a burden.
卸 衣 to undress.
卸 貨 to unload cargo; to deliver goods.
¹⁵卸 責 to lay down responsibility; to put the blame on others.
卸 車 to unload a cart; to unhitch the animals.
卸 載 to unload and reload.
卸·開 to take off; to remove.
卸 除 軍 械 to disarm.
²⁰卸 頭 to let down the hair.
交 卸 hand over to a successor.
推 卸 to shirk responsibility; to lay blame on others.

寫
寫
2627

To write; to sketch.

寫·下 write it down.
寫·不 來 unable to write it; cannot write.
寫·不 得 it must not be written; do not write it.
寫 信 or 寫 書 to write a letter.
⁵寫 字 to write.
寫 字 端 楷 to write evenly and carefully.
寫 實·的 realistic, as contrasted with romantic. 「well.
寫·得 好 well written; can write
寫 意 impressionist outlines.
¹⁰寫 文·章 to write a literary essay.
寫 明 to write plainly; to set forth clearly.
寫 本 a draft; manuscript.
寫 法 style of handwriting; penmanship.
寫 生 to draw living objects.
¹⁵寫 生 逼 眞 drawings almost rivalling nature.
寫 眞 or 傳 眞 to draw a portrait.
寫 眞 器 photographic camera. (Jap.).
寫 眞 版 photographic process-block.
寫 立 to draw up—as a document.
²⁰寫·着 is writing.

(a) To unburden; to dispel. To drain, for which the next is now used.

寫 憂 to dispel anxiety or sorrow.
寫 水 to drain off the water—from fields.
我 心 寫 兮 my heart is now free from anger.
洩 寫 to relieve the mind.

瀉 ⁴   **To drain off; to leak.**
2628

瀉 土 barren land that will not retain moisture.
瀉 底 事 a matter without foundation.
瀉 水 to drain off water.

(a) Read hsieh⁴. **To purge; diarrhoea.**

瀉 火 to reduce a fever by purging.
瀉 肚 子 to have diarrhoea.
瀉 藥 purgatives.

榭 ⁴   **A kiosk.**
2629

謝 ⁴   **To thank; to be grateful for. Thanks.**
2630

謝 候 to reward.
謝 儀 a return present; doctor's fees.
謝 別 to take leave.
謝 孝 to visit and thank friends after a parent's funeral.
⁵謝 帖 a card of thanks; a notice of reward offered.
謝 恩 to give thanks for favours.
謝 步 or 謝 踵 to return a call.
謝 神 to thank the gods.
謝 表 (or 章) memorial of thanks to the throne.
¹⁰謝·謝 thanks; much obliged.
謝 賞 thanks for a gift.
謝 辭 to take leave.
謝 酒 to make a call after a feast; an after-dinner call.
謝 金 doctor's fees.
¹⁵謝 錢 to give a reward in money.
鳴 謝 many thanks — for subscriptions.

(a) To decline.

謝 客 not at home to visitors.
謝 病 to decline office on account of sickness.
謝 絕 to decline an offer.
謝 老 to decline on account of age.

(b) To confess faults.

謝 罪 to acknowledge a fault.
謝 過 or 謝 咎 to confess a fault.
謝 道 to apologize for.

(c) To die; to fade.

謝 世 to die.
謝 暑 fading of the summer.
謝 落 to fade and fall, as flowers.
代 謝 alternation of seasons.
凋 謝 to fade—as flowers.

(d) To hand over.

謝 任 to hand over a charge or office.

HSIEH.   (ㄒ一ㄝ)

俠 ¹·⁵.   **Generous; bold. Pron. hsia²·⁵.**
2631

俠 客 a knight-errant.
俠 氣 magnanimity; heroism; disinterestedness.
俠 烈 brave; resolute; heroic.
遊 俠 a knight-errant, one who seeks to right wrongs.

挾 ²·⁵.   **To clasp under the arm. To put in the bosom.**
2632   Also read hsia²·⁵

挾 仇 or 挾 恨 to nurse a grievance.
挾 佐 to protect; to assist.
挾 帶 to carry under the arm.
挾 持 to have ability to manage affairs.
⁵挾 有 微 嫌 to cherish resentment.
挾 泰 山 以 超 北 海 to clasp Mt. T'ai under the arm and step over the Northern Sea—an impossibility.
挾 纊 to feel warm when offered sympathy on account of the cold—wadded garments.
三 軍 之 士 皆 如 挾 纊 the soldiers (though cold) were as if clad in wadded garments.

懷挾 to carry a crib into an examination.

(a) To pinch; to presume; to extort.

挾制 to intimidate; to oppress; to coerce.

挾告 to lay a malicious accusation.

挾故 to presume upon acquaintanceship.

挾求 to presume upon an advantage and demand something.

挾私妄作 recklessly to carry out one's selfish plans.

挾貴 to presume upon rank.

挾長 (chang³) to presume on account of greater age.

(b) Read chieh¹·⁵. u.f. 浹 No. 787.

挾日 a cycle of ten days from 甲 to 癸.

(c) Also occurs u.f. 梜 No. 612.

叶 2.5. To harmonize; to rhyme. To unite.
2633

叶韻 or 叶音 a sound given to a character specially for rhyming purposes.

叶時月 to rectify the calendar.

絜 2.5. A marking line. To adjust. To regulate.
2634

絜度 to adjust; to limit.

絜矩之道 rules of proper behavior; mutual obligations—the golden rule.

絜靜 tranquil.

絜齊 to make even; to regulate.

(a) Pure; similar to 潔 No. 772.

絜爾牛羊 the oxen and sheep are all pure.

頡 2.5. To fly upwards; to soar.
2635

頡之頏之 now flying up and now down; fluttering about.

(a) The neck.

頡頏 stiff-necked.

挺頡 to stretch forth the neck.

(b) Vague, ambiguous.

頡滑 specious; having a double meaning.

(c) Read chia²·⁵. To rob.

盜頡資糧 plundered the military supply.

擷 2.5. To collect; to take up. u.f. 襭 No. 2638. To gather up the skirts, a lapful. Also read yeh.
2636

尋芳擷秀 to seek and gather the lovely fragrant—flowers.

纈 2.5. To tie up silk into skeins. To tie a knot; a knot.
2637

打個纈 to tie a knot.

死纈 a knot that will not slip.

襭 2.5. To tuck the skirts into the girdle. The fold of a robe.
2638

做襭次哺 she opened her robe to give suck.

協 2.5. United in. Agreement; mutual help. To aid; to help. Inter. 脅 No. 2641.
叶
2639

協力 co-operation; united effort.

協力合作 co-operation.

協助 to aid; to sympathize with.

協助與合作 mutual assistance and co-operation.

⁵協同 participation; united action.

協同動作 united action.

協同巡警 together with the police.

協定憲法 conventional constitution.

協定稅則 conventional tariff. (legal).

¹⁰協定行爲 conventional act. (legal).

協揆 designation of a former Assistant Grand Secretary.

協會 a society or association.

協比讒言予一人 to form parties to defame the one man—the Emperor.

協治 to assist in ruling.

¹⁵協濟 to lend assistance.

協理 a sub-manager.

協爾幫 Commissioner of Justice—Tibet.

協約 alliance; agreement.

協約內容 terms of an alliance.

²⁰協約國 allied nations.

協約局外中立 conventional neutrality. (legal).

協統 former title for a commander of a brigade.

協緝 to assist in the search for.

協解 to forward money to assist the revenue of another province.

²⁵協謀 to consult together; to conspire.

協議 or 協商 conference; discussion; mutual consent.

協議離婚 divorce by consent.

協贊 consent; to second.

協辦 assistance in managing.

³⁰協辦大學士 former Assistant Grand Secretary; cabinet-minister.

協進會 used for the National Christian Council.

協鎭 or 協守 Colonel in the former Imperial Army.

協餉 to render financial assistance to another province.

(a) To harmonize; to be in accord.

協和 to harmonize.

協和萬邦 he brought all the States into harmony.

協奏 to perform music in harmony.

協從 in agreement; in harmony with each other.

⁵協心 of one mind.

協時 to regulate the calendar; in accord with the times.

協音 having the same sound as.

相協 in harmony with.

恊 2.5. To intimidate, to coerce.
2640

脅 2.5. The ribs; the flank.
脇
2641

脅下 below the ribs; the flank.

脅生 born between the ribs, as Laotzŭ was fabled to have been.

脅骨 or 兩脅 or 脅·巴骨 the ribs.
短脅 false ribs.

(a) To coerce. To be forced. Also inter. 協 No. 2639.

脅 勒 to terrify and oppress.
脅 取 to take by force.
脅 從 罔 治 those who were coerced into taking part are not to be executed.
脅 息 panting with fright.
脅 權 to abuse power.
脅 迫 persecution; coercion.

(b) Read *hsi*[1.5]. To shrug the shoulders.

脅 肩 諂 笑 to shrug the shoulders and laugh with another—to play the sycophant.

(c) To gather; to collect together, similar to 翕 No. 2475.

動 靜 翕 脅 motion and rest, repulsion and attraction.

歇 [1.5]. To rest; to stop. To desist.
2642
[-*hsiu*[3].

歇 一 宿 to stay over a night.
歇 一 歇 罷 take a rest! Wait a while!
歇 下 to cease; to stop.
歇 乏 to rest when weary.
[5]歇 住 口 to hold one's peace; to desist from eating.
歇 嘴 hold your tongue! to stop talking.
歇 夏 or 歇 伏 to go away for the summer.
歇 客 a guest at an inn.
歇 工 to take a holiday; to stop work.
[10]歇 店 an inn; to stay at an inn.
歇 後 語 phrases of which the first part only is quoted, leaving the hearer to draw his own conclusions; e.g., one might describe a person as being 禮 義 廉 omitting 恥 the last word of the phrase, the inference being that the said person is without shame. *See* 貽 No. 2967-2.
歇 心 or 放 心 to set the mind at rest.

歇 息 to rest; to wait; to suspend operations.
歇 手 to rest from work; to desist.
[15]歇 擔 to put down a load.
歇 晌 noonday rest.
歇 業 or 歇 生·意 to fail in business; to go out of business.
歇·歇 rest for a while; take it easy.
歇 氣 or 歇 止 to rest; to leave off.
[20]歇 涼 to rest and cool off.
歇·罷 Stop! Take a rest.
歇 脚 to rest when weary.
歇 至 uneven; irregular.
歇 覺 to take a nap. (-*chiao*[4])
[25]歇 馬 primarily used of getting off a horse to rest him, used fig., to suspend operations, etc.
不 歇 其 味 had not lost its flavour.
芳 草 亦 未 歇 the flowers had not lost their fragrance.

(b) Read *ho*[4.5]. (*hoh*[4]) A short-nosed hunting dog. u.f. next.

歇 驕 (*hsiao*[1]) a short-nosed hunting dog.

猲 [1.5]. A fierce dog. Also read *ho*[4.5].
2643

蠍 [1.5]. A scorpion.
2644

蠍·子 scorpions.
蠍 虎·子 the house-lizard or gecko.
蠍 螫 (or 勾 or 刺) sting of a scorpion.

薤 [4]. Shallots or scallions.
2645

薤 白 the bulb of a shallot.
薤 葉 篆 a form of the *seal* style of Chinese characters.
薤 露 dew on the shallots—brevity of life; a dirge or elegy.

炧 [4.5]. The remnants of an expiring candle. Also read *to*[4].
2646

餘 炧 猶 明 the flaring up of an expiring flame.

紲 [4.5]. To fasten with cords. A bridle. To remove.
2647

媟 [4.5]. To commit an outrage on a woman. To lust after.
2648

媟 狎 indecent behaviour.
媟 黷 to take indecent liberties with a woman.

洩 [4.5]. To leak, to drip, to ooze; thus:—to divulge. Inter. 泄 No. 2950.
2649

洩 底 or 漏 底 to betray one's antecedents; to lose caste.
洩 忿 (or 恨) to work off one's spleen.
洩 氣 to lose smell or virtue as through exposure to the air; to vent the feelings; to be appeased. 洩·氣 disappointing; annoying.
洩 漏 to leak; to divulge.
洩 漏 天 機 to disclose the secrets of nature, or the hidden springs of Heaven's plans.
洩 漏 密 事 to divulge a secret.

(a) Read *i*[1]. Leisurely.

緤 [4.5]. Bonds. To tie up.
2650

縲 緤 in bonds; bound.
繫 緤 bonds and fetters.

楔 [1.5]. A wedge. To wedge.
2651

楔·子 a wedge; a preface.
楔·起·來 to wedge.

屑 [4.5]. A fragment; a crumb. To powder; to break in pieces.
2652

屑 塵 very fine dust.
屑 桂 與 薑 powdered cassia and ginger.
屑 榆 爲 粥 gruel made from elm, used in famines.
屑 涕 to weep.
屑 物 waste material.
屑 金 powdered gold—the stars.

木 屑 waste wood, carpenter's refuse. (-hsüeh[1])

煤 屑 ashes from coal. (-hsüeh[1])

(a) **To take pains for; to condescend; to consider as worth while.**

不 屑 to disregard.

不 屑 去 not worth while going.

不 屑 就 not fit to go to or to associate with.

不 屑 爲 之 事 not worth doing.

(b) **Lightly; triflingly. Vexatious.**

屑 播 天 命 lightly to set aside the decrees of Heaven.

往 來 屑 屑 constantly coming and going.

瑣 屑 vexatious.

輕 屑 to depreciate.

薛
2653
1.5. **A large kind of marsh grass. A small feudal State. A surname.**
Pron. hsüeh[1,5]

薛 國 a small feudal State in what is now Shantung.

蹩
2653a
3.5. **To limp.**

褻
褻
2654
4.5. **Dirty, ragged. Undress; thus:—to treat with irreverence.**

褻 瀆 to blaspheme; to profane.

褻 瀆 神 明 to blaspheme the gods.

褻 器 a chamber-utensil.

褻 慢 to treat with contempt.

褻 服 in undress; mourning clothes.

褻 狎 輕 佻 undue familiarity.

褻 穢 indecent; filthy.

褻 臣 a favourite of royalty who has improper intimacy.

燮
2655
4.5. **To blend; to harmonize; to adjust.**

燮 伐 大 商 in accordance with (the decree of Heaven) he destroyed the great Shang dynasty.

燮 理 陰 陽 to adjust the dual powers.

燮 和 or 調 燮 to arrange equably; to harmonize.

躞
2656
4.5.
To walk.

躞 蹀 to walk; walking.

HSIEN.   (ㄒㄧㄢ)

祆
2657
1 **A term used during the T'ang dynasty to denote the god of the Zoroastrians; it was also adopted by the Manicheans. Distinguish 祆 No. 7281.**

祆 敎 or 二 元 敎 or 拜 火 敎 Zoroastrianism.

祆 正 an official appointed during the T'ang dynasty to take charge of the worship in Mongolia and the outer dependencies.

火 祆 the fire-god of Zoroastrianism.

枚
2658
1 **A shovel. Read hsien[2]. A trough to carry off water.**

掀
2659
1 **To lift to one side; to raise up; to open. To whisk away.**

掀·不 動 unable to move it or lift it up.

掀·不 開 cannot lift—the lid or cover.

掀 脣 to open the lips—in speaking.

掀 天 揭 地 lifting the heavens and pulling up the earth—describing extraordinary ability.

⁵掀 房 頂 to take the roof off a house.

掀 發 to escape; to fly out.

掀 簾·子 to pull aside or raise a bamboo screen-blind.

掀 翻 桌·子 to tip a table over.

掀 腫 a swelling.

¹⁰掀 被 to throw off a coverlet.

掀·起·來 to raise; to lift up, as a curtain, or lid of a box, etc.

掀·開 書 本 to open a book.

掀·開 黑 幕 to draw aside the black curtain—to reveal hidden deeds of evil.

掀 風 播 浪 to raise the wind and waves—to make a great stir; to raise an agitation.

¹⁵木 掀 a wooden shovel used by farmers.(-hsüan[1])

鐵 掀 an iron shovel.(-hsüan[1])

(a) **High; proud.**

掀 轟 a great noise as of a storm.

掀 顚 proud boasting.

首 掀 掀 to raise the head high.

(b) **Read hên[2]. To lead; to guide.**

掀 引 to guide.

軒
2660
1 **A porch or balcony. A pavilion, a side-room.**
Pron. hsüan[1]

軒 檻 railing of a balcony.

臨 軒 to go to the pavilion—said of the Emperor.

舍 軒 or 書 軒 a study or library.

茶 軒 a tea-house.

(a) **A carriage formerly used by high officials. A carriage or chariot with a high front.**

軒 車 a high carriage.

軒 輊 high and low chariots—u.f. comparison of relative merits.

魚 軒 a carriage decorated with shagreen.

(b) **High, soaring, lofty.**

軒 尾 to cock the tail.

軒 峻 lofty.

軒 昂 dignified; imposing; grand; high-priced.

軒 爽 spacious.

軒 翥 to soar on high.

軒 鶱 to soar.

(c) **Merry, laughing, pleasant.**

軒 渠 laughing with satisfaction.

軒 然 仰 笑 with a pleasant smile.

軒 眉 to raise the eyebrows with satisfaction.

軒 軒 然 smiling; satisfied.

軒 軒 自 得 delighted; merry.

(d) **A surname.**

軒 轅 a name for Huangti or the Yellow Emperor, said to be from the place where he was born, near the present 新 鄭 縣 in Honan.

軒 岐 *Hsien Yüan,* as above, and *Ch'i Pê. See* No. 522-4. Founders of Chinese medicine.
軒 羲 *Hsien Yüan* and *Fu Hsi.*

弦 **2661** The string of a musical instrument. The chord of an arc. The first and last quarters of the moon. A crescent. Also read *hsüan².* See 絃 No. 2663.

弦·子 a lute. = 2663.9.
弦 柱 the post to which the strings of a lute are fastened.
弦 歌 之 聲 music and singing.
弦 索 stringed instruments.
⁵弦 誦 music and chanting.
弦 韋 silk string and leather girdle, one to urge and the other to restrain. *See* 佩 No. 5015—3, 9.
上 弦,下 弦 first and last quarters of the moon.
弓 弦 string of a bow.
斷 弦 to break a string—to lose a wife.
¹⁰正 弦 sine. (*math.*).
續 弦 to repair the string—to re-marry, to take a second wife.
餘 弦 cosine. (*math.*).

(a) A thready pulse.

脈 弦 長 a thready pulse.

痃 **2662** Indigestion, faintness at the stomach.

痃 癖 dyspepsia.

(a) Buboes.

橫 痃 buboes.

絃 **2663** The string of a musical instrument. A musical chord. Also read *hsüan².*

絃 索 stringed instruments.
絃 馬 the bridge of a violin.
二 絃 the two-stringed violin, in which the bow passes between the strings.
四 絃 提 琴 a violin.
⁵擊 絃 to pluck the strings.
斷 絃 to break a string—to lose a wife.
理 絃 to tune the strings.
續 絃 to repair the string—to marry a second wife.
三 絃 a three-stringed plucked instrument.

舷 **2664** The bulwarks or sides of a boat.

蚿 **2665** The millipede or galley-worm.

咸 **2666** Together, all, completely. To unite. The 31st diagram of the *Book of Changes.* Also read *han².*

咸 共 all, altogether.
咸 同 all alike.
咸 因 此 故 all were on this ac-count.
咸 我 績 all the merit belongs to me.
⁵咸 思 a general wish or thought.
咸 集 all gathered together.
咸 知 咸 聞 everybody knows it.
咸 見 all saw it.
咸 豐 *Hsien Feng*—style of the reign of the emperor who ruled China from A.D. 1851—1862.

(a) Music of *Yao.*

咸 英 韶 濩 the various kinds of music of the emperors *Yao, Shun,* and *Ch'eng-T'ang.*

諴 **2667** Sincerity; union. To bring into accord. Distinguish 誠 No. 381.

至 諴 感 神 perfect sincerity will move the gods.

鹹 **2668** Salt; brackish. Also read *han².*

鹹 土 salt-land.
鹹 水 salt water; the sea.
鹹 汁 brine.
鹹 泉 salt-springs.
⁵鹹 津 津·的 very salt indeed.
鹹 淡 salt and fresh.
鹹 湖 salt lakes.
鹹 肉 salt meat; bacon.
鹹 腥 brackish and smelly.
¹⁰鹹 苦 salt and bitter—used fig.
     不 知 鹹 苦 not to know what is salt or bitter—not having had experience of the bit-terness of life.
鹹 菜 pickled vegetables.
鹹 蛋 salted eggs.
鹹 酸 salt and sour.

¹⁵鹹 魚 salt fish.
鹹 鹺 salt used in sacrifices.

嫌 **2669** To dislike, to suspect. To object to; to reject. Jealousy, suspicion, dislike.

嫌 事 太 多 objected to there being too much to do.
嫌 以 君 子 自 居 did not like to style himself a superior man.
嫌 名 names which are taboo (as those of a ruler, father or senior) which may not be used. *See under* 諱 No. 2357.
嫌 多 嫌 少 either too much or too little,—hard to please.
⁵嫌 小 to object to a thing as being too small.
嫌 少 to consider an amount too small.
嫌 忌 to be jealous of.
嫌 怨 enmity; grudge.
嫌 惡 to hate; to dislike.
¹⁰嫌 棄 to reject; to despise.
嫌 氣 dislike; jealousy; repug-nance.
嫌 煩 to consider anything too troublesome.
嫌 畏 suspicious and fearful.
嫌·疑 suspicion; dislike; jealousy.
¹⁵嫌·疑 犯 a suspected criminal.
避 嫌·疑 to avoid suspicion.
嫌 繁 瑣 to complain of tediousness.
嫌 貧 愛 富 to slight the poor and pay attention to the rich.
嫌 醜 嫌 好 to take exception to good and bad alike; to talk at random about anything.
²⁰嫌 隙 ill-will; a breach.
嫌 髒 to object to anything as being dirty.
勿 嫌 輶 褻 do not regard it as too trifling—to accept.

蒹 **2670** Half-grown beans.

賢 賢 **2671** Virtuous, worthy, good. To esteem as worthy. Ex-celling.

賢 人 a man of excellent virtues; a worthy.

賢其賢 regarded as worthy that which (*Wên Wang* 文王 and *Wu Wang* 武王) regarded as worthy.

賢勞 admirably industrious.

賢叔 your uncle—complimentary.

⁵賢名 a good reputation.

賢君 an excellent ruler.

賢員 officers worthy of confidence.

賢哲 virtuous and wise.

賢善 worth and excellence.

¹⁰賢契 my worthy young friends—term of respect to juniors.

賢女 a woman of the highest character.

賢姊 your elder sister—complimentary.

賢妻 or 賢內助 worthy wife—in addressing her.

賢子·賢孫 worthy descendants.

¹⁵賢孝 virtuous and filial.

賢弟 my good brother—spoken to a brother or friend.

賢彥 a worthy.

賢德 high moral character.

賢惠 kind and good.

²⁰賢愚 wise and foolish—all classes.

賢慧 virtuous and sagacious.

賢才 pre-eminent ability.

賢明 of high character and clear intelligence; enlightened.

賢書 the list of successful graduates for the second degree under the former system.

²⁵賢淑 good and virtuous—of women.

賢相 an able and virtuous statesman.

賢者辟世 worthies retire from the world.

賢能 good and able.

賢良 good and virtuous.

³⁰賢良祠 temple erected to the memory of good and virtuous officials.

賢英 a man of super-excellence.

賢賢易色 to love the virtuous and turn the heart from lust.

賢路 the career of the virtuous.

賢達 worthy and well-informed.

³⁵先賢 former worthies.

自賢 self-righteous.

(a) Used in transliterating.

賢豆 a name for India.

閒² Leisure, idleness, unoccupied. Distinguish 閉 No. 835, of which this character is the older form; and 閑 No. 2679, with which it is now interchanged, though it was formerly a different word. [2672]

閒·不住 or 不閒 or 不得閒 busy; having no spare time; fully occupied.

閒事 unimportant matters; private affairs.

好管閒事 fond of meddling in other people's business.

閒人 or 閒民 loafers; intruders; unemployed persons.

⁵閒人免進 "No admittance except on business."

閒冗 not much business—of an easy official post.

閒園 unoccupied property.

閒地 or 閒田 vacant land.

閒官 an official who has an easy post.

¹⁰閒居 or 閒住 living alone; in retirement; unemployed.

閒居獨處 while I was quite alone.

閒得兒 or 閒等兒 beggars.

閒懶人 a loafer, an idler.

閒手 an idler; a lazy fellow.

¹⁵閒打牙 idle talk to pass the time.

閒散 to take relaxation; disbanded—as troops.

閒是閒非 it is not my business; idle gossip.

閒時 leisure and quiet.

閒暇 unoccupied; at leisure; in peace.

²⁰閒書 light literature; novels.

閒月 the slack season of the farmer.

閒步 or 閒行 or 閒遊 to take a stroll.

閒氣 anger at what is not one's business.

閒燕 when at leisure in private.

²⁵閒田 unalloted lands under the feudal system.

閒看 looking idly on.

閒空 (*k'ung*) or 清·閒 or 閒常 or 得閒 or 有閒時 at leisure; nothing to do.

閒站 to stand idle.

閒耍 to waste time.

³⁰閒茶 drinking tea in idleness; hanging around a teashop.

閒處 to live in retirement.

閒裝 ordinary dress.

閒言閒語 idle talk.

閒話 chit-chat; pleasant talk; gossip.

³⁵閒談 to chat.

閒逛 to stroll around.

閒逸 easy.

閒適 leisurely and quietly, in accord with one's desires.

閒錢 spare cash.

⁴⁰閒門 a side-door, a private entrance.

閒雅 easy, self-possessed manners.

閒雜人等 loafers; idlers.

閒雲 merely a passing cloud.

閒靜 leisure and quiet.

⁴⁵閒飯 food for which one has given no equivalent; food got by sponging.

偷閒 to make time for a little relaxation.

心安閒放 the mind at peace and free from anxiety.

抽閒 to find leisure for.

(a) Read *chien*¹. A crevice, a space between; now usually written 間 See No. 835.

閒至 nearly arrived.

閒隙 a crack; a breach.

(b) Read *chien*¹. To separate; to put a space between, see No. 835—B, now usually written 間

閒候 or 閒諜 a spy.

閒出 to go and spy.

閒斷 to shut off, to separate; to block up.

閒歲 every other year.

閒道 a byway.

閒隔 separated; to set apart; at intervals.

僩³ Courageous, martial; dignified. [2673]

嫻｜² Elegant, accomplished. 嫺｜ Refined. [2674]

嫻於禮 well-versed in etiquette.

嫻熟 skilled in.

嫻習 adept at.

嫻雅 polished; cultured; apt.

憪 [2] Composed, contented, peaceful.

2675

憪 然 pleased; tranquil.

(a) Read *hsien*[3]. Disquieted, stern, wrathful.

憪 然 sternly.
憪 然 念 人 之 有 非 sternly pondering the fact that men were full of faults.

撊 [3] Wrathful, valiant.

2676

撊 然 wrathfully.

癇 [2] Fits, convulsions.

2677

癇 症 or 癲 癇 fits, epilepsy.
羊 癇 瘋 or 羊 角 瘋 epilepsy.
風 癇 convulsions of children.

瞯 [2] To watch narrowly, to spy. Also read *chien*[4].

2678

瞯 窺 to peep at.
使 人 瞯 夫 子 [3] set a man to watch the sage—Mencius.

(a) Read *hsien*[1]. Cornea of the eye; a wall-eyed horse. Also occurs u.f. fits of children.

閑 [2] A bar, a barrier, a fence, an enclosure; thus:—to defend.

2679

閑 先 聖 之 道 to defend the doctrines of the ancient sages.
閑 邪 存 誠 keep out depravity and foster sincerity.
閑 阻 to embarrass; to hinder; to prevent.
不 踰 閑 not to go beyond the bounds, i.e., not to transgress.

(a) Stables. A corral.

天 子 [3] 有 十 二 閑 the Emperor had twelve corrals for rearing horses.

(b) Large.

旅 楹 有 閑 "large are the many pillars."

(c) Trained.

閑 習 軍 事 well-trained in military arts.
四 馬 既 閑 "his four horses display their training."

(d) u.f. 閒 No. 2672. Leisure, etc.

閑 人 混 擾 idlers creating a disturbance.
閑 地 自 養 "an easy post in which one could recuperate."
閑 坐 idle.
閑 安 leisure, quietness.
[5]閑 客 an idler; the silver pheasant.
閑·得 不 耐 煩 bored with inaction.
閑 放 at leisure.
閑 散 to take relaxation.
閑 暢 at ease and contented.
[10]閑 暮 the leisure of old age.
閑 步 to take a stroll.
閑 淑 reserved and modest.
閑 清 at leisure.
閑 獨 living quietly in retirement and alone.
[15]閑 肆 free and unrestrained—not cramped as by bonds and rules —of poetry.
閑 豫 pleasurable ease.
臨 衝 閑 閑 "the engines of onfall and assault were gently plied." *Shih ching*, Legge 455.

鷳 [2] The silver pheasant, formerly worn as a badge by civil officials of the fifth grade.

2680

銜 [2] A bit, thus:—to hold in the mouth, to gag, to control.

2681

銜 冤 to cherish a grievance.
銜 勒 a bit; to be gagged.
銜 命 to act according to orders received.
銜 哀 致 誠 "control my grief and collect my thoughts." *Giles*.
[5]銜 塊 to hold a lump of earth in the mouth as a token that one deserves death.
銜 尾 to hold the tail in the mouth —both ends meet.
銜 恨 to control one's anger.
銜 恤 to carry grief—i.e., to lose one's parents.
銜 感 or 銜 恩 to feel grateful.
[10]銜 枚 to be gagged; to refrain from talking;—from the custom of gagging soldiers on a night-attack.
銜 泣 to weep without making a noise.
銜 環 以 報 to carry a bracelet as a recompense. *See* 結 No. 782 —A.37.
銜 繮 bit and bridle.
緊 銜 to hold a horse in.
馬 銜 a bit for a horse.

(a) Rank, official title; brevet rank.

銜 名 or 官 銜 official title of an officer.
上 校 銜 with the title of "Colonel."
加 銜 brevet rank.
加 有 少 [4] 將 銜 to hold brevet rank of Major-general.
升 銜 brevet rank.
海 軍 上 將 [4] 銜 with the title of "Admiral."
虛 銜 brevet rank.
階 銜 ranks and titles.

嗛 [2]
啣 To hold in the mouth. Also read *han*[2].

2682

嗛 命 receiving instructions.
嗛·在 嘴·裏 to hold in the mouth.
嗛 糖 欖 to suck a sugared olive— well pleased.

峴 [3] A steep hill. Name of mountains in various places.

2683

現 [4] The glitter of gems, thus: —to manifest, to appear, to see.

2684

現·了 原 形 he has shown his real feelings.
現·出·來 or 現·出 to appear; to manifest.
現 實 the actual as contrasted with the ideal.
現 實 主 義 realism.
[5]現 實 人 生 the actual in human life.
現 實 性 actuality.
現 形 to become manifest—as a supernatural being.
現 活 life-like.
現 狀 symptoms. *See below* A.31.
[10]現 相 [4] appearance.

現 象 phenomenon.
現 身 說 法 manifested himself and explained the principles of Buddhism—used of setting an example by life and conduct.
現 醜 to make an object of oneself, attempting that which one is not able to do.
現 露 to disclose; to divulge.

(a) Now, at present.

現 世 (or 代) 主 義 secularism or modernism.
現 世 報 retribution in the present life.
現 今 之 用 present usage.
現 付 cash-payment.
⁵現 代 the present generation.
現 代 情 形 present-day conditions.
現 代 精 神 spirit of the times.
現 任 the present incumbent.
現 值 at this juncture.
¹⁰現 價 present worth. (arith.).
現 兌 店 a cash-store.
現 制 the existing system.
現 務 the business in hand.
現 勢 the trend of the times.
¹⁵現 吃 現 做 prepare the food as you require it; to prepare meals as they are ordered. (hsüan⁴-)
現 售 簿 cash-sales book.
現 在 or 現 今 or 現 時 or 現 當 or 現 刻 now, at present, at this time.
現 在 式 present tense.
現 在 裏 面 in the present.
²⁰現 在 農 業 present-day conditions of agriculture.
現 存 in stock; subsisting; in existence.
現 役 on active service.
現 成 物 ready-made goods.
現 成 的 ready-made.
²⁵現 成 話 stock phrases.
現 有 on hand.
現 有 貨 stock in hand.
現 款 結 存 cash-balance.
現 洋 ready money in Mexican dollars.
³⁰大 批 現 洋 large sum in ready money.
現 狀 the present state of affairs; the status quo. See above.—9.
現 狀 之 下 in the existing state of affairs.

維 持 現 狀 to maintain the status quo.　[(hsüan⁴-)
現 用 現 買 buy as required.
³⁵現 眼 to make a fool of oneself.
現 種 現 吃 to have no stock of grain, having to wait until the crops are ripe. (hsüan⁴-)
現 行 for the time being; temporary.
現 行 法 則 laws in operation; existing laws.
現 行 犯 a criminal caught in the act.
⁴⁰現 行 規·則 existing regulations; temporary regulations.
現 設 or 現 行 functioning for the present; at present in force.
現 銀 or 現 錢 or 現 金 ready money.
現 銀 交 貨 cash on delivery.
現 銀 定 價 cash price.
⁴⁵現 銀 折 扣 discount for cash.
現 銀 換 取 證 書 cash against document.
現 錢 不 賒 no credit given.
現 錢 交·易 ready-money business.

睍 ³ Goggle-eyes. Eyes agog with fear.
2685

睍 惡 dangerous; treacherous.
睍 睆 pleasant; melodious.
睍 睍 a scared look.

莧 ⁴ Edible greens of various sorts. Amarantus, Chenopodium, etc.
2686

莧 荣 greens used like spinach.
馬 齒 莧 purslane or portulaca.

蜆 3.4.　Small, smooth bivalves.
2687

蜆 塘 a pond for rearing shellfish.
蜆 妹 a young girl of the Tanka or boat population of Canton. See 蛋 家 No. 6050—A.
蜆 肉 shelled clams, etc.
蜆 蛤 raw clams seasoned.

(a) A small, black insect with a red head; it suspends itself while making its cocoon. See 縊 女 No. 3055—1.

憸 ¹ Artful, crafty. Flattering, having a specious tongue.
2688

憸 人 specious flatterers.

險 ³ A narrow pass, thus:— dangerous, danger, risk.
2689

險 傷 a dangerous wound.
險 固 secure; strongly defended.
險 岸 a steep declivity.
險 得 很 or 險 中 in the midst of danger; imminently dangerous.
⁵險 惡 evil; malicious.
險 症 a dangerous illness.
險 處 danger, a dangerous position.
險 詐 to backbite.
險 語 startling words.
¹⁰險 要 dangerous and important, as a strategic post.
險 象 a crisis.
險 道 dangerous courses.
險 釁 grave difficulties and calamities.
險 阻 in difficulties or straits.
¹⁵險 隘 or 險 口 a dangerous pass.
險 韻 a rhyme which is exceedingly difficult to make.
保 險 insurance, See 保 No. 4946-B.41.ff.　　　[accident.
出 險 out of danger; to have an
危 險 dangerous; precipitous.
²⁰心 險 a treacherous heart.
出 危 險 to have an accident.

(a) Almost; nearly.

險 些 nearly; almost.
險·險 死·了 nearly died.

檻 ³ A railing; bars. A cage. Also read chien³.
2690

檻 車 or 囚 車 a cart with a cage for prisoners.
花 檻 a garden-fence.

(a) Read k'an³. A door-sill; threshold.

門 檻 threshold; a door-sill.

爢 ³ Motes in a sunbeam, thus: —minute, impalpable.
2691 Bright. Fibrous.

顯
顯
2692
To manifest, to display. To be illustrious. Evident. To seem; to appear.

顯 亮 clear; evident.
顯 係 it is evidently...
顯 像 (or 景) development of a photographic image.
顯 像 藥(or 水)or 顯 影 藥 photographic developer.
⁵顯·出·來 to be revealed; to be made manifest.
顯·出 榮 耀 to show forth his glory.
顯 士 a distinguished scholar.
顯 妣 a deceased mother.
顯 官 illustrious officials.
¹⁰顯 弄 or 顯 排 to show off.
顯 微 化 學 micro-chemistry.
顯 微 鏡 microscope.
合 成 顯 微 鏡 compound microscope.
簡 單 顯 微 鏡 simple microscope.
¹⁵顯 微 音 器 microphone.
顯 應 or 靈 顯 a divine manifestation.
顯 威 to make a show of power; to show severity in order to intimidate.
顯 手·段 to show off one's skill; to "show what one can do."
顯 揚 to spread abroad; notable; famous.
²⁰顯 明 or 顯 然 or 顯 著 to set forth clearly; manifest; prominent; apparent.
顯 晦 brightness and shadow.
顯 榮 honours; tokens of distinction.
顯 猷 a brilliant plan.
顯 現 to display; to manifest.
²⁵顯 現 日 Epiphany.
顯 示 to manifest; to display to view.
顯 祖 one's ancestors.
顯 考 a deceased father.
顯 而 易 (i⁴) 見 obvious.
³⁰顯 職 to fulfil the duties of a position.
顯 能 or 顯 本 事 to make a display of ability; to show off.
顯 親 揚 名 to bring glory to one's parents.
顯 證 prima facie evidence.
顯 赫 illustrious; glorious.
³⁵顯 達 illustrious; successful.

顯 違 to manifest a disregard for.
顯 露 to disclose; apparent.
顯 靈 to display divine efficacy—said of an idol, a tree, or any place, etc.
顯 面 業 主 prima facie proprietor.
⁴⁰顯 顯 令 德 How illustrious is his virtue!

臽
4
2693
A pit, a hole. Distinguish 舀 No. 7299.

坎 臽 pitfall.

陷
4
2694
To sink. To involve, to beguile, to betray. Also read han⁴.

陷 井 to fall into a well.
陷 人 不 義 to lead men to do wrong.
陷 入 to sink into.
陷 地 獄 to sink into hell.
⁵陷·在 泥 裏 sunk in the mud.
陷·在 罪·裏 to involve in sin.
陷 堅 to attack the enemy's centre.
陷 害 to betray; to get another into trouble; to involve.
陷 敵 to enter the enemy's lines.
¹⁰陷·於 水 深 火 熱·之 境 involved in the deepest difficulties.
陷 於 臆 斷 deeply imbued with prejudice.
陷 水 to fall into water.
陷 沙 河 to sink in the quicksands.
陷 沒 sunk into; overwhelmed in.
¹⁵陷 溺 overwhelmed in; sunk in—as vice.
陷 給 to submit; to surrender.
陷 罪 to lead others into crime; to be involved in crime.
陷 阱 or 陷 坑 a trap or pitfall; to entrap.
陷 阱·之 中 fallen into the pit—sunk in vice.
²⁰陷 陣 to break through the enemy's lines.
坑 陷 to entrap; to involve in.
城 陷 the city has fallen.

餡
4
2695
The fruit, meat, sugar, etc., put in pastry as stuffing. A secret.

肉 餡 meat for putting into pasties.
露·了 餡 the stuffing is visible—the secret is out. (lou⁴-)

餅 餡 things put into cakes, etc., as stuffing.

限
4
2696
A boundary, a limit. A fixed time. To limit; to regard as a limit.

限 令 to give one a certain time-limit.
限 價 price-limit.
限 內 within the limit.
限·制 a restriction; a fixed measure.
⁵限·制 主 權 國 nation with a limited sovereignty.
限·制·的 競 試 limited competition.
限·制 解·釋 limited interpretation. (legal).
限·制 辯 論 limited debate.
限·制 軍 備 restriction of armaments, etc.
¹⁰限·制 童 工 restriction of child-labour.
限 外 beyond the limit.
限 定 to fix a limit to.
限 幾 日 how many days do you set? limited to how many days?
限 度 standards; qualification required; a restriction; a limit.
¹⁵限 於 篇 幅 owing to limitations of space—as in a magazine or paper.
限 日 the appointed day or term.
限 期 a set period; a limit of time.
限 止 to limit; to check.
限 滿 at the expiration of the appointed time.
²⁰限 界 or 界 限 a boundary; a fixed limit.
限 碗 to diet; to limit one's appetite.
限 量 a limit; an estimate.
大 限 the great boundary—death.
寬 限 to extend a time-limit.
²⁵年 限 limit of years.
有 限 there is a limit; not very much or not very many, etc.
有 限 公·司 limited-liability company.
有 限 責·任 limited responsibility or liability.
權 限 limit of authority.
³⁰滿 限 matured.
無 限 unlimited; boundless.
過 限 to exceed the bounds; to exceed a time-limit.

(a) A threshold; a door-sill.
門 限 a door-step or threshold.

憲[4] An example; a law; a pattern. Regulations; a constitution.
2697

憲 兵 military police.
憲 典 the statutes of government.
憲 政 constitutional government.
憲 政 時 期 period of constitutional government.
[5]憲 書 a calendar.
憲 法 constitution of a State.
憲 法 原 理 theory of the constitution.
憲 法 大 綱 general outline of a constitution.
憲 法 起 草 draft constitution.
[10] 成 文 憲 法 written constitution.
憲 禁 government prohibitions.
憲 章 orders issued by the authorities.
憲 章 文 武 he modelled himself upon *Wên Wang* and *Wu Wang*.

(a) A ruler; formerly a complimentary title of address for highest officials.

憲 天 the highest authorities.
憲 恩 your excellency's favour.
憲 庭 your excellency's abode.
憲 臺 your excellency.
憲 裁 your excellency's decision.
上 憲 high provincial authorities.

(b) Pleased; complacently.

憲 憲 然 complacently; elated.

(c) Read *hsien³*. Illustrious.

憲 憲 令 德 displaying his illustrious virtue.

幰[3] A curtain at the front of a carriage.
2698

獻
献
2699
[4] To offer up; to present.

獻 上 or 進 獻 or 奉 獻 to offer up to a superior.
獻 俘 to present captives, taken in war, at the temple.
獻 功 to report one's services.
獻 媚 to toady; to ingratiate oneself with.

[5]獻 堂 禮 dedication of a hall or church.
獻 寶 to present valuables.
獻 捷 to present captives, taken in war.
獻 歲 the beginning of a year.
獻 祭 to offer sacrifices.
[10]獻 禮 物 to offer gifts.
獻 策 to submit plans; to offer advice.
獻 芹 獻 曝 I offer you parsley and the warmth of the sun—depreciatory phrase for a present.
獻 茶 to hand tea.
獻 計 to give advice.
[15]獻 諛 懷 詐 presenting flattery and cherishing craftiness — acting the hypocrite.
獻 身 to devote oneself to.
獻 酒 to offer wine.
獻 酬 to help to food, etc., at a dinner.
獻 馘 to present the left ear, (cut from a captive taken in war.)

(a) To show.

獻 勤 to show industry when the master is by—eye-service.
獻 醜 to make an object of oneself, by attempting what one is unfitted for, etc.

縣[4] A District, formerly a subdivision of a Prefecture or *fu* 府 No. 1928.
2700

縣 丞 a former assistant Magistrate.
縣 令 title of District Magistrate.
縣 佐 assistant County Magistrate.
縣 城 chief town of a County District.
[5]縣 塾 former name for a District School.
縣 官 or 縣 太 爺 or 縣 尊 ┌ 縣 長 popular terms for a district magistrate.
縣 敎·育 會 District Educational Council.
縣 法 庭 County court.
縣 知 事 County Magistrate.
[10]縣 立 學 校 County School under official control.
縣 考 or 縣 試 the former examination by the District Magistrate, under the old system.
縣 議 會 a local council.

(a) Read *hsien²* or *hsüan²*. u.f. 縣 No. 2887. Suspended. To hang.

縣 空 suspended in mid-air.
縣 解 to cut down a hanging man.

騫[1]
2701　　To soar.

HSIEN. SIEN　(ㄙ一ㄢ)

先[1] First, foremost. Before, former. In front.
2702

先 不 先,後 不 後 neither too early nor too late, just in the nick of time.
先 世 previous generations; one's ancestors.
先 事 豫 備 preliminary preparations.
先 事 豫 防 to be prepared beforehand.
[5]先 事 防 止·的 方 法 precautionary methods.
先 今 then and now.
先 例 precedents.
先 偏 "I have already eaten,"—in reply to a question.

先 兆 an omen.
[10]先 入 爲 主 he who gets the first hearing has the best opportunity; preoccupied.
先 到 to arrive first.
先 到 先 得 first come, first served.
先 前 or 原 先 formerly.
先 取 得 權 preferential rights.
[15]先 史 人 prehistoric men.
先 史 期 prehistoric period.
先 占 occupation. (*legal*).
先 古 of old; in ancient times.
先 天 a good constitution; natural physical endowments; the former heaven, a technical Taoist term for the previous invisible existence of all things,—it is contrasted with 後 天 or latter heaven, which is used for the present state of existence; the arrangement of the *Eight Diagrams* 八 卦 by 伏 羲.
[20]先 天 不 足 a weak constitution.
先 容 to make an introduction for another.
先 導 predecessor; forerunner; to take the lead.

先 巳 having previously.

先 後 before and after; first and last; at various times; successive; to assist, as a minister of State.

25 先 後 矛 盾 contradictory; inconsistent. *See* 矛 No. 4570.

先 從 preliminary.

先 意 承 志 to anticipate and attend to the wishes of another.

先 支 an advance; to advance—payment, etc.

先 是 at first; before; prior to this.

30 先 時 or 先 日 or 先 年 or 先 期 before; previously; last time.

先 有 所 本 there must be an original.

先 期 聲 明 to give due notice.

先 機 foreboding; presage; premature.

先 民 the ancients.

35 先 決 判 決 preliminary decision.

先 烈 or 前 烈 our worthy predecessors; previous martyrs.

先 王 the ancient rulers.

先·生 teacher; sir; Mr.; a doctor.

先 生 饌 (the young) set the food before their elders.

40 先 發 to have a start of another.

先 發 制 人 he who makes the first start rules others.

先 發 後 聞 make arrangements first and afterwards report them to the prince.

先 知 *a priori* knowledge; to know beforehand; used for a prophet.

先 知 先 覺 的 men of foresight and vision.

45 先 祖 or 先 人 ancestors; forefathers.

先 秦 before the destruction of the books by *Ch'in Shih-huang*.

先 聖 Confucius.

先 聲 a harbinger; preliminary announcement.

先 聲 奪 人 his fame is sufficient to intimidate others.

50 革 命 的 先 聲 harbinger of the revolution.

先 行 antecedent.

先 行 其 言 而 後 從 之 he first acts, and then speaks according to his actions.

先 行 知 照 to give notice.

先 要 primary requirements.

55 先 見 anticipation; a sign; to foresee.

先 見 之 明 far-seeing; intelligent.

先 買 權 right of option.

先 賢 the ancient worthies.

先 走 一 步 go ahead a little.

60 先 路 one who has experience.

先 農 壇 Temple of Agriculture in Peiping. (Peking).

先 進 preceding; those who have gone before.

先 進 於 禮 樂 野 人 也 the former men are now judged to have been uncultivated persons as regards ceremonies and music.

先 達 an elder; one of a preceding generation; a scholar.

65 先 鋒 the vanguard of an army; thus:—a pioneer, forerunner, leader, etc.

先 頭 or 先 頭 裏 at the beginning.

先 馬 or 先 騙 a forerunner.

(a) Deceased.

先 君 or 先 父 or 先 考 or 先 子³ my late father.

先 嚴 先 慈 my late father and mother, respectively.

先 夫 my late husband.

先 妣 my late mother.

先 室 my late wife.

先 祖 my late grandfather.

(b) Read *hsien*⁴. To put first; to take preference.

先 之 勞 之 lead the people and work for them.

先 事 後 得 put your work itself first, and success in it afterwards.

先 己 後 人 put self first and others afterwards.

先 有 司 let the officials first deal with affairs.

(c) Transliterating, as in 先 令 shilling.

剃 ⁴ 2703

To castrate a fowl; also written 鐟 No. 5422.

剃 鷄 a capon.

筅 ³ 2704

Bamboo brush.

筅 帚 small bamboo brush or pot-scrubber.

(a) A halberd.

猥 筅 a halberd with long, bamboo handle.

跣 ³ 2705

Barefooted.

跣 足 barefooted.

徒 跣 to go barefooted.

銑 ³ 2706

A small chisel. Burnished, bright.

銑 鐵 cast iron.

(a) The two projecting rims at each side of the mouth of a Chinese bell.

鐘 口 兩 角 謂 之 銑 the two projecting sides of the mouth of a bell are called *sien*.

(b) Chilly and raw. Metal ornaments on a bow.

仙 僊 ¹ 2707

An immortal. a fairy, a genie.

仙 人 or 仙 師 or 仙 郎 or 仙 班 those who attain immortality by elimination of desire, etc.

仙 人 掌 a cactus; the prickly pear.

仙 人 跳 a confidence trick or scheme in which a woman is used as a decoy, and other such tricks.

仙 仗 insignia carried before the Emperor.

5 仙 境 Elysium; Fairyland.

仙 姑 or 仙 女 a fairy; an elf; one of the Eight Immortals of Taoism, who was a woman. *See below*—24.

仙 姿 light and graceful like a fairy.

仙 家 Taoists.

仙 才 extraordinary talent, said of *Li Po* the poet.

10 仙 景 beautiful scenery like Fairyland.

仙 法 magic.

仙 童 fairy messenger.

仙 筆 the pen of a genius or immortal, said of *Li Po* the poet.

仙藥 or 仙丹 the elixir of life.
15 仙遊 or 登仙 to become an immortal—to die.
仙釋 Taoism and Buddhism.
仙風道骨 a person having immortal characteristics, said of *Li Po* the poet.
仙馭升遐 to mount and ride away to Elysium—to die.
仙骨 having an immortal frame; light; graceful, fairy-like.
20 仙鶴 or 仙禽 the white crane.
仙鼠 bats.
人仙 human beings who have attained to immortality by asceticism, etc.
修仙 to strive to eliminate the grosser elements and become an immortal.
八仙 the Eight Worthies or Immortals of Taoism:—張果老, 鍾離權, 呂洞賓, 曹國舅, 李鐵拐, 韓湘子, 藍采和, 何仙姑,
25 八仙桌 table for eight persons, so named after the Eight Immortals of the Winecup.
半仙 a clever medium or fortune-teller.
天仙 celestial beings who have attained to purity.
水仙花 the narcissus.
神仙 fairies, e l v e s ; benignant spirits ; deified genii.

秈 粙 ¹
2708
Common rice, as distinguished from the glutinous variety or 糯米.

秈米 common rice.

翩 ¹
2709
To soar as a bird.

蹮 ¹
2710
To walk round and round.

銛 ²
2711
Sharp; acute.

銛利 keen-edged.
銛筆 a sharp pen—fig.

(a) A sort of spear for fishing.

(b) Read *t'ien*³ or *hsien*³. A kind of hoe. To take. To cut or hew.

暹 ¹
2712
The sun rising. To advance.

暹羅國 Siam, in imitation of the native word.

撏 ²
2713
To take. To pull out hair. To select.

撏撦 to pull out; to select and copy; to drag in.
撏撦細故 to drag in trifling objections.

涎 次 ²
2714
Spittle, saliva. Also read *nien*², *yen*², *ch'ien*².

涎沫 saliva.
口涎 mouth watering.
垂涎 water running from the mouth—fig., of intense desire for.
流涎 to have the mouth watering.

(a) Read *yen*⁴, *hsien*⁴. Appearance of water.

洒涎 water flowing.

羨 ⁴
2715
To covet; to long for; to admire.

羨人 to covet the things of others.
羨慕 to admire; to desire; to long for.
羨殺 desperate longing for.
羨門 a genii, said to have lived in ancient times.

(a) To praise.

稱羨 to praise and admire.
欽羨 to praise; to extol.

(b) A surplus.

羨偹 or 奇 (*chi*¹) 羨 a surplus.
以羨補不足 to make the surplus of one supply the deficiency of another.
有羨 ample; more than enough.

鮮 魚 鱻 ¹
2716
Fresh, as flowers, fruit, etc., just killed, as meat, etc. New. Delicious.

鮮味 a nice, fresh flavour.
鮮明 new, fresh.
鮮明貨物 brand-new goods.
鮮湛湛的 perfectly fresh.
5 鮮甜 very sweet.
鮮紅 bright red.
鮮肉 fresh meat.
鮮花 freshly-cut flowers.
鮮菓子 fresh fruit, as contrasted with dried or preserved fruits.
10 鮮血 fresh blood.
鮮衣 new clothes.
鮮食 fresh food.
鮮魚 fresh fish.
海鮮 fresh marine-fish.

(a) A Tartar tribe.

鮮卑 a tribe which occupied S. E. Mongolia; it was a branch of the 東胡 which took its name from a mountain in that region. Another branch belongs to the Coreans 朝鮮.

(b) Read *hsien*³. Rare, few, seldom.

鮮乏 impoverished, not sufficient.
鮮少 very few.
鮮探其奇 rarely investigate its curiosities.
鮮矣仁 seldom associated with true virtue.
鮮覯 seldom seen.

癬 ³
2717
Ringworm. U s e d f o r various diseases of the skin. Pron. *hsiian*¹.

環癬 ringworm.
疥癬 itch and ringworm—annoyances.
腰帶癬 herpes zoster, shingles.

蘚 ³
2718
Mosses on damp walls.

蘚帽 calytra of mosses, etc.
蘚書 lichens growing on rocks and forming into the appearance of letters.
蘚斑 patches of lichen.
蘚痕 a moss scar—traces, vestiges.
苔蘚 moss, lichen.

燹 [3]
2719　A fire.　Also read *hsi*[4].

兵燹 ravages and burning committed by soldiers.

孅 [1]
2720　Slender, sharp-pointed; thus:—cunning and artful. Inter. next.

孅介之事 a trifling matter.
孅弱 slight and delicate.
孅悉 intelligent.
孅趨 artful; cunning.

纖 [1]
2721　Small, fine, delicate. Inter. preceding.

纖人 a delicate person.
纖介 minute; the least.
纖兒[2] a small child.
纖妍 slender and handsome.
[5]纖小 small, weak.
纖屑 vexatious; paltry.
纖巧 slender; delicate, fine work.
纖弱 fine and delicate.
纖手 (or 指) slender fingers or hand of a woman.
[10]纖條 slender—as twigs.
纖毛 cilia.
纖毛蟲 infusoria.
纖毫 very little; minute.
纖疵 slight faults.
[15]纖維 fibre; cellulose.
纖纖 fine, s l e n d e r, delicately formed.
纖腰瘦項 slender waist and delicately formed neck.
纖鉅 small and great.

(a) Fine silk embroidery. Fine silk with black woof and white warp.

(b) Niggardly.

纖悋 niggardly.

(c) Read *chien*[1]. To prick. u.f. 殲 No. 864.

其刑罪則纖剸 (*chuan*[1]) their punishment was mutilation and dismemberment.

獮 [3]
2722　To hunt. To kill. Autumn hunting of ancient emperors.

獮田 to hunt.
獮薙 to exterminate.

線 [4]
綫
2723　Thread; cotton; wire. Distinguish 綿 No. 4506.

線步 stitches.
線綢 corded silk.
線縷 hemp; unspun thread.
線脚 stitches.
[5]線花 cotton for spinning.
線蟲 thread-worms; nematodes.
線路 a narrow path.
線輪 electric coil.
線香 slender sticks of incense.
[10]線麻 flax; hemp; ramie fibre.
紡線 to spin thread.
絲線 silk thread.
針線 needlework.
鐵線 iron wire.

(a) A line. A clue. A fuse. Length.

線人 a spy.
線索 a clue.
一線之光 one ray of light.
一線之望 one thread of hope.
[5]一線之路 only one way.
作線 to play the spy.
光線 rays of light.
八線 trigonometry. = 三角[2.3]
單線雙線 single and double lines respectively.
[10]地平線 the horizon.
射線 line of fire. A.c. 火線.
導火線 a fuse.
平行線 parallel lines.
幹線支線 main line and branch lines respectively.
[15]底線 base-line.
曲線 a curved line.
測鉛線 lead-line for sounding.
界線 boundary-line; division; difference. 防(禦)線 defense line.
直線 a straight line.
[20]航線 sea-routes.
邊線 frontier-line.
電線 telegraph or telephone lines.
前線 the front. A.c. 戰線,陣線.

腺 [4]
2724　A gland.

腺細胞 gland cells.

霰 [4]
霓
2725　Sleet.

霰雪 sleet.

HSIN.　(ㄒㄧㄣ)

昕 [1]
2726　Early morning. Daylight.

昕夕從公 morning and night busy with public business.

欣 [1]
忻
2727　Joy, delight; happy.

欣企 pleasurable expectations.
欣厭兩具非 neither moved to pleasure nor loathing.
欣喜 or 歡欣 or 欣義 or 欣悅 to rejoice; pleased.
欣待 to welcome with pleasure.
[5]欣從 joyfully to comply with.
欣悉 or 欣審 am glad to learn that....
欣愉 exceedingly pleased.
欣感 gratified.
欣想 pleasurable memories.
[10]欣慰 satisfied; comforted; contented.
欣嘉 to admire; to be pleased with.
欣暢 or 欣快 elated; happy.
欣服高義 joyfully to respect his high ideals.
欣欣向榮 j o y o u s reviving—after drought.
[15]欣欣然 with pleasure; joyfully.
欣歎 or 欣讚 deep admiration of.
欣瞻 to regard with feelings of pleasure.
欣賞 to delight in; to find pleasure in—as literature, studies, etc., appreciation.
欣賞善之價值 appreciate the value of goodness.
[20]欣躍 dancing with glee.
欣願 delighted to....
上下欣嘉 all approved and were glad.

訢 [1]
2728　Joy and pleasure. Inter. preceding.

訢戴 pleased to honour him.
訢然 joyful; cheerful.
天下訢訢 the whole empire is pleased. *See below*—B.

(a) Read *hsi*[1]. Vapour rising from the earth.

天 地 訢 合 the breath (or influence) of earth and heaven mingle (in music).

(b) Read *yin*[2]. Respectful.

訢 訢 如 也 attentive and respectful.

歆 [1] To accept the fragrance of sacrifice.
2729

歆 享 to be pleased with—as an offering.

歆 響 grateful odours.

上 帝 居 歆 God is well pleased with the sweet savour.

(a) To quicken.

履 帝 武 敏 歆 she trod in the great footprint and conceived. (footprint of God. *Giles*).

(b) To like.

歆 羡 to desire; to long for.

焮 1.4.
2730   Flames, fire. To heat.

焮 天 heat; intense fire, scorching the heavens.

(a) Swelling, inflammation.

焮 腫 swelling.

廞 [1] To prepare horses and chariots for battle before
2731 going out. To begin the music. To stop up.

鑫 [1] A character not in *K'anghsi*
2732 —used in names.

胂 [4]
痻   Erysipelas. Sloughing
2733   of an ulcer.

釁 [4]
衅   To offer blood in sacri-
2734 fice; to smear sacrificial vessels with blood.

釁 鐘 to consecrate a bell with the blood of a victim—an ox.

釁 鼓 to consecrate a drum before going into battle.

(a) To anoint oneself for worship. To embalm.

釁 浴 to bathe and anoint with fragrant essences—before worship.

釁 面 to smear the face; to blacken the face.

釁 鬯 to anoint a body with fragrant wine.

(b) A rift, cause of quarrel; a grievance; a wrong.

釁 瑕 a defect; cause of offence.

釁 端 an offence; an occasion for variance; an act of violence.

釁 隙 a pretext for strife.

尋 釁 to seek a quarrel.

起 釁 the beginnings of a quarrel; to begin strife.

開 釁 to commence hostilities.

HSIN. SIN.   (ㄙㄣ)

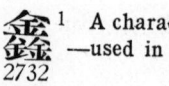
2735

The heart. The moral nature, the mind, the affections. Intention.

心 上 人 a lover; a great friend.

心 不 在 absent-minded.

心 不 在 焉 inattentive; the mind running on other things.

心 不 屬 the heart is not in the matter.   [plaining.

[5] 心 不 平 disquieted, anxious; com-

心 不 正 a depraved mind.

心 不 死 not *dead* to anything—the intention still holds good.

心 中 保 留 mental reservation.

心 中 態 度 mental attitude.

[10] 心 中 無 物 a heart free from the control of outward things.

心 之 全 體 大 用 the mind in its entire substance and relation to things.

心 之 用 the action of the mental powers.

心 之 體 the mental constitution.

心 亂 confused in mind.

[15] 心 事 matters of the mind; cares; concerns.

心 傳 a secret passed on by a teacher.

心 全 於 中 形 全 於 外 when the heart is right within, the manifestation of the heart is right without. "As a man thinketh in his heart so is he."

心 力 mentality; vigor of mind.

心 動 to move the mind; agitated; nervous; to start thinking.

[20] 心 勞 mental labour.

心 匠 planned out in the heart, as a workman plies his trade.

心 化 to influence and change the heart.

心 印 the heart's seal—the swastika on the heart of Buddha.

心 口 疼 heartburn; pain at the pit of the stomach.

[25] 心 口 相 應 plain spoken; to say what one thinks.

心 向 inclination.

心 君 the heart as the ruler of the whole body.

心 喪 三 年 the heart mourns for the period of three years,—even if there were no outward signs of mourning.

心 囊 the pericardium.

[30] 心 囊 炎 pericarditis.

心 地 or 心 田 the moral nature; motive.

心 地 不 亂 undisturbed in heart; presence of mind.

心 地 光 明 purehearted; open-minded.

心 地 性 王 in the region of the mind, the disposition is ruler.

[35] 心 地 齷 齪 having a dirty mind; impure motives.

心 坎 or 心 口 or 心 窩 the pit of the stomach; the recesses of the mind.

心 .... 塞 滿 deep feeling; a full heart.

心 境 (or 景) moods.

心 塵 the dust of the heart—impurities of the mind.

[40] 心 多 capricious; suspicious.

心 如 刀 扎 pierced to the heart; extremely painful.

心 如 懸 鐘 the heart is like a bell suspended (in an empty hall).

心 如 旋 磨 驢 my heart is like an ass turning a millstone—anxiously turning a matter over in the mind.

心 如 虎 面 如 豺 heart like a tiger and face like a wolf—

smiling and treacherous, a wolf being said to smile on seeing a man.

[45]心安無夢 a heart at rest has no dreams—to disturb it.

心安理得 my conscience is void of offence.

心定 the mind at rest; calm; cool.

心定自然涼 if the mind is settled one naturally will be cool.

心寒毛豎 the heart shudders and the hair stands on end—from fear.

[50]心寒膽怯 shuddering and fearful.

心巧 clever; smart.

心府 the inner treasury of the heart.

心底 the bottom of the heart; one's intentions.

心廣體胖 a liberal mind and a well-nourished body.

[55]心強命不強 his will is strong but his destiny is against him.

心形 cardiform; heart-shaped.

心得 that which one gains—as from intense study or long practice.

沒有心得 have got nothing out of it.

心心懷念 or 心心念念 constantly thinking of; persevering; set on doing.

[60]心心相印 our opinions exactly tally.

心志 the will; determination.

心怯 fearful; timid.

心性 disposition; temper; moral nature.

心·思 thoughts; opinions; anxieties.

[65]心·思才力 intellectual faculties.

心恨 animosity.

心悸 nervous; palpitating heart.

心情 affection; mood.

心感 very grateful.

[70]心意 ideas; aims.

心慌 flurried; confused; nervous.

心懷意念 thoughts and intents of the heart; heart and mind.

心裁 mental decision.

心戰 mental conflict; double-minded; indecision.

[75]心房 or 心室 ventricles.

心房大 dilation of the heart.

心手相應 mind and hand in accord.

心折 extremely partial to.

心散 a distracted heart or mind.

[80]心旌 heart fluttering like a flag.

心旨 determination.

心曲 the complexities of the mental processes.

心有餘力不足 more than willing but lacking power.

心服情願 heartily willing.

[85]心機 expedients; powers of the mind; anxiety; trouble.

心正不怕影邪 a man whose heart is upright does not fear what others may say.

心死·了 dead to a thing; indifferent to it.

心氣 mind; disposition; temper.

心滿意足 mind and heart perfectly satisfied; self-confident.

[90]心火 enthusiasm or anger.

心灰意冷 discouraged; dispirited.

心灰意懶 utterly despondent.

心焦 worried; vexed.

心焦·起·來 to begin to worry.

[95]心照 quick of apprehension; to anticipate the wishes of another.

心煩意亂 restless and disquieted.

心狠性悍 fierce and obstreperous.

心猿意馬 the heart of an ape and the mind of a horse—restless and unsettled.

心理 bent of mind; taste; inclination.

[100]心理上 mental; mentally.

心理作用 mental action; function of the mind; auto-suggestion.

心理學 psychology; mental philosophy.

應用(的)心理學 applied psychology.

普通(的)心理學 general psychology.

[105] 構造(的)心理學 structural psychology.

機能(的)心理學 functional psychology.

生理(的)心理學 psycho-physiology.

行·爲 (or 動·作) 心理學 behaviour psychology.

變態(的)心理學 abnormal psychology.

[110]心理學之趨勢 psychological tendencies.

心理廣度 mental span.

心理狀態 mentality.

心理現象 psychic phenomena.

心理發育律 laws of mental development.

[115]心理能力 mental power or ability.

心理零點 point of mental indifference.

心略 plans and devices of the mind.

心理病態 morbid state of mind.

心病(症) heart-disease. 心病 sick conscience.

[120]心病難醫 "Who can minister to a mind diseased?"

心癢 itching heart—intense desires.

心目中 in the mind's eye.

心盲 mental or psychic blindness.

心直口快 blunt and outspoken, but honest.

[125]心直·的人 a straightforward man.

心眼 disposition; character; eyes of the mind; the heart's core; holes of intelligence supposed to be in the heart.

心眼儿不通 holes of the heart blocked—unintelligent, stupid.

心知 to be aware.

心神 mind; mentality.

[130]心神不定 a restless mind; a changeable spirit; not quite sane.

心神惝恍 perturbed in spirit; flurried; absent-minded.

心竅 the intellect; powers of understanding; comprehension—said to be holes in the heart which give intelligence.

心算 mental arithmetic.

心·緒 sequence of thought; thoughts; state of mind.

[135]心耳 auricles.

心聾 mental or psychic deafness.

心肝 heart and liver—sweetheart, from a writing of T'ang dynasty.

心胸 heart, mind, will.

心脈 pulsations of the blood.

[140]心能 faculty.

心膂 a confidential assistant or minister.

心·腸 the affections; sympathies.

心腹 confidential; secret; sympathetic.

心腹友 bosom-friend.

[145]心腹腎腸 the inner man—internal organs.

心腹話 confidential talk.

(organ).

心 臟 endocardium; the heart

心 臟 瓣 valves of the heart.

心 花 開 the heart blossoming, i.e., expectations realized.

150 心 若 寒 灰 heart like cold ashes —hopeless and apathetic.

心 若 懸 天 地 之 間 as if the heart were suspended between heaven and earth.

心 若 湯 my heart is poured out like water—of extreme agitation.

心 蕩 unable to control the emotions.

心 藥 stimulants; tonics.

155 心 虛 afraid; agitated lest a matter be found out; undogmatic.

心 血 來 潮 suddenly to think of a thing; to come to a sudden comprehension of any matter.

心 行 性 生 when the mind moves the nature is revealed.

心 術 devices of the mind; plans and schemes.

心 術 壞 evil in heart.

160 心 裏 or 心 內 or 心 中 or 心 上 at heart; in the mind.

心·裏 不 安 disquieted; ill at ease.

心·裏 想 to think; to be of opinion.

心·裏 明·白 clear-minded; intelligent.

心·裏 難 過 distressed in mind.

165 心·裏 萬 分 難 過 very deeply distressed in heart.

心 解 力 行 he opens his heart and exerts his strength.

學 不 心 解 則 忘 之 易 what is studied without mental elucidation is easily forgotten.

心 計 clever schemes; plans, etc.

心 許 pleased; elated; mental agreement.

170 心 象 mental image.

心 跳 pulsations; palpitations; fearful and apprehensive.

心 軟 tender-hearted; lenient; credulous.

心 迹 frame of mind; intentions.

心 迷 captivated.

175 心 酸 to feel sick at heart, from grief.

心 醉 infatuated with; intoxicated with.

心 靈 natural intelligence; mentality; also u.f., the soul.

心 靈 論 psychism; immaterialism; spiritualism.

心 非 false at heart.

180 心 韻 the rhythm of the heart.

心 領 my heart receives it—phrase used when declining an invitation or a present.

心 頭 or 心 胸 the heart or mind.

心 頭 恨 concealed animosity.

心 頭 肉 a person greatly beloved.

185 心 願 wish; desire; aspiration.

心 饜 珍 饈 the mind set on good living; gluttonous.

心 驕 氣 傲 haughty; arrogant.

心 驚 膽 戰 palpitating with fear or anxiety.

心 高 ambitious.

190 心 魂 遠 相 隨 my spirit followed you afar.

一 心 with undivided heart. [mind.

回 心 to repent; to change one's

存 心 one's frame of mind; a disposition; intentionally.

放 心 to rest assured.

195 有 心 intentionally; cheerfully.

本 心 one's original intention.

無 心 unintentionally.

無 心 是 道 to be without thought is wisdom. [fully.

用 心 to apply the mind to, care-

200 留 心 to keep in mind; to take care.

當 心 or 小 心 be careful; take care; with care.

自 心 是 佛 your own mind is Buddha.

良·心 conscience; goodness of heart.

(a) The centre or middle. Generally a suffix.

中 心 點 the central point.

向 心 centripetal.

地 心 the centre of the earth.

手 心 the palm of the hand.

5 江 心 the middle of a river.

空 心 empty; hollow.

通 心 tubular; hollow.

離 心 centrifugal.

芯[1]
2736

Lamp pith or 燈 芯 草.

新[1]
2737

New, recent. Fresh. Distinguish 親 No. 1107.

新 世 界 the New World.

新 交 a new friend.

新 人 bride or bridegroom.

新 人 生 觀 new viewpoint of life.

5 新 任 a new incumbent; newly appointed.

新 修 recently repaired.

新 兵 recruits.

新 出 版 new publications.

新 刻 newly issued.

10 新 制 new regime.

新 劇 modern-style play.

新 加 坡 Singapore.

新 國 民 citizens of the New Republic.

新 大 陸 the new continent—America.

15 新 奇 novel; extraordinary.

新 娘 or 新 婦 a bride.

新 婚 旅 行 a wedding-trip.

新 學 new style of learning; first beginnings of study.

新 學 理 new theories or doctrines.

20 新 客 newcomers (among the Chinese immigrants in the Straits Settlements.)

新 局 a new arrangement; new era.

新 局 面 new aspect of affairs.

新 布 new cloth.

新 年 or 新 喜 or 新 春 the new-year.

25 新 式 new pattern or type; new style; recent fashions.

新 式 標 點 modern punctuation.

新 式 的 國 家 a modern nation.

新 式 電 碼 new telegraph-code.

新 思 潮 new tide of ideas; new thought; renaissance.

30 新 房 bride-chamber.

新 手 a new hand; raw, inexperienced; newcomer.

新 授 designate—of official appointments.

新 故 交 接 the meeting of old and new—as on the last day of the year.

新 教 Protestantism (as opposed to Roman Catholicism.)

35 新 文 化 modern culture.

新 文 化 運 動 movement towards modern culture.

新 方 面 a new aspect.

新 曆 the new calendar or solar calendar.

新 月 new moon.

40 新 村 a modern village.

新 柔 young and tender—of vegetation.

新 樣 new style or pattern.

新 正[1] the first month of the year.

新 民 to renew the people.

45 新 法 recent methods; improved processes.

新 派 new school; modernists.

新 派 學 說 modernism.

新 潮 renaissance.

新 潮 流 new movements.

50 新。疆 or 新 土 the new frontier —Chinese Turkestan.

新 發 展 new or recent developments.

新 發 明 new discoveries, (in the sense of invention.)

新 禧 new-year congratulations.

新 竹 young bamboos.

55 新 節 the new-year—the 15th of the lst lunar month.

新 節·目 new features; new items.

新 紀 元 a new era.

新 約 The New Testament.

新 組 織 newly organized.

60 新 義 new interpretation.

新 聞 news; intelligence.

新 聞 學 journalism.

新 聞 招 待 處 Press Gallery.

65 新 聞 界 the press.

新 聞 紙 (or 報) newspapers.

新 聞 記 者 reporters for the press.

新 腔 舊 調 old and new tunes.

新 舊 old and new.

70 新。色[4] new styles, etc.

新 西 蘭 New Zealand.

新 要·求 new demands.

新 親 newly related—as by marriage.

新 近 or 新 來 near to; adjacent; recent.

75 新 造 new creation; recently constructed.

新 進 succeeding, as contrasted with preceding.

新 都 市 modern cities.

新 郎 or 新 女·壻 or 新 姑 爺 a bridegroom.

新 金 山 a name for Australia.

80 新 關 the Maritime Customs.

新 陳 代 謝 assimilation of the new and excretion of the old.

新 需 recent requirements.

新 體 new forms—especially of literature, etc.

新 體 詩 new style of free verse.

85 新 鬼 a newly-deceased person.

新·鮮 fresh.

出 新 to renew; to renovate.

從 新 再 作 do it over again.

日 新 daily renewal or reformation.

90 自 新 self-improvement; reformation.

重 (ch'ung[2]) 新 anew, over again.

(a) To gather fuel, see the next.

薪[1] Fuel; firewood.
2738

薪 俸 salary.

薪 傳 handed down from teacher to pupil.

薪 工 wages—of servants.

薪 木 or 柴 薪 firewood.

5 薪 桂 米 珠 firing (as dear as) cassia and rice (as dear as) pearls —of the high cost of living.

薪。水 firing and water—used for salary of teachers, etc.

薪 炭 charred remnants of wood.

薪 燎 fuel gathered for use at the ancient sacrifices.

薪 米 爲 憂 anxiety regarding food and firing.

10 薪 者 a wood-cutter.

薪 芻 益 高 the price of fuel still continued to rise.

薪 草 grass for fuel.

薪 蘇 or 薪 樵 grass or wood for firing—formerly used at night for lighting.

薪 費 payment for services rendered.

15 抽 薪 to withdraw the fuel—also used fig.

束 薪 faggots.

火·上 加 薪 adding fuel to the fire.

負 薪 to carry faggots on the back.

辛[1] Bitter, acrid; from which comes the idea of distressing,
2739 toilsome, grievous. Radical 160. Distinguish 幸 No. 2764.

辛 勞 exertions; trouble.

辛 勤 industry; toil.

辛 味 acrid; bitter.

辛 夷 or 辛 雉 *Magnolia kobus.* A deciduous flowering tree.

5 辛 楚 bitterness and sorrow.

辛 痛 painful and distressing.

辛 盤 a plate of bitter things— garlic, onions, shallots and other things, once eaten to welcome the new-year.

辛 艱 toil and difficulty—used of a hard mountain-climb.

辛 芥 a small kind of rape-turnip.

10 辛·苦 tired; suffering; hardship. "You have put yourself out for me."

辛 螫 a painful sting.

辛 辣 pungent; peppery.

辛 酸 grievous; disappointing.

辛 金 or 辛 俸 or 辛 工 workmen's wages; pay.

喫 辛 受 苦 to endure hardship and toil.

(a) The 8th of the *Heavenly Stems* 天 干.

辛 亥 之 役 or 辛 亥 革 命 the revolution of the *Hsin-hai* year, i.e., 1911.

莘[1] A marshy plant, known as
莘 細 辛, or *asarum*, a name
2740 derived from the bitterness of the root which is used in medicine.

(a) Long and straggling. Numerous.

有 莘 其 尾 "showing their long tails," said of fishes.

俎 豆 莘 莘 the dishes and plates were numerous.

鋅[1] Zinc.
2741

氧 化 鋅 zinc oxide.

鋅 板 sheet-zinc.

鋅 版 zinc blocks for printing.

鋅 腐 蝕 版 zinc etching.

鋅 華 (or 白) zinc white; zinc oxide.

硫 酸 鋅 zinc sulphate.

(a) Read *tzŭ*[3]. Hard.

鐔[2] A sword-blade. Knob on the guard of a sword. Also
2742 read *t'an*[2]. A surname.

鑐[2] A caldron or boiler.
2743

尋 [2] To investigate; to search for; to seek.
2744 Pron. *hsün*[2] exc. (d).

尋 不 着 or 尋 不 見 unable to find.

尋 事 to seek an occasion for meddling; to look for employment.

尋 仇 or 尋 隙 to seek a quarrel; to take the offensive.

尋 出 to find out.

[5]尋 味 to go into the niceties of a thing—as literature, etc.

尋 問 to make inquiries about.

尋 奪 to seek for and seize.

尋 幽 to investigate abstruse theories; to seek for a place of retirement from public life.

尋 思 or 尋 想 to ponder; to consider.

[10]尋 情 to request a favour.

尋 找 or 尋 覓 to seek; to look for.

尋 探 to search for; to seek after.

尋 東 西 to look for a thing.

尋 查 or 尋 察 to investigate things thoroughly; to look into; to examine.

[15]尋 根 究 底 to make a thorough investigation; to sift a matter to the bottom.

尋 樂 to seek for pleasure; to amuse oneself.

尋 死 to commit, or attempt to commit, suicide.

尋 求 to seek after; to entreat.

尋 究 to follow up; to search into.

[20]尋 章 摘 句 老 雕 蟲 the old pedant (lit., carver of insects) cares only for punctuating texts.

尋 索 to demand.

尋 緝 to seek for and arrest.

尋 繹 to investigate abstruse theories.

尋 花 問 柳 to seek flowers and amuse onself with the willows —to frequent the company of harlots.

[25]尋 見 found; to find.

尋 討 to worry; to make trouble.

尋 訪 to make inquiries about.

尋 路 to find the way; to seek the way.

尋 香 to seek the company of women.

[30]自 尋 煩 惱 to bring trouble upon oneself.

(a) A measure of 8ft. Chinese, whence comes the idea of commonly, usual, ordinary.

尋 丈 length, measurement.

尋 常 ordinary; commonplace; routine.

尋 常 咫 尺 measurement; a 常 is equal to two 尋, thus it means measured, regular; ordinary.

尋 常 慣 例 precedent; normal methods.

尋 引 a measuring instrument used in building.

尋 矩 a rule; a measure.

(b) To renew.

尋 盟 to renew a covenant.

(c) Subsequently.

尋 爲 商 賈 subsequently they became traders.

尋 至 subsequently arrived.

(d) Pron. *hsin*[2]. To ask for (trifles, as salt, matches, etc.)

潯 [2] A steep bank by the deep stream. A river near Kiukiang. Also read *hsün*[2].
2745

潯 關 Kiukiang Customs.

潯 陽 Kiukiang.

燖 [2] To warm up food. To scald, to boil. Also read *ch'in*[2].
2746

燖 溫 to warm up.

燖 毛 to scald off the hair—as of pigs.

鱘 [2] The sturgeon. Also read *hsün*[2].
2747

信 [4] To believe in; to trust. Truth, sincerity, confidence. A pledge or token.
2748

信 之 則 有 if you believe it, it is so!

信 乎 is it true?

信 人 a man of sincerity; to believe in another.

信 仰 belief; trust.

[5]信 仰 之 遺 傳 traditional beliefs.

信 任 to trust; to accredit.

信 任 投 票 vote of confidence.

信 士 a Buddhist disciple.

信 奉 to believe and serve.

[10]信 女 female Buddhist disciple.

信 守 to keep faithfully.

↑信 仰 自 由 freedom of faith.

信 實 trustworthy.

信 徒 a disciple, a believer.

信 從 to follow; to believe and obey.

[15]信 德 faith; sincerity.

信 心 faith.

信 念 faith, confidence.

信 據 a guarantee.

信 敎 religious belief.

[20]信 敎 自 由 religious toleration.

信 服 to trust; to accept in faith.

信 條 a creed; statement of belief.

信 然 it is true indeed.

信 物 a pledge.

[25]信·用 credit.

信·用 借 欵 fiduciary loan; open credit.

信·用 匯 兌 blank credit.

信·用 單 bill of credit.

信·用 往 來 credit in business.

[30]信·用 昭 著 their credit is good.

信·用 破 壞 了 their credit is lost; cannot get credit.

信·用 票 bills drawn on a letter of credit.

信·用 證 券 trust bonds.

信·用 證 書 trust deed.

[35]信·用 買·賣 credit sale or business.

信·用 透 支 credit facilities.

國 家 信·用 national credit.

對 人 信·用 personal credit.

信 眞 belief; credence.

[40]信 約 a covenant.

信 經 a confession of faith.

信 義 "justification by faith,"—used as a prefix by some Lutherans.

信 義 會 Norwegian Lutheran Mission.

信 行 verified; approved.

[45]信 行 君 子 a man of honour.

信 衣 Buddhist robes.

信 託 credit; to entrust to; a business agency.

信 託 公 司 trustee company.

信 託 業 trust business.

[50]信 託 權 利 power conferred by trust.

信 託 物 a trust; goods entrusted to another.

信 託 者 a trustee.

信 託 證 書 trust deed.

信 託 財 產 trust estate.

[55]信 近 於 義 言 可 復 也 if agreements are made in accordance with what is right, the words spoken can be made good.

信靠 or 信準 to believe and trust in.

信驗 experience.

不信 incredible; to doubt.

可信 credible; worthy of belief.

⁶⁰失信 to break faith.

相信 mutual confidence.

背信 to go back on one's word.

自信 self-confidence.

輕信·的 credulous.

(a) A letter, a token of confidence. An envoy. News. Symptoms. Indications.

信使 an envoy; a faithful messenger.

信函 or 書信 a letter.

信天翁 the albatross.

信局 a post office.

⁵信差 a postman; a courier. (-ch'ai¹)

信·息 news; intelligence.

信挾 a letter-clip.

信札 a note, a letter.

信片 a postcard. = 4534.2.

¹⁰信砲 a signal-gun.

信票 postage stamps; a warrant to arrest.

信稿 draft of a letter.

信筒 or 信封 or 信皮 or 信套 an envelope—the first also means a pillar-box.

信箱 letter-box.

¹⁵信簿 a chit-book.

信紙 or 信箋 letter-paper; note-paper.

信號 signals.

信袋 mail-bag.

信風 prevalent winds of various seasons, monsoons; a poetical fancy gives names to the winds according to the flowers which blossom at the periods.

²⁰印信 impression of a seal.

口信 verbal message.

安信 a home-letter.

密信 private letter.

快信 express-letter.

²⁵掛號信 registered letter.

送信 to deliver a letter; to take a message.

通信 news-letter from any place.

通信員記者 news correspondent.

(b) Free, easy, aimless.

信口胡扯 to talk at random.

信口說 to say whatever comes into one's mind.

信步行 or 信脚走 aimless wandering; sauntering.

信筆寫 to dash off a piece of writing without hesitation or premeditation.

(c) To stay for two nights.

信宿 to stay over two nights.

有客信信 the honourable guest will stay twice two nights.

(d) Arsenic.

信石 arsenic.

(e) Read shen¹. u.f. 伸 No. 5713. To stretch out.

不我信兮 "we cannot make good—our word."

屈而不信 (his finger) was bent and could not be straightened.

(f) Read shen¹. u.f. 身. A figure.

信圭 a token held by a 侯—it was about 7 inches in length and ornamented by having a human figure engraved on it.

汛 ⁴ A military post. To guard.
2749 Pron. hsün⁴. The titles given below are obsolete. Distinguish 汎 No. 1773.

汛兵 the police.

汛地 or 汛所 a guard-station.

汛城 to guard a city.

汛官 police officials of a District.

汛弁 petty officials—local.

(a) To sprinkle water.

汛掃 to sprinkle and sweep.

(b) High water. Menses.

秋汛 or 春汛 autumn and spring floods.

訊 ⁴ To make judicial investiga-
2750 tion. To inquire into. To announce to. To admonish. Pron. hsün⁴.

訊供 oral testimony at a trial; evidence.

訊取 to extort evidence.

訊問 to interrogate judicially.

訊據 according to the evidence.

⁵訊明 to try; to investigate.

訊案 or 審訊 to hear a case; to examine.

訊檢 to make an investigation.

訊結 the close of an investigation.

訊認 to admit on examination.

¹⁰訊辦 or 訊理 to hear and deal with a case.

訊鞫 to take depositions.

刑訊 to examine with the torture; to compel evidence.

堂訊 to hear in open court.

執訊 to arrest and interrogate.

¹⁵音訊 news, information.

迅 ⁴ Quick, swift. Pron.
2751 hsün¹.

迅即 immediately.

迅捷 prompt.

迅步追踪 make haste and follow him.

迅流 a rapid current.

⁵迅疾 swiftly; promptly.

迅羽 swift as an eagle.

迅走 to hasten.

迅速 fleet; quickly.

迅逝如飛 to fly past.

¹⁰迅邁 swiftly passing—of time.

迅雷 quick as thunder; a sudden clap of thunder.

迅雷不及掩耳 as swift as a clap of thunder which gives no time to cover the ears.

迅風 a smart breeze.

凶 ⁴
顖 The top of the head.
顦 The skull.
2752

凶帽 the common skull-cap of the Chinese.

凶門 the fontanel on a baby's head.

HSING. (ㄒㄧㄥ)

興 ¹ To prosper. To begin.
凼 To increase; to rise; to
2753 raise. Flourishing. Distinguish 輿 No. 7615.

興作 to begin a piece of work.

興修 to repair; to construct.

興兵 or 興戎 to begin military operations.

興利除弊 to promote that which is profitable and abolish that which is evil.

5 興 動 to act; to begin to move.

興 嗟 to give a sigh or groan.

興 奮 to stimulate; to rouse to effort. *See below*—A.2.

興 奮 劑 stimulants.

興 家 立 業 to prosper; to establish a competency.

10 興 寢 "downsittings and uprisings."

興 居 motion and rest:—state, condition, circumstances.

興 居 納 福 may you be happy under all circumstances.

興 工 to commence work.

興 市 政 promote municipal government.

15 興 師 to mobilize troops.

興 建 to re-establish; reconstruction.

興 復 to revive.

興 敗 or 興 亡 or 興 衰 prosperity and adversity; success and failure; vicissitudes.

興 旺 or 興 隆 prosperity; to flourish; to prosper; to increase.

20 興 替 or 興 亡 rise and fall—as of a State.

興 業 公 司 a syndicate.

興 業 銀 行 Industrial Bank.

興 滅 繼 絕 to revive the extinguished States, and restore families whose line of succession had been cut off,—to rise from its ashes.

興 發 to multiply; to issue.

25 興 盛 to increase prosperity.

興 積 to collect together.

興 立 to stand up.

興 訟 to commence litigation.

興 走 to prosper; to flourish.

30 興 起 to raise; to begin; to rise.

興 起 來 to begin to flourish.

興 辦 to put into effective operation.

興 雨 beginning to rain.

興 革 to promote the new and do away with the old.

35 新 興 a new vogue.

時 興 fashionable.

(a) Read *hsing*⁴. Joyful, merry, elated. Passion, appetite.

興 味 interest; pleasure.

興 奮 exuberance of spirits; excitement. *See above*—7.

興 會 pleasure.

興 致 pleasure; high spirits; glee.

5 興 致 減 少 了 the pleasure was taken out of it.

興 趣 merriment; pleasure; interest.

興 酣 exhilarated.

興 頭 joyful; merry; bustling.

興 高 采 烈 full of spirits and elated; in high spirits.

10 乘 興 take advantage of the enthusiasm, etc., of the moment.

掃 興 dispirited; to take all the exhilaration out of.

敗 興 to spoil one's pleasure; to take the joy out of a thing.

沒² 興 lack of enthusiasm.

起 興 the rising of sexual desire.

15 高 興 exhilarated; in good spirits; merry; glad to.

行²
2754 Originally the character represented the picture of a crossroad. To walk, to do, to act, to travel. Radical 144.

行 三 軍 則 誰 與 if you had to control three armies, whom would you have with you?

行 不 去 or 不 行 this will not do! it can't be done!

行 不 履 閾 in walking he did not tread on the threshold.

行 不 行 will it do or not? is it practicable? can you do it or not?

5 行 不 由 徑 do not take short cuts.

行 主 one in charge of a travelling party.

行 事 to act.

行 事 為 人 conduct, behaviour, "walk."

行 交 to forward to.

10 行 人 a traveller; official in charge of travelling envoys under *Chou* dynasty.

行 人 子 羽 修 飾 之 *Tzŭ Yü*, the official in charge of foreign intercourse, corrected and polished it.

行 人 情 to send a complimentary present.

行 仁 to live a life of kindness and goodness.

行 令 to issue orders to underofficers; to impose a forfeit in wine-drinking.

15 行 使 to employ; to use; to exercise functions, etc.

行 使 公 權 to act in accord with civic rights.

行 侶 or 行 伴 travelling-companions.

行 像 to carry an idol in procession.

行 具 travelling-requisites.

20 行 准 to receive a despatch.

行 刑 or 動 刑 to administer punishment.

行 刑 場 execution-ground.

行 刺 to assassinate.

行 刺 不 遂 failure of an attempted assassination.

25 行 動 deportment; bearing; to journey—of the Emperor.

行 動 自 由 liberty of action.

行 千 步 to walk a thousand steps —to walk to and fro.

行 吟 to hum or chant while walking.

行 了 that will do! fine! splendid!

30 行 善 or 行 好 事 (or 心) to practice good deeds.

行 囊 travelling-bag; baggage; knapsack.

行 國 nomads, referring in the books to the 月 氏 and other nomad tribes.

行 媒 to act as marriage go-between.

男 女 非 有 行 媒 不 相 知 名 if there has been no go-between, men and women should not know each other's name.

35 行 子³ a traveller.

行 宮 the Emperor's travelling-lodges.

行 寓 halting-place on a journey.

行 實 facts.

行 將 on the point of; about to.

40 行 尸 走 肉 a walking-corpse— fig.

行 巫 術 的 a sorcerer.

行 己 也 恭 humble in his own actions.

行 己 有 恥 in governing oneself to maintain a sense of shame.

行 常 ordinarily; usual.

45 行 年 四 歲 four years of age.

行 幸 an Imperial progress—wherever the chariot of the Emperor came there was good fortune.

行 廚 culinary arrangements by the way.

行 役 to go on active service; away at the wars.

行 徑 a path; way of life; course of action.

50 行 必 果 will certainly carry out their actions.

行 息 bearing interest.

行 惡 過 分 excessive wickedness.

行 成 to sue for peace.

行 所 無 事 to act as if it was no concern of his.

55 行 房 sexual intercourse.

行 操 military evolutions.

行 政 administration of government. *See* 政 No. 355—69ff.

行 政 事 件 administrative matters.

行 政 作 用 function of the administration.

60 行 政 制 裁 administrative restraint.

行 政 區 畫 administrative districts.

行 政 司 法 權 judicial administrative powers.

行 政 命 令 administrative laws, such as control of publications, quarantine, etc.

行 政 官 administrative officer.

65 行 政 官 署 office of the administration.

行 政 方 畧 methods of administration.

行 政 機 關 organ of the administration.

行 政 權 限 limitations of the executive authority.

行 政 法 administrative law.

70 行 政·的 administrative.

行 政 秘 書 secretary of the executive.

行 政 管 理 administration.

行 政 處³分⁴ administrative measure.

行 政 行 爲 administrative action.

75 行 政 裁 判 administrative decision.

行 政 規·則 administrative regulations, as in schools, etc.

行 政 解 釋 administrative interpretation.

行 政 訴 訟 administrative legal procedure.

行 政 部 the executive.

80 行 政 院 the Administrative *Yüan* or Department.

行 教 to teach; to propagate a faith, as missionary work, etc.

行 文 despatches between officials; to send a despatch; to write.

行 旅 a traveller.

行 旌 a flag—used for travellers.

85 行 星 the planets.

行 書 the correspondence style of Chinese writing.

行 期 date of departure.

行 木 to examine timber and trees.

行·李 or 行 裝 baggage; luggage; the first primarily meant a traveller.

90 行·李 之 往 來 the coming and going of travellers.

行·李 房 baggage-room.

行·李 票 baggage-checks.

行·李 車 baggage-car.

行 檢 economical; self-restrained; temperate.

95 行 權 to act according to circumstances, *see* No. 1663. B.; to act from compulsion; to submit to circumstances; to act irregularly on account of the peculiar exigencies of the case.

行 止 moving and stopping:—behaviour, conduct under all conditions; plans as to travel.

行 止 舉·動 behaviour, deportment and manner of life.

行 蓮 starved to death by the roadside.

行 水 moving water; to go by water; to inspect streams for conservancy purposes.

100 行 淫 lewd and dissolute conduct.

行 火 to use fire; to start a fire.

行 營 military camp when on the march.

行·爲 actions; way of life; used as a suffix (in legal terms) for an act, etc.

商 行·爲 a commercial act, or transaction.

105 基 本 商 行·爲 fundamental commercial transaction.

有 賞 行·爲 act of consideration.

法 律 行·爲 a legal act.

犯 罪 行·爲 a criminal act.

行 爲 不 正 not upright in conduct; to misbehave.

110 行·爲 能 力 capacity for taking action.

有 行·爲 能 力 人 capable persons. (*legal*).

行 犯 to transgress the law.

行·理 baggage.

行 用 to make use of.

115 行 疫 (or 瘟) an epidemic.

行 百 里 者 半 九 十 to stop at ninety *li* when attempting to walk one hundred — although almost there it is as bad as not starting—used of the difficulty of completing a project.

行 省 provinces of China.

行 知 to notify; to give information officially.

行 神 the god of travellers.

120 行 禮 to salute; to perform acts of ceremony.

行 私 to act selfishly.

行 租 periodical rent.

行 竊 未 成 failure of an attempted robbery.

行 竈 a travelling-stove.

125 行 縢 puttees.

行 纏 to pack the baggage.

行 義 to work righteousness; to be a righteous man.

行 者 之 赴 家 the coming home of a traveller.

行 者 言 之 實 actions are the reality of words.

130 行 聘 to send betrothal presents.

行 脚 僧 an itinerant Buddhist priest.

行 至 on reaching....

行 臺 a hotel.

行 船 to travel by boat; to embark.

135 行 色 circumstances and conditions of travel.

行 藏 conduct, from 用 之 則 行 舍³之 則 藏 "when called to office, undertake its duties; when not so called, retire."

行 虐 於 民 to treat the masses with oppression.

行 行 且 止 inconstant; now stopping, now moving.

行 行 重 (*ch'ung²*) 行 行 repeated efforts—used of gradual advance.

140 行 術 or 行 狀 or 行 畧 biography; brief records of a career.

行 許 possibly.

行 詐 to cheat; to deceive.

行 詣 to visit.

行 貨 goods carried around for sale. *See below* B.1.

145 行 販 or 行 商 itinerant traders; pedlars.

行 貸 to lend on interest.

行 資 fund for travelling-expenses.

行 賄 or 行 賂 to bribe.

行 走 to walk; to be employed at; duties, etc.

150 行 趣 to hasten to; hurry to get on.

行 路 or 行 程 or 出 行 to travel.

行 蹤 traces; footsteps.

行 蹤 無 定 vagrant; to have no fixed abode.

行 車 時 間 表 railway time-table.   [army cot; canvas cot.

¹⁵⁵行 軍 troops on the march 行 軍 牀

行 軍 椅 a camp-stool.

行 轅 temporary residence for high officials on tour.

行 辟 人 可 也 when (an officer) is on the road, he may cause people to be removed from his path.

行 道 to travel; to follow the right way.

¹⁶⁰行 遯 to retire from the world.

行 酒 to pass around the wine-cups.

行 醫 to practice as a doctor.

行 銷 to have free sale; may be sold everywhere.

行 鍼 to practice acupuncture.

¹⁶⁵行 險 to walk in dangerous courses; hazardous occupation.

行 險 倖 倖 之 機 熟 well versed in the chances of dangerous courses.

行 雲 流 水 travelling clouds send down rain—said of open-hand-ed men.

行 露 the dew on the road.

行·頭 actor's garments and pro-perties.

¹⁷⁰行 食 food for the road.

行 香 to burn incense.

行 馬 a *cheval de frise.*

行 駛 to sail; a vessel plying between certain places for trade.

行 高 nobility of conduct; lofty aims.

¹⁷⁵五 行 the five elements of Chinese philosophy, 金, metal, 木 wood, 水 water, 火 fire, 土 earth.

施 行 or 實 行 to carry into effect.

旅 行 to travel.

獨 行 to walk alone.

閒 行 leisurely walking.

¹⁸⁰開 行 to set forth; to sail.

風 行 天 下 spread all over the empire.

(a) Read *hsing⁴.* **Actions; conduct; behaviour, etc.**

行 之 過 an error in conduct.

行 同 倫 for conduct there are the same rules.

行 者 心·之 發 actions are prompted by the heart.

行 高 excellence of conduct.

⁵修·行 to regulate the conduct to moral standards.

品·行 disposition, temper.   [isms.

德 行 virtuous ways. 德·行 manner-

損 行 to injure the character by evil deeds.

無 行 之 人 a bad character.

素 行 usual habits or practices.

(b) Read *hang².* **A business firm.**

行 作 or 行 貨 inferior goods made for the market.

行 員 shop-assistant.

行 商 merchants.

行·家 an expert in any line; a business man; profession, trade, etc.

⁵行·市 or 行 價 market rates; rate of exchange, etc.

行 店 a shop; a business house.

行 情 market prices; customs of the trade.

行 戶 or 行 號 a firm; a business house.

行 東 head of a firm.

¹⁰行 棧 a warehouse.

行·業 business or occupation.

行 當⁴ a man's business or occupa-tion.

行 號 註 冊 章·程 rules for re-gistration of companies, etc.

行 規 regulations of a firm; com-mission.

¹⁵行 話 trade terms.

不 在 行 not in the trade; inex-pert, does not understand the business.

內 行, 外 行 an insider and an outsider respectively; expert and amateur.

當 行 one of the same trade or business.

洋 行 foreign firms.

(c) Read *hang².* **A row, a line, a series. N.A.**

行 伍 ranks of an army.

行 伍 出 身 rose from the ranks.

行 列 in a row.

行 幾 which brother are you?

⁵行 款 column in a book.

行 衣 服 to stitch garments.

行 輩 in the same rank.

一 行 樹 a row of trees.

八 行 書 ordinary Chinese note-paper ruled with eight lines to a page.

¹⁰排 行 the sequence of sons in a family.

數 行 字 "a few lines."

雁 行 in a column, like geese on the wing.

(d) Read *hang¹.* **Bold, determined.**

行 行 如 也 a bold, martial air.

刑² A law. To punish; punish-ment.

2755

刑·事 a criminal case.

刑 事 事 件 criminal cases. 罪 學

刑 事 人 類 學 criminology.= 犯

刑 事 庭 or 刑 庭 criminal court.

⁵刑 事 法 or 刑 律 criminal law.

刑 事 裁 判 criminal trial.

刑 事 裁 判 所 criminal court.

刑 事 訴 訟 criminal action.

刑 事 訴 訟 法 code of criminal procedure.

¹⁰刑 具 or 刑 械 instruments of punishment or torture.

刑·名 former term for criminal law, punishments, etc.

刑 問 or 刑 訊 or 刑 求 to ex-amine by torture.

刑 戮 capital punishment.

刑 措 不 用 punishments were put on one side as unnecessary—because the people were law-abiding.

¹⁵刑 房 former criminal department in a *yamen.*

刑 期 term of punishment.

刑 期 無 刑 punishment is de-signed in the hope that there will be no punishment—as a deterrent.

刑 杖 a rod of correction.

刑 法 criminal law, criminal code.

²⁰刑 牲 to slaughter victims for sacrifice.

刑 網 the meshes of the law.

刑·罰 punishment; to punish; pen-alty.

刑·罰 之 目 的⁴ object of punish-ment.

刑 罰 權 criminal jurisdiction.

²⁵刑 罰 法 penal code.

刑 莫 威 焉 (*Ch'in* 秦) could not show any severer punishment (than that of subjugating *Chin* 晋).

刑 部 the former Board of Pun-ishments.

刑 餘 eunuchs, those who had suffered castration.

五 刑 the five punishments of ancient times, *see* No. 1198-5.

³⁰名 譽 刑 to disfranchise.

寬 刑 to mitigate punishment.

非 刑 illegal punishment or tortures.

身 體 刑 corporal punishment.

(a) An example. To imitate.

刑 于 寡 妻 his example influenced his wife.

刑 於 四 海 be a model for all the empire.

型² A mould of earth for castings. A statute, a law, in which sense it is used with No. 2755, above.
2756

型 模 a mould for casting metals.

儀 型 裕 後 an example for the benefit of posterity.

典 型 a statute.

砌² A whetstone, a hone.
2757

鉶² A sacrificial caldron.
2758

鉶 鼎 a sacrificial tripod.

鉶 羹 sacrificial broth.

形² Figure, form, appearance. To take shape. The body.
2759

形 下 real, visible.

形 下 之 學 material sciences.

形 人 之 醜 to reveal the defects of others.

形 似 apparently; to purport; an outline.

⁵形 便 natural defences or barriers.

形 凋 敝 a state of decay.

形 勝 之 地 natural barriers or frontiers.

形 勢 the outline—as of hills; the aspect; the state of; conditions; semblance; circumstances.

形 單 solitary.

¹⁰形 單 影 隻 one form, one shadow—solitary, lonely; single.

形 天 a being who is said to have fought against the Supreme, who cut off his head, making eyes in his breasts and a mouth in his navel,–from 山 海 經.

形 學 geometry. = 幾 何 (學).

形·容 to describe.

形·容 兇 惡 having an evil aspect or appearance.

¹⁵形·容 出·來 to express clearly—by acting or otherwise.

形·容 失 實 misrepresentation; caricature; distorted description.

形·容 詞 an adjective.

形 家 geomancers.

形·式 a model or figure; aspect, appearances, externals.

²⁰形·式 上·的 formal. (*philos.*).

形·式 主 義 formalism.

形·式 科 學 formal science.

形·式 觀 formalistic view. (*logic*).

形·式 訓 練 formal discipline.

²⁵形·式 雖 存 作·用 已 失 although the form remains, it has ceased to function.

有 形·式 而 無 精·神 having the form but lacking the spirit.

形 形 色 色 many varieties.

形 影 相 弔 only my form and shadow to console each other—said by one who was sadly bereaved and lonely.

形 影 相 隨 inseparable, as form from shadow.

³⁰形 態 status; manner; form.

形 成 formation; formed; to materialize.

形 成 素 form-element.

形 景 prospect; outlook; status.

形 格 勢 禁 in an unfavourable situation.

³⁵形 狀 appearance; form; shape; condition.

形 相 form.

形 者 神 之 質 the body is the material form of the spirit.

形 而 上 學 or 純 正 哲 學 metaphysics.

形 諸 紙 筆 to commit to writing.

⁴⁰形 貌 the countenance; the appearance of.

形 質 likeness; form.

形 跡 traces; objective existence.

形 跡 之 富 貴 material wealth and honour.

形 跡 可 疑 he is not to be trusted —said of one who is a suspicious character.

⁴⁵ 不 拘 形 跡 not to stand on ceremony.

形 蹤 詭 秘 of suspicious ante-

cedents; not an upright character.

形 骸 formal.

形 體 or 形 像 the substance of; resemblance; a likeness; an image; the body.

情·形 circumstances of a matter; things as they are.

⁵⁰有 形·之 輸 入 輸 出 visible imports and exports.

無 形 formless.

邢² Name of a State in what is now Hopei or Chihli.
2760

邢 臺 縣 the chief city of the former *Shuntehfu* in Chihli, (Hopei).

莖² The stalk of a plant. A stem. The hilt of a sword. Also read *ching*¹.
2761

木 莖 trunk of a tree.

玉 莖 or 陰 莖 the penis.

陘² A defile, a gorge, a pass. Niche near the kitchen stove.
2762

竈 陘 a niche near the kitchen fireplace.

杏⁴ The apricot, the almond; often read *heng*³.
2763

杏 仁 almonds; apricot kernels.

杏 仁 茶 almond-tea, drunk at feasts.

杏 兒 or 杏·子 apricots.

杏 壇 the Apricot Altar, name of ·the place where Confucius had his school, in the present 曲 阜 縣, Shantung.

⁵杏 月 the second lunar month,(on account of the blossoms.)

杏 桃 a variety of plum like a greengage.

杏 梅 a kind of plum.

杏 眼 almond-eyes.

杏 酪 a drink made from almonds.

銀 杏 the gingko, from the Japanese sound of these characters.

幸⁴ To rejoice. Fortunate, prosperous. Distinguish 辛 No. 2739.
2764

幸 其 成 if haply they may grow up.

幸 勿 推 却 I hope that you will not refuse.

幸 勿 有 緩 I trust that there will be no delay.

幸 得 fortunately succeeded; a lucky hit.

[5]幸 承 had the pleasure of.

幸 有 fortunately there is.

幸 未 致 命 fortunately it did not involve life.

幸 災 不 仁 to take pleasure in calamity is inhuman.

幸 災 樂 禍 to take pleasure in the calamity of others.

[10]幸 甚 or 幸 極 very lucky; fortunate indeed.

幸 福 happiness, blessings.

幸 福 之 石 the philosopher's stone.

幸 福 說 eudemonism.

幸·而 or 幸·虧 fortunately; happily; thanks to....; but for...

[15]幸·而 免 he escapes by mere good luck.

幸 臣 favorite courtier.

幸 運 good fortune.

幸·頭 good fortune; good luck.

得 幸 to get imperial favours.

(a) An Imperial progress.

巡 幸 an Imperial progress.

倖 [4] Lucky; fortunate. Inter. preceding.
2765

倖 位 favourites.

倖 免 a lucky escape.

倖 獲 or 倖 得 luckily acquired.

佞 倖 sycophantic.

儌 倖 a fortunate coincidence; a lucky chance.

悻 [4] Anger, vexation. Quarrelsome.
2766

悻 悻 然 enraged; angry.

悻 悻 自 好 quarrelsome and fond of self.

悻 直 upright; blunt and outspoken.

涬 [4] A watery expanse. To drag, to lead.
2767

涬 溟 the Infinite, defined as 自 然 之 氣.

溟 涬 然 most honourable.

擤 [3] To blow the nose with the fingers.
2768

馨 [1] Fragrant; fragrance.
2769

馨 氣 sweet fragrance.

馨 逸 exceeding great fragrance.

馨 香 禱 祝 fragrant prayers.

HSING. SING. (ㄙㄧㄥ)

姓 [4] A surname. A clan. People.
2770

姓 名 surname and personal name.

姓 李 my surname is *Li*.

姓 氏 the surname, the clan name.

姓 譜 a family register; genealogical record.

[5]姓 高·的 a person named *Kao*.

不 知 姓 甚 名 誰 I do not know who he was.

出 姓 to change the surname.

同 姓 不 宗 of the same surname but of a different ancestry.

敝 姓.. or 賤 姓... my humble surname is....

[10]百 姓 one hundred names—many names, i.e., the people.

百 家 姓 the book of 438 surnames, compiled early in the *Sung* dynasty.

萬 姓 all names, mankind.

複 姓 or 雙 姓 surnames with two or more characters.

貴 姓 or 尊 姓 What is your surname?

隱 姓 to hide one's name; to be anonymous.

性 [4] Nature, disposition, spirit, temper. A property or quality. Sex.
2771

性 交 sexual intercourse.

性 分 individuality.

性 向 propensity.

性·命 life.

[5]性 善 the theory of Mencius that men are born naturally good.

性·子 如 何 what sort of a temper has he?

性·子 躁 impatient; quick-tempered.

性 急 hasty; impetuous.

性 悍 refractory; obstinate.

[10]性·情 or 性·子 natural temperament; mind; habit of mind; disposition; temper.

性 惡 the theory of *Hsün tzǔ* 荀 子 that the nature of man is inherently evil.

性(慾)之 衝 動 sex impulse.

性(慾)教·育 sex education.

性 慢 sluggish disposition.

[15]性 成 life habits; natural tendency.

性 拙 stupid; dull.

性 擇 sexual selection.

性 暴 fierce disposition; fiery temper.

性 本 善 the nature of man is good—at birth.

[20]性 氣 impatience.

性 烈 irritable and violent.

性 理 mental philosophy; metaphysics; propensities; intellect.

性 生 temper; disposition.

性·的 進 化 evolution of sex.

[25]性 相 近 也 習 相 遠 也 in natural disposition they are similar, but in practice they differ widely.

性 神 spirit.

性 空 無 性 my nature, being vacancy, is in fact no nature at all. (*Budd.*).

性 能 sense.

性 行 conduct.

[30]性 質 or 性 格 temperament; disposition; spirit; temper.

多 血 質·的 性 質 sanguine temperament.

憂 鬱 質·的 性 質 melancholic temperament.

粘 液·的 性 質 phlegmatic temperament.

膽 汁 質·的 質 性 bilious temperament.

[35]性 靈 intelligent.

個 性 individuality.

兩 性 問 題 sex questions.

兩 性 差 異 sex differences.

天 性 natural gifts.

[40]本 性 inherent properties or qualities.

無 定 性 flighty.

特 性 characteristics; specific properties.

牽 性 to follow one's natural bent.

索 性 might as well ...

生 性 natural disposition.
45 男 女 特 性 sex characteristics of man and woman.
確 實 性 trustworthy qualities.
藥 性 properties of medicines.
見 性 成 佛 in perceiving what the nature of man is, the state of Buddha is arrived at.
記·性 memory.
悟·性 power of apprehension.
慢 性 chronic (med.)

星 ¹ A point of light. Stars, planets. A spark.
2772

星 使 former Imperial Commissioner; a Literary Chancellor.
星 卜 astrology and divination.
星 君 the zodiacal star that rules the year.
星 命 the star under which a man is born.
⁵星 士 or 星 者 or 星 丈 先 生 or 占 星 家 astrologer; astronomer.
星 夜 night.
星 夜 奔 馳 to travel by night.
星 奔 to travel by night.
星 學 or 天 文 學 astronomy.
¹⁰星·宿 the constellations; stars(-𝑕siu⁴).
星·宿 海 the sea of stars—name of the source of the Yellow River.
星 工 one well acquainted with astronomy.
星 座 a constellation.
星 散 scattered like stars; sprinkled over—as g o l d - l e a f on lacquer-ware.
¹⁵星 斗 the stars.
星·星 the stars; 星 星 numerous; scattered and few.
星 星 點 點 a few, sparse; scattered.
星 曆 the sidereal calendar.
星 期 a week.
²⁰星 期 日 Sunday.
星 期 一 Monday,—o t h e r d a y s similarly.
星 次 the position of the stars.
星 氣 or 星 圑 dense star-clusters.
星 河 the Milky Way.
²⁵星 火 desperately urgent; small, insignificant.
星 火 燎 原 "how great a matter a little fire kindleth!"
星 球 planets; stars.
星 眼 bright, starry eyes.
星 移 斗 轉 the movements of the

stars—the flight of time.
³⁰星 算 astronomical calculations; astrological reckonings.
星 羅 棋 布 scattered about like stars or like the pieces on a chess-board.
星 翳 white spots on the cornea.
星 臺 an observatory.
星 芒 star-like rays.
³⁵星 落 地 a star fallen to the earth.
星 處 the starry dwelling—Buddhist term for Magadha in India.
星 術 astrology.
星 象 stars; heavenly bodies; constellations.
星 辰 stars, planets.
⁴⁰星 貨 鋪 a general store.
星 迴 the circuit of the stars during the year—a year.
星 速 as quick as the stars.
星 院 The Star Chamber.
星 隕 a meteorite or aerolite.
⁴⁵星 雲 or 星 霧 nebula.
星 雲 說 or 星 霧 說 the nebular hypothesis.
星 霜 the stars (complete their course year by year, and) the frost descends,—used to express years.
星 飯 to eat by night.
星 蝕 an occultation.
⁵⁰星 馳 a fleet courier who travels by night.
星 駕 to yoke animals to a cart and travel by night.
星 魚 or 海 盤 車 the starfish.
一 星 之 火 a tiny spark of fire; a point of light.
冒 星 to send forth sparks; "to see stars."
⁵⁵北 極 星 The Polar Star.
土 星 Saturn.
壽·星 the star of old age—portrayed as a very old man with a large head; a person on his birthday.
天 王 星 Uranus.
小 星 your concubine.
⁶⁰彗 星 or 長 星 a comet. stars.
恒 星 the fixed stars or permanent
救 星 an unexpected deliverer.
明 星 the morning star.
晦 氣 星 an evil star.
⁶⁵木 星 Jupiter.
水 星 Mercury.
海 王 星 Neptune.
流·星 meteors.
火 星 Mars.
⁷⁰火 星·子 sparks.

福 星 a lucky star.
賊 星 a meteor; a robber.
行 星 planets.
金 星 Venus.
零 星 odds and ends; miscellaneous.
冥 王 星 Pluto.

惺 悎 ¹·³ Intelligent; to comprehend. Still, passionless.
2773

惺 悟 to recall to mind; to awaken to; to become conscious of.
惺 惺 alert; astute; the cry of a bird; startled.
惺 憁 astute; shrewd.
惺 忪 flickering; twinkling.

猩 ¹ Orang-outang.
2774

猩·猩(猴) a chimpanzee.
猩 脣 apes' lips—a rare delicacy.

(a) Red.

猩 猩 菓 a wild jujube-plum.
猩 紅 scarlet.
猩 紅 氈 small scarlet hair-rugs.
猩 紅 熱 scarlet fever. (Jap.).

腥 ¹ Measly flesh. Rank; frowsy; strong-smelling.
2775

腥 味 an evil, frowsy smell.
腥 氣 the smell of newly-killed meat; fishy smell.
腥 羶 the smell of sheep and goats.
腥 聞 a malodorous reputation.
腥 臭 foul smelling; rancid.
魚 腥 fishy smell.

醒 ³ To wake up; to be aroused. To startle. To become sober.
2776

醒 世 之 言 words to arouse the age.
醒 世 圖 startling pictures.
醒 悟 to awake; to perceive; to come to oneself.
醒 悟 過 來 to realize the error of one's ways.
⁵醒 獅 the w a k i n g l i o n—China aroused.
醒 目 or 醒 眼 to catch the eye; to attract attention.

醒脾 to tone up the stomach.
醒着 awake. ⌈(-chiao⁴)
醒覺 to pay heed to; to be awake.
[10]醒豁 clear; alert.
醒轉 to rouse; to awaken.
醒·過來 to awake, actually or figuratively.
醒鐘 an alarum-clock.＝鬧鐘.
喚醒 to rouse with a call.
[15]復醒 to revive; to return to consciousness.
醉醒 to recover from drunkenness—also used figuratively.

騂[1]
2777 Red. Bay.

騂剛 hard red soil; also a red bull, when 剛 is u.f. 犅.
騂牡 a red bull, for sacrifice.
有騂有騏 "there were bay horses and there were piebald."
面汗騂 flushed, perspiring face.

(a) Fashioning of a bow.

騂騂角弓 "well-fashioned is the bow adorned with horn."

錫錫[2]
2778 Malt-sugar. Sweetmeats. Second form is also read *t'ang*². Sugar.

錫餅 sugar-cakes.
飴錫 malt-sugar sweets.

HSÜEH. (Hsioh)(ㄒㄩㄝ)

埕 [2.5.] Stiff, hard clay or rocky strata. A crack in a jar.
2779

學學 [2.5.] To study; to learn, to imitate. To train up. A branch of learning. Also read *hsüeh*².
2780

學·不上來 cannot learn it.
學·不會 unable to learn how to do it.
學之弗能弗措也 if he studies anything and cannot grasp it, he does not relax his efforts.
學位 academic degree.
[5]學伴 or 學友 a fellow-student. *See below*—11.

學制 educational system.
學力 scholarship; scholarly attainments.
學力根深 scholarship that is deeply rooted.
學力到 to give application to one's studies and be successful.
[10]學務 educational matters.
學友 enquirers, catechumens. *See above*—5.
學名 a name given by one's teacher on beginning school-life; scientific names, as in botany, zoology, etc.
學員 scholars; students.
學·問 to study and inquire—learning.
[15]學嘴學舌 to imitate the speech of another.
學壞·了 to imitate the depraved; to go to the bad; to follow depraved ways.
學士 a scholar; former sub-chancellor of the Grand Secretariat; a B.A.
學如不及猶恐失之 study as if you could not attain your aim, and were afraid you should lose it.
學好 to learn what is good; to follow after the right.
[20]學宮 a college; a Confucian Temple.
學官 formerly a Provincial official who directed the studies of candidates for the preliminary degrees; a District Examiner of schools.
學師 or 學正 former Director of Studies attached to a *Chou* District.
學干祿 studying with a view to emoluments.
學年 school-year; period of school-course.
[25]學年考試 annual examination.
學廟 or 學宮 Confucian Temple.
學役 a fag.
學徒 a pupil; an apprentice.
學徒制度 apprenticeship.
[30]學房 or 學館 or 學塾 or 學堂 a school.
學手·藝 to serve an apprenticeship; to learn a trade.
學政 or 學憲 or 學臺 or 學院 the former Provincial Literary Chancellor.
學文 studies for one seeking the accomplishments of culture.

學時髦 to follow the fashions.
[35]學曆 school or college-calendar.
學會 a literary society; learned how to do it.
學期 school-term.
學期考試 term-examination.
學校 a school.
[40]中學(校) middle or secondary school; high school.
夜課學校 night-school.
半日學校 half-day schools.
國民學校 primary schools.
官立學校 government schools.
[45]實業學校 technical school.
專門學校 school for the study of special subjects—any term may be prefixed to this, showing the nature of the special studies undertaken in such a school, e.g., 法科專門學校 School of Laws.
工業學校 technical or industrial school.
師範學校 normal school.
省立學校 provincial school.
[50]私立學校 private school.
縣立學校 county school.
職工學校 industrial school.
鄉立學校 district school.
高等小學校 higher primary schools.
[55]學校保育 matron of a school.
學校儀式 school-ceremonial.
學校制服 school-uniforms.
學校劇 school-plays.
學校化 educated by the schools.
[60]學校園 school-yard or grounds.
學校基金 school-endowments.
學務委員會 commission on schools and education.
學校市 the school-municipality, a system of organizing pupils into a small municipality.
學校建築 school-architecture.
[65]學校教·育 school-education as contrasted with home-training, etc.
學校新聞 school-news.
學校日誌 daily record of the work of a school.
學校生·活 school-life.
學校用書 text-books for schools.
[70]學校精·神 the spirit of a school.
學校管理 school-management.
學校系統 school-system.
學校組·織 school-organization.

學校衛生檢驗 medical inspection of schools.
[75]學校設備 fittings, furniture, etc., of a school.
學校風潮 school-agitations; pupils' lawlessness—strikes, etc.
學業 proficiency in scholarship.
學樣 to follow a pattern; to imitate an example.
學步邯鄲 slavishly to imitate others and lose one's own originality. See 邯 No. 2036—3.
[80]學殖 to advance in learning as plants grow in the fields.
學海 (streams) follow to the sea—used of persevering in studies until one reaches the goal, as streams flow ceaselessly until they reach the sea; a name given to 何休 i.e., sea of learning.
學派 a school of thought.
學潮 school-boy agitations such as strikes, etc.
學無老少 in scholarship there is no account taken of age—it is the achievement that counts.
[85]學理 scientific principle; doctrine; theory.
學理解釋 explanation or interpretation of a theory.
學・生 or 門・生 a pupil; a student; a disciple; term of depreciation, I.
學・生團 student-body.
學・生聯合會 Student Association.
[90]學田 land, the produce of which is used for school-purposes.
學界 the school-world; educational circles; literary circles.
學監 dean of a college; a proctor.
學科 course or department of studies. See 科 No. 3389—42, 46.ff.
學程 course of study; curriculum.
[95]學究 a pedant.
學究派 scholastic pedants.
學窮 an indigent scholar.
學章 school-badge.
學童 primary-school pupils.
[100]學籍 school or college-register.
學級 school-grade or form.
學習 to study; to acquire by constant practice.
學者 one of high scholastic attainments; scholar.

學而不思則罔 learning without thought is vain.
[105]學・而時習之 to study with constant perseverance and application.
學・而知之 wisdom acquired by studies—not by natural gifts.
學否 or 學說 to repeat what has been said.
學舍 school-premises.
學藝 polite accomplishments.
[110]學藝會 exhibition of pupils' work, etc.
學行 scholarship and character.
學術 art; learning; scholarship.
學規 the rules of a school; discipline; fees formerly paid on taking the first degree.
學說 theory; thesis.
[115]學語 technical terms.
學課 lesson; task; subject; curriculum.
學・識 knowledge derived from studies.
學・識造詣 scholarly attainments.
學費 school fees; tuition.
[120]學資 teacher's fees.
學買・賣 to learn business.
學道・理 to study doctrines.
學部 former Board of Education, now changed to 教育部.
學長 seniors in a school; dean of a department of study.
[125] 神學科學長 dean of the theological faculty.
學院 academy.
學院的理 academic theories.
學額 number of pupils received in a school; formerly the number of degrees to be awarded in any one district.
學風 the atmosphere or special characteristics of a school.
[130]學齡保險 insurance for the period of school-age.
學齡兒童 children of school-age.
學齡期 school-age.
勤學 to study with diligence.
博學 extensive learning.
[135]同學 schoolmates; fellow-pupils.
大學 university; *The Great Learning*.
求學 to seek scholarship.
無學識 unlettered; ignorant.
留學 to study abroad.
[140]義學 free schools.
逃學 to play truant.

(a) Used as a suffix, it combines with other words as a term for various branches of study, etc. Examples of these will be found under various characters, only a few are given below.

力學 dynamics.
文學 literature, arts.
哲學 philosophy.
地文學 physical geography.

鶯 2.5.   Oriental bullfinch.
2781

糒 4.5.   Grits of rice, etc., left after hulling.
屑
2782

糒末 rice-grits.
粉糒 grits in flour.

翯 2.5. The glistening plumage of birds. Reflection of the sun upon water.
2783

懼 2.5. To be in awe of. To fear. Also read *chüo*[2.5].
2784   *kuo*[4.5].

驚懼 startled.

(a) Read *kuo*[4.5]. Suddenly.

懼然 suddenly; hastily.

HSÜEH. (Hsioh) (ㄒㄩㄝ)

削 [4.5] To pare, to scrape; to delete from tablets by scraping; to sharpen to a point.
2785 To seize territory. Pron. *hsiao*[1] in compounds marked "x."
×削到薄 scraped or pared thin.
削則削 what should be deleted, he deleted.
×削・去 to do away with.
削地 to seize territory.
×削字 to engrave characters.
×削平 to raze, to scrape level.
×削成四方 cut into a rectangular form.
×削・掉 to slice off; to pare.
削正 or 斧削 to amend writings, etc., as when asked to do so by a friend.
[10]削減 to cut off; to exterminate.

削 牘 to prepare tablets for use by scraping.

× 削 皮 to scrape off the skin.

削 籍 to remove the name, etc., from the register,—of a degraded official.

削 職 to remove from office.

[15]削 趾 適 屨 to trim the toes to fit the shoes—used fig. = 削足

削 跡 to remove traces. ｜適履

× 削 鉛 筆 to sharpen a lead-pencil.

削 除 to cut short.

削 而 光 此 to lose face.

[20]削 骨 難 填 I could not make up the amount even if I scraped my bones.

削 髮 to cut the hair—and become a priest.

× 針 尖 上 削 鐵 to scrape iron from the point of a needle—mean, stingy; difficult.

(a) Sloping; sheer, as a cliff.

削 肩 sloping shoulders.

削 壁 a precipice.

HSIU. (ㄒㄧㄡ)

休[1] **To rest. To cease. To desist. To resign. Used imperatively—do not, etc.**
2786

休 休 upright; frugal.

休 假[4] a holiday; to have a holiday.

休 假 日 期 school-holidays.

休 怪 do not think it strange.

[5]休 怕 他 don't be afraid.

休 息 to cease; to rest.

休 息 在 此 rest here.

休 息 所 a resting-place; a place for refreshment.

休 憩 to stop for a breathing space.

[10]休 戰 a truce; armistice.

休 戰 紀 念 Armistice Day.

休 手 to leave off work.

休 敎 走 了 don't let him go away.

休 業 to close a business; to have a holiday; a recess.

[15]休 止 to desist from; to stop.

休 止 符 sign of rests in staff-notation.

休 沐 to take leave of absence for bathing—as was done every ten days by officials in *T'ang* dynasty.

休 糧 辟 穀 to abstain from or-

dinary food with a view to attaining immortality.

休 職 to resign from office.

[20]休 致 to resign.

休 題 起 don't mention it.

休 養 生 息 to nourish the people.

告 休 to ask for leave to retire.

天 地 同 休 enduring as long as the heavens and the earth.

[25]就 休 罷 there's an end to it.

罷 休 to finish; to give up.

萬 休 all things cease—death.

(a) To separate from; divorce.

休 妻 or 出 妻 to divorce a wife.

休 書 a bill of divorcement.

休 棄 to repudiate; to renounce.

(b) Blessings; prosperity; good-fortune.

休 咎 good fortune and ill.

休 徵 favourable signs.

休 戚 joy and sorrow; good fortune and ill.

休 明 at peace—after disturbance and trouble.

休 祥 or 休 嘉 or 休 美 fortunate; excellent; very good.

天 休 blessings from Heaven.

(c) Read *hsü*[3]. Similar to next, sound of grief or pain.

懊 休 之 grieved exceedingly for him.

咻[1] **To call out; to shout. To jeer.**
2787

咻 咻 sound of breathing, or of speaking with defective mouth.

衆 楚 人 咻 之 with the babble of all the men of *Ch'u* around him confusing him.

(a) Read *hsü*[3]. To groan, to shriek.

噢 咻 to groan in pain or remembrance.

庥[1] **Shade, shelter, protection. Kindness. Inter.** 休 **No.**
2788 2786—B.

天 庥 the blessings of Heaven.

庇 庥 protection; shelter.

神 庥 divine blessings.

鴻 庥 your great favour.

貅[1] A fabulous fierce beast—
2789 thus:—fierce, valiant, heroic, brave.

貔 貅 the fierce beast as above.

鵂[1] An owl; a bird of ill-omen.
2790

鴟 鵂 the white horned-owl.

朽[3] Rotten, decayed, useless.
2791 Distinguish 朽 No. 7174.

朽 壞 or 朽 敗 or 朽 爛 worthless; decayed; spoilt.

朽 斃 rent asunder—broken in pieces, as rocks or mountains.

朽 折 decayed and broken—of beams.

朽 散 decayed and scattered.

[5]朽 木 不 可 雕 也 decayed wood cannot be carved—said of a useless man.

朽 木 糞 土 from the above,—decayed wood and a wall of filthy earth—a worthless man.

朽 材 unserviceable—conventional term of self-depreciation.

朽 株 a rotten stump of a tree—used fig.

朽 物 worthless, rotten things—term of abuse.

[10]朽 穢 之 物 a rotten, filthy thing—said about a relic.

朽 索 馭 六 馬 like driving six horses with rotten reins—very anxious.

朽 老 筋 力 盡 old and worthless, strength exhausted.

朽 腐 復 化 爲 神 奇 decomposed things by chemical changes may be transmuted into rarities.

朽 邁 a worthless old man—term of self-depreciation.

[15]朽 骨 decaying bones.

天 地 同 朽 滅 will endure as long as the heaven and the earth.

死 而 不 朽 they die but do not perish—their works survive them.

萬 古 不 朽 an imperishable memory.

嗅[4] **To smell; to scent.**
2792

嗅 嗅 看 to smell; smell it.
嗅 花 to smell flowers.
嗅 覺 the sense of smell.

齅 [4]
2793
To smell.

HSIU. SIU. (ㄙㄡ)

修 [1]
2794
To repair; to regulate; to cultivate. To reform. To prune. Inter. next.

修 仙 to seek to become an immortal.
修 備 to prepare.
修 其 天 爵 cultivated their heavenly nobility (i.e. virtues).
修 刺 to prepare a visiting-card—formerly a wooden tablet.
[5]修 合 to mix; to compound—as drugs.
修 品 行 to regulate one's behaviour.
修 城 to repair a city wall.
修 好 to do good deeds; to foster friendly relations.
修 學 旅 行 to take pupils for a walk for the purpose of special study.
[10]修 容 toilet operations; to improve the appearance.
修 廟 宇 to repair temples.
修·得 到 attained—to bliss.
修 德 to cultivate virtue.
修 心 to cultivate the heart.
[15]修 志 to prepare a topography.
修 性 保 眞 to cultivate the divine element within oneself.
修 成 metamorphosed into. (Budd.).
修 房·子 to build a house.
修 持 steadfastly to maintain—a principle.
[20]修 改 to revise; to amend; to reform.
修 文 to cultivate literary skill.
修 書 or 修 函 to write a letter.
修 業 to study at school.
修 業 文 憑 certificate of attendance.
[25]修 樹 to prune trees.
修 橋 補 路 to repair or build bridges and mend roads—works of merit.
修 正 to rectify; to ratify; to revise; to amend.
修 正 主 義 revisionism

修 正 司 法 制 度 reform of the judicial system.
修 正 案 an amendment.
[30]修 正 議 案 the motion as amended.
修 河 to repair canals; river conservancy.
修 濠 to dig a moat or a trench.
修 煉 to practice asceticism.
修 燈 to trim lamps.
[35]修·理 or 修 補 or 修 整 or 修 復 to repair; to regulate; to prune.
修 理 鐘 表 to repair clocks and watches.
修 直 to make straight.
修 省 (hsing[3]) to examine one's moral character with a view to reformation.
修 眞 to cultivate the divine element within. See above—16.
[40]修 睦 to foster harmonious relations.
修 禊 to remove evils by a ceremony of purification.
修 禮 to cultivate propriety.
修 脚 to pare the toe-nails, etc.
修 舊 怨 to revive an old grievance.
[45]修 船 to repair a boat.
修 船 渠 a dock.
修 葺 花 園 to prune and trim up a garden.
修·行 to cultivate morality. (Budd.); to become a Buddhist.
修 表 文 to write a despatch.
[50]修 訂 to make an amendment.
修 訂 條 約 to revise a treaty.
修 詞 學 rhetoric.
修 譜 to revise the family register.
修 費 expenses incurred in repairs.
[55]修 路 機 a road-roller.
修 身 to cultivate oneself; to practice moral culture; ethics; moral culture.
修 身 學 ethics, as taught in the primary grades; in the higher grades it is called 倫 理.
修 造 or 修 盖 or 修 築 to repair; to construct; to build.
修 道 to cultivate Tao—to strive for virtue, to seek by culture and asceticism, etc., to become an immortal.
[60]修 道 院 a monastery.
修 金 corruption of 2795.3
修 陰 功 to do good in secret.
修 飾 to adorn; to beautify.
修 飾 品 articles of adornment.

[65]修 養 to take care of oneself, as when convalescent; to cultivate, to train; to seek the best.
修 髮 to dress or trim the hair.
復 修 前 好 to renew a former friendship.

(a) Long.

修 久 very long time.
修 廣 long and stout—said of horses.
修 眉 覆 目 heavy eyebrows hanging over the eyes.
修 竹 tall bamboos.
[5]修 遠 distant.
命 之 修 短 有 數 long life or short is all a matter of fate.

(b) Used for transliterating.

修 多 羅 a Buddhist sutra.
修 羅 abbreviation for Asuras, the giant demons of Buddhism. See 阿 1—B.7.

脩 [1]
2795
Dried meat, used in ancient times as a teacher's salary.

脩 敬 a respectful present.
脩 脯 or 束 脩 dried strips of meat—salary for a teacher.
脩 金 a teacher's salary; tuition fees.

(a) Inter. preceding. To do; to act; to restore; to regulate; to cultivate.

脩 慝 to get rid of secret evil.
脩 成 changed into... (Budd.).
脩 持 steadfastly to maintain a principle.
脩 治 regulated; to govern.
脩 禊 to remove evils by a ceremony of purification.

(b) Far, long, distant.

脩 久 for a long time.
脩 遠 very far distant.
脩 長 to make longer; drawn-out.
脩 阻 kept apart—by distance.

潃 [1]
2796
Water in which rice has been boiled.

羞 [1] Shame, to feel ashamed; to blush. Distinguish 差 No.
2797   105.

羞 人 mortified; ashamed.
羞 口 afraid to open the mouth; bashful.
羞 客 mortified; ashamed.
羞 容 bashfulness.
[5] 羞 得 面 紅 過 耳 blushing to the ears.
羞 怯 bashful and nervous.
羞 恨 交 加 shame and resentment mingled.
羞 恥 or 羞 慚 or 羞 愧 a sense of shame; mortified; chagrined.
羞 惡 (wu[4]) ashamed of one's evil deeds and hating those of others.
[10] 羞 惡 之 心 義 之 端 也 the feeling of shame and dislike is the principle of righteousness.
羞 愧 流 汗 perspiring with shame.
羞 手 羞 脚 bashful, afraid to move hand or foot.
羞 明 afraid of the light, (from affection of the optic nerve.)
羞 死 了 to die with shame; mortified.   [bashful.
[15] 羞 澀 ashamed because of poverty;
羞 癢 覺 tickling sensation.
羞 稱 afraid to mention it.
羞 與 爲 伍 ashamed to be in the same rank with him.
羞 花 閉 月 causes the flowers to blush and the moon to hide her face—said of a beautiful woman.
[20] 羞 袒 a shirt.
羞 赧 to blush.
羞 辱 shame; disgrace; to insult.
不 知 羞 no sense of shame.
含 羞 to feel ashamed; to blush.
害 羞 bashful; to feel bashful.

(a) Food, delicacies. To nourish.

羞 耇 to nourish the aged.
時 羞 seasonable delicacies.
珍 羞 delicacies.
羣 鳥 養 羞 the birds are kept for food.
膳 羞 viands; dainties.

(b) To bring forward.

今 我 旣 羞 告 爾 now I have brought forward and announced to you.

(c) Sacrifice; offerings.

進 羞 to make an offering.

饈 膮 膌 [1] Delicacies, savoury food. Inter. preceding.
2798

饈 膳 dainties.
進 饈 to offer delicacies as a gift.

泅 [2] To swim, to float. Also read ts'iu[2].
2799

泅 水 to swim.
泅 泳 to float.

岫 [4] A cavern in a mountain cliff. Mountain peak.
2800

窓 中 列 遠 岫 the distant peaks stand as it were framed by my window.

袖 [4] A sleeve. To put a thing in the sleeve.
2801

袖 中 up one's sleeve.
袖 出 to produce from the sleeve.
袖 刀 a dagger hid in the sleeve.
袖 刺 to carry a visiting-card (anciently a wooden tablet) in the sleeve.
[5] 袖 劍 to conceal a sword in the sleeve.
袖 口 the wristband; the mouth of a sleeve.
袖 手 to put the hands in the sleeves—to have nothing to do with a matter.
袖 手 旁 觀 to put the hands in the sleeves and look on—to have nothing to do with a thing. to take no part in a matter.
袖 狗 or 袖 巴 狗 Pekingese dogs.
[10] 袖 珍 日 記 pocket-diary.
袖 珍 本 pocket-edition.
袖 章 sleeve-badge or stripes.
袖 箭 poisoned arrows fired from a kind of tube with a spring.
袖 而 藏 之 concealed it in his sleeve.

[15] 袖 頭 a cuff.
領 袖 collar and cuffs—a leader.
馬 蹄 袖 horse-shoe shaped sleeve-cuffs.

褎 褏 [4] Ancient form of the preceding. Also read yu[4]. Ample flowing robes. The appearance of growing grain. Laughing.
2802

秀 [4] Grain in the ear. Flowering, luxuriant.
2803

秀 了 穗 to put forth ears.
秀 穗 ears of corn.
秀 而 不 實 flowering but producing no fruit.
秀 茂 luxuriant, as vegetation.

(a) From the above comes:— Elegant, flourishing, accomplished, refined, graceful.

秀 士 an accomplished scholar; a graduate of the former first degree.
秀 女 girls employed as servants in the palace.
秀 才 cultivated talents—a graduate of the former first degree or hsiu ts'ai.
秀 氣 fine manners; talent; lucky influences—as of a place; elegant.
[5] 秀 流 refined; elegant.
秀 眼 a yellowish-green warbler with a white ring round its eyes.
秀 色 可 餐 she is beautiful enough to eat.
秀 衣 fine clothes.
秀 雅 accomplished; graceful.
[10] 秀 項 a graceful neck.
秀 麗 or 秀 美 fine-looking; beautiful.

琇 [4] A coarse jade or jasper called 琇 陽 石.
2804

琇 瑩 a whitish variety of the above used for ornaments.

綉 繡 [4] To embroider. Embroidery. Ornamented; embellished; variegated; illustrated.
2805

繡·出 花 紋 to work flowers in embroidery.

繡 墩 an embroidered cushion.

繡 女 a young lady; a spinster.

繡 工 embroidery work.

⁵繡 房 or 繡 閣 a young lady's chamber.

繡 服 or 繡 裳 embroidered garments.

繡 毬 an embroidered ball; the hydrangea.

繡 畫 to embroider designs.

繡 線 菊 spiræa.

¹⁰繡 花 or 刺 繡 to embroider.

繡 貨 embroideries.

繡 金 to spangle with gold.

繡 面 to tattoo the face.

顧 繡 embroideries.

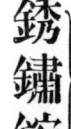

2806

Rust. To rust, to corrode.

銹·住 rusted in; rusted together.

銹 壞 corroded; spoilt by rust.

生 銹 to rust.

銅 銹 verdigris.

HSIUNG. (ㄒㄩㄥ)
(Hsiong)

兄 ¹ A brother, an elder brother. A senior. Used as a term of respect.

2807

兄 事(之) treat (another) as an elder brother.

兄 台 a conventional phrase—Sir!

兄 寬 弟 忍 brotherly forbearance.   [See 16, 17.

兄·弟 or 弟 兄 brethren, brother.

⁵兄 弟 如 手 足 brothers are like hands and feet.

兄 長³ a senior. Sir.

令 兄 your elder brother.

內 兄 wife's elder brother.

同 胞 兄 弟 uterine brothers.

¹⁰堂 兄 弟 cousins of the same surname.

女 兄 elder sister.

家 兄 my elder brother.

盟 兄 sworn brothers.

表 兄 弟 cousins of a different surname.

長 兄 an elder brother.

兄·弟 younger brother; I (in speeches).

弟·兄(們) soldiers, brothers in arms.

凶 ¹ Cruel. Unfortunate. Sad. Inter. next.

2808

凶 事 unlucky affairs—deaths, funerals, etc.

凶 人 a bad person.

凶 俠 bold and intractable; cruel.

凶 信 or 凶 報 or 凶 耗 bad tidings.

⁵凶 兆 an evil omen.

凶 刀 weapon with which a murder was committed.

凶 命 a bitter fate; a sad destiny.

凶 器 weapon with which murder was committed.

凶 宅 a haunted house.

¹⁰凶 年 year of famine; a bad year.

凶 徒 a murderer.

凶 德 an evil aspect; evil influence.

凶 悖 evil and refractory.

凶 惡 evil; cruel.

¹⁵凶 戾 fierce and cruel.

凶·手 a murderer.

凶 日 a black day—on which everything done is unlucky.

凶 星 a malevolent star.

凶 暴 vindictive; malignant.

²⁰凶 服 者 式 之, 式 負 版 者 he would bow on the crossboard of his carriage to anyone in mourning, and to the bearer of the census-boards.

凶 殃 misfortune; evil.

凶 殺 to kill; murder.

凶 毒 malignancy.

凶 煞 malignant; ill-omened.

²⁵凶 禮 funeral rites.

凶 終 隙 末 the end of it is evil—said of those whose friendship has come to an end.

凶 荒 famine.

凶 虐 cruel and malignant.

凶 身 a murderer.

³⁰凶 邪 malignant and evil.

凶 門 white hangings at a door when there is a death.

凶 險 danger; hazardous.

凶 黨 bad characters; desperadoes.

化 凶 to avert calamities.

吉 凶 good and evil fortune.

兇 ¹ Cruel, fierce, violent. Truculent; inhuman. Used with preceding.

2809

兇 悍 passionate and violent.

兇 惡 or 兇 殘 or 兇 報 or 兇 猛 or 兇 狠 or 兇 橫 evil, cruel, savage, wicked, malignant.

兇 手 a murderer.

兇 死 died a violent death.

⁵兇 殺 cruel murder.

兇 毒 cruel; malevolent.

兇 淫 醜 惡 overflowing with evil; utterly unscrupulous.

兇 氣 an evil manner; evil influences.

兇 犯 or 兇 徒 or 兇 賊 persons concerned in a case of murder.

¹⁰兇 言 threats; bad language.

兇 頑 cross-grained; intractable.

行 兇 to do murder; to act violently.

恟 ¹ Nervous, startled.

2810

洶 ¹ The rush of water. Tumultuous, clamorous; a din.

2811

洶 洶 clamour; panic; noise of rushing waters.

洶 湧 the dashing of waves; the rush of a torrent.

胸 ¹
匈
胷
The thorax; the breast; the bosom. The mind; the intelligence.

2812

胸 中 in the breast; on the mind.

胸 中 懷 刀 concealing a knife in the bosom—treacherous.

胸 中 甲 兵 an army in the bosom—a man who is full of strategic plans is as good as ten thousand troops.

胸 中 邱 壑 obstinate and stubborn prejudices.

⁵胸 中 鱗 甲 a man with a crocodile or similar creature in his bosom—i.e., a dangerous, treacherous person.

胸 前 on the breast.

胸 口 or 胸 膛 the breast; the chest.

胸 如 墨 塊 weighed down by anxiety and foreboding.

胸 宇 the mind; the bosom.

¹⁰胸 廓 the thorax.

胸 懷 or 胸 臆 the feelings; the affections.

胸 有 城 府 a fortress in the mind —reticence; reserved manner.

胸 有 成 竹 See 竹 No. 1373—21. To have an idea in the mind before giving expression to it.

胸 椎 thoracic vertebra.

[15] 胸 次 the bosom.

胸 次 不 凡 of no ordinary intelligence.

胸 次 悠 然 his intelligence was far-reaching.

胸 無 城 府 open and unreserved.

胸 無 宿 物 utterly simple and unreserved.

[20] 胸 無 芥 蔕 nothing at all on the mind—free from anxiety.

胸 甲 a breast-plate.

胸 痛 pleurodynia.

胸 翅 pectoral fins.

胸 腔 the chest.

[25] 胸 膜 the pleura.

胸 膈 the diaphragm; the feelings.

胸 膈 嶔 滯 indigestion; heartburn.

胸 衣 corsets.

胸 襟 the mind.

[30] 胸 襟 闊 broad-minded; liberal in outlook.

胸 骨 the sternum.

聽 胸 器 a stethoscope.

(a) Name of a tribe.

匈 奴 *Hsiung nu,* a name given to certain Turki tribes under the *Han* dynasty, when these people occupied Mongolia. They were divided and the northern group travelled westwards as the *Huns.*

匈 牙 利 Hungary.

(b) Hubbub. See next.

天 下 匈 匈 the whole land is in an uproar.

詾 訩 [1]　To brawl; to scold. Inter. 洶 No. 2811.

2813

天 下 詾 訩 the whole land is in an uproar.

(a) Calamity; trouble. To go to law; to judge.

降 此 鞠 訩 ... has sent down

these judgements—of disorder and anarchy.

雄 [2]　The male of birds—thus:— virile, strong, brave, martial.

2814

雄 健 vigorous; able-bodied.

雄 偉 brave; strong; capable; imposing.

雄 兒 [2] a fine man.

雄 兵 or 雄 師 brave soldiers.

[5] 雄 冠 劍 佩 fully armed from head to foot.

雄 力 great strength.

雄 勁 vigorous and muscular.

雄 勝 a hazardous pass; a strategic post.

雄 圖 an ambitious plan.

[10] 雄 壯 well-proportioned; handsome; strong.

雄 壯 氣 概 a vigorous attitude or determination.

雄 大 great, vigorous, imposing.

雄 姿 outstanding; bold appearance.

雄 峻 imposing; grand; inaccessible.

[15] 雄 心 ambition.

雄 才 大 畧 a man with clever strategy.

雄 文 vigorous writings.

雄 斷 a stern decision.

雄 武 martial.

[20] 雄 闊 spacious, vast.

雄 花 sterile flowers, male flowers.

雄 蕊 stamens.

雄 藩 a strong frontier post.

雄 視 or 虎 視 to look on fiercely; to glare at.

[25] 雄 豪 virile.

雄 軀 a robust frame.

雄 辯 a vigorous debate or argument.

雄 鎮 a strong outpost.

雄 長 [3] "the cock of the walk."

[30] 雄 霸 一 方 to seize a region by force.

雄 風 or 雄 威 martial; awe-inspiring.

雄 飛 ambitious, lit., to fly up like a cock.

雄 飛 突 進 a vigorous ambition forcing its way.

雄 駝 鳥 the emu.

[35] 雄 鷄 a cock.

雄 黃 realgar; flowers of sulphur.

雌 雄 female and male of birds— used figuratively of other things,

e.g., 分 出 雌 雄 see who is the better man.

熊 [2]　A bear. Distinguish 態 No. 6024.

2815

熊 人 or 人 熊 the brown bear.

熊 掌 bear's paws, a delicacy.

熊 羆 different names for the bear—used to express martial valour.

熊 羆 入 夢 may you see bears in your dreams—may you have sons.

[5] 熊 耳 山 a high peak near 盧 氏 縣 in Honan, where *Yü* the Great began his survey.

熊 膽 bear's gall—used as a medicine.

狗 熊 the Tibetan bear—a small performing bear.

(a) Brilliant glare.

熊 熊 青 色 有 光 the bright reflection from the blue.

其 光 熊 熊 the glare is very trying.

夐 [4]　Pre-eminent; superior. To aim high; to scheme.

2816

夐 乎 尙 矣 "he stood alone and peerless!"

夐 哉 特 立 he stood alone, pre-eminent.

夐 莫 與 京 there is no place comparable to the capital.

詗 [4]　To give information about; to spy. To gossip. Shrewd, clever. Also read *ch'eng* [4].

2817

詗 察 to spy.

詗 悟 sharp; intelligent.

詗 邏 to patrol and spy.

窺 詗 to watch and report.

HSÜ.　　(ㄒㄩ)

吁 [1]　An interjection. Alas! To sigh. Also read *yü* [1].

2818

吁 嗟 or 吁 嗟 乎 alas!

吁 好 出 奇 it is very strange.

吁 是 何 言 也 Fie! What are you saying?

長吁短歎 with sighs and groans.

吁¹ To open the eyes wide; to gaze in astonishment.
2819

吁吁 staring about.

吁瞑 gazing into the dim distance.

吁衡 to open the eyes, as when trying to see distant objects; glaring in anger.

吁衡厲色 staring in anger.

⁵吁衡當世 to have open eyes and know what is going on—to have knowledge of the times.

(a) Anxious, vexed.

云何其吁 Why am I kept in this state of anxiety?

云何吁矣 How I long for them!

(b) Similar to the next:—Great, etc.

怡吁 cheerful, happy.

訏¹ To boast. Great, important.
2820

訏誇 to make a boast; boastful.

(a) Read hsü³. Great, large.

訏訏 great.

訏謨 important plans; great schemes.

虛¹ False; untrue; unreal. Hollow; empty. Vacant; insubstantial; figurative; abstract.
2821

虛中 hollow. See below—A.1.

虛位 to leave a seat vacant; to reserve a seat for another.

虛來謊去 hollow intercourse.

虛假 false; unreal.

⁵虛傳 legendary; a false account.

虛像 virtual image.

虛僞 false; a fallacy.

虛價 overcharge.

虛名 a reputation without the facts to support it.

¹⁰虛名虛利 vain is a good name; empty, profits.

虛君 mere figure-heads.

虛器 an empty vessel; a man with capacity but no office.

虛坐以待 a vacant seat awaits.

虛報 false report.

¹⁵虛士 a pretended scholar.

虛套 mere conventionalities; polite phrases.

虛妄 vain; dissolute.

虛好看 mere empty show.

虛字 particles.

²⁰虛實 abstract and concrete; hollow and solid; general and particular, etc.

虛左 kept the left seat (of honour) vacant; to leave room for a more worthy man.

虛幻 false; visionary; illusory; unreal.

虛度 to pass—the years—in vain.

虛度三十六歲 I have lived in vain for 36 years—conventional way of stating one's age.

²⁵虛弱 weak; decrepit.

虛張聲勢 to make a demonstration; to make a display; to pretend to power and influence.

虛影 an empty shadow; invisible; shadowy.

虛恭 making a pretence of showing respect.

虛情 hollow affection; false sympathy.

³⁰虛想 fancy; imagination.

虛應故事 a mere formality; routine practice.

虛掩 partly open; ajar.

虛捏 to concoct a statement.

虛擬 supposition.

³⁵虛數 or 虛量 imaginary number or quantity.

虛文 conventional phrases.

虛有其表 mere show,—no reality in the claim.

虛望 vain hopes; delusive.

虛本 nominal capital.

⁴⁰虛構 to trump up.

虛榮 empty glory; vanity.

虛榮心 a desire for glory and wealth.

虛浮 light; trifling; treacherous.

虛火 an empty fireplace—hungry; inflammation.

⁴⁵虛無 empty; visionary; false.

虛無主義 Nihilism.

虛無寂滅 vacant and quiet, as the mind absorbed in Buddhist meditation.

虛無縹渺 utterly visionary, no reality whatever.

虛無黨 Nihilists.

⁵⁰虛牝 a bottomless pit.

虛用 a figurative use.

虛留 to make a show of pressing one to stay.

虛癆 consumption.

虛發 to miss the target.

⁵⁵虛禮 formal ceremony.

虛空 hollow; empty.

虛糜 useless waste; extravagance.

虛線 imaginary line; dotted line.

虛聲 mere empty sound; false reputation.

⁶⁰虛與委蛇 (-i²) to pretend interest and sympathy.

虛船 an empty boat.

虛花 to waste.

虛華 vain; empty show.

虛衍 empty; unreal.

⁶⁵虛設 an empty spread—to make provision in vain, a conventional phrase used to guests.

虛詐 false; treacherous.

虛話 unfounded statements; idle prating.

虛誇 mere empty boasting.

虛誣 visionary; illusory.

⁷⁰虛誕 lying; vain.

虛談 empty talk.

虛訛 false.

虛謊 lying; false.

虛譽 empty reputation.

⁷⁵虛讚 hollow compliments.

虛負 to regard lightly; to look upon as a sinecure.

虛負光陰 to waste time.

虛軟 weak; feeble.

虛辭 empty talk; vain words; false statements.

⁸⁰虛邪 weak and affected by noxious influences.

虛飄飄 fickle, light and unstable.

虛飾 affected; got up to appear in false colours; put on.

虛驚 empty fears.

虛體 a delicate constitution.

⁸⁵六虛 everywhere.

太虛 the great void; space; the Illimitable.

心虛 apprehensive.

房虛昴星 the names of four constellations in the list of 28 which are found in calendars; they are the 4th, 11th, 18th, and 25th respectively,-the days which are represented by these stars are always Sundays.

空虛 unoccupied; empty.

(a) Pure, unprejudiced, humble.

虛中 humble minded. See above —1.

虛 己 to empty oneself.
虛 己 下 人 to humble oneself.
5 虛 己 說 Theory of the Kenosis.
虛 徐 quiet and dignified.
虛 心 "poor in spirit," unprejudiced, meek, humble.
虛 心 下 氣 meek and submissive.
虛 心 研 審 to make an unprejudiced investigation.
虛 憍 to humble oneself.
10 虛 懷 聽 納 to receive the information in a humble manner.
虛 懷 若 谷 a mind open to instruction.
虛 明 clear and unprejudiced—mind.
虛 沖 unassuming and complaisant.
虛 衷 diffident; unprejudiced in heart.
15 虛 靜 humble and quiet; abstracted.
虛 靈 不 昧 an unclouded mind.
自 虛 to empty oneself.
謙·虛 diffident and modest; unassuming.

噓 2822 1.4. Slow expiration of the breath. A deep sigh.

噓 吸 breathing; used to describe the movements of the atmosphere; like the breathing of some great creature.
噓 嘺 a deep sigh.
噓 噫 belching; hiccoughing.
噓 枯 吹 生 warm breath that would cause dying things to revive.
噓 氣 to belch.

(a) From the above comes the idea of:—To praise, to recommend, to flatter, to puff.

吹 噓 to praise; to puff; to recommend.

墟 2823 1 Old burial grounds. Wild, waste land. A fair, a market.

墟 塲 the site of the fair.
墟 墓·之 間 among the old tombs.
墟 期 the date of the fair or market.
歸 墟 to go to the grave—to die.

歔 2824 1 To snort. To blow through the nose.

歔 欷 to sob and sigh with sniffing.

許 2825 3 To promise, thus:—to betroth, to allow.

許(下)·了 promised in marriage.
許 人 to promise; betrothed to.
許 信 to put faith in.
許 允 to accede to.
5 許 其 所 已 能 agreed with what he had already attained.
許 可 to sanction; approval.
許 可 規 定 sanctioned.
得 許 可 to get permission; sanctioned.
衆 皆 許 可 by common consent.
10 許 婚 betrothed; affianced.
許 嫁 to betroth a daughter.
許 纓 to receive the betrothal presents from the bridegroom's family.
許 字 to promise in marriage.
許 神 or 許 佛 to vow to the gods or to Buddha—to make a faithful promise.
15 許 約 to make an agreement with.
許 聘 to betroth.
許 與 to promise to.
許 諾 or 應 許 or 許·下 to promise; to assent to.
許 賜 to promise to bestow.
20 許 送 鬼 a promise never intended to be fulfilled.
許 進 to permit to enter.
許 配 to betroth.
許 配 良 緣 a felicitous betrothal.
許 願 to vow.
25 不 許 will not allow; will not consent to.
則 王 許 之 乎 would your majesty allow what he said?
可 復 許 乎 could you hope to accomplish such results — as achieved by *Kuan Chung?*
必 許 it must be granted; most certainly.
自 許 conceited.

(a) Perhaps.

許 得 it may be; most probably is.
許·阿 most likely; probably.
也 許 有 most probably there is.
管 許 possibly; most likely, quite probable.

行 許 probably.

(b) Excess, surplus. Very. About.

許 久 a long time.
許 多 very many; much.
三 十 許 thirty odd; over thirty.
少 許 a little.

(c) Final particle.

奈 何 許 but for a time.
如 許 such; so; like this.
心 思 如 許 "so sympathetic is his heart."
幾 許 how much; not far.

(d) A place, like 所.

何 許 人 (did not know) where he came from.
出 何 許 where did he come from?

(e) Read *hu*[3]. A sound.

伐 木 許 許 the sound of the axes on the trees.
邪 (*ye*) 許 sing-song of carriers.

栩 2826 3 A species of oak. Pleased.

栩 栩 然 a state of happiness.
栩 栩 自 得 well-pleased.

詡 2827 3 To brag; to boast.

誇 詡 to boast; to exaggerate.

(a) To spread, to make known.

德 發 揚 詡 萬 物 "his goodness extends to every creature."
遍 詡 everywhere.

(b) Harmony.

和 詡 in harmony.
魴 鱮 詡 詡 the bream and the tench dwell there together.

(c) Bold, vigorous.

會 同 主 詡 when *princes* meet, a firm and courteous manner is essential.

(d) To flatter, to toady to.

呴 2828 3.4. To breathe on; to yawn.

呴 嘘 to breathe on; to yawn.
呴 鏡 to breathe on a mirror.
相 呴 以 濕 to breathe—on a dry fish—to revive it.

(a) Read *hou³*. To roar, similar to 吼 No. 2148.

雷 呴 而 電 發 the roar of the thunder and the flash of the lightning.

姁[1] Handsome.
2829

姁 媮 handsome, elegant, graceful; a pleasant face.

(a) Read *hsü³*. Cheerful.

姁 姁 然 happy and cheerful.

(b) Read *hsü³*. To chatter like an old woman. u.f. 嫗 No. 7655.

言 語 炮 姁 he chattered like an old woman.

昫[1] Warmth of the rising sun. Inter., next and read *hsü³*. 2830 Genial.

昫 嫗 覆 育 萬 物 to give warmth to and nurture all things—as nature in producing.

煦[3] Genial, warm. To boil, to heat. Kind, gracious. Inter. 2831 preceding.
Distinguish 照 No. 238.

煦 仁 孑 義 from 煦 煦 爲 仁, 子 子 爲 義 little acts of benevolence and isolated deeds of righteousness—are not the great principles of love and righteousness.

煦 伏 之 恩 to treat kindly—lit., to warm and cover, as a bird its eggs.

煦 嫗 萬 物 to stimulate nature—by the genial warmth.

煦 日 a warm day.
煦 育 to rear; to nourish.
和 煦 genial, kind.

欨[1] To blow or breathe upon. To smile. Inter. 呴 No. 2828 2832 and 煦 next.

欨 愉 smiling; contented.

(a) Read *hsü³*. Cheerful.

欨 欣 欣 cheerful; elated.

煦[4.3] To breathe upon. Inter. 呴 No. 2828 and 欨 above.
2833

吹 煦 to blow.

(a) To smile.

煦 煦 趄 趄 smiling and chuckling.

(b) To soothe.

煦 之 若 子 he pacified them as if they were his children.

(c) To report to superiors.

酗[4] Drunk.
2834

酗 酒 滋 事 drunk and disorderly.
沈 酗 dead drunk.

HSÜ. SÜ. (ㄙㄨ)

胥[1] All, together, mutually.
2835

胥 匡 以 生 to render mutual assistance in order to preserve their lives.
胥 在 是 矣 all depend upon this.
胥 失 之 they were mutually wrong.
胥 皆 all; every one.
胥 靡 tied together—convicts.
胥 徒 prisoners,—similar to preceding entry.
載 胥 及 溺 you will only go with it to ruin.

(a) A final particle, meaning all.

君 子 樂 胥 all these princes are to be rejoiced in.

(b) To store.

儲 胥 to accumulate.

(c) To assist.

相 胥 mutually assisting.

(d) To wait. To expect.

胥 命 wait for orders.

(e) To spy, to examine.

于 胥 斯 原 he had surveyed the plain where he dwelt.
聿 來 胥 宗 they came together and chose the site for settlement.

(f) Distant.

胥 胥 separated.
無 胥 遠 矣 they should not be treated distantly—said of near relatives.

(g) A clerk or writer.

胥 吏 or 胥 鈔 clerks in a *yamen*.
胥 役 *yamen* runners.

(h) Crabs, minced and salted.

蟹 胥 crabs salted down and minced.

壻
婿[4] A son-in-law.
2836

夫 壻 a husband.
女 壻 a son-in-law.

湑[3] To strain spirits.
2837

飲 此 湑 矣 let us drink this clear wine.

(a) Abundant.

其 葉 湑 兮 "How luxuriant are the leaves!"

(b) Bright.

零 露 湑 兮 "with the bright dew upon it."

糈[1.3] Sacrificial rice. Rations —official pay.
2838

諝[3.1] Knowledge; discrimination; prudence.
2839

才 諝 ability.
智 諝 wisdom, prudence.
謀 無 遺 諝 if there is no lack of discernment in the plans.

(a) Deceit; treachery.

詐 諝 treacherous; unreliable.

醑 ³ To strain spirits. Inter. 湑 No. 2837.

2840

祝 醑 prayers and offerings—of wine.

徐 ² A composed, dignified step. Grave, slow, dignified.

2841

徐 圖 carefully considered.

徐 徐 tardy.

徐 徐 而 來 approaching with slow and dignified steps.

其 臥 徐 徐 his sleep was sound and peaceful.

5 姑 徐 徐 云 爾 "Gently, gently if you please."

徐 步 with slow steps.

徐 綏 之 let them relax—and recuperate.

徐 而 日 出 slowly and majestically rises the sun.

徐 行 後 長 (chang³) 者 proceed slowly behind your seniors.

10 徐 速 slow and fast—rate, speed.

增 加 之 徐 速 rate of increase—as of population.

徐 雨 gentle rain.

安 徐 placid and quiet.

沖 而 徐 盈 it bubbles up and slowly fills.

清 風 徐 來 the refreshing breeze gently blows.

濁 而 徐 清 turbid water gradually becomes clear.

舒 徐 at ease; having leisure.

(a) Surname.

徐 娘 an elderly woman whose beauty is fading—from a woman named *Hsü* who carried on amorous intrigues when old; she was a concubine of *Liang Yüan Ti* 梁 元 帝.

徐 州 one of the divisions of China under *Yü* the Great, *see under* 九 No. 1198—15; it extended from *T'ai Shan* in Shantung to the sea, south to the Yangtze River, and west to the *Poyang* Lake. Now a city in North Kiangsu.

敘 ⁴ To converse, to chat;
敍 to state. An interview, a meeting.

2842

敍 事 to discuss facts; explanatory notes.

敍 事 詩 a narrative poem; an epic.

敍 別 to take leave of.

敍 寒 溫 to discuss the weather—ordinary conversation.

5 敍 情 a private friendly conversation between two people.

敍 明 or 細 敍 to state explicitly.

敍 會 a meeting, an interview.

敍 舊 to talk over old times.

敍 話 to have an interview.

10 敍 談 or 相 敍 to chat.

敍 述 to quote from; to narrate; description.

全 敍 to quote the whole—of a despatch.

暢 敍 a pleasant conversation.

節 敍 partly quoted—in a despatch.

15 議 敍 to discuss; to deliberate.

(a) To arrange; to place in order. Details. Rank, series.

敍 勳 條 例 rules for granting rewards and decorations.

敍 功 to reward a worthy man with a decoration or rank.

敍 等 rank.

敍 論 to discuss in order and detail.

5 敍 錄 to copy out in order.

獎 敍 a reward, decoration, honours, etc.

(b) A preface. Inter. 序 No. 2851.

溆 ⁴ A river in Hunan.

2843

需 ¹ To require; to need. Essential.

2844

需 次 = 2136.10

需 求 claim; demand.

需 用 的 indispensable.

需 用 經 費 necessary expenses.

5 需 索 obstinately bent on; to get by any means; to extort.

需 要 necessity; demand—as in supply and demand.

需 要 品 necessities.

需 要 額 the necessary amount; the required number.

些 需 a little.

10 急 需 urgently required.

軍 需 military expenditure. *See* No. 1722—98 ff.

(a) Stopped by the rain, hence:— To doubt, to hesitate, to procrastinate.

需 事 之 賊 也 procrastination is the thief of time.

(b) Read *juan³.* Pliant, supple.

(c) Read *nuan⁴.* Weak.

(d) Read *ju².* Pliant and slippery.

需 弱 者 來 使 when the plausible envoys come.

繻 ¹ Fine gauze. Frayed edges of silk. Silk torn into two pieces, one of which was given as a credential and the other retained. Also read *ju².* A leak.

2845

鑐 ¹ The bolt of a Chinese lock.

2846

須 ¹ Necessary. Must. Inter.
須 需 No. 2844. Second form is common but not strictly correct; it is read *hui³* or *mei⁴.*

2847

須 人 a man is indispensable; must have the assistance of a man.

須 如 must be like...

須 用 necessary.

須 知 that which it is essential to know; take note.

5 須 票 an indispensable document.

須 簽 名 蓋 章 之 銀 票 cheque payable to order.

須 至 執 照 者 this is the due document—phrase closing a despatch.

須 至 照 會 者 let this despatch come to... phrase used at end of despatches.

須 要 or 必 須 or 須 當 or 須 定 or 須・得 must ; absolutely necessary. (得 pron. *tei³*)

¹⁰須 要 小 心 you need to exercise great care.

務 須 it is absolutely necessary.

相 須 mutually dependent.

終 須 after all, it is necessary to....

(a) A moment.

須 臾 for a moment ; a little while.

須 搖 an instant.

其 須 之 間 in a little while ; in a moment.

少 須 just a little.

(b) To wait; to expect.

須 女 a waiting-maid. Star in Aquarius.

須 暇 to wait for with indulgence.

須 留 to wait ; to hesitate.

(c) Whiskers; the beard. See next, No. 2848.

(d) u.f. Foreign sounds.

須 彌 座 or 須 彌 樓 Sumeru— the central mountain peak of the Buddhist universe; by some referred to as a transliteration for Himalayas.

鬚¹ The beard and whiskers; whiskers of animals ; awns of grasses; used of anything beardlike.
2848

鬚 根 fine rootlets of certain grasses.

鬚 梳 a moustache comb.

鬚 眉 beard and eyebrows—a handsome man, as male beauty is thought to reside in these.

鬚 髯 如 戟 beard bristling with fury, like the blade of a halberd.

⁵剃 鬚 to shave the beard.

撚 鬚 to fondle the beard, as the Chinese do.

留 鬚 to allow the beard to grow, generally after forty.

禾 鬚 beard of grain.

鎖 鬚 the bolt of a Chinese lock.

絮⁴ Refuse silk or cotton, from which comes the idea of:— woolly and fluffy.
2849

絮 帽 a fleecy cap—clouds on a mountain.

絮 棉・花 to line with cotton-wool.

絮 綿・子 silk-wadding in sheets.

絮 繒 silken fabrics.

⁵絮 纊 unpicked cotton.

絮 花 raw cotton.

絮 衣 coarse garments.

絮 被 a wadded quilt.

(a) From the above:—catkins and similar blossoms.

柳 絮 willow catkins.

蘆 絮 the fluffy flowers of reeds.

(b) Also from the above:—long-drawn-out; interminable.

絮 煩 to bother ; tired of it ; talkative.

絮 絮 叨 叨 (*tao¹*) jabbering, loquacious ; prosy repetition ; constant nagging.

絮 聒 chattering.

絮 話 ceaseless chatter.

休 休 絮 絮 ceaseless nagging.

(c) Read *ch'ü*⁴. To stir.

毋 絮 羹 do not stir—condiments —into the soup ;—if a guest did this, it was taken as a suggestion that the soup was not properly seasoned.

緒⁴ The end of a ball of thread. A clue. To connect.
2850

緒 業 business or calling.

緒 正 律 歷 to adjust the standard pitch for music and regulate the rules of mathematics.

緒 言 (or 論) an introduction or preface.

緒 餘 a remnant ; surplus.

就 緒 to follow a clue ; to proceed in due order.

心 緒 the thread of one's thoughts ; thoughts, intentions.

接 緒 to connect.

頭 緒 the clue to anything.

序⁴ Precedence, order, orderly.
2851

序 事 妥 當 to arrange everything properly.

序 次 series, order ; in due sequence.

序 爵 to arrange according to rank.

序 齒 in order of age.

失 序 to get out of order.

次・序 (serial) order

(a) A preface. Inter. 敍 No. 2842.

序 (文) a preface.

序 傳 or 書 序 a preface.

自 序 preface written by the author.

(b) An east and west wall; side-rooms. Screen-walls to private rooms of the palace. Ancient school which was also an asylum for aged scholars.

東 序 西 序 special apartments in the palace set apart under the *Han* dynasty for aged scholars.

庠 序 an ancient school where aged scholars found asylum.

芧⁴ The chestnut oak. Also read *yü²*.
2852

芧 栗 a small chestnut.

(a) Read *chu³*. Similar to 苧 No. 1367. China grass or Ramie fibre.

嶼⁴ An islet. Also read *yü⁴*.
2853

孤 嶼 a solitary islet.

鱮³ The tench.
2854

魴 鱮 bream and tench.

HSÜ.　　(ㄒㄩ)

(Hsüh)

旭⁴·⁵ The dawn. The rising sun.
2855

旭 卉 dark, mysterious, difficult to comprehend.

旭 日 始 旦 at daybreak ; very early.

旭 日 旗 Japanese national flag.

(a) Pleased with oneself.

旭 旭 蹻 蹻 proud and pleased with oneself.

嘻 嘻 旭 旭 flushed with success — contemptuous.

(b) Drumming.

泃 泃 旭 旭 the booming of surf.

洫 1.5. A ditch, a gutter, a drain, a moat. To overflow.
2856

溝 洫 drains and ditches.

欻 4.5. Suddenly, abrupt. To sniff. Also read *ch'ua*[1],
2857 *hu*[4.5].

欻 吸 to breathe quickly; to sniff up.
欻 忽 suddenly; quickly.
欻 欻 而 動 shaking; trembling.
欻 欻 聲 a whizzing sound; whirring.
欻 火 the spirit of lightning.
欻 起 to rise up suddenly.

勖 4.5.
勗 To excite; to stimulate. Distinguish 最 No. 6858.
2858

勖 哉 勖 哉 rouse yourselves!
勖 哉 夫 子[3] exert yourselves, my heroes!

頊 1.5. Anxious, worried.
2859

頊 頊 不 自 得 uneasy in mind.

蓄 4.5. To store; to collect. Used with 畜 No. 1412—A.
2860

蓄 力 to husband the strength.
蓄 力 器 accumulator.
蓄 念 to harbour certain thoughts.
蓄 怨 to cherish a grievance.
[5]蓄 氣 槽 (or 器) gasometer.
蓄 疑 to harbour suspicion.
蓄 積 or 蓄 聚 to accumulate; to hoard; to lay by.
蓄 縮 to contract; to curl up.
蓄 謀 to continue plotting.
[10]蓄 電 器 leyden jar; accumulator.
蓄 電 槽 electric accumulator.
蓄 電 池 storage battery.
蓄 音 器 or 留 聲 機 a phonograph or gramophone.
蓄 髮 to allow the hair to grow.

(a) To rear; to breed.

蓄 丫 頭 to bring up slave-girls.
蓄 養 to bring up; to rear.
蓄 馬 to breed horses.

HSÜ. SÜ. (台)
(Hsüh)

戌 1.5. The eleventh of the Twelve Branches 地 支.
2861 Distinguish *shu* 戍 No. 5873, *jung* 戎 No. 3181, and *wu* 戊 No. 7197.

戌 時 7—9 p.m.
戌 月 the ninth lunar month.

恤 4.5.
卹 Sympathy, pity.
2862

恤 典 regulations for honouring the dead.
恤 匱 to relieve the distressed.
恤 嫠 to assist widows.
恤 孤 to pity orphans.
[5]恤 宅 the room where the emperor mourns.
恤 恤 distressed; sorrowful.
恤 政 a benevolent government.
恤 欵 indemnity for life lost.
恤 民 to assist the masses.
[10]恤 病 to pity one who is deformed or afflicted.
恤 老 to pity the aged.
恤 貧 to relieve the poor.
恤 賞 to relieve by grants, etc.
恤 金 compensation; indemnity.
[15]撫 恤 to soothe and pity.
賑 恤 to relieve the needy.

賉 4.5. To give alms. Inter. preceding.
2863

賉 孤 to help orphans.

訹 4.5.
To beguile by false stories.
2864

引 訹 to lead on; to beguile.

續 4.5. To connect, continuous. To join on; to add to.
2865

續 一 點 水 add a little water.

續 上 supplementary to the above.
續 信 a supplementary letter.
續 假[4] 數 日 extended leave of absence for several days.
[5]續 嗣 to adopt an heir.
續 增 or 續 添 to add to; supplementary.
續 斷 to splice.
續 會 an adjourned meeting.
續 油 add a little oil—as to a lamp.
[10]續 煩 prosy; wearisome.
續 祀 to continue the ancestral worship.
續 約 supplementary agreement or treaty.
續 絃 to join the guitar string—to marry another wife.
續 議 additionally agreed upon—as clauses.
[15]續 繼 配 or 續 娶 to marry a second wife.
續 開 談 判 to continue negotiations.
續 領 to renew—as a license, etc.
續 骨 to set a fracture.
續 麻 to splice a rope.
接 續 to continue; to carry on.
繼 續 continuous; unbroken.
陸 續 in succession; one after another in continuity.

HSÜAN. (T̤)
(Hsüen)

晅 [3] Glorious; majestic.
2866

赫 兮 晅 兮 "How commanding and distinguished!"

(a) Read *hsüan*[1]. Slow and circuitous.

晅 1.3.
烜 The light of the sun. Brilliant.
2867

晅 明 splendour; brilliant.

(a) To dry; to parch.

烜 肉 to smoke meat.
烜 魚 to cure fish.
日 以 晅 之 dry it in the sun.

貒 [1] A badger. Also read *huan*[2].
2868　See 貛 No. 2267.

貒豬 a name for the porcupine
or 豪豬.

喧 [1] Clamour, noise.
2869

喧傳 to spread rumours.
喧呼 loud crying; clamour.
喧啾 hubbub.
喧塵 noise and dust—this present
　life.
[5]喧天震地 to disturb nature; to
　upset heaven and earth with the
　noise.
喧歌 loud singing.
喧爭 wrangling and altercation.
喧競 striving; noisily contesting.
喧紛 noisy bustle.
[10]喧繁 noisy clamour — describing
　waterfowl.
喧聒茅簷下 noisy chattering
　under the thatched eaves.
喧聲震耳 an ear-splitting noise.
喧㕊 sound of altercation.
喧譁 or 喧嚷 or 喧吵 or 喧嘈
　clamour; hubbub.
[15]喧闐 a rumbling, roaring sound.
喧鬧 altercation; w r a n g l i n g;
　quarreling.

暄 [1] Genial and warm.
2870

日暄 the genial warmth of the
　sun.

楦 [1.4.] A last for making shoes.
楥   To turn in a lathe.
2871

楦圓 to turn; to make round in
　a lathe.
楦鞋 to fit a shoe to the last.
楦·頭 or 楦椿 a last; boot-trees.

縇 [1] Bright colour.
2872

縇紅 bright red.

萱 [1] A day-lily—*hemerocallis*
萲   *flava*. The dried flowers
2873　are used for food and are
known as 金銀菜. The
names of this plant are
many, 忘憂 'to forget sor-
row,' 宜男 'should have a
son,' 療愁 'curer of sorrow,'
etc. Japanese call it 忘草.
諠 No. 2875 is also u.f. this
plant.

萱堂 your mother.　See 椿 No.
　1494—2.
萱堂之靠 the assistance and
　support which a mother can
　give.
萱草忘憂 the day-lily causes
　one to forget sorrow—so a
　son is a comfort to his mother.

諠 [1.3.]
2874　　To bawl. u.f. 喧 No. 2869.

諠呼滿道 shouting filled the
　streets.
諠譁 shouting and hubbub.
諠駭 to frighten with bawling.

(a) Deceitful; to forget, (for which
　the next is used.)

諠弄 to befool.

諼 [1] Deceitful, false.
2875

詐諼之策 a r t f u l schemes;
　crafty stratagems.

(a) Inter. 萱 No. 2873.

諼草 or 忘憂草 the plant of
　forgetfulness.
焉得諼草 "How shall I get the
　plant of forgetfulness?"

(b) From the above:—to forget.

以誌勿諼 as a token of my
　lasting remembrance.
永矢弗諼 "he swears that he
　will never forget."
終不可諼兮 can never be for-
　gotten.

儇 [1] Ingenious, clever, dexter-
2876　ous, nimble.

儇子 an active, nimble person.
儇性 expert, alert, dexterous.
儇薄 alert, lively; practical joking.

(a) Read *hsüan*[2].　The name of a
　State.

嬛 [1] Apt, clever.
2877

嬛佞 seductive in speech.
便嬛綽約 clever, p r e t t y and
　modest.

(a) Read *huan*[2].　See below.

娜嬛 or 嫏嬛 the place where
天帝, the Supreme, is said to
　bestow his books.

(b) Read *ch'iung*[2].　Solitary;
　lonely.　Similar to 惸 No.
　1249, and 煢 No. 1250.

嬛嬛在疚 "solitary and full of
　distress."

懁 [1] Anxious, distressed.
　　Inter. 悁 No. 1629.
2878

懁急 anxious, desperate.

蠉 [1] Crawling of insects. Larvæ
　　of mosquitoes. See 孑 No.
2879　784—B.3.

蜎蠉 various larvæ found in
　water.

鋗 [1] A small basin.　Rings on
　　a cart or carriage.　Tinkling
2880　of jade.　Read *chüan*[1].　u.f.
涓 No. 1631—A.　Ascetic,
　pure.

鋗人 an ascetic.

玄 [2]
玄　　Dark, sombre; black.
玆　　Deep, profound, abstruse,
2881　subtle.　Radical 95.

玄仗 the *tao*—principles of right.
玄元皇帝 title u n d e r which
　Laotzǔ was canonized in A.D.
　666 by *Kao Tsung*.

玄冥 dark and mysterious—a water-spirit, the attendant on the ruler of winter.

玄化 incorporeal.

5 玄厲 black stone.

玄圃 Taoist name for paradise.

玄堂 the sombre hall—"The Grand Fane." (Legge). Place occupied by ancient emperors in second month of winter.

玄天 the northern heavens; a high mountain. See below—13.

玄女 a female who is said to have instructed the Yellow Emperor in military arts.

10 玄妙 or 玄奧 abstruse; mysterious.

玄孫 a great-great-grandson.

玄學 Taoism. Occultism.

玄帝 or 玄天上帝 the God of the Profound Heavens.

玄德 secret, hidden virtues.

15 玄悟 able to comprehend mysteries and abstruse doctrines.

玄教 Taoism.

玄旨 abstruse; mysterious.

玄明粉 salts; sulphate of soda.

玄月 the ninth lunar month.

20 玄根 the foundations of the Tao. (Taoism).

玄機 magic; skilful contrivance.

玄武 the constellations numbered 8—14 in the list of 28 given in appendix.

玄武岩 black basalt.

玄混之世 the mythical ages.

25 玄牝 "the hidden mother"—mysterious mother of all things. (Taoism).

玄牝之門 "the abode of the hidden mother,"—the universe.

玄狐 the black fox.

玄玉 black jade.

玄理 abstruse principles.

30 玄石 loadstone; magnetic rock.

玄秘 mysterious; profound.

玄秘主義 occultism.

玄穹 the profound vastness; the sky.

玄策 deep, subtle plans or strategies.

35 玄精石 carbonate of lime.

玄聖 Confucius.

玄色 dark, sombre colours.

玄英 the winter.

玄著 abstruse or occult writings.

40 玄衣 dark garments.

玄談 abstruse speculations, as in Laotzŭ.

玄謀 deep schemes; dark plots.

玄都 Fairyland.

玄酒 water.

45 玄門 Taoism; the state before birth.

玄關 the sombre entrance to the Way—(Budd.); a narrow door.

玄駒 a colt; ants; a name for the carp.

玄鱧 the snake-fish, also called black fish.

玄鳥 the swallow.

50 玄鶴 the crane, said to change into grey at 1,000 years of age, and into black at 2,000.

玄黃 heaven and earth, see below.

玄黃未判 before the earth received its form.

天玄地黃 heaven is black and earth is yellow.

玄默 silent meditation.

55 上玄 heaven, the sky; used by Taoists for God.

通玄 versed in abstruse doctrines —of Taoism.

泫⁴ To glisten; to sparkle. To weep.
2882

泫泫 copious tears.

孔子泫然流涕 Confucius' tears fell freely.

淚泫泫兮 the tears fell fast.

露泫花上 the dew sparkles on the flowers.

(a) Read hsüan². A deep, wide expanse of water.

淵泫 a waste of waters.

炫⁴ Bright, shining. Splendid.
2883

炫人耳目 to dazzle; to confuse the senses.

炫光 brilliant; splendid.

炫晝縞夜 dazzling in the day, white at night—said of plum blossoms.

炫炫上天 the (stars) sparkled in the sky.

炫燿 to illuminate.

(a) To make a display; to show off. Inter. 衒 No. 2885.

炫怪 to show off; to make a display of.

炫耀於人 to show off before others.

矜炫 to show off; to boast.

自炫 self-praise; showing off.

眩⁴ Confused vision; dizzy; giddy.
2884

眩仆 to fall down from vertigo.

眩暈 vertigo.

眩死 to die from suffocation.

眩疾 nervousness; dizziness.

目眩 eyes confused through dizziness.

頭·眩 dizzy.

(a) Mistaken; deceived; deluded.

眩于名實 to confuse the real and the unreal, the nominal and the actual.

衒⁴ To praise; To recommend. To expose, as for sale. To show off.
2885

衒天衒地 boastful exaggeration.

衒女 a coquette.

衒玉求售 to offer jade for sale —to recommend oneself.

衒鬻自信 to pass oneself off as trustworthy.

矜衒 to boast; to show off.

自衒 to show off.

鉉³ Rings or ears on a tripod by means of which it was carried. Also defined as:— a wooden pole decorated with metal for carrying a tripod.
2886

懸² To hang up; to suspend.
2887

懸乩 the planchette.

懸在空中 suspended in mid-air —in suspense.

懸雍垂 or 小舌 the uvula.

懸壺 to hang a pot—once the sign of a druggist's.

5 懸寄 to leave behind temporarily.

懸崖 or 懸疊 overhanging cliffs.

懸崖勒馬 to rein in the horse on the brink of the precipice— said of a profligate reforming before it is too late.

懸 弧 in ancient times, when a son was born, a bow was hung on the left of the door,—from which comes the next—

懸 弧 令旦 congratulatory phrase on a man's birthday.

[10]懸 掛 or 懸 上 to suspend.

懸 揣 之 詞 ambiguous expressions; guesses; having a double meaning.

懸 斷 to decide without evidence.

懸 旗 to hoist flags.

懸 梁 to tie to a beam.

[15]懸 河 a flowing stream—unending.

懸 泉 a cascade.

懸 瀨 (or 溜) a waterfall.

懸 燈 結 彩 to hang lamps and festoons—to decorate.

懸 牌 to hang up a sign.

[20]懸 空 suspended in space—unfounded; guesswork.

不 是 懸 空 生 的 it hasn't come from nothing.

懸 節 to leave one's post; to resign.

懸 磬 an empty vessel—illustrative of poverty.

懸 肘 or 懸 腕 to write without resting the arm or wrist on the table.

[25]懸 膽 a hanging gall-bladder; a nose with a bulbous tip; also :— a reminder. See 菁 No. 229-8,9.

懸 象 the sun and moon.

懸 賞 or 懸 金 to offer a reward.

懸 賞 緝 拿 reward for arrest.

懸 車 to hang up the carriage—an indication that he was not going out—of an official arriving at his post; also used of twilight.

[30]懸 軍 an army cut off from assistance.

懸 針 a hanging needle—the upright stroke in writing seen in the character for ten, etc.

懸 頭 to study with much earnestness, from a story of one who tied his head to a beam to keep him from dozing.

懸 首 to hang the head of a decapitated criminal in the market or over the gate.

倒[4]懸 hanging upside down; hanging by the heels. See below —A.6.

[35]案 懸 不 結 the suit is still unsettled.

(a) **To be in suspense; anxious.**

懸·得 很 very precarious.

懸 心 in suspense.

懸 念 or 懸 想 to think anxiously about.

懸 懸 於 吾 也 be very anxious about me.

懸 望 to hope for anxiously.

倒[4]懸 之 際 in the last extremity; a critical juncture.

(b) **Distant from; separated.**

懸 絕 very unlike.

懸 隔 separated from; distant.

絢[4] Silken pouch hung at the girdle. Stylish, adorned, variegated, ornamental.
2888

絢 彩 elegant; adorned.

素 以 爲 絢 兮 the plain ground to receive the colours.

(a) **Swift.**

絢 練 to hasten; swift.

HSÜAN. SÜAN. (台丩)

(Hsüen)

亘[1.4.] **To revolve. Distinguish** 亙 **No. 3344, for which it**
2889 **is sometimes wrongly used.**

宣[1] **To proclaim; to display;** wide, comprehensive.
2890

宣 付 to hand over orders, etc.

宣 來 to summon, to call.

宣 傳 to declare; propaganda.

宣 傳 品 propaganda material.

[5]宣 傳 家 propagandists.

宣 傳 赤 化 to propagate "Red" doctrines or communism.

宣 傳 過 激 to propagate Bolshevism.

宣 傳 隊 bands of propagandists.

宣 判 to declare a judgement.

[10]宣 力 (or 勞) to exert oneself to great efforts on behalf of another.

宣 力 軍 a "dare-to-die" regiment.

宣 募 to call for enlistment.

宣 化 to make known certain principles of reformation.

宣 召 to summon—as to court.

[15]宣 吐 to disclose.

宣 告 a formal declaration; to pronounce a sentence.

宣 告 戒 嚴 to declare martial law.

宣 告 書 or 宣 言 書 a manifesto; a statement.

宣 告 無 效 to declare null and void.

[20]宣 告 破 產 to declare bankruptcy.

宣 命 to issue commands.

宣 哲 penetrating wisdom.

宣 四 the fourth year of Hsüan T'ung—last of Manchu rulers.

宣 室 the palace.

[25]宣 導 to lead; to open up; penetrating.

宣 布 休 會 to declare the meeting adjourned.

宣 布 政 策 statement of government policy.

宣 布 政 見 a declaration of policy.

宣 布 死 刑 capital sentence declared.

[30]宣 布 疑 義 to express dissent.

宣 布 罪 狀 statement of a condemnation.

宣 布 軍 令 declaration of martial law.   A.c. 戒 嚴 令

宣 徧 to publish everywhere.

宣 慰 使 Pacification Commissioner.

[35]宣 威 to extend one's power or sovereignty.

宣 戰 declaration of war.

宣 揚 or 宣 布 or 宣 徧 or 宣 開 or 宣 示 or 誥 宣 to publish; to declare; to proclaim.

宣 撫 使 司 former title of chieftains among the frontier tribes of Yunnan.

宣 敎 to proclaim any religion; to preach.

[40]宣 敎 師 a missionary.

宣 敎 會 a missionary society.

宣 猷 to render great service to the country.

宣 福 音 to preach the Gospel.

宣 紙 or 宣 城 紙 a fine white paper from Ningkuo in S. Anhwei, specially used by artists, etc.

[45]宣 績 to do one's utmost for another.

宣 聖 Confucius.

宣 言 a statement.

宣 詔 or 宣 旨 to proclaim the Imperial will.

宣 誓 to take an oath of allegiance or of office.

50 宣 誓 典 禮 formal inauguration.

宣 誓 就 職 formally took office by swearing in.

宣 誓 釋 放 liberation on parole.

宣 謀 to make known a scheme; far-reaching devices.

宣 講 to preach; to proclaim.

55 宣 讀 to read out, as a sentence or a proclamation.

宣 讀 判 詞 to read a decision or judgement.

宣 赦 to proclaim a pardon for an offender.

宣 露 to divulge.

宣 髮 grey hair.

(a) To drain.

宣 泄 to leak out—to divulge.

宣 洩 to leak away, to leak out.

宣 洩 積 水 to drain off stagnant water.

揎 [1]
To pull up the sleeves and stretch out the arms.
2891

揎 袖 to pull up the sleeves—as for work.

(a) To strike with bare fists.

(b) Read hsüan[1]. To cram.

渲 [4]
To add repeated washes of colour in a drawing.
2892

渲 染 to make a certain colour stand out in relief by shading.

瑄 [1]
Ornamental piece of jade, described as being six inches in diameter with a hole in the centre.
2893

瑄 玉 the above.

旋 [2]
To revolve; to move in an orbit. To come back.
2894

旋 乾 轉 坤 to move heaven and earth—having great power and authority.

旋 反 to turn back.

旋 旋 a whirlpool or eddy.

旋 旆 flag-signal for return home —of soldiers.

5 旋 暈 giddy.

旋 曲 serpentine; winding.

旋 止 to stop for a while.

旋 歸 to return.

旋 毛 the hair turned back, as on some horses.

10 旋 毛 蟲 trichina.

旋 沫 the whirling foam.

旋 泉 a deep whirlpool.

旋 渦 an eddy; a whirlpool.

旋 淵 the deep pools—where the dragon lies hid.

15 旋 紋 whirling ripples; concentric circles.

旋 繞 to encircle; to go round.

旋 至 to come round.

旋 花 bindweed.

旋 螺 spiral.

20 旋 蟲 the knob by which a bell is hung.

旋 覆 花 the convolvulus.

旋 踵 to return at once, in the turning of a heel—See No. 1513—9.

旋 轉 or 旋 輪 or 回 旋 to revolve.

旋 里 or 鄉 旋 to return home to one's native place.

25 旋 風 a whirlwind.

旋 風 筆 a whirlwind-pen—incomparable style.

旋 飆 a cyclone.

周 旋 to be very attentive to; to wait on with every attention.

盤 旋 to make a circuit; to stroll around.

(a) Thereupon; forthwith; subsequently.

旋 值 just then.

旋 准 thereupon receiving—a despatch in reply.

旋 即 forthwith.

旋 得 旋 失 to lose a thing as soon as it is got.

旋 查 further examination.

旋 經 then there were.

漩 [4]
An eddy.
2895

漩 兒 or 水 漩 an eddy.

漩 渦 a vortex; an eddy or whirlpool—also used fig.

璇 璿 [2]
A fine kind of jade.
2896

璇 室 the Jade Palace—one of the extravagant luxuries of *Chou* and *Chieh*, the infamous tyrants.

璇 瑰 a fine kind of jasper.

璇 璣 圖 a palindrome, worked on a piece of satin by a woman 蘇 蕙, for her husband 竇 滔 who was banished to Tartary at the close of the 4th century A.D. There were 840 characters which could be read in either direction. *See* 廻 No. 2315—4.

璿 璣 玉 衡 ancient astronomical instruments of the time of *Shun* 舜, 2255—2205 B.C. The 璣 is described as the gear of a rotating instrument; some have thought that it was an armillary sphere, but there is no certainty of this.

鏇 [4]
A pewter heater for keeping spirits warm.
2897
A lathe. To turn in a lathe. A thread in a screw.

選 [3]
To select; to choose; to elect. Choice.
2898

選 人 officials waiting for appointment.

選 侍 girls selected for the palace.

選 備 chosen and prepared.

選 出 to pick out; to select.

5 選 勝 to visit places of scenic beauty.

選 募 to enlist picked men.

選 取 selection; to select; to pick out.

選 召 to select and summon.

選 品 a choice lot.

10 選 定 elected.

選 德 to select men of virtue.

選 手 able men selected from a number of others—a team.

選 擇 or 選 下 or 選 拔 or 選 中 to choose; to select.

選 擇 權 right of selection. (*legal*)

15 選 擇 行 動 selective act. (*legal*)

選 於 衆 to select from all the people.

選 日·子 to choose a day.

選 民 the elect; the chosen race; those who have electoral rights.

選 派 to depute; to appoint to a post.

²⁰選 用 to select for use or employment.

選 科 elective course of studies.

選 舉 to elect; election.

選 舉 人 a voter.

選 舉 侯 Elector—as in German States.

²⁵選 舉 制 suffrage.

選 舉 區 electoral district.

選 舉 會 election meeting.

選 舉 權 suffrage; right to vote.

選 舉 法 laws relating to elections.

³⁰選 舉 票 ballot-paper; votes.

選 舉 競 爭 election contest.

選 舉 資 格 qualification for election or for voting.

選 輯 compilation; editing.

選 補 chosen to fill a vacancy.

³⁵選 議 員 candidate for election.

選 集 an anthology.

(a) A little wnile.

選 間 or 少 選 a little while.

(b) Ancient weight, similar to No. 2262.

白 選 a piece of silver ornamented with a dragon, used as money under *Han* dynasty.

(c) Read *süan*[1]. Selected, as by a board for appointment.

選 授 selected for appointment.

(d) Read *hsüan*[1] or *suan*[1]. To enumerate, to count up.

世 選 爾 勞 for generations your laborious services have been noted.

何 足 選 how can they be numbered?

弗 去 懼 選 he would not go, as he feared the enumeration—of his faults.

(e) Read *sun*[1]. Peaceful, mild. similar to 巽 No. 5550.

選 懦 gentle, kind and timorous.

選 懦 之 恩 gentle, kind and good; unwilling to decide a case.

選 奱 weak and gentle; timorous.

(f) Read *shua*[1.5]. Ancient weight.

金 選 之 品 money — as weighed out,—for redemption in lieu of punishment.

(g) u.f. 萬 10,000. The ancient sounds being similar.

十 選 ten times ten thousand.

HSÜEH. (ㄒㄩㄝ)

穴 ^{4.5.} A cave, a den, a hole. A lurking-place. Underground dwellings. To bore a hole. Radical 116.

2899

穴 出 to find its way out—as water finding its level.

穴 壁 to bore a hole through a wall—in order to steal.

穴 居 野 處 to dwell in caves in the wilds.

穴 木 而 居 to make a hollow in a tree and live in it.

⁵穴 蟲 rats.

穴 見 a limited outlook; a narrow viewpoint.

穴 道 an underground channel; influences which affect the health and good fortune of a region. *See below* B.1.

穴 隙 a crack, a cranny.

穴 鼻 a rabbit.

¹⁰孔 穴 a cavity; a hole.

巢 穴 a nest; a lurking-place for robbers, etc.

窟 穴 to dig a hole.

鑽 穴 to bore a hole.

陶 穴 kiln-like huts used in ancient times.

(a) A grave.

穴 塋 site for a grave.

穴 堬 site for a grave.

穴 情 the geomantic surroundings of a grave.

吉 穴 a lucky site for a grave.

同 穴 buried in one grave.

墓 穴 a vault; the place for the coffin in a tomb.

(b) A sinus in the body.

穴 道 spots on the body suitable for acupuncture.

眤 ^{2.5.} Looking about with eagerness.

2900

眤—眣 to take a glance, to look around.(*dial.*)

眤 目 to have a look.

血 ^{3.4.5.} Blood. Blood relationship. Radical 143. Also read *hsieh*[3]. Distinguish 皿 No. 4536.

2901

血 之 運 行 the circulation of the blood.

血 凝 coagulation of the blood.

血 刃 a bloody knife.

不 血 刃 而 克 復 to recover —a city—without using weapons or losing a life.

⁵血 友 病 hæmophilia.

血 嗣 posterity.

血 塊 or 血 栓 thrombus.

血 塞 thrombus.

血 崩 menorrhagia.

¹⁰血 弱 pale; delicate.

血 心 warm-heartedness; sympathy.

血 忌 days on which the slaughter of beasts is unlucky.

血 性 violent temperament; rough-mannered; resolute disposition.

血 性 漢 子 a rough-tempered person; a manly man.

¹⁵血 戰 or 衃 戰 a bloody battle.

血 族 or 血 統 blood relatives.

血 族 結 婚 consanguineous marriage.

血 晶 blood-red quartz crystal.

血 書 a letter in blood—an application for relief in the last extremity.

²⁰血 本 hard-earned capital.

血·氣 animal desires; vigour; constitution.

血 氣 之 勇 brute force or courage.

血 氣 所 使 in bondage to the animal nature.

血 氣 未 定 the physical powers are not yet stabilized; the passions are not yet under control.

²⁵血 氣 虛 弱 lack of animal spirits; lacking in vigour. ⌠sweat.

血 汗 to sweat blood; blood and

血 汗 工 夫 strenuous efforts.

血 汗 的 錢 wages earned by the hardest toil.

血 流 漂 杵 blood flowed so as to float a pestle—said of a dreadful carnage.

³⁰血 液 the blood.

血液學 hæmatology.
血淋 blood in the urine.
血淚 tears of blood—extreme grief.
血清 serum.
[35] 血清療法 serum treatment of disease.
血漿 blood deprived of corpuscles, etc.
血熱度 blood-heat.
血玉髓 blood-stone.
血珀 deep-red amber.
[40] 血球 or 血輪 corpuscles.
血球素 hæmoglobin.
白血球 white corpuscles.
紅血球 red corpuscles.
血痂 a scab; dried blood on a wound.
[45] 血痕 marks of blood; marks of a wound.
血祭 sacrifice of blood to the gods.
血石 hæmatite.
血竭 dragon's blood, a red gum from a species of palm, used as an astringent, etc.
血肉 flesh and blood.
[50] 血肉橫飛 lit:—blood and flesh flying in every direction—describes a carnage.
血胤 posterity.
血脈 pulse—relationship, consanguinity.
血脈貫通 one argument pervades the whole.
血膽 or 血管 arteries, blood-vessels.
[55] 血色 scarlet, the colour of blood.
血色質 red colouring-matter in the blood.
血虛 (or 虧) anæmia. = 5274.19.
血行器 organs of circulation.
血表 blood relatives having a different surname.
[60] 血誠 or 血忱 intense sincerity.
血跡 blood stains.
血食 to partake of a sacrificial offering—of the gods.
血餅 clots of blood.
血點紅 to add red to blood—useless labour, unnecessary.
[65] 吐血 hæmatemesis.
泣血 tears of blood—mourning for parents.
熱血 warm-hearted; enthusiasm.
瘀血 extravasation of blood.
補血 to nourish the blood by tonics, etc.

靴]
鞾]
[2902]

Boots. Also read hsü[1].

靴子 boots.
靴夾 or 靴袯子 a pocket-book for papers, carried in the leg of the boot.
靴笏 boots and tablet—articles of official usage.
靴衫 ancient riding-jacket.
靴袍 long garment that was worn with official boots.
[5] 官靴 official boots.
快靴 thin-soled boots.
皮靴 leather boots.
穿靴 to put on boots.
脫靴 to take off boots.
[10] 隔靴搔癢 to scratch an itchy place through the boots—not very effective.

HSÜEH. SÜEH. (ㄒㄩㄝ)

雪
[2903]

3.5. Snow, ice. Also read sieh.

雪上加霜 adding frost to snow —one disaster after another.
雪中送炭 to send fuel in cold weather—timely assistance.
雪光 glare from the snow.
雪兆豐年 a fall of snow gives promise of a fruitful year.
[5] 雪冷 bitterly cold.
雪化了 the snow has melted.
雪堆 snowdrifts.
雪客 the egret. See 鷺 No. 4187.
雪散 melting; disappearing.
[10] 雪景 a snowy scene.
雪梨 fine pears from Hweichow in Anhwei.
雪白 white as snow.
雪眼 the sun shining through a cloudy haze when snow is imminent.
雪等伴 said when a fall of snow occurs before a previous fall has melted.
[15] 雪線 the snow-line.
雪肌 snow-white flesh.
雪花 or 雪片 snow-flakes.
雪衣娘 a white cockatoo.
雪霜 snow and frost; hoar-frost.
[20] 雪青 pale mauve colour.
雪鞋 snowshoes.
雪髯 white beard.

下雪 to snow.
大雪 Solar period, about Dec. 7—21.
[25] 小雪 Solar period, about Nov. 22—Dec. 6.

(a) To whiten. To wipe out a grievance.

雪[4]冤 to clear a person from a false charge.
雪[4]忿 to avenge; to appease one's anger.
雪[4]恥 to avenge an insult; to wipe out a disgrace.
雪洗 to whiten; to wash clean.
(b) used in transliterating.
雪茄 cigar.

鱈
雪
[2904]

[5] The codfish. Commonly called 鰵魚 See No. 4518.

HSÜN.　　　(ㄒㄩㄣ)

(Hsüin)

煮
[2905]

[1] Fumes from sacrifice.

煮蒿 a subtle vapour from sacrifices.
煮蒿悽愴 the odours of the sacrifice affect (the offerer).

熏
燻]
[2906]

[1] Smoke; fog; vapour. Miasma. To scent, to fumigate, to smoke. To suffocate.

熏乾 to dry at the fire.
熏人 to bluff another into action by loud talk.
熏出來 to force (flowers) with heat.
熏夕 dusk; evening.
[5] 熏天氣焰 their breath blazes up to heaven—an expression indicating great power and influence.
衆口熏天 the clamour rose to heaven.
熏死 suffocated—as by fumes of charcoal.
熏灼四方 to usurp authority and oppress on every side.
熏炙 to cauterize; to be contaminated by evil company.
[10] 熏烝 steam; hot vapour.
熏烘 to fumigate.

熏 熏 pleased; harmonious; numerous.

熏 爐 a brazier.

熏 籠 a frame, made to fit over a brazier, used for drying clothes.

15 熏 肉 to smoke meat previously boiled.

熏 臘 a shop-sign indicating the sale of hams and other smoked meats.

熏 蒸 消 毒 to fumigate against disease.

熏 蚊 子 to smoke out mosquitoes.

熏 衣 to fumigate clothing.

20 熏 透 ·了 thoroughly smoked.

熏 風 a south-west wind.

熏 魚 smoked fish; bloaters.

熏 黃 a deep orange colour.

熏 黑 smoked black.

25 熏 鼠 to smoke out rats.

勳
勛 } 1 Merit. Loyal efforts rendered to the State.
2907

勳 位 an order of merit,—it has degrees, and carries a salary.

勳 業 or 勳 勞 honours conferred for loyal services.

勳 烈 merit earned by loyal service.

勳 爵 rank conferred for merit.

5 勳 猷 meritorious plans.

勳 祉 or 勳 安 well-deserved happiness.

勳 章 a decoration.

勳 臣 a patriotic statesman; an official whose services deserve recognition.

勳 襲 ennobled for merit.

10 勳 賜 to bestow—as a decoration.

壎
塤 } 1 Ancient wind-instrument, shaped like an egg, made of porcelain; something like the ocarina.
2908

曛 1 Twilight; sunset.
2909

曛 夕 or 曛 暮 evening; the gloaming.

曛 映 the setting sun.

獯 1 A tribe of Scythians which invaded China during the *Hsia* dynasty.
2910

獯 鬻 the above tribe,–they were known as the *Hsiung nu* in the *Ch'in* and *Han* dynasties.

纁 1 Crimson, dark red.
2911

薰 1 A fragrant plant. Fragrance. To becloud. u.f. 熏 No. 2906.
2912

薰 心 to becloud the mind— through lusts; greed of gain.

薰 染 to be imbued with.

薰 沐 to bathe; to disinfect.

薰 爐 an incense burner.

5 薰 籠 a brazier, a frame for placing over a brazier.

薰 草 general name for fragrant plants.

薰 蕕 fragrant and foetid—plants.

薰 衣 ·裳 to put camphor or perfumed plants among clothes.

薰 赫 honoured and respected.

10 薰 陶 culture.

薰 風 southerly winds, warm breezes.

薰 香 fragrance of plants; to fumigate by burning herbs, etc.

醺 1 Helplessly intoxicated.
2913

訓 4 To instruct, to advise, to admonish. Counsel.
2914

訓 令 instructions from superiors.

訓 典 moral maxims; wise sayings.

訓 卒 to train soldiers.

訓 子 to train one's son.

5 訓 導 former title of a Sub-Director of Studies in a district.

訓 戒 to warn.

訓 政 時 期 period of political tutelage.

訓 示 instructions.

訓 ·練 to drill; to train; discipline.

10 訓 練 機 關 training-institutions.

訓 育 practical culture.

訓 蒙 to train the young.

訓 言 precepts.

訓 詁 (or 故) to comment on.

15 訓 詞 official speech, as in opening parliament, etc. Practical advice.

訓 誨 or 訓 教 to instruct.

訓 誨 諄 諄 line upon line, precept upon precept.

訓 誘 to lead on by instruction.

訓 諭 injunctions.

20 訓 責 to caution and punish.

訓 辭 instructions; injunctions.

訓 迪 to open up a man's intelligence.

訓 飭 to instruct and admonish.

古 訓 lessons of antiquity.

HSÜN. SÜN. (台宀)

(Hsüin)

旬 2 A period of ten days. Sometimes used for ten years.
2915

旬 內 within ten days.

旬 日 ten days.

旬 歲 a full year.

上, 中, 下 旬 the three decades of a month.

七 旬 70 years; 70 days; also u.f. the seven periods of seven days each in the mourning for parents.

六 旬 60 years.

(a) Wide-spreading.

來 旬 來 宣 you have diffused— my instructions—everywhere.

(b) Read *chün*[1]. Forced labour.

公 旬 levy of labour on public works.

峋 2 Ranges of hills stretching one beyond another. Irregular peaks.
2916

徇 4 To follow, to accord with. Inter. 殉 No. 2920.
2917

徇 人 to fall in with another's ideas.

徇 庇 to uphold another; to protect.

徇 從 to comply with; to accord with.

徇 情 to be influenced by feelings in giving a decision; favouritism.

[5]徇 情 故 縱 to show favour and connive at wrong.

徇 照 according to.

徇 私 favoritism; nepotism.

徇 義 to follow rectitude.

徇 財 to seek for gain.

[10]徇 隱 to connive at.

(a) Quick.

徇 疾 speedily.

徇 齊 quick of apprehension.

(b) Read *hsün²*. Pervading, comprehensive. All around.

徇 通 to comprehend fully.

恂 [2]
2918
Sincere; reverently careful.

恂 實 sincerely honest.

恂 恂 如 也 simple and sincere.

恂 恂 自 下 modest.

恂 慄 tremblingly attentive.

恂 達 intelligent.

栒 籚 [3]
2919
The cross-beam of a bell or drum-frame. A tree.

殉 狥 徇 [4]
2920
To be buried with the dead.

殉 君 to die with one's prince.

殉 國 to die for one's country.

殉 夫 to be buried with her husband.

殉 母 to die with one's mother.

[5]殉 節 to die in defence of her virtue.

殉 節 自 盡 to commit suicide rather than remarry—of a widow.

殉 義 martyrdom.

殉 葬 to bury the living with the dead.

殉 裝 grave-clothes.

[10]殉 難 to die—as for one's country; to commit suicide to escape from the hands of the enemy.

(a) To desire with ardour. To be greedy for. To comply with. Inter. 徇 No. 2917.

殉 利 greedy for gain.

殉 情 or 殉 私 favouritism; to be influenced by feelings in making a decision; to act according to another's wishes.

殉 於 貨 色 addicted to lust and gain.

殉 求 to seek after.

殉 衆 to agree with all; to fall in with the wishes of others.

殉 財 殉 名 to covet gain and glory.

殉 隱 to screen; to connive at.

洵 [2]
2921
To weep.

洵 涕 to shed tears in silence.

(a) Really, truly.

洵 堪 quite suitable.

洵 是 it is indeed!

洵 美 且 仁 truly admirable and humane.

洵 美 且 異 truly elegant and rare.

(b) Distant, remote.

吁 嗟 洵 兮 Alas, how remote!

(c) Water flowing out from a whirlpool. A river in Shensi.

荀 [2]
2922
A plant with a yellow flower and a red fruit.

詢 [2]
2923
To inquire about; to deliberate; to consult.

詢 事 to consult about affairs.

詢 以 何 軒 asked what he was about!

詢 取 asked for.

詢 商 to take counsel with.

[5]詢 問 to interrogate.

詢 問 代 詞 interrogative particle.

詢 察 to investigate by inquiry.

詢 悉 to make full investigations.

詢 明 to ascertain by inquiry.

[10]詢 據 to examine with the help of.

詢 訪 to make inquiries.

詢 請 to inquire about and request.

逈 [4]
2924
To be the first to begin a quarrel.

郇 [2]
2925
An ancient feudal State in Shensi. Used for transliterating sounds.

郇 廚 the kitchen of a duke of that name in the *T'ang* dynasty; he was given to lavish hospitality, hence the expression comes to signify:—Your excellent entertainment.

循 [2]
2926
To follow; to comply with. In order.

循 其 性 之 自 然 to act in accordance with his natural disposition.

循 吏 upright official.

循 序 gradually; step by step.

循 序 漸 進 to follow in proper sequence and make gradual progress.

[5]循 循 然 methodically; orderly.

循 方 針 to take a given direction.

循 法 to observe the law.

循 照 according to; accordingly.

循 物 無 違 never to break an agreement with others.

[10]循 牆 而 走 he followed the wall and got away.

循 理 reasonable; in accord with principle.

循 環 to revolve; to come round in order.

循 環 器 organs of circulation.

循 環 小 數 recurring decimals.

[15]循 環 往 復 to follow in a circle.

循 良 docile.

循 規 蹈 矩 to follow precedent; law-abiding.

循 途 守 轍 to follow the tracks and keep to the ruts—to keep to the beaten path; to follow precedent.

循 階 to advance by regular steps.

[20]循 順 tractable.

(a) Tethered.

走 踚 踚 如 有 循 dragging his feet as if they were held to the ground.

巡 巡
2927

To go on circuit; to cruise; to patrol.

巡 丁 or 巡 役 or 巡 差 watch-men; police.

巡 兵 soldiers on patrol.

巡 哨 or 巡 遊 to patrol.

巡 夜 night-watching.

⁵巡 守 (or 狩) an imperial tour of inspection.

巡 幸 imperial tour.

巡 按 使 civil governor—a former title.

巡·捕 a policeman.

巡·捕 房 a police-station.

¹⁰巡 撫 former title of the Governor of a Province.

巡 更 or 巡 邏 or 巡 察 to go the rounds—as a watchman or a constable on his beat.

巡 查 to inspect.

巡 檢 former title of a sub-District Deputy Magistrate.

巡 歷 or 巡 閱 to go on a round of inspection.

¹⁵巡 洋 艦 a cruiser.

巡 營 outposts; night-guards.

巡 緝 to patrol and seize.

巡 船 revenue cruiser.

巡 警 policemen.

²⁰巡 警 總 監 Inspector-general of Police.

巡 迴 圖 書 官 circulating library.

巡 迴 文 庫 circulating library.

巡 迴 法 院 Court of Assize.

巡 迴 講 演 團 travelling lecture-party for educational purposes.

²⁵巡 邏 隊 military police.

巡 邊 to patrol the frontier.

巡 長 Inspector-in-chief of Police.

巡 閱 使 High-Inspecting Commissioner.

鄩
2928

An old name for the present Wei-hsien 濰 縣 in the east of Shantung.

馴
2929

Tame, from which comes:—mild, docile, well-bred.

馴 和 quiet and docile.

馴 狐 the horned-owl.

馴 畜 tame, trained animals.

馴 良 harmless; tractable; tame; gentle.

馴 鹿 the reindeer.

(a) To attain gradually.

馴 至 to reach to gradually.

I. (一)

已
2930

³ Already; finished. Sign of the past. To come to an end. Distinguish 己 No. 429. 巳 No. 5590.

已 久 for a long time.

已 前 before; formerly. ≡ 以 前

已 去 already gone.

已 定 already fixed.

⁵已 往 bygone; already passed.

已 後 hereafter; subsequently.*

已 滿 already full; expired—as a time-limit.

已 然 past.

已 畢 already finished.

¹⁰已 矣 乎 it is all over.

已·經 or 業 已 or 早 已 already; some time ago. A.c. 已 竟.

已 足 sufficient.

不 得 已 cannot help it; obliged to.

無 已 endless; before long.

* ≡ 以 後

(a) Very, excessive.

已 極 the utmost; the extreme limit.

已 甚 extremely; excessive.

病 之 已 甚 his illness is very severe.

(b) Intensive final particle, gives emphasis to what precedes.

已 而 or 而 已 or 已 耳 that's all! simply that, and no more!

也 已 Indeed! Yes, certainly!

亦 不 足 畏 也 已 he will then indeed not be worth respect.

可 謂 好 學 也 已 it may be said that he indeed loves to learn.

可 知 已 certainly may be known.

圯
2931

³ A bridge; a bank. Distinguish 圮 No. 5141.

圯 橋 三 進 履 three times going down for the shoe at the bridge.

以 以
2932

³ By, through, with. An instrumental preposition. A sign of the object which it precedes. Can often be translated by take.

以 事 實 證 之 illustrate this with some facts.

以 人 治 人 to rule men by that which is common to all men.

以 仁 存 心 he cherishes benevolence in his heart.

以 何 市 而 反 what shall I purchase with the money and bring back with me?

⁵以 其 病 之 所 切 took that which applied to his weak point.

以 冷 靜 之 頭 腦 判 定 之 came to a decision about it in a cool, deliberate manner.

以 利 言 之 speaks of it as gain.

以 力 服 人 cause men to submit by force.

以 如 是 之 偉 人 that such a man of parts—points out the object.

¹⁰以 實 告 之 told him the truth.

以 工 代 賑 to give relief by providing labour.

以 己 爲 問 made himself the object of inquiry.

以 德 報 怨 recompense injury with kindness.

以 威 力 嚇 散 羣 衆 caused the crowd to disperse by intimidation.

¹⁵以 方 徧 諸 侯 he visited all the feudal chiefs with his magical formulae.

以 方 見 上 came with magic formulae to see the emperor.

以 書 相 分 gave him a letter of introduction as he parted from him.

以 狀 白 縣 notified the magistrate.

以 禮 節 之 regulate it by means of the rules of propriety.

²⁰以 管 窺 天 look at the sky through a tube.

以 約 失 之 者 鮮 矣 few are the mistakes of those who use caution.

以 訛 傳 訛 to transmit errors; to perpetuate mistakes.

以 身 教 者 從 they will follow one who teaches by example.

以 身 體 之 felt for them in his own person.

²⁵以 道 事 君 served their prince with right principles.

以 隸 使 之 use them as slaves.

以 首 承 之 supporting it on its summit.

以 鼓 進 以 金 退 advanced at the sound of the drum, and retreated at the sound of the gong.

敎 以 人 倫 teach them the relations of humanity.

³⁰生 事 之 以 禮 when living serve them with propriety.

給 以 米 粉 一 碗 gave him a basin of rice-gruel.

道 之 以 政 lead the people by laws.

(a) Because; on account of.

以 告 者 過 也 this is because those who reported it went beyond the truth.

以 此 on this account; hence.

以 言 舉 人 to promote a man merely on his own statements.

不 以 辭 害 志 do not insist on one sentence so as to do violence to the general tenor of the passage.

⁵問 其 所 以 asked the cause of it.

必 有 以 也 there surely will be a reason.

故 以 wherefore; therefore.

是 以 wherefore, because, on this account, for this reason.

是 以 不 往 見 也 it is on this account that I have not gone to see him.

¹⁰此 以 沒 世 不 忘 也 it is on this account that they are not forgotten after they leave the world.

誠 不 以 富 亦 祇 以 異 it may not be because she is rich, yet you come to make a difference.

辭 以 病 declined on account of illness.

(b) So as to; in order to.

以 便 商 民 or 以 便 商 旅 so as to accommodate merchants.

以 便 照 辦 in order to act accordingly.

以 便 輸 餉 in order to facilitate the payment of duties.

以 備 稽 査 in order to provide for examination; for future reference; for future identification.

⁵以 免 兩 歧 辦 理 to avoid divergent methods of procedure.

以 免 參 差 爭 論 in order to prevent misunderstanding.

以 免 周 章 in order to avoid useless trouble.

以 免 推 諉 in order to avoid the shirking of responsibility.

以 免 曠 悞 in order to avoid delay.

¹⁰以 免 舛 悞 so as to avoid mistakes.

以 冀 so as to give reason for hope.

以 善 其 後 in order to effect future improvement.

以 況 之 也 so as to make a comparison.

以 實 之 in order to substantiate it.

¹⁵以 專 責 成 in order to impose responsibility.

以 己 及 物 仁 也 to impart yourself to others is benevolence.

以 平 其 氣 to tranquilize their spirits; to keep the peace.

以 弭 後 患 in order to forestall calamities.

以 息 浮 議 in order to stop idle discussions.

²⁰以 憑 on the ground of which; provided with which.

以 憑 査 驗 on the ground of which examination may be made.

以 憑 核 辦 in order to have proof for acting.

以 致 to cause; so as to bring about;—indicates result.

以 致 於 the result of which was ...; which resulted in ....

²⁵以 旌 其 所 爲 to honour their deed; to make their deed known.

以 昭 so as to exhibit; in token of.

以 昭 信 實 in order to show good faith; "in witness thereof."

以 昭 公 允 or 以 昭 平 允 for the sake of justice; in the interests of fair play.

以 昭 周 備 for the sake of greater completeness.

³⁰以 昭 激 勸 for the sake of encouragement.

以 服 to bring to submission.

以 期 so as to hope; so as not to interfere with.

以 期 妥 善 in order that matters may be properly arranged.

以 期 相 安 so that mutual peace may be hoped for.

³⁵以 杜 偏 累 in order to prevent partiality.

以 歸 畫 一 in order to attain uniformity.

以 耗 時 力 whereby time and strength is wasted.

以 求 眞 是 in order to ascertain the truth.

以 清 界 限 so that the limits may be clearly defined.

⁴⁰以 爲 郵 商 in order to facilitate trade.

以 爲 食 in order to get a living.

以 用 委 員 會 so as to bring committees into use.

以 發 子 貢 之 疑 so as to elicit an inquiry from *Tzŭ Kung*.

以 示 儆 as a warning.

⁴⁵以 示 優 獎 to indicate special merit.

以 示 區 別 to show the distinction.

以 示 限 制 so as to draw a limit; to cause restrictions.

以 符 原 案 so as to accord with the original arrangement.

以 符 舊 制 so as to agree with the old rule.

⁵⁰以 篤 周 祜 so as to consolidate the prosperity of *Chou*.

以 自 快 足 於 己 in order to be satisfied with oneself.

以 舉 例 to make a comparison.

以 若 所 爲 to act as you have done.

以 見 上 文 取 辟 之 意 in order to render obvious the meaning of the illustrations selected above.

⁵⁵以 資 in order to afford...; by means of which one may...

以 資 參 考 to assist further investigation.

以 資 比 較 for the sake of comparison.

以 資 鼓 勵 so as to encourage.

以 遂 其 姦 混 in order to prolong their evil ways.

⁶⁰以 重 稅 課 so as to show due respect to the interests of the revenue.

以 防 so as to guard against.

以 鳴 聲 氣 in order to get a reputation.

(c) According to.

以 其 道 得 之 to obtain them in the proper way.

以 貌 取 人 to choose by outward appearances; to show favouritism.

以 道 事 君 不 可 則 止 to serve a prince according to righteousness and to quit the service when this cannot be done.

使 民 以 時 employ the people according to the seasons—using them when free from farm labour.

禮 以 行 之 he performs it according to propriety.

(d) To regard as; to think; to consider. Often used in combination with 爲. Introduces the subject.

以 公 利 爲 期 to hope for just profits; having due regard to public interests.

以 其 外 之 because he considers it as something external.

以 反 經 合 道 爲 權 considered *ch'üan* as that which, in order to make things agree with right, deviated from fixed principles.

以 我 爲 隱 乎 do you think that I have any hidden teachings?

⁵以 技 能 及 義 蘊 勝 it is remarkable in point of craftsmanship and profundity of ideas.

以 此 爲 記 look on this as a token.

以 氣 韻 勝 vitality and refinement are regarded as excellences—"rhythmic vitality." *Giles.*

以 爲 不 可 regarded it as impracticable, unjustifiable.

以 爲 迂 to regard as impracticable.

¹⁰以 爲 遠 其 子³ thought that he was distantly reserved towards his son.

以 義 爲 利 to regard righteousness as profit.

以 難(之) to ask a difficult question; to stump. 「tion.

以 齒 爲 序 precedence by age.

吾 以 女 爲 死 矣 I thought that you had died.

¹⁵毋 吾 以 也 do not think that of me!

自 以 爲 是 they think themselves right.

(e) To have. To use. To do.

以 不 敎 民 戰 是 謂 棄 之 to use an untaught people in fighting may be called throwing them away.

以 意 構 drawn from the imagination.

以 能 問 於 不 能 以 多 問 於 寡 possessing ability and yet asking those who do not possess it, having much and yet asking of those who have little.

以 自 限 to impose a limit on oneself.

怨 乎 不 以 murmur because they do not employ him.

我 以 吾 仁 I have my goodness.

雖 不 吾 以 Although I am not used—in office.

(f) Until, when, where. Often joined with other expressions of time and place.

以 上 above.
以 下 below, beneath.
　中 人 以 下 those below mediocrity.
　十 八 以 下 those under 18 years of age.
⁵以 來 all along; till the present.
　自 古 以 來 from of old till now.
　自 有 生 民 以 來 since there were living men until now.
以 前 before.
以 南 北 統 一 之 後 since the north and south have been unified.
¹⁰以 告 則 殺 之 when he was informed, he had the slanderers executed.
以 外 outside; beyond.
以 如 江 南 went to *Kiangnan.*
以 待 來 年 wait until next year.
以 待 將 來 until some future time.
¹⁵以 待 秦 命 while awaiting the mandate of *Ch'in*—to return the captive prince of *Chin.*
以 後 afterwards.
以 至 相 蹙 until they appeared to crowd in on each other.

所 以 whence; wherefore. *See* No. 5465-2.ff.

自 今 以 往 from now on.

(g) Although. And.

以 吾 一 日 長³乎 爾 although I am a day or so older than you.

富 以 苟 不 如 貧 以 譽 riches and obscurity are not equal to poverty and fame.

生 以 辱 不 如 死 以 榮 life and shame are not equal to death and glory.

聞 一 以 知 二 I hear one point and know the second.

(h) Or.

當 克 以 否 will the war be successful or not?

(i) Used for transliteration.

以 弗 所 Ephesus.

以 色 列 Israel.

以 脫 (or 太) Ether.

苡 苢 ³ 2933　Name of a plant.

苡 米 or 薏 苡 仁 the seeds of Job's tears, (*coix lachryma*). Sometimes used for pearl-barley. Usually called 薏 仁 米.

乂 ⁴ To regulate; to bring into order. To aid. Distinguish 2934　乂 No. 7539. Also read *ngai*⁴ and inter. 艾 No. 19.

保 乂 to protect.

夾 介 乂 我 co-operate with us.

安 乂 peaceful.

有 能 俾 乂 Is there one capable of regulating this—evil?

(a) Able men.

俊 乂 在 官 men of eminence will hold office.

天 生 聰 明 時 乂 Heaven raised a man of intelligence to regulate matters at the right time.

刈 ⁴ 2935　To mow.

刈 禾 機 a reaping-machine.

刈 穫 to reap.
刈 草 機 a mowing-machine.

伊[1] A personal pronoun:—he, she, it, that one. A particle.
2936 inter. next.

伊 人 that man.
伊 家 he or she.
伊 已 年 老 無 用 she is old and useless.
伊 年 that year.
[5]伊 等 they; those.
伊 誰 之 辜 whose fault is it?
伊 誰 云 何 what was it that man said?
伊 邇 presently; soon; a little way.
其 效 伊 何 what was the result of it all?
實 維 伊 何 who are these persons?
非 伊 朝 夕 not only for that occasion.

(a) Used in names.

伊 尹 a famous minister of *T'ang* the Completer. 1766 B.C.
伊 犂 the province of Ili or Chinese Turkestan.
伊 索 Æsop.

咿
唔[1]

Used to represent sounds.

2937

咿 啞 creaking sounds; laughter.
咿 唔 hum of voices.

(a) Also read *Itsi*[4]. to moan.

矣[3] A final particle denoting that the sense has been fully
2938 expressed.

也 矣 or 已 矣 gives great emphasis to the preceding sentence.
亦 各 言 其 志 也 已 矣 they *simply* told each one his wishes.
可 謂 好 學 也 矣 it may be said (of such) that he *indeed* loves to learn.
可 謂 明 也 已 矣 may be called intelligent *indeed*.
可 謂 至 德 也 已 矣 may *indeed* be said to have reached the highest point of virtuous action.

吾 末 如 之 何 也 已 矣 I can *really* do nothing with such a person!

(a) Simply; only; merely.

而 已 矣 or 爾 已 矣 only this, nothing more.
則 日 月 至 焉 而 已 矣 on some days or in some months they may attain to this, but nothing more.
可 謂 云 爾 已 矣 it may simply be said of me.
無 所 苟 而 已 矣 simply that there may be nothing incorrect.
耳 矣 simply; merely.

(b) Has exclamatory force, often used with 夫.

吾 已 矣 夫 It is all over with me!
吾 死 矣 夫 I am a dead man!
已 矣 乎 Alas, it is all over with me!
秀 而 不 實 者 有 矣 夫 there are instances where a plant may flower but produces no fruit.

(c) Gives emphasis to individual words.

子 曰 清 矣, 曰 仁 矣 乎 The Master replied,—"He was pure." "Was he perfectly virtuous?"
鮮 矣 仁 seldom associated with true virtue.

肄[4] To become skilled in a pro-
2939 fession. To practise.

肄 業 to learn a profession or trade.
肄 習 to practise.

(a) Toil, distress.

既 詒 我 肄 you only cause me pain.
莫 知 我 肄 they know not my toil.

(b) The remnant. Descendants.

而 夏 肄 時 屏 the remnant of *Hsia* is cut off.

(c) Twigs which have sprouted after pruning.

伐 其 肄 條 I cut down the branches and the twigs.

疑[2] To doubt; to distrust. To
2940 suspect. Doubt, suspicion.

疑 人 不 用 do not use a man if you suspect him.
疑 似 doubtful.
疑 似 之 間 doubtful; it may be or may not be.
疑 兵 soldiers placed so as to deceive the foe.
[5]疑 問 a query; a difficult question.
疑 團 suspicions.
疑 團 冰 解 doubts and suspicions cleared away.
疑·心 a suspicious mind; doubtful.
疑·心 生 暗 鬼 a suspicious heart will see ghosts—suspicions create imaginary fears.
[10]疑·心 病 hypochondria.
疑 忌 suspicions and jealousy.
疑·惑 to be in doubt; to suspect.
疑·惑 論 scepticism.
疑 閟 之 際 a state of doubt and uncertainty.
[15]疑 意 hesitation.
疑 慮 suspicions; doubts; misgivings; hesitancy.
疑 慮 不 決 doubtful and unable to come to a decision.
疑 懼 or 疑 畏 apprehensions; misgivings.
疑 昧 equivocal.
[20]疑 案 a disputed case; an open question.
疑 爲 to wonder if.
疑 獄 a doubtful case at law.
疑 義 doubtful interpretation.
毫 無 疑 義 no ground at all for hesitation.
[25]疑 若 as if; it seems as if.
疑 謗 suspected (wrongfully) and slandered.
疑 貳 double-minded from suspicion and doubt.
疑 辭 particles indicating doubt; a negative interrogative.
疑 難 之 事 a matter of doubt and difficulty.
[30]勿 疑 do not doubt; you may be sure of this.
令 人 生 疑 calculated to arouse suspicion.

可 疑 suspicious; doubtful.
因 此 致 疑 because of this, suspicions will be aroused.
多 疑 full of suspicion—mental hesitancy and distress.
[35] 思 疑 to suspect; to doubt.
懷 疑 to harbour suspicions or doubts; skeptic.
見 疑 to be suspected.
解 疑 to elucidate doubts; to resolve suspicions.

沂[2] Name of a river in S. E. Shantung.
2941　　A sunken line in a carved border.

沂 鄂 the sunken and raised lines of a moulding or border.

(a) Also read yin[2]. Name of a place.

匜[2] A washbasin with a tubular handle to let the water run off.
2942

訑[2] Arrogant, overbearing; mean.
2943

訑 訑 之 顏 色 an air of self-satisfaction.
訑 訑 自 得 overbearing; assuming.
訑 謾 to cheat or deceive.

(a) Read tan[4]. u.f. 誕 No. 6051.

慢 訑 contemptuous, arrogant.

貤[2] A series. Steps, grades. To promote; to reward.
2944

貤 封 三 代 ennobled his ancestors for three generations.
貤 贈 to present; to bestow.
一 貤 a grade; a step.
益 貤 gradually increasing.

迤[3] To walk awry. Adjoining, connected.
2945

迤 邐 adjoining—as fields.

㑸[2] A tribe of savages in South China.
2946

迻[2] To walk out of the straight path. Extending to. Connected. Inter. 迤 No. 2945.
2947

迻 南 going south; towards the south.
迻 邐 to travel; to follow on.
迻 邐 一 碧 a winding path of green.

椸[2] A clothes-horse.
2948

椸 架 a clothes-horse.

枻[4] A rowing-sweep. Read hsieh[4,5]. A stand for bending a bow.
2949

洩[4] A small tributary of the River Hwai. To disperse.
2950　　To slight. Leisurely.

洩 洩 leisurely; at one's ease.
洩 洩 其 羽 lazily flapping its wings.
俾 民 憂 洩 to dispel the sorrows of the people.

(a) Read hsieh[4,5]. u.f. 渫 No. 2649. To leak out; to flow.

洩 出 to leak out.
洩 憤 to vent the spleen.
洩 沓 a babble of incoherent words.
洩 涕 to weep; to shed tears.
[5] 洩 漏 (or 露) to leak out; to cause secrets to become known.
洩 漏 秘 密 to divulge secrets or confidences.
洩 用 promiscuous use.
洩 痢 diarrhoea.

勩[4] Toil, affliction.
2951

莫 知 我 勩 you do not know my suffering.

易[4] Easy. To be at ease.
2952

易 事 而 難 說 (yüeh[4,5]) easy to serve and yet difficult to please.
易 人 one who is easy to get on with.
易 信 credulous, trustful.

易 剖 別 easily distinguished.
[5] 易 如 反 掌 as easy as turning over the palm of the hand.
易 學 easy to learn. See below —C.9.
易 得 者 易 失 easy come, easy go.
易 怒 prone to anger.
易 於 傷 損 easily damaged.
[10] 易 於 核 算 easily calculated.
易 於 着 潮 liable to become damp. (-chao[1]-ch'ao[2])
易 於 變 幻 changeable; fickle.
易 於 進 行 to go along smoothly.
易 曉 intelligible and clear.
[15] 易 爲 力 not very difficult.
易 知 easily understood.
易 知 由 單 a list prepared so that taxpayers may readily ascertain what is their amount.
易 破 fragile.
易 簡 simple and brief.
[20] 易 致 病 predisposed to sickness.
易 與 easily managed; to treat lightly.
易 見 obvious; conspicuous.
易 解 easily understood.
易 辦 easily managed.
[25] 容 易 easy.
淺 易 simple and easy.

(a) Lenient; to treat lightly.

易 之 to regard as insignificant.
易 怠 careless and indifferent.
易 物 to despise a thing.
慢 易 to treat lightly; to disregard.
輕 易 carelessly; to treat lightly. See 輕 No. 1156—B.9.

(b) To clear the fields. To cultivate.

易 其 田 疇 to clear and cultivate the fields.
喪 與 其 易 也 寧 戚 in the ceremonies of mourning it is better that there be deep sorrow rather than a minute attention to observances.
禾 易 長 畝 the grain is well cultivated in the fields.

(c) Read i[4,5]. To change. The Book of Changes.

易 主 to change owners; to change hands.
易 位 to transpose; to move to another position.
易 卦 the Diagrams of the Book of Changes.

↓ 易言之 in other words.
易名 to change one's name; to be canonized.
⁵易地則皆然 it will be the same if you change your circumstances.
易地而處 to change one's place and manage affairs. [surname.
易姓 to change the dynasty, the
易學 the science of divination according to the diagrams of the *Book of Changes*. *See above* —6.
易手 to change hands; to pass from one to another.
¹⁰易換 to exchange—a banknote.
易服 to change the prevailing style of dress.
易簀 to change the bed-mat—about to die,–from the story of 曾參 a disciple of Confucius, who had his mat changed for the sake of propriety and died soon after.
易經 the *Book of Changes*.
易置 to put a thing in another place.
¹⁵易道之無窮 the illimitable doctrine of the *Book of Changes*.
互易 interaction; exchange.
交易 to barter.
卜易 to divine by means of the *diagrams*.
天命不易 the decree of Heaven is unchangeable.
²⁰數易寒暑 several years had passed.
移風易俗 to change the evil customs of a place.
萬古不易 unchangeable by time.
變易 to transform.
貿易 to trade.
交易所 stock exchange.

倚 ³ To rely on; to trust to; to lean towards. Similar to
2953 依 No. 2990.

倚仗 or 倚憑 or 倚恃 to depend on; to take advantage of.
倚伏 rely on (happiness) and submit to (calamity)—, shows how these are interacting.
倚勢 to presume on power or authority.
倚勢仗力 to trust to power or influence.
⁵倚勢欺人 to presume on authority to browbeat others.
倚己 self-reliance; self-con-

fidence.
倚度 (*to*⁵) carefully to estimate.
倚廬 the hut by a grave.
倚情 to rely on influence.
¹⁰倚托 to engage one to do; to ask a favour.
倚於衡 attached to the yoke.
倚欄 to lean against the railing.
倚牆牆崩 lean on the wall and it falls—nothing to trust to.
倚瑟而歌 to sing to the accompaniment of a lute.
¹⁵倚畀 to rely on one's help.
倚老賣老 to presume on old age to despise others.
倚肩並立 standing shoulder to shoulder.
倚財 to trust to wealth.
倚酒撒瘋 under the influence of liquor he becomes wild.
²⁰倚門望子 leaning against the door looking for the return of their son. *See next.*
倚閭 leaning against the gate—*see preceding illustration*—u.f. parental affection.
倚靠 or 倚賴 to trust to; to rely on.
倚馬可待 immediately; hastily: –refers to one who wrote a document, using the side of his horse for a table.

椅 ³ A chair, a couch or seat.
2954

椅墊子 chair-cushions.
椅子 a chair; chairs.
椅披 or 椅搭 a piece of red cloth hung over the back of a chair.
椅靠 the back of a chair.
交椅 an arm-chair.
搖椅 a rocking-chair.

(a) Read *i*¹. The catalpa.

椅梓 the catalpa.

犄 ¹ Horns of an ox—thus:— the wing of an army.
2955 Pron. *chi*¹.

犄角 a horn; a projection; the wing of an army. (–*chiao*)
犄角之勢 the wing of an army; horns; mutual help.

猗 ¹
欹 A fierce dog. An interjection of pleasure:— Bravo! Good!
2956

猗嗟 alas! ah!
猗與那與 how complete and elegant!

(a) A final particle.

河水清且直猗 the river waters flow clear and even.

(b) Read *i*³. To pull on one side.

猗枝 a leaning branch.
偏猗不正 leaning to one side.

(c) Read *o*¹. Pliant; luxuriance of growth.

猗儺其枝 "soft and pliant are its branches."
有實其猗 "vigorously grows the vegetation."

漪 ¹ The ripples on water.
2957

漪瀾盪漾 rippling and curling as it flows.
淪漪 rippling water.

齮 ³ To bite.
2958

齮齕 to backbite.

旖 ¹ Gracefully waving; fluttering of flags.
2959

意 ⁴ An idea; an opinion; a sentiment; a thought. Meaning. Wish, will, purpose.
2960

意下 in mind; an idea.
意不自主 vacillating.
意中事 something that is very probable.
意中人 the person of one's heart, the loved one.
⁵於意中 intentional; implied.
意匠 design; device; creative idea of a craftsman.
意味 idea and beauty—as of music, poetry, etc.

意 向 object, intention.
意 合 agreeing in opinion.
10意 圓 而 語 滯 者 也 the meaning was perfect but the expression of it was awkward.
意 圖 to plan; intention.
意 在 intention; with a certain end in view.
意 在 言 外 having a meaning beyond the mere words.
意 外 unexpected; beyond thought.
15意 外 事 accidents; unexpected events.
意 外 障 礙 unexpected hindrance or obstacle.
意 外 風 波 an unexpected change in the state of affairs.
意 密 close, affectionate feelings.
意 志 will, purpose.
20意 志 優 勝 the ascendancy of the will.
意 志 敎 育 training of the will.
意 志 自 由 freewill.
意 念 or 意·思 thought; idea; meaning; sentiment; design.
意·思 表 示 declaration of intention. (legal).
25意·思 說 that is to say.
不 好 意·思 in an awkward position; rather ashamed to; not nice to do.
小 意·思 a little thought—depreciatory term for a present.
有 意·思 it has point; with intent; interesting.
意 意 思 思 irresolute; as if about to speak yet keeping silent.
30意 想 to think.
意 想 不 到 unexpected; unthinkable.
意 態 demeanour; bearing.
意 態 自 然 a cool, calm demeanour. —natural, graceful.
意 慮 consideration.
35意 指 view; to mean.
意 料 to suppose; to anticipate.
意 旨 will, desire, purpose.
意 智 ability to deal with problems.
意 會 or 會 意 to form a mental conception.
40意 會 心 謀 to form a mental conception.
意 有 不 洽 disagreement.
意 欲 to wish; to desire.
意 氣 spirit; bearing; feelings; a sense of duty. 意·氣 emotion.
意 氣 揚 揚 in high spirits.

45意·氣 用 事 to act without due consideration.
意 氣 相 許 a loyal spirit.
意 氣 驕 滿 bearing themselves with pride.
意 消 to get rid of a grudge from one's mind.
意 緒 the thread of one's thoughts.
50意 義 meaning; signification.
意 義·的 生 活 a life with a purpose.
意 義 相 彷 之 字 synonyms.
意·見 views; opinions.
意·見 不 同 of different views; clashing of opinions.
55意·見 書 a prospectus.
意·見 相 投 their opinions agreed.
陳 述 意·見 to state one's opinions.
意 譯 a paraphrase; free translation.
意·識 consciousness; discernment.
60意·識 世·界 the sphere of consciousness.
意·識 作·用 the function of discernment.
意·識 流 the stream of consciousness.
意·識·的 發 展 the expansion and development of consciousness.
意 象 appearance of the thoughts on the countenance; imagination.
65意 趣 mind; thoughts; intent; soul.
意 願 a wish or desire.
意 馬 心 猿 the intents of the mind and heart are like the horse and the ape—very difficult to bring under control; undecided.
不 以 爲 意 gave it no thought; disregarded it.
不 意 unawares; did not expect.
70作 意 to make up the mind.
加 意 see 3137.30.
如 意 all as one wishes. 大·意 careless.
大 意 the general scope or idea. 大
失 意 to be disillusioned; out of favor.
75得 意 gratified; jolly; to get one's wish; proud.
特 意 or 故·意 purposely.
當 意 suitable; according to one's idea.
立 意 to decide.
會 意 ideographic formation of a character; to understand

(a) Used in transliterating.

意 大 利 Italy.
意 大 利 體 字 italics.

噫¹
2961

To belch. Interjection.

噫 嚏 to belch.
噫 嘻 alas! dear me!

薏⁴
2962

Seeds of a small waterplant.

薏 苡 仁 the seeds of Job's tears, (coix lachryma) sometimes used for pearl-barley. See 苡 No. 2933.

鷾⁴
2963

A swallow.

怡²
2964

Harmony. Mutual pleasure. Pleased, delighted.

怡 和 delightful harmony; true accord.
怡 怡 如 也 giving the impression of satisfied relief.
怡 悅 taking delight in.
怡 情 to cheer the heart.
5怡 情 理 性 cheers the heart and regulates the disposition—said of music.
怡 愉 a look of gratification.
怡 然 自 得 happy and satisfied.
怡 穆 pleasant and harmonious.
怡 聲 a pleasant tone in speaking
10怡 色 a pleasing expression of countenance.
怡 蕩 gratifying the passions.
怡 衍 complaisant; to be pleased.
怡 謹 盡 孝 pleasant and fulfilling her filial duties.
怡 顏 a cheerful countenance.
15怡 養 healthy.

眙²
2965

To gaze at. Also read ch'ih⁴.

詒²
2966

To bequeath. To send. Inter. next.

詒 傳 to hand down; to bequeath.
詒 孫 子³ to transmit to descendants.
詒 情 to send greetings.
詒 罹 to cause grief and sorrow.
詒 爾 多 福 confer many blessings upon thee.

詒 謀 to hand down good plans to posterity.

饋 詒 to send a present of food.

(a) Read *t'ai*[4]. To deceive. To ridicule. Inter. 紿 No. 5991.

狎 侮 欺 詒 to treat with disrespect and rudeness.

貽[2] To hand down; to leave to; to give to. Inter. preceding.
2967

貽 人 以 口 實 to give occasion for scandal.

貽 厥 descendants, posterity:—from the next, an example of 歇 後 語 (*See* No. 2642—11)—the word for descendants being understood.

貽 厥 孫 謀 to leave plans for posterity.

貽 害 羣 生 to bring calamity upon the masses.

[5]貽 悞 後 人 to mislead posterity.

貽 書 to send a letter to.

貽 殃 to bring down misfortune.

貽 禍 子[3]孫 to entail calamity on one's posterity.

貽 笑 大 方 to become a laughing-stock by showing inability.

[10]貽 範 to bequeath a good example.

貽 累 to involve others.

貽 累 國 家 to involve the State.

貽 羞 to hand down shame—to leave a bad reputation.

貽 訓 traditional teachings, proverbs, etc.

[15]貽 謀 to set a good example to posterity.

貽 誤 to cause any delay.

貽 贈 to leave—a legacy; to make a parting present.

貽 送 知 己 to give to an intimate friend.

貽 遺 to bequeath; to leave behind.

飴[2] Sweet cakes; sweetmeats; sugar; to feed.
2968

飴 糖 or 甘 飴 sugar-plums; sweetmeats.

飴 訓 pleasant counsels.

飴 鹽 rock-salt.

苦 飴 bitter and sweet; joy and sorrow.

頤[2] The chin, the jaws. To nourish, to rear.
2969

交 頤 to kiss.

支 頤 to rest the chin on the hands.

期 頤 a centenarian.

解 頤 語 a joke.

頤 養 to nourish.

顊[3] A pleasing, respectful manner.
2970

禕[1] Rare, excellent; precious.
2971

嫛 嫛[4] Compliant, yielding. Easy-going. The first also means a newborn child.
2972

嫛 婗 a baby.

欙[1] Ebony.
2973

瑿[1] A black stone like jade; jet. Also read *hsi*[1].
2974

瑿 珀 a kind of jet.

瑿 紅 described as if it was black opal or a similar substance,—black in daylight, but shining red under strong light.

瞖[4] A cataract or film over the eye.
2975

瞖 瞙 a cataract.

繄[1] An interjection. A sighing sound.
2976

繄 我 獨 無 Alas! I alone have not!

翳[4] A feather screen; a shade. To screen, to shade.
2977

翳 形 to vanish.

翳 毛 eyelashes.

翳 眼 之 幻 optical illusions.

翳 翳 obscurely.

翳 障 to screen off.

(a) A film over the eye.

翳 瞙 white film on the eye.

(b) Dead trees that have fallen.

醫 医[1] To heal, to cure. A doctor.
2978

醫·不·來 incurable.

醫 不 對 症 the treatment is not suitable.

醫 事 medical work.

醫 匠 ancient term for a doctor.

[5]醫 國 to regulate the State.

醫 壞·了 to treat a case improperly so that death or injury results.

醫 好 cured.

醫 學 the science of medicine.

醫 學 博 士 Doctor of Medicine. M.D.

[10]醫 學 士 Bachelor of Medicine. M.B.

醫 官 medical officer.

醫 家 or 醫 門 the medical profession.

醫 家 器·具 medical instruments and appliances.

醫·得 身 醫·不·得 心 the body may be healed, but who can minister to a mind diseased?

[15]醫 手 skill in healing.

醫 救 to bring round—from insensibility.

醫 方 a medical prescription.

醫 治 or 醫 療 or 醫 調 to cure diseases.

醫 治 不 效 the treatment is not efficacious.

[20]醫 法 the art of healing.

醫 理 principles of medicine.

醫 生 or 醫 師 a doctor.

醫 科 department of medicine.

醫 病 to heal disease.

[25]醫 舘 or 醫 院 a hospital; a dispensary.

醫 藥 healing medicines.

醫 藥 團 體 the medical profession.

醫 藥 服 務 團 Army Medical Corps.

醫 藥 無 靈 doctors and medicine will not avail.

[30]醫 術 methods of treatment.

醫 道 system of medicine; medical science; a physician's skill.

醫 金 doctor's fees.

醫 門 寒 暑 表 clinical thermometer. = 體温表.

醫 院 船 or 醫 船 hospital ship.

[35] 不 可 醫 治 irremediable.

世 醫 one whose ancestors have been doctors.

包 醫 to guarantee a cure.

可 醫 amenable to treatment.

名 醫 a famous physician.

[40] 外 科 醫·生 a surgeon.

女 醫·生 a female doctor.

庸 醫 a quack or charlatan.

獸 醫 a veterinary surgeon.

神 醫 a skilful physician.

良 醫 a skilful doctor.

行 醫 to practise medicine.

謝 醫 to pay medical fees.

鷖[1] The widgeon. Sometimes referred to the phoenix.
2979

移
逸[2] To move across. To shift. To transmit, to convey. To influence; to change.
2980

移·下 carried forward.

移 人 若 此 it influenced one to such an extent.

移 借 to borrow.

移 則 番 代 changed them in rotation.

[5]移 咨 to inform in a despatch.

移 寵 to withdraw favour from.

移 尸 to lay a corpse at the door of another—to involve him in trouble.

移 居 or 移 遷 or 移 徙 to move one's residence; to change one's abode.

移 山 倒[4]海 casting away mountains and upsetting the sea—magic.

[10]移 年 over a year.

移 往 to migrate.

移 復 to reply to.

移 情 to stir the emotions.

移 提 to summon for trial.

[15]移 換 to change.

移 文 a despatch to an equal.

移 易[4,5] to change; to vary.

移 時 after the lapse of a short time.

移 書 to send a letter.

[20]移 植 to transplant.

移 交 to transfer a position, an administration, to a successor.

移 民 墾 荒 to open up waste lands by colonization.

移 民 政 策 colonization policy.

移 注 to lend.

移 泊 to change anchorage.

[25]移 玉 to invite a friend—to an entertainment.

移 病 (or 疾) to resign on account of illness.

移 知 to inform by despatch.

移 禍 他 人 to shift trouble to another.

移 種 to remove a plant.

[30]移 縣 to forward to the local magistrate.

移 船 to move a boat.

移 花 接 木 grafting,—also used fig.

移 行 to communicate to ....

移 解[4] to send up for trial.

[35]移 調[4] to transfer—as troops.

移 請[4] to request, in a despatch.

移 軍 to move troops.

移 轉[3] to transfer; to revolve.

移 轉[3]馬 首 to turn the horses' heads—to come back.

[40]移 近 to move nearer.

移 送 or 移 交 or 移·給 to transmit; to hand over to.

移 錨 to drag anchor.

移·開 or 移 動 or 移 離 or 移 去 to remove to one side; to put away.

移 附 abandonment.

[45]移 頃 after a little time.

移 風 易[4,5]俗 莫 善 於 樂 for improving the public morals there is nothing better than music.

移 飭 to request that orders be given.

不 移 言 not to alter one word.

更 移 to alter.

[50]爲 物 所 移 influenced by externals.

黟[1] Black and shining. Ebony.
2981

黟 縣 a district in the former *Hweichowfu* of S. Anhwei.

夷
夸[2] Barbarous tribes on the east. Often used for any foreigner.
2982

夷 人 a foreigner; a barbarian.

夷 則 a classical pitch correspond-

---

ing in function to G-sharp.

夷 戶 Yunnan tribes.

夷 狄 barbarians, those tribes on the east and north of ancient China.

夷 船 foreign ships.

夷 陵 now 宜昌, Ichang, a port on the Upper Yangtze.

南 夷 Southern tribes.

東 夷 old name for Korea.

(a) To squat on the heels.

夷 居 to remain squatting—a useless life.

(b) Peaceful, pleased; at ease.

夷 悅 ease.

夷 然 quietly and calmly.

云 胡 不 夷 he asked, "Who would not be pleased?"

我 心 則 夷 my heart will then be at rest.

(c) Level, even; just.

夷 險 levels and hills.

化 險 爲 夷 making the rough places smooth.

君 子 如 夷 if the superior man acts with justice.

大 道 甚 夷 the Way is very smooth—but it is neglected.

平 夷 level, even.

有 夷 之 行 there were level roads leading to it.

(d) Common, usual, ordinary.

民 之 秉 夷 the usual disposition of the people.

(e) To kill, to exterminate. Injured.

夷 九 族 to exterminate the race.

夷 於 左 股 injured in the left thigh.

(f) Grades, classes. Inter. next.

夷 人 ordinary men.

貴 賤 等 夷 nobles and others of all grades.

(g) Flying animals.

夷 由 the flying squirrel.

侇[2] A class, a category. A corpse.
2983

侇 衾 the shroud placed over a corpse before it is placed in the coffin.

儒 侇 the literati.

咦² An exclamation of fear. Also read *hsi*¹. An interjection of sorrow. A shout.
2984 Now used as interjection of surprise and pron. *yeh*³.

姨² A wife's sister; a mother's sister.
2985

姨·夫 husbands of wife's sisters.
姨娘 a mother's sister; a concubine of one's father.
姨母 or 娘媽 one's mother's married sisters.
姨爹 or 姨丈 husbands of maternal aunts. A.c. 姨·父
姨老表 male maternal cousin.
姨表姊妹 female maternal cousins.
大姨子，小姨子 a wife's elder or younger sister.

洟² Mucus from the nose.
2986

洟涕 to weep and snivel.

(a) Read *t'i*¹. To blow the nose.

垂洟 to spit and blow the nose.

痍² A wound, bruise or sore.
2987

瘡痍 sores, bruises; ill-treatment.

胰² The omentum. Soap.
脶
2988

胰·子 or 肥·皂 soap.
胰·子沫兒 soap-lather.
胰皂舖 soap-chandler's shop.

衣¹ Clothing.
衤
2989

衣不稱 (*ch'ên*⁴) 身 ill-fitting garments.
衣冠 full dress—the gentry.
衣冠禽獸 a dressed-up beast.
衣取蔽寒 my clothing was chosen merely to avoid the cold.
⁵衣刷 a clothes' brush.

衣帽 clothes and hat—full dress.
衣帽不周 in undress; not having sufficient clothes.
衣廚 a wardrobe.
衣料 material for clothing.
¹⁰衣·服 or 衣·裳 or 衣襟 clothing; garments.
衣·服各件 all kinds of wearing apparel.
衣·服爲階·級之符號 clothing as a mark of class-distinction.
衣架 a clothes-horse.
衣架飯囊·的材料 mere material for a clothes-horse and a food-bag—useless, lazy persons.
¹⁵衣業 clothing-industry.
衣物 clothing and other effects.
衣祿食祿 the blessings of raiment and food.
衣衫 clothing.
衣衾 burial garments.
²⁰衣衾棺槨 clothing and coffins—funeral requisites.
衣裙雜襲 women's clothes of all descriptions.
衣褶 clothing.
衣食 clothing and food—necessities.
衣飾以爲優劣之別 clothing and ornament as a mark of distinction.
²⁵內衣 under garments.
大衣 an overcoat.
成衣 ready-made garments.
更¹衣 to change the clothing—euphemy for easing nature, used by women.
號衣 uniforms.
³⁰青衣 black garments—a servant, a student.

(a) Read *i*⁴. To dress, to wear.

衣敝縕袍與衣狐貉者立·而不恥 though wearing an old garment quilted with hemp, he was not ashamed to stand with those who wore fine furs.
衣繡夜行 to wear embroidered robes and walk by night—hidden talent.
衣錦尚絅 to wear a plain garment over a fine one.

依¹ To follow; to comply with. To trust to, to depend on.
2990 To obey. To be near to. According to.

依人作活 dependent upon others for a living.
依人門下 dependent upon others.
依依不捨 unwilling to part from.
依實說 a true statement.
⁵依序 or 依次 in order; according to rank.
依從 to follow; to obey.
依戀 or 依慕 to be desirous of; to long for.
依據 proof; evidence.
依於仁 to cleave to virtue.
¹⁰依期 or 依時 according to the stated time.
依樣畫葫·蘆 sketch the gourd according to the pattern—follow the beaten track.
依歸 a pattern.
依然故我 I am just as of old.
依照 in obedience to.
¹⁵依禮·而行 act according to propriety.
依稀 similar; few; trifling; uncertain.
依稀之間 in an uncertain condition.
依舊 or 依然 as before; in the usual way.
依言 or 依口 as you say; according to the statement.
²⁰依議 according to the agreement. Let it be as recommended! a phrase conveying Imperial sanction.
依賴 or 依靠 to trust; to depend on.
依賴性 submissive disposition.
依近 close to; adjoining.
依道 according to eternal principles.
²⁵依附 to be close to; to agree with.
依限 within the time-limit.
依隨 to assent to; to agree with.
依順 agreeable; willing.

(a) To regard with favour.

不依 not pleased with.
上帝是依 God regarded her with favour.

(b) Luxuriant.

依彼平林 "dense is that forest in the plain."
楊柳依依 the willows were fresh and green.

辰[3]
2991 A silken screen ornamented with a design in hatchets, used in the Imperial audience chamber.

斧 辰 the name of the above.
負 辰 with the back to the screen.

裔
裔[4]
2992 The hem of a robe. A border, a frontier. Border tribes.

四 裔 之 地 the bounds of the empire.
夷 裔 frontier tribes; barbarians.

(a) Descendants, posterity.

來 裔 posterity.
後 裔 posterity.
絕 裔 descendants cut off.

宜
宜[2]
2993 Right, fitting, seemly, to be fit. Ought, should. To order rightly. Suitable.

宜 乎 an initial phrase—no wonder that; surely, etc.
宜 乎 不 宜 Is it right or not? Will this do?
宜 人 former title given to wives of officials of the fifth degree; to delight men.
宜 兄 宜 弟 they act correctly towards their elder and their younger brothers.
[5]宜 其 事 也 a matter that should be completed; something fitting.
宜 其 遐 福 enjoying the lasting happiness which is his right.
宜 家 from 宜 其 家 室 ordering well her house and home—to act as becomes a wife.
宜°於 出 外 fit to go out.
宜 昌 the port of Ichang on the Upper Yangtze.
[10]宜 春 May it always be spring with you—felicitous wish pasted up at 立春.
宜 服 special costume or dress.
宜 業 其 家 者 不 蒙 其 澤 矣 ".... the hope of the family, survives not to continue the tradition of his house." *Giles*.
宜 此 proper; fit for this use.
宜 然 or 合 宜 fitting; proper; suitable.

[15]宜 爾 子[3] 孫 it is right that your posterity....
宜 男 should have a son—a name for the day-lily. See 萱 No. 2873, also used of women who have had several sons.
宜 興 壺 a kind of teapot made of earthenware—named after the city where it is made, a place in Kiangsu.
宜 若 小 然 there seems to be a small principle in this.
不 宜 not fitting; it is not right to....
[20]便·宜 cheap, convenient. (*p'ien²·i*)
合 宜 proper; fitting.
時 宜 in accord with the times—fashionable.
相 宜 fitting, expedient.

誼
誼[4]
2994 That which is suitable; right, proper. Inter. preceding. Also u.f. 義 Righteousness.

誼 不 容 辭 public duty will not admit excuse, or, will not take a denial.
誼 士 a righteous man.
行 誼 to act with justice and righteousness.

(a) Related, connected; friendships.

誼 同 手 足 (brotherly) relationship is like that of hand and foot.
世 誼 connected for generations—when the families have been friends for many generations.
友 誼 friendship; goodwill.
情 誼 a favour.
親 誼 relatives of a wife.
雅 誼 friendly courtesies.

(b) To discuss, to deliberate. Inter. 議. No. 3006.

論 誼 考 問 to deliberate and investigate.

遺
遺[2]
2995 To bequeath; to hand down; to leave behind. Distinguish 遣 No. 901.

遺·下 bequeathed; left to another.
遺·下 一 子[3] he left one son behind.
遺·下·來 handed down; left behind.

遺 世 to leave this world of cares.
[5]遺 俗 之 累 the encumbrance of inherited customs.
遺 傳 transmitted; heredity.
遺 傳 學 study of heredity.
遺 傳 性 heredity.
遺 傳 性·的 公 例 general principles of heredity.
[10]遺 傳 病 hereditary disease.
遺 像 photograph of deceased.
遺 光 spare light—to ask a favour that will not cost the giver anything. See 分 No. 1851—56.
遺 囑 or 遺 命 or 遺 言 dying commands; a command handed down; a will.
遺 囑 執 行 人 executor of a will. (*legal*).
[15]遺 囑 自 由 主 義 principle of the right to bequeath by will. (*legal*).
遺 址 remains; ruins.
遺 大 投 艱 to undertake a grave responsibility.
遺 存 remnants; remains.
遺 弊 inherited disease or trait.
[20]遺 志 a wish handed down from those who have gone before.
遺 念 a souvenir; a memento.
遺 恨 regrets.
遺 愛 love passed on by one who has gone.
遺 意 traditional.
[25]遺 憾 regrets.
遺 掛 articles left by deceased.
遺 族 those who are left of the clan or family when the head dies.
遺 書 a will.
遺 本 or 遺 表 valedictory memorial by a high official.
[30]遺 業 business left by deceased.
遺 毒 transmitted evil; an inheritance of evil.
遺 民 those who refuse to accept office under a new dynasty; the "remnant."
遺 澤 a token of remembrance.
遺 烈 the merit of one who has gone before.
[35]遺 產 inherited property.
遺 產 受 取 人 a legatee. (*legal*).
遺 產 承 受 人 an heir. (*legal*).
遺 產 稅 legacy duty. (*legal*).
遺 產 管 理 人 executor or trustee. (*legal*).
[40]遺 產 繼 承 succession of property. (*legal*).
遺 留 to leave; to hand down.

遺留產業 to bequeath possessions.

遺稿 MSS. left by deceased.

遺笑全球 to be a laughing-stock for the whole world.

[45]遺策 (or 計) policy or plans handed down.

遺緒 business or profession left by deceased.

遺聞 hearsay; tradition.

遺腹子 a posthumous child.

遺臣 or 遺老 statesman or minister of the previous dynasty.

[50]遺臭 of infamous memory.

遺規 tradition.

遺訓 instructions or teaching of one who has died.

遺跡 historical traces; vestiges.

遺風 customs which have been handed down.

[55]遺餘 or 遺剩 overplus; surplus.

遺骸 remains of deceased person.

遺體 the body handed down—by our parents.

不遺餘力 spare no efforts.

無遺類 no one left.

(a) To lose or neglect. To abandon. To forget.

遺卻 neglected; discarded.

遺失 or 遺落 lost; gone.

遺失物 lost articles. (legal).

遺尿 or 遺溺 to urinate in the sleep.

[5]遺忘 forgotten; long out of mind.

遺愎 to make a mistake.

遺棄 to abandon.

遺棄罪 the crime of abandonment. (legal).

遺棄行為 abandonment—as of a family or home.

[10]遺漏 or 遺逸 to miss or omit.

遺漏點 deficiencies; omissions.

遺珠 a discarded pearl—a talented man who is not used.

遺矢 to ease nature.

小遺 to urinate.

[15]遺算 (or 計) to make a miscalculation and fail.

遺編 lost records.

遺精 involuntary emissions.

遺行 misconduct; irregular ways.

(b) Read wei[4]. To send a present.

遺贈 a present.

曀[1] The sun hidden by clouds. Obscure.
2996

曀日光 the sun is obscured.

陰曀 dark and gloomy.

殪[4] To kill; to exterminate. A file of ten soldiers.
2997

殪戎殷 to exterminate the Yin dynasty.

饐[4] Cooked food which has become mouldy. Sour, as food.
2998

臭饐 rancid; foul.

懿[4] Virtuous, especially of women. Admirable, esteemed, excellent.
2999

懿德 admirable virtue.

懿懿 fragrant.

懿旨 the commands of the empress.

懿範 a worthy example.

懿行 admirable conduct.

懿親 the closest relatives.

懿鑠 full and admirable virtue.

(a) Read i[4.5]. u.f. 抑 No. 3031. To curb.

懿戒 to restrain.

羿[4] Name of a famous archer, 后羿.
3000

羿善射 I was clever at archery.

彝[2] Cups or vases used in libations. A rule, a law. Regular; constant. The normal nature of man.
3001

彝倫 social relationships.

是彝是訓 "let this be your rule and guide."

民之秉彝 the people hold their natural disposition.

義[4] Right conduct. Righteousness. Morality. Duty to one's neighbour. Public spirit. Patriotic. Loyal, faithful.
3002
See also 主 No. 1336—76.

義不容辭 public duty admits of no excuse.

義之與比 to follow what is right.

義人 or 義士 a righteous man; a fair-minded person.

義俠 chivalrous.

[5]義僕 a faithful servant.

義兵 or 義勇隊 volunteers.

義勇佈道團 Student Volunteer Movement.

義務 duty, responsibility, obligation—especially when the service is voluntary.

義務員 honorary workers.

[10]義務學校 public schools— schools for the masses, common schools, free schools.

義務心 faithfulness; loyalty to duty.

義務教育 free education, or compulsory education.

義務會員 active members.

義務職員 officers of a society not in receipt of salary.

[15]義和 harmonious; friendly.

義和團 (or 拳) The Boxers, whose name is connected with the uprising of 1900.

義夫 a widower who does not re-marry.

義婦 a virtuous wife.

義憤 righteous indignation; imbued with public spirit.

[20]義戰 a fight for the right.

義所當為 bound in honour.

義捐 donation for public use.

義斂貲財 there would be public contributions.

義方 just and righteous methods.

[25]義氣 public spirit; patriotism; integrity; uprightness; righteous indignation; personal loyalty.

義犬 a faithful dog.

義理昭著 the principles of righteousness are clearly manifested.

義祠 an ancestral temple.

義節 etiquette; right rule of conduct.

[30]義舉 a movement in public interests.

義襲 incidental acts of righteousness.

義賑會 Famine Relief Society.

義路 the road of righteousness— just ways.

義重如山 his integrity is as firm as the hills.

[35]義鳥 the wild goose.

人 不 學 不 知 義 if a man does not learn, he will not know his duty to his neighbour.

以 義 爲 利 regard right conduct as profitable.

仗 義 疎 財 devoted to public interests and distributing wealth for this purpose.

申 明 大 義 appealing to a man's sense of right.

信 義 integrity.

(a) Public, free, open to all. Some of the preceding illustrations might be included here.

義 倉 a public granary.

義 井 a public well.

義 地 or 義 田 or 義 莊 land tilled for the benefit of the poor; public ground.

義 塚 or 義 山 a public or free cemetery.

義 學 a free school.

義 渡 a free ferry.

(b) Meaning, purport, interpretation.

義 例 the outline or scope of a book.

義 意 meaning; purport.

義 未 詳 也 the purport of the passage is not clear.

義 理 the scope or sense of a passage.

義 闕 the meaning is not known.

(c) False, adopted.

義 女 adopted daughter, a slave-girl.

義 子³ adopted son.

義 手 (or 足) false hand or foot.

義 父 adopted father.

義 髮 false hair.

義 齒 artificial teeth.

儀² Ceremonies, usages. A rite, a rule. Deportment, manners.
3003

儀 仗 insignia carried before the Emperor.

儀 則 rules, usages.

儀 制 forms, ceremonies.

儀 型 a good pattern.

⁵儀 容 端 好 correct in manners and bearing.

儀 賓 men who married imperial connections.

儀 度 or 儀 容 demeanour, bearing.

儀 式 deportment, outward appearance; ceremony.

儀 態 posture, attitude—as of a figure, etc.

¹⁰儀 文 outward ceremonial; manners; style; arrangement.

儀 監 于 殷 take warning from the Yin dynasty.

儀 禮 one of the 13 classics:—The Book of Ritual.

儀 節 ceremonial usages and rules.

儀 表 outward forms; rites and ceremonies.

¹⁵儀 註 rules of propriety; ceremonies.

儀 門 the middle gate of a yamen, between the entrance gate and the door which leads to the private apartments.

二 儀 Yin and Yang:—See No. 1751—7.

三 儀 the three powers—Heaven, earth and man.

失 儀 to be impolite and brusque.

²⁰威 儀 dignified bearing; rules of deportment.

平 儀 ordinary rules of etiquette.

禮 儀 rules of ceremony.

(a) A present.

儀 物 or 謝 儀 a present; an acknowledgement of service.

儀 目 a list of presents.

程 儀 presents sent to one going on a journey.

行 儀 presents given to a traveller.

香 儀 or 奠 儀 presents given to assist friends in the celebration of the rites at their parents' funeral.

(b) Instruments; apparatus.

儀°器 demonstrating apparatus, maps and other things in schools; scientific instruments, etc.

地 平 經 儀 azimuth instrument.

天 體 儀 armillary sphere.

子 午 儀 transit instrument.

⁵方 位 儀 azimuth compass.

紀 限 儀 or 六 分 儀 a sextant.

赤 道 儀 equatorial instruments.

高 度 儀 altitude instrument.

艤³ To moor a boat to the bank.
3004

蟻³ An ant. A conventional term used in petitions for "I" and "We".
3005

蟻 冢 ant-hill.

蟻 動 running about like ants.

蟻 合 (or 集) gathered together in great numbers like ants.

蟻 孔 ant-hill.

⁵蟻 寇 a petty robber.

蟻 封 small hills.

蟻 封 穴 the ants close their hill—as when rain threatens.

蟻 植 物 plants which are benefited by ants.

蟻 民 or 蟻 等 we; your petitioners.

¹⁰蟻 潰 scattering like ants.

蟻 獸 ant-eater.

蟻 瘍 formication.

蟻 聚 gathered together like ants—of robbers, etc.

蟻 術 to study the ant (as incentive to industry.)

¹⁵蟻 視 to regard with contempt.

蟻 酸 formic acid.

蟻 附 ants swarming on a carcase—used of greed.

蟻 陣 ants on the march.

蟻 頭² or 蟻 穴 or 蟻 丘 or 蟻 壤 an ant-hill.

²⁰白 蟻 white ants.

飛 蟻 flying ants.

螞 蟻 ants generally.

(a) Scum on wine.

浮 蟻 scum on wine.

議⁴ To discuss; to talk over; to consult; to deliberate. To criticise.
3006

議 事 員 councillor.

議 事 日 程 order of the day; agenda.

議 事 會 a council.

議 事 規 則 rules of debate.

⁵中 止 議 事 to adjourn a debate.

議 准 agree to sanction.

議 和 peace-negotiations.

議 和 會 Peace Conference.

議 員 member of parliament.

¹⁰議 士 a councillor.

議 奏 to deliberate and memorialize the throne.

議 定 settled after deliberation; to decide.

議擇賢者 to deliberate upon the selection of the best men.

議會 parliament.

¹⁵議會立法 statutes.

地方議會 Provincial Assemblies.

議案 proposals; motions; a bill.

執照議案 licensing bill.

理財議案 bill to regulate finance.

²⁰議決 to decide by vote; a resolution.

議決保留 decided to reserve for further consideration.

議決分頭 a division.

議決權 deciding authority; power to vote in discussion.

議竣 decided; discussed; fixed.

²⁵議結 to close a discussion.

議罰 to consider the punishment.

議覆 to deliberate and report.

議訂 to agree upon; to regulate.

議・論 to talk over; to discuss a matter; to criticize.

³⁰議・論・的 critical.

議謀 to plan.

議辦 to make arrangements.

議長 speaker, chairman at a parliamentary discussion.

議長取決 chairman's casting-vote.

³⁵議院 parliament.

議院法 parliamentary standing orders.

議題 subject of debate; resolution.

提議 or 動議 to propose or move a resolution.

會議 to meet and negotiate a matter; to hold a conference.

⁴⁰補行開議 to re-open a discussion.

贊成提議 to be in favor of a 「motion.

開議 to open a debate.

附議 to second a motion.

(a) An agreement; article of agreement.

議單 or 議約 a written agreement.

鵣²
3007
The crow-pheasant.

曳)⁴
拽)
3008
To trail; to drag after; to pull.

曳尾 to wag the tail.

曳弦 to draw—as a bow.

曳踵 to drag the heels; to shuffle.

往前曳 to drag forward.

(a) Read *chuai*¹. To throw. See No. 1419.

拽泥 to throw mud.

異⁴
3009
Strange; extraordinary. Other, different; foreign. Heterodox.

異乎常人 different from the ordinary run of men.

異事 a peculiar affair; different duties of office.

異人 an extraordinary man; a stranger.

異俗 different customs; evil customs.

⁵異兆 an omen; a portent.

異化 katabolism.

異口一詞 different persons gave the same story.

異同 difference; not unanimous.

異味 uncommonly nice flavours.

¹⁰異地 another place.

異域 a strange country.

異姓 a different surname.

異字同義 synonyms.

異客 a stranger.

¹⁵異寶 a rarity; a special treasure.

異常 abnormal; exceptional; anomalous.

異心 alienated.

異志 inclined to revolution, etc.

異想天開 a brilliant idea; sudden thought; fantastic.

²⁰異態 strange bearing or manner.

異才 exceptional talents.

異教 heretical sects; heresy.

異教徒 heretics.

異數 difference; remainder. (*arith.*).

²⁵異於 different from.

異日 another day.

異書 strange or heterodox writings.

異服 strange or different clothing.

異極 opposite poles.

³⁰異樣 unusual.

異母兄弟 brothers having a different mother.

異民 foreigners; strangers.

異㸑 to live apart, having separate cooking arrangements.

異相 peculiarly strange physiognomy.

³⁵異稟 extraordinary endowment of talents.

異種 or 異族 an alien race.

異端 strange principles; heresy.

異等 above the average man in talents.

異聞 special or unusual news.

⁴⁰異能 uncommon ability.

異花受精 cross-fertilization.

異草奇花 rare plants and curious flowers.

異見 dissenting views.

異言 or 異詞 discrepancy; misunderstanding.

⁴⁵異說 objections.

異象 signs; wonders.

異質 (or 性) of a different nature. 異性 heterosexual.

異趣 a different aim.

異蹟 wonders, signs; miracle.

⁵⁰異道 sectarianism; heresy—from a Confucian point of view.

異邦 or 異國 other countries; heathen.

異鄉 another village or district; belonging to another place.

異類 of a different species or class.

異香 a rare perfume.

⁵⁵異點 point of difference or contrast.

無異 invariably; no difference.

毅⁴
3010
Firm, resolute, intrepid, bold. Fortitude.

毅力 an untiring effort; energy.

毅勇 brave.

毅心 or 毅志 firm and resolute in heart.

毅然 resolutely.

弘毅 of great courage.

果毅 fixed purpose.

溫毅 gentle and yet resolute.

詣⁴
3011
To reach a place; to go to.

詣謁 to pay a visit.

親詣 to visit personally.

造詣 to make progress in studies.

瘞⁴
3012
A retired place. To bury; to sacrifice to. [of a woman.

瘞玉 a departed friend; the burial

收瘞 to gather (dead bodies of horses) and bury them.

奠瘞 to sacrifice to the dead.

剸 劓 4
3013

To cut off the nose.

劓 割 夏 邑 he harshly treated the people in the cities of *Hsia*.

劓 滅 無 遺 he maimed or destroyed them all.

藝 埶 秇 萟 4
3014

Skill, ability in handicraft. A craft, an art, a calling, a trade, an accomplishment. Also read *ni*[4].

藝 員 artists; actors.
藝 徒 apprentices.
藝 文 literary pursuits.
藝 業 a profession.
[5]藝 翠 skill and forethought.
藝 術 the arts; art.
藝 術 敎 育 training in craftsmanship.
學 藝 to learn a trade.
才 藝 ability; dexterity; skill.
手 藝 handicraft.

(a) To plant.

藝 樹 to plant trees.

(b) Measure, standard. A limit or boundary.

藝 貢 to allot the amount of tribute due from each chief.
貪 欲 無 藝 there is no limit to lust and covetousness.

囈 4
3015

To talk in the sleep.

I. (一)
(Ih)

一 弌 壹 1.5.
3016

One. Unity. The first. A, an, the. The same. Uniform. To unify, to unite. All. Radical 1.
In the sense of 'a, an' either (1) pron. *i*[2] before 4th tone and *i*[4] before other tones, or (2) pron. ·*i*. In the sense of one, etc., pron. *i*[1].

一 一 each one; one and all; each separately; one by one.
一 一 講 明 explained each point clearly.
一 丁 one person; one character of Chinese.
不 識 一 丁 字 he does not recognise a character.
[5]一 下ₙ once.
一 下 (*ha*) ·子 once; at once.(*dial.*)
一 下 手 a blow of the hand.
一 不 做 二 不 休 either do not begin, or having begun, do not give up.
一 不 拗 衆 one cannot override the majority.
[10]一 丘 之 貉 like the badgers from one mound—very much the same.
一 串 院 ·子 a courtyard.
一 之 爲 甚 其 可 再 乎 once is too much, how can it be repeated?
一 了[3] 百[3] 了[3] one finished all is finished—when a man is dead everything is finished.
一 事 無 成 not a thing completed.
[15]一 事 蓋 一 時 to judge the times by a single occurrence.
一 二 one or two; a few; we.
一 五 一 十 的 告 訴 ·他 he told him the whole story.
一 些 some, few.
一 些 些 scarcely any; very few.
[20]一 人 不 敵 二 人 智 two heads are better than one.
一 人 不 敵 衆 人 智 one man's wisdom cannot compete with that of the majority.
一 人 之 所 需 百 工 斯 爲 備 the requirements of one man are met by the labours of a hundred.
一 人 作 事 一 人 當 a man must bear the consequences of his own acts.
一 人 傳 虛 百 人 傳 實 one man tells an idle story and it becomes fact in the mouths of a hundred.
[25]一 人 難 如 千 人 意 one man can hardly meet the wishes of everybody.
一 以 貫 之 one unity pervading all things.
一 伙 兒 all together—as when several are travelling together.

一 件 東 ·西 an article, a thing.
一 似 quite like.
[30]一 位 one; a—gentleman.
一 來 二 來 firstly, secondly.
一 例 one rule; consistently; uniformly; alike.
一 例 看 待 act in a uniform manner to all.
一 例 科 員 first-class departmental clerk.
[35]一 個 半 個 the least amount; one or two.
   給 我 一 個 半 個 就 行 just give me one or two.
一 個 指 頭 a finger.
一 個 時 辰 a period of two hours.
一 個 牌 a tablet; a sign.
[40]一 個 統 一 點 ·子 a point of unification.
一 倂 wholly; all.
一 元 a common denominator.
一 元 復 始 萬 象 更 新 the year returns to its beginning, all things are renewed.
一 元 方 程 式 a simple equation.
[45]一 元 論 Monistic theory of origins. Monism.
一 兩 個 人 one or two people.
一 再 repeatedly; once and again.
一 刀 兩 斷 to sever it at one blow.
一 分 a tenth; one-hundredth; a part; a fraction; one cent.
[50]一 分[4] 子[3] a division; a part.
一 切 the whole of; all.
一 刻 a quarter of an hour; a short time.
一 刻 不 容 少 緩 not a moment to be lost.
一 刻 千 金 every moment is precious.
[55]一 刹 那 間 in a moment. *See* 110—2.
一 則 in the first place.
一 副 對 ·子 a pair of scrolls.
一 副 環 ·子 a pair of ear-rings.
一 力 with one effort; united; with the whole strength.
[60]一 力 擔 承 to give the whole of one's energy to a certain effort.
一 利 the same benefit; something good.
一 勞 永 逸 by one supreme effort to win eternal ease.
一 匹 驢 an ass, a donkey.
一 匡 天 下 united and corrected the whole empire.
[65]一 千 萬 ten million — a large number.

一 牛 a half.
一 牛 成 功 half the battle.
一 卯 a period.
一 口 unanimous voices; a mouth.
[70] 一 口 人 one person.
一 口 兩 舌 double-tongued.
一 口 同 音 with united voice; of the same sentiments.
一 口 咬 定 fix it with one bite—said of obstinately positive statements.
一 口 應 許 to agree without excuse or demur.
[75] 一 口 氣 in one breath; quickly; smartly; of one mind; a slight affront; an insult; provocation.
一 口 氣 做 完·了 finished in one attempt.
一 口 氣 答 應·了 gave an immediate answer.
一 口 氣 跑 到 came at once, without taking a "breather."
他 和 洋 人 是 一 口 氣·的 he is one with the foreigners.
[80] 一 口 水 a mouthful of water.
一 句 a sentence; an expression; a chapter.
一 句 是 一 句 a sentence is a sentence—no shuffling; to mean what is said.
一 句 話 a saying; a sentence.
一 向 up to the present; heretofore.
[85] 一 向 作 甚 麼 事·情 what have you been doing hitherto.
一 向 如 此 it was like this.
一 同 together.
一 味 uniformly; habitually; invariably; entirely.
一 呼 百 諾 when he gives a call, a hundred respond—of a wealthy man.
[90] 一 品 當 朝 the first rank; a high official.
一 唱 百 和 (ho⁴) one sings, all follow—agreement.
一 回 or 一 次 or 一 會 兒 an occasion; a time.
一 團 a collection; a mass.
一 團 和 氣 the embodiment of good nature; harmony.
[95] 一 團 孩 氣 quite a childish spirit.
一 團 泥 a ball of mud.
一 團 糟 everything in a hopeless muddle.
一 團 高 興 full of good spirits; quite elated.
一 坏 土 a clod of earth—a grave.
[100] 一 堆 a group; a heap or pile.

一 報 還 一 報 one recompense after another.
一 塊 兒 altogether; all at once.
一 塊 地 a piece of land.
一 塊 田 地 a field.
[105] 一 塊 石·頭 a stone; a piece of stone.
一 塊 銀·子 a piece of silver.
一 場 事 the whole business.
一 場 夢 merely a dream.
一 場 無 結 果 from first to last there was no good result.
[110] 一 場 雨 a shower of rain.
一 塵 不 染 unstained by even a particle of dust; not contaminated by the world—of an honourable official whose record is clean.
一 夕 暴 卒 one evening he died suddenly.
一 夥 a group; a gang.
一 大 些 a good many.
[115] 一 天 到 晚 a whole day—said of a whole day's work without intermission.
一 夫 a man; a tyrant.
一 夫 一 妻 monogamy.
一 夫 多 妻 polygamy.
一 套 (or 一 副) 衣·服 a suit of clothes.
[120] 一 妻 主 義 monogamy.
一 妻 多 夫 polyandry.
一 孔 不 見 unable to see a hole—of limited experience and outlook.
一 字 一 淚 a weep at every character—of pathetic writings.
一 字 值 千 金 one character is worth a thousand ounces of gold.
[125] 一 官 半 職 an unimportant official.
一 宗 one item; the special subject of...; a special line of....
一 定 or 一 定 的 certainly; decidedly; surely; without fail.
一 定 方 式 a fixed method.
一 客 不 煩 二 主 one visitor does not trouble two hosts—to invite a person to undertake sole responsibility.
[130] 一 家 人 口 the whole of a family.
一 家·子 通 罵·了 cursed the whole family.
一 實 with perfect truth.
一 對 a brace—of birds; a pair.
一 小 部·分 a small part.
[135] 一 尺 一 寸·的 進·步 step by

step advancing; gradual progress.
一 層 a layer; a storey.
一 工 a day's labour by a workman.
一 差 二 錯 a sudden slip; a mistake.
一 己 oneself.
[140] 一 帆 風 順 May you have favourable winds in your sails!
一 帖 藥 a dose of medicine.
一 幇 or 一 幇 船 a fleet.
一 席 地 a very small piece of land.
一 席 話 a conversation.
[145] 一 帶 all along; in the neighbourhood of.
一 帶 地 方 a district; a belt of country.
一 年 到 頭 from one year's end to another; all year round.
一 年 度 one year.
一 年 生 植 物 annual plants.
[150] 一 座 城 a city.
一 座 棚 a tent or booth.
一 座 樓 an upper building; a storey; a tower.
一 座 壇 an altar.
一 張 一 弛 stretching and relaxing—work and play; fast and loose.
[155] 一 往 無 前 to carry all before one.
一 往 直 前 to go straight forward.
一 律 uniformly; one law.
一 律 斷 絕 to break off all connection.
一 律 無 效 altogether ineffective.
[160] 一 得 之 見 I have only attained to one line of thought—my poor opinion.
一 心 with all the heart; of like mind.
一 心 一 意 of one heart and mind.
一 心 一 計 one mind and one object.
一 心 念 佛 with undivided attention to repeat prayers to Buddha.
[165] 一 心 歸 路 to put the whole heart into it.
一 息 尙 存 as long as there is any breath remaining.
一 意 unanimously.
一 扇 門 a one-leaved door; a door.
一 打 one dozen.

170 一 抑 一 揚 now a loss and now a gain; up and down, high and low—as musical notes.

一 把 柴 or 一 箍 柴 a faggot.

一 把 鎖 a lock.

一 拃 a span.

一 拳 一 脚 a succession of kicks and blows.

175 一 拳 難 敵 四 手 with one fist it is not easy to oppose four hands.

一 捆 柴 a bundle of firing.

一 掃 光 swept clean.

一 掃。而 空 swept clean at one attempt.

一 搬 合。攏 來 all brought together.

180 一 搖 一 擺 staggering along.

一 擊 之 下 at one blow.

一 敗 塗 地 wiped out at one blow—utterly routed.

一 文 不 値 not worth a cash.

一 方 行。爲 one field of action; one phase of activity.

185 一 方 面 on the one hand; one phase or side; one viewpoint.

一 日 三 秋 one day seems like three years—when separated from a friend.

一 日 之 間 in the course of a day.

一 日 千 里 a thousand *li* in a day—rapid advance.

一 日 快。活 勝 千 年 a day of happiness is better than a life of a thousand years.

190 一 日 打 柴 一 日 燒 to burn one day's gathering of fuel on the same day—living from hand to mouth.

一 日 清 閑 一 日 仙 if a man has leisure for a day he enjoys one day's experience as an immortal.

一 旦 at some time or other; suddenly; one morning.

一 早 very early.

一 時 a time; at once; in a little while; inadvertently; suddenly; off-hand.

195 一 時 間 hastily; on the spur of the moment.

一 會 兒 a brief space of time.

一 木 焉 能 支 大 廈 how can a single beam support a great mansion?—of the difficulty of unaided efforts.

一 本 之 所 以 萬 殊 也 that by which one origin produces a myriad diversities.

一 本 書 one book.

200 一 束 a bunch of.

一 板 三 眼 one strong and three weak beats to the bar — said of one who is bound by precedent inelasticity; very careful of rules.

一 枝 軍 a detachment of troops.

一 根 草 a blade of grass.

205 一 根 葦 。子 a reed.

一 根 頭 。髮 a hair of the head.

一 條 a length.

一 條 街 or 一 道 街 a street; a thoroughfare.

一 條 褲 (or 褲 。子) a pair of trousers.

210 一 條 通 則 a general principle.

一 條 針 a needle. A.c. 一 根 針.

一 模 一 樣 exactly similar.

一 樣 the same kind; alike.

一 椿 事 a matter; an affair.

215 一 概 to sum up; all included; collectively.

一 段 話 a speech; a saying or quotation.

一 般 the same; common; general.

一 般 人 a certain class.

一 般 法 general law.

220 一 般 社 會 ordinary society.

一 毛 不 拔 unwilling even to pluck out a hair for another.

一 毫 挫 於 人 the slightest push from a person.

一 氣 like-minded; of the same spirit; in collusion; in one breath; in anger.

一 派 浮 言 the whole is a made-up story.

225 一 流 (or 溜) of one class; connected.

一 溜 房 。子 a row of houses.

一 溜 烟。而 去 he was gone like a puff of smoke.

一 滴 液 體 a drop of liquid.

一 滿 多 少 what is the total amount?

230 一 炷 香 a stick of incense.

一 無 所 有 without a single thing.

一 無 所 知 absolutely ignorant.

一 無 所 長 no special ability; having no special superiority.

一 煞 兒 (or。子) a brief space of time; a short period.

235 一 片 光 明 a ray of light.

一 片 好 心 a good heart.

一 片 胡 言 all nonsense.

一 片 烟 雲 a dark cloud.

一 物 不 留 not a thing left.

240 一 物 不 知 utterly ignorant.

一 理 貫 通 one principle runs through it all.

一 生 一 世 a lifetime.

一 甲 子 a cycle of sixty years.

一 番 once; an occasion.

245 一 畫 a line; a stroke of the pen.

一 百 萬 a million.

一 盤 散 沙 a plate of loose sand—utterly lacking cohesion.

一 盤 棋 or 一 局 棋 a game of chess.

一 目 十 行 to read ten lines at a glance.(-hang²)

250 一 目 瞭 (or 了) 然 to see all at one glance.

一 直 走 to go straight on.

一 知 半 解 very limited knowledge; smattering

一 神 敎 monotheism.

一 程 子 for quite a while; a spell.

255 一 窩 一 拖 bag and baggage.

一 窩 蜂 a swarm of bees or hornets—a crowd of persons rushing forward.

一 竅 不 通 not one cavity open —utterly stupid and dense.

一 筐 線 one hank of thread.

一 等 勳 位 order of merit of the first rank.

260 一 等 國 a first-class power.

一 等 大 使 plenipotentiary; an ambassador.

一 等 書 記 官 a first-class secretary.

一 等 親 first degree of kinship.

一 筆 勾 銷 cancelled with one stroke of the pen.

265 一 筆 抹 倒 cancelled with one stroke.

一 筆 鉤 cancelled; done away with; forgotten entirely.

一 管 筆 or 一 枝 筆 a pen.

一 篇 之 體 要 the substance of the whole work or paragraph.

一 箭 之 地 a bowshot.

270 一 箭 雙 鵰 two birds with one arrow.

一 紅 一 白 first red and then white.

一 紙 書 a letter.

一 統 令 act of uniformity.

一 絲 不 掛 utterly naked, not a stitch on.

275 一 絲 半 縷 the least thread.

一 網 打 盡 to capture all in one net (draught).

一 群 人 or 一 干 人 or 一 起 人 or 一 夥 人 or 一 叢 人 a crowd; a group; a party; a knot of people.

一 群 猪 a herd of swine.

一 而 再 once and again; repeatedly.

一 聯 a collection.

280 一 股 土 匪 a band of brigands or robbers.

一 股 氣 a breath; of the same spirit.

一 股 水 a body of water.

一 脚 踏 兩 船 a foot on each boat—"between two stools."

一 臂 之 力 an exhibition of strength; help.

285 一 致 unanimously; uniformly; as one man.

一 致 一 說 unanimity in every word.

一 致 對 外 one attitude towards foreign relations.　[(-wu⁴)

一 致 憎 惡 to hate as one man.

一 致 行 動 unanimous action.

290 一 致 起 來 to rise up as one man.

一 舉 一 動 every movement; every action—behaviour.

一 舉 兩 得 to attain two advantages at one move.

一 色 (的) of one complexion; of one party; flush in mahjong.

一 葉 a leaf—fig:—a tiny skiff.

295 一 葦 a reed—fig:—a small boat.

一 落 千 丈 to drop 10,000 feet in one fall—rapid declension or retreat; utter failure.

一 表 人 才 a man of great talents.

一 見 便 知 to take it all in at a glance.

一 見 如 故 friendly at the first meeting, love at first sight.

300 一 視 同 仁 to be equally kind to all; impartial kindness or favour.

一 覽 表 a chart; a table; a brief list of contents, etc.

一 言 一 行 every word and action.

一 言 不 洩 not a word leaked out.

一 言 以 蔽 之 one sentence can cover the whole—of the Odes.

305 一 言 僨 事 one word can spoil a matter.

一 言 蓋 一 人 to judge a man by one of his sayings.

↓ 一 髮 千 鈞 see 1725.1.

一 言 難 盡 it is a long story.

一 誤 再 誤 one fault leads to another.

一 諾 千 金 one promise is worth a thousand ounces of gold.

310 一 路 來 的 to come at the same time; to travel together.

一 路 福 星 May a happy star illuminate all your path!

一 輛 車 a cart.

一 輩 子 a lifetime; during a lifetime; a long time.

一 連 successively; connectedly; joined.

315 一 連 三 個 three in succession; three joined together.

一 週 a cycle; a week; a period; a year.

一 週 間 during the week; a period.

一 部 主 權 國 a State having partial sovereignty.

一 部 分 a part of the whole; a section; a department.

320 一 部 判 決 partial decision.

一 間 車 a compartment in a railway carriage.

一 限 a limit; a set time.

一 院 制 the Single-Chamber System.

一 霎 時 an instant; a short time.

325 一 面... 一 面 while...; at the same time...; on the one hand... on the other hand...

一 面 之 詞 one-sided statements.

一 面 的 事 a one-sided matter.

一 類 的 of the same class.

一 體 one body; the whole; uniformly.

330 一 體 一 用 one doctrine and one application.

一 點 a little; a point; a dot.

一 點 一 畫 a dot and a stroke.

一 黨 的 人 of the same company or class.

一 齊 together; all at once.

(a) As soon as.

一 來 就 說 he spoke as soon as he arrived.

一 俟 議 決 as soon as definite conclusions are reached.

一 去 不 返 once it goes it will not return.

一 成 不 變 once completed it cannot be altered; invariable.

5 一 望 one look; as soon as he saw....

一 病 不 起 once he took to his bed he never left it.

一 經 as soon as....

一 聞 as soon as heard.

一 聞 警 訊 as soon as the alarm was heard; as soon as the warning was given.

10 一 見 as soon as seen; on seeing.

乙 1.5. One. The second of the Ten Stems 天 干, thus used 3017 for "the second," "so and so," etc. See No. 610—B. Bent, curved. Radical 5.

乙 乙 one by one; each. See below C.

乙 夜 the second watch at night.

乙 科 or 乙 榜 the former 2nd degree or Chü jen.

乙 覽 the studies of the emperor, to which the second watch was supposed to be devoted.

某 乙 "so and so," a certain other person.

甲 乙 1st and 2nd, A and B, etc.

(a) A black bird, a swallow, also u.f. a duck.

乙 鳥 a swallow.

道 佛 兩 殊 非 鳧 則 乙 the difference between Buddhism and Taoism is very much like the difference between one duck and another.

(b) Guts of a fish.

魚 去 乙 the guts of fish should be thrown away.

(c) Twisted, bent, crooked.

乙 乙 twisted and tortuous; difficult to express.

(d) A caret or mark indicating omissions.

乙 其 處 to mark the place where one leaves off reading.

塗 乙 to erase.

弋 4,5. A dart. A sharpened stake. To shoot with bow 3018 and arrow. Radical 56. Distinguish 戈 No. 3358.

弋 不 射 宿 he would not shoot at birds perching—Confucius.

弋 鳧 與 雁 to shoot wild ducks and geese.

時 亦 弋 獲 a bird is sometimes struck or captured.

(a) **To arrest.**

弋 利 to get gain from.

弋 取 to extort, to seize.

弋 獲 to catch—as thieves.

(b) **Black.**

身 衣 弋 綈 he was dressed in thick, black silk—spoken of the economy of 文 帝 of the *Han* dynasty.

(c) **A perch for fowls.**

雞 棲 於 弋 fowls roost on the perch.

杙 4.5. **A post for tethering animals. A boundary-mark**
3019 **or fence.**

默 4.5.
3020 **Black. Inter 弋 No. 3018**

亦 4.5. **And, also, moreover,**
3021 **likewise, further, however, then.**

亦 不 必 問 亦 不 敢 言 you need not ask for I dare not tell.

亦 不 復 存 are no longer present.

亦 且 moreover.

亦 係 it is also....

5 亦 好 very well; also good.

亦 孔 之 昭 it is clearly seen.

亦 學 人 奔 (the mountains) also appeared to imitate our running.

亦 屬 is also....

亦 已 衆 矣 are also numerous.

10 亦 復 quite....; perfectly....

亦 復 不 少 by no means few.

亦 曷 所 失 it also loses nothing.

亦 有 there are also; I also have.

亦 步 亦 趨 step by step following the Master—*See No. 1618-35.*

15 亦 然 just so; in accordance with.

亦 無 如 何 then there 's no help for it.

亦 若 是 it is also thus.

亦 足 以 成 I can well effect it.

亦 運 而 已 矣 it will do quite as well if he goes another way.

---

20 亦 附 屬 之 also belong to this class.

奕 4.5. **Great; abundant; grand.**
3022 **Graceful, u.f. next.**

奕 奕 梁 山 How great is Mt. *Liang!*

奕 禩 great and lasting—as a dynasty.

奕 葉 or 奕 世 abundant leaves, or many generations—an old family.

新 廟 奕 奕 How grand is the new temple!

萬 舞 奕 奕 the different dances were gracefully performed.

(a) **Anxious, unsettled.**

憂 心 奕 奕 their sorrowing hearts are all unsettled.

(b) **In order, in sequence.**

萬 舞 有 奕 the various dances were each performed in their proper sequence.

(c) **Slack and careless.**

弈 4.5. **A Chinese game, played**
3023 **on a chequered board, called 圍 棋. See No. 7082.**

弈 秋 a famous player of the above game.

佾 4.5. **A row of dancers employed at the ancestral sa-**
3024 **crifices under the *Chou* dynasty.**

佾 生 dancer; an undergraduate who failed to get the degree of *Hsiu ts'ai* owing to there being insufficient vacancies.

八 佾 舞 于 庭 eight rows of dancers performed in the hall.

佚 4.5. **Idleness; ease. To err.**
3025 **Out of office.**
Inter 逸 No. 3045.

佚 女 a beautiful girl.

佚 罰 to err in the application of punishment.

佚 蕩 easygoing; slow; idle indulgence. *See below* A.

佚 道 the way of ease.

---

5 佚 遊 idle sauntering.

淫 佚 lewd indulgence.

遏 佚 to end; to suppress.

遺 佚 to go into retirement from office.

(a) Read *tieh*4.5. **Alternating; successively. Inter. 迭 No. 6311. Exceedingly.**

佚 蕩 exceedingly profligate.

泆 4.5. **To overflow. To be dis-**
3026 **sipated; licentious. Excessive. u.f. 溢 No. 3054.**

泆 陽 a fabulous animal, said to have the head of a leopard and the tail of a horse.

蕩 泆 overflowing; excessive.

軼 4.5. **To come from behind, as**
3027 **when one carriage overtakes another. To rush forth. To surpass. Exceeding. Also read *tieh*4.5. u.f. 迭 No. 6311.**

軼 倫 towering above his generation.

軼 態 demeanour and bearing rather above the average.

軼 材 having talents that excel.

軼 羣 excelling the masses of men.

(a) **To disperse, scatter.**

軼 事 anecdotes.

軼 詩 irregular poems.

散 軼 scattered; dispersed.

(b) **To make a surprise attack.**

侵 軼 to surprise; to seize.

(c) **To put in order.**

整 齊 而 軼 之 to arrange in order.

誰 能 軼 who can arrange—my disordered papers?

役 4.5. **A jailor; a policeman.**
3028 **To serve as a servant. Also read *yü*5.**

役 人 underlings in a magistrate's office.

役 卒 lictors, runners.

役 耳 目 a slave to the senses.

下 役 menial service.

⁵力 役 personal service.
天 役 the servant of Heaven.
夫 役 a servant.
捕 役 constables in a *yamen*.
職 役 duty; office; function.

(a) To employ as a servant.

役 使 to employ as a servant.
役 志 to bring the will into submission.
役 母 如 婢 treated her mother as a servant.
役 萬 物 to make all things serve him.
役 鬼 神 to bring supernatural beings under his control.

(b) To guard the frontiers; military service. War.

君 子³于 役 my husband is away on active service.
應 役 fit for active service.
行 役 to go to the wars.

疫 ^{4.5.} **Pestilence, epidemic. Also read** *yü*⁵.
3029

疫 氣 傳 染 the disease is infectious.
疫 症 an epidemic.
疫 癘 a plague.
疫 鬼 the demon of pestilence.

揖 ^{1.5.} **To bow; to salute. A bow or salutation.**
3030

揖 讓 而 升 下 而 飲 he bows complaisantly to his competitors and ascends the hall, he descends and exacts the forfeit of drinking.
作⁴揖 to make a low bow with the hands in front.
還 揖 to return a salute.
長 揖 a very low bow, performed very slowly, showing deep respect.

(a) Read *chi*^{4.5}. **u.f.** 輯 **No. 503. To gather together; to cluster.**

抑 ^{4.5.} **Or, or if, else, either, still.**
3031

抑 亦 可 矣 this may possibly be.
抑 再 or 抑 且 furthermore; again.

抑 或 or else; otherwise.
抑 或 如 此 it may be like this.
⁵抑 或 無 歟 can it be that there are none?
抑 或 負 焉 or there is failure and defeat.
抑....抑. whether....or....
抑 而 強 與 or is it your own energy?
抑 與 之 與 or is it given to him?

(a) Interrogative particle.

有 不 同 歟, 抑 Is there any difference? or....
焉 有 寃 抑 how can there be grievances?

(b) To press down with the hand. Repress. To restrain, to curb. To settle.

抑 塞 to repress and hinder.
抑 塞 之 才 talents that lack opportunity for display.
抑 強 扶 弱 curb the violent and support the weak.
抑 揚 rising and falling in cadence.
⁵抑 揚 反 覆 going over a thing again and again.
抑 揚 太 過 the sentiment is exaggerated.
抑 搔 to allay irritation.
抑 損 to injure; to oppress.
抑 遏 or 抑 制 or 抑 勒 to restrain; to press down; to coerce.
¹⁰抑 配 to extort and oppress illegally.
抑 音 機 damper—on a musical instrument.
抑 鬱 grieved; despondent; depressed.

(c) Handsome. Elegant.

威 儀 抑 抑 their manners are most elegant.

掖 ^{4.5.} **To support under the arms. Armpits. Also read** *yeh*^{4.5}. **u.f.** 腋 **No. 3034.**
3032

掖 之 上 岸 assisted them up the bank.
扶 掖 to uphold.

(a) Side-apartments in the palace.

掖 垣 the wall around the palace.
掖 庭 side-apartments in the palace. Imperial concubines.

(b) Read *yeh*¹. **To stick in.**

掖·起·來 tuck it in.

液 ^{4.5.} **Fluid secretions; juices; sap.** Also read *Yeh*⁴.
3033

液 化 liquefaction.
液 淲 a name for Peking.
液 洽 to dissolve.
液 量 liquid measure, volume of liquids.
⁵液 金 to smelt metals.
液 體 liquids; essences; juices.
液 體 重 學 the mechanics of liquids.
涎 液 saliva.
潤 液 humid, moist.
¹⁰玉 液 dew.
血 液 blood.

腋 ^{4.5.} **The arm-pits; the part under the forelegs of animals.** Also read *yeh*⁴.
3034

腋 下 under the arms.
腋 氣 the smell under the arm-pits.
腋 臭 the smell under the arm-pits.
腋 芽 axillary buds.
集 腋 成 裘 collecting little bits of fur from under the forelegs in order to make a robe. *See* No. 508-24.

場 ^{4.5.} **A border; a limit; a dike; a frontier; a boundary.** Distinguish 場 No. 218.
3035

田 場 boundary of a field.

蝪 ^{4.5.} **A chameleon.**
3036

蜥 蝪 a small lizard.

邑 阝 ^{4.5.} **A District city or** *hsien* 縣 **No. 2700. A region. The contracted form is written to the right of characters. Radical 163.**
3037

邑 人 those of the same *hsien*.
邑 侯 former title of a city magistrate.
邑 子³ fellow citizens of the same city.

邑宰 or 邑尊 or 邑令 or 邑主 a District Magistrate.
邑庠 the graduates of a District under the old examination system.
邑落 the villages in a *hsien* District.
邑豪 a village-bully.

(a) Shortness of breath. To choke. Depressed.

邑邑 depressed; weak.
邑邑待數百年 wait several hundred years in uncertainty.
於邑 melancholy and sad.
鬱邑 depressed and anxious.

唈 3038 4.5. Short and asthmatic breathing. Palpitation.

悒 3039 4.5. Anxiety, unrest.

悒怏 upset through grief.
悒悒 depressed; sad and anxious.
悒憤 disquieted and uneasy with anger.

挹 3040 4.5. To bale out; to decant liquids

挹注 to draw from one to make good the deficits in another.
挹酌 to pour out wine.
挹酒漿 to ladle wine, etc.

浥 3041 4.5. Damp, moist, soaked.

浥浥 heavy with fragrance.
浥潤 humid, wet.
浥濕 soaked through.

億 3042 4.5. A hundred thousand.

億兆 100,000,000,000.
億兆之衆 myriads of people.
億萬 numberless.

(a) To contrive, calculate.

億中 to calculate.
億度 to calculate; to plan; to estimate. (*-t.o*⁴·⁵)

億測人情 to estimate a man's character; to fathom one's motives, intentions, etc.

(b) Quiet, at rest.

供億 to satisfy the heart.
心億 the mind at rest.

憶 3043 4.5. To recall, to bring to mind, to reflect upon, to remember.

憶念 or 憶思 to consider; to remember.
憶恨 to cherish ill-will.
憶懷 to bear in mind.
憶昔 to think of old times.
憶記 to remember.
憶起 to recall to mind.
回憶 to recollect; to recall.
復憶 to recall to mind.
相憶 mutual remembrance.
記憶力 memory.
記憶薄弱 a weak memory.

臆 3044 4.5. The breast, the heart. The thoughts; the feelings; opinions, views.

臆對 to get a judgement or opinion from another.
臆度 (*to*⁴·⁵) to guess.
臆撰之文 an original composition.
臆斷 decided views; prejudices.
臆測 to form one's own opinion of.
臆見 or 臆說 opinion; notion without foundation.
臆造 trumped up; concocted.

逸 3045 4.5. Ease, idleness. Excess, to exceed. Inter. 佚 No. 3025.

逸事 an extraordinary affair.
逸則淫 ease leads to vicious ways.
逸勞 fresh or worn-out; confident or dispirited.
逸厥逸 carried his dissipation to excess.
逸居偃息 to live in luxurious indolence.
逸居無教則近於禽獸 to dwell in idleness without instruction is a life akin to that of the birds and beasts.
逸志 an easy-going manner; modest; not desirous of fame.

逸材 talents above the average.
逸樂 indolence and pleasure.
逸欲 indolence and lust.
逸興太豪 too bold a manifestation of hilarity.
逸言 or 逸口 boasting.
逸豫 idleness and pleasure; ease.
逸足 swift of foot.
罔遊于逸 do not seek enjoyment in indulgence and ease.
安逸 peaceful leisure.
縱逸 to give the reins to.

(a) In retirement; to withdraw from.

逸士 a retired official.
逸民 cultivated persons living in retirement.
隱逸 to be out of office in retirement.

(b) To let go. To loose. To lose.

逸出 to get out—of a cage.
逸囚 a released prisoner.
逸虎 an escaped tiger.
逸響 floating sounds of music.

(c) Order and sequence.

逸逸 in order.

痷 3046 4.5. Sickness. Repeated.

痷瘵 able to sit up a little—in convalescence.

翊 3047 4.5. To assist. To stand. Ready to fly.

翊贊 to assist; to support.
輔翊 to assist, an assistant.

(a) To respect.

翊戴 to venerate.
翊翊 respectfully.

翌 3048 4.5. Bright; dawn. Tomorrow.

翌日 to-morrow.
翌朝 to-morrow morning.

熠 3049 4.5. Bright and sparkling.

熠燿 the glow-worm.
熠熠其羽 flapping its wings.

襛 3050 4.5. The duration of a dynasty or reign.

萬襛 a long reign.

翼 3051 4.5. The wings of a bird; the flanks of an army. To assist. To shelter.

翼室 a side-room.
翼庇 to shelter—as with wings.
翼房 a gaol in a *yamen*.
翼日 the next day.
⁵翼翅 or 羽翼 wings; aids; assistants.
翼翼 r e g u l a r movements, like those of wings.
小心翼翼 very careful and reverent.
疆場翼翼 t h e boundaries carefully delimited.
翼護 to shelter.
¹⁰剪翼 to clip wings.
四翼 four wings—i.e., two birds, conventional term for such a present.
折翼 to break a wing—to lose a brother.
拍 (or 撲) 翼 to flap the wings in preparation for flight.
覆翼 to screen with wings.

益 3052 4.5. Advantage; profit; benefit. To increase; to progress. To benefit.

益之不寧 my d i s q u i e t was greatly augmented.
益之曰.... added a word, saying....
益劇 increasing; aggravated.
益加 to increase.
⁵益友 a useful friend.
益壽 to add years to one's life.
益多 or 益衆 or 益益 more and more.
益智 the *lungan* or dragon's eye, a fruit grown in South China.
益智圖 wooden blocks which may be built into many different forms.
¹⁰益發 growth; advancement.
益矢公忠 most just and loyal.
益知 to increase knowledge.
益者三友 there are three kinds of friendship which are useful.
益者與 Is he one who has made progress?

¹⁵益算 to add.
益臻敦睦 to augment friendly relationships.
益處 advantage; profit; benefit.
益蟲 insects which both directly and indirectly are advantageous to man.
益覺因難 things became increasingly difficult.
²⁰益足 ample; sufficient.
益鳥 insectivorous birds—useful to the community.
公益 public welfare.
利益 benefit; profit.
有益 advantageous.
²⁵無益 useless; of no benefit.

嗌 3053 4.5. The throat.

溢 3054 4.5. Full; abundant. To spread; to overflow. A handful.

溢出 to overflow; to be in excess.
溢惡 to overstate the evils of another.
溢數 an overplus.
溢滿 full; abundant.
⁵溢目 to dazzle the eyes.
溢美 fulsome praise.
溢譽 flattery; fulsomeness.
外溢 to leak out and be lost
流溢 to overflow

縊 3055 4.5. To strangle oneself. To hang.

縊女 a small insect with black body and red head; it suspends itself when making its cocoon.
縊死 to die by hanging.
縊殺 to kill by strangling.
縊牛 to tie up an ox.
縊頸 to hang; to execute by strangling.
自縊 suicide by hanging.

艗 3056 4.5. The bow of a Chinese boat.

鎰 3057 4.5. A piece of gold of twenty *taels* weight. Wealth.

鷁 3058 4.5. A fabulous sea-bird painted on the prow of junks. A fishhawk.

睪 3059 4.5. To spy. To lead on.

嶧 3060 4.5. Name of hills in Shantung and Kiangsu.

懌 3061 4.5. To rejoice; pleased.

懌悅 rejoicing.
懌然 elated.

斁 斁 3062 4.5. To put away; to be weary of.

服之無斁 "I will wear it without getting tired of it."

(a) To explain.
解斁 to explain; to elucidate.

(b) Read *tu⁴*. To ruin, to destroy.
耗斁下土 wasting and destroying our land.

繹 3063 4.5. To unravel silk; to get the clue. To explain. Unceasing; continuous. Inter, next.

繹之爲貴 it is important to seek out the meaning.
繹其義 unravelled the meaning of it.
繹昧 to seek out the meaning.
繹思 ever thinking of.
繹續 continuous.
繹繭爲絲 to unwind a cocoon—to explain.
絡繹不斷 in a continuous line.

(a) u.f. 驛 No. 3065.
繹繹 to travel well.

譯 3064 4.5. To explain; to interpret; to translate.

譯出漢文 to translate it into Chinese.
↓譯音 transliteration.

譯務 translation-work.
譯官 an official interpreter.
譯密碼電報 to decode a telegram.
[5]譯文 a translation.
譯書 translating books.
譯署 Bureau of Translation.
譯述 interpreter.
譯電 translated foreign cables—in the press.
[10]意譯 a free translation.
直譯 literal translation.
翻‧譯‧繙譯 to translate; an interpreter.

驛
3065 [4.5.] **A government post; a station where couriers rested or were changed. The former government service for the transmission of despatches.**

驛傳 or 驛遞 to send by courier.
驛務 the postal service.
驛卒 couriers; posts.
驛吏 officers in charge of courier-stations or posting-houses.
[5]驛站 post-stages.
驛舍 or 驛館 post-houses.
驛馬 post-horses; destiny.
驛馬性 fidgety; in a hurry.
驛馬星進命 born under the star of a post-horse—never at rest.
驛驛其達 the blades are springing up rapidly.

噎
3066 [4.5.] **A stoppage in the throat. To choke. Hiccough.**

噎喉 the throat obstructed.
噎塞 or 噎食 or 噎隔 unable to swallow food; to choke.

(a) Read *yeh*[4]. To swallow.

JAN.   (ㄖㄢ)
(Ran)

冉
冄
3067 [3] **Tender; weak. Gradually, alternating.**

冉冉 gradually; imperceptibly.
光陰冉冉 alternations of light and shade—the passing of time.

老冉冉其將至 old age is gradually coming on.
冉有 name of a favourite disciple of Confucius.

苒
3068 [3] **Luxuriant herbage. By turns; successively. Inter. preceding.**

苒荏 alternating, passing.
時去苒荏 time is rapidly passing.

蚺
蚦
3069 [2] **A boa constrictor.**

蛅
3070 [2] **A caterpillar.**

蛅蟖 caterpillars.

染
3071 [3] **To dye; to infect; to catch a disease. To apply colour in painting.**

染布 to dye cloth.
染店 or 染坊 a dyer's shop.
染患 to suffer from; to be infected by.
染惡習 stained by evil habits or customs.
[5]染指 to dye the fingers; to have a finger in the pie; to receive bribes.
染指擇肥 to receive a coveted share of what is not one's due.
染料 dye-stuffs.
染毒 infected with poison.
染污 to get a bad name; soiled; dirtied.
[10]染病 to catch a disease.
染痘 to become infected with small-pox.
染票 a receipt for goods left to be dyed.
染綢拿‧不出白布‧來 white cloth cannot be taken from a dyer's vat—a good name is ruined by evil associations.
染耦 harmony.
[15]染色 or 沾染 to dye.
染着 dyed; affected by.
染術 art of dyeing.
染黑 to dye black.
傳染病 infectious disease; contagious diseases.

---

[20]有染 to have illicit intercourse with.
沾‧染 imbued with; infected by.

(a) Soft.

荏染 soft woods.

然
3072 [2] **Yes, certainly. Really. Still, nevertheless; but; although; on the other hand. An adversative particle.**

然且 moreover.
然也 it is so.
然亦 yet also; nevertheless.
然則 hence, but, then.
[5]然則從之者與 in that case they will follow their chief?
然後 afterward, by and by.
然猶 but, still.
然猶有 at the same time, there is as it were.
然而 still; notwithstanding; however.
[10]然諾 to give assent to; promise.
然贊 to assent to.
不然 not so; on the contrary; were it not so.
以爲然 regard as right; give heed to.
俱然 wholly; in every way.
[15]其然豈其然乎 So! But is it so with him?
卒然 suddenly.
天然 natural.
將然 about to.
對曰然 he answered, "Yes!"
[20]已然 accomplished.
必然 certain; it has to be so.
所以然 the reason for; the cause; the circumstances of.
未必然 not necessarily so.
未然 not yet completed.
[25]果然 naturally; eventually so.
當然之理 a natural or self-evident principle.
自然 naturally; of course.
雖然 although.
當然 of course.

(a) To burn; to blaze—the primary meaning of the character. Inter. next.

若火之始然 like a fire that has begun to burn.

燃
3073 [2] **To burn; to light a fire.**

燃 料 fuel.
燃 料 油 oil for fuel.
燃 燭 to light a candle.
燃 燒 to catch fire; to burn.
⁵燃 燒 物 combustibles.
燃 燒 點 point of combustion.
燃 犀 clear-sighted. *See* No. 2463—2.
燃 眉 之 急 a crisis as imminent as when the eyebrows are singed in trying to save a fire.
↑燃 燒 彈 incendiary shell or bomb.

頹² 3074
Beard, whiskers.

髯² 3075
The whiskers; the beard.

髯 如 戟 者 whiskers bristling like a halberd.
髯 翁 an old man.

JANG. (ㅁㄤˇ)
(Rang)

勷² 3076
To assist. Urgent. In haste.

勷 執 to support oneself by means of—as a trade.
劻 勷 hurried, hastily.

嚷³ 3077
To make an uproar. To brawl.

嚷 罵 to scold; to abuse.
嚷 道 to shout; to bawl out.
嚷 鬧 to quarrel.
別 嚷 Stop your noise!
吵 嚷 bawling; altercation.
↑嚷·嚷 to bawl, to brawl.

壤³ 3078
Rich, as soil. Mould, earth, soil. A place, a region, land.

壤 子³ a favourite, well-nourished child.
壤 地 territory.
壤 奠 produce of a place.
同 壤 of the same place.
⁵天 壤 heaven and earth—wide apart.
平 壤 level land.
接 壤 adjoining places.
沃 壤 rich soil.
異 壤 different places.

¹⁰蓋 壤 heaven and earth.
黃 壤 yellow soil.

攘² 3079
To seize; to take; to steal.

攘 善 to seize the best.
攘 奪 to seize; to clutch.
攘 竊 to steal; to pilfer.
攘 羊 to steal a sheep.
月 攘 一 雞 to steal one fowl a month—instead of one a day, from Mencius; gradual improvement.

(a) To reject; to drive out.

攘 夷 狄 to drive out the barbarians.
攘 災 to drive off evil—by charms or incantations.
攘 辟 to avoid; to move aside and allow the carriage to pass.
攘 除 to discard; to reject.

(b) To lay bare.

攘 臂 to bare the arms—for a fight.
攘 袂 to pull up the sleeves—for a fight.

(c) Read *jang⁵*. To throw into confusion.

天 下 擾 攘 the empire was thrown into confusion.

(d) Read *jang⁴*. u.f. 讓 No. 3085. To yield, etc.

盛 揖 攘 之 with a deep bow he yielded place.

(e) Read *jang⁴*. u.f. 餉 No. 2551. To take.

攘 其 左 右 he takes (of the food) from left and right.

(f) Read *jang⁴*. u.f. 禳 No. 3082. To sacrifice.

九 門 磔 攘 at the nine gates animals are torn in pieces in deprecation—against pestilence.

瀼² 3080
Flowing of water. Name of a river in Szechwan. Heavily bedewed.

零 露 瀼 瀼 heavily wet with dew.

瓤² 3081
The pulp; the pith; the core; the kernel. Cartilage; membrane.

瓤 子 flesh of melons, etc; a letter, as being the inside of the envelope.
果 瓤 the flesh of fruits.
瓜 瓤ㄦ the pulp of a melon.

禳² 3082
To pray; to sacrifice.

禳 星 禮 斗 to pray to one's natal star and worship the *Dipper*.
禳 禍 or 禳 災 to seek to avert calamities by sacrifices.
禳 解 to get release from calamity by sacrifice or prayer.
禳 除 瘟 殃 to pray or sacrifice for the removal of pestilence.

穰² 3083
The stalks of grain. Luxuriant; abundant. Ten billions. u.f. No. 3081, 3082.

盛 穰 prosperous; flourishing.
降 福 穰 穰 sending down blessings in abundance.

(a) u.f. preceding No. 3082. To sacrifice.

穰 田 sacrifices to beseech for a good harvest.

蘘² 3084
A kind of wild ginger.

讓⁴ 3085
To yield; to resign; to cede. Polite; yielding.

讓 人 to yield to others.
讓 付 surrender—as of property, etc.
讓 以 爲 得 to yield in order to gain.
讓 位 to give up a seat; to abdicate; to take a lower place.
⁵讓 受 acquisition. (*legal*).
讓 受 人 assignee. (*legal*).
讓 坐 to invite to take a seat.
讓 多°少 how much will you take off—the price?
讓·我 過·去 kindly allow me to pass.
¹⁰讓 授 to hand over; to surrender.

讓 步 to yield place to another; to give in; to compromise.

讓 渡 assignment; to concede. (*legal*).

讓 王 to abdicate the throne.

讓 稿 to surrender the copyright.

15讓 能 give a place to those of ability.

讓 與 to cede to; assignment; to surrender privileges, etc. (*legal*).

讓 與 人 transferor.

讓 與 證 書 deed of transfer or surrender.

讓 走 to request one to go—as when a superior, as host, lifts his teacup to his lips.

20讓 路 or 讓‧開 to yield the road; to make way.

讓 酒 to invite to drink wine.

不 讓 unwilling to yield; no humility.

克 讓 able to yield.

責 讓 to reprimand.

25退 讓 to decline in favour of another.

JAO. (ㄖㄠ)
(Rao)

嬈²
3086 Graceful; fascinating.

嬌 嬈 graceful and slender.

(a) Read *niao*³. To sport with.

鬼 嬈 the haunting ghost of a murdered man.

(b) Read *jao*³. u.f. 擾 No. 3092.

除 苛 解 嬈 remove oppressive burdens and regulate disturbances.

(c) Read *yao*³. Tender and weak.

嬈 嬈 slender and delicate.

橈²
3087 An oar. To row.

橈 船 to row a boat.

停 橈 to hold the oars.

(a) Read *nao*⁴. Crooked; bent wood. Unjust.

橈 骨 the radius of the forearm.

枉 橈 unjust; crooked in dealing.

(b) Read *nao*⁴. Weak, soft.

柔 橈 delicate and weak.

(c) Read *nao*⁴. To disperse. Scattered; defeated.

橈 敗 defeated and dispersed.

橈 萬 物 to scatter things.

繞 遶 }³,⁴
3088 To surround; to wind round. To make a detour. To coil.

繞⁴一 次 bind it around once.

繞⁴住‧了 made fast—as by binding something round.

繞⁴口 令 a jingle that is difficult to repeat, like, "She sells seashells."

繞⁴指 柔 so pliable as to be twisted around the finger.

⁵繞⁴日 to revolve round the sun.

繞³⁴梁 encircles the beams—said of good clear singing.

繞⁴灣ㄦ to go round a corner; to make a detour.

繞³⁴纏 to bind; to encircle.

繞‧起‧來 to wind up.

10繞⁴越 circuitous; to evade—as the customs, etc.

繞⁴路 or 繞⁴道 or 繞³⁴行 to make a detour.

繞⁴過 to wind around—as a path.

繞⁴避 to evade; to avoid by a detour.

繞⁴遠 a long way round.

15圍 繞³⁴to encircle.

環 繞³⁴to enclose; to encircle.

蕘²
3089 Grass, rushes, stubble, fuel. Also read *nao*².

火 蕘 fuel for kindling.

薪 蕘 faggots; fuel.

蟯²
3090 Worms in the bowels.

饒²
3091 To forgive; to spare; to overlook. To be liberal; to be indulgent.

饒‧了‧他‧罷 let him off this time!

饒 人 不 是 癡 漢 he who considers the feelings of others is no fool.

饒 命 to spare life.

饒‧恕 to forgive; to pardon.

⁵饒 手 no more fighting; to allow an adversary to win the game.

饒 一 兩 子³ to give a piece or two to an opponent in chess.

饒 舌 to wrangle; to complain.

饒 過 to forgive an error.

饒‧過 數 次 has been let off several times.

10白 饒 trouble in vain.

討 饒 to plead for mercy.

(a) Abundant; plentiful.

饒 侈 extravagance.

饒 歲 plentiful year.

饒 沃 rich soil.

饒 給 rich; well supplied.

⁵饒 衍 abundant; having ample.

饒 裕 or 富 饒 or 豐 饒 abundant; plentiful.

饒 頭 a surplus.

擾³
3092 To disturb; to annoy; to give trouble.

擾 亂 or 擾 累 or 擾 害 or 騷 擾 to disturb; to give trouble; to annoy; to vex.

擾 亂 國 政 to introduce disorder into the State.

擾 動 to disturb; to unsettle.

擾 害 治 安 to break the peace; rioting.

⁵擾 攘 or 擾 攪 to create a disturbance.

喧 擾 noise and disturbance.

有 擾 I have given you a great deal of trouble—conventional expression said to a host.

煩 擾 to trouble another; to bother.

打‧擾 to disturb. cf. 699.10.

(a) Docile. To train to obedience.

擾 兆 民 to train the masses to obedience.

擾 於 有 帝 obedient to the Supreme.

擾 而 毅 docility combined with firmness.

六 擾 the six domestic animals,— the horse, ox, sheep or goat, pig, dog and fowl.

JÊ.　(曰廿)

(Reh, Rae)

嗻[3] Respectful reply of assent to superiors. Also read *no*[4,5] and *êrh*[4].
3093

唱 嗻 used for a low bow or 作揖.

惹[3] To provoke; to exasperate. To rouse; to incite or induce. To tease.
3094

惹 不 得 not to be provoked.
惹 事 to make trouble gratuitously.
惹 人 注 目 to cause others to take notice.
惹 人 笑 to provoke to laughter.
[5]惹 他 不 起 or 我 不 敢 惹 他 I dare not provoke him.
惹 出 事 來 to cause trouble; to provoke mischief.
惹 動 to provoke; to stir up.
惹 脈 to turn the stomach; to incur dislike.
惹 嫌 to provoke dislike.
[10]惹 我 想[1]思 aroused my amorous thoughts.
惹 是 招 非 to make mischief.
惹 氣 or 惹 怒 or 惹 惱 to provoke a quarrel; to irritate.
惹 火 燒 身 to stir a fire and burn oneself—to bring trouble upon oneself.
惹 禍 to bring evil on oneself.
[15]惹 草 招 風 to get oneself into trouble.
惹 草 拈 花 to be of a lascivious tendency and fond of women.
惹 蝶 to attract the butterflies.
惹 起 人 注 意 to attract attention.
引 惹 to urge; to provoke.
[20]招 惹 to stimulate; to excite.

熱 熱[4,5]. Hot. Fever. To heat. Earnest.
3095
Distinguish 熟 No. 5895. The first form is more commonly used in printed books.

熱 中 to burn within—desiring the regard of his sovereign.
熱 之 傳 導 體 conductor of heat.
熱 力 caloric; heat.
熱 勢 having power and influence.
[5]熱 地 important place.
熱 天 hot weather.
↑熱 力 學 thermodynamics.

熱 學 heat—as a branch of science.
熱 官 an official with power and influence.
熱 客 a visitor who braves the heat; one who brings power and influence; a constant visitor.
[10]熱 帶 the tropics.
熱 度 temperature; degree of heat.
熱 得 打 鐵 hot enough to beat iron.
熱 心 or 熱 腸 or 熱 心 腸 enthusiastic; earnest; zealous.
熱 心 人 士 enthusiasts.
[15]熱 心 從 事 to put the heart into a matter.
熱 念 enthusiasm.
熱 念 已 經 整 個 吞 了 他 his enthusiasm has already swallowed him whole.
熱 惱 burning with anxiety.
熱 望 ambitions; longings.
[20]熱 死 sweltering heat.
熱 氣 烝 人 the muggy weather is enough to steam one.
熱 水 瓶 hot-water bottle; thermos flask.
熱 河 Jehol—summer retreat of the emperors, north of Peking.
熱 泉 hot springs.
[25]熱 漲 expansion caused by heat.
熱 烈 fiery; red-hot.
熱 熟 on very familiar terms.
熱 狂 fanatic.
熱 病 fever.
[30]熱 管 子 hot pipes.
熱 線 heat rays.
熱 血 hot blood; enthusiasm.
熱 誠 earnestness; enthusiasm.
熱 誠 奉 公 earnestness and sincerity in the public welfare.
[35]熱 量[4] quantity of heat.
熱 鬧 interesting; bustling; noisy; busy
熱 霧 hot, steamy vapours.
熱 飯 hot food.
傳 熱 to conduct heat.
[40]悶 熱 hot and muggy.
暑 熱 steamy heat.
殺 熱 to lower the temperature.
溫 熱 tepid.
炎 熱 scorching heat.
[45]燥 熱 steaming, muggy heat.
發 熱 to be feverish.
白 熱 or 紅 熱 white and red heat respectively.
虛 熱 症 typhus fever.
黃 熱 症 yellow fever.
↑比 熱 specific heat.

爇 爏[4,5].
3096
To burn; to heat.

爇 山 林 以 逐 豺 狼 to burn the forests on the hills in order to drive out the wolves.
爇 燋 to scorch—tortoise shell for divination.
爇 茶 to heat tea.

JÊN　(叧)

(Ren)

人 亻[2] Man; mankind. Others, when used in contrast. Radical 9.
3097

人 一 能 之 what others can do by one effort.
人 丁 an individual.
人 丁 很 旺 his descendants are numerous.
人 不 勸 不 善 man, if not urged by example, does no good.
[5]人 不 可 貌 相 a man cannot be known by his looks.
人 不 堪 其 憂 others could not bear his sufferings.
人 不 知 nobody knows.
人 不 知 己 過 a man is unconscious of his own faults.
人 不 足 與 適 也 政 不 足 間 也 it is not sufficient to remonstrate with (a prince) about the men (he employs) nor to rebuke him about his government.
[10]人 不 間 others do not differ from.
人 世 mortals; the world of mortal men.
人 中 the raphe of the upper lip.
人 之 常 事 an ordinary matter; everyday occurrence.
人 之 易 其 言 也 無 責 耳 矣 men are careless about their words, simply because they have not been rebuked.
[15]人 之 生 也 直 there is uprightness in the essence of man's life.
人 事 human affairs; a present.
人 事 不 省 insensible; unconscious. (-*hsing*[3])

人事勝天 art excels nature.

人事訴訟 personal process. (*legal*).

[20] 人云亦云 merely repeating what is said by others.

人人 or 人民 all men; everybody. *See below*—102.

人仰馬翻 men and horses all overturned—utter defeat.

人倫 human relationships.

人倒不錯 he is not a bad sort.

[25] 人們 the people; others.

人傑地靈 may the men be heroes and the soil productive!—the birth of heroes makes the place glorious.

人其人 make men of their men—i.e., the celibate priests.

人其舍諸 will others let them alone?

人力 human strength.

[30] 人力車 a ricksha, from the Japanese sound of the word,—*see* 黃 No. 2297—4.

人參 ginseng, a tonic medicine; it takes its name from the shape of the roots.

人口 members of a family; individuals; population.

人口稅 poll-tax

販賣人口 to traffic in human beings.

[35] 人名計算 personal account.

人命 human life; a life.

人命官司 a case of murder or manslaughter.

人和 popular; pleasing.

人品 a man's disposition; his moral or intellectual standing.

[40] 人員 officers and others; personnel.

人地相宜 the right man in the right place.

人在人情在 while a man lives his favors are remembered.

人境 human habitations; where there are human beings.

人壽保險 life insurance.

[45] 人多口雜 babel of many voices.

人多手雜 too many cooks.

人多掣肘 hampered by having no freedom of action.

人天 a prince or ruler, from 君 爲人天.

人天小果 small fruits of men and *devas;* i.e. building monasteries and making many copies of Buddhist literature, these being accounted as small attainments.

[50] 人夫 servants.

人妖 a human bogy—one who does not act in orthodox ways.

人子 a man; son of a man; The Son of Man.

人字樣 shaped like the character for 'man.'

人定勝天 human determination will overcome destiny.

[55] 人定時候 when all was settled and at rest.

人客 guests; visitors.

人家 people; persons; someone else.

一家人家 all the family.

是人家的 it belongs to someone else.

[60] 是個老人家 it is an old man.

人寰 the world of men.

人山人海 crowded conditions.

人山人海的羣衆 the masses of mankind.

人工呼吸 artificial respiration.

[65] 人工孵卵器 an incubator.

人工火食 labour and means of existence.

人工的 artificial.

人師 a leader and teacher of men.

人形 human form.

[70] 人形化 anthropomorphism.

人微言輕 my position is lowly and my words carry no weight—self-depreciatory.

人心 opinion; sentiment.

人心不古 men are not what they were in the times of long ago.

人急智生 in a crisis a man becomes wise.

[75] 人性 human nature; personality.

人情 human feelings; favour; kindness; sympathy; human nature; the expression of goodwill, as by presents, etc.

不近人情 unreasonable.

作個人情 grant a favour; speak a word for me.

說人情 to appeal on behalf of another.

[80] 人我之見 individual opinion.

人所不見 out of sight; unobserved by others.

人所共知 what is known to all men.

人才 talents; men of ability.

人才教育 vocational education.

[85] 人才輩出 each generation produces its talented men.

人手一編 a copy in the hand of every man.

人擇 artificial selection.

人文 human knowledge or inquiry. 人文主義 humanism.

人文地理 or 政治地理 political geography.

[90] 人日 the 7th day of the 1st lunar month; the birthday of mankind.

人有同俗而爲 a person acts so as to please the vulgar.

人望 those to whom the masses look up.

人未自致者 a man may not have exerted himself to the full.

人本說 homocentric theory.

[95] 人格 personality; stature; character.

人格化 personify; personification.

人格差律 the personal equation.

人棄我取 I pick up what others discard.

人權 human rights.

[100] 人欲 human desires and passions.

人欲日消 human desires daily lessen.

人民 the people. *See above* 21.

人民之權利與義務 the rights and obligations of the people.

人民私有 private ownership.

[105] 人海 a sea of men,—fig:—great numbers gathered together.

人浮於事 there are more men than there are vacancies.

人浮於食 there are more mouths than there is food to fill them.

人滿 full of people; well-populated.

人滿之患 danger of over-population.

[110] 人無遠慮必有近憂 if a man takes no thought about what is distant, he will certainly have anxiety and sorrow near at hand.

人烟 men and smoke—human habitation, population.

人烟稠密 crowded conditions.

人烟絕跡 no trace of human habitation.

人爲 man-made; artificial.

[115] 人爲品 artificial productions.

人爲法 human laws as opposed to natural laws.

人爲淘汰 artificial selection.

人爲·的 artificial.

人爲·的 工·夫 human efforts.

120 人爲萬物之靈 man is the spiritual part of creation.

人爲記憶法 artificial mnemonics.

人爲⁴財死鳥爲⁴食亡 men die in the hope of gain, birds perish in the search for food.

人牙·子 a kidnapper; dealer in human beings.

人物 a man of mark; men and things; people; personage.

125 人犯 criminals awaiting trial.

人理 human experience.

人琴俱亡 the man and his lute are both dead—used of the death of a friend. 王獻之 died, his brother took up the dead man's lute but could not make it come into tune, hence he uttered the above lament.

人生 human life; man.

人生之定命 human destiny.

130 人生哲學 philosophy of human life.

人生如夢 man's life is but a dream.

人生地理 anthropological geography.

人生朝¹露 man's life is like the morning dew.

人生·的 pertaining to human life.

135 人生行·爲 human actions.

人生觀 view of life; philosophy of life.

人生面不熟 he is an utter stranger.

人相學 physiognomy.

人稱代名詞 personal pronoun.

140 人種 races of mankind.

人種仇視 race-hatred.

人種偏見 race-prejudice.

人種學 ethnology. [7509.20.

人種改良學 eugenics. See

145 人種·的性·質 race-disposition.

人種自盡 race-suicide.

人種誌 ethnography.

人種起原學 ethnogeny.

150 人窮志短 when a man is very poor, his ambition is not far-reaching.

人立 to stand erect like a man.

人算不如天算 human calculations are not equal to God's plans.

人籟 the human voice.

人緣 luck; affinity; destiny; influence; popularity.

155 人羣 the masses; society.

人老心不老 a man may be old in years but his heart need not be old.

人能弘道非道弘人 a man can expand the truths which he follows, these truths do not expand him.

人莫不知之 obvious to all.

人莫之非 men did not blame him.

160 人行便道 footpath; side-walk.

人言 human speech; criticisms by others.

人言 or 信石 arsenic,—the first is from the construction of the character hsin.

人證 testimony of witnesses.

人豕 the human sow—said of 戚夫人 who was mutilated by her rival.

165 人豪 a hero; a man among men.

人財兩空 both the person and the money are lost—when a kidnapper fails to get the money for the girl whom he has sold.

人貧犬也欺 when a man is poor even the dogs insult him.

人跡罕經 unfrequented by man.

人身一小天 the body of man is the universe in miniature.

170 人輪·子·裏 surrounded by a crowd.

人造 artificial.

人造氷 artificial ice.

人造橡皮 synthetic rubber.

人造皮 artificial skin.

175 人造石 concrete.

人造絲 artificial silk; rayon.

人造語言 artificial language.

人造象牙 artificial ivory; celluloid.

人造金 artificial gold; gilt.

180 人道 principles of humanity; moral law.

人道學 humanitarianism.

人道敎 humanism; Comptism.

人道敏政地道敏樹 good men cause a rapid growth of government, as good soil does of vegetation.

人道正義 human rights.

185 人采 a personage.

人銀並保 a surety in both men and money.

人間 among mortals; in the world.

人難與天鬬 men cannot struggle against Heaven.

人面獸心 having the face of a man but the heart of a beast.

190 人類 mankind.

人類不齊 all kinds of men.

人類公權 human rights.

人類學 anthropology.

人類幸福 human happiness.

195 人類生活 the life of man.

人類的 human; pertaining to the race.

人類社會 human society.

人類起原 human origins.

人類進化 human evolution.

200 人馬 N.A. for troops, etc; centaur.

多少人馬 how many troops?

人體模型 model of the human form; manikin.

人體組織 the physical structure of man; histology.

人體解剖學 study of human anatomy; anthropometry.

205 不能人 to be impotent.

做人 to act like a man.

爲人 to be a man; as a man.

豈能爲人 can he be reckoned as a man?

儿² Man. Radical 10.
3098

仁² Perfect virtue, free from selfishness, the ideal of Confucius. See below—38. The inner love for man which prompts to just deeds. See below—22. Benevolence, charity, humanity, love.
3099

仁不可以爲衆也 against a benevolent ruler they do not reckon as a large number.

仁之實 the fruit of benevolence.

仁之於父子也 the exercise of love between father and son.

仁之而弗親 he loves the people generally, but is not intimately affectionate. See below —36.

⁵仁者人也　jên is man—humanity.

仁人之安宅 benevolence is the peaceful habitation of man.

仁人心也,義人路也 benevolence is man's mind, righteousness is his path.

仁 人 無 敵 於 天 下 the *bene-volent* man—as a ruler—has no one under Heaven who can oppose him.

仁 兄 or 仁 台 Kind Sir! My good Sir!

[10] 仁 孝 filial affection.

仁 心 kind-hearted; benevolent.

仁 愛 or 仁 惠 or 仁 慈 or 仁 德 merciful; mercy; kindness; benevolence; humanity.

仁 懷 compassion; good-will.

仁 政 a good administration.

[15] 仁 民 而 愛 物 he *loves* the people and is kind to creatures.

仁 父 an adopted father.

仁 義 love and righteousness—the *principle of love* and its manifestation in conduct.

仁 義 充 塞 full of *humanity* and justice.

仁 義 禮 智 信 the Five Constant Virtues—love, justice, propriety, wisdom and sincerity.

[20] 仁 者 其 言 也 訒 the words of a *virtuous* man are slow.

仁 者 無 不 愛 也 the *perfectly virtuous* embrace all in their love.

仁 者 義 之 本 *unselfish love* ·is the foundation of right conduct.

仁 者 靜 ... 仁 者 壽 the *virtuous* are tranquil...they are long-lived.

仁 而 下 士 benevolent and willing to humble himself before the learned.

[25] 仁 聞 famed for benevolence.

仁 術 a kindness; an act of good-will.

仁 言 不 如 仁 聲 之 入 人 深 也 kindly words do not enter so deeply into a man as a reputation for kindness.

仁 賢 men of virtue and stability.

仁 風 a benevolent, magnanimous air.

[30] 仁 里 a *well-disposed* neighbourhood.

人 之 所 以 靈 於 萬 物 者 仁 也 that which gives man a spiritual eminence above the beasts is *jen*.

其 趨 一 也 ... 曰 仁 也 their aim was one....i.e., to be *perfectly virtuous*.

夫 仁 者 己 欲 立 而 立 人 now the man of *perfect virtue*, wishing to be established himself, seeks also to establish others.

彊 恕 而 行 求 仁 莫 近 焉 if a man makes a vigorous effort to act according to the law of reciprocity, when he seeks for the realization of *perfect virtue*, nothing can be closer than his approximation to it.(*ch'iang*³-)

[35] 惻 隱 之 心 仁 也 the feeling of commiseration comes from *jen* —loving goodwill.

愛 之 而 弗 仁 he is kind to (inferior creatures) but not *loving*. *See above*—4.

愛 人 不 親 反 其 仁 if a man loves others and no responsive attachment is shown to him, let him turn inwards and examine his own *benevolence*.

愛 人 無 私 者 謂 之 仁 to love men without selfishness may be called *jên*.

我 必 不 仁 者 I must have been lacking in the spirit of *true love*.

[40] 求 仁 而 得 仁 they sought to act *virtuously* and they did so.

能 近 取 譬 可 謂 仁 之 方 也 已 to be able to judge of others by what is near in ourselves, may be called the *art of virtue*.

親 親 而 仁 民 he is affectionate to his parents and *lovingly disposed* to the people generally.

(a) Sensitive, as hands or feet. Used with a negative.

痲 木 不 仁 numbed, lacking feeling or sensation.

痿 痲 (or 痹) 不 仁 numbed, without sensation.

(b) A kernel.

仁 兒 a kernel, as of a nut.

瞳 仁 the pupil of the eye.

鰕 仁ㄦ shelled shrimps.

壬² The ninth of the *Ten Stems*, 天 干. North.
3100

壬 丙 坐 向 facing north and south.

(a) Artful.

壬 人 a specious deceiver.

巧 言 令 色 孔 壬 fine words, an insinuating countenance and great artfulness.

(b) Great.

有 壬 有 林 with grandeur and with completeness.

(c) u.f. next two.

任⁴ An official position. An office. To employ, to put in
3101 office.

任 事 to perform the duties of a post.

任 事 股 東 managing partner.

任 內 included in the duties of the office; during the jurisdiction of; within the scope of the position.

任 務 public duty.

[5] 任 免 hiring and firing.

任 免 權 power of appointment and dismissal.

任 命 appointment; nomination.

任 命 制 度 appointment by nomination.

任 命 狀 certificate of appointment; proxy; power of attorney; credentials.

[10] 任 官 惟 賢 之 制 the merit system of appointing to office.

任 期 term of office.

任 期 無 定 the term of office is not fixed.

任 滿 term of office expires.

任 用 to engage; to employ.

[15] 任 賢 to employ worthy men.

上 任 to take over the duties of a post; last administration.

信 任 狀 credentials.

兼 任 to fill two offices.

初 任 a first appointment.

[20] 前 任 the former occupant of the position.

勝 任 qualified for the position.

委 任 to commission.

才 不 勝 任 his abilities are not adequate for the position.

授 任 to receive appointment to a post.

[25] 接 任 to take over the seals of office.

新 任 a new incumbent.

歷 任 文 簿 a list of appointments held previously.

現 任 the present incumbent.

再 任 a reappointment.

[30] 知 任 to take up an appointment.

簡 任 directly appointed.

繼 任 to succeed to a post.

↑ 特 任 specially appointed. ⌈tion.

↑ 薦 任 appointed on recommenda-

聘 任 appointed by invitation.
調 任 to be transferred to another post.
賀 任 喜 congratulations on an appointment.
[35] 赴 任 to take office.
赴 任 執 照 credentials.
連 任 to continue in office for another term.
重 任 an important post.
革 職 留 任 degraded but kept in office.

(a) To allow; to tolerate.

任 人 觀 覽 open to inspection.
任·他 let him do as he pleases.
任 何 any.
任·你 作 主 leave the decision to you.
[5] 任·你 是 誰 不 能 依 從 I do not care who you are, I cannot allow it.
任 便 to use one's own convenience; at liberty to.
任 便 隨 時 at one's own discretion.
任 其 取 捨 permit him either to choose or reject.
任 其 如 何 as the case may be.
[10] 任 口 胡 說 reckless talk.
任 從 你 as you please.
任 性 to do as one pleases; headstrong.
任 性 縱 欲 to give rein to the lusts.
任 情 to indulge the passions.
[15] 任 意 according to one's wish; arbitrarily; voluntarily.
任 意 公 積 金 voluntary public subscription.
任 意 共 犯 voluntary co-operation in crime. (legal).
任 意 往 來 to come and go at will.
任 意 揮 擺 reckless scattering—of money.
[20] 任 意 放 蕩 reckless profligacy.
任 意 清 算 voluntary liquidation.
任 意·的 活 動 freedom of action.
任 意 而 待 treat as you like.
任 意 而 行 do as one likes.
[25] 任 意 行 動 arbitrary action.
任 意 規 畫 draw up any scheme as they may please.
任 意 買 賣 voluntary sale. (legal).
任 憑 or 任 聽 to let a person take his course.

任 憑 名 醫 高 手 也 治 不 好 no matter how famous a doctor you get, it cannot be cured.
[30] 好 壞 任 憑 你 罷 whether good or bad, it rests with you.
任 我 所 為 let me do as I please.
任 所 欲 為 to do as one pleases.
任 氣 敢 為 or 任 性 妄 為 to give rein to the passions; to act recklessly.
任·甚²·麼 or 管·甚²·麼 no matter what; anything at all.
[35] 任 由 at the option of.
任 船 飄·去 allow the boat to drift.
任 說 惡 言 indulge in evil speaking.
任 達 unrestrained; indulgent.
任 風 颳·去 allow it to drive before the wind.

(b) Read jên². To bear; to be responsible for. To confide in. Burdens.　Now read jên⁴.

任 人 家 事 to mind other people's business.
任 俠 chivalrous.
任 償 to be responsible for payment.
任 勞 任 怨 to bear responsibility and blame.
[5] 任 咎 to bear responsibility for a fault.
任 天 to trust in God.
任 警 備 之 責 to bear responsibility for emergency measures.
任 運 to rest in one's destiny.
任 重 道 遠 the burden is heavy and the way is long.
[10] 保 任 to go bail for.
信·任 to trust in.
責·任 responsibility.

(c) Read jên². Artful, cunning.

任 人 a flatterer, a man of plausible tongue.
任 恤 sympathizing.

(d) Read jên². u.f. next:—pregnant, etc.

(e) Read jên². A surname.

妊²
姙
3102
To be with child.

有 妊 to be with child; pregnant.
懷 妊 to be pregnant.

恁¹　Thus, so, in this way. To consider, to think.
3103　Distinguish 您 No. 4722.

恁 地 like this; thus.
恁 地 便 凶 if like this, it is an unlucky omen.
恁 地 便 吉 if like this, it is a lucky omen.
恁 樣 or 恁 生 in this way.
恁·的 不 是 他·麼 of course it is he.
恁·麼 in this way; like this.

絍²　To lay the warp; to weave.
3104

織 絍 to weave.

荏³　A plant, the seeds of which produce an oil used for oiling paper, etc. (Perilla ocimoides). A large kind of bean. The Wu-tung tree.
3105

荏 胡 麻 perilla ocimoides.
荏 桐 a name for the Wu-tung tree 梧 桐, aleurites cordata.
荏 菽 large beans; broad beans.

(a) Soft, pliant.

荏 弱 soft and weak.
荏 染 柔 木 soft, easily-worked wood.
荏 柔 soft and pliant.

(b) In course of time; alternating.

荏 苒 至 今 we have, in course of time, come to the present.

衽⁴
袵
3106
The lapel of a coat, buttoned under the right arm.

四 夷 左 衽 the barbarian tribes whose garments fasten on the left side.
斂 衽 to bring the sleeves together, as a Chinese woman in making a bow.

(a) A sleeping-mat.

衽 席 a place to sleep.

衽 席 之 安 the comforts of a peaceful resting-place.
衽 席 炊 爨 to spread the mat and cook the food—to dwell.
衽 金 革 to lie down armed.

賃[4] To rent; to lease. Pron. *lin*[4].
3107

賃 作 hired for work.
賃 借 物 hired articles.
賃 房·子 to rent a house.
賃 書 one hired to write.
[5]**賃 舂** employed to hull rice.
賃 費 hiring-expenses.
出 賃 to lease; to hire out.
招 賃 to let!—an advertisement.
永 賃 a lease in perpetuity.
[10]**租 賃** to take on lease or rent.

餁[3]
肝} To cook food thoroughly.
3108

餁 熟 well-cooked.
失 餁 不 食 Confucius—did not eat ill-cooked food.

鳺[4] A hoopoe, a bird with a crest.
3109

刃[4] An edge. A two-edged weapon or tool; a sword.
3110 To kill.

刃 傷 事 主 wounded the leader.
刃 牛 to kill an ox.
兵 刃 weapons.
刀 刃 the edge of a knife or sword.
手 刃 其 子 killed her son with her own hand.
白 刃 naked weapons.
迎 刃 而 解 splitting open as it meets the knife—like bamboo; a successful campaign. *See* 竹 No. 1373—20.

仞[4] A measure of eight feet. To measure.
3111

仞 溝 洫 measured the depth of the moats and ditches.
壁 立 千 仞 a sheer precipice of 8,000 feet.
高 仞 lofty.

(a) To fill.

充 仞 其 中 filled it full.

忍[3]
忉} To endure; to bear; to forbear; to repress.
3112

忍 不 住 unable to bear it.
忍 事 to put up with things; patient.
忍 事 敵 災 星 patiently bearing up against calamity.
忍 人 a man of no feeling.
[5]**忍 冬** bears the winter—the honeysuckle.
忍 力 patience.
忍 受 to endure patiently.
忍 嘴 不 欠 債 he who restrains his lips will not get into debt.
忍 字 家 中 寶 forbearance is a family treasure.
[10]**忍 字 心 頭**[2] **一 把 刀** the character *jên* has a knife over the heart—do not provoke a man's patience too far.
忍 尤 含 垢 to suffer shame and obloquy.
忍 弗 能 予 to begrudge giving.
忍 心 unfeeling; hard-hearted; to give way to feelings.
忍 心 下 毒 手 he acted malignantly with an unfeeling heart.
[15]**忍 心 害 理** to harden the heart and do violence to principles.
惟 彼 忍 心 there is a hard-hearted man.
忍 忍 hard and impatient.
忍 性 patient; a patient disposition.
忍 恥 to bear shame.
[20]**忍 情** to restrain the emotions.
忍 於 言 to forbear speaking.
忍 氣 to restrain one's anger.
忍 氣 吞 聲 to restrain one's temper and say nothing.
忍 涕 to restrain the tears.
[25]**忍 痛** to bear pain.
忍 笑 to repress laughter.
忍 耐 to bear with; patience; to have patience.
忍 耐 一 下 wait awhile; put up with it for the present.
忍 耐 處[3]**置** patiently settle the matter.
[30]**忍 苦·了** to bear suffering.
忍 辱 報 仇 to bear disgrace but revenge it—in the future.

忍 餓 to bear hunger.
含 忍 to restrain the emotions.
得 忍 且 忍 when you can forbear, do so.

認[4] To recognize; to know. To confess, to acknowledge.
3113

認 一 個 不 是 to make an apology.
認 不 出 來 unable to recognize.
認 不 清 or **認 不 眞** unable to recognize clearly. [take as.
認 作 to agree to act as. **認·作** to
[5]**認 保** to guarantee; to go surety for.
認 准 to recognize and give effect to.
認 可 assent; official sanction.
認 可 狀 certificate of sanction.
認 字 to recognize Chinese characters.
[10]**認 定** to be confident; to recognize for a certainty; sanguine.
認 左·了 mistaken recognition.
認 弱 acknowledgement of weakness.
認 恩 推 過 to claim merits and reject faults.
認 明 to acknowledge; let it be clearly understood.
[15]**認·爲 正·當** to acknowledge the justice of; justification.
認 狼 爲 犬 to mistake a wolf for a dog—to take a scoundrel for an honest man.
認 眞 conscientiousness; in earnest; painstaking; take it seriously.
認 眞 保·護 afford effective protection.
認 眞 監·督 to give effective superintendence.
[20]**認 眞 辦 事** to give conscientious attention to the business.
辦 事 不 認 眞 lacking in thoroughness.
認 知 recognition; acknowledgement.
認·繳 to agree to pay over—a fixed sum.
認 罪 to confess sin; to acknowledge a fault.
[25]**認 虧** to accept the loss.
認 見 to recognize.
認 親 to acknowledge relationship.
認 識 or **認·得** to recognize; to know; to be acquainted with.
認·識 力 cognition.

30 認 賊 作 子 to treat a thief as a son.

認 賬 to acknowledge a debt, or an account.

認 輸 to acknowledge defeat.

認 還 to be responsible for the payment of.

認 錯 to confess a fault.

35 認 領 to establish identity.

認 餉 接 辦 to farm taxes—to pay a sum for the right to collect the taxes.

不 認 to deny; to disown.

不 承 認 to disclaim; non-acceptance. for ownership of.

冒 認 pretence to knowledge of,

40 承．認 to acknowledge or confess.

招 認 口 供 to acknowledge the truth of the depositions.

擔 認 to act as security for; to be responsible for.

朋 認 or 直 認 to acknowledge.

自 認 to own up to.

45 錯 認 mistaken recognition.

物⁴
3114
To stuff; to fill up.

充 物 stuffed full.
實 物 filled full; stuffed tight.

紉² ⁴
3115
To thread, as a needle; to join together; to string. To sew, to stitch.

紉 佩 to appreciate fully; to wear as an amulet.
紉 絲 to make floss-silk into thread.
紉 荷 to bear in remembrance.
紉 謝 grateful thanks.
紉 針 or 穿 針 to thread a needle.
縫 紉 to stitch together.

朋⁴
3116
Tough, strong, hard.

朋 心·腸 obdurate; hard-hearted.
朋 皮 tough skin or hide.
鐵 朋 as hard as iron.

訒⁴
3117
Slow of speech; to hesitate in speech. Cautious in speech.

訒 訥 slow of speech; to stammer.

軔⁴
3118
To skid a wheel; to stop. A catch, a skid, an impediment.

發 軔 to remove the skid—i.e. to start a cart, to begin a journey on the road.

(a) u.f. 仞 No. 3111. Length of eight feet.

掘 井 九 軔 dig a well of nine jên or 72 feet.

(b) Hard, firm, tough.

攻 堅 則 軔 to attack that which is hard one must use hard tools.

(c) Pliable, lazy.

靭
靭
3119
Pliable but strong—like leather.

靭 性 an obstinate disposition.
靭 皮 flexible, fibrous inner-bark of limes and other trees, called bast.
堅 靭 pliable but tough.

稔³
3120
Ripe grain. A harvest. Also read shen³. nien³.

稔 年 or 歲 稔 a good harvest.
稔 熟 a ripe and abundant harvest. See below B.3.
稔 穀 harvest; grain in the ear.
稔 頭 sorghum with mildew on it.

(a) To accumulate.

暗 稔 to hoard in secret.
積 稔 to hoard.

(b) Practised in; familiar with.

稔 悉 thorough knowledge of.
稔 惡 familiar with evil ways; very evil.
稔 熟 familiar with. See above. —2.

(c) Read jên³·⁴. Only. A year, a season.

不 及 五 稔 in less than five seasons.
甫 及 一 稔 scarcely a year ago.

JÊNG. (ㄖㄥ)

(Reng)

仍²
3121
As before; usual. Still, yet again.

仍 世 successive generations.
仍 仍 disappointed; numerous.
仍 似 as before; similar to.
仍 係 it is still so.
5 仍 在 still in existence.
仍 孫 or 礽 孫 a descendant of the seventh generation below oneself; also referred to as a grandson.
仍 復 如 是 it is still the same.
仍 然 如 此 still the same old thing.
仍 舊 or 仍 然 as before; as usual.
10 仍 舊 貫 let the affair go on as before; in the same old way.
仍 行 again.
仍 蹈 前 轍 he continues at his old practices.

扔¹·³·
3122
To throw away; to reject.

扔·掉·了 to throw away.
扔 棄 throw it away.
扔 石 to throw stones.
扔．開 to dismiss it from consideration.

礽²
3123
Blessings. To draw near to. Inter. 仍. See No. 3121—6.

JIH. (ㄖ)

(Rih)

日⁴·⁵·
3124
The sun. A day. Daily. Radical 72. National Phonetic letter for j, written ㄖ.

日 上 三 竿 the sun is as high as three poles—the day is advancing, about 8 or 9 a.m.
日 下 the emperor; name for Peking; the past few days; under the sun.
日 三 四 人 three or four men daily.
日 中 the sun in the midst—the equinox.

5 日 中 則 昃 as soon as the sun reaches the meridian it declines.

日 久 in process of time; at length; as time went on.

日 久 厭 生 in course of time dislike may arise.

日 來 recently; frequently.

日 光 sunlight; sunshine.

10 日 光 之 下 under the sun.

日 光 浴 a sun-bath.

日 光 曬 黑·的 tanned through exposure to the sun.

日 再 食 two meals daily.

日 凡 數 起 several times a day.

15 日 出 以 前 before sunrise.

日 刊 daily publications.

日 利 interest reckoned daily.

日 前 formerly; in the past; on a former occasion.

日 力 gradual proficiency through giving time and effort.

20 日 加 沉 重 daily increasing in severity.

日 升 月 恆 daily increasing in prosperity—as the rising sun and the waxing moon.

日 即 烟 滅 being destroyed daily.

日 圍 主 水 a solar halo indicates rain.

日 域 where the sun rises—in ancient times u.f. the extreme east.

25 日 報 月 刊 dailies and monthlies —the papers.

日 增 月 益 increase of days and months—the flight of time.

日 夕 day and night.

日·子 a day.

日·子 滿 足 the time is fully up.

30 日·子 短 the days are short.

日 家 fortune-tellers.

日 就 月 將 daily progress and monthly advance.

日 常 daily; ordinary; usual.

日 常 生·活 the daily round; daily life.

35 日 往 月 來 days went and months came—of the flight of time.

日 後 after; in the future; by and by.

日 支 daily expenses.

日 斑 sun-spots.

日 數 百 通 電 several hundred telegrams daily.

40 日 新 之 要 the important points in daily reform.

日 新 月 異 new every day, different every month.

日 日 daily.

日 日 新 daily renovation, or reformation.

日 日 社 daily telegraph-agency.

45 日 昨 or 昨 日 yesterday.

日 晡 sunset.

日 晷 a sun-dial.

日 景 (or 影) s h a d o w s cast by the sun. *See* No. 1129—B.

日 曜 日 used by some for Sunday.

50 日 月 sun and moon—the times.

日 月 如 梭 days and months fly like a weaver's shuttle.

日 月 星 辰 sun, moon and stars.

日 月 經 天 as the sun and moon in the heavens—fig:—eternally unchanging.

日 月 逝 矣 歲 不 我 與 the days and months pass away, the years do not wait for us.

55 日 有 孳 孳 daily diligence.

日 有 廩 稍 之 供 there are daily supplies of food sent to the students by the officials.

日·期 a period; a date.

日 期 滿·了 the time has fully come; the period expires.

日 歷 a calendar.

60 日 照 sunshine.

日 理 萬 幾 busy with a myriad affairs every day.

日 甚 increasing every day.

日 用 or 日 給 or 日 費 daily expenses.

日 用 之 間 the ordinary matters of life.

65 日 用 品 articles in everyday use.

日 用 常 事 things that happen necessarily every day.

日 益 明 顯 increasingly obvious every day.

日 程 daily agenda.

日 系 the solar system. *See* No. 2423—A. 5.

70 日 者 one who selects lucky days; a former day; the other day.

日 脚 a day, (used in the 吳 dialects.)

日 至 the solstices.

日 華 the glory of the sun.

日 落 or 日 平 西 or 日 入 or 日 暮 sunset.

75 日 薄 西 山 the sun is pressing on the western hills—her days are rapidly declining.

日 行 事 宜 the daily round; daily business.

日 行 通 用 in general use every

day.

日 表 a calendar; beyond the sun —a very great distance.

日 見 其 衰 it was daily growing more delapidated.

80 日 見 繁 昌 every day saw further expansion and prosperity.

日 見 興 旺 daily increasing in prosperity.

日 角 the protuberances on the crowns of Buddhist saints.

日 計 daily reckoning.

日 記 a diary.

85 日 課 daily lessons.

日 趨 羸 弱 daily becoming thinner and weaker.

日 趨 下 流 rapid declension and failure; degenerating daily.

日 躔 the orbit of the sun.

日 射 病 sunstroke.

90 日 輪 the disc of the sun.

日 近 drawing nearer daily.

日 迫 getting near the end of the year; pressing nearer daily.

日 進 daily advancement; constant improvement.

日 進 分 文 a small profit coming in every day.

95 日 進 斗 金 May bushels of gold come in every day!

日 道 the path of the sun.

日 重 一 日 daily becoming more serious.

日 錄 a daily record.

日 長 the days are lengthening.

100 日 長 一 線 the day has increased by a thread—the day after the winter solstice.

日 長 如 歲 every day seems as long as a year.

日 間 during the day.

日 闢 益 廣 daily development and expansion.

日 陽 sunshine.

105 日·頭 or 太·陽 the sun.

日·頭 暴 曬 the sun shone with great fierceness.

日 蝕 or 日 食 solar eclipses.

日 體 the body of the sun.

一 個 日 子 a date.

110 一 日 千 里 a thousand *li* a day —tremendous forward strides.

不 日 shortly; in a day or so— not fixing any definite date.

不 日 不 月 not within any definite period; indefinitely.

今 日 to-day.

前 日 the day before yesterday.

115 吉 日 a lucky day.

平 日 an ordinary day; everyday.
往 日 formerly.
後 日 the day after to-morrow.
惡 日 an evil day; unpropitious; unlucky.
¹²⁰明 日 to-morrow.
昔 日 in days gone by.
有 日 there will be an opportunity.
永 日 or 長 日 an eternally long day—as when bored with inaction.
無 日 shortly; in a day or so; sunless.
¹²⁵白 日 daylight.
破 日 an unlucky day.
終 日 all day long.
計 日 圖 功 to carry out the daily programme.
近 日 recently; lately.
¹³⁰連 日 several days consecutively.
除 日 last day of the year.
隔 一 日 every other day.

(a) Used for names of places; Japan, etc.

日 俄 戰 爭 Russo-Japanese War.
日 內 瓦 Geneva.
日 國 for 日 斯 巴 尼 亞 former name for Spain, now 西 班 牙.
日 本 the east. Japan.

日 方 之 仇 視 態 度 the antagonistic attitude of Japan.
日 清 Sino-Japanese, during the Manchu rule.
日 耳 曼 Germany.
日 英 同 盟 Anglo-Japanese alliance.
日 貨 Japanese goods.

(b) Oblong.

日 字 the character *jih*—oblong.

駬 4.5. Mounted couriers formerly used for carrying despatches.
3125

JO. (얃)
(Roh)

若 4.5. And. If, as if, as to, supposing. Also read *yao*⁴.
3126 Distinguish 苦 No. 3493.

若 不 是 if it were not so....; had it not been for....

若 不 然 or 若 不 及 if not so; if otherwise.
若 乃 梁 as for *Liang*.
若 何 how then? what then?
⁵若 固 有 之 as if they were his as a matter of course.
若 夫 with regard to.
若 干 a certain amount; so much.
若 彼 若 此 皆 可 爲 也 either this way or that way will do.
若 數 而 見 疏 if after several times there be estrangement.
¹⁰若 斯 such.
若 是 if; if so, thus, so, in this way.
若 是 其 甚 與 Is it as bad as that?
若 有 不 豫 色 然 as if he was displeased.
若 果 然 if really.
¹⁵若 果 如 此 if such be the case.
若 此 such is.
若 民 則 喜 as to the people, they were pleased.
若 無 可 言 in case there is nothing to refer to.
若 然 if such is the case.
²⁰若 爲 how then? What then?
若 知 生 命 爲 重 if you know the value of life.
若 禁 緩 之 if I restrained them and made them go slowly.
若 老 若 幼 both old and young.
若 要 if it is to be; in case of.
²⁵若 要 不 知 if you wish it not to be known.
若 許 so long; so many.
若 論 if we speak of....
若 非 if not.
倘 若 supposing.
³⁰如 若 if; supposing.

(a) Like, to be like.

若 合 符 節 like the agreement of the two halves of a seal.
若 生 子 like a child of fifteen.
不 若 人 not like others.
相 若 just like.
視 難 若 易 to look upon a difficulty as easy.
自 若 as before; like himself—self-possessed. *See* No. 6960.
莫 己 若 也 no one like himself.
莫 若 nothing like; cannot do better than.

(b) To conform to; to accord with.

時 寒 若 seasonably cold.

曾 孫 是 若 the desire of the great-grandson is gratified.
欽 若 昊 天 reverently in accord with the will of Heaven.

(c) Approved.

若 否 approved or otherwise; good or bad.
邦 國 若 否 those rulers in the states, either good or bad.

(d) You, u.f. 汝 No. 3142. This one, that one.

若 人 that person; the said.
若 個 that one.
若 入 前 爲 壽 you go forward and pay him birthday-honours.
若 居 深 禁 you dwell in deep seclusion.
若 曹 you.
若 胡 弗 效 Why do you not follow the example?
若 父 your father.
若 而 人 that person.
若 輩 you.

(e) A plant.

若 木 a fabulous tree with luminous leaves.
杜 若 a plant like turmeric.

(f) A sea-god.

望 洋 向 若 而 歎 to gaze into the distance and sigh to the god of the sea.
For 望 洋 (or 羊), cf. 7043.34.

(g) u.f. transliterating Sanskrit words.

箬 4.5. The cuticle of the bamboo. A broad-leaved bamboo, the leaves of which
3127 are used for mats, hats, boat-covers, packing tea, etc. Inter. 篛 No. 3129. Also read *yao*⁴.

箬 竹 the variety of bamboo, as above; it grows about three feet high.
箬 笠 a wide, conical hat used by labourers, chair-bearers, etc.; it is made of bamboo splints interwoven with the broad leaves of this variety of bamboo,—these render it rain-proof.
箬 (or 篛) 篷 covering, made in the form of an arch, used over

boats; it is constructed from bamboo splints and lined with these broad leaves,—it is rain-proof.

弱 3128 4.5. Weak; yielding. To treat as weak. To weaken. The young. Deficient, weak constitution.

弱 不 勝 強 the weak cannot resist the strong.
弱 不 勝¹衣 too weak to bear the weight of the clothing.
弱 力 weakness.
弱 冠 a young man of twenty; one who was not yet capped.
⁵弱 半 the smaller half.
弱 弟 a little brother.
弱 息 my children; my son or daughter
弱 戸 a simpleton; one who is easily deceived.
弱 水 a fluid between air and water—found in Fairyland.
¹⁰弱 肉 強 食 the weak are the prey of the strong.
弱 行 to limp.
弱 質 weak, of feeble constitution.
弱 點 the weak point; vulnerable point; point of deficiency
使 衰 弱 to enfeeble.
¹⁵志·氣 弱 slack, unambitious, lacking firmness of purpose.
柔 弱 flexible; pliable; supple; weak.
疲 弱 feeble and tired.
老 弱 feebleness of senility.
脆 弱 fragile.
²⁰軟 弱 weakly.

篛 3129 4.5. A broad-leaved bamboo. See 箬 No. 3127.

蒻 3130 4.5. A water-plant, a wild arum.

叒 3131 4.5. Obedient; united.

叒 木 a tree, supposed to grow in Fu-sang 扶桑, see No. 1909—27.

JOU.　　　　(柔)
(Reo)

禸 3132 ³ A footprint. Radical 114.

柔 3133 ² Soft, pliant. Yielding, gentle. To overcome by kindness.

柔 之 勝 剛 the soft overcoming the hard.
柔 光 a soft light.
柔 和 soft, gentle.
柔 嘉 tender and beautiful.
⁵柔 媚 attractive; effeminate.
柔 嫩 tender—as plants.
柔 握 soft grasp—a woman's hand.
柔 情 soft and sentimental.
柔 懦 weak, lacking backbone.
¹⁰柔 日 the days that bear the even-numbered signs of the *stems* 天 干, i.e. 乙、丁、己、辛、癸.
柔 曼 softness of the stem.
柔 橈 a weak constitution of body.
柔 毛 sheep's wool; the sheep.
柔 然 ancient tribe destroyed by the Turki.
¹⁵柔 甚 How tender!
柔 綿 accommodating.
柔 翰 a Chinese writing-brush.
柔 色 a pleasant countenance.
柔 荑 the soft, white hand of a lady.
²⁰柔 術 or 柔 道 jiujitsu, or jujutsu.
柔 語 soft speech.
柔 弱 mild, soft, meek.
柔 軟 組 織 soft substance of an organ, parenchymatous tissue.
柔 軟 體 操 physical exercises.
²⁵柔 道 the principle of yielding and humility. *See also above*—20.
柔 遠 人 be gracious to strangers.
柔 韌 pliable, yet tough—like leather.
柔 順 yielding, agreeable.
柔 麻 to macerate hemp.
³⁰剛 柔 hard and soft; flexible and rigid
温·柔 gentle; meek.

揉 3134 2.4. To bend, to twist. To subdue.

揉 搓 to crush together in the hand; to bully.

揉 此 萬 邦 to subdue all these countries.
揉 球 to roll metal balls (in the hands in order to keep the fingers supple.)
揉 碎 to twist to pieces.
揉 輪 to bend wood for wheels.
錯 揉 mixed up.

(a) To rub.

揉·出 淚·來 to force tears by rubbing the eyes.
揉 捼 to massage.
揉 眼·睛 to rub the eye.

蹂 3135 2.4. To tread out grain; to trample.

蹂 去 粃 糠 to tread the grain from the chaff.
蹂 若 to trample under foot.
蹂 踐 to trample under foot.
蹂 躪 the trampling of animals; oppressive exactions; the devastations of the military.

輮 3136 ³ The felloe of a wheel. Inter. 揉 No. 3134.

JU.　　　　(如)
(Ru)

如 3137 ² Like, if, as. As good as, equal to. An initial particle: —if, supposing, etc.

如 一 much alike; similar.
如 一 日 as at the present time; as one day.
如 下 as below; as follows.
如 之 the like; such as this.
⁵如 之 何 勿 思 How can I not think of him?
無 如 之 何 there is no help for it.
如 今 or 目 今 now, at this time.
如 何 How? Why?
如 何 是 了 What will be the outcome?
¹⁰如 何 是 好 What is the best thing to do?
其 如 我 何 What can they do to me?
如 使 人 之 所 欲 if among the things which men like....

如 來 a term applied to every Buddha. *See* 佛 No. 1982—35, 36.

如 來 滿 山 the hills were covered with images of Buddha.

¹⁵如 保 赤 子 act as if you were looking after an infant.

如 兄 如 弟 terms of address used to each other by elder and younger sworn-brothers.

如 出 一 口 with one voice.

如 切 如 磋 如 琢 如 磨 as you cut and then file, as you carve and then polish.

如 初 as at the first.

²⁰如 同 like to; resembling.

如 夫·人 or 如 君 your concubine—lit:—as your wife.

如 失 一 臂 like losing an arm—a brother.

如 實·地 描 寫 portray the picture in accord with reality.

如 寶 very precious; very dear.

²⁵如 左 as follows; as below—of writing.

如 常 or 照 常 as customary; according to routine.

如 干 or 若 干 a certain quantity.

如 影 歷 歷 like shadows passing before me.

如 心 爲 恕 *shu* is made up of 如 and 心—forgiveness refers to the action of the heart.

³⁰如 意 as you wish; a kind of sceptre, used as a symbol of Buddha and his doctrines.

如 意 草 clover; trefoil.

不 得 如 意 could not get it according to his wishes.

如 愛 己 然 like loving themselves.

如 或 if perchance; or if.

³⁵如 或 知 爾 則 何 以 哉 suppose some ruler knew (and employed) you, what would you do?

如 所 擬 as suggested.

如 故 as before; as of old.

如 數 like the amount; in full.

如 數 家 珍 like the precious treasure of every family—very clear and lucid.

⁴⁰如 日 月 之 食 like the eclipses of the sun and moon—seen by everybody.

如 是 like this.

如 … 是 也 such as....

如 月 the second lunar month.

如 有 if there be; if any one has; should it happen that.

↑ 如 坐 針 氈 uncomfortable as sitting on a rug of needles.

⁴⁵如 有 復 我 者 if you should seek me again.

如 有 所 立 卓 爾 as if something stood erect before me.

如 期 punctually; at the time appointed.

如°果 or 若 果 or 如 然 if; what if.

如 柴 like a stick—very thin.

⁵⁰如 此 thus; like this.

如 此 看 來 looked at in this way.

如 此 這 般 and so on; it was like this.

如 歸 like returning home—said of death.

如 法 泡 製 compounded according to the correct rules—of drugs, etc., now used to indicate:—done according to instructions.

⁵⁵如 湯 沃 雪 like hot water on snow—easily made to disappear.

如 狂·地 like mad; wildly.

如 獲 石 田 like acquiring stony land—getting what is useless.

如 矢 as straight as a dart.

如 約 according to agreement or treaty.

⁶⁰如 膠 似 漆 like glue and varnish—closely attached.

如 蛾 赴 火 like a moth to a candle.

如 許 such are:—implies greatness in the comparison.

如 詳 according to the details of the report.

如 話 而 成 completed according to orders.

⁶⁵如 遇 whenever; if ever; should it happen.

如 須 if it shall be necessary.

如 願 as one wishes.

如 願 以 償 fulfilled my utmost ambitions.

如 饑 如 渴 as if hungering and thirsting.

⁷⁰如 飛 like flying—swiftly.

如 魚 得 水 like a fish getting to water—readily, pleased.

二 二 如 四 twice two is four.

不 如 cannot do better than; not to be compared; not equal to.

不 如 不 去 you had better not go.

⁷⁵夭 夭 如 也 pleased looking; happy.

申 申 如 也 self-possessed; comfortable.

深 如 海 as deep as the sea.

空 如 也 cleaned out; quite empty.

突 如 其 來 to come unexpectedly.

(a) To go to; to proceed; to follow. Sometimes read *ju*⁴.

以 如 江 南 went to Kiangnan.

如 吳 went to *Wu*.

公 如 棠 the chief went to *T'ang*.

(b) Should, ought.

則 如 亡 then he should die.

洳^{2.4.} Damp. Marshy.
3138

茹² To eat. Also read *yü*².
3139

茹 其 拳 sucked his fist.

茹 古 合 今 to feed on the ancients and taste the moderns—well read.

茹 毛 飲 血 to eat the hair and drink the blood—to be a savage.

茹 氣 to eat wind—hidden hatred.

茹 素 to abstain from meats and things forbidden.

茹 素 念 經 fasting from meats and chanting the Buddhist books.

茹 苦 to eat bitterness—to suffer.

茹 草 to eat herbs.

茹 葷 to eat meats.

啜 茹 to gobble up.

貪 茹 to gorge.

(a) Putrid.

茹 魚 putrid fish.

(b) Roots which are connected.

拔 茅 連 茹 to root out entirely.

(c) To reckon, to calculate.

不 可 以 茹 not able to guess what it is.

(d) General name for vegetable food. A kind of madder.

茹 藘 madder. *See* 茜 No. 929.

袽^{2.4.} Old rags, old clothing. Caulking.
3140

鴽² 3141 A bird resembling a quail.

汝³ 3142 You, your. Often written like 女 No. 4776. Used alone, generally in the singular of address, implies familiarity. See 爾 No. 1754.

汝其于予治 you manage them for me.
汝曹 you—plural.
汝輩 like 你們 you—plural.

(a) Name of two tributaries of the River *Huai* 淮河.

粀³ 3143 Cakes made from rice-flour and honey.

粔粀 fried cakes of fine rice-flour; pastry.

乳³ 3144 Milk. The breasts; a teat, a nipple. To suckle.

乳下 unweaned, at the breast.
乳名 the pet-name given to children.
乳哺 to suckle.
乳媼 or 乳嫗 a wet-nurse.
⁵乳子 a sucking-child.
乳房 the udder; breasts.
乳核 a teat.
乳榨器 milking-machine.
乳母 or 乳娘 a wet-nurse.
¹⁰乳氣 childish.
乳汁 or 乳奶 milk.
乳汁不足 destitute of milk.
乳油 butter. = 黃油,牛油.
乳熱症 milk-fever.
¹⁵乳球 globules of milk.
乳癌 cancer of the breast.
乳癰 abscess of the breast.
乳皮 cream.
乳糖 lactose, milk-sugar.
²⁰乳糜 chyle.
乳糜管 lacteals.
乳腺 mammary gland.
乳臭 smell of milk—young and inexperienced.
乳酪 curds, junket.
²⁵乳酸 lactic acid.
乳金 liquid gold—used in painting.
乳頭 a nipple, a teat.
乳餅 cheese, esp. goats' cheese of Yunnan.

乳養 to rear—as a young child.
³⁰乳香 frankincense; gum olibanum.
乳齒 milk-teeth.
喂乳 to give suck.
斷乳 to wean.
石鐘乳 stalactites.
³⁵竹乳 tabasheer, a concretion found in the joints of bamboo.
腐乳 a milky preparation from beans.
馬乳酒 koumiss.
驗乳器 lactometer.

(a) The young of animals, birds, etc.

乳燕 young swallows.
乳虎 a sucking-tiger.

(b) To give birth.

婦人免乳九死一生 child-birth is exceedingly dangerous to the life of a woman.
乳醫 ancient term for a midwife.

(c) To triturate.

乳碎 to triturate in a mortar.
乳鉢 a mortar used by druggists.

(d) To brood over eggs. Also read *jou*⁴.

雄雛雞乳 the pheasants crow and the hens brood.

儒² 3145 The learned, defined as one to whom everything is known. See —24 below. A scholar. Confucianists.

儒吏 an educated official.
儒墨 Confucius and Micius 墨子.
儒學 a former Director of Studies.
儒教 Confucianism.
⁵儒服 dress of a scholar.
儒林 a collection of the writings of Confucian scholars.
儒為人 to study so as to get the praise of others.
儒為己 to study so as to improve oneself.
儒玄 Confucianism and Taoism.
¹⁰儒者 or 儒士 or 儒生 or 儒家 a scholar of the Confucian school.
儒醫 a learned doctor of the Chinese school.

儒釋道三教 the religions of Confucianism, Buddhism, and Taoism.
儒門 Confucianism.
儒雅 elegant; stylish.
¹⁵侏儒 a dwarf.
名儒 a famous scholar.
君子之儒 scholarship of the superior man.
大儒 a great scholar.
宿儒 an aged scholar of wide reputation.
²⁰寒儒 a scholar in poor circumstances.
鴻儒 a man of wide reading.
腐儒 a scholastic pedant.
通儒 wide learning.
通天地人曰儒 to be conversant with the things of Heaven, earth and man is called *ju*.

嚅² 3146 Noise of chattering.

喁嚅 chattering, talking.

孺²·⁴ 3147 A suckling, a child. Dependent, as a child. Childlike.

孺人 title given to wives of former officials of the seventh grade. Used on tombstones for "a deceased wife."
孺子 a child; my lad.
孺子可教 the lad is worth teaching.
孺慕之私 my longing affection.
和樂且孺 happy as a child.

擩⁴ 3148 To stain, to dye. Inter. next.

耳擩目染 ears and eyes imbued with learning.

(a) Read *jui*³. To place the hand on; to feel.

擩嚌 to enter deeply into—the hands feeling and the mouth tasting.

(b) Read *juan*¹. To rub between the hands.

濡² 3149 To immerse; to moisten. Damp, moist, glossy.

濡 化 imbued with and transformed.

濡 染 or 沾 濡 to dye.

濡 溺 immersed in; to dip; to soak.

濡 潤 imbued with.

濡 濕 to soak, to make wet.

濡 首 very drunk.

如 濡 glossy, as if wet.

(a) Patient, enduring. Dilatory.

濡 忍 to be patient; to bear with.

濡 滯 dilatory, slow; embarrassed.

濡 迹 to linger; to be detained.

濡 需 brief enjoyment.

含 濡 to endure, to be patient.

(b) Soft—as boiled meats.

濡 肉 齒 決 boiled meats for those whose teeth are lacking.

(c) Read *êrh*². Boiled, stewed.

濡 豚 boiled sucking-pig.

濡 鷄 stewed fowl with gravy.

襦²
3150
    A short coat; a jacket.

襦 袴 jacket and trousers.

汗 襦 a shirt or singlet.

顬²
3151
    The temporal bone.

顳 顬 the temporal bone.

顳 顬 筋 temporal muscle.

JU.   (日ㄨ)
(Ruh)

入
3152
    4.5. To enter; to make to enter. To put in.
Radical 11.
Distinguish 人 No. 3097;
八 No. 4845.

入 不 敷 出 income does not meet expenditure.

入 主 以 來 from the time when they obtained the mastery.

入 伍 to enlist.

入 信 credible; worthy of trust.

⁵入 值 to be in waiting.

入 冊 registered.

入 口 to import; entrance; way in; to enter the mouth.

入 口 稅 import duty.

入 口 貨 imports.

¹⁰入 告 to bring to the royal notice.

入 味 interested in.

入 味 就 好 if it is appetizing it will do.

入 坐 to take a seat at the table.

入 城 治 喪 (to permit the body of an official, who has died in office elsewhere, to be brought home and) enter the city for the funeral.

¹⁵入 場 to enter the arena; to go in for the examinations.

入 場 券 ticket of admission.

入 場 費 price of admission.

入 塢 to go into dock.

入 境 問 禁 on entering a country inquire about the prohibitions.

²⁰入 夜 nightfall; at night.

入 奏 to present a memorial to the throne.

入 官 to be confiscated; to enter official life.

入 定 to enter into the contemplative state—as a Buddhist priest.

入 寇 to invade—of rebels.

²⁵入 室 well advanced in scholarship.

入 局 to gamble together.

入 山 to retire into the mountains; to become a recluse.

入 幕 to act as secretary.

入 彀 well enough; done well—as a piece of work; capable; adequate to.

³⁰入 息 income.

入 手 to begin with; elementary.

爲 入 手 as a preliminary step.

入 敎 to become a church member.

入 數 to put into the account; to be reckoned among the number.

³⁵入 會 to join a society.

入 會 典 禮 initiation rites or ceremonies.

入 月 beginning of the menses.

入 朝² to go to court.

入 木 三 分 to enter well into the timber—to put energy into a thing; vigorous efforts.

⁴⁰入 格 suitable; agreeable to one's plan.

入 梅 (or 霉) beginning of the mildew period, being about June 10th.

入 棧 憑 單 warehouse receipt.

入 欵 or 入 賬 or 入 銀 or 入 項 receipts.

入 此 類 it falls into this class.

⁴⁵入 殮 to prepare a corpse and place it in the coffin.

入 水 捉 水 泡 to enter the water and grasp the foam—useless.

入 泮 to take the former first degree of *Hsiu ts'ai*.

入 港 稅 port dues.

入 涅 盤 to enter Nirvana.

⁵⁰入 班 to enter the ranks of; to become a member of.

入 理 reasonable; proper.

入 眼 pleasing to the eyes; within [eyesight.]

入 祀 to place the ancestral tablet in the temple.

入 神 to go into a trance; to be absent-minded.

⁵⁵ 正 聽 得 入 神 he sat listening with entrancement.

入 禀 to file a petition.

入 籍 to be enrolled as a citizen; to acquire citizenship.

入 耳 之 言 words of wisdom.

入 耳 著² 心 it enters my ear and illumines my heart.

⁶⁰入 聖 to be of the orthodox faith.

入 聲 the tone commonly called the fifth in Chinese speech.

入 肚 to remember—as a pupil his lessons.

入 股 to become a shareholder.

入 腦 to get an impression.

⁶⁵入 腦 太 深 made a deep impression.

入 英 籍 to be naturalized as a British subject.

入 華 to enter China

入 調⁴ in tune; spoken in season.

入 貢 to bring tribute.

⁷⁰入 贅 to enter the family of his wife.

入 射 角 angle of incidence.

入 迷 captivated; fascinated.

入 道 to become a Buddhist or Taoist.

入 選 to be placed on the selected list.

⁷⁵入 邪 途 to enter on depraved courses.

入 門 to enter the door; to make a beginning; introductory.

入 閣 to become a Cabinet Minister.

入 闈 to compete at the former public examinations under the old system.

入 隊 to join the ranks.

⁸⁰入 骨 to enter the bone; to be influential with.

恨 得 入 骨 very deep hatred.

入 黨 to join a party; to take a side.

不 入 俗 眼 not for the vulgar gaze.

不 相 入 incongruous.

⁸⁵出 入 相 抵 to make both ends meet.

收 入 to receive.

故 入 人 罪 to charge an innocent person knowing him to be not guilty.

肉 / 月
3153 — 4.5.

Flesh; meat. Fleshy. The pulp of fruit, etc. Radical 130. Also read jou⁴.

肉 丸·子 or 肉 圓·子 meat-balls.

↓ 肉 餅·子 flat piece of minced meat.

肉 刑 mutilation as a punishment, such as castration, etc.

肉 動 眼 跳 palpitation; thrills; a sensation of creepiness.

肉 品 meat.

⁵肉 好 fat and flourishing. See below—A.

肉 山 脯 林 extensive quantities of fresh and dried meats—unlimited extravagance.

肉 市 the meat market.

肉 慾 sensuality.

肉 攫 之 鳥 birds of prey.

¹⁰肉 桂 cinnamon.

肉 案·子 or 肉 架·子 a butcher's stall.

肉 片 slices of meat.

肉 球 一 般 的 as fat as a ball.

肉 疔 an ulcer.

¹⁵肉 痛 suffering pain—as in separation.

肉 瘤 a fleshy tumour.

肉 癢 討 打 your flesh is itching for a thrashing.

肉 白 骨 to put flesh on dry bones; to bring the dead to life.

肉 眼 a carnal view; stupid.

²⁰肉 眼 不 識 英 雄 his fleshy eyes cannot tell a hero.

肉 眼 凡 夫 an ordinary mortal with no spiritual conception.

肉 眼 無 珠 carnal eyes without pupils—stupid, dull.

肉 票 captives held for ransom.

肉 色 flesh-coloured.

²⁵肉 莖 the main stalk of a flower; peduncle.

肉 菓 or 荳 宼 nutmegs.

肉 薄 skin-tight, as wet clothing; close contact.

肉 袒 to strip off the upper garments as a token of submission, asking for punishment; u.f. making humble apology.

肉 跳 creepy feelings; apprehensive.

³⁰肉 鞍·子 hump of a camel.

肉⁴頭²a lout, a stupid. (S. dial.)

肉 食 carnivorous.

肉 食 植 物 carnivorous plants.

肉 食 獸 類 carnivorous animals.

³⁵肉 食 鳥 carnivorous birds.

肉 體 or 肉 身 the body; the mortal frame.

肉 體·的 carnal, pertaining to the body.

肉 鬆 dried meat in very fine silky threads.

肉 麻 creepy feelings.

⁴⁰割 肉 療 親 to cut off a piece of one's flesh and cook it for the cure of one's parents.

打 肉 to sell meat.

生 肉 or 長 肉 to put on flesh.

腐 肉 rotting flesh.

臘 肉 dried, salted meat.

⁴⁵親 骨 肉 parents and children.

飛 肉 game, poultry.

魚 肉 fish.

(a) The disc of a jade ring or other circular, perforated object such as a *cash*.

肉 好 names given respectively to the disc and the hole of any flat, circular, perforated object, such as a *cash*.

辱
3154 — 3,4.5

To disgrace, to defile. To abuse. Disgrace; to be disgraceful.

辱 命 you demean yourself to command me; to dishonour one's commission.

辱 國 to bring shame on the nation —as high officials who only seek their own ends.

辱 家 敗 門 to bring disgrace on a family.

辱 承 見 召 I have been honoured by your invitation.

⁵辱 沒 to reproach; to insult; to scold. (-mo⁴)

辱 罵 to curse and revile.

辱 臨 敝 舍 I disgrace you by making you come to my humble abode.

辱 莫 大 焉 there is no greater shame.

辱 親 to disgrace one's parents.

¹⁰辱 身 to disgrace oneself.

含 辱 to swallow an affront.

忍 辱 to bear an insult.

挫 辱 humiliation.

榮 辱 glory and shame.

¹⁵汚 辱 to defile—a woman.

玷 辱 to violate; to defile.

羞 辱 insult; disgrace.

↑ 侮 辱 insult.

溽
3155 — 4.5.

Damp, muggy.

溽 暑 humid, hot weather.

溽 氣 蒸 騰 the muggy vapour rises.

溽 熱 muggy weather; sultry.

(a) Rich, savoury, greasy.

飲 食 不 溽 simple, plain living.

縟
3156 — 4.5.

Adorned; beautiful. Gay, elegant.

縟 禮 tiresome ceremonial.

縟 節 over-formal and ceremonious.

縟 細 fine.

繁 縟 gay, with variegated colours.

(a) To reckon with.

蓐
3157 — 4.5.

Suckers, shoots, sprouts. Rushes.

蓐 收 the Spirit of Autumn, which inflicts punishment.

竹 蓐 fungus on bamboo.

(a) A mat for bedding.

蓐 母 a mid-wife.

蓐 瘡 bed-sores.

蓐 食 to take meals in bed.

坐 蓐 in childbed.

臨 蓐 nearing confinement.

茵 蓐 a cushion of grass.

落 蓐 birth; to be born.

(b) Name of ancient State.

褥 4.5. A thick, stuffed mat; a mattress; a cushion; bedding.
3158

褥套 bed-bag for a journey.
褥子 or 床褥 or 睏褥 a mattress.
褥草 short, smooth grass like a mat.

JUAN. (曰ㄨㄢ)

(Ruan)

奬 3 Soft, weak. Pliable. Inter. 輭 No. 3165.
3159

奬國 a weak State.
奬梯 a light ladder; rope-ladder.
奬輪 wheel of a light carriage.
奬體 a weak constitution.

堧 2 Empty spaces enclosed by a city wall. Fields near the bank of a river.
3160

愞 4 Timid, apprehensive.
3161

愞弱 timid and weak.

挼 2 To dip, to soak. Inter. 挪 No. 3166. To rub in the hands.
3162

瑌 3 A white opaque quartz used for ornaments.
3163

蠕 3 Ancient tribe in Central Asia, destroyed by Turks in 6th century.
3164
Read ju[2]. To wriggle as a worm.

蠕動 wriggling.

輭 3 Soft, yielding, pliable. Weak.
軟
3165

輭包 a soft person.
輭化 to melt; to bring into submission.
輭半 the lesser half.

輭和 comfortable; pliable, easy; accommodating. (--huo)
[5]輭壳蛋 soft-shelled egg.
輭弱 weak; sickly.
輭怯 nervous; apprehensive.
輭木 soft woods; cork.
輭木塞 corks for stoppers.
[10]輭木皮 cork-bark.
輭水 soft water.
輭洋紗 very fine cambrics or lawns.
輭煤 soft or bituminous coal.
輭熟 very affable and pliable.
[15]輭牀 a litter or stretcher.
輭片子 a silk robe; materials that can be folded without injury. 輭片 photographic film.
輭玉 nephrite.
輭皮 soft leather; soft skin; cork.
輭硬 soft and hard.
[20]輭簀 flexible mats.
輭紅塵 soft, red dust—Vanity Fair.
輭聲 a soft, pleasing voice; fascinating tones.
輭脚 a welcome feast to a returned traveller.
輭脚病 or 脚氣 Beri-beri.
[25]輭膏 ointments.
輭芽 tender shoots.
輭語 soft words; gentle speech.
輭身 lissome, supple; weakly; delicate.
輭風 a light breeze.
[30]輭飽 light refreshment; to drink wine.
輭骨 cartilage.
輭體動物 molluscs.
伸輭腰 to stretch oneself.
心輭 a soft heart.
[35]柔輭 pliable, flexible, soft.
細輭 fine and soft.

挪 2 To rub between the hands. Also read no[2]. Inter. 挼 No. 3162.
3166 3162

挪挱 to rub in the hands.

JUI. (曰ㄨㄟ)

(Rui)

枘 4 The handle of tools. Distinguish 柄 No. 5286.
3167

枘鑿不入 to fit a (square) handle into a (round) socket—

not fitting, not in sympathy with, used fig.
不鑿枘 not in harmony, not fitted well together.

汭 4 Junction of two streams. The winding of streams. River in Kansu.
3168

蜹 4 A kind of mosquito; a gnat.
蜹
3169

蚊蜹 mosquitoes and gnats.

(a) A venomous snake.

芮 3.4. Small plants budding. Thongs of a shield.
3170

芮芮 flourishing vegetation.

緌 1 Strings of a cap. Also read sui[1]. Inter. 綏 No. 5520.
3171

蕊 3 The stamen or pistil of a flower. Buds, unopened flowers. Sap, juice.
蕋
3172

蕊心 stamens and pistils.
蕊汁 viscid juices of plants.
燭蕊 wick of a candle.
發蕊 to put forth buds.
花蕊 stamens or pistils.
陰蕊 pistil.
陽蕊 stamens.

蘂 3 Stamens or pistil of a flower. Inter. preceding.
3173

銳 4 A sharp-pointed weapon. Acute, zealous, valiant.
3174

銳任 to accept responsibility.
銳兵 or 銳師 or 銳卒 well-drilled troops.
銳利 sharp and pointed.
銳志 or 銳意 valiant, keen determination; keen-spirited.
[5]銳氣 ardent spirit.

銳眼 sharp-eyed.
銳角 an acute angle.
銳身救人 to rush forward and save another.
銳達 quick.
[10] 口銳 pert speech.
失銳 crestfallen.
尖銳 sharp-pointed.

(a) Trifling, insignificant.

不亦銳乎 Is it not a trifle?

㷊[2]
㷊
3175
Drooping leaves; fringe. Soft, delicate. Also read *sui*[3]. Inter. 蕤 No. 3172.

㷊賓 the fifth lunar month; luxuriant vegetation; a classical pitch corresponding in function to F-sharp.

睿[4]
叡
3176
Shrewd, discreet, astute. Quick of perception. The divine sagacity of sages.

睿哲 profoundly wise.
睿智 intuitive wisdom.
睿藻 essay by the emperor.

JUN.　　(ㄖㄨㄣ)
(Ruen)

閏[4]
3177
Extra, inserted between others, as a day or month. To intercalate. Also read *yüin*[4].

閏位 dynasty not in the direct line of succession.
閏壽 a birthday in an intercalary month.
閏日 the intercalary day in leap-year. February 29th.
閏月 an extra month inserted seven times in nineteen years to make up the deficiency between the solar and the lunar years; intercalary month.
七閏爲一章 seven intercalations make a cycle of nineteen years.

潤[4]
3178
To moisten, to enrich, to fatten, to benefit, to adorn. Shining, sleek.

潤劑 demulcent medicines.
潤寡 to give to the poor.
潤心養眼 to comfort the heart and please the eye—as with good cheer.
潤滑 smooth, shining, glossy, slippery.
[5] 潤澤 agreeable; kind-hearted; to enrich by favours; glossy; moist; to modify.
潤筆 a present given for writing.
潤雨 a soaking rain.
分潤 to share the good things.
滋潤 to moisten; to do good to.
肥潤 to fatten, to enrich.

瞤[2]
3179
To blink or twitch the eyes.

JUNG.　　(ㄖㄨㄥˊ)
(Rong)

冗[3]
宂
3180
Scattered, mixed. Affairs; duties; occupation; business.

冗冗 a crowd; busy; numerous.
冗從 a great retinue.
冗繁 busy with many different matters; no leisure.
冗賦 miscellaneous taxes.
[5] 冗雜 mixed, confused, miscellaneous.
公冗 public business.
撥冗 to put business aside—for a visit.
會務冗冗 very busy with the business of the church.

(a) Extra, supernumerary.

冗兵 superfluous troops.
冗官 or 冗吏 officials out of office; supernumeraries.
冗費 unnecessary expense.

(b) Tramps.

流冗 tramps; vagrants.

戎[2]
3181
Weapons of war; warlike; war, military, soldiers. Military chariots. Distinguish 戍 No. 2861, 戌 No. 5873.

戎伍 or 軍戎 the army, the ranks.

戎作 war, aggressive attack.
戎兵 weapons.
戎政 military organization.
[5] 戎機 the needs of the army.
戎行 warfare, the army.
戎衣 armour.
戎裝打扮 martial array; in military dress.
戎車 a war-chariot.
[10] 興戎 to commence hostilities.
從戎 to follow a military career.

(a) Your.

戎有良翰 "You have a good support."
以佐戎辟 in order to assist your sovereign.

(b) Great.

戎毒 great evils.
戎疾 great disorders.
念茲戎功 "thinking of this great service."

(c) To come to the help of; to assist.

烝也無戎 none of them willing to give help.

(d) General name for the tribes on the western frontier.

戎狄 tribes to the west and the north of China.
戎狄是膺 he smote the *Jung* and the *Tih* barbarians.
戎菽 the garden pea; also defined as broad beans.
西戎 Tibetans. Western frontier-tribes.

毧[2]
3182
Fine, soft fur or hair; down. Felt. Camel's hair.

毧帽 felt caps.
毧毯 felt rugs.
毧鞋 felt shoes.

絨[2]
3183
Sponge; velvet. Wool; woollen. Floss; nap; down.

絨子 flannel; velvet.
絨字 characters of velvet.
絨布 woollens; flannels.
絨毛 wool.
[5] 絨氈 or 絨被 blankets.
絨線布 woollen and cotton mixtures.

絨 線 woollen yarn; floss for embroidering. *See* 茸 No. 3185—2.

絨 花 embroidered flowers done with silk.

絨 車 a reel for winding silk.

[10]絨 頭 rough surface.

大 絨 broadcloth.

天 鵝 絨 velvets.

小 絨 flannels.

斜 絨 twills.

[15]法 蘭 絨 flannels.

洋 絨 velvet.

火 絨 tinder.

石 絨 asbestos.

羢[2]　The wool of sheep.
3184

茸[2.3]　The luxuriant growth of plants. Soft, downy, fluffy. In disorder, confused.
3185

茸 毛 大 如 斗 the tuft (on a lion's tail) is as big as a bushel.

茸 線 flossy silk for embroidery.

茸 茸 luxuriance of growth.

叢 以 龍 茸 growing closely together in luxuriance.

狐 裘 尨 茸 our fox-furs are all ragged and worn.

紫 茸 purple shoots.

(a) Horns, antlers.

茸 墊 the base of the antler.

茸 片 horn shavings.

茸 膠 hartshorn jelly; glue.

鹿 茸 the soft core of the young antlers of the deer.

(b) To repair.

茸 成 repairs completed.

毧[3]　Down or fine hair; nap; floss; u.f. 氈 No. 3182.
3186

毧 毛 fine, soft fur.

毧 羽 down.

毧 鷄 newly-hatched chickens.

KA.　　(ㄍㄚ)

尬[4]　A staggering gait. Also read *chieh*[4].
3187
尷 尬 *kan*[1]-*ka*[4] in an embarrassing situation. (*Wu-dial.*)

KAI.　　(ㄍㄞ)

垓[1]　A boundary; a limit. Wilds beyond the frontier.
3188

垓 埏 the farthest limit, the bounds of the earth.

垓 極 the distant wilds beyond the frontier.

垓 限 a limit, a frontier.

兼 垓 all the bounds; everywhere, the world.

(a) A hundred million.

萬 萬 爲 垓 ten thousand times ten thousand is called *kai*.

(b) Read *chiai*[1]. A class, step, ledge.

垓 級 a degree, a step.

挍[4]　To move; to shake; to excite. Also read *hai*[4].
3189

荄[1]　Roots of plants.
3190

根 荄 roots.

邪 荄 evil roots—fig.

該[1]　Ought, should. Fated to be. What is proper. To owe.
3191

該 下 to owe.

該 他 如 此 it is his fate!

該 他 多 少 How much do you owe him?

該 備 prepared; ready.

[5]該 博 extensive knowledge.

該 曉 having full knowledge of.

該 應 fated; should be.

該 應 該 應 you deserve it! your own fault!

該 死 he ought to die—a term of abuse.

[10]該 班 to be on-duty.

該 當 or 應 該 or 該 派 ought; should; fit; right.

該 當 該 當 it's nothing more than I ought to do; merely my duty to treat you thus.

該 衰 lucky and unlucky; flourishing and fading.

該 贍 extensive—learning.

[15]該 錢 or 該 欠 or 該 賬 to owe money.

不 該 ought not; should not.

命 該 如 此 it is so ordained.

本 該 it is incumbent on.

(a) The said, the respective, that, the, to belong to.

該 人 the said person.

該 大 臣 the said high official.

該 犯 the said prisoner.

該 管 under the control of; belonging to the jurisdiction of; his business.

該 處 the place in question.

該 部 知 道 let the proper board take note.

(b) To have.

他 很 該 錢 he has plenty of money. (*S. dial.*)

賅侅[1]　To give. Prepared for, included in; embraced in.
3192

賅 備 to be provided for.

賅 括 to involve; to include in; classification.

賅 載 written in; on record. . . .

(a) Rare, uncommon.

賅 事 an unusual affair.

賅 物 a rarity.

奇 賅 extraordinary.

陔[1]　A step, a terrace, a grade, a ledge.
3193

九 陔 之 上 above the nine terraces—in heaven.

丐匄匃[4]　To beg for alms. A beggar. Distinguish 丏 No. 4489; 匈 No. 2812.
3194

丐 子 or 丐 者 or 乞 丐 a beggar.

丐 戶 beggars.

丐 頭 chief of the beggars.

丐 飯 to beg for food.

鈣[4]　Calcium.
3195

改 3196

改[3] To alter, to change. To correct. To repent. To reform.

改之爲貴 reformation is the important matter.
改了裝 to change the style of dress; to disguise.
改元 to change the year-title of a dynasty.
改任 changing to another post.
[5]改判 amended judgement.
改制 to change the system—as of administration, etc.
改削 to amend; to obliterate and alter an error in writing.
改包 to re-pack goods for re-shipment, etc.
改名 to change one's name.
[10]改善觀 meliorism, doctrine that the world can be changed for the better by human effort.
改圖 to change the plans.
改土歸流 to change the authority over tribes-people from local chiefs to regular officials.
改塗 change to another road.
改天 another day.
[15]改嫁 or 再醮 to marry a second husband.
改字之事 the matter of a girl's changing her betrothal.
改定 amended.
改官制 to change the official system.
改容 to change one's appearance.
[20]改常 to change from the normal.
改弦易轍 to tune the string, to get out of the old rut—to alter the laws.
改弦更張 to tune the strings—to reform the laws.
改形 to change one's appearance, style, etc.
改悔 to regret; to reform.
[25]改悔福隨 blessings follow repentance and reformation.
改惡從善 to leave the evil and follow the good—to reform.
改換一新 wholly changed for the better.
改換門閭 to change the position of a door.
改政體 to alter the form of the administration. 「改革．
[30]改敎 The Reformation.＝宗敎
改日再來 I'll come on another day.
改期 to change the date.

風雨改期 weather permitting.
改格 reduction. (logic).
[35]改樣 to alter the style.
改正 to correct; amendment.
改正改正 to revise, to correct.
改正敎會 reformation of the church.
改正案 amendment to a resolution.
[40]改正行動 to reform the conduct.
改歲 next year; the new-year.
改照 alter in accordance with.
改爲 change to; alter to.
改竄 revision, correction.
[45]改組 reorganization.
改組內閣 reorganization of the cabinet.
改組軍隊 reorganization of the army.
改編 reorganization.
改良 reform; to change for the better; improve.
[50]改良市政 municipal reform.
改良政俗 reformation of the methods of the government.
改良會 Reform Society.
改良社會 reformation of society.
改良私塾 modern private schools.
[55]可改良 may be improved.
改色 to change countenance.
改葬 or 遷葬 to re-inter a body.
改行 (hang[2]) 改業 to change one's calling. 「costumes.
改裝 to re-pack goods; to change
[60]改裝易服 to disguise oneself.
改觀 change its appearance.
改訂 to revise.
改變 or 改換 or 改易 or 改移 to alter, to change.
改變形像 to change its appearance; to be transfigured.
[65]改變態度 an attitude of change; to change one's attitude.
改轍 to get out of the old ruts.
改造 to reconstruct; to rebuild.
改過 to reform.
改過不吝 to reform without any begrudging.
[70]改過所 a reformatory.
改過自新 to make a new start; to turn over a new leaf.
改過遷善 to reform one's errors and revert to good deeds.
改進 progress; advance.
改道 changed its course.

[75]改選 re-election.
改邪歸正 forsake evil ways and return to the right.
改革 a reform, a radical change.
改頓再吃 another time I shall accept your invitation—to a meal.
改頭換面 to disguise.
[80]改風水 to alter the geomantic conditions—with a view to improving the luck.
痛改前非 earnestly repent and reform former faults.
風雨不改 no alteration will be made on account of the weather.

劃 3197

劃[1.4]. To sharpen a knife. Carefully. Fully. To influence.

劃切曉諭 let all clearly understand this.
劃動民心 to move the hearts of the people.

戤 3198

戤[4] To infringe a trade-mark. To pledge an article.

蓋 3199

蓋蓋葢[4] To cover. To hide. A cover. An umbrella.

蓋上蓋子 put on the cover.
蓋不了 it will not cover it, it cannot be hidden.
蓋不嚴 not covered completely. See below—8.
蓋世之才 talents overshadowing the age.
[5]蓋世英雄 the hero of the age.
蓋住面 to cover the face.
蓋愆 to cover the faults of the past by good deeds.
蓋掩 to screen; to hide from.
蓋棺論定 when his coffin is covered all discussion about him can be settled.
[10]蓋碗 or 蓋盅 a covered teacup.
蓋笠 the sky.
蓋纏 involved; entangled by custom.
蓋藏 to secrete; to put away securely.
蓋被窩 to cover with a quilt.

[15]蓋·起·來 or 蓋·上 to cover over.

蓋 輿 cover and floor—heaven and earth.

蓋 頭[2] to cover the head; a cover for the head.

圓 蓋 a round cover—the heavens.

地 蓋 earth's umbrellas—mushrooms.

[20]天 靈 蓋 the forehead; the fontanel.

房 蓋 roof of a house.

車 蓋 covering for a cart.

(a) To seal; to affix a seal.

蓋 印 to stamp; to affix a seal.

蓋 印 署 名 under hand and seal.

蓋 戳 to affix a seal; to stamp; to seal.

蓋 用 關 防 to affix an official seal.

蓋 章 to seal—as a document.

(b) To build, to erect.

蓋 房 or 蓋 屋 to build a house.

蓋 瓦 to lay tiles.

蓋 造 to build; to erect.

蓋 頂 to put the roof on.

(c) Initial particle:—Now; the above. Particle indicating doubt. For, because. cf. 3201.

蓋 傷 失 (or 離) 本 such sorrow is not warranted by the facts.

蓋 因 ....because that....

蓋 時 at the time.

蓋 曰 now it is said that.

[5]蓋 有 之 矣 possibly there is such a case.

蓋 有 非 常 之 功 now to perform an extraordinary service.

蓋 聞 now I have heard that.

蓋 赤 苟 至 乏 now if Ch'ih were really in need.

顋 [4]
3200　The top of the skull.

概
槩 [4] A piece of wood used to strike off grain in a measure, thus:—All, to level, to adjust. Generally, for the most part.
3201

概 乎 不 論 all these are beside the question.(lamenting the loss of fundamental principles.)

概 免 all is pardoned; all are exempt.

概 免 重 征 universally exempted from a second levy.

概 況 in general—at the end of a sentence.

[5]概 則 general regulations.

概 同 all alike; the same.

概 念 concept; idea; abstraction.

概 念 論 conceptualism.

概 括 generalization.

[10]概 括 名 義 general definition.

概 括 法 a comprehensive law.

概 略 generally speaking; in general.

概 算 a rough estimate; inventory.

概 算 書 a prospectus.

[15]概 算 預 計 a budget.

概 行 免 稅 all are exempt from duty.

概 行 寬 免 all are forgiven—a general pardon.

概 要 principles.

概 見 it is evident throughout that.

[20]概 觀 view, conception, idea.

概 言 之 to sum up.

概 論 summary.

一 概 the whole; altogether.

大 概 probable; for the most part.

[25]梗 概 abridged summary.

氣 概 resolution; bearing; energy.

風 概 a fine manner or bearing.

溉
摡 [4]
3202
To irrigate; to flood. Water flowing. To scour.

灌 溉 to irrigate.

滌 溉 to scour.

K'AI. (ㄎㄞ)

揩 [1]
3203
To rub, to wipe, to dust.

揩 乾 淨 to wipe clean.

揩 排 to run up against a person.

揩 油 to wipe oil—to gain some advantage.

揩 癢 to rub an irritable place.

揩 眼 淚 to wipe away tears.

揩 磨 to rub; to scour off.

揩 面 to wipe the face.

開 [1]
3204
To open. To explain. To state. To begin. To found.

開 一 張 單 子 to make out a bill.

開 三 天 弔 mourning rites extending over three days.

開·不 動 cannot open it.

開·不 開 cannot be opened; no opening it; will you open it or not?

[5]開 井 機 well-boring apparatus.

開 交 to get clear from; to settle up.

開 以 廣 塲 opening up into broad spaces, parks and gardens.

開 仗 to commence a battle.

開 例 to make a rule.

[10]開 信 to write a letter.

開 價 opening prices; to state a price.

開 光 to paint the pupils in the eyes of an idol—thought to endow it with life.

開 先 at the first.

開 具 to draw up a document.

[15]開 凍 to thaw.

開 出 acquitted.

開 刀 to attack with edged weapons; to perform an operation.

開 列 to set forth; to state; to arrange in order or in a row.

開 列 于 後 in order as follows.

[20]開 列 清 單 to draw up a clear account or balance sheet; table.

開 到 leave: arrive — as in a timetable.

開 創 to found—as a State; to originate; to commence.

開 化 civilizing process; development.

開 化 國 civilized nation.

[25]開 卯 to make a first payment.

開 印 to open the seal—to re-open the yamen for public business after new-year.

開 去 to cancel.

開 卷 有 益 there is profit in unrolling the scroll—i.e., in reading books.

開 口 to open the mouth; to begin to speak; to burst the banks—of a river, etc.

[30]開 口 不 如 緘 口 穩 it is safer to keep silence than to speak.

開 名 to make a list of names.

開 呈 to present—in a document.

開 胃 to give an appetite; to enjoy; to like.

開 啟 to instruct.

[35]開 單 to make out a bill, a list, or a pass, etc.

開 善 門 to practice benevolence.

開 國 to found a State.
開 國 元 勳 the founder of the State—used for The Founder of the Republic.
開 國 紀 念 national anniversary.
[40]開 地 to open up new land.
開 基 to found—an enterprise, etc.
開 堂 dinner is now on—in some places such a notice is put outside restaurants; to commence proceedings.
開 報 to make a written report.
開 塲 to open negotiations; to open a gambling establishment,*
[45]開 墾 to break up fallow ground; to till; to open up waste land.
開 始 to commence to.
開 始 營 業 to open up industries.
開 審 宣 判 to declare a judgement.
開 導 to guide; to enlighten.
[50]開 導 旗 flag in front of a procession.
開 展 to manifest; to develop.
開 山 to bring under cultivation; to dig a grave.
開 山 斧 a pioneer; one who opens up the way.
開 山 祖 師 a founder, primarily a priest who collects subscriptions to build a temple, etc.
[55]開 工 to begin work.
開 工·錢 to pay wages.
開 差 to send runners. (-ch'ai[1])
開 市 to open the market.
開 幕 the curtain rises—to open; has a wide usage.
[60]開 年 or 開 歲 next year.
開 庭 to open court.
開 廓 to enlarge; to extend.
開 廣 to open wide; to extend; to enlarge.
開 弓 不 放 箭 to draw the bow but not loose the arrow—empty threats; appearance of severity.
[65]開 弔 to open the funeral rites.
開 張 to open out—as goods; to begin doing business; to sell; to re-open.
開 彩 drawing of a lottery.
開 往 to start for—as a boat.
開·得 can open it; may be opened.
[70]開 復 to restore—a degraded official.
開 徵 to begin taxation.
開 心　　to feel happy; to make fun of another.
開 心 見 誠 perfect sincerity.
開 泰 to be successful.
　*to open performance, in a theatre.

[75]開 恩 to show favour; to be lenient.
開 恩 免 債 graciously to remit a debt.
開 懷 or 放 懷 to relax the mind; to throw off cares; to be at ease.
開 成 立 大 會 to hold an inaugural meeting.
開 戒 to break an abstinence.
[80]開 戰 outbreak of war; commencement of hostilities.
開 手 to begin; at the outset.
開 折 舊 賬 to compound old debts.
開 拆 to break open—as a letter.
開 拔 to move; to start out for; to advance troops.
[85]開 拓 to stretch the arms in order to take the measure of anything; a big piece of land.
開 挖 河 湖 to dredge rivers and lakes.
開 摺 to draw up a despatch.
開 擴 to enlarge.
開 支 to pay; disbursements.
[90]開 放 to release; to let go; to open—to the public.
開 放 門 戶 the *open-door* (policy).
開 敏 intelligent.
開 敞 to expand; to extend.
開 方 evolution. (*math.*)
[95]開 方 便 to begin deeds of charity. *See* No. 1802—C.1.
開 方·子 (or 藥 方) to write a prescription.
開 明 to list clearly; enlightened.
開 明 國 an enlightened nation.
開 映 to start showing — as a film
[100]開 曙 light breaking in the east.
開 會 to open a conference; to begin a meeting.
開 會 歡 迎 to give a reception.
開 會 程 序 procedure for opening a meeting.
開 會 詞 opening speech.
[105]開 步 走 Quick(or forward)march!
開 水 boiling water.
　水 開·了 the water boils.
開 河 the river opens—after frost.
開·消 to spend; expenses.
[110]開 源 節 流 open the fountains and restrict the outflow—study ways of profit and limit expenditure.
開 濬 to dredge rivers.
開 滾 如 鍋 to boil like a pot.

開 演 to begin performance.
開 燈 to light a lamp—to take to opium smoking or start serving opium.
[115]開 發 to pay—as wages; to disburse; to develop; development; to discharge (servant).
開 發 敎 授 teaching by questioning.
開 發 實 業 to open a business or industries.
開 盤 and 收 盤 opening and closing prices, respectively.
開 眉 to open the eyebrows—to look satisfied.
[120]開 眼 to see sights; to learn by experience.
開 眼 界 enlarge the field of vision, to see new things.
開 示 to show details for.
開 票 to write a cheque; to open ballot papers; to draw(lottery).
開 禁 to relax restrictions; to abrogate laws.
[125]開 端 first principles; the beginning—of trouble, etc.
開 筆 to commence the study of composition.
開 筵 to spread a feast.
開 缺 to vacate a post.
開 罪 to offend.
[130]開 耳 受 訓 to open the ear and receive instruction.
開 胃 口 to stimulate the appetite—as by condiments.
開 脫 acquitted.
開 腔 to begin to sing; to speak. 我 沒 有 開 腔 I didn't say a word.
[135]開 腿 to stretch the legs; to run fast.
開 臉 to remove the fine hair from the face and prepare for marriage—before a girl leaves home.
開 舖(子) to open a shop.
開 船 to set sail; to cast off the moorings.
開 艙 准 單 permit to break bulk.
[140]開 花 to bloom; to flower.
開 花 彈 shells—projectiles.
　大 炸 力 開 花 彈 high-explosive shells.
　子 母 開 花 彈 shrapnel.
開 花 放 香 to blossom into fragrance.
[145]開 茅 塞 to enlighten the mind.
開 荒 to reclaim neglected fields; to open up waste lands.

開荒佈道 pioneer evangelism.
開蒙 to give the first lesson; to enter school for the first time.
開行 (*hang²*) to open a business, etc.
150開行 (*hsing²*) to start on a journey.
開襟 opening or vent at the sides of a garment.
開解 to elucidate a meaning; to console.
開言 to begin speaking.
開設 to establish—as a business.
155開誠布公 to maintain mutual sincerity; to lay all cards on the table.
開談判 to open negotiations.
開誘 to entice.
開講 to explain; to expound; to commence to preach.
開譬 to explain an illustration—to exhort from a parable.
160開賬 to open accounts—to begin business; to make out the bill.
開路 to open a road; to make a beginning.
開路先鋒 the vanguard; a pioneer.
開路神 effigy in front of coffins in funeral processions.
開車執照 driver's license.
165開車的 a driver—of a train, car, etc.
開辦 to put into operation.
開辦費 promotion expenses.
開送 to forward.
開‧通 to open intercourse with; to open a way through; to make clear; judicious.
170開通風氣 to advance civilization.
開釋 to resolve difficulties; to set free.
開‧銷 expenses; an account of expenses.
開錄 to record.
開鎗 to fire a gun. Fire!
175開鎖 to open a lock.
開門 to open a door.
開門七件事 the seven necessities of life, i.e., firing, rice, oil, salt, soy, vinegar, and tea.
開門揖盜 to invite trouble upon oneself.
開間 the width of a *chien* in a Chinese house.
180開闢 to open a barrier or water-way.
開關 to open the Customs—as

after a holiday; to open and shut; a switch.
開‧關 to open; to develop; to extend.
開天闢地 creation.
開除 to deduct; to abrogate; to dispense with; to expel from school.
185開隊 to move troops.
開陽 to enter on the second half of the year; dried shrimps.
開雲見日 the clouds disperse and the sun appears.
開電門 to open an electric switch.
開革 dismissal; to degrade.
190開頭 in the beginning; at first; to start.
開顏 to smile.
開飯 to serve up a meal.
開首 at the beginning.
開驗 to open and examine—as the Customs.
195開齋 to break vegetarian vows.

(a) An auxiliary verb indicating action.

剖‧開 to lay open; to split open.
劈‧開 to split open.
打‧開 to open.
張‧開 to open wide.
5撥‧開 to put on one side; to reject.
擺不開 no room to place them.
走‧開 Move on! Stand aside!
離‧開 to leave.

凱 3 A victory, triumphant return of an army.
3205 Distinguish 剴 No. 3197, 獃 No. 5986.

凱旋 to return in triumph.
凱旋門 a triumphal arch.
凱樂 rejoicings over a victory.
凱歌 songs of triumph.

(a) Balmy, soothing, gentle.

凱風 a south wind.

愷 3 Joyful; contented. Good, kind.
3206

愷悌君子 a kindly gentleman.
愷惻 generous; kind.
愷澤 benevolent; kind.

(a) Used for transliterating.

愷撒 Cæsar.

鎧 3.4. Armour; mail.
3207

鎧甲 armour.
鐵鎧 a coat of mail.
首鎧 a helmet.

闓 3 To loosen; to open. A thumb-ring.
3208

闓大關 open great barriers.

(a) Inter. 愷 No. 3206. Kind, etc.

闓澤滂流 his grace extended in every direction.

嘅 4 To sigh, to regret.
3209

嘅其嘆矣 sighed regretfully.
嘅嘆 to mourn.
嘅然 mournfully.

慨 4 Generous, noble-minded; loyal.
3210

慨允 to consent readily.
慨然 impulsive; warm-hearted.
意氣慨然 full of a fine spirit of fearlessness.
慷慨 magnanimous; noble-hearted; chivalrous.

(a) Inter. preceding. Sad, regretful.

慨念時歎 sighing constantly with sad memories.
慨歎 sad, melancholy.

KAN. (ㄍㄢ)

干 1 To oppose. To offend against. A shield. Radical 51.
3211

干城 to resist the foe and protect the besieged—a great leader.
干戈 or 干櫓 weapons of war, warfare.
干戈戚揚 shields, spears and battle-axes.
動干戈 to go to war.
5干法 or 干例 to break the law.
干犯 to transgress; to offend intentionally.

干 犯 名 義 to offend against well known principles of right.

干 盾 a shield; weapons.

干 觸 to offend against; to oppose or attack.

(a) The bank of a river.

江 (or 河) 干 a river bank.

(b) A stem.

干 支 the system of the *Stems* and *Branches* which makes the cycle.

天 干 the *Ten Heavenly Stems,* ten characters which, in combination with the *Twelve Earthly Branches,* 地 支, make a cycle of sixty.

干 旄 staff and pennon of high office.

(c) To attend to, to concern. To involve. Consequences, results.

干 你 甚 事 what business is it of yours?

與 你 何 干 what has it got to do with you?

干 己 to concern oneself.

干 政 to interfere in politics.

5 干 涉 or 干 係 c o n c e r n ; consequences; responsibilities.

干 涉 態 度 attitude of intervention.

干 涉 的 必 要 necessity for intervention.

我 不 干 涉 I'll have nothing to do with it.

干 礙 to concern; to affect; compromised.

10 干 與 to interfere; intervene.

干 証 a witness; to depose.

干 連 implicated.

干 預 intervention.

干 預 世 事 intervention in world affairs.

15 不 相 干 no matter.

非 干 我 事 it is no business of mine.

(d) To seek.

干 時 seeking to keep up with the times.

干 求 to entreat; to beg.

干 祿 seeking official emolument.

干 祿 豈 弟 in seeking emolument he was self-possessed.

干 諛 富 貴 to wheedle rich grandees.

干 謁 to pay a call with the object of seeking personal advantage.

干 譽 seeking fame and reputation.

干 進 seeking official advancement.

(e) To arrange.

干 休 to arrange; to bring a quarrel to an end.

又 是 一 干 人 another class of people.

若 干 so much or so many; a certain sum, or amount.

忓 1
3212
Concerned about. Similar to preceding—No. 3211-C.

與 我 無 忓 it is no concern of mine.

旰 4
3213
Sunset, dusk; evening. See 宵 No. 2607-5.

旰 食 a late meal—too busy to eat before.

日 旰 evening; late in the day.

杆 1.3.
3214
The shaft of a spear; a pole. N.A. for guns, pipes, etc.

杆 子 a pole, a rod.

一 杆 秤 a steelyard.

一 杆 鎗 a gun or rifle.

便 杆 a walking-stick.

旗 杆 flagstaff.

桅 杆 a mast.

欄 杆 a railing, a balustrade.

秤 杆 beam of a steelyard.

玕 1
3215
Inferior kind of gem.

竿
樺 1
3216
A pole, a staff. The stem of the bamboo; a cane, a slender rod.

竿 子 a rod or pole.

竿 牘 a letter, from ancient use of slips of bamboo.

竿 頭 end of a pole.

插 竿 to stick in a pole.

日 上 三 竿 the sun is three rods high—between eight and nine.

竹 竿 bamboo poles.

筆 竿 the stem of a pencil.

釣 竿 a fishing rod.

箭 竿 兒 (arrow) shaft.

肝 1
3217
The liver.

肝 氣 有 餘 多 怒 fulness of the liver produces anger.

肝 氣 痛 a pain in the liver.

肝 油 cod-liver-oil. = 7668.42.

肝 火 inflammatory conditions in the liver; weak of body; easily angered.

5 肝 火 盛 easily angered.

肝 腸 寸 斷 internal organs cut into pieces—greatly afflicted.

肝 腦 塗 地 the liver and brains spilt on the ground—as on the battlefield.

肝 腦 碎 裂 entire energies exhausted—in the service of the country.

肝 膽 liver and gall—intimate.

10 肝 膽 義 氣 real friendship.

肝 色 liver-coloured.

肝 藏 魄 the liver is the seat of the animal soul.

肝 蛭 flukes.

心 肝 heart and liver—intimate; sweetheart; disposition.

骭 4
3218
The shin-bone.

桿 3
3219
A staff, a handle, a pole. N.A. Inter. 杆 No. 3214.

桿 棒 Indian clubs.

桿 秤 scales.

稈
秆 3
3220
The stalk of grain; straw.

稈 人 a straw effigy.

稈 頭 stubble.

稈 篲 a straw broom.

掔 1
3221
Name of a place in Honan.

趕 / 赶 [3222]

趕 | 赶 } To follow, to expel. To drive, to pursue.

趕·上·去 to pursue and overtake.
趕·不·上 unable to overtake; inferior to.
趕·不·上 城 cannot reach the city before the gates close.
趕·不·及 will not be there on time.
⁵趕·他 回·來 bring him back.
趕·出·去 or 趕 逐 to drive out; to expel.
趕 到 無 路 driven into a corner; no resource left. cf. 6807.77.
趕·去 to pursue.
趕·回·來 hurry back.
¹⁰趕·工 生·活 to make up time on a job—as when promised within a certain time.
趕·得 上 can overtake.
趕 忙 to put in extra work for nothing; to hurry.
趕·快 in a hurry; to hasten.
趕 快 走 go faster; make haste.
¹⁵趕 攏 to gather together; to bring together.
趕 散 to scatter.
趕 會 to attend a fair, such as is held in North China and elsewhere.
趕 集 or 趕 墟 or 趕 市 to go to market or fair.
趕 站 to hurry to the end of a stage—when travelling.
²⁰趕 賊 to pursue a thief.
趕 脚·的 a donkey-boy.
趕 赴 to repair to; to hurry to.
趕 路 to hurry on; to go faster.
趕 車 to drive a cart.
²⁵趕 車·的 a carter; a driver.
趕 開 to drive away.
趕 鬼 to exorcise demons.

(a) As soon as; by the time; to avail oneself of.

趕 早 起·來 you must get up early.
趕·緊 speedily; at once.
趕·着 拿·出·來 be quick and take them out.
趕 順 水 to avail oneself of the tide.
趕 黑 就 到 we shall be there by dark.

甘 [3223]

甘 ¹ Sweet; pleasant, thus:— voluntarily; willingly.
Radical 99.

甘 休 willing to come to an agreement; willingly to let it go.
甘 願 效 勞 willing to offer for arduous service.
甘 受 willing to submit to it.
甘 味 sweet, luscious.
⁵甘 居 人 下 willing to fill a humble position.
甘 心 or 甘 願 pleased, contented, willing.
甘 心 情 願 perfectly willing.
甘 心 樂 意 freely; cordially.
死 也 甘 心 even if I die I am quite willing.
¹⁰甘 心 to satisfy the desire for revenge.
甘 拜 下 風 willing to take an inferior position.
甘 於 willingly.
甘 旨 delicacies—for aged parents.
甘 松 valerian. ⌈water from kitchen.
¹⁵甘 水 fresh water. 甘·水 waste
甘 汞 or 輕 粉 calomel.
甘 油 glycerine.
甘 煖 sweet (food) and warm (clothing).
甘 甜 sweet; smooth, fair—as words.
²⁰甘 結 a willing bond; a voluntary agreement.
甘 罪 無 辭 willing to take punishment without shrinking.
甘 美 luscious; delicious.
甘 者 a smooth-tongued person.
甘·肅 the province of Kansu.
²⁵甘 脆 sweet and crisp—delicacies.
甘 自 吃 虧 to suffer willingly.
甘 芳 sweet and fragrant.
甘 苦 sweet and bitter; prosperity and adversity.
甘 苦 備 嘗 to have tasted both prosperity and adversity.
³⁰甘 苦 同 受 to share both the sweet and the bitter.
甘 草 liquorice root. See 苷 No. 3228.
甘 茶 hydrangea.
甘 菊 camomile.
甘·蔗 糖 sugar cane.
³⁵甘 蕉 the banana. = 香 蕉.
甘 薯 or 紅 薯 sweet potatoes.
甘 藍 kohl-rabi. = 5218½.1.
甘 言 a kind answer; soft words.
甘 貧 contented with poverty.
⁴⁰自 甘 貧 賤 content to be abased and in poverty.

甘 雨 seasonable rains.
甘 霖 timely rain after long drought.
甘 露 sweet dew—favours.

柑 [3224]

柑 ¹·² The loose-skinned orange, (Citrus nobilis); there is some variation in the use of this word, some refer it to other varieties.

柑 皮 orange-peel.
柑·子 the orange, as above; a large tangerine.
(a) Read ch'ien². u.f. 鉗 No. 899. A wooden gag for mouths of horses.

泔 [3225]

泔 ¹ Water from washing rice. To boil thick, as gruel.

米 泔 水 water from washing rice. cf. 3223.15
(a) Read han³. Full.

泔 淡 overflowing.

疳 [3226]

疳 ¹ A disease of children.

疳 積 rickets; swelling of the belly and limbs of children.
疳 積 糖 worm-tablets for children.
疳 黃 a form of anæmia.

(a) Sores, ulcers.

疳 氣 poison; virus.
疳 瘡 venereal ulcers.
牙 疳 gum-boil.

紺 [3227]

紺 ⁴ Violet or purple.

紺 宇 purple sides to a house—nobleman's residence.
紺 珠 purple pearl or bead—u.f. good memory, from a story of 張 說 of T'ang dynasty, whose memory was helped by looking at such a pearl or bead.
紺 瞳 violet eyes.
紺 緅 飾 ornaments of purple or puce colour.
紺 燕 a name for the turquoise kingfisher.

甘[1]
3228   Liquorice.

甘 草 liquorice root.

敢[3]
3229   To dare, to presume, to venture.

敢 作 敢 爲 afraid of nothing.
敢 來 I venture to approach.
敢 保 to guarantee; to aver.
敢 則 or 敢 自 really, certainly, no doubt; as a matter of course.
[5]敢 問 I venture to ask.
敢 問 所 安 I venture to ask in which class you will place yourself.
敢 存 攘 臂 之 心 dare to bare the arms—not afraid of a fight.
敢 強 to oppose, to resist; to argue.
敢 怒 不 敢 言 daring to be angry, but not daring to show it in speech.
[10]敢 怕 I dare say; perhaps so.
敢 惹 to dare; to dare to provoke.
敢·情 certainly; no wonder.
敢·情 他 有 好 意 doubtless he means well.
敢 攀 I have ventured to drag you —to my house.
[15]敢 是 certainly; it seems as if.
敢 死 隊 'dare-to-die' corps.
敢 求 I venture to beseech.
敢 用 玄 牡 敢 昭 告 于 皇 皇 后 帝 I venture to offer a dark victim and to announce to Thee, the Great Sovereign Ruler.
敢 當 I dare to do.
[20]敢 竟 as a matter of course; no doubt.
不 敢 當 thank you,— ("I do not deserve").

橄[3]
3230   The olive.

橄·欖 olives.
橄·欖 油 olive oil.
橄·欖 泥 a condiment made from salted olives.

澉[3]
3231   To wash. Name of a place.

澉 浦 the port of Hangchow.

感[3]
3232   To influence, to move; to affect. To touch.
Distinguish 惑 No. 2403.

感 佩 appreciation.
感 傷 or 感 懷 to be deeply affected.
感 傷 主 義 sentimentalism.
感 光 affected by light—as photoplates.
[5]感·冒 influenza, a cold.
感·冒 假 sick-leave.
感 冒 風 寒 to catch a cold.
感 力 influence.
感 動 or 感 化 to influence; to move; to act on.
[10]感 動 力 inspirational force.
感 歎 詞 interjection.
感 化 to move; to influence; to convert.
感 化 人 心 to move the hearts of men.
感 化·得 來 able to influence or convert.
[15]感 化 敎·育 reformatory instruction or training.
感 化 院 a reformatory.
感 受 affected by; impressed with.
感 受 不 便·利 to suffer inconvenience.
感 受 其 影 響 felt the effects of; moved by.
[20]感 受 性 sensitivity.
感 嘆 moved to sighing.
感 孕 to conceive—by supernatural means.
感 官 the organs of sense.
感 性 emotional. ⌜aestheticism.
[25]感 性 論 epistemological
感 性 障 礙 disorders of the sensibilities.
感 悟 suddenly to come to an understanding or consciousness of.
感 悼 grieved.
感·情 influence, emotion, sentiment, affection.
[30]感·情 作 用 the function of emotion or sentiment.
感·情 用 事 stirred into action merely by the emotions; biased.
感·情 衝 動 emotional impulse.
傷 感 情 to hurt the feelings of.
感 想 impressions.
[35]感 愁 moved to sorrow.
感 慕 to think of with longing.
感 慨 melancholy; painful recollections; lament.

感 應[4] moved to response through the feelings and affections; induction.
感 應[4] 篇 Book of Rewards and Punishments. A popular work in the form of a tract.
[40]感 應[4] 電 流 induced current.
感 應[4] 電 流 器 induction coil.
感 格 moved by the earnestness of another; the response of the gods to good works, etc.
感 物 而 易 動 者 莫 如 怒 there is nothing like anger for influencing and moving others.
感 痛 sensation of pain; conscious of pain.
[45]感 發 to influence, to move or disturb.
感 舊 to think of old times.
感 覺 feelings; sensations; impressions.
感 覺 器 organs of sense.
感 覺 性 sensibility.
[50]感 覺 無 思 想 是 瞎·的 perception without conception is blind.
感 覺·的 機 能 the function of the emotions.
感 覺 神 經 sensory nerves.
感 覺 訓 練 sense training.
感 覺 論 sensationalism.
[55]感 覺 運 動 the movements of the sensations.
感 覺 遲 鈍 dullness of sensibility.
思 想 無 感 覺 是 空·的 thought without emotion is empty.
感 觸 stirrings of emotion; stimulated; moved to sorrow or anger; to dawn in the consciousness.
感 觸 器 organs of touch—in molluscs.
[60]感 觸 運 動 irritable movements.
感 銘 so moved that it is engraved on the heart.
感 頌 to express one's deep sense of.
交 感 mutual interaction.
傷 感 moved to commiseration.
[65]易 感 susceptible.

(a) From the above:—moved to thanks; gratitude.

感 德 深 deeply thankful for your goodness.
感 心 grateful; gratitude.
感 念 grateful for; to think of with gratitude.

感 恩 grateful for kindness.
5 感 恩 圖 報 grateful for kindness and seeking a way to recompense it.
感·情 無 盡 extremely grateful.
感 慰 moved to gratitude.
感 戴 深 恩 grateful for special favours.
感 激 之 至 exceedingly grateful.
10 感 激 涕 零 so moved to gratitude that—words fail—and the tears fall.
感 謝 or 感 激 grateful for; many thanks.
感 謝·他 替 死·的 恩 情 thankful for His grace in dying for us.

乾 ¹ Dry. Dried, as opposed to fresh.
3233

乾 嘔 to retch.
乾 圓 潔 淨 dry, whole and clean —the best rice; cleaned right out.
乾 土 dry land.
乾 季 a dry season, a drought.
5 乾·巴 巴·的 extremely dry.
乾 性 油 a drying oil.
乾 旱 drought; dry weather.
乾 枯 dried up; withered.
乾 柴 近 火 dry wood near a fire —imminent danger.
10 乾 汞 mercury.
乾 涸 or 乾 竭 dried up; needy.
乾 渴 thirsty; parched.
乾 溜 dry distillation.
乾 灰 lime, dry ashes.
15 乾·燥 feverish; dry; parched.
乾·燥 劑 driers for paint, drying substances like lime, etc.
乾 燥 療 法 dry rubbing and warmth as a curative.
乾 爽 airy, dry and clean.
乾 片 dry photographic plates.
20 乾 瘦 shrunk; shrivelled.
乾 癟 dry and withered; shrunken.
乾 癬 tetter.
乾 笑 a dry laugh without mirth.
乾·糧 dry provisions.
25 乾 脆 clear, crisp; clear-cut; straightforward; to the point.
乾 脩 strips of dried meat,—in ancient times these were given to a teacher in lieu of salary, thus the phrase has come to mean a teacher's salary.

↑ 乾 杯 empty the glass.
乾 花 dried flowers.
乾 草 hay.
乾 菓·子 dried fruits.
30 乾 薑 dry ginger.
乾 裂 split from dryness.
乾 裱 (or 鰾) lit:—pasted up and dried—neither taking action nor relinquishing control, so as to give trouble to another.
乾 貨 dry goods.
乾 酪 cheese.
35 乾 量 dry measure.
乾 電 池 dry-cells.
乾 飯 cooked rice, without gravy, etc.
乾 魚 dried fish.
乾·麪 flour.
40 揩 乾 wipe dry.
曬 乾 dry in the sun.
杏 乾 dried apricots.
漏 乾 drain dry.
炕 乾 dry by a fire.
45 通 乾 thoroughly dry.
陰 乾 dry in the shade.
餅 乾 biscuits.
風·乾 to dry food in the wind.

(a) Clean. Exhausted.

乾·淨 clean; all gone.
賣 得 乾 淨 all sold out.

(b) To hold the name without the true relationship. To hold a position merely in name.

乾 俸 advantage or profit.
乾 兄·弟 sworn brothers.
乾 兒·子 an adopted child taken without formal deeds, etc.
乾 回 報 to report falsely.
5 乾 娘 乾 爹 mother and father of an adopted child, not in the regular form of adoption; it is a relationship somewhat like that of godparents.
乾 工 a sinecure; unrequited labours.
乾 折 to substitute; to exchange for.
乾 沒 to take unfair advantage or profit.
乾 發 急 to sit fretting and fuming when in trouble, but taking no action.
10 乾 老·子 an adopted father, as above—5.
乾 脩 gratuities; salaries drawn without due equivalent in service.
乾 館 a sinecure.

(c) Read *ch'ien²*. Heaven. Male. A father, a sovereign. Ist of the *diagrams*, 八 卦.

乾 元 heaven.
乾 坤 male and female; heaven and earth.
乾 宅 the bridegroom's home.
乾 綱 the power of the sovereign.
5 乾 造 male destiny.
乾 道 the way of heaven.
乾 道 變 化 the transformation of the way of heaven.
體 乾 to embody the way of heaven.

(d) Read *ch'ien²*. Lasting; continuous.

終 日 乾 乾 "respectfully attentive all day long."

皸 ⁴ Sunrise; dawn.
3234

日 光 皸 皸 the sun's light is dawning.

幹 ⁴ The trunk of a tree, or of the body.
3235

幹 本 trunk and root; essentials, fundamentals.
幹 枝 trunk and branches.
幹 綫 main line; trunk-lines—of railway.
幹 路 trunk-line of railway.
幹 路 國 有 nationalization of trunk-lines.
幹 骨 the skeleton.

(a) Business. To attend to business. To manage. Capable, skilful.

幹 不 下 去 or 幹 不 來 unable to undertake; not capable of managing.
幹·不 了³ unable to manage or to complete an affair.
幹 事 or 幹 事 情 to do business; to manage affairs.
幹 事 executive secretary.
幹 事 員 members of executive committee.
5 幹 事 部 executive council; secretarial staff.
主 任 幹 事 president of a society; chief of the executive.
↓ 總 幹 事 general secretary.

專務幹事 departmental secretary.

幹任大事 to manage important matters.

幹員 a capable official.

[10]幹局 a clever player; a man of ability.

幹得來 can be put through.

幹旋 common corruption of 3570 A.1.

幹甚麼 What are you up to? What is your business?

幹略 executive abilities.

[15]幹蠱 to cover up a parent's failings.

幹練 experienced in managing affairs.

幹辦 to manage; to transact.

幹長 to keep a thing going for some time.

不結幹 not durable.

[20]公幹 public affairs.

才幹 ability; talents.

能幹 competency; capable.

貴幹 What is your honourable business?

幹麻 what are you doing? Why?

擀 [3] **To roll along. To open out, as a roll. To stretch out with the hand.**
3236

擀麪杖 a rolling-pin.

擀麪條子 to roll out dough for vermicelli.

榦 [4] **The trunk of a tree. A handle.**
3237

榦枝 trunk and branches.

(a) Boards used in making adobe walls.

槙榦 or 貞榦 planks and post for making adobe walls. *See* No. 346—A.5. and No. 349—1.

(b) A support.

榦不庭方 "be a support against those princes who do not come to court."

(c) Railing round the mouth of a well. Also read *han*[2].

井榦 the railing as above.

(d) A tree suitable for making bows. Sugar-cane.

淦 [4] Water leaking into a boat. A small river in Kiangsi.
3238

贛 [4] Region south of the Po-yang Lake, u.f. Province of Kiangsi.
3239

贛省 Kiangsi Province.

(a) Read *kung*[4]. u.f. 貢 No. 3715. To offer tribute.

子贛 (or 貢) a disciple of Confucius.

灨 [4] The River Kan in Kiangsi. Inter. preceding.
3240

K'AN. (ㄎㄢ)

凵 [3] A receptacle. Radical 17.
3241

刋 [1] **To hew. To cut; to carve; to engrave; thus:— to erase by cutting away.**
刊
3242

刊例 regulations, etc., of newspaper offices regarding advertising.

刊刷 to engrave blocks and print books.

刊刻文字 to prepare blocks and engrave characters.

刊印 to print.

[5]刊字 to engrave letters.

刊定 corrected and authorized.

刊布 to publish.

刊木 to hew timber.

刊本 to cut and print a book.

[10]刊板 to cut blocks for printing.

刊發 to publish; to issue.

刊發日報 to issue a daily newspaper.

刊碑立石 to carve and set up stone tablets.

刊行 publication.

[15]刊誤 to amend errors in printing.

名論不刊 an unalterable reputation.

坩 [1] An earthen vessel.
3243

坩堝 a crucible.

欻 [1] Irregular.
3244

欻鼓 uneven; irregular.

坎 [3] A pit, a hole, a snare, a danger. A crisis. A mortar. Inter. 砍 No. 3247.
㤼
3245

坎坷 (or 軻) irksome; difficulties of the way; bad luck.

坎子 a pot-hole or break in the road.

坎穴 or 坎坑 a pit, a hole, a cave.

坎陷 to set a pit; to involve a person maliciously.

心坎 the pit of the stomach.

掘坎 to dig a pit.

灰坎 pit for lime or mortar.

舂坎 a pestle and mortar.

(a) A small wine-vessel.

小罍謂之坎 a small *lei* or drinking-cup is called *k'an*.

(b) The second of the *diagrams*, 八卦. It represents water.

(c) Sound of striking.

坎其擊鼓 How you beat your drums!

坎坎伐檀兮 "Chop! chop! go his blows on the sandalwood."

扻 [3] **To strike; to run against. To throw, as a stone.**
㧊
3246

扻爛 or 掀破 to shatter.

扻狗 to throw a stone at a dog.

扻碰 to collide.

砍 [3] **To hack, to chop, to fell. Inter. 坎 No. 3245.**
3247

砍下來 to chop down—as trees.

砍伐樹木 to fell trees.

砍傷 to wound by cutting.

砍刈 to cut down and kill.

[5]砍斷 to cut in two.

砍斷木偶 to cut down images of wood.

砍斫 to cut and hack.

砍 肩 兒 or 背 心 a Chinese waistcoat.
砍 腦 袋 to behead.
[10] 砍 落 to cut down.
砍 開 to split open.
刀 砍 cut with a sword or knife.

(a) A mortar. Inter. No. 3245.

灰 砍 a lime-pit for mortar.
舂 砍 pestle and mortar.

欿 [3] Discontented with oneself. Humble.
3248

欿 然 而 餒 dissatisfied and hungry.
自 視 欿 然 discontented when one examines oneself.

嵌 [1] A deep valley. To fall into. Also read *ch'ien*[1].
3249

嵌 巖 dangerous cliffs.

(a) To inlay

嵌 寶 inlaid with gems.
嵌 銀 匠 a jeweller.
嵌 鑲 to inlay; to set.

侃 [3.4.] Straightforward; bold.
3250

侃 侃 with confidence and boldness.
侃 侃 如 也 straightforward.

看 [4] To see; to look at; to observe; to examine. To look in the direction of. To consider, to think.
3251

看 一 看 have a look.
看 上 了 to think highly of; to approve; to take a fancy to.
看 不 上 眼 to look on with contempt; to look down upon.
看 不 中 意 rather inclined to disfavour.
[5] 看 不 出 來 unable to perceive; illegible.
看 不 分 明 cannot see distinctly.
看 不 得 unfit to be seen; cannot see it; disgusting, ugly and coarse.
看 不 清 楚 cannot see clearly; cannot see what it is; indistinct.

看 不 眞 cannot clearly distinguish; it is not distinct.
[10] 看 不 見 unable to see; invisible.
看 不 起 to hold in disregard.
看 不 過 to have no high opinion of; unable to bear the sight of.
看 不 遠 cannot see very far.
看 不 佻 with insatiable gaze.
[15] 看 中[4] to like; to prefer.
看 了 看 had a look or two at it.
看 事 行 事 act as the occasion warrants.
看 人 眉 睫 to watch the eyebrows of another—to be subservient.
看 他 面 上 look on his face—do it for the sake of another.
[20] 看 作 to regard as.
看 來 as it seems; thus; from the appearances.
以 我 看 來 in my opinion.
這 樣 看 來 looking at it thus.
看 光 景 see what the circumstances are.
[25] 看 冷 炮 look at a cold cannon—to look coldly on and take no action.
看 嘴 臉 watching the lips and countenance—subservience.
看 外 貌 取 人 to select a man according to appearances.
看 官 a reader. Reader!
看 得 明 白 understand clearly.
[30] 看 得 眼 花 eyes becoming blurred through excessive use.
看 得 見 can see it; able to see.
看 得 輕 to regard lightly.
看 情 面 to regard with partiality.
看 慣 了 accustomed to seeing.
[35] 看 我 薄 面 for my sake.
看 承 to act towards.
看 掌 文 palmistry.
看 書 to read; to look through a book.
看 望 to pay a visit; to look at.
[40] 看 板 a sign-board. (*Jap*.).
看 呆 了 gazing with admiration.
看 東 西 好 歹 it depends on the quality.
看 機 會 to watch the opportunity.
看 法 way of looking at a thing.
[45] 看 準 了 to take in a situation; to see accurately.
看 燭 ornament made like a candle.
看 熱 鬧 looking on; seeing the fun.
看 熟 了 accustomed to see; familiar with the sight.
看 燈 to see the illuminations.

[50] 看 病 to attend sickness; to diagnose a disease; to practice medicine; to see a doctor.
看 看 Look! Let's see! Gradually.
看 相 (*hsiang*[4]) to practice physiognomy.
看 相 (*hsiang*[4]) 的 a physiognomist.
看 破 to see through a thing.
[55] 看 破 紅 塵 to see through the vanities of this life.
看 穿 to see through.
看 紅 了 眼 to be jealous; to covet.
看 着 不 理 pay no heed to; act as if one does not see.
看 着 辦 to do as one sees fit.
[60] 看 脉 or 診 脉 or 搭 脉 to feel the pulse.
看 脚 路 see that the entrance and exit are good—as is done by thieves.
看 茶 來 bring in some tea!
看 戲 to attend a theatrical performance.
看 西 南 in a south-westerly direction; looking south-west.
[65] 看 見 saw; seen; to see.
看 詢 to examine.
看 輕 lightly esteem.
看 透 to see through; to understand a matter thoroughly.
看 透 世 界 to see the vanity of this life.
[70] 看 過 seen; experienced; versed in.
看 重 to honour; to regard as important.
看 野 眼 give a side-glance at.
看 頭 a sight; something to look at; something worth seeing.
沒 有 甚[2] 麼 看 頭 there's nothing to see here.
[75] 看 風 水 to study the geomantic conditions of a place.
看 風 色 see which way the wind blows.
好 看 pretty; nice to look at; beautiful.
說 起 來 看 say it over for me to hear.
重 看 to have great regard for.
[80] 難 看 ugly; pitiable.

(a) Read *k'an*[1]. To watch; to look after; to guard.

看 一 看 give an eye to it.

看 孩·子 to mind a child.
看·守 to guard; to keep watch.
看 守 所 lock-up for prisoners awaiting trial.
[5]看 家 to mind the house.
看 家 狗 a watch-dog.
看 待 to behave towards.
看 更 to be in charge of the night-watches.
看 牧 to shepherd.
[10]看 管 to care for; to attend to.
看 船 to look after a boat.
看·護 to look after; to watch.
看·護(婦) a hospital nurse.＝護 士
看 財 奴 a miser.
[15]看 門·的 a gate-keeper.
看 馬 to look after horses.

衎 [4] To be pleased; to give pleasure.
3252

衎 我 烈 祖 to please our honoured ancestors.
衎 然 而 作 he arose joyfully.

勘 [4] To investigate officially.
3253

勘 丈 or 勘 度 to measure; to make a survey.
勘 估 to estimate.
勘 問 or 查 勘 to examine; to cross-question.
勘 斷 to investigate and decide.
[5]勘 災 to investigate a disaster.
勘 破 to elicit; to bring to light.
勘 船 to overhaul a boat.
勘 量 to measure—as a ship.
勘 辦 or 勘 理 to inquire into a matter and act accordingly.
[10]磨 勘 to make a searching investigation.
覆 勘 re-investigation.
驗 勘 to hold an inquest.

(a) To compare; to collate.

勘 對 or 校 勘 to compare, as papers or texts.
勘 誤 to correct errors.
勘 誤 表 corrigenda.

堪 [1] To sustain, to bear. Able, adequate for, worthy of, fit for.
3254

堪·不 住 unable to endure; too weak to sustain.
堪 久 enduring for a long time.
堪 以 is fit for; suitable.

堪 任 fit for an official post.
[5]堪 克 adequate for; fit for.
堪 勝 重 任 fit for heavy responsibilities.
堪 可 委 用 fit for the post.
堪 嗟 involving grave anxiety.
堪 室 of marriageable age.
[10]堪 用 useful; serviceable.
堪 當 worthy of.
堪 議 satisfactory.
不 堪 unfit for; unbearable.
不 堪 其 苦 not able to bear these difficulties.
[15]不 堪 回 首 cannot bear to mention things that are past.
品·行 最 不 堪·的 人 a most insufferable person.
破 爛 不 堪 utterly ragged and disreputable.
人 不 堪 其 憂 others could not have endured such distress.
情 以 何 堪 How can I sustain such a weight of kindness?
[20]難 堪 intolerable; unbearable.
受 苦 難 堪 suffering bitterly things that are hard to bear.

(b) A covering.

堪 輿 a cover and a support—heaven and earth, u.f., geomancy.
堪 輿 先·生 a geomancer.
堪 坏 K'an p'i—a god mentioned by Chuangtzŭ.

磡 [4] A dangerous bank; a ledge; a cliff. A step.
礁
3255

磡 邊 edge of a cliff.
井 磡 the edge round a well.
山 磡 a mountain cliff.
石 磡 a bund.
石 磡 子 a stone door-sill.
門 磡 a door-sill.

戡 [1] To pierce, to stab, to kill. To suppress, to subdue.
3256 Inter. 戡 No. 3254.

戡 亂 to suppress a riot or insurrection.
戡 天 主 義 conquest of nature.
戡 定 厥 功 fully settled their achievements.
戡 定 長 江 has successfully

---

swept the Yangtze valley—of insurgents.
戡 己 self-mortification.
戡 敗 victory and defeat; success and failure.

轗 [3] Unlucky, unable to reach one's aim.
3257

轗 軻 unable to attain; hindered; bad luck.   cf. 3245.1.

龕 [1] A niche for an idol; a shrine. To contain.
3258

龕 受 to contain—as a shrine.
佛 龕 a niche for an idol; a shrine.
禪 龕 mausoleum for the ashes of Buddhist priests.

闞 [4] To peep. A pavilion. Name of a city in the ancient State of Lu.
3259

鬼 闞 其 室 demons watch their homes.

(a) Read han[3]. The growl of a savage beast.

闞 如 虓 虎 as savage as an angry tiger.
闞 闞 仰 仰 bold appearance of troops.
吼 怒 闞 闞 (the hungry tiger fighting for its meat) growls with fierce anger.

矙 [4] To spy, to watch.
瞰
3260

矙 孔 子[3] 之 亡 也 he watched to know when Confucius was away from home.
瞰 臨 城 中 they gazed down into the city.
魚 瞰 open-eyed.
鳥 瞰 a bird's-eye view.

KANG   (ㄍㄤ)

扛 [1] To carry on the shoulders—of two or more men.
3261

扛 嗓·子 an altercation.
扛 幫 to help; to render assistance.
扛·得 起 來 able to bear the weight.

扛 抬 to carry on a pole-between two men.
扛 轎 to carry a sedan-chair.
扛 重 機 a crane or derrick.
扛 鼎 to lift a tripod (a very heavy weight)—an extraordinary feat of strength.

(a) Read *k'ang*[2]. **To carry on the shoulder-of one person.**

扛 不 動 cannot lift it.
扛 鋤 to carry a hoe over the shoulder.

杠 [4] A cross-bar, a yard-arm. A stout carrying-pole; poles
3262 of a bier. Inter 槓 3716.

單 杠 a single line placed at the side of a row of characters to indicate names of places.
雙 杠 a double line placed at the side of a row of characters to indicate names of persons.

(a) Read *kang*[1] or *chiang*[1]. A foot-bridge.

杠 梁 foot-bridge.
徒 杠 a foot-bridge.

矼 [1] Stone bridge, stepping-stones. Reliable. Also
3263 read *chiang*[1].

徒 矼 foot-bridge.
德 厚 信 矼 his substantial virtue and his firm sincerity.
跨 石 矼 to step across stepping-stones.

缸 綱 堈 [1] A cistern; an earthenware jar of large dimensions; a vat; a crock.
3264

缸 口 mouth of a jar or vat.
缸 面 酒 early, newly-matured wine.
坑 缸 receptacle for nightsoil.
水 缸 a large open-mouthed jar for holding water.

肛 [1] The large intestine.
3265

肛 門 the rectum.
脱 肛 prolapse of the rectum.

罡 [1] The name of certain stars. The god who is supposed to
3266 live in them.

罡 風 a high wind.
四 大 金 罡 (or 剛) the four guardian idols at the entrance of Buddhist temples.
天 罡 the bowl of the *dipper,* consisting of four stars.

港 [3] A port or creek. Also read *chiang*[3].
3267

港 內 in port.
港 務 局 Harbour Bureau.
港 口 a port; a harbour.
港 稅 port dues.
[5]港 脚 the mouth of a river.
入 港 稅 harbour dues.
卸 貨 港 port of discharge.
收 港 to remain in port.
商 港 a treaty port.
[10]封 港 to blockade a port.
本 港 船 native boats.
無 稅 港 口 a free port.
船 籍 港 口 port of registration.
起 貨 港 port of discharge.
[15]載 貨 港 port of loading.
領 港 船 pilot-boats.
香 港 Hongkong.

剛 [1] Hard; unyielding. Constant, enduring.
3268

剛 健 robust, in good health.
剛 勁 hardy; stubborn; vigorous.
剛 勇 or 剛 大 courageous, valiant.
剛 性 pig-headed; rigidity.
[5]剛 性 憲 法 a hard and fast constitution.
剛 愎 obstinate; stubborn; hardened.
剛 日 and 柔 日 the odd and even days of the month, respectively.
剛 柔 hard and soft; energetic and slow; positive and negative, etc.
剛 正 or 剛 直 upright; firm in principle.
[10]剛 毅 or 剛 志 resolute; firm of purpose.
剛 毅 木 訥 the resolute, the enduring, the simple, the slow.
剛 烈 or 剛 強 or 剛 暴 overbearing; wilful; violent.
剛 硬 hard, stubborn.

花 剛 石 hard stone, as granite.
金 剛 石 the diamond.

(a) Recently; just now.

剛 一 來 as soon as he comes.
剛 到 just arrived.
剛 剛 擺 下 just put it down.
剛 巧 just at the right moment.
剛 纔 a short time ago; just now.

崗 岡 [1,3] Ridge of a hill; a mound. Distinguish 閬 No. 7045.
3269

崗 亭 police-box.
崗 位 beat of a policeman.
崗 警 police.
崗 陵 a high mound.
站 崗 to go on duty—as a sentry or policeman.
血 崗 weals made by a blow with a stick.

鋼 [4] To temper steel.
3270

綱 [1] The large rope of a net; thus:—Laws, principles. A
3271 bond, a tie. Distinguish 網 No. 7047.

綱 佐 principal and subordinate.
綱 常 the constant obligations of morality.
綱 目 a general outline; subject and predicate; text and commentary.
綱 紀 principle—as of government; fundamental; to control.
[5]綱 紀 四 方 gave laws to the whole realm.
綱 紀 大 壞 public morality was in a state of corruption.
綱 紀 布 也 the laws are spread abroad.
綱 維 a ruling Buddhist priest; the ruling of a temple.
綱 要 a summary.
[10]綱 鑑 a chronological view of history; a narrative; annals.
綱 領 a principle running through a book; heads—as of a discourse, etc., the leading thought.
三 綱 the three bonds—the relation between prince and minister, father and son, husband and wife.

提綱 to bring out the leading theme.

大綱 an outline; a summary.

鋼 [1] Hard; strong, tough. Steel.
3272

鋼勁 lusty; vigorous.

鋼版 a steel-engraving.

鋼玉 corundum.

鋼玉砂 corundum; emery-powder.

[5]鋼琴 a piano.

鋼筆 a steel-pen.

鋼筆畫 pen-and-ink drawing.

鋼筆頭 a pen-point or nib.

鋼螺絲 steel bolts.

[10]鋼襯圈 steel washer.

鋼鍵 a steel die.

鋼鐵 iron of superior quality;

鋼鑽 a steel drill.

鋼骨三和土 reinforced concrete.

[15]純鋼 pure steel.

純鐵無鋼 dull iron which cannot be tempered.

K'ANG.   (ㄎㄤ)

亢 [4] Overbearing, violent, strong. To oppose, to attack. High.
3273

亢宗 to exalt the family name; to promote the interests of the clan.

亢排 a bully.

亢旱 or 亢陽 hot, dry weather.

亢氣 domineering; violent temper.

亢直 straightforward in dealing with another, without any compromise.

亢禮 to treat each other as equals, without regarding formal etiquette, ceremonials, etc. *See next* A-3.

(a) The second of the 28 constellations of the Chinese zodiac.

亢宿 or 亢金龍 the above constellation.

(b) Read *kang*[1]. The throat or neck, Inter. 吭 No. 2055.

伉 [4] To compare, to match. A pair.
3274

伉儷 a pair, husband and wife.

伉儷甚篤 a devoted couple.

(a) To oppose. To dislike. Inter. 抗 No. 3276.

伉俠 strong, chivalrous in assisting others.

伉敵 to oppose, to compete against.

伉禮 to disregard etiquette and treat each other as equals. *See* 亢 No. 3273—6, and 抗 No. 3276—20.

(b) High and lofty.

皐門有伉 the gate of the enclosure was high.

庎 [4] The divan or couch at the head of a reception room.
3275

庎几 or 庎桌子 the table used on the *k'ang.*

庎牀 a divan or couch for two persons.

抗 [4] To oppose, to resist. Inter. 伉 No. 3274.
3276

抗傳 to refuse to obey a summons.

抗力 resistance.

抗吞 or 抗霸 refusing to give up the property of another.

抗告 to lodge an appeal against a decision; to protest.

[5]抗告人 one who lodges an appeal.

抗告期限 time-limit within which protests must be lodged.

抗官 to oppose the government.

抗性 or 抗頸之人 a stiff-necked person.

抗拒 to resist; to repulse; to protest. 抗戰 to resist by war.

[10] 極力抗拒 resist to the utmost.

抗捐 to refuse to pay—as taxes.

抗敵 to oppose, to resist; to treat as equals. *See below*—20.

抗斷 to oppose a judgement.

抗旨 to resist the Imperial will.

[15]抗欠 to refuse to pay a debt.

抗爭 to resist; opposition.

抗疏 to address a remonstrance to the throne.

↑抗日 to resist Japanese aggression.

抗直 firm, unyielding and straight-forward.

抗禦 to oppose, to resist.

[20]抗禮 to treat as equals without regard to ceremonial and etiquette. *See* 伉 No. 3274—A.3.

分庭抗禮 negotiated with them as with equals.

抗節 to maintain moral integrity and not submit to disgrace.

抗糧 to refuse to pay the land-tax.

抗聲 opposing voices.

[25]抗衡 to contend; to struggle against—as in trade competition.

抗論 to speak fearlessly without any subserviency; to oppose in discussion.

抗議 remonstrance; protest.

抗議書 form of protest.

抗逆 to thwart; to resist.

[30]抗顏 to show an unyielding countenance.

反抗 to revolt against.

違抗 to disobey; to rebel.

(a) To raise. To set up.

抗價 to keep up the prices.

抗墜疾徐 (the music) now rising, now falling, now rapid, now smooth and slow.

抗策 to raise the horsewhip.

抗舉 to raise up.

抗首 to raise the head.

(b) To screen. To secrete.

抗·起·來 hide it. (*Wu-dial.*)

未報楚惠而抗宋 you have not recompensed the kindness of *Ch'u* and yet you protect *Sung.*

(c) Read *k'ang*[2]. Inter. 扛 No. 3261—A.

抗口袋 to carry bags on the shoulder.

炕 [4] To dry. A brick-bed warmed by a fire.
3277

炕布 to dry cloth.

炕桌 a small table for the *k'ang.*

炕氣眼 ventilating holes in the side of a *k'ang.*

炕沿 the edge of a *k'ang.*

⁵炕 洞 the flue of a *k'ang*.
炕 牀 a warmed brick-bed; to warm a bed.
炕 陽 or 炕 旱 very dry weather.
炕 面·子 the surface of a *k'ang*.

康¹ Ease, vigour. Health. Peace; repose.
3278 Distinguish 庚 No. 3339.

康°健 or 康 強 robust; hale, vigorous; healthy.
康 寧 health and peace; repose.
康 居 living in retirement. Sogdiana.
康 年 a year of peace and plenty.
⁵康 泰 in good health.
康 樂 和 平 health, happiness and peaceful harmony.
康 熙 *K'anghsi,* style of the second emperor of the Manchu dynasty A.D. 1662—1723.
康 莊 or 康 衢 a great highway.
康 誥 the announcement of *Wu Wang* to *K'ang*.
¹⁰康 阜 peaceful happiness and abundance.
太 康 excess of enjoyment. District in Honan, an ancient capital.
小 康 之 家 a wealthy family.

慷¹·³ Generous; magnanimous; public-spirited; noble.
3279

慷 慨 noble, disinterested; generous; liberal; chivalrous; energetic; public-spirited.
慷 慨 悲 吟 to chant in a mournful tone.
慷 慨 解 囊 to give liberally.

糠
穅¹ Chaff, bran, husks of grain, from which comes:—Poor, remiss.
3280

糠 市 residences of the poor.
糠 粃 chaff, husks.
木 糠 saw-dust.
麥 糠 wheaten bran.

躿¹ Tall.
3281

KAO.　　(ㄍㄠ)

羔¹ A lamb, a kid. Distinguish 羌 No. 7250.
3282

羔 羊 a lamb—fig., for worthy statesmen and high officers—purity.
踏 羔 羊 之 義 walk in the righteous ways of the virtuous high officers.
羔 雁 a lamb and a wild goose—ancient presents of ceremony from high officers.
珍 珠 羔 astrakhan.
黑 羔 皮 black lambskin.

糕
餻¹ Cakes; pastry; baked or steamed dumplings.
3283

糕 粉 or 米 粉 rice-flour.
糕 餅 a cake; a pudding.
糕 餅 店 a pastry shop.
糕 點 cakes; pastry.
年 糕 cakes for the new-year.
雞 蛋 糕 sponge-cakes.

杲³ The sun shining brightly.
3284

杲 日 升 空 the bright sun rises into the void.
杲 杲 出 日 the sun shines forth with brightness.

皋
皐
皋¹ To praise; to bless. High. Eminent.
3285

皋 原 a plateau.
皋 月 the fifth lunar month.
皋 比 (*p'i³*) a tiger's skin—a teacher's mat, thus used for a teacher.
皋 門 a palace gate.

(a) A marsh; banks of a marsh; pool in a marsh.

漢 皋 bank of the Han. Hankow.
江 皋 a river bank.

(b) To announce. A long drawn-out sound.

皋 魚 之 痛 the grief of *Kao Yü.* See 風 No. 1890—25, the lines of which are attributed to him; u.f. sorrow for lack of further opportunity to serve one's parents, grief at the death of parents.

(c) The testicles.

睪 丸 the testicles.
睪 丸 炎 orchitis.
割 睪 丸 castration.

橰¹ A spar.
3286

枯 橰 a well-sweep.

告⁴ To tell, to inform, to announce to.
3287

告 令 an order—as from the President.
告 休 or 告 退 to resign office.
告 便 to ask for permission to retire for personal convenience.
告 借 to ask for a loan.
⁵告 假 (*chia⁴*) to ask for leave of absence.
告 備 to announce the completion of any work.
告 免 ask to be excused.
告 回 to take leave of a person after escorting him some distance.
告 奮 勇 to announce willingness to put forth every effort.
¹⁰告 密 to give information concerning secret matters.
告 成 之 禮 dedication ceremony of a new building.
告 朔 之 餼 羊 the sheep offered when announcing the new moon.
告 病 to ask for sick leave.
告 白 an advertisement; a notice.
¹⁵告 知 to inform; to notify.
告·示 a proclamation.
告 祖 to inform one's ancestors—by prayer.
告 窆 to announce a funeral.
告 竣 or 告 成 to announce the completion—as of a building, etc.

²⁰告終養 to apply for leave to go home and care for one's parents for the rest of their lives.

告老 to apply for leave to resign on account of old age. A.w. 告·懇

告·訴 to tell. *See below—A 12.*

告誡 to warn; to enjoin.

告諸往而知來者 I told him one point and he knew its proper sequence.

²⁵告謝 to thank. 告·迻 to tell.

告貸無門 unable to b o r r o w money anywhere.

告辭 or 告別 or 辭行 to leave; to take leave; to say good-bye.

告饒 or 告罪 to apologize; to seek pardon.

不告而去 to take i n f o r m a l leave.

³⁰報告 to inform; to announce.

廣告 advertisements.

(a) To lay an accusation; to indict.

告·下·你·來 I have entered an accusation against you.

告人 to accuse a person.

告·他 to accuse him.

告倒 successful prosecution.

⁵告官 to bring a case before the officials.

告寃 to make a complaint.

告狀 to accuse at law; an indictment.

告發 an information. (*legal*).

告發人 an informer.

¹⁰告知參加 notice of intervention. (*legal*).

告訟 to accuse before a court.

告訴 an accusation. *See above—22.*

告訴主體 subject of accusation; the injured person.

告賬 to sue for debt.

¹⁵告進 to give official notice of an indictment.

上告 to appeal to a higher court.

原告 prosecutor.

控告 to accuse; to bring an indictment against.

無告 the poor and helpless—those who have none to appeal to.

²⁰被告 accused; the defendant.

(b) Read *ku*^{4.5.} **To announce.**

出必告 on leaving home—a son —must inform his parents.

嘉告 to announce in a blessing.

(c) Read *chü*^{2.5.} **To deal with judicially.** u.f. 鞫 No. 1591.

亦告于甸人 such a case was also handed over to the forester's department for execution.

誥 ⁴ To grant, as a title of honour. A patent, a title of nobility.
3288

誥命 the patents by which titles are conferred.

誥封 to bestow a title on a wife, living parents, etc.

誥封三代 to bestow titles of honour for three generations.

誥授 to grant a title to an official.

誥書 patent for a title of nobility.

誥贈 to bestow a title after death.

金花誥 patent of nobility given to the wife of an official.

(a) To enjoin, to order, to inform a superior.

誥誡 solemnly to enjoin.

誥誓 Imperial commands.

郜 ⁴ Name of a fief in Shantung bestowed on the eldest son
3289 of *Wên Wang* 文王.

高 ¹ High, exalted, tall, lofty. Noble, eminent. High in
3290 price; loud in tone; good in quality. Radical 189.

高下 reduction in height or value.

高世 above the average of the age.

高亢 proud and unbending.

高人 a man of superior attainments.

⁵高位 a high seat; high station.

高低 high and low; quality, rank.

高傲 proud, haughty; arrogant.

高利貸者 those who lend on usury.

高升 promotion.

¹⁰高升高升 add a little more—to a gratuity.

高原 a high plateau.

高及諸天 as h i g h as the heavens.

高及天象 as high as the stars.

高名 celebrated, famous. May I ask your name?

¹⁵高命 fortunate, lucky.

高地 upland.

高城深池 high walls and deep moat—security.

高堂父母 both parents living.

高壓手段 oppressive treatment.

²⁰高壘 a high military wall, a defence.

高壽 or 年高 aged. What is your exalted age? said of and to those over fifty—first example only.

高大 great, eminent; lofty.

高姓 What is your surname?

高尚 high-minded; magnanimous; of superior attainments.

²⁵高尚思想 high-mindedness.

高就 a high position.

高山 a high mountain.

高山景行 to look up to a worthy man, as one looks up to a mountain.

高山絕頂 lofty m o u n t a i n s whose summits are hidden.

³⁰高峯 a peak, used fig;—of a peak period or a crisis in one's life.

成結的高峯 had reached the pinnacle of his career.

高峻諸門 a gate higher than all the others.

高師 abbreviation for H i g h e r Normal School.

高度 height.

³⁵高底 thick soles to shoes.

高弟 an able scholar.

高張 in an exalted station.

高強 pre-eminent; excellent.

高得頂天 r e a c h i n g up to heaven.

⁴⁰高志 a lofty spirit.

高手 a clever person; to lift the hand—i.e., to forgive.

高抬時價 to raise the current prices.

高抬自己 to exalt oneself.

高抬貴手 raise your honourable hand—do not be too hard on me this time.

⁴⁵高抬身價 to put a high price on oneself.

高掛 to hang up high.

高·明 lofty and intelligent—said to one whose attainments are high; of excellent quality.

高昂 rising higher; having ambitions.

高材疾足 skilful and l i v e l y, alert.

⁵⁰高枕而寐 to sleep on a high pillow—in quietness, without care

↑高射炮 anti-aircraft gun.

高 枕 酣 睡 soundly asleep on a high pillow—free from care or anxiety.

高 架 鐵 路 elevated railroad.

高 梁 冠 a hat with high crown worn at funerals.

高 梢 quite lofty.

55高 標 a high beacon—excelling the average.

高 樓 大 廈 a great mansion.

高 深 的 思 想 lofty and deeply rooted ideals.

高 照 燈 lanterns used in processions or temples.

高 燥 high and arid.

60高 爵 顯 位 those high nobles in prominent positions.

高 登 advancement; exalted; to rise high.

高 矮 tall and short.

高 矮 不 等 tall and short together.

高 祖 great-great-grandfather.

65高 等 advanced; higher—of education.

高 等 動 物 animals having complex organisms.

高 等 學 堂 junior college.

高 等 小 學(校) higher primary school.

高 等 師 範(學 校) higher normal school.

70高 等 批·評 higher criticism.

高 等 文 官 a high civil official.

高 等 會 議 Supreme Council.

高 等 檢 察 廳 High Court of Procuration.

高 等 法 官 judges of the high court.

75高 等 法 庭 higher courts.

高 等 法 院 high court.

高 等 華 人 high-class Chinese—upper circle; used derisively.

高 等 顧 問 higher grade advisor.

高 第 a high place on the lists.

80高·粱 common sorghum.

高·粱(酒) spirits made from sorghum.

高 級 high class. [ghum.

高 級 所 得²稅 super-tax.

高 級 書 記 官 chief clerks.

85高 義 (or 誼) to make every effort to assist another in distress.

高 而 又 高 higher and higher.

高 聳 lofty; high.

高 聲 a loud voice.

高 脚 or 高 翹 stilts.

90高 脚 擔·子 a load tied close to the carrying-pole.

高 臥 to sleep high—i.e., a life of ease and freedom from anxiety.

高 自 位 置 to have a very high opinion of oneself.

高 至 一 半 reaching as high as to the middle.

高 臺 倒 塌 the lofty terrace collapses. [glad to . . .

95高 興 (hsing⁴) delighted; elated;

高 舉 lifted high; raised to honours; to take a long journey.

高·處 height; altitude.

高 行 (hang²) high prices.

高 見 your opinion.

100高 言 boasting; bombast.

高 言 大 智 great eloquence and much wisdom.

高 談 闊 論 high-flown talk.

高·貴 costly; valuable.

高 超 to excel.

105高 足 the best pupil—your scholar.

高 跳 high jumping.

高 跟 鞋 high-heeled shoes.

高 蹈 to go on a long journey.

高 蹤 your footstep; noble deeds.

110高 姚 子 a tall and spare person.

高 過 一 切 overtopping everything.

高 過 人 頭 above a man's head.

高 逾 尋 丈 higher than could be measured.

高 遠 high and distant; lofty.

115高 遠·的 思 想 lofty and far-reaching thought.

高 邁 aged; superior to; higher than.

高 門 a family of high degree.

高 陞 promotion; large double fire-crackers.

高 隱 之 談 high-flown, obscure talk of impracticable things.

120高 音 high notes; soprano; tenor.

高·頭 top; thereon. (S. mand.)

上·頭 above; top.

高 額 high forehead.

高 顴 high cheek-bones.

高 風 a great reputation.

125高 騫 soaring; raising its head high.

高 高 低 低 rugged; uneven.

高 高·的 very lofty.

高 點 the apex; acme.

高 鼻 a prominent nose.

唱 高 調 visionary.

(a) used in transliterating.

高 加 索 Caucasus.

高 加 索 人 種 Caucasians.

高 爾 夫 golf.

高 盧 Gaul.

高·麗 Korea. A.c. 朝 鮮 Chosen. See 233.22.

槁³
3291
Dry. Rotten, as wood; withered.

槁 木 朽 廢 a worthless fellow.

槁 木 死 灰 (body) like a dry stick (and heart) like cold ashes—utterly without desire to live (through suppression of the mental faculties.)

槁 梧 another name for the 琴 or lute.

瘑³
3292
A scabby, itching disease.

瘑 疥 eczema.

稿
稾
3293
The stalk of grain; thus:—A rough draft or copy; a proof.

稿 人 a straw effigy.

稿 公 a clerk of the records.

稿 子 a rough draft; a first copy; MS.

稿 房 record-office.

5稿 案 official papers.

稿 薦 a straw mattress.

稿 葬 a rough and ready burial without rites.

打 稿 to prepare a rough draft.

文 稿 draft or rough copy of a despatch; MS.

10草 稿 a rough draft.

篙¹
3294
A bamboo pole; a pole for punting a boat.

篙 人 a boatman.

篙·子 a boat-pole.

篙 工 or 篙 師 one who has charge of the poling of a boat.

撐 篙 to pole a boat.

縞³
3295
Plain white silk.

縞 冠 white silk caps.

縞 素 plain white silk—mourning.

膏[1] 3296

Ointment; plaster. Fat, grease. To grease. From which comes:—Rich, sleek.

膏 恩 rich favours, abundant grace.

膏 沐 bandoline and cosmetics for the use of women.

膏 油 oil, grease.

膏 澤 sleek, fat—favours, kindness.

[5]膏 火 allowance for candles; support for students.

十 年 讀 易 費 膏 火 to study for ten years wastes many candles.

膏 火 自 煎 fat burns and fries itself—those who have talent incur misfortune.

膏 粱 rich fare—the wealthy.

膏 粱 子[3]弟 sons of the wealthy.

[10]膏 紅 rouge.

膏 羶 fat from sheep or goats, tallow.

膏 肥 fat, greasy.

膏 脂 grease, fat.

膏 腴 fertile; rich—as soil.

[15]膏 腥 fat from fowls.

膏 臊 fat from dogs.

膏 薌 fat from oxen.

膏·藥 a plaster.

膏 露 fertilizing dew.

[20]民 膏 血 所 爲 made from the blood and the fat of the masses.

石 膏 gypsum; plaster of Paris.

藥 膏 or 公 膏 opium.

(a) The region below the heart.

膏 肓 the region below the heart. See 肓 No. 2274.

(b) The white grain of certain woods, as the poplar and willow.

(c) Read k'ao[4]. To fertilize.

陰 雨 膏 之 much rain has made it fertile.

藁[3] 3297

Straw; a straw mat.

藁 砧 or 槀 砧 instrument for chopping straw—a chopper and block, also called a fu 鈇; this sounds like 夫 a husband, hence the expression is a cryptic word for husband.

K'AO. (ㄎㄠ)

尻 𡱝 [1] 3298

The end of the spine; the rump, the buttocks.

尻 坐 to squat on the haunches; to crouch.

黑 尻 the heron.

考 攷 [3] 3299

To examine, to test. Distinguish 孝 No. 2601.

考 中 (chung[1])·了 passed the examination, (under the old system.)

考 亭 學 派 the school of thought led by *Chu Hsi,* also known as that of the *Sung* dynasty. *See* 程 No. 375—C.

考 例 or 歲 考 a triennial examination at which former first-degree graduates were tested to ascertain whether they had maintained their scholarship.

考 卜 to search out by divination.

[5]考 功 to investigate merits.

考 勤 to examine into one's diligence.

考 取 人 才 to examine and select men of talent.

考 古 學 archæology.

考 塲 examination halls.

[10]考 官 former examiners.

考·察 to search into; judicial examination.

考 察 商 業 investigation of industries.

考 察 團 investigating commission.

考 工 廠 a commercial exhibition.

[15]考·慮 attention; consideration; to give thoughtful attention; to weigh.

考 成 formerly used of the settlement between superior and subordinate; now used of examining into the results of the work of teachers and others.

考 成 條 例 regulations governing the investigation of school returns, for the rewarding or punishment of teachers, etc.

考 掠 to elicit answers by flogging.

考·掉 to fail in examinations.

[20]考·據 to seek for proofs or examples; textual research.

考 查 to investigate.

考 核 judicial investigation.

考 案 畫 creative art.

考 案 首 first on the list for first degree under former system.

[25]考 格 standard of the examination.

考 正 to put right; to adjust.

考 求 to discover by examination or investigation.

考 究 to investigate.

考 績 periodical examination of the services of officials.

[30]考 覈 to investigate; to scrutinize.

考 試 examinations.

考 試 不 及 格 to fail in examinations.

考 試 合 (or 及) 格 to pass an examination.

考 試 官 examiners.

[35]考 試 官 吏 Civil Service examinations.

考 試 法 method of examination.

考 試 章 程 rules and conditions of examination.

考 試 答 案 examination papers.

考 試 紙 examination paper.

[40]考 試 院 Examination *Yüan* or Council.

入 學 考 試 school entrance-examination.

受 考 試 to sit for an examination.

學 年 考 試 annual school examinations.

學 期 考 試 term examinations.

[45]定 期 考 試 periodical examinations.

每 月 考 試 monthly examinations. A.c. 月 考.

畢 業 考 試 graduation examinations.

考 語 the character, etc., of pupils given at end of school course.

考 課 periodical examination of the services of officials.

[50]考 證 verification; to prove.

考 證 學 textual criticism.

考 較 to compare.

考 辨 to examine into and discriminate between.

考 院 examination halls.

[55]考 鞫 judicial investigation of a criminal.

考 題 or 試 題 examination papers or subjects.

出 考 題 to set an examination paper.

考 驗 to examine; to test.

考 驗 合 格 to pass the test.

⁶⁰考 驗 輿 地 geographical exploration.

扣 考 excluded from the examinations.

此 事 無 考 there is no record of this.

赴 考 to present oneself for examination.

(a) Long life, aged. A deceased father.

考 妣 deceased father and mother.

考 妣 三 年 three years' mourning for parents.

考 終 to enjoy life to its allotted span; to die a natural death in old age.

先 考 my late father.

壽 考 to enjoy long life.

祖 考 grandfather and father—ancestors.

(b) To strike.

考 考 sound of drums.

考 鐘 to strike a bell.

考 鼓 to beat a drum.

(c) To complete.

考 仲 子 之 宮 celebrate the completion of the shrine for *Chung Tzŭ.*

考 室 之 禮 celebrate the completion of the house.

考 槃 completed his hut.

(d) Flaws in jade.

不 能 無 考 cannot be without a flaw.

拷 ³ To examine by torture; to flog.
3300

拷 問 or 拷 訊 to elicit evidence by flogging.

拷 打 to beat in order to extort a confession.

拷 脚 眼 to beat the ankles.

拷 貝 *k'ao³-pei⁴* copy, esp. of *

栲 ³ A tree producing a kind of varnish-sap. The mangrove.
3301

栲 皮 foreign mangrove-bark.

* motion-picture films.

栲 紬 pongee dyed with mangrove-bark.

烤 ⁴ To warm, to roast, to bake.
3302

烤 ‧ 一 ‧ 烤 to warm a thing.

烤 手 to warm the hands at a fire.

烤 木 to bend wood by means of heat.

烤 火 to warm oneself at the fire.

⁵烤 焦 burned in roasting or baking.

烤 煳 ‧ 了 burnt black.

烤 爛 over-roasted.

烤 肉 to roast meat.

烤 餅 to bake a cake.

¹⁰烤 饅 ‧ 頭 to bake steamed bread.

烤 麵 包 to bake bread; toast.

筹 3.4. A basket.
3303

筹 栳 a wicker basket.

銬 ⁴ Manacles.
3304

熇 3.4. To dry at the fire; to
熇 toast; to roast. Also read *hu²·⁵.*
3305

熇 乾 to dry before a fire.

熇 肉 to roast meat.

(a) Read *ho¹·⁵.* Heat of fires.

熇 暑 very hot weather.

熇 熇 intensely hot.

多 將 熇 熇 will multiply like flames—said of difficulties, trouble, etc.

犒 ⁴ To feast victorious soldiers on their return. Bounty money. Gratuities. To entertain.
3306

犒 以 金 reward with money bounties.

犒 勞 or 犒 軍 a feast to soldiers or workmen.

犒 工 to feast workmen.

犒 資 a prize.

犒 賞 to reward, a reward.

犒 農 official grants to farmers.

薧 ³ Dried fish. A cemetery.
3307

靠 ⁴ To depend on; to trust to; to lean on. Near to.
3308

靠 ‧ 不 住 unreliable; not to be trusted.

靠 傍 resources; one who can be relied on.

靠 天 吃 飯 to depend on Heaven for food.

靠 山 leaning against a hill, as a grave or a hut. *See below—A-1.*

⁵靠 ‧ 得 住 trustworthy; reliable.

靠 枕 to rest on a pillow.

靠 此 生 意 dependent upon this for a living.

靠 海 爲 業 dependent upon the sea for a living.

靠 父 名 來 to come in the Father's name.

¹⁰靠 着 自 己 to trust to one's own efforts.

靠 背 椅 a chair with a high back.

靠 着 trusting; leaning on.

靠 託 to entrust a matter to another.

靠 賴 to confide in; to rely on.

¹⁵靠 ‧ 頭 a support; something to trust to.

倚 靠 to trust in.

終 身 之 靠 a lifelong trust—as a husband or a son.

(a) Near to; adjoining.

靠 山 吃 山 靠 水 吃 水 if a man lives on the mountains, he must get his living there; if near the water, from the water—must depend on his environment.

靠 火 to warm oneself by getting near the fire.

靠 近 near to.

KO. KÊ.   (ㄍㄜ)
(Keh)

格 ² To reach; to come or go to; thus:—to influence, to investigate.
3309

格 于 上 下 reaching from heaven to earth.

格 于 皇 天 he became equal to High Heaven.

格 汝 舜 "Come, you Shun!"
格 物 the investigation of affairs and things.
⁵格 物 學 science. = 科 學.
格 知 天 命 to attain to a knowledge of the will of Heaven (God).
格 致 researches; natural science.
感 格 to be influenced.
神 之 格 思 the approaches of spiritual beings.

(a) To correct.

格 心 a regulated heart.
惟 先 格 王 the king must first be corrected.
有 恥 且 格 having a sense of shame they will correct themselves.
能 格 君 心 之 非 can rectify what is wrong in the mind of the sovereign.

(b) A rule, a limit, a pattern, a frame.

格 位 personality.
格 例 a rule or statute.
格 外 beyond the rule—unusually; extraordinary; extra.
格 外 大 extra large.
⁵格 外 重 賞 extra heavy reward.
格·子 a trellis; a pattern or form.
格·字 紙 ruled paper.
格 守 faithfully observe.
格 局 style, manner.
¹⁰格·式 a style, a pattern; ruled lines for writing.
格 律 metre of poetry.
格 應 于 圖 up to standard.
格 率 maxims, precepts.
格 的⁴不 中 failed to hit the bull's-eye.
¹⁵格 眼 blanks left in documentary forms, for filling in.
格 調 metre, tune, rhythm, style.
格 蹬 to hop.
不 入 格 without any style.
人 格 personality.
²⁰俗 格 conventional style.
品 格 habits, disposition, character, quality of.
書 架 中 格 the middle shelf of a bookcase.
空 格 a blank space above a name in writing.
窗 格 window frame.
²⁵資·格 rank, qualifications.
跳 一 格 miss one space.

間⁴格 (to write on) alternate lines.
離 格 not according to the pattern, or the lines, rule, etc.
風 格 style—in writing or painting; air, manner, disposition.
骨 格 physical frame.

(c) To resist; to attack.

格 戰 to fight without weapons.
格 殺 勿 論 to slay a man who is resisting (lawful authority) will not be accounted murder.
格 者 不 赦 those who resist will not be pardoned.
格 虎 to attack a tiger.
格 鬭 to fight without weapons.
↑格 格 不 入 repulsive; incongruous.

(d) Wise, intelligent.

格 人 a man of great intelligence.
格 言 wise sayings, maxims, mottoes.

(e) Noise of birds.

格 格·的 叫 chirruping of birds; squawking.

(f) Used in transliterating.

格 林 威 池 Greenwich.
格 林 礮 Gatling guns.
格 林 蘭 Greenland.
蘇 格 蘭 Scotland.
↑格 拉 斯 哥 Glasgow.

胳
肐
肐 1.5.
3310

The armpit; the arm. The side.　Also read *ko*⁵.

胳 肢 窩 or 胳 肋 底 the armpit.
胳·膊 折，往 袖·裏 藏 if your arm is broken, hide it in your sleeve —wash your dirty linen at home. (-*shê*²)
胳 臊 人 a rank-smelling man.
胳 髆 the upper arm, the arm.
胳·臂 the arm.

疙 1.5.　A pimple, a boil, a sore.
3311

疙·瘩 a pimple; a knot.
疙·裏 疙·瘩·的 troublesome, difficult, lit:—full of knots.

虼 4.5.　A flea. Species of beetle.
3312

虼·蚤 or 虼·子 a flea.

矻 1.5.
3313　To jolt.

矻 蹬 矻 蹬 jolting along in a cart.

革 2.5.　Hides deprived of the hair. Human skin. Radical 177.
3314

革 囊 a skin-bag—the human body.
革 履 leather shoes.
革 帶 a leather belt.
革 船 a coracle.
革 衣 石 斧 clad in skins and using stone axes—barbarians.
兵 革 armour.
皮 革 leather.
製 革 廠 a tannery.
齒 革 ivory and hides.

(a) Wings of a bird.

如 鳥 其 革 like a bird with its wings.

(b) To moult or cast hair.　Old and ragged appearance of an animal's coat.

鳥 獸 希 革 the feathers of birds and the fur of animals are thin in summer.

(c) To remove.

革 俸 or 罰 俸 to stop the salary.
革 其 舊 to get rid of the old; to renovate.
革 出 to expel.
革 剗 to get rid of.
⁵革 名 to strike off a name.
革 命 to deprive a ruling dynasty of the divine mandate to rule,—from the next. Used for revolution, or any reform which, strictly speaking, is not a revolution.
湯 武 革 命 *T'ang* and *Wu Wang* both took away the mandate to rule from the reigning dynasties.
革 其 王 命 deprived them of the divine mandate to rule.
革 命 勢 力 the force of the revolution.
¹⁰革 命 同 志 comrades of the revolution.
革 命 思 想 revolutionary convictions.
↑革 命 家 revolutionist.

革命戰爭 revolutionary war.
革命暴發 the revolution broke out.
革命曆 (French) Revolutionary Calendar.
[15]革命徵象 revolutionary symptoms.
革命裁判所 (French) Revolutionary Tribunal.
革命觀念 revolutionary conceptions.
革命軍 revolutionary army.
革命風說 revolutionary talk.
[30]革命黨 The Revolutionary Party.
家庭革命 domestic revolution; changes in family arrangements.
工業革命 industrial revolution.
種族革命 racial revolution.
經濟革命 economic revolution.
[25]革心 to change the thoughts and intents of the heart.
革換 to exchange.
革故鼎新 to drop old habits and reform.
革新 innovations; new ideas; to take a new line.
革新世界 the modern world.
[30]革新運動 reform movement.
革旦 the next morning.
革條 notice of dismissal or of excommunication.
革正 to reform.
革聖餐 to discipline a church member by witholding the privilege of the Lord's Supper.
[35]革職 or 革頂 or 革官 to degrade from office; to cashier.
革職留任 to degrade but retain in office.
革責 to dismiss and punish.
革軍 the people's or revolutionary army.
革退 to dismiss from employment.
[40]革酒 to break off wine.
革除 to deduct; to expel; to get rid of.
革除名籍 to strike off the roll.
革面洗心 lit:—to change the skin of the face and wash the heart—to reform.
天地革而四時成 the universe is subject to changes and thus the four seasons are completed.

改革 to alter, to change; to break with the past.

(d) The ends of reins.

(e) Read *chi*[2.5]. Urgent, anxious.
疾革 very ill.
病革 dangerously ill.

扇扇 [4.5.] A large earthen pot. A large iron cauldron. Radical 193. Also read *li*[4.5.]
3315

嗝 [2.5.] Cackling of fowls. To gag, to vomit.
3316
嗝噎 to choke.

翮 [2.5.] Pinions, quills. The root of a feather. Also read *ho*[2.5.]
3317
六翮 principal feathers of the wing.
振翮 to flap the wings for flight.
整翮 to preen the feathers.
羽翮 quills, feathers.

膈 [2.5.] The diaphragm. Any thin separating membrane or pellicle. Inter. next.
3318
膈肢 to tickle.
膈膜 the diaphragm, any separating membrane.
膈食 or 不下膈 unable to digest food.
打膈 to belch.
↑打冷膈兒 to hiccough.

隔 [2.5.] To separate. Divided by. A partition. To divide. To filter.
3319
隔一條河 divided by a stream.
隔一道街 separated by one street.
隔三跳二 doing things by fits and starts.
隔世 (or 代) 遺傳 atavism.
[5]隔別多年 I have not seen him for years.
隔壁 next door; a partition wall; neighbours.
隔壁戲 to give imitations of animals, voices, etc., behind a screen, one man ringing the changes on the voices.

隔壁鄰居 next-door neighbours.
隔夜 left over night; a night intervening.
[10]隔年皇曆 last year's calendar—something that is past.
隔得遠 very far apart.
隔感 telepathy.
隔房 the adjoining room.
隔扇門 partition made of doors.
[15]隔斷 severed; cut off.
隔日 every other day.
隔日來 come on alternate days.
隔日可取 may be taken away the next day.
隔板 partition-boards; panelling.
[20]隔母 step-brothers or sisters.
隔水 separated by a stream.
隔渣盤 a filtering-dish.
隔火 covering for incense burner.
隔牆抓癢 to scratch an itchy place through a wall—labour in vain. *See below*—36.
[25]隔牆有耳 walls have ears.
隔絕 cut off from; broken off—as friendship.
隔着敎 belonging to different religions.
隔膜 u.f. the diaphragm; to have no dealings with; lack mutual understanding.
隔行 (*hang*[2]) 如隔山 different trades are separated as by mountains.
[30]隔裁 cut off.
隔開 separated; to divide.
隔閡 no dealings with: alienated.
隔離 to set apart; to keep apart.
隔電帶 insulating tape.
[35]隔電線 insulated wire.
隔靴搔癢 to scratch an itchy place through the boot—not very effective. *See above*—24.

(a) A bar in music.
準隔 a bar in music.

K'O. K'Ĕ (⿱)
(K'eh)

克 [4.5.] To be able to. Competent. Adequate. Also read *k'o*[5].
3320
克享 able to enjoy; in good health.
克勤克儉 diligent and frugal.
克家 able to take charge of the family affairs.

克 明 德 able to make his virtues illustrious.

[5]克 當 or 克 堪 fit for; adequate to.

何 以 克 當 How can I sustain such honour?—conventional phrase.

克 繩 祖 武 able to follow the footsteps of one's ancestors.

克 諧 以 孝 (Shun) by his filial piety was able to live in harmony with his—father, step-mother and step-brother.

克 讓 able to yield.

[10]克 配 上 帝 they were able to please the Supreme.

克 食 a dole; bounty.

不 克 分 身 I am not able to get away.

弗 克 如 願 unable to attain my wishes.

惟 克 天 德 they attained to divine virtue.

(a) To subdue.

克 制 感 情 to subdue the emotions.

克 制 萬 物 to bring all things under control.

克 己 to deny self.

克 復 to recapture a fallen city.

[5]克 服 to conquer, to subdue.

克 滅 俗 情 to bring the passions under control.

克 欲 to master the passions.

克 私 to subdue the appetites.

不 測 不 克 inscrutable and unconquerable.

攻 克 to break through the forces of the foe.

(b) Love of superiority.

克 伐 怨 欲 to love pre-eminence and be boastful, to hate and be covetous.

(c) To fix upon. Certain. Inter. next two.

克 日 within a certain time.

克 日 彙 報 make a classified report within a certain time.

克 期 告 成 to be completed within a certain time.

(d) Used in transliterating.

克 冷 grain—in English weights.

克 勒 特 Celt.

克 蘭 母 gramme. See 3701.93.
克 虜 佰 Krupp.

剋
尅 [4.5.]
3321
To subdue, to destroy. to overcome. Also read k'o[4.5]. Inter. preceding.

剋 制 to restrain, to prevail against.

剋 復 to recover—as a city that has been taken.

剋 扣 軍 餉 to reduce army supplies for personal gain.

剋 煞 凶 神 to drive off malicious demons.

相 生 相 剋 mutually producing and destroying each other.

(a) Inter. next. To fix on. Certain.

刻 [1.5.]
3322
To engrave.

刻 印 to engrave and print.

刻 圖 書 to engrave a seal.

刻 在 心 裏 engraven on the heart.

刻 字 to carve characters.

[5]刻 字 刀 graving tool.

刻 念 to think of.

刻 明 clearly engraved.

刻 板 to cut blocks for printing; fixed, certain.

刻 畫 carved and painted—laboured style of writing.

[10]刻 石 engraved stones.

刻 花 to carve ornamental work.

刻 鏤 to inlay.

刻 骨 銘 心 engraven on the memory; to remember without fail.

彫 刻 to carve or engrave.

[15]深 刻 次 骨 it cuts to the bone.

重 刻 to re-engrave—a second edition.

(a) Close, stingy, oppressive. k'o[4.5]

刻 己 利 人 to benefit others at personal expense.

刻 待 or 刻 勒 or 刻 毒 to treat harshly; to oppress.

刻 求 to be particular.

刻 苦 oppressive; to suffer hardships.

刻 薄 stingy; to treat harshly.

(b) A quarter of an hour; in ancient reckoning, a quarter of a 時 辰 or half an hour. Already. To fix. Now.　　k'o[4.5]

刻 今 or 刻 下 or 此 刻 at present; now.

刻 已 already.

刻 日 at an early date.

刻 期 to fix a date.

[5]刻 漏 a clepsydra.

一 刻 工 夫 in a short time.

時 刻 constantly; from time to time.

虛 刻 an interval.

限 刻 a fixed period.

咳
欬 [2.5.]
3323
To cough up. To cough.

咳 唾 the words of an older generation; to utter fine phrases.

咳 嗽 to cough.

咳 痰 to cough up phlegm.

咳 血 to cough up blood.

咳 頃 in the time of a cough—in a moment.

百 日 咳 whooping cough.

(a) Read hai[2]. An exclamation. Laughter of a child.

咳 嬰 a child of two or three.

客 [4.5.]
3324
A guest, a visitor. A traveller, a travelling merchant, a stranger. A customer.

客 人 a guest, a customer, a trader.

客 作 an employee or servant.

客 兵 troops from other garrison areas; allied foreign troops. A.c. 客 軍

客 卿 foreigner in an official position.

[5]客 商 or 商 賈 travelling merchants.

客 堂 or 客 房 a reception room.

客 套 話 conventional greetings.

客 妻 a kept mistress.

客 家 customers. The Hakkas of S. China.

[10]客 居 temporary residence.

客 廳 a reception room.

客 戶 an alien or stranger.

客 旅 or 賓 客 strangers; lodgers.

客 星 a strange star.

[15]客棧 or 客店 or 客寓 an inn, hotel.

客次 place for visitors; lodging-place for strangers.

客·氣 formality; politeness.

不客·氣 do not stand on ceremony.

客目 a list of guests.

[20]客籍 a stranger; a visitor from another province or district.

客股 subscribed capital.

客舍 lodging place, an inn.

客觀 objective. *See* No. 3575—A.4 ff.

客觀敎育 objective teaching.

[25]客觀·的 objectively.

客販 travelling merchants.

客貨 goods bought on account for others; goods from other places.

客車 a passenger train.

主客 host and guest.

[30]堂客 lady visitors.

拜客 to pay calls.

生客 a stranger.

↑ (款) 待客 to entertain guests.

發客 on sale to customers.

[35]茶客 merchants who go into the interior to purchase tea.

說客 an envoy sent in ancient times to talk over treaties, etc.

請客 to entertain.

貴客 an honoured guest; a son-in-law.

送客 to see a visitor off.

(a) Last year.

客歲 last year.

喀 [3.5.] Used for transliterating, *k'a* or *k'o*.
3325   To cough.

搭 [2.5.] To seize. Also read
3326   *ch'ia* [1.5.]

搭出去 drag him away.

KÊN. (ㄍㄣ)

艮 [4] A limit. Hard. Perverse, obstinate. Seventh of the
3327 *Eight Diagrams.* Radical 138.
Distinguish 良 No. 3941.

根 [1] A root; a base. A beginning. A cause. A founda-
3328 tion. N.A.

根塵 the six bases of sensation:—eye, ear, nose, tongue, body and mind; and the six worldly environments:— form, sound, smell, taste, touch and perception. (*Budd.*). *See* 六 No. 4189—8, 13.

根·子 antecedents.

根必盤深 the foundations must be broad and deep.

根性 nature, disposition.

[5]根據 a basis, authority, evidence; in accord with.

根據互惠精·神 based on a spirit of reciprocity.

根據古義 conforms to the ancient ways of righteousness.

根據地 fundamental grounds; military base of operations.

根據條約 according to treaty; based on the treaties.

[10]根據法律 according to law.

根本 or 根由 or 根·基 or 根·底 root; origin; the reason for things; foundation; basis.

根本·上 radically; fundamentally.

根本不知 knows nothing at all about it.

根本剷·除 a radical clearance.

[15]根本哲學 fundamental philosophy.

根本問題 a fundamental question.

根本改革 a radical change; fundamentally changed.

根本放棄 let it go root and branch.

根本要道 the most fundamental doctrines.

[20]根本覺悟 thoroughly roused.

根本觀念 a radical conception.

根本解決 settled in accord with fundamental principles; a radical solution.

根本辦·法 basic principles of action.

根本錯誤 a fundamental error.

[25]根末 or 根梢 root and branches—altogether, throughout.

根查 thorough investigation.

根株盡絕 to destroy utterly.

根毛 fine roots.

根氣 intrinsic quality.

[30]根治 radical treatment—as of disease.

根深蒂固 the root is deep and the branches strong.

根深葉茂 the root is deep and the leaves flourishing.

根源 source; foundation.

根生點 growing-point.

[35]根究 thorough investigation.

根脚 a base of operations; foundation.

根苗 roots and shoots—origin, source.

根莖 root-stock; rhizome.

根蒂 root and stem—regular arrangement.

[40]根號 radical sign. (*math.*)

根起 from the beginning.

根追 to trace to a source or origin.

有根器 having a foundation,—able to study *Tao*.

歸根 to revert to first principles; [after all.

[45]絕·了根 exterminated; cut off.

除根 to eradicate.

有根 smart. (*slang*)

詪 [3] Difficulty in speaking. Wrangling.
3329

跟 [1] The heel. To follow; to accompany; to imitate.
3330

跟丁 a servant of an official.

跟·不上 or 趕·不上 inferior to; cannot overtake.

跟人做 to do as others do.

跟·前 in front of, in company of.

[5]跟壞品 to follow bad examples.

跟好人學好人 follow the good and learn their ways—a man is known by his company.

跟從 or 跟隨 or 跟著 to follow, to go with.

跟手去做 do it at once.

跟·我去 follow me; come with me.

[10]跟班 a footman; servant of an official.

跟輯 to trace, to follow the track of.

跟·着又是雨 following this, there was more rain.

跟·着學 to follow an example.

跟·着衆人 with the crowd.

[15]跟誰學·的 under what teacher did you study?

跟踪 to follow a clue.

跟轎 a runner to a sedan-chair.

跟·進·去 go in with the others.

(a) With, to.

跟·他 說 speak to him, tell him.

K'ÊN.　　(ㄎㄣ)

硍⁴ A stone with a flaw in it.
3331

硍 晶 rock crystal.

(a) Rumbling noise.

硍 雷 之 聲 rumbling, as of heavy things being rolled about.

裉⁴
褙⎱ A seam in a garment.
3332

繚 裉 to stitch a seam.

齦³ To gnaw; to bite. To bark—a tree.
3333

齦 聲 a gnashing sound.
齦 骨 to gnaw a bone.

(a) Read *yin*². The gums.

肯³ Willing; to consent to. To permit. To wish; to choose to. Also read *k'êng*³.
3334

肯·不·肯 are you willing or not?
肯 吃 苦 willing to endure hardship.
肯 幹 willing to do it.
肯 構 肯 堂 willing to put on the roof as well as to build—a son willing to carry on his father's ambitions.
肯 許 or 允 肯 to agree, to assent.
不 肯 unwilling; cross, peevish—of children.

啃³ To bite, to gnaw.
3335

揯³ To oppress; to extort; to take by force.
3336

揯 勒 to levy blackmail.

揯 口 說 話 abusive talk; to speak indistinctly.
揯 吞 to monopolize.
揯 手 to catch the hand—to delay: not dexterous.
⁵揯 留 forcible detention.
揯 贖 to interfere and prevent redemption of a mortgage.
揯 阻 to obstruct.

墾³ To open new soil. To reclaim land.
3337

墾 力 with all one's might.
墾 地 稅 duties on newly-cleared land.
墾 種 (*chung*⁴) to plough and sow.
墾 荒 to open up barren lands.
開 墾 事 reclamation works.

懇³ To beseech; to supplicate. With earnestness.
3338

懇 乞 to entreat.
懇 准 to ask permission.
懇 切 earnestly; importunate.
懇 啟 to draw up a written appeal for assistance.
⁵懇 恩 to beg a favour.
懇 惻 sincerity; good faith.
懇 懇 earnestly; eager.
懇 求 or 懇 請 or 懇 祈 to implore; to entreat.
懇 爲 過 信 I beg you to believe me.
¹⁰懇 給 to beg; to ask for.
懇 親 會 parent-teacher association or meeting.
懇 諫 earnest admonitions.

KÊNG.　　(ㄍㄥ)

庚¹ Seventh of the *Ten Stems* 天 干, thus used for age.
3339

庚 子 年 the year of the cyclical characters *kêng tzŭ*, i.e., 1900— the Boxer outbreak.
庚 帖 or 庚 柬 a document in which is written the four pairs of cyclical characters indicating the hour, day, month and year of birth; this is sent as a formal proposal of marriage, the sending of a return document constitutes a formal betrothal.

庚 欵 Boxer indemnity.
同 庚 of the same year.
⁵年 庚 八 字 the four pairs of cyclical characters as in—2 above.
貴 庚 what is your honourable age?

(a) A path. An orbit.

以 塞 夷 庚 in order to block the main highways.

(b) The west. The evening-star.

呼 庚 癸 *kêng* refers to the west and grain, *kuei* to the north and water,—to call for grain and water :—term used by troops in ancient times in order to prevent the knowledge of their shortage from reaching the enemy.
長 庚 the evening-star.—it lengthens the day.

(c) To change or restore, u.f. 更 No. 3346.

(d) To reward.

賡¹ To continue, as a song.
3340

賡 和 to carry on the melody.
賡 揚 功 績 proclaimed his merits.

鶊¹ The oriole.
3341

鶬 鶊 the oriole.

羹¹
羮⎱ Soup, broth.
3342

羹 匙 or 調 羹 a spoon, a ladle.
羹 湯 soup.
如 沸 如 羹 like the bubbling of soup in a pot—popular discontent.

耕¹
畊⎱ To plough, to till.
3343

耕 夫 a ploughman.
耕 牛 an ox trained to the plough.
耕 田 or 耕 地 to plough the fields. (also pron. *ching*[1]-)
[5]耕 種·的 one who ploughs and sows—a farmer.
耕 耘 收 穫 farming operations.
耕 耡 or 耕 作 to cultivate the soil.
耕 道 得 道 if you cultivate *Tao*—the right Way—you will attain to it.
目 耕 to plough with the eyes—i.e., to read extensively.
[10]筆 耕 ploughing with the pen—to live by writing.

亙 [4] An extreme limit. To fill. Universal. Connected. Distinguish 亘 No. 2889, 亙 No. 2152.
3344

亙 古 一 人 from of old the only man—refers to Confucius, or the God of War 關 帝.
亙 古 以 來 from of old.
亙 古 至 今 from of old till now.

絚
絙 A rope.
3345

絚 梯 a rope-ladder.

更
叓 To change, to alter.
3346

更 代 to change and substitute.
更·加 to change and add—*See below* D-4.
更 勳 to transfer—officers.
更 名 to change one's name.
[5]更 始 to make a new beginning.
更 定 to amend or revise; to change.
更 張 to relax.
更 換 to replace; to substitute.
更 改 to alter, to change; substitution.
[10]更 新 to make a fresh start; to reform.
更 新 之 時 a new era.
更 易 to exchange; to alter.
更 替 to interchange.

更 正 to reform; to correct; to amend or alter.
[15]更 番 many times; repeatedly.
更 番 迭 次 to have altered repeatedly.
更 移 to remove; to go back on.
更 衣 to change the dress—euphemism used by women for visiting the lavatory.
更 訂 to revise, to amend.
[20]更 變 to effect a change; entirely different.
更 迭 to alternate.

(a) To attend to; to be experienced in.

更 事 者 experienced man.
少 不 更 事 he is too young to take responsibility.

(b) A night-watch.

更 夫 or 更 練 or 打 更·的 a watchman. A.p. *ta*[3]-*ching*[1]·*tê*.
更 樓 a watch-tower.
更 次 two hours—the interval between the watches.
更 深 late at night.
[5]更 漏 a clepsydra for regulating the length of the watches.
更 香 sticks of incense for indicating the night watch.
更 鼓 a watchman's drum or bamboo.

(c) Mutual, similar to 互 No. 2152.

更 相 爲 命 mutually dependent.

(d) Read *kêng*[4]. More, much more. Still, again.

更 不 still less, much less.
更 兼 in addition, besides.
更 利·害 more severe; still worse.
更·加 still more. *See above*—2.
[5]更 宜 still more fitting.
更·宜 注 意 still more important.
更 多·了 still more.
更 大 still greater.
更 好 better; preferable.
[10]更 形 重 要 still more important.
更 其 一 件 there is still another point; in addition.
更 有 一 說 a further remark.
更 甚 still more.

哽 [3] Choking,—either from grief or anger.
3347

哽 咽 choking with sobs.
哽 塞 the throat choked and unable to speak.

埂 [3] A channel for irrigation.
3348

梗 [3] A thorny tree. Thorny; prickly. Stem of a flower.
3349

枝 梗 a stalk or stem.
脖 梗·子 the neck.
花 梗·子 stem of a flower.

(a) Strong, stubborn. Straight.

梗 性·子 an obstinate disposition.
梗 直 blunt, honest, upright.
頑 梗 obstinate, perverse.

(b) Distress.

至 今 爲 梗 which have brought about the present distress.

(c) To ward off calamity.

招 梗 禬 禳 prayers and sacrifices to ward off calamities.

(d) An outline, general summary.

梗 概 on the whole, generally speaking; a rough outline.

(e) To obstruct.

梗 化 to hinder civilization or culture.
梗 道 making the road difficult.
路 梗 obstructions.

粳
秔
稉 Non-glutinous rice.
3350

粳 米 or 粳 籼 or 籼 米 ordinary rice as distinguished from the glutinous variety or 糯 米 *See* No. 4751.

綆 [3] A well-rope. A rope.
3351

綆 短 不 可 汲 深 if the rope is short, it cannot reach the deep water. Used fig.

骾 鯁 3352

Fish-bones, things that stick in the throat. Unyielding, blunt of speech.

骾 直 straightforward and blunt.
骾 訐 blunt of speech.
小 骾 a trifling thing; a trifling cause of enmity.
骨 骾 outspoken.

耿 3353

Bright.

耿 介 greatness and glory; resolute; straightforward.
耿 光 dazzling light; glory.
耿 直 firm, correct, upright.

(a) Disquieted. Getting bright.

耿 耿 不 寐 disquieted and unable to sleep.
河 曙 耿 耿 the light on the river is increasing.

K'ÊNG (ㄎㄥ)

坑 阬 3354

A pit, a hole, a gully. To involve, to entrap.

坑 人 to injure another.
坑 儒 to bury the literati in a pit, as was done by *Ch'in Shih-Huang* 秦 始 皇
坑 其 民 involved his people in great disaster.
坑 坎 a pit, a hole.
⁵坑 埋 to bury deeply.
坑 害 to involve in difficulties; to injure, to harass.
坑 死 人 to involve in great trouble.
坑 渠 a sewer.
坑 田 rice-fields.
¹⁰坑 谷 a valley.
坑 降 (*hsiang*²) 卒 he killed the soldiers who surrendered.
坑 騙 to over-reach; to defraud.
火 坑 a fiery pit—conditions of great suffering.

硻 3355

The shank bone of an ox.

硜 硜 3356

The sound of pebbles or stones knocking together. Obstinate.

硜 然 小 人 哉 obstinate, petty men.

鏗 3357

The jingling of metals. To strike.

鏗 鏗 有 聲 tinkling as they go.
鏗 鏘 the jingle of bells, etc.
鏗 鐘 to strike a bell.

KO. (ㄍㄛ)

戈 3358

A spear, a lance. Radical 62. Distinguish 弋 No. 3018.

倒 戈 相 向 they betrayed their own party.
干 戈 war. *See* No. 3211—2 ff.

(a) Used for transliterating.

戈 壁 Gobi or the Desert.
戈 登 Gordon.

舸 3359

A stake to which a boat may be moored. A rope or painter.

舸 3360

A barge.

哿 3361

Excellent. To commend. To be able to. Also read *k'o*³.

哿 矣 富 人 哀 此 煢 獨 "The rich may get through *life well*; but alas for the miserable and solitary!"

菏 3362

A marsh drained by *Yü* the Great.

菏 澤 縣 place in Shantung.

哥 3363

An elder brother.

哥·哥 or 大 哥 or 哥 兒 or 哥 郎 an elder brother.

哥 嫂 an elder brother's wife.
哥 老 會 a powerful secret society.
八·哥 the mynah.
↑哥 倫 比 亞 Columbia.

歌 謌 3364

Songs. To sing.

歌 唱 to sing, to chant.
歌 曲 ballads, to sing ballads.
歌 本 a song-book.
歌 笑 singing and laughter.
⁵歌 聲 the sound of singing.
歌 詞 poetry; verses of song.
歌 詩 to sing poems; songs.
歌 謠 folk-songs; popular ballads.
歌 頌 to sing praises.

鴚 3365

A goose.

個 箇 个 3366

A numerary adjunct. This; this one.

個 中 人 one of us; one of the same calling; the initiated.
從 個 中 from an inside viewpoint.
個 人 individual; personal.
個 人 主 義 individualism; egoism.
⁵個 人 佈 道 personal work, individual evangelism.
個 人 倫 理 personal ethics.
個 人 名·譽 personal reputation.
個 人 權 personal rights.
個 人 自 由 權 personal rights; individual liberty.
¹⁰個 人 衛 生 personal hygiene.
個 人 資·格 personal qualifications.
個 個 如 此 all are like this.
個 個 都 有 each one possesses it.
個 別 教 育 individual teaching.
¹⁵個 性 individuality.
個 性 原 理 principle of individuality.
個 性 心 理 學 psychology of the individual.
個 體 the individual as contrasted with the group 團 體.
個 體 獨 立 主 義 particularism.

[20]一个 one.

有·個我在 to have individual personality.

這·個那·個 this one, that one.

噶 [1] Transliterating sounds, ko, ka.
3367

KO. (ㄍ)
(Koh)

各 [4.5.] Each, every; All.
3368

各一 one of each; one to each.

各[4]人 each person. 各[2]人 each himself.

各人各見 each one has his own opinion.

各以其類而應 each answers to his class.

[5]各住 to live apart.

各個 each, every.

各·個人 everybody, per head.

各各 each one, singly.

各因其材 each according to his ability.

[10]各國 each nation.

各執己見 each cleaves to his own opinion.

各就其重處言之 shows what is most important in each case.

各屬 all his subordinates.

各等因 sums up the various communications under acknowledgement, or the different items dealt with.

[15]各得其所 each in its proper place.

各從其道 each after its own order; each according to its own order; each according to its own way.

各從其類 each after its kind.

各方面 from every viewpoint; all sides.

各有一説 each has his own story.

[20]各有不同 each different.

各有所長 each one has his own gift.

各樣 or 各色 or 各項 or 各種 each sort, every kind.

各樣具全 all kinds kept in stock.

各皆 all, both.

[25]各盡所長 each exhausted his special ability.   [one.

↑ 各個撃破 to knock out one by

各自 or 各自各兒[3] each one.

各色貨 all sorts of goods.

各處 or 各地方 or 各路 every place.

各適其宜 each is as it should be.

[30]各適其用 each is suitable for the purpose intended.

各門各戸 each separate household.

各類 different species; separate orders.

各顧各 each for himself.

閣 [2.5.] A council-chamber. A pavilion.
3369

閣下 you sir—polite address.

閣令 orders from the cabinet.

閣員 cabinet ministers.

閣老 secretary of State during *Ming* dynasty.

閣議 meeting of the cabinet.

內閣 the cabinet.

(a) Women's apartments, vestibule. Screen.

出閣 to leave the women's apartments; to go to her marriage.

在閣上 upstairs.

坐閣 seclusion of girls before marriage.

(b) A bookcase. A shelf.

置高閣 put it on a high shelf—ignore it.

擱 [1.5.] To place, to put; to put down.
3370

擱一邊 to put aside; to neglect.

擱·下 put it down; drop it.

擱·不下 cannot find room for it.

擱·在外·邊 put it down outside.

[5]擱·在心·裏 take it to heart.

擱平 put it down flat.

擱木 or 托木 the wooden plate over a door or window.

擱板 a shelf, a mantel.

擱筆 to put down the pen.

[10]擱·着·罷 put it aside just now.

擱·開 to put a thing aside. *See below* A-1.

(a) To delay, to hinder.

擱·開 to delay, to defer.

延擱 to dally; to hinder.

就·擱 to hinder, to delay.

(b) To run aground.

擱·了淺 to go ashore; stranded on the shallows; also used fig.

骼 [2.5.] Frame or skeleton of man or animals.
3371

骨骼 the skeleton; the build of a man.

胳 [2.5.] The ribs. Also read hsieh[2.5.]. Originally written as 脅 No. 2641.
3372

蛤 [2.5.] A frog; a lizard. Also read ha[2].
3373

蛤蚧 a red-spotted lizard.

蛤蜥 the gecko.

蛤蟆 frogs. (ha[2]-)

蛤·魚 edible frogs.

(a) Bivalves.

蛤·子 clams.

蛤·子肉 the flesh of shellfish.

蛤粉 powder from oyster-shells.

蛤蚌 oysters.

蛤蜊 a species of clam.

蛤蜊板 boards halved at the edges for flooring, etc.

閤 [2.5.] A small side-door. Inter 閣 No. 3369.
3374

頜 [1.5.] The jowl. Also read ho[1.5.].
3375

鴿 [1.5.] A dove, a pigeon.
3376

鴿·子 pigeons or doves.

鴿鈴 whistles fastened on pigeons.

傳書鴿 carrier pigeons.

地鴿·子 a humming-top.

野鴿 wood-pigeons.

葛 [2.5.] A creeping, edible bean, from the fibres of which cloth is made.
3377

葛布 a coarse, yellowish cloth for summer wear.

葛粉 a fine white powder like arrowroot, made from the roots of a plant.

葛籐 creepers, tendrils,—complications, difficulties.

葛籐立斷 immediately stop all further complications.

(a) Relatives, connections.

瓜葛 creeping vines, i.e., relationships, things involved, connections.

瓜葛之愛 love of relatives.

揢 4.5.
3378
To scrape or grate.

輵
輵 2.5.
Great array of spears and chariots.
3379

割 1.5. To cut, to hack, to reap. To buy—meat in small quantities.
3380

割一斤肉·來 buy a pound of meat.

割下·來 to cut down.

割傷 an incised wound.

割價 to reduce the price.

⁵割八兩猪肉 buy half a catty of pork.

割勢 castration.

割口 to make an incision.

割地 to cede territory.

割工·錢 to reduce wages.

¹⁰割席 to cut the mat—i.e., to separate from association with an unworthy friend.

割情 to break off intercourse.

割愛 to give up what one treasures.

割捨 to be loth to give up.

割損 to injure.

¹⁵割數 to deduct part of an account; to force to take less.

割斷 to cut apart; to divide.

割烹 what is cut off and prepared—victuals.

割眼 to cut a hole.

割禮 circumcision.

²⁰割禾 to reap grain.

割穫 or 割稻 to reap; to harvest.

割肚 cut to the heart—as by evil tidings.

割臂之盟 vows of eternal friendship, love.

割與 to cede to.

²⁵割草 to mow.

割術 art of surgery.

割裂 to sever; disruption.

割袍斷義 to break off all intercourse with a friend.

³⁰割鐵絲鉗·子 cutting-pliers.

割開 to cut open.

割雞焉¹用牛刀 in killing a fowl why use an ox-knife?

割首 to behead.

割麥·子 to reap wheat. (-mai⁴-)

K'O. (코)

可 ³ May, can, might, able; sign of potential mood.
3381

可一而不可再 may be done once, but may not be repeated.

可·不·可 may it be done or not?

可·不·是·麼 to be sure it is; can it be?

可也 it will do—a final phrase.

⁵不知其可也 I do not know what use such a man is!

可也簡 "He will do! He does not trouble about small affairs."

可了³不·得 dreadful; how horrible! [charming.

可人 a capable man; pleasing;

可人意 acceptable to others.

¹⁰可·以 may; an expression of assent—very well; that will do, etc.

可·以不必 not necessary.

可·以人而不如鳥乎 can it be that man is not equal to a bird?

可·以做·得 allowable; it may be done.

可·以取可·以無取 to appear (at first) as if a thing may be taken, and (afterwards) as if it may not be taken.

¹⁵可·以羣 (by them) we may become sociable.

可·以觀 can use them to ascertain.

不可·以風 cannot bear much wind.

可仗 reliable.

可使南面 is fit to sit facing the south—to be a ruler.

²⁰可依 to fall back upon.

可信 credible.

可兒² a charming lad.

可分性 divisibility.

可厭·的 disgusting.

²⁵可及 within reach; accessible.

可取 worthy; having qualities that make it worth using.

可口 palatable; delicious.

可吃·的 eatable.

可否 will it do or not? is it practicable?

³⁰可咒詛 accursed.

可嘉 joyful.

可大可小 elastic.

可獎 commendable.

可好 fortunately; may I . . . ?

³⁵可容 admirable.

可貴 honourable.

可·就晚·了 it is now too late, however.

可巧 luckily; as it fortunately happened.

可怪 wonderful; how strange! horrible!

⁴⁰可怕 may be dreaded; an object of fear.

可恃 dependable.

可恥·的 something to be ashamed of.

可恨 detestable; abominable.

可恨天氣不好 unfortunately the weather is bad.

⁴⁵可惜 Too bad! Unfortunately!

可愛 lovable.

可想而知 having a fair knowledge of; no need to go into details.

可意 suits one's ideas.

可惱 irritable; provoking.

⁵⁰可惡 (wu⁴) detestable; hateful.

可惡之至 utterly detestable.

可慘 tragic; pitiable.

可慮 giving rise to worry or anxiety.

可憑 reliable.

⁵⁵可憎 abominable.

可憐 to pity; pitiable.

可懼 fearful; to be dreaded.

可掬 feelings showing in the face.

笑容可掬 with a broad smile.

⁶⁰可敬 worthy of all respect; respectable.

可·是 but, however; is it that . . . ?

可·不·是 sure enough! that is so; really; now I think of it.

可·是不能答·應 but one could not agree to that!

可·是他做·的 was it his doing?

可望而不可卽 can gaze but cannot approach.

⁶⁵可期 one may hope for.

可 欺 也 不 可 罔 也 (the superior man) may be imposed upon, but he cannot be fooled.

可 歎 Alas!—expresses sympathy.

可 止 may be dispensed with.

可 決 can be passed; may be accepted.

[70]可 容 性 solubility.

可 無 慮 nothing to fear.

可 燃 性 inflammability.

可 畏 awful; dreadful.

可 異 how peculiar!

[75]可 當 作 it may be taken as....

可 知 it is evident; it may be seen that.

可 疑 suspicious; doubtful.

可 笑 laughable.

可 羞 shameful.

[80]可 能 able; possibility; potentiality; possible.

可 能 性 possibility.

有 成 的 可 能 there is a possibility of completion.

可 著 頭 做 帽 子 make the cap to fit the head—stiff, lacking elasticity.

可 行 allowable; it may be done.

[85]可 行 的 理 想 practicable idealism.

可 見 it is evident; obvious.

可 觀 worth inspection or worth seeing.

大 有 可 觀 well worth seeing.

可 託 trustworthy.

[90]可 謂 云 爾 已 矣 you may say just that and no more!

可 變 mutability.

可 賀 worthy of congratulation.

可 身 well fitting.

可 進 可 退 can either advance or retire.

[95]可 達 capable of attainment.

可 體 a good fit.

不 可 not permissible; not practicable.

不 我 可 no affair of mine.

小 可 a trifling matter. *See below* —101.

[100]有 何 不 可 what objection can there be?

非 同 小 可 no trifling matter.

(a) Used for transliterating.

可 汗 (*k'o⁴ han²*) u.f. Khan. A Mongol chief.

可 蘭 The Koran.

↑可 可 cocoa; a.c. 蔲 蔲.

坷 [4] Uneven; rugged. Unfortunate.
3382

坎 坷 uneven ways of life; bad luck.

敤 [1.4.] To thump; to beat.
3383 ≡ 3405.

敤 敤 乾 淨 了 knock—a box—till it is clean.

敤 打 烟 灰 knock out the ashes from a pipe.

敤 打 臭 蟲 knock out the bed-bugs.

柯 [1] An axe-handle. An agent or go-between. See 伐 No.
3384 1765—B.

伐 柯 之 敬 a present to the go-between.

執 柯 伐 柯 grasp an axe-handle while cutting another—the pattern is not far off.

斧 柯 an axe-handle.

(a) A stalk or branch. N.A.

一 柯 白 菜 a head of cabbage.

千 頃 地 一 柯 (or 科) 苗 only one sprout in a vast estate—dying out.

珂 [1] An inferior kind of jade. A small shell. Used in transliterating.
3385

珂 羅 版 Collotype.

苛 [1] Small plants; thus:—petty, vexatious, troublesome. To reprove. Also read *ho¹*.
3386

苛 刻 very harsh; to domineer; to bully.

苛 屬 cruel and harsh.

苛 嚴 cruel, severe.

苛 察 fault-finding.

[5]苛 待 to treat with harshness and severity.

苛 性 caustic.

苛 性 蘇 達 caustic soda.

苛 政 harsh government.

苛 政 猛 於 虎 an oppressive government is worse than a tiger.

[10]苛 求 to make excuses.

苛 派 severe exactions by officials.

苛 疾 dangerous illness.

苛 擾 petty, vexatious.

苛 評 hypercriticism.

軻 [1] A pair of wheels. An axle-tree. The personal name of Mencius.
3387

齣可 [4] To gnaw or bite.
3388

科 [1] A class, an order or series. A rule, a line. A department. Classification of second-degree graduates under the former system.
3389

科 任 制 the educational system of having special teachers for certain branches of study, as opposed to the system of having one teacher in charge of a class and teaching all subjects.

科 則 rate, classification.

科 收 to levy; to assess.

科 名 honours gained at the examinations under the former system.

[5]科 員 clerks.

科 塲 examination hall.

科 學 science.

科 學 儀 器 scientific instruments.

科 學 家 scientists.

[10]科 學 常 識 scientific knowledge of a general character.

科 學 式 的 批 評 scientific criticism.

科 學 方 法 scientific methods.

科 學 智 識 scientific knowledge.

科 學 的 實 驗 scientific tests.

[15]科 學 的 管 理 scientific control.

科 學 的 精 神 the scientific spirit.

科 學 研 究 scientific research or investigation.

不 科 學 的 unscientific.

科 征 taxation; to assess a tax.

[20]科 房 or 房 科 the six departments in a *yamen*.

科 斂 to collect taxes or levies.

科 條 orders, laws.

科 派 to levy; to assess without authority.

科 班 literary men; former second-degree graduates.

[25]科 目 list of subjects for study.

科目出身 or 科甲出身 to get a degree and hold office by graduation—not merely by purchase.

科稅 an extra tax ; to levy a tax.

科籃 basket of necessities taken into the old examination halls.

科第 or 科甲 graduates of the former second and third degrees.

[30]科舉制·度 (under) the old examination-system.

科試 or 科考 preliminary examination of candidates for the former triennial examinations.

科配 extra taxes and levies.

科長 head of a department.

併科 together with.

[35]內科外科 medical and surgical practice.

力不同科 people's strength is not equal.

幼科 treatment of children's ailments.

庶務科 department of general affairs.

文牘科 secretariat.

[40]易科 in lieu of.

正科 compulsory subjects.

犯科 to offend the law.

總務科 chief department ; head office.

衛生科 health or sanitation department.

[45]豫科 preparatory department.

選科 elective or optional subjects.

醫科 department of medicine.

(a) A hole.

盈科而後進 it fills every hole and then flows on.

(b) To judge or decide.

科斷 to decide a case according to law.

科罪 to deal with a crime.

科罰 fines, punishments.

科金 fines.

(c) Movement, stage business.

科白 simple acting without singing.

(d) Hollow timber. N.A. for stalks, etc.

竹數科 several bamboos.

(e) To do the hair in a knot.

科結 the hair tied in a knot.

科頭 bare-headed—at leisure.

(f) Inter. next. A tadpole.

科斗·子 tadpoles.

科斗文 tadpole characters of ancient times.

蝌 [1] 3390   The tadpole.

蝌斗·子 tadpoles.

棵 [1] 3391   A numerary adjunct for trees, etc.

一棵樹 one tree.

稞 [4] 3392   Grain ready for grinding.

窠 [1] 3393   A hole, a nest, a burrow.

蜂窠 beehive ; wasp's nest.

鼠鳥同窠 the rat and the bird in the same hole—on good terms.

(a) A rule or line for engraving. To carve. The engraved face of a seal.

窠木 woodcarving.

擘窠 to arrange characters in a seal so that each column is even.

(b) An indentation.

窠臼 or 科臼 a ready-made pattern or rule.

落窠臼 to fall into the old ruts or ways.

(c) N.A. for plants, trees, etc. Inter. with others of similar sound.

課 [4] 3394   A task ; a lesson.

課員 departmental staff.

課堂 class room.

課外活動 extra-curricula activities.

課文 to criticise compositions.

[5]課期 the time for examinations.

課本 text books. ⌈in former times.

課業 the profession of literature.

課畢 after lessons.

課程 curriculum.

[10]課程之變遷 changes in curriculum.

課程表 syllabus ; schedule—of studies, etc.

課級 course, class, etc.

課長 head of a department.

上課 to go to classes.

[15]功·課 tasks ; lessons.

學·生罷課 schoolboy-strikes.

日課 daily tasks.

(a) To exhort, to counsel.

課勸 to exhort.

(b) To examine.

課筒 tube used by fortune-tellers.

課試 to experiment ; to test.

占課 to tell fortunes.

起課 to divine.

(c) To levy taxes.

課稅 custom's duties.

課館 a revenue office.

鹽課 salt-tax.

錁 [3] 3395   A grease-pot for carts. Small ingots of silver. Mock ingots for idolatry.

顆 [1.3.] 3396   A kernel. N.A. of small things as pearls, etc., also of trees.

一顆珠 a pearl.

一顆樹 one tree.

有幾顆 how many are there ?

騍 [4] 3397   Female of horses, mules, etc.

騍馬 a mare.

騍騾 a she-mule.

髁 [3] 3398   Socket of hip-joints. Thigh-bone. Read k'ua[4]. Crooked.

課髁無任 knowing his unfitness he occupied no office.

藹 [1]　Empty, hungry-looking.
3399

藹 軸 hunger and sickness,—straitened.

藹 軸 之 疾 已 消 his anxieties are now dispelled.

藹 軸 有 懷 於 求 祿 when a person is pressed by anxious cares he tries to seek emoluments.

碩 人 之 藹 that great man with such a look of hunger.

K'O.　　　(흐)

(K'oh)

恪 4.5.　Reverent; respectful. To reverence. Also read
3400　ch'ioh[4.5].

恪 守 準 繩 faithfully to keep the correct way.

恪 守 規 範 reverently to observe the rules of conduct.

恪 恭 己 職 respectfully to attend to the duties of one's office.

恪 遵 to render respectful obedience.

謹 恪 very respectful.

渴 2.5.　To thirst. Thirsty, parched. Also read k'eh[2.5].
3401

渴 仰 longing to see another.

渴 想 or 渴 念 or 渴 慕 to long for—as for an absent friend.

渴 想 之 極 How I have longed for you?

渴 懷 ardent longing.

[5]渴 欲 aspired to.

渴·死 dying of thirst; extremely thirsty.

渴 病 or 消 渴 病 diabetes. See 糖 No. 6121—2.

渴 睡 漢 a very sleepy person.

渴 葬 to bury in haste without selecting a lucky day, etc.

[10]渴 賞 thirsting for rewards.

渴 雨 prolonged drought.

口 渴 thirsty.

嗜 義 如 渴 thirsting for righteousness.

解 渴 to allay thirst.

飲 鴆 止 渴 to drink poison to allay thirst.

(a) Read chich[4.5].　**Water dried up.**

渴 澤 a dried-up lake or marsh.

水 渴 water dried up.

搕 1.5.　To strike. To take in the hand. ≡ 3405.
3402

搕 扁 to flatten.

搕 碎 to smash to pieces.

(a) Read o[1.5].　**To cover.**

溘 4.5.　Suddenly; from whence comes:—to die.
3403

溘 死 to die.

溘 然 suddenly.

溘 逝 to die.

形 神 溘 謝 his form and his spirit have passed away.

朝 露 溘 至 the morning dew comes suddenly.

(a) To bump against. Inter. 磕 No. 3405.

塘 水 聲 溘 溘 the sound of the water against the sides of the pond.

(b) Used to express intense cold.

沙 堤 十 里 寒 溘 溘 for ten li along the sandy embankment in the bitter cold.

瞌 2.5.　Sleepy from fatigue.
3404

瞌 眼 the eyes heavy with sleep.

瞌 睡 to doze.

瞌 睡 來·了 he is getting drowsy.

磕 1.5.　To strike stones together. To hit against, to bump. Also read k'êh[1.5].
3405

磕 出 to knock out.

磕 打 to clean a box by knocking it.

磕 烟 灰 to knock the ashes from a pipe.

磕[4] 瓜 子[3] to crack and eat melon-seeds.

[5]磕 碰 to clash; to bump against.

磕 絆 hindrances; obstacles.

磕 頭[6] the ceremony of the kotow, made by prostrating and knock-

---

ing the head on the ground—the phrase often means, "Many thanks."

殼 壳 殼 1.5.　The husk, skin or shell of fruits; the shell of eggs; the exuviæ of snakes, insects, etc., the shells of molluscs.
3406

殼 灰 lime made from burnt shells.

空 殼 an empty shell—a fraud.

蛋 殼 egg-shell.

表 殼 a watch-case.

面 殼 a mask.

㲄 1.5.　Egg-shell.
3407

KOU.　　　(쑷)

(Keo)

亅 [1]　A barb. Vertical stroke ending in a hook. Radical 6. Read chüeh[2]. To mark off.
3408

勾 亅 to mark off criminals for execution.

勾 [1]　To hook, to entice, to inveigle; thus:—to arrest.
3409　Distinguish 句 No. 1541, note No. 1541-A.

勾·上 我·的 心·事·來 you have anticipated my idea.

勾 使 messengers sent to bring souls to Hades.

勾 引 or 勾 挑 to entice illicitly.

勾 情 intrigue, illicit intercourse.

[5]勾·搭 to form an illicit connection; to entice others.

勾 欄 the balustrade to a bridge built over the Yellow River by the 吐 谷 渾—later used to designate the prostitutes' quarter.

勾 欄 甚 嚴 飾 the balustrade, as above, was very imposing.

勾 生·意 to fish for custom.

勾 留 to be detained.

[10]勾·當 business, affairs; to manage affairs.

勾·當 公 事 回 returned after attending to his public business.

勾 結 警 隊 got the police in league with them—brigands.

勾 股 弦 the shorter and longer sides of a triangle and the base, respectively.

勾 脂 粉 entangled with women.

[15] 勾 芒 神 to worship an agricultural god at the beginning of spring.

勾 見 to have illicit intercourse with.

勾 通 or 勾 串 to join in a plot; secretly connected.

勾 魂 to bewitch.

(a) To mark off; to punctuate.

勾·去·了 to mark off a passage.

勾 決 to mark names in a list of criminals indicating those to be executed.

勾 消 (or 銷) to cancel.

一 筆 勾 消 cancelled by a stroke of the pen.

勾 除 to mark off for rejection.

峋 [3]
3410
A hill in Hunan.

峋 嶁 山 the main peak of 衡 山. *See* 嶁 No. 4141.

拘 [1]
3411
To collect; to join together. See 拘 No. 1542. Inter. 勾 No. 3409, 鉤 No. 3417.

拘 手 to join in collusion.
拘 賬 to check an account.
拘 通 to be in collusion.
拘 連 to unite; to connect; to rabbet together.

(a) To grasp. To hook.

拘 執 to seize.
拘 拿 to seize.
拘 束 to restrain; to coerce.
拘 牽 to drag along.
拘 留 to detain.

枸 [3]
3412
A kind of aspen, etc.

枸 杞 (or 忌) *Lysium chinense*.

(a) Read *chü*[3]. A tree, see below.

枸 櫞 or 香 櫞 *Citrus medica*, an acid variety of orange.

枸 櫞 酸 citric acid.
枸 骨 holly.

狗 [3]
3413
A dog. Term of contempt.

狗 不 嫌 家 貧 dogs do not despise a poor home.
狗 偷 a petty theft.
狗 叫 or 狗 吠 dogs barking.
狗 咬 破·的 dogs bite the ragged—beggars.
[5] 狗 嗄 vomiting of dogs.
一 隻 狗 a dog.
狗 寶 bezoar from dogs.
狗 尾 續 貂 to join a dog's tail to sable—incongruous.
狗 屠 a dog-butcher.
[10] 狗 熊 the small black Tibetan bear.
狗 牙 (齒) dog-toothed—of patterns, irregular.
狗 獾 the badger.
狗 癲 (or 瘋) rabies.
狗 腿·子 nickname for *yamen* runners.
[15] 狗 苟 exceedingly easy-going; improper.
狗 荳·子 dog-ticks.
狗 蚤 fleas.
狗 蠅 dog-flies.
狗 賊 a pilferer; thief.
[20] 狗 醫 veterinary surgeon for dogs.
狗 頭 鷹 a vulture.
狗 馬 dog and horse—term formerly used by statesmen of themselves.
下 狗 to have puppies.
哈·吧 狗 Pekingese dogs; bulldogs.
[25] 善 狗 a gelded dog.
喪 家 之 狗 a dog without a home—miserable and distressed.
海 狗 a kind of seal.
牙 狗 male dog.
獵 狗 hound, hunting-dog.
[30] 瘋 狗 mad dog.
走 狗 term of abuse, the hunting-dog—henchman, satellite, underling.

騍 狗 a bitch.

笱 [3]
3414
A basket trap for fish, placed in the opening of a weir.

耇 [3]
3415
Old, wizened.

耇 老 infirm; in second childhood.
耇 長 (*chang*[3]) elders.
羞 耇 to care for the aged.
黃 耇 gray and wizened.

苟 [3]
3416
Illicit. Careless. Of small importance.

苟 且 careless; carelessness; improper; lacking foresight.
苟 且 了[3]事 to do a thing carelessly, slovenly.
苟 免 to shirk.
苟 合 illicit intercourse.
[5] 苟 同 without a mind of one's own; easily agreeing with the opinions of others.
苟 安 improper ease; fool's paradise.
苟 安 度 日 a quiet, lazy life.
苟 延 to delay; to waste time.
苟 得 to obtain by foul means.
[10] 不 爲 苟 得 也 not willing to seek life by improper means.
苟 政 bad government.
苟 求 to seek pretexts for quarrels. 「life.
苟 活 a careless and dishonorable
苟 犯 to give offence recklessly.
[15] 苟 生 my life—of little value.
苟 磯 an obstacle, as a rock in a stream.
苟 笑 silly giggling without cause.
苟 簡 insignificant.
苟 言 easy, careless speech.
[20] 苟 賤 low, sordid, base, mean.
苟 進 heedlessly blundering in.
苟 難 (*nan*[4]) to shirk danger.

(a) If, only, if indeed.

苟 不 然 if it is not so.
苟 志 於 仁 矣 無 惡 也 if the will be truly set on virtue there will be no wicked actions.
苟 患 失 之 無 所 不 至 矣 if they are afraid of losing it, they will stick at nothing.
苟 日 新 日 日 新 if you can renovate yourself for one day, let there be daily renovation.
苟 能 如 此 if it can be thus.
苟 非 if it were not that....; unless there be.

鈎 鉤 [1]
3417
A hook, a barb, a sickle. To entice, to connect. Distinguish 鈎 No. 6279, 鉤 No. 1725.

鈎·住·了 hooked, detained.
鈎·出·來 hook it out.
鈎 帶 to fasten the girdle.
鈎。搭 or 勾。搭 to hook together; to inveigle.
⁵鈎 搭 連 環 closely l i n k e d; intimately associated.
鈎 格 or 鈎·子 a hook.
鈎 橾 a scaling-ladder.
鈎 止 or 鈎 留 to detain; to keep.
鈎 爪 talons.
¹⁰鈎 生 魂 to invoke spirits.
鈎 誘 to beguile; to entice.
鈎 針 a crochet hook.
鈎 黨 to form cliques.
帳 鈎 curtain hooks.
雙 鈎 double hooks—bound feet.

(a) To draw in outline.

鈎 勒 drawing or writing in outline.
鈎 勒 形 廓 to trace a design in outline, in the style of an etching or engraving.
鈎 染 to draw an outline and fill in the colour afterwards.
鈎 描 to trace an outline.
雙 鈎 字 form of character like 字

(b) To search into.

鈎 深 致 遠 to go deeply into abstruse subjects.
鈎 稽 to audit; to search into.
鈎 索 義 理 to search out the principles of a thing.

雊⁴
3418　　The crowing of a pheasant.

够⁴
夠　　Enough, fully; quite. Inter. next.
3419

够·不·够·呢 is there enough?
够·得 很 abundantly sufficient.
够 纏·的 a troublesome man.

彀⁴　Enough, adequate. Fully, quite. Used with preceding.
3420　Distinguish 穀 No. 3490.

彀 一 斤 fully a catty.
彀 三 里 地 quite three *li*.
彀 sufficient; enough.
彀 受·的 enough to bear; bad enough for once.

⁵彀 數 enough for the purpose.
彀 用 enough for use.
不 彀 本 not sufficient to pay the cost.
不 彀 用 insufficient.
不 能·彀 unable to.

(a) To shoot, to draw a bow to the full.

彀 者 archers.

垢⁴
3421　　Dirt, filth, disgrace.

垢 穢 or 垢 汚 dirty, foul.
含 垢 to endure shame.
洗 垢 to cleanse away filth—to reform.
無 垢 free from stains—a pearl, a symbol of Buddha.

姤⁴　To pair, to copulate. One of the eight diagrams.
3422　Distinguish 妒 No. 6503.

姤 交 sexual intercourse.

(a) Good.

其 人 彝 姤 they are inclined to goodness.

詬
詢⁴　A sense of shame; to shame.
3423

詬 感 之 情 sentiments of shame and thankfulness.
詬 病 ashamed; mortification.

(a) To abuse, to rail at.

詬 厲 to abuse harshly.
詬 怒 to speak angrily.
詬 詈 to vilify.
詬 罵 to curse.
相 詬 vituperation.

緱¹　The cord-binding on the hilt of a sword.
3424

冓⁴
3425　　Ten billions. A room.

媾⁴　A second marriage; to wed. Love, favour.
3426

媾 合 coition.
媾 和 to negotiate for peace.
媾 精 sexual fertilization.
交 媾 sexual intercourse.
⁵媒 媾 a go-between.
昏 媾 marriage alliance.

搆⁴　To pull; to drag. To reach to, to implicate. Inter. next.
3427

搆·不 着 I cannot reach it.
搆 兵 to be at war; to move troops.
搆 和 to negotiate peace.
搆 廬 節 Feast of Tabernacles.
⁵搆 思 to puzzle about; to meditate.
搆 怨 to contract dislike.
搆 文 to compose literature.
搆 禍 to bring disaster upon oneself.
搆 訟 to go to law.
¹⁰結 搆 connection, sequence; a composition.

構⁴　To roof with beams; thus: —to unite. Inter. preceding.
3428

構 木 to roof with boughs.
構 火 to take fire.
構 精 sexual fertilization.

(a) To plot, to implicate.

構 亂 to stir up disorders.
構 怨 to arouse animosity.
構 煽 to incite to mischief.
構 陷 to scheme in order to bring another into trouble, to implicate another.

(b) To complete.

構 成 to complete.
構 成 分 constituent part.
構 約 to complete an agreement.
構 造 to build; a frame.
構 難 to bring trouble upon oneself.

溝¹　A water-course; a drain; a ditch; an aqueduct.
3429

溝 中 瘠 died of starvation in the ditch.
溝·子 or 溝 眼 a ditch, a drain, a gutter.
溝 渠 a ditch

溝 滿 濠 平 watercourses full—abundant rain.
陰 溝 a covered drain.
陽 溝 an open drain.

(a) Penetrating.

溝 通 今 古 to have a thorough knowledge of past and present.

覯 [4] To see or meet suddenly. To see. Unforeseen.
3430

覯 見 to meet with.
罕 覯 rarely seen.

(a) Inter. 構 No. 3428—B.

覯 成 其 事 to complete the business.

購 [4] To buy, to hire.
3431

購 入 bought in.
購 拿 or 購 緝 offer rewards as an inducement for capture.
購 捕 to offer a reward for the arrest.
購 料 to buy material.
[5]購 求 to offer a reward.
購 用 to purchase for use.
購 綫 to buy a clue—to the capture of criminals.
購 貨 之 定 錢 earnest money.
購 買 to buy.
[10]購 買 力 purchasing power.
購 辦 to buy up wholesale.
購 運 to purchase and forward goods.
自 購 寃 仇 to bring enmity upon oneself.

遘 [4] To meet with; to come upon suddenly.
3432

遘 疾 to meet with sickness.
遘 遇 or 遘 逢 a chance meeting; to fall in with.

韝 [1] The armlet and glove of a falconer.
3433

射 韝 armguard of an archer.

口 [3] An opening; a mouth; a hole; an aperture; a port.
3434 Speech, talk. Radical 30. N.A.

口 不 應 心 speech not agreeing with the heart—false.
口 不 穩 當 an unstable mouth—one who cannot keep secrets.
口 中 雌 黄 yellow ochre in the mouth—ochre was formerly used for erasing, thus the phrase signifies a person who has no mind of his own, and is always changing his ideas.
口 令 word of command; military password.
[5]口 供 depositions.
口 信 a verbal message.
口 傳 tradition, report, hearsay.
口 內 炎 stomatitis.
口 北 Mongolia.
[10]口 占 to dictate; to improvise.
口 吃 to stammer.
口 吻 自 然 ease in speaking.

口 味 taste.
口 器 mouth of insects.
[15]口 外 outside the Great Wall; Mongolia; outside the port.
口 外 引 費 pilotage.
口 子 an opening; a mouth.
口 蜜 腹 劍 a honeyed mouth but a sword in the belly.
口 實 things to eat; cause for talk.
[20]口 小 a young mouth—of horses.
口 岸 a port.
口 徑 diameter of the mouth of things; calibre of guns, etc.
口 德 to speak well of.
口 快 quick and thoughtless in speech; blunt.
[25]口 才 eloquence.
口 技 to imitate; to mimic.
口 授 verbal instruction without books; to dictate.
口 是 心 非 to say one thing and mean another—hypocrisy.
口 業 mischief-making; to live by stirring up trouble, etc.
[30]口 操 河 南 口 音 his speech has a Honan accent.
口 氣 talk; expression; tone: a sigh.
口 氣 不 好 the style is not good.
口 渴 thirsty.

口 率 *per capita* rate.
[35]口 痰 saliva.
口 瘡 a sore in the mouth.
口 皮 skins from Mongolia.
口 碑 public sentiment—the mouths of the people commemorate his virtue, there is no need for stone tablets. [to eat.
[40]口 福 luck in having good things
口 答 verbal answers.
口 糧 or 口 食 rations; provisions.
口 給 smart speech.
口 腔 cavity of the mouth.
口 腹 mouth and stomach—necessities of life.
[45]口 腹 主 義 epicureanism.
口 腹 之 奉 being a slave to appetite.
口 腹 之 累 the trouble of getting enough of the necessities of life.
口 若 懸 河 his speech flows like a cataract.
口 蓋 the palate; roof of the mouth.
[50]口 號 a signal; password; slogan.
口 血 未 乾 before the blood of the oath is dry—breaking an oath almost before it is made.
口 袋 a sack; a bag.
口 角 or 口 舌 wrangling; altercation.
口 角 春 風 to say a good word for another.
[55]口 訣 secret passed on orally.
口 詞 depositions; evidence.
口 試 oral examinations.
口 說 無 憑 mere verbal agreement is not evidence—used in deeds, etc.
口 調 denunciations.
[60]口 譯 to construe a passage. [soned.
口 賦 poll-tax. 口 輕 lightly sea-
口 輕 的 easy-mouthed—of horses. Also young-mouthed.
口 述 oral method.
口 過 faults of speech.
[65]口 錢 poll-tax.
口 音 accent; enunciation.
口 頭 oral communication.
口 頭 交 mere outward friendliness.
口 頭 審 理 oral examination.
[70]口 頭 禪 mere conventionalisms; empty talk; platitudes; slogans.
口 頭 證 據 oral proof or evidence.
口 風 breath; sentiment; air.
↑ 口 紅 lip-stick; a.c. 唇 膏.

口 風 琴 harmonica or mouth-organ.

口 鼻 mouth and nose—features.

75 口。齒 好 clear enunciation.

一 口 兩 舌 double-tongued.

一 口 櫥 a cupboard.

一 口 水 a mouthful of water.

一 口 煙 a smoke.

80 一 口 缸 a water-jar.

人。口 number of persons.

借 口 to offer as a pretext.

利 口 of shrewd, sharp speech.

兩 口·子 a married couple.

85 可 口 pleasant to the taste.

每 口 計 算 *per capita* calculations.

海 口 a port on the coast.

牲·口 domestic animals, especially horses, donkeys or mules.

還 口 to retort.

90 門 口ㄦa doorway.

開·了 口·子 burst its banks; made an opening.

開 口 to open the mouth; to make an opening; to sharpen a knife; unrounded. (*phonetics*)

叩 3435 3.4. To knock, to bump the head. To ask, to pray for.

叩 其 姓 名 asked his name.

叩 其 脛 struck him on the shin.

叩 問 to ask for.

叩 喜 I implore every joy for you.

5 叩 徑 with all respects.

叩 恩 to plead for mercy.

叩 拜 to worship; to pay respects to.

叩 求 or 叩 乞 to beg for; to beseech.

叩 稟 to make a humble petition.

10 叩 見 to visit a superior.

叩 請 to implore.

叩 謁 to pay a visit of respect.

叩 謝 to offer earnest thanks.

叩 辭 to take leave of a superior.

15 叩 門 to knock at a door.

叩 關 to knock at a closed door; to invade.

叩 頭 蟲 snap-beetles.

叩 首 or 叩 頭 to knock the head in reverence, *kotow.*

叩 馬 to whip up a horse.

(a) To set forth; to display.

叩 其 兩 端 而 竭 焉 to " set it forth from beginning to end and exhaust it."

扣 3436 3.4. To rap, to knock.

扣 其 背 slapped him on the back.

扣 捄 to pound.

扣 邊 to invade the frontier.

扣 門 to knock at a door.

扣 關 to invade a country.

(a) To rein in; to fasten; to button; to buckle. N.A.

扣·上 to fit on.

扣·下 to detain.

扣·住 stopped; held.

扣·子 a button.

5 扣 帶 to fasten a belt.

扣 留 to detain; to intern; to confiscate.

扣 留 關 棧 to detain in bond.

扣 繫 to make fast.

扣 衣·服 to button garments.

10 扣·起·來 fasten it back.

扣 針 safety-pin.

扣 鈕 to fasten buttons.

扣 馬 to rein in a horse.

一 扣 線 a skein of silk.

(b) To deduct, to discount.

扣 回 to deduct from, to repay.

扣 折 or 扣 算 or 扣 出 or 扣 計 扣 抵 to discount.

扣 數 to reduce an account; money deducted.

扣 色 discount on account of quality of silver.

扣 除 to subtract; to deduct.

扣 錢 to deduct money; the total; the amount charged.

扣·頭 or 扣 水 discount.

扣 錢 三 角 the total charge is 30cts.

八 五 扣 15% discount.

(c) Name of native cotton cloth.

扣 布 narrow cotton cloth, T-cloths.

扣 牯 3437 4 Domesticated animals.

紐 3438 4 A button; a plaited knob. To fasten; to hook back.

紐·上 鈕·子 loop on the button.

釦 3439 3.4. To engrave; to chase. A button or clasp. Inter. 扣 No. 3436.

釦 口 a button-hole.

釦·子 or 鈕 釦 buttons.

剾 3440 1 To pick out with a knife.

彄 3441 1 The nock at the end of a bow.

彄 環 archer's thumb-ring.

摳 3442 1 To raise. To feel for.

摳·不 出 來 unable to get a grip on a thing.

摳 衣 升 堂 lifted his dress and ascended the hall.

(a) To scrape.

摳 破 to scrape a hole in anything.

摳 鑿 scraping and cutting—persistence.

膒 3443 1 Deeply-sunk eyes.

寇 寇 3444 4 Tyrannical, cruel. To rob, to plunder. Banditti; thieves; highwaymen.

寇 攘 to rob and steal.

寇 盜 or 寇 賊 insurgents; outlaws; banditti.

司 寇 ancient Minister of Crime.

海 寇 pirates.

蔲 3445 4 Cardamom seeds.

蔲 仁 or 荳 蔲 nutmeg.

草 荳 蔲 Chinese cardamoms.

荳 蔲 花 mace.

彀 3446 4 Fledglings.

彀 音 the chirping of fledglings.

KU.　(ㄍㄨ)

古[3] Ancient; antique; old. Distinguish 右 No. 7541.
3447

古之學者爲[4]己 in ancient times men studied in order to improve themselves.

古之聞人 an ancient of great reputation.

古事 an old story; a legend.

古人 the ancients; a dead man.

[5]古今 ancient and modern.

古代 antiquity.

古來 from of old.

古典 or 典故 an allusion; a quotation. 古典主義 classicism.

古刹 ancient monastery.

[10]古制 ancient regime.

古古·的 ancient; old-fashioned.

古史 ancient history.

古字 ancient characters.

古帝壙 the pyramids.

[15]古·怪 strange; peculiar; very.

古文 ancient writings; ancient essays.

古文學 paleography.

古昔 of old; in times gone by.

古時 or 古朝 in ancient times.

[20]古木 ancient trees.

古板 bigoted.

古樸 primitive and simple.

古磁 ancient porcelain.

古禮 ancient customs.

[25]古稀 seventy years old. *See* No. 2421—B.8.

古翠 patina which comes through age.

古老 an aged man; antiquated.

古·董玩器 curios; antiques.

古訓是式 the lessons of antiquity are his pattern.

[30]古語 archaisms.

古象 the mammoth.

古蹟 relics; sacred places; ancient remains.

古道 old paths; reserved; retiring.

古鄉 or 古里 one's old home-district.

[35]古銅 ancient bronzes.

古風 primitive ways.

上古 earliest times.

歸古 to go to his fathers—to die.

古巴 Cuba. (transliteration)

估[3] To estimate; to value; to consider; to guess.
3448

估中 to make an accurate guess.

估值 to value; value.

估價 to estimate a price.

估定 to value; to decide a price.

[5]估客 a trader.

估摸 to conjecture; to imagine.

估猜 to guess; to conjecture.

估算 to estimate.

估計 to calculate; to estimate; to give an opinion.

[10]估量 to suppose; to give an estimate.

估量單 estimate; pro-forma invoice.

估需 estimated cost.

照估價 *ad valorem.*

(a) Read *ku*[4]. Old.

估衣 secondhand clothes.

估衣舖 secondhand-clothing shop.

咕[1] To mutter, to chatter or hum.
3449

咕咕唧唧 whispering.

咕°囔 to mutter.

咕°嚕 to mumble.

固[4] Firm, strong, established. Assuredly, decidedly. Originally, obstinately. Chronic.
3450

固也 assuredly.

固亂 to strengthen misrule.

固力 rigidity.

固可 can surely.

[5]固哉高叟 How stupid was old *Kao!*

固國 to strengthen the nation.

固城 the defences of a city.

固·執 obstinate; self-opinionated; perverse.

固·執不移 fixed in his own ideas.

[10]固·執不通 obstinate and perverse.

固多 very many.

固存 to strengthen the things that remain.

固守 to persist; to guard carefully.

固宜 assuredly so; it should be so.

[15]固定 firm, fixed, stationary.

固定資本 fixed capital.

固形體 solid masses.

固應 positively; must.

固所願也 certainly, it is what I want.

[20]固持己見 holding fast to his own opinion.

固有權 inherent rights.

固然 really; unquestionably; of course; to be sure.

固疾 chronic disease.

固窮 to endure poverty.

[25]固結 to strengthen; consolidate.

固結團體 a consolidated body.

固而如此 it certainly is so.

固請 a strong invitation.

固質 solids.

[30]固辭 a firm refusal.

固陋 vulgar; rustic.

固體 solids—not liquids.

堅·固 firm; secure; strong and lasting.

疾固也 I detest obstinacy—said by Confucius.

閉固 closely shut up.

痼|[4]
痞| Chronic disease.
3451

痼疾 a chronic complaint.

錮[4] To run metal into cracks; to close; to stop; to restrain.
3452 Inter. preceding.

錮疾 chronic disease.

錮蔽 stopped up.

錮身 to fetter a prisoner.

禁錮 to confine; to keep in custody.

姑[1] A girl. A paternal aunt. A maiden.
3453

姑丈 or 姑·夫 husband of father's sister.

姑·娘 a young lady; Miss; a girl.

姑婆 sisters of a husband's father.

姑嫂 sisters-in-law.

[5]姑媽 a father's sister.

姑母 or 姑·姑 father's sisters; paternal aunts.

姑爺 a son-in-law.

姑祖爹娘 grandparents on the mother's side; aunt's husband's parents.

姑舅 uncle on the mother's side.

[10]姑表兄弟 first cousins when the father of one and the mother of the other are brother and sister.

↑姑洗 (-*hsien*[3]) a classical pitch corresponding in function to E.

大 姑 小 姑 father's elder and younger sisters.
尼·姑 Buddhist nuns.
道 姑 Taoist nuns.

(a) **To be lenient. To tolerate. To act under pressure.**

姑 妄 carelessly.
姑 寬 forbearing; lenient.
姑 念 indulgent towards; having kindly feelings.
姑 恕 to forbear; to be lenient.
姑 息 or 姑 容 indulgent; easy with; to spoil a child.
姑 息 養 姦 over-indulgence nourishes evil.

(b) **Meanwhile.**

姑 不 具 論 we will not go into the matter.
姑 且 for the time being.
姑 舍³ 是 let us drop the subject.
姑 待 明 日 just wait till tomorrow.

(c) **Euphonic particle.**

菇¹
3454　**Mushrooms, fungus.**

土 菇 or 草 菇 mushrooms.
蘇 菇 mushrooms.

故⁴
3455　**A reason, a cause, a pretext. Consequently.**
Inter. 古 No. 3447.

故 以 wherefore; therefore.
故 入 said when the apportioned punishment is heavier than the crime.
故 出 said when the apportioned punishment is lighter than the crime.
故 失 said when a decision does not fit the case, either being too light or too heavy.
⁵故°意 of purpose; with intent.
故°意 殺 人 罪 premeditated murder.
故 時 措 之 宜 也 hence whenever he employs—those virtues —they will be right.
故 此 or 是 故 or 故 而 on this account; therefore.
故 殺 intentional murder.
¹⁰故 民 不 失 望 hence the people are not disappointed.

故 犯 or 故 違 wilful offence.
故 發 此 歎 hence he uttered this lament.
故 設 此 問 hence he asked him about this supposititious case.
何 故 for what cause?
¹⁵無 故 without a cause.
細 故 trifling matters.
緣·故 a cause; a reason.

(a) **Old, ancient, formerly. To die.** Inter. 古 No. 3447.

故·了 died.
故·事 a story.
故 人 or 故 交 an old friend; a deceased friend.
故 典 a quotation, a precedent; anecdote.
⁵故 吾 my former self.
故 土 one's native place.
故 在 is still in existence.
故 墟 one's home-land.
故 夫 my late husband.
¹⁰故 家 my home; ancient family.
故 常 customary.
故 態 usual attitude.
故 智 old schemes and tricks.
故 物 old things.
¹⁵故 知 an old acquaintance.
故 紙 waste paper.
故 老 old; aged ministers of State.
故 舊 old; of standing; an old friend; long.
故 舊 不 遺 not to be neglectful of old friends.
²⁰故 蹈 前 轍 continuing to walk in the old ruts.
故 鄉 (or 里) my native village.
如 故 as of old; like old friends.
大 故 death of a parent or a ruler.
病 故 died of disease.
²⁵身 故 died. A.c. 已 故.

(b) **Fact, phenomena.**

故 實 former facts.
故 者 以 利 爲 本 the value of a phenomenon is in its being natural.

沽¹
3456　**To buy and sell.**

沽 名 釣 譽 to fish for praise and reputation.
沽 激 to do something to attract attention in order to get a reputation.

沽 物 inferior articles, as being hawked for sale.
沽 酒 to deal in spirits; wine bought from stores.

牯³
3457　**A bull; a male.**

牯 牛 a bull.
牯 嶺 Kuling, mountain resort in Kiangsi.

罟³
3458　**A net for birds or fish. To snare, thus:—to implicate.**

網 罟 fishing-nets.
罪 罟 the net for crime.

羖³
3459　**A ram; a sheep of a black and white colour.**

羖 羊 a ram.

蛄¹
3460　**The mole-cricket.**

螻 蛄 or 蟪 蛄 the mole-cricket.

詁 3.4.
3461　**To explain; to comment.**

詁 傳 (chuan⁴) commentary.

轂¹
3462　**A wheel; to revolve.**

轂 轆 a wheel.

辜¹
3463　**Crime, a fault; guilt. To be ungrateful for.**

辜 恩 ungrateful for kindness.
辜 月 the eleventh lunar month.
辜·負 ingratitude; to be ungrateful.
辜 負 恩 典 insensible to favours.
無 辜 the innocent.

酤⁴
3464　**To deal in spirits.**

鈷³ 3465 A flat-iron for warming. Used for Co, the symbol for Cobalt.

鴣¹ 3466 A partridge. See No. 262.

股胍³ 3467 The thighs; the haunches; the rump; thus:—a share, a portion, a division.

股份 shares in a company.
股份兌換 exchange of stocks.
股份公司 joint-stock corporation.
股份掮客 stock-brokers.
⁵股份有限公司 limited-liability company.
股份讓與 transfer of shares.
股份銀行 joint-stock bank.
股分 or 股子 a share; a part in.
股利 dividends.
¹⁰股夥 a partner.
股弁 very scared.
股息 dividend.
股息票 dividend-warrants.
除股息 ex-dividend.
¹⁵股戰而慄 trembling with fear.
股掌 an assistant.
股本 share-capital.
股東 shareholder.
股東總會 general meeting of shareholders.
²⁰股栗欲墮 shuddering with fear, about to fall.
股款 share-capital.
招募股款 to call for share-capital.
股票 share-certificates.
股票更換 transfer of shares.
²⁵股票經記 stock-broking.
股肱 legs and arms—assistants, ministers.
股金 share-capital.
股長³ (or 員) head of a department.
優先股 preference-shares.
³⁰派股 to allot shares.

(a) N.A. for a puff; a band, etc.
一股熱氣 a blast of hot air.
一股匪徒 a band of robbers.

嘏³ 3468 Felicity, prosperity. Large and strong. Also read chia³.

祝嘏 to offer a felicitous wish on birthdays.

盬³ 3469 A pot, an earthen pot.

盬子 or 砂盬子 an earthen pot.

孤¹ 3470 Fatherless; lonely; solitary; an orphan. Alone.

孤介 self-confident, unwilling to submit to others; unwilling to toady to others.
孤兒² or 孤子³ a fatherless child.
孤兒院 orphanage.
孤另 solitary; alone.
⁵孤哀子 father- and mother-less orphan, used on obituaries. Cf. 3.10.
孤單 or 孤獨 or 孤寒 solitary, alone, neglected.
孤單無二 the only one.
孤城 a city which has been cut off from communications.
孤墳 a lonely grave.
¹⁰孤孀 orphan and widow.
孤子歸宗 a son going back to his father's family, when his mother re-marries.
孤孤單單的 single; all alone.
孤家 I, the emperor.
孤寂 solitary; lonely.
¹⁵孤山 a solitary rock or hill.
孤峭 a solitary peak—an outstanding man.
孤微 poor and humble.
孤忠 an honest, loyal-hearted man.
孤恩 ungrateful.
²⁰孤憤 a pessimistic spirit; misanthropic.
孤懸 completely cut off from all places.
孤拔 isolation; outstanding.
孤掌難鳴 one palm cannot clap and make a sound—cannot do without assistance.
孤本 a rare volume; a book of which there is only one copy.
²⁵孤枕 to sleep alone.
孤標 a solitary tree.
孤樹不成林 one tree does not make a forest.
孤注一擲 stake all on a single throw.
孤燈 lonely, only the lamp for company; a solitary lamp.
³⁰孤癖 (or 僻) eccentric, peculiar.
孤種 orphaned; lonely.

孤立 solitary; single-handed.
孤孽 an orphan.
孤老 forlorn; desolate.
³⁵孤臣 a minister in whom the ruler has no confidence.
孤舟 a solitary boat.
孤苦人 a lonely, wretched man.
孤虛王相 unlucky and lucky—terms used in divination.
孤負 to be ungrateful.
⁴⁰孤身一人 solitary.
孤迥 an exceptional man.
孤門獨戶 to dwell alone.
孤陋 scholarship and experience very limited.
孤雲野鶴 a recluse.
⁴⁵孤零 scattered; isolated.
孤露 to lose both parents when young.
孤高 to think too highly of oneself; far from the madding crowd.
孤魂 a spirit for whom there is none to offer sacrifices.
孤魂節 festival of orphaned spirits on the 15th of the 7th lunar month.
⁵⁰撫孤 to comfort and support the fatherless.
託孤 to commit an orphan to the care of another.

箛¹ 3471 Name of a bamboo. Trumpet used as a signal for chariots to start and stop.

箛聲 the sound of the trumpet as above.

罛¹ 3472 A large fishing-net.

觚¹ 3473 A goblet. Angular; an angle, a corner. A law, a rule. A writing-tablet.

觚法 tactics; rule or plan.
觚不觚觚哉觚哉 A goblet that is not a goblet! (i.e., it being without corners) A goblet! A goblet!—name without reality.

箍¹ 3474 A hoop, a belt. To surround. To wind round. Also read k'u¹.

箍子 or 篏箍 a hoop, a fillet.

箍 嘴 muzzle over the mouth of an animal.
箍 桶 to put a hoop on a bucket.
箍 綻 the hoop has broken.
打 箍 to work as a cooper.
花 箍 a floral wreath.

蠱 **3 Internal worms. Insanity. Poison, see below—5.**
3475

蠱 惑 之 疾 insanity caused through sexual exhaustion.
蠱 惑 人 心 to seduce men.
蠱 毒 poisonous; noxious.
蠱 脹 or 蠱 腹 dropsy.
⁵埋 蠱 to put all sorts of poisonous insects, etc., into a vessel, cover it up and leave it for a year; the insects devour each other until one only is left, this is *ku*,—there are also other explanations.
埋 蠱 厭 人 to resort to magic in order to get rid of others—either by poison as above, or by making a straw figure of a man and pouring water upon it or sticking knives, etc., into it—it may be summed up as witchcraft.

賈 **3 A resident-trader. To trade.**
3476

賈 售 to sell.
賈 市 a market.
賈 買 to purchase.
商 賈 mercantile men.

(a) Read *chia*³. **The price of anything. A name. A surname.**

賈 請 見 而 解 之 *Kia* asked that he might see (Mencius) and relieve (the king's feeling of shame).

雇 僱 **4 To hire, to engage.**
3477

雇 主 employer.
雇 人 to hire persons; a hireling.
雇 備 employed for wages.
雇 募 to engage—as soldiers.
⁵雇 員 underlings in government offices.

雇 定 to arrange for the employment of.
雇 工 a hired labourer; to hire labour.
雇 搭 to take a passage on a boat.
雇 用 to engage; to charter—as a boat.
¹⁰雇 約 contract of employment.
雇 脚 夫 to hire coolies.
雇 船 to hire or charter a boat.
雇 船 證 書 deed of charter of a ship.
雇 賃 to rent a house.
¹⁵雇 車 to hire a cart or barrow.
雇 備 兵 mercenary troop.

(a) **Also read *hu*⁴. A bird akin to the quail.**

顧 顧 **4 To care for, to look after. To regard. To turn the head round to look.**
3478

顧 不 住 I cannot look after it.
顧 兔 to look at the moon.
顧 全 大 局 in order to come to a satisfactory arrangement of the whole matter.
顧 及 to take into account.
⁵顧 問 to think of; to advise; an advisor.
顧 問 質 an advisory capacity.
顧 嘴 to have regard only for things to eat; burdened with the struggle to live.
顧 守 to care for and guard.
顧 客 a customer.
¹⁰顧 家 to care for the home.
顧 己 to care for oneself and one's own interests.
顧 影 to turn and admire one's own shadow; to have a good opinion of oneself.
顧 後 to reflect upon the after effects; to lay by—as money.
不 顧 後 regardless of the consequences.
¹⁵顧 復 to care for.
顧 忌 to fear; to avoid; scruples.
顧 念 to think of; to care for; regarding.
顧 恤 to have compassion on; to pity.
顧 惜 to shield; to screen; to pity.
²⁰顧 慮 consideration.
顧 慮 時 世 looking with anxiety at the present-day trend of affairs.

顧 指 a glance back and a move of the finger—instantly, quickly done.
顧 本 to be careful of one's capital; to give attention to things fundamental.
顧 盼 to gaze around.
²⁵顧 看 or 顧 視 to look after, to care for.
顧 瞻 to look after.
顧 繡 embroidery, from the famous woman of that name.
顧 臉 to care for one's reputation or "face."
顧 諟 天 之 明 命 he contemplated and studied the lucid decrees of Heaven.
³⁰顧 門 戶 caring for the reputation of the family.
顧 面 子 to have regard for good name or "face."
顧 頭 不 顧 尾 to act with no regard for consequences; to see only one aspect of an affair.
顧 體 面 having a regard for appearances.
主 顧 to patronize or deal regularly with; a regular customer.
³⁵內 顧 means of livelihood; to turn round and look in (the carriage when driving.)
反 顧 to look back.
四 顧 on all sides.
相 顧 in accord; in harmony.

(a) **An adversative particle, on the contrary; then; therefore.**

顧 上 先 下 後 耳 but it must first flow from those above to those below.
顧 如 是 乎 Is it indeed?
顧 忘 之 耶 Have you then forgotten it?
顧 而 and yet....

鼓 鼓 皷 **3 A drum. To drum, from whence comes:—to rouse; to swell; to bulge. Radical 207. (not the third form).**
3479

鼓 動 to rouse, to incite, to instigate.
鼓 勵 or 勉 勵 to stimulate; to encourage.
鼓 吹 to drum and blow—to incite; to encourage; to praise.

鼓 吹 革 命 to foment the revolution.
[5]鼓 感 to excite uncertainty or alarm.
鼓 手 or 鼓 使 or 吹 鼓 手 drummers.
鼓 掌 to clap the hands—to approve.
鼓 板 musical instruments.
鼓 架 a drum-stand.
[10]鼓 桴 a drumstick.
鼓 樓 a drum-tower.
鼓 樂 to play music. (-yüeh[4])
鼓 火 to blow up a fire.
鼓 瑟 drums and lutes; to play the lute.
[15]鼓 盪 to excite.
鼓 腹 well-fed and care-free.
鼓 膜 or 耳 鼓 the ear-drum.
鼓 舌 to speak evil; to flatter; to gossip.
鼓 舞 to exert oneself; to dance; to excite.
[20]鼓 行 to advance—drums beat the advance and gongs the retreat.
鼓 譟 a great hubbub; an uproar.
鼓 ·起 ·來 filled out—as a hose with water.
鼓 鐘 to strike a bell.
鼓 鑄 to melt metals.
[25]鼓 琴 一 聲 響 a hollow, reverberating sound.
打 鼓 or 擂 鼓 to beat drums.
擊 鼓 to beat a drum.
蘇 鼓 kettle-drums.

臌 [3] Dropsical swelling; puffy; bloated.
3480

臌 脹 swollen; puffed out.
臌 膨 膨 bloated.
水 臌 dropsy.

瞽 [3] Blind. Blind musicians.
3481

瞽 惑 to blind and mislead.
瞽 目 院 blind asylum.
瞽 瞍 Ku Sou, the name of Shun's father.
瞽 者 a blind man.
[5]瞽 言 (or 說) absurdities.
瞽 議 stupid discussions.
以 瞽 相 瞽 blind leading the blind.
盲 瞽 手 摸 識 字 finger-reading of the blind.

盲 瞽 拼 音 字 母 Braille letters for blind readers.
胎 瞽 born blind.

KU. (ㄍㄨ)
(Kuh)

汩 [4.5.] To float. Confused. To throw into disorder.
3482　Distinguish 汨 No. 7695.

汩 汩 sound of waves.
汩 沒 floating and sinking—up and down.
汩 於 私 欲 confused by lusts.
汩 陳 其 五 行 he threw the five elements into disorder.
汩 陳 是 非 to confuse right and wrong.

(a) Read mi[4.5]. A river in Hunan.

谷 [3.5.] A valley, a ravine. A hollow. Difficult. Radical
3483　150.

谷 口 a gorge.
谷 樹 the paper-mulberry, from the bark of which paper is made.
谷 水 a mountain stream.
谷 穴 the hollow behind the ankle.
[5]谷 風 the east wind.
山 谷 a ravine.
幽 谷 a dark valley.
窮 谷 utterly cut off; hemmed in.
進 退 維 谷 advance and retreat both difficult—in a dilemma.

(a) Read yü[4.5]. Name of a branch of the Hsien pei. See 鮮 No. 2716—A.

吐 谷 渾 a tribe which flourished during the T'ang dynasty and afterwards settled around Lob Nor.

梏 [4.5.] Manacles; fetters.
3484

梏 亡 fettered in mind by lusts.

(a) Read chio[4.5]. Straight.

鵠 [3.5.] The snow-goose. Hoary; white-haired.
3485

鵠 立 to stand on the lookout like a wild goose—said of sentinels.
鵠 面 菜 色 pale, emaciated.
鵠 面 鳩 形 haggard, emaciated.
鵠 髮 童 顏 white hair and a young countenance.

(a) A target.

鵠 的 [4] a target.
不 失 正 鵠 to hit the target.

骨 [3.5.] A bone. A framework, as of a fan or an umbrella.
3486　Anything hard enclosed in a soft covering. Radical 188.

骨 力 strength; firmness.
骨 學 osteology.
骨 尸 or 骨 屍 a corpse.
骨 折 fractures. (-shê[2])
[5]骨 架 frame; the skeleton.
骨 格 大 a large frame—as of a man.
骨 氣 breeding; nurture; inborn disposition; moral integrity.
骨 炭 animal-charcoal.
骨 牌 dominoes.
[10]骨 瘦 如 柴 thin and emaciated like a stick.
骨 盤 the pelvis.
骨 相 學 phrenology.
骨 立 stiff—of cloths; bony.
骨 節 joints; articulations of the bones.
[15]骨 肉 bone and flesh—kindred.
骨 肉 之 親 blood-relationship; near of kin.
骨 肉 兄 弟 brothers; blood-relatives.
骨 膜 periosteum.
骨 血 bone and blood—relations; children.
[20]骨 質 bone-substance.
骨 頓 enervated; weak. [fied.
骨 酥 肉 麻 paralyzed; electri-
骨 醉 helplessly intoxicated.
骨 霜 the bones were whitened.
[25]骨 ·頭 bone.
骨 ·頭 脫 節 dislocation of the joints.
骨 骼 a skeleton.
骨 髓 marrow.
傲 骨 a proud, stiff and unbending manner.
[30]反 骨 the prominence behind the ear; bump of pugnacity or rebellion.

忠骨 bone of a man killed in battle.
白骨 dry bones.
結骨 to set bones.
續骨 to unite a fracture.

3487 **楛**$^{2.5.}$ **A fine, white wood used for arrows.**

楛柮 (*tu*^{5}) short sticks used for burning into charcoal.

3488 **蓇**$^{4.5.}$ **Follicles of plants.**

3489 **鶻**$^{4.5.}$ **A migratory bird resembling the crested-lark. A falcon.**
Also read *hu*$^{4.5}$.

鶻眼 hawk-eyed.
鶻突而來 to pounce down like a hawk.
鶻落 the swoop of a falcon.

3490 **穀 / 穀**$^{3.5.}$ **Grain, corn.**
Distinguish 彀 No. 3420.

穀人 a farmer.
穀倉 a granary.
穀場 a threshing-floor.
穀子 spiked-millet.
5 穀實 grain.
穀槍 the awn of grain.
穀物進口法 corn-laws.
穀田 rice-fields.
穀秀 ripening crops.
10 穀種 (*chung*^{3}) seed-corn.
穀穗 an ear of corn or wheat.
穀草 rice-straw.
穀蟲 weevils.
穀道 the alimentary canal.
Also = 5172 H5.
15 穀雨 Grain Rains—a solar period, about April 20th—May 4th.
穀食饒足 foodstuffs in abundance.
五穀 cereals in general.
收穀 to harvest grain.
義穀 freely-distributed grain.
20 辟穀 see above—14.

(a) Lucky, good, happy.

穀善 good, excellent.
穀旦 a lucky day.
民莫不穀 the people are all happy.
不穀 a former depreciatory term [for "I" (by kings, etc.)

(b) Salary. To nourish.

穀育 to nourish.
穀祿 salary.

(c) Alive.

穀則異室 while alive we are dwelling apart.

3491 **轂**$^{3.5.}$ **The nave or hub of a wheel.**

轂·轆 or 輪轂 a wheel.
推轂 to give a man a push on; to assist.

K'U. (ㄎㄨ)

3492 **枯**^{1} **Withered, rotten, decayed. Dried wood.**

枯乾 or 枯焦 dried up.
枯朽 rotten.
枯株 a dry stump.
枯楊生稊 a dried poplar sends forth a shoot—an old man marries a young wife and has a son.
5 枯槁 decayed; attenuated.
形容枯槁 dried and wizened.
枯樹生花 a withered old tree puts forth flowers—rejuvenation.
枯瘠 thin and emaciated.
枯索 dead, lifeless.
10 枯竭 dried up—as a river.
枯腸 mentally dried up.
枯草 dried, withered grass.
枯萎 to decay; to fail in vigor.
枯葉蝶 the leaf-butterfly, which when resting looks exactly like a withered leaf.
15 枯骨 dried bones.
枯魚 a fish dying out of water—illustrative of poverty and great straits.
摧枯拉朽 to push decayed stumps down—easily done.

3493 **苦**^{3} **Bitter; thus:—sorrow, suffering; in bad circumstances; painstaking, earnest.**
Distinguish 若 No. 3126.

苦上加苦 adding sorrow to sorrow.
苦不堪言 unspeakable sufferings.
苦中作樂 joy in sorrow.
苦主 the injured person.
5 苦况 unhappiness.
苦人 a poor, wretched person.
苦似黃連 bitter as wormwood.
苦像 an unhappy appearance.
苦刑 torture; severe punishments.
10 苦力 to put forth severe effort, u.f. coolie, though it is not the origin of the word.
苦功 strenuous efforts—in study, etc.
苦勒 to oppress, to be harsh to.
苦勸 earnest exhortations.
苦口 bitter to the taste; faithful in exhortation.
15 苦口利於病 bitter to the taste but good for the complaint.
苦口婆心 faithful in remonstrance and kindly in heart.
苦味 a bitter flavour.
苦味丁幾 a bitter tonic medicine; bitter tincture.
苦命 a bitter fate; hard lot in life.
20 苦境 places suffering from distress; distressing circumstances.
苦學 hard studies.
苦害 to injure grievously.
苦寒 to fear the cold; poor, in straits.
苦工 hard labour.
25 苦差 hard service. (-*ch'ai*^{1})
苦役 toilsome drudgery.
苦待 to treat harshly.
苦心 a feeling of pain; distressed in mind; great pains taken in a pla
苦志 firm; desperately resolved.
30 苦忱 very earnestly.
苦急 urgent.
苦患 calamity; hardship.
苦惱 trouble, distress.
苦戰 a desperate battle.
35 苦打 a severe thrashing.
苦楚 misery, suffering, bitterness.
苦業 a hard lot in life.
苦樂不均 misery and happiness are not equally divided.
苦^{3}死 in great distress; to die of misery.

⁴⁰苦 毒 bitter; distressed.

苦 水 hard water; bitter water.

苦 活 hard work; struggle to live.

苦 海 (or 河) the bitter sea—life, the world.

苦 海 無 邊 回 頭 是 岸 the bitter sea has no bounds; only repent and the shore is at hand.

⁴⁵苦 熱 bothered by heat.

苦 瓜 a small, yellow gourd.

苦 留 to urge a person to stay.

苦 盡 甜 來 after the bitter is finished comes the sweet.

苦 節 to maintain moral integrity through suffering and trial.

⁵⁰苦 累 grievously to involve.

苦 膽 the gall.

苦 船 seasick. = 7762.5.

苦 苦 哀 求 to implore urgently.

苦 草 a bitter herb given to women after childbirth.

⁵⁵苦 菜 bitter herbs, a name given to various plants.

苦 藥 良 鍼 bitter medicine and good surgery—painful but salutary.

苦 處 or **苦 情** hardships; sufferings.

苦 行 to accomplish things, beyond the powers of others, by strenuous efforts.

苦 行 制 慾 mortification of the passions.

⁶⁰苦 言 (or 語) earnest and faithful remonstrance.

苦 諫 earnest admonitions.

苦 貧 or **苦 極** very poor; in straitened circumstances.

苦 辛 hardship; suffering.

苦 辣 a bitter taste.

⁶⁵苦 酒 bitter wine—vinegar.

苦 難 calamity; hardship.

苦 雨 凄 風 bitterly cold winds and rain.

何 苦 What's the use? Why did I?

(a) Read *hu⁴*. **The name of a place.**

苦 邑 birthplace of Laotzŭ B.C. 604. A place in Hupeh.

骷 ¹ **The skeleton. Bones. The shoulder blade.**
3494

骷 髏 a skeleton.

刳 ¹ **To cut open; to rip up; to cut out.**
3495

刳 剔 孕 婦 to rip up pregnant women.

刳 心 to cleanse the heart.

刳 木 to scoop out a block of wood.

刳 皮 to slice off the skin.

庫 ⁴ **A treasury; a storehouse; a granary; an armoury.**
3496

庫 倫 name for Urga.

庫 收 former treasury-bill or draft.

庫 大 使 former treasury-keeper of a Provincial *yamen*.

庫 官 official in charge of treasury.

⁵庫 平 treasury-scale for silver.

庫 房 a treasury.

庫 緞 a very fine kind of satin from Chekiang.

庫 貨 articles from the palace stores.

庫 銀 silver according to the treasury-scale.

¹⁰庫 項 stores in a treasury.

司 庫 a treasurer.

國 庫 national treasury.

土 庫 a cellar.

武 庫 an arsenal.

關 庫 customs revenue.

褲
袴 ⁴
绔 ~ **Trousers; breeches; leggings; drawers.**
3497

褲 子 trousers; leggings.

褲 帶 子 girdle to fasten trousers round the waist.

褲 腿 legs of trousers.

褲 襠 seat of trousers.

套 褲 leggings drawn over the trousers.

矻 1.5. **To toil.**
3498

矻 矻 窮 年 to toil the whole year round.

終 日 矻 矻 toiling the livelong day.

圣 1.5. **To work in the fields. u.f. an abbrev. of 聖 No. 5753.**
3499

哭 1.5. **To weep; to cry; to wail; to mourn for.**
3500

哭 不 出 好 處 來 weeping brought no good.

哭 之 慟 wailed with excessive grief.

哭 喊 to cry out in pain; to weep aloud.

哭 哭 啼 啼 的 tearful, whimpering.

⁵哭 喪 to wail for the dead.

哭 喪 棒 (or 杖) a staff held by chief mourners.

哭 天 哭 地 or **哀 哭** or **痛 哭** to weep bitterly.

哭 子 喪 明 lost his sight through crying for his son.

哭 得 可 憐 crying piteously.

¹⁰哭 泣 to weep.

哭 涕 to weep and snivel.

哭 甚 麼 what are you crying for?

哭 的 甚 痛 wept bitterly.

哭 皇 天 to weep and call upon God.

¹⁵哭 瞎 to cry oneself blind.

哭 祭 to mourn and offer sacrifice for ancestors.

哭 號 to weep with much noise.

哭 訴 to tell a tale of woe; to state with tears.

哭 踊 to cry and jump about with grief.

酷 4.5. **Tyrannical; cruel, oppressive.**
3501

酷 吏 rapacious underlings.

酷 氣 蒸 人 the air is stifling.

酷 法 cruel laws.

酷 烈 fierce.

酷 虐 oppressive, cruel.

(a) **Very, extremely.**

酷 似 very like.

酷 喜 very fond of.

酷 好 or **酷 愛** devoted to; addicted to.

酷 寒 bitter cold.

酷 熱 exceedingly hot.

酷 肖 very similar.

譽借 3502
4.5.
To inform quickly; an urgent communication.

窟 3503
1.5.
A hole, a cave. A dwelling.

窟 室 a cave-dwelling.
窟·竉 a hole, a cavity.
窟·竉 橋 a bridge with a hole in it—deceitful, treacherous tricks.
挖 窟 to make a hole—for burglary.
禪 窟 Buddhist cloisters.
鼠 窟 a rat-hole.

KUA. (ㄍㄨㄚ)

瓜 3504
[1] Melons, gourds, cucumbers, etc. Radical 97.

瓜 代 one official relieving another, from—8 *below*.
瓜 分 annexation; to divide a country like a melon.
瓜 分 之 端 the beginning of dismemberment.
瓜 分 豆 剖 to divide (territory) like a melon, or split it in two like a bean.
[5]瓜·子ⁿ melon-seeds.
瓜·子 臉 a fine, oval face—like a melon-seed.
瓜 時 a term of service—from the next.
瓜 時 而 往 曰 及 瓜 而 代 it was the time of melons when they went. He said, "When the melons are in season again I will relieve you."—from the *Tso chuan*.
瓜 月 the seventh lunar month.
[10]瓜 期 a term of service, *see above*—8.
瓜 熟 蒂 落 when the melon is ripe it falls—at the right time things are easily managed.
瓜 瓞 spreading like melon-vines—large posterity.
瓜 田 不 納 履 don't tie your shoes in a melon-patch—avoid the appearance of evil.
瓜 田 李 下 from the above and adding—(neither adjust your hat) under a plum tree.

[15]瓜 皮 帽 the small round skull-cap of the Chinese.
瓜 皮 艇 small skiffs used on the West Lake.
瓜 秧·子 melon-plants for planting out.
瓜 菓 fruits.
瓜 葛 melon-vines—complications; involved in; relatives.
[20]瓜 蔓 pumpkin-vines—complication of affairs.
瓜 蔓 抄 to make a record of the property of a criminal and involve those who are innocent.
倭 瓜 a crooked kind of squash.
冬·瓜 a large white-frosted kind of preserving-melon.
南·瓜 a pumpkin.
[25]木·瓜 the quince.
絲·瓜 the loofah or snake-gourd.
甜·瓜 the sweet melon; musk-melon.
西·瓜 the water-melon, said to have been introduced from the west by the Kitans who got the seed from the Ouigours.
香·瓜 musk-melons.
黃·瓜 and 胡 瓜 cucumbers and vegetable-marrows.

(a) Used in transliterating.

瓜 哇 Java. = 爪 哇 240.2.

刵 3505
[1]
To cut; to slice.

剐 3506
[3]
To cut the flesh from the bones. Distinguish 另 No. 4073.

咼 3507
[1]
A wry mouth.

剮 3508
[3]
To cut a criminal in pieces; to hack.

剮 死 to hack to death.
剮 骨 刀 a knife which hacks the bones—lust.

蝸 3509
[1]
A snail. Also read *wa*[1].

蝸 牛 the common snail.
蝸 舍 my snail-shell of a house—my humble abode.

蝸 角 虛 名 the fable of the snail's horns—that there is a kingdom on each horn of a snail,—from *Chuangtzŭ*.

騧 3510
[2] A piebald horse. Also read *wa*[2].

罣 3511
[4] A hindrance. To be anxious. To fall into a snare.

罣 念 to be anxious about.
罣 慮 anxiety.
罣 礙 to hinder; to impede.
結 罣 full of anxiety.

絓 3512
[4] Coarse silk from refuse cocoons. To fasten.

絓 於 大 樹 he was caught in a large tree—as he fell.

(a) Anxious, inter. preceding.

詿 3513
[4] To impose upon; to deceive; to disturb.

詿 亂 to distract; to disturb.
詿 誤 to mislead.

卦 3514
[4] To divine. A diagram of the *Book of Changes*.

卦 位 a divination diagram.
卦 命 先 生 a fortune-teller.
卦 盒 lottery box.
卦 衍 河 圖 the diagrams illustrating the River Plan—said to have been revealed to *Fu Hsi*.
八 卦 the *Eight Diagrams* consisting of an arrangement of single and divided lines in eight groups of three lines each; these are said to have been derived by *Fu Hsi* from the design on the back of a tortoise. *See* 二 No. 1751—7.
占 卦 or 卜 卦 or 算 卦 to cast a horoscope; to tell fortunes.

掛 挂 3515
[4]
To hang up; to suspend, thus:—suspense; anxious; to think of. N.A.

掛 上 to hang up; hang it up.

掛·不·下 there is no room to hang it.

掛·不·住 it is not hung securely.

掛 名 only in name; nominally.

[5] 掛 單 to put up for one night—as Buddhist priests at temples.

掛 壁 to hang on a wall.

掛 孝 to put on mourning.

↑ 掛 冠 to leave office.

掛 念 or 掛 心 or 掛 慮 or 掛 肚 or 記·掛 to be anxious; to be in suspense; thoughtful for.

[10] 掛 意 undecided; in suspense.

掛 扁 to hang up a tablet; to start a medical practice.

掛 旗 or 升 旗 to hoist a flag.

掛 望 anxiously to hope for.

掛 欠 to record one's debts—to get goods on credit.

[15] 掛 漏 omissions. Abbr. from 29.

掛 燈 to hang up lanterns.

掛 牌 to hang out a signboard.

掛 畫 to hang pictures.

掛 礙 anxiety.

[20] 掛 綠 to dress in green; to dress up.

掛 花 to dress up in gay garments.

掛 號 to register; to enter—as arrivals, etc.

掛 號 信 registered letter.

掛 誤 embarrassments; to implicate.

[25] 掛·起·來 to hang up.

掛 鐘 to hang a wall-clock; a hanging-clock.

掛·麪 a kind of vermicelli made by hanging dough-strings to dry on a frame.

不 足 掛 齒 not worth hanging on the teeth—a mere trifle.

↑ 掛 一 漏 萬 to record one item while omitting 10,000 — incomplete.

褂 [4]
3516   An outer jacket; a coat.

褂·子 a jacket or coat; outer garment.

寡 [3]
3517   Few, little. Friendless, alone. A term of deprecia-tion used by princes of themselves. To lessen.

寡 不 敵 衆 the few cannot withstand the many.

寡 交 having few friends; unsociable.

寡 人 恥 之 I consider it a disgrace, a shame.

寡 兄 I, your unworthy brother.

[5] 寡 君 or 寡 人 I, the ruler.

寡 妻 the legitimate wife; a rare woman.

寡·婦 or 孀 婦 or 孀 寡 a widow.

寡 少 very few.

寡 尤 few occasions for blame.

[10] 寡·居 to live alone—as a widow.

寡 悔 few occasions for regrets.

寡 慾 few desires.   [formed.

寡 聞 of little experience; ill-in-

寡 言 taciturn.

多 寡 many or few.

↑ 寡 過 to lessen one's faults.

KUA.   (ㄍㄨㄚ)

(Kuah)

刮 [1.5.]
3518   To pare away; to scrape; to shave; to brush away.

刮 刀 a scraping knife.

刮 削 to scrape; to trim; to oppress.

刮 削 價 錢 to reduce the price.

刮 垢 to scrape off the dirt.

[5] 刮 字 to erase a writing.

刮 平 to level; to raze.

刮 擦 to rub off; to scrape.

刮 斗 a striker used in measuring grain.

刮 木 to plane wood.

[10] 刮 漿 to stiffen by starch.

刮 痧 to scarify for cholera.

刮 目 相 看 to rub the eyes and look at each other—to see if there is any change.

刮 磨 to rub off; to scrape off.

刮·着 scraping—we shall knock against each other—cry of coolies or carters. (-∘chao[2])

[15] 刮 臉 or 刮 鬍·子 to shave the face.

刮 腿 to strike legs—as two horsemen colliding.

刮 舌 to scrape the tongue.

刮 衣·裳 to brush clothes.

刮 面 光 lit:—to scrape the light off one's face—to lose one's good name, to lose *face*.

↑ 刮 地 皮 to exact money from the people.

括 [1.5.]
3519   To include, to enclose, to embrace. To come to. Also read k'uo[4].

括 囊 to tie up in a bag—to say little; taciturn.

括 弧 brackets; parentheses.

括 水 to bale a boat.

括 號 brackets, in writing or mathematics.

[5] 括 要 comprehensive.

括 髮 ancient form of mourning head-dress, to bind up the hair with hemp.

包 括 to contain; included in.

機 括 ingenious mechanism.

栝 [1.5.]
3520   A builder's frame for measuring. Also read *kuai*[4]. Juniper.

聒 [1.5.]
3521   A clamour, a din, hubbub.

聒 擾 clamorous; to make a disturbance.

聒 耳 ear stunned by the hubbub.

聒 聒 a din, a noise.

蛙 聒 croaking of frogs.

适 [1.5.]
3522   To hasten. Quickly.

适 疾 to drive on; to hasten.

颳 [1.5.]
3523   To blow, as the wind.

颳 北 風 a north wind blew.

颳·得 滿 天 飛 (the dust) was blown sky-high.

颳·起 風·來 the wind arose.

颳·開·了 blown open by the wind.

颳 風 or 起 風 the wind blows; to blow—as the wind.

髻 [4.5.]
3524   The hair dishevelled, as in mourning.

鴰 [1.5.]
3525   A kind of wader, allied to the crane. Cawing of crows.

鴰 鹿 the black crane.

老·鴰 crows.

K'UA.   (ㄎㄨㄚ)

夸 [1]
3526   To brag; to talk big.

夸 口 to brag.

夸 奢 自 大 to boast oneself.

夸 [3] 3527 To revile.

嫇 [1] 3528 Fascinating and pretty.

嫇 修 elegant.
嫇 節 refined.

胯 [4] 3529 The thighs, the legs.

胯 夫 a coward.
胯 間 or 胯 下 between the legs.

誇 [1] 3530 To boast, to brag. To praise, to commend.

誇 勝 to boast of victory or of pre-eminence.
誇 口 or 誇 嘴 to boast.
誇 大 to swagger; to exaggerate; to boast.
誇·獎 or 誇 讚 or 誇 說 to praise; to extol.
[5] 誇 張 to boast.
誇 揚 to talk big.
誇 海 口 to talk grandiloquently.
誇 耀 to show off.
誇 能 to boast of one's ability.
[10] 誇 許 praised; boasted of.
誇 詐 boasting deception.
誇 誇 earnest; really.
浮 誇 to give oneself airs.
自 誇 self-praise; boasting.

(a) Ample.

誇 布 ample; wide-spreading.

(b) Read k'ua[3]. A brogue.

誇·子 one who speaks a brogue—a northerner.

跨 [4] 3531 To straddle, to bestride. To encroach upon. To pass over. To surpass, to excel.

跨 刀 to wear a sword.
跨 坐 to sit astride.
跨·子 a long and narrow boat, used on the Upper Yangtze.
跨 梁 a cross-beam.
[5] 跨 海 to cross the sea.
跨 竈 to bestride the fireplace—to excel a father.

跨 考 to sit for examinations in two districts.
跨 越 to excel; to surpass.
跨·過·來 to clamber over; to bestride.
[10] 跨 馬 to ride; to bestride a horse.

KUAI.   (ㄍㄨㄞ)

乖 [1] 3532 Cunning, crafty. Perverse, obstinate. Good — as a child. Distinguish 乘 No. 398.

乖 令 unseasonable.
乖 僻 or 乖 張 or 乖 戾 or 乖 謬 unreasonable; perverse.
乖·兒[2]·子 a mischievous child; a term of endearment.
我·的 乖·乖 my little dear.
[5] 乖 口 glib-tongued; plausible.
乖 巧 tricky; wily; clever.
乖 忤 perverse.
乖 異 odd, eccentric; intractable.
乖 棼 to pervert all reason; confounded.
[10] 乖 舛 mistaken; bad luck.
倫 常 乖 舛 the human relationships are all out of course.
乖 覺 precocious.
乖 錯 errors.
乖 離 to bend; to deviate from.

拐 [3] 3533 To kidnap, to decoy. To swindle.

拐·子 a kidnapper.
拐 孩·子 to kidnap children.
拐 帶 to make off with; to kidnap.
拐 販 to kidnap and sell.
拐 騙 or 拐 誘 to swindle; to decoy.

(a) To turn.

拐·回·來 to turn back.
拐 彎 to turn a corner; a corner, as of a road; to change—fig.
拐 肘 the elbow.
拐 角[3] to turn a corner; a corner.
拐 跌·了·他 pushed him over.
拐·過·去 to follow round a corner.

(b) Inter. next. A staff.

拐·杖 an old man's staff.

枴 [3] 3534 An old man's staff.

枴·杖 or 枴 棍 an old man's staff.
枴 棒 a staff, a stick.

夬 [4] 3535 Parted. To fork. Certain. Distinguish 央 No. 7239. Read chüch[1,5]. Secret signs made with the fingers.

怪 恠 [4] 3536 Strange, uncanny. Wonderful.

怪·不·得 no wonder! that accounts for.... See below A-1.
怪 事 extraordinary! a strange affair.
怪 人 a peculiar person.
怪 僻 之 行·爲 an eccentric manner.
[5] 怪 劇 strange.
怪 哉 How strange! How uncanny!
怪 幻 whimsical.
怪 性 eccentric disposition.
怪 模 怪 樣 queer appearance and manner.
[10] 怪 物 a monstrosity; an apparition.
怪 特 extraordinary; strange.
怪 現 狀 (or 象) strange phenomenon; uncouth; disagreeable occurrence.
怪 異 or 鬼 怪 uncanny; supernatural.
怪 病 an abnormal disease.
[15] 怪 石 a peculiar piece of stone.
怪 祟 ghost; supernatural appearance.
怪 笑 sardonic laughter; laughter without cause.
怪 精 a ghost or bogy.
怪 詭 or 奇 怪 or 古·怪 wonderful; strange; peculiar; weird.
[20] 怪 說 absurdities.
怪 誕 wild, fabulous stories.
怪 誕 不 經 something entirely out of the common.
怪 談 weird talk.
怪 象 發 生 strange portents have appeared.
[25] 怪 道 strange to say! no wonder that! the wrong path, unorthodox.
怪 魅 a bogy; an apparition.

妖·怪 an apparition; a spook; a bogy.

子 不 語 怪 Confucius did not talk about extraordinary things.

行 怪 to practise sorcery, etc.

[30]難·怪 no wonder!

(a) To blame.

怪·不·得 我 do not blame me!

怪 責 to reprimand.

不·要 見 怪 do not take offence.

別 怪 or 莫 怪 do not be offended; do not blame me.

(b) Unusually, very; rather.

怪 可 憐 pitiable indeed!

怪 好 quite good, very good.

怪 澀·的 quite astringent—to the taste.

怪 熱 very hot.

怪 難 very difficult.

噲[4] A man's name. Read k'uai[4]. To swallow. Greedy.
3537 Strange. Pleasant, bright.

檜[4] The Chinese juniper. Also read kuei[4].
3538

檜 柏 the Chinese cypress.

澮[4] Streams flowing. A drain. A water tank. Also read
3539 kuei[4].

溝 澮 irrigation-channels.

獪[4] Mischievous, crafty. Also read kuei[4].
3540

狡 獪 cunning, mischievous.

膾[4] Flesh or fish hashed fine; minced meat. Also read kuei[4].
鱠[4]
3541

膾 殘 魚 Chinese white-bait.

膾 炙 人 口 to please all tastes.

鄶[4] Name of a small feudal State in what is now the
3542 province of Honan.

旝[4] A signal flag. Also read kuei[4].
3543

K'UAI. (ㄎㄨㄞ)

喎[1] A wry mouth.
3544

搲[3] To rub, to scratch.
3545

搲 攘 to scratch an irritated place.

搲 破 to scratch and break the skin.

搲 破 臉 to scratch the face; to cut an acquaintance.

(a) To carry on the arm.

搲 籃·子 to carry a basket on the arm.

儈[4] A broker; a middleman. Distinguish 僧 No. 5453.
3546 Also read kuei[4].

儈 費 brokerage.

牙 儈 a broker.

(a) To hint. To tip a wink.

儈 心 to communicate by a nod or sign.

快[4] Quickly, fast, hasty, soon. Sharp, keen. Indicates the
3547 future.

快·些 a little quicker.

快 人 a sharp man.

快 作·罷 make haste and do it!

快 來·了 he will soon be here.

[5]快 信 an express letter.

快 刀 a sharp knife.

快 刀 斬 亂 麻 chopping a mass of tangled hemp with a sharp knife— cut the Gordian knot.

快 利 sharp, keen; "quick returns."

快 到·了 nearly there.

[10]快 口 鉗 cutting-pliers.

快 完 it will soon be done.

快 快 quickly; instantly.

快 慢 fast and slow—rate of speed.

快 手 yamen runners; dexterous.

[15]快 捷 promptly; at once.

快 板 quick time in music.

快 機 砲 quick-firing guns.

快 班 or 馬 快 policemen; runners of a yamen.

快·當 prompt; quick.

[20]快 跑 to trot; to run quickly.

快 車 express train.

快 鎗 or 盒·子 鎗 magazine rifle.

快 馬 a fleet horse.

快 馬 一 鞭 快 人 一 言 a fast horse only needs one touch of the whip,—an intelligent man only needs a hint.

(a) Cheerful. In good health.

快 壻 a good son-in-law.

快 慰 glad; pleased.

快 暢 happy; pleased.

快 樂 happy; joyful.

[5]快 樂 說 hedonism.

快·活 happy.

↓ 爽·快 satisfying; decisive.

心 裏 不 快 a little out of sorts.

(b) Chopsticks. Inter. next.

快·子 the pair of slender sticks used to convey food to the mouth. Chopsticks.

一 雙 快 a pair of chopsticks.

象 牙 快 ivory chopsticks.

筷[4] Chopsticks.
3548

筷·子 chopsticks.

駃[4] Fast, swift—as a good horse.
3549

駃 流 如 竹 箭 its waters are as swift as an arrow.

駃 馬 a fast horse.

塊[4] A lump. A piece of. A fraction. N.A.
3550

塊·把 兩 塊 one or two—dollars.

塊 然 一 物 a blockhead.

塊 然 無 偶 alone, without a wife.

塊 然 無 知 ignorant and stupid.

[5]一 塊 兒 all together; in a lump.

一 塊 地 a piece of land.

一 塊 肉 a piece of meat.

一 塊 錢 a dollar.

蒯[3] A rush, of which various things are made.
3551

蒯 屨 rush sandals.

蒯 索 rush ropes.

蒯 蓆 rush mats.

KUAN.　(ㄍㄨㄢ)

官[1] An official, a mandarin. Public. A term of respect.
3552 Distinguish 官 No. 2238.

官 事 a public matter.

官 事 不 攝 the officers did not perform double duties—were not pluralists.

官 況 conditions of official life.

官 人 official underling; term of respect for a husband; prostitute.

[5]官 俸 official salary.

官 僚 fellow officials; officialdom; officials.

官 僚 政 治 officialism; bureaucracy.

官 價 officially fixed price.

官 兵 government troops.

[10]官 利 guaranteed rate of interest to bond-holders, apart from division of profits.

官 制 official system; function of officials.

官 勢 power and authority of officials.

官 印 seal of office; pottery stamp.

官·司 an officer; a lawsuit.

[15]官·司 打 贏 to win a lawsuit.

官 名 one's official name.

官 吏 懲 戒 法 laws relating to delinquent officials.

官 員 錄 register of government officers.

官 商 合 辦 subsidized industries.

[20]官 地 public lands.

官 場 official circles; officialdom.

官 場 中 among officials; an official style of things.

官 報 official reports or gazette.

官 契 officially-stamped deed.

[25]官 媒 matron of a jail.

官 守 to hold office; one's offices.

官 官 相 護 one official will protect another.

官 客 male visitors or guests.

官 宦 statesmen; officials.

[30]官 宦 人 家 highly connected families.

官 尺 official foot-measure.

官 居 極 品 attained to the highest rank.

官 差 underlings of officials; official service. (-ch'ai[1])

官 帖 license granted to commission-agents.

[35]官 廨 government offices.

官 廳 government offices.

官 憲 high officials; the authorities.　[ment; the authorities.

官 方 official dignity; of the govern-

官 星 顯 his official star shines forth—he will soon be in office.

[40]官 曆 official calendar.

官 服 official dress.

官 本 official subsidy; a book containing the official calendar of lucky days, etc.

官 板 books printed and issued by the authorities.

官 業 government undertakings, railways, posts, salt-monopoly, etc.

[45]官 樣 文·章 official formalities; red tape.

官 權 official authority.

官 欠 shortage in official funds.

官 次 official residence; official precedence; duties, etc., of officials.

官 法 the law of the land.

[50]官 治 official jurisdiction.

官 河 a public stream.

官 渡 public ferry.

官 爵 official rank.

官 用 for official use.

[55]官 田 government lands.

官 界 official circles; officialdom.

官 盛 任 使 the officers are numerous so that the various orders may be carried out.

官 眷 family of an official.

官 督 商 辦 subsidized industry under government supervision.

[60]官 祿 official salary.

官 秩 official grades or precedence.

官 程 term of office.

官 窰 government porcelain works.

官 立 學 校 government schools.

[65]官 章 regalia.

官 等 official grades and ranks.

官 米 government rice.

官 結 official certificate of character.

官 紳 officials and gentry.

[70]官 署 a government office.

官 職 official title; office or rank.

官 銜 full title of an official.

官 規 official regulations; red tape.

官 許 official permission.

[75]官 話 the official language or "Mandarin."

官 說 官 話 to speak without regard for the facts.

官 誥 rank conferred on women.

官 課 taxes.

官 謗 objections to an incompetent official.

[80]官 資 qualification of an official.

官 費 生 officially supported students.

官 費 留 學 government support for students abroad.

官 賣 sale of tobacco, wine, etc., under official license.

官 路 a highway; public road.

[85]官 途 in official ways; official career.

官 運 official preferment.

官 逼 民 變 misgovernment drives the masses to revolution.

官 邪 official corruption.

官 邸 official residence.

[90]官 醫 medical officer for prisons.

官 長 or 官 府 or 官 吏 or 官 員 or 官 曹 officials; a mandarin; magistrates.

官 門 official entrance.

官 階 official rank.

官 項 (or 款) public monies.

[95]官 體 or 官 樣 official dignity.

官 鹽 salt on which duty has been paid.

做 官 to be an official.

入 官 to confiscate.

捐 官 purchased office.

[100]文 官 武 官 civil and military officials.

清 官 an incorrupt official.

當 官 = above 97.

看 官 Reader!—as spoken by the author in a book.

行 政 官 administrative official.

貪 官 corrupt official.

(a) The senses.

官 感 sensation.

官 能 faculties, senses.

官 能 之 作 用 function of the senses.

官 覺 sense perception.

五 官 the five senses, five planets.

覺 (or 感) 官 sense organs.

(b) Excellent; standard quality.

官 粉 carbonate of lead for face-powder.

官 紗 superior kind of light crape.

官 燕 best quality swallow's nests —for soup.

官 醬 standard quality soy.

倌[1] A groom. Imperial chari-
3553 oteer. Assistant in a wine-
shop.

棺[1] A coffin; an inner coffin.
3554

棺·材 or 棺木 a coffin.
棺·材餡兒 stuffing for a coffin—a
corpse; also said of one about
to die.
棺·材鑿 a coffin-chisel—body-
snatcher.
棺椁 inner and outer coffins in
ancient times.
[5]棺殮 coffin and grave-clothes.
棺罩 a funeral pall.
施棺 to give coffins for charity.

瑄[3] Stone tube.
3555

瘝[3] Exhausted, worn out.
3556

四牡瘝瘝 the four horses were
exhausted.

管[3] To govern, to care for,
莞 to control; thus:—a key.
3557

管下 under the jurisdiction of.
管·不住 or 不能管 unable to
control.
管事 to manage; a manager.
管事·的 "number one boy," housekeeper; manager.
[5]管○保 to guarantee.
管守 to garrison; to keep watch
over.
管家 to manage the house; a
steward.
管帶 to have the control of; to be
in authority.
管帳 (or 賬)的 a book-keeper.
[10]管店 a shop-boy.
管庫 a treasurer.
管待 to look after one.
管戒 to warn; to prohibit.
管·我·呢 or 你管·你·的·罷 mind
your own business!
[15]管押 to keep in custody.
管掌 to control; to oversee.
管攝 to oversee; to manage.

管教 to correct; to teach; to manage.
管數 or 管賬 to keep accounts.
[20]管束 to control; to restrain.
管·理 to a d m i n i s t e r; administration; to control; to manage.
管理事務 business management.
管理員 overseer; manager.
管理局 administration department.
[25]管理權 authority over. (legal).
管理稅務 control of the government revenue.
託·他管理 put it under his
control; asked him to take
charge of it.
管筵席·的 ruler of the feast.
管籥 a key for a lock.
[30]管船·的 head-boatman.
管記 secretaryship.
管誰都是 no matter who, all
are....
管財人 administrator. (legal).
管車 woman in charge of silk-
reeling.
[35]管輪 marine engineer.
管輪正 or 總管輪 chief en-
gineer of a steamer.
管轄 to have rule over; to govern.
管轄區域 jurisdiction.
管轄地 jurisdiction.
[40]管轄權 authority over. (legal).
管轄範圍 sphere of competen-
cy. (legal).
管轄錯誤 beyond the jurisdic-
tion of. (legal).
受人管轄 under his control
or jurisdiction.
管鍵 the catch of a lock—the key
to the situation, the crux, the
important point. Cf. 3751.38.
[45]管閒事 to be a busybody.
管領 to govern; to control.
不管·他 never mind him!
只○管做 go on and do it, never
mind!
只○管說 say on—do not mind
him.
[50]我不管 it's none of my business;
I don't care.
總管 manager; in general control
of.

(a) A reed, a tube, a duct, a flute.
N.A. for tubular things.
管中窺豹 to look at (the spots
of) a leopard through a tube
—limited experience; partial
knowledge.

管口 mouth of a pipe or tube.
管城子 a Chinese pen.
管形橋 tubular bridge.
[5]管狀 tubular.
管狀細胞 tracheal cells.
管狀珊瑚 tubular coral.
管穴 the hole of a tube—limited
view.
管窺 or 管見 to see through a
tube—limited experience, my
humble opinion. See above—1.
[10]管絃 musical instruments—wind
and strings.
管蠡之見 limited views,—
abbrev. for below—13.
管足 tube feet.
管闚蠡測 to look (at the sky)
through a tube, and measure
(the sea) with a calabash—
limited outlook.
一管筆 a Chinese pen.
[15]傳聲管 speaking tube.
呼吸管 bronchial tubes.
氣管 the windpipe.
汽管 steam-pipes.
洩水管 drain-pipe.
[20]筆管 stem of a Chinese pen.
起水管 hydrant.
食管 gullet.

(b) Surname.

管葛 Kuan Chung and Chu-ko
Liang, two famous leaders.
管鮑 Kuan Chung and Pao Shu-
ya, two famous friends—used
as Damon and Pythias, or
David and Jonathan.

脘[3] A duct in the body.
脘 Core of a boil.
3558

水脘 urethra.
漏脘 fistula.
血脘 blood-vessels.

館[3] A private dwelling. A
舘 public office, a hall. A
tavern, restaurant, tea-
house, etc. To lodge.
3559

館地 a position in an office; opening for employment.
館·子 a restaurant; an inn.
館舍 an inn; hotel.

公 館 rest-house for travelling officials; a residence; public hall.

⁵客 館 an inn; lodging-place.
會 館 guild-hall.
茶 館 tea-house.
酒 館 wine-shop; restaurant.

癏¹ To render useless; to cause distress. Vicious.
3560

癏 官 neglect of duties as an official.
智 藏 癏 在 the wise are left to live in obscurity while the corrupt hold office.

鰥¹ Huge fish found in the Yellow River, said to be unable to close its eyes.
3561

鰥 魚 the fish, as above.
愁 似 鰥 魚 夜 不 眠 in grief one is like the fish, and cannot close one's eyes all night.
目 鰥 鰥 wide-open eyes.

(a) A widower, unmarried man. Solitary.

鰥 夫 or 鰥 棍 a widower, a bachelor.
鰥 寡 孤 獨 the widower, the widow, the orphan and the childless.
鰥 居 to live alone (without wife).
鰥 民 aged widower, lonely.
鰥 身 漢·子 a lonely man, without kith or kin.

丱⁴ The two tufts made in dressing a child's hair.
3562

絴¹ To run the threads through a web in weaving.
3563

冠¹ A cap. The comb or crest of a bird.
3564 Distinguish 寇 No. 3444.

冠 履 cap and sandals—high and low.
冠 巾 head-dress.
冠 帶 cap and sash—the literati.
冠 冕 a crown. 冠·冕 ceremonious; elegant.

⁵冠 毛 downy appendage on seeds of thistles, dandelion, etc.—pappus.
冠 章 badge on cap.
冠 緌 comb and wattles of a cock; strings of a cap.
冠 蓋 cap and chariot or carriage —high officials.
冠 蓋 相 屬 continuous messengers back and forth.
¹⁰冠 裳 cap and robes—dress.
冠 首 to dress a lady's hair. See A—6.
下 冠 wattles that hang below the beak of a cock.
免 冠 to raise the hat; term of respect.
素 冠 white mourning-cap.
¹⁵道·士 冠 square hat of the Taoists.
雞 冠 cock's comb.

(a) Read kuan⁴. To cap; thus:— a youth. To be married. To excel.

冠 場 cock of the walk.
冠 禮 capping ceremony of youths in ancient times; used sometimes for coronation.
冠 絕 to excel.
冠 詞 article, distinguishing adjective.
⁵冠 軍 first in the lists for the former first degree of Hsiu ts'ai; a general in ancient times.
冠 首 the best.
冠 首 字 體 capital letters.
及 冠 reached the age for capping —twenty.
弱 冠 a youth, not yet capped.

祼⁴ To pour out libations. Distinguish 裸 No. 4109.
3565

祼 將 于 京 they poured out the wine offering and assisted in the capital.
祼 酒 or 祼 奠 to pour out a libation.

貫⁴ A string of 1,000 cash; to string on a thread, thus:—to go through, to implicate. Inter. next.
3566

貫 中 going through the bull's-eye.
貫 串 to thread together; to connect.

貫 址 or 籍 貫 a person's antecedents.
貫 徹 to see clearly through.
⁵貫 注 to concentrate on.
貫 珠 to string pearls.
貫 甲 to put on armour.
貫 衆 the whole together.
貫 習 accustomed to
¹⁰貫 穿 the thread of; to thread; to pass through.
貫 通 to go through; is pervaded by; to have a thorough understanding.
貫 錢 to string cash.
惡 貫 滿 盈 the measure of their iniquity is full.
直 貫 到 底 extends right through to the end.
籍 貫 one's parentage; one's native place.

慣⁴ Accustomed to; experienced in; addicted to. Inter. preceding.
3567

慣 便 familiar with the use of.
慣 例 custom; habit.
慣 壞·了 to spoil—as a petted child.
慣 弄 practised in.
⁵慣 性 or 惰 性 inertia.
慣 愛 specially fond of; addicted to.
慣 戰 veteran in war.
慣 會 practised in.
慣 熟 expert in; habitual; used to.
¹⁰慣 用 usage.
慣 用 句 idiom.
慣 用 語 法 idiom.
慣 習 or 習 慣 custom; habit.
慣 習 法 customary law. (legal).
¹⁵慣 能 able through practice; specially skilled in.
慣 行 habituated.
慣 行 犯 habitual criminal.
作 慣·了 accustomed to doing the thing; practised.
成 慣 becomes a habit.

摜⁴ To be familiar with. To take. To throw down.
3568

摜 瀆 鬼 神 to treat the gods with irreverence.
摜 珓 盃 to throw down the divining blocks.

盥⁴ To wash, especially the hands. Also read k'uan⁴.
3569

盥 手 to wash the hands.
盥 櫛 to wash and comb—to make one's toilet.
盥 洗 or 盥 沐 or 盥 濯 to wash.
盥 浴 to bathe.
盥 漱 to wash and rinse the mouth.
盥 誦 having washed my hands, I read—your letter.

幹 3 3570

To manage. To lead.

幹 官 title of an official under the *Han* dynasty.

(a) Read *wo*[4.5]. A handle, a wheel by which to turn a machine. To revolve, to circulate. A striker for grain measures.

幹 旋 to revolve; to intercede.
如 輪 幹 to revolve like a wheel: to circulate.

3571
1

A frontier pass or gate: thus:—to shut or close. A Custom-house. Suburbs of a city.

關 ·不 住 will not keep closed.
關 中 within the passes—Shensi.
關 人 officer in charge of the passes.
關 俸 salary.
5 關 內 within the passes, within the *Han-ku Kuan* 函 谷 關 i.e., Shensi.
關 卡 or 關 廠 a Customs barrier.
關 口 a pass; a Customs station.
關 外 beyond the *Shan-hai Kuan*, i.e., Manchuria; beyond the *Han-ku Kuan*, i.e., *eastwards*, Shansi; outside the suburbs of a city.
關 ·子 paper money under the *Sung* dynasty; blank pass or order.
10 關 市 譏 而 不 征 strangers were examined at the outposts and markets, but no imposts were levied.
關 平 銀 *Hai-kuan* taels,—the Customs scale for silver.
關 征 Customs dues.
關 捩 mechanism.
關 提 to send a warrant to arrest

a person in a district beyond one's jurisdiction.
15 關 文 a passport.
關 暇 to forbid leave of absence; detention.
關 書 indentures; engagement, as for teacher or secretary.
關 東 Manchuria. *See above*—8.
關 棧 bonded warehouse.
20 關 汛 a guard-station.
關 津 guard-houses at fords.
關 ·照 a passport; to look after.
關 禁 to confine.
關 税 Customs dues.
25 關 税 會 議 Tariff Commission.
關 税 自 主 Tariff autonomy.
關 章 Customs regulations.
關 糧 米 military rations or pay.
關 船 revenue cruiser.
30 關 ·裏 in the suburbs.
關 西 beyond the *Han-ku Kuan*, i.e., Shensi and Kansuh.
關 費 customs' dues.
關 道 or 海 關 道 Customs' Tao-tai.
關 部 a designation of the *Hoppo* at Canton, i.e., the former Superintendent of Customs at Canton.
35 關 針 or 別 針 a safety pin; a pin.
關 銀 *Hai-kuan* taels.
關 鎖 locked.
關 ·鍵 catch for a lock, pivot of a door—key to a situation; pivot, crux of the matter.
關 鍵 a door catch, pivot, or key; —also used fig.
40 關 門 shut the door.
關 閉 to close.
關 閘 a pass or barrier; to shut a gate. [passes.
關 防 oblong official seal; frontier
關 防 嚴 密 to take secret precautions.
45 關 餘 Customs surplus.
出 關 to go beyond the Great Wall.
守 關 to guard the passes.
常 關 the Native Customs (as contrasted with the Maritime Customs.)
海 關 Maritime Customs.

(a) To connect, to implicate, to involve. Concerned with.

關 ·平 concerned with.
關 事 implications.

關 ·係 relation ; consequences: to involve:
關 係 民 生 it involves the welfare of the masses.
5 關 係 益 密 intimate relationships.
關 切 to concern ; relating to.
關 心 to give attention to; to be affected by.
關 心 照 ·料 to look after carefully.
關 情 kindness.
10 關 懷 to be affected by ; concerned with.
關 注 to use interest on behalf of another.
關 涉 concern ; connected with.
關 礙 concern ; hindrance ; relation to.
關 節 collusion ; suborning. *See below* D-1.
15 關 繫 responsibilities ; concern.
關 託 to seek another's influence on behalf of a friend.
關 說 to make arrangements ; to use influence on behalf of a friend.
關 通 an understanding ; collusion.
關 顧 to look after ; to have a care for.

(b) A crisis, a juncture.

關 煞 crises in the life of a child.
關 煞 開 通 may the crisis be got through in safety.
關 頭 [2] crisis ; juncture.
取 命 關 crisis when a demon may snatch the life of a child.
5 度 關 to pass the crisis.
撞 門 關 for a child to get a disease, or come into danger, etc., through visiting a neighbour.
斷 橋 關 the crisis of the broken bridge.
短 命 關 short-life crisis—to die before the age of twelve, or within 100 days of birth.
落 水 關 danger of a child's drowning.

(c) To inform.

關 白 to give public notice.

(d) The important parts of the body.

關 節 articulations of the joints. *See above* A-14.

關 脉 the centre pulse.

三 關 three places to be guarded—like passes, i.e., ear, eye and mouth.

五 關 the ear, eye, mouth, nose and body. Corrupt. of 3552 A5.

(e) Sound made by an osprey.

關 雎 the title of the first of the *Odes*—used for marriage, happy union.

關 雎 之 亂 洋 洋 乎 盈 耳 哉 how splendid the singing of the last clause of the *Kuan chü!* How it filled the ears!

關 關 the sound of the above bird.

(f) A surname.

關 羽 *Kuan Yü,* originally a seller of beancurd who in A.D. 184 joined himself to *Liu Pei* 劉備 and became a famous hero during the period of the Three Kingdoms.

關 帝 or 關 公 or 關 聖 or 關 老 爺 or 關 夫 子 the above, canonized as the God of War.

關 張 the above and Chang Fei 張 飛, another hero of the same period—used to illustrate heroism.

(g) Read *wan*[1]. **To bend a bow.**

關 弓 to bend a bow.

鸛
3572   A heron. Small cup.

灌
3573   To pour into, to pour on. To force to drink; to force down or into.

灌 地 to pour a libation on the ground.

灌 域 course of a river; river valley.

灌 奠 to pour a libation of wine.

灌 救 to save life by forcing medicine down the person's throat.

⁵灌 ·死 to kill by pouring water into the mouth, or by holding the head under water.

灌 水 to blow water into—as into meat, to make it weigh heavier.

灌 注 to pour out or into.

灌 漿 to pour liquid mortar into crevices—of a pavement or a wall; to fill, as a pustule.

↓ 灌 片 ·子 to record a phonograph record.

灌 溉 to irrigate; to water.

¹⁰灌 灌 rushing of water; perfect sincerity; forlorn and fearful.

灌 耳 dinned into the ears.

灌 腸 to give an enema.
滋 養 灌 腸 nutrient injections.

灌 花 to water flowers.

¹⁵灌 藥 to force a person to take medicine.

灌 輸 poured into; imported, as culture or civilization, etc.

灌 醉 to make a man drunk.

灌 頂 a Buddhist form of baptism.

(a) To assemble.

灌 木 shrubs, trees growing closely together.

灌 聚 to assemble together.

灌 叢 shrubs; thick undergrowth.

爟
3573a   To light a fire; to set fire to.

罐 礶
3574   A jug, a pitcher, a jar, a pot.

罐 ·頭 食 物 tinned goods.

罐 ·子 a pot, jar or pitcher.

水 罐 water-pitcher.

瓦 罐 earthenware pitchers or pots.

茶 罐 tea-canister.

觀 观
3575   To behold; to gaze on; to travel for pleasure.

观 光 to see the good example of another; to travel for pleasure; to see your brightness—to meet you.

观 光 團 party of sight-seers.

观 兵 to inspect troops.

观 其 所 由 mark a man's motives.

⁵观 其 鄉 面 而 順 宜 (the Sage) observed the ways of the place and followed what was fitting.

观 天 文 or 观 星 斗 to practise astrology, or astronomy.

观 如 塔 牆 the spectators stood around like a wall.

观 客 spectators.

观 察 to look into; observation; former designation of a Taot'ai or Intendant of a Circuit.

¹⁰观 察 自 然 之 能 力 his natural powers of observation.

观 察 點 point of observation.

观 審 to act as an assessor.

观 往 知 來 by examining the past we may know the future.

观 念 a concept; an idea; view.

¹⁵观 念 力 force of ideas.

观 念 表 ·出 動 ·作 motor-activity displayed by ideas.

观 念 論 idealism.   [pression.

观 感 to be moved by a sight; im-
观 成 to expect to succeed.

²⁰观 摩 to see the good in another and strive to emulate it.

观 星 (or 象) 臺 observatory.

观 星 ·的 astronomers.=6361.42.

观 ·望 to gaze at; looking on; hesitating.

观 止 to look and find satisfaction,—no need to look further.

²⁵观 海 to gaze on the sea—breadth of vision.

观 潮 to see the tidal bore at Hangchow.

观 火 to see the fire—clear apprehension of.

观 玩 to enjoy.

观 看 to behold; to inspect.

³⁰观 相 (*hsiang*[4]) to practise physiognomy.

观 瞻 attractive.

观 美 to look on the beautiful.

观 者 an onlooker.

观 色 to observe the countenance.

³⁵观 色 為 務 crafty opportunist—one who regards the observation of the countenance as of prime importance.

观 花 to enjoy a flower garden.

观 覽 to examine, to read.

观 賞 to view; to enjoy any special sights.

观 過 知 仁 by examining a man's faults it may be known whether he is truly virtuous.

⁴⁰观 陣 to review troops.

观 音 or 观 世 音 the Goddess of Mercy—the one who hears the prayers of the world—formerly represented as a man.

观 風 to examine into the customs of a place; to watch the development of things in order to act accordingly.

由 是 觀 之 from this it appears; looking at it from this standpoint.

(a) As a suffix—aspect, view, etc., according to the context.

主 觀 subjective; subjectivity. *See* No. 1336—90ff.
主 觀 感 覺 subjective sensations.
主 觀 觀 察 subjective observation.
客 觀 objective. *See* No. 3324—23ff.
5客 觀 觀 察 objective observation.
客 觀 論 objectivism.
容 觀 deportment.
悲 觀 家 pessimists.
抽 象 觀 abstraction; abstract ideas. *See* No. 1314—19ff.
10政 治 觀 political aspect.
樂 觀 家 optimists.
美 觀 beautiful, elegant.
通 觀 a conception.
達 觀 optimism.

(b) Read *kuan*⁴. Taoist monastery.

寺 觀 Buddhist and Taoist monasteries.

鑵⁴
3576
A jar. Inter. 罐 No. 3574.

鸛⁴
3577
The crane; the stork.

鸛 鳴 the cry of the crane.

K'UAN.   (ㄎㄨㄢ)

寬¹
3578
Broad, spacious, wide; thus:—liberal; forgiving; lenient. To extend.

寬 仁 kindness, clemency.
寬 以 律 己 indulgent to oneself.
寬 免 to forgive; to remit.
寬 則 得 眾 kindness wins the heart of the people.
5寬 厚 broad and thick—generous.
寬 和 kindly, genial.
寬 大 or 寬 闊 or 寬·敞 or 寬 宏 or 寬 廣 vast, liberal; broad, ample, spacious.
寬 容 toleration; leniency.
寬 展 explicit.
10寬 度 width.

寬 廣 vast.
寬 待 to treat liberally.
寬 徵 to extend the time for payment of taxes.
寬 心 耐 守 patient and forbearing.
15寬 忍 to bear with; to endure.
寬 恕 or 寬 宥 or 寬 貸 to remit; to forgive; forgiving; lenient.
寬 恩 to extend kindness to.
寬 慰 to console; to comfort.
寬 懷 or 寬 心 to be easy in mind; pleased.
20寬 房 大 屋 roomy apartments; a spacious house.
寬 洪 大 量 liberal-minded; magnanimous.
寬 洪 惻 怛 liberal-minded and compassionate.
寬 海 大 量 broad-minded and magnanimous.
寬 牛 之 憂 to allay the anxiety of *Niu*.
25寬 猛 並 濟 severity tempered with gentleness.
寬·的 broad; wide.
寬·窄 broad and narrow—width.
寬·綽 wealthy; ample; spacious; liberal. (--*ch'ao*)
寬 緊 elastic.
30寬 緩 lenient; gentle; slow.
寬 縱 easy-going.
寬 舒 relaxation; lenient.
寬 衣 to remove the upper coat; ample, wide garments.
寬 裕 well-to-do; comfortably off.
35寬 讓 making allowances for; yielding.
寬 釋 to release as an act of grace.
寬 長 breadth and length—area.
寬 門 the broad door; broad, as theology.
寬 限 to extend a time-limit.
40寬·餘 abundant; overplus.
寬 饒 to act with lenience towards offenders.
寬 鬆 loose.

款 欵³
3579
To treat well; to detain.

款 冬 花 coltsfoot.
款 客 to entertain a visitor.
款 密 affectionate, intimate.
款·待 to entertain; to treat with cordiality.

5款 接 to receive; to usher.
款 曲 to receive with expressions of cordiality.
與 人 不 款 曲 unsociable.
款 洽 courteous.
款 留 to detain a visitor.
10款 語 words of welcome to a visitor.

(a) An item, an amount; article in a treaty.

款 式 pattern; style; article.
款 案 records of cases.
款 目 items; expenses.
款 項 a sum; items of expenditure.
5借 款 a loan.
入 款 debit side—receipts.
公 款 public funds.
各 款 all kinds; all sorts.
存 款 deposit, credit account.
10支 款 credit side—payments.
條 款 clause, article, section—in a treaty or agreement.
歸 款 to repay a loan.
籌 款 to raise funds.
約 款 articles of agreement.
15賠 款 indemnity.
進 款 income.

(b) Sincere. Real, true. Desire or wish.

款 伏 to confess guilt and submit to punishment.
款 引 (or 服) to confess the truth and submit to justice.
款 懷 sincere.
款 款 loyal, sincere; gently.
5款 然 according to one's wishes.
款 要 the facts of the case; crux of the matter.
款 附 sincere return to allegiance.

(c) To knock at.

款 塞 to approach the frontiers offering submission.
款 門 to knock at a door.
款 關 請 見 knocked at a closed door and asked for an interview.

(d) To carve or engrave. Inscription. Intaglio letters.

款 居 內 而 凹 (on ancient vessels) the *k'uan* was on the inside and in intaglio.
款 識 primarily the *k'uan* was an inscription in intaglio, engraved on the inside of a vessel, and

shih was an inscription engraved in *rilievo* on the outside—now used generally for any inscription.

題 款 to write an inscription.

(e) Slowly.

款 動 slow movements.
款 斟 to pour wine slowly.
款 款 飛 flying slowly.
款 步 with slow steps.
款 段 馬 a quiet slow horse.

(f) To extend to; to reach.

款 牛 首 reached *Niu shou*.

(g) Empty.

款 言 不 聽 do not listen to empty talk.

窾 ³
3580　Hollow; ignorant; empty.

窾 啓 uninformed; ignorant.
窾 坎 a hollow place.
窾 櫃 an empty cupboard.
窾 空 a vacuum.
⁵窾 竅 an empty hole.
窾 要 the facts, the crux of the matter.

鐬 ⁴
3581　A branding-iron.　To solder.

鐬 刻 to brand.
鐬 縫 to seal a seam.

梡 ³
3582　A small wooden stand having four legs; it was used in sacrifice. Faggots. Also read *huan²*. A kind of tree.

KUANG.　(ㄍㄨㄤ)

光 ¹
3583　Light; favour; brightness; honour. To illumine. Glossy.

光 之 分 散 diffusion of light.
光 之 反 射 reflection of light.
光 之 吸 收 absorption of light.
光 之 速 度 velocity of light.
⁵光 亮 or 光 明 clear, bright; glorious.
光 光 堂 堂 的 in good order; tidy.

光 分 器 spectroscope. A.c.分 光 鏡
光 前 裕 後 to glorify ancestors and enrich posterity.
光 力 brightness or intensity of light.
¹⁰光 回 reflection of light. 回 光, 反 光
光 圖 spectrum.
光 圖 分 析 spectrum analysis.
光 圖 鏡 spectroscope.
帶 光 圖 band spectrum.
¹⁵光 大 glorious and great.
光 天 化 日 times of prosperity and peace; in broad daylight.
光 學 light as a science, optics.
光 學 器 具 optical instrument.
光 宗 耀 祖 to reflect glory on one's ancestors.
²⁰光 帶 spectrum.
光 度 intensity of light; illuminating power.
光 度 表 photometer.
光 強 度 intensity of light.
光 彩 brilliance; splendour.
²⁵光 復 return of light—the restoration; revolution of 1911.
光 復 紀 念 Commemoration of the Revolution of 1911.
光 復 軍 the army of the revolution.
光 怪 a strange light.
光 折 refraction.＝折 光
³⁰光 散 astigmatism.＝散 光
光 昌 splendid; brilliant.
光 明 磊 落 a conscience at peace and void of offence.
光 映 sparkling, gleaming.
光 景 prospect; circumstances; probably.
³⁵光 景 可 以 就 來 probably able to come soon judging by the circumstances.
光 景 很 難 times are very bad.
三 塊 錢 的 光 景 about three dollars.
看 光 景 judge by the circumstances.
光 榮 glory, splendour.
⁴⁰光 浪 waves of light; light-waves.
光 源 source of illumination.
光 潔 bright and clean.
光 澤 or 光 潤 glossy, shining, lustrous.
光 焰 flame.
⁴⁵光 照 to shine; to illumine.
光 燿 magnificence; illustrious.
光 球 the photosphere.
光 環 the rings of Saturn.
光 素 elements of light—the spectrum.

⁵⁰光 線 ray of light.
光 線 不 足 the light was insufficient.
光 臨 brightness approaching—the arrival of a visitor.
光 芒 a flash of light, as an electric spark.
光 花 splendid, bright.
⁵⁵光 華 or 光 輝 glorious; splendid; gay.
光 行 差 aberration of light.(-*ch'a¹*)
光 覺 light-sensation.
光 角 angle of light.
光 射 a sunbeam; gleam of light; radiation of light.
⁶⁰光 輪 halo, aureole.
光 道 the ecliptic.
光 降 the light descends—you have come to visit me.
光 陰 light and shade—time.
光 陰 似 箭 time flies like an arrow.
⁶⁵光 風 a light, warm breeze.
光 風 霽 月 light breeze and clear moon—of a man's clear virtue.
光 體 luminous body.
光 鮮 bright and new.
候 光 to await a visitor.
⁷⁰叨 光 to beg a little light—ask a favour; to enjoy a favour.
回 光 反 照 the dying flicker of a man's life.
圓 光 lunar halo.
夜 光 a pearl.
日 光 月 光 sunlight and moonlight.
⁷⁵發 光 to emit light; to radiate.
絲 光 lustre of silk.
豪 光 aureole round the head of a saint.
閃 光 glittering; to glisten.

(a) Smooth, bare, naked.　Alone.

光 手 with bare hands.
光 棍 a bare stick—swindler, rogue, pettifogger; a bachelor.
光 溜 溜 的 quite smooth and bare; naked, stripped.
光 滑 bright, shining, polished, smooth.
⁵光 着 脊 梁 upper part of the body stripped bare.(-*niang*)
光 脚 bare feet.
光 蛋 a slippery egg—a treacherous man.
光 身 naked.
光 身 來 to come without presents, etc.

¹⁰光 頭 or 光 禿 bald-headed.
花 光·了 all spent.

(b) Only.

光 有 一 個 there is only one.
光 說 話 不 行 mere talk is of no use.

桄¹ A coir-palm.
3584

桄 榔 coir-palm.

洸¹ Sparkling water. Bold.
3585

胱¹ The bladder.
3586

膀 胱 the bladder.

觥¹
觵 } A cup made of horn. Obstinate. Also read huang¹.
3587

觥 羊 a large ram.
觥 觥 obstinate, determined.

鈁¹ Used for Ra, the symbol of Radium.
3588

逛⁴ To ramble, to wander about, to stroll, to roam.
3589

逛·一·逛 or 遊 逛 or 開 逛 to go for a walk.
逛 廟 to visit temples.
逛 景 to go sight-seeing.
逛·的 腿 酸 I've walked till my legs ache.
逛 窰·子 to visit brothels.
逛 街 to stroll along the streets.

廣³ Extensive, wide, broad. Area. The province of Kwangtung. Canton. Broadminded.
3590

廣 交 an extensive acquaintance.
廣 博 wide, vast, extensive.
廣 廈 spacious mansions.
廣 告 advertisements.

⁵廣 告 欄 advertising column.
廣 告 經 理 人 advertising agent.
廣 告 部 advertising department.
廣 嗣 numerous posterity.
廣 坐 ample seating accommodation.
¹⁰廣 大 large; vast; profound.
廣 大 眼 光 wide vision; breadth of vision.
廣 寒 宮 the palace in the moon.
廣 學 會 Christian Literature Society.
廣 布 天 下 to circulate through the empire.
¹⁵廣 揚 to diffuse far and wide.
廣 文 former designation of the prefectural Director of Studies.
廣 東 人 or 廣·東 仔 Cantonese.
廣 淵 vast and deep.
廣 演 慈 悲 far-reaching compassion.
²⁰廣 漠 (or 莫) boundless, vast.
廣 濟 to do good on a large scale.
廣 狹 broad and narrow—breadth.
廣 益 great advantage.
廣 目 天 王 one of the four kings —Virupaksha, he rules in the west. (Budd.).
²⁵廣 眉 broad eyebrows.
廣 知 extensive knowledge.
廣 義 broad definition; liberal interpretation.
廣 莫 風 North wind.
廣 行 abundantly; widespread.
³⁰廣 行 善 事 widespread benevolence.
廣 被 —grace—extending to all.
廣 袤 breadth and length—area.
廣·西 Kwangsi Province.
廣 見 聞 to increase one's knowledge.
³⁵廣 貨 Cantonese goods.
廣 軌 broad gauge—railway.
廣 輪 area.
廣 運 area, dimensions; covering a wide area.
廣 野 the desert, wilds.
⁴⁰廣 量 (liang⁴) 多 少 what is the area?
廣 銷 a wide sale.
廣 長 舌 eloquence.
廣 闊 vast; broad; extensive.
廣 韻 rhyming dictionary published under the Sung dynasty.
⁴⁵兩 廣 Kwangtung and Kwangsi Provinces.
推 廣 to extend.
量⁴ 廣 of great capacity; liberalminded.

獷³ Fierce, rude, uncivilized. Also read k'uang⁴, kung³.
3591

獷 俗 barbarous customs.
獷 悍 ferocious.
獷 獷 難 近 dangerous to approach.

鄺³ A surname.
3592

K'UANG.　　(ㄎㄨㄤ)

匡¹ To deliver, to correct. To assist, to relieve. Square.
3593

匡 人 其 如 予 何 what harm can the people of K'uang do to me?—said by Confucius when in peril.
匡 其 不 及 to make up any deficiencies—of conduct, etc.
匡 助 to support; to assist.
匡 天 下 to put the empire in order.
⁵匡 復 to save the State and restore its prestige.
匡 扶 to re-organize; to correct.
匡 救 correcting and preserving.
匡 方 square, placed properly; on the square.
匡 時 to reform and deliver from the perils of the age.
¹⁰匡 正 to reform; to put in order.
匡 輔 to aid; to assist.
以 匡 不 逮 in order to make up any deficiencies—of conduct.

(a) The bulging as of a barrel or drum.

匡 當 tne bulging of the body of anything.

劻¹ Zealous, prompt.
3594

劻 勷 quick, hasty.

恇¹ To fear, apprehensive.
3595

恇 恇 apprehensive; timid.
恇 懾 fearful.

框[1] The end of a coffin where it can be opened. A frame, a framework; the skeleton of a lantern.
3596

框 檔 a window-sash or door-frame.
門 框 door-frame.

眶[1] Socket of the eye.
3597

筐[1] An open basket. A couch. A chest.
3598

筐·子 an open basket.
筐 牀 a square couch.
筐 球 basket-ball.
筐 篋 a long, narrow box or chest.
管 闚 筐 舉 limited outlook and experience.

誆[1.4.] To swindle; to mislead.
3599

誆 哄 or 誆 誘 to cheat.
誆 駕 I have misled you in bringing you here—said when a host has to leave a guest.
誆 騙 to cheat.

閶[1] The frame of a door or window fixed in a wall.
3600

門 閶 a door-frame.

狂[2] Wild, mad, overbearing; cruel, violent. Also read huang[2].
3601

狂 且 (chü[1]) a crazy person; flippant foolish person.
狂 信·的 a fanatic.
狂 傲 haughty; domineering.
狂 勃 violent manner.
[5]狂 吠 wild words like the barking of a dog.
狂 喜 frantically overjoyed.
狂 士 or 狂 儒 a pedant.
狂 夫 a dissolute man.
狂 奔 running like mad.
[10]狂 妄 disorderly; ill-behaved; arrogant.
狂 徒 a profligate.
狂 性 headstrong, violent disposition.
狂 恣 to give reins to.
狂 悖 acting in defiance of right.

[15]狂 想 extravagant thoughts.
狂 態 a proud bearing.
狂 放 unrestrained; profligate.
狂 易 changed (in disposition) through madness.
狂 暴 wild, violent.
[20]狂 瀾 severe floods.
狂 熱 fanatical enthusiasm.
狂 犬 a mad dog.
狂 狷 ardently devoted to, yet cautious.
狂 生 a profligate.
[25]狂 病 lunatic; mad.
狂 疾 a mad fit.
狂 癡 crazy; demented.
狂 瞽 wild and blind—stupid; crazy.
狂 童 a young fool.
[30]狂 笑 foolish laughter.
狂 簡 ambitious and impetuous.
狂 者 進 取 an ardent man advances and lays hold—of the truth.
狂 而 不 直 ardent but not upright.
狂 草 a very free form of scribbling.
[35]狂 蕩 profligate.
狂 藥 wine.
狂 行 going to extremes.
狂 言 nonsense; lies.
狂 詈 vile abuse.
[40]狂 躁 eccentric; crazy.
狂 風 a gale of wind.
狂 飲 greedy drinking.
今 之 狂 也 蕩 the ambitious of the present day give way to wild license.
古 之 狂 也 肆 the ambitious of past days showed a disregard for small matters.
[45]書 狂 bibliomania.
發 狂 to go crazy.
酒 狂 dipsomania.

誑[2] Lies; to deceive.
3602

誑 之 以 理 之 所 有 deceived by what has reason in it.
誑 言 or 誑 語 wild talk; lies.
誑 騙 to cheat.

況
况[4] In addition; moreover. How much more? An initial particle. To compare. The first is also read huang[4].
3603

況 乎 moreover, further.
況 兼 or 況 且 or 況 復 or 況 又 further, still more, in addition, besides.
況 味 flavour; character; quality.
何 況 how much more? still less?
景°況 affairs; things in general.
近 況 recent affairs; recent life.

貺[4] To give, to bestow; to confer. Inter. preceding. Also read huang[4].
3604

貺 儀 a present.
貺 施 or 貺 賜 to grant to; to confer.
天 貺 有 德 Heaven (God) has bestowed virtue upon him.

壙[4] A vault; a tomb, a brick grave.
3605

壙 地 an open space.
壙 野 a wilderness of graves.
進 壙 to inter.
開 壙 to dig a grave.

曠[4] A desert, a wilderness.
3606

曠 野 a desert, a wilderness.
開 曠 to open up waste lands.

(a) Waste, empty. To waste. To vacate, to neglect.

曠 功 to neglect duties; to idle.
曠 學 to neglect studies.
曠 工 to neglect business.
曠 延 時 日 delayed for some time.
[5]曠 日 to waste the day.
曠 日 持 久 they were inactive for many days.
曠 職 to be remiss in office.
曠 課 to neglect classes in school.
曠 責 neglectful of the duties of one's office.

(b) Unmarried, alone.

曠 夫 an unmarried man.

(c) Distant; far-reaching.

曠 然 無 崖 boundless.
曠 遠 distant; widely separated.
曠 邈 far from home.
曠 隔 wide apart; separated.

礦 鑛 3607
[4] The ore of metals. A mine. Also read *kung*[3].

礦 丁 a miner.
礦 井 a mine-shaft.
礦 務 mining matters.
礦 務 局 Bureau of Mines.
[5]礦 區 mining areas.
礦 坑 a mine-shaft.
礦 夫 a miner.
礦 學 mineralogy.
礦 山 a mine.
[10]礦 山 技 師 mining expert.
礦 師 mining engineer.
礦 朴 ores.
礦 業 mining industry.
礦 業 權 mining rights.
[15]礦 油 mineral oils.
礦 泉 mineral spring.
礦°物 minerals.
礦°物 學 mineralogy.
礦°物 界 mineral kingdom.
[20]礦 產 minerals.
礦 產 富 有 rich in minerals.
礦 石 ores.
礦 砂 metallic ores.
礦 科 department of mining.
[25]礦 脈 vein of ore.
礦 苗 outcrop of mineral or ore.
礦 銅 copper ore.
礦 鐵 iron ore.
煤 礦 coal mine.
[30]開 礦 to open a mine.

纊 絖 3608
[4] Fine floss-silk.

纊 中 引 線 to draw a thread of silk from a confused mass of floss—to bring order out of disorder.
纊 絮 unsorted cotton.
絲 纊 silks.

KUEI. (ㄍㄨㄟ)

圭 珪 3609
[1] A jade tablet or baton conferred upon feudal princes by the emperor, as a symbol of dignity and authority. It varied in shape with the rank.

圭 田 a piece of land given to officials, the produce of which supplied the means for sacrifice.
圭 璋 a jade tally—as sign of authority for an envoy—honourable.
圭 臬 ancient measure—a pattern or model.
圭 角 sharp corner—correct, honest, incorrupt.
執 圭 to grasp the symbol—to hold office.
白 圭 之 玷 a flaw in a white symbol of office.

(a) The smallest measure, less than a pinch.

圭 勺 the least amount.

桂 3610
[4] The cassia or cinnamon.

桂 圓 dried longans 龍 眼.
桂 子[3] cassia buds.
桂 子[3] 蘭 孫 famous posterity.
桂 宮 palace built at *Si-an,* Shensi by *Han Wu-ti* 漢 武 帝.
[5]桂 月 the eighth lunar month.
桂 枝 twigs of cassia.
桂 林 府 Kweilin in Kwangsi.
桂 江 Cassia River in Kwangsi.
桂 皮 cassia bark.
[10]桂 皮 油 or 桂 花 油 cassia oil.
桂 粉 face-powder from Kweilin.
桂 花 the *Osmanthus fragrans.*
桂 花 布 figured calicoes.
桂 輪 the moon.
[15]桂 魄 the moon.
折 桂 to pluck the cassia—to gain the former third degree or 進 士.
肉 桂 cinnamon.

硅 3611
[1] Used for Si, the symbol for Silicon.

硅 藻 diatom.

邽 3612
[1] Ancient name for districts in Kansu and Shensi.

閨 3613
[1] Women's apartments; private quarters in official or family residences. Lady-like, feminine.

閨 女 or 閨 秀 a virgin, a young lady. 閨·女 daughter.
閨 門 or 閨 閣 or 閨 中 the women's apartments.
深 閨 處[3] 女 a virgin of the inner apartments.

鮭 3614
[1] The fresh-water porpoise. Also read *hsi*[2]. See also 鯰 No. 6599.

劮 3615
[1] Wearied, exhausted.

足 劮 tired, footsore.

皈 3616
[1] To follow, to comply with. Used by Buddhists for the next.

皈 依 佛 to take refuge in Buddha.
皈 依 僧 to take refuge in the priesthood.
皈 依 法 to take refuge in the law.
三 皈 the three refuges, as above.

歸 归 3617
[1] The marriage of a woman. To return to; to revert to; to go back. To belong to. To restore. To send back.

歸 主 to return to the Lord—conversion.
歸 于 上 to die.
歸 人 a dead man.
歸 伍 to return to the ranks.
[5]歸 休 to return home for recuperation.
歸 你 管 it is under your charge.
歸 併 to re-unite; to compound; to blend.
歸 依 or 依 歸 to put confidence in.
歸 佳 城 or 歸 土 to die.
[10]歸 償 to refund; to compensate.
歸 元 to restore to health.
歸 入 to make part of; to enter in.
歸 到 本 家 to return to one's native place.
歸 化 to be naturalized as a citizen.
[15]歸 化 人 a naturalized person.
歸 化 條 件 regulations governing naturalization.
歸 原 主 revert to the original owner.
歸 去 to go back.
歸 古 or 歸 世 dead; to die.

²⁰歸 向 to yield to; to go towards.
歸 咎 to lay the blame on another.
歸 命 to submit to; to trust in.
歸 回 to return.
歸 國 to return to one's native land.
²⁵歸 坐 to take one's seat.
歸 天 to return to God; to die.
歸 妻 to bring home a wife.
歸 官 to confiscate; to be confiscated.
歸 宗 to revert to the original stock, as when an adopted child returns to the original family.
³⁰歸 家 to go home.
歸 宿 the final resting-place.
歸 甯 a bride's visit to her parents 3 days after wedding,—or any other time.
歸 市 those who return to allegiance are as numerous as those going to market.
歸 從 to follow; to obey.
³⁵歸 心 thoughts of returning; to submit in heart.
歸 心 似 箭 a mind bent on returning is like an arrow.
歸 於 to attribute to; to revert to.
歸 於 一 to unite into one.
歸 於 烏 有 to come to nothing.
⁴⁰歸 服 or 歸 降 (hsiang²) to submit; to yield.
歸 期 date of one's return; ultimately; date of marriage.
歸 本 to return to the former state; to repay principal.
歸 根 at last; finally; in the end; to revert to the original condition.
歸 款 to repay; to pay for goods.
⁴⁵歸 歟 歸 歟 Let us return! Let us return!
歸 正 to revert to purity; to come back to the right way.
歸 正 敎 (American) Reformed Church.
歸 泉 to die.
歸 烏 the returning crows.
⁵⁰歸 無 to be annihilated; to die.
歸 爲 to belong to.
歸 田 to return to one's fields—to retire from public life.
歸 省 to visit one's parents.
歸 眞 finally; in the end. To die —(Budd.).
⁵⁵歸 究 in the end; finally; after all.
歸 納 inductive—reasoning.
歸 納 式 敎 法 inductive methods of teaching.

歸 納 推 理 inductive reasoning.
歸 納 法 inductive methods.
⁶⁰歸 結 to terminate; to wind up.
歸 給 to give to; to return to.
歸 總 collectively; in a lump; on an average.
歸 罪 to inculpate; to lay the blame on another; to bring a crime home to.
歸 義 to return to right principles.
⁶⁵歸 老 to resign on account of age.
歸 耕 to return to farming—to retire from public life.
歸 葬 to bring home the remains for burial.
歸 趙 to return the (gem) to Chao,—send a thing to its proper owner.
歸 路 the way of retreat.
⁷⁰歸 途 the return path; the way home.
歸 遺 to take home a present.
歸 還 to return; to send back; to go back.
歸 附 to return to allegiance; to attach oneself to.
歸 隊 to return to the army; fall in!
⁷⁵歸 順 to submit; to surrender.
歸 類 to arrange; to classify.
歸 首 to lay an information against oneself; to confess.
歸 骨 to bring remains home for burial.
歸 點 point of convergence.
⁸⁰殊 途 同 歸 to arrive at the same conclusions by different means.
總 歸 always.

(a) To divide, as in arithmetic.

歸 法 the rules of division by any number up to nine inclusive.
歸 除 division and subtraction; division by any number above ten.

(b) Read kuei⁴. To send a present of food.

歸 孔 子³ 豚 he sent Confucius a present of a pig.

規 ¹ A pair of compasses. A circle or disc, thus:—a custom; usage; regulation. Fees.
3618

規 例 or 規 制 a regulation; a by-law.
規 元 the Shanghai scale for silver. See below—32.

規 則 principle; rule; law.
規 勸 to reprimand; to admonish.
⁵規 定 to regulate according to rule.
規 定 權 限 limited by law.
規 平 銀 Shanghai scale for silver.
規 戒 to warn; to admonish.
規 條 regulations.
¹⁰規 模 a pattern; model; scale.
規 模 卑 狹 mean; sordid.
規 模 狹 隘 his pattern was narrow.
規 正 to adjust; to correct.
規 求 無 度 unbounded covetousness.
¹⁵規 爲 scheme; plan.
規 田 a piece of land divided into nine portions.
規 畫 scheme; contrivance; to mark out.
規 矩 compass and square—custom; usage. 規·矩 rule; true (carpentry).
規·矩 人 well-behaved person.
²⁰規 矩 方 圓 之 至 by the compass and the square the perfections of round and square are obtained.
規 矩 準 繩 compass, square, level and plumb-line—exact; fixed laws.
規 程 rules and regulations.
規 章 rules; regulations.
規 範 model; standard.
²⁵規 約 an agreement.
規 行 矩 步 in every act and movement to be guided by rule —strictly upright and correct.
規 規 inexperienced; bewilderment.
規 諫 to remonstrate with a superior.
規 費 fees; customary gratuities.
³⁰規 過 to correct one's faults; to reprove.
規 避 to pervert or evade the law.
規 銀 Shanghai scale for silver. See No. 5303—B.7.
規 鑑 to take warning by the example of another.
規 院 Hall of Admonition. (Budd.).
³⁵定 規 to fix rules.
日 規 sun-dial; disc of the sun.
月 牛 規 half full-moon.
行 (hang²) 規 trade-custom.

嬀 ¹ Name of a river in Shansi. Crafty.
3619

瀉 [1] Name of a river.
Also read *wei*[1].
3620

龜 [1] The tortoise. Longevity.
龟 Used as a term of abuse
—a cuckold. Radical 213.
3621

龜兆 the marks on the seared tortoise-shell—for divination.

龜公 a cuckold.

龜卜 divination by the shell of the tortoise.

龜子 a term of abuse—cuckold; illegitimate.

[5]龜從 to divine by the tortoise-shell.

龜板 the shell of the tortoise.

龜殼 tortoise-shell.

龜爪 or 龜家 a procurer.

龜玉 valuables.

[10]龜玉毀於櫝中 if a tortoise or jewel be injured in its case.

龜筴 tortoise-shell and stalks of a certain grass—divination.

龜紐 knob on a seal.

龜背 arched like the back of a tortoise.

龜胸 bulging like the breast of a tortoise.

[15]龜脚 a sea-anemone.

龜貝 tortoise-shell and cowries—ancient coinage.

龜貨 valuables.

龜趺 base for a stone tablet, made in the form of a tortoise.

龜鑑 (or 鏡) a magic mirror—the tortoise foretells, the mirror reveals—an example.

[20]龜鶴 tortoise and crane—longevity.

龜鼎 the throne.

龜齡 longevity.

(a) Read *chün*[1]. Chapped.

龜坼 cracks in the soil through drought; crackly like the shell of a tortoise—used for chapped hands.

龜手 chapped hands.

龜裂 chapped.

(b) Read *chiu*[1].

龜茲 A country of Central Asia: Kuchah.

伔 [3] Crafty, treacherous.
Inter. 詭 No. 3626.
3622 Almost attained to. Suddenly.

伔伔成 not to succeed at first; almost achieved.

伔得伔失 suddenly gained and suddenly lost.

塊 [3] Dilapidated, ruined.
3623

塊垣 a ruined wall.

(a) A stand for goblets.

媿 [3] Quiet and nice.
3624

恑 [3] To change; to alter; to
3625 accommodate oneself to.

恑異 strange; marvellous; to change one's form.

恑變 to trim—as an opportunist.

詭 [3] To feign, to cheat. Cunning. Perverse.
3626

詭名 to falsify names.

詭嘴 artful tongues.

詭戾 treacherous and perverse.

詭激 not in accord with right.

[5]詭祕 secret.

詭計 an artful device.

詭計多端 full of schemes and tricks.

詭詐 or 詭譎 crafty; cunning; treacherous.

詭謀 treacherous devices.

[10]詭辯 (or 辨) sophistry; paradoxes.

詭辯學派 sophism.

詭辭 lies; pretended excuse.

詭道 perverse ways; heterodox.

詭遇 to get by cunning.

[15]詭銜竊轡 to eject the bit and gnaw the reins—the more you force a horse, the more he resists.

詭隨 cunning and obsequious.

(a) To oppose; to offend.

有所詭于天之理與 Have I offended in anywise against the laws of God?

詭毀 to slander; to defame.

(b) Odd, strange.

詭狀殊形 fantastic shapes and strange forms.

詭特 strange; extraordinary appearance.

詭異 odd; uncommon.

跪 [4] To kneel; to bow down to.
3627

跪下 or 跪倒 to kneel down.

跪奏 to memorialize the throne.

跪官 to kneel before an official.

跪拜 to kneel and make obeisance.

[5]跪接 to receive kneeling.

跪稟 to make a humble petition.

跪謝 humble thanks.

跪送 to kneel and bid goodbye—as a mark of respect.

跪鍊 to kneel on chains—a torture.

[10]跪香 to kneel and hold a stick of incense—in penitence or punishment.

羊有跪乳之恩 the lamb has the grace of kneeling to suck,—filial piety.

癸 [3] The last of the *Ten Stems*
天干. Refers to the north
3628 and water.

天癸 menstruation.

晷 [3] A shadow. The gnomon
of a sun-dial. Time, the
3629 day.

晷刻 a short time.

晷形電話機 dial telephone-instrument.

晷面 a dial.

日晷 a sun-dial.

[5]移晷 the movement of the shadow—a little while.

繼晷 to lengthen the day.

飛晷 the flying shadow—time.

宄 [3] A traitor; a villain.
Distinguish 究 No. 1199.
3630

寇盜 …. 起外爲宄 when rebels and bandits arise from without they are called *kuei*.

軌 [3] A rut, a track, a path. An
orbit. The axle of a wheel:
3631 —thus—a rule or law.

軌 則 laws; regulations.

軌 度 laws; statutes.

軌 模 pattern; rule.

軌 法 or 軌 範 a rule; regular mode of action.

[5]軌 漏 ancient instrument for telling the time.

軌 物 rules; laws.

軌 線 line of railway.

軌 謀 to plot.

軌 轍 a rut.

[10]軌 道 a constant path; orbit; groove; railway; tramway.

不 軌 irregular; unusual; illegal; rebellious.

同 軌 axle-trees all one width.

欲 謀 不 軌 to plot sedition.

車 軌 cart-ruts.

鐵 軌 rails.

匭 [3]
3632
A casket, a small box.

簋 [3]
3633
A square basket of bamboo for holding grain used at sacrifices, feasts, etc. It is also defined as a round vessel of wood and a square or round vessel of metal, but the first seems to be the strictly correct use.

簋 簠 square and round vessels for grain and fruits.

鬼 [3]
3634
Disembodied spirits. Demons. Spirits of the dead. Ghost, goblin. See below 34, 39, 42, 43, 46. Radical 194.

鬼 卒 demon attendants.

鬼 商 量 mutual agreement to do evil.

鬼·子 or 洋 鬼·子 or 番 鬼 foreign devil—term of abuse.

鬼 密 secret.

[5]鬼 弊 secret understanding for dishonest purposes.

鬼 怪 bogy; ghost; sprite.

鬼 打·算 to make a private decision—to do evil.

鬼 拿 鬼 a rogue catching a rogue.

鬼 斧 神 工 supernatural workmanship.

[10]鬼 混 to live an idle, slovenly life.

鬼 火 will-o'-the-wisp.

鬼 物 demons; ghosts.

鬼 王 ruler of the demons.

鬼 祟 demoniacal; devilish tricks.

[15]鬼 神 demons and gods; spiritual beings good or evil.

鬼 神 其 違 天 乎 would the lower and higher spiritual beings dare oppose God?

鬼 神 福 善 the spiritual beings reward the good.

鬼 神 難 欺 it is difficult to deceive the spiritual beings.

事 鬼 敬 神 而 遠 之 serve the demons, respect the gods, keeping them at a distance.

[20]敬 鬼 神 而 遠 之 respect the demons and the gods but keep them at a distance.

鬼 節 the festival to demons on the 15th of the 7th lunar month.

鬼 籍 record of the dead in Hades.

鬼 胎 a womb that does not bring forth; evil plots; dark schemes.

鬼 蜮 secret danger to a man; treacherous persons.

[25]鬼 話 false words; to whisper; to speak with privately.

鬼 車 a goatsucker. 鬼 臉 兒 a mask.

鬼 迷 possessed by demons.

鬼 附·着 possessed by demons.

鬼 頭 風 a whirlwind.

[30]鬼 頭 鬼 腦 hiding and peeping; ludicrous; outlandish.

鬼 魂 ghosts; disembodied spirits.

鬼 魅 a bogy; sprites.

鬼 厲 demons; evil spiritual beings.

人 死 曰 鬼 when a man dies he is called a kuei.

[35]冒 失 鬼 a heedless, reckless person.

弄 鬼 to play tricks; to scare people; to indulge in illicit practices.

憑 鬼 to have intercourse with demons.

掉 鬼 to play pranks.

未 能 事 人 焉 能 事 鬼 you are not able to serve the living, how can you serve the spirits of the dead?

[40]禱 鬼 to mutter to oneself; to whisper.

禳 鬼 to quieten evil spirits.

非 其 鬼 而 祭 之 諂 也 for a man to sacrifice to a spirit which does not belong to him is flattery.

餓 鬼 hungry demons, the spirits of those who have not been buried with proper rites, or those who have no one to offer sacrifices for them; an uninvited guest.

[45]魔 鬼 The Devil. Satan.

鴉 片 鬼 an opium fiend.

眾 生 必 死.... 此 之 謂 鬼 all must die... and they are then called kuei.

扮 鬼 臉 to make a grimace.

瑰 [1]
3635
A kind of jasper. Extraordinary. Admirable.

瑰 意 琦 行 just ideas and admirable actions.

瑰 瑋 extraordinary; pre-eminent.

(a) Read kuei[4]. The rose.

玫 瑰[4]花 roses.

貴 [4]
3636
Honourable. Expensive, costly. Prized, high-class. To hold in honour. "Your." Distinguish 貴 No. 3566.

貴 主 a princess.

貴 人 a man of high position. See below—10.

貴 介 a nobleman.

貴 以 專 give importance to thoroughness.

[5]貴 仕 a high official.

貴 合 於 秦 to approve of a league with Ch'in.

貴 器 precious things; children.

貴 國 Your honourable nation?

貴 士 (or 地) Your honourable home district?

[10]貴 妃 and 貴 人 imperial concubines of the third and fourth rank respectively.

貴 姓 or 尊 姓 Your honourable surname?

貴 妾 in ancient times a concubine with children was so called.

貴 官 a high official.

貴 客 an esteemed customer; honoured guest, etc.

[15]貴 州 Province of Kweichow.

貴 庚 or 貴 甲 子 What are the characters of your honourable place in the cycle? i.e., Your age?

貴·得 很 very expensive.

貴 德 a virtuous man of high rank.

貴 戚 relatives by marriage of the imperial family.

[20]貴 族 the nobility; imperial clan.

貴 族 團 the aristocracy.
貴 族 政 治 aristocracy.
貴 族 院 House of Lords.
貴 治 Your jurisdiction.
25 貴 相 (*hsiang*[4]) a noble face—indicating success in life.
貴 細 elegant—as manners; delicate.
貴 冑 a nobleman; princes of the blood.
貴 臣 honourable official.
貴 自 勉 to put emphasis on self-exertion.
30 貴 要 influential official with much authority.
貴 貴 to honour the honourable.
貴 賤 noble and base; patrician and plebeian; dear and cheap.
貴 近 high statesmen with access to the throne.
貴 鄉 Your home district or village.
35 貴·重 weighty; valuable; to prize.
貴 金 precious metals.
貴 門 Your family.
貴 顯 honourable and glorious; held in high esteem.
富 貴 riches and honour.
40 尊 貴 honourable; to honour.

愧 [4]
3637
Troubled, anxious. Dazed. Also pron. *k'uei*[4].

愧 亂 confused; dazed.
愧 愧 confused; stupid.

櫃 匱 鑕 [4]
3638
A cupboard; a press; a wardrobe. Shop-counter.

櫃 圍 or 櫃 檯 counter in a shop.
櫃·子 a cupboard.
櫃 房 a counting house.
櫃 桶 a drawer or till.
5 押 櫃 a deposit.
掌 櫃·的 manager of a shop, used as general term of address to tradesmen, etc., in the north.
書 櫃 bookcase.

(a) Read *k'uei*[4]. (of second character only) Exhausted, failing, deficient.

劊 [4]
3639
To cut, to amputate. Also pron. *k'uai*[4].

劊·子 手 an executioner.

劌 [4]
3640
To cut, to wound, to injure.

鱖 [4]
3641
A kind of perch with large mouth, small scales and black stripes.

鱖 魚 the mandarin fish.

K'UEI. (ㄎㄨㄟ)

刲 [1]
3642
To cut open and clean—as fish. To kill, to sacrifice. To stab.

奎 奞 [2]
3643
The stride made by a man.

奎 星 閣 a hall devoted to the worship of the God of Literature.
奎 宿 the 15th constellation, which has sixteen stars, supposed to resemble a person striding.
奎 蹣 to hop about.

跬 [3]
3644
To step. A stride equal to half a pace.

跬 步 a step.
跬 譽 a brief reputation.

(a) Read *hsieh*[4.5]. Exhausted.

悝 [1]
3645
To laugh at. Read *li*[2]. To pity; afflicted, sad.

喟 [4]
3646
To breathe heavily. Also read *wei*[1].

喟 然 而 嘆 to sigh deeply.

盔 [1]
3647
A helmet. Block on which caps are made. A basin.

盔 甲 helmet and mail.
盔·頭 a cap or hat-block.
頭 盔 a helmet.

窺 [1]
3648
To pry into; to watch; to spy. Inter. next.

窺 事 to watch and see how things will turn out.
窺 佔 to encroach on.
窺 伺 to watch the doings of a home in order to avail oneself of an opportunity to enter.
窺 天 鏡 a telescope. = 7043.47.
5 窺 察 to look into; to ferret out.
窺 探 (*t'an*[4]) to pry into.
窺 涉 concerned with.
窺 測 to make observations.
窺 看 or 窺 見 or 窺 視 to spy on; to peep at.
10 窺 聽 to listen stealthily.
窺 豹 一 斑 can spy one spot of a leopard—only get a limited view.

閱 [1]
3649
To peep; to observe; to spy. Inter. preceding.

閱 視 to spy out; to peep at.
閱 覢 to have a peep at.

虧 [1]
3650
To lose, to fail. Failure; loss, deficiency.

虧 人 to annoy, to wrong another.
虧 倒 to go bankrupt.
虧 價 to underpay.
虧 心 a bad conscience; ingratitude.
5 虧 心 之 人 an ungrateful person.
虧 心 事 a discreditable matter.
虧 折 to be deficient; to lose.
虧 損 to injure; injury.
虧 數 the amount of deficit.
10 虧 本 loss of capital; to fail in business.
虧 欠 deficiency; loss; in arrears.
虧 短 deficient; deficit.
虧 空[4] debt; deficit; bankrupt.
虧 累 to involve in losses.
15 虧 缺 to fall short of; deficiency.
虧 耗 to lose money.
虧 負 to wrong; to be ungrateful; to give less than is due.
虧 賠 to make up a deficiency.
虧 蝕 to cause another financial losses. *See below* A—1.
20 吃 虧 to suffer loss; to be victimized; to be deceived—this term has a wide range of usage.

無 虧 心 a conscience void of offence.
血 虧 anæmia.

(a) To wane.

虧 蝕 an eclipse. *See above*—19.
不 虧 不 崩 never waning, never failing.
月 滿 則 虧 when the moon reaches the full, it begins to wane.

(b) Happily, fortunately; owing to.

虧·了 你 thanks to you; I have troubled you.
虧·得 thanks to....; fortunately.
幸·虧 fortunately; happily.

逵[2] Cross-roads; a thorough-fare.
3651

馗[2] A centre from which nine roads lead out. Inter. pre-ceding. The cheek bones. High.
3652

馗 廚 mushrooms.
中 馗 mushrooms.

傀[1] Great, gigantic, monstrous. Wonderful. Also read *kuei*[1].
3653

傀 人 a giant.
傀 偉 a powerful man; a giant.
傀 然 獨 立 he was without an equal.
大 傀 異 災 an extraordinary ca-lamity.

(a) Read *k'uei*[3]. A wooden pup-pet.

傀 儡 puppets; Punch and Judy; Quisling.

愧 媿 } [4] Ashamed; conscience-stricken; bashful.
3654

愧 心 conscience-stricken.
愧 忿 shame and anger.
愧 恥 ashamed; abashed.
愧 恨 to be ashamed and grieved.
[5]愧 汗 perspiring on account of deep mortification.

羞 愧 modest, shy.
愧 赧 to blush with shame.

魁[2] The head; the chief; best. Monstrous, eminent, great.
3655

魁 偉 of great stature; stalwart.
魁 士 an eminent scholar.
魁 岸 imposing in stature and appearance.
魁 帥 a general; a leader.
[5]魁 手 the best man; a head; chief.
魁 柄 the power of the throne.
魁 梧 stalwart, gigantic stature.
魁 武 stalwart; great stature.
魁 頭 to do the hair in a knot on top.
[10]魁 首 or 元 魁 best, first, chief; first on list of candidates for the former second degree of 舉 人.
文 魁 亞 魁 first and second on list for second degree of 舉 人.
罪 魁 the chief of sinners.

(a) The four stars of the Dipper.

魁 星 the chief star of the Dipper, worshipped as god of literature.
魁 杓 the second star of the Dip-per.

餽[4] To make a present of food. To offer in sacrifice.
3656 Inter. 饋 No. 3669.

餽 送 to present.
餽 餞 food presented to one start-ing on a journey.

戣[2] A lance.
3657

揆[3.4] To consider; to guess; to calculate.
3658

揆 之 以 日 he determined — its location — by the sun.
揆 度 (*to*[4.5.]) to estimate, to con-sider.
揆 席 ancient designation of a prime minister.
揆 情 度 (*to*[4.5.]) 理 to estimate the bearings of a principle or case.
揆 手 the master-mind; the best hand.

百 揆 ancient designation of a prime minister—the one who plans for and manages every-thing.

暌[1] In opposition; distant from; separated.
3659

暌 別 一 月 separated for a whole month.
暌 違 日 久 long separated.
暌 隔 sundered; estrangement; isolated.

睽[2] To squint; to stare at. Unusual; strange.
3660

萬 目 睽 睽 everybody staring.

葵[2] The mallow; the sunflower.
3661

葵 傾 to lean towards—as the sunflower to the sun—longing affection.
葵 扇 palm-leaf fans.
葵 篷 palm-thatch.
葵 花 sunflowers.
[5]葵 菜 edible mallows.
葵 表 a letter,—from early use of palm-leaves for writing.
葵 黃 sunflower-yellow.
日 葵 or 向 日 葵 the sunflower.
秋 葵 a hibiscus.
蜀 葵 the hollyhock.

(a) u.f. 揆 No. 3658. To calculate.

天 子[3] 葵 之 the emperor examin-ed them—for merits.

夔[2] A one-legged monster; a walrus. Grave, respectful.
3662

夔 夔 齊 慄 he looked grave and awestruck.

瞶[4] Dim sight of the aged. Distinguish 瞶 No. 3666. Also read *hui*[4].
3663

簣 蕢 } [4] A basket for carrying earth.
3664

功虧一簣 to fail of completion by one basketful; almost successful.

績[4] To draw; to embroider. Red strings for hats.
3665

聵[4] Deaf; born deaf. Also read *wai*[4].
3666

蕢[4] A straw-basket. A plant.
3667

荷蕢 to carry a basket on the shoulder.

闠[4] Gate of a market. Also read *hui*[4].
3668

饋[4] Provisions; food. To make a present. To offer food to a superior.
3669

饋人 a butler.
饋奠 to offer sacrifice.
饋禮 to make presents.
饋糧 to transport grain.
[5]饋給 to transport supplies.
饋路 transport-road for supplies.
饋送 to make a farewell present.
饋食 to offer food.
饋饌 to bring in food to a superior, [in the house,— the wife.
↑ 中饋 one who manages the cooking

歸[1] A group of small hills. Grand. Read *kuei*[4]. Solitary.
3670

歸然 alone; by itself.

KUN. (ㄍㄨㄣ)
(Kuen)

丨[3] A perpendicular stroke. Radical 2.
3671

棍[4] A stick, a cudgel.
3672

棍·子 a stick, a club.
棍成 natural.
棍徒 or 棍脚 or 棍匪 or 光棍 villains; rowdies; ruffians, etc.
棍棒 a club.

[5]棍香 sticks of incense.
棍騙 to wheedle out of; to cheat.
訟棍 a man who foments litigation; a pettifogger.
鐵棍 an iron bar.

緄[3] An embroidered sash. To sew. A cord or thong.
3673

緄帶 embroidered sash.
緄邊 embroidered border.

輥[3] To revolve; to turn round. A stone roller.
3674

輥·子 a stone roller used on the threshing floors, or for rolling in seed.
輥動 rotatory.
輥轉之速 the quick turning of a wheel; speed of rotation.

衮
袞[3] Robes worn by the emperor and feudal princes, during the *Chou* dynasty. Royal. Imperial.
3675

袞冕 a robe and crown—full dress.
袞龍袍 an imperial robe.

滾[3] Water flowing rapidly. Boiling.
3676

滾水 boiling water. ＝開水.
滾滾東流 floods rolling eastward.
滾熱 boiling hot.
滾燙 burning hot; in high fever.
[5]滾·起·來 to boil up.
滾開 or 沸滾 boiling, bubbling up.
財源滾滾 may the fountains of wealth bubble up!

(a) To roll, to roll over.

滾亂 to disarrange; to turn topsy-turvy.
滾·來 to come rolling along.
滾刀筋 or 滾刀肉 a desperado; one lost to a sense of shame.
滾木 to resort to force.
[5]滾濁 to make water muddy.
滾盤 to roll about.
滾 or 滾蛋 be off! begone!—term of abuse.

滾落 to fall down and roll away.
滾鞍下馬 he rolled off his horse.

(b) Commonly used in error for 緄 No. 3673.

滾邊 embroidered border.

鯀[3] A great fish. Name of the father of *Yü* the Great.
3677

K'UN. (丂ㄨㄣ)
(K'uen)

昆[1] An elder brother.
3678

昆玉 your brother.
昆季 or 昆弟 or 昆仲 elder and younger brothers.

(a) Posterity. Afterwards.

昆孫 the sixth generation below oneself.
昆裔 posterity.
後昆 after ages; posterity.

(b) Together. A multitude; hence used for insects.

昆羣 a multitude.
昆蟲 insects generally.
昆蟲學 entomology.

(c) Inter. next.

昆侖 Koulkun Mts. in Tibet.

(d) Read *hun*[1]. Used in tribal names.

昆邪 a branch of the *Hsiung nu* 匈奴 See No. 2812—A.

崑[1] High mountain in Tibet.
3679

崑崙山 Koulkun Mts. in Tibet.

琨[1] A fine kind of jade. A precious stone resembling a pearl. Also read *kun*[1].
3680

蜫
蚰[1] Insects. See 昆 No. 3678—B.
3681

蚰蟲 or 昆蟲 insects generally.

鯤[1] A sea-monster, leviathan. Young of fishes. Also read
3682 *kun*[1].

鯤 化 而 爲 鵬 the leviathan changes into the roc.

鵾[1] A jungle-fowl. Also read *kun*[1].
3683

坤
堃)[1] Inferior, subordinate. The earth as contrasted with heaven. Female, feminine. The *Eighth Diagram*.
3684 South-west.

坤 儀 earth.
坤 宅 the bride's family.
坤 母 mother-earth; a mother.
坤 角 an actress.
坤 造 a girl's horoscope.
坤 道 women; the action of the earthly principle.
乾 (*ch'ien*[2]) 坤 Heaven and Earth; superior and inferior; male and female; sun and moon, etc.

髡[1] To make the head bald.
3685

褌[1] Drawers; loose trousers. Also read *kun*[1].
3686

壼[3] A corridor in a palace; Apartments.
3687 Distinguish 壺 No. 2187.

困[4] Distress; difficulty; anxiety; poverty. Surrounded by. Weary, tired.
3688 Distinguish 囷 No. 7407.

困 乏 or 困·倦 tired; exhausted.
困 住 to restrain; to surround.
困 城 a besieged city.
困 守 or 圍 困 or 被 困 besieged; hemmed in.
[5]困 急 or 困 極 in straits; in extremities.
困 惱 vexed, bothered.
困 愁 城 besieged in a city of distress,— a heart full of grief.
困 憊 exhausted; worn out.
困 於 心 distressed in mind.
[10]困 於 酒 色 enslaved by wine and women.

困 死 worried to death.
困 獸 猶 鬭 even pent-up wild beasts try to fight.
困 眼 nodding, drowsy, tired.
困 窮 extreme poverty and distress.
[15]困 而 學 之 to learn in spite of difficulties.
困 苦 poverty; in great distress.
困 難 difficulty; distress; difficult.
困 難 之 時 hard times.
困 難 問 題 a difficult question.
[20]困 頓 tired; exhausted.
困 鬱 grieved; deeply anxious.

悃[3] Sincere, loyal, genuine.
3689

悃 實 simple, genuine.
悃 款 simple, genuine, single-hearted.
悃 誠 earnest and sincere; genuine.
謝 悃 sincere thanks.

捆[3] To bind; to plait; to tie up. Used with 綑 No. 3694.
3690

捆·上 to bind up.
捆·住 tied up.
捆 屨 to bind shoes.
捆 屨 織 席 to make hemp sandals and weave mats.
[5]捆 押 to put under restraint.
捆 綁 to bind.
捆 緻 to make fine; well plaited.
捆 紲 bound, tied.
捆·起·來 to tie up.
[10]捆 鎖 to chain; to fetter.
一 捆 a bundle.

梱[3] A moveable door-sill.
3691

梱 外 之 事 things outside the door—none of my business.

睏[4] To nod; to take a nap; sleep.
3692

睏·了 sleepy.
睏 着[2]了 to go to sleep; fast asleep. (*S. dial.*) = 睡 着[2]了

綑[3] To bind, as faggots or sheaves.
3693

綑[3] To bind, to cord. To plait, to braid. To hem. A border or trimming on the edge of a garment. A coil, a roll, a bundle. N.A.
3694

綑·在 一 塊 tie them together.
綑 倒[2]to throw down and bind.
綑 籐 to bind with rattans—as a chest.
綑 綁 or 綑·起·來 to bind.
綑 織 to weave.

裍[3] A border or band on the edge of a dress.
3695

閫[3] A threshold. Door leading to the women's apartments.
3696

閫 內 or 閫 外 within and without the women's apartments.
閫 安 peace; quiet.
閫 範 a pattern of female decorum.

KUNG.　(ㄍㄨㄥ)

(Kong)

工[1] Labour. A labourer; a workman. A job. The time occupied in doing a piece of work. Radical 48.
3697

工 不 信 度 those in office pay no regard to the proper rules.
工 事 塲 studio.
工 人 or 工 丁 a labourer.
工 人 保 險 workers' insurance.
[5]工 人 團 體 body of workmen—labour.
工 人 契 約 labour-contract.
工 人 子 弟 學 校 school for children of workers or employees.
工 人 結 合 問 題 problems of the union of workers.
工 人 義 務 敎 育 free education for workers.
[10]工 人 聯 合 會 labour-union.
工 人 騷 擾 labour-agitation.
工 作 to work; activities; labour.
工 作 日 a working-day.
工 作 時 間 hours of labour.
[15]工 作 物 products of labour.
工 具 tools; instruments of labour.
工 力 work.
↓工 合 Indusco, abbr. of 輕 工 業 合 作, q.v.

工 力 悉 敵 the workmanship of each vies with the other.

工 力 準 個 unit of work.

20 工 務 matters concerning labour.

工。匠 an artisan; a mechanic.

工 友 fellow-workman; factory and shop-hands.

工 品 manufactured articles.

工 商 事 業 trade.

25 工 商 友 誼 會 Friendly Association of Industry and Commerce.

工 商 學 聯 合 會 United Association of Industry, Commerce and Students.

工 商 局 Bureau of Industry and Commerce.

工 商 法 規 commercial and industrial laws and regulations.

工 商 界 the world of industry and commerce.

30 工 商 調 查 員 Inspector of Industry and Commerce.

工 商 部 Board of Industry and Commerce.

工 商 部 部 長³ Minister of Industry and Commerce.

工 團 labour-body.

工 團 主 義 syndicalism.

35 工 場 制 度 workshop or factory system, regulations, etc.

工 夫 time, leisure; labour—as devoted to an art.

工。夫 茶 Congo Tea.

他 很 有 些 工。夫 he has had very much experience in ....

沒 有 工。夫 I have no time or leisure.

40 費 點 工。夫 put forth an effort; take a little pains.

工 女 or 女 工 (or 紅) female-labour.

工 學 engineering. =77.

工 尺 字 name of a Chinese musical scale 五 六 凡 工 尺³ 上 乙 四 合 (-ch'ĕ³-)

工 巧 skill; art; craftsmanship.

45 工 師 engineer of public works.

工 廠 factory or mill.

工 廠 產 品 mill or factory-products.

工 律 labour-legislation.

工 徒 apprentices.

50 工 戰 industrial war.

工 手 artisan; workman.

工 料 labour and materials.

工 方 及 半 the work was only half-completed.

工 書 to study.

55 工 會 labour-union.

工 會 主 義 trades-unionism.

工 會 議 會 Trades Union Congress.

工 楷 well executed.

工 業 industries.

60 工 業 化 學 industrial chemistry.

工 業 國 industrial nations.

工 業 地 帶 industrial zone.

工 業 學 校 technical school.

工 業 時 代 industrial age.

65 工 業 用 具 industrial equipment.

工 業 進 步 industrial progress.

工 業 都 市 industrial towns or cities.

工 業 革 命 industrial revolution.

工 欲 善 其 事 必 先 利 其 器 a workman must first sharpen his tools if he wishes his work to be well done.

70 工 正 former chief of public works.

工 潮 發 生 rise of labour agitations.

工 率 rate of work; amount of energy put forth. (-lü⁴·⁵)

工 用 for use; employed in labour.

工 界 industrial world.

75 工 監 superintendent of works.

工 科 technical course or department. [engineering.

工。程 labour; construction work;

工 程 兵 sappers and miners.

工 程 師 an engineer.

80 工 程 處 department of public works.

工 程 隊 engineer corps.

工 竣 the work is finished.

工 競 labour-competition.

工 筆 畫 fine, delicate drawings.

85 工 緻 fine, skilful work.

工 藝 學 technology.

工。課 a task; literary or other employments, apart from manual labour. =3698.27.

工 讀 主 義 education for workers.

工 讀 互 助 團 Association for Education of Workers.

90 工 費 expenses of labour.

工 資 wages for workmen.

工 資 之 最 低 額 minimum wage.

工 資 標 準 率 standard rate of wages. (-lü⁴·⁵)

工 部 former Board of Works.

95 工 部 尺 Chinese standard foot-measure.

[Council.

工 部 局 Shanghai Municipal

工·錢 or 工 銀 or 工 值 or 工 價 wages.

工 雀 the tailor-bird.

工 頭 a foreman.

100 工 食 rations for workmen.

工 黨 Labour Party.

工 黨 聯 盟 labour-federation.

工 黨 舉 動 labour-movements.

件 工 piece-work.

105 借 工 營 私 exploitation of labour.

備 工 unskilled labour.

包 工 contract work; work by the job.

收 工 to cease work.

小 工 unskilled labour.

110 手³工 handicraft.

散³工 odd jobs.

日 工 work paid by the day.

百 工 all kinds of skilled labour; many officials.

省 工 機 labour-saving contrivances.

115 短 工 temporary employment.

童 工 child-labour.

粗 工 poor workmanship.

精 工 fine workmanship.

罷 工 strike.

120 論 工·by the job.

費 工 troublesome.

長 工 constant employment.

開 工 to start work.

功¹ Merit, achievement; meritorious. Efficacy; good results.
3698
Distinguish 攻 No. 3699.

功 令 regulations of the government for the selection of officials by merit.

功 作 task; labour.

功 利 主 義 utilitarianism.

功 力 merits; efficacy.

5 功·勞 or 功 勳 merit; worthy service.

功·名 honour, rank.

功·名 心 ambition.

功 同 再 造 you have, as it were, made me anew.

功·夫 ability; work; service.

10 功 封 promotion or title awarded for merit.

功 布 strip of white cloth carried on a pole before a coffin.

功 德 merit; excellence.

功 成 身 退 to retire after meritorious service.

功 效 result; merit; efficacy; beneficial outcome.

[15] 功 效 如 神 divine efficacy.

功 服 mourning, 大 功 for nine months, 小 功 for five months.

功 果 outcome; finale.

功 業 achievement; exploit.

功 烈 enterprising; dashing.

[20] 功 牌 a badge of merit given to soldiers; a medal.

功 用 meritorious services; power in action; beneficial result or operation; function.

功 績 achievement.

功 績 大 a great stock of merit.

功 能 merit and ability; skill; function.

[25] 功 臣 meritorious statesmen.

功 虧 一 簣 to fall short of success by one basket—of earth, when making a mound.

功 行 a successful achievement.

功·課 lessons; a task.

功·課 時 間 表 time-table of lessons.

[30] 功 賜 to bestow a reward for service.

功 過 merits and demerits.

功 難 補 過 merit cannot make up for faults.

成 功 to achieve success.; succeed.

有 功 meritorious.

[35] 無 功 unworthy; lack of merit.

用 功 to work hard, to study with diligence.

立 功 to do some act of merit.

記 功 to record merits.

誇 功 to boast of one's services.

攻[1] To attack; to assault. To apply oneself to; to work at. 3699 Distinguish 功 No. 3698.

攻·下 to batter down.

攻 乎 異 端 斯 害 也 已 to apply oneself to heretical doctrines is injurious indeed.

攻 人 之 過 to attack the faults of others.

攻 佔 to occupy; to seize.

攻 克 to overcome; to vanquish.

攻 克 自 己 to subdue the body.

攻 剿 to put to rout.

攻 勢 the offensive.

攻 勢 防 禦 to defend by assuming the offensive.

[10] 攻 匪 to repress bandits.

攻 取 to occupy by attack.

攻 圍 to surround; to besiege.

攻 城 to lay siege to a city.

攻 城 砲 siege guns.

[15] 攻 堅 to attack the strong.

攻 守 之 具 weapons of offence and defence.

攻 守 同 盟 alliance for offence and defence.

攻 心 to conquer the hearts.

攻 打 or 攻·擊 to attack; to fight against; to besiege; attack.

[20] 攻 拔 or 攻 刦 or 攻 殺 to take by storm; to capture by assault.

攻 書 to study hard.

攻 滅 to assault and wipe out.

攻 獲 城 池 to capture a city.

攻 發 人 之 陰 私 to ascertain and make known the secrets of others.

[25] 攻 破 to carry by assault.

攻 訐 to bring a charge against.

攻 退 to drive back; to rout.

攻 錯 to attack one's faults—by observing the goodness of others.

攻 風 to expel bad humours—by drugs.

[30] 不 攻 而 得 to capture without an attack.

反 攻 to return the attack; counterattack.

釭[1] Tire of a wheel. Read *kang*[1]. A bowl for a hanging-lamp or for fish. 3700

公[1] Public; open to all. 3701

公 丈 a *décametre*. *See below*—69.

公·事 or 公 幹 or 公 務 or 公 冗 public business; public matters.

公·事 房 office.

公·事 話 diplomatic language; the language of public business.

[5] 公 估 局 a valuation office.

公 使 minister; ambassador.

公 使 權 right of legation.

公 使·的 ministerial.

公 使 館 legation.

[10] 公 使 館 書 記·官 private secretary to a minister or embassy.

代 理 公 使 chargé d' affaires.

全 權 公 使 minister plenipotentiary. (11 = 5996.70.)

公 例 regulation; universal rule.

公 信 public confidence.

[15] 公 倍 數 a common multiple. (*math.*)

公 債 public debt.

公 債 條 例 regulations regarding the public debt.

公 債 票 government bonds.

公 共 public.

[20] 公 共 事 務 public matters.

公 共 事 務 之 絕 對 完 整 absolute integrity in public affairs.

公 共 事 業 public business.

公 共 利 用 品 public utilities.

公 共 博 物 館 public museum.

[25] 公 共 團 體 public body.

公 共 地 public land.

公 共 塲 所 a public place.

公 共 安 寧 public peace, safety.

公 共 意·思 public sentiment.

[30] 公 共 意·見 public opinion. = 輿 論.

公 共 支 配 under control of the public.

公 共 機 關 public organ.

公 共 生·活 life in common; communal life.

公 共 租 界 International Settlement, Shanghai.

[35] 公 共 秩·序 public order.

公 共 花 園 public parks, or gardens.

公 共 衛 生 public health.

公 出 to go out on public business.

公 函 official letter; circular letter.

[40] 公 務 public service; public matters.

公 務 無 線 電 台 public service radio-stations.

公 升 a litre—from this descending by decimals to 公 合, 公 勺, 公 撮, and ascending decimally to 公 斗, 公 石.

公·司 public company.

公 司 員 director of a company.

[45] 公 司 律 company-law.

公 司 條 例 Companies Act.

公 司 發 起 人 company-promoter.

公 司 輪 船 mail-steamer.

股 份 有 限 公 司 limited-liability company.

[50] 公 同 conjointly; impartial; altogether.

公 同 共 有 joint-ownership.

公 同 擬 定 jointly-drafted

公 呈 public appeal to official, etc.

公 告 public notification.

[55] 公 告 所 place for public notices.

公 回 return after absence on public business.

公 園 public park or gardens.

公 團 public body.

公 堂 a law court.

公 報 bulletin; official report.
公 報 今 日 發 表 bulletin issued today.
公 學 public school.
公 安 public safety.
公 安 局 Bureau of Public Safety.
65 公 安 處 Department of Public Safety.
公 家 government.
公 家 財 力 government wealth.
公 差 bearer of despatch (-ch'ai[1]);*
公 尺 a metre—descending by decimals to 公 寸, 公 分, 公 釐, and ascending by decimals to 公 丈, 公 引, 公 里.
70 公 局 an office; a bureau or board.
公 布 public proclamation; promulgated.
公 布 法 令 public proclamation of an order.
公 府 public court.
公 度 數 a common factor. (math.) = 公 因 數
75 公 庭 or 公 堂 a court.
公 式 a general formula; an example, as in mathematics.
公 式 解 釋 formal interpretation.
代 數 公 式 algebraic formula.
公 役 public servant.
80 公 役 公 司 Public Service Company.
公 德 public morality; regard for public welfare.
公 心 a public spirit.
公 意 public sentiment.
公 憤 public indignation.
85 公 所 a public place; an office.
公 拍 賣 public auction.
公 捐 public subscription.
公 摺 public documents or records.
公 敵 public enemy.
90 公 文 public documents.
公 文 宣 布 to publish an official despatch.
公 文 書 official despatch.
公 斤 a kilogram—descending by decimals to 公 兩, 公 錢, 公 分, 公 釐, and ascending by decimals to 公 衡, 公 石, 公 噸.
公 暇 leisure after public duties.
95 公 有 owned by the public.
公 有 物 public property.
公 有 船 隻 publicly owned vessels.
公 有 財 產 public property.
公 東 a feast at which everyone pays his share.
100 公 案 magistrate's table—cases in court.

* common difference (math.) (-ch'a[1]).

公 業 publicly-run industry or business undertaking.
公 權 civic rights.
公 正 之 外 交 方 式 proper diplomatic procedure.
公 民 citizen; the public; civics.
105 公 民 大 會 civic convention.
公 民 幸 福 public welfare.
公 民 權 rights of a citizen.
公 比 例 a common ratio. (math.)
公 水 public waters.
110 公 決 decided by the majority; passed.
公 決 緩 議 to defer discussion of a measure; to lay on the table.
公 法 public law; international law.
公 法 學 civics.
公 海 the high seas.
115 公 海 自 由 freedom of the seas—outside territorial limits.
公 烟 the best opium.
公 然 openly; publicly.
公 然 承 認 generally recognized.
公 牘 局 public record office.
120 公 理 right; common rights; universal principle.
公 理 會 Congregational Church.
公 產 public property.
公 用 for the use of all.
公 用 事 業 public utilities.
125 公 用 徵 收 法 law of compulsory surrender of land.
公 用 物 public property.
公 用 處 department of public utilities.
公 用 設 備 public utilities.
公 田 public fields.
130 公 畝 an are—metric unit of square measure, a square whose side is 10 metres.
公 益 public interests or welfare.
公 益 事 業 public welfare; things that promote the interests of the public.
公 益 工 程 public works.
公 眾 事 務 public matters.
135 公 眾 人 士 the public.
公 眾 大 會 public meeting.
公 眾 衛 生 public health, sanitation.
公 示 public notification.
公 示 催 告 public summons.
140 公 示 送 達 service by public notification.
公 私 public and private; govern-

mental and personal; fair and selfish.
公 私 訴 訟 public and private litigation.
公 積 reserves.
公 積 金 reserves.
145 公 立 publicly established.
公 立 學 校 public schools.
公 立 實 業 publicly established industries.
公 約 數 common factor. (math.) = 公 因 數.
公 罪 crime against the public.
150 公 署 public offices.
公 而 忘 私 to forget selfish considerations in the interests of the public.
公 職 public duty.
公 膏 or 公 土 Patna opium.
公 舉 public nomination.
155 公 見 concensus of opinion.
公 訴 law suit.
公 訴 之 銷 滅 abolition of lawsuits.
公 訴 權 right of appeal.
公 認 public recognition and approval.
160 公 認·的 表 示 manifestation of approval.
公 認·的 風 俗 recognized customs.
公 論 or 公 議 public discussion or opinion.
公 誼 會 Society of Friends or Quakers.
公 證 public register.
165 公 證 人 notary public.
公 議 會 public meeting.
公 費 public expenditure.
公 賣 public sale.
公 路 highway.
170 公 辦 public management.
公 門 a public office; law court.
公 里 a kilometre.
公 開 public opening; open; unrestrained; open to the public.
公 開 之 法 庭 open court.
175 公 開 地 public place.
公 開·的 方 式 open-handed methods, in a public manner.
公 開 表 演 public demonstration—as of a machine, etc.
公 開 選 舉 open election.
公 項 or 公 欵 public funds.
180 公 餘 之 暇 leisure from official duties.
公 館 a government or public office; a residence.

(a) Just, fair, equal.

公 事 公 辦 public affairs should be managed with equity.

公 允 fair and just.

公 判 arbitration decision.

公 判 條 約 arbitration treaty.

⁵公·平 fair and honest.

公·平 交 易 fair trade.

公·平 工 資 fair wages.

公·平 的 旁 觀 fair and independent opinion.

公 斷 to arbitrate.

¹⁰公 斷 人 arbitrator.

公 斷 決 定 arbitration decision.

公 斷 法 院 arbitration court.

情 願 公 斷 voluntary arbitration.

公 明 just and wise.

¹⁵公 正 just; impartial; fair; equitable.

公 正 人 arbitrator.

公 義 just, fair.

公 行 to act with fairness.

公·道 equitable; honest; a fair price.

(b) A duke, highest title of nobility. A gentleman, sir. A male. Husband's father.

公 主 a princess.

公 侯 nobility; a prince.

公 侯 伯 子³ 男 the five orders of ancient nobility in China in their proper sequence.

公·公 father-in-law, father of husband.

⁵公 婆 husband's father and mother.

公 子³ a gentleman's son; young gentleman.

公·家 imperial family.

公 母 cock and hen; male and female of animals.

公·爵 or 公 爺 a duke; my lord duke.　⌐= 陽 性

¹⁰公 生 類 masculine (grammar).

公 等 You, Gentlemen!

公 郎 your son; a young gentleman.

張 公 Mr. Chang—in speaking of him.

相⁴公 a young gentleman; a catamite; ancient designation of Secretary of State.

¹⁵辟 公 feudal princes.

蚣¹
3702
An insect.

蜈·蚣 a centipede.

弓¹
3703
A bow. Curved. Radical 57.

弓 人 a bow maker.

弓 冶 or 弓 裘 to carry on the father's profession. See 箕 No. 402—4.

弓 弦 bow-string; a chord; a straight road.

弓 形 arched; a segment.

⁵弓 手 an archer. See below A-2.

弓 杸 a rest for the arm of an archer.

弓 矢 斯 張 their bows and arrows were displayed.

弓 箭 or 弓 矢 bows and arrows; archery.

弓 背 arched, like the back of a bow; a curving road.

¹⁰弓 袋 a bow-case.

弓 規 bow compasses.

弓 足 or 弓 脚 feet of a Chinese woman when bound.

弓 鞋 shoes for the bound feet of a woman.

弓 頭 ends of a bow.

彈 棉 弓 a bow for fluffing out cotton into wadding.

拉 (or 開 or 張) 弓 to draw a bow.

虎 弓 spring-snare for wild beasts.

(a) A land measure of five Chinese feet.

弓 丈 or 弓 步 a wooden frame measuring five feet, (Chinese) used for land measures.

弓 手 underlings who measure land. See above—5.

躬²
軀 }
3704
The body; oneself. Personally.

躬 桑 the plucking of mulberry-leaves by the empress in person.

躬 耕 the ploughing by the emperor in person.

躬 自 厚 而 薄 責 於 人 則 遠 怨 矣 he who makes liberal demands upon himself and small demands on others, will keep resentment far from himself.

躬 行 to do a thing personally.

⁵躬 親 personally.

躬 親 其 事 to attend to a matter oneself.

躬 詣 to go in person.

躬 身 下 拜 to bend the body in obeisance.

躬 造 .... 第 go in person to call on ....

反 躬 自 問 self-examination.

宮¹
3705
A palace; a temple; a college. A dwelling.

宮 主 a princess.

宮 保 guardian of the heir-apparent.

宮 刑 castration for men, banishment to secluded quarters for women.

宮 城 the imperial city—the forbidden city.

⁵宮 妃 or 宮 娥 or 宮 女 or 後 宮 imperial concubines; maids-of-honour.

宮 室 a mansion; a dwelling.

宮 寢 or 宮 禁 private apartments of the emperor.

宮 掖 apartments in the palace.

宮 敎 palace rules and regulations.

¹⁰宮 殿 or 宮 庭 or 皇 宮 a palace; a hall.

宮 碗 half-sized bowl as compared with bowls in general use.

宮 詹 Chief Supervisor of Education to the Heir Apparent.

宮 車 晏 駕 death of the Emperor.

宮 錦 紅 a deep red peony.

¹⁵宮 門 抄 Court Circular.

宮 闕 gate of the palace.

子³宮 the womb.

守 宮 the gecko.

東 宮 the Empress; Heir Apparent.

²⁰老 宮 a eunuch.

行 宮 rural palace. Imperial lodging-place.

西 宮 highest imperial concubine.

(a) First note in ancient musical scale.

宮 商 the two first notes of the scale—music, harmony.

宮 商 角 徵 羽 the notes of the ancient pentatonic scale,—do, re, mi, sol, la.

厷 肱 3706] 1 The fore-arm. Most Chinese-English dictionaries give:—the upper-arm. Also read *hung*[1].

肱 膂 arms and backbone—most important and secret.

肱 臂 the arms.

曲 肱 而 枕 之 to bend the arm for a pillow.

股 肱 legs and arms—ministers, assistants.

自 肘 至 腕 謂 之 肱 from the elbow to the wrist is called *kung*.

廾 3707 ³ Hands joined. Radical 55.

孑 3708 ³ Larvae of the mosquito.

孑 孓 larvae of the mosquito.

(a) Read *chüeh*[2:5] Short and straight.

共 3709 ⁴ All, the whole; collectively. To share; to work together.

共 事 to work together; to participate.

共 井 a well open to all; people of the same place.

共 享 to enjoy together.

共 助 mutual assistance.

⁵共 勖 combined effort.

共 同 all; collective; co-operating.

共 同 原 理 a general principle.

共 同 奮 鬥 to strive unitedly.

共 同 存 在 collective existence.

¹⁰共 同 權 利 common rights.

共 同 海 捐 general average.

共 同 生 活 collective life.

共 同 的 精 神 spirit of co-operation.

共 同 結 婚 communal marriage.

¹⁵共 同 行 為 a joint-act. (*legal*).

共 同 被 告 co-respondent in a suit.

共 同 訴 訟 joint-litigation.

共[1]和 united in purpose; republican.

共[1]和 主 義 republicanism.

²⁰共[1]和 制 republican system.

共[1]和 原 理 republican principles.

共[1]和 告 成 establishment of the Republic.

共[1]和 國 republics.

共[1]和 政 治 republican legislation.

²⁵共[1]和 政 體 republican form of government.

共[1]和 精 神 spirit of the Republic.

共[1]和 黨 Republican Party.

共 鳴 resonance.

共 鳴 裝 器 resonator. (*wireless*).

³⁰共 夥 accomplices; companions.

共 存 co-existent.

共 學 to study together.

共 宿 to lodge in the same place.

共 振 resonance.

³⁵共 政 to share in the government.

共 敦 cordially united.

共 曉 all know.

共 有 joint-possession.

共 有 權 common rights.

⁴⁰共 有 物 common property.

共 濟 united activities; co-operation. 共 榮 "co-prosperity."

共 濟 會 aid-society. ⌊(*Jap.*)

共 犯 co-operation in crime.

共 犯 罪 joint crime.

⁴⁵共 生 or 共 接 symbiosis, permanent union between organisms, each of which depends for its existence upon the other.

共 產 public property; all things in common; communism.

共 產 主 義 Communism.

共 產 份 子 communistic elements.

共 產 原 理 communistic principles. 共 產 國 際 Comintern.

⁵⁰共 產 社 會 communistic society.

共 產 黨 Communist Party.

共 總 or 共 有 or 一 共 the whole; altogether; the total.

共 襄 盛 舉 united assistance in a great cause.

共 計 or 共 合 or 共 算 the sum total; to sum up; in all.

⁵⁵共 計 算 the sum total; joint-account.

共 軛 conjugate.

共 軛 焦 點 conjugate foci.

共 軛 角 conjugate angles.

共 軛 點 conjugate points.

⁶⁰共 通 common; universal.

共 通 對 象 common objective.

共 點 性 of a concurrent nature.

不 共 戴 天 will not live under the same sky—as the man who slew his father; inveterate hatred.

(a) Read *kung*[1]. To fulfil one's duties. Respectful.

共 工 superintendent of works under *Yao*.

靖 共 爾 位 quietly fulfil the duties of your office.

(b) Read *kung*[3]. To hold. To fold the hands. Inter. 拱 No. 3712.

眾 星 共 之 all the stars turn towards it and bow.

供 3710 ¹ To supply; to contribute to.

供 不 應 求 the supply is not equal to the demand.

供 事 copying-clerks.

供 備 to supply.

供 口 to furnish food; to get enough to eat.

⁵供 差 official servants; to return to duty. (-*ch'ai*[1])

供 帳 to arrange; to set out.

供 役 to furnish feudal service.

供 應[4] or 供 支 to furnish; to supply.

供 應[4] 部 supply department.

¹⁰供 求 supply and demand.

供 物 offerings.

供 獻 or 供 奉 to offer to; to minister to; to supply.

供 用 to give for use.

供 給 to supply; to equip; to outfit; supply and demand. (-*chi*)

¹⁵供 給 過 多 oversupply.

供 給 需 要 supply and demand.

一 批 供 給 to get a supply of . . . .

日 常 供 給 daily supplies.

牀 舖 供 給 beds, food and service.

²⁰供 職 to hold an appointment; to resume duties.

供 酒 to set out wine.

供 養 to nourish; to support; to make presents to superiors.

(a) To give evidence.

供 情 the particulars of the evidence.

供 招 to confess in evidence.

供 指 to indicate in evidence.

供 據 evidence.

⁵供 攀 to implicate others in giving evidence.

供 狀 depositions in writing.
供 稱 he gave evidence, saying....
供 詞 depositions.
供 認 to confess on trial.
[10]供 送 to forward the evidence.
供 開 to state in evidence.
反 供 to retract a statement.
口 供 verbal evidence; deposition.
畫 供 to sign or make a mark on one's depositions.

(ㄴ) Read *kung*[4]. **To offer in worship.**

供 佛 to offer to Buddha.
供 桌 table for setting out sacrifices.
供 祖 to worship ancestors.
供 神 to worship the gods with offerings.
供 飯 to offer food—in sacrifice.

恭[1] **To reverence; to respect. Reverent; respectful.**
3711

恭 人 wives of officials formerly classed as the fourth rank.
恭 候 to await respectfully.
恭 叩 we respectfully pray—in petitions.
恭 喜 or 恭 賀 to congratulate.
[5]恭 奉 to receive with reverence.
恭 恭 敬 敬 very reverently.
恭 摺 respectfully to memorialize.
恭·敬 to respect; to venerate.
恭 敬 不 如 從 命 obedience is better than outward reverence.
[10]恭 敬 不 寧 respectful and uneasy.
恭 祝 to tender respectful congratulations.
恭·維 to flatter; to praise.
恭 者 不 侮 人 the respectful man does not insult others.
恭 而 無 禮 則 勞 respect shown, but not in accord with the rules of propriety, leads to troublesome labour.
[15]恭 肅 reverential demeanour.
恭 行 to execute orders with care.
恭 謁 or 恭 踐 to pay one's respects.
恭 謝 humble thanks.
恭 近 於 禮 遠 恥 辱 也 if respect is shown according to what is proper, one will keep shame and disgrace far from him.

[20]恭 迓 or 恭 迎 to welcome; to await—a visitor.
恭 遜 reverential submission.
恭 錄 to copy respectfully.
恭 順 submissive; complaisant.
恭 默 reverent and quiet.

拱[3] **To fold the hands on the breast, as when making a bow. To bow, to salute.**
3712

拱 別 to bow and take leave.
拱 北 or 拱 辰 to bow to the North Star, as the other stars are said to do—used of the influence of a good ruler.
拱 手 to salute with the hands folded; to fold the hands and look on.
拱 手 自 服 you can fold your arms and they will submit—very easy.
拱 立 to stand in a reverent posture.

(a) **To encircle; to span with the hands. An arch.**

拱 璧 a large circular token of jade—something to be prized.
　珍 如 拱 璧 esteemed it as precious as a large jade token.
拱 瓦 curved tiles.
拱 衛 to surround; to guard.
拱 頂 a dome.
橋 拱 arch of a bridge.

棋[3] **A post, a prop; a pillar; the short posts between the beams and the roof timbers.**
3713

龔[1] **To give; to present to. Decorous; reverential. An old name for the south-east part of the province of Kwangsi.**
3714

貢[4] **To offer as tribute. The best quality; superior. To levy a tax. Revenue.**
3715

貢 上 to offer to a superior.
貢 使 a tribute-bearer.
貢 品 articles of tribute.
貢·士 graduates who succeed at the preliminary examination for the former 3rd degree.
[5]貢 燭 tribute-candles—the best quality.

貢 獻 an offering; contribution; to offer.
貢·生 a senior licentiate of the former regime.
貢 稅 or 貢 賦 taxes; revenue.
貢 紬 tribute-silk; the best silk.
[10]貢 船 ship bearing tribute.
貢 茶 tribute-tea—fine quality tea.
貢 言 to offer a word—of advice.
貢 賜 to permit.
貢 銀 tribute-silver.
[15]貢 院 former Provincial examination-hall.
進 貢 to bring tribute.

槓[4] **A pole, a lever. Also read** *kang*[4]. **Inter. 杠 No. 3262.**
3716

槓·子 a bar, carrying-pole. (*kang*[4])
槓 桿 a lever.

蟈[3] **To wriggle. To work through, as smoke through a crevice.**
3717

蟈 來 蟈 去 dodging in and out.
蟈 地 to root up the ground.
蟈 孔 to go into a hole—as a snake.

鞏[3] **To strengthen; to guard. Firm, strong.**
3718

鞏 固 well-guarded; secure; firm.
鞏 固 國 基 strengthen the foundations of the State.
鞏 固 地·位 a firm basis.
鞏 鞏 不 夷 bound in heart and not at ease.
鞏 膜 the white of the eye; sclerotic membrane.
無 不 克 鞏 there is nothing which (昊 天, God) cannot strengthen.

(a) **To dry at a fire.**

鞏 乾 to dry by a fire.

(b) **To bind with thongs.**

鞏 用 黃 牛 之 革 to bind use ox-hide.

熲[3] **The blaze of fire.**
3719

K'UNG.　　(丂ㄥ)

(K'ong)

孔 [3] An opening, a hole. Touch-hole; hole of a flute, etc. To penetrate.
3720

孔 性 of a porous nature.
孔 方 the square hole—copper cash.
孔 穴 or 空 孔 a hole, a cave, a hollow.
孔 竅 openings; pores.
[5]孔 道 a thoroughfare; a drain.
毛 孔 pores of the skin.
眼 孔 small holes in things.
面 孔 the countenance. (Wu-dial.)
鼻 孔 nostrils.

(a) Great. Very.

孔 亟 very urgent; pressing.
孔 修 great perfection.
孔 壬 great artfulness.
孔 德 great virtue.
[5]孔 懷 great mutual sympathy.
孔 明 great brightness. Style of Chu-ko Liang.
孔 明 燈 bull's-eye lanterns.
孔 昭 widely known—as a doctrine.
孔 棘 urgent, in great stress.
[10]孔 樂 very pleased; joyful.
孔 樹 a great tree.
孔 殷 urgent; needed; busy.
孔 碩 very great—of articles. etc.
孔 靜 exceedingly quiet.

(b) A surname. Confucius.

孔 佛 (or 釋) Confucius and Buddha.
孔 周 Confucius and Chou kung.
孔 子 or 孔 夫 子 the sage Confucius.
孔 子 然 之 Confucius accepted it as true.
[5]孔 子 生 日 Birthday of Confucius, 27th of 8th lunar month.
孔 孟 Confucius and Mencius.
孔 廟 Confucian temples.
孔 教 Confucianism.
孔 林 the tomb of Confucius.
[10]孔 父 攸 歎 Confucius gave a deep sigh.
孔 老 Confucius and Laotzŭ.
孔 聖 人 Confucius the Sage.
孔 門 Confucianism.

(c) The peacock.　　--ch'iao)

孔 雀 the peacock.　　(-ch'üeh or

孔 雀 屛 peacock-feather screens.
孔 雀 扇 peacock-feather fan.
孔 雀 石 malachite.
孔 雀 領 the peacock-feather decoration, formerly granted for merit in government service; the grade was distinguished by the number of eyes in the feather.

恐 恐 [3] Fearful, apprehensive. To fear. Lest. Distinguish 恐 No. 5875, 怨 No. 7714.
3721

恐 不 贍 to fear there will be insufficient.
恐 喝 罪 crime of blackmail.
恐 嚇 to terrify.
恐 嚇 一 番 gave him a scare.
[5]恐 怖 frightened.
恐 怖 世 代 reign of terror.
恐 怕 probably; perhaps.
恐 怕 他 不 來 perhaps he will not come.
恐 惶 fear, suspicion.
恐 慌 panic, crisis.

空 [1] Empty, hollow. Insincere. To be impoverished; reduced to extremities.
3722

空 中 space, emptiness; in the air.
空 中 偵 察 air-patrol.
空 中 樓 閣 castles in the air.
↑空 中 堡 壘 Flying Fortress.
[5]空 中 航 路 air-lanes or routes.
空 (中) 襲 (擊) air-raid.
空 中 巡 邏 air-patrol.
空 中 郵 船 air-mail ships.
空 中 陷 窂 air-pockets.
[10]空 中 魚 雷 air-torpedoes.
空 前 (絕 後) unprecedented.
空 勞 無 益 I have spent all my efforts in a fruitless attempt.
空 匱 poor, in need—an empty cupboard.
空 口 無 憑 a verbal statement is no proof or evidence.
[15]空 口 講 to speak without evidence.
空 回 to return empty; to fail and return.
空 地 vacant ground.
空 孔 a hollow; a hole, a cave.
空 寂 abstraction and seclusion.
[20]空 屋 an empty house.
空 幻 illusory; visionary.
空 心 disinterested; humble; hollow, tubular.

空 心 大 老 官 a man of vain pretensions.
空 心 湯 團 a hollow dumpling — an impossibility.
[25]空 想 to wish for in vain; fantasy.
空 手 or 空 拳 empty-handed; poor.
空 明 reflection of the moon in water.
空 曠 vast; cannot see the bounds of.
空 望 vain hopes.
[30]空 架 子 a humbug; one who is all empty pretension.
空 歡 喜 baseless rejoicings.
空 氣 air
空 氣 制 動 機 an air-brake.
空 氣 囊 air-bag.
[35]空 氣 外 套 air-casing.
空 氣 室 air-chamber.
空 氣 寒 暖 表 air-thermometer.
空 氣 浴 air-bath.
空 氣 流 通 airy; circulation of the air.
↓[40]空 話 empty talk.
空 洞 a large hollow; a cave; vast, broad, obscure.
空 濛 appearance of rain.
空 王 Buddha.
空 理 empty theory.
[45]空 碧 之 中 between the sky and the blue sea.
空 盒 晴 雨 or 風 雨 表 aneroid barometer.
空 盤 speculation.
空 空 utterly empty; unlearned.
空 空 如 也 as if entirely empty.
[50]空 空 落 落 的 or 空 空 洞 洞 的 in vain; empty.
空 羣 之 選 all the best have been selected—said of a man of great ability, from a story of one who had selected all the good horses from a mob.
空 翠 the blue sky.
空 肚 an empty stomach.
空 腸 the jejunum.
[55]空 花 (or 華) vain imaginations.
空 處 or 空 所 empty space.
↓ 眞 a vacuum.
眞 空 制 動 機 vacuum-brake.
眞 空 掃 除 機 vacuum-cleaner.
眞 空 管 vacuum-tubes.
[60]眞 空 管 檢 波 器 radio-detector valves.
空 虛 empty; a state of abstraction.

↓ 空 襲 air raid.
空 行 to labour in vain; unencumbered, without luggage.
空 談 fanciful; impracticable.
空 談 學 理 merely theoretical.
⁶⁵空 谷 足 音 the sound of footsteps in a deserted valley, used of persons and things that are not easily met with.
空 跑 一 趟 to have had a journey for nothing.
空 身 to have no impedimenta.
空 門 Buddhism.
空 間 space.
⁷⁰空 閒 vacant; unoccupied; leisure.
空 闊 vast, broad.
空 際 the firmament.
空 靈 clever—the apertures of the mind being open.
空 響 內 貯 full of reverberations.
⁷⁵空 響 彈 blank cartridges.
空 頭² 人 情 empty sympathy.
一 場 空 all gone; a clean sweep.
中 空 hollow; tubular.
太 空 the great void; the sky; nothingness; interstellar space.
⁸⁰抽 個 空 籤 to draw a blank.
航 空 aerial navigation. *See* No. 2059—14ff.
買 空 賣 空 speculation on the markets.

(a) Read *k'ung⁴*. Leisure. To leave a blank. A deficit.

空 乏 wanting; impoverished.
空 兒 an occasion; an opportunity; a blank space.
  抽·個 空 兒 to find time for anything—when busy.
  沒·有 空 兒 I have no time for it.
⁵空 白 blank; not filled in.
空 白 單·子 a blank form.
空 白 定 單 blank order-forms.
空 白 帳 簿 blank account-book.
空 白 式 樣 empty forms.
¹⁰空 白 本·子 blank book.
空 白 背 署 endorsed in blank.
空·開 寫 leave a space and then write.
空 餘 vacant; unoccupied.
房·子 空 了 the house is unoccupied.
虧。空 deficit; bankruptcy.

倥⁴ Boorish, ignorant. Urgent; pressing.
3723

倥 偬 pressing, urgent.

崆¹ Mountain in Kansu.
3724

崆 峒 mountains in Kansu and Honan.

悾¹ Ignorant, simple; guileless.
3725

悾 悾 而 不 信 simple and yet insincere.
悾 憁 downcast, depressed.
悾 誠 truly sincere.

控⁴ To accuse.
3726

控 瀆 to demand justice.
控 告 to charge; to appeal to a higher court.
控 告 事 件 a charge, a plaint.
控 官 to inform the authorities.
⁵控 案 to accuse; to lay a charge.
控 理 to charge; to accuse.
控 詞 a charge, a plaint.
控 訴 to appeal; to charge.
控 訴 人 appellant.
¹⁰控 訴 狀 letter of appeal.
控 訴 院 Court of Appeal.
  國 際 控 訴 最 高 法 庭 International Supreme Court of Appeal.
控 追 to take proceedings for recovery....
上 控 appeal to a higher court.
¹⁵上 控 權 right of appeal.
捏 控 to trump up a charge.
暗 控 to inform.

(a) To control.
控 馬 to rein in a horse.
抑 轡 控 忌 now he gives the horses the rein, now he reins them in.

(b) To draw a bow.
控 弦 to draw a bow.

(c) Read *ch'iang¹*. To beat.
控 其 頭² hit him on the head.

箜¹ Ancient kind of lute.
3727

鞚⁴ A bridle, reins. To rein in a horse.
3728

KUO. (《乂ㄛ)
(Ko)

堝¹ A crucible.
3729

坩 堝 a crucible.

過 过⁴ To pass, to pass through or by; to cross over. Sign of past or perfect tense. Beyond the ordinary or proper limit.
3730

過·一·會兒 in a minute or two.
過·不 來 unable to cross; it disagrees with me.
過·不 去 cannot be passed—used of anything one does not feel easy about; intolerable.
過·不·得 眼 cannot stand inspection.
⁵過 世 deceased.
過 之 必 趨 if he had to pass them he would do so quickly.
過·了 dead—as a parent.
過·些 年 後 after some years.
過 人 to surpass others.
¹⁰過 付 overpaid.
過·來 人 one who has come over that road—a man of experience.
過 入 brought forward.
過 冬 to pass the winter.
過 分 (*fen⁴*) to exceed the limit; excessive
¹⁵過·到 to pass to...
過 半 more than half.
過 半 數 the majority.
過·去 to pass over or away.
過 去 式 past tense.
²⁰過·去·的 事 things that are past.
過 去 經 驗 past experience.
過 去 與 現 在 past and present.
過 問 to interfere; to inquire into.
過 嗣 to adopt; to be adopted.
²⁵過 堂 to come before the court.
過 境 to cross the frontier.
過 多 too much; too many.
過 夜 to pass the night.
過 子 to be adopted—of those who are related on the father's side.
³⁰過 存 to inquire after.
過 客 a passing stranger.
過 家 to pass from house to house gossiping; to keep house.
過 寬 too lenient.
過 屠 門 而 大 嚼 when passing the butchers to chew a large mouthful—to act as if one had a mouthful when one has none.
↑過 家·家 兒 to play house.

85 過 山 礮 mountain guns.

過 年 to pass into the new-year; new-year period.

過 度 excess; beyond measure.

過 往 passing by.

過 後 next in order; finally; afterwards.

40 過 得 去 or 過·得 what can be done; passable; can make ends

過 從 to ask after; to be with. meet.

過 忙 or 過 急 over-hasty; over anxious.

過·意 不 去 to feel ill at ease—I am obliged to you; your goodness makes me uneasy.

過 慮 over-anxious.

45 過 戶 to transfer.

過 戶 登 記 簿 transfer-book.

過 房 to adopt the son of a brother or one of the same clan.

過 支 overdraft.

過·於 to exceed, more than.

50 過·於 小 心 too particular; too cautious.

過·於 秘 密 too retiring; too close; too secretive.

過·於 自 信 over-confident.

過·於 重 視 to esteem too highly.

過 日·子 to pass the days—to live.

55 過 時 behindhand; past the time.

過 時 再 來 to come again after a little time.

過 期 passed the time; over-due.

過 期 支 票 out-of-date cheque.

過 橋 抽 板 to pull away the plank after using it as a bridge—ingratitude for past help.

60 過 水 竹 筒 a bucket for carrying the water over—said of taking a message for another.

過 江 or 過 河 to cross a river or stream.

過 河 拆 橋 to break the bridge after crossing the river—to leave others in difficulty; ingratitude. *See above*—59.

過 活 to make a living; to live.

過 渡 transition; transference; to cross a ferry.

65 過 渡 時 代 a period of transition.

過 渡 期 中 during the period of transition.   [B2.

過 激 黨 Bolshevist Party. = 5364.

過 火 excessive; beyond limits; extravagance.

過 貓 to give birth to kittens.

70 過 猶 不 及 excess is as bad as deficiency.

過 當 beyond what is fitting.

過 癮 to satisfy a craving—as for opium.

過 盛 too abundant; too much.

過 目 to give it a glance.

75 過 目 不 忘 not to be forgotten after being once seen.

過 衆 too numerous.

過 秤 to weigh.

過 程 a stage; a process—as in psychology.

心 之 過 程 past and present mental processes.

80 過 稱 overpraise; overstatement.

過 節 to observe a holiday; to keep a festival.

過 細 查 查 make a careful investigation.

過·繼 to adopt, (as a child).

過 聘 or 過 禮 to send the bridal presents.

85 過 訪 to pay a visit.

過 話 to pass on a message; to pass on a story.

過 謙 over-modest.

過 費 to go to overmuch expense.

過 路·的 a passer-by; a traveller.

90 過 身 to have gone past; dead.

過 載 to tranship cargo; to load into another cart or boat.

過·過 目 to look over; to glance at.

過 重 too heavy; excess (baggage).

過 量 beyond measure.

95 過 門 to marry—of girls.

過 關 to pass the customs.

過 雨 after the rain.

過 雲 雨 a passing shower.

過 飯 to assist the food down—by savoury dishes and condiments.

100 不 過 如 此 nothing more than this.

不 過 意 uncomfortable, as by the favours of another.

不 過·是 merely; only; not more than.

難 過 hard to get on; in trouble, difficulty, or grief.

↑° 不·過 but.

(a) **From the above comes:—transgression, error, fault. To blame.**

過 則 勿 憚 改 if you have faults do not fear to abandon them.

過 失 faults, errors, mistake, culpability.

過 失 傷 害 罪 unintentional injury.

過 失 致 死 罪 unintentional homicide.

---

5 過 惡 evil; excessively wicked.

過 犯 transgressions, sins.

過 生 於 輕 慢 error grows out of lightness and carelessness.

過·處 a fault.

過 錯 an error.

知 過 改 過 when you know your faults, reform.

鍋[1] A cooking-pot, a saucepan.
3731

鍋 圈 the iron ring to make the hole of a stove smaller; a ring to stand a round-bottomed cooking-pot on.

鍋·巴 the burnt rice that adheres to the sides of the pot.

鍋 蓋 the cover of a pot.

鍋 窰 or 鍋 坊 or 冶 坊 a foundry for cooking-pots.

5 鍋 臺 or 鍋 竈 a cooking-stove or range.

鍋 鏟·子 a shovel or slice used in cooking; a spatula.

鍋 鑪 a boiler.

沙 鍋 an earthenware saucepan.

補 鍋 to mend pots and pans. stuffing.

↑ 鍋 貼 兒 fried pastry with meat

果[3] Certainly, surely, really, truly. Consequences.
3732 Inter. 菓 next.

果 否 whether really so or not...

果 報 the consequences of actions in a previous state.

果 如 or 如 果 if; supposing that.

果 實 result. *See below A-3.*

5 果 得 realized.

果 有 之 乎 Is it actually so?

果 然 certainly; in deed and truth; if indeed. *See below C-3. D-1.*

果 然 如 此 so it has turned out as was expected.

果 眞 really.

10 因 果 cause and effect. *See* 因 No. 7407.

於 是 不 果 so it has not come about as expected.

若 果 if, supposing that; if really.

(a) **Fruit of trees. Inter. next.**

果 品 fruits.

果 園 orchard.

果 實 fruits, kernels. *See above* —4.

果 木 fruit trees.

5 果 林 orchard.

果 梗 (or 柄) stem of fruit.
果 皮 (or 被) the pericarp or outer covering of the seed.
中 果 皮 the fleshy, juicy part of fruits.
內 果 皮 the hard covering in contact with the seeds.
10 外 果 皮 the outer skin or peel.
乾 果 dried fruits.
時 果 fruits in season.
水 果 fruits.
百 果 all kinds of fruit.
15 結 果 to bear fruit; to finish up; results, etc. *See* No. 782—C-8.
鮮 果 fresh fruits.

(b) Obstinate; determined.

果 勇 daring, courageous.
果 勁 firm and unyielding.
果 哉 末 之 難 矣 How fixed is his resolve! There is nothing difficult to him.
果 悍 determined and fierce.
5 果 敢 having decision and daring to carry it out.
果 敢 而 窒 firm and daring, yet without understanding.
果 斷 decision, to decide.
果 毅 daring, courage.
果 決 brave; daring, having determination.
果 銳 determined and ardent.

(c) Satisfied, full.

果 腹 satisfied, full (in eating).
未 嘗 果 腹 he had never eaten to the full.
腹 有 果 然 satisfied, having eaten enough.

(d) A monkey.

果 然 a long-tailed black monkey with a white face. *See above* —7.

菓 3 Fruit, berries, nuts, etc. Inter. Preceding—A.
3733

菓 仁 a kernel.　[A.c. 7515.12.
菓 子 fruits, berries, nuts, etc.
菓 盒 a covered box in which fruit is sent.
菓 餅 fruit and cakes, refreshments.
糖 菓 crystallized fruits.

螺 3 The solitary wasp.
3734

螺 蠃 the wasp which imprisons caterpillars in a cell to feed its young.

裹 3 To wrap, to bind, to bandage.
3735 Distinguish 裏 No. 3865.

裹 來·的 鴿·子 a decoy-pigeon.
裹 創 to bind up a wound.
裹 尸 to wrap up a corpse.
裹 糧 to pack up rations for travelling.
5 裹 而 又 纏 to roll up and bind tightly.
裹 肚 a stomacher; a band worn round the loins.
裹 脅 to coerce; to force to take part.　⌈cloth so used.
裹 脚 to bind the feet. 裹·脚(布)
裹 腹 to eat to the full. *See* 果 No. 3732—C.
10 裹 腿·子 gaiters, leggings.
裹·著 wrapped up; bound.
裹·起·來 wrap or bind it up.
裹 足 to stop, not daring to advance; to bind the feet.
裹 足 不 入 秦 unwilling to advance into the territory of *Ch'in.*
15 裹 載 to wrap up.
裹 革 to wrap (the body of a soldier) in the skin (of his horse).
裹 頭 巾 a turban.
裹 飯 to wrap up food and take it to someone.

輠 3 Grease-pot hung under the axle of a cart.
3736

餜 3
粿 Cakes, biscuits, pastry.
3737

餜 餅 biscuits, cakes.

KUO. (𡜡)

(Kueh or Kuoh)

國 2.5.　A kingdom; a nation. A State; a country; a dynasty. The capital.
3738

國 丈 第 home of the Emperor's father-in-law.
國 中 in the city; in the capital.
國 之 典 章 the social order of the country.
國 事 government or national affairs.
5 國 事 犯 political offender.
國 交 national intercourse.
國 使 an ambassador; an envoy.
國 債 national debt.
國 債 用 途 the expenditure of national loans.
10 國 債 票 government bonds.
國 光 national glory.
國 內 公 債 internal public loan.
國 法 national law.
↓ 國 境 national border. *See below* 117.
15 國 內 製 造 home manufacture.
國 內 貿 易 internal trade.
國 公 債 domestic loans.
國 利 民 福 national prosperity and welfare of the masses.
國 制 the rule of the State; the government.
20 國 務 State affairs.
國 務 卿 Secretary of State.
國 務 總 理 Prime Minister.
國 勢 state of the nation; national conditions.
國 勢 調 查 a census.
25 國 化 nationalization.
國 史 national history.
國 史 館 Bureau of National History.
國 命 government orders; national life.
國 喪 national mourning.
30 國 土 a land—as "there is a land"; national territory.
國 地 稅 national land-tax.
國 基 漸 拔 the country gradually falling into decay.
國 士 a leading scholar esteemed by all.
國 外 貿 易 foreign trade.
35 國 姓 surname of the reigning family.
國 姓 阿 or 鄭 成 功 Koxinga.
國 子 heir-apparent of a prince.
國 子 監 The Imperial Academy.
國 定 稅 則 authorized tariff.
40 國 家 a State, nation, or country as having territory, population and complete sovereign-rights.
國 家 主 義 nationalism.
國 家 主 權 national sovereignty.
國 家 代 表 national representative.

國家信用 national credit.
[45] 國家圖書館 National Library.
國家政策學 political economy.
國家稅 national taxes.
國家純益 national dividend—the net income of the State.
國家觀念 national sentiment.
[50] 國家資本主義 nationalization of capital.
國賓 copper cash.
國帑 national treasury.
國幣 national currency.
國府 the government.
[55] 國度 or 國政 the administration of a State; a nation.
國庫 the treasury.
國庫證券 treasury-notes.
國徽 national emblem.
國性 national characteristics.
[60] 國恥 national humiliation.
國恥紀念日 National Day of Humiliation—May 7th, the anniversary of the Chinese yielding to the 21 demands of Japan.
國情 national traits or characteristics.
國慶 national celebrations.
國慶日 Anniversary of the Republic. October 10th.
[65] 國慶紀念 national celebration.
國憲 national constitution.
國威 national prestige.
國手 an expert; national champion.
國故 ancient learning.
[70] 國政 State affairs; policy, administration.
國教 State religion.
國文 national literature; Chinese.
國旗 national flag.
國是 national policy.
[75] 國書 national credentials; communication from one State to another.
國朝 the dynasty.
國會 parliament.
國會召集 to summon parliament.
國會政治 parliamentary government.
[80] 國會籌備處 Bureau of Preparation for Parliament.
國會議員 member of parliament.
國會選舉 parliamentary election.
國有 nationally owned (railways, etc.).
國有政策 policy of State ownership.

[85] 田地國有 nationalization of land.
鐵道國有 nationalization of railways.
國本 foundation of a State—the masses.
國柱 or 砥柱 pillar of State.
國權 national sovereignty.
[90] 國歌 national anthem.
國步 the fortunes of a nation.
國母 the Empress.
國民 citizen.
國民保險 national insurance.
[95] 國民協會 National Association.
國民大會 a national congress.
國民學校 national primary schools.
國民感情 national sentiment.
國民憤激 popular unrest and indignation.
[100] 國民捐 poll-tax.
國民權 people's rights.
國民眼光 democratic view.
國民精神 national spirit.
國民自決 plebiscite.
[105] 國民軍 national army; citizen forces.
國民銀行 national bank.
國民黨 Nationalist Party.
國法 national legislation :—laws.
國法學 study of public law.
[110] 國泰民安 May the State prosper and the people enjoy peace!
國營事業 government enterprise.
國父 father of his country.
國王 or 國主 a king.
國璽 seal of State.
[115] 國產 national products.
國用 national expenditure.
國界 national boundary.
國祚 or 年祚 the prosperity of the State.
國禩 the Emperor's reign.
[120] 國稅 national taxes.
國立事業 State enterprises.
國立大學 government university.
國立學校 government schools.
國策 national policy.
[125] 國節 national holidays.
國籍 register of nationality.
國籍取得 acquirement of nationality.
國籍喪失 loss of nationality.
國籍回復 restoration of nationality.
[130] 國籍法 naturalization laws.
↑國民革命 national revolution.

國籍抵觸 contradiction of nationality.
國粹 the special excellencies of art or literature, peculiar to a nation.
國粹存亡 preservation or ruin of nationally characteristic products of art, etc.
國粹工業 our splendid native industries.
[135] 國紀 national statistics.
國聞通訊社 national news-agency.
國色 a national beauty.
國花 national flower as an emblem.
國葬 State funeral.
[140] 國號 style of the reigning dynasty.
國計 politics.
國計民生 national economy and the livelihood of the masses.
國語 national language; mandarin.
國語教育 teaching in the national language.
[145] 國語統一 unification of the language.
國課 national revenue.
國謂君何 what does your State say with regard to your captive prince?—shall he be slain or released?
國變 a revolution.
國貨 native goods.
[150] 國賊 traitor to his country.
國軍部隊 government forces.
國運 fortunes of the State.
國道主管機關 Organization for the Nationalization of Roads and Transport.
國都 the capital, metropolis.
[155] 國防 national defence.
國防費 expenditure on defence.
國防軍 National Defence Forces.
國際 international.
國際主義 internationalism.
[160] 國際事務局 Bureau of International Affairs.
國際交易 international exchange.
國際交涉 international intercourse.
國際交誼 international comity.
國際仲裁裁判 international arbitration.
↑國殤 death for the sake of one's country.

¹⁶⁵國際保障 international guarantee.

國際價值 international value.

國際公法 international public law.

國際公法原則 principles of international law.

國際公道之原理 principles of international justice.

¹⁷⁰國際共同發展中國實業 international development of China's industries.

國際共產黨 Communist Internationals. A.c. 共產國際.

國際制·度 international standards.

國際勞動者協會 International Working Men's Association.

國際合作 international co-operation.

¹⁷⁵國際同盟 (or 聯盟) League of Nations. A.c. 國聯.

國際和平 international peace and goodwill.

國際問題 international question.

國際嘉禮 international courtesy.

國際團體 international group.

¹⁸⁰國際地位 international status.

國際委員會 International Commission.

國際婦女會 International Women's Association.

國際感情 international goodwill.

國際戰爭 international conflict.

¹⁸⁵國際政局 International Political Bureau.

國際會議 International Congress.

國際條約 international treaty.

國際法 international law.

國際法刑法 international criminal law.

¹⁹⁰國際法庭 international court of justice.

國際爭辯 international dispute.

國際版權 international copyright.

國際·的 international(ly).

國際·的性格 international character.

¹⁹⁵國際睦誼 (or 友誼) international comity or goodwill.

國際禮讓 international courtesy.

國際私法 international private law.

國際糾紛 international complications.

國際聯合會 International Association.

²⁰⁰國際聯盟主義 international unionism.

國際調·停 international arbitration.

國際財政劃賬所 clearing house for the world.

國際貿易 international trade and commerce.

國際關·係 international relation.

²⁰⁵國際高度 international pitch. (music). A.c. 國際音高.

國電 national telegraphs.

國霸諸侯 his State became the chief of all the feudal dominions.

國音 standard national pronunciation.

國風 national customs.

²¹⁰國香 the *epidendrum*.

國體 national constitution; national prestige.

國魂 spirit of the nation.

喎 4.5. To chatter. Read ku⁴. Name of a secret society.
3739

喎匪 robbers and secret-society rebels in Szechwan.

喎嚕·子 secret-society rebels in Szechwan.

幗 1.5. A cap worn by women. Feminine. Read kuei⁴.
3740 Mourning cap worn by women.

摑摝 1.5. To slap; to box the ears.
3741

摑一把 a slap or smack.

蟈 1.5. A small green frog. A cicada.
3742

蟈·蟈 a large kind of green cricket.

螻蟈 the small green frog.

馘 職 4.5. To cut off the left ears of the slain.
3743

馘首級 to behead.

獻馘 to present the left ears of the slain—to tender allegiance.

(a) Read hsü¹·⁵. The face.

槁項黃馘 a withered neck and a sallow face.

虢 2.5. Name of an ancient feudal State in Shensi and Honan.
3744

虢國夫人 title given to the sister of *Yang Kuei-fei* 楊貴妃.

崞 4.5. Mountain in Shansi.
3745

郭 1.5. An outer wall of fortifications. Suburbs; from which comes the meaning of:—a rim.
3746

郭公 puppets; the cuckoo.

郭外 wastes outside the city.

郭索 to walk like a crab.

城郭 the suburbs.

輪郭 outer rim of a coin, wheel, etc.

槨椁 3.5. An outer-coffin. A brick vault.
3747

钁 4.5. A mattock. A billhook.
3748

K'UO. (ㄎㄨㄛ)
(K'ueh or K'uoh)

蛞 1.5. See below.
3749

蛞蝓 the garden-slug.

蛞螻 or 蛞蟖 the mole-cricket.

闊 潤 3750
4.5.
Broad, ample. Indulgent. Rich; well-off.

闊 大 capacious, liberal.
闊 家 well-to-do family.
闊 少 rich young man.
闊·得 很 very broad; extravagant; well-off.
5 闊 步 to take big strides.
闊 落 coarse, as contrasted with fine.
闊 論 high-flown talk.
寬 闊 breadth.
深 闊 depth and breadth—area.
胸 襟 闊 magnanimous.

(a) Separated, distant.

久 闊 long-parted.
疏 闊 parted, separated.

彏 3751
4.5.
To draw a bow to the full.

彏 騎 emperor's night body-guard —T'ang dynasty.

擴 3752
4.5.
To expand, to stretch.

擴 充 to extend; to enlarge.
擴 充 心 欲 to enlarge the desires.
擴 其 心 胸 to enlarge the heart.
擴 大 to enlarge. 擴 大 器 amplifier. I(elec.)
5 擴 張 expansion; to expand; to amplify; to enlarge upon.
擴 張 公 共 事 業 expansion of public works.
擴 張 營 業 expansion of business.
擴 張 計 畫 plans for expansion.
領 土·的 擴 張 territorial expansion.
10 擴 散 diffusion.
擴 眼 界 to enlarge the vision.

廓 3753
4.5. To enlarge; to make great. Wide, extensive.

廓 土 a large, vacant area.
廓 然 大 公 a fair field and no favour.
廓 落 broad; large-minded.
廓 開 to enlarge.

憎 其 式 廓 hating the great—States.

(a) Empty, alone.

廓 廓 無 事 矣 all quiet, no disturbance.
廓 清 quiet, undisturbed; swept away—as rebels.
廓 然 獨 居 to stand alone.

(b) To pare, to trim.

(c) Used in transliterating.

廓 爾 喀 Gurkhas.

鞹 鞟 3754
4.5.
Leather; hides with the hair removed.

虎 豹 之 鞹 猶 犬 羊 之 鞹 the hide of a tiger or leopard stripped of its hair, is like the hide of a dog or goat stripped of its hair.

LA.   (ㄌ)

垃 3755
5
See below.

垃 圾 rubbish, such as is thrown on a dust-heap or dust-bin.
垃 圾 堆 a rubbish-heap.
垃 圾 夫 or 清 道 夫 scavenger, dustman.
垃 圾 箱 dust-bin.
垃 圾 車 rubbish-cart, dust-cart.

拉 3756
1.5. To drag, to pull. To seize. To draw a bow.

拉·不 出 來 I can't pull it out.
說·的 拉 不 出·的 he speaks well, but there is nothing to be pulled out of him.
拉·不 動 cannot make it move; cannot pull it—a heavy cart.
拉·不 開 cannot pull it open.
5 拉 主 顧 to attract customers.
拉·住·了 held fast.
拉倒·了 never mind; there's an end to it—say no more about it.
拉倒·了 罷, 不 要 追 究 that's enough, don't go further into the matter.

拉·到 死 地 taken to the execution ground.
10 拉 口·子 to offer bribes.
拉 壞·了 spoilt by pulling about.
拉 夫 to impress men for military coolie-service—to carry the baggage of soldiers, etc.
↓ 拉 拉 扯 扯·的, 拖 拖 拉 拉·的 to pull and drag, — diffuse talk; to work into each other's hands.

拉 屎 to go to stool.
拉 弓 to draw a bow.
15 拉 手 to take the hand; to shake hands. 拉·手 a door-knob.
拉·扯 to pull; to drag; to implicate; to work into each other's hands.
拉 拽 to drag; to compel to go.
拉·攏 to associate with; acquainted with; to bring a thing about; to dally, to dawdle.
拉·攏 半 天 delayed for some time.
20 拉 替·身 兒 to seize a substitute —as the ghosts of the drowned are said to do.
拉 洋 片 to run a peep-show.
拉 煤 to work in a coal-mine.
拉 琴 a concertina or accordion.
拉 生·意 to bring in business; to ply, as a hired cart.
25 拉 疲 lazy, slow, dilatory.
拉 皮·條 to act as a procurer; a pimp.
拉 短 兒 to tell a man's failings; to take a hire for a short distance—of a cart.
拉 硬 弓 to pull a stiff bow—he is hard to manage, said of a stiff, intractable person.
拉 空 to run into debt.
30 拉 篷 haul up the sail.
拉 結·實 pull tight; it drags heavily.
拉 絲 to draw out silk—to dally about a matter.
拉 縴 to track a boat.
拉·着 to pull; pulling.
35 拉 胡·琴 to play a Chinese fiddle.
拉 舌·頭 to gossip; to slander.
拉 買·賣 to ply for hire—as a cart.
拉 賬 to run into debt; to run an account.
拉·起·來 pull it up.
40 拉 車 to haul a cart.
拉 車·的 a ricksha-puller.
拉·過·來 pull it over here.

拉 鋸 to pull a two-handed saw.
拉·開 to pull open; pull apart.
⁴⁵拉 雜 confused; all of a heap.
拉 風 扇 to pull a punkah.
拉 儀·荒 to go into debt when there is no hope of paying.
一 拉 就 斷 one pull and it will break.

(a) Used for transliterating.

拉 丁 Latin.
拉 伯 蘭 Lapland.
拉 薩 Lhassa.
↑拉 特 維 亞 Latvia.

刺
3757
2.5. To cut in two. To slash. Distinguish 刺 No. 6985.

刺·下 to cut off.
刺。去 to cut away.
刺 屍 to mutilate a corpse.
刺 手 to cut the hand.
刺。開 to cut open.

(a) Wicked, perverse, intractable.

刺 戾 perverse, wicked.
乖 刺 perverse, intractable.

(b) Inter. next. *la³.*

刺·麻 Tibetan Lamas, priests of Tibetan Buddhism.
刺·麻 敎 Lamaism.
達 賴 刺·麻 Dalai Lama.

喇
3758
3.5. A final particle. Character used in names when transliterated.

喇·叭 a trumpet.
喇·嘛 Lama, priest of Tibetan Buddhism.

(a) To chatter.

喇 喇 不 休 always chattering.
喇 嘴 to boast.

捋
攋
3759
1.5. To clutch; to grab at. To rub or scrape. To tear.

捋 去 pull it off.

癩
3760
4.5. Severe; poisonous; dangerous. Itch and other skin-diseases.

癩 痢 scald-head.

痢 痢 頭 a head bald from scald-head.

辢
辣
3761
4.5. Bitter, pungent, acrid.

辢 口 a pungent remark.
辢 味 pungent, peppery taste.
辢 實 dangerous; bitter; cruel.
辢 手 cruel, harsh in treatment; rough handling.
⁵辢 椒 or 紅 辢 capsicum.
辢 蓼 *polygonum.*
辢 詞 sharp words.
老 辢 experienced and severe.

攦
擸
3762
4.5. To hold, to grasp. Also read *lieh⁴·⁵.* To hold the hair; to pull at.

攦 持 to lay hold of; to grasp firmly.
攦 攦 sound of breaking branches.
攦 破 to break.

臘
臈
腊
3763
4.5. The winter sacrifice, held three days after the solstice. To sacrifice. A year. The twelfth lunar month.

臘 先 祖 to sacrifice to ancestors.
臘 八 粥 gruel eaten on 8th of the 12th lunar month.
臘 日 day of the winter sacrifice, three days after the solstice, about Dec. 25, when sacrifice is offered to the gods, 臘 祭 百 神.
臘·月 the twelfth lunar month.

(a) The number of years that a man has been a Buddhist priest.

僧 臘 seniority of Buddhist priests.
老 臘 an aged priest.

(b) Dried or salted meats.

臘 味 preserved foods.
臘 肉 dried or salted meat.
臘 腸 sausages made of salted meats.

臘 鴨 dried salted ducks.

(c) The edge of a sword.

劍 臘 the edge of a sword.

蠟
蜡
3764
4.5. Wax. Waxy; glazed. A candle.

蠟 丸 wax-coated pills.
蠟 像 wax-figures.
蠟 嘴 the wax-bill.
蠟 梅 the *Chimonanthus fragrans.*
⁵蠟 樹 the wax-tree—*Ligustrum lucidum.*
蠟 油 the drip from candles.
蠟 淚 guttering of a candle.
蠟 燭 or 腊 燭 candles.
蠟 石 yellow quartz.
¹⁰蠟 紙 or 蠟 箋 glazed paper.
蠟 臺 a candlestick.
蠟 餅 tapers curled in a flat coil.
嚼 蠟 to chew wax—insipid.
白 蠟 white wax, from the insect deposits on the wax-tree.
¹⁵白 蠟 蟲 the insects which deposit the wax as above.
石 蠟 paraffin-wax.
耳 蠟 ear-wax.
黃 蠟 bees-wax.

襤
袛
3765
4.5. Old, or badly fitting clothes. Untidy.

邋
3766
4.5. To exceed; to pass by. Slovenly.

邋 在 後 頭 to dawdle behind.
邋 遢 or 邋 裡 邋 遢·的 slovenly, neglected, dirty.
邋 遢 從 事 careless and negligent in business.
邋 雜 mixed; confused.

鑞
3767
4.5. Hard tin.

錫·鑞 pewter, solder.
白 鑞 pewter.

LAI. (ㄌㄞ)

來[2] To come; coming. A complement of verbs. See 出
3768 No. 1409; 起 No. 548-4.

來·不·來 will you come or not? are you coming?

來·不·及 too late.

來世 or 來生 the life to come; future state of existence.

來人 or 來手 or 來使 the bearer; a messenger.

[5] 叫 來人 等 tell the bearer to wait.

來來 come on—to fight, to begin work, etc.

來來往往 coming and going in great numbers.

來信 letter to hand; inward correspondence.

來函 your letter to hand.

[10]來到·了 come, arrived.

來勢甚兇 of very savage aspect.

來去分明 no secret about his movement; everything clear and aboveboard.

來去無定 coming and going without any definite time.

來·呀 Come!

[15]來回 there and back; to come and go.

來回·的走 walking to and fro.

來回票 return ticket.

來回郵片 return postcard.

一天打兩·個來回 make two trips in one day.

[20]來因 or 來由 cause; reason of; origin; source.

來孫 the fourth generation below oneself.

來賓 visitors; guests.

來就耶穌 come to Jesus.

來年 or 明年 next year.

[25]來·往 intercourse; coming and going.

來往不絕 ceaseless coming and going.

來往存款 current account.

沒有來往 no intercourse with.

來·得 able to do it; over and above; it is all right to come.

[30] 很可以來·得 well able to do it; it's quite right to come.

比他來得貴些 it comes a little dearer than that one.

來·得勤 constantly coming.

來·得及 there is time; one can make it in time.

來·得早 to arrive early.

[35]來·得湊巧 just arrived in the nick of time.

來復 a week,—from a phrase in the *Book of Changes* 七日來復·

來復日 Sunday.

來文 the despatch under reply; an incoming despatch.

來日 tomorrow; by and by.

[40]來·得遲 or 來晚·了 to come late; to be behind-hand.

來朝 to come to court; to pay respects. 來朝 tomorrow morning.

來格 to arrive.

來·歷 antecedents; notices of; annals; history; foundation.

來歷不明 of questionable antecedents.

[45] 沒有來歷 no foundation for it.

來源 source; origin.

來稿 contributed articles in a paper.

來者猶可追 the future may yet be saved—there is still time to retire.

來臨 to come down to.

[50]來自 to come from....

來至 come, arrived.

來茲 afterwards.

來訊 letter received.

來·路 the source; the way by which anything comes.

[55]來路貨 imported, not local goods—good quality articles.

來頭 a source; aspect of; appearance.

上·來 come up.

下·來 come down.

做·不·來 it cannot be done; impossible; I cannot do it.

[60]原來 as a matter of fact; originally; in the beginning.

回·來 to return; to come back.

後來 afterwards. |回·來 by-and-by.

日來 lately; recently.

本來 originally; in the beginning; as a matter of fact.

[65]說·不·來 cannot say; may not be uttered; I cannot explain, or, dare not say.

辦·不·來 cannot manage it.

過·來 to come across; to come to.

(a) Read *lai*[4] or *li*[4,5]. To encourage by reward.

來百工 to encourage artisans to come.

(b) Read ·*la(i)* After a number it is equivalent to:—more than, and some over, odd, etc.

三·十·來·個人 a few more than thirty persons.

十·來·個 ten or a dozen.

四·十·來·歲 forty odd years.

(c) Used in transliterating and read *lai*[2].

來因 The Rhine.

來復 (or 福) 鎗 a rifle.

來頓瓶 a Leyden jar.

(d) Wheat. A sheaf.

來牟 wheat and barley.

倈
徠[4]
勑
3769

To induce to come; to encourage.

倈獸臭 to be laughed at.

招倈 to induce the people to come.

淶[2] A brook, ripples. Name
3770 of a river in Shantung and Chihli or Hopei.

睞[4]
3771

To squint; to look at.

盼睞 fondly gazing—favours.

萊[2] Goosefoot; wild herbs.
3772 Fields lying fallow.

賚[4] To confer; to bestow on
an inferior. To reward.
3773 Distinguish 賫 No. 464.

賚我思成 the realization of our thoughts is granted to us.

周有大賚 *Chou* conferred great gifts.

鯠[2]
3774 A kind of eel.

犝[1] Child of an old man.
Also read *nai*[2].
3775

賴
頼[4] To trust to; to rely on.
3776

賴仗 or 倚賴 or 仰賴 to rely on; to trust to.
賴厚朋友 an intimate friend.
賴·得此耳 trusting in this....; fortunately, but for this....
無賴之徒 a vagabond.

(a) To repudiate. Shameless.

賴·不過去 no chance for repudiation—with the evidence all there.
賴人情 to repudiate favours.
賴債 to repudiate a debt.
賴婚 to repudiate a marriage contract.
[5]賴學 or 逃學 to play truant.
賴·得很 very bad; roguish.
賴皮 a man who has no shame; a rogue.
賴臉 shameless.
賴詞 lies.
[10]一齊賴·掉 repudiate the whole thing.

(b) To accuse falsely.

賴別人 to blame another; to accuse another falsely.

瀨[4] Water flowing over shallows. Name of a river in Kwangsi.
3777

癩[4] Skin disease; blotch; leprosy; mange.
3778

癩仙 a scabby fellow.
癩大蟲 or 癩團 a toad.
癩狗 a mangy dog.
癩瘡 or 癩·子 sores caused by scabies.
[5]癩癬 ringworm.
癩蛤蟆 the toad.
癩蛤蟆想吃天鵝肉 the toad thought to partake of the meat of the swan—vain hopes, foolish imaginings.
癩頭 a scabby head.

過癩 to pass on a skin disease.
長[3]癩 to become leprous.

籟[4] A musical pipe consisting of three reeds. Music.
3779

萬籟都寂 all sounds are hushed.

LAN.   (ㄌㄢ)

婪[2] Covetous; avaricious.
3780

婪索 to extort from.
貪婪 avaricious; greedy.

潵[3] To pickle fruits. To divine by dripping water through the shell of a tortoise.
3781

惏[2] Avaricious; greedy.
Read *lin*[2]. Cold.
3782

惏慄 cold; chilly.

嵐[2] Vapour, mist. A mountain in Shansi.
3783

嵐氣 vapour or mists.
山嵐 mountain mists.

壈[3] Disappointed.
3784

壈坎難歸來 it is difficult to return after a failure.
坎壈 to miss one's mark; to fail.

燗[2.3] To toast; to roast.
3785

燗一燗 toast it for a while.
燗焦 to roast; to burn.
燗脆 to toast crisp.
燗黃 to brown.

嬾[3] Lazy. Inter. next.
3786

嬾婦 the cricket.

懶[3] Lazy, indolent. Reluctant.
3787

懶吃 disinclined for food.
懶怠 loath; disinclined to.
懶惰 lazy; idle.
懶懶·的 leisurely; reluctantly.
[5]懶散 careless and remiss.
懶洋洋·的 reluctantly, in a slow and listless manner.
懶筋 disinclined to move, out of sorts, failing and weak.
懶走 disinclined to walk.
懶骨 lazybones.
[10]伸懶腰 to stretch oneself.
偷懶 to be idle.

(a) Read *lai*[4]. Evil.

罱[3] A kind of spring fishing-net.
3788

闌[2] A door-screen. To cut off. Inter. 欄 No. 3792.
3789

有河山以闌之 rivers and mountains bar the way—from *Chin* to *Liang*, two feudal States.

(a) Late, the evening.

夜闌 late at night.
歲闌 late in the year.

(b) Few. Decline.

廚人夜語闌 the chatter of the servants in the kitchen lessens as the night comes on.
酒闌 the wine drinkers have gone.

(c) Exhausted; finished.

闌單 tired, worn out; in disorder; untidy in dress.
闌殫 utterly weary.
闌珊 decayed; worn out; in confusion.

(d) Reckless, abrupt.

闌入 to enter the palace without a pass; to bring in extraneous matters.
闌出 recklessly leaving a place without pass or permission.

(e) A railing. Inter. 欄 No. 3792.

闌干 a railing to a balcony; the socket of the eye; horizontal; athwart; across.
北斗闌干 the Dipper lies across the sky.

(f) A bracelet.

腕 闌 a bracelet for the wrist.

(g) Large intestine.

闌 尾 炎 appendicitis. *See* 蕋 No. 1519—5. Pop. called 4346.9½.

闌 門 mouth of the large intestine.

攔[2] **To hinder; to obstruct; to cut off.**
3790

攔 勸 to remonstrate with.

攔 截 to hinder; to cut off; to intercept.

攔 搶 to commit highway robbery.

攔 擋 to intercept; to check; to restrain.

[5]攔 擋 不 住 unable to hinder.

攔 櫃 a shop-counter.

攔 腰 抱 住 to seize a man by the waist from behind.

攔 擧 to obstruct—a scheme.

攔 街 blocking up the street.

[10]攔 路 to block the road.

攔 路 虎 a sign hung across the street.

攔 輿 遞 稟 to stop the chair of an official and hand in a petition.

攔 轎 to stop the chair of an official—as above.

攔°開 to separate; to part.

攔 阻 or 攔 住 to obstruct; to hinder; to stop—as a way.

斕[2] **Variegated; parti-coloured.**
3791

欄[2] **A railing, a balustrade. A pen for animals.**
3792

欄·杆儿 a railing; a baluster; silk trimmings, etc. *Inter.* 闌 No. 3789—E.

欄 架 wooden *chevaux-de-frise*.

扶 手 欄·杆儿 a banister.

牛 欄 a pen for cows.

(a) A column in a newspaper.

文 學 欄 literary column.

答 問 欄 inquiry column.

瀾[2] **Swelling water; billows, waves.**
3793

瀾 汗 great waves.

瀾 漫 to overflow; an inundation.

瀾 瀾 weeping bitterly.

瀾 翻 overflowing waves—exuberant style of writing.

爛[4] **Rotten; over-ripe. Broken, smashed. Ragged.**
3794 **Very.**

爛·了 rotten; spoilt.

爛 命 a hard lot; suffering.

爛 嘴 or 爛 口 a blackguard; may your mouth rot!

爛 好 人 a goody-goody (person.)

[5]爛 小 人 a low-down blackguard.

爛·得 很 very muddy; cooked to rags; very ragged; utterly rotten.

爛 泥 soft mud.

爛 漫 retired; at ease and light-hearted; fast asleep. *See below* A—1.

爛 熟 thoroughly cooked; over-ripe. *See below* A—3.

[10]爛 眼 邊 sore eyelids.

爛 紙 waste paper.

爛 肉 meat cooked till very tender.

爛 芝·麻 spoilt sesamum—something useless or rotten.

爛 衣 ragged garments.

[15]爛 賖 惡 討 to give credit loosely and press hard for payment.

爛 醉 dead drunk.

打 爛 beaten to a pulp.

煮 爛 boil till tender.

破 爛 ragged.

[20]蛀 爛 worm-eaten.

(a) Bright; glistening.

爛 漫 (or 縵) brilliant. *See above*—8.

星 爛 縵 the stars are glittering

爛 熟 very well versed in. *See above*—9.

爛 然 bright; brilliant.

爛 爛 brightness—of eyes.

爛 門 an illuminated doorway.

蘭[2] **The epidendrum. Used figuratively in the sense of**
3795 **fragrant, elegant, refined, numerous, etc.**

蘭 交 sweet relations—an intimate friend.

蘭 兆 prognostication of the birth of a son.

蘭 兄 a sworn brother.

蘭 夢 a fragrant dream—foretells the birth of a son.

[5]蘭 姐 a sworn sister.

蘭 孫 many grandchildren.

蘭 客 a loved friend.

蘭 形 棘 心 beautiful in form but a villain at heart.

蘭 心 refined.

[10]蘭 情 a fragrant and pure disposition.

蘭 摧 玉 折 death of a virtuous man.

蘭 桂 orchids and cassia—fragrance.

蘭 炷 incense.

蘭 玉 abbreviation for fragrant and beautiful plants and trees—your beautiful children.

[15]蘭 盆 a bath-tub; to save the souls of those who have no one to care for their graves, etc.—from 盂 蘭 盆 transliteration of the Sanskrit *ullambhama*, deliverance.

蘭 石 fragrant and strong—excellent moral virtues.

蘭 秋 the 7th lunar month.

蘭 膏 fragrant ointments.

蘭 臭 agreeable fragrance.

[20]蘭 艾 epidendrum and artemisia—high and lowly.

蘭 花儿 orchids.

蘭 若 a hermit's cell.

蘭 草 general name for orchid-like plants.

蘭 薰 桂 馥 fragrance disseminated around—of virtue.

[25]蘭 言 your fragrant speech; words with which one agrees.

蘭 訊 a letter.

蘭 譜 the genealogical records of those who have sworn brotherhood.

蘭 質 蕙 心 a refined nature.

蘭 缸 a fragrant lamp.

[30]蘭 閨 a maiden's boudoir; girls.

蘭 鮑 fragrant (as flowers) and malodorous (as dried fish)—dissimilar.

蘭 麝 sweet fragrance.

吊 蘭 orchids with aerial roots.

玉 蘭 *magnolia conspicua.*

芝 蘭 the epidendrum.

襴[2]
3796 **Gown of former graduates.**

讕 [2.4.]
3797　To make a false charge.

讕 誣 to lay a false accusation.

躝 [2]　To pass; to step over. To
3798　creep; to twine round.

躝 地 to run over the ground—as melons, etc.
躝 藤 creeping plants, vines, etc.
躝 踰 to pass over.

韊 [2]
3799　A case for a bow.

濫 [4]　To overflow; to go to excess.
3800

濫 交 to form undesirable companionships.
濫 保 to give security carelessly; to recommend without full knowledge.
濫·出·來 to overflow.
濫 刑 excessive punishments.
[5]濫 取 to take too much.
濫 委 to shirk responsibility and pass it on to others.
濫 寫 to write without regard to facts or proper sequence; to scribble.
濫 支 lavish expenditure.
濫 收 to receive too much.
[10]濫 淫 debauchery.
濫 溢 to overflow.
濫 用 to go to excess; to use extravagantly.
濫 用 職 權 wide misuse of official authority.
濫 發 紙 幣 to flood the market with paper money.
[15]濫 竽 to pretend to play the *yü*—of a pretender who joined the orchestra of *Hsüan Wang* of *Ch'i* 齊 宣 王; he was unnoticed in the crowd, but discovered when the son, who preferred solos, came to the throne.
濫 竽 充 數 to hold an office without having the requisite skill; to make up the number—from the preceding phrase.
濫 與 to lavish upon.
濫 觴 it would overflow a goblet, —of the source of the Yangtze

—yet it becomes a great river; used of the beginning of things.
濫 言 excessive talk.
[20]濫 費 to waste; profuse expenditure.
濫 錢 waste of money.
濫 開 數 目 to overcharge an account.

籃 [2]
3801　A basket.

籃·子 a basket.
籃 球 basket-ball.
籃 筐 baskets generally.
籃 細 工 fine basket-work.
[5]籃 輿 a bamboo sedan.

藍 [2]
3802　Blue, indigo.

藍 光 blue light.
藍 寳·石 sapphire.
藍 布 blue cloth.
藍 帶 a blue ribbon.
[5]藍 榜 or 紫 榜 the list, at the former public examinations, of candidates who have been deprived of their chances for some breach of the regulations.
藍 澱 indigo.
藍 皮 書 *a blue-book.*
藍 色 blue colour.
藍 色 照 相 a blue-print.
[10]藍 花 荳 or 蠶 荳 broad beans.
藍 草 the indigo plant.
藍 蔚 azure.
藍 衫 a graduate, 秀·才.
藍 青 dark, indigo blue.
[15]藍 靛 indigo.
洋 藍 foreign indigo.
淺 藍 light blue.
翠 藍 kingfisher blue.
老 藍 blue-black.

襤 [2]
3803　Ragged garments.

襤 褸 tattered garments; shabby.

覽 [3]
覧
3804　To look at; to inspect; to perceive. Distinguish 賢 No. 2671.

覽 勝 to visit scenic resorts.

覽 悉 to take in at a glance—as the details of a letter.
覽 視 to examine; to look at; to witness.
覽 觀 今 古 wide reading.
一 覽 無 遺 the whole may be seen at a glance.
一 覽 盡 知 understood it all with one glance.
博 覽 extensive reading.

攬 [3]
擥
3805　To grasp; to seize. To monopolize.

攬 取 or 攬 采 to seize.
攬 契 a cargo receipt; an insurance contract.
攬 得 過 able to get one's arms round anything.
攬 權 to grasp at authority.
[5]攬 榜 the last on the list of second-degree graduates under the old system.
攬 貨 to corner goods; to buy up the market.
攬 頭 the head of—as a guild.
包 攬 to monopolize.
承 攬 to undertake for.

欖 [3]
3806　The Chinese olive.

欖 仁 olive seeds.
橄·欖 the olive.

纜 [4]
3807　A hawser, a cable; a rope.

纜 索 cordage; thick ropes.
篾 纜 a bamboo hawser.
鐵 纜 a wire-rope.

LANG.　　　(ㄌㄤ)

朗 [3]　Clear, bright. Distinct
3808　utterance.

朗 抱 雲 the bright clouds embracing—the moon.
朗 月 or 月 朗 a bright moon.
朗 朗 如 日 月 as bright as the sun or moon.
聲 朗 朗 the sounds were clear and distinct.

[5]朗 烈 clear; perspicuous.
朗 照 to shine brightly——your brightness shines on me.
朗 聲 a clear voice.
朗 若 列 眉 as distinct and clear as the eyebrows.
朗 誦 to read in a clear voice.
[10]朗 鑒 Your clear intelligence—to a friend.
清 朗 limpid; clear.

梆[2] A species of palm, the pith of which produces a sago.
3809

浪[4] A wave.
3810

浪 動 wave-motion.
浪 木 a see-saw.
浪 橋 a swinging bridge.(gymnast.)
浪 花 the foam of breaking waves.
[5]浪・頭 a wave, the crest of a wave.
浪・頭 大 high-crested waves.

(a) Wasteful; extravagant; profligate.

浪 人 a vagabond; a disorderly person; ronin. (Jap.)
浪 傳 carelessly spreading a story.
浪 子 a prodigal.
浪 漫 romance.
[5]浪 漫 主 義 romanticism.
浪 漫・的 青 年 a romantic youth.
浪 用 reckless expenditure.
浪 蕩 dissipated; prodigal.
浪 語 reckless talk.
[10]浪 費 extravagance.
浪 遊 to travel far; wandering; roaming.

狼[2] The wolf; thus:—cruel, fierce; poisonous.
3811

狼 人 to swindle a person.
狼 吞 虎 咽 a wolfish, tiger-like appetite; grasping.
狼 子 野 心 a wolf-cub has a wild disposition—of an intractable person.
狼 心 cruel, vindictive, savage, brutal.
[5]狼 心 犬 肺 cruel and fierce disposition.
狼 戾 greedy and cruel; abundance; abundant.
狼 戾 無 親 merciless, cruel, without natural affection.

狼 抗 merciless, cruel, savage.
狼 星 or 天 狼 Sirius.
[10]狼 木 viburnum.
狼 毒 merciless; savage.
狼 烟 smoke from wolf-dung burnt in beacons as a warning.
狼 牙 (or 子) a poison— potentilla cryptotaeniae.
狼 狽 helplessly dependent; ill at ease; ruined. The wolf is said to have short hind legs, and the pei to have short forelegs, so that the latter is said to ride on the back of the wolf. Used to express indecision, distress, etc.
[15]狼 狽 不 堪 very much troubled; in great distress; in disorder.
狼 狽 爲 奸 banded together, in collusion for seditious purposes.
狼 狽 萬 狀 in utter confusion.
狼 疾 人 "a man like a hurried wolf."
狼 巔 lycanthropy.
[20]狼 羣 a wolf pack.
狼 藉 scattered about; profusion.
聲 名 狼 藉 a bad reputation.
狼 貛 the wolverine.
狼 貪 虎 視 insatiable covetousness, like a wolf or tiger.
[25]狼 顧 looking round like a wolf, nervous or brutal looks.
黃 鼠 狼 a weasel.

琅[2] A kind of white cornelian.
瑯
3812

琅 函 your esteemed favour.
琅 玕 a reddish kind of jade.
琅 琅 tinkling of pendants.
琅 瑯 王 title of the heir-apparent.
琅 瑯 郡 ancient name for the eastern portion of Shantung.
琅 璫 pendant ornaments, tinkling things.

稂[2] Grass; weeds.
3813

稂 莠 weeds, tares—worthless, injurious things.

筤[2] Young bamboos.
3814

蒼 筤 竹 green bamboo shoots.

莨[2] A marsh grass.
3815

莨 菪 (tang[4]) Henbane.

(a) Read liang[1]. A plant which produces a brown dye.

薯 莨 a plant which produces a dark brown dye for silk.

蜋[2] A mantis. Dung-beetle.
螂
3816

螳 蜋 the mantis. = 刀 螂
蜣 蜋 the dung-beetle.

駺[2] Tall.
3817

鋃[2] An ornament. Inter. 琅 No. 3812.
3818

鋃 鐺 tinkling; chains for prisoners.
以 鐵 鋃 鐺 其 頸 put an iron chain about his neck.

閬[3] A high door. Lofty. Bright.
3819

閬 閬 lofty, exalted. See below A—3.
高 閬 a lofty entrance.

(a) Deserts. Vacant. The outlying wastes beyond the city outskirts.

閬 苑 a park; elysium.
閬 苑 奇 才 a man of remarkable talents.
閬 閬 boundless wastes. See above —1.
土 閬 the outlying wastes.

郎[2] A young gentleman. Term of respect.
3820

郎・中 a doctor; senior secretary of a board—obsolete.
郎 君 or 才 郎 a husband.
郎 子 a young gentleman.
郎 署 a high official.

合 郎 your son.
員 外 郎 former title of a second-class secretary to a board.
新 郎 a bridegroom.

郎² 　See below.
3821

郎 環 the place where the Supreme 天 帝, stores his books.

廊² 　A verandah; a porch; a corridor.
3822

廊·子 or 廊 房 a porch; verandah; corridor. = 廊 檐.
廊 廡 corridors; passages; verandah.
明 廊 暗 廊 open and covered ways.
遊 廊 corridors.

榔² 　Name given to various trees.
3823

榔 楡 an elm—*ulmus parvifolia.*
檳 榔 the areca palm or betel nut.

LAO. 　(ㄌㄠˊ)

牢² 　A pen for cattle. A prison.
3824

牢 戶 a prison.
牢 桟 a pen for animals.
牢 籠 a pen; a prison.
牢 籠 人 心 to captivate the minds of men.
⁵牢 籠 計 a scheme to entrap another.
牢 頭 禁·子 a jailer.
牢 間 a prison.
坐 牢 to be in prison.
監 牢 or 獄 牢 a jail or prison.

(a) Firmly, securely.

牢 不 可 改 unalterable.
牢 不 可 破 impregnable; unalterable.
牢 固 firm, secure.
牢 記 make a point of remembering.
牢°靠 firm, trustworthy.

不 牢 insecure; fragile; easily damaged.

(b) Troubled.　Inter. 勞 No. 3826. Lonely.

牢 愁 worried, anxious.
牢 落 lonely.
牢 騷 grumbling; disturbed; discontented.

(c) Sacrificial animals.

少 牢 sacrificial sheep.
太 牢 sacrificial ox.

哞² 　Incoherent chatter.
3825

哞 叨 chattering.

勞² 　To toil, to suffer.　Weary. To give trouble to.
3826

勞 乏 or 勞 困 wearied; worn out.
勞 人 a worker; a man of suffering and toil.
勞 働 labour. *See below*—7.
勞 備 a hired labourer.
⁵勞 力 者 those who toil with their hands.
勞 務 a task.
勞·動 labour generally; to give trouble to.
勞 動 主 義 proletariatism.
勞 動 問 題 the labour question.
¹⁰勞 動 團 體 the labour body.
勞 動 家 labourer; worker; labour agitator.
勞 動 政 府 labour government.
勞 動 日 working days; week days.
勞 動 時 間 hours of labour.
¹⁵勞 動 權 rights of labour.
勞 動 界 the labour world.
勞 動·的 組 合 labour union.
勞 動 社 會 proletariat.
勞 動 紀 念 日 Labour Day.
²⁰勞 動 組 合 會 議 Trades Union Congress.
勞 動 者 the worker.
勞 動 規·則 labour regulations.
勞 動 過 度 overwork.
勞 動 運·動 labour movement.
²⁵勞 動 階·級 the labouring classes.
勞 動 黨 Labour Party.
勞 嘈 clamour and noise.

勞 工 factory work; labour.
勞 工 會 labour union.
³⁰勞 工 神 聖 divinity of labour.
勞 工 領 袖 labour leader.
勞 形 appearance of weariness.
勞 役 toilsome service.
勞 心 mental labour; anxious.
³⁵勞 民 to employ the people on toilsome service. *See below*—B.2.
勞 生 a life of toil.
勞 瘁 wearied and worn.
勞 瘵 (or 症) consumption. *See* 癆 No. 3831.
勞 碌 or 勞 力 weary toil; bodily labour.
⁴⁰勞 神 to weary oneself; wearied in mind.
勞 累 involved; entangled; weary.
勞 績 meritorious achievement.
勞 苦 labour; fatigue.
勞 苦 患 難 distress and difficulties.
⁴⁵　不 辭 勞 苦 not afraid of toil; indefatigable.
勞 資 兩 方 之 衝 突 clash between capital and labour.
勞 資 兩 方 爭 執 hostility between capital and labour.
勞 資 糾 紛·的 事 件 disputes between capital and labour.
勞 費 labour and expense.
⁵⁰勞 農 會 Workers' and Peasants' Union.
勞 金 or 酬 勞 a reward; fee; recompense.
勞 頓 labour and weariness.
勞 煩 or 煩 勞 worried; anxious; to trouble one—to do something.
勞 駕 conventional phrase—I have troubled you; excuse me.
⁵⁵徒 勞 labour in vain.

(a) To make to labor.

勞 而 不 怨 he lays tasks (on the people) without their repining.

(b) Read *lao⁴*.　To reward; to recompense; to encourage.

勞 兵 or 勞 軍 to reward troops.
勞 民 to encourage the masses.
勞 賚 to encourage by rewards.

嘮² 　To chatter.
3827

嘮 叨 chattering; loquacious.

憥[4]
3828
To regret.

撈[1,2]
3829
To drag for; to fish up; to dredge for; to drag out of the water.

撈取 salvage.

撈 (or 牢) 什·子 something useless or troublesome.

撈回·來 to get back.

撈屍 to drag for a dead body.

[5]撈摸 to feel about in the water; to grope for.

撈獲 to recover from the water.

撈·起 or 撈·上·來 to pull out of the water.

撈魚 to scoop up fish—as by a landing-net.

海底撈針 to drag up a needle from the depths of the sea—vain effort.

澇[4]
3830
A torrent. Great waves. Inter. 潦 No. 3836.

癆[2]
3831
Wasting away from toil or anxiety. Consumption. Injurious.

癆人之物 injurious things.

癆傷 sprained; injured—as by over-exertion.

癆·病 or 癆瘵 or 癆症 consumption.

蒡[4]
3832
To weed. Read lao[2]. A plant.

老[3]
3833 Radical 125.
Old, aged. Venerable. Term of honour and respect.

老·了 old, grown old.

老·人·家 an aged person; a title of respect.

老伯 respectful address to a friend of one's father, or the father of one's friend.

老兄 elder brother—polite form of address.

[5]老先·生 venerable sir—title of respectful address.

老公 an old man; a crow.

老友 an old friend.

老叟 an old man; venerable sir.

老君 or 老子[3] the philosopher Laotzǔ.

[10]老圃 an aged market gardener.

老大 a skipper of a boat; old chap! elder brother; old.

老天爺 Venerable Heavenly Ruler—used by some for God.

老夫 I, me—used by an old man.

老太·太 an old lady; your mother.

[15]老奸巨猾 an old rogue.

老姊 my elder sister—in address.

老娘 an old lady; maternal grandmother; a midwife.

老婆 an old woman; a wife.

小老婆 a concubine.

[20]老媽 an old woman; a nurse; or amah.

老·子 a father. See above—9.

老·子娘 father and mother.

老學究 an old pedant.

老宮 an old eunuch.

[25]老家 the old home; one's native place.

老·實 honest; well-disposed; simple; trustworthy; good-tempered—of animals.

老·實頭 a simpleton.

老少 (shao[4]) old and young.

老居民 an old resident.

[30]老師 an instructor; a professor; a journeyman; a chief among Mohammedans; a teacher.

老師宿儒 aged masters and scholars.

老幼 old and young.

老弱 the aged and weak.

老弱饋食 the old and feeble carried food to the labourers.

[35]老態 his old manner.

老手 an old hand.

老拙 old and stupid—depreciatory phrase referring to oneself.

老拳 the fist.

老昏 senility.

[40]老書·生 an aged scholar.

老朽 old and worthless.

老板 master of a Chinese boat; proprietor of a shop; a husband, etc. This term is not reckoned as respectful in North China.

老氏之流 a follower of Laotzǔ.

老江湖 an old traveller; a man who lives by his wits.

[45]老·爺 old gentleman—term of respect; a district magistrate; a god; an object of reverence.

老牛舐犢 the old cow licks her calf—maternal or paternal love.

老王 old Mr. Wang; Wang!

老生常談 (or 譚) the platitudes of an old scholar.

老相識 an old acquaintance.

[50]老眊 dim sight of the aged.

老老[3] to treat the aged as they should be treated.

老者安之 to give rest to the aged.

老聃 Laotzǔ.

老·虎 a tiger.

↑老·老 mother's mother.

[55]老蚌生珠 a pearl from the old oyster—a son in late life.

老行 (hang[2]) 長 (chang[3]) an old customer.

老衲 aged Buddhist priest.

老身 term of depreciation used by women in speaking of themselves.

老酒 old wine.

[60]老遠·的 a long way off.

老邁 aged, old.

老頭·子 an old man, a husband.

老馬識途 the old horse knows the way—used of experience.

識途老馬—permit me—as an experienced man—to....

[65]老驥伏櫪 the old horse in the stable—still has plenty of spirit—of the ambitions of the aged.

老鴉 a crow.

老鴇 a procuress.

老鵠 a crow.

老·鼠 a rat.

[70]老鼠刺 holly.

(a) For a long time. Old-established.

老·是不要 for a long time I did not want it; really had no need for it.

老沒看·見 I have not seen him for a good while.

老牌·子 the old-established brand.

(b) Hard-boiled. Well cooked. Extremely. Very. Experienced in.

老成 experienced; sincere, honest.

老早 very early.

老練 experienced in; experience.

老色 deep colour.

[5]老辣 decisive, firm in action.

老長 very long.

老饞 gluttonous.

煮 老 to boil eggs hard; to cook thoroughly.

咾³
3834   A noise; a sound.

栳³
3835   A basket.

栲 栳 a bucket made of willow.

潦⁴
3836   Heavy rains. Roads flooded.

潦·死 drowned.
水 潦 降 the rain poured down.

(a) Read *lao*⁴. Inter. 澇 No. 3830. Floods.

潦 漫 floods, overflowing.
潦 壞·了 ruined by floods.

(b) Read *lao*². Unlucky.

潦 倒 unlucky in life; to fail; disappointed.

(c) Read *liao*². Careless.

潦○草 careless in managing affairs.

(d) u.f. 遼 No. 3981. River in S. Manchuria.

嫪⁴
3837   Lustful.

戀 嫪 lustful longings for.

醪²
3838   The lees of wine or spirits.

LÊ.   (ㄌㄜ)
(Leh)

了 v. 3958.
仂⁴·⁵
3839   A surplus or excess. A tithe.

喪 用 三 年 之 仂 "for mourning use one tenth of three years' income."
祭 用 數 之 仂 "for offerings use one tenth of the annual expenditure."

肋⁴·⁵
3840   The ribs, the side.

肋 傍 or 肋 門 the side.
肋 把 骨 or 肋 條 骨 a rib.
肋 條 or 脊 肋 the ribs.
肋 膜 the pleura.
⁵肋 膜 心 胞 炎 pleuro-carditis.
肋 膜 炎 pleurisy.
肋 膜 肺 炎 pleuro-pneumonia.
軟 肋 the floating ribs.

勒⁴·⁵
3841   To bridle; to restrain.
[(*lei*¹-)]

勒·不 住 unable to check—a horse.
勒 兵 to check the advance of troops.
勒 口 to gag; to bridle.
勒 死 to strangle. (*lei*¹-)
勒 馬 to rein in a horse.

(a) To extort; to force. To coerce.

勒 令 to insist on; to force.
勒 休 to force an officer to vacate his post.
勒 佔 to usurp; to seize on.
勒 充 兵 役 to compel military service.
⁵勒 捐 enforced subscriptions.
勒 索 or 勒 揩 or 勒 收 to demand; to extort.
勒 贖 held for ransom.
勒 逼 or 苦 勒 to extort; to force; to coerce.

(b) To engrave. A horizontal stroke in writing.

勒 名 碑 上 to carve a name on stone.

鰳⁴·⁵
3842   A fish, a kind of shad. Spermary of a fish.

泐⁴·⁵
3843   To write; to indite.

泐 此 奉 覆 I write this in reply to yours.
泐 覆 to reply to a letter.
泐 達 to inform by letter.
名 別 泐 my name is separately written—enclosed on a card.
手 泐 with my own hand.

(a) To split, as rocks.
石 泐 splitting of rocks.

LÊNG.   (ㄌㄥ)

冷³
3844   Cold. Indifferent.

冷 不 防 suddenly; unforeseen.
冷·他 一 程·子 treat him with indifference.
冷 冰 冰·的 cold as ice.
冷 却 器 refrigerator.
⁵冷·子 sleet.
冷 字 an unfamiliar character in writing or reading.
冷 孤 丁·的 unexpectedly; a lonely person.
冷 客 to treat a visitor with indifference.
冷 宮 the cold palace—place to which discarded favourites were banished.
¹⁰冷 峭·的 問·他 asked him quite sharply.
冷 布 very coarse cloth used in North China for screening windows.
冷·得 利·害 exceedingly cold.
冷 心 indifferent.
冷 情 indifference.
¹⁵冷 暖 自 知 I know when it is cold or hot—no need to tell me anything about the matter.
冷 板·凳 a cold bench—a post without much inducement, the position of a poor teacher.
冷 水 浴 a cold bath.
冷 汗 cold perspiration.
冷 河 the headwaters of the Yellow River.
²⁰冷 淡 distant; cool—as friends; insipid—as a book; dull—as trade. *See below*—A.3.
冷 淡 待 人 to treat a person with indifference.
生·意 冷 淡 business is dull.
冷 瘡 chilblains. =凍 瘡
冷 眼 to look coldly on; to look askance; without prejudice.
²⁵冷 眼 旁 觀 to look on as a disinterested bystander.
冷 眼 熱 心 affected indifference.
冷 竈 a cold stove—a man who is unlucky and in poor circumstances.
冷 笑 a cold, heartless laugh; sarcastic grin.
冷 節 the cold-food festival, *See* 寒 No. 2048—56.

[80] 冷箭 an arrow shot from an ambush; a shot at a venture.

冷罨法 cold-compress method of treatment.

冷葷 cold meats.

冷藏室 cold-storage chamber.

冷血 cold blood.

[35] 冷血動物 cold-blooded animals.

冷言冷語 mocking words; to talk at a person; sarcasm.

冷貨 unsaleable goods.

冷靜態度 dispassionate attitude.

冷靜見解 a dispassionate view.

[40] 冷面 to show disregard.

冷颼颼的 chilly; raw.

冷飯菜 cold food.

覺冷 it feels cold.

(a) Solitary, quiet.

冷僻 lonely; deserted; obsolete.

冷冷清清 quiet, still.

冷淡 lonely—See above—20.

冷清 or 冷落 or 冷靜 quiet, comfortless, lonely.

冷巷 a deserted lane.

楞 [2] Mountain range; u.f. Ceylon in Buddhist books.
3845

楞伽 Ceylon; name of a Buddhist sûtra.

楞嚴經 a famous Buddhist sûtra.

崚 [2] Hilly, mountainous.
3846

棱 [2] Squared or hewn timber; beams. An edge. Angular.
3847 Inter. 稜 No. 3849.

棱角 a projection.

棱角峭厲 the sharp, dangerous corners of beams.

棱起來 stand it on its edge.

剛棱 unyielding.

模棱 (or 稜) vacillating, undecided.

睖 [4] To stare straight ahead.
3848

睖瞪 to stare at.

稜 [2] A corner, an angle, an edge. Inter. 棱 No. 3847.
3849

稜光 diffracted light.

稜稜 protuberant.

稜稜霜氣 thoroughly chilled by the frost.

稜角 a right angle; a corner; a person who is difficult to get on with.

稜錐體 a pyramid.

三稜體 a prism.

觚稜 the turned-up corners of Chinese roofs.

(a) The awe of the gods.

稜威 or 威稜 awe, dignity.

(b) Read leng[4]. N.A. of fields.

蔆 [2] Spinach,—an old name for it.
3850

菠蔆菜 spinach. = 菠菜.

踜 [2] To stumble; to slip; to fall.
3851

LI.　　　　(ㄌ)

李 [3] Plums. Distinguish 季 No. 435.
3852

李下不整冠 do not adjust your hat under a plum tree—avoid suspicion.

李代桃僵 to change this for that.

李子 plums.

李樹 a plum tree.

行李 baggage—anciently, a traveller; official retinue.

(a) A surname.

李唐 the T'ang dynasty, as Li was the family name of the reigning house.

吏 [4] An officer, a deputy; a government servant.
3853 Distinguish 史 No. 5769.

吏房 an office in a yamen corresponding to the former Board of Civil Office.

吏治其國 to administer the affairs of the nation.

吏目 head constable and keeper of the jail.

吏部 the former Board of Civil Office.

書吏 a clerk in government offices.

戾 [4] To do violence. Perverse; rebellious. Calamities; tribulations; miseries; crime; sin.
3854

戾愆 or 罪戾 sin, crime.

戾旋 to go contrary to; perverse.

戾蟲 the tiger.

乖戾 perverse; rebellious.

暴戾 cruel, savage.

獲戾 to offend.

(a) To come to; to stop.

戾天 to soar to the sky.

戾止 to come and stop.

民之未戾 the people were not settled.

(b) Read lieh[4.5]. To turn back; to twist.

戾手 to turn the hand.

唳 [4] The cry of a crane, wild goose, etc. See 風 No. 1890 —52.
3855

捩 [4] A plectrum for stringed instruments.
3856

插捩舉琵琶 inserted the plectrum and raised the guitar.

(a) Read lieh[4.5]. To turn around; to twist; to snap.

捩手覆羹 "he jerked his hand round and upset the soup."

里 [3] A lane; a street. A neighbourhood. The country. Radical 166.
3857

里俗 rustic, vulgar.

里宰 headman of a village.

里居 to live in retirement.

里巷小人 the masses.

[5] 里社 a village altar.

里耳 the ears of the rustics.

里落 a country village.

里諺 rustic songs and sayings.

里豪 village bully.

[10] 里長 (or 正) a village elder—25 families was reckoned a li.

里 門 gate of a village; the old home.

里 閭 gate of a village.

里 魁 head of a village under the *Han* dynasty—a village was 100 families.

故 里 the old home district.

[15]鄉 里 one's old home.

(a) A measure of length reckoned at 360 paces, or about 1890 feet English measure.

一 里 路 one *li* distant.

千 里 眼 a telescope; long-sighted.

千 里 鏡 a telescope.

(b) Melancholy, sorrow.

云 如 何 里 why have I such sorrow as this?

俚[3]
3858
Unpolished, rustic, vulgar.

俚 俗 rustic and vulgar.

俚 歌 rustic songs.

俚 言 vulgar expressions.

(a) Resources. To support.

俚 賴 resources.

無 俚 no one to trust to; without resources. ≡ 3960.B4

(b) Aboriginal tribes.

俚 人 aborigines in Hainan.

哩[4]
3859
A final particle. Used in transliterating names.

娌[3]
3860
A brother's wife; a sister-in-law. See 姒 No. 1377.

梩[2]
3861
A basket for removing earth. A spade.

浬[3]
3862
A nautical mile, equal to 3.22 Chinese 里.

狸 }
貍 }[2]
3863
The fox; the wild-cat; the raccoon.

狐·貍 the fox.

野 貍 a wild-cat.

靈 貍 the civet.

理[3]
3864
Reason, principle; the fitness of things. Right, as an abstract principle.

理 之 所 無 contrary to right principles.

理 信 rational belief.

理 化 abbreviation: physics and chemistry.

理 化 學 科 Department of Physics and Chemistry.

[5]理 化 家 physicist and chemist.

理 合 in duty bound; as a matter of course.

理 學 metaphysics; moral science.

理 宜 reasonable; fitting.

理 屈 詞 窮 to twist one's principles in order to finish an argument.

[10]理·性 reason.

理·性 動·物 reasonable beings; rational creatures.

理 性 派 rationalists.

理 性·的 光 the light of reason.

理 性·的 批 評 rational criticism.

[15]理 想 ideal; idea; theory.

理 想·上 完 全·的 the ideally perfect.

理 想 主 義 idealism.

理 想 化 idealize.

理 想 派 idealists.

[20]理 想·的 ideally.

理 想·的 確 當 the practicability of his ideals.

理 想 社 會 ideal society.

理 想 觀 an ideal.

理 想 論 idealistic theory.

[25]理 應 in duty bound; as a matter of course.

理 所 應 當 that which should be.

理 所 當 然 in accordance with what is right.

理 所 當 為 that which should be done.

理 智 intelligence; intellect.

[30]理 由 reason, cause, rational motive; ground of right; argument; cause, etc.

理 由 書 affidavit.

理 當 as a matter of fact; in duty bound.

理 直 氣 壯 to be in the right and confident.

理 科 science department.

[35]理 解 兒 童 to understand a child.

理 解 能 力 faculty of understanding.

理 說 doctrine. ⌈theoretically.

理 論 theory; to discuss. 理 論·上

理 論 科 學 pure sciences.

[40]不 近 理 論 illogical.

天 理 eternal principles of right; divine justice.

心 理 學 psychology.

物 理 學 physics.

講 理 to discuss pros and cons.

(a) To regulate, to arrange, to manage; to regard.

理 七 or 做 七 to perform certain funeral rites every seventh day until the forty-ninth day after the decease.

理·事 to transact business; to attend to a matter; member of a directors' board.

理 勸 to reason with.

理 喪 to manage the funeral ceremonies.

[5]理 家 to manage the affairs of the family.

理 書 to go over what one has learnt. |A.p. *lü*[3].

理·會 to regard; to take note of.

理 枉 to right a wrong.

理 結 or 理 妥 or 理 明 to arrange; to settle.

[10]理 繁 to manage difficult affairs.

理 繁 治 劇 to manage difficulties and cure the trouble.

理 財 之 道 the matter of finance.

理 財 家 financier.

理 財 議 案 finance bill.

[15]理 處 (*ch'u*[3]) to settle, to arrange.

理 髮 to dress the hair, hair-cut

不 理·他 disregard him; pay no attention to him.

代 理 to act in place of.

修 理 to repair; to put in order.

署 理 to act in place of an official.

(b) To polish gems. Streaks, veins, grain of wood.

堅 而 有 理 hard and streaked with veins.

脈 理 皆 斜 the grain is all crooked.

裏 }
裡 }[3.4]
3865
Within, inside. A lining. Distinguish 裏 No. 3735.

裏 外 within and without; internal and external.

裏·子 a lining.

裏 海 the Caspian Sea.

裏 舵 or 推 舵 port the helm.

[5]裏 衣 under-garments.

裏 言 confidential words; sincere talk.

裏 面 表 面 inward and outward; essential and external.

裏·頭 or 裏·邊 inside.

表 裏 outer and inner; external and internal.

鯉[3] The carp.
3866

鯉 化 龍 or 鯉 魚 跳 龍 門 the carp has become a dragon, or has leaped the dragon's gate—success at the former public examinations.

鯉 庭 to obey the instructions of a father—鯉 was the name of the son of Confucius. See *Analects* Bk. 16, ch. 13.

鯉 素 a letter,—from the story of a man who found a letter inside a carp.

鯉 魚 the carp.

利 私[4] Profit, gain, advantage. Interest on money.
3867

利 上 加 利 compound interest.

利 人 主 義 altruism.

利 令 智 昏 blinded by the lust for gain.

利 他 主 義 altruism.

[5]利 便 easy; speedy; convenient; handy.

利 便 運 輸 to facilitate transport.

利 名 or 名 利 wealth and fame.

利 子 interest on money.

利 害 profit and injury— 利·害 severe, injurious. A.w. 厲害.

[10]利 害·的 興[4]趣 the interest of mere matters of profit and loss.

利 害 關·係 a matter of life and death, of extreme urgency, of profit and loss.

利 己 to benefit oneself.

利 己 主 義 selfishness.

利 己 害 人 to benefit oneself at the expense of others.

---

[15]利·市 prosperous trade; a good market.

利·息 profit; interest.

利 權 economic rights; vested interests.

保 本 國·的 利 權 protect our national interests.

利 欲 covetousness; lust for gain.

[20]利 毒 gluttonous, mean.

利 源 source of profit or advantage.

利 濟 事 profitable matters.

利 率 (*liü*[4.5.]) rate of interest, bank-rate.

利·用 utility; utilization; to make a tool of; to use for one's own ends.

[25]利 用 厚 生 provide abundant means of support.

利·用 器·具 useful implements or tools.

利·用 時 機 opportunism.

利·用 適 當 properly utilized.

利·益 advantage; benefit; profits; rights; privileges.

[30]利 益 均 沾 equal rights.

利 薄 there is little advantage or profit.

利 誘 to beguile another with money.

利 路 means of making profits.

利 達 favourable; auspicious; successful.

[35]利·錢 or 利·銀 profit, interest.

↑利 弊 advantage and disadvantage.

(a) Sharp, cutting. Witty.

利 口 sharp speech; fluency.

利 器 edged tools, cutlery—a cat's paw.

利 嘴 talkative.

快 利 sharp.

俐[4] Intelligent; sharp, clever; active.
3868

俐·儸 handy, orderly; able, facile.

俐 索 settled, in order, tidy.

伶·俐 sharp, clever; active.

唎[4] Sound, noise. Final particle.
3869

梨 黎[2] A pear.
3870

梨 園 子[3]弟 play-actors,—because a pear-garden was set apart for this purpose during the *T'ang* dynasty.

梨(-子)pear.

梨 棗 pear and date—wood used for cutting printing-blocks—thus used to express, "blocks for printing purposes."

沙 梨 a small pear which has hard sand-like specks in its flesh.

[5]白 梨 a small white pear.

雪 梨 a large white juicy pear.

犁 犂[2] A plough. To plough.
3871

犁 刀 a ploughshare.

犁 溝 plough-furrows.

犁 田 or 扶 犁 to plough.

犁 脊 the ridges of the furrows.

[5]犁 鈀 a plough.

犁 鑱 or 犁 頭[2]the coulter of a plough.

(a) Brindled.

犁 牛 之 子[3]騂 且 角 if the calf of a brindled cow be red and properly horned....

猁[2] A kind of monkey.
3872

痢[4] Dysentery, diarrhoea.
3873

痢·疾 or 血 痢 dysentery.

白 痢 diarrhoea.

紅 痢 dysentery.

莉[4] The white jasmine.
3874

蜊[2] A kind of clam with thick white shells.
3875

黎[2] Black; black-haired. Many.
3876

黎 人 or 黎 母 the aborigines of Hainan. *See* 俚 No. 3858—B.

黎 元 the masses.
黎 明 early dawn.
黎 民 or 群 黎 or 黎 衆 or 黎 庶 the black-haired people, Chinese.
[5]黎 獻 a virtuous, wise man from among the people.
黎 祁 or 來 其 a name for bean-curd.
黎 老 an old man.
黎 蒸 the masses.
黎 首 black-heads—the people.
黎 黑 black.

(a) Light, as soil.

厥 土 青 黎 the soil was greenish and light.

藜[2] A weed, *chenopodium*. A kind of bramble.
3877

藜 杖 a staff of *chenopodium*.
藜 蘆 hellebore.

黧[2] A dark, sallow colour.
3878

犁[2] To split, to chap, to crack.
3879

嫠[2] A widow.
3880

嫠 婦 a widow.

氂[2] A tuft of hair, a tail.
3881

牛 氂 tail of a yak used as a fly-brush.

犛[2] A black ox. The yak.
3882

釐[2] The thousandth part of a Chinese foot, 尺. The thousandth part of a *tael* 兩. Small; minute.
3883

釐 分 minute, scanty, few.

釐 分 之 間 very trifling.
公 釐 millimetre.
毫 釐 不 錯 not the least particle of error.

(a) The *likin* tax, the name of which is derived from the above.

釐 卡 a *likin* barrier.
釐 照 a *likin* pass.
釐 稅 *likin* and customs duties
釐 金 or 釐 捐 the *likin* tax, originally voluntarily imposed upon themselves by the people, to make up the deficiency in the land-tax caused by the Taiping rebellion; it was nominally a tax of one cash per *tael* on all sales, but was raised.
釐 金 局 a *likin* office.

(b) To regulate.

釐 制 to regulate.
釐 勘 carefully collated—as articles from magazines.
釐 定 to arrange; to put in order.
釐 正 to reform.
[5]釐 訂 to edit, to collate for publication.
釐 革 to make radical reformation —in civil offices and appointments.
允 釐 百 工 regulated all the various offices.

(c) To give.

釐 爾 圭 瓚 I give you a large jade vessel for libations.
釐 降 二 女 … 嬪 于 虞 he sent down his two daughters to be the wives of *Yü*. (舜 *Shun.*)

(d) Twins.

釐 孳 twins.

豊[3] A sacrificial vessel.
3884

澧[3] Name of a river in Hunan.
3885

禮
礼[3] Propriety, good manners. Politeness. Ceremony. Worship. The external exemplification of eternal principles; the feeling of respect and reverence. See below—12, 41, 59, 63.
3886

禮 之 用 和 為 貴 in carrying out the rules of propriety, ease of manner is to be prized.
禮 之 體 主 於 敬 the embodiment of *li* is headed up in reverence.
禮 云 禮 云 玉 帛 云 乎 哉 they say, Propriety! Propriety! Does Propriety consist in gems and silk?
禮 儀 ceremonies; ceremonial.
[5]禮 儀 卒 度 every form according to rule.
禮 制 ritual.
禮 單 an inventory of presents sent.
禮 堂 chapel, hall of assembly in schools; auditorium.
禮 多 formal, obsequious.
[10]禮 多 人 不 怪 nobody blames one for being too polite.
禮 宜 courtesy; good feeling.
禮 履 也 所 以 事 神 致 福 也 *li* is a step or act whereby we serve spiritual beings and obtain happiness.
禮 帖 list of presents sent; acknowledgement of wedding presents.
禮 帽 a tall silk hat; a top-hat.
[15]禮 式 rules of etiquette.
禮 性 propriety; good behaviour.
禮 意 a feeling of courtesy.
禮 懺 a Buddhist ritual.
禮 所 生 that which springs from propriety.
[20]禮 所 當 然 etiquette requires it.
禮 房 the department in a *yamen* which dealt with such matters as were dealt with by the Board of Rites.
禮 拜 worship; to worship; week.
禮 拜 六 Saturday.
禮 拜 堂 a place of worship; a church or chapel.
[25]禮 拜 寺 a mosque.
禮 拜 日 Sunday.
禮 數 or 禮 法 politeness; etiquette.
禮 文 courteous; ceremony.
禮 星 拜 斗 to worship the stars.
[30]禮 書 documents sent by parties arranging a marriage.
禮 服 full dress.
大 禮 服 full ceremonial dress.
常 禮 服 informal dress.
禮 燭 candles of ceremony for weddings.
[35]禮 物 a present, an offering.

禮生 master of ceremonies at the worship in a Confucian temple.

禮礮 a salute fired by guns.

禮節 requirements of etiquette; formality.

禮義 decorum.

40 禮義廉恥 propriety, morality, modesty, and a sense of shame.

禮者天理之節文 li is the external exemplification of eternal principles.

禮與其奢也寧儉 in (festive) ceremonies it is better to be sparing than extravagant.

禮衣 ceremonial dress.

禮記 the *Book of Rites.*

45 禮讓 courteousness; modesty.

禮貌 manners; politeness; etiquette.

禮貌待人 to treat others with politeness.

禮貴得中 the thing most to be prized in *li,* is a happy medium.

禮賢下士 courteous to the worthy and condescending to the scholarly.

50 禮輕人意重 the present is a trifle, but the intention is weighty. [with courtesy.

禮遇 to do honour to; to treat

禮部 the Board of Rites.

禮金 or 聘禮 money paid at a betrothal.

禮防 restrained by propriety.

55 禮體 decorum; propriety.

不招禮 do not stand on ceremony.

仁義禮智非由外鑠我也 benevolence, righteousness, propriety and knowledge are not infused into us from without.

失禮 wanting in politeness.

恭敬之心禮也 the feeling of reverence and respect is *li.*

60 行禮 to salute; to bow, etc.

送禮 to send presents.

還禮 to return a salute.

辭讓之心禮之端也 the feeling of modesty and courtesy is the principle of *li.*

醴³ Sweet wine; must. A wine made overnight. A fountain of sweet water.
3887

醴泉 a sweet spring.

醴酒不設 neither sweet nor alcoholic wine is set out—rudeness to a guest.

鱧³ The snake-fish.
3888

沴⁴ Foul, poisonous.
3889

沴氣 miasma; poisonous exhalations.

(a) Read *t'ien³.* Out of harmony. *See* No. 6376.

沴戾 counteracting each other.

例⁴ A regulation; a law; a custom; a precedent; a usage.
3890

例假 a statutory holiday.

例則 statutes and regulations; laws and by-laws.

例外 unusual; abnormal; exception.

例外辦法 exceptional measures.

5 例如 for example; thus.

例應完稅 subject to duty.

例會 regular meeting.

例案 precedents; recorded decisions.

例條 or 律條 regulations; rules.

10 例率 (*lü⁴·⁵.*) rate.

例禁 prohibitory by-laws.

例薄 register of officials.

例行公事 to do routine work.

例規 precedent; the correct thing.

15 例言 introduction to a book.

例證 evidence; circumstantial evidence.

不以爲例 not to be taken as a precedent.

不合事例 contrary to general usage.

先例 or 前例 a precedent.

20 公例 a general principle.

凡例 introduction to a book; directions to the reader.

判例 a legal precedent.

定例 a fixed rule.

循例 to conform to rule; to follow a precedent.

25 成例 a precedent; to become a precedent.

舉一個例 to give an example.

詈⁴ Railing; to scold; to curse.
3891

詈罵 to swear at.

詈謗 to slander.

詈辱 to scold; to blame.

罹² Sorrow, grief, troubles. To happen to; to incur.
3892

罹其凶害 I suffered from his malice.

履³ A shoe. To walk; thus:—actions, conduct, ceremonies.
3893 Pron. *lü³.*

履仁 to act kindly.

履任 to enter on a post.

履底 the sole of a shoe.

履德 to walk in the path of virtue.

5 履新 to take up a new appointment.

履歷 a record of conduct; statement of one's antecedents.

履端於始 begin with uprightness,—from which 履端 is used for the first day of the year.

履約 to keep an agreement.

履薄冰 treading on thin ice—needs caution.

10 履行 one's conduct; to walk; to carry out an agreement.

履行義務 to carry out obligations.

履行預約 to carry out a former agreement.

履霜 to walk on hoar-frost.

蠡³ A wood-boring insect; worm-eaten.
3894

彭蠡 old name for the Poyang Lake in Kiangsi.

(a) Read *li².* A calabash.

以蠡測海 to measure the sea with a calabash—impossible; used of a man of limited experience.

覽芷圃之蠡蠡 looking down on the rows of plants in the vegetable garden.

(b) Read *lo².* A shellfish.

蠡蚌閉戶 the mussel and the oyster close their doors.

(c) Read *lo³.* A skin disease of cattle.

劙³ To divide, to partition.
3895

离² A bogy. Bright. Elegant. To oppose.
3896

漓² Water dripping; the pattering of rain or hail.
3897

淋漓 dripping of rain.

璃² Glass; a glassy substance.
3898

篱² A skimmer or scoop used by cooks.
3899

縭² A bridal ornament.
3900

結縭 to tie the bridal ornament—married.

醨² Dregs of wine.
3901

離² To leave; to retire; to separate. Distant from; apart from.
3902

離·不開 no getting away from; always.
離世 to leave the world—to die.
離乳 to wean.
離·了 to leave; left.
⁵離人 an absent husband.
離任 to leave one's post.
離俗 to abandon secular ways; not at all commonplace; elegant, refined.
離別 to part from; to bid goodbye.
離叛 opposition; rebellion.
¹⁰離合 partings and meetings.
離城三里 three li from the city.
離境 evacuation of territory.
離奇 eccentric; warped.
離婚 divorce.
¹⁵離孫 sons of a sister's sons.
離官 lodge for the emperor when on tour; name of a star.
離家 to leave home.
離局 to leave a post.
離席 or 離櫈 to leave the table.
²⁰離得有多遠 how far off is it? (-to¹,²-)
離心力 centrifugal force.
離心·的 centrifugal.

離思 thought during separation.
離愁 grief at separation.
²⁵離憂 the sorrow of separation.
離披 scattered.
離散 to disperse; scattered.
離書 or 離婚書 a bill of divorce.
離本題 wandering from the subject.
³⁰離棄 to reject; to forsake; to give up.
離水 high and dry.
離父子 a posthumous child.
離目的 beside the mark.
離絕 to leave entirely; to break away from; separated.
³⁵離經 strayed from the path; wayward; absurdly.
離經叛道 wayward and rebellious.
離縫 separated.
離羣 to forsake society.
離落 opposition in heart.
⁴⁰離襟 to separate.
離詞 contradiction of what has been said.
離貳 divided in heart.
離遏 separated by a distance.
離道反敎 apostacy.
⁴⁵離那裏遠 a long way from there.
離門離戶 far from home.
離開 to leave; to separate.
離間計 the trick of sowing dissension and thus defeating the foe.
離間 (chien⁴) 骨肉 to sow discord among relatives.
⁵⁰離離 unconsciously.
離魂病 somnambulism.

(a) To fall into. To meet with. To pass through.

不離于裏 did I not pass through—my mother's womb?
雉離于罦 (fu²) the pheasant has got into the snare.
魚網之設鴻則離之 the net was set for fish but the wild goose fell into it.

(b) Paired.

離坐 to sit in pairs.
離立 to stand in pairs.

(c) To set out; to divide off. To decide.

一年視離經 in the first year

it was seen whether they could read the texts intelligently.
陳離 to set in order and spread out.

(d) The oriole, described as a bird of a brilliant yellow plumage.

離黃 the oriole.

(e) Brightness. One of the diagrams of the 八卦.

二離 the sun and moon.

(f) Inter. 籬 No. 3903. A fence.
(g) Inter. 蘺 No. 3904. Weeds.
(h) Inter. 縭 No. 3900. A sash.
(i) Read li³. Unbroken, continuous.

離麾 unbroken; continuous.

籬² A wattle or bamboo fence.
3903

籬竹 bamboos for wattle-fences.
籬·笆 a bamboo fence.

蘺² Grass and weeds. Read lo³, a fragrant plant.
3904

江蘺 a fragrant plant.

隷⁴ Attached to; belonging to. To control; to rule.
3905

隷人 a vagabond; a criminal.
隷卒 or 皂隷 lictors; official servants.
隷圉 a servant.
隷屬 attached to.
隷書 the square plain style of Chinese writing.

厲⁴ A whetstone. To grind; thus, to discipline; harsh; severe; stern. To oppress. Cruel; oppressive.
3906

厲兵 to drill troops; to sharpen weapons.
厲民 to oppress the people.
厲治 harsh rule.
厲疾 a serious illness.
⁵厲目而視 to look with a fierce glare.

厲 禁 severe prohibitions.
厲 聲 而 言 talking harshly.
厲 色 a stern countenance.
厲 行 法 律 rigorous enforcement of the laws.
¹⁰厲 行 禁 烟 to enforce opium prohibitions.
厲 階 calamities; disasters.
厲 風 a cruel custom.
厲 鬼 a malicious spirit.
嚴 厲 stern; severe.
↑厲·害 severe; terrible.

(a) To cross water with the clothes on.

深 則 厲 if it is deep I shall cross with my clothes on.

勵 ⁴ To urge; to incite; to encourage.
3907

勵 志 to bend the mind to.
勵 志 實 行 determined to put it into operation.
勵 民 to encourage the people.
勵 精 to strengthen the spirits; to brace oneself up.
勵 行 forceful action.
勉 勵 to incite to effort.

癘 ⁴ A sore, an ulcer; swelling and sores caused by varnish-poisoning.
3908

癘 疾 不 降 pestilence does not descend.

(a) To kill.

無 癘 雛 殼 do not kill fledglings.

礪 ⁴ A coarse whetstone. Sandstone. To grind.
3909

礪 石 sandstone.

糲 ⁴ Coarse—of grain.
3910

糲 食 coarse food.
精 糲 fine and coarse.

蠣 ⁴ Rock-oysters.
3911

蠣 殼 oyster shells.
乾 蠣 dried oysters.
↑蠣 蠔 oyster.

涖 莅 蒞 ⁴ To overlook, to manage. To exercise the duties of office; to rule. The seat of office.
3912

涖 事 to attend to official duties.
涖 任 or 涖 位 to exercise official functions; to come into office.
涖 任 宣 言 書 inaugural statement.
涖 止 to arrive at a place.
⁵涖 治 to rule; to govern.
涖 民 to govern the people.
涖 黑 籍 to become an opium smoker.

荔 梿 ⁴ The lichee, a fruit which grows in South China.
3913

荔 枝 核 lichee kernels. (-hur²)
荔 枝 菓 the lichee.
番 荔 枝 the custard-apple.

麗 ⁴ Beautiful, elegant.
3914

麗 人 a beauty.
麗 服 well-dressed; beautiful dress.
麗 爾 or 靡 麗 extravagant; elegant.
麗 都 beautiful; magnificent.
⁵麗 辭 elegant phrases.
美 麗 beautiful.
華 麗 ornamental.

(a) To be connected with; to depend on.

麗 刑 liable to punishment.
麗 澤 mutual assistance between friends.
附 麗 joined to; connected with; attached.

(b) Number.

其 麗 不 億 in number more than hundreds of thousands.

(c) To tie to; to tether.

麗 于 碑 tethered (the beast) to a stone tablet.

(d) Inter. next.

儷 ⁴ A pair, a couple.
3915

伉 儷 a married couple.
失 儷 to lose a wife.

邐 ³ To walk in crowds. Winding.
3916

酈 ⁴ Name of a place in the State of Lu 魯.
3917

驪 ² A good horse; a black horse. To use a pair of horses in a carriage.
3918

驪 駕 a pair of horses.
驪 龍 a black dragon—See 探 No. 6054—A.49.

鸝 ² The oriole.
3919

鸝 子 or 黃 鸝 the yellow oriole.

LI.　　　(ㄌ)
(Lih)

力 4.5. Strength, force, power. Feats of strength. A unit of strength for testing bows, one li being equal to 10 *catties*. Radical 19.
3920

力 不 支 strength insufficient to support it.
力 不 從 心 the strength is not equal to the will.
力 不 能 勝 beyond my power.
力 之 所 及 to the best of one's power.
⁵力 作 do it with all one's might.
力 倦 worn out; fatigued.
力 圖 earnestly to strive for.
力 圖 改 良 improved methods should be energetically devised.
力 圖 自 強 plucked up one's strength.
¹⁰力 士 a strong man.
力 壯 or 力 強 or 力 健 robust, vigorous.
力 學 to study with diligence; dynamics.
動 力 學 dynamics.
靜 力 學 statics.

¹⁵力 守 to strive to observe.

力 役 personal service to the State, etc.

力 戰 to fight with zeal and vigour.

力 政 to govern by force.

力 本 to devote the energies to things fundamental.

²⁰力 求 to strive for.

力 求 進 步 to advance by vigorous effort.

力 爭 to strive mightily.

力 田 industry; to cultivate the fields.

力 疾 從 事 to exert oneself to duty even when weak and ill.

²⁵力 盡 (or 竭) strength exhausted.

力 積 impulse. (*dynamics*).

力 索 forcible demands.

力 能 扛 鼎 able to carry a great tripod.

力 舉 百 鈞 strength sufficient to raise a weight of 3,000 *catties.*

³⁰力 薄 deficient in strength.

力 行 近 乎 仁 to practice with earnestness is to attain nearly to goodness.

力 衰 weak and feeble.

力 辯 to argue with force.

力·量 or 力·氣 strength; vigour; resources.

³⁵力 阻 forcible interference.

力 難 挽 回 beyond one's power of recall.

力 顧 regarding with earnestness.

力 點 point of application of force.

(a) Used as a suffix to indicate:— power, strength, movement, etc. A selection is given in alphabetical order.

愛 力 affinity,

補 助 力 auxiliary force.

浮 泛 力 buoyancy.

遠 心 力 centrifugal force.

⁵求 心 力 centripetal force.

化 合 力 chemical affinity.

協 力 co-operation.

功 力 efficacy.

發 展 力 expansive force.

¹⁰火 力 strength of(cooking fire; firing power.

吸 力 gravitation.

地 球 引 力 gravitation—terrestrial.

重 力 gravity.

馬 力 horse-power.

¹⁵感 化 力 influence.

不 可 抗 力 irresistible force.

省 力 labour-saving.

記 憶 力 memory.

精 神 力 mental force.

²⁰發 動 力 motive force.

體 力 physical force.

可 能 力 potentiality.

權·力 privilege; rights.

攙 力 resistance, power of.

²⁵分 力 resolution of forces.

靜 力 statics.

才 力 strength of materials.

結 合 力 uniting force; crystallization.

目 力 vision, strength of.

³⁰活 力 vital force.

費 力 waste of force, strength or effort.

水 力 water, force of.

財 力 wealth, power of.

壓 力 weight; pressure.

³⁵風 力 wind, force of.

酒 力 wine, strength of.

角 力 wrestling, trial of strength.

筆 力 writing, vigor of.

立   4.5.   **To stand up; to establish. Radical 117.**

3921

立 人 the raphe.   Radical 9: 亻.

單 立 人 ㄦ Radical 9: 亻.

雙 立 人 ㄦ Radical 60: 彳.

立 停 to come to a standstill.

⁵立 則 見 其 參 於 前 也 when standing let him see them spread out before him.

立 勢 a standing position.

立 場 a standing.

立·得 住 able to stand.

立 方 cube; cubic.

¹⁰ 整 立 方 a perfect cube.

立 方 尺 度 solid measure.

立 方 根 or 三 乘 根 cube roots.

立 方 積 contents of a solid.

立 方 量 cubic measure.

¹⁵立 方 體 a cube.

  正 立 方 體 a regular solid.

立 枷 the cangue.

立 止 to come to a standstill.

立 正 to stand at attention; attention!

²⁰立 脚 地 a foothold; standing-room.

立 足 之 地 standing-room; a standing.

立 選 to elect by a rising vote.

立 體 a solid.

立 體 度 量 solid measure.

²⁵立 體 幾 何 solid geometry.

立 體 形 學 solid geometry.

中 立 neutral.   孤 立 派 isolationist.

孤 立 independent; standing alone.

無 立 錐 之 地 not even enough land in which to stick an awl—very poor.

³⁰自 立 independent.   *See under* 自 No. 6960.

起 立 to rise; to stand up.

遠 立 standing at a distance.

(a) To set up; to fix; to establish; to draw up.

立 之 斯 立 道 之 斯 行 綏 之 斯 來 he planted the people and they were established, led them and they followed, made them happy and they came to him.

立 像 to erect a statue.

立 具 to execute—as a document.

立 冬 a solar term.   Beginning of Winter, about November 7—21.

⁵立 功 to establish one's merit—the second of the three imperishable features of a man. *See below*—32, 55.

立 合 同 to draw up an agreement or trust deed.

立 名 to make a name for oneself.

立 同 盟 to make an alliance.

立 和 約 to make a treaty.

¹⁰立 品 or 立 人 品 to reform; to become a respectable member of society.

立 嗣 承 繼 to adopt an heir.

立 國 to found a State.

立 基 to fix the groundwork; to draw up a basis.

立 壇 to set up an altar.

¹⁵立 夏 a solar term.   Beginning of Summer, about May 5—18.

立 妾 to take a concubine.

立 婚 書 to draw up a marriage contract.

立 字 印 to draw up an agreement.

立 定 to decide.

²⁰立 定 主 意 to make a resolve.

立 定 單 to make an agreement, fixing the amount of deposit to be paid.

立 定 心 志 to resolve.

立 室 to take a wife.

立 家 to establish a family.

²⁵立 寨 to pitch a camp.

立 憲 to establish a constitution.

立 憲 制 the constitutional system.

立 憲 國 constitutional State.

立 憲 政 體 constitutional form of government.

[30] 立 憲 黨 the constitutional party.

立 後 to take an heir.

立 德 to establish one's virtue, the first of the three imperishable features of a man. *See above —5, and below—55.*

立 志 or 立 心 or 立 意 to make up the mind; to determine.

立 春 a solar term. Beginning of Spring, about February 5—18.

[35] 立 會 to found a society.

立 期 票 to draw up an agreement fixing the date of payment.

立 案 to register; to make a record of.

立 業 to get property together; to establish a competency.

立 法 to draw up laws; to legislate.

[40] 立 法 事 業 legislative matters.

立 法 制 legislative system.

立 法 團 legislative bodies.

立 法 家 legislator.

立 法 手 續 legislative procedure or process.

[45] 立 法 機 關 legislative organ.

立 法 權 legislative authority.

立 法 部 the legislative.

立 法 院 Legislative Yüan.

立 泉 a waterfall.

[50] 立 碑 to set up a monument.

立 秋 a solar term. Beginning of Autumn, about August 7—21.

立 章·程 to draw up rules and regulations.

立 約 to draw up an agreement or contract, etc.

立 規 條 to draw up by-laws.

[55] 立 言 to establish one's words, teachings, etc., the third of the three imperishable features of a man. *See above—5 and 32.*

立 說 to make a scientific explanation of; to set up a theory; a statement.

立 誓 or 立 願 to take an oath.

立 證·據 to establish proof.

立 賣 契 to draw up a deed of transfer or sale.

[60] 立 賢 無 方 he employed worthy men regardless of the clan to which they belonged.

立 身 to establish oneself in life.

立 限 to fix a limit.

立 黨 to form a clique or party.

(b) Immediately; forthwith.

立 卽 下·來 came down immediately.

立 地 on the spot, at once.

立 打 立 死 died directly he was beaten.

立 日 on the same day.

[5] 立 時 or 立 刻 or 立 卽 or 立 等 immediately; at the time; at once.

立 決 summary execution.

立 行 to proceed at once (to).

立 速 quickly; at once.

(c) Used in transliterating.

立 特 a litre.

立 陶 宛 Lithuania.

笠 4.5.　A rain-hat of bamboo splints worn by coolies.
3922

一 笠 一 瓢 a bamboo hat and a gourd—all a man really needs.

戴 笠 to wear a bamboo hat—to be a servant.

(a) A basket.

秧 笠 baskets for rice-plants when transplanting.

粒 4.5.　A grain, a kernel. N.A. of seeds, grains, etc.
3923

粒 米 狼 戾 the grain lies about in abundance.

一 粒 米 a grain of rice.

顆 粒 不 收 not a grain gathered —in famine.

苙 4.5.　A pig-sty. Open basket for carrying pigs.
3924

栗 4.5.　The chestnut tree. Distinguish 粟 No. 5500.
3925

栗·子 or 風 栗 or 板 栗 chestnuts.

栗 房 a chestnut-burr.

栗 色 chestnut-colour.

栗 鼠 a squirrel.

麻 栗 木 teak.

(a) Firm, durable. Full, as grain when ripe.

積 之 栗 栗 set (the sheaves) up solidly.

縝 密 以 栗 fine and close texture for durability.

(b) Inter. 慄 No. 3927. Fearful.

戰 戰 栗 栗 trembling with fear.

(c) Dignified.

寬 而 栗 gentle and yet dignified.

(d) To step over.

栗 階 不 過 二 等 do not miss more than two steps—in ascending a stair.

(e) Cold, chilly.

栗 烈 cold and chilly. *See No. 3926.*

(f) Ancestral tablet, also written 慄.

栗 背 the back of the tablet.

溧 4.5.　Cold.
3926

溧 烈 chilly; bleak.

慘 溧 piercing cold.

慄 4.5.　Afraid, trembling.
3927

慄 慄 危 懼 fearful and trembling.

戰 慄 trembling with fear.

溧 4.5.　River in Kiangsu.
3928

篥 4.5.　Bamboos suitable for poles. A horn.
3929

觱 篥 the Tartar horn or pipe— a mournful sound.

曆 厤 4.5.　To calculate. The calendar. The original form of the next.
3930

曆 尾 the end of the almanac— close of the year.

曆 書 (or 本) an almanac.

曆 法 astronomy, calculations of the stars and times.

曆 頭 the beginning of the almanac—new-year.

歷 4.5. **To calculate. The calendar.**
3931

歷 家 astronomers.
歷 數 calculations of the calendar—destiny.
歷 書 an almanac.
歷 法 astronomy; calculations of the calendar.
歷 象 to calculate the movements of the heavenly bodies.
陽 歷 陰 歷 the solar and the lunar calendar respectively.

(a) To pass through.

歷 世 to pass through the world.
歷 人 harbourers of criminals.
歷 經 to have been through.
歷 練 to have passed through; to have had the experience.
歷 覽 名 山 travelled to see famous mountains.

(b) In order; successive.

歷 世 以 來 through successive generations.
歷 世 歷 代 ages and generations.
歷 久 long since; for past years.
歷 亂 in confusion.
5 歷 例 to mention in order.
歷 代 successive generations.
歷 來 from the first; hitherto.
歷 來 行 動 consistent course of action.
歷 來 辦 法 a long-continued practice.
10 歷 劫 successive *kalpas*.
歷 史 history.
歷 史 哲 學 philosophy of history.
歷 史 地 理 historical geography.
歷 史 學 science of history.
15 歷 史 家 historians.
歷 史 的 historical.
歷 史 的 事 實 historical facts.
歷 史 的 態 度 historical attitude.
歷 史 眼 光 in the light of history.
20 歷 史 派 the historical school.
歷 學 chronology.
歷 屆 successively; repeatedly.
歷 屆 宣 言 successive statements of policy.
歷 奉 periodically received,— as orders.
25 歷 年 以 來 for many years past.
歷 年 福 樂 years of pleasure and happiness.
歷 日 successive days; a diary.

歷 時 in the course of time.
歷 歷 敍 述 to set forth in detail.
30 歷 歷 可 數 every one may be counted.
歷 歷 可 考 every detail may be verified.
歷 歷 在 目 every detail as if before the eyes.
歷 程 process; step; stage.
歷 節 according to rule.
35 歷 落 disorder; continued, as a sound; above the average.
歷 述 narrated in detail.
歷 陳 to narrate in order.
歷 階 successive steps; progressive.

嚦 4.5. **Sounds of splitting or cracking. A crash.**
3932

櫪 4.5. **A species of oak. A stable. Frames.**
3933

櫪 樕 sticks or frames to torture the fingers by squeezing.
蠶 櫪 silkworm-frames.
馬 櫪 a stable.

瀝 4.5. **A drop. To drip, to trickle, to strain.**
3934

瀝 瀝 sound of wind or of waters.
瀝 膽 to manifest great loyalty and bravery.
瀝 血 to drip blood.
瀝 青 pitch, gum, resin, etc.

(a) Inter. 歷 No 3931. Detail, in order, etc.

瀝 情 稟 求 beseeching with earnestness.
瀝 懇 to implore earnestly.
瀝 申 to state the details.
瀝 陳 to state in detail.

癧 4.5. **Scrofulous lumps or swellings.**
3935

瘰 癧 a swelling of the glands. A lump.

靂 4.5. **A clap of thunder.**
3936

櫟 4.5. **The chestnut-leaved oak.** *Quercus chinensis* and *serrata*.
3937

礫 4.5. **Small stones, gravel, shingle.**
3938

瓦 礫 broken tiles, rubble.

躒 4.5. **A step, a pace.** Read *lo*4.5. **Surpassing.**
3939

卓 躒 surpassing talents.

轢 4.5. **A wheel-rut**
3940

倆 3 LIA. *See 3954 A.*
3940½

LIANG. (ㄌㄤ)

良 2 **Good, excellent. Peaceful. Virtuous.**
3941

良 人 my goodman, my goodwife.
良 以 or 良 由 for that reason; in consequence of; owing to.
良 劑 a good remedy.
良 匠 a good workman.
5 良 友 or 益 友 or 好 友 a good friend.
良 善 good; law-abiding.
良 善 風 俗 a good custom.
良 士 a good man.
良 夜 a clear night; late at night.
10 良 子 a good son.
良 家 honourable families, whose members have not engaged in trade, business, or any dishonourable calling.
良 將 a skilful general.
良 導 體 a good conductor.
良 工 skilful workman or workmanship.
15 良 心 conscience.
良 心 常 存 to maintain a good conscience.
良 心 有 愧 conscience-stricken.
良 心 發 現 the conscience is moved.
良 感 cordial relations.
20 良 才 outstanding ability.
良 方 a good prescription; the best remedy.
良 日 a lucky day.
良 月 the 10th lunar month.

良 朋 密 友 intimate friends.
25 良 朋 益 友 worthy friends.
良 機 a favourable opportunity.
良 死 a peaceful death.
良 民 loyal subjects; law-abiding people.
良 沃 the best fields.
30 良 法 a good remedy; an equitable law.
良 濟 法 poor-laws.
良 田 fertile fields; good land.
良 知 innate knowledge; instinct.
良 策 a good policy or proposal.
35 良 終 a peaceful death.
良 緣 a harmonious union; a happy match.
良 能 natural ability; instinct.
良 藥 good medicine.
良 謀 a good plan or scheme.
40 良 辰 or 良 時 a lucky moment; a seasonable hour.
良 醫 a skilful doctor.
良 食 good food.

(a) Very.

良 久 for a good while.
良 多 very many.
良 有 之 very much so.
良 深 very much; deeply.

跟 2 To jump. Read liang⁴ or lang⁴. Hurriedly; to walk crookedly.
3942

跟 跟 蹌 蹌 to hurry; to press on rapidly; to stagger.
跟 蹡 urgent; hurriedly.

量 2 To measure. To deliberate. To buy, as grain.
3943

量 一 量 to measure.
量 入 爲 出 measure expenditure by income.
量 力 to measure one's strength.
量 力 而 行 to calculate one's strength and resources.
5 量 地 to measure land.
量 度 or 度 量 to reckon the measure of; to estimate.
量 才 to estimate abilities.
量 米 to buy rice; to measure out rice.
量 行 to consider the feasibility of any action.
10 量 見 to measure.
丈 量 to measure an area.

(a) Read liang¹. A measure, a limit.

量 乳 表 a lactometer
量 器 a measure of capacity.
量 天 尺 a sextant.
量 帶 measuring-tape.
5 量 杯 a measuring-glass.
量 肺 表 a spirometer.
量 角 規 a protractor.
量 雨 表 rain-gauge.
大 量 liberal-minded.
10 酒 量 capacity for wine.
限 量 a limit.

糧 2 Provision, grain, food, rations. Taxes in kind.
粮
3944

糧 儲 豐 足 an abundant supply of grain.
糧 秣 provisions, grain for troops.
糧 米 government rations.
糧 米 行 (hang²)·市 market-price of grain.
5 糧 臺 commissariat.
糧 船 grain-junks.
糧 草 fodder.
糧 行 (hang²) a corn chandler's.
糧 賦 the land-tax.
10 糧 道 or 督 糧 道 or 糧 儲 道 the former commissioner who collected the revenue of a province.
糧 重 provisions and baggage.
糧 食 grain, food, provision.
糧 食 市 grain-market.
糧 餉 rations.
15 乾 糧 provender.
兵 糧 rations for troops.
口 糧 rations.
吃 (or 食) 糧 的 one who eats rations—a soldier.
日 糧 月 糧 daily or monthly rations respectively.
20 糴 糧 to buy grain.
糶 糧 to sell grain.
納 錢 糧 to pay the land-tax.
錢 糧 the land-tax.

晾 4 To dry in the air; to hang in the wind to dry.
3945

晾 一 晾 to air—clothing, etc.
晾 乾 to dry in the air.
晾 開 to spread out to air.
陰 晾 to dry in the shade.

涼 2 Cool, cold. To cool.
涼
3946

涼 一 涼 to allow to cool.
涼 亭 or 花 亭 a summer-house.
涼 友 a cool friend—a fan.
涼 國 name of several short-lived States in N.W. China. A.D. 400—420.
5 涼 帽 a summer hat.
涼 德 having very little virtue.
涼 快 cool.
↓ 涼 爽 refreshing.
涼 棚 an awning.
涼 水 cold water.
10 涼 汗 a cold perspiration.
涼 涼 cool, indifferent towards.
涼 粉 兒 jelly made from agar-agar, a kind of seaweed.
涼 薄 看 待 to treat with coolness.
涼 血 cold blood.
15 涼 血 動 物 cold-blooded creatures.
涼 風 a cool breeze.
冰 涼 ice-cold.
乘 涼 to take advantage of the coolness; to enjoy the coolness.

(a) Read liang⁴. To assist.

涼 彼 武 王 assisting Wu Wang.

(b) Sincere. Inter. next.

諒 4 To excuse; to consider.
3947

諒 不 我 怪 I trust that you will not blame me.
諒 必 most likely; probably.
諒 必 如 此 I think it must be so; most probably it is so.
諒 情 to bear the circumstances in mind.
5 原 諒 to excuse; to make allowance for.
祈 爲 諒 之 pray, excuse me!
約 諒 to consider; to bear in mind the circumstances.
見 諒 to excuse.
體 諒 to make allowance for.

(a) Faithful, sincere. To believe in.

友 直 友 諒 friendship with the upright, friendship with the sincere.

(b) Obstinate. Credulous.

匹 夫 匹 婦 之 爲 諒 也 the small fidelity of a common man or woman.

君 子 貞 而 不 諒 the superior man is firm from the consideration of the facts, not merely firm from obstinacy.

(c) Mourning-shed.

諒 陰 (*an*[1]) imperial mourning; the mourning-shed.

諒 闇 imperial mourning.

辌 [2]
3948
A hearse. A carriage.

亮 [4]
3949
Light, bright, brightness. Clear, transparent.

亮·一·亮 to put out to air.
亮 光 light, bright.
亮 堂 堂·的 flourishing.
亮 壳 表 open-faced watch.
[5]亮 察 for your perusal.
亮 明 clear and bright.
亮 然 clear, lucid.
亮 白 a transparent white.
亮 節 clear, bright principles.
[10]亮 紗 transparent gauze.
亮 轎 an open sedan.
亮 陰 (*an*[1]) imperial mourning.
亮 青 布 glazed cotton-cloth.
亮 䰀 roomy, light and bright.
[15]光 亮 bright, clear.
天 亮 dawn; daylight.
月·亮 moonlight; the moon.
清 亮 clean, tidy.
響·亮 clear and sweet(sounds); bright and airy.

(a) Faith, confidence in. Firm, straightforward.

亮 直 straightforward.
君 子[3] 不 亮 惡 乎 執[1] if a man of virtue have not faith, how shall he take a firm grasp of things? (-*wu*[1])
公 亮 just, firm, fair, straightforward.
便 亮 brusque, trustworthy.

(b) To assist. To spread the wings.

亮 翅 䯄 to spread the wings.
翼 亮 三 世 assisted three generations.

嘹 唡 [4]
3950
The crying of infants. Also read *lang*[2].

梁 樑 [2]
3951
A bridge over a brook. A beam. A ridge. Joists. Distinguish 粱 No. 3952.

梁 上 君 子[3] gentlemen of the beams—burglars.
梁 孟 abbreviation for 梁 鴻 and 孟 光, a married couple of the *Han* dynasty,— she was ill-favoured but virtuous, and they lived in harmony, holding each other in respect—used in praise of any married couple.
梁 洲 one of the nine provinces into which China was divided under *Yü* the Great. It included Hupeh and part of Szechwan. *See* 九 No. 1198-15.
梁 朝 the *Liang* Dynasty. A.D. 502—556.
[5]梁 木 beams, timbers.
梁 頭 a cross-beam.
橋 梁 bridges.
魚 梁 dam to retain fish.
鼻 梁 bridge of the nose.
脊 梁 the back. (-·*niang*)

粱 [2]
3952
The spiked or common millet; canary-seed.
Distinguish 梁 No. 3951.

粱 米 or 膏 粱 子[3] millet-seed.
高 粱 sorghum.

兩 兩 両 [3]
3953
Two. A pair, a couple, both.
Distinguish 雨 No. 7662.

兩 下 both sides or parties.
兩 三·個 人 two or three persons.
兩 不 相 照 gave no heed to each other.
兩 世 一 身 two generations represented by but one body.
[5]兩 便 convenient for both parties.
兩 便·罷 let us drop ceremony.
兩·個 two.
兩 儀 the two powers—*yin* and

yang, heaven and earth, sun and moon. *See* 二 No. 1751—7.
兩 全 complete in both respects.
[10]兩 凹·的 double-concave.
兩 凸·的 double-convex.
兩 可 alternative; ambiguous.
兩 口·子 husband and wife.
兩 可 之 間 between two possibilities.
[15]兩 君 之 好 a friendly meeting between two princes.
兩 大 heaven and earth.
兩 套 衣·服 two suits of clothes.
兩 家 two families; both parties.
兩 屬 類 common gender.
[20]兩 廣 Kwangtung and Kwangsi Provinces.
兩 性 問 題 sex questions.
兩 意 insincere; equivocal.
兩 方 面 both sides; the two sides.
兩 曜 sun and moon.
[25]兩 本 位 制 bi-metallic system.
兩 極 the poles.
兩 極 性 polarity.
兩 樣 different; two kinds.
兩 次 or 兩 回 twice; on two occasions.
[30]兩 歧 two alternatives; contradictory.
兩 歧 語 double-entendre; ambiguity.
兩 歲 two years; two years old.
兩 江 Kiangnan Provinces, i.e., Kiangsi, Kiangsu, and Anhwei
兩 淮 the region between the Yellow River and the Yangtze in Anhwei and Kiangsu.
[35]兩 清 both sides clear—as of an account.
兩 相 mutually, both parties.
兩 相 對 立 standing in pairs, opposite each other.
兩 相 情 願 both parties are willing.
兩 端 two ends or extremities.
[40]兩 老 father and mother.
兩 脚 書 廚 a two-legged bookcase—one who cannot make use of his learning.
兩 脚 規 compasses.
兩 舌 double-tongued.
兩 袂 軒 翥 both sleeves lifted high.
[45]兩 親 both parents.
兩 訖 both sides clear.
兩 造 the plaintiff and defendant.
兩 造 對 質 cross-examination of plaintiff and defendant.

兩 道 two ways; two principles.
50 兩 院 two houses of parliament.
兩 院 制 the two-chamber system.
兩 難 之 間 in a dilemma.
兩 面 two sides; double-faced.
兩 面 三 刀 a person who slanders another behind his back.
兩 面 有 光 both parties coming off creditably.
兩 黨 合 併 amalgamation of two parties.

(a) An ounce, Chinese. A *tael* or ounce of silver.

兩 換 exchange.
兩 替 exchange, sign of a money-changer.
一 兩 one *tael,* one ounce.
半 斤 八 兩 eight ounces and half a *catty,*-six of one and half a dozen of the other.

(b) A body of 25 soldiers.

(c) Inter. 輛 No. 3956.

(d) Inter. 魎 No. 3957.

俩³
3954
Clever at, skilled.

伎 俩 craft, ability, cleverness.

(a) Read *lia³.* Two.

俩 人 two persons.
俩 月 two months.
俩 錢 一 個 two cash each.
夫 婦 俩 a married couple.

裲³
3955
A waistcoat.

輛⁴
3956
A pair of wheels. N.A. for vehicles.

一 輛 車 a cart or barrow.

魎³
3957
A sprite, a fairy.

LIAO.   (ㄌㄧㄠ)

了³
3958
To complete, to f i n i s h. Distinguish Y No. 7213.

了³ 不 了³ cannot be brought to an end.
了³ 不 得 startling, wonderful; it's no go; whatever can be done!
好 得 了³ 不 得 extraordinarily good.
了³ 不 成 cannot be brought to a satisfactory issue.
5 了³ 事 to settle up a matter. *See below*—A.2.
了³ 債 to wipe off a debt.
了³ 卻 = No. 8.
了³ 局 or 了³ 結 to end; finished; to settle.
了³ 得 a consequence; terrible; what can be done?
10 這 還² 了³ 得 can such a thing as this be done? (-hai²-)
了³ 心 願 to fulfil one's desires.
了³ 手 to end one's task; to leave off; to abandon.
了³ 斷 to decide; the end of a matter.
了³ 案 to wind up a case.
15 了³ 無 not in the least.
了³ 無 懼 怕 did not show the least fear.
了³ 當 satisfied; settled.
了³ 賬 the account is settled—he is dead.
了³ 願 to realize one's wishes.
20 了³ 饑 荒 to settle up accounts; to clear off a debt.
罷 了³ enough! that will do.

(a) Intelligent.

了³ 了³ clear and distinct.
了³ 事 to understand the matter. *See above*—5.
了³ 亮 sensible, intelligent.
了³ 悟 to understand thoroughly.
5 了³ 然 clearly, fully.
了³ 然 明 白 to understand fully.
了³ 解 to comprehend.
一 目 了³ 然 seen at a glance.
(b) Pron. ·*lė.* Perfective particle. 他 吃 了 飯 就 走 *l* having eaten, he went away.

料⁴
3959
Materials; ingredients.

料 物 materials; stuff.
原 料 raw material.
工 料 labour and material.
廢 料 waste material—a useless person.
5 木 料 lumber.
材 料 materials for use.
衣 料 materials for garments.

(a) Coloured glass-ware.

料 器 glass-ware, imitation jade, etc.
料 手 鐲 glass bracelets.
料 球 glass beads.
料 貨 glass-ware; a cheap counterfeit.

(b) Provender.

不 餵 料 嗎 are you not going to give it any beans, etc,—only feeding it on straw?
草 料 straw and beans, etc., for animals.

(c)   To consider. To estimate. To arrange. To calculate.

料 中⁴ to make a good guess.
料 事 不 到 a contingency unprovided for; to fail in one's estimate. [if seen.
料 事 如 見 to predict things as
料 估 to estimate; to conjecture.
5 料 力 to estimate one's strength.
料 得 it may be so!
料 想 to consider; to reckon; to anticipate; to imagine.
料 理 to arrange; to manage; to put in order.
料 量 to measure.
10 不 出 所 料 it turned out as expected.
不 料 unexpectedly.
照 料 to look after.
詎 料 who'd have thought it!
逆 料 to forecast, to conjecture.

聊²
3960
A particle indicating purpose; an expletive.

聊 以 行 國 I think I must travel over the State.
聊 圖 with a view to....
聊 與 之 謀 I will consult with them.

(a) Moreover, in some degree, merely.

聊 且 moreover; therefore.
聊 勝 於 無 it is merely better than nothing at all.
聊 復 爾 爾 merely to be like this.

(b) To depend on.

聊 生 something on which to live.

聊 資 to depend on as, for.
聊 賴 to trust to ; to depend on.
無 聊 dejected, without help or resources ; cheerless ; ennui ; silly.

(c) Careless, reckless.

聊 且 粗 略 careless, indifferent.
聊 浪 wild and careless.

(d) Noises in the ears.

聊 啾 buzzing in the ear.

敹² To sew. To keep tidy and repaired.
3961

敹 縫 to sew a seam.

蓼² The sound of the wind. Read *liu⁴*, *liao⁴*. To soar.
3962

寥² Empty, solitary, silent.
3963

寥 寥 無 伴 lonely and desolate.
寥 寥 無 幾 very few.
寥 廓 boundless, vast ; unconventional.
寥 戾 clear and sounding afar.
寥 落 deserted, unoccupied ; few.
寥 闊 the expanse of heaven.

廖² Name of a small ancient State.
3964

憀² To rely on. u.f. 聊 No. 3960.
3965

蓼³ Smartweed. Polygonum.
3966

蓼 灘 a place where smartweed grows.
蓼 糾 surrounded.
水 蓼 water-pepper.
辣 蓼 smartweed.

(a) Read *lu⁴·⁵*. Luxuriant growth.

蓼 莪 one of the odes—a filial son thinking of his parents.
蓼 蓼 者 莪 luxuriant is the growth of the artemisia.

飂² Wind in high places. Also read *liu²*.
3967

飂 戾 sound of high wind.
飂 飂 wind in lofty places.

尞²·⁴ Fuel used in sacrifices.
3968

僚² A companion, a colleague. Official associate. A clique.
3969

僚 友 a comrade.
僚 壻 husband of a sister.
僚 屬 officials.
同 僚 a colleague.
官 僚 officials.

(a) Read *liao³*. A pretty face.

佼 人 僚 兮 How pretty is that lady!

嘹² A note, a cry, a sound.
3970

嘹 唳 cry of the heron, crane, etc.
嘹 嘵 loud and clear—of sounds.
嘹 嚦 a cry—as of a bird.

寮² A fellow-official. Inter. 僚 No. 3969.
3971

寮 房 a room in a *yamen* where petty officials can meet.
同 寮 colleagues.

(a) A small window.

看 斜 暉 之 度 寮 see the slanting rays of the sun pass the window.

(b) A shanty, a hut.

僧 寮 a Buddhist priest's hut.
妓 寮 a brothel.
打 寮 a hut on the mountains.
茶 寮 a tea-house.

憭³ Intelligible, sympathetic.
3972

明 憭 intelligent.

(a) Read *liao²*. Empty.

憭 慄 disappointed and sad.

撩²·⁴ To manage. To lay hold of.
3973

撩 亂 in disorder.
撩 弄 to intrigue ; to seize, to grasp.
撩 治 or 撩 理 to control ; to manage ; to put in order.

(a) To excite, to stir up, to tease.

撩 人 to pull a person about ; to tease.
撩 動 肝 火 to stir up one's wrath.
撩 情 to arouse the passions.
撩 戰 to challenge to a fight.
⁵撩 火 to stir the fire.
撩 醒 to awaken.

(b) To pull up   To throw.

撩 石 頭 to throw stones.
撩 衣 裳 to pull up the garments.
撩 起 來 to pull up.

(c) To fall.

撩 臉 their faces fell.

嘹² Bright, shining.
3974

嘹 然 而 明 bright and splendid.

燎²·⁴ To burn. To illuminate. A signal light ; brilliant.
3975

燎 亮 clear, bright, intelligent.
燎 原 之 火 a great prairie-fire.
燎 如 指 掌 as plain as pointing to the palm of the hand.
燎 朗 luminous.
⁵燎 泡 blister raised by a burn.
燎 炬 a torch.
燎 燎 clear, plain, apparent, brilliant.
燎 薪 blazing faggots.
燎 髮 to singe the hair—easily done.

獠²
獟² To hunt at night by torches.
3976

獠 牙 long projecting teeth ; fierce.
獠 獵 to hunt.

(a) Read *lao*³. Tribes-people in Kweichow and Yunnan.

獠·子 aboriginal tribes in S. W. China.

獠面 ugly.

療² To heal, to cure.
3977

療 劑 medicines.
療 國 to heal national troubles.
療 妬 to stop jealousy.
療 法 therapeutics.
⁵水 療 法 hydropathy.
療 治 to cure; to heal.
冷 水 療 治 cold-water treatment.
戶 外 療 治 open-air treatment.
療 病 to heal diseases.
¹⁰療 瘳 convalescent.
療 貧 to relieve poverty.
療 饑 to appease hunger.
療 養 convalescence.
療 養(病)院 sanatorium.

瞭³·⁴ Bright, clear-sighted.
3978

瞭 亮 clear, intelligent.
瞭 如 指 掌 as clear as pointing to the palm of the hand.
瞭 望 to keep a look-out—as at sea.
瞭 望 臺 a look-out post.
瞭 然 it is quite clear.

繚² To bind, to wrap, to wind round. Fetters.
3979

繚 亂 in disorder; confused.
繚 戾 the noise of a whirlpool.
繚 繞 to wind around; involved.
繚 辮·子 to wind the queue round the head.
⁵繚 遶 to saunter; to look about.
繚 鈕 to wind or tie in a ball, to make knots for buttons.
一 繚 髮 a lock of hair.

(a) Lines for a sail.

繚 絲 lines for a sail.
鬆 繚 to slack off the sail.

膫
營² The fat covering the intestines. The omentum.
3980

膫 油 the fat covering the intestines.

遼² Distant.
3981

遼 望 to see from afar.
遼 落 far-distant—as hills.
遼 遠 a long way off.
遼 闊 extensive; vast.
⁵遼 闊 誕 漫 far-fetched and absurd.
遼 隔 widely separated.

(a) Name of a territory, State, etc.

遼 國(or 紀) the *Liao* dynasty—Kitan Tartars 契 丹 A.D. 907—1125.
遼 東 半 島 the Liaotung Peninsula.
遼 東 豕 Liaotung pigs—an expression similar to "carrying coals to Newcastle." Pigs in Liaotung were black, but a sow once brought forth young ones having white heads; these were regarded as a rarity and worthy of being presented to the Court, but on the way thither the owner discovered that all the pigs in the region of the Court were white, and returned home disheartened.
遼 河 a river which flows into the Gulf of Chihli.

鐐² Manacles, fetters.
3982

手 鐐 (or 銬) handcuffs.
脚 鐐 fetters.

(a) Pure silver. A furnace.

鐐 (or 燎)·子 a cook.

鷯² Small birds—the wren, tit, etc.
3983

鷦 鷯 a wren; the tailor-bird.

列⁴·⁵· To arrange in order. To enumerate; to classify. Each one. A file or rank. A series.
3984

列 下 as follows; enumerated below.
列 位 or 列 公 or 列 位 兄 台 Gentlemen!
列 傳 biographies.
列 入 to enter; to embody in proper order.
⁵列 單 to draw up a memo.
列 國 all countries; various kingdoms.
列 坐 其 次 each one sitting in his proper place.
列 子³ a philosopher who is said to have lived in the age immediately after Confucius; his writings are classed as Taoist classics. Giles regards him as a creation of Chuangtzǔ.
列 席 旁 聽 to stand by and listen.
¹⁰列 席 權 right of entry.
列 席 者 those in attendance.
列 強 the Powers.
列 強 均 勢 the balance of power.
列 成 arranged in order.
¹⁵列 摺 to draw up a memorial or despatch.
列 於 左 or 開 列 於 後 written below; as follows.
列 族 all ancestors.
列 祖 successive ancestors.
列 稅 則 as enumerated in the tariff.
²⁰列 肆 many shops.
列 舉 introduced item by item.
列 車 a train. (Ry. term)
列 陣 or 行 (*hang*²) 列 drawn up in array.
列 隊 to dress ranks.
列 寧 Lenin. (transliteration)

冽⁴·⁵· Cold and raw.
3985

冽 風 a biting blast.
霜 風 冽 冽 the cold frosty winds.

咧⁴·⁵· A final particle.
3986

洌 3987 ⁴·⁵· Pure, clear. To wash clean.

烈 3988 ⁴·⁵· Burning, ardent, violent, impetuous. Meritorious, high-principled, eminent. Chaste. Brightness. Majestic, imposing.

烈 丈·夫 a hero, a bold man.
烈 士 a patriot; a noble statesman; a hero.
烈 女 a woman who prefers to die rather than re-marry, or marry after the death of her betrothed.
烈 山 澤 burned the brushwood on the hills and in the low levels.
⁵烈 性 an ardent disposition.
烈 怒 fierce anger.
烈 日 the fierce heat of the sun.
烈 暑 a hot summer.
烈 火 a fierce fire.
¹⁰烈 烈 majestic, ardent. *See below* A.
烈 烈 征 師 majestic was the advance of our host.
烈 烈 轟 轟 with much imposing array and noise; loud roaring; angry noise.
如 火 烈 烈 as fierce as a fire.
烈 焰 a fierce flame.
¹⁵烈 猛 fierce, violent.
烈 祖 an eminent ancestor.
烈 考 my illustrious father.
烈 風 a violent wind.

(a) Cold. Sad.

冬 日 烈 烈 bitter and cold is the wintry day!
南 山 烈 烈 "cold and bleak is the southern hill."
憂 心 烈 烈 our hearts are sad and disconsolate.

茢 3989 ⁴·⁵· Sedges. Rushes.

裂 3990 ⁴·⁵· To split, to crack. To rend, to rip open.

裂 帛 tearing silk—a sharp, clear sound.
裂 果 the splitting of fruits, seed vessels, etc.
裂 爲 兩 半 rent in two.

裂 牙 or 酸 牙 to set the teeth on edge.
⁵裂 痕 a fissure.
裂 眥 to open the eyes wide in anger.
裂 破 broken; torn; cracked.
裂 紋 cleavage.
裂 縫 a crack; a rent.
¹⁰裂 膚 chapped skin.
裂 衣 to tear the clothing.
裂·開 to split open.
打 裂 to split; to tear.
爆 裂 to burst; to explode.

趔 3991 ⁴·⁵· Not progressing; to be checked.

鬣 3992 ⁴·⁵· A mane; bristles, as on a hog; dorsal fins.

獵 3993 ⁴·⁵· To hunt; field-sports.

獵 戶 huntsmen; foresters.
獵 戶 星 Orion.
獵 狗 a pointer; a hunting-dog.
獵 獵 sound of the wind.
獵 艦 a torpedo-boat destroyer.
獵 較 to "struggle for the game taken in hunting."

(a) To hunt up a quotation.

獵 其 菁 華 to search out the elegant extracts.

躐 3994 ⁴·⁵· To stride over; to step across.

躐 山 越 嶺 to skip over the hills.
躐 席 to occupy a wrong place at table.
躐 等 to skip over; irregular.

LIEN.   (ㄌㄢ)

恰 3995 ² To pity. u.f. next.

憐 3996 ² To have compassion on; to pity; to sympathize.

憐 孤 惜 寡 to have compassion on the widow and orphan.
憐 愛 to pity; to regard; fond of.
憐 憫 or 憐 恤 or 憐 念 or 憐 惜 to sympathize; to commiserate.
憐 貧 to pity the poor.
可 憐 pitiable; Have pity on me!
相 憐 mutual sympathy.

(a) To envy.

風 憐 目 the wind envies the eye—which travels fast and far without moving.

奩 3997 ² A lady's dressing-case. A bridal trousseau.

奩 儀 money given to a bride.
粧 奩 a trousseau; a mirrored dressing-case.

帘 3998 ² The flag-sign of a tavern. A booth.

門 帘 a cloth screen hung before a door.

斂 3999 ³·⁴· To gather, to accumulate. Distinguish 歛 No. 2052.

斂 嗇 parsimonious; miserly.
斂 存 to lay up; to store.
斂 怨 以 爲 德 you deem it a virtue to get the hatred of people.
斂 錢 to hoard money.
收 斂 to gather in the harvest.

(a) To arrange. To compose the features. To control oneself. To withdraw.

斂 事 to be patient with; not to meddle.
斂 容 to wear a serious expression.
斂 形 to become invisible.
斂 手 to stay the hand; to draw the hands up the sleeves.
⁵斂 翼 to fold the wings.
斂 聲 with bated breath.
斂 脚 or 斂 跡 to stay at home; to give up evil ways.
斂 膝 to draw up the knees.
斂 足 to refuse to advance.
斂 身 to control oneself.

(b) u.f. 殮 No. 4001.

入 斂 to prepare a body for the coffin and place it within it.

蘝 4 A wild vine. *Vitis penta-phylla.*
4000

殮 4 To dress a corpse for burial.
4001

殮 具 articles used for wrapping a corpse.
殮 埋 or 殮 葬 to shroud and bury.
小 殮 to dress a person newly dead.
大 殮 to put the deceased into coffin.

臉 3 The face. Reputation, character. Also read *chien*³.
4002

臉·上 下·不 來 or 下·不 來 臉 haven't the face to.
臉·上 不 好 看 discreditable; shameful.
臉·上 抹·不 開 mortified; ashamed; unable to face the world.
臉·上 掛 招·牌 his face is a signboard.
⁵臉·上 無 光 out of countenance; having lost prestige.
臉 冷 and serious.
臉 厚 不 挨 餓 a thick-skinned person need not starve.
臉 嫩 or 臉 皮 薄 diffident; bashful.
臉 旦 兒 or 顋 巴·子 cheeks.
¹⁰臉 熱 anxious to do what is asked.
臉 皮 厚 thick-skinned; brazen; shameless.
臉 盆 a face-basin.
臉 紅 blushing; flushed with anger.
紅 漲·了 臉 a blush overspread his face.
¹⁵臉 罕 shameless.
臉 色 expression; colour; countenance.
臉 蛋 兒 the cheeks. ⌈spoken
臉 軟 soft-hearted; lenient; soft-
臉 酸 sour-visaged.
²⁰臉 面 the face; appearance; reputation; *face*.
臉 面 大 having great influence.
臉 面 發 光 a bright countenance.
不 要 臉 shameless; having no regard for reputation or *face*.
丟 臉 to lose *face*.

²⁵掉 臉 to change countenance; to turn the face; to be angry.
沒 有 臉 *face* lost; disgraced.
看·他·的 臉 to beg a thing as a favour from another.
笑 臉 a smiling face.
翻 臉 to become angry towards another; to be estranged.
³⁰轉 臉 in the turning of the face—at once; to come out of a matter with success.
鬼 臉ᵢ a mask; a scowl.

廉 2 Pure, modest, incorrupt. Not avaricious—thus:—reasonable in price.
4003

廉 俸 salary.
廉 價 cheap, reasonable prices.
廉 吏 a pure-handed officer.
廉 士 a pure official.
⁵廉 恥 modest; bashful.
廉 明 pure and intelligent—of officials.
廉 潔 honest; purity; not corruptible.
廉 節 sparing, frugal; not avaricious.
廉 靜 寡 欲 pure and of few desires.

(a) An angle or corner.

廉 隅 angular—thus:—punctilious; scrupulous.

(b) To investigate, to examine.

廉 察 to investigate.
廉 按 to examine into.
廉 訪 or 廉 使 designation of the former Provincial Judge.

濂 2 A waterfall. River in Hunan.
4004

濂 泉 a waterfall.

簾 幨 2 A loose hanging-screen; window-screens; curtains, blinds.
4005

簾 內 簾 外 private and public.
簾·子 a curtain; a hanging-screen.
下 簾 to let down a screen.
垂 簾 to let down a screen,*
布 簾 a curtain; a cloth screen.
竹 簾 a screen of bamboo splints.
*esp., when an empress dowager is on the throne.

臁 2 The calf of the leg. Spleen of animals.
4006

鐮 鎌 2 A sickle, a reaping-hook.
4007

鐮 刀 a sickle.

聯 2 To connect, to unite. Joined, connected, associated. Scrolls.
4008

聯 保 mutual security.
聯 句 couplets, as on scrolls.
聯 合 to join; joined; to confederate; to affiliate.
聯 合 作 用 combined function.
⁵聯 合 債 欵 consolidation of debt.
聯 合 國 the United Nations.
聯 合 會 a united association.
聯 合 組 織 a merger.
聯 名 joint signatures.
¹⁰聯 姻 connection by marriage.
聯 宗 to join clans having the same surname but different ancestors.
聯 居 to dwell side by side—as in a row of houses.
聯 席 會 議 joint conference.
聯 帶 關·係 affiliations; associated relationships.
¹⁵聯 心 合 作 to act with united purpose.
聯 志 united purpose.
聯 想 association of ideas.
聯 想 派 心 理 學 association psychology.
聯 手 in united strength.
²⁰聯 棺 和 塚 to bury husband and wife side by side.
聯 甲 a union of ten families; a tithing.
聯 省 會 議 inter-provincial conference.
聯 盟 allied.
聯 盟 會 會 員 members of the League.
²⁵聯 禱 圑 prayer-circles.
聯 絡 joined to; in fellowship with; to affiliate.
聯 絡 一 片 to combine into one whole.
聯 絡 不 斷 unbroken—as a line of people.
聯 絡 員 liaison officer.

³⁰聯 群 a flock; to crowd together.
聯 行 (hang²) a trade combine.
聯 袂 side by side.
聯 貫 to string together.
聯 軍 allied armies.
³⁵聯 邦 政 體 a confederated form of government.
聯 銜 to join titles—in a despatch, etc.
聯 黨 to form cabals; to join in a clique.
上 聯 下 聯 right hand and left hand scrolls.
對 聯 scrolls for hanging on walls, consisting of rhymed antithetical couplets.
⁴⁰輓 聯 funeral scrolls.

連² To connect; to join.
4009

連 不 上 unconnected; lacking sequence.
連 不 貫 incoherent. = 不 連 貫.
連 任 a re-appointment to office.
連 合 or 連 同 connected; joined; banded together.
⁵連 名 joint signatures.
連 坐 involved in.
連 夜 day and night; throughout the night.
連 夥 in partnership.
連 天 for successive days; joined to the sky—very high.
¹⁰連 姻 allied by marriage.
連 屬 connected.
連 帶 債 務 joint obligations in debt.
連 帶 債 權 joint credit.
連 帶 地 closely connected with.
¹⁵連 帶 子 a step-son.
連 帶 義·務 joint obligation.
連 帶 責·任 joint liabilities or responsibility.
連 帶 進 行 joint procedure.
連 帶 關·係 direct succession; affiliated relationship; associations.
²⁰連 年 for successive years.
連 忙 without delay; at once.
連 成 joined so as to form....
連 捷 one success after another.
連 搖 帶 按 shaken together and pressed down.
²⁵連 日 or 連 天 successive days.
連 枝 brothers, relatives.
連 架 a flail.
連 理 枝 trees whose branches interlock.

連 環 links; connected together.
³⁰連 環 保 mutually responsible for.
連 環 計 a plan that effects two or more objects successively.
連 璧 sun and moon.
連 皮 ...with the packing; gross weight.
連 累 or 牽 連 to implicate; to involve.
³⁵連 絡 joined; connected.
連 絡 不 絕 unbroken connection.
連 綴 joined into one.
連 綴 貫 串 linked up together.
連 綿 挺 拔 continuous succession of stiffly-standing peaks.
⁴⁰連 線 不 斷 continuous; unbroken.
連 續 罪 continuous offence.
連 背 abreast.
連 號 consecutive numbers; branch establishments.
連·襟 (or 袂) husbands of sisters.
⁴⁵連 親 consanguineous association.
連 記 投 票 voting-paper with a series of names.
連 辭 a conjunction.
連 連 or 接 連 unceasingly; connected.
連 連 不 斷 incessant.
⁵⁰連 連 懇 求 importunate entreaty.
連 連 滴 漏 constant dripping.
連 阡 累 陌 in every direction.
連 陰 continuous cloudy weather.
相 連 adjoining.

(a) A company of soldiers. Nominally 126 men.
連 長 officer in charge of a *lien*.

(b) Even, and, together with, including.
連 三 倒 四 one thing after another.
連 他 也 在 內 even he is included.
連 底 凍 even the bottom is frozen—irrevocable, unalterable.
連 手 也 不 洗 he does not even wash his hands.
⁵連 打 帶 罵 with both beating and cursing.
連 本 帶 利 both principal and interest.
連 草 帶 根 root and branch.

嗹² Chattering, loquacious.
4010

嗹 嘍 chattering.

(a) u.f. Denmark. 丹 麥.

挮³ To transport; to remove. To take.
4011

挮 來 挮 去 to take backwards and forwards.
挮 稭 a flail.
挮 過 人 to hand over to another.
挮·開 曬 to take out and dry in the sun.

漣² Flowing water. River in Hunan.
4012

泣 涕 漣 漣 her tears flowed unceasingly.

璉³ A vessel used to hold grain at the imperial sacrifice.
4013

蓮² The lotus or water-lily.
4014

蓮 塘 a lotus-pond.
蓮 步 lady-like steps.
蓮 炬 ornamental candles.
蓮 燈 lantern in the shape of a lotus-flower.
⁵蓮 的 lotus-seeds—bitter at heart.
蓮 米 or 蓮 子 or 蓮 肉 lotus-seeds.
蓮 花 lotus-flowers.
蓮 花 池 a lotus-pond.
蓮 花 經 a Buddhist *sûtra*.
¹⁰蓮 蓬 or 蓮 房 the seed-case of the lotus.
蓮 鉤 or 金 蓮 the small feet of Chinese women, when bound.
蓮 青 色 a purple colour.
蓮 駕 or 蓮 座 the lotus-seat—a name of the goddess of mercy.
西 番 蓮 the passion-flower; the dahlia.

褳² A pouch, a pocket.
4015

褡·褳 a pouch worn at the girdle.

鏈² A chain. A cable.
4016

鏈 尺 surveyor's chain.
鏈 索 or 鏈·子 chains, fetters.
鏈 着 chained; in chains.
測 鏈 a surveyor's chain.

(a) Lead or tin ore.

錫鏈 (or 連) tin ore.

鰱[2] A kind of bream.
4017

楝[4] Pride of India. *Melia azederach.*
4017a

涷[4] To boil raw silk. Inter. 練 No. 4020.
4018

煉[4] To smelt, to refine. To purify.
4019

煉丹 to refine the pill—of immortality.
煉乳 condensed milk.
煉氣 to imbibe energy—a Taoist practice.
煉淨銀·子 to refine silver.
[5]煉獄 or 練獄 purgatory—a Romanist term.
煉糖 to refine sugar.
煉金術 alchemy.
煉鋼場 steel foundry.

練[4] To practise. To drill. To select.
4020

練兵 or 練武 or 練軍 to drill troops.
練冠線纓要経不除 the mourning hat, collar and girdle are not put away.
練勁 to exercise the muscles.
練勇 or 練丁 or 團練 home guards.
[5]練在一處 gathered together in one place.
練布 coarse sackcloth for mourning.
練服 one year's mourning.
練·習 to practise.
練·習簿 exercise-book.
[10]練·習體操 physical training.
練船 a training-ship.
練若 monasteries.
練達 versed in; experienced.
練閱 to hold a review.

(a) To select.

練時日 to select a day.

(b) To soften raw silk by boiling.

練熟絲 dressed silk.

鍊[4] To smelt, to refine. To discipline.
4021 Inter. 煉 No. 4019.

鍊仙 to become an immortal.
鍊氣 to practise breathing, as a religious exercise, to imbibe energy. (*Taoist*).
鍊熟 well smelted; matured in; accustomed to.
鍊金 to refine gold.

(a) A chain.

鍊·子 a chain.
解鍊 to unchain.

LIN. (ㄌㄧㄣ)

林[2] A forest; a grove; a copse. A grave,—from the trees planted about it.
4022

林下 to retire to the country—i.e., from official life.
林下風氣 the breath of the forest—said in praise of a woman
退歸林下 to retire from public life and return home.
林坰 the wilds and solitary places.
[5]林·子 or 樹林 a grove, a clump of trees; a forest.
林木 a forest.
林林而羣 crowded together as trees in a forest.
林業 forestry.
林檎 (*ch'in*[2]) small red apples.
[10]林泉 forest and spring—place for a recluse.
林烟 the mists of the forest.
林立 numerous—as a forest of masts.
林莽 the jungle.
林薄 forests and dense undergrowth—jungle.
[15]林鐘 a classical pitch corresponding in function to G.
林霏 the driving rain in the forest.
森林 a dense forest.
深林 in the depths of a forest.
竹林 a bamboo grove.
[20]綠林暴客 men of the greenwood—robbers, bandits.

(a) A collection of books, literary extracts, etc.

儒林 a collection of the writings of Confucian scholars.
文林 literary body; a literary collection.

淋[2] To drip; to rain heavily. To soak through.
4023

淋巴 lymph.
淋巴管 lymphatics.
淋巴腺 lymphatic glands.
淋漓 dripping wet.
[5]淋漓盡致 thoroughly imbued with.
淋濕 wet through by rain.
淋症 gravel, strangury, etc. *See* 痳 No. 4025.
淋花 to sprinkle flowers.
淋透 soaked through by rain.

(a) Read *lin*[4]. To strain, to filter.

淋水罐 a filter for water.
淋淨 to filter.
過淋 to strain; to filter.

琳[2] A gem.
4024

琳國 a country near the Caspian Sea which produced topazes.
琳宇 or 琳宮 Buddhist monastery.
琳琅 tinkling of gems; valuables; gems, etc.

痳[2] Diseases of the bladder; gravel, stone, etc.
4025 See 淋 No. 4023—7.

痳症 strangury; diseases of the bladder.
五痳 various diseases of the bladder.
急痳 strangury.
石痳 stone in the bladder.
砂痳 gravel.
血痳 blood in the urine.

霖[2] Long-continued rain. Inter. 淋 No. 4023.
4026

霖雨 continuous rains.
霖霖 continuous rains.
甘霖 timely rains.

臨² To descend; to come to. Near to, on the point of.
4027

臨了兒 after all; at last.

臨下無戾 do not be harsh to subordinates.

臨世 or 臨凡 to come into the world—as Jesus did.

臨之以莊 to govern with gravity.

臨事 when the matter is at hand; in a crisis.

⁵臨事堅決 firm in action at a crisis.

臨事而懼 full of anxiety and fear in the crisis of an affair.

臨別 on the point of departure.

臨·到 to approach.

臨危 on the brink of danger.

¹⁰臨夜 at nightfall; eventide.

臨大節 in a great emergency; in a grave crisis.

臨大節而不可奪 even in great emergencies he cannot be driven from his principles.

臨席 present at meetings.

臨年 in declining years.

¹⁵臨御 to take over government; to rule.

臨急 or 臨忙 to hurry oneself.

臨時 provisional; temporary; special; extraordinary—as a meeting—contrasted with 永久 permanent.

臨時任命 provisional appointments.

臨時作文 improvisation.

²⁰臨時借債 temporary loan.

臨時列車 special train.

臨時執政 provisional chief executive.

臨時執照 provisional charter.

臨時大會 extraordinary general meeting.

²⁵臨時契約 provisional contract.

臨時抱佛脚 to expect impossible immediate effect. Cf. 4938.5.

臨時悮事 to fail at the critical moment.

臨時戒嚴 temporary martial-law.

臨時政府 provisional government.

³⁰臨時會 a special session.

臨時會議 extraordinary general meeting..

臨時期內 during the provisional period.

臨時期間 provisional time-limit.

臨時法院 provisional court.

³⁵臨時發票 provisional invoice.

臨時籌備處 temporary office for the arrangement of ways and means.

臨時經費 extraordinary expenses.

臨時處分 provisional arrangement.

臨時處置 provisional disposition.

⁴⁰臨時設法 a provisional plan.

臨時證券 provisional certificates.

臨時證書 provisional charter.

臨時鐵路 construction line of railway.

臨時預算特別費 extraordinary budget.

⁴⁵臨朝 to give audience. to hold a levee.

臨機應變 to be guided by the turn of events.

臨死垂絕 at the point of death.

臨民 to rule the people.

臨水 near the water; overlooking a stream.

⁵⁰臨水人家 near neighbours.

臨深履薄 cautious—abbreviation for "as if on the brink of the abyss, as if treading on thin ice."

臨渴掘井 to dig a well when one is thirsty—too late.

臨牀講議 clinical lecture.

臨牀醫學 clinical medicine.

⁵⁵臨產 near childbirth.

臨界壓力 critical pressure. (physics).

臨界密度 critical density. (physics).

臨界·的 critical. (physics).

臨界過度 critical temperature. (physics).

⁶⁰臨界速度 critical speed. (physics).

臨界點 critical point. (physics).

臨症下藥 administer medicine according to the diagnosis.

臨盆 parturition.

臨睡 before going to sleep; at bedtime.

⁶⁵臨終 or 臨危 or 臨死 near the end—at the point of death.

臨終奉教 death-bed conversion.

臨蓐 to be brought to childbed.

臨行 or 臨去 or 臨走 on the point of departure; just going.

臨街 abutting on the street.

⁷⁰臨財毋苟得 in getting wealth do not be unscrupulous.

臨近 drawing near to.

臨陣 about to go into battle.

臨陣退縮 to skulk when going into battle.

臨雍拜老 came into the imperial schoolroom and bowed to the teacher.

⁷⁵臨顧 or 臨存 to pay a visit.

下臨 to come down.

五福臨門 May every happiness visit you!

親臨 to come in person.

降臨 advent; to come from above.

(a) To copy, to imitate.

臨帖 to write from a copy-slip.

臨本 a copy.

臨摹 to copy, as pictures—not tracing them.

粦
燐
㷠²

A will-o'-the-wisp; a flitting light. Phosphorous, See 磷, No. 4074.
4028

㷠光 phosphorescence.

㷠光性·的 phosphorescent.

㷠寸 matches.

㷠素 phosphorous.

⁵㷠酸 phosphoric acid.

嶙³ Precipitous.
4029

嶙峋 rugged.

瞵² To stare at.
4030

轔²·³ Rumbling of vehicles. A threshold, u.f. 鄰 No. 4033. Neighbours.
4031

遴² To choose; to select for appointment.
4032

遴員任理 to appoint an official to attend to the management.

遴才 to choose talented men.

遴柬 to select.

遴派 to choose and depute.

遴選 to select.

(a) Read *lin⁴*. **Difficult.**

不可以 遴 you must not regard the difficulty—and shirk it.

(b) Inter. 吝 No. 4040. Stingy.

性實遴嗇 his is a truly stingy nature.

鄰 / 隣 ² A neighbour. Near to, connected.
4033

鄰人 a neighbour.
鄰國 or 鄰邦 neighbouring States.
鄰舍 or 鄰居 or 鄰家 neighbours.
鄰近 contiguous, near at hand.
⁵鄰鄉 neighbourhood; near-by village.
鄰里 a neighbourhood.
近鄰 a near neighbour.

鱗 ² The scales of a fish. Scaly; overlapping like scales.
4034

鱗介 the scaly or finny tribes.
鱗傷 covered with scars like scales.
鱗次 in orderly rows, like scales on a fish.
鱗集 to herd together.
⁵鱗毛 scales and fur—a class of paintings which includes birds, animals, fish, etc.
鱗鴻 fish and wild goose—they are said to carry letters,–u.f. a letter.
鱗爪 scales and claws—trifles.
鱗物 or 鱗部 all scaly animals—reptiles, fish, etc.
鱗甲 scales; armour-plates; tortoise, turtles, etc.
¹⁰鱗芽 scaly buds of certain trees.
鱗莖 bulbs of lilies, onions, etc.—in layers.
鱗鱗 ripples on water.

 ² The female of the Chinese unicorn. See 麒 No. 534.
4035

鱗趾呈祥 may the unicorn's hoof bring you good luck!—may you have many sons.

凜 ³ To shiver with cold or fear. Inter. 懍 No. 4038.
4036

凜冽 piercingly cold.
凜然 stern, harsh manner; severity.
凜遵 tremblingly obey!

廩 ³ A government granary. A stipend.
4037

廩俸 salary; stipend.
廩·生 a former salaried graduate of the first or *Hsiu ts'ai* degree.

懍 ³ Fear, to fear; to tremble at. Inter. 凜 No. 4036.
4038

懍之慎之 tremble at this! beware!
懍懍 trembling with fear.
懍懍 fearful.

檁 / 标 ³ The bole of a tree. A cross-beam. The combing round the hatches of a ship.
4039

檁·子 purlins.

吝 / 悋 / 恡 ⁴ Stingy, sparing of; close-fisted.
4040

吝惜 or 吝嗇 niggardly, miserly.
吝情 a parsimonious spirit.
吝色 to show unwillingness in the face.
吝財 parsimonious.

(a) To repent; to regret.

悔吝 to repent.

藺 ⁴ Kind of rush used for mats.
4041

藺石 stones placed to throw down from a city wall on besiegers.

躪 ⁴ A cart-rut. To run over. To trample down.
4042

蹂躪 to trample under foot.

令 ⁴ To command. To tell. To cause. An order.
4043

令人厭·惡 cause men to be disgusted. (-ₒwu⁴)
令人生氣 it makes men angry.
令·他來 tell him to come.
令旗 a military signal-flag.
⁵令旨 a command of the empress-dowager.
令箭 an arrow with a triangular flag attached, bestowed by the emperor as a token of conferred authority.
三令五申 repeated orders and injunctions.
命令 a command, an order.
批令 mandate embodying a decision in reply to matters which have been referred to high authority.
¹⁰敕令 separate orders embodying laws, rules, etc., which have been preceded by the 申令.
申令 a mandate proclaiming new laws, etc.
此令 such is the order!
法令 a legal order.
策令 mandate conferring honours or notifying an appointment.
¹⁵訓令 orders or instructions from higher to lower officials.

(a) Good, honourable. A term of respect.

令似 your sons.
令儀 excellent deportment.
令兄令弟 your elder or younger brothers.
令名 a good name.
⁵令坦 your son-in-law.
令堂 or 令慈 your mother.
令妹 your sister.
令媛 or 令千金 your daughter.
令尊 your father.
¹⁰令德 excellent virtue.
令正 your wife.
令終 a good death.
令開令望 a subject of praise, a source of hope—to the people.

令 聞 廣 譽 a good reputation and wide-spreading praise.

15令 郎 your son.

令 親 your parents.

(b) A district magistrate.

令 尹 prime minister of a feudal State; a district magistrate.

縣 令 a district magistrate.

(c) A season.

令 節 a time, a festival.

伏 令 the hottest season.

時 令 a season.

春 令 夏 令 spring and summer seasons respectively.

(d) Insinuating, i.e., pretending to goodness as above under—A.

巧 言 令 色 fine words and an insinuating countenance.

伶² A musician.
4044

伶 人 a musician; an actor.

伶 使 a servant.

伶 優 an actor.

伶 官 master of the musicians.

⁵伶 界 actors, musicians, etc.

伶 長 (chang³) a chief musician.

(a) Clever, sprightly.

伶 便 lithe, active.

伶·俐 shrewd; clever; smart and quick.

伶 分 active, smart.

伶 牙 俐 齒 glib, fluent of speech.

(b) Lonely.

伶 仃 lonely, sad.

囹² A prison, an enclosure.
4045

囹 圄 prisons, jails.

拎¹ To lift, to raise. To take.
4046

拎·他 一 把 to lend a helping hand.

拎·起 一 桶 水 to draw a bucket of water.

玲² Tinkling of gem-pendants.
4047

玲 玎 clear sound as of stones when struck.

玲 玲 如 振 玉 a clear sound like jade when struck.

玲 琅 sound of jade when struck.

玲 瓏 elegant; fine and regular; openwork; splendid.

玲 瓏 望 秋 月 gaze through—a crystal screen—at the autumn moon.

玲 瓏 然 tinkling like pendants.

映 竹 見 玲 瓏 the light of the setting sun on the bamboos, gave them the appearance of carved openwork.

瓴² Concave channels of tiling. A long-necked jar.
4048

羚² A species of antelope.
4049

羚 羊 the antelope.

翎² A wing. A plume, a feather.
4050

翎·子 a feather.

翎 扇 a feather-fan.

翎 筒·子 jade-holder for the peacock-feather decoration.

翎 雙 the peacock-feather decoration worn on the hats of former officials, awarded for merit under the Manchus.

箭 翎 feather on an arrow.

花 翎 the peacock-feather decoration.

聆² To hear; to listen; to apprehend.
4051

聆 悉 to make oneself acquainted with—the contents of a letter.

聆 教 to listen to your instructions —used in reply to invitations.

舲² A small boat for passengers.
4052

苓² A fungus; a tuber.
4053

茯 苓 China-root, a fungus growing on the roots of fir-trees.

(a) u.f. 零 No. 4057.

苓 落 the fall of the leaf.

蛉² A kind of mosquito; a sandfly.
4054

蜻 蛉 the dragon-fly.

詅².⁴. To sell.
4055

鈴² Small round bells used on horses, etc.
4056

鈴·子 a pedlar's gong struck by swinging knobs as he twirls it.

鈴 釘 a pike or halberd.

鈴·鐺 a hand-bell.

鈴·鐺·似·的 globular like a small bell. (--shih·tê)

馬 鈴 bells on horses.

零² Fragments; fractional. Used to express a cipher in 4057 a numerical series.

零 丁 solitary, lonely.

零 傭 僕 役 man hired for odd jobs.

零 剪 tailor's cuttings.

零 賣 店 retail shop.

⁵零 數 fractions; odd numbers.

零 度 zero degrees.

零 星 物 品 a job lot.

零 殘 remnants.

零 物 odds and ends.

10零 用 錢 pocket-money.

零 碎 or 零 星 fragments; odds and ends; miscellaneous; fractions.

零 碎 工·夫 odd jobs.

零 碎 生·意 retail trade.

零 碎 銀·子 odd pieces of silver used to make up the weight.

15零 落 to be stripped of leaves; scattered; standing alone; poverty-stricken.

零 貨 retail goods.

零 賣 sold retail.

零 錢 small change.
零 傜 a surplus; superfluity.
²⁰二 百 零 三 203.
五 百 有 零 over five hundred.

(a) To fall as rain or dew.

零 雨 drizzling rain.
零 露 heavy with dew.

領³ The throat, a collar—thus: —to lead, to guide, to direct.
4058 To have control of. N.A. for mats, coats, etc.

領·事 consular; a consul.
領·事 團 the consular body.
領·事 官 a consul.
領·事 署 consulate.
⁵領·事 裁 判 權 extraterritoriality; consular jurisdiction.
領 人 to guide or lead others.
領 兵 to lead troops.
領 去 to lead away.
領 土 territory.
¹⁰領 土 保 全 to preserve territorial integrity.
領 土 權 territorial rights.
領 地 dependency.
領 域 a realm.
領·子 or 領 緣 a collar; a necktie.
¹⁵領 帶 a necktie.
領 師 or 統 領 a general.
領 江·(的)river-pilot.
領 海 territorial waters.
領 港 a pilot.
²⁰領 港 費 pilotage.
領 盤 or 羅 盤 a compass.
領 章 collar-badges of rank, etc.
領 結 a necktie.
領·袖 collar and sleeves—a manager; a headman; the leader.
²⁵領 袖 公 使 doyen of the diplomatic body.
領 頭 or 領 首 a leader; a guide.
帶 領 to conduct; to guide.
引 領 to stretch out the neck.
首 領 a leader.

(a) To receive

領 下 to receive from a superior.
領 受 to receive; to accept; to suffer; receptive capacity.
領 名 to receive a name.
領 命 to receive commands.
⁵領 回 to receive back.
領 帖 or 領 單 or 領 照 to take out—as a certificate, etc.
領 悟 to apprehend.

領 情 to receive a favour; to be obliged; to be under obligation.
領 悉 received and contents noted.
¹⁰領 收 to take out.
領 教 to receive instruction; conventional reply when one's question is answered, etc.
領·會 to comprehend.
領 洗 or 受 洗 to receive baptism.
領 狀 permit to receive goods; receipt.
¹⁵領·略 to gain experience of; to comprehend; to appreciate.
領 罰 to be fined.
領 訖 all received.
領 諾 to assent to.
領 謝 received with thanks.
²⁰領 賞 to be rewarded.
本 領 ability.

嶺³ A mountain range.
4059

嶺 南 south of the pass—Kwangtung and Kwangsi.
嶺 頭 or 嶺 表 the highest peak in the range.
分 水 嶺 a watershed.

鴒² A wagtail, a lark.
4060

百 鴒 a lark.
角 鴒 the skylark.

齡² The front teeth. The age of a person. Years.
4061

齡 苗 infantile; very young.
年 齡 the age of a person.

凌² Ice, pure, chaste. Distinguish 淩 No. 4063.
4062

淩 人 official in charge of icehouse in ancient times.
淩 兢 shivering with the cold.
淩 室 or 淩 陰 an ice-house.
淩 牀 a sledge.

(a) To insult; to maltreat, to put to shame.

淩 厲 to oppress, to maltreat.
淩 弱 to oppress the weak.
淩 虐 to oppress; to treat harshly.

淩 辱 to put to shame; to deflower; to humiliate.
淩 逼 to treat with cruelty; to coerce.
淩 遲 to put to death by the slow process of slicing the limbs, etc., before beheading.
淩 駕 to oppress another in order to advance oneself.

(b) To advance; to aspire to; to rise.

淩 出 excelled; advanced.
淩 空 to tower aloft; to guess.
淩 雲 or 淩 霄 to reach the clouds —pre-eminent.
淩 霄 花 tecoma grandiflora.

(c) To cross, to traverse.

淩 波 微 步 like crossing the waves with tiny steps—describing the carriage of a beautiful woman.
淩 波 汎 水 to cross the seas.

(d) To tremble. Inter. 陵 No. 4067.

淩 慄 trembling with fear.

淩² To pass over, to traverse. Distinguish 凌 No. 4062, which was the original form.
4063

淩 山 to cross the mountains.

綾² Damask. Thin silk.
4064

綾 絹 or 綾 羅 or 綾·子 silk gauze.
綾 錦 silk brocade.

菱² The water-chestnut.
4065

菱 粉 flour made from the waterchestnut.
菱 花 米 kernel of the waterchestnut.
菱·角 the water-chestnut—trapa bicornis. (··chiao)
菱 雞 the egret.

輘² A cart-rut. Rumbling of a cart.
4066

輘 輷 a rut; to oppress; to crush.

陵[2] A mound; a tumulus.
4067

陵 夷 to deteriorate—as a mound tends to become level, so kingdoms decay.

陵 寢 imperial tombs; sepulchres.

陵 谷 變 遷 mounds and valleys change—the changes in worldly affairs during the course of time.

陵 遲 to deteriorate; decadence—as the high mounds are reduced in the course of time, so a dynasty, after long years becomes effete.

[5]孝 陵 Ming tombs at Nanking.

武 陵 name for Hangchow.

金 陵 name for Nanking.

(a) **To insult, etc., in which sense it is inter. 凌 No. 4062.**

陵 轢 to oppress.

侵 陵 to usurp.

(b) **To cross, to traverse.**

陵 波 to walk on the water.

鯪[2] A dace.
4068

土 鯪 魚 a kind of dace.

(a) **Ant-eater.**

鯪 鯉 scaly ant-eater or pangolin.

霝[2] Drops of rain; to fall in drops.
4069

酃[2]
鄏
4070
District in S. E. Hunan.

靈[2] The spirit of a being, which acts upon others. Spirit; spiritual; divine. Supernatural. Efficacious.
4071

靈 丹 elixir of immortality.

靈 修 devotion; spiritual nurture.

靈 修 會 a devotional retreat.

靈 勝 marvellous scenery.

[5]靈 化 spiritualization.

靈 媒 a spiritualistic medium.

通 靈 媒 介 a medium; to act as a medium.

靈 宮 a spiritual dwelling-place.

靈 府 the home of the spirit—Hades; the mind, the faculties.

[10]靈 德 spiritual virtues.

靈 性 spiritual nature.

靈 性 之 生 活 spiritual life.

靈 性 的 人 a spiritual man.

靈 應 efficacious; able to produce the result intended; virtue; energy.

[15]靈 氣 subtle influences; force; supernatural power; ethereal.

靈 物 spiritual beings.

靈 界 pertaining to spiritual matters; the spiritual realm.

靈 界 景 感 a spiritual atmosphere.

靈 神 a god who answers his worshippers.

[20]靈 籤 divination tallies in temples.

靈 育 spiritual nurture.

靈 臺 a tower built by *Wen Wang;* the reasoning faculties.

靈 藥 efficacious medicine.

靈 解 spiritualization.

[25]靈 通 communicating with each other.

靈 雨 timely rains.

靈 驗 responsive; fulfilling expectations; efficacious.

靈 體 a spiritual body.

靈 魂 the soul.

[30]靈 魂 不 滅 論 theory of the immortality of the soul.

靈 魂 創 造 說 theory of the creation of a soul for every person at birth.

靈 魂 生 殖 說 theory that the soul as well as the body is propagated; traducianism.

亡 靈 departed spirits.

先 靈 one's ancestors.

[35]唯 靈 論 spiritualism.

心 靈 one's spirit.

生 靈 living beings.

聖 靈 the Holy Spirit.

(a) **Ingenious, smart, intelligent.**

靈 便 clever, handy.

靈 動 skilful, dexterous; an ingenious mind.

靈 妙 subtle, ingenious.

靈 巧 ingenious; subtle.

[5]靈 慧 quiet perception.

靈 敏 ingenious, clever.

靈 敏 的 電 具 an ingenious electric appliance.

靈 明 intelligent.

靈 機 a clever contrivance.

[10]靈 活 bright and lively.

靈 活 敏 捷 lively, active and intelligent.

靈 秀 refined, elegant, exquisite.

靈 竅 smartness, cleverness.

靈 警 active and clever; alert.

[15]靈 變 versatile, handy.

(b) **A coffin containing a corpse.**

靈 位 or 靈 牌 the wooden tablet placed before a coffin to show that it contains a corpse.

靈 屋 paper houses burnt for the dead.

靈 柩 a coffin containing a corpse.

靈 轎 the chair in which the tablet of a dead man is carried.

櫺[2] The lattice of a window. A sill, a lintel.
4072

櫺 星 門 gate of a Confucian temple.

窗 戶 櫺 子 a window-sill.

另[4] Separate; besides; another; in addition; extra. Separately; again.
4073
Distinguish 另 No. 3506.

另 來 he came alone.

另 加 additional.

另 在 別 處 in another place.

另 外 in addition; besides; by itself; exclusive.

[5]另 外 一 方 面 there is another side to it.

另 定 or 另 議 to make a special arrangement.

另 寫 一 張 write another copy; write it separately.

另 居 to live apart.

另 日 another day.

[10]另 有 一 家 there is another family.

另 有 多 少 how many more are there?

另 欵 a separate item.

另 照 a separate certificate.

另 眼 看 待 to pay special regard to.

[15]另 立 to draw up a special agreement; to stand by itself.

別 自 or 別 行 by itself; apart: proceed separately.

別 起 爐 竈 set up another kitchen range—find some other way of doing it; to start all over again.

磷[2] A thin stone. To become thin. Used as symbol for phosphorous. See 燐 No. 4028. Also read *lin*[4].

4074

病 骨 磷 磷 he is reduced to a bag of bones by illness.

(a) Read *lin*[2]. Water flowing over stones. Noise of a rapid, or of carts.

LÜEH. LIOH (ㄌㄩㄝ)
(Lioh)

略 畧 4.5. Slightly, a little. A summary. Outline or sketch.

4075

略 取 幾 個 take some.

略 可 perhaps it will do.

略 同 much alike; very similar.

略 字 abbreviations.

[5]略 少 rather few.

略 式·的 訪 問 informal interview.

略 暫 for a little while.

略 曉 得 slightly acquainted with.

略 略·的 a little; slightly.

[10]略 知 一 二 I understand a little.

略 視 to despise.

略 薄·的 but slightly; very slightly.

略 見 一 斑 received a glimpse ot one spot—a rapid survey.

略 言 大 段 give the general outline.

[15]略 誌 a summary of events.

略 談 一 二 a short talk about it.

略 謂 the gist of it being....

大 略 a summary of.

節 略 general outline of.

(a) A plan, strategy. To put in order.

戰 略 strategy of a battle or war.

戰 略 之 重 要 of strategic importance.

戰 略·的 要 害 strategic point.

策 略 policy; strategy.

謀 略 clever plans; to devise plans.

軍 略 military strategy.

(b) To define.

略 界 to define a boundary.

略 道 principles.

(c) To seize. To plunder. Inter. 掠 No. 4077.

略 人 to seize and sell people.

略 地 to seize territory.

略 誘 forcible abduction.

略 賣 to kidnap and sell.

(d) Sharp.

有 略 其 耜 sharp are their ploughshares.

掔[4.5.] To take by force. To throw aside. Also read *liao*[4].

4076

掔·下 to lay aside; to cast off.

掔·開 手 to shake something off the hand.

掠[4.5.] To rob, to plunder. Also read *liao*[4], *liang*[4].

4077

掠 取 or 搶 掠 to seize, to rob.

掠 奪 制 度 the plundering system of government—sarcastic.

掠 提 to seize with violence.

掠 美 市 恩 to purchase popularity by claiming the good deeds of another as one's own.

掠 食 to forage; to seize food.

抄 掠 to seize and confiscate.

(a) To flog.

掠 笞 to flog with the bamboo.

(b) A stroke to the left in writing.

LIU. (ㄌㄧㄡ)

旒[2] A cap with pendants.

4078

旒 旒[2] Fringes of pearls on crowns. A pennant.

4079

冕 旒 gems on a crown.

流[2] To flow, to drift, to circulate. A current. To descend. Unstable, weak.

4080

流 不 絶 ceaseless flow.

流 丐 vagrant beggars.

流 亡 to flee, to desert.

流 俗 prevalent customs.

[5]流 傳 to hand down, tradition.

流 傭 one who has left home for employment elsewhere.

流 光 the passing of time like a flowing stream.

流 冰 floating ice.

流·出·去 to flow out.

[10]流·出 水·來 water flows forth.

流 利 movable; lively; not at all hide-bound.

流 動 書 庫 circulating library.

流 動 資 本 floating capital.

流 丢 worthless.

[15]流 口 折 pat phrases.

流 域 a river valley or basin.

流 娼 a prostitute.

流 寓 residents in foreign lands.

流 寇 bandits.

[20]流 布 to spread; to diffuse.

流 平 地 level ground.

流 年 idly passing years.

流 弊 spreading of corrupt practices.

流 彈 a stray bullet.

[25]流 戸 vagrants.

流 支 rivulets; headwaters.

流·星 a meteor.

流 毒 flowing poison—wide-spread injury.

流 民 vagrants; tramps.

[30]流 氓 vagrants; loafers; vagabonds.

流 氛 昌 熾 the spreading disorders went like a flame over the land.

流 水 running water; to flow.

流 水 不 腐 flowing water never becomes putrid.

流 水 席 succession of guests.

[35]流 水 簿 a journal.

流 水 賬 current account.

流 汗 to perspire freely.

流 沙 shifting sands.

流 注 no fixed place of abode; a disease with inflammatory swellings.

[40]流 沫 floating foam.

流 泊 without any fixed stopping-place.

流 波 bright glances.

流 浪 floating about; drifting.

流 浪 生·活 a vagrant life.

[45]流 流·的 風 a gentle breeze.

流 淚 or 流 眼 淚 to shed tears.

流 淚 狀 a lachrymose expression.

流 湎 a confirmed habit of drunkenness.
流 涎 to drivel.
[50]流 湧 to overflow; to spring up.
流 溢 to overflow; to inundate.
流 產 to miscarry.
流 瘠 starving refugees.
流 目 a shifty gaze.
[55]流 盼 to make sheep's eyes at.
流 礦 槽 sluices.
流 精 or 遺 精 involuntary emissions.
流 芳 百 世 to hand down a fragrant reputation to all generations.
流·落 to drift away; to emigrate; outcast.
[60]流 蕩 to wander; to stray.
流 蕩 忘 返 to wander away and forget to return—unsettled and contrary.
流 蘇 tassels.
流 血 to shed blood.
流 行 prevalent, as an epidemic.
[65]流 行 性 感 冒 epidemic influenza.
流 行 病 epidemic.
流 行·的 prevalent; fashionable.
流 覽 to take a glance at.
流 覽 勝 景 to go about sight-seeing.
[70]流 言 hearsay; rumour.
流 質 liquids.
流 質 重 率 (liŭ4.5.) specific gravity of fluids.
流 轉 to circulate; to spread; glancing here and there.
流 通 to circulate freely; circulation; interchange.
[75]流 通 之 貨 幣 circulating medium.
流 通 額 limit of circulation—as of bank notes.
流 逛 to stroll; to roam.
流 連 to give oneself up to pleasure.
流 連 忘 返 fond of roaming so as to forget to return home—unsettled disposition.
[80]流 連 荒 亡 they flow with the stream, or they work against it; they are wild, they are lost.
流 量 volume of flowing water.
流 金 鑠 石 hot enough to—melt metals and fuse rocks.
流 離 vagabond; wandering.
流 離 失 所 homeless vagrants.
[85]流 離 遷 徙 scattered; vagrant.

流 離 飄 蕩 tossed about.
流 電 lightning—quickly, in an instant.
流 電 表 voltameter.
流 霞 scattered clouds.
[90]流 露 to divulge; to leak out.
流 風 prestige.
流 體 fluids.
流 鼻·涕 running at the nose.
直 流 direct (electric) current.
[95]如 流 fluently; glibly.
小 流 a small stream.
氣 流 air-currents.
間 流 indirect (electric) current.
風 流 given to gaiety and pleasure; amorous; romantic.

(a) To transport, to banish.

流 放 to banish.
流 罪 transportation for life.
流 配 banishment.

(b) A class. A kind. A set of persons.

流 亞 one class of person.
流 別 classes.
流 品 standing in society.
流 輩 of the same class or standing.
[5]一 流 人 one class of people
上 流 人 士 the classes as contrasted with the masses.
上 流 社 會 upper classes of society.
下 流 人 the lower classes.
中 流 社 會 the middle classes.
[10]九 流 nine schools of philosophy. *See* No. 1198-25.
儒 家 者 流 Confucianists.
女 流 a woman; womankind; womenfolk.

琉 ﹜
瑠 ﹜   A precious stone.
4081

琉 球 國 The Lewchew or Ryukyu Islands.
琉·璃 an opaque, glass-like substance; porcelain.
琉·璃 珠 glass beads.
琉·璃 瓦 glazed tiles.

硫 ²
   Sulphur.
4082

硫 強 水   sulphuric acid.

硫·礦 粉 or 硫·礦 sulphur.
硫·礦 華 brimstone-sticks.
硫 苦 sulphate of magnesia.
[5]硫 酸 sulphuric acid; sulphates—used with various words as prefix.
硫 酸 鎂 sulphate of magnesia.
↑硫 化 sulphides.

留 ﹜²
雷 ﹜   To detain. To entertain. To keep; to put by.
4083

留·下 put it by.
留·不 住 unable to detain.
留 任 to retain in office—of an official who has lost his rank, but is allowed an opportunity to retrieve his character. Also = ⌊4009.3
留 候 to detain.
[5]留 兵 to garrison; to detain troops.
留 別 a parting gift; a keepsake.
留 城 to keep the city gate open, as for a benighted visitor.
留 學 to study abroad.
留 學 生 students abroad.
[10]留 客 or 留 賓 to entertain.
留 宿 or 留 歇 to keep over-night.
留 尿 retention of urine.
留 居 to give shelter.
留 心 to pay attention to.
[15]留 心 辦 事 mind what you are about; be careful in the management of the business.
留 意 to give attention; to give the mind to.
留 戀 to hanker after; to begrudge.
留 版 新 聞 stop-press.
留 神 be on the look-out; to give heed.
[20]留 空 to keep a berth open; to leave a space in writing.
留 連 to stop at.
留 門 keep the gate or door open.
留 難 or 留 滯 to put obstacles in the way of departure.
留 飯 to detain to a meal.

(a) To restrain. To leave behind. To transmit.

留·下·來·的 handed down; bequeathed.
留·下 話 to leave word.
留 名 to leave a good reputation behind.
留 命 to spare a man's life.

[5]留·在 這·裏 leave it here.

留 步 don't trouble yourself to come out—said by a visitor to the host on leaving.

留 種[3] to leave a seed; to reserve a nucleus.

留 級 to leave in the same class without promotion.

留 辮·子 to wear a queue.

[10]留 聲 機 a phonograph.

留 聲 機 片 phonograph records.

留 落 handed down; relinquished; to leave behind.

留 訣 dying request; parting words.

留 遺 to leave behind; to abandon.

[15]留 遺 命 to leave a will.

留 都 a subordinate capital.

留 音 器 a phonograph.

留 餘 地 to leave some ground— do not press a man too hard.

留 髮 to allow the hair to grow— as a Taoist.

[20]留·點ㄦ火 leave a little fire.

榴[2]
4084   The pomegranate.

榴 彈 shrapnel.

榴 彈 礮 howitzer.

榴 月 the 5th lunar month.

榴 齒 even teeth like the seeds of a pomegranate.

石·榴 the pomegranate.

↑手 榴 彈 hand-grenade.

溜[4]
4085   A current; a stream.

溜 通 to flow through.

滴 溜 to drip.

順 溜 to go with the stream.

(a) Read *liu*[1]. To glide. To prowl. Inter. 遛 No. 4087.

溜 冰 to skate.

溜 打 to go for a stroll.

溜 頭 the end—as of a street.

溜 黑·的 to prowl about at dusk in order to steal, or to mark things for stealing.

(b) Read *liu*[1]. Smooth, glossy.

溜 光 very smooth.

溜 㳰 to flatter.

溜 溜·的 眼 睛 crafty, shifty eyes.

瘤[2]
4086   A tumour, a wen, a swelling.

瘤·子 or 贅 瘤 a tumour.

遛[1,4]
4087   To linger, to dawdle, to saunter. To lead. Inter. 溜 No. 4085—A. Also read *liu*[1,4].

遛·打 遛·打 to ramble, to take a stroll.

遛+馬 to lead a horse up and down.

霤[4]
4088   Dripping of rain from the eaves. To drip

屋 霤 eaves.

飀[2]
4089   Soughing of the wind.

餾[4]
4090   To steam food.

餾 飯 to steam rice.

餾 饌 to steam bread.

駠[2]
4091   A bay horse with a black mane.

鶹[2]
4092   A large horned-owl.

劉[2]
4093   A battle-axe. To kill. To destroy. A surname.

劉 兵 驚 敵 to put soldiers to death as a warning to the enemy.

懰[3]
4094   Lovely.

佼 人 懰 分 How lovely is that lady!

(a) Read *liu*[2]. Melancholy.

懰 慄 melancholy.

瀏[2,3]
4095   Clear, deep water.

瀏 其 清 矣 showing their clear, deep pools.

(a) Sound of wind in the trees.

瀏 莅 the wind in the trees.

(b) Bright and clear.

瀏 亮 clear and bright weather.

鏐[2]
4096   Pure gold.

柳[3]
4097   The willow tree. Pleasure, dissipation, gaiety.

柳 媚 beautiful but not virtuous.

柳 條 willow wand.

柳 條 布 striped cottons.

柳 條 身 a willowy figure.

[5]柳 楊 the willow; the poplar.

柳 眉 arched eyebrows, like a willow-leaf.

柳 絮 willow catkins.

柳 綠 willow green.

柳 腰 a slender, willowy waist.

[10]柳 巷 the willow-lane—brothels.

柳 谷 the valley where the sun sets.

三 春 柳 or 垂 絲 柳 or 檉 (*ch'eng*[1]) 柳 the tamarisk.

絡[3]
4098   A skein of silk. A pocket.

小 絡·子 a cutpurse; pickpocket.

LO.   (ㄌㄛ)

羅[2]
4099   Gauze, a thin kind of silk. Netting. To sift or bolt.

羅 傘 a state silk umbrella carried in procession.

羅 布 netting; gauze used for curtains. *See below* B.2. C.2.

羅 帷 gauze curtains.

羅 帷 孤 冷 in the curtained bed alone and cold—a deserted wife.

[5]羅 星 stars dotted like gauze.

羅 櫃 a frame for bolting flour.

羅 織 to weave; to involve an innocent person in a criminal charge.

羅 襪 silk socks.

羅 麵 to sift or bolt flour.

¹⁰一 疋 羅 a piece of silk gauze.

(a) A net to catch birds.

羅 取 to net; to enclose.

羅 捕 to seize.

羅 掘 or 羅 雀 掘 鼠 to net birds and dig out rats—to contrive ways and means to live when in straits.

羅 網 nets.

大 羅 the canopy of heaven.

(b) To arrange; to spread out.

羅 列 to set out in order.

羅 布 to display; to arrange. *See above—2, below-C.2.*

羅 拜 to surround and kneel before.

羅 致 men of talent coming together.

⁵羅 文 to place the impress of a finger, hand or foot upon a document.

羅 盤 or 羅 經 a compass.

羅 紋 the lines of the hand or face.

羅 經 變 差 variation of the compass. (-ch'a¹)

羅 續 紀 存 to keep a detailed record.

¹⁰羅 羅 清 疏 arranged neatly and in order.

羅 針 the compass-needle.

羅 針 子³午 線 the line of the magnetic needle north and south, as contrasted with the true north and south.

羅 鍋 humpbacked,-as if a round-bottomed cooking-pot had been placed on the back.

(c) Used in transliterating *l* or *r* in foreign words.

羅 刹 *Rakshas*, demons who devour men.

羅 布 Rouble. *See above—2, B.2.*

羅 ○漢 *Lohan* from *Arhan* or *Arhat* —the 500 disciples of Buddha, often used of those who enjoy an easy life.

十 八 羅 漢 the 18 *Lohan*— the personal disciples of Buddha, whose images are

---

seen in temples; two are Chinese, the others are Hindu.

⁵羅 ○漢 台 堦 ○兒 a series of steps decreasing in width.

羅 ○漢 果 the mangosteen.

羅 ○漢 松 the Chinese yew.

羅 ○漢 椅 ·子 an easy chair.

羅 ○漢 牀 a dais for guests.

¹⁰羅 ○漢 錢 a special lot of cash minted during the reign of *K'anghsi*, Manchu Dynasty.

羅 ○漢 頂 a shaven head. ⌈dish.

羅 ○漢 Rome. 羅 ○漢 齋 a mixed vegetable

羅 馬 制 the Roman system.

羅 馬 字 Roman letters; romanization.

¹⁵羅 馬 尼 亞 Roumania.

羅 馬 帝 國 The Roman Empire.

羅 馬 敎 Roman Catholicism.

羅 馬 敎 皇 The Pope of Rome.

羅 馬 數 字 Roman numerals.

²⁰羅 馬 法 Roman law.

↑羅 宋 a Russian. 羅 斯 國 Russia.

(d) Name given to certain independent tribes in West China.

羅 羅 wild independent tribes in W. Szechwan and Yunnan; also a tiger-like fabulous beast; a black tiger.

儸² Smart, clever.
4100

僂 儸 the rank and file of a robber band.

囉² A note in singing. Prattle, chattering.
4101

囉 唆 or 囉¹·裡 囉¹ 唆·的 prosy; complicated; annoying.

囉 嗦 verbose, loquacious.

囉 囉 to grunt.

攞³·⁴ To split, to rend. To choose. To rub, to wipe.
4102

攞 汗 to wipe off the perspiration.

欏 The horse-chestnut.
4103

籮² Deep open baskets without handles or covers. Crates.
4104 A sieve.

羅 圈 circular.

羅 筐 large baskets.

蘿² Creeping plants.
4105

蘿 藤 to entwine.

蘿 萬 creepers of various kinds.

蘿 ·蔔 turnips and similar roots.

白 蘿 ·蔔 white turnips.

紅 蘿 ·蔔 radishes.

蘿 藤 the wistaria. 胡 蘿 蔔 carrots.

邏² To patrol, to make a circuit. To watch.
4106

邏 察 to cruise in search of.

邏 繞 to surround.

邏 輯 transliteration for *logic*.

巡 邏 to go the rounds.

鑼² A gong.
4107

鑼 槌 a stick to beat a gong.

打 鑼 or 鳴 鑼 to beat a gong.

LO   LUO. (ㄌㄛ)

(Lo)

倮³ Naked. See next.
4108

裸│ Naked. To strip; to unclothe.
躶│ Distinguish 裸 No. 3565.
4109

裸 曬 exposed naked to the sun.

裸 葬 buried naked.

裸 蟲 the naked animal—man.

裸 裎 or 裸 身 naked.

裸 體 naked.

摞⁴ To pile up.
4110

摞 起 書 來 pile up the books.

(a) Read *lo²*. To manage; to arrange.

摞 頭 to dress the hair.

螺[2] A spiral univalve shell. A conch. Spiral.
4111

螺·殼 univalve shells in general.
螺·絲 a screw, a spiral.
　　陰·螺·絲 female thread.
　　陽·螺·絲 male thread.
[5] 扁 頭 螺·絲 thumb-screw.
螺·絲 彈 簧 spiral spring.
螺·絲 擺 a screw-driver.
螺·絲 板 (or 搬) a spanner.
螺·絲 樓 梯 a spiral staircase.
[10]螺·絲 蓋 兒 screw-top.
螺·絲 起 重 器 screw-jack.
螺·絲 釘 or 螺 旋 screw-nails.
螺·絲 鋼 板 screw-plate.
螺·絲 鐵 柱 a screw-pile.
[15]螺·絲 鑽 an auger.
螺·絲 鑽 頭 bits for boring holes.
螺·線·的 spiral.
螺 距 the pitch of a thread.
螺 輪 to screw; a propeller.
[20]螺 髻 a spiral head-dress.
田 螺 snails.

騾[2]
贏　A mule, the offspring of an ass and a mare.
4112

騾·子 a mule.
騾 店 inn with accommodation for mules, etc.
騾 綱 a mob of mules.
騾 馬 mules and horses.
[5]騾 馬 以 報 I will be to you as your horse or mule by way of recompense—for your kindness.
騾 馬 車 a cart drawn by mules or horses.
騾 馱 (to[4])·子 a mule's load.
騾 駒 子 a mule colt.
騾 駝 轎 a mule-litter,—kind of sedan supported by mules.

硧[3] Piles of stones.
4113

磊 硧 piled up—eminent.

覼[2] To look about. Order, sequence. Complicated thought
4114 which is not easy to express. Inter. next.

覼 縷 involved; complicated; difficult to express.

覼[2] See preceding.
4115

羸[4] Animals with short hair.
4116

臝[3] Naked.
4117

臝 物 animals with short hair.

蠃[3] The solitary wasp. See 蜾 No. 3734.
4118

蓏[3] Fruit of plants as contrasted with that of trees.
4119

LO.　　(ㄌㄛ)
(Loh)

咯[4.5]. A final particle. Inter. 了 No. 3958.
4120

好·咯 finished.
是·咯 that is so!

(a) Read k'ê. Inter. 咳 No. 3325. To cough.

咯 吱 creaking sound.
咯 血 pulmonary hemorrhage.

洛[4.5] Two tributaries of the Yellow River, rising in
4121 Shensi.

洛 學 or 洛 黨 the school of 程 顥 and 程 頤 in the Sung dynasty; these men were born in Loyang.
洛 書 mystic markings said to have been revealed to Yü the Great, 大 禹, on the back of a tortoise from the River Lo. These marks showed the numerals from one to nine, the accepted diagram shows them in the form of a magic square. See 河 No. 2111-10.
洛 洛 clear water.
洛 陽 ancient name for Honanfu; it was the capital under the Eastern Han dynasty.

洛 陽 紙 貴 paper is dear at Loyang—said in praise of a man's writings, from the story of 左 思 during the 晉 dynasty. He wrote some poetry which others copied to such an extent that the price of paper rose.
洛 陽 花 the white peony.

落[4.5]. To fall, to drop, to let drop. To lose, to scatter.
4122 Scattered. To die. Coll. lao[4].

落·下·來 to drop down; to fall, as leaves. (lao[4]-)
落·了 空 the effort has failed; come to nought. (lao[4]-)
落 井 to fall into a well.
落 井 下 石 to drop stones on a man who has fallen into a well—to take a mean advantage.
[5]落 伍 者 one not fit for the ranks—a useless person.
落 價 the price has fallen.
落 卷 rejected essays. ⎡(lao[4]-)
落·在 地·下 to fall to the ground.
落 地 to fall to the ground—to be born. See below B.1. (lao[4]-)
[10]落 地 稅 local tax on goods which have already paid duty. (lao[4]-)
落 孫 山 後 to come after Sun Shan—he was last on the examination lists—to fail in the examination.
落 定 銀 to pay earnest-money.
落 差 to come off duty. (lao[4]-ch'ai[1])
落 帆 to lower the sail.
[15]落 後 to fall behind; backward.
　　工 業·的 落 後 backward condition of industries.
落·得 領 受 to receive gratuitously or without effort.
落 成 completed—as a building.
落 托 spiritless, disheartened; disconnected: things going badly.
[20]落 拓 unhampered; unrestrained.
落 日 落 月 setting sun or moon.
　　日 落 sunset; daily decreasing.
落 暉 (or 照) the rays of the setting sun.
落 水 to fall into the water; to launch; to become a prostitute.
[25]落 泊 spiritless, disheartened.
落 淚 to weep.
落 漠 (or 寞) quiet, calm, hushed; disordered; discontented.
落 潮 or 落 水 or 退 潮 a falling tide.

落 皮 毛 to get free from this earthly frame. (*Buddhist*)

[30]落 第 to fail in the examinations.

落 籍 to be disenrolled.

落 肚 swallowed.

落 胎 a miscarriage.

落 膽 discouraged; disheartened; terrified.

[35]落 船 tò go aboard a vessel. (*lao⁴-*)

落 色 to lose countenance; to fade in colour.(*lao⁴-shai³*)

落 花 flowers falling.

落 花 生 the ground-nut or peanut.

落 英 fallen flowers.

[40]落 葉 樹 deciduous trees.

落 落 穆 穆 disheartened and dispirited.

落 薄 reduced; decayed; poor.

落 蘇 name for the brinjal or eggplant.

落 墊 貶 to come in for censure.

[45]落 西 山 or 太 陽 落 sunset.(*lao⁴-*)

落 貨 to ship cargo. (*lao⁴-*)

落 貨 單 bill of lading.

落 霜 frosty. (*lao⁴-*)

落 頭 to fall into distress.

[50]落 馬 to fall off a horse.

落 髮 to cut off the hair and become a Buddhist priest or nun.

落 魄 (*t'o⁴*) spiritless; in reduced circumstances. *See above*—19.

家 貧 落 魄 a family whose circumstances have been reduced to poverty.

(a) To enter, as in a book.

落 墨 to begin to write.

落 欸 to write the designation or inscription.

落 筆 to put pen to paper.

落 紙 to put pen to paper.

(b) A dwelling-place. A village.

落 地 a place; a location. *See above*—9.

落 寓 an inn; to rest in an inn.

落 實 to find a solid resting-place; at rest.

下 落 whereabouts; a place of residence.

[5]村 落 a village.

着 落 an arrangement; definite settlement; place of residence; whereabouts. *See No.* 1258—A.12ff.

不 知 着 落 do not know their location.

(c) To stand apart. Unconventional.

落 落 大 方 generous; magnanimous.

落 落 清 可 數 all clearly distinguished, so that it was possible to count them.

落 落 難 合 difficult to bring them together; keeping aloof.

烙 ^4.5. To brand, to burn. To iron. Pron. *lao⁴*.
4123

烙 到 焦 or 烙 焦 了 roasted brown, burnt.

烙 印 to brand; a brand.

烙 慣 seared; cauterized.

烙 煳 了 burnt in cooking, scorched.

[5]烙 紅 了 red-hot.

烙 衣 裳 to iron clothes.

烙 鐵 a branding-iron; a kind of flat-iron.

烙 餅 a wheaten cake baked on a plate; to bake such a cake.

珞 ^4.5. Ornaments for the neck.
4124

珞 瓔 brooches; a necklace.

絡 ^4.5. Unreeled silk; hemp; cotton fibre. A cord. To spin silk, etc.
4125

絡 新 婦 the garden-spider.

絡 絡 絲 hanging in a fringe.

絡 綢 a kind of sarsenet.

絡 絲 (or 緯) 娘 a cricket.

麻 絡 unspun hemp.

(a) To connect; continuous.

絡 繹 不 絕 unbroken; continuous.

綱 絡 古 今 to bind past and present in one.

連 (or 聯) 絡 connected, joined, allied.

(b) Blood-vessels.

脈 絡 greater and lesser blood-vessels.

(c) A halter.

絡 馬 頭 a halter; to halter a horse.

(d) Fibrous covering of seeds, as cotton, loofah, etc.

酪 ^4.5. Cream; cheese; koumiss.
4126 Pron. *lao⁴*.

酪 漿 butter-milk; whey.

酪 餅 cheese.

杏 酪 almond tea or gruel.

駱 ^4.5. The camel. White horse with a black mane.
4127

駱 駝 a camel.

駱 駝 絨 camel's hair.

雒 ^4.5. Black horse with white mane. Inter. 洛 No. 4121.
4128 A river in Honan. To read.

雒 誦 to read—as a letter.

雒 雒 然 fearful and trembling.

樂 ^4.5. Happy, pleased. To laugh. Joy. Pron. *lê⁴*.
4129

樂 不 可 支 insupportable joy.

樂 不 可 極 pleasure should not be pursued to its limit.

樂 不 可 言 inexpressible pleasure or joy.

樂 主 發 散 在 外 *lo* indicates the outward manifestation.

[5]樂 之 所 由 生 the source of pleasure.

樂 事 pleasures; joys.

樂 人 之 樂 to rejoice with those who rejoice.

樂 何 如 之 What pleasure can be equal to this?

樂 利 pleasure and profit.

[10]樂 則 樂 矣 be happy while you may!

樂 只 君 子 ³ let the princes be rejoiced in.

樂 善 pleased to do good.

樂 園 the garden of pleasure—Paradise.

樂 土 a place free from sorrow.

[15]樂 境 joys; pleasures.

樂 天 主 義 optimism.

樂 天 知 命 to accord with the decree of Heaven.

樂 幸 well-pleased.

樂 得 gratified; to have the luck to.

²⁰樂 得²的 or 樂 得²乎 How lucky! Just the thing!

樂 從 very pleased to do so.

樂 心 contented; happy.

樂 意 willingly; gladly; cheerfully.

樂 施 bounteous to those in distress.

²⁵樂 易 pleasure and ease—easy-going.

樂 是 苦 源 pleasure is the fountain of sorrow.

樂 業 content with one's lot.

樂 極 生 悲 extreme joy gives rise to sadness.

樂 歲 prosperous years.

³⁰樂 禍 to take pleasure in the calamities of others.

樂 而 不 淫 pleasure without licentiousness.

樂 聞 to show willingness.

樂 育 to lead; to instruct.

樂 處 pleasures; joys.

³⁵樂 觀 optimistic view.

樂 觀 主 義 optimism.

樂 觀 家 optimists.

樂 輸 voluntary contributions.

作 樂 to make merry.

⁴⁰何 樂 之 有 What pleasure is there in it?

取 樂 to seek amusement.

淫 樂 carnal pleasure; sensuality.

(a) Read yüeh⁴·⁵. **Music.**

樂 之 卒 章 the last part of the musical service.

樂 云 樂 云 鐘 鼓 云 乎 哉 they say music! music! Does music consist of bells and drums?

樂 亭 a bandstand.

樂 人 a musician.

⁵樂 典 treatise on music.

樂 則 韶 舞 let the music be the shao with its dancing.

樂 器 or 樂 具 musical instruments.

樂 工 奏 曲 the musicians performed.

樂 府 collection of tunes.

¹⁰樂 戶 singing-girls—wives of those whose estates were confiscated.

樂 歌 music and singing—as a course in schools.

樂 理 theory of music.

樂 生 musicians.

樂 曲 a tune; musical composition.

¹⁵樂 表 the staff in notation.

樂 譜 book of tunes.

樂 部 Board of Music—a department of the former Board of Rites.

樂 音 music; tunes.

作 樂 to play music.

²⁰奏 樂 to perform, to play music.

(b) Read yao⁴. **To take pleasure in.** Now pron. lê⁴·⁵ except B4, 5.

樂 節 禮 樂 (yüeh⁴·⁵) to enjoy the study of the various ceremonies and music.

樂 羣 fond of those of his own class.

樂 道 人 之 善 to enjoy speaking of the goodness of others.

仁 者 樂 山 the good find pleasure in the hills—for quiet retirement.

知 者 樂 水 the wise find pleasure in streams—to watch their movement, etc.

濼 ⁴·⁵.
4130
A river in Shantung.

犖 ⁴·⁵. A brindled ox. Manifest. Open.
4131

犖 犖 clearly; evident.

卓 犖 不 羣 eminent; above the average.

LO LUO. (ㄌㄛ)
(Loh)

寽 ⁴·⁵. A handful; a pinch. Also read lieh.
4132

埒 ⁴·⁵. An enclosure. An embankment. A dike.
4133

馬 埒 an enclosure for horses; a racecourse.

(a) Alike; of one kind.

才 相 等 埒 their abilities were much alike.

捋 ⁴·⁵. To pluck; to gather in the fingers; to rub. To scrape off.
4134

捋 乾 淸 to clean up—as rubbish with a shovel.

捋 取 to take by force or fraud.

捋 奶 to milk—as a cow.

捋 膏 to scrape off the fat.

⁵捋 起 袖·子 to turn up the sleeves.

捋 采 to pluck.

捋 鑊 to scrape a boiler or pan.

捋 鬚 to stroke the beard.

酹 ⁴·⁵. To pour out a libation. To sprinkle. Also read lai⁴.
4135

酹 花 to water flowers.

酹 奠 to pour out a libation.

LOU. (ㄌㄡ)
(Leo)

婁 ² To wear. A constellation. A surname.
4136

離 婁 a man mentioned by Mencius,—he was of the period of Huang Ti, and could see a hair at a hundred paces.

(a) Read lü³. **To tether.**

牛 馬 維 婁 the oxen and horses were tethered.

(b) Read lü². **To trail along. To wear.**

弗 曳 弗 婁 you will not wear them.

(c) Read lü³. **Frequently. Inter.** 屢 No. 4288.

婁 遭 凶 爸 frequently met with great calamities.

(d) Read lou⁴. **Annoying.**

婁 驕 troublesome and proud.

僂 ² Hunchback, bent, deformed. Also read lü³.
4137

僂 偏 misshapen.

僂 儸 the rank and file of a band of robbers.

僂 兵 brigands; soldiers in ambush.

(a) Read lü⁴. **To bend.**

僂 指 to count by bending down the fingers.

劃[2] 4138 To carve; to hollow out.

嘍[2] 4139 To chatter. To mutter.

嘍 啒 twittering of birds.

塿[3] 4140 A small mound. A tumulus.

嶁[3] 4141 A mountain in Hunan, associated with the memorial tablet to *Yü* the Great 大禹.

岣 嶁 山 a peak of the *Hêng shan* in Hunan, as above.

摟[3] 4142 To drag, to pull. To embrace, to hug.

摟·住 to hold in the arms.
摟 抱 to embrace; to put the arms round a person's neck.
摟 挽 to detain.
摟 處 女 to elope; to carry off a virgin.
摟 衣·裳 to hold up the skirts.

樓[2] 4143 An upper storey; a tower; a two-storied house.

樓·上 upstairs.
樓 上 樓 storey above storey; many-storied.
樓 下 ground-floor; downstairs.
樓 廂 a gallery.
[5]樓 房 an upper storey; a loft.
樓 月 the moon seen from an upstairs window.
樓 板 flooring to an upper storey.
樓 梯 a staircase.
樓 櫓 a look-out turret without a roof.
[10]樓 窻 a staircase window.
樓 臺 a stage for theatricals; a gallery.
樓 車 a chariot with a turret.
城 樓 tower over a city gate.
望 樓 a look-out.
[15]牌·樓 honorary arch or portal.
玉 樓 the shoulders.

茶 樓 a tea-house.
青 樓 a brothel.
酒 樓 a wine-shop; a restaurant.

簍[3] 4144 A hamper. a basket.

簍·子 a basket; a crate.
油 簍 wicker oil-baskets.

耬[2] 4145 A kind of drill for sowing grain.

蔞[2] 4146 A kind of artemisia; the young leaves are eaten. Also read *lü*[2].

蔞 蒿 southernwood.

螻[2] 4147 The mole-cricket.

螻 蛄 a mole-cricket.
螻 蟈 a small green frog.
螻 蟻 mole-crickets; ants.

鏤[4] 4148 To engrave; to chase; to carve.

鏤 刻 or 雕 鏤 to carve or engrave.
鏤 心 engraved on the heart.
鏤 板 to cut a block for printing.
鏤 空·的 花 兒 fret-work.
鏤 花 elegant style; ornamental engravings.
(a) Hard steel; a boiler.

髏[2] 4149 A skull.

髏 骨 or 髑 髏 a skull.

囡[4] 4150 To retire into obscurity.

陋[4] 4151 Vile, low. Rude, rustic, vulgar.

陋 儒 illiterate pretender to scholarship.
陋 劣 vile, detestable, sordid.
陋 巷 a mean alley.
陋 室 a humble house.
[5]陋 淺 mean, low, humble.
陋 習 low practices.
陋 規 bribes, illegalities in taking fees.
陋 識 vulgar outlook and experience.

漏[4] 4152 To leak, to drip. To disclose, to leak out. To smuggle. A funnel.

漏·下 or 失 漏 to leave out; to lose track of.
漏·出·來 to leak out.
漏 勺 a strainer, a colander.
漏 包 a vessel for straining.
[5]漏 去 一 字 a character is left out.
漏 報 to evade declaration of dutiable goods.
漏 夜 or 夜 漏 by night.
漏·子 or 漏 斗 a funnel for liquids.
漏 天 to leak, as a roof; open to the sky.
[10]漏 屋 a leaking house.
漏 底 to betray one's antecedents; to lose caste.
漏 卮 a falling off; to run to waste; a syphon.
漏 數 left out; omitted, as in an account.
漏 斗 形 funnel-shaped.
[15]漏 泄 leakage.
漏 現 to disclose; to become apparent.
漏 症 an issue of blood.
漏 瘡 fistula.
偏 漏 fistula *in ano*.
[20]漏 稅 to lose revenue through smuggling.
漏 空 to reveal a weak spot.
漏 網 to escape the net—evade punishment.
漏 縫 (*fêng*[4]) to open—as a joint or seam; to lose; to slip through the fingers.
漏 脯 putrid meat.
[25]漏 規 losses—as of money; defalcations.
漏 風 to leak out, as a secret.
漏 鼓 to announce the watches,—from the custom of using the clepsydra 更 漏.
不 漏 氣 air-tight.
屋 漏 a skylight.
[30]洩 漏 to divulge.
補 漏 to repair a leak.

LU.   (ㄌ)

鹵 [3] Natural salt. Rock-salt. Alkaline soil. Radical 197.
4153

鹵 地 salt-land.
鹵 斫 a mattock.
鹵 餅 a steamed wheaten cake.
鹵 鹹 salt; nitrous.
鹵 鹽 natural salt.

(a) Inter. 魯 No. 4176. Rude, common, vulgar; dull.

鹵 莽 careless—as in writing.
鹵 莽 rash, careless; abrupt, rude.
鹵 莽 滅 裂 careless and haphazard in one's undertakings—as a farmer in sowing and weeding.
頑 鹵 dull and stupid.

(b) Inter. 櫓 No. 4178. A large shield.

鹵 簿 insignia of the emperor—various explanations are given, the most likely being that the 鹵 or large shield was first on the list, 簿, of articles carried when on tour.
流 血 漂 鹵 blood flowed so as to float the shields.

(c) Inter. 擄 No. 4175. To carry captive.

鹵 掠 to capture; to plunder and carry away captive.

摅 [1] To strip off; to wipe, to rub. Similar to 攦 No. 4102.
4154

摅 汗 to wipe off perspiration.
摅 樹 皮 to peel off the bark.

(a) Read *lu*[3]. Violent, aggressive. To sway.

滷 [3] Salt, alkaline soil. Salt, bitter. Brine.
4155 Inter. 鹵 No. 4153.

滷 水 lye used in making beancurd.
滷 湯·子 lye.
滷 蝦 salted shrimps.
滷 鷄 salted fowl.

(a) Thick gravy.

滷·子 thick gravy.

滷 豢 肉 stewed meat with thick gravy.
滷 麵 vermicelli served with thick gravy.

盧 [2] Black. This character carries many meanings and is interchanged with several having a different radical,—see below.
4156

盧 弓 a black bow.
呼 盧 to call *lu,* i.e., black—five blacks being the best throw in dice.

(a) A vessel for holding cooked rice.

(b) A hound. Inter. 獹 No. 4161.

(c) A brazier. Inter. 爐 No. 4160.

(d) A wine-shop. Inter. 壚 No. 4157—A.

(e) The pupil of the eye. Inter. 矑 No. 4163.

(f) Used for transliterating.

盧 布 Rouble.   [(onomatopoeic)].
盧 胡 而 笑 laughter in the throat
盧 梭 Rousseau.
盧 比 rupee.

壚 [2] Stiff black clods of earth.
4157

黃 壚 yellow clay—the grave.

(a) A shop. A hut.

壚 邸 a wine-shop.
草 壚 my cottage.
酒 壚 a wine-shop.

(b) A stove.

茶 壚 烟 起 the smoke rises from the tea-stove.

廬 [2] A thatched hut; a booth, a hovel. To pass the night.
4158 Inter. preceding—A. Also read *lü*[2].

廬 墓 to dwell in a hut by the grave of a parent.
廬 帳 a tent.
廬 舍 or 廬 房 a cottage; a hut.

廬 落 a tent.
清 廬 a Buddhist monastery.

瀘 [2] River in Kiangsi, also in Szechwan.
4159

瀘 水 tributary of the Yangtze.

爐 **炉** [2] A stove, a fireplace. A censer, a brazier. Inter. 鑪 No. 4170.
4160

爐 坑 a brick-bed or *k'ang* heated by a stove.
爐·子 a stove.
爐 房 a mint, government assay shop.
爐 格·子 or 爐 柵 grate of a stove.
[5] 爐 條 fire-bars, grate of a stove.
爐 灰 ashes from a stove.
爐 瓶 a censer.
爐 籠 a cooking-range.
爐 齒 grate for a stove.
[10] 手 爐 or 脚 爐 a hand- or foot-stove, containing charcoal covered with ashes.
煤 氣 爐 a gas-stove.
茶 爐 small stove for heating water to make tea.
電 爐·子 electric stove.
風 爐 a small portable fire-pot for cooking.

獹 [2] A hound.
4161

瓤 [2] A gourd.
4162

壺 瓤 the bottle-gourd; a jar shaped like a bottle-gourd.

矑 [2] The pupil of the eye. To see.
4163

纑 [2] Hempen thread. To dress flax or hemp for weaving.
4164

罏 [2] A squat, wide-mouthed jar, used for wine.
4165

膚² 4166 The skin; the belly.

膚脹 dropsy.

(a) To arrange in order; to state; to intimate to.

膚列 to state *seriatim;* to set out in order.

膚句 messages—from a superior are called *lu,* and from an inferior are called *chü.*

膚敍 to narrate in detail.

膚歡萬姓 to cause rejoicing among the masses.

⁵膚陳 to state; to arrange.

傳膚 or 膚唱 to carry a message; title formerly given to candidates who graduated at the head of the 2nd class *Hanlin* examinations.

艫² 4167 The stem of a boat; prow of a ship.

蘆² 4168 Rushes, reeds.

蘆柴 rush faggots.

蘆田 sandy fields where reeds grow.   [asparagus.

蘆筍 edible shoots of young reeds;

蘆管 reed-pipe or whistle of the Tartars.

⁵蘆粟 the sweet sorghum.

蘆荻 a kind of reed.

蘆蓆 coarse rush mats.

蘆葦 reeds.

蘆薈 aloes.

¹⁰蘆衣 rushes for clothing—unable to give warmth.

蘆課 taxes on reed lands along the banks of a river.

轤² 4169 A windlass; a pulley.

鑪² 4170 A brazier; a hand-stove; a stove. u.f. 爐 No. 4160.

鑪鼎 a tripod used in temples.

顱 } 髗 } ² 4171 The skull; the forehead.

顱頂骨 parietal bones.

顱頭 a skull.

頭顱 the pate.

鱸² 4172 The sea-perch.

鸕² 4173 The fishing cormorant.

鸕鷀 the fishing cormorant.

嚕³ 4174 Cry used in calling pigs. Also read *lo¹.*

擄 } 虜 } ³ 4175 To take captive; to seize. A prisoner; a slave. Also read *lo³, lou³.* Distinguish 攎 No. 5858.

擄人勒贖 to hold captives for ransom.

擄刦 to rob.

擄勒 to extort.

擄掠 to take captive; to plunder.

擄禁 to carry off and keep prisoner.

(a) To tuck up.

擄·起袖·子 to roll up the sleeves.

魯³ 4176 Stupid, common, vulgar.

魯朴 stupid, unlettered.

魯鈍 or 魯惘 or 魯莽 dull of understanding.

粗魯 coarse, rude, rough-mannered.

(a) Name of the State in which Confucius was born. Now u.f. Shantung.

魯一變至於道 the State of *Lu* by one change would become a country of true principles.

魯人爲長府 some men of *Lu* were about to rebuild the *Ch'ang* treasury.

魯班 *Lu Pan,* a man of the above State, now deified as the god of carpenters, etc.

魯魚亥豕 clerical or typographical errors—these characters being easily confused.

嚕³ 4177 Speech. To flatter. To pout.

櫓 } 艣 } 艫 } 㯭 } ³ 4178 A lookout turret on a city wall. Moveable wooden tower for archers. A scull. a sweep, an oar.

櫓棒 the pivot for a scull.

搖櫓 to work the sculls of a Chinese boat.

氌³ 4179 Rough serge made from yak's hair. Also read *lo³.*

賂⁴ 4180 To give a present; to bribe.

賄賂 bribes.

路⁴ 4181 A road, a path, a way. A journey.

路·上 on a journey; on the road.

路不通行 no thoroughfare.

路人 or 陌路人 a stranger.

路兵 patrols.

⁵路口 the entrance to a road or street.

路室 an inn.

路徑 a short cut; roads.

路截 or 截路 to be intercepted; a highwayman.

路斃 or 路倒³ to die by the roadside—as a tramp.

¹⁰路次 on the road; by the way.

路死路埋 may you die and be buried by the roadside—a curse.

路滑 the road is slippery.

路燈 street-lamps.

路爛 a muddy road; the road is muddy.

15路 癩 a bad road; the road is bad.

路 祭 a sacrifice by the way, before a funeral.

路 票 a waybill; passport.

路 科 Department of Civil Engineering.

路 程 a road; a journey.

20路 程 單·子 a list of places, traveller's guide; itinerary.

路 線 a line, as of railroad.

路 費 travelling expenses.

路 過 to pass by or through a place *en route*.

一 路 平 安 May you enjoy peace all the way! Bon voyage!

25十 字 路 cross-roads.

小 路 a byway; a path.

引 路 a guide.

旱 路 roadways.

死 路 dangerous ways; dead end.

30水 路 waterways.

生 路 a means of livelihood.

門·路 a trade; a way of life; clue.

趕 路 to hasten on.

(a) A chariot.

路 車 ancient chariot.

(b) Great. Loud.

路 寢 孔 碩 vast rose the great inner chambers.

路 門 the innermost door of an ancient palace.

厥 聲 載 路 his voice was loud.

(c) Used in transliterating.

路 透 電 Reuter's telegrams.

瞈 4 Used for sounds only.
4182

潞 4 Name of a river in Shansi, and another in Yunnan.
4183

璐 4 Beautiful variety of jade.
4184

鏴 4 To plug a hole.
4185

鋼 鏴 to mend a crack or a hole with molten metal.

露 4 Dew.
4186

露 宿 風 餐 to sleep on the dew and sup the wind—hardships of travel; homeless; miserably poor.

露·水 dew, scent.

花 露 水 scents.

露·水 珠 dewdrops.

5露 電 dew and lightning—transient.

露 點 dew-point.

寒 露 Cold Dew—a solar term, about October 8—22.

甘 露 sweet dew—favours.

白 露 White Dew, a solar term, about September 8—22.

10間 露 transient.

(a) Read *lou*4 in 2, 3, 4, 23; *lu*4 or *lou*4 in 15, 17, 20, 21, 22; *lu*4 in others. To disclose. To expose.

露 井 an open well.

露·出·來 to disclose; to reveal.

露·出 破 綻 revealed the open seams—the matter is divulged.

露·出 馬 脚 the horse's hoof shows—the plot is out.

5露 天 open to the sky; out at elbows.

露 天 大 會 an open-air meeting.

露 天 學 校 open-air school.

露 布 to proclaim victory; a manifesto; to display, to exhibit; an unsealed letter.

露 形 to show the real form.

10露 次 in the open.

露 營 open-air camp for troops.

露 田 open fields with no trees.

露 相 (*hsiang*4) to show by the facial expression.

露 積 ricks of grain in the open air.

15露 胸 to expose the bosom.

露 脊 鯨 the whale.

露 臂 to bare the arm.

露 臺 a drying stage, open to the air.

露 車 an uncovered cart.

20露 面 to appear in public; to take the lead; to be forward.

不 敢 露 面 dare not show one's face; or, dare not appear in the matter.

露 頭 to show the head; to appear—as the sun over the horizon; prominent; a mineral outcrop.

露 風 divulged; known.

露 骨 emaciated, showing the bones; the bones of the dead when unburied; undisguised.

25露 體 出 醜 shamefully exposed.

露 體 受 辱 naked and disgraced, suffering.

露 齒 prominent teeth.

敗 露 spoiled, ruined—as by secrets leaking out.

鷺 4 An egret, a paddy-bird.
4187

鷺 序 in order, in a line, like paddy-birds.

鷺·鷥 or 白 鷺 the eastern egret.

鷺·鷥 毛 egret feathers.

輅 4 A chariot; a state carriage.
4188

LU. (ㄌㄨ)
(Luh)

六 4.5. Six. Usually pron. *liu*4.
4189

六 六 thirty-six; double-six.

六 出 花 six-petalled flowers—snowflakes.

六 十 sixty.

六 十 花 甲 the sexagenary cycle.

5六 合 the six points—north, east, south, west, the zenith and the nadir,—everywhere; the universe.

六 呂 the six lower pitch-pipes of ancient music.

六 國 the six States which combined to overthrow the State of Ch'in 秦, 240 B.C.

六 塵 the six worldly environments:—form, sound, smell, taste, touch, and perception of character, 色, 聲, 香, 味, 觸, 法.

六 尺 之 孤 a young orphan-prince.

10六 律 the six upper musical pitch-pipes of ancient music.

六 德 the six virtues—wisdom 智, benevolence 仁, sincerity 信, righteousness 義, moderation 中, and harmony 和.

六書 the six classes into which Chinese characters are divided.
象形 No. 2568-A.6,
指事 No. 959-A.1,
會意 No. 2345-B.5,
諧聲 No. 2546-9,
假借 No. 599-5,
轉注 No. 1431-34.
六根 the six roots of sensation— eye, ear, nose, tongue, body and mind. (*Budd.*).
六根不全 defective in person.
[15]六氣 the six influences of the *Yin* 陰, and *Yang* 陽:—cold 寒, heat 暑, drought 燥, moisture 濕, wind 風, and fire 火. Also *Yin* 陰, and *Yang* 陽, (which do not change), wind 風, rain 雨, darkness 晦, and light 明.
六爻 the six lines of the hexagrams, 重卦, formed from the diagrams 八卦.
六畜 the six domestic animals, horse, ox, goat, pig, dog and fowl.
六(百)零六 salvarsan.
六藝 the six arts—propriety 禮, music 樂, archery 射, charioteering 御, writing 書, and mathematics 數.
[20]六行 the six obligations of conduct—filial piety 孝, friendship 友, kindness 睦, love of kin 婣, endurance on behalf of others 任, and charity 恤.
六親 the six relationships—parents, brothers, wife and child.
六言六蔽 the six words with the six becloudings in them.
六道 the six paths of metempsychosis—*devas* 天, man 人, *asuras* 修羅, beasts 畜生, hungry ghosts 餓鬼, and hell 地獄.
六部 the six boards which were abolished after the revolution of 1911—Civil Office 吏部, Rites 禮部, Revenue 戶部, War 兵部, Punishments 刑部, and Works 工部.
[25]六院 imperial harems.
六面形 or 六角形 hexagonal.
六面體 a hexagon.

奎 [4.5.]
4190   A clod of earth; land.

陸 [4.5.]
4191   Six, in documents or accounts to prevent forgery. Dry land.
Distinguish 陵 No. 4067.

陸兵 land forces.
陸地 dry land.
陸戰 land operations in war.
陸棲 creatures that live on dry land.
[5]陸沉 engulfed, swallowed up—as a nation.
陸海 an elevated, fruitful spot—as productive as the sea
陸產 productions of the dry land.
陸田 dry fields, as opposed to paddy fields.
陸行 to travel by land.
[10]陸路 by road; a land journey.
陸路礮 field-guns.
陸軍 the army.
陸軍刑律 military criminal law.
陸軍部長 minister of war.
[15]陸軍軍長 commander-in-chief.
陸軍部 ministry of war.
陸運 to forward by road.
陸風 land winds.
↑陸戰隊 marine corps.
(a) Continuous.
陸續 in succession.
陸續就獲 they were arrested one after the other.
陸續有來 coming one after the other.
陸陸 continuous.
陸離 in confusion.

彔 [4.5.]
4192   To carve wood.

睩 [4.5.]
4193   Indistinct nasal utterance.

睩睩 to mumble: to mutter.

淥 [4.5.]
4194   Tributary of the River *Hsiang* in Hunan. To drip; to strain.
氯[4194b] chlorine. A.w. 綠.

碌 [4.5.]
4195   Green jasper. Rough, uneven. Laborious, toilsome.

碌碌 rough; irregular.
碌碌塵土 to toil along in the world.
碌碌庸人 a man with no ability.
碌碌無奇 commonplace.

祿 [4.5.]
4196   A favour or gift. Happiness; prosperity. Official pay; salary.

祿位 salary and rank.
祿命 a man's lot of happiness.
祿足以代其耕也 emolument equal to what they would have got by cultivating the land.
祿食 emoluments.
俸祿 official salary.

綠 [4.5.]
4197   Green. Chlorine. Usually read *lü*[4].
Distinguish 緣 No. 7741.

綠化 chlorides; any character indicating the nature of the compound may be added.
綠化鈉 sodium chloride.
綠化銀 chloride of silver.
綠寶石 emerald.
[5]綠林客 men of the greenwood —brigands.
綠毛龜 the moss-terrapin.
綠氣 chlorine gas.
綠水 chlorine water.
綠沸銅 malachite.
[10]綠營 former name for certain military camps of Chinese, as distinguished from Manchu, troops.
綠玉 beryl; emerald.
綠瑪瑙 chalcedony.
綠礬 copperas, sulphate of iron.
綠篔 green bamboos.
[15]綠耳 a famous horse, one of *Mu Wang's* steeds.
綠膏 a sap-green dyestuff.
綠膠 a green dye.
綠茶 green tea. ＝青茶.
綠荷 the green of lotus leaves.
[20]綠豆 green lentils.
綠豆蠅 large blue-bottle flies.
綠車 ancient name for the carriage of the heir-apparent.
綠輀 a green sedan-chair only used by high officials.
綠野 grassy plains.
[25]綠陰 green shade of trees.
綠雲 dark clouds—said of the abundant hair of a beauty.
綠青 malachite.
綠頭巾 green-turbaned—a cuckold.
綠頭鴨 the mallard-duck.
[30]墨綠 very dark green.
瓜皮綠 melon green.
碧綠 a bright green.
青綠 grass green.

蓫 4.5. A kind of lentil. Green. A reed. Also read *lü*⁴·⁵.
4198

蓫竹猗猗 How fresh and bright are the green bamboos!
蓫 萓 芽 lentil sprouts used as a vegetable.
蓫穀 or 六穀 maize.

遼 4.5. To go carefully. To advance.
4199

錄 4.5. To record; to make an entry.
4200

錄 三 次 recorded three times—of a deserving official.
錄 事 to detail an affair; to narrate; to record; a recorder.
錄 供 to take down evidence.
錄 呈 to forward a copy to a superior.
⁵錄 囚 徒 to revise a sentence against a criminal.
錄 案 to draw up a formal statement of a case.
錄 籍 one's native place; the district in which a person is registered.
錄 詩 一 首 to copy a verse of a poem.
錄 請 to send a copy with request.
¹⁰錄 送 to send a copy of.
錄 錄 ordinary; like the generality.
抄 錄 to make a copy of.
目·錄 an index; table of contents.
記°錄 recorded.
附 錄 appendix.

(a) To choose.
錄 用 to select for appointment
取 錄 to select for a degree.

籙 4.5. A map, a chart. Memorandum; a list.
4201

籙 璽 a signet, a seal.

騄 4.5. Name of one of *Mu Wang's* steeds.
4202

鹿 4.5. A deer, a stag. Radical 198.
4203

鹿 尾 deer's tail—a precious delicacy.
鹿 死 不 擇 音 (== 陰) a stricken deer does not select its retreat. *See* 擇 No. 276-13.
鹿 死 誰 手 at whose hand did the deer die?—after all who got it?
鹿 王 the deer-king.—*Shakyâmuni*, as he was supposed to have been a deer in a former life.
⁵鹿 筋 deer's sinews.
鹿 茸 deer's antlers.
鹿 角 deer's horns.
鹿 豕 rustic, vulgar, unlettered.
鹿 車 a small, narrow carriage.
¹⁰鹿 鳥 the cassowary.
家 鹿 the rat.
↓逐 鹿 to chase after the deer — to fight for the palm, the sovereignty.
牝 鹿 a doe.

漉 4.5. To strain liquids. Inter. 漊 No. 4194.
4204

簏 4.5. A box, a basket.
4205

筐 簏 a crate or hamper.

轆 **槤** 4.5. A pulley, a windlass, a wheel, a block.
4206

轆 轆 rumbling of wheels.
轆 轤 a windlass or pulley.
轆 轤 轉 to revolve; repetition.

麓 4.5. The foot of a hill.
4207

僇 4.5. To despise, to treat with contempt. u.f. 戮 No. 4210.
4208

勠 4.5. To unite; u.f. next.
4209

勠 力 to join forces.

戮 4.5. To kill in war, to massacre. To disgrace. Distinguish 戳 No. 1283.
4210

戮 人 於 社 to put people to death at the altars.
戮 尸 梟 示 to behead a corpse and expose the head.
戮 民 to oppress the people.
戮 誅 or 戮 殺 to massacre

LUAN. (ㄌㄨㄢ)

孿 ¹ To tie together. To manage.
4211

圝 ² Round, spherical.
4212

團 圝 circular, spherical.

孿 ² To bear twins. Also read *shuan*⁴.
4213

孿·子 or 孿 伴 兒 twins.
孿·生 to bear twins; twins.(*shuan*⁴·)

巒 ² Mountain peaks.
4214

欒 ² Name of a small tree called 欒 華; said to have yellow flowers.
4215

朱 欒 the pumelo.

(a) The two corners at the mouth of a Chinese bell.
鐘 口 兩 角 爲 欒 the two corners at the mouth of a bell are called *luan*.
兩 欒 謂 之 銑 the two corners are called *sien. See* No. 2706-A.

(b) Emaciated appearance.
棘 人 欒 欒 兮 the sincere mourner—keen to observe all the rites—has worn himself thin.

灤 ² To drip.
4216

灤 河 River in Chihli. (Hopei.)
灤 州 a district at the mouth of that river.

鑾 ² Bells hung on the imperial chariot. A carriage. Imperial, a term of respect.
4217

鑾 鈴 tinkling bells.

變駕 or 玉變 the imperial chariot.

恭迓變輿 I respectfully await your chariot — conventional phrase in invitations.

鸞² A fabulous bird. Bells supposed to give the same note as this bird.
4218

鸞箋鳳束 marriage papers of bride and bridegroom.

鸞聲將將 sound of tinkling bells.

鸞鳳 female and male—sexual relations.

鸞鳳和鳴 female and male in harmony—of marriage.

鸞鷄 the argus pheasant.

卵³ An egg. The roe of fishes. Testicles. Also read *luo³*.
4219

卵·子 the testes; an egg.

卵形 ovate.

卵巢 ovaries.

卵生 produced from an egg.

⁵卵白 albumen.

卵翼 to brood, to cherish.

卵育 to brood.

卵袋 the ovisac; the scrotum.

亂⁴ } Disorderly; reckless. Rebellion. To confuse.
乱 }
4220

↓亂·起·來 got into trouble.

亂世 times of anarchy and disorder.

亂·七八蹧 in confusion; topsy-turvy.

亂來 to act capriciously.

⁵亂倫 incest.

亂命 the confused orders of a dying man, as in 結 No. 782-A.36, where the son preferred to regard his father's wish to have the concubine buried with him, as such an order.

亂嚷 to clamour; hubbub.

亂坐 to sit without regard to precedence.

亂如麻 like tangled hemp.

¹⁰亂·子 a disturbance.

亂定之後 after the riot was settled.

亂性 injurious to the disposition.

亂戰 trembling and upset.

亂招胡攀 to give evidence wildly and implicate others.

¹⁵亂搞 in disorder; disorderly conditions; to pound carelessly.

亂政 misgovernment.

亂戮 to intrude upon rudely.

亂機 occasion of disorder.

亂殺 ruthless and reckless slaughter.

²⁰亂民 a disorderly mob; rebels.

亂流 flowing irregularly—as when a river changes its course.

亂用 to use recklessly.

亂眞 it rivals the reality—of a good imitation of nature, as in a picture, etc.

亂石 rocks scattered about.

²⁵亂絲頭 ravelled silk.

亂線 ravelled thread.

亂臣賊子 rebellious statesman and bad son. *See below* A.3.

亂萌 incipient rebellion.

亂言 wild talk; to talk wildly.

³⁰亂說 to speak foolishly.

亂謀 seditious plots.

亂走 running away in disorder.

亂跑 to run all over the place; to play truant.

亂道 foolish or disorderly talk; to injure morals.

³⁵亂邦不居 he will not dwell in a country where disorder prevails.

亂階 origin of trouble, calamity or disorders.

亂隊伍 to break rank.

亂雜 or 雜亂 confused, disorderly.

亂頭緒 tangled, without a clue.

⁴⁰亂黨 reactionaries; rebels; anarchists.

作亂 to create a disturbance.

心亂 disturbed in mind.

擾亂 turmoil; riot.

紛亂 disorder and confusion.

↑搞亂 to spoil; to play a trick.

(a) To bring about order. To govern.

亂而敬 having capacity to rule and yet reverent.

亂越我家 to secure the good government of our State.

予有亂臣十人 I have ten able ministers; 亂 said to have been written 紒 an ancient form of 治 to rule. *See above*—27.

(b) The finale of a musical performance.

關雎之亂 the finish of the performance of the *Kuan chü*.

(c) A ferry.

亂于河 ferried over the river.

涉渭爲亂 crossed the River *Wei* by means of the ferry.

LEI   LUI   (ㄌㄟ)
(Lui)

累²·³· To tie, to bind. To accumulate.
4221

累世勳舊 enduring merit, extending through several generations.

累仁 to accumulate goodness by works of merit.

累卵 a pile of eggs—hazardous.

累宵 night after night.

⁵累德 to accumulate virtue.

累戰皆捷 victorious in successive battles.

累次 repeatedly.

累日 for many days.

累時 for a long time.

¹⁰累月經年 month after month and year after year.

累石 to pile up stones.

累積 or 積累 to accumulate.

(a) Read *lei⁴* To implicate, to involve, to embarrass. Verbose. tiresome. Tired, weary.

累·了 tired.

累事 an embarrassing affair.

累人 to tire one; fatiguing.

累人物 embarrassments—wife and family.

⁵累及人 to implicate others.

累及無辜 to involve the innocent.

累墜 troublesome; unmanageable; difficult.

累墮 embarrassed; harassing; annoying.

累·得·慌 very tired; overburdened.

¹⁰累心 bothering; troublesome.

累步 I have troubled you to accompany me.

累病·了 ill with overwork.

累·著 to embarrass.

累贅 verbose; repetition; tiresome.

[15]累 重 heavy embarrassment—wife and family.

累 雜·的 事 multifarious affairs and bothers.

受 累 to suffer hardship; involved in.

帶·累 to implicate; to involve.

拖 累 to involve.

[20]掛 累 anxieties.

賠 累 to suffer loss.

連 累 to implicate; implications.

嫘[2]
4222

A surname.

瘰[3]
4223

Scrofula, swellings.

瘰 癧 scrofulous swellings.

縲[2]
4224

To bind; a bond.

縲 紲 之 中 in bonds.

磊 }[3]
礌 }
4225

A heap of stones. Boulders.

磊 塊 lumpy, uneven ground; a grievance; uneven—as writings that are not in good style.

以 寫 其 磊 塊 in order to vent his spleen.

磊 磊 plenty of rocks and stones; to roll round.

磊 磊 堆 堆·的 lumpy, confused —stupid person.

[5]磊 磊 落 落 clear and distinct; intelligent.

磊 落 confused; numerous; also, open-hearted.

畾[2]
4226

Fields divided by dikes.

傫[3]
4227

To injure; to destroy.

壘[3]
4228

A military wall; a rampart. To pile up. A pile.

壘 塊 a pile of clods—a grievance. See 磊 No. 4225—1,2.

壘 塹 wall and trench before a camp.

壘 字 characters consisting of repeated radicals.

壘 石 a pile of stones.

壘 肩 crowded together.

軍 壘 an entrenchment.

(a) Read lü[4,5]. A name.

鬱 壘 ancient warrior deified as a guardian door-god with his elder brother 神 荼 No. 6526-A; their effigies or names are pasted up on doors.

擂[4]
4229

To beat a drum. Inter. 擂 No. 4237.

儡[4]
4230

To roll stones down hill. Piles of stones. Inter. preceding.

Read lui[3]. A boulder.

纍[2]
4231

To join, to bind. To creep, to wind about. u.f. 縲 No. 4224.

纍 囚 a bound prisoner.

纍 垂 to hang down; to suspend.

纍 繫 bound; to tie; entwined.

纍 纍 strung together like pearls or beads.

(a) Dispirited, purposeless, emaciated.

纍 纍 若 喪 家 之 狗 aimless, like a dog which has lost his home.

喪 容 纍 纍 emaciated from mourning.

(b) A large rope.

以 劍 斫 絕 纍 with his sword he hacked through the rope.

儽[4]
4232

Lazy. Tired out, worn, fatigued. =4241.A.

儽·了 一 生 I have wearied out my whole life.

儽 得 很 or 儽 得 慌 quite fatigued.

儽 憜 weakly.

儽·的 發 喘 so wearied that he panted.

虆[2]
4233

A creeper, a bramble. Basket for carrying earth.

虆 梩 a dirt-basket.

罍[2]
4234

A jar. Ornamental drinking-cup made of wood.

藟[2]
4235

Climbing plants. Brambles.

雷[2]
4236

Thunder. Distinguish 電 No. 6358.

雷·公 or 雷 神 the god of thunder, who strikes those who are guilty of secret evils.

雷 劈 struck by lightning—thunder.

雷 動 like thunder rolling—of applause.

雷 厲 terrible as thunder.

[5]雷 同 one peal of thunder is like another—to re-echo, to copy.

雷 同 前 人 a mere follower of predecessors.

不 見 雷 同 no tautology.

雷 鳴 the roll of thunder.

雷 子[3] Sons of Thunder.

[10]雷 打 眼 前 報 to be struck by lightning—thunder—is a recompense here and now—without waiting till the next life.

雷 擊 struck by lightning—thunder.

雷 火 the marks of lightning; lightning.

雷 聲 or 雷 轟 sound of thunder.

雷 車 隆 隆 the hollow rumbling of the thunder chariot.

[15]雷 雨 a thunder shower.

雷 雲 thunder clouds.

雷 電 thunder and lightning.

雷 電 交 作 a thunderstorm.

雷 震 struck by lightning—thunder.

[20]雷 霆 thunder.

雷 霆 之 怒 thundering mad.

雷 鞭 a streak of lightning.

雷 鼓 to beat a drum.

地 雷 a land-mine.

[25]打 雷 to thunder.

水 雷 a sea-mine.

炸 雷 a clap of thunder.

魚 雷 a torpedo.

魚 雷 艇 a torpedo-boat.

擂[2] 4237　To triturate; to pound.

擂 研 to rub down on a slab.
擂 鎚 a pestle for triturating.
擂 顏 料 to grind colours.

(a) Read *lui*[4]. To beat a drum; to roll down stones.

擂 鼓 to beat a drum.

蕾[3] 4238　Unopened flower buds.

鐳[2] 4239　A pot. Small copper coins. Radium. See 鎇 No. 3588.

鐳 錠 Radium, from the sound.

羸[2] 4240　Bound; entangled. Lean, emaciated, thin. Distinguish 贏 No. 7480.

羸 其 角 caught by the horns.
羸 疾 consumption, wasting disease.
羸 瘦 emaciated.

耒[3] 4241　A plough. Name of a tributary of the River Hsiang in Hunan. Radical 127.

耒 耜 ploughs and plowshares—agriculture.

誄[3] 4242　To eulogize the dead. A speech or ode in praise of the dead. To confer an honorary posthumous title.

誄 功 to narrate the merits of a person.
誄 文 eulogistic prayers for the dead, burned at the grave.
誄 曰 禱 爾 于 上 下 神 祇 the Book of Prayers says, "Prayer has been made for you to the upper and lower gods."
誄 述 to write a biography.

淚
泪[4] 4243　Tears. To weep, to cry.

淚 如 湧 泉 the tears flowed like a fountain.

淚 注 汪·的 to weep bitterly; tearful.
淚 河 tears like a river.
淚 珠 teardrops.
[5]淚 痕 traces of tears.
淚 竹 the speckled bamboo, *see* 湘 No. 2565-1.
淚 蠟 guttering of a candle.
收 淚 to stop weeping.
拭 淚 to wipe away tears.
[10]泣 淚 to weep with tears.

(a) Read *li*[4]. Water flowing rapidly.

類
類[4] 4244　A class, a species, a kind.

類 人 形 in form something like a man.
類 似 or 類 同 similar; alike.
類 典 books of quotations arranged under subjects for reference.
類 化 assimilation, as of an old idea with a new one.
[5]類 推 to reason by analogy.
類 族 grouped according to species or kind.
類 書 books of reference arranged according to subjects.
類 次 to classify.
類 此 in this manner; thus.
[10]類 犬 like a dog.
類 聚 grouped in classes, species, etc.
不 相 類 dissimilar.
不 類 a monstrosity; unlike.
人 類 human beings.
[15]同 類 of the same kind; fellow creature.
各 從 其 類 each after its own kind.
善 類 the good.
畜 類 beasts.
等 類 and similar kinds.

(a) A fabulous kind of wild cat.

(b) A special sacrifice.

類 于 上 帝 I have offered a special sacrifice to God—上 帝 is here defined as 天 Heaven.

類[4] 4245　A flaw; a knot.

倫[2] 4246　To arrange. To think.

倫[2] 4247　Constant, regular, ordinary. Natural relationships. Right principles.

倫 常 or 人 倫 or 五 倫 or 天 倫 moral obligations; the five human relationships,— between prince and minister 君 臣, father and son 父 子, husband and wife 夫 婦, brothers 兄 弟, and friends 朋 友.
倫 理 moral principles.
倫 理 上 morally.
倫 理 學 ethics; moral philosophy.
[5]倫 理·的 ethical; ethically.
亂 倫 incest.
逆 倫 to violate human obligations.

(a) Degrees, as of comparison. In order.

倫 次 in order, a series, sequence.
無 倫 beyond compare.
等 倫 of the same class.
絕 倫 beyond compare.
超 倫 excelling them all.

(b) Used in transliterating.

倫 敦 London.

圇[2] 4248　Complete, whole.

囫 圇 complete, whole. *See* No. 2191.

崙[2] 4249　*See* 3679.

掄
䢂[2] 4250　To choose, to select. In turn. Also read *liin*[1].

掄 元 to come out first in the examinations.
掄 才 to select men of talent.
掄 材 to select timber.
掄 選 or 掄 擇 to select fit persons.

掄 魁 to head the list at the former examinations.

(a) To wave. To brandish. To swing—as the hand.

掄 手 攻·他 raise the hand and attack him.

掄 打 to raise the hand to strike.

掄·起 手·來 to wave the hand.

掄 鎚 to swing a sledge-hammer.

淪 2 Ruined, engulfed, lost. Eddying water.
4251

淪 亡 ruined, lost.

淪 於 骨 髓 to enter into a man's very being.

淪 沒 淪 喪 ruined, lost, destroyed.

淪 淪 ripples, eddies.

⁵淪 落 sinking into—vicious ways.

淪 迴 an eddy; shoal water.

沉 淪 sunk; lost; perdition.

綸 2 Silken threads. To twist or wind silk.
4252

綸 扉 the silken door—the palace.

綸 絮 a clue, a thread.

綸 繩 a fishing-line.

綸 音 silken sounds—words of the emperor.

絲 綸 silken cords; fishing-line; learning.

(a) To adjust, classify.

彌 綸 to put in order; to supply deficiencies.

經 綸 to put in order; to classify; political ability; learning.

(b) Read kuan¹. A kind of silk kerchief.

綸 巾 silk kerchief as used by 諸·葛 亮 Chu-ko Liang.

論 4 To discuss. To arrange. To reason, to argue, to speak of.
4253

論·不·得 not to be reasoned or talked about.

論 云 to discuss.

論 人 to talk about others; to judge.

論 人 所 長 to speak of the excellencies of others.

⁵論 來 論 去 to talk on; prolonged discussion.

論·到 to speak of; with reference to.

論 功 論 過 to estimate the merits and demerits of officials.

論 勢 cogency of an argument.

論·及 to talk about; as regards; with reference to.

¹⁰論 天 by the day—as when engaging labour.

論 定 to settle by discussion.

論 工 by the piece or job—of work.

論 據 data; ground of proof.

論 料 data.

¹⁵論 斤 賣 sold by the catty.

論 斷 to discuss; to judge.

論 月 or 按 月 monthly; by the month.

論 法 logic of.

不 合 於 論 法 illogical.

²⁰論 理 logic.

論 理 上·的 logical.

論 理 學 logic as a science.

論 理 學 家 logicians.

²⁵論 理·的 必 要 logical necessity.

論 理·的 推 論 logical reasoning.

論 理·的 斷 定 logical conclusion.

論 理·的 議·論 logical reasoning or argument.

論 篤 是 與 to praise a man because his discourses are sincere.

論 調 (tiao⁴) the tone or sentiment —as of a newspaper; its general platform.

³⁰論 證 proof; argument for.

論·起 to talk about; with reference to.

論 道 to discuss the truth; with reference to.

不 論 or 無 論 no matter what; it does not matter.

不 論 大 小 either large or small, it does not matter.

³⁵不 論·是 誰 no matter who he is; whoever it is.

對 論 opposite views.

無 論 如 何 in any case; at all events.

理 論 to reason; to discuss.

罷 論 drop the matter; end the discussion.

⁴⁰討·論 to dispute; to argue.

談 論 to converse; to talk over.

議·論 to discuss; to debate.

輿 論 public opinion.

(a) An essay; an article.

論 文 an essay.

論 文 家 essayists.

論² 語 discourses—the Analects of Confucius, one of the Four Books.

論 說 an essay; a leading article.

⁵論 述 pamphlets.

論 題 a thesis.

作 論 to write an essay or leading article.

社 論 a leading article in a newspaper or magazine; editorial.

輪 2 To revolve; a wheel. A revolution, a turn.
4254

輪 值 to take turns of duty.

輪 充 to serve in turn.

輪 匠 a wheelwright.

輪 囷 spiral.

⁵輪 姦 violation of a woman by several men in turn.

輪·子 a wheel.

輪 廻 transmigration.

輪 流 or 輪 班 to take turns; in rotation; in order.

輪 流 電 力 alternating electric current.

¹⁰輪 王 or 轉 輪 聖 王 a Buddha who is supposed to rule the world, the king of the wheel.

輪 班 替·換 to take turns in rotation.

輪 盤 賭 roulette.

輪 種 rotation of crops.

輪 船 a steamship.

¹⁵輪 葉 blade of a propeller.

輪 軸 wheel and axle.

輪 輞 felloe of a wheel.

輪 輻 spokes of a wheel.

輪 轂 nave of a wheel.

²⁰輪 轉 to turn round; to revolve.

輪 道 a circuit—of electricity.

閉 輪 道 closed circuit.

開 放 輪 道 open circuit.

輪 飲 to drink in turns at a banquet.

²⁵卡·子 輪 escapement wheel.

兩 心 輪 eccentric wheel.

擺 輪 a balance-wheel, as of a clock, etc.

水 輪 water-wheel.

舵 輪 steering-wheel.

³⁰通 力 輪 balance-wheel.

飛 輪 fly-wheel.

齒 輪 cog-wheel.

LUNG.　(ㄌㄨㄥ)

(Long)

隆[2] Eminent, surpassing; abundant. To exalt, to
4255 magnify. Prosperous.

隆 儀 a valuable present.
隆 冬 時·候 cold weather.
隆 厚 generous; substantial.
隆 多 abundant.
[5]隆 恩 imperial favour or bounty.
隆 情 great favours.
隆 暑 the great heat of summer.
隆 準 a prominent nose.
隆 盛 affluent; abundant.
[10]隆 窮 (u.f. 穹) the hair dressed so as to increase the height.
隆 薄 generous and mean.
隆 貴 noble; of high rank.
隆 起 to swell up.
隆 重 impressive.
[15]隆 重 禮 儀 impressive ceremony or ritual.
隆 隆 or 興 隆 prosperous.
隆 顏 the imperial countenance.

(a) Rumbling of thunder.

隆 隆 然 rumbling like thunder.

癃[2] Weakness, infirmity.
　 Retention of urine.
4256

癃 病 infirmity of old age.
癃 閉 retention of urine.

窿[2]
4257 A cavity. A hole.

窟·窿 a hole.

龍[2] The dragon, associated with rain, floods, and geo-
4258 mancy. An emblem of imperialism. Radical 212.

龍 不 離 潭 the dragon does not leave its pool—mind your own business.
龍 井 a kind of green tea from Hangchow.
龍 位 or 天 位 the imperial throne.
龍 吟 the flute.
[5]龍 團 a fragrant kind of green tea.
龍 城 ancient name for Sianfu 西 安 府·

龍 孫 bamboo shoots.
龍 尾 硯 fine stone ink-slabs from Wu yüan in Hweichow, S. Anhwei.
龍 忌 the day on which fire was forbidden—the day before Tsing ming 清 明.
[10]龍 戶 the Tanka 蛋 家 or boat-population of Canton.
龍 抬 頭 the dragon raises his head—on the 2nd of the 2nd lunar month.
龍 旗 the dragon-flag—the former Chinese national flag.
龍 樓 鳳 閣 the imperial apartments.
龍 氣 favourable geomantic influences.
[15]龍 池 Peking. (Peiping).
龍 洋 a dollar minted at the close of the Manchu Dynasty, having the emblem of a dragon.
龍 涎 香 ambergris.
龍 漦 dragon's saliva—said to have caused the birth of 襃 姒 in the Chou dynasty.
龍 潛 the dragon is hidden in the depths—the emperor has not yet ascended the throne.
[20]龍 爪 the emperor's hands.
龍 牌 the imperial tablet.
龍 王 the god of rain and water.
龍 生·日 birthday of the dragon—13th of the 5th lunar month.
龍 生 龍 鳳 生 鳳 dragons beget dragons, the phœnix begets a phœnix—each after its own kind.
[25]龍 盾 a shield.
龍 眼 a fruit, the Longan, which when dried is called 桂 圓.
龍 神 the ruling powers of nature—gods of waters and springs.
龍 種 the imperial family.
龍 穴 dragon's den—lucky site on a hill where the geomantic influences are assembled.
[30]龍 章 鳳 姿 noble and handsome.
龍 筆 the imperial autograph.
龍 脈 dragon's pulse—geomantic influences or magnetic currents.
龍 腦 Baroos camphor.
龍 膽 草 gentian.
[35]龍 船 a dragon-boat, used on the 5th of the 5th lunar month for races.
龍 茲 a mat made of rushes 龍 鬚.
龍 葵 black nightshade.

龍 虎 dragon and tiger—water and fire elements.
龍 虎 榜 published list of successful candidates for the degree of 舉 人.
[40]龍 蛇 dragons and snakes—flourishes in penmanship.
龍 蝦 large prawns; lobsters.
龍 蟠 虎 踞 where the dragon is coiled and the tiger crouches—dangerous places.
龍 蟠 鳳 逸 a man of no ordinary talents.
龍 衣 or 龍 袍 the imperial robe.
[45]龍 跳 天 門 usurping authority.
龍 跳 虎 臥 free and vigorous style of writing.
龍 金 魚 the variety of goldfish with prominent eyes and very large waving tail.
龍 鍾 之 年 the period of senility.
龍 門 the dragon-gate—the attainment of success is described as entering this. 龍 頭 a faucet.
[50]龍 頭[2] 蛇 尾 dragon's head and snake's tail—dwindling away to nothing after an initial display of greatness.
龍 頭[2] 鳳 尾 good from beginning to end.
龍 顏 大 悅 the imperial countenance showed signs of great pleasure.
龍 類 the dragon class—lizards, serpents, dragons, etc.
龍 飛 the emperor ascends the throne.
[55]龍 馬 精 神 vigorous old age—like that of a dragon or a horse.
龍 馬 負 圖 the dragon-horse bore the diagrams 八 卦 on his back.
龍 駒 dragon's colt—a fine horse; a talented young scholar.
龍 驤 虎 步 with dragon-like prancing and tiger-like steps——majestic steps.
龍 驤 虎 視 with dragon-like prancing and tiger-like glances——awe-inspiring.
[60]龍 骨 keel of a boat; dragon's bones.
龍 體 person of the emperor.
龍 鬚 rushes used for making mats.
龍 鬚 菜 asparagus.
龍 鳳 呈 祥 prosperity brought by the dragon and the phœnix—excellent good fortune.

65龍 鳳 帖 betrothal cards.
乘 龍 to mount the dragon—to get married.
地 龍 the earth-worm; a top.
放 龍 入 海 let the dragon escape to the sea—give a man a chance to show his ability.

攏² Rude; barbarous.
4259

攏 侗 unpolished; rustic.

嚨² The throat.
4260

壟³ A mound of earth. A tumulus.
4261

壟 斷 mound on which a trader stood to look out for trade; hence, a place favourable for trade; to monopolize.
壟 斷 專 賣 monopoly of sales.
壟 斷 獨 登 to create a monopoly.
壟 斷 資 本 monopoly of capital.

攏³ To collect. To grasp. To take action.
4262

攏·住 口 to muzzle.
攏·在 袖 裏 put it in his sleeve.
攏 掠 to plunder; to rob.
攏 攏 to crowd together.
⁵攏 統·的 空 說 a lot of empty talk.
攏 總 都 來·了 they have all come; everything is here.
聚 攏·來 assembled together.

(a) To draw near to.

攏 前·來 to come forward.
攏 岸 to approach the shore.
攏 碼°頭 to come alongside a jetty.
攏 近 to draw near to.
⁵攏 進·去 to work towards the entrance—as a boat.
還 沒·有 攏 he has not yet arrived.

(b) To comb.

攏·子 a woman's comb; a long bag for carrying things.
攏 髮 or 攏 頭 to comb the hair.

曨² The rising sun obscured.
4263

朧² The rising moon.
4264

櫳 }² A cage, a pen, a grating, bars.
櫳 }   Inter 籠 No. 4271.
4265

櫳·子 a cage, a pen.
門 櫳·子 bars across a doorway.

瀧² River in Kwangtung.
4266

爖² Fire.
4267

瓏² A gem cut like a dragon.
4268

玲 瓏 elegant.

礱 }2.4. To grind. To sharpen.
礱 }   A mill.
4269

礱 利 to grind sharp.
礱 坊 a miller's; grain dealer's.
礱 穀 to hull grain.

窿³ A hole; a cleft. Empty.
4270

窿 口 a mine, a coal·pit.
孔 窿 a hole.
空 窿 empty.
穿 窿 to bore a hole.

籠² A cage, a basket, a noose.
4271

籠·住 口 to muzzle.
籠 嘴 a muzzle.
籠 括 to contain; to embody.
籠 紗 gauze covering of lanterns.
⁵籠 絡 toils; in the clutches of; to victimize.

籠 通 general; of broad application.
籠 頭 a halter.
燈·籠 a lantern.
蒸 籠 a steamer for cooking.
雀 籠 a birdcage.

聾² Deaf.
4272

聾·子 a deaf person.

蘢² A species of water-weed: Polygonum.
4273

蒙 蘢 overgrown with weeds; obscured.

襱² Legs of trousers. Overalls worn by workmen.
4274

躘² To walk.
4275

躘 蹱 to toddle.
躘 蹱 to turn on the heel.

隴² A dike; a bank.
4276

隴 溝 dikes and ditches.
隴 畝 之 間 among dikes and fields—busy farming.

(a) Used for Shensi Province.

隴 西 old name for the south-east corner of Kansu.
得 隴 望 蜀 having got Shensi, to look towards Szechwan—insatiable grasping.

韓 }² A halter.
韄 }
4277

韃 頭 a halter.

弄⁴ To do, to make; to act. Also read nung⁴.
4278

弄 之 traced its winding course.
弄·了·來 to get hold of.

弄假成眞 to fulfil what was promised in joke.
弄·出事·來 to cause a squabble; to make trouble.
[5]弄·出·去 to make away with.
弄壞 to spoil; to put out of order.
弄媚 coquetry; to make eyes at.
弄巧反拙 to try to be clever and fail.
弄性尙氣 arrogant; hot-headed.
[10]弄慣·了 thoroughly acquainted with the use of; accustomed to make or do.
弄權 to abuse power.
弄·死 to put to death; to cause the death of.
弄火 to light a fire.
弄·的不好 badly done; to make a muddle of.
[15]弄神弄鬼 to rouse ghosts and demons—as by incantations.
弄翻·了 tipped over; spilled.
弄聳 to dupe; to befool.
弄舌 to tattle; to jabber.
弄草 to cut grass.
[20]弄錢 or 弄銀·子 to make money; to make money dishonestly.
弄飯 to prepare food.

(a) To play with; to handle.

弄兒[2] to play with a child for one's own amusement.
弄玩意兒 to play with toys.
弄璋 to play with a sceptre—to bear a son.
弄瓦 to play with a tile—to bear a daughter.
弄蛇 to play with snakes.

(b) u.f. 衕 No. 2554. An alley.

佛侤 [4]
To make a fool of. Simple, stupid.
4279

佛愚人 to impose upon a simpleton.

LÜ. (ㄌㄩˇ)

呂 [3]
A tube. A musical note.
4280

六呂 the six lower pipes of the standard ancient musical scale of China.

(a) An ancient State. The Philippines.

呂宋 Luzon, a native name for the Philippines.
呂·宋烟 Manila cigarettes or cigars.
呂宋菓 St. Ignatius' bean.
呂祖巷 a Taoist nunnery.

(b) The backbone.

心呂之臣 a devoted, loyal minister.

(c) A kind of sword.

侶 [3]
A companion, a mate. To associate with.
4281

侶伴 a comrade.
侶行 to travel with a mate.
結侶 to form a companionship.

梠 [3]
A small beam supporting the rafters at the eaves.
4282

榮梠 turned up eaves of Chinese architecture.

鋁 [3]
Aluminium.
4283

鋁金 aluminium bronze.

閭 [2]
The gate of a village; a village of 25 families. Also read lu[2].
4284

閭伍 a village.
閭巷 a lane or alley.
閭里 rural population; the country.
閭里童稚 a village youth.
門閭 a dwelling.

櫚 [2]
A palm.
4285

椶櫚 a coir-palm.

旅 [3]
A guest, a stranger. To travel, to lodge.
4286

旅夜 in an inn at night.
旅客 or 商旅 strangers, travellers, merchants.

旅寄 to lodge at.
旅店 or 旅舘 or 旅寓 or 旅舍 or 旅邸 a lodging-house; an inn, a hotel.
[5]旅居 temporary lodging.
旅次 an inn.
旅行 to take a journey; to travel.
旅行商人 commercial traveller.
旅費 lodging expenses.
[10]旅食 to eat in an inn.

(a) A multitude; all.

旅力 the strength of numbers. *See below* G.
旅見天子[3] they all saw the emperor.
旅進旅退 they advance and retire together.
亞旅—the great officers 大夫—all ranked as inferior—to the nobles.

(b) A body of 500 troops in ancient times, now a brigade. Troops generally.

旅長[3] commander of a brigade.
師旅 troops.
混成旅 mixed brigade.
軍旅之事 military matters.

(c) Order, sequence. To arrange.

旅酬下爲上 "in the general pledging, the inferiors handed the cup to the superiors."
殽核維旅 "with the sauces and the kernels arranged in them."

(d) Younger members of a family. The children.

侯亞侯旅 the younger sons and their children.

(e) A sacrifice to the mountains.

旅於泰山 about to sacrifice to *T'ai shan.*
王大旅上帝 the king sacrificed to *Shangti*—here defined as the ancient sacrifice on the round mound.

(f) Self-sown.

野穀旅生 wild self-sown grain.

(g) u.f. next. The backbone.

旅力方剛 while my backbone retains its strength.

膂 [3] The backbone; strength.
4287

膂力絕羣 he excels all others in strength.

屢 [3] Frequent; constantly; repeatedly; often. Also read
4288 *lui*[3].

屢屢 again and again; repeatedly.
屢年 for a series of years.
屢次 or 屢番 often; many times.
屢空 he is often in straits.
[5]屢蒙過愛 I have repeatedly enjoyed your favours.
屢試屢驗 as often as it is used it proves efficacious.
屢豐年 successive good harvests.
迭屢 frequently; many times.

瘻瘤 [2] A purulent tumour; a running sore; an ulcer.
4289

瘻癘 a malignant tumour.
瘰瘻 scrofulous swellings.

縷 [3] Hempen or silken threads. A hank or knot. A strand
4290 or lock of hair.

縷伸妥·了 the threads are unravelled.
縷切 to cut into fine shreds.
縷金 gold thread.
一縷絲 a hank of floss silk.
頭·髮數縷 several strands or locks of hair.

(a) To state in detail.

縷布 to state item by item.
縷晰 clearly set forth.
縷述 to go into particulars.
縷陳 to state in detail.

(b) Read *lou*[2]. Ragged.

褸 [3] The lapel of a coat. Tattered; soiled. Also read *lou*[2].
4291

褸裂 torn and ragged.
襤褸 ragged clothing.

慮 [4] Anxiety; to be anxious. To plan.
4292 Distinguish 盧 No. 4156.

慮事 to make plans for.
慮以下人 anxious to humble himself to others.
慮·到 to forecast; to anticipate.
慮·及 to have anticipated.
[5]慮後 to take thought for the morrow.
慮念 or 思慮 to think anxiously about.
慮患 to take precautions against calamity.
慮深 wise, having forethought.
慮無 the pennant carried before the army.
[10]慮遠 long foresight.
不掛慮 do not be anxious.
無遠慮 no foresight; improvident.

(a) Read *lu*[4.5.] u.f. 錄 No. 4200.

慮囚 to revise sentences on prisoners.

(b) Read *lii*[4]. Indefinite numbers.

亡慮 about; no matter how many.

濾 [4] To strain, to filter. Also read *lu*[4].
4293

濾·出·來 to strain out.
濾去渣 strain off the sediment.
濾布 or 濾水羅 a cloth through which things may be strained.

蘆 [4] Madder.
4294

鑢鐦 [4] A file, a rasp, a polishing tool. To burnish.
4295

鑢成槽 a groove worn by friction.
自鑢 to restrain oneself.

驢馿 [2] An ass. A donkey.
4296

驢不喝水強飲不能 if a donkey will not drink, you cannot force him.
驢叫 the bray of an ass.

驢鳴狗吠 ass braying and dog barking—poor style of writing.
驢·子 a donkey.
[5]驢皮 obstinate; mulish.
驢脣不對馬嘴 a donkey's lips do not match a horse's mouth—incongruous.
驢駒 foal of a donkey.
叫驢 a jackass.
蹇驢 a lame donkey.
[10]騲驢 a she-ass.

LÜ.   (ㄌ)
(Lüh)

律 [4.5.] A law, a statute, a rule.
4297

律例 statutes and laws; a code of laws.
律典 a precedent; an example
律師 a barrister. Buddhist ascetic.
律師公會 law association; the bar.
[5]律師與訟師 barrister and solicitor.
最高律師 solicitor-general.
律書 law book.
律條 regulations.
律法 law; laws; statutes.
[10]報律 press laws.
本地律 local laws.
民律 civil law.
海律 maritime law.
用與失用律 law of use and disuse.
道德律 moral law.

(a) To follow, to copy.

上律天時 "above, he imitates the regularity of the seasons."

(b) See below

律呂 or 十二律 a series of standard bamboo pitch-pipes used in ancient music; the twelve semitones represented by these pitch-pipes

(c) A stanza of eight lines.

律詩 stanza of eight lines with certain rules about rhymes, tones, and antitheses.
五律七律 eight-line verse having five or seven characters to the line, respectively.

(d) Uniform; according to rule.

律 律 uniformly; entirely.
一 律 看 待 treat all in the same way.
一 律 辦 理 to act according to precedent.
一 律 裁 撤 uniformly abolished.

LÜAN. (ㄌㄨㄢ)
(Luan)

變[3] Beautiful; handsome; admirable. Also read *lien*[3].
4298

變 童 a catamite; effeminate.
靜 女 其 變 How beautiful is that modest girl!

戀
恋 [4] To hanker after; to dote on; to be fond of. Also read *lien*[4].
4299

戀 主 attached to one's master.
戀 土 難 移 fond of one's home and loath to leave it for other parts.
戀 妓 lusting after prostitutes.
戀 家 fond of staying at home.
[5]戀 愛 love between the sexes.
發 生 戀 愛 fell in love.
戀 慕 or 眷 戀 strongly attached to; to think of fondly.
戀 戀 不 忘 a strong attachment which one cannot forget.
戀 戀 不 捨 unable to part from; unwilling to give up.
[10]戀 枕 fond of his pillow—lazy.
戀 職 ambitious to retain office.
戀 色 lecherous.
戀 酒 fond of strong drink.
相 戀 mutual attachment.

攣 [4] To bend; to warp. Bent, crooked; winding.
4300

攣 其 手 足 hands and feet bent —as with rheumatism.
攣 毛 curly hair.
攣 曲 crooked, bent, curved, winding.
攣 腰 or 攣 躬 bent; hunch-backed.

(a) Read *liian*[2]. To bind or tie. To take hold of; to drag along.

臠 [3] Sliced meat.
4301

臠 割 dismemberment.
臠 殺 to chop a man up.
臠 肉 sliced meat.

LIEH. LÜEH. (ㄌㄧㄝ)
(Lieh)

劣 [4.5] Vile, degraded, bad. Inferior, inadequate.
4302

劣 兄 self-depreciatory term—I.
劣 德 little ability; inferior virtue.
劣 才 inferior abilities.
劣 把 stupid, dull.
[5]劣 根 生 come of a bad stock.
劣 等 low class; low grade.
劣 衿 scholars who misapply their talents.
劣 貨 low-grade goods—used in boycott slogans.
劣 跡 a bad reputation.
劣 馬 a vicious horse.

MA. (ㄇㄚ)

麻 [2] Hemp. Radical 200.
4303

麻·俐 or 麻 麻 俐 俐 quick-witted; clever, ready, expert.
麻·子 hemp-seed.
麻·子 油 hemp-seed oil.
麻 布 hempen fabrics; linen.
[5]麻 布 粗 衣 clad in coarse hempen garments—very frugal.
麻 杆·子 a hempstalk.
麻 栗 木 teak wood.
麻·煩 troublesome.
麻 稭 hemp stalks.
[10]麻 線 linen thread; twine.
麻 縷 hemp and silk.
麻 繁 troublesome; complicated.
麻 繩 兒 hemp cordage.
麻 綹 or 麻 刀 caulking; old rope chopped up for strengthening mortar.
[15]麻 花 a twist of dough; three strands of anything twisted together.
麻 達 布 sacking.
麻 衣 mourning garments.
麻 袋 sacks.
麻 雀 or 瓦 雀 the house-sparrow.(-*ch'üeh*[4], -*ch'iao'r*[3])
↑麻 將 *mahjong*.

[20]麻 鞋 hempen sandals.
亂 麻 tangled hemp.
大 麻 油 castor oil.
胡 麻 linseed; flax.
芝·麻 sesamum.

(a) Numb. Drugged. Inter. 痲 No. 4305.

痲·子 pock-marks.
痲·木 or 木 痲 numbed.
痲 藥 anæsthetic.
痲 醉 drugged; doped. See 局 No. 1584-10.
[5]痲 醉 劑 drugs, narcotics.
痲 醉 藥 narcotics.
肉 痲 the flesh creeping; nauseating.

嘛 [2] What. u.f. 甚 麼.
4304

幹 嘛 What are you doing? Why?

痲 [2] Numbness; paralysis. Distinguish 癜 No. 4025.
4305 Inter. 麻 No. 4303.

痲·子 pock-marks.
痲·木 numbed; without sensation of feeling.
痲 瘋 leprosy.
痲 瘋 院 leper asylum.
[5]痲 痹 numbness.
發 痲 to become numbed.

曆 [2] To see indistinctly.
4306

曆 督 indistinct vision; blurred.

蔴 [2] Hemp. Applied to other plants furnishing textile fibres.
4307 Inter 麻 No. 4303. q.v.

蔴 刀 chopped old rope used to strengthen mortar.
蔴 布 hempen cloth; linen.
蔴 油 oil expressed from the seeds of hemp or sesamum.

糢 [2] Blurred, indistinct.
4308

糢·糊 blurred; dim.

蟆 [2] A frog. Also read *mo*[1].
4309

馬[3] A horse. A piece in Chinese chess. Radical 187.
4310

馬 不 背 主 a horse does not turn its back on its master.
馬 乳 mare's milk—koumiss; a variety of grape.
馬 兵 or 馬 隊 mounted troops.
馬 刀 a shellfish something like a mussel.
[5]馬 刷·子 a horse-brush.
馬 力 horse-power.
　公 稱 馬 力 nominal horse-power.
　實 馬 力 indicated horse-power.
馬 勃 lycoperdon or puff-ball.
[10]馬 匹 horses.
馬 匹 踢 跳 horses prancing.
馬 口 鐵 or 洋 鐵 or 白 鐵 tin-plates.
馬 鳴 (or 嘶) the neighing of a horse.
馬 圖 the plans which were said to be revealed to *Fu Hsi.* *See* 河 No. 2111-10.
[15]馬 埒 a track for racing horses.
馬·夫 a groom.
馬 尾 a horse's tail.
馬 尾 纂 wig worn by women.
馬 尾 羅 a fine hair-sieve.
[20]馬 後 砲 wise after the event.
馬 快 a detective.
馬 戲 a circus.
馬 房 or 馬 號 a stable.
馬 把 勢 a horse-breaker.
[25]馬 掌 a horseshoe.
馬 撓·子 a curry-comb.
馬 撒 歡 兒 the horse is capering about.
馬 政 rules for the management of horses.
馬 極 a camp-stool.
[30]馬 棚 a stable.
馬 桶 or 馬·子 a night-stool.
馬 椿 a hitching-post.
馬 槽 a manger or horse-trough.
馬 步 a god that injures horses.
[35]馬 流·子 a vagrant.
馬 牛 襟 裾 a dressed-up horse or ox—a man without manners.
馬 生 角 when a horse produces horns—never.
馬 甲 a long sleeveless waistcoat worn over the gown by women.
馬 矢 (or 糞) horse-dung.
[40]馬 策 a riding-whip.
馬 絡·頭 a halter.

馬 肚 帶 a saddle-girth.
馬 肝 liver of a horse—said to be poisonous.
馬 膺 a breast-plate.
[45]馬 蘭 the aster.
馬·蜂 hornets; the gadfly.
馬 蟥 or 馬 蜞 the horse-leech.
馬 蚰 a name for the dragon-fly.
馬 術 horsemanship.
[50]馬 衣 (or 袀) a horse-cloth.
馬 褂 兒 a riding-jacket — outside jacket with wide sleeves.
馬 褲 riding-breeches.
馬 褥 seat of a saddle; saddle-pad.
馬 販·子 dealer in horses.
[55]馬 賊 mounted highwaymen.
馬 路 macadam road.
馬 蹄 hoof of a horse; a kind of baked biscuit.
馬 車 a carriage.
馬 軍 mounted troops.
[60]馬 通 horse-dung.
馬 道 a track for horses to run in.
馬 醫 a veterinary surgeon for horses.
馬 鈴 horse-bells.
馬 鈴 薯 potatoes.
[65]馬 錢 doctor's fees.
馬 錢 子 nux vomica.
馬 鐙 or 鞍 馬 stirrups.
馬 陸 or 馬 蚿 the millipede.
馬 面 the horse-faced demon messenger from purgatory.
[70]馬 革 horse's hide—in which the body of a soldier was wrapped —u.f., death on the battle field.
馬 勒 or 馬 韁 a bridle, reins.
馬 鞭 草 vervain.
馬·頭 or 碼·頭 a jetty, a landing-place.
馬 頭 費 wharfage.
[75]馬 餼 provender for horses.
馬 鬃 a horse's mane.
馬 鬣 封 a rounded tomb.
馬 鹿 the red-deer.
馬 齒 莧 *portulaca.*
[80]備 馬 to saddle a horse.
兒 馬 or 公 馬 a stallion.
東 風 吹 馬 耳 like the wind blowing a horse's ear—to pay no heed to it.
生 馬 an unbroken horse.
競 馬 or 賽 馬 horse-races.
[85]良 馬 a steady horse.
華 馬 skewbald horse.
野 馬 a wild horse; a mirage, mote in a sunbeam.
騍 馬 or 草 馬 a mare.
騸 馬 a gelding.

(a) At once; immediately; rapidly.
馬·上 without delay.
馬·上 來·了 will be here in a minute.
馬·上 就 做 I will do it immediately.
馬 利 quickly.
馬 到 成 功 it will be arranged for at once—used when guaranteeing work, etc.

(b) Used in transliterating.
馬 來 Malay.
馬 來 遜 競 走 Marathon race.
馬 克 a mark—German coinage.
馬 克 丹 Macadam.
[5]馬 克 斯 Marx.
馬 克 斯 主 義 Marxism.
馬 司 電 Morse code.
馬 賽 Marseilles.
馬 尼 剌 Manila.
馬 達 motor.

嗎[4] An interrogative particle. Also used in transliterating.
4311
嗎 啡 morphine.

媽[1] Ma. An old woman; a mother. A waiting woman. a nurse.
4312
媽·媽 a mother, a nurse; mamma.
乾 媽 a procuress; a kind of god-mother.
奶·媽 wet-nurse.
老 媽 a nurse, old woman. [(S. dial.)
阿 媽 amah, a woman servant.
↑老 媽·子 a woman servant.

榪[4] The head-board of a bed. A board, a panel. To clamp. A clamp.
4313
榪·子 a clamp.
榪 桶 a commode. *See* 馬 No. 4310-31.

瑪[3] Cornelian; agate.
4314
瑪·瑙 agate.
瑪 瑙 文 veins in cornelian.
瑪 瑙 珠 agate or cornelian beads.

(a) Used in transliterating.
瑪 可 尼 Marconi.
瑪 哥 波 羅 Marco Polo.
瑪 那 manna.

碼³ Weights for money or goods. An English measure
4315 of one yard. A form of Chinese numerals.

碼·子 the business form of numerals. *See appendix* viii.

碼號 a distinguishing number; a number.

碼頭 or 馬頭 a jetty; a wharf; a mart.

密碼電報 code telegram.

明碼電報 a telegram in the ordinary numerals used to represent Chinese characters.

起碼 opening price; minimum.

禡⁴ Sacrifice to the god of war
4316 before a campaign.

罵 ⎱ ⁴
碼 ⎰ To curse, to revile, to abuse. To scold.
4317

罵不絶口 to curse without ceasing.

罵人 to abuse or curse people.

罵人·的話 abusive expressions; cursing.

罵·他 curse him!

⁵罵·他一頓 give him a good scolding; he gave him a cursing.

罵名 a bad reputation.

罵爹打娘 to curse father and beat mother—unfilial.

罵街 to curse from one end of the street to another.

螞³ A leech. A locust. An ant.
4318

螞蚱 grasshoppers.
螞·蜂 a hornet.
螞蟥 a leech.
螞蟥釘·住鷺鷥脚 the leech fastens itself to the legs of the egret—to rise in life by means of someone else.
螞蟻 ants.

MAI.   (ㄇㄞ)

埋² To bury. To secrete. To
lie in wait. Also *man²* in 6.
4319 Distinguish 理 No. 3864.

埋·伏 an ambuscade; ambush.
埋·伏兵馬 to dispose forces in ambush.
埋名 to conceal one's name—to retire into obscurity.
埋堆 to heap up.
⁵埋幽 interment.
埋怨 or 懷怨 to bear a grudge against; to blame; to grumble; to brood over a grievance.
埋憂地下 to bury one's grief.
埋書 to bury a covenant, ancient form of oath.
埋根 firm; obstinate.
¹⁰埋水雷 to lay mines. [cognition.
埋沒 to conceal; without due recognition.
埋沒人心 to disappoint another; to snub a person.
埋玉 death and burial of a beautiful woman.
埋葬 to bury.
¹⁵埋藏 or 收埋 to hide; to conceal.
埋蠱 to work evil on another by magic. *See* No. 3475-5, 6.
埋設地雷 to lay mines.
埋身隴畝 to retire to the country—giving up official life.
埋頭埋腦 to pretend ignorance.
²⁰埋香 burial of a beautiful woman.
埋骨不埋名 inter the bones, but not his fame.

薶² To bury. Inter. preceding.
Read *li²*. To stop up.
4320 Read *wei¹*. Dirty, filthy.

塵垢弗能薶 dirt and dust cannot soil.

霾² A dust-storm. Misty,
foggy.
4321

陰霾濁霧 a dense fog.
風雨霾晦 wind and rain darken the sky.

買³ To buy, to purchase.
To win over. To suborn.
4322 Cost, value.

買·不來 cannot be purchased for money.
買·不到 cannot be bought.
買·不起 cannot afford to buy it.
買主 the purchaser.
⁵買來·了 purchased.
買價 purchasing price.
買入 to purchase.

買到 purchased and taken delivery of.
買·去·了 he has gone to buy it.
¹⁰買受 to acquire by purchase.
買名 to purchase fame; to become notorious.
買嘴吃 fond of eating good things.
買囑 to suborn; to bribe.
買奉 to toady to.
¹⁵買契 deed of purchase.
買存 to buy and stock.
買定 purchased and paid a deposit on.
買官 to purchase official position.
買客 a customer.
²⁰買家 purchaser.
買山 to retire to the country and give up public life.
買·得昂貴 paid dearly for.
買服民心 to win the hearts of the people—by favours, etc.
買業 to purchase an estate.
²⁵買櫝還珠 to buy the casket and return the pearls—not to know the value of a thing.
買爵 to purchase high rank.
買·的便·宜 bought it cheaply.
買盤 current prices. [(p'ien²·i)
買空賣空 speculation on the rise and fall of the markets.
³⁰買笑 to buy smiles—associate with prostitutes.
買菜求益 in buying vegetables to ask for more—driving a hard bargain.
買譽 to try and get a reputation.
買貴·了 to buy at high prices—a bad bargain.
買賄 to bribe.
³⁵買賣 buying and selling; trade.
作買·賣 to do business; to open a shop.
買賣不見面 underhanded dealings; bribery.
買賣人 a trader.
買賣倒·了 failed in business.
⁴⁰買賣證書 contract note.
買賣賠·了 failed in business.
買賤 to buy cheaply.
買路錢 blackmail paid for immunity from robbers.
買·辦 a comprador; purveyor.
⁴⁵買通·了 to bribe—as the servants of a place by robbers.
買鄰 to select a good neighbourhood.
買醉 to buy intoxicants for one's own consumption.

買 關 to purchase a permit for a ship to pass through before the customs opens.

買 關·子 in teaching another, to keep the most important secret to oneself.

50買 骨 very desirous to obtain men of talent—from a story of one who desired to buy a splendid horse and failing, purchased its bones.

承 買 to contract for purchase.

採 買 to choose and purchase.

現 錢 買 to buy for ready money.

賒 買 to buy on credit.

賣 ⁴ To sell. To show off.
4323

賣·不 動 stagnant market, things will not sell.

賣 主 seller.

賣 乖 to talk glibly; to boast.

賣·了 or 賣·出·去 sold.

5賣 交 to betray a friend.

賣 人口 to sell human beings—as girls for brothels.

賣 人 情 to curry favour.

賣 俏 to show oneself off—as a meretricious woman.

賣 冷 to excite compassion by shivering.

10賣 出 證 書 sale-note.

賣 劍 買 牛 selling their swords and purchasing oxen for farming—reformation of brigands.

賣 力 to hire out for odd jobs.

賣 卜 to practice fortune-telling for a living.

賣 友 to betray a friend for personal gain.

15賣 名 to boast oneself.

賣 唱 to sing along the streets for a living.

賣 魯 to sell.

賣 嘴 to live by one's wits and glibness of speech.

賣 國 奴 (or 賊) traitor to his country.

20賣 契 a deed of sale.

賣 婚 to demand a large dowry.

賣 客 seller.

賣 巧 to show off one's skill.

賣 弄 to show off; to put on airs.

25賣 弄 手 段 to show off one's ability.

賣 弄 風 情 flirtation; coquetry.

賣·得 貴 sold at a high price—a profitable transaction.

賣 恩 to show favours for one's own ends.

賣 惡 to put the blame upon another.

30賣 房·子 to dispose of house property.

賣 放 罪 人 to release a criminal for a bribe.

賣 文 to sell one's writings.

賣 本·事 to make a display of one's ability.

賣 呆 to idle away time; to loiter or dawdle.

35賣 李 鑽 核 to sell plums and bore a hole through the stones —to prevent their growing—utter meanness.

賣 武·的 an acrobat.

賣 油·的 dealer in oil.

賣 清 to sell off.

賣 田 to sell fields.

40賣 瘋 to infect another with leprosy.

賣 眼 to sell a glance—a prostitute.

賣 破 綻 pretended carelessness and remissness in order to hookwink another.

賣 票 所 ticket office.

賣 笑 to sell smiles—a prostitute.

45賣 罄 to sell off.

賣 聲 to boast oneself.

賣 臉 to sell one's face—shameless importunity.

賣 舌 to live by one's wits, as fortune-tellers, etc.

賣 藝·的 an acrobat.

50賣 貨 手 salesman.

賣 賤 to sell cheaply.

賣 賴 to lay the blame upon another.

賣 身 to sell one's body—prostitution.

賣 面 光 or 賣 風·流 to show oneself off; to make oneself attractive.

55賣 飯 to sell cooked food.

公 賣 public sale.

出 賣 for sale.

底 貨 賤 賣 cheap clearance-sale.

拍 賣 sale by auction.

60現 賣 cash sales.

發 賣 to sell to the trade.

訂 賣 contract of sale.

轉 賣 re-sale.

非 賣 品 not for sale—often written on propaganda leaflets, etc.

勘 ⁴ To put forth effort.
4324

用 勘 相 我 國 家 put forth effort on behalf of one's nation.

邁 ⁴ To go on a journey; to pass by. To surpass.
4325

邁 一 步 to take a step.

邁·不 開 步 unable to take a step.

邁 大 步 行 to walk with great strides.

邁 種 超 羣 he surpassed them all.

邁 進 or 邁 往 to make progress; to go forward.

高 邁 excelling.

(a) To grow old.

年 邁 growing old.

老 邁 aged.

MAN. (ㄇㄢ)

滿 ³ Full, satisfied. Self-sufficient. The whole of. Complete.
4326

滿 世·界 the whole world.

滿·了 full.

滿 任 at the expiration of the term of office.

滿 假 at the expiration of a leave.

5滿 分 a full quota.

滿 口 應 承 made profuse promises.

滿 口 春 風 fluent; eloquent.

滿 口 胡 言 full of stupid talk.

滿 嘴 to keep on saying.

10滿 地 all over the ground.

滿 天 星 covered with stars.

滿 天 香 氣 the whole air was filled with fragrance.

滿 實 quite full.

滿 屋 the whole house.

15滿 帆 with full sails.

滿 座 the whole audience.

滿 心 whole-heartedly.

滿 心 喜 樂 filled with joy.

滿 心 憂 愁 a heart full of grief.

20滿 心 毒 惡 full of viciousness.

滿 意 satisfactory; satisfied.

滿 把 or 滿 握 a full handful.

滿 招 損 haughtiness invites disaster.

滿 日 on the expiration of the term.

[25]滿 月 a whole month; the month after childbirth; to pull a bow to the full; full moon.

滿 服 or 滿 孝 at the expiration of mourning.

滿 期 at the expiration of the period.

滿 杯 a full cup.

滿 流 the full tide.

[30]滿 溢 full to overflowing.

滿 盈 full; filled up.

滿 腔 熱 血 full of sympathetic feelings.

滿 腹 經 綸 profoundly learned.

滿 臉 俗·氣 a coarse facial expression.

[35]滿 臉 晦 氣 to have an unfavourable countenance.

滿 臉 風 塵 face covered with the dust of the road.

滿 處 everywhere; all over.

滿 足 satisfied.

滿 足 人 民 to satisfy the people.

[40]滿 路 the whole way; all along the road.

滿 身 the whole body.

滿 身 事 務 very fully occupied.

滿 身 病 症 full of infirmities.

滿 載 fully laden.

[45]滿 載 而 歸 return home fully laden—felicitous wish.

滿 錢 full amount of cash on the strings.

滿 門 the whole family.

滿 限 expired.

滿 面 or 滿 臉 the whole face; all over the face.

[50]滿 面 春 風 beaming with pleasure.

滿 額 a full allowance; the full allowance.

滿 願 而 已 fully satisfied—as having attained one's object.

滿 飲 drink a bumper.

塞 滿 stuffed full.

[55]裝 滿 packed full.

(a) Manchu.

滿 族 the Manchus.

滿 洲 Manchuria.

滿 漢 Manchu and Chinese.

瞞 [2] To deceive; to blind; eyes half-closed.
4327

瞞 得 過 人 瞞 不 過 神 you may deceive men, but you cannot deceive the gods.

瞞 心 昧 己 to deceive oneself.

瞞 目 to throw dust in the eyes of.

瞞 藏 to conceal.

[5]瞞 驅 or 瞞 哄 or 欺 瞞 to cheat; to take advantage of.

蹒 [2] To jump over—as a wall. Read *p'an*[1,2]. To limp.
4328

蹒 跚 的 走 to limp around; to walk with a waddle.

顢 [1,2] A large face. Dawdling.
4329

顢 頇 vacillating, dawdling.

曼
曼 [4] Long, extended. Large.
4330

曼 倩 偷 桃 May you have long life!—from the story of 曼 倩 who was said to have stolen peaches from 西 王 母; these peaches took 3,000 years to blossom and 300 years to mature.

曼 壽 long life.

曼 延 wide-spreading; endless.

曼 綽 high, falsetto notes.

[5]曼 死·了 killed—as a tree by climbers.

曼 漶 not recognizable; indecipherable.

曼 羨 spacious; flourishing.

曼 衍 to spread; endless.

(a) Read *man*[4], or *wan*[4]. Fine. Well cared for. Handsome.

曼 澤 sleek, well-favoured.

曼 煖 light and warm.

曼 辭 elegant language.

曼 陀 羅 stramonium; *datura alba.*

曼 靡 light and fine.

曼 麗 plump and beautiful.

墁 [4] To plaster. To pave.
4331

墁 地 板 or 鋪 地 板 to lay a board flooring.

墁 牆 to plaster a wall.

墁 磚 to pave with bricks.

嫚 [4] To insult; to affront. Inter. 慢 No. 4334.
4332

憎 嫚 to despise.

褻 嫚 to treat with contempt.

幔 [4] A curtain, a screen.
4333

幔·子 a curtain.

幔 室 a kind of tent.

幛 幔 to screen off.

慢 [4] Slow; slowly; dilatory. Gradually.
4334

慢 些 slower; not so fast.

慢 令 致 期 to give orders without urgency, and yet expect them to be finished in a set time.

慢 性 easy-going; chronic—of disease.

慢 慢 slowly; don't be in a hurry.

[5]慢·慢 來 come slowly; take your time; slower; slowly.

慢 慢[1]·的 all in good time; gently.

慢 慢[1]·走 go slowly; don't hurry away!

慢 手 慢 脚 slow in movements.

慢 板 slow time in music.

[10]慢 藏 誨 盜 slackness in putting things away properly teaches others to steal.

慢 行 do not hurry away!

慢 說 speak slowly; not quite so fast.

(a) To treat rudely.

慢 待 to treat with rudeness.

怠 慢 rudely.

輕 慢 with contempt.

漫
漫 [4] Water overflowing. Diffused; spreading.
4335

漫 失 disappeared.

漫 汗 wide-spreading; boundless.

漫 浪 wild, reckless.

漫 滅 to vanish; to disappear.

[5]漫 漫 far and wide.

漫 漫 大 霧 a dense fog.

漫 漶 單 簡 indecipherable except for a few characters here and there.

漫 無 限 制 with no restrictions whatever.

漫 種 to sow broadcast.

¹⁰漫 荒 the open country.

漫 道 如 此 do not talk like that!

彌 漫 boundless. 浪◦漫 unconven-[tional; romantic.

↑ 漫 畫 cartoons.

縵 4336 ² Silk thread. Thin silk, plain and unadorned.

縵 田 untilled fields.

(a) Read man⁴. Slow and stately.

縵 立 遠 視 to stand and gaze afar.

縵 縵 the slow rolling—as of the clouds.

(b) Mingled sounds in a musical performance.

縵 樂 harmony of mingled instruments.

蔓 4337 ⁴ To creep, as a plant.

蔓 子 a tendril; a creeper.

蔓 延 to spread about; diffusive.

爬 蔓 子 creeping plants.

(a) Read man². A kind of turnip.

蔓 青 the rape-turnip.

謾 4338 ² To deceive; to insult. Cf. 4327.

謾 上 不 謾 下 deceiving the superiors but not deceiving one's fellows.

謾 天 謾 地 deceiving those above and those below.

謾 語 exaggerated talk.

詐 謾 to deceive.

誕 謾 to brag; to boast.

(a) Read man⁴. Inter. 慢 No. 4334, 漫 No. 4335. Slow.

鏝 4339 ² A trowel. Inter. 墁 No. 4331.

鏝 刀 or 坭 鏝 a trowel for plastering.

饅 4340 ² Steamed bread; bread of any kind.

饅◦頭 steamed bread.

鰻 4341 ² Eels.

鰻 鱔 general term for eels.

靴 4342 ² Sides or uppers of shoes. To stretch a skin on a frame for a drum.

蠻 4343 ² Barbarous tribes in the south of China. Fierce, savage, uncivilized.

蠻 力 herculean strength.

蠻 夷 savages, wild tribes.

蠻 子 southerners.

蠻 性 ungovernable; wild.

⁵蠻 悍 rowdy.

蠻 橫 barbarous, savage.

蠻 石 conglomerate.

蠻 貊 tribes of the south and the north.

蠻 賴 talking like a barbarian.

蠻 邦 barbarous countries.

(a) A python found in S. China.

(b) In some parts used as a superlative.

蠻 好 excellent.

蠻 蠻 大 very large.

MANG.   (ㄇㄤˊ)

忙 4344 ² Hurried, in haste. Anxious. Busy. Flustered.

忙 中 有 錯 haste causes errors.

忙◦不 過 來 more on hand than one can accomplish; too busy.

忙 亂 flurried; anxious.

忙 卒 all in a bustle.

⁵忙 工 workers engaged during a press of work—as for rice-planting, harvest, etc.

忙◦得 很 very busy.

忙◦月 the busy months—for the farmer.

忙◦甚²麼 what are you in a hurry about? what is all this bustle?

忙 忙 碌 碌 fully occupied; flurried.

¹⁰忙 迫 pressed with work and flurried.

忙 速 or 急 忙 or 慌 忙 confusedly; hastily.

不 要 忙 don't be in a hurry; don't get flustered.

㝱 4345 ² Ridge-pole in a roof.

盲 4346 ² Blind; deluded, blind in heart.

盲 人 騎 瞎 馬 a blind man riding a blind horse—imminent danger.

盲 啞 學 校 school for the blind and dumb.

盲 年 a year which has no 立 春 term in it.

盲 從 (附 和) blindly following.

⁵盲 斑 (or 點) the blind spot.

盲 於 心 blind in heart.

盲 目◦的 lacking definite aim or lacking decision.

盲 眼 blind.

盲 腸 the cœcum. 盲 腸 炎 appen-[dicitis.

¹⁰盲◦蜘 蛛 the shepherd-spider.

盲 風 a violent wind.

↑盲 動 to act blindly, foolishly.

芒 4347 ² A sharp-edged grass. The awn or beard of wheat, etc.

芒 刺 在 背 having prickles down the back—of a man who sits stiffly and ill at ease.

芒 神 the clay figure of the driver of the clay ox used at the spring festival in honour of agriculture.

芒 種 a solar term. Grain in Ear, about June 6—20.

芒 鞋 straw sandals.

(a) A sharp point; a ray of light.

芒 刃 a sharp-pointed knife.

芒 角 sharp corners or edges.

光 芒 a ray or flash of light.

鋒 芒 a sharp point,—also used fig.

(b) Extensive. Numerous. Weary.

芒 芒 其 稼 "far and wide he sowed his crops."

芒 芒 然 歸 returning home weary and worn.

洪水芒芒 the flood waters spread widely abroad.

(c) Used for transliterating.

芒果 the mango.
芒硝 sodium sulphate.

(d) Read *huang²*. **Dispirited.**

芒芴 dispirited, disappointed.

茫² Vast, vague.
4348

茫然 on a sudden; surprising.
茫然不知 utterly ignorant of the matter.
茫無界·限 boundless.
茫茫堪輿 illimitable as creation.
茫茫大海 the boundless ocean.

硭² A crude saltpetre.
4349

硭硝 saltpetre.

鋩² A sharp point.
4350

邙² Name of a hill near Loyang in Honan.
4351

厖² Abundant. Mixed.
4352

厖洪 great favours.
政厖 the government is in confusion.
敦厖 simple, straight; to multiply.

狵
尨² Blended; variegated; striped. Inter. preceding.
4353

尨服 parti-coloured clothes.

(a) A shaggy dog, the Tibetan mastiff.

無使狵也吠 do not cause the dogs to bark.

(b) Read *mêng²*. **Confused.**

尨茸 confused and disordered.

莽³ Confused, disorderly. Undergrowth; jungle. Rude.
4354

莽大·夫 a term of reproach used by *Chu Hsi* in his history with reference to *Yang Hsiung* 楊雄 because he served the usurper 王莽.
莽撞 rude, rough.
莽漢 or 粗莽 a coarse fellow.
莽草 a poisonous plant.
莽蒼 the blue indefinite atmosphere of wide spaces.

漭³ Vast, expansive.
4355

蟒³ A python; a boa-constrictor.
4356

蟒蟲 or 蟒蛇 or 王蟒 a python.
蟒袍 ceremonial robes embroidered or woven with dragons having four claws.
蟒裙 skirt of former ceremonial dress.
蟒龍 a dragon; a monster.

MAO. (ㄇㄠ)

毛² The hair of an animal. Fur, down, feathers, nap.
4357 Rough, coarse. Radical 82.

毛·子 or 大毛·子 a foreigner—term of contempt.
　二毛·子 term of contempt for Chinese Christians.
毛孔 pores of the skin.
毛布 ginghams.
⁵毛息 small interest on deposits.
毛手毛脚 a busybody; a lively boy; a tease.
毛氈 felt.
毛氈苔 the sun-dew.
毛物 beasts.
¹⁰毛猶有倫 there are degrees even in hairs.
毛玻·璃 frosted glass.
毛·病 originally refers to examining the hair of a horse, in order to tell his condition—a fault, a defect, disease; an idiosyncrasy.

毛皮 furs, pelts.
毛稍 the tip of a hair—a trifle.
¹⁵毛竹 a large variety of bamboo.
毛筆 a Chinese writing-brush.
毛筆畫 wash-drawings.
毛管 a quill.
毛細管 capillaries.
²⁰毛織物 woollen goods.
毛羽 fur and feathers.
毛羽同類 classed with the furry and the feathery—a mere beast.
毛舉細故 to bring up many irrelevant and petty matters.
毛茛 crow-foot.
²⁵毛落皮單 when the hair falls the skin is insufficient for protection—without protection one is in danger.
毛蟹 the crab-louse.
毛蟲 caterpillars; beasts.
毛血 feathers and blood—offered in sacrifice.
毛製 woollen.
³⁰毛道 the class or quality of furs.
毛邊紙 a quality of Chinese writing-paper.
毛重 the gross weight—tare.
毛錢 small, worn cash; dime.
毛錐 a Chinese writing-brush or pencil.
³⁵毛錐·子 a mere penman; a copyist.
毛穎 a name for a Chinese writing-brush.
毛·頭 the hair of furs.
毛頭兒 a newly-born infant.
毛驢 a young donkey.
⁴⁰毛骨 the whole frame.
毛骨竦然 horror-stricken.
毛髮森立 the hair standing on end.
不毛之地 without any growth—sterile soil.
刺毛 stinging-hairs.
⁴⁵圓毛 round hairs—fur, animals.
扁毛 feathers—birds.
柔毛 soft hair—sheep, etc.
汗毛 fine hairs on the body.
理毛 to preen the feathers.
⁵⁰發毛 to grow mildewed.
白毛 mildew.
脫⁴毛 or 掉毛 to moult.

(a) Used in transliterating.
　A surname.

毛嬙 a famous beauty about 465 B.C.
毛瑟鎗 Mauser pistol.
毛詩 the Book of Odes, as edited by 毛亨 and 毛萇.

牦 2
4358
A wild yak.

眊 4
4359
Dim-sighted; dull, bewildered. Inter. next.

眸 子 眊 然 the eye will be unsteady.

耄 4
4360
An old man of eighty. Aged.

耄 耋 a very old man.
耄 期 a centenarian.

芼 4
4361
Greens, vegetables. To select, to gather.

芼 羹 a stew of meat and greens.

(a) Read *mao²*. Grasses, etc., growing up.

髦 2
4362
Hair on the head; long hair.

髦 馬 a horse with a long mane.

(a) Eminent; excellent.

髦 士 eminent men.

(b) A western tribe of the Ch'iang 羌 No. 666.

(c) A kind of asparagus.

旄 2
4363
The tail of an animal, used as a banner.

旄 戈 a spear with a tail-tassel.
旄 牛 the yak or grunting-ox.
旄 頭 a name for the Pleiades.

(a) Read *mao⁴*. Inter. 耄 No. 4360.

旄 倪 old and young.

茅 2
4364
(--*ssŭ*)
Reeds, rushes, grasses. Poor.

茅 厠 or 茅 鬮 or 茅 房 a privy.
茅 屋 a hut; a thatched house.
茅 棚 or 茅 寮 a shed in a field.
茅 舍 my humble cottage.

⁵茅 草 grass, thatch, rushes.
開 茅 塞 remove the obstructing rushes—open up the mind for instruction.

蝥 2
蟊
4365
A fly which is used similarly to cantharides.

斑 蝥 the fly, as above.

(a) Read *mao²*. A grub which eats growing grain.

蝥 賊 grubs which eat grain; the former eats the roots, the latter the joints—injurious persons.

貓 2
猫
4366
The cat. Also read *miao²*.

貓 兒 嘴 dainty as a cat in feeding.
貓 叫 to mew.
貓 哭 耗 子 假 慈 悲 like the cat weeping for the rat—false sympathy.
貓·子 or 貓 兒 a cat. (*dial.*)
⁵貓 狸 a striped fox; wild cat.
貓 眼 石 cat's-eyes.
貓 頭 鷹 the horned-owl.
貓 鼠 同 眠 the cat and the rat are asleep together—officials and bandits working in collusion.
淨 貓 a castrated cat.
¹⁰郎 貓 or 公 貓 a male cat.
↑母 貓 a female cat.

錨 2
4367
An anchor. Also read *miao²*.

錨 漂 (or 桴) a mooring-buoy.
錨 纜 or 錨 繩 an anchor-rope or hawser.
錨 鍊 a cable.
下 錨 or 抛 錨 to drop anchor.
⁵落 錨 to drop anchor—to settle a matter.
起 錨 to weigh anchor.

貌 4
兒
4368
Manner, appearance, form, face, bearing.
Distinguish 兒 No. 1759.

貌 作 to appear to....
貌 似 而 神 虧 the appearance is there but the spirit is lacking.
貌 合 心 離 apparently of one accord, but divided in heart.
貌 善 防 心 毒 his face is good, but watch his treacherous heart.
⁵貌 執 to treat with ceremony.
貌 形 form, figure.
貌 敬 respectful demeanour.
貌 爲 to pretend; to make an appearance.
貌 狀 appearance, expression.
¹⁰貌 甚 寢 very ugly.
貌 言 unreliable statements.
貌 醜 ugly; plain.
不 可 貌 相 do not judge a person by his looks.
以 貌 取 人 to judge by appearances.
¹⁵外 貌 outward appearance.
容 貌 appearance, expression of the face.
月 貌 round-faced—beautiful.
美 貌 handsome.
面·貌 face, features, mien.

(a) Read *mo⁴·⁵*. To draw portraits.

命 工 貌 妃 he ordered the artist to paint a picture of his concubine.
能 貌 able to draw portraits.

卯 3
4369
The fourth of the *Earthly Branches*—the period from 5—7 a.m. A period or term.

卯 刻 or 卯 時 5—7 a.m.
卯·子 工 or 卯·子 活 work done by the day.
卯 月 the second lunar month.
卯 期 the fixed dates at which a muster is made.
⁵卯 簿 the muster-roll.
卯 鐘 the matin-bell in a monastery.
慌 卯 to miss the muster.
應 卯 to answer to the muster.
點 卯 to call the muster-roll.

(a) A mortise.

榫 卯 mortise and tenon.

昴 3
4370
The eighteenth of the Chinese zodiacal constellations, answering to the Pleiades; it is one of the four that always mark a Sunday

in the calendar. See 虛 No. 2821-88.

昴 星 the Pleiades.

泖 ³ Still waters. River in Kiangsu.
4371

茆 ²·³· Water-mallows.
4372

冒 ⁴ To go forward with eyes covered. To risk, to rush upon. To put forth, to issue forth.
4373

冒 侵 to encroach.
冒 冒 失 失 suddenly.
冒 瀆 to trespass; to annoy.
⁵冒·失 abruptly; recklessly.
冒·失 鬼 a blundering rash sort of person.
冒 嫌·疑 to brave suspicion.
冒 寒 to brave the cold; to take a cold.
冒 往 遭 禍 to go forward rashly and meet with disaster.
¹⁰冒 撞 rude, rough mannered.
冒•昧 ignorant; rash; headstrong.
冒 死 to brave death.
冒 火 fig., to get ang.y; to throw out sparks.
冒 烟 to smoke—as a chimney.
¹⁵冒 犯 to insult; to give offence.
冒 犯·的 罪 presumptuous sin.
冒 猛·的 hastily; rashly.
冒 觸 to behave rudely to; to offend.
冒 險 to brave danger;to take risks.
↓²⁰冒 險 精·神 the spirit of adventure.
冒 險 事·業 a risky business.
冒 險 家 adventurers; explorers.
冒 險 性·質 foolhardy temperament.
冒 險 投 資 reckless investment.
²⁵冒 險 進 行 reckless advance.
冒 雨 to brave the rain.
冒 風 to catch cold; to face the weather.

(a) To feign; to assume falsely; to imitate.

冒 充 to pretend to be; to assume.
冒 充 字·號 to use the name of a firm with criminal intent.

冒 名 to take the name of another falsely.
冒 名 頂 替 See 9.below.
⁵冒 告 to lay a false accusation.
冒 姓 to take another surname.
冒 官 to pretend to be an official.
冒 捏 to counterfeit.
冒 替 to assume; to take the place of another under false pretences; false names, etc.
¹⁰冒 混 to be underhand; false pretences; to deceive.
冒 牌 to imitate or forge a trademark.
冒 籍 to enter for an examination under false pretences; to pretend to be of another district.
冒 認 to lay a false claim to.
冒 頂 to assume; to pretend to be.
冒 騙 人 財 to rob by false pretences.

(b) To cover.

下 土 是 冒 ..... which overshadows this lower earth.

(c) Inter. next. Jealous.

冒 嫉 以 惡 之 her jealousy made her hate her. (-wu⁴-)

(d) Read mo⁴. Covetous. Name of a Hsiung-nu chieftain.

娼 ³·⁴· Envious; jealousy. Dislike.
4374　Distinguish 娼 No. 209.

帽 ⁴ A cap, a hat.
4375

帽·匠 a hatter.
帽·子 a cap or hat.
帽 帶 hat-strings.
帽 店 or 帽 舖 hat-shop.
⁵帽 架 hat-rack or stand.
帽 沿·子 brim of a hat.
帽 盒 hat-box.
帽 章 badge for a cap.
帽 襻 hat-band.
¹⁰帽 頂 or 帽 結 兒 the knob on a Chinese skull-cap.
大 禮 帽 a tall silk hat.
筆 帽 cap for protecting the point of a Chinese writing-brush.
脫 帽 to raise the hat; to remove the hat.
銅 帽·子 a percussion-cap.

銅 盆 帽·子 the ordinary felt or Homburg hat, from its shape.

髳 ³ Restless.
4376

髳 氄 restless, melancholy.

湏 ⁴ To ooze out. Inter. 冒 No. 4373.
4377

湏·出·來 oozing out.
湏 熱 氣 giving forth steam or heat.

瑁 ⁴ A kind of jade. Read mei¹. Tortoise shell.
4378

玳·瑁 tortoise shell.

MO MÊ. (ㄇㄛ)
(Meh)

麥 ⁴·⁵· Wheat. Radical 199. Usually pron. mai⁴.
4379

麥 信 風 the north-east wind in the 5th month.
麥 四 米 六 40% wheat and 60% rice—as in dieting.
麥 塲 threshing floor for wheat.
麥 奴 smut in wheat.
⁵麥·子 wheat or barley.
麥 浪 the appearance of a wheat-field during the passing of a breeze.
麥 燒 whisky; distilled spirits.
麥 田 a wheat-field.
麥 秀 兩 歧 two ears on every stalk of wheat—a year of plenty.
¹⁰麥 秋 the wheat-harvest—fourth lunar month.
麥 穗 ears of wheat.
麥 芒 the awn of wheat.
麥 芽 wheat-sprouts; malt.
麥 芽 糖 malt-sugar.
¹⁵麥 苗 young growing wheat.
麥 英 a name for cherries.
麥 角 ergot.
麥 酒 beer.
麥 門 冬 asparagus.
²⁰麥 飯 boiled wheat.
麥 餅 wheaten cakes.
麥 餘·子 chaff.
麥 麩·子 or 麥 糠 bran; chaff.

麥 麵 wheaten flour.
25 大◦麥 barley.
小◦麥 wheat.
打 麥 to thresh wheat or barley.
油 麥 or 燕 麥 oats.
烏 麥 or 蕎◦麥 buckwheat.

(a) Used in transliterating.

麥 克 沁 礮 Maxim gun.

貃 4.5. Wild tribes of the north.
4380   Also read *mai*[4].

蠻 貃 wild tribes of the south and the north respectively.

(a) To grow up silently.

貃 其 德 音 the fame of his virtue silently grew.

陌 4.5. A raised path going east
4381   and west between fields. A street, a road.

陌 上 in the street.
陌 路 人 or 陌 生 人 a stranger.
阡 陌 交 通 roads in every direction.

脈
脉
衇 4.5.
The pulse. The veins or arteries. Also read *mai*[4].
4382

脈 伏 a low pulse.
脈◦息 the beating of the pulse.
脈◦息 微 弱 a weak pulse.
脈 氣 充 足 a good constitution.
5 脈 理 the philosophy of the pulse.
脈 絡 相 連 the veins and arteries are connected—joined, conterminous.
脈 門 the pulse at the wrist.
動 脈 the arteries. 靜 脈 the veins.
命 脈 the life of a thing.
10 山 脈 a mountain range.
爭 脈 the veins.
診 脈 or 評 脈 to feel the pulse.
點 脈 to hit the pulse.
脈 脈 full of tacit affection.

霢
霂 4.5.
Drizzling rain. To soak—used fig. of favours.
4383

貘 4.5.
4384   The tapir.

驀 4.5. To leap on or over.
4385   Suddenly.

驀 波 to ride on the waves.
驀 越 to spring over; to flash past.

墨 4.5. Ink. Black; dark. A
4386   measure of five feet.

墨 丈 之 間 between five and ten feet long.
墨 刑 tattooing on the face—an ancient punishment.
墨 壺 an inkstand.
墨 守 conservative.
5 墨 客 a literary man.
墨 戲 drawing pictures.
墨 斗 兒 a carpenter's ink-cup and line for marking.
墨 晶 smoky quartz.
墨 板 block for printing.
10 墨 水 liquid ink.
墨 水 規 bow-pen.
墨 池 the hollow for water on a Chinese ink-slab.
墨 油 printing ink.
墨 滾 printer's roller.
15 墨 牀 a stand for ink.
墨 硯 slab for rubbing up Chinese ink.
墨 綠 a blue-black colour.
墨 線 a marking-line.
墨 迹 original copy of writings.
20 墨 頭◦子 stumps of Chinese ink.
墨 魚 the cuttle-fish.
墨 黑 jet black.
近 墨 者 黑 those who use ink get black—beware of associations.

(a) Silent, lonely.
Inter. 默 No. 4388.

墨 墨 no sound nor smell, uneventful.

(b) Covetous.

墨 吏 an official greedy for bribes.
貪 墨 covetous.

(c) To be gloomy and disconsolate.

面 深 墨 crestfallen; of sad countenance.

(d) Used in transliterating. A surname.

墨 子 or 墨 翟 the philosopher whose name has been Latinized into Micius. His date is uncertain but it is generally placed between the 4th and 5th centuries B.C. His doctrines were assailed by Mencius.

墨 子 兼 愛 the philosopher Micius loves all without distinction.
墨 西 哥 Mexico.
墨 銀 Mexican dollars.

纆 4.5.
4387   A cord. To bind.

纆 索 bonds; cords.
糾 纆 bound up together.

默 4.5. Dark, secret. Silent.
4388

默 佑 to protect secretly.
默 坐 to sit in silence.
默 契 tacit understanding.
默 存 to have a fit of absent-mindedness.
5 默 寫 to write from memory.
默 念 or 默 想 to reflect on.
默 書 to write from memory.
默 會 intuitive understanding.
默 為 贊 助 tacit support.
10 默 示 to instruct secretly; to reveal.
默 禱 to pray in secret.
默 約 tacit understanding.
默 而 識 之 silently to remember what one has learned.
默 許 tacit permission.
15 默 諾 tacit consent.
默 識 心 融 with a clear heart he silently treasured up knowledge.
默 陰 gloomy; retired.
默 默 無 聲 perfectly silent.
20 默 默 靜 聽 silently listening.

(a) Used for transliterating.

默 伽 Mecca.
默 德 那 Medina.

MEI.   (ㄇㄟ)

枚 2 The stalk of a shrub. A
4389   piece; one of anything. N.A. for coins, fruits, etc.

枚 數 the number of.

枚 舉 to reckon up one by one.
   不 勝 枚 舉 too many to be counted.
   難 以 枚 舉 difficult to deal with each one.
幾 枚 How many?
條 枚 branches and stems.
猜 枚 the game of *mora* or guess-fingers.

(a) A gag for troops when making a night attack.
衡 枚 疾 走 hastening forward with gagged mouths.

(b) To cast lots. To divine.
枚 卜 功 臣 to cast lots among the worthy statesmen.
枚 筮 to divine.

(c) Fine workmanship.
枚 枚 實 實 solid and well-finished—as a building.

玫
玫 } ² A sparkling red gem.
4390
玫 瑰 油 attar of roses.
玫 瑰 花 the pink or red cultivated rose.

眉 ² The eyebrows.
4391
眉 來 眼 去 exchanging glances.
眉 史 a courtesan.
眉 壽 long eyebrows which indicate old age; longevity.
眉 如 新 月 crescent-shaped eyebrows.
⁵眉 宇 the eyebrows—like a penthouse.
眉 心 space between the eyebrows.
眉·毛 the eyebrows.
眉 清 目 秀 beautiful, handsome.
眉·目 eyebrows and eyes—arrangement, order, sequence; very close; clue to a problem. [nomy.
¹⁰眉 眼 arrangement; order; physiog-
眉 睫 eyebrows and lashes—close; imminent.
   近 在 眉 睫 at a crisis; imminent.
眉 語 speaking with the eyebrows—giving a hint.

眉 邊 the temples.
¹⁵眉 間 白 毫 white hairs between the eyebrows—mark of every Buddha.
眉 開 眼 笑 a beaming countenance.
眉 雪 white eyebrows.
眉 頭 the eyebrows.
眉 黛 black for the eyebrows—thus used to describe the eyebrows of a beauty.
²⁰倒³眉 bad luck; to have things go all wrong.
愁 眉 frowning eyebrows.

(a) The edge of a well. The top of a book.
眉 批 or 題 眉 comments at the head of the pages of Chinese books.
居 井 之 眉 dwelling on the edge of a well.

媚 ⁴ To flatter; to fawn on. To love, to coax. Attractive.
4392 Fascinating, seductive.
媚 上 驕 下 acting like a snob.
媚 人 to fawn on a person.
媚 人 意 to humour a person; to seek to please another.
媚 外 to toady to foreigners.
⁵媚·子 a favourite—concubine.
媚 態 the seductive appearance of a pretty woman.
媚 竈 to play up to the officer who has power—from the *Analects*:
   寧 媚 於 竈 better to pay court to the furnace—i.e., the important place.
媚 眼 bewitching eyes.
媚 藥 aphrodisiacs.
¹⁰媚·裏 媚 氣·的 smiling and smirking.
側 媚 toadying.
狐 媚 seductive; bewitching.
諂 媚 to flatter and toady to.
↑妖 媚 glamorous.

嵋 ² Name of a mountain in Szechwan.
4393
峨 嵋 a famous mountain in Szechwan — *O mei*.

楣 ² The lintel of a door or window.
4394

倒³楣 之 事 an unpleasant or unlucky matter. *See* 眉 No. 4391 —20.

湄 ² The brink of a stream; the margin of a lake.
4395 See 眉 No. 4391—A.
湄 湖 a lake in Hunan.

郿 ² A district in Shensi.
4396

媒 ² A go-between. A match-maker. A decoy.
4397
媒·人 or 媒 賓 or 媒 妁 a matchmaker; a go-between.
媒 介 a go-between; to negotiate or mediate.
媒 介 物 a flux.
媒 介 體 a medium.
⁵媒 婆 a female go-between.
媒 蘗 to cause gradual injury to come to another.
媒 怨 to arouse hatred.
媒 束 betrothal papers.
媒 染 劑 a mordant.
¹⁰作 媒 to act as a go-between.
傳 染 之 媒 agents of infection.
自 媒 to advertise oneself.
誘 媒 to decoy; to lead into trouble.
酒 媒 a ferment for liquors.

煤 ² Coal; charcoal.
4398
煤 井 the shaft of a coal mine.
煤 坑 a coal-pit.
煤 屑 cinders.
煤 山 Coal Hill, Peking. (Peiping).
⁵煤 廠 a coal-depôt.
煤 根 石 jet; fossil lignite.
煤 業 the coal industry.
煤·氣 gas.
煤 氣 機 gas-engine.
¹⁰煤 氣 燈 gas-lamp.
煤 氣 爐 gas-stove.
煤 氣 表 gas-meter.
煤 油 kerosene.
煤 油 燭 paraffin-wax candles.
¹⁵煤 渣 兒 cinders; small coal.
煤 炱 soot.
煤 炭 charcoal; coal.

煤 炭 桶 coal-scuttle.
煤 烟 soot; lampblack.
20 煤 爐 stove for burning coal.
煤 球 ㄦ or 煤 基·子 coal-balls—made of coal-dust and clay.
煤 田 coal-fields.
煤 磚 briquettes.
煤 礦 or 煤 籠 a coal-mine.
25 煤 窰 a coal-pit.
煤 精 brimstone.
煤 艙 coal-bunkers.
煤 艙 門 coaling port.
煤 車 coal-trucks.
30 煤 餅·子 cakes of coal-dust and clay.
煤 黑 油 gas or coal-tar.
木 煤 brown coal; lignite.
烟 煤 or 油 煤 bituminous coal.
石 煤 or 白 煤 or 紅 煤 anthracite.
裝 煤 to take in coal—as a ship.

禖 2 Sacrifice held to supplicate for a son.
4399

脄 2 Quickening of the fœtus.
4400

脄 胎 to quicken.

每 3 Each, every.
4401

每 下 愈 况 or 每 况 愈 下 to go from bad to worse.
每 人 一 分 (*fen*[4]) to each man a share.
每 人 每 one to each person—to serve one dish to each person instead of having the common bowls in the centre as is customary in Chinese meals.
每 件 every article.
5 每 個 三·十 文 thirty cash each.
每 兩 年 一 回 once every two years.
每 到 節 期 at every festival.
每 受 人 欺 he is always deceived by others.
每 口 之 資 度 *per capita* wealth.
10 每 口 計 算 *per capita* calculations.
每 回 on each occasion.
每 常 whenever.
每 年 every year.
每 日 or 每 天 every day.

15 每 日·裏 daily.
每 時 every time.
每 有 there are constantly....
每 次 on each occasion.
每 每 always; invariably.
20 每 百 by the hundred.
每 種 各 出 少 許 would take a little of each kind and offer it.
每 逢 or 每 到 on each occasion; every time; whenever.

(a) Read *mei*[2]. Beautiful.

原 田 每 每 beautiful are the fields and plains.

梅 2 Plums; prunes.
4402

梅 占 百 花 魁 the flowering plum stands first among the flowers.
梅 妻 鶴 子 plum trees for my wife and cranes for my children—said by a recluse who had neither, but cultivated the plum and reared the cranes for his pleasure.
梅 嶺 the range of mountains lying between Kiangsi and Kwangtung.
梅 月 the tenth lunar month.
5 梅 毒 venereal virus.
梅 花 椿 bamboos or stakes driven in as a palisade for a military camp on the march.
梅 花 疔 venereal sores.
梅 花 瓣 形 five-pointed star-figure.
梅 花 骨 瘦 slim and emaciated.
10 梅 雨 or 霉 雨 the rainy season—from about the end of May to early July.
梅 香 a slave girl.
楊 梅 the arbutus; syphilis.

痗 4 Disease caused by worry, anxiety, etc.
4403

痗 氣 bad luck.
心 痗 heart ache.

苺
莓 2 Edible berries, as the blackberry, strawberry, etc.
4404

莓 苔 moss; lichen.

霉 2 Damp, mouldy; mildewed.
4405

霉 天 the rainy season, from about the end of May to early July.
霉 氣 damp; mildew.
霉 爛 or 霉 壞 spoiled by damp and mildew.
發 霉 to grow mildewed.

美 3 Beautiful, comely. Admirable. Delicious. Good.
4406

美 中 不 足 happiness incomplete.
美 之 觀 念 conception of beauty.
美 事 a praiseworthy matter.
美 人 a beauty. 美 人 計 to use a pretty woman in order to ensnare a person.
5 美 人 蕉 a beautiful flowering variety of plantain.
美 俗 good customs.
美 備 good and perfect; above criticism.
美 利 handsome profits.
美 名 a good name.
10 美 味 well-flavoured; delicacies.
美 哉 Admirable! How beautiful!
美 善 excellent.
美 地 fertile land.
美 士 an excellent scholar.
15 美 女 a pretty girl.
美 如 冠 玉 as beautiful as the jade ornaments of a cap.
美 學 aesthetics.
美 學 史 history of aesthetics.
美 少 年 a young fop; a beau.
20 美 德 excellent virtue.
美 意 a kind intention.
美 情 love of the beautiful.
美 感 taste; emotions stirred by the beautiful.
美 才 fine talents.
25 美 政 good government.
美 景 beautiful scenery.
美 服 fine clothes.
美 樂 不 可 勝 言 inexpressibly happy. (-*lê*[4]-)
美 滿 on the best of terms with; superb; splendid; perfect.
30 美 盛 貌 the appearance of great beauty.
美 目 attractive eyes—the black and white clearly defined.
美 盻 to gaze with longing.
美 秀 而 文 elegant, cultivated and talented.

美 育 aesthetic culture.

[85] 美 舉 a good action; a benevolent deed; an excellent proposal

美 色 or 美 貌 handsome; female beauty.

美 術 art.

美 術 品 works of art.

美 術 學 會 artists' society.

[40] 美 術 家 artists.

美 術 展 覽 會 exhibition of fine arts.

美 術 工 業 學 校 school of applied art.

美 術 思 想 aesthetic taste.

美 術 意 味 artistic taste.

[45] 美 術 明 信 片 picture postcards.

美 術 界 the world of art.

美 術 科 department of fine arts.

美 術 館 art gallery.

美 觀 fine appearance; stylish looking.

[50] 美 談 an interesting anecdote.

美 譽 splendid reputation.

美 質 good qualities.

美 辭 choice speech; rhetoric.

美 辭 法 laws of rhetoric.

[55] 美 酒 肥 肉 wine and meat of the best quality.

美 除 promoted to a good post.

美 食 excellent food; delicacies.

美 麗 beautiful, excellent.

(a) Used in transliterating.

美 利 堅 United States of America.

美·國 United States of America.

美 國 各 省 the states of the U.S.A. A.c....州.

美 國 聯 邦 United States of America.

美 棉 American cotton.

美 總 統 the President of U.S.A.

↑美○洲 or 亞 美 利 加 America.

渼 [3]
4407
River in Shensi.

鎂 [3]
4408
Magnesium.

浼 浼 [3]
4409
To request; to ask a favour of.

浼 中 說 合 to invite middlemen and arrange a bargain.

浼 托 or 拜 浼 to be obliged for; to ask a kindness of.

浼 求 to implore.

(a) To defile.

爾 焉 能 浼 我 哉 How can you defile me?

(b) Read *mien*[3]. Water flowing.

河 水 浼 浼 the river flows on.

妹 [4]
4410
A younger sister. Distinguish 妹 No. 4547.

妹·夫 or 妹 丈 or 妹·婿 husband of a younger sister.

妹·子 or 妹·妹 or 小 妹 a younger sister.

↑妹 喜 or 妺 喜 *See* 4547.

昧 [4]
4411
Obscure, dark. Colour-blind. To suppress, to appropriate.

昧 之 以 理 之 所 無 deceived by what is unreasonable.

昧 心 or 昧 良·心 to blind the mind; to go contrary to conscience.

昧 旦 a dull dawn.

昧 昧 我 思 之 I have given it deep consideration.

[5] 昧 昧 芒 芒 然 sound and wide-spreading, as doctrines; 昧 昧 has the meaning of 純 厚 here.

日 昧 昧 其 將 暮 the day darkened towards evening.

昧 死 to risk death; to do a thing at the risk of one's life.

昧 沒 ambiguous—of writings.

昧 爽 just before daylight.

[10] 昧 瞀 stupid and ignorant—a dark mind.

昧 莫 之 垌 a wide expanse of waste land.

昧 覛 to examine a thing in the dark.

昧 谷 the valley where the sun sets.

昧 起·來 to cover a thing up.

(a) To cut.

昧 雉 to kill a pheasant—ancient form of oath.

沬 [4]
4412
Name of a river. Name of a town in the State of *Wei*.

Distinguish 沫 No. 4549.

眛 [4]
4413
Colour-blindness.

眛 於 事 實 blind as to facts.

眛 於 本 國 情·形 blind as to the conditions of one's nation.

魅 [4]
4414
A demon with a man's face and four legs, the exhalation of the mountains and forests.

黴 [2]
4415
Mouldy and black. Dirty. To rot; bacteria; lichens.

黴 毒 or 梅 毒 syphilitic virus.

黴 瘠 swarthy and emaciated from hunger.

黴 菌 bacteria.

黴 黑 grimy; dark-complexioned.

寐 [4]
4416
To sleep soundly. See 假 No. 599-17.

寐 息 to sleep, to rest.

失 寐 insomnia.

媺 [3]
4417
A slight, elegant woman. Handsome, similar to 美.

MÊN.   (ㄇㄣ)

門 [2]
4418
A door, a gateway, an opening. Radical 169. N.A.

門 丁 or 看 門·的 or 門 公 a doorkeeper.

門·上 or 門·子 an attendant in a *yamen*.

門 下 retainers—*see below*—A.1.

↓門·巡 an opening; opportunity.

[5] 再 沒 有 門·巡 there is no other way.

門 刺 or 名 刺 a visiting-card.

門 包 or 門 規 or 門 敬 fees to doorkeepers; perquisites.

門 口ㄦ a doorway; an entrance; at the door.

門 可 羅 雀 birds may be snared at the door—of a deserted house.

[10] 門 吏 petty officer in charge of a gate.

門 堂 the entrance-hall.

門 橛 a door-sill.

門 墩 the stone block at each side of the steps, outside the door of a Chinese house.

門 外 outside the door.

15 門 客 retainers.

門 巷 door and street—one's address.

門 市 to sell retail over the counter.

門 帖 a name for couplets pasted on doors, etc.

門 心 the panel of a door.

20 門 戶 a door. *See below*—A.4:—B.2.ff.

門 戶 開 放 the open-door (policy).

門 房 a porter's lodge.

門 扇 the leaf of a door.

門 插 關 the bolt of a door.

25 門 斗 former attendants on a district inspector of schools.

門 框 door-frame.

門 楣 the lintel of a door.

門 橝 a door-post.

門 樞 the pivot on which a Chinese door hangs.

30 門 樓 rooms over a city gate.

門 檻 a threshold; a door-sill (-*k'ar³*)

門 無 雜 賓 there are no irregular visitors—care being taken in making acquaintances.

門 牌 a door-plate giving particulars of residents, number, occupation, etc.

門 牙 (or 齒) front teeth.

35 門 牡 the bolt of a door.

門 狀 a notice pasted on the right of a door, giving the date of birth and death of one recently deceased; ancient term for a visiting-card.

門 環 子 a ring on a door used as a knocker.

門 神 door-gods—either paper effigies or the names of the gods pasted on the doors.

門 禁 restrictions as to entrance.

40 門 禮 fees to a door-keeper.

門 簾 子 hanging-screens before doors.

門 簿 visitor's book.

門 籠 子 posts to bar the shutters of shops.

門 者 a door porter.

45 門 聯 antithetic couplets pasted on doors and doorposts at new year.

門 脈 the portal vein.

門 衛 door-porter.

門 診 to see patients at home, as contrasted with visiting them in their homes.

門 鈴 door-bell.

50 門 鎖 上 了 the door is locked.

門 閂 the bar or bolt of a door or gate.

門 閭 paternal dwelling.

門 限 threshold, doorsill.

門 隙 中 a crack in a door.

55 門 面 a shopfront; frontage of a house; the appearance of things.

門 面 語 mere outside talk, having no real reliability, not from the heart.

維 持 一 點 門 面 leave him a little chance to keep up his appearance.

門 領 door-keeper.

門 首 a porch; a doorway.

60 上 門 to close a door; to fail in business; to visit.

便 門 a private entrance.

叩 門 to seek entrance.

大 門 main entrance.

球 門 the goal in football, etc.

65 耳 門 side-entrance.

腰 門 a side door.

(a) A profession. A sect. A school or party.

門 下 受 業 to study under a certain person.

門 人 or 門 徒 a disciple.

門 外 漢 an outsider, not in the trade or profession.

門 戶 成 見 party prejudice.

5 門 生 a pupil; a disciple.

門 路 an occupation; an opening; an introduction.

門 門 曉 得 to know something of everything.

門 類 various branches.

佛 門 Buddhism.

10 入 門 to enter; introductory studies.

分 門 to classify; to form cliques.

孔 門 Confucianism.

專 (門) 家 a specialist; an expert.

(b) A family.

門 婿 a son-in-law.

門 戶 a family. *See above*—20.

門 戶 不 對 an unsuitable alliance.

門 氏 the married and maiden surnames of a woman.

5 門 當 戶 對 well-matched—of a matrimonial alliance.

門 第 reputation; social position.

門 衰 祚 薄 the family had declined in prosperity.

門 風 reputation of a family.

(c) N.A. for cannons, etc.

幾 門 砲 several pieces of ordnance.

們² Sign of the plural.
4419

人 們 persons; human; mankind.

娘 們 women.

弟 兄 們 brethren; brothers in arms.

我 們, 你 們, 他 們 we, us; you; they, them.

↑ 咱 們 you and I; you and we.

悶 惆 懑 ⁴
4420

Mournful, sorrowful, melancholy, depressed. To stupefy.

悶 倦 wearied and depressed.

悶 坐 to sit in silent melancholy.

悶 得 慌 or 悶 得 很 very depressed.

悶 悶 不 樂 melancholy; sad and depressed. (-*lê⁴*)

5 悶 甑 stifling—as the weather.

悶 死 了 to be down in the dumps.

悶 殺 了 人 bored to death.

悶 氣 low spirits.

悶 熱 or 懊 熱 sultry weather; hot and close.

10 悶 空 氣 foul, stifling air.

悶 酒 wine drunk when alone.

悶 香 stupefying perfume.

悶 默 solitary and depressed.

愁 悶 melancholy.

15 憂 悶 sad and grieved; melancholy.

煩 悶 to feel dull and listless or depressed.

解 悶 or 遣 悶 to dispel melancholy.

(a) To cover.

悶 上 茶 cover the tea—to draw a while.

悶 了 口 to shut up the mouth; to cease chattering.

悶 住 了 puzzled, unable to reply.

悶 火 to cover a fire with ashes.
⁵悶 礶 a sealed jar.
悶·葫·蘆 a closed gourd—something difficult to comprehend.
悶 表 a watch with a cover to protect the glass—a hunter.

煟 1.4 **To cook in a close vessel and steam.**
4421

燜 肉 meat cooked *en casserole*.

捫 2 **To feel, to lay the hand on; to hold. To cover.**
4422

捫 心 自 問 self-examination.
捫 書 皮 to cover a book.
捫 紗 to cover with gauze.
捫 緊 to stretch tight—as a cover.
⁵捫 虱 to kill lice between the thumb nails.
捫 開 to smooth out with the hands.
捫 黑 路 to feel the way in the dark.
捫 鼓 to cover a drum.

虋 2 Asparagus,–also called 天 門 冬.
4423　 A variety of red-stalked millet.

MÊNG.　　(ㄗ)

氓 2
虻 }　The people; vassals. Also read *mang²*.
4424

流 氓 vagrants. (-*mang²*)

䖟 2
虻 }　A gadfly.
4425

䖟 蟲 or 蚊 蟲 gadflies and mosquitoes.
牛 䖟 a horsefly.
蜚 䖟 a gadfly.

(a) A plant. *Fritillaria,*-also called 貝 母.

盟 2 A solemn declaration before the gods. An oath, a covenant, an alliance, a contract. To swear. A Mongol tribe or league. Also read *ming²*.
4426

盟 主 the person who administers an oath.
盟 兄 弟 sworn brothers; members of a secret society.
盟 國 allied States.
盟 府 the place where records of covenants were kept.
⁵盟 心 or 盟 情 sworn devotion.
盟 書 or 盟 詞 a form of oath; the papers signed by the contracting parties.
盟 約 a treaty or agreement.
盟 誓 to swear an oath; oath or covenant.
盟 長 ³ the leader in a covenant.
¹⁰盟 首 the first to sign a covenant.
背 盟 to break a covenant.
請 盟 to seek an alliance.
金 石 同 盟 a perpetual alliance.

萌 2 **The budding of plants, the sprouting of seeds. To germinate, to shoot forth. The first risings of.**
4427

萌 作 to sprout.
萌 兆 warnings of coming events.
萌 動 budding; risings of discontent, etc.
萌 蘖 incipient germ of rebellion.
⁵萌 於 再 to sprout again.
萌 條 young shoots or twigs.
萌 生 numerous, like sprouting grasses.
萌 芽 to sprout; to put forth buds; early growth.
萌 芽 時 代 period of growth and development; initial stages.
¹⁰萌 萌 remaining; present.
復 萌 to revive—as old affections or plans.

(a) To destroy by ploughing.

春 始 生 而 萌 之 in the spring when it begins to grow, destroy it by ploughing.

(b) Inter. 氓 No. 4424. The people.

萌 黎 or 萌 隸 the masses.

孟 4 **Great, eminent. Senior, eldest, first, chief. Mencius.**
4428

孟 仲 季 first, second and third—sons or daughters.
孟 侯 the heir-apparent at eighteen years.
孟·夫 子 ³ or 孟 軻 Mencius.
孟 婆 goddess of the winds.
⁵孟 春 the first month of spring—the other seasons are similarly spoken of.
孟 月 the first, fourth, seventh, and tenth lunar months.
孟 母 三 遷 the mother of Mencius changed her abode three times.
孟 陬 or 孟 陽 the first lunar month.

(a) Rough and rude.

孟 浪 rude; rough manner; careless speech.
孟 浪 之 言 careless speech.
　勿 嫌 孟 浪 do not dislike me because I am rough and rude.
孟 行 arbitrary action.

(b) To press forward.

孟 晉 to advance with zeal.

(c) Used in transliterating.

孟 祿 主 義 Monroe Doctrine—other characters are also used for this expression, esp. 門 羅 主 義.

猛 3 **Fierce, savage, cruel, violent, courageous.**
4429

猛 力 strength, force.
猛 勇 valiant, bold.
猛 勢 cruel use of power.
猛 卯 tribal headman in Yunnan.
⁵猛 士 a valiant man.
猛·孤 釘·的 suddenly, unexpectedly.
猛 將 ⁴ a fierce general; a god worshipped by farmers.
猛 性 violent disposition.
猛 戾 fierce, intractable.
¹⁰猛 撞 to burst in suddenly.
猛 擊 a furious attack.
猛 攻 a furious assault.
猛 於 虎 也 is worse than a fierce tiger.

猛 水 滔 滔 wild waters.
[15]猛 汞 vapor of mercury.
猛 火 a fierce fire.
猛 烈 brave; fierce.
猛 然 suddenly.
猛 爪 claws of savage beast.
[20]猛 狗 a savage dog.
猛 獸 wild beasts.
猛 省 (*hsing*[3]) suddenly to call to mind.
猛 禽 birds of prey.
猛 藥 potent drugs.　　　　[advance.
[25]猛 進 radical reform; a striking
猛 風 a blustering gale.
扎 猛 子 to dive (in swimming).

艋[3]　A small boat.
4430

蜢[3]　A small grasshopper or locust.
4431

蜢 蟲 midges; gnats.
蚱 蜢 grasshoppers.

錳[3]　Manganese.
4432

MÊNG　MUNG. (ㄇㄥ)

夢
夣[4]　A dream; to dream. Visionary. Stupid.
4433

夢 不 到 or 夢 想 不 到 I should never have dreamt it!
夢 中 夢 a dream within a dream.
夢 中 行 走 somnambulism.
夢 兆 prognostic from a dream.
[5]夢 卜 to divine from a dream.
夢 境 the things seen in a dream.
夢 寐 之 事 visionary matters; vague ideas.
夢 幻 泡 影 utterly visionary; illusory.
夢 想 day dreams; vain hopes.
[10]夢 景 things dreamt of; illusory visions.
夢 洩 or 夢 遺 nocturnal emissions.
夢 熊 夢 羆 to dream of bears—omen of bearing a son.
夢 虺 夢 蛇 to dream of great serpents—omen of bearing a daughter.

夢 見 to see in a dream.
[15]夢 話 humbug; to talk nonsense.
夢 醒 to wake from a dream.
夢 間 or 夢 中 in a dream.
夢 魘 nightmare.
一 場 夢 all a dream.
[20]作 夢 to dream.
噩 夢 a terrifying dream.
詳 夢 to explain a dream.A.c.圓 夢

甍[2]　Rafters which support the tiles.
4434

瞢[4]　Eyesight obscured. To feel ashamed.
4435

瞢 瞢 darkened and obscured.
瞢 容 to look ashamed : conscious of loss of face.

懵
懜[3]　Dull, stupid, doltish.
4436

懵 懂 foolish, stupid.
懵 懵 無 知 ignorant and dull.
(a) Read *mêng*[1].　To cover.
懵 蔽 眼 to cover the eyes.

蒙[2]　To cover; to conceal.
4437

蒙 上 一 層 cover it with a layer —as of paper.
蒙 不 潔 to cover the head with something filthy.
蒙 塞 to cover over and stop up.
蒙 塵 covered with dust—the emperor losing the throne and taking flight to another place.
[5]蒙 氣 the atmosphere.
蒙 灰 to cover with ashes.
蒙 羞 to hide one's shame; ashamed.
蒙 臉 帕 子 a veil.
蒙 蔽 hidden; obscured.
[10]蒙 衝 a covering of green hide put over boats in ancient warfare.
蒙 身 披 肩 to cover the body and shoulders—a shawl.
蒙 頭 蓋 臉 to cover the head and face.
蒙 首 冠 a cap that envelops the head.

(a) Dull, stupid. An untaught child.

蒙 以 養 正 cultivate responsible behaviour while a child.
蒙 士 or 蒙 童 an untaught child; a pupil.
蒙 學 primary school.
蒙 戎 confused.
[5]蒙 昧 heedless; wilful; stupid.
蒙 昧 無 知 stupid and ignorant.
蒙 汗 藥 chloroform.
蒙 混 dull, confused; to hoodwink.
蒙 稚 the young.
[10]蒙 蒙 indistinct.
蒙 館 primary school.
蒙 養 作 聖 early training will make a man into a sage.
蒙 養 園 former name for kindergarten school,—now 幼 稚 園 is used.
啟 蒙 to enlighten the dullness—of a child; to commence teaching.
[15]訓 蒙 to teach a child.

(b) To receive from a superior. Depreciatory term—I, my. Indicates the passive. To meet with, to leave.

蒙 不 測 之 事 to meet with something unexpected and dreadful.
蒙 大 難 to suffer great disaster.
蒙 恩 to receive a favour with gratitude.
蒙 恩 寵 to be greatly favoured.
[5]蒙 指 示 to be instructed.
蒙 教 to receive instruction—thank you for the information.
蒙 死 to face death.
蒙 福 or 蒙 祐 to be blessed; grateful for blessing.
蒙 劄 to receive orders.
[10]蒙 記 念 to be remembered.
蒙 辜 to suffer misfortune.

(c) Read *mêng*[1].　To cheat.

蒙 哄 人 to swindle another.

(d) Read *mêng*[2,3] Mongolia. Used in transliterating.

蒙 古 人 Mongols.
蒙 古 利 亞 Mongolia.
蒙 台 梭 利 敎 育 法 The Montessori System.
蒙 特 尼 格 羅 Montenegro.

蒙²藏事務局 Bureau of Mongolian and Tibetan Affairs.

幪² A covering, a screen. To protect, to cover.
4438

幪上 to cover up.

曚² The sun below the horizon. Inter. next.
4439

曚曨 the dim light of early dawn.

朦² To humbug, to deceive. Dim, indistinct.
4440

朦·上 to cover over; to hoodwink.
朦人 to swindle.
朦作 to pretend.
朦朧 to deceive; obscure; ambiguous.
⁵朦朦亮兒 earliest dawn; just getting light.
朦·混 to cajole; to hoodwink.
朦瞢 to hoodwink.
↑朦光 dimout.

檬² A kind of locust or acacia. The lemon.
4441

檬菓 the mango.
檸檬 the lemon.

濛
霿
4442
² Drizzling, fine rain. Mist.

濛鴻 or 鴻濛 nebulous, misty.
濛雨 or 濛濛小雨 misty rain; mist.

矇² Dim-sighted; blind. Ignorant.
4443

矇曨的觀察 a blind investigation.
矇蔽 to hoodwink.

艨² A war-boat.
4444

艨艪 war-vessels of ancient times.

蠓²·³ Midges. Sandflies.
4445

蠓蜟 gadflies.

MI.　　(二)

米³ Hulled rice; uncooked rice—also used of other grains.
4446

米·湯 rice-water—flattery.
米潘 rice washings.
米牛 a weevil.
米珠薪桂 rice like pearls and firing like cassia (for value)—in times of famine.
⁵米穀 rice and grain.
米粉 or 米麵 rice-flour.
↓米粒兒 a grain of rice.
米粒之大 of the size of rice-grains.
米粥 rice-gruel.
¹⁰米糠 paddy chaff.
米糧 provisions.
米袋 rice-bag.
米飯 or 大米飯 cooked rice.
小米 spiked millet or canary-seed.
¹⁵江米 glutinous rice.
爆米 puffed rice. A.c. 炒米.
粳米 ordinary hard rice.
糯米 glutinous rice.
紅穀米 red rice.
²⁰花生米 shelled pea-nuts.
蝦米 dried shrimps.
西米 sago.
香米 fragrant rice—used for flavouring.
黃米 glutinous millet.

(a) Used in transliterating.

米·突 metre—of length.
米突頓 a metric ton.
米突法 Metrical System.

宷² Universal. Deep.
4447

宷入其阻 penetrated deeply into the fastnesses.
宷增兢惶 in the greatest fear.

救
俅
4448
³ To soothe, to pacify. To settle, to establish. Also read mei³.

救匪 to put down rebels.

救定 to bring about peaceful conditions.
救平 to tranquilize the country.

眯³ Blind, as with dust. Nightmare.
4449

眯·了眼睛 the eyes blinded—as with dust.

迷² To deceive, to delude, to confuse. To lead or go astray. Error. Fascinated, infatuated.
4450
Distinguish 迷 No. 5890.

迷亂 bewildered.
迷·了心 deceived in heart; infatuated.
迷信 superstition.
迷信神話 superstitious myths.
⁵迷夢 a confused dream—illusory.
迷失 lost; astray.
迷失物件 to mislay or lose a thing.
迷岸 the shore of error.
迷·惑 confused; deceit; to deceive.
¹⁰迷拐人口 to drug and kidnap people.
迷昏·了 enchanted.
迷昧 blinded in mind; stupid.
迷暗 in the dark.
迷朦 confused; befooled.
¹⁵迷樓 a labyrinth or maze.
迷津 to miss the ferry—to go astray from the right path.
迷溺 infatuated.
迷漫 indefinite; confused.
迷症 weak-mindedness.
²⁰迷眩 or 迷瞢 dazed; giddy.
迷·糊 muddled.
迷惘 stupid, foolish.
迷蒙藥 anæsthetics.
迷謬 false, erroneous.
²⁵迷迷 a spell or charm.
迷迷濛濛 overcast; cloudy; drizzling.
迷途 or 迷路 the path of error; to lose one's way; in error.
迷離 indistinct; confused.
迷離道路 lost the way.
³⁰迷雲 in the clouds—muddled; bemused.
迷魂 infatuated; bewildered; fooled.
迷·魂湯 waters of oblivion—given to souls that are about to be re-born, so that they will forget their past lives.

迷·魂 陣 a fish-trap of wicker.

執 迷 不 悟 obstinately foolish and deluded.

[35]色 迷 infatuated with women.

財 迷 crazy for wealth.

鬼 迷 bewitched.

謎 [2.4.] A riddle, a conundrum. To puzzle.
4451

謎 語 a riddle or conundrum.

謎 隱 a conundrum.

燈 謎 riddles hung on lamps.

麋[2] The tailed deer.
4452

麋 茸 deer's horns.

(a) The bank of a river.

居 河 之 麋 dwelling on the bank of the river.

糜[2] Rice-gruel. Dissolved.
4453

糜 粥 rice-gruel; congee.

糜 爛 reduced to a pulp—by oppression.

(a) Wasted. Inter. 靡 No. 4455.

糜 敝 altogether ruined.

糜 滅 destroyed.

糜 費 extravagance.

縻[2] A halter for an ox. To tie up.
4454

靡[3] To divide, to scatter. To be extravagant. To waste.
4455 Also read *mi*[2].

靡 敝 weak; ruined, declining.

靡 時 to waste time.

靡 漫 diffusive; indefinite.

靡 然 從 風 to go with the fashion.

[5]靡 草 decayed growth of vegetation.

靡 衣 媮 食 living in luxurious extravagance.

靡 費 extravagant expenditure.

靡 靡 slowly; reckless.

靡 麗 luxurious.

(a) A negative. Not.

靡 不 有 初 there is none that has not a beginning.

靡 常 not constant.

天 命 靡 常 the decrees of Heaven are not unalterable.

靡 既 limitless.

[5]靡 日 不 思 not a day without thinking of it.

靡 有 there are not.

靡 有 孑 遺 there was not half a person left.

靡 涯 boundless.

靡 然 emphatic negative.

[10]靡 足 insufficient.

靡 遺 without any omission.

袂[4] The sleeve of a robe. Also read *mei*[4].
4456

分 袂 to part from a friend.

連 袂 side by side.

弭[3] The ends of a bow. To desist; to stop. To repress.
4457

弭 兵 an armistice.

弭 兵 會 Peace Conference.

弭 忘 to repress and forget.

弭 暈 to stop giddiness.

[5]弭 止 釁 端 to allay hostility.

弭 盜 安 良 to repress the seditious and pacify the law-abiding.

消 弭 to remove; to dispel.

麛[2] A fawn. Young of animals.
4458

麛 卵 the young and eggs.

彌[2] To fill. To stop; to close up; to complete.
4459

彌 六 合 to fill the universe.

彌 加 still further.

彌 多 very many.

彌 天 大 罪 crime that fills the universe.

[5]彌 封 to conceal—a name—by pasting a slip of paper over it.

彌 年 a whole year.

彌 彌 abundant.

彌 日 the whole day.

彌 昌 to prosper; prosperity.

[10]彌 月 a whole month; the first month after childbirth.

彌 深 profound.

彌 漫 boundless.

彌 滿 filled full.

彌 甥 a daughter's grandson.

[15]彌 留 之 際 a crisis in a disease when there is no hope of recovery.

彌 留 遺 言 dying injunctions.

彌 綸 to restore; to meet deficiencies.

彌 縫 to make up for; to rectify.

彌 補 to repair; to make good.

彌 遠 still further.

(a) Used in transliterating.

彌 賽 亞 The Messiah.

彌 撒 The Mass of the Roman Catholic Church.

瀰[2] A watery expanse.
4460

渺 瀰 a watery waste.

(a) Read *mi*[3]. Overflowing.

河 水 瀰 瀰 the river is overflowing.

獼[2] A female monkey.
4461

MI.   (二)
(Mih)

冖 [4.5.] A cover; to cover. Radical 14. Nat. Phon.
4462 letter for *m*, written ㄇ.

宓 [4.5.] Still, silent. To stop. Also read *fu*[2.5.]. Name of a certain person in ancient history.
4463

密
密 [4.5.] Secret, confidential. Intimate. Thorough.
4464

密 事 a private affair.

密 交 intimate friendship.

密 使 secret envoy.

密 保 secretly to recommend a man of ability.

密(偵)探 private inquiry agent.
密切 closely connected in prin-
　ciple; intimate; secret.
密切關·係 intimate relation-
　ships; closely connected with.
密勿 important matter of State;
　to do things thoroughly and
　with urgency.
密厚 intimate; close—as friend-
　ship.
10密友 an intimate friend.
密口 keep silent. Hush!
密咨 secret communication or
　despatch.
密坐 to sit in private conversation.
密房 or 密室 a private room.
15密日 a term formerly used in
　Amoy almanacs for every
　seventh day. See 虛 No. 2821·
　88.
密書 or 密函 a private letter.
密會 secret conclave; clandestine
　meeting.
密札 secret orders or letters.
密派 to depute secretly.
20密碼 codes.
密碼電報 code telegram.
密禱 secret prayer.
密·秘交·涉 secret diplomacy.
密約 secret treaty; assignation.
25密言 a secret.
密訪 secret inquiries about; to
　make careful search for.
密語 tête-a-tête, confidential talk.
密談 whispering; private conver-
　sation.
密謀 secret schemes; secret plot.
30密諭 a secret decree.
密議 secret discussion.
密通 illicit connection with.
密陳 a secret memorial.
密電 code telegram.
35密飭 instructions given secretly.
封密 closely sealed.
機密 occult; secret; a secret
　moving-cause.
秘·密 secret; hidden.
秘·密結婚 secret marriage.
40親密 very intimate; closely re-
　lated.
近密 familiar; intimate.
靜密 still, secret, close.

(a) Close, dense, fine—texture.

密如蛛網 as fine as a spider's
　web.
密密實實 very dense; thick;
　close.

密密層層 covered closely, with
　no seam or gap.
密布 closely spread over; covered
　completely.
5密度 (or 率 lii⁴·⁵·) density.
密接 very closely connected.
密枝 close branches; dense
　growth.
密集 massed; close together.
密集隊 massed formation of
　troops.
10密石 hard, finely-grained stone.
密網 a close net—the meshes of
　the law.
密緻 close, dense, compact.
密邇 very closely related; intim-
　ately connected.
密雲 dense clouds.
15人口稠密 dense population.
細密 delicate, fine—as texture.
緊密 compact.

(b) Used for transliterating.

密理克蘭姆 milligramme.
密理密突 millimetre.
密達 a metre.
密達制 Metric System.
密達尺 metric foot.

蜜 ⁴·⁵·　Honey; sweet.
4465

蜜嘴 honeyed lips.
蜜屈律 the *hovenia dulcis*.
蜜房 or 蜜窩 a honey-comb;
　cells in a beehive.
蜜果 or 無花果 the fig.
5蜜棗 honey-dates—the fruit of
　the *zizyphus vulgaris* preserved
　in sugar and dried.
蜜橘 or 蜜柑 sweet oranges
　from S. China.
蜜汁 syrup.
蜜漿 honey syrup—drunk in sum-
　mer.
蜜漬 honey-preserves.
10蜜煎 honey-preserves.
蜜父 the Chinese pear.
蜜王 the queen bee.
蜜甘 (or 草) liquorice.
蜜筒 the sweet melon or 甜瓜.
15蜜塘 or 蜂蜜 honey.
蜜腺 the nectary of flowers.
蜜菓 preserved fruits.
蜜蜂 bees.
蜜蠟 beeswax.
20蜜語 smooth speech; honeyed
　words.

蜜酒 sweet wine.
蜜餞 honey-sweetmeats.
蜜餞 confections.
蜜餞砒礵 sweetmeats made with
　arsenic—false speech.
25甜如蜜 as sweet as honey.
石蜜 rock-honey.
花蜜 nectar or honey from
　flowers.
野蜜 wild honey.

鼏 ⁴·⁵·
4466　　Cover of a tripod kettle.

冪
羃 ⁴·⁵·　A cover of cloth for
4467　　food; a veil.

羃法 superficial measure.

謐 ⁴·⁵·　To whisper. Quiet.
4468　　Inattentive.

謐然清靜 peaceful and still.

覓
覔 ⁴·⁵·　To search for; to look
4469　　after.

覓人 to look for a person.
覓保 to find securities—persons.
覓僱 to engage labour.
覓利 to look for employment.
5覓句 to seek for a suitable phrase.
覓有 to find out.
覓汗 to hire labour.
覓索 to demand; to strive to get.
覓致 to seek and procure.
10覓見·了 sought and found.
覓訪 to inquire after.
覓路 to seek the right road.
覓飲食 to seek for a living.

MIAO.　(ㄇㄠ)

苗 ² Sprouts; growing corn. A
4470　　flame, a jet. Posterity; pro-
　　geny.

苗末 progeny; descendants.
苗·條 slender and graceful—car-
　riage.

苗 稼 grain before flowering and while in flower, respectively.

苗 緒 posterity; descendants.

⁵苗 而 不 秀 者 有 矣 夫 there are some which spring up but never flower.

苗 胤 distant descendants.

苗 裔 descendants; progeny.

火 苗ㄦ flame of a lamp.

禾 苗 young rice-plants.

¹⁰鑛 苗 outcrop of minerals.

魚 苗 the fry of fish.

黎 苗 prolific.

(a) Tribes-people.

苗·子 the *Miao* tribes of Kwei-chow and Yunnan.

苗 戶 tribes which have come under control.

熟 苗 tribes brought under control.

生 苗 wild tribes not controlled by the government.

(b) A summer hunting-expedition. To hunt.

之 子 于 苗 those officers in charge of the hunting.

喵¹
4471   The mew of the cat.

描²
4472   To trace; to draw; to design; to sketch; to depict.

描 像 to paint portraits.

描。出 to portray; to depict.

描 字 to trace writing.

描 寫 to describe well; word-painting.

⁵描 情 to describe emotions.

描 摹 to copy; to imitate.

描 摹 一 樣 to take an exact copy.

描 畫 to paint; to sketch.

描 眉 to pencil the eyebrows.

¹⁰描 金 to paint in gold; to gild.

心 描 to picture in the mind.

廟庿⎰⁴
4473   A temple; a shrine.

廟 堂 之 上 in the presence of the emperor.

廟 塔 temples and pagodas.

廟 宇 temples.

廟 祝 a temple curate—one who assists in reading prayers, etc., for the dead.

⁵廟 算 or 廟 略 the emperor's policy or councils.

廟 號 title conferred on an emperor after his death.

廟 見 a bride's worship of her husband's ancestors three months after marriage, announcing the formal assumption of her duties.

廟 謨 the counsels or policy of the emperor.

廟 貌 the likenesses of ancestors stored in the temples.

¹⁰廟 貨 inferior goods purchased at temple fairs.

廟 食 worthy of being deified and thus enjoying the temple sacrifices.

九 廟 the imperial ancestral temples.

宗 廟 an imperial ancestral temple.

家 廟 ancestral hall or temple.

¹⁵聖 廟 a Confucian temple.

瞄²
4473a   To take aim. See 眇 No. 4476.

瞄 準 to take aim.

妙玅⎰⁴
4474   Beautiful, excellent. Wonderful. Mysterious. Subtle.

妙 事 a fine matter.

妙 化 supernatural.

妙 境 a wonderfully pleasing place.

妙 想 subtle, abstruse thought.

⁵妙 手 a skilled artist or physician.

妙 才 excellent capabilities and talents.

妙 技 wonderful skill; excellent technique.

妙 極 Excellent! Wonderful!

妙 理 mysterious, abstruse doctrines.

¹⁰妙 甚 Clever! Admirable!

妙 用 admirably suited for use; marvels.

妙 算 an excellent plan.

妙 絕 Admirable! Wonderful!

妙 義 of excellent purport; an admirable idea.

¹⁵妙 舌 smart in speech.

妙 藥 wonderful remedy.

妙 行 法 術 clever practice of the black art.

妙 計 or 妙 法 or 妙 術 a capital plan; excellent scheme.

妙 語 clever talk; interesting words.

²⁰妙 蹟 marvels.

妙 音 sweet sounds; harmony.

(a) Young, small.

妙 年 or 妙 齡 the young; youthful.

杪³
4475   The tip of a small branch. The limit.

杪 冬 end of the winter—other seasons are spoken of in a similar manner.

杪 末 the tip; the point.

杪 杪 very tiny.

杪 歲 end of the year.

⁵月 杪 end of the month.

眇³
4476   Having one eye smaller than the other. One-eyed. Gazing into distance. To take aim. See 瞄 No. 4473a.

眇 一 目 one-eyed.

眇 中 (*chung⁴*) 紅 心 to hit the bull's-eye.

眇² 準 to sight a gun; to aim.

眇² 準 於 碪 to aim and fire a gun.

⁵眇 能 視 a one-eyed man can see.

眇² 靶 to aim at a target.

(a) Subtle, insignificant. Minute.

眇 少 dwarf; short.

眇 微 small, minute.

眇 然 有 身 the insignificance of a mere individual—in the vastness of creation.

眇 身 my insignificant self.

渺³
4477   Vague; vast; boundless.

渺 不 相 涉 has not the slightest relation to it.

渺 渺 乎 How boundless!

渺 漫 expanse of water.

渺 溔 vast expanse of water.

[5]渺 然 vast.

渺·茫 misty; not susceptible of proof; doubtful; vague; indistinct.

渺 軀 獨 立 世 上 a tiny mite standing alone in the world.

緲[3] Indistinct. Minute, infinitesimal. Inter. 眇 No. 4476.
4478

緲 微 infinitesimal.

縹 緲 obscure; misty; dimly seen.

秒[3] The beard of grain. Minute. A second of time
4479 or of a degree. One tenthousandth.

秒 忽 the smallest fraction.

藐[3] To slight; to treat with contempt. Small, petty.
4480

藐 妄 ill-mannered; stupid discourtesy.

藐 孤 a frail orphan.

藐 小 insignificant.

藐 法 to despise the law.

[5]藐 玩 to despise; to treat with lightness.

藐 視 to treat with contempt.

輕 藐 to treat with indifference.

(a) Read mo[4.5]. or miao[3]. Vast; distant. Inter. 邈 No. 4564.

藐 藐 昊 天 Great and mighty Heaven!

既 成 藐 藐 when completed it was spacious and magnificent.

聽 我 藐 藐 you—listened to me without paying attention.

MIEH.　　　(ㄇㄧㄝ)

乜[1] To squint. Distinguish 也 No. 7312.
4481

乜 斜 to squint, screwed up eyes.

(a) Used in transliterating.

乜 攝 Moses—used on the Jewish Synagogue memorial slab at Kaifengfu, Honan.

咩[1] The bleating of sheep.
4482

咩 羊 bleating of a sheep.

羊 咩 a lamb.

滅| [4.5.]
威|　To destroy; to exterminate. To extinguish. Distinguish 威 No. 7051.
4483

滅·了 destroyed; gone out (fire).

滅 亡 to destroy.

滅 其 類 exterminated the race.

滅 口 to slay a man to prevent his betrayal of a secret.

[5]滅 度 to die, to save,—(Budd.), i.e., to destroy care and trouble and ferry souls over the sea of death.

滅 性 to destroy life.

滅 息 to extinguish.

滅 掉 destroyed utterly—as robbers.

滅 搗 to exterminate.

[10]滅 族 to wipe out a clan.

滅 沒 to kill; destroyed.

滅 火 to put out a fire.

滅 燈 to extinguish a lamp.

滅 種[2] extinction of a race.

[15]滅 絕 淨 盡 utterly exterminated.

滅 罪 to do away with sin.

滅 良·心 to destroy the conscience.

滅 裂 careless, lacking thoroughness. See 鹵 No. 4153-A.3.

滅 裂 之 學 superficial study, lacking thoroughness.

[20]滅 跡 to destroy all traces of.

滅 門 to exterminate a family.

滅 頂 to overwhelm, the waters covering the head.

勦 滅 to blot out; to exterminate.

撲 滅 to put out a fire.

篾[4.5.] Splints; slats; laths.
4484

篾·匠 a worker in bamboo.

篾 尺 a bamboo-splint measure for taking the girth of timber.

篾 片·子 a splint; a sponger.

篾 箍 bamboo-splints twisted into a hoop for coopering.

[5]篾 箱 a bamboo box.

篾 蓆 mats made of bamboo-splints.

篾 青 or 竹 篾 bamboo-splints.

蔑[4.5.] Not, to be without.
4485

蔑 以 加 矣 nothing could be better.

蔑 有 none at all.

蔑 法 in contempt of the law.

蔑 無 destitute of.

蔑 然 無 言 he did not utter a word.

蔑 禮 without manners.

(a) Minute, worthless. To throw away.

蔑 如 也 not worth mentioning; worthless.

蔑 星 minute stars—fine, small.

蔑 棄 to throw away; to neglect.

蔑 視 to look down upon; to despise.

蔑 資 wasting capital and property.

(b) Subtle, abstract.

蔑 德 abstract virtues.

蠛[4.5.] Flies, small insects produced in damp places.
4486

蠛 蠓 minute flies.

衊[4.5.] Defiled with blood. To calumniate.
4487

汙 衊 宗 室 he defiled his ancestral hall.

MIEN.　　　(ㄇㄧㄢ)

宀[2] A roof. Radical 40.
4488

冂[4] Curtain to ward off arrows. Hidden.
4489 Distinguish 冋 No. 3194.

沔[3] A flood. Branch of the River Han.
4490

眄[3.4.] To ogle.
4491

眄 睞 to give sidelong glances.

免³ To avoid, to escape, to evade. To remit, to spare, to excuse, to forego.
4492　Distinguish 兔 No. 6534.

免·不 了³ unavoidable; no help for it.
免·他 discharge him.
免 例 to evade the law.
免 傷 損 之 虞 to avoid injury or damage.
⁵免 債 to remit a debt.
免 冠 to take off one's hat; anciently as an acknowledgement of a fault, now as a sign of respect.
免 勞 to avoid trouble.
免 却 to decline.
免。去 to avoid.
¹⁰免 去 利·息 to remit the interest.
免 啓 to avoid.
免 官 dismissed from office.
免 官 令 order of dismissal—walking-ticket.
免 害 to escape from peril unhurt.
¹⁵免 役 immunity from compulsory service.
免 役 租 quit-rent, paid in lieu of compulsory service.
免·得 or 免 致 lest; to avoid; so as not to; to escape from.
免 後 患 to avoid future trouble.
免 愁 煩 to put cares and anxieties on one side.
²⁰免 戰 to decline battle; to cease fighting.
免 戰 牌 or 免 戰 旗 flag of truce.
免 房 租 rent-free.
免 拆 驗 exemption from customs examination.
免 捐 exemption from likin.
²⁵免 收 to exempt—from duty.
免 照 duty exemption certificate.
免 狀 dismissal notice—walking-ticket.
免 疫 性 immunity from infection.
免 票 free pass.
³⁰免 禮 do not stand on ceremony.
免 稅 duty-free; to exempt from taxes or duties.
免 稅 口 岸 free ports.
免 稅 品 duty-free goods.
免 稅 單 exemption certificate.
³⁵免 稅 放 行 to release without payment of duty.
免 稅 港 a free port.
免 稅 遞 送 to frank.
免 究 to acquit.
免 糧 to remit taxes.

⁴⁰免 罪 to pardon sins; to escape punishment.
免 罪 符 dispensation of indulgence.
免 而 無 恥 to avoid—punishment—and yet to have no sense of shame.
免 職 to dismiss from office; to resign and have the resignation accepted.
免 脫 to get rid of.
⁴⁵免 致 後 患 to avoid future trouble.
免 行 舊 法 to abrogate the old laws.
免 見 to decline to see—a visitor.
免 許 to concede.
免 許 主 義 principle of concession. (company law).
⁵⁰免 試 to admit without examination.
免 試 資·格 to forego test of qualifications.
免 課 to be absent from classes.
免 費 free of expense.
入 場 免 費 admission free.
⁵⁵船 上 免 費 free on board. F.O.B.
免 費 學 額 free tuition scholarships.
免 費 發 送 to frank.
免 費 送 信 to frank letters.
免 跌 倒 to avoid stumbling.
⁶⁰免 追 to forego prosecution.
免 釐 to exempt from likin.
免 除 to give quittance; to relieve from obligations.
以 免 周 折 in order to avoid complications.
以 免 懸 望 in order to relieve anxiety.
⁶⁵幸 免 luckily avoided it; had a lucky escape.
放 免 to discharge a prisoner.
未 免 not able to avoid; will certainly; not without.
除 免 to dispense with; to excuse.

(a) Read wên⁴.　Mourning attire.
袒 免 服 mourning for relatives of the fifth degree.

(b) Read wên⁴.　To bear a son.
免 身 生 男 to bear a son.

(c) Read wên⁴.　Fresh.
免 蠡 fresh and dried—provisions.
陳 免 stale and fresh.

俛³ To make an effort. Used with 勉 No. 4495.
4493　Also read fu³. To hang down the head. Inter. 俯 No. 1929.

俛 仰 looking down and looking up.
俛 僂 to stoop; to bow the head; hunchbacked.
俛 啄 to stoop and peck.
俛 拾 地 芥 as easy as—stooping to pick up straws.
俛 首 to bow the head—in acquiescence.

冕³ A crown, a ceremonial cap.
4494

冕 旒 crown gems.
加 冕 coronation; to cap.

勉³ To urge; to constrain; to exert oneself.
4495

勉 其 所 未 至 to urge him on to positions not yet attained.
勉 力 to exert one's strength.
勉 勉 industrious; active.
勉·勵 to incite; to urge.
⁵勉·勵 會 Christian Endeavour Society.
勉 勸 to exhort to action.
勉 強 to compel; to constrain; forced—as an interpretation. *
勉 強 飲 食 compel himself to eat.*
勉 思 企 及 to press on with the hope of reaching.
¹⁰勉 旃 exert yourself.
勉 礪 爲 善 矣 exert oneself to reform and do good.
勉 行 to make strenuous efforts.
勉 詞 words of exhortation.
* (-ch'iang³)

挽³ To bear a son. Also read wên⁴. See 免 No. 4492—B.
4496

分 挽 parturition.

面⁴ The surface. The face. Personally; in person. Verbally. The front, before. A plane surface. Radical 176. N.A. of mirrors, etc.
4497

面·上 the surface.
面·上 無 光 having lost prestige.
面 云 to say to one's face.

面 交 to give to personally.
⁵面 交 之 友 casual acquaintances.
面 似 桃 花 face like peach-blossoms.
面 像 a portrait.
面 具 the face; countenance; a mask.
戴 上 科 學 ·的 面 具 wearing the appearance of scientific scholarship.
¹⁰面 ·前 before, in front of.
面 友 a mere acquaintance.
面 叙 to chat.
面 向 上 this side up.
面 告 to inform personally.
¹⁵面 命 personal orders.
面 商 to consult personally.
面 善 (your) face looks familiar.
面 囑 personal instructions.
面 團 團 a round full face.
²⁰面 壁 face to the wall—sitting in meditation and self-examination; to spend time in acquiring.
面 奏 to state to the emperor in person.
面 如 土 色 a ghastly livid countenance.
面 如 死 灰 a face like ashes.
面 如 滿 月 a full round face.
²⁵面 ·子 a surface; character; social standing; the outside, or facing of a garment; face.
面 ·子 情 mere outward friendliness.
面 ·孔 the face; the countenance.
面 容 or 面 光 appearance; countenance.
面 對 面 face to face.
³⁰面 巾 face-towel; covering over the face of the dead.
面 龐 the countenance.
面 從 mere verbal acquiescence.
面 ·情 intercourse; friendship.
面 授 personal teaching.
³⁵面 斥 to rebuke severely.
面 會 to meet face to face.
面 朝 裏 inside out.
面 柔 bashful; shy.
面 ·湯 water for washing the face.
⁴⁰面 無 人 色 to look aghast.
面 熟 to know by sight; familiar with.
面 熟 陌 生 a person whose face one may recognize, but with whose name one is not acquainted.
面 牆 face to a wall—unable to see through a thing, as a person

with no education.
面 珠 the cheeks.
⁴⁵面 生 unacquainted with.
面 生 可 疑 a strange suspicious-looking face.
面 生 討 保 identification of strangers is required—as by banks.
面 皮 厚 thick-skinned; shameless.
面 皮 皺 a wrinkled face.
⁵⁰面 ·目 or 面 ·貌 the face; the countenance; social standing; appearance.
面 ·目 可 憎 a repulsive appearance.
面 相 (hsiang⁴) likeness; physiognomy.
面 稟 or 面 陳 to make a verbal report.
面 稱 to state in person.
⁵⁵面 ·積 surface; area.
面 絡 (or 衣) a veil.
面 聆 to hear from personally.
面 般 the four sides of the face.
面 色 the complexion; the countenance.
⁶⁰面 藥 complexion mixture, a lotion to prevent chaps, etc.
面 西 facing the west.
面 見 a personal interview.
面 角 the facial angle.
面 託 to make a request personally.
⁶⁵面 訴 to make a verbal complaint.
面 試 oral examination.
面 諛 flattery to the face.
面 請 to request in person.
面 諭 verbal orders.
⁷⁰面 談 or 面 商 or 面 論 or 面 議 to speak face to face; to discuss verbally.
面 謝 to thank in person.
面 譽 人 to flatter a man before his face.
面 赤 a red face.　　⌈spoken.
面 軟 bashful; soft-hearted; soft-
⁷⁵面 辭 to take leave in person.*
面 遞 to hand over personally.
面 部 the face.
面 門 the forehead.
面 面 相 覰 looking at each other, at a loss what to do.
⁸⁰面 領 to receive personally.
面 飾 making up the face—of women.
一 面 …. 一 面 on the one hand …., on the other hand.
上 面 the upper side; on the surface.
*to decline in person.

下 ·面 the under side of anything flat.
⁸⁵世 面 state of affairs.
前 ·面 before, in front of.
南 ·面 facing the south; the emperor.
反 ·面ㄦ the reverse; to turn the back.
四 面 all sides.
⁹⁰失 面 to lose face.
對 ·面 opposite; face to face.
情 面 kindness; favour; face.
方 面 a square surface; a side, bearing, phase, etc.
横 裁 面 transverse section.
⁹⁵正 ·面 the right side; the face of.
歪 面 a grimace. A.c. 鬼 臉.
當 面 face to face.
縱 剖 面 longitudinal section.
背 ·面ㄦ the back of; behind the back.
¹⁰⁰裏 ·面 inside.

恓⁴ To look towards. To turn the back on; to oppose.
4498

恓 規 越 矩 to commit a breach of etiquette.

勔³ To stimulate; to urge.
4499

愐³ Bashful. To consider.
4500

愐 念 fond thoughts.
愐 愐 modest, bashful.

湎³ Flushed with drink.
4501

湎 于 酒 addicted to intoxicants.
天 不 湎 爾 以 酒 it is not Heaven that flushes you with wine!

(a) Changing and confusion.

湎 湎 紛 紛 constantly making great changes.

緬³ To think of; to remember.
4502

緬 思 or 緬 想 to think of with fondness.

緬 懷 to think of with affection.

緬 然 引 領 南 望 longingly to stretch the neck and gaze towards the south.

緬 訴 to describe in detail.

(a) Name of places.

緬 甸 Burma.

(b) Distant.

邈 緬 in the far distance.

麵 麪 [4]　Flour. Vermicelli. Dough.
4503

麵 包 a loaf of bread; bread.

麵 杖 rolling-pin.

麵 案 board for kneading dough.

麵 湯 gruel.

[5] 麵 灰 slaked lime.

麵 片 or 麵 條 dough-strips or slices.

麵 筋 gluten of wheat.

麵 粉 or 麥 麵 wheaten flour.

麵 粉 機 器 flour-milling machine.

[10] 麵 酵 yeast; leaven.

麵 食 wheaten food.

麵 餅 biscuits.

切 麵 vermicelli freshly made and cut with a knife.

掛 麵 thin vermicelli that has been hung to dry.

眠 [2]　To sleep; to close the eyes.
4504

眠 臥 to lie down to sleep.

眠 思 to dream.

眠 牀 a couch; a sofa.

眠 牛 地 a sleeping cow's form—regarded as a lucky spot for a grave by geomancers.

[5] 眠 目 to close the eyes. Cf 4531.1.

眠 睡 to sleep.

眠 花 臥 柳 passing the nights in brothels.

不 眠 症 insomnia.

同 眠 to sleep together.

長 眠 the long sleep—death.

棉 [2]　Cotton. The cotton-plant. Inter. next.
4505

棉 子 cotton-seeds.

棉 屑 cotton waste.

棉 布 cotton cloth.

棉 紗 cotton yarn.

[5] 棉 絮 waste cotton.

棉 綫 cotton thread.

棉 織 工 業 cotton-weaving industry.

棉 花 cotton; cotton wadding.

棉 花 子 油 cotton-seed oil.

[10] 棉 花 稭 cotton-stalks used for firing.

棉 衣 cotton garments.

棉 袍 a wadded gown.

棉 被 a wadded coverlet.

棉 褲 wadded trousers.

[15] 棉 襖 wadded jacket.

淨 棉 花 cleaned cotton, free from seeds.

生 棉 raw cotton.

絲 棉 floss silk.

綿 緜 [2]　Soft, downy. Floss silk. Inter. preceding.
4506

綿 力 or 綿 薄 not strong; delicate.

綿 子 silk wadding or quilting.

綿 柔 or 綿 軟 delicate, soft.

綿 紗 cotton yarn.

[5] 綿 絮 floss silk.

綿 綢 a kind of silk.

綿 綫 cotton thread.

綿 羊 a sheep.

綿 羊 毛 wool.

[10] 綿 美 beautiful and soft—as a voice.

綿 花 火 藥 gun-cotton.

綿 裏 針 a needle in wool—a soft appearance but a dangerous heart.

綿 襖 a wadded coat.

綿 鞋 wadded shoes.

(a) Drawn-out; continuous; prolonged.

綿 亙 continuous; unbroken.

綿 代 successive generations.

綿 延 or 綿 連 continuous; prolonged—as descendants.

綿 綿 不 絕 continuous; unbroken.

綿 長 long drawn-out; protracted.

澠 [3]　Name of a river in Honan.
4507

澠 池 縣 a district in West Honan.

(a) Read *shêng*[2]. Name of a river in Shantung.

MIN.　(ㄇㄧㄣ)

民 [2]　The people; mankind. Distinguish 氏 No. 5785.
4508

民 不 堪 命 the people find your rule intolerable.

民 主 democracy.

民 主 主 義 democratic theory.

民 主 制 democratic system.

[5] 民 主 國 a democratic country.

民 主 政 治 democratic government.

民 主 政 體 democratic form of government.

民 主 潮 流 the rising tide of democracy.

民 主 黨 Democratic Party.

[10] 民 之 不 予 者 the people who did not follow him.

民 事 a civil suit.

民 事 愈 悴 distress on account of the economic conditions of the people.

民 事 處 Bureau of General Affairs.

民 事 裁 判 civil judgment.

[15] 民 事 訴 訟 action in a civil suit.

民 事 訴 訟 法 law relating to civil suits.

民 俗 學 folk lore.

民 兵 militia; citizen forces.

民 具 而 瞻 the people all look to you.

[20] 民 力 the strength—i.e., the wealth of the people.

民 勇 volunteer forces.

民 國 republic.

民 國 公 會 democratic congress.

民 國 成 立 the establishment of the republic.

[25] 民 國 軍 the army of the republic.

民 團 militia; volunteers.

民 壯 militia; volunteers.

民 天 the heaven of the masses—food,—from the next.

民 以 食 爲 天 the masses regard sufficient food as their heaven.

[30] 民 夫 coolies; peasants.

民 害 public evil.

民 庭 Civil Court.

民 律 Civil Law.

民 德 public standards of morality.

³⁵民 心 popular sentiments.

民 心 離 散 disaffection among the people.

民 怨 popular enmity.

民 情 popular sentiment or feelings.

民 意 will of the people.

⁴⁰民 所 棄 也 what the people reject.

民 房 private houses.

民 政 civil administration.

民 政 司 magistracy.

民 政 廳 or 民 政 署 head-office of provincial administration.

⁴⁵民 政 機 關 organ of civil authority.

民 政 長 civil magistrate, having no judicial powers.

民 教 the people and converts (to Christianity) as opposed to each other in lawsuits, etc.

民 族 race; peoples; tribe; the nation, in the sense of the people.

民 族 主 義 Principle of Nationalism.

⁵⁰民 族 主 義 之 啟 發 the growth of nationalism.

民 族 學 ethnography.

民 族 心 理 學 race psychology.

民 族 意 旨 the will of the nation —as a people.

⁵⁵民 族 的 覺 悟 race consciousness; national consciousness.

民 族 自 決 self-determination of peoples.

民 軍 運 動 nationalistic movements.

民 時 the busy times of the farmer.

民 望 the hope of the masses.

⁶⁰民 極 a popular leader.

民 權 rights of the people; authority of the people.

民 權 主 義 Principle of Democracy.

充 分 的 民 權 perfect democracy.

發 達 民 權 further the cause of democracy.

⁶⁵民 氣 public sentiment; tone of the masses.

民 氣 斲 喪 the spirit, or morale, of the people is broken.

民 法 Civil Law.

民 治 主 義 democracy.

民 無 德 而 稱 焉 the people found no good action of his for which to praise him.

⁷⁰民 無 所 措 手 足 the people have no place for their hands and feet—they live in constant terror.

民 爲 邦 本 the people are the foundation of the State.

民 父 母 the magistrates, under the former system.

民 生 the livelihood of the people.

民 生 不 遂 the people are not prosperous.

⁷⁵民 生 主 義 Principle of National Livelihood.

民 生 卽 是 共 産 the welfare of the people is communism.

民 生 困 苦 the hardships and difficulties in the livelihood of the people.

民 生 於 三 事 之 如 一 the people were begotten for the three —i.e., prince, parent and teacher —and served them as one.

民 用 for the use of the people.

⁸⁰民 衆 the masses; a mob, a crowd.

民 衆 之 堅 決 the determination of the people.

民 衆 大 會 mass meeting.

民 衆 的 造 反 popular rising.

民 衆 運 動 mass movements.

⁸⁵民 瘼 the sufferings of the masses.

民 社 a community.

民 稅 land-tax.

民 種 迥 殊 great differences in the races of men.

民 籍 a register of the population.

⁹⁰民 約 論 doctrine of the Social Contract.

民 脂 民 膏 the revenue—i.e., the fat of the people.

民 船 native boats.

民 謠 folk-songs.

民 變 insurrection.

⁹⁵民 賊 robbers of the people; public enemies—i.e., leaders in high places who feather their own nests.

民 質 characteristics of the people—of any nation.

民 部 former name for the Board of Revenue.

民 隱 the hardships and toil of the masses.

民 風 popular customs; national character.

¹⁰⁰民 食 the food of the people.

民 鮮 久 矣 for a long time but few have attained this.

民 黨 People's Party.

人 民 mankind.

公 民 citizens.

¹⁰⁵四 民 the four classes, scholars 士, farmers 農, artisans 工, and merchants, 商.

失 業 民 the unemployed.

居 民 inhabitants.

平 民 the masses.

庶 民 the masses.

¹¹⁰愚 民 the illiterate masses.

游 民 vagrants; idlers.

良 民 law-abiding citizens.

黎 民 the masses of Chinese.

刉 ³ To scrape. To pare.
4509

刉 子 or 油 刉 a narrow spatula of horn used by women in dressing their hair.

岷 ² Mountains in N. W. Szechwan.
4510

岷 江 a river which flows from these mountains through Chengtu to join the Yangtze at Suifu.

泯 ³·⁴ To be destroyed; to put an end to.
4511

泯 平 階 級 obliterate class distinction.

泯 棄 neglected; ignored; disregarded.

泯 沒 or 泯 滅 dead; blotted out; destroyed.

泯 沒 而 無 聞 dead and utterly forgotten.

泯 絕 utterly destroyed.

(a) Confusion. Inter. 湣 No. 4515.

泯 亂 anarchy.

泯 泯 紛 紛 all in confusion.

(b) A sheet of water. To flow.

春 流 泯 泯 the spring freshets roll down.

珉 砇 碈 [2] 4512

A stone resembling jade.

珉 玉 a pure white stone of very fine texture.

珉 玉 雜 淆 other stones and jade mixed together—scholars of various talents.

珉 石 common alabaster.

暋 愍 [3] 4513

Strong; robust; vigorous.

暋 不 畏 死 brave men do not fear death.

(a) Read *min²*. Sorry, anxious.

慰 暋 沉 屯 (*chun¹*) soothe my anxious distress.

揗 抿 [3] 4514

To smooth, to stroke. To pucker, to contract.

揗 嘴 or 揗 口 to purse up the lips.

揗 頭 to smooth the hair.

湣 [3] 4515

To mourn. Inter. 閔 No. 4520.

湣 王 prince *Min* of *Ch'i* 齊, a feudal State.

(a) Read *mien⁴*. Turbid, foul. Confused.

(b) Read *hun¹*. Confusion.

緍 [2] 4516

A fishing-line. A cord. A string of cash.

緍 錢 strings of cash in ancient times.

釣 緍 a fishing-line.

(a) To cover with one's clothing—as bedding.

緍 被 to cover with clothing for a quilt.

(b) Ancient town in Shansi.

敏 勄 [3] 4517

Active; clever; prompt; witty; smart. Earnest; diligent. To hasten.

敏 力 energetic.
敏 慎 clever and cautious.
敏 慧 sagacious; quickness of perception.
敏 慧 的 judicious.
[5]敏 捷 quick-witted; sharp.
敏 於 事 而 慎 於 言 earnest in action and cautious in speech.
敏 求 to beg earnestly.
敏 治 clever, nimble.
敏 而 好 (*hao⁴*) 學 clever and fond of study.
[10]敏 辯 clever at argument or disputation.

(a) The great toe. See 歂 No. 2729—A.

鰵 [3] 4518

A kind of perch. The cod. See 鱈 No. 2904

鰵 魚 肝 油 cod-liver oil.

旻 [2] 4519

The appearance of the sky in autumn. Merciful. Distinguish 昊 No. 2072.

旻 天 autumn; compassionate Heaven as overshadowing all things below—Heaven pities the fall of all things into winter decay.

號 泣 于 旻 天 cried with tears to the compassionate Heavens—God.

旻 序 the autumn festival.

閔 [3] 4520

To mourn; to weep. To encourage.

閔 其 苗 之 不 長 sorry that the young corn was not growing more quickly.

閔 勉 從 事 to urge to duty.

憫 愍 [3] 4521

To sympathize with; to pity; to grieve.

憫 不 畏 法 grieved that they did not fear the laws.
憫 恤 or 憐 憫 to befriend; to pity.
憫 惜 to pity.
憫 惆 to have sympathy with.

閩 [3] 4522

A sort of snake. Fukien Province.

閩 江 the River *Min*.
閩 浙 Fukien and Chekiang.
閩 粵 Fukien and Kwangtung.

黽 [3] 4523

A toad. A tree-frog. Radical 205.

蛙 黽 frogs and toads.

(a) To put forth an effort.

黽 勉 to urge to effort.

MING.   (ㄇㄧㄥ)

名 [2] 4524

A name. Reputation. Fame. N.A. for persons.

名 下 under the name; in the name of.
名 不 符 實 the name and the reality do not tally.
名 不 虛 傳 his reputation is well-deserved.
名 世 famous.
[5]名 世 者 men noted in their time.
名 之 必 可 言 也 the names he uses may certainly be spoken with propriety.
名 人 notables.
名 人 欄 "who's who" column.
名 位 reputation.
[10]名 內 具 the name is written inside.
名 冊 list of names; muster-roll.
名 分 (*fen⁴*) obligations; relative rank; title.
名 利 fame and wealth.
名 刺 a visiting-card.
[15]名 勝 famous places of scenic resort.

名另渼 my name is written separately—my card is enclosed.

名叫 called; named.

名單 list of names; personnel.

名器 rank, degree.

[20]名場 former examination for degrees.[centric, free from formalities.

名士 famous scholars; scholarly ec-

名·子 a name.

名字 official name and courtesy names. 名·字 name.

名學 or 論理學 logic. See No. 4253-21, ff.

[25]名宦 distinguished officials.

名家 celebrated families.

名宿 well-known scholar.

名實 the name and the reality.

有名無實 nominal; having the name without the reality.

[30]名山 celebrated mountains.

名帖 or 名片 a visiting-card.

名手 a well-known hand—as of an artist.

名教 obligations and teachings of the sages—Confucianism.

名數 a concrete number.

[35]名·望 reputation; fame. A.c. 名氣

名次 position in a list of names.

名正具 my name is given—on a separate card.

名氏 name and surname; family name.

名流萬世 his fame reaches to myriad generations.

[40]名為 under the name of; called.

名·目 name; reputation; designation.

名稱 appellation.

名筆 a masterpiece of art.

名節 reputation; moral integrity.

[45]名籍 name and native place.

名籤 a tag for luggage.

名·義 titles, names, definitions.

名聞天下 world-famous.

名·聲 reputation; fame.

[50]名肅片 respectfully enclosing my card.

名脚兒 famous actors; theatrical stars.

名臣 celebrated statesman.

名色 reputation, fame; a famous beauty.

名花 well-known courtesan; [first 23.

[55]名號 a designation; an epithet. =

名言 to give a name; famous say-[ings.

名詞 a noun; terminology.

固有名詞 proper noun.

普通名詞 common noun.

[60]集合名詞 collective noun.

無形名詞 or 抽象名詞 abstract noun.

名·譽 honour; reputation.

名·譽刑 degradation; to cashier; to disfranchise.

[65]名·譽書記 honorary secretary.

名·譽會員 honorary member.

名·譽會長[3] honorary president.

名·譽職 honorary office.

名·譽著[4]開 his name and praise are spread abroad.

名·譽董·事 honorary director, trustee, etc.

[70]名·譽領·事 honorary consul.

名貴 valuable.

名跡 famous places or resorts.

名醫 a famous doctor.

名門 notable families.

[75]名頭 reputation.

名額 the full number of names.

乳名 infantile name, used by parents.

借名 to assume the name of another.

冒名 to forge a name.

[80]出名 to become celebrated.

別名 alias; also known as.

匿名 anonymous.

單名 a name with only one character; usually there are two.

學名 or 書名 name given on going to school.

[85]官名 person's official name.

托名 assumed name.

求名 to seek fame.

混名 a nickname.

無名 nameless; anonymous. See No. 7180.

[90]無名指 the third finger.

簽名 to sign one's name.

買名 to seek for fame.

點名 to call a roll.

↑筆名 pen name; nom de plume.

茗[2]
4525   Tea. The tea-plant.

茗具 tea-utensils.

茗坊 tea-shop.

茗戰 tea-drinking contest.

茗果 light refreshments.

[5]茗椀 tea-cups.

茗汁 tea—as a drink.

茗粥 boiled-tea gruel.

茗芽 tea-buds.

茗飲 tea—as a drink.

酩[2]
4526   Strong spirituous liquor.

酩酊無所知 helplessly intoxicated.

銘[2]
4527   To engrave; to carve.

銘佩 grateful remembrance.

銘刻 to engrave.

銘功 to record merit.

銘心 engraved on the heart.

[5]銘感五內 held in my grateful remembrance :—lit., engraved on my five viscera.

銘文 engraved inscription.

銘旌 flag with an inscription, bestowed on worthy people.

銘肌鏤骨 engraved on the bones—everlasting gratitude.

銘記在心 engraved on the heart.

[10]銘誌 an obituary; epitaph.

銘諸肺腑 engraved on my innermost being.

銘識 an inscription.

銘謝 or 銘感 deeply grateful.

銘鼎相傳 engraved on a tripod and handed down.

[15]碑銘 inscription on a stone tablet.

冥[2]
4528   Dark; obscure. The unseen world. Hades.

冥吏 messengers from Hades.

冥報 recompense in the next life.

冥婚 a marriage ceremony for those who are already dead.

冥府 or 冥間 Hades; the underworld.

[5]冥搜 to grope in the dark.

冥物 or 冥器 paper articles burnt at funerals—boxes, human figures, houses, even steamers and cars.

冥王星 the planet Pluto.

冥福 bliss in the next world.

冥誚 punishment from Hades.

[10]冥衣 paper clothes burnt for the use of the dead.

冥途 the road to Hades.

冥錢 or 冥寶 paper money burnt for the use of the dead.

(a) Deep, profound. High; distant.

冥想 in absent-minded reverie.

冥 海 the deep sea.
幽 冥 obscure; profound.
青 冥 the blue depths of the sky.

(b) Dark in mind, stupid. Confused.

冥 然 罔 覺 stupid; without misgivings.
冥 頑 dull; stupid.

瞑 [2] Dark.
4529 Read *ming*[1]. Night.

溟 [2] Vast, deep. Boundless.
4530 Inter. 冥 No. 4528.

溟 涬 然 most honoured.
北 溟 有 魚 there are fish in the vast Arctic regions.

(a) Drizzling rain.

溟 沐 gradually wet through with fine rain.
溟 溟 drizzling, fine rain.

瞑 [2] To close the eyes.
4531

瞑 目 to close the eyes—death.
甘 心 瞑 目 to depart in peace.
瞑 瞑 blinded, vision obscured.

(a) Read *mien*[4]. To disturb.

瞑 眩 to cause a disturbance—as drastic medicines do internally.

(b) Read *mien*[2]. Inter. 眠 No. 4504. To sleep.

蓂 [2.4.] An auspicious fabulous
4532 plant, called 蓂 莢, which grew in the palace of the Emperor *Yao*. It produced a leaf on the first of the lunar month, and one each day till the full moon, after which it lost a leaf each day till the end of the month.

(a) Read *mi*[4,5] A kind of shepherd's purse or greens.

螟 [2] Various groups of moths
4533 which produce destructive caterpillars. *Pyralidae, heliothidae,* etc.

螟 蛉 caterpillars which destroy rice and other plants; some of these caterpillars are taken by the sphex as food for its larvae.
螟 蛉 之 子 [3] an adopted son.
螟 蟊 a wasp which deposits its eggs in the caterpillars, as above.
螟 蝗 caterpillars and locusts—destructive insects.

明 [2] Bright, clear, intelligent.
朙 Light, brilliant. To understand. To illustrate. To
4534 cleanse.

明 人 a man who is above-board in his dealings.
明 信 片 a postal card.
明 信 花 片 picture-postcard.
明 倫 堂 hall in a Confucian temple.
[5]明 光 or 明 亮 or 明 朗 clear; evident; brilliant.
明 兒(個) tomorrow.
明 公 master of an art or science; a professor of geomancy; ancient term of respect.
明 分 (*fen*[4]) proper status.
明 前 tea picked before *Ts'ing ming.*
[10]明 口 袋 outside pockets.
明 哲 sagacious; shrewd.
明 哲 保 身 a wise man protects his body.
明 堂 hall used under the *Chou* dynasty for sacrifice to 上 帝; imperial ancestral hall; hall in which the feudal princes had audience with the emperor. Spots for acupuncture. Open space before a grave—geomantic term. Centre courtyard of a dwelling.
明 天 or 明 日 or 明 朝[1] tomorrow.
[15]明 天 再 說 we shall discuss this again tomorrow.
明 天 見 (or 會) I'll see you again tomorrow—said in parting—good-bye; good-night.
明 媚 bright; attractive.
明 察 秋 毫 able to examine the tip of an autumn hair—discerning intelligence.
明 年 or 開 年 or 來 年 next year.
[20]明 度 degree of brilliancy.
明 心 迹 to make one's intention clear.
明 悟 talent; intellect; intelligence.
明 據 clear proof.
明 敏 quick-witted.
[25]明 文 clearly stated in writing—as in a treaty or agreement.
明 斷 to decide openly.
明 日 黃 花 things that are past their time.
明 早 or 明 旦 tomorrow morning.
明 明 上 天 the bright and high heaven.
[30]明 明 德 to illustrate illustrious virtue.
明 明 是 你 without a doubt it was you!
明 星 the morning star.
明 時 times of peace.
明 暗 之 奄 映 chiaroscuro.
[35]明 曉 clearly to understand; to have a clear perception of.
明 月 the bright moon.
明 朝 [2] or 大 明 the Ming Dynasty —A.D. 1368—1644.
明 棄 暗 取 rejecting a thing openly while taking it in secret.
明 槍 暗 劍 both open and covert attack.
[40]明 欺 open swindling.
明 正 clear and pure-minded; a Tibetan chief.
明 決 clear and decided.
明 河 the Milky Way.
明 淨 clear; bright.
[45]明 滅 可 見 where it was in view and where it was hidden could be clearly traced.
明 溝 an open drain.
明 火 fire obtained by a burning-glass, used in ancient sacrifices; highway-robbers.
明 火 執 仗 a raid with torches and weapons—evil deeds cannot be hidden.
明 燈 a light; fires.
[50]明 玕 the bamboo.
明 珠 bright pearls—a person who is much esteemed.
明 珠 闇 投 a bright pearl thrown into darkness—a discarded man of talents; a good man who

descends to shady practices; a good man fallen among evil companions, etc.

明 理·的 人 a man of clear principles; an intelligent person.

明 瑟 clear and fresh.

⁵⁵明 璫 pearl ear-ring.

明 瓦 or 雲 母 石 mica.

明 發 the day is dawning.

明·白 to understand; clear, plain.

明 目 張 胆·的 undaunted; fearlessly; openly; shamelessly.

⁶⁰明 睿 clear wisdom.

明 瞭 perspicuous.

明 知 to know quite well.

明 知 故 問 to feign ignorance and ask questions; to draw a person out.

明 知 故 犯 presumptuous crime; wilful offence.

⁶⁵明 碼 plain language—not code.

明 確 clear and definite; self-evident.

明 礬 alum.

明 示 to issue explicit instructions.

明 神 the sun and moon, hills and streams—an ancient designation.

⁷⁰明 細 書 specifications.

明 經 familiar with the classics; a senior graduate under the old system.

明 膠 clear glue.

明 若 觀 火 as clear as looking at a fire.

明 處 in the light; openly.

⁷⁵明 衣 cotton garment worn in fasting; garments given to the dead.

明 見 clear view—your opinion.

明 見 萬 里 far-sighted capacity.

明 視 a name for the hare.

明 視 距 離 the distance of distinct vision.

⁸⁰明 訂 to define clearly.

明 詔 特 下 when the imperial mandate was issued.

明 證 clear evidence.

明 貺 your valuable present.

明 買 明 賣 an open transaction.

⁸⁵明 輪 a paddle-wheel steamer.

明 通 intelligent.

明 透 perspicuous; to have a thorough understanding of.

明 達 or 明 悉 to understand thoroughly.

明 都 a clear mirror.

⁹⁰明 鏡 the south—an ancient term.

明 鏡 高 懸 a clear mirror hung on high—clear intelligence.

明 鑑 perspicacious.

明 顯 evident; clearly manifest.

不 明 not clear; not quite sure.

⁹⁵分 明 clearly; manifestly.

發 明 to invent.

鳴² To sound. A sound. The cry of a bird or animal.
4535

鳴 嘶 or 鳴 叫 to neigh.

鳴 冤 to cry out for redress.

鳴 得 意 crowing over one's success.

鳴 旦 the herald of the dawn—a cock.

⁵鳴 礮 示 敬 to fire a salute.

鳴 管 eustachian tube; the song organ of birds.

鳴 鑼 or 鳴 金 to beat a gong.

鳴 鼓 to beat a drum.

鳴 謝 to express thanks.

¹⁰自 鳴 鐘 striking-clock.

皿³ A vessel; a utensil. Radical 108.
4536 Distinguish 血 No. 2901.

器 皿 utensils; vessels.

命⁴ The will of God. A command; a decree. To command. Fate, destiny. Life. To name. Government notification.
4537

命 不 該 死 not fated to die.

命 不 足 道 righteousness is of more importance than one's position in life.

命 世 famous.

命 中 to hit a mark.

⁵命 之 所 招 caused by fate.

命 之 曰 he called it the....

命 也 如 何 Alas, such is destiny!

命·介 a command; orders.

命 分 or 分 數 fractions.

¹⁰命 名 to name; to term; to distinguish.

命 好 having good luck.

命 婦 wives of former officials.

命 定 destiny; fixed fate; to decide; to decree.

命 定 主 義 fatalism. Cf. 6393.21.

¹⁵命 意 meaning or purpose implied.

命 案 a law-case involving life.

命 根 or 命 本 one's own life; inmost self.

命 矣 夫 Alas, it is the appointment of Heaven!

命 窮 in poor circumstances; fated to be poor.

²⁰命 紙 a divination paper. [matter.

命 脈 the pulse of life; important

命 若 懸 絲 life hanging by a thread.

命 薄 如 紙 my luck is as thin as paper!

命 該 如 此 this is my appointed lot.

²⁵命 賈 means of livelihood; fees of a fortune-teller.

命 辭 a proposition.

命 途 one's lot in life.

命·運 a horoscope; destiny; fate.

命 門 the gate of life—the womb; the right kidney.

³⁰命 題 a subject set for an essay; a proposition.

命 駕 to order the carriage.

償 命 life for a life.

喪 命 to lose one's life.

天 命 the will of God; the decree of Heaven.

³⁵性·命 life.

怨 命 to murmur against one's lot.

拚 命 to risk one's life as a gambler risks his stake; desperate.

救 命 Help! Help! to save life.

短 命 a short life.

⁴⁰算 命 to tell fortunes.

義 命 one's rightful lot.

致 命 fatal.

苦 命 a miserable fate.

要 命 hazardous; critical; alarming.

⁴⁵覆 命 to report on a commission.

逃 命 to escape for one's life.

非 命 a sudden or violent death.

MIU.   (ㄇㄡ)

繆⁴ To mislead. In error. Errors. Inter. next.
4538

繆 爲 恭 敬 pretended to show respect.

紕 繆 faulty, erroneous; having deficiencies.

(a) Read *mou²*. To wind round.

綢 繆 to bind round and round—married union. *See* No. 1318-B.

(b) Read *chiu¹* or *liao³*. To cord. To bind.

自 繆 死 strangled herself.
衣 衰 而 繆 經 when wearing the sackcloth with the edges evenly bound.

(c) Read *mu⁴˙⁵*. Inter. 穆 No. 4601.

壯 繆 martial awe and dignity.

謬 4 Falsehood, error, exaggeration. Also read *niu⁴*.
4539

謬 傳 a false report.
謬 妄 untrue; to make wrong use of.
謬 悮 an error; a blunder.
謬 愛 to love wrongly.
↓⁵謬 誤 百 出 hundreds of errors; the mistakes are numerous.
↓ 荒 謬 絕 倫 absurd beyond compare.
謬 見 mistaken views.
謬 解 warped or twisted interpretations.
謬 言 lies.
謬 說 nonsense; crooked ideas.
¹⁰謬 誤 到 極 點 utterly erroneous.
謬 論 fallacious reasoning.
大 謬 great error.
差 謬 mistaken ideas; errors.
心 謬 false-hearted.
¹⁵狂 謬 wild exaggeration.

MO.   (ㄇㄛ)

4540

1.3.

An interrogative particle.

他 去·了·麼 Has he gone? (··*ma*)
甚·麼 or 什·麼 What? (··*mê*)
那·麼 or 這·麼 thus; under these or those circumstances; then; hence, etc. (··*mê*)

(a) Read *ma¹*. Insignificant. Small.

摩 2 To feel with the hand. To rub. To scour, to polish. To
4541 grope for. The interaction of one thing upon another.

摩·一·摩 give it a rub.
摩 厲 以 須 to grind weapons sharp in preparation.
摩 崖 之 碑 places for inscriptions, made by smoothing the face of a cliff.
摩 弄 to handle; to play with.
⁵摩 戞 friction; knocking of things together.
摩 拳 to rub the hands together.
摩 挲 to stroke, to fondle; to grope for. Usually pron. *ma¹.sa*.
摩 擦 發 電 機 frictional electric apparatus.
摩 民 以 義 to influence the people to righteousness.
¹⁰摩 煉 to discipline.
摩 牙 to grind the teeth—altercation.
摩 盪 operations of nature.
摩 肩 to rub shoulders—as in a crowd.
摩 阻 力 friction.
¹⁵摩 頂 受 戒 Buddhist initiation rites.
摩 頂 放 踵 to wear the whole body smooth from head to foot —to give oneself to save others.
拊 摩 to pat; to soothe.

(a) Used in transliterating.

摩 尼 or 末 尼 used for *Mâni* and the Manichæans. The former is also a pearl, from the Sanskrit, *mani*.
摩 尼 敎 Manichæism.
摩 托 車 motor-car.
摩 拉 維 亞 Moravia.
⁵摩 揭 佗 Magadha—a kingdom in Central India, formerly the chief centre of Buddhism.
摩 洛 哥 Morocco.
摩 納 哥 Monaco.
摩 西 Moses.
摩 耶 *Mâyâ*, the mother of Buddha.
¹⁰摩 門 Mormons.
摩 鹿 加 Moluccas.

蘑 2
蘑
4542

Edible mushrooms.

蘑·菇 mushrooms; edible fungoid growth on trees.

磨 2 To grind, to rub, to sharpen.
4543

磨·不 開 cannot move, — unsuccessful. (cf. A *below*)
磨·不 開 臉 to have a feeling of shame—loss of face. (cf. A *below*)
磨·了 泡 hands or feet rubbed into blisters.
磨 人 troublesome; wearing.
⁵磨 光 or 磨 明 to burnish.
磨 刀 to grind a knife.
磨 利 or 磨 快 to grind sharp.
磨 功 夫 to dawdle over work.
磨 勁 to stick at the task.
¹⁰磨 勘 to revise selected essays, under the former examination system, before pronouncing them successful.
磨 勵 to encourage.
磨 嘴 磨 舌·的 to haggle; to bandy words.
磨 墨 to grind ink.
磨·得 尖 利 sharpen to a fine point.
¹⁵磨 快 擦 亮 ground sharp and polished bright.
磨 折 to bow very low; to check; misfortune; trials; ordeals.
磨 拳 擦 掌 rubbing the hands together—eager to get at a thing.
磨 耗 frayed and worn.
磨 淬 to grind and temper.
²⁰磨 滅 rubbed out; obliterated; to crush—as a movement or spirit.
磨 煉 or 磨 鍊 to discipline.
磨 牙 to grind the teeth.
磨 琢 to grind and polish.
磨 璞 to grind off the roughnesses of a gem.
²⁵磨·的 鋒 快 ground very sharp.
磨 石 a whetstone.
磨 研 to grind; to investigate.
磨 磚 bricks made smooth by rubbing.
磨 礪 to discipline. ⌐ rubbing.
³⁰磨 究 to make a thorough investigation.
磨 穿 鐵 硯 to wear through an iron ink-slab—denotes ardent attention to literary work.
磨 舌 active with the tongue.
磨 難 (*nan⁴*) tribulations; sufferings.
磨 顏·色 to grind colours.
³⁵磨 麵 to grind flour.

(a) Read *mo*[4]. A mill. To turn. An occasion, a turn.

磨·房 or 磨·坊 a mill.
磨·煩 to worry; to annoy.
磨·盤 石 a millstone.
磨·過·來 to turn round—as a cart.
推 磨 to turn a mill.
水 磨 a water-mill.

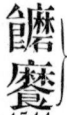

饡 [2]   To feed an infant by
饝   hand. Steamed bread.
4544

饝 饝 steamed loaves.

魔 [2]   A malignant spirit. A
4545   demon. Correctly written
   as below.

魔 力 fascination; glamour; power of personality; influence.
魔 媼 a woman who pretends to have intercourse with spirits and demons—a witch.
魔 媚 fascinating; bewitching.
魔 民 the wicked angels of *Mâra*. *See below*—7.
[5]魔 氣 demoniacal afflatus; demon-possession.
魔 王 the prince of evil.
魔 羅 or 天 魔 the evil one of Buddhism—*Mâra*.
魔 術 magic.
魔 道 injurious courses.
[10]魔 障 b e w i t c h e d; obscured in vision.
魔 鬼 the Devil.
妖 魔 mischievous spirits.
病 魔 delirium.
酒 魔 delirium tremens.

MO. (ㄛ)
(Moh)

末 [4.5.] The end; finally, as op-
4546   posed to 本 No. 5025.
   Mean, insignificant. Dust,
   powder.
   Distinguish 未 No. 7114.

↓末了兒 *See below* 21.
末 世 the last days; the end of a dynasty; the end of the world.
末 作 inferior occupation—artisan or trading, as compared with farming.
末 位 the lowest seat.

末 俗 modern customs. (abusive)
[5]末·利 wealth acquired through trade. *See above*—2.
末 命 dying injunctions.
末 回 the final occasion.
末 如 之 何 也 已 矣 in the end there is no help for it.
↑末 兒 or 末·子 dust; fragments.
[10]末 學 self-depreciatory—I.
末 學 膚 受 superficial scholarship.
末 官 a very petty official.
末 富 wealth acquired through trade—reckoned inferior to farming. *See above*—2, 5.
末 尾 at the last; in the rear.
[15]末 帝 the last ruler of a dynasty.
末 年 the closing years of life, etc.
末 座 or 末 席 the lowest seat.
末 弁 petty officials—military.
末 後 or 過 後 afterwards; finally.
[20]末 日 the last day; the last age; the end of. 「末了兒」or 末 拉
末·末·了 finally; in the end. A.c.
末 梢 神 經 nerve-endings.
末 次 the last occasion.
末 殺 to obliterate; to wipe out.
[25]末 流 modern customs.
末 減 to lighten a punishment.
末 生 trade and industry—as compared with farming, are inferior modes of life. *See above*—2, 5, 13.
末 疾 dizziness, headache.
末 策 the final resource.
[30]末 節 a tip of a twig—fine details.
末 著 the last resource.
末 葉 the last years.
末 藝 skill in trifles.
末 行 petty details of conduct.
[35]末 計 last ideas or plans; second thoughts.
末 議 petty discussions.
末 路 the end of the journey; the end drawing near.
末 造 decadent period, as the last years of a dynasty.
四 末 the four extremities of the body.
[40]本 末 beginning and ending; fundamentals and incidentals.

(a) A negative.

末 之 覩 也 I had not seen it.
末 之 也 已 Don't go! and there's an end to it.
末 由 也 已 but there is no way.

妹 [4.5.] Wife of *Chich* 桀, the last
4547   ruler of the *Hsia* dynasty.
   A.c. 妹 喜

抹 [3.5.] To smear. To rub over,
4548   to wipe clean. To obliterate.

抹·下 臉·來 to straighten one's countenance.
抹·了 良 心 obliterated all moral sense.
抹 他 眼·睛 daubed his eyes.
抹 兌 to settle accounts for another.
[5]抹○去 to wipe out.
抹·子 a trowel for plaster.
抹 布 a dish-cloth; a duster. (*S. dial.*)
抹 掉 to wipe out; cleared off.
抹 數 to wipe out an account.
[10]抹 棹·子 to wipe down a table.
抹 涙 to wipe away tears. (*S. dial.*)
抹 滅 to wipe out.
抹 煞 or 抹 殺 ≡ 4546.24
抹 牌 to play cards.
[15]抹 粉 to make up the face.
抹 胸 a tight garment worn over the breasts; a stomacher.
抹 角 to go round a corner.
抹 銷 to deface and cancel.
抹 頸 or 抹 脖·子 to cut one's throat.
[20]塗 抹 to erase; to blot out—as sins, etc.

沫 [4.5.] Saliva; froth. To finish.
4549

沫·子 or 浮 沫 foam, froth, scum.
吐·沫 spittle.

秣 [4.5.] To feed a horse with grain.
4550

秣 馬 to feed a horse.
秣 陵 ancient name for Nanking District.

茉 [4.5.] The white jasmine.
4551

茉·莉 花 white jasmine flowers, used for scenting tea.

袜 [4.5.] Girdle. Kerchief.
4552

襪 胸 a stomacher; tight garment worn over the breasts.
襪 腹 a stomacher.

(a) Read *wa*[4.5.] or *ma*[4.5.]. Socks. Inter. 襪 No. 7000.

韎 [4.5.] Socks, stockings. See 襪, preceding—A.
4553　　A tribe, see below.

韎 鞨 a tribe which occupied Manchuria. Tunguses, variously known as 肅愼, 勿吉.

歾 [4.5.] To end, to die. The dead. Old form of the next.
4554

歾 世 不 忘 I shall never forget.
歾 存 均 感 the dead and the living will both thank you.
歾 於 陣 died in battle.

沒 [4.5.] To die. Dead. Sunk, gone, drowned. Also read
4555　*mu*[4.5.].

沒 世 不 忘 I shall never forget.
沒 人 a diver.
沒 入 to confiscate.
沒 收 to confiscate; to withhold.
[5]沒 地 buried; interred.
沒 官 confiscated by the government.
沒 沒 無 聞 buried and unheard of—a busy man who does not get preferment.
沒 溺 drowned.
沒 而 有 知 if there is knowledge after death!
[10]沒 飲 constant intoxication with liquor—as if drowned in it.
沒 齒 till all my teeth are lost—throughout my whole life.
乾 沒 to embezzle; to squeeze.
出 沒 appearing and disappearing. *See* No. 1409-D.3ff.

(a) No, not:—opposite to 有, to have. Read *mei*[2].

沒 下 梢 having no good ending; no harvest or result.
沒 事 nothing the matter.
沒 事 人 one who keeps himself out of a matter.
沒 二 句 話 there are no two ways about it!
[5]沒 交 涉 no dealings with; no relation to.

沒 作 理 會 處 difficult to plan for.
沒 來 由 without any cause or reason. ⌈thing.
沒 出 息 unprofitable; good for nosomething.
沒 味 兒 insipid; to have no pleasure in.
[10]沒 命 regardless of life; dead.
沒 商 量 difficult to come to agreement; done carelessly without consultation.
沒 奈 何 no help for it; no alternative. A.c. 莫...
沒 字 碑 one who does not recognize any characters.
沒 影 兒 not a sign of it.
[15]沒 得 impossible; cannot be done; there is not.
沒 心 眼 without twists and turns; simple-minded.
沒 志 氣 without decision of character. ⌈tional.
沒 意 思 uninteresting; unintensomething-
沒 把 鼻 nothing to take hold of; not fixed. A.c. 沒 把 柄.
[20]沒 數 innumerable.
沒 有 there is not;—he—has not.
沒 有 准 兒 not at all certain; undecided; not sure.
沒 有 甚 麼 not in the least; none at all; nothing whatsoever.
沒 有 的 話 no such thing.
[25]沒 有 空 兒 I have no time; I am very busy.
沒 有 臉 no face, ashamed.
沒 有 這 個 道 理 no such thing; nothing of the kind!
沒 根 兒 groundless; having no foundation in fact.
沒 法 子 or 無 法 no help; no remedy; cannot be helped. A.c.
[30]沒 王 法 lawless. ⌈沒 法 兒.
沒 用 or 無 用 useless.
沒 的 there are not.
沒 眼 色 rigid, unable to fit in with changing conditions.
沒 禮 犯 分 without manners, going beyond one's proper position.
[35]沒 精 打 彩 dispirited and discouraged; listless.
沒 良 心 ungrateful; without sense of right and wrong.
沒 行 止 no starting and stopping—unprincipled, i.e., without decent conduct.
沒 規 沒 矩 without manners.

沒 趣 uninteresting; unpleasant; awkwardness of situation
[40] caused by tactless words or action.
沒 頭 帖 anonymous placard.
沒 頭 沒 腦 stupid; heedlessly; thoughtlessly; incoherent.
沒 食 子 蜂 the gall-fly.
沒 骨 氣 spiritless; lacking decision of character.
[45]沒 骨 畫 a form of wash-drawing in which definite outlines are not first drawn.

(b) Used in transliterating.

沒 藥 myrrh.

眿 [4.5.]
4556　To gaze; to ogle.
Distinguish 脈 No. 4382.

眿 眿 to look at.

莫 [4.5.] A negative; not; do not; there is not.
4557

莫 不 perhaps; probably; absolutely.
莫 不 成 can it be that....?
莫 不 是 it must be so; is it not so? surely it is.
莫 不 髮 指 there were none whose hair did not stand on end.
[5]莫 之 致 而 至 者 that which comes without being caused.
莫 來 you need not come.
莫 信 do not believe.
莫 名 cannot be expressed.
莫 吾 猶 人 也 possibly I equal others!
[10]莫 大 之 恩 unbounded grace.
莫 大 於 天 there is nothing greater than Heaven.
莫 如 cannot do better than; rather.
　知 子 莫 如 父 no one knows a son like his father.
莫 定 it is uncertain.
[15]莫 往 莫 來 neither goes nor comes; no intercourse.
莫 愁 do not be grieved; name of a famous singing-girl.
莫 想 do not suppose, expect
莫 或 不 難 perhaps it may not be difficult.

莫 我 知 也 夫 no one knows me, alas!

²⁰莫 明 其 妙 or 莫 名 其 妙 very mysterious and abstruse; very strange; peculiar.

莫 爲 or 莫 作 do not do it.

莫 甚 於 此 nothing beyond this.

莫 知 nobody knows.

莫 知 其 鄉⁺者 you cannot tell the trend of it.

²⁵莫 管 閒 事 do not meddle in the affairs of others—mind your own business.

莫 若 better; cannot do better than.

莫 見 怪 or 莫 怪 do not take offence.

莫 說 do not say; not to mention; it is needless to remark.

莫 逆 之 交 uninterrupted friendship.

³⁰莫 過 於 此 nothing more than this.

莫 道 ... do not say that....

莫 非 a strong affirmative; *

莫 非 他 it can be nobody else.

莫 非 寫 錯 了 could it be that it was written wrongly?

³⁵莫 非 己 也 it certainly touches oneself.

莫 非 此 理 之 用 it is nothing but the application of this principle.

莫 非 王 臣 the king's power and officers reached everywhere.

莫 須 有 it is not certain that there is; is there not?

* a conjectural interrogative.

(a) To decide; to fix. To plan for.

求 民 之 莫 seeking—on every hand—to find someone to give settlement to the people.

聖 人 莫 之 the sages planned for them.

(b) Extensive, great—when repeated:—flourishing.

廣 莫 之 野 a great expanse of waste land.

維 葉 莫 莫 "its leaves are luxurious and dense."

(c) To shave, to pare.

刀 可 莫 鐵 the knife could shave iron.

(d) Inter. 瘼 No. 4562.

莫 此 下 民 the distress of the masses.

(e) Inter. 幕 No. 4559.

莫 府 military headquarters.

(f) Read mu⁴·⁵. Evening; late.

莫 夜 late at night.

莫 春 者 in the last month of spring.

歲 莫 the close of the year.

(g) Read mo⁴·⁵. Quiet, tranquil.

君 婦 莫 莫 "the presiding wives are still and reverent."

(h) Used in transliterating.

莫 斯 科 Moscow.

窸 4558 4.5. Still, silent. Lonely.

寂 寞 the stillness of solitude.

索 寞 desolate and lonely.

幕 慔} 4559 4.5. A curtain, a screen. Also read mu⁴·⁵.

幕 天 席 地 to have the sky for curtains and the earth for a mat.

幕 幃 or 幃 幕 a curtain.

幕 府 an encampment. See below —A. [story.

內 幕 behind the scenes; the inside

⁵啟 幕 to raise the curtain—to open a person's eyes.

戲 幕 the drop-screen of the stage.

閉 幕 to drop the screen.

開 幕 to raise the curtain—to begin anything; to open a sale, business, etc.

黑 幕 dark screen—things that are dark and shady; hidden evils.

(a) A private secretary.

幕 友 or 幕 賓 or 幕 僚 private secretary to a official; an advisor.

幕 府 secretary to high official.

(b) Read man⁴. The reverse of a coin, as the obverse is 文.

摸 4560 1.5. To feel for or after; to grope. To guess. A. p. mao¹. Distinguish 幕 No. 4588.

摸·一·摸 to rub or feel; to give a rub.

摸·不 清 not quite clear about it.

摸·不 著² I cannot find it out.(-chao²)

摸 手 to feel another's hand—up the sleeve in bargaining.

⁵摸 東 摸 西 feeling about for.

摸 水 to grope about in water.

摸 瞎·子 to grope like a blind man.

摸·稜 to feel the corners—undecided; lacking decision; ambiguous. (mo²-) A.w. 模 稜

摸·索 to grope for; to stroke; to feel. (mo¹-)

¹⁰摸·着 門 found the way—to do anything, or of livelihood, etc.

摸·著 groping; feeling for.

摸 頭 緒 to find the clue.

摸 魚 to grope for fish.

摸 黑ʲ to be belated on the road.

(a) To trace, for which 摹 No. 4588, is generally used.

摸 本 a traced copy.

漠 4561 4.5. A sandy desert.

漠 然 vast, boundless.

(a) Careless; indifferent.

漠 不 相 關 of no consequence to.

漠 然 無 所 動 unmoved; indifferent.

瘼 4562 4.5. Sickness; distress.

民 瘼 the sufferings of the masses.

膜 4563 4.5. Any thin membrane in plants or animals.

膜·子 a membrane; the inner lining of the bamboo.

膜 翅 類 hymenoptera.

膜 視 to disregard; to ignore.

眼 膜 the sclerotic.

⁵置 諸 膜 外 disregard it entirely.

視 同 膈 膜 regard it with indifference.

(a) Read *mu²* To make a prostration.

膜 拜 to make a long prostration; to go on a pilgrimage.

邈 3.5. Far off, remote. Profound, abstruse. Also read
4564 *miao²*.

邈 然 不 可 復 求 irrecoverably gone.
邈 邈 sorrowful.

糢
蘪 4.5. Broken grain.
4565

糢 屑 crumbs.

MOU. (ᒫ)
(Meo)

牟
麰 ² Barley.
4566

牟 麥 barley.
來 牟 wheat and barley; *lai* is the original form for wheat.

(a) To low like an ox.

牟 然 而 鳴 to low like an ox.

(b) To encroach on. To take.

牟 利 起 見 mercenary motives.
牟 大 利 to make large profits in trade.
侵 牟 to usurp; to prey upon.

(c) To double.

(d) Used in transliterating.

牟 尼 from the Sanskrit, *Muni,* a hermit, an ascetic; u.f. *Shâkyamuni.*

侔 ² Equal, similar, alike.
4567

侔 莫 to urge; to force.
不 相 侔 dissimilar.

眸 ² The pupil of the eye. The eye.
4568

眸 子 ³ the pupil of the eye.
眸 子 不 能 掩 其 惡 the pupil of a man's eye cannot hide his evil.

蛑 ² A marine crab.
4569

矛 ² A lance, a spear. Radical 110. Pron. *mao².*
4570

矛 勇 irregulars armed with spears.
矛 盾 spear and shield—mutually opposed; u.f., inconsistency, from the story of a man who boasted that he could supply shields which nothing could pierce, and spears which could penetrate anything.
矛 盾 之 謂 blame of inconsistency.
矛 盾 衝 突 a clash.
自 相 矛 盾 he contradicts himself.

敄 ⁴ To put forth effort. Also read *wu⁴.*
4571

瞀 ⁴ To look at closely. Nearsighted; dim; indistinct vision.
4572

瞀 亂 confusion—as of right and wrong.
瞀 瞀 然 bashful.
瞀 視 confused sight; to see dimly.

鍪 ² An iron pan; a metal cap.
4573

袤 ⁴ Measurement from north to south, as that from east to west is 廣.
4574

廣 袤 breadth and length—area.

(a) A long robe.

袤 服 long garments.

懋 ⁴ To exert the mind; to be energetic. To be great; to make great. Pron. *mao⁴.*
4575

懋 典 great celebrations.
懋 力 to urge to effort.
懋 庸 to reward the meritorious.
懋 修 earnest efforts to reform.
⁵懋 績 great meritorious achievement.
懋 賞 to reward in order to encourage further effort.
懋 遷 trade and commerce.
德 懋 懋 官 to those of great virtue he gave great office.

牡 ³ The male of animals and of some birds. Bolt of a door. Also read *mu³.*
4576

牡·丹 茶 a large variety of camellia.
牡·丹 花 the peony.

某
厶 ³ A certain person or thing; formerly used to avoid giving its proper sound to a tabooed character.
4577 So-and-so; such-and-such.

某 人 or 某 甲 a certain person—one whose name is unknown, or which it is not desirable to mention.
某 何 爲 哉 what does So-and-so do?
某 在 斯 So-and-so is here.
某 城 a certain city.
⁵某 月 某 日 a certain month and a certain day.
某 某 certain others; a certain person named....
某 種 常 識 a certain kind of general knowledge.
某 種 技 能 a certain class of ability.
某 處 a certain place.

謀 ² To scheme; to plot; to devise. A device.
4578

謀 主 ringleader of a plot; the one who devised the plan.
謀 事 在 人 成 事 在 天 man proposes but God disposes.
謀 反 or 謀 叛 to plot against the State.
謀 士 a counsellor; a strategist.
⁵謀 害 to plot to injure.
謀 幹 ability; resourceful.
謀 府 the leader of a plot.
謀 盧 to plan; to scheme.
謀 權 a plot to usurp authority.

[10]謀 殺 to plot murder.
謀 求 to seek.
謀 活 to strive for a living.
謀 泄 the plot leaks out.
謀 為 power to plan; ability to bring a matter to pass.
[15]謀 生 or 營 謀 to plan to get a living.
謀 生 乏 術 having no means of getting a livelihood.
謀 略 a plan; military strategy; to plot.
謀 畫 to plot; to plan.
謀 算 to devise; to scheme.
[20]謀 計 or 謀 議 to plan; to plot.
謀 財 to scheme to acquire wealth.
謀 陷 to plot in order to injure another.
謀 面 to be acquainted with; to meet each other.

畝 畒 [3]
4579
A Chinese land-measure of area; it varies in different provinces, but for general purposes it is reckoned as 240 sq. paces 步, or 733½ sq. yds.: thus 6.6 *mou* or *mow* equal one acre.
Fields, arable land.
More commonly pron. *mu*[3].
畝 丘 a hill cultivated in terraces.
畝 數 acres.
幾 畝 地 a few *mow* of land.
田 畝 fields.

茂 [4]
4580
Exuberant, flourishing. Elegant. Healthy, vigorous, strong.　Pron. *nao*[4].
茂 勳 excellent merits.
茂 密 close; rank growth.
茂 年 the prime of one's years.
茂 才 fine, varied talents.
[5]茂 林 a dense forest.
茂 業 flourishing business.
茂 正 其 德 he sedulously cultivated his virtue.
茂 猷 excellent plans.
茂 生 to grow luxuriantly.
[10]茂 盛 luxuriant; exuberant; abundant.
茂 繁 or 茂 衍 numerous—as progeny.
茂 草 luxuriant growth; jungle.
茂 蔭 shady.
茂 行 virtuous conduct.

貿 [4]
4581
To barter, to trade.
Pron. *mao*[4].

貿 利 to strive for gain.
貿 名 to purchase fame.
貿 易 trade; exchange of goods.
貿 易 之 差 額 balance of trade.
[5]貿 易 事 務 官 commercial agent.
貿 易 景 象 trade prospects.
貿 易 集 中 concentration of trade.
貿 易 風 the trade winds.
國 內 貿 易 internal trade.
[10]國 外 貿 易 foreign trade.
自 由 貿 易 free-trade.

(a) Rashly. Many.

貿 然 recklessly; heedlessly.
貿 貿 recklessly; many; much; dull vision.
貿 首 to rise as a mob and behead one against whom there is a grievance.

MU.　　(ㄇㄨ)

母 [3]
4582
A mother; a dam; female. Distinguish 毋 No. 7193.

母 儀 an example for mothers—a pattern of motherhood.
母 兄 uterine elder-brother.
母 后 the empress.
母 國 mother country.
[5]母 姨 maternal aunts.
母 子 [3] mother and son; principal and interest.
母 子 [3] 之 情 maternal love.
母 弟 uterine younger-brother.
母 慈 maternal tenderness.
[10]母 敎 the teachings of one's mother.
母 數 or 分 母 denominator of a fraction.
公 母 common denominator.
母 會 mother-church or society.
母 校 Alma Mater.
[15]母 權 maternal authority.
母 氏 mother.
母 胎 a mother's womb.
母 舅 mother's brother.
母 親 a mother.
[20]母 財 capital.
母 錢 principal; capital.
母 雞 a hen.
母 難 日 one's birthday.
母 音 or 元 音 or 主 音 vowels.
[25]母 黨 mother's relatives.
乳 母 or 奶 母 a wet-nurse.
出 母 a divorced mother.
外 母 mother-in-law.

契 母 adopted mother.
[30]字 母 the letters of the alphabet; one of the initial sounds of ancient Chinese.
家 母 my mother—in speaking to others.
岳 母 mother-in-law.
水 母 a jelly-fish.
繼 母 or 後 母 a step-mother.
[35]親 母 one's own mother.
酒 母 yeast; ferment.
雲 母 mica; mother-of-pearl.

姆 姥 [3]
4583
A matron; a dame. The second form is also read *lao*[3].

姆 姆 or 大 姆 the title by which a younger brother addresses the wife of his elder brother.
姆 師 a governess or matron.

拇 [3]
4584
The thumb; the great toe.

拇 戰 to play guess-fingers or *mora*.
大 拇 指, 大 拇 哥 the thumb.
駢 拇 joined toes.

募 [4]
4585
To summon; to levy; to raise.

募 兵 to raise troops.
募 勇 to enlist irregular troops.
募 化 to collect subscriptions—as Buddhist priests.
募 化 桶 box for offerings in a temple.
[5]募 化 重 [2] 修 to collect subscriptions for the repair of a temple.
募 捐 to appeal for subscriptions.
募 緣 to ask for subscriptions for idolatry.
募 補 to enroll so as to make up the quota.
招 募 to call for troops.

墓 [4]
4586
A grave, a tomb.

墓 域 the boundaries of a grave.
墓 所 a cemetery.　A.c. 公 墓
墓 木 trees near a grave.
墓 碑 a tombstone.

⁵墓 誌 an epitaph.
墓 道 the path before a grave.
墓 門 the door of a tomb.
修 墓 to repair a tomb.
掃 墓 to sweep the graves—at *Ts'ing Ming.*

慕⁴ To desire; to long for; to be fond of. To think of
4587 affectionately. To admire.

慕 勢 to toady to those in power.
慕 名 to emulate the good name of another.
慕 名 利 to long for fame and fortune.
慕 德 to long after virtue.
⁵慕 效 to look up to another with affection and copy his example.
慕 父 母 affection for one's parents.
慕 義 to emulate a good action.
慕 藺 to emulate a worthy man—as 司 馬 相 如 of *Han* dynasty, who so respected 藺 相 如 that he took his name.
仰 慕 to look up to with admiration.
¹⁰愛 慕 to love with ardent affection.

摹² To follow a pattern; to copy. A pattern.
4588

摹 仿 to copy a pattern.
摹 古 to copy the old style.
摹 寫 to write from a copy.
摹 效 imitations.
摹 本 a copy from a tracing; figured satin.

暮⁴ The evening; sunset. The end of a period of time.
4589

暮 年 aged; in the evening of life.
暮 春 the end of spring.
暮 景 a sunset sky.
暮 歲 or 歲 暮 the end of the year.
⁵暮 鐘 the evening bell.
旦 暮 morning and evening.
昏 暮 the gloaming.
薄 暮 the evening.

模² A mould, a pattern. A style. Pron. *mo²* exc. 3.
4590

模 仿 性 an imitative disposition.

模 型 機 器 models of machinery.
模 子 a mould; a pattern or example; a model. (*mu²-*)
模 形 (or 型) models; a matrix.
⁵模 擬 to imitate; to copy.
模 楷 a pattern.
模 樣 a style; a manner; a fashion.
模 碑 rubbing of an inscription.
模 稜 indecision; ambiguity. *See* 摸 No. 4560-8.
¹⁰模 糊 blurred, indistinct, confused.
模 範 a pattern; an example; model; exemplary.
模 範 小 學 model primary school.
模 範 監 獄 model prison.
模 範 軍 隊 model army.
¹⁵模 結 a deed on which a man has placed the print of his hand or foot.
模 表 an example; a pattern.

謨⁴ A plan; a course of action. To imitate. False.
4591 Also read *mo⁴.*

僞 謨 false.
聖 謨 the plans of the sages.

(a) Read *mo⁴·⁵.* To practice.

謨 先 聖 之 大 猶 to practice the maxims of the ancient sages.

MU. (ㄨ)
(Muh)

殳 ⁴·⁵.
4592 To dive; to disappear.

木 ⁴·⁵. Wood; wooden. Timber. Trees—thus:—numb, without feeling. Radical 75.
4593

木 主 or 神 主 tablet of a deceased person.
木 乃 伊 or 木 默 a mummy—from the sound.
木 了 or 麻 木 了 numb; palsied.
木 人 an image; a blockhead.
⁵木 俑 a wooden image; a puppet.
木 偶 an idol; a wooden image.
木 偶 人 a blockhead; a puppet.
木 公 a name for the pine-tree.
木 勺 a wooden dipper.
¹⁰木 化 石 opal.
木 匠 or 木 工 or 木 作 a carpenter.

木 器 wooden vessels.
木 客 timber dealers.
木 屑 sawdust.
¹⁵木 屜 pattens; clogs.
木 已 成 舟 the wood is already made into a boat—the thing is done.
木 廠 a timber yard.
木 強 inflexible; blunt.
木 排 a timber raft.
²⁰木 摺 尺 folding boxwood rule.
木 料 timber; lumber.
木 星 or 危 星 the planet Jupiter.
木 曜 日 used in some calendars for Thursday.
木 木 子 the stump of a tree.
²⁵木 本 woody plants, shrubs, trees—used in classifications.
木 板 planks; boarding.
木 架 a wooden framework; a gallows.
木 桂 or 肉 桂 cinnamon.
木 栓 cork.
³⁰木 業 the timber industry.
木 椿 wooden piles.
木 槿 the hibiscus.
木 油 wood-oil.
木 炭 or 柴 炭 charcoal.
³⁵木 煤 brown coal or lignite.
木 片 chips of wood.
木 版 blocks engraved for printing.
木 犀 the *Osmanthus fragrans* or 桂 花 *See* No. 3610.
木 狗 the stocks.
⁴⁰木 王 the king of trees—*Catalpa Kaempferi* or 梓 No. 6951.
木 理 the grain of wood.
木 瓜 the quince; the papaya.
木 皮 bark.
木 石 wood and stone—dull, lifeless, stupid.
⁴⁵木 立 to stand like a post.
木 筆 the *Magnolia Kobis.*
木 簡 wooden tablets or slips.
木 精 wood-alcohol.
木 紋 the grain of wood.
⁵⁰木 索 instrument of torture for squeezing hands or feet.
木 絲 wood-shavings.
木 綿 cotton.
木 耳 edible fungus from trees.
木 舌 the tongue of a bell; to speak without opening the mouth.
⁵⁵木 葉 蝶 the dried-leaf butterfly.
木 蘭 deciduous magnolias; a famous heroine who personated her sick father at the wars for

twelve years without betraying the secret of her sex,— *circa* A.D. 500.

木 虱 a wood-louse; bed-bug.

木 蠟 wood-wax; known commercially as Japan wax.

木 訊 using-a wooden instrument of torture to extort a confession. [eloquence!

60 木 訥 inflexible; honest; lacking

木 貓 a wooden cat—a rat-trap.

木 賊 a rough, hollow-stemmed rush-like plant—*Equisetum hiemale*—used for smoothing fine cabinet work, etc.

木 通 the clematis.

木·部 trees—in classifications.

65 木 鐸 a bell with a wooden clapper used to call people together.

木 陣 wooden sleepers.

木·頭 timber; wood.

木 香 putchuck, the root of a species of thistle found in Cashmere.

木 香 花 banksia roses.

70 木 馬 wooden horse—for gymnastics.

木 魚 the wooden fish—a skull-shaped block on which priests beat time when chanting.

沐 4.5. To wash, to bathe, to cleanse. To enrich by kindness; to receive favours; to be steeped in.
4594

沐 恩 steeped in your bounty.

沐 手 謹 序 I washed my hands and respectfully indited this.

沐 日 a holiday—in ancient times officials had periodical holidays for bathing, etc.

沐 浴 or 沐 洗 to wash; to bathe; to receive much favour.

5 沐 浴 清 化 enriched by your kindness and transformed by your purity.

沐 猴 而 冠 a monkey washed and dressed up—no sort of a man.

沐 雨 櫛 風 bathed by the rain and combed by the wind—the hardships of toil and travel.

霂 4.5.
     Fine rain; drizzle.
4595

目 4.5. The eyes. To regard, to look on. Radical 109.
4596

目·下 or 目 前 before the eyes—now, in the present.

在 目 下 (or 前) before the eyes; imminent.

目 下 十 行 (*hang²*) to take in ten columns of characters at a glance. = 一 目 十 行

目 不 忍 視 could not bear the sight.

5 目 不 識 丁 an ignoramus—one who does not even recognize the character *ting,* i.e., a single character, the 丁 being originally 个.

目 不 轉 睛 a fixed gaze.

目 不 邪 視 his eye does not look upon things evil.

目 中 無 人 supercilious; contemptuous.

目 仁 or 瞳 人 the pupil of the eye.

10 目 今 now; the present.

目 使 頤 令 to give orders by hints of the eyes and movements of the cheeks.

目 光 如 炬 eyes like flaming torches—anger; also u.f. far-sightedness.

目 光 如 豆 his circle of vision is as large as a bean—very limited outlook.

目 光 無 神 dull eyes, lacking lustre.

15 目 光 之 圈 the circle of vision.

目 光 銳 利 eagle-eyed.

目 前 現 象 the present aspect of affairs.

目 力 strength of vision.

目 往 神 授 by looking at them the mind became receptive.

20 目 想 the expression of the eyes.

目 成 to give a hint with the eyes.

目 所 未 覩 eye hath not seen.

目 擊 to strike the eye; to witness.

目 擊 耳 聞 之 情 what one hears and sees for oneself.

25 目 標 objective.

目 波 bright glances—like dancing waves.

目 無 法 紀 he does not regard the laws.

目 為 to look upon as....; to regard as....

目·的 4 the aim, object—lit:—the target before the eyes.

30 目 的 4 因 final cause.

目 的 4 地 destination.

目 的 4 格 object—in grammar.

目 的 4 物 objective; aim.

目 的 4 達 到 to attain the object.

35 目 眩 dizzy; giddy.

目 眶 the socket of the eye.

目 眦 eyes staring with fright.

目 睟 (or 睟) having the eyes fixed on an object.

目 瞪 口 呆 dumbfounded.

40 目 禁 to restrain by a glance.

目 空 一 世 the world is too mean for his notice.

目 空 四 海 everything is beneath his regard—superciliousness.

目 笑 to smile.

目 聽 to hear with the eyes—to know what a man says from the expression of his face.

45 目 視 to gaze at.

目 視 眼 見 to see with one's own eyes.

目 逃 glancing here and there in fear or nervousness; to wince.

目 送 to follow with the eyes.

目 迷 blurred vision.

50 目 迷 五 色 bewildered by a multitude of articles and unable to decide which is best.

目 清 眉 秀 handsome.

目 食 耳 視 to eat with the eye and see with the ear— of indulgence in fancy dishes and fashionable dress.

反 目 to turn the eyes—to quarrel; to regard with unfriendliness.

怒 目 angry glances.

55 注 目 to fix the attention on.

(a) Chief. The most important. An index. A list, an item. Headings or chief points.

目 兵 a corporal.

目·錄 a catalogue.

價·目 price-list.

數·目 numbers.

5 條·目 list of articles.

科·目 list of successful candidates under the former examination system.

題·目 a theme; topic for discussion.

(b) Used in transliterating.

目 連 戲 the play of *Moginlin*—a disciple of Buddha who descended into hell to release his mother.

苜 4597 4.5.
Clover.

苜蓿 lucerne.

鉬 4598 4.5.
Molybdenum

牧 4599 4.5.
To tend as a shepherd. Former official designation of a Department magistrate or 州.

牧人 herdmen.
牧伯 an overseer; a governor.
牧圉 those engaged in horse-breeding.
牧地 grazing areas.
⁵牧師 a pastor.
牧放 to tend animals; to lead to pasture.
牧民 to shepherd the people.
牧牛 to tend cattle; a cowherd.
牧畜業 pastoral industry.
¹⁰牧豬奴戲 gambling and dice.
牧童 or 牧羊·的 a shepherd.
牧野 name of the battle-ground where *Wu Wang* 武王 defeated *Chou Hsin* 紂辛.
牧養 to shepherd.

睦 4600 4.5.
Friendly; peaceful; harmonious; kind. To promote peace.

睦誼 friendly feelings.
睦誼會 Friendly Association.
睦鄰 friendly neighbours.

穆 4601 4.5.
Majestic; reverent. Profound. Solemn.

穆然 profound—as in meditation.
穆穆 exciting wonder; to be profound.

(a) Used in transliterating.

穆民 Mohammedans.
穆罕默德 Mohammed.
穆迦 Mecca.

鶩 4602 4.5.
Ducks, either wild or tame. Also read *wu⁴*.

趨之如鶩 rush to it like ducks—taking to water.

NA. (ㄋㄚ)

拏拿挐 4603 2
To bring, to take, to apprehend, to grasp. Sign of the objective. With, by.

拏·不住 cannot be grasped.
拏·不到 not able to lay hands on.
拏·不動 cannot move it.
拏·不完 cannot take them all.
⁵拏·不準 uncertain.
拏·不穩 unable to get a firm grasp.
拏·不着²I cannot get it. (-*chao²*)
拏·不起來 cannot lift it.
拏人票 warrant for arrest.
¹⁰拏他·的錯 to pick out his shortcomings.
拏住 to lay hold of.
拏·來 bring it here.
拏·出·來 to take out.
拏·去 take it away.
¹⁵拏取 to select; to take out of.
拏問 to arrest and examine.
拏大價 to overcharge; to raise the price of.
拏定主²意 to resolve upon; to make up the mind; to decide.
拏小事當 (*tang⁴*) 大事辦 much ado about nothing.
²⁰拏·得定 certain; assured.
拏手 to grasp the hand; dexterous; expert; specialty.
拏把 to oppress; to coerce.
拏捕 capture. (*legal*).
拏搯 to manipulate.
²⁵拏東忘西 to take one thing and forget another.
拏獲 to apprehend.
拏盜賊 to arrest thieves and robbers.
拏私 to seize smugglers.
拏究 to arrest and deal with an offender.
³⁰拏衣食養·活·他 to feed and clothe him.
拏解⁴ to arrest and take to court.
拏辦 to seize and deal with.
拏·過·來 bring it over here.
拏錢不當 (*tang⁴*) 錢用 to use money recklessly.
³⁵拏開 to take away.

(a) Used in transliterating.

拿破崙 Napoleon.

那 4604 4
That. There. ×*na⁴* or *nei⁴*. *nê⁴*

×那·些 those.
×那·個 that; used indefinitely to avoid mentioning a name or a thing that is unpleasant.
那·是一定·的 that's a fact; that's so; that is certain.
⁵那·是不用說·的 that goes without saying; of course.
×那·末 or ×那·麼 thus; so; hence.
那樣不妥 that kind is not satisfactory; that's not quite right.
那自然 that is a matter of course.
那處 or 那兒 or×那邊兒 or 那·裏 there.
¹⁰那還問 Why ask that? of course not, or, of course. (-*hai²*-)
×那·麼多 as much as that.
×那·麼·樣 thus; in that way.

(a) Read *na³*. Interrogative particle. Where? Who? What? Which?   ×*na³*, *nai³*, or *nei³*

×那一件事 which affair?
×那(一)個 who? who is it? which?
那兒來·的 where is it from?
那兒·的話 what nonsense; what do you mean by such talk?
⁵那堪如是 how can this be borne?
那年那月 which year and which month?
那怕 no matter if....; never mind how.... even if ...
那知 strange to say.
那能彀 how can it be? how is it possible?
¹⁰那裏 or 那塊 or 那(一)塊 where? in which place?
那·裏·去 or 那兒·去 or 上那兒 where are you going?
那·裏知道他必來 who could know that he would come?

(b) Read *nai⁴*. Inter. 奈 No. 4615.

無那 little wonder.

(c) Read *no²*. Name of an ancient State in the present *P'ing liang* district of Kansu. Much, many. How then?

受福不那 "will they not receive much happiness?"
棄甲則那 if the armour is discarded, what then?

(d) Read *no²*. Tranquil.

有 那 其 居 dwelling in quietness.

哪¹ A final particle. Read *no²*. The name of a supernatural
4605 being.

NA. (ㄋ)
(Nah)

捺 ⁴·⁵· To press heavily downwards. A downstroke in
4606 writing, slanting towards the right.

按 捺 to press down firmly.

(a) To mend. To stitch.

捺 鞋 底 to stitch shoe-soles— made of cotton cloth, pasted rags, etc., and stitched through and through to make them firm and hard.

納 ⁴·⁵· To give. To receive. To enter; to be appointed. To
4607 insert.

納 交 to receive and accept one as a friend.

納 人 之 意 to accept the opinions of others.

納 女 to present a daughter to the emperor.

納 妾 or 納 寵 to take a concubine.

⁵納 幣 to send silk as a betrothal present.

納 悶ㄦ in anxiety; puzzled.

納 日 the declining sun.

納 欵 to submit and pay tribute; to make an offering.

納 涼 to get the cool breezes.

¹⁰納 福 to enjoy oneself. May you be happy!

納 稅 or 納 錢 糧 or 納 餉 to pay the land-tax.

納 稅 華 人 會 Chinese Ratepayers' Association.

納 糧 to pay taxes in grain.

納 罕 to be surprised.

¹⁵納 職 to buy official rank.

納 諫 to receive a reprimand.

納 貢 to pay tribute.

納 賂 to receive bribes.

納 采 to send presents to the bride's home and fix the betrothal.

²⁰受 納 to receive; to accept.

納 粹 Nazi. (transliteration.)

衲 ⁴·⁵· To patch; to line; to
4608 quilt. A robe, a cassock.

衲·子 a Buddhist cassock; a priest.

皮 衲 fur lining.

老 衲 the old priest—I.

訥 }
吶 } ⁴·⁵· To raise the voice; to blurt out.
4609

訥 一 聲 喊 to burst out in a loud voice.

訥 喊 to shout in triumph; the noise of shouting in battle.

訥 嘴 to pout.

(a) Read *no⁴·⁵·* To speak cautiously.

訥 口 to stammer.

訥 於 言 而 敏 於 行 slow in speech but quick in action.

訥 澀 to stammer.

訥 舌 to have an impediment in speech.

軜 ⁴·⁵· The inner reins of a
4610 four-horse team.

鈉 ⁴·⁵· To sharpen wood. To
4611 hammer iron to a point; u.f. Na, the chemical symbol for Sodium.

NAI. (ㄋㄞ)

乃 }
廼 }³
迺 }
4612

Conjunctive and disjunctive particle. But, if, namely. Also, and, however, then.

乃 今 然 后 henceforth.

乃 克 成 行 and was able to go.

乃 可 it will then do.

乃 因 but; because of.

⁵乃 如 or 乃 若 but; as to.

乃 所 願 but what I desire....

乃·是 but; which is....

乃 爾 thus; and so on; just so.

乃 異 質 哉 changes its nature.

¹⁰乃 者 formerly.

(a) Possessive pronoun—Your; their. That, those. It is.

乃 公 your father.

乃 功 your meritorious service.

乃 夫 that man.

乃 父 your father.

⁵乃 祖 your grandfather.

乃 積 乃 倉 he had his ricks of grain and granaries.

乃 翁 your father.

乃 聖 乃 神 乃 武 乃 文 he was altogether wise and divine, brave and accomplished.

廼 裹 餱 糧 bound up his provisions and grain.

(b) Read *ai³*. A sound.

欸 乃 (*ao³-ai³*) sound made by a boatman as he works his oars.

奶 }
嬭 }³
妳 }
4613

Milk. The breasts of a woman. To suckle. Term of respect for women.

奶 名 pet name given to a child, used by his parents.

奶 奶 a grandmother; a woman; to suckle.

奶·媽 or 乳 母 or 奶 娘 a wet-nurse; a foster-mother.

奶·子 milk; the breasts; a wet-nurse.

⁵奶·子 茶 tea with milk.

奶 油 butter; cream.

奶 猪 a sucking-pig.

奶 皮 cream.

奶·着 孩·子 to suckle a child.

¹⁰奶 豆·腐 cheese—as made by the Mongols.

奶 頭² the nipple; the breasts.

鼐 ³·⁴· Incense tripod.
4614

奈 }
柰 }⁴
4615

But, how. A remedy, a resource. To bear. To endure.

奈·不 過 or 奈·不 住 unable to bear it.

奈 何 what remedy or alternative is there?—there is none. what shall I do then?

奈 何 夫 to feel angry with Providence.

奈 何 我 不 得 he cannot do anything against me!

5奈 何 橋 a bridge in purgatory which all departed spirits are forced to cross.

奈 我 何 what can he do to me?

奈 援 車 不 至 unfortunately the reinforcements did not arrive.

奈 隔 一 水 but alas! the stream lies between.

無 奈 or 無 奈 何 or 無 可 奈 何 there is no alternative; only that...

(a) A crab-apple, for which the second form is strictly used.

耐
耏⁴
4616

　Patient. To bear, to endure. Enduring.

耐·不 久 cannot last long.
耐·不 住 cannot bear it.
耐·不(得) 長 it cannot last long.
耐 久 or 耐 長 durable; to last a long time.[pregnant with meaning.
5耐 人 尋 味 intensely interesting;
耐 冬 to bear the cold.
耐 冷 to bear the cold.
耐 勞 able to endure.
耐 口 forbearing threatening.
10耐 守 時·候 bear the present conditions patiently.
耐·心 patience.
耐·心 煩 to bear annoyance patiently.
耐·心 聽 to listen with patience.
耐·性 a patient disposition.
15耐 慣 to be accustomed to.
忍 耐 patience.
能·耐 ability; skill.

罷⁴
4617

　Stupid and dull.

NAN.　(ㄋㄢ)

囡¹
4618

　One's daughter. Also read nieh². To filch. To secrete.

男²
4619

　Man; male as distinguished from female 女, No. 4776. A son. A baron.

男 丁 an adult man.
男 人 a husband; a man.[manliness.
男 兒² a son; men, emphasizing the
男 女 men and women.
5男 女 公 權 平 等 equality between the sexes in public affairs.
男 女 同 校 co-education.
男 女 平 權 equal rights for both sexes.
男 女 授 受 不 親 men and women in giving and taking things should not touch hands.
男 子 漢 men, as distinguished from women.
10男 家 the husband.
男 性 masculine nature.
男 爵 the rank of baron.
男 盜 女 娼 May your sons be robbers and your daughters harlots!
男 胎 to be with man-child.
15男 風 or 男 色 sodomy.

南²
4620

　The south. The region of fire and vegetation.

南·京 Nanking. 南 昌 Nanchang.
南 冰 洋 Antarctic Ocean.
南 向 has a southern aspect.
南 回 歸 線 Tropic of Capricorn.
5南 方 or 南·邊 the south.
南 柯 一 夢 the dream of Nan k'o—of a man who thought he was made governor of Nank'o, a place which did not exist—u.f. an empty dream.
南 極 South Pole.
南 極 光 Aurora Australis.
南 極 圈 Antarctic Circle.
10南 洋 羣 島 South Sea Islands.
南 海 the Southern Sea or Indian Archipelago.
南 滿 鐵 路 South Manchuria Railway.
南 牢 a jail.
南·瓜 the pumpkin.
15南 緯 southern latitudes.
南 針 a compass—a guide.
南 面 facing the south—the ruler; officials. [ing in function to A.
↑南 呂 a classical pitch correspond-
(a) Read na³. Used in transliterating.
南 無 (mo²) or 南 謨 to trust in

—the ave of Buddhism, from Sanskrit namah.

南 無 佛, (or 法 or 僧) I put my trust in Buddha, (or in his law, or in his church).

南 無 師 priests who use formulas and spells.

南 無 阿 彌 陀 佛 I put my trust in Amida Buddha.

喃²
諵
4621

　To gabble; to chatter. To mumble in repetition as when memorizing.

喃 喃 呐 呐 muttering, grumbling.

楠
枏
4622

² An even-grained, yellowish, fine wood used for furniture; commonly known as cedar. The Machilus nanmu. Common in W. China.

楠·木 the wood, as above.

蝻²
4623

　Immature locusts. Also read an².

蝻·子 or 蝗 蝻 unfledged locusts.

赧³
4624

　To blush; to turn red.

赧 赧 然 blushing.
赧 顏 blushing.

難
难²
4625

　A kind of bird. Difficult; grievous; troublesome. To overtax. To contend with.

難 上 加 難 extremely difficult.
難 不 住 他 it will not bother him very much.
難 乎 免 於 今 之 世 矣 it is very difficult to escape in the present world.
難 乎 爲 繼 difficult to carry on.
↑難 乎 爲 情 embarrassing. See 29. below.
5難 事 an awkward business.
難 交 distressed; having difficulty in getting friends.
難 人 a man in difficulty; to cause a man difficulty.

難 以 ... hard; difficult to....

難 以 出 口 not easy to speak about it; difficult to export.

10 難 以 測 度 difficult to comprehend.

難 以 爲 情 to regard as inappropriate; difficult to regard as the correct thing.

難 以 相 處³ difficult to live or deal with.

難 任 a difficult post or office.

難·任·了 stumped.

15 難 保 hard to say; difficult to guarantee.

難 做 difficult to do.

難 免 cannot be helped, unavoidable; cannot but. [able.

難 受 not easy to bear; uncomfort-

難 字 difficult characters—in a book.

20 難 容 hard to put up with; in-excusable.

難 得 hard to get; hard to meet with; rare; good for him!

難 忍 or 難 耐 hard to bear.

難 怪 no wonder; difficult to blame for.

難 成 hard to bring about.

25 難 擔 difficult to bear.

難 朋 obscure; difficult to clear up.

難·爲 to trouble; to vex; "I have put you to trouble."

難·爲 人 to give trouble; burdensome.

難·爲 情 it troubles your kindness—conventional expression: —"You are too kind."

30 難 甘 reluctant; unwilling.

難 産 difficult labour. See below —A.8.

難 當 or 難 堪 intolerable; in-supportable.

難 看 repulsive; ugly.

難 色 appearance of reluctance.

難 纏 difficult to get on with, or to deal with.

35 難 聽 unpleasant to hear; discordant.

難 能 可 貴 what is difficult to achieve is estimable—when one man does something quite out of the ordinary.

難 處 suffering, difficulty.

難 計 其 數 a vast number; beyond computation.

難 說 話 —he is—difficult to deal with.

↑難 說 hard to tell, predict; who knows but that . . .

40 難 走 difficult to travel over—as a bad road.

難 辨 difficult to distinguish.

難 辦 difficult to manage.

難 過 sad; in trouble; finding it difficult to get through the days.

難·道 Is it possible? Is it conceivable? Do you mean to say...?

45 難·道 你 忘 了 Can you have forgotten it?

難·道 說 我 偷·了 你·的 不 成 Do you mean to say that I have stolen your things?

難 關 difficult to pass over—like a mountain pass—as when things are burdensome and poverty makes it difficult to pass the new-year season and pay the debts.

↑難 聞 smells bad.

難 題 (目) a difficult problem.

難 養·活 difficult to rear.

(a) Read *nan*¹. Difficulty, trouble, suffering, hardship.

難 民 people in distress, from famine, etc; refugees.

事 在 兩 難 in a dilemma.

何 難²之 有 What difficulty can there be?

受 難 to endure distress.

5 大 難 踵 至 great disasters coming one after another.

患 難 夫 妻 a husband and wife who have been through trouble together.

災 難 or 患 難 calamity; disasters —flood, fire, famine, oppressive government, etc.

産 難 the sufferings of childbirth. See above—31.

臨 難 to be involved in difficulty.

10 落 難 to fall into calamity or distress.

(b) Read *nan*¹. To rebuke. To contend with.

於 禽 獸 又 何 難 焉 Why should a mere brute be reprimanded?

(c) Read *no*². To drive away pestilence.

季 春 命 國 難 in the last month of spring, orders are given for the ceremonies against pestilence throughout the city.

季 冬 命 有 司 大 難 in the last month of winter, orders are given to the proper officers to conduct, on a grand scale, all ceremonies against pestilence.

(d) Read *no*². Many, luxuriant.

其 葉 有 難 their leaves are luxuriant.

難³ To stand in awe of. To reverence.
4626

不 難 不 竦 neither terrified nor excited.

NANG.   (ㄋㄤ)

囊² A bag; a purse; a sack; a case.
4627

囊 中 之 錐 an awl in a bag—will work its way out:—genius cannot be hid.

囊 中 物 things in one's bag— easily got at.

囊 括 to contain; to include.

囊 泡 spongy; porous.

5 囊 罄 my purse is empty.

囊 螢 映 雪 one bagged the fire-flies and another reflected the light from the snow—in order to study.

囊 袋 a bag; a sack; a skin.

空 囊 an empty purse.

行 囊 baggage; travelling-bag.

10 解 囊 unloose the purse-strings.

儾⁴ Slow, dull. Irresolute.
4628

倭 儾 slovenly; weak.

嚷² Muttering, indistinct speech.
4629

嘟 嚷 muttering and grumbling.

攮³ To fend off. To stab.
4630

攮 死 人 stabbed to death.

推 攮 to fend off.

瀼⁴ Muddy. Thick, muddy water.
4631

瀼 泥 sloppy mud.

精 瀼 very muddy.

齉 Stoppage of the nose. To speak with a nasal twang.
4632

齉鼻 stoppage of the nose.

曩³ In former times; of old; previously.
4633

曩昔 or 曩日 anciently; formerly; in days gone by.
曩者 old times; ancient events.

NAO.   (ㄋㄠ)

呶² Clamour, hubbub.
4634

呶呶 ceaseless hubbub.
呶讓于道 to brawl in the street.

惱³ Vexed, grieved, irritated. To dislike. Anger.
4635

惱人 irritating, provoking.
惱心 irritation.
惱怒 rage; anger.
惱恨 annoyed at; to be vexed at; to hate.
⁵惱悶 grieved and sad.
惱氣 vexation.
煩惱 vexed; distressed.
苦惱 distressed.

殙⁴ To poison.
4636

殙死 death from poison.

**瑙
碯**³ Agate; cornelian.
4637

**腦
匘**³ The brain.
4638

(腦)中⁴風 apoplexy.
腦充血 congestion of the brain.
腦出血 or 腦溢血 effusion of blood on the brain; apoplexy.
腦力 brains; mental vigour; mental energy.

⁵腦力衰弱 neurasthenia.
腦室 ventricles of the brain.
腦橋 the *pons varolii*.
腦水腫症 hydrocephalus.
腦海 the brain—as the organ of the mind.
¹⁰腦漿 or 腦·子 or 腦髓 the substance of the brain.
腦漏 catarrh with offensive discharge from the nose.
腦炎症 brain-fever.
腦狀珊瑚 brain-coral.
腦病 brain-trouble.
¹⁵腦疲 brain-fag.
腦神經 cranial nerves.
腦筋 nerves of the brain.
腦筋簡單 simple-minded.
腦筋靈敏 nerves in a healthy state; alert and active.
²⁰腦細胞 brain-cells.
腦經震動 concussion of the brain.
腦網 brains—the mind.
腦膜 or 腦衣 the covering membranes of the brain.
腦膜炎 or 腦脊膜髓炎 cerebro-spinal meningitis.
²⁵腦葉 lobe of the brain.
腦蓋 the top of the skull.
腦血衣 *pia mater*.
腦·袋 or 腦瓜·子 the head.
腦·袋疼 or 腦殼疼 headache.
³⁰腦質敏活 mental activity.
腦門·子 the forehead.
腦骨 the skull.
腦體變軟 softening of the brain.
腦體震撞 concussion of the brain.
³⁵主腦 the leader; the 'brain' of a cause; the leading idea.
大腦 cerebrum.
小腦 cerebellum.

**撓
拗**² To scratch; to vex; to disturb.
4639

撓亂 to confuse.
撓心 to annoy the mind.
撓擾 to make a disturbance.
撓癢 to scratch an itching spot.
⁵撓破 to scratch and tear open.
撓菜 to scrape vegetables.
撓頭 to scratch the head—to be at a loss what to do.

(a) To bend. To yield; to flinch.

撓敗 utterly routed.
不屈不撓 without bending or flinching.

譊² Wrangling, contention. To dispute.
4640

譊譊者天下皆訟也 the whole country was filled with the wrangling of litigants.
誼譊 noisy disputation.

鐃² Hand-bells, formerly used in the army to stop the sound of the drums. Cymbals.
4641

鐃鈸 small cymbals.
鐃鉤 a double-pronged hook.

猱² A monkey with yellow hair.
4642

猱升 to climb a tree like a monkey.
猱雜 playing dissolute pranks; restless monkey-tricks.

獂² Fierce dog with long shaggy hair.
4643

獂苗 a tribe in Kwangsi.

撋⁴ To handle; to play with.
4644

淖⁴ Slush, mud.
4645

淖人 to nauseate; to make one feel bilious.
淖沙 quicksands.
淖泥 mud.
淖濘 slushy mud.
淖糜 gruel, congee.

(a) Read *chao*⁴. Peace.

(b) Read *cho*⁴·⁵. Gentle.

淖約如處³子³ gentle and submissive as a young maiden.

鬧 鬧 [4]

To make a disturbance. Noise, bustle.
To suffer from; to be troubled by.

4646

鬧 亂·子 to cause trouble; to start a riot.

鬧·了一身·的水點 spattered all over.

鬧 事 to make trouble.

鬧 人 to scold; disturbing—as a noise.

[5]鬧·出事·來 to cause a disturbance; to make trouble.

鬧 嗓·子 an epidemic of throat trouble; to have a sore throat.

鬧 壤 noisy; clamorous.

鬧 壞·了 spoiled; terribly noisy.

鬧 天·氣 unseasonable weather. *

[10]鬧 妖·精 the ghosts are about.

鬧 市 a busy market.

鬧·得兜 making a great disturbance.

鬧 性 restive.

鬧 意·見 wrangling over conflicting opinions; to be on bad terms.

[15]鬧 戲 noisy, improper farces.

鬧 房 or 鬧 新 房 rough horse-play at weddings, often of a suggestive nature.

鬧 敎 to annoy converts.

鬧 昏·了 to lose one's head.

↓熱·鬧 busy; bustling; lively; interesting.

[20]鬧 玩 to play; to romp.

鬧 羊 花 Rhododendron sinense.

鬧 肚·子 bowel-trouble.

鬧 脾·氣 to show temper; to get into a passion.

鬧 起 來 to begin to make trouble.

[25]鬧 酒 a carouse; a drinking bout.

鬧 鐘 an alarm-clock.

鬧 風°潮 to cause trouble; to make a disturbance.

鬧 饑·荒 to suffer(from, or disturbance created by) famine, scarcity.

鬧 駕·子 to play the fop Cf. 4864.12.

[30]鬧 鬼 to have devils about; to play tricks; to humbug.

瞎 鬧 or 胡 鬧 to make a row over nothing.

*to suffer from the inclemency of the weather.

臑 [4]

The shoulder blade. Outer bone of the arm.

4647 NEI, NÊN see p. 661.

NÊNG. (ㄋ)

能 [2]

Able to; may; can. Power, talent, ability.

4648

能 一不能二 capable in one direction only.

能 事 competent; able for affairs.

能 人 or 能 手 a capable person.

能 以 禮讓爲國乎何有 what difficulties are there to one who is able to rule the country by the complaisance proper to the rules of propriety?

[5]能 使 物 able to invoke demons.

能 做 able to do.

能 力 power; ability; energy.

能 力 不 滅 energy cannot be destroyed—conservation of energy.

能 力 就 是 公 理 might is right.

[10]能 吏 an able officer.

能 名 one who is well known for his talent and ability.

能 否 Is it possible?

能 品 pictures that show ability—but not exceptional, as 神 品.

能 士 a man of ability.

[15]能 官 an able official.

能 容 to hold; to tolerate.

能 耐 久 able to continue; the gift of continuance.; endurance.

能·幹 or 能 爲 or 才 能 ability; capacity; talent.

能·彀 able; able to; competent.

[20]能 有 以 察 其 幾 able to possess that whereby he can discern his motives.

能 閒 之 周 波 數 audio-frequency.

能 言·的 人 an eloquent person.

能 詩 able to write poetry.

能 說 不 能 行 able to say but unable to perform.

[25]能 近 取 譬 able to think of others according to what is near to us—in ourselves.

能 量 capacity.

不 能 impossible; unable; it cannot be; cannot.

何 能 how can....?

全 能 almighty.

可 能 possible.

(a) Read nai[2]. A surname. Read nai[4]. Inter. 耐 No. 4616. To endure.

能 寒 to stand the cold.

NI. (ㄋ)

你 佽 [3]

Thou, you.

4649

你·們 you—　(plural)

你·們·的 your, yours.

你 先·生 or 您　you, Sir.

你 我 兩·個 人 we two persons.

[5]你 敬 我 愛 mutual respect.

你·的 thine, your.

你·老 人 家 my dear sir; you, my friend; old gentleman!

你 自 己 yourself.

你 走·你·的 you go your way; mind your own business.

[10]你 這·個 人 you fellow—in reproach.

瀰 [3]

To overflow. To level up. Many. Also read mi[3]. Inter.

4650 瀰 No. 4460.

瀰 迤 平 原 the floods fill up the plain.

禰 [3]

A term applied to a deceased father after his tablet has been placed in the ancestral temple.

4651

禰 其 祖 treated his ancestor's tablet as if it were his father's.

NI. (ㄋ)

(Nih)

溺 氼 [4.5]

To sink; to drown. To be given over to.

4652

溺 女 female infanticide.

溺 愛 lovesick; to dote on.

溺 愛 不 明 to love foolishly; foolishly fond.

溺 於 利 欲 to be absorbed in profits and desires.

[5]溺 於 名 利 ambitious for fame and wealth.

溺 死 to drown a person.

溺 水 submerged; drowned.

溺 職 to neglect official duties.

溺 酒 given over to intoxicants.

[10]溺 魂 the spirit of a drowned person.

(a) Read *niao*[4]. To urinate.

溺 器 chamber-vessel.

愵 4.5. **To think of with sorrow. To feel hunger.**
4653

愵 思 to think of with fondness.

NI.   (广)

尼[2] A nun.
4654

尼·姑 or 尼 僧 or 女 尼 a Buddhist nun.

(a) A mountain.

尼 丘 the mountains after which Confucius was named.

尼 父 Confucius.

(b) Read *ni*[3.5]. To stop. To approach from behind.

止 或 尼 之 the hindering (of his progress) may possibly result from the efforts of others.

(c) Read *ni*[4.5]. Near.

尼 遠 咸 安 near and far, all is at peace.

(d) Used in transliterating.

尼 亞 格 拉 Niagara.

尼 古 丁 nicotine.

尼 尼 微 Nineveh.

尼 羅 the Nile.

伲[3] Used in parts of Kiangsu for the first personal pronoun.
4655

伲 自 家 we ourselves.   A.w.
     倪 (*Soochow dial.*)

呢[2] Interrogative and emphatic particle. Read ·*nê*.
4656 Used when a new point is raised in a subject under discussion.

何 必 憂 慮 呢 Why should you be anxious?

何 等 大·呢 How great it is!

有 甚[2]麼 長·處·呢 Wherein is it any better—than others?

還 沒 去·呢 he has not yet gone.

(a) Foreign woollen cloth.

厚 呢 meltons.

哈 喇 呢 fine woollens from Russia.

大 呢 broadcloth.

平 厚 呢 beavers.

[5]毛 棉 呢 union shirtings.

細 呢 vicunas.

軍 呢 army cloths.

(b) A low sound, murmuring.

呢 喃 twittering of swallows; to whisper; to murmur.

妮[2] A slave-girl; maid of all work.
4657

怩[2] To blush; to look ashamed.
4658

忸 怩 to blush with shame.

柅[2.3] A tree with hard wood. Chock for stopping a cart. To stop. Handle of a distaff.
4659

柅 杜 to cut off; to separate finally.

(a) To investigate.

捷 柅 姦 冒 make prompt inquiries into treachery and fraud.

(b) Flourishing.

泥 [2] Mud, mire. To paste, to plaster.
坭
4660

泥 人 ㄦ(or 偶) clay-figures.

泥 兜·子 a bag used by bricklayers instead of a hod.

泥 刀 a trowel for plaster.

泥 地 clay soil; muddy.

[5]泥 塑 木 雕 modelled in clay or carved from wood—idols.

泥 塗 in the mire—out of office; in troubles.

泥 墻 mud walls; to plaster a wall.

泥 封 to seal; to paste.

泥·巴 or 泥 土 mud; earth.

[10]泥 水 活 bricklayer's work.

泥 沙 mud and sand—of little value.

失 路 委 泥 沙 to lose the way and fall into the mud—depraved ways, perdition.

泥 滓 silt; filthiness.

泥 溝 a gutter or drain.

[15]泥 濘 諸 澤 mire in all the marshes.

泥 火 山 a mud volcano.

泥 炭 peat.

泥 牛 入 海 a clay-ox enters the sea—never to return.

泥 水 匠 or 泥 瓦 匠 bricklayer.

[20]泥 磚 mud bricks; adobe.

泥 腿 a bare-footed labourer; a loafer.

泥 路 a muddy road; earthen path.

泥 醉 dead drunk.

泥 金 splashed with gold—as fancy paper, etc.

[25]泥 鏟 a shovel for mud.

泥 鏝 a trowel for plaster.

泥 首 to dirty the head—by kotowing.

泥·鰍 or 泥 魚 the loach.

拖 泥 to drag through the mire.

[30]撈 泥 to dredge.

白 泥 white clay.

黑 泥 black soil.

(a) Soft; weak. A jelly-fish.

泥 泥 grass wet with dew; soft, glossy—leaves.

(b) Read *ni*[4]. Bigoted.

泥 古 ultra-conservative.

泥 於 風 水 bigoted belief in geomancy.

泥 飲 addicted to intoxicants.

拘 泥 bigoted.

旎[3] Fluttering of flags.
4661

旖 旎 fluttering flags.

倪[2] To distinguish; to glance at. Also read *i*[2].
4662

倪 小 大 to distinguish small from great.

倪 貴 賤 to distinguish noble from ignoble.
俾 倪 to give a sidelong glance.
左 倪 右 倪 glancing right and left.

(a) A beginning. A limit, a bound.

天 倪 the Infinite. "Obliterating unity—God." (*Giles*).
和 之 以 天 倪 embraced in the realm of the Infinite. "Embraced in the obliterating unity of God." (*Giles*).
端 倪 a clue, a beginning, an origin; the least point; definite issues.

(b) Young.

反 其 旄 倪 he sent back the decrepit and the young.

婗² A new-born child. The whimper of an infant.
4662a

猊² The lion. A wild beast or a wild horse which can do 500 *li* a day, 狻 猊.
4663

猊 座 a lion's den.
猊 糖 sugar made into the shape of the above.

睨⁴ To look askance. To glance at. Also read *i*⁴.
4664

睨 而 視 之 to look at it askance.

輗² The cross-bar at the end of a carriage-pole.
4665

霓² A rainbow. Variegated, coloured. Also read *i*².
4666

霓 現 雨 止 when the rainbow appears the rain ceases.
彩 霓 variegated.
虹 霓 the rainbow.

鯢² A large amphibious creature, something like the newt but very much larger.
4667

大 鯢 魚 the giant salamander.

(a) Small fish, fry.

鯢 鮒 small fry.

(b) The female whale.

鯨 鯢 whales.
取 其 鯨 鯢 而 封 之 take these oppressors—who swallow up small States like great monsters —and slay them, burying their bodies.

麑² A fawn. Also read *i*².
4668

麑 裘 deer-skin robes.

齯² Teeth grown in old age. Also read *i*².
4669

齯 齒 teeth growing in old age; ninety years of age.

衵⁴ Women's under-garments. Read *jih*⁴
4670

嶷⁴ Range of mountains in Hunan. Also read *i*².
4671

嶷 然 不 少 屈 he proudly refused to humble himself.
嶷 然 有 異 —among the boys—I was uncommonly prominent.
嶷 然 自 若 stood firm and self-possessed—when others fled.

擬³ To determine. To intend. Also read *i*³.
4672

擬 作 to propose.
擬 具 to draw up a proposal.
擬 奏 to sentence and report the case to the throne.
擬 定 or 擬 妥 to decide. ｛draft.
⁵擬 就 decided; settled; finish the
擬 度 (*to*⁴·⁵) to think over; to form an opinion.
擬 稿 to draw up a draft.
擬 結 final judgement.
擬 罪 to sentence to; to fix the punishment.
¹⁰擬 舉 a proposal.
擬 請 to suggest that; it is proposed.
擬 議 to decide after deliberation.

擬 軍 罪 to sentence to transportation and service in the army.
擬 辦 to arrange to settle; to make a proposal for settlement; to sentence to.

(a) To compare. To resemble. To estimate, to guess.

擬 古 to imitate the ancients.
擬 態 mimicry—in insects.
比 擬 to compare.
相 擬 to resemble each other.

膩⁴ Grease; fat. Oily, smooth, glossy.
4673

膩 友 a very close friend.
膩·味 to loathe; loathsome.
膩·子 grease; composition; putty.
膩 滯 indigestion.
⁵膩 煩 tired with; sick of; disgusted.
膩 粉 to make up—the face.
膩 細 smooth; glossy.
膩·胃 to cause biliousness; to turn the stomach.
油 膩 rich; oily; greasy.

犠³ Rings on the yokes. Also read *i*³.
4674

NI.　　(宀)
(Nih)

疒4.5. Disease. Radical 104. Also read *ch'uang*². To rest, as when ill.
4675

屰4.5. Disobedient.
4676

逆4.5. To disobey; to rebel; to oppose. Refractory; contrary; rebellious.
4677

逆 倫 atrocious; unnatural; violating human obligations.
逆 匪 or 逆 黨 rebels.
逆 叛 to rebel.
逆 取 順 守 to keep by right methods that which was first obtained by wrong.
⁵逆 命 to rebel.
逆 囚 prisoner convicted of sedition.

逆 境 adverse circumstances.
逆 天 行 道 in defiance of nature.
逆 子³ a disobedient child.
¹⁰逆 惡 perverse; refractory.
逆 數 unseasonable times.
逆 旅 an inn.
逆 旅 主 landlord of an inn.
逆 水 a head tide; against the stream.
¹⁵逆 流 adverse current.
逆 耳 unpleasant truths which—grate on the ear.
逆 處 obstinacy; perverseness.
逆 行 perverse; to go backwards.
逆 謀 to plot rebellion; seditious schemes.
²⁰逆 風 a contrary wind.
逆 鱗 reversed scales—said to be found under the throat of the dragon; it was death to come into collision with them—u.f., the wrath of a prince.

(a) **To meet; to accord with.**

逆 志 to put one's mind to—understand the meaning.
敬 逆 天 命 reverently to fall in with the will of Heaven.

(b) **To anticipate.**

逆 備 to prepare for.
逆 料 to conjecture; to decide about.
逆 知 to know beforehand.
逆 覩 to see beforehand; to forecast.
逆 詐 to anticipate deceit.

匿 4.5. A wine-jar. To hide; to abscond. Hidden, clandes-
4678 tine.

匿 名 anonymous; an alias.
匿 名 帖 anonymous placard.
匿 名 投 票 secret ballot.
匿 名 書 anonymous writings.
⁵匿 單 少 報 to make a false declaration of quantity by withholding a document.
匿 喪 to conceal the fact of a parent's death—in order to avoid retirement from office.
匿 怨 而 友 其 人 to cherish a secret grudge while pretending to friendship with the man.
匿 拐 to kidnap and secrete.
匿 避 or 逃 匿 or 藏 匿 to hide; to run away.

惄 3.5. Mortified; ashamed.
4679

暱 昵 4.5. Familiar; intimate. To approach.
4680

暱 就 draw near to.
暱 愛 familiarity.
暱 比 罪 人 to be familiar with rascals.
暱 近 to be familiar with.
私 暱 intimate with.

瞑 4.5. To blink; to half-close the eyes.
4681

翻 翻 4.5. Glue. A kind of cement made of hemp, lime and oil.
4682

翻 封 to paste or seal.

NIANG. (广尢)

娘 ² A girl; a woman; a mother; a wife.
4683

娘 兒·們 women.
娘·娘 an empress.
太 后 娘·娘 empress dowager.
娘 姨 maidservant.
⁵娘 媽 or 天 后 Taoist Queen of Heaven.
娘·子 a young lady; a wife; a woman.
娘°子 軍 a female general, like Joan of Arc; amazons.
娘·家 a wife's family.
娘·家 姓 李 her maiden name was Li; née Li.
¹⁰娘 親 a mother.
伴 娘 bridesmaids.
大 娘 paternal aunt; term of respect for any elderly woman.
奶 娘 a wet-nurse.
姑·娘 unmarried girls; younger sisters of husband.
¹⁵師 娘 wife of a journeyman; in Northern China;—Mrs.
新 娘 a bride.

爹 娘 father and mother.
送 娘 a woman who attends to the ceremonies, etc., at a wedding.

孃 ² Troubled; careworn. Fat; u.f. preceding.
4684

耶 孃 哭 子³ father and mother weeping for their son.
辭 爺 孃 去 said goodbye to her father and mother.

釀 ⁴ To brew; to ferment—thus:—to cause, to excite, to foment. Also read jang⁴.
4685

釀 亂 to excite rebellion.
釀 命 to cause loss of life—to persons.
釀 奸 to foment conspiracy.
釀 成 to excite; to bring about.
⁵釀 成 事 端 to cause trouble to arise.
釀 成 糾 紛 to cause confusion or riot.
釀 母 or 酵 母 the yeast, etc., used to cause fermentation.
釀 母 菌 or 酵 母 菌 the yeast plant.
釀 疑 起 釁 to excite suspicion and strife.
¹⁰釀 禍 to bring about disaster.
釀 膿 suppuration.
釀 膿 菌 germs which cause suppuration.
釀 膿 藥 medicines that promote suppuration.
釀 蜜 to make honey—by bees.
¹⁵釀 酒 to ferment spirits.
酒 釀 sweet fermented rice.

NIAO. (广ㄠ)

尿 ⁴ Urine. To urinate. Also read sui¹.
4686

尿 壺 or 尿 罐·子 or 尿 盆ㄦ a chamber-vessel.
尿 滴 瀝 症 or 尿 截 or 急 淋 strangury.
尿 牀 to wet the bed.
尿 淋 症 or 尿 崩 症 diabetes. See 消 No. 2607a—47.
⁵尿 管 the urethra.
尿 缸 a jar for public convenience.
尿 胞 the bladder.
尿 道 the urethra.
撒 尿 to pass urine. [niao⁴ sui¹.)
↑尿 尿 to pass urine. (niao⁴ niao⁴ or

[10]流 尿 incontinence of urine.

遺 尿 involuntary passage of urine.

嬝[3]
4687   Slender and delicate.

嬝 娜 fascinating; bewitching; slender and willowy.

嬝 嬝 waving in the wind; curling up like smoke.—*See* 裊 No. 4690.

嬝 嬝 柳 垂 條 long and slender hung the willow branches.

餘 香 嬝 嬝 the dying sounds were carried far.

鳥[3]
4688   Birds. Radical 196. Distinguish 鳥 No. 7166.

鳥 信 the north-east wind in the 3rd lunar month.

鳥 則 擇 木 the bird chooses its tree—a man chooses whom he will follow.

鳥 哨 the twittering of birds.

鳥 喙 a beak—a mouth like a bird.

[5]鳥 鳴 the cry of a bird.

鳥 嘴 the beak of a bird.

鳥 媒 a decoy-bird.

鳥 學 ornithology.

鳥 巢 or 鳥 窩 a bird's-nest.

[10]鳥 爪 bird's-claws—used to describe fine, delicate finger tips.

鳥 爲 食 亡 a bird will perish in its attempts to get food.

鳥 獸 散 scattered like birds and beasts—in disorder.

鳥 獸 般·的 like birds and beasts.

鳥 獸 行[4] beastly conduct—not fitting for human beings.

[15]鳥 盡 弓 藏 when the birds have gone the bow is put away—to discharge a worthy officer in times of peace.

鳥 篆 ancient form of the *seal* character—like bird-tracks.

鳥 胃 a gizzard.

鳥 葬 exposure of a corpse to the vultures.

鳥 蛋 or 鳥 卵 eggs.

[20]鳥 語 gabbling; the talk of strangers which is not understood.

鳥 跡 bird's-tracks—a fancy style of penmanship.

鳥 道 a winding path.

鳥 里 measurement as the crow flies.

↑鳥 人 the bird man; aviator.

↑鳥 瞰 bird's-eye view.

鳥 銃 a fowling-piece.

[25]鳥 雀 or 雀 鳥 birds, generally.

鳥 集 鱗 萃 a great number gathered together—like birds or fishes.

鳥 面 鵠 形 gaunt and emaciated —from famine.

鳥 革 翬 飛 like a newly moulted bird, like a flying pheasant— graceful and handsome—of buildings.

夜 鳥 nocturnal birds.

[30]如 鳥 出 籠 like a bird escaped from the cage.

玄 鳥 a swallow.

鬼 鳥 night-hawks.

蔦[3]
4689   The convolvulus. Parasitic plants like mistletoe, etc.

蔦 蘿 之 親 closely bound like the convolvulus to a tree—of marriage relations.

裊[3]
4690   Curling up, as smoke.

裊 垂 楊 the graceful, drooping willows.

裊 娜 莖 graceful, slender stems.

裊 空 floating like gossamer.

裊 窕 graceful, elegant.

嫋[3]
4691   To dally with; obscene.

NIEH.   (广廿)

埕 皇[3]
4692   [1.5.]   To fill up, as a hole.

捏 捏[3]
4693   [1.5.]   To fabricate; to trump up.

捏 住·了 to catch a thing.

捏 手 捏 脚 stealthily.

捏 控 or 捏 稱 to lay a false accusation.

捏 病 to feign sickness.

[5]捏 稟 or 捏 報 to present a false petition or report.

捏 詞 告 人 to fabricate evidence and lay a charge.

捏 造 or 捏 飾 or 捏 做 to fabricate; to trump up.

捏 造 壞 話 to fabricate slanders.

捏 造 惡 事 to devise evil.

[10]捏 造 謠 言 to spread false rumours.

捏 陷 or 誣 捏 to involve by groundless accusations.

(a) To knead with the fingers.

捏·一 把 to take a pinch.

捏·一 把 冷 汗 to break out into cold perspiration.

捏 像 moulded images of clay.

捏 弄 to knead or mould.

涅[4.5.]
4694   Black mud; slime. Also read *ni*[4.5.].

涅 字 to rub ink into tattooed characters.

涅 白 an opaque white.

涅 而 不 緇 it may be steeped in a dark fluid without becoming black.

涅 面 to tattoo characters on the face.

(a) Name of a river in Honan.

(b) Used in transliterating.

涅 盤 Nirvana—the state of complete absence of sensation, the goal of Buddhism.

隉[1.5.]
4695   In disorder; a dangerous condition of the State.

捻 扭[1.5.]
4696   To nip with the fingers; to take a pinch; to take up, as with tongs. A pinch. Also read *nien*[4].

捻·一·捻 take a pinch.

捻 手 to snap the fingers.

捻 手 捻 脚 stealthily; lightly.

捻·着 鼻·子 to lead by the nose.

捻 花 to pluck flowers.

(a) Read *nien*[3]. Inter. 撚 No. 4715. To twist.

捻 匪 mounted bandits who arose during the reign of 嘉 慶 in the

Manchu dynasty; they operated in Shantung, Anhwei, and Kiangsu.

捻 燈 to turn up a lamp.

捻 珠 to finger a rosary; to tell one's beads.

捻 綿 to twist thread.

紙 捻·子 paper spills for lighting pipes.

臬 4.5. A rule, a law. A limit. A small post.

4697　Distinguish 臭 No. 1331.

臬 司 or 臬 臺 or 臬 憲 former designation of a provincial judge.

臬 限 an impediment; a boundary

鎳 4.5. Nickel.

4698

闑 4.5. A threshold. A side door.

4699　Distinguish 闑 No. 1627.

闑 以 內 寡 人 制 之 I, the emperor, will manage my own domestic affairs.

臲 4.5. Unsteady.

4700

臲 卼 tottering; dizzy; unsteady; anxious.

孽 孼 Sin, evil, retribution. The son of a concubine. Also read yeh⁴·⁵.

4701

孽 債 retribution in kind; curses coming home to roost.

孽 子³or 孽 種 son of a harlot—abusive.

孽 根 the root of misfortune—a perverse child.

孽 緣 a predestined connection—of evil.

⁵孽 障 retribution for evil which a person has committed; wicked children are supposed to be the medium of this retribution.

孽 鬼 the demon of retribution—bringing retribution for previous misdeeds.

天 作 孽 calamities sent by God.

罪 孽 sin and retribution.

自 作 孽 calamities brought upon oneself by way of retribution.

檗 蘗 4.5. The stump of a tree.

4702

檗 木 a large tree, from the bark of which a yellow dye is produced.

生 檗 shoots from an old stump.

蘖 4.5. Fermenting grain. Grain which has sprouted. Yeast.

4703

齧 嚙 4.5. To gnaw; to bite.

4704

嚙 合·子 or 嚙 接·子 a clutch.

嚙 噬 to eat, to bite.

嚙 岸 erosion of a bank.

嚙 桑 a grub that eats mulberries.

⁵嚙 牙 to bite on something hard.

嚙 骨 to gnaw bones.

嚙 齒 類 rodents.

聶 4.5. To whisper. Occurs u.f. 攝 No. 5710.

4705

聶 耳 語 whispers.

(a) To pick up one's skirts.

聶 許 co-ordination.

(b) Read chê⁵. To slice meat into thin strips.

聶 而 切 之 爲 膾 sliced thin and chopped up, it is called kuei.

(c) Read chê⁵. To close up.

聶 合 宵 炕 — its leaves — close during the day and open at night.

囁 4.5. To move the mouth as in speaking. To chatter.

4706

囁 嚅 to be about to speak but to refrain from doing so.

躡 蹑 4.5. To tread; to step. To ascend.

4707

躡 手 躡 脚·的 stealthily; to walk lightly.

躡 景 (ying³) to follow up the sun's shadow—to be in a hurry.

躡 登 to go up.

躡 草 履 to wear straw sandals.

⁵躡 足 不 前 not to move a step forward.

躡 足 行 伍 之 間 on active service with the army.

躡 踪 to track; to pursue a trail.

躡 蹀 mincing steps.

鑷 4.5. Forceps, pincers, tweezers. To pull out; to nip.

4708

鑷 子 a pair of tweezers, etc.

鑷 毛 to pull out hairs.

顳 4.5. The temporal bones.

4709

顳 顬 骨 the temporal bones.

顳 顬 筋 the temporal muscles.

NIEN.　(广/马)

廿 卄 ⁴ Twenty. See 念 No. 4716-B.

4710

廿 多 人 more than twenty persons.

年 ² A year. Age. Harvest.

4711

年·下 the close of the year.

年 不 等 歲 of varying ages.

年 事 the age of a man.

年 代 or 世 代 a generation; an age.

⁵年 代 湮 沒 oblivious of the passing of the years.

年 伯 father of one who graduated at the same time as oneself—under the old system.

年 來 for a number of years; recent years.

年 例 annual customs.

年 俸 annual salary.

¹⁰年 假⁴ new-year vacation.

年 兄 graduate of the same year as oneself—under the old system.

年 入 annual income.

年 內 within the year.

年°分 (*fen*⁴) the year of a cycle; time; a man's age.

¹⁵年 前 before last new-year.

年 力 就 衰 with his years his vital force is declining.

年 功 the meritorious service of many years.

年 報 annual report; year-book.

年 壽 age.

²⁰年 夜 last night of the year.

年 姪 said to one of the same generation as one's father—in speaking of oneself.

年 家 子³ son of a fellow-graduate —under the old system.

年 富 in the prime of life.

年 將 就 木 his years were approaching their close—lit:—drawing near to the wood, i.e., the coffin.

²⁵年 尾 the close of the year.

年 年 yearly; year by year; every year.

年 幼 or 少 年 youthful; juvenile.

年 度 an arbitrarily fixed period called a year, as a school-year, etc.

會 (*k'uai*³) 計 年 度 fiscal year.

³⁰年 度 預 算 annual budget.

年 庚 八 字 the eight cyclical characters of a horoscope— two each for the year, month, day, and hour of birth.

年 底 the end of the year.

年 德 並 高 their age and standing are equal.

年·成 harvest; crops.

³⁵ 十 二 分 年 成 a super-abundant harvest.

年 所 years; a period of years.

多 歷 年 所 in the course of many years.

年 數 歲 several years old.

年 方 二 八 he was only just sixteen.

⁴⁰年 日 years; seasons.

年 時 during the year.

年 景 harvest; crops.

年 月 日 時 seasons; periods.

年 望 一 年 year after year.

⁴⁵年 期 annual session.

年 歲 years; age; a harvest.

年 登 花 甲 to complete the cycle of sixty years.

年 矢 the arrow of the years—the swift passing of time.

年 祚 length of a dynasty; length of a man's life.

⁵⁰年 禮 new-year presents.

年 租 annual rental.

年 穀 amount of grain harvested in the year.

年 等 者 of the same age.

年 節 the holiday season at the new year.

⁵⁵年 糕 cakes of glutinous rice eaten at the new-year.

年·紀 age.

年·紀 老 邁 of advanced age.

年·紀 長 (*chang*³) aged; growing old.

年 級 classes in a school according to the years of the curriculum, as 低, 中, 高 年 級 first, second, and third year classes.

⁶⁰年 終 the close of the year.

年 至 八 十 to reach 80 years of age.

年 荒 a year of scarcity.

年 華 years; time.

年 華 虛 度 I have vainly spent the best of my days.

⁶⁵年 號 the style of an emperor's reign.

年 表 historical table of dates and events.

年 誼 friendships formed with fellow-graduates—under the old system.

年 譜 a biography arranged according to the successive years of a man's career.

年 貌 age and appearance—in registrations.

⁷⁰年 輕 youthful; young.

年 輪 rings indicating the growth of a tree.

年 輩 age and generation.

年 近 歲 逼 drawing near to the close of the year.

年 逾 耳 順 over sixty years of age—*from* 六 十 而 耳 順 at sixty my ear was an obedient organ for the reception of truth.

⁷⁵年 邁 old; aged.

年 金 annuity.

年 鑑 year-book; annual report.

年 間 the times; years.

年 關 the end of the year—when all accounts have to be settled; so called because it is like a mountain pass, not easy to cross.

⁸⁰年 限 a limit of years.

年 陳 日 久 in the course of time.

年 頭 the beginning of a year; part of a year; the crops.

三 個 年 頭 between two and three years.

年 額 annual number or amount, etc.

⁸⁵年 首 the first month of the year.

年 高 advanced in years.

年 鬢 old age with grey hair.

年 齡 the age of a person.

不 上 幾 年 before many years had elapsed.

⁹⁰今·年 this year.

全 年 a whole year.

前·年 the year before last.

去·年 or 往 年 last year.

壯 年 the prime of life.

⁹⁵天 年 the allotted span of a man's life.

學 年 a school-year.

常 年 ordinarily; ordinary years.

拜 年 to pay respects at the new-year.

按 年 by the year.

¹⁰⁰新 年 the new-year.

明·年 or 來 年 next year.

星 年 sidereal year.

流 年 the passing years.

現 年 the current year.

¹⁰⁵舊·年 last year.   (*S. dial.*)

賀 年 new-year congratulations.

連 年 year after year.

閏 年 leap year.

這 年 頭 兒 nowadays.

拈²   To draw lots; to pick out; to take in the fingers.
4712

拈 書 to turn over the leaves of a book.

拈 筆 to take up a pen.

拈 花 to pluck a flower.

拈 花 惹 草 lascivious, fond of women.

⁵拈·起·來 pick it up.

拈 轉 to twist in the fingers.

拈 題 to select a theme for an essay.

拈 香 to offer incense; to worship.

拈 鬚 to finger the beard.

¹⁰拈 鬮 to draw lots.

拈 鼻 to seize by the nose.

鮎²   The sheat-fish.
4713

黏[2] Sticky; glutinous. Paste. Inter. 粘 No. 129.
4714

黏 力 adhesive power.
黏 合 to cohere; to adhere.
黏 土 clay.
黏·得 很 very sticky.
[5]黏 油 heavy oils.
黏 液 腺 mucous glands.
黏 液 質 phlegmatic temperament.
黏 米 glutinous rice.
黏 膜 mucous membrane.
[10]黏 附 to append; to paste on something additional.
黏 韌 tenacious; tough.

撚[3] To twist with the fingers; to play with. A twist of paper.
4715

撚·不 動 cannot be twisted.
撚 乾 手 巾 to wring a face-towel dry.
撚 指 間 while you can twist your finger—in a moment.
撚 毛 to work wool into felt.
[5]撚 紙 撚·子 to twist paper strips into spills.
撚 錢 to spin a coin.
撚 鬚 to finger the beard.

念[4] To think of; to remember; to recall.
4716

念 念 不 忘 constantly to bear in mind.
念 念 自 見 by constant thinking you will come to know yourself.
念 怨 不 休 incessant brooding over grievances.
念 想 a keepsake.
[5]念·着 父 母 to remember one's father and mother.
念 舊 情 to remember old times.
念 茲 在 茲 fix your attention upon what you are doing.
念·頭 thoughts; desires.
一 念 不 動 utterly unmoved.
[10]不 念 舊 惡 he did not remember old evils.
不 復 置 念 do not think any more about it.
卦 念 to think of with anxiety.
思 念 to remember; to think of.
惡 念 evil thoughts.
[15]意 念 the desires of the heart.
懷 念 to bear in mind.

(a) To chant; to intone; to read aloud; to repeat from memory.

念 一 遍 read it over once.
念 佛 to repeat the name of Buddha.
念 口 供 to read over the depositions.
念 咒 治 鬼 to utter charms in order to exorcise demons.
[5]念 書 to read aloud; to study.
念 法 a plan of reading.
念 熟·了 learned by heart.(-shou[2]-)
念 珠 a rosary; to tell beads.
念 經 to chant a liturgy.
[10]念 誦 to recite; to intone.

(b) Twenty. See 卄 4710.

念 五 twenty-five.

舲 綸[3] To caulk.
4717

舲 船 to caulk a boat.

(a) Read nien[4]. A tow-rope.
舲 索 a hawser.

趂[3] To pursue; to follow up.
4718

趂·不 上 他 unable to catch him.
趂·他·回 來 follow him and bring him back.

碾[3] A stone roller used for husking grain, etc. To roll.
4719

碾·掉·他·的 頭 —a wheel—passed over his head.
碾 房 a mill for husking grain.
碾 柁 a fluted roller.
碾 盤 the nether mill-stone.
[5]碾 碎 to pulverize.
碾 穀 or 碾 米 to husk grain or rice.
碾 米 廠 a rice-hulling mill.
碾 盤 or 藥 碾·子 an iron trough in which runs a wheel for pulverizing drugs, etc.
碾 輥·子 the roller on a mill.

輦[3] An easy chair used as a hand carriage. The emperor's carriage. The court. To push.
4720

輦 下 at court; in the capital.
輦 道 paths within the palace grounds; the imperial highways.
玉 輦 the imperial carriage.

攆[3] To expel; to drive out.
4721

攆·不 開 not able to drive away.
攆·他·出·去 drive him out; drive him away.
攆 走·了 driven away.
攆 跑·了 driven off with a run.
攆 逐 to drive away; to drive out.

您[2] A respectful form of 你 No. 4649. You, thou.
4722

您 納 you, Sir. (< 您 阿)

佞[4] Eloquent; persuasive; insinuating. Artful talk; flattery; fluency.
4723

佞 口 eloquent; plausible.
佞 婦 a clever-tongued woman.
佞 臣 a deceitful minister.
佞 黨 traitors.

寍 寗[2] Peaceful. Inter. next.
4724

寗 波 Ningpo.
寗 綢 good quality silks from Kiangning. (Nanking).
寗 靜 tranquil; in peace.

寧 寗 甯[2] Used as a term of comparison:—rather; it is better. Would that.
4725

寧 可 rather.
寧 可 信 其 有 不 可 信 其 無 it is better to believe that it exists than that it does not.

寧 可 濕 衣 不 可 亂 步 rather wet the robes than hasten in an undignified manner—in the rain.

寧 折 不 彎 it may break, but it will not bend.

⁵寧 有 當 乎 Is it fitting? Is it right?

寧 樸 毋 華 simple and plain rather than ornamented.

寧 死 不 去 rather die than go.

寧 死 不 辱 to prefer death to disgrace.

寧 爲 玉 碎 莫 爲 瓦 全 rather be a smashed piece of precious jade than an unbroken tile.

¹⁰寧 疏 毋 密 well spaced rather than crowded together.

寧 肯 or 寧 自 would rather; would prefer to.

寧 願 I had rather; I prefer.

(a) Inter. preceding. Peaceful, repose.

寧 時 a time of rest.
安 寧 peace and quiet.
康 寧 good health.

儜² Weak; wearied. In distress.
4726

嚀² To enjoin; to charge; to order.
4727

叮 嚀 to enjoin.

擰²,³ To pull about; to cause confusion about. To twist; to sprain.
4728

擰 一 下 子 or 擰 一 把 give it a twist.

擰 乾 了 wring it dry.
擰 壞 to spoil by twisting.
擰 手 to sprain the wrist.
擰 脚 to sprain the ankle; to twist the foot.
↑擰 了 too bad! it's all over!

檸² A tree, from the bark of which a medicinal tincture is made. Used for the lemon.
4729

檸 檬 the lemon.
檸 檬 水 lemonade.
檸 檬 酸 citric acid.
檸 頭 a tenon.

濘⁴ Miry; mud.
4730

獰² Fierce appearance. Hair of dogs.
4731

獰 惡 可 怖 fierce and repulsively ugly.

凝²,⁴ To freeze; to congeal; to coagulate; to curdle Frozen; stiffened.
4732

凝 冰 to freeze.
凝 喜 or 凝 祥 May felicity collect about this place!
凝 固 congealed; hard; freezing.
凝 固 點 freezing point; point of solidification.
⁵凝 寒 very cold; freezing.
凝 思 默 想 profoundly meditating.
凝 據 stern; rigorous; adhering to the old usage; unaccommodating.
凝 水 櫃 a condensing engine.
凝 澀 congealed and weak.
¹⁰凝 眸 a fixed gaze.
凝 神 遠 視 gazing fixedly into distance.
凝 結 or 凝 住 or 凝 聚 to freeze; to congeal; to curdle.
凝 結 力 chemical affinity.
凝 結 器 a condenser.
¹⁵凝 聚 力 cohesion; cohesive force.
凝 聚 器 a condenser—in microscopy.
次 級 凝 聚 器 sub-stage condenser.
凝 胎 an embryo.
凝 脂 congealed fat.
²⁰凝 質 crystals.
凝 阻 congestion from indigestion.
凝 集 凸 鏡 condensing lens.
凝 電 器 condenser—electric.
凝 霜 stiff with frost.
凝 點 freezing point; point of congelation.

(a) To accomplish. To bring to pass.

苟 不 至 德 至 道 不 凝 焉 only by perfect virtue can the perfect path be made a fact.

NÜEH   (ㄋㄩㄝ)

(Nioh)

搦⁴,⁵ To seize. To take hold of. Also read nuo⁴.
4733

搦 筆 or 搦 管 to take up a pen.

虐⁴,⁵ Unfeeling, harsh, cruel. Tyrannical. To maltreat; to oppress.
4734

虐 取 to extort unjustly; to fleece.
虐 待 to ill-treat.
虐 打 maltreatment.
虐 政 tyrannical government.
虐 民 to oppress the masses.
天 作 大 虐 Heaven sent down great calamities.

瘧⁴,⁵ Fevers—remittent or intermittent. Also read yao⁴, yo⁴,⁵.
4735

瘧 媒 蚊 the *anopheles* mosquito.
瘧 母 enlarged spleen from malarial diseases.
瘧 疾 intermittent or remittent fevers.
發 瘧 子 to have an attack of malarial fever. (- yao⁴ -)

謔⁴,⁵ To ridicule; to jest; to mock. Also read hsüeh⁴,⁵.
4736

謔 浪 笑 敖 with scornful words and jeering smiles.
劇 謔 jokes; banter.
戲 謔 to play tricks on; obscene sporting.

NIU.   (ㄋㄧㄡ)

牛² An ox, a cow. Radical 93. Distinguish 午 No. 7177.
4737

牛 人 or 牛 兵 a farm-hand.
牛 公 or 牡 牛 a bull.
牛 刀 割 鷄 using a large knife to kill a fowl—unnecessary.
牛 刀 小 試 waste of energy.
⁵牛 鳴 or 牛 吼 the lowing of an ox.
牛 圈 a cow-pen.
牛 女 the constellations of the Herd-boy and the Spinning Damsel.
牛 女 和 合 the union of the constellations of the Herd-boy and the Spinning Damsel—7th of the 7th lunar month.
牛 奶 cow's milk.

¹⁰牛 奶 棚 a dairy. = 牛 奶 公 司.
牛 奶 皮 cream.
牛 奶 餅 cheese.
牛 崽 a calf.
牛 後 buttocks of an ox—used in derision of those who are content to follow the great. See 鷄 No. 428—2.
¹⁵牛 性 stubborn; obstinate.
牛 梭 or 牛 軶 yoke for an ox.
牛 椎 or 椎 牛 to kill an ox.
牛 毛 hair of an ox—numerous; many.
牛 毛 雨 fine drizzling rain.
²⁰牛 油 butter.
牛 溲 馬 勃 urine of cattle, and horse-dung—very inferior articles.
牛 犢 a calf.
牛 痘 calf-vaccine.
牛 瘟 or 牛 疫 rinderpest.
²⁵牛 皮 燈 籠 an ox-hide lantern—a dull, stupid person.
牛 皮 膠 ox-glue.
牛 眠 地 a lucky spot for a grave—according to geomancy.
牛 羊 cattle and sheep.
牛 羊 子³ 於 其 中 the cattle and sheep breed there.
³⁰牛 耳 the ear of an ox—refers to a covenant of blood. See 執 No. 996—18.
牛 肉 beef.
牛 (肉) 扒 beef-steak. (-p'a²)
牛 膝 草 hyssop.
牛 舌 頭 ox-tongue; the common dock.
³⁵牛 莊 Newchwang.
牛 蒡 burdock.
牛 蜂 a hornet.
牛 蝱 horse-fly; gad-fly.
牛 衣 rough hempen rugs for cattle.
⁴⁰牛 車 an ox-cart.
牛 郎 or 牽 牛 the constellation of the Herd-boy—some stars in Aquila.
牛 酪 butter.
牛 革 hides.
牛 頭² 不 對 馬 臉 the head of an ox will not match the face of a horse—things that do not agree; incongruous.
⁴⁵牛 頭² 馬 面 the ox-headed, and horse-faced demon-messengers from purgatory.
牛 飲 to drink like an ox.
牛 馬 走 depreciatory expression —I'll be of service to you like

your ox or your horse.
牛 鬼 蛇 神 demons with the head of an ox and spiritual beings with bodies of serpents—supernatural, weird; also u.f. an ugly fellow.
牛 黃 cow bezoar.
⁵⁰牛 鱉 leeches.
牛 鼎 烹 鷄 to boil a fowl in the great cauldron made for cooking an ox—great talent used in petty things.
宧 牛 a bullock.
牡 牛 or 牝 牛 a cow.
水 牛 a water-buffalo.
⁵⁵黃 牛 the common yellow cattle.

妞¹
4738 A little girl.

忸³
4739 Perverse, obstinate. Inter. 狃 No. 4741. Also read *nŭ⁴*.
忸 惡 the mind set on evil.

(a) To blush. To be ashamed.
忸 怩 to blush.

扭³
4740 To wrench, to twist. To turn round. To seize, to grasp.
扭·一·扭 give it a twist.
扭 乾 wring it dry.
扭·了 脖·子 he twisted his neck round; to strain the neck.
扭 傷 to sprain.
⁵扭 壞 spoilt by a wrench.
扭 扭 踢 踢 twisting and squirming; coy; coquettish.
扭 揑 to fidget; to put on coquettish airs.
扭 毆 to squabble.
扭 禀 or 扭 送 to seize a man and bring him to justice.
¹⁰扭 紋 木 cross-grained wood.
扭 結 to grapple; to twist; to struggle together.
扭 肚 colicky pains.
扭 脚 to sprain the ankle.
扭 轉 to turn over; to twist about.
¹⁵扭 轉 心 腸 to reform; to change one's feelings.
扭·過 臉 去 he turned his face away.
扭 鎖 a door-knob.
扭 頸 to crick the neck.

狃³
4741 Inclined to evil; perverse. Familiar with. Accustomed to. Inter. 忸 No. 4739.
狃 於 姦 宄 practised in guile.
狃 於 陋 習 habituated to low practices.
狃 習 familiar with; versed in.

紐³
4742 A knot; a fastening. To tie.
紐 別 perverse; contrary; unhappy; cross-grained.
紐 結 to fasten, so as to untie readily.
紐 解 鼎 遷 severed connections with the established basis.

(a) Used in transliterating.
紐 約 New York.
紐 芬 蘭 Newfoundland.
紐 西 蘭 New Zealand.

鈕³
4743 A knob; a button.
鈕 口 a button-hole.
鈕·子 buttons.
鈕 絆 loops for buttons.
鈕 耳 a button-hole.
鈕 襻 loops for buttons.
瓜 鈕 the newly-formed fruits on melon and similar vines.
銅 鈕 brass buttons.

糅²·³·
4744 Mixed; assorted.

NO. (⽳)

娜²
4745 Elegant; courteous; fascinating.
萬 柳 枝 娜 娜 long and graceful were the myriad willow branches.

儺² / 單
4746 To exorcise demons; to drive away pestilence.
儺 神 a god which drives away pestilence.

(a) Soft and delicate.

猗儺其枝 "soft and pliant are its branches."

猗儺其實 "soft and delicate is its fruit."

(b) Read *no*[3]. Walking with measured steps.

佩玉之儺 "how the pendants swing to the measured steps!"

諾 嗒   4.5.   4747

To respond; to answer. To promise. The second form is also read *êrh*[3].

諾諾 answer of assent in response to a call.

應[4]諾 to respond; to assent; to answer.

許諾 to promise.

(a) Used in transliterating.

諾脫邁爾 a nautical mile.

NO. NUO   (ㄋㄛㄜ)

挪 [2]   4748

To move; to shift on one side.

挪·不動 cannot move it.

挪·不開 cannot get away.

挪借 to borrow of, to embezzle.

挪·到別人身上 shift the blame —to another's shoulders.

[5]挪動 to move.

挪用 to misappropriate funds.

挪移 to move from one place to another.

挪移地界 to remove a landmark.

挪·開 or 搬·開 to set aside; to move.

(a) To rub.

搓挪 to rub between the hands.

挼 挼 [2]   4749

To rub; to crumple.

挼手 to rub the hands.

挼挲 to crumple up in the hands.

雙脚挼挲 rubbing its two legs together—as a fly.

挼油 to rub on paint—as Chinese do in painting houses, etc.

挼穗 to rub ears of corn between the hands.

(a) Read *hui*[2] or *sui*[2]. Food offered to the gods.

挼祭 food offered in sacrifice.

懦 [4]   4750

Weak; timid; imbecile. Also read *lo*[4].

懦夫 a weak, spiritless man; a coward.

懦弱 without energy.

懦鈍 weak and dull.

糯 粳 [4]   4751

Glutinous, sticky. Also read *lo*[4].

糯米 glutinous rice.

糯米糕 cakes made from glutinous rice.

糯米臀 epithet for a lazy man who sticks to his seat.

糯米酒 sweet spirits made from glutinous rice.

NOU.   (ㄋㄡ)   (Neo)

耨 鎒 [4]   4752

To hoe; to weed.

耨草 to hoe up weeds.

NU.   (ㄋㄨ)

奴 [2]   4753

A slave; a servant. Term of depreciation.

奴僕 a male slave.

奴婢 female slaves.

奴家 a slave; formerly used by women for I.

奴役 slavery.

[5]奴性 a servile disposition.

奴才 a bondman; a slave; formerly used by officials, of themselves, in addressing the emperor; also used in abuse.

奴欺主 inferiors behaving offensively towards their superiors.

奴產子[3] sons born in slavery.

奴籍 slavery.

[10]奴輩 You slave! Term of abuse.

奴顏婢膝 servile behaviour; also a term of abuse.

奴◦隸 slaves.

奴◦隸生活 a life of slavery.

奴◦隸貿易 the slave trade.

[15]燭奴 a candlestick.

狸奴 an otter.

看財奴 a miser.

竹奴 a bamboo bed-rest—a Dutch wife.

飛奴 a carrier-pigeon.

↑木奴 another name for 橘.

伮 [2]   4754

To make a great effort.

伮力爭強 to strive with all the might.

努 [3]   4755

To exert; to strive.

努傷 injured through over exertion.

努力 to put forth effort.

努力加餐 to make an effort to eat.

努力實施 energetically carry it out.

[5]努力行善 to do good with all one's energies.

努嘴 to pout the lips in giving directions; to make signs with the lips; to pout.

努·着勁兒 put your back into it!

孥 [2]   4756

A child, children.

孥戮 punishment involving the death of the whole family.

孥稚 a young child.

妻孥 wife and children.

弩 [3]   4757

A cross-bow.

弩弓 a cross-bow.

弩彈 pellets for cross-bows.

怒[4] Anger; passion; rage.
Distinguish 恕 No. 5875.
4758

怒 不 能 回 too angry to reply.
怒 容 滿 面 the face flushed with rage.
怒 忿 忿 的 full of anger; highly wrathful.
怒 恨 full of rage and spite.
[5]怒 氣 wrath; anger.
怒 氣 傷 肝 anger injures the liver.
怒 氣 冲 冲 in a great rage.
怒 氣 塡 胸 anger filled his breast.
怒 潮 a raging tide; tide of wrath
[10]怒 濤 raging billows.
怒 目 angry looks; to look angrily.
怒 目 相 視 they eyed each other angrily.
怒 罵 angry cursing.
怒 臂 to raise the arms in anger.
[15]怒 色 flushed with rage.
怒 號 roaring with rage.
怒 視 to give black looks.
怒 言 angry words.
怒 起 to spring up and stand erect —as the hair when one is angry or alarmed.
[20]怒 鄰 不 義 to anger one's neighbour is unrighteous.
怒 馬 spirited, proud horses.
怒 髮 衝 冠 his rage lifted his cap.
易 怒 easily provoked to anger.
暴 怒 fierce anger.
[25]發 怒 to get in a temper; to be angry.
盛 怒 full of anger.

(a) To put forth.

怒 生 之 草 flourishing grasses and herbage.
怒 華 covered with blossoms.

獠[4]
4759
A tribe in South China.

獠 夷 a tribe in S. W. Yunnan.

砮[3]
4760
Flint arrow-heads.

篗[2]
4761
A bird-cage.

駑[2] Worn-out old horses—used by analogy of one whose talents are becoming weak.
4762

駑 下 very inferior.
駑 散 very ordinary; commonplace.
駑 鈍 a bad horse and a blunt (knife)—not of much use.
駑 鉛 a worn out horse and a lead (knife)—not of much use.
[5]駑 馬 戀 棧 豆 the old horse hankers after his stall and his beans.

駑 駘 竭 力 I am but a jaded horse, but I'll do my best.

NUAN. (ㄋㄨㄢ)

煖
暖[3]
4763
Warm, genial, of weather.

煖 和 warm; genial.　(--huo)
煖 壺 a vessel for keeping wine, etc., warm; a thermos bottle.
煖 壽 to celebrate a birthday. *
↑煖 喪 feast given on the eve of the funeral. (hist.)
煖 房 (or 屋) a house-warming.
[5]煖 手 to warm the hands.
煖 氣 warm vapour.
煖 洞 子 places for storing or forcing plants.
煖 流 warm ocean-currents.
煖 爐 a radiator. A.c. 煖 氣 管 (子)
[10]煖 牀 to warm the bed—to celebrate a wedding.
煖 眼 to look upon with favour.
煖 翠 the green of the hills in spring.
煖 衣 warm clothing.
煖 鍋 a vessel of copper for keeping food hot.
[15]煖 風 genial breezes.
煖 飽 warm and well-fed.
* Usually before the actual date.
(a) Read hsüan[1]. Delicate; pliable; soft.

煖 姝 attractive, beautiful—of a girl.

餪[3] To send a present of a feast.
4764

餪 女 feast sent to a daughter three days after her wedding.
餪 席 a bridal feast.

NUN or NÊN. (ㄋㄨㄣ)

(Nuen)

嫩[4] Tender; delicate. Immature; young. Lightly boiled, as an egg.
4765

嫩 手 soft hands.
嫩 皮 soft furs; a soft skin.
嫩 細 small and delicate.
嫩 肉 tender meat.
[5]嫩 色 a soft, delicate shade of colour.
嫩 芽 a tender shoot.
嫩 葉 young and tender leaves.
嫩 藍 light blue.
嫩 骨 頭 small bones.
[10]嫩 鷄 a chicken.
嬌 嫩 delicately nurtured.
年 紀 嫩 of tender years.
煮 得 太 嫩 boiled too lightly—of eggs.

NEI. NUI. (ㄋㄨㄟ)

(Nui)

內[4] Within; inside; inner; among—hence:—a wife.
4766

內 中 among; within.
內 中 有 幾 個 there were some among them.
內 丹 a pill supposed by Taoists to confer immortality.
內 亂 civil war; anarchy.
[5]內 亂 犯 those guilty of insurrection.
內 云 or 內 開 or 內 稱 in which it is said; the above mentioned —of a despatch under acknowledgement.
內 人 or 賤 內 my wife.
內 侍 臣 a chamberlain; official in waiting.
內 傷 an internal injury.
[10]內 債 domestic loans.
內 兄 弟 a wife's brothers.
內 函 enclosure; inclusion.
內 助 wife.
內 務 home affairs.
[15]內 務 次 長 Assistant Home Secretary or Assistant Minister of Home Affairs.
內 務 科 Bureau of Civil Affairs.

↓ 內 政 部 Ministry of the Interior.

↓ 內 政 部 長 Minister of the Interior.

內 勤 indoor service—as in the customs.

[20] 內 史 the censorate—during the *Han* dynasty.

內 含 or 內 在 immanence.

內 國 公 債 internal national debts.

內 地 the interior—of a country.

內 地 土 產 native products.

[25] 內 地 子³口 稅 transit duties.

內 地 居 民 natives of a place.

內 地 收 稅 局 Inland Revenue Office.

內 地 會 China Inland Mission.

內 地 流 域 inland river basins.

[30] 內 在·的 目 的 the immanent purpose.

內 城 Tartar City of Peking. (Peiping.)

內 堂 or 內 庭 inner room or court.

內 外 inner and outer; internal and external; native and foreign; home and abroad; inclusive and exclusive, etc.

內 外 交 養 a cultivation of both interior and exterior.

[35] 內 外 賓 主 之 辨 the difference between the permanent and the transitory.

內 奸 disaffection; disloyalty.

內 姪 son of a wife's brother.

內 嬖 concubines; favourites.

內 宅 the inner apartments—women's quarters.

[40] 內 室 or 內 幃 women's apartments.

內 容 contents; details; internal economy; within; before a list it signifies—as follows.

圖 畫 之 內 容 included in fine arts, pictures and drawings, are....

內 寢 private rooms.

內 幕 behind the scenes; inner circles.

[45] 內 心 the affections. ⌈columnist.

內 應 treachery within; fifth

內 憂 外 亂 internal anxiety and external disorder.

內 房 the women's apartments.

內 抵 抗 internal resistance.

[50] 內 援 influence behind the scenes.

內 政 home administration.

↑內 戰 civil war.

內 服 to be taken internally.

內 櫃 behind the counter of a shop.

內 河 小 輪 launches that ply on the inland rivers.

[55] 內 治 peace at home—either national or private.

內 海 inland seas.

內 港 inland waters.

內 燃 機 器 internal-combustion engine. [science.

內 疚 ashamed in heart; sick con-

[60] 內 症 internal complaints.

內 痔 or 外 痔 internal or external piles.

內 省 不 疚 to find no fault in examining one's heart.

內 相 or 內 公 or 內 侍 a eunuch.

內 眷 止 步 Women's apartments. Stop !

[65] 內 石 sterility of a woman.

內 科 and 外 科 medical and surgical practice.

內 耳 the inner ear.

內 臣 or 內 監 eunuchs.

內 自 訟 者 one who inwardly accuses himself.

[70] 內 蒙 古 Inner Mongolia.

內 行 (*hang²*) skilful; an expert; in the know; versed in.

內 行 ways and conduct of the inner apartments.

內 親 a wife's relations.

內 角 inner angle.

[75] 內 訌 internal strife.

內 證 internal evidence.

內 部 internal section; interior.

內 部 結 合 internal unification.

內 部 關·係 internal relation.

[80] 內 閣 the Cabinet; former Grand Secretariat.

內 閣 制 the Cabinet system of government.

內 閣 總 理 Prime Minister.

內 顧 無 憂 no anxiety about the home or family.

不 在 內 not included.

[85] 五 內 the viscera.

分⁴內 within one's duty.

懼 內 to fear one's wife; henpecked.

(a) Read *na⁴⁵*. Inter. 納 No. 4607. To enter.

若 己 推 而 內 之 溝 中 as if he himself pushed them into a ditch.

餒 餒
[4767]

Hungry, famished. Feeble. See No. 7103.

餒 在 其 中 hunger will be found therein—when the crops fail.

餒 怯 weak and timid.

不 慊 於 心 則 餒 矣 if the mind does not feel complacency in the conduct, the nature becomes starved.

民 氣 餒 the spirit of the masses is cowed; the morale is low.

無 是 餒 也 without it—man—is in a state of starvation.

(a) Putrid fish.

餒 爛 putrid; rotten.

NUNG. (ㄋㄨㄥ)
(Nong)

農 農
[4768]

To farm; a farmer. Agriculture.

農 事 or 農 工 agricultural operations.

農 作 ploughing and sowing.

農 具 agricultural implements.

農 功 farming operations.

[5] 農 商 部 Board of Agriculture, Industry and Commerce.

農 夫 or 農 丁 or 農 人 a farmer.

農 學 agricultural science.

農 家 子³ a farmer.

農 工 商 學 兵 聯 合 會 United Association of Peasants, Artisans, Merchants, Students, and Soldiers.

[10] 農 工 銀 行 Bank of Agriculture and Industry.

農 忙 the busy season for farmers.

農 時 the season for farming—ploughing in spring, weeding in summer, and reaping in autumn.

農 會 Agricultural Society.

農 月 the busy season for farmers.

[15] 農 末 farming and the inferior occupations such as trade or business, etc. *See* 末 No. 4546-2.

農 村 師 範 學 校 Village Normal Schools.

農 林 業 agriculture and forestry.
農 林 試 驗 場 Government Experimental Farm and Nursery.
農 林 部 Board of Agriculture and Forestry.
20 農 桑 agriculture and sericulture.
農 業 agriculture.
農 業 保 險 agricultural insurance.
農 業 化 學 agricultural chemistry.
農 業 學 校 School of Agriculture.
25 農 業 機 器 agricultural machinery.
農 殖 嘉 穀 widely cultivate the best kinds of grain.
農 民 協 會 Peasants Union.
農 父 a farmer; Minister of Agriculture in ancient times.
農 產 物 agricultural produce.
30 農 界 the agricultural world.
農 科 agricultural course in a college.
農 隙 the slack season for farming operations.

儂 2 Anciently used as the first personal pronoun. I, me.
4769 Now used in Kiangsu, etc., for the second person. Thou, you. Also used for 'they.'

儂 自 家 You yourself.(*Shanghai dial.*) I myself.
勸 儂 莫 上 高 峯 I exhort you not to ascend that high peak.
渠 儂 they; he; so-and-so.

噥 1 Garrulous. To chatter; to gabble.
4770

噥 噥 然 talking in a low tone.
唧 噥 muttering.

濃 2 Thick, strong—of liquids. Dark, deep—of tints. Dense.
4771 Also read *nêng²*.

濃 厚 thick—as fluids.
濃 厚 的 興 趣 intensely interesting.
濃 密 close; dense.
濃 度 viscosity.
5 濃 情 great kindness.
濃 愁 deep anxiety or grief.
濃 抹 heavily got-up—of a woman's face.

濃 淡 light and shade; rich and thin; strong and weak.
濃 湯 thick soup.
10 濃 濃 heavy with dew.
濃 烟 strong tobacco.
濃 眉 heavy eyebrows.
濃 睡 deep sleep.
濃 粧 a rich attire—as of a bride.
15 濃 翳 gloom, shade.
濃 茶 strong tea.
濃 郁 strong—as wine, etc.
濃 酒 strong wine.
濃 陰 a dense shade.
20 濃 雨 heavy rain.
濃 黃 sienna colour.

穠 2 Thickly clustered, as blossoms or plants and trees.
4772 Stout.

穠 密 dense vegetation.
穠 纖 stout and slender.

膿 2 Pus. Also read *nêng²*.
4773

膿 水 pus.
膿 潰 suppurating freely.
膿 瘡 an abscess.
膿 眼 症 purulent opthalmia.
5 膿 胞 pustules filled with pus.
膿 腫 purulent swellings.
膿 血 bloody pus.
結 膿 to suppurate; to come to a head.
釀 膿 to suppurate.

醲 1.2. Generous, as wine. Strong, rich.
4774 Inter. 濃 No. 4771.

醲 于 用 賞 liberal in bestowing rewards.
醲 郁 rich, strong—as wines.
醲 酒 strong wines.

齈 2 Cold in the head. Catarrh of the nose.
4775

齈 鼻 a cold in the head; stoppage of the nasal passages.

NÜ.   (ㄋㄩˇ)

女 3 A woman; feminine.
    Radical 38.
4776

女 中 丈 夫 an unusually capable woman.

女 主 lady; mistress; a queen.
女 主 人 mistress.
女 事 women's duties or employments.
5 女 人 or 婦 人 a woman; females.
女 人 心 weak-minded; feminine.
女 人 短 見 women are short-sighted.
女 伶 or 女 優 an actress.
女 僧 Buddhist nun.
10 女 兄 女 弟 elder and younger sisters.
女 兒 a daughter.
女 子 3 a daughter; womankind.
女 公 husband's elder sister.
女 公 子 your daughter.
女 冠 a Taoist nun.
15 女 叔 husband's younger sister.
女 史 a learned woman.
女 司 機 female operative or machinist.
女 君 or 女 主 a queen; a superior woman.
女 基 督 節 制 會 Women's Christian Temperance Union.
20 女 壻 a son-in-law.
女 士 female teacher; a lady. Miss. (The last is now the commonest meaning.)
女 奴 female slaves.
女 媧 氏 the sister and successor of *Fu Hsi* 伏 義.
女 子 3 參 政 團 suffragettes.
25 女 子 3 經 濟 獨 立 economic independence of women.
女 子 3 解 放 emancipation of women.
女 子 3 選 舉 權 female suffrage.
女 孩 兒 a daughter; a girl.
女 孫 grand-daughter.
30 女 宗 a pattern of womanliness.
女 工 or 女 紅 women's employments; needlework.
女 巫 a witch.
女 幹 事 female secretary.
女 徒 or 女 弟 子 3 female disciples.
35 女 德 the virtues due from a woman.
女 德 尚 柔 the estimable virtue in women is yieldingness.
女 性 的 feminine.
女 會 吏 a deaconess.
女 校 長 3 a woman school principal.
40 女 樂 (*yüeh⁴·⁵*) female musicians.
女 權 women's rights.
女 流 women generally.
女 牆 a parapet or battlements.

女 生 外 向 a woman is born with an outward tendency—she leaves the home to be married.

⁴⁵女 界 women's world.

女 界 革 命 revolution in the status of women.

女 眞 *Nüchên* Tartars who founded the *Chin* dynasty 金 朝 A.D. 1115—1235.　(A.p. *ju³-*)

女 神 a goddess.

女 科 gynæcology.

⁵⁰女 職 員 female officer.

女 色 venery.

女 英 雄 a heroine.

女 蘿 dodder.

女 訪 員 female reporter.

⁵⁵女 貞 evergreen shrub; privet, *ligustrum japonicum.*

女 郎 a young woman; a very able woman.

女 陰 the vagina.

女 革 命 軍 women's revolutionary force—Chinese Amazons.

侍 女 a maid; waiting woman.

⁶⁰怨 女 an old maid; woman with a grievance.

烈 女 a virtuous woman.

處³女 a virgin.

童 女 a young woman.

養 女 foster-daughter.

(a) Read *nü⁴.* **To give a daughter in marriage.**

女 于 鄰 國 he married her into a neighbouring State.

(b) Read *ju³.* u.f. 汝 No. 3142. **Thou, you.**

女 何 人 Who are you?

女 則 異 于 彼 Are you, then, different from them?

女 弗 能 救 與 Can you not save him?

女 得 人 焉 爾 乎 Have you got any eminent men?

衄 ⁴
衂 ｝ **To bleed at the nose. Also read *niu⁴·⁵.***
4777

衄 鼻 to bleed at the nose.

(a) **A check in battle. To damp ardour. To shrink from; to treat harshly.**

小 衄 a slight check in battle.

挫 衄 to be damped; to suffer defeat.

驚 衄 scared to death.

O. NGO.　(ㄜ)
(O)

我 ³ **I, my, me, we, our. Subjective. Distinguish** 找 **No.**
4778 242.　**Pron.** *wo³.*

我 不 管 I don't care; I'll have nothing to do with it.

我 何 與 焉 what has it to do with me?

我 個 人 myself; individually.

我·們 or 我 等 or 我 曹 we; us.

⁵我·們·的 ours; our.

我 儂 I, myself.

我 儕 we; us; our set.

我 兄·弟 a polite expression for *I.*

我 郎 爾 誅 I am come to consult with you.

¹⁰我 同 你 去 I will go with you.

我 意 my private opinion.

我 方 my point of view; our side.

我 欠 你 I. O. U.

我 欲 selfishness.

¹⁵我 武 惟 揚 I will spread abroad my powers.

我 毒 秦 we injured *Ch'in*—by refusing to give grain in their time of famine.

我 生 my manner of life; my generation.

我 生 不 辰 I was born out of my time.

我·的 my; mine.

²⁰我·的 生·活 觀 my view of life.

我 知 罪 矣 I acknowledge my fault.

我 耕 人 獲 I plough but others reap—used fig.

我 自 己 I myself.

我 見 as I see it; my opinion.

²⁵我 見 猶 憐 even I, on seeing her, love her and pity her—said by the wife of 桓 溫 when she saw the beauty of the concubine whom he had taken; she had taken a weapon to slay her, but threw it down when she saw her beauty.

俄 ² **Suddenly; momentarily; sudden. To lean to one side.**
4779

俄 倫 袋 a kind of jacket which buttons on the side.

俄 然 or 俄 爾 suddenly.

俄 頃 a short time; in a moment; presently.

(a) **Used in transliterating.**

俄·國 or 俄 羅 斯 國 Russia.

哦 ² **To intone; to chant; to hum. An exclamation.**
4780

哦 有 的 Ah! there is.

哦 詩 to hum poetry.

娥 ² **Good, beautiful.**
4781

娥 女 a beautiful woman.

娥 皇 one of the two daughters of the Emperor *Yao.*

娥 眉 beautiful eyebrows—a beauty. *See* 蛾 No. 4784—3.

峨
峩 ｝ 2.3. **High; commanding.**
4782

峨 冠 a high hat.

峨 峩 兮 若 泰 山 Lofty indeed! like Mount *T'ai.*

峨 眉 山 Mount *Omei*—a Buddhist resort in Szechwan.

莪 ² **A variety of artemisia, the young stems of which are cooked and eaten.**
4783

莪 蒿 the artemisia, as above.

蛾 ² **A moth.**
4784

蛾·子 or 蛾 蟲 a moth.

蛾 式 飛 機 Moth Aeroplane.

蛾 眉 moth-eyebrows—the eyebrows of a beautiful woman.

女 眉 細 如 蠶 蛾 觸 鬚 fine and delicate eyebrows on a woman, like the antennæ of the silkworm moth.

蛾 眉 月 the crescent moon.

蛾 綠 a dark pencil once used for the eyebrows.

(a) Read *i³.* u.f. 蟻 No. 3005. **The ant.**

蛾³子 larvæ of ants.

蛾 術 the methods of the ant.
蛾 賊 robbers as numerous as ants.

餓[4]
4785   **Hungry; starved.**

餓·不·餓 Are you hungry?
餓·了 hungry.
餓·了 一 日 went hungry for a whole day.
餓 倒 to fall down from hunger.
[5]餓 壞·了 prostrated from starvation.
餓·死·了 starved to death.
餓 殍 the bodies of the starved.
餓 瘦·了 emaciated from hunger.
餓 眼 a hungry eye.
[10]餓 肚·子 吃 take it on an empty stomach.
餓 虎 a hungry tiger—rapacious officers of the government.
餓 蚊·子 見·了 血 the hungry mosquito has seen blood.
餓 鬼 hungry ghosts, who are propitiated on the 15th of the 7th lunar month; an uninvited guest.

鵝[2]
4786   **The domestic goose.**

鵝 口 瘡 thrush.
鵝 掌 the foot of a goose.
鵝 毛 down of a goose—petty trifles.
鵝 毛 片 snowflakes.
[5]鵝 眼 goose-eyes—small cash; small.
鵝 絨 down of the goose; velvet.
鵝 翎 筆 goose-quill pen.
鵝 翎 管 goose-quills.
鵝 蛋 臉 an oval face.
[10]鵝 酒 禮 the present of a goose and wine—at a wedding, the goose is an emblem of conjugal fidelity.
鵝 黃 a fine yellow, like that of a gosling.
塘 鵝 the pelican.
天 鵝 the crane; the wild swan.

鵞[兒鵝]
4787   4.5.   **Cackling of geese.**

鵞 鵞 cackling of geese.

(a) Read *i*[4.5]. Inter. 鸖 No. 3058. A fish-hawk.

鵍 鸖 the tiger-bittern or chestnut-heron.

囮[2]
[鳥]
4788   **To inveigle; to decoy.** Also read *yu*[2].

囮·子 or 鳥 囮 a decoy-bird.

(a) **To transform.** u.f. 化 No. 2211.

囮 育 produced and nurtured.

訛[2]
[譌]
4789   **To extort, to cheat. To deceive. False, erroneous.**

訛 人 to extort by false pretensions.
訛 奪 mistakes in a book; wrong characters and omissions.
訛 字 wrong characters in a book.
訛 索 to defraud; to extort money from.
[5]訛 言 or 訛 語 false stories; lies.
訛 詐 to deceive; to cheat.
訛 詐 人 錢 to extort money by false pretences.
訛 誤 to misrepresent.
訛 謬 erroneous.
[10]訛 錯 an error.
訛 頭 or 囮 頭 to extort by false pretences, as one bird is decoyed by another.

(a) **To change; to transform; to move.** u.f. 化 No. 2211.

訛 訛 如 懸 旌 fluttering like a banner.
式 訛 爾 心 if you would but change your heart!
或 寢 或 訛 some lying down and some moving about.

(b) **A will-o'-the-wisp.**

訛 火 a will-o'-the-wisp; a prairie fire.

O. NGO.   (꼴)

(Oh)

咢[4.5]
4790   **To beat a drum; to startle.**

堮[4.5]
4791   **A boundary. A border.**

圻 堮 to carve in relief; carved in relief on one side.

愕[4.5]
4792   **To be startled.**

愕 然 alarmed; startled.
愕 視 staring with fright.
愕 顧 startled glances; glancing round in fear.

腭[齶腭][4.5]
4793   **The roof of the mouth. The palate.**

腭 腺 the glands of the palate.
上 腭 the roof of the mouth.

萼[4.5]
4794   **The stem and calyx of a flower. A younger brother:—one who helps the elder brother as the calyx helps the flower.**

花 萼 the calyx of a flower.

諤[諤謁][4.5]
4795   **Honest speech.**

一 士 之 諤 諤 the honest criticism of a scholar.

鄂[4.5]
4796   **Name of an ancient State which occupied the site of the present province of Hupeh. Hupeh. Used for transliterating.**

鄂 博 *Obo*—a Mongolian frontier post or cairn used to indicate a boundary.
鄂 爾 多 斯 *Ordos*—a district of Inner Mongolia.

(a) **Inter. with preceding. Blunt, honest.**

周 舍 之 鄂 鄂 the straight-forward rebukes of *Chou Shê*.

(b) **Inter.** 愕 No. 4792. **Startled.**

驚 鄂 alarmed; startled.

齶 [4.5.] High cheek-bones
4797

上 下 齶 骨 upper and lower maxillary bones.

鶚 [4.5.] The osprey or fish-eagle. Also called 鵰鶚 and 魚鷹
4798

鶚 展 鵬 程 the osprey has spread his wings to follow the roc on his journey—of a successful graduate.

鶚 立 to wait patiently—as the osprey does for his prey.

噩 [4.5.] Startling; serious.
4799

噩 夢 a dreadful dream.
噩 音 startling news—as of a death.

鱷
鰐 [4.5.] The crocodile; the alligator. Rapacious, cruel.
4800

鱷 紳 劣 吏 rapacious gentry and unscrupulous underlings.
鱷 魚 an alligator; a crocodile.

OU NGOU. (兀又)

(Eo)

偶 [3] An image; an idol. A mate; to mate. Inter. next.
4801

偶 像 or 偶 人 an image; an idol.
偶 戲 Punch and Judy show.
偶 數 even numbers.
偶 視 to look at each other.
[5] 偶 語 to talk together.
佳 偶 a happy couple; a good wife.
喪 偶 to lose one's wife.
失 偶 to lose one's mate.
木 偶 images; dolls; puppets.

(a) Accidental.

偶 或 if by chance.
偶 殺 人 manslaughter.
偶 然 or 偶 爾 by chance; to happen casually; unforeseen.
偶 然 犯 罪 to sin inadvertently.
[5] 偶 聞 to overhear.

偶 見 accidental meeting.
偶 遇 or 偶 逢 to happen to meet.

耦 [3] A pair, a mate. Inter. preceding.
4802

耦 居 to dwell together as man and wife.
配 耦 a mate; to pair or match.

藕 [3] The root-stock of the lotus. Arrowroot.
4803

藕 斷 絲 連 the lotus-root breaks but the fibres hold together—outwardly the alliance is broken, but the illicit affection remains; also used in other ways.
藕 粉 arrowroot.
藕 色 pale lilac colour.
藕 芽 tapering fingers of a woman.

O. (呂)

(See also p. 664)

婀 [1] Unstable. Graceful.
4804

婀 娜 graceful; elegant.

屙 [1] To ease nature.
4805

屙 尿 to urinate.
屙 血 to pass blood.

疴
痾 [1] Sickness. Pain. Also read k'o[4].
4806

疴 嘔 diarrhœa and vomiting.
疴 痢 dysentery.
疴 癢 pain and itching—ailments.

蹉 [1] To slip and sprain a limb. Pron. wo[1].
4807

蹉 脚 to sprain the ankle.
蹉 腿 to wrench the leg.
蹉 折 了 (-shê[2]-) bent and broken.

See No. 1 C-G. **O.** (呂)

(Oh)

堊 [4.5.] To whitewash. To plaster.
4808

堊 土 white clay for porcelain.
堊 壁 to whitewash walls.

惡 [4.5.] Evil, wicked, wrong, foul.
4809

惡 事 malpractices.
惡 作 劇 practical jokes.
惡 俗 an evil custom.
惡 俗 花 紙 vile, vulgar pictures.
[5] 惡 勢 力 subversive influences.
惡 口 foul-mouthed.
惡 名 ill fame; notoriety.
惡 報 an evil recompense.
惡 姻 緣 a bad match—when a couple do not get on well together.
[10] 惡 寒 the cold before a fever—as in malaria.
惡 少 [4] evil youths.
惡 德 evil conduct and ways.
惡 心 feeling of nausea or disgust; nauseating.
惡 念 evil thoughts; malice.
[15] 惡 感 ill-feelings; a bad impression; a depressing influence.
惡 意 evil-minded; bad intentions.
惡 態 an evil appearance or manner.
惡 打 cruel beating.
惡 月 the fifth lunar month.
[20] 惡 有 惡 報 evil has an evil recompense.
惡 木 poisonous trees.
惡 札 my unworthy screed—depreciatory term for one's own letter.
惡 棍 or 惡 徒 roughs; rowdies.
惡 欲 evil desires; lusts.
[25] 惡 歲 a bad year.
惡 毒 viciousness.
惡 氣 noxious air.
惡 濁 foul, unclean.
惡 犬 a fierce dog.
[30] 惡 獸 fierce beasts.
惡 疾 an incurable complaint—usually denotes leprosy.
惡 瘡 foul ulcers; venereal sores.
惡 結 果 evil results.
惡 習 evil practices or habits.
[35] 惡 耗 bad tidings.
惡 聲 至 必 反 之 if any evil words were spoken to him he would certainly repay them.
惡 臭 foul odours; putrid food.
惡 草 or 野 草 weeds.
惡 處 bad points; evil characteristics.

⁴⁰惡 衣 菲 食 poor clothing and meagre diet.

惡 言 bad language.

惡 貫 the measure of wickedness.

惡 貫 滿 盈 the measure of their iniquity is full.

惡 賴 utterly depraved; very bad.

⁴⁵惡 逆 unfilial; rebellious; refractory.

惡 道 or 惡 趣 the evil way—Buddhist expression for the lowest transmigrations—hell, hungry ghosts, and beasts.

惡 運 規 定 his evil fate decided it.

惡 風 evil customs.

惡 鬼 an evil demon.

⁵⁰惡 魔 an evil demon; one who seduces others.

(a) Read *wu*⁴. To dislike, to hate. Hateful.

惡 徼 以 爲 知 者 I hate those who think that their prying into matters is wisdom.

惡 紫 之 奪 朱 也 I hate the purple for taking the place of the vermilion.

惡 訐 以 爲 直 者 I hate those who betray secrets and judge this to be uprightness.

可 惡 hateful; abominable.

恨 惡 or 憎 惡 to loathe; to hate.

↑惡 惡 (*wu*⁴ *o*⁴) to hate evil.

(b) Read *wu*¹. Where? How? In what? An interjection.

惡 乎 How? Wherein? By what means?

惡 在 其 爲 民 父 母 也 Wherein can he be called the father and mother of the people?

惡 得 賢 How can he be deemed worthy!

惡 是 何 言 也 O! what words are these?

扼 扼 搤 ⁴·⁵· To clutch; to grasp.
4810

扼 制 交 通 control of communications.

扼 吭 to choke; to throttle.

扼 吭 之 地 a strategical position.

扼 守 to hold—as a strategical position.

⁵扼 腕 to hold a person's wrist—as indicating affection, unwillingness to part; to seize by the wrist.

扼 虎 to throttle a tiger.

扼 要 to hold a strategical position.

扼 險 to hold the key of a position.

阨 阸 ⁴·⁵· Distress; difficulty.
4811

阨 窮 in great distress; very poor.

艱 阨 in serious difficulties.

(a) Read *ai*⁴, *yai*⁴. Inter. 隘 No. 18. A defile, a pass.

阨 狹 a defile; a mountain pass.

遏 ⁴·⁵· To stop; to check; to prevent. To ruin; to extinguish.
4812

遏 亂 to repress rebellion.

遏 其 萌 芽 nip it in the bud.

遏 制 to put down—as rebellion, etc.

遏 惡 揚 善 to repress evil and encourage good.

⁵遏 慾 難 it is hard to curb the passions and lusts.

遏 抑 to restrain; to check.

遏 病 to check disease.

遏 禁 to prevent.

遏 糴 to stop the purchase of rice.

¹⁰遏 絶 to cut off—as a retreat.

遏 訟 to repress litigation.

遏 防 to prevent.

遏 阻 to hinder.

頞 ⁴·⁵· The brow; junction of the nose and forehead.
4813

閼 ⁴·⁵· To shut. To stop. To obstruct. To conceal. An impediment.
4814

天 閼 a natural obstacle.

遮 閼 to conceal.

(a) Read *yen*¹. A surname.

閼 氏 a princess of the *Hsiung nu* tribes.

OU. (ㄨ)
(Eo)

嘔 ³ To vomit.
4815

嘔 吐 to vomit.

嘔·回·出·來 to disgorge—as ill-gotten gains.

嘔 心 a feeling of sickness from disappointment, etc.

嘔 氣 to vent one's anger or spleen.

嘔 絲 to spin cocoons.

嘔 血 to spit blood.

(a) To prattle. Sounds. *ou*¹.

嘔 啞 prattle of children; creak of a barrow; sound of instruments.

嘔 唳 cry of wild geese, ducks, etc.

嘔 嗄 twitter of swallows.

(b) Read *hsü*¹. Kind words.

言 語 嘔 嘔 cordial and consoling words.

(c) Read *yü*⁴. Cordial, kind.

嘔 喩 受 之 receiving with cordiality.

慪 ⁴ To excite; to irritate.
4816

慪 氣 to exasperate.

(a) Read *kou*¹. Stingy, mean.

慪·得 很 excessively close and mean.

歐 ¹ To vomit; to retch.
4817

歐 泄 vomiting and diarrhœa.

(a) Used in transliterating.

歐 亞 Europe and Asia.

歐 人 European.

歐 几 里 得 Euclid. [ropeanize.

歐 化 European civilization; Eu-

⁵歐 姆 Ohm—(*electric*).

歐 洲 Europe.
歐 羅 巴 Europe.
歐 風 European customs.
↑ 歐 戰 World War I.

毆 敺 1.3. To fight with sticks or the fists; to beat; to brawl.
4818

毆 傷 to wound by beating.
毆 打 to maul; to beat.
毆 斃 or 毆 死 or 毆 殺 to beat to death; to kill in a brawl.
毆 逐 to drive out forcibly.

漚 4 To soak; to steep.
4819

漚 柔 to soften by soaking.
漚 漬 to macerate.
漚 爛 rotted by water.
漚 透 soaked through.
漚 霉 mouldy; damp.

(a) Read *ou*[1]. Bubbles on water.

漚 釘 large round-headed nails used to stud doors.
浮 漚 or 泡 漚 bubbles; f r o t h; foam.

熰 1 Great drought. Heat.
4820

甌 1 A bowl, a cup.
4821

甌 窶 a small eminence.
甌 脫 entrenchments on the frontiers.
木 甌 a wooden bowl.
茶 甌 a tea-cup.

(a) Name of a river near Wênchow, Chê.

褊 1 An infant's bib.
4822

謳 謳 1 To sing ballads. Songs, ballads.
4823

謳 吟 or 謳 咏 to sing songs.

謳 歌 ditties; ballads; songs.
棹 謳 song of the boatman.

鷗 1 Seagulls; terns, etc.
4824

PA.   (ㄅㄚ)

叭 1 The mouth open. A trumpet.
4825

喇·叭 a trumpet.
↑叭 兒 狗 *See* 4826.2.

巴 1 Name of an ancient State which occupied part of what
4826 is now Szechwan.

巴 且 the plantain or banana. *See* 芭 No. 4836.
巴 狗 a Pekingese pug-dog.
巴 蜀 two ancient States, now used to denote the province of Szechwan.
巴 蛇 a python—fabled to swallow elephants.
巴 豆 the croton-oil bean.
↑巴 縣 Chungking.

(a) Sign of the optative.

巴 不 得 or 巴 不 能 Would that! May it be so!
巴 望 earnestly to hope for.
眼 巴 巴·的 expectantly; hopefully desirous of.

(b) The open hand. See 把 No. 4829.

巴·掌 the palm of the hand; a smack with the hand.
打 嘴 巴 to smack on the mouth; to slap in the face.
巴·結 to curry favour; to toady; to flatter; to exert oneself.
巴·結 到 手 to get into a person's favour by toadying.

(c) Crust on a pot.

巴·巴 a crust; also u.f. unintelligible speech, *see next*: No. 4827.
鍋·巴 crust on the rice-boiler.

(d) Used in transliterating.

巴 他 戈 拿 Patagonia.
巴 克 特 里 亞 Bactria.
巴 圖 魯 *Baturu*—Manchu term

for an order conferred for military service.
巴 布 亞 Papua.
5巴 威 略 Bavaria.
巴 拉 圭 Paraguay.
巴 拉 馬 u.f. palms; palm trees.
巴 拿 馬 Panama.
巴 比 倫 Babylon.
10巴 爾 幹 Balkans.
巴 西 Brazil.
巴 黎 Paris.
巴 達 維 亞 Batavia.

吧 1 Large-mouthed.
4827

吧 吧 loquacious; unintelligible speech.
吧 呀 wrangling of infants; large-mouthed.
瘂·吧 dumb.

(a) Used in transliterating.

吧 嗎 油 *dammar*—a kind of pitch or resin from Borneo.
吧 國 Java, for which 爪 哇 is now used.

(b) Final particle, = 4841 A.

弝 4 The part of a bow grasped when shooting.
4828

把 3 To take; to hold. N.A. for things with handles or
4829 things which are taken hold of.

把·勢 匠 a strong man; an acrobat.
把 卷 to hold a book and open it.
把 守 to stop; to guard; to hold fast.
把 家 人 a housekeeper; a doorkeeper.
5把 戲 a c r o b a t i c performances; juggling, etc.; also used in some places for young children.
把 持 to use undue influence; to control; to monopolize.
把 持 不 定 irresolute; undecided.
把 捉 to arrest; to seize.
把·握 to take hold of; authority for taking action; security; guarantee.
10把 穩 to hold firmly; to maintain with firmness.
把 總 a former title for a sergeant in the Chinese army.
把 臂 arm in arm; clasping hands; very intimate.

把 舵 to steer.

把 袂 to grasp the sleeve—in friendly intercourse.

[15] 把 袂 之 時 times of friendly intercourse— old times.

把 酒 to pass round the wine; to take up the wine-cup.

把 門 to watch a door.

把 關 to guard a pass; former title of an officer in charge of the passes.

把 風 to spy; to scout.

[20] 二 匪 在 下 把 風 two robbers kept watch below.

一 把 a bundle; a handful; a grasp of the hand.

一 把 傘 an umbrella.

一 把 刀 a knife.

一 把 扇 a fan.

[25] 一 把 汗 a flow of perspiration.

一 把 眼 淚 a flood of tears.

火 把 a torch.

(a) Read *pa*³ or *pai*⁴ Sign of the object. Used in the colloquial instead of 將 No. 656.

把 怨 報 怨 to recompense evil with evil.

把 手 撥 開 push it aside with your hand.

把 這·個 給·他 give this to him.

把 門 關·上 shut the door.

(b) Read *pa*⁴. A handle.

把·子 or 把 兒 a handle.

把·柄 a handle; also used fig. for anything that gives occasion for talk, etc.

話 把 an occasion for scandal.

杷 杁 }¹ A kind of rake without teeth, used to smooth seed-plots. The first is also u.f. 耙 No. 4835.

4830

爸 }⁴ A father—a Mohammedan term.

4831

爸·爸 or 阿 爸 papa.

疤 }¹ A scar; a birth-mark.

4832

疤 痕 or 疤 癩 a scar.

疤 眼 兒 a scar from a sore on the eyelid.

疤 臉 a scarred face.

笆 }¹ A fence. A kind of bamboo.

4833

笆 城 a stockade.

籬·笆 a bamboo fence or hedge.

弝 }¹ Dried meat.

4834

耙 鈀 }⁴ A drag; a harrow. Also read *p'a*².

4835

耙 地 to harrow.

耙·子 or 犁 耙 a rake; a harrow.

耙 齒 teeth of a rake or harrow.

芭 }¹ A fragrant plant. The plantain.

4836

芭 蕉 or 香 蕉 the banana; the plantain.

芭 蕉 扇 or 芭 蕉 葉 a palm-leaf fan.

靶 }⁴ A target. The splash-board of a chariot.

4837

靶·子 a target.

靶·子 場 rifle-range.

打 靶 target-practice.

鈀 欛 }⁴ A handle.

4838

筢 }² A bamboo rake with teeth. Pron. *p'a*²

4839

筢·子 or 九 齒 竹 筢 a bamboo rake.

葩 The corolla of a flower. Also read *p'a*¹.

4840

葩 經 the *Book of Odes*.

罷 }⁴ To cease, to finish. Finished.

4841

罷·了³ finished; that is enough; an expression of satisfaction or of trouble. (-*liao*³ or ·*lê*)

也 還·罷²·了 It will do! It is enough! (-*hai*²-)

罷 休 or 罷 息 to finish; to have done with.

罷 免 to remove from office.

[5] 罷 兵 to withdraw troops.

罷 官 to resign office; to be dismissed from office.

罷 工 to go on strike; to stop labour.

罷 工 風 潮 trouble of strikes.

醞 釀 罷 工 to foment strikes —as by labour-agitators.

[10] 罷 市 to refuse to do business; to shut up shops, etc., in protest against the authorities.

罷 手 to cease; to discontinue.

罷 斥 to be dismissed from office.

罷 職 to suspend from office.

罷 試 to refuse to attend an examination.

[15] 罷 論 to end the matter; to drop the discussion.

罷 課 or 罷 學 schoolboy strikes.

(a) A sign of the imperative. Final particle of emphasis, sometimes interrogative, implying probability.

不 暈 船·罷 You don't get sea-sick?

也 許 買·了·罷 I suppose he has bought it?

去·罷 Be off! Get out of this!

坐·一 回 兒·罷 sit down for a while.

[5] 好·罷 All right!

我·們 走·罷 let us go!

改 日 見·罷 I'll see you another day!

算·了·罷 that's an end of it! Enough!

請 進 去·罷 kindly step inside.

飯 好·了·罷 Is the dinner ready? —implying that the speaker thinks that it is.

(b) Read *p'i*². Weary; fatigued.

罷 勞 great weariness.

罷 病 infirm; weak.

霸 [4] To be chief. To rule by
4842 might rather than by right.
A tyrant; a usurper.

霸 佔 to infringe on; to usurp.
霸 佔 地 土 to infringe on territory; to occupy territory.
霸 勒 to intimidate.
霸 天 下 to rule the country by
force.
[5]霸 市 to corner the market.
霸 政 之 餘 習 the prevalent custom of usurpation.
霸 權 tyranny.
霸·氣 audacity; fearless disregard
of right.
霸·王 one who rules by force; the
chief among several princes.
[10]霸 者 a dictator.
霸 諸 侯 to lead the feudal princes.
霸·道 to act unreasonably or violently; to intimidate; the way
of might, as contrasted with the
way of right 王 道; fierce.

壩 [4]
垻 ｝ An embankment; a slope
over which boats pass.
Distinguish 垻 No. 1558.
4843

壩 埠 an embankment or bunding.
壩 頭 a mart; a port.
打 壩 to make an embankment.

灞 [4]
Name of a river in Shensi.
4844

PA.   (ㄅ)

(Pah)

八 1.5. Eight. Radical 12.
Distinguish 入 No. 3152.
4845

八 元 the eight sons or descendants
of the Emperor K'u 帝 嚳 who
assisted 舜 in the government.
八 仙 the eight immortals of Taoism, *see* No. 2707—24.
八 仙 桌 子 a table for eight
persons.
八 佾 the eight rows of dancers
mentioned in the second book
of the *Analects*.
[5]八·[1.2]個 eight (things).
八 八 sixty-four.

八 分 書 a form of the 隸 書 or
square style of writing.
八 到 the four points of the compass and the four intermediate
points.
八·十 eighty.
[10]八 卦 the Eight Diagrams. *See*
No. 3514—5.
八·哥 the mynah.
八 大 八 小 eight large and eight
small dishes of a feast.
八 字 the character *pa;* the cyclic
characters for the year, month,
day, and hour of the birth of
betrothed persons.
開 八 字 to prepare the horoscope, as above.
[15]八 字 不 合 the horoscopes do not
agree.
八 字 牆 門 a double door partly
open, and thus resembling the
character *pa.*
八 字 形 shaped like the character
pa; spreading fan-wise; slanting.
八 字 沒 見 一 撇 the first stroke
of the character *pa* not yet
visible—nothing has been done
so far.
八 字 眉 sloping eyebrows.
[20]八 寶 the Eight Treasures—carried
in the hands of the Eight Immortals. *See above*—2.
八 小 時 工 作 制 the Eight
Hours System of labour.
八 成 or 八 分 or 八 就 eight-
tenths—probably; most likely.
八 成 之 譜 about 80%.
八 成 要 下 雨 most probably it
will rain.
[25]八 成 賬 almost complete.
八 成 餘 over 80%.
八 擡 轎 a sedan-chair with eight
bearers.
八 斗 才 eight bushels of talent—
very gifted.
八 旗 the Eight Banners in the
former Manchu Army.
[30]八 景 eight classes of scenery.
八 節 the Eight Festivals—i.e., the
beginning of the four seasons,
the equinoxes, and the solstices.
八 股 文 章 the "eight-legged
essay" of the old examination
system. A.c. 時 文.
八 荒 in every direction; everywhere.
八 蜡 the eight imperial thanks-
givings made at the close of the

year, for the harvest, etc.
[35]八 行 (*hang*[2]) 書 Chinese letter-
paper with eight lines to the
page.
八 角 octagonal; eight corners.
八 角 形 octagonal figure; octagonal.
八 角 油 oil of aniseed.
八 角 渣 broken star-aniseed.
[40]八 角 茴 香 star-aniseed.
八 開 ten-cent subsidiary coins.
八 面 or 八 方 the eight points of
the compass.
八 面 威·風 an awe-inspiring reputation extending in every
direction.
八 面 玲 瓏 well finished and
elegant throughout.
[45]八 面 週 全 all complete.
八 音 eight kinds of musical
sounds, as produced from—the
calabash, earthenware, stretched
hides, wood, stone, metal, silk
strings, and bamboo.
八 音 琴 or 八 音 盒 a music
box.

唎 1.5.
The cry of a bird.
4846

唎·哥 兒 the mynah, *see preceding*
—11.

捌 1.5. A form of scraper for
levelling a seed-plot.
4847 A form of 八 No. 4845.
Eight. Used in accounts
to prevent fraud.

拔 2.5.
To pluck up; to root up.
4848

拔·上·來 to pull up.
拔·乎 其 萃 to rise above the common level.
拔 俗 far above the common standard; not at all vulgar or trite.
拔·出·來 to pluck up; to draw out;
to extract.
[5]拔 刀 or 拔 劍 to draw a sword.
拔 力 to exert the strength.
拔 地 rising above the ground.
拔 城 to capture a city.
拔 寨 or 拔 營 to break up a
camp.
[10]拔 尤 to promote men of outstanding ability.

拔 山 to root up a mountain—extraordinary strength.

拔 擢 or 拔 取 or 提 拔 to raise; to promote; to bring forward.

拔 根 to eradicate.

拔 椿 to pull up the stakes—to have done with a thing; to return home.

[15]拔 毒 to draw out the poison.

拔 毛 to pluck out hairs.

拔 河 a tug of war.

拔 牙 to extract a tooth.

拔 睫 毛 to pluck out the eyelashes.

[20]拔 秧 to pull up young rice-plants for transplanting.

拔 羣 said of one who has outstanding ability.

拔 草 to weed.

拔 萃 人 才 a man of outstanding talents.

出 類 拔 萃 pre-eminent above his fellows.

[25]拔 身 to recover one's liberty.

拔 釘 to pull out nails.

拔 釘 鐵 錘 a claw-hammer.

拔 除 to pull out; to uproot.

拔 隊 to withdraw troops.

[30]拔 麥 子 to pull up wheat by the roots.

跋 [2.5.] **To walk; to travel. The heel. Also read** p'o[4.5.]
4849

跋 倒 to stumble and fall.

跋 扈 to tread down legal rights; recalcitrant.

跋 本 the root; the base.

跋 涉 to travel over land and water.

[5]跋 涉 勞 苦 the hardships of travel.

跋 足 the heel.

跋 馬 to turn a horse round.

(a) The conclusion of a book. A colophon. An epilogue.

題 跋 to write a colophon; a colophon.

(b) Used in transliterating.

跋 陀 or 跋 達 virtuous and wise—title applied to every Buddha; Sanskrit, *bhadra*.

鈸 [2.5.] **A small bell. Cymbals. Also read** po[2.5.]
4850

魃 [2.5.] The drought demon. See
4851 旱 No. 2023-18,19. Also read po[2.5.]

鮁 [4.5.] The bonito. Also read
4852 po[2.5.]

P'A.   (ㄆㄚ)

扒 [2] **To scratch.**
4853

扒 手 a pickpocket.

(a) Read p'a[1]. To crouch; to crawl. Inter. next.

扒 灰 to crawl on the ashes—incest with a daughter-in-law.

(b) Read pa[1]. To strip. To pull out. To eradicate. To climb.

扒 房 子 to pull down a house.

扒 牆 上 catching hold of the top of a wall.

扒 皮 to peel.

扒 衣 裳 strip off his clothes.

扒 載 to jettison cargo.

趴 [2] To crawl; to creep.
4854 Inter. 爬 No. 4857.

趴 上 去 to climb up.

趴 在 地 下 to crawl on the ground.

趴 山 to climb a mountain.

趴 牆 to climb a wall.

趴 牆 虎 Virginia creeper.

趴 起 來 to climb up; to get out of bed.

(a) Read p'a[1]. To crouch.

趴 下 to crouch; to fall on hands and knees.

趴 着 老 虎 a crouching tiger.

帕 [4] A turban; a kerchief; a veil.
4855

帕 子 a veil; a handkerchief.

手 帕 a handkerchief.

頭 帕 a turban.

怕 [4] To fear; to apprehend; to
4856 dread. Lest, perhaps.

怕 事 nervous of what might happen.

怕 他 不 來 I fear that he will not come.

怕 前 怕 後 afraid of everything.

怕 得 罪 人 fearful of giving offence.

[5]怕 懼 fearful; apprehensive.

怕 死 to be afraid of death; very scared.

怕 甚 麼 What are you afraid of? Don't be afraid!

怕 的 是 .... it is to be feared that....

怕 羞 to fear shame; bashful.

[10]怕 老 婆 hen-pecked.

怕 臊 shy; bashful.

爬 [2] To scratch, to scrape. To
4857 crawl, to creep. To climb, to clamber, to scale. Inter. 趴 No. 4854.

爬 上 to climb up.

爬 上 樹 去 to climb a tree.

爬 不 動 cannot crawl.

爬 不 起 來 unable to get up from bed.

[5]爬 出 來 to crawl out.

爬 剔 to extract; to draw out.

爬 山 虎 or 爬 牆 虎 Virginia creeper.

爬 癢 to scratch an itchy place.

爬 羅 all embracing.

[10]爬 行 to crawl.

爬 起 來 to creep; to get out of bed.

爬 飯 to shovel one's rice.

琶 [2] A guitar. Also read pa[2].
4858

琵 琶 a guitar.

湴 [1] Name of a certain river.
4859

PAI.   (ㄅㄞ)

拜 [4] To do obeisance; to pay
4860 one's respects to; to visit. To salute.

拜 上 帝 to worship God.

拜 伏 to prostrate oneself.

拜 佛 to worship Buddha.

拜˙候 to call on; to visit.
[5]拜偶像 to worship idols.
拜別 to take leave.
拜匣 a card-case.
拜印 to salute the official seal—on taking over office.
拜台 the broad pedestal at the base of a tombstone.
[10]拜嘉 respectful thanks—for your present.
拜堂 to worship Heaven and Earth—at a wedding.
拜墊 kneeling-mats.
拜墓 to worship at a tomb.
拜墳 or 拜掃 to worship at the graves.
[15]拜壽 to visit a person on his birth-day.
拜天地 to worship Heaven and Earth.
拜官 to accept an office.
拜客 to pay a visit; to make a call.
拜帖 a visiting-card.
[20]拜師 to pay respects to a teacher or master.
拜年 to pay new-year calls.
拜廟 to worship at a temple.
拜懇 to request; to implore.
拜懺 Buddhist worship.
[25]拜手 to salute with the hands raised together.
拜把˙子 to become sworn broth-ers.
拜˙拜 to bring the hands together and bow—as a Chinese woman does.
拜斗 to worship the *Dipper*.
拜旗 to salute the flag.
[30]拜會 or 拜˙望 to pay a visit; to make a call.
拜月 to worship the moon.
拜服 to submit to; to own al-legiance to.
拜本 to burn incense and salute a memorial before sending it off to the emperor.
拜火敎 Fire-worshippers.
[35]拜物 a fetish.
拜物敎 Fetishism.
拜留 courteously to detain.
拜相 (*hsiang*[4]) to become a minister of state.
拜祖˙宗 to worship ancestors.
[40]拜祝 to worship.
拜神 to worship the gods.
拜神儀式 ritual of worship.
拜禱 to request; to pray.
拜答 to reply with thanks.

[45]拜表 or 拜章 to send in a memorial.
拜見 to pay a visit.
拜親 to pay respects to the parents of one's friend, or to the parents of one's wife.
拜託 to request—as a favour.
拜訪 to call and inquire after.
[50]拜謁 to make a call.
拜謝 to thank.
拜賀 to congratulate.
拜賜 respectful thanks—for your present.
拜辭 to take leave.
[55]拜金主義 worship of Mammon.
拜門下 to acknowledge as one's teacher.
拜除 to confer official rank.
拜領 accepted with thanks.
回拜 to return a call.

捭[3] To open. To spread out. Inter. 擺 No. 4864.
4861

捭闔 to open and to close; to make trouble and to settle dis-putes.

(a) Read *p'ai*[1.3]. To clap the hands; to strike with both hands.

拉捭摧藏 to pull and strike, push and break.

(b) Read *po*[4.5]. To roast on heated stones.

燔黍捭豚 they roasted millet and pieces of pork on heated stones.

稗[4] Tares. Weeds. Small.
4862

稗˙子 darnel; tares.
稗草 darnel; weeds.
稗說 or 稗官野史 novels; romances; fictitious histories.
稗販 a pedlar.

粺[4] Cleaned, polished rice or millet.
4863

擺[3] To place; to spread; to set in order.
4864

擺上酒 to make a banquet.
擺供 a sacrificial offering.

擺˙不開 unable to arrange things—for lack of space.
擺列 to display; to exhibit; to place.
[5]擺卦攤子 to set out a fortune-telling stall.
擺執事 to arrange things—for a procession.
擺宴 to spread a feast.
擺布 to place; to display.
擺布˙他 to injure a person; to throw difficulties in his way; to *do* him.
[10]擺撥 to put on side.
擺攤˙子 to spread a stall for trade. or 一兒.
擺架˙子 to make a display; to put on airs.
擺桌 to lay the table for a meal.
擺樣˙子 to make a display; to show off.
[15]擺治 to torture; to injure; to ar-range; to fix up.
擺空架˙子 to make an empty show.
擺˙脫 to get rid of.
擺臺 to lay a table for meals.
擺花街 to decorate a street.
[20]擺設 to display; to exhibit; to place; ornaments.
擺賣 to expose for sale.
擺酒席 to spread a banquet.
擺˙開 to place; to exhibit.
擺陣 to draw up in line of battle; to dispose troops.
[25]擺隊˙伍 to parade troops.
擺飯 to spread a meal.
擺齊 to arrange evenly.
擺龍門陣 to arrange troops ac-cording to the *Dragon-Gate* tactics—to tell yarns, to gossip.

(a) To wave to and fro. To shake, to move.

擺動 to oscillate; to swing.
擺˙子 a pendulum.
擺唆 to induce; to coax.
擺尾 to wag the tail.
[5]擺˙弄 to do; to manage; to play with.
擺手 to wave the hand—in dis-sent.
擺˙渡 to ferry across; a ferry.
擺針 the pivot of scales; the balance in machinery; the axis.

唄[4] To recite; to chant over.
4865

敗退 [4] 4866

To ruin, to destroy, to spoil. Defeat; to be defeated. Bad, as meat.

敗 事 to baffle an attempt; to spoil an affair.
敗 亡 loss; disgrace; dead.
敗 人 名·譽 to injure a man's reputation.
敗 仗 defeated in battle.
[5] 敗 倫 to behave in a way contrary to human obligations.
敗 北 defeated in battle.
敗 名 節 to injure a moral reputation.
敗 壞 ruined; to corrupt.
敗 子 a spendthrift.
[10] 敗 家 to ruin a family.
敗 家 蕩 產 to squander a patrimony and ruin the family.
敗 德 loss of virtue.
敗 挫 to thwart; to frustrate.
敗 殘 routed; destroyed.
[15] 敗 沒 ruined; destroyed.
敗 滅 or 敗 盡 ruined; destroyed.
敗 盟 a broken covenant.
敗 筆 a spoilt pencil; bad style in painting or writing.
敗 絮 cotton waste.
[20] 敗 績 utterly defeated.
敗 肉 putrid meat.
敗 興 to be a wet blanket.
敗 葉 fallen leaves.
敗 落 in reduced circumstances; defeated.
[25] 敗 血 effused blood.
敗 衄 routed.
敗 訴 to lose a case at law.
敗 謀 to bring a plot to nought.
敗 走 routed.
[30] 敗 門 風 to disgrace the good name of the family.
敗 陣 a defeat in battle.
敗 露 to be ruined by discovery —of a plot.
敗 類 a bad class; to disgrace.
敗 風·俗 to corrupt public morals.
[35] 勝 敗 victory and defeat.
成 敗 success and failure.

挈 [1] 4867

To open out; to separate.

挈 鋸 to set a saw.
挈·開 to break apart.

俳 [2] 4868

P'AI (ㄆㄞ)

Sport or amusement. An actor.

俳 優 a comedy actor.

徘 [1] 4869

To walk. Also read p'ei[2].

徘 徊 flying about, like swallows; walking to and fro; irresolute.

排 [2] 4870

A row, a line, a rank. To place in order; to dispose. To push.

排 兵 or 排 隊 to dispose troops.
排 列 to arrange in series; permutations.
排 列 兩 行 (hang[2]) arranged in two rows.
排 列 次 序 arranged in a series.
[5] 排 列 法 method of arrangement.
排 卦 to arrange the diagrams—for divination.
排 印 to set up and print from type.
排 單 a form, on which was entered the hours of arrival and departure of a government courier. ⌈red tape.
排·塲 stylish; elaborate; showy;
[10] 排 字 to set up type.
排 字 人 a compositor.
排 字 機·器 a type-setting machine; a linotype machine.
排 字 盤 a composing-stick.
排 字 術 typography. ⌈theatricals.
[15] 排 戲 to arrange or rehearse
排 排 坐 to seat in rows.
排·揎 to set out in order the faults of another.
排 斥 to reject; to expel; to reprimand.
排 比 arranged in order and connected together.
[20] 排 球 volley-ball.
排 當 to arrange everything beforehand—as for a feast.
排 簫 a kind of ancient pan-pipes.
排·着 placed; arranged.
排 行 (hang[2]) 第 幾 What is your seniority among your brothers?
[25] 排 衙 to arrange the court and open proceedings.
排·起·來 to stack up in order—as timber.
排 鎗 a volley.
排 長 a lieutenant.

排·開 to spread out; to open.
[30] 排 陣 to deploy troops.
排 隊 游 行 to parade, as a demonstration.
排 飯 to set out a meal.
排 香 案 to set out the incense table.
排 骨 the ribs.
[35] 羊 排 骨 mutton-chops.
排 鬚 fringes or tassels.
排 齊 all arranged in order.
子 彈 一 排 a clip of cartridges.

(a) To push. To clear out.

排 外 anti-foreign.
排 外 運·動 anti-foreign movement.
排 外 主 義 anti-foreign policy.
排 山 倒 海 to overthrow a mountain and upset the sea—of great ability.
[5] 排 悶 to dispel melancholy.
排 患 to get rid of trouble.
排 氣 機 an air-pump.
排 氣 鐘 a bell-jar.
排 水 量 displacement of water.
[10] 排 水 噸 數 displacement—in tons.
排 沙 簡 金 to pick gold out of sand—skilful in selecting.
排 泄 elimination, excretion.
排 泄 作 用 excretory functions.
排 泄 器 excretory organs.
[15] 排 泄 物 output; excreta.
排 泄 管 excretory duct.
排 滿 anti-Manchu.
排 異 端 to stamp out heterodoxy.
排 遣 to push away; dissipate.
[20] 排 闥 而 入 he pushed open the door and went in.

(b) To open out. To settle.

排·解 to explain; to make peace.
排 難 to arrange difficulties.
排 難 解 紛 to settle difficulties; to clear up misunderstandings.

(c) A raft. Also written 簰.

木 排 a timber raft.
竹 排 a bamboo raft.

簰簿 [2] 4870a

A raft. The first also means the stern of a junk. A shield.

牌[2] A sign-board; a placard;
a tablet. A permit, a war-
4871 rant. A badge. A shield.

牌·位 or 靈 牌 an ancestral tablet.
牌·匾 a sign-board.
牌·坊 or 牌·樓 an honorific arch
  or portal.
牌·子 or 牌·號 a label; a trade-
  mark.
[5]牌照 a commission; a certificate.
牌·盾 a shield.
牌·示 a notice.
牌·票 or 火 票 or 牌·單 a war-
  rant.
牌·長 (*chang*[3]) head of ten households.
[10]出 牌 to issue a warrant.
執照號·數牌 number-plate, as
  on a car or bicycle, etc.
打·牌 to play cards, dominoes,
招·牌 a sign-board. [or *mahjong*.
牙·牌 dominoes.
[15]籐·牌 a shield of rattan.
紅·牌 customs clearance.
紙·牌 playing-cards.
肩·牌 epaulettes.   A.c. 肩章.
骨·牌 dominoes.

辰[4]
4872   To branch off.

派[4]
4873   To depute; to send.

派·他 去 depute him to go.
派 代·表 appoint delegates or representatives.
派·令 deputed.
派 兵 防·堵 to despatch troops to
  defend a certain place.
[5]派·出 to depute; to appoint.
派·司 a pass. (*transliterated*).
派·員 to appoint an officer.
派·委 to depute; to send on official
  duty.
派·定 to decide upon.
[10]派·差 to send runners. (*-ch'ai*[1])
派·撥 to allot; to apportion; to
  detach troops.
派·立 to send and appoint; to depute.
派·籌 to give out tickets.

(a) To branch off. To distribute.
A clan, a party or school of
thought. N.A.

派·別 to divide into branches; a
  category.

派·名 name given to members of
  a clan or family, each generation
  having a particular character
  which is put into the name of
  each person of that generation.
派·頭 the scale of the household
  arrangements.
分·派 to distribute; to allot.
[5]厭 世 派 pessimists.
同·派 of the same generation in
  the clan; of the same school.
和 平 派 peace party.
唯 心 派 idealists.
唯 物 派 materialists.
[10]學 究 派 pedants.
宗·派 a sect or denomination.
對·派 to divide equally.
常 識 派 the common-sense school.
懷 疑 派 sceptics.
[15]折 衷 學 派 eclectic school.
支·派 a branch or clan.
樂 天 派 optimists.
正·派 direct descent; orthodox.
非 國 敎 派 Nonconformists.
↑正·派 serious-minded.

湃[4]
4874   The sound of waves.

澎 湃 the roaring of the billows.

PAN.   (ㄅㄢ)

半[4] Half; to halve.
    Distinguish 平 No. 5303.
4875

半·不道 兒 not half-way there.
半 世 人 middle-aged.
半 中 腰 the waist; in the midst.
半 人 半 鬼 half man, half demon
  —ugly, deformed.
[5]半 信 半 疑 doubtful, suspicious.
半·個 時·辰 half a Chinese hour;
  an hour.
半·個 月 half a month.
半·俸 half-pay.
半 價 票 half-price ticket.
[10]半·允 half-consenting.
半·刻 a little while.
半 吊·子 a half-witted person; a
  scoundrel; a profligate; amateurish.
半 吞 半 吐 to tell a part only;
  to hum and haw.
半 圓 semicircle; half a dollar.
[15]半 塊 錢 half a dollar.
半·壁 on one side.
半 夏 *Penellia tuberifera*—a medicine.
半 夏 稻 late rice.

半·佼 midnight.
[20]半·佼 三 更 midnight.
半 天 half a day—a considerable
  time.
半 子[3] a son-in-law.
半 官 消·息 semi-official news.
半·島 a peninsula.
[25]半 工 half a day's work.
半·影 penumbra.
半·徑 the radius.
半 意·識 or 下 意·識 sub-con-
  sciousness.
半·憨·子 a half-witted person.
[30]半·截 half; half-way.
下 半 截 the lower half.
半 打 half a dozen.
半 推 半 就 between refusal and
  consent.
半 斤 八 兩 half a *catty* and eight
  ounces—six of one and half a
  dozen of the other.
[35]半 新 不 舊 things not new, but
  not regarded as quite old.
半 日 假 half-holiday.
半 日 學·校 half-day schools.
半 旬 half a decade.
半 明 半 暗 half-light, half-obs-
  cure; veiled.
[40]半 晌 half a day; a long time; for
  the most part.
半 月 報 fortnightly periodical.
半 月 形 crescentic.
半 月 瓣 semi-lunar valves.
半 有 半 無 half-visible and half-
  invisible.
[45]半 死 不 活 half-dead.
半 流 動 體 semi-fluid.
半·球 hemisphere.
半 瓶 醋 half a bottle of vinegar
  —a half-educated man.
半 生 不 熟 half-raw; half-cooked.
[50]半·癡·子 or 半 獃·子 an eccentric
  person; half-crazy person.
半 百 fifty—years of age.
半·直 half-priced.
半·稅 half duty—coast trade duty;
  transit dues.
半 空 中 in mid-air.
[55]半·絲·線 silk and cotton mixtures.
半·袴 knickers.
半·規 semi-circular.
半 角 印 (documents) stamped
  with one seal, half on each.
半 語·子 a stammerer.
[60]半·路 half-way.
半·路 夫 妻 a couple married in
  later life.
半·路 棄 妻 to divorce a wife in
  the middle of life's journey.
↑半 公·開 semi-open.

半 身 不 遂 paralysed on one side.
半 身 像 half-length portrait.
65 半 身 入 土 one foot in the grave.
半 載 half a year; a long time.
半 輪 明 月 the quarters of the moon.   [half a life.
半 輩·子 a middle-aged person;
半 頓 半 硬 half soft, half hard —an appearance of severity.
70 半 途 而 廢 to stop half-way; to fail to complete a thing.
半 透 明 translucent.
半 邊 on one side.
半 醒 half-awake·
半 開 化·的 人 half-civilized people.
75 半 開 半 掩 half-open; ajar.
半 面 形 profile.
半 音 semitones.
半 音 階 the chromatic scale.
半 點 half a dot—the least amount; infinitesimal.
80 半 點 鐘 half an hour.
一 半ル一 半ル half-and-half.
大 一 半 one half again as large.
大°半 or 多°半 the greater half; the majority; most probably.
對 半 half-and-half; half each.
85 折 半 broken in half.
↑半 殖 民 地 semi-colony.

伴[4] A comrade, an associate. To keep another company.
4876

伴 君 如 伴 虎 to company with a prince is like companying with a tiger—dangerous.
伴 娘 a maid who accompanies a bride.
伴 婆 female warders or assistants at inquests.
伴 耦 or 伴 侶 or 同 伴 a partner; a companion.
5 伴 讀 to study together.
伴 靈 柩 to keep watch by a corpse the night before burial·
伴 食 a boon companion; an official who neglects his duties for pleasure, etc.
陪 伴ル to accompany a person.

絆[4] A fetter; a loop; a catch. To trip over; to be hampered
4877 by.

絆·住 detained; hindered.
絆 倒[3] to trip and fall.
絆 拘 to restrain; to keep in order.
絆 脚 to trip up; to be hindered.

5 絆 跌 to stumble.
絆 馬 索 a rope for tying a horse's legs when training him to amble.
鈕 絆 loop for a button.

扮[4] To dress; to dress up; to disguise. Dress, style of
4878 dress.

扮·作 to dress up; to feign to be.
扮 古 事 to dress up in the old style—as in processions.
扮 戲 to dress up—as an actor.
扮 攙 閣 to carry dressed-up children in procession.
5 扮 民 核 訪 to dress as a commoner and make inquiries.
扮 演 to dress for a part on the stage.
打·扮 style of dress; to dress up; to adorn.
(a) Read *fen*[4]. To mix. To join.

以 椒 薑 扮 之 seasoned it with pepper and ginger.
於 秦 扮 之 joined in alliance with *Ch'in*.

頒[1] To bestow; to make known. To promulgate.
4879

頒 定 憲 法 to promulgate the constitution.
頒 布 to proclaim; to promulgate.
頒 犒 to give rewards—as to soldiers.
頒 發 or 頒 下 to make known to subordinates; to issue orders.
5 頒 行 to publish by authority.
頒 詔 an imperial proclamation.
頒 諭 to decree.
頒 賜 or 頒 給 to confer upon—by authority.
頒 賞 to give rewards or bounties.
10 頒 送 to confer.

(a) Striped, variegated; u.f. 斑 No. 4890.

頒 斌 promiscuous association.
頒 白 者 a grey-haired man-aged.

(b) Read *fên*[2]. A fish with a large head. Numerous.

有 頒 其 首 —the fish—showing their large heads.

分鳥[1]   The wild pigeon.
4880

鷐 鳩 the wild pigeon.

般[1]   Sort; manner; class; kind.
4881

般 分 to distribute.
般 般 or 百 般 or 萬 般 all kinds; every sort.
般 賜 to bestow.
一 般 exactly alike; the average . . .
一 般 大 the same size.
多 般 many kinds.

(a) Read *p'an*[2]. To go round and round. Pleasure.

般 樂·怠 敖 to give oneself up to pleasure and indolence.
般 遊 to roam for pleasure.
般 還 to go round and round; to go back and forth.

(b) Read *po*[1]. Used in transliterating.

般 若 wisdom—a Buddhist term from the Sanskrit, *prajnâ*.
般 若 湯 from the above—a Buddhist euphemism for wine.

搬[1] To remove; to shift; to transport.
4882

搬 下·來 bring them down.
搬·不 倒[3] a small figure, weighted at the base so that it always comes upright when knocked over.
搬 來 搬 去 to carry hither and thither.
搬·動 to move; to shift.
5 搬 取 to shift; to transfer.
搬 嘴 to wrangle; to carry tales.
搬 場 to remove household goods, etc.(*Wu-dial.*)
搬 場 公 司 removal contractors.
搬 家 or 搬 屋 to move from one dwelling to another.
10 搬 弄 是·非 to carry tales; to make mischief.
搬 徙 to remove from one dwelling to another.
搬 指 a thumb-ring.
搬 撥 to arrange.
搬 東·西 to move things from one place to another.

[15]搬 移 or 搬 挪 to r e m o v e; to transfer.

搬 讓 to vacate.

搬 貨 to remove goods.

搬 送 to transport under escort.

搬 運 糧 餉 to transport a r m y stores.

[20]搬 運 費 carriage-expenses.

搬 遷 to remove; to transfer.

搬 鬪 to egg on to fight.

搬 駁 to overcome in argument; to argue.

瘢[1]
4883 A mark or scar on the skin.

瘢 疹 a sort of carbuncle.

瘢 痕 a scar.

雀 瘢 moles or dark spots on the face; freckles.

蝨[1]
4884 A striped, poisonous fly.

蝨 螯 or 斑 蝨 the Chinese cantharides.

板[3]
4885 Boards, planks. Blocks for printing from. A slab; a plate of iron, etc. Stiff.

板·凳 or 長 凳 a bench; a form.

板 單 a printed form.

板 執 不 通 obstinate.

板 壁 a wooden partition.

[5]板·子 a board; a flat bamboo for beating criminals.

板·子 好 the typography is good.

板 屋 a wooden structure; place of detention.

板 本 book printed from wooden blocks; edition.

板 橋 a wooden bridge; a plank-bridge.

[10]板 滯 not apt to take a hint; formal; precise.

板 片 pieces of planking.

板 牙 or 槽 牙 molars. 「music.

板 眼 or 板 路 a rest or beat in

板 蕩 lawlessness.

[15]板·起·了 面 孔 hardened his countenance.

板 魚 the sole.

古 板 conservative; old fashioned.

地 板 flooring on the ground-floor.

壽 板 boards for a coffin; a coffin.

[20]天 花 板 (wooden)ceiling.

太 板 too precise.

套 板 to print in colours.

木 板 planks; wooden blocks.

呆 板 wooden, stiff, obstinate.

[25]樓 板 upstairs flooring.

石 板 stone slabs; lithography.

老 板 a shop-keeper; head-boat-man—in some places this term is disrespectful, especially in North China.

黑 板 a blackboard.

版[3]
4886 Blocks for printing. Type. An edition. A schedule, a register. Inter. preceding.

版 圖 a plan; a map; population land territory.

版 權 copyright.

版 權 使 用 費 royalties for books.

版 權 所 有 "All rights reserved."

[5]版 法 laws of planetary motion.

版 稅 royalties on books.

版 籍 a census; register of the population; jurisdiction.

版 部 the former Board of Revenue.

出 版 to be published; publication.

[10]活 版 movable types.

石 版 lithography; stone slab.

翻 版 to infringe a copyright.

鋅 版 zinc blocks.

魪[3]
4887 Sole or flounder.

褊[1]
4888 Variegated. Striped. Marbled.

班[1]
4889 A class, a company. Inter. 般 No. 4881.

班 列 to be arranged according to rank.

班·子 or 戲 班 a company of actors.

班 師 to withdraw troops.

班 次 or 班 位 relative r a n k; order.

[5]班 班 rumble of carts; clear and in order.

班 行 (hang[2]) arranged in a row.

班 輩 a colleague; rank; status.

班 門 弄 斧 to wield an axe before *Lu Pan* 魯 班, the god of carpenters—to be conceited.

班 頭[2] a headman; a boss.

[10]一 班 人 a certain class of persons.

上 班 下 班 to go on or come off duty respectively.

大 班 a *Taipan,* head of a firm.

捐 班 class of officials who purchased their rank.

站 班 to stand on duty.

(a) To distribute; to spread.

班 荊 相 對 to treat with courtesy. —*See next entry.*

班 草 or 班 荊 to spread rushes or straw and sit down.

(b) Variegated; of different colours. Inter. next.

班 猫 (or 蝨) cantharides. *See* 蝨 No. 4884.

班 白 者 the grey-headed.

班 色 variegated.

班 駁 of various colours.

班 鳩 the turtle dove; a pigeon.

(c) To leave.

班 馬 之 聲 the neighing of a horse that has been left alone.

(d) Used for transliterating.

班 禪 喇 嘛 Panchan Lama.

斑[1]
4890 Variegated, striped, streaked, mottled.

斑 文 mottled; streaked.

斑 白 grey—of hair.

斑 竹 mottled bamboo. *See* 湘 No. 2565.

斑 色 variegated.

[5]斑 衣 theatrical costumes.

斑 馬 the zebra.

斑 駁 v a r i e g a t e d; of different colours.

斑 駁 之 石 片 coloured tiling, for a floor.

斑 鳩 the turtle-dove; a pigeon.

[10]斑 點 spots.

辦[4]
4891 To manage; to do business; to transact; to do; to provide.
Distinguish 辨 No. 5240.

辦 不 來 cannot be obtained; cannot be done; impracticable.

辦 不 到 unable to accomplish; impracticable.

辦 事 to manage an affair; to transact business. ⌠ clerk.

辦 事 員 the staff of a concern; a

⁵**辦 事 整 齊** to manage an affair in a proper manner; to arrange in proper order.

辦 事 章·程 by-laws.

辦 交·涉 to negotiate.

辦 公·事 to transact official business.

辦 公 處 an office.

¹⁰**辦 公 廳** place for transaction of public business.

辦 報 to run a newspaper.

辦 妥 to manage satisfactorily.

辦 後 事 to prepare a body for the coffin.

辦·得 不 好 badly managed; muddled the business.

¹⁵**辦·得 好** well managed.

辦·得 妥·當 well arranged; satisfactorily managed.

辦 案 to deal with lawsuits, etc.

辦 法 method of transacting the business; the way to manage; the conditions.

辦 理 to undertake; to do.

²⁰**辦 生·日** to celebrate a birthday.

辦 結 to settle a case.

辦 罪 to punish.

辦 貨 to buy or import goods.

辦 賑 to give relief—in famine, etc.

²⁵**辦 酒** to prepare a feast.

代 辦 to act in place of.

備 辦 to provide; to make ready.

創 辦 to promote—a company or business; to buy for use.

查 辦 make inquiries and take action accordingly.

瓣⁴ A division; a section—as of an orange, etc. Petal of a
4892 flower. The pulp of melons, etc.

瓣 香 to burn a stick of incense in honour of a person—used to indicate extreme desire to follow the ways of another.

花 瓣 petals.

萱 瓣 the two halves of a bean.

(a) From the above, it is used for valves.

瓣 膜 valves of the heart.

心 臟 瓣 膜 病 valvular disease of the heart.

滑 瓣 a slide-valve.

P'AN.　　(ㄆㄢ)

判⁴ To cut in two. To divide. To judge; to decide.
4893

判 例 legal precedents.

判 別 to distinguish; to divide.

判 牛 to divide in halves.

判 合 to join; to separate and unite.

⁵**判 官** ancient term for a judge; a judge in Hades.

判 押 to sentence to imprisonment.

判·斷 or **判 定** to decide; to judge; to give judgement.

判·斷 力 powers of jurisdiction.

判 書 a record of decisions.

¹⁰**判 決** a judgement; a decision.

判 決 公 平 an equitable judgement.

判·給·他 命 運 to settle his fate.

判 若 difference between.

判 苔 兩 人 the difference between the two men.

¹⁵**判 若 天 淵** the difference is as great as that between the heavens and the depths.

判 袂 to part; to separate.

判 語 or **判 言** or **判 詞** a sentence; a judgement.

審 判 to judge.

裁 判 to judge; to arbitrate.

拌⁴ To separate; to throw away. Often read *pan*⁴.
4894

拌 命 to throw away one's life.

拌 石 to throw a stone.

把 他 拌·了 throw it away; discard it.

(a) Read *pan*⁴. To mix.

拌·上 草 料 to mix fodder and beans, etc.

拌 勻 to mix properly.

拌 嘴 to wrangle; bickering.

拌 水 to mix water with the fodder.

拌 麩·子 to mix bran in with the fodder.

泮⁴ A semi-circular pool within the precincts of a former
4895 provincial college. The chief college of an ancient State. Pool in a Confucian temple.

泮 宮 the outermost of the three courts in a Confucian temple.

泮 池 the pool in the Confucian temple.

遊 泮 池 to cross the (above) pool—to take the first degree under the former system.

(a) To melt. To disperse.

迨 冰 未 泮 before the ice is melted.

(b) A shore, a bank. Inter. next.

泮 汗 apparently boundless expanse of water.

隰 則 有 泮 the marsh has its banks.

畔⁴ A path dividing fields; a side-walk; a bank.
4896 Also read *pan*⁴.

畔 岸 a bank; a boundary.

畔 道 a path by the side of the road. *See below*—A.4.

河 畔 the bank of a river.

(a) To leave; to rebel; to reject. To overstep a boundary; to transgress.

畔 官 離 次 to leave one's official post.

畔 援 —to follow the fancy—rejecting this and holding to that.

畔 約 to break an agreement.

畔 道 to deviate from the true path. *See above*—2.

叛⁴ To rebel; to revolt.
4897

叛 亂 rebellion.

叛 亂 無 統 no connection in their rebellions.

叛 臣 a rebellious minister.

叛 賊 or **叛 匪** rebels.

⁵**叛 逆** to revolt.

背 叛 to revolt.

謀 叛 to plot sedition.

(a) Brilliant, shining.

環 北 極 叛 赫 ..... as they circle the North Pole in their brilliance.....

拚[4] **To disregard; to reject.** Also read *p'in*[1]. Wrongly 4898 used for 抨 No. 4894.

拚去 or 拚棄 or 拚除 to reject.
拚命 to disregard life; to do a thing at the risk of one's life.
拚財 to make rash speculations.

(a) Read *p'in*[1]. Inter. 拼 No. 5294—A.

拼命 to risk one's life.
拼爛 to act recklessly; to venture.

(b) Read *pien*[4]. Inter. 抃 No. 5221. **To tap. To lay the hand on.**

歌拚 singing and clapping the hands.

(c) Read *fên*[4]. **To sweep.**

拚箕 a dust basket.
掃席前曰拚 to sweep before the mats—whereon they sat—was called *fên*.

(d) Read *fan*[1]. Inter. 翻 No. 1796. **To turn over.**

拚飛 tumbling in flight as a tumbler-pigeon.

攀 扳 [1]　**To drag down; to seize. To pull. To hold to.**
4899

攀下來 pull it down.
攀戀 to seize the carriage of an official who is popular, in order to detain him.
攀扶 to hold on for support.
攀桂 to pluck the cassia—to take the second degree under the former system; to take a wife.
[5]攀留 to detain—as a friend.
攀索 to heave on a rope.
攀轅臥轍 to hold the shafts of the carriage and lie down in the ruts—manifesting unwillingness to allow a popular magistrate to depart.

(a) **To climb up; to clamber.**

攀不起 cannot afford to aspire—to such acquaintances.
攀援 to clamber along; to climb up; to climb by sycophancy.

攀援出坎 he climbed out of the pit.
攀登 to climb; to scramble up.
[5]攀禽 climbing-birds—the woodpecker, etc.
攀緣 to climb up.
攀緣莖 stems of climbing-plants.
攀親 to aspire to marriage with.
攀鞍上馬 climbed into the saddle.
[10]攀龍附鳳 to mount the dragon and cleave to the phœnix—to follow a famous leader in order to establish oneself.

(b) **To involve; to implicate.**

攀扯 or 攀累 to involve; to implicate.
供攀 to involve another in giving evidence.

(c) Read *pan*[1]. **To take away; to pull out.**

攀下來了 pulled out—of teeth, etc.
攀不動 cannot pull it out—of a tooth, etc.
攀弓 to draw a bow.

襻 [4]　**A loop. A belt or band.**
4900

襻帶 a girdle.

媻 [2]　**To move.**
4901

媻姍孛窣 to crawl slowly forward on hands and knees.
媻媻 going to and fro.

(a) Read *p'o*[2]. A form of 婆 No. 5347. **An old woman. Extravagant**

(b) **Used for foreign sounds.**

媻藪天 a Buddhist name for the Hindu *Vishnu*.

槃 [2]　**A tray; a kind of dumb-waiter. Inter. next.**
4902

槃匜 a washing-bowl.
少者奉槃 the younger ones will bring in the stand for the washing-bowl.
托槃 a tray.

(a) A hut for retirement—thus:—happiness.

考槃在澗 completed his happiness (i.e., his hut for quiet seclusion) on the *Chien*.

(b) **To stop. To coil up.** Inter. next.

槃停 to stop and go no farther.
槃旋 to go round; hesitating; circumlocution.
槃礴 to sit cross-legged.
槃錯 embarrassment.

盤 [2]　**A plate, a dish, a tub for bathing, a vessel. A tray.**
4903

盤子 a dish; a plate; a tray.
盤子碗 "plates and dishes."
盤子秤 scales with pans.
盤子球 billiards. = 彈子.
[5]盤盂 a basin or bowl.
盤銘 inscription engraved on a bath-tub.
和盤托出 put the vessels together and carry them out—tell the whole story; give the details.
水晶盤 a crystal bowl—poetical for the Yangtze River.
算盤 the abacus.
[10]銅盤 a brass bowl; a lamp.

(a) **To interrogate. To examine. To estimate.**

盤倒 to upset a person's story by cross-examination.
盤問 to interrogate officially.
盤庫 to audit the treasury.
盤查 to examine judicially; to search out.
[5]盤查奸究 to interrogate bad characters.
盤算 to make a mental calculation.
盤訪 to examine official balances of accounts.
盤詰 to interrogate closely.
盤貨 to take stock.
[10]盤賬 to examine the account; to make an audit.

(b) **To coil up. To wriggle. To turn, as a wheel. A pulley. To wind around.**

盤上 to coil up; to wind up.
盤屈 coiled like a snake.
盤旋 uncertain; hesitating; roundabout.

盤 旋 交 互 interlaced; interlocked.

⁵盤 旋 竹 林 路 to go round by the bamboo grove.

盤 曲 coiled like a snake.

盤 桓 to take relaxation; to stroll about; undecided; hesitating.

盤 根 錯 節 twisted roots and gnarled branches.

盤 槓·子 to perform on the horizontal bar.

¹⁰盤 渦 a whirlpool. (-kang⁴-)

盤 空 to wheel in the air—as birds.

盤 紆 winding; circuitous.

盤 繞 to wind round.

盤 繞 機 器 winding-apparatus.

¹⁵盤 膝 or 盤 脚 to sit with the legs crossed.

盤 螭 a coiled dragon.

盤 蠅 flies circling round.

盤·起 辮·子 to coil the queue round the head.

盤 踞 to squat with the legs doubled under.

²⁰盤 踞 山 谷 to hold a strong position; to maintain a hold on territory.

盤 身 to coil oneself up.

盤 輪 a pulley—for machinery.

兩 盍 盤 輪 a split pulley.

死 皮 帶 盤 a fast pulley.

²⁵活 皮 帶 盤 a loose pulley.

階 級 皮 帶 盤 a cone-pulley for changing speeds.

盤 辟 coiled; perverse.

盤 遊 to stroll around for pleasure.

盤 道 a winding road.

³⁰盤 錯 wound around—embarrassed; in misfortune.

盤 香 coiled incense.

(c) Expenses. Costs. The market rate.

盤·子 the bottom—the market rate.

盤 川 travelling-expenses.

盤 纏 expenses for the road.

盤°費 or 盤 資 travelling-expenses.

⁵盤 錢 travelling-expenses.

和 盤 current prices.

大 放 盤 great reduction in prices; clearing-sale.

成 盤 a completed transaction.

收 盤 to wind up accounts; to close the books.

¹⁰錢 盤 the money-market.

開 盤 to open the market.

(d) To transfer. To tranship.

盤 店 to transfer a business.

盤 運 to remove; to tranship; to convey.

盤 駁 to tranship.

交 盤 to transfer.

召 盤 to transfer a business.

(e) To hamper; to involve—from the meaning under B.

盤 剝 to fleece; to involve a person in financial difficulties.

盤 剝 重 利 exorbitant usury.

盤 弄 to harass; to squeeze; to extort.

(f) A name.

盤 古 氏 P'an Ku—a legendary being, said to have been evolved from chaos; in dying he gave birth to the universe. The accounts vary.

(g) u.f. next. Firm. A rock.

盤 石 a great rock.

磐²   A rock; firm, stable.
4904

磐 桓 hesitating. See No. 4903—B.7.

磐 牙 to league together, as bandits.

磐 石 a great rock; fig., stable, enduring.

磐 石 之 安 a stable peace—like that of a great rock.

磐 礴 vast; imposing; extensive.

蹩 蹣²   To bend the feet under one.
4905

蹩·着 腿 to sit with the legs crossed.

蹩 膝 而 坐 to sit cross-legged.

盼⁴   The black and white of the eye clearly defined. To gaze. To hope for; to expect.
4906   Distinguish 盻 No. 2415.

盼 切 to hope for anxiously.

盼 慕 to look for; to desire.

盼·望 or 盼 念 or 盼 想 to long for; to hope for.

盼 睞 fondly gazing at.

⁵多 蒙 盼 睞 I am greatly indebted for your favours.

盼 禱 to entreat.

盼 詣 to wait for one's coming.

盼 雨 or 望 雨 hoping for rain.

美 目 盼 兮 How beautiful her eyes, so clearly defined!

轉 盼 to glance at; to turn the eyes.

¹⁰顧 盼 to watch for.

潘¹   An affluent of the River Han. Water in which rice
4907   has been washed.

磻²   A tributary of the River Wei in Shensi.
4908

蟠²   To coil; to curl round. Curling, encircling.
4909   Inter. 盤 No. 4903—B.

蟠 屈 to coil like a snake.

蟠 據 to encroach upon; to occupy.

蟠 木 a large, twisted tree.

蟠 桃 the flat peach.

⁵蟠 桃 會 a festival held on the 3rd of the 3rd lunar month in honour of the goddess 西 王 母.

蟠 繞 to encircle; spirally.

蟠 踞 to occupy—as a squatter; to sit cross-legged.

極 乎 天 而 蟠 乎 地 they reach to the height of heaven and embrace the earth—ceremonies and musical rites.

(a) Read fan². Wood-lice; insects found in damp places.

PANG.   (夊ㄤ)

邦¹   A State; a country; a nation.
4910

邦 交 friendly intercourse between nations.

邦 人 the people; compatriots.

邦 其 傾 矣 the country is overthrown.

邦 君 ruler of a nation.

⁵邦 國 States; nations.

邦 基 foundation of the State.

邦 家 the State; the nation.

邦 有 道 不 廢 when the country is well governed he is not out of office.

邦 有 道 則 見 (*hsien*⁴) a State prospers by observing righteousness.

¹⁰邦 有 道 穀 to set the heart upon emoluments when the country is well governed.

邦 有 道 貧 且 賤 焉 恥 也 poverty and a mean position are a shame in a well-governed State.

邦 無 道 富 且 貴 焉 恥 也 wealth and honour are a shame in a badly-governed State.

邦 畿 the imperial domain.

邦 禁 the prohibitions of a State.

¹⁵友 邦 a friendly power.

聯 邦 united States.

萬 邦 all nations.

鄰 邦 neighbouring States.

捄¹ To propel a boat. To beat.
4911

梆¹ A watchman's rattle.
4912

梆·子 or 更 梆 a watchman's rattle.

梆·子 腔 the Shensi style of dramatic singing.

梆 皷 a kettle-drum.

綁³ To bind; to tie.
4913

綁·上 to bind.

綁·去 carried away captive.

綁 票 a person held for ransom by brigands; to seize for ransom.

綁 票 匪 brigands.

⁵綁 緊 or 綁 結·實 tie it tightly.

綁 縛 手 足 bound hand and foot.

綁 腿·子(women's) leggings or gaiters.

綁 赴 市 曹 bind him and take him to the execution ground.

綁·起·來 to tie up.

帮
幇¹
幫
4914

To help. To defend.

帮 一 句 話 say a word in favour of.

帮 佐 to help; to assist.

帮·助 to assist; to lend a hand.

帮 口 one who speaks for another.

⁵帮 嘴 to help in an altercation.

帮 夥 assistant in a shop.

帮 套 an extra animal in a team.

帮 工 an assistant; to assist.

帮 忙 to help; to give assistance.

¹⁰帮 手 a helper; one who lends a hand.

帮 扶 to assist; to lend a hand; to aid.

帮 補 or 帮 貼 or 帮 錢 to eke out; to render monetary assistance.

帮 襯 to patronize; to assist.

帮 護 to help and protect.

¹⁵帮 辦 to assist in managing; a sub-manager.

相 帮 mutual help.

↑帮 兇 an accomplice in a crime.

(a) N.A. for a class, a group, a fleet, etc.

帮 腔 a chorus; a choir.

一 帮 船 a fleet of boats.

大 帮 or 貨 帮 a caravan.

頭 帮 first-class—as tea.

(b) A class, a group, a fraternity.

榜³ A list of successful candidates in the examinations. A placard.
4915

榜·上 無 名 or 落 榜 to fail in an examination.

名 榜 What is your name?—to a literary man.

榜 文 a notice; a placard.

榜 眼 the "eye of the list"—a graduate who came out second on the list at the former palace examination 殿 試.

⁵榜 示 to make a public notification.

榜 額 a tablet with a horizontal inscription.

同 榜 fellow-graduates.

開 榜 to publish the list of successful graduates.

(a) An example—from the above.

榜 樣 an example; a pattern.

(b) Read *pêng*⁴. To row a boat.

榜 人 a boatman.

榜 女 boat-women

榜 歌 songs of the boatmen.

(c) Read *pêng*¹. To beat.

榜 掠 to beat; to flog.

牓³ A tablet; a register.
4916

磅⁴ The noise of stones crashing. Also read *p'ang*².
4917

磅 唐 to occupy great space; extensive.

磅 礡 extensive; filling everywhere.

(a) Read *pang*⁴. A pound avoirdupois, in imitation of the sound. See 鎊 No. 4920.

磅 秤 a scale which gives the weight in avoirdupois.

過 磅 to be weighed. (A.p. -*pêng*⁴)

艕⁴ Two boats fastened side by side.
4918

艕 人 boatmen. See 榜 No. 4915-B.

謗⁴ To speak ill of; to detract, to slander.
4919

謗 佛 to vilify Buddha.

謗 訕 to backbite; to slander.

謗 是 非 to talk of the faults of others; to defame.

謗 書 a scurrilous letter; a defamatory publication.

⁵謗 木 See 誹 No. 1833-3. A board set up by the wayside on which the people could record the errors in the public administration.

謗 讟 or 毀 謗 to defame; to slander.

鎊² To scrape. To level.
4920

鎊 地 to rake the soil level. (*p'ang*³)

(a) Read *pang*⁴. A pound sterling, in imitation of the sound. See 磅 No. 4917.

鎊 虧 loss on sterling exchange, as in a loan.

鎊 金 or 金 鎊 pounds sterling.
鎊 傺 gain on sterling exchange, as in loans, etc.

鞺[1] The lining of a shoe; the vamp or upper part of a shoe or boot.
4921

髈[3] Defined as the pelvis, the hip-bone; now used for the humerus.
4922   Inter. 膀 No. 4931.

髈 臂 shoulders and arms—assistance.
肩 髈 the shoulder.

棒[4] Cudgels. A staff, a stick. The "bang" of a gun.
4923

棒·他 出 drive him out with a stick.
棒 喝 to arouse a person from his folly. See 當 No. 6087-B.27.
棒·子 a drumstick; a cudgel. Indian corn.
棒·子 麵 corn-meal.
[5]棒 槌 a washerman's baton.
棒 球[2] baseball.
棒 頭[2]出 孝 子[3] from the end of the stick comes the filial son."

蚌[4]
蜯   Oysters; mussels. Also read pêng[3].
4924

蚌 胎 the conception of an oyster —a pearl, anciently believed to be thus produced.
蚌 蛤 an oyster.

P'ANG.   (ㄆㄤ)

乒[1] Used for the sound.
4925

乒 乓 ping-pong.

旁[2] By the side of. Near. Other. Inter. next.
4926

旁○人 a bystander; an outsider.
旁 出 diverging.
旁 午 in confusion; crosswise; transverse; coming and going; multifarious.

使 者 旁 午 the attendants went in different directions.
[5]旁 坐 implication; punishment of the family members and relatives of a criminal.
旁 妻 a concubine.
旁 眷 father's brothers.
旁 岔 的 話 a digression; irrelevant talk.
旁 唐 extensive; on a large scale.
[10]旁 引 collateral evidence.
旁 招 俊 乂 to seek for able men.
旁 批 marginal notes.
旁 方 by the side of.
旁 旁 in constant motion—as a string of animals.
[15]旁 死 魄 the 2nd day of the moon. See 既 No. 453—A.8-10 and 魄 No. 4988—B.
旁 求 俊 彥 to look around for men of refinement.
旁 燭 無 疆 shedding unlimited lustre all around.
旁 牌 a shield.
旁·的 不 要 嗎 do you want nothing else?
[20]旁 皇 to wander around irresolute; several other pairs of similar-sounding characters are thus used.
旁 眛 a sidelong glance.
旁 礴 to embrace in one; to fill immensity; extensive; on a grand scale; to spread far and wide.
旁 系 collateral branch—of a family. [audit (a course).
旁 聽 a visitor at a meeting; to
[25]旁 聽 席 visitors' seats.
旁 聽 權 right to visit and listen, but having no power to speak or to vote.
旁 聽 生 pupils not regularly enrolled as part of the class.
旁 舍 a small side-room.
旁 若 無 人 as if there was nobody near—proud.
[30]旁 行 to traverse; horizontal writing.
旁 觀 a looker-on; to look on.
旁 觀 態 度 attitude of non-interference.
旁 觀 者 清 the mind of the on-looker is clear.
旁 言 gossip.
[35]旁 訓 running commentary, notes, etc., in a book.
旁 證 circumstantial evidence.

旁 路 a side-walk; a branch-road.
旁 近 adjoining; near.
旁 通 running into from the side—as a road; a by-way.
[40]旁 邊 by the side of; the side.
旁 門 a side-door.
旁 門 左 道 heterodox paths.
旁 題 a side issue.
旁 魄 to spread far and wide; extensive; on a grand scale. See above—22. /

(a) Read pang[4]. Near to. Inter. next—A.

旁 明 near dawn.
旁 晚 near evening.

傍[2] By the side of; the side. To depend on. Inter. preceding.
4927

傍 不 相 干 nothing to do with anyone else.
傍 人 a bystander; to depend on a person.
傍 徨 walking back and forth; irresolute. See 旁 No. 4926-20.
傍 立 standing by the side.
[5]傍 系 collateral descent.
傍·着 to lean on. (pang[4]-)
傍 處 another neighbourhood or place.
傍 邊·的 人 a bystander.
近 傍 approximating to.

(a) Read pang[4]. Near to.

傍 人 門 戶 to follow in the steps of, as a disciple.
傍 明 near dawn.
傍 晚 near evening.

(b) Read pêng[1]. Coming and going; restless.

王 事 傍 傍 the king's affairs do not permit of any rest.

謗[3] To boast. To speak figuratively.
4928

謗 喩 sound of singing.
亂 謗 wild exaggeration.

鎊[2] To walk alongside of. Inter. 傍 No. 4927.
4929   Read p'ang[2]. Perturbed, fearful. Similar to 彷 No. 1805—A.

徬徨無計 agitated, not knowing what to do.

滂² Heavy rain.
4930

滂沛 or 滂沱 大雨 copious rains.
滂洋 extensive; vast.
滂浡 convulsed; agitated.

膀² The groin; the loins. Also read pang³, and used
4931 for the shoulders and upper arm. See 髈 No. 4922.

膀·子 the upper arm. (pang³-)
膀胱 the bladder.
膀胱炎 inflammation of the bladder.
膀胠 the lower ribs.

螃² A crab.
4932

螃·蟹 the swimming-crab.

胮
胖²　To swell.
4933

胮·不起來 it will not swell.
胮肛 to swell—as with a tumour, etc.
胮脹 dropsical.
胮腫 to swell up.

逄² A surname.
4934

厖² A high house. Confused.
4935

厖眉皓髮 shaggy eyebrows and hoary head—aged.
厖錯 in disorder—used of the times.
厖雜 disorderly; confused; not observing proper distinctions.

(a) Read lung². Great. Fat. Full.

四牡厖厖 the four stallions were fat and sleek.
湛恩厖洪 under very great obligations; great grace and favour.

胖⁴　Fat, stout. In comfort.
4936

胖·子 a fat person.
胖病 obesity.
肥胖 corpulent.

(a) Read p'an⁴. Half of a carcase. The meat from the ribs.

PAO.　(ㄅㄠ)

包
勹
4937
¹ A parcel. To wrap; to include.
Radical 20.
(2nd form only). National Phonetic letter for p, written ㄅ.

包·上 wrap it up.
包元 to include them all.
包件 parcels—in the mails.
包·含 or 包·涵 to contain; enclosed; to be lenient; to make allowances for; to endure wrong; magnanimous; to bear with patience.
⁵包含萬有 embracing all things.
包圍 hemmed in; surrounded; blockaded.
包圍敵翼 to execute a flanking movement.
包·在裏·面 included in.
包·子 a meat-patty or dumpling.
¹⁰包封 to wrap up and seal.
包得廣 wide; embracing.
包括下文 it includes the following text.
包滿·着 conceited.
包皮 the wrapper or packing of merchandise; tare; the prepuce.
¹⁵包瞞 to conceal from.
包種茶 Powchong tea.
包米 or 包穀 maize or Indian corn.
包總 included; contained in.
包羅 to wrap up; to monopolize.
²⁰包羅萬象 all-embracing—said of a man with wide learning.
包脚 to bind the feet.
包荒 broad-minded; liberal.
包莊 a warehouse.
包著帕·子 wrapped in a napkin.
²⁵包藏 to conceal; to store up.
包藏禍心 to hide a malicious intent under a fair countenance.
包衣 the placenta.
包·袱 a small cloth-wrapper.
包裹 to wrap up; a parcel.

---

³⁰包·起·來 to wrap up.
包金 to gild; to plate.
包·頭 a fillet; a headband.
包頭·的 actors who impersonate women.

(a) To undertake; to contract; to manage; to guarantee.

包來回 will be exchanged if not satisfactory.
包償 to guarantee compensation.
包含徧覆 to be lenient to all.
包妓 a kept mistress.
⁵包完銀糧 to farm or contract for the payment of the land-tax.
包定 to engage—as a seat, etc.
包容 to be patient with; to make allowance for.
包工制 the piece-work system.
包工料 to contract for labour and materials.
¹⁰包工活 contract-work.
包席館 a large restaurant which contracts for feasts.
包庇 to screen; to harbour; to countenance.
包廂 stalls or boxes in a theatre.
包修 to guarantee repairs.
¹⁵包房間 to engage a room.
包抽 to be responsible for a certain fixed sum.
包探 or 包打·聽 detectives.
包換 to guarantee to change—unsuitable goods.
包攬 to take the responsibility of; to monopolize.
²⁰包攬詞訟 to conduct a lawsuit.
包攬閒事 to act as a busy-body; to meddle in other people's business.
包月車 cart or vehicle, ricksha, etc., engaged by the month.
包治 to guarantee a cure.
包牌·子 to monopolize the sale of certain brands.
²⁵包用 guaranteed suitable.
包·管 to guarantee that....
包·管無事 to guarantee that there will be no trouble.
包船 to engage a boat for one's own use.
包賠 guarantee to make good.
³⁰包車 a private vehicle or ricksha; a cart engaged for one's own use. See 黃 No. 2297-4.
包辦 or 承包 to undertake.
包辦酒席 to contract for feasts.
包退回換 guarantee to exchange if returned as unsuitable.

包 醫 guarantee a cure.
35 包 銷 monopoly of sales.
包 領 to go security for a person.
包 飯 to contract to supply food at a fixed price ; to board.
包 餼 to contract for the feeding of animals.

抱 4 To embrace; to enfold; to carry in the arms:—thus, to
4938 harbour; to cherish. To brood over eggs.

抱 一 to attend to the important matter.　⌈wrong.
抱 不 平 to bear a grudge for a
↓ 打 抱 不 平 to take up the cudgels against an injustice.
抱·住 to embrace; enfolded.
　雙 手 抱·住 to embrace with both arms.
5 抱 佛 脚 to clasp the feet of Buddha---when in distress—used to illustrate getting into difficulties through lack of due preparation, and then seeking help at the critical moment.
抱 其 弓 與 龍 顂 號 grasped the bow of the emperor and the dragon's whiskers and wept.
抱 冰 to cherish grievances and embitter oneself, as if carrying ice in the bosom.
抱·出·來 to hatch out.
抱 厦 small out-buildings encircling a larger one.
10 抱 告 or 抱 呈 to present a petition for another.
抱 告 人 one who pleads for the plaintiff; a proxy in a suit.
抱 娃·子 to nurse a baby.(S.mand.)
抱 孩·子 to nurse a child.
抱 屈 to bear a grudge against.
15 抱 屈 含 冤 to cherish wrongs.
抱 忌 bigotry.
抱 念 甚 深 to cherish deeply.
抱·怨 or 抱 恨 to bear a grudge against.
抱 恨 終 身 I shall hate him as long as I live.
20 抱 悲 觀 to be pessimistic.
抱 感 to cherish deep feelings.
抱 愧 ashamed; to feel ashamed.
抱 憾 to deplore.
抱 憾 終 身 he regretted it all his life.
25 抱 承 to act on behalf of.
抱 攬 to pick up in the arms; to

monopolize.　See 包 No. 4937-A.19.
抱 於 懷 中 folded to his bosom; to cherish; to harbour in the mind.
抱 柱 to keep one's promise faithfully.
抱 柱 對 wooden tablets, with couplets written or engraved on them, curved so as to fit the pillars.
30 抱 樂 觀 to be optimistic.
抱 樸 to preserve one's natural state of purity—free from passions and desires.
抱 歉 to deplore; to be deficient; to regret; to feel sorry.
抱 殘 守 缺 to cherish broken and worn -out things—to be fond of antiquity.
抱 牘 to receive a letter.
35 抱 牽 obstinate.
抱 病 or 抱 恙 sick; to be ill.
抱 義 to maintain the right; to cherish righteousness.
抱 罪 to be conscious of guilt; to apologize.
抱 膝 to nurse the knees.
40 抱·著 embraced; embracing.
抱 薪 救 火 to add fuel to a fire—when trying to put it out.
抱 蛋 to brood over eggs.
抱 負 one's aims and ambitions.
抱 負 不 凡 a genius; a clever man.
45 抱 關 to guard or hold the gates.
抱 頭² 痛 哭 to hold the head and weep bitterly.
抱 頭² 鼠 竄 to hold the head and skulk away in shame.
抱 養 to adopt and bring up.
合 抱 an armful.
50 挾 抱 to hold under the arms.

菢
勹
毲
4939
To incubate; to brood; to hatch.

菢 窩 to sit on a nest.
菢 蛋 to hatch eggs.

胞 ¹
4940
The womb. A bladder.

胞 兄 or 胞 弟 brothers by the same mother.
胞 姪 one's own brother's sons.
胞 胎 the womb.
胞 衣 the placenta=衣 胞
5 同 胞 brothers by the same mother ; fellow-countrymen.
細 胞 cells.

苞 ¹
4941
The husk of grain. A kind of rush.

苞 屨 mourning-sandals of straw.
苞 稂 bushy grasses.
苞 苴 presents of food ; bribes ; to wrap up.
苞 茅 sedge.
苞 蟲 a caterpillar which is injurious to rice-plants.

(a) Firm; enduring.

苞 桑 firmly bound to the mulberry-tree—used figuratively of enduring strength.
如 竹 苞 矣 firmly bound together like the roots of bamboos.

(b) Springing of plants from seed. To burst forth.

苞 符 the mystic diagrams—from the next.
天 苞 地 符 the plan from the Yellow River and the book from the River Lo.　See 河 No. 2111-10.
開 苞 to blossom; to deflorate.

鉋
刨
4942
A plane. To plane; to level off.

鉋 削 to correct; to polish—as a literary style.
鉋 子 a plane; a curry-comb.
鉋 木 to plane wood.
鉋 煙 to plane tobacco into fine shreds.
鉋°花 or 鉋 柴 shavings.

(a) Read p'ao². To deduct. To dig.

鉋·出·來 to dig out.
鉋 去 零 頭² discard the fractional amount—the odd cents.
鉋 地 to dig the ground.

鉋 坑 to excavate a hole.
⁵鉋 挖 to excavate.
鉋 根 問 底 to ferret out the details.
鉋 窖 to dig a cellar or vault.

飽³ To eat to the full. Satisfied.
4943

飽 之 則 颺 不 飽 則 噬 fed, they will fly; not full, they will bite.
飽 和 溶 液 saturated solution.
飽 和 蒸 氣 saturated steam.
飽 和 點 point of saturation. (chem.).
⁵飽 學 鴻 儒 a well-read, learned man.
飽 帆 a full sail.
飽 德 filled with your goodness—phrase used on a card sent after dinner—Thanks!
飽 暖 well-fed and well-clad.
飽 暖 思 淫 慾 lewd thoughts arise from fullness of food and the comfort of warm clothing, i.e., easy living.
¹⁰飽 滿 full—as a face; inclusive; complete.
飽 滿 子³粒 well-filled seeds.
飽 滿 豐 盈 fully satisfied.
飽 看 一 回 to take a good look at.
飽 脹 swollen; a sense of distension.
¹⁵飽 足 fully satisfied.
飽 食 a hearty meal.
飽 飯 to eat to repletion.
飽 飫 satisfied with food; satiated.
飽 食 終 日 eating to the full every day.
²⁰發 飽 flatulence after eating

鮑⁴ Dried fish; pickled or salted fish.
4944

鮑 人 a tanner.
鮑 魚 shell-fish; dried fish; the abalone.

齙² Projecting teeth.
4945

保³ To protect. A guardian.
4946

保·佑 to protect; to guard.

保 全 to preserve intact.
保 全 外 貌 to save appearances.
保 全 榮 譽 to preserve intact one's good reputation.
⁵保 全 領 土 to preserve territorial integrity.
保 和 會 Universal Peace Society.
保 存 to preserve; to maintain; to conserve.
↓保 守 主 義 conservatism.
保 存 古 蹟 to preserve ancient relics and ruins.
¹⁰保 存 國 粹 preserve national treasures.
保 存 生 命 to preserve one's life.
保 安 to preserve peace and safety.
保 安 刀 片 safety-razor blade.
保 安 手 段 active measures for preserving public safety.
¹⁵保 安 林 conservation of forests.
保 安 燈 safety-lamp.
保 安 警 察 police for the preservation of safety.
保 安 針 safety-pin.
保 安 隊 local volunteers.
²⁰保 守 to maintain; to keep watch over.
保 守 國 權 preserve national rights.
保 守 態·度 a conservative attitude.
保 守 黨 Conservative Party.
保 守 黨 政 府 maintain the Nationalist-Party government.
²⁵保 庇 to protect; to guard.
保 持 hold fast; keep intact. See below A.2.
保 持 秩 序 to maintain order.
保 標·的 escorts; guards to convoy travellers. See below—50.
保 甲 局 the tithing-office—an office charged with the maintenance of public order.
³⁰保 眞 to care for the divine element within one.
保·祐 to bless; to care for.
保 種 preservation of the race.
保 管 to keep safely—as valuables which have been entrusted.
保 菌 人 (or 動 物) carriers—of disease.
³⁵保 衛 to protect; to guard.
保 衛 團 local militia.
保·護 to protect.
保·護 不 力 ineffectual protection.
保·護 人 a guardian.
⁴⁰保·護 作 用 protective functions.
保·護 國 a protected country.
保·護 治 安 to preserve the peace.

保·護 炮 擊 protective barrage.
保·護 狀 Habeus Corpus.
⁴⁵保·護 稅 or 保·護 制·度 protective tariff.
保·護 色 protective colouring.
保·護 貿 易 protection of trade and commerce.
保·護 金 bounties.
保·護 鳥 protected birds.
⁵⁰保 鏢 armed escort for a bank-messenger, etc. See above—28.
保 障 a defence; to defend the frontiers; a capable minister.
保 障 和 平 計 plans for the preservation of peace.
保 障 工 人 之 生 活 safeguard the livelihood of the workers.
保 障 物 defensive weapons.
⁵⁵保 障 農 民 利 益 safeguard the interests of the farmers.

(a) To nourish; to care for.

保 姆 (or 母) a kindergarten teacher; a governess.
保 持 康 健 to maintain the health.
保 育 to nourish and care for.
保 重 保 重 take care of yourself—said in parting.
⁵保 重 身 體 to take care of the health.
保 養 to nourish.
保 養 所 a sanatorium.

(b) To guarantee. To go bail or security for. To insure.

保·不 住 or 保·不 定 unable to protect or to answer for.
保·人 a guarantor; one who goes bail.
保 債 to be security for a debt.
保 充 to guarantee a person as fit for a certain position.
⁵保 其 無 罪 guarantee his innocence.
保·出·來 to bail out—of custody.
保 升 to promote; to recommend.
保 商 security merchants; insurance business.
保 固 限 time-limit within which a contractor guarantees a building.
¹⁰保 奏 to recommend to the throne—for reward.
保 家 a surety; one who goes bail for another.
保 山 a security; a guarantee.

保 師 a surety for candidates at a public examination.

保 息 premium.

[15] 保 惠 師 The Comforter. Paraclete.

保 戶 the insured.

保 條•子 a bond; a guarantee.

保 正 or 保 長 (*chang*[3]) the headman of a ward.

保 狀 a bond; a guarantee.

[20] 保 留 to retain—as officials; to reserve—as a discussion.

意 中 保 留 mental reservation.

保 留 一 切 權 利 "all rights reserved."

保 留 事 項 reserved subjects.

保 留 地 a reservation—as territory set apart for a certain class of people.

[25] 保 留 案 reservation—as in a treaty.

保 留 條 件 a reservation—as in a treaty, etc.

保 票 a bond or guarantee.

保 結 a guarantee; a bond.

保 舉 to recommend; a recommendation.

[30] 保 薦 to recommend and guarantee.

保•證 guaranty.

保 證 書 deed of security.

保 證 股 guarantee stock.

保 證 責 任 reserve liability.

[35] 保 證 金 security; bail.

保 辜 限 a time-limit, fixed by the magistrate, during which a badly wounded person is handed over to the family of the person who is charged with the injury; if the wounded person dies within that time-limit, the accused is held responsible for the death.

保 釋 to release on bail.

准 保 釋 to admit to bail.

保 釋 人 one who goes bail.

[40] 保 銀 guarantee money.

保 險 insurance.

保 壽 險 to insure one's life; life-insurance.

保 水 險 or 保 海 險 marine insurance.

保 火 險 fire-insurance.

[45] 不 測 保 險 accident-insurance.

償 資 保 險 endowment-insurance.

死 亡 保 險 insurance till death.

疾 病 保 險 insurance during a period of illness.

買 保 險 to take out an insurance policy.

[50] 保 險 人 underwriter.

保 險 信 insured letter.

保 險 價 額 value of the thing insured; the sum which anything is insured for.

保 險 公 司 insurance company.

保 險 刀 safety-razor. *See above* —13.

[55] 保 險 商 underwriters.

保 險 單 or 保 險 約 insurance-policy.

保 險 期 間 period of insurance.

保 險 業 insurance-business.

保 險 法 laws relating to insurance.

[60] 保 險 箱 a safe.

保 險 證 券 insurance-policy.

保 險 費 premium on insurance.

保 險 金 額 the sum insured.

保 領 to receive on giving security.

[65] 交 保 to hand over the security.

堡[3] A walled village. An earthwork; a petty military station. Subdivision of a township; a ward in a city. A.p.*
4947

堡 內 升 平 Peace be within thy walls!

堡 寨 a fort, a camp.

堡 甲 the tithing system. *See* 保 No. 4946-29.

堡 障 a defence; a wall.

* *p'u*[3,4]

㷀[1] To heat; to boil. A saucepan.
4948

㷀 水 to boil water.

葆[3] Luxuriant foliage.
4949

葆 葆 luxuriant growth.

頭 如 蓬 葆 head like a bramble-bush.

(a) To cover; to conceal.

葆 光 to contain light within oneself.

羽 葆 a feather screen.

翟 葆 a pheasant-feather screen.

(b) To extol. See 襃 No. 4951.

葆 大 great mark of distinction.

(c) To nurture, etc.
Inter. 保 No. 4946.

葆 其 天 眞 to care for the divine element within one.

遁 世 以 葆 眞 withdrew from the world in order to care for the divine element within him.

(d) u.f. 堡 No. 4847. A tithing; a rampart, etc.

葆 塞 a frontier military station.

(e) u.f. 寶 No. 4956. Precious.

葆 祠 之 regarded it as a precious keepsake.

褓[3] A swaddling-cloth.
緥
4950

襁 褓 swaddling-clothes—infancy.

襃[1] Long robes conferred by the emperor upon deserving officials—thus:—To praise; to overlook a person's defects.
襄
4951

襃 卹 忠 裔 to reward the children of patriots who have given their lives for their country.

襃 獎 or 襃 美 to praise; to be lenient towards.

襃 章 a decoration given as a reward.

襃•貶 to criticise.

(a) Read *pao*[4]. To prostrate oneself.

襃 拜 a double prostration.

垺[3] A tithing.
4952

鴇[3] A bird said to be like the wild goose. The bustard.
4953 A procuress.

鴇 母 or 老 鴇 a procuress.

豹[4] A leopard; a panther; a kind of wild cat.
4954

豹•子 or 金 錢 豹 the leopard.

豹 死 留 皮 the leopard dies but leaves his skin—as a man leaves his reputation.
豹 略 clever strategy.
豹 眼 to look fierce.
⁵豹 變 the leopard's versatility—a poor man getting on in life.
豹 騎 fierce cavalry.

報 ⁴ To announce. To inform; to report to; to declare.
4955 A newspaper.

報 人 a messenger; a journalist.
報 信 to notify; to give information.
報 函 a written report.
報 到 to report one's arrival.
⁵報 勘 to give information; to inform of.
報 名 上 冊 to enroll; to register names.
報 告 to inform; to announce; to report.
報 告 文 件 a report.
報 告 書 a report in writing.
¹⁰報 命 to respond to an order or command.
報 喜 to announce good news; to announce a birth.
報 單 a notice; a report; application to pass goods through the customs.
報 單 費 application fee.
報 喪 to announce a death.
¹⁵報 子 a messenger; a placard.
報 官 to notify the magistrates.
報 客 to announce a visitor.
報 律 laws relating to the press.
報 房 the department that announced the success of students at the examinations.
²⁰報 故 to announce a death.
報 故 單 certificate of death given by a doctor.
報 明 to state clearly; to declare goods.
報 曉 to announce the dawn—a cock.
報 案 to give information about a suit.
²⁵報 條 a notice.
報 死 憑 單 notification of death.
報 消 息 to communicate intelligence.
報 清 to declare goods.
報 災 to report a calamity, famine, etc.
³⁰報 界 the press.

報 界 往 訪 the press sought an interview.
報 病 to plead sickness as an excuse for returning home and giving up office.
報 盜 to report a robbery.
報 知 to inform.
³⁵報 稅 to declare goods for duty.
報 稅 單 bill of entry.
報 章 newspapers.
報 紅 to bring good news.
報 紙 newspapers.
⁴⁰報 老 to plead age as an excuse for retiring from office.
報 荒 to report famine or failure of crops.
報 覆 to reply.
報 貨 單 application to pass goods through the customs.
報 道 to inform; to report to.
⁴⁵報 銷 to send in accounts.
報 關 to declare at the customs.
報 關 行 (hang²) Customs Broker.
報 館 newspaper office.
報 館 主 筆 editor of a newspaper.
⁵⁰報 館 自 由 liberty of the press.
報 馬 a courier.
報 驗 to declare goods for examination.
京 報 Peking Gazette.
回 報 a reply.
⁵⁵日 報 daily newspaper.
月 報 monthly periodical.
畫 報 illustrated paper.
通 報 notification for general information.
週 報 weekly paper.

(a) To recompense. To requite. A reward; retribution.

報 仇 to avenge a grievance.
報 仇 雪 恨 to wipe out a grievance.
報 償 to avenge.
報 復 to revenge; to pay out.
⁵報 怨 to avenge a grievance.
報 怨 以 德 recompense injustice with kindness.
報 恩 to show gratitude.
報 本 追 源 to requite one's ancestors by sacrifice.
報 答 or 報 應 or 報 寃 to requite; to recompense; a recompense; retribution; to pay off a grudge.
¹⁰天 報 divine retribution.

果 報 just recompense.
現 報 immediate retribution.
陰 報 secret retribution in the hereafter.
陽 報 present retribution in this life.

寶 宝 宝 ³ Precious; rare; valuable. Treasure; bullion. A jewel. Used conventionally as "your."
4956

寶 光 an unusual brightness.
寶 刀 a short sword; a dagger.
寶 剎 a monastery; your monastery.
寶 劍 a double-edged sword.
⁵寶 善 to esteem the good; to appreciate goodness.
寶 器 or 寶 物 precious things; valuables.
寶 塔 a pagoda.
寶 奇 precious, rare.
寶 局 gambling-saloon.
¹⁰寶 座 or 大 寶 a throne.
寶 庫 a treasury.
寶 星 a decoration.
寶 玉 a precious gem.
寶 産 valuable productions.
¹⁵寶 盒 a casket; a cup used in gambling.
寶 眷 your wife.
寶 石 precious stones.
紅 寶 石 rubies.
藍 寶 石 sapphires.
²⁰寶 砂 emery powder.
寶 箋 your letter.
寶 舟 your boat.
寶 莊 your firm.
寶 藍 a bright, sapphire-blue.
²⁵寶 號 what is the style or name of your firm? your firm.
寶 觀 your monastery. (Taoist).
寶 訓 precious teaching—your advice.
寶 貝 or 珍 寶 precious; valuables.
寶 貨 valuable merchandise.
³⁰寶 貴 valuable; precious.
寶 重 to set store by; to value.
國 寶 national currency; national emblems; good men.
無 價 之 寶 a priceless thing.
通 寶 coins; currency.

暴 踈 }⁴
4957

Cruel, passionate. A scorching heat. Sudden, abrupt.

暴 主 a tyrant.
暴 亡 sudden death.
暴 作 to burst forth—as a sudden noise.
暴 傷 sudden injury.
⁵暴 動 riot; insurrection.
暴 動 民 rioters.
暴 卒 violent, sudden death.
暴 客 robbers; brigands.
暴 徒 份 子³ desperadoes.
¹⁰暴 性 a violent temper.
暴 怒 very angry; violent anger.
暴 戾 fierce; violent.
暴 掠 looting and robbery with violence.
暴 斂 橫 征 extortionate and illegal taxes and levies.
¹⁵暴 棄 to injure one's own interests.
暴 橫 cruel; tyrannical.
暴 死 sudden, violent death.
暴 殄 天 物 reckless misuse of God's gifts.
暴 漲 to rise suddenly—as a flood.
²⁰暴 烈 terrific—as a storm.
暴 然 suddenly; severely.
暴 狠 hatred; malice.
暴 猛 or 兇 暴 savage; cruel.
暴 病 a sickness that carries people off suddenly. [upstart.
²⁵暴 發 sudden wealth. 暴 發 戶 an
暴 虎 馮 河 to attack a tiger without weapons, and to cross a river without a boat.
暴 虐 to harry; to treat harshly.
暴 行 violent conduct.
暴 貴 or 暴 富 or 暴 財 主 a parvenu.
³⁰暴 跳 to dance with rage.
暴 躁 hot-tempered; to exasperate.
暴 醃 a quick process of salting meat.
暴 雨 a heavy shower; a squall.
暴 雷 heavy thunder.
³⁵暴 風 a fierce wind.

(a) Read p'u⁴·⁵ To dry in the sun. To exhibit. Inter. 曝 No. 5403.

暴 之 于 民 to show it to the people.
暴 尸 to exhibit a corpse.
暴 揚 to show forth; to exhibit.
暴 曬 to dry in the sun.

---

⁵暴 著 to manifest.
暴 露 exposed; left uncovered.
暴 面 to expose the face.
暴 骨 dry, exposed bones of the dead.

㸑 ⁴
4958

To be on duty.

㸑 直 a censor on duty for a few days.

瀑 ⁴
4959

A heavy rain after a thunderstorm. Read p'u⁴·⁵. A cascade; a waterfall. Froth.

瀑 布 飛 泉 a cascade like a strip of calico.
瀑 水 or 飛 瀑 or 瀑 布 a waterfall; a cascade.
瀑 沫 froth; foam.

爆 ⁴
4960

To crackle; to pop; to explode. To burst; to crack. Crackers.

爆 了 burst.
爆 仗 crackers.
爆 子³ 音 or 爆 音 explosive consonants; plosives.
爆 性 quick-tempered.
⁵爆 火 a crackling fire.
爆 炸 to explode.
爆 發 to burst by explosion—used fig. for any sudden disorder or riot.
爆 發 力 explosive force.
爆 發 性 ·的 explosive.
¹⁰爆 穀 popped grain; pop-corn.
爆 竹 or 串 爆 or 花 爆 crackers.
爆 裂 chapped; cracked; to explode.
爆 裂 品 explosives.

P'AO.   (ㄆㄠ)

脬 ¹
4961

A bladder. Used with 胞 No. 4940.

尿 脬 the bladder.
氣 脬 air-bladder.

抛 ¹
4962

To cast; to throw; to throw away; to reject. To deduct.

抛 出 selling margin.

抛 別 to leave; to desert.
抛 却 to cast away.
抛 去 to throw away.
⁵抛 家 to desert one's home.
抛 撒 to cast abroad; to scatter.
抛 撒 父 母 to leave one's parents.
抛 擲 to cast; to throw.
抛 梭 or 擲 梭 to throw the shuttle.
¹⁰抛 棄 or 丢 棄 or 抛 捨 to reject; to cast aside; to abandon.
抛 物 線 a parabola.
抛 球 to play ball; to throw a ball.
抛 盤 to fix prices for goods to arrive; to speculate.
抛 碎 to throw down and smash.
¹⁵抛 磚 引 玉 cast a brick to get a gem—throw a sprat to catch a mackerel.
抛 空 盤 to speculate on the market.
抛 網 to cast a net.
抛 繡 球 to throw the embroidered ball—to choose a husband.
抛 荒 to discard; to abandon.
²⁰抛 費 to spend recklessly; extravagance.
抛 車 ancient ballista.
抛 進 buying margin.
抛 錨 to cast anchor.
抛 閃 to abandon.
²⁵抛 除 多 少 How much do you deduct?
抛 離 to separate, as from a friend.
抛 頭 露 面 to expose oneself in public—said of women.

咆 ²
4963

To roar; to bluster.

咆 勃 to put on bravado.
咆 哮 to roar.
咆 哮 公 堂 disorderly behaviour in court.

庖 ²
4964

A kitchen. Shambles.

庖 人 or 庖 丁 a cook.
庖 代 a substitute.
庖 廚 a kitchen.

泡 ⁴
4965

To soak; to dip. To infuse.

泡 濕 to dip; to soak.

泡 茶 to infuse tea.
泡 壞 spoiled by soaking.
泡 透 thoroughly soaked.
泡。開 to soak dried things till they open up.

(a) Bubbles; froth; foam. A blister.

泡。子 blisters; bubbles.
泡 幻 empty bubbles—visionary.
泡 影 a bubble—unreal.
泡 氣 froth.
⁵泡 沫 foam; froth.
泡 泡 foaming—as a stream.
水 泡 a blister.
燙。了 一 個 泡ㄦ raised a blister by scalding.
脚 泡ㄦ blisters on the feet.
¹⁰起 泡ㄦ to raise a blister.; to bubble.

炮²
4966
To bake or roast.

炮 烙 之 刑 the punishment of the hot pillar—in the Chinese purgatory.
炮 製 to decoct Chinese medicine.

(a) Inter. 礮 No. 4969. A cannon, etc. Read *p'ao*⁴.

炮 手 a gunner.
炮 擊 a bombardment.
炮 轟 to bombard · noise of guns.
號 炮 signal-gun.

匏²
瓟
4967
The bottle-gourd.

匏 瓜 the bitter gourd.
匏 瓠 gourds and calabashes.
匏 繫 a hanging gourd—a useless fellow.

疱⁴
皰
4968
A pustule or pimple.

砲⁴
礮
礟
4969
Ancient ballista for throwing heavy stones. A cannon, a gun. A piece in Chinese chess.

礮 兵 artillery.
礮 口 速 度 muzzle-velocity.
礮 壘 a fort.
礮 子³or 礮 碼 shot; cannon-balls.
⁵礮 廠 an arsenal.
礮 手 a gunner.
礮 械 guns and equipments.
礮 樓 gun-turret.
礮 眼 a port-hole for guns; touch-hole.
¹⁰礮 線 firing line; line of fire.
礮 臺 a fort.
礮 臺 門 embrasures for guns.
礮 船 or 礮 划。子 small native gunboats.
礮 艦 a gunboat.
¹⁵礮 艦 政 策 the *Gunboat Policy*.
礮 術 gunnery.
礮 車 or 礮 架 a gun-carriage.
礮 門 port-holes—for guns.
礮 門 the breech-block, etc., of a gun.
²⁰礮 隊 a company of artillery.
礮 響 report of a gun.
機 關 礮 a quick-firing gun; a machine-gun.
短 礮 a howitzer. [mortar.
臼 礮 a mortar. 迫 擊 礮 trench
²⁵開 礮 to open fire.
高 射 礮 an anti-aircraft gun.

袍²
4970
A long gown; a robe.

袍 哥 sworn brother; member of certain secret societies.
袍。子 a robe; a wadded gown.
袍 料 material for a gown.
割 袍 to break off a friendship.
同 袍 to share a robe; close friendship.

跑²
4971
To run; to gallop; to hurry.

跑。不 動 unable to move.
跑。來 to come running.
跑 來 跑 去 to run to and fro.
跑 信。的 a messenger; a letter-carrier.
⁵跑 冰 to skate.
跑 冰 鞋 skates.
跑 出。去 to rush out.
跑 堂。a waiter.
跑 報 to carry news or letters.
¹⁰跑 外。的 a commercial traveller.
跑 得 快 to run fast.
跑 文。書 to carry official despatches; a courier.

跑 海。的 travellers; carters.
跑 狗 場 a dog-racing course.
¹⁵跑 狗 限 制 limitation of dog-racing.
跑 肚 or 屙 肚 looseness of the bowels.
跑 街。的 a commercial traveller.
跑 賬。的 a debt collector.
跑 走 to run.
²⁰跑 路 or 跑 道 to journey.
跑 開 or 跑 脫 or 逃 跑 to abscond; to run away.
跑 風 to run before the wind.
跑 馬 場 a racecourse.
跑 馬 廳 grandstand on a racecourse.
²⁵賽 跑 to run a race.

鞄²
4972
To tan and soften leather.

麅²
4973
A small, spotted deer found in N. China.

麅 鹿 the roebuck.

PO.   PE.   (ㄅㄛ)
(Peh)

北 4.5.
4974
The north. Usually pron. *pei*³.

北 京 or 北 關 Peking.
北 冰 洋 Arctic Ocean.
北 半 球 Northern Hemisphere.
北 口 外 beyond the Great Wall.
⁵北 回 歸 線 Tropic of Cancer.
北 堂 one's mother.
北 嶽 Mt. *Hêng* 恆 山 in Chihli. (Hopei).
北 斗 the Dipper.
北 星 the Polar Star=北 極 星
¹⁰北 極 the North Pole.
北 極 光 Aurora Borealis.
北 極 圈 Arctic Circle.
北 極 熊 the polar bear.
北 極 犬 Esquimaux dogs.
¹⁵北 洋 大。臣 Superintendent of Trade for Northern Ports.
北 海 the Gulf of Chihli; the Arctic Regions.
北 溟 the far north; Arctic Regions.
北 滿 州 North Manchuria.
北 直 the province of Chihli.
²⁰北 緯 northern latitudes.

北·邊 or 北 方 in the north; northern regions.

北 鄙 殺 伐 之 聲 an air descriptive of the fighting on the northern frontiers.

北 里 brothels.

北 面 而 朝 to have an audience with the emperor—who always sat facing the south.

(a) To be defeated.

三 戰 三 北 took part in three battles and was thrice defeated.

佯 北 to pretend to flee.

敗 北 to be routed.

追 北 to pursue a defeated army.

(b) Read pei⁴. To separate.

白   2.5. White. To consider as white. Radical 106.
4975   Usually pron. pai².
Distinguish 自 No. 1202.

白 下 old name for Nanking.

白 丹 white lead.

白 乎 湼 而 不 緇 Is it really white? Then you can dye it with dark dye and not make it black.

白 事 a funeral—from the colour of mourning.

白 亮 亮¹的 brightly white.

⁵白 化 病 chlorosis.

白 叟 a white-haired old man.

白 可 以 受 采 colours can be put on a white ground.

白 喉 or 喉 痧 diphtheria.

白 土 white clay.

¹⁰白 地 a white ground. 白天 daytime.

白 契 a deed which has not been stamped officially—the stamped deeds are called 紅契.

白 宮 the White House.

白 屋 朱 門 a house thatched with white grass, and a door painted with vermilion—the homes of the rich and poor.

白 布 white calico.

¹⁵白 描 outline drawings.

白 摺·子 plain white writing-paper.

白 日 or 白 晝 broad daylight.

白 日 昇 天 to ascend in broad daylight—to become an immortal.

白 日 見 鬼 to see demons in broad daylight— of a strange, absurd, impossible thing.

↑白 俄 White Russian.

²⁰白 日 鬼 a confidence trickster.

白 晳 white, as of complexion, etc.

白 晳 晳·的 dazzlingly white.

白 楊 the aspen; Populus alba or p. tremula.

白 殭 a disease of silkworms.

²⁵白 毛 mould; mildew; white hair.

白 沫 white froth or foam.

白 浪 white-capped waves.

白·淨 a fair and clear complexion.

白 濁 gonorrhœa.

³⁰白 灰 lime.

白 烏 a white crow.

白 煤 anthracite.

白 熊 the white bear.

白 熱 燈 incandescent lamp.

³⁵白 燕 best quality bird's nests—for soup.

白 玉 微 瑕 a tiny flaw in a white gem—small faults.

白 癜 leuchorrhœa. A.w. 白 帶.

白 眉 white eyebrows—a man who excels his fellows; from a man named 馬 良 who had white hairs between his eyebrows; he was extolled as excelling his four brothers.

白 眼 相 看 to look upon with disdain—to turn the whites of the eyes upon.

⁴⁰白 皮 書 a White Book.

白 礬 alum.

白 種³the white race.

白 筆 chalk for the blackboard.

白 米 white, polished rice.

⁴⁵白 粉 chalk; whiting.

白 糖 white sugar.

白 紵 fine white linen.

白 練 white silk.

白 蛉·子 sand-flies.

⁵⁰白 耗·子 white mice.

白 脖 老·鴰 white-necked or parson-crows.

白 臉 white-faced; the villain—in Chinese plays.   [ror.

白 色 white.白 色 恐 怖 White Ter-

白 色 人 or 白 屑 an albino.

⁵⁵白 芨 a mucilaginous root used in mixing red ink.

白 茫 茫·的 dazzlingly white.

白 萱 white peas or beans.

白 菜 cabbage.

白 菓 the gingko tree. Gingko biloba.

⁶⁰白 莊 or 白 鳥 the egret.

白 蓮 敎 the White-Lotus Sect—a secret society for seditious purposes.

↑白 旗 white flag — for surrender.

白 蟻 white ants; 白 螞 蟻.

白 蠟 white wax from the wax insect.

白 血 球 white corpuscles in the blood.

⁶⁵白 衣 white garments; anciently a commoner without rank.

白 衣 道 or 在 禮 a temperance society common in North China.

白 金 silver; now used for platinum.

白 鉛 zinc.

白 銅 white brass.

⁷⁰白 銀 silver.

白 錫 pewter.

白 鐵 tin-plates.

白 鐵 絲 galvanized-iron wire.

白 雲 石 white marble.

⁷⁵白 雲 蒼 狗 the white clouds change into a grey dog—from a line by 杜 甫; used to illustrate the unexpected in the changing conditions of the times.

白 露 White Dew. A solar term, about September 8—22.

白 面 書·生 a pale-faced youth—having no experience.

白 頭²or 白 首 white-haired.

白 頭²偕 老 to grow old together.

⁸⁰白 頭²如 新 to maintain an acquaintanceship till the hair is white, without coming to any real understanding with each other, just as if the acquaintance was newly-formed.

白 額 a white forehead—on a horse.

白 駒 過 隙 the white colt passes the crack—i.e., a sunbeam passing a crack—time flies.

白 骨 bones of the dead.

白 髮 蒼 蒼 hair streaked with grey.

⁸⁵白 魚 the silver-fish that destroys books, clothing, etc. See 蠹 No. 6507.

白 鴿 domestic pigeons.

白 鴿 眼 to regard with disdain.

白 麵 white wheaten flour.

白 黑 分 明 make a clear distinction between black and white—or right and wrong.

⁹⁰使 白 to bleach; to make white.

漂 白 to bleach.

潔 白 white and clean.

穿 白 to wear white—in mourning.

蛋 白 white of an egg; albumen.

(a) Clear, obvious. Simple, easy to understand. Spoken parts in a play. To explain, to inform, to tell, to express.

白 字 characters wrongly written for others of the same sound.

白 文 the simple text—without commentary.

白 是 or 明 是 it is clear that ....; evidently.

白 話 vernacular.

[5]白 話 報 a newspaper in the colloquial.

不 能 自 白 unable to clear himself.

以 狀 白 縣 notified the magistrate, of the facts.

含 冤 莫 白 to be unable to redress one's wrongs.

告 白 a notice or advertisement.

[10]明·白 clear; intelligible.

(b) Empty; vain. Naked. Free; gratis. Plain.

白 佔 to take without payment; to occupy without adequate return.

白 來·了 to have come in vain.

白 充 數 to fill up the number to no purpose—as by adding those who are incompetent, merely to make up the full number.

白 刃 naked blades.

[5]白 効 勞 to toil for another without reward.

白 勞 神 labour in vain; useless effort.

白 坐 to sit idle.

白 得·了 I got it for nothing.

白 忙 all my trouble for nothing.

[10]白 手 empty-handed.

白 手 成 家 to rise in life by one's own efforts; self-made.

白 抄 or 白 頭 帖·子 a libel; an anonymous placard.

白 撞 a loafer.

白 水 plain water.

[15]白 白 的 freely; in vain.

白 白 給·你 I freely give it to you.

白 瞧 to have a look for nothing.

白 空 unoccupied.

白 肉 plain meat, cooked without sauce or seasoning; white meat.

[20]白 說 to speak in vain.

白 費 事 (or 工 夫) to take trouble in vain.

白 長 (chang[3]) to grow old uselessly; to do nothing in life.

白 食 a free meal.

白 饒 to take pains to no purpose.

(c) Common, ordinary. A commoner.

白 人 or 白 衣 人 or 白 丁 a commoner; one without a degree or official standing.

白 身 a man with no official standing.

(d) used in transliterating.

白 蘭 地 brandy.

百 佰 } [2,4,5] A hundred. All, every, etc. Usually pron. pai[3]

4976

百 中 無 — not one in a hundred.

百 之 to do a hundred times.

百 事 all sorts of things.

百 事 不 問 he concerned himself about nothing; took no responsibility.

[5]百 事 俱 廢 everything going to ruin.

百 事 通 expert in everything.

百 事 順 利 May you prosper in everything!

百 五 the day before 清·明, it being 105 days after the winter solstice.

百 倍 a hundred-fold.

[10]百 六 the festival of 清·明. See above—8.

百 凡 all; the whole of.   [(ch'a[1]-)

百 分 差 誤 percentage of errors.

百 分 法 percentage. (arith.).

百 則 a little under a hundred.

[15]百 十 about a hundred; round about one hundred.

百 千 萬 hundreds of thousands—a vast number.

百 口 難 辨 difficult to get at the truth.

百·合 (花) the lily.

百 叫 百 應 unfailing obedience.

[20]百 善 孝 爲 先 of all virtues, filial piety is chief.

百 夫 長 a centurion.

百·姓 the people; population, lit., a hundred surnames.

百 子 全 書 the complete set of the writings of various philosophers and others which are not included in the Classics.

百 子 圖 pictures of numerous young children either drawn or embroidered, given as a present

with the wish that the recipient might have a numerous progeny.

[25]百 官 all officials; rulers generally.

百 官 總 己 all the officers managed their own business.

百 家 姓 the Book of Family Names.

百 家 衣 garment for a child made from pieces begged from many homes—to bring good luck.

百 寮 all the officials.

[30]百 川 會 海 all rivers meet in the sea.

百 工 all sorts of crafts; all kinds of workmen.

百 工 居 肆 all mechanics shall dwell in the place set apart for their trade by the government.

百 巧 the various laws and regulations; all kinds of devices; every move on the board.

百 度 表 Centigrade thermometer.

[35]百 戰 百 勝 ever-victorious.

百 折 不 回 obstinate; unbending; stubborn.

百 折 不 撓 unmoved by a hundred difficulties, unflinching, unbending.

百 揆 a high statesman; a general supervisor.

百 摺 裙 a pleated skirt.

[40]百 方 調 治 every effort was made to restore health.

百 日 咳 whooping cough.

百 日 紅 or 紫 薇 the crêpe-myrtle. Lagerostroemia.

百 日 草 the zinnia.

百 會 the sea, from above—30; the crown of the head from which the hair seems to grow.

[45]百 業 停 頓 all industries ceased.

百 歲 a hundred years of age—death, as a man's years rarely reach a hundred.

百 歲 之 後 after a hundred years of age—i.e., after death.

百 歲 羹 the shepherd's purse.

百 無 一 失 never a failure in many trials.

[50]百 無 可 爲 nothing can be done.

百 無 禁 忌 nothing to be superstitious about—no restrictions of any kind here, in the way of taboo or things to be avoided.

百 物 all things.

百 獸 all animals.

百 發 百 中 (chung[4]) to hit the mark every time.

[55]百 盤 all kinds—as of speculation.

百 福 駢 臻 May all blessings settle here!

百 科 全 書 an encyclopædia.

百 穀 all kinds of grain.

百 端 交 集 many thoughts crowded in upon him.

60百 結 衣 ragged garments.

百 聞 不 如 一 見 to hear about a thing many times is not equal to a single look at it.

百 舌 the Chinese blackbird.

百 般 all sorts; every kind.

百 花 開 放 all the flowers are blooming.

65百 菓 all kinds of fruit.

百 萬 a million.

百 葉 tripe; a many-petaled flower; many generations; a kind of bean-curd.

百 葉 窗 Venetian-shutters.

百 蟲 insects generally; all small animals.

70百 行 all sorts of conduct.

百 計 圖 謀 to devise all sorts of schemes.

百 貨 公 司 a department-store.

百 足 the centipede.

百 辟 其 刑 之 all the princes imitate it.

75百 週 紀 念 centenary celebration.

百 里 俟 a former District Magistrate.

百 里 才 a man with no great ability.

百 體 all the members of the body.

百 鴒 or 百 靈 the Mongolian lark.

伯
4977

2.5. A father's elder brothers; an uncle. Senior; elder. A title of respect. An earl. Also read *pai*³.

伯 主 chief; the leading man.

伯 仲 之 間 not much difference in age.

伯 仲 叔 季 first, second, third and fourth—of brothers.

伯 公 or 伯·父 a paternal uncle.

5伯 勞 a shrike.

伯 叔 uncles on the father's side.

伯 姊 an elder sister.

伯 母 wife of father's elder brother.

伯 氏 the elder of two friends.

10伯 爵 the rank somewhat equivalent to that of earl.

伯 父 叔 父 uncles, being the elder and younger brothers of one's father, respectively.

伯 爺 an elder brother.

伯 牛 之 疾 a fatal illness, from the illness of a disciple of Confucius of that name.

大 伯·子 husband's elder brother (-*pai*³-)

啪
4978

2.5.

Used in transliterating.

帛
4979

4.5. Silk, thus:—wealth, property. A.p. *pai*².

寶 帛 valuables.

財 帛 wealth.

賜 帛 to make a present of silk cord to a statesman in order that he might strangle himself in lieu of execution.

柏
栢
4980

2

The cypress; the cedar. To crowd. Also read *pai*³.

柏 子³ 油 oil from juniper seeds— used in red ink for seals.

柏 府 the Censorate.

柏 操 (*ts'ao*¹) chaste widowhood.

柏 香 樹 the cedar—used for incense.

刺 柏 the Chinese juniper.

舶
4981

2.5. An ocean-going junk. Also read *po*⁴˙⁵.

舶 物 or 舶 來 品 imported goods.

迫
廹
4982

4.5. To persecute; to oppress. In difficulties; embarrassed. Pron. *p'o*⁴˙⁵.

迫 于 勢 力 compelled by force of circumstances.

迫 促 to urge on; to hurry.

迫 倒 to ruin.

迫 切 or 急 迫 urgent; pressing; to urge a point; to press.

5迫 害 to persecute and injure; to annoy.

迫 從 to compel compliance.

迫·得 forced to....

迫 斯 可 以 見 矣 if urgently requested, such a person may rightly see the prince.

迫 服 to force submission.

10迫 脅 to intimidate; to coerce.

迫·著·他 要 compelled him to take it.

迫 虎 傷 人 a tiger when pressed will injure a person—to harass a man until he turns on his persecutor.

迫 趕 to expel.

迫 近 imminent.

15危 迫 critical juncture.

壓 迫 to oppress; to wrong; to persecute.

窘 迫 in great distress.

逼 迫 to compel; to persecute.

勃
4983

2.5. Suddenly. To change, as the countenance. Also read *p'o*⁴˙⁵.

勃 然 大 怒 all at once he flew into a great rage.

勃 然 興 起 to arise suddenly.

勃 然 變 色 he suddenly changed countenance.

勃 發 suddenly to issue forth.

5勃 谿 to quarrel.

勃 起 不 良 he suddenly conceived a malicious purpose.

浡
4984

2.5. Full. Opening-out, as a plant. Copious, as a fountain. Also read *p'o*⁴˙⁵.

浡 潏 bubbling of a fountain.

渤
4985

2.5.

An arm of the sea.

渤 海 the Gulf of Chihli.

渤 澥 the expanse of ocean.

擘
4985a

4.5. To break; to open; to tear. Pron. *pai*ⁿ.

擘 交 情 to break a friendship.

擘 父 兄 面 to make one's elders blush.

擘 紙 to tear paper.

擘 開 to break off; to break open.

擘 餅 to break bread.

(a) A thumb.

巨 擘 the thumb. (-*po*⁴)

P'O.   P'E. (ㄆㄛˊ)

(P'eh)

拍 4.5. To strike with the hand; to pat; to clap.
4986   Usually pron. *p'ai*[1].

拍○去 to pat away or off.
拍和 to act as a peacemaker; to make peace.
拍張 a shuttlecock.
拍手 to clap the hands.
[5]拍·打 to pat; to tap.
拍掌 to clap the hands.
拍板 to beat time; castenets.
拍案 to slap the table—a gesture of anger, surprise, or admiration.
拍照 to take a photograph.
[10]拍照印刷版 photo-process block.
拍發消·息 to send the news by telegram.
拍網·子 a snare for birds.
拍肩 to slap on the shoulder.
拍胸 to smite the breast.
[15]拍花·的拐·子 kidnappers of small children.
拍賣 to sell by auction.
拍賣佣金 (or 規費) auctioneer's commission.
拍醒·了 to awaken by patting or slapping.
拍門 to knock at a door.
[20]拍電 to tap the telegraph instrument—to send a wire.
拍馬屁 to flatter obsequiously.

泊 4.5. To be at leisure.
4987   Pron. *p'o*[2].

泊然無所求 quiet and tranquil without desires.
澹泊 calm, tranquil, without desires; abstracted in mind.

(a)   To anchor a vessel.

泊泊 ripples.
泊界 harbour-limits.
泊船 or 灣泊 to anchor a vessel.
泊船章程 regulations for mooring vessels.
停泊 to moor; to anchor.

魄 4.5. The animal or inferior soul; the animal or sentient
4988   life which inheres in the body—the body in this sense; the animal spirits; this soul goes to the earth with the body. See below —4. See 魂 No. 2365.

魄也者鬼之盛也 the *p'o*[4] or sentient soul is of the *kuei* nature, and shows that nature in its fullest measure—*kuei* is defined as that which on dying returns to the ground.
魄·力 animal courage; power.
形體魄也，死則魄之靈爲鬼 the physical form is the *sentient* part; when death comes, the spiritual part of the *sentient soul* becomes spirit or ghost.
精魄返於地 the *animal or sentient essence* returns to the earth.
[5]附形之靈爲魄 the spiritual part which inheres in the body is the *p'o*[4].
魂氣而魄精 the *hun* is the breath and the *p'o* is the essence.
魂神而魄靈 the *hun* is the divine part and the *p'o* is the spiritual.
魂魄死者之神靈 the *hun* and the *p'o* are the spirit of the dead.

(a) Form, shape.

形魄 form, shape.

(b) The dark portion of the moon's disc. See 旣 No. 453—A. 7ff.

月魄生光 the moon begins to show brightness.
死魄 the first day of the moon. *See* 旁 No. 4926-15.

(c) Grains in distilled spirits. Also written 粕 No. 5353.

糟魄 grains in liquors.
魄門 the anus.

(d) Read *t'o*[4]. Dispirited; desolate.

家貧落魄 a poor and wretched family.
落魄 disheartened and discouraged; to fail in one's profession or aim; poverty-stricken.

(e) Read *po*[2.5]. Extensive. u.f. 薄 No. 5326.

旁魄 or 旁薄 extensive.
旁魄而無用 extensive—as ability—but of no practical use.

PEI. (ㄅㄟ)

背 4   The back; behind.
4989

背人 clandestinely. *See below—* B.2.
背倒 a backfall.
背兒 or 錢背 the reverse of a coin.
背厚 stout.
[5]背口言 to talk behind a person's back.
背地 in the background; quiet; secluded; behind one's back.
背地·裏 on the quiet; in secret; underhanded.
背境 a background.
背壓 back-pressure.
[10]背巷 a quiet, back lane.
背後 behind the back.
背後說人 to backbite.
背心 a vest; a sleeveless jacket.
背景 or 遠景 the background.
[15]背染 to define an object by painting the background in a darker shade, leaving the object in relief.
背榜 last on the list—under the former examination system.
背痛 backache.
背筋 the muscles of the back.
背累 bowed—as with cares.
[20]背·着手 to place the hands behind the back.
背脊 or 脊梁背 the back; the backbone.
背褡 a vest or sleeveless jacket.
背視 a back-sight.
背陰 a shady spot not reached by the sun.
[25]背集 a day on which there is no market.
背面 the back; the rear.
背風岸 a sheltered shore.
佗背 or 駝背 hunchbacked.
刀背 the back of a knife.
[30]屈背 to stoop; to bend the back.
手背 the back of the hand.
轉背 to turn the back.

(a) To turn the back on. To disavow. To memorize.

背·不 出 來 unable to repeat it from memory.
背 主 to desert a master.
背 井 離 鄉 to turn the back on one's native-place.
背 信 to be unfaithful; perfidy.
[5]背 倚 to lean against.
背 却 前 言 to go back on one's word.
背 叛 to revolt.
背 命 to disobey orders.
背 城 一 戰 a fight with the back to the city—a death-struggle.
[10]背 念 insubordinate.
背 敎 to apostatize.
背 施 幸 災 to turn the back upon those that rendered you assistance, and take pleasure in their calamities.
背 施 無 親 to turn the back upon those who were kind to you is to be without natural affection; (the State of *Chin* refused to give grain to the State of *Ch'in*, though *Ch'in* had given it to them when they were distressed).
背 日 性 plants that turn from the sun.
[15]背 書 or 背 出 來 to repeat a lesson; to repeat from memory.
背 望 to despair.
背 本 to turn the back on one's parents.
背 棄 to reject; to desert.
背 水 陣 to fight to the death. *See above*—A.9.
[20]背 理 unreasonable; irrational.
背 約 to be unfaithful to an agreement; to discard treaty obligations.
背·著 to turn the back on; to carry on the back.
背 誓 to forswear oneself.
背 誦 to repeat from memory.
[25]背 謬 falsehood; error.
背 軍 to desert from the army.
背 逆 disobedient; unruly.
背 道 to forswear; to renounce.
向 背 opposed to.
[30]相 背 back to back; contradictory.
違°背 to oppose; to disobey.

(b) Read *pei*[1]. **To carry on the back.**

背·不 動 too heavy to carry on the back.
背 人 過 河 to carry a person on the back across a river.
背·子 a load carried on the back.
背 負 to bear; to carry on the back; to be ungrateful.
[5]背 負 肩 挑 manual labour.
背 馬 to saddle a horse.
↑背 帶 suspenders. A.c. 吊 帶

褙 [4] **Cloth or paper pasted together; pasteboard.**
4990

裱 褙 pasteboard.
隔 褙 pieces of cloth pasted together into a kind of pasteboard, used to form the base of shoe-soles.

輩 輩 [4] **A row of carriages. A generation. A class, a series, a kind. Denotes the plural.**
4991

輩 出 to come out in succession; numerous.
輩·數 the scale or degree of the generation; the position of the generation in a series.
輩 流 of the same generation, sort.
輩 行 order of seniority.
[5]輩 輩 generation after generation.
一 輩·子 a lifetime.
上 輩 下 輩 seniors and juniors.
先 輩 or 前 輩 seniors.
同 輩 the same generation.
[10]後 輩 after generations.
我 輩 or 吾 輩 we; our class.
晚 輩 juniors.
無 輩 without a peer.
班 輩 colleagues; generation.
[15]老 輩 ancestors.

悲 [1] **Grieved; sorry; sad. To lament. To sympathize.**
4992

悲 不 幾 時 this sorrow is but for a little while.
悲 傷 or 悲 哀 grieved; melancholy; to be sad; grievous.
悲 切 mournful, sad.
悲 劇 a tragedy.
[5]悲 哉 or 悲 夫 Alas! How sad!
悲 嘯 sobbing with grief.
悲 喜 交 集 grief and joy intermingled.

悲 嘆 to sigh with sadness.
悲 悼 to lament for.
[10]悲 惻 to feel sympathy with grief.
悲 愁 melancholy; sad; grievous.
悲 慟 sad; mournful; to pity.
悲 慘 grievous; sad; melancholy; to commiserate.
悲 憫 to commiserate; to feel for.
[15]悲 懷 sorrowful in heart.
悲 戚 mournful; grieved.
悲 歡 grief and joy.
悲 淒 mournful; sad.
悲 痛 之 懷 the mood of grief and pain.
[20]悲 秋 to lament the autumn—to regret the passing of the summer of life.
悲 號 (*hao*[2]) to weep grievously; to cry bitterly.
悲 觀 pessimistic views.
悲 觀 主 義 pessimism.
悲 辛 sadness.
[25]悲 離 其 實 也 lamenting that the truth is distorted.

卑 卑 [1] **Low, inferior, lowly, humble. Used conventionally for "I", "my".**
4993

卑 下 base; mean; humble.
卑 以 自 牧 retiring; humble.
卑 卑 不 足 道 not worth mentioning.
卑 小 inferior; low; insignificant.
[5]卑 屈 cringing; servile.
卑 幼 a junior.
卑 弱 lowly and weak.
卑 微 lowly; humble.
卑 汚 base; mean; humble.
[10]卑 濕 lowlying and damp.
卑 禮 厚 幣 he humbled himself and sent generous presents.
卑 職 I; the humble subordinate.
卑 視 to slight.
卑 諂 辯 給 flattery and specious talk.
[15]卑 賤 base; humble; mean.
卑 遜 modest; retiring.
卑 鄙 mean; vulgar; humble; base.
卑 陋 mean; humble; vulgar.

(a) Read *pi*[1] **u.f. 萆 No. 5071.**
卑 蔴 油 castor oil.

婢 [4] **A female slave; a maid-servant.**
4994 **Also read** *pi*[4].

婢 作 夫 人 the maid acts the mistress—subordinate taking first place.
婢 女 a maid; the maids.
婢 媼 female servants, young and old.
婢 子 a term used by women when speaking of themselves.
婢 學 夫 人 the maid copies her mistress—a poor attempt to be somebody.

碑[1] A large stone tablet; a gravestone.
4995

碑 帖 rubbings from tablets.
碑 樓 a pavilion over a stone tablet.
碑 碣 stone tablets.
碑 記 or 碑 文 the inscription on a tablet.
[5]碑 銘 carved on stone.
碑 陰 the back of a tablet.
碑 額 the head of a tablet.
勒 碑 to engrave on a stone tablet.
口 碑 the mouths of the people are as tablets recording the merits of a good magistrate.
墓 碑 a tombstone.

杯[1]
盃 A cup, a tumbler, a glass.
4996

杯 中 物 wine.
杯 子 a cup; a wine-cup.
杯 弓 蛇 影 he sees the reflection of a bow as a snake's shadow in the cup—said of a very suspicious person, from a story.
杯 棬 wooden cups and bowls.
[5]杯 水 車 薪 a cup of water to put out a load of burning firewood —utterly inadequate.
杯 爵 盌 盞 cups, goblets, basins, and plates.
杯 盤 a salver; a waiter.; dishes.
杯 茗 候 敍 with cups—for wine —and tea, I await your conversation—phrase used in invitations.
杯 酒 a cup of wine—conventional in invitations to a feast.

備
偹 [4] To prepare; to provide; to put in order; to complete. Perfection; completeness; ready.
4997

備 下 or 預 備 or 准 備 to prepare; to make ready.
備 亂 to prepare against disorder.
備 價 to find the necessary amount.
備 全 completely prepared; to prepare for the whole of.
[5]備 兵 or 備 戰 to prepare for war.
備 具 呈 文 prepared a despatch for submitting.
備 呈 to submit for investigation.
備 嘗 辛 苦 to have experienced bitterness and trouble.
備 官 to act as, or to fulfil the duties of an official.
[10]備 忘 錄 memorandum(book).
備 悉 纖 微 he knows it all minutely.
備 情 由 to draw up a statement of details.
備 文 to prepare a despatch.
備 於 一 人 perfection in one man.
[15]備 札 to draw up instructions.
備 查 to keep for future reference.
備 案 to serve as a record; to keep on record.
備 歷 安 危 he knows both prosperity and misfortune.
備 用 for use.
[20]備 由 to draw up a statement.
備 移 to write a despatch to.
備 細 completely.
備 緩 急 ready for emergencies.
備 考 to submit for investigation; an appendix for reference.
[25]備 聆 to make oneself acquainted with.
備 虞 preparedness.
備 質 to call as witness; to be prepared to give evidence.
備 足 to provide fully.
備 辦 to make ready; to be in readiness to act.
[30]備 送 to get ready for sending.
備 閱 to keep for future reference; to keep for inspection.
備 馬 to saddle a horse.
出 其 不 備 take him unawares.
告 備 to announce the completion of.
[35]戒 備 on the alert.
準 備 all ready; to be ready for.

憊 [4] Exhausted; worn out.
4998

憊 倦 tired; fatigued.
憊 懶 listless.
憊 累 得 很 utterly exhausted.

被 [3.4.] A coverlet, a quilt. A scarf.
4999

被 單 sheets for a bed.
被 套 a large bag for holding bedding or clothing.
被 巾 a woman's scarf or kerchief.
被 服 bedding and clothes—something from which a man is not easily parted—to cleave to.
[5]被 服 聖 教 cleave to the teaching of the sages.　[coverlet.
被 窩 a coverlet. 綿 被 a quilted
被 胎 or 被 綿 a cotton-wool quilt without a cover.
被 褥 bedding. 被 窩 兒 bed made
被 鋪 bedding.　[up to sleep in.
[10]單 被 a single coverlet.
夾 被 a double coverlet.
覆 被 to pull the coverlet over oneself.
鋪 被 單 to make a bed. A.c.
鋪 牀.
(a) Sign of the passive. To suffer, to be the object of.

被 了 盜 to be robbed.
被 人 欺 負 cheated by others.
被 保 護 國 a protectorate.
被 傷 injured.
[5]被 具 all has been prepared.
被 判 sentenced.
被 動 passivity.
被 動 的 心 passive mind.
被 取 上 升 to be received up; to be taken up.
[10]被 告 者 the accused; the defendant.
被 害 injured; misused.
被 害 者 the injured party.
被 家 所 累 harassed by family affairs.
被 屈 wronged.
[15]被 情 所 感 moved by the emotions; or affected by circumstances.
被 拿 to be arrested.
被 掛 to be involved.
被 接 上 升 to be received up.
被 搶 to be robbed.
被 迫 降 落 forced landing — as of planes.

被攎 to be carried captive.
被殺 to be killed.
被水災 to suffer from floods.
被浪搖撼 tossed by the waves.
被祿 or 回祿 to have had a fire; to suffer from a fire. *See* No. 2309-60.
²⁵被約拘束 bound by a covenant.
被累 harassed; careworn.
被誣 falsely charged.
被誘惑 to be deceived.
被請 to be invited.
³⁰被議 discussed; talked about.
被負 to sustain.
被逼 coerced into.
被選舉人 the elected.
被選舉權 elegibility for election.
³⁵被風吹着 blown by the wind.
↑被難⁴ to be killed in an accident or an uprising
(b) Read *p'i*¹. To wear on the back.

被堅執銳 dressed in strong armour and armed with sharp weapons.
被衣 to carry the clothes on one's back.
被褐懷玉 wearing rough garments but carrying a precious gem in the bosom—used fig.
被髮 the hair hanging dishevelled down the back.

倍⁴ **Double; to double. Joined to a numeral—a time,—fold.**
5000

倍利 double profit.
倍加整備 to have a thing put into extra good order.
倍地 doubled his territory.
倍增 doubled.
⁵倍增惆悵 a double load of care and worry.
倍·數 a multiple.
倍日并行 forced marches.
倍牽 (*lii*⁴·⁵·) 100 per cent.
倍益 to increase; to add to.
¹⁰倍稱之息 100 per cent profit.
倍蓰 twice or five times as much —to increase several fold.
倍道 double stages; forced marches.
一倍多·的利·息 over one hundred per cent profit.
十倍 ten-fold.
加倍 double; to double.

(a) To act contrary to. To rebel. Impropriety.

倍世離俗 to turn the back upon worldly things.
倍其師說 ran counter to the sayings of their teacher.
倍叛 to rebel.
倍殯柩 turned their backs on the coffin (and wept facing the north).
⁵倍約 to repudiate an agreement or a treaty.
鄙倍 vulgar; low.

蓓⁴ **A bud. Also read *p'ei*³·⁴.**
5001

蓓蕾 flower buds.

焙⁴ **To dry over a fire in a utensil. To hatch artificially.**
5002

焙乾 to dry; to cure by drying.
焙卵 to hatch eggs artificially.
焙燒爐 an oven.
焙茶 to fire tea.
焙鴨苗 to hatch ducklings.

悖⁴ **Perverse; contrary to what is right. To rebel. Inter.**
5003 **next.**

悖亂 rebellion; sedition.
悖入悖出 gains, which come in a wrong way, will leave in a wrong way.
悖叛 to revolt.
悖德 not loving those to whom one is bound by natural ties.
⁵悖戾 to act contrary to all rule; perverse behaviour.
悖棄 to reject; to break off—as friendship.
悖狂 outrageous behaviour.
悖理 opposed to principle.
悖禮 uncivil; contrary to etiquette.
¹⁰悖言 falsehood; perverse speech.
悖謬 perverse and erroneous; false.
悖逆 rebellious; refractory.
悖逆反常 to act in a way contrary to all received usage; perverse conduct.

誖⁴ **Obstinate; disorderly; perverse. Inter. preceding.**
5004

誖亂 revolutionary; sedition.
誖謬 wrong; unreasonable.

貝⁴ **Cowries, shells, formerly used as currency; thus:—**
5005 **valuables, precious. Radical 154.**
Distinguish 具 No 1556.

貝胄 a helmet ornamented with shells.
貝勒 *Beileh*, a Manchu title bestowed on the sons of the imperial princes.
貝·子 the sons of a *Beileh*.
貝子³ cowries—anciently used as currency.
⁵貝殼學 conchology.
貝殼投票 ostracism.
貝母 a fritellaria.
貝玉 or 寶貝 valuables; gems.
貝葉 Buddhist religious books.
¹⁰貝貨 cowries, as currency.
貝資 wealth; property.
貝錦 embroidery worked in a shell pattern.
寶·貝 treasures, valuables; precious.

棋⁴ **A palm-tree.**
5006

棋多羅 the palm, of which the leaves were used for writing material—from the Sanskrit, *pattra*.

狽⁴ **An animal with short fore-legs, supposed to ride on the wolf.**
5007 **See 狼 No. 3811-14ff.**

P'EI.　　(ㄆ)

坏¹
坯
Unburnt bricks or tiles. Also read *p'i*¹.
5008

坯塊 or 泥坯 unburnt bricks.
坯模·子 mould for making bricks.
土坯 sun-dried bricks.

(a) A hill.

(b) Read p'ei². The back-wall of a house. To use mud for stopping cracks in walls.

坏 城 郭 the city and suburban walls are put in repair.

蟄 蟲 坏 戶 hibernating insects stop up the entrances to their holes.

鑿 坏 而 遁 knocked a hole through the back-wall and escaped.

秠¹ 5009 Ancient name for a dark kind of millet used to make a spirituous liquor used in sacrifices.

胚 胚 } ¹ 5010 An embryo; a fœtus a month old. Also read p'i¹.

胚 球 ovule.

胚 胎 a pregnant womb; in embryo.

胚 膜 blastoderm.

培² 5011 To bank up with earth. To nourish; to strengthen.

培 土 or 培 壅 to bank up with earth.

培 植 to cultivate by banking up; to assist; to support.

培 植 起 來 to straighten up by banking; used fig., to assist.

培 磚 to bank up with bricks.

培 育 to cherish.

培 養 or 培 補 to invigorate; to nourish.

(a) Read p'ou². A mound.

培 塿 small mounds of earth.

賠² 5012 To make good; to restore; to indemnify. To apologize.

賠 不 是 to apologize for a fault.

賠 不 起 unable to make good.

賠 償 to compensate; to repay.

賠 償 兵 費 to pay a war indemnity.

⁵賠 償 名 譽 indemnity for defamation.

賠 償 損 失 indemnity for damage or loss.

請 索 賠 償 to claim compensation.

賠 反 定 銀 to restore the earnest money.

賠 墊 to pay—as a surety; to make up, as a deficiency in public funds.

¹⁰賠 情 to make an apology.

賠 找 to find a sum of money for compensation.

賠 本 to lose one's outlay; to get less than the capital invested.

賠 款 an indemnity.

賠 款 執 照 letter of indemnity.

¹⁵ 要 求 賠 款 to demand an indemnity.

賠 禮 to make apologies; to do something to appease another.

賠 累 to incur liabilities.

賠 繳 to repay; to make good a loss; to compensate.

賠 罪 to make an apology.

²⁰賠 虧 to fail; to suffer loss.

賠 補 or 賠 墊 to compensate; to make up a deficiency.

賠 話 to say a word in apology.

賠 貼 to lose money in business.

賠 賺 losses and gains.

²⁵賠 送 to give without a return; dowry given to a daughter.

賠 還 to repay.

賠 錯 to make an apology.

賠 錢 貨 goods on which money is lost—daughters.

醅¹ 5013 Unstrained spirits.

陪² 5014 To accompany; to keep another company.

陪 乘 to ride with a person of rank.

陪 你 出 門 I'll go out with you.

陪 伴 a companion; to bear company to.

陪 侍 to wait upon.

⁵陪 助 to take part in; to assist.

陪 哭 to assist in weeping.

陪 坐 to keep a guest company.

陪 嫁 dowry given to a daughter.

陪 客 or 陪 賓 to entertain a visitor.

¹⁰陪 審 an assessor.

陪 審 員 jurymen.

陪 審 官 an assessor.

陪 審 裁 判 制 the jury system.

陪 弔 to attend to the mourners at a funeral.

¹⁵陪 從 to follow.

陪 房 a maid who accompanies a bride to her new home.

陪 祭 one who assists at a sacrifice.

陪 笑 to greet with a smile.

陪 臣 an officer of a tributary State.

²⁰陪 臺 servants; retainers.

陪 襯 to praise or blame by allusions; to bring forward an illustration.

陪 貳 an assistant or deputy.

陪 送 to see a guest out; to escort.

陪 都 a secondary capital.

²⁵陪 隸 retainers; servants.

少 陪 excuse my leaving you—when a host has to go, or when one of the guests has to leave sooner than the rest.

佩⁴ 5015 To wear at the waist.

佩 劍 or 佩 刀 to wear a sword.

佩 帶 to wear at the girdle; to wear—as an order.

佩 弦 to use a bowstring as a girdle—to stimulate his sluggishness—used to indicate the taking heed to friendly admonitions. See below—9.

佩 戴 to wear; to adorn.

⁵佩 文 韻 府 a book of phrases, rhymes, etc., in 212 vols.; 卷, compiled during the reign of K'ang-Hsi, A.D. 1711.

佩 玉 ornament worn as a pendant.

佩 經 a charm.

佩 身 to wear on the person.

佩 韋 to wear a girdle of leather—to restrain his rash ardour—used to illustrate friendly admonitions. See above—3.

(a) To respect. To remember.

佩 慰 gratefully to appreciate.

佩 服 to respect; to have confidence in.

感 佩 to remember with gratitude.

欽 佩 to respect.

珮⁴ 5016 Girdle ornaments. Inter. preceding.

珄[3] A string of five hundred pearls.
5017

裴[2] Long robes. Inter. 徘 **No. 4869.** To walk.
5018 Distinguish 婓 No. 1824.

裴回 flying to and fro like swallows; to walk up and down.

(a) Read *fei*[2]. An old name for the district of 合肥 in Anhwei.

配[4] Worthy; fit. To match; to pair.
5019

配·一·個·來 bring another to match it.
配·不·上 it does not match; unsuitable.
配享 to be admitted to membership in the Confucian temple.
配享千秋 May you enjoy your honours for a thousand years!
[5]配偶 to mate; to make a pair.
配備充實 fully prepared.
配儷 a pair; a couple—as man and wife.
配分器 a measure; measuring-glass.
配·合 to mate; to pair.
[10]配天地 the equal of Heaven and Earth.
配婚姻 to make a marriage contract.
配存摺 bank pass-book.
配室 a betrothed woman.
配對 to couple; to mate; copulation of animals.
[15]配·布 to arrange.
配·得·過 suitable; worthy of.
配成 mixed—as colours or paints.
配·搭 supplementary; to add to; to adjust.
配景法 law of perspective.
[20]　並行配景 parallel perspective.
　幾何配景 geometrical or linear perspective.
　登眺配景 bird's-eye perspective.
　直線配景 linear perspective.
　色影配景 aerial perspective.
[25]配用 fittings; gear.
配當 matched; suitable.
配置 arrangement; to arrange.
配給 to give in marriage.
配色 to match colours.

[30]配藥 to compound medicines.
配製 to compound—as drugs, etc.
配製假體 to fit artificial limbs.
配貨單 an invoice.
配貨摺 pass-book for goods.
[35]配鑰·匙 to fit a key.(--*shih*)
配頭 accompaniment to a dish.
配食 a general sacrifice to ancestors.
不配 matchless; unworthy; incongruous; not qualified for.
合配 well-matched.
[40]相[1]配 matched; suitable; equal to.
許配 to consent to a marriage.

(a) To be loaded with. To be charged with. To suffer punishment.

配兌 to transfer.
配格 the standard of punishment for banishment—whether near or far, according to the offence.
配流 to be banished.
配軍 banished to the frontiers.
配運 to carry a cargo of....

(b) Used in transliterating.

配客 a peck—measure.

沛[4] Copious. Abundance. To flow. Sudden.
5020

沛澤 thickets and marshes.
沛然下雨 it rained in torrents.

(a) Tall, high. Great.

沛然自大 self-conceit; vain-glorious.
沛艾 tall, handsome, proud appearance.

(b) To fall prostrate.

顛沛必於是 when he falls, he still cleaves to it—his virtue.
顛沛流離 vagrant on account of poverty.

霈[4] Torrents of rain. Rain.
5021

霈霈 the sound of colliding waters.
甘霈之流 sweet rains flowing down—used also for beneficence.

雲油雨霈 the clouds gathered darkly and the rain came in torrents.

旆
旆[4] A pennon; a streamer. Also read *pei*[4].
5022

旆旆 waving—as a flag in the wind.
旟旆飛揚 the flags are waving.

孛[4] The shooting up of plants. A comet. Also read *po*[4.5].
5023

孛星 a sudden star—a comet.
孛羅 to pop glutinous rice in a pan.

轡[4] Reins; a bridle.
5024

轡頭[2] reins; a halter.
執轡 to hold the reins.
按轡 to draw the reins.

PÊN.　(ㄅ)

本[3] Root; source; origin. Rooted in; to find the origin in; essential; original. From these comes the idea of principal or capital.
5025

本上文而言 has its origin in the preceding sentence.
本不如此 originally it was not so.
本主 the original owner.
本乎 inherent in; consisting in.
[5]本乎此 it has its origin in this.
本·事 ability; capacity; resources.
本人 the man himself.
本人情該物理 (the *Odes*) have their root in the emotions of man, and include the principles of all things.
本位 the place originally occupied; standard; unit; basis.
[10]本位貨幣 standard coin.
本來 originally; as a matter of fact; properly; the truth is; in fact.
本來面·目 the original expression; the natural form.

本 利 or 本 息 principal and interest.

本 利 之 盈 虧 profit and loss on capital and interest.

[15] 本 刑 punishment according to the code.

本 務 duty.

本 可 may certainly....

本 合 what is proper; requisite.

本 始 the origin; the beginning.

[20] 本 富 wealthy through the primary industry—farming.

本 屆 之 祝 典 the celebration this year.

本 屬 really is or belongs to; comes under the category of ....; on the basis of.

本 屬 可 惡 (wu⁴) it is truly detestable.

本 年 the present year.

[25] 本 影 umbra.

本 性 natural disposition.

本 息 對 清 to square the accounts, both principal and interest.

本 應 what is proper; it is properly my duty to....

本 於 神 權 based on divine right.

[30] 本 日 today; the same day.

本·是 was originally....; always was.

本 月 the current month.

本 木 水 源 or 木 本 水 源 the root of wood and the source of water—the foundation of things —ancestors.

本 末 first and last; essential and non-essential, etc.

[35] 本 業 original (hereditary) occupation; one's business.

本 洋 the Spanish dollar.

本 流 the main stream—of a river.

本 源 cause.

本 無 定 體 originally having no fixed bias.

[40] 本 當 should; ought to.

本 科 regular fixed courses in a curriculum.

本 素 original elements.

本 義 the original meaning; literal meaning.

本 能 instinct; faculty.

[45] 本 能 上 感 情 instinctive emotions.

本 能 動 作 instinctive movements.

本 能 欲 求 instinctive cravings.

本 自 naturally; as a matter of course.

本 色 the natural colour.

[50] 本 色 敎 會 a church adapted to Chinese thought.

本 色 文 字 native literature.

本 草 a Chinese materia medica.

本·著 according to.

本 行 normal action; profession.

[55] 本 該 what is proper; requisite; it is properly my duty to.

本 質 essence.

本 部 headquarters.

本 量 capacity.

本·錢 capital in trade.

[60] 本 靈 ability.

本 音 the key-note; the air.

本 領 ability; capacity.

本 題 the topic under discussion.

本 體 論 ontology.

[65] 不 彀 本 not enough to repay my cost price.

務 本 to give attention to what is radical.

原 本 primitive form.

報 本 to show gratitude to one's ancestors.

忘 本 forgetful of one's ancestors.

[70] 折 本 to encroach upon one's capital.

根 本 the root; fundamental.

虧 本 to lose one's capital.

(a) Native. I, my, our, we.

本·分 (fen⁴) one's duty or obligations.

本 商 we, the merchants.

本 國 native country.

本 圖 宦 達 my intention was to go into official life.

[5] 本 地 native; local.

本 地 人 natives of a place; aborigines.

本 地 貨 local or native products.

本 地 貿 易 local trade.

本 地 銷 路 local consumption.

[10] 本 大 臣 I, the minister.

本 家 one's own family.

本 心 or 本 意 my first intention; my original idea.

本 族 one's own clan.

本 罪 one's own sin.

[15] 本 處 I, the officer; I, the writer.

本 行 or 本 號 our firm; my *hong*.

本 要 my original intention was; I was going to.

本 身 I, myself.

本 院 I, the governor.

[20] 本 領 事 I, the consul.

(b) N.A. for books, documents, drawings etc.

本 章 fair copy of a memorial.

一 本 書 a book.

上 本 to send in a memorial.

字 本 a copy-book.

監 本 a revised edition.

藏 本 an edition for library purposes, to be kept as a specimen, not for general use.

笨 ⁴
怂 } Awkward; clumsy. Stupid; dull.
5026

笨 人 or 笨 才 a dolt; a stupid.

笨 伯 a dull, simple person.

笨 工 an unskilled workman.

笨 手 笨 脚 clumsy of hand and foot.

[5] 笨 拙 unskilful, awkward, clumsy.

笨 漢 a simpleton; an awkward, clumsy fellow.

笨 貨 a clumsy lout.

笨 賊 clumsy thief—abusive.

笨 車 a heavy cart.

[10] 笨 重 heavy and clumsy person.

賁 ¹
5027   Energetic, strenuous.

賁 育 the names of two ancient heroes 孟 賁 and 夏 育—used as a comparative term for great bravery.

(a) Read *fên*¹. Large.

賁 鼓 large drums.

(b) Read *p'i*⁴. Bright. Ornamental. To honour.

賁 然 brightly.

賁 臨 Your lustrous visit—conventional.

賁 若 草 木 beautiful and bright as trees and plants.

(c) Read *fên*⁴. Defeated.

賁 敗 routed.

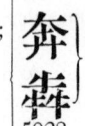
奔 ¹
犇 } To run away; to be in a hurry; urgent.
5028

奔 來 奔 去 running about; busy.
奔 北 defeated; routed.
奔 告 an urgent notice; to inform without delay.
奔 命 to flee for one's life.
⁵奔 喪 to hasten home to bury a deceased relative.
奔 天 涯 to travel everywhere.
奔 忙 busy; to fag; to toil.
奔 投 to repair to; to fly to—for help.
奔 放 to bolt—as a horse; fig., of a free style of writing.
¹⁰奔 敗 to flee; routed—troops.
奔 散 to scatter hurriedly in all directions.
奔 星 meteors.
奔 波 fag; toil; disquieted; restless waves.
奔 波 勞 苦 the toil and anxiety of life.
¹⁵奔 程 to hasten on a journey.
奔 竄 to fly and hide; to be routed.
奔 競 in haste and fear; eager to get positions.
奔 而 殿 kept the rear in a retreat.
奔 走 or 奔 逃 or 奔 跑 to travel quickly; to hasten.
²⁰奔 踶 不 遜 untamed; wild.
奔 軼 to hasten forward from the rear.
奔 逐 to drive out.
奔 逸 to flee, routed—as troops.
奔 馳 to travel quickly; to hasten.
²⁵奔 騰 to scatter—as beasts and birds.

(a) To marry without the preliminary customs.

奔 女 a fallen woman.
奔 者 不 禁 do not prohibit those who marry irregularly—without the preliminary formalities.
淫 奔 lewdness—of women; elopement.

捹 4
5029
To throw into confusion.

逩 1
5030
To run quickly. Used with 奔 No. 5028.
逩 命 to flee for one's life.

錛 1
5031
An adze. To adze.

錛 了 去 to cut away with an adze.
錛 子 an adze.

畚 3
5032
A basket or hod used by bricklayers and farmers for earth, manure, grass, etc. A bin.

畚 斗 a dust-basket.
畚 畬 之 勞 the toil of a farmer.

P'ÊN. (ㄆ)

坌 4
5033
Dust, earth. A bank of earth. To dig. To bring together.
Also read fên⁴.

坌 息 breathless haste.
坌 集 京 師 to collect at the capital.
坌 身 to smear the body with paint—as savages.
坌 鬆 to loosen soil by digging.

盆 2
5034
A basin, a tub, a pot, a bowl.

盆 堂 a bath-house where the bathers have separate tubs in the same room.
盆 盂 a bowl, a tub.
盆 頭 the percentage taken by gambling-house keepers.
傾 盆 雨 torrents of rain—as if a bowl had been overturned.
⁵浴 盆 a bath-tub.
臨 盆 nearing her confinement.
花 盆 flower-pots.
臉 盆 a face-basin.

湓 2
5035
An affluent of the River Yangtze near Kiukiang.

湓 城 old name for Kiukiang.

噴 歕 味 1
5036
To spurt; to blow out; to puff out. To snort.
Also read fên¹.

噴 壺 a watering-pot.
噴 布 to spurt water over cloth—as tailors do.
噴 氣 to snort; to fume.

噴 水 to spurt water out of the mouth—as Chinese do when damping clothing.
⁵噴 水 井 artesian well.
噴 水 池 a fountain.
噴 泉 a fountain; a geyser.
噴 符 水 to spurt holy water.
噴 糞 to abuse with foul language.
¹⁰噴 雲 吐 霧 to smoke opium.
噴 霧 器 atomizer.
噴 飯 to spurt out the food—when laughing; hence, 令 人 噴 飯 funny, humorous, laughable.
(a) Read p'ên⁴. To emit.

噴 筒 a rocket.
噴 香 to emit fragrance.

PÊNG. (ㄆ)

伻 1
5037
To send, to cause. A messenger.

崩 1
5038
To fall in ruins; to slip down, as a bank of earth.

崩 厥 角 稽 首 bowed their heads to the ground like the horns of animals falling off.
崩 口 a hare-lip.
崩 坍 the collapse of a wall or a bank.
崩 墜 to fall into ruins.
⁵崩 壞 collapsed in ruins.
崩 山 裂 石 convulsions of nature.
崩 折 to snap.
崩 敗 to be ruined.
崩 滅 destroyed.
¹⁰崩 裂 to fall in—as a landslip; to break open—as a sore or cut.
崩 騰 furious—as a hurricane.
崩 解 disintegration.
山 崩 a landslide.

(a) The death of an emperor.
崩 駕 or 崩 殂 the death of an emperor.

(b) u.f. 痭 No. 5040. Menorrhagia.
崩 帶 leuchorrhœa.
崩 漏 menorrhagia.
血 崩 flooding.

弸 1
5039
A bow stretched to the full. Full, substantial. To stretch.

弸 中 彪 外 a man of talent and fine exterior.

弸 弓 to stretch a bow to the full.
弸 緊 stretched tightly.

癞[1] Menorrhagia, for which 崩 No. 5038—B. is also used.
5040

血 癞 flooding.

繃
繃 [1]
} A cloth to carry an infant on the back. To tie, to bind.
5041

繃 孩 子 to wrap a baby in swaddling-clothes. See 倒 No. 6134—A.24.
繃 帶 a bandage.
繃 緊 bind it tightly.
繃 鼓 taut.

浜 [3] A creek, a ditch, a canal.
5042

弮 [1] To draw a bow to the full. See 弸 No. 5039.
5043

弮 緊 了 pulled taut.

絣 [1] To baste for sewing. To connect. Inter. preceding.
5044

迸 [4] To scatter. To expel. To crack, to split. To jump.
5045 Also read ping[4].

迸 出 來 to jump out.
迸 散 or 迸 逃 to dissipate; to flee in all directions.
迸 泉 fountains; geysers.
迸 淚 a flood of tears.
[5]迸 裂 to split.
迸 跳 to jump about.
迸 逐 to drive away.
迸 開 to split open.
亂 迸 flying in all directions.

(a) A superlative. Very, extremely.

迸 乾 as dry as tinder.
迸 脆 very brittle.

踍 [4] To jump; to bound. u.f. 迸 No. 5045.
5046

踍 起 來 jumped into the air.
踍 跳 to jump; to frisk about.

罋 [4] A squat jar for holding wine, sauces, etc. Also read p'êng[1].
5047

甭 [2] 〈不用 .need not.
5047½

P'ÊNG. (ㄆ)

鲆 [1] Noise of waters.
5048

鲆 匐 the roar of billows or surf.

怦 [1] Ardent, impulsive.
5049

心 怦 怦 分 諒 直 loyal and earnest; faithful and straightforward.
心 怦 怦 欲 動 keen to be doing something.
急 怦 eager and impulsive.

抨 [1] To grasp. To follow. To cause. Inter. 怦 No. 5037. Also read pêng[1].
5050

抨 彈 to impeach.
抨 擊 to attack a person's faults.

砰 [1] The crash of falling rocks.
5051

砰 然 如 雷 with a crash like thunder.
砰 匐 一 聲 with a mighty crash.
砰 轟 之 聲 the roaring sound—of the cataract.

烹 [1] To boil; to cook.
5052

烹 宰 boiling and killing—the work of a cook.
烹 湯 to boil soup.
烹 滅 to exterminate.
烹 煉 to seethe; to decoct.
[5]烹 茶 or 烹 茗 to make tea.
烹 調 to boil and mix the ingredients for medicines. (-t'iao[2])

烹 飪 之 事 the business of a cook.
烹 飪 班 a cooking-class.

埄 [2] Whirling of dust in the wind.
5053

埄 起 塵 土 causing the dust to rise in clouds.

(a) Read keng[3]. An irrigation ditch.

朋 [2] A friend, an acquaintance, a companion. To match, to pair.
5054

朋 僚 fellow officials; colleagues.
朋·友 friends.
朋 儕 friends and companions.
朋 從 friends and associates.
[5]朋 比 爲 奸 to associate for treasonable purposes.
朋 酒 two cups of wine.
朋 黨 a cabal; a clique.
好 朋 情 great friendliness.
患 難 朋 友 a friend in need.
[10]酒 肉 朋 友 friends in prosperity.

棚 [2] A tent; an awning; a booth; a shed.
5055 Used with 篷 No. 5067.

棚·匠 a builder of mat-sheds, awnings, etc.
棚 廠 a shed for storing things.
棚 民 people who live under booths—woodcutters, etc.
棚 鋪 a mat-shop.
[5]涼 棚 an awning.
天 棚 a tent or awning.
洋 棚 a steamer-office on the Yangtze River.
茶 棚 a booth for tea.
頂 棚 the ceiling.

硼 [2] Borax.
5056

硼 砂 borax from Tibet.
硼 酸 boric acid.

鬅 [2] Dishevelled hair hanging down the back.
5057

首 髮 鬅 鬙 his hair all unkempt and dishevelled.

鵬 ² A fabulous bird of enormous size—the roc.
5058

鵬程萬里 the roc's journey of 10,000 *li*—said of those who early attain office.

潀 ¹ The noise of dashing water.
5059 See 澎 No. 5061.

潀湃 noise of waters.

彭 ² To be strong and handsome. A surname.
5060

彭亨 proud, contemptuous.
彭年 an advanced age.
彭祖 or 老彭 P'eng Tsu—the Methuselah of China.

(a) Read *p'ang*¹. To be numerous. Unceasing. Strong.

以車彭彭 rumbling go the carriages.
四牡彭彭 my four steeds never halt.
行人彭彭 many persons on the road.
駟騵彭彭 four splendid bay carriage-horses.

澎 ² The sound of waves.
5061

澎湃 the roaring of breakers.

膨 ² Fat, bloated, swollen.
5062

膨漲 expansion.
膨脖 obese; puffed out; swollen.
澎脹 expansion.
三段澎脹機關 triple-expansion engines.
澎脹力 power of expansion.

蟛 ² A land-crab.
5063

蟛蜞 a land-crab.

碰
撞　⁴
砰
　　To run against; to collide.
　　To meet, to come across.
5064

碰·不着 not to come across a person. (-*chao*²)
碰命 to run the risk; to take one's chances.
碰壞 or 碰破 to damage by collision.
碰巧 accidentally; fortunately.
⁵碰撞 to run up against.
碰機·會 to meet with an opportunity; to take a chance.
碰沒 to sink by collision.
碰礁 to strike a rock.
碰着 to hit against; take care we do not collide—a street-cry.
¹⁰碰·見 to meet—as an acquaintance.
碰運·氣 it depends upon my luck.
碰釘·子 to meet with a refusal.
碰頭²聚飲 to meet together and drink—as friends.
碰鼻轉灣 turn when you get to the cross-street.

P'ĒNG.　　(ㄆㄥ)

芃 ² Bushy, luxuriant growth.
5065

芃芃其麥 luxuriant grows the wheat.

捧 ³ To hold up in both hands. To offer respectfully. To scoop up.
5066

捧·住 grasp it carefully; hold it firmly.
捧托 to hold up with both hands.
捧水飲 to drink out of the hands.
捧場 to applaud, cheer or show interest in a performance. (*sat.*)
⁵捧腹 to hold the sides with laughter.
捧讀 to hold up and read; to read carefully.
一捧 a double handful.

篷
簰　²　A sail, an awning. A covering. Mats woven from bamboo and other leaves.
5067

篷廠 a mat-shed for temporary use.
篷寮 mat-huts or shanties.
篷帆 sails; sail-cloth.
篷窗 window in a boat.
⁵篷腳索 the sheet of a sail.
篷茅 a thatched hut.
篷船 a sailing-vessel.
篷襴 the covering of a sail.
篷過腳 to gibe a sail.
¹⁰扯篷 hoist the sail.
搭篷 to put up an awning.
落篷 to drop the sail. (*lao*⁴-)

蓬 ² A species of raspberry or *Rubus* found growing sporadically among hemp. Overgrown, tangled, luxuriant. Dishevelled.
5068

蓬戶 or 蓬門 a poor scholar's house; my humble house.
蓬星 a baleful star.
蓬牖 an overgrown window.
蓬萊仙境 or 蓬萊山 Fairyland.
⁵蓬頭垢面 with dishevelled hair and grimy face.
蓬首 dishevelled hair.
蓬鬆 dishevelled.

PI.　　(ㄅ)

俾 ⁴ To cause, to enable. That, so that, to the end that. To follow, to accord, to employ. Also read *pei*¹.
5069

俾不通 to be the cause of others not getting on.
俾予從欲 so that I follow my own desires.
俾免 in order to avoid.
俾各懷遵 so that all obey with trembling.
⁵俾得 or 俾之 so that; so as to enable.
俾得安焉 that he may be quieted.
俾應需要 to meet important demands.
俾晝作夜 to turn day into night—idle during the day, busy at night.
俾爾職守 to enable you to fulfil your duties as an official.
¹⁰俾知 for the information of.
俾速施工 so that the work may be carried out quickly.

(a) Read *p'i*[4]. u.f. 睥 No. 5163. To look askance.

俾 倪 or 睥 睨 to look askance; to cast sidelong glances.

庳[4]　A low-built house. Also read *pei*[3].
5070

宮室卑庳 "his own palace was low and small."

(a) Read *pi*[4].　Short, low.

其民豐肉而庳 the people were stout and short.
陂塘污庳 the embankment is low and under water.

(b) Read *p'i*[4].　Name of a place.

有庳 a fief conferred by Shun 舜 on his brother 象; it was in the province now called Hunan.

萆 蓖 蔥[4]　The castor-oil plant. Also used for other plants. Also read *pei*[1].
5071

萆 蔴 油 castor oil.
萆 蔴 草 the castor-oil plant.

裨[4]　To benefit; to aid; advantageous.
5072　Also read *pei*[1].

裨 益 of great advantage.
裨 補 to second; to support; to aid; to make up a deficiency.
裨 襦 a long garment.

(a) Read *p'i*[2].　Small.

裨 冕 a little cap.
裨 官 野 史 fictitious stories purporting to be history. Cf.4862.3.
裨 將 a colonel or adjutant-general. (*obs.*).
裨 海 a small sea.
裨 王 a petty ruler.
裨 販 small traders; pedlars.

髀[4]　The buttocks. The thigh.
5073

髀 樞 or 髀 臼 the socket of the thigh-bone.

髀 肉 復 生 putting on flesh again —a sigh of regret at his inactivity.
髀 骨 os innominata.
髀 胝 the tough, coloured skin of a monkey's buttocks.
拊 髀 or 撫 髀 to slap the thigh.

鼙[2]　A war-drum used on horseback.
5074

屄[1]　The vagina.
5075

匕[3]　A spoon or ladle. Radical 21. Distinguish 七 No. 579.
5076

匕 首 a dagger.

比[3]　To compare. Radical 81.
5077

比 一 比 to make a comparison.
比 不 上 not to be compared with; inferior to.
比 不 得 incomparable; not to be compared with.
比 並 to compare; to treat in a similar manner.
[5]比 他 大 greater than he.
比 作 to compare.
比 例 to compare; ratio; a parallel case.
　反 比 例 inverse ratio.
　同 理 比 例 proportion.
[10]　增 比 例 increasing ratio.
　大 比 例 ascending ratio.
　小 比 例 decreasing ratio.
　常 比 例 constant ratio.
　正 比 例 direct ratio.
[15]　等 比 例 equal ratio.
比 例 尺 a scale, as on a map; instrument for drawing to scale.
　按 比 例 尺 所 畫 drawn to scale.
　每 寸 爲 十 里 的 比 例 a scale of one inch to ten *li*.
比 例 法 law of proportion.
[20]比 例 符 號 sign of proportion— (::). (*math.*)
比 例 規 proportionate dividers.
比 依 according to; analogous to.
比 典 metaphor and allusion.
比 喻 a metaphor; a comparison; an allegory.

[25]比 如 for instance; let us suppose.
比 對 to pair; to match.
比 差 or 比 捕 to punish policemen for failing to produce thieves or stolen property. (-*ch'ai*[1])
比 得 不 好 inaptly illustrated.
比 我 強 he is better or stronger than I.
[30]比 手 說 to indicate with the hands—as a size, etc.
比 擬 to compare; to treat in a similar manner.
比 方 for instance; by way of illustration.
比 於 compared with.
比 梭 更 快 swifter than a shuttle.
[35]比 武 contests of strength.
比 準 的 well-aimed.
比 照 according to; analogous to; contrasting.
比 熱 specific heat.
比 萬 有 大 greater than all things.
[40]比 號 the sign of comparison— (:). (*math.*)
比 評 to criticize.
比 試 to compete with.
比 語 a comparison; an illustration; a simile.
比 論 argument from analogy.
[45]比 賽 to race; to compete—as at an exhibition.
比 賽 會 competitive meeting. The Olympic contests.
比 賽 表 score-sheet.
比 較 to compare; to classify; comparative.
比 較 上 之 多 數 relative majority.
[50]比 較 土 俗 學 comparative folk-lore.
比 較 心 理 學 comparative psychology.
比 較 生 理 學 comparative physiology.
比 較 的 comparative.
比 較 研 究 法 comparative methods of study.
[55]比 較 神 學 comparative theology.
比 較 級 comparative degree.
比 較 表 comparative chart or table.
比 較 解 剖 學 comparative anatomy.
比 較 起 來 to compare them; to make a comparison.
[60]　不 足 與 比 較 not to be compared with; no comparison.

以 原 本 與 譯 文 比 較 to compare the translation with the original.

比 這 大 得 多 much larger than this.

比 重 specific gravity.

比 重 計 specific-gravity chart.

⁶⁵比 量 intelligence.

比 類 to compare.

比 體 of equal rank; a married couple.

克 順 克 比 able to bring about submission and effect a union.

可 比 may be compared to.

⁷⁰無 比 incomparable.

(a) Read *pi⁴*. **To associate with. To follow. To be near. Neighbours. A group of five families under the** *Chou* **dynasty. Intimate.**

比 匪 to associate with low persons.

比 化 者 the dead.

比 周 partisan and catholic, respectively.

比 密 close; intimate.

⁵比 物 matched—as horses.

比 目 魚 pair-eyed fish—flat-fish, as the sole, plaice, etc.

比 目 魚 筋 the soleus muscle of the leg.

比 翼 鳥 birds that had only one wing each, and thus had to fly in pairs—used for husband and wife.

比 肩 matched in height, quality...

¹⁰比 親 familiar with.

比 鄰 neighbours.

比 閭 five families were reckoned as one 比, and five 比 as one 閭.

比 附 to append.

君 子 周 而 不 比 "the superior man is catholic and not partisan."

¹⁵洽 比 其 鄰 they gather the neighbours together.

義 之 與 比 what is right, he will follow.

(b) Read *pi⁴*. **To arrive. Recently. When.**

比 于 as to; with regard to; respecting.

比 來 in recent years, months.

比 其 反 也 when he had returned.

比 到 continuously to....

⁵比 及 when; by the time.

比 及 三 年 in three years time.

比 及 到 家 when they reached home.

比 年 the year of the former triennial examination for the third degree; every year; successive years.

比 時 by that time.

¹⁰比 歲 successive years.

歲 比 不 登 there had been successive famines.

比 經 札 行 and then I instructed ....

比 聞 I have recently heard.

比 至 when they arrived; as soon as I arrived.

¹⁵比 見 when he saw.

比 長 不 倦 indefatigable.

(c) Read *pi⁴*. **For, on behalf of.**

比 死 者 洒 之 by one blow to wipe out the disgrace on behalf of the dead.

(d) Read *pi⁴*. **Each, every.**

比 屋 皆 然 every house is similarly provided.

比 戶 慶 賀 every household visits and congratulates—at the New Year.

比 比 然 也 every one is the same.

↑ 比 比 repeatedly, frequently.

(a) Read *p'i³*. **See below.**

皋 比 a tiger skin—used as a seat by ancient tutors—a teacher.

(f) Read *pi³*. **Used in transliterating.**

比 國 or 比 利 時 Belgium.

(g) Read *pi⁴*. **Used in transliterating.**

比 丘 a Buddhist mendicant, from *bhiksha*.

比 丘 尼 female Buddhist mendicant, from *bhikshuni*.

毕⁴ **To compare; to match; to equal.**
5078

栍⁴ A stockade.
5079

猚⁴ A kind of tapir. A fierce beast depicted on the door of prisons.
5080
       Also read *p'i³*.

猚 狅 the beast as above—a prison.

陛⁴ The steps to the throne. The emperor.
5081

陛 下 under the steps—the emperor; first applied to the official attendants, then, as ministers did not dare to address the throne directly, they spoke to these officers, and thus the term came to be used for the emperor himself.

陛 殿 the audience chamber.

陛 見 to have an audience with the emperor.

陛 辭 to retire from an audience.

陛 陛 abundant, many.

升 陛 to ascend steps.

妣³ A deceased mother. Also read *p'i³*.
5082

先 妣 my deceased mother.

祖 妣 deceased grandparents.

庇⁴ To protect; to shelter; to screen.
5083

庇 民 to protect the people.

庇 短 to screen faults.

庇 祐 divine aid; to countenance.

庇 護 or 護 庇 secretly to help; to shelter.

秕
粃} ³ Grain not fully grown. Chaff, husks. Also read *p'i³*.
5084

秕 政 bad government.

秕 糠 chaff; husks; annoying; trifling.

蚍² Mussels; various shellfish.
5085

毖[4] To guard against; to take care. Caution.
5086

毖後患 to guard against future disaster.

(a) Laborious. To be distressed.

無毖于恤 do not be distressed with sorrow.

泌[4] To gush forth, as water. Also read *mi*[5].
5087

泌之洋洋 a whirling stream.

祕秘[4] Mysterious; secret; abstruse. Usually pron. *mi*[4·5].
5088

祕不宣洩 to keep a matter dark.
祕傳 secretly handed down—as a prescription or formula; made known secretly.
祕受 to receive privately—as a bribe.
祕守 to keep secret.
[5]祕密 or 隱密 close; secret.
祕密主義 Occultism.
祕密投票 a secret ballot.
祕密會 a secret society.
祕密會議 a secret conclave.
[10]祕密消息 confidential information.
祕密結社 a secret society.
祕寶 valuables; esoteric doctrines.
祕府 a secret repository.
祕授神方 an infallible recipe or prescription which has been privately received.
[15]祕文 writings of a secret or mysterious character.
祕方 nostrums.
祕書 private secretary.
祕書員 private secretary.
祕書官 official private secretary.
[20]祕書廳 secretariat of the cabinet · Bureau of Secret Affairs.
祕書長 private secretary to high officials.
祕法 secret methods.
祕液 internal secretions.
祕而不宣 to keep one's own counsel.
[25]祕製 prepared from a secret recipe.

祕要 secret and important.
祕計 intrigues.
祕訣 a secret; a mystery.
祕起 to keep secret.

閟[4] To hide. Hidden, close, secret.
5089

閟匿 to abscond; to keep out of the way.
閟慎無洩 be very careful not to let the matter leak out.

篦笓[4] To comb. A fine-toothed comb.
5090

篦子 a fine-toothed comb; a grid on which things are placed in a steamer.
篦髮 to comb the hair.
鐵篦子 a gridiron.

鎞[2] A ploughshare. A barb. A lancet.
5091

鐵鎞 a crowbar.

閉[4] To close; to stop up; to obstruct.
5092

閉口 to shut the mouth.
閉口無聲 nothing to say.
閉塞 to close up.
閉幕 to drop the curtain—the thing is ended.
[5]會議已閉幕 the conference had already closed.
閉息行氣 to hold the breath. (Taoist).
閉戶 or 閉門 to shut a door; closed doors.
閉房 a private room.
閉會 to close a session.
[10]閉月羞花 causes the moon to hide her face and the flowers to blush—of great female beauty.
閉果 indehiscent fruits.
閉歇 or 倒閉 to become bankrupt.
閉死 to smother.
閉氣 obstruction of the breath; to hold the breath.

[15]閉氣彈 asphyxiating bombs.
閉目合睛 to close the eyes.
閉眼 or 閉目 to close the eyes; to die.
閉糴 to restrict the purchase of grain.
閉結 constipation.
[20]閉經 stoppage of the menses.
閉藏 stored up; laid by.
閉蟄 hibernating creatures.
閉門不納 to refuse visitors.
閉門思過 to reflect on one's misdeeds in private.
[25]閉門羹 to refuse visitors.
閉門謝客 to close the door to visitors.
閉門造車, 出門合轍 please yourself in private, but follow the beaten track in public.
閉關不通 to close the communications at the borders.
閉關政策 policy of exclusion.
[30]閉關時代 the period of exclusion.
閉關自守 to close the country to trade.
閉靈 a notice of death indicating that visitors are not received.
瞞閉 to deceive.
禁閉 to prohibit.

彼[3] That, the other, another, those, there.
5093

彼人 that person.
彼以行言此以知言 that was spoken in reference to conduct; this, in reference to knowledge.
彼天子固然 as he was emperor, what he did was a matter of course.
彼姝者子 That beautiful girl!
[5]彼時 at that time.
彼有取爾也 there can be gathered from that remark....
彼此 that and this; there and here; then and now; you and I; both parties, etc.
彼此之間 between this one and that one: among them.
彼此交盡 an exhaustive comparison.
[10]彼此唱和 to sing responsively.
彼此對說 speaking to one another.
彼此推讓 yielding to one another.
彼此有錯 faults on both sides.

彼 此 相 愛 to love one another.
[15]彼 此 相 顧 to care for one another.
彼 自 he himself.
彼 蒼 者 天 "O, ye blue heavens!" *Giles*.
彼 處 there; in that spot.

髲[4]
5094   A wig.

鄙[3]   Rustic, low, mean. Vile.
5095   To despise. Also read *p'i*[3].

鄙 俚 之 詞 vulgar expressions.
鄙 劣 mean; base.
鄙 吝 or 鄙 嗇 parsimonious; niggardly.
鄙 哉 硜 硜 乎 How vulgar the persistence!
[5]鄙 夫 a rustic.
鄙 夫 可 以 事 君 也 與 哉 Can one serve his prince in company with those mean fellows?
鄙 夷 to despise; to scorn.
鄙 意 my humble opinion.
鄙 瑣 paltry; petty-minded.
[10]鄙 薄 to despise; to speak ill of.
鄙 誠 my sincere—desire.
鄙 賤 humble; rustic.
鄙 陋 base, mean.
不 鄙 not to disdain.
[15]可 鄙 despicable.

(a) A border town; a town of 500 homes.

邊 鄙 之 邑 a border town.

畀[4]
5096   To give to; to confer on.

痹 痺[4]
5097   Rheumatism.

瘋 痹 不 仁 numb, having no sense of feeling.

糒[4]
5098   Food for a journey; cakes.

輔 紼[4] To harness a horse. The
5099   second is also read *fu*[2]. A board in front of a carriage for the driver to lean on.

鼻[2.4]
5100   The nose. Radical 209.

鼻 哂 to snigger.
鼻 塞 the nose stuffed up—as with a cold.
鼻 子 the nose.
鼻 子 眼 the nostrils.
[5]鼻 孔 or 鼻 竇 the nostrils.
鼻 息 the breath.
   仰 外 人 鼻 息 to be at the beck and call of the foreigner.
鼻 息 春 雷 吼 snores like thunder in spring.
鼻 樑 the bridge of the nose.
[10]鼻 泣 to snivel.
鼻 涕 mucus from the nose; snivel.
鼻 淵 nasal catarrh.
鼻 準 the tip of the nose.
鼻 烟 snuff.
[15]鼻 烟 壺 a snuff-bottle.
鼻 環 nose-ring.
鼻 界 the cartilage of the nose.
鼻 痔 nasal polypus.
鼻 祖 the first ancestor of a family.
[20]鼻 端 the tip of the nose.
鼻 管 nasal ducts.
鼻 腔 the nasal cavity.
鼻 膩 a shiny nose.
鼻 蛇 nasal polypus.
[25]鼻 衄 to bleed at the nose.
鼻 觀 the nostrils.
鼻 音 nasal sounds.
鼻 飲 to snuff up liquid through the nose.
鼻 骨 the nasal bone.
[30]鼻 鼾 to snore.

敝[4] Poor, unworthy, vile.
5101 Worn out. A modest term for "my"; "our".
Distinguish 敝 No. 225.

敝 之 而 無 憾 not to be angry if they spoil them.
敝 俗 our native customs.
敝 前 任 my predecessor in office.
敝 友 my friend.
[5]敝 國 my country.
敝 壞 ruined.
敝 姓 王 or 賤 姓 王 my humble surname is *Wang*.

敝 東 my master.
敝 衣 old clothes.
[10]敝 屣 worn-out shoes—useless.
敝 鄉 my native place.

弊 獘[4]   Distressed. Fraud; cor-
5102   ruption; evil practices.

弊 害 injurious practices.
弊 病 or 弊 端 or 弊 混 abuses; corrupt practices.
作 弊 to practice fraud.
利 弊 merits and demerits.
[5]情 弊 abuses; irregularities.
無 弊 不 生 every kind of abuse sprang up.
疲 弊 fatigued; worn-out; in extremities.

幣[4]   Silk. Presents; wealth.
5103   Coin; a token.

幣 之 未 將 before any offering of gifts.
幣 制 currency.
幣 制 問 題 the currency question.
幣 制 局 national mint.
[5]幣 制 改 革 currency reform.
幣 制 畫 一 unification of currency.
幣 帛 presents—of silk.
幣 鏟 an ancient coin shaped like a spade.
楮 幣 paper-money used in idolatry.
金 幣 gold standard.

蔽[4]   To conceal, to hide. To
5104   shade, to darken.

蔽 上 to deceive superiors.
蔽 匿 to hide oneself.
蔽 塞 to close up; stupid, dull.
蔽 容 to hide the face.
[5]蔽 形 術 the art of rendering the body invisible.
蔽 掩 concealed; hidden.
蔽 於 世 俗 之 見 blinded by a long-standing custom.
蔽 日 to hide the sun.
蔽 目 to shade the eyes.
[10]蔽 膝 an apron.
蔽 護 to protect; to cover or screen.

蔽 賢 to keep the virtuous from becoming known.

蔽 野 covering the whole place—as undergrowth.

蔽 錮 to impede.

[15]蔽 障 to keep in obscurity.

不 足 蔽 障 insufficient to hide the crime.

蔽 風 雨 to shelter from the storm—used fig.

一 言 以 蔽 之 may be summed up in one word—said of the *Odes*.

利 慾 昏 蔽 covetousness and lust obscured his mind.

[20]蒙 蔽 to mislead; to hoodwink.

雲 蔽 月 the clouds obscure the moon.

斃
斃[4] **To die a violent death; to kill; to fall down dead.**
5105

斃 命 to die a violent death.

斃 而 後 已 to continue till death.

倒 斃 to fall down dead.

束 手 待 斃 to fold the hands and wait till death—as in famine.

[5]淹 斃 drowned.

猝 斃 sudden death by accident.

自 斃 to ruin oneself by depraved courses.

鎗 斃 killed by shooting.

嬖[4] **Partial; a favourite; a parasite. Lecherous, depraved.**
5106

嬖 人 or 愛 嬖 a favourite.

嬖 子 配 嫡 for the sons of concubines to be reckoned legitimate.

嬖 妾 a favourite concubine.

嬖 童 or 嬖 倖 a catamite.

便 嬖 favourites.

臂[4]
The arm. Also read *pei*
5107

臂 助 a helping hand.

臂 環 bracelets.

臂 肘 the arm.

臂 上 骨 the humerus.

[5]前 臂 the forearm.

助 一 臂 之 力 lend a hand.

反 臂 to throw the arms backward.

攘 臂 to bare the arms.

羊 臂 shoulder of mutton.

避[4] **To shun, to evade, to avoid, to hide.**
5108

避 世 to go into retirement.

避 事 to shirk work.

避 債 to avoid creditors.

避 債 臺 a place in which to avoid creditors.

[5]避 免 to get clear; to avoid; to escape from.

避 免 衝 突 to avoid a clash.

避 入 to seek a refuge.

避 凶 to avoid anything that is ill-omened.

避 匿 to abscond.

[10]避 去 to run away.

避 坑 落 井 to escape one difficulty only to fall into another.

避 姙 to avoid conception; birth-control.

避 嫌 疑 to avoid suspicion.

避 寢 to live alone.

[15]避 席 to leave the table; to vacate one's seat.

避 役 the chameleon.

避 忌 to guard against jealousy.

避 是 非 to avoid scandal.

避 煞 to avoid evil influences, demons, etc.

[20]避 熱 or 避 暑 to take a summer holiday.

避 稅 to evade payment of duty.

避 繁 就 簡 for the sake of conciseness.

避 罪 to avoid punishment—for a crime.

避 而 不 犯 to avoid encroachment.

[25]避 艱 險 to flee from danger.

避 諱 之 字 characters to be avoided—*see* 諱 No. 2357.

避 諱 不 說 to avoid the mention of.; taboo.

避 讓 to give way—to traffic.

避 過 一 次 險 he escaped the danger one time.

[30]避 邪 to avoid evil influences.

避 邪 符 a charm against evil influences.

避 重 就 輕 to shirk the difficult and take the easy.

避 難 or 避 禍 to run away from trouble; to escape calamity.

避 難 趨 易 to take the easy way.

[35]避 電 針 lightning-conductor.

避 面 to avoid meeting a person.

避 風 to avoid draughts; to escape or hide from trouble.

避 風 所 a refuge from the storm—fig.

逃 避 to get out of the way.

[40]遠 避 to keep far from.

PI.　　　　　(ㄆ)
(Pih)

必
4.5. **An emphatic particle. Certainly. must, will, necessarily.**
5109

必 世 而 後 仁 it would take a generation before virtue thoroughly penetrated.

必 也 射 乎 if he must—contend—is it in archery?

必 也 狂 狷 乎 I must have the ambitious and the cautious.

必 也 聖 乎 Must he not certainly be a sage?

[5]必 也 臨 事 而 懼 I must certainly have one who is cautious in entering on affairs.

必 以 類 應 it will be responded to without fail, by those in the same class.

必 修 科 compulsory course—in a curriculum.

必 如 此 must be like this.

必 定 or 必 須 or 必 然 or 必 得 certainly; must; bound to; it is necessary.

[10]必 居 一 於 此 must accept one of these alternatives.

必 殺 不 赦 certain death without respite.

必 然 之 事 a necessity.

必 然 之 勢 stern necessity.

必 然 性 necessity.

[15]必 祭 he certainly would offer it.

必 至 論 necessitarianism.

必 表 而 出 之 he would wear it on the outside of another garment.

必 要 certainly; bound to; a necessity; an essential.

必 要 來 he certainly will come.

[20]必 要 物 necessaries.

必 須 品 necessaries.

不 必 not necessarily; need not.

何 必 What is the necessity?

未 必 it is not likely; not necessarily.

柲
4.5. **To give a playful blow. To strike against.**
5110

攍 拟 to obstruct—as a rock in a stream.

瑟 4.5. A gem or ornament on a scabbard.
5111

苾 4.5. Fragrant.
5112

苾 勃 strongly fragrant.
苾 芬 孝 祀 fragrant has been your filial sacrifice.

(a) Used in transliterating.

苾 芻 a *Bhikshu* or mendicant Buddhist. See 比 No. 5077-G.

壁 4.5. A partition-wall; the wall of a house; a screen-wall; a cliff.
5113

壁 上 觀 an onlooker.
壁 壘 a military breast-work.
壁 子 a partition; a party-wall.
壁 燈 lamps hung on a screen-wall.
⁵壁 立 to stand bolt upright.
壁 虎 or 壁 宮 the gecko or house-lizard.
壁 蝨 ticks.
壁 錢 or 壁 蟢 a flat spider. *See* No. 2441.
影 壁 a screen-wall in front of an entrance.
¹⁰絕 壁 a precipice.[A.p. *chieh⁴-piēr³*
隔 壁 a partition-wall—next door.
↑壁 報 bulletins posted on the wall.

擗 2.5. To beat the breast. Also read *p'i²·⁵*.
5114

擗 踊 to beat the breast and stamp the feet—indicating great grief.

(a) Read *p'i¹·⁵*. To split open. Inter. 劈 No. 5174.

璧 4.5. A piece of jade with a round hole in it, once used as a badge of rank.
5115

璧 璽 or 玉 璽 the State Seal.
璧 謝 to return—a present—with thanks.
原 璧 歸 趙 to return the jewel to the State of *Chao*—to return a thing to its rightful owner.

甓 4.5. Glazed tiles. Also read *p'i⁴·⁵*.
5116

罾 4.5. A kind of fishing-net.
5117

襞 4.5. Folds; pleats.
5118

襞 積 the pleats in a skirt.
襞 衣 中 有 刀 斧 手 some armed men were concealed among the women.
襞 褶 folds or pleats in a garment.

躄 4.5. Lame. Also read *p'i⁴·⁵*.
5119

躄 踊 to stamp with grief—as at the death of a parent.

畢 2.5. To finish; concluded. All, together.
5120

畢 世 a lifetime.
畢 來 they have all come.
畢 命 to end the life.
畢 業 to graduate.
⁵畢 業 年 限 time-limit for graduation.
畢 業 文 憑 a diploma.
畢 業 生 a graduate.
畢 竟 after all; in the end; finally.
畢 竟 何 如 what will be the outcome of it?
¹⁰畢 集 all gathered together.

(a) A hand-net.

畢 之 羅 之 the birds are taken in the various nets.

(b) A constellation. The Hyades.

畢 星 the Hyades.

嗶 4.5. Used in transliterating.
5121

嗶 嘰 beiges.

篳 4.5. A bamboo or wicker fence. Wicker-work.
5122

篳 篥 a whistle used by the Tartars.

篳 路 a cart for faggots.
篳 路 襤 褸 riding on a firewood cart in ragged clothes—i.e., beginning life in a humble way.
篳 門 a wicker gate.

蓽 4.5. A variety of pulse; beans. Used for the preceding.
5123

蓽 澄 茄 Chinese cubebs.

蹕 4.5. To keep persons off the route of the emperor, when on tour. Imperial halting-place.
5124

蹕 臨 the approach of the emperor.
駐 蹕 imperial halting-place.

韠 4.5. Knee-pads of leather worn with ancient court dress.
5125

驆 4.5. Used in transliterating Buddhist books.
5126

弼 4.5. To aid; to assist, as in the government.
5127

弼 傅 imperial tutor.
輔 弼 a support; an assistant.

碧 4.5. Jade. Green or blue.
5128

碧 桃 a double-flowering peach.
碧 樹 a tree of jade, said to grow in the K'un-lun Mountains.
碧 海 the blue-green sea.
碧 清 very clear; lucid.
⁵碧 漢 the blue sky.
碧 玉 green jade.
碧 眼 blue-green eyes—said of foreigners.
碧 空 the blue sky.
碧 紗 green gauze.
¹⁰碧 紗 廚 a gauze tent or room as protection against mosquitoes.
碧 綠 的 bright, clear green.
碧 翳 天 日 the green shades obscured the sky and sun.
碧 色 a greenish blue or bluish green.
碧 落 or 碧 霄 the blue sky.
¹⁵碧 血 a man named 萇 弘 of *Chou* dynasty died in battle in Sze.;

after three years his blood turned to jade—the expression was used afterwards to indicate loyalty to the death.

碧 雲 azure clouds.

碧 霞 元 君 a Taoist goddess, said to be the daughter of 東 嶽 大 帝.

愎 4.5. Perverse; self-willed; obstinate. Also read *p'i*⁴·⁵.

5129

愎 諫 to reject admonitions.

剛 愎 obstinate; perverse.

筆 **笔** 3.5. A pen, a pencil. A stroke of the pen. Straight, direct. To write.

5130

筆 下 under the pen—what one writes.

筆 之 於 書 commit it to writing.

筆 削 to correct a composition.

筆 力 vigour and boldness of the strokes in writing.

⁵筆 勢 style of penmanship or drawing.

筆 墨 pen and ink—stationery.

筆 墨 生 涯 the teaching profession; the profession of a writer.

筆 套·子 sheath to protect the point of a pen.

筆 寫 to put it down in black and white.

¹⁰筆 尖 the tip of a writing-brush or pencil.

筆 帽 a sheath to protect the point of a pencil.

筆 底 生 花 flowers spring up under his pen.

筆 意 handwriting; style of writing.

筆 據 written evidence; in black and white.

¹⁵筆 札 stationery; writing-materials.

筆 架 or 筆 格 a pen-rest; stand for pens.

筆 氣 壯 勁 bold and vigorous handwriting.

筆 法 style of handwriting.

筆·書 strokes in writing characters.

²⁰筆 直 perfectly straight—as straight as a pencil.

筆 直 走 go straight ahead.

筆 硯 pen and ink-slab—writing-materials.

筆 竿 shaft of a pen or pencil.

筆 筒 case for pens; point-protector.

²⁵筆 算 arithmetic worked out on paper, as opposed to that worked out on the abacus.

筆 耕 餬 口 to make a living by writing—lit., to plough with the pen for a living.

筆 記 to take down in writing.

筆 試 written examination.

筆 誤 a slip of the pen.

³⁰筆 資 writer's fees.

筆 走 龍 蛇 dragons and snakes follow his pen—of fine writing.

筆 跡 handwriting; style of handwriting.

筆 金 writer's fees.

筆 鉛 graphite.

³⁵筆 鋒 the tip of a pen or pencil.

筆 頭 a pen-nib or pen-point.

下 筆 to commence to write.

大 筆 large characters; your penmanship.

排 筆 a pencil which spreads the point.

⁴⁰旱 筆 or 乾 筆 brushes with white hairs, requiring less water than those with coloured hairs.

水 筆 brushes for water-colours.

濡 筆 to moisten the pen.

畫 筆 small brushes used by artists.

石 筆 slate-pencil.

⁴⁵粉 筆 chalk for the blackboard.

鉛 筆 lead pencil.

鋼 筆 steel pen.; fountain pen.

開 筆 to begin to study composition.

潷 4.5. To strain off liquid.

5131

潷 乾·了 to drain dry—by pouring off liquid.

潷 藥 to strain a decoction of drugs.

湢 4.5. A public bath-house.

5132

煏 4.5. To dry by the fire.

5133

逼 偪 1.5. To annoy. To press. To compel. To crowd. Near.

5134

逼 不 得 巳 to be obliged to do it.

逼 于 無 奈 forced into a position in which there is no alternative.

逼 人 to overawe.

逼·他 要 compelled him to take it.

⁵逼 令 改 嫁 to force a widow to marry again.

逼 供 to extort evidence.

逼 前 to press forward.

逼 勒 or 逼 令 to compel by force; to constrain.

逼 勒 錢 財 to extort money.

¹⁰逼 取 to extort; to blackmail.

逼 問 to interrogate; to demand an answer.

逼 壓 to browbeat; to keep down.

逼 姦 rape.

逼 嫁 to force a woman to marry.

¹⁵逼·死 or 逼 命 to ill-use so as to force suicide.

逼 窄 narrow; confined.

逼 索 to get by threats.

逼 近 bordering on; to draw near.

逼 迫 to persecute.

²⁰逼 鄰 neighbouring.

荸 2.5. The water chestnut— *Scirpus tuberosus*.

5135

荸·薺 the water-chestnut.

觱 4.5. The Tartar horn or pipe, used to frighten the horses of their foes. Whistling of wind.

5136

觱 篥 the Tartar pipe which has a mournful sound.

(a) Read *pi*². A whistle.

吹 觱 to blow a whistle.

P'I. (ㄆ)

丕 1 Great, distinguished.

5137

丕 丕 vast.

丕 基 a great heritage.

丕 子 the emperor.

丕 承 哉 武 王 烈 great in the carrying out of these plans was the brilliant work of King *Wu*.

5不 時 a time of great prosperity.
不 績 a vast achievement.
不 顯 哉 文 王 謨 great and splendid were the schemes of King *Wên*.

呸[1] To give a snort of contempt. Pron. *p'ei*[1].
5138

邳[1] A department in the State of *Lu*, in what is now Shantung or North Kiangsu.
5139

痞[3] A stoppage; constipation; indigestion.
5140

痞 匪 rebels or marauders; obstructionists.
痞 塊 or 痞 症 a swelling of the abdomen from constipation.
痞 滿 indigestion.
痞 積 constipation.
土 痞 local villains.

圮[3] Destroyed, ruined. To subvert. To injure.
5141 Distinguish 圯 No. 2931.

圮 毀 ruined, destroyed.
傾 圮 collapsed in ruins.

皮[2] Skin, leather, bark, fur, peel, outer covering, wrapping. Tare. Weight of wrapping, etc. Radical 107.
5142

皮 之 不 存 毛 將 安 傅 if the skin be lost, how can the fur be laid on?
皮 包 wrapping of packages; small handbag or valise.
皮 包 骨 emaciated.
皮・匠 a tanner.
5皮・卷 parchment manuscripts.
皮 器 leather goods.
皮 囊 the skin-bag—the body.
皮 夾 a wallet, a portfolio.
皮・子 skin; wrapping.(人皮 兒.)
10皮・帶 a leather belt; belting for machinery.
皮 扯 手 straps in tramcars, etc.
皮 板 the skin side of furs.
皮・條 leathern thongs. *See* 拉 No. 3756-26.
皮 毛 skin and hair; fine hairs on the body; body, as opposed to the soul; superficial.

15但 知 皮 毛 不 知 內 容 he has only a superficial knowledge of the matter, he does not know the inner bearings of the case.
皮 油 tallow from the tallow-tree.
皮 症 skin diseases.
皮 相 (*hsiang*[1]) the style or appearance of a person; superficial.
皮 硝 tannin.
20皮 箱 a leather box.
皮 紙 tough paper made from the bark of the paper-mulberry.
皮 統 unlined fur garment.
皮 肉 skin and flesh; the flesh.
皮 肉 生 涯 prostitution.
25皮 脂 oil on the skin.
皮 脂 腺 sebaceous glands.
皮 臉 shameless.
皮 膠 glue.
皮 膚 the skin.
30皮 色 complexion; quality of furs.
皮 蛋 duck's eggs preserved in lime. A.c. 變 蛋.
皮 衣 fur clothing.
皮 袍・子 a fur gown.
皮 袋 leather purse or small bag.
35皮 貨 furs; skins.
皮 開 肉 綻 effects of a severe thrashing.
皮 革 leather.
假 冒 皮 imitation leather.
奶 皮 cream.
40書 皮 cover of a book.
油 漆 皮 patent leather.
熟 皮 dressed leather.
生 皮 raw hides; undressed leather.
眞 皮 the true skin.
45硝 皮 to tan and dress leather.
表 皮 the epidermis.
除 皮 deduct the tare.

劈 劃[1] To peel, to pare, to trim, to split.
5143

劃 削 to scrape or shave off.
劃 手 甲 to pare the finger nails.
劃 橙 to peel an orange.

帔[4] A skirt. Long robe for women, having no sleeves and fastened down the front. Inter. next, to throw over the shoulders.
5144 Also read *p'ei*[4].

披[1] To open; to unroll; to spread out. Also read *p'ei*[1].
5145

披 卷 to open a scroll or a book.
披 屋 an outhouse.
披 展 to open out—as a map or a letter.
披 廈 an outhouse; a lean-to.
5披 心 or 披 懷 to be open and sincere, telling all one's heart.
披 拂 to wave; to turn over, as the leaves of a book.
披 摩 to open out and smooth; to give minute explanation.
披 書 to open a book.
披 瀝 to speak without reserve.
10披 猖 to run wild.
披 肝 瀝 膽 I open my liver and empty my gall-bladder—I speak without reserve.
披 荒 to open up untilled lands.
披 襟 to open the bosom of the gown.
披 覽 to open and read.
15披 讀 to open and read.
披 開 to open up.
披 閱 to open and note the contents, as of a letter.
披 離 tangled, as branches.
披 露 to make an announcement; to publish.
20披 露 心 曲 to unburden the mind; to tell the innermost thoughts.
披 靡 blown about by the wind; scattered, as troops.
披 髮 dishevelled hair.

(a) To wrap, to throw on, as a garment.

披・上 衣・服 to throw on the clothing. (*p'ei*[1]-)
披 剃 to put on the cassock and shave the head—to become a Buddhist priest or nun.
披 帶 to wear; to carry.
披 掛 to put on full uniform.
5披 星 戴 月 to cloak oneself with the stars and wear the moon—to travel by night.
披 枷 帶 鎖 manacled and wearing the cangue.
披 甲 to wear armour.
披 簑 衣 to throw on a coir rain-cloak.
披・肩 a kind of cape.
10披・著 to throw on. (*p'ei*[1]-)

披 風 a woman's cloak.
椅 披 a cover for the back of a chair.

疲 [2] Tired, weary, exhausted.
5146

疲 倦 or 疲 乏 or 疲 困 fatigued, weary and weak.
疲 勞 utterly weary in body and spirits.
疲 弊 weakness.
疲 怯 nervous; dispirited.
[5]疲 懶 dilatory; inert.
疲 敗 wearied; used up.
疲 根 dyspepsia.
疲 民 an exhausted population.
疲 玩 remiss; lazy; dilatory.
[10]疲 瘠 barren and poor—soil.
疲 癃 aged and prone to illness.
疲 神 energies exhausted.
疲 緩 remiss; dilatory.
疲 輭 fatigued; weak.
[15]疲 鈍 fatigued; weary.
疲 難 缺 a wearisome and difficult post—official posts were classified into groups according to the nature of the work.
疲 馬 a jaded horse.

詖 [4] To flatter. Half the truth; one-sided.
5147   Also read *pi*[4].

詖 辭 知 其 所 蔽 when his words are partial, I know—his ideas—are clouded.
詖 辯 to argue for the wrong; to toady.

庀 [3] To prepare. To regulate. To hand up.
5148

庀 賦 to provide levies.
官 庀 其 司 officials fulfil their duties.

仳 [3] To part.
5149

仳 離 to separate from—as a husband.

(a) Read *p'i*[2]. A plain woman.

仳 傀 (*hui*[1]) ugly.

屁 氣 [4]
5150   To break wind.

屁·股 the buttocks.
屁·股 眼 the anus.
打 屁·股 to flog on the buttocks.
狗 屁 What rot! Bosh!

批 搋 [1]
5151   To criticize; to comment upon.

批 判 論 criticism.
批 子 a comment.
批 改 correction—by a teacher on pupil's work.
批 明 to comment on; to give clear instructions.
[5]批 正 or 批 削 to correct; to revise.
批·評 or 批 註 criticisms; a critique; to criticize; to censure.
批·評 家 critics.
批·評 會 criticism lessons—in a normal school.
批·評·的 功 用 the critical function.
[10]批 評 論 criticism.
批 評 論 文 critical essays; a critique.
批 誌 to make critical notes on the margin of a book.
批 講 to explain.
批 點 to criticize; to revise.
[15]旁 批 notes at the side.
頂 批 critical notes at the top of the page.

(a) To endorse a petition. To reply officially to an inferior. To make an order of court. Officially authorized.

批 令 a rescript.
批 准 to assent to a petition; to sanction; approved.
批 准 主 義 the policy of making concessions.
批 判 呈 詞 to give an official decision about a petition.
[5]批 回 official reply to a petitioner, or a subordinate.
批 斥 to reprimand.

批 斷 or 批 判 to decide a case; to endorse a judgement.
批 示 to publish a case; official reply to a petition; proclamation.
批 答 reply to a petition.
[10]批 繳 official reply to a petitioner or a subordinate.
批 行 to sanction.
批 覆 official reply to a subordinate or to a petition.
批 諭 a rescript; official authorization.
批 銷 to write off; to endorse as correct.
[15]批 飭 to sanction.
批 駁 to reverse the decision of a lower court; to note disapproval of a course of action.

(b) To lease. To arrange for the purchase of.

批 出 to lease out.
批 單 agreement for a time-bargain.
批 地 to lease land.
批 定 to buy goods to arrive.
[5]批 帖 a deed; a lease.
批 約 a lease; an agreement.
批 與 to lease to.
批 辦 to grant a trading-privilege to.
批 限 period of a lease.
[10]批 貨 to buy goods to arrive.

(c) To sell wholesale. A shipment of goods, or a number of men, etc., sent in batches—each batch is called a *p'i*.

批·發 wholesale trade.
批·發 價 wholesale price.
批·發 商 人 wholesale dealers.
批·發 生 意 wholesale trade.
[5]一 大 批 軍 火 a large batch of munitions.
前 一 批 到·了 the first batch has arrived.
大 批 的 wholesale; a large batch.
整 批 出 售 to sell by wholesale.

(d) To slap, to smack.

批 嘴 巴·子 [4] to slap a person on the mouth.
批 殺 to beat to death with the hands.
批 面 or 批 頰 to slap the face.

(e) To shave to a point. Pointed.

竹 批 雙 耳 峻 their ears sticking up like sharp-pointed bamboos.

枇 2
5152

The loquat.

枇·杷 the loquat.
枇 杷 門 巷 brothels.

(a) Read *pi*³. A ladle used in sacrifices.

𥓋 1
5153

To split. Cracked.

砒
礜 1
5154

Arsenic.

砒 信 or 砒 礵 or 砒 石 or 砒 毒 arsenic.

紕 1
5155

Spoilt silk.

紕 繆 erroneous.

(a) Read *p'i*². Tassels, silk fringes.

素 絲 紕 之 tied with a twist of white silk.
縞 冠 素 紕 a white silk cap with white silk tassels.

邳 4
5156

Name of a feudal State in the north of what is now Honan. Also read *pei*⁴.

琵 2
5157

A musical instrument, known as the balloon-guitar.

琵·琶 the guitar, as above.
琵·琶 別 抱 carrying her guitar to another boat — said of a widow or a concubine who remarries.
琵 琶 撥 a plectrum. [remarries.
琵 琶 精 or 琵 琶 蟲 name for a louse.
琵 琶 骨 the collar-bone.
琵 琶 魦 a species of ray.

毗
毘
毗 2
5158

Adjoining, near, having the same boundary.

毗 倚 to lean on.
毗 連 adjacent.

(a) Used in transliterating.

毗 佛 略 one of the twelve divisions of the Buddhist Canon.
毗 沙 門 a Hindu god, worshipped by Buddhists as the god of wealth.
毗 舍 闍 vampire-like demons, (Budd.), from the Sanskrit, *pisâtcha*.

媲 4
5159

To pair; to match.

媲 美 a pair.

貔 2
5160

A white fox. A kind of leopard.

貔 貅 the male and female respectively, of a fabulous, fierce beast like a leopard—used as descriptive of brave troops.
貔 虎 a fierce beast.

啤 2
5161

Used in transliterating.

啤 酒 beer.

埤 2
5162

A low wall; a parapet. Inter. 陴 No. 5165.

埤 堄 (*i*⁴) parapets. *See next* No. 5163.

(a) Increasingly. To add to.

政 事 一 埤 益 我 the affairs of government increasingly devolve upon me.

(b) Read *p'i*³. Low-lying.

埤 濕 marshy places.

睥 4
5163

To glance around. To look askance. Also read *pi*⁴.

睥 睨 to look upon with disdain; battlements,—because the defenders looked down from them.

脾 2
5164

The spleen, the stomach. Temper; disposition.

脾 寒 a chill; malaria.
脾·氣 temper; disposition.
脾 泄 bowel troubles.
脾 病 or 脾 疬 enlargement of the spleen.
脾 胃 the stomach; appetite.
脾 臟 the spleen.

陴 2
5165

A parapet. Inter. 埤 No. 5162.

守 陴 to guard the ramparts.

羆 2
5166

A kind of bear.

譬 4
5167

To compare; to suppose. A simile.

譬·不 得 incomparable.
譬·喻 a simile; for instance.
譬 如 or 譬 若 for instance; may be compared with; is like.
譬 比 for instance.
譬 況 之 言 symbolic language.
譬 類 to make comparison.

贔 4
5168

Able to support a great weight. Also read *pi*⁴.

贔 屓 a river-god figured as a tortoise and used as a base for heavy stone tablets.

P'I.   (ㄆ)

(P'ih)

疋 3.5.
5169

Anciently read *shu*¹. The foot. A roll of cloth. N.A. for such things. Radical 103.

疋·數 number of pieces.
疋○頭 舖 a piece-goods store.
一 疋 布 a piece of cloth.

(a) Read *ya³*. Used for 雅 No. 7222.

匹 3.5. One of a pair; a mate. A common or ignorant man.

5170

匹偶 or 匹配 a married couple.
匹夫 a husband; an ordinary man.
匹夫不可奪志也 you cannot take the will, even from an ordinary person.
匹婦 a married woman.
⁵匹嫡 the first wife.
匹配之際 at the time of marriage.
匹雛 a duckling.
匹鳥 the mandarin-duck.

(a) N.A. for horses; also used for pieces or rolls of cloth, etc. See preceding No. 5169.

一匹¹馬 a horse.
半匹³紅紗 half a roll of red silk.
馬匹¹ horses.

鴄 3.5. Wild duck or mallard.

5171

辟 4.5. To punish; to put to death. To beat the breast.

5172

辟以止辟乃辟 to punish in order that punishment may prevent further punishment.
辟踊 to beat the breast and leap about—indicating extreme grief.
大辟 capital punishment.
宮辟 castration as a punishment.
致辟 to execute.

(a) Perverse; specious; partial. Inter. next.

辟名 merely nominal; false; pretended.
辟陋 rustic; mean.
便辟 a flatterer; a sycophant; specious.
是以非辟之心無自入也 in this way evil and depraved thoughts found no entrance into his mind.
放辟邪侈 self-abandonment, moral deflection, depravity, and wild license.

(b) To remove.

行辟人 to remove people out of the roads when on tour.

(c) To spin, to twist thread.

妻辟纑 the wife twists hempen threads.

(d) Used as 闢 No. 5177. To open up; to develop.

辟土地 to enlarge the territories.
辟草萊任土地者次之 those who open up the grassy lands and make—the people—cultivate them should receive the next punishment.
田野不辟 the cultivated areas not being extended.

(e) Read *p'i⁴*. To compare. Used as 譬 No. 5167.

辟如天地—Confucius—may be compared with Heaven and Earth.
辟若掘井 may be compared to one digging a well.

(f) Read *p'i⁴* or *pi⁴*. The emperor. A sovereign or prince.

辟不辟 to be the sovereign in name only.
辟公 the feudal princes.
辟王 a prince or ruler.
辟雝 the hall in Peking where the Hanlin graduates were examined.
⁵先辟 my deceased husband.
后辟 the empress.
皇辟 an emperor; a deceased husband.
復辟 to restore the monarchy.

(g) To summon to court. To appoint to office.

辟召 to summon to court.
辟命 appointments to office.
辟引 to call to court.
辟除 to appoint to office.
來辟 to appear before the ruler.
徵辟 to summon to court.

(h) Read *pi⁴*. Used as 避 No. 5108.

辟世 to withdraw from the world; to retire from office.
辟席 to vacate one's seat.

辟患 to avoid distress or sorrow.
辟易 to flee in all directions; to shy and swerve, as a horse; to disperse, as troops or mists.
⁵辟穀 to abstain from cereals in order to attain to immortality; to starve.
辟邪 to ward off evil influences; a fabulous animal with two horns, placed at the graves of feudal princes.

(i) Read *p'i* or *pi⁴*. Used as 睥 No. 5163. To glance down; to look with disdain.

辟倪 to look with disdain; to glance down.

(j) To incline the head.

辟咡 (*êrh⁴*) 而對 to turn the head and answer.

(k) Used in transliterating.

辟支 or 辟支迦 or 辟支佛 a Buddha who appears between the disappearance of one and the arrival of the next true Buddha—self-intelligence.

僻 4.5. Mean; low; rustic. Secluded.

5173

僻倪 battlements, *see* Nos. 5162, 5163.
僻儒 perverted and decadent scholarship.
僻地 a secluded place.
僻左 sinister practices; corruptions.
⁵僻巷 a side-lane.
僻脫 or 撇脫 alert and active; prompt in action; getting things done.
僻處 or 僻居 to reside; to dwell privately.
僻見 prejudiced; a partial view.
僻陋 rustic; untaught.
¹⁰僻·靜 out-of-the-way; lonely. (*pei⁴-*)
乖僻 dissolute.
偏僻 eccentric; heterodox; out-of-the-way.
怪僻 eccentric.
放僻 dissolute.
¹⁵荒僻 out-of-the-way places.
邪僻 depraved; heterodox; mean.
隱僻 remote; obscure—of writings.

劈 1.5.
5174　To split open; to rend.

劈 分 to divide.
劈 手 to thrust forth the hand.
劈·柴 to split firewood; split firewood.
劈 歷 一 聲 a clap of thunder; a rending sound. *See* 霹 No. 5178.
⁵劈 水 scull used in the front of a boat when descending rapids.
劈 破 to break open; to split in two.
劈 碎 to split into fragments.
劈 空 to fabricate; to make up a story.
劈 臉 or 劈 頭² to aim blows at the face.
¹⁰劈·開 to split open—as with a hatchet.

澼 4.5. To bleach. To wash
5175　clean.

以 泭 澼 絖 爲 事 were engaged in silk washing.

癖 3.5. Indigestion. Morbid ap-
5176　petite; a weakness for; a craving.

癖 性 one's weakness for any particular thing; eccentricity; propensity.
癖 病 indigestion; constipation.
癖 疾 dyspeptic; hysteric.
書 癖 excessive fondness for study; bibliomania.
⁵衣 癖 excessive fondness for dress.
錢 癖 avarice.
食 癖 craving for food; morbid appetite.

闢 4.5. To split open; to cleave.
5177　To burst forth; to develop.

闢 土 植 穀 to open up the land and cultivate cereals—agriculture.
闢 戶 to open the door.
闢 牖 取 明 to open the windows and get more light—fig.
闢 田 to open up land for agriculture.

透 闢 to see through a thing; poignant.
開 天 闢 地 the creation of the universe.

(a) To dispute, to controvert.

闢 佛 老 to expose the fallacies of Buddhism and Taoism.
闢 邪 to expose heretical teachings.

(b) To avoid; to retire.

闢 處 海 濱 retired to the seashore.

霹 4.5.
5178　The crash of thunder.

霹 雷 a clap of thunder.
霹 靂 sound of thunder; a rumbling noise.
霹 靂 一 聲 a clap of thunder; a startling sound—used fig.

PIAO.　　(ㄆㄠ)

摽 ³ To strike. To throw down.
　　To push off. Inter. next.
5179. Also read *piao*¹.

摽 出 門 外 turn him out of doors.
摽 梅 the plum drops when ripe—girls should be married when they are of age.
摽 榜 mutually publishing each other—as men of talents.
摽 落 底 下 throw it down.

(a) Read *piao*¹. To wave.

摽 使 者 to motion to the messenger.
摽 幟 a sign, a mark, an indication.
摽 旗 to signal with a flag.

標 ¹ The topmost branch. A
　　mark, a beacon, a signal, a
5180　flag, a streamer, a signboard;
　　to put up a notice. A warrant, a notice.

標 名 to publish the names of successful candidates.
標 布 T-cloths.
標 幟 a mark, a label, a sign.
標 揚 to exhibit.
⁵標 旗 a signal flag.

標 旗 幟 to raise a standard.
標 本 specimens; samples; example.
　動·物 標 本 zoological specimens.
標 本 買·賣 sale of goods by samples.
¹⁰標 格 the appearance; the countenance.
標 槍 a spear with a flag—used by escorts.
標 榜 to publish the list of successful candidates.
標 榜 沽 名 to trade on one's reputation.
標 樣 an example.
¹⁵標 準 a mark to aim at—an example, normal standard, basis of comparison; as a prefix—standard.
　以 作 標 準 to serve as a standard.
標 準 一 致 standardization.
標 準 判 定 standardization.
標 準 化 standardization.
²⁰標 準 品 質 standard quality.
標 準 差 standard deviation. (-*ch'a*¹)
標 準 時 standard time.
標 準 樣 子 standard sample.
標 準 權 度 standard weights and measures.
²⁵標 準 氣 壓 standard air-pressure.
標 準 燭 光 standard candle-power.
標 準 語 standard speech.
²⁷½標 準 音 standard pronunciation.
標 的⁺ or 目 的 aim; object.
標 示 to publish.
³⁰標 秀 to flourish—as grain.
標 程 model; example.
標 章 sign.
標 竿 a signal post.
標 籤 a magistrate's warrant.
³⁵標 緻 handsome, beautiful, pretty.
標 舉 to extol; to raise to high honours.
標 記 marks—for navigating; distinguishing marks.
標 語 notices; slogans.
標 語 口 號 slogans.
⁴⁰貼 標 語 to paste up written slogans.
標 識 labelled.
　航 路 標 識 navigation buoys or beacons.
標 車 convoy carts, hired to protect travellers.
標 金 gold bars.
⁴⁵標 題 a heading—in a newspaper.

大字標題 large-type headings.
標題員 caption writer.
標麵 the best flour.
標點 punctuation.
[50]標點符號 punctuation marks.
投標承攬 to tender for a contract.
警船浮標 a warning buoy.
開標 to draw (a lottery.)
頭標 first prize.
↑音標 phonetic symbols.
(a) A body of troops.
標下 under the banner of.
標統 a colonel.
鎮標 troops under a former Brigade-general.

彪[1] A tiger-cat. Stripes, streaks, veins. Ornamental.
5181

彪子 a mischievous person.
半彪子 a fool.
彪炳 or 文炳 elegant.
彪煥 brilliant; elegant; showy.

5182
Hair, shaggy. Radical 190.

5183
A whirlwind.

飇影星馳 as rapid as a whirlwind or a star.
飇風暴雨 a violent storm of wind and rain.

麃[1] To weed.
5184

綿綿其麃 many were the weeders.

(a) Martial appearance.

駟介麃麃 the team with its mail has a martial air.

(b) Read p'iao[3]. To moult, to change colour.

鳥麃色而沙鳴 when birds are moulting and their voices harsh.

臕[1] Fat, gross, sleek.
5185

臕滿 or 肥臕 plump.
上臕 to get fat.

鑣[1] Bit for a horse. An iron-pointed spear.
5186　Used with 鏕 No. 5204.

表[3] To manifest; to display.
5187

表冊 statements.
表出 to make manifest; to make known.
表句 a proposition. (logic).
表同情 to show sympathy; to show agreement.
[5]表同意 to manifest agreement.
表奏 to memorialize the emperor.
表彰 to show forth clearly.
表德 to exhibit virtue.
表徵 proofs.
[10]表情 expression of emotion.
表拒 to protest.
表拒狀 form of protest.
表拒之完稅 to pay duty under protest.
表揚善行 to publish a man's good deeds.
[15]表文 or 表本 a memorial to the throne.
表明 to manifest; to make clear.
表明中立 to manifest neutrality.
表樣 an example.
表決 to manifest an opinion; to show by a vote.
[20]　反表決 negative vote.
　正表決 affirmative vote.
　起立表決 rising vote.
表演 to demonstrate the use of—as machinery, instruments, etc.; [perform(ance).
表物 a keepsake.
[25]表率 an example; a leader.
表現 to reveal; to exhibit; becomes manifest.
表現感情 manifesting emotion.
情緒之表現 expression of emotion.
表異 to mark out the difference—as between talented and ordinary people.
[30]表發意見 to express an opinion.
表白 to show plainly; defence; vindication.

表示 to represent; to signify; a sign or emblem; expression; superscription.
表示同意 an expression of unanimity.
表示否認 to express disagreement.
[35]表示意見 to express an opinion.
表禮 a present given on first seeing a child.
表章 a memorial to the throne.
表著 or 顯著 to manifest.
表號 a symbol.
[40]表表 noted people; rare things.
表記 a keepsake.
表象 expression—in teaching, etc.
表達其意 to express the meaning of.
表道樹 trees marking the road—finger-posts.
[45]表音法 phonetic methods.
表題 a motto.
以表寸忱 as a token of my feelings (friendship, affection).
代表 a representative; a delegate.
旌表建坊 a gateway or arch erected to commemorate the virtues of a person.
[50]發表 released for publication.
自表 to distinguish oneself.

(a) Outside, external.

表壯 external vigour.
表皮 epidermis.
表綱 outline.
表裏 coat and lining; outside and inside; used fig.
[5]表裏[3]如一 outside and inside the same—sincere.
表裏[3]爲奸 in treacherous collusion.
表面 appearance; outward expression; surface.
表面上 outwardly; superficially.
表面上看來 looking at the thing superficially.
[10]表面張力 surface tension. (physics).
表面觀 superficial view.
表面觀之 looking at the matter superficially.
僅屬表面 only on the surface.
僅觀人物之表面 only looks at the surface of men and things.
[15]現於表面 manifest on the surface.

(b) Applied to descendants of female relatives on the father's side, and to descendants of the mother's brothers.

表 兄 弟 male first cousins of another surname.

表 姐 妹 female first cousins of another surname.

表 姪 grandchildren of paternal aunts.

表 親 relatives on the mother's side.

(c) A "style" or fancy name.

表 字 a fancy name or "style."
貴 表 What is your "style?"

(d) An index. A chart. A watch. Used as a suffix indicating meters, gauges, etc.

表 列 to catalogue; to index or tabulate.

一 覽 表 a chart or table.

九 九 表 the multiplication table.

光 力 表 actinometer.
[5]壓 力 表 pressure gauge.
天 氣 表 weather-glass or barometer.

寒 暑 (or 暖) 表 thermometer.

列 氏 寒 暖 表 Réaumur thermometer.

攝 氏 寒 暖 表 Celsius thermometer.

[10] 最 高 寒 暑 (or 暖) 表 maximum thermometer.

百 分 度 寒 暑 表 centigrade thermometer.

空 氣 寒 暖 表 air thermometer.

自 記 寒 暖 表 self-registering thermometer.

華 氏 寒 暖 表 Fahrenheit thermometer.

[15]手 表 a wrist-watch.
時 表 a watch.

最 準 時 辰 表 a chronometer.

時 間 表 time-table.
晴 雨 表 a barometer.
[20]更 次 表 a telltale clock for watchmen.

核 算 表 calculating machine.
水 力 表 hydraulic gauge.
水 程 表 ship's patent log.
汽 表 steam-gauge.
[25]浮 表 a float-gauge.

漏 沙 分 時 表 hour-glass.
測 火 表 pyrometer.
煤 氣 表 gas-meter.
算 數 表 calculating machine.
[30]自 停 表 stop-watch.
記 數 表 register of attendance.
速 力 表 speedometer.
量²力 表 dynamometer.
量²水 表 water-meter.
[35]量²電 表 electric-units meter.
量²風 表 wind-gauge.
鐘 表 匠 watchmaker.
雨 量⁴表 rain-gauge.
電 力 表 meter for measuring electric power.
[40]電·氣 表 meter for measuring electricity consumed.
預 算 表 a budget.
風 力 表 wind-gauge; anemometer.
驗 濕 表 hygrometer.

俵³
5188
     To distribute.

俵 散 to disperse; scattered.
俵 給 to distribute; to divide.

婊³
5189
     A prostitute.

婊·子 a prostitute.
婊·子 養·的 you son of a harlot!

裱³
5190
     To mount maps or scrolls. To paste.

裱 畫 舖 shop where mounting work is done.
裱 糊 匠 a paper-hanger.
裱 褙 to paste paper into pasteboard.

P'IAO.   (ㄆㄧㄠ)

殍 3.4.
5191
   To die of hunger; to perish. 莩 No. 1940 is also used for this.

殍 殣 to die of starvation.

票⁴
5192
   A warrant. A bill, a bank note; a ticket; a certificate; a document. A slip of bamboo or paper.

票 劵 a ticket.
票 夾 a wallet for notes.

票·子 a ticket; a warrant; a cashnote.
票 存 cash reserves against notes issued.
[5]票 摺 a share-certificate and the corresponding dividend-warrant.
票 據 a certificate.
票 根 a counterfoil—as of a cheque or ticket.
票 背 簽 字 to endorse a cheque.
票 號 a bank for the issue of drafts, etc.
[10]票 面 價 值 face-value of a note.
票 額 sum due on a bill.
串 票 certificate for payment of taxes.
來 回 票 return ticket.
信 票 or 差 票 a warrant for arrest.
[15]傳 票 a summons.
公 債 票 stocks; government bonds.
出 票 to issue a warrant.
匯 票 a bill of exchange; a draft. See No. 2353—A.
半 票 half-ticket.
[20]多 票 制 plural-voting system.
存 票 a drawback for duties paid.
彩 票 or 發 財 票 a lottery-ticket.
憑 票 draft or note payable to bearer.
投 票 to ballot.
[25]橫 線 紙 票 a crossed cheque.
流 通 錢 票 circular note.
火 票 warrant for immediate arrest.
火 車 免 票 railway pass.
當 票 pawn-ticket.
[30]發 票 an invoice.
季 票 season-ticket.
船 票 steamer-ticket; boat-license.
認 票 不 認 人 payable to bearer.
路 票 a passport.
[35]頓 票 women and children held for ransom.
鈔 票 bank notes.
銀 票 a cheque; a bank note.

僄 4.1.
5193
   Light, airy.

僄 悍 supercilious and hasty.
僄 狡 smart, prompt, alert, roguish.
僄 遨 alert, prompt in action.

剽 ⁴
5194
   To stab, to puncture; to cut. To rob. Swift, alert.

勡 掠 to rob with violence.
勡 疾 or 輕 勡 nimble, active.
勡 竊 to plagiarize.

嫖² To visit prostitutes.
Lewd, lustful. Fornication.
5195

嫖 妓 or 嫖 娼 to visit prostitutes.
嫖 婊·子 to visit prostitutes.
嫖 客 a frequenter of brothels.
嫖 舍 a brothel.
嫖 賭 prostitution and gambling—profligacy.

(a) Read *p'iao¹*. Military title.

嫖 姚 (*yao⁴*) Military title under the *Han* dynasty.

漂¹ To float; to drift; to be tossed about.
5196 Used with 飄 No. 5205.

漂 來 漂 去 drifting hither and thither.
漂 搖 tossed about; rocking.
漂 撞 to collide—ships.
漂 沒 floating and sinking—as things on the water; used fig.
⁵漂 泊 without fixed abode.
漂 泊 江 湖 to travel all over the country; a vagrant life.
漂 流 drifting about.
漂 流 浪 子 a dissipated vagabond.
漂 流 無 定 wandering aimlessly.
¹⁰漂 海 or 漂 洋 to take a voyage; to cross the ocean.
漂 蕩 wandering; vagrant.

(a) Read *p'iao³* To bleach.

漂 去 顏 色 to bleach out the colour.
漂 布 to bleach linen.
漂 布 匠 a fuller; a bleacher.
漂·得 亮 bleached very white.
⁵漂 晒 to bleach in the sun.
漂 洋 布 white shirtings.
漂 白 to bleach.
漂 白 粉 bleaching powder.

(b) Read *p'iao¹*. To look fresh.

漂·亮 bright; smart; fresh; sleek and glossy; good-looking.

藻² Duck-weed.
5197

藻 萍 or 浮 藻 duck-weed.

瓢² A calabash or gourd, used for a ladle.
5198

瓢 蟲 the lady-bird.

瘭¹·⁴ A whitlow.
5199

瞟³ To look askance; to squint; one-eyed.
5200 Also read *p'iao¹*.

瞟·了 一 眼 to cast a glance; to give a wink.
瞟 眇 to see indistinctly.

縹³·⁴ Clear, bright colour.
5201

縹 白 a clear white.
縹 碧 bright, clear green.
縹 青 or 縹 色 the blue-green colour of nature.

(a) Read *p'iao³*. Misty, indistinct.

縹 緲 misty, obscure, impressionistic paintings.
縹 縹 soaring.

膘¹ Fat, swollen—used of a sleek horse
5202

膘 肥 fat.

(a) Read *p'iao³*. The flanks of an animal.

蟉¹ A chrysalis.
5203

鏢¹ The point of a sword; a weapon. Also read *piao¹*.
5204

鏢 師 armed escort for bank messengers.
鏢 鎗 iron pointed spear.

飄¹ To whirl, as the wind. Floating. Graceful.
5205 Used with 漂 No. 5196.

飄 僻 地 方 a deserted spot.
飄 動 moved; fluttering in the wind.

飄 寓 to be a stranger in a strange land.
飄 布 or 票 布 a cloth badge as a token of membership.
⁵飄 帶 a pennant.
飄 忽 fluttering; speedy; suddenly.
飄 揚 blown into the air; to waft.
飄 搖 rocking in the wind; drifting about.
飄 泛 the movement of a vessel on the water.
¹⁰飄 流 floating about; hither and thither; dissipated.
飄 潑 大 雨 to rain excessively.
飄 疾 swiftly.
飄 眇 long and clear sounds.
飄 落 blown down—as leaves.
¹⁵飄 蕩 to rock; to roll.
飄 雪 snow whirled by the winds.
飄 雲 floating clouds.
飄 零 fallen—as leaves from the trees; ruined—as a family.
飄 零 一 身 a lonely wanderer.
²⁰飄 風 a whirlwind.
飄 飄 然 airy and graceful; sylph-like.
輕 飄 light; floating.

驃⁴ A charger.
5206

驃 勇 a valiant horseman.
驃 國 name given under the *T'ang* dynasty to the eastern part of Burma.
驃 騎 cavalry.

鰾⁴ The swimming-bladder of fishes.
5207

鰾 膠 fish-glue.

PIEH.   (ㄅㄝ)

別²·⁵ To separate; to part.
5208

別·了 to leave; to say goodbye.
別 來 一 載 since we parted a year ago.
別 來 已 三 秋 it is already three years since we parted.
別 來 無 恙 since we parted, have you been well?
⁵別 去 to part; to separate. Cf. C 1½
別 後 after we parted.

別 後 正 深 渴 慕 since we parted, I have deeply longed for you.

別 敬 a parting present.

別 筵 a parting feast.

[10]別 緒 the ties which bind when separated.

別 離 to leave; to depart from.

別 離 愁 the sorrow of separation.

告 別 to take leave.

小 別 a short absence.

[15]留 別 to linger at parting as unwilling to separate.

訪·別 a farewell call.

話 別 to bid farewell.

送 別 to see a person off.

餞 別 to give a farewell party.

(a) To discriminate; to distinguish.

別 字 眼 to argue; to dispute; to find fault.

別 擇 to adjudicate.

別 異 to discriminate.

別 白 to discriminate clearly.

[5]別 除 權 right of discrimination. (legal).

分 別 to discriminate; to distinguish.

區 別 discrimination; a great difference.

特 別 special.

識 別 to discriminate.

(b) Other, another.

別 下 毒 手 he will find some other way to do injury.

別·人 others.

別·的 人 some other person.

別 具 肺 腸 having other aims and outlook. (condemnatory)

[5]別 史 a name given to histories, reckoned as inferior to the dynastic histories but superior to the historical romances.

別 向 to change one's viewpoint or opinions.

別 名 a different name; another name; a separate name.

別 墅 a country villa.

別 外 in some other way.

[10]別 往 to go to another place.

別 徑 another road.

別 情 other circumstances.

別 意 of another opinion.

別 房 or 別 室 a concubine.

[15]別 才 unusual ability.

別 於 禽 獸 differing from the birds and beasts—because of the knowledge of propriety.

↓別 本 different copy; replica.

別 是 一 天 we were in another world.

別 時 another time; other times—the past.

[20]別 有 天 地 another state of existence altogether.

別 有 意 思 ulterior motives.

別 業 houses or land not used personally by the owner.

別 樣 other kinds.

別 歲 a feast at the close of the year.

[25]別 派 of another school or class.

別 無 他 法 there is no other alternative.

別 無 所 有 has nothing else.

別 生 枝 節 other shoots will sprout—disorders will spread; other contingencies may arise.

別 的 other; another.

[30]別 科 a special course.

別 種 用 意 ulterior motives.

別·紐 contrary; perverse; stubborn; awkward. A.w. 彆 扭

別·致 (or·緻) new and unusual; obstinate.

別·處 another place.

[35]別 號 another name, an alias.

別 調 (tiao⁴) another tune—something different; unusual.

別 趣 opinions, thoughts, etc., quite different.

別 針 a pin.

別 開 生 面 to do a thing in an unusual way.

[40]別 集 a collection of poems, etc., by one author.

別 項 different sorts.

別 體 another style of penmanship.

(c) Do not.

別 動 don't move! 別 去 don't go!

別·家 do not.

別 就·他 do not follow him.

別 忙 Steady! Don't fluster yourself!

[5]別 怕 人 笑 Don't be afraid of ridicule!

別 急 Don't be anxious! Don't get in a flurry!

別 怪·我 Don't blame me! Do not think me rude.

別 忝 聲 or 別 作 聲 Hold your noise! Be quiet!

別 生 氣 Now don't get angry!

[10]別 管·我 Don't you interfere with me!

別 見 笑 Don't laugh at me—my ignorance.

別 說 話 Be quiet! Hold your peace!

別 過 獎 Do not flatter me so!

(d) To twist around.

別·過 頭·來 to turn the head around.

懊 憋 4.5. Irritable; testy.
5209

懊·怩 unwilling; surly; snappish.

懊 性 nervous; hasty; irritable.

懊 腸 狗 態 an irritable temper and a snappish manner.

(a) Read p'ing¹. Mournful.

懊·悶 melancholy; mournful.

癟 1.5. An ulcer which has begun to suppurate. To repress.
5210   To choke.

癟·不·住 or 忍·不·住 unable to retain—of easing nature.

癟·子 a urinal.

癟·死 to suffocate.

癟 氣 to hold the breath.

癟·着 一 肚·子 委·曲 to brood over a bellyful of grievances.

蹩 1.5. To limp. Also read p'ieh⁵.
5211

蹩 蹩 踽 踽 limping along; going round and round.

蹩 蹩 爲 仁 "tripping people over charity." Giles. Giving intense mental application to the doctrines of benevolence.

跛 蹩 lame. (Wu-dial.)

蹩 脚 inferior in skill or quality

鼈 鱉 1.5. A turtle. The freshwater turtle.
5212

鼈 湯 turtle soup.

鼈 甲 turtle-shell.

鼈 縮 頭 the turtle withdraws its head—to hide oneself from danger.

鼈 蛋 a turtle's egg—a bastard.

(a) Ticks, etc.

狗 鼈 dog-ticks.
馬 鼈 a horse-leech.

䐑 **3.5. To dry fruit, etc., in the sun.**
5213

癟 **3.5. Shrivelled up; empty; limp. Also read pi⁵.**
5214

癟 嘴·子 a person whose cheeks have fallen in from loss of teeth.
癟 皮 shrivelled and wrinkled skin.
乾 癟 shrivelled.
↑癟·子 a dent or depression.

P'IEH. (ㄆㄧㄝ)

丿 **1.5. A dash; a downstroke to the left in writing. Radical 4. See next—B.**
5215

撇 擎 **1.5. To desert; to cast away; to reject; to abandon.**
5216

撇 下 to desert; to leave.
撇·不 過 could not refuse to.
撇 個 孩·子 an orphan child.
撇 回 馬 頭 to turn a horse's head.
⁵撇·得 孤 苦 left without kindred.
撇 斷 to divide.
撇 棄 to cast away.
撇 清 to leave off; to abandon.
撇 脫 to cast aside; prompt in action.
¹⁰撇 邪 to jeer at; supercilious.
撇·開 to set aside; to push away from.
撇 離 to abandon.

(a) To skim.

撇 沫·子 to skim off scum.
撇 油 to skim off fat.

(b) A downstroke in writing, as in Radical 4. A.p. p'ieh³.

一 撇 一 捺 a stroke to the left and another to the right.
兩 撇 鬍·子 a pair of moustaches like downstrokes in writing.

澈 **4.5. Rippling. Pure.**
5217

澈 洌 dancing, like rippling waves.
澈 淨·了 pure, as water.

瞥 **1.5. To blink; to glance at.**
5218

瞥 不 可 見 to vanish away in a twinkling.
瞥 眼 to glance at.
瞥 瞥 然 blinking.
瞥 見 to catch a glimpse of.
瞥 觀 to catch a glimpse of.
一 瞥 之 時 in the twinkling of an eye.

苤 **苤 藍 (-la) kohl rabi.**
5218½

PIEN. (ㄅㄧㄢ)

卞 **4 Hurried; excitable. A law, a rule.**
5219 Distinguish 卡 No. 616.

卞 急 testy, excitable.
牽 循 大 卞 complying with the great principles.

忭 昇 **4 Delighted; pleased.**
5220

忭 喜 extreme joy.
忭 躍 to dance for joy.
忭 頌 良 殷 you have my sincerest wishes for your happiness.

抃 **4 To strike, to tap. To keep time by tapping.**
5221 Inter. 拚 No. 4898—B.

抃 以 爲 節 to beat time.

汴 **4 A branch of the River Han in Hupeh.**
5222

汴 梁 an old name for K'ai-feng-fu in Honan.

弁 **4 A conical cap worn under the Chou dynasty. A military cap. Military officers of a low grade.**
5223

弁 兵 petty officers and privates.
弁 冕 ancient cap of ceremony—a leader; the topmost.
弁 目 petty officers.
弁 置 to cast aside, as no longer wanted. See below—5.
⁵弁 髦 the cap worn by children, discarded when capped at coming of age—from which comes the meaning:—to reject; to despise.
視 如 弁 髦 regard it as useless.
弁 髦 命 令 to set orders at naught.
皮 (or 革) 弁 ancient military cap of leather.

(a) A heading. Introductory note.

弁 言 introductory note in a book.

(b) To move hurriedly; agitated.

弁 行 to move hurriedly.
更 皆 股 弁 all the officials knocked their knees with fear.

(c) To rub the hands.

(d) Read p'an². Happy.

弁 彼 鸒 斯 with flapping wings, the jackdaws....

便 **4 Convenient, handy. Ordinary, plain. Advantageous.**
5224 Distinguish 使 No. 5770.

便 中 at your convenience.
便 中 就 說 say it at your convenience.
便 人 a convenient person—to send a letter by; to benefit others.
如 有 便 人 if there is anyone coming this way.
⁵便·利 serviceable; profitable; convenient.
便 坐 to sit without ceremony.
便 壺 a chamber utensil.
便 娟 graceful and easy in deportment or posturing.
便 宜 advantageous; fitting. See below—C.
¹⁰便 宜 主 義 utilitarianism.
便 宜 從 事 or 便 宜 施 行 to act as circumstances may require.
便 宜 行 事 大 臣 a Minister Plenipotentiary.
便 家 a wealthy family.

便 捷 convenient.
[15]便 於 他 人 of advantage to others.
便 易 convenient; easy.
便 服 or 便 衣 ordinary dress as contrasted with full dress or uniform.
便 溺 to urinate. *See below* A.
便 用 for use as required.
[20]便·當 suitable; comfortable; convenient.
便 章 "no dress,"—in invitations.
便 箋 memorandum.
便 道 side-road for slow traffic; a place for convenience. Cf. B 8.
便 酌 a simple meal—conventional phrase.
[25]便 門 a side door.
便 附 take this opportunity to enclose.....
便 面 a fan—it being convenient for covering the face.
便 飯 an ordinary, plain meal.
不 便 not convenient.
[30]就 便 when it is convenient.
方 便 convenient; handy; suitable.
未 有 便 I have no leisure.
簡 便 brief; concise; handy.
自 便 one's own convenience.
[35]請 便 do not stand on ceremony.
輕 便 light; easily-handled.
隨 便 please yourself; at your convenience.
順 便 at convenience.

(a) To ease nature.

便 所 a place of convenience.
便 旋 to urinate.
便 桶 a commode.
便 毒 venereal ulcers; buboes.
[5]便 秘 constipation.
便 閉 constipation.
告 便 ask to be excused.
大 便 to go to stool.
小 便 to urinate.

(b) Then, in that case. Even if. (*old mand.*)

便 了 a final expression—very well, etc.
便 卽 then; in that case.
便 是 or 便 可 just so; that is it; just the thing—a final expression.
便 是 如 此 it must be so.
便 有 so if there is; and even if there were.

便 罷 there's an end to it.
便 若 likely as.
便 道 then said . . .

(c) Read *p'ien²*. Cheap; advantageous.

便·宜 cheap.
太 便·宜 too easily; too cheaply.
小 便·宜 petty advantages.

(d) To describe

便 佞 口 給 glib-tongued.
便 便 言 唯 謹 爾 he spoke minutely but carefully.
便 嬖 attendants and favourites.
便 辟 to curry favour; specious.

篾 [1] A bamboo sledge.
5225

緶 [3] To sew. A hem. A plait. Inter. 編 No. 5231.
5226

鞭 [1] A whip. To flog. The penis of a horse.
5227

鞭·子 or 馬 鞭 a horse-whip.
鞭 打 to flog with a whip.
鞭 撻 or 鞭 笞 or 鞭 背 to chastise; to whip.
鞭 杆 a whip-stock.
[5]鞭 梢 a riding-switch; the end of a whip.
鞭 策 to lash.
鞭 爆 fire-crackers.
鞭 長 莫 及 even a long lash will not reach him—beyond the reach of the law.
鳴 鞭 to crack a whip.
[10]執 鞭 to hold the whip; to act as a groom—reckoned low by Confucius.
掌 鞭·的 a carter.

扁 [3] A tablet; a sign-board. Flat. Inter. next.
5228

扁 倉 skilful in medicine—from the names of two famous doctors of ancient times—扁 鵲 and 倉 公.
扁 嘴·子 flat-billed—a duck.
扁 嘴 鉗 flat-nosed pliers.

扁·擔 the flat stick—a carrying-pole.
[5]扁·擔 戲 Punch and Judy—because it is carried around on a coolie-pole.
扁 桃 the flat-peach.
扁 桃 腺 (or 體) the tonsils.
扁 菓 melon-seeds.
扁 蝨 ticks.
[10]扁 蟲 tapeworm.
扁 豆 a kind of bean.
扁 頭 螺·絲 a thumb-screw.
扁 額 a horizontal tablet before a hall, etc.
扁·食 or 燒 餃 meat-dumplings.
[15]扁 魚 a bream.
扁 鼻 a flat nose.
壓 扁 crushed flat.

(a) Small.

扁 舟 a skiff.

匾 [3] A tablet. Used with preceding.
5229

匾 聯 horizontal and upright tablets.
匾 額 or 牌 匾 a votive tablet with a horizontal inscription.

(a) A flat bamboo basket or sieve.

徧
遍 [4] Everywhere. The whole. A time, a turn. Also read *p'ien⁴*. Distinguish 偏 No. 5246.
5230

徧 世 界 the whole world.
徧 告 or 徧 諭 to inform everybody.
徧 國 中 to travel through the country; throughout the country.
徧 地 the whole earth; everywhere.
[5]徧 布 to spread far and wide.
徧 數 series.
徧 滿 to fill every part.
徧 爲 爾 德 universally practise your virtue.
徧 處 everywhere.
[10]徧 街 the whole street.
徧 贊 賓 客 he introduced him to all the guests.
徧 走 or 徧 行 or 徧 歷 to travel extensively.
徧 身 or 徧 體 the entire body.
徧 遊 to travel for pleasure.

[15]一 徧 once; one time or turn.
述 說 一 徧 to tell a narrative.

編[1] To plait; to weave. To fabricate.
5231

編 作 冕 to plait into a crown.
編 匠 a weaver in bamboo.
編 工 plaiting.
編 木 a raft.
[5]編 物 crochet work.
編 結 to tie; to bind.
編 織 機 a knitting-machine.
編 輿 a bamboo sedan.
編 造 謊 言 to fabricate lies.
[10]編 連 to continue; to piece together.
編 髮 to plait the hair.

(a) To arrange in order; to compile. To enroll, to register.

編 伍 之 間 enrolled in the rank and file.
編 修 to edit; a second-class Hanlin compiler.
編 入 to include; to enroll.
編 冊 a list; a register.
[5]編 列 字 號 to register—as a trading-firm, etc.
編 制 to codify; to compile; to devise plans.
編 制 法 organization of; arrangement.
編 制 軍 隊 to organize an army.
編 削 to arrange; to edit.
[10]編 劇 家 dramatists.
編 史 家 historians.
編 定 compiled.
編 定 法 典 codification of laws.
編 定 統 計 compilation of statistics.
[15]編 年 annual registers; to arrange under years.
編 年 史 history arranged according to the years; chronicles.
編 愁 to brood over one's griefs.
編 成 to compile.
編 戶 a registered person.
[20]編 排 to vilify.
編 次 or 編 列 to dispose in a series; to arrange.
編 氓 the people.
編 笆 in league; to conspire together.
編 纂 to compile.
[25]編 級 試 驗 examination for the formation of classes—on entering a school.

編 綴 to compile.
編 號 to classify; to arrange under numbers, etc., a *hong* list.
編 號 印 字 機 a numbering-machine. [= 32.]
編 譯 所 translation department;
[30]編 ‧ 輯 to edit; to arrange; to put together; an editor.
編 ‧ 輯 人 an editor.
編 ‧ 輯 部 editorial department or staff.
主 任 編 ‧ 輯 managing editor.
國 內 電 報 編 ‧ 輯 editor of inland telegrams.
[35]國 外 電 報 編 ‧ 輯 cable editor.
夜 編 ‧ 輯 night editor.
總 編 ‧ 輯 editor-in-chief.
編 述 to narrate.
編 造 to write a book; to compose.
[40]編 遣 會 議 re-organization and disbandment conference.
編 鐘 a set of sixteen bells, hung in two rows.

蝙[1,3] The bat, called 蝙 蝠. Used as an emblem of happiness or 福.
5232

褊[3] Cramped, narrow. Petty, mean.
5233

褊 小 mean; contracted.
褊 心 timid; anxious; petty-spirited.
褊 淺 limited; petty; shallow.
褊 激 petty-spirited; irritable.
褊 窄 cramped; straitened; small.
褊 陋 cramped and mean.

鯿[1] The bream; the carp.
5234

藊[3] A kind of bean with flat pods.
5235

砭[1] A stone probe. To pierce.
5236

砭 人 肌 骨 piercing to the bones.
砭 炙 to puncture and cauterize.

窆[3] To put a coffin in a grave.
5236a

窆 器 funeral requisites.
窆 所 place of burial.

貶[3] To censure, to disparage. To diminish. To dismiss; to cashier; to send away.
5237

貶 下 or 貶 謫 to degrade.
貶 人 功 勞 to detract from a person's merit.
貶 官 爲 民 to reduce an official to the ranks of the people.
貶 損 to disparage.
[5]貶 減 to diminish.
貶 評 to pass adverse judgement.
貶 詞 an expression of censure.
貶 辱 to bring low; to put down.
貶 黜 or 貶 退 to dismiss from office.

釆[4] To separate; to distinguish. Radical 165.
5238

辡[4] Recrimination; wrangling.
5239

辨[4] To discriminate; to distinguish between.
5240

辨 ‧ 不 出 來 or 辨 ‧ 不 開 not able to discriminate.
辨 別 or 分 辨 to discriminate; to see the differences between.
辨 別 是 非 to distinguish between right and wrong.
辨 別 高 低 to discriminate between good and bad, superior and inferior, etc.
[5]辨 味 to distinguish between flavours. 辨 士 penny, pence.
辨 明 to distinguish clearly.
辨 異 to distinguish between things that differ.
辨 白 to distinguish clearly; to clear up.
辨 色 to distinguish colours.
[10]辨 認 or 辨 識 to recognize; to distinguish.
辨 論 to discuss; to argue.
辨 護 to defend.

辮[4] To plait; to braid. A queue.
5241

辮 子 a queue.
辮 捷 子 false queue.

辮 綫 silk cord plaited into the queue.

辯 [4] To argue; to dispute; to discuss; to explain.
5242

辯 人 one skilful in debate.
辯 佞 specious arguments.
辯 倒 to overturn in an argument.
辯 勝 to gain a point in an argument.
[5]辯 口 eloquent.
辯 問 to ask in argument.
辯 士 a disputer.
辯 學 dialectics.
辯 慧 or 才 辯 ability to argue; skilled in debate.
[10]辯 才 ability in debate.
辯 明 to show a matter clearly; to show a thing in the right light.
辯 明 證 實 to defend and vindicate.
辯 給 eloquent.
辯 解 to palliate; to make excuses for.
[15]辯 訴 to explain in detail; to make a defence.
辯 論 or 辯 理 to dispute; to debate.
辯 論 之 範 圍 the field of inquiry or controversy.
辯 論 會 a debating-society.
辯 論 條 理 points of a debate or controversy.
[20]辯 論 終 結 to sum up a debate.
辯 護 to defend a case as a barrister.
辯 護 士 or 律 師 a barrister.
辯 護 家 apologists.
公 辯 a public debate.
[25]好 辯 captious.
多 辯 flippancy; glibness.
無 可 辯 beyond all dispute.
爭 辯 quarrelsome

邊  [1] A side, a border, an edge, a margin, a bank, a boundary. The frontier.
边
5243

邊 側 or 旁 邊 at the side.
邊 務 frontier-matters.
邊 地 the frontier.
邊 坐 to sit at the side.
[5]邊 城 the outer Great Wall.
邊 外 beyond the frontier.
邊 套 the side-mule in a team.

「邊兒」
邊 子 braid; fancy trimming. A.c.
邊 疆 the frontier.
[10]邊 患 trouble on the frontier.
邊 沿 the edge; along the bank; the margin.
邊 牙 a horse's side-teeth.
邊 界 the frontier.
邊 線 a boundary-line.
[15]邊 緣 a rim; a raised edge.
邊 門 a side door; a frontier-pass.
邊 關 or 邊 塞 or 邊 隘 a frontier-pass.
邊 防 frontier-defence.
邊 隅 the frontier.
[20]天 邊 the horizon.
花 邊 embroidered border; laces.
裏 邊 外 邊 inside and outside.
身 邊 about the person.

籩 [1] A splint-basket with a cover, used to contain fruits
5244 offered in worship.

變  [4] To change; to alter; to
变 transform. Rebellion.
5245

變 不 來 it cannot be changed.
變 亂 or 大 變 revolution; rebellion.
變 了 顏 色 or 變 色 to change colour.
變 位 displacement. (*physics*).
[5]變 兵 mutinous troops.
變 制 change of regime.
變 力 transforming power.
變 動 excitement; to alter; to move; to change; rearrangement.
變 動 形 conjugations.
[10]變 化 to transform; to undergo a change; evolution; metamorphosis.
變 化 律 the law of variation.
變 卦 to retract; to change; change of circumstances.
變 壞 了 to change for the worse; spoiled.
變 多 了 to increase in changing.
[15]變 局 change in the state of affairs.
變 幻 illusions.
變 形 to transform; metamorphosis.
變 形 法 transformation. (*logic*).
變 形 蟲 amœba. [one's mind.
[20]變 心 to alter one's views; to change

變 性 transmutation.
變 態 transformation; abnormality.
變 態 心 理 學 abnormal psychology.
變 成 or 變 爲 to become; to change into.
[25]變 戲 法 legerdemain; juggling, etc.
變 換 to change—as money.
變 故 calamity; misfortune.
變 易 mutations.
變 易 方 針 to change one's objective.
[30]變 星 variable or periodic stars.
變 更 to change.
變 樣 variation.
變 法 reform.
變 法 之 際 the reform crisis.
[35]變 流 機 electric transformer.
變 產 to realize property.
變 異 or 災 變 a calamity—as a flood, etc. [in disguise.
變 相 changes; metamorphosis;
變 種 variation.
[40]變 節 to reform; to condescend to inferiors; apostasy.
變 約 to alter an agreement.
變 臉 to change countenance; to sulk.
變 調 (*tiao*[4]) to change the tune —used fig.
變 賣 to realize; to sell.
[45]變 通 accommodating; to fall in with. [situdes.
變 遷 variations; changes; vicissitudes.
事 態 變 遷 the aspect of affairs has changed.
時 世 變 遷 the changes of the times.
變 革 revolution.
[50]變 體 altered form of writing characters.
不 知 機 變 lacking in tact; unaccommodating.
不 變 invariable.
天 變 changes in the weather.
權 變 versatile.
[55]順 變 to accept the inevitable changes—of bereavement.

P'IEN. (ㄆㄧㄢ)

偏 [1] Inclined to one side; leaning. Partial, prejudiced. De-
5246 termined, in a bad sense.

偏 不 湊 巧 unexpectedly.
偏 倚 to lean on.

偏 値 it so happened that....; as luck would have it.

偏 側 生 心 one-sided: prejudiced. 「that...

[5]偏 偏 unfortunately it happened

偏 偏 這 個 this of all things...

偏·僻 eccentric; depraved; out of the way.

偏 助 to take sides.

偏 勞 Thanks for your trouble! To get one person to take charge of arrangements, etc., for an undertaking.

[10]偏 南 inclined towards the south.

偏 厦 a side-room.

偏 向 deflection; bias.

磁 力 偏 向 magnetic deflection.

偏 口 魚 the sole.

[15]偏 國 an out-of-the-way country.

偏 坐 to sit on one side.

偏 執 己 見 bigoted.

偏 好 a hobby; predilection.

偏 安 partial peace, as when a ruler is acknowledged only by a section of the nation.

[20]偏 巧 it so happened; as luck would have it.

偏 度 degrees of longitude.=經 度

偏 廢 deformed; to do one thing and forget another.

偏 待 人 to treat others with favouritism.

偏 從 to follow wrong courses; unfair.

[25]偏 心 眼 partiality.

偏 心 輪 an eccentric. (mechanics).

偏 愛 or 偏 疼 undue partiality; to love one more than another.

偏 房 or 偏 室 a concubine.

偏 拗 perverse; bigoted.

[30]偏 斜 slanting; oblique.

偏 斷 an unjust decision; a partial judgement—as in law.

偏 旁 one side of a character.

讀 偏 旁 to pronounce or mispronounce a character according to its phonetic.

偏 是 is specially; is notwithstanding.

偏 會 fortunately; it so happened that.

[35]偏 曲 wilful; a side issue.

偏 枯 paralysed on one side; prejudiced; partial.

偏 棱 形 rhomboid.

偏 理 one-sided argument.

偏 生 it so happened that; unexpectedly.

[40]偏 盲 blind of one eye.

偏 私 bias; partiality.

偏 罰 unequal punishment—a parent's death.

偏 聽 to hear one side only.

偏 背 to enjoy a thing by oneself.

[45]偏 舉 to bring forward one only; inadequate explanation.

偏 袒 biassed; to give improper protection to; to screen.

偏 要 bent on having.

偏 見 a partial view; prejudice.

爲 偏 見 所 蔽 blinded by prejudice.

[50]偏 角 declination.

偏 東 之 方 位 角 eastern declination.

偏 謬 utterly unreasonable statements or doctrines.

偏 護 to favour.

偏 過 了 a polite reply in the affirmative to the question, "Have you taken your food?"

[55]偏 遇 to happen unexpectedly; as luck would have it.

偏 邪 depraved.

偏 重 旣 往 unduly to esteem the past or those that have gone before.

偏 重 現 在 unduly to esteem the present.

偏 阿 partiality; favouritism.

[60]偏 陂 one-sided.

偏 隅 an out-of-the-way place.

偏 墜 swelling of one of the testicles; hernia.

偏 離 divergence.

偏 頗 unjust; partial; biassed.

[65]偏 頭 風 hemicrania.

偏 駕 the conveyances for followers.

不 偏 不 倚 without partiality.

無 偏 無 黨 without prejudice.

(a) A group of twenty-five chariots in ancient warfare.

偏 伍 chariots and infantry.

剐[4] To pare; to cut into slices.

5247

剐 刀 a carving-knife.

篇[1] A leaf of a book; a section; an essay; a book. A tablet of bamboo formerly used for writing on. **N.A.**

5248

篇 什 a name for *The Odes*.

篇 幅 a chapter; a section.

篇 章 sections and chapters.

一 篇 大 話 a great boast.

一 篇 書 one book.

翻 篇 兒 to turn over the leaves.

翩[1] To run to and fro. To flutter; fluttering.

5249

翩 翩 fluttering; moving to and fro; elegant.

翩 翩 公 子 an elegant young man, a dandy.

翩 翩 巍 巍 imposing; stately.

翩 翩 fluttering about—as a bird or a butterfly.

艑[1.3.] A skiff.

5250

諞[3] Plausible, specious talk.

5251

諞 言 quibbling.

蹁[1] To walk with a limp.

5252

蹁 躚 swaggering gait.

騙[4] **扁馬** To swindle; to cheat.

5253

騙·了·去 swindled out of.

騙 人 to swindle.

騙·子 手 a swindler.

騙 局 a plan for cheating; a confidence trick.

[5]騙 淨 or 騙 沒 swindled out of everything.

騙 術 tricks; wiles; swindles.

騙 賴 to repudiate.

欺 騙 or 哄 騙 to humbug; to swindle.

(a) To mount a horse.

騙 馬 to mount a horse.

胼[2] Callosities on the hands or feet. Also read *pien*[2].

5254

駢² A pair of horses; from which comes:—to associate; joined together. **5255** Also read *p'in¹*.

駢 字 two-word expressions.
駢 拇 the great toe joined to the next.
駢 枝 superfluous, as a double toe or finger.
駢 比 numerous.
駢 田 associated together.
⁵駢 肩 shoulders together—a crowd.
駢 脅 the ribs joined together; plump, so that the ribs cannot be seen.
駢 誅 to execute criminals in a batch.
駢 識 cohabiting with.
¹⁰駢 首 with two heads.
駢 (體) 文 euphuistically antithetic style.
駢 齒 two front teeth united.

片⁴ A splinter; a slice; a strip; a slip; a flake. N. A. Radical 91. **5256** Distinguish 爿 No. 672.

片 交 memorandum; a note handed in for consideration.
片 假 名 the square form of the Japanese syllabary, or *katakana*. Cf.5303.4.
片 函 a note; a chit—usually written on a visiting-card.
片 刻 a short space of time; a little while.
⁵片 務 契 約 unilateral contract.
片 善 or 片 長 one very little point of excellence.
片 奏 to send in a memorial.
片·子 or 名 片 a visiting-card.
片 影 毫 無 there is no trace of it.
¹⁰片 方 one-sided.
片 時 a little while; an instant.
片 段 clauses and sentences.
片 烟 leaf-tobacco.
片 的 in flakes and slips (or slices.)
¹⁵片 白 gonorrhœa.
片 石 slate.
片 紙 a visiting card.
片 紙 隻 字 a scrap of written paper.
片 言 a few words.
²⁰片 言 折 獄 to settle litigation with half a word.

片 詞 隻 義 a formula.
片 辭 a few words.
片 雲 a little cloud.
片 面 *ex-parte*.
²⁵片 面 條 約 unilateral treaties.
一 片 一 片 的 in layers or slices.
一 片 婆 心 a kind motherly heart.
一 片 紙 a piece of paper.
切 片 to slice.
³⁰投 片 子 to send in a visiting-card.
瓦 片 broken tiles.
附 片 a supplement; an enclosure.
↑唱 片 or 留 聲 機 片 a phonograph record.

PIN. (ㄅㄧㄣ)

斌 彬 Ornamental, refined. **5257**

文 質 彬 彬 the ornamental and the fundamental combined.

邠 豳 豳 Name of a small principality in what is now Shensi, the home of the founder of the *Chou* dynasty. **5258**

賓 賓 A visitor, a guest. To submit. The second form is also used as phonetic in each of the following characters: Nos. 5260—5270. **5259**

賓 主 guest and host; servant and master; secondary and principal, etc.
賓 事 to treat a person as a visitor.
賓 位 the guest's seat; predicate.
賓 天 to die—of emperors.
⁵賓 客 or 賓 朋 guests; friends.
賓 服 to submit; to respect.
賓 東 guest and host.
賓 次 the guest's place.
賓 白 dialogue and monologue, respectively, in Chinese plays.
¹⁰賓 禮 the rules of hospitality.
賓 至 如 歸 visitors came as if they were returning home.
賓 萌 people from other places.

賓 賓 to show respect to.
賓 辭 predicate.
¹⁵賓 雀 the sparrow. [able guest.
大 賓 a marriage go-between; honor-
西 賓 a private tutor. = 西 席.

(a) u.f. 鑌 No. 5270. Steel.
賓 鐵 fine steel.

儐⁴ To entertain a guest. To arrange, to set in order. **5260**
儐 其 宗 器 to set out the ancestral vessels.
儐 接 to receive guests with respect.
儐 相 (bridegroom's) best man, or, (bride's) maid of honor.

嬪¹ A concubine. To become wife to. Also read *p'in²*. **5261**
嬪 婦 a wife.
嬪 御 imperial concubines.

擯⁴ To expel; to reject. **5262**
擯 棄 or 擯 斥 to reject; to find fault with.
擯 逐 出 境 to drive out of the country.
擯 錮 終 身 kept him out of office all his life.

(a) Inter. 儐 No. 5260. To set in order.
擯 相⁴ master of ceremonies at weddings, etc.

檳 榔 The areca-nut; the betel-nut. Also read *ping¹*. **5263**

檳 榔 or 檳 子³ the betel-nut.
檳 資 betel-nut money—gratuities for carrying letters, etc.

殯⁴ To carry to burial. Funerals. To encoffin a corpse. **5264**
殯 天 to die.
殯 殮 to prepare a corpse for burial.

殯儀館 funeral parlour.
殯 葬 to inter.
出 殯 to carry to the grave; to hold a funeral procession.

濱
瀕 } ¹

A bank, a brink, a shore, a beach. Also read p'in².

5265

濱 危 之 際 a crisis; on the verge of danger.
濱 死 on the brink of death.
濱 臨 大 海 I had nearly reached the ocean.
濱 行 on the point of going.
海 濱 the sea-shore.

獱 ¹

A kind of otter.

5266

獱 獺 the otter.

繽 ¹

Mixed colours; in confusion.

5267

繽 亂 or 繽 分 confused; mixed.
繽 紛 confused.

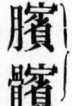

臏
髕 } ⁴

The knee-cap.

5268

臏 脚 to cut off the feet.
鑽 臏 to cut off the knee-cap as a punishment.

蠙 ¹

The pearl-oyster.

5269

鑌 ¹

Fine steel, the best quality.

5270

鬢
鬓 } ⁴

The hair on the temples.

5271

鬢 角 the temples. (--chiao)
鬢 霜 frosted temples.
雲 鬢 the hair puffed out at the sides.

稟 ³ To petition; to state. Distinguish 禀 which is really the correct form. Also read ping³.

5272

稟 候 to petition and await—action on the part of the authorities.
稟 假 to apply for leave of absence.
稟 准 to request permission.
稟 告 to petition.
⁵稟 命 to ask—as of a parent.
稟 報 or 稟 呈 or 稟 陳 or 稟 稱 to report to a superior.
稟 奏 or 稟 蒙 to receive the answer to a petition.
稟 安 to pay one's respects.
稟 官 to notify an official.
¹⁰稟 審 or 稟 究 to apply for an investigation.
稟 帖 or 稟 詞 an official statement to a superior; a petition.
稟 擬 to suggest or propose to a superior.
稟 明 to state clearly.
稟 書 a petition.
¹⁵稟 核 to report for the decision of a superior.
稟 知 to report to a superior.
稟 祈 to apply for.
稟 神 to pray to the gods.
稟 覆 or 回 稟 to petition in reply.
²⁰稟 覆 察 核 to report in reply for the consideration and decision of a superior.
稟 見 to apply for an interview.
稟 訴 to file a plaint.
稟 詢 to inquire of a superior.
稟 請 or 稟 求 or 稟 懇 or 稟 叩 to report requesting; to apply for.
²⁵稟 請 賠 補 to appeal for compensation.
稟 辦 to report proceedings.
稟 辭 to announce one's departure.
稟 追 to bring an action for the recovery of.

(a) To receive commands. Natural endowment.

稟 受 to be endowed with.
稟 性 or 氣 稟 disposition; natural endowment.
稟 賦 to be endowed by nature.

禀 ³ To receive commands. Disposition, natural endowment. Original form of the preceding. Also read ping³.

5273

禀 於 有 生 之 初 a fixed endowment at the beginning of life.

(a) Read lin³. A government granary, allowance of grain.

禀 俸 salary, stipend.

P'IN. (ㄅㄧㄣ)

貧 ² Poor, impoverished. Distinguish 貪 No. 6055.

5274

貧 不 勝 言 indescribable poverty.
貧 人 or 貧 民 a poor man; poor people.
貧 兒 院 a home for poor children.
⁵貧 嘴 spiteful lips.
貧 困 in distressed circumstances.
貧 士 or 寒 士 a poor scholar.
貧 家 子 a person of lowly birth.
貧 寒 or 貧 窮 or 貧 乏 poverty-stricken; in straits.
貧 富 poverty and wealth; relative wealth; rich and poor.
¹⁰貧 富 老 少 poor and rich, old and young.
貧 戶 a poor family.
貧 民 學 校 school for the poor.
貧 民 車 4th class on the railways.
貧 病 相 連 poverty and sickness are closely associated.
¹⁵貧 襄 累 其 心 distress disturbed his heart.
貧 而 無 諂 富 而 無 驕 to be poor and yet not flatter, to be rich and yet not proud.
貧 而 樂 poor yet happy.
貧 苦 無 告 bitterly poor.
貧 血 症 anæmia.
²⁰貧 賤 in humble circumstances.
貧 賤 交 the friend of one's humble days.
貧 賤 驕 poor but proud.
貧 道 I, a poor Taoist priest.
貧 陋 mean, humble.
²⁵貧 齒 類 edentata, animals without incisors or canine teeth.
貧 如 洗 as poor as though everything was washed away.

赤 貧 utterly destitute.
食 貧 to eat poor food.

頻 [2] Urgent, hurried, incessant. Inter. next two.
5275

頻 仍 as before.
頻 來 頻 往 coming and going; hurrying to and fro.
頻 依 於 人 always trusting to others.
頻 催 incessantly urging.
[5] 頻 巽 importunate.
頻 年 year after year.
頻 數 repeatedly. (*shuo*⁴·⁵)
頻 氣 repetitious; fussy.
頻 添 additionally.
[10] 頻 速 urgently; hurriedly.
頻 顧 uneasy; to frown.
國 步 斯 頻 the kingdom hastens to its doom.

(a) A shore, a bank. Imminent. Similar to 濱 No. 5265.

頻 行 on the point of going.

嚬 顰 [2] To knit the brows; to look distressed.
5276

嚬 笑 不 苟 do not frown or smile to order.

櫇 [2] Name of a fruit. Inter. next.
5277

櫇 菓 the apple.

蘋 [2] Duck-weed.
5278

蘋 菓 the apple.
蘋 婆 *sterculia lanceolata.*

矉 [2] An angry glare. To open the eyes with anger.
5279

牝 [4] The female of animals and some birds.
5280

牝 戸 the vagina.
牝 牛 a cow.
牝 牡 female and male.

牝 羊 a ewe.
牝 馬 a mare.
牝 鷄 司 晨 the hen rules the morning—the wife wears the breeches.

(a) A deep gorge.

虛 牝 the bottomless pit.

品 [3] Actions, conduct.
5281

品 性 temper; feelings; disposition.
品 格 or 品 度 carriage; bearing; manners.
品 行 (*hsing*⁴) conduct; disposition.
品 貌 the countenance; the expression.
品 質 disposition; capabilities.

(a) A kind, a class, a series, an order. Degree, rank. To classify, to estimate. Thing. Quality.

品 之 最 上 者 of the very best sort.
品 位 status; rank.
品 名 name and description of articles.
品 味 delicacies; flavour.
[5] 品 品 味 try the flavour.
品 嘗 食 the officer would taste the food.
品 流 or 流 品 classes; grades.
品 物 articles; things classified.
品 物 陳 列 場 show-room; exhibition.
[10] 品 目 name and description of article.
品 秩 or 品 銜 or 班 秩 official rank or precedence.
品 端 學 美 morally upright and highly educated.
品 竹 or 品 簫 to play the flute.
品 第 to classify; to criticize.
[15] 品 節 to regulate the details of; regulation.
品 紅 rosaniline.
品 級 grade; rank; status.
品 茶 to sip tea.
品 藍 a brilliant blue; aniline blue.
[20] 品 評 or 品 題 to classify; to arrange; to criticize.
品 質 quality; character; condition.
品 質 優 良 of sound quality.

品 類 to classify; classes.
上 品 first class, grade or rank.
[25] 下 品 bass. See—A. 30, 33.
九 品 the former official grades or ranks.
佳 品 good quality.
低 品 low grade.
劣 品 inferior grade.
[30] 副 品 alto. See—A. 25, 33.
普 通 品 ordinary quality, average grade.
極 上 品 superfine quality.
正 品 soprano. See—A. 25, 30.
消 閒 品 something to while away the time.
[35] 物 品 commodities.
神 品 inspired—of paintings.
製 造 品 manufactured articles.
農 産 品 agricultural products.
食 品 foodstuffs.
[40] 點 綴 品 accessories; ornaments.

(b) Used in transliterating.

品 脫 a pint.

PING.   (ㄆㄧㄥ)

兵 [1] A soldier, troops, military. A piece in Chinese chess.
5282 Arms, weapons.

兵 丁 or 兵 卒 or 兵 士 soldiers.
兵 亂 troops in revolt.
兵 事 hostilities.
兵 制 military regime.
[5] 兵 力 military strength.
兵 勢 warlike demonstrations.
兵 反 mutiny of troops.
兵 器 or 兵 械 or 兵 刃 or 兵 戈 military weapons.
兵 威 military prestige.
[10] 兵 家 soldiers; military strategists.
兵 工 廠 arsenal.
兵 庫 armoury.
兵 式 體 操 military drill.
兵 役 military service; a soldier.
[15] 兵 戎 military forces.
兵 房 or 兵 舍 barracks.
兵 書 books on tactics.
兵 機 tactics, strategy.
兵 法 military tactics.
[20] 兵 燹 匪 患 ravages of soldiery and brigands.
兵 禍 distress caused by the military.
兵 站 司 令 部 base head-quarters.

兵 端 hostilities.
兵 符 military tally for despatches, etc.
25 兵 策 military tactics.
兵 籍 military register.
兵 船 a gun-boat.
兵 釁 hostilities.
兵 衣 or 軍 衣 military uniform.
30 兵 變 troops in mutiny.
兵 輪 a transport.
兵 部 former Board of War.
兵 隊 troops.
兵 險 war risks.
35 兵 餉 or 兵 糧 soldiers' rations.
交 兵 to go to war.
伏 兵 ambuscade.
傳 令 兵 an orderly
動 兵 to go to war; to mobilize.
40 團 練 兵 volunteers; militia.
守 兵 or 哨 兵 a sentry.
常 備 兵 standing-army.
息 兵 truce; cessation of hostilities.
招 兵 or 募 兵 to enlist troops.
45 操 兵 to drill soldiers.
散 兵 or 退 伍 兵 disbanded troops.
新 兵 recruits.
步 兵 infantry.
殘 兵 or 敗 兵 defeated troops.
50 水 兵 bluejackets; marines.
目 兵 privates
短 兵 side-arms.
礮 兵 artillery.
精 兵 trained troops; picked troops.
55 罷 兵 to cease hostilities.
調 兵 to remove troops to another place.
逃 兵 deserter(soldiers).
退 兵 to withdraw troops.
進 兵 to advance troops.
60 閱 兵 to review troops.
預 備 兵 reserve troops.
馬 兵 or 騎 兵 mounted troops.
點 兵 to muster troops.

冫 冰 氷 ¹

5283

Ice, icicles. Cold, frost. Crystallized. Radical 15. (First form only).

冰 人 or 代 冰 人 or 冰 斧 a marriage go-between.
冰 冷 or 冰 得 慌 as cold as ice.
冰 凍 frozen hard.

冰 凌 an icicle.
5 冰 囊 an ice-bag.
冰 壺 a pot of ice—clear-minded.
冰 天 the icy regions.
冰 室 or 冰 窖 an ice-house.
冰 山 an iceberg; fig., that which is not trustworthy.
10 冰 山 不 可 靠 do not trust to an iceberg.
冰 島 iceberg.
冰 床 a sledge.
冰 廠 ice manufactory.
冰 心 chaste; chastity; noble-[minded.
15 冰 戲 or 溜 冰 skating.
冰 排 an ice-floe.
冰 柱 icicles.
冰 桶 ice-cream freezer.
冰 橇 ice-sledge.
20 冰 水 ice-water.
冰 河 or 冰 川 a glacier.
冰 洲 Iceland.
冰 洋 the Arctic Ocean.
冰 消 or 冰 化 the ice is melting.
25 冰 消 瓦 解 finished; collapsed.
冰 淇 淋 or 冰 其 冷 ice-cream (called 雪 糕 in Cantonese).
冰 清 玉 潔 人 an incorrupt person.
冰 炭 ice and charcoal—incompatibles.
冰 片 Baroos camphor from Borneo.
30 冰 玉 father-in-law and son-in-law.
冰 生 于 水 而 寒 于 水 ice is produced from water but it is colder than water—the pupil excels his tutor. *See* 青 No. 1168-1.
冰 田 ice-fields.
冰 筋 or 冰 著 ice-chopsticks—icicles.
冰 箱 an ice-box; refrigerator.
35 冰 糖 crystal-sugar in lumps.
冰 紀 or 冰 川 時 代 the glacial period; the ice age.
冰 脂 hard animal-fat.
冰 解 the ice is melting.
冰 車 a sledge.
40 冰 輪 the icy wheel—the moon.
冰 釋 solved; ended; leaving little trace.
冰 野 or 冰 原 an ice field.
冰 鉗 ice-tongs.
冰 雪 ice and snow.
45 冰 雪 聰 明 clear in mind.
冰 雹 hail.
冰 霜 ice and frost.
冰 鞋 skates.

冰 魚 frozen fish.
50 冰 點 freezing point; zero.
伐 冰 to break ice—for storing.
堅 冰 之 漸 the gradual hardening of ice—used of gradual development.
結 冰 to freeze.

丙 ³

5284

The third of the Ten Stems 天 干, referring to the south and fire. A fish's tail.

丙 丁 John Doe and Richard Roe; C. and D. as persons contrasted with A. and B.
付 於 丙 丁 or 付 丙 burn it —as a letter when read.
其 日 丙 丁 the days are then hot.
丙 丁 火 the heat of the sun.
丙 夜 midnight—the third watch.

昺 ³

5285

Bright, glorious.

柄 棅 ³·⁴

5286

A handle. To have control of. Power; authority.

國 柄 authority of the State; control of the country.
執 柄 to hold the power.
把 柄 a handle; to grasp a handle.
斗 柄 the handle of The Dipper.
5 曲 柄 a crank.
權 柄 authority.
笑 柄 something to laugh at.
話 柄 something to talk about—a matter for scandal.

炳 ³

5287

Luminous; bright.

炳 炳 麟 麟 brilliant, glorious.
炳 然 evident.
炳 燭 a bright candle-light.

病 ⁴

5288

Sickness, disease. To be ill. A fault, a defect, a vice. To regard as a defect. To disparage. Distressed about.

病 世 之 學 harmful studies.
病 中 胡 言 delirium.
病 人 a sick man.

病倦 sick and weak.
[5]病假 sick leave.
病入膏肓 the disease has entered the vital region—there is little hope of recovery.
病勢 the aspect of a case of sickness.
病勢陡重 the disease suddenly became very serious.
病原 or 病根 the root of the disease.
[10]病原論 aetiology.
病國 to injure the State.
病室 a ward in a hospital.
隔離病室 isolation ward.
病容 a sickly appearance.
[15]病得很重 or 病得利害 dangerously ill.
病從口入 diseases enter by the mouth.
病復發 a relapse.
病徵 symptoms of disease.
病愈了 or 病瘥 convalescent.
[20]病招人 diseases are catching.
病故 to die from disease.
病於亢旱 suffering from drought.
病日重 daily getting worse.
病死 or 病沒 to die from disease.
[25]病民 to cause the people distress.
病災保險 sickness and accident insurance.
病狀 symptoms of disease.
病狂 delirious; raving.
病理學 pathology.
[30]病甚麼 what is the matter with you?
病病痛痛 ailing; out of sorts.
病症 or 病疾 or 患病 to be ill; sickness; disease.
病痛 suffering; illness.
病瘦如柴 as thin as a stick after illness.
[35]病臥在牀 sick in bed.
病舍 infirmary.
病象 symptoms of disease.
病閒 during a remission of the disease.
病院 a hospital.
[40]病革 dangerously ill.
病體學 pathological anatomy.
告病 to ask for sick-leave.
心病學 mental pathology.
患病 to be ill.
[45]推病 or 托病 to plead illness as an excuse.
暴病 a sudden, violent illness.
死病 a mortal disease.

舊病 an old complaint; an old fault.
通病 a universal defect or shortcoming.

芮 [5289] [3]
Bright, shining, splendid.

邴 [5290] [4]
Name of a city in the ancient State of Sung 宋, in what is now Shantung. Pleased.

邴邴乎 to smile.

秉 [5291] [3]
To grasp, to hold, to maintain.

秉公辦理 to act with justice.
秉願 to act in accord with one's desires.
秉國之均 he holds in his hands the balance of the State.
秉夷 or 秉彝 the constant laws of nature.
[5]秉心無競 kept their hearts free from strife.
秉性 or 稟性 the natural disposition.
秉性愚蒙 his natural disposition was stupid.
秉持 to grasp.
秉政 to hold political power.
[10]秉權 to wield power; holding full power.
秉正 to hold to correct principles.
秉燭待旦 to hold a candle and wait for dawn—to avoid suspicion.
秉直 to maintain correct principles.
一秉至公 perfectly just.

(a) A handful of grain. Ancient grain measure of two 石.

禾秉 a handful of grain.
與之粟五秉 gave him 5 ping of millet.
遺秉 handfuls of corn left for gleaners.

並 弁 竝 [5292] [4]
And, also, or, at the same time; together with. United; together.

並下文 and the following.
並且 moreover.
並力 mutual assistance; with united strength.
並合 united.
[5]並在一塊兒 all together in one place.
並坐 to sit together.
並存 continuing together; co-existent.
並成 united together.
並排 or 並行 to walk abreast; to place in a row.
[10]並日 two days.
並皆 alike; together.
並目其所長 to record together their excellent parts.
並肩 shoulder to shoulder; side by side; to be an equal or friend.
並蒂蓮 two lotus blossoms on one stalk—united; copulation.
[15]並行界尺 parallel ruler.
並行線 parallel lines.
並起 to rise at once; to begin together.
並踵頂而臥 to lie close together, heads to heels.
並車 in the same carriage.
[20]並轡爭馳 racing together, bridle to bridle.
並重 equally heavy or important.
並頭 in an even row.
並馬 to ride abreast.
並駕齊驅 advancing in line; to ride abreast; to compare with; on equal terms; to keep abreast with.
[25]比並 to compare.

(a) Intensive particle before a negative.

並不必禁 must not, on any account, be prohibited.
並不是 or 並非 by no means; in no sense.
並不至於 it surely has not come to....
並未 it has by no means as yet.
並無不合 there is really no disagreement, not anything wrong.
並非如此 it is really not so.

併 偋 [5293] [4]
On a level with; even; equal. All. Used for preceding.

併吞 to swallow up entirely.

併 地 to absorb territory.
併 糧 to put the victuals of two together to make enough for one.
併 進 to advance together.
一 併 在 内 all included.

(a) To put aside.

併 日 而 食 ate on alternate days.
併 絕 己 私 to set aside one's private opinions.

拼
摒 } ⁴
5294
To drive off; to expel. To arrange. Also read *p'in*¹.

拼⁴ 擋 to arrange; to put in order.
拼 法 spelling. (*p'in*¹-)
拼 音 to spell phonetically. (*p'in*¹-)

(a) Read *p'in*¹. **To risk.** Inter. 拚 No. 4898—A.

拼 命 to risk the life.
拼 死 抵 抗 resist to the death.

(b) Read *pêng*¹. **The recoil, as of a bowstring.**

拼 破 了 手 the string, in recoiling, cut his hand.

鉼 ³
5295
A thin plate of gold or silver, formerly used as money in offerings.

餅 ³
5296
Cakes, biscuits, pastry.

餅 乾 biscuits.
餅 子 cakes, pastry.
餅 屑 crumbs.
餅 師 pastry-cook.
⁵餅 金 cake - money — presents to servants.
餅 食 pastry; cakes.
餅 餡 the stuffing of pastry.
月 餅 moon-cakes, eaten at the Mid-Autumn Festival.
牛 奶 餅 cheese.
¹⁰番 餅 念 貫 Twenty Dollars — 貫 is the N.A. for images, etc., and as dollars have an image, this is applied to them here.

P'ING.   (ㄆㄧㄥ)

姘 ¹
5297
Illicit intercourse, especially with a maid-servant. Also read *p'in*¹, *p'êng*¹.

姘 夫 a paramour.
姘 識 to have illicit sexual relation with.

屏 ²
5298
A screen; an ornamental tablet. A protection. To screen.

屏 列 set out and arranged, as a screen.
屏 帳 screen-curtains.
屏 立 a guard or a servant — one who stands like a screen.
屏 藩 之 臣 a minister who is as a screen-wall to his country.
⁵屏 衛 a folding screen.
屏 障 or 屏 蔽 to screen; to shield; barriers.
屏 障 智 識 hindrance to knowledge.
屏 風 or 屏 門 a movable door-screen.
圍 屏 a folding screen.
¹⁰壽 屏 birthday-scrolls given to an elderly person.
桌 屏 ornamental tablets of stone, framed to stand on the table.
開 屏 to open a screen, i.e., to spread the tail — of a peacock.
鏡 屏 an upright mirror standing in a frame.

(a) Read *ping*³. **To put aside, to reject**

屏 人 耳 目 to cause people to retire — in order to be private.
屏 居 to live in retirement — out of office.
屏 息 觀 之 held his breath and watched.
屏 斥 其 非 blamed him for his faults.
⁵屏 棄 to reject; to dismiss.
屏 氣 to hold the breath — as when before a superior.
屏 氣 似 不 息 者 he held his breath as if he dared not breathe — of Confucius at an audience.
屏 氣 凝 神 with bated breath not able to move.
屏 當 to arrange; to settle.
¹⁰屏 簇 scattered arrow-points.
屏 絕 to break off intercourse.

屏 聲 with bated breath.
屏 聲 色 to have nothing to do with music or women.
屏 語 to speak in private.
¹⁵屏 迹 to avoid, to keep at a distance.
屏 退 左 右 ordered the retainers to retire.
屏 逐 to drive out.
屏 除 to get rid of — as a bad habit.
屏 黜 to dismiss.

(b) Read *ping*¹. See below.

屏 營 nervous, agitated.

軿 ²
5299
A screen, an awning, a shelter. Also read *pêng*¹.

軿 幪 之 下 under your protection.

泙 ²
5300
To wash, to bleach.

泙 澼 絖 the washing of silk.

(a) Read *p'êng*². **The noise of waters.**

瓶
餅 } ²
5301
A pitcher, a jug, a vase, a bottle.

瓶 塞 a stopper or cork for a bottle.
守 口 如 瓶 keep the mouth (as one keeps the mouth of a bottle).
水 瓶 a pitcher.
花 瓶 a flower-vase.
酒 瓶 a wine-jar.

乒 ¹
5302
Used for the sound.

乒 乓 ping-pong.

平 ²
5303
Level, even. Just, equal. Average, ordinary, common, usual. Brief for 北 平 Peiping.

平 人 an innocent person. *See below,*—A.2.
平 價 par.
平 允 or 公 平 fair, just.
↑平 假 名 the cursive form of the Japanese syllabary, or *hira-*

gana.

平 光 plain spectacles,— zero diopter.

⁵平 其 政 to give equal justice.

平 凡 的 話 very commonplace talk.

平 分 to divide equally; to bisect.

平 原 a plain.

平 品 of equal rank.

¹⁰平 圓 a circle.

平 地 level ground; the ground of a carving.

平 地 登 天 to spring to heaven from the level—to make a sudden rise in life.

平 地 風 波 unexpected disturbance.

平 坐 to sit on terms of equality.

¹⁵平 均 average; equilibrium.

平 均 地 權 equalization of right of land property.

平 均 數 average number.

平 均 計 算 general average.

平 均 速 度 average speed; mean velocity.

²⁰平 均 高 度 average height.

平 坦 之 地 level land.

平 天 冠 the ancient flat-topped caps of the Chinese.

平 定 to arrive at a just settlement.

平 常 usually; in the ordinary course of things; daily; commonly; constantly.

²⁵平 常 無 奇 very ordinary; nothing remarkable.

平 平 的 average; middling.

平 庸 分 子 an ordinary person.

平 房 a level roof; a house of one storey.

平 排 uniformly arranged; placed side by side.

³⁰平 斷 equitable decision.

平 方 a square. (*math.*)

平 方 根 square root.

平 日 or 平 時 usually; daily; ordinarily; constantly; commonly.

平 明 the dawn; very early.

³⁵平 權 equal rights.

平 正 level; even; just.

平 民 大 學 higher education for the masses.

平 民 政 治 popular government.

平 民 百 姓 the common people.

⁴⁰平 民 精 神 the spirit of the masses.

平 浪 a smooth sea.

平 淡 insipid, ordinary, commonplace.

平 滅 to destroy utterly; to raze.

平 準 a system of grain purchase that enabled the government to retail it cheaply in times of scarcity.

⁴⁵平 滑 smooth and even.

平 版 測 器 plane table.

平 班 of equal rank.

平 生 the whole life.

平 生 絕 冠 unsurpassed in my experience.

⁵⁰平 白 trumped up; gratuitously.

平 白 人 the ordinary people.

平 直 level and straight.

平 空 empty; unfounded; suddenly.

平 等 of equal rank.

⁵⁵平 等 主 義 theory of legal and economic equality.

平 等 互 惠 reciprocity based on equality.

平 等 待 遇 equal treatment.

國 際 地 位 平 等 equal standing in international affairs.

政 治 地 位 平 等 equal standing in politics.

⁶⁰ 經 濟 地 位 平 等 equal standing in economic life.

平 素 usually; in the ordinary course of events.

平 經 度 mean longitude.

平 聲 the even tone in Chinese speech.

平 肩 行 to walk side by side.

⁶⁵平 臥 汽 機 horizontal engine.

平 行 of equal rank; on a footing of equality; parallel.

平 行 方 形 parallelogram.

平 行 界 尺 parallel ruler.

平 行 稜 體 parallelopiped.

⁷⁰平 行 線 parallel lines.

平 衍 a fine, level plain.

平 衡 evenly balanced.

平 西 level with the west—sunset.

平 角 a straight angle. (*math.*)

⁷⁵平 輩 of the same generation.

平 陽 大 路 an open level highway.

平 面 a plane.

平 面 三 角 術 plane trigonometry.

平 面 幾 何 plane geometry.

⁸⁰平 頭 螺 絲 flat-headed screw.

平 齒 輪 a spur-wheel.

公 平 fair; just; equitable.

(a) Peaceful; tranquil.

平 世 times of peace.

平 人 a person in good health. *See above*—1.

平 和 at peace; all settled; moderate—of prices.

平 和 會 Peace Society.

⁵平 善 satisfactory; in good circumstances.

平 天 下 to tranquilize the empire.

平 安 peace; peaceful; contented.

平 安 康 泰 great peace and well-being.

平 安 無 事 perfect tranquillity; freedom from anxiety; in peace.

¹⁰平 安 醮 an idolatrous service held in an infected region after an epidemic.

平 康 quiet and peaceful—prosperous.

平 復 recovered—as health or tranquillity.

平 心 calm; self-possessed.

平 心 而 論 to discuss candidly.

¹⁵平 息 quiet; peaceful.

平 時 編 制 peace established.

平 服 to subjugate; to reduce to order; recovered.

平 治 a peaceful rule; to rule fairly.

平 脈 pulse of a healthy person.

²⁰平 靜 peaceful and quiet; calm.

平 靜 安 穩 peace and security.

平 靜 安 逸 peace and tranquillity.

平 風 a gentle breeze.

(b) To weigh, as silver. Standard weight.

平 兌 to weigh.

平 出 五 百 兩 銀 子 weigh out Tls. 500 of silver.

平 政 院 Administrative Court.

天 平 scales for silver.

⁵庫 平 Treasury Scale for silver. Tls.100.＝Shanghai Tls.104 in weight, and Tls.109.6 in value.

曹 平 Standard scale for silver. Tls.100.＝Shanghai Tls.102.

規 平 Shanghai scale for silver. Tls.100.＝Treasury Tls.98.

關 平 Haikwan or Customs scale for silver. Tls.100.＝Shanghai Tls.110.4

(c) To control. To regulate.

平 章 or 辨 章 to control; to reg-

ulate; official title during the *T'ang* dynasty.

平 章 政 事 Minister of State during the *Chin* dynasty.

平 章 百 姓 to control and regulate the people.

王 道 平 平 the kingly way is just. (-*p'ien²-p'ien²*)

↑平 糴 or 平 糶 official control of ⌐ rice.

坪² A plain, a level place.
5304

萍² A kind of artemisia or southernwood.
5305

萍 萍 luxuriant.

食 野 之 萍—the deer—eat the artemisia in the wilds.

(a) Duck-weed. See 萍 No. 5307.

七 月 生 萍 the duck-weed grows in the seventh month.

(b) Read *p'ien²*. A screen.

萍 車 a chariot with a screen for the soldiers.

評² To arrange; to criticize. To comment on. A running
5306 commentary.

評 事 judge of the Administrative Court. *See* 平 No. 5303. B.3.

評 估 to adjudicate; to estimate a value.

評 價 to appraise; to valuate.

評 判 criticism; review or critique.

⁵評 判 其 得 失 critically decide the merits and demerits of a case.

評 判 員 judge or umpire in a debate.

評 判·的 態·度 critical attitude.

評 判 習 慣 a habit of criticism.

評 判 過 於 刻 覈 hypercritical.

¹⁰主 觀·的 評 判 subjective criticism.

咬 文 嚼 字·的 評 判 pedantic literary criticism.

客 觀·的 評 判 objective criticism.

評 劇 員 dramatic critics.

評 品 to criticize—works of art.

¹⁵評 斷 or 評 定 to decide; to arbitrate.

評 理 to discuss; to settle.

評 脈 to examine the pulse.

評 註 comments; critical notes.

評 論 to discuss.

²⁰評 論 家 critics.

評 議 to deliberate.

評 議 會 Senate of University.

評 量 to discuss.

評 閱 詩 文 to review poems and essays.

²⁵評 點 to prepare notes and punctuation for a new edition of an old book.

批 評 to criticize.

苛 評 家 or 酷 評 家 hypercritics.

萍² Duckweed. Wandering, travelling.
5307

萍 散 篷 飄 like floating duckweed or seeds blown by the wind—no fixed abode.

萍 水 a casual acquaintance.

萍 水 之 人 a chance stranger.

萍 水 相 逢 patches of duckweed meeting—unexpected meeting of friends abroad.

萍 浮 南 北 floating from · north to south like duckweed—no fixed abode.

萍 蹤 無 定 duckweed has no certain tracks to leave—it is uncertain where he is now.

浮 萍 or 水 萍 duckweed.

溯¹ The sound of dashing waves. Also read *p'êng¹*.
5308

凭²·⁴· To lean against; to trust to; to rely on. Inter. next.
5309 Also read *ping⁴*.

凭 几 托 腮 leaning on the table with his head in his hands.

凭 欄 to lean on a railing.

乾 柴 凭 火 a dry stick leaning against the fire—imminent danger.

依 凭 to rely on; to lean on.

挨 凭 to lean against; to rest on.

憑²
馮
凴
5310

According to. As.

憑 你 說 it is as you say.

憑 口 說 mere talk; unfounded statements.

憑 眼 見 as the eye sees.

憑·著 自 己 according to one's own idea.

憑·著 良 心 according to conscience; to act conscientiously.

(a) Evidence; proof.

憑 單 or 憑 照 a certificate; a voucher.

憑 帖 a card sent as an acknowledgement of receipt.

憑 據 evidence; guarantee; proof.

憑 文 official credentials.

⁵憑 證 evidence; proof; guarantee.

以 物 爲 憑 to take something as a pledge.

恐 口 無 憑 word of mouth is no evidence or proof—of a transaction.

文 憑 a diploma or certificate.

修 業 文 憑 certificate of attendance.

¹⁰學 位 文 憑 diploma for a degree.

畢 業 文 憑 graduation diploma.

(b) To rely on　To depend on. To lean.

憑 中 in the presence of a middleman; through an intermediary.

憑 仗 to lean on; to rely on.

憑 依 or 憑 附 means of support; to trust to.

憑 信 trustworthy.

⁵憑 其 理 智 經 驗 relying on his wisdom and experience.

憑 几 leaning on the table.

憑 天 發 誓 to swear by Heaven.

憑 弔 moved to grief by the sight of something connected with the departed.

憑 票 note or money order payable to bearer; a pawn-ticket.

¹⁰憑 票 入 內 admission by ticket.

憑 票 取 銀 payable to bearer.

憑 空 unfounded; without proof.

憑 空 臆 測 之 譚 exaggerated boastings founded upon nothing.

憑 肩 to lean on one's shoulder.

¹⁵憑 藉 to recline on.

憑 陵 to rely on the influence of others to browbeat a man.

(c) Used for 馮 No. 1895. To mount, to ascend.

憑眺 to gaze about from an eminence.
憑高 to look down from a height.

(d) No matter what.

憑·他·罷 let him do as he likes; don't bother about him.
憑·你 as you please.
憑渠所往 let him go where he will.
任·憑·他·們 let them go their own way; do not mind them.

(e) A small bird.

憑霄 a kind of lark.

傳[4] To trust to; to pass on a message.
5311

傳俠持權 having both courage and authority—to take action.

娉[1] Graceful.
5312

娉婷 elegant and graceful, gentle.

(a) Read *p'ing*[4]. Inter. next.

遣人娉問 to send a proposal of marriage.

聘[4] To invite by presents. To betroth. Also read *p'in*[4].
5313

聘則爲妻 a wife is espoused by betrothal—not bought, as a concubine.
聘姑·娘 or 聘女·兒 to betroth a girl or daughter.
聘定 or 聘下 betrothed; engaged.
聘請 to engage—as a teacher.
[5]聘賢 to engage worthy men.
聘選 to choose and betroth.
聘金 money paid at a betrothal.
下聘 or 定聘 to send the betrothal presents.
却聘 to refuse the betrothal presents.
[10]待聘 awaiting betrothal.
過聘禮 to send the presents for a betrothal.

(a) To inquire about.

聘問鄰國 an embassy of inquiry to a neighbouring State.

PO   (ㄛ)

波[1] Breakers; waves.
5314

波丘 crest of a wave.
波動 undulatory movements, as of a field of grain in the wind.
波動面 undulating surface.
波及於人 to be involved in.
[5]波平浪靜 calm waters.
波沫 foam; surf.
波浪 breakers.
波浪洪濤 boisterous breakers.
波浪滔天 great upheavals.
[10]波浪澎湃 waves roaring.
波濤 waves and billows.
波瀾 dashing—of literary style.
波稜蓋 or 波羅蓋 the knee-cap.
波紋 ripples.
[15]波累 to involve; to compromise.
波谷 the trough of the waves.
波長 wave-length.
奔波 hurrying here and there.
檢波器 wave-detector. (*radio*.).
[20]減幅波 damped waves. (*radio*.).
測波器 wave-meter. (*radio*.).
連續波 continuous wave. (*radio*)
↓長波短波 long and short waves.
金波 bright moonlight. (*radio*)
↑週波 cycles. (*radio*).

(a) Used in transliterating.

波士頓 Boston.
波斯 Persia.
波瀾 Poland.
波羅蜜 the jack-fruit.
[5]波羅蜜多 moral and intellectual perfection, Sanskrit: *pâramita*.
波羅菓 or 鳳梨 the pineapple.
波羅門 Brahman.
↑波利維亞 Bolivia.

菠[1,2] General name for spinach and similar greens.
5315

波荣 spinach, etc.

玻[1] Glass. Also read *p'o*[1].
5316

玻·璃 or 玻·璃片 window-glass.
玻·璃杯 a tumbler.

玻·璃板 plate-glass.
玻·璃珠 glass beads.
[5]玻·璃的 glassy.
玻·璃體 (or 質) vitreous humour.
吹玻·璃 glass-blowing.
鑲玻·璃 to glaze—a window.

跛[3] To walk lame.
5317

跛·子 or 瘸·子 a lame person.
跛能履 the lame can walk.
跛脚 or 跛腿 lame.
跛鼈千里 a lame tortoise walks a thousand *li*—perseverance and patience accomplish much.

(a) Read *pei* or *p'i*[4]. To lean on; to be partial.

跛倚 to lean against.
跛向不明 an unreasoning partiality.

簸[4] A winnowing fan.
5318

簸·箕 a winnowing fan; a basket for dust, etc.
簸·籮 an open, flat basket for grain, etc. (*p'o*[3]-)

(a) Read *po*[3]. To winnow. To rock.

簸弄 to spread rumours; to deceive.
簸穀 to winnow unhulled rice or paddy.
簸米 to winnow rice.
簸頓 to dally with or trifle with.
[5]簸颺 to clean grain in the wind.
擺簸 to rock; to totter.
顚簸 unsteady, rocking—as a boat.

嶓[1] A mountain in Shensi.
5319

播[4] To sow. To publish, to make known. To broadcast.
5320

播傳 to disseminate; to spread abroad—as doctrine.
播種 to scatter seed; to sow.

播 迻 to carry—as disease; to broadcast.

無線電播迻臺 wireless broadcasting-station.

播 音 to go on the air. (radio)

廣 播 to broadcast. (radio)

(a) To stimulate and encourage.

播 民 和 stimulated the harmony of the people.

(b) To reject. To cast away.

播 棄 犁 老 "he has cast away the time-worn sires."

爾 乃 屑 播 天 命 do you triflingly reject the ordinances of Heaven?

(c) To separate. To distribute. To flee. To banish.

播 五 行 于 四 時 the five elements were distributed through the four seasons.

播 散 to flee; scattered.

播 流 banishment.

播 爲 九 河 (the stream) was distributed and became the Nine Rivers.

⁵播 臣 transported ministers.

播 蕩 to flee; to abscond; to be homeless and vagrant.

播 越 homeless and vagrant.

播 遷 to remove to another region; to change one's place of abode.

(d) Read po³. To winnow. To shake. To agitate.

播 揚 to winnow; to promulgate.

播 米 to winnow rice.

播 精 to sift and clean—rice.

播 鼗 to shake the hand-drum.

(e) Read po¹. To humbug.

播 亂 to throw into disorder.

播 弄 to dupe; to humbug; to dally with.

播 弄 是 非 to pervert the truth.

PO. (ㄅㄛ)
See also 4974.
(Poh)

癶 4.5. Back to back. Radical 105.
5321

博 博 2.5.
5322

Extensive; ample. Distinguish 傅 No. 1446, 傅 No. 1948.

博 勞 a shrike.

博 古 家 archaeologists.

博 古 通 今 acquainted with things ancient and modern.

博 物 館 a museum.

⁵博 士 a doctor—as of science, etc. *See* No. 5776·14ff.

博 學 extensive learning; well informed.

博 學 於 文 約 之 以 禮 he widely studies learning, and restrains himself by the rules of propriety.

博 學 鴻 儒 an exceedingly well-informed man.

博 愛 love without distinction.

¹⁰博 愛 主 義 philanthropy.

博 採 to select from a large number.

博 施 濟 眾 liberal gifts to relieve the masses.

博 淵 wide and deep—learning.

博 濟 于 民 universal kindness to the people.

¹⁵博 物 學 natural sciences.

博 物 家 naturalists.

博 物 院 natural-history museum.

博 而 不 精 wide but shallow knowledge.

博 聞 extensive learning; well informed.

²⁰博 聞 廣 識 encyclopedic knowledge.

博 聞 強 記 wide learning and a powerful memory.

博 覽 會 an exposition.

博 觀 having wide experience.

博 證 to procure corroborative evidence.

²⁵博 識 to add to one's knowledge.

博 雅 learned and accomplished.

(a) To gamble. To play games, as chess.

博 奇 揥 played in a strange contest.

博 局 gambling-house; a chessboard.

博 弈 to play at 圍 棋 or the game in which one tries to surround the opponent's pieces.

博 徒 a gambler.

博 戲 gambling.

六 博 playing with dice.

賭 博 to gamble.

(b) To barter.

博 貨 to barter goods.

博 金 to sell for money.

以 博 一 笑 to cause a laugh.

搏 2.5. **To spring upon; to seize; to strike with the fist; to box.**
5323

搏 取 to seize.

搏 挽 to be drawn together.

搏 擊 to strike; the office of a censor in past times.

搏 虎 to attack a tiger with the hands.

搏 襲 to seize—as prey.

膊 4.5. **The upper arm; the shoulder.**
5324

膊 甲 the shoulder-blade.

胳 膊 the arms.

轉 膊 to change shoulders when carrying a load.

(a) To slice; to dismember.

殺 而 膊 諸 城 上 they slew him and dismembered the corpse on the city wall.

(b) The crowing of cocks.

膊 膊 sound of cocks crowing.

鎛 4.5. **A large bell suspended from a frame. A hoe.**
5325

錢 鎛 small hoes for weeding.

薄 2.5. **Thin, slight, poor, mean. Ungenerous, stingy; contemptuous; careless.** A.p. *pao²*. Distinguish 簿 No. 5375.
5326

薄 人 a prostitute.

薄 倖 lacking in right feeling.

薄 冰 thin ice.

薄 切 cut into thin slices.

⁵薄 命 unfortunate in life.

薄 官 a petty official.

薄 小 poor, small.

薄 弱 weak, sickly, ailing.

薄 待 to treat badly.

¹⁰薄 情 no sense of gratitude; destitute of right feeling.

薄 惡 contemptuous.
薄 懲 to punish lightly.
薄 產 a small estate.
薄 瘠 sterile—of land.
15 薄 祚 poor.
薄 福 a poor fate; unlucky.
薄 禮 shabby presents.
薄 罪 於 人 to punish a person leniently.
薄 荷 peppermint. (po⁴-)
20 薄 荷 油 oil of peppermint. (-po⁴)
薄 落 人 a prostitute.
薄 行 人 a heartless person.
薄 視 to regard with contempt.
薄 觀 to take a mere glance at.
25 薄 餅 wafer cakes; "doilies" (pao²-)
刻 薄 mean; unsympathetic.
厚 薄 thick and thin; liberal and stingy. (-pao²)
淡 薄 dull, as trade; stinted.
臉 皮 薄 bashful. (-pao²)
30 菲 薄 meagre.
輕 薄 contemptuous; frivolous.

(a) **Dense growth.**

匿 叢 薄 中 hid in the thick growth.

(b) **To reach to, to extend to, to approach, to cleave to.**

薄 城 to besiege a city.
薄 暮 evening; towards dark.
外 薄 四 海 extending to the limits of the empire.
日 薄 食 the sun is almost eclipsed.
直 薄 城 下 he came right up to the city wall.

(c) **A curtain or screen.**

帷 薄 不 修 the curtains are not kept repaired—the women are allowed too much freedom.
帷 薄 之 外 不 趨 outside the curtain or screen the visitor should not hasten his steps.

(d) **To collect together.**

相 薄 gathered together; mixed together; blended.
雷 風 相 薄 the noise of the thunder and the wind together.

(e) **Initial particle. Ah, so.**

薄 澣 我 衣 therefore I washed my garments.
薄 言 采 之 薄 言 有 之 thus we selected them and now we have got them.

(f) Read po¹. **A noise.**

載 驅 薄 薄 the noise of the carts and carriages.

礴 4.5.
5326a
To fill. To extend.

脖 2.5.
5327
The neck, the back of the neck. The navel.

脖 臍 or 脖 胦 the navel.
脖 頸 子 or 脖 梗 子 or 脖 子 the neck.

餑 1.5.
5328
Cakes, biscuits.

餑 餑 cakes.

鵓 2.5.
5329
A wood-pigeon.

鵓 鴿 pigeons.
鵓 鴣 a wood-pigeon.

茇 4.5.
5330
Grass; stubble.

茇 舍 a thatched cottage.

葍 2.5.
5331
A term applied, in combination, to such roots as the carrot, turnip, radish, etc.

蘿 葍 carrots, turnips, etc.

駒 2.5.
5332
Noise of tramping feet. Read pao⁴. To leap.

鉢 1.5.
5333
An earthenware basin. A Buddhist priest's alms-bowl.

鉢 多 羅 the alms-bowl of the Buddhist. Sanskrit: pâtra.
鉢 子 or 鉢 頭 an earthenware bowl.
鉢 盂 a priest's dish, shaped like a flattened globe.
傳 衣 鉢 to hand down the cassock and bowl,—to appoint a successor; to communicate one's doctrines to a pupil.

鉑 2.5.
5334
A thin sheet of metal. Mock-metal. Used for platinum.

金 鉑 gold-leaf.
錫 鉑 tin-foil.

箔 2.5.
5335
Door-screen of bamboo; u.f. preceding, and 薄 No. 5326. A sheet, a leaf. Frame for silkworms.

葦 箔 a reed-screen.
蠶 箔 a frame on which silkworms spin.
錫 箔 tin-foil.

亳 4.5.
5336
A district in North Anhwei. Distinguish 毫 No. 2066.

剝 1.5.
5337
To flay, to peel. To strip, as clothes or badges of office. u.f. 駁 No. 5342. A.p. pao¹.

剝 削 to fleece: to cut down, as wages.
剝 啄 to tap at a door; dilapidated and knocked about.
剝 奪 to strip; to divest.
剝 奪 公 權 to deprive of civil rights.
5 剝 奪 淨 盡 fleeced; stripped bare.
剝 極 則 復 when things are at their worst, they begin to mend.
剝 權 deprived of one's rights.
剝 殼 to strip off the husk.
剝 民 to oppress the people.
10 剝 皮 to skin; to flay; to fleece; to extort.; to rob the clothes off.
剝 皮 的 one who fleeces others unmercifully.
剝 脫 下 來 to strip off.
剝 膚 to strip the skin—an imminent calamity.
剝 落 dilapidated.
15 剝 面 皮 to skin the face; to make ashamed.

雹 2.5.
5338
Hail. Pron. pao².

雹 子 or 冰 雹 hail. (pao². tzŭ)
下 雹 子 to hail.

撥 1.5. To distribute. To spread.
5339 To make appropriations.
To allot. To disperse. To
get rid of. To transfer, as
money.

撥亂 to disperse rebellion.
撥亂反正 to turn from hetero-
doxy to the right path.
撥交 to hand over to.
撥兵 to detach troops.
[5]撥冗 to put one's affairs on one
side.
撥出 to distribute; to allot.
撥收 received—as a deposit.
撥土 to turn over the soil.
撥弓 to draw a bow.
[10]撥款 to appropriate a fund.
撥歸一邊 to put on one side;
partial.
撥正 to correct; to make straight.
撥·浪鼓 a pedlar's drum which
is twirled in the hand.
撥準了 distributed evenly.
[15]撥用 to appropriate for.
撥發 to distribute.
撥給 to give out; to set aside for.
撥船 a lighter; to transfer goods
from one boat to another.
撥落 to ward off.
[20]撥蚊 to drive away mosquitoes.
撥身金 to allot one's wages.
撥轉 to transmit; to cause a thing
to turn; to hand over.
撥送 to despatch.
撥錢 to set aside a sum; to transfer money.
[25]撥開 to reject; to open out; to
prise open.
撥開烟 to disperse the smoke.
撥雲見日 to scatter the clouds
and see the sun—to dissipate
error, or redress grievances.
撥項 to transfer a sum of money.
撥馬 to turn a horse round.

(a) **To stir up. To poke. A
plectrum. To thrum strings.**

撥剌 the twang of a bowstring or
a similar sound.
撥動 to move; to wind up—as a
spring; to pluck—as strings.
撥壞·了 pulled to pieces.
撥弄 to fiddle with; to play with.
[5]撥捌 to poke; to turn over; to
sift.
撥擱 to stir up; to push away.
撥火 to poke a fire.

襏 4.5. Garment of coarse cloth
5340 —a rain-coat.

襮 4.5. An embroidered collar.
5341 To expose.

駁
駮 2.5. To argue; to contradict.
To annul, to reverse a
5342 decision.

駁·不倒[3] unable to overcome in
argument.
駁人 to contradict a person.
駁人不過 unable to convince a
man.
駁倒[3] worsted in argument.
[5]駁價 to cavil at the price.
駁勘 to reverse a decision—as by
a higher authority.
駁口 to contradict.
駁回 or 批駁不准 to reject
a petition.
駁斥 to expose an error; to find
fault with.
[10]駁正言語 to criticize words.
駁爲虛空 to disprove.
駁罪 to find fault with the punishment.
駁詰 to browbeat; to cross-question.
駁語 a reversal of sentence on
appeal.
[15]駁議 to dispute.
駁辯 to argue; to dispute.
駁飭 to express disapproval.

(a) **To transfer; to tranship. To
graft.**

駁樹 to graft trees.
駁渡 to transport across a ferry.
駁船 a lighter; to transfer goods
to another boat.
駁貨 to tranship goods.
[5]駁賣 to sell retail.
駁·過·去 to tranship goods into a
lighter.
駁運 to transport; to tranship.
接駁 to tranship.

(b) **A piebald horse. Parti-
coloured. Miscellaneous.**

駁犖 a parti-coloured ox—parti-
coloured; variegated.
駁色 variegated.

駁錯 confused; miscellaneous.
駁雜 mixed; confused, miscellaneous.
駁馬 parti-coloured horses.

(c) **Suddenly.**

駁然大怒 he suddenly grew
angry.

(d) A fierce beast, fabled to eat
tigers and panthers.

P'O.　　　　　(파)

坡 1 A bank; a slope.
5343

下坡 a slope; downhill.
山坡儿 the slope of a hill.
斜坡儿 a declivity.

破 4 Broken; ruined. To break;
5344 to rend; to solve. To take
by storm. To see through.
To lay bare. To destroy.
To begin.

破一塊錢 to break into a
dollar.
破人婚姻 to break off the marriage betrothal of others.
破例 to break a precedent.
破傷風 tetanus.
[5]破口之城 city walls that have
been breached.
破口大罵 to abuse freely.
破土 to open the ground—to
commence building operations;
to make a grave.
破地獄 to get souls out of Purgatory. (Budd.).
破壁飛去 broke the wall and
flew away—a man named 張僧
繇 painted a picture of four
dragons; he was asked why he
had not painted in their eyeballs; he replied that if he did
so they would immediately fly
away; on being pressed he added the eyeballs, and sure
enough, they fled.
[10]破壞 spoilt by a rent; to pull
down; to destroy.
破壞中立 violation of neu-
trality.
破壞交通 to destroy the com-
munications.

破壞名舉 libel; defamation.
破壞黨 disturbers of the peace.
¹⁵破天荒 to begin a thing; to get a degree after long waiting; lit., to break up the wilderness. for the first time; unprecedented.

破失 broken down.
破家 to break up a family by extravagance.
破家子³弟 he is the ruin of the family.
破屋 a ruined house.
²⁰破廟 a ruined temple.
破戒 to break a vow—as for fasting or total abstinence.
破扉 a partly-open door.
破扉·的缺處 a small opening.
破折號 a dash (—).
²⁵破損 breakage. (commerce).
破敗 ruined; defeated.
破斷 to snap; to break.
破日 an unlucky day.
破曉 the break of day; dawn.
³⁰破板 to cut timber into planks.
破案 to clear up a case; to find out the offenders; the secret has leaked out.
破柴 to split firewood.
破格 to break through the rule.
破死忘魂 reckless of life and person.
³⁵破法 to match and neutralize a scheme.
破法術 to break a charm.
破涕爲笑 to change tears into laughter.
破浪 to dash through the waves.
破爛 ragged---as clothes; broken.
⁴⁰破獄 to break prison.
破獲 to discover and arrest.
破獲圖害 to unearth a plot.
破瓜之年 sixteen years of age—of a girl; also used of sixty-four years, from the idea that the character kua divides into two eights.
破產 bankruptcy.
⁴⁵破產人 a bankrupt.
破產債權人 creditor in a bankrupt estate.
破產原因 causes of bankruptcy.
破產法 insolvency laws.
破產程序 bankruptcy proceedings.
⁵⁰破產管財人 administrator in a bankrupt estate.

破產財團 bankrupt estate.
有破產之勢 on the verge of bankruptcy.
強制破產 involuntary bankruptcy.
申請破產 voluntary bankruptcy.
⁵⁵破·的 broken; 破的⁴ to pierce the bull's-eye — used fig.
破皮 broken skin; to break the skin.
破眼 perforations;holes.
破碎 smashed; broken to shivers.
⁶⁰破空 suddenly; unexpectedly.
破竹 splitting bamboo—easily done.
破竹之勢 irresistible force.
破約 to break an agreement; breach of promise. [flaw.
破綻 a rent; an inconsistency; a
破腹 to lay bare one's heart; to make a clean breast of it.
⁶⁵破膽 to burst the gall---very scared.
破舊 old and shabby.
破船偏遇打頭²風 one trouble coming on top of another.
破落戶 a vagabond; a decayed family.
破衣·裳 ragged garments.
⁷⁰破裂 cracked; torn; split.
破解詳細 to explain most carefully.
破計 to detect a scheme; to break up a plan.
破謎 to guess a riddle.(A.p.-mêr⁴)
破貞 to deflower a maid.
⁷⁵破財 to squander property.
破賊 to break down rebels.
破費 to waste; to spend recklessly.
破身 to begin sexual indulgence; to deflower.
破釜沉舟 to smash the cooking vessels and sink the boats—as 項羽 ordered his men to do, after crossing the river; indicates determination to succeed, or cutting off all retreat.
⁸⁰破鈔 to break into a note—to change it; extravagance.
破鈔幇人 to give liberal assistance.
破鏡重圓 the broken mirror is round again—said of a second marriage.
破開 split it open; to split open.
破除 to eliminate; to remove.
⁸⁵破除積習 to break through a

long-standing custom.
破除迷信 to break down superstitions.
破除障礙 to remove hindrances.
破陣 to break through the ranks.
破顏 to smile.
⁹⁰破題 to broach a theme.
破題兒 the beginning of a thing.
破體字 a character written in an irregular or unauthorized form.
攻破 to take by storm.
看破 to see through a thing.

陂¹ A slope. Inter. 坡 No. 5343.
5345

陂陀 a declivity.
世運平陂 the ups and downs of fortune.

(a) Read pci¹, or p'i¹. A dam, an embankment, a shore, a bank.

陂塘 a dam; a pond.
陂池 artificial pond.
彼澤之陂 by the shores of the marsh.

(b) Read p'i². Inclined; uneven.

陂曲 bent; crooked.
偏陂 biassed.

頗¹ Inclined to one side; partial; uneven.
5346

偏頗 partial.

(a) Read p'o¹,³ A little; somewhat; rather; quite; very.

頗久 rather too long a time.
頗佳 very good.
頗切 exceedingly.
頗可 it will answer very well.
⁵頗呈寂靜 very quiet and lonely.
頗多 too much; very many.
頗好 (hao⁴) rather fond of.
頗形接近 close; in touch.
頗有 rather too much.
¹⁰頗有錯簡 a confusion of documents.
頗欲以風雅自見 greatly desired to appear as refined and elegant.
頗知一二 I know a thing or two about it.

頗 稱 may be said to....

頗 表 同 情 had expressed great sympathy.

[15]頗 資 affords some ground for...

頗 願 very desirous of.

頗 饒 與 味 of considerable interest.

婆[2] An old woman; a step-mother; a mother-in-law.

5347 Used for the female of some animals.

婆 娘 or 老 婆·婆 or 婆·子 an old woman.

婆·婆 or 婆 母 husband's mother.

婆·家 a husband's mother's family.

　有 婆·家 she is already betrothed.

[5]婆 心 苦 口 a compassionate heart and importunate words.

仙 婆 a fairy.

公 婆 husband's father and mother.

媒 婆 a marriage go-between.

小 老 婆 a concubine.

[10]師 婆 a witch; a medium.

接 生 婆 or 穩 婆 a midwife.

湯 婆 a bed-warmer.

漁 婆 a fish-wife.

牙 婆 a procuress.

[15]紡 線 婆 the spinning-woman—a kind of cicada.

樂 婆 a female quack.

虔 婆 a female villain; a wicked woman.

(a) Used in transliterating.

婆 羅 吸 摩 Brahmâ.

婆 迦 婆 the most meritorious—a term applied to every Buddha. *Sanskrit: bhagavat.*

婆 那 娑 the jack-fruit—from *panasa.*

珀[4.5] Amber.

5348

珀 末 amber-dust—used as medicine.

琥 珀 amber.

叵
匭[3] Not; cannot. Then; forthwith. Following. Distinguish 叵 No. 1544.

5349

匚 信 unworthy of belief.

匚 耐 心 煩 I cannot bear the inconvenience.

匚 平 諸 國 therefore he reduced the feudal barons to subjection.

匚 欲 討 之 he thereupon wished to reduce him.

匚 測 unfathomable; unexpected.

筥[3] A flat basket-tray for grain.

5350

筥 籮 a flat tray for grain; a flat work-basket.

皤[2] White; grey.
Also read *po*[2].

5351

皤 然 white, silvery.

皤 皤 雪 snowy white.

(a) Corpulent.

皤 腹 corpulent.

鄱[2] A district in North Kiangsi.

5352

鄱 陽 湖 the Poyang Lake.

P'O. (至)
See also 4986
(P'oh)

粕[4.5]
5353　　　Grains in distilled liquor.

樸
朴[3.5] Sincere. Plain, simple. The substance of things; things in the rough. Also
Pron. *p'u*[2.3.4.5]

5354

樸 儉 or 簡 樸 frugal.

樸 塞 uninformed; unintelligent.

樸 實 or 樸 厚 simple-minded; honest; sincere.

樸 拙 stupid; dull.

[5]樸 淳 simple; pure and honest.

樸 素 simple and plain.

樸 素 家 風 simple family habits.

樸 質·的 unornamented; plain.

樸 重 simple; honest and sincere.

[10]樸 野 simple; rustic.

樸 鈍 blunt—of tools; dull—of intelligence.

樸 馬 an unbroken horse.

(a) A tree.

樸 樕 a tree described as of the elm family—the leaves when dried are used as sand-paper. —*Aphananthe aspera.*

樸 樹 a kind of oak: *Quercus dentata.*

璞[4.5] The crust of a gem; an unpolished gem.

5355　　Pron. *p'u*[4.5]

璞 玉 uncut jade.

潑[1.5] To sprinkle; to scatter. To dissipate; to waste.

5356

潑 剌 the splash of a rising fish.

潑 墨 a splash of ink—to scribble; a form of impressionistic painting.

潑 天 drenching rain.

潑 失 生 意 to lose custom—as by rudeness.

[5]潑 息 to extinguish by throwing on water.

潑 水 難 收 spilt water cannot be gathered.

潑 瀉 to spill.

潑 街 to water the street.

散 潑 to dissipate or waste.

[10]活 潑 潑·的 lively, bustling, active; naive, ingenuous.

↑活·潑 lively.

(a) Violent, vigorous. Malignant.

潑 婦 a shrew; a termagant.

潑 怪 noxious; malicious.

潑 悍 a shrewish temper.

潑 皮 or 潑 賴 roughs; rascals; rowdies.

潑 辣 saucy; spiteful.

P'OU. (至)
(P'eo)

抔[1.2] To take up in both hands.
Also read *p'ei*[1].

5357

抔 土 a double handful of earth—very small; a grave.

抔 錢 濟 貧 to give generously to assist the poor—lit., in double handfuls.

抔 飲 to drink from the hands.

剖 [3] To split; to cut in two. To lay open; to disclose.
5358 To decide. Also read *p'o*[3].

剖 分 to divide.

剖 判 or 剖 斷 to give judgement in a case.

剖 割 to rip open.

剖 字 to dissect a Chinese character.

[5] 剖 屍 to dissect a corpse.

剖 心 紂辛 to cut out a man's heart as did to his faithful minister 比干.

剖 心 破 膽 to open one's heart.

剖 明 to decide intelligently.

剖 析 to divide; to distinguish; to solve.

[10] 剖 析 曉 諭 a proclamation explaining the minutest details.

剖 瓜 to divide a melon.

剖 白 to explain away—as false reports; to exonerate.

剖 白 良 心 to clear one's conscience.

剖 符 to divide the token or seal of office, one half being kept by the emperor and the other given to the officer appointed.

[15] 剖 腹 明 心 to disclose the real feelings.

剖 腹 藏 珠 to rip open the stomach to hide a pearl—to die for the sake of gain.

剖 解 to dissect.

剖 解 學 anatomy.

剖 訴 前 因 it clearly sets forth the aforesaid details.

[20] 剖 開 to rip open.

剖 驗 post-mortem examination.

掊 [2] To exact. Also read *peo*[1], *p'ei*[2].
5359

掊 克 在 位 exactors in office.

(a) To get salt from sea-water.

掊 坑 而 得 鹽 they worked the salt-pans for salt.

(b) Read *p'ou*[3]. Inter. preceding. To break up; to injure.

掊 擊 於 世 俗 injured by worldly entanglements.

掊 斗 折 衡 break the measure and destroy the scales—to prevent wrangling over them.

棓 [2.3.] To strike. Read *pang*[3]. A flail, a club. Inter. 棒
5360 No. 4923. Read *p'ei*[1]. Planks.

五 棓 子 galls.

五 棓 子 蟲 the gall-fly.

甂 [3] A jar or pot.
5361

徒 以 共 覆 甂 之 用 only fit for covering pickle jars—of worthless writings.

瓦 甂 an earthenware jar.

裒 [2] To collect; to assemble. Distinguish 衰 No. 5908.
5362

裒 多 益 寡 take from the surplus to supply the deficit.

裒 聚 to gather together.

PU.   (ㄆㄨ)

步 [4] A step, a pace. A land measure of five local feet;
5363 240 square *pu* being equal to one *mow* 畝. To follow in the footsteps of. On foot.

步 下 to go on foot.

步 他 父 親 的 後 塵 he followed in his father's footsteps.

步 伐 整 齊 to march in order.

步 位 space; room.

[5] 步 兵 or 步 軍 or 步 勇 infantry.

步 哨 a sentry.

步 士 infantry.

步 屈 a name for the looper caterpillar.

步 履 to go on foot.

[10] 步 履 之 間 while walking a few paces—in a very little while.

步 師 to move an army.

步 帶 ambulacral area of sea-urchins, star-fish, etc.

步 弓 a land measure of five feet, shaped like a fork.

步 從 人 attendants.

[15] 步 態 gait, stride, step.

步 月 to walk in the moonlight.

步 檐 a porch or verandah.

步 歐 美 的 後 塵 to run after western ways—European and American.

步 步 or 一 步 一 步 a step at a time; gradually.

[20] 步 步 為 營 to take precautions at every step.

步 步 留 心 careful of every step.

步 步 高 陞 he gradually rose to eminence.

步 武 to tread in the footsteps of another; a very short distance; lit., a pace and a half.

步 水 to walk on water.

[25] 步 漲 gradual increase—in prices.

步 箭 foot-archers.

步 虛 聲 chanting Taoist liturgies.

步 行 to go on foot.

步 調 marching orders.

[30] 步 趨 to keep step with a person. *See* No. 1618-35.

步 足 or 步 腳 ambulacral feet of the star-fish and other creatures.

步 跑 to go on foot.

步 路 a step.

步 踏 to step off; to measure by pacing.

[35] 步 軍 統 領 Commandant of Gendarmerie in Peking.

步 輦 imperial hand-carriage.

步 道 a foot-path.

步 金 or 謝 步 doctor's or geomancer's fees.

步 鎗 rifles—infantry.

[40] 步 隊 infantry.

步 障 a bamboo screen or fence against the dust.

步 頭 a landing-place.

步 驟 rate of progress; sequence; order; series.

信 步 walking slowly without aim—as when in deep thought.

[45] 回 步 to retrace the steps.

國 步 the fortunes of a State.

天 步 the way of Heaven.

寸 步 難 行 even one step is difficult.

徐 步 to walk slowly.

[50] 急 步 with rapid strides.

散 步 to go for a walk.

止 步 Stop!

留 步 please come no further; stop!

進 步 progress.

布 [4] Calico, cotton cloth, shirtings, linen.
5364 Distinguish 市 No. 5792; 希 No. 2416.

布 疋 cloth or cotton goods; piece-goods.

布 商 piece-goods merchants.

布 店 linen-drapers.
布 衣 cotton garments—the common people.
⁵布 衣 之 交 friendship of the days when one was in humble circumstances.
布 袋 a calico sack for grain, etc.
布 被 之 譏 ridiculed for wearing cotton garments,–as being a pretended humility.
印 花 布 prints.
原 色 布 unbleached goods.
¹⁰帆 布 canvas, sailcloth.
夏 布 grass-cloth, linen.
斜 紋 布 twills.
橡 皮 布 rubber-cloth.
檯 布 tablecloth.
¹⁵油 布 oiled calico.
火 浣 布 asbestos.
白 布 calico.
羽 布 bunting.
紫 花 布 native cotton cloth made from a whitey-brown cotton.
²⁰緞 布 damask.
花 布 fancy cottons.

(a) To notify. To publish. To spread out. To display.

布 列 to arrange in order.
布 列 左 右 to arrange in position.
布 告 天 下 to publish throughout the land.
布 局 arrangement.
⁵布 政 司 (or 使) former Provincial Treasurer; former Provincial Governor.
布 散 to distribute.
布 施 to give liberally.
布 景 stage-scenery.
布 種 to disseminate, as doctrines.
¹⁰布 穀 the cuckoo.
布 網 to cast nets.
布 置 to arrange; to deploy—as troops.
布 置 得 宜 well-arranged; all done to suit.
布 訂 to name a date or time.
¹⁵布 達 to announce—as by a notice; to advise.
布 陣 to set in battle.

(b) Used in transliterating.

布 丁 pudding.
布 爾 施 維 克 Bolshevik.
布 黨 Bolshevik Party.

佈 ⁴ To extend; to diffuse; to inform. Used for preceding.
5365

佈 告 to announce; to declare.
佈 寢 to give hush-money.
佈 散 謠 言 to scatter evil rumours.
佈 置 to arrange; to put in order.
⁵佈 聞 for your information.
佈 覆 an answer in return; in reply.
佈 請 to present one's best wishes for . . . .
佈 道 to preach; evangelize.
　文 字 佈 道 dissemination of doctrine by means of literature.
¹⁰　逐 家 佈 道 house to house evangelism.
佈 道 團 evangelistic group—as in a school, etc.
佈 道 會 evangelistic society—generally home mission.
公 佈 to make public.
散 佈 to disseminate.

怖 ⁴ Afraid, surprised. To frighten.
5366

怖 悸 perturbed.
怖 慄 trembling.
怖 畏 to dread.
怖 禍 dreading danger or calamity.
⁵海 內 怖 駭 the whole country was alarmed.
犬 馬 怖 懼 之 情 the affection of your dog or your horse, expressed by fear.

哺 ⁴ To feed by hand; to chew food for infants; to feed as a bird does. To sit on eggs. Also read p'u⁴.
5367

哺 乳 to suckle.
哺 乳 類 mammalia.
反 哺 to disgorge to feed—its parents, as crows are said to do.
受 哺 to receive food—as fledglings.

圃 ³·⁴ A vegetable garden; an orchard. Also read p'u³.
5368

園 圃 gardens.
老 圃 a gardener.

埔 ³ A plain, an arena. A port. A mart. Used for 浦 No. 5369 5390. Also read p'u³.

埔 頭 a mart, a port.

捕 ³·⁴ To seize; to apprehend; to catch.
5370

捕 差 or 捕 役 or 捕 快 constables.
捕 廳 or 典 史 or 右 堂 former Police Master and Gaol Warden.
捕 房 a police-station.
捕 拿 to arrest; to catch.
⁵捕 獲 to arrest; to take prisoner, as in war.
捕 獲 物 a prize in warfare.
捕 獲 船 隻 prize-vessel.
捕 獲 裁 判 所 Prize Court.
捕 獲 賞 金 prize-money.
¹⁰捕 盜 to arrest robbers.
捕 緝 to arrest; to catch.
捕 蠅 紙 fly-papers.
捕 頭 a head-constable.
捕 風 捉 影 to grasp at shadows; to trump up a story.
¹⁵捕 魚 to catch fish.
捕 鯨 船 whale-boat.
捕 鳥 to catch birds.

晡 ¹ 3—5 p.m.
5371

下 晡 towards sunset.
日 晡 afternoon.

補 ³ To repair; to patch; to add to; to mend. To help. To fill a vacancy.
5372

補 上 to add to.
補 償 compensation.
補 充 to supplement; to recruit.
補 充 兵 territorial forces.
⁵補 充 物 supplementary things; subsidiary things.
補 充 的 supplementary; subsidiary.
補 其 缺 漏 to repair the omissions.
補 力 to strengthen.
補 助 to assist; to subsidize.
¹⁰以 公 款 補 助 to subsidize from public funds.
助 以 補 金 to subsidize.
政 府 補 助 金 government subsidies.

補 助 力 auxiliary force.

補 助 商 行 爲 subsidiary commercial transactions.

[15]補 助 條 件 supplementary items or clauses.

補 助 貨 幣 subsidiary coins.

補 助 費 subsidy.

  經 常 補 助 費 permanent subsidy.

  臨 時 補 助 費 temporary subsidy.

[20]補 助 金 subsidy.

補 品 tonics.

補 報 to repay—as a kindness.

補 增 to make a supplementary payment.

補 平 頭 to make up for light-weight silver.

[25]補 情 to make a return for kindness done.

補 拙 to supplement one's stupidity—by work.

補 授 to fill an appointment.

補 救 to rectify shortcomings and reform abuses; to save the situation.

補 救 辦 法 means to save the situation.

[30]補 整 compensation.

補 整 振 子[3] compensating pendulum.

補 正 解 釋 supplementary explanations—as of a law.

補 氣 to restore to health; to reinvigorate.

補 添 物 complement.

[35]補 漏 to stop a leak.

補 滿 to make up the full amount.

補 滿 缺 欠 to make good all defects.

補 滿 額 數 to make up the required number.

補 用 to employ as a supernumerary; expectant—of office.

[40]補 發 to issue; to pay.

補 益 to help; to benefit.

補 窮 的 a woman who goes about doing mending for poor men.

補 筆 to give further details.

補 築 to repair—a wall.

[45]補 網 to repair nets.

補 綻 or 補 修 or 打 補 to patch; to mend.

補 經 to stop a crack.

補 缺 or 補 放 to supply a vacancy.

補 習 敎 育 supplementary education.

---

[50]補 習 科 course for backward pupils.

補 色 complementary colours.

補 苴 rectification; to repair.

補 苴 罅 漏 to make good any omissions; to repair; to correct.

補 葺 to thatch; to repair.

[55]補 藥 tonics.

補 血 氣 to recruit the vital energies; to strengthen the powers.

補 衣 服 to patch garments.

補 補 釘 to put on a patch.

補 角 supplementary angle.

[60]補 諫 君 王 to aid and reprove a ruler.

補 足 to make up a deficiency.

補 足 語 complement. (grammar).

補 路 to repair the roads.

補 身 to build up the body; to recruit the vital powers.

[65]補 遺 to supplement omissions—an appendix.

補 還 to make good; to restore; to compensate.

補 銀 水 or 補 色 to make up the difference between an inferior silver and that of a better quality.

補 鞋 匠 a cobbler.

補 領 to receive anew — as a lost document, salary overdue, etc.

[70]修 補 to repair.

抵 補 to make up a deficit.

賠 補 to make reparations.

(a) Read *p'u*[3]. **Official insignia.**

補 服 the embroidered robes formerly worn by officials or mandarins.

補 子 insignia of office; the badges of former officials.

逋[1]
5373   **To flee, to abscond.**

逋 臣 disloyal officials.

逋 逃 or 逋 竄 to abscond; to skulk.

逋 逃 藪 a refuge for criminals.

(a) **To owe, especially to the government.**

逋 負 or 逋 欠 a debt; to owe.

逋 賦 in debt to the tax-collectors.

餔[1]
5374   **The time of the evening meal.**

餔 時 the time of the evening meal.

日 餔 時 evening.

(a) Read *pu*[3]. Inter. 哺 No. 5367. **To eat.**

餔 餟 food and drink.

簿[4]
5375   **A register; a memorandum book; a blank book; an account-book.**
     Distinguish 薄 No. 5326.

簿 册 lists; registers.

簿 子 an account-book.

簿 書 books in general.

簿 正 祭 器 to correct the sacrificial vessels according to the records.

[5]簿 籍 books and records.

簿 記 book-keeping, accountant.

簿 記 學 book-keeping.

  復 式 簿 記 book-keeping by double-entry.

  單 式 簿 記 book-keeping by single-entry.

[10]上 簿 to enter in the account-book.

信 件 底 簿 copying-book for letters.

原 簿 or 總 賬 簿 a ledger.

收 支 簿 cash-book.

存 貨 簿 stock-book.

[15]小 賬 簿 petty-cash book.

捐 簿 subscription book.

日 記 簿 diary.

樣 子 簿 pattern-book.

流 水 簿 journal.

[20]簽 名 簿 register of attendance.

練 習 簿 exercise-book.

賬 簿 account-books.

賣 出 賬 簿 sales-book.

送 信 簿 chit-book.

(a) A token or tablet similar to 笏 No. 2193.

以 簿 擊 頰 struck him on the face with the tablet.

(b) Read *po*[5]. u.f. 箔 No. 5335.

部[4]
5376   **A class, a division, a section, a sort, a genus. A public court. A board.**

部。下 those under a certain command.

部 位 position or place in a series, etc.

部·分 a part; a division; a section; a group.

部 務 affairs of a board.

[5] 部 員 officers of a department.

部 堂 a former Governor-General or Viceroy; title of the President of one of the government boards.

部 居 divided into groups—as under the radicals.

部 屬 the personnel of a board.

部 屬 會 議 meeting of a board.

[10] 部 族 a tribe.

部 曹 member of one of the former six boards.

部 照 a commission—formerly issued by the Board of Civil Office.

部 置 to arrange the parts; to assign places to.

部 臣 a ministry; a government.

[15] 部 落 aboriginal tribes.

部 長 head of a board; a minister.

部 院 the former Governor of a Province; Vice-President of a Board.

部 隊 army corps.

部 頒 issued by a Board.

[20] 部 類 a section; a class.

部 首 or 字 部 radicals for Chinese characters.

上 部 下 部 the upper and lower parts of the body respectively.

交 通 部 Ministry of Communications.

內 務 部 Ministry of Home Affairs. 參 謀 部 Staff Headquar-

[25] 司 令 部 Head-quarters. [ters.

司 法 部 Ministry of Justice.

外 交 部 Ministry for Foreign Affairs. 經 濟 部 M. of Economics.

實 業 部 Ministry of Industry, Agriculture and Commerce.

敎 育 部 Ministry of Education.

[30] 財 政 部 Ministry of Finance.

軍 政 部 Ministry of War.

鐵 道 部 Ministry of Railways.

↑ 衞 生 部 Ministry of Health.

(a) Read *p'ou*³. A hillock.

部 婁 a hillock.

埠 ⁴ A port, a mart on the river or on the sea. Also read *fou*⁴.

5377

埠 商 wholesale salt-merchants.

埠 頭 or 埠 口 or 埠 子 a port; a mart.

埠 頭 稅 wharfage.

商 埠 a treaty port.

PU.   (ㄆ)

(Puh)

卜 3.5. **To divine; to foretell. Radical 25.**

5378

卜 人 or 卜 士 a fortune-teller.

卜 卦 to divine by the Diagrams.

卜 宅 to divine about a locality.

卜 居 to divine about a dwelling place.

[5] 卜 年 or 卜 世 to forecast the length of a dynasty.

卜 晝 卜 夜 all day and night carousal.

卜 筮 偕 止 I have divined by the tortoise-shell and the straws.

卜 課 the diviner's art; fortune-telling.

卜 鄰 to select a neighbourhood by divination.

[10] 卜 魚 a wooden block like a skull, used by priests to beat time when chanting.

卜 龜 to divine by means of tortoise-shell.

問 卜 to seek divination.

不 4.5. **Not; a negative.**

5379

不 一 phrase used at the end of letters, indicating that many things have been left unsaid.

不 一 而 足 one is too many. (in derogatory descriptions)

不 三 不 四 neither one thing nor the other; insolent, formless.

不 上 算 it does not pay.

[5] 不 下 帶 do not go below the girdle; near; easily seen.

不 不 no, no! not un-.

不 中 (*chung*¹) will not do; useless.

不 中 (*chung*¹) 用 or 無 用 useless; not useful for the purpose.

不 久 before long; in a short time.

[10] 不 乾 性 油 non-drying oil.

不 了 解 unable to understand.

不 事 will not attend to.

不 二 價 uniform prices—a shop notice.

不 亞 其 主 not inferior to his master.

[15] 不 亞 於 not inferior to....

不 亢 不 卑 neither cringing nor rude—a happy medium.

不 亦 樂 乎 will not that also be pleasant? what a mess!

不 以 爲 恥 did not regard it as shameful.

不 以 爲 然 to come to a different conclusion; to disagree.

[20] 不 令 而 行 they will do it without being ordered.

不 任 其 責 neglected the responsibility.

不 住 的 incessantly.

不 作 爲 犯 offence of omission. (*legal*).

不 作 聲 keep silence.

[25] 不 依 to disallow; to withstand; to demand satisfaction.

不 値 得 說 not worth mentioning.

不 俟 經 宿 he did not wait till he had passed the night.

不 倒 翁 a small weighted doll that cannot be pushed over: *

不 備 phrase used at the end of a letter indicating the there is much more to be said which must be taken for granted.

[30] 不 傳 導 物 non-conductor.

不 像 話 improper; unpresentable; nonsense: undignified.

不 允 to refuse—as a petition.

不 充 分 insufficient.

不 內 顧 did not turn his head quite round—when riding.

[35] 不 公 開 not open to the public; to hear a case *in camera*.

不 共 戴 天 irreconcilable enemies; not able to live together under the same sky.

不 具 insufficient.

不 准 招 貼 Post no Bills!

不 凡 uncommon; not mortal.

[40] 不 出 所 料 not unexpected: not surprising.

不 分 高 低 unable to distinguish between; obtuse.

不 切 於 身 之 弊 no relation to his natural defects.

不 加 思 索 without thinking.

不 助 No—in a vote; dissent.

[45] 不 動 產 real estate.

不 動 心 dispassionate.

* a roly-poly.

不勞而得 obtained without labour.

不勝任 inadequate for the post.

不卽不離 neither instantly nor remotely—reasonably; moderately; a middle course.

⁵⁰不反抗 non-resistance.

不反芻類 non-ruminants.

不及 not so good as; not so good.

不及之處 wherein he comes short.

不及人的 to fall behind others.

⁵⁵不及於你 inferior to you.

不及格 not up to the standard.

不及物的 or 自動的 intransitive.

不占而已 they merely ignore the divination.

不可以風 I must avoid the wind; unable to stand the wind.

⁶⁰不可入性 impenetrability.

不可分物 indivisible things. (legal).

不可勝用也 you cannot exhaust the use of; more than can be called into practice.

不可勝言 beyond description; it cannot be told.

不可思議 inconceivable.

⁶⁵不可思議論 Agnosticism.

不可抗力 irresistible force; "act of God."

不可救藥 too far gone for medicines; irremediable.

不可知的 cannot be known; agnostic.

不可礙 unable to endure the slightest interruption.

⁷⁰不可紀極 innumerable.

不可能 impossible.

不召之臣 ministers who are not called to go to the sovereign.

不合 not in agreement.

不合作主義 principle of non-co-operation.

⁷⁵不合作的團體 non-co-operative association.

不合時宜 untimely.

不合時用 not adapted to modern use.

不合格 not up to the standard.

不合算 not economical.

⁸⁰不合論理的 illogical.

不同意 non-concurrence.

不同道 not in the same way as I am.

不名譽 dishonour.

不名譽行爲 dishonourable act.

⁸⁵不告不理 no condemnation without accusation.

不告而去 left without announcing his departure.

不咖 no, not so. (‑chieh)

不問 no matter; no matter whether.

不啻 not otherwise than; not less than.

⁹⁰不因人熱 not dependent upon others.

不在 not present; not at home; dead.

不在乎 nonchalant; indifferent.

不在意 neglectful; unconcerned.

不報無道 not to recompense that which is evil.

⁹⁵不堪 unendurable.

不堪置想 could not bear to think of it.

不外 not beyond; included in; nothing more than.

不多幾日 in a few days.

不大離 or 不大支離 or 不大訛 or 不大離經 not far out (about the thing)(S. Mand.)

¹⁰⁰不奪不厭 not satisfied unless they snatch all.

不如 not equal to; cannot do better than.

不如意 not to one's liking; dissatisfied.

不好意思 ashamed to; embarrassed; reluctant to.

不好過 unwell; out of sorts.

¹⁰⁵不妨 might as well; it doesn't do any harm to; harmless.

不妥當 unsatisfactory; unsuitable; not settled; not quite right.

不存在 non-existence.

不完備格 incomplete; imperfect. (grammar.)

不完全局外中立 imperfect neutrality.

¹¹⁰不完全行爲 incomplete action. (legal).

不完全證據 incomplete evidence.

不完全變態 incomplete transformation.

不定 or 不一定 or 未定 uncertain; not yet settled.

不定期的 irregular dates—as of issue.

¹¹⁵不宣 phrase used at the end of a letter, indicating that there is a lot more that has not been said.

不容 to disallow.

不審 ignorant of; I wonder ...

不耐煩 impatient of; cannot be bothered with.

不耐站立 cannot stand still.

¹²⁰不對勁 uncongenial; ill-mated.

不導體 non-conducting body.

不屑就己 it was not inconsistent with purity to go with them.

不已 endless; without ceasing.

不干涉 non-intervention.

¹²⁵不平等條約 unequal treaties.

不幸 unluckily.

不幸事件 unfortunate incident.

不彀人格 not up to the standard of a man.

不彀本 less than cost price—I shall lose on it.

¹³⁰不彀用 insufficient for use.

不待勉強 spontaneously; without effort.

不待教而誅 to punish by death without giving a warning by teaching.

不徑不竇 he would not travel by bypaths or narrow lanes.

不得 unattainable; following a verb is equivalent to:—may not; must not.

¹³⁵不得不 or 不得不然 cannot but....; bound to....

不得以言勿求於心 what you do not understand in words, do not seek for in the mind.

不得其死 an untimely end.

不得受用 uncomfortable; out of sorts.

不得已 no alternative; the only thing possible.

¹⁴⁰不得時 out of season; out of favour.

不得要領 nothing to the point.

不復容喙 to admit of no further discussion.

不必屢說 no need for a lot of talk.

不忍其求 could not tolerate his ambitions.

¹⁴⁵不忍的 unendurable.

不念舊惡 forgetting old grievances.

不忮不求 neither perverse nor fawning.

不恥下問 not ashamed to inquire of those beneath him.

不惜 not to spare—labour.

¹⁵⁰不惜工本 to spare neither labour nor money.

不悱不發 I do not unfold to those who are not anxious to express themselves.

不情 unfeeling.

不意之中 in a moment of carelessness; unexpectedly.

不想吃 no liking for food; no appetite.

155 不愛 averse to; do not care for.

不憚所難為 do not fear difficulties.

不憤不啟 I do not explain to those not in earnest.

不成 incomplete; forms an interrogative final particle, it follows 難道. See 難 No. 4625-46.

不成事實 not materialized.

160 不成問題 out of the question.*

不成器 unfit for anything; good-for-nothing.

不成常 profligate; dissipated.

不成才 useless; stupid.

不成文法 ungrammatical; unwritten law.

165 不成文憲法 unwritten constitution.

不成話 or 不成句 it makes no sense. (First also＝31.)

不戒視成 to look for completion without giving previous warning.

不我足 do not look upon me as fulfilling their wishes.

不才 devoid of talent.

170 不抵抗主義 non-resistance.

不拘 or 不用拘 no matter; no matter whether; don't be formal.

不拿當事 took no account of.

不挾貴 not to presume on rank.

不提 to make no mention of.

175 不揚 awkward; ugly.

不敢當 not equal to the honour—a polite phrase.

不敬之處 indignities.

不敷用 insufficient.

不料 unforeseen; unexpected.

180 不旋踵 before one could turn round.

不日 before long; in a few days; quickly.

不時 shortly; in a little while.

不是 not; no; a fault; a failing.

不服教 headstrong; intractable.

185 不服法術 not yielding to incantations.

*beyond question.

不期然而然 to happen unexpectedly; not as one thought it would happen.

不欺暗室 be not deceitful in your secret abode—in acts which are unseen be as careful as in those which are seen.

不止 not only; not to stop at.

不正當 not proper.

190 不正行為 a wrong action.

不殖貨 do not be avaricious.

不毛 sterile, barren—of soil.

不求人 no need to seek the help of others—a back-scratcher.

不注意 inattention.

195 不法的事 unlawful matters.

不法行為 illegal act.

不消提 don't speak of it; let that pass; that goes without saying.

不減 not inferior to.

不滲透質 non-porous.

200 不澈底的 not thorough.

不濟 not up to the mark; worthless.

不濟於事 ineffective.

不無辛苦 to take great trouble; it was very difficult.

不無裨益 decidedly of use.

205 不然 not so; if otherwise.

不爭主義 pacificism.

不為罪 not criminal. (legal).

不爽 unfailing; certain.

不爾 otherwise.

210 不特 not merely; not alone; not only.

不犯 not worth while.

不獲乎上 do not obtain—the confidence of—the sovereign.

不牽 undisciplined.

不理 or 不睬 to disregard; to despise.

215 不甚好 only tolerable; not very good.

不生利 not bearing interest.

不生効力 invalid.

不生產 unproductive.

不用我輩操心 there is no need for our generation to worry over it.

220 不由得 unconsciously; involuntarily.

不當利得² illegal profit; ill-gotten gains.

不痛不癢的 unfeeling; ineffective.

不盈科不行 does not pro-

ceed till it has filled up the hollows.

不盡 a phrase used at the end of a letter indicating that there are many more things to be said which must be taken for granted.

225 不盡然 hardly so; not altogether so.

不目逃 his eyes did not flinch from a thrust made at them.

不省人事 unconscious; insensible. (-hsing³-)

不省所怙 "without a father's care." Giles. (-hsing³-)

不相倫 having no relationship.

230 不相入 not suited one to the other; in disagreement.

不相宜 unsuitable; unfitting.

不相干 of no moment; beside the question.

不相符 the parts do not match; there is a discrepancy.

不知不覺 unconscious; unawares.

235 不知其可也 I do not know how he can get on.

不知好歹 not to know good from bad.

不知死活 or 不顧死活 heedless of consequences; reckless; no idea of the fitness of things.

不知道 or 不曉得 or 知不到 I don't know; not acquainted with.

不碍事 it is no matter; don't be alarmed.

240 不稱 (ch'ên⁴) unsuitable; not in correspondence.

不符 to disagree; not to accord with.

不答應 not to reply; not to agree to.

不等 unlike; a variety.

不等號 sign of dissimilarity. (math.)

245 不第如此 not merely thus.

不約而同 acting in concert without previous arrangement.

不素餐兮 he would not eat the bread of idleness.

不經事 inexperienced.

不置真名 anonymous.

250 不羈暫刻 not detained for any length of time.

不聞不問的態度 an attitude of indifference.

不 聽 勸 not to listen to advice.

不 肖 not like; degenerate--as a son; to fall short of a conventional standard.

不 能 以 髮 cannot be separated by a hair.

²⁵⁵不 能 必 其 有 無 could not be certain whether he had or not.

不 能 白 事 they are not able to manage the business.

不 膚 撓 he did not flinch when struck.

不 自 愛 lacking in self-respect.

不 至·於 so as not; not necessarily to....

²⁶⁰不 至·於 外 馳 not involved in outside fleeting things.

不 致 not so as to....

不 舍³晝 夜 not ceasing day or night.

不 良 導 體 non-conductor.

不 虔 不 義 irreligious and unjust.

²⁶⁵不 虞 之 譽 unexpected praise.

不 行 cannot be done; out of the question; will not do; no good.

不 行·為 a negative act.

不 行·為 犯 negative offence.

不 要 忙 don't be in a hurry; all in good time.

²⁷⁰不 要 緊 unimportant; never mind.

不 要 臉 shameless; without self-respect.

不 要 見 怪 don't feel angry; don't be annoyed.

不 見 好 not any better.

不 見·得 or 不 見 其 by no means certain; not at all evident.

²⁷⁵不 規 則 irregular.

不 許 to forbid; to refuse; "thou shalt not."

不 許 可 to disapprove.

不 認 支 non-acceptance.

不 論 no matter.

²⁸⁰不 謹 愼 careless; lazy.

不 變 塞 焉 he does not change the principles he held when in retirement.

不 變 未 達 之 所 守 does not change that which he held when he was unknown.

不 負 責 does not accept responsibility; irresponsible.

不 貳 過 not to repeat a fault.

²⁸⁵不 賴 勇 而 裕 如 者 he does not depend on valour, and yet

---

he has it in abundance.

不 贊 成 to oppose; to disapprove; not to support—as a motion before a meeting.

不 起 unable to get up—very ill.

不 足 or 不 穀 insufficient.

不 足 介 意 of no consequence; not worth a thought.

²⁹⁰不 足 觀 not fit to be looked at; not worth attention.

不 足 輕 重 not fit to be considered.

不 足 道 not worth mentioning; inadequate; not up to the mark.

不 踐 前 言 to break a promise.

不 速 之 客 an uninvited guest.

²⁹⁵不 逮 unequal to.

不 透 光 opaque.

不 過 only, merely; ∘不∘過 but.

不 過 時 日 問 題 merely a question of time.

不 違 如 愚 he made no objection, as if he were stupid.

³⁰⁰不 適 宜 inappropriate; inapt.

不 適 用 之 條 約 treaties which have become unsuitable.

不 遺 餘 力 to spare no efforts.

不 配 unworthy; unfit; incongruous.

不 關 心 unconcerned; indifferent.

³⁰⁵不 防·備 unawares.

不 隨 和 to refuse to agree to others; not in accord; aloof.

不 雅 inelegant; ungraceful; ill-mannered.

不 離 not far out; nearly right.

不 離 左 右 never to leave; to be in close attendance.

³¹⁰不 需 要 unnecessary.

不 靈 inefficacious; unresponsive; dull of apprehension.

不 顧 to neglect; not to care for.

不 顧 信·用 abuse of trust.

不 顧 性·命 careless of one's life.

³¹⁵不 顧 羞 恥 shameless.

不 食 周 粟 hunger-strike.

不 齊 incomplete; deficient; uneven.

(a) Between two verbs it makes an interrogative.

來·不·來 Will he come?

要·不·要 Do you want it or not?

(b) With another negative or following 好 it makes a strong affirmative. See No. 2062—B.

好 不 歡 喜 full of rejoicing.

無 不 or 莫 不 strong affirmatives.

(c) Read fou³. u.f. 否 No. 1902. Not, etc.

襆 2 5.   A hood or cowl.
5380   Pron. p'u².

蹼 4.5.   Webbed feet of water-fowl. Also read po⁵.
5381

醭 2.5.   Mould on liquids, scum.
5382

濮 2.5.   Name of a river in Shantung. Name of an ancient tribe in Hupeh.
5383   Pron. p'u²

P'U.   (ㄆ)

普 ³ General, universal, everywhere. All.
5384 Distinguish 晉 No. 1088.

普 傳 天 下 proclaim to all the world.

普 及 extending to all; universal; made widely available.

普 及 敎·育 universal education; education for all.

普 同 one and all.

⁵普 告 to make widely known.

普 天 下 all under heaven; the whole land of China; the world.

普 天 同 慶 the whole world joins in congratulation.

普 度 to get souls out of torment.

普 揚 to make widely known.

¹⁰普 救 衆 生 to save all living beings—said of the goddess *Kwan Yin.*

普 施 to disburse to all; liberal gifts.

普 旱 a general drought.

普 渡 慈 航 all may cross in the barge of mercy.

普 濟 院 a hospital; a poor-house.

↑普 洱 茶 tea produced in Pu-êrh, Yunnan.

¹⁵普 照 to illuminate all things; to shed light on.

普 通 universal; general; current; in ordinary use.

普 通 任 用 ordinary appointment.

普 通 收 電 機 receiving sets for radio.

普 通 品 ordinary quality.

²⁰普 通 學 general education.

普 通 定 理 a universal axiom.

普 通 官 話 current Mandarin speech.

普 通 折 扣 usual discount.

普 通 敎·育 general elementary education.

²⁵普 通 條 件 usual terms.

普 通 法 common law.

普 通 生·活 低 度 之 時 when the general standard of living was low.

普 通 知·識 general knowledge.

普 通 稅 則 general tariff.

³⁰普 通 程 度 general standard.

普 通 章·程 general regulations.

普 通 話 current speech; language generally understood.

普 通 認 支 general acceptance.

普 通 選 舉 universal suffrage.

³⁵普 通 電 台 broadcasting station.

普 選 運 動 universal suffrage movement.

普 門 大 士 name for the goddess *Kwan yin* 觀 音·

↑普 遍 universal, widespread.

(a) Used in transliterating.

普 法 戰 爭 Franco-Prussian war.

普 魯 士 Prussia.

氆³ A thick, rough serge from Tibet.
5385

譜³ A register; a genealogical table; a treatise.
5386

譜 入 to make rhymes agree.

譜·子 a standard; something to go by; after numbers = about; nearly.

譜 第 or **譜 牒** a family register or genealogy.

譜 系 or **家 譜** a family register.

⁵譜 錄 scientific repertories and similar works.

修 譜 to revise a register, especially the clan register.

樂 譜 music book. (*yüeh*⁴-)

琴 譜 music for the lute.

菩² A herb. Transliteration of a Sanskrit sound.
5387

菩 提 intelligence; enlightenment. Sanskrit: *bôdhi.*

菩 提 子³ beads of a rosary.

菩 提 樹 the *Ficus religiosa,* often called the *Bo* tree; also used for the linden.

菩 提 畫 leaf pictures.

菩·薩 or **菩 提 薩 埵** *Bôdhisatva* —"he whose essence is intelligence;" one who has become ready for Nirvana, but who refrains from the next step in order to remain and benefit mankind—commonly used for idols.

匍² To crawl; to lie prostrate.
5388

匍 匐 哀 求 to fall prostrate and beseech.

匍 匐 莖 creeping stems of plants.

匍 匐 行 to crawl on hands and knees.

匍 叩 to prostrate oneself and beg.

葡² The vine; a grape.
5389

葡·萄 grapes.

葡·萄 乾 兒 raisins; sultanas.

葡·萄 果 the cherry-apple.

葡·萄 糖 grape-sugar.

⁵葡·萄 酒 or **葡·萄 汁** grape-wine or grape-juice.

葡·萄 酸 tartaric acid.

(a) Used in transliterating.

葡 萄 牙 Portugal.

浦³ The bank of a river; a reach in a river.
5390

浦 東 opposite Shanghai.

黃 浦 the Whangpoo River at Shanghai.

溥³ Extensive; pervading;· universal.
5391

溥 仁 universal benevolence.

溥 儀 the personal name of the last emperor of the Manchu dynasty.

溥 博 extensive and vast; all embracing.

溥 徧 to extend on all sides.

溥 漠 vast—as the sea.

蒲² A kind of rush from which mats, bags, etc., are made. Also used for the vine. See 葡 No. 5389.
5392

蒲 劍 the rush-sword, hung at the doors of houses on the 5th of the 5th lunar month,

蒲 包 a rush-bag for packing.

蒲 墊 or **蒲 團** rush kneeling-mats.

蒲 扇 rush-leaf fans.

⁵蒲 月 the 5th lunar month.

蒲 笋 edible shoots of certain rushes.

蒲 節 the rush-festival — 5th of the 5th lunar month.

蒲 草 rushes.

蒲 蓆 rush-mats.

莆² Name of a place in Fukien.
5393

舖⁴ A shop, a store. The correct form is 鋪 No. 5396.
5394

舖 保 guarantee for a person, given by a shopkeeper.

舖 夥 shop-assistants.

舖·子 a shop or place of business.

舖 家 tradesmen.

⁵舖 店 a shop or an inn.

舖 底 shop-fixtures.

舖 戶 shopkeepers.

舖 東 or **財 東** the moneyed partner.

舖 規 shop-rules.

¹⁰舖 面 shop-front.

當 舖 a pawn-shop.

開 舖·子 to open a shop.

雜 貨 舖 a general store.

酺² To drink heavily; to drink in company.
5395

鋪 [1] 5396   To spread out; to arrange.

鋪 地 to spread on the ground.
鋪 墊 to spread a cushion; household furniture.
鋪 席 to spread a feast.
鋪 張 to extend; to make much of a little.
[5]鋪 叙 to state in detail.
鋪 牀 to make a bed.
鋪 滿·了 overspread—as with clouds.
鋪·蓋 bedding.
鋪 設 or 鋪 陳 or 鋪·排 to lay in order; to arrange; to set out; to plan.
[10]鋪·開 to spread out.

(a) Read p'u[4]. A bed; a sleeping-place; a bunk; a berth. A shop —for the latter see No. 5394.

打 地 鋪 to make up a bed on the ground.
牀 鋪 a bed.

鯆 [2] 5397   The skate or ray.

蒲 [2] 5398   Sedges. u.f. 蒲 No. 5392. Old gambling-game. Dice.

摴 蒲 gambling; dice.

P'U.   (夂)
(P'uh)

攴 攵 [3.5] 5399   To rap; to tap. Radical 66. Nat. Phon. letter for p'. Written 攵.

業 [2.5] 5400   Thickets. A copse.

僕 [2.5] 5401   A slave; a servant. Used conventionally for oneself. A charioteer.

僕 之 先 人 my ancestors.
僕 人 a slave; a menial; I.
僕 僕 爾 annoyed; troubled.
僕 婢 male and female slaves.
[5]僕 婦 women servants.

僕 隸 the lictors in a yamen; servants; retainers.
公 僕 public servants.
奴 僕 slaves.
家 僕 domestic servants.

撲 扑 [1.5] 5402   To beat; to pound. To strike; to rush on.

撲·了·來 they came rushing on.
撲 交 to wrestle.
撲 作 敎 刑 the rod is the punishment in teaching.
撲 朔 迷 離 unable to distinguish male and female—from a poem which says:—the feet of the male hare rush on, the eyes of the female hare are not discriminating; how can they tell whether I am a man or a woman?
[5]撲 滅 火 to beat out a fire.
撲 燈 to fly at a lamp, as a moth.
撲 生 to seize living creatures, as a beast of prey.
撲 空 a fruitless errand.
撲 翼 to flap the wings.
[10]撲 過·了 to rush on; to close in upon—as a robber.
撲 食 to seize for prey.
撲 馬 an untrained horse.
撲 鼻 to strike the nostrils—as a smell.

(a) Used in imitation of sounds.

撲 通 一 聲 sound as of a heavy body falling; a splash.

曝 [4.5] 5403   To sun; to air.

曝 背 to labour in the hot sun; to sun oneself for warmth.
曝 衣 to air clothes.

(a) Read pu[4.5]. To dry in the sun; u.f. 暴 No. 4957—A.

SA.   (ㄙY)
(Sah)

卅 [4.5] 5404   Thirty.

颯 [4.5] 5405   The sound of wind. A gust; suddenly.

颯 戾 clear and cool.
颯 沓 numerous; abundant; gathered together—as clouds.
颯 灑 blown by the wind.
颯 然 the sound of a gust of wind.
[5]颯 然 來·了 he came suddenly.
颯 爽 lively.
颯 爾 涼 風 吹 the cold wind blows in gusts.
颯 纚 long-sleeved.
颯 辣 untamed—of a horse.
[10]颯 颯 soughing of the wind.

(a) Melancholy. Decadent.

衰 颯 depressed and melancholy.
鬢 毛 颯 已 蒼 the hair on the temples is thin and grey.

(b) Read li[5]. A gale of wind.

撒 [1.5] 5406   To cast away; to sow; to distribute; to disperse; to let loose. Distinguish 撒 No. 286.

撒·下 網·去 to cast a net.
撒·不·得 嬌 not to act pettishly.
撒 俐 tidy; smartly dressed.
撒·出·來 to leak out.
[5]撒 嬌 to tease—of spoilt children.
撒 尿 or 屙 尿 to˙ urinate.
撒 手 to lose control of.
撒 手 不 及 unexpectedly; before he had time to go.
撒 手 不 理 to wash the hands of a matter.
[10]撒 放 to let loose—as a bird.
撒 村 to blackguard; to abuse; to retail scandal.
撒 歡 to frisk—as a horse.
撒 潑 to make an effort; to get in a tantrum, as a pettish child.
撒 災 to scatter calamity.
[15]撒 種 to sow seed.
撒 米 to throw rice on a bridal chair.
撒 蠻 reckless; rude and aggressive.
撒 謊 or 扯 謊 to tell lies.
撒 賴 to implicate another; to trump up a charge; to pretend to be injured.
[20]撒 野 to act impudently; to bluster.
撒·開 to disperse; to let go; to quit; to arrange amicably.

(a) Used in transliterating.

撒 但 Satan.

瞅 1.5.
To glance at.
5407

跋 1.5.
To tread on; slipshod.
5408

跋·拉·着 鞋 to wear the slippers in a slipshod manner.

跋 脚鞋 slippers without backs for the heels.

靸 1.5.
Slippers, shoes.
5409

薩 1.5. Used in transliterating. See 菩 No. 5387.
5410

薩 布 *Sabu*—the neutral strip between two lines of boundary stones on the Mongolian frontier.

SAI.　　(ㄙㄞ)

挱 1
To shake.
5411

顋
腮 1
The lower part of the face; the jaws. The gills of a fish.
5412

顋 頰 or 顋 臉 or 顋 巴·子 the cheeks.

顋 骨 the jawbone.

脹·起 顋 to puff out the cheeks.

鰓 1
The gills of a fish.
5413

鰓 蓋 the gill-covers.

(a) Read *hsi³*. Timid, cautious, apprehensive.

鰓 鰓 然 cautiously; pettishly.

鰓 鰓 過 計 over cautious.

賽 4 To compete; to contend for mastery; to emulate; to rival.
5414

賽 膝 or 賽 比 or 對 賽 to compete with.

賽 燈 to show off lanterns—as at the Feast of Lanterns.

賽 珍 會 or 賽 會 an exhibition.

賽 眞 兒·的 珠·子 it rivals the real pearls.

⁵賽 神 or 賽 會 processions got up to thank the gods; an idolatrous procession in which the gods are carried.

賽 牲 獸 會 cattle show.

賽 船 a regatta.

賽 跑 foot-racing; to run a race.

接 力 賽 跑 relay race.
¹⁰跳 欄 賽 跑 hurdle race.
障 礙 賽 跑 obstacle race.

賽 過 to surpass; to excel.

賽 雪 rivals the snow,—for whiteness.

賽 馬 or 賽 走 馬 to race horses.
¹⁵賽 馬 場 a racecourse.

報 賽 to give a thank-offering to the gods.

比 賽 competition.

賭 賽 to bet on races.

SAN.　　(ㄙㄢ)

三
叄 1
Three. The second form is used in accounts to prevent fraud.
5415

三 七 the mourning-ceremony three weeks after death; a plant which is used as a medicine.

三 七 二 十 一 three sevens are twenty-one—six of one and half a dozen of the other.

三 三 五 五 all at sixes and sevens.

三 三 兩 兩 in crowds.
⁵三 三 見 九 three threes are nine.

三 不 朽 the three imperishables—one's virtue 德, meritorious achievements 功, and one's teachings 言.

三 不 求 three things not to be had for the asking—offspring, wealth, and a long beard.

三 不 知 to know neither the beginning, the middle, nor the end of a matter.

三 不 幸 the three greatest misfortunes—in youth to lose one's father 少 年 喪⁴父, in middle-age to lose one's wife

中 年 失 妻, and in old age to have no son 晚 年 無 子³.

¹⁰三 世 如 來 Buddha of the past, present and future.

三 五 four or five; the 15th of the lunar month.

三 五 天 four or five days.

三 人 行 必 有 我 師 焉 if three of us are walking together, there will certainly be a teacher for me.

三 令 五 申 repeated orders and injunctions.

¹⁵三 仙 丹 or 汞 養 red oxide of mercury.

三 仙 出 洞 a fortunate result.

三 代 the three ancient dynasties.—*Hsia* 夏, *Shang* 商, and *Chou* 周. See also No. 5996-2, 3.

三 代 之 所 以 直 道 而 行 也 the ground by which the three dynasties could follow the correct path.

三 代 迭 用 之 the three dynasties used them alternately.

²⁰三 伏 the three decades of summer; the "dog-days."

三 位 一 體 the Trinity.

三 位 一 體 主 日 Trinity Sunday.

三 個 three.

三 倍·的 or 三 份·的 triplicate; three-fold.

²⁵三 傳 the three commentaries on the *Spring and Autumn Annals*.

三 元 the three great principles—essence 精, breath 氣, and spirit 神; or the three primordial powers—heaven, earth, and water. (*Taoist*).

三 元 及 第 the three highest graduates of the former third degree.

三 光 the three lights—sun, moon and stars.

三 兩 in two or three days; shortly.

³⁰三 冬 the three winter months.

三 分 之 一 one third.

三 力 穩 定 equilibrium of forces.

三·十 thirty.

三 協 約 triple entente.

³⁵三 危 given as a mountain with three overhanging peaks in the *Tun Huang* district of N. W. Kansu; also as Eastern Tibet,

and the Hunan-Kwangsi region.

三 叉 a trident.

三 反 四 覆 fickle; changeable.

三 友 or 歲 寒 三 友 the three friends of winter as depicted by artists, i.e., the pine, the bamboo and the *mei* flower; also—mountains and streams, pines and bamboos, and the lute and wine.

益 者 三 友 損 者 三 友 there are three friendships which are advantageous, and there are three which are injurious.

40 三 司 the former Provincial Treasurer, Provincial Judge and the Salt Commissioner.

三 台 the three terraces—six stars forming part of the constellation of Ursa Major.

三 合 土 a native concrete of lime, earth and sand, etc.

三 合 星 a triple star.

三 合 會 The Triad Society—a secret society.

45 三 同 式 紙 triplicate copies.

三 同 盟 The Triple Alliance.

三 吳 Soochow, Changchow and Huchow.

三 呼 萬 歲 three cheers.

三 四 丈 thirty or forty feet.

50 三 國 the Three States which divided China from A.D. 222-265.

三 國 同 盟 Triple Alliance.

三 國 志 Annals of the Three States.

三 境 the three highest regions. (*Taoist*).

三 墳 五 典 the books of the Three Emperors and the Five Rulers.

55 三 夏 三 秋 the three months of summer and autumn respectively.

三 多 i.e., 多 福, 多 壽, 多 男 子 abundance of blessings, abundance of years, and abundance of offspring.

三 夥 the third officer of a ship.

三 大 憲 the three highest provincial officials of former times.

三 姑 六 婆 a bevy of strolling women.

60 三 媒 六 證 the proofs required in marriages.

三 字 經 the Trimetrical Classic, formerly the first primer in schools.

三 家 the three departments of a man—body 身, heart 心, and mind 意. (*Taoist*).

三 家 村 a small hamlet.

三 寶 the Buddhist Trinity; three essentials of a State—territory, population and government.

65 三 寸 金 蓮 three inch golden lilies—the bound feet of Chinese women.

三 尺 法 the laws.

三 屬 gender.

三 年 喪 three years mourning for parents.

三 從 the three degrees of dependence observed by a woman—dependent upon her father first, then her husband, and later upon her son. (*hist.*)

70 三 心 二 意 undecided; changeable.

三 思 or 再 三 思 think again and again.

三 態 the three states of physics—solid, liquid and gaseous.

三 成 獻 捐 the three-tenths land-tax.

三 戶 three families—a very small number.

75 三 才 the three powers—Heaven, Earth and Man.

三 拳 難 敵 四 手 three fists are not equal to four hands.

三 敎 Confucianism, Buddhism, and Taoism.

三 斗 three bushels — Chinese measure.

三 斷 法 trichotomy.

80 三 族 the three kindreds--father's, mother's and wife's.

三 旬 the three decades of a month.

三 旬 九 食 nine meals in thirty days—very poor.

三 春 the three months of spring.

三 星 happiness, emolument, and long-life.

85 三 時 three o'clock; spring, summer and autumn, the times for agriculture; the fifteen days after the summer solstice are divided into three periods of three, five and seven days respectively, i.e., 頭 時, 中 時, 三 時.

三 晋 the three States of Wei 魏 Chao 趙, and Han 韓.

三 更 or 三 鼓 the third watch.

三 板 a sampan.

三 極 球 radio-valves.

90 三 權 分 立 separation of the legislative, executive, and the judicial functions. = 三 權 鼎 立

三 歎 deep sighs and regrets.

三 歧 出 trichotomy.

三 歸 the threefold refuge of Buddhism—a profession of faith in *Buddha, Dharma* or the Law, and *Sangha* or the Priesthood.

95 三 段 論 式 a syllogism.

三 民 主 義 *San Min Chu I*, or the Three Principles of the People advocated by Dr. Sun Yat-sen.

三 清 the Taoist trinity.

三 漲 汽 機 triple-expansion engines.

三 牲 fowl, fish and pig's head—used in idolatrous ceremonies.

100 三 生 the three lives of re-birth; past, present, and future.

三 生 有 幸 the good fortune of three lives; a stroke of luck; a fortunate meeting.

三 界 the threefold division of the universe into the regions of desire, form, and formlessness. (*Budd.*).

三 番 or 三 次 or 三 回 on three occasions; three times.

三 皇 the Three Emperors—*Fu Hsi* 伏 羲, *Shen Nung* 神 農, and *Huang Ti* 黃 帝; or *T'ien Huang* 天 皇, *Ti Huang* 地 皇, and *Jên Huang* 人 皇.

105 三 眠 the three changes of skin made by the silkworm, during which it seems to sleep.

三 稜 鏡 prism.

三 等 third class.

三 等 九 級 the three ranks and nine grades of former officials.

三 絃 琴 a trichord instrument.

110 三 綱 the three net-ropes—the duties of a prince, father, and husband; the bands of human society.

三 綱 五 常 the whole duty of man.

三 羣 二 隊 small groups of people.

三 色 tricolour.

三 色 旗 The Tricoloured Flag.

115 三色板 three-colour blocks for printing.
三苗 ancient tribal dominion which occupied the present Hunan, part of Hupeh, etc.
三葉形飾 trefoil decoration.
三萬 thirty thousand.
三角尺 angle gauge.
120 三角形 a triangle.
不等邊三角形 scalene triangle.
二等邊三角形 isosceles triangle.
直角三角形 right-angled triangle.
等邊三角形 equilateral triangle.
125 鈍角三角形 obtuse-angled triangle.
銳角三角形 acute-angled triangle.
三角戀愛 a love affair in which three persons are involved.
三角方程式 trigonometrical equation.
三角板 a set square.
130 三角洲 a delta.
三角測量 trigonometrical survey.
三角術 trigonometry.
平面三角術 plane trigonometry.
弧面三角術 spherical trigonometry.
135 三角規 triangular compasses.
三角釘 caltrops.
三角鏡 angle mirror.
三角頂 a pediment.
三言兩語 a few words; in short.
140 三讓 to yield time and again.
三足凳 a three-legged stool.
三足架 a trivet; a tripod.
三足鼎 a tripod—used in ancient worship.
三跪九叩首 the prostrations before the emperor.
145 三通 the three famous encyclopedic works.
三軍 an army; the enemy.
三軍可奪帥也 the commander of three forces may be captured.
三辰 three regulators of time—the sun, moon and stars, or the Dipper.
三連單 or 三單 a transit-memorandum or transit-pass.
150 三連星 a triple star.
三還九轉 or 三灣九轉 adapted to circumstances; resources.
三陽神 the three *yang* spirits of Taoism—the original spirit 元神, the spirit that knows 識神, and the real spirit 眞神.
三陽開泰 the opening of nature in spring; lucky; happy.
三電極眞空管 radio vacuum-tubes or valves.
155 三隻手 a pickpocket.
三鞠躬 the three bows of modern ceremony.
三音節語 trisyllable.
三頭[2]六臂 three heads and six arms—clever, tricky, full of schemes.
三頭[2]政治 a triumvirate.
160 三頭[2]筋 the triceps muscle.
三餘讀書 the three periods of leisure, i.e., winter, evening and wet days, to be used for study.
三魂 the three souls of a man,—one ascends to heaven, one goes to earth, and one stays with the corpse.
三魂七魄 the three souls and seven animal spirits of Taoism.
三黨 father's, mother's and wife's kindred.
165 三鼓 the third watch.

(a) **Read** *san*[4]. **Thrice; to treble.**

三思而行 think thrice before you act.
三已之 retired from office three times.

(b) **Often read** *sa*[1], **when it means three:** 三個.

姍[1]
5416
To jest; to ridicule. Pron. *shan*[1].

姍笑 to ridicule.

(a) **Read** *hsien*[1]. **To proceed slowly.**

姍姍·地走 walked slowly on; to walk with a womanish gait.

珊[1]
5417
Coral. Pron. *shan*[1].

珊瑚 coral.
珊瑚島 coral islands.
珊瑚頂 a red coral button formerly worn by officials of the 1st and 2nd grades.

(a) **Tinkling of pendants.**

珊然 to give forth a tinkling sound.
雜珮聲珊珊 the pendant ornaments of her girdle give forth a tinkling sound.

跚[1]
5418
To limp. Pron. *shan*[1].

蹣跚·的走 waddled along.

糝[3]
5419
Rice-gruel mixed with meat. Fried cakes of rice and meat. Scattered.

糝於雞之肩腋 scattered under the cock's wing.
糝粉 to mix powder with.
石青糝之 done with a dark green colour.

傘[3]
繖
5420
An umbrella, a parasol.

傘蓋 a sunshade.
打傘 to put up an umbrella.
萬民傘 a presentation umbrella of red silk or satin inscribed with the names of the donors in gold—given to a popular official.
開傘 or 抽傘 to open an umbrella.
雨傘 an umbrella for rain.
↑傘兵 paratroops.

散[4]
5421
To scatter; to disperse; to break up or separate for a time; to dismiss. Miscellaneous.

散·了 ended; all gone; dismissed.
散住 scattered.
散佈 to scatter; to promulgate.
散値 came off duty.
5 散[3]光 astigmatism.
散光鏡 a diverging lens; spectacles for astigmatism.
散兵 disbanded soldiers; orderlies or messengers not regularly enrolled.

散 勇 disbanded troops.

散 地 to resign office; to live in retirement.

¹⁰散 場 to separate—as an audience; to break up a gathering.

散 夥 to dissolve partnership.

散 學 to break up school; to dismiss school.

散 居 各 處 living in different places.

散 徧 四 方 scattered in every direction.

¹⁵散 心 to cheer up; to take some recreation.

散 悶 to dissipate care; to get rid of melancholy.

散 播 傳 單 to distribute handbills.

散 擱·着 put things down anywhere.

散 放 or 發 散 to scatter; to distribute.

²⁰散 會 to dismiss a meeting; to close a conference.

散 步 to go for a stroll.

散 沙³⁴ scattered sand—used fig.

散 漫 無 紀 desultory.

散 熱 to disperse heat; refrigeration.

²⁵散 班 to go off duty; to break up—as a troupe.

散 給 to distribute—as alms.

散 臺 the play is finished.

散 逛 recreation and travel.

散。開 to scatter; to separate; to dismiss.

³⁰散 隊 Dismissed!

散 音 discord; false notes through wrong fingering of the strings.

散 館 Hanlin graduates who failed to reach high appointments; to dismiss school.

散 髮 dishevelled hair.

分 散 dispersed; divergence; to distribute.

³⁵失 散 missing; scattered.

聚 散 meeting and parting.

(a) Read *san³*. To fall to pieces. To break up an association; medicinal powders.

散·了 loosened, as a shoestring.

散 人 a man out of employment; a good-for-nothing fellow.

散 儒 a man who has no talents as a scholar.

散 工 odd jobs; desultory work.

散 布 村 落 scattered villages.

⁵散 木 odd pieces of wood; useless trees.

散 秩 official out of a regular office.

散 藥 medicinal powders.

散 見 seen at different times.

散 鹽 powdered salt.

戲 班 散·了 the troupe is broken up.

鐵⁴ The trigger of a crossbow. A cross-bow.
5422
Read *hsien⁴*. To castrate a fowl, for which 制 No. 2703 is now used.

饊³ Fried round cakes of wheaten flour.
5423
饊·子 fried puffy shredded ⌊dough.

SANG   (ㄙㄤ)

桑¹ The mulberry-tree.
5424

桑 中 之 約 illicit intercourse—from a line in the *Odes*.

桑 園 a mulberry-orchard.

桑 土 (*tu⁴*) the skin from the roots of the mulberry-tree—a medicine.

桑 子³ or 桑 黮 or 桑 棗 or 桑 椹⁴ the mulberry. (-*jêr⁴*).

⁵桑 寄 生 a kind of mistletoe that grows on the mulberry.

桑 扈 (or 鳸 *hu⁴*) the haw-finch.

桑 果 berries, as the mulberry, raspberry, etc.

桑 梓 the mulberry and the lindera—one's native place, because these trees, planted by the parents, grow around the old home.

桑 梓 之 情 the friendship of fellow-countrymen.

¹⁰桑 榆 the west, because the dying rays of the sun light up the tops of these trees—old age.

桑 榆 暮 景 the evening of life.

桑 樹 the mulberry-tree.

桑 田 a mulberry-orchard.

桑 白 皮 the bark of mulberry-roots—a diuretic.

¹⁵桑 皮 紙 paper made from the bark of the mulberry.

桑 蠅 a fly which lays its eggs on the leaf of the mulberry, from which they are transferred to the silkworms, doing much damage.

桑 蠖 a looper caterpillar.

桑 蠶 or 蠶 桑 silkworms.

桑 間 濮 上 *Sang Chien* on the River *P'u*, a place notorious for profligacy, for which idea the phrase is now used.

²⁰桑 飛 the wren.

桑 鳩 the cuckoo.

白 桑 the white mulberry.

探 桑 to pick mulberry-leaves.

嗓³ The throat, the larynx.
5425

嗓·子 啞·了 hoarse, through much speaking.

嗓·子 眼 the gullet.

嗓 門 or 嗓·子 the throat; the voice.

搡³ To push over; to push back.
5426

搡 在 地·下 he tipped it on to the ground.

磉³ The stone base or plinth of a pillar.
5427

磉 柯 the stone base of a pillar.

顙³ The forehead.
5428

廣 顙 a broad forehead.

喪⁴ To lose; to die. To destroy.
5429

喪·了 夫·人 he lost his wife.

喪 其 元 to lose his head.

喪 名 to lose one's good name.

喪 命 or 喪 亡 to lose life; to die.

⁵喪 國 he lost his kingdom.

喪 失 to lose by death.

喪 失 政 府 之 作 用 the government has lost its function.

喪 失 自 由 loss of liberty.

喪 家 失 業 to bring a family to ruin.

¹⁰喪 家 狗 a dog that has lost its home—outcast.

喪 師 to lose the confidence of the people.

喪 心 病 insanity; loss of mental balance.

喪 志 to lose courage.

喪 無 日 it will be destroyed in no time.

[15]喪 明 blind; to lose sight.

喪・氣 melancholy; downcast; down on one's luck.

喪 膽 to lose heart; to be discouraged.

喪 良・心 to lose conscience; to be dead to right feeling.

喪 良 無 恥 shameless depravity.

[20]喪 魄 to lose one's wits—scared to death.

喪 邦 to lose one's country.

中 年 喪 偶 to lose one's wife in middle life.

似 喪 其 耦 as if he had lost part of himself—in a fit of abstraction.

何 患 於 喪 Why are you distressed at—your master's—loss of office?

[25]天 喪 予 Heaven is destroying me! said by Confucius on the death of his favourite disciple *Yen Hwei.*

(a) Read *sang*[1]. To mourn for parents.

喪 主 chief mourner.

喪 主 素 吉 主 玄 white is the mourning colour, black the festive.

喪 事 funeral affairs.

喪 服 mourning garments.

[5]喪 禮 funeral rites.

喪 與 其 易 也 宁 戚 in mourning, deep sorrow is worth more than minute observances.

喪 葬 a funeral.

喪 輿 a hearse.

出 喪 to carry to the grave.

[10]國 喪 national mourning.

守 喪 to observe mourning rites.

居 喪 to be in mourning.

弔 喪 to mourn.

送 喪 to escort a funeral.

SAO.　　(厶幺)

憟[1]
5430
Agitated.

搔[1]
5431
To scratch; to irritate.

搔 破 臉 to scratch the face till it bleeds.

搔 頭 to scratch the head—in perplexity.

搔 首 問 靑 天 to scratch the head and appeal to Heaven—in a dilemma.

搔 首 踟 躕 to scratch the head in perplexity.

(a) Inter. 騷 No. 5433.　Disturbed.

搔 擾 disturbed; annoyed.

(b) Read *chao*[3].　Finger or toe-nails.

搔 𤓾 to trim the nails—after a bath.

颼[1]
5432
Blowing of the wind.

颼 爛・了 blown to pieces.

颼 風 雨 storm of wind and rain.

騷[1]
5433
To annoy.　Sad, grieved.
Moved.　Lascivious.

騷 亂・的 狀 態 agitated, discontented manner.

騷 動 to stir up; to excite.

騷 動 家 agitators.

騷 擾 to vex; to irritate.

[5]騷 殺 fluttering in the wind.

騷 然 disturbed.

騷 騷 fluttering in the wind; agitated; irritable.

騷 體 poems written in the style of the *Li sao*,—see next entry.

離 騷 getting into trouble—name of a famous poem by 屈 原, 4th cent. B.C., written before his suicide on the 5th of the 5th lunar month.　[plaints

牢 騷 grieved; miserable; com-

風 騷 屑 以 搖 木 the whistling of the wind as it shakes the trees.

(a) On heat.

發 騷 to be on heat.

(b) Poetic; elegant.

騷 人 墨 客 a poet; a writer.

騷 國 a country where literature flourishes.

騷 賦 poetry.

(c) Inter. 臊 No. 5442.　Frowzy.

騷 鼠 a polecat.

嫂[3]
5434
An elder brother's wife; married woman.

嫂。夫・人 your wife—said to intimate friends.

嫂・子 or 嫂・嫂 an elder brother's wife.

嫂 溺 援 之 以 手 者 權 也 to use the hand to rescue a sister-in-law from drowning is to act according to emergency.

令 嫂 your wife; your elder brother's wife.

大 嫂 wife of the eldest brother—term of respect for women.

艘[1]
5435
A boat, a junk.　N.A.

兵 船 數 艘 several war-vessels.

掃[4]
5436
A broom.　Inter. next.

掃 星 a comet.

掃 眉 to paint the eyebrows.

掃 除 to sweep away.

(a) A dike or embankment.

堤 埽 a dike.

掃[3]
5437
To sweep; to clear away.
To exterminate.

掃・乾・淨 to sweep clean.

掃 地 to sweep the ground.

五 經 掃 地 trailing the classics in the dust—neglectful of scholarly dignity.

威 風 掃 地 dragged his reputation in the dust.

[5]掃 地 以 盡 make a clean sweep.

掃 地 夫 a scavenger.

掃 墳 or 拜 墳 to sweep the graves; to worship at the graves.

掃 平 or 掃 淸 to quell a disturbance; to bring about peaceful conditions.

掃 房 to sweep the house—in preparation for new-year.

[10]掃 數 to clear off an account.

掃 榻 以 待 I shall sweep the couch and await you—conventional phrase in invitations.

掃 海 mine-sweeping.

掃聽掃聽 to make thorough inquiries.

掃興 (*hsing*⁴) to disappoint one's hopes.

¹⁵掃艙 the sweepings of the hold—as the leakings of rice bags.

掃落 swept down; to fall from.

掃蕩摧清 to make a clean sweep.

掃蕩軍閥 make a clean sweep of the militarists.

掃邊關 to clear the frontiers.

²⁰掃除奸黨 make a clean sweep of seditious factions.

掃靖海氛 to sweep away the sea-mist—to wipe out pirates.

打²掃 to sweep.

(a) Read *sao*⁴. A broom.

掃愁帚 the broom that sweeps away grief—wine.

掃把 a broom.

掃把星 or 掃箒星 a comet.

掃箒 a broom.

⁵椶掃 a coir broom.

禾稈掃 a straw broom.

竹掃 a bamboo broom.

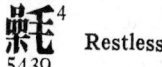
5438

梟噪啼 }

The chirping of birds; the hum of voices.

蟬梟 chirping of cicadas.

鴉梟 the cawing of crows, rooks, etc.

鼓梟 a great clamour.

氉 4
5439

Restless.

氄氉 restless, melancholy.

燥 4
5440

Dry, scorched, parched. Also read *tsao*⁴.

燥渴 parched with thirst.

燥灼 worried; harassed.

燥烈 fierce; raging.

燥熱 fiery; very hot.

乾燥 dried up; drought.

口燥 mouth parched.

繰繅 } ¹
5441

To reel silk from cocoons. Also read *ch'ao*¹.

繰絲 to reel off silk.

繰絲廠 silk filature.

繰繭 to wind off cocoons.

(a) The first is also read *tsao*³. Elegant, of compositions, paintings, etc. u.f. 藻 No. 6727.

(b) The second is also read *tsao*³. or *ch'ao*³. Crimson silk.

臊臊 } ¹
5442

Rank-smelling; rancid; frowzy, fetid.

臊氣 rank; the smell of perspiration.

臊狐 the smell of foxes.

臊聲 a foul reputation.

臊肉 tainted meat.

臊腥 frowzy.

臊陀 a parrot,—from the Sanskrit sound.

(a) Read *sao*⁴. Bashful, ashamed.

臊死 utterly ashamed; to die of shame.

臊的滿面通紅 so bashful that her face was suffused with blushes.

害臊 very bashful.

譟 4
5443

The noise of a crowd; a disturbance. Also read *tsao*⁴.

譟擾 to disturb.

譟讓 altercation; a row.

鼓譟而起 they rose in mutinous clamour.

髞 4
5444

High, imposing. Eminent.

SÊ.　　　(ㄥˋ)
(Seh)

色 4.5.
5445

Colour. Beauty, looks, appearance. Lust, lewdness. Sort, kind, quality. Radical 139. Also *shai*³, or *shai*³ when marked "x".

色卽是空空卽是色 everything is emptiness, and emptiness is everything.

色厲而內荏 firmness in the countenance, but weakness within.

色取仁而行違 he gathers virtue in his countenance, but his actions are opposed to it.

色差 chromatic aberration. (-*ch'a*¹)

⁵色布 dyed cotton piece-goods.

色彩 colour; style, as of dress, art, etc.

色慾 passion; lust.

色斯舉矣翔而後集 seeing the face (is fierce) it rises, then flies round, then settles.

色暈 aureola.

¹⁰色氣 or 色樣 or 顏色 colour; tint; shade.

色水低 alloyed; an inferior colour—generally said of silver.

色澤 glossy; shining; tinge.

色界 the world of vision. (*Budd.*).

色癆 sexual debility.

¹⁵色盲 colour-blindness.

色相 (*hsiang*⁴) form and substance; aspect and reality.

色笑 a smiling face.

色粒 grains of colour.

色素 pigments.

²⁰色素細胞 pigment cells.

色膽如天 heaven-daring in his lewdness.

色色俱全 every sort is kept in stock.

色莊者 a man whose gravity is only a matter of appearance.

色覺 sense of colour.

²⁵色身 a material body.

色迷 given up to lust.

色難 "it is difficult to define—filial piety." *Giles.* "the difficulty is with the countenance." *Legge.*

色鬼 or 色中餓鬼 a man given up to lewdness—like a hungry demon for lust.

³⁰×五色 the five colours, i.e., blue or green 青, yellow 黃, red 赤, white 白, and black 黑—all colours.

作色 to show anger.

出色 a fine colour; outstanding.

×原色 primary colours.

名色 a pretext; an end.

³⁵喜色 a pleased look.

均厲一色 all tarred with the one brush.
失色 to lose colour; to change countenance; to turn pale.
女色 lust for women.
好^{4}色 given to lust.
40 ×嫩色 light, delicate colours.
彩色 variegated.
成色 the fineness of silver—its quality.
扮色 to dress up for a pageant.
×暗色 dull colours.
45 景色 view, aspect, scenery.
×本色 natural colour; personality; features. *See* No. 5025—49ff.
正色 standard colours; sedate.
減色 to lose colour by fading; to deteriorate. =×掉色
×濃色 full, rich colouring.
50 物色 substance; colour.
百色 all colours; all kinds.
×老色 deep colours.
聲色 sound and appearance; music and women.
諸色人等 all kinds of men.
55 起色 improvement—as of the market for goods.
未有起色 no improvement in the conditions—of trade.
足色 full or standard purity of silver, or gold.
閃色 changing colours.
間色 secondary colours.
×雜色 variegated colours; miscellaneous.

塞 1.5. **To stop up; to block. To cork. A cork or stopper.**
5446 Pron. *sai*^{1} when marked "x" *se*^{4} when unmarked.

×塞·了鼻·子 the nose stuffed up.
×塞·住 to stop up.
×塞口 to stop a hole; to gag or bribe; to put down by argument.
×塞嚴·了 corked tight.
5 ×塞·子 a cork or stopper.
×塞實 stuffed full.
塞淵 deep feeling, sincerity of heart.
×塞漏 to stop a leak.
×塞滿 to stuff full.
10 ×塞狗洞 to stop the dog's hole—to give secret bribes.
(×)塞耳不聽 to stop the ears and pay no heed.
塞職 to shirk one's duties.
塞胸 choked—as with rage.
×塞·著心 to harden the heart; to resist conviction.
15 塞責 perfunctory performance of duties; evasion of responsibility.
塞道 to block the roads.
×塞鑽^{4} corkscrew.
×塞頭兒 stoppers; corks, etc.

(a) Read *sai*^{4}. A pass. The northern and eastern frontiers. In retirement.

塞外 or 塞北 beyond the borders; Mongolia.
塞翁失馬 blessing in disguise—lit., the old man of the frontier lost his horse—the horse returned with another which his son mounted, and falling broke his thigh; through this injury he escaped the battle in which all his fellows were slain.
出塞 to pass the frontiers.

(b) Used for transliterating.

塞爾維亞 Servia. (*sê*^{4}-)

嗇 4.5. **Miserly.**
5447

嗇刻 or 嗇吝 or 省嗇 stingy; mean; miserly; grasping.
嗇夫 a petty official; a miser.
嗇言 sparing of words.
吝嗇 miserly; stingy.

(a) Stopped up.

澀嗇 constipation.

(b) Inter. 穡 **No. 5449. The harvest.**

濇 澀 4.5. **Rough; astringent; harsh. Uneven.**
5448 The second form is more commonly used.

濇味 a harsh flavour.
濇滯 stopped; obstructed.
濇肚 constipation.
濇·著嘴 to leave an astringent taste in the mouth.
言語艱濇 unpolished speech.

穡 4.5. **To gather in the harvest. Husbandry.**
5449

穡事 harvesting; reaping.
穡夫 a husbandman.
稼穡 agriculture.

轖 4.5. **Framework of lattice on a cart; a leather covering for a cart.**
5450

瑟 4.5. **A large horizontal musical instrument, usually having 25 strings which pass over bridges for tuning; anciently this instrument had 50 strings, but the number varies.**
5451

琴瑟和調 the instruments are in tune—conjugal harmony.

(a) Dignified. Massive. Dense. Numerous. Pure.

瑟兮僴兮 How grave and dignified!
瑟彼柞棫 Numerous are the oaks.
瑟彼玉瓚 How pure and fine that libation cup of jade.

(b) Chilly. Soughing of the wind.

瑟瑟 the sound of wind.
瑟瑟縮縮 weakly; feeble; chilly.
瑟索 to tremble; disquieted.
瑟縮不達 numbed and stiff from cold.
蕭瑟 chilly; desolate; lonely.

(c) A gem.

瑟瑟 a kind of gem—a turquoise.

虱 蝨 1.5. **A louse; parasites of various kinds. Pron.** *shih*^{1}.
5452

虱·子 or 人虱 a louse.
虱蟣 nits.
木虱 bedbugs.
跳虱 a flea.

森 5452½ **SÊN.** *See* 5722.

SÊNG. (ㄙㄥ)

僧 1 **A Buddhist priest. Buddhism—from the Sanskrit sound.**
5453

僧人 a Buddhist priest.

僧 伽 the assembly of priests. *Samgha.*

僧 伽 婆 羅 *Samgapâla,* a Burmese priest, who in A.D. 506 introduced into China the first a l p h a b e t for transliterating Sanskrit.

僧 伽 祇 the double robe of a priest. *Samghâti.*

[5]僧 侶 a Buddhist priest; a monk; the clergy.

僧 俗 the Buddhist clergy and laity.

僧 家 or 僧 門 the Buddhist priesthood; Buddhism.

僧 尼 Buddhist priests and nuns.

僧 帽 a priest's head-dress.

[10]僧 房 or 僧 伽 藍 a monastery or nunnery.

僧 敎 Buddhism.

僧 綱 司 a Buddhist bishop.

僧 道 無 緣 no affinity with Buddhists or Taoists—notice on doors to keep away mendicants.

僧 錄 司 an office in Peking for the general control of the Buddhist priesthood.

5454

Short hair. Unkempt.

For *SH-* see p. 771ff.

SO. (ㄛ)

娑[1] To dance; to frisk. To lounge; to saunter.
5455

娑 娑 free, careless.

(a) Used in transliterating.

娑 娑 世 界 the world of suffering. Sanskrit: *Saha.*

娑 羅 王 a title given to every Buddha, meaning most victorious over vice and passion; Sanskrit: *Sâlarâja.*

娑 訶 a Buddhist amen. Sanskrit: *Svâha.*

↑娑 發 sofa.

5456

To finger; to feel.

摩 挱 to grope; to toy with; to stroke; to fondle.

梭[1]
5457
A horse-chestnut.

梭 欏 the horse-chestnut; the Sanskrit:—*Sâla*—the tree under which Buddha was born and died.

莎[1] A species of sedge. A kind of grass anciently used for rain-coats. Also u.f. 蓑 No. 5456. To feel.
5458

SO. (ㄛ)
(Soh)

索 絲 索 3.5.

A large rope. To bind. A rule or law. Distinguish 素 No. 5490.
5459

索 力 tension—as of a rope.

索·子 ropes.

索 結 or 索 連 connected; bound together.

索 解 to loosen; to explain.

一 根 索 a large rope.

(a) To demand. To ask; to exact.

索 償 to claim damages or indemnity.

索 命 to demand one's life.

索 取 or 勒 索 to extort forcibly.

索[2]性 to make a point of; to determine; may as well; simply; forced to act contrary to one's nature.

[5]索[2]性 死·了 he made up his mind to die.

索 捐 to demand payment of the *likin* tax; forcible subscription to "loyal benevolences."

索 擾 to maltreat.

索 欠 or 索 賬 to demand payment of a debt.

索 求 to importune.

[10]索 筆 和[4]之 he asked for a pen and rhymed them.

索 詐 or 索 討 or 逼 索 to extort; to get a thing forcibly; to demand from.

索 謝 to demand a gratuity.

索 賠 to demand compensation or indemnity.

索 費 to "squeeze."

(b) To search into. To inquire. To think.

索 句 to think of a good idea.—as in writing.

索 引 an idea; to introduce; to lead; index.

索 思 or 思 索 to comprehend; to think out.

索 途 to find the way.

[5]索 隱 to trace out the hidden meanings of a book; a commentary on the *History* in 50 vols.

搜 索 to ponder over; to think about.

玩 索 而 得 焉 to explore with delight until he has apprehended it.

(c) Exhausted. Scattered. Isolated.

索 寞 desolate and lonely.

索 居 to live apart, away from one's friends.

索 然 無 味 insipid; flavourless.

索 瑟 desolate and sad.

(d) Disquieted; apprehensive.

索 索·的 抖·着 tremblingly.

震 索 索 startled and agitated.

挱[4.5.] To feel with the hand.
5460

摸 挱 to feel; to finger.

(a) u.f. preceding—To inquire.

挱 隱 to investigate hidden things.

鎍[3.5.] Wire. Chains.
5461

鎍·子 chains; the mainspring of a watch.

SO SUO. (ㄛ)
(So)

唆[1] To make mischief; to incite.
5462

唆 事 to make mischief; to sow discord.

唆 來 唆 去 to carry tales back and forth.

唆 使 or 使 唆 to instigate to evil.

唆 慫 or 唆 哄 to enrage; to provoke.

唆 訟 to foment litigation.

調 唆 to make mischief.

梭[1] A weaver's shuttle. To and fro; swift.
5463

梭 布 a kind of native cloth.

梭 織 飛 報 to maintain constant and rapid communications.

梭 巡 to patrol.

抛 梭 to throw the shuttle.

日 月 如 梭 days and months fly like a shuttle.

蓑[1] A rain-cloak of leaves, grass, coir, etc.
5464

蓑 笠 a rain-cloak and leaf hat.

蓑 衣 rain-clothes.

蓑 衣 鶴 a crane with pendent neck-feathers.

所[3] That which; who; what; whatsoever. A cause; whereby.
5465

所 之 a tendency; a direction.

○所 以 hence; therefore; that by which certain things are effected.

視 其 所 以 see what a man does.

所 以 文 之 that by which it is adorned.

[5]所 以 然 for this cause; the why and wherefore; the reason why.

所 以 爲 方 者 an instrument for squaring.

所 以 示 不 當 與 也 by this he showed that it should not be given.

所 以 者 何 Why is this?

所 以 行 之 者 一 也 that by which they practise them is the same.

[10]所 司 何 事 What is your business? What does he do?

所 屬 all under one; all one's subordinates.

所 得 what one gets or attains; must.

所 得 稅 income tax.

↓所 爲[2] that which one does, be- [havior.

所 性 不 存 焉 what his nature enjoys is not here.

[15]所 推 定 者 that which is assumed.

所 有 the; the subject under consideration; whatever there is.

所 有 權 proprietorship; ownership.

所 有·的 whatever there is.

所 有 者 possessor.

[20]所 有 章·程 列 後 the regulations are as follows.

所 爲[4] 何 來 How comes this about? what for?

所 由 是 也 was the cause of.

視 其 所 由 mark a man's motives.

所 當 辦 that which should be done.

[25]所 繫 all that is implied in or connected with the matter.

所 自 or 所 從 whence it comes; the cause or origin of a thing.

所 致 the effect of.

所 謂 as it is said; that which is called; so-called.

所 載 that which is included; or that which is stated.

[30]所 部 under the command of.

所 長[2] the merits; the strong points. See A. 3.

所 須 that which is necessary.

察 其 所 安 examine that in which a man is contented.

無 所 不 知 nothing which is not known; omniscient.

[35]無 所 不 能 nothing which cannot be done; omnipotent.

所 不 至 extending everywhere.

(a) A place. A land measure of 130 *mow*. N.A. for houses, etc.

所 在 a place.

所 在 地 location.

所 長[3] head of an office.

公 所 a public place; an office.

[5]得 其 所 got into its proper place.

無 所 不 在 omnipresent.

處 所 or 房 所 a place.

瑣[3] Fragments. Petty, troublesome, annoying.
5466

瑣 尾 流 離 people who have drifted; refugees.

瑣 瑣 fidgety; petty; contemptible.

瑣 碎 or 瑣 屑 trifling; vexatious; annoying.

瑣 聞 rumour; tattle.

不 務 瑣 末 do not bother about trifles.

繁 瑣 vexatious.

璅[3] Inter. preceding. Also read *tsao*[3]. A stone like jade.
467

鎖 鏁[3] A lock. To lock. Fetters, chains.
5468

鎖·上 門 to lock the door.

鎖·不 住 unable to keep under restraint; cannot lock.

鎖 匙 or 鎖 鑰 a key.

鎖 匠 a locksmith.

[5]鎖 子 甲 chain-armour.

鎖 子 錦 chain-pattern embroidery.

鎖(·子)骨 the collar-bone.

鎖 押 or 鎖 禁 to confine in chains.

鎖 拏 to apprehend; to manacle.

[10]鎖 殼 the body of a Chinese lock.

鎖 港 to blockade ports.

鎖 眉 頭 to knit the brows; to frown.

鎖 累 fettered; curbed.

鎖 絆 to chain up; to lock up.

[15]鎖·起·來 to lock.

鎖 鍊 chains; fetters.

鎖 鑰 之 勳 the merit of keeping well the key of the country—of high officials.

鎖 頭 or 一 把 鎖 a lock.

鎖 鬚 or 鎖 簧 the wards of a Chinese lock.

[20]寒 烟 鎖 柳 the cold mists envelop the willows.

寧 鎖 to turn a key in a lock.

跪 鎖 to kneel on chains—a cruel form of torture.

SOU. 　　(수)

(Seo)

蒐[1] To search out; to come across; to hunt up.
5469

蒐 羅 to search out and gather together; to hunt up—a quota-

tion; to meet with accidentally —as a rare phrase, etc.

蒐·輯 to search out and arrange together.

(a) The spring hunt in ancient times; to assemble for a hunt; to prepare troops for war.

蒐索擇取不孕者 in the spring hunt, pregnant animals were not taken.

蒐 練 to drill.
春 蒐 the spring hunt.

(b) To hide; hidden.

蒐 慝 hidden iniquities.

(c) A plant allied to madder. *Rubia cordifolia.*

叟 | 3
叜
傁
5470   An old person.

老 叟 Venerable Sir! an old man.

廋 | 1 To secrete; to be concealed.
     To search; to examine into.
5471 Distinguish 搜 No. 5848.

廋 人 a superintendent of education during the *Chou* dynasty.
廋 求 to search for; to investigate.
廋 辭 a euphemism.
人焉廋哉 How can a man conceal his character?

搜 | 1
捜   To search for; to inquire into; to investigate.
5472

搜·出·來 to search out; to find; to recover—as stolen goods.
搜 剔 to make a vexatious search.
搜 尋 or 搜 查 to search for.
搜 檢 to search a person.
⁵搜 求 to seek.
搜 票 a search-warrant.
搜 索 to search for; to think out; to hunt up; investigation.
搜 索 枯 腸 to ransack one's brains.
搜 索 狀 a search-warrant.

---

¹⁰搜 輯 or 搜 拿 or 搜 捕 or 搜 獲 to search for and seize.
搜 羅 to hunt up; to make researches.
搜 身 to search the person.
搜·集 論 料 to collect data.
搜·集 證 據 collecting evidence.
¹⁵搜 驗 to examine—as at the Customs.
窮 搜 to make a thorough search; exhaustive researches.

(a) Swift. The sound of an arrow discharged from the bow.

搜 然 quickly.

溲 | 1
5473   To soak in water—as meal.

溲 溲 sound of washing grain.
溲 酒 to make spirits.

(a)   To urinate.

溲 便 to urinate.
溲 器 a chamber-vessel.

瞍 | 3
瞍
5474   Blind, having no pupil to the eye.

蟫 | 3
5475   The spider millipede.

謏 | 4 To scold, to censure. Also
5476 read *hsiao¹*. To induce people to virtuous ways. Small.

謏 說 novels.

鎪 | 1 To engrave on metal or
5477 wood.

颼 | 1
飅   To blow chilly. A whizzing sound.
5478

颼 飅 whizzing of an arrow; soughing of the wind.
颼·得·慌 —the wind—makes me shiver.

餿 | 1
5479   Rancid, soured, as food.

餿 味 a frowzy smell; sour—of rice.

擻 | 3
5480   To shake.

擻·下·來 to shake and sift.
抖·擻 毛 to shake its feathers.
抖·擻 精·神 to pull oneself together; to rouse the energies.

藪 | 3 A marshy preserve for game or fish. A place of
5481 concourse.

利 藪 a great centre for commerce.
盜 藪 a robbers' retreat.
蜂 藪 swarming of bees.
逃 藪 a refuge; a harbour for criminals.

(a) Read *shu³*. A pad for the head.

塞 藪 a straw pad for the head used by porters.

嗽 | 4
漱   To cough; to expectorate. A cough. Inter.
瘶   next.
5482

嗽 口 to rinse the mouth. (*shu⁴-*)
咳·嗽 to cough. (*k'ê²·sou*)

漱 | 4 To rinse the mouth; to
5483 scour. Pron. *shu⁴*.

漱 口 to rinse the mouth.
漱 浣 to wash and purify oneself.
漱 盂 a hand spittoon.
漱 石 枕 流 "to rinse one's mouth (with the beauty of) rocks, and pillow one's head on (the murmur of) streams." *Giles,—* living in seclusion.

嗾 | 3 To urge; to incite. To set
5484 a dog on. Also read *so⁴*.

嗾 狗 to set a dog on.

SSŬ. *See* p. 765.

SU. (ㄙㄨ)

練[1] A kind of sackcloth. Also read *shu*[1].
5485

酥[1] Cheese. Flaky, crisp, short.
5486

酥 土 spongy soil.
酥 油 butter.
酥 燈 lamps burning before an image of Buddha.
酥 脆 花 生 crisp ground-nuts.
酥 酪 koumiss.
酥 餅 short-cakes.

穌
甦[1] To revive; to rise again. To rest. To collect. Inter. next.
5487

甦 涸 鮒 to revive a dry fish—to relieve distress.
甦 軟 out of sorts; tired; apathetic; limp.
甦 醒 or 甦 轉 to revive; to arouse; to awaken.
甦 醒 過 來 to recover consciousness.
耶 穌 Jesus. (*yeh*[1]-)

蘇[1] Soochow. To revive. Cheerful, plentiful. Inter. preceding. Abbr. for Kiangsu.
5488

蘇 息 to rest.
蘇 杭 Soochow and Hangchow.
蘇 活 to revive.
蘇 相 (*hsiang*[4]) the Soochow type of face.
蘇 蘇 nervous; fearful; uneasy.
以 蘇 民 困 in order to relieve the distress of the masses.

(a) A species of thyme. To gather grass. Name of certain trees and plants as below.

蘇 合 香 rose-storax, a gum derived from the *Liquidambar orientalis*.
蘇·子 or 蘇 麻 *Perilla ocymoides* —the seeds of which are used for canaries, and the leaves of which are eaten.
蘇·子 油 oil from the seeds of the above, used for lamps.
蘇 木 or 蘇 枋 Sapan-wood.

樵 蘇 to gather firewood and grass.
紫 蘇 *Perilla nankinensis*.
落 蘇 a name for the egg-plant.

(b) Used in transliterating.

蘇 丹 Soudan.
蘇 俄 Soviet Russia.
蘇 俄 政 府 Soviet Government.
蘇 彝 士 Suez.
⁵蘇 打 or 蘇 達 soda.
蘇 格 拉 底 Socrates.
蘇 格 蘭 Scotland.
蘇 維 埃 Soviet.
蘇 維 埃 化 or 赤 化 Sovietized.
¹⁰蘇 聯 abbreviated form of U. S. S. R.
蘇 門 答 臘 Sumatra.

嗉[1] Loquacious.
5489

嚕 嗉 gabbling; loquacious.

素[4] Plain; unornamented. White. Ordinary. Simple. The original constitution of things. Matter. Distinguish 索 No. 5459.
5490

素 人 a layman.
素 啟 者 opening phrase in letters written by one in mourning.
素 因 predisposition.
素 娥 fancy name for the moon.
⁵素 官 a clean-handed official—therefore a poor man.
素 尺 or 尺 素 a letter—lit., a foot of white silk, once used for writing on.
素 性 a uniform character; one's ordinary disposition.
素 手 empty-handed; a white hand.
素 手 無 憑 empty-handed and nothing to depend on.
¹⁰素 數 prime numbers.
素 服 white garments—mourning.
素 楮 note-paper.
素 湍 淥 潭 foaming white torrents and clear pools.
素 王 the throneless king—Confucius.
¹⁵素 珠 or 念 珠 a Buddhist rosary.
素·的 plain; unadorned; vegetarian [(food).
素 祭 the Meal Offering.

素 紗 white crape.
素 絲 white silk.
²⁰素 聯 or 輓 聯 funeral couplets hung up during mourning.
素 粲 vegetarian dishes.
素 裝 simply dressed.
素 質 elements—chemistry.
素 酒 non-alcoholic wine.
²⁵素 門 a poor family.
素 面 a face that has not been made up with powder, etc.
素 食 vegetable diet.
  食 素 to partake of vegetarian diet; to fast.
素 食 主 義 vegetarianism —rather from hygienic than from religious motives.
³⁰素 餐 to eat the bread of idleness.
素 餐 尸 位 a sinecure position.
素 髮 white hair.
元 素·的 elemental.
原 素 chemical elements.
³⁵樸 素 simple; plain.
葷 素 meat and vegetable dishes respectively.

(a) Formerly; usually, commonly. Heretofore. As a rule.

素 不 相[1] 識 we have not known each other hitherto.
素 交 old acquaintances.
素 來 or 素 本 up till now; originally; heretofore.
素 其 位 attends to the duties of his station.
⁵素 富 貴 行 乎 富 貴 if you are rich and noble act accordingly.
素 常 or 平 素 or 素 日 or 素 昔 commonly; usually; habitually; generally.
素 愛 to be in the habit of.
素 所 擁 護 it has been upheld in practice.
素 持 之 政 府 established policy of the government.
¹⁰素 有 不 臣 之 心 he never had the feelings of a statesman.
素 有 之 敬 之 inherent honour.
素 稱[1] well-known as.
素 行[1] general behaviour; conduct.
素 諳 has long known.
¹⁵素 識 or 素 稔 well acquainted with.
素 貧 always poor.
素 隱 行 怪 to live in retirement and yet work marvels.
素 願 original intention or desire.

5491 嗉膆 [4]

膆·子 the crop of a bird.

膈·勒膆 (ko²-) Adam's apple.

5492 塐塑 [4]

To model in clay.

塑 像 to make an idol.
塑 繪 to model and paint.
泥 塑 人 a clay image—a stupid.

5493 愫 [4]

Guileless, sincere, honest.

5494 訴愬 [4]

To tell, to inform, to state. To accuse, to lay a plaint. To complain. Slander. Distinguish 訴 No. 2728.

訴 呈 a plea in reply; a counter-statement.
訴 冤 or 訴 苦 to state one's grievances.
訴 帋 a plea in reply.
訴 情 to state in detail.
[5]訴 權 right of action.
訴 毀 to defame; to slander.
訴 求·的 眼 光 the appeal in his eyes.
訴 瀝 a counter-statement.
訴 狀 a plaint; to file a plea.
[10]訴 病 to report as sick.
訴 稱 to state in answer.
訴 稟 to accuse another; to file a plea.
訴 罪 to state one's case in such a way as to escape punishment.
訴 行 accusation; slander.
[15]訴 訟 or 投 訴 or 赴 訴 to lay an accusation.
訴 訟 代 理 人 legal representative.
訴 訟 參 加 intervention. (legal).
訴 訟 案 件 a law case.
訴 訟 法 law of procedure.
[20]訴 訟 當 事 人 persons in a case at law.
訴 訟 目 的 object of procedure.
訴 訟 程 序 legal procedure.
訴 訟 費 用 law-costs.
訴 訟 輔 佐 人 legal counsel.
[25]訴 詞 defence.

訴 說 to state in detail.
訴 辭 to state a case.
訴 願 a vow.

5495 溯溯 [4]

To trace up to a source. To go against the stream. Water. Inter. next.

溯 查 to inquire into the origin of; I find that....
溯 洄 to go against the stream.
溯 源 to trace to the source; to search out the origins.
溯 自 ever since.

5496 遡泝 [4]

To go against the stream; to go up; to trace the source. Formerly.

遡 洄 to go against the stream.
遡 流 而 行 to go against the current.
遡 游 to go down stream.
遡 自 since then; it appears that ever since....
遡 風 to go against the wind.

SU. (ㄙㄨ)
(Suh)

5497 俗 2.5.

Vulgar, common. Worldly. Unrefined. Lay, in contrast to clerical.

俗 事 common affairs.
俗 人 a layman; an ordinary person.
俗 傳 common tradition.
俗 套 conventional.
[5]俗 字 眼ₙ non-classical expressions; common phrases.
俗 學 ordinary studies.
俗 家 姓 名 the lay surname and name of a Buddhist priest.
俗 格 conventional style—of writing.
俗·氣 a nuisance; an annoyance; commonplace; vulgar.
[10]俗 物 everyday matters; unrefined things; philistines.
俗 筆 commonplace style of writing.
俗 緣 the common lot of man.
俗 話 colloquial; common expressions.

俗 語 common sayings; proverbs.
[15]俗 謂 there is a common saying.
俗 識 common sense.
俗 辭 vulgar expressions; commonplaces.
俗 陋 vulgar; low.
不 俗 not at all commonplace.
[20]世 俗 customs of the times.
土 俗 local customs; provincial.
塵 俗 the world. (Budd.).
太 俗 too commonplace.
還 俗 to return to the laity.
[25]鄙 俗 base; vulgar mannered.
風·俗 customs.

5498 宿宿 4.5.

A halting place; to lodge for the night. To keep over night. To cherish. Asleep and perching.

宿 主 host—of a parasite, etc.
宿 娼 to company with harlots.
宿 宿 or 信 宿 or 再 宿 to lodge for two successive nights.
宿 舍 a dormitory, in a school.
[5]宿 諾 to sleep over a promise.
宿 雨 night rain.
宿 露 morning dew.
宿 鳥 birds going to roost.
住·宿 to pass a night in a place.
[10]借 宿 to ask for a night's lodging.
寄 宿 to lodge.
求 宿 to seek lodgings.
留 宿 to keep a visitor for the night.
露 宿 to sleep in the open air.

(a) Stale, old. In the past.

宿 世 from a former generation; an old quarrel; Buddhist phrase for a former life.
宿 儒 an old scholar.
宿 命 論 fatalism.
宿 嫌 hereditary grievance; grudge handed on from a previous existence.
[5]宿 孽 predestined retribution.
宿 將 an aged general.
宿 怨 an old grudge from a previous life; hereditary grievance.
宿 恨 an old enmity; grudge handed on from a former existence. Last two also used verbally.
宿 日 former days.
[10]宿 背 formerly.
宿 有 formerly had....

宿 肉 meat kept overnight.
宿 貨 damaged goods; old stock.

(b) Read *hsiu³*. **A night.**

(c) Read *hsiu⁴*. **A constellation.**

星 宿 constellations.
二 十 八 宿 the 28 Chinese zodiacal constellations. (*see* p. 1177)

蓿 4.5.
5499   Clover; lucerne.

粟 4.5. Grain. Millet; maize or
5500   Indian corn. Rent in kind;
tithes. Distinguish 栗 No.
3925.

粟 布 proportion; rule of three.
粟 米 maize.
太 倉 一 粟 a mere grain in the barn.
屋 粟 rent or tax of a house.
脫 粟 frugal fare.
輸 粟 to pay taxes in kind.

窣 4.5. **To rush out of a den.**
5501   **Rustling; whispering.**

夙 4.5. Dawn; early in the morn-
5502   ing Inter. 宿 No. 5498.

夙 夜 morning and evening; early and late.
夙 夜 在 公 at earliest dawn he is at business.
夙 早 early in the morning.
夙 興 to rise early.
夙 興⁴ 兢 兢 anxiety morning and night.
夙 遭 閔 凶 early met with distressing misfortune.

(a) **Belonging to a previous state of existence. Formerly.**

夙 世 冤 家 enemies in a former existence.
夙 仇 or 夙 恨 enemies in a former life.
夙 好⁴ predilection.
夙 孽 retribution for evil in a previous existence.
夙 慧 naturally intelligent.
夙 昔 of old.
夙 緣 pre-ordained in a former state of existence to be friends.

涑 1.5. Name of a river in
5503   Shansi. Read *sou¹*. To
rinse the mouth; u.f. 漱
No. 5483.

觫 4.5. To start; to tremble with
5504   fear.

速 4.5. Hurried; quickly. To
5505   urge.

速 交 speedy payment.
速 力 acceleration; speed; velocity.
速 力 限 制 speed-limit.
速 力 增 進 機 accelerator.
⁵速 度 speed; velocity.
速 度 表 speed indicator.
速 成 to finish quickly; quickly completed.
速 成 科 special short course.
速 於 置 郵 quicker than the posts.
¹⁰速 步 rapid strides.
速 爲 辦 理 to put through without delay.
速 率 (*lü*⁴·⁵·) velocity.
速 行 to hasten.
速 記 人 a stenographer.
¹⁵速 記 打 字 員 stenographer and typist.
速 記 符 號 shorthand-script.
速 記 術 (or 法) shorthand-writing.
速 記 錄 shorthand report.
速 議 for immediate consideration.
²⁰速 速 來 to come quickly.
速 達 rapidity and freedom—of communication.
速 飭 to give immediate instructions.
加 速 機 accelerator.
疾 速 as quickly as possible.

(a) **To invite.**

速 客 函 invitation to dinner.
速 玉 a second invitation, as a reminder.
不 速 之 客 an uninvited guest.

餗 4.5.
5506   A pot of cooked rice.

簌 4.5. Luxuriant and dense
5507   vegetation. A fine sieve.

簌 簌 ·的 眼 淚 tears flowing in streams.

蔌 4.5.
5508   Vegetables.

蔌 蔌 mean in appearance; looking as if blown about.
蔌 蔌 作 記 scribbled a note.

肅 4.5. Respectful; reverential;
5509   majestic; awful. To write.
The province of Kansu.

肅 函 respectfully to write a note.
肅 客 而 入 he bowed to his guest and they both entered.
肅 復 respectfully to reply.
肅 愼 a Tungusic tribe—ancestors of the Manchus.
⁵肅 拜 to bow.
肅 敬 respectful.
肅 會 to call a meeting to order.
肅 此 this respectfully....
肅 殺 之 氣 awful, stern, forbidding air.
¹⁰肅 清 tranquillized—as after a revolt.
肅 然 起 敬 reverently to rise.
肅 立 to stand in an attitude of reverence.
肅 肅 decorous; stern; quick; severe—as an officer; adjusted.
肅 衣 to adjust the dress.
¹⁵肅 靜 an awed silence.

(a) **Sound of birds flying.**

肅 殺 飛 過 whirring sound of birds flying over.

驌 4.5.
5510   Name of a famous horse.

鷫 4.5.
5511   The turquoise kingfisher.

鷫 鷞 the kingfisher as above.

SUAN.   (ㄙㄨㄢ)

狻 1
5512   A fabulous beast.

狻 猊 a lion; a wild horse which can do 500 *li* in a day.

痠[1] Aching of the limbs; muscular pains.
5513

痠疼 painful; aching—as from over-fatigue, etc.

痠覩 a pricking, aching feeling; uncomfortable.

腿痠 aching legs.

骨痠 rheumatic pains.

酸[1] Sour; acid. Distressed; grieved; afflicted. Used as a suffix with various words to indicate the names of different acids.
5514

酸人 a misanthrope.

酸切 painful and distressing.

酸心 sick at heart; grieved; heartburn.

酸性反應[4] acid reaction.

[5]酸楚 grieved and sad.

酸漿氣 a sour smell.

酸溜溜的 very sour.

酸牙 teeth on edge.

酸甜苦辣 sour, sweet, bitter, astringent—the cares of life.

[10]酸菜 or 酸菜 pickles.

酸辛 misfortunes.

酸迷 sorrel.

酸醋 vinegar.

酸類 acids.

[15]酸鼻 cold; shivering; snuffling; sorrowful; grieved.

寒°酸 poor.

發酸 to turn sour.

蒜[4] Garlic.
5515

蒜瓣 the quarters of a head of garlic.

蒜頭[2] or 卵蒜 heads of garlic.

算
籌[4] To reckon; to calculate. To consider as. To plan; to scheme. A scheme; a reckoning.
5516

算不了[3] cannot be reckoned as; of no consequence.

算·不·得 of no special value; no account.

算了 that will do; to have had enough of it.

算來算去 full of schemes; taking everything into consideration; trying to devise something.

[5]算卦先·生 a fortune-teller.

算命 or 算卦 to tell fortunes.

算命先·生 a(blind) fortune-teller.

算差 out in one's calculations.(-ch'a[4])

算度 to calculate; to estimate.

[10]算式 mathematical formula.

算·得是 is regarded as.

算·得甚[2]麼 or 算·不·得·甚[2]·麼 of no special account; it's a mere nothing.

算數[4] to take as final, in earnest.

算法 = 算學 mathematics.

[15]算清 or 算明 clearly reckoned —as accounts, etc.

清算 liquidation.

算減則貧 when their period of life is curtailed they become poor and needy. *See below*—19, 40, 42.

算理 mathematical principles.

算盡則死 when his allotted span is complete, death claims him. *See below*—40, 42.

[20]算盤 the abacus.

打算·盤 to calculate on the abacus; calculating.

打小算·盤 mean; close-fisted; petty.

算·盤密 or 算·盤利害 very sharp; close-fisted.

算·盤珠 the balls of an abacus; a person who is too wooden to move of his own accord.

[25]算結 to settle accounts.

算術 arithmetic.

十進算術 decimal arithmetic.

算·計 to calculate; to plan; to estimate.

算·計不到 unskilful financing.

[30]算·計人 to counterplot; to scheme against another.

算賬 or 計賬 to reckon accounts.

算·起·來 to reckon up.

算進在內 all reckoned in.

算錯 out in one's estimate or calculations.

[35]算除 to deduct.

算題 mathematical problems.

不上算 it does not pay.

不出所算 it does not exceed the calculations—it is as was expected.

不由人算 beyond human calculations.

[40]以奪人算 to shorten a man's
period of life by one hundred days. [pays.

合算 to reckon up altogether; it

小則奪算 lighter offences are punished by a deduction of one hundred days from the allotted span.

打·算 to plan to.

推算八字 to calculate a horoscope.

[45]暗算 treachery; secret schemes.

概算 a rough estimate.

無算 numberless; incalculable.

筆算 arithmetic.

誤算 miscalculation.

[50]預算 an estimate; a budget.

SUI.   (ㄙㄨㄟ)

夊[1] Moving slowly. Radical 35. Distinguish 夂 No. 962.
5517

睢[1] To gaze at. Distinguish 雎 No. 1580.
5518 A district in Honan.

萬衆睢睢 the multitude stared —with astonishment and terror.

雖[1.2] Supposing. Though; even if; still.
5519

雖不吾以 although I am not employed as a government official.

雖則 nevertheless.

雖多亦奚以爲 although he has learned much, what does it amount to?

雖是這°樣 though it be so.

[5]雖然 although; notwithstanding; albeit.

雖然如此 be that as it may.

雖狎必變 although it were a familiar acquaintance, he would change his countenance.

雖若丘陵 enough to make a hill.

雖褻必以貌 although in ordinary dress, he would salute them properly.

[10]雖請退可也 if he does invite you, you can decline.

雖賞之不竊 although you reward them to steal, they will not.

(a) To dismiss.

吾雖之不能 I am not able to dismiss him.

(b) Only, used like 惟.

(c) A large ground lizard.

(d) Read *wei*[4]. A name for the probocis monkey; it is said to have a forked tail with which it stops its nostrils when hanging from a branch in the rain.

綏 [1,2] To tranquilize; to soothe; to comfort. To retreat, as
5520 from a battle.

綏其不足 comfort those who have insufficient — of this world's goods.

綏厥士女 gave peace to the men and women.

綏和 peace and quiet.

綏定 to restore peace.

[5]綏宥 to soothe and comfort.

綏萬邦 there is peace in all the empire.

綏軍 to draw off troops; to retreat.

綏靖 to restore peace.

撫綏 to pacify.

(a) The traces of carriage-harness; a strap to hold on by.

必正立執綏 he would stand erect grasping the cord—in mounting his carriage.

(b) A flag.

則下小綏 they lowered their small flag.

(c) Also read *shui*[1]. Prowling alone.

有狐綏綏 there was a fox prowling around.

(d) Read *sui*[3], or *hui*[3]. A sacrifice.

(e) Read *t'o*[3]. u.f. 妥 No. 6454.

大夫則綏之 carry that which belongs to a great officer lower than the heart.

 荽 [1]
5521　　Coriander.

芫荽 coriander.

隋 [2]　Name of a dynasty.
5522

隋紀 the *Sui* Dynasty: A.D. 589 —618.

(a) Read *to*[4], *t'o*[3]. Strips of meat. To fall.

隨 [2]　To follow; to accord with;
5523　together; to accompany. Forthwith; instantly; subsequently. In the course of time.

隨下隨凍 it freezes as it falls.

隨事酌情 to decide according to circumstances.

隨事隨在 at home in all things.

隨·他去 let him go! take no notice! (A.p. *ts'ui*[2]-)

[5]隨·你 as you please. (A.p. *ts'ui*[2]-)

隨侍 attendants; servants.

隨來隨花 spend the money as it comes in.

隨俗 to fall in with prevailing customs.

隨便 at your convenience; please yourself; at will; at pleasure.

[10]隨其所在 wherever he may be.

隨分 (*fen*[4]) content with one's lot.

隨勢 according to circumstances.

隨即 immediately; forthwith.

隨口說 to talk at random; extempore speech.

[15]隨同 to follow; to obey; to accompany.

隨·和 to act as others do; pliable.

隨員 suite; retinue.

隨喜 to wander for one's pleasure, to find pleasure in.

隨在 any place; according to where you are.

[20]隨地 anywhere.

隨坐 to be jointly incriminated; to involve an innocent person in joint punishment for a crime.

隨寓而安 to feel at ease wherever one dwells; happy anywhere.

隨封 a small gratuity for the servants, sent with a present.

隨就 forthwith; without delay.

[25]隨常 common; ordinary.

隨帶 decorated with.

隨後 by and by; afterwards; in due course.

隨得隨失 lost as soon as gained.

隨從 or 追隨 to follow; to obey; to accompany.

[30]隨復 again; immediately.

隨心所出 just as fancy suggests.

隨意 at your convenience; please yourself; at pleasure.

隨意契約 informal agreement.

隨意科 optional course.

[35]隨意筋 voluntary muscle.

隨感而應 as soon as they were affected they responded.

隨我來 come after me.

隨手 at once; while the hand is in; without hesitation; freely; ready at hand.

隨方就圓 adapting oneself to circumstances.

[40]隨時 at all seasons.

隨時支欵 current account.

隨時過機 opportunities afforded from time *to* time.

隨時開會 holding occasional meetings.

隨時隨地 at all times and in all places.

[45]隨機 or 隨事 according to circumstances.

隨機應變 to adapt oneself to circumstances.

隨波逐流 to follow the current —to do as others; a time-server.

隨筆 to make notes at the time.

隨緣樂助 give such assistance as you can freely afford.

[50]隨·着意·思吹 "it bloweth where it listeth."

隨羣 or 隨衆 to do as the crowd does.

隨習 to follow the crowd; to do as others do.

隨處 in all places.

隨處說長道短 everywhere talking of the faults of others.

[55]隨行 or 相隨 to obey; to follow; to accompany.

隨護 to escort.

隨跟之 to follow after; at once.

隨身帶·的 carried on the person; carried with one.

隨車雨 rain follows his carriage —鄭弘 of the Later *Han* dynasty was such a good ruler that rain followed his carriage during a period of drought— used for beneficent government.

[60]隨 辨 to assist in the settlement of.

隨 鄉 入 鄉 not to stand on precedent; to do what is done by others—in Rome do as Rome does.

隨 長[3] 隨 下 rising and falling.

隨 陽 鳥 migratory birds.

隨 風 使 帆 to sail with the wind—to follow the line of least resistance.

[65]隨 風 倒 following the wind—without a mind of one's own.

隨 風 行 to go with the wind.

各 隨 所 好[4] each following his own inclination.

灕[2]
5524
Slippery.

髓[3]
5525
Marrow. The essence of a thing.

髓 海 the brain.

恨 入 骨 髓 his hatred has penetrated his bones and his marrow.

筆 下 滴 滴 文 章 髓 from his pen dripped the very essence of elegant composition.

穗[4]
5526
An ear of grain; the flower of grasses.

穗 子 an ear of corn; a tassel.

穗 狀 花 a spike of flowers.

一 禾 九 穗 nine ears on the stalk—abundant harvest.

燭 穗 the snuff of a candle.

繐[4]
5527
Fine cloth loose in texture.

碎[4]
5528
Fragments; small pieces; odds and ends. Broken.

碎 務 trifling, petty affairs.

碎 嘴 子 a chatterbox.

碎 塊 bits; fragments; odd pieces.

碎 工 odd jobs.

[5]碎 景 small views of scenery.

碎 浪 breakers.

碎 煤 slack coal.

碎 爛 broken, smashed.

碎 磁 crackle ware.

[10]碎 膽 to burst the gall-bladder—great fear.

碎 裂 to take to pieces; to pull to pieces.

碎 貨 retail goods; driblets.

碎 金 bits of gold—fragmentary pieces of literature having special excellence.

碎 銀·子 silver in small pieces.

[15]心 碎 heartbroken.

打 碎 or 破 碎 to break into fragments.

煩 碎 numerous trifling matters.

零 碎 fragmentary; odds and ends.

粹[4]
See No. 6878. u.f. preceding.

誶[4]
5529
To vilify; to scold; to rail at; to abuse; to accuse. To interrogate.

誶 罵 to vilify; to abuse; to curse.

誶 語 to blame; to reprimand.

凌 誶 to disgrace.

恣 誶 angry abuse.

詬 誶 to curse; abusive language.

遂[4]
5530
To comply with; to follow; to proceed to; to prolong. To complete. Consequently; and then; thereupon; next.

遂 不 住 could not forbear.

遂 中 止 stopped halfway—come to naught.

遂 事 不 諫 it is useless to remonstrate about matters that have had their course.

遂 初 to fulfil one's natural bent—as when a man is out of public life, living in retirement.

[5]遂 卽 thereupon; forthwith.

遂 古 ancient times; long ago.

遂 從 to follow.

遂 意 or 遂 心 or 遂 願 as one likes; agreeable to one's wish.

遂 至 如 此 and so it came to this.

[10]遂 路 an open highway.

遂 非 to persist in a false statement.

不 遂 unfulfilled; not to comply.

謀 姦 不 遂 an attempt at criminal intercourse failed.

得 遂 to get one's wish.

[15]百 事 乃 遂 May everything be as you wish!

自 遂 to follow one's inclinations.

順 遂 compliant.

篩 非 遂 過 to gloss over faults.

(a) Territory one hundred li from the capital.

遂 土 territory as above.

燧[4]
5531
A speculum. Fire, flame. A beacon fire of brushwood. A torch.

燧 人 氏 a fabulous ruler who is said to have discovered fire.

燧 木 a tree, the branches of which, when bored, produced fire.

燧 石 flint.

木 燧 a piece of wood for producing fire by friction.

烽 燧 之 警 alarm of beacon-fires.

金 燧 a speculum for producing fire from the rays of the sun.

璲[4]
5532
Pendant girdle-ornaments.

穟[4]
5533
Ripe grain.

邃[4]
5534
Deep; abstruse. In the rear, far-off.

邃 遠 far-off; out of sight.

繸[4]
5535
The hem or border of a garment. A tassel.

襚[4]
5536
Grave-clothes.

隧
邃[4]
5537
The path to a tomb, underground passage. A tunnel. A mine.

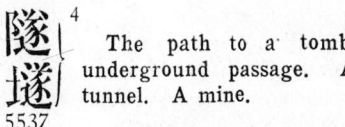

隧 道 the tunnel to a grave; a tunnel; entrenchments.

出 入 不 當 門 隧 do not use the main path in going in and out.

(a) To turn.

若 磨 石 之 隧 turning round like a millstone.

歲 崴 山二歳 A year. Age. The harvest.
5538

歲 不 我 與 the years do not wait for me.
歲 俸 or 年 歲 annual salary.
歲 入 annual income.
歲 入 歲 出 現 計 書 annual statement of receipts and expenditure.
⁵歲 入 預 算 annual budget.
歲 凶 or 歲 荒 a bad year.
歲 出 annual expenditure.
歲 口 age of a horse.
歲 將 闌 the year is drawing to a close.
¹⁰歲 差 the precession of the equinoxes. (-ch'a¹)
歲 底 the close of the year.
歲 成 the harvest; end of the year.
歲·數 or 年 歲 age.
歲 星 or 太 歲 the planet Jupiter; the year star.
¹⁵歲 時 times and seasons.
歲 晚 New Year's Eve.
歲 暮 the close of the year.
歲 月 times and seasons; years and months.
歲 月 如 流 the months and years run by like a stream.
²⁰歲 月 裴 葛 之 遺 there are annual supplies of furs and summer garments sent—by parents.
歲 杪 the close of the year.
歲 次 the order of the year, according to the cycle.
歲 比 successive years.
歲 登 大 有 or 大 有 年 May you have a prosperous year!
²⁵歲 稔 a good year.
歲 考 or 歲 試 former prefectural test-examinations held every three years to test first-degree graduates.
歲 計 yearly accounts.

歲 首 or 歲 律 更 新 the beginning of the year.
千 歲 a thousand years—a prince.
³⁰守 歲 or 別 歲 to see the old year out.
客 歲 or 去 歲 last year.
幾 歲 How old? (of a child).
舊 歲 or 隔 歲 last year.
萬 歲 ten thousand years—the Emperor. Long live . . . !
³⁵週 歲 a full year; anniversary.

祟 Calamities. An evil spirit; evil influences of a spiritual nature. Distinguish 崇 No. 1528.
5539

祟 怪 a bogy; a goblin.
作 祟 to act like one possessed.
鬼 祟 evil spirits.
鬼 鬼 祟 祟 mischievous, devilish.

巂 Ancient name of a district in Szechwan, comprising the present 甯 遠 and 會 理 districts.
5540

SUN. (울)
(Suen)

孫 A grandson; a grandchild. Descendants, posterity. Second growth of plants.
5541

孫·女 a granddaughter.
孫·子 a grandson. 2nd generation below oneself.
曾 孫 or 重 孫 great-grandson. 3rd generation as above.
元 孫 or 玄 孫 son of a great-grandson. 4th generation as above.
⁵來 孫 5th generation as above.
昆 孫 6th generation as above.
仍 孫 7th generation as above.
雲 孫 8th generation as above.
耳 孫 9th generation as above.
外·孫 son of a daughter.
姪 孫 grandnephew.

(a) Read sun⁴ or hsün⁴. u.f. 遜 No. 5545. Prudent, reserved, docile.

孫 以 出 之 he brings it forth in humility.

搎 To rub with the hand. To stroke.
5542

捫 搎 to feel; to stroke.

猻 A kind of monkey.
5543

蓀 A flower. Iris.
5544

遜 To yield. Humble. To accord. To be obedient. To withdraw. Also read hsün⁴.
5545

遜 于 汝 志 in accord with your own mind.
遜 位 to abdicate.
遜 志 a humble determination.
遜 讓 to give up to others.
遜 順 yielding; complaisant.

飧 An evening meal. Supper. To eat. Used for No. 6694.
5546

笋 筍 The tender shoots of the bamboo; a sprout; a shoot.
5547

笋 席 mats made from the sheath of bamboo-shoots.
笋 芽 or 竹 笋 bamboo-shoots.
笋 輿 a bamboo sedan.
笋 鞭 the root of the bamboo.
笋 鞵 shoes made from the sheath of bamboo-shoots.
乾 笋 dried bamboo-shoots.

(a) A tenon. Conical, pointed.

笋 峯 a conical peak.
笋 眼 a mortise.
笋 頭 a tenon, a dovetail.
作 笋 to circumcise.

損 To injure; to destroy; to spoil. Injury; disadvantage. Distinguish 捐 No. 1630.
5548

損 人 利 己 to injure others in order to benefit oneself.
損 傷 or 損 壞 to damage; to spoil; damaged.
損 傷 元 氣 to weaken the constitution.

損 價 出 售 to sell at a loss.

[5] 損 友 an injurious friend.

損 名·譽 to injure one's good name.

損 增 to diminish and to increase.

損 壽 to shorten one's life.

損·失 injury or loss; casualties.

[10] 全 部 損 失 actual total loss.

損·失 精 神 loss of vigour or energy.

損·失 總 數 total amount of loss.

損 害 or 損 破 to damage; damaged; to injure.

損 害 保 險 accident insurance.

[15] 損 害 賠 償 compensation for damage.

損 德 to outrage morality; to injure one's virtue.

損 書 your letter—i.e., the letter which you have been at so much trouble to write.

損 有 餘 補 不 足 to cut off the excess and make up the deficiency.

損 毀 信 用 injury to credit.

[20] 損 氣 to destroy the health.

損 益 diminution and increase; profit and loss, etc.

損 益 帳 profit and loss account.

損 過 以 就 中 to cut off the excess in order to reach the mean.

有 益 無 損 altogether advantageous.

榫
榫 } [3]
5549

To fit into. A tenon.

榫·子 or 榫·頭 a tenon; a dovetail; a wooden pin.

榫 卯 tenon and mortise.

榫 牙 a dovetailed edge.

巽 [4]
5550

The 5th of the Eight Diagrams, 八 卦. South-east. Mild, bland, insinuating.

巽 位 to resign the throne.

巽 與 之 言 能 無 說 (yüeh[5]) 乎 Can you not be pleased with words of gentle advice?

巽 言 peaceful words.

噀 [4]
5551

To spirt out of the mouth.

SUNG.　(ㄙㄨㄥ)

(Song)

松 [1]
5552

The pine-tree; the fir-tree. An emblem of longevity.

松 兒 石 or 綠 松 石 turquoise.

松 子 or 松 塔 pine seed-vessels; fir-cones.

松 明 resin; pine-splints used for lighting.

松 木 or 松 板 deal-boards.

[5] 松 柏 後 彫 the leaves of the fir and cypress are the last to fall—of honest officials.

松 柏 節 操 (tsao[4]) a vigorous old age.

松 柏 類 conifers.

如 松 柏 之 茂 May you flourish as the pine and the cypress.

歲 寒 松 柏 the pine and the cypress endure the cold together—constancy.

[10] 松 楸 the pine and the catalpa-trees around a graveyard; a grave.

松 樹 the pine-tree.

松 毛 pine-needles.

松 漠 pine-forests on the plains.

松 濤 the soughing of the wind in the pines compared with the roar of the surf.

[15] 松 炬 pine-torches.　[soot.

松 烟 墨 Chinese ink from pine

松 煤 soot from pine-smoke.

松 球 pine or fir-cones.

松 竹 梅 the pine, bamboo, and the flowering-plum. See 三 No. 5415—38.

[20] 松 籟 the sound of the wind in the pines.

松 脂 pitch.

松 花 江 the Songari River.

松 菊 猶 存 the pine and the chrysanthemum endure—when other things have faded.

松 菌 or 松 蕈 an edible fungus which grows under pines.

[25] 松 蘿 name of a tea produced in Hweichow, S. Anhwei.

松 針 pine-needles.

松 風 之 韻 the soughing of the wind in the pines.

松·香 or 松 樹 膠 resin.

松·香 油 turpentine.

[30] 松 鷄 the ptarmigan or hazel-grouse.

松 黃 the flowers of the pine.

松 鼠 the squirrel.

水 松 Codium macronatum.

瓦 松 roof-pines—Cotyledon japonica.

[35] 白 松 the lace-bark pine: Pinus Bungeana.

石 松 Lycopodium clavatum.

節 操 (tsao[4]) 方 松 篤 moral integrity like the pine—for endurance—and the bamboo-skin—for toughness.

落 葉 松 the larch.

赤 松 Pinus densiflora.

[40] 金 松 the Umbrella pine.

黑 松 Pinus Thunbergii.

淞 [1]
5553

Dew-drop. Icicle.

嵩
崧 } [1]
5554

The highest of the Five Peaks, 五 嶽; it is situated in Honan. Eminent; lofty.

嵩 呼 萬 歲 Exalted is His Majesty!

嵩 嶽 效 靈 to be hailed emperor.

嵩 高 維 嶽 How majestic and grand are the lofty peaks!

淞 [1]
5555

Name of a river.

吳 淞 Woosung—near Shanghai.

菘 [1]
5556

A variety of cabbage.

鬆 [1]
5557

Loose; lax; slack. To let go; to relax.

鬆·了 勁 兒 to relax one's efforts; to take things easy.

鬆·些 or 鬆·點 兒 loosen it a little.

鬆·動 to loosen; slacken it a little.

鬆 口 to give assent to.

[5] 鬆 性 of a porous nature; of a loose nature.

鬆 手 Let go!

鬆 散 loosely arranged; to get rid of melancholy.

鬆 爽 or 鬆 快 contented; pleased; hilarious.

鬆綁 or 鬆·開 to loosen; to untie; to slack.
[10]鬆緊 fast and loose.
鬆緩 to loosen; to untie.
鬆脆 doughy and crisp, respectively.
鬆軟 loose, soft, flexible — of things.
鬆鬆肩兒 rest the shoulders a while—as carriers or porters.

訟 [4] Litigation. To dispute. To demand justice.
5558

訟人者殃 wretched is he who charges others.
訟告 to accuse.
訟庭 a law court.
訟心者祥 fortunate is he who charges himself.
[5]訟案 a case at law.
訟案之要點 the matter of the charge.
訟棍 or 訟師 pettifoggers; those who foment litigation.
訟獄 or 訟事 litigation; lawsuits.
訟詞 an indictment.
[10]訟費 costs in law.
息訟 to settle a case.
構訟 to bring an action.
涉訟 to go to law.
自訟 self-reproach.

頌 [4] To praise; to commend. Hymns. Odes.
5559

頌德 to commend virtue.
頌揚 to laud; to praise.
頌揚載道 everybody sang his praises.
頌日祉 May you have daily joy! —salutation closing a letter.
[5]頌榮 Doxology.
頌祝三多 May you have every blessing—wealth, longevity and posterity.
頌言 praises; odes.
頌詞 commendatory odes.
頌讚 to commend; to eulogize.

娀 [1] Name of a concubine of 帝嚳 the father of the Emperor Yao.
5560

有娀 name of an ancient State.

悚 慄 [3] Frightened; terrified.
5561

悚惕 trembling; fearful.
悚慄 or 悚懼 or 悚惶 to tremble at.
悚然 timorous; affrighted.

竦 [3] To stand. To raise. To incite. Respect. Horrified; alarmed.
5562

竦動 excited; aroused; agitated.
竦勵 to incite; to encourage.
竦善 to incite to goodness.
竦敬 to respect.
[5]竦立 or 竦然 to stand trembling; terrified.
　毛骨竦然 hair rising and flesh creeping.
　毛髮竦然 his hair stood on end—for fear.
竦翅而上也 to clap the wings and soar aloft.
竦骨 flesh creeping from fear.

慫 [3] To alarm. To arouse. Also read tsung[3].
5563

慫動 to excite; to arouse.
慫通 to egg on.
慫然 to excite; to arouse.

聳 [3] To excite; to egg on; to raise up; to stir up.
5564

聳人耳目 to arrest the attention.
聳動 to egg on; to stir up.
聳惡打仗 to urge to go to war.
聳惑 to excite suspicions.
[5]聳惕 to cause to tremble.
聳懼 terrified.
聳聽 to excite one to listen.
聳肩 high shoulders.
聳起 to stick up; to emit; to rise out of suddenly.
[10]聳起肩來 to shrug the shoulders.
　山峰聳起 the peaks of the mountains stick up.
高聳 lofty—as mountain peaks.

宋 [4] Name of a feudal State. Name of a dynasty. To dwell.
5565

宋儒 the school of philosophers under the Sung dynasty.
宋國 a feudal State, dating from 1113—285 B.C.
宋朝 or 宋紀 or 趙宋 the Sung dynasty which reigned from A.D. 960—1280. It had its capital at Kaifeng in Honan.
宋朝 or 劉宋紀 the Sung dynasty which reigned from A.D. 420—479. It had its capital at Nanking.
宋體字 the form of characters in which this book is printed.

送 [4] To accompany; to escort.
5566

送一程 to go with a person for a short distance.
送三 the ceremonies on the third day after death.
送別 to see a friend off; a farewell visit.
送別會 valedictory meeting.
[5]送夢 to appear in a dream.
送娘·子 bridesmaids.
送客 or 送賓 to escort a visitor to the door.
送往迎來 speed the parting and welcome the coming guest.
送殯 or 送喪 to attend a funeral.
[10]送竈 to dismiss the kitchen-god to report to his superior.
送老 or 送終 to attend a parent in the last extremity; to bury a parent.
送舊迎新 speed the old and welcome the new.
送行 to see a person off.
送親 to see a bride to her husband's house.
[15]送鬼·的 an exorcist.
恕不送 excuse my not seeing you off.
莫送 or 別送 don't trouble to see me off.

(a) To send. To give to. To hand over.

送上 to send to a superior.
送·了命 to give up one's life; to run risks.
送交 to hand over to.
送信 to send a letter or a message.

5送信·的 letter-carrier.
送信薄 chit-book.
送·出 to send away. [destination.
送·到 to send to. 送到 to send to his
送·到·他口 conveyed it to his mouth.
10送呈 to submit to—as a statement.
送命差·事 dangerous government-service. (-ch'ai¹-)
送回 or 送還 to send back.
送子娘娘 the goddess of child-bearing.
送官 to hand over to the magistrates.
15送帖 to send a card to.
送懲 to hand over for punishment.
送日 to ask for a date to be fixed for a marriage.
送案 to hand over to the magistrate.
送禮 to send presents.
20送究 to hand over to the officials for punishment.
送納 to send—in payment.
送·給·你 I give it to you.
送至 to send to.
送花圈 to send a wreath.
25送請 to send with a present.
送達 to deliver to.
送貨 to send goods to the purchaser.

誦⁴ To hum over; to intone; to recite. A song.
5567

誦經 to chant a liturgy.
誦習 to get by heart—through repetition.
誦說 to relate.
誦論 to discourse.
誦讀 to read aloud; to hum over.
背誦 to turn the back and repeat from memory—as schoolboys.

SZŬ or SSŬ.　　(ㄙ)
(Sï)

厶
5568　Selfish, private. Used as the sign of a blank to be filled up. Radical 28. Written 厶 Nat. Phon. letter for s.

私
5569　¹ Private, personal. Selfish, partial, unfair. Secret, contraband, underhand, illicit. The private parts.

私·下 privately; secretly.
私·下議·論 privately, criticize.
私事 private affairs.
私人 a private individual.
5私人之筆記 private notes.
私人住屋 private residence; private houses.
私人資·格 personal character.
私人間之匯票 private bill or draft.
私充 illicit substitution.
10私兒²·子 = 私生子³ an illegitimate, a natural child.
私刑 or 私加刑 illegal punishment; lynching.
私剋 to take a squeeze—from wages, etc.
私印 private seal.
私受 to receive in secret.
15私合 illicit intercourse; to settle a quarrel out of court.
私同 in collusion.
私名號 a line at the side of characters in a book indicating proper names.
私和 to arrange a case privately.
私和公案 to hush up public crimes.
20私地 in secret; in private.
私塾 private school (of the old style) with one teacher.
私奔 to elope; illicit intercourse between the sexes.
私娶 clandestine marriage.
私宅 private residence of an official.
25私室 private room.
私帶 to smuggle; to carry contraband.
私座 private property.
私德 personal virtue.
私徵稅餉 to levy unauthorized taxes.
30私弊 bribery and corruption.
私心 partial; unfair; selfish.
私怨 private malice.
私悃 or 私忱 one's inmost feelings.
私情 private feelings; personal preference; illicit love.
35私意 private idea; secret purpose.
私愛 favour.
私慾 lust; desire.
私拿東·西 to pilfer.
私收入 private income.
40私改 to falsify—accounts, etc.
私敵 private enemy.
私書 private letters.
私有 privately owned.

私有財產 private property.
45私有鐵路 private railroad.
私業 private enterprise.
私權 private right. (legal).
私法 civil law; private law.=民法
私派 sent secretly; self-sent.
50私淑艾 privately cultivate and correct themselves.
私濫逮捕監禁 unlawful arrest and imprisonment.
私物 private goods. (legal).
私生子³ a natural child.
私生子³認領 acknowledgement of a natural child. (legal).
55私產 personal estate or effects.
私用 for private use.
私·的 secretly; secret.
私益 private interests.
私相 privately.
60私窺 to peep at; to steal a glance.
私立公立 private and public respectively—as applied to schools, institutions, etc.
私立學校 private school.
私第 private residence.
私約 a private treaty or agreement.
65私結條約 to conclude a treaty or an agreement in private.
私罰 illegal punishment; to lynch.
私自 privately.
私處 the privates; a private place.
私行 privately; illicitly; to travel incognito; private life.
70私行下貨 to ship goods without a permit.
私衷 my private opinion; my humble opinion.
私見 private view or opinion; prejudice.
私覿 private audience.
私訪 to make secret inquiries.
75私設寄宿所 private boarding-house.
私訴 private lawsuit.
私訴關係人 party in a private suit.
私話 private talk.
私謀 to plot in secret.
80私貨 smuggled goods.
私販 to smuggle.
私販酒商 bootleggers; sellers of illicit liquors.
私費生 self-supporting pupils.
私賣 private sale. (legal).
85私起 or 私行起貨 to land goods without a permit.
私逃 to abscond.
私造 illicit manufacture.

私通 illicit intercourse; treacherous; secretly to inform.

私通別國 in treacherous collusion with another State.

⁹⁰私運進口 to smuggle goods into a port.

私銷 to dispose of without a licence.

私錢 base coin.

私鑄 to coin base money.

私阿 or 阿私 favouritism; partiality. (-o¹, o¹-)

⁹⁵私願 one's private aspirations.

私鹽 smuggled salt.

一人之私言 the private opinion of an individual.

勝己之私謂之克 to overcome one's lusts may be termed conquest.

君之私也 favourite of the prince.

¹⁰⁰家私 private property; personal effects.

必有私故 he must have private reasons.

無私 impartial; unselfish.

退而省其私 he has retired, and I have examined his conduct when away from me.

(a) Depreciatory term; used by a woman for the husband of her sister.

私屬 one's household.

某也夫子³之賤私 I am merely the humble servant of a minister.

譚公維私 the ruler of T'an was her sister's husband.

糸
糸
5570

¹ Silk, etc. Used with the next.
Read mi⁴·⁵. Floss silk. Fine, delicate. Radical 120.

絲
5571

¹ Silk. Thread, wire, fibre, strings of musical instruments.

絲商 silk merchants.

絲帶 silk ribbons, braid or sashes.

絲廠 silk filatures.

絲斤 silk in bulk—as cargo, etc.

⁵絲桐 a lute.

絲·瓜 the loofah gourd.

絲禽 the egret. See 鷥 No. 5573.

絲竹 stringed and wind instruments, respectively.

絲管 stringed instruments and pipes, respectively.

¹⁰絲經 thrown silk.

絲綿 silk wadding.

絲綿雜貨 silk and cotton mixtures.

絲綫 silk thread for sewing.

絲緞 silk and satin.

¹⁵絲羅 gauze; silk crape.

絲蘿 intertwined; marriage relations.

絲衣 the gentry.

絲音 stringed musical instruments.

吐絲 to spin silk—of the silkworm.

²⁰命若懸絲 life hanging by a thread.

土絲 native silks.

料絲 spun glass.

獨絲 a single fibre.

生絲 raw silk.

²⁵節絲 knotted silk.

粉絲 vermicelli made from beans.

紡絲 or 抽絲 to reel silk from the cocoon.

肉絲 shredded meat.

銅絲 copper or brass wire.

飛絲 or 游絲 gossamer.

(a) The hundred thousandth part of a tael, 兩. Small, minute.

絲忽之間 the minutest fraction.

絲來毫去 just the least bit.

絲毫不留 not a trace left.

絲毫不錯 or 分絲不差 without error; exact; no difference at all; exactly right.(-ch'a¹·⁴)

嘶¹
5572

To hiss; a call to come.

鷥¹
5573

The egret.

鷺·鷥 the eastern egret.

斯¹
5574

This, these, thus, such. Distinguish 期 No. 526.

斯事 this matter.

斯人 this person.

斯已而已矣 let it end!

斯文 elegant; scholarly; courteous; literati; culture.

⁵斯文掃地 scholastic dignity trails in the dust.

斯文敗類 polished rascals.

斯文模樣 in a polished, gentlemanly manner.

斯昭昭之多 just this spot of brightness.

斯時 this time.

¹⁰斯焉取斯 When did this man get this virtue?

斯須之間 in a twinkling.

(a) A connecting particle.

斯仁至矣 then virtue is at hand.

斯天下之民至焉 then from all the empire people will come to you.

斯得天下矣 then the empire is secured.

斯民服 then the people will submit.

(b) A final particle; a particle which gives emphasis or strength to the sentence.

彼何人斯 What sort of a man is he?

有兎斯首 "there is but a single rabbit."

清斯濯纓 if it is clear, he will wash his cap-strings in it.

湛湛露斯 heavy lies the dew.

濁斯濯足 if it is muddy, he will wash his feet in it.

(c) To lop.

斧以斯之 take an axe and lop it off.

(d) Read ts'ŭ⁴.

王赫斯怒 the king blazed with wrath.

(e) Read szŭ¹. Used in transliterating.

斯拉夫 Slav.

斯巴達 Sparta.

斯
廝
傂
5575

¹ A servant; a menial. A woodcutter.

厮 下 a person of lowly birth; a servant.

厮 守 to wait for; to wait on.

厮 徒 or 厮 僕 or 厮 隸 servants; menials.

厮 會 to meet.

[5] 厮 濫 a common, ordinary person.

厮 舍 servant's quarters.

厮 身 together.

厮 輿 firewood-cutters and grooms.

厮 鑼 a brass face-basin.

[10] 厮 養 卒 woodcutters, servants.

女 厮 a maid-servant.

小 厮 (my) servant.

(a) To rend. To make a disturbance. Similar to 撕 No. 5577.

厮 吵 altercation.

厮 殺 or 厮 打 a mêlée, a scrimmage; to kill.

厮 混 horse-play; altercation over trifles.

嘶[1] The neighing of a horse. Noise, din. Also read *hsi*[1].
5576

嘶 喊 to roar; to cry out.

嘶 殺 din of battle.

馬 嘶 neighing of a horse.

撕[1] To rip; to tear; to rend.
5577

撕·下·來 to tear down—as papers from a wall.

撕 口 to wrangle.

撕 打 a scrimmage.

撕 撕 拉 拉·的 gripping—in a wrestle; struggling together.

[5] 撕 攞 to pull a tangle apart; to bring into order.

撕 殺 to fight fiercely; to fight to the death.

撕 破 or 撕 爛 to tear up.

撕 碎 to tear to pieces.

撕 票 tear up the ticket—to kill one who is held for ransom by soldier brigands.

[10] 撕 臉 to tear the face—as in a brawl.

撕 衣·裳 Mind your clothes!—said by carriers.

撕·開 torn; to rip open.

(a) Read *hsi*[1]. To arouse to attention.

提 撕 to manage; to arouse to attention; business matters.

澌[1.4.] To exhaust. To drain dry.
5578

澌 滅 to extinguish—a fire.

澌 盡 run dry; exhausted—of the death of a man who has come to a good end.

(a) Read *hsi*[1]. Noise of breaking. Similar to 嘶 No. 5576.

廝[1] An amphibious beast resembling a tiger, having one horn. Read *chai*[4]. Uneven, rough. Read *i*[2]. Name of an ancient district in Shansi.
5579

思[1] To think; to contemplate; to consider.
5580 Distinguish 恩 No. 1743.

思 不 出 其 位 does not consider things outside his position.

思 之 質 料 food for thought.

思 前 to think of former days.

思 家 to think of home.

[5] 思 家 病 home-sickness.

思 忖 to consider; to turn over in the mind.

思 念 之 間 in a moment; while meditating.

思 患 to be anxious for.

思 患 預 防 anticipate danger and prepare for emergency.

[10] 思 悟 to understand as a result of thought.

思 惟 meditation.

思 想 or 思 念 to meditate; to think; to consider; to take into consideration; theory; ideal; thought.

思 想 之 主 因 the subject of thought.

思 想 力 or 思 力 the compass of one's thoughts.

[15] 思 想 哲 學 speculative philosophy.

思 想 太 幼 稚 the thought is too immature.

思 想 家 thinkers.

思 想 活 潑 active thought.

思 想 界 the world of thought;

the thinking world.

[20] 思 想 自 由 freedom of thought.

奇 特 思 想 striking thoughts.

思 慕 or 思 戀 to long for.

思 慮 anxiety; to brood over.

思 懷 往 事 thinking of the past.

[25] 思 欲 to wish to; to have such an intention.

思 服 to cherish in the heart.

思 潮 the flood of ideas; stream of thought; popular ideas.

革 命 思 潮 the flood of revolutionary ideas.

思 理 學 logic.=論 理 學, 邏 輯

[30] 思 索 to meditate on; to think over.

不 假[3] 思 索 without any thought.

竭 力 思 索 exhaustive thinking.

思 維 thought; thinking; turning over in the mind.

思 緒 a train of thought.

[35] 思 維 再 四 to think over and over again.

思 考 thought; thinking; to inquire into.

思 考 之 法 則 the laws of thought.

思 考 能 力 the power to think.

思 議 to conceive; a conception.

[40] 不 可 思 議 inconceivable; beyond conception.

思 路 the path of one's thought.

思 辨 speculation.

思 辨 哲 學 speculative philosophy.

思°量[2] to meditate; to think; to consider.

[45] 思 齊 to wish to be equal to.

回 思 recollections.

幽 思 contemplative retirement.

熟 思 mature thought.

熟 思 後 after mature consideration.

[50] 再 思 second thoughts.

想 思 病 lovesickness.

(a) A particle—final particle to round off the expression.

思 樂 泮 水 pleasant is the college pool.

不 可 方 思 it cannot be traversed by a raft.

不 可 求 思 it is vain to solicit her.

不 可 泳 思 cannot be dived across.

神之格思不可度思 the approaches of the gods you cannot surmise. ⌈sound.

其聲哀思 mournful was its

(b) To lament.

吉士思秋 scholars lament over autumn.

(c) Read *ssu*[4]. Thoughts.

↓鼠思泣血 painful are my innermost thoughts and I weep blood. Cf. 5871 A1

思無邪 have no depraved thoughts.

孝思 filial thoughts.

秋思 melancholy thoughts.

詩思 poetic thoughts.

(d) Read *sai*[1]. The jaw, the jowl.

于思 a beard.

偲[1] Talented. Urgent.
5581

緦[1] Coarse, cotton cloth, used for mourning.
5582

緦麻 or 緦麻服 a degree of mourning—worn for three months for distant relatives.

罳[1] A screen. See 罘 No. 1904-1.
5583

颸[1] The cool breezes of autumn. The south-west wind.
5584

司[1] An officer. To control; to manage; to preside. A subdivision of a district.
5585

司事 a manager; clerks in law department.

司令 command issued by high officer of the army or navy to those officers in charge. Commander.

司令塔 conning-tower.

司令官 Commandant.

[5]司令權 right of command.

司令部 headquarters of the army, navy, etc.

總司令 Commander-in-chief.

司務 service; servant.

司務長[3] General Army Superintendent.

[10]司匠 overseer to the former Board of Works.

司命 the Arbiter of human destiny.

司命神 the god of the kitchen.

司員 or 司官 secretaries to the former Six Boards.

司寇 Minister of Crime; Criminal Judge. (*ancient*).

[15]司帳 cashier.

司帳員 accountant.

司庫 treasurer.

司徒 Minister of Education under the *Chou* Dynasty.

司敎 former District Director of Studies.

[20]司更卒 night-watchman; night-patrol.

司書生 clerk; copyist.

司會 leader of a meeting.

司業 Tutor in the former Imperial Academy.

司機 engine driver; chauffeur.

[25]司法 judicature.

司法事務 judicial business.

司法制度 judicial system.

司法參議會 Judicial Council.

司法官 a judge.

[30]司法年度 a judicial year.

司法手續 judicial procedure.

司法會 Legal Association.

司法會議 judicial committee.

司法權 jurisdiction.

[35]司法次長[3] vice-minister of Justice.

司法獨立 independence of the judiciary.

司法界 the legal profession.

司法籌備處 department for the drafting of laws.

司法部長[3] Minister of Justice.

[40]司法職務 judical functions.

司法行政 judicial administration. 司法院 Judicial Yuan.

司法行政權 judicial administrative authority.

司法裁判所 Court of Justice.

司法解釋 judicial interpretation.

[45]司法警察 judicial police.

司法部 Ministry of Justice.

司法部註冊 registered in the Ministry of Justice.

司牧 a shepherd—a ruler, one

divinely appointed to care for the masses of the people.

司獄官 officer of a prison.

[50]司理 to oversee; to manage.

司空 Minister of Works under the *Chou* Dynasty.

司空見慣 used to indicate—accustomed to seeing such things, they are not regarded as strange; familiar.

司筆札者 correspondent clerk.

司簿 a book-keeper.

[55]司藥 Military Druggist.

司道 the former Provincial Treasurer. the Provincial Judge, the Salt Commissioner, and the Grain Commissioner.

司鐸 a Roman Catholic priest.

司馬 the Minister of War under the *Chou* Dynasty; designation of the former sub-Prefect and Department magistrate.

各有所司 each has his own duties.

[60]官·司 litigation.

有司 civil authorities.

有限公·司 limited-liability companies.

百司 various officials.

笥[4] A hamper; a box or trunk.
5586

笥匵罍空 empty cupboards and boxes—destitute.

書笥 a book-box.

飼
飤[4] To feed; to nourish. Provisions; food.
5587

飼料 fodder.

飼養 to nourish.

嗣[4] To connect; to inherit. Heirs, posterity. Afterwards.
5588

嗣位 to succeed to the throne.

嗣因別故 following from other causes.

嗣子 heirs; an adopted son.

嗣後 hereafter; subsequently.

[5]嗣徽音 to inherit a good reputation.

嗣業 to inherit a property.

嗣歲 the succeeding year.

嗣 王 the new king.

嗣 續 or 後 嗣 descendants; posterity.

10 嗣 適 the heir-apparent.

絕 嗣 the male line of a family coming to an end.

繼 嗣 to carry on.

死[3] To die; dead; inanimate. Death.
5589

死 不 明 the cause of death not clear—when foul play is suspected.

死 地 不 肯 to die rather than....

死 事 death; to lay down the life.

死 亡 to die; death.

5 死 亡 保 險 life insurance payable at death.

死 亡 率 (lü[4,5].) death-rate.

死 仇 implacable enmity.

死 傷 數 人 there were several casualties.

死 其 長[3] willing to die for their elders.

10 死 刑 capital punishment.

死 則 不 得 飯 含 when dead, could not have the due rites performed—placing rice in the mouth of the corpse was called 飯, and placing a pearl was called 含.

死 力 with all the force at command.

死 去 活 來 to come round after fainting; to revive when apparently dead.

死 口 話 that which is said definitely; for certain.

15 死 地 place of execution; place of death.

死 喪 funeral; death and burial.

死 守 to defend to the last—as a fort; to remain unmarried—as a widow.

死 尸 a corpse.

死 巷 a cul-de-sac.

20 死 心 眼 兒 wedded to his own way; obstinate.

死 心 蹋 地 to give up all hope.

死 性 不 改 death will not make him change—of an unchangeable disposition.

死 數 a deadly fate.

死 於 非 命 to die a premature death.

25 死 有 餘 辜 death would not expiate all his crimes.

死 期 將 至 death is imminent.

死 板·的 a wooden person.

死 樣 stupid; doltish; stereotyped.

死 水 stagnant water.

30 死 海 The Dead Sea.

死 灰 dead ashes.

死 無 遺 書 to die intestate.

死 物 inanimate objects.

死 生 death and life; dead or alive.

35 死 生 問 題 a question of life and death.

死 生 有 命 富 貴 在 天 death and life are pre-determined, riches and honour are in the hand of Heaven.

死 產 still-birth.

死·的 dead; inert.

死 盡 to die out.

40 死 節 臣 a minister who dies for his country.

死 結 a fast knot, as opposed to a slip knot.

死 絕 to die out.

死 罪 a capital crime.

死 而 不 亡 dead but not destroyed.

45 死 而 後 已 only with death does his course end.

死 而 復 活 to die and rise again.

死 而 有 知 if there is consciousness after death.

死 而 湮 沒 dead, and gone into oblivion.

死 肉 dead flesh—a dull person; a bore.

50 死 胎 still-born.

死 色 deadly pale; cadaverous.

死·裏 逃 生 a very narrow escape from death.

死 詞 dead language.

死 路 a dangerous road; deadly habits.

55 死 難[4] to die for the country.

死 馬 當[4] 活 馬 醫 to doctor a dead horse as if it were alive—to try to win an apparently lost cause by making all humanly possible efforts.

死 骸 mortal remains.

死 鬼 a dead person.

死 黨 sworn confederates.

60 不 得 其 死 to come to an untimely end.

不 知 死 regardless of life.

不 知 死 活 said of a fool—he does not even know the difference between life and death.

九 死 一 生 extremely hazardous—only one chance of life in ten.

半 死 不 活 half-dead.

65 善 死 a peaceful death.

垂 死 at death's door.

暴 死 sudden death.

氣·死 人 to drive a man to desperation; mortified.

病 死 to die of disease.

70 縊 死 to die by hanging.

老 死 to die of old age.

(a) Used as an intensive or superlative.

死 工 夫 intense application; continuous work without intervals.

死 等 to wait indefinitely; bored with inaction.

死 辣 intensely pungent.

死 鹹 intensely salty.

冷·死·了 as cold as death; intensely cold.

好·死·了 terribly good; the very best.

一 死 兒 (·的) to insist on.

巳[4] The sixth of the *Twelve Branches*, 地 支. The period from 9 a.m. to 11 a.m. Distinguish 己 No. 429, 已 No. 2930.
5590

巳 初 9 to 10 a.m.

汜[4] A stream which leaves the main branch, and afterwards flows into it. Distinguish 汜 No. 1777.
5591

祀[4] To sacrifice. Sacrifices to the dead.
5592

祀 典 sacrificial rites.

祀 天 the sacrifice to Heaven on the winter solstice.

祀 孔 the sacrifice to Confucius.

祀 祖 or 祀 先 人 to sacrifice to ancestors.

祀 神 to sacrifice to the gods.

祀 竈 the sacrifice to the kitchen god on the 23rd of the 12th lunar month; in ancient times it was offered in early summer.

祭 祀 to sacrifice.

(a) A year.

元 祀 the first year of a reign.

似 [4] Resembling; like; as if; to seem.
5593

似 不 能 as if unable.

似·乎 as though; as if; fancy!

似·乎 有 理 or 似 覺 合 宜 it looks somewhat reasonable.

似 可 might; it might be as well to.

[5]似 宜 perhaps it might be as well.

似 形 resembling in form.

似 是 而 非 like the reality, but not so; apparently; seemingly.

似 有 there seems to be.

似 此 thus; like this.

[10]似 無 there would probably not be.

似 膠 如 漆 like glue and varnish—attracted to each other.

似 這 等 看·來 judging by these.

似 非 apparently not.

好 似 very much alike.

[15]宛 似 analogous.

涼 似 水 cool as water.

無 似 incomparable.

相 似 alike; similar.

類 似 like to; to take after.

↑·似·的 (·shih·tê) used at the end of

(a) To continue by inheritance.

似 續 不 承 not to carry on the line of descent.

似 續 妣 祖 he took the inheritance of his ancestors.

姒 [4] Wife of an elder brother. An elder sister.
5594

姒 娣 sisters-in-law; wives of elder and younger brothers.

俟 涘 [4] To wait for. Until, when, as soon as.
5595

俟 下 月 wait till next month.

俟 候 or 等 候 waiting for.

俟 卽 when....; then....

俟 至 于 後 by and by.

涘 [4] The banks of a river.
5596

河 涘 the banks of the Yellow River.   ⌈etc.

* a clause with "as if", "seems",

寺 [4] A hall; a court; a public office. A Buddhist monastery. A mosque.
5597

寺 承 a secretary in one of the imperial courts.

寺 人 or 宦 寺 eunuchs.

寺 觀 monasteries and temples.

寺 門 Buddhism; a Buddhist monastery.

寺 院 temples; mosques.

府 寺 a public office.

禮 拜 寺 a mosque.

四 肆 [4] Four. The second form is used in documents, etc., to avoid forgery.
5598

四 下 the four quarters; on all sides.

四 不 像 unlike everybody; a monstrosity; nondescript; outlandish; the elaphure.

四 令 the four seasons.

四·個 four things; four.

[5]四·分 之 一 one fourth.

四·十 多 歲 more than forty years old.

四 周 圍 on all sides; in every direction.

四 合 the four quarters.

四 四 four times four.

[10]四 國 four corners of the State—the State.

四 圍 all round.

四 址 the four boundaries.

四 堵 the four walls.

四 境 or 四 界 four boundaries; all round.

[15]四 大 the four elements of Buddhist teaching—Earth, Water, Fire, and Air; also of Taoism—Tao, Heaven, Earth and the Sovereign.

四 大 天 王 or 四 大 王 the Four Demon Kings whose images are placed at the entrances of Buddhist temples.

四 季 or 四 時 the four seasons.

四 乳 four births.

四 寶 the four treasures—pencil, paper, ink and ink-slab.

[20]四 寸 之 目 a four-inch mesh.

四 川 the Province of Szechwan.

四 平 八 穩 very firm; well done; satisfactory; very safe.

四 庫 全 書 the encyclopædia.

四 德 of women—right behaviour 德, proper speech 言, proper demeanour 容, proper employment 功.

[25]四 手 類 quadrumana.

四 摺 木 尺 four-fold folding foot-rule.

四 教 the four studies—literature 文, conduct 行, loyalty 忠, good faith 信.

四 散 scattered in all directions; routed.

四 方 on all sides; foursquare.

[30]四 方 木 a blockhead.

四 方·的 four-sides; square.

四 更 時 分 the fourth watch.

四 書 五 經 the four Books and the Five Canons or Classics—the *Great Learning* 大 學, *Confucian Analects* 論 語, *Doctrine of the Mean* 中 庸, and *Mencius* 孟 子; with the *Book of Changes* 易 經, the *Book of History* 書 經, the *Odes* 詩 經, the *Book of Rites* 禮 記, and the *Spring and Autumn Annals* 春 秋.

四 望 無 人 nobody in sight.

[35]四 極 the four points of the compass.

四 民 the four classes—scholar, farmer, artisan and merchant.

四 海 the four seas, anciently supposed to surround China.

四 海 之 內 in the world.

四 海 爲 家 finding a home anywhere.

[40]四 瀆 the four streams—the Yellow River, the Yangtze, the River Hwai, and the River Tsi.

四 直 straight on all sides; square; quite straight.

四 眞 the four disciples of *Laotzŭ* 老 子[3]—*Chuangtzŭ* 莊 子, *Wêntzŭ* 文 子, *Liehtzŭ* 列 子[3], and —*Kêng-sangtzŭ* 庚 桑 子.

四 眼 人 a pregnant woman.

四 科 the four classes of the chief disciples of Confucius—德 行, 言 語, 政 事, 文 學, the first, distinguished for virtue; the second, for able speech; the third, for administrative abilities; and the fourth, for literary attainments.

[45]四 端 the four fundamental principles—humanity 仁, rectitude 義, propriety 禮, and wisdom 智.

四 維 the four social bonds—禮義廉恥; the cardinal points.

四 聖 the four sages—*Shun* 舜, *Yü* 禹, *Choukung* 周公, and Confucius 孔子.

四 肢 the four limbs.

四 肢 百 體 the members of the body; the body.

50 四 至 all around; the four sides; the cardinal points.

四。處 on every side; the four quarters.

四 角 four-cornered; rectangular.

四 象 the four secondary figures formed from the two primary symbols of the *diagrams, See* 二 No. 1751-7.

四 起 rising up from all sides.

55 四 路 無 門 no resource in any direction.

四 通 八 達 to open out on all sides; communicating in all directions.

四 週 all round; on every side.

四 鄰 the neighbourhood; the neighbours on each side.

四 隅 the four corners.

60 四 靈 畢 至 the four supernatural creatures — unicorn, phœnix, tortoise, and dragon — will arrive.

四 面 four sides; everywhere.

四 面 八 方 on every side.

四 面 楚 歌 enemies on every side. *See* 楚 No. 1393-11.

四 面 體 a four-sided solid.

65 四 體 the head, trunk, arms and legs of the human frame.

四 體 不 勤 your limbs are not accustomed to toil.

肆 隸
5599

4 An initial particle—now, though, thus, so, thereon, therefore. Distinguish 肄 No. 2939. u.f. 四, see preceding.

肆 不 殄 厥 慍 though he did not remove their wrath.

肆 予 以 爾 衆 士 therefore have I gathered you soldiers together.

肆 類 于 上 帝 he thereupon offered a special sacrifice to the Supreme.

(a) To set forth. To display.

肆 伸 to stretch out.

肆 德 to display virtue.

肆 祀 to set the sacrifice in order.

肆 筵 設 席 to make a great feast.

肆 陳 to arrange; to dispose in order.

(b) Greatly; excessive.

肆 口 大 罵 outrageous abuse.

肆 念 to reflect upon.

(c) Reckless, dissolute.

肆 剁 to plunder.

肆 意 recklessly; unscrupulously.

肆 掠 to rob with violence.

肆 筆 careless writing.

肆 虐 reckless and oppressive.

肆 行 無 忌 to care for nobody; outrageous in behaviour.

放 肆 or 恣 肆 to act disorderly.

(d) To exhaust; to put forth.

肆 力 to put forth all the energies.

肆 目 to use the eyesight to the utmost.

(e) A market-place. A shop.

肆 諸 市 朝 to expose a corpse—after execution—in the market place or court.

市 肆 a market place.

酒 肆 a wine shop.

閉 肆 to close a shop.

(f) To take heart. To be at ease. To let go.

肆 赦 to pardon.

肆 哉 Take heart!

(g) Read *i*[4] u.f. 肄 No. 2939. Surplus.

肆 束 及 帶 when the ends of the fastening strings reached to the girdle.

(h) Read *t'i*[5]. To cut up a carcase.

(i) Read *kai*[1]. A song.

肆 夏 ancient marching song.

泗
5600

4 Mucus. Name of a river in Shantung.

泗 明 an old name for Ningpo.

駟
5601

4 A team of four horses.

駟 不 及 舌 four horses cannot overtake the tongue.

駟 馬 難 追 a team of four horses cannot overtake—a spoken word.

傂
5602

4 Small; minute. Lacking sincerity.

救 傂 莫 若 以 忠 "against insincerity there is no better safeguard than loyalty."

兕 兕
5603

4 A bovine animal, described as having one horn, said to be the female of 犀 No. 2463.

兕 中 a wooden vessel shaped like a reclining buffalo used for receiving counters in ancient archery competitions.

兕 牛 the female rhinoceros.

兕 觥 a rhinoceros-shaped (old bronze) vessel.

耜
5604

4 A plough; a ploughshare.

SHA. (ㄕㄚ)

㘞
5605

4 A small cavity.

㘞 眼 pores.

沙
5606

1 Sand, gravel, pebbles. Granulated. Inter. 砂 No. 5610.

沙 丘 sand-hills.

沙 人 a tribe in Yunnan.

沙 包 sandbags.

沙 參 a plant with a root like ginseng—*Adenophora polymorpha.*

5 沙 噀 or 海 參 sea-slugs; bêche-de-mer, trepang.

沙 囊 sandbags.

沙 土 sandy soil; gravel.

沙 堆 sand-hills.

沙 場 the desert; a battle-field.

10 沙 塵 騰 播 clouds of dust rising.

沙 子 sand; small shot.

沙 布 emery-cloth.

沙 方 wood from the fir cut into planks suitable for coffins.

沙·木 a tree similar to the fir. *Cunninghamia sinensis.* See 桬 No. 5607. A.w. 杉·木

[15] 沙果 the crab apple.

沙梨 a small russet pear, with hard particles in the flesh from which it gets its name.

沙民 squatters on the uncultivated river foreshores.

沙河 quicksands; desert.

沙泉 a spring in the sand.

[20] 沙洲 a shoal.

沙漏 a sand filter.

沙漠 desert.

沙灘 quicksand; a sandbank; the bar at the mouth of a river.

沙狐 the fox of the steppes.

[25] 沙猛 the file-fish.

沙田 sand-flats; tidal lands.

沙甲 the dragonet fish.

沙石 pebbles; sandstone.

沙磨 to sand-paper a thing.

[30] 沙磧 a sandbank.

沙礫 small pebbles.

沙籐 rattans.

沙粉 emery powder.

沙糖 granulated sugar.

[35] 沙紙 sand-paper.

沙船 sand-junks.

沙蟲 the larvæ of mosquitoes.

沙角 or 沙尾 a sandspit.

沙錢 ancient cash, very thin.

[40] 沙錐 the sandpiper; the snipe.

沙鍋 an earthenware cooking pot.

沙陣 a sand-storm.

沙面 a sandbank; the Island of Shameen at Canton.

沙面輪 emery-wheel.

[45] 沙魚 the shark. *See* 鯊 No. 5613.

沙鷄 a sand-grouse.

一片散沙 a lot of loose sand, — lack of internal unity in a country.

流沙 quicksands.

(a) To sift.

沙汰 to sift and reduce the number.

(b) Used for transliterating.

沙彌 or 沙僧 a Buddhist novice, male or female.

沙爾 a city.

沙門 or 桬門 a Buddhist monk or priest. *Shaman.*

(c) Read *sha⁴*. To neigh.

沙鳴 sounds made by animals.

桬[1]
5607　**Name of various trees.**

桬木 *Cunninghamia sinensis.*

桬棠 a kind of wild pear.

痧[1]
5608　**Cholera. Colic.**

痧氣丸 cholera pills.

痧神娘娘 goddess prayed to when children have measles.

絞腸痧 colic.

紗[1]
5609　**Coarse.**

粆糖 coarse sugar.

砂[1]
5610　**Pebbles, coarse sand, gravel; gritty. Inter.** 沙 **No. 5606.**

砂仁 inferior cardamoms or grains of Paradise.

砂囊 the gizzard of a fowl.

砂子 gravel; pebbles.

砂布 emery-cloth.

[5] 砂浴 sand-bath.

砂淋 stone in the bladder; gravel.

砂石 sandstone.

砂殺米 sago. =西米

砂箱 frame for casting.

[10] 砂輪 emery-wheel.

硃砂 cinnabar.

金鋼砂 corundum.

鐵砂 iron ore.

靈砂 sulphide of mercury.

紗[1]
5611　**Gauze, thin silk. Untwisted thread, yarn.**

紗廠 cotton mills.

紗錠 spindles in a cotton mill.

紗業 cotton-spinning industry.

紗燈 a gauze lantern.

[5] 紗燈罩 a Welsbach gas-mantle.

紗窻 a gauze window to keep out insects.

紗衫·子 a gauze shirt.

亮紗 glazed gauze.

洋紗 cambric; lawns.

綿紗 cotton yarn.

5612　**A Buddhist cassock.**

5613　**The shark family; it includes some rays and skates.**

鯊綠色 a bright, slate blue.

鯊魚 a shark; a small fresh-water fish with a round body and a large head, which buries itself in the mud.

鯊魚皮 shagreen.

琵·琶鯊 the spotted ray.

鋸鯊 a saw-fish.

傻[3]
5614　**Foolish; thoughtless; stupid.**

傻人 a fool.

傻·子 a simpleton.

傻睡 the heavy, dull slumber of a sick person.

傻話 nonsense.

SHA.　　(ㄕㄚ)

(Shah)

殺[1,5]
5615　**To kill; to destroy; to murder.**

[½] 殺人 to kill a person;

--殺人 as a superlative — enough to kill one.

殺伐用張 my work of punishing will spread out.

殺害 to destroy; to slaughter.

殺戮 to kill.

[5] 殺手 an executioner.

殺敗 to kill and defeat; to put to flight in battle.

殺斃 death by violence.

殺機已啟 the bloodthirsty spirit is already aroused.

殺氣 a violent temper; murderous.

[10] 殺無道以就有道 to kill the lawless for the benefit of the law-abiding.

殺生 to slaughter animals.

殺盡了 exterminated; all killed.

殺神 the Destroying Angel.

殺罪 the punishment of beheading.

15殺蟲 to drive out worms; to kill bugs, etc.
殺身成仁 sacrifice of one's life to preserve one's integrity.
殺退 to kill and disperse; to rout.
殺◦開一條路 to cut one's way out—as in a battle.
殺頭 to behead.
20偶殺 accidental homicide.
屠殺 massacre; butchery.
故殺 wilful murder.
暗殺 assassination.
毆殺 to kill in a fight.
25自殺 suicide; self-destruction.
誤殺 to kill by mistake for some other person.
謀殺 to plot murder.

(a) **To add up.**

殺個總兒 to bring various items under one heading.
殺數 to add up totals.

(b) **Very, exceedingly.**

殺^{4}尾 the very last.
殺緊 too tight—as a rope.
好·殺 very good. (*dial.*) ≡好煞
急·殺 worried to death. (*dial.*)

(c) **Read** *shai*^{4}. **To pare off; to reduce; to clip. To decrease.**

殺縫 to cut a piece of stuff away and then sew up the opening.
殺青 to take off the green—from tablets of bamboo to prepare them for writing purposes.
其聲噍殺 "his voice was broken and confused."
親親之殺 behaviour towards kindred on a graduated scale.

𧝬 4.5. **To fell a seam.**
5616

煞 4.5. **To strike dead, as by evil influences. Baleful; detrimental; noxious. Inter. preceding.**
5617

煞凶 noxious; baleful.
煞星 a malignant star—one that brings pestilence, etc.
煞氣 malaria; the active spirit of death; baleful influences which destroy good fortune.

(a) **Very, exceedingly.**

煞尾字 the last word.
煞是有味 very tasty.
煞脚 the last sentence.
煞費苦心 went to a great amount of trouble.
5煞近 very near.
令人笑·煞 very laughable.
收煞 to conclude.
費煞工·夫 to take much trouble.

(b) **To sew a seam.**

煞䙊 to sew a seam.

歃 4.5. **To smear the mouth with the blood of a victim when taking an oath. Also read** *ch'a*^{4}.
5618

翣 4.5. **Feathers used to adorn coffins. Large wooden fan carried in a procession. A fan.**
5619

霎 4.5. **An instant. Passing; for a season. Also read** *sa*^{5}.
5620

霎時 momentarily; for a little while.
霎然間 in a moment; suddenly.
霎眼 to dazzle the eyes.
霎雨 a passing shower.
霎霎雨聲 the sound of rain.

SHAI. (ㄕㄞ)

篩 簁 簛 1 **A sieve. To sift; to strain.**
5621

篩之 to sift.
篩·出粃糠 to sift the chaff—from the wheat.
篩·子 or 篩箕 a sieve.
篩沙器 sand-sifter
5篩管 sieve-vessel in plants.
篩籮 silk strainers.
篩米 to sift rice.
篩粉器 bolter for flour.
篩粉雨 a drizzling rain.
10篩糠狀 like a person sifting with a sieve—shaking with malaria.
篩酒 to strain wine; to pour out liquor.
篩錢板 a board with grooves for cash.
篩鑼 to beat a gong.
篩骨 the ethmoid bone.
15細篩 or 密篩 a fine sieve.

(a) **Read** *shih*^{1}. **A variety of bamboo.**

揌 1 **To strike; to beat. Inter. preceding.**
5622

揌鑼 to beat a gong.

曬 晒 4 **To dry in the sun; to dry. To get a sunstroke.**
5623

曬·不透 impervious to the sun's rays; not thoroughly dried.
曬乾 to dry in the sun.
曬暖 to bask in the sun.
曬棚 or 曬臺 a drying-terrace or frame, often erected on the house-top.
5曬糧·食 to dry grain in the sun.
曬衣·服 to sun garments.
曬迷·糊·了 to get a sunstroke.
曬陽 to sun oneself.
曬鹽 to evaporate salt.
10曬黑 sunburnt.
吹曬 to dry in the wind.
生曬 to dry fresh fruit.

灑 洒 3 **To sprinkle; to scatter; to throw. Free. Distinguish 酒 No. 1208. Pron.** *sa*^{3}.
5624

灑掃應對 sprinkling, sweeping, and answering questions—the earlier steps in education.
灑水 to sprinkle water.
灑灑 continuous.
灑淚 to shed tears.
5灑濕衣 to get the clothing wet with rain.
灑灰·水 to whitewash.
灑綉衣 embroidered robes.
灑◦脫 untrammelled; reckless; free and easy.
灑花 flowered—as material.
10灑落 free, vigorous brushwork—in paintings.

灑 金 sprinkled with gold—as fancy paper.
灑 釣 to cast a hook.

(a) The second form is also read *hsi³*. To wipe away. Similar to 洗.

灑 濯 其 心 to cleanse the heart.
願 比 死 者 一 灑 之 I wish to wipe away (the shame) on the account of my departed predecessors.

(b) Read *hsin⁴*. To shiver. Alarmed.

灑 灑 時 寒 shivering with the cold.
灑 然 alarmed.

(c) Read *hsien⁴*. Grave and dignified.

色 灑 如 也 with a grave countenance.

(d) Read *ts'ui³*. Lofty. New and fresh.

新 臺 有 灑 high and fine is the new terrace.

SHAN.　(ㄕㄢ)

彡 ¹ Feathers; streaky. Radical 59.
5625

杉 ¹ A name given to various species of fir and pine. Also read *sha¹*.
5626

杉 木 deal; pine-boards.
杉 木 靈 牌 an ancestral tablet made of pine—worthless.
杉 板 sometimes written for 三 板 a small boat.
杉 桴 a raft.
杉 樹 *Cunninghamia sinensis*; also the *Cryptomeria*.

衫 ¹ A shirt; a robe; a gown.
5627

衫 裙 gown and skirt—women's clothes.
汗 衫 under-shirt.
衣 衫 garments generally.
長 衫 a long gown. = 5943.263.

删 ¹ To cut; to cancel; to efface. To geld.
5628

删 削 to pare off.
删 去 to expunge.
删 改 to erase and alter; to revise.
删 減 or 删 繁 to abridge.
⁵删 潤 to revise and polish up—literary efforts.
删 牲 口 to geld animals.
删 節 to expunge—certain portions of books.
删 節 號 marks to indicate ellipsis....
删 簡 to condense.
¹⁰删 荒 to clear away a rank growth of weeds.
删 訂 to revise.
删 詩 書 定 禮 樂 he edited the odes and settled the Ritual and Music.
删 鐮 刀 a sickle; a pruning knife.
删 除 to expunge.

潸 ¹ To weep.
5629

山 ¹ A mountain, a hill. A range of mountains. An island. A grave. Radical 46.
5630

山 丹 the lily.
山 人 wild tribes; a mountaineer; a recluse or hermit.
山 兔 the Mongolian hare.
山 兜 a mountain-chair.
⁵山 公 monkeys.
山 勢 the appearance of a mountain.
山 口 or 山 峽 a mountain pass.
山 向 aspects of a grave according to geomancy.
山 君 the ruler of the hills—a tiger.
¹⁰山 呼 萬 歲 three kotows and three hails to the emperor.
山 嘴 子 the spur of a hill.
山 地 hilly country.
山 坡 the slope of a hill; a declivity.
山 堂 水 殿 煙 寺 相 望 the scenery of the mountains, streams, and mists looked like magnificent architecture.
¹⁵山 塢 waste places on a hill.

山 外 主 義 ultra-montanism.
山 妻 my wife.
山 客 a mountaineer; the rhododendron.
山 寨 a hill fortress for temporary defence.
²⁰山 居 to dwell in retirement.
山 岳 mountain peaks.
山 崗 a peak; a summit.
山 崖 a precipice; a ledge.
山 崩 a land-slide.
²⁵山 嵐 mountain mist.
山 嶽 or 山 峯 a lofty mountain peak.
山 嶺 a range of mountains; a pass; the highest peak of a range.
山 巖 a cliff.
山 川 or 山 河 or 江 山 hills and streams; the country; one's country. China.
³⁰山 川 其 舍 諸 Would the gods of the hills and streams reject it?
山 左 or 山 右 terms for Shantung and Shansi respectively, having reference to Peking.
山 庭 a nose with a high bridge.
山 庭 異 表 a lucky physiognomy.
山 徑 mountain path.
³⁵山 得 有 半 mountains and hills occupied half the area of the city.
山 斗 an exemplar,—one who is looked up to like a mountain or the Dipper.
山 東 the Province of Shantung.
山 林 a mountain grove; a wooded hill; retreat of a recluse.
山 梁 the crest of a hill—a prostitute, from:—山 梁 雌 雉 the pheasant on the crest of the hill—these women being sometimes called pheasants.
⁴⁰山 椒 the peak of a hill.
山 楂 or 山 裏 紅 or 紅 菓 子 the hill haw.
山 楂 糕 jelly made from hill haws.
山 歌 rustic songs; boatmen's songs.
山 民 those who live in the hills; recluses.
⁴⁵山 氣 mountain mists.
山 水 landscape; prospect.
山 水 之 費 travelling expenses.
山 水 畫 landscape painting.
山 水 相 逢 to meet in the course of travels.

50 山河國寶 hills and rivers are national treasures.
山河日月 (an exemplar, to be looked up to as) the hills, the sun or the moon.
山河破裂 the country is ruined.
山洞 or 山穴 or 山窟 caves.
山海關 Shanhaikwan—a town near which the Great Wall touches the coast; the Newchwang Customs.
55 山澗 a mountain torrent.
山珍海錯 delicacies from the hills and seas.
山用鐵路 mountain railway.
山畫眉 the song-thrush.
山百合 *Lilium auratum.*
60 山盟海誓 a solemn oath.
山碓 mill for hulling grain, worked by a mountain stream.
山祇 the god of the hills.
山禽 wild fowl.
山窮水盡之境 circumstances of extreme need.
65 山立 to stand erect like the hills.
山節藻梲 he carved hills on the pillars and duckweed on the joists—extravagance.
山系 mountain system.
山羊 goats.
山脊 a mountain ridge.
70 山脈 a mountain range; a watershed.
山脚[3] or 山根 the base of a hill.
山腰 or 山腹 half-way up a hill.
山芋 or 地瓜 the sweet potato.
山茶 wild tea.
75 山莊 a home in the hills; a country house; burying ground for strangers.
山·藥 the yam—*Dioscorea sativa,* etc. (-·*yao*)
山蠶 the wild silk-worm.
山·西 the Province of Shansi.
山谷 a valley; a ravine.
80 山貨 wood and bamboo-ware—baskets, tubs, etc.
山路 mountain paths.
山都 a monkey; a mountain deity.
山門 Buddhist monastery or temple.
山野 mountain wilds; rustic; unsophisticated.
85 山陵 hills, mounds; grave of an emperor.
山隘 a mountain pass.
山頂 or 山頭 or 山尖 a mountain peak or hilltop.
山高水長 the hills are high and the rivers long—an enduring reputation.
山鬼 the spirit of the hills.
90 山鴉 the white-necked crow.
山鷄 the ringed pheasant.
名山 famous mountains or famous temples on mountains.
孤山 a solitary peak.
童山 a hill without vegetation.
95 開山 to open up hills for cultivation; to make a grave.

汕[4] **A basket for catching fish.**
5631

汕頭 Swatow.

疝[4] **Rupture; hernia.**
5632

疝氣 hernia; stricture.
小腸疝氣 hernia.
腎囊疝氣 scrotal hernia.
心疝 angina pectoris.

舢[1] **A small boat.**
5633

舢板 or 三板 a sampan or small boat.

訕[1.4.] **To abuse; to revile.**
5634

訕上 to revile superiors.
訕言 slander; backbiting.
訕謗 to backbite.

芟 / **剗**[1] **To mow; to cut down. scythe. Sometimes u.f. 剷 No. 5628.**
5635

芟刀 a scythe.
芟割 to cut down.
芟夷 to exterminate.
芟草除根 to exterminate root and branch.
芟薙 to mow.
芟鋤 to root out.
芟除 to exterminate.

摻[1] **A delicate hand; tapering; beautiful. Also read** *sien*[3]
5636

摻摻女手 the bride's delicate fingers.

(a) **Read** *shan*[3]. **To grasp.**

摻去 to expurgate.
摻執 to grasp.

(b) **Read** *ts'an*[1]. **To mix; to adulterate.**

摻假 to adulterate.
摻和 to blend together—as ingredients.
摻雜 to mix up; to adulterate.

陝[3] **Mountain passes. The Province of Shensi.**
5637

陝·西 Shensi Province.
陝甘 Shensi and Kansu.

閃[3] **To flash, as lightning. A flash.**
5638

閃亮 gleaming; early dawn.
閃亮·的刀 a glittering sword.
閃光 a flash.
閃光燈 flash-light.
5 閃光電筒 electric flash-torch.
閃爍 in glimpses; flashing.
閃眼 to dazzle the eyes.
閃綢 shot silk.
閃見 to see for an instant.
10 閃射 to flash; to gleam.
閃閃 twinkling.
閃電 lightning; to flash.
打閃 the lightning flashes.

(a) **To evade; to dodge; to shun.**

閃·了脚 to slip.
閃在一邊 to slip to one side; to avoid a person.
閃腰 to twist the back.
閃道 Clear the way!
5 閃避 to dodge; to move out of the way.
閃閃縮縮 dodging in and out.
閃·開·點兒 get on one side; move out of the way a little.

掞[4] **Easy, quiet, smooth.**
5639

掞舒 comfortable; in repose.

睒³ To glance at; to peep. Glittering, flashing.
5640

睒 目 to take a look at.
睒 睒 lustrous; glittering.
太 白 睒 睒 How brightly Venus shines!

苫¹ To cover with grass; to thatch. A straw mat. Also read *chan⁴*.
5641

苫 塊 之 戚 the sorrow of the clod and the mat—alluding to the death of a parent.
苫 次 in mourning for parents.
在 苫 in mourning.

扇⁴ A fan. The leaf of a door. N. A. Read *shan¹* when used as a verb.
5642

扇 墜 兒 a pendant from a fan-case.
扇·子 or 一 把 扇 a fan.
扇 形 窗 a fan-light.
扇 絡 or 扇 套 子 a case for a fan.
⁵扇 袋 a case for a fan.
扇 車 a winnowing machine.
扇 面·子 the covering of a fan.
扇 骨·子 the framework of a fan.
單 扇 門 a single-leaf door.
¹⁰圓 扇 a round fan.
打 扇 to use a fan.
秋 後 扇 a fan after the autumn —discarded; used of a deserted wife.
紗 扇 a gauze fan.
紙 扇 or 摺 扇 a folding fan.
¹⁵羽 扇 or 翮 扇 a feather fan.
芭 蕉 扇 palm-leaf fans.
電 扇 electric fan.
風 扇 a punkah.

搧¹ To fan; to strike.
5643

搧 一 搧 fan it a little.
搧 動 to agitate; to stir up.
搧 展 to flap the wings.
搧 扇 to fan with a fan.
搧 打 to flog.
搧·開·了 brush it aside.
搧 風 to move the air.

煽¹ To excite. To delude. To blaze up; to fan into a flame.
5644

煽 亂 to stir up revolt.
煽 亂 爭 端 to arouse controversy.
煽 動 to incite; to instigate.
煽 動·了 世·界 stirred the whole world.
⁵煽 動 平 民 to arouse the masses.
煽 動 者 or 煽 惑 者 agitators.
受 煽 動 之 害 injured through agitators.
煽 惑 to deceive.
煽 惑 人 心 to agitate the minds of the people; to cause suspicion.
煽 火 to light a fire.

諞⁴ To beguile; to cajole.
5645

騗⁴ To geld a horse or ass, etc.
5646

騗 樹 to graft a tree.
騗 牯 a bullock.
騗 羊 a wether.
騗 馬 a gelding.
騗 鷄 a capon.

墠⁴ A smooth hard spot made level for sacrifices.
5647

嬋² Beautiful; graceful. Also read *ch'an²*.
5648

嬋 娟 attractive; lady-like; graceful; beautiful; pretty.
嬋 連 relatives; of the same clan.

燀³ To make a fire.
5649

禪² To sit in abstracted contemplation, as the Buddhists do. Contemplation, abstraction, meditation. Pron. *chan²*.
5650

禪 堂 room in Buddhist monastery set apart for meditation.
禪 定 in fixed contemplation.
禪 師 Buddhist priests.
禪 廟 or 禪 林 a Buddhist temple.
⁵禪 延 the fabled palace of Indra on Mt. Meru.

禪 心 an abstracted mind.
禪 機 Buddhist spells.
禪 法 Buddhism.
禪 經 Buddhist scriptures.
¹⁰禪 舍 rooms in a temple.
禪 那 or 定 禪 a state of abstraction.
參 禪 to enter into meditation— to become a Buddhist priest.
坐 禪 to sit in abstraction.

(a) Read *shan⁴*. To level an area for an altar. To sacrifice to the hills and the fountains. To abdicate.

禪 以 帝 位 to abdicate.
禪 代 the succession to the throne.
禪 位 to resign the throne.
禪 讓 to abdicate.

蟬² The cicada or broad locust. Also read *ch'an²*.
5651

蟬 不 知 雪 the cicada knows nothing of snow—ignorance.
蟬 吟 or 蟬 噪 the chirp of the cicada.
蟬 聯 a pair of scrolls; connected.
蟬 脫 the exuviæ of the cicada.
蟬 鬢 hair on the temples dressed so as to resemble the eyes of the cicada.
寒 蟬 a cicada in cold weather— dumb and silent.

嬗⁴ Changes and succession. Inter. 禪 No. 5650-A.
5652

嬗 代 the succession to the throne.
相 嬗 succession.

擅⁴ To act on one's own responsibility; to act without authority. To dare.
5653

擅 便 to consult one's own convenience only.
擅 利 to monopolize.
擅 加 to make unauthorized additions.
擅 取 to take without authority; to arrogate.
⁵擅 呼 聖 諱 to dare to use the private name of the emperor.
擅 塲 monopolizing the arena; having special talents so that others have no chance.

擅 定 to take upon oneself to decide.

擅 專 to usurp power; to act on one's own authority; to presume to.

擅 敢 to have the presumption to.

10擅 權 to assume authority.

擅 殺 to slay without authority.

擅 用 to use on one's own account.

擅 用 私 刑 to take the law into one's own hands.

擅 自 作 主 to act without authority.

15擅 自 專 權 to usurp authority.

擅 自 辦 事 to dare to act on one's own authority.

擅 行 to act without authority.

擅 進 to enter without leave.

擅 違 wilful transgression.

20擅 長² skilled; versed in.

擅 離 職 守 to leave one's official post without authority to do so.

澶² Still water.
5654

澶 淵 name of a branch of the River Hwai.

(a) Read *tan*⁴. Sluggish.

澶 漫 vast—as an expanse of water.

禪⁴ To sacrifice to heaven.
5655 The imperial power, as only the emperor was allowed to offer these sacrifices.

讓 禪 to resign the imperial authority.

羶 }¹
羴 } The rank odour of sheep or goats; frowzy.
5656

羶 氣 musty; a rank odour.

羶 腥 the rank smell of fresh meat or fish.

羣 蟻 附 羶 swarms of ants attach themselves to what is rank and foul—used fig.

善⁴ Good, virtuous. Apt, expert. Familiar with. Whole.
5657 To perfect, to make good.

善 事 a good act; a virtuous deed.

善 人 good people.

善 俗 to reform popular customs.

善 價 a good price.

5善 勸 good exhortations.

善 哭 to cry easily.

善 善 靜 靜 fair and serene—as the sky.

善 堂 a benevolent institution; a charity.

善 士 an eminent scholar; a good man.

10善 始 善 終 a good beginning makes a good ending.

善 居 室 managed his household well.

善 形 容 聖 人 處 a happy sketch of the manners of the Sage.

善 待 to treat well.

善 後 reconstruction; to supplement a set of rules, to make good what comes after.

15善 後 事 宜 negotiations for rehabilitation or for remedying the conditions.

善 後 會 議 reconstruction conference.

善 後 條 約 or 善 後 章 程 the rules appended to the tariff.

善 後 策 remedial measures.

善 心 good-hearted.

20善 性 a good disposition.

善 意 good intention; goodwill.

善 感 good impulses.

善 惡 good and evil.

善 戰 者 服 上 刑 the skilful fighters should endure the highest punishment.

25善 手 a good hand—an expert.

善 政 good government.

善 敗 success and failure.

善 於 應⁴對 good at retort.

善 於 施 教 skilful in imparting knowledge.

30善 於 敎 導 apt in giving instruction.

善 於 說 辭 skilful at making a story sound well; able to speak without giving offence.

善 於 辦 事 a good manager.

善 書 good books; moral tracts.

善 會 a charitable organization.

35善 會 交 友 apt to make friends.

善 有 善 報 goodness has a good recompense.

善 果 good fruit; outcome of a good life.

善 棍 one who pretends to charitable deeds in order to gain his own ends.

善 欲 人 知 不 是 眞 善 good deeds done for mere show are not really good.

40善 歲 a prosperous year.

善 死 or 善 終 a peaceful end.

善 氣 迎 人 to meet a man with warmth of feeling.

善 法 a clever scheme; a good plan.

善 治 good administration; a good cure for.

45善 爲⁴我 辭 kindly make my apologies.

善 理 to manage well.

善 用 to make good use of.

善 男 信 女 Buddhist devotees—good men and believing women.

善 策 a clever scheme; a good plan or policy.

50善 能 well able to.

善 舉 a good move; a good act; virtuous deeds.

善 良 well-disposed; loyal; good.

善 處³逆 境 to make the best of a bad job.

善 行⁴ good actions.

55善 記 well able to remember things.

善 謀 a good device; a clever scheme.

善 走 good at walking.

善 遣 to dismiss a person who is not wanted, with good words.

善 門 a philanthropic family.

60善 門 難 開 it is difficult to begin to dispense charity—because one cannot leave off easily.

善 類 loyal, good citizens.

善 飯 having a large appetite.

善 馬 a quiet horse.

僞 善 hypocrisy.

65完 善 thorough; whole; perfect.

爲²善 to do good.

相⁴善 familiar with; acquainted.

行 善 to perform acts of merit; to give to charitable causes.

面 善 (your) face looks familiar.

(a) Read *shan*³. To approve.

善 善 to approve the good.

帝 善 其 言 the emperor approved his words.

繕⁴ To mend. To copy; to write out.
5658

繕 修 to put in repair; to be prepared.

繕 備 or 修 繕 to put in repair; to make ready.

繕 具 節 略 write out and submit a summary.

繕 寫 文 件 copying of documents.

⁵繕 就 effected.

繕 抄 to write out; to transcribe.

繕 正 to correct and copy; to make a fair copy.

繕 治 宮 館 prepared residences.

繕 立 to write out; to place on record; to note—as a protest.

¹⁰繕 錄 to transcribe; to write out.

膳
饍
5659
⁴ Provisions; viands; savoury food; delicacies.

膳 夫 授 祭 the cook would bring in the sacrifice.

膳 宿 生 boarding pupils.

膳 宿 費 charge for board and lodging.

膳 廳 dining hall.

⁵膳 房 the imperial kitchen; dining room.

膳 正 or 膳 長 (chang³) a king's butler; the chief cook.

膳 費 fees for board.

膳 饌 delicacies; good food.

午 膳 tiffin; midday meal.

¹⁰早 膳 breakfast.

晚 膳 evening meal; supper.

5660
⁴ The earthworm.

鄯
5661
⁴ Name of a district in Kansu under the T'ang dynasty. A country situated in what is now Sinkiang.

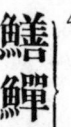
5662

鱔 籠 an eel-pot.

黃 鱔 the small yellow eel.

蟾
5663
⁴ A striped toad, supposed to live in the moon. The moon. Also read ch'an².

蟾 光 moonlight.

蟾 兔 "the man in the moon"—a hare is supposed to live there, hence the black marks.

蟾 宮 the moon.

蟾 彩 moonlight.

⁵蟾 蜍 the toad that lives in the moon.

蟾 輪 the moon.

蟾 酥 a juice from the warts of a toad—used for medicine.

蟾 魄 the moon.

贍
5664
⁴ To give; to supply; to aid. To be sufficient for.
Distinguish 151, 6047.

贍 助 to supply deficiencies.

贍 補 to help the poor.

贍 貧 to meet the needs of the poor.

贍 身 support for oneself.

贍 逸 fresh and vigorous — of literary composition.

力 不 贍 也 not having sufficient strength.

SHANG.　(ㄕㄤ)

剔
5665
¹ To injure; to wound.

傷
5666
¹ To injure; to wound. To grieve. Distressed.

傷 亡 to die of wounds.

傷 亡 數 number of casualties.

傷 亡 枕 藉 the dead and wounded were lying around on each other.

傷 元 氣 debilitating.

⁵傷 創 a wound.

傷 勢 無 大 礙 not injured to any great extent.

傷 化 injurious to public morals.

傷 及 父 母 to cause grief to parents.

傷 口 the mouth of a wound.

¹⁰傷 名 to injure one's reputation.

傷 命 to kill; mortal; fatal.

傷 和 氣 to wound good feeling.

傷 壞 to spoil; to ruin.

傷 害 to wound.

¹⁵傷 寒 (病) typhoid fever.

傷 弓 之 鳥 the bird that has been injured by the bow—similar to:—"the burnt child dreads the fire."

傷 心 grieved; heart-broken.

傷 心 事 a heart-breaking affair.

傷 性 to lose one's life.

²⁰傷 情 grieved; to wound the feelings; wounded in spirit.

傷 感 emotional; deeply moved; touched in heart.

傷 感·情 to hurt the feelings.

傷 感·情·的 光。景 touching circumstances.

傷 慘 sad; tragic; mournful.

²⁵傷·掉 to injure.

傷 損 to injure; to damage.

傷 時 to lament over (the morals of) the times.

傷 暑 to suffer from the heat.

傷 殘 支 體 to maim.

³⁰傷 生 injurious to life.

傷 病 to be ill.

傷 痕 scars of wounds.

傷 痛 the pain of a wound; to mourn.

傷 科 the treatment of injuries, as a department in surgery.

³⁵傷 老 to grieve over old age coming on.

傷 胎 to injure a pregnant womb.

傷 臉 to injure one's reputation.

傷 處 the wounded place; wounds.

傷 財 to waste money or property.

⁴⁰傷·起 心 來 to begin to feel grieved

傷 身 to wound the body: to injure the health.

傷 風 to catch a cold.

傷 風 化 a breach of morality.

傷 風 敗 俗 injurious to public morality.

⁴⁵傷 風 時 症 influenza.

何 傷 What does it matter? What objection is there to it?

打 傷 to injure by a blow.

無 傷 of no consequence; no matter; no hurt.

殤
5667
¹ To die young; to die.

下 殤 to die between the ages of eight and eleven.

中 殤 to die between the ages of twelve and fifteen.

夭 殤 or 短 殤 premature death.

無 服 之 殤 death (before the age

of eight) for which no mourning is worn.

長 殤 to die between the ages of
sixteen and nineteen.

觴¹ A goblet. A feast.
Also read *ch'ang*².
5668

傳 觴 to circulate the wine-cup.

潔 觴 or 滌 觴 to wash the cups
—to prepare for a feast.

稱 觴 to pledge.

舉 觴 to raise the goblet—to drink.

酒 觴 a wine-cup.

上⁴ Above. Supreme. Top,
summit; on, above. First;
5669 best. Previous, before.

上 丁 the day which has the *ting*
character, in the first decade of
the 2nd and 8th lunar months.

上 上 or 頂 上 the best quality;
tiptop.

上 下 above and below; superior
and inferior; up and down;
about; more or less; on the one
hand and on the other hand;
heaven and earth; ruler and
people; to go up and come
down, etc.

五 百 人 上 下   about five
hundred persons.

⁵上 下 其 手 to distort facts to
suit one's private ends—from a
story of a man who made one
statement with his hand raised,
and another with it down.

上 下 文 the context.

上 下 畫 a picture that can be inverted.

上 下 通 氣 upper and lower
classes in accord.

不 相 上 下 not much differ-
ence between them.

¹⁰自 上 而 下 from top to bottom; from the ruler down-
wards.

上 世 remote antiquity.

上 中 下 top, middle, bottom;
best, medium, inferior; first,
second, third.

上 乘 the Great Conveyance.
(*Budd.*). *See* No. 398-E.

上 人 a superior, as parents, em-
ployers, etc. 上 人 monk.

¹⁵上 代 a former generation.

上 來 to come up—an auxiliary
verb.

喘 不 上 氣 來 cannot get
my breath.

想 不 上 來 cannot call it to
mind.

拉 上 來 haul it up.

²⁰說 不 上 來 he cannot pro-
nounce it; cannot get the
words out.

上 元 the first full moon or the
fifteenth of the first lunar
month.

上 冬 last winter.

上 瀆 to worry and annoy a
superior.

上 列 the upper row.

²⁵上 午 noon; the forenoon.

上 半 天 the forenoon.

上 半 夜 before midnight.

上 半 截 the upper half.

上 古 remote antiquity.

³⁰上 司 or 上 憲 former designation of government officials in
high positions.

上 吐 下 瀉 vomiting and
purging.

上 告 to appeal to a higher court.

上 回 on a former occasion; the
previous occasion.

上 國 the capital; the sovereign
State of feudal kingdoms.

³⁵上 坐 the place of honour; take
the upper seat.

上 壓 力 upward pressure of
liquids.

上 士 superior officers; first sergeant.

上 壽 extreme old age—100 to
120 years. *See below*—B.16.

上 天 the heavens above. God.

⁴⁰上 天 下 地 the heavens above
and the earth beneath.

上 天 作 成 的 God's handiwork.

上 天 鑒 臨 I call God to witness.

上 如 揖 下 如 授 as high as
when making a bow, as low
as when giving anything to a
person—of the hands.

上 好 的 the best; first class;
superior quality.

⁴⁵上 官 your honour—used by
underlings.

上 客 distinguished guests.

上 尉 lieutenant commander—
navy; captain—army.

上 將 admiral; general; field-
marshal.

上 屆 a previous occasion, term.

⁵⁰上 巳 the 3rd of the 3rd lunar
month.

上 巳 被 除 washing—for sins—

on the 3rd of the 3rd lunar
month.

上 帝 the Supreme Ruler—God.
See below—A.

上 平 聲 the upper even tone in
Chinese speech.

上 年 former years; last year.

⁵⁵不 上 一 年 before a year had
elapsed.

上 庠 an ancient academy.

上 座 the upper seat.   「month.

上 弦 the first quarter of the lunar

上 絃 的 弓 a strung bow.

⁶⁰上 律 天 時 下 襲 水 土 he
conformed to the laws of
nature.

上 怒 the emperor was angry.

上 愚 an utter stupid.

上 房 the best room; the upper
room at the end of a Chinese
courtyard.

上 手 to begin; at the outset; a
higher seat; a head partner.

⁶⁵一 上 手 就 弄 錯 了 as
soon as he put his hand
to it he made a mess of it.

上 控 to appeal to a higher court.

上 方 Heaven; high places.

上 日 the other day; the first day.

上 旬 the first decade of a month.

⁷⁰上 早 very early.

上 智 the Sage.

上 月 last month.

不 上 一 月 before a month
had elapsed.

上 柱 國 ancient title of great
honour for a meritorious
statesman.

⁷⁵上 校 captain — navy; colonel —
army.

上 梁 不 正 下 梁 歪 if the upper
beam is crooked the lower ones
are out of plumb—example of
those in high places.

上 次 on a previous occasion.

上 江 the Upper Yangtze.

上 江 下 江 the Upper and
Lower sections of Kiangnan—
i.e., Anhwei and Kiangsu respectively.

⁸⁰上 浮 力 buoyancy.

上 流 the upper reaches of a
stream.

上 流 社 會 the upper circles of
society.

上 海 or 上 洋 Shanghai.

上 浣 or 上 澣 the first decade
of the lunar month.

⁸⁵上 游 upper reaches of a river.

上 半 年 first six months of a year.

上 漏 下 濕 leaking above and wet beneath—uninhabitable.

上 無 道 揆 the rulers have no principles to consider.

上 玄 Heaven.

上 界 Heaven.

90 上 略 a portion omitted—as in a quotation, etc.

上 皇 father of the emperor; the late emperor.

皇 上 the emperor.

上 知 (*chih*⁴) 與 下 愚 不 移 the highest of the wise, and the lowest of the stupid cannot be altered.

上 禮 拜 last Sunday; last week.

95 上 禮 拜 四 last Thursday.

上 等 first-class.

上 等 人 a superior person.

上 等 牌 子 a superior brand.

上 節 last term or quarter.

100 上 算 for a thing to pay; a good speculation.

不 見 得 上 算 there was no profit in it.

上 級 superior grades; superior classes.

上 級 官 廳 the higher authorities.

上 結 last term or quarter.

105 上 緊 promptly; without delay; urgently.

上 者 爲 營 窟 in the high parts they made caves to dwell in.

上 聯 the first of a pair of scrolls.

上 肉 superior quality of meat.

上 肢 the arms; upper limbs.

110 上 色 the best quality. (-*s*³⁴)

上 蒼 the firmament; heaven.

上 虛 下 實 hypothesis — in composition.

上 行 下 效 the doings of superiors are imitated by inferiors.

上 行 星 the four superior planets, i.e., those outside the earth's orbit.

115 上 衣 upper garments.

上 訴 to appeal to a higher court; to state to a superior.

上 訴 權 right of appeal.

上 諭 an imperial decree.

上 議 院 Upper House or Senate.

120 上 賞 1st prize.

上 輩 earlier generation; one's seniors.

上 達 to notify; for the information of.

上 門 牙 the upper incisors.

上 面 or 上 邊 the upper surface; the top; above; on the one hand.

125 上 頭 above; the top of; the upper circles. *See below*— B.60.

上 風 the superior wind which gives one an advantage, as in sailing or shooting, etc.

佔 上 風 to hold the position of advantage.

由 上 風 來 了 coming up before a wind.

上 首 the place of honour.

130 上 駟 a fine horse—a man of superior talents and abilities, able to bear heavy responsibilities.

君 上 or 主 上 the emperor.

天·上 in heaven.

河 上 by the river.

看·上 to take a fancy to.

135 經·上 in the classics.

聖 上 the emperor.

街·上 on the street.

身·上 on the person.

(a) Quotations, etc., to illustrate the meaning and application of 上 帝—above—52.

See 皇 No. 2283-5, 17, 26-28.
    玄 No. 2881-13.
    類 No. 4244-B.
    帝 No. 6204-32, 35ff.

上 帝 之 耿 命 the bright ordinance of the Supreme.

上 帝 垂 恩 諸 祉 the Supreme bends down in grace and manifold blessing.

上 帝 天 也 *Shangti* is Heaven.

上 帝 居 歆 The Supreme (God) well pleased, smells the sweet savour.

5 上 帝 是 依 The Supreme regarded her with favour.

上 帝 時 歆 The Supreme (God) will always enjoy your offerings.

上 帝 引 逸 The Supreme guideth to rest.

上 帝 臨 女 "God is near you."

克 配 上 帝 they could appear before The Supreme (God); explained here as 天 之 主 宰 The Lord of Heaven.

10 則 惟 上 帝 降 格 whereupon

The Supreme visited him with corrections.

夢 上 帝 賚 以 良 弼 in a dream The Supreme bestowed on him an able and virtuous helper.

天 神 之 大 者 曰 昊 天 上 帝 The Great One among the gods in heaven is called, "The Sovereign on High of the Vast Heavens."

姜 嫄 與 帝 禋 上 帝 而 生 棄 *Chiang Yüan* together with the Emperor sacrificed to The Supreme and gave birth to *Ch'i.*

弗 事 上 帝 神 祇 "not serving God nor the spirits of Heaven and Earth." *Giles.*

15 惟 上 帝 不 常, 作 善 降 之 百 祥, 作 不 善 降 之 百 殃. (the favour of) The Supreme is not invariable; on the good He sends down manifold blessings, but on the evil manifold calamities.

惟 時 上 帝 不 保 wherefore The Supreme no longer protected him.

我 畏 上 帝 不 敢 不 正 "I fear God, and dare not but rectify" —the conditions by punishing him.

敢 祗 承 上 帝 以 遏 亂 略 dare to approach The Supreme in order to put an end to disorderly ways.

明 昭 上 帝 迄 用 康 年 The Bright and Glorious Supreme will give us a good year.

20 昭 事 上 帝 聿 懷 多 福 (*Wên Wang*) served The Supreme with intelligence and secured abundant blessings.

玉 皇 上 帝 "The Gemmeous Sovereign on High"—title under which a favourite court magician was deified by the Emperor *Hui Tsung,* (A.D. 1101—1125).

皆 上 帝 諸 神 之 賜 (all these blessings) are gift of The Supreme and all the gods.

祀 上 帝, 接 萬 靈, 布 政 教 焉. (*Huangti*) sacrificed to the Supreme, gathered the populace together, and diffused among them the principles of government and religion.

雖有惡人齋戒沐浴則可以祀上帝 though a man be wicked, yet if he adjust his thoughts, fast, and bathe, he may sacrifice to The Supreme. (God).

[25]郊之神, 莫尊于上帝 of the gods worshipped at the border sacrifice none are higher than *Shangti*. See also 郊 No. 714-A. 5.

(b) Read *shang*[3]. To ascend; to go up; to go to; to go on. To send to. To pay in. This rising tone is not used except in the Cantonese dialect.

上·上門 bolt the door.
上·不上 cannot put the thing on —as a hammer-head, etc.
上·不來 he cannot come up.
上·不去 cannot ascend it; cannot go up.
[5]上·不得臺盤 cannot go on the stage—said of a person unfit for the task.
上·了年紀 getting on in years.
上京 to go to the capital.
上任 to enter on the duties of an office; to take up an official appointment.
上供 to offer in worship.
[10]上凍 to freeze.
上前 to go on in front; to go ahead.
上·去下·來 ascending and descending.
上吊 to hang oneself.
上坡 to ascend a slope.
[15]上場瘟 stage-fever.
上壽 to attend or celebrate a person's birthday. See above —38.
上天 to ascend to heaven.
上天無路, 入地無門 no road by which to ascend to heaven, no door by which to enter the earth—in desperate straits.
上學 to go to school.
[20]上山 to go up a hill; silkworms going on to the frame for spinning.
上岸 to go ashore.
上岸准單 landing permit.
上岸碼頭 a landing-stage.
上岸費 landing charges.
[25]上工 to begin work; to go to work.

上市 to go to market.
上店門 to put up the shutters; to shut up shop. See below— B. 29.
上本 to present a memorial.
上板 to go to press; to put up the shutters for the night.
[30]上樓 to go upstairs.
上水 to go up stream.
上水船 up-river boats—a dull, slow-going person.
上火 to get feverish.
上牀 to go to bed.
[35]上班 to go on duty.
上當 to be swindled; to be taken in.
上當學乖 when one has been deceived one learns to be wary.
上癮 to get a craving for—as opium or alcohol.
上稟 to send in a petition.
[40]上稅 to pay taxes; to pay duty.
上稅單 a duty memo.
上糧 to pay taxes in kind.
上聲 the rising tone or third tone in Chinese speech.
上膘 or 長 (*chang*[3]) 膘 to put into condition; plump.
[45]上臺 to go on the stage—to begin a thing.
上臺容易下臺難 it is easy to take a matter in hand, but not so easy to get rid of it.
上船 to go on board a vessel.
上街 to go on the street; to go to market. 上色 to color(-*shai*[3])
上衙門 to go to the magistrate's office.
[50]上表鏈 to wind up a watch.
上課 to commence lessons in a school; to have a class.
上轅 to go to the office of a superior.
上轎 or 升轎 to get into a sedan-chair.
上進 to make progress; to advance.
[55]上那兒去 Where are you going?
上銹 to rust; to get rusty.
上銀子 to pay taxes in money.
上門 to fasten a door; to go to a house.
上陣 to go into battle.
[60]上頭 to dress the hair—putting it up for marriage. See above —125.
上馬 to mount a horse.
上駛 to go up stream in a boat.

(c) To esteem. To exalt. A wish.

u.f. 尚 No. 5670.

上慎旃哉 May he be careful!
上親上齒 honour parents and esteem the aged.
上賢上貴 exalt the worthy and honour the honourable.
上首功 to give promotion to those soldiers who brought in the head of an enemy.

尚[4] Still; yet; and besides; in addition to. To add, to append to.
5670

尚不可知也 we cannot tell yet.
尚不滿意 still unsatisfied.
尚且 still; however; for all that.
尚係舊式 still following the old pattern.
[5]尚可 still possible.
尚在兩可 still a matter of doubt.
尚屬平允 may still be considered as fair and just.
尚屬疑問 still a matter of doubt.
尚屬緩慢 the advance is but slow.
[10]尚希 still hopes....
尚有 still there is....
尚有典刑 there still remain the laws and the penalties.
尚未妥當 not yet satisfactorily settled.
尚未能預知 cannot yet foretell.
[15]尚為周到 may still be considered as complete.
尚祈 and he would beg....
尚能 still able to....
尚衣盛服 dressed in their best.
尚詳洽 clear and satisfactory enough.
[20]尚遠之又遠 still farther off than ever.
尚還 still; as before.
尚須稍待 must have a little patience.
衣錦尚絅 she puts a plain, single garment over her embroidered robes.

(a) To honour; to esteem. To surpass.

尚主 or 尚公主 to wed a

princess—as she is of high rank, she is to be honoured, therefore 娶 is not used.

尚 享 at the end of a prayer Let this be accepted! Mayest thou enjoy this!

尚 其 前 者 esteem the former.

尚 勇 to esteem valour.

⁵尚 姓 What is your honoured surname?

尚 年 to respect old age.

尚 德 to respect virtue.

尚 心 to set the mind on.

尚 志 to aspire to.

¹⁰尚 武 bellicose.

尚 武 精 神 militarism; to encourage a military spirit.

尚 節 儉 to set store by economy.

尚 繁 華 to love pomp and vanity.

尚 義 to love uprightness.

¹⁵尚 論 fond of discussion; to praise. See below—B. 1.

尚 赤 尚 黑 to esteem red or to esteem black.

尚 饗 deign to accept this offering—said at the end of prayers to the gods. See above—A. 2.

尚 齒 to esteem the aged.

俗 尚 prevailing fashions or customs.

²⁰好 仁 者 無 以 尚 之 he who loves virtue will not regard anything as superior to it.

相 尚 mutual rivalry.

自 尚 其 功 praises his own deeds.

(b) To ascend. To go to. To proceed.

尚 論 古 人 he proceeds to discuss the ancients.

是 尚 友 也 this is to go and make friends—of the men of old.

舜 尚 見 帝 Shun went up and saw the emperor.

(c) To be in charge of, as a chamberlain.

尚 冠, 尚 食, 尚 沐, 尚 席, 尚 書, 尚 衣. officers in the imperial household—lords-in-waiting.

尚 方 official apothecary.

尚 方 令 persons who make things "by appointment."

尚 書 the Canons of Yao and Shun—the Book of History; high officials in ancient dynasties.

⁵尚 書 史 Grand Historiographer of the Chou dynasty.

尚 書 郎 Secretary of State.

六 部 尚·書 Presidents of the former Six Boards of State.

尚 衣 ancient office—keeper of the robes; the imperial robes.

(d) Used like 倘 or 徜.

尚 佯 to and fro; hesitating; unsteady.

裳 ² Clothes; garments, especially the lower ones.
5671 Also read ch'ang².

衣·裳 garments generally.

(a) Beautiful appearance.

裳 裳 者 華 How beautiful are the flowers! (ch'ang²-)

賞 ³ To reward, to grant, to bestow, to give to an inferior. Rewards. To praise. An award.
5672

賞 以 勸 善 to reward in order to stimulate virtue.

賞 以 酒 肉 presented him with wine and meats.

賞 假 (chia⁴) to grant leave of absence.

賞 功 or 賞 勞 to reward meritorious service.

⁵賞 勳 章 to award a decoration.

賞 品 a prize.

賞 善 罰 惡 reward the good and punish the evil.

賞 封 a present given to children or to servants.

賞 帖 a placard offering a reward.

¹⁰賞 收 to condescend to accept.

賞 格 a reward; bounty given to troops.

出 賞 格 to offer a reward.

賞 牌 a prize-medal; a decoration.

賞 筵 to give an entertainment.

¹⁵賞 給 to bestow; gifts; to bestow a reward.

賞 罰 在 我 recompense is Mine.

賞 臉 to favour with one's presence; to condescend; to give face to.

賞 謝 花 紅 to pay the reward offered.

賞 賚 to reward; a reward.

²⁰賞 賜 to bestow gifts; to bestow; to give rewards; a gift.

賞 還 be so good as to return—something lent.

賞 銀 牌 to distribute silver medals.

賞 錢 to bestow money; 賞·錢 tips.

賞 鑒 to bestow a glance on. See below—A. 8.

²⁵賞 首 winner of the first prize.

得 賞 to take the prize.

恩 賞 a gracious award.

懸 賞 文 prize-essay.

懸 賞 百 元 to offer a reward of $100.

³⁰懸 賞 競 技 prize-fight.

捕 獲 賞 金 prize-money—for naval captures.

犒 賞 軍 士 to give bounties to troops.

(a) To enjoy; to appreciate.

賞 嘆 to regard with wonder.

賞 心 to take delight in.

賞 月 to enjoy the moonlight.

賞 玩 to enjoy oneself.

⁵賞 稱 to prize.

賞 花 to enjoy the flowers.

賞·識 to appreciate—as the qualities or kindness of another, or as literature; to prize.

賞 鑒 to appreciate; to criticize—as art. See above—24.

商 賚 ¹
5673

To discuss; to deliberate. Distinguish 商 No. 6209.

商 准 to agree to after consultation.

商 同 to confer with; joint deliberation.

商 定 to deliberate and decide; to come to a decision.

商 榷 to consult with; negotiations; to revise after consultation.

⁵商 擬 to propose to; to suggest.

商 明 to come to a clear understanding after consultation.

商 略 negotiations.

商 訂 to arrange; to settle on.

商·議 to deliberate; to consult; to talk over.

¹⁰商 議 中 under consideration.

商 議 定 了 definitely agreed upon.

商 辦 to consult and take action; to discuss ways and means.
商·量 or 商 酌 to deliberate; to consult.
商·量 停·當 satisfactorily arranged.
¹⁵協 商 to negotiate.
磋 商 to negotiate.

(a) Trade or commerce. A merchant. To trade.

商 事 business matters.
商 事 公 斷 處 trade arbitration office.
商 事 訴 訟 trade disputes.
商 人 or 商 戶 or 商 民 merchants.
⁵商 人 階 級 the merchant class.
商 價 不 定 fluctuation of prices.
商 價 騰 貴 appreciation of market prices.
商 務 commerce. 商 務 印 書 館*
商 務 參 贊 commercial attaché to a legation.
¹⁰商 務 局 Board of Trade.
商 務 日 衰 trade is daily declining.
商 務 條 約 commercial treaty.
商 品 goods; merchandise.
商 品 陳 列 所 show-room.
¹⁵商 團 volunteer corps organized by merchants for mutual protection.
商 埠 a port.
商 塲 emporium; a mart.
商 店 a shop; a business firm.
商 情 details of commerce; current rate.
²⁰商 戰 commercial war.
商 數 quotient. (arith.).
商 旅 or 客 商 travelling merchants.
商 旗 merchant-service flag.
商 會 Chamber of Commerce.
²⁵商 會 聯 合 會 Associated Chambers of Commerce.
商 會 長³ Chairman of the Chamber of Commerce.
商 本 capital for trading purposes.
商 業 business; trade, commerce.
商 業 中 心 點 commercial centre.
³⁰商 業 使 用 人 persons engaged in trade.
商 業 信 用 欵 commercial credits.
商 業 公 所 commercial guild or exchange.
* the Commercial Press.

商 業 同 盟 trust; syndicate.
商 業 地 理 commercial geography.
³⁵商 業 報 告 trade returns.
商 業 學 校 commercial school.
商 業 恐 慌 commercial crisis.
商 業 教 育 commercial education or training.
商 業 數 學 commercial arithmetic.
⁴⁰商 業 時 代 commercial age.
商 業 歷 史 history of commerce.
商 業 登 記 commercial registration.
商 業 社 會 commercial community.
商 業 組 合 a syndicate or corporation.
⁴⁵商 業 習 慣 trade usages.
商 業 調⁴ 度 business arrangements.
商 業 證 劵 business vouchers, etc.
商 業 通 信 or 商 業 書 札 commercial correspondence.
商 業 銀 行 Bank of Commerce.
⁵⁰商 業 關·係 business relationships.
商 標 trade-mark.
商 標 權 trade-mark privileges.
商 標 法 trade-mark regulations.
商 法 or 商 律 commercial law.
⁵⁵商 港 open ports.
商 用 航 空 事 業 commercial aviation.
商 用 略 字 commercial abbreviations.
商 界 commercial world.
商 科 Department of Commerce in a university.
⁶⁰商 競 commercial competition.
商 約 commercial treaty or agreement.
商 習 慣 trade usages.
商 股 shares.
商 船 mercantile marine.
⁶⁵商 船 塢 dock for mercantile marine.
商 船 學 校 school for mercantile marine.
商 船 隊 mercantile marine fleet.
商 董 directors.
商 號 trade name of a firm.
⁷⁰商 行·爲 commercial transaction. (legal).
商 販 主 義 commercialism.
商 販 制·度 commercial control.
商 賈 traders; resident and travelling merchants. (-ku³)

商 部 Board of Trade.
⁷⁵商 隊 caravan.
商 電 commercial telegrams.
以 保 商 局 in the interests of trade.
出 口 商 exporter.
招 商 局 China Merchants Steamship Company.
⁸⁰洋 商 華 商 foreign and Chinese merchants.
通 商 international commerce.
進 口 商 importer.

(b) Name of a dynasty.

商。朝² or 商 紀 or 殷 紀 the Shang Dynasty founded by T'ang the Completer, 成 湯, 1766 B.C. and destroyed by Wu Wang, 武 王, 1122 B.C.
商 紂 the last ruler of the Shang Dynasty.
商 風 the west wind.

(c) The second note in the ancient pentatonic scale.

商 秋 the autumn.

諦¹ To consult; to deliberate. Inter. preceding.
5674

扃³ The large ring on a front door, used as a knocker.
5674a　See 扃 No. 1239.

SHAO. (尸幺)

少³ Few, a little. Short of, scarce. Seldom, briefly.
5675

少·不 了³ cannot do without; you won't get too little.
少·不 了³ 也 有 件 把 事 兒 doubtless there will be a few matters.
少·不 免 it cannot but be that; obliged to.
少·不·得 indispensable; most likely; probably; bound to.
⁵少·不·是 probably.
少 了 不 賣 I won't sell it for less.
少·些 a little less; fewer.
少·他·不·得 he is indispensable.
少 候 to wait awhile; I have failed

in calling on you—conventional phrase.

[10] 少刻 in a little while; a short time.

少可 it is but seldom.

少吃儉用 frugality.

少吃多甜 the less you have to eat the nicer it tastes.

少吃沒穿 lacking food and clothing—necessities.

[15] 少家無業 utterly poor and destitute.

少待 or 少停 wait awhile.

少微 in the smallest degree.

少憩 rest a little while.

少教·訓 ill-bred; uncouth in manners.

[20] 少數 a few; the minority.

少時 in a little while. See below—A. 17.

少有 there are few; rare; rarely.

少有日苟完矣 when he had a little more he said, "Here's perfection!"

少有·的事 a rare thing.

[25] 少欠 short of the proper number.

少禮 wanting in manners.

少等片時 wait a little while.

少算 to cheapen; to reckon less.

少給錢 to give less than agreed.

[30] 少興 cast down; low-spirited.

少見多怪 things seldom seen are strange—lack of experience.

少見多聞 little experience.

少見少見 I have seen very little of you—I am glad to see you again.

少許 a very little; a trifle.

[35] 少說·兩·句 say a little less.

少調失教 ill-bred.

少請安 I have made but few inquiries about your health—conventional phrase.

少選 an instant.

少錢 to owe; to deduct from a sum.

[40] 少間 in a little while; a little better—of sickness.

少陪 I have been poor company, used in parting; also used as "Excuse me."

少頃 in a little while; a short time.

少頭缺尾 imperfect; unfinished.

少飲 to sip.

[45] 多少 how many?

稀少 seldom; rarely.

至少 at least.

(a) Read shao[1]. Young.

少事僞朝 in earlier years I served the usurping dynasty.

少保 Junior Guardian of the Heir-Apparent.

少傅 Tutor to the Heir-Apparent.

少卿 a censor—obsolete.

[5] 少君 your son.

少壯 young and vigorous.

少妾 a concubine.

少婦 young married woman.

少子 the youngest son.

[10] 少孤 was orphaned when young.

少尉 second-lieutenant—army; midshipman—navy.

少將 major-general; rear-admiral.

少年中國 Young China.

少年人 or 少年 a young person.

[15] 少年裁判所 Juvenile Court.

少年親進 the rising generation.

少時 in youth. See above—21.

少林 the name of a monastery, the members of which were famous for boxing—a bully.

少校 major; commander.

[20] 少·爺 a young gentleman; your son.

少牢 sheep or pigs—as offerings.

少者懷之 carefully tend those that are young.

少而不勉老而無聞 if in youth you do not press on, you will have no reputation in old age.

少艾 or 少女 young women. See 艾 No. 19-B.

哨[4]

An encampment; an outpost.
5676

哨下 stationed on guard.

哨人 a sentry.

哨兵 sentinel.

哨堡 an entrenchment; an outpost.

[5] 哨官 a military lieutenant.

哨探 to spy; to scout; a scout; a spy.

哨望 a sentry.

哨總 officer in charge of a patrol.

哨船 revenue cruiser.

[10] 哨長 a petty military officer.

哨馬 mounted sentinel in advance of an outpost.

前軍哨 an advance patrol.

守哨 sentry.

左哨 or 右哨 a guard of honour.

[15] 步哨 to patrol; sentry.

營哨 guard stations.

巡哨 to patrol.

關哨 tide-waiters.

(a) A whistle; to whistle.

哨哨 loquacious.

哨·子 a whistle. = 哨兒

吹哨·子 to blow a whistle.

帶哨·子 to carry a whistle—of pigeons.

(b) Read hsiao, siao[1]. A wry mouth.

哨兒 the mouth of a trumpet.

哨口 a wry mouth.

陗[1]

The ends of a bow.
5677

捎[1]

To select; to take; to carry; to send when occasion offers.
5678

捎信 to send a letter.

捎在背後 to put the arms behind the back.

捎帶貨物 to carry goods—as a ship.

捎手 to fold the arms.

捎掠 to seize.

梢[1]

The tip of a branch; a twig. Musician's staff.
5679

梢末 the tip of anything.

區區梢梢 trifles; petty, insignificant.

樹梢 the top of a tree.

鞭梢 a riding-whip.

(a) A rudder. The stern of a boat.

梢公水手 helmsman and crew of a boat.

梢子 boatmen.

(b) Sound of wind. Sticking up. hanging like a tail.

竹馬梢梢搖綠尾 the bamboo horse hangs down his green tail.

風梢梢而過樹 the wind sighs as it passes the trees.

(c) Read *hsiao*[1]. **Erosion.**

梢 溝 trench made by running water.

稍[1] 5680   **Slightly; a little. To diminish slightly. Rather.** The word, esp. when used alone, is rather literary.

稍 乾 somewhat dried.
稍 事 an unimportant matter.
稍 加 to make some additions.
[5]稍 可 卽 止 stop after being moderately successful—do not be too ambitious.
稍 好 rather good.
稍 寬 其 禁 slightly relax the prohibitions.
稍 小 rather small.
稍 微 somewhat; slightly.
[10]稍 微 不 利 rather unlucky.
稍 戢 to lay aside gradually.
稍 暇 a little leisure.
稍 有 不 合 not exactly the thing; not quite suitable.
稍 有 誤 會 a slight misapprehension.
[15]稍 殊 somewhat different.
稍 涉 to trench upon; to tend towards.
稍 濃 rather too strong—as tea; rather thick.
稍 爲 to be somewhat.
稍 獲 微 利 to make a little profit.
[20]稍 申 to explain somewhat.
稍 知 to have some knowledge of.
稍 稍 蠶 食 之 gradually nibbling it like a silkworm—of gradual encroachment.
稍 緩 not too fast.
稍 能 or 稍 可 tolerable; perhaps it will do.
[25]稍 食 grain from the granary for rations.

潲[4] 5681   **Driving rain. To sprinkle. To dash water.**

潲 水 to sprinkle water.
潲 濕·了 wet through by driving rain.
雨 潲·進·來 the rain is beating in.

筲[1] 5682   **A basket; a bucket.**

筲 箕 a large basket for holding cooked rice.
斗 筲 之 人 people who are mere utensils.

艄[1] 5683   **The stern of a vessel. See** 梢 **No. 5679—A.**

艄 工 or 舵 工 (or 公) a helmsman.

蛸[1] 5684   **A long-legged spider.**

髾[1] 5685   **Tail of a comet. Read** *shao*[3]. **Long hair.**

旓[1] 5686   **The serrated edges on a Chinese flag.**

劭[4] 5687   **To stimulate to effort. Excellent; admirable.**

劭 才 fine talents.
劭 農 to encourage husbandry.

卲[4] 5688   **Eminent; lofty.**

紹 召 [4] 5689   **To connect; to join; to hand down; to continue.**

紹 介 or 介 紹 one who serves as a medium or go-between; to introduce a person.
紹 位 to succeed to the throne.
紹 天 明 to be put in relation with the intelligence of Heaven.
紹 復 to re-establish—as an inheritance.
[5]紹 我 周 王 見 休 will serve our king of the *Chou* Dynasty and so see prosperity.
紹 箕 裘 to carry on the father's trade or profession. *See No. 402-4.*
繼 紹 to continue; to carry on.

(a) Name of a place. Abbreviation for Shaohsing in Chekiang.

紹 酒 wine from Shaohsing—the best quality.

邵[4] 5690   **Name of a place.**

邵 子[3] 神 數[4] *Shao* knew the auguries of the gods.

韶[2] 5691   **The name of the music of the legendary Emperor** *Shun.* **Harmonious; excellent.**

韶 秀 blooming—of beauty.
韶 華 or 韶 光 splendid; glorious. 韶 光 spring time.
子 聞 韶 三 月 不 知 肉 味 for three months after Confucius had heard the *Shao*, he did not know the taste of meat.

燒[1] 5692   **To burn. To heat. To roast, to bake. Fever.**

燒 丹 alchemy.
燒 化 or 燒 燬 to consume by fire; to melt.
燒 山 to burn the grass on the hills—in order to fertilize them.
燒 拜 香 to supplicate the gods for a parent's recovery.
[5]燒 料 clouded glass.
燒 杯 a beaker.
燒 湯 to heat liquids.
燒 火 or 生 火 or 興 火 to light a fire.
燒 烟·火 = 放 烟·火 to let off fireworks.
[10]燒 烤 to bake and roast; baked and roast meats.
燒 煉 alchemy.
燒 爐 to burn to ashes.
燒 猪 a roast pig.
燒 瓶 a flask.
[15]燒 磚 to burn bricks.
燒 神 福 to burn paper, etc., as an offering to the gods before starting on a boat journey.
燒 窰 a kiln.
燒 紅 heated to redness; red-hot.
燒 紙 to burn paper for the dead.
[20]燒 絕 棧 道 to burn the plankwalk along a precipice—committed to a certain course of action.
燒 着·了 to catch fire; to set on fire. (-*chao*[2])
燒 肉 roast meat.
燒 茶 to boil water for tea.
↑燒 夷 彈 incendiary shell or bomb.

燒 路 頭 to worship the god of wealth.
²⁵燒 酒 *samshoo*—spirits that will burn.
燒 鍋 to light the fire for cooking.
燒·餅 a baked cake.
燒·香 or 拈 香 or 行 香 to burn incense.
燒 點 ignition point.
³⁰發 燒 to have a fever.

(a) Read *shao*⁴. Prairie-fire.

燋¹ To smelt.
Read *shao*⁴. Prairie-fire.
5693   Read *yao*⁴. Glorious.
u.f. 燿 No. 7306.

SHÊ.   (ㄕㄜ)
(Shæ)

佘² A surname.
Distinguish 余 No. 7605.
5694

賒¹ To buy or sell on credit.
5695
賒 借 無 門 no way of getting credit.
賒○去 to sell on credit.
賒 貨 to get credit for goods.
賒 貸 credit.
概 不 賒 貸 no credit given!
賒 買 to buy on credit.
賒 賬 or 賒 欠 to give credit.

(a) Distant.
去 國 賒 to go to a distant place.
尚 賒 still distant.

(b) To shirk. To put off.
賒 死 to shirk death.

奢¹ Extravagant; wasteful.
5696
奢·侈 or 奢 費 wasteful; prodigal.
奢·侈 品 article of luxury.
奢·侈·的 習 慣 luxurious habits.
奢·侈 稅 luxury tax.
⁵ 生 活 奢·侈 luxurious living.
耽 於 奢·侈 reclining in the lap of luxury.
奢 則 不 孫 extravagance begets rebelliousness.

奢 想 extravagant hopes or fancies.
奢 望 extravagant hopes.
¹⁰奢 華 showy.
奢 華 宴 樂 extravagant feasting.

厙⁴ A surname.
5697   Distinguish 庫 No. 3496.

蛇² A snake.
5698
蛇 吞 象 the snake would swallow an elephant—inordinately greedy.
蛇 文 石 serpentine.
蛇 殼 the slough of a snake.
蛇 牀 or 蛇 米 or 蛇 蛋 果 *Selinum japonicum*.
⁵蛇 皮 snake's skin.
蛇 皮 身·子 a disease of the skin like eczema.
蛇 苺 *Duchesnea indica*.
蛇 落 竹 筒 節 節 難 like a snake in a bamboo tube, every joint is difficult—meeting one difficulty after another.
蛇 蠍 snakes and scorpions—venomous things, things to be dreaded.
¹⁰蛇 行 moving like a snake; to advance in column.
蛇 行 而 進 he glided in.
蛇 豕 from 貪 害 如 蛇 豕 as injurious as snakes and boars—used of encroachments, etc.
蛇 足 snake's feet—superfluous.
蛇 頭 瘡 a whitlow.
¹⁵蛇 頭 鼠 眼 a snake's head and rat's eyes—crafty, wily.
蛇 魚 an eel.
蛇 麻 hops.
蛇 黃 iron pyrites—thought to be vomited by snakes when they appear after hibernation.
一 條 蛇 a snake.
²⁰打 草 驚 蛇 to beat the grass to frighten the snakes—to make an example of one to warn others.
雷·公 蛇 the gecko.
響 尾 蛇 the rattlesnake.

(a) Read *i*², *t'o*². At ease.
蛇 蛇 or 委 蛇 easy, contented, self-possessed. *See* 佗 No. 6439—A.

舍⁴ A cottage; a shed. To lodge; to reside at. A neighbour. In speaking of junior relatives it means:—my.
5699
舍 下 or 寒 舍 my poor residence.
舍 人 an official secretary; a retainer; son of a nobleman.
舍 居 or 舍 止 to lodge; to stop
舍 弟 my younger brother.
⁵舍 息 to rest awhile.
舍 次 place to camp for the night.
舍 監 dormitory master.
舍 親 my humble relatives.
舍 長 head of a dormitory.
¹⁰舍 軍 to halt an army.
客 舍 or 傳 舍 a wayside inn.

(a) A march of 35 *li*,—some give it as 30.
其 辟 君 三 舍 three stages distant from you.

(b) Used in transliterating.
舍 伯 領 Zeppelin.=徐 伯 林.
舍 利 Buddhist relic, from the Sanskrit; also a mynah.
舍 利 別 syrup.

(c) Read *shê*³. To put away. To release. To set aside. To bestow. To omit. Inter. next.

舍 利 取 義 sacrifice profit to duty.
舍 匿 to abscond.
舍 己 從 人 to yield one's wishes to those of another.
舍 然 clear, intelligent.
⁵舍 生 to give up one's life.
舍 矢 to shoot an arrow.
舍 短 取 長 reject his shortcomings and select his excellencies.
舍 身 to yield up one's life.
舍 近 圖 遠 to sacrifice the near for the distant.
¹⁰不 舍 晝 夜 never ceasing day nor night—of a stream.
施 舍 to bestow in charity.

捨³ To give alms; to bestow; to part with; to forsake. To reject. To spend.
5700   Distinguish 拾 No. 5809.

捨·不·得 or 捨·不 丁³ to grudge; to be loth to part with.
捨·不·得 去 loth to go.

捨·不·得用 loth to use it.
捨·不·得給人 loth to part with it.
[5] 捨·了·他·罷 forgive him!
捨○去 to part with; to give away.
捨·命 to give up life for others.
捨·得 to give up; not to withhold from; to part with.
捨·掉 parted with; given up.
[10] 捨·本 to give up one's capital; to fail in business.
捨·棄 or 捨·了 to forsake; to abandon.
捨死拼命 to resist to the death.
捨置 to put aside.
捨臉 to put on a bold face; brazen-faced.
[15] 捨財 to abjure riches; to give money in charity.
捨身 to give up the world; to devote the person; to commit suicide—as by throwing oneself over a precipice.
捨身入寺 to devote oneself and become a priest.
捨身爲道 a martyr.
捨飯 to give away food.
[20] 施捨 to dispense charity.

社 [4] The earth, as a god. The god of the soil. The altars to this god; sacrifices to the local gods.
5701

社五土之神能生萬物者 *Shê* is the god of the soil, the one who produces all things.
社公 an albino.
社公社母 the local gods of the soil or 土地神·
社壇 an altar.
[5] 社廟 a temple to a local deity.
社日 two festivals, in honour of local deities, known as 春社 and 秋社·
社樹 a tree which is worshipped as the earth-god.
社火 illuminations in favour of local deities.
社燕 the swallow—because its migration accords with the 社日, *above*—6.
[10] 社祭 sacrifice to the earth-spirit.
社稷 gods of the soil and grain—one's country, the national altars.
社稷之臣 a minister under the direct control of the sovereign.
主社稷 to reign.

利社稷 advantageous to the commonwealth.
[15] 失守社稷 to neglect his duties as a sovereign.
社翁雨 spring rains.
夏至祭地曰社 the sacrifice to Earth at the summer solstice is called *shê*.
擇元日命民社 the fortunate day is chosen and the people are ordered to sacrifice at their altars to the spirits of the soil (local gods).
郊社之禮 the rites of the sacrifice to Heaven and Earth.

(a) A village or hamlet, i.e., a group of 25 families which had an altar to the local earth-gods. A company or society.

社交 social intercourse.
社交婦女 a society woman.
社交性 sociability.
社交教會 an institutional church.
[5] 社交服裝 society style of dress.
社交界之領袖 leaders of society.
社交·的歡樂 social enjoyment or pleasures.
社交聚會 a social.
社債 municipal debt.
[10] 社友 fellow-member of a society.
社員 a partner; member of an association.
社團 society; community.
社○會 a sacrificial festival—in modern use:—society, a community; social order; an organized society.
社會上 social.
[15] 社會上之義務 social obligations.
社會上的 socially.
社會中人 a member of society.
社會主義 Socialism(in theory.)
社會主義的國 a socialistic State.
[20] 社會交通 social intercourse.
社會保險 social insurance.
社會倫理學 social ethics.
社會公論 opinion of society; public opinion.
社會制·度 the social system.
[25] 社會問題 social problems.
社會學 sociology.
社會平等 social equality.

社會心理學 social psychology.
社會改良 social reform.
[30] 社會改造 reconstruction of society.
社會政·策 socialism as a government policy.
社會敎·育 community education, i.e., of all those under twelve.
社會服務 social service.
社會民主同盟 Social Democratic Federation.
[35] 社會生·活 social life.
社會·的 pertaining to society.
社會·的傳說 social traditions.
社會·的科學 social science.
社會·的職務 social duties.
[40] 社會經濟 social economics.
社會觀 aspect of society.
社會進化 evolution or progress of society.
社會階·級 caste; social grades.
社會黨 Socialists.
[45] 上流社會 the upper classes.
下流社會 the lower classes.
中級社會 the middle classes.   「A.c. 社評
社論 editorials; leading articles.
社長 president of an association, newspaper, etc.
[50] 文社 literary club.

赦 [4] To forgive; to remit; to pardon.
5702

赦免 or 赦放 or 赦宥 to forgive; to remit.
赦回 to pardon and restore.
赦罪 to forgive sins.
大赦 general pardon or amnesty.
寬赦 to act in a lenient manner.
法無可赦 the law cannot remit offences.
罪在不赦 unpardonable offence.

射 [4] To project; to shoot out. To aim at. Also read *shih*[2,5].
5703

射不主皮 shooting through the leather is not the chief point in archery.
射中 (*chung*[4]) to hit the bull's eye.
射來射去 darting hither and thither.
射光 to emit light; dazzling; luminous.

5射·出 radiating.
射 利 to aim at gain.
射 地 雷 機 a mine thrower.
射 影 imaginary demon that spurts sand at the shadow of a man walking on the shore, thus causing his death—to implicate in trouble. *See* 蜮 No. 7680.
射 影 燈 magic-lantern.
10射 御 書 數 four of the *Six Arts*—archery, charioteering, writing and mathematics.
射 擊 to fire a gun; bombardment.
射·死 killed by an arrow.
射 熱 radiation of heat.
射 父 the musk-deer.
15射 生 to shoot at living creatures.
射 目 to dazzle.
目 射 flashing eyes.
射 箭 archery.
射 藥 針 hypodermic needle.
20射 言 to joke with one.
善 射 skilful archery.
放 射 radiation.
注 射 to inject—fluids.
相 射 opposite to each other.

(a) Read *yü*[4.5]. **To dislike; to be disliked.**

好 爾 無 射 I will love you for ever.
矧 可 射 思 Can you treat—the gods—with indifference?

(b) Read *yeh*[4.5]. **A servant.**

僕 射 a major-domo.
(c) Read *i*[4.5]. 無 射 a musical note.

麝
5704
4 See 7180.106½
The musk-deer.

麝 牛 the musk-ox.
麝 臍 the bag of the musk-deer.
麝·香 musk.
麝 鼠 the musk-rat.

SHÊ. (尸`)
(Sheh)

舌
5705
½
2.5. The tongue; the clapper of a bell; the tongue of a buckle, etc. Radical 135.
舌 人 interpreter.
舌 刺 papillæ of the tongue.
舌 尖 the tip of the tongue.
舌 戰 tongue warfare—argument.
舌 本 the root of the tongue—the palate.

5舌 根 the root of the tongue.
舌 狀 tongue-shaped.
舌 短 thick of speech; to have no answer to make.
舌 耕 to plough with the tongue—to teach.
舌 腺 lingual glands.
10舌 苔 fur on the tongue.
舌 鈍 mumbling as if the tongue was thick. [sives and liquids.
舌 音 lingual sounds; dental plo-
舌·頭 the tongue.
舌·頭 尖 利 sharp-tongued.
15舌 骨 the hyoid bone.
刮 舌 to scrape the tongue.
劍 舌 sharp-tongued.
口 舌 mouth and tongue—altercation.
吐 舌 put out the tongue.
20在 舌·頭 尖兒上 on the tip of the tongue.
插 舌 to intrude on an argument.
捫 舌 to hold the tongue.
滑 舌 smooth-tongued.
白 舌 slanderous tongues.
25結 舌 to stutter; tongue-tied.
鐘 舌 tongue of a bell.
長 舌 long-tongued; loquacious.
饒 舌 loquacious.

賒
5706
2.5. To lose in trade. To lose in weight or measure.

賒 了 虧 to be swindled.
賒 分·兩 or 賒 秤 to lose weight—as by shrinkage.
賒 收 a scanty harvest.
賒 斗 斛 to lose measure.
賒 本 to lose in trade; to fail in business.

涉
5707
4.5. To ford a stream. To pass through; to be connected with. To involve; to concern; to implicate.

涉 世 to pass through the world—to gain experience.
涉 世 人 a man acquainted with the world; liberal.
涉 事 to state; to narrate.
涉 于 春 冰 to cross on spring ice—dangerous.
5涉 及 非 禮 involving a breach of etiquette.
涉 水 to wade through water; to ford.
涉 水 鳥 wading-birds.

涉 獵 書 籍 to wade and hunt through books—w i d e b u t shallow reading; to browse.
涉 訟 to involve in legal proceedings.
10交·涉 negotiation.
干 涉 to interfere with.
牽 涉 to implicate; to involve.
與 我 無 涉 no concern of mine.
關 涉 to concern.

揲
5708
2.5. To sort out the divining stalks.

揲 蓍 to divine by stalks of grass.
占 揲 to divine.

(a) Read *t'ieh*[2.5]. **To fold.**

韘
5709
4.5. Archer's thumb-ring of leather.

攝
5710
4.5. To unite in one person; to assist.

攝 乎 大 國 之 間 harassed between two States.
攝 事 to attend to an affair; to manage.
攝 位 to administer the government during a regency.
攝 政 to be associated in the government.
5攝 政 王 Prince-Regent.
攝 理 in the meantime.
攝 生 hygiene; sanitation.
攝 行 or 攝 篆 to act for another in an official capacity.
攝 衛 to take care of one's health.
10攝 護 腺 the prostate gland.
兼 攝 to assist temporarily in another office as well as one's own.

(a) To take up. To hold up. To take.

攝 力 attraction.
攝 影 to take a photograph.
攝 弊 衣 冠 w e a r i n g poor clothing.
攝 持 to take up.
5攝 石 a loadstone.
攝 衽 抱 儿 carrying mats and tables—m a k i n g g r e a t preparations.

攝 齊 升 堂 he held up his lower robes and descended the hall.

(b) Read *nieh*[2.5]. To pacify.

攝 然 at peace.

鎮 攝 to keep the peace.

設 [4.5]. To establish; to found; to arrange; to devise.
5711

設 下 to set up; to establish.

設 下 圈 套 to set a snare.

設 主 to place an ancestral tablet in position.

設 伏 to lay an ambush.

[5]設 佈 to set up; to establish.

設 假[3]見·證 to bring forward false evidence.

設 備 equipment, to make preparation.

設 備 簡 陋 poorly equipped.

設 奠 to set the sacrifice in order.

[10]設 官 分 職 to establish an official post and define its duties.

設 宴 or 設 酒 or 設 席 to make a feast.

設 局 to establish a board or public company.

設 帨 to hang out a handkerchief at the right of a door—done in ancient times to announce the birth of a girl—a woman's birthday. *See below*—16.

設 序 to arrange in order.

[15]設 建 rehabilitation.

設 弧 to hang out a bow—as was done in ancient times to announce the birth of a son—a man's birthday. *See above*—13.

設 惡 計 to concoct a wicked scheme.

設 擺 to prepare; to spread out; to arrange.

設 擺 盛 筵 to spread a sumptuous feast.

[20]設 教 to open a school; to begin teaching.

設 新 章 to introduce new regulations.

設 施 plans; methods; programmes; arrangements; institutions.

設 有 established.

設 法 to devise means; to plan.

[25]設 疑 to have doubts; to harbour suspicions.

設 立 to set up; to establish.

設 立 學 堂 to establish a school.

設 計 or 設 謀 to devise means; to plan; to scheme.

設 誓 to take an oath.

[30]設 險 to place soldiers in important positions.

設 饌 to set out food; to give a feast.

(a) Supposing that; what if?

設 想 to imagine; supposing.

設 或 or 設 使 or 設 若 suppose that; if; what if?

設 有 不 測 in the event of anything unforeseen.

設 身 處[3]地 將 若 之 何 if you were in my place, what would you do?

設 辭 hypothetical particles; words denoting condition or supposition.

SHÊN.　(ㄕㄣ)

申 [1] To state to a superior; to report; to notify. To give orders.
5712

申 令 Presidential mandate.

申 信 to convey information.

申 其 不 平 to protest.

申 告 complaint. (*legal*).

[5]申 呈 to send up a statement; to report to a superior.

申 報 to report to a superior. *See below*—D. 1.

申 守 to warn and make ready for defence.

申 冤 to redress a grievance.

申 救 to redress a grievance and deliver.

[10]申 敬 to show esteem.

申 文 a report to a superior.

申 斥 to reprimand; a rebuff.

申 明 to explain clearly.

申 理 to show that one is right.

[15]申 示 to promulgate.

申 祈 have the honour to beseech.

申 稱 to send up a statement or report.

申 繳 to hand back a report to a superior.

申 覆 to reply to a superior.

[20]申 解 to explain.

申 訴 to state to a superior.

申 詳 to send up a report to a superior.

申 請 to request a superior.

申 謝 to beg to thank.

[25]申 警 to caution.

申 送 to forward to a superior.

彙 齊 申 送 to submit collectively.

申 達 to make a report to a superior.

申 飭 to reprimand; to caution.

(a) To extend. To repeat.

申 命 to give further injunctions.

申 命 記 The Book of Deuteronomy.

申 旦 until morning.

申 重 repeatedly.

福 自 天 申 blessings come from Heaven.

(b) Easy, relaxed.

申 申 如 也 easy, self-possessed.

(c) The 9th of the *Twelve Branches* 地 支. 3—5 p.m.

申 初 about 3 p.m.

申 月 the 7th lunar month.

申 正 4 p.m.

申 牌 時 分 about 4 p.m.

(d) Old name for the River Whangpoo at Shanghai.

申 報 the Shanghai Newspaper—the first Chinese newspaper to be published in Shanghai. *See above*—6.

申 州 old name for 信 陽 州 in Honan.

申 江 the river now called the Whangpoo, Shanghai.

(e) To make up the deficit of scale or quality in weighing silver.

申 水 to receive the difference in the scale or touch of silver, as 貼 水 is to pay the difference.

伸 [1] To stretch out; to extend. To straighten out. To redress. To report to. Inter. preceding.
5713

伸·不 直 not able to straighten out the matter or to get redress.

伸·不 起 來 cannot straighten up.

伸·出 to bring out—as the meaning of a phrase; to extend; to stretch forth.

伸·出·來 to stretch forth.
[5]伸·出 脖·子 to stretch out the neck.
伸 寃 to redress a grievance.
伸 展 to expand; to develop.
伸 張 to widen; to stretch out.
伸 志 to carry out one's purpose.
[10]伸 愬 to state one's grievances.
伸 懶 腰 to stretch—as when yawning.
伸 手 to stretch out the hand.
伸 手 不 見 掌 cannot see the hand before the face.
伸 手 摸 天 to stretch out the hand and touch the heavens—ambitious attempts.
[15]伸 明 to give a full, clear explanation.
伸 理 to get redress; to show oneself to be in the right.
伸 直 to straighten.
伸 直 脚 to stretch out the legs—to die; dead.
伸 眉 to show gratification in the countenance.
[20]伸 縮 to expand and to contract; contraction.
伸 縮 力 elasticity.
伸 縮 距 規 a sliding gauge.
伸 舌·頭 to put out the tongue.
伸 訴 to present a complaint.
[25]伸 謝 to present one's thanks.
伸·開 腿 to stretch the legs.
伸 陳 to state to a superior officer.
伸 雅 懷 to express beautiful sentiments.
引 伸 to infer; to stretch out.
[30]欠 伸 to stretch when tired.

呻[1] To groan. To hum; to drone.
5714

呻 吟 to hum over—as lessons from a book; to groan.

砷[2] Arsenic.
5715

神[2] A spirit; a god. Spiritual, inscrutable, divine, supernatural. The soul.
5716

神 主 an ancestral tablet.
神 之 憑 格 divine inspiration.
神 之 格 思 不 可 度 思 you cannot calculate the coming of the spiritual beings.

神 事 祭 祀 the business of the gods, that is, sacrifices.
[5]神 人 並 誅 punished by both gods and men.
神 人 共 悅 gods and men rejoice together.
神 人 共 鑑 for the inspection of gods and men.
神 人 同 形 說 anthropomorphism.
神 人 相 通 communication between gods and men.
[10]神 佛 a Buddha.
神 位 divine seat or throne; tablet or altar before which gods and the spirits of ancestors are worshipped.
神 像 an image or idol.
神 出 鬼 沒 movements of supernatural beings—evil practices.
神 力 superhuman strength.
[15]神 嗜 飲 食 the gods tasted your sacrifice.
神 器 a divine utensil; the throne; the soul; the empire, as a trust from God; Imperial regalia.
傷 其 神 器 injured his divine nature.
神 在 男 曰 覡 when a man is possessed by a spirit he is called a sorcerer.
神 女 goddesses.
[20]神 妙 無 方 passing all human comprehension.
神 學 or 神 道 學 theology.
神 學 院 theological seminary.
神 學 博 士 Doctor of Divinity.
神 學 派 theologians.
神 實 司 之 it is wholly in the hands of the gods.
[25]神 將 伺 之 the gods will search into the actions of men.
神 師 divine teacher.
神 庥 divine care and aid.
神 廟 temple of the gods.
神 性 the divine nature. Godhead.
[30]神 意 the divine purpose or mind.
神 政 主 義 Theocracy.
神 明 the gods.
神 明 之 昭 示 the forewarning of the gods.
神 明 享 其 禱 the gods will accept his prayer.
[35]神 明 有 報 the gods will punish him.
尊 重 神 明 卽 告 于 祖 宗 reverentially honouring the gods, he thus made the announcement to his ancestors.

敬 之 如 神 明 reverencing him as they do the gods.
暗 祝 神 明 secretly invoke the gods.
神 智 敎 Theosophy.
[40]神 嘗 見 人 人 不 見 神 the gods always see men, but men see not the gods.
神 格 divine personality, as opposed to 人 格 human personality.
神 權 divine power; divine right.
神 父 a Roman Catholic missionary; a Catholic father.
神 牌 an ancestral tablet.
[45]神 異 miraculous; marvellous.
神 福 仁 而 禍 淫 the gods bless the good and punish the wicked.
神 秘 mysterious; mystic.
神 秘 主 義 Mysticism.
神 秘 敎 派 mystics.
[50]神 秘 的 mystical.
神 聖 sacred. See 勞 No. 3826—30.
神 聖 不 可 侵 犯 what is sacred cannot be violated.
神 聖 主 義 the sacred principle.
神 聖 之 權 利 sacred privileges.
[55]神 聖 權 sacred rights.
神 聖 盟 約 a sacred compact.
神 聖 羅 馬 帝 國 The Holy Roman Empire.
神 聖 義 務 sacred duty.
神 聖 高 尙 的 職 業 a high and holy calling.
[60]神 自 來 享 the gods will still come and accept it.
神 視 力 divine perception; spiritual insight.
神 話 myths.
神 話 學 mythology.
神 誕 festival of the birthday of a god.
[65]神 譜 theogony.
神 跡 divine traces or footsteps—miracles.
神 通 supernatural powers.
神 道 the avenue leading to a grave; the Way of the gods—Shintoism, the ancient religion of Japan; the black art.
神 降 之 嘉 福 the gods sent him down estimable blessings.
[70]神 靈 the soul; the gods; supernatural manifestations; divine.
神 餕 food that has been offered to ancestors.
神 饗 offerings to the gods.

神 鬼 仙 佛 gods, demons, immortals and Buddhas.

神 鬼 保 佑 gods and demons protecting you.

[75]神 鬼 具 知 the gods and demons all know it.

神 鬼 昭 彰 放 過 誰 Who has ever escaped the manifest retribution of the gods and demons?

神 鬼 難 欺 gods and demons cannot be deceived.

上 下 神 祇 the gods of Heaven and Earth.

五 帝 爲 次 神 the Five Rulers are inferior gods.

[80]事 神 to serve the god as a priest.

人 死 成 神 而 位 較 卑 men at their death become *Shên*, but their status is comparatively humble.

以 交 神 爲 主 communion with the gods is the chief element of it—worship.

以 禮 神 也 in order to worship the gods.

以 道 事 神 to serve the gods as they should be served.

[85]司 命 神 guardian deity of the family.

地 之 神 曰 祇 the god of the Earth is call *Ch'i*.

城 隍 神 guardian deity of the city.

夕 夢 神 責 he was reproved in a dream by a god.

天 惟 一 神 Heaven is Only One God.

[90]天 神 the highest classification of spiritual beings; used by some for angels.

天 神 引 出 萬 物 者 也 all things have been developed by the gods of Heaven.

太 歲 之 神 the god of the years.

家 神 the family gods—the ancestral tablets.

帝 神 The Sovereign God—i.e., Shangti 上 帝

[95]拜 神 to worship the gods.

救 助 於 神 sought help of the gods.

暗 中 虧 心 神 目 如 電 the evil deeds done in darkness flash in the eyes of the gods like lightning.

正 直 無 私 是 神 to be upright and without partiality is—the

nature of—the gods.

死 後 難 不 見 神 after death it will be difficult to avoid facing the gods.

[100]生 物 便 是 神 也 He who produced all things is divine.

皇 天 有 神 不 Is there a god in heaven or not?

祈 禱 神 祇 he prayed to the gods of Heaven and Earth.

祭 神 如 神 在 worship the gods as if they were present.

禮 神 謂 祭 天 也 by worshipping *Shên* is meant sacrificing to Heaven.

[105]聖 而 不 可 知 之 謂 神 when the Sage is beyond our knowledge, he is what is called a god.

至 誠 如 神 the man possessed of complete sincerity is like a god.

至 誠 感 神 perfect sincerity moves the gods.

誓 神 to swear by the gods.

酬 神 to thank the gods.

[110]陰 陽 不 測 之 謂 神 the inscrutable operations of *Yin* and *Yang* are called *Shên*.

鬼 神 無 形 無 聲 the spiritual beings have neither form nor sound.

鬼 神 者 造 化 之 功 也 *Kwei-Shên* is the efficient agency in creation—defined here as the dual divine essence.

鬼 神 非 其 族 類 不 歆 其 祀 the gods will not accept the offerings of those who are not of their own class.

(a) The mind. Animal spirits. Genius. Expression. Nerves. Energy.

神 不 守 舍 scared out of one's wits; delirious.

神 似 the expression of the face.

神 彩 countenance; looks.

神 彩 不 俗 there was an air of refinement about him.

[5]神 往 者 my thoughts go back; I visit it in spirit.

神 志 昏 亂 clouded and confused in mind.

神 思 thought; intellect.

神 情 affectionate spirit; air, manner.

神 情 恍·惚 nervousness; delirium.

[10]神 情 活 現 having the air of a living person; vivid.

神 情 眉 目 facial expression.

神 態 bearing; manner.

不 安 的 神 態 not at ease.

欲 睡 的 神 態 as if wanting to go to sleep; drowsy.

[15]神 我 the spiritual ego of Buddhism.

神 搖 目 眩 he trembled in spirit and became dizzy.

神 散 解 the energy is exhausted.

神 明 不 測 之 號 —the Sage— is the designation of one whose spirit and intelligence may not be fathomed.

神 明 未 衰 his faculties were not dissipated.

[20]心 之 神 明 也 the divine intelligence of the mind.

神 昏 氣 濁 the mind confused and turbid.

神·氣 the vital principle; the appearance or expression; the style—as of literature.

神·氣 過·來·了 his appearance has changed for the better.

神 清 氣 爽 the mind clear and vigorous.

[25]神 爲 之 奪 infatuated.

神 經 nerves—used as below.

交 感 神 經 sympathetic nerve.

聽 神 經 auditory nerve.

視 神 經 optic nerve.

[30]顏 面 神 經 facial nerves.

神 經 中 樞 nerve centres.

神 經 叢 plexus.

神 經 器 nervous organs.

神 經 學 Neurology.

[35]神 經 炎 neuritis.

神 經 病 nervous diseases; insanity.

神 經 痛 neuralgia.

神 經 系 the nervous system.

神 經 細 胞 nerve cells.

[40]神 經 纖 維 or 神 經 節 ganglion of nerves.

神 經 衰 弱 neurasthenia.

神 經 質 nervous substance; nervous temperament.

神 經 過 敏 sensitive; nervous.

神 經 部 位 nerve centres.

[45]神 經 錯 亂 nerves in disorder.

震 人 神 經 to jar the nerves.

神 能 飛 形 the mind can fly beyond the limits of the body.

神 色 the mind; the expression.

神 色 不 定 timid, nervous, unsettled.

[50]神 色 慘 淡 the energy all dissipated.

神色自若 the expression of his face was quite normal.

神觀 air, bearing, manner.

神迷意奪 infatuated.

神馳 the thoughts are far away.

55神魂 the vital principle; the soul; the faculties.

傳神 to paint a portrait; to make a life-like portrait; life-like.

凝神 to concentrate the mind.

出神 in a fit of absent-mindedness.

勞神 to exhaust the mind or energies.

60失神 to be absent-minded; to get a fright.

安神 to tranquilize the mind.

心神 the mind.

收回心神 to recover one's wits.

用神 or 留神 to keep one's wits about one; to be careful.

65眼神 the expression of the eyes.

精神 animal spirits; energy. *See* No. 1149—C. 11ff.

豐神 fairy-like; graceful.

費神 to expend and waste the vitality or mental force.

鍊神 to refine the faculties or soul.

70養神 to nourish the vital energies —by rest.

(b) Used as an adjective.

神人 a prophet; man of God.

神人無功 the divine man seeks not merit.

神光 divine glory.

神兵 a marvellous soldier.

5神劍 a magic sword.

神化 divine transformations.

神奇 rare, valuable.

神妙不測 inscrutable; beyond comprehension.

神巧 remarkable; ingenious.

10神怪 prodigy.

神悟 divine intelligence.

神效 wonderfully efficacious—as a prescription.

神明者先勝者也 he who has divine intelligence is the first to gain the victory. *See above*—32-38,—A. 18ff.

神機 extraordinary strategy or devices.

15神物 things for divination having supernatural powers.

神獸 a supernatural beast.

神異 divinely wonderful—a prodigy.

神童 a divine youth.

神算 a very clever plan.

20神藥 divine drugs.

神術 a divine art.

神速 marvellously quick.

神馬 a divine horse.

神龜 a supernatural tortoise.

(c) Used as an exclamation.

神乎神乎 Wonderful, wonderful!

神矣妙矣精矣微矣 Divine! Mysterious! Subtle! Inscrutable!

神哉 How divine! How wonderful!

不亦神乎 Is it not divine?

何其神也 How remarkable! How extraordinary!

(d) Used in names.

神州 old name for China.

神者 or 神京 Peking.

神農 *Shên Nung*—the legendary emperor 2838 B.C., the supposed teacher of husbandry, etc.

(e) Read *shên¹.* **A name.**

神荼 (*t'u²*) one of the two figures painted as door-gods. *See* 壘 4228—A, 荼 No. 6526—D.

紳 ¹ A girdle. To bind. The gentry.
5717

紳商 gentry and merchants.

紳士 the gentry.

紳宦 the gentry and retired officials.

紳束 to bind.

紳衿 or 紳耆 or 鄉紳 or 紳董 the gentry, officials out of office; educated classes.

官紳 officials and gentry.

身 ¹ The body. The person. The hull. Oneself; I, me.
5718 A lifetime. Radical 158.

身丁錢 poll-tax.

身上 or 身中 on or about the person.

身不由主 hampered or constrained by circumstances.

身世 the experience of a lifetime.

5身價 a person's status or rank.

身入公門 to work in the magistrate's offices.

身分 (*fên⁴*) rank; position; quality.

身前身後 previous to and subsequent to the attainment of the human form.

身受 to receive in person; personally to endure.

10身命 the body and the life.

身在心馳 the body is present but the spirit is far away.

身外 not one's own affair; not connected intimately with oneself.

身子 the body; the trunk; the hull.

身孕 to be pregnant.

15身家 or 本身 oneself.

身家性命 one's person, family and life; position in society.

身家清白 of honourable parentage—those whose families have not been engaged in undesirable pursuits, such as those of actors, lictors, etc., such pursuits being a barrier to the former examinations for degrees.

身居 he was by rank a....

身廢 to ruin the health.

20身後 or 善後 after death and burial.

身後事宜 funeral affairs.

身後蕭條 to die without heirs or money left for them.

身心之適合 body and mind in co-ordination.

身懷六甲 to be pregnant.

25身懶肚飽 lazy and gluttonous.

身手 dexterity, skill.

身操 engaged in.

身故 or 身亡 or 身死 to die.

身敗名裂 down and out.

30身是道場 you yourself are the hall of worship.

身材 the person.

身材合中 medium height.

身材窈窕 a graceful figure.

身段 physique; figure

35身火 the passions.

身當其衝 to stand in the breach.

身章 the clothing.

身老習成 when the body is old, habits are already formed.

身肩 to undertake responsibility.

40身臨 to visit in person.

身邊 by the side of a person; in

another's company; on the person.

身 邊 人 an attendant.
身 量 stature; height.
身 量 未 足 not yet fully grown.
[45] 身 量 高 tall.
身 金 salary; wages; price of a slave.
身 長 height of the body; rather tall.
身·體 or 身 軀 the person.
身 體 刑 corporal punishment.
[50] 身·體 檢 驗 表 physical chart.
身 體 權 right of the person.
身·體 輕 健 active, alert and strong.
一 身 wholly; all one's life.
一 身 衣·服 a suit of clothes.
[55] 下·一 身 the lower parts of the body; the privates.
不 顧 身 regardless of danger.
以 身 作 則 he in himself sets up a standard.
元 身 virility.
出 身 to begin a career; to come forward; one's antecedents.
[60] 分 身 to get away—as from duties, etc.
動 身 to start on a journey.
周 身 the whole body.
捨 身 救 親 to give up the life for parents.
有 身 pregnant.
[65] 樹 身 trunk of a tree.
河 身 bed of a river.
法 身 the immortal body. (Budd.).
渾 身 the whole body.
發 身 puberty.
[70] 立 身 to establish personal character.
終 身 the whole life.
色 身 the material body. (Budd.).
賣 身 to sell oneself; prostitution.
赤 身 naked.
[75] 起 身 to rise; to start on a journey.
轉 身 the body in which a person is re-born after death. (Budd.).
過 身 to die.
開 身 to set sail.
防 身 self-defence.
[80] 隨 身 on the person.

(a) Read *yüan*[2] Due to a misinterpretation of the commentary 身 音 捐 (i.e. *yüan*[2]), also read *chüan*!

身 毒 a name for India.

深 [1] Deep, profound, abstruse. Intimate. Long. Old. Very, 5719 extremely.

深 不 可 測 unfathomable.
深 久 a very long time.
深 交 intimate relationships.
深 似 海 as deep as the sea.
[5] 深 信 to have implicit faith in.
深 信 不 疑 to be profoundly convinced of.
深 僻 retired.
深 入 to penetrate deeply into.
深 切 intensely; profound and apposite.
[10] 深 則 厲 淺 則 揭 you must wade deep water with the clothes on, shallow water with the clothes held up—act according to circumstances.
深 厚 on very good terms with.
深 呼·吸 deep breathing.
深 坑 a deep pit.
深 奧 or 深 微 profound; deep; abstruse.
[15] 深 好 very fond of.
深 妙 admirable; first rate!
深 學 profoundly learned; deeply versed in.
深 宮 之 中 within the palace.
深 密 thick; dense.
[20] 深 居 簡 出 dwelling in deep seclusion, rarely coming out.
深 山 古 洞 ancient grottoes deep in the mountains.
深 度 depth.
深 思 contemplation; deep thought.
深 恩 great kindness.
[25] 深 恨 deep hatred.
深 悉 to have a profound knowledge of.
深 意 profound significance.
深 房 邃 室 a secluded dwelling.
深 揖 a profound bow.
[30] 深 敬 profound respect.
深 文 奧 義 abstruse writings.
深 於 情·的 人 a person deeply in love.
深 林 the deep forests.
深 染 deeply imbued with.
[35] 深 沉 crafty; scheming.
深 沾 deeply indebted.
深 海 魚 deep-sea fish.
深 淺 deep and shallow—depth.
深 淺 不 知 not to know deep from shallow—inexperienced.
[40] 深 扎 根 take deep root.
深 深·的 感 動 deeply moved.

深 深·的 見 地 insight.
深 渺 far-distant.
深 淵 an abyss.
[45] 深 潛 純 粹 profound and pure.
深 睡 deep sleep.
深 知 profound knowledge.
深 禱 earnestly beseech.
深 穴 a deep cave.
[50] 深 究 or 深 查 to make a thorough investigation.
深 色 deep colours.(-*shai*[3] or -*sê*[4])
深 荷 or 深 蒙 deeply indebted for.
深 藍 deep blue.
深 處 a deep place.
[55] 深 衣 garments that come down longer than the court robe.
深 表 同 情 to show the deepest sympathy.
深 訪 to explore.
深 謀 遠 慮 thoughtful and far-seeing.
深 資 of great assistance.
[60] 深 通 to understand thoroughly.
深 進·的 眼 deep-set eyes.
深 遠 far distant; remote.
深 銘 五 內 deeply engraved on my heart.
深 闊 length and breadth—in square measure.
[65] 深 青 揚 赤 色 a deep azure flushed with carnation.
深 靜 profound silence.
深 體 deeply sympathizing.
深 黑 dense darkness.
更 深 夜 靜 in the stillness of midnight.
[70] 有 幾 尺 深 How many feet deep is it?

姺 [1] Name of an ancient small State. Also read *hsin*[1].
5720

駪 [1]
侁 A large crowd.
5721
駪 駪 往 來 many coming and going.

森 [1] Luxuriant vegetation; overgrown. Dark. Dignified. 5722 Usually read *sên*[1].

森 列 rising in ranks—of mountain peaks.

森 嚴 stern.
森 森 in ranks; deep, leafy luxuriant.
頭 目 森 森 dizzy.
森 樹 Pride of India—*Melia Azedarach.*
森 羅 rigorous; majestic; severe.
森 鬱 stern; forbidding; severe harsh.

澲 [1]
5723
Ginseng.
人 澲 or 人 參 ginseng.

甚 [4]
5724
What? Who? Any. Very; extremely. More important than
甚 不 相 宜 extremely unsuitable.
甚 大 big; huge.
甚 如 quite so; unlikely.
甚 好 very good.
[5]甚 少 無 幾 very few indeed.
甚 屬 or 甚 為 is indeed; is very....
甚 或 or what is worse....
甚 是 quite right; just the thing.
甚 為 凄 涼 very desolate; solitary.
[10]甚 矣 吾 衰 也 great is my decay!
甚 而 so much so that....
甚·至 or 甚·至 於 even to; even as far as to; at the worst; culminating in.
甚 至 不 然 if in no other way; otherwise; if not.... then....
甚²麼 or 甚²麼 事 What? What's the matter?
[15]甚·麼 人 Who is it? Who is he?
甚²麼 話 What talk! Bosh!
沒·有 甚²麼 there is nothing.
太 甚 excessive.
↑甚 麼 的 and things; and so forth

葚 [4]
5725
The fruit of the mulberry. Also read *jên*[4].

諶 訦 [2]
5726
Sincere; faithful; to trust to.
More commonly read *ch'en*[2].

伈 [3]
5727
Nervous, fearful. Also read *hsin*[3].

哂 吲 [3]
5728
To smile; to sneer at.
哂 之 smiled at him—at his folly.
哂 存 or 哂 納 receive with a smile—a present.
哂 笑 to smile at.

審 [3]
5729
To judge; to hold an official inquiry; to investigate; to examine.
審 供 to hear evidence.
審 其 機 to inquire into his secret motives.
審 判 judgement; to judge.
審 判 公 開 to hear in open court.
[5]審 判 廳 Court of Justice.
審 卦 to inquire by divination with the *diagrams.*
審 奪 to examine and decide.
審 定 to decide a case at law; to come to a conclusion; to authorize—as publications.
教 育 部 審 定 Authorized by the Ministry of Education.
[10]審 定 書 decision in writing.
審 察 or 審 問 or 審 訊 or 審 究 or 審 明 to investigate; to inquire into a case.
審 察 其 源 to trace the origins; to find out the cause.
審 實 a final judgement.
審 度 to estimate the pros and cons.
[15]審 度 情 境 look into the circumstances.
審 慎 to take into account; to give due weight to; careful.
審 擇 所 處 to examine well before acting.
審 斷 or 審 結 to hear and decide a case; to give final judgement; final settlement of a case.
審 時 度 世 to observe the times.
[20]審 時 觀 變 examine the signs of the times and mark the changes of affairs.
審 查 to examine; to investigate.
審 查 員 inspector.
審 查 會 examining committee.
審 核 judicial inquiry.
[25]審 案 to try a case.
審 理 to deal with a case.
審 級 stages of trial; judicial procedure.

審 美 æsthetics; to search for the best.
審 美 學 æsthetic studies.
[30]審 美 觀 念 æsthetic conceptions.
審 覆 前 後 re-examine the whole matter.
審 視 to make a close inspection.
審 解 to try a case and send on the parties.
審 計 法 law relating to the Audit Department.
[35]審 計 院 Audit Department.
審 賊 to examine a criminal.
審 辦 to deal with a case.
審 追 to get at the truth of a case; to enforce a decision.
審 量 to deliberate on; to consider.
[40]審 音 to distinguish tones in music, or niceties in phonetics.
季 審 會 Quarterly Sessions.
對 審 to confront witnesses with one another.
小 審 會 Petty Sessions.
[45]提 審 to carry up a case.
會 審 公 堂 Mixed Court.
調 審 to carry up a case.
質 審 to examine in the presence of one another.
陪 審 官 an assessor.
預 審 廳 Preliminary Court.

嬸 [3]
5730
Wife of a father's younger brother.
嬸·子 or 叔 嬸 wife of father's younger brother.
嬸 嬸 aunt—complimentary title applied to the wife of the younger brother by the wife of the elder brother.
嬸 母 or 嬸 娘 wife of father's younger brother.

瀋 [3]
5731
To pour out water. To leak.

矧 訒 [3]
5732
Still more. How much more? How much less? Also.
矧 伊 人 矣 不 求 友 生 Shall a man not seek to have his friends?
矧 可 射 (*i*⁴·⁵) 思 Can you ignore them?—the supernatural beings.

剡 如 是 乎 How much more then?

剡 惟 不 孝 不 友 he is also unfilial and unfriendly.

剡 是 樞 機 this is the controlling force.

(a) The gums.

笑 不 至 剡 when laughing, do not show the gums.

諗 3 **To consult carefully with; to counsel. To announce.**
5733

諗 告 to conjure; to urge upon.
諗 念 to reflect on.
諗 諫 百 端 admonish him by every argument.

愼 4 **To act with care; to be cautious. Also read** *ch'en.*
5734

愼 之 Beware!
愼 其 獨 也 careful of himself when alone.
愼 勿 怠 荒 take heed, be not idle.
愼 密 secret, reticent.
5**愼 微** careful in the minutest particulars.
愼 思 明 辨 discriminate wisely.
愼 終 追 遠 carefully attend to the funeral rites of parents and follow them when gone with due sacrifices.
愼 而 無 禮 則 葸 carefulness without the rules of propriety begets fearfulness.
愼 行 careful in action.
10**愼 言 其 餘** be careful how you speak of the rest.
愼·重 to be very careful; to give heed to; to attach weight to.
愼·重 執 行 proceed with great care.
不 可 不 愼 great caution is necessary.

滲 4 **To leak; to soak through. Also read** *ch'en*4.
5735

滲 漏 to leak.
滲 灕 to run off; to flow away.
滲 透 osmosis.

(a) **Read** *shên*1. **The downy appearance of growing feathers.**

腎 4 **The kidneys. The testes. A gizzard.**
5736

腎 上 腺 supra-renal glands.
腎 主 智 the kidneys are the seat of wisdom.
腎 囊 the scrotum.
腎 子 the testicles.
5**腎 水 虧** incontinence of urine.
腎 臟 炎 nephritis.
腎 葉 lobes of the kidney.
內 腎 the kidneys.
外 腎 the testicles.
鴨 腎 a duck's gizzard.

蜃 4 **A marine monster which can change its shape. Water-spouts. The Chinese sea-serpent. General name for clams. Also read** *ch'en*2.
5737

蜃 市 a mirage.
蜃 樓 buildings seen in a mirage—sea-serpent stories.
蜃 氣 a water-spout; a mirage.
蜃 炭 clam-shells burnt to lime.
蜃 車 a hearse.

SHENG.　(ㄕㄥ)
(Seng)

生 1 **To produce; to bring forth; to beget. To be born.**
5738 **Life, living. Radical 100.**

生·下 begotten.
生 不 帶 來 死 不 帶 去 we brought nothing into this world and we shall carry nothing out.
生 世 to be born into the world.
生 之 者 衆 食 之 者 寡 let the producers be many, the consumers few.
5**生 亂** to create a disturbance.
生·了 杈 兒 sending out a branch—to meet with something awkward or unfortunate.
生 事 to make a disturbance.
生 人 a mortal; a living person. *See below*-B. 1.
生 來 from birth; to produce.
10**生·來 是 這·樣** it is naturally like this.

生·來·的 性·情 the natural disposition.
生·出 枝 葉 leads to complications.
生·出 芽 來 sending forth shoots.
生 分 at variance; estranged.
15**生 利** profit; to make profit.
生 利 者 producers.
生 前 死 後 during life and after death.
今 日 生 前 now in this life.
生 則 不 得 事 養 could not be served with propriety while living.
20**生 剖 動 物** vivisection. *See below* —173.
生 動 life-like.
生 勞 不 如 死 逸 better dead and at ease than alive and unhappy.
生 口 captives in war. Sometimes used wrongly for **牲·口**, horses, mules, etc.
生 吞 活 剝 flayed and swallowed alive—determined to have him killed; mere plagiarisms, fitting stock expressions into one's compositions. *See* **活** No. 2401—8.
25**生 命** life.
生 命 保 險 life insurance.
生 命 刑 capital punishment.
生 命 哲 學 philosophy of life.
生 命 帶 life-belt.
30**生 命 權** right of life.
生 壙 tomb prepared during one's life.
生 好 結 果 productive of good.
生 子 to beget children; a child of fifteen.
生 子 立 後 to beget sons and establish a posterity.
35**生 存** existence; survival; preserved alive.
生 存 力 vitality.
生 存 競 爭 struggle for existence.
生 孩 六 月 when only a child, six months old.
生 平 or **平 生** habitually; through life.
40**生 平 之 力** the entire strength.
生 平 之 萬 幸 it will be the greatest good fortune of my life.
生 平 無 病 never ailing.
喪 其 生 平 lost all sense of propriety.
如 平 生 as usual.

45 平生終日別 parted for ever in this life.

生弊竇 gives rise to corrupt practices.

生徒 pupils.

生·得天然 made so naturally; born so.

生得²觀念 innate ideas.

50 生心 the passions and emotions; mental activity.

生性 natural disposition.

生息 to bear interest; to make profit.

生恐 to become fearful.

生·意 trade, business, livelihood, vitality, desires.

55 終無生意 but he had no desire to live.

生意滿 satisfied the heart's desires.

生·意發達 business prospering.

生愛 to show great kindness.

生態學 or 生·活狀態變化學 the study of animal and plant life—ecology.

60 生成 second nature; innate; to grow to; to become.

生成人家 to help others to get on.

生擒 to take alive.

生敗子³ to bear a profligate son.

生數ᵃ a factor.

65 生於憂患死於安樂 life springs from sorrow and calamity, death comes from ease and pleasure. (-lê⁴)

生·日 or 生辰 a birthday.

生旦净末丑 five classes of actors.

生有日死有時 there is a time to be born and a time to die.

生根 to take root.

70 生業 occupation; calling.

生機 vitality; principle of life.

生機素 vitamines.

生機論 vitalism.

生死 life and death; alive and dead.

75 生死之際 a life and death crisis.

生死之交 life and death friendship.

生死大事 the important matters of life and death.

生殖 reproduction.

生殖作用 the reproductive function.

80 生殖器 reproductive organs.

生殖細胞 reproductive cells.

生殺之權 the power of life and death.

生民 or 民生 people; population.

生氣 to get angry; the spirit of life.

85 沒有生氣 no living breath—quite dead.

生氣主義 animism.

生氣勃勃 full of vitality.

生沒遷徙 births, deaths, and removals.

生法 means of livelihood.

90 生法子 to devise means.

生活 life; to endow with life.

91½ 生·活 livelihood.

生活問題 problems of life; problems of a livelihood.

生·活機能 vital function.

生·活漸其度 the standard of living gradually rose.

95 生·活程·度 the standard of living.

生·活狀·況 conditions of living.

生·活競爭 struggle for a livelihood.

生·活要素 necessities of life.

生·活費 living expenses; cost of living.

100 生·活需用 necessities of life.

生津 to cause a flow of saliva.

生涯 trade; business; livelihood.

以筆墨爲生涯 to earn a living by means of the pen.

生火 to light a fire.

105 生物 living things; animal and plant life.

生物化學 bio-chemistry.

生物學 biology.

生物學·的人類學 biological anthropology.

生物界 the world of living creatures.

110 生物·的團體 a group of living things.

生物進化中之一級 .... is only one step in the evolution of living creatures—referring to man.

生理 physiology; trade: livelihood.

生理·上 physiologically.

生理上的病 physical defects.

115 生理冷淡 business is dull.

生理學 physiology.

生理心理學 physiological psychology.

生理·的 physiological.

生生不已 age after age; unceasing succession.

120 生生不息 ever producing without rest.

生生世世 from generation to generation, without end.

生產 to give birth to; parturition; produce; production.

生產三要素 three essential elements of production—raw material, labour, and capital.

生產制 productive system.

125 生產協社 productive co-operation.

生產方法 methods of production. 生產過剩 over-production.

生產物 products.

生產者 producer.

生產行·爲 a productive action.

130 生產費 cost of production.

生疏 estranged; at variance. *See below*—B. 19.

生疑 to create doubts or suspicions.

生病 to fall ill.

生瘡 to break out in sores; to get boils or ulcers.

135 生發 to develop; to spring up; to get on; to put forth.

生端 to cause trouble or disturbance.

生者寄也死者歸也 life is a lodging place, death is returning home.

生知 intuitive knowledge.

生知之亞 one stage below intuitive knowledge.

140 生祠 shrine in honour of a living person.

生稟 heredity.

生稟之異 constitutional differences.

生而知之 knew it when he was born—intuitive knowledge.

生而知者 one who knows intuitively.

145 生而瞽 born blind.

生肖 the animal which rules the year in which one was born.

生育 to bear; to rear.

生自 to be produced from; to come forth from.

生花 to have smallpox; to blossom.

150 生華陀 a living *Hua T'o*—a famous surgeon who lived in the 3d century A.D. — said of a clever doctor.

[words.

生 蟲 to breed worms, etc.
生 觀 view of life.
生°計 livelihood; plans for getting a living.
生 計 問 題 problem of a livelihood.
155生 計 困 難 difficult economic conditions; hard to make a living.
生 財 有 道 there is a way to become wealthy.
生 資 means of a livelihood.
生 質 the natural constitution of.
生 質 之 美 the beauty of the natural disposition.
160生 身 父 母 one's father and mother.
生 辰 八 字 the eight characters of a horoscope, giving the pairs of characters indicating the year, month, day and hour of birth.
生 逢 聖 代 I was born under a worthy ruler.
生 道 the way of life.
生 金 profits. 生 銹 to get rusty.
165生 長 (chang³) to be born and grow up.
生 長³律 general law of growth.
生 離 死 別 悲 哀 最 切 to be separated in life and parted at death is the bitterest sorrow.
生 電 to generate electricity.
生 靈 living beings.
170生 類 之 羣 the multitude of living beings.
生 養 to bring up; to beget.
生 兒 養 女 begat sons and daughters.
生 體 解 剖 vivisection. See above—20.
生 髮 油 oil to make the hair grow.
175生 齒 the people.
一 生 a whole life; a lifetime.
三 生 past, present, and future—three states of existence.
今 生 this life.
來 生 the life to come; future existence.
180偸 生 to steal a life—to escape a capital sentence.
先°生 elder-born; title of courtesy—Sir. 先°生 Mr.
再 生 to come to life again.
半 生 mid-life.
四 生 four kinds of birth, i.e.,
185胎 生 birth from the womb—viviparous.

卵 生 birth from an egg—oviparous.
濕 生 birth from damp—as insects are supposed to be.
化 生 birth by transformation—as moths, etc., or as reincarnations.
天 生 innate.
190如 生 life-like. 後°生 young.
後 生 or 晚 生 late-born—used of oneself in address to elders.
復 生 to arise from the dead.
托°生 reborn in the body of another.
投 生 to be born again.
195接 生 or 收 生 to attend child-birth.
放 生 to liberate living creatures—for merit.
無 一 爲 生 nothing to support life.
畜 生 brute beasts.
重 生ᶻ a new-birth; regeneration.

(a) A scholar. A graduate. Term used by pupils of themselves. Young male characters in plays.

生 員 a first-degree licentiate under the former system.
儒 生 the literati.
學°生 pupils; students.
寄 宿 生 boarding pupils.
5文 生 or 童 生 a pupil who had received a certificate from the local magistrate permitting him to compete at the examinations for the former first degree.
書°生 a literary man.
畢 業 生 a graduate.
監²生 a first-degree graduate under the former system.
通 學°生 a day scholar.
10醫°生 a doctor.
門°生 a pupil; a disciple.

(b) Raw, unworked, uncooked. Fresh, unfamiliar, uncivilized, unacquainted with.

生 人 or 生 臉 人 a stranger. See above—8.
生°來°的 spontaneous; newly-arrived.
生 冷 raw fruits.
生 分 estranged; unripe.
5生 力 軍 fresh troops.
生 吃°了 eaten alive or eaten raw.
生 地 unopened lands; a medicine, the root of Rehmannia glutinosa.

生 字 unfamiliar characters; new
生 客 a stranger.
10生 小 when young and inexperienced.
生°得°很 very unfamiliar with; very much out of practice.
生 手 a raw hand; a new comer.
生 書 books which one has not studied.
生 棉 raw cotton.
15生 油 peanut-oil.
生 漆 unboiled varnish.
生 牛 皮 raw hides.
生 番 wild savages.
生 疏 out of practice; strange. See above—131.
20生 石 灰 quicklime.
生 筋 uncooked dough.
生 絲 raw silk.
生 紙 unsized paper; uncalendered paper.
生 芻 sacrificial gift at a funeral.
25生 菜 raw vegetables; salads.
生 菓 unripe fruit; raw fruits.
生 薑 green ginger.
生 藥 herbs; simples.
生 賣 to sell a standing crop.
30生 銅 copper ore; unmanufactured copper or brass.
生 銀 lump silver.
生 鐵 cast iron; raw iron.
生 面 a stranger. See 別 No. 5208—B. 39.
面 生 unfamiliar face; a stranger.
35認 生 to be shy; to recognize as strange or unfamiliar.

(c) Used as an intensive.

生 怕 very fearful; apprehensive.
生 拉 硬 拽 to drag a person to an affair rather against his will.
生 生°的 嚇°死°了 absolutely scared to death.
生 痛 or 生 疼 intensely painful.
5好°生 be careful. See No. 2062—A. 19, 20.
怎 生 是 好 What is the best thing to do?
白 生 生²的 very white.

(d) Used in transliterating.

生 丁 centime.
生 的 克 蘭 姆 centigramme.
生 的 立 脫 爾 centilitre.
生 的 米 突 centimetre.
生 脫 cent.
生 脫 爾 cental.

牲[1] Animals; sacrificial beasts; cattle.
5739

牲 犢 a calf.
牲 畜 or 牲·口 animals; cattle.
三 牲 fish, pork and fowl.
六 牲 six domestic animals—the horse, ox, goat or sheep, pig, dog, and fowl.
犧 牲 a sacrificial beast; to sacrifice.

牲[1] A multitude; a crowd; numerous.
5740

牲 牲 其 鹿 How numerous the deer!
牲 衆 numerous.

眚[3] A disease of the eyes; a film. A crime, a fault. To injure.
5741

眚 沴 poisonous exhalations.
眚 災 肆 赦 inadvertencies and crimes caused by misfortune might be forgiven.
眚 病 a disease in which the hands, nails, and lips turn green; to be possessed by demons.
不 以 一 眚 掩 大 德 do not allow one error to obscure great merits.

笙[1] A small musical instrument consisting of a number of pipes of different lengths; it has a spout through which the player blows out or sucks in the air, while fingering the keyholes.
5742

笙 歌 music and singing.
笙 磬 同 音 harmony—used fig.
笙 管 the pipes of the above.
笙 簧 the reeds of the above.
笙 簧 迭 作 the music struck up.

甥[1] The children of a sister. A son-in-law.
5743

甥 兒[2] or 甥 女 son or daughter of a sister.
外·甥 or 外·甥 女 nephew or niece, children of a sister.
外(甥)孫 son of a daughter.

省[3] A province.
5744

省·分 (fên[4]) a province.
省 制 provincial system.
省 城 or 省 會 the provincial capital.
省 政 府 Provincial Government.
[5]省 政 府 委 員 會 Provincial Government Committee.
省 敎 育 會 Provincial Educational Association.
省 界 provincial boundaries.
省 立 學 校 Provincial School.
省 議 員 member of a Provincial Assembly.
[10]省 議 會 Provincial Assembly.
省 長 Provincial Governor.
省 黨 部 Provincial Nationalist Party Bureau.

(a) Frugal. To diminish. To save. To reduce.

省·不 下 unable to economize further.
省 事 or 省 工 to save trouble or labour; to avoid doing it over again.
省 儉 frugal; sparing.
省 刑 罰 to be sparing of punishment.
[5]省 力 to save strength.
省 却 to spare; to save.
省 吃 儉 用 very frugal.
省·得 lest; to avoid.
省·得 我 去 to save my going there.
[10]省 文 terse; an abridged expression; elliptical.
省 料 to save material.
省 易 abbreviated; simplified.
省 減 to reduce; to lessen; to diminish.
省 用 to economize.
[15]省 略 法 ellipsis.
省 約 to abridge; to be sparing of.
省 約 其 言 sparing of words.
省 處 terse passages.
省 訟 to save litigation.
[20]省 費 to save expense.
省 費 心 to save oneself trouble.
省 釋 to release.
省 錢 to save money.

(b) Read hsing[3], sing[3]. To examine; to watch. To be on the alert.

省 于 其 君 to report everything to one's sovereign.

省 其 私 亦 足 以 發 I have examined his conduct when he is away from me, and have found him able to show forth—my teachings.
省 墓 to visit the graves of parents or relations.
省 安 to keep the country quiet.
[5]省 察 to look into; to scrutinize.
省 心 or 省 悟 to comprehend; to be sensible of.
省 斂 to examine the harvest.
省 書 to study.
省 省 uneasy.
[10]省 自 己 過 self-examination.
省 親 to visit one's parents.
省 覺 to comprehend; to be sensible of.
不 省 unable to comprehend; not able to make out the meaning.
不 省 人 事 insensible; unconscious.
[15]定 省 to bid one's parents good-morning or good-night.

升[1] To ascend; to arise; to advance in office; to promote. Inter. next. Distinguish 卅 No. 1143; 卉 No. 5223.
5745

升 任 to be promoted to a post.
升 冠 raise your hat!
升 化 作 用 sublimation. See below—No. 5746-5.
升 堂 to enter court; to sit on the bench; to enter the inner hall.
[5]升 堂 入 室 entered into the inner apartments—said of one whose scholarship is profound. See below—6.
升 堂 奕 未 入 於 室 也 he has ascended the hall, but he has not entered the inner rooms—not fully entered into the profundities of the teaching.
升 天 to ascend to heaven.
升 天 日 Ascension Day.
升 學 promoted to a higher school.
[10]升 安 promotion and peace—conventional close to a letter.
升 平 peaceful—times.
升 座 to take the chair.
升 座 公 位 took his seat on the bench.
升 旗 to hoist a flag.
[15]升 旗 繩 flag-halyards.
升 沉 已 定 promotion and degradation are already fixed.

升法 or 機升法 sublimation. *See below*—No. 5746-5.

升班 to be promoted.

升登 to go up; to get up.

20 升硫磺 sublimated sulphur.

升祉 promotion and happiness—conventional close to a letter.

升科 to enter newly opened or reclaimed land as being available for taxation.

升級 to be promoted.

升·過·來 transferred on promotion.

25 升遐 to ascend to the distant regions—to die.

升遷 promoted; to transfer on promotion.

升降 to ascend and descend; promotion and degradation.

升降機 an elevator or lift.

升降舵 elevator on an aeroplane.

30 升階 to go up steps; an honorary title.

升騰 to ascend.

(a) A pint, a measure equivalent to 31.6 cubic inches. 10 *shêng* equal one *tou* 斗.

升斗 pints and pecks—dry measure.

一升米 a pint of rice.

昇

5746　To ascend. Peaceful.

昇天 to ascend to heaven.

昇平之代 a transformed age of peace.

昇平盛世 a tranquil and plenteous age.

昇汞 corrosive sublimate.

5 昇華作用 sublimation.

昇華物 sublimates.

昇降 to rise and fall.

陞

5747 Inter. 升 No. 5745.　To ascend; to rise, as in office.

陞啟 to be handed to ....to open—put at the bottom of an envelope beneath the name of the addressee.

陞官 to be promoted.

陞賦 to enter for taxation—waste lands, etc.

陞轎 to get into a sedan chair.

SHÊNG. (ㄕㄥ)

聲 声

5748　1 A sound; a voice; a tone. Music. Reputation; fame. To state, to make known.

聲價甚高 great reputation.

聲其罪以責之 make known his faults in order to reprove them.

聲利 fame and profit.

聲勢 display; majesty.

5 聲勢大 powerful; influential.

聲勢相倚 mutually dependent forces.

虛張聲勢 to make an empty demonstration—as a bluff.

聲叉 a tuning-fork.

聲及 mentioned.

10 聲敘理由 explain the circumstances.

聲名 fame; reputation.

聲名狼籍 his reputation is ruined.

聲妓 singing-girls.

聲學 acoustics.

15 聲容 voice and facial expression.

聲實 a substantial reputation.

聲帶 vocal cords.

聲張 to noise abroad; to disclose.

聲影片 "talking films."

20 聲律 laws of sound.

聲威 prestige.

聲拒 to protest.

聲援 to come to the relief of—as troops.

聲敎 a ruler's name and influence.

25 聲明 to report clearly about; to state in detail.

聲明事由 explain the details.

聲望 fame, reputation, prestige.

聲東擊西 to let it be known that an attack is proposed on the east, while the real advance is on the west.

聲母 initials in phonetics.

30 聲氣 voice; sound.

聲浪 sound waves.

聲淚具下 bitter weeping with loud noise.

聲稱 to state verbally; to declare.

聲聞 disciples who listen to the utterances of Buddha; reputation; it is rumoured that ....; the sound heard in ....

35 聲聞於我 it has been reported to me.

聲聲相應[4] every sound was re-echoed; to echo the opinions of another.

聲色 demeanour; countenance; music and women.

不動聲色 unmoved.

聲色者敗德之具 music and sensual pleasures are destructive to virtue.

40 聲華 a glorious reputation.

聲裂天地 the sound rent the skies.

聲言 to say; to express a thing.

聲調 (*tiao*[4]) voice or tune in singing; the tones (of Chinese).

聲請 to make a verbal request.

45 聲請表揚 verbal request to make it widely known.

聲門 the glottis.

聲·音 a tone; a sound; a voice.

聲音學 phonetics.

聲音尖 high, shrill tones.

50 聲·音幽雅 refined accents.

聲·音意識 sound consciousness.

聲·音洪亮 clear sounds.

聲韻 sound and echo; tones and finals for rhyming in the Chinese dictionaries.

聲響 a sound; a report.

55 同聲相應 the echo answers.

四聲 the four tones of the Chinese literary style.

平聲 the even tone.

上[4]聲 the rising tone.

去聲 the departing tone.

60 入聲 the entering tone.

繩

5749　2 A cord, a rope, string, a marking-line:—thus—to measure, to estimate, to restrain.

繩之以法 restrain them by law.

繩其祖武 to imitate one's ancestors.

繩墨 a marking-line—rule of conduct.

不拘繩墨 not bound by hard and fast rules.

5 繩·子 rope; twine; cordage.

繩愆糾繆 to correct faults or shortcomings.

繩樞 rope for hinges—a poor man's house.

繩正 to rectify.

繩牀 a rope-bed.

10 繩盜 to punish robbers.

繩直 straight as a stretched cord.

繩繙 ropes; cordage.

子³孫 繩 繩 a continuous line of posterity.

打 繩 to twist ropes.

¹⁵赤 繩 繫 足 the red cord binds the feet—of those destined to marry each other; to betroth.

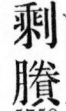

剩
賸

5750

Residue; overplus; remains; remnants.

剩 ·下·的 left over; surplus.

剩 三·百·個 錢 a balance of three hundred cash.

剩 ·了 一 半 one half remains over.

剩 多·少 How much is left over?

⁵剩 有 限 there is not much left.

剩 貨 remnants of goods; driblets.

剩 錢 money remaining; balance.

剩 飯 left over food.

剩 餘 價·值 surplus value.

晟

5751

⁴ The brightness of the sun. Light; splendour.

盛

5752

⁴ Abundant, flourishing, plenteous. Used conventionally for "your."

盛 世 a prosperous age or period.

盛 事 a generous action; a grand affair.

盛 京 Shêngking—an old name for the province of Liaoning.

盛 典 Imperial favour or kindness.

⁵盛 名 難 副 his fame is greater than he deserves.

盛 大 very great.

盛 年 in the prime of life.

盛 德 great virtue.

盛 心 kindheartedness; good feeling; kindness.

¹⁰盛 怒 great anger.

盛 恩 great favour; your kindness.

盛 意 your generous intentions.

盛 惠 or 盛 情 great favour; grace; kindness.

盛 時 prosperous times.

¹⁵盛 服 full dress.

盛 極 必 衰 when prosperity reaches its height it begins to wane.

盛 業 thriving trade; prosperous.

盛 氣 in a great rage.

盛 氣 陵 人 to put on airs and insult others.

²⁰盛 治 a prosperous administration.

盛 衆 very numerous.

盛 福 profusion of blessings.

盛 禮 profuse politeness.

盛 筵 a sumptuous feast.

²⁵盛 美 excellent; admirable.

盛 與 prosperous; thriving.

盛 行 (hang²) your firm.

盛 衰 thriving and declining; robust and failing, etc.

盛 裝 gaily dressed.

³⁰盛 設 plentiful spread—of dishes.

盛 開 in full bloom.

盛 饌 abundance of delicacies—as at a feast.

(a) Read ch'êng². To hold; to contain.

盛 ·不 住 話 unable to keep a secret; to tell all that one hears.

盛 ·不 起 來 will not hold it.

盛 水 不 漏 close-fisted; trustworthy; able to keep a secret.

盛 滿 ·了 filled to the full.

盛 酒 to fill with wine; to contain wine.

盛 飯 to help to rice; to serve up the meal.

聖
圣

5753

⁴ Holy, sacred, reverend. Divine. Used for "saint." Imperial.

聖 主 or 聖 上 or 聖 君 the Emperor.

聖 京 the Holy City—Jerusalem.

聖 人 a sage; Confucius—one divinely inspired and intuitively wise.

主 保 聖 人 patron saint.

⁵聖 供 地 consecrated ground.

聖 像 sacred effigies; images; idols.

聖 品 Holy Orders.

聖 善 goodness; holiness.

聖 地 holy ground; holy places; The Holy Land.

¹⁰聖 壽 the Emperor's birthday.

聖 安 his Majesty's health.

聖 廟 the Confucian Temple.

聖 徒 saints.

聖 徒 交 通 communion of saints.

¹⁵聖 戰 the Crusades.

聖 所 The Holy Place.

聖 教 Confucianism.

聖 旨 an Imperial decree.

聖 書 or 聖 經 The Bible; the Confucian Canon.

²⁰聖 母 title of a goddess; term for the Virgin Mary used by Roman Catholics.

聖 水 holy water.

聖 潔 holy; pure.

聖 牌 charms worn on the person.

聖 王 Yao and Shun.

²⁵聖 王 之 瑞 the auspicious omens of a sage king.

聖 神 sages and spiritual men.

聖 秩 制 度 hierarchy.

聖 經 外 傳 Apocrypha.

聖 經 研 究 會 Bible-Study Classes.

³⁰聖 經 類 編 a concordance to the Bible.

聖 裁 Imperial decision.

聖 裔 descendants of Confucius.

聖 誕 or 寶 誕 the birthday of a god, sage, etc.

聖 誕 節 festival of the birthday of a god—used by some for Christmas. See No. 6051-5 ff.

³⁵聖 諭 an Imperial Edict.

聖 賢 saints and worthy men; sages.

聖 都 the Holy City—Jerusalem, Mecca, Rome, etc.

聖 鑑 or 聖 覽 the sacred glance—of the Emperor's eye.

聖 門 the disciples of Confucius—literati.

⁴⁰聖 靈 the Holy Spirit.

聖 靈 降 臨 日 Whitsunday.

聖 馬 太 S. Matthew.

聖 餐 Holy Communion; the Lord's Supper.

吃 聖 餐 to partake of the Lord's Supper.

⁴⁵領 聖 餐 者 a communicant.

勝

5754

⁴ To overcome; to vanquish; to excel. Superior to.

勝 ·了 世 界 overcame the world.

勝 人 to have an advantage over others.

勝 仗 a victorious battle.

勝 似 much better than; superior to.

⁵勝 利 victory—not only in battles.

勝 利 ·的 結 果 the fruits of victory.

勝 國 a defeated State; a superseded dynasty.

勝 如 more than; better than.

勝 強 much superior; much stronger than.

[10]勝 常 better than usual—a good wish.

勝 情 emotion.

勝 意 your valued opinion.

勝 敗 未 分 the issue is still doubtful.

勝 敵 to overcome the foe.

[15]勝 於 superior to.

勝 於 飲 食 more than food or drink.

不 勝 於 走 獸 no better than the beasts.

較 勝 於 無 better than nothing.

勝 日 fine days.

[20]勝 會 a gala.

勝 流 the upper classes.

勝 績 victory.

勝 訴 to win a lawsuit.

勝 負 or 勝 敗 to win or lose; to succeed or fail.

[25]勝 過 (much) better than; superior to.

克 勝 or 制 勝 to master; to overcome.

好 勝 always must be first.

得 勝 to get the victory.

德 行 勝 人 his virtue excels that of others.

[30]戰 勝 to win a battle.

連 勝 successive victories.

遠 勝 in a great degree; far surpassing.

(a) Place of scenic beauty.

勝 地 beautiful place.

勝 景 scenic resort.

勝 概 beautiful scenery.

勝 踐 or 勝 游 to visit places of scenic beauty.

勝 迹 famous ruins

江 山 之 勝 the beauty of the scenery.

(b) Read *shêng*[1]. To be equal to; to sustain; to bear. To be worthy of.

勝 任 equal to the duties of the office.

勝 住 to take the responsibility.

勝 其 任 to fulfil its intended purpose.

勝 衣 able to wear clothes—as a child that is growing.

[5]勝 選 eligible.

勝 防 able to fend.

不 勝 欣 喜 overcome with joy.

不 可 勝 言 beyond description.

力 不 能 勝 unable to lift it.

膡 [4]
5755　Sesame.

苣 藤 sesame.

SHIH.　(ㄕ)
(Shǐ)

尸 [1] A corpse. One who im-personates the dead at a
5756　sacrifice. Radical 44.
Distinguish 戶 No. 2189. 「ㄕ.
National Phonetic letter for *sh*.

尸 位 a corpse on the throne; an idler, one who does nothing for his bread; the person who represents Confucius in sacrifices; one who impersonates the dead.

尸 位 素 餐 to neglect the duties of an office while taking the pay.

尸 婆 子 female exorcists.

[5]尸 居 餘 氣 at the point of death.

尸 祝 one who impersonates a deceased person at funerals.

尸 祿 to draw the salary but neglect the duty.

尸 解 death of a Taoist who be-comes an immortal.

尸 諫 rebuked his prince by means of his corpse.

尸 首 or 尸 身 a corpse.

[10]尸 骨 a corpse.

三 尸 神 three spirits supposed to reside in the body, controlling the body, heart, and mind, i.e., the material, the emotions, and the reason or will; they are supposed to reside in the head, belly, and feet respectively.

(a) To arrange. To manage or superintend.

尸 盟 the person who administers an oath.

尸 臣 an officer in charge of certain matters.

誰 其 尸 之 Who attends to the matter?—the cooking.

(b) To expose the corpse of an executed person.

尸 諸 朝 exposed the corpse in the court.

屎 [3]　Filth, ordure, excrement.
5757

屎 坑 or 茅 鋼 a public convenience.

屎 桶 a commode.

屎·蜣 蜋 the dung beetle.

拉 屎 to go to stool.

眼 屎 the secretion from the eyes.

鳲 [1]　The turtle-dove or wood-pigeon.
5758

鳲 鳩 the cuckoo; the wood-pigeon.

屍 [1]　A corpse, a carcase.
5759

屍 圖 the diagram of a corpse—showing the vital and the non-vital spots.

屍 姓 the deceased man.

屍 所 or 屍 場 or 屍 棚 the place of death.

屍 格 a printed form enumerating the parts of a corpse—used at inquests.

[5]屍 橫 屋 倒 corpses lying around and houses overturned.

屍 親 relatives of the deceased.

屍·首 or 屍 身 or 屍 骸 a corpse; the remains of the dead.

屍 骨 bones of the dead.

屍 體 解 剖 post-mortem examination.

[10]以 屍 移 害 to get a person into trouble by placing a corpse at his door.

剝 屍 to strip a corpse.

驗 屍 to hold an inquest.

師 [1] A teacher, an instructor. To imitate. Distinguish 帥
5760　No. 5909. Also read *szŭ*[1].

師 事 to treat a person as a teacher.

師·傅 a teacher; an expert; a master workman.

大·師·傅 a cook; a head servant.

師 兄 弟 schoolmates; fellow-students.

[5]師 公 a male instructor.

師·姑 a Buddhist nun.

師 娘 and 師 母 a wife; wife of one of the middle classes. Mrs.,

in North and South China, respectively. [ther of one's teacher.

師 婆 a female instructor; the mo-
師 尊 a teacher; a chief.
10 師 心 自 用 self-opinionated.
師 比 fastening of a leather girdle.
師 父 a teacher; a master; term of respect sometimes applied to women.
師 爺 secretaries in a *yamen*.
師 範 學 校 Normal School.
15 師 表 patterns to be imitated—as former worthy men. *See below*—A. 4.
師 資 a teacher.
師 長 (*chang*³) a superintendent. *See below*—A. 5.
律 師 a legal advisor; barrister.
法 師 a Buddhist priest.
20 測 量 師 a surveyor.
老 師 a teacher; a journeyman.
舵 師 a pilot on an aeroplane.
醫 師 a physician.

(a) **The people. A multitude. All. An army. Capital city. A division in the Chinese army.**

師 團 a division in the Jap. army.
師 旅 a body of 2,500 troops—ancient.
師 船 a war-vessel.
師 表 call to arms. *See above*—15.
5 師 長 (*chang*³) a divisional commander.
京 師 the capital.
出 師 to go on a campaign.
大 師 the masses.
居 師 to settle the people.
10 水 師 marines.
班 師 to withdraw forces.

獅¹
5761
A lion. Also read *szŭ*¹.

獅 口 the lion's mouth.
獅 子 a lion.
獅 子 吼 the roar of the lion—the preaching of Buddha.
獅 子 國 Ceylon. [stellation Leo.
5 獅 子 座 Buddha's seat; the con-
獅 子 狗 Pekingese dogs.
獅 子 鷹 the screech-owl.
獅 子 鼻 a short, flat nose.
獅 身 人 面 the Sphinx.
石 獅 stone lions at entrance gates.

螄¹
5762
A spiral shell. Also read *szŭ*¹.

螄 蛤 scallop-ribbed shells.

筮⁴
5763
To divine by stalks of plants.

筮 人 a fortune-teller.
筮 仕 to be appointed by lot to an official post.

噬⁴
5764
To bite; to gnaw. An initial particle.

噬 指 棄 薪 she bit her finger and he dropped the firewood—alludes to a youth, who, while out gathering brushwood, was conscious of his mother's pain; she had bitten her finger in order to let him know that a visitor had come.
噬 狗 a dog that bites people.
噬 臍 何 及 How can a man bite his navel?—impossibility; too late to repent.

澨⁴
5765
A river in Hupeh. A bank; a foreshore. Also read *shê*⁴.

豕³
5766
A pig; a hog. Radical 152.

豕 苓 a root resembling China-root.
豕 鬃 pig's bristles.

弛³
5767
To unstring a bow. To relax; to annul; to do away with.

弛 力 slack; to become remiss.
弛 放 or 解 (*hsie*⁴) 弛 to loosen; to weaken.
弛 禁 to rescind a prohibition; to abrogate.
廢 弛 obsolete; worn out and useless.

施¹
5768
To bestow; to grant. To act; to do. To exhibit. Used to strengthen the verb which it precedes.

施 主 a benefactor—a title given to all who support Buddhism

by acts of charity.
施 于 中 林 —the net is—set in the forest.
施 佈 to give in charity.
施 力 to put forth effort; to exert oneself.
5 施 勞 to make a display of merit.
施 展 to expand; to open; to display.
施 展 大 恩 to bestow great favours.
施 工 to employ labour; to labour.
施 張 to expand; to display; to open; to bestow.
10 施 恩 to show favour; to be kind to.
施 恩 所 the "mercy-seat."
施 威 to show severity.
施 捨 or 施 濟 to do alms; to bestow in charity.
施 擺 to boast; to make a show.
15 施 放 to discharge—as a gun.
施 政 根 據 basis of administrative activities.
施 敎 to teach; to instruct; to propagate doctrines.
施 救 to save; to give relief.
施 散 to distribute.
20 施 於 有 政 —these qualities—are displayed in government.
施 施 從 外 來 to come in jauntily.
施 洗 or 行 洗 to baptize.
施 爲 actions; behaviour.
施 禮 to perform acts of ceremony.
25 施 粥 廠 a soup-kitchen, for charity.
施 脂 粉 to use cosmetics for making up the face.
施 與 to grant to; to bestow.
施 行 grant that it be so; allow it; let it be thus; to act; to put into operation; to enforce.
施 行 公 理 to act with justice.
30 施 行 審 判 to execute justice.
施 行 手 續 procedure necessary to put a thing into effect.
施 行 拯 救 to effect salvation.
施 行 期 fixed date for putting into effect.
施 行 符 咒 to use spells or charms.
35 施 行 鬆 免 to grant a generous pardon.
施 諸 己 而 不 願 亦 勿 施 于 人 what you do not wish done to yourself, do not do unto others.
己 所 不 欲 勿 施 於 人 a variant of the above.

施 醫 院 or 醫 館 a hospital.
施 食 to feed the poor.

(a) Read *shih*[3]. To relax; to do away with. See No. 5767.

君 子[3]不 施 其 親 the virtuous prince does not neglect his relations.

(b) Read *i*[4], or *i*[2]. To extend to.

施 于 中 谷 extending to the middle of the valley.
施 從 良 人 之 所 之 she privately followed her husband wherever he went.

史[3] History; chronicles; annals. A historian.
5769 Distinguish 吏 No. 3853.

史 乘 annals.
史 學 家 historians.
史 官 a censor; historiographer.
史 料 historical data.
[5]史 書 historical books; annals.
史 臣 a chronicler; a historian.
史 記 The Historical Records—one of the Dynastic Histories of China.
史 遷 or 司 馬 遷 the historian *Szŭ Ma Ch'ien*.
野 史 romances; stories with a basis of supposed historical data.

使[3] To employ; to use. To send; to order. To cause;
5770 to allow.
Distinguish 便 No. 5224.

使 不 得 unserviceable; useless; not allowable.
使 不 通 will not pass current.
使 之 降 服 to cause to surrender.
使 乖 弄 巧 to use cunning or trickery.
[5]使 人 也 器 之 he uses men according to their capacity.
使 人 證 明 to call to account.
使 令 or 使 命 to summon; to order.
使 作 商 品 made a matter of merchandise.
使 利 to cause profit to; to benefit.
[10]使 利 便 to facilitate.
使 勁 to exert one's strength.
使 喚 to use; to call—as a servant.
使 壞 了 spoilt in using.

使 好 意 思 to mean well.
[15]使 己 爲 政 pushed himself into the government.
使 得 or 做 得 so that; allowable; very well; it will do; to cause.
使 心 用 意 to take pains.
使 性 子 sulky; cross; to act in a contrary manner.
使 於 四 方 to be sent in any direction on government business.
[20]使 有 to occasion....to be.
使 民 以 時 employ the people at the proper season—so as not to interfere with agricultural operations.
使 用 outlay; needful expenses; to employ; to use.
使 的 東 西 things in use.
使 眼 色 to ogle; to make signs with the eyes.
[25]使 知 to acquaint; to cause to know.
使 罪 得 赦 that sin may be forgiven.
使 脾 氣 or 使 氣 sulky; peevish; to act in a contrary manner.
使 臂 使 指 to use the arms and fingers—fig., untrammelled.
使 費 expenditure; outlay; charges.
[30]使 費 預 付 charges prepaid.
使 賄 賂 to use bribes.
使 錢 to use money; to bribe; to "squeeze."
使 門 人 爲 臣 he caused the disciples to act as household ministers—to the Sage.

(a) Read *shih*[4]. A messenger. A commissioner. See 公 No. 3701-5ff.

使 君 an envoy.
使 團 the diplomatic corps.
使 女 or 使 婢 a maid-servant.
使 役 a servant.
[5]使 徒 an apostle.
使 徒 時 代 the Apostolic Age.
使 節 a tally given as credentials.
使 者 a messenger.
使 臣 an envoy; a legate; ministers accredited to foreign courts.
[10]使[3]館 a legation; an embassy.
使[3]館 界 the legation quarter.
大 使[3]館 ambassador. 大 使[3]館 an embassy.
天 使 angels.
↑ 公 使 minister. 公 使[3]館 a legation.

駛
駛[3]
5771 To sail a vessel. To hasten; to proceed to.

駛 入 to sail into.
駛 勾 風 to beat against the wind.
駛 回 to sail back.
駛 往 何 處 Where are you bound for?
[5]駛 攏 to come alongside of.
駛 法 rules of navigation.
駛 河 a rapid current.
駛 船 to sail a ship.
駛 行 to go; to run; to proceed.
[10]駛 赴 to sail to; to be bound for.
(駛) 車 夫 car driver.
駛 錯 港 口 to miss reaching port.
駛 風 to run before the wind.
駛 馬 to drive a horse.
[15]在 行 駛 中 under way.
開 駛 to set sail.

始[3] The beginning. To start, to begin; to be the first.
5772

始 作 to initiate; to begin to make.
始 來 origin.
始 初 or 起 初 or 元 始 the beginning; the commencement; at first.
始 則 at first.
[5]始 創 or 始 制 to be the first to make or to do.
始 可 then only can you....
始 基 the basis; the commencement.
始 有 曰 苟 合 矣 when he began to have wealth, he said, "Here's a collection"!
始 條 理 者 commencement of the blended harmony."
[10]始 業 式 commencement exercises; inauguration.
始 皇 帝 the First Emperor—of a united China, 221-209 B.C.
始 祖 the founder of a family; the first ancestor.
　始 遷 祖 the first ancestor that moved into the region.
始 終 or 始 末 beginning and end; throughout; in any case; sooner or later.
[15]始 終 其 事 managed it from first to last.
始 終 如 一 the same from beginning to end; consistent.

始 終 甚 暢 flourished from its inception.

有 始 無 終 abortive.

始 而 at first.

[20]始 行 and then proceeded to.

漦[2] Mucus, spittle, slime. Also read *li*[2].
5773　Read *lai*[2]. Used in names of places.

縰[3] A band or fillet for the hair. Also read *hsi*[3]. Similar to
5774　the next.

縰 縰 莘 莘 numerous; a crowd.

纚[3]　Long, dangling.
5775

飌 纚 flapping and dangling.

(a) Also read *hsi*[3], or *li*[2]. To bind. A rope.

冠 纚 cap strings.

士[4] A scholar; a gentleman. An officer, a soldier. A piece
5776　in Chinese chess. Radical 33. Also read *szŭ*.

士 卒 foot soldiers.

士 君 子[3] the upper classes.

士 大 夫 gentry; officials; upper classes. A.p. (-*tai*[4]·*fu*.)

士 子[3]or 士 人 a scholar.

[5]士 女 men and women.

士 師 the Chief Criminal Judge. The Judges.

士 林 or 士 類 the literati.

士 民 literati and people. [morale.

士。氣 spirit of courage in a soldier;

[10]士 窮 見 節 義 poverty shows up the purity and goodness of a scholar.

士 農 工 商 scholar, f a r m e r, a r t i s a n, and merchant—all classes of people.

士 馬 infantry and cavalry.

勇 士 a warrior.

博 士 doctor, *used as below*.

[15]哲 學 博 士 D o c t o r of Philosophy. Ph.D.

文 學 博 士 D o c t o r of Literature. Litt.D.

法 學 博 士 D o c t o r of Laws. LL.D.

理 學 博 士 D o c t o r of Science. D.Sc.

神 學 博 士 D o c t o r of Divinity. D.D.

[20]醫 學 博 士 D o c t o r of Medicine. M.D.

壯 士 valiant soldiers.

學 士 Bachelor of Arts. B.A.

女 修 士 Sister of Mercy.

女 士 Miss—general term for a professional w o m a n, a s a teacher, etc.

[25]寒 士 a needy scholar.

居 士 a country gentleman; retired scholar.

愛 國 士 a patriot.

文 士 a student.

道 士 a Taoist priest.

[30]碩 士 Master of Arts. M.A.

仕[4] To fill an office; to be a government servant.
5777

仕 商 officials and merchants.

仕 宦 之 家 official family.

仕 宦 行 臺 temporary residence of an official.

仕 版 register of officials.

[5]仕 者 爲 通 to take office in order to share in the schemes of the prince.

仕 途 or 仕 路 an official career.

仕 途 偃 蹇 unfortunate in one's official career.

出 仕 to enter on an official career.

致 仕 to resign office.

侍[4]　To serve; to wait upon.
5778

侍 奉 or 服 侍 or 侍 候 to at-tend on.

侍 女 or 侍 婢 or 侍 姜 waiting-maids.

侍 從 or 侍 僕 followers; at-tendants; servants.

侍 御 a Censor.

[5]侍 生 seniors; elders.

侍 立 or 侍 側 to be in at-tendance.

侍 臣 officials in attendance.

侍 衞 the Imperial Body-Guards.

侍 親 to wait on one's parents.

[10]侍 講 學 士 an Expositor of the Hanlin College.

侍 讀 學 士 a Reader of the Hanlin College.

侍 郎 Vice-President of one of the Six Boards. (obs.).

侍 食 to be in attendance at dinner.

內 侍 or 常 侍 eunuchs.

[15]親 侍 to wait on in person.

恃[4] To depend on. To pre-sume upon. To trust to.
5779

恃 刁 or 恃 橫 to rely on violence.

恃 力 to rely on force; to depend on one's strength.

恃 勢 to presume upon one's position or influence.

恃 寵 to presume on being a favourite.

[5]恃 強 壓 制 to intimidate by show of force.

恃 愛 presuming upon your kind-ness—phrase in letters.

恃 才 傲 物 self-conceited a n d insolent on account of one's ability.

恃 有 手 足 he relies on his brothers.

恃 氣 empty pride.

[10]恃 衆 to presume on numbers.

恃 籍 or 仗 恃 or 依 恃 or 倚 恃 to rely on; to depend on.

恃 蠻 to rely on force.

恃 衿 to presume on one's position as a graduate.

恃 財 to rely on one's wealth.

[15]恃 貴 presuming on nobility.

嚴 恃 a father.

失 恃 to lose a mother.

慈 恃 a mother.

時[2]　Time. A season; a period. Opportunity.
5780

時 不 可 失 must not lose the opportunity.

時 不 虛 擲 time was not wasted.

時 中 at the right moment.

時 乖 inconvenient; a w k w a r d moment; inopportune.

[5]時 事 current events; news of the day.

時 享 the seasonable sacrifice of ancient times.

時 人 contemporaries.

時 令 times and seasons; divisions of time.

時 令 不 好 a bad season—for disease, etc.

時令風 the monsoons.
時代 age; period; epoch; date of.
時代精神 spirit of the age.
時作時止 intermittent action.
時使薄斂 employ the people when they are at leisure and make the taxes light.
時值 the season being....; it happened to be the time of....
時·候 time; a period.
時·候壞 the times are bad.
時價 current prices; time value of musical notes.
時光 time; opportunity.
正當時光 just at the opportune moment.
時其亡也 watched for a time when he was not at home.
時其墐發 arrange for the—swarming of the bees—according to the season.
時分 (fên⁴) a period; time.
時刻 time; at once; incessantly.
時務 timely topics; businesses.
時勢 times; conditions of affairs; circumstances.
時勢不佳 the times are unfavourable.
時勢境地不同 the times and conditions are different.
時異勢殊 times and circumstances are widely different.
時君 the princes of that time.
時夜 the cock.
時失事 present loss.
時女 a girl; a maiden.
時好 the fashion of the times.
時安 the compliments of the season.
時宜 what is right at the time.
時宜之言 a word in season.
不得時宜 out of season; inopportune time.
因時制宜 act in accord with the times.
時尚 fashionable; in vogue.
時尚早 it is yet early.
時局 conditions; aspect of the times; present situation.
時局平靖 peaceful conditions.
時局艱險 a critical situation.
時差 time equation. (-ch'a¹)
時常 constantly; often.
時不常 occasionally.
時序 seasons; times.
時序易遷 the change of the seasons.

時弊 present-day evils.
時式 fashions.
時忌 things to be avoided at certain times—from superstitious taboo.
時憲書 the Imperial Calendar.
時或 at times.
時措之宜 always to adjust matters rightly.
時放時止 intermittent, as a spring.
時效 prescription. (legal).
時效之中斷 interruption of prescription.
時效停止 suspension of prescription.
時文 current literature; the eight-legged essay of the former examination system.
時日 the date; the time of; lucky days; suitable time; duration.
時時 habitually; often; from time to time.
時時刻刻 continually.
時·辰 a Chinese hour—two English hours.
時會變遷 changing conditions.
失此時會 lose this opportunity.
時有 there are constantly....
時有改革 there have been changes at times.
時期 period; season; time.
私有時期 the period of private ownership.
時機 opportunity.
時機已至 the time has come.
時機成熟 the opportunity was ripe.
時機至矣 Now's the time!
仲裁時機 opportunity for arbitration.
時樣 fashion of the day.
時流 people of fashion.
時災 epidemic.
時然後言 to speak when it is time to speak.
時球 time-ball.
時用 the present juncture.
時疫 epidemic.
時症 epidemic.
時礮 time-gun.
時禑 the compliments of the season.
時節 occasion; time.
時節到來 the time has come.
時經 was over and over again....
時羞 seasonable delicacies.
時興 fashionable; in vogue.

時行品 things in vogue.
時衰 inconvenient; inopportune; awkward.　　in style.
時裝 styles in dress, or dresses
時見 an occasional interview—of a prince.
時評 present-day criticisms; articles on the affairs of the day.
時論書 tracts for the times.
時譽 prestige, fame of the time.
時貨 things for daily use, grain, money, domestic animals, etc.
時辰香 incense sticks which mark the hours as they burn away.
時·辰表 a watch.
時迫 pressed for time.
時運 luck; fortune.
時運不齊 the times are unpropitious.
時運盛衰 the fluctuations of fortune.
時運亨通 the luck is good.
時道 fashion of the times.
時醫 a fashionable doctor.
時針 the hour-hand of a clock or watch.
時鐘 hour-bell.
時間 time; period; the interim.
時間之卡片 time-card—for workers.
時間信號 time-signal.
時間甚準 exactly on time.
時間·的 of, belonging to, time.
時間·的問題 a question of time.
時間·的試驗 the test of time.
時間盡矣 Time! Time's up!
時間簿 time-book.
時間表 time-table; time-sheet.
時間記錄 time-sheet—in workshops, etc.
營業時間 business hours.
辦公時間 office hours.
授課時間 school hours.
測定時間 to time—races, etc.
時限 a time-limit.
時雍 times of peace.
時雨 seasonable rain; the prevailing style.
時雨之潤 the moistening influences of seasonable rain.
時雪 timely snow.
時態 tense. (grammar). A.c.式
時髦 fashionable.
時髦人物 men of fashion.
時髦女郎 a fashionable

girl.

[135] 時髦話 fashionable talk.

時鮮 seasonable things—as flowers, fresh fruit, etc. [while.

一時 an hour; at once; for a

一時就來 I'll come at once.

一時流行的書 a book of the hour; best-seller.

[140] 一小時 one hour.

不合時 unseasonable.

不時 unseasonably; unexpectedly.

不時不食 (Confucius) would not eat food out of its proper season.

乘時 seize the chance.

[145] 何時 at what time? When?

依時 at stated times; regular.

冠時 prominent; distinctive.

前時 formerly.

即時 instantly.

[150] 古時 ancient times.

合時 in good time; seasonable.

同時 at the same time.

四時 the seasons.

天時 the weather.

[155] 天文時 astronomical time.

太陰時 lunar time.

太陽時 solar time.

失時 to miss the opportunity.

定時信管 time-fuse. 幾時 when?

[160] 平均時 mean time.

得時 to hit the favourable moment; popular; successful.

應時而至 to come in time.

暫時 for the time being.

有時 occasionally; sometimes.

[165] 標準時 standard time.

每時步度 hourly rate.

片時 a little while.

現時 just now.

當從時世 must conform to the times.

[170] 臨時 temporarily; provisionally.

隨時 at any time.

(a) Used for 是, this.

時日害喪 when will this sun expire?

蒔 [2]
5781

To plant; to erect.

蒔秧 to plant rice.

(a) Name of a plant.

蒔蘿子 [3] cummin seeds.

鰣 [2]
5782

A fish called Samli; it is something like a shad, it enters the rivers in May and returns in September, hence the name.

詩 [1]
5783

Poetry; an ode.

詩中有畫,畫中有詩 in his poems there are pictures, and in his pictures there are poems.

詩人 or 詩家 poets.

詩以言志 poetry expresses the feelings, or sentiments.

詩仙 a poetic genius—said of *Li T'ai-po*.

[5] 詩伯 a great poet.

詩債 unable to versify on the given rhyme.

詩天 weather that would inspire a man to write poetry.

詩奴 a low grade of poet.

詩妖 folk-songs—prophesying evil.

[10] 詩律 rules of metrical composition.

詩思 poetic thoughts.

詩才 the poetic gift.

詩文 poems and essays.

詩料 matter for composing poetry.

[15] 詩書 the *Book of Odes* and the *Canon of History;* literature.

詩本性情 the *Odes* have their root in human affections.

詩格 poetical forms and metre.

詩派 classes of poets.

詩癖 (or 癡) a passion for poetry.

[20] 詩眼 the vision of a poet.

詩社 a club, the members of which meet to write poetry, etc.

詩章 poetry; compositions.

詩篇 The Psalms.

詩經 the *Book of Odes*.

[25] 詩聖 the Sage of the poets—*Tu Fu* 杜甫.

詩興 the poetic fervour.

詩虎 riddles in the form of verse —*hu* is a sigh at their difficulty.

詩詞歌賦 the four orders of Chinese poetry; poetry generally.

詩話 critical reviews of poems.

[30] 詩集 collection of poems.

詩韻 the rhyme of the verse.

詩體 poetical form.

五言的詩體 five-character verses; pentametric.

一首詩 a poem.

[35] 作詩 to write poetry.

史詩 an epic poem.

和詩 to compose verses to a given rhyme.

劇詩 dramatic poetry.

敘事詩 narrative poetry.

[40] 抒情詩 lyrics.

敎訓詩 didactic poetry.

散文詩 a prose poem.

獨行 (*hang* [2]) 詩 a poem in a single line. [torals.

田園詩 or 詠景詩 idylls; pastorable to write poetry.

[45] 能詩 able to write poetry.

詠詩 to recite verses.

譏諷詩 or 諷刺詩 an epigram.

題詩 to write a poetical inscription.

矢 [3]
5784

A dart, an arrow. To aim at. Radical 111.

矢人 a maker of arrows.

矢心已久 has long been my aim.

矢服 a quiver.

矢直 as straight as an arrow.

矢石 to throw stones; archery and slinging.

一矢之地 a bow-shot.

流矢 a stray arrow.

(a) An oath.

矢以天日 he swore by the sun in the heavens.

矢口不移 to abide by one's oath.

矢志不移 he swore that he would not change his mind.

矢言 a solemn protestation.

[5] 矢誓 to take an oath.

之死矢靡他 I swear that till death I will have no other husband.

之死矢靡慝 I swear that till death I will not do this evil thing—a widow against remarriage.

永矢勿諼 he swears that he will never forget.

永矢弗過 he swears that he will never pass—from this spot. *See* 諼 No. 2875—B. 2.

(b) To marshal.

矢于牧野 marshalled in the wilderness of *Muh*.

無 矢 我 陵 they arrayed no forces on our hills.

(c) To set forth. To display.

矢 其 之 德 Let him display his virtues in civil—government.

矢 詩 不 多 I have made a few verses.

以 矢 其 音 thereupon I gave forth my song.

(d)　　　Ordure. Original form of 屎 No. 5757.

埋 之 馬 矢 之 中 buried him amidst the horse-dung.

如 矢 斯 棗 these dates are like —sheep—droppings.

氏 4 A family, a clan. A woman's maiden name; a female.
5785 Radical 83.
Distinguish 民 No. 4508.

氏 族 or 姓 氏 of such a family or clan.

因 以 爲 氏 he thereupon adopted it as his family surname.

王 馬 氏 or 王 門 馬 氏 Mrs. Wang, *née* Ma.

該 氏 the said female.

釋 氏 Buddhists.

(a) Read chih[1].

大 月 氏 and 小 月 氏 ancient divisions of a tribe said to be of the same race as the *Ch'iang* 羌; they were driven out of their original home, to the N. of N. W. China, by the *Hsiung nu;* the former branch migrated west into Transoxania, the smaller branch turned south and found refuge in the mountains.

舐 舐 舓 4　To lick; to lap.
5786

舐 犢 to lick her calf—parental love.

舐 痔 to lick piles—sycophancy.

舐 窗 以 窺 to lick a hole in a paper window and peep through.

事 4 An affair; a matter; an undertaking; business.
5787 Also read *szŭ*[1].

事 不 兩 施 cannot do two things at once.

事 不 宜 遲 the matter should not be delayed.

事 不 干 己 no concern of mine.

事 不 量 力 to attempt something beyond one's strength.

[5]事 主 the principal person concerned in any matter.

事 事 周 到 everything is well done.

事 事 如 意 May everything be as you wish!

事 件 matters; a case; an incident.

不 幸 事 件 an unfortunate affair.

[10]瑣 屑 事 件 trifling matters.

着 手 之 事 件 the matter in hand.

事 出 有 因 there are grounds for believing that it did happen.

事 出 權 宜 a course of action dictated by circumstances.

事 到 其 間 the matter has come to this stage—there's no help for it.

[15]事 到 臨 頭 the matter is coming to a crisis.

事 前 before the event; before something happens.

事 前 從 犯 accessory before the fact.

事 務 business; affairs.

事 務 家 a man of affairs.

[20]事 務 所 office for business.

事 務 管 轄 the control of affairs.

事 務 長 (*chang*[3]) purser; business manager.

事 勢 state of affairs; general trend of events.

事 半 功 倍 half the work with double the result.

[25]事 多 busy.

事 如 屬 實 the affair seems genuine; if these things are so.

事 宜 the fitness of things; conditions; interest; requirements; the necessary arrangements.

敎 育 事 宜 educational matters.

事 實 facts; an accomplished fact; actual; real.

[30]事 實 上 之 關 係 actual connection with the matter.

事 實 不 符 the facts did not tally.

事 實 問 題 a matter of fact.

事 實 如 此 such being the case.

不 可 爭 之 事 實 indisputable facts.

[35]已 成 的 事 實 an accomplished fact.

有 最 近 的 事 實 可 證 the most recent facts prove.

事 屬 創 始 the matter is in the initial stages.

事 序 單 agenda.

事 後 從 犯 accessory after the fact.

[40]事 忙 very busy.

事 急 the matter is urgent—no time to lose.

事 情 matters; business; circumstances; details; events; affairs

事 情 黃 了 the business has miscarried. (*dial*).

事 態 aspect of affairs.

[45]事 態 嚴 重 the aspect of affairs is serious.

事 故 occasion of trouble.

事 變 accidents and emergencies; disturbances.

事 業 calling; occupation; profession; career.

合 法 事 業 legitimate business.

[50]事 業 年 度 fiscal year. Cf. 2345

事 機 policy; political motives. [D5

事 權 power; authority.

事 物 things in general.

事 理 principles of action; facts and principles involved; way of doing business.

[55]事 由 an affair; the origin of a matter; circumstances; particulars.

事 皆 拂 意 everything going contrary to one's wishes.

事 禮 the conventionalities.

事 端 occasion of trouble.

事 緩 有 變 when a matter is delayed there may be a change.

[60]事 績 actions; deeds.

事 繢 traces; results; evidences.

事 行 而 不 悖 affairs will go smoothly and not contrarily.

事 跡 history; facts of a case.

事 蹟 a man's record—a biography.

[65]事 過 境 遷 the matter is past and the circumstances have changed.

事 雖 小 不 作 不 成 although it is a trifling matter, if you do not begin it cannot be accomplished.

事 體 concerns; matters; affairs.

不 成 事 體 it is not a proper matter—an impropriety or irregularity.

不 事 遷 延 not to allow any further delay.

[70]供 事 a clerk.

公 事 public business.

多 事 officious; meddlesome.

大 事 important matters—death, marriage, change of governments, etc.

家 事 household matters.

[75]小 事 a trifling matter.

差 事 public business; special errand. (ch'ai[1].)

從 事 to engage in; to set about; to take in hand.

急 事 urgent business.

故 事 an anecdote.

[80]敗 事 to fail in an undertaking.

有 事 busy; engaged.

本 事 talent; ability.

無 濟 於 事 will not help the matter.

私 事 private business.

[85]萬 事 everything that men do.

通 事 an interpreter.

金 錢 之 事 money matters.

閒 事 idle matter.

(a) To serve.

事 半 古 之 人 to do half the work of the ancients.

事 君 數 斯 辱 矣 constant remonstrance when serving a prince brings disgrace.

事 天 饗 帝 to serve Heaven and sacrifice to the Supreme.

事 舉 to serve; to attend; to wait on.

事 父 母 to serve one's parents.

不 事 二 君 cannot serve two masters.

示 示 示
5788

An omen. To manifest; to proclaim; to exhibit. Radical 113.

示 下 or 訓 示 to instruct; to order.

示 之 而 已 矣 simply made it known by....

示 仰 to issue a proclamation with a view to; expect you to; will you be so good as to.

示 仰 中 西 官 商 人 知 悉 expect all foreigners and Chinese business men to know.

[5]示 仰 各 商 民 ... look to all you merchants to know.

示 威 to awe; to make a demonstration.

示 威 游 行 demonstration by making a procession.

示 威 運 動 a demonstration.

排 隊 游 行 示 威 to hold a parade and make a demonstration.

[10]示 寂 death of a Buddhist priest.

示 弱 to show weakness.

示 悉 to notify; to apprise.

示 意 to demonstrate, as affection; to make known one's wishes.

以 目 示 意 to give a hint with the eyes.

[15]微 示 其 意 to give a person to understand.

招 手 示 意 to give a hint by a movement of the hand.

輕 觸 示 意 to nudge.

示 懲 as a mark of punishment.

示 我 周 行 and show me the perfect path.

[20]示 我 顯 德 行 show me how to display a virtuous conduct.

示 教 a demonstration—in teaching.

實 物 示 教 者 a demonstrator.

實 驗 的 示 教 practical demonstration.

示 敬 as a mark of respect; to show deference to.

[25]示 明 to notify; to inform.

示 期 to fix a date.

示 求 救 to make signals of distress. [revelation of miracles.

示 異 showed itself different; a

示 衆 to make known to the public.

[30]示 知 or 給 示 to notify; to inform.

祈 爲 示 知 I beg you to inform me.

示 禁 to proclaim a prohibition.

示 範 法 the method of teaching by example.

示 罰 as a warning.

[35]示 覆 give instructions in reply.

請 卽 示 覆 asking the favour of a reply.

示 訂 to fix; to indicate.

示 諴 proclamation.

示 諭 to issue a proclamation; a mandate.

[40]出 示 曉 諭 to issue a proclamation; to inform.

示 警 to warn.

示 遵 to give instructions to.

來 示 or 手 示 your letter; your favour.

告 示 a public proclamation.

[45]指 示 代 名 詞 demonstrative pronoun.

指 示 形 容 詞 demonstrative adjective.

指 示 說 明 to demonstrate, as in anatomy, etc.

暗 示 to hint at.

言 示 之 事 "showed the difference by appealing to affairs."

[50]韻 示 a proclamation in simple rhyme so as to be easily understood.

(a) To see; u.f. next.

如 示 諸 斯 乎 like looking at this—pointing to his palm.

如 示 諸 掌 as easy as looking into his palm.

(b) Read ch'i[2]. u.f. 祇 No. 538. Earth personified as a god.

視 眎
5789
[4]

To look at; to regard; to inspect.

視 事 to examine; to attend to business.

視 人 猶 己 to regard others as oneself.

視 作 等 閒 may be regarded as negligible.

視 其 所 以 look at what a man does.

[5]視 力 power of vision.

視 力 表 optometer.

視 動 visual motion.

視 孔 or 窺 孔 a sight-hole.

視 學 to inspect schools.

[10]視 學 員 Inspector of Schools.

視 官 sense of sight; vision.

視 察 to investigate; to look into.

視 察 員 investigating deputies.

視 察 團 delegation for making investigations.

15 經濟視察團 economic delegation.

視差 parallax. (-ch'a[1])

視息 to exist—merely seeing and breathing; an idle life.

視望 to gaze at.

視朝[2] to hold a court.

20 視死如歸 to look upon death as going home.

視法古人 to imitate the ancients.

視為具文 to regard as a mere document—of regulations not in actual operation.

視為重要 to attach great importance to.

視界 the field of vision.

25 視界之外 out of the field of vision.

視神經 the optic nerve.

視網膜 the retina.

視線之外 out of the line of vision.

視繁若寡 to make a complex matter simple.

30 視義之可否 sees whether the thing is right or no.

視而不見 to look at but not pay attention to.

視聽言動 to see, hear, talk and move.

視能 visual function.

視膳 to wait on parents or superiors.

35 視若無物 to regard as nothing.

視覺 sense of vision.

視覺器 organ of vision.

視角 visual angle.

視財如命 to regard wealth as one's life.

40 視險如夷 to regard hazardous places as level ground—no fear of difficulties.

視養 to care for and nurture.

視點 end in view; point of sight.

一視同仁 to regard all with equal favour.

俯視 to look down on.

45 偷視 to steal a glance.

側視 to look askance.

淩空俯視 to take a bird's-eye view.

凝視 to stare in amazement.

善視 to treat well.

50 斜視 to leer at; to ogle.

檢視 to look over; to check.

正視 to look straight forward.

注視 to fix the gaze on.

眇視 to look askance at.

55 細視 attentive vision.

輕視 to despise; to look lightly upon.

遠視眼 or 近視眼 far- or near-sightedness.

重視 to take care of, to esteem.

(a) Equal to.

受地視侯 received an amount of territory equal to that of a *Hou.*

(b) To show. u.f. 示 No. 5788.

丕視功載 freely display the record of merits.

世 [4] An age. A generation of
5790 thirty years. From generation to generation.

世世代代 from generation to generation; successive ages.

世世無窮 from generation to generation without end; from age to age without end.

世亂識忠臣 loyal officers are known in troublous times.

世交 a friendship of many generations.

5 世仇 enmity of several generations; ages.

世代 generations; ages.

世代交替 alternation of generations.

世代交番 atavism.

世代書香 a literary reputation sustained through several generations.

10 極盛世代 the Golden Age.

游牧世代 pastoral ages.

退化世代 age of degeneracy.

進化世代 age of progress.

開化世代 age of dawning civilization.

15 世伯 or 世叔 friends, older or younger, of one's father.

世傳 handed down from generation to generation.

世兄 or 世弟 terms of address between friends whose fathers have also been friends.

世好 family acquaintance.

世姪 son of an old friend.

20 世子[3] the eldest son of a prince.

世守 must be kept from generation to generation—i.e., the kingdom.

世家 an old and honourable family.

世官 officials whose ancestors were officials.

世族 a friendship of many generations.

25 世母 paternal aunt.

世爵 hereditary rank or nobility.

世父 father's elder brother.

世祿 hereditary emoluments.

世系 a genealogy; successive generations.

30 世紀 a century.

世職 hereditary office or title.

世臣 hereditary officials.

世襲罔替 hereditary rank for ever—conferred as a reward for military services only.

世襲子[3]爵 a hereditary viscount.

35 世運 the changes of the times.

世醫 doctors in the family for generations.

一世 one generation.

七世後裔 descendant of the seventh generation.

中世 the Middle Ages.

40 亂世 age of anarchy and confusion.

末世 or 季世 last period of a dynasty.

當[1]世 the present age.

蓋 (or 冠) 世 to overtop the age.

(a) The world. Society.

世上的 worldly.

世之快樂 worldly pleasure.(-lê)

世之終盡 the end of the world.

世事 the affairs of life.

5 世事無常 the affairs of the world are not constant.

通曉世事 to have a knowledge of the world.

世況 world conditions, or conditions of the age.

世人 or 世上人 mankind.

世人咸知 all the world knows.

10 世俗 the customs of the world; the ordinary course of affairs.

世俗的 worldly.

世務 the affairs of this life; the customs of the world.

世務纏身 entangled by the affairs of this life.

不識世務 unacquainted with the world.

15 世尊 one honoured by the world —Buddha.

世情 worldly affairs; ordinary events; common sense.

不近世情 out of touch with the world.

世 態 人 情 the way ot the world.
世 態 炎 涼 the way of the world, now hot, now cold.
²⁰世 慾 worldliness.
世。故 the way of the world; shrewd
世 業 a calling; an occupation.
世 無 其 匹 no equal in the world.
世·界 the world; life; society: past, present, and future.
²⁵世 界 不 好 a bad state of society.
世·界 主 義 cosmopolitanism.
世·界 傾 向 trend of the times; world tendency.
世·界 史 universal history.
世·界 同 一 federation of the world.
³⁰世·界 商 塲 world markets.
世·界 大 同 Utopia.
世·界 大 舞 臺 the world's stage.
世·界 如 輪 轉 the affairs of the world go round like a wheel—constantly changing.
世·界 市 塲 world markets.
³⁵世·界 情 勢 變 遷 changed world situation.
世·界 戰 爭 world war.
世·界 政 論 world politics.
世·界 潮 流 trend of the times.
世·界 眼 光 worldly wisdom.
⁴⁰世·界 知 識 worldly wisdom; wide experience.
世·界 精 神 world spirit.
世·界 觀 world view—the larger vision.
世·界 語 Esperanto.
世·界 趨 勢 world tendencies.
⁴⁵世·界 進 步 world progress.
世·界 革 命 world revolution.
新 世·界 the New World.
舊 世·界 the Old World.
世 路 the way of the world; the ·course of events.
⁵⁰世 路 羊 腸 the ways of the world are as twisted as the entrails of a sheep.
世 道 the way of the world; the course of events; manners and morals.
世 道 日 衰 the way of the world is daily getting worse.
世 間 the world.
世 面 state of the world; conditions of the times.
⁵⁵ 沒 有 見 個 世 面 very unsophisticated.
今 世 this world or age.
來 世 the future world or age.
塵 世 this life of care.

早 世 to die prematurely.
⁶⁰棄 世 or 違 世 or 去 世 to die.
涉 世 to pass through the world.
舉 世 the whole world.
處³世 to be in the world.
過 世 or 辭 世 to leave the world—to die.
⁶⁵陰 世 the invisible world; the next world.
陽 世 the visible world; this life.
離 世 to leave the world—to die.

貰⁴ To buy on credit; to borrow. To let on hire.
5791 Also read shê⁴.

貰 器 皿 to hire out furniture.
貰 貸 to borrow.
貰 酒 to get wine on trust.

(a) To pardon.

貰 赦 to pardon.

市⁴ A market; a fair. To trade. An execution ground.
5792 Distinguish 布 No. 5364; 希 No. 2416.

市·上 on the market.
市·上 不 易 消 賣 goods that are a drug on the market.
市 井 or 市 口 兒 a market-place.
市 井 中 間 among the ordinary rank and file.
⁵市 井 主 義 commercialism.
市 井 之 流 tradespeople.
市 井 匪 類 riff-raff of the market-place.
市 井 徒 unlettered shopkeepers.
市 俗 vulgar; unrefined.
¹⁰市 債 municipal bonds.
市 價 or 時 值 the market price.
市 價 表 list of market quotations.
市 儈 a broker; term of abuse for those who have purchased official rank; a sharp dealer.
市 化 municipalization.
¹⁵市 區 municipality.
市 塲 market for goods.
市 塲 價 格 market rates.
市 平 local scale of weights; market rates.
市 府 municipal government.
²⁰市 廛 a bazaar.
市 恩 or 市 義 to parade one's goodness.
市 情 報 告 market reports.

市 政 municipality; street regulations.
市 政 廳 municipal offices; town hall.
²⁵市 政 改 良 municipal reform.
市 政 機 關 municipal organizations.
市 政 衛 生 局 Municipal Health Bureau.
市 政 長³Chairman of a Municipal Council.
市 曹 or 菜·市 口 兒 an execution-ground.
³⁰市 會 議 士 municipal councillor
市 有 municipally owned.
市 朝²public place.
市 歡 to get advantage from.ling.
市 民 大 會 citizens' mass meeting.
³⁵市 法 municipal laws.
市 立 學 校 municipal schools.
市 米 to buy rice.
市 聲 the hawking of pedlers.
市 虎 rumours; wild stories.
⁴⁰市 語 market- or shop-slang.
市 議 會 municipal council.
市 鄉 subdivisions of a hsien 縣
市 鄉 制 municipal system of government.
市 門 a market-place.
⁴⁵市 面 the state of trade.
市 面 之 盛 衰 fluctuations of the market.
市 面 清 淡 a depressed market.
市 面 穩 固 the market is firm.
市 面 轉 機 the turn of the market.
⁵⁰市 面 頓 形 恐 惶 panic of a falling market.
市 頭³a market or market-place.
夜 市 night markets.
早 市 early markets.
罷 市 to cease trade as a protest against the government, etc.
⁵⁵行 (hang²)·市 the current prices on
都 市 a capital city.　market.
鎮·市 a commercial centre.
開 市 to resume business—after the New Year; to open the market.　「the 營造尺 (7467.36.
↑市尺 the municipal foot, which supersede

柿
棘 }
The persimmon or China fig. Also read szŭ⁴. Note 柿 No. 1842, which is commonly used for this.
5793

棘·子 persimmons.
棘 霜 sugar obtained from persimmons.

栟 餅 or 乾 栟 dried persimmons.

是 ⁴ Yes. Right. The verb to be.
5794

是·不·是 or 是 否 isn't it so? is it so or not?
是 之 to approve of a thing.
是 否 可 信 May we believe it or not
是 否 無 誤 Is it correct or not?
⁵是 己 非 人 to consider oneself right and others wrong.
是 必 surely; certainly.
是 我 to approve of my actions; it is I.
是 爲 is; it is.
·是·的 or 是·了 yes; right; it is so.
¹⁰是 眞·的 是 假·的 Is it true or false?
是 與 不 是 true or not.
是 要 or 是 爲 至 要 which is very important.
是 這·樣 是 那·樣 Is it this way or not? Whether it be this way or not....
是 非 yes and no; right and wrong; positive and negative.
是·非 gossip; scandal.
¹⁵是 非 不 當 failing to assign the right and wrong to their proper places.
是 非 之 心 人 皆 有 之 the power of distinguishing right and wrong belongs to all men.
是 非 之 心 智 也 the feeling of approving or disapproving implies the principle of wisdom.
是·非 人 a wrongdoer.
是 非 場 a situation in which a person cannot give satisfaction.
²⁰是 非 學 ethics; moral philosophy.
是 非 自 有 公 論 right or wrong, let the public decide.
是 非 難 逃 it is hard to escape criticism.
似 是 而 非 it seems right, but it is wrong.
來 說 是·非 者 便 是 是·非 人 he who comes with a tale about others is a wrongdoer himself.
²⁵口 是 心 非 the mouth is right but the heart is false.
各 有 是 非 each has its right and wrong.

惹 是·非·的 人 a mischief maker.
搬 弄 是·非 to carry tales.
是 則 是 非 則 非 right is right and wrong is wrong.
³⁰論 人 是·非 to discuss the failings of others.
不 是 it is not so; a fault.
是 我·的 不 是 it is my fault.
卽 是 namely; that is.
自 以 爲 是 to regard oneself as right.

(a) This, that, which.

是 也 and that is so; a final emphatic particle; also used as a final particle indicating, for example, for instance.
　如 金 屬 是 也 as metals, for example.
　所 謂 世 界·的 國 是 也 as that which is called a world State, for instance.
　詩 之 國 風 是 也 the "Lessons from the States" in the Odes are an example.
⁵是 以 therefore; by this means; hence.
是 則 然 矣 this is so.
是 可 忍 也 孰 不 可 忍 也 if this may be endured, what may not?
是 幸 for which I shall be much obliged.
是 故 on this account; for this reason.
¹⁰是 所 至 禱 for which I earnestly pray.
是 日 on that day; at the time spoken of.
是 皆 基 於 this is all founded on....
是 美 堯 德 this is extolling the virtues of Yao.
是 荷 for which I shall be grateful —closing phrase in letters, etc.
¹⁵是 道 也 何 足 以 臧 How can this point suffice for the highest virtue?
怨 是 用 希 thereby resentments were few.

諟 ⁴ To examine whether a thing is right; to judge; to consider. Inter. preceding.
5795

顧 諟 天 之 明 命 he contemplated and studied the illustrious decrees of heaven.

鍉 匙 ² A spoon. A key. Also read ch'ih².
5796

匙·子 a spoon. (ch'ih²-)
鑰·匙 a key. (-shih)
門 匙 a door-key.

弑 ⁴ To murder a superior.
5797

弑 其 主 he killed his master.
弑 君 to kill one's sovereign.
弑 父 parricide.

試 ⁴ To test, to try, to experiment. To examine; examination. To use. Trained; disciplined.
5798

試·一·試 or 試·試·看 to attempt; make a trial and see; try.
試 以 to take for an example.
試 兒 ² to test a child on his first birthday by placing certain objects before him and allowing him to seize what he fancies. See 周 No. 1293—A. 5.
試 其 能 to test his ability.
⁵試·出 眞 情 the test revealed the truth.
試 問 let me ask; allow me to put it to you; to see how.
試 問·他 put a test question to him.
試 卷 ⁴ examination papers.
試 妝 to try on the bridal array.
¹⁰試 巧 to show one's skill; to test a child. See above—3.
試 思 just think!
試 想 to think; to consider.
試 手 to try; to practise.
試 探 to tempt; to test.
¹⁵試 敎 teaching tests.
試 晬 to test a child. See above -3.
試 嘗 to taste and try.
嘗 試 to test as by tasting; to try whether something prohibited could be attempted.
試 演 to practise; to try; to attempt.
²⁰試 煉 to prove; experience.
試 用 on probation—as an official.
試 用 期 間 during probation.
試 用·的 人 probationer.
試 用 期 限 period of probation.

²⁵試 目 力 表 test-type for eye-sight.

試 看 to take a look at.

試 筒 (or 管) test-tubes. *See below*—49.

試 茶 tea-tasting.

試 藥 re-agents.

³⁰試 行 tentative; experimental; tests; to practise.

試 行 四 權 to exercise the four prerogatives—of suffrage. recall, initiative, and referendum.

試·試 大 小 try the size.

試 賣 trial sale.

試 辦 to make the experiment.

³⁵試 辦 再 議 to put into operation provisionally for future discussion.

試 辦 章·程 experimental regulations.

試 運 轉 test working of machinery.

試 金 石 a touchstone; used fig.

試 金 術 assaying.

⁴⁰試·驗 to prove; to verify; examination.

試·驗 假 釋 allowed out on probation.

試·驗 塲 experimental station.

試·驗 室 laboratory.

試·驗 家 experimenters; assayers.

⁴⁵試 驗 局 assay office.

試 驗 時 代 experimental period.

試·驗 機 器 testing machine.

試·驗 物 test for gold, iron, etc.

試·驗 管 test-tube. *See above*—27.

⁵⁰試·驗 紙 or 試 紙 test-paper.

試·驗 論 理 學 experimental logic.

試·驗·過 examined.

受 試 鍊 to pass through trials.

考 試 examinations.

⁵⁵殿 試 former examination of 3rd degree graduates for admission to the Hanlin Academy.

會 試 former triennial examination for the 3rd degree held in Peking.

鄉 試 former triennial examination for the 2nd degree held in the provincial capitals.

勢 ⁴ Power; influence; authority; strength. Aspect, circumstances, conditions.
5799

勢 不 佳 affairs are looking serious, bad.

勢 不 兩 立 impossible for both to exist together.

勢 不 行 circumstances are against it.

勢 交 friendships based on power or influence.

⁵勢 佔 to seize unlawfully.

勢 兇 fierce; desperate.

勢 分 (*fên*⁴) prospect; aspect.

勢 利 之 徒 sycophants; snobs.

勢 利 常 情 common affairs of influence and profit.

¹⁰勢·力 strength; influence; power.

勢·力 圈 sphere of influence. *See* 範 No. 1780-2ff.

勢·力 平 均 balance of power.

勢·力 範 圍 sphere of influence. *See above*—11.

海 軍 勢·力 naval strength.

¹⁵勢 壓 to put down with authority.

勢·子 figure; bearing; attitude; the male organ.

割 勢 to castrate.

勢 如 破 竹 their strength is like splitting bamboo—once it starts it is sure to go on.

勢 家 influential families.

²⁰勢 將 will or may; probably or apparently.

勢 將 成 就 it looks like being a success.

勢 弱 難 敵 when the strength is weak resistance is difficult.

勢 必 necessarily; inevitably.

勢 所 不 能 impossibility.

²⁵勢 所 必 然 circumstances compel it.

勢 殊 事 異 the conditions are very different.

勢 派 scale—as of living, building, etc.

勢 餤 fury; ferocity.

勢 熾 their power was fierce.

³⁰勢 窮 力 竭 strength and energy exhausted.

勢 絀 position of embarrassment.

勢 處 兩 難 to be in a dilemma.

勢 要 high and influential persons.

勢 難 保 持 an untenable position.

³⁵勢 難 從 命 circumstances make it difficult for me to accede to your request.

勢·頭 好 the prospect is good.

乘 勢 to take advantage of the occasion.

無 勢 可 乘 no chance for taking action.

事 勢 course of events.

⁴⁰仗 勢 to trust to one's influence.

在 勢 in actual authority.

地 勢 the physical features of the earth.

大 勢 the country; general situation.

威 勢 pomp; majesty.

⁴⁵形 勢 figure; appearance of; situation, as of a grave.

得 勢 to get a footing in; to have a hold on; to be in power.

手 勢 signs made with the hands.

權 勢 authority; power.

附 勢 to toady to those who have power or influence.

⁵⁰騎 虎 之 勢 conditions from which there is no backing down.

嗜 ⁴ To desire; to lust after; to be fond of.
5800

嗜 口 腹 fond of good living.

嗜·好 (*hao*⁴) to be fond of—as of eating; addicted to—as vice, sensuality, etc.

嗜 慾 addicted to lust.

嗜 慾 薰 心 lustful desires becloud the heart.

⁵嗜 痂 to have low tastes.

嗜 義 如 嗜 利 as fond of duty as of making gain.

嗜 賭 addicted to gambling.

嗜 酒 色 addicted to women and wine.

嗜 音 fond of music.

¹⁰不 嗜 殺 人 者 能 一 之 he who takes no pleasure in killing can so unite it—the kingdom.

蓍 ¹ A plant, the stalks of which were used in divination. Milfoil.
5801

諡
謚 ⁴ A posthumous title conferred upon emperors and eminent officials. To confer such a title.
5802

諡 名 or 諡 號 the posthumous title.

諡 法 rule for conferring such titles.

誓 ⁴ An oath, a vow. To take an oath; to swear.
5803

誓 不 兩 立 I swear that both of us shall not stand.

誓 不 承 認 to deny with an oath.
誓 墓 to resign office and return home for good.
誓 師 to harangue troops.
⁵誓 必 報 仇 to vow vengeance.
誓 願 a vow.
誓 書 an oath; an affidavit.
誓 死 勿 去 to swear to hold on, even till death.
誓 死 守 swore to remain un-married, or to defend, until death.
¹⁰誓 章 a written oath.
誓 約 to contract.
誓 絕 to abjure.
誓 言 an oath.
當 天 立 誓 to call Heaven to witness.
¹⁵發 誓 to take an oath.
背 誓 or 違 誓 to break an oath.
起 誓 to take an oath.

逝 ⁴ To pass away; to depart; to die.
5804

逝 世·了 he has died.
逝 水 flowing water.
逝 者 其 亡 it will pass away and we shall be dead.
逝 者 如 斯 it passes away like this—said of a stream.
偕 逝 to die together.
日 月 逝 矣 the days and months pass away.
長 逝 the long journey—death.

豉 ⁴ Salted fruits, etc. Also read ch'ih³.
5805

豉 油 soy. (Cantonese.) = 醬 油.
薑 豉² salted beans, eaten with rice gruel, etc.

SHIH.   (ㄕ)
(Shïh)

失 ¹·⁵· To lose; to slip; to neglect; to miss; to err. An omission. Distinguish 矢 No. 5784.
5806

失 中 to err on the one side or the other; to miss the happy medium.
失 主 the loser of property.
失 之 交 臂 to lose an opportunity or chance.

失 之 東 隅 收 諸 桑 榆 what is lost in the morning is gained in the evening. *See* 桑 No. 5424-10.
⁵失 之 毫 釐 謬 以 千 里 to diverge the slightest fraction will mean an error of a thousand *li*.
失·了 體 統 to lose dignity; to be disgraced.
失 事 loss; to lose; to get into trouble; to meet with an ac-cident, etc.
失 人 one who has certain ability, but is not known.
失 位 or 失 國 or 失 天 下 to lose the throne.
¹⁰失 信 to break faith.
失 信 用 to lose credit.
失 值 to lose its value.
失 傳 to lose the record of; to lose the tradition of—as an art.
失 儀 to commit a breach of etiquette.
¹⁵失 入 punishment altogether too heavy for the offence. (*legal*).
失 出 punishment inadequate to the crime. (*legal*).
失·去 lost; to lose.
失 口 a slip of the tongue—to apologize for what one has said.
失 名 name unknown—as an author of a poem, etc.
²⁰失 名·譽 to lose reputation or good name; disgraced.
失 命 to lose life.
失 味 lost its flavour.
失 和 to disgrace; to fall out.
失 和·氣 to fail to keep on good terms.
²⁵失 單 claim for goods lost.
失 喪 to lose; destroyed.
失 守 to lose the command of—as territory; to fall into the hands of the enemy.
失 宜 lacking in fitness; improper.
失 容 to change countenance.
³⁰失 察 to neglect to inquire into; to be careless.
失 實 inaccurate.
失 寵 to lose favour.
失 常 out of its usual order.
失 常 度 to go beyond the bounds.
³⁵失 德 lost to virtue.
失 心 瘋 stupidity; idiocy.
失 志 氣 to lose ambition or spirit.
失 怙 bereaved of one's father.
失 恃 bereaved of one's mother.
⁴⁰失 悞 loss and hindrance.
失 慎 careless—to have a fire.

失 意 not at all pleased; dis-appointed. 失 態 *See* 6246,B2.
失 愛 out of favour.
失 憶 to forget.
⁴⁵失 所 to lose one's home—as of those who have been evicted; to make a failure of; out of place.
失 手 to lose control of the hand; accidentally.
失 手 打 碎 to break by accident.
失·掉 lost; to lose.
失 措 to lose one's head; flustered.
⁵⁰手 足 失 措 to lose the use of one's limbs with fright.
失 損 injury and loss.
失 政 maladministration of government.
失 效 lost its efficacy.
失 敎·訓 uninstructed; to let a chance of education slip.
⁵⁵失 敗 defeat and failure.
外 交 失 敗 diplomatic failure.
失 散 scattered; dispersed.
失 敬 disrespectful; wanting in regard—I beg your pardon.
失 於 to be deficient in; to err on the side of.
⁶⁰失 於 調 養 careless of one's health.
失 明 to lose the sight.
失 時 to lose the chance; to miss the opportunity; defeated.
不 失 時 機 not to lose a moment.
失 望 to lose hope; disappointed.
⁶⁵失 期 to miss an appointed time.
失 本 to lose capital; to fail in business.
失 業 to be out of work; loss of time—as in business.
失 業 之 人 the unemployed.
失 業 恐 慌 fear of unemploy-ment.
⁷⁰失 機 to lose the chance; to miss an opportunity; to fail.
失 檢 lacking in care.
失 權 loss of authority and power.
失 次 to lose sequence or order; bewilderment.
失 步 to saunter.
⁷⁵失 民 心 to lose the affection of the people.
失 漏 to omit.
失 火 or 走 水 to catch fire; to have a fire.
失 物 to lose property.
失 物 不 管 not responsible for anything lost.

80 失 當 irregular; improper—of conduct.

失 目 blind.

失 眠 insomnia.

失 眼 to be deceived.

失 知 覺 beside oneself.

85 失 神 absent-minded; inattentive; abstracted.

失 禮 wanting in politeness—I beg your pardon.

失 笑 s u d d e n, uncontrollable laughter.

失 策 a faulty policy.

失 算 miscalculation.

90 失 節 to incur disgrace; to lose one's virtue—as a woman; to lose caste.

失 約 to be unfaithful to an agreement. [(-cho¹)

失 着⁴ to make a wrong move.

失 而 復 得 lost and found again.

失 聲 (to weep until) voiceless.

95 失 聲 望 to fall from one's position; to suffer in reputation.

失 職 delinquent; negligent of duty.

失 脚³ or 失 足 to slip; to lose one's footing.

失 良 心 conscience dead.

失 色⁴ to change colour.

100 失 落 to lose; lost.

失 血 to lose blood.

失 行⁴ to make a false move; misdemeanour.

失 行 (hang²) 伍 to break rank.

失 覺 to fail to perceive; to be neglectful.

105 失 言 to commit oneself by a statement; a slip of the tongue —to apologize for what one has said.

失 計 to miscalculate.

失 記 to forget.

失 誤 blunder; fault; omission.

失 賊 or 失 盜 to have had a robbery committed.

110 失 路 to go astray.

失 踪 disappearance.

失 蹤 lost traces of.

失 蹄 to cast a shoe.

失 身 to lose virtue—as a woman; to incur disgrace.

115 失 載 to omit.

失 迎 I am sorry that I was out when you called.

失 迷 lost; astray.

失 道 to lose the way.

失 錯 fault; mistake.

120 失 防 neglectful of precautions.

失 陷 to lose the command—as of territory; to fall into the hands of the enemy.

失 陪 excuse my leaving you.

失 音 loss of voice.

失 風 foundered; to be wrecked.

125 失 飪 不 食 he would not eat badly-cooked food.

失 體 面 disgraced; unbecoming.

失 魂 stupid; inattentive; witless.

失 鹿 共 逐 when (the House of Ch'in, 秦) lost its deer, the whole empire pursued it—downfall of a dynasty.

失 黏 poems in which the even and oblique tones are out of their proper sequence.

130 亡 失 to die.

得 失 gain and loss.

自 失 absent-minded.

萬 無 一 失 not the least mistake about it.

過·失 faults; errors.

十 2.5. Ten. Complete. Radical 24.
5807

十 一 eleven.

十 不 全 incomplete; lacking; crippled.

十 二 分 in abundant measure.

十 二 分 年·成 super-abundant harvest.

⁵ 十 二 宮 the twelve divisions of the ecliptic—the zodiac.

十 二 打 a gross.

十 二 支 or 地 支 the Twelve Branches,-see appendix.

十 二 禽 the twelve animals corresponding to the Twelve Branches, as above.

十·個 ten persons or things.

10 十 全 entire; perfect.

十 八 變 constant changes—as of a growing girl, or of the weather.

黃 梅 天 十 八 變 i n t h e rainy season the weather is fickle.

十 分 (fên⁴) ten shares.

十 分³ extremely.

十 分⁴之 一 a tenth.

15 十 分⁴好 superlatively good.

十 哲 the ten noted men who were disciples of Confucius.

十 多 歲 or 十·來 (la¹) 歲 between ten and twenty years of age; more than ten years old.

十 姊 妹 Rosa multiflora. Ten girls of different surnames who have sworn not to marry.

十 字 布 embroidery canvas.

20 十 字 架 the Cross.

十 字 縫⁴ cross-stitch.

十 字 花 cruciferous flowers.

十 字 街 cross-roads.

十 字 路 or 十 字 口 cross-roads.

25 十 字 路 口 the junction of cross-roads.

十 字 軍 The Crusaders.

紅 十 字 The Red Cross.

十 室 九 空 nearly all the houses empty—after a raid.

十 尖 ten points—the fingers.

30 十 州 ancient name for the abode of the immortals.

十 干 or 天 干 the Ten Stems—ten characters which with the 地 支 are used to form a cycle of sixty years,- see appendix.

十 年 樹 木 it takes ten years to g r o w trees—a far-sighted policy.

十 幾 個 or 十·來 個 between ten and twenty.

十 幾 天 between ten and twenty days.

35 十 惡 不 赦 the ten unpardonable crimes--rebellion; conspiracy against the person of the ruler; treason; parricide, etc.; inhuman offences, as murder or mutilation; sacrilege; unfilial behaviour; lack of harmony; insubordination; and incest.

十 成 complete; the full number.

十 拿 九 穩 the matter is well in hand.

十 指 有 長 短 fingers are unequal in length—men are not all perfect.

十 方 the ten positions—the four cardinal points, the intermediate points, and above and below.

40 十 有 八 九 eight or nine chances in ten.

十 樣 錦 the Amarantus gangeticus; used also of a man who cannot make a success in business; also of a deformed person.

十 死 一 生 ten to one he will die.

十 無 其 一 not even one in ten.

十 甲 牌 a register of ten families.

45 十目十手 ten eyes, ten hands—things done in secret cannot be hid, ten eyes see and ten hands point to it.

十義 the ten moral obligations—benevolence of the ruler and loyalty of the minister 君仁臣忠; tenderness of the father and filial respect of the son 父慈子³孝; friendliness and respect between older and younger brothers 兄友弟恭; harmony between husband and wife 夫昌婦隨; graciousness of seniors and submission of juniors 長惠幼順.

十脡爲束 ten strips of dried flesh make a bundle.

十角形 a decagon.

十誡 The Decalogue.

50 十足 complete; pure—as gold; 100 per cent.

十進法 the decimal system.

什 **2.5.** A file of ten soldiers. Ten. Sundry, miscellaneous. Inter. preceding
5808

什一 one tenth.

什件 sundries; miscellaneous goods; giblets, edible internal parts.

什·麼 or 甚·麼 What? (shên²-)

什物 or 什貨 or 什器 sundries, miscellaneous goods; things.

5 什百 ten-fold; one hundred-fold.

什襲 carefully wrapped up.

什錦小菜 condiments; garnishing.

什長³ the corporal of a file of ten.

拾 **2.5.** To pick up; to collect. To tidy; to put to rights.
5809

拾人牙慧 to plagiarize.

拾執 to arrange things.

拾·得 to put in order.

拾·掇 to put in order; to make tidy. (-·tou)

5 拾撫 to put to rights.

拾取 to pick up.

拾芥 to pick up a straw—easily done.

拾·起·來 to pick up; pick it up.

拾遺 to pick up things that have dropped; to repair omissions; official under T'ang dynasty.

收·拾 to tidy up; to repair; to collect together; to put in order.

(a) Ten. The form of No. 5807 used in documents to prevent fraud.

(b) Read shê⁵. To ascend.

拾級而入 ascended the steps and entered.

食 **2.5.** Food. To eat; to drink. Radical 184.
5810

食不知味 to eat but not have any taste for it.

食井 a well of good water for drinking.

食俸 allowance of grain.

食前方丈 about a square chang of provisions set before one—luxurious extravagance.

5 食力 to eat by means of one's own labour.

食厭 to disrelish food.

食取充腹 my food was selected simply with a view to satisfy hunger.

食品 provisions; victuals.

食單 bill of fare.

10 食土之毛 eating the produce of the soil.

食地 arable lands. [sites.

食客 retainer; hangers on; para-

食復 a relapse of any disease caused through eating unsuitable food too soon after recovery.

食德 to receive the kindness of another.

15 食息 eating and resting.

食指 the forefinger.

食指衆多 those that wait to eat are many.

食指不甘 he eats delicacies, but they are not pleasant.

食母 a wet-nurse.

20 食氣 to enjoy the fragrance of; Taoist breathing exercises.

食水 or 吃水 to draw water — as a ship.

食火雞 the cassowary.

食烟 to smoke. (Cantonese)

食無求飽居無求安 in his food he does not seek merely to gratify his appetite, nor in his dwelling-place does he seek mere ease.

---

25 食物 eatables; provisions.

食犬 edible dog.

食玉炊桂 to eat (rice as dear as) gems, and burn (fuel as dear as) cassia.

食用 provisions; edible.

食用蛙 edible frogs.

30 食祿 to draw pay; to live on a salary.

食租衣稅 to live on the taxes of the people—as officials and others.

食管·子 the œsophagus or gullet.

食籮 food-basket.

食粥麤衰 (ts'ui¹.) to eat gruel and wear coarse mourning apparel.

35 食糧 to eat rations—as a soldier.

食而嗜之 to eat and be fond of.

食肉寢皮 to eat the flesh and sleep on the skin—of an enemy; savages.

食肉獸 carnivorous animals.

食自己 to find oneself in food.

40 食蟲植物 insectivorous plants.

食蟲椿象 insectivorous beetles.

食蟲類 insectivora.

食蟻獸 ant-eater.

食言 to eat one's words—to retract a promise.

45 食言而肥 to grow fat from eating one's words.

食譜 a dietary.

食道 the gullet.

食邑 or 食土 a place granted in ancient times to a meritorious person.

食酒 to drink wine.

50 食量 capacity for eating.

食頃 for the space of a single meal.

食鹽 table-salt.

食齋 to abstain from meat for religious reasons.

伙·食 board.

55 共食 to eat together. [board.

寄食 to sponge on others; to

日食 an eclipse.

耳食不化 to hear without understanding.

血食 a sacrifice.

60 隔食 indigestion.

鳥吃食 the bird eats its feed.

(a) Read szŭ⁴. Food; rice. To feed. But see 61 above.

食不厭精 he did not object to having his rice finely cleansed.

食志乎食功乎 do you re-

---

munerate a man's intention, oɪ do you remunerate his service

食饐而餲 rice which had beer injured by heat or damp anc turned sour.

一簞食 a single bamboo dish of rice.

⁵可食而食之矣 he deserves tc be supported and should be supported.

有酒食 to have wine and food.

殺雞爲黍而食之 killed a fowl, prepared m i l l e t and feasted him.

治人者食於人 those whc govern others are supported by them.

飯疏食 with coarse food to eat.

(b) Sometimes read *i²*. A man's name.

蝕 2.5. To eat up slowly. An eclipse.
5811

蝕刻 or 腐刻 to etch.
蝕壞 to eat away, as insects moth-eaten; to corrode.
蝕既 the moment of full eclipse.
蝕損 to injure or diminish by encroachment.
⁵蝕本 to encroach upon one's capital.
侵蝕 to encroach upon.
全蝕 total eclipse.
日蝕月蝕 eclipse of the sun and moon, respectively.
缺蝕 or 分蝕 partial eclipse.
¹⁰(金)環蝕 annular eclipse.

飾餙 4.5. To adorn; to set off. To gloss over; to deceive. Ornaments.
5812

飾僞 false.
飾口 to gloss over a fault.
飾器 ornamental articles; ornamented weapons.
飾延 pretexts for delay.
⁵飾擢 to flatter and select—for office.
飾智 to show off; to pretend to scholarship.
飾玩 ornaments and toys.
飾裝 to prepare one's baggage.
飾觀 to decorate the exterior.

¹⁰飾言 ornamental words—used to gloss over faults, etc.
飾詞 to trump up a story.
飾諱 to conceal.
飾辭偸漏 a pretext for evading payment of duties.
飾非 to gloss over one's wrong-doings.
¹⁵飾非文過 to gloss over faults.
修飾 to adorn; to brighten.
外飾 ostentation; outside show.
掩飾 to conceal.
粉飾 to stop up cracks; to decorate.
²⁰身飾 articles of personal adornment.
首·飾 head ornaments; jewelry.

石 2.5. Stone; rock; mineral. Barren. Radical 112.
5813

石交 deep, firm friendship.
石人石馬 stone figures of men and horses.
石化 to petrify.
石·匠 or 石工 a stone-mason.
⁵石印 lithography.
石友 a trustworthy friend.
石器時代 the stone age.
石國 Tashkend.
石堆 a heap of stones.
¹⁰石塊 stone in pieces.
石墩 blocks of stone placed before gates.
石墨 graphite.
石壁 a precipice.
石女 a barren woman.
¹⁵石子ㄦ³ or 石·頭子ㄦ³ small stones; pebbles.
石室 a stone house—firm, enduring; home of a hermit in the hills.
石拒 or 章魚 the octopus.
石料 unhewn stone.
石本 rubbings from stone inscriptions.
²⁰石松 *Lycopodium clanata.*
石板 slabs of stone.
石果 drupes.
石柱 stone pillars.
石棉 asbestos. *See below*—57.
²⁵石·榴 the pomegranate.
石·榴石 garnets.
石民 the fundamental stone-pillar of a State—scholars, farmers, artisans, and merchants.
石決明 sea-ear—*Haliotis.*

石油 or 煤油 petroleum; kerosene.
³⁰石油機 oil-engine.
石洞 a rock-cave.
石淋 stone in the bladder.
石漆 bitumen.
石灰 lime.
³⁵石灰乳 milk of lime.
石灰岩 limestone.
石灰燈 limelight.
石灰質 calcareous substance.
石灰酸 phenol; carbolic acid.
⁴⁰石淋 stalagmite. *See below*—54.
石版 slate; stone slabs.
石版術 or 石版印刷 lithography.
石版石 lithographic stone.
油畫石版·術 c h r o m o - lithography.
⁴⁵影印石版術 p h o t o - lithography.
石狐 stone fox.
石田 stony, barren land.
石畫 mosaic.
石破天驚 a great concussion oɪ shock.
⁵⁰石硫·黃 crude sulphur.
石礁 hidden rocks.
石礫 gravel.
石竹 pinks, carnations.
石筍 stalagmites. *See above*—40.
⁵⁵石筆 slate-pencil.
石粉 chalk.
石絨 asbestos. *See above*—24.
石經 the stone slabs engraved with the classics.
石綠 malachite.
⁶⁰石缸 a stone water-butt.
石耳 lichens.
石聾 stone deaf.
石胎 a barren womb.
石脈 vein of mineral.
⁶⁵石腦油 naphtha.
石腦油精 naphthalene.
石膏 gypsum; plaster of Paris.
石船 a stone-junk.
石花菜 edible sea-weed; agar-agar.
⁷⁰石苔 lichens; moss.
石英 quartz.
石英斑岩 porphyry.
石華表 stone pillars at a grave.
石蠟 paraffin-wax.
⁷⁵石蠶 madrepore.
石衣 moss.
石斛 dendrobium.
石貂 stone-marten.
石路 a stone-paved road.
⁸⁰石隙 a cleft in a rock.

石 青 dark green.
石 青 糝 之 done with dark green colouring.
石 頭 a stone.
石 首 魚 or 黃 花 魚 or 黃 魚 species of *Sciæna*.
[85]石 髮 stalactites; moss or lichens.
石 鹻 washing-soda.
石 鹽 rock-salt.
石 黃 orpiment.
石 龍·子 a lizard.
[90]浮 石 pumice.
滑 石 soap-stone.
磁 石 or 吸 鐵 石 a loadstone.
紅 石 red-sandstone.
鐘 乳 石 stalactites.
[95]青 石 granite.

(a) A liquid measure. A dry measure for grain. A weight of 120 catties—a picul of 100 catties or 133⅓ lb., avoirdupois. Sometimes it is written 石 and read *tan*[4].

一 石 米 a picul of rice.
食 酒 一 石 to drink a gallon of wine.

祏 [2.5.] Stone shrine in a family temple.
5814

碩 [2.5.] Great; eminent. Large. Full. Ripe.
5815 Also read *shuo*[4].
碩 人 之 寬 that large man at his ease—a recluse.
碩 人 其 頎 beautiful was she and tall.
念 彼 碩 人 thinking of that great man.
碩 儒 an eminent scholar.
[5]碩 勇 brave; valorous—a term bestowed as a title.
碩 士 a worthy scholar.
碩 士 學 位 M.A.
碩 大 無 朋 great and peerless.
碩 學 高 才 of great learning and exalted talents.
[10]碩 彥 eminent; talented.
碩 果 things that are durable.
碩 畫 great designs.
碩 老 an aged scholar of wide knowledge.
碩 膚 greatly admirable.
[15]碩 苗 grain full in the ear.
碩 言 boastful talk.

碩 輔 an eminent statesman.
碩 量 liberality; broad-mindedness.
碩 鼠 large rats—oppressive officers of the government; a squirrel.
[20]孔 碩 very large—describing male animals in hunting.

(a) u.f. 石. A picul.

鼫 [2.5.] The long-tailed marmot.
5816
鼫 鼠 a squirrel.

式 [4.5.] A form, fashion, rule, pattern, model. To imitate; to set an example.
5817
式·子 a sample; a formula.
公 式 a formula.
圖 解 式 a graphic formula.
定 式 a formula.
[5]構 造 式 constitutional formula.
示 性 式 rational formula.
算 式 a formula. (*arith.*).
式 樣 an example; a model; a pattern.
式 樣 品 specimens.
[10]式 類 a class; a category.
儀 式 上·的 conventional; formal.
古 訓 是 式 taking the ancients as a model.
合 式 suitable; in accordance with the pattern.
各 式 all kinds.
[15]字 式 copy-slip.
時 式 fashionable styles.
格·式 a pattern or copy.
欵 式 form—as of a document.
正 式 formally.
[20]正 式 陳 述 to formulate.
衣 式 style of dress.

(a) To employ; to use. To cause.

式 廓 疆 圉 to employ in enlarging the borders of the empire.
式 爾 purposely.
式 靖 亂 階 to employ in pacifying incipient disorder.
惟 天 式 教 我 用 休 Heaven therefore taught us and thereby was excellence.

(b) To reverence. To bow forward to the front bar of a carriage.

式 和 民 則 reverently seek to bring the people and their duties into harmony.
式 如 金 式 如 玉 regard them as gold and as gems.
式 敬 爾 由 獄 reverently dealt with all the criminal matters which came before him.
式 黃 髮 to reverence hoary heads.
凶 服 者 式 之 to any person in mourning he bowed forward to the cross-bar of his carriage.

(c) An initial particle; a conjunction:—only, and, thereby.

式 固 爾 猶 only lay your plans securely.
式 序 在 位 he has regulated the positions of the princes.
式 微 reduced in circumstances; decadent.
女 界 式 微 the status of women is low.
[5]式 救 爾 後 and it will save your posterity.
式 遄 其 歸 and he will soon return.
式 遏 寇 虐 and to repress robbers and oppressors.

拭 [4.5.]
帗   To wipe; to rub; to dust; to clean.
5818
拭 桌 to wipe a table.
拭 涕 or 拭 淚 to wipe away tears.
拭 淨 to rub clean.
拭 目 to wipe the eyes.

軾 [4.5.] A stretcher in a sedan-chair to lean on when bowing.
5819

室 [4.5.] A house; a mansion; a home; an apartment.
5820
室 女 an unmarried girl; a virgin.
室 如 懸 磬 house as empty as a musical stone—desperately poor.

室 宇 rooms; chambers.
室 家 or 家 室 household; a home.
⁵室 家 不 寧 an unquiet home.
世 室 ancestral home.
交 際 室 social hall.
兵 室 barracks.
宮 室 a mansion; a palace.
¹⁰宗 室 the Imperial family.
延 賓 室 or 會 客 室 reception room.
教 授 室 class-room.
暗 室 dark-room.
更 衣 室 dressing-room.
¹⁵未 入 室 not yet entered into the inner apartments—has still something to learn. See 升 No. 5745—5, 6.
機 械 室 engine-room.
浴 室 bath-room.
無 陳 設 之 室 an unfurnished room.
皇 室 Imperial house.
²⁰考 試 室 examination-hall.
試 驗 室 laboratory.

(a) A wife.

室 人 a wife—used in announcements of death for "my late wife."
側 室 or 配 室 a concubine.
受 室 to take a wife.
未 有 室 not yet taken a wife.
⁵正 室 a wife.
繼 室 to marry again; a second wife.

實 寔

2.5. Solid; substantial; hard. Real; true; truly; really. Authentic. Sincere; genuine. Reality.

5821　Distinguish 寶 No. 4956

實 不 瞞 你 I really do not deceive you.
實 事 an actual thing; a fact.
實 事 求 是 by verification of the facts to get at the truth.
實 事·的 practical.
⁵實 況 real state of affairs.
實 以 藥 彈 loaded it with powder and shot.
實 任 or 實 缺 a substantive appointment.
實 係 really is; really belongs to.
實 係 為 難 it is really a difficult matter.
¹⁰實 值 real value.

實 像 the real image.
實 價 the net price; the true value.
實 利 having practical value.
實 利 主 義 Utilitarianism.
¹⁵實 則 有 truly there is....
實 力 actual strength; real, unequivocal.
實 口 to fill the mouth of a corpse with rice, tea, and incense.
實 吐 to tell the truth.
實 噸 位 dead weight,—in tons.
²⁰實 在 really; truly; actually; reality.
實 在 情 形 actual state of affairs.
實 在 論 Realism.
　　墨 肉 實 在 The Real Presence.
實 地 terra-firma.
²⁵實 地 應 用 practical application.
實 地·的 觀 察 actual observation.
實 地 試 驗 actual tests.
實 境 the real thing.
實 存 the actual balance; net total.
³⁰實 字 concrete words as opposed to 虛 字, particles, etc.
實 學 solid learning; practical knowledge.
實 實 solid; real.
實 實 落 落 real; plain; substantial.
實 屬 really belongs to....
³⁵實 彈 藥 筒 ball-cartridge.
實 心 honestly; heartily.
實 心 奉 行 to carry out honestly.
實 心 實 意 unfeigned; purposely.
實 心 彈 solid shells—non-explosive.
⁴⁰實 心 眼 extremely simple and honest.
實 念 論 realism.
實 情 the actual facts of the case.
實 感 real emotion.
實 意 the real meaning; honestly; faithfully.
⁴⁵實 打 實 perfectly true.
實 打 實 摜 unbreakable; firm—as a price, etc.
實 授 substantive appointment.
實 據 substantial evidence or proofs.
實 收 official receipts.
⁵⁰實 收 資 本 paid-up capital.
實 效 results; effects; outcome.
實 數 real numbers; concrete numbers; multiplicand or dividend.

實 施 practical application; to realize; to give effect to; to enforce.
實 是 it truly is....
⁵⁵實 有 其 事 it truly is a fact.
實 業 industry; labour, trade, etc.
實 業 中 心 點 industrial centre.
實 業 主 義 industrialism.
實 業 部 Ministry of Industries.
⁶⁰實 業 部 長 Minister of Industries.
實 業 團 industrial circles; industrial group.
實 業 學 校 technical schools.
實 業 家 business men; industrialists.
實 業 展 覽 會 industrial exhibition.
⁶⁵實 業 戰 爭 industrial warfare.
實 業 界 the industrial world.
實 業 界 領 袖 captains of industry.
實 業 發 展 expansion of industries.
實 業 競 爭 industrial competition.
⁷⁰實 業 蕭 索 industrial depression.
實 業 計 畫 industrial programme or measures.
實 業 調 察 會 industrial commission. ＝工 業 革 命
實 業 變 遷 industrial revolution.
實 業 首 領 captains of industry.
75
世 界 實 業 勞 動 者 團 體 Industrial Workers of the World or I.W.W.
公 立 實 業 public industries.
分 俵 實 業 distributive industries.
初 級 實 業 primary industries.
大 宗 實 業 staple industries
80
進 級 實 業 secondary industries.
實 濟 real use or advantage.
實 焦 點 real focus.
實 為 really is or belongs to ...
實 為 公 便 truly both just and expedient.
⁸⁵實 物 substance; solid matter.
實 物 教 授 object lesson.
實 狀 real condition.
實 現 practical realization; practical manifestation; practical evidence.
實 生·活 real life as opposed to fiction.
⁹⁰實 用 practical use.
實 用 主 義 pragmatism.

實 用 其 力 to use genuine endeavours.

實 科 practical course.

實 習 to practise—as an art, etc.

95實 行 to put into operation; applied.

實 行 印 花 稅 put the stamp duty into operation.

實 行 未 遂 actual attempt without result. (*legal*).

實 話 the truth.

實 證 論 positivism.

100實 貼 to post up—as a notice or proclamation.

實 質 physical; real; solid.

實 質 上 in reality; physically.

實 質 主 義 materialism.

實 質 科 學 material sciences.

105實 質·的 really; physically.

有 實 質·的 substantial as contrasted with nominal.

實 足 年 齡 actual age.

實 跡 the fact; the reality.

110實 踐 倫 理 學 practical ethics.

實 踐 哲 學 practical philosophy.

實 踐·的 practically.

實 踐 社 會 學 practical sociology.

實 斦 斦 really and truly the very thing.

實 重 the real weight.

115實 銀 the real amount.

實 錄 a true narration; faithful transcript.

實 際 practical; actuality.

實 際·上 practically; in substance; in reality.

實 際·上·的 效 果 practical results.

120實 際 主 義 realism.

實 際 之 精 神 a practical spirit.

實 際 之 經 驗 practical experience.

實 際 情 次 face to facts

實 際 生·活 practical life.

125實 際·的 practical.

實 際 神 學 practical theology.

實 際 言 之 practically speaking.

沒 有 一 些 實 際·的 價 值 not of the least practical value.

實 驗 test, experiment; to test.

130實 驗 哲 學 positivism.

實 驗 室 laboratory.

實 驗 家 investigator; experimentalist.

實 驗 心 理 學 experimental psychology.

實 驗 法 experimental methods.

135實 驗 社 會 學 experimental sociology.

實 驗 論 positivism.

實 驗 馬 力 effective horsepower.

一 個 實 驗 a test.

實 體 substance; material substance; physical.

140實 體 上 substantially.

實 體 法 substantial law.

實 體 論 realism.

實 體 鏡 stereoscope.

寫 實 主 義 realism in writing.

145其 實 as a matter of fact; in reality.

其 實 一 也 are actually the same thing.

言 過 其 實 exaggeration.

名 實 the name and the reality.

名 不 副 實 the reality does not agree with the name.

150 有 名 無 實 merely nominal, without reality; a sham.

着·實·的 it really is.... (*chao²-*)

誠·實 honest; sincere.

軍 實 military stores.

(a) Small, hard fruits.

實 小 墨 而 圓 the kernel was small, black and round.

其 實 纍 纍 its fruits are overhanging.

秀 而 不 實 者 those which blossom but do not come to fruition.

結 實² to bear fruit; 結·實 solid; sturdy.

適 4.5 To go to; to reach. A
5822 bride going to her husband's house; to marry—of women.

適 嫁 to marry a husband.

適 往 to go to.

適 從 何 來 where have you come from now?

無 所 適 從 not knowing which way to turn.

5適 陳 家 married into the *Ch'ên* family.

不 貳 適 no double aims.

可 與 適 道 we may go on with them as to principles.

子 適 衛 the master went to *Wei*.

(a) To suit. To succeed. To be blessed with. Pleasure. Amusement. Agreeable.

適 中 之 數 moderate quantity.

適 中 地 點 central location.

適 人 嗜·好 suit people's fancies.

適 任 fit for the post.

5適 切 to the point.

適 口 palatable.

適 合 fitting; suitable; to adapt itself to.

適 合 時 勢 adapted to present conditions.

適 宜 fitting.

10適 宜 存 在 survival of the fittest.

適 宜·的 境 地 suitable environment.

適 度 moderately; measurably.

適 意 agreeable; in good health; in accordance with one's wishes.

適 應 adaptation.

15適 應 環 境 adaptation to environment.

適 應 說 theory of adaptation.

不 能 適 應 現 時·的 要 求 does not meet the demands of the times.

適 我 願 it meets my wishes.

適 於 初 學 者 suitable for beginners.

20適 於 食 用 fit for food.

適 法 in accordance with the law.

適 用 sufficient for use; answers the purpose; application; applicability.

適 用 條 例 applicable rules.

適 用 的 applied.

25 不 適 現 今 之 用 not suited to present requirements.

適 當 adequate; appropriate.

適 當 之 外 交 手 段 proper diplomatic procedure.

適 當 方 法 a suitable method.

適 當 機 關 an appropriate instrument.

30不 適 當 inapt; inappropriate; unfitting.

適 相 反 對 the exact opposite.

適 者 生 存 survival of the fittest.

適 輕 適 重 the circumstances being extenuating and aggravating, respectively.

適 體 to fit the body.

35取 適 to seek pleasure.

從 所 適 let him go where he pleases.

(b) To happen. To fall in with. Suddenly; just now.

適 來 此 地 he had just come to this place.

適値其時 happened just right; opportune; precisely at that time.

適因 just because....

適因此故 just for this very reason.

[5]適有客來 just then a visitor arrived.

適然 or 適爾 suddenly; accidentally.

適竟其事 the affair had just been concluded, when....

適纔 just now.

適纔說·的話 what has just been said.

[10]適臨 it falls on....

適間 just now.

寧適不來 it is better that something should happen to keep them from coming.

(c) Only.

則口腹豈適爲尺寸之膚哉 how should his mouth and belly be considered as no more than an inch of skin?

(d) Read ti[4.5]. **The legitimate heir.**

天位殷適 Yin's rightful heir to the heavenly seat.

(e) To be bent on. To take the lead. To preside over.

君子[3]之於天下也無適也無莫也 the superior man in the world, does not set his mind either for anything or against anything.

存適莫之見 prejudiced views.

誰適爲容 for whom should I give my attention in adorning myself?

誰適與謀 who devised their schemes for them?

(f) Read chê[2.5]. **u.f.** 謫 **No. 279. To reprove; to remonstrate.**

人不足與適也 it is not enough to remonstrate with—a sovereign.

勿予禍適 do not punish us or reprove us.

濕溼 1.5.

5823

Wet, damp, moist.

濕·了 wet.

濕地 swampy land.

濕度 degree of humidity.

濕度表 hygrometer.

[5]濕氣 humid exhalations; damp air; moist.

濕水貨 damaged goods.

濕漚 steeped; soaked.

濕·漬漬[1]·的 or 濕·拉拉·的 quite wet; dripping wet.(--chi-chi[1]-)

濕潤 to moisten; to benefit.

[10]濕熱 damp heat.

濕生 damp birth—insects supposed to be spontaneously generated in damp places.

濕禮 or 水禮 presents of eatables—not money.

濕窪 marshy; swampy.

濕透 wet through.

[15]潮·濕 damp.

發濕 to be damp.

風濕 rheumatism.

(a) Read chê[2.5]. **Flapping of the ears of cattle.**

爾牛來思，其耳濕濕 your cattle come, flapping their ears.

(b) Read t'a[4.5]. **u.f.** 漯 **No. 5984. A river in Shantung.**

釋 4.5. **To release; to unloose; to open out. To explain.**

5824

釋分明 to explain clearly.

釋回 to liberate—as from exile, or from evil.

釋回增美 to forsake evil ways and improve the disposition.

釋嬈 to lay aside ill-feeling.

[5]釋恨 or 釋冤 to get rid of ill-will and hatred.

釋悶 to shake off melancholy; to get relief of mind.

釋憾 to dispel hatred of heart.

釋手 to unhand; to let go one's hand.

釋放 or 開釋 to liberate.

[10]釋服 to leave off mourning apparel.

釋本末 to explain fully.

釋然於心 to set the mind at rest.

釋甲 to lay down arms; to surrender.

釋紛 to settle a lawsuit for others.

[15]釋縛 to uncord; to loose the bonds.

釋罪 to let off; to pardon.

釋義 to explain the meaning.

釋褐 to doff the rough serge—to assume official robes.

釋言 to make a verbal explanation or excuse.

[20]釋釋 dispersed; released; free.

釋難攻易 to avoid the difficult and attempt the easy.

如釋重負 as if released from a heavy burden.

解·釋 to console; to explain.

註釋 commentary; notes on the text.

(a) Used in transliterating. Buddhism.

釋像 Buddhist images.

釋子[3] Buddhist priests.

釋旨 Buddhism.

釋氏 Buddha. Buddhists.

[5]釋老 Buddhism and Taoism.

釋迦帝婆 Indra.

釋迦牟尼 Shâkyamuni—Buddha.

釋道 Buddhism and Taoism.

釋門 or 釋敎 Buddhism.

識 4.5. **To recognize; to know; to be acquainted with. To distinguish.**

5825

識丁 to know characters—to be able to read.

識人 to know a person thoroughly.

識別 to discriminate.

識[2]字 to recognize characters—to be able to read.

[5]識禮 acquainted with the rules of etiquette.

識荆 or 識韓 first acquaintance with a person, from a poem by Li Po.

識貨 to know goods—their quality, etc.

識趣 knowledge; tactful.

識透 or 識破 to see through; to be fully aware of.

[10]識量之淺狹 small ability.

識面 to know by sight.

常識 general knowledge; common sense. See No. 221-52, 53.

無知·識 ignorant.

熟·識 intimate with.

[15]見·識 knowledge; experience.

認·識 to recognize; to be acquainted.

(a) Read *chih*[4]. To remember. To record. Inscriptions cast on bronzes. u.f. 誌 No. 973.

識 文 inscriptions, as on bronzes.
神 識 衰 耗 mental faculties declining.
醒 而 識 之 on waking, she recalled it.

螫 [4.5.] To poison; to sting. Venomous. Troublesome; oppressive. Also read *chê*[1.5] [(*chê*[1.])]
5826

螫 了 手 it has stung my hand.
螫 蟲 a poisonous insect; the scorpion.

赨 [4.5.] To be angry. Red.
5827

襩 [4.5.] A rain-coat. Also read *ch'ih*[4.5.]
5828

襏 襩 a rain-coat.

SHUO. SHO (ㄕㄛ)
(Shoh)

勺 [4.5.] To ladle out with a spoon. A spoon, a ladle. The tenth of a 合. Also read *shao*[2].
5829

勺·子 a spoon. (*shao*[2]-)

妁 [4.5.] A go-between; a matchmaker. Also read *cho*[2.5].
5830

媒 妁 a go-between in a marriage.
女 妁 a female go-between.

杓 [4.5.] A handle, as of a cup, ladle, etc. Also read *shao*[2]. Inter. 勺 No. 5829.
5831

斗 杓 the handle of the *Dipper*.
木 杓 a wooden ladle. (-*shao*[2])

(a) Read *piao*[1]. Name of a constellation.

汋 [2.5.] Water bubbling up. Also read *ts'u*[4.5.]
5832 Read *cho*[2.5.] To pour, etc. Similar to 酌 No. 1257.

芍 [4.5.] The Chinese water-chestnut—*Scirpus tuberosus*.
5833 Also read *shao*[2].

芍·藥 the peony, the roots of which are used as medicine. (*shao*[2]·*yao*)

爍 [4.5.] Bright; splendid; brilliant. Inter. next.
5834

爍 閃 or 閃 爍 to reflect light.
灼 爍 luminous; brilliant.

鑠 [4.5.] To melt. To polish. Lustrous; shining.
5835

鑠 目 brilliant eyes.
鑠 石 流 金 to melt stones and fuse metals—intense heat.
鑠 金 to fuse metals.
鑠 鑠 bright; lustrous.
衆 口 鑠 金 public opinion will fuse metals.

蟀 [4.5.] A cricket. Also read *shuai*[1], *hsi*[2].
5836

蟋 蟀 crickets.

SHOU. (ㄕㄡ)
(Sheo)

收收抴 1 To receive what is due; to gather together. To harvest. To collect; to put away. To close, to bind, to restrain.. To bring to an end.
5837

收 入 income.
收·下 or 收·入 to receive; to receive from; to gather in.
收·不 回 來 cannot be recalled—as words.
收 主 consignee.
收·了 買 賣 the business is closed.
[5] 收 儲 to put by; to lay in store.
收 元 to change the "style" of a reign.
收 入 版 圖 to annex a territory.
收 兵 to recall troops.
收 刀 入 鞘 to return the sword to the scabbard.
[10] 收 到 received.
收 割 to gather in the harvest.
收 受 to receive; to accept.
收 取 to receive and select.

收 口 closing of a wound; to put into port.
[15] 收 單 a receipt.
收 回 to take back.
收 回 利 權 to restore rights and privileges.
收 回 會 審 公 廨 rendition of the Mixed Court.
收 回 紙 幣 to call in bank-notes.
[20] 收 埋 to gather up and bury.
收 執 to receive as a receipt; to hold in possession.
收 塲 to bring to an end—as a performance.
收 存 to lay by; to put aside.
收 字 a receipt.
[25] 收 守 to receive and guard.
收 容 to receive and make a place for—as a patient in a hospital, etc.
收 審 to confine awaiting trial.
收 工 to stop work.
收 帶 to carry on the person.
[30] 收 得 [2] received.
收 復 to recover; to re-capture.
收 心 世 務 to withdraw the thoughts from mundane affairs.
收 成 harvest; return—for trouble, etc.
收 房 to be taken in as a concubine.
[35] 收 拆 to receive and open—as a letter.
收 押 to confine; to imprison; to receive pledges—as a pawn-broker.
收·拾 to make ready; to put in order; to mend; to gather together; to tidy up.
收·拾 三 軍 回 朝 [2] got ready the army and returned to the capital.
收·拾·你 I'll fix you! I'll settle your business!
[40] 收·拾·行·李 to get the baggage ready.
收·拾·起·來 to gather things together.
收 掌 to take over the management of.
收 據 a receipt.
收 攬 to work up a business.
[45] 收 支 receipts and disbursements.
收 支 員 teller; cashier.
收 效 to have effective results.
收 敎 友 to receive church members.
收 斂 to gather the harvest; to gather together.

50 收 斂 劑 astringents.
收 明 received in full.
收。服 to win back to allegiance.
收 束 to bind.
文 條 a receipt.
55 收 梢 the end of a thing; the outcome.
收 欵 人 receiving teller.
收 欵 票 bills receivable.
收 殮 to prepare a corpse for burial.
收 歸 國 有 nationalization of property.
60 收 沒 to confiscate.
收 淸 received in full.
收 潔 淨 費 者 collector of fees for street cleaning.
收 熱 to conserve heat.
收 生 or 收 生 婆 or 接 生 a midwife.
65 收 用 to take for use.
收 留 to detain; to harbour.
收 畢 received in full.
收 監 to confine in prison.
收 碗 to clear away after a meal.
70 收 禁 to keep in detention.
收 科 or 收 塲 to finish; to complete.
收 租 to collect rents.
收 稅 to receive taxes.
收 稅 免 照 an exemption certificate.
75 收 稅 單 a duty-paid certificate.
收 穫 to gather in the crops.
收 管 to take over the management of.
收 納 to receive; to accept.
收 縮 to contract.
80 收 繫 to keep in confinement.
收 羅 to haul in a net.
收 脚 to stop running.
收 葬 to gather up and bury.
收 藏 to lay up in store.
85 收 藏 家 curio collectors.
收 規 to collect fees.
收 訖 received in full.
收 貨 人 consignee.
收 買 人 心 to win the hearts of the people—by presents, etc.
90 收 買 玩 器 curios bought here.
收 賬 to collect accounts.
收 贖 to redeem; to take out of pawn; to raise a mortgage.
收·起·來 to take up; to put away; to keep safely.
收 足 received in full.
95 收 辦 to take over and deal with.
收 進 to take in.

收 銀 單 bills receivable.
收 鋪 to close a shop; to shut up shop.
收 錢 to receive money; to take bribes.
100 收 門·生 to receive pupils.
收 隊 to recall troops.
收·集 to gather things together in one place.
收 霧 氣 to clear up—as fog or mist.
收 領 to receive.
接 收 to receive.

(a) The front and rear of a carriage.

小 戎 儇 收 his short war-chariot.

(b) A cap worn at sacrificial rites during the *Hsia* dynasty.

手
才 } 3　The hand. A "hand."
Radical 64.
5838

手 下 under the hand; under the power or control of.
下 手 to commence anything; to set the hand to a thing; an assistant.
先 下 手 give the first blow.
手 下 人 servants; underlings.
5 手 下 留 情 to make allowances for a person.
手 不 停 披 turning over the pages without ceasing—diligent study.
手 不 穩 light-fingered.
手 不 老 實 light-fingered; given to pilfering.
手 中 in the hand.
10 手 串 a bead bracelet.
手 乏 in want of money; hard up.
手 代 a clerk.
手 作 an art; handicraft; workmanship.
手 信 號 hand-signalling.
15 手 凹 the inside of the elbow.
手 到 成 功 when he sets his hand to it, it is done.
手 力 印 刷 機 a hand-press for printing.
手 動 制 動 機 a hand-brake.
手 動 磨 機 hand-mill.
20 手 勢 gestures.
手 勤 diligent.

手 印 the impression of the hand or thumb as a signature.
打 手 印 to make a hand or thumb-print.
手 卷 a scroll or picture that is too long to hang up; a book in MS.
25 手 口 相 應 actions and words agree—to carry out one's promises.
手 囊 a wallet; a small handbag.
手 困 hard up; in want of money.
手 圈 a bracelet.
手 大 遮·不 過 天 even if your hand is large, it will not cover up the sky—your ability is not equal to the task.
30 手 套 gloves; mittens.
半 手 手 套 mittens.
手 工 handicraft; manual training.
手 巧 or 手 頭 巧 dexterous; skilful with the hands.
手·巾 or 手 帕 a handkerchief.
35 手 帖 the visiting-card of a subordinate official.
手 底·下 under one's hand; in hand; at hand.
手 弄 to handle.
手 式 sign language.
手 心 the palm of the hand.
40 手 忙 脚 亂 very busy.
手 懶 lazy.
手 扣 handcuffs.
手 抄 manuscript; a copy made by oneself.
手 技 handicraft.
45 手 招 to beckon to.
手 拏 to grasp in the hand.
手 指 or 手 指 頭 the fingers.
手 指 凍 僵 fingers stiff and numb with cold.
手 指 目 逤 pointing and staring —as at a passing crowd or show.
50 手 捧 to hold up in the hand.
手 掌 the palm of the hand.
手 援 to lead by the hand.
手 提 器·具 portable instrument.
手 提 燈 a hand-lantern.
55 手 提 行·李 hand-baggage.
手 搖 車 a hand-trolley.
手 攏·子 a muff.
手 摺 a small note-book; notes; memoranda.
手 擲 炸 彈 hand-grenade.
60 手 文 lines of the palm.
手 書 your letter; personal handwriting.

手 本 the visiting-card of a sub-ordinate official.

手 杖 or 手 拐 a walking-stick.

手 植 personally planted—as a tree.

[65] 手 模 the impression of the hand or thumb as a signature.

手 機 關 鎗 Lewis-gun.

手‧段 skill; knack; power; ability; schemes or plans.

好 手‧段 good craftsmanship.

強 硬 手‧段 to carry things with a high hand.

[70] 強 迫 手‧段 violent methods.

恫 嚇‧的 手‧段 threatening, over-bearing methods.

操 縱 手‧段 wire-pulling.

美 人 計‧的 手‧段 the trick of using a pretty woman to ensnare a person.

高 壓 手‧段 high-handed methods.

[75] 手 毒 dangerous; vicious.

手 民 a compositor; an engraver of blocks for printing.

手 法 sleight of hand.

手 泐 written with one's own hand.

手 渡 to hand from one to another.

[80] 手 淫 masturbation.

手 溜 彈 hand-grenades.

手 澤 如 新 his relic is still fresh and new.

手 球 hand-ball.

手 琴 an accordion.

[85] 手 生 inexperienced.

生 手 a raw-hand.

手 甲 the finger-nails.

手 眼 device; wire-pulling.

手 笠 mittens or gloves.

[90] 手 筒 a muff.

手 筆 one's handwriting.

手 節 the knuckles.

手 簡 your letter; your favour.

手 紋 the lines on the palm.

[95] 手 緊 stingy; in financial difficul-ties.

手 縫 (fèng⁴) spaces between the fingers.

手 織 機 hand-loom.

手‧續 process; procedure; meth-ods.

手‧續 便‧利 the method of pro-cedure is simple.

[100] 手‧續 法 auxiliary law.

手‧續 繁 重 the various pro-cesses involved are onerous.

手‧續 費 auxiliary expenses; overhead expenses.

訴 訟 手 續 legal procedure.

迅 速 之 手 續 expeditious methods.

[105] 手 肘 the elbow.

手 背 the back of the hand.

手‧脚 hands and feet—assistants; tricks. *See* No. 1177—B. 3.

手 脚³ 不 閑 always on the bustle.

手 脚³ 快 便 active; dexterous; handy.

[110] 手 脚³ 穩‧當 trustworthy a n d careful—as a good servant.

大 手 大 脚³ wasteful; free-handed.

好 手 脚³ skilful; dexterous.

費‧了 我 許 多 手 脚³ it has given me a lot of trouble.

手 腕‧子 the wrist.

[115] 手 臂 the arm.

手 自 筆 錄 transcribed t h e m with his own hand.

手 舞 足 蹈 capering about; gesticulating with hands and feet.

手 荷 物 hand-baggage.

手‧藝 a trade or handicraft.

[120] 手 虎 口 space between finger and thumb.

手 表 wrist-watch.

手‧術 operation—as in surgery; skill of handicraft.

手 記 a finger-ring.

手 詔 edict written b y t h e emperor.

[125] 手 語 to talk on the fingers—as deaf-mutes.

手 談 to play *wei-ch'i,* cards, etc.

手 足 hands and feet—brothers.

手 足 不 相 爭 brothers do not fight.

手 足 並 行 to go on all fours.

[130] 手 足 分 離 separation of brothers.

手 足 無 措 no room to move hand or feet—busy and bust-ling.

手 足 相 依 hands and feet are m u t u a l l y dependent,—as brothers should be.

手 足 至 親 brotherly affection.

手 足 重 繭 hands and f e e t heavily calloused and rough like a cocoon—hard-labour.

[135] 手 跡 autographs; handwriting.

手 辣 hard-dealing; malicious.

手 選 elected by a show of hands.

手 鈴 hand-bell.

手 銬 hand-cuffs.

[140] 手 錐 a hand-drill.

手 鎗 a pistol; a revolver.

手 鏡 hand-mirror.

手 鐲 or 手 釧 bracelets.

手 鑪 stove for warming the hands.

[145] 手 鑽 a gimlet.

手 長 greedy.

手 長 袖 短 the hand is long but the sleeve is short—the inten-tion is good but the ability is limited.

手 面₂ the palm of the hand.

手 頭₂ the hand; the grasp of the hand.

[150] 手 頭² 不 寬‧綽 close-fisted; not well off. (‑‑*ch'ao*)

手 頭² 好 dexterous; skilful.

手 頭² 巧 skilful with the hand.

手 頭² 緊 close-fisted; short of cash.

手 頭² 鬆 lack of grip—wanting in energy; to give too much.

[155] 手 風 琴 accordion or concertina.

手 鬆‧的 人 a spendthrift.

手 鼓 a tambourine.

假³ 手 to procure assistance.

到 手 come to hand.

[160] 動 手 to start on anything; to commence work; to fight.

垂 手 可 取 able to take it with hands down—very easily.

執 手 or 拉 手 or 握 手 to shake hands.

好 手 a good hand at anything.

巧 手 dexterous; neat-fingered.

[165] 換 手 to change hands.

放 手 to let go.

束 手 to draw back the hand.

棘 手 a thorny matter.

洗 手 to wash the hands—also used fig.   [(*shu²*‑)

[170] 熟 手 an old experienced worker.

縮 手 to draw back the hand.

罷 手 to cease; to stop.

起 手 to begin operations.

遊 手 a vagrant.

[175] 還 手 to return a blow.

閒 手 having leisure.

順 手 or 帶 手 at convenience.

首 [3] The head. A chief, a leader. First. Radical 185.
5839 N.A. of poems, plays, etc.

首 丘 (the fox's) original home.

歸 正 首 丘 to return home to die—to bring a body home for burial.

首事 a leader; one who takes charge.

首位 the chief seat.

[5]首倡 to start; to originate.

首先 first; in the first place.

首創 the founder; the original manufacturer; to originate.

首功 first-class merit. *See* 上 No. 5669—C. 4.

首匪 brigand chiefs.

首句 the opening sentence.

[10]首名 or 魁首 the first or leading name; chief.

首善 the very best; the highest.

首尾 beginning and end; sum and substance.

首尾相應 beginning and end correspond with each other.

[15]首尾相顧 front and rear supporting each other.

首席 (or 座) the head of the table; chief place at a feast.

首府 the head prefecture; capital of a province.

首從 (*tsung*[1]) principal and accessory.

首惡 the chief sinner; first in evil.

[20]首揆 the Prime Minister.

首服 head-dress. *See below*—A. 3.

首歲 the 1st month of the lunar year.

首生 or 初生·的 the first-born.

首痛 headache.

[25]首相 or 首宰 chief Minister of State.

首祚 the beginning of the year.

首秋 the 7th lunar month.

首級 the decapitated heads of criminals; a step in rank given to soldiers who bring in such heads.

首縣 the leading county city.

[30]首罪 the chief sinner; first in evil. *See below*—A. 5.

首肯 to nod assent.

首虜 heads of the enemy and captives of war.

首要 the principal; head; chief.

首謀 the first plan.

[35]首路 to start on a journey.

首途 to set forth on a journey.

首選 head of the poll.

首重 what is of chief importance.

首都 the capital. Nanking.

[40]首頁 a title-page.

首領 head and neck; a leader; chief eunuch.

保得首領 saved his neck.

首·飾 women's ornaments.

首鼠兩端 like a rat looking both ways—of a suspicious person, or of one who is in two minds. Cf. the prefaces to 辭

[45]一首詩 a poem; a stanza. 通

元首 the emperor; chief.

分首 to part.

泥首 to dirty the head by kotowing.

稽首 to knock the head in prostrations.

[50]自首至足 from head to foot.

門首 an entrance.

(a) Read *shou*[1]. **To come forward. To confess guilt.**

首告 to turn informer.

首報 to turn informer.

首服 to accuse oneself. *See above*—21.

首狀 a charge; an accusation.

[5]首罪 to confess a crime. *See above*—30.

出首 to turn informer.

投首 to give oneself up.

自首 to accuse oneself.

降 (*hsiang*[2]) 首 to submit.

受[4] **To receive; to endure; to suffer. Indicates the passive.**
5840 Distinguish 愛 No. 9.

受·不·得 or 受·不·住 unendurable; hard to bear.

受之於天 received from heaven.

受享 to enjoy.

受人之託 to receive a commission from another.

[5]受人籠絡 to be imposed on.

受信機 receiver—telegraph.

受信用 to be credited.

受俸給之權利 right to salary—of officials.

受傷 to be injured; wounded.

[10]受刑 to be punished.

受動主義 passivism.

受動態 or 受動調 passive voice.

受動·的 passive.

受動詞 passive verb.

[15]受吃受喝 eatable and drinkable, respectively.

受命 to be content with one's lot.

受報酬 to be recompensed.

受天之命 received a divine appointment—to rule.

受室 to take a wife.

[20]受害 to suffer injury.

受寄物 thing received in trust.

受寒 to suffer from cold.

受審 to be judged.

受寵若驚 receive favours as with fear.

[25]受封 to be ennobled.

受屈 or 受委·屈 to be deceived; to be imposed upon; to be wronged.

受徒 to receive pupils or disciples.

受恩 to receive grace; to be benefited.

受戒 to do penance; to be initiated into the Buddhist priesthood.

[30]受損 or 受壞 to suffer loss; to sustain damage.

受教 docile; to receive instruction.

受於.. received from....

受業 to receive instruction; your pupil—in letters.

受榮耀 to receive glory.

[35]受毒 to be poisoned.

受氣 to suffer indignity; to be scolded; to be the object of a person's anger; abused; ill-treated.

受洗 or 領洗 to be baptized.

受熱 to suffer from heat; to get a fever.

受·用 comfortable; at ease; gratification.

[40]受用不盡 more than can be used.

受用慣·了 accustomed to comforts.

受病 to be ill.

受益 to be benefited.

受看 or 受瞧 worthy of regard; passable.

[45]受禍 to endure calamities.

受福 to be blessed.

受禮 to receive a salutation.

受窄 hampered; oppressed.

受窘迫 to suffer extreme poverty.

[50]受精 to be fertilized.

受納 to be accepted.

受累 to be involved.

受罪 to endure the consequences of sin; to be punished.

受罰 to be fined.

[55]受聘 to be betrothed; to receive wedding presents.

受聽 pleasant to hear.

受胎 or 受孕 to become pregnant.

受苦 or 吃苦 to suffer; to be treated badly.

受託人 a trustee.

⁶⁰受話器 telephone receiver.

受貨人 recipient of goods.

受賄賣放 to release prisoners for a bribe.

受辦 possible to carry out, administer, or rule.

受辱 to be shamefully treated or disgraced.

⁶⁵受造 to be created.

受遺人 heir.

受難 (nan¹) to be in difficulties.

受風 to get a chill.

受騙 to be taken in; to be deceived.

⁷⁰受驚 to get a fright; to suffer a shock.

大受 great responsibility or trust.

容受 to contain.

忍受 to endure; to bear.

承受 to accept; to undertake; to inherit.

⁷⁵樂受 to take a thing in good part.

買受 to purchase.

難受 uncomfortable; depressed; feeling unhappy.

授⁴ To give to; to confer. To transmit.
5841

授之以手者權 to rescue (her) with the hand outweighs considerations of etiquette.

授之以政不達 if he is used in the government service and knows not how to act....

授位 to confer a dignity.

授受 to give and to receive.

⁵授命 to sacrifice the life for the State.

授室 to take a wife.

授意 to intimate; to hint at.

授業 to give an education to.

授田 fields received from the ruler at coming of age, and which at death reverted to the State.

¹⁰授職 to confer the rank of.

授課 to teach.

授首 to be killed.

傳授 to deliver over to.

口授 to communicate orally.

¹⁵祕授 to impart a secret.

綬⁴ The cord or ribbon on a seal; a cord; a band.
5842

印綬 ribbon attached to a seal; a seal of office.

組綬 tassel on a cap.

解綬而去 he took off the seal and went—resigned the office.

售⁴ To sell; to dispose of.
5843

售主 the purchaser.

售價 or 售値 the price; the proceeds of sale.

售底貨 clearance sale.

售現 cash sale.

⁵售虧 to sell at a loss.

售貨清單 account sales.

售賣 or 出售 to sell.

售賣所得總數 gross proceeds.

↑售票處 ticket office.

守³ To guard; to protect. To observe; to keep, as observances; to attend to. To hold on to; to maintain.
5844

守·不住 unable to keep, hold or maintain, etc.

守中立 to observe neutrality.

守信 to maintain good faith; to remain faithful.

守候 to wait for a person.

⁵守備 to defend; former title of a second captain in the Chinese army.

守冢 to watch over graves.

守制 to be in mourning for a parent.

守取回音 waiting for an answer.

守口 to guard a pass; to close up, as a sore.

¹⁰守口如瓶 keep the mouth closed like a bottle.

守喪 to watch by a corpse.

守土 the local authorities.

守城 to guard a city.

守夜 to keep watch at night.

¹⁵守孝 to be in mourning for a parent.

守宇 territory.

守定了 to maintain firmly; to persevere in; to keep to.

守宮 a eunuch; the gecko.

守寡 to remain a widow.

²⁰守屍 to watch by a corpse.

守己 self-control.

安分守己 to mind one's own business.

守府 former title of a second captain in the Chinese army.

守成尚文 when times are quiet, civil rule ranks first.

²⁵守得住 able to hold on to.

守得緊 to guard securely; to keep close watch over.

守拙 to hold to one's stupidity.

守持 to maintain one's ground.

守更 (keng¹) to keep the watches at night.

³⁰守更望風 to keep watch and wait for the dawn.

守望 to keep watch.

守望相助 mutual aid and protection.

守本分 to mind one's own business; to be content with one's lot.

守株待兎 to wait by a stump for a hare—a farmer of the State of Sung was ploughing and saw a hare dash itself against a stump and fall dead; he thereupon left his work and waited for another hare—used fig.

³⁵守業 to keep to one's calling.

守業難 it is difficult to keep one's patrimony.

守正不阿 to maintain fairness without favour.

守歲 to see the old year out and the new year in.

守死善道 holding on even to death in order to perfect his way.

⁴⁰守汛 to guard a military post.

守法 to be law-abiding.

守犬 a watch-dog.

守瓜 pumpkin-beetle.

守眞 to take care of one's original constitution; to cherish the divine nature within. See No. 297-A.

⁴⁵守祕·密 to keep a secret.

守禁 to guard; to watch over.

守禮 to be free from irregularities.

守禮拜 to observe the Day of Rest.

守節 to keep a holiday; to remain unmarried after the death of a betrothed or a husband.

⁵⁰守約 to attend to that which is of the most importance; to keep one's engagements.

守終喪 to observe the last rites.

守經行權 or 守經達權 holding right principles, but

acting according to circumstances.   [= 4946.23

守 舊 黨 Conservative Party.
守 舍 to take care of a house.
[55]守 行 (hang[2]) 伍 to keep rank.
守 衞 to guard; to protect.
守 規 矩 to observe the proprieties; well-behaved.
守 護 or 看 守 or 保 守 to guard; to protect.
守 貞 to maintain chastity; to remain a virgin—as a girl whose betrothed has died.
[60]守 身 如 玉 to keep oneself as pure as jade.
守 邊 to guard the frontier.
守 錢 虜 a stingy man; a miser.
守 門 使 a name for the dog.
守 靈 to watch by a corpse.
[65]守 領 to receive into one's charge.
守 風 to wait for the wind. [emy)
失 守 to lose control of (to the en
有 守 to have a firm resolve and keep themselves from evil.

(a) Official designation.

太 守 a prefect.

(b) Read shou[1]. Territory under a feudal prince. Also inter. next

巡 守 an Imperial tour of inspection.

狩[4] A hunting-dog. To hunt in winter. Imperial tour.
5845

狩 獵 條 例 game laws.
巡 狩 Imperial tour of inspection.

壽[4] Old age; long life.
5846

壽 世 良 醫 a clever physician who lengthens the lives of men.
壽 七 十 六 歲 aged seventy-six —said of a deceased person.
壽 元 number of years; old age: length of life.
壽 命 a man's allotted span.
[5]壽 器 a coffin.
壽 城 a cenotaph, tomb prepared during the lifetime.
壽 域 a tomb prepared during a man's lifetime; the Golden Age.
壽 山 福 海 May your age be as Mount (T'ai), and your happiness as the (Eastern) Sea!

壽 帳 a scroll given to old people on their birthdays.
[10]壽 數 a man's alloted span; old age; number of years.
壽 · 星 公 or 老 壽 · 星 the God of Longevity. Canopus.
壽 木 a coffin; boards for a coffin.
壽 板 or 壽 材 boards for a coffin.
壽 桃 old-age peaches—cakes made in the shape of a peach and presented on birthdays.
[15]壽 比 南 山 May your age be as the Southern Mountain!
壽 物 or 壽 禮 birthday presents.
壽 穴 a tomb prepared during the lifetime.
壽 終 to die in old age.
壽 考 or 長 壽 long life; old age.
[20]壽 聯 birthday scrolls.
壽 藏 a tomb or a coffin prepared during a man's lifetime.
壽 衣 grave-clothes.
壽 誕 an old man's birthday feast; a birthday.
壽 辰 a birthday; birthday feast for an old man.
[25]壽 酒 birthday feast.
壽 鈴 · 鐺 long-life bells—worn by children on their caps.
壽 錢 coin given by old people to children for amulets.
壽 險 life-insurance.
壽 高 德 重 of a ripe old age and great virtue.
[30] 高 壽 what is your venerable age?
壽 麵 vermicelli eaten on birthdays —fig., long life.
上 壽, 中 壽, 下 壽 one hundred, eighty, and sixty years of age respectively.
享 壽 aged....; at the age of....
冥 壽 birthday of a deceased person.
[35]拜 壽 or 賀 壽 to offer birthday congratulations.

獸[4] Wild beasts; brutes.
5847

獸 中 之 王 the king of beasts— the tiger.
獸 性 作 用 the animal functions.
獸 慾 animal passions.
獸 疫 檢 查 quarantine for infected animals.
[5]獸 醫 veterinary surgeon.

獸 頭[2] animal figures on the ends of a roof, etc.
獸 類 beasts.
獸 馬 wild horses.
走 獸 quadrupeds.

瘦[4] Lean, emaciated, poor, thin. Also read sou[1].
5848

瘦 削 emaciated.
瘦 · 子 a thin person.
瘦 小 thin; emaciated.
瘦 弱 wasted away.
[5]瘦 影 lean as a shadow.
瘦 損 thin and emaciated.
瘦 枯 lean and shrivelled.
瘦 田 or 瘦 地 barren land.
瘦 肉 lean meat.
[10]瘦 貨 goods on which no profit is made.
消 瘦 to lose flesh.

SHU. (ㄕㄨ)

殳
殳[1] To kill. A spear. Radical 79. (1st form only).
5849

殳 書 a style of writing used on ancient weapons.

姝[1] A pretty woman. Elegant. Also read ch'u[1].
5850

姝 色[4] beauty.
彼 姝 者 子[3] that lovely maiden; that admirable gentleman.

殊[1] To kill; to exterminate.
5851

殊 戰 to kill in battle.
殊 死 刑 the extreme penalty of the law.
殊 死 戰 to fight to the death.

(a) To distinguish; to define.

殊 厥 疆 里 to define the boundaries of hamlets.

(b) Different; unlike. Really. Very; extremely.

殊 不 介 意 do not concern yourself about it at all.

殊 不 可 解 I really cannot understand—your meaning.

殊 不 得 知 who would have thought it? it was impossible to know.

殊 不 思 surely does not bear in mind.

[5] 殊 不 然 certainly not so; not at all so.

殊 俗 strange customs.

殊 別 very different.

殊 力 extraordinary strength.

殊 功 special merits.

[10] 殊 域 a strange land.

殊 堪 詫 異 most extraordinary.

殊 尤 most strange.

殊 屬 不 成 事 體 the arrangement is not at all a proper one.

殊 屬 可 憐 truly lamentable.

[15] 殊 常 extraordinary.

殊 形 is very; seems very.

殊 技 remarkable skill.

殊 方 various regions; strange lands.

殊 有 is surely.

[20] 殊 榮 special honours.

殊 深 extremely; profoundly.

殊 無 本 事 not the least ability.

殊 爲 is greatly.

殊 特 specially.

[25] 殊 珍 very rare and valuable.

殊 異 or 逈 殊 very different.

殊 等 a different class or status.

殊 色 special beauty; also = 20.

殊 途 同 歸 by different roads to the same conclusion.

[30] 殊 遇 to meet with special kindness.

萬 殊 一 本 all things, though different, have a common origin.

洙 [2]
5852　A small stream in Shantung. Also read chu[1].

茱 [1]
5853　Dogwood. Also read chu[1].

山 茱 萸 dogwood—*Cornus officinalis*.

抒 [1]
5854　To strain, to pour out. To take out, to exclude.

抒 恨 to allay anger; to put aside hate. 抒 情 詩 lyric.

抒 情 素 to unburden the mind.

抒 挹 to remove; to bale out.

紓 [1]
5855　Slow, remiss; little by little.

紓 緩 to procrastinate.

彼 交 匪 紓 "there is no remissness in the demeanour."

(a) To loosen. To free from. u.f. next.

紓 君 敬 to free himself from the responsibility demanded by respect for his prince.

紓 禍 to dispel calamity.

紓 難 to give relief in time of difficulty.

紓 革 非 心 to get rid of evil in the heart.

舒 [1]
5856　To stretch out; to unroll; to expand. Comfortable.

舒 伸 to stretch out.

舒 勃 to expand—the countenance.

舒 坦 in good health; comfortable.

舒 展 to open; to expand.

[5] 舒 張 to open; to expand.

舒 情 to express one's feelings.

舒 懷 to set the mind at rest.

舒 揚 to relax.

舒 散 to dismiss—as care.

[10] 舒 暢 in good spirits; cheerful.

舒 服 easy; in good health; happy; comfortable.

舒 眉 開 眼 to relax the eyebrows—to wear a pleased expression.

舒 筋 藥 anti-spasmodics.

舒 緒 a clue.

[15] 舒 緩 remiss.

舒 着 翅 膀 to spread the wings.

舒 舒 徐 徐 to do things leisurely and orderly. (*Wu-dial.*)

舒 蕊 to open—as flowers.

舒 身 to stretch oneself.

[20] 舒 遲 quiet; leisurely; refined—expression of countenance.

舒 長 (*chang*[3]) to expand and grow.

舒 鳧 wild duck.

卷 舒 to roll and unroll.

晨 舒 昏 合 opening in the morning and closing in the evening—as flowers.

書 [1]
5857　Books; writings. To write.

書 上 in a book.

書 不 盡 言 I cannot write all that I would say.

書 中 義 蘊 contents of the volume.

書 云 the *Book of History* states....

[5] 書 信 a letter; an epistle.

書 冊 records; books.

書 卷 books; rolls.

書 名 to sign one's name.

書 吏 actuary; clerks in law courts.

[10] 書 啓 letters; notes; correspondence. 書 包 a satchel for books.

書 啓 先 生 or 書 禀 師 爺 correspondence secretary in a *yamen*.

書 坊 a book-shop.

書 墨 records; books.

書 案 to begin writing to....

[15] 書 契 documents; deeds; contracts.

書 套 子 a cover for binding several volumes in one.

書 子 a letter. (*dial.*)

書 封 or 書 套 envelopes.

書 寫 to write.

[20] 書 局 a book-shop.

書 房 a library or study.

書 據 documentary proofs

書 札 or 書 柬 or 書 牘 letters.

書 林 a book-shop.

[25] 書 架 子 book-shelves.

書 案 a writing desk; a study table.

書 櫃 a bookcase.

書 氣 or 詩 書 氣 the air of a literary man.　[raphist.

書 法 calligraphy. 書 法 家 calligraphist.

[30] 書 狂 biblio-mania. A.c. 書 淫.

書 獃 子 a bookworm. A.c. 書 蟲.

書 班 clerks in the law courts.

書 生 scholars; pupils.

書 生 之 見 a pedantic view.

[35] 書 畫 books and pictures.

書 癖 biblio-mania.

書 目 index to a book; catalogue of books.

書 社 a literary club.

書 禀 to write a petition.

[40] 書 符 念 咒 to write charms and recite incantations.

書 籤 label on a book.

書 籍 records; books.

書 經 the *Book of History*.

書 舖 a book-shop. A.c. 書 店.

[45] 書 館 a library or study.

書 衣 cover for binding several volumes into one.

書 記 clerk; secretary; writers.

書 記 的 clerical.

↑書 庫 stack (in a library).

書 諸 紳 wrote it on the part of his girdle that was hanging down.
50書 證 documentary evidence.
書 辦 clerks in law courts.
書 院 a college; a school. (old)
書 面 in written form.
書 香 literary fame.
55書 香 之 家 a literary family.
書 齋 a library or study.
代 書 to write for another; a writer of accusations, etc.
保 證 書 a security.
功 書 to study with diligence.
60國 書 credentials—as of an ambassador.
宣 告 書 a manifesto.
家 書 a home letter. [your letter.
手 書 in one's own handwriting;
敎·科 書 text books.
65文·書 official despatches.
楷 書 the orthodox style of Chinese writing.
淫 書 obscene books.
祕 書 private secretary.
背 書 to recite lessons from memory.
70草 書 the very free, running style of handwriting.
行 書 the correspondence style of handwriting.
診 斷 書 medical certificate.
說·書·的 a story-teller.
請 願 書 a petition.
75證 明 書 evidence.
離 書 or 休 書 bill of divorce.
隸 書 the square, ornamental style of Chinese writing.

攄[1] To spread; to set forth; to unroll.
5858 Distinguish 攎 No. 4175.

攄 所 見 to set forth one's views; to express one's ideas.
獨 攄 意 乎 宇 宙 之 外 let the thoughts stray beyond the bounds of the universe.

(a) To prance.

樞[1] A pivot; an axis; the central point. Indispensable;
5859 fundamental; cardinal.
Also read ch'u.

樞 務 affairs of State.
樞 密 affairs of State.

樞 密 院 Privy Council of the Sung dynasty.
樞 機 the controlling power; the moving spirit; the guiding mind.
5樞 紐 the central part on which a machine works; a pivot or axis.
樞 臣 ministers of State.
樞 衡 to manage affairs of State.
樞 要 a pivot or axis; a focus.
樞 軸 the control of affairs.
10天 樞 the North Star.

梳[1] To comb. A coarse comb.
5860

梳 刷 羊 毛 to card wool.
梳 好·的 麻 well-carded hemp.
梳·子 a comb. = 木·梳.
梳 棉 機 rotary carding machine.
5梳 洗 to comb and wash—toilet.
梳 粧 the toilet of a lady.
梳 粧 盤 paper toilet requisites to burn for the dead.
梳 粧 臺 a set of toilet requisites —for a bride; dressing table.
梳 頭 to comb the hair.
10梳 齒 the teeth of a comb.

疏[1] Distant. To separate.
疎｜ Usually pron. su[1].
5861

疏 不 間 親 distant relatives may not come between near ones.
疏 以 廣 大 之 園 林 divided by broad, extensive parks and gardens.
疏 傲 distant and haughty.
疏 宕 parted; separated.
5疏 宕 不 拘 free, unconventional.
疏 密 有 行 they were spaced in even rows. (-hang[2])
疏 屬 distant connections.
疏 影 scattered shadows.
疏 散 scattered, dispersed—as civilians from a combat-zone.
10疏 數 之 交 intercourse between distant and near—as marriage relationships.
疏 枝 scattered branches.
疏 林 a grove of trees thinly planted.
疏 棄 cast away and neglected.
疏 淡 estranged, on cool terms.
15疏 瘦 如 削 as thin as a pared stick.

疏 眉 目 wide eyebrows.
疏 眼 a crevice; open-worked.
疏 窗 an open lattice.
疏 簾 a door curtain.
20疏 索 distant; estranged.
疏 落 few; sparse.
疏 親 to treat relatives distantly; a distant relative; distant and near.
親 疏 near and distant relatives.
疏 豁 broad, spacious.
25疏 遠 distant—as relatives.
疏 闊 far apart; separated—as friends.
疏 雨 sprinkling of rain.
疏 髮 sparse hair.
情 誼 愈 疏 more estranged than ever.
30見 疏 to become estranged.

(a) To distribute. To spread out.

疏 網 to spread a net.
疏 財 仗 義 to give generously and show devotion to duty.
疏 銷 to carry to other places to sell.

(b) Careless, lax, remiss. Rude.

疏 失 remiss.
疏·忽 careless; neglectful.
疏 惰 lazy and indifferent.
疏 愚 careless stupidity.
5疏 慢 covetous.
疏 慵 careless and lazy.
疏 懶 or 疏 懈 idle, careless; rude.
疏 於 防 範 heedless about taking due precautions.
疏 於 聽 斷 remiss in the performance of his judicial functions.
10疏 放 careless; lax; remiss.
疏 漏 careless, inaccurate—as history.
疏 狂 rude and brusque; disregarding all etiquette.
疏 率 careless; lax; heedless.
疏 略 careless; negligent; inaccurate; unreliable.
15疏 節 remissness.
疏 縱 lax, careless.
疏 薄 indifferent.
疏 虞 carelessness; negligence.
疏 防 neglectful of all precautions.
20疏 頑 careless; heedless.

(c) To dredge. To clear out.

疏 導 to remove obstructions.

疏 濬 河 道 to dredge a river.
疏 理 to make matters clear; to come to an understanding.
疏 穢 clear away evil thoughts.
[5]疏 通 to make matters clear; to try and bring about an understanding.
疏 鑿 to cut away obstructions; to cut through—as a mountain.
禹 疏 九 河 *Yü* dredged the nine rivers.

(d) Coarse.

疏 糲 coarse food.
疏 裳 coarse garments.
疏 食 coarse food.
疏 鬆 coarse in texture.

(e) Read *shu*[4], or *su*[4]. To state to a superior. To lay before. A statement; a running commentary.

疏 去 矣 the memorial has already gone to the emperor.
疏 文 a prayer written out and burnt before the gods.
疏 請 to pray the throne to....
疏 頭 or 疏 紙 a prayer written and burnt before the gods.
上 疏 to send in a memorial to the throne.
註 疏 to explain as in a commentary.

蔬 [1] Vegetable food. Usually pron. *su*[1].
5862

蔬 油 vegetable oil.
蔬 糲 wild vegetables and coarse rice.
蔬 菜 vegetables.
蔬 菓 vegetables and fruits.
蔬 食 vegetable diet.
蔬 飯 rice with only vegetables as an accompaniment.

樗 [1] *Ailanthus glandulosa*—it is of no use as timber; commonly known as 臭 椿 樹. Also read *ch'u*[1].
5863

樗 櫟 之 材 timber of ailanthus and chestnut-oak—useless.

輸 [1] To pay, as tribute, etc. To bring in what is due. An offering. Read *shu*[4] as a noun.
輸
5864

輸 亥 to pay up—as taxes.
輸 稅 or 輸 餉 to pay duty or taxes.
輸 納 to pay up—as taxes.
輸 財 助 邊 to contribute from one's own resources in order to assist at the frontier.
捐 輸 to subscribe.

(a) To transport. To introduce.

輸 入 to import; to introduce.
輸 入 價 值 import price.
輸 入 品 imports.
輸 入 外 資 to introduce foreign capital.
[5]輸 入 稅 率 import tariff.
輸 入 額 amount of imports.
輸 出 to export.
輸 出 商 號 shipping house.
輸 出 折 口 export duty.
[10]輸 出 稅 export duty.
輸 出 許 可 書 export permit.
輸 出 額 amount of exports.
輸 將 to transport.
輸 尿 管 ureter.
[15]輸 送 to transport.
輸 運 transportation.

(b) To lose. To be beaten. To exhaust. To be wanting. To submit.

輸 了 to lose—as a wager, game, etc.
輸 敗 discomfited; defeated.
輸 服 to confess, without torture; to submit to a superior.
輸 氣 to lose caste.
[5]輸 盡 to exhaust.
輸 給 人 家 去 了 gambled (his wife) away to others.
輸 誠 to turn State evidence.
輸 賭 or 打 賭 to bet.
輸 贏 loss and gain—to gamble; a wager.
[10]輸 身 to fall; to lose her virtue.
輸 錢 to lose money.

(c) To report to a superior.

輸 而 孚 when (a case) is reported (the sovereign) will have confidence—in the judgement.

(d) To overturn.

載 輸 爾 載 your load will be overturned.

數 [3] To count; to calculate; to estimate. To enumerate.
5865

數 一 數 count them.
數 一 數 二 的 one of the very best.
數 不 清 cannot be reckoned; cannot count them clearly.
數 不 過 來 too numerous to be counted.
[5]數 九 the nine-times-nine days following the winter solstice.
數 典 忘 祖 he counts the records but he has forgotten his ancestors.
數 多 少 how many do you reckon?
數 數 看 count and see.
數 算 to count and reckon.
[10]數 米 而 炊 to count the grains of rice before cooking them—parsimony.
數 過 了 counted; numbered.
數 錢 to count coin.
數 錯 了 you have counted wrongly.
數 點 to reckon up; to count up. *See below*—C. 15.

(a) To scold. To reprimand.

數 罵 to scold; to curse.
數 而 責 之 censured him.
數 落 to scold, enumerating one thing after another.
數 過 or 數 說 to enumerate a person's faults—to scold.

(b) To discriminate.

往 來 行 言 心 焉 數 之 what other men have in their minds as they come and go, I can measure by reflection.

(c) Read *shu*[4]. A number. Several.

數 十 several tens.
數 十 百 人 a hundred or more people.
數 口 之 家 a family of several persons.
數 學 mathematics; theory of numbers.
[5]數 學 儀 器 mathematical instruments.
數 學 家 mathematicians.
數 學 表 arithmetical tables.
數 尾 the balance of an account.
數 日 several days.

[10]數 次 several times.

數·目 the amount; number; amounts; accounts.

數·目 字 figures, numerals.

數 碼 numbers; figures; numerals.

數 量 number.

[15]數 點 several points—See above—14.

上 數 put it to the account.

不 可 勝 數 innumerable.

不 在 其 數 not in the reckoning.

乘 數 multiplier.

[20]偶 數 even numbers.

充 數 to be a stop-gap; to make up the required number.

公 倍 數 common multiple.

最 小 公 倍 數 least common multiple.

分 盡 之 數 aliquot parts.

[25]因 數 a factor.

奇 數 odd numbers. (chi[1])

定 數 a fixed number. [rithms.

對 數 to balance accounts; loga-

序 數 ordinal numbers. 歲·數 age.

[30]收 數 to collect accounts.

有 數 not many; limited number.

本 數 cardinal numbers.

法 數 divisor. 次·數 no. of times.

清 數 to settle an account.

[35]減 得 之 數 difference.

短 數 a shortage.

積 得 數 product.

等 差 級 數 arithmetical progression. (-ch'a[1])

等 比 級 數 geometrical progression. 答 數 an answer. (math.)

[40]約 得 之 數 quotient.

級 數 progression.

素 數 prime numbers.

餘 數 complement.

(d) Read   shu[4].   Fate; destiny.

數 奇 (chi[1]) bad fortune.

數 有 所 不 逮 fate has its deficiencies.

數 盡 his days are numbered.

劫 數 a cataclysm, calamity.

[5]命 數 fate, destiny.

在 數 難 逃 it is fate and cannot be avoided.

天 數 fate, destiny.

天 之 曆 數 the Heaven-determined order of succession. See No. 3931-2.

有 定 數 it is a matter of destiny.

[10]氣 數 destiny, fate.

(e) Read shu[4].   An art.

今 夫 弈 之 爲 數, 小 數 也 now wei-ch'i as an art, is but a small art.

(f) Read shuo[4·5].   Frequently.

數 四 over and over again.

數 數 frequently.

數 至 空 匱 often in straits.

數 見 不 鮮 what is frequently seen is not strange.

[5]事 君 數 斯 辱 矣 in serving a prince frequent reproofs lead to disgrace.

朋 友 數 斯 疏 矣 between friends, frequent reproofs lead to estrangement.

祭 不 欲 數 數 則 煩 sacrifices should not be frequently repeated; such frequency indicates importunity—inconsistent with reverence.

(g) Read shuo[4·5].   To annoy. Worried, bothered.

數 而 見 疏 to annoy and then be treated distantly.

煩 數 or 頻 數 worrysome.

(h') Read ts'u[4·5].   Close-meshed, as a net.

數 罟 不 入 汚 池 if nets of close mesh are not allowed in the pools and ponds....

暑 [3] The heat of summer. Distinguish 署 No. 5867.
5866

暑 伏 the hot season.

暑 假 summer vacation.

暑 天 the dog-days.

暑 暍 heat apoplexy.

[5]暑 月 the 6th lunar month.

暑·氣 heat; the rays of the sun.

暑 氣 迫 人 the heat is very oppressive.

暑 源 hot and steamy.

暑 熱 very hot.

[10]中 暑 to get sunstroke; to suffer from the heat.

避 暑 to go to a cool place to avoid the heat of summer.

署 [3] A public office. Distinguish 暑 No. 5866.
5867

公 署 a public office; a yamen.

衙 署 a yamen or magistrate's office.

部 署 to adjust; to arrange.

領 事 署 a consulate.

(a) To write, to sign.

署 函 an envelope or cover.

署 券 to draw up a deed.

署 名 to sign one's name—especially on official documents.

署 書 to write a title for a book.

[5]署 第 一 this name was written first on the list.

署 簽 to write an inscription for a title-label on a book.

押 署 to sign.

(b) Read shu[4].   Acting; temporary appointment.

署 任 an acting appointment.

署 理 to hold as an acting appointment.

署 欽 差 an acting minister; a chargé d'affaires.

署 領 事 官 an acting consul.

曙 [4] Bright, luminous. The light of the rising sun.
5868

曙 光 the light of dawn—hopeful conditions.

曙 後 星 孤 after the dawn there shines a solitary star—to die and leave an only daughter.

曙 日 in the morning.

曙 色 the light of early dawn.

薯 藷 [3] A term for plants with tubers; a tuber; a potato; a yam.
5869

薯 仔 (Cant.) or 馬 鈴 薯 the common potato.

薯 粉 sweet-potato flour.

薯 芋 or 大 薯 the common yam.

薯 莨 a dye-plant used for dark brown; it is grown in Fukien and Kwangtung.

薯 蕷 or 山 藥 the Chinese yam.

紅 薯 or 番 薯 the sweet potato.

[1]百 薯 or 白 薯 the sweet potato.

黍 [3] Glutinous, panicled millet. A unit of weight, dry measure, and length. Radical 202.
5870

黍·子 or 黍 稷 varieties of millet.

黍 酒 a measure of wine containing 3 升—about 3 pints.
玉 蜀 黍 maize or Indian corn.
百 黍 爲 銖 二 十 四 銖 爲 兩 100 grains of millet equal one *shu*, 24 *shu* equal one *tael*.
縱 黍 百 當 十 寸 100 grains of millet placed lengthwise equal 10 Chinese inches.
蜀 黍 or 高 粱 sorghum.

鼠 [3] A rat, a mouse. Squirrels. Moles, etc. Also read *ch'ü*[3].
5871 Radical 208.

鼠 伏 to hide like a rat.
鼠 壤 vegetable or garden plots.
鼠 姑 a name for the peony; the wood-louse.
鼠 婦 or 鼠 負 the wood-louse.
[5]鼠 子 rats—occurs as a term of abuse in ancient histories.
鼠 尾 草 *Salvia japonica*.
鼠 技 rat's ability—small talents and misapplied.
鼠 梓 or 女 貞 an evergreen shrub—*Ligustrum lucidum*.
鼠 牙 雀 角 litigation.
[10]鼠 狼 or 黃 鼠 狼 a weasel.
鼠 疫 the plague.
鼠 瘻 scrofulous, running sores.
鼠 目 rat's eyes—sharp, cunning; also short-sighted or timorous.
鼠 眼 timorous; villainous.
[15]鼠 穴 a rat-hole.
鼠 竄 to flee like rats; to skulk.
鼠 竊 狗 偸 pilfering—like rats and dogs.
鼠 肚 雞 腸 paltry; petty; willing to suffer affronts without resentment; lacking courage or endurance.
鼠 肝 蟲 臂 rat's liver and insect's legs—worthless things.
[20]鼠 詭 cunning—as a rat.
鼠 輩 thieves.
倉 鼠 a hamster.
松 鼠 the squirrel.
渠 鼠 a water-rat.
[25]老 鼠 a rat.
跳 鼠 the jerboa.
銀 鼠 the ermine.
飛 鼠 the bat; flying squirrel.
騷 鼠 the polecat.
[30]鼮 鼠 a variety of marmot.

(a) Hidden, secret.

鼠 思 泣 血 my secret thoughts make me weep blood.

蜍 蟖 [2]
5872
A toad, called 蟾 蜍.
Also read *ch'u*[2].
Read *yü*[2]. A spider.

戍 [4] To guard the frontiers.
5873 Distinguish 戌 No. 2861; 氏 No. 7701; 戎 No. 3181.

戍 卒 soldiers on guard at the frontier.
戍 所 a garrison.
戍 邊 關 a frontier customs barrier.

庶 [4] A multitude. The whole, all, a great number. The
5874 people, the masses.
Distinguish 度 No. 6504.

庶 人 commoners; ordinary people.
庶 佰 君 子 [3] all ye noble chiefs.
庶。務 general affairs.
庶 務 員 business manager.
[5]庶 務 科 department of general affairs.
庶 士 the various gentlemen; all the officers of State.
庶 多 very many.
庶 常 吉 士 all the worthy officers and their subordinates.
庶 常 館 an academy for 3rd degree graduates, 進 士, under the Manchus; it was conducted by a Hanlin official; examinations were held every three years.
[10]庶 吉 士 a Hanlin bachelor, or graduate of the lowest degree.
庶 府 their treasurers.
庶 彙 all things.
庶 徵 the "various verifications" —one of the divisions of the *Great Plan of Yü*; the meteorological phenomena of rain, sunshine, heat, cold, wind, and seasonableness.
庶 政 numerous affairs of state.
[15]庶 正 or 庶 尹 ancient title for "heads of departments."
庶 殷 丕 作 all the people of *Yin* arose with vigour to do the work.
庶 民 or 黎 庶 the masses.
庶 物 all things; every kind of creature.
庶 績 a great achievement.

[20]庶 績 咸 熙 all will be fully performed.
庶 羞 all kinds of delicacies.
庶 羣 自 酒 the masses abandoning themselves to drunkenness.
庶 老 all aged men—who were cared for in the 庠 No. 2576.
庶 頑 讒 說 the obstinately stupid and calumniating talkers.
[25]庶 類 every kind of creature.
惟 茲 臣 庶 that if these my ministers and people....

(a) Nearly; about; so that; thus; it may be; with a view to.

庶 乎 not far from; almost; probably; so that to some extent; nearly; it may be.
庶 保 in order to ensure.
庶 免 in order to prevent.
庶 可 so that....; so as to enable.
[5]庶 屬 允 當 so as to be in accordance with justice and right.
庶 幾 [1] almost; nearly; probably; not far from; so that to some extent; it may be.
庶 幾 [1] 乎 not far from....
庶 幾 [1] 夙 夜 from day to day and from night to night.
庶 幾 [1] 無 疾 病 he seems to be free from all sickness.
[10]庶 有 事 there will probably be some business to do.
庶 有 格 命 in which, it may be, you will receive a most important charge.

(b) A concubine.

庶 出 son of a concubine.
庶 子 [3] son of a concubine; tutor to the heir-apparent.
庶 室 a concubine.
庶 孽 son of a concubine.
庶 母 a concubine—so called by her sons.
庶 長 [2] eldest son of a concubine; title of honour under the *Ch'in* and *Han* dynasties.

恕 [4] The principle of reciprocity, making our own feel-
5875 ings a rule whereby we are guided in dealing with others. To forgive; to show mercy; to excuse.
Distinguish 怒 No. 4758.

恕 報 不 週 excuse us if we have not notified anyone—of a death.

Notice posted up at the front door.

恕 宥 or 赦 宥 to excuse; to forgive an error; to reprieve.

恕 容 to excuse; to make allowance for others.

恕 己 恕 人 forgive others as you forgive yourself.

[5]恕 怪 don't blame; don't think me rude.

恕 我 不 陪 excuse me for leaving you—said to a visitor.

恕 物 to treat others on the principle of reciprocity.

恕 直 lenient and straight dealing.

恕 罪 to forgive a fault.

[10]恕 迸 excuse my not accompanying you—to visitors on leaving.

恕 速 excuse haste! a formal phrase closing an invitation.

恕 過 to forgive a fault.

恕 道 reciprocity; considerate.

其 恕 乎 己 所 不 欲 勿 施 於 人 "Is not reciprocity such a word?" "What you do not want done to yourself, do not do to others"—Confucius in reply to a question, "Is there one word which may serve as a rule of practice for all one's life?"

[15]寬 恕 lenient; to pardon.

疆[3]恕 而 行 求 仁 莫 近 焉 "If one acts with a vigorous effort towards reciprocity, when he seeks perfect virtue, nothing can be closer than his approximation to it."

忠 恕 達 道 不 遠 when one cultivates to the utmost the principles of his nature, and exercises them on the principle of reciprocity, he is not far from the path. *See* No. 1506-11.

祈 恕 I beg your pardon.

行 恕 to be generous and lenient.

墅 [4]
5876

A villa; a country-house.

別 墅 a villa; a country-house

豎 竪 [4]
5877

To set up; to establish. Upright, perpendicular, vertical. A perpendicular stroke in writing. Distinguish 堅 No. 825.

豎 幅 an upright, hanging inscription.

豎 旗·竿 to plant a flag-staff.

豎 桅 or 起 桅 to step the mast.

[5]豎 毛 the hair standing on end.

豎 直 perpendicular; upright.

豎 眼 to stare in anger or contempt.

豎 碑 to erect a monument.

豎 立 to raise; to establish.

豎·起 to raise; to establish.

[10]豎·起 脊·梁 to get one's back up; to pull oneself together.(--*niang*)

橫 豎 horizontal and vertical. *See* No. 2106-41, 42.

(a) A servant.

豎 儒 a mean and worthless scholar.

豎 婢 male and female slave children.

豎 子[3] a stupid person; a catamite.

豎 宦 eunuchs.

內 豎 a page.

牧 豎 a herd boy.

褈 [4]
878

Coarse clothing of camel's hair.

樹 [4]
5879

A tree, a plant.

樹 大 招 風 high trees attract the wind.

樹 幹 trunk of a tree.

樹 心 pith.

樹 懶 the sloth.

[5]樹 掛 or 樹 杈 the fork of a tree.

樹·木 trees; a tree. *See below—A.*

樹 末 tip of a tree.

樹 枝 boughs; branches.

樹 林 a grove of trees.

[10]樹 株 trees; a forest.

樹 根 or 樹 本 the root of a tree.

樹 栽·子 saplings; cuttings of trees for planting.

樹 條·子 twigs.

樹 梢 or 樹 杪 the tip of a tree; the topmost bough.

[15]樹 樁 a stump; a bole.

樹 汁 sap; juice.

樹 皮 bark.

樹 脂 or 樹 膠 resin; gum.

樹 腰 the girth of a tree.

[20]樹 葉 leaves of trees.

樹 陰 the shade of a tree.

樹 雞 a fungus that grows on trees; the hazel-grouse.

樹 頭 a stump; a bole.

(a) To plant; to erect. To sow grain.

樹 之 風 聲 establishing their reputation and virtue.

樹 人 to nurture men of talent.

樹 其 樹 以 蔭 行 人 plant trees to shade wayfarers.

樹 勳 to establish one's merit.

[5]樹 屏 to put up a screen; to appoint men as bulwarks.

樹 德 to establish one's virtue.

樹 旗 to set up a flag.

樹 木 to plant trees. *See above—*6.

樹 立 to erect; administrative talent.

[10]樹 立 政 治 基 礎 to establish the basis of a government.

樹 穀 to sow grain.

樹 藝 forestry.

樹 藝 五 穀 to sow and cultivate the five kinds of grain.

樹·起 to set up.

[15]樹 黨 to form a clique or party.

同 樹 之 時 the time of sowing is the same.

地 道 敏 樹 the growth of vegetation in the earth is rapid.

(b) To appoint. Appointed; legitimate.

樹 后 王 君 公 appointing of sovereign kings, princes and dukes.

樹 子[2] the legitimate heir of a feudal prince.

(c) A screen.

樹 塞 門 a screen intercepting the view at the gates.

澍 [4]
5880

Water running. Saturated. Also read *chu*[4].

澍 濡 saturated; enriched.

澍 生 萬 物 rain causes all things to grow.

SHU. (ㄕㄨ)
(Shuh)

叔 未
5881

25. Younger of brothers. Father's younger brother. Younger brother of a husband.

Pron. *shu*[1] after 大, 二, 三, etc.

叔 世 end of a period.

叔 伯 uncles; a term prefixed to many relationships on the father's side.

叔 公 a father's uncle.

叔 台 an uncle—used conventionally; a friend.

[5] 叔 姪 uncles and nephews—a father's relatives.

叔 季 之 世 a time of general decadence.

叔 母 or 叔 嬸 an aunt—wife of a father's younger brother.

叔·父 or 叔 叔 or 亞 叔 an uncle—father's younger brother.

(a) To gather.

九 月 叔 苴 in the ninth month we gathered the hemp seed.

俶 [4.5.] **To begin. A beginning. Also read** ch'u[4.5]

5882

俶 裝 to arrange the baggage.

俶 載 to commence—as agricultural operations.

(a) Read t'i[4.5]. **Similar to** 倜 **No. 6266. Unrestrained.**

俶 儻 energetic; masterful; unhesitating; easy and free.

淑 [2.5.] **Clear, pure. Virtuous, especially of women.**

5883

淑 人 title of wives of former 3rd grade officials.

淑 女 a virtuous young woman.

淑 媛 a good, clever woman.

淑 德 female virtue.

[5] 淑 性 a good disposition.

淑 慎 careful, cautious.

淑 慝 殊 途 the virtuous and the evil take different ways.

淑 秀 modest, virtuous.

淑 範 a good example.

[10] 淑 美 virtuous and beautiful.

淑 訓 teaching suitable for women.

(a) Fine, good.

淑 氣 fine, genial weather.

淑 清 clear and fine.

(b) Skilful.

淑 哲 good and talented.

淑 問 skilful at asking questions.

菽 [2.5.] **Pulse; leguminous plants.**

5884

菽 乳 a name for bean-curd.

菽 水 pulse and water—poor fare.

菽 水 不 贍 he only lived on pulse and water.

倏 倐 [4.5.] **Hastily; suddenly. Distinguish** 條 **No. 6301.**

5885

倏 忽 very suddenly.

倏 爾 不 見 it suddenly vanished.

倏 起 倏 滅 rising and sinking, of flames.

朮 [2.5.] **Name of a plant.**

5886

朮 律 草 *Podophyllum versipelle*.

沭 [2.5.] **River in Shantung.**

5887

秫 [2.5.] **Glutinous variety of millet. See** 黍 **No. 5870.**

5888

秫 稻 a name for glutinous rice.

秫 稭 millet stalks.

術 [4.5.] **A device; an artifice. A trick, a mystery. Art; method.**

5889

術 士 a conjurer; a magician.

術 家 a trickster; a geomancer.

術 數 magical calculations.

術 智 prudence in affairs.

[5] 術 計 clever plan or device.

術 語 technical terms.

術 語 學 terminology.

仁 術 an artifice of benevolence.

催 眠 術 hypnotism.

[10] 劍 術 fencing.

妖 術 enchantment; magic.

學 術 learning.

心 術 one's moral principles.

戰 術 art of strategy.

[15] 彫 刻 術 the art of engraving.

手 術 surgery.

外 科 手 術 surgical operations.

技 術 sleight of hand.

招 魂 術 spiritism.

[20] 拳 術 boxing.

權 術 the art of complying with circumstances.

氣 管 切 開 術 tracheotomy.

法 術 or 魘 術 the black art.

無 線 電 報 術 wireless telegraphy.

[25] 照 相 術 photography.

相 術 phrenology.

算 術 arithmetic.

罰 術 punishment—as from God.

美 術 art. *See* No. 4406-37 ff.

[30] 航 海 術 navigation.

航 空 術 aviation.

藝 術 art.

觀 水 有 術 there is an art in the contemplation of water.

解 剖 術 anatomy.

[35] 迷 魂 術 enchantment.

道 術 magical arts; arts, devices.

邪 術 miracles; tricks of magic.

醫 術 the art of healing.

電 話 術 telephony.

[40] 驅 邪 術 exorcism.

齒 醫 術 dentistry.

(a) A profession. Occupation.

術 不 可 不 慎 you may not be careless about the profession you choose.

(b) Similar to 述 **next.**

而 術 省 之 and was continually examining himself.

(c) A group of ten hamlets or 里.

(d) Read sui[4]. **Similar to** 遂 **No. 5530. District of 12,500 families.**

術 有 序 for the larger districts there was the *hsü*—a school.

述 [4.5.] **To narrate; to tell the details; to state. To transmit, to hand down. Distinguish** 迷 **No. 4450.**

5890

述 人 之 言 to speak in the words of another—plagiarism.

述 作 to compose.

述 古 詞 to tell old legends.

述 命 to declare the will—as the result of divination.

[5] 述 職 the appearance at court of the feudal princes once every six years.

述 而 不 作 信 而 好 古 a recorder and not a creator, I believe in and love the ancients.
述 說 to give a detailed account.
述 陳 to set forth.
行 述 a biographical sketch of the deceased.

束 4.5. **To bind; to control; to restrain; to keep in order.**
5891 Distinguish 束 No. 6986.

束 傷 to bind up a wound.
束 儀 a teacher's salary.
束 帶 to wear a girdle.
束 手 待 斃 with tied hands waiting for death—without resource; nothing further can be done; helpless.
⁵束 手 無 策 without resource.
束 擱 to put away.
束 笴 piled up in heaps.
束 細 to tie up.
束 縛 to bind; to tie; to control; obligations.
¹⁰束 繫 to gird; to bind on.
束 脩 a teacher's salary.
束 芻 presents sent to a funeral for sacrifice.
束 裝 to pack up—for a journey.
束 身 to control oneself.
¹⁵束 躬 自 愛 to practice discipline and self-respect.
束 金 a teacher's salary.
一 束 之 絲 a hank of silk.
無 拘·束 without restraint.
管 束 to control; to restrain.
²⁰約 束 to control; to coerce.

嗽 4.5. **To imbibe; to suck in. Also read** *sou*⁴. **See** 嗽 No.
5892 5482.

嗽 口 to rinse the mouth.
嗽 奶 to suckle.
嗽 氣 to suck in the breath.
嗽 濕 to absorb moisture.

(a) Read *tsui*³. **Beak of a bird.**

孰 2.5. **Who? Which? What?**
5893

孰 不 可 忍 也 what can he not bear to do?
孰 不 知 禮 who does not know propriety?
孰 先 傳 焉 孰 後 倦 焉 what is there of first importance to be taught, and what of secondary importance to be idle about?

孰 從 而 聽 之 which side is one to take?—in a controversy.
⁵孰 爲 來 哉 why has he come?
孰 能 一 之 who can so unite it?
孰 能 與 之 who can give it to him?
孰 若 另 籌 一 法 what better than to devise another plan?
孰 誰 who?
¹⁰孰 賢 who is the superior?
孰 輕 孰 重 which is the lighter?
事 孰 爲 大 of services, which is the greatest?
未 知 孰 是 I do not know which is right.

(a) Ripe—original form of 熟 **No. 5895.**

孰 復 well studied.
孰 慮 mature consideration.

塾 2.5. **An ante-room or vestibule. A village school.**
5894 Distinguish 塾 No. 6359.

塾 師 a private tutor.
塾 門 outer porch of the palace.
家 塾 a family school.
義 塾 a free school.

熟 2.5. **Ripe. Cooked, prepared, manufactured—as opposed to raw. Experienced; apt; accustomed to. Intimate; well acquainted. To cook. Distinguish** 熱 **No. 3095.**
5895 Pron. *shou*² when marked "x".

x 熟·了 ripe; thoroughly cooked; experienced.
(x)熟 人 a person one knows well.
(x)熟 人 是 個 寶 a familiar person is a treasure.
熟 商 to discuss thoroughly.
⁵熟 寐 sound sleep.
熟 思 to ponder well; to consider.
(x)熟 悉 practised in; conversant with; experienced.
熟 慮 mature consideration.
熟 成 or 成 熟 to ripen.
¹⁰熟 手 an old hand; experienced person.
熟 於 versed in; proficient in.
x 熟 烟 prepared tobacco.
x 熟 牛 皮 dressed hides; leather.
(x)熟 番 savages who have submitted to Chinese rule.
¹⁵熟 睡 or 熟 眠 to sleep soundly.
x 熟 石 灰 slaked lime.

x 熟 米 to hull rice in a mortar; hulled rice.
熟 精 well versed in; experienced.
熟 練 well tried; accustomed to.
²⁰熟·習 practised in; conversant with.
熟 能 生 巧 practice makes perfect.
x 熟 膏 prepared opium.
(x)熟 苗 Miao tribes that have submitted to the Chinese domination.
x 熟 藥 prepared drugs.
²⁵熟 視 to look at for a long time; accustomed to the sight of.
熟 計 a well-matured plan.
(x)熟 記 to commit to memory.
熟 諳 practised in; experienced; conversant with.
(x)熟·識 to be well acquainted with; familiar with.
³⁰熟 讀 詳 味 to study earnestly and search out the essence.
x 熟 貨 manufactured goods, as opposed to raw materials.
x 熟 路 a familiar road. *See* 輕 No. 1156-31.
x 熟 透·了 thoroughly ripe; over-ripe; over cooked.
x 熟 銅 wrought brass or copper.
³⁵熟 鐵 wrought iron.
x 熟 食 cooked food.
x 爛 熟 thoroughly cooked.
(x)相 熟 intimately acquainted.
(x)讀 熟 thoroughly mastered—the studies.

屬 3.5.
屬 **To belong to; to be subject to; connected with. Depending upon. Class, kind.**
屬
5896

屬 下 subordinates; under the jurisdiction of.
屬 乎 belonging to; of the same class.
屬 乎 地 earthly.
屬 人 法 the law of the realm as applied to its nationals everywhere. *See below*—11.
⁵屬 僚 fellow-officials; colleagues.
屬 員 or 屬 吏 subordinate officials.
屬 國 a tributary State; colonies.
屬 國 於 resigned the kingdom to....

屬 在 相¹ 好 intimate; friendly.
¹⁰屬 地 dependencies.
屬 地 法 the law of the realm as applied to all within its territorial limits. *See above*—4.
屬 地·的 earthly.
屬 客 visitors.
屬 性 attributes; qualities.
¹⁵屬 於 belonging to.
屬 星 satellites.
屬 民 subjects; nationals.
屬 物 belongings.
屬 甚·麽·的 what (animal) do you belong to?—how old are you?
²⁰屬·相⁴ the animals associated with the different years; a totem.
屬 血 氣·的 carnal.
屬 誰 管 under whose jurisdiction?
屬 陰 hidden; dark; female.
屬 靈·的 spiritual.
²⁵實 屬 it really is....
親 屬 or 族 屬 or 家 屬 relatives.

(a) Read *chu*³·⁵. **To be connected with; to be near to; to assemble. To entrust to.**

屬 其 耆 老 而 告 之 assembled the old men and announced to them.
屬 垣 to apply the ear to the wall —eaves dropping.
屬 意 to fix the attention upon.
屬 文 to compose.
⁵屬 望 aspect.
屬 毛 離 裏 a man's connection with his parents—from a passage in the *Odes*.

不 屬 于 毛 不 離 于 裏 have I not a connection with the hairs (of my father)? did I not pass through (the womb of my mother)?

屬 目 to give attention to.
屬 纊 to apply cotton-wool to the mouth or nostrils of the dying —on the point of death.
¹⁰屬 者 recently.
屬 草 to make a rough draft.
屬 託 to entrust to; to commission.

(b) Read *chu*³·⁵. u.f. 囑 No. 1386. **To enjoin.**

縮 **1.5. To draw in; to draw back. To coil up; to shrink; to shorten. To**
5897
bind fast. **Straight, up-right. Pron.** *so*¹·⁵.

縮 不 進 去 unable to draw in.
縮 伏 to draw back.
縮·住 relaxed; stopped; drawn in.
縮 印·的 書 books printed on a reduced scale by photo-lithography.
⁵縮 囊 gradually getting into a poverty-stricken condition.
縮 回 to draw back.
縮 圖 器 a pantagraph.
縮 地 to contract space—by magic.
縮 寫 shorthand; abbreviation.
¹⁰縮 小 t o restrict; narrowing; tapering; to shrink.
縮 尺 scale rule.
縮 屋 to keep to one's room.
縮 成 一 閛 huddled up in a heap; to keep close.
縮 手 to pull in the hand; to decline to aid in an affair.
¹⁵縮 攏·來 to shrink up.
縮 本 a copy on a reduced scale.
縮 短 to shrink up; to shorten; to abridge.
縮 短 國 際 間 之 距 離 bring the nations closer together.
縮 短 年 限 reduce the number of allotted years.
²⁰縮 緊 shrunk tight.
縮 縮 shrinkingly—as from fear.
縮 縫 a straight seam.
縮 肩 to shrug the shoulders.
縮 腮 shrunken cheeks.
²⁵縮 衣 節 食 to economize in food and clothing.
縮 酒 to strain liquor.
縮 頭 縮 腦·的 faint-hearted; fidgetty.
縮 額 to wrinkle the brow—in anxiety.
縮 鼻 to turn up the nose; to ridicule.
³⁰伸 縮 stretching and shrinking.
局 縮 confined; hampered; i n straits.
收 縮 量 shrinkage—as of woollens.
瑟 縮 to shrink.
畏 縮 shrinking from fear.
³⁵退 縮 to retract.

踰 **4.5. To walk carefully.**
5898
Also read *so*⁴·⁵.

踰 踰 如 有 循 (Confucius) dragged his feet as if they were

attached to the ground—when carrying his official token.

摴 **Dice. Also read** *ch'u*⁵.
5899
摴 蒱 dice; gambling.

謖 **4.5. To raise. To rise.**
5900　**Also read** *su*⁵.

謖 然 斂 袂 而 興 drew his sleeves suddenly together and rose.
謖 謖 the soughing of wind; keen, stern.

蜀 **3.5.**
5901　**Szechwan.**

蜀 布 fine cloth from Szechwan.
蜀 椒 a wild pepper from Szechwan.
蜀 漢 紀 the Minor *Han* dynasty —one of the "*Three Kingdoms*", established in what is now Szechwan. A.D. 221.
蜀 犬 吠 日 Szechwan dogs bark at the sun—because they see it so rarely—used of limited experience.
⁵蜀 葵 the mallow.
蜀 道 難 the way into Szechwan is difficult.
蜀 鳥 or 子³ 規 the goatsucker or night-jar.
蜀 黍 sorghum.
巴 蜀 or 西 蜀 Szechwan.

(a) A caterpillar. See next.

(b) Alone. u.f. 獨 No. 6512.

蠋 **3.5. A large, green cater-**
5902　**pillar, originally written** 蜀.
　　　Read *chu*²·⁵.

贖 **2.5. To redeem; to ransom;**
5903　**to atone for.**

贖·不 回 來 unable to redeem.
贖 價 price of ransom.
贖 刑 punishment redeemable by money.
贖 命 to redeem one's life.
⁵贖 回 or 取 贖 or 收 贖 to redeem.

贖 回 金 a ransom.
贖 愆 祭 the Trespass Offering.
贖 死 to ransom one's life.
贖 當 to get a pledge out of pawn.
[10]贖 罪 to atone for sin; redemption.
贖 罪 所 the Mercy Seat.
贖 罪 祭 the Sin Offering.
贖 身 to ransom oneself.

SHUA. (ㄕㄨㄚ)

耍 3 **To play; to trifle. To loaf. To gamble.**
5904 Distinguish 耍 No. 7300.

耍 人·的 one who lives by his wits.
耍 傀 儡 to play Punch and Judy.
耍 光 棍 to act the blackguard.
耍 刀 to do sword exercise.
[5]耍 勢·力 to make a show of power and influence.
耍 嘴 to joke; to show off one's ability in speech.
耍 孩 兒 dolls.
耍 弄 人 to deceive; to befool.
耍 戲 to sport; to romp; to waste one's time.
[10]耍 戲 法 to juggle; to do tricks.
耍 懶 or 耍 惰 to spend time in idleness; to loiter.
耍 手·藝 to work at a trade.
耍 拳 to box.
耍 拳 腳 to do gymnastics.
[15]耍 棍 or 耍 棒 to play at singlesticks.
耍 猴 兒·的 to play monkeytricks.
耍 獅·子 to act the lion—in processions, etc.
耍 獃·子 to chaff a bumpkin.
耍 盤 or 耍 碗 to juggle with plates or bowls.
[20]耍 笑 to joke; to chaff.
耍 罈·子 to juggle with a large jar.
耍 脾 氣 to provoke; to show temper.
耍 花 鎗 to brandish spears—as a conjurer; to quarrel.
耍 虛·子 or 耍 匪 類 to act the blackguard.
[25]耍 話 jokes.
耍 貨 toys.
耍 錢 to gamble.
耍 鎗 to practise with a gun.
耍 馬 前 三 刀 to do eye-service.

[30]耍 骨 頭 to be frivolous in speech and action; to act in an unreliable manner.
耍 鬧 to sport; to romp; to create a disturbance.
耍 鬼 or 耍 錢 鬼 an inveterate gambler.
不 是 耍·的 it is no joke!

刷 厮 1.5. **A brush. To brush; to cleanse; to scrub. To print, especially from blocks.**
5905

刷 刨 a curry-comb.
刷 刮 to do a job cleanly and smartly.
刷 刷·的 寫 to write rapidly.
刷 印 or 刊 刷 to print.
[5]印 刷 所 printing establishment.
刷 子 a brush.
刷 布 to size or starch cloth.
刷 恥 to wipe away disgrace.
刷 招 帖 to post bills.
[10]刷 新 精·神 to brush up the spirits.
刷 書 to print.
刷 洗 to brush and wash; to clean.
刷 牙 to brush the teeth.
牙 刷 a toothbrush.
[15]刷 白 to whitewash.
刷 箒 a scrubbing brush.
刷 衣·裳 to brush clothes.
刷 鍋 to clean the cooking-pot.
刷 鞋 to brush shoes.
[20]刷 馬 to groom a horse.

涮 4.5. **To wash; to scour. Also read shuan⁴.**
5906

涮 一·涮 rinse it out.
涮 洗 to rinse; to scour.
涮 涮 大 雨 a heavy rain.
涮 蔴 to soak and rot hemp.
涮 羊 肉 sliced mutton eaten from a chafing dish.

SHUAI. (ㄕㄨㄞ)

甩 1.3. **To cast away; to throw. (An unauthorized character.)**
5907

甩 在 底 下 fling it down.
甩 在 外 頭 throw it outside.
甩 瓦 to toss tiles up.
甩 脫 throw it away.

衰 1 **To decrease; to decline. Small, decayed, weak.**
5908 Distinguish 哀 No. 3.

衰 世 an age of decadence.
衰 喪 failing; dying out.
衰 壞 degeneracy.
衰 弊 decadent and corrupt.
[5]衰 弱 failing; declining; debilitated.
衰 彫 died down—as vegetation.
衰 微 to decline.
衰 敗 to decrease.
衰 暮 feeble; debilitated.
[10]衰 朽 decayed; rotten.
衰 枯 withered—as foliage.
衰 殘 failing; decaying; debilitated; feeble.
衰 沒 faded away.
衰 老 feeble; decadent; decrepit; debilitated.
[15]衰 草 寒 烟 the fading plants and chilly mists—of autumn.
衰 落 decayed; failing.
衰 退 decadent.
衰 運 fortunes declining.
衰 邁 feeble; decrepit; diseased; debilitated; failing.
[20]衰 頽 feeble; debilitated; failing; declining.
德 衰 morals declining.

(a) Read *ts'ui*[1]. **Mourning garments. u.f. 縗 No. 6870.**

衰 経 coarse, hempen garments for mourning—mourning generally.
斬 衰 coarse, hempen garments with frayed edges—deepest mourning.

(b) Read *ts'ui*[1]. **Cyanogen.**

衰 化 物 or 青 化 物 cyanides.
衰 化 鉀 potassium cyanide.
衰 質 or 青 質 cyanogen.
衰 酸 cyanic acid.

(c) Read *ch'ui*[1]. **Order, series.**

衰 分 fellowship—of numbers. (*math.*).
衰 征 to levy taxes, etc., in due proportion.
等 衰 order of precedence.

帥 4 **A leader; a commander. Distinguish 師 No. 5760.**
5909

帥 旗 flag of a commander-in-chief or admiral.

帥 領 a leader; a general; a commander-in-chief.

元°帥 or 將⁴帥 a commander-in-chief.

(a) Read *shuo*⁴·⁵. To lead on.

帥 天 下 以 仁 to lead the country by benevolence.

帥 師 征 伐 to lead an army to battle.

率 ⁴ **To lead. To follow and obey. Universally; all; generally; for the most part. Also read *shuo*⁴·⁵.**
5910

率 作 to take the initiative.

率 先 to take the lead; to go on before.

率 兵 to lead troops.

率 同 to take with one; accompanied by.

⁵率 土 within the boundaries of the national territory.

率 多 in large quantities.

率 天 下 而 路 to keep all the people on the move with no time for rest.

率 師 to lead troops.

率 常 generally; in general.

¹⁰率 從 to follow—a leader.

率 性 to adhere to one's opinion; to follow one's natural disposition; arbitrary.

率 意 to follow one's bent; to put forth every effort.

率 敎 to follow a line of teaching.

率 易 easy-going disposition.

¹⁵率 然 suddenly; hastily.

率 由 to go by; to follow.

率 由 典 常 follow and observe the proper statutes.

率 由 舊 章 to observe the old rules.

率 直 straightforward.

²⁰率 眞 to speak the truth.

率 衆 to lead a mob.

率 禮 to observe propriety.

率 稱 是 焉 all exactly corresponding.

率 素 simple and plain.

²⁵率 職 to fulfil one's duties.

率 臆 to follow one's own ideas.

率 西 水 滸 he followed the banks of the west waters.

率 規 矩 to follow the established usage.

率 言 to speak without thinking.

³⁰率 部 to lead troops.

率 錢 to collect money—for an entertainment, etc.

率 領 to lead; to take with one.

表 率 an example; a leader.

(a) Read *lü*⁴·⁵. A term in a series. Used as a suffix to indicate measure or rate.

兌 換 率 rate of exchange.

利 率 rate of interest.

增 率 rate of increase.

密 率 density.

⁵常 率 normal rate.

年 利 率 annual rate. (*arith.*).

死 率 death-rate.

生 率 birth-rate.

稅 率 rate of duty.

¹⁰速 率 velocity; rate of speed.

(b) Read *lei*⁴. To calculate.

率 更 an officer who attended to the clepsydra or water-clock.

捽 ³·¹. **To throw or dash down; to fall down. To cast at.**
5911

捽 下·來·了 thrown, as from a horse.

捽 倒³ thrown over; turned over.

捽 子³ or 下 子³ to lay eggs—of insects; to spawn—of fishes.

捽³ 手 to swing the arms; chair-bearer without a chair.

⁵捽¹ 打 to dash down; to swagger.

捽¹ 折 to snap off; to break.

捽¹ 掉 thrown down; cast away.

捽³ 捽¹ 打 打 dashing things about in a temper.

捽³ 東·西 to flip a thing away.

¹⁰捽¹ 死·了 dashed to death.

捽¹ 破·了 broken—as by slamming.

捽¹ 碎 thrown down and smashed to pieces.

捽 筋·斗 (*kên*¹·*t'ou*²) to fall head over heels.

捽³ 袖·子 to flick the sleeve.

¹⁵捽¹ 跤 to wrestle.

SHUAN.　　　　(ㄕㄨㄢ)

拴 ¹ **To tie up; to fasten.**
5912

拴·不·住 心 unable to keep the mind fixed; wanting in purpose.

拴·住·了 made fast.

拴 娃·娃 to tie a string round the neck of a clay baby with a view to procuring offspring

拴 扣 兒 to make a noose or knot.

⁵拴 捆 to tie up; to bind.

拴 繫 to tie up; to fasten.

拴 著 tied up; standing in the stable.

拴 車 to keep a cart or a carriage.

拴 鎖 to bind; to restrain.

¹⁰拴 馬 to tie up a horse.

拴 馬 椿 a post for tying up a horse.

栓 ¹ **A wooden pin or peg; a stopper for a bottle.**
5913

閂
扂
櫳 ¹ The bolt or beam used to bar a door.
5914

閂 栅 to bar street-gates.

閂 門 bar the door.

閂 鎖 to lock up—as a door.

SHUANG.　　　　(ㄕㄨㄤ)

雙 ¹
双 A pair; a couple. Both. Two. Double. Even, as opposed to odd.
5915

雙 亡 both dead—as parents.

雙 作 機 關 double-acting machine.

雙 全 both complete; complete in every respect.

雙 六 double sixes—dice, gambling.

⁵雙 凸·的 bi-convex.

雙 凹·的 bi-concave.

雙 刀 two swords in one sheath.

雙 務 契 約 bilateral contract.

雙 十 節 the *Double Ten Festival*, i.e., October 10th, the anniversary of the Republic of China.

¹⁰雙 口 鎗 double-barrelled gun.

雙 喜 doubled joys; two happy events; a wedding—also written 囍

雙 姓 a double surname—as 歐 陽

雙 宿 to sleep two in a bed.

雙 小 葉·的 bi-foliate.
15 雙 尖 齒 bicuspids.
雙 層 兒·的 doubled; in folds.
雙 層 花 a double flower.
雙 式 電 報 法 duplex telegraph system.
雙 弓 米 a name for rice-gruel; it describes the character 粥.
20 雙 手 both hands.
雙 掛 號 registered letter with return receipt.
雙 數 an even number.
雙 料 thick; firm—said of goods or people.
雙 料 炸 藥 explosive compound.
25 雙 斧 伐 孤 樹 felling a tree with two axes—given to women and wine.
雙 方 two sides; both parties. *See* 解 No. 626—A. 26.
雙 方 同 意 by mutual consent.
雙 方 堅 持 both parties unyielding.
雙 方 平 等 equality of both parties.
30 雙 方 滿 意 mutual satisfaction.
雙 方 聯 手 both join hands.
雙 方 行 爲 bilateral action.
雙 日 days of the month having an even number.
雙 星 double stars; the constellations of the *Herdboy* and the *Spinning Damsel*.
35 雙 晶 composite crystals.
雙 曲 線 hyperbola.
雙 月 the even months—2nd, 4th, etc.
雙 本 位 a double standard.
雙 棲 to roost together—marriage.
40 雙 殼 貝 bivalve shells.
雙·生 twin birth; twins. (*shuan*[4]-)
雙·的 單·的 odd and even—lit., even and odd.
雙 目 失 明 blind in both eyes.
雙 眼 both eyes.
45 雙 眼 鏡 binoculars.
雙 管 (or 筒)·的 double-barrelled.
雙 管 齊 下 to draw with two pencils at once—used also to express,-having a double meaning.
雙 翼 飛 艇 a biplane.
雙 耦·的 bi-conjugate.
50 雙 聲 格 alliteration.
雙 胎 or 雙 胞 twin birth; twins.
雙 葉 飛 機 a biplane.
雙 螺 輪 twin propellers.
雙 視 作 用 binocular vision.

55 雙 親 both parents.
雙 身·子 pregnant.
雙 軸·的 bi-axial.
雙 鈎 drawings in outline only.
雙 鈎 字 characters in outline only.
60 雙 關 語 a pun; a phrase with a double meaning.
雙 雙 in pairs; both.
雙 頭 筋 the biceps.
雙 飛 flying in pairs—close union, as in marriage.
雙 餉 double allowance for victorious troops.
65 雙 騎 馬 having a double meaning.
雙 鯉 a letter, from the shape into which ancient letters were folded.

艭[1]
5916   A boat.

爽[3]
5917   Lively; quick. Comfortable; in good health; agreeable.

爽 利 smart; brisk.
爽 塏 a high, dry place.
爽 德 distinguished virtue.
爽 心 grateful to the heart.
5 爽·快 brisk, in good spirits; comfortable; straightforward.
爽 手·的 事 something that can be done easily.
爽 撒 brisk, vigorous.
爽 旦 on the following morning.
爽 昧 or 昧 爽 at daylight.
10 爽 氣 smart; vigorous.
爽 爽 above the average.
爽 當 ready; brisk and smart.
爽 目 悅 心 it pleases the eye and gladdens the heart.
爽 直 straightforward; candid.
15 爽 神 in good health and spirits.
爽 脆 smart; ready; cheerful.
爽 甜 crisp and sweet.
爽 邁 vigorous; energetic.
乾 爽 fine, dry—of weather.
直 爽 = 14.
(a) To fail. To miss the mark. To make a mistake.

爽 信 or 爽 言 to fail in one's promise.
爽 然 若 失 it flashed upon him that he had made a mistake.
爽 約 to fail to keep an appointment.

分 文 無 爽 not a fraction out.

鶒[1]
5918   The turquoise kingfisher.

霜[1]
5919   Frost. Crystallized; candied, as fruits. Bloom, efflorescence. Grave, frigid. A year.

霜 下 傑 a name for the chrysanthemum.
霜 信 the frost messenger—a name for the wild-goose.
霜 刀 a bright, keen blade.
霜 威 dreaded, as frost—of a harsh ruler.
5 霜 月 the 7th lunar month.
霜 殺 to kill by frost.
霜 毛 describing the whiteness of feathers or furs.
霜 毫 white down.
霜 毳 white down.
10 霜 烈 cold, bleak and distressing.
霜 畦 vegetable plots under frost.
霜 菓 crystallized fruits.
霜 降 one of the Solar Terms, about October 23—November 6.
霜 雪 frost and snow.
15 霜 鬢 hoary temples.
三 千 霜 3,000 years.
傲 霜 to defy the frost—said of evergreens.
拒 霜 to resist the frost—as certain plants.
粉 霜 acetate of lead.
20 經 霜 to go through the frost—as plants.
落 霜 frosty.

(a) u.f. 孀 next. A widow.

霜 妻 a widow.

孀[1]
5920   A widow.

孀 婦 or 孀 居 a widow.
守 孀 or 居 孀 to live in widowhood.

礵[1]
5921   Arsenic.

砒 礵 arsenic.

SHUI. (ㄕㄨㄟ)

水 ㇏ 3
氵

Water. Fluid; liquids.
Radical 85.

5922

水上保險 marine insurance.

水上飛機 a hydroplane.

水丞 a small vessel to hold water for use on the ink-slab.

水中炸彈 a depth-charge.

[5] 水中球戲 water-polo.

水丹 or 油灰 putty for caulking boats, etc.

水亮 clear and shining.

水人 one familiar with swimming.

水仙花 the narcissus.

[10] 水利 water conservancy; irrigation schemes.

水利局 Conservancy Bureau.

興辦水利 improve the waterways and promote irrigation.

水到渠成 when the water flows the drain is completed—after much labour the work is completed.

水力 water power; freight charges.

[15] 水力學 hydraulics.

水力摩托 a hydraulic motor.

水力昇降機 a hydraulic lift.

水力發動機 a hydraulic motor.

水力起重機 a hydraulic crane.

[20] 水力電機 a hydro-electric machine.

水勢 the appearance of the water.

水化物 hydrates.

水印 or 壓印 a water-mark, as in paper.

水厄 drowned; discomfort from drinking too much tea.

[25] 水口 the place where a stream discharges; the meeting of waters—a term used in geomancy; the amount of moisture in fruits.

水國 the watery region.

水土 climate.

水土不服 the climate does not agree; unused to a place.

水土動植 climate, fauna and flora.

[30] 水坑 a pond.

水塔 a water-tower.

水塘 a tank; a pool or pond.

水墨畫 wash drawings.

水壓力 hydraulic pressure.

[35] 水壓撞壽 a hydraulic ram.

水壓機 a hydraulic press.

水大 the water is rising; flood tide.

水夫 or 挑水的 a water-carrier.

水宋 a name for the *Liu Sung* dynasty, — 劉宋紀.

[40] 水客 a sailor; a man sent to buy up goods.

水官 ancient title for an official in charge of conservancy works and the receiver of taxes for that purpose.

水宿 to sleep on a boat.

水工 boatmen; river conservancy works.

水匜 a syphon.

[45] 水平尺 a water-level—sometimes used for a spirit-level.

水平的 horizontal.

水平面 water-level.

水府 the god of the waters.

水底撈月 to dredge up the moon from the bottom of the water—impossible.

[50] 水底電線 submarine cable.

水彩 water-colours.

水彩畫 water-colour painting.

水心 the middle of the water.

水性楊花 unstable; fickle.

[55] 水手 a sailor.

水拉拉的 or 水漬漬的 soaking wet. (--*chi-chi*[1]-)

水族 aquatic animals, fishes, etc.

水旱 flood and drought; wet and dry.

水星 or 伐星 the planet Mercury.

[60] 水晶 crystal.

水曜日 used by some for Wednesday.

水曲 a place near the water.

水月鏡花 the moon reflected in the water, and flowers reflected in a mirror—insubstantial; unreal.

水月電燈 an acetylene lamp.

[65] 水月電石 carbide of calcium.

水木兩作 both bricklaying and joinery done.

水柱 a water-spout.

水柵 a weir.

水栗 a name for the water-chestnut.

[70] 水桶 a bucket for water.

水楊 the water-willow.

水槽 a water-tank.

水標準 water-mark.

水樣液 aqueous humour.

[75] 水機學 hydraulics.

水次 by the water.

水正 ancient title for an official in charge of conservancy works.

水死 drowned.

水母 the jelly-fish.

[80] 水氣 water-gas.

水池 a tank; a pool or pond.

水注 a vessel for holding water to use on the ink-slab.

水沉 or 沉香 lign-aloes.

水泥 cement; concrete.

[83] 水泄不通 not the least leakage—of a closely-kept secret.

水泡 bubbles.

水沫子 froth; foam.

水泉 or 水源 a fountain or spring.

水油 water and oil—incompatible.

[90] 水波 waves; ripples.

水波紋 ripples on the surface of the water.

水涌 a canal.

水流 the current of a stream.

水流破布 rags floating on the stream—a vagabond.

[95] 水涸 water-shallows; the drying up of rivers.

水深火熱 plunged into deep water and tormented by the heat of fires—the oppression of the masses by government officials.

水深計 a hydro-barometer.

水淺魚現 in shallow water the fish are seen—plain facts.

水清 the water is clear.

[100] 水清無魚 when the water is clear there are no fish—used of a pure-minded official; he is pure and has no evil practices; also:—too clever a person has no friends.

水清石見 when the water is clear the stones are seen—used fig.

水溝 a drain; a ditch.

水溝管 drainpipes.

水準 water-gauge.

[105] 水漏 a clepsydra or water-clock.

水漬貨 water-damaged cargo.

水漚 bubbles.

水滴石穿 dripping water wears through a stone.

水漲 flood tide; the water is rising.

[110] 水漲船浮 when the water rises the boat floats—things are easily done when the right method is used.

水澤 submerged; fertilized by water.

水瀉 diarrhoea.

水火無情 water and fire have no sympathy.

水火相敵 water and fire are antagonistic—mutual aversion.

[115] 水災 floods; inundations.

水烟 or 生烟 tobacco for the water-pipe.

水烟袋 a water-pipe; a hubble-bubble.

水燕·子 the sand-martin.

水牌 a small painted board used for making notes which can be washed off easily.

[120] 水牛 a water-buffalo.

水狗 the kingfisher; the otter.

水獺 the common otter.

水王 the ruler of the waters—the sea.

水玉 crystal.

[125] 水玻·璃 water-glass, silicate of potassium.

水理工學 hydraulic engineering.

水瓢 a calabash used as a water-ladle or dipper.

水瓶 a pitcher or water-jar.

水甕 a large earthenware vessel for water.

[130] 水產 marine products, fish, etc.

水田 fields which can be inundated; lowlying lands; tidal lands.

水田衣 a Buddhist cassock, from its cut.

水疝 hydrocele.

水痕跡 high-water mark.

[135] 水痘 water-pox.

水療法 hydropathy.

水盡草枯 bankrupt; resources exhausted.

水盡鵝飛 when the water is exhausted the geese fly away—utterly bankrupt, without resource.

水石灰 hydraulic lime.

[140] 水碓 a mill for hulling rice, worked by water power.

水磨 a water-mill.

水磨玻·璃 cut-glass.

水礶·子 a water-jar; a pitcher.

水禮 presents of food—as opposed to money.

[145] 水秤 a hydrostatic balance.

水稅 or 水捐 water-rates.

水程 a voyage.

水管 water-pipes; water-mains.

水管汽鍋 a water-tube boiler.

[150] 水簾 a waterfall like a curtain before a cliff.

水精匕首 crystal daggers—icicles.

水紅 a light red.

水素 Japanese term for hydrogen.

水綠色 a pale green like that of a duck-egg.

[155] 水線 water-level; the water-line.

水缸 a large earthenware vessel for holding water.

水老鴉 the cormorant.

水脈 the course of a stream.

水脚 freight or passage money.

[160] 水腫 dropsy.

水膠 liquid glue.

水臌 dropsy of the abdomen.

水色 complexion—of women.

水芝 a name for the lotus; the melon.

[165] 水芹 Chinese celery.

水花 the lotus; spray.

水苔 duckweed.

水草 water-plants.

水菜 vegetables such as greens, melons, etc.

[170] 水菓 fresh fruits.

水蒽 the bulrush.

水落 a down-pipe.

水落石出 when the water falls, the stones are revealed—hidden things will surely be brought to light in due season.

水葬 burial by throwing the body into the river or sea.

[175] 水蒸汽 steam or vapour.

水蒼玉 aquamarine or beryl.

水蓼 water-pepper.

水藻 algæ

水蛇 water-snakes.

[180] 水蛭 leeches.

水蠟 insect wax produced by insects on certain trees in Szechwan.

水衣 moss.

水營察 water-police.

水賊 pirates.

[185] 水質 fluids.

水路 waterways.

水車 a water-wheel for irrigating; a fire-engine; water-cart.

水軍 marines.

水輪 water-wheel.

[190] 上擊水輪 or 上沖水輪 overshot wheel.

下擊水輪 or 下沖水輪 undershot wheel.

水巡捕 water-police.

水退 ebb tide; the water is falling.

水道 waterways; the fairway.

[195] 水量標 water-mark to register the depth of water.

水量計 or 水表 water-meter.

水銀 mercury.

水銀劑 mercurial preparations.

水銀漬 mercurial amalgam.

[200] 水鑽 name for a diamond when used on a drill.

水長 (chang) 船高 as the water increases the boat rises—a rise in cost demands higher prices.

水閘 an aqueduct; a sluice; a waste-weir with gates.

水陸並棲·的 amphibious.

水陸平安 May you have peace by land and water! I wish you a safe journey.

[205] 水陸飛艇 a hydroplane.

水際 the water-front.

水雷 submarine mines; torpedoes.

水雷艇 a torpedo boat.

水電池 wet-battery cells.

[210] 水電發展 development of hydro-electric schemes.

水面 the surface of the water; nautical.

水音 acquired dialects.

水頭 depth of water.

水飯 a name for rice-gruel.

[215] 水蝕 erosion by water.

水馬 the hippopotamus.=河馬

水駱·駝 the bittern.

水髮 duckweed.

水鴨 teal.

[220] 水鷁 (cha) the grebe; the snipe.

水龍 a fire-engine.

一滴水 a drop of water.

沖水 to infuse; an infusion.

如水乳不分 mixed like water and milk—inseparable.

[225] 山水 scenery; landscape.

打水 to draw water.

扣水 discount.

投水 to jump into the water; to throw into the water.

死水 stagnant water.

[230] 洪水 a great flood.

活 水 running water: living water.*

淡 水 fresh water.

清 水 clear water.

溫 水 warm water; tepid water.

235 濁 水 turbid water.

絕 水 to cross streams.

苦 水 alkaline water.

藥 水 ㄦ liquid medicines.

覆 水 難 收 spilt water cannot be gathered up.

240 逆 水 to go against the current.

開 水 or 滾 水 boiling water.

順 水 with the current.

頭 水 first-class quality.

誰[2] Who? Which? Whose? Anyone. Also pron. *shei*[2].
5923

誰 不 做 who doesn't do that?

誰 不 知 who doesn't know that?

誰 也 who?

誰 也 不 敢 no one dares do it.

5 誰 人 who?

誰 家 門 口 能 掛 無 事 牌 at whose door can a 'no-trouble' sign be hung?—what family has no trouble?

誰 想 who would have thought it?

誰 敢 who dare?

誰 料 who knows? who would have thought it?

10 誰 毀 誰 譽 whom do I censure or praise beyond due?

誰·的 whose?

誰 知 who knows? who would have thought....?

誰 肯 who is willing?

誰 能 做 who can do it?

15 誰 能 執 熱 逝 不 以 濯 who can lay hold of anything that is hot without first putting his hand in water?

誰 都 趕·不 上·他 nobody could equal him.

誰·阿 who's there?

爲[4]誰 for whom?

(a) An initial particle.

誰 昔 然 矣 "long time has it been thus with him."

瑞[4] A jade tablet given to feudal princes on their investiture, as a sign of authority and rank. A keepsake. A
5924

happy omen. Auspicious, lucky. Pron. *jui*[4].

瑞 世 瓊 瑤 a gem indicating a prosperous age.

瑞 日 an auspicious day.

瑞 氣 auspicious influences—as of the sovereign.

瑞 色 a lovely colour.

瑞 草 an auspicious plant; a name for the tea-plant.

瑞 雪 seasonable snow.

(a) Used in transliterating.

瑞 典 國 Sweden.

瑞 典 體 操 Swedish drill.

瑞 士 國 Switzerland.

睡[4] To sleep; to doze.
5925

睡·不 合 眼 to sleep with the eyes open.

睡·不 寧 uneasy sleep.

睡·不 着 unable to sleep. (-*chao*[2])

睡 以 醒 醉 to sleep off a debauch.

5 睡 午 覺 (*chiao*[4]) to take a siesta.

睡 椅 an easy-chair.

睡 熟 to sleep soundly.

睡 眠 to sleep.

睡 眠 劑 a sleeping-draught.

10 睡 眠 病 sleeping-sickness.

睡 眼 eyes heavy with slumber.

↑睡·的 跟 死 一 樣 he sleeps as though he were dead.

睡 臥 to lie down and sleep.

睡 藥 soporifics.

15 睡 行 somnambulism.

睡 衣 night-dress; pajamas.

睡 覺 (*chiao*[4]) to sleep.

睡 車 or 臥 車 sleeping-car.

睡 鄉 the Land of Nod.

20 睡 醒 to awake.

睡 長 覺 (*chiao*[4]) to sleep the long sleep—death.

睡 魔 night-mare.

小 睡 a nap.

欲 睡·的 drowsy.

帨[4] A handkerchief.
5926

設 帨 之 辰 a woman's birthday,—from the next:—

設 帨 于 門 右 to hang a handkerchief at the right of the door —when a girl was born.

稅[4] Taxes; revenue; duty on goods.
5927

稅 制 taxation.

稅 則 the tariff.

稅·務 matters connected with the Customs.

稅·務 司 Commissioner of Customs.

5 稅·務 處 revenue office.

稅 印 to procure the official seal on payment of the regular fee.

稅 口·子 a station where duties are levied.

稅 單 transit pass for imports.

收 稅 單 duty-paid certificate.

10 正 稅 單 full-duty certificate.

稅 吏 tax-gatherers.

稅 地 land assessed for taxation.

稅 契 official fee for registering documents, deeds, etc.

稅 捐 duties, taxes, etc.

15 稅 率 (*lü*[4,5].) tariff; rate of duty.

稅 舘 or 稅 局 a revenue office.

稅 課 taxes.

稅 課 銀 a fee paid for the stamping of deeds, etc.

稅 費 fees in general; expenses of taxation.

20 稅 聲 regular taxes and *likin*.

稅 鈔 dues.

稅 銀 revenue; duties.

稅 關·上 the Custom-House.

稅 項 revenue; duties.

25 稅 額 the stated or legal revenue of a place.

稅 餉 revenue, duties.

人 頭[2] 稅 poll-tax.

佔 稅 to assess.

保 護 稅 protective tariff.

30 內 國 稅 excise duties.

出 口 稅 export duties.

印 花 稅 stamp duty.

噸 稅 tonnage dues.

國 內 關 稅 inland customs dues.

35 國 境 關 稅 frontier customs dues.

國 稅 national revenue.

土 貨 稅 or 土 產 稅 excise duties.

地 稅 land-taxes.

常 稅 native customs dues, as opposed to those of the Maritime Customs.

40 從 價 稅 *ad valorem* duty.

應 稅 liable to duty.

所 得 稅 income-tax.

抽 稅 to levy taxes.

正 稅 full amount of duty.
⁴⁵港 稅 port dues.
漏 稅 to evade duty; to smuggle.
燈 塔 稅 lighthouse dues.
直 接 稅 direct taxation.
碇 泊 稅 anchorage dues.
⁵⁰科 稅 extra duties.
苛 稅 exactions; levies.
返 稅 customs drawback.
進 口 稅 import duties.
通 過 稅 transit tolls.
⁵⁵遺 產 稅 probate duty.
重 稅 heavy taxes.
間 接 稅 indirect taxation.

(a) **To halt, as at a post. To put up at.**

稅 駕 to put up the carriage—to rest.

(b) **Read** *chuan*⁴. **Black, as garments.**

稅 衣 black garments.

(c) **Read** *tui*⁴. **To change into mourning garments after the allotted period has passed.**

小 功 不 稅 in a case where mourning should be worn for five months, if the death is not heard of till after the lapse of that time, and then no mourning is worn....

(d) **u.f.** 脫 No. 6468. **To take off.**

不 稅 冕 而 行 he went away without taking off his cap of ceremony.

蛻 ⁴ **The exuviæ of insects or reptiles.**
5928

蛻 殼 or 蛻 委 the skins of insects, etc.

SHUN. (ㄕㄨㄣ)
(Shuen)

吮 ³ **To suck, to lick. Also read** *chüin*³.
5929

吮 乾·淨 to suck dry.
吮 味 to test the flavour.
吮 癰 舐 痔 to lick ulcers and piles—sycophancy.

純 ² **Pure. Simple. Of one colour; unmixed; sincere.**
5930　**Inter.** 淳 No. 5932, 醇 No. 5933.　**Pron.** *ch'un*².

純 一 unmixed; simple; sincere.
純 一 不 二 unmixed; unadulterated; uniform.
純 一 不 雜 uniform, of one colour; unadulterated.
純·平 perfectly; solely.
⁵純 全 pure; spotless.
純 厚 sincere; sound.
純 吏 an honest officer.
純 品 人 a man of high moral integrity.
純 善 unmixed goodness.
¹⁰純 嘏 unalloyed happiness.
純 孝 truly filial.
純 忠 perfectly loyal.
純 收 入 net income.
純 明 pure intelligence.
¹⁵純·是 is purely....
純 樸 pure and upright; sincere.
純 正 simple; honest.
純 正 化 學 pure chemistry.
純 正 哲 學 metaphysics.
²⁰純 正 數 學 pure mathematics.
純 淨 pure; unmixed.
純 潔 clean; unadulterated.
純 然·的 pure; unadulterated; purely.
純 理 主 義 rationalism.
²⁵純 白 pure white; a pure heart.
純 益 net profit.
純 直 free from affectation.
純 種·的 pure-bred.
純 粹 unadulterated; clear; beautiful.
³⁰純 粹 理 智 pure reason.
純 素 pure white.
純 臣 an honest, loyal minister.
純 良 good, sincere.
純 色 unspotted; of one colour.
³⁵純 血 pure-blooded—stock.
純 誠 perfectly sincere.
純 質 unadulterated substance.
純 金 pure gold.
純 銅 pure or solid copper.
⁴⁰純 麗 beautiful; pure; clear.
純 黑 all black.

(a) **Great. To enlarge.**

純 大 great.

(b) **Silk.**

今 也 純 but now a silk—cap is worn.

(c) **In harmony.**

純 如 也 they should be in harmony--musical instruments.

(d) **Read** *chun*³. **A border, as to a mat.**

玄 紛 純 a dark, mixed border.
畫 純 a border of painted silk.
綴 純 a variegated border.
黼 純 striped borders of white and black silk—to mats.

(e) **Read** *t'ien*¹. **To tie.**

茅 純 束 it is bound round with white grass.

蓴 ²
蒓 }　**An edible water-plant—** *Brasenia purpurea.* **Pron.** *ch'un*².
5931

蓴 菜 the above.
蓴 香 the fragrance of a dish of this plant.

淳 ²
湻 }　**Pure, unmixed, genuine. Honest. Pron.** *ch'un*². **Inter.** 純 No. 5930.
5932

淳 厚 pure and honest.
淳 和 sincere and affable.
淳 樸 之 鄉 a pure and honest neighbourhood.
淳 氣 a sincere, friendly spirit.
⁵淳 深 deeply honest and sincere.
淳 清 pellucid; pure.
淳 潔 pure, clean, pellucid.
淳 白 clear.
淳 粹 pure and unadulterated.
¹⁰淳 良 good and honest; open.
淳 茂 unadorned and beautiful.
淳 質 unadulterated; unalloyed.
淳 魯 simple, honest and plain.

(a) **Salt lands.**

淳 鹵 salt, barren lands.

(b) **A pair of chariots.**

淳 十 五 乘 fifteen pairs of war chariots.

(c) **Flowing.**

禍 福 淳 淳 calamity and blessing alternating.

(d) **Read** *chun*^{1}. **Rich, fertile.**

淳毋 a dish prepared by placing fried pickled meat over millet, and enriching it with melted fat. (ancient).
淳沃 rich, fertile.
淳熬 a dish prepared by placing fried pickled meat over rice which has been grown on dry soil, and enriching it with melted fat. (ancient).

(e) **Read** *chun*^{3}. **A border, as of a mat. See 純 No. 5930. D.**

醇 醕 ^{2} **Rich, good, as wine. Pure. Unmixed. Pron.** *ch'un*^{2}. **Inter. 純 No. 5930, 淳 No. 5932.**
5933

醇備 excellent and perfect.
醇儒 a sincere scholar.
醇化 to idealize; outlet for emotion, as by the drama, etc., the catharsis of Aristotle.
醇厚 pure-minded and honest.
5醇樸 pure and honest.
醇粹 pure, unadulterated.
醇美 excellent; pure.
醇謹 careful; observant.
醇酒 good wine.
10醇酒婦人 wine and women—profligacy.
醇醨 strong and light wines.
醇醪 strong wines.
醇醴 very rich wine.
精醇 unadulterated; pure.

楯 ^{3} **The horizontal bar of a railing; a parapet. Also read** *t'un*^{3}.
5934

楯梯 scaling ladders.
欄楯 a railing.

(a) **A light shield. Similar to 盾 No. 6578.**

甲楯 armour and shield.

(b) **To draw forth. To excite.**

引楯 to draw forth; to excite; to animate.

順 ^{4} **Favourable; prosperous. To obey; to agree. In accordance with; to go with.**
5935

順乎天應乎人 "obedient to Heaven, well-pleasing to men."
順事 a thing that happens at a favourable time; a satisfactory matter.
順便 favourable; suitable; when convenient.
順候 I avail myself of this opportunity to present my kind regards, etc.—used at the end of letters.
5順其自然 in accordance with its natural tendencies.
順利 prosperous; no trouble with; easy; successful; easy to manage.
順口說 to say what comes first.
順命 obedience to orders; to follow one's destiny.
順嘴·子 one who agrees with everything said.
10順境 prosperous.
順天者存 he who obeys Heaven is preserved.
順天者昌 he prospers who obeys Heaven.
順姦 criminal connection, in which the woman is a consenting party.
順帶 to take along with one.
15順序 in proper sequence.
順延 to proceed in due sequence.
順從 to obey; to comply with; to follow the wishes of another.
順德人 a mild person.
順心 suitable to one's wishes; according to one's mind.
20順志 an obedient will.
順性 according to nature.
順情 reasonable; in harmony with one's feelings.
順情順理 proper; reasonable; regular; systematic.
順應潮流 to go with the tide—of affairs.
25順應環境 to accord with one's environment.
順應環境·的要求 to comply with the demands of one's environment.
順成 to complete an affair without hitch or hindrance.
順手 by the way; while the hand is in; at your convenience.
順時 timely.
30順時聽天 follow the times and obey the will of God.
順服 submissive.
順次 to follow in due sequence.
順正 prosperous; favourable; in accord with what is fitting.
順毛 straight hair—of animals.
35順民 good citizens.
順水 with the stream; a fair tide.
順水推舟 to drift with the current—to go with the crowd.
順流 with the tide—prosperous, as one would wish; with the nap.
順理 reasonable.
40順·當 prosperous; favourable; proper; smooth.
順症反症 curable and incurable diseases respectively.
順直 perfectly straight.
順筆寫 to write for another while the pen is in hand; to write offhand.
順絲順絡 methodical, systematic; properly arranged.
45順緒 the right way; pleasantly.
順義 in accord with what is right and fitting.
順耳 an obedient ear.
順職 to fulfil one's duty.
順請 I take this opportunity to wish you my kind regards, etc., —at the close of letters.
50順路 by the way; doing it if convenient; (doing something) on the way-as when passing through a place, etc.
順輿情 to accord with public opinion.
順辰 timely.
順逆 direct and inverse; fair and foul; mild and perverse, etc.
順遂 without hindrance.
55順運 a lucky chance.
順道 to go by the way of....
順道走 to follow the road.
順遜 agreeable; affable.
順適 prosperous; everything going smoothly; favourable.
60順適作用 adjustment.
順隨 to agree with; to follow others; to comply.
順頌 With kind regards, etc.,—closing a letter.
順頌升旗 I avail myself of the occasion to wish you high advancement—in official notes.
順風 a favourable wind; pig's ears. (*Shanghai*).
65順風打旗 set your flag according to the breeze.
順風相送 may fair winds accompany you!

順 風 耳 an ancient kind of megaphone; fond of listening to gossip.

文 理 不 順 the style is not at all smooth.

(a) To persist in.

過 則 順 之 if they have faults, they persist in them.

(b) To allow. To indulge.

上 帝 弗 順 God will no longer indulge them.

舜[4] Name of a legendary Chinese ruler, said to have ruled
5936 from 2255—2205 B.C. Wise; good.

舜 發 於 畎 畝 之 中 *Shun* came forth from the furrowed fields —to rule.

虞 舜 *Yü Shun*—the Emperor *Shun*.

(a) A name for the hibiscus. See 蕣 No. 5938.

瞬
瞚[4] To glance; to wink.
5937

瞬 息 之 間 or 一 瞬 眼 in the twinkling of an eye.

蕣[4] The hibiscus.
5938

蕣 英 the hibiscus—used fig., for things that are transitory.

SHUO.   (ㄕㄨㄛ)
(Shoh)

說[1.5.] To speak; to say; to tell;
5939 to talk. To scold.

說 一 是 一 to speak definitely without prevarication.

說·不 上 來 cannot get the words out; cannot say.

說·不 下 去 it was no use speaking.

說·不 了[3] it is too long to tell; I cannot settle it.

說·不 來 may not be spoken; it is no use talking; cannot get on together.

說·不 出 來 unable to express—either because of the difficulty of the subject, or the inability of the speaker.

說·不·得 must not be mentioned —as something secret, or something improper.

說·不 清 unable to explain clearly.

說·不 清·楚 to speak indistinctly.

說·不 盡 more than can be said; too long a story to tell.

說·不 過·他 unable to talk him down.

說·了·一·聲 he said a few words.

說·了·一·說 say a word for.

說 事 人 a mediator; a middleman; an arbitrator.

說 人 to scold; to find fault with.

說 人 是·非 to backbite; to discuss the failings of others.

說·他·一·句 give him a hint; give him a good talking to.

說·來 話 長 it is a long story to tell.

說 來 說 去 to repeat over and over again; to talk about a matter without coming to the point; to ramble; to beat about the bush.

說·個 人·情 to appeal to a person on behalf of another.

說°出 to divulge; to reveal; to speak out.

說·出 心 事 to speak what is in one's mind.

說·到 to mention; to speak of.

說 反·了 to speak ironically; to say the opposite to what is fact.

說 合 to arrange; to come to a conclusion.

說 和 to make up a quarrel; to act as a mediator.

說 嘴 to brag; to boast.

說 夢 話 to tell dreams; to talk nonsense; to gammon; to talk in one's sleep.

說 大 話 to boast; to lie.

說 好 settled; come to an understanding; agreed upon.

說 好 說 歹 to speak good or bad; to discuss a person.

好 說 好 說 very kind of you to say so—conventional reply to congratulations, etc.

那 還 好 說 that is easily arranged. (-*hai*[2]-)

說 媒 to act as a marriage go-between.

說 完 to finish speaking; when he had finished speaking.

說 完·了 settled; agreed upon; engaged to be married.

說 帖 a specification, as attached to a contract.

說·得 是 well said; spoken to the point.

說·得 有 理 to speak reasonably; to speak to the point.

說·得 活 現 word painting; described to the life.

說·得 過 去 that explanation will do; it will meet the case; it bears that meaning.

說·得 響 亮 to speak with a clear voice.

說 情 to solicit a favour; to apologize.

說 成·了 settled; agreed upon.

說 成 就 成 when he speaks it is done.

說 故·事 to tell yarns.

說 敎 to preach.

說 文 to explain characters—the name of a famous dictionary compiled about A.D. 100.

說 方 便 to say a good word for. *See* 方 No. 1802—C. 1.

說 明 to come to an understanding; to explain; to clear up; explanation.

說 明 書 explanatory document; instructions.

說 明 理 由 to tell the reason; to account for.

說 明·白 to come to a clear understanding—as in a bargain, etc.

說·是 那 麼°樣 it's all very well to say so, but....

說 書 to tell yarns—as itinerant story-tellers.

說 書·的 an itinerant story-teller.

說 曹·操 曹·操 就 到 speak of *Ts'ao Ts'ao*—a famous usurper —and he is sure to appear—used like "talk of the devil and he will appear."

說 服 to bring into submission by importunity; to persuade.

說 法 a way of speaking; an idiom; a mood; to preach Buddhism.

使 令 說 法 imperative mood.

可 能 說 法 potential mood.

未 定 說 法 or 附 屬 說 法 subjunctive mood.

條 件 說 法 conditional mood.

無 限 說 法 infinitive mood.

65 直 說 法 or 準 定 說 法 indicative mood.

說 現 成 話 to give ready-made criticisms; Monday morning quarter-backing.

說 理·的 rational.

說 略 a summary.

說 異 言 to speak in a strange tongue.

70 說 白 to give the spoken part in a play (in contrast to that part which is sung or chanted).

說 白 話 to tell white lies.

說 相·聲 to mimic sounds and voices—as showmen.

說 睡 語 to talk nonsense; to talk in one's sleep.

說 瞎 話 to tell lies, nonsense.

75 說 知 to inform; to make a statement.

說 破 to divulge.

說 破 嘴 to speak until one's mouth is sore—to use every argument until weary.

說 神 說 鬼 to talk of supernatural beings—wild talk.

說 笑·話 to jest; to tell jokes.

80 說 胡 話 to talk rubbish; to talk as in a delirium.

說 話 to speak; to talk; to converse.

說 話 粗·了 to speak coarsely.

這 句 (說) 話 this sentence.

這 樣 說 話 this manner of speech.

85 說 說 聽·聽 talking and listening.

說 謊 to tell lies.

說 謊 掉 白 to lie and play the fool.

說 譫 話 to talk in the sleep; to talk nonsense.

說 豫 言 to prophesy.

90 說·起·來 to tell the truth; as a matter of fact.

說 通 to discuss thoroughly—with a view to avoid misunderstanding.

說·道 to speak of; to say.

說 長 道 短 to find fault with; to backbite; to discuss the failings of others; to gossip.

說 開 to explain; to enlarge upon; to have it out with.

95 說 開 價 錢 to agree upon a price.

說 項 to mention favourably; to say a good word for—from a story of one who praised a man named 項 斯.

說·頭 something to talk about; something to boast of.

說 鬼 話 to lie; to whisper.

不 必 說 or 不 消 說·的 that goes without saying.

100 口 說 orally.

對 人 說 to tell others.

把 話 說·下 make an explanation; let him know.

無 言 可 說 nothing to be said; he had nothing to say.

(a) Used as a suffix—theory, view, —ism. Especially used when the subject is abstruse.

主 德 說 moralism.

主 情 說 emotionalism.

主 意 說 voluntarism.

主 知 說 intellectualism.

5 主 美 說 aestheticism.

主 觀 說 subjectivism.

互 働 說 interactionism.

人 本 說 homocentric theory.

人 格 說 theory of personality.

10 個 人 快 樂 說 individualistic hedonism.

倫 理 說 ethical theories.

假 說 hypothesis.

充 實 說 plenum theory.

公 衆·的 快 樂 說 universalistic hedonism.

15 動 力 說 dynamical theory.

原 子 說 atomic theory.

學 說 a theory.

完 全 說 perfectionism.

宿 命 說 fatalism.

20 宿 罪 說 theory of original sin.

小 說 novels.

幸 福 說 eudemonism.

必 然 說 necessitarianism.

快 樂 說 hedonism.

25 惟 我 說 egoism.

折 衷 說 eclecticism.

機 械 說 mechanical theory or view.

淺 說 elementary language.

混 合 說 syncretism.

30 淘 汰 說 theory of selection.

理 學 說 theory—in logic.

直 覺 說 intuitionism.

相 制 說 interactionism.

社 說 leading article in a newspaper, etc.

35 社 會 契 約 說 doctrine of the social contract.

神 話 說 mythical theories.

經 濟 學 說 economic theories.

自 動 說 automatism.

自 由 說 libertarianism.

40 表 象 說 or 直 覺 說 presentationism.

複 演 說 theory of recapitulation.

進 化 說 theory of evolution.

邪 說 heretical doctrines.

開 展 說 preformation theory.

45 靈 魂 創 造 說 traducianism.

(b) Read shui[4]. To influence; to persuade.

說 大 人 則 藐 之 those who give counsel to the great should despise them.

說 客 intriguing persons; persuasive politicians. A.p. shuo[1].

說 而 罷 之 persuade him to cease hostilities.

故 就 湯 而 說 之 he therefore went to T'ang and urged him.

遊 說 列 國 he went about persuading the different States.

(c) Read shui[4] To halt. To stop u.f. 稅 No. 5927—A.

說 于 桑 田 stop among the mulberry trees and fields.

說 于 株 野 I will rest in the country about Chu.

說 于 農 郊 halted in the cultivated outskirts of the city.

召 伯 所 說 under it the chief of Shao halted.

於 我 歸 說 would they but come and lodge with me.

(d) Read yüeh[4,5]. To take pleasure in. Pleased. u.f. 悅 No. 7702.

說 之 不 以 道 不 說 也 if you attempt to please him in any way that is not right he is not pleased.

說 懌 女 美 I delight in the beauty of the girl.

不 亦 說 乎 is it not a source of pleasure?

庶 幾 說 懌 they may then be happy and glad.

5 我 心 不 說 my heart is dissatisfied.

我 心 則 說 my heart will then be pleased.

民 莫 不 說 the people are all pleased.

無 所 不 說 nothing in which he does not delight.

近 者 說 those near are made happy.

¹⁰非 不 說 子³之 道 it is not that I do not delight in your doctrines.

(e) Read *yüeh*⁴·⁵. To number. u.f. 閱 No. 7703.

與 子³成 說 with you we will complete the number in our ranks—or according to *Legge*:—to our wives we pledged our word.

(f) Read *t'o*¹·⁵. To take off. u.f. 脫 No. 6468.

說 桎 梏 take off the manacles and fetters.

朔 4.5. The first of the lunar month. New moon.
5940

朔 政 plans of administration promulgated by the emperor on the first of the month and carried out by the feudal princes.

朔 日 the first day of the lunar month.

朔 月 the 10th lunar month.

朔 望 new moon and full moon, 1st and 15th of the lunar months.

⁶朔 氣 a festival.

正 朔 New Year's Day,—in the lunar calendar.

賀 朔 to offer new-year congratulations.

(a) The north. Northern.

朔 吹 the northern blast.

朔 方 the northern regions.

朔 漠 the northern deserts.

朔 風 the north wind.

河 朔 north of the river.

捌 4.5. To daub; to thrust.
5941

槊 4.5. A long lance, described as being 18ft. (Chinese) in length. A kind of checkers or chess.
5942

握 槊 to play checkers or chess, etc.; also defined as playing dice.

棊 槊 a game of chess.

TA.　(夕)

大 4 Great; big; tall; vast; extensive. Noble; high in rank.
5943 Very; much. Full-grown. To make great. Radical 37.

大 丈·夫 a hero; a virtuous man.

大·不 了³多 出·幾·個 錢 at the worst, put out a few more cash—disrespectful.

大 不 列 顚 Great Britain.

大 不 可 totally impossible.

⁵大 不 同 very unlike.

大·不·大 is it large or not?

大 不 對 very unsuitable.

大 主 筆 editor-in-chief.

大 乘 敎 the form of Buddhism prevalent in China.

¹⁰大 事 an important matter.

大 事 記 record of important events.

大 亮 the day has fully dawned.

大·人 a mandarin of rank; a full-grown person; Your Excellency.↑大 主 敎 Cardinal.

大 人 不 記 小 人 過 a great man does not remember the faults of smaller men—he is lenient to them.

¹⁵大 人 物 an important personage.

大 佔 勢·力 to hold a position of great advantage.

大 伙 chief officer of a ship. *See below*—39.　[piece.

大 作 your composition, master-

大 伯 father's eldest brother.

²⁶大 使 ambassador.

大 俠 great integrity; high principles; heroic personality.

大 便 great convenience—euphemism for going to stool.

大 便 不 通 constipation.

大 信 unchangeable; constant.

²⁵大 倫 the social relationships of prince and minister, father and son, husband and wife, elder and younger brothers, and friend with friend.

大 借 欵 the great loan borrowed in 1913.

大 元 帥 a generalissimo.

大 兄 elder brother—my friend.

大 兒·子 the eldest son.

³⁰大 內 ancient name for the palace

of a ruler.

大 公 disinterestedness.

大 公 無 私 just, without partiality.

大 共 all; the whole.

大 典 great affairs of State; great ceremonial.

³⁵大 凡 all; generally; for the most part.

大 刀 闊 斧 a great knife and a broad axe—to deal with a matter summarily without regard to details.

大 刀 會 Great Sword Society—a name for the Boxers, a secret society.

大 前·天 three days ago.

大 副 chief officer of a ship. *See above*—17.　[an original idea.

⁴⁰大 創 見 great discovery; a find.

大 功 great meritorious service; nine months' mourning—for relationships of the third degree, worn for brothers and sisters, etc. *See* 服 No. 1999-2.

大 動 脈 the aorta.

大 勢 circumstances; conditions.

大 勳 位 highest decoration for merit.

⁴⁵大·半 or 多·半 the greater part; for the most part.

大 司 務 a master-workman; a cook.

大 司 馬 or 大 司 空 or 大 司 徒 former titles of Presidents of the Boards of War, Work, and Revenue.

大 同 harmony of sentiment; universal harmony.

大 同 世 界 a world where harmony and equality prevails—Utopia.

⁵⁰大 同 小 異 for the most part alike; not very different.

大 同 社 會 the ideal society—Utopia.

大 名 a name given to a boy by his parents; your great name.

大 名 鼎 鼎 a famous name.

大 呼 or 大 叫 great howling; loud-voiced.

⁵⁵大 呢 broadcloth. (-*ni*²)

大 和 Japan; *yamato*.

大 和 民 族 the Japanese race.

大 哉 Great!

大 員 a high official. Heaven.

⁶⁰大 喜 過 望 pleased beyond expectation.

↑大 呂 a classical pitch corresponding in function to C-sharp.

大哭 to cry bitterly.

大器 a man of talents; great capacity; the throne.

大器晚成 great vessels are long in reaching completion—talent matures slowly.

大堂 principal hall in a *yamen*.

[65]大塊 nature. (*Taoism*).

大多數 the greater part; a large majority.

大夥ㄦ we all; the whole of; all of us.

大大的 greatly; deeply.

大大的福氣 extreme bliss; the highest happiness.

[70]大如拳 as big as your fist.

大姐 or 大姐姐 an elder sister.

大姓 a noted family or surname.

大娘 a paternal aunt; Mrs.

大嫂 elder brother's wife; term of respectful address to women—Mrs.

[75]大學 university; the *Great Learning*—one of the *Four Books*.

大學士 former title of a Grand Secretary.

大學校 university.

大學院 special post-graduate college for research work, etc.

大學院生 Fellow of a University.

[80]大宇之內 in the universe.

大安 your health.

大宗 mostly; for the greater part.

大宗包裹 parcels in bulk.

大家 we all; all of us; men generally.

[85]大家公用 for general use; used in common.

大家相爭 general strife.

大富由天 great wealth comes from Heaven.

大寫 the large style of writing the numerals.

大寫字母 capital letters.

[90]大將 a general; military commander.

大小 large and small; size; of all sizes.

大小方脈 general practice in medicine.

大局 the great scheme—i.e., public affairs; public welfare; great matters; the main aspect of affairs; matters of general interest.

大屈必有伸 great humiliation is sure to be followed by great enlargement.

[95]大工 a master-workman.

大布 coarse cloth.

大師 term of respect for a Buddhist priest; great masters.

大師傅 a head cook; a chef.

大帽子 to make some one do a thing by having his superior (who is the "big hat") order him to do it.

[100]大帽釘 large-headed nails.

大幫 a caravan.

大年夜 the last day of the lunar year.

大庇探 Great Britain.

大庭廣衆 a great crowd.

[105]大廳 the main hall or reception room of a large house.

大建小建 lunar months having thirty and twenty-nine days, respectively.

大張威勢 to assume great authority.

大彎花 the convolvulus.

大後天 three days hence.

[110]大得多了 very much larger.

大循環 the great circulation—of the blood.

大志 high aims.

大怒 great anger; in a great rage.

大恭 great respect—euphemism for going to stool.

[115]大悟 a great awakening.

大慈大悲 great mercy and compassion—the Goddess of Mercy, *Kuanyin*.

大意 heedless; careless; 大意 the drift (of); the scope (of).

大憲 the high authorities.

大憲章 Magna Charta.

[120]大慶 great congratulations—on a birthday.

大成殿 the main hall of a Confucian temple.

大成至聖 Confucius—from the next:—

孔子之謂集大成 in Confucius we have what may be termed a complete orchestra.

大戒于國 issued a proclamation throughout the whole empire.

[125]大戶人家 or 大門戶 great households; well-to-do families.

大房 residence of the eldest brother when a family separates.

大才槃槃 said in praise of another's great ability.

大手大脚 extravagant.

大手筆 a great literary work.

[130]大抵 probably; for the most part; in general.

大挑一等 an examination for former graduates who have been up and failed thrice at the metropolitan examination for the third degree.

大指 or 巨指 the thumb.

大掃除 a great clearance.

大排 a great mass—as of troops, etc.

[135]大搖大擺 swaggering along.

大擺 to swagger.

大放無拘 recklessly, without restraint.

大故 death of a parent.

大敎 Confucianism; your valued instructions.

[140]大赦 amnesty.

大數 one's allotted destiny.

大斂 to cover the coffin ready for interment.

大文豪 a famous literary man.

大斗小秤 unequal weights and measures; crooked.

[145]大料 most probably; generally speaking; a kind of spice.

大方 liberal; on a large scale; generous-minded; dignified.

大方家 great philosophers.

大方釘 a spike.

大早 very early.

[150]大旨 the sum of; the general drift of; the gist (of).

大明 the great Ming dynasty.

大智若愚 great wisdom seems like folly.

大會 synod—Presbyterian; a plenary assembly.

大有 abundant; prosperous.

[155]大有之年 an abundant year.

大有名聲 having a great reputation.

大有爲 of great ability.

大有造於其國 of great benefit to the nation.

大本營 military headquarters.

[160]大本領 extraordinary ability.

大札 your valued favour.

大材小用 large material for small uses—waste of talents, misuse of material; to use a talented man in an inferior capacity.

大棉二棉 first and second quality cotton respectively.

大模大樣 haughty; bombast.

165 大概 probably; generally speaking; for the most part.

大武 name for an ox.

大段著力 to put forth strength and make great strides. (-cho²-)

大殿 main hall in a Buddhist temple.

大母 grandmother.

170 大比之年 years of the former triennial examination.

大比例 ascending ratio. (math.)　大氅 overcoat.

大氣 the atmosphere; great anger; 大氣 generous; in good taste.

大江 or 長江 the Great River or the Long River—the Yangtze.

大決 the great assizes.

175 大法 fundamental law.

大洋 the ocean.

大活動 a great movement.

大海 the high seas.

大清 the great Ch'ing dynasty—the Manchu dynasty.

18 大減價 great reduction in prices—great sale.

大漢 a tall man.

大災難 great calamity—as pestilence, flood or famine.

大烟 opium.

大烹 high living.

185 大無畏的精神 a dauntless, fearless spirit.

大熟 a good harvest.

大父 grandfather.

大父母 Heaven and earth; the Sovereign.

大爺 father's elder brother.

190 大猩猩 the gorilla.

大率 on the whole; generally.

大班 head of a firm—taipan.

大理寺 former Grand Court of Appeal.

大理石 marble from Talifu in Yunnan—varieties with mountain-like markings are used for ornamenting chairs, etc.

195 大理院 Supreme Court.

大理院推事 judge of the Supreme Court.

大甘草 liquorice.

大畏民志 a great awe on the minds of the people.

大略 probably; for the most part; a summary; generally speaking; in general.

200 大略相符 agreeing in the main.

大痲瘋 leprosy.

大發狗狂 got into a rage like a mad dog.

大發發的 extra large.

大發財源 to open a great source of wealth.

205 大發雷霆 raised a great thunder storm—got into a fearful rage.

大盆 a woman's confinement.

大相懸遠 widely different.

大相逕庭 far apart.

大衆 we all; all of us; the whole; people.

210 大衆公論 public opinion.

大礮打雀 to use a cannon to shoot a sparrow—waste of talents on petty matters.

大祀 national anniversary.

大神通 supernatural ability and power.

大祥 sacrifice offered to deceased parents two years after death when the tablets are removed to the ancestral temple.

215 大禘 an Imperial sacrifice formerly offered once in five years.

大禮帽 silk top-hat.

大禮服 formal or full dress.

大禹 Yü the Great.

大秦 ancient name for the Roman Empire; also defined as Syria.

220 大稔 a prosperous year.

大端 the main division; a great affair.

大筆 a large brush for writing; large characters.

大節 great emergency; the important affairs of life—as birth and death, etc.

大節目 matters of great importance that cannot be dealt with carelessly.

225 大米 rice as opposed to millet.

大約 probably; for the most part; generally; to sum up.

大約摸 approximately.

大紅色 crimson.

大索 to search everywhere; a great rope.

230 大絨 broadcloth.

大經 the Five Relationships, see above—25; the Six Arts, see 六 No. 4189-19.

大綱 principles; chief points.

大綬 sash to hold insignia of rank.

大總統 President of the Republic.

235 大總統選舉會 Electoral College.

大着臍子 to pluck up courage.

大義 duties of importance which probably involve the life; the general meaning of; the tenor of.

大義滅親 unmitigated punishment for offenders, even if blood relations.

大老爺 former official term of address for magistrates.

240 大考 final examination in a semester or a year.

大而可畏 great and terrible.

大聲疾呼 to shout with desperation—as for help.

大肉 pork.

大腸 the large intestine.

245 大腦 the cerebrum.

大腿 the thigh.

大膽 very courageous.

大臣 a high official.

大致相同 practically the same.

250 大舉 a great undertaking; a large force.

大舅 elder brother of a wife.

大荒 great famine; scarcity.

大荳 or 黑荳 or 黃荳 the soya bean.

大著 your composition.

255 大號 a name or "style" taken by educated men.

大蟲 a name for the tiger.

大行 progress; to prevail; to be in vogue; the death of a sovereign or parent.

大行其道 made his principles widely known.

大行皇帝 His late Majesty.

260 大街 the main street.

大街小巷 streets and lanes.

大衣 full-dress; an overcoat.

大襟 the large lapel of a Chinese garment. 大褂兒 a man's gown.

大西洋 Atlantic Ocean.

265 大要 the essential points; the gist of the matter.

大觀 a great sight; fine appearance; flourishing.

大解 to go to stool.

大言 to assert too much; boastful words.

大話 bragging; a tall story.

270 大諒 most likely; probably.

大譜 approximately; for the most part; probably.

↓大驚小怪 much a d o about nothing; extraordinary behaviour.

↓大驚小怪之觀 alarmist views.

大資本家 great capitalists; millionaires.

275 大·起膽量 to pluck up courage.

大趾 the great toe.

大路 the main road; generosity.

大車 chief engineer; a baggage cart.

大較 the greater part; probably; for the most part.

280 大辟 capital punishment.

大逆不道 rebellion a n d sedition, great crimes.

大連灣 Dalny.

大道 the highway; the main road; the Way.

大道生財 the right way produces wealth. ⌈demerit.

285 大·過 greater than. 大過 great

大·部·分 the greater part; the majority.

大都 probably; for the most part; in general.

大都會 great cities.

大量⁴ of great capacity; magnanimous.

290 大針 the minute hand of a clock or watch.=長針. 大銲 welding.

大銀條 silver bars.

大門 the main entrance.

大開門做·的 do it with open doors; done in public.

大閱 a grand review—of troops.

295 大閹之亂 the disorders under the great eunuchs.

大關 the native customs—as opposed to the Maritime Customs.

大關節目 the principal heads and divisions; the general outline.

大限 the great limit—death.

大陪審官 grand jury.

300 大陸 a continent.

大陸性 a dry climate with great differences of temperature.

大隊人馬 a large body of troops; a great concourse.

大雁 the wild goose.

大雄氏 honourable term for Buddha.

305 大雨 heavy rain.

大革命　great revolution.

大頁紙 foolscap.

大頭²菜 salted turnips.

大題 an important case.

310 大風 a typhoon; great gale of wind.

大食 Arabia—from the Persian *Tazi* or *Tadjik*.

大飲 to drink heavily.

大餐 a banquet.

大體 the main principle; morality; scope. 大體上 in the main.

315 從其大體爲大人 those who follow that part of themselves which is great are great men.

大麥 or 粗麥 barley. (·· *mai*)

大麻 hemp.

大黃 rhubarb.

大黃蜂 a hornet.

320 大黑幕 deeds o f darkness, things done in deep secrecy—lit., a great black screen.

大鼓書 to sing or tell stories with occasional musical accompaniment.

大齋節 Lent.

大齋首日 Ash Wednesday.

四大 four great things—earth, fire, water, and wind.

325 更大 bigger; larger. ⌈31) days.

月大 a lunar (or solar) month of 30 (or

自大 conceited; puffed up.

行大事 to strike a good blow; to make a good impression.

(a) Read *tai⁴*. A physician.

大·夫 a physician; great officers of State in ancient times.

(b) Read *t'ai⁴*. u.f. 太 No. 6020.

大一 the primordial condition of all things before the evolution of the dual powers.

大上 God. Heaven. The ancient sages—title of reverence.

無已大康 but let us not go to great excess.

無俾大怠 prevent the others from going to such great abandonment.

鈦⁴ Fetters. To fetter. u.f. Yttrium. Also read *ti⁴*.
5944

打³ To strike, to beat, to hit. To fetch. To buy. To make, to do, to cause. To go or
5945

---

come by way of. It takes its meaning from the accompanying words.

打一·個字 the answer is a certain character—to a riddle.

打·下 to cut off; to prepare.

打·下·來 to purge.

打·不到 will not reach; no match for.

5 打·不·得 must not be struck.

打·不遠 will not carry far—as a gun or telescope.

打·不·開 will not open; cannot open it; will not clear up.

打主²意 to think of a plan.

打·了中火 to have eaten lunch.

10 打交·道 to mediate. ⌊(*dial.*)

打仗 to fight; to go to war.

打他一頓 give him a beating; to give a person a thrashing.

打他幾個耳光 boxed his ears a few times. (*S. dial.*)

打伙·食 to mess together.

15 打住·了 stopped work.

打倒³ to knock down; down with!

打倒³資本家 Down with capitalists! 打倒³軍閥 Down with the militarists! 打倒³帝國主義 Down with imperialism!

打個磴 or 打個艮 to hold back; to hesitate.

20 打個纈 tie a knot.

打個轉兒⁴ take a turn.

打傘 to open an umbrella.

打傷 wounded by a blow.

↓打點 to bribe. See below 207.

25 打冷戰 (or 驚) to shudder; suddenly; all at once.

打劫 to take by force; to plunder.

打前失 or 打磕絆 to slip: to stumble.

打勝仗 to gain a victory; to win

↑打價 to bargain. ⌊in a battle.

打包 to bud; to pack.

30 打包·的 a packer.

打千 to bend one knee in salutation.

打協同 to co-operate; to join with another officer.

打卦 or 占卦 or 卜卦 to cast lots; to divine.

打印 to stamp.

35 打印·子 small loans at exorbitant rates of interest paid back in instalments; to buy on time-payment.

打丟 to lose.

打呼·嚕 to snore; to purr.

打 呵·欠 to yawn.

打 哈·息 to yawn.

[40]打 哨 to whistle.

打 罩 to blackmail.

打 喳·喳 or 打 耳 唧 to whisper.

打 嚏·嘖 to sneeze.

打 嘴 巴 to beat on the lips; 打 嘴 靶·子 to slap on the face.

[45]打 圈 to draw a circle.

打 地 脚 to lay a foundation.

打 地 舖 to make up a bed on the ground or on the floor.

打 坐 to sit in meditation—as Buddhists.

打 坑 to dig a pit or a grave.

[50]打 場 to thresh and winnow grain.

打 夜 作 to do night work.

打 夥 to go into partnership.

打 字 to use a typewriter.

打 字 機 a typewriter.

[55]打 字·的(書·記)typist.

打 官·司 to go to law.

打 小 算·盤 to use a small abacus —penurious; mean.

打 尖 to stop for refreshment when travelling.

打 岔 to interrupt.

[60]打 彈。子 to play billiards.

打 彩 a lottery.

打 影 格 to draw or rule lines to put under a sheet when writing.

打·得 火 熱 very intimate with.

打 恭 to salute with folded hands.

[65]打·成 to make into.

打 戰 to tremble.

打 手·勢 to gesticulate; to talk on the fingers.

打 手 印 to sign by making an impression of the hand.

打·扮 or 裝·扮 style of dress; to dress gaily.

[70]打 把·式 to do acrobatic feats; to live by one's wits.

打 折 to break off.

打 折·頭 還 to square a debt by paying a percentage of the amount owing.

打 拔 to play tipcat.

打 招·呼 give him a call; let him know; to nod; to beckon.

[75]打 抽·搭 to sob.

打 捆 to bind; to make into bundles or sheaves.

打·掉 knocked down; to knock down.

打·掃 to sweep up.

打 探 to make inquiries.

[80]打·擊 to strike; a shock; to injure

a cause; to put down.

他·受·了·一·個 打·擊 he received a shock.

打 攪 打 攪 I have incommoded you—said by a visitor when leaving.

打 敗 仗 defeated; vanquished.

打 斧 頭 to cheat.

[85]打 斷·了·他·們·的 話 cut off their conversation.

打 斷 念·頭 to give up the thought.

打 暗 號 to give a hint; to signal.

打 更 (kêng[1] or ching[1]) to beat the night watches.

打 更·的 a night watchman who patrols the streets.

[90]打 板·子 to flog with the bamboo.

打 板 臺 imposing stone for type.

打 板 殿 to strike an iron plate— to summon to worship or to meals, etc.

打 架 to fight; to quarrel.

打 柴·的 a woodcutter.

[95]打 樣 to draw a design or plan, as for a building, etc.; to shut up shop for the night. (Shanghai).

打 樣 筆 a drawing-pen.

打 椿 to drive piles.

打 欠 to yawn; the noise of yawning.

打·死 or 打·殺 to kill.

[100]打 毽 to play shuttlecock.

打 水 to draw water.

打 油 to buy oil.

打 油 詩 to make rhymes in colloquial,—from a man of the T'ang dynasty named 張 打 油.

打 消 to destroy; to cancel; to abolish.

[105]打 消 辭 意 to withdraw a resignation.

打 渾 to joke; to chaff.

打 溜 a vagabond.

打 滾 to roll on the ground —as a mule.

打 火 to strike a light.

[110]打 烙 印 to brand by burning.

打 燈 籠 to carry a lantern.

打 爺 罵 娘 to strike father and curse mother—unfilial.

打 牌 or 鬥 牌 to play cards, etc.

打 獵 to hunt.

[115]打 生 to sit in meditation as a Buddhist.

打 當 or 出 典 to sell off unredeemed pledges.

打·當 to arrange; to put in order.

打 疊 to set out in order.

打 疊 精 神 to arouse one's faculties.

[120]打·發 to send.

打 皮 毯 to tickle.

打 睏 to doze.

打 眼 to perforate; to make holes.

打 瞌 睡 nodding with sleep.

[125]打 石 頭 to cut stone; to throw stones.

打 破 to break, as precedents, taboos, etc.

打 碎 to smash; to break in pieces.

打 破 迷 關 to come to a realization of one's mistake.

打 磨 to polish; to rub up.

打 磚 to knock a brick—to beg.

[130]打 礬 水 to settle water with alum.

打 禮 to make a bow; to salute.

打 秋 風 to raise the wind; to appeal for help to return to some distant place; to make a small present with a view to some substantial recompense. See 抽 No. 1314—A. 7.

打 稻·子 to thresh rice.

打 種 to sow seeds; to copulate —as animals.

[135]打 穀 to thresh grain.

打 稿·子 to take a proof; to make a rough draft. (-kên[1]-)

打 筋·斗 to turn head over heels.

打·算 to calculate; to reckon; to plan; to purpose; to resolve.

打 算·盤 to calculate; to reckon on the abacus; to be economical.

[140]打·算·着 intending to.

打 節 to pay by instalments.

打 箍 to put a hoop—on a bucket or tub.

打 篷 to put up the sail.

打 籠 to set a trap for a bird.

[145]打 糨·子 or 打 糨·糊 to make paste or starch.

打 紙 眼 機 a punch for making holes in paper.

打 網 球 to play lawn-tennis.

打 辮·子 or 梳 辮·子 to plait the queue.

打 罵 to revile; to abuse.

[150]打·聽 to make inquiries.

打 胎 to procure abortion.

打 膈 兒 to hiccough; to belch.

打 舒 張 to stretch oneself.

打 草 to mow grass.

[155]打 草 稿 to make a rough draft.

打 草 驚 蛇 to beat the grass and startle the snakes—to frighten out of cover; to cause undesired agitation.

打 茶 圍 to go the round of the brothels.
打 落 to knock down—as fruits from a tree; to haggle — without intending to purchase.
打 藥 purgatives; to buy medicines.
160 打 號·子 to signal.
打 裂 to break; to crack; cracked.
打 補·釘 to put on a patch—used fig.
打 診 to feel the pulse.
打 賭 to bet.
165 打 賬 to square up one's accounts.
打 贏 to conquer; to gain the victory.
打 赤 脚 to bare the feet; to go bare-footed. (S. dial.)
打³起 to raise.
打 翅 趄 to trip up; to stumble.
170 打 躬 to make a bow.
打 躺·下·來 knocked down.
打 造 to work—as in iron.
打 通 to knock through; to bribe; to make a hole in.
打 這 兒 走 go by this path.
175 打 連 環 to fire a volley.
打 道 to send a circular around.
打 選 to select.
打 那³裏 來 by which road did you come?
打 酒 to buy wine.
180 打 醮 or 建 醮 or 設 醮 to celebrate the festival of All-Souls; a public idolatrous service.
打·量 to suppose; to consider; to estimate.
打 針 inoculation; hypodermic injection.
打 鋪·蓋 to roll up bedding and tie in a bundle.
打 鎗 to fire a gun.
185 打 鐵·的 a blacksmith.
打 鑽 to drill a hole.
打 鑼 or 敲 鑼 or 撣 鑼 to beat a gong.
打 門 to knock at a door.
打 門 前 經 過 he passed by the door.
190 打 閃 to flash (lightning).
打·開 to break open; to open.
打 閒 to loaf.
打 雜·的 a man of all work; a house coolie.
打 雷 to thunder.
195 打 電 報 to send a telegram.
打 電 話 to speak by telephone.
打 靶 競 賽 shooting competition; rifle match.

打 鞦·韆 to swing.
打 頭²風 a head-wind.
200 打 飽·膈 兒 to belch after eating.
打 饑·荒 in distress; wanting supplies; borrowing money; to pretend to be in want.
打 高 興 (hsing⁴) or 打 興 (hsing⁴) 頭 to spoil the fun; to take the wind out of one's sails.
打 鬧 to create a disturbance; to fight.
打 魚 to go fishing.
205 打 麻 將 to play mahjong.
打 黃 昏 to be belated; to travel in the gloaming.
打·點 to make ready; to look after; to put in order; to check off the number of.
打·點 行·李 to get the baggage ready.
打 鼓 to beat a drum.
210 打 鼾 to snore.
打 齋 to fast; penance.
不 打 緊 unimportant.
不 打 誑 話 not to tell lies.
攻 打 to attack.
215 痛 打 to give a severe beating.

(a) Used in transliterating.

一 打 a dozen.
打 拉 dollar.

TA.　(ㄉㄚ)
(Tah)

姐 2.5. Concubine of *Chou hsin*, the last ruler of the *Shang* dynasty.
5946

妲 己 the above.

怛 2.5. Grieved; distressed.
5947

怛 傷 moved by emotions.
中 心 怛 兮 my inward heart is pained with sorrow.
勞 心 怛 怛 your toiling heart will be grieved.

(a) To startle; to alarm.

怛 化 death; to die—from the next:—
　無 怛 化 do not be alarmed at death.

笪 2.5. A coarse mat of rushes or bamboo. Also read *tan⁴*.
5948

竹 笪 heavy mats of bamboo used for sheds, etc.
輭 笪 flexible mats.

(a) A blow.

鞭 笪 一 百 gave him a hundred blows.

靼 2.5. Dressed leather. Used for sounds.
5949

韃 靼 Tartars.

軬 1.5. Ears hanging down.
5950

軬·拉·着 dragging; slovenly.

答 2.5. To reply; to respond to; to echo. To return, as a salute, etc. To recompense.
5951

答 不 上 cannot give the answer.
答 之 以 不 同 也 answered him in order to point out the difference.
答 對 or 回 答 to answer; to reply.
答 情 to return a kindness.
5 答·應 to answer; to respond; to assent to.
不 答 應·他 do not comply with his demands.
答 拜 ceremonial return visit.
答 數 answer to a sum.
答 曰 said in reply.
10 答 書 a written answer.
答 案 reply in writing; also answer to a sum.
答 理 to answer a person.
不 答 理 他 take no notice of him.
答 禮 to make return presents or salutations.
15 答 稱 official reply, as to question in parliament.
答 聘 to make an acknowledgement for betrothal gifts.
答 覆 to respond; to answer.
答 覆 信 to acknowledge a letter.
答 覆 訴 狀 dealing with complaints.
20 答 言 said in reply.
答 詞 response—as to an address of congratulation.

答 話 or 答 語 a reply.

答 謝 to return thanks; to send a return present.

答 辯 to refute; to rebut

25 答 道 said in reply.

問 答 question and answer; a catechism.

報 答 to recompense.

無 言 可 答 at a loss for a reply.

解 答 explanation.

(a) Thick, coarse.

答 布 a kind of coarse cloth. *See next.—B.*

荅 2.5. **A species of pulse. To undertake.**
5952

奉 荅 天 命 to carry out the will of God.

(a) Original form of 答 No. 5951. To reply.

(b) Similar to 疊 No. 6325. Coarse, thick.

白 荅 a thick, white cotton cloth.

(c) Iron spikes.

布 渠 荅 to set out iron spikes as *chevaux de frise.*

(d) A concretion found in animals.

鮓 荅 a kind of bezoar; calculi.

(e) u.f. 合. A small dry measure, about one tenth of a pint.

搭 1.5. **To raise; to build—of temporary structures only.**
5953

搭 寮 to put up a shed.

搭 彩 to decorate with lanterns, hangings, etc.

搭 彩 匠 scaffold builders.

搭 架 子 to put up scaffolding.

5 搭 桴 橋 to throw a floating bridge across.

搭 棚 to put up a shed or awning.

搭 脚 手 scaffolding.

(a) To take a passage.

搭 客 passengers.

搭 搭 脚 to rest the legs—as by taking a ride.

搭 船 to take a passage on a boat.

搭 車 to ride in a cart; to travel by train.

搭 載 to carry passengers.

(b) To add to; to hang over; to suspend.

搭 上 to add to.

搭 單 to add to a list.

搭 在 繩 子 上 hang them on the line.

搭 拉 hanging down; a latch.

5 搭 拉 下 來 hanging down; peeling off and hanging, as paper from a wall.

搭 拉 尾 巴 with the tail drooping.(-i³ pa)

搭 拉 貨 damaged goods.

搭 界 to bound; to form the frontier.

搭 箭 to fit an arrow to the string.

10 搭 解 to pay in addition.

搭 訕 to give heedless replies.

(c) To join together.

搭 住 to take a house together and share it; to lodge temporarily.

搭 伴 to accompany another.

搭 夥 to join in partnership; to club together.

搭 夥 吃 飯 to mess together.

5 搭 夥 計 to live as man and wife without regular marriage.

搭 幫 走 to travel in company.

搭 脚 connected with; implicated.

搭 配 to match; to copulate—of animals.

(d) To help.

搭 手 to assist. *See below—E.*

搭 救 to assist in rescuing; to save.

(e) A disease.

搭 手 abcess between the shoulders or in the small of the back.

瘩 2.5. **A sore, a boil, a scab An unauthorized character.**
5954

疙 瘩 a pimple; a boil; a lump; a knot.

褡 1.5. **A girdle; a loin-cloth.**
5955

褡 子 a sack; a bag sewn up at each end and opening in the middle.

錢 褡 子 a bag, as above, for carrying over the shoulder.

褡 連 a purse or pouch carried hanging over the girdle.

褡 連 布 drills.

達 2.5. **Intelligent; successful. To succeed. To obtain advancement. To be in office. To apprehend. Prominent.**
5956

達 不 離 道 when he has achieved success, he does not depart from his right path.

達 也 者 the man of distinction.

達 人 an intelligent, successful man; a well-informed person.

達 人 知 命 an intelligent man recognizes the decree of Heaven.

5 達 人 自 玉 a wise man takes care of himself.

達 其 目 的 attained his object.

達 其 辭 to comprehend his words.

達 則 兼 善 天 下 if advanced to dignity, they made the whole realm virtuous as well.

達 於 事 理 conversant with the fundamental principles of human affairs.

10 達 旨 to achieve one's ambition.

達 權 to understand the art of adapting oneself to circumstances.

丘 未 達 I do not know it—said Confucius.

富 貴 利 達 riches, honour, gain and advancement.

授 之 以 政 不 達 entrusted with a charge of government he knows not how to act.

15 是 聞 也 非 達 也 this is notoriety, not distinction.

發 達 to succeed in life; to develop a business or industry.

辭 達 而 已 矣 in language it is simply required that it conveys the meaning.

(a) Free from the trammels of environment.

達 士 a man who is not bound by outward phenomena.

達 觀 的 人 one who is above the emotions stirred by environment.

(b) To notify; to make known.

達 信 or 函 達 to communicate by letter; to send a letter.

達 復 to inform in reply.

達 意 to express one's desire; to make one's meaning clear.

達 知 to inform.

[5]達 部 to inform the Ministry.

達 鑒 to bring to the distinguished notice of.

上 達 天 聽 for the information of the gods.

(c) To penetrate. To reach to. To pass through. Thorough. To carry out. To have access to.

達 乎 四 境 reached to the four boundaries of the State.

達 于 河 flowing into the river.

達 四 聰 to hear with the ears of all. See 6916.12.

達 旦 until daylight.

[5]達 觀 于 新 邑 營 thoroughly surveyed the plans for the new city.

達 道 the universal path.

不 成 章 不 達 "does not advance to them but by completing one lesson after another."

不 達 於 天 子[3] could not have access to the sovereign.

中 心 達 於 面 目 the emotions of their hearts affected their faces and their eyes.

[10]其 達 孝 矣 乎 how far-extending was the filial piety—of King *Wu* and the Duke of *Chou*.

君 子[3] 上 達 小 人 下 達 the progress of the superior man is upwards, the progress of the mean man is downwards.

有 達 尊 三 there are three things universally acknowledged to be honourable.

欲 速 則 不 達 the desire to have things done quickly prevents their being done thoroughly.

泉 之 始 達 a spring which has begun to find vent.

[15]自 天 子[3] 達 於 庶 人 from the sovereign to the common people.

行 義 以 達 其 道 practising righteousness in order to carry out their principles.

(d) Appearance of growing grain.

莫 遂 莫 達 could make no progress, no growth.

驛 驛 其 達 in unbroken lines rises the blade.

(e) A lamb.

先 生 如 達 her first-born son— came forth—like a lamb—in birth.

(f) Used in transliteration.

達 因 Dyne—unit of force, the amount that, acting for one second on a one-gramme mass, gives it a velocity of one centimetre per second.

達 塔 海 峽 the Dardanelles. *See below*—F. 11.

達 姆 達 姆 彈 dum-dum bullet.

達·子 Tartars.

[5]達 摩 *Bodhidharma,* the Buddhist missionary who came to China in A.D. 526.

達 曷 the Tigris.

達 爾 文 Darwin.

達 爾 文 主 義 Darwinism.

達 磨 the law of Buddha— *Dharma.*

[10]達 賴 喇 嘛 Dalai Lama.

達 達 尼 爾 the Dardanelles.

(g) Read *t'a*[5]. To be dissipated.

挑 兮 達 兮 how volatile are you and dissipated!

噠[2.5]
5957

Name of a country.

嚈 (*yeh*) 噠 or 挹 怛 a branch of the 大 月 氏 which lived in Central Asia; their customs were similar to those of the Turkish tribes; they flourished in the early part of the sixth century.

縫[2.5]
5958

A knot.

紇·縫 a knot.

蓬[1.5]
5959

Plantago major.

韃[2.5]
5960

A nomadic tribe which formerly dwelt in the north-west.

韃·子 or 臭 韃·子 the Tartars; a term of contempt applied to the Mongols.

韃 靼 Tartar.

T'A.   (ㄊㄚ)

他
她
牠
5961

[1] A pronoun. He, she, it. That. Other, another. The second and third forms are modern, and indicate the genders, representing feminine and neuter respectively. Also read *t'o*[1] in the sense of 'other'.

他 不 具 論 without bringing forward other examples—let this suffice.

他 人 others; another person.

他·們 they; them.

他·們 自 己·的 their own.

[5]他 兩·個 人 those two persons.

他 力 the strength of another— i.e., of Buddha.

他 動 字 or 他 動 詞 transitive verbs.

他 國 other nations.

他 山 之 助 trust in the help of another—to rectify oneself.

[10]他 往 to go elsewhere.

他 心 通 universal perception of the thoughts of others. (*Budd.*).

他 志 of a different mind; alienated.

他 意 with another intent; a different opinion.

他 故 other reasons.

[15]他 方 another region.

他 日 another day; other days; at another time.

他 書 other books.

他 歧 之 惑 the deception of vacillation.

他 用 to use for other purposes; other uses.

[20]他 異 different.

他·的 his. 她·的 hers. 牠·的 its.

他 端 other plans.

他 自 己 himself. 她 自 己 herself.

他 花 受 接 (or 受 精) cross-fertilization.

[25]他 處 another place; elsewhere.

他·那 個 人 that fellow!

他 鄉 another countryside.
他 項 another kind; other items.
之 死 矢 靡 他 I swear that till death I will have no other—husband.
[30]豈 有 他 哉 was there any other reason for this?
此 無 他 this is from no other reason.
無 他 焉 was there no other but this?
無 他 說 there is nothing more to be said.
王 顧 左 右 而 言 他 the king looked to the right and left, and spoke of other matters.

T'A.　　　(ㄊ)
(T'ah)

沓 [4.5.] Joined, connected. Piled up, crowded together. Repeated, reiterated. Greedy. Distinguish 杳 No. 7297.
5962

沓 合 to pile up.
沓 杯 a set of cups that fit into each other.
沓 沓 babbling flow of talk; running rapidly. *See below*—A.
沓 潮 a meeting place of two tides.
[5]沓 至 coming one after another; coming in great numbers.
　紛 至 沓 來 coming in great crowds.
沓 雜 or 雜 沓 complex.
沓 風 a form of paralysis from indulgence in liquor.
天 與 地 沓 heaven and earth are connected.

(a) Read *t'o*[4]. Dilatory.

沓 沓 dilatory; negligent. *See above*—3.

幝 [4.5.] A covering; an awning; a screen.
5963

幝 幔 the tester and curtains of a bed.

踏 [4.5.] To tread; to plant the feet; to walk.
5964

踏 勘 to make a personal investigation.
踏 定 to tread firmly.
踏 實 地 步 a safe footing; a firm foundation.
踏 扁 了 to tread flat; trodden flat.
[5]踏 月 to walk in the moonlight.
踏 板 a treadle.
踏 歌 to beat time with the feet to a song.
踏 水 to walk on the water.
踏 破 to break by stepping on.
[10]踏 破 鐵 鞋 to wear out iron shoes—to spare no effort, as in a search for truth.
踏 碓 a pestle for hulling rice, worked by the foot.
踏 [3]脚 板 running board of a car; footboard of a railway carriage.
踏 跋 slow and dilatory. (*Shanghai*).
踏 踐 to trample on; to trespass.
[15]踏 軟 索 to walk the slack rope.
踏 雪 尋 梅 to go out in the snow looking for flowering plum trees—to get an inspiration for a poem.
踏 青 to walk on the green grass—to worship at the graves at *Ts'ing ming* in spring. 清 明 節.
脚 踏 兩 頭 船 to stand on two boats at once—to attempt to profit in two different ways at once; to waver; to seek favour with opposing parties; to fall between two stools.

鐋 [4.5.] To encase the end of anything with metal.
5965

鐋 鉅 to put metal spurs on a fighting cock.
筆 鐋 a brass top to protect a pen-point.

翂 [1.5.] The rushing sound of wings.
5966

塌 [1.5.] To fall in ruins; to collapse. To sink down.
5967

塌 下 去 了 sunk down; sunken; given way—as a bank of earth.

塌 天 大 禍 a great disaster—as of the heavens falling.
塌 颯 disappointed; disheartened.
塌 翼 to droop the wings.
[5]塌 車 a sack truck; a large hand-truck as used in Shanghai, etc.
塌 陷 to collapse.
塌 鼻 子 a flat nose.
例 塌 to collapse.
遭 塌 to waste.

搨 [4.5.] To rub. To take a rubbing of an inscription on stone. A fac-simile; an impression.
5968

搨 冒 stupid; easily imposed upon.
搨 地 錢 a tax on tea levied under the *T'ang* dynasty; a present made to servants or gate-keepers; bribes at a *yamen*.
搨 摸 to rub over.
搨 本 a rubbing of an inscription.
搨 板 a shelf.

榻 [4.5.] A couch; a bed.
5969

上 榻 to go to bed.
下 榻 to lodge at.
楊 妃 榻 a long sofa or couch.
登 榻 to go to bed.

(a) u.f. 鐋 No. 5965.

筆 榻 a metal cover to protect the point of a pen.

毼 [4.5.] A coarse, woollen serge.
5970

濕 [1.5.] To moisten; to soak through.
5971

濕 透 了 soaked through—as with perspiration.
汗 濕 [几] a singlet. *See next.*

褟 [1.5.] Inner shirt or singlet.
5972

汗 褟 [几] a singlet.

蹋 **蹾** [4.5.] To tread on; to stamp; to walk. Inter. 踏 No. 5964.
5973

蹋 伏 to crawl along the ground.
蹋 倒 to slip down when walking.
蹋 撒 to shuffle with the feet.
蹋 鞠 to kick a kind of football.

遢 4.5. Careless; negligent; untidy.
5974　See 遢 No. 3766.

遢·拉 鞋 shoes down at the heel.

闒 4.5. Door or window in an upper storey.
5975

鳎 4.5. The sole or plaice.
5976

嗒 1.5. Absent-minded. Also read ta⁵.
5977

嗒 然 forgetful of care.
嗒 喪 sick at heart; downcast.

塔 3.5. A tower; a pagoda; a spire; a lighthouse.
5978

寶 塔 a pagoda.
燈 塔 a lighthouse.

撻 4.5. To flog.
5979

撻 其 背 beat him on the back.
撻 罰 to punish by flogging.

(a) Rapid.

撻 彼 般 武 rapid was the warlike energy of—our king of —Yin.

澾 4.5. Slippery, as a road.
5980

躂 4.5. To slip when walking.
5981

躂 倒 to slip down.
躂 足 to slip; to slide.

闥 4.5. The door of an inner room.
5982

遝 4.5. Mixed, abundant, assorted. Repeated.
5983

卒 遝 mixed; assorted.

濼 4.5. Ancient name of a stream in the north of Shantung. Read lo⁴. Name of a market town in Central Honan,—(this reading is not given in the dictionaries.)
5984

濼 灣 河 a town near Yench'êng 郾 城 縣 in Honan.

獺 4.5. An otter. Also read t'a³.
5985

獺 公 獺 婆 a name given by the Cantonese to the Tanka, 蛋 家, or boat-people.
獺 皮 冠 otter-skin cap.
獺 皮 領 otter-skin collars.
獺 祭 魚 the otter sacrifices fish—"simply a superstitious misinterpretation of its habit of eating only a small part of its prey, and leaving the rest on the bank." Legge.
山 獺 the beaver.
水 獺 the common otter.
海 獺 the sea-otter.

TAI.　　(ㄉㄞ)

獃 呆 1 Foolish, silly, simple, idiotic. Also read ngai².
5986

獃·住 to linger about; to loiter in the streets; to foist oneself on another.
獃·子 a simpleton; a fool.
獃 意 astonished.
獃 板 a failure; a wooden person.
⁵獃 氣 stupidity.
獃 獃·的 vacant; stupid.
獃 立 to stand amazed.
獃 笑 a silly laugh; an inane smile.
獃·着 to stay; to rest.
¹⁰獃 臉 gaping; staring.
獃 視 to look at in an absent-minded way.
獃 話 nonsense.
獃 進 不 獃 出 one who pretends to be a fool for his own profit.

獃 頭²獃 腦 looking like an idiot.
¹⁵癡 獃 idiotic; stupid.
詐 獃 to pretend stupidity.

懛 1 Alarmed, scared. Stupid. Inter. preceding.
5987

歹 } 3 Vicious, depraved, bad. Radical 78. See 好 No. 2062-31ff.
歺 }
5988

歹 人 a bad man.
歹 意 malicious intent.
歹 毒 malicious.
歹 竹 出 好 筍 a bad bamboo putting forth good shoots—evil parents having good children.
不 知 好 歹 to have no sense of right or wrong—as a stupid or a child.

怠 4 Idle, remiss. Disrespectful, insolent.
5989

怠 倦 or 倦 怠 tired of a task.
怠 工 'lazy-strike'; sabotage.
怠 廢 lazy and unthrifty.
怠 忽 negligent; remiss.
⁵怠 息 to rest for a while.
怠 情 養 性 to take things easy; easy-going disposition.
怠 惰 lazy; negligent; remiss.
怠 惰 放 肆 careless and lax.
怠 惰 自 安 idle and self-indulgent.
¹⁰怠 慢 disrespectful; to treat rudely; rash; unwary; unguarded.
怠 散 indolent; neglectful.
怠 於 聽 斷 remiss in hearing cases in law.
怠 業 sabotage; 'lazy-strikes.'
怠 玩 remiss; idle; negligent.
¹⁵怠 緩 lazy; negligent; procrastinating.
怠 遑 idle.
怠 驚 disrespectful; insolent; unguarded.

殆 4 Dangerous; perilous. To endanger; to be in danger.
5990

殆 哉 perilous indeed!
危 殆 perilous; imminent.

多見闕殆 see much and put aside the things which seem doubtful.

思而不學則殆 thought without learning is perilous—or, is a weariness to the flesh; or, is doubtful.

車殆馬煩 horses and carriage are weary.

(a) About; at the limit; nearly; only; merely; even; almost. An introductory particle.

殆不可復 I apprehend that you will not do so a second time.

殆以此歟 probably it was because of this.

殆及 nearly; drawing near; until.

殆存而已 just existing and that's all.

[5]殆於不可 appears to us to be improper.

殆有甚焉 yes, and it is even worse.

殆無 scarcely any; next to nothing.

殆至一載 nearly a whole year.

殆非也 I apprehend not.

紿[4] To mock at; to fool. To pretend. To cheat. Also read t'ai[2.4].
5991

紿之 fooled him.

乃紿爲謁 pretended to make a call on him.

絲勞即紿 silk thread if much handled becomes tangled.

予昔紿若 I was only fooling you,

(a) To bind.

迨
逮[4] Until; when. See 殆 No. 5990-A. Also pron. tai[3].
5992

迨今 until now.

迨其今兮 now is the time.

迨其吉兮 while it is the lucky moment.

迨其謂之 if they would only come and speak about it.

[5]迨冰未泮 before the ice is melted.

迨天之未陰雨 before the sky was dark with rain.

迨夫 when.

迨後 subsequently.

迨經 when afterwards....

[10]迨至其時 up to that period.

(a) To seize. To follow up. To arrest. To come to; to reach.

逮捕 to follow up and arrest.

逮繫 to seize and imprison.

不逮 not seemly; not up to the standard.

莽云不逮 they are made to say, "It is no use."—to carry on.

被逮 to be arrested.

追逮 to pursue and arrest.

隶[4] To reach to. Radical 171. Read shih[4]. Surplus.
5993 Read ti[4]. A fox-cub.

埭[4] A dam, a lock. Inclined plane on a canal, where boats
5994 can be hauled up or down.

埭格 the scale of charges at a lock.

靆[4] Cloudy sky. See 靉 No. 13.
5995

代[4] A generation; a dynasty. Distinguish 伐 No. 1765.
5996

世代 generations.

三代 three generations of great-grandfather, grandfather, and father. See also No. 5415-17ff.

三代不清 his three preceding generations have been engaged in certain employments which disqualify him as a candidate for the examinations, and for official life,—to which the examinations were an entrance.

先代後代 former and succeeding generations.

歷代 successive generations.

當代·的思想 present-day thought.

(a) A substitute; in place of; for; instead of.

代人受過 vicarious suffering; to suffer for the faults of another.

代人經手 to act as agent for another.

代任 to act as a substitute or deputy.

代位 subrogation, as of a debt.

[5]代倩 for; on behalf of; to act as a substitute.

代作 to act for; to take the place of.

代價 equivalent price: satisfaction; cost.

代勞 to do something for another; to lend a hand.

代印 temporarily to hold the seal of another official.

[10]代名詞 a pronoun. See below—14, 62.

代塡 to advance money for another.

代墊 to pay money for another.

代奏 to send in a memorial for another.

代字 a pronoun. See above—10.

[15]代客 a broker.

代客買賣 buying and selling on commission.

代庖 to act for another.

代席 money in lieu of a feast as a reward, etc.

代手 to do something for another; to lend a hand.

[20]代抱·不平 to take up the cudgels for another.

代拆代行 to open letters and act for another.

代換 to exchange; to put one thing in place of another.

代數學 algebra.

代數式 algebraical formula.

[25]代書 an attorney; a copyist; a clerk in a yamen.

代替 on behalf of; in place of.

代替物 substitute commodity.

代月 a name for a lantern.

代權 to hold delegated authority; to act for another.

[30]代步 substitute for walking—as a horse, vehicle, etc.

代求 to intercede for.

代爲致意 give my regards to.

代爲辦理 to act on behalf of another.

代理 to act as locum-tenens or deputy; a substitute.

[35]代理人 representative; attorney; agent.

代理人扣取用金 commission.

代理公使 Chargé d'affaires.

代理店 agency.

代理會長³acting president.
⁴⁰代理權 proxy; power of attorney.
代理處 an agency.
代理行為 to act by proxy.
代理貿易商 commission agent.
代理領‧事 acting-consul.
⁴⁵ 副代理 a sub-agent.
法律代理人 an attorney.
總代理人 general agent.
載貨代理 shipping agent.
代用品 substitute articles.
⁵⁰代用學校 temporary building used for a school.
代用敎員 an unqualified teacher as a substitute.
代用貨幣 substitutionary coinage.
代當 to take the place of; to act on behalf of.
代筆 a writer; to write for another.
⁵⁵代署 a deputy official.
代脚 to give a person a lift—as in a cart, etc.
代舘 to act as a substitute teacher.
代表 representative; representation; to represent another.
代表團 representative body.
⁶⁰代表輿論 represents public opinion.
代訴 to plead on behalf of.
代詞 a pronoun. See above—10, 14.
代詢 to ask on behalf of.
代請 to intercede for.
⁶⁵代議制 parliamentary representative system.
代議制政府 representative government.
代議士 member of the House of Representatives.
代議院 House of Representatives.
代贖 to redeem another.
⁷⁰代辦 to act for; chargé-d'affaires.
代辦郵政櫃 sub-agency of the post office in a shop.
代面 a mask; to send a letter as a substitute for a face to face talk.
代食維好 they love this substitute for—official—emolument.

(b) Successively. Repeatedly.

代序 succession—as of the seasons.

代脈 irregular pulse.
代與 continuance as oppressors or usurpers.
代舞 dancing in relays.
⁵代謝 to supersede.
人事有代謝 human affairs are always in a state of transition.
新舊代謝之際 a time of transition.
春秋之代謝 the change from spring to autumn.
日月之代明 successive shining of the sun and moon.
¹⁰暴君代作 oppressive sovereigns arose one after the other.

(c) Name of a place in Shansi. Used also in transliteration.

代赭石 red raddle from a place in Shansi.
代那模 dynamo.
代那美脱 dynamite.

岱⁴ The eastern one of the Five Sacred Mountains, situated in Shantung.
5997
岱山 or 岱宗 or 泰山 the above mountain, the most important of the five.

玳瑇⁴ Tortoise-shell.
5998

玳瑁殼 tortoise-shell.

袋代帒⁴ A bag, a sack. A case. A pocket, a pouch.
5999

袋‧子 or 口‧袋 a sack or bag.
袋獸 marsupials.
袋鼠 the kangaroo.
布袋 a bag or sack.
⁵書袋 a satchel for books.
書信袋 a despatch bag.
烟袋 a tobacco pipe.
皮袋 a leather bag.
表袋 a fob pocket.
¹⁰襯袋 a pocket in the waist-band.
馬口‧袋 a nose-bag.

貸⁴ To lend on interest. To borrow.
6000 Distinguish 貸 No. 2398.

貸主 the lender.
貸借 a loan; to borrow or lend.
貸借對照表 a statement of assets and liabilities.
貸入 to borrow; to seek for a loan.
⁵貸出 to lend.
貸出圖書館 a lending-library.
貸出文庫 a lending-library.
貸‧子 a debt.
乞貸 to beg for a loan.
¹⁰告貸 to ask for a loan.
賒貸 to give credit.

(a) To forgive; to pardon.

貸減 to diminish.
寬貸 to be lenient to; to show mercy.
責罰不貸 to punish without leniency.

(b) Read t'ê⁴˙⁵ or êrh⁴. An error.

宿離不貸 so that there be no error in the astronomical calculations of the conjunctions.
無或差貸 without error or change. (-ch'a¹)

黛⁴ To blacken the eyebrows. Black; a sombre colour.
6001

黛環 black hair of a girl.
黛眉 black eyebrows.
黛黑 to blacken the eyebrows.
畫黛 pencilled eyebrows.
青黛 a deep purplish blue—as of distant hills; sombre.

待⁴ To treat; to behave.
6002

待下 attitude towards inferiors.
待人 attitude towards others.
待人厚道 to treat others with generosity.
待人如己 to treat others as yourself.
⁵待人親熱 to treat a person with cordiality.
待好 to treat well.
待客不周到 to treat a visitor improperly.
待承 to undertake for.

待物之洪如此 he treats outsiders in this liberal manner.
10待稱 to attend to—guests.
待。遇 to treat; behaviour towards.
公平待遇 to treat fairly.
厚待 liberal treatment.
善待 to treat well.
15寬待 liberal dealing.
慢待 to treat with contempt.
招待員 an usher.
接待 to receive—as visitors.
柔待遠人 treat strangers from a distance with kindness.
20相待 to treat; behaviour towards.

(a) **To wait for.**

待[1]一·會兒 wait a little while.
待[1]·了半天 waiting for a considerable time.
待來年 wait for next year.
待價 waiting for prices—to watch the market.
5待[1]·兩·天 wait a day or two.
待分[4] waiting to receive presents, as an engagement to teach.
待怎·的 what about it? how? in what way? what do you expect?
待我 wait until I come.
待斃 waiting for death.
10待旦 to wait for the morning.
待時 to bide one s time.
待時而動 wait until the right moment and then take action.
待有暇 waiting till one has leisure.
待沽 to get a good price in the market.
15待決於命而後泰然 he waits for the decision of fate and then is at peace.
待等 or 等待 to await.
待罪 I wait for punishment—an apologetic phrase.
待聘 waiting for an engagement.
待要 to be about to.
20待質 detained to give evidence.
久待 waiting for a long time.
少待片刻 wait for a little while.
屏息以待 waiting with bated brea

戴[4] **To wear on the head or on the nose.**
6003

戴·不上 unable to wear it.
戴冠冕 to wear a crown.
戴勝 the hoopoe; feather head-dress.
戴帽·子 to wear a hat.
5戴德 to crown with goodness; thankful for kindness.
戴日 to have the sun overhead.
戴星而出 left before the dawn.
戴星而往 travelled there by night.
戴月披星 to wear the moon and wrap in the stars—to travel by night.
10戴白 hoary-headed.
戴盆望天 to wear a bowl and look up to the sky—cannot do two things at once.
戴眼鏡兒 to wear spectacles.
戴笠 to wear a bamboo rain-hat.—peasant dress.
戴綠頭巾 to wear a green turban—to be a cuckold.
15戴翎·子 to wear the official feather-insignia.
戴雞佩豚 dressed in an outlandish, barbarous style.
戴頂·子 to wear a button—as was done by officials under the empire.
戴高帽 to wear a high hat—to put oneself forward; to be fond of flattery.
不共戴天 will not live under the same sky with—the murderer of his father.
20負戴 to bear burdens on the back or on the head.

(a) **To uphold. To honour. To bear; to sustain.**

愛戴 to love and honour.
擔戴 to undertake.
民之戴商厥惟舊哉 the honouring of *Shang* by the people is a thing of long existence.
衆非元后何戴 if the masses had no sovereign, whom would they be able to honour?

襶[4] **Ignorant; inexperienced.**
6004

褦襶 unsophisticated.

帶 䌖[4] **A girdle; a tape; a sash or scarf. A belt. A belt of country. A district.**
6005

帶·子 tape; a girdle or sash, etc.
帶圍 a belt.
帶弦 girded on a bow-string—to urge himself to effort.
帶甲 to wear armour—a soldier.
5帶蟲 tape-worm.
帶鈎 buckle of a belt.
帶頭[2] buckle or fastening of a belt.
帶魚 the hair-tail fish. *Trichiurus chinensis.*
一帶地·方 a region; a neighbourhood; a stretch of country.
10一帶草地 a piece of meadow land.
光帶 band of light.
劍帶 sword-belt.
夾帶 to smuggle—as papers into an examination.
寒帶 the Frigid Zone.
15束帶 to gird on a belt; to wear a girdle.
海帶 edible seaweed; kelp.
温帶 the Temperate Zone.
無掛帶 without anxiety.
熱帶 the Torrid Zone.
20皮帶 a leather belt.
肩帶 a shoulder-belt.
腰帶 a waist-band; a belt.
色帶 the spectrum.
裹傷帶 bandages.
25襪帶 garters.
馬肚帶 belly-band for a horse.

(a) **To bear; to carry to or from, to take or bring with. To involve. See 連 No. 4009-B.5ff.**

帶·上 to take with; to concern; to touch.
帶人爲質 to take men as hostages.
帶·來 to bring; to bring with.
帶信 to carry letters.
5帶·個人·去 take a man with you.
帶·個好兒去 give them my greetings.
帶候 to keep in charge till....
帶傷 to be wounded.
帶兵 to lead or have charge of troops.
10帶到縣 to take to the magistrates.
帶到那[4]邊去 take it over there.
帶·去 to carry off.
帶口音 to speak with an accent.
帶同 or 隨帶 to lead; to take with one.
15帶哭 crying.
帶喜色[4] wearing a pleased expression.

帶·回·來 to bring back.

帶 壞 to lead astray; to pull apart; to involve in ruin.

帶 往 to take to.

[20] 帶 息 interest included; bearing interest.

帶 愁 容 looking very unhappy.

帶 手 to do at the same time.

帶 書 to carry letters.

帶 案 to bring before the court.

[25] 帶 氣 人·的 樣·子 has an exasperating manner.

帶 水 to pilot; including water.

帶 水 人 a pilot.

帶 病 with his illness upon him.

帶°累 to involve; to impede.

[30] 帶 着 to carry; carrying.

帶·着 傲 慢·的 樣·子 with an air of arrogance.

帶·着 恐 怖·的 精·神 with a spirit of nervous dread.

帶 肚·子 pregnant.

帶 至 to take to.

[35] 帶 見 to introduce to a superior.

帶 赴 to take to.

帶 送 to take to.

帶 道·的 a guide.

帶 酒 in liquor.

[40] 帶 門 to shut the door on leaving.

帶 陷 to involve; to encumber.

帶 隊 to lead or have charge of troops.

帶 領 to take in one's charge; to lead.

你 託 我 帶·的 東·西 the things which you asked me to bring for you.

[45] 拐 帶 to kidnap.

挾 帶 to carry under the arm.

捎 帶 to carry—letters, etc.

癗 [4]
6006
A discharge or flux.

白 癗 leucorrhoea.

赤 癗 uterine discharge.

(a) Read *chih*[4] or *ti*[4]. Dysentery; severe diarrhoea. The head half covered with sores.

蔕 [4]
6007
Roots of grass, etc. Inter. 蔕 No. 6207 and read *ti*[4]. A peduncle, a stem. A base or foundation.

蔕 芥 or 芥 蔕 trifling; a grudge, enmity.

從 無 芥 蔕 without the least disagreement.

心 存 芥 蔕 cherishing a grudge.

細 故 蔕 芥 trifling matters.

胸 無 芥 蔕 no enmity; no grudge in the mind.

T'AI. (ㄊㄞ)

台 [2]
6008
Three stars in Ursa Major are known as 三 台, also the three highest dignitaries of State, from which comes the meaning:— eminent; exalted.

台 函 your note.

台 吉 lowest order of Mongol nobility—*Taiji*.

台 命 your orders.

台 安 your welfare—used at the end of letters.

[5] 台 從 your Honour.

台 啟 for your information.

台 敎 what you have to say.

台 槐 or 三 公 chief ministers under the *Chou* dynasty. *See below*—15.

台 照 for your Honour's inspection—opening phrase in letters.

[10] 台 甫 是 那[3] 兩·個 字 which two characters form your honoured "style."

台 祺 or 台 祉 your welfare—used at the end of letters.

台 端 your Honour—you.

台 號 your "style."

台 駕 your Honour; you.

[15] 台 鼎 or 三 公 *See above*—8. Said to be derived from the three stars in Ursa Major, or from the three legs of a tripod.

兄 台 honoured elder brother—Sir.

(a) Read *t'ai*[2]. u.f. 臺 No. 6016. A terrace, a raised platform or steps, etc.

台 前 before the seat of justice.

台 秤 platform-scales.

台 站 a border patrol-station.

台 階 steps leading up to a house, etc.

(b) u.f. 鮐 No. 6015. The globe-fish.

台 背 the rounded back of the aged.

(c) Read *i*[2]. I, me.

祇 台 德 先 "let me go before the empire with reverent attention to my virtue."

非 台 小 子[3] 敢 稱 亂 "it is not I, the little child, that dares undertake *what seems to be a* rebellious enterprise."

予 恐 來 世 以 台 爲 口 實 "I am afraid that in future ages men will fill their mouths with me."

(d) Read *i*[2]. u.f. 怡 No. 2964. Pleased.

虞 舜 不 台 the Emperor *Shun* was not pleased.

(e) Read *i*[2]. An exclamation of surprise.

夏 罪 其 如 台 What can be done about the crimes of *Hsia*? *Legge* translates 台 as the personal pronoun—"What are the crimes of *Hsia* to us?"

炱 [2]
6009
Soot.

炱 黑 blackened with soot.

胎 [1]
6010
The pregnant womb.

胎 仙 the white crane. *See below*—21.

胎 元 an embryo.

胎 兒[2] an embryo.

胎 前 産 後 before and after confinement.

[5] 胎 動 the quickening of the womb.

胎 墮 abortion.

胎 孕 or 懷 胎 or 有 胎 or 受 胎 to be pregnant.

胎 座 placenta. (*botany*).

胎 形 the form of the foetus.

[10] 胎 敎 pre-natal influences.

胎 敗 death in the womb.

胎 毒 congenital disease.

胎 濕 卵 化 the four classes of birth, according to the Chinese philosophers. *See* 生 No. 5738-184 ff.

胎 生 viviparous.

[15] 胎 生 學 or 胎 育 學 embryology.

胎 生 魚 viviparous fish, as certain sharks.

胎 產 child-birth.
胎 甲 in the womb.
胎 盤 the placenta.
20 胎 瞽 born blind.
胎 禽 the white crane, said to be born from the womb. *See above* —1.
胎 胞 the womb.
胎 衣 the placenta.
胎·裏·帶·來·的 congenital.
25 胎 記 a birth-mark.
胎 誨 pre-natal influence.
一 胎 三 子 or 品 胎 triplets.
安 胎 to quiet the womb.
懷 鬼 胎 to cherish evil schemes or dark plots; to be conscious of guilt.
30 打 胎 to procure abortion.
投 胎 to pass into a womb; to take possession of a foetus.
石 胎 a barren womb.
禍 胎 pregnant with evil.
私 胎 illegitimate conception.
35 結 聖 胎 得 長 生 to attain to immortality by a mystic conception.
脫 胎 換 骨 to get rid of one's mortal frame; to make a radical reformation.
落 胎 miscarriage; premature birth.
複 胎 multiple birth.
頭 胎 the firstborn.

苔² Moss; lichen.
6011

苔 封 wrapped up in moss.
苔 岑 a like-minded friend.
苔 扉 a moss-covered door.
苔 梅 a moss growing on flowering plums.
5 苔 甃 the mossy brickwork of a well.
苔 痕 lichens.
苔 癬 lichens.
苔 砌 or 苔 階 mossy steps.
苔 碑 a stone tablet overgrown with moss or lichens.
10 苔 磴 滑 難 步 the mossy steps are slippery and difficult to ascend.
苔 色 the colouring of lichens.
苔 茵 a cushion of moss.
苔 草 沒 階 moss and weeds hide the steps.
苔 菜 edible seaweed.

15 苔 衣 mosses and lichens generally.
苔 錢 lichens like cash.
苔 鬚 the moss hangs like hair.
蒼 苔 moss.
青 苔 moss.
↑舌 苔¹ fur on the tongue.

跆² To trample.
6012

跆 藉 (*chi*⁴·⁵·) in confusion; trampled.

邰² Name of a small feudal State in Shensi.
6013

駘² A worn-out horse.
6014

駑 駘 a worn-out old horse.
駘 背 humpbacked.

(a) Tired; jaded.

朽 駘 weary; fatigued.

(b) A horse free of its bit.

馬 駘 其 銜 the horse lost its bit.

(c) *See below*

駘 蕩 broad expanse.
駘 鈍 blunt; dull.
相 駘 藉 now appearing, now disappearing.

鮐² The globe-fish or tetraodon. See 河 豚 No. 2111-48.
6015

鮐 背 rounded shoulders like the globe-fish.

臺² A lookout, a tower. A terrace, a platform, a stage.
6016 Inter. 台 No. 6008.
Distinguish 壹 No. 3016.

臺 地 a table-land.
臺 布 a table-cloth.
臺 榭 open-air pavilion in a garden.
臺 灣 Taiwan—the island of Formosa.
5 臺 磴 steps up to a house.
臺 站 a frontier patrol station.
臺 門 gate of the forbidden city.
臺 閣 towers and pavilions. *See below* —A. 8.

臺 階 steps; ascent.
10 一 臺 戲 a performance on the stage.
下 臺 to come off the stage; to retire. *See No.* 2520-3.
債 臺 高 築 heavily involved in debt.
天 文 臺 an observatory.
戲 臺 or 舞 臺 a stage for theatricals.
15 收 臺 to drop the curtain.
晒 臺 a drying stage—often on the roof.
月 臺 a platform as on a railway station or a car.
望 臺 or 瞭 望 臺 the bridge of a steamer.
演 臺 a platform for a speaker. *See below* —25.
20 登 臺 to go on the stage or platform.
砲 臺 a fort.
蠟 臺 a candle-stick.
觀 臺 a lookout or observatory.
觀 象 臺 an observatory. *See above* —13.
25 講 臺 platform for a speaker; a pulpit. *See above* —19.
開 臺 to begin the performance on the stage.
靈 臺 The Marvellous Tower of King *Wên*.

(a) A title of respect. See 台 No. 6008.

臺 下 conventional phrase equivalent to your Honour.
臺 函 your favour.
臺 前 conventional phrase—your Honour.
臺 官 or 臺 臣 censors under the *Yuan* dynasty.
5 臺 示 your instructions.
臺 翁 your Honour,—conventional phrase.
臺 諫 censors.
臺 閣 high metropolitan official under the *Han* dynasty.
臺 院 or 御 史 臺 the censorate.
10 臺 電 for your glance—introductory phrase in letters:—kindly give this your attention.
制·臺 former designation of a Viceroy.
撫·臺 former designation of a Governor.
臬·臺 former designation of a Provincial-Judge.

蕃·臺 former designation of the Treasurer of a Province.

[15]道·臺 former designation of an Intendant of a Circuit.

(b) A low-class office, a servant. See No. 6017.

僕 臣 臺 my servant.

自 是 臺 無 餽 也 from that time a servant was no longer sent with the presents.

輿 臺 low mean servants.

(c) A kind of sedge. *Cyperus rotundus*, used in ancient times for raincoats, etc. Also called 莎 草 or 夫 須.

臺 笠 rain-hats made of sedge.

南 山 有 臺 on the southern hills are the sedges.

儓[2]
6017
A servant.

輿 儓 之 鬼 a menial devil.

(a) Read *tai*[4]. Appearance of stupidity.

儓 儗 (*hai*[4]) foolish-looking.

擡
抬
6018
To carry between two or more persons. To raise.

擡·不·動 unable to lift or carry.

擡 價 or 擡 高 時 價 to raise the prices.

擡·出·去 to carry out; carry it out.

擡·回·去 carry it back.

擡 手 動 脚 gesticulating with hands and feet.

擡 扛 to carry on a pole; to wrangle; to quarrel.

擡 摃 to carry on a stretcher; to wrangle.

擡 摃 辯 嘴 to wrangle as bearers do.

[10]擡·舉 to advance; to recommend; to exalt; to extol.

擡·著 to carry; carrying.

擡 貴 to extol another.

擡 貴 手 lift your honoured hand —to beg pardon.

擡·起·來 to lift up.

[15]擡 身 to get up from a stooping position.

擡 轎·子 to carry a sedan; to run a gambling game so as to cause strangers to lose.

擡 轎·的 or 轎·夫 chair-bearers.

擡 閣 to carry dressed-up children on high frames in a spectacular procession.

擡 頭[2] to raise the head; to raise the weight on the steelyard— good weight; to be encouraged.

[20]擡 頭[2]—看 lift up the head and take a look.

擡 頭[2]字 characters which are raised one or two spaces above the column as a mark of distinction.

擡 三 頭[2] or 三 擡 to raise three characters.

擡 雙 頭[2] or 雙 擡 to raise two characters.

擡 頭[2]見 喜 may you see joy when you raise your head!

[25]擡 高 身 價 to put a high value upon oneself.

薹
6019
[2] A kind of sedge. *Cyperus rotundus.* See No. 6016-C. Also *Carex dispalatha*.

薹 菜 or 薹 薹 or 油 菜 rape— *Brassica campestris.*

太
6020
[4] Very, much, too, excessive.

太 不 及 quite insufficient; will not come up to the mark.

太 不 成 話·了 what he said was too outrageous altogether.

太 不 自 愛 altogether lacking in self-respect.

太 乙 the Great Monad from which all things sprang.

[5]太 初 in the beginning; the beginning of all things.

太 古 in very early days; extreme antiquity.

太 和 universal harmony; harmony of the duel powers, *Yin* and *Yang;* the essence of all things.

太 多 too much.

太 好 better than I wish.

[10]太 始 the beginning of form. (*Taoist*).

太 小 too small.

太 少 too few.

太·平 peace; peaceful; the title chosen by the Taiping rebels.

太·平 圈 a life-belt; life-buoy.

[15]太·平 梯 safety ladder.

太·平 洋 the Pacific Ocean.

太·平 洋 會 議 the Pacific Conference.

太·平 衣 safety-jacket; life-belt.

太·平 車 a flat, four-wheeled cart used by farmers in north China.

[20]太·平 錢 coins issued by the Taiping rebels, having the inscription 太·平 天 國.

太·平 門 safety-exit in theatres, etc.

太·平 鼓 a tambourine.

太 息 a heavy sigh.

太 拘 禮 too punctilious.

[25]太 數 the hypothetical or absolute quantity. (*algebra*).

太 早 too early.

太 易 the invisible. (*Taoist*).

太 極 the Absolute—the ultimate principle of Chinese philosophy.

太 極 圖 diagram representing the *Yin* and the *Yang* elements.

[30]太 歲 the planet Jupiter.

太 沖 abstraction, inaction; the harmony resulting from the principle of non-interference.

太 無 禮 too rude altogether.

太 牢 sacrificial animals—the ox, sheep or goat, and the pig.

太 甚 excessive; excessively.

[35]太 白 星 the evening star—Venus.

太 眞 the original substance of which a thing is composed; gold. (*Taoist*).

太 硬 too hard; too firm.

太 空 the sky; the great void.

太 素 the beginning of substance. (*Taoist*).

[40]太 虛 the great void; the universe; illimitable.

太 過 excessive; to be beyond the mark.

太 阿 or 泰 阿 (*o*[1]) name of a famous sword.

太 陰 the moon.

太 陽 the sun.

[45]太·陽 帽 sun helmet.

太·陽 年 the solar year.

太·陽 斑 點 sun spots.

太·陽 穴 the temples.

太·陽 系 the solar system.

[50]太 項 an absolute term. (*algebra*).

↑太 簇 (-*ts'ou*[4]) A.w. 大 簇, 泰 簇, etc. a classical pitch corresponding

in function to D.

(a) A term of respect, used in titles.

太 上 heaven; a title of respect.

太 上 皇 the father of the emperor.

太 上 老 君 a title of Laotzŭ.

太 傅 Assistant Grand Tutor,—*Chou* dynasty.

[5]太 先·生 teacher of one's father; father of one's teacher.

太 公 a great-grandfather; ancestors.

太 卜 chief prognosticator.

太 史 a second-class compiler of the *Hanlin Academy;* one who selects lucky days. [historian.

太 史 公 chief astronomer and
[10]太·后 mother of the emperor.

太 君 your mother.

太 夫 人 mother of an official; your mother. [Mrs.

太·太 wife of an official; a lady;

太 婆 a great-grandmother.

[15]太 子³ or 儲 君 the heir-apparent.

太 子³ 太 保 Senior Guardian of the Heir-Apparent.

太 子³ 少 保 Junior Guardian of the Heir-Apparent.

太 守 a Prefect.

太 宰 President of the former Board of Civil Offices; a chief minister.

[20]太 師 Grand Tutor under the *Chou* dynasty.

太 廟 the Imperial Ancestral Temple.

太 歲 a star god who presides over the year. *See above*—30.

太 爺 your Worship—used in addressing a district magistrate; title of respect to an elderly gentleman.

太·監 a eunuch.

[25]太 祖 the first emperor of a dynasty; oldest ancestor of a clan.

忕 [4]
6021   Extravagant.

汏 [4] **To rinse. To scour. To wash out.**
6022

汏 揀 to sift out and make a choice.

淘 汏 to wash out; to select.

(a) Excessive.

汏 侈 wasteful excess.

泰 [4] Exalted; honourable; extensive; liberal; prosperous.
6023 Extreme.
Inter. 太 No. 6020.

泰 一 or 太 一 *See* 太 No. 6020-4.

泰 初 or 太 初 the origin of all things; primeval.

泰 半 the greater portion.

泰 始 primeval; the beginning of all things.

[5]泰 山 Mt. T'ai in the west of Shantung—the eastern sacred mountain, worshipped as a god.

泰 山 其 頹 乎 the great mountain must crumble—Confucius before his death.

泰 山 壓 卵 to use Mt. T'ai to crush eggs—when the extremely powerful crush the extremely weak, the result is certain.

泰 山 梁 木 said in praise of the good and wise.

泰 山 and 泰 水 terms used in speaking of another man's father-in-law and mother-in-law respectively.

[10]泰 山 石 敢 當 a stone from Mt. T'ai will dare to resist—evil influences; often cut on a stone and let into a wall, or set up on a road opposite the place where a side-street comes in.

泰 山 鴻 毛 a great mountain and goose-down—comparison of extremes in weight.

泰 平 great peace; peaceful.

泰 斗 abbrev. 泰 山 北 斗 Mt. Tai and the Dipper—both are high and looked up to—said in praise of worthy men, notables, etc.

泰 日 days of peace.

[15]泰 東 Japan; the Orient.

泰 清 the sky.

泰 然 calm and composed; dignity.

泰 社 the Imperial family.

泰 而 不 驕 having a dignified ease without being proud.

[20]泰 西 occidental; the Occident.

泰 西 國 European nations; western nations.

泰 運 a good destiny.

泰 遠 the Orient.

泰 適 excellent—health.

---

[25]泰 辰 times of peace.

泰 風 the west wind.

國 泰 民 安 the State is prosperous and the people are in peace.

約 而 爲 泰 straitened and yet affecting to be at ease.

(a) Arrogant. Extravagant.

不 以 爲 泰 is not to be considered extravagant.

今 拜 乎 上 泰 也 now the practice is to bow only after ascending the hall; this is arrogant.

昊 天 泰 憮 (*hu*[1]) (the terrors of) Great Heaven are very excessive.

驕 泰 以 失 之 by pride and extravagance he will fail—in his course.

(b) Used in transliterating.

泰 晤 士 報 the *Times* newspaper.

↑泰 國 Thailand, Siam.

態 [4] **Manner, bearing, behaviour. Policy. Attitude.**
6024 Distinguish 熊 No. 2815.

態·度 behaviour; attitude towards; demeanour.

態·度 之 嫻 雅 refined manners and deportment.

態·度 和 平 a friendly attitude.

態·度 失 當 improper behaviour.
[5]取 反 對·的 態·度 to assume an attitude of opposition.

對 本 會·的 態·度 attitude towards our organization.

清 醒 態·度 a clear, sober attitude.

精 神 態·度 spirit and attitude.

觀 望·的 態·度 a waiting attitude.

[10]飛 行 態·度 attitude of flying.

態 臣 a plausible, flattering statesman.

主 動 態 active voice.

形 態 deportment or bearing.

情 態 sentiment.

[15]感 情·的 狀 態 attitude of mind.

狀 態 posture or attitude.

靜 態 quiet attitude.

體 態 bearing; deportment.

艜 [4] **A long, narrow vessel with two masts.**
6025

艜 公 a fisherman.

TAN. (ㄉㄢ)

丹 [1] A pill. A decoction that confers immortality.
6026

丹 方 an excellent prescription.
仙 丹 the pill or drug of immortality.
靈 丹 an efficacious pill.

(a) Cinnabar. Red.

丹 參 salvia.
丹 墀 the Court; the palace; an open space in a Confucian temple.
丹 娘 a firefly.
丹 家 or 丹 爐 家 alchemists.
[5]丹 心 a sincere heart—lit., a red heart. See 赤 No. 1048-11.
丹 朱 red.
丹 桂 cinnamon.
丹 灶 the pomegranate flower.
丹 田 the pubic region. (Taoist).
[10]丹 田 不 足 his constitution was not strong.
丹 穴 the tropics.
丹 砂 cinnabar.
丹 紅 red.
丹 色 red.
[15]丹 訣 alchemy.
丹 詔 Imperial Decrees—written with the vermilion pencil.
丹 誠 sincere—red-hearted.
丹 鉛 cinnabar and white lead powder—formerly used in revising books, etc.; thus it comes to mean, revision, etc.
丹 青 colours; painting.
[20]丹 青 人 an artist; a painter.
丹 頂 鶴 the crane.
丹 鳥 a firefly.
丹 鳳 the phœnix.
丹 黃 red and yellow—once used for critical notes in the margin of a book.
[25]丹 鼎 an alchemist's crucible.
內 丹 the mental process of sublimation which freed the body from the impurities of earth and made it fit for immortality.
卷 丹 the tiger-lily.
外 丹 the elixir of immortality.
煉 丹 to prepare the elixir of life; to fit oneself for immortality.
[30]紅 丹 red lead.
金 丹 the elixir of gold—the philosopher's stone; the compound by which base metals could be transmuted into gold and immortality conferred.

(b) Used in transliterating.

丹 第 Dante.
丹 麥 Denmark.

聃 聅 [1] Ears without rim.
6027

老 聃 a name for Laotzǔ.

耽 [1] Pendent ears. Addicted to pleasures. Doting.
6028

耽 惑 besotted with excessive indulgence.
耽 酒 besotted with drink.
耽 溺 sunk in pleasure.
耽 習 不 倦 continued study without weariness.
[5]今 日 耽 樂 today I will indulge in pleasure.
士 之 耽 兮 猶 可 說 也 when a gentleman indulges in pleasures of a licentious character, something may still be said for him.
女 之 耽 兮 不 可 說 也 when a woman goes astray nothing can be said for her.
惟 耽 樂 之 從 they only sought after excessive pleasures.
無 與 士 耽 seek no licentious indulgence with a gentleman.

(a) The glare of a tiger. Sometimes written 眈.

虎 視 耽 耽 glaring like a tiger watching its prey—covetous longing.

躭 眈 [1] To delay; to loiter; to hinder. u.f. preceding.
6029

躭 延 to delay; to hinder; to impede; to loiter.
躭 悞 工 夫 to waste time; to impede the execution of work.
躭 擱 to hinder; to delay; to loiter.
躭 時 日 to procrastinate; to waste time.
[5]躭 誤 to delay; to impede; to loiter; to hinder.
躭 誤 不 了 [3]there will be no delay; it will not be neglected.
躭 貸 一 二 make some little allowance.

單 单 [1] Odd, as a number. Single, alone. Only. Simple, as opposed to complex or compound.
6030

單 一 simple—not complex or compound.
單 一 化 simplification.
單 一 神 論 henotheism.
單 丁 one alone; a man without brothers.
[5]單 人 a single person.
單 人 獨 馬 a solitary horseman—alone; single-handed.
單 住 to live alone.
單 位 a unit; a standard, as of weights and measures.
以 個 人 爲 單 位 regard the individual as the unit.
[10]基 本 單 位 fundamental unit.
實 用 單 位 practical unit.
海 關 金 單 位 Customs gold-unit.
絕 對 單 位 absolute unit.
單 個 的 single, as opposed to double.
[15]單 傳 only one descendant.
單 價 the simple price.
單 元 a complete unit, as opposed to a portion or section.
單 刀 直 入 to attack with a single weapon—fearless; independent energy displayed in studies.
單 利 simple interest.
[20]單 動 機 關 single-acting engine.
單 句 a simple sentence.
單 單 的 specially; purposely; for one thing only.
單 夫 雙 妻 a childless couple.
單 套 車 a one-horse cart.
[25]單 子 獨 立 standing utterly alone.
單 層 飛 艇 monoplane. = 82.
單 己 individual.
單 式 教 授 system of teaching in schools where pupils of the same grade or school year are assembled in the same class for single subjects.

單 式 簿 記 single-entry book-keeping.
[30] 單 弱 weak and delicate.
單 心 single-hearted; with a single purpose.
單 性 生 殖 parthenogenesis.
單 性·的 unisexual.
單 思 病 or 相 思 病 love-sickness.
[35] 單 戀 苦 love-sickness.
單 扇 殼 univalve shells.
單 扇 門 a single-leaf door.
單 數 odd numbers; singular number in grammar.
單 料 poor materials.
[40] 單 方 a simple prescription; unilateral.
單 方 契 約 unilateral contract or agreement.
單 日 the odd days of the month.
單 是 but; however; merely.
單 月 the odd months of the year.
[45] 單 本 位 制 single standard; monometallism.
單 果 simple fruits produced from a single flower.
單 根 simple roots. (bot.).
單 桅 single-masted.
單 比 例 simple-proportion. (arith.).
[50] 單 為 especially; only for.
單 獨 or 孤 單 alone; solitary.
單 獨 制 one-man control.
單 獨 國 a simple State, as opposed to a federation of severa States.
單 獨 營 業 a private business, as opposed to a joint-stock company.
[55] 單 獨 行 動 independent action.
單 獨 行·為 unilateral action (legal).
單 瓣 花 single-petalled flowers.
單 瓣 貝 univalve shells.
單 相 思 one-sided thoughts, as in a lovesick person.
[60] 單 科 大 學 single-course college—as a medical college, etc.
單 稅 制 single tax system.
單 稱 判 斷 singular judgement.
單 竭 exhausted.
單 簡 unadulterated; homogeneous; simple, not complex.
[65] 單 級 小 學 校 primary schools where all pupils gather into one class under a single teacher.
單 純 unmixed; unadulterated; absolute; simple.

單 純 人 種 a pure, unmixed race of people.
單 純 化 simplification.
單 純 分 子 a unit; an integer.
[70] 單 純 局 外 中 立 simple neutrality. (legal).
單 純 換 位 simple conversion. (logic).
單 純 概 念 singular concept.
單 純 泉 a pure spring, without minerals.
單 純 贈 與 simple gift without conditions. (legal).
[75] 單 細 胞 動 物 single-cell organism.
單 絲 羅 the finest gauze. [107.
單 綴 語 monosyllable. See below
單 舍 利 別 simple syrup—transliterated.
單 色 畫 monochrome.
[80] 單 花 single flowers.
單 落 solitary; alone.
單 葉 飛 機 monoplane.
單 行 to act alone; independent action.
單 行 (hang²) single file.
[85] 單 行 本 books published singly—as opposed to those published in sets.
單 行 犯 crime committed by a single person.
單 行 章·程 regulations issued independently, as by local officials.
單 襟·的 上 衣 a single-breasted coat.
單 要 to want nothing but....
[90] 單 記 投 票 single balloting, where only one name is voted for.
單 記 法 single-entry—book-keeping.
單 調·的 monotonous.
單 買 一 樣 buy one kind only.
單 走 to go alone.
[95] 單 跪 to kneel on one knee.
單 身 one alone.
單 身 漢 a bachelor.
單 軌 鐵 路 monorail.
單 軟 膏 simple ointment.
[100] 單 辭 statement without proof.
單 金 本 位 制 gold-monometallism. See above—45.
單 鎗 匹 馬 a single horse and a solitary gun—facing danger alone.
單 門 a poor, solitary family.
單 雙 single and double; odd and even.
[105] 單 音 monotone.
單 音 唱 歌 singing in unison.

單 音 字 monosyllable.
單 音 節 語 monosyllabic language.
單 項 式 monomial expression. (math.)
[110] 單 顯 微 鏡 simple microscope.
單 騎 a single horseman riding alone.
單 體 simple substance, composed of one element.
餉 竭 兵 單 insufficient number of troops and lack of supplies.

(a) Unlined, as a garment.

單 寒 or 單·薄 thinly-dressed; poverty-stricken; insufficient.
單 衣·裳 unlined garments.
單 衫 a shirt without lining.

(b) A document. A single sheet of paper. A bill, a cheque.

單·子 a list; a memo; a bill.
開 一 張 單·子 make out a bill or a list.
單 帖 a memo; a bill or list.
單 式 blank forms.
[5] 單 據 receipt; documentary evidence.
單 票 a certificate.
信 用 單 bill of credit.
借 單 a receipt for a loan.
免 稅 單 exemption certificate.
[10] 出 清 單 to show a clear statement of accounts, etc.
出 貨 單 bill of sales; invoice.
匯 單 bill of exchange.
原 貨 憑 單 certificate of origin.
報 死 憑 單 certificate of death.
[15] 存 欠 憑 單 certificate of balance.
失 單 list of missing articles.
帳 目 單 a bill; account of goods sold.
提 (貨) 單 bill of lading.
攬 載 單 bill of lading.
[20] 支 單 order to pay money.
收 單 a receipt; a mate's receipt for cargo.
收 稅 單 duty-paid certificate.
有 病 憑 單 doctor's certificate of illness.
棧 單 warehouse warrant.
[25] 無 病 憑 單 bill of health.
生 產 憑 單 certificate of birth.
總 單 cargo certificate.
菜 單 bill of fare. 被 單 sheets.
裝 載 單 bill of lading.
[30] 貨 單 an invoice.
開 具 清 單 to draw up a clear statement.

(c) Read *ch'an²*. Name of a chief of the Huns. A chieftain.

單 閼 the years of the cycle which have 卯 in them.
單 于 a chieftain; a Khan.

(d) Read *shan⁴*. A surname.

憚 ⁴ To dread; to shrink from; to shirk.
6031

憚 勞 dislike to taking trouble.
憚 煩 dislike to taking trouble.
過 則 無 憚 改 if you have faults, do not fear to correct them.

殫 ¹ The utmost; entirely; quite.
6032

殫 力 with the whole energy.
殫 思 極 慮 deeply meditated upon it.
殫 悶 suffocated—as in a fit.
殫 殘 to destroy.
⁵殫 洽 thoroughly investigated.
殫 究 to make a thorough investigation.
殫 竭 exhausted; used up.
殫 精 with all one's energies.
殫 褚 the purse is empty.
¹⁰耗 思 殫 神 used all his energies upon it.

癉 ⁴ Disease arising from overwork. Wearied. To afflict; to be distressed. Severe.
6033

癉 疽 a malignant ulcer.
下 民 卒 癉 the masses are put to distress.
彰 善 癉 惡 distinguishing the good, so as to make it ill for the evil.

(a) Inter. 疸 No. 6040. Biliousness.

黃 癉 jaundice.

(b) Read *tan¹*.

火 癉 a disease of children, described as feverishness with red spots and patches.

簞 ¹ A small basket for holding cooked rice. A hat-box.
6034

簞 瓢 屢 空 the baskets and gourds were repeatedly empty —in famine.

一 簞 食 a single dish of food— very poor.

襌 ¹ A garment without a lining. Single.
6035 Distinguish 禪 No. 5650.

鄲 ¹ Name of a place.
6036

邯 鄲 a district in Hopei—Chihli. *See No.* 2036.

旦 ⁴ The morning; the dawn. See 卿 No. 1155-B.3.
6037

旦 不 保 夕 in the morning not able to guarantee the evening— not to know what a day may bring forth; in imminent danger.
旦 夕 morning and evening.
旦 夕 且 死 death was imminent.
旦 夕 之 間 between the morning and the evening; during the day.
⁵旦 夕 可 至 it can be reached in a day.
旦 夕 間 耳 imminent; between dawn and sunset.
危 在 旦 夕 the danger is imminent.
旦 日 tomorrow.
旦 旦 every morning. *See below* —A.
¹⁰旦 明 just at dawn.
旦 晚 morning and evening.
旦 暮 morning and evening; imminent—illustrates the passage of time.
旦 望 1st and 15th of the lunar month.
旦 氣 the air of the early morning.
¹⁵旦 晝 the forenoon.
一 旦 one morning; suddenly.
一 旦 分 離 sudden separation.
元 旦 New Year's Day.
坐 以 待 旦 to sit and wait for the dawn.
²⁰始 旦 just dawn.
平 旦 at dawn.
穀 旦 a lucky day.
自 夜 達 旦 from night till early morning.
自 旦 及 昏 from dawn till evening—all day long.

(a) Clearly.

信 誓 旦 旦 clearly were we sworn to good faith.
昊 天 曰 旦 High Heaven is intelligent.

(b) An actor who personates female parts.

小 旦 an actor who takes the part of young females.
旦 兒 or 旦 角 actors who personate females.
花 旦 female personators.

(c) Used in transliterating.

震 旦 ancient Buddhist name for China—said to be derived from 秦 *Ch'in* and *suan*—land, the land of *Ch'in*.

但 ⁴ But; only; merely. Yet; still. Singly.
6038

但 不 知 but I do not know.
但 不 過 not more than; merely.
但 係 the fact is; except that; but.
但 其 notwithstanding.
⁵但 凡 whoever; whatever; all; whenever; however.
但 則 but.
但 取 眼 前 福 only seeking the happiness of the present moment.
但 只 not only so; but.
但 只 恨 I only regret that...
¹⁰但 坐 不 妨 you may as well sit down.
但 憑 天 理 不 信 地 理 only trust in Divine justice, put no faith in geomancy.
但·是 but; the fact is that; except that.
但·是 有 一 件 or 但 還 有 一 件 .... but there is one thing ....; it must be borne in mind that....
但 求 塞 責 only seeking to evade responsibility.
¹⁵但 特 無 匹 without a mate.
但 知 其 一 I only know one point.
但 託 空 言 it was all mere talk.
但 說 不 怕 come, speak out boldly.
但 願 a formula expressive desire—Oh that! etc.

²⁰但 願 如 此 would that it might be so.

不 但 如 此 not only so....

(a) Used in transliterating.

但 以 理 Daniel.

但 以 里 電 池 Daniell's cells.

↑但 丁 Dante.

担³ To brush off; to dust. A duster. Inter. 撢 No. 6062-A, and 撣 No. 6073-B.

6039

担 一 担 give it a dusting.

担 塵 to brush off the dust—to welcome a returning traveller. See No. 328-11.

担·子 a feather duster.

担·担 衣·服 to dust clothes.

⁵担 撢·子 a duster made of strips of cloth fastened to a handle.

担 灰 to dust.

(a) Inter. 擔 No. 6044. To carry, etc.

疸⁴ Disorders of the stomach, liver, etc. Also read *tan*³.

6040

女 勞 疸 chlorosis.

胃 疸 to have a feeling of hunger after eating to the full.

酒 疸 disease of the liver from alcoholism.

黃 疸 jaundice.

鴠⁴ A kind of nightingale.

6041

儋¹ A small jar. Read *tan*⁴. To bear a burden. A load of two *piculs*.

6042 Inter. 擔 No. 6044.

憺⁴ Tranquil; easy; satisfied.

6043

憺 然 ... 欲 satisfied, having few desires.

(a) 　　　　To stir; to move.

憺 乎 鄰 國 stirred up the neighbouring States.

憺 畏 fearful; afraid.

擔¹ To carry with a pole over the shoulder (by one person). To take responsibility; to undertake; to sustain.

6044

擔·上·來 to take up—as a burden.

擔·不·動 cannot carry it—on the pole over the shoulder.

擔 不 是 to bear the blame.

擔·不 起 unequal to the burden.

⁵擔 事 or 問 事 to undertake to do a thing; to bear responsibility.

擔 代 to take upon oneself to do.

擔·任 to bear; to take responsibility; to put up with.

擔 任 義·務 to shoulder one's responsibilities; to give assistance.

擔 任 補 助 to undertake to give assistance.

¹⁰擔 保 to go bail for; to insure; to be responsible for.

擔 保 人 a guarantee.

擔 保 信 託 公 司 guaranty trust company.

擔 保 品 security.

附 屬 擔 保 品 collateral security.

¹⁵擔 架 牀 stretcher

↑擔 架 兵 stretcher-bearers.

擔·待 to put up with; to bear with.

擔 待·不 起 cannot put up with; cannot bear.

擔·得 起 擔·不 起 can you take the responsibility?

擔 心 or 操 心 to be anxious.

²⁰擔 心 事 a matter for which one bears responsibility; a weighty affair; to be worried over anything.

擔 心 害 怕 anxious and alarmed.

擔 憂 to bear sorrow; to be grieved.

擔 擔 (*tan*⁴)·子 to carry a burden.

擔 是 不 擔 錯 to accept the credit and repudiate the blame.

²⁵擔 水 to carry water.

擔 當 to bear; to take responsibility for; to put up with.

擔 當 不 起 unable to take the responsibility; cannot endure.

擔 當 罪 名 to bear the guilt; to become involved in the guilt.

擔 盤 the betrothal presents.

³⁰擔 荷 or 擔 承 to undertake; to shoulder a responsibility.

擔 處·分 to undertake responsibility.

擔 說 to rely on the statements of others.

擔 負 to bear; to sustain. See below—A. 5.

擔 負 責·任 to bear responsibility.

³⁵擔 賣 商 a pedlar.

擔·這·個 箱·子 carry this box.

擔 遲 不 擔 錯 risk being blamed for delay rather than be blamed for mistakes.

擔 錯 to bear the blame.

擔·閣 to delay; to hinder. See 耽 No. 6029-3.

⁴⁰擔 險 to brave danger; to run the risk.

擔 風 to endure the hardships of the weather.

擔 驚 to be alarmed.

(a) Read *tan*⁴. A burden or load. A *picul*.

擔 任 responsibility. See above —7ff.

擔·子 a load; a burden.

擔 杆 a carrying-pole used by coolies.

擔 荷 responsibility. See above—30.

⁵擔·負 liability; responsibility. See above—33.

重 擔 a heavy burden.

扁·擔 a carrying-pole used by coolies.

澹⁴ Tranquil; placid.

6045

澹 容 a placid countenance.

澹 泊 爲 德 (regards) tranquility of heart as virtue.

澹 泊 自 如 frugal and contented; quiet in mind with few desires.

澹 漠 dispassionate; placid; calm.

澹 雅 quiet and refined.

(a) Similar to 淡 No. 6053. Insipid, watery, etc.

澹 味 flavorless; insipid.

澹 澹 colourless; light-coloured.

(b) Agitation, as of water.

澹 心 disturbed in mind.

澹 淡 (*yen*⁴) rushing away of waters.

隨 風 澹 淡 tossed by the wind.

(c) Read *t'an*².

澹 臺 a double-surname.

(d) Read *tan*[1].

澹 林 name of an ancient tribe.

礜[3] A silicate substance from
6046 the salt-wells in Szechwan; it
is used as a wash for hardening plaster, etc., also for
certain skin diseases, like
ringworm.

石 礜 or 石 礬 sulphate of copper.

膽[3]
胆] The gall, said to be the
seat of courage. Bravery.
6047

膽 作 膽 爲 daring; not afraid to
tackle difficulty.

膽 力 courage.

膽 喪 魂 消 at the wit's end
through fright.

膽 囊 the gall-bladder. *See below*
—28.

[5]膽 壯 brave; fearless.

膽 大 心 小 brave but cautious.

膽 大 於 身 his gall-bladder is
greater than his body—of great
courage.

膽·子 or 膽 兒 courage.

放 開 膽·子 to pluck up cour-
age.

[10] 沒 有 膽·子 without courage;
craven.

膽 寒 lacking in courage; fearful.

膽 志 moral courage; determination.

膽 怯 fearful.

膽 戰 to tremble with fear.

[15]膽 戰 心 驚 in terror.

膽 敢 to have the audacity.

膽 氣 courage; bravery.

膽 水 bile.

膽 液 質 choleric; bilious temperа-
ment.

[20]膽 玩 to venture to trifle with.

膽 瓶 a vase having a straight neck
and a bulging belly—like a
suspended gall-bladder.

膽 生 毛 his gall grows hairs—
dauntless, audacious.

膽 畧 bravery and resource.

膽 石 biliary calculus.

[25]膽 破 to burst the gall-bladder—
from fear.

膽 礬 sulphate of copper. *See*
No. 6046.

膽 管 the bile-duct.

膽 胞 the gall-bladder. *See above*
—4.

膽 落 or 喪 膽 courage failing;
white-livered.

[30]膽 虛 craven; courage failing;
white-livered.

膽 識 intelligent and determined.

膽·量 courage.

膽·量 小 or 膽ₙ小 timid; fearful.

膽 青 bile.

[35]嘗 膽 to taste gall—to nurse vengeance. *See No.* 229-9.

壯·着 膽ₙor 伏·着 膽ₙto pluck up
courage.

肝 膽 liver and gall—dependent
upon each other.

亶[3]
6048　Sincere; real; true.

亶 不 聰 you have indeed acted
without discrimination.

亶 候 多 藏 all of them indeed of
great wealth.

亶 其 然 乎 will you not find it
really so?

[5]亶 時 in its due season—of the
fragrance of sacrifices.

亶 父 *Tan Fu*—the progenitor of
the House of *Chou*, 14th cent.
B.C.

亶 翔 wheeling and soaring—of
birds flying together.

不 實 于 亶 you have no reality
in your sincerity.

勯[1]
6049　Exhausted.

蛋[4]
蜑]　An egg.
6050

蛋 卵 eggs.

蛋 坊 or 蛋 行 (*hang*[2]) an egg
merchant's business.

蛋 壳 兒 the shell of an egg.

蛋 清 the white of an egg.

[5]蛋 白 the white of an egg.

蛋 白 石 opal.

蛋 白 石 光 opalescence.

蛋 白 質 albumen.

蛋 黃 the yolk of an egg.

[10]地 蛋 used in some places for
the potato.

壞 蛋 or 渾 蛋 a bad egg—term
of abuse.

生 蛋 or 下 蛋 to lay an egg.

皮 蛋 or 變 蛋 eggs preserved in
lime.

鷄 蛋 hen's eggs.

[15]鹹 蛋 salted eggs.

(a) Name of a southern tribe.

蛋 人 or 蛋 戶 the boat-people of
Canton.

蛋 家 or 蛋 民 the Tanka or
boat-people of Canton—they
have been excluded from public
examinations, and are under
social disabilities similar to
those of the 小 戶 of Chehkiang
and South Anhwei.

誕[4]
誔] A birthday. To bear
children.
6051

誕 子 to bear a son.

誕 日 or 誕 時 or 生 誕 a birthday.

誕 育 to nourish; to bring up.

誕 辰 or 壽 誕 a birthday.

[5]聖 誕 the birthday of a god.

五 瘟 聖 誕 birthday of a
Taoist priest who died in
battle.

孔 子 先 師 聖 誕 birthday
of Confucius—27th of the
8th lunar month.

玉 皇 上 帝 聖 誕 birthday
of *Yühwang*, a Taoist
deity—9th of the 1st lunar
month.

齊 天 大 聖 誕 the birthday
of a Buddha, originally
an ape.

↑ 耶 穌 聖 誕 Christmas.

(a) To extend. To make great.
To increase. To be widely
separated.

誕 以 爾 衆 士 by the powerful
help of you, all my officials.

誕 厭 逸 increase his indolent
luxury.

誕 告 萬 方 to proclaim far and
wide.

誕 大 to extend; to enlarge.

[5]誕 敢 紀 其 敘 greatly dares to
take in hand its *broken* line.

誕 敷 文 德 diffusing his accomplishments and virtue more widely.

誕 膺 天 命 received the great decree of Heaven—to rule.

誕 闓 to extend; to enlarge.

何 誕 之 節 how wide apart *are now* its joints—said of a creeper.

[10]汝 誕 勸 憂 you greatly encourage one another in what must prove to be your sorrow.

(b) **Boastful talk. To brag. Disorderly.**

誕 妄 to talk extravagantly.

旣 誕 and become quite disorderly.

放 誕 to boast.

(c) **An initial particle.**

誕 先 登 于 岸 so h e grandly ascended, before others, the heights—of virtue.

誕 實 匍 匐 when he was able to crawl.

誕 彌 厥 月 when she had fulfilled her months.

啖 啗 啖 }　3.4.
To eat; to chew; to bite. To entice; to lure.
6052

啖 以 利 乎 can he entice him by gain?

淡 [4] **Insipid; tasteless; flavour-less. Weak, as liquids. Light**
6053 **in colour. Dull, of trade. Lonely.**

淡 墨 light ink—not well rubbed up on the slab.

淡 如 水 as insipid as water.

君 子 之 交 淡 如 水 there is no familiarity i n t h e friendship of the superior man.

淡 妝 濃 抹 either plainly dressed or richly attired—she looks well.

[5]淡 定 indifferent.

淡 容 a placid countenance; impassive expression.

淡 得 狠 very insipid; utterly lacking interest.

淡 心 indifferent.

淡 愁 slight grief.

[10]淡 掃 蛾 眉 lightly pencil in the moth eyebrows.

淡 描 to sketch.

淡 收 poor receipts—in business.

淡 月 a pale moon.

淡 氣 nitrogen.

[15]淡 水 fresh water. Tamsui—a port in the north of Formosa.

淡 水 湖 fresh-water lakes.

淡 沱 on the waves, flowing with the stream.

淡 泉 fresh-water spring.

淡 泊 dispassionate; calm; indifferent; frugal, content with little.

[20]淡 泊 主 義 Stoicism. Indifferentism.

淡 淡 清 霜 a light, clear frost.

潰 淡 淡 flowing full and quietly.

淡 漠 calm; nonchalant; without passion; stranger to a person.

淡 漠 態 度 an air of nonchalance.

[25]淡 潔 clear and pure.

淡 碧 a pale, greenish colour.

淡 竹 a kind of bamboo, useful for making things; the shoots are e d i b l e. *Phyllostachys puberula.*

淡 紅 light red; pink.

淡 色 a light colour.

[30]淡 菜 dried mussels.

淡 薄 insipid; profitless; tasteless; poor.

淡 酒 weak wine.

淡 雅 quiet and refined.

淡 靄 light mists.

[35]淡 青 plain blue.

淡 食 粗 衣 simple f o o d and coarse clothing.

淡 飯 poor food.

淡 黃 玉 topaz.

先 淡 喫 first eat some plain rice.

[40]冷 淡 cold; indifferent; dull, as trade.

(a) **Read** *yen*[4]. *See* 澹 No. 6045-B.2.

T'AN.　　　(ㄊㄢ)

探 [1]　**To try; to tempt; to essay.**
6054

探 囊 取 物 (as easy as) feeling for things in a bag.

探 天 之 威 bring upon yourselves the wrath of Heaven.

探 湯 to thrust the hand into boiling water—something to be dreaded.

探 虎 口 to tempt Providence.

探 賾 索 隱 to investigate t h e hidden mysteries of things.

(a) **Read** *t'an*[4]. **To spy; to search out; to inquire after.**

探 一 個 確 信 get some authentic information.

探 一 探 make inquiries.

探 伺 to spy; to be on the watch.

探 信 to inquire; to seek information about.

[5]探 先 beforehand; in anticipation.

探 前 in anticipation; beforehand.

探 友 to ask after or visit friends.

探 問 to inquire about; to pick up information.

探 喪 to inquire about mourning ceremonies.

[10]探 報 to find out and report.

探 子 a spy.

探 察 to examine into; to explore; to search out.

探 差 a spy; a confidential messenger. (-*ch'ai*[1])

探 悉 to ascertain.

[15]探 悉 敵 情 to reconnoitre.

探 抉 遯 隱 to make a thorough investigation of hidden things.

探 捕 detectives and policemen.

探 探 口 氣 to ascertain a person's opinions or feelings.

探 春 to go into the country for an excursion in the early spring.

[20]探 望 to interview; to visit.

探 本 to make a fundamental investigation.

探 檢 to explore. *See below*—44. (*Jap.*).

探 水 to take soundings.

探 求 to seek; to search into; to look into.

[25]探 海 燈 a searchlight.

探 深 淺 to sound; to take soundings.

探 測 to measure; to survey; to ascertain the depth—as of a well or spring.

探 病 to inquire after a sick person.

探 看 seeking out.

[30]探 知 to ascertain.

探 究 to make a thorough investigation.

探 端 知 緒 investigate the beginning and you will know the end.

探 聞 to ascertain.

探·聽 虛 實 verify the facts by inquiry.

35 探·花 title of the third graduate on the list at the finals for the *Hanlin Academy*.

探·花 紅 a name for the *lichi*.

探 見 電 燈 electric torch. *See* 閃 No. 5638-5.

探 親 to visit one's parents.

探 訪 to inquire about; to pick up information.

40 探 訪 員 a reporter.

探 試 or 試 探 to essay; to experiment.

探 討 or 探 詢 or 打 探 to inquire about; to pick up information.

探 身 to stretch forward.

探 險 to explore; to make an adventure; venturesome.

45 探 險 家 explorers; discoverers.

探 險 隊 exploration party.

探 馬 a spy.

探 騎 mounted spy.

探 驪 得 珠 under the black dragon's *jaws* he obtained a pearl—his composition expounded the very essence of the theme; he grasped the point of the theme.

50 探 闔 to draw lots; to play a game by drawing out a lot; to judge, by any occurrence, the feasibility or otherwise of any propsal.

偵 探 a detective.

報 探 軍 情 to spy and report on military matters.

洞 探 to make a clear discovery.

貪 ¹ To covet; to desire. Avaricious. Name of a beast
6055 painted on the wall outside a *yamen,* as a warning against avariciousness.

貪 人 敗 類 the covetous man injures his fellows.

貪 便·宜 折²大 本 being covetous of petty advantages, one loses large profits. (-*shê²*-)

貪 利 keen for gain; avaricious.

貪 前 eager to be first.

5 貪 叨 addicted to.

貪 吏 grasping officials.

貪 吃 gluttonous.

貪 名 greedy for fame.

貪 客 covetous; avaricious.

10 貪 嘴 gluttonous.

貪·圖 to seek after; to scheme for.

貪 墨 to covet booty; grasping.

貪 多 務 得 insatiable covetousness.

貪 多 嚼 不 爛 desirous of much but unable to make use of it— "bite off more than one can chew."

15 貪 天 之 功 爲 己 功 he desires to take the merit that belongs to Heaven as his own.

貪 婪 covetous; avaricious.

貪 婪 成 性 extortion becomes a second nature.

貪 官 汚 吏 avaricious government officials, and grasping underlings.

貪 小 失 大 by petty meanness he lost a great—battle. *S. above*-2.

20 貪 得²無 厭 insatiable greed.

貪 心 covetousness.

貪 心 不 足 insatiable—used in abuse.

貪 心 狠 very covetous indeed.

貪 情 greediness; covetous desires; desirous of getting at the facts of a matter.

25 貪 愛 or 貪 想 or 貪 慾 to be fond of; to long for; to desire.

貪 懶 seeking only for ease; lazy and greedy.

貪 戀 to hanker after; lustful.

貪 望 to long for; to desire.

貪 樂 given to pleasure. (-*lê⁴*)

30 貪 求 無 厭 insatiable.

貪 汚 avaricious.

貪 泉 a spring, to drink the water of which was supposed to make even good men covetous.

貪 泥 女 色 familiar with women; given to debauchery.

貪 淫 好 色 debauched; viciously sensual.

35 貪 爵 慕 位 coveting rank and office.

貪 玩 fond of play.

貪 生 怕 死 clinging to life.

貪 睡 fond of sleep.

貪 紅 塵 desirous for the things of time and sense; worldly.

40 貪 羨 to be fond of; to long for; to desire.

貪 色⁴ given to sexual indulgence

貪 財 covetous for wealth.

貪 財 害 命 to lose the life in desire for wealth.

貪 賕 or 貪 賄 covetous; grasping.

45 貪 賕 枉 法 to pervert justice for a bribe.

貪 賕 賣 法 corruption and bribery—of government officials.

貪 酒 addicted to alcoholic liquors.

貪 酷 avaricious and cruel.

貪·頭 the object of desire.

50 貪 食 好 (*hao⁴*) 酒 gluttonous and drunken.

貪 食 醉 酒 gluttonous and drunken.

貪 饕 greedy; gluttonous.

圮 ¹ To fall into ruins; to collapse.
6056

圮·了 半 截 one face of the wall has fallen—of walls that are only faced with brick.

圮·了 堤 has broken down the dike.

圮 倒³ to collapse—as a building.

圮 塌 to fall into ruins.

↑ 圮 台 disgraceful failure.

坦 ³ Level; smooth. Satisfied: peaceful.
6057 Distinguish 垣 No. 7724.

坦 夷 peaceful and quiet; at ease.

坦 平·的 路 a level road.

坦 然 自 若 self-possessed.

坦 腹 or 坦 婚 a son-in-law.

5 坦 蕩 蕩 contented and composed.

坦 途 a level road.

舒 坦 comfortable; easy.

(a) To lay bare. Open.

坦 然 無 懼 boldly; without fear.

坦 然 無 疑 confidently; without suspicion.

坦 率 frank; straightforward.

坦 白·的 說·出·來 s p o k e out quite freely without any reserve.

坦 直 open and straightforward.

(b) Used in transliterating.

坦 克 tanks; armoured land-ships.

袒 ³ To lay bare; to strip;
禤 to throw off garments. Bared; naked.
6058

祖兔 (*wên*⁴) mourning worn for three months—to bare the left shoulder and take off the head-dress, wearing a white band in the hair.

祖左祖右 to throw off every-thing.

祖幘 in undress.

祖服 partially to slip off a garment.

⁵祖縛 to bare the shoulder and bind the arms behind—token of submission.

祖而示之背 he stripped and showed his back.

祖膊 to bare the shoulder.

祖裼裸裎 with naked arms and exposed body.

祖裸 naked.

¹⁰右祖 to bare the right shoulder—in punishment.

左祖 to bare the left shoulder—in ancient ceremonies of mourning, etc.

肉祖 half-naked, with bared back.

(a) To screen.

祖庇 to give improper protection to; to screen.

祖縱 to give license to and screen—subordinates.

祖護 or 偏祖 to give improper protection to; to screen.

壇坛 } An altar, generally of earth. An arena. An examination hall.
6059

壇塲 an arena.

壇墠樹木 altars and groves.

元壇 Taoist altar.

地壇 the Altar to Earth.

⁵天壇 the Altar to Heaven.

文壇 examination hall.

築壇 to build an altar of earth.

花壇 a flower-bed.

設壇 to prepare the altar for sacrifice.

醮壇 altar for masses for souls in purgatory.

檀 ² A hard, tough wood; san-dalwood.
6060

檀色 a reddish-brown.

檀越 the benefactors of a convent; an alms-giver—from Sanskrit:—*dânapati*.

檀香山 Honolulu.

檀香木 common sandalwood.

檀香爐 a censer.

紫檀木 red sandalwood.

覃 ² Enduring; extensive; vast; long; prolonged.
6061   This character is the correct way of writing the phonetics of Nos. 6062-67.

覃及鬼方 extends to foreign countries—from the *Odes*.

覃恩 great graces; to grant an amnesty.

實覃實訏 his cry was long and loud.

葛之覃兮 how the dolichos spread itself out!

(a) Read *yen*¹. Sharp.

以我覃耜 we take our sharp plough-shares.

撢 ³·⁴ To feel for with the hand. u.f. 探 No. 6054.
6062

撢人 ancient official under the *Chou* dynasty, who was appointed to inform the feudal States of the Imperial mandates.

撢攘 to scratch—of animals.

(a) Read *tan*³. To dust, u.f. 擔 No. 6039.

撢帚 or 撢子 a feather duster.

潭 ² Deep; vast. A pool or lake.
6063

潭府 your house—your secluded and extensive residence.

屓潭之府 a deep pool.

潭潭府中居 dwelling in an extensive, secluded house.

潭恩下逮 his great kindness reached to the lowest.

潭水 deep water.

潭第 your house—*See above*—1.

↑潭吉 regards to your family.

(a) Name of a river in Hunan.

潭州 a name for Changsha, Hunan.

(b) Read *yen*².

浚潭 absorbed in; devoted to—as music.

燂 ² To dry at the fire; to scorch; to burn; to heat.
6064   Also read *hsien*².

燂水 to heat water.

燂湯請浴 heat water and ask *her mother-in-law* to have a bath—a dutiful wife was expected to do this once every five days.

燂船 to burn off the barnacles, etc., from the bottom of a boat.

(a) Also read *hsün* or *hsin*². To scald; to heat anything.

禫 ³ Sacrifice offered at the close of the period of three years mourning for parents.
6065

禫服 to lay aside mourning apparel.

譚 ² To boast. Extravagant. Inter. 談 No. 6078.
6066

參譚不絕 continuing without cessation.

老生常譚 the common talk of an old scholar.

(a) Name of a small feudal State lying to the east of the present Tsinanfu in Shantung.

譚公維私 the viscount of *T'an*, also her brother-in-law.

醰 ² Bitter taste in wine. Rich; full flavoured.
6067

醰粹 pure and excellent.

良醰醰而有味 good and rich flavoured.

曇 ² Dark clouds.
6068

罎罈壜 } An earthenware jar; a jug.
6069

酒罎子 a jar for wine—a toper.

蕁[2] **The nettle.**
6070
蕁麻 a variety of nettle.
蕁麻疹 urticaria.

嘽[1] **To snort.**
6071
嘽嘽駱馬 "They panted and snorted, the white steeds black-maned."

(a) **Numerous.**
徒御嘽嘽 numerous were his war-chariots and footmen.
戎車嘽嘽 numerous were his war-chariots.
王旅嘽嘽 numerous were the royal legions.

彈[2] **To play on stringed instruments. To snap the fingers.**
6072
彈冠 to fillip one's cap—to remove the dust—preparing for official life.
彈唱 to play and sing.
彈墨 to sprinkle with ink; figured in black.
彈墨線 to strike a line with an inky string—as a carpenter does.
5彈奏 to play; to strike up the strings.
彈指 to snap the fingers; to fillip.
彈指須臾 during the snapping of the fingers—a very brief space of time.
彈染 to dye by sprinkling.
彈棉·花 to bow cotton and make it fluffy.
10彈琴 or 搊琴 to play the harp, organ, piano, etc.
彈琵·琶 to play the guitar.
彈瘡 to open an ulcer or boil.
彈空說嘴 boastful talk.
彈粉·線 to strike a line with a string and white powder, as Chinese tailors do.
15彈絃·子 to play the three-stringed lute.
彈絲竹 to play musical instruments.
彈詞 to put stories into rhyme for singing; having a spoken part and musical accompaniment.
彈鋏而歌 tapping the hilt of his sword and singing—poor, but waiting for an opportunity to advance in life. *See* No. 770-2.

(a) **To rebound.**
彈·出·去 bounced away.
彈力 tension; force of elasticity.
彈力性 elasticity.
彈回 rebound; recoil, as of a bow-string.
5彈·子臺 a spring-balance.
彈性 elasticity.
彈性軟骨 elastic cartilage.
彈條 springs.
彈條秤 hanging spring-balance.
10彈機 springs.
彈簧 springs.
匝線彈簧 spiral springs.
螺狀彈簧 volute springs.
彈簧圈 a spring-ring.
15彈簧夾鉗 a spring-clip.
彈限 limit of elasticity.

(b) **To press down; to accuse.**
彈劾(案) impeachment.
彈劾權 power of impeachment.
彈劾訴訟 official accusation.
彈壓 or 鎮壓 to press down; to repress.
5彈文 an impeachment.
彈章 an impeachment.
彈糾 to bring charges against; to accuse.
彈違 to repress those who rebel.

(c) **Read** *tan*[4]. **A bullet; a pellet; a shot or shell; a pill; a cross-bow.**
彈丸 a pill.
彈丸之地 a small piece of ground; a little country.
彈°子[3] a bullet.
彈°子[3]房 billiard-saloon.
5彈°子[3]臺 billiard-table.
彈殼 cartridges.
彈界 range of a shot or shell.
彈藥 ammunition.
彈雨 a hail of bullets.
10手榴彈 hand-grenade.
榴彈 or 榴霰彈 shrapnel. *See* 開 No. 3204-143.
炸彈 a bomb.
鉛彈 leaden bullets.

撣[3] **To grasp. To hit against. To butt.**
6073
動撣 to shake; to move.

(a) u.f. 禪 *shan*[4]. **To abdicate.**
堯舜撣讓 *Yao* and *Shun* abdicated.

(b) **Read** *tan*[3]. **To dust. See 担 No. 6039.**

(c) **Read** *t'an*[2]. **Name of a country on the Irrawady River, beyond the eastern frontiers of the present Burma.**

忐[3] **Timorous; nervous.**
6074
忐忑 vacillating; timid.

(a) **Read** *k'en*[3].
心心忐忑 (*tao*[4]) most sincere and earnest.

毯[3] **Rugs; carpets.**
6075
毯·子 a rug or carpet.

痰[2] **Phlegm.**
6076
痰喘 asthma.
痰堵·住嗓·子·了 phlegm has blocked the windpipe.
痰壅 the death-rattle.
痰·氣 asthma.
5痰涎 spittle; phlegm.
痰瘀 choked by phlegm.
痰盂 or 痰盒 a spittoon.
痰罐 a spittoon.
化痰藥 expectorants.
10吐痰 to expectorate.

菼[3] **A rush or sedge.**
6077
葭菼 rushes and sedges.

談[2] **To chat; to converse.**
6078
談何容易 how easy to talk about it!—how difficult to achieve.

談 公 事 to discuss business matters.

談 兵 to discuss military matters

談 判 an informal conference; to confer; negotiations.

⁵新 商 約 之 談 判 negotiations for a new commercial treaty.

談 助 matter for conversation.

談 及 talking about....

談 叢 or 談 藪 a collection of conversations.

談 吐 to discuss; to talk.

¹⁰談 吐 風 生 light, bright, interesting talk.

談 天 chatting about things in general.

談 天 論 地 to talk on all kinds of subjects.

談 宗 one skilful at discussion, who is trusted by all.

談 客 person with the gift of speech—a mediator.

¹⁵談 屑 ceaseless chatter—falling like the sawdust from the movement of the saw.

談 心 to converse; tête-à-tête.

談 政 to talk politics.

談 柄 a topic of conversation.

談 次 in the course of conversation.

²⁰談 空 or 空 談 to spin yarns.

談 空 說 有 discussing the formless and the real—philosophizing; from discussing the two forms of Buddhism, 空 and 有.

談 笑 to laugh and talk; to tell jokes.

談 笑 封 侯 enobled for telling a joke—rank easily obtained.

談 虎 變 色 speaking of tigers makes one pale—nervous fears make things seem real.

²⁵談 言 微 中 to use an expression which hits the mark.

談 話 an interview—as by a reporter.

談 話 影 片 "talkies," moving pictures with talking = 7533.158½

談 話 會 a conversazione.

談 講 or 談 論 or 談 談 to discuss; to chat; to converse.

³⁰談 鋒 vigorous, voluble speech.

交 談 conversation.

妄 談 senseless talk.

常 談 common talk.

虛 談 empty talking; mere talk.

³⁵街 談 巷 語 common talk on the street.

鄉 談 local patois.

閒 談 idle gossip.

高 談 loud-voiced talk.

鄒² (6079) Name of a small ancient principality which was situated in what is now part of Shantung and Kiangsu.

餤² (6080) To advance; to increase.

亂 是 用 餤 disorders are thereby increased.

(a) A cake; a bait.

餤 餌 a bait; temptation.

餅 餤 a meat-cake.

歎⁴ / 嘆⁴ (6081) To sigh; to lament.

歎 一 口 氣 to heave a sigh.

歎 不 出 氣 來 unable to get one's breath.

歎 息 to sigh.

歎 惜 sighing with regret.

⁵歎 氣 to sigh.

歎 美 or 歎 羨 or 讚 歎 to admire and praise; to commend.

歎 美 辭 expression of admiration.

歎 辭 an interjection; a phrase implying regret.

歎 道 he said, with a sigh....

¹⁰可 歎 Alas! How sad!

悲 歎 to mourn and lament.

攤¹ (6082) To open and spread out, as for sale. To apportion; to divide amongst; to distribute. A stall or mat on which goods are displayed for sale.

攤 償 to make a composition with creditors.

攤 分 (fēn⁴) to pay a share; to divide up—money.

攤 子 or 攤 兒 a street stall.

攤 手 攤 脚 to gesticulate; to throw the arms and legs about.

⁵攤 派 to assess; to rate proportionately; to apportion.

攤 繳 to pay by instalments.

攤 賠 to pay equal shares; to make up a loss by assessments.

攤 還 to pay by instalments.

攤 錢 to divide money; to allot money; to share.

¹⁰攤 開 to spread out; to unfold.

攤 館 a gambling den.

公 攤 to pay equal shares.

擺 攤 to spread out goods for sale.

賣 攤 to put on a stake in a gambling game.

灘 / 潬¹ (6083) A rapid. A sand-bank; a foreshore.

灘 師 or 放 灘 的 a pilot through the rapids.

灘 頭 小 調 songs of the boatmen.

坭 灘 a mud-bank.

沙 灘 a sand-bank.

癱¹ (6084) Palsy; paralysis.

癱 子 a paralytic.

癱 手 癱 脚 palsied hands and feet.

癱 瘓 paralytic.

癱 瘋 病 paralysis.

偏 癱 partial paralysis.

炭⁴ (6085) Charcoal. Coal. Carbon (A.w. 碳).

炭 化 作 用 carbonization process.

炭 化 器 carburettor.

炭 化 物 carbides.

炭 化 輕 hydrocarbons.

⁵炭 坑 coal-pit.

炭 塼 briquettes for fuel.

炭 層 coal-seam.

炭 氣 carbon dioxide.

炭 水 化 合 質 carbo-hydrates.

¹⁰炭 火 a charcoal fire.

炭 灰 or 碎 炭 charcoal ashes.

炭 田 coal-fields.

炭 畫 charcoal drawings.

炭 筆 a charcoal pencil for drawing.

¹⁵炭 精 pure carbon.

炭 精 紙 carbon-paper for manifolding.

炭紙 carbon-tissue for carbon prints. (*photo.*).

炭紙曬相法 carbon-process of photography.

炭結 small cakes of compressed charcoal used in footstoves, etc.

²⁰炭質 carbon.

炭質發話器 carbon transmitter.

炭酸鹽 carbonates.

炭酸鈉 sodium carbonate.

炭酸鉀 potassium carbonate.

²⁵炭養氣 carbonic acid gas.

二炭贏質 ethylene gas.

木炭 charcoal.

桴炭 soft charcoal.

煤炭 coal.

醃
膽 } ³ Brine from pickled meat; condiments.

6086

醃膽 the brine of pickled minced meat.

髣 ³ Hair hanging down over the forehead.

6086a

TANG. (ㄉㄤ)

當 ¹ Ought; should; must. Suitable; correct.

6087

當務之急 a pressing obligation; earnest about what is of greatest importance.

當斷不斷 to neglect what should be decided; to be hesitant when decision is needed.

當如後患何 what future misery have they and ought they to endure—who talk of the failings of others.

當死的罪 offence punishable with death.

⁵當然 natural; self-evident; should; ought.

當然之理 a self-evident principle; what ought to be, according to the nature of things; right.

理所當然 it is quite reasonable; only as it should be.

當眞 in good earnest. *See below* —F. 17.

當自照辦 must necessarily take

---

action accordingly.

¹⁰當道 the right path. Cf. A. 27, H. 3.

不相當 out of place; not fitting.

應當 fitting; proper; ought; should.

正當 exactly what should be.

相當 suitable; matching each other.

¹⁵該當 ought to; should.

(a) To undertake. To act as. To fill an office. To occupy a position. To be equal to.

當不了 or 當不得 not competent to.

當不起 unequal to the responsibility; unable to endure.

當中人 to act as middleman.

當事 to have the management of.

⁵當事者 the person or party concerned *(legal)*; the manager or head of.

當仁不讓 make virtue your burden.

當兵 to be a soldier.

當國 to rule a State.

當地方 the head of a tithing.

¹⁰當夕 to take her turn as a concubine.

當大事 to manage the great business—a parent's funeral.

當娼 to be a prostitute.

當官 the officer or magistrate in charge. *See below*—B. 11.

當家 to be the head of; to take charge of; to oversee; to keep up a household.

¹⁵當家的 the head of the family; my husband.

當局 the person responsible for the matter; the authorities. *See below*—B. 12, 13.

中國當局 the Chinese authorities.

當差 to be employed as messengers or runners. (-*ch'ai*¹).

當差使 employed in government business. (-*ch'ai*¹-).

²⁰當得起 able to assume responsibility.

當月 to take one month's duty—as an official.

當權 to exercise authority.

當番 to act as magistrate in turn.

當直 or 當值 to take one's turn on duty.

²⁵當路於齊 have the ordering of the government in *Ch'i*.

當軸 one on whom the business turns—the officials in charge.

當道 the responsible officials; the authorities. *See below*—H. 3.

當選 to be elected.

當選人 candidates for election.

³⁰當選者 the elected person. *(legal)*.

當關 a door-keeper; to guard a pass.

不敢當 I dare not venture to—occupy such a high place, or undertake such responsibility, etc., a conventional reply—"You do me too much honour."

勾當 to intrigue; to act in secret. *See* No. 3409-10.

擔當 to take responsibility for.

³⁵難當 hard to bear; not easy to manage.

(b) In the presence of. At the place. In. At.

當中 in the midst.

當人前 before others.

當先 in front. *See below*—D. 5.

當口 a juncture; a space between two objects; an interval; a gap.

⁵當地 on the spot; at the place in question.

當堂 in open court; publicly; formally.

當堂畫押 sign before the magistrate, or before any official.

當場 on the spot.

當場被獲 caught on the spot.

¹⁰當天 out of doors; in the open. *See below*—D. 10,—F. 5.

當官 in the presence of the magistrate or official. *See above*—A. 13.

當局者迷 when it is one's turn to move, one is easily confused—as in chess.

當局者 a participant.

當暑 hot weather.

¹⁵當洒掃 in sprinkling and sweeping the ground.

當爐 before the fire—to get warm; to sell wine.

當衆 or 當着衆人 in the presence of all.

當衆宣布 bring it before the public.

當眼 before the eyes; in full view.

²⁰當着百姓 before the people.

當街 in the streets; abroad.

當 面 in the presence of; face to face.

當 面 言 明 it was agreed at a personal interview that..; it was clearly stated in the presence of...

當 面 說 謊 to lie to one's face.

²⁵當 陽 on the throne; in the sun.

當 頭 right overhead.

當 頭 棒 喝 to tap a person on the head with a stick and make him cry out—a Buddhist phrase:—a man sitting in meditation asked a question when speaking was forbidden; he was rapped on the head for it and cried out; he asked a second and a third time before he realized his mistake—used to express:—to arouse a person from his stupidity.

罪 當 朕 躬 弗 敢 自 赦 the evil that is in myself, I dare not forgive.

(c) To match.

文 王 何 可 當 也 How can King *Wên* be matched?

(d) A temporal particle—then, at that time.

當 下 at the time; then.

當 世 the present age; now.

當 代 now; that period; the present age.

當 今 at present; now.

⁵當 先 formerly. *See above*—B. 3.

當 其 盛 時 at their most flourishing period; when they were at their best.

當 初 in the beginning.

當 卽 thereupon; at once.

當 夜 that night.

¹⁰當 天 the day in question. *See above*—B. 10, *below*—F. 5.

當 始 in the beginning.

當 尚 未 ... 之 時 before....; previous to....

當 已 at that time; when; in due course.

當 年 years ago. *See below*—F 7.

¹⁵當 日 in those days; in the day when; the said day; up to date *See below*—F. 10.

當 日 立 契 on the day the deed is executed...

當 時 at the time in question. *See below*—F. 12.

當 經 I have thereupon; thereupon I....

當 茲 at present; now.

(e) To withstand.

彼 惡 敢 當 我 哉 "How dare he withstand me?"

(f) Read *tang*⁴. To treat as; to regard as; thus:—to pawn. A pledge. To represent; to stand in the place of.

當 作 to use one thing as the equivalent of another; to represent; to regard as; to consider as being.

當 作 上 帝 make himself equal with God.

當 個 成 字 講 it has the same meaning as the character *ch'êng*.

當 十 the equivalent of ten—as ten-cash coppers.

⁵當 天 in one day; on the same day. *See above*—B. 10,—D. 10.

當 店 a legal pawn-office.

當 年 this year. *See above*—D. 14.

當 心 Take care!

當 成 to treat as.

¹⁰當 日 on the same day. *See above*—D. 15.

當 日 不 能 回 來 you cannot return the same day.

當 時 now, at once, immediately. *See above*—D. 17.

當 本 the amount advanced on a pledge.

當 爲 無 事 to make light of; to regard it as nothing.

¹⁵當 物 something pawned.

當 當 to put something in pawn.

當 眞 的 麼 is it a fact? is it really true? *See above*—8.

當 票 a pawn-ticket.

當 稅 pawn-office license fees.

²⁰當 耍 的 to regard as a mere plaything—trifling.

當 耳 旁 風 to look upon it as a wind blowing past the ear—as of no importance; in one ear and out of the other.

當 舖 a legal pawn-office.

當 衣 裳 to pawn garments.

當 頑 意 兒 to regard as a mere plaything; trifling.

²⁵當 頭 or 押 頭 a pledge. *See above*—B. 26.

上 當 to fall into a trap; to be taken in.

只 當 merely regard as; to pretend to.

贖 當 to redeem a pledge.

錢 不 當 事 money is not regarded as anything.

(g) Read *tang*⁴. Fitting, just, right.

不 當 unfair; improper.

四 時 當 the seasons are in proper sequence.

失 當 improper.

甚 當 quite in keeping; very proper.

⁵的 當 proper; right.

穩 當 settled; firm; solidly placed.

(h) Read *tang*³. To ward off. *See next*.

當 煞 to ward off noxious influences.

當 路 to bar the way. *See above*—A. 25.

當 道 to bar the way. *See above*—A. 27.

擋 攩 攪 ³　To resist; to ward off; to oppose. To stop; to impede.

6088

擋 不 住 cannot resist them.

擋 住 to prevent; to stop effectually.

擋 眼 to obstruct one's view.

擋 路 to obstruct the road; to rob on the highway.

⁵擋 頭 陣 the vanguard.

擋 風 to keep off the wind.

擋 駕 to stop the carriage—of a visitor; to decline to receive; "not at home."

攔 擋 to hinder.

阻 擋 to hinder; to oppose.

檔 檔 ⁴　A cross-piece, as the round of a ladder, the rail of a chair. Shelves; pigeon-holes.

6089

檔 冊 records; archives.
檔 卷 archives.
檔 房 the registry department—of a Board.
檔 案 to put away among the records of cases; archives; files.

(a) u.f. 當 No. 6087-F.26. A snare.

璫[1] Pendant ornaments. Earrings. A name for eunuchs in the *Latter Han* dynasty.
6090

襠[1] Breeches; trousers; the seat of a pair of trousers.
6091

輈[1] Vertical pegs of wood, used to keep the axle-tree of a cart in its place.
6092

鐺[1] Small gong struck by pedlars; the sound of a gong. A lock.
6093

鐺 戶 those who evaporate salt. (*ancient*).
鐺 鐺 the sound made by striking a gong.
鋃 鐺 an iron chain; a lock or clasp; tinkling.

(a) Read *ch'êng*[1]. A vessel with feet, used for warming wine.

茶 鐺 vessel for keeping tea warm.
藥 鐺 a vessel for warming medicines.

党[3] Ancient family name. u.f. next.
6094

黨[3] A village of 500 families. A clique, a faction, a gang, a party, an association— anciently regarded as always in opposition to the government.
6095

黨 之 訓練 the disciplines and training of a party.
黨 人 member of the same party.
黨 化 to make conform to the propaganda and platform of a party.
黨 化 敎·育 education in the platform of a party.

[5]黨 友 member of a party.
黨 同 伐 異 unite with those of the same ideas and punish those who differ.
黨 員 member of a party.
黨 員 充 當 filled by members of the party.
黨 國 party government, esp. the nation under the government of the Nationalist Party.
[10]黨 國 人 員 the Nationalist Party and government officials.
黨 德 party spirit.
黨 惡 to associate with evil men.
黨 朋 adherents; mutual helpers.
黨 正 a headman or village elder.
[15]黨 治 國 one-party government.
黨。派 parties; cliques; factions.
黨。派 問題 problem of parties.
黨 爭 party strife.
黨 禁 a proscribed party.
[20]黨 禍 political intrigue.
黨 策 policy of a party.
黨 籍 party register.
黨 綱 platform of a party.
黨 義 party principles.
[25]黨 羽 adherents; partisans.
黨 與 members of the same party.
黨 見 party views.
黨 費 party expenses.
黨 部 Local Councils of the Nationalist Party.
[30]黨 錮 proscribed party.
黨 附 to side with; to join with.
黨 類 a class; a species.
黨 魁 leader of a party.
君 子 不 黨 the man of complete virtue is not partisan.
[35]結 黨 to form cliques or parties.

(a) Used as a suffix to indicate a party, association, clique, etc. The illustrations are given alphabetically.

無 政 府 黨 Anarchists.
過 激 黨 Bolshevists. Cf. 5364. B2.
守 舊 黨 Conservative Party.
憲 政 黨 Constitutional Party.
[5]民 主 黨 Democratic Party.
父 黨 母 黨 father's and mother's families.
騎 墙 黨 Independent Party—railsitters.
工 黨 Labour Party.
自 由 黨 Liberal Party.
[10]漸 進 黨 Liberal Party.
宗 社 黨 Royalist Party.

國 民 黨 Nationalist Party.
虛 無 黨 Nihilists.
反 對 黨 Opposition Party.
[15]在 野 黨 Party out of office.
和 平 黨 Peace Party.
民 黨 People's Party.
政 黨 Political Parties.
進 步 黨 Progressive Party.
↑共 產 黨 Communist Party
[20]急 進 黨 Radical Party.
維 新 黨 Reform Party.
共 和 黨 Republican Party.
革 命 黨 Revolutionary Party.
叛 黨 Revolutionary factions.
[25]賊 黨 Robbers or brigands in bands.
社 會 黨 Socialist Party.
保 皇 黨 Tory Party.
統 一 黨 Union Party.

(b) u.f. next. Counsel, etc.

黨 論 counsels; remonstrance.

讜[3.4] Counsels; advice; remonstrance.
6096

讜 論 remonstrances; counsels.

盪[4] To move; to disturb.
6097

盪 激 to agitate; to disturb.
八 卦 相 盪 the Eight Diagrams act and react upon each other.
動 盪 血 脈 it stirs the pulses— speaking of music.
推 盪 interacting influences—as of the elements.
跳 盪 troops sent to throw the enemy into disorder before the actual battle commences.
震 盪 to startle.
震 盪 播 越 driven abroad in terror and agitation.

(a) Great.

廓 盪 盪 其 亡 雙 vast, great and matchless—of Heaven and Earth.

(b) To allay.

盪 意 平 心 to compose the thoughts and quiet the mind.

(c) Vain, empty.

求 之 盪 盪 besought him in vain —like grasping the wind.

(d) To withstand; to resist.

盪 寒 to keep out the cold.

盪 風 to keep out the wind—by taking a stiff dram.

(e) Read *t'ang*[1]. **To propel a boat over dry land. To row.** Older char. for 6113.

盪 槳 to row.

盪 舟 to propel a boat by hand — rowing.

盪 船 to propel a boat; to row.

(f) Also read *t'ang*[4]. **A bathing tub. To cleanse.**

盪 垢 滌 瑕 to reform.

盪 口 to rinse the mouth.

盪 盤 a bath-tub.

盪 碗 to rinse bowls, etc.

滌 盪 to scour; to rinse.

(g) A tailor's chalk-line.

盪·子 a chalk marking-line.

蕩 [4]
6098
Vast. Large. Magnificent.

蕩 蕩 上 帝 How vast is God!

蕩 蕩 乎 How vast!

蕩 蕩 懷 山 襄 陵 in their vast extent they embrace the mountains and overtop the hills —of vast floods.

(a) Easy and plain. Level. Broad and long. Peaceful.

君 子[3] 坦 蕩 然 the superior man is peaceful and composed.

王 道 蕩 蕩 the royal road is broad and long.

魯 道 有 蕩 the way to *Lu* is easy and plain.

(b) Unsettled; vagrant. Dissipated. Licentious. Reckless.

蕩 婦 a dissolute woman.

蕩 子[3] a profligate; a vagrant.

蕩 志 to dissipate and becloud the mind.

蕩 意 a reckless air.

[5]蕩 析 離 居 dispersed and obliged to leave their homes.

蕩 檢 踰 閑 to violate rules and overstep all bounds.

以 蕩 陵 德 they became dissolute and did violence to virtue.

今 之 狂 也 蕩 the ardour of the present day shows itself in wild license.

其 蔽 也 蕩 the beclouding here, leads to a dissolute mind.

[10]放 蕩 heedless; careless; dissipated; dissolute.

浪 蕩 idle and vagrant.

(c) To squander. To waste. To destroy.

蕩 失 lost; squandered.

蕩 寇 to destroy rebels.

蕩 平 to reduce rebels to submission.

蕩 沒 submerged.

[5]蕩 然 無 存 all spent; wasted entirely.

蕩 為 灰 燼 reduced to ashes.

蕩 產 to squander one's inheritance.

蕩 盡 to waste; to exhaust.

掃 蕩 to destroy; to make a clean sweep—of rebels.

[10]焚 蕩 to destroy by fire.

(d) Agitated; disturbed.

蕩 懸 unsettled, in suspense.

蕩 漾 the rippling of water.

以 惑 上 心 蕩 disturbed the mind of the emperor.

心 蕩 agitated in mind; unsettled.

(e) To cleanse.

蕩 天 下 之 陰 事 purifying everything that belonged to the feminine sphere throughout the kingdom.

蕩 滌 其 邪 穢 to purge away his depravity.

(f) Read *tang*[3]. **To drain.**

以 溝 蕩 水 to drain off water by ditches.

(g) Read *t'ang*[1]. **Ancient name of a river in S. W. Chihli. (Hopei.)**

(h) Read *t'ang*[1]. **To move backwards and forwards as in rowing.**

碭 [4]
6099
A brilliantly coloured stone with veins running through it. To overflow. To exceed.

碭 溢 to overflow.

宕 [4]
6100
A covered way; a passage. Inter. 蕩 No. 6098.

宕 子[3] a vagrant.

宕 戶 a person who runs a bad debt. *See below*-A.

宕 渠 name of a river; a mountain in E. Szechwan.

宕 管 an overseer—as in a spinning mill.

[5]宕 賬 bad debts.

延 宕 to put off—as payment of accounts.

懸 宕 in suspense.

拖 宕 to put a thing off.

推 宕 to expatiate.

[10]放 宕 dissolute; profligate.

跌 宕 to speak recklessly; to vary one's style.

(a) A stone quarry. A cave dwelling.

宕 戶 a worker in a stone quarry.

T'ANG.   (ㄊㄤ)

湯 [1]
6101
Hot water; soup; gravy. To scald; to heat.

湯 傷 a scald.

湯 兜 a soup-tureen. 湯 兒 juice.

湯 匙 a soup-spoon.(-*ch'ih*[2]) ⌊gravy

湯 圓 or 湯 團 dumplings.

[5]湯 引 vehicle for a drug—supposed to guide it to the affected organs.

湯 池 hot springs; a hot-water moat—impregnable city. *See* 金 No. 1057—A. 4.

湯 沐 a hot bath.

湯 泉 hot springs.

↑湯 婆·子 a metal hot-water bottle.

[10]湯 澆 雪 (like) hot water poured upon snow—it soon melts; fig., something easily done.

無 義 錢 財 湯 潑 雪 ill-gotten wealth is but snow sprinkled with hot water— soon gone.

湯 碟 or 湯 盤 soup-plates.

湯 肉 soup-meat.

湯 藥 medicine in draught—as opposed to pills or powders.

[15]湯 鑊 a large cauldron used in ancient times for boiling to death.

湯 頭 ingredients in a prescription.

湯 餅 flat dumplings.

湯 餅 筵 a feast formerly given

on the third day after the birth of a child.

湯 麪 noodles in soup.

[20]清 湯 clear soup.

熬 湯 to boil soup.

熱 湯 hot water; hot soup.

牛 肉 湯 beef tea.

赴 湯 蹈 火 to go through hot water and fire—to suffer for another.

(a) Dissipated. u.f. 蕩 No. 6098.

子 之 湯 兮 How dissipated you are!

(b) Founder of the *Shang* Dynasty. 1766 B.C.

湯 孫 之 緖 such was the fitting achievement of the descendants of *T'ang*.

湯 有 天 下 *T'ang* being in possession of the kingdom.

天 乃 佑 命 成 湯 Heaven favoured and charged *T'ang* the Successful.

於 赫 湯 孫 O majestic is the descendant of *T'ang*!

(c) Read *shang*[1]. **Waves in motion. Appearance of water in flood.**

湯 湯 洪 水 方 割 destructive in their overflow are the waters of the great inundation.

其 流 湯 湯 roll on in their swollen flood.

淇 水 湯 湯 the full waters of the *Ch'i*.

燙 [4] To scald. To heat by placing in hot water.
6102

燙 一 燙 heat it up.

燙 了 泡 兒 raised a blister by scalding.

燙 人 it scalds!

燙 手 to scald the hand.

[5]燙 滾 scalding hot.

燙 炸 了 cracked by heat.

燙 藥 to make a decoction of medicines.

燙 蠟 to fill cracks with wax.

燙 酒 to heat wine in hot water.

電(機)燙(髮)permanent wave.

(a) **To smooth. To iron.**

燙 斗 a chafing-dish; a flat-iron.

燙 衣 服 to iron clothes.

錫 [4]　A plane. To smooth.
6103

趯 [1] To wade; to get the feet wet.
6104

趯 一 脚 的 泥 I waded in mud as deep as my foot.

趯 半 身 的 水 to wade waist-deep.

趯 渾 之 泉 a spring fouled by trampling.

趯 濕 了 wet through wading.

趯 過 去 to wade across.

踼 [3] To fall flat. To fall on the face.
6105　Distinguish 踢 No. 6264. Also read *tang*[4].

踼 倒[3] 了 stumbled and fell flat.

跌 踼 to stumble and fall; irregular—as the time of music; reckless; heedless.

倘
儻 [3]　If; supposing; in the event of.
6106

倘 其 不 願 if he be unwilling.

倘 如 supposing; if; should it be.

倘 或 supposing; if.

倘 或 可 得 if it can be obtained.

[5]倘 敢 if they venture to.

倘 有 in the event of; supposing that.

倘 然 不 行 if it will not do; if it cannot be.

倘 能 if possible; if one can.

倘 若 supposing; should it be; if.

[10]倘 遇 in the event of; supposing that.

(a) **Unforeseen. Accidental.**

儻 來 之 物 things that come unexpectedly.

儻 儻 vacillating; nervous; agitated.

儻 蕩 不 備 careless and unprepared.

堂 [2] A hall; a reception room; a meeting-place. A court
6107　of justice.

堂 上 your parents; magistrates.

上 堂 to appear before the court.

堂 下 at a court or office.

下 堂 to take one's seat on the bench as a magistrate.

[5]堂 中 in the hall.

堂 伯 叔 father's male first cousins of the same surname.

堂 倌 a waiter in a restaurant or tea-shop.

堂 兄 弟 or 堂 姊 妹 male and female first cousins on the father's side.

堂 判 the finding of the court; order of the court.

[10]堂 前 before the court; the main hall of the house.

堂 印 the seal of a prime minister.

堂 口 ability to plead a case in court.

堂 名 the family-hall name—usually consisting of two characters followed by 堂; the name given in Kiangsu and Chehkiang to a band of musicians, from the above.

堂 唱 the singing, etc., of singing-girls.

[15]堂 坳 hollows; lowlying places.

堂 塗 the path from the hall to the entrance gate.

堂 奥 the innermost recess of the home—profound.

堂 子 a bath-house; a waiter. Manchu place of sacrifice.

堂 官 Presidents and Vice-Presidents of the Six Boards and of the superior Courts; the authorities. (*obs*.).

[20]堂 客 a lady; female guests or visitors.

堂 屋 a hall; the middle room of a Chinese house.

堂 廉 the sides of a hall.

堂 廡 the side rooms of a hall.

堂 族 relatives of the same surname but not of the same generation.

[25]堂 會 to get famous actors for a performance. Presbyterian Session.

堂 構 to carry on a father's inheritance. See 肯 No. 3334-4.

堂 牓 the tablet bearing an inscription with the name of the hall.

堂 票 a warrant.

堂 諭 an order of court; a judgement.

[30]堂 費 legal expenses.
堂 選 appointed as prime minister.
堂 限 limited time for appeal.
堂 除 steps down from the hall; to be made a prime minister.
堂 鞫 to have a hearing of a case.
[35]令 堂 your mother.
佛 堂 Buddhist shrine.
升 堂 to take a seat on the bench as judge.
善 堂 benevolent institution.
坐 堂 to sit as a magistrate.
[40]大 堂 or 公 堂 the principal hall in a *yamen*.
拜 堂 the worship of the bride and bridegroom in the hall.
敎 堂 a mission station; a church.
朝 (*ch'ao*[2]) 堂 the audience chamber.
正 堂 title of a district magistrate.
[45]浴 堂 a bath-house.
父 母 在 堂 both parents living.
玉 堂 the *Hanlin Academy*.
當 堂 publicly; in open court.
祠 堂 an ancestral hall.
[50]福 音 堂 a mission station; preaching chapel.
禮 拜 堂 a place of worship; a church building.
講 堂 a lecture hall; a place for preaching.
退 堂 to retire from the bench— at the end of a sitting.
過 堂 to have a hearing of a case.

(a) Venerable; grave.

堂 堂 乎 grave and dignified.
堂 皇 dignified bearing; spacious; polite.

(b) An open level space on the hills.

有 紀 有 堂 there are nooks and open glades.

膛[2] Fat. The swelling belly of a jar. The capacity of a vessel.
6108

膛 口 the mouth of; the muzzle.
膛 子 大 it has a great capacity.
上 膛 the roof of the mouth.
淚 膛 the space just below the eye.
胸 膛 the breast; the pit of the stomach.
開 膛 to remove the entrails.

螳[2]　The mantis.
6109

螳 斧 the mandibles of the mantis.
螳 臂 當 車 the mantis would try to stop a chariot with its feelers —fig., great rage and puny strength.
螳 螂 the praying mantis.
螳 螂 捕 蟬 不 知 黃 雀 在 後 the mantis seized the cicada, not knowing that the oriole was just behind it—warning against covetousness.

鏜[1]　Noise of drums; other loud booming noises.
6110

棠[2]　The crab-apple. The wild plum.
6111

棠 梨 *Pyrus assuriensis; pyrus betulaefolia.*
棠 棣 *Prunus japonica.*
棠 陰 the shade of the pear. *See below*—7.
海 棠 *Pryus spectabilis.*
秋 海 棠 *Begonia evansiana.*
甘 棠 a wild, sweet pear.
甘 棠 之 意 love for the tree under which 召 伯 lodged— used to illustrate a fondness for ancient relics.

淌[3]　To flow; to drip.
6112

淌 出 水 來 the water is leaking out.
淌 水 to drip; to leak.
淌 汗 dripping with perspiration.
淌 溝 an eaves-gutter; a water-channel.
淌 眼 淚 to shed tears.

(a) Read *ch'ang*[4]. Great waves; billows.

趟[4]　A time; an occasion. See 輄 No. 6115.
6113

去 過 幾 趟 I have been there several times.

躺[3]　To lie down; to recline.
6114

躺 下 to fall flat; down.
躺 在 床 上 to lie on a bed.

躺 椅 子 a lounge.
躺 箱 a long box for clothing.
躺 臥 or 躺 著 to recline.
躺 躺 歇 歇 lie down and rest awhile.

輄[4]　An axle.
6115

輄 軸 an axle.

(a) A time, a turn; an occasion. A row; a ruled line.

一 輄 字 a column of characters.
一 輄 瓦 a row of tiles.
走 了 一 輄 went once.

(b) A track for training horses to gallop.

輄 兒 的 馬 a horse trained by military students to gallop at full speed without guidance, so that both hands of the rider were free for archery.

唐[2]　Name of a dynasty.
6116
　　　　　　　[(Cantonese)
唐 人 the men of *T'ang*—Chinese.
唐 國 an ancient State in the south-west of the present Chihli —Hopei.　　[(Cantonese)
唐 山 the hills of *T'ang*—China.
唐 朝 the *T'ang* dynasty—A.D. 618 —907.
唐 詩 poems of the *T'ang* dynasty.
唐 話 Chinese language. (*Cantonese*)

(a) Name of the Emperor *Yao*.

唐 虞 之 世 the halcyon days of *Yao* and *Shun*—the Golden Age.
唐 皇 great—from the name of *Yao*, coupled with *huang* for the *Han* dynasty.

(b) Hasty; bold; rude. Boastful.

唐 突 abrupt; unceremonious.
唐 花 or 堂 花 flowers, the opening of which has been hastened by heat.

(c) The path from the entrance gate of a temple to the raised platform, or to the main hall.

中 唐 有 甓 the middle path of the temple is covered with its tiles.

(d) Dodder.

唐 蒙 dodder.

爰 采 唐 矣 I am going to gather the dodder.

(e) A tree called the sparrow-plum or aspen-plum, identified as *Prunus japonica* or *Amelanchier asiatica*.

唐 棣 之 華 偏 其 反 而 the flowers of the aspen-plum quiver and turn over.

(f) u.f. next. A dike, etc.

唐 堤 an embankment.

(g) Used in names.

唐 古 忒 Tangut.

塘 2 A square pool; a pond; a tank. A bund; an embank-
6117 ment.

海 塘 a sea-wall.
蓮 塘 a lotus-pond.
魚 塘 a fish-pond.

搪 偪 2 To ward off; to parry; to keep out, as wind, rain, or cold.
6118

搪·不 住 風 cannot keep out the wind.

搪·不 過 去 unable to parry.

搪·他 幾 天 put him off a few days.

搪 塞 to evade; to put off; to decline politely; to perform duties perfunctorily; to do as little as possible.

藉 端 搪 塞 to bring forward as an excuse.

搪 拖 or 搪 抵 to evade; to postpone; to impose upon by false promises.

搪 突 or 唐 突 unceremoniously; impudently.

搪 賬 to evade the payment of debts.

溏 2 A pool. Free, not con-
6119 gealed.

便 溏 not constipated.

煻 2 To warm; to toast.
6120

糖 煨 to warm before the fire.
糖 煨 池 an inflammable spring in the north of Liao-tung.

糖 餹 2 Sugar; sugared; candy. Crystallized sweetmeats.
6121

糖 人 兒 sugar men—given to children.

糖 尿 病 diabetes. *See* 渴 No. 3401-7.

糖 果 preserved, crystallized fruits.

糖 楓 the sugar-maple.
糖 水 molasses; syrup.
糖 汁 syrup.
糖 漿 syrup. 糖 精 saccharin.
糖 瓜 sugared melons.
糖 薑 preserved ginger.
糖 蘿·葡 sugar-beet.
糖 醯 molasses; syrup.
糖 霜 crystallized sugar.
糖 食 sweetmeats.
糖 餅 sugared cakes.
冰 糖 clear, rock-candy.
塊 糖 loaf-sugar.
蜜 糖 honey.
沙 糖 granulated sugar.
白 糖 white, cane-sugar.
精 糖 refined sugar.
紅 糖 or 赤 糖 brown sugar.
蔗 糖 cane-sugar.

螗 2 A kind of cicada.
6122

帑 3 A treasury.
6123

帑 藏 a treasury.

(a) Read *nu*[2]. Children of a legal wife. u.f. 孥 No. 4756.

樂 爾 妻 帑 rejoice in your wife and children.

TAO.　　(ㄉ幺)

刀 刂 1 A knife; a sword; a razor. Radical 18. National Phonetic letter for *t*, written ㄉ. Distinguish 力 No. 3920.
6124

刀 俎 魚 肉 fish and flesh for the sacrificial vessels—used of the oppression by government officials.

刀 兵 swords and soldiers—military troubles; war.

刀 刃 儿 the edge of a knife or sword.

刀 劍 swords.
刀 口 the edge of a knife.
刀 口 鈍 the edge is dull.

刀 圭 ancient small measure for medicines—a pinch.

刀 墨 tattooing—an ancient punishment.

刀 尖 the point of a knife.

刀 尺 scissors and rule—a tailor's implements.

刀 山 劍 樹 hills of knives and forests of swords—difficult to get through.

刀 布 ancient coins shaped like a knife.

刀 把 儿 handle of a knife or sword.

刀 斧 手 an executioner.

刀 柄 the handle of a knife.

刀 棒 swords and staves.

刀 沒 有 口 the knife is dull.

刀 無 鋼 an untempered sword.

刀 筆 ancient writing-instruments —a knife for erasing and a stylus for inscribing upon bamboo tablets.

刀 筆 先 生 a writer of indictments. 刀·蠅 the mantis.

刀·筆 吏 scribes, clerks who draw up indictments, etc.

刀 背 the back of a knife.

刀 豆 a large kind of French-bean. *Canavalia ensiformis.*

刀 身 blade of a knife or sword.

刀 鋒 the point of a sword.

刀 錢 ancient coins shaped like a knife.

刀 錐 petty profits.

刀 鎗 棍 棒 swords, spears, staves, and cudgels.

刀 鞘 a scabbard; a sheath.

刀 頭 to return—from :—

何 當 大 刀 頭 when will you return—a sword has a ring, 環, on the hilt; this character has the same sound as 還, to return.

刀 頭 蜜 or 刀 上 蜜 honey on the edge of a knife—he who licks it will cut his tongue; used to illustrate the danger of greed or lust.

刀 魚 the mullet.
一 把 刀 a knife or sword.
³⁵兩 面 刀 a two-edged sword—two-faced.
切 肉 刀 a carving-knife.
刮 刀 a scraper.
刻 字 刀 engraver's tool.
剃 刀 a razor.
⁴⁰剪 刀 scissors. = 剪子.
割 肉 刀 a chopper.
單 刀 a broad sword.
大 刀 a long-handled sword.
尖 刀 a dagger.
⁴⁵屠 刀 a chopper.
洋 刀 a pocket-knife; a table-knife.
腰 刀 a dagger.
舞 刀 fencing; sword-juggling, etc.
菜 刀 a kitchen-chopper.
⁵⁰鎗 頭 刀 a bayonet. = 刺刀.
鐮 刀 a sickle; reaping hook.

(a) A quire, or one hundred sheets of paper.

(b) A small, narrow boat.

曾 不 容 刀 it would not admit a small boat.

忉¹ Grieved; distressed in mind.
6125

忉 恒 grieved; distressed.
勞 心 忉 忉 your toiling heart will be grieved.

(a) Used in transliterating.

忉 利 天 one of the 33 heavens of Buddhism—the paradise of a city of pure gold.

魛¹ The mullet.
6126

壔² A mound, a tumulus.
6127

幬⁴ The canopy of heaven; the sky. Also read t'ao².
6128

無 不 覆 幬 there is nothing which it does not cover.

(a) Also read ch'ou². A curtain; a canopy.

素 幬 a plain curtain for a carriage.

懤³ Grieved, pained. Also read ch'ou².
6129

懤 恨 不 釋 my grief and rage have not been put away.

禱
禂｝ To pray. Prayer.
6130

禱 切 to pray earnestly that...
禱·告 to pray.
禱·告 文 a form of prayer.
禱·告 會 a prayer-meeting.
⁵公 衆 禱·告 public prayer.
私 室 禱·告 private prayer.
默 禱·告 silent prayer.
禱 念 to pray; to read prayers.
禱 文 form of prayer; prayers.
¹⁰主 禱 文 The Lord's Prayer.
早 禱 文 Morning Prayer—matins.
晚 禱 文 Evening Prayer—evensong.
禱 祝 to pray.
禱 神 不 效 prayers to the gods were ineffectual.
¹⁵禱 者 悔 過 遷 善 以 祈 神 之 佑 也 to pray is to repent and reform in order to beseech the protection of the gods.
是 禱 this is my prayer or request—phrase closing a letter asking for a favour. A c. 爲禱.
當 殺 人 以 禱 a man must be offered as a sacrifice with our prayers.

島³ An island in the sea.
6131

島 國 an island kingdom.
島 夷 barbarians; islanders.
島 嶼 large and small islands.
島 民 islanders.
牛 島 a peninsula.
南 海 島 South Sea Islands.
羣 島 archipelago.

搗
擣｝ To beat; to pound; to ram down. To attack.
6132

搗 亂 to throw into confusion; to cause a disturbance.
搗 亂 份 子 one who gives trouble; a disturbing element.
搗 出 汁 pound out the juice.
搗 到 作 紙 make into pulp for paper.
⁵搗 實 to beat down solidly.
搗 爛 to pound to a pulp.
搗 白 to gossip; to chat.
搗 碎 to pound to pieces; to smash to fragments by pounding.
搗 碓 to pound—as when hulling rice.
¹⁰搗 米 to hull rice in a mortar.
搗 絲 to wind silk.
搗 翻 to pound to pieces; to thwart.
搗 藥 to pound drugs.
搗 虛 to make a surprise attack.
¹⁵搗 衣 to beat clothes when washing them.
搗 鬼 to pound the devil—to play tricks.
怒 焉 如 搗 I think till I feel as if pounded all over.

(a) Close, dense.

上 有 搗 蓍 above were the thickly growing divining-stalks.

到⁴ To arrive at; to reach; to attain to; to go to. To (a place).
6133

到·不 了 unable to reach; no getting there.
到·不 了 底 it will not reach the bottom.
到 了 having arrived; reached.
到 了 任 to arrive at an official post.
⁵到 了 兒 in the end; after all.
到·了·沒·有 has he arrived?
到 來 to arrive at; to receive.
華 水 捕 到 來 the Chinese river police came on the scene.
到 口 to reach port.
¹⁰到 塲 to be present at.
到 境 to arrive in the jurisdiction of....

到 如·今 until now.
到 家 to reach home; f u l l y; thoroughly; "at home" in anything.
沒 有 做·到 家 not done at all well.
15 說·到 家 drove the argument home.
釘 打·到 家 drive the nail well home.
到 底 after all; in the end; to the bottom.
到 底 怎·麼 樣 how will it turn out after all? what are the facts of the matter?
到·得 until; on arriving; when; as soon as.
20 到 手 to come to hand.
到 日 付 清 to be paid in full at the appointed time.
到 會 present at the meeting.
到 月 頭 兒 at the end of the month.
到 期 at the appointed time.
25 到 期 日 due date.
到 末 了 兒 or 到 臨 了 兒 in the end; finally.
到 案 to come before the court.
到 極 點 to the last degree; the very limit.
到 次 日 till next day.
30 到 此 停 步 Stop here!
到 船 行 (hang²)·去 go to the boat-office.
到·處 everywhere.
到·處 一 樣 it is everywhere the same.
到·處 都·是 水 you've got t h e water all over the place.
35 到·處 流 行 to wander everywhere.
到·處 都 有 they are everywhere; you can get it anywhere.
不 到 之 處 shortcoming.
到 達 地 destination.
到 達 目 的 objective.
40 到·過·了 I have been there.
到 那·裏·去 where are you going?
到 頭 in the end; at the end; thoroughly.
搆 不 到 頭 it will not reach to the end—too short.

(a) Sign of the past tense or the potential mood.

作·不 到 cannot be done.
來 到 he has come.
想·不·到 unexpected.

想·得·到 thought of it.
5 找·到·了 found it.
收 到 received.
看·到·了 seen it.

倒³ **To fall over; to lie down. To knock down.**
6134

倒·不·了³ it will not fall; it cannot fall.
倒 借 or 挪 借 to borrow of one to pay another.
倒 倒 險 險 tottering; unsteady.
倒 嚼 to chew the cud.
5 倒 圈 an epidemic among cattle, sheep, pigs, etc.
倒 地 葫·蘆 rolling on the ground like a gourd—a toper.
倒 塌 or 倒 坍 to collapse—as a building; to fail—as a firm.
倒 床 to take to one's bed.
倒 店 to vacate an inn for another guest.
10 倒 扣 to deduct unfairly.
倒 換 to exchange for; to substitute for.
倒 換 班 to work in relays or shifts.
倒 敗 to squander; to ruin.
倒 斃 to fall dead.
15 倒 旗 to haul down the colours.
倒 欠 bankrupt. Cf. B.10.
倒 盤 to become bankrupt.
倒 空 still to have a deficiency.
倒 竈 to overturn the stove—fallen upon unlucky days.
20 倒 罷 to become bankrupt.
倒 臥 to fall dead.
倒 芻 to chew the cud.
倒 草 to chew the cud.
倒 行 to go insolvent. (-hang²)
25 倒 裝 to unpack; to open up goods.
倒 賠 to find or repay money due to another. [turn over business.
倒 賬 to become bankrupt; to
倒 身 下 拜 to make a prostration.
倒·過·來 to purchase the goodwill —as of a business.
30 倒 運 or 倒 造 unfortunate; unlucky.
倒 閉 to go insolvent.
倒 陰 to fall on one's face.
倒 陽 to fall on one's back.
倒 韻 out of rhyme.
35 倒 頓 slack trousers for pulling over others.

倒 頭 經 a mass performed on the day of death.
打 倒 to knock down; down with!
拉 倒 to pull down—the end of a matter.
推 倒 to push over.
40 捧 倒 to throw down.
栽 倒 to slip and fall.
跌 倒 to stumble and fall.
辯 倒 to bowl over in an argument.

(a) Read *tao⁴*. To pour out. To invert.

倒 句 法 inversion. (*gramm.*).
倒 垂 蓮 the tiger lily.
倒 好 to cry down a performance; to "hiss."
倒 屣 迎 賓 to receive a visitor with the shoes on back to front —from haste to welcome him.
5 倒 座 seats facing the rear of a train, etc.
倒 弔 to suspend upside down.
倒 彩 to cry down actors, etc., to "hiss."
倒 懸 to hang upside down; to be in suspense; an unfinished affair; in great straits; suffering severely.
倒 戈 相 向 to mutiny; to attack one's own men. (a.p. *tao³-*)
10 倒 抽 一 口 氣 to give a gasp of astonishment.
倒 抽 涼 氣 to give a shudder.
倒 押 韻 inversion of the usual order of a pair of characters to suit the exigencies of rhyme.
倒 拱 inverted arches.
倒 掛 鳥 the love-bird of Formosa.
15 倒 掛 龍 a dragon suspended upside down—nimbus clouds heavy with rain.
倒 捲 to roll up backwards.
倒 景 the highest heavens. (*Tao.*).
倒 果 爲 因 putting cause f o r effect.
倒 栽 葱 an onion planted upside down—to fall head over heels.
20 倒 氣 to gasp.
倒 溜 兒 a syphon.
倒 滿 fill full.
倒 生·的 inverted; inverse.
倒 繃 孩 兒 to swaddle a child upside down — (after being a midwife for thirty years).
↑倒 欠 to owe (after expecting to have a credit)
25 倒 置 to place upside down; inversion; to invert.

倒背 着手 to put the hands behind the back.

倒茶 to pour out tea.

倒茶·來 pour out and hand round the tea.

倒行逆施 to act in opposition to right principles; perversely.

[30]倒裝句法 inversion. (*gramm.*).

倒車 to back up a vehicle.

倒轉·的 inverse.

倒退 to shirk; to skulk; to hang back.

倒·過 to transpose.

[35]倒·過·來 turned over.

倒針·脚 to backstitch. (--*chiao*)

倒開水 pour out some boiling water.

倒騎驢 to ride a donkey with the face towards the tail.

顛倒 turned upside down; topsy-turvy. (a.p.-*tao³*)

(b) Read *tao¹*. On the contrary; but; and yet; nevertheless.

倒不如 but you can't do better than.

倒不如大雨 it is not so good as a heavy rain after all.

倒也罷了³ very well; let it pass; nothing more need be said about it.

倒也說·得不錯 nevertheless what he says is quite correct.

[5]倒像 why it is like....; but it seems....; on the contrary it seems.

倒反 or 反倒 but; on the contrary.

你·倒說不好 nevertheless you say it is not good.

想省事倒費·了大事 thinking to avoid trouble, you have given yourself a great deal of bother.

那。倒不要緊 well, that doesn't matter much.

悼 [4] Wounded in spirit; afflicted; grieved. To die early.
6135

悼亡詩 a monody; mournful poem on the death of a friend.

悼哭 or 悲悼 to bewail; to compassionate.

悼嘆 to sigh for.

悼道無傳 he grieved that there was no one to hand his doctrine down.

道 [4] A road; a way; a path.
6136 From which comes the idea of The Way; the Truth. A doctrine. A principle. Reason.

道一而已矣 there is only one Way.

道不同不相爲謀 there can be no mutual plannings between those whose principles differ.

道不拾遺 no one picked up things that were dropped on the road.

道不行 my doctrines make no way.

[5]道不通 the way is impassable.

道之至矣 the most essential of all truth.

道也者不可須臾離也 the Path may not be left for a moment.

道光 the light of morality; reign name of Emperor Hsüan *

道力 the effort necessary to attain —*Tao*.

[10]道可道非常道也 the way that can be traversed is not the Way.

道周 by the side of the road.

道味 the flavour of moral truth.

道地 or 地道 local; genuine.

道地藥材 genuine native drugs.

[15]道大 having broad views.

道學 the orthodox school of ethics as taught by the 宋儒, or *Sung* dynasty philosophers.

道學先生 a person who carried out the teaching of the orthodox school of Confucianism.

道學院 a Bible Institute; theological school.

道德 morality.

[20] 商業道德 commercial morality.

思考·的道德 reflective morality.

本能·的道德 instinctive morality.

習尚·的道德 customary morality.

道德·上 morally.

[25]道德主義 Moralism—natural system of morality.

道德之制裁 moral sanction.

道德之勇力 moral courage.

道德哲學 moral philosophy.

道德問題 moral questions.

[30]道德墮落 moral decadence; demoralization.

* Tsung of Ch'ing dynasty.

道德學 moral science; ethics.

道德官 a moral sense.

道德家 moralists.

道德律 moral law.

[35]道德心 a moral sense.

道德思想 a moral purpose.

道德意識 moral consciousness.

道德教授 teaching of morality.

道德教育 moral education.

[40]道德敗壞 moral decadence; demoralization.

道德標準 moral standards.

必然·的道德標準 imperative moral standards.

習俗·的道德標準 customary moral standards.

自覺·的道德標準 individual moral standards.

[45]道德狂 moral insanity.

道德·的進化 moral progress.

道德知覺 moral sense or consciousness.

道德義·務 moral obligations.

道德能力 moral faculty.

[50]道德自由 moral liberty.

道德觀念 moral concept.

道心 spiritual nature.

道心惟微 the principle of right in the heart is but small.

道揆 principles by which a ruler examines his administration.

[55]道根 moral foundations; the source of truth.

道次 by the way; on the road.

道殣 those who die of starvation by the roadside.

道法自然 *Tao* imitates that which is natural, i.e., it has no need to imitate anything else.

道無常名 *Tao*—the truth, has no constant designation.

[60]道·理 doctrine; the rights of things; principles; reason; argument.

道眞 truth; the right.

道眼 the eye that can perceive the truth; a channel made in the road by rains.

道統 the succession of those who preached the truth; according to the *Sung* dynasty philosophers, it began with *Fu Hsi* 伏羲, and ended with *Chu Hsi* 朱熹.

道線 line of a road; a way.

[65]道義 reason and right; sense of right and honour.

道義上 morally.

有道義心的 a moral agent.

道 義 學 moral science.

道 義 感 情 moral sentiment.

70 道 聽 而 塗 說 to tell on the road what you have heard by the way—gossip.

道 與 一，神 之 強 名 也 *Tao* and *Unity* are approximate designations for God.

道 藝 genius and technical ability; moral principles and artistic skill—in music, literature, archery, etc.

道 行 高 潔 high moral attainments.

道 衝 a thoroughfare.

75 道 謀 to consult with casual way-farers.

道 路 a road; a way.

道 路 以 目 signified their anger by their looks as they met by the way—not daring to speak openly about the oppression of the government.

道 路 通 達 a prosperous way; prosperous.

道 途 a road; a way.

80 道 遠 the way is long; a long distance.

道 里 計 distance between places.

道 隆 道 汚 a doctrine in favour or in disrepute—according as it is accepted or rejected by the people.

不 以 其 道 得 之 if it cannot be obtained by proper means, or in the right way.

人 能 弘 道，非 道 弘 人 a man can enlarge the moral principles which he follows, those principles do not enlarge the man.

85 各 行 其 道 let each go his own way.

吾 道 一 以 貫 之 my doctrine is that of an all-pervading unity.

天 下 無 道 the kingdom is without principles of truth and right; bad government prevails.

就 有 道 而 正 焉 he resorts to men of principle in order to correct himself.

形 而 上 者 謂 之 道 the immaterial principle is called *Tao*.

90 志 於 道 the mind set on truth.

率 性 之 謂 道 accordance with the nature conferred by Heaven is called the Path.

通 萬 物 而 謂 之 道 that which, as pervading all things, is called

Tao—reason.

(a) Used as a suffix to indicate—roads, principles, ways, the nature of, religion, etc.

不 道 wicked; unnatural; not in accordance with what should be.

世 道 the general aspect of the times; the prevailing fashion, etc.

中 道 the middle path; the happy mean; half-way.

乾 道 pertaining to males; the Way of *Yang*, 陽. *See below* —16.

5 人 道 the state of being a human being; moral law; sexual intercourse.

佛 道 Buddhism.

入 道 to enter upon *Tao;* to become a Buddhist priest.

公 道 fair; impartial; reasonable.

分 道 to take different ways.

10 右 道 the right-hand or orthodox Way.

前 道 the road ahead.

味 道 a flavour; the flavour of a thing.

和 道 the way of domestic harmony.

善 道 virtue; a good way.

15 地 道 the way of the Earth; a subway; genuine.

坤 道 pertaining to females; the Way of *Yin*, 陰. *See above—* 4.

大 道 the highway; the Right Path.

夫 婦 之 道 the state of matrimony.

天 道 the Way of Heaven; the weather.

20 失 道 to go astray.

奇 道 a clever trick.

官 道 a public highway.

家 道 the condition of a family; the social status, etc.

小 道 small, petty ways; ignoble arts; a by-way.

25 左 道 the sinister path; heterodox.

徑 道 a short-cut.

從 道 to follow the way—of truth.

得 道 to obtain *Tao*—to become a *Lo-han*.

成 道 attainment to perfect spiritual knowledge. (*Budd.*).

30 撞 道 to encounter a person whom one does not wish to meet.

數 道 several times; several rounds.

日 道 月 道 the orbit of the sun and the phases of the moon.

易 道 an easy way.

曲 道 crooked ways; winding paths.

35 枉 道 crooked, evil ways; partiality.

正 道 the Right Way—orthodoxy.

死 道 the Way of Death.

水 道 the current of a river; water-ways; a journey by water; the general nature of water itself.

河 道 river-ways; the course of a river.

40 海 道 sea-routes.

父 道 fatherhood.

王 道，霸 道 the rule of right, and the rule of might.

生 道 means of preserving life; the Way of Life.

盤 道 covered ways.

45 直 道 impartiality; moral uprightness.

眞 道 the Truth.

知 道 to know.

祖 道 a farewell feast.

神 道 the Way of God.

50 禽 獸 道 the nature of birds and beasts.

穀 道 the alimentary canal.

穴 道 vital places on the body; spots for acupuncture.

繞 道 a circuitous way.

至 道 the Perfect Way.

55 花 道 harlotry.

血 道 the circulation; veins and arteries.

行 道 to do justice; to act according to *Tao*.

要 道 important doctrines or principles; strategic district.

變 化 之 道 the philosophy of transformation.

60 赤 道 the equator.

軌 道 ruts; rails; orbit of the heavenly bodies.

迂 道 a by-way.

通 道 a thoroughfare; a trade-route.

避 道 to avoid a person on the road—as a superior official.

65 邪 道 heterodoxy.

鐵 道 a railway.

階 道 steps; stair-way.

隧 道 tunnel to a grave.

馬 道 ramps leading on to the city wall.

⁷⁰鬼 道 the way of demons.

鳥 道 the way of the birds—a difficult way.

黃 道 the ecliptic. *See* No. 2297-85ff.

(b) Taoism.

道 人 an expert in *Tao;* a Taoist priest; an immortal; a member of the Taoist sect.

道 俗 Taoist priests and laity.

道 兄 respectful term of address to a Taoist priest.

道 塲 place where Taoist ceremonies for delivering a soul from purgatory are performed.

⁵道 士 a Taoist priest.

道 姑 or 道 妮 Taoist nun.

道 官 Taoist leaders.

道 山 the hill of the immortals.

歸 道 山 to return to the hill of the immortals—to die.

¹⁰道 岸 the shore of Truth.

道 德 經 a work attributed to *Laotzŭ*, but most probably of a much later date.

道 敎 Taoism.

道 末 conventional term by which a Taoist priest speaks of himself.

道 正 a Taoist superior.

¹⁵道 流 Taoist followers.

道 經 Taoist classics, etc.

道 藏 Taoist books, etc.

道 號 Taoist priest's name in religion.

道 術 magical arts.

²⁰道 裝 Taoist robes.

道 觀 Taoist monastery.

道 門 Taoism; the Portal of Truth.

道 院 Taoist temple.

老 道 a Taoist priest.

(c) A district; a political division of a province.

道 台 *Taotai*—the former intendant of a circuit.

道 契 deeds for land in Shanghai concessions, stamped by the *Taotai*.

道 尹 Intendant of a Circuit under the Republic.

(d) To speak; to tell. Words.

道 乏 to thank a person for his trouble.

道 吾 惡 者 是 吾 師 he who

---

tells me my faults is my instructor.

道 古 今 to tell tales; talking of past and present.

道 喜 congratulations; to congratulate.

⁵道 惱 or 改 惱 to condole with.

道 故 to tell stories of the past.

道 歉 to apologize.

道 解 to explain.

道 談 to converse.

¹⁰道 謝 or 申 謝 or 聲 謝 to express one's thanks.

道 賀 to congratulate; congratulations.

道 達 to inform; to state.

不 可 勝 道 beyond the power of expression.

莫 道 do not say....

¹⁵說 道 said as follows....

難 道 can it be....; you do not mean to say....

(e) N. A. or classifier for various things,—as under.

一 道 a time; an occasion, etc., a stripe.

一 道 光 a ray of light.

一 道 公 文 an official despatch.

一 道 氣 a current of air.

⁵一 道 油 a coat of paint.

一 道 河 a river.

一 道 灰 a coat of plaster.

一 道 烟 a wreath of smoke or mist.

一 道 菜 a course of a dinner.

¹⁰頭 道 菜 first course.

一 道 街 a street.

一 道 諭 旨 an Imperial mandate.

(f) Read *tao³·⁴*. **To lead; to guide. u.f. next.**

道 之 以 德 齊 之 以 禮 if you lead the people by virtue and make them uniform by the rules of propriety....

道 之 以 政 齊 之 以 刑 if you lead the people by laws, and make them uniform by punishments....

道 引 to lead; the practice of Taoist breathing exercises.

(g) Read *tao⁴*. **Used in transliterating.**

道 爾 頓 制 The Dalton Plan—of education.

導　³·⁴ To lead; to guide. To instruct.

6137

導 入 室 to show into a room.

導 器 a vehicle or excipient.

導 尿 管 catheter.

導 師 a guide — a director.

⁵導 引 Taoist breathing exercises.

導 江 river conservancy.

導 淮 委 員 會 Huai River Conservancy Board.

導 火 線 a fuse; also used fig.

導 管 a pipe; a duct; meatus.

¹⁰導 線 exciting cause; line of advance.

導 言 introduction; preface or foreword.

導 誘 to instruct.

導 體 a conductor.

不 導 體 non-conductor.

¹⁵先 導 a forerunner.

指 導 員 a guide.

開 導 to point out the right way; to undeceive; to enhearten.

盜　⁴ To rob; to steal. A robber, a bandit, a pirate.

盜

6138

盜 亦 有 道 there is *Tao* even in robbery.

盜 劫 to rob; to plunder.

盜 匪 robbers; bandits.

盜 取 to rob.

⁵盜 名 to steal a person's name or trade-mark; to gain a reputation to which one is not entitled.

盜 寇 bandits; rebels.

盜 帑 to rob the treasury; to misappropriate public funds.

盜 案 a case of robbery.

盜 殺 to plunder and murder.

¹⁰盜 汗 or 自 汗 night-sweats.

盜 泉 a polluted spring.

盜 淫 to rape.

盜 用 to purloin and make use of.

盜 神 像 to take out an idol.

¹⁵盜 竊 to plunder.

盜 賊 robbers and thieves.

盜 賊 淵 藪 a robbers' retreat.

盜 賊 蠭 起 robbers arose in swarms.

盜 賣 to sell fraudulently.

²⁰盜 風 the practice of thieving.

盜 首 chief of a robber gang.

盜 驚 alarm of thieves or robbers.

盜 魁 chief of a robber gang.

失 盗 to have had a robbery, theft.
²⁵小 盗 a pilferer; a thief.
強·盗 highway robbers; bandits.
海 盗 pirates.
被 盗 to have been robbed.

稻⁴ Rice growing in the field; paddy.
6139

稻 塲 a floor on which rice is dried.
稻·子 rice in the husk.
稻 草 rice straw.
割 稻 to reap rice.
旱 稻 or 陸 稻 rice grown in dry fields.
水 稻 rice grown in flooded fields.

蹈⁴ To tread on; to violate; to disregard. To follow.
6140

蹈 危 地 to be in a place of great danger.
蹈 平 to raze to the ground.
蹈 常 襲 故 to follow mere routine.
蹈 法 to violate the law.
蹈 虎 尾 to tread on the tail of a tiger—dangerous.
蹈 襲 to plagiarize.

T'AO. (玄)

叨¹ To desire; to be in receipt of; to enjoy. Distinguish 叨 No. 6269; similar to 饕 No. 6147.
6141

叨 光 to desire your favour; to receive advantage from.
叨 在 同 志 I am favoured by having you for a friend—conventional, in letters.
叨 在 知 己 I shame you by being your friend.—conventional, in letters.
叨 忝 I am ashamed to receive so many favours.
⁵叨 恩 to receive favour.
叨 慣 日 欽 he daily honoured the covetous and the cruel.
叨 擾 I have put you to great trouble—conventional form of thanks for entertainment.
叨 敎 多 年 I have been in receipt of your instructions for many years.

叨 沐 I am greatly indebted to you.
¹⁰叨 濫 my desires are insatiable.
叨 蒙 thank you for your favours.

(a) Read *tao¹*. Garrulous.

叨 叨 人 nagging at a person.
叨 嘮 loquacious; chattering; to nag at; to scold.
叨 叨 念 念 chattering; muttering and grumbling.

慆¹'². Excessive; reckless; insolent.
6142

慆 德 insolent disposition.
慆 心 reckless; careless.
慆 慆 不 歸 long were we there without returning.
慆 淫 insolent dissoluteness.
慆 閒 leisurely.

(a) To pass by.

日 月 其 慆 the days and months will have passed by.

(b) To conceal.

以 樂 慆 憂 burying all grief in pleasure.

(c) To doubt.

天 命 不 慆 the will of Heaven (God) is certain.

掏¹ To pull out; to take out. To clean out. Used with 淘 No. 6153.
6143

掏 井 to clean out a well.
掏·出 價·錢 to pay the price.
掏 水 to bale out water.
掏 溝 to clean out a drain.
⁵掏 籌 to give out bamboo tallies—to carrying porters.
掏 耳 聹 to clean the ears.
掏 花 to pick flowers.
掏 虱·子 to crack a louse.
掏 錢 to take out some cash.

滔¹ To overflow. A torrent; rushing water.
6144

滔 天 to dash to the skies—of foaming billows.

滔 天 大 禍 a terrible disaster.
滔 德 or 慆 德 insolent disposition.
滔 滔 不 斷 古 今 流 it has never ceased to roll on, in this great stream.
滔 滔 者 天 下 皆 是 也 there is a ferment throughout the whole empire.
滔 濫 to overflow.
滔 風 the east wind.

韜 弢¹ A bow-case; a scabbard. To sheathe. Just, liberal.
6145

韜 光 used of an able man living in retirement—hiding his light under a bushel.
韜 光 養 晦 to hide one's light.
韜 弓 to put a bow into its case.
韜 晦 to hide one's light—under a bushel.
⁵韜 畧 military tactics; strategy.
韜 筆 to put away one's pen—to give up writing.
韜 藏 to conceal.
韜 鈐 the science of military strategy.
韜 面 to cover up the face.

條 絛¹ A sash; a band; a cord.
6146

條·子 辮·子 silk braided in the queue.
打 條·子 to twist a cord.

饕¹ Gluttonous; rapacious; covetous; greedy.
6147 Inter. 叨 No. 6141.

饕 戾 covetous and cruel.
饕 腹 a glutton.
饕 餮 avaricious and gluttonous—name of a greedy man who was banished by Shun, 舜; a fierce animal having a head and no body; a fabulous race of men who were fierce savages.
饕 餮 成 性 gluttony and covetousness has become a fixed habit.
貪 財 爲 饕 covetousness is called *t'ao*.

桃² The peach. Profligacy. Marriage.
6148

桃 人 ancient figures of peach-wood, used to scare demons—the door-gods. *See* 荼 No. 6526-D.

桃 仁 peach-kernels.

桃 園 結 義 the compact made in a peach orchard by *Liu Pei* 劉備, *Kuan Yü* 關羽, and *Chang Fei* 張飛, in which they swore everlasting fidelity to each other.

桃 墜 a peach-stone pendant.

⁵桃 夭 合 harmony of marriage—from the next.

桃 之 夭 夭 之 子 于 歸 How graceful and slender yonder peach-tree stands! The maiden comes to her husband's home.

桃 奴 dried peaches remaining on the tree through the winter.

桃 兒 a peach.

桃 乳 peach-gum.

¹⁰桃 弧 a peach-wood bow anciently used to repel demons and sinister influences.

桃 月 the third lunar month.

桃 李 peaches and plums—pupils; disciples.

桃 李 得 陰 蒺 藜 得 刺 the peach and the plum repay you with shade (and fruit); the calthrop returns you (neither shade in summer, nor fruit in autumn, but) mere prickles.

桃 李 無 言 下 自 成 蹊 the peach and the plum do not speak, yet a path is worn beneath them.

¹⁵桃 枝 a kind of bamboo with a red skin; it is used for fine mats and other purposes.

桃 林 a peach-orchard.

桃 根 桃 葉 a wife and concubine—from the names of two sisters beloved by Wang Hsien-chih 王獻之.

桃 核 peach-stones. (-*hur²*)

桃 梗 a peach-wood figure.

²⁰桃 梟 dried peaches remaining on the tree through the winter.

桃 樽 invitation to a birthday feast.

桃 源 Arcadia—from a story of a man who went through a peach orchard and discovered a secluded valley in which people were living in peace, quite ignorant of passing events and changes of dynasty.

世 外 桃 源 Arcadia—a harbour of refuge from oppressive governments.

桃 符 peach-wood charm—hung over the lintel at New-Year; now used of the paper scrolls pasted at the sides of doors, etc.

²⁵桃 紅 colour of peach-blossoms; pink.

桃 絲 竹 a large bamboo which grows in south China.

桃 肉 shelled walnuts.

桃 腮 杏 眼 rosy cheeks and oval eyes—the fair features of a woman.

桃 膠 peach-gum.

³⁰桃 花 peach-blossoms.

桃 花 水 spring freshets—the snow melting in spring when the peach is in blossom.

桃 花 汛 spring freshets.

桃 花 浪 a profligate.

桃 花 粉 pink face-powder.

³⁵桃 花 粧 thickly painted—of a woman's face.

桃 花 臉 rosy cheeks.

桃 花 運 popularity, or good luck, in adventures with women.

桃 茢 branches of peach-wood and broom of rushes used to expel demons.

桃 蟲 a wren.

⁴⁰桃 諸 pickled peaches.

桃 金 孃 myrtle.

桃 雀 a wren; the tailor-bird.

佛 桃 a fragrant citrus.

夾 竹 桃 the oleander.

⁴⁵核 桃 the walnut. (*ho²-*)

楊 桃 the carambola or willow-peach.

櫻 桃 the cherry.

碧 桃 花 double-flowering peach.

蟠 桃 the flat peach.

⁵⁰金 絲 桃 St. John's wort.

香 桃 a lemon. ＝檸檬.

洮² Name of a large affluent of the Yellow River. To cleanse.
6149
Inter. 淘 No. 6153.

洮 汰 to cleanse; to scour or rinse, used fig., to clear out useless elements.

逃 逃² To escape; to abscond; to flee.
6150

逃 不 出 去 cannot get away—as from besiegers.

逃 世 to retire from the world as a recluse.

逃 亡 to run away; to abscond.

逃 人 a deserter; a fugitive.

⁵逃 兇 an escaped murderer.

逃 兵 a deserter.

逃 出 去 fled away out of it.

逃 匿 to shirk; to skulk; to hide; to keep out of sight.

逃 名 to avoid fame.

¹⁰逃 命 to fly for one's life; to escape with one's life.

逃 城 City of Refuge.

逃 墨 必 歸 於 楊 escaping (the errors of) *Motzŭ*, they naturally turn to *Yang Chu*.

逃 奴 a runaway slave.

逃 嫁 to desert a husband and re-marry.

¹⁵逃 學 to play truant.

逃 席 to leave one's place at a feast without making one's excuses.

逃 往 to abscond to....

逃 捨 to desert.

逃 散 to flee in all directions.

²⁰逃 法 網 to escape the net of the law.

逃 犯 an escaped criminal.

逃 生 to fly for one's life; to escape with one's life.

逃 瘧 to move to another place to avoid malaria, it being thought that in another house the attack may be averted.

逃 監 to escape from prison.

²⁵逃 祿 to refuse emoluments.

逃 禪 to retire and become a Buddhist; to offend against the ritual when drunk.

逃 竄 to shirk; to hide from; to skulk; to keep out of sight.

逃 罪 to escape punishment.

逃 脫 to cast off; to get clear of.

³⁰逃 荒 to flee from famine districts.

逃 課 to play truant; to dodge classes.

逃 走 to run away; to escape.

逃 跑 to escape; to run away.

逃 躲 to dodge; to hide from; to skulk.

[33]逃軍 to desert one's troops and flee alone.

逃逸 broke loose and got away.

逃避 or 逃遁 to shirk; to hide from; to keep out of sight.

逃閃 to run away; to escape.

逃難 (nan[4]) to flee from calamity.

目逃 to turn away the eyes from an attack; to flinch.

鞀
鞉}[2] Hand-drum used by ped-
鼗   lars; it is sounded by twirl-
6151   ling it backwards in the
       hand, so that two swinging
       knobs can strike the face
       of the drum.

啕
咷}[2] To wail; to weep.
6152

號啕痛哭 bitter weeping and wailing.

淘[2] To scour; to wash in a
6153 Inter. 掏 No. 6143. sieve; to clean out. To sift.

淘乾·淨 to clean thoroughly—as rice.

淘井 to clean out a well.

淘汰 to make a selection; to cleanse; to weed out superfluous elements.

淘汰作用 the selective process.

[5]淘汰說 theory of natural selection.

人爲淘汰 artificial selection.

天演淘汰 natural selection.

意識·的淘汰 conscious selection.

生殖·的淘汰 germinal selection.

[10] 自然·的淘汰 natural selection.

雌雄淘汰 sexual selection.

淘沙 to wash sand.

淘河 to scour a river; name for the pelican.

淘溝 to clean out a drain.

[15]淘米 to wash rice.

淘金 to wash for gold.

淘陽溝 to clean out an open drain.

(a) To excite. To play.

淘氣 to excite; mischievous; annoying; irritating.

淘神 worrying; troublesome; irritating.

綯[2] To bind; to braid; to
6154   twist. A cord.

綯住 to tie up—as a dog.

索綯 to twist ropes.

匋
匋}[2] See 匋 No. 5389.
6155

陶
匋}[2] A kiln for burning pot-
6156   tery or earthenware.

陶人 or 陶窰·的 a potter.

陶冶 potters and founders; to mould; used fig.

陶匠 a potter.

陶化 to transform; to convert.

[5]陶器 pottery; earthenware.

陶土 clay suitable for pottery.

陶塲 a potter's field.

陶成 to refine; to harden by burning.

陶朱公 title taken by an ancient millionaire,—his name was Fan Li 范蠡;—used for good fortune, etc.

[10] 陶猗 the above and 猗頓, another very wealthy man—used as above.

陶染 to influence; to mould; to transform.

陶正 title of official in charge of potteries under the Chou dynasty.

陶煉 to refine; to harden by burning.

陶犬瓦鷄 pottery dogs and cocks—useless; they can neither bark nor crow.

[15]陶瓦 to make tiles.

陶甄 to mould—used fig.

陶硯 a pottery inkslab.

陶鈞萬品 to mould and bring all things into order.

陶鍊 to refine; to fashion.

[20]陶鎔 to melt; to transform.

陶鑄 to smelt; to mould and fashion.

(a) To be pleased.

陶兀 obstinately perverse when intoxicated.

陶寫 to amuse oneself.

陶情 friendly after taking liquor.

陶暢 happy and jolly.

[5]陶然 jolly, contented and happy.

陶遂 to amuse oneself.

陶陶自得 well pleased with oneself and others.

鬱陶 anxieties.

(b) Read yao[2]. Name of a man in ancient history.

討[3] To beg; to demand; to dun.
6157

討·不出好·來 you will get no good out of it.

討人喜·歡 to seek the favour of men.

討保 to seek bail; to find security.

討便 (p'ien[2])·宜 to seek advantage.

[5]討個公道 I only wish to get justice.

討債 to dun for debts.

討債鬼 the demon who comes for the debt—an unpaid creditor who is born again as the son of his debtor.

討厭 annoying; disagreeable; to incur dislike.

討取 to exact; to demand.

[10]討命鬼 the demon of one who has been wronged, coming to revenge itself; one who gets himself into difficulties.

討問 to ask for an opinion.

討好 to toady; to get advantage from; to ingratiate oneself.

討嫌 to incur dislike; disagreeable; annoying.

討巧 to get an advantage without making an effort for it.

[15]討情 to intercede for; to ask favours; to appeal on behalf of another.

討愧 to be ashamed.

討戰 to challenge to battle.

討打 you are itching for a thrashing.

討新婦 to seek a wife for one's son. (Wu-dial.)

[20]討替 to seek for a substitute.

討求 to seek; to beg for.

討 沒 趣 to invite something disagreeable on oneself; to do something that will only bring one into dislike or that will bring a rebuke.

討 源 to trace out the origins of things.

討 生 活 to seek for a livelihood.

²⁵討 究 to investigate, as a scientist.

討 索 to lay claim to; to exact.

討 臊 to cover oneself with confusion.

討 要 to demand.

討 親 to marry a wife. (*Wu-dial.*)

³⁰討 論 to discuss a question; to debate.

討 論 最 後 辦 法 discuss the final arrangements.

討 論 會 meeting for discussion.

討 賬 to dun; to apply for debts.

討 賞 to ask for a gratuity.

³⁵討 錢 to ask for money; to dun.

討 限 to ask an extension of time.

討 頭 路 to seek employment.

討 飯 to beg for food.

討 飯 的 a beggar.

⁴⁰討 饒 to seek forgiveness.

自 討 苦 吃 you are only bringing trouble upon yourself.

(a) To punish. To put to death, to exterminate.

討 亂 to suppress rebellion or disorders.

討 伐 to reduce to submission; to punish.

討 伐 令 punitive command.

討 伐 方 式 punitive methods.

⁵討 伐 軍 a punitive force.

討 其 君 put their sovereign to death.

討 平 內 亂 to settle internal disorders by punishment.

討 罪 to punish.

天 討 有 罪 Heaven punishes the guilty.

¹⁰討 賊 to exterminate rebels.

天 子 討 而 不 伐 the sovereign commanded the punishment, but did not inflict it.

檮 ² A block of wood; a blockhead.
6158

檮 昧 ignorant; stupid.

檮 杌 one not fit to associate with others; a blockhead—name

given to the annals of the State of *Ch'u* 楚; a fabulous beast described as being like a tiger, having hair like a dog, the face of a man, feet of a tiger, and the tusks of a boar; its length was about two feet, but it had a tail eighteen feet long.

濤 ²
6159   Billows; great waves.

松 濤 wind in the pines.

波 濤 great waves.

套 ⁴ A case; a wrapper; a covering; a snare. To encase;
6160 to slip over. To harness. N.A. for things worn or slipped on, etc.

套 上 衣 服 to put on one's garments.

套 包 子 or 護 肩 a collar for a horse.

套 夾 棍 to put on instruments of torture.

套 子 a loop; a noose; a snare.

⁵套 拳 to box.

套 數 the whole number; the whole set; number of times.

套 板 blocks for printing in two or more colours.

套 杯 a set of cups that fit into each other.

套 棺 an outer coffin.

¹⁰套 氣 = 客 氣 formality; conventionality.

套 用 or 通 套 formal; conventional; in common use.

套 禮 conventionalities.

套 索 a lasso.

套 繩 a noose; a lasso.

¹⁵套 衣 outer garments.

套 褲 overalls; leggings.

套 言 不 叙 dispense with conventionalities—and get on with the business.

套 話 or 客 套 話 conventional phrases.

套 調 to plagiarize.

²⁰套 車 to get a cart ready; to harness up the animals and put them in the cart.

套 連 inseparably connected; involved.

套 進 去 put one inside the other.

套 間 a small room opening off another.

套 鞋 galoshes; rubber-shoes.

²⁵套 頭 an act of politeness; a polite phrase.

套 馬 to lasso a horse; to harness a horse.

套 馬 杆 a noose for catching horses.

一 套 傢 伙 a set of tools, etc.

一 套 衣 服 a suit of clothes.

³⁰二 套 車 a two-horsed cart.

俗 套 common; vulgar; ordinary.

圈 套 a snare; a trap.

外 套 overcoat. = 大 氅.

封 套 an envelope.

³⁵手 套 gloves.

書 套 case for a set of books.

河 套 the great bend of the Yellow River.

脫 套 to get out of a snare.

落 套 to fall into a snare.

⁴⁰虛 套 formalities; conventionalities.

褥 套 or 被 套 a bag for bedding.

TÊ.   (勺)
(Teh)

得 ²·⁵ To obtain; to acquire; to gain. To effect; to at-
6161 tain. Can, may; able to be done.

得 一 望 二 to get one and look for another.

得 不 償 失 the gain does not recompense for the loss.

得 不 着 unable to obtain. (-*chao*²)

得 中 to win.

⁵得 享 安 靜 to enjoy peace and quietness.

得 人 to be popular; to get hold of the right men—for subordinates.

得 人 意 to be popular.

得 以 to be able; in order that; so that.

得 位 or 得 天 下 to get the throne.

¹⁰得 便 at convenience.

得 便 (*p'ien*²) 宜 to get an advantage.

得 做 doing; in the process of making.

得 其 實 情 get at the facts.

得 其 所 he has got to his place.

¹⁵得 准 having a certainty.

得 利 to obtain profit or advantage.

得 力 competent; capable; to be of service.

得 勁 to get a purchase; to get a grip; the advantageous application of strength.

得 勝 to obtain a victory; to overcome.

20得 勝 有 餘 more than conquerors.

得 及 within reach.

得 君 寵 obtain favour with a king.

得 味 palatable.

得 咯 that's all! enough! etc.

25得 善 價 to get a good price.

得 因 以 爲 利 has an opportunity to get an advantage.

得 地 步 to get a base for operations; to gain a vantage ground.

得 失 gain and loss; success and failure; errors.

得 奉 to have received.

30得 子 to have children.

得 宜 satisfactory.

得 實 to get at the facts of a matter under trial.

得 寵 to find favour; to be in favour; to win a husband's love.

得 寸 得 尺 to get an inch and then a foot—to acquire and retain territory.

35得 轂 capable of; able to.

得 心 應 手 what the mind wishes the hand is able to do; to get a suitable helper.

得 志 to attain one's purpose.

得 志 海 內 to have one's (political) ambition in the nation realized.

得 悉 to become acquainted with —as the contents of a letter.

40得 情 to get at the facts.

得 意 to get one's desires.

得 意 洋 洋 quite elated.

得 意·的 很 exceedingly well satisfied; just what I wanted.

得 手 to get into one's hand; to obtain; to make sure of.

45得 救 to obtain salvation.

得 數 answer to a problem in arithmetic.

得 新 望 古 to obtain the new and look with longing to the old.

得 於 心 acquisition in the heart.

得 時 at a convenient time; in favour; in luck.

50得 眼 to have leisure.

得 本 又 得 利 to obtain both principal and interest.

得 樣 suitable; to look well.

得 民 心 to be popular.

得 民 情 to get the goodwill of the people; popular.

55得 法 to have got the knack of doing a thing; comfortable; easy.

得 生 to obtain life; to regain life.

得 用 fit for use; suitable for use.

得 當 fitting; suitable; proper.

得 病 to get ill.

60得 益 處 to obtain advantage; to be benefited.

得 知 to become acquainted with —as a fact.

得 神 life-like—as a portrait.

得 稱 爲 義 justification; to be justified.

得 空 兒 to have leisure for.

65得 竅 got the knack of it.

得 缺 to obtain an appointment to a vacant post.

得·罪 to offend. "I have offended." "Excuse me." "I beg pardon."

得 聞 to have heard—as a rumour.

得 色 an appearance of satisfaction.

70得·著 風·就·是 雨 gets the wind and immediately expects the rain—illustrates hasty conclusions, etc. (-chao-)

得 衛 巫 he called a wizard from Wei.

得 見 to get an interview.

得 解 to understand the rights of a matter, etc.

得 財 to obtain wealth.

75得 達 can be reached.

得 過 can pass—comes up to a conventional standard.

得 過 且 過 easy going; to make do; to be satisfied with; to make shift with.

得 道 to become perfect and enter Nirvana.

得 采 to win a lottery prize.

80得 銷 路 to get a good market for goods.

得 閒 to find leisure for.

得 閑 to get leisure.

得 附 列 之 supplementary to it.

得 項 profits; perquisites; emoluments.

85得 風 便 轉 to shift with the wind; to adapt oneself to circumstances.

得 體 proper in deportment, etc.

得 魚 忘 筌 when the fish is caught there is no more need to remember the trap.

不 得 must not.

復 得 to get back again.

90應 得 worthy of.

獲 得 to get; to capture.

未 得 have not been able to.

目 瞪·得 圓·了 his eyes grew large and round.

相 得 mutually agreeable.

苟 得 to obtain by improper means.

(a) **Following an adjective equals very, greatly; an auxiliary verb; an adverb.**

·得 不 得 了 again and again; time after time.

·得 利·害 very severe; extremely —used after verbs.

·得 多 sign of comparison—much more; many more, etc.

·得 很 very; exceedingly; extremely.

5得·慌 or.的·慌 very; excessive— used after words indicating weariness, sorrow, or things unpleasant.

·得 緊 exceedingly.

(b) **Read tei³. Ought; should; must.**

得 甚·麼 時·候 去 at what hour must we start?

得 用 多·少 how much is needed?

(c) Particle indicating potentiality.
看·得 見 can see.

德 惪 }
6162

2.5. **Virtue; moral excellence; goodness. Conduct; behaviour—not always good. Energy; power. To repay kindness. See below—40.**

德 不 孤 必 有 鄰 virtue does not stand alone; it will attract neighbours.

德 之 不 忘 ever grateful for it.

德 便 proper and convenient.

德 力 moral strength.

5德 勝 才 爲 君 子 he whose virtue exceeds his talents is the good man.

德 士 name for a Buddhist priest.

德 己 to take merit to oneself.

德·性 morality; virtue.

德 政 good government.

¹⁰德政碑 stone tablet erected to the memory of a virtuous official.

德星 a lucky star.

德水 a name given to the Yellow River by *Ch'in Shih huang*.

秦始皇.

德潤身 virtue adorns the person.

德禽 the cock.

¹⁵德耀 the fame of one's merits.

德育 moral culture; ethical training.

德能 virtue and ability.

德色 a self-satisfied air after doing good deeds.

德莫厚焉 could not show greater virtue than by—pardoning them.

²⁰德行 upright conduct; virtuous character; 德行 mannerisms.

德輶如毛 virtue is as light as a hair.

德配 your wife.

德門 a virtuous family.

德隆望尊 his lofty virtue was worthy of respect.

²⁵德音 a wise answer.

德音不瑕 there was no flaw in his virtuous fame.

德音孔昭 whose virtuous fame is grandly brilliant.

德音莫違 while I do nothing contrary to my good name.

二三其德 ever varying in his conduct.

³⁰修德 to give attention to conduct; to cultivate virtue; to give in charity.

喪德 to blunt the moral sense.

夏德若茲 such is (the evil) course of the (rule of) *Hsia*.

惡德 an evil disposition.

有德 worthy; virtuous.

³⁵淑德 female virtue.

用降我凶德 thereby he removed our evils—conditions of suffering, famine, etc.

盛德 great, abundant virtue.

神德 spiritual efficacy.

穢德彰聞 their filthy deeds are known on high.

⁴⁰行道而得於心謂之德 the practice of truth and the acquisition thereof in the heart may be termed *tê*.

陰德 secret deeds of merit.

(a) Used in transliterating.

德人 a German.

德國 Germany.

德干 the Deccan.

德律風 telephone. = 電話.

德意志 Deutschland.

德黑蘭 Teheran.

↑德謨克拉西 democracy.

T'Ē.　　　(특)

(T'eh)

忒 ^{4.5.} Excessive; too; very—usually of objectionable
6163　 things. To err; to mistake. Changeable.

忒兇猛 very furious.

忒小 too small.

忒晚 very late.

忒殺 or 忒煞 excessive.

↑⁵忒年輕 too young.

享祀不忒 his offerings are all without error.

其儀不忒 there is nothing wrong in his deportment.

差忒 errors; mistakes.

忮忒 hurtful and deceitful.

⁰昊天不忒 Great Heaven—God—makes no mistakes.

衍忒 errors; excesses.

忑 ^{4.5.} Fearful; nervous; timid.
6164

忐忑 timid; vacillating; palpitating.

特 ^{4.5.} On purpose; special;
6165　 specially; eminent; prominent; alone.

特交 specially handed over to....

特任 special appointments by the President—as heads of Boards, etc.

特任代理人 special agent.

特來 to come purposely.

⁵特例 a special act.

特使 special envoy.

特價 special price.

特典 a mark of distinction.

特別 special; distinctive; particular; unique.

¹⁰特別事件 special items or matters.

特別事務 special business.

特別任務 special service.

特別刑事訴訟 special criminal action.

特別制限 special restrictions. (*legal*).

¹⁵特別區域 special administrative districts.

特別定制 specifically fixed.

特別定貨 special order for goods.

特別密碼 special code.

特別專車 special train.

²⁰特別待遇 special treatment; special behaviour towards.

特別快車 express train.

特別性質 special characteristics.

特別情形 special conditions.

特別手續 special procedure.

²⁵特別折扣 special discount.

特別教室 special buildings for lectures, etc., as in colleges.

特別會議 special conference for discussion; special meeting.

特別權利 preferential rights; special privileges.

特別注意 special notice.

³⁰特別法庭 special courts.

特別法律 special law; particular enactments.

特別海損 particular average.

特別犯 special offenders, as those who break special regulations, military law, etc.

特別理由 special reasons.

³⁵特別破產 special bankruptcy.

特別經理 special agent.

特別考試 special examination.

特別行政 special executive.

特別行為 exceptional action. (*legal*).

⁴⁰特別裁判 special court.

特別製貨 special make.

特別要事 particularly important business.

特別記者 special editor or reporter.

特別負擔 particular responsibility.

⁴⁵特別費 extraordinary expenses; special expenses.

特別開支 specialization.

特別預算 extraordinary budget.

特受權 special legal privilege.

特地 on purpose; designedly; specially.

⁵⁰特報 special edition of a paper.

特定 particular.

特定事實 particular facts.

特定物 particular thing.

特定遺贈 special legacy.

⁵⁵特宥 special pardon or leniency.

特專 specially; for that very reason.

特待生 remission of school fees to special pupils.

特徵 special features, marks, etc., characteristics.

宗敎·的特徵 special characteristics of religion.

[60] 特性 distinguishing features; characteristics; individuality.

有特性·的 specific.

特恩 special favour.

特意 for this very reason; on purpose; specially.

特愛·的 a particular favourite.

[65] 特指 specially alluding to; with special reference to.

特授 specially appointed.

特揀 specially selected.

特效 specific result.

特效藥 specifics.

[70] 特赦 special pardon.

特時 at given or particular dates.

特有之嗜好 a particular hobby or fancy.

特有·的 specific.

特有財產 entailed property.

[75] 特權 special rights or privileges.

特此卽請 specially sent to wish you....

特此懇祈 I therefore specially pray that....

特此通知 specially sent for your information.

特殊 characteristic; special.

[80] 特殊敎·育 special education, as for the blind, etc.

特殊·的勢·力 special spheres of influence.

特殊盟結 special alliances.

特殊關·係 special relations.

特派員 special reporter appointed for interviews, etc., special commissioner.

[85] 特派訪員 special reporter.

特。爲 for this very reason; specially because of.

特特歸我 to be specially mine.

特班 special class or course of studies outside the regular curriculum.

特產 products peculiar to any place.

[90] 特用 for special use; special expenditure.

特留財產 legal property. (legal).

特異 singular; peculiar; sui generis.

特異之人 a marked man.

特異性 a special nature.

[95] 特發准單 special permit.

特白 a special notification.

特示 special notification; special proclamation.

特種 special kinds.

特種條欵 special provision. (legal).

[100] 特種營業稅 special tax—as on wine, tobacco, etc.

特種·的 specific.

特種病 specific disease.

特種目的 special purpose or aim.

特種義務 special obligation.

[105] 特種背書 special endorsement.

特種計畫 specific schemes.

特稱 special description.

特稱命題 particular proposition. (logic).

特竊自異之耳 he merely thought that it was peculiar.

[110] 特立 to stand up for bravely.

特立獨行 independent action.

特等 a class just above the first.

特劄 special instructions.

特簡 specially selected—officials.

[115] 特約 special agreement or contract.

特約通記員 special correspondent of a newspaper.

特約電 special cablegrams supplied by contract to particular papers.

特色 unique feature; distinctive; exceptional.

特製品 speciality.

[120] 特要 I specially desire it.

特記 remarkable.

特許 special permit; license; patent.

特許其淸 praises his purity only.

特許局 patent office.

[125] 特許權 patent rights; special privileges; special concession.

特許證書 patent certificate.

特許護照 special passport.

特調 specially transferred—to a post.

特諭 a special proclamation or notification.

[130] 特買權 patent rights; right of monopoly.

特貸 special leniency or pardon.

特質 idiosyncrasy; characteristics.

有特質·的 specific.

特起 outstanding.

[135] 特達 outstanding.

特遣 specially despatched.

特選 specially selected—of officials.

特錯大錯 = 大錯特錯 gross mistakes; glaring errors.

特長 outstanding: specialty.

[140] 特開會議 special session.

特點 special characteristics; peculiarities; special features.

(a) A male animal. A bull. A stallion. A three-year old beast.

特牲 a sacrificial bull.

有縣特兮 How do we see those —three-year olds—hanging in your courtyards?

格于藝祖用特 he went to the temple of the Cultivated Ancestor and offered a single bullock.

(b) A mate. An eminent man.

特夫 my husband.

特婦 my wife.

實維我特 he was my only one.

求爾新特 seek to please your new relative.

百夫之特 a man in a hundred.

(c) Grain growing straight up.

有菀有特 luxuriantly in it rises the springing grain.

(d) Used in transliterating.

特卡克蘭姆 decagramme.

特卡立脫爾 decalitre.-

特母特姆彈 dum-dum bullet.

特西克蘭姆 decigramme.

特西立脫爾 decilitre.

特里 Delhi. A.c. 德里德利得利.

慝 4.5. Evil. To do evil in secret.
6166 Distinguish 慞 No. 4679. Also read t'i[5].

匿慝 to conceal one's wickedness.

引慝 to take the guilt on oneself.

民乃作慝 the people proceeded to do evil.

TÊNG.　　(ㄉ)

登¹ To rise; to mount. To advance. To step up. To commence.
6167

登 仙 to ascend and become an immortal.
登 位 to ascend the throne; to begin a reign.
登 基 to ascend the throne.
登 堂 to visit; to go up into a hall.
⁵登 壇 拜 將 the ceremony of appointing a general.
登 壇 拜 懺 to ascend the altar and recite the Buddhist ritual.
登 天 to ascend to heaven—difficult.
登 對 suitably matched.
登 山 to ascend a mountain.
¹⁰登 岸 to go ashore; to succeed at the examinations.
登 峯 造 極 to reach the summit—to attain to perfection.
登 庸 to be employed.
登 徒 子 a lecherous man.
登 梯 to climb a ladder.
¹⁵登 極 to ascend the throne.
登 榜 to graduate; to be announced as a successful candidate.
登 殿 to ascend the throne.
登 眞 to become an immortal.
登 碓 to work a pestle with a treadle.
²⁰登 科 or 登 科 甲 to graduate under the former examination system.
登 程 to start on a journey.
登 稼 to reap the harvest.
登 空 to fly aloft.
登 臨 to go up and come down—to travel; to roam.
²⁵登 腿 to stretch the legs—to die.
登 臺 to mount the stage.
登 臺 演 說 to give an address from the platform.
登 臺 說 法 to preach Buddhism.
登 舟 to go on board ship.
³⁰登 車 to get up into a carriage.
登 退 to die.
登 進 to be promoted.
登 遐 to ascend to the far-away regions—to die, of the sovereign.
登 門 to enter a house; to go through a gateway.
³⁵登 門 拜 謝 to go to the house and return thanks.

登 門 認 錯 to go and make an apology.
登 閎 imposing; high and vast.
登 陴 to ascend the city wall.
登 陴 to mount the wall—on guard.
⁴⁰登 陸 to journey overland.
登 青 雲 梯 to mount to the clouds—to take one's degree.
登 高 to ascend heights—as is done on the 9th of the 9th lunar month with a view to longevity.
登 高 必 自 卑 to reach the heights one must begin from the bottom.
登 龍 門 to win sudden success—to graduate.
⁴⁵五 穀 不 登 the five grains will not flourish.
五 穀 豐 登 an abundant harvest.

(a) To record. To make an entry. To publish.

登 冊 to enter in a register.
登 出 to publish.
登 告 白 to publish an advertisement in the press.
登 報 to put it in the papers; to publish in a periodical.
⁵登 報 聲 明 to make the matter widely known through the press.
登 塡 to enter in a register.
登 帳 to enter in the accounts.
登 簿 to enter in the account books.
登 記 to enrol; to register; to make an entry.
¹⁰登 記 法 the law of registration.
登 載 to be inserted—as in a newspaper.
登 錄 商 標 registered trade-mark.
登 鬼 錄 entered in the register of the demons—to be deceased.

(b) As soon as. Specially. At that time.

登 動 to move at once.
登 卽 at that time; at once.
登 時 forthwith; at that time.
登 時 變 相 (hsiang⁴) he forthwith changed countenance.

(c) Used for sounds.

登 丁 sound of felling trees.
登 登 the sound of beating foundations.

氉⁴ Coarse serge. See 罷 No. 5970.
6168

燈 ¹
灯
6169
A lamp; a lantern.

燈 下 in the evening; beneath the lamp-light.
燈 塔 a light-house.
燈 山 numerous lamps arranged to make a hill of light.
燈 心 lamp-wick.
⁵燈 挺 the shaft of a candlestick.
燈 掛 椅 a high-backed chair.
燈 樓 a light-house.
燈 毬 a number of lights arranged like a globe.
燈 油 lamp-oil.
¹⁰燈 火 or 燈 光 the light of a lamp; the flame of a lamp.
燈 炷 the wick of a lamp.
燈 燭 輝 煌 brilliant lights.
燈 盞 the saucer of the old-fashioned Chinese lamp;*
燈 節 the Feast of Lanterns on the 15th of the 1st lunar month.
¹⁵燈 籠 a lantern.
燈 籠 褲 子 very baggy trousers.
燈 罩 子 a lamp-glass or lamp-shade.
燈 臺 a lamp-stand; a lamp-post.
燈 船 a light-ship.
²⁰燈 花 the snuff of a wick.
燈 苗 the flame of a lamp-wick.
燈 苗 放 高 些 turn the lamp up a little.
燈 草 or 燈 心 草 a grass, the pith of which furnishes a wick for native lamps.
燈 虎 riddles written on lamps—hung at the street door.
²⁵燈 號 signalling with lights.
燈 蛾 moths that circle around a lamp.
燈 語 light signalling.
燈 謎 riddles written on lamps, a prize is offered for the solution.
↑燈火管制 blackout or dimout.

瞪 ⁴
瞠
6170
To stare at. Also read ch'êng¹.

瞪 眼 or 瞪 目 gazing at fixedly; staring in anger.

* lamps collectively.

瞪 神 a vacant stare.

磴 嶝 [4]
6171
A ledge on a precipice; stone steps; a cliff, a stone plinth.

磴 道 road over a mountain.
石 磴 stone steps.

澄 [4]
6172
Swept away, as by a flood. Soaked, saturated. To settle, as with alum; to strain; to drain off. A.w. 澄

澄 倒 overflowed and swept away.
澄·出·來 to strain off.
澄·得 清 to strain clear—as liquid. 澄沙 puree of beans.
澄 米 湯 or 澄 飯 to drain the water from cooked rice.
澄 落 海 swept out to sea.

簦 [1]
6173
Large umbrella with a long handle, used for street stalls.

蹬 [1.4.]
6174
To step; to treat. To go on. To lose one's energy. To struggle on with little success.

蹭 蹬 dilatory; baffled; dispirited; unsuccessful.

鄧 [4]
6175
A small feudal State in what is now Hupeh.

鐙 [4]
6176
A stirrup. u.f. 燈 No. 6169.

鐙·子 a stirrup.
鐙 骨 the stirrup bone in the ear.

(a) Read têng[1]. A sacrificial dish made of earthenware, sometimes written 豋.

橙 凳 [4]
6177
A stool, a bench, a form. The small characters below are not strictly correct.

櫈·子 or 板·櫈 a stool; a form; a bench.
方 櫈 or 斗 櫈 a square stool.

梯 櫈 a step-ladder.
脚 櫈 a footstool.

等 [3]
6178
To wait.

等(一)等兒 or 等·一·下 or 等·一·會 兒 wait a little.
等·不 及 unable to wait.
等 候 or 等 俟 to wait; to wait for.
等·到 明 天 wait until tomorrow.
[5]等·到 老·了 to wait until old age.
等 待 to wait; to wait for.
等·得 許 久 I have waited a long while.
等·我 作 let me do it.
等 煩 weary of waiting.
[10]等 緊 用 wanted at once.
等·着 要 waiting for it.
↑等·着 waiting.

(a) A step—of a staircase. A class, a rank, a sort. To grade, to classify, to arrange. A comparison. Equal to.

等 人 men of the same class or standing.
等 伏 線 isoclinic line.
等 位 of similar standing.
等 倫 of the same generation.
[5]等 倍 數 equimultiple.
等 價 物 equivalent in value.
等 儲 力 equipotence.
等 分 equal quantities, as in a prescription.
等 分 桿 equalizing bar.
[10]等 分 級 數 geometrical series.
等 列 of the same rank or class.
等 壓 線 isobars.
等 夷 mutual equality.
等·子 a small balance for weighing medicines, etc. ≡6179.1.
[15]等 差 difference between.(-*ch'a*[1] or-*tz'u*·)
等 差 級 數 arithmetical progression. (-*ch'a*·-)
等 式 an equation.
等 威 已 辨 the styles befitting the various ranks were distinct.
等 數 消 cancelling of equal numbers.
[20]等 於 equals to; amounts to.
等 時 性 isochronism.
等 次 in order; place in a series.
等 比 例 equal ratio.
等 氣 壓 線 isobars.
[25]等 温 線 isotherms.

等 熱 線 isotherms.
等 百 世 之 王 to arrange the kings of all ages according to merit.
等 磁 線 isomagnetic lines.
等 秤 equilibration.
[30]等 第 in proper sequence; order; series.
等 等 不 一 of various kinds; assorted.
等·級 standards; steps; grade; rank.
等 級 選 舉 class election where there is a property or other qualification.
等 而 論 之 to treat in a similar manner; and so with the others.
[35]等 色·的 isochromatic.
等 號 the sign for equality,=.
等 角·的 equiangular.
等 角 畫 法 isometric projection.
等 賦 taxation by a sliding scale, under which the rich pay more in proportion.
[40]等 距 離 equidistance.
等 距 離 點 equidistant points.
等 身 書 a pile of books as high as himself.
等 速 運 動 uniform motion.
等 邊 三 角 形 equilateral triangle.
[45]等 邊·的 equilateral.—
等 量 equal quantities.
等 長 of equal length.
等 閒 ordinary; common.
萬 事 付 等 閒 all things become commonplace.
[50]等 震 線 isoseismal line.
等 面 形 two surfaces equal in area but having unequal sides and angles.
等 韻 classification of rhymes.
等 高 曲 線 contour lines.
上 等 first-class; the best.
[55]下 等 inferior.
不 等 uncertain; inferior; not of the same class.
中 等 medium.
何 等 大 how great!
初 等 elementary. *See* No. 1390-37ff.
[60]同 等 of the same class.
平 等 of the same rank; equality. *See* No. 5303-54ff.
機 會 均 等 equal opportunity.
相 等 similar; of the same rank or class.
與 人 對 等 on an equal footing with.
[65]頭 等 first-class.

高 等 advanced. *See* No. 3290-65ff.

(b) Used as a sign of the plural; to mark the end of a quotation in official documents; it is often equivalent to *et cetera*.

等 事 and such matters—as the foregoing; a phrase used as a plural termination.

等 件 and so on—a phrase used after an enumeration of things; *et cetera*.

等 因 and like arguments—closing a quotation from a document written by a superior or an equal, and followed by 奉此 or 承准此.

等 屬 and other places within the jurisdiction of.

⁵等 弊 and such malpractices.

等 情 such circumstances—used when quoting a document written by an inferior; it is followed by 據此.

等 樣 of the same species; such articles; "etc., etc."

等 由 marks the end of a quotation in communications between officials of equal standing or slightly inferior rank; it is followed by 准此.

等 等 and so forth; and so on; "etc."—it follows a list.

¹⁰等 處 and such places; the above-mentioned places.

等 語 such words—as those quoted; marks a quotation.

等 類 or 等 項 or the same species; such articles; "etc., etc."

我 等 we.

文 武 等 官 the various civil and military officials.

¹⁵牛 馬 等 cattle, horses, etc.

爾 等 you.

該 犯 等 the aforesaid criminals.

戥³ A small steelyard for weighing money, etc.
6179

戥·子 a small steelyard.

戥 星 the dots on the beam of the steelyard.

戥 盒 the small case in which the above is carried.

戥 盤 the plate on which the thing to be weighed is placed.

T'ÊNG.　　ㄊㄥ)

疼² To ache. Pain, soreness. Affection. To love.
6180

疼 愛 to love passionately; very fond of.

疼 痛 pain; to ache.

疼 絲 絲·的 or 疼 肌 肌·的 a continued pain; very painful.

疼 苦 pain; agony.

疼 顧 very kind to inferiors.

心 疼 pained at heart. 心·疼 to love or to pet; to grudge (spending, etc.)

滕² Water bursting forth. To open the mouth wide when talking.
6181

滕 六 降 雪 the god of snow sends down a snowstorm.

滕 口 說 也 to open the mouth wide when speaking.

(a) Name of an ancient State in what is now Shantung.

籐² 藤 General name for climbing plants. Rattan; cane.
6182

藤 席 a rattan mat.

藤 條 split rattans.

藤 椅·子 a cane chair.

藤 牌 a cane shield.

⁵藤 竿 or 沙 藤 rattans.

藤 絲 rattan shavings.

藤 繞 involved; complicated.

藤 肉 split rattans.

藤 葛 or 葛 藤 creepers; complications.

¹⁰藤·蘿 or 紫 藤 wistaria.

藤 黃 gamboge.

長 春 藤 ivy.

縢² To bind; to tie up. A cord.
6183

行 縢 to bind the legs with cord.

螣² A wingless dragon of the clouds.
6184

螣 蛇 a flying serpent—the above dragon.

(a) Read *t'ê*⁴·⁵. A destructive insect which attacks rice plants.

去 其 螟 螣 remove the insects that eat the heart, and those that attack the leaf.

謄² To copy; to transcribe.
6185

謄·出·來 make a copy of it.

謄·出 底 稿 make a copy from the original.

謄 寫 to copy.

謄 抄 to copy.

謄 清 to make a fair copy.

謄 眞 make a fair copy.

謄 錄 to copy.

騰² 驀 To mount; to ascend. To move; to turn out. Inter. preceding.
6186

騰·出 傢·伙 turn out the furniture.

騰 房 to move out of a house for another to take it.

騰 挪 to remove; to transfer.

騰 掉 nimble; active; 騰·掉 to

⁵騰 揑 flying swiftly. [empty out.

騰 空 to soar; to mount to heaven; to empty out.

騰 笑 loud laughter.

騰 蛟 起 鳳 mounting dragon and soaring phœnix—a rising man; describes great talents.

騰 貴 very expensive.

¹⁰騰 起 to rise—as a mist.

騰 跳 to bounce; to jump up and down.

騰 踴 to leap up; to mount—as prices.

騰 躍 to prance; to rear; to bounce.

騰 辯 to discuss warmly.

¹⁵騰 達 to prosper; to get on in life.

騰 閃 to evade; to dodge.

騰 降 rising and falling.

騰 雲 駕 霧 to mount the clouds and ride the mists—absurd, improbable.

騰 馬 to cover a mare.

²⁰騰 驤 to prance.

沸 騰 bubbling and boiling—of dissension and trouble.

飛 騰 to soar; to mount to heaven.

TI. (ㄉ)

氐 [3] A foundation. A constellation.
6187

維 周 之 氐 the foundation of the House of *Chou*—said of a worthy minister.

(a) Read *ti*[1]. Name of an ancient tribe.

氐 羌 a tribe which, in the *Shang* dynasty, occupied a region on the upper waters of the River *Wei* in Kansu.

(b) Inter. next. To hang down.

氐 賤 low in price.
氐 首 bowed their heads in submission.

(c) Read *ti*[n]. Inter. 抵 No. 6192. On the whole, etc.

大 氐 for the most part; on the whole; generally speaking.

低} [1] To hang or bow the head; to droop; to lower. Low; beneath.
伍}
6188

低 一 格 or 低 一 頭[2] put it a line lower down.
低 一 級 a step lower.
低 下 人 menials.
低 三 下 四·的 at the beck and call of everybody—low-class persons.
[5]低 僞 counterfeit; fictitious.
低 價 low in price.
低 原 a lowlying plain.
低 品 low-class.
低 回 or 低 徊 to bow the head and look round in meditation or hesitation.
[10]低 地 lowlying lands.
低 垂 to hang down.
低 屋 a low-built house.
低 年 級 the first-year class in a school or college.
低 徊 久 之 pondered for a long time; lingering fondly.
[15]低 徊 欲 絕 walking backwards and forwards meditating suicide.
低 微 low; base; lowly.
低 拉 拉·的 overcome with grief.

低 昂 low and high; fluctuating.
低 潮 low-tide.
[20]低 眉 to be servile; merciful.
低 稅 to lower the duty.
低 窪 low-lying.
低 而 又 低 lower and lower.
低 聲 in a low voice.
[25]低 聲 下 氣 meek and submissive.
低 色[+] depreciated; low-grade—of silver.
低 處 a lowlying place.
低 言 whispers.
低 迷 muddled.
[30]低 音 in a low tone; contralto; bass.
低 頭[2] to bow the head.
低 頭[2] 服 小 to bow the head and submit.
低 首 下 心 to bow and submit.
低 首 無 言 he hung his head and said nothing.
[35]出 身 低 of lowly birth.

呧 [3] To vex. Vexatious. To slander. u.f. 詆 No. 6196.
6189

底 [3] The bottom; the base. Underneath; low; below. A foundation—thus, a rough draft, a constitution.
6190

底·下 below; lower down.
底·下·人 underlings; servants of a wealthy man.
底·子 a foundation; a shoe-sole; a rough draft of a document; the mode of entering public service.
好 底·子 comes from a good stock.
[5]打 個 底·子 to make out a rough draft.
打 底·子 to lay a foundation; to put on a coat of priming.
底·子 錢 gate-money paid by venders.
底 定 to calm—as disorders.
底 數 or 對 數 底 base—in logarithms.
底 本 the base; capital; the general tenor of.
[10]底 根 the root; the base; originally.
底 極 extremities.
底 歉 endowment fund, of which the interest only is to be used; reserve fund.
底 片 a negative—for photographs.

底 稿 rough draft.
[15]底 簿 book for drafts of letters, documents, etc.
底·細 the gist of; the real story.
底 線 base—geometry.
底 蘊 the true cause; the inside story.
底·裏 the sum and substance of.
[20]不 知 底·裏 do not know the details.
底 金 funds of which the interest only is to be used.
底 面 the under surface.
底 類 base—chemistry.
到 底 at bottom; after all.
[25]地 底 the underworld; Hades.
家 底 family possessions.
小 底 servants; menials.
後 底 last; the rear; behind.
根 底 base; origin; root.
[30]河 底 river-bed.
海 底 the bottom of the sea.
澈 底 radically; thoroughly.
無 底 深 潭 a bottomless gulf.
眼 底 無 人 supercilious; treating others as if they were beneath his notice.

(a) To come to. To end.

底 止 to come to a stop.
底 豫 brought to find delight in.
伊 于 胡 底 what will they come to? what will be the outcome of it?

(b) A whetstone. See 砥 No. 951.

周 道 如 底 the way to *Chou* is level like a whetstone.

(c) An interrogative like 何. What?

底 事 來 why do you come?
底 處 where?
成 底 事 what have I accomplished?

(d) A sign of the genitive, similar to 的.

信 仰·底 內 容 the content of a belief.
動 物·底 身 體 animal bodies.
原 素·底 變 化 the changes in chemical elements.
[5]心·底 分 析 mental analysis.
罷 工·底 理 由 the reason for strikes.

道德·底影響 a moral effect.
那時代·底精神 the spirit of that age.

弤³ The bow of the Emperor *Shun*.
6191

抵³ To resist; to oppose. To knock. To butt.
6192

抵·不·住 unable to sustain or resist; not equivalent in value.
抵冒 inconsiderate and shameless.
抵·住 to hold up; to stop—from falling.
抵几 to slap the table.
⁵抵制 to oppose; to boycott.
抵制力 resistance; opposition.
抵制外貨 boycott foreign goods. 「＝高射砲.
抵制飛機砲 anti-aircraft guns.
抵力 power of resistance.
¹⁰低抵力 low resistance. (*electric*).
內抵力 internal resistance. (*electric*).
高抵力 high resistance. (*electric*).
抵力箱 resistance-box. (*electric*).
抵·得·住 able to sustain; able to resist.
¹⁵抵抗 to oppose; to resist; to withstand; antagonism.
抵抗力 power of resistance.
抵抗器 rheostat.
抵抗圈 resistance-coil. (*electric*).
抵抗性 resistibility.
²⁰最小抵抗線 the line of least resistance.
消極抵抗 passive resistance.
抵掌 to clap the hands; to gesticulate.
抵擋 to resist; to ward off; to parry.
抵擋關係 to bear the consequences.
²⁵抵敵 to resist an enemy.
抵破 to break with a blow.
抵禁 to break prohibitions.
抵禦 to withstand; to resist.
抵突 to clash.
³⁰抵觸 to butt; to infringe upon; to come into conflict with; to collide with.
抵賴 to repudiate.

抵逐 repulsion.
抵針 a thimble.
抵門 to knock at a door.

(a) To substitute. To give as an equivalent. To make good.

抵代稅 commuted taxes.
抵付 to repay; to make good.
抵借 to pledge against a loan.
抵償 to make good; to ransom; to atone for; to forfeit one's life.
⁵抵兌 to give an equivalent for.
抵典 to mortgage.
抵命 to forfeit one's life.
抵完 to pay up—as taxes.
抵·得·兩·個 equivalent to two.
¹⁰抵°押 to pledge; to mortgage.
抵押品 pledges; securities.
抵·換 to barter; to exchange one thing for another.
抵據 a mortgage-deed.
抵數 to balance an account.
¹⁵抵欵 a mortgage-loan.
抵消 a set-off.
抵當權 right over the property of a debtor.
抵給 to pledge to.
抵罪 to atone for crime; to bear the blame.
²⁰抵質 to mortgage.
抵賬 to settle a debt; to compound for a money payment by an equivalent.
抵還 to repay; to make good.
抵銷 to make compensation; to commute.
大抵 on the whole; generally.

(b) To arrive at. To reach.

抵上海 arrived at Shanghai.
抵任 to reach one's post.
抵至 or 抵到 to arrive at.

柢³ Root; foundation; base.
6193

根深柢固 deeply and firmly rooted.

牴³
觝 To gore; to butt. To resist; to push.
6194

牴挑異端 to oppose heresies.

牴牾 to resist; to oppose; contradictory.
牴觸 to butt; to gore.
角牴 to butt with the horns.

羝¹ A ram or he-goat.
6195

羝羊觸藩 like a ram butting a hedge—he is held by his horns. *See* 觸 No. 1416-3.

詆³·¹ To slander; to defame.
6196

詆毀 to calumniate.
詆訶古人 to disparage the ancients.
詆謗 to disparage; to slander.
詆陷人 to incriminate a person falsely.
見詆 to suffer insult.

邸³ Place where feudal princes lodged when visiting the capital, hence it means the capital. A lodging-house. A screen.
6197

邸報 or 邸抄 the Peking Gazette.
邸舍 or 旅邸 a lodging-place.
官邸 official residence.

地⁴ The earth. Earth, soil, ground. A place, locality, territory, position, situation.
6198

地丁 the land-tax.
地上·的 terrestrial.
地上莖 aerial stem.
地·下 on the floor; on the ground.
⁵地·下莖 subterranean stems.
地·下跑 (or 走) to go on foot.
地不出產 the land produces nothing; the earth does not yield her increase.
地不改辟 there is not the necessity for opening up the country.
地中 subterranean.
¹⁰地中海 The Mediterranean Sea.
地主 a landowner; a landlord.
地位 a site; a position or situation.
地保 local constables or headmen who are responsible for good order.
地價稅 assessment tax.

15 地 出 寶 the earth produces precious things.

地 利 productions; produce; advantages of situation.

地 券 a title-deed.

地 力 學 dynamical-geology.

地 動 an earthquake.

20 地 勢 physical features of a place.

地 勢 學 physical geography.

地 卜 geomancy.

地 史 historical geography.

地 圖 a map.

25 地 土 soil; locality; territory; earth.

地 址 locality; position; a site; a plot of land.

地。基 land; property; a foundation.

地 堂 space before the steps of a grave.

地 域 district; region.

30 地 境 boundaries.

地 壇 The Temple of Earth.

地 壯 the soil is fertile.

地 契 title-deeds for land.

地 學 geography.

35 地 學 協 會 Geographical Society.

地 層 strata.

地 峽 isthmus.

地 師 one who practices geomancy.

地 帶 zones.

40 地 平 horizontal.

地 平 線 the horizon. ⌈(-ch'a¹)

地 平 視 差 geocentric parallax.

地 府 the grave; the next world.

地 形 topography.

45 地 心 centre of the earth.

地 心 吸 力 or 地 心 引 力 gravitation.

地 心 經 度 geocentric longitude.

地 心 緯 度 geocentric latitude.

地 攤 stall; mats spread out with goods for sale.

50 地 支 the *Earthly Branches*, used in calculations with the *Heavenly Stems* 天 干.*

地 文 學 physical geography.

地。方 local; a local constable or headman who is responsible for order; a place.

地 方 主 義 localism.

地 方 保 衛 團 local militia.

55 地。方 公 債 local public loans.

地 方 公 益 local public utilities.

地。方 分 權 decentralization.

地。方 制 local-government system.

地。方 官 local officials.

60 地。方 審 判 廳 local courts.

* *See App. IV. p. 1176.*

地。方 法 院 local courts.

地。方 稅 local taxes.

地。方 自 治 local self-government. 地方色彩 local color.

地。方 行 政 local administration.

65 地。方 財 政 local finances. ·

地 望 position and influence.

地 板 flooring; a boarded floor.

地 極 the ends of the earth.

地 棍 local bullies or rowdies.

70 地 楊 梅 name coined for the strawberry.

地 業 landed property.

地 權 rights of property.

地·步 position; state; condition; place; footing.

地 段 a piece of ground.

75 地 殼 the crust of the earth.

地 氈 a carpet.

地 氣 climate; a subtle essence that is supposed to animate the earth.

地 洞 車 underground railway.

地 瀝 青 asphaltum.

80 地 炕 to make up a bed on the ground in lieu of a *k'ang*.

地 然 炬 火 lit a great fire on the ground.

地 無 立 錐 not even enough land in which to stick an awl.

地 爐·子 a hot-air furnace; a ground-stove.

地 牛 轉 肩 the earth-ox changes his load to the other shoulder—an earthquake.

85 地 獄 hell; a prison.

地 球 the earth; the globe.

地 球 儀 a terrestrial globe.

地 球 對 足 the antipodes.

地 球 引 力 terrestrial gravitation.

90 地 球·的 terrestrial.

地 理 geography.

人 文 地 理 political geography.

人 種 地 理 ethnological geography.

天 然 地 理 physical geography.

95 宗 敎 地 理 geography dealing with the distribution of religions.

政 治 地 理 political geography.

經 濟 地 理 economic geography.

地 理 先·生 or 堪 輿 先·生 a geomancer.

地 理·的 geographical.

100 地 理 術 geomancy.

地 瓜 sweet potatoes.

地 產 productions of the soil; landed estate; real-estate.

地 產 公 司 real-estate agency.

地 甲 the former tithing system; petty local officers.

105 地 界 boundary of a place; a place.

地 畝 the land; earth; acreage.

地 瘠 barren soil.

地 皮 the surface of the land.

地 盤 position; place; site; place occupied by usurpation.

110 地 石 學 structural geology.

地 磁 氣 terrestrial magnetism.

地 祇 the god of the earth.

地 租 ground rent; land tax.

地 穴 a grave; a hole.

115 地 窖 or 地 窖·子 a cellar.

地 精 a name for ginseng; also *Polygonum multiflorum*.

地 緯 度 geographical latitude.

地 脉 the earth-pulse—lucky signs in the earth, which according to the geomancers indicate good fortune, etc.

地 脚 堅 固 the foundation is firm. ↑地 線 ground wire.

120 地 蓆 floor matting.

地·藏 (*tsang*⁴) 王 a Buddha who saves souls.

地 蛋 sweet potatoes; potatoes.

地 蠟 paraffin-wax.

地 血 a kind of madder—*Rubia cordifolia*. Also *Lithospermum officinale*.

125 地 衣 lichens.

地 表 surface of the earth.

地 角 the corner of a field; a cape.

地 解 (*chiai*¹) to send under guard from one jurisdiction to another.

地 誌 topography.

130 地 質 上 or 地 質·的 geologically.

地 質 化 學 geo-chemistry.

地 質 學 geology.

地 身 surface; area.

地 軸 the earth's axis.

135 地 輿 geography.

地 輿 圖 or 地 理 圖 a map of the world, or of China.

地 載 the earth supports—as the heavens cover.

地 道 a subway. See 6136 A. 15.

地 醜 德 齊 equal territories and similar abilities.

110 地 金 land rent.
地 鋪 to make up a bed on the floor.
地 門 冬 asparagus.
地 閣 the chin.
地 闢 於 丑 earth appeared at the period *Ch'ou.*
145 地 雷 land mines used for military purpose.
地 電 流 earth currents. (*electric*).
地 震 earthquakes.
地 震 學 seismology.
地 震 表 seismoscope; seismometer.
150 地 震 計 seismograph or seismometer.
地 面 territory.
地 頸 an isthmus.
地 頭² local; native; belonging to the place; destination.
地 頭² 蛇 the local snake—rascals familiar with the place.
155 地 頭² 鬼 local rowdies who bring in robbers from outside, etc.
地 體 the body of the earth.
地 髓 the foxglove—*Rehmannia lutea.*
地 黃 the foxglove, as above.
地 點 position; location.
160 地 鼠 the shrew-mouse.
地 龍 the earth-worm.
人 地 abilities; talents.
保 護 地 a protectorate.
后 地 Earth—personified as a goddess.
165 在 甲 地,在 乙 地 in one place, in another place.
大 地 the whole world; the earth.
實 地 terra-firma; practically.
就 地 正 法 deal with the offender on the spot.
心 地 one's disposition. *See No. 2735—31ff.*
170 暗 地 in secret; behind one's back.
本 地 local; native.
根 據 地 a base for operations.
此 地 here.
殖 民 地 a colony.
175 白 地 waste lands.
空 地 waste lands; unoccupied land.
置 地 to purchase land.
荒 地 uncultivated lands.
落 地 to fall to the ground—to be born; place; locality.

180 餘 地 a margin; a reserve; a little space.
黑 地 a black background.

(a) Used like 的 with adjectival or adverbial force. Read *ti*⁴, spoken as ·tê.
低 聲·地 說 whispering said....
哈 哈·地 笑 gave a great laugh.
實 實·地 說·出·來 speak out truthfully.
緊 緊·地 裹 tightly bound.

枕⁴ Standing alone.
6199
有 枕 之 杜 there stands a solitary russet-pear tree.

棣⁴ A mountain tree like the cherry. A plum—*Prunus japonica.*
6200
棣 棠 a shrub with yellow flowers—*Kerria japonica.*
棣 鄂 (or 萼) the flower and its calyx—elder and younger brothers.
常 棣 之 華, 鄂 不 韡 韡 the flowers of the cherry-tree, are they not gorgeously displayed?—from the *Odes,* refers to the relation and affection of brothers, from which the characters 常 棣 or 棣 華 are used for an elder brother.

(a) Read *tai*⁴. Dignified.
威 儀 棣 棣 my deportment has been dignified.

弟⁴ A younger brother; a junior. Used conventionally by a speaker of himself.
6201 Distinguish 第 No. 6203.
弟·兄 or 兄·弟 brothers; brethren.
弟 兄 官 officials of equal rank.
弟 妹 younger brother and sister.
弟·婦 or 弟 媳 a younger brother's wife.
5 弟 子³ a disciple; a junior.
弟 子³ 服 其 勞 the young endure toil—for their elders.
弟 男 子³ 姪 younger members of a family.
弟 郎 younger brother.

令 弟 your younger brother.
10 小 弟 or 愚 弟 your little brother or foolish brother—I, me.
舍 弟 my younger brother.

(a) Read *t'i*⁴. To act in a submissive manner, as a younger brother should. u.f. 悌 No. 6248.
孝 弟 filial piety and brotherly submission.
弟 子³ 出 則 弟 a youth (*ti*) when abroad should be respectful (*t'i*) to his elders.

(b) Read *t'i*⁴. Easy and self-possessed. *See* 豈 No. 544-A.
豈 弟 君 子³ easy and self-possessed are my noble guests; O happy and courteous sovereign! easy and self-possessed was our prince.
齊 子³ 豈 (*k'ai*³) 弟 the daughter of *Ch'i* is delighted and complaisant.

(c) Read *ti*⁴. u.f. 第 No. 6203. Order, sequence, etc.
弟 一 弟 二 first, second.

娣⁴ A younger sister; wife of a younger brother.
6202
娣 姒 brother's wives—both older and younger.
娣 婦 wife of a younger brother.

第⁴ A series; a grade; a degree; a class. Order; sequence. Placed before numerals it forms the ordinal numbers.
6203 Distinguish 弟 No. 6201.
第 一 number one; the first; the best.
第 一 二 三 身 first, second, and third person.
第 一 件 the first article; in the first place.
第 一 原 因 first cause.
5 第 一 層 the first storey; first division.
第 一 手 the best player, worker, etc.
第 一 權 first right. (*legal*).
第 一 流 the first class.

第 一 等 of the highest class; first-rate.
[10]弟 一 義 務 first obligation. (*legal*).
第 一 要 緊 的 the first in importance.
第 一 身 代 名 詞 first personal pronoun.
第 三 人 (or 者) third party. (*legal*).
第 三 人 稱 third person. (*gramm.*).
[15]第 三 債 務 人 third debtor. (*legal*).
第 三 國 際 會 議 Third Internationale.
第 三 方 (or 造) third party. (*legal*).
第 三 日 on the third day.
第 三 紀 tertiary period.
[20]第 二 篇 the second—hymn.
第 二 道 防 線 the second line of defence.
第 五 號 number five.
第 六 覺 a sixth sense.
第 幾 節 which verse is it?
[25]次 第 order; precedence; sequence.

(a) A house. State apartments for successful *Hanlin* graduates in ancient times. A degree. To take a degree.

第 主 head of the house.
及 第 to take a place among the first three successful candidates for the third-degree examinations.
宅 第 a dwelling-house.
得 第 to be among the first three successful candidates for the highest degree.
[5]甲 第 the third or highest degree under the old system.
科 第 the second class of graduates under the old system.
落 第 to fail in the examinations for the highest degree.
詩 書 門 第 a literary family.
賜 第 to confer a mansion—on a deserving official.

(b) But. Only. However.

第 今 日 之 人 but the men of today.
第 每 值 夜 漁 but whenever he had a night of fishing.
第 求 安 逸 they only seek ease and comfort.

第 能 can only.
第 至 明 年 夏 日 only wait until next summer.
不 第 如 此 not only thus.

帝 [4] The Supreme Ruler, often interchanged with 天. A ruler; the emperor; a god; a deified being.
6204

帝 京 the capital—Peking.
帝 典 the statutes of Yao, 堯.
帝 制 monarchy.
帝 制 派 imperialists.
[5]帝 力 何 有 於 我 what is the strength of the Emperor to us?
帝 君 a title of reverence added to the names of gods.
　文 昌 帝 君 the god of literature.
　關 聖 帝 君 the god of war.
帝 命 不 時 the appointments of the Supreme came at the right time. (the 不 時 being defined as an affirmative.)
[10]帝 命 不 違 the favour of the Supreme did not leave—the *Shang* dynasty.
帝 命 率 育 God appointed *the wheat and barley* for the nourishment of all—without distinction of territory or boundary.
帝 國 an empire.
帝 國 主 義 Imperialism.
帝 城 the capital.
[15]帝 女 a goddess.
帝 室 the Imperial clan.
帝 居 the Imperial capital.
帝 弓 or 天 弓 the bow of God—the rainbow.
帝 王 or 皇 帝 the Emperor.
[20]帝 用 不 臧 the Supreme viewed him with disapprobation—the preceding sentence uses 上 天 High Heaven, in the same connection.
帝 畿 the capital.
帝 省 其 山 God surveyed the hills.
帝 祚 the Imperial throne.
帝 籍 the fields ploughed in person by the emperor.
[25]帝 者 天 之 用 *ti* signifies the activity of Heaven.
帝 號 the style of an emperor's reign.
帝 車 the chariot of God—the Dipper, part of Ursa Major.

帝 遷 明 德 The Supreme brought about the removal thither of this intelligent ruler.
帝 都 the Imperial capital.
[30]帝 鄉 Heaven; the home of the ruler.
帝 闍 the door of the Imperial palace—Peking.
上 帝 不 寧 不 康 禋 祀 Did not the Supreme comfort her? Had He not accepted her offering and sacrifice?
五 帝 the Five Rulers of the earliest ages of China—太昊, 炎帝, 黃帝, 少昊, 顓頊.
天 帝 the Heavenly Ruler.
[35]恭 默 思 道 夢 帝 賚 予 良 while I reverently and silently pondered on the Right Way, I dreamt that God gave me a worthy assistant.
惟 簡 在 上 帝 之 心 I will examine these things in harmony with the mind of God—said by *T'ang*, 成湯, when praying for rain; in other sentences he uses 天 Heaven.
昭 上 帝 迄 用 康 年 the bright and glorious Supreme will, in these, (wheat and barley,) give us a good year.
有 皇 上 帝 伊 誰 云 憎 there is the Great Supreme, does He hate anyone?—on the two lines preceding this, the commentaries speak of 天 Heaven, in a personal way.
皇 矣 上 帝 臨 下 有 赫 Great is God, beholding the lower world in majesty!
[40]神 之 聲 者 稱 帝 the venerable among the gods is called *Ti*.
蕩 蕩 上 帝 下 民 之 辟 How vast is God, the Ruler of men below!

渧 [4] To drop, as liquids. A drop.
6205

渧 下 水 來 the water is dripping.
渧 哭 crying and weeping.

禘 [4] The Imperial Sacrifice; offered of old, by the emperor alone, to the remotest ancestor from whom the founder of the reigning dynasty traced his descent.
6206

禘 嘗 the various ancestral sacrifices.

禘 自 旣 灌 而 往 者 吾 不 欲 觀 之 矣 I have no wish to look at the great sacrifice after the libation is poured.

或 問 禘 之 說 子 曰 不 知 也 someone asked the meaning of the great sacrifice; Confucius replied, "I do not know."

蒂[4]
6207

A stem; a base; a peduncle or footstalk of a flower or fruit.

蒂 固 a firm support.
蒂 盤 the stem and green calyx.

諦[4]
6208

To judge; to examine into; to make researches; to discriminate.

諦 毫 末 to investigate minute things.
諦 視 to scrutinize.

(a) Buddhist term for The Truth.

(b) u.f. 啼 To cry; to wail.

哭 泣 諦 號 weeping and wailing.

遞 遞[4]
6209

To hand to; to pass over; to forward; to transmit.

遞 傳 or 傳 遞 to transmit; to forward; to send by post; to hand down—as traditions.
遞 具 to hand in—as documents.
遞 到 sent; forwarded to.
遞 名 to hand in one's name.
[5]遞 夫 a courier.
遞 奏 to memorialize the emperor.
遞 手 本 to hand in a personal statement—of one's services, etc.—sent in to a superior to inform him regarding the petitioner.
遞 束 to hand a letter to a person.
遞 片 子 to hand in a card.
[10]遞 眼 色[4] to tip a wink.
遞 禀 to hand in or file a petition.
遞 籍 to deport; to send back to his native place.
遞·給 to hand to.
遞·給 我 hand it to me; bring it here.

[15]遞 至 sent; forwarded to.
遞 與 to hand to.
遞 解 to send; to forward; to deport.
遞 解 回 籍 to deport a criminal back to his native place.
遞 貨 單 to present a ship's manifest.
[20]遞 送 to send; to forward.
遞·過·來 to pass over.
飛 遞 by express.
馬 遞 post courier.

(a) To substitute; to change. To alternate. Proportional. For; instead of.

遞 代 substituted for; instead of; to take the place of.
遞 加 to add pro rata; to add a certain proportion.
遞 加 無 已 to add to continually.
遞 加 稅 progressive taxation.
[5]遞 增 proportionate increase; continually increasing.
遞 年 one year following another.
遞 更 to change—as the seasons, etc.
遞 減 continual decrease; proportionate decrease.
遞 相 往 還 alternating; going backwards and forwards.
[10]遞 算 to calculate proportionately.
遞 補 to fill a vacant position on a committee, etc.
遞 起 脚 to change step—when marching.
遞 進 progress; advance.
遞 進 之 庸 progressive wages.
[15]遞 進 事 級[2] progressive steps.
遞 進 所 得 稅 progressive income tax.

隄[1]
6210

To guard against. A barrier; a dike. Also read t'i[2].
Inter. 堤 No. 6231.

隄 埈 an embankment.
隄 岸 a dike.
隄·防 to be careful of; to watch against.
築 隄 to raise an embankment or dike.

蝃[4]
6211

A secondary rainbow.
Inter. next.

蝀[4]
6212

The rainbow.

蝃 蝀 the rainbow.

TI.　　　(ㄉ)
(Tih)

的[4.5]
6213

Bull's-eye of a target.

中 的 to hit the bull's-eye.
準 的 a mark; standard; object to be attained.
發 彼 有 的 I shall hit that mark.
目 的 aim; object, etc. See No. 4596-29ff.

(a) Clear; evident. Genuine; real.

的 保 a satisfactory guarantee.
的 係 it is really.
的 信 trustworthy.
的 名 the real name.
[5]的 歷 fresh and bright—as flowers.
的 決 to receive the actual number of blows ordered in punishment.
的 準 accurate; reliable.
的 然 openly; publicly; notoriously.
的 然 可 信 may be really accepted as true.
[10]的 然 而 日 亡 displayed forth, but daily diminishing.
的 當 careful; proper.
的 的 detailed; circumstantial; clearly manifested.
的 皪 bright, shining, lustrous—as a pearl.
的[2]確 reliable; trustworthy; genuine.
[15]的 筆 autograph.
的 細 the exact details.
眞 的 true; a fact.
端 的 really and truly.

(b) Subordinative particle, corresponding in translation to 's, relative pronoun, that, which, etc. Pron. ·tê.

他·的 書 his book.
↓ 我·的 衣 裳 my clothing.
他 穿·的 草 鞋 the straw sandals which he wore.
他 說·的 有 理 what he says is reasonable.

傳 道·的 an evangelist.
好·的 歹·的 good and bad.
⁵大·的 小·的 large and small.
是·的 it is so; yes.
有·的 there are; there is some.
書 上·的 what is in the book.
送 信·的 a postman; a messenger.

(c) Used like 得 to indicate manner or possibility. Pron. *te*.
他 說·的(or 得)有 理 he talks reasonably.
看·的 (or 得) 見 can see.

鞉 1.5.　Reins. A bridle.
6214

狄 2.5.　Northern barbarians—the *Hsiung Nu* and others.
6215

夷 狄 wild tribes.
北 狄 the wild tribes of the north.

(a) Menials employed about the Court.

狄 人 menials; attendants on musicians in ancient times.
狄 設 黼 扆 servants set out the screens ornamented with figures of axes.

(b) A stag; an elk.

(c) Read *t'i²*. To drive away. u.f. 逖 No. 6265.

狄 彼 東 南 to drive away the tribes of the east and the south.

荻 2.5.　A kind of reed with a pithy stem.
6216

荻 筆 a reed-pen.

笛 2.5.　A flute; a fife. A whistle.
6217

笛·子 or·兒 a flute.
低 音 大 笛 a bassoon.
口 笛 a whistle.
吹 笛·子 or·兒 to play the flute.
⁵小 笛 a piccolo.
横 笛 the common flute.
汽 笛 a steam-whistle.
竹 笛 a bamboo flute.
簫 笛 pipes.
¹⁰羌 笛 shepherd's flute.
號 笛 a siren.
軍 笛 the fife.
響 笛 flageolet.
↑笛膜 the thin membrane over one of the holes of a Chinese flute.

迪\\迪 2.5.　To follow the right path. To bring forward; to direct. The right path.
6218

迪 哲 carried their knowledge into practice.
迪 屢 未 同 notwithstanding my frequent leading of them
迪 我 高 后 tread in the steps of my High Ancestor.
迪 果 毅 advance with determined boldness.
⁵迪 民 康 led the masses to tranquility.
迪 畏 天 顯 manifested a reverential awe of the bright principles of Heaven.
迪 知 上 帝 命 obeyed and knew the decree of God.
迪 簡 to be chosen and promoted.
迪 高 后 intimate to my High Sovereign.
¹⁰不 吉 不 迪 bad and unprincipled men.
不 迪 率 典 there is no obedience to the statutes.
允 迪 厥 德 if (a ruler) sincerely pursues the course of his virtue.
允 迪 茲 if you really follow this course.
各 迪 有 功 these all pursue the right path, and are meritorious.
¹⁵弗 求 弗 迪 he is not sought nor employed.
啓 迪 後 人 to guide his posterity.

商 4.5.　The stalk; the stem; the foot; the base.
6219　Distinguish 商 No. 5673.

嫡 2.5.　The legal wife, as opposed to a concubine.
6220

嫡 傳 a phrase used of an accomplishment learnt direct from a master.
嫡 兄 or 嫡 弟 the elder and younger brothers—as distinguished from the sons of a concubine.
嫡 堂 兄 弟 the sons of two brothers, who were the offspring of the legal wife.
嫡 妻 or 嫡 室 the legal wife.
⁵嫡 子³ eldest son of the legal wife.
嫡 母 term of address used to the

wife by the children of a concubine.
嫡 派 親 枝 blood relatives.
嫡 親 blood relatives.
嫡 配 the legal wife.

敵 2.5.　To oppose; to be a match for. An opponent; an enemy; an equal.
6221

敵 不 住 風 unable to make headway against the wind; will not keep out the wind.
敵 人 or 仇 敵 a competitor; an adversary; an enemy.
敵 住 to oppose; to resist.
敵 兵 the troops of the enemy.
⁵敵 勢 大 挫 the morale of the foe was broken.↑敵 僑 enemy aliens.
敵 國 a hostile nation; the enemy's country.
敵·得 住 to be a match for.
敵 意 行·爲 intentional hostile act. (*legal*).
敵 愾 (*k'ai⁴*) to wreak vengeance; hatred.
¹⁰敵 戰 to fight against in battle.
敵 手 a rival; a competitor; an adversary.
敵 擋 to resist; to oppose.
敵 樓 a watch-tower.
敵 軍 戰 地 the firing line.
¹⁵敵 頭 an enemy; an opponent.
敵 體 同 尊 both equally honourable.
匹 敵 well-matched.
對 敵 in array; hostile; enemies.
無 敵 matchless; unequalled.
↑敵 情 intelligence about the enemy

滴 1.5.　To drip; to drop. A drop.
6222

滴·下 to drip.
滴·出 to leak; to drip out.
滴 在 地·上 to drip on the ground.
滴 字 滴 血 every word drops blood—said of pathos in literature.
⁵滴 打 or 滴 搭 to drip.
滴。水 water dripping; a drip-tile.
滴 水 成 冰 the dripping water forms into ice--the cold is intense.
滴 水 石 a drip-stone.
滴 水 穿 石 constant dropping wears away a stone.
¹⁰滴 油 器 oil-stand.

滴溜溜ㄦ的 round; bulging; staring.

滴溜滴溜 going round and round.

滴漏 to leak; to drip out.

滴滴金 elecampane.

[15]滴瀝 to drip.

滴瓶 a dropping-bottle.

滴管 medicine dropper.

滴血 to drop blood—a test used to decide relationship.

甋 [2.5.] A jar without ears.
6223

鏑 [2.5.] The barb of an arrow; the head of a javelin.
6224

鏑鏑·的聲 a shrill sound.

鳴鏑 a whistling arrow.

翟 [2.5.] The Tartar pheasant. Plumage; feather trimming. Name of a feudal State. Also read *chai*[2].
6225

翟羽飾車 pheasant feathers decorated the chariot.

右手秉翟 the right hand held the plumes.

夏翟 the pheasant.

籊 [2.5.] Long bamboos used for fishing-rods.
6226

糴 [2.5.] To lay in grain; to buy grain.
6227

糴米 to buy rice.

糴糧 to buy grain.

踧 [2.5.] Level, as a road.
6228

踧踧周道 the road to *Chou* is level and easy.

(a) Read *ts'u*[4.5]. Appearance of uneasiness.

踧踖如也 uneasiness caused by respect.

滌 [2.5.] To wash; to scour; to cleanse; to purify. To reform. To sweep.
6229

滌去 to wash away.

滌場 to sweep the yards.

滌塵 to wash off the dust.

滌慮 to free the mind from anxieties.

[5]滌煩子 the one that washes away care—a name for tea.

滌瑕 to cleanse away the stains—fig.

滌硯 to wash the ink-slab—to prepare for study.

(a) A pen or stable for fattening beasts.

在滌三月 keep it in the stall for three months.

(b) Appearance of the country during a drought.

滌滌山川 parched are the hills and the streams are dried.

覿 [2.5.] To see face to face; to be admitted to an audience.
6230

覿面相失 they did not recognize each other when face to face.

覿面過 to meet face to face.

T'I. (ㄊ)

堤 [2] A dike; a barrier; an embankment. Also read *ti*[1].
6231 Inter. 隄·No. 6210.

堤堰 a bund; a dike.

河堤 river embankment.

媞 [2] At ease. Fascinatingly beautiful.
6232

提 [2] To lift in the hand; to raise; to pull up; to pick up.
6233 To mention; to bring forward; to suggest. Inter. 題 No. 6238.

提·不動 cannot lift it.

提交 to hand over to the custody of; to submit to another body for discussion.

提供 to offer for acceptance or rejection. (*legal*).

提供全部財產 general assignment. (*legal*).

[5]提供物 the thing offered. (*legal*).

提倡 to bring forward; to introduce; to promote; to originate; to pioneer; to initiate; to stimulate; to advocate.

提倡善舉 to promote good causes.

提倡文學 to promote learning.

提倡民權 promote democracy.

[10]提倡民氣 rouse the spirit of the masses.

提倡藝術 to promote arts and crafts.

提傀儡 to work marionettes.

提兵 to lead troops; to bring troops forward.

提·出 proposals; demands; to bring forward.

[15]提·出·他·來 bring him up for trial.

提·出·來 to bring forward; to refer to.

提·出抗議 to enter a protest.

提出者 mover of a resolution.

提·出質問 to state a case.

[20]提·出辭職書 to hand in one's resignation.

提刑 or 臬·臺 the former title of a Provincial Judge.

提到 summoned; brought forward; noticed.

提前 to give precedence to.

提包 a portmanteau or suitcase.

[25]提升 to promote; to advance.

提及 to mention; to allude to; to suggest.

提取 to fetch; to select.

提名選舉 to nominate for election.

提命 suggestive instructions.

[30]提問 to bring up and examine.

提單 or 提貨單 a bill of lading; delivery order; invoice.

提回 to summon back.

提壺 to take the pot for wine.

提夾 a hand-bag.

[33] 銀絲手提夾 a silver-thread hand-bag.

提存 assignment. (*legal*).

提孩 or 孩提 a child-in-arms.

提學司 Provincial Superintendent of Education.

提審 to bring forward for trial.

[40]提將 to carry (the young) and take (the aged) by the hand.

提心吊膽 timidly; nervously.

提手躡脚·的走 creeping along stealthily.

提·拔 to raise up; to promote; to advance.

提 押 to bring to jurisdiction and retain in custody.

⁴⁵提 挈 mutual support.

提 掖 to lead and support—a person.

提 控 to exercise authority over; to control.

提 握 to take in the hand.

提 攜 to take in the arms; to carry; to nourish; to help on.

⁵⁰提 撕 to manage; to attend to; to get a person on by teaching.

提 撥 to remind.

提 擎 to raise in the hands.

提 擊 to pick up and throw at; to strike.

提 撕 to arouse; to stimulate.

⁵⁵提 撕 精·神 to rouse to action; to reinvigorate the energies.

提 叙 to speak of.

提 案 to bring before a court; a proposition; a motion.

提 梁 the handle of a basket.

提 條 件 to enter a protest; to bring forward certain conditions.

⁶⁰提 標 the main body of troops under a provincial Commander-in-chief. (obs.).

提 槧 small tablets of wood for writing memoranda.

提 氣 to rouse the energies.

提 法 司 a Provincial Commissioner of Justice.

提 淨 to separate pure metal from alloy.

⁶⁵提 減 權 the right to reduce the amount of a legacy if the estate has decreased in value.

提 煉 to refine.

提 燈 會 a lantern or torchlight procession.

提 爐 a censer for carrying in the hand.

提 牢 吏 Superintendent of a prison.

⁷⁰提 犯 to bring a criminal before the court.

提 琴 a violin.

提·目 or 題·目 a text; a subject; theme.

提·督 or 提·臺 title of a former Provincial Commander-in-chief.

提 督 學 政 a Literary Chancellor attached to each province. (obs.).

⁷⁵提·督 軍 務 with control over the forces—part of the title of former Viceroys and Governors.

提 示 to indicate; presentation of new ideas as related to what a pupil already knows.

提 神 to stimulate one's energies.

提 票 or 拘 票 a summons.

提 究 to bring up and examine.

⁸⁰提 筆 to lift the pen—to write.

提 筆 忘 字 to forget the characters when one lifts the pen.

提 箱 a suitcase.

提 籃 a hand-basket.

提·給 to hand over to the custody of.

⁸⁵提 綱 挈 領 to select and bring forward the important points.

提 腕 to exercise the wrist for writing.

提 花 to weave flowers, etc., on fabrics.

提 花 布 figured brocades.

提 衡 to raise the beam of the scale—of justice and equity in government.

⁹⁰提 袋 a hand-bag.

提 要 to bring forward the important points.

提 解 to forward to a court for trial.

提 詞 to prompt (in a play).

提 訊 to call—as witness.

提 訴 to go to law.

⁹⁵提 調 former title of official.

提 議 to propose; to bring forward; to make a suggestion; a proposal or motion.

提 議 人 the mover of a resolution.

提 議 通 過·了 the motion is carried.

提 貨 摺 pass-book for goods. See No. 6030—B. 18.

¹⁰⁰提 質 to summon and confront.

提。起 to mention; to raise; to allude to; to suggest.

不 要 提 起 do not mention it.

提 轉 面 耳 to incline the ear; to give a favourable hearing.

提 送 to forward to a court for trial.

¹⁰⁵提 醒 to remind; to arouse.

提。開 to carry away; to introduce.

提。防 to take precautions against.

提 集 to summon all the parties to a case.

提 鞋 to pull on one's shoes.

¹¹⁰提 頭² to raise the characters above the column of writing, in order to show respect.

提 驗 to bring forward for examination—as a wounded man.

提 高 to raise—as prices; to uplift.

提 高 人 民 uplift the masses.

提 高 智 慧 上·的 地 位 raise the intellectual status.

¹¹⁵理 想 之 提 高 sublimation of ideals.

提 點 to reprove; to remind of a fault.

言 提 其 耳 I held you by the ear—as a father teaching his child, holding the child by the ear in order to maintain his attention— 言 is merely a particle.

(a) To send; to remit.

提 塘 courier posts.

提 歸 to remit to a given place or for a given purpose.

提 運 to have things removed officially.

提 運 汽 車 motor trucks.

提 項 remittances.

(b) Descriptive of gentlemanly ease.

好 人 提 提 wealthy, he moves about quite at his ease. (好 人 = a great and noble man.)

(c) A drum.

師 帥 執 提 the officers take up the drum.

(d) Read ti³. To throw at. To cut out.

牛 羊 之 肺 離 而 不 提 心 in separating the lungs of oxen or sheep, they did not cut out the central portion of them.

(e) Read shih². Describes birds flying in a flock.

歸 飛 提 提 (the crows) come back, flying all in a flock.

(f) Name of a place in Szechwan.

朱 提 a place in Szechwan where silver is produced—a name for silver.

禔[2] 6234　Repose; peace; rest.

禔 福 happy; happiness.
禔 躬 good health; well-being.

(a) Read *chih*[3.5]. Only, etc.
u.f. 祇 No. 952.

禔 取 辱 耳 to get nothing but disgrace.

緹[2] 6235　Light red silk.

緹 騎 mounted officers dressed in red silk, sent to escort prisoners.

踶[2] 6236　To tread on; to kick. Inter. 蹄 No. 6244.

奔 踶 to gallop.

(a) Read *ch'ih*[3]. To urge.

踶 跂 爲 義 to urge to righteous actions.

醍[2] 6237　The essential oil of butter.

醍 醐 a rich liquor skimmed from boiled butter—used to describe the goodness of Buddha, or the excellence of a man's talents.

醍 醐 灌 頭 to pour the rich liquor on a man's head—to increase his wisdom. (*Budd.*).

(a) Read *t'i*[3]. A dark, red wine.

粢 醍 a rich, reddish spirit distilled from millet.

題[2] 6238　The forehead:—hence, a heading, a theme, a subject, a proposition. To bring to notice.
u.f. 提 No. 6233.

題 主 the person who is invited to write the name, etc., of the deceased on the ancestral tablet.
題 區 to write an inscription for a tablet.
題 句 a motto; an inscription.
題 名 to get a degree; to nominate.
[5]題 名 錄 a record of one's name, age, address, etc.
題 壁 to write on a wall.

題 曰 the theme was as follows ....
題·目 a theme; a subject; a heading; a text.
　大 題·目 a great theme—an important matter.
[10]　難 題(·目)a difficult problem.
題 簽 the title printed in a book.
題 紙 paper for an essay.
題 綱 to prompt; to give a hint.
題 署 an inscription.
[15]題 評 to criticize.
題 詩 to write impromptu verses, as for an inscription on a vase, picture, etc.
題 說 to mention.
題 贈 or 題 記 to write an inscription by way of dedication.
題 跋 a colophon; summary at the end of a book, giving the author, printer, etc.
[20]題 辭 a summary of the topic of a book, written as an introduction.
題 醒 to remind one of.
題 面 to prompt; to give a hint.
題 頭 to prompt.
題 額 to write an inscription for a tablet.
[25]不 消 題 you had b e t t e r not mention it. ≡提.
出 題 to assign a theme for a composition; to sum up at the close of an essay.
在 題 外 irrelevant.
小 題 大 作 great fuss about a small matter.
承 題 to enlarge upon the theme—in an essay.
[30]破 題 to open up the theme—in writing essays.
門 題 inscription over a door or gateway.

騠[2] 6239　A spirited horse.

鯷[2] **鮧** 6240　The sheat fish.

鶗[2] 6241　A kind of hawk.

鶗 鴃 the goat-sucker.

啼[2] **嗁** 6242　To cry; to mourn; to howl. To twitter; to crow. Distinguish 嚃 No. 1041.

啼 叫 to scream—as birds.
啼 哭 to lament.
雞 啼 cockcrow.

締[2] 6243　A knot; closely joined; a connection. Pron. *ti*[4].

締 交 closely allied, as friends; bound closely.
締 好 之 由 the origin of their friendship.
締 姻 陋 俗 c o a r s e marriage customs.
締 成 betrothed; engaged; allied.
[5]締 盟 to form an alliance.
締 約 an alliance; a treaty.
締 結 betrothed; engaged; allied.
締 結 條 約 to make treaties.
締 造 composed of; to construct.
[10]締 造 國 家 to build up a nation.
取 締 to control; to suppress.

蹄[2] **蹏** 6244　A hoof. A horse.

蹄·子 a hoof.
蹄 聲 隆 隆 the h o r s e-h o o f s sounded loud.
蹄 腿 a whole leg—of pork, etc.
蹄 角 hoofs and horns—cattle.
[5]失 蹄 to stumble—of a horse.
豬 蹄 pig's pettitoes.
馬 蹄 horse's hoofs; the water-chestnut—*Scirpus tuberosa*.

荑[2] 6245　Sprouts. Tares. A kind of white grass. Read *i*[2]. To weed.

體[3] **体** 6246　The body. The whole person. The trunk; the limbs. A class or body of persons. The essentials of; the substance of. Real. Solid substance. Thickness. Style.

體 不 安 not very well; indisposed.

體之充 fills the whole body.
體例 form—as of literature; regulations.
體健 physical well-being.
⁵體刑 corporal punishment.
體制 regulation; system; fundamental rules.
體力 physical strength.
體勢 style—as of painting, etc.
體學 anatomy.
¹⁰體容 or 容體 appearance.
體局 the general appearance.
體式 a pattern.
體息 something valuable; a secret.
體態 deportment; form; attitude.
¹⁵令有體之感覺 gives the impression of solidity—in perspective drawings.
體操 physical exercise; drill.
兵式體操 military drill.
游戲體操 physical drill as distinct from military drill.
體操器械 gymnastic apparatus.
²⁰體操塲 drill-ground.
體操室 (or 堂) gymnasium.
體有貴賤 in the body there are both noble and ignoble parts.
體格 physique.
體格之美 physical beauty.
²⁵體格檢查 physical examination.
體格的 physically.
體段 principles. 「there.
體段已具 the principles are
體氣 or 體理 style—of writing or painting.
³⁰氣體 physical vigour.
體法 a fixed rule or regulation.
體溫 temperature of the body.
體溫本度 normal temperature of the body.
體溫表 clinical thermometer or chart.
³⁵體狀 form.
體用 theory and practice; doctrinal and practical.
體用之謂 a designation of the mental constitution and its activities.
體積 volume; cubic contents of.
體範 model or pattern.
⁴⁰體系 system.
體統 dignity; decorum; propriety; general state of affairs—as of a State.
體罰 corporal punishment.
體育 physical culture.
體育會 athletic club.

⁴⁵體育部 physical culture department. 體育館 gymnasium.
體胖 fat; corpulent.
體腔 cavity of the body.
體裁 style of literature; format.
體要 the gist; substance.
⁵⁰體角 the corner of a solid.
體註 a running commentary.
體貌 body and appearance.
體質 substance; elements of; bodily constitution.
體質上之原因 physical causes.
⁵⁵體面互見 both solid and surface are shown—as in sculpture.
一體 the whole of; all; equally or uniformly.
主體 the subject. (gramm.).
事體 a matter.
六體 the six styles of Chinese writing— 篆 the form used in seals, 隸 the square form used in former official documents, 楷 the ordinary orthodox form, 行 the running hand used in correspondence, 草 the rapid running hand, 宋 the form used in printed books. Disting. 六書.
⁶⁰全體 the whole body of.
具體 the complete thing.
四支百體 the four limbs and all the members of the body—the whole body.
四體 the four limbs.
大體 the scope of; real parts of; principle. 大體上 in the main.
⁶⁵實體 a solid. (physics).
立體 a solid; cube.
聖體 the sacred person.
質物體 a material object.
身體 the body.

(a) To embody. To show consideration. To put oneself in the place of another.

體人意 to interpret the desire of another.
體合 adaptability; sympathy.
體國經野 to administer the empire.
體察 to investigate thoroughly.
⁵體己 to treat as though it was a personal matter; to flatter; private.
體恤 or 體念 to sympathize with; to pity.
體會 to comprehend; to take in an idea.

體物情 in sympathy with nature.
體物而不可遺 embodied in things and inseparable from them.
¹⁰體羣臣 to show consideration for all officers.
體行 to embody in one's personal actions.
體諒 to excuse.
體貼 to have sympathy with; to show appreciation of; to act in conformity with; to show solicitude or consideration for.
體貼人情 in consideration of friendship; out of sympathy for others.
¹⁵體量 to sympathize with; to pity.

(b) Handsome. Good form.

體面 handsome; honorable.
粧體面 to pose as being well off, or well up in polite ways.
失體 to do something dishonourable; faux pas.

剃 4 To shave.
6247

剃得乾淨 shaved smooth.
剃頭 to shave the head.
剃(頭)刀 a razor.
剃頭店 or 剃頭舖 a barber's shop.
⁵剃頭擔子 an itinerant barber's kit.
剃頭的 or 剃頭匠 a barber.
剃鬚 or 剃鬍子 to shave the beard.
剃髮修行 to shave and turn Buddhist priest.

悌 4 To do one's duty as a younger brother.
6248

悌弟 to act in a brotherly manner.

(a) Read li³ or t'i⁴. Easy and self-possessed.

愷悌 kind and courteous.

梯 1 A ladder; steps; stairs. To lean against.
6249

梯几 to lean on the table—as in deep thought.

梯·子 a ladder or steps.
梯·子脚連·着地 the foot of the ladder rests on the ground.
梯山 to scale the mountains.
⁵梯櫈 or 梯·子檔 the rungs of a ladder.
梯階 steps of a ladder; means whereby a thing is accomplished, etc.
梯雲 or 雲梯 to mount to the clouds—to take a degree.
亂梯 steps to rebellions—things that stir the anger of the masses, such as oppressive taxation; corruption in the law-courts, etc.
塔梯 a winding staircase.
¹⁰天梯 a long ladder.
板梯 a step-ladder.
樓梯 stairs to an upper storey.
軟梯 a rope-ladder.
雲梯 scaling-ladder used in attacking walled cities.

涕 / 鯷 ⁴
6250
Tears; snivel; mucus. To weep; to snivel.

涕出而女⁴於吳 his tears flowed as he gave his daughter in marriage to the prince of *Wu*.
涕泗 tears; snivel.
涕泣 to weep.
涕洟 tears and snivel.
涕淚 to weep.
涕零如雨 the tear-drops fell like rain.
鼻涕 mucus from the nose.

睇 ²
6251
To stare; to look at. To glance at. Also read *ti*⁴.

睇而弗識 to look at without recognition.
睇視 to stare.
審睇 to scrutinize.

稊 / 穊 ²
6252
Tares. Grass.

稊稗 a panic grass cultivated in Chihli for its grain.

稊米在田亂生 tares grow all over the field.

(a) A new shoot from a dried stem. *See* 枯 No. 3492—4.

綈 ²
6253
A coarse, thick, greenish-black pongee. Used in modern times for a kind of artificial silk material.

綈袍之意 remembrance of a silk-robe—old acquaintance.
弋綈 thick, black silk.

鍗 ¹
6254
Antimony.

鍗沙 antimony ore.
鍗酒 or 鍗劑 antimonial wine.
生鍗 crude antimony.

鵜 / 鶗 ²
6255
The pelican.

鵜鶘 the pelican.

薙 ⁴
6256
To shave. To weed.

薙髮 to shave the head.
燒薙 to burn off the undergrowth.

替 ⁴
6257
For; instead of; in place of. To substitute; to change. Used in some places for 給 as a sign of the dative.

替人做事 to act for another.
替人死 to die for mankind.
替人贖罪 to atone for the sins of mankind.
替·他說 speak for him.
⁵替代 in place of another; for.
替·工 or 替·手 a workman who fills the place of another; a temporary substitute workman or servant.
替·換 to change; to change in order.
替·換賽跑 relay race.
替·換·着 alternately.
¹⁰替死人作墓誌 to write an epitaph.

替死鬼 a substitute for a criminal sentenced to capital punishment.
替活人上條陳 to send in a memorial for the living. *See above*—10.
替爲 on behalf of; in place of.
替·身 a substitute.
¹⁵頂替 fraudulent substitution for another.

(a) To discontinue. To intermit. To supersede. To deteriorate.

不敢替上帝命 dare not disregard the charge received from God.
不敢替厥義德 did not dare to supersede his righteous and virtuous men.
公勿替刑 let not the example you have afforded me be intermitted.
勿替敬典 do not disregard the statutes which you should reverence.
無替厥服 not to neglect their duties.
興¹替 prosperity and decline—fluctuation.

嚏 / 齂 ⁴
6258
To sneeze; a running at the nose.

嚏·嚏 or 打嚏 to sneeze.

屜 / 屜 ⁴
6259
A tray; a drawer; a pad; a screen.

屜·子 a drawer; a tray in a box.
屜·子抽不開 this drawer will not pull open.
抽屜 a drawer.
籠屜 tray in a steamer for cooking food.
鞍屜·子 saddle-pad.

髢 ⁴
6260
A switch of false hair.

遰 ⁴
6261
To go away. To migrate, as birds.

T'I.　　(ㄊ)
(T'ih)

剔 6262 1.5. To cut the flesh from the bones; to scrape off; to pick out; to get rid of.

剔 出 to pick out; to get rid of.
剔 刀 butcher's scraper.
剔 燈 棍 a wire to pull up the wick of a Chinese lamp.
剔 翎 to preen their feathers.
剔 骨 to bone meat before it is sold.
剔 齒 or 剔 牙 to pick the teeth.
挑·剔 to sort out and reject; to find fault with.

惕 慄 6263 4.5. Respect; regard. To stand in awe of; to be alarmed.

心 焉 惕 惕 my heart is full of trouble.

踢 6264 1.5. To kick. Distinguish 踼 No. 6105.

踢·死 人 to kill by a kick.
踢 球 to play football.
踢·着 he kicks—of a horse or mule.
踢 燕 to kick the shuttlecock.
踢 斛 淋 尖 to kick the rice measure and cause the grain to shake down, and to strike off the top of the measure lightly, allowing grain to remain on the top—to get more rice than is legal measure.
踢 達 sound of footsteps.
踢·開 to kick open—a door.

邌 逖 6265 4.5. To remove far away; to send off; to keep at a distance from.

用 邌 蠻 方 keep at a distance from the southern barbarians.
離 邌 爾 土 get far away from your country.

倜 6266 4.5. Unrestrained; unoccupied.

倜 儻 energetic; masterful; unrestrained; free and easy of manner.

擿 6267 4.5. To select; to pick out from; to discard.

擿 伏 to bring to light the inner workings of a case at law; to expose evil.
擿 抉 to extract.
擿 耳 俛 首 to cleanse the ears and incline the head—to listen intently.

(a) Read *chih*[5]. To throw. u.f. 擲.

TIAO.　　(ㄉㄠ)

刁 6268 1 Perverse; knavish; artful; wicked.

刁 乖 knavish; perverse; rascally.
刁 健 obstinate; perverse; overbearing.
刁 刁 gusty; the wind coming in gusts.
刁 婦 a virago; a shrew.
⁵刁 悍 arrogant; obstinate.
刁 惡 outrageous; wicked; depraved.
刁 抗 obstinate.
刁 斗 a soldier's cooking-pot; it was used for beating alarms at night. (*ancient*).
刁 棍 perverse; knavish.
¹⁰刁 民 the rabble.
刁 滑 perverse; knavish; rascally.
刁 狡 unscrupulous.
刁 筆 rabid or caustic writings.
刁 脾 outrageous; depraved; wicked.
¹⁵刁 蠻 barbarous; violent.
刁 詐 knavish; rascally.
刁 話 violent language.
刁 賴 to repudiate; to accuse recklessly.
刁 野 barbarous; violent.
²⁰刁 鑽 shifty; intriguing; crafty.
刁 險 outrageous; wicked; depraved.
刁 難 obstructive.
刁 頓 obstructive.
刁 頑 unscrupulous; rascally; rowdy.
²⁵刁 風 depraved manners; evil customs.

叼 6269 1 To hold in the mouth; to seize.
Distinguish 叼 No. 6141.

凋 6270 1 To be exhausted; faded; withered.

凋 卸 fallen—as blossoms; withered; faded.
凋 敝 destitute.
凋 殘 declining—as trade.
凋 腐 decaying; to wither.
⁵凋 萎 to shrivel; to decay.
凋 落 fallen—as blossoms; faded; withered.
凋 謝 faded and fallen—as blossoms.
凋 零 fallen—as scattered leaves; rare.

琱 6271 1 To engrave gems; to work jade and other stones. To draw a sketch.
Inter. 雕 No. 6273.

碉 6272 1 Stone house, used by Tibetans.

雕 鵰 彫 6273 1 To engrave; to carve; to tattoo.

雕 作 engraver's work.
雕 像 to carve an idol.
雕 刀 a graving tool.
雕 刻 to engrave—as blocks for printing; to carve; sculpture.
⁵雕 字 to cut characters on blocks, etc. 雕 刻 家 sculptor.
雕 工 or 雕 匠 a carver; an engraver.
雕 文 tracery.
雕 板 to cut blocks for printing.
雕 梁 carved beams—wealth.
¹⁰雕 漆 carved lacquer-ware.
雕 牆 an ornamented wall.
雕 琢 to cut and polish gems.
雕 花 to carve figures or pictures.
雕 蟲 小 技 engraving insects and such things with poor skill—making a living as a hack writer.
¹⁵雕 蟲 篆 刻 ability in small things, as a carver of insects and reptiles.

雕 題 to tattoo the forehead.
雕 龍 to carve a dragon—skilled in debate.

(a) Occurs used for the next.

鵰 ¹ The eagle; the vulture; also used for hawks; buzzards, etc.
6274

鵰 悍 brave and fierce—as an eagle.
鵰 扇 a fan of eagle's feathers.
鵰 翎 eagle plumes—an arrow.
鵰 鷄 an osprey.
皂 鵰 the vulture.

貂 ¹ The sable.
6275

貂 帽 a hat trimmed with sable.
貂 尾 sable tails.
貂 璫 furs and jewels—wealth.
貂 皮 sable skins.
貂 袖 sable cuffs.
貂 裘 a sable robe.
紫 貂 undyed sables.

弔 ⎫
　⎬ ⁴ To condole with; to mourn. To pity, to console.
吊 ⎭
6276

弔 友 to mourn for a friend.
弔 古 to speak with regret of the ancients.
弔 唁 to condole with.
弔 問 to make inquiries—after a death.
⁵弔 喪 to condole with on a bereavement.
弔 孝 to condole with on the death of a parent.
弔 客 visitors who come to condole. See below—A. 1.
弔 慰 to sympathize; to condole.
弔 文 a kind of funeral oration written on paper, and burnt at the grave of a friend.
¹⁰弔 民 伐 罪 to console the people and punish the rebellious.
弔 祭 to mourn and sacrifice to the dead.
弔 紙 to condole with and (burn) paper—a visit of condolence.
不 弔 pitiless.
開 弔 to begin mourning ceremonies.

(a) To suspend. To hang. To droop. A string of cash.

弔 客 or 弔·死 鬼 the ghost of a person who has hanged himself.
弔 帶 suspenders.
弔 床 a hammock.
弔 掛 to hang up—as by a string.
⁵弔 桶 a well-bucket.
弔 橋 a suspension-bridge.
弔 水 to draw water from a well.
弔 睛 to turn up the eyes—so as to look fierce.
弔 綫 a plumb-line.
¹⁰弔 角 to go round a corner.
弔·起·來 to suspend; to hang up.
弔 鎖 a padlock.
弔 頸 to hang by the neck.
一 弔 錢 a string of cash—nominally one thousand.

(b) To demand. To ask for.

弔 案 to bring forward a case; to revise a case.
弔 照 or 弔 看 to cause (documents) to be produced in court.
弔 銷 差 票 to cancel a warrant.
弔 驗 or 弔 覈 to ask for in order to verify—as a passport.

(c) Read ti¹·⁵. To come to; to proceed.

弔 由 靈 only used the best—of the plans.
惟 弔 兹 as to those who proceed to such—wickedness.
無 敢 不 弔 presume not to have any of these (weapons) but in perfect order.
神 之 弔 矣 the s p i r i t s are present.

捄 ⁴ To take; to carry away.
6277

掉 ⁴ To fall. To move; to shake. To change.
6278 Inter. 調 No. 6298.

掉·下·來 fallen down.
掉 動 to issue orders; to administrate; to agitate.
掉 包 to substitute inferior articles (when exchanging)—a swindling trick.
掉·在 地·下 to fall to the ground.
⁵掉 尾 to wag the tail.

掉 手 to change from hand to hand.
掉·換 to exchange.
掉·換·過·來 to turn around; to invert.
掉 槳 to pull the oars.
¹⁰掉 歪 to befool; to play jokes.
掉 猴 a slippery fellow—one who will play monkey tricks; a game played with dice.
掉 磬 to strike stones together—to impeach one another, as two hostile officials.
掉 秤 or 賍 秤 to lose weight.
掉 綫 to take aim.
¹⁵掉 胎 to have a miscarriage.
掉 脚 to change from one foot to the other—as shoes.
掉 脾 obstinate; perverse; cunning; untrustworthy.
掉 臉 to turn the head; to look round.
掉 臂 to brace the arms; to stand defiantly.
²⁰掉 舌 to chatter; to go back on one's word.
掉 船 to row a boat.　[or -shar³
掉 色 to lose colour; to fade.(-shai³
掉 誕 to lie; mischievous; deceitful.
掉·過 頭·來 or 掉 轉³ to turn the head; to turn end for end.
²⁵掉 頭 不 顧 to turn the head away.
掉 頭 之 罪 decapitation.
掉 陷 to fall down into.
掉 鬼 to play tricks; to act in a strange manner.
掉 魂 to lose one's wits.

(a) An auxiliary verb, may be substituted for 去 in similar positions e.g.,1848.5,21.
去·得 掉 you can remove it.
去·掉 get rid of.
失·掉 lost. 掉·掉 dropped; lost.
殺·掉 to kill.
洗·不 掉 it will not wash out.
滅·掉 to exterminate.
賣·不 掉 unsaleable.

釣 ⁴ To fish with a hook and line. A fish-hook.
6279 Distinguish 鈞 No. 3417; 鉤 No. 1725.

釣 不 獲 to fish without success.
釣 名 fishing for fame.
釣 徒 an angler.
釣 竿 a fishing-rod.

⁵釣船 fishing-boat; a long fish-shaped boat.
釣譽 to fish for praise.
釣鈎 a fish-hook.
釣魚 to fish with a rod and line.
釣魚翁 an angler.
¹⁰釣魚郎 a kingfisher.
子³釣而不綱 in fishing the Sage used a hook, but not a net.

窵⁴
6280
Deep; distant; profound.

窵不可測 deep and unfathomable.
窵窅 or **窵窌** dark and deep; cave-like.
窵角 a secluded spot; a quiet corner.
窵遠 far off; distant.

T'IAO.　　(ㄊㄠ)

佻²·³·
6281
Weakly; unsteadily; frivolous.

佻佻公子³ a delicately-nurtured young gentleman.
佻健 loose; impudent; frivolous.
佻天以爲己力 to claim merit for the great deeds of others—lit.:—to claim the work of Heaven as his own.
佻脫 frivolous; unsteady.
佻薄 frivolous; impudent; worthless.

(a) Read *tiao*⁴. To provoke. To treat lightly. To act furtively.

佻巧 furtive ways; tricky; fraudulent.

(b) Read *yao*². To delay. Dilatory; slow.

佻其期日 to put off the date.

挑¹
6282
To carry on the shoulder with a pole, (by one person).

挑·不·起 or **挑·不·動** too heavy to carry.
挑·夫 a coolie.
挑擔 to carry a load.
挑水·的 a water-carrier.
挑賣 to sell—as a huckster.

肩挑貿易 the business of a pedlar who carries his stock-in-trade on a carrying-pole.

(a) To pick out. To choose. To find fault.

挑三窩四 to make mischief.
挑五挑六·的 fault-finding.
挑·剔 to pick out; to take out; to cavil; to find fault with.
挑·剔字眼 to find fault with the diction.
⁵挑募 to select for enlistment.
挑取 to select for enlistment.
挑好日·子 to select a lucky day.
挑好·的 pick (a) good one(s).
挑弄 to work—as puppets.
¹⁰挑引 to lead into evil.
挑揀 or **挑擇** to select; to choose.
挑·撥 to find fault with. See below—D. 9.
挑攀線 cat's-cradle.
挑斥 to blame.
¹⁵挑燈 to raise the wick of a Chinese lamp.
挑眼 to pick holes; to find fault.
挑禮 to find fault with the behaviour of others.
挑秀女 to select beautiful girls for the Imperial harem.
挑缺 to appoint to a vacant post.
²⁰挑選 to select; to choose.
挑錯 to pick flaws.

(b) To clear out; to open up.

挑·開 to open—as a boil; to clear out—as a channel.

(c) Inter. 調 No. 6298. To dally with, etc.

挑情 to dally with.
挑戲 to trifle with; dalliance.

(d) Read *t'iao*¹·³ To provoke; to stir up. To turn over.

挑之使戰 defied him to the combat.
挑事 to embroil; to stir up trouble.
挑事·的 a mischief-maker.
挑動 to disturb; to excite suspicion; to sow strife.
⁵挑唆 to stir up; to make mischief.
挑戰 to challenge to battle; to provoke a fight.

挑戰行·爲 provocative action. (*legal*).
挑戲 Punch and Judy.
挑撥 to incite to contention. See above—A. 12.
¹⁰挑旺·起·來 to arouse; to stir up —as zeal.
挑花 to embroider; to work flowers.
挑釁 to provoke hostilities.
挑釁舉動 provocative action.

(e) Read *t'ao*¹. Light; frivolous and dissipated.

挑達 frivolous and dissipated.

朓⁴
6283
The moon seen in the west before sunrise, as at the end of the lunar month.

眺⁴
6284
To gaze at.

眺望 to gaze at.
遊眺 to give a glance around.

祧¹
6285
An ancestral hall.

宗祧 an ancestral hall.
承祧 one person taking the place of son in two ancestral halls, as when a nephew takes the leading part for a deceased uncle who has left no sons.

窕³
6286
Secluded; elegant; refined. Also read *tiao*⁴.

窈窕 modest and retiring; secluded; apart.
窈窕淑女 the modest, retiring young lady of virtuous conduct.

(a) Flippant; frivolous.

輕窕 levity; frivolity.

跳⁴
趒
6287
To jump; to climb over; to leap; to posture. A gangway.

跳上架·子 to put on airs.
跳下·去 to jump down.

跳 丸 to juggle with balls—used to illustrate the rapid flight of time.

跳 凳 a long form.

⁵跳 出 to leap out; to raise the characters above the column of writing to indicate respect.

跳·出 樊 籠 escaped from the cage—used fig.

跳·出 火 坑 escaped from grave danger.

跳·到 海·裏·去 to jump into the sea.

跳 勤 to move.

¹⁰跳 板 or 跳 架 scaffolding; the first is also a gangway-plank.

跳 梁 to jump on to the beams—a burglar.

東 西 跳 梁 jumping from right to left—among the boughs.

跳 梁 小 醜 petty lawbreakers; mischief-doers.

跳 槽 to go from one employ to another; to throw up a situation.

¹⁵跳 欄 競 走 a hurdle-race.

跳 水·裏 to jump into the water.

跳 河 to jump into the river.

跳 火 坑 to leap the fiery pit—great daring.

跳 牛 to cover a cow.

²⁰跳 白 a small fishing-boat.

跳 盪 troops used to throw the foe into confusion before the battle commences.

跳 神 to leap before the gods; to practise exorcism.

跳 神·的 exorcists.

跳 粉 牆 to leap a whitewashed wall—an assignation.

²⁵跳 繩 to skip rope.

跳 舞 to dance.

跳 蟲 or 跳 蚤 or 跳 虱 a flea.

跳 行 (hang²) to raise the characters above the column of writing as an indication of respect.

跳·起·來 to jump up; to skip about; to begin to jump.

³⁰跳 跟 to hop about; to fling oneself about in temper.

跳 躍 or 夏 跳 to dance; to leap—as for joy, etc.

跳 擲 to hop; to jump.

跳 迸 to leap; to dance.

跳 進·去 to jump in.

³⁵跳 過·來 to jump across.

跳 遠 the broad jump.

跳 鑽 to jump about in high spirits.

跳 馬 to cover a mare.

跳 高 the high jump.

⁴⁰跳 鼠 a jerboa.

跳 龍 門 to leap the dragon's gate.—to graduate.

嚇 (hsia⁴)·了 一 跳 gave me quite a start.

心 跳 the heart in a flutter.

躰 ³ The appearance of height in a person.
6288

銚 ² A spear. To burn, as in a kiln.
6289

長 銚 利 兵 long spears and sharp swords.

(a) Read t'iao⁴ or tiao⁴. A pan with a long handle.

(b) Read yao². A weeding-implement; A surname.

頫
覜 ⁴ To have an audience, as the feudal princes did once every three years. The first form is also read fu³, see 1929.
6290

岧 ² A lofty peak.
6291

笤 ² A broom; a besom.
6292

笤 把 a long broom, usually made of bamboo.

笤·箒 a broom or besom.

笤·箒 星 a comet.＝掃·箒星.

苕
芀 ² Name of a plant.
6293

陵 苕 Tecoma grandiflora.

迢 ² Remote.
6294

迢 遞 far off.

迢 遠 distant.

髫 ² The tufts of hair on the heads of children.
6295

髫 齡 or 髫 年 young; about seven years of age.

髫 髮 勵 志 while still young strengthen the will.

齠 ² To shed the milk teeth—young.
6296   Inter. preceding.

蜩 ² The cicada or broad locust.
6297

蜩 甲 the exuviæ of the cicada.

蜩 螗 a cicada.

調 ² To stir up; to mix. To blend; to harmonize; to adjust. To train.
6298

調 伏 to moderate and subdue the passions.

調·停 to arrange; to mediate; to compromise; to reconcile; to adjust.

調·停 和 局 to mediate for peace.

調·停 勞 資 糾 紛 arbitration in disputes between labour and capital.

⁵調·停 機 關 Arbitration Bureau.

居 間 調 停 to act as a mediator.

調 劑 to even off; to arrange; to compensate; to mix—as colours; to make up—a disagreement.

調 劑 術 pharmacy.

調 劑 金 融 to regulate the currency.

¹⁰調 匀 or 攪 匀 to stir up thoroughly; to mix in equal proportions.

調 合 to mix; to compound.

調 味 to season; to blend flavours.

調 和 to mix; to blend; to make peace; to tune up; in tune—as instruments.

調 和 五 味 to blend the flavours nicely, so that no one flavour predominates.

¹⁵調 和 意·見 to reconcile opinions.

調 和 爭 端 to compromise differences.

調 和 級 數 harmonical progression. (arith.).

居 中 調 和 to act as a mediator.

時序調和 the seasons are regular.

20 琴瑟調和 domestic harmony —the lutes are in tune.

琴瑟不調 the lutes are out of tune—domestic discord.

調字聲 or 調韻 to make the sounds of words suit or rhyme —as in poetry.

調攝 to recuperate.

調敎 education; teaching.

25 調桌 to arrange a table.

調整 to regulate; to tune.

調治 to attend to; to cure.

調°理 to arrange—as a business; to heal; to repair; to adjust.

調節 to regulate.

30 調絃 to tune a stringed instrument.

調經 to regulate the menses.

調羹 a spoon; to season soups.

調習 to train; to tame.

調良 well mixed and excellent.

35 調色板 a palette.

調處 to arrange matters between persons who have quarrelled.

調製 to edit—books.

調解 to come to an agreement.

調詩 to compose an ode.

40 調說 to effect a compromise; to adjust differences.

調護 to protect; to take care of.

調音 to harmonize; to tune.

調養 to nurse one's health; to take care of oneself.

調馬 to train horses.

(a) To stir up. To provoke. To instigate.

調三窩四 to set by the ears.

調唆 to stir up; to instigate.

調弄 to dupe; to make fun of.

調情 to make love; to dally with.

5 調戲 lewd dalliance; to flirt.

調笑 to ridicule; to provoke.

調脾 or 調皮 artful; cunning; unscrupulous; shifty.

(b) Read *tiao*⁴. **An air, a tune.**

調°子 or 曲調 a tune.

調°子不合 out of tune.

不殼調°子 out of tune. 「mode.

小 調 ditties, folk tunes; the minor

樂 調 a tune. (*yüeh*⁴-)

氣 調 rhythm. 短 調 the minor mode.

轉調 to modulate.

長調 or 大調 the major mode.

(c) Read *tiao*⁴. **To transfer. To change. To move.**

調任 or 調充 to transfer an official from one post to another.

調兵 to move troops.

調·動 to shake; to transfer.

調員 to transfer an officer.

5 調換 to transpose; to exchange.

調撥 to distribute—troops between stations.

調撤 to withdraw—troops.

調用 to transfer an official to another post.

調簾 to be detached for duty at the former provincial examinations.

10 調署 to transfer to another post as Acting....

調補 to transfer an official to another post.

調白 or 調包 to substitute an inferior article when exchanging—common trick of swindlers.

調赴 to transfer to another post.

調轉 to change about; to turn end for end.

15 調·過·來 to turn the opposite way.

調·過·來說 to transpose a phrase.

調遷 to transfer to another post.

調開 to separate.

調·頭 a figure of speech; a tune.

20 調驗 to transfer for the purposes of an inquest—as magistrates may not hold inquests on deaths occurring in their own gaols.

(d) Read *tiao*⁴. **To investigate; to arrange.**

調人 an arbitrator. (*t'iao*²-)

調度 to calculate; to consider; to arrange; calculation; tactics.

調查 to send for to examine—as a document, etc., to investigate.

5 調查員 inspector; auditor.

調查委員會 Commission of Inquiry.

調查戶口 census.

調查書 report of a Commission of Inquiry.

調查海軍 to investigate naval matters.

調查表 record of investigation.

10 出產調查 census of production.

鯛³

6299 General name for perch, etc.

條² A length; a section. A clause; an item. A branch,

6300 a twig. Orderly; regular; regulated.

條°件 sections; divisions; clauses; articles; terms; conditions.

依此條°件 upon these conditions.

有條°件 conditional.

附條°件 conditionally.

5 條件句 conditional clause. (*gram.*).

條件法 conditional mood.

條件·的 conditional.

條件附 supplementary clause.

條例 or 律條 or 規條 laws; regulations; rules.

10 條條有理 there is reason in every clause; orderly.

條條蛇咬人 every snake will bite—every position has its difficulty.

條几 or 書几 a sideboard; a long narrow table.

條分縷析 to arrange the points and speak in order.

條·子 a twig; a chit; a poster; an unfolded strip of paper.

15 條對 to reply point by point.

條文 text of a treaty.

條暢 clear; perspicuous.

條桑 to strip the mulberry-tree of its leaves.

條欵 clauses; sections—as of a treaty.

20 條狼 a scavenger.

條理 sequence; reasonable; logical; method; regularity.

條痕 streaks.

條目 particulars; details; clauses; articles.

條答 to reply item by item.

25 條約 regulations‚ treaties.

條約之保障 treaty protection.

條約之因果關·係 relation of cause and effect in the treaties.

條約制度 the treaty system.

條約國 Treaty Powers.

30 條約期限 time limit of a treaty.

條約權 treaty rights.

條約滿限 the time limit of the treaty has expired.

公斷條約 arbitration treaty.

通商條約 commercial treaty.

³⁵條 紋 stripes; streaks.
條 編 plaited basket-work.
條 脫 a bangle.
條 規 laws; regulations; rules.
條 誡 laws; regulations, etc.
⁴⁰條 達 straightforward; reasonable.
條 陳 lucid statement of; to present in detail.
條 項 provisions; conditions.
條 風 the north-east wind.

(a) High; tall.

厥 木 惟 條 the trees grew tall.

(b) N.A. for dogs, roads, snakes, fishes, and long narrow things.

一 條 性·命 a life.
一 條 狗 a dog.
一 條 綫 a piece of string; a length of thread.
一 條 繩 a piece of rope.
⁵一 條 腿 a leg.
一 條 蛇 a snake.
一 條 街 a street.
一 條 裙·子 a skirt.
一 條 褲·子 a pair of trousers.
¹⁰一 條 路 a road.
一 條 魚 a fish.
皮 條 strip of leather.
紙 條 a strip of paper.

篠 莜 ⁴
A bamboo basket.
6301

鯈 ²
A long narrow fish.
6302

糶 ⁴
To sell grain.
6303

糶 糧 to sell grain.

TIEH.   (ㄉㄝ)

爹 ¹
A father; a grandfather.
6304

爹 娘 father and mother.
爹·爹 daddy; father.
乾·爹 an adopted father.

凸 ⁴·⁵· Protuberant; jutting; convex. To protrude. Also read t'u⁴·⁵, and ku³.
6305 See 凹 No. 7268.

凸 凹·的 convexo-concave.
凸·出 to project; bulging; protuberant.
凸·出·的 protuberant.
凸 嘴 凹 鼻 projecting lips and a sunken nose.
⁵凸 圓 形 convexity.
凸 圓 體 a convex body.
凸 字 letters cut in relief.
凸 然 出 水 suddenly rising out of the water.
凸 牙 projecting teeth.
¹⁰凸 狀 convex.
凸 瘇 a protuberant swelling.
凸 眼 protruding eyes.
凸 紋 in relief.
凸 花 embossed figures.
¹⁵凸 起·的 projecting; convex.
凸 路 a raised road.
凸 鏡 convex lenses.
凸 面·的 convex.
凸 額 prominent forehead.

跕 ⁴·⁵·
To fall. To swoop down.
6306

飛 鳶 跕 跕 墮 水 中 the flying hawk swoops down into the water.

(a) Read t'ieh⁴·⁵. To tap with the foot. To allow the slipper to hang loosely.

鳴 瑟 跕 屣 playing the psaltery and tapping with her slipper.
女 子³ 彈 絃 跕 躧 strumming the strings and beating time with her slipper.

(b) Read tien³. To stand on tiptoe. To be lame.

跕·着 脚 standing on tiptoe; lame.

昳 ⁴·⁵· The declining sun in the west.
6307

日 昳 sunset.

(a) Read i³. Bright.
昳 麗 dazzling.

瓞 ²·⁵·
Young melons just forming.
6308

眣 ²·⁵· Prominent eyes. Distinguish 眣 No. 5937.
6309

跌 ¹·⁵· To stumble; to slip; to fall down. ˣA.p. tsai¹.
6310

ˣ跌 一 跤 to have a fall.
ˣ跌 倒 or 打 跌 or ˣ跌·了 腿 or 跌·着 to fall; fallen.
ˣ跌 傷 injured by a fall.
跌 價 the price has fallen.
⁵股 票 跌 價 the price of shares has dropped.
跌 墮 to decline; to fall.
跌 宕 unrestrained; reckless.
跌 撞 to fall and collide with.
ˣ跌·死 to be killed by a fall; to drop down dead.
¹⁰跌 破 or 跌 爛 broken by a fall.
跌 落·下·來 to lose one's position; to fall.
價 值 跌 落 prices have fallen.
跌 蕩 放 言 to speak at random; wild talk.
跌 足 to stamp the feet; to slip.
¹⁵跌 足 大 驚 jumped up with fright.
跌 跌 躞 躞 reeling—when tipsy.
跌 跟·頭 to fall head over heels.
跌 踼 to stumble; reckless; unrestrained.
跌 蹼 to stumble and fall.
²⁰漲 跌 rise and fall—as of prices.

迭 ²·⁵· To alternate; to change. Repeatedly.
6311 Distinguish 送 No. 5566.

迭 屢 frequently; repeatedly.
迭 擊 repeated attacks.
迭 變 successive changes.
迭 次 again and again; repeatedly.
⁵迭 爲 賓 主 they treated each other as host and guest.
迭 用 to use in rotation.
迭 用 柔 剛 to employ kindness and severity alternately.
迭 經 照 會 I have repeatedly addressed you officially.
迭 興 迭 廢 now prospering, now declining.
¹⁰迭 費 淸 神 I have troubled you repeatedly.
迭 起 frequently rising.
迭 運 alternate rotation.

(a) To attack.

迭 我 殽 地 he attacked our land of *Hsiao*.

(b) To succeed. Satisfactory.

迭 不 得 去 I cannot spare time to go.
迭 當 satisfactory.
逃 命 不 迭 failed to escape with his life.

(c) Occurs u.f. 軼 No. 3027.

(d) Used in transliterating.

迭 更 斯 Dickens.

垤[2.5.]   A mound. An ant-hill.
6312

丘 垤 mounds and hillocks.

絰[2.5.] White hempen cloth worn by mourners.
6313

喪 絰 mourning garments.

耋[2.5.] Seventy or eighty years of age. Aged; infirm.
6314

戜[4.5.]   To scrape. Advantageous.
6315

喋[2.5.]   To chatter.
6316

喋 聑 ceaseless chattering.

(a) Flowing blood. To smear or to taste blood in taking oaths.

喋 血 flowing blood.

(b) Read *cha*[5]**. Noise of ducks feeding.**

嗘 (*sha*[5]) 喋 乎 蓱 (the ducks are) noisily feeding in the duckweed.

堞[2.5.] Battlements; battlement-ed walls.
6317

城 堞 or 雉 堞 a parapet.

渫[2.5.]   Rolling billows.
6318

長 波 浃 渫 great billows roll by.

(a) Intelligent.

憒 眊 不 渫 dull and stupid.

(b) Read *hsieh*[4.5.]**. To get rid of. To scatter.**

粟 有 所 渫 there will be grain for distribution.

(c) Read *hsieh*[4.5.]**. Turbid, muddy. Unsettled. To ooze.**

渫 惡 evil, degraded—men.
井 渫 不 食 do not drink from a tainted well.

(d) Read *hsieh*[4.5.]**. To rest.**

爲 歡 未 渫 he could not rest for joy.

牒[2.5.] Tablets for writing on; records; official instruc-tions; documents; a des-patch; a warrant.
6319

牒 文 an official despatch.
牒 稱 to state in a memorial.
呈 牒 to hand in a report.
簡 牒 tablets; memoranda.
譜 牒 genealogies.

碟[2.5.] A plate; a small dish, a saucer.
6320

碟·子 a plate; a saucer.
碟 架 a plate-rack.
菓 碟 dishes of fruits.

蝶[2.5.]
蜨 A butterfly. Also read *t'ieh*.
6321

蝶 蝀 the rainbow.
蝶 銨 關 節 hinge-joints.
蝶 骨 the sphenoid bone.
蝴 蝶 a butterfly.

諜[2.5.]   To spy.
6322

諜 報 to spy and report.
諜 賊 a spy; a traitor.
間 諜 a secret agent; a spy.

(a) To chatter. u.f. 喋 No. 6316.

諜 諜 loquacious.

(b) A genealogy. u.f. 牒 No. 6319.

譜 諜 a genealogy.

蹀[2.5.] To skip; to dance. To put the foot down.
6323

蹀 足 to stamp the foot.
蹀 蹀 恐 顚 墮 stepping lightly, fearing a fall.
躍 蹀 to dance about.

褶[2.5.]   A lined coat.
6324

褶 衣 lined garments.

(a) Read *hsi*[2]**. Breeches; overalls.**

袴 褶 riding breeches.

(b) Read *chê*[5]**. Pleats.**

褶 襇 embroidered pleats in a robe.

叠[2.5.]
疊 To fold up. To repeat. To duplicate.
曡
6325

叠 句 a repeated sentence.
叠 次 repeatedly.
叠 言 tautology.
叠·起·來 to fold up.
叠 騎 to ride double.
重 重 叠 叠 layer upon layer; fold upon fold; repetition, etc.

(a) To fear.

震 叠 to tremble with awe.

(b) A kind of white cotton cloth.

攝[2.5.] To pile on; to fold up.
6326

攝 四 摺 兒 to fold into four folds.

T'IEH. (去廿)

帖 4.5. To taste. To sip.
6327

帖 血 之 盟 an oath ratified by drinking blood.

(a) Petty; small. Vulgar.

帖 帖 小 人 a mean, petty fellow.

(b) Read ch'ê⁴. To whisper.

帖 囁 耳 語 to whisper in the ear.
帖 囁 to whisper in the ear.

帖 1.5. A label; a card; a placard; a document.
6328

帖³ 套 a card-case.
帖³ 子 a card which has something on it more than the name.
帖¹ 存 to record the numbers and particulars of bank-notes received.
帖 寫 a clerk; a style of penmanship which is not according to rule, but which has some famous writer's authority for it.
⁵帖¹ 括 a term used under the T'ang dynasty for an essay; a 2nd degree graduate.
帖¹ 欠 to record the numbers and particulars of bank-notes paid out.
全 帖 a sheet of red paper folded into five leaves with a different salutation on each—used on great occasions.
勾 帖³ a warrant—death summons from Hades.
匿 名 揭 帖³ anonymous placard.
¹⁰名 帖³ a visiting-card.
喜 帖³ invitation to a wedding.
喪 帖³ invitation to a funeral.
回 帖³ card sent in acknowledgement of a present.
字 帖⁴ a copy-slip.
¹⁵招 帖⁴ a notice—as of a house to let, etc.
招 生 帖³ notice calling for pupils.
拜 帖³ a visiting-card.
法 帖⁴ a copy-slip.
白 帖³ anonymous placard.
²⁰碑 帖⁴ rubbing taken from a stone tablet.

設 帖³ a prospectus; specifications.
請 帖³ card of invitation.
謝 帖³ a card of thanks.
賞 帖³ notice of reward offered.
²⁵軍 帖³ military despatch.
領 帖³ a card acknowledging receipt of a present.

(a) Settled; decided.

妥 帖⁴ settled.
帖⁴ 然 certain; sure.

(b) To submit.

帖⁴ 伏 to tame.
帖⁴ 尾 to put the tail between the legs.
帖⁴ 服 to be submissive.
帖⁴ 耳 to droop the ears—as a tamed animal, to be submissive.

帖 1.5. Peaceful. Quiet.
6329

帖 服 resigned.
帖 靜 retired and quiet.

貼 1.5. To stick up; to paste. To stick to; attached.
6330

貼 伏 attached to; to submit to.
貼 住 上 膛 sticks to the palate.
貼 切 apposite.
貼 告 示 to post proclamations.
⁵貼 在 牆 上 paste it on the wall.
貼 報 條 to post up notices.
貼 寫 clerks; copyists in a yamen.
貼 對 子 to paste up scrolls.
貼 己 intimate; private.
¹⁰貼 席 to stick to the mat—to sleep soundly.
貼 店 to reserve an inn for an official.
貼 座 to reserve seats.
貼 心 intimate; attached to; fellow-feeling.
貼 心 貼 意 amiable and obliging.
¹⁵貼 服 intimate; attached to.
貼 書 copying clerks; writers.
貼 梗 海 棠 Pyrus spectabilis.
貼 耳 to be ready to listen to.
貼 背 風 岸 to hug the lee shore.
²⁰貼 膏 藥 to stick on a medicated plaster.
貼 船 to impress boats for official use.

貼·著 attached; to make up; to go along by the side of.
貼 身 next to the body—attached to, as a servant, or one's children.
貼 近 to keep close to; contiguous.
²⁵貼 邊 a wide hem or facing to strengthen the edge for holding buttons, etc.
貼 金 to gild; to praise oneself.
貼 附 joined; to keep close to.
貼 靠 to depend on; to trust to.
貼 靠 牆 press close to the wall.
³⁰貼 食 to eat in company with; to be a diner-out.
膠 貼 to glue up.
體 貼 to accommodate oneself to another. See No. 6246—A. 13.

(a) To make up, as a deficiency.

貼 匯 水 discount on exchange.
貼 戶 those who were not strong enough for military service and paid a levy instead—under the Yuan dynasty.
貼 旦 (or 貼) a supernumerary actor.
貼 本 to lose money in a business.
⁵貼 水 to pay the difference in the value of silver when the quality is not up to standard; discount; commission.
貼 現 discount on exchange.
貼 現 票 據 discount on cheques.
貼 納 to assist with money.
貼 色 to pay the difference in value between alloyed silver and standard quality.
¹⁰貼 補 to make up a deficiency; to help, as with money; to subsidize.
貼 賠 to lose in a business.
貼 錢 to pay up money; to give monetary assistance.
津·貼 subsidy; gratuities; bonus, etc. See No. 1081—A. 5.
米 貼 supplementary wages paid to meet the high cost of living.

(b) Settled.

貼 妥 or 妥 貼 properly arranged; adjusted.

饕 4.5. Gluttonous.
See 饕 No. 6147.
6331

鐵
鉄｝
鈇｝
6332

3.5.

Iron; used as a symbol of strength, firmness, etc. Firm, decided.

鐵 中 錚 錚 an outstanding man among ordinary persons.

鐵 主 意 a fixed resolve; an iron will.

鐵 價 不 二 our prices are unalterable.

鐵 公 鷄 or 鐵 沙 梨 an iron cock, or an iron pear—a mean fellow.

⁵鐵 具 iron implements.

鐵 券 metal tokens given to meritorious statesmen in ancient times.

鐵·匠 a blacksmith.

鐵 十 字 the Iron Cross; an anchor.

鐵 口 or 鐵 嘴 determined, but fair and just speech.

¹⁰鐵 商 iron-merchants.

鐵·器 hardware; iron tools.

鐵·器 店 ironmongery; hardware store.

鐵。器 時 代 the Iron Age.

鐵 壁 iron walls—impregnable.

¹⁵鐵 夾 櫃 an iron safe.

鐵 尺 a short, iron staff.

鐵 工 iron-workers.

鐵 床 架 iron bedstead.

鐵 廠 ironworks.

²⁰鐵 心 石 腸·的 人 a hard, unfeeling person.

鐵 手 桶 an iron bucket.

鐵 搭 an iron cramp; a kind of rake.

鐵 政 局 ordnance office.

鐵 板 sheet-iron.

²⁵鐵 案 an irrevocable decision.

鐵 枴 李 Mr. Li of the iron staff —one of the Eight Immortals.

鐵 條 rod-iron.

鐵 條 網 wire entanglements.

鐵 槓 iron horizontal bar.

³⁰鐵 樹 開 花 when the iron tree blossoms—never; an impossibility.

鐵 泉 a chalybeate spring.

鐵 漢 a hard, determined man; a strong fellow.

鐵 牆 銅 壁 walls of iron and brass—impregnable.

鐵 片 條 hoop-iron.

---

³⁵鐵 牛 iron ox; placed by the side of rivers, they are supposed to prevent floods.

鐵 甲 汽 車 armoured motor cars.

鐵 甲 船 an ironclad.

鐵 甲 車 armoured car.

鐵 石 人 a hard man; a determined person; a mulish man.

⁴⁰鐵 砂 iron filings.

鐵 硯 磨 穿 he rubbed through an iron ink-slab—by his application to study.

鐵 磚 pig-iron.

鐵 窗 風 味 the flavour of prison-bars.

鐵 筋 土 reinforced concrete.

⁴⁵鐵 筆 a burin.

鐵 筆 不 改 an unalterable writing.

鐵 箍 iron hoops.

鐵 算·盤 the iron abacus—a trick by means of which one is swindled out of money.

鐵 管 iron piping.

⁵⁰鐵 箱 a safe.

鐵 離 wire entanglements.

鐵 索 iron chains.

鐵 紗 窗 wire screens for windows.

鐵 紅 散 red oxide of iron.

⁵⁵鐵 絲ㄦ or 鐵 線 iron wire.

鐵 絲 網 wire entanglements.

鐵 絲 草 maiden-hair fern.

鐵 葉 sheet-iron.

鐵 蒺 藜 caltrops.

⁶⁰鐵 血 手 腕 the mailed fist.

鐵 血 政·策 or 鐵 血 主 義 the Blood and Iron Policy.

鐵 血 會 a bomb-throwing society.

鐵 衣 rust; armour.

鐵 裁·縫 a sewing-machine.

⁶⁵鐵 證 proof strong as iron.

鐵 路 a railway.

鐵 路 交 站 railway clearing-house.

鐵 路 人 員 railroad officials.

鐵 路 則 例 railway by-laws.

⁷⁰國 有 鐵 路 National Railways.

鐵 路 權 railway concessions.

鐵 路 軌 道 railroad track.

鐵 軌 道 iron rails.

鐵 道 實 業 railway enterprise.

⁷⁵鐵 道 局 railway offices.

鐵 道 幹 線 trunk railroad.

鐵 道 部 Ministry of Railways.

鐵 釘 iron nails.

鐵 鍫 or 鐵 銑 an iron shovel or spade.

---

⁸⁰鐵 鋼 or 純 鋼 steel; pure steel.

鐵 鍊 iron chains.

鐵 鍬 an iron shovel.

鐵 鐺 an iron bell.

鐵 鑛 iron mines.

⁸⁵鐵 鑛 石 iron ore.

鐵 鑽 a bit; an iron auger.

鐵 門 door of a strong-room.

鐵 門 限 rigid restrictions.

鐵 靑 iron-grey.

⁹⁰鐵 面 無 私 describes a man of integrity and justice; inflexibly just.

鐵 馬 or 鐵 騎 strong mounted forces. Cf. 7351.4,7.

鐵 鬼 a black-faced rascal.

接 鐵 to weld iron.

熟 鐵 wrought-iron.

⁹⁵洋 鐵 tin-plates.

生 鐵 cast-iron.

白 鐵 tin-plates.

↑鐵 屑 or 廢 鐵 scrap iron.

TIEN. (ㄉㄧㄢ)

摃｜
6333

¹

To beat. To winnow.

摃 米 to winnow rice.

滇｜
6334

¹

The province of Yunnan.

or Kunming

滇 池 a lake south of Yunnanfu

滇 省 or 古 滇 the province of Yunnan.

(a) Read t'ien². Vast.

滇 㴉 vast and boundless.

滇 滇 overflowing.

癲
癩｝
6335

¹

Mad; crazy. Fits; convulsions.

癲 氣 hot-headed; rashness.

癲 狂 or 瘋 癲 wild; mad; delirious.

行 止 癲 狂 to act as if crazy.

癲 狗 a mad dog.

⁵癲 症 insanity.

癲 癇 epilepsy.

多 喜 爲 癩 excess of joy causes madness.

發 癩 to become insane; to go crazy.

色迷酒巔 crazy for women and wine.

趯[1] To go unequally. To trot; to jog; to jolt.
6336

趯和·着走 to go at a trot.
趯散[3]了骨[2]頭 shaken to pieces, as by a jolting cart or a trotting horse.
趯·的慌 jolting terribly.

顛[1] To upset; to turn over. To fall. Upside down.
6337

顛三倒[4]四 awkward; topsy-turvy.
顛仆 to fall down.
顛倒[34] upside down.
顛倒[3]是非 to confound right and wrong.
[5]顛倒[3]黑白 to confound black and white—right and wrong.
七顛八倒[4] topsy-turvy; all in confusion.
晨昏顛倒[34] to turn night into day.
顛危困頓之時 a critical and distressing time.
顛撲 upside down.
[10]顛撲不破 if it falls it will not break—very strong; used fig., of strong principles.
顛沛 to fall utterly; in difficulties; danger; upset.
顛沛流離 in difficulties; in confusion.
顛覆 to be overthrown; to overthrow; ruined; reduced to poverty.
顛覆政府 to overthrow the government.
[15]顛越 to fall down.
顛跌 to stumble and fall.
顛蹶 to overthrow.
顛躓 to fall.
顛連 in trouble; in confusion; at sixes and sevens; helplessly dependent.
[20]顛險 dangerous; difficulties; misfortunes.

(a) The top. The summit. The crown. The forehead. The beginning of.

顛末 from beginning to end.
　事有顛末 everything has a beginning and an end.

能詳知顛末 can know all the details, from first to last.
顛頂 the top; the crown.
白顛馬 a horse with a white forehead.

(b) u.f. 巔 No. 6335. Crazy, etc.

顛冥 dull, stupid, idiotic; confounded.
顛狂 wild; crazy; insane; throwing off all restraint.
顛癇 epilepsy.
顛飲 to drink without restraint.

(c) To jolt. To joggle. To trot.

顛·得穩 it trots smoothly.
顛播 to shake; to jolt.
顛簸 to jolt; to joggle.
顛馬 a trotting horse.
大顛小顛 a fast and a slow trot respectively.

巔[1] The peak of a hill or range of mountains.
6338 Occurs u.f. 巓 No. 6335.

巔疾 madness.

坫[4] A stand on which to replace goblets after drinking.
6339

塾[4] To steady by putting something underneath. To shore up; to prop.
6340

塾平 to level off—ground; to make of the same level—as by propping.
塾穩 to steady—by a proper wedge.
塾高 to raise higher.

店[4] An inn; a shop; a tavern.
6341

店主 landlord of an inn; proprietor.
店務 matters connected with the shop.
店員 employees in a shop or warehouse.
店夥 shop-assistants.
[5]店客 travellers; guests at an inn.
客店 an inn.

店·家 shop-keepers; shop-assist-·ants.
店底 stock-in-trade.
店檯 or 櫃檯 a shop-counter.
[10]店肆 a shop; a place of business.
店鋪 a shop.
店錢 inn expenses; cost of lodging.
店面 a shop-front.
下店 or 住店 to stop at an inn.
[15]守店 to mind the shop.
投店 to stop at an inn.
收店 to shut up the shop.
飯店 a restaurant; a modern style [hotel.
黑店 a thieves' inn.

惦[4] To remember; to think about.
6342

惦念 to ponder; to reflect on.
惦·記 or 惦懷 or 惦掛 to bear in mind; to think of.

掂[1]
戡 To weigh in the hand; to estimate. To shake.
6343

掂·掇 or 掂量 to estimate the weight of anything held in the hand.
掂·掂有多[12]重 take it in your hand and guess the weight.
掂搭 to shake in the hand.
掂敠 to weigh; to estimate the weight of.
掂算 to estimate; to weigh; to form an opinion.

玷[4] A flaw in a piece of jade, thus—a defect, a flaw, a blemish. To disgrace.
6344

玷缺 a flaw; a defect.
玷辱 or 玷汚 to bring discredit on; to disgrace; to debauch.
玷辱祖宗 to disgrace one's ancestors.
玷辱處女 to dishonour a maiden.
白珪之玷 the flaw in a white jade-token.

疷[1.4.] Malarial fever.
6345

點 点 [3] A dot, a spot, a speck. A point. A little, a mite. To count; to check one by one. To punctuate.
6346

點 主 to consecrate an ancestral tablet by dotting the character 王 and making it 主.

點 主 官 the Master of Ceremonies at the consecration of an ancestral tablet.

點 交 to check and hand over.

點 勘 to verify; to compare.

[5]點 化 to reform; to educate.

點 卯 to call the muster-roll.

點 句 讀 (*tou*[4]) to punctuate.

點 名 to call a roll.

點 名 冊 a roll.

[10]點 單 a list of names submitted to a superior to tick off the ones he selects.

點·子 a spot; a dot.

點 字 Braille type.

點 定 to select.

點 定 文 句 to punctuate; to mark off into paragraphs.

[15]點·心 confectionery; sweets; pastry; refreshment.

點 戲 to tick off, on a list, the performances which one desires to see.

點 手 to beckon with the hand.

點 掇 to tidy up; to put in order.

點 接 to check and receive.

[20]點 收 to check and receive.

點 數·目 record the number; check the number—of pieces, etc.

點 明 to explain; to mark off; to reckon over.

點 書 to punctuate a book.

點 染 to portray in painting.

[25]點 檢 to check; to count over a list, etc.

點 派 to appoint to duties.

點 漆 black.

點 狀 元 to be marked by the emperor as first graduate of the *Hanlin* Academy.

點 畫 to outline; to draw.

[30]點 看 to check; to inspect.

點 眼 to fill in the eyes—of an effigy, etc.; to make clear.

點 石 成 金 it changes stone into gold—as when a phrase is altered in a composition.

點 破 or 點 穿 to explain abstruse teaching by analogy; to make explicit. — as a deliberate obscurity.

點 穴 to select a good site for a grave. (*geomancy*).

[35]點 空 to point out deficiencies; to find fault.

點 竄 to strike out and alter—a phrase in a composition.

點·綴 accessories; to add accessories; to adorn.

點 翠 to put on feathers; to imitate feather-work in enamel.

點 翰 林 to be marked off by the Emperor as a member of the *Hanlin* Academy.

[40]點 脈 to hit the pulse—Chinese think that an enemy can destroy health in this way.

點 脚 to limp.

點 苔 to dot trees, grasses, etc., in a landscape painting.

點 菜 to select the dishes one desires at a restaurant.

點 號 a comma.

[45]點 記 to punctuate.

點 註 to fill in—as a form, etc.

點 較 to review.

點 金 to transmute into gold.

點 金 乏 術 no means of getting money—utterly without resources.

[50]點 金 成 鐵 I have turned your gold into iron—depreciatory phrase when correcting or revising compositions for another.

點 鐵 成 金 it changes iron into gold—as when a phrase is altered in a composition. *See above*—32.

點 頭 to bow; to nod assent.

點 頭 示 意 to convey a meaning by a nod.

點 頭 禮 the ceremony of bowing.

[55]點 額 to mark the forehead of a child with a red spot—for beauty.

點 驗 to tick off and examine—as goods.

點 點 to punctuate; to check; to count over; small and numerous.

點 點 滴 滴 drop by drop.

點 齊 all present—at roll-call.

[60]一 點 兒 a speck; a dot; a little.(-*tiar*[3])

多·一 點 兒 a little more; a little too much.

(a) To light.

點 上 燈 light the lamps.

點·不 着 it will not light.(-*chao*[2])

點 火 to light a fire.

點 燈 to light a lamp.

(b) The stroke of a clock.

六 點 鐘 six o'clock.

幾 點 鐘 what is the time?

(c) Used as a suffix to indicate a point, as of degree or departure, etc.

中 心 點 the centre.

主 要·的 點 the important point.

交 叉 點 point of intersection.

交 點 juncture; point of intersection.

[5]元 點 an atom.= 原 子[3].

出 發 點 point of departure.

切 點 point of contact.

劣 點 depravity; bad points.

差 點 point of divergence or difference.(*ch'a*[2]-)

[10]微 點 a molecule. = 分 子[3].

打 點 to put in order.

指 點 to point out; to show.

汚 點 its bad points; a flaw; a defect.

焦 點 focus.

[15]等 距 點 equidistant points.

細 密 之 點 minute points.

要 點 essential points.

視 點 view-point.

誤 點 errors.

[20]起 點 starting point.

集 中 點 point of focus.

缺點 defect; shortcoming.

典 [3] A statute; a law; a code; a canon. Documents; records.
6347

典 刑 laws and penalties.

典 型 a model; a pattern; an example.

典 奥 profound; abstruse.

典 常 a constant rule.

[5]典 故 or 古 典 a quotation; an allusion.

典 禮 ritual; ceremony.

典 章 regulations; rules; a pattern; a constitution, as of a society.

典 簿 a recorder in the government offices at Peking. (*obs.*)

典 籍 books; records; the canon, as of Scripture.

[10]典 要 authoritative; classical.

典 雅 well-bred; refined.

五 典 the *Five Relationships. See* 倫 No. 4247-1. The books of the *Five Emperors.*
入 典 to bring in classical allusions.
國 典 the laws of the land.
[15] 恩 典 grace; favour.
經 典 precedent; authority; classics.

(a) **To be in charge of; to control.**

典 儀 Assistant Major-domo in the palace of the Imperial princes at Peking. (*obs.*).
典 制 to control.
典 史 a District Police-Master and Gaol-Warden. (*obs.*).
典 守 to keep in charge; to have special charge of.
典 獄 官 a gaoler.
典 試 委 員 會 Examining Commission.

(b) **To mortgage. To give in pledge.**

典 主 the mortgage.
典·出·去 to mortgage to.
典 契 a deed of mortgage.
典 房·子 to mortgage a house.
[5] 典 田 to mortgage agricultural fields.
典 當[4] or 典 押 or 典 質 or 典 賣 to mortgage; to pledge; to pawn.
典 身 to mortgage one's person—to work for the mortgagee.
典 鋪 a pawn-shop.
出 典 to mortgage.

碘[3] **Used as a symbol for Iodine.**
6348

碘 酒 tincture of iodine.

佃[2,4] **To till. To hunt. A farmer.**
6349

佃 戶 門 or 佃 夫 or 佃 丁 husbandmen; agriculturists.
佃 田 to till fields.

(a) **To lease.**

佃 字 a lease.
佃 批 to lease to.

旬[4] **The Imperial Domain. To rule; to govern.**
6350

旬 服 the Imperial Domain.
旬 萬 姓 to govern the people.

蜎[4] **Inlaid shell-work.**
6351

淀[4] **Shallow water. Name of a lake in Hopei. (Chihli.)**
6352 Occurs u.f. 旬 No. 6350.

靛[4] **Indigo, or any of the blue native dyes found in China; an indigo colour.**
6353

靛 坊 an indigo warehouse.
靛 池 an indigo tank.
靛 花 the scum on an indigo tank.
靛 青 or 藍 靛 indigo.
洋 靛 foreign Prussian blue.
漚 靛 to macerate the indigo leaves.

殿[4] **A temple; a palace; a hall.**
6354

殿 下 a title of the Heir-Apparent.
殿 宇 temple buildings.
殿 定 to establish firmly.
殿 庭 or 宮 殿 palaces and halls; a palace.
[5] 殿 廊 the temple porch.
殿 廷 a palace.
殿 板 an edition of a book prepared for Imperial use.
殿 試 examination for the admission of 進士 into the *Hanlin* Academy. (*obs.*).
殿 閣 halls; pavilions.
[10] 殿 陛 恩 濃 the gracious kindness of the Emperor.
殿 頂 上 the roof of the temple.
便 殿 side-halls.

(a) **To protect; to bring up the rear of an army.**

殿 天 子[3] 之 邦 to defend the Imperial Domain.
殿 後 to bring up the rear; the rear.
殿 最 inferior and superior merit.
殿 軍 the rearward of an army; to bring up the rear.
奔 而 殿 being in the rear on an occasion of flight.

澱[4] **Sediment; dregs; precipitate. Indigo.**
6355

澱 粉 starch; glucose.
沉 澱 物 precipitates.

癜[4] **Erythema.**
6356

奠[4] **To offer libations.**
6357

奠 土 to offer a drink-offering to the God of the Earth.
奠 敬 or 奠 儀 an offering sent to mourners—usually of money.
奠 禮 contributions of money sent to friends on the occasion of a funeral.
奠 酒 to pour out a libation of wine.
[5] 奠 醊 to offer libations to the gods.
奠 雁 to pour out a libation to geese at a marriage; to present a goose—by the bridegroom, to indicate conjugal fidelity.
拜 奠 with condolences—when no present is sent to the funeral.
釋 奠 to offer a sacrifice.

(a) **To determine. To settle.**

奠 厥 攸 居 he settled their places of abode.
奠 定 quiet; settled; well-governed.
奠 定 民 生 to secure the welfare of the masses.
奠 枕 to put the pillow straight—to rule in peace.
奠 高 山 大 川 he determined the high hills, and the great rivers—of *Yü* the Great in his work of reclamation.
奠 鼎 to consolidate the empire.

(b) **To put down.**

奠 之 而 後 取 lay it down and then (she) will take it up—as men and women may not touch hands.

電[4] **Lightning. Electricity.**
6358

電 位 electric potential.
電 信 a telegram.
電 信 住 址 telegraphic address.
電 傳 照 相[4] 法 transmission of photographic images by telegraphy.

[5]電 光 the glare of lightning.
電 光 影 戲 cinematograph.
電 光 照 相 flashlight photography.
電 光 閃 flashes of lightning.
電 刺 鰩 the electric ray.
[10]電 力 electric power; voltage.
電 力 火 車 electric trains.
電 動 力 electro-motive force.
電(動)機 electric motor.
電 勢 electric potential.
[15]電 匯 telegraphic transmission of money.
電 化 electrolysis.
電 化 學 electro-chemistry.
電 呈 telegraphic despatches.
電 吸 力 electric attraction; polarity.
[20]電 告 telegraphic information.
電 周 electric circuit.
電 商 to consult by telegraph.
電 器 公 司 firm which supplies or manufactures electric appliances.
測 電 器 electrometer.
[25]積 電 器 accumulator.
轉 電 器 commutator.
阻 電 器 interrupter.
驗 電 器 electroscope.
電 報 a telegram.
[30]電 報 司 機 telegraph operator.
電 報 局 a telegraph office.
電 報 生 telegraphist.
電 報 發 電 匙 sending-key for a telegraph instrument.
電 報 的 telegraphic.
[35]電 報 紙 telegraph form.
電 報 費 fees for sending a telegram.
暗 碼 電 報 code-telegram.
自 動 電 報 機 automatic telegraphic instrument.
轉 送 電 報 deferred telegram —sent by mail from the nearest post office.
[40]電 墢 electric field.
電 壓 力 electric pressure.
電 奏 to wire to the throne.
電 子[3] electrons.
陽 電 子[3] or 質 子[3] protons.
[45]電 子[3] 單 位 electronic units.
電 學 electricity as a science.
電 學 家 electricians.
電 學 科 electricity as a course of study.
電 容 electric capacity.
[50]電 察 deign to examine—opening phrase in correspondence written by inferiors.

電 弧 燈 arc lamp.
電 影 事 務 motion-picture industry. 電 影(兒) motion picture.
電 影 場 cinemas.
電 影 明 星 movie-stars.
[55]電 影 發 聲 片 sound films.
五 彩 電 影 technicolour motion picture
有 聲 電 影 talkies.
無 線 電 影 television. =電視.
↑電 化 教 育 education through the motion picture and the radio.
[60]電 性 the nature of electricity.
電 感 inductance.
感 電 圈 inductance coil.
電 扇 electric fan.
電 扣 (or 紐) electric button.
[65]電 抵 力 electric resistance.
電 擊 electric shock.
電 政 telegraph administration.
電 政 司 Telegraph Administration Bureau.
電 政 局 Telegraph Administration Office.
[70]電 文 text of a telegram or cable.
電 映 術 television.
電 梯 electric lift.
電 極 端 electrodes.
電 槽 storage battery.
[75]電 機 electric machine; motor.
發 電 機 a dynamo.
電 斃 electrocution.
電 母 the Goddess of Lightning.
電 氣 electricity.
[80]電 氣 分 路 器 electric switch.
電 氣 塞 子 electric plug.
電 氣 烘 爐 electric oven.
電 氣 烘 麵 包 器 electric toaster.
電 氣 燈 electric light.
[85]白 熱 電 燈 incandescent electric light.
電 氣 熨 斗 electric iron.
電 氣 爐 electric stove for cooking.
電 氣 行 刑 椅 electrocution chair.
電 氣 表 electric meter; electrometer.
[90]電 氣 調 整 鐘 electric clock.
電 氣 風 扇 electric fan.
電 氣 鑴 刻 術 electro-engraving.
上 電 氣 to charge with electricity.
電 池 electric battery.
[95]乾 電 池 dry-cell battery.
蓄 電 池 storage battery.

電 波 (or 浪) electric waves.
電 流 electric current.
直 流 電 direct current.
[100]交 流 電 alternating current.
變 電 器 or 變 壓 器 transformer.
電 流 繼 續 continuous current.
電 流 表 galvanometer.
電 照 or 台 電 deign to inspect this—opening phrase in correspondence from an inferior.
[105]電 熱 的 electro-thermal.
電 燈 electric lamp; electric light.
電 燈 泡 electric-light bulb.
電 版 electrotype.
電 瓶 insulator.
[110]電 療 electro-therapeutics.
電 磁 學 electro-magnetism as a science.
電 磁 浪 electro-magnetic waves.
電 磁 石 electro-magnet.
電 碼 numeral telegraph code.
[115]電 示 to wire instructions.
電 稱 to state by telegram.
電 筒 electric torch or flash-lamp.
電 絲 圈 electric coil.
電 線 electric wires; telegraph-wires.
[120]隔 電 線 insulated wires.
電 線 杆[3] 子 telegraph-poles.
電 線 總 開 關 switch-board panel. 電 網 electrified barbed wire.
海 底 電 線 submarine cable.
電 纜 electric cable.
[125]電 聲 筒 electric buzzer.
電 花 塞 spark plugs.
電 表 electricity meter. [television.
顯 電 表 electroscope. 電 視
電 視 機 visagraph—an instrument for teaching the blind.(rare.)
[130]電 解 electrolysis.
電 話 telephone.
電 話 交 換 所 telephone exchange.
電 話 傳 音 器 telephone transmitter.
電 話 局 telephone exchange.
[135]電 話 接 音 器 telephone receiver.
電 話 的 telephonic.
電 話 簿 telephone directory.
電 話 號 數 telephone number.
電 警 鈴 electric alarm.
[140]電 賀 congratulations sent by telegram.
電 赴 to go with great rapidity.
電 路 electric circuit.
電 車 electric tramcar.

電 鈴 electric bell.
145 電 鍍 器 electroplated goods.
電 鍍 術 electroplating.
電 鍍 赤 金 gold electroplate.
電 錐 electric needles.
電 鑄 electrotyping.
150 電 鎖 electric lock.
電 鑒 deign to examine—opening phrase in correspondence from inferiors.
電 離 electrolytic dissociation.
電 鰻 the electric eel.
乾 電 瓶 dry battery-cells.
155 動 物 電 animal electricity.
動 電 dynamic electricity.
急 電 an urgent telegram.
接 觸 電 contact electricity.
摩 電 frictional electricity.
160 無 線 電 wireless telegraphy. *See* No. 7180.
片 電 sheet-lightning.
生 電 to generate electricity.
發 電 to send a telegram.
積 流 電 箱 rheostat.
165 空 氣 電 atmospheric electricity.
繼 換 電 力 器 relay instrument.
釋 電 free electricity.
↑ 電 阻 箱 resistance box.
陰 電 negative electricity=負電.
170 陽 電 positive electricity=正電.
隱 電 latent electricity.
雷 電 atmospheric electricity;*
靜 電 static electricity.
↑ 電 機 激 發 permanent wave.
      * thunder and lightning.

墊 4 To fill up; to make good.
To steady, as by a support.
6359 A cushion.
Distinguish 墊 No. 5894.

墊 套 cushion cover.
墊 子 or 椅 墊 chair-cushions.
墊 平 to fill up and make even.
墊 穩 to steady—as by a wedge.
5 墊 鋪 a cushion-shop.
墊 頭 a cushion; anything to fill up, etc.
榻 墊 coir mat-frame for a bed.
籐 墊 rattan mats for the table.

(a) To make up. To advance money. To pay for another.

墊 上 to fill up; to advance money.
墊 不 出 unable to advance the money.
墊 付 to advance money on security.
墊 債 to pay another's debts.

5 墊 本 to advance capital—for a business.
墊 欵 advances in cash.
墊 賬 to settle another's account.
墊 辦 to arrange for an advance of money.
墊 錢 or 墊 銀 to advance money.
10 代 墊 to advance money for another.
賠 墊 to make good a loss.

(b) To sink into. To be overwhelmed. Erosion.

墊 沒 to sink; to be overwhelmed.
墊 陷 collapsed.
墊 隘 in straits, as if confined in a narrow gorge.
下 民 昏 墊 the people were bewildered and overwhelmed.

簟 4 A species of bamboo from which fine mats may be
6360 made.

簟 席 fine mats made from bamboo splints.
簟 茀 (or 第) a chequered bamboo screen used in ancient times for the back of a carriage.

T'IEN. (ㄊㄧㄢ)

天 顛 1 The material heavens, the firmament. The sky. Heaven. The weather. A
6361 day.
Distinguish 夭 No. 7277.
The second form is found in the rationalist Taoist books.

天 上 heaven.
天 上 石 麟 the stone unicorn in the skies—of a bright boy.
天 下 under heaven; the empire; the world.
天 下 一 家 all under heaven are one family
5 天 下 之 本 fundamental occupation of the country—refers to agriculture.
天 下 之 達 道 principles of universal obligation.
天 下 和 局 the peace of the world.
天 下 從 風 the masses all followed his commands as if swayed by the wind.

天 下 歸 仁 焉 all will ascribe virtue to him.
10 天 下 歸 心 throughout the kingdom the hearts of all turned to him.
天 下 無 雙 unequalled in all the world.
天 下 爲 公 a public spirit ruled all under the sky.
天 下 爲 官 to attain to the throne by merit, not by hereditary succession.
天 下 爲 家 to attain to the throne by inheritance.
15 天 下 響 應 the country relies on him; the empire turns to him.
天 井 the small courtyard in certain Chinese houses; a light-well.
天 亮 daylight; the day breaks.
天 冷 the weather is cold.
天 勢 the heavenly bodies; the powers of heaven.
20 天 南 地 北 far distant.
天 喜 small-pox. *See below*—78.
天 地 heaven and earth. *See below*—A. 28.
天 地 之 藏 the hidden treasures of the universe—minerals, etc.
天 地 比 壽 May your age be as that of heaven and earth !
25 別 有 天 地 another state of existence; fairyland.
天 堂 heaven.
天 壤 heaven and earth—things widely apart or vastly different.
天 外 the firmament.
天 大 的 as large as the heavens.
30 天 天 兒 or 每 天 every day.
天 孫 the *Weaving Damsel*, a star in Lyra.
天 宇 the firmament; the world; the Imperial capital.
天 容 the look of the weather.
天 容 日 光 sky and sunlight.
35 天 崩 地 塌 nature is overthrown —dreadful calamities; death of the emperor.
天 幕 a tent.
天 心 the zenith. *See below* A. 58.
天 戒 warnings in the heavens; portents, such as eclipses, etc.
天 變 portents in the heavens— refers to an eclipse; changes in the weather; meteorological phenomena.
40 天 文 astronomy.

天 文 圖 a star-atlas.

天 文 家 astronomers.

天 文 臺 astronomical observatory.

天 日 the sun; the light of day.

⁴⁵天 旱 dry weather; drought.

天 明 daylight; dawn.

天 昏 地 暗 gloom above and darkness beneath—hopeless outlook.

天 星 the heavenly bodies.

天 星 牢 落 the stars in the heavens were few and scattered.

⁵⁰天 時 the seasons; the weather.

天 時 不 如 地 利 advantages of time are not equal to those of situation.

天 晚 evening; drawing to a close.

天 朗 氣 清 fine, bright weather.

天 棚 an awning.

⁵⁵天 極 the poles.

天 樞 the axis of the heavens; the navel.

天 氣 vapours; air; weather; climate.

天 水 相 際 sky and water meeting.

天 河 or 雲 漢 or 銀 河 the Milky Way.

⁶⁰天 津 Name of a constellation; 天·津 (--ching or --chin) Tientsin

天 涯 the horizon.

天 涯 地 角 the ends of the earth.

天 涼 cool weather.

天 淵 相 隔 as far apart as the sky and sea.

⁶⁵天 漏 heavy rains.

天 火 lightning.

天 狼 星 Sirius.

天 球 the celestial globe.

天 發 亮 day is breaking.

⁷⁰天 空 the firmament; the void of ether; the weather.

天 空 地 闊 boundless capacity—used of broad-mindedness.

天 窗 a skylight; a dormer-window.

天 經 地 義 unalterable principles.

天 羅 地 網 surrounded by difficulties like nets above and snares below.

⁷⁵天 翻 地 覆 a condition of utter disorder, as if the universe was overthrown.

天 脚 the horizon.

天 色 the weather; the look of the weather.

天 花 small-pox. *See above*—21.

天 花 亂 墜 flowers falling from the skies—extravagant description.

⁸⁰天 花 板 a ceiling.

天 蠍 宮 Scorpio.

天 表 the firmament.

天 覆 地 載 all under heaven and upon earth; the heavens cover and the earth sustains.

天 象 celestial phenomena; the heavenly bodies.

⁸⁵天 邊 the horizon.

天 酒 heavenly wine—the dew.

天 長 地 久 lasting; enduring as long as the universe.

天 陰 a dull day.

天 露 dew; moisture.

⁹⁰天 青 plum colour; a purplish black.

天 體 the heavenly bodies.

天 高 地 厚 the immensity of the universe.

天 高 星 遠 the skies are high and the stars are distant—no one to appeal to.

天 高 皇 帝 遠 heaven is high and the emperor is far away—it is difficult to get justice.

⁹⁵天 黑 了 after dark.

一 天 a day; one day.

今·天 today.

前·天 the day before yesterday.

後·天 the day after tomorrow.

¹⁰⁰夏·天, 冬·天 summer, winter.

明·天 tomorrow.

昨·天 yesterday.

見 天 daily.

間 一 天 every other day.

¹⁰⁵隔 一 天 every other day.

(a) Nature,—often used in combination with earth 地. Providence. The Supreme Ruler. God. Celestial. Divine. See below—A. 110.

天 主 a term for God used by Roman Catholics and others. *See* 主 No. 1336-111.

天 主 教 Roman Catholicism.

天 之 所 助 雖 小 必 大 those whom Heaven aids, though small, become great.

天 之 所 違 雖 成 必 敗 those whom Heaven disregards, though successful, must suffer defeat.

⁵天 之 方 蹶 無 然 泄 泄 when Heaven intends to destroy, do not be so dilatory.

天 之 曆 數 the divine order of the succession—to the throne.

天 之 至 私 用 之 至 公 the extreme partiality of Heaven, in practice, is extreme justice.

天 之 至 高 聽 之 至 卑 Heaven is most high, yet listens to the lowliest.

天 人 one who has attained to *Tao*; an angel. God and man; one whose talents are above the average; a beautiful woman.

¹⁰天 仙 a Mohammedan term for angels.

天 何 言 哉 does Heaven speak?

天 使 angels.

天 公 God; the Lord.

天 功 heaven-sent success.

¹⁵天 即 理 也 Heaven is the principle of right.

天 厭 棄 之 rejected by Heaven.

天 敍 天 秩 relationships and rank as appointed by Heaven; social order.

天 口 a skilful debater; to speak on behalf of Heaven.

天 吏 也 he is the minister of Heaven.

²⁰天 后 or 天 后 聖 母 the Queen of Heaven; the Goddess of Seamen.

天 命 the decree of Heaven; fate.

天 命 之 謂 性 what Heaven has conferred is called The Nature.

天 命 靡 常 the decrees of Heaven are not unchanging.

天 和 divine harmony, as in nature.

²⁵天 啓 revelation.

天 喪 予 Heaven is destroying me.

天 國 the Kingdom of Heaven.

天 地 Heaven and Earth, as nature, etc. *See above*—22, *below*—C. 1.

天 地 不 通 there is no intercommunion between heaven and earth—in the winter.

³⁰天 地 人 the *Three Powers*—Heaven, Earth, and Man.

天 地 位 焉 Heaven and Earth will get their proper place—a happy harmony will prevail throughout the universe.

天 地 儲 精 the collected essence of heaven and earth.

天 地 絪 縕 the generative influences of heaven and earth by which all things are produced.

天 地 自 位 heaven and earth will get their proper positions.

[35]天 地 萬 物 父 母 heaven and earth are the parent of all things.

天 地 陰 陽 之 神 也 the divine essence of the dual principle (when embodied) is heaven and earth.

無 天 無 地 fearing neither God nor man.

與 天 地 參 矣 (he who is possessed of complete sincerity) may form one of three with heaven and earth.

贊 天 地 之 化 育 able to assist the nourishing and transforming powers of heaven and earth.

[40]天 壇 the Altar of Heaven at Peking.

天 大 過 神 Heaven is greater than the gods.

天 女 a female *Dêva.*

天 娘·娘 the Goddess of Small-pox.

天 子 the Son of Heaven—the Emperor.

[45]君 天 下 曰 天 子 he who rules over the whole land is called Son of Heaven or Emperor.

天 字 第 一 號 the very best; A.1.

天 官 former title of the President of the Board of Civil Office; a god—the Heavenly Ruler.

天 尊 or 天 宮 a god.

天 工 人 其 代 之 the work is Heaven's, it is man's to act for it.

[50]天 帝 God, the Supreme.

天 師 or 張 天 師 the head of the Taoist sect.

天 干 the *Ten Heavenly Stems,* used with the *Twelve Earthly Branches* to form a cycle of sixty. *See appendix. III, p. 1176*

天 平 scales—such as are used for weighing silver.

天 年 age; one's allotted span.

[55]天 幸 lucky; fortunately.

天 弓 or 帝 弓 the bow of God-the rainbow.

天 德 divine virtue.

天 心 難 測 the ways of Providence are inscrutable.

天 怒 the wrath of God, or of the

Emperor.

[60]天 意 fate; the decree of Heaven.

天 意 人 緣 Providence and natural affinity.

天 威 不 違 顏 咫 尺 Heaven's majesty is not far from me, not even a cubit's length.

天 數 fate.

天 曉·得 Heaven knows—said when one is suffering without any hope of redress.

[65]天 書 Taoist books; unrecognized characters.

天 曹 or 陰 曹 the powers of the lower world.

天 朝 the Celestial Dynasty—a term for China.

天 機 fate; destiny; the decree of Heaven; the hidden plans of Providence.

天 殃 calamities from Heaven.

[70]天 爵 nature's nobility; dignity conferred by Heaven.

天 父 Heavenly Father.

天 王 星 the planet Uranus.

天 理 moral rectitude; moral principles; divine justice.

天 生 natural; produced by Heaven.

[75]天 生 天 養 produced and nourished by Heaven.

天 生 蒸 民 Heaven produced all people.

天 眞 the divine element within one. *See below*—B. 31.

天 眼 通 clairvoyance.

天 知 powers of intuition.

[80]天 神 a Roman Catholic term for angels.

天 神 也 Heaven is divine.

天 神 天 明 Heaven is intelligent.

天 神 貴 者 太 一 the most exalted of the gods in heaven is the Primary Unity.

天 秩 or 天 序 the social relationships.

[85]天 精 天 粹 Heaven is subtle, Heaven is refined. 天 線 aerial.

天 網 恢 恢 疏 而 不 漏 the net of Heaven stretches everywhere, its meshes are wide, but nothing escapes them.

天 緣 湊 合 a lucky chance.

天 縱 之 Heaven has let him loose—has given him great powers.

天 老·爺 The Ruler of the Heavens—commonly used in the sense of Providence.

---

[90]天 者 人 之 始 也 Heaven is man's origin.

天 開 如 雷 like thunder in the ears of God.

天 職 calling; duty; Heaven-appointed office.

天 聾 地 啞 the unconscious powers of nature; also used to describe an utterly stupid person.

天 荒 地 老 describes the decadence of nature.

[95]天 行 自 若 the operations of nature go on as before.

天 見 久 遠 Heaven sees what is far distant.

天 討 有 罪 Heaven punishes the guilty.

天 誅 a divine judgement.

天 貺 節 a festival on the 6th of the 6th lunar month, when clothing is aired and dried meats are eaten.

[100]天 賦 人 權 natural prerogatives; innate rights of man.

天 軍 a heavenly host; heavenly spirits.

天 造 地 設 created by Heaven and put in their place by Earth—the hills and mountains.

天 道 Providence; the ways of Heaven.

天 道 福 善 禍 淫 the way of Heaven is to reward the good and punish the wicked.

[105]天 錫 純 嘏 May Heaven grant you perfect blessing!

天 開 於 子 Heaven was opened at the period of *Tzŭ.*

天 開 眼 Heaven has observed it.

天 降 下 民 Heaven produced the masses of mankind.

天 顏 the Emperor's countenance.

[110]天，顛 也，至 高 在 上，從 一 大 也 *T'ien* is the apex, the Most High over all; it is constructed from one and great.

上 不 怨 天 he does not murmur against Heaven above.

上 天 之 載 無 聲 無 臭 the doings of the Supreme Heavens have neither sound nor smell.

不 怨 天 不 尤 人 neither murmur at Heaven nor hate men.

事 由 天 定 不 由 人 算 events depend upon the appointment of Heaven, not upon the planning of men.

[115] 仰 不 愧 於 天 looking up, he has no occasion for shame before Heaven.

故 曰 配 天 therefore he is called "the equal of Heaven."

瞞 不 過 天 you cannot deceive God.

獲 罪 於 天 無 所 禱 也 he who offends against Heaven has none to whom he can pray.

(b) Natural, as opposed to artificial. Divinely endowed.

天 倫 the natural relationships of man.

天。分 (*fen*[4]) 高 high natural abilities; noble endowments.

天 塹 the natural moat, i.e., the River Yangtze between north and south. *See below*—44, 45.

長 江 天 塹 古 來 限 隔 南 北 the River Yangtze is the natural boundary which from of old has been the dividing line between north and south.

[5] 天 壽 the natural term of existence.

天 姿 natural beauty—unadorned.

天 性 natural disposition.

天 性 誠·實 honest by nature.

天 才 natural genius.

[10] 天 擇 natural selection.

天 演 之 變 更 evolutionary changes.

天 演 論 theory of evolution.

天 演 進 化 natural evolution.

天 然 naturally; inherent; essential.

[15] 天 然 之 理 the course of nature; an evident principle.

天 然 力 natural forces.

天 然 原 因 natural causes.

天 然 地 理 physical geography.

天 然 崇 拜 natural-worship.

[20] 天 然 變 化 natural evolution.

天 然 果 實 natural productions.

天 然 消 滅 natural elimination.

天 然 淘 汰 natural selection.

天 然 煤 氣 natural gas.

[25] 天 然 產 物 natural productions.

天 然 界 nature; the natural world as distinct from the spiritual.

天 然 磁 石 natural magnet.

天 然 結 果 the natural outcome.

天 然 色 照 相 術 photography

in natural colours; autochrome process of photography.

[30] 天 理 良 心 fairness; justice.

天 生 羽 翼 natural wings—brothers,-said to one who sought to get wings and become an immortal by magic and drugs.

天 癸 menstruation.

天 眞 爛 漫 childish; simple and unaffected, as a child.

天 眞·的 快·樂 natural happiness, as of a child. (--*lê*)

[35] 天 老 兒 or 陰 天 樂 兒 an albino—one who is glad of dull days because of the weakness of his eyes. (-*lêr*[4])

天 良 natural goodness; conscience.

天 資 natural endowments or disposition.

天 賦 才 能 natural ability.

天 質 natural ability.

[40] 天 足 natural, i.e., unbound, feet.

天 足 會 Anti-Foot-binding Society.

天 道 難 違 nature must be obeyed.

天 閹 naturally impotent.

天 限 南 北 the natural or divinely-appointed boundary between north and south, i.e., the River Yangtze.

[45] 天 險 a natural barrier for defence, as high mountains, great rivers, etc.

(c) A husband.

天 地 man and wife.

夫 者 妻 之 天 也 the husband is the heaven of the wife.

早 失 所 天 early lost her husband.

(d) Describes that which is indispensable.

民 以 食 爲 天 the people regard food as their one necessity.

王 者 以 民 爲 天 rulers regard the people as indispensable.

(e) Used in names, anatomical terms, etc.

天 中 the top of the forehead.

天 仙 菓 *Ficus japonica*.

天 元 ancient term for a science similar to algebra.

天 南 星 *Arisaema japonica*.

[5] 天 君 the heart.

天 君 泰 然 the heart at rest without anxiety.

天 山 the Celestial Mountains, a range between Russia and Chinese Turkestan.

天 庭 the forehead.

天 方 Arabia.

[10] 天 泡 草 *Solanum nigrum*, etc.; also *Physalis alkekengi*.

天 牛 a class of destructive beetles—*Apriona rugicollis*, etc.

天 狗 猴 the proboscis monkey.

天 祿 a fabulous creature, something like a deer, with a single horn.

天 竹 or 南 天 竹 the Heavenly bamboo—*Nandina domestica*.

[15] 天 竺 國 ancient name for India.

天 竺 牡 丹 the dahlia.

天 羅 or 天 絲 瓜 the loofah gourd—*Luffa cylindrica*.

天 花 粉 bryonia.

天 茄·子 *Solanum nigrum*.

[20] 天 葱 the narcissus.

天 門 冬 asparagus.

天 靈 蓋 the forehead.

天 香 百·合 *Lilium auratum*.

天 鵝 the crane; the wild swan.

[25] 天 鵝 絨 velvet.

天 麻 裏 *Hydrangea hortensia*, etc.

田 [2] Fields; land; landed property. Radical 102.
6362

田 主 landlord of agricultural land.

田 假[4] holiday for schools granted during the busy season for farmers.

田 功 the work of the farmer.

田 單 a paper, stating particulars of a plot of land, issued by the District Magistrate.

[5] 田 園 fields and gardens—cultivated land.

田 地 arable land; position; condition; state of things.

這·步·田·地 these circumstances, etc.

田 坎 a raised path through the fields.

田 夫 agricultural labourer.

[10] 田 字 面 a square face.

田 客 a tenant who cultivates the land.

↑田 徑 賽 track and field sports.

田·家 farmers.
田 岸 the banks of a rice-field.
田 庄 a farm-house.
[15]田 底 secondary crops, the produce of which is not included in the rental.
田 溝 agricultural drains.
田 父 an aged farmer.
田 產 agricultural products.
田 產 家 業 lands and estates.
[20]田 產 房 屋 lands; property and houses; possessions.
田 田 然 arranged in an orderly manner.
田 畝 or 土 田 or 田 疇 cultivated lands; property.
田 畦 small plots of ground.
田 畯 an officer of agriculture.
[25]田 盪 a kind of rake.
田 祖 神 農 *Shên Nung*—the God of Agriculture.
田 禾 growing rice.
田 租 rent for fields.
田 舍 a farm-house.
[30]田 螺 fresh-water snails.
田 角 the corners of the fields.
田 賦 land-taxes.
田 野 fields; cultivated lands.
田 隴 a bank of earth; a path in the fields.
[35]田 雞 the edible frog.
田 面 the regular crops, such as rice or wheat, of which a certain percentage is paid as rental.
田 鼠 the mole.
田 賽 field-sports.
心 田 the heart, as the inner man.
[40]書 田 fields of literature.
桑 田 a mulberry orchard.
歸 田 to retire from public life.
水 田 plots of land that can be flooded for growing rice.
石 田 stony lands; barren fields.
[45]硯 田 the fields of the inkslab—literature.
福 田 fields of happiness.
籍 田 field ploughed by the emperor in person during the early spring.
荒 田 neglected fields.

(a) **To hunt.**

田 犬 a hunting dog.
田 獵 to hunt.
公 田 the duke was hunting.

(b) Read *tien*[4]. **To cultivate.**

無 田 甫 田 (*t'ien*[2]) "do not try to cultivate fields too large."

畋 [2] To cultivate land. To hunt.
6363

畋 獵 to hunt.
畋 食 to live by agriculture.

鈿 [2] Silver or gold filagree. Hairpin. Also read *tien*[4].
6364 Inlaid work.

鈿 合 case for head-ornaments.
鈿 尺 an inlaid foot-rule.
鈿 帶 ornamented girdle.
鈿 螺 椅·子 a chair inlaid with mother-of-pearl.
[5]鈿 車 carriage ornamented with fine metal-work.
螺 鈿 mother-of-pearl.

恬 [2] Quiet; peaceful.
6365

恬 裕 dignified and liberal.
恬 靜 or 恬 淡 tranquil; quiet; undisturbed.
↑恬 不 知 恥 calm and devoid of any sense of shame.

甜 [2] Sweet; agreeable; pleasant.
6366

甜 蜜·的 承 受 sweetly receive it.
甜 水 sweet—as opposed to brackish-water. ⌠ musk melon.
甜 瓜 sweet melons. 甜·瓜 the
甜 甘 very sweet.
[5]甜 睡 a sweet sleep.
甜 笑 a sweet smile.
甜 美 sweet; pleasant.
甜 絲 絲·的 or 甜 蜜 蜜·的 very sweet.
甜 脆 sweet and crisp.
[10]甜 苦 sweet and bitter—the ups and downs of life.
甜 言 蜜 語 sweet honeyed words —flattery.
甜 話 specious statements.
甜 醇 pleasant to the taste—as wine.
甜·頭 a bait; a lure; sweetness.
[15]黑 甜 鄉 the land of sweet darkness—sleep.

舚 [4] To put out the tongue.
6367

舚 唇 to lick the lips.

忝 [3]. Ashamed. To disgrace. Used in depreciatory phrases
6368 of oneself.
Inter. 覥 No. 6380.

忝 不 知 羞 brazen-faced; shameless.
忝 厥 祖 to disgrace one's ancestors.
忝 在 相 好 I disgrace you by my intimacy—conventional phrase.
忝 帝 位 to disgrace the throne.
[5]忝 眷 I shame you by seeking relationship—conventional phrase in marriage papers.
忝 累 I disgrace the office.
忝 蒙 敎 誨 I have unworthily received your instructions.
忝 辱 家 門 to disgrace one's family.

挑 [4] To manipulate. A pricker for a lamp-wick.
6369

挑 燈 to raise the wick of a Chinese lamp.
燈 挑 a pricker for a lamp-wick.
挑 筆 to bring the writing-brush to a fine point when preparing to write.
挑 鎖 to pick a lock.

添 [1] To add to; to increase; to make good.
6370

添 丁 or 添 人 口 to have an increase in one's family; to increase the population.
添·上 to add to.
添·了 一·個 to add one extra.
↑添·點 兒 add a little.
[5]添 價 to raise the price.
添 兵 to add reinforcements.
添 募 to enrol.
添 多 to increase the number of.
添 少 許 add a little more.[(-ch'ai[1]-)]
[10]添 差 使 to add to official duties.
添 房 to take a concubine.
添 改 to make additions and alterations.
添 本 to increase the capital.
添 枝 葉 to add a few branches and leaves—to embellish a story.
[15]添 注 to add a note on the margin.
添 油 器 a lubricator.

添 派 to appoint or send additional....

添 病 to grow worse.

添 福 添 壽 May you increase in happiness and longevity!

20 添 箱 ·的 禮 wedding presents given to a bride.

添 築 屋 an annex.

添 續 to add to.

添 補 to make up a deficiency; to supplement.

添 製 to construct—roads, etc.

25 添 襯 to add something to; to supplement.

添 設 to establish additional....

添 註 to fill in—a blank form.

添 財 to become wealthy.

添 購 to buy additional....

30 添 造 to construct—as a road.

添 錢 to add money; to give more.

添 附 additional; supplementary.

添 ·雙 筷 ·子 add another pair of chopsticks—another guest has come.

添 ·頭 something to be added; something to fill up.

舔 餂 3.4.

To lick; to taste.

6371

餂 ·一 ·餂 taste it.

餂 乾 ·淨 to lick clean.

餂 ·破 ·了 窗 紙 to lick a hole in a paper window.

(a) To catch; to inveigle.

是 以 言 餂 之 也 by *guile of speech* seeking to gain some end.

菾 2

Beet.

6372

塡 窴 2.

To fill up; to fill in. To make good.

6373

塡 債 to pay a debt.

塡 具 to fill in—as a blank form.

塡 冊 to fill in a list; to enrol one's name in a list.

塡 命 to give one's life for another.

---

5 塡 咽 blocked,—with the crowds.

塡 塞 to stuff up; or fill in—as a pillow with hair, etc.

塡 大 計 to be recorded as superannuated, etc., of officials under the dynasties.

塡 寫 to fill in—as particulars in a document, etc.

塡 履 歷 to note in the register the age, residence, etc., of officials.

10 塡 平 to level up—as inequalities in the ground, holes, etc.

塡 房 to take a new wife after the death of the first one. *

塡 明 to fill in—as particulars.

塡 格 to fill up a form—as the details and report of the coroner at an inquest.

塡 湊 crowding together.

15 塡 滿 to fill up level.

塡 漆 to varnish.

塡 發 to fill in and issue—as a document.

塡 窟 ·窿 to fill up a hole.

塡 築 to fill up in building.

20 塡 簿 to fill in a register.

塡 給 to fill in and issue—as a document.

塡 膺 it fills my breast.

塡 街 塞 巷 crowded all the streets and lanes.

塡 補 to make up a deficiency.

25 塡 註 to fill in—as particulars.

塡 詞 to make verses on a given rhyme.

塡 載 to fill in—as particulars.

塡 造 to make up a deficiency.

塡 還 to pay back.

30 塡 鴨 to stuff and fatten ducks.

塡 齊 to level up—as inequalities in the ground, etc.

* 塡 ·房 new wife.

(a) A crashing sound. Rumbling, as of drums.

塡 然 crashing or rumbling.

(b) Read *ch'ên*2. For a long time.

孔 塡 不 寧 very long have we been disquieted.

(c) Read *tien*1. u.f. 瘨 No. 6335.

哀 我 塡 寡 Alas for the distressed and solitary!

(d) Read *chên*4. u.f. 鎭 No. 299. To settle.

塡 國 家 settle the kingdom.

(e) Read *tien*4. Sound of thunder. To move quietly.

其 行 塡 塡 they moved quietly.

雷 塡 塡 兮 the thunder rolled.

闐 2 To fill up; to stuff. Inter. preceding.

6374

賓 客 闐 門 visitors thronged the door.

(a) Rumbling sounds.

轟 轟 闐 闐 rumbling and rolling.

(b) Read *tien*4. Name of a place.

于 闐 or 和 闐 Khoten.

殄 3. To terminate; to root out; to exterminate; to cease.

6375

殄 戮 to destroy; to slaughter.

殄 殲 to extirpate; to cut off.

殄 滅 to cut off; to extirpate.

殄 瘁 to be entirely ruined—of the country.

5 殄 絕 to bring to an end.

殄 草 to injure the grasses.

不 殄 厥 慍 he could not prevent the rage (of his foes).

不 殄 心 憂 it is an unceasing sorrow in my heart.

戎 疾 不 殄 he could not prevent (some) great calamities.

10 餘 風 未 殄 the other evil customs have not yet been got rid of.

(a) Good. Inter. 腆 No. 6379.

遷 篠 不 殄 this vicious bloated mass.

殄 3.4. In confusion. Out of harmony.

6376

殄 戾 counteracting each other.

(a) Read *li*4. Foul air. See 3889.

殄 氣 foul air; miasma.

怏 3 Bashful; shy.

6377

怏 墨 countenance darkened with shame.

怏 愧 to be bashful; ashamed.

涊³ Turbid, muddy.
6378

涊 染 defiled and stained.

醍³ To make strong—as liquors.
6379

自 洗 (*hsien*³) 醍 致 酒 then you may set forth your spirits, clear and strong.

(a) Good; virtuous.

不 醍 unworthy.
辭 無 不 醍 there was nothing in his speech that was not proper.

(b) Prosperous.

殷 小 醍 little as the prosperity of *Yin* is....

(c) To go to excess.

不 醍 于 酒 indulge in no excess of liquors.

靦
覥³ To see face to face. To blush. Ashamed.
6380

靦 色 bashful countenance.
有 靦 面 目 when you are face to face.
面 覥 to blush.

TING. (ㄉㄥ)

丁¹ An individual; a person; a male adult. To incur.
6381

丁 內 憂,丁 外 憂 to mourn for a mother and father respectively. (Cf. C *below*)
丁 口 people; population.
丁 壯 in the full vigor of young manhood.
丁 子 a tadpole.
⁵丁 年 in the prime of early manhood.
丁 役 attendants.
丁 憂 or 丁 艱 to be in mourning for parents three years. (Cf. C)
丁 男 a full-grown man.
丁 稅 a poll-tax.

¹⁰丁 財 兩 壯 prosperous both in family and in wealth.
丁 賦 a poll-tax which was in force from the *Han* dynasty until the reign of *K'ang Hsi* in the Manchu dynasty.
丁 銀 a poll-tax.
人 丁 冊 a census.
六 丁 a Taoist god who has power over demons. *See below*—A. 3.
¹⁵兵 丁 soldiers.
地 丁 the incorporated land and poll-taxes.
家 丁 domestic servants.
小 丁 a minor.
年 不 上 丁 not yet sixteen years of age.
²⁰庖 丁 a cook.
成 丁 to become an adult—generally reckoned at sixteen years of age.
抽 丁 to levy soldiers.
神 丁 attendants upon the gods.
門 丁 a gate-keeper.
²⁵零 丁 lonely; disconsolate.

(a) The fourth of the *Ten Stems* 天 干.

丁 夜 in the fourth watch of the night.
丁 祭 Spring and Autumn Sacrifices to Confucius, being offered on the first 丁 day of the 2nd and 8th lunar months respectively.
六 丁 the six combinations of 丁 with characters of the *Twelve Branches* 地 支.

(b) From the shape of the character, used for T-shaped.

丁 倒 to turn upside down.
丁 字 尺 a T-square.
丁 字 斧 a pickaxe.
丁 字 街 a street which ends in another at right-angles to it.
⁵丁·香 cloves.
丁·香 油 oil of cloves.
丁·香 花 lilac.

(c) To fall upon. To incur.

寧 丁 我 躬 would that it fell (only) upon me!

(d) u.f. 玎 No. 6384. Imitation of tinkling sounds.

丁 東 or 丁 當 tinkling of things striking together in the wind.

(e) u.f. 叮 No. 6383. To enjoin.

丁 寧 to give repeated injunctions.

(f) Read *chêng*¹. Sound of blows on trees, etc.

伐 木 丁 丁 on the trees go the blows, *chêng, chêng*.
椓 (*chu*¹) 之 丁 丁 clang, clang, go the blows on the pegs.

(g) Used in transliterating.

丁 幾 tincture.

仃¹ Alone.
6382

冷 孤 仃·的 alone and solitary.

叮¹ To reiterate; to give charge to; to order. To sting; as a mosquito.
6383

叮 嚀 or 囑 咐 or 叮 囑 to repeat an order; to reiterate; to enjoin on; repetition.
叮 嚀 告 戒 repeatedly bade him take heed.

玎¹ A jingling or tinkling noise.
6384

玎 玲 jingling; tinkling.
玎 璫 a small hand-gong used by hawkers.

疔¹ A boil; a venereal ulcer; a bubo; syphilitic sores.
6385

疔 墜 syphilitic sores.
疔 瘡 boils; ulcers; buboes.
口 疔 apthæ.
指 疔 a whitlow.

訂⁴ To arrange; to settle; to fix. To edit; to collate.
6386

訂 問 to come to an agreement beforehand.
訂 報 to subscribe for a newspaper, etc.
訂 定 to conclude—as a treaty, etc.
訂 定 日 期 to fix a certain date.
⁵訂 密 約 to appoint a secret meeting.

訂 明 to settle clearly.
訂 時 to let one know the time for.
訂 期 to set a time; to fix a date.
訂 正 or 較 正 or 訂 書 to revise; to edit; to prepare for publication.
¹⁰訂 盟 to make a treaty.
訂 立 to fix on; to draw up.
訂 約 to conclude a treaty.
訂 訊 to fix a date for trial.
修 訂 to make amendments to.

酊¹
6387　Intoxicated.

酩 酊 helplessly drunk.

釘¹
6388　A nail; a spike.

釘 倒 a name for the larvæ of the mosquito.
釘·子 a nail.
釘 帽 head of a nail.
釘 痕 the print of a nail.
⁵釘 耙 a toothed harrow.
釘 靴 nailed boots for wet weather.
釘 頭 a nail.
三 角 釘 caltrops.
大 方 釘 a spike.
¹⁰好 鐵 不 打 釘 good iron is not made into nails.
棗 核 釘 a nail pointed at both ends.
拔 釘 to extract a nail.
木 釘 a wooden peg.
尖 頭 短 釘 tacks.
¹⁵無 頭 小 釘 brads.
眼 中 釘 a nail in the eye—something or some person who is objectionable.
螺 旋 釘 bolts.
螺·絲 釘 a screw-nail; bolts.
鍋 釘 rivets.

(a) Read ting⁴. To nail. To bind, as books.

釘 不 住 the nail will not hold; impossible to nail it.
釘·住 to nail securely.
釘·在 架 上 nailed to a frame or a cross.
釘 封 a despatch nailed up in boards; an important despatch.
⁵釘 心 to take a thing to heart.
釘 書 or 裝 釘 to bind a book.

釘 死 or 釘 牢 to nail securely.
釘 (ting⁴) 釘 (ting¹)·子 to drive nails.
釘 鈕·子 to sew on buttons.
¹⁰釘 馬 掌 to nail on horse-shoes.
安 釘 to nail down a coffin.

靪¹
6389　To cobble; to patch.

靪 底 to mend a sole.
補 靪 a patch.

頂
6390　³ The top. A button formerly worn on the hat to indicate rank. To wear on the head. To push the head against. Topmost, very, extremely.

頂 上 the very best; to carry on the head.
頂 上 圓 光 a nimbus—as on divine personages.
頂 中 (chung⁴) 意 it exactly hits my fancy.
頂 充 to assume the name of.
⁵頂 名 to take the name of another.
頂 嘴 to contradict.
頂 天 立 地 his head reaches to heaven and his feet are on earth—talented; a hero.
頂 好 or 頂 上 the very best.
頂·子 or 頂 兒 a knob or button formerly worn on the hat to indicate official rank.
¹⁰頂 尖 the acme; the apex; the very best.
頂 德 receiving your kindness on my head—conventional expression of gratitude.
頂 心 the crown of the head.
頂 戴 to carry on the head.
頂 手 to take the place of.
¹⁵頂 批 critical notes at the top of a page.
頂 拜 to bow in deep obeisance.
頂 換 or 頂 包 to substitute inferior articles when exchanged—a swindling trick.
頂 撞 to run against; to oppose; to offend.
頂 替 a substitute.
²⁰頂 柱 a prop.
頂 棚 the ceiling.
頂 水 or 頂 流 against the tide.
頂 當⁴ (tang⁴) or 定 當⁴ to substitute one pledge for another at a pawnshop.

頂 盔 貫 甲 clothed in armour.
²⁵頂 盤 to take over the goodwill, etc., of a business.
接 頂 to take over a business.
頂 磚 to carry a brick on the head—a punishment for schoolboys.
頂 禮 to bow; bowing.
頂 笠 to wear a bamboo hat.
³⁰頂 缸 to carry a vessel on the head—to receive the blame due to another.
頂 脫 to become bald.
頂 芽 a terminal bud. (bot.).
頂 角 the angle opposite the base of a triangle.
頂 賬 set-off against an account.
³⁵頂 趾 the crown of the head and the heels.
頂·針 a thimble.
頂 銀 adulterated silver.
頂 頭 opposing; contrary; face to face.
頂 (頭) 風 or 逆 風 or 迎 風 a head wind.
⁴⁰頂 馬 outriders.
頂 香·的 a witch.
頂 高 the highest.
頂 點 the vertex. (geom.).
山 頂 summit of a mountain or hill.
⁴⁵屋 頂 roof of a house. 房頂 儿
自 頂 至 踵 from head to heels.
露 頂 bare-headed.

(a) N.A. for hats, sedan-chairs, etc.

一 頂 帽·子 a hat.
一 頂 轎·子 a sedan-chair.

飣
6391　⁴ To set out fruit, etc., in plates arranged only for show.

餖 飣 fruit, etc., merely arranged for show, not to be eaten.

鼎
6392　³ A tripod of bronze with two ears; a caldron; a sacrificial vessel regarded as a type of imperial power. The Empire. Radical 206.

鼎 力 great strength—able to lift a tripod.
鼎 力 玉 成 I humbly entreat your powerful influence—to accomplish the matter.
望 祈 鼎 力 I beg the assistance of your powerful influence.

鼎 士 a powerful person.
⁵鼎 實 food, especially that of the nobility.
鼎 峙 standing firmly, like a tripod.
鼎 彝 sacrificial vessels engraved with inscriptions to worthy men.
鼎 折 足 a tripod with a broken foot—a minister who ruins the State.
鼎 新 to renew.
¹⁰鼎 族 a great family.
鼎 業 rule; sway.
鼎 沸 bubbling like a caldron—used fig., of seething insurrection, etc.
鼎 湖 name of a place—the death of an emperor.
鼎 甲 the three highest graduates at the former palace examination for the *Hanlin* Academy.
¹⁵鼎 盛 prosperous and flourishing.
鼎 祚 the destiny of a State.
鼎 臣 a high minister of State.
鼎 言 words of grave importance.
鼎 足 之 勢 consisting of three parts.
²⁰鼎 足 而 三 divided into three parts.
鼎 輔 three chief ministers of State.
鼎 運 the destiny of a State.
鼎 遷 於 周 the Imperial power was tranferred to the House of *Chou*.
鼎 鐘 bells and vessels engraved with inscriptions to worthy men.
²⁵鼎 鑊 a caldron without feet.
鼎 革 後 after the change of dynasty.
革 鼎 to overthrow a dynasty.
鼎 食 food of the nobility.
鼎 鼎 flourishing; great.
³⁰鼎 鼐 the administration of a State.
定 鼎 to establish a dynasty.

定 ⁴ To fix; to settle; to arrange; to decide. Decided;
6393 certainly. A state of abstraction.

定·下 to determine; to settle for goods by payment of bargain-money.
定·不 住 cannot be decided definitely.

定·了 主·意 to make up the mind.
定·了 案 to decide a case at law.
⁵定 于 一 settle them by uniting them into one whole.
定 位 to assign positions to.
定 例 fixed rules or regulations.
定 做 to make to order.
定 做·的 made to order.
¹⁰定 備 車 a reserved car.
定 像 液 fixing bath. (*photo.*).
定 價 to fix the price; the fixed price.
定 全 局 to make the final settlement.
定 分 a certain position or duty.
¹⁵定 則 a formula; fixed rules or regulations.
定 制 fixed rules or regulations.
定 力 resolution; determination; power of abstraction and contemplation. (*Budd.*).
定 南 針 the compass; also used fig.
定 卜 to have no doubt that.
²⁰定 向 direction; course.
定 命 主 義 fatalism.
定 單 a contract; an agreement; order-form.
定 地 段 to divide a country into sections.
定 報 to subscribe for a newspaper.
²⁵定 奪 finally decided—as a lawsuit, etc.
定 妥 satisfactorily settled; to settle on a satisfactory basis.
定 婚 to betroth; affianced.
定 局 to settle finally.
定 居 to settle in a place.
³⁰定 座 to book seats.
定 式 a fixed pattern; a formula.
定 律 the statute law.
定 心 to settle the mind.
定 志 to make up one's mind.
³⁵定 性 分 析 (化 學) qualitative analysis.
定 性 程 序 the settling process.
定 情 to fasten the affections on.
定 意 to determine; to decide.
定 擬 to decide upon; to fix upon, as a penalty.
⁴⁰定 數 a definite amount; fate, etc.
定 數 論 determinism.
定 斷 finally settled on; to decide, as a lawsuit.
定 日 a fixed date; to fix a date.
定 旨 先 見 purpose and foreknowledge.

⁴⁵定 是 非 to decide between good and evil.
定 時 a fixed time; to fix a time.
定 更 to set the watch—at sundown.
定 期 a fixed period; to fix a time or date; periodic.
定 期 不 改 the fixed date will not be changed.
⁵⁰定 期 交 易 time-bargains.
定 期 儲 蓄 fixed savings deposits.
定 期 存 欵 fixed deposits.
定 期 票 (or 劵) season ticket.
定 期 考 試 periodic examinations.
⁵⁵定 期 試 驗 periodic examinations.
定 本 stereotyped.
定 根 axial roots.
定 歸 agreed upon; decided.
定 準 decided; certain; to settle; to settle definitely.
⁶⁰定 準 不 移 undoubtedly.
定 準 數 a determinate number.
定 然 certainly; surely; positively.
定 燒 pottery or chinaware made to order.
定 理 theorem.
⁶⁵定 率 standard; rate. (*-lü*⁴·⁵)
定 當 (*tang*⁴) to substitute one pledge for another at a pawnshop.
定 盟 to enter into a covenant; to arrange a sworn confederacy.
定 盤 星 the marks on the balance of a steelyard.
定 目 的⁴ to fix one's purpose.
⁷⁰定 省 to inquire after the health of one's parents. (*–hsing*³)
定 眼 to fix the eyes upon.
定 睛 to look at fixedly.
定 睛 望 天 gazing into heaven.
定 神 to compose oneself.
⁷⁵定 禮 to fix the marriage ceremonies; to settle the amount of the betrothal presents.
定 立 to fix upon and draw up—as rules.
定 章 fixed rules or regulations.
定 等 to classify.
定 罪 to condemn; to decide upon the punishment.
⁸⁰定 義 scientific definitions; to define; the true explanation.
定 而 后 能 靜 fix the mind and then you will attain to perfect repose.

定 聘 to betroth.

定 芽 normal bud. (*bot.*).

定 被 to quilt.

[85]定 製 made to order.

定 製 品 article made to order.

定 見 decided views; fixed opinions.

定。規 to decide; agreed upon; rules or regulations.

定 視 to gaze at; to look at fixedly.

[90]定 親 to betroth.

定 親 書 a marriage contract.

定 計 to decide upon a plan.

定 論 or 定 評 to come to a decision; to settle finally.

定 謀 to decide upon a plan.

[95]定 識 (*chih*) fixed marks.

定 議 to decide upon ultimately.

定 貨 to contract for goods; to buy goods to arrive.

定 貨 單 order-form.

定 貨 簿 order-book.

[100]定 買 to give a contract for the purchase of.

定 質 solids.

定 酪 cream.

定 量 quantity.

定 量 分 析 化 學 quantitative analysis.

[105]定 銀 or 定·錢 earnest money.

定 限 fixed limit.

定 關 節 fixed joints.

定 額 a fixed number.

定 點 restriction; limit.

[110]定 鼎 to found a dynasty.

一 定 certainly.

不 定 uncertain; unsettled.

保·不 定 cannot guarantee it.

入 定 to enter upon a fixed state of contemplation. (*Budd.*).

[115]商 定 to come to an understanding after discussion.

必 定 absolutely certain.

未 定 not yet settled.

決 定 certain; resolved to.

注 定 to be under the necessity of.

(a) The forehead.

麟 之 定 the forehead of the *lin*.

(b) One or two stars in Pegasus.

定 之 方 中 when the star *Ting* (Markab) was on the meridian.

碇[4]　　Large stone for an anchor.
6394

錠[4]　An ingot. A slab; a cake.
6395

一 錠 墨　a cake of Chinese ink.

一 錠 銀·子 a small ingot of silver, about Tls. 10.

元 寶 錠 gold and silver paper ingots burnt for the use of the dead.

錠 硃 cakes of vermilion.

[5]粉 錠 a cake of cosmetic.

糊 錠 to paste tinfoil-paper into ingots.

紫 金 錠 ointment used for sores.

金 錠 an ingot of gold.

(a) An anchor.

寄 錠 to drop an anchor.

TING.　　　(ㄊㄥ)

杕[1]　A post or stake.
　　　Also read *chêng*[4].
6396

楔 杕 door-posts.

(a) Name of a place in the ancient State of *Sung*.

會 於 虛 杕 they had a meeting in *Hsü ting*.

(b) Read *chêng*[1]. Sound of chopping. *See* 丁 No. 6381-F.

汀[1]　A bank. A spit of land.
　　　A beach.
6397

汀 曲 a bend in a stream.

汀 洲 a sand-bank; an islet in a stream.

汀 渚 an islet.

汀 濘 a mud-bank; slime.

[5]汀 瀅 a clear brook.

汀 線 上 昇 elevation of the coast-line.

汀 線 下 落 depression of the coast-line.

沙 汀 a sand-spit.

町[3]　A raised path between fields. A piece of waste
6398　land.

町 畦 a boundary; a bank between fields; bounds—used fig.

町 畽 vacant land by the side of a house; a paddock.

町 畽 鹿 場 our paddocks would be deer-fields.

(a) A Japanese measure of length =119 yards.

町 人 a townsman.

町 村 land division.

町 步 unit of square measure= 2.45 acres.

亭[2]　An arbour; a pavilion; a shed; a kiosk.
6399

亭·子 an arbour; a rest-house.

亭 戶 salt-workers.

亭 臺 pavilions and terraces.

亭 長 (*chang*[3]) 亭 父 or 亭 公 an ancient term for a headman, or village constable.

[5]亭 障 a shelter erected for those in charge of important places on a city wall.

八 角[3] 亭 an octagonal pavilion;

涼 亭 a summer-house; rest-houses by the roadside, usually about ten *li* apart.

碑 亭 a shelter erected over a stone tablet.

茶 亭 a roadside tea-house.

驛 亭 rest-houses for couriers.

(a) Erect; standing alone. A mountain in Shantung.

亭 亭 聳 立 standing alone, as a mountain peak.

(b) To reach.

亭 午 to reach midday—noon.

(c) To harmonize. Even. Level.

五 味 亭 the various flavours were blended.

平 亭 to adjust matters.

(d) Occurs u.f. 蜓 No. 6412. A dragon-fly.

停[2]　To stop; to desist; to delay.
6400

停·一·會 兒 take a rest; stop for a while.

停 付 to refuse advances; to suspend payment.

停·住 to stop; to cease.
停 体 to stop a salary.
⁵停 公 or 停 辦 公 事 to suspend public business—as on a holiday.
停 刋 to suspend publication.
停 利 stoppage of interest.
停 口 to cease speaking.
停 學 rustication.
¹⁰停 屍·首 to lay out a corpse—said of the interval before it is put into the coffin.
停 工 to cease from work.
停 戰 armistice; cessation of hostilities.
停 息 to stop; to cease.
停 手 to stop work.
¹⁵停 支 to suspend payments.
停 放 Cease fire!
停 會 to suspend a meeting; prorogation.
停 柩 a coffin containing a corpse awaiting interment.
停 止 to cease; to stop.
²⁰停 止 交 通 stoppage of communications.
停 止 兌 現 a moratorium.
停 止 公 權 suspension of civic rights.
停 止 投 票 disfranchisement.
停 止 法 律 施 行 to suspend a law.
²⁵停 止 議 事 suspend proceedings.
停 止 軍 事 行 動 to cease military operations.
停 止 過 付 命·令 a stop-order.
停 泊 to anchor.
停 泊 地 點 port of call.
³⁰停 泊 所 anchorage; a berth.
停 泊 日 期 lay-days.
停 滯 to obstruct; to delay; indigestion.
停 火 Cease fire!
停 牀 a death-bed.
³⁵停 版 to suspend publication.
停 班 to be suspended from school.
停 留 to cause to stop; to delay.
停 給 to stop—as salary, etc.
停 緩 to defer; to put off.
↑⁴⁰停 擺 to stop, as a clock.
停 職 to suspend a person from office.
停 薪 to stop payment of salary.
停 訊 to stop judicial proceedings or business.
停 車 to stop a vehicle; stoppage on a railway; to park a car.
⁴⁵停 輪 to slow down or stop, of a steamer.
↑停 車 場 parking lot.

停 陞 to delay promotion.
停 雲 to stay the clouds—to think of a friend.
停 靈·柩 to delay the burial of a coffin.
停 飲 indigestion.
⁵⁰停 頓 to stop for a while; stoppage of business.
按 停 表 a stop-watch.
暫 停 temporary stoppage; to suspend.
活 狀 暫 停 suspended animation.
盡 停 to come to a standstill.

(a) Suitable. Satisfactory. An integral part.

停 勻 even; to blend; well proportioned.
停 當 or 停 妥 well arranged; satisfactorily settled; accomplished; able.
　　收 拾 停 當 all well prepared —as baggage, etc.
三 停 forehead, nose, and chin—in physiognomy; head, trunk and lower limbs.
十 停 人 家 ten families.
十 停 去 九 停 take away nine-tenths.

婷²
6401

Graceful and ladylike.

娉 婷 elegant and gentle.

聽 听¹
6402

To hear; to listen to; to understand.

聽·不 到 unable to hear—through distance or lack of familiarity with the sound in question.
聽·不 明·白 I do not quite understand; I did not hear well.
聽·不 眞 unable to hear accurately.
聽·不 見 unable to hear.
⁵聽·不 足 cannot hear enough.
聽 事 an attendant; an office servant; a messenger.
聽 信 to be moved by the incitement of others; to wait for further orders.
聽 勸 言 to take heed to advice.
聽 喚 to attend on.
¹⁰聽 官 sense of hearing.

聽¹⁴差 attendants; messengers.(-ch'ai¹
聽·得 出 I can understand; to hear and distinguish.
聽·得 見 I can hear; I have heard.
聽 戲 to listen to a theatrical performance.
¹⁵聽 熒 to doubt; to be suspicious.
聽 界 range of hearing.
聽 界 外 beyond the range of hearing.
聽 衆 the audience.
聽 神 經 the auditory nerve.
²⁰聽 管 the acoustic duct.
聽 而 不 聞 to hear and pay no attention.
聽 聞 to hear about; to hear—as a rumour.
聽·聽 說·說 hearing and speaking.
聽 能 power of hearing.
²⁵聽·著 listened; listening.
聽·見 heard; to hear.
聽 覺 the sense of hearing.
聽 覺 器 organs of hearing.
聽 診 器 stethoscope.
³⁰聽 話 to obey.
　他 不 聽 話 disobedient; he gives no heed to what is said to him.
聽 說 to hear say; to be obedient.
聽 道·理 to listen to preaching.
聽 錯·了 I heard wrongly; I misunderstood.
³⁵聽 音 器 audiphone.
聽·頭 something worth hearing.
不 中 聽 unpleasant to hear.
可 聽 worth listening to.
打·聽 to make inquiries.

(a) Read t'ing¹. To comply with; to allow; to let. To acknowledge. To await. To hear, as a lawsuit.

聽 之 可 也 make no bother about it; that does not matter.
聽·他 來 let him come.
聽·他 良·心 leave it to his conscience.
聽 令 to obey orders.
⁵聽 任 to allow; to suffer.
聽 候 to await.
聽 候 批 示 to wait for the answer of the magistrate to a request that a case be tried.
聽 允 to allow; to permit; to fall in with.
聽 其 自 便 let him consult his own convenience.

10聽 其 自 然 let it take its own course.

聽 准 to grant.

聽 受 to heed; to receive instruction.

聽 命 to accept a command; to accept one's fate.

惟 命 是 聽 I cannot but obey.

15聽 天 由 命 to submit to Providence.

聽 察 to try and find out by listening.

聽 審 to abide by the result of the trial; to leave the case in the hands of the judge; to hear a case.

聽 待 to await.

聽 從 to obey; to heed; to fall in with.

20聽 憑 as one pleases; let it be at the option of.

聽 政 to administer the affairs of State.

聽 斷 to accept a legal decision.

聽 罪 to own one's offence; to leave one's punishment to the judge.

聽 訟 to hear a lawsuit.

25聽 重 (ch'ung²) deaf—having to be spoken to several times.
= 重 聽

廳¹ A hall; a court; a lodge; a room. A Sub-Prefecture.
6403

廳 事 the court-room of a magistrate.

廳 堂 or 大 廳 the great hall.

廳 房 or 客 廳 a reception room.

廳 票 subpœna; a warrant.

5國 稅 廳 National Taxation Bureau.

官 廳 a public office or court.

審 判 廳 a court of justice.

市 廳 municipal offices.

檢 察 廳 Court of Procuration.

10理 船 廳 Harbour-Master.

神 廳 hall for ancestral tablets.

縣 廳 a county office.

門 廳 porter's lodge.

飯 廳 a dining hall.

↑廳 長 provincial commissioner of...

廷² The court of the palace; the Court. Inter. next.
6404

廷 寄 a confidential letter sent direct from the palace to the highest provincial officials.

廷 尉 former title for the Governor of a gaol.

廷 杖 to flog a statesman in the audience chamber.

廷 毀 to reprimand a statesman in the presence of the Court.

5廷 爭 to wrangle in the Imperial presence.

廷 臣 Court officials; courtiers.

廷 試 final examinations in the palace, under the old system.

廷 議 discussions at Court.

廷 魁 the first on the list at the palace examination for the third degree, under the old system.

10天 廷 the top of the forehead. (physiog.).

朝 廷 the Court; the sovereign.

庭² A hall. The audience-chamber; the Court; the palace. A courtyard; a house; a court of justice. A family. Inter. preceding.
6405

庭 丁 court-police.

庭 澤 icicles hanging from the eaves.

庭 參 ancient ceremonial at an interview with a superior.

庭 實 presents given in the audience-chamber.

5庭 幃 women's apartments.

庭 房 or 大 庭 the principal hall in a Chinese building.

庭 決 summary execution.

庭 燎 beacon-fires used as warning in ancient times.

庭 舍 or 庭 堂 a house.

10庭 訓 paternal instruction.

庭 趨 ancient ceremonial at an interview with a superior.

庭 辱 to disgrace a person in public.

庭 長 superintendent.

庭 闈 outer and inner apartments —one's father and mother.

15庭 除 the outer porch before the hall of a house.

出 庭 to appear before the court.

刑 事 庭 Criminal Court.

天 帝 之 庭 the throne of God.

天 庭 the forehead.

20家 庭 the home; the family.

民 事 庭 Civil Court.

禁 庭 or 丹 庭 the private apartments of the Emperor.

開 庭 to open the court.

(a) Read t'ing⁴.

大 相 逕 庭 very unlike; very improbable.

(b) Read t'ing¹. To grow up straight.

既 庭 且 碩 which grow up straight and large—speaking of grain.

挺³ To stick out; to straighten. To exert. To thrust forward. To move. To pull up. To hold rigidly to. Eminent; prominent. Rigid. Rather; pretty.
6406

挺·不 住 unable to stand a flogging.

挺 佔 refusing to leave a place where one has no right to be.

挺 出 to project; to bulge.

挺 刃 to stretch out a sword.

5挺 刑 to bear punishment without flinching or confessing.

挺 嚴 tight; strict.

挺 坐 to sit up straight.

挺 拔 stiff and upright.

挺 撞 to oppose; to try conclusions with; to gainsay.

10挺 撻 to bear punishment without flinching or confessing.

挺 然 outstanding; excellent.

挺 生 to raise up specially; begotten for a special purpose.

挺 硬 very hard.

挺 秀 prominent; excellent.

15挺 立 to stand up straight.

挺 節 冰 心 rigidly chaste.

挺 粗 挺 奘·的 very coarse and bulging—as a water-jar.

挺 緊 to pull tight.

挺·着 脛 項 to stiffen the neck.

20挺 胸 to thrust forward the chest.

挺 胸 凸 肚 strutting around in a bullying manner.

挺 腰·子 to put on airs.

挺·起 腿·來 stiffened the legs.

挺 身 to straighten the body; to put oneself forward.

25挺 身 昂 首 to stand erect and hold up the head.

挺 身 而 立 to stand erect.

挺 身 而 走 to walk erect.

挺 項 to stiffen the neck.

周 道 挺 挺 the great highway is straight.

30直 挺 挺·的 stiff and rigid.

梃³ A club; a stick; a cudgel.
6407 A stalk. Inter. preceding.

梃斡之人 an efficient man.

珽³ A sceptre.
6408

脡³ Strips of dried meat. Stiff
6409 and straight.

脡脡然 standing erect.
鮮魚曰脡祭 fresh fish are
called "The Straight Oblation."

艇³ A small boat; a punt; a
6410 skiff.

花艇 a large pleasure-boat.
飛艇 aeroplane.
魚雷艇 torpedo-boat.

莛² Stalks of grasses, etc.
6411

麥莛 wheaten straw.

蜓² A dragon-fly.
6412

蜻蜓 a dragon-fly.

(a) Read t'ien³. A chameleon.

蝘蜓 the chameleon.

鋌³ Iron or copper ore. Ingots.
6413 Bars of metal.

鋌子茶 a name for brick-tea.
黃金四十鋌 forty bars of
gold.

(a) The barb of an arrow.

箭鋌 the barb of an arrow.

(b) To run with haste.

鋌而走險急何能擇 a deer
driven to its death, does not
choose the best place to shelter
in.

(c) Exhausted. Hollow.

霆² Thunder; the noise of
6414 thunder.

雷霆 thunder.

TIU.　(ㄉㄡ)

丟¹ To cast away; to reject;
6415 to get rid of. To lose.

丟下 to throw down; to lay aside.
丟下去 to leave behind.
丟下水 thrown into the water.
丟不下 I cannot get it off my
hands; unable to get rid of.
⁵丟了一匹馬 he has lost a
horse.
丟人 to lose face; to disgrace.
丟你的人 put you to shame.
丟兒²溺女 infanticide.
丟到九霄雲外 cast it beyond
the clouds—utterly disregard
the matter; do not give it any
thought.
¹⁰丟包 to drop the parcel—a
Chinese confidence trick.
丟失 to lose.
丟官 to lose office.
丟掉 to lose; to cast away.
丟東西 to lose things.
¹⁵丟棄 to reject; to discard.
丟監¹ to cast into prison.
丟眼色 to give a hint with the
eyes.
丟石頭 to cast stones.
丟空兒⁴ leave every other space a
blank.
²⁰丟繩子 to heave a rope.
丟臉 to lose face; to disgrace.
丟醜 to disgrace oneself.
丟開 to put on one side; not to
mention.
丟開手 hands off; let it alone;
leave off.

TO.　(ㄉㄛ)

多¹ Much; too much; many;
6416 numerous. Often; mostly.

多不多 are there many; is it too
much?
多不得幾個 not many over.
多事 officious; interfering; meddling.
⁵多係 the majority is....
多個冷 how cold it is!
多像 polymorphism.

多元論 pluralism.
多出來 to exceed.
多分 extremely; in a great
degree.
¹⁰多半 the greater part.
多口 loquacious.
多口舌 to quarrel.
多咱 when?
多嘴 loquacious.
¹⁵多報 to overstate; to state more
than the actual quantity.
多多少少 a great number.
多多的 large quantities.
多多益善 the more the better.
多大 how great? however big;
huge.
²⁰多大年紀 how old are you?
多夫主義 polyandry.
多妻主義 polygamy.
多寡 how much? how many? a
certain quantity; many or few.
多少 how much? how many? a
certain quantity? much or little.
²⁵多少留幾個 keep a few.
多少起碼 what is the lowest
(price, etc.)
多年 many years.
多年生植物 perennial plants.
多心 to be suspicious.
³⁰多情 affectionate; emotional.
多憂多慮 always in trouble and
distress.
多才多藝 great ability.
多手 a meddlesome person.
多收 to receive too much.
³⁵多故 many difficulties and
troubles.
多數 the majority; many; plural.
多數決議 decided by the
majority.
多數表決 a majority vote.
多數贊成 the majority ap-
proved.
⁴⁰多方 many places; by all means;
in every way.
多早 or 多早晚兒 or 多會
兒 when?
多有 are (or have) mostly....
多次 many times.
多疑 to be suspicious.
⁴⁵多病 prone to illness.
多神教 polytheism.
多禮 very polite.
多端 many parts; in many ways;
artful.
多管閒事 to be a meddlesome
busybody.
⁵⁰多索 to extort.
多義 ambiguity.

多 聞 擇 其 善 者 而 從 之 to hear much and to follow the good picked out from it.

多 聞 闕 疑 hear much and cast aside the doubtful points.

多 肉 果 a berry.

[55] 多 胞 狀 cellular.

多 虧 Thanks to.

多 血 質 sanguine temperament.

多 見 多 聞 well-informed; of considerable experience.

多 親 寡 友 many relatives but few friends.

[60] 多 言 or 多 說 話 loquacious.

多 謝 much obliged; many thanks.

多 足 動 物 *Myriapoda*.

多[1,2] 重 的 皮 "What is the tare?"

多 量[4] a large amount.

[65] 多 · 餘 superfluous; unnecessary.

多 餘 之 財 富 surplus wealth.

多[1,2] 高 very high; how high?

多[1,2] 麼 好 how good!

三 多 i.e., 多 福, 多 壽, 多 男 子[3], the three abundancies—much happiness, long life, and many sons.

[70] 不 多 · 幾 · 個 only a few; not very many.

太 多 too many; too much.

好 多 very many.

許 多 a great many.

過 多 in excessive numbers; a quantity.

(a) Only.

多 見 其 不 知 量[4] 也 he only shows that he does not know his own capacity.

(b) A little.

一 勺 之 多 but a spoonful.

一 卷 石 之 多 appears as a mere stone.

一 撮 土 之 多 is but a handful of soil.

(c) Used in transliterating for the next.

哆[1]
A broad woollen cloth.
6417

哆 · 囉 呢 woollens.

(a) Also read *ch'ih*[3]. To open the mouth wide.

哆 兮 哆 兮 成 是 南 箕 a few diverging points may be made out to be the *Southern Sieve*.

舵[4]
A rudder; a helm. Also read *t'o*[4].
6418

舵 尾 the lower portion of a rudder.

舵 工 or 舵 師 a helmsman.

舵 杷 or 舵 杆 the tiller.

舵 梃 the rudder-post.

[5] 舵 行 汽 球 dirigible balloon.

舵 車 or 舵 輪 a steering-wheel.

舵 車 把 手 the hand-grips of a steering-wheel.

外 舵 starboard the helm.

掌 舵 or 把 舵 to grasp the tiller.

[10] 裏 舵 port the helm.

轉 舵 機 steering-engine.

TO. TUO. (ㄷ)

朵 朵[3]
A cluster of flowers or fruits; a bud. The lobe of the ear. Used conventionally for "your." N.A.
6419

朵 殿 halls to the right and left of the main building—like ears.

朵 翰 your favour—your letter.

朵 雲 your valued favour.

朵 頤 the movement of the jaws in eating.

[5] 一 朵 花 a flower.

一 朵 雲 a cloud. [(--*tou*, --*t'ou*)

耳 · 朵 the lobe of the ear; ears.

花 朵 a flower-bud.

剁[4]
To chop; to mince; to hash.
6420

剁 成 肉 醬 chopped him to mincemeat.

剁 排 骨 to cut up chops.

剁 碎 · 了 to chop small—as meat.

垛[4]
A target. A battlement. To add up; to pile up.
6421

垛 · 上 or 垛 · 起 · 來 to pile up.

垛 口 embrasures.

垛 子 or 射 垛 a target.

垛 數 兒 add up the amounts.

垛 柴 · 火 to stack firewood.

垛 錢 to pile up money.

城 垛 · 子 battlements on a city wall.

稞[4]
A heap; a stack; a pile.
6422

堆 成 一 稞 pile it up in a heap.

跺[3,4]
To take a step.
6423

跥 脚 to stamp the feet.

躲 躲[3]
To hide; to secrete; to withdraw; to shun; to avoid.
6424

躲 · 不 脫 or 躲 · 不 開 no escape from.

躲 債 to avoid one's creditors.

躲 匿 to avoid; to get out of the way of meeting anyone.

躲 學 to play truant.

[5] 躲 懶 to shirk work; to loiter.

躲 空 (*k'ung*[4]) to take a holiday.

躲 藏 to escape from; to withdraw; to avoid meeting a person; to hide from.

躲 身 to hide from; to slip away; to escape from; to withdraw.

躲 道 to get out of the way.

[10] 躲 避 to avoid; to withdraw; to hide from; to escape from.

躲 閃 to dodge out of sight.

躲 開 to withdraw; to hide from; to avoid a meeting with any person.

躲 難[4] to flee from trouble.

躲 雨 to take shelter from the rain,—used fig., to shelter from troubles.

惰[4]
Indolent; careless; lazy.
6425

惰 力 feeble remnant of exhausted energies.

惰 性 inertia.

惰 遊 or 遊 惰 to loaf about; to lounge.

惰 鉗 lazy-tongs.

髡[3]
Tufts of hair left on the heads of children after shaving.
6426

墮[4]
To fall; to sink; to let fall; to set.
6427

墮 五 里 霧 中 plunged into a dense fog. (fig.)

墮 其 術 中 fell into his snare.

墮 後 to fall behind.

墮 民 fallen people—a class of people in Chekiang and South Anhwei, also called 小 戶 or 小 姓; they suffer from various social disabilities.

⁵墮 胎 a miscarriage.

墮 落 to sink; to fall; decadent.

墮 落 戶 a fallen family.

墮 落 風 塵 to fall into the dust—to become a prostitute.

墮 行 to misdemean oneself.

¹⁰墮 馬 a fall off a horse.

夕 陽 西 墮 the sun was sinking in the west—evening.

(a) Lazy. u.f. preceding.

民 氣 解 墮 the people are indolent.

TO.　　(ㄉㄛ)
(Toh)

憜 4.5.　　To estimate; to calculate.
6428

踱 4.5.　　To walk; to step.
6429

踱 來 踱 去 walking backwards and forwards.

閒 踱 to stroll.

澤 2.5.　An icicle.
　　Distinguish 澤 No. 277.
6430

鐸 2.5.　A bell with a clapper.
　　To incite to.
6431

鐸 德 to incite to virtue.

天 將 以 夫 子 ³爲 木 鐸 God is about to use the Master as a bell with a wooden clapper—to arouse the age.

TO. TUO.　　(ㄉㄛ)
(Toh)

咄 4.5.　　To cry out.
6432　　Also pron. tu⁴.

咄 咄 alarmed; surprised.

咄 咄 而 去 went away offended.

咄 嗺 insulting; reproachful.

咄 嗟 而 辦 done at once.

咄·的 一 聲 cried, "Oh!"

奪 2.5.　To snatch; to grasp; to take away. To settle; to decide. To surpass.
6433

奪 人 心 目 prepossessing.

奪 人 算 to take one hundred days from a person's life.

奪 佔 to usurp.

奪 倫 discordant; out of place; to usurp the function of.

⁵奪 其 志 to break a person's determination.

奪 其 權 利 to deprive another of his privileges or rights.

奪 利 grasping for gain.

奪 功 勞 to assume the merit due to another.

奪·去 to snatch from.

¹⁰奪 取 to carry off; to wrest from.

奪 名 to take the name that belongs to another.

奪 命 金 丹 a golden pill that snatches life from death.

奪 囚 to break open a prison.

奪 回 to recover by force.

¹⁵奪 天 地 造 化 to wrest from nature.

奪 寵 to snatch the affection due to another.

奪 彩 to win the prize; to reach the goal.

奪 情 to do violence to one's feelings.

奪 春 魁 to come out first in the former spring examinations—held triennially for the third degree.

²⁰奪 標 to take the prize—as in a race.

奪 權 to deprive of rights.

奪 氣 to gasp for breath.

奪 獲 to capture.

奪 理 to wrest justice.

²⁵奪 生 計 to deprive of the means of a livelihood.

奪 目 to dazzle the eyes.

奪 秀 氣 to carry off literary fame.

奪 紀 to take twelve years from a person's life.

奪 職 to dismiss from office.

³⁰奪 胎 to drive off the soul of a foetus and take its place.

奪 胎 換 骨 to imitate the compositions of another.

奪 路 to take the road—in front of another.

奪·過·來 to take from.

奪 魄 to lose one's nerve.

搶 奪 to rob with violence.

(a) To determine. To decide.

定 奪 to settle; to determine.

察 奪 to examine into and decide upon.

酌 奪 to deliberate and come to a decision.

(b) Read tui⁴. Name of a place.

洈 4.5.　　To let drop.
6434

滴 洈 to drip.

剟 2.5.　To prick. To cut blocks; to engrave.
6435

掇 4.5.　To arrange; to gather up; to pluck.
6436

掇 弄 to arrange; to look after.

掇 拾 to gather up.

掇 探 to gather; to pluck.

掇 提 to fondle in the arms.

⁵掇 環 rings whereby a thing is lifted.

掇 石 to practise heavy weight-lifting.

掇 芹 to pluck cress—to take the former first degree.

敠 1.5.　To weigh a thing in the hand.
6437

掂 敠 to estimate the weight of a thing by balancing it in the hand.

裰 2.5.　　To mend clothes.
6438

補 裰 to patch and mend.

T'O.　　(ㄊㄛ)

它 1.2.
佗]　　That; another; he.
6439　　Inter. 他 No. 5961.

它 如 besides; again.

它 如 故 約 the rest to be according to the old agreement.
無 它 or 非 它 nothing more than...; no other.

(a) Easy and self-possessed in manner. Inter. 蛇 No. 5698-A.

委 委 它 它 easy and elegant in her movements.

(b) Hump-backed. Inter. 駝 No. 6448.

它²子 a humpback.
它²背 hump-backed.

(c) Read t'o³. Hanging loose.

它 髮 the hair hanging loose.

(d) Read t'o⁴. To impute; to add to.

今 彼 有 罪 予 之 它 矣 he does not interfere with the guilty and imputes guilt to me.

扡 拖 6440

¹ To drag after; to drag out; from which comes:— to involve; to delay; to implicate.

拖 到 城 外 to drag out of the city.
拖 尾 鳥 or 拖 白 練 the Paradise fly-catcher.
拖 帶 to track; to drag; to tow.
拖 延 to put off; to procrastinate.
⁵拖 手 hand in hand.
拖 拉 to delay—as payments.
拖 欠 to delay payments; to be in arrears.
拖 欠 之 息 defaulted interest.
拖 泥 帶 水 dragged through mud and water—muddled, as a style of writing or acting.
¹⁰拖 累 to implicate; involved.
拖 紳 ends of a girdle hanging low; an official.
拖 罟 船 a fishing-smack which drags a net after it.
拖 船 a tugboat; a fishing-smack.
拖 花 翎 to wear the peacock's feather.
¹⁵拖 輪 a steam-tug.
拖 重 汽 機 traction engine.
拖 鈎 tug of war.
拖 長² long-drawn-out.
拖 鞋 slippers.

柂⁴ 6441

Large tie-beams.

柂 頭² the ends of the beams which project outside the houses.

(a) u.f. 舵 No. 6418. A rudder.

沱 澢 6442

² Water diverging into streams. Flowing of water. Name of a river.

俾 滂 沱 矣 which will bring still greater rain.
出 涕 沱 若 from my eyes and nose the water streams.
江 有 沱 the Great River has its branches which take a different course, but ultimately rejoin the main stream.

疴 6443

² Hump-backed.
See 佗 No. 6439, and 駝 No. 6448.

疴 子 a hunchback.
疴 背 hump-backed.

砣 碢 鉈 6444

2.4.

A stone roller. A heavy stone; a weight; a plummet.

秤 砣 the weight on a steelyard.

跎 6445

² To slip; to miss one's footing; to stumble.

蹉 跎 to stumble; to slip. See No. 6791.

酡 6446

² Flushed. Rubicund.

醉 酡 flushed with liquor.
顏 酡 a flushed face.

陀 陁 6447

² A steep bank; a declivity.

陀 螺 a top.
沙 陀 sandy steppes.
陂 陀 a declivity.
鹽 陀 a salt-mound.

(a) Used in transliterating.

陀 羅 尼 Buddhist charms and magic formulas—Sanskrit:— dhârani.
頭² 陀 a Buddhist recluse or priest; Buddhist relics—Sanskrit:— dhâtu.

駝 6448

² The camel.

駝 子 a humpback.
駝 峯 the hump of a camel.
駝 背 hump-backed.
駝 負 to carry a burden on the back.
⁵駝 轎 a mule litter.
駝 雞 a name for the ostrich.
駝 鳥 the ostrich; sometimes used for the emu.
駱 駝 the camel.

鮀 6449

² A kind of fish which burrows in the sand.

鴕 6450

² The ostrich. The emu.

鴕 鳥 the ostrich.
澳 州 鴕 鳥 the emu.

鼧 6451

² The marmot.

鼧 鼤 (pa⁵) the marmot found in Manchuria and Mongolia; also called 土 撥 鼠.

馱 馱 6452

² To carry on the back; to bear.
Inter. 駝 No. 6448.

馱 不 住 too heavy for the beast.
馱 不 動 too heavy to carry.
馱 上 to load a pack-animal.
馱 上 山 去 carry it up the hill.
馱 着 carrying a load on the back.
馱 轎 a mule litter.
背 馱 to carry on the back.

鼉[2] A large water-lizard. An iguana, the skin of which 6453 was used for drums.

鼉更 to strike the watches—in the Drum Tower.

鼉鼓逢逢矇瞍奏公 "the lizard-skin drums rolled harmonious, as the blind musicians performed their parts."

T'O. T'UO. (ㄊㄛ)

妥[3] Firm, secure. Satisfactory. Safe; settled. Ready; pre-6454 pared.

妥·了 settled; finished; safe.
妥便 safe and convenient.
妥先靈 to quiet the spirits of one's ancestors.
妥協 satisfactory; suitable; fit; co-operation; to compromise.
[5]妥員 a reliable officer.
妥商 to consult; to negotiate about.
妥善 satisfactory; properly arranged for; well-managed.
妥妙 satisfactory; well suited.
妥定 to settle; definitely.
[10]妥實 reliable.
妥帖 everything satisfactorily arranged; properly arranged in order; firmly placed.
妥幹 competent.
妥捷 expeditiously.
妥極 or 極妥 extremely satisfactory.
[15]妥派 to send out; to commission.
妥爲商辦 to come to a satisfactory decision and act accordingly.
妥理 to make satisfactory arrangements.
妥當 or 穩妥 everything right; properly done; on a sound basis; well arranged.
妥籌 to make suitable arrangements for.
[20]妥結 to make a satisfactory settlement.
妥練 experienced; trustworthy.
妥設良法 to adopt satisfactory measures.
妥議章·程 to decide upon satisfactory rules and regulations.
妥辦 to transact satisfactorily.
[25]妥速 safe and prompt; without delay.

不妥 unsettled; unsatisfactory.
事未妥 the matter has not been satisfactorily arranged.
低頭妥尾 they (three black lions) hung their heads and put their tails between their legs.
欠妥 unreliable; not quite right.

毻[3.4.] To moult. To change the coat—of animals.
6455

撱[3] To shorten; to clip. To throw away.
6456

橢[3] Tubular. Oval. Elliptical.
6457

橢圓形·的 oval; elliptical.
橢圓畫規 elliptical compasses.
橢圓體 an oval figure; an ellipsoid.

唾 **涶** [4] To spit. Saliva. Also read t'u[4].
6458

唾人 to spit on a person—also used fig.
唾口水 to spit.
唾·沫 spittle. (t'u[4]-)
唾·沫盒 a spittoon. (t'u[4]-)
唾罵 to spit on and revile.
唾腺 salivary glands.
唾面 to spit in one's face.

T'O. (ㄊㄛ)
(T'oh)

乇[4.5] To depend on; to entrust with.
6459

托 [1.5]
拓 [4.5] To carry on the palm; to support with the hand. Inter. 託 next The second form means also to expand.
6460

托一層紙 to lay a thickness of paper underneath.
托·不住 unable to support—as a weight.
托付 to entrust to; to commit to the care of.

托件 the person who takes the money for a band of strolling players.
[5]托住萬有 upholds all things; sustains the universe.
托命 I owe my life to....
托在手 (or 掌) 中 bear it upon the palm of the hand.
托塔天王 the god who supports a pagoda in his hand.
托·子 a waiter or tray; the satin lining of a fur robe.
[10]托孤 to entrust with the care of an orphan.
托故 to make a pretext.
托於其友 given into the charge of his friend.
托病 to plead sickness as an excuse.
托·盤 a waiter or tray.
[15]托腮 to lean the head upon the hand.
拓落 mortified; reduced to poverty; alone, helpless; intelligent and clever.
托襟 or 托領 the round collar on a woman's garment.
托足之地 a foothold.
托身 to dwell in.
[20]托鉢 to carry the wooden bowl—to beg.
推托 to make excuses.

(a) Read t'a[5]. u.f. 搨 No. 5968. To take rubbings.
拓本 a rubbing from a stone tablet.

(b) Read t'o[1.5]. Used in transliterating.
托立克 Toric—lens.
托辣斯 trust—as a trust company.
拓跋氏 Toba—the founder of the Northern Wei dynasty.
拓都 total.

(c) A fathom—the length of both arms outstretched.

託 **侂** [1.5.] To commission; to entrust to; to depute. To request; to ask. Inter. preceding.
6461

託之空言 the matter fell through; the proposals came to nothing.

託 交 to become friends.

託 人 to request the good offices of a person.

託 人 情 to engage the aid of another; to appeal to a man's feelings; to seek the good offices of another.

[5]託 付 to entrust to.

託 你 一 件 事 I will entrust you with this affair.

託 六 尺 之 孤 entrusted with the care of a young orphan prince.

託 名 in the name of another; to infringe the name of another.

託 夢 to appear to in a dream.

[10]託 大 to be arrogant and despise others.

託 始 the origin; the beginnings.

託 孤 to entrust an orphan to the care of; to appoint a guardian.

託 寄 to commission one to send.

託 實 straightforward, without any conventionalities.

[15]託 帶 to ask a person to bring.

託 庇 "many thanks;" "much obliged;" "it is kind of you;" etc. *See below* 23.

託 庇 外 人 to seek foreign protection.

託 心 to believe in another.

託 情 to ask a favour.

[20]託 故 to make excuses.

託 生 to become incarnate.

託 疾 to make a pretext of illness.

託 福 thanks to the spreading of your good luck, I am (we are) very well.

託 處 one's dwelling.

[25]託 言 to make excuses.

託 諷 to make one's purpose and ideals known by writings.

託 買 to ask a person to buy; to purchase on commission.

託 賴 to rely on; to repudiate.

託 足 to dwell in.

[30]託 足 遠 方 to seek asylum abroad.

託 身 文 墨 to trust to literature for a living.

託 辭 to make excuses; to entrust with a commission.

託 迹 to be trusted.

託 附 to set oneself forth as a person of importance, by relying on the power and influence of another.

[35]託 音 to send news.

託 食 to sponge upon another.

不 可 託 untrustworthy.

受 人 之 託 to have received a commission from another.

寄 子[3] 託 妻 to entrust one's wife and child to another.

析[4.5.] A watchman's rattle. Distinguish 析 No. 2488.
6462

跅[4.5.] Careless; lax.
6463

跅 弛 之 士 careless and incompetent officers.

跅 落 disorderly and careless.

庹[1.5.] The length of one's two outstretched arms, for which 托 No. 6460-C, is now used.
6464

橐[2.5.] A sack; a bag opening at both ends.
6465

橐 橐 sacks with and without bottoms.

橐 筒 a satchel; a bag.

橐 駝 the camel; a humpback.

(a) Tube for blowing the fires of a furnace.

橐 籥 a tube for blowing up the fires of a furnace.

(b) Sound of footfalls. Noise of pounding.

履 聲 橐 橐 the sound of footsteps.

椓 之 橐 橐 *t'o-t'o* went on the pounding—of building earthen walls.

籜[4.5.] Sheath which envelops the joints of the bamboo. The first leaves of bamboo shoots.
6466

蘀[4.5.] Fallen leaves and bark.
6467

T'O. T'UO. (토)
(T'oh)

脫[1.5.] To undress; to take off; to strip. To cast off; to abandon; to renounce; to escape from; to get out of. To omit. To slip off, as an axe-head.
6468

脫 下 to take off—as garments.

脫 不 開 身 cannot get away from; cannot get leisure for it.

脫 了 圈 套 slipped out of the snare.

[5]脫 使 可 行 perhaps it can be done.

脫 俗 to drop ceremony—as among friends; free from mere conventionality; refined in manner, taste etc.

脫 光 said of a dark day.

脫 免 to avoid; to get free from.

脫 兔 an escaped hare—alert, sharp, nervous.

[10]脫 凡 胎 to disembody; to escape from the trammels of the flesh.

脫 卸 to unload.

脫 卻 to discard; to cast off entirely.

脫 去 to throw off.

脫 名 to abscond.

[15]脫 套 to escape a snare; not to conform to; eccentric; peculiar.

脫 孝 to go out of mourning.

脫 屣 to slip off the shoes—to do something that is easily accomplished.

脫 帽 to raise the hat.

脫 帽 三 鞠 躬 to raise the hat and make three formal bows—the modern ceremonial.

[20]脫 帽 歡 呼 to wave the hat and cheer.

脫 手 to slip out of the hand; to finish a matter; to sell out.

脫 捐 omissions and errors—as in historical records.

脫 掉 renounced; left off; take off

脫 易 easy-going disposition.

[25]脫 案 to escape a trial.

脫 死 逃 生 to enter Nirvana.

脫 殼 to cast the shell—as insects.

脫 水 dehydration.

脫 漏 leaked out; to miss; gone; to omit; omissions.

³⁰脱 灑 free from trammels, original; lofty in thought—as a composition.

脱 然 無 累 to get away without being implicated.

脱 班 not up to schedule—as a train.

脱 生 to be reincarnated; transmigration.

脱 皮 to cast the skin; to peel.

³⁵脱 皮 不 脱 毒 cast off the skin but not the poison—external reformation.

脱 盡·了 completely freed from.

脱 稿 to complete a work ready for the printer.

脱 空 to put all one's energies into a thing and yet fail; to tell lies.

脱 節 to dislocate a joint.

⁴⁰脱 籍 to resign membership.

脱 籠 to get out of the cage—to slip away; to deceive.

脱 粟 rice that has just been imperfectly hulled.

脱 素 unconventional and simple.

脱 累 to get rid of a burden; a hiatus; a lacuna.

⁴⁵脱 略 liberal; unrestrained; to make a résumé.

脱 網 to escape from the net—from troubles.

脱 肛 prolapsus of the rectum.

脱 肩 to uncover the shoulder—to shake off a burden, as of responsibility.

脱 胎 to get free from one's shackles—as a new-born child; to have a miscarriage. See No. 6010-36.

⁵⁰脱 臼 dislocation, as of a joint.

脱 若 if.

脱 落 to cast; to shed; to drop.

脱 落·下·來 to fall off.

脱 衣 市 易 took off their garments and sold them.

⁵⁵脱 衣·服 to undress.

脱 誤 omissions and errors.

脱 謬 omissions and mis-statements.

脱 走 to escape from.

脱 身 to dodge; to slip away; to escape; to withdraw; to find leisure; to give birth to a child.

⁶⁰脱 身 之 計 a plan of escape.

脱 逃 to escape from.

脱²開 or 脱 閃 to slip away; to escape; to withdraw; to retire; to find leisure.

脱 除 to get rid of; to remove.

脱 險 removed from danger.

⁶⁵脱 離 to cast off; to escape from.

脱 離 束 縛 to escape from bonds.

脱 離 關·係 to escape the consequences.

脱 難 (nan⁴) to escape troubles.

脱 非 unless; were it not for.

⁷⁰脱 頂 a bald head.

脱 穎 而 出 the sharp point has come out—real talent will show itself, like the point of an awl coming through a bag.

脱 黨 to leave the party; to apostatize.

出 脱 to part with; to escape.

失 脱 lost.

⁷⁵推 脱 to make excuses.

放 脱 to release; to liberate.

TOU. (夂)
(Teo)

兜¹　A helmet; a head-covering.
6469

兜·子 a woman's head-dress. See below—A. 5.

兜 鍪 or 兜 盔 a helmet.

風 兜 a hood for cold weather.

(a) To wrap up in a cloth. To put into the bosom of one's garments. A sack or bag.

兜·住 拿·罷 wrap them up in a cloth and take them.

兜 剿 to surround and slay—brigands or rebels.

兜 嘴 to muzzle.

兜 圈·子 to take a stroll around.

⁵兜·子 a piece of cloth with a string at each corner, used as a bricklayer's hod. See above—1.

兜 拏 to stop or seize.

兜 截 to cut off an enemy.

兜 東·西 to wrap things up in a cloth for carrying.

兜·肚　or 肚 兜 a stomacher; a kind of corset; a pocket worn round the waist.

¹⁰下 巴 兜 the chin.

銀 兜·子 a money-bag; a purse.

(b) To obtain in an unlawful or irregular manner.

兜 搭 provoking; dawdling.

兜 攬 生·意 to make unlawful gains.

兜 轉²來 to come by a roundabout way.

兜 風 to take the air; to go joy-riding.

兜 風 逛·逛 to go out for a stroll and get some fresh air.

(c) Used for transliterating.

兜 率 天 the dwelling of 太 上 老 君 in heaven. (Tao.).

兜 率 陀 Tushita, the heaven in which Bôdhisattvas dwell before coming down to earth.

兜 羅 a tree which produces seeds containing cotton—Sanskrit: tûla.

兜 羅 綿 手 the soft white hands (of Buddha).

兜 羅 綿 雲 fleecy-white clouds like cotton-wool.

(d) Inter. 篼 No. 6471. A mountain-chair.

兜 轎 a mountain-chair.

山 兜·子 a mountain-chair.

挽¹　To lift up; to take in the hand. To control. To open.
6470　Inter. preceding.

挽 攬 to grasp after; to be affected by.

挽 起 轎·子 to tilt the poles of a sedan-chair so that the passenger can get over them.

挽·開 to lift aside; to put elsewhere.

篼¹　A basket-work muzzle. A bag. A mountain-chair. Inter. 兜 No. 6469.
6471

篼 轎 or 山 篼 a mountain-chair.

驢 篼·子 a nose-bag for a donkey.

斗³　A dry measure, often called a peck in translation; the size varies considerably, but it has been standardized to contain 316 cubic inches. The cup of an acorn, etc. Radical 68.
6472

斗 城 a very small city.

斗 大 字 very large characters.

斗·子 or 灰 斗 a rag with strings at each corner, used as a hod by Chinese bricklayers.

斗帳 a small canopy like an inverted bushel measure.

[5] 斗底下 under a bushel.

斗底房 or 斗室 a small house.

斗方 sheets of paper about a foot square, often used for pasting inscriptions on doors, etc.

斗方名士 a pretender to refinement and elegance.

斗棋 or 斗·子 the square peck-shaped box half-way up a Chinese flagstaff.

[10] 斗秤 weights and measures.

斗笠 or 一頂斗笠 a wide rain-hat.

斗筲之人 peck and hamper people—mere utensils.

斗·篷 a cape; a great-coat; a straw rain-hat.

斗紋 the circular markings on the finger-tips.

[15] 斗級 official measurer of grain.

斗絕 completely isolated—of a place.

斗膽 great courage—a peck of gall, i.e., courage.

斗斛 pecks and bushels.

斗僻 out-of-way; isolated.

[20] 斗酒百篇 a hundred stanzas to a gallon of wine, from a line of Tu Fu 杜甫, alluding to the drinking capacity of the poet Li T'ai-po 李太白.

斗量 to measure by pecks.

斗門 a sluice gate in a weir.

斗食 a daily allowance of a tou of grain—used for clerks in a yamen who were given this allowance.

倉斗 a peck of 6.5 catties or 1.13 gallons.

[25] 墨斗·子 a carpenter's marking-line with its box for ink.

市斗 or 十斤斗 the market peck holding 10 catties of rice, or 1.63 gallons.

水斗 a ladle or dipper.

(a) The *Dipper*—a part of Ursa Major. A zodiacal constellation.

斗南一人 the only man in the world.—lit., the one man south of the *Dipper*.

斗柄初昏 when the handle of the *Dipper* first becomes obscured.

斗柄建此三辰之月 the handle of the *Dipper* establishes the months of these three constellations 子, 丑, 寅 — by pointing at them.

斗極 the Pole-star.

[5] 斗折蛇行 crooked like the *Dipper* and winding like a serpent.

北斗 the *Dipper*—seven stars in Ursa Major.

北斗神君 the Spirit Ruler of the *Dipper*—the Controller of Destiny.

北斗神君誕 the feast held on the 3rd of the 8th lunar month in honour of the birthday of the above.

南斗 the *Southern Dipper*, a constellation consisting of six stars in Sagittarius.

拜斗 to worship the *Dipper*.

(b) Inter. next. To shake up. To rouse.

斗擻 to arouse the energies; to shake off the dust.

(c) Inter. 阧 No. 6477. Suddenly.

斗覺 suddenly became aware.

抖 [3] To shake; to rouse. To tremble.
6473

抖·一·抖 to shake up; give it a shake.

抖·下·去 to shake off.

抖抖擻擻·的 cringing; awkward...

抖抖縮縮·的 trembling; shaking.

[5] 抖·擻 to shake out.

抖·擻塵埃 to shake off the dust.

抖·擻毛 to shake the feathers.

抖·擻精神 to pull oneself together; to make an effort; to rouse one's energies.

抖攬 to get business; to make unlawful or irregular gains. *See* 兜 No. 6469—B. 2.

[10] 抖晾 to air—as books or clothing.

抖膽 to pluck up courage.

發抖 to tremble.

枓 [3] The square peck-shaped box half-way up a Chinese
6474 flagstaff.

枓棋 or 旗杆枓·子 the square box, as above.

(a) Read *chu*[3]. A ladle with a long handle.

沃水用枓 to ladle out water to wash a corpse.

蚪 [3]　A tadpole.
6475

蝌蚪·子 tadpoles.

斜 [3]　A wine flagon. Also read *to'u*[3]. A surname.
6476

阧) [3]
陡)　　Sloping; steep. Suddenly; abruptly.
6477

陡坡兒 a steep bank.

陡峭 or 陡峻 precipitous.

陡然 all at once; suddenly; unexpectedly.

陡發 to burst forth or grow up suddenly.

[5] 陡起不良 an evil intention straightway entered his mind.

陡重 suddenly to become very serious—as a disease.

陡長 (*chang*[3]) to grow up suddenly.

陡門 locks in a canal.

陡險 very dangerous—also used fig.

豆 [4]　Beans, peas; for which 荳
6478　No. 6481 is generally used. Radical 151.

豆剖瓜分 to be partitioned, as a bean, into two sections, or as a melon, into slices.

豆·子 beans; peas. 豆沙 = 6172.3½.

豆油 oil expressed from beans.

豆皮 husks of beans and peas.

[5] 豆科 leguminous plants.

豆腐 bean-curd, a preparation which, in its liquid state, is almost identical with cow's milk as regards its nutritive constituents.

豆芽兒 bean-sprouts, used as a vegetable.

豆莢 the pods of beans or peas.

豆萁 bean-stalks. *See* 煮 No. 1356-6.

↑豆乳 = 豆漿 juice from beans.

¹⁰豆 蔲 nutmegs; cardamoms.
豆 蟹 the oyster-crab.
豆 餅 bean-cake.
紅 豆 the seeds of *Abrus precatorius*, known as love-seeds. *See* 相 No. 2562-68.

(a) A vessel like a platter, made of wood, bronze, or porcelain, used for holding food in sacrifices, etc. A dry measure; a peck. A small weight equal to 16 grains of millet.

乾 豆 a stirrup-shaped sacrificial vessel.
揭 豆 plain wooden trenchers.
木 豆 wooden platters.
獻 豆 a carved platter.
籩 豆 之 事 matters relating to sacrifices.

痘 ⁴ Smallpox.
6479

痘·子 smallpox.
痘 母 or 痘 神 娘 娘 Goddess of Smallpox.
痘 毒 smallpox virus; deeply pitted.
痘 汁 the pus of smallpox.
⁵痘 漿 vaccine virus.
痘 疤 smallpox scabs.
痘 疹 smallpox pustules.
痘 瘡 pustules.
痘 皮 pockmarked.
¹⁰出 痘 to have smallpox.
染 痘 to be infected by smallpox.
種 牛 痘 to vaccinate.
種 痘 to inoculate for smallpox.

脰 ⁴ The throat; the neck.
6480

脰 頸 the neck.
絕 脰 to break the neck.

荳 ⁴ Peas, beans, pulse. See also under 豆 No. 6478.
6481

荳·子 beans; peas, etc.
荳 油 oil expressed from beans.
荳 瓣 the halves of a bean.
荳 秧 young bean-plants.
⁵荳 稭 bean-stalks.
荳 粉 bean-flour.

荳·腐 bean-curd. *See* 豆 No. 6478-6.
荳·腐 乾 dried cakes of bean-curd, usually flavoured with soy.
荳·腐 官 underlings—bean-curd officials.
¹⁰荳·腐 心 soft-hearted.
荳 芽 bean-sprouts → used as a vegetable.
荳 蔲 nutmegs; cardamoms.
荳 蔲 花 mace.
荳 規 銀 a name for Shanghai silver or *taels*.
¹⁵荳 角 bean-pods.
荳 醬 soy.
荳 靑 a bright green.
荳 餅 bean-cake.
刀 荳 horse-beans; a bean with a large, flat pod.
²⁰大 荳 or 黑 荳 or 烏 荳 or 黃 荳 various kinds of soya beans, used for making bean-curd, soy, etc. *Glycine hyspida*.
扁 荳 a flat-bean. *Dolichos lablab*.
絲 荳 green lentils.
胡 荳 broad-beans.
蠶 荳 broad-beans; house-beans.
²⁵芸 荳 or 雲 扁 荳 French or kidney-beans.
豇 荳 a small kidney-bean.
豌 荳 green peas.

逗 ⁴ To loiter; to skulk.
6482

逗 住 dawdled; delayed.
逗 遛 loitering about.

(a) To excite; to arouse. To tempt.

逗·弄 to disturb; to tease; to fidget.
引 逗 to beguile.

(b) To avoid, as an enemy.

逗 橈 to take a circuitous course in order to avoid the foe.

餖 ⁴ To set out food.
6483

餖 飣 fruit, etc., merely arranged for show, not to be eaten; to plagiarize.

鬥 鬦 鬬 ⁴
6484

To quarrel; to contest; to fight; to provoke. Radical 191. Distinguish 門 No. 4418.

鬥 三 板 boat-racing.
鬥·上 一 合 to fight one round.
鬥·不 過·你 (he is) no match for you.
鬥 傷 a wound; a bruise received in a fight.
⁵鬥 兵 to fight—as two armies.
鬥 力 wrestling; a trial of strength.
鬥 勁 a trial of strength; to chaff.
鬥 勝 to strive for mastery.
鬥 口 or 鬥 嘴 to squabble; to wrangle.
¹⁰鬥 口 角 to chaff.
鬥 合·的 地 方 the place where the two sides met.
鬥 富 rivalry in wealthy display.
鬥 心 事 to debate about.
鬥 心·思 a battle of wits.
¹⁵鬥 志 a pugnacious disposition.
鬥 意·見 wrangling over conflicting opinions; arguments; discussions.
鬥 成 一 起 to unite; to join in one.
鬥 拳 to fight with the fists.
鬥 智 a battle of wits.
²⁰鬥 毆 assault and battery; to fight.
鬥 氣 to quarrel; pugnacious.
鬥 狠 to fight; quarreling; making an uproar.
鬥 眉 眼 to give a hint with the eyes.
鬥 眼 to squint.
²⁵鬥 笑 to have a battle of wits.
鬥 紙 牌 to play cards.
鬥 而 鑄 兵 to make weapons after the fight has begun—to begin preparations when it is too late.
鬥 脚 to wrestle.
鬥 蟋 蟀 to fight crickets.
³⁰鬥 趣 to have a battle of wits.
鬥 閒 氣 to wrangle about nothing.
鬥 雞 坑 a cock-pit.
鬥 雞 走 狗 cock-fighting and dog-racing.
鬥 鵪 鶉 to fight quails.
³⁵鬥 駁 to dispute; to argue.
鬥 龍 船 to race dragon-boats.

格 鬬 to fight without weapons.
械 鬬 to fight with weapons.
死 鬬 a fight to the death.
決 鬬 a duel.

(a) To gather things together. To collect; to agree.

鬬 分⁴子 to subscribe.
鬬 榫 to fit together nicely, as a mortise and tenon—used of affairs, etc.
鬬 縫 to fit nicely, as seams—used fig., of affairs.

 竇⁴ A hole; a drain; a sluice.
6485

竇 路 a narrow path; a gorge.
塞 竇 a sluice-gate.
水 竇 a drain.
狗 竇 a hole for a dog to go in and out by—used of a person whose front tooth is missing.

(a) A corrupt practice. An error.

弊 竇 corrupt practices.
疑 竇 suspicious practices.

T'OU. (㐄)
(T'eo)

上² Above. Radical 8.
6486

㗊³ A flagon.
6487

 偷 偷 ¹ To steal; to pilfer. Stealthily; clandestine. Distinguish 倫 No. 4247.
6488

偷 人 to have a paramour; to commit adultery—of a woman.
偷 作 to do a thing on the sly.
偷 佔 to pilfer; to steal.
偷 偷 摸 摸 secretly; clandestinely; privately.
⁵偷 入 to enter slyly.
偷 冷·的 unexpectedly.
偷·去 to steal.
偷 嘴 to steal food; to take food on the sly.

偷 女·人 to seduce a woman.
¹⁰偷 安 to take one's ease; to shirk work.
偷 寒 送 煖 to do everything to please others.
偷 工 to scamp work.
偷 巧 to adopt artful methods.
偷 情 illicit intercourse.
¹⁵偷 懶 to loaf on a job; to be idle.
偷 捐 to, evade payment of *likin*.
偷 暇 to take a vacation.
偷 書 看 不 爲 賊 to steal a book in order to read it, is not being a thief.
偷 東·西 to steal things.
²⁰偷 棺 掘 墓 to rob graves.
偷 漏 to smuggle.
偷 漢·子 to have a paramour; to commit adultery—of a woman.
偷 營 to surprise an enemy's camp.
偷 生 to save one's life by ignoble means; to have a child secretly.
²⁵偷 看 or 偷 眼 to steal a glance.
偷 稅 or 偷 私 to smuggle.
偷 空 to avail oneself of a leisure moment.
偷·窺 to steal a glance.
偷·竊 to steal; to pilfer.
³⁰偷·着 secretly; privately.
偷·着 引 進 stealthily introduced.
偷 聽 to listen secretly.
偷 薄 vicious; depraved; remiss; negligent. *See below* (a)
偷 視 to steal a glance.
³⁵偷 走 or 偷 跑 to skulk off; to steal away.
偷 長 head of a band of thieves.
偷 閒 to loaf; to waste time when on a job.
忙·裏 偷 閒 to snatch a rest when busy.
偷 雞 摸 狗 to pilfer; also used of crooked dealings.
⁴⁰偷 雞 貓 不 改 性 a cat that steals chickens will not change its nature.
偷 雨 不 偷 雪 偷 風 不 偷 月 robberies are committed on rainy nights, but not when snow has fallen; on windy nights, but not when the moon is shining.
偷 青 to steal growing crops, cotton, melons, etc.
偷 香 to have illicit intercourse.
偷 龍 轉 鳳 to steal a male child and substitute a female one— to make a secret substitution.

(a) Mean; low.

故 舊 不 遺 則 民 不 偷 when old friends are not neglected by them, the people are preserved from meanness.

頭² The head; the top. Chief. First; the most important;
6489   the best. The end; ends; odd pieces. N.A. noun suffix.

頭·一·個 the first one; the chief.
頭·一 日 the first day.
頭·一 條 the first—commandment.
頭·上 above; on the head.
⁵ 上·頭 above.
下·頭 beneath.
頭·上 光 禿 bald.
頭·上 安 頭 to try and fit on a head where there is a head already—superfluous; complications.[an end of an elongated object.
頭 兒 the head of an organization;
¹⁰頭 出 角 his head has put forth horns—he has become fierce.
頭 前 formerly; a while ago; on ahead; once upon a time.
頭 口 horses, cattle, etc.
頭 名 the first on a list; the first rank or quality.
頭 品 the best quality; formerly the highest official rank.
¹⁵頭·回 the first occasion.
頭 垢 dandruff.
頭 家 one who takes a percentage from a gambling party.
頭 尖 the apex; the acme; the very best.
頭 尾 head and tail—beginning and ending; the whole.
²⁰ 有 頭 有 尾 having a head and tail; methodical; systematic; complete.
有 頭 無 尾 it has a beginning but no ending—something left half accomplished.
無 頭 無 尾 without head or tail—incomplete; incomprehensible; nonsensical.
頭 屑 dandruff.
頭 巾 or 頭 帕 a turban; a kerchief.
²⁵頭·年 last year.
頭 彩 first prize in a lottery.
頭 役 or 差 (*ch'ai*¹) 頭² a head underling.
頭 挑 to select first-class goods.

頭 暈 or 頭 昏 headache.

³⁰頭 會 箕 斂 to assess taxes according to the population, and collect the grain for them as in a sieve—of taxation for military supplies.

頭 枕 刀 劍 the head pillowed on a sword—ready for action.

頭 桅 the foremast.

頭 次 the first time; the first occasion.

頭 殼 the skull; the head.

³⁵頭 殼 皮 pericranium.

頭 毛 hair of the head.

頭 水 commission taken from the winnings of a gambling party.

頭 生·的 the first-born.

頭 痛 headache.

⁴⁰頭 白 寶 first-class silver; pure sycee.

頭 盔 a helmet.

頭 目 a chief; a headman.

頭 目 暈 眩 one's eyes swim in one's head; dizzy.

頭 童 齒 豁 hair gone and teeth falling out—old age.

⁴⁵頭 等 first quality; first class or rank.

頭 等 國 the Great Powers.

頭 等 貨 first-class goods.

頭 筋 the muscles of the head.

頭。緒 the clue; the point at which to make a start; way; means.

⁵⁰頭 緒 紛 繁 bewilderment; perplexity and embarrassment.

頭 繩 cord worn in the queue by children; red cord.

頭 胎·的 the first-born child.

頭 腦 a chief; headman; the head.

頭 臉 the facial appearance—usually with the idea of ugly.

⁵⁵頭 蓋 腔 the cavity of the skull.

頭 蓋 計 (or 測) craniometer.

頭 蓋 骨 the cranium.

穿·開 頭 蓋 術 craniotomy.

頭 號 number one; the best; first class.

⁶⁰頭 蝨 head-lice.

頭 衛 full official rank and title.

頭 衣 head-dress.

頭 裏 on ahead.

頭 角 崢 嶸 a noble brow—outstanding appearance.

⁶⁵頭 貨 first-class goods; mules and donkeys.

頭 足 異 處 head and feet in different places—beheaded.

頭 足 類·的 Cephalapoda.

頭 路 an opening; a way; a cause; a vocation.

頭 迷 dizzy.

⁷⁰頭 道 the first occasion.

頭 達 insignia carried before an official on tour.

頭 遭 the first time.

頭 酸 滴 醋 the head soured until it drips vinegar—nervous and fearful on account of trouble and anxiety.

頭 錢 subscription made by members of a society.

⁷⁵頭 門 the principal gate or entrance.

頭 難 保 his life is in danger.

頭 面 women's head-ornaments, etc.

頭 頂 the top of the head.

頭 頂·着 overhead.

⁸⁰頭 領 a leader; the head.

頭 頭 是 道 everything clear and straightforward—on the high road to success.

頭 額 the forehead; the brow.

頭 顱 the skull; the head.

頭 風 headache.

⁸⁵頭 骨 the cranium.

頭 骨 學 craniology.

頭 髮 human hair.

頭 髮 上 指 his hair stood on end.

一 頭² 牛 an ox.

⁹⁰一 頭² 蒜 a head of garlic.

一 頭² 重 heavy at one end—as a coolie-load.

出 人 頭² 地 to come to the front.

出 頭² to appear in a matter; to come to the front.

分 頭² 探 索 to search in every direction.

⁹⁵分 頭² 逃 散 to flee in every direction.

分 頭² 追 捕 to pursue in all directions.

到 頭 come to a head; come to the crisis.

千 頭 萬 緒 all issues.

包 頭² a fillet or headband.

¹⁰⁰回 頭² to turn the head; later on.

埋 頭² to bow the head.

宿 頭² a place to rest the head at night—an inn.

市 頭² the market-place.

拏 頭² something to take hold of—an opportunity.

¹⁰⁵收 頭² to come to an end.

昂 頭² to raise the head.

無 想 (or 望)·頭 without hope.

無 頭 公 案 a charge against a person or persons unknown.

牀 頭² the head of a bed.

¹¹⁰碼 頭² a wharf; a landing-place.

說·頭 something to talk about.

開 頭² the beginning of a matter.

點 頭² to nod the head.

投² To throw at or into. To jump into. To cast, as a vote.
6490

投 劾 to give up an official position.

投 井 to drown oneself in a well; to throw into a well.

投 入 to plunge into.

投 命 to throw away one's life.

⁵投 壺 ancient game of pitching arrows into a pot—the loser had to drink a forfeit.

投·在 海·裏 to jump into the sea; to be cast into the sea.

投·子 dice. (S. dial.)

投 擲 to throw away; to reject.

投 杼 to throw down the shuttle—and cease weaving.

¹⁰投 棄 to reject; to throw away.

投 水 to throw into the water; to jump into the water.

投 河 or 跳 河 to throw into a river; to drown oneself in the river.

投 火 to throw into the fire; to jump into the fire.

投 灰 於 道 to throw rubbish on the roads.

¹⁵投 炸 彈 to throw a bomb.

投 石 問 路 to drop a stone to ascertain whether anyone is about—done by thieves.

投 石 打 狗 to throw a stone at a dog.

若 卵 投 石 like an egg thrown at a rock—hopelessly ruined.

投 礫 to fling pebbles.

²⁰投 票 to cast a vote; to ballot.

無 記 名 投 票 to ballot.

秘 密 投 票 secret ballot.

投 票 人 a voter.

投 票 多 數 majority vote.

²⁵投 票 所 polling place.

投 票 檢 查 人 scrutineers.

投 票 櫃 (or 箱) ballot-box.

投 票 權 the franchise; right to vote.

投 票 法 laws governing voting.

³⁰投票紙 ballot-paper.
投票表決 to decide by ballot.
投票選舉 to elect by ballot.
投竿 a fishing-rod.
投竿釋褐 to throw away the fishing-rod and cast off one's rough garments—to become an official.
³⁵投筆從戎 to throw away the pen and follow the battle—to give up literature for a military career.
投綸 to cast a line—when angling.
投繯 to hang oneself.
投羅 to fall into a snare.
投翰 to throw down the pen.
⁴⁰投艱 to have heavy responsibility thrown upon one.
投袂 to flick the sleeves—in anger.
投鑰 to put the key in the lock—shut the doors and refuse admittance.
投鞭斷流 if they throw their whips into the river, they would be sufficient to stem its flow—speaking of his numerous forces.
投鼠忌器 to throw at a rat and fear for the vase—afraid to impeach a corrupt statesman for fear of involving the prince.
⁴⁵自投網羅 fell into his own snare.

(a) To present. To hand over to.

投交 to take to; to give over to.
投供 to present one's credentials.
投函 correspondence—as in the newspapers.
投剌 to send in one's card.
⁵投報 to send in a report; to make an application; to report—for payment of duty; to recompense.
投帖 to send in one's card.
投收 to hand over to; to take to.
投文書 to hand in a despatch.
投明 to lay before an official.
¹⁰投桃報李 to get a peach and send a plum—to return present for present.
投標 to tender for a contract.
投知 to notify.
投稟 to present a petition.
投稅 to pay duty or a legal fee.
¹⁵投稿 a contributed article; to send

in an article—to a newspaper, etc.
投繳 to deliver up; to hand over to.
投親 to visit one's relatives.
投詞 to present a statement or plaint.
投謁 to present when visiting—as letters of introduction.
²⁰投資 to subscribe capital; to invest.
投資塲 field for investment.
投資事業 investment interests.
投·進·去 to send in—as a card.
投遞 to take to; to hand over to.
²⁵投順 to tender allegiance.
投首 to lay an accusation.

(b) To fit in with; to join. To submit to. To offer oneself to.

投交甚契 their intimacy was very close.
投允 to offer one's services to.
投其所好 to play the sycophant; to agree to whatever another is pleased with.
投分 friendly; on good terms.
⁵投到 to surrender oneself to.
投効 to offer one's services.
投契 friendly feeling; mutual attraction.
投懷 in harmony with feelings.
投機 to agree in opinion; to see the point; to get the clue; to speculate.
¹⁰投機事業 speculative business.
投機份子 an opportunist.
投機取巧者 an opportunist.
投機失敗 failure in speculation.
投機家 speculators; opportunists.
¹⁵話不投機半句多 half a sentence of irrelevant talk is too much.
投緣 pleased with; suited to each other; fitting.
投託 placed in the care of another.
投誠 to return to allegiance.
投身 to give oneself to, as a servant.
²⁰投軍 to enlist; to enter the army.
投降 (hsiang²) to surrender; to submit.
無條件投降 unconditional surrender.
投降媚外·的態度 the attitude of surrender to, and fawning upon foreigners.

自投 to give oneself up.

(c) To go in the direction of.

投下處 to seek a lodging.
投奔 to hurry up; to abscond; to fly to for refuge.
投奔救主 fly to the Saviour.
投宿 to seek a lodging; to go to an inn.
⁵投審 to appear before a court.
投店 to seek a lodging.
投案 to appear before a court.
投止 to take refuge—from impending peril.
投穴 to return to their dens—as wild beasts.
¹⁰投老 to retire on account of old age.
投荒 to flee to distant places.
投行 to repair to.
投西 going westwards.
投訊 to go before a court.
¹⁵投門 to go into a house; to get the good offices of a person.
投門·路 to find an opening—for employment, etc.

(d) To project.

投出 to project.
投射 projection; incidence.
投射光線 rays of incidence.
投射器 projector.
⁵投射物 a projectile—thrown by hand.
投射角 angle of incidence.
投射電燈 electric projector.
圓錐投射 conical projection.
等角投射 isometric projection.
¹⁰配景投射 perspective projection.
投影 projection.
投生 rebirth into another state of existence.
投胎 to quicken; to be reborn into another state of existence.

骰² Dice.　Also read *shai³*, or *ku³*.
6491

骰·子 dice.(*S. dial.*)
骰·子筒 a dice-box.
擲 (or 耍) 骰·子 to throw dice.

音⁴　**To spit out.**
6492

透[4] To pass through; to penetrate. To understand. Transparent. Thoroughly; fully.
6493

透·了 penetrated; thoroughly.
透亮 to be transparent.
透信 to convey news; fully believing.
透光 transparent.
[5] 不透光 opaque.
透光性 transparent nature; transparent.
透光鏡 lenses.
透光體 transparent bodies.
透化人心 to make a thorough reformation of the hearts of men.
[10] 透味 well-flavoured; appetizing.
透地說 to make a clean breast of a thing.
透家子[3] a shrewd fellow.
透寒 penetrating cold; chilled to the bone.
透射力 powers of penetration—of certain rays.
[15] 透度 degree of transparency.
透徹 thoroughly.
透心涼 chilled through.
透性 permeability.
透情講 to tell one's inmost feelings; to make a clean breast of it.
[20] 透支 to overdraw.

透明 to penetrate; transparent.
半透明 translucent.
透明質 transparent substances; of a transparent nature.
透明體 transparent bodies.
[25] 透氣 to let the air in or out; pervious—as an ill-fitting cork or cover.
透汗 a very heavy perspiration.
透消息 to convey news.
透漏 to divulge.
透濕 wet through.
[30] 透畫 a transparency—as used on windows, etc.
透芽 to put forth shoots.
透視力 clairvoyance.
透觀 clairvoyance.
透說 to explain matters.
[35] 透識 to be thoroughly acquainted with.
透越 to pass through.
透身 the entire person; the whole body.
透過 to pass through; to penetrate.
↑透視 perspective.

透重的病 very serious illness.
[40]透鏡 lenses.
凹面透鏡 concave lens.
凸面透鏡 convex lens.
收斂透鏡 converging lens.
消色透鏡 achromatic lens.
[45]發散透鏡 diverging lens.
透關 to see through; to expose fallacies, etc; pungent.[to rain.
透雨 a penetrating rain; pervious
透露 to leak out; to reveal; to divulge.
透頂 penetrated to the head—when venereal disease appears in the head; also used of anything that comes to the surface, or leaks out.
[50]透風 to let the wind through; a through current—of air.
密不透風 kept very secret.
透骨 to penetrate to the bones.
壞透·了 utterly bad; utterly ruined.
浸透 soaked through.
[55]測不透 cannot fathom it.
熟透 thoroughly ripe.
看透 to see through—a person, etc.
飢透食有味 when one is extremely hungry any food has a fine flavour.
For TS- see p. 912 ff.

TU.　(ㄉㄨ)

稌[3] Ancient term for glutinous rice. Also read t'u[2].
6494

杜[4] To shut out; to restrict; to impede; to stop; to prevent.
6495

杜口 to silence.
杜弊 to put an end to corrupt practices.
杜撰 to restrict; to impose upon. See below—A. 1.
杜漸防微 to nip the matter in the bud.
[5]杜私運 to stop secret traffic or smuggling.
杜絕 to suspend intercourse with; to cut off.
杜絕文契 or 杜絕官契 a deed of irrevocable sale or transfer.
杜釁端 to remove causes of strife.

杜賣 to sell out and out; an irrevocable sale.
[10]杜門不出 to shut the door and not go out.
杜門謝客 to refuse to see visitors.

(a) To fabricate; to trump up.

杜撰 not according to the rules of prosody; not classical; fictitious; trumped up. See above—3.
杜造 fabrication; forgery; trumped up.

(b) The russet pear. Also used for other plants.

杜仲 a tree, the bark of which is used in medicine—Eucommia ulmoides.
杜梨 or 甘棠 a pear-tree which bears small fruit—Pyrus betulœfolia.
杜·鵑 or 杜宇 the cuckoo; the goatsucker or nightjar.
杜鵑花 the red azalea.
白杜鵑 the white azalea.

(c) Locally produced.

杜布 coarse cotton cloth produced by local mills.
杜米 locally-grown rice.

肚[3,4] The stomach; the belly.
6496

肚內有火 to be bilious.
肚·子 the belly; the entrails.
肚·子疼 or 肚痛 to have a belly-ache.
肚帶 girths.
[5]肚皮 the skin of the abdomen; the abdomen.
肚脾 the stomach.
肚臍 the viscera.
肚脹 dropsy; swelling of the abdomen.
肚腹 the abdomen; the bowels.
[10]肚腹軟 indigestion; heart-burn.
肚腸·子 the viscera.
肚臍 the navel.
肚袋獸 marsupials.
肚·裏明·白 of clear perception; intelligent.
[15]肚量大 liberal-minded; forbearing; magnanimous.
肚飽 a full stomach.

一 肚·子 火 (or 氣) full of anger.
小 肚 the pubic region.
有 肚·子 pregnant.
20 瀉 肚·子 or 走 肚·子 to have diarrhoea.

堵[3] **To stop up; to block up; to shut off. To guard; to**
6497 **invest.**

堵·住 to block up; to stop.
堵 勦 to obstruct and scatter—as rebels.
堵 口 to gag; to stop the mouth.
堵 塞 to stop up; to close against.
5 堵 截 to guard; to cut off approach to.
堵 死 to suffocate to death.
堵 禦 to ward off; to guard against.
堵·著 耳 to stop the ears.
巡 堵 to patrol and guard—against an army.

(a) **A wall fifty cubits in length.**

堵 牆 a wall.
環 堵 surrounding walls.

(b) **Also read** *chê*[2]. **Name of a district.**

覩
睹[3]   **To observe; to gaze at.**
6498

覩 此 情 形 in view of these circumstances.
覩 而 不 見 to gaze at without seeing.
目 所 未 覩 what the eye has not seen.

賭[3] **To gamble; to bet; to**
6499 **stake; to risk.**

賭 假 咒 to take a false oath.
賭 債 gambling-debts.
賭 具 things used in gambling, as cards, dice, etc.
賭 勝 to try one's luck.
5 賭 博 to gamble for money.
賭 博 場 a gaming-house.
賭 命 to risk one's life.
賭 咒 to take an oath; to vow.
賭 客 a gambler.

10 賭 局 a gaming-house.
賭 彩 to try for a prize.
賭 很 to fight without weapons.
賭 押 賬 a pledge for a gambling-debt.
賭 攤 gambling-booths.
15 賭 東·道 or 賭 東 東 to bet on something for which the loser has to pay a forfeit—as a dinner, etc.
賭 棍 a gambler. A.c. 賭徒
賭 氣 to get in a rage and insist on doing something regardless of the consequences; for spite.
賭 當[4] 頭 a pledge for a gambling-debt.
賭 眼 力 to decide the relative merits of various things.
20 賭 約 a wager.
賭 館 a gaming-house.
賭 誓 to take an oath.
賭 賬 gambling-debts; debts of honour.
賭 賽 to compete.
25 賭 輸 to lose in gambling.
賭 近 盜 gambling is akin to robbery.
賭 錢 to gamble for money.
賭 鬼 an inveterate gambler.

都[1] **The metropolis. A sub-**
6500 **division of a 縣 district.**

都 下 or 都 中 the capital; Peking.
都 事 an assistant secretary.
都 司 or 都 府 a captain in the Chinese army; a commander in the navy. (*obs*·).
都 城 the capital.
5 都 察 院 or 都 憲 or 都 老 爺 the former Court of Censors at Peking. Censors. (*old*)
都 尉 a title of the 6th and 7th orders of nobility.
都 會 a city or town.
都 督 or 都 統 military-governor of a province.
都 鄙 有 章 there were regulations for the government of cities.
10 都 門 the capital. Peking.
上 都 i.e., Xanadu, the residence of Kublai Khan near the present Jehol.
天 都 Paradise.
建 都 to establish a city as the capital.

東 都 a name for Loyang or Honanfu in ancient times.
15 遷 都 to make another city the capital.
酆 都 城 Hades—the city of the dead or of ghosts; a city in Szechwan near to which is said to be the entrance to the infernal regions.
陪 都 a subordinate capital.

(a) **All. The whole. Every one. Abundant, full. Also read** *tou*[1].

都 來·了 they have all arrived.
都 收 到·了 all received.
都 是 一 樣 all are alike.
都 有 have them all.
大 都 on the whole; for the most part.
大 都 如 是 on the whole they are so.

(b) **Elegant; refined. Beauty; excellence. An exclamation of admiration.**

都 雅 well-bred.
洵 美 且 都 very beautiful and excellent—of a woman.
衣 服 麗 都 elegant and beautiful garments.

嘟[1]   **To mutter and grumble.**
6501

嘟·嚕 (or 嚕) to swear; to mutter.
嘟 囔 to scold; to mutter.

(a) **A bunch or cluster, for which the preceding character is sometimes used.**

嘟·嚕 a bunch—as of grapes.

闍[1] **The tower over a city-**
   gate. Also read *shê*[2]. **Used**
6502 **in Buddhist transliterations.**

闍 棃 or 阿 闍 棃 a pastor; a Buddhist priest—Sanskrit:— *āchārya*.
闍 維 or 闍 毗 or 茶 毗 or 闍 鼻 多 cremation of Buddhist priests, from *djapita*, burnt.

妬
妒[4]   Jealous; envious.
   Distinguish 娔 No. 3422.
6503

妒·婦 a jealous woman.
妒 心 a jealous mind.
妒·忌 envy; jealousy.
妒 賢 嫉 能 envious of the worthy and able.
因 妒 損 身 to fret oneself with envy.

度[4] A rule; a law. A limit; a measure. An interval in music. A degree, as in geography, astronomy, etc.
6504

度 外 beyond the estimate.
度 弧 器 spherometer.
度 標 準 standard.
度·數 certain times, periods or distances; number of degrees of latitude or longitude, etc.
[5]度 曲 to keep time in playing.
度 法 superficial measure.
度·量 (liang[4]) measure; capacity; view; judgement; considera- tion. See below—B. 6.
度·量 大 broad-minded.
度·量 狹 sordid; petty-minded.
[10]度·量 衡 length, capacity, and weight.
中 度 the happy mean.
制·度 system; regime; institution.
四 度·的 世 界 a world of four dimensions.
失 度 out of proportion.
[15]密 度 density.
尺 度 linear measure.
局 度 capacity; views; demean- our; bearings.
強 度 intensity.
氣 度 manner and bearing; de- meanour.
[20]法 度 laws and statutes.
溫 度 temperature.
無 度 reckless; unrestrained; without limit.
程·度 standard; pitch; grade; degree of attainments or quali- fication.
第 四 度 the fourth dimension.
[25]節 度 economy. See No. 795— A. 2.
角 度 angular measure.
過 度 excessive; beyond measure; intemperate; extravagant.
風 度 bearing and manner, etc.

(a) To pass; to cross over. Inter. next.
度 世 法 Buddhist way of salva- tion.

度 亡 to save the lost from hell.
度 卒 to die.
度 命 to live; to make a living.
[5]度 日 to pass the day; to make a living.
度 牒 diploma of a Buddhist priest.
度 衆 生 to save all living creatures.
度 脫 to deliver from human form.
度 覓 to search for.
白 度 光 陰 to lead a useless life.

(b) Read to[4.5]. To calculate; to estimate; to guess.

度 不 可 奈 何 he thought that there was no help for it.
度 其 時 可 矣 he reckoned that there would be sufficient time.
度 必 禍 己 he reckoned that there would be trouble for him- self.
度 支 to estimate expenditure.(to[4]-)
[5]度 支 部 Board of Revenue and Finance. (old) (to[4]-)
度 量 (liang[4]) consider; to mea- sure.
以 己 度 人 to measure others by oneself.
揣 情 度 理 to weigh the pros and cons; to take all things into consideration.

渡[4] A ferry. To ferry over; to cross over.
6505 Inter. preceding—A.

渡 化 人 to make a convert—to Buddhism.
渡 口 a ford.
渡 夫 or 渡 人 a ferryman.
渡 江 or 渡 河 to cross a river.
[5]渡 法 means to an end.
渡 淺 to ford shallows.
渡 生 to go through life.
渡 船 a ferry-boat.
渡 過 海 to cross the sea.
[10]渡 頭 or 擺·渡 a ferry.
喚 渡 to hail the ferryman.
引 渡 罪 犯 to hand over a prisoner.(Jap.)
競 渡 to race boats.
過 渡 transition. See No. 3730- 64ff.

鍍[4] To gild; to plate.
6506

鍍 一 層 金 washed once with gold.
鍍 金 to plate with gold; to gild.
鍍 金 作 a gilder's shop.
鍍 金 面 gilt.
[5]鍍 銀 to plate with silver.
鍍 首·飾 gilt head-ornaments.
電 鍍 electro-plating.
電 鍍 品 electro-plated goods.

蠧[4] Grubs in wood; worms in books, clothes, etc. Used figuratively of corrupt of- ficials.
6507

蠧 吏 or 蠧 役 or 蠧 差 rapacious underlings.
蠧 國 害 民 to prey upon one's country and injure the people.
蠧 毛 蟲 hairy caterpillars.
蠧 魚 worms in books; silver-fish; "a book-worm."
蠧 蝕 主 義 rapacious schemes— preying on the people.
生 蠧 to breed weevils, etc.

TU.   (ㄉ)
(Tuh)

督[1.5] To oversee; to superin- tend; to direct. To reprove. A Viceroy or Governor- General.
6508

督 人 作 工 to act as overseer of work.
督 促 to enforce.
督 催 to urge on; to keep a per- son up to the mark.
督 催 所 office for the payment of grain-taxes.
[5]督 兵 to lead troops.
督 勸 to admonish.
督 同 to act as leader; to direct; to lead; to conduct.
督 堂 a Viceroy; Governor- General.
督 字 despatch from a Governor- General.
[10]督 學 局 a Provincial Department of Education.
督 官 an overseer.
督 宰 ministers; high officials.
督 工 人 to superintend labourers.
督 帥 to lead troops.
[15]督 帶 to direct; to lead; to act as leader.

督憲 or 總·督 or 總·督部堂 a Governor-General or Viceroy. (*obs.*).

督戰 to lead in battle.

督撫 Governor-General and Governor.

督撫司道 the former high Provincial authorities—Viceroy, Governor, Treasurer, Judge, Salt-Commissioner, and Intendant of Grain.

20 督撫大院 the highest officials. (*obs.*).

督斥 to reprove.

督會 presbytery.

督查 to oversee; to manage; to direct; to superintend.

督牽 to act as leader; to lead; to conduct; to direct.

25 督理 to manage; to direct; a military superintendent.

督管 an overseer.

督糧道 an Intendant of Grain.

督臣 Your minister the Governor-General.

督責 to reprove; to restrain; to admonish.

30 督軍 *Tuchun*, a military Governor of a Province.

督軍團 the *Tuchunate*.

督辦 to control; to manage; Commissioner.

督過 to reprove faults.

督陣 to lead troops.

35 督飭 to take part with one's subordinates in....

監·督 to oversee; to superintend; an overseer; a director.

(a) The centre. The middle seam in the back of a coat.

緣督以爲經 pursue a middle course.

毒 2.5. Poison. Poisonous; cruel; evil; hurtful. Malicious;
6509 malevolent.

毒刺 a sting, as of wasps, bees, etc.

毒劑 poisonous drugs.

毒口 a spiteful tongue.

毒害 to injure dangerously.

5 毒害人心 to poison the minds of the people.

毒心 malicious; cruel; spiteful.

毒恨 to hate; to abominate.

毒手 a malicious person.

毒打 a cruel beating.

10 毒日 a fierce sun.

毒月 a name for the fifth lunar month.

毒根 a root of bitterness.

毒·死人 or 毒斃 to poison a person.

毒氣 poison; virus; miasma.

15 毒氣彈 poison-gas bombs.

毒牙 poison-fangs, as of a snake.

毒物 poison; venom.

毒瘡 an ulcer.

毒癘 poisonous miasma.

20 毒箭 poisoned arrows.

毒腺 poison-glands.

毒藥 poisons.

毒虐 malicious and cruelly over-bearing.

毒蛇 or 毒虺 a poisonous snake.

25 毒蟲 poisonous insects, reptiles, etc.

毒言 malicious, harmful words.

毒計 a malicious proposal or scheme.

毒質 poisonous.

毒鈎 a fang; a sting.

30 毒霉 poisonous mildew.

中⁴毒 to take poison accidentally.

中⁴魚毒 to be poisoned with fish.

以毒攻毒 to attack one poison with another.

便毒 venereal ulcers.

35 惡毒 cruel; brutal.

服毒 to take poison intentionally.

消毒 to counteract poison; sterilize.

流毒 baneful influences.

置毒 to envenom; to place poison, as in water, food, etc.

40 腐化毒 ptomaine poisoning.

解毒 to counteract poison.

解毒藥 antidotes.

邪毒 heresies; evil ways; moral poison.

鴆毒 deadly poison.

碡 2.5. A stone roller.
6510

纛 2.5. A banner; a streamer. Also read *tao*⁴.
6511

祭纛 to sacrifice to the flag.

獨 2.5. Only; single; alone; solitary.
6512

獨一不死 he alone is immortal.

獨一無二 the only (God).

獨一眞神 the only true God.

獨享利權 individual privileges.

5 獨人 a solitary or single person; an egotistical person.

獨任制 system of single authority, as that of a magistrate, administration, etc.

獨任推事 a magistrate with sole authority.

獨何與 how is an exception to be made?

獨出乎衆 standing alone, above all.

10 獨出心裁 ingenious; original.

獨力 individual effort.

獨只 merely; simply.

獨占 monopoly; to monopolize.

獨占事業 monopolies; corporations.

15 獨占鰲頭² perched alone on the Leviathan's head—first at the final *Hanlin* examination.

獨唱 to sing a solo.

獨善其身 attended to their own virtue in solitude.

獨在一處 alone in a place.

獨坐 to sit alone.

20 獨夫 the lone man—an evil ruler who is deserted by all.

獨奏 a solo performance.

獨子³留養 only this son left to nourish—his parents.

獨孤臣孼子³ a friendless minister and concubine's son.

獨學 to study alone, without companions.

25 獨害 selfish; egotistical.

獨家經理人 sole agents.

獨居 to dwell alone.

獨峯駝 a dromedary.

獨弦哀歌 to chant a melancholy song while strumming on a single string—"to play in a key to which nobody can sing so as to spread his reputation abroad."

30 獨往獨來·的精·神 a free and independent spirit.

獨房 to have a room to oneself.

獨持異議 to maintain an independent attitude—to stand alone on a debated question.

獨斷 to dogmatize; dogmatism.

獨斷之意·見 dogma.

35 獨斷之辭 dogmatic expressions.

獨斷獨行 to come to a decision and act on one's own responsibility.

獨斷論 dogmatism.

獨有 sole; unequalled; by itself.
[40]獨木不成林 one tree does not make a forest—it cannot be done single-handed.
獨木橋 a single-plank bridge.
獨木舟 a dug-out canoe.
獨木難支 a single stick cannot prop it up—individual effort cannot sustain it.
獨木難行 a bridge consisting of a single plank is not easy to cross.
[45]獨柴難燒獨子[3]難敎 a single stick is difficult to burn; an only son is not easy to train.
獨樂 to find pleasure alone.(-le[4])
獨樹 a solitary tree.
獨樹一幟 or 獨出心裁 to set up a separate flag; to take one's own course.
獨步 going on alone; to be without a rival.
[50]獨清獨醒 I alone am pure, I alone am sober.
獨特·的發明 unique discovery.
獨獨·的 only...; none but...; alone.
獨生子[3] the Only-begotten Son.
獨當[1]一面 able to undertake the sole responsibility for one matter.
[55]獨異 a peculiarity.
獨立 to stand alone; independent.
獨立不移 standing alone unmoved.
獨立不羈 independence—of spirit, etc.
獨立之價值 an independent value.
[60]獨立命·令 independent orders, as issued by a ruler or administrator, independent of parliament, etc.
獨立國 an independent nation.
獨立存在 independent existence.
獨立工黨 Independent Labour Party.
獨立性質 an independent nature.
[65]獨立思想 independent thought.
獨立敎派 independent sects; Congregationalists.
獨立權利 independent rights.
獨立精·神 a spirit of independence.

獨立紀念日 Independence Day.
[70]獨立自治 independent and self-governing.
獨立謀生活 to seek an independent livelihood.
獨立財產 independent income.
各敎會獨立主義 Independency or Congregationalism.
宣佈獨立 to declare independence.
[75]獨脚[3]戲 a play with one actor—also used fig., of undertaking the whole responsibility.
獨自 by oneself.
獨自得盡 to obtain for one's sole use.
獨自擅 to set up for oneself—as a professional.
獨處[3] to live alone.
[80]獨行 independent actions—of one who does not slavishly follow customs or fashions.
獨行 (hang[2]) a firm which has a monopoly.
獨裁 dictatorial; arbitrary.
獨裁政治 autocracy.
獨裁政體 absolute dictatorship.
[85]獨見 one's own opinion.
獨覺其進 (the Sage) alone was aware of his progress.
獨角 a unicorn.
獨語 soliloquy. A.c.獨白.
獨身 alone; single-handed; celibacy.
[90]獨門 to dwell alone.
獨院 a small independent house.
獨霸一方 usurped authority in the whole neighbourhood.
獨馬小車 a light chariot drawn by a single horse.
獨鹿 a whirlwind; a snare or trap.
[95]不獨 not only.
單獨 only; single-handed.
孤獨 orphaned; friendless.
故君子懷其獨也 therefore the superior man is watchful of himself when alone.

(a) A particle of emphasis, used to strengthen an interrogative.

汝獨不知 do you not know that...?
奚獨後予 "why does he make us alone the last?"

(b) Meditative. Lost in thought.

獨若不聞 as if he had not heard.

獨遊 to roam about lost in contemplation.

(c) A kind of baboon.

髑 [2.5.] The bones on the top of the head; a skull.
6513

髑髏 a skull.

篤 [3.5.] True; genuine; magnanimous; sincere; generous.
6514 To attach importance to; to respect.

篤信 to believe truly.
篤信之效 an outcome of strong faith.
篤厚 honest; straightforward.
篤學 diligent in study.
[5]篤守 to guard carefully; to give careful attention to.
篤宗族以昭雍睦 give due weight to kinship with a view to the display of concord.
篤實 sincere; real.
篤志力行 earnest resolutions and strength to carry them out.
篤性 a magnanimous disposition.
[10]篤恭 sincerely respectful.
篤愛 warm-hearted affection.
篤敦友誼 to consolidate amicable relations.
篤於親 faithful to relatives.
篤行不倦 to work sedulously without weariness.
[15]篤誠 sincere.
碩大且篤 is large and generous.

(a) Serious, as an illness. Very. Largely.

篤疾 or 病篤 a dangerous illness.
篤老 very old.
危篤 very dangerous—illness.

(b) Specially favoured by Heaven.

篤生武王 she was blessed in giving birth to Wu Wang.
篤降若人 was incarnated—speaking of 上天.

瀆 [2.5.] To be rude to; to annoy; to profane. To trouble; to harass.
6515 u.f. 瀆 No. 6518.

瀆犯聖境 to commit sacrilege.

瀆聽 or 瀆聰 to importune one to listen—to certain representations, etc.

冒瀆 to annoy with petitions, etc.

褻瀆 to blaspheme; to annoy by one's persistence.

圓櫝 2.5. A casket; a case; a sheath; a coffin; a box.
6516

殰 2.5. An abortion. Stillborn.
6517

瀆 2.5. A ditch; a sluice; a drain; a river. Correct form of 瀆 No. 6515.
6518

四瀆 the four great rivers of China, i.e., the Yangtze 江, the Yellow River 河, the River Huai 淮, and the River Chi or Tsi 濟.

犢 2.5. A calf; a victim for sacrifice.
6519

犢不畏虎 the calf does not fear the tiger—ignorant and foolish.

舐犢之愛 the love of the cow for its calf, shown by licking it—parental love.

牘 2.5. Boards or writing tablets; documents; books; archives; registers.
6520

公牘 official documents.

尺牘 a letter—a letter-writer.

案牘 records; archives.

讀 2.5. To study; to read.
6521

讀·不起書 unable to afford an education.

讀·出病·來 he studied till he became ill.

讀夜書 to study by night.

讀報慾 a passion for reading the newspapers.

5 讀完·了 to have finished reading.

讀書 or 念書 to study; study.

讀書五車 has read cartloads of books—a profound student.

讀書人 or 念書人 a scholar; the literati.

讀書治愚 the study of books will cure ignorance.

10 讀本 a reader—for schools.

讀祭文 to read sacrificial prayers.

讀禮 reading the ritual—a notice put at the door when mourning for parents.

讀稿 to read proofs.

讀者 he who reads this—the reader.

15 讀賦 to recite irregular metres.

讀音統一 unification of the spoken language.

夜讀 to study by night.

對讀 to read and compare.

默讀 to read silently.

(a) Read *tou*[4]. A clause. A sentence.

點清句讀 punctuate the clauses distinctly.

讟 2.5. To slander; to murmur.
6522

黷 2.5. To blacken; to dirty; to insult. Black; soiled.
6523

黷濁 dirty; defiled.

狎黷 to take liberties with; to insult.

(a) Constantly.

黷武 soldiers disposed for war; excessive use of soldiers to prolong warfare.

T'U.　　　(ㄊㄨ)

涂 2 Name of certain rivers in Shansi, Shantung, and Szechwan. Inter. next and 途 No. 6527.
6524

塗 2 To smear; to daub. To erase; to blot out. Mud, mire.
6525

塗之 erase it.

塗乙 to blot out wrong characters, and make a note where there are omissions, 乙 being used for a caret.

塗塵 mire and dust—the world.

塗抹 to erase; obliteration.

5 塗改 to alter; to blot out.

塗改形蹟 to cover up traces—of crime.

塗改添注 to erase errors and add omissions—to revise.

塗毒人民 to oppress the people—by taxes, etc.

塗汚 to daub or smear; to besmirch.

10 塗泥 soft and miry; to plaster a wall with mud.

塗漆 to varnish; to lacquer.

塗澤 to paint and powder the face.

塗炭生靈 to oppress the masses.

坐於塗炭 (as if he) sat amid mud and coals—in his official robes, disgracing himself.

15 民墜塗炭 the people were fallen amid mire and coals—they were in great distress.

生民塗炭 the people suffered great misery.

塗牆 to plaster a wall.

塗畫·的 artists; painters.

塗竄 to alter; to blot out.

20 塗粉 to powder the face.

塗脂抹粉 to rouge and powder.

塗膏 to make up the face.

塗銷 to cancel; to erase; to strike out.

塗銷作廢 cancelled and regarded as waste paper.

25 塗面 to daub the face; to make up the face.

塗飾 to plaster in colours.

塗鴉 to write badly; to scribble.

一敗塗地 utter loss; complete failure and defeat.

如塗塗附 like adding mire to one already down in the mud—fig.

30 糊塗 stupid; muddled; blundering; blockhead.

(a) A road. Inter 途 No. 6527.

塗之人 the man in the street.

塗有餓莩 there are people dying from famine on the roads.

塗說 to tell what one has heard on the roads.

五塗 the Imperial highways; the world.

遇諸塗 met him on the road.

(b) Read *ch'a*[2]. u.f. 搽 No. 102. To smear, etc.

塗 藥 to smear on ointment.

荼[2] A bitter edible plant; the sow-thistle.
6526 Distinguish 茶 No. 101.

荼 毒 bitter and poisonous; calamities; sorrows.
　　寧 爲 荼 毒 finding enjoyment in bitter, poisonous ways.
　　弗 忍 荼 毒 unable to endure the bitterness and poison.
荼 炭 the distress of the masses. *See* 塗 No. 6525-13.
荼 苦 affliction.
荼 草 a bitter grass.

(a) A flowering rush.

有 女 如 荼 there were girls like flowering rushes.
予 所 将 荼 (through) the rushes which I gathered—said of a bird building its nest; its beak was sore through gathering the materials.

(b) A kind of smartweed.

以 薅 荼 蓼 clearing away the smartweed on the dry land and on the wet.

(c) Anciently used for 茶 No. 101. The tea-plant.

苦 荼 ancient name for the tea-plant.

(d) Also read *shu*[1]. Name of a god.

荼 與 or 神 荼 the elder of two brothers, of whom the younger was called 鬱 壘 Yü Lü; they were renowned for their power over evil spirits which they caught, bound with rushes and threw to tigers. Their effigies or their names written on squares of paper are pasted on the entrance-doors as door-gods.

(e) u.f. 舒 No. 5856. A jade tablet.

諸 侯 荼 上 圓 下 方 feudal lords had the *shu*; it was round

at the top and square at the base.

途[2] A road; a path; a journey. A career; a pursuit.
6527 Inter. 塗 No. 6525.

途 中 on the roads.
途 人 a traveller; a stranger.
途 次 a stage; a halting-place.
途 程 a road; a journey.
[5]途 路 a road; a journey.
途 間 on the road. ⌈Cf. 919.62.
前 途 the road ahead—the future.
前 途 多 荊 棘 there is a thorny path ahead.
半 途 而 廢 to give up when only half-way.
[10]命 途 one's fate.
宦 途 official career.
殊 途 同 歸 to return by different roads, all leading to the one end.
沿 途 along the side of the road; along the road.
當 途 or 當 道 to be in an official position. ⌈tance.
[15]長 途 a long journey; long dis-

酴[2]
6528 Leaven; yeast; barm.

屠[2] To butcher; to kill and dress animals.
6529

屠 刀 a butcher's knife.
屠 城 to slaughter the inhabitants of a captured city.
屠 塲 slaughter-house.
屠 夫 or 屠 戶 a butcher.
[5]屠 宰 to slaughter—animals.
屠 宰 稅 tax per head on slaughtered animals.
屠 戮 to slaughter; to slay—as an enemy.
屠 沽 butchers and wine-sellers—degrading employments.
屠 滅 to exterminate.
[10]屠 燒 to massacre and burn.
屠 狗 dog-butcher—used of any degrading employment.
屠 門 大 嚼 to stand before a butcher's shop and masticate v i g o r o u s l y—of one who, ardently desiring the unattainable, sought to solace himself in this manner.

禁 屠 to prohibit the slaughter of animals in times of drought, pestilence, etc., in order to propitiate the gods.

(a) Read *ch'u*[2]. A name.

休 屠 name of a chief of the *Hsiung nu,* father of 金 日 磾.

瘏[2] To be ill.
6530

我 馬 瘏 矣 my horses were disabled.
予 口 卒 瘏 my mouth was quite sore—of a bird after gathering twigs, etc., for its nest.

圖[2] A map; a picture; a diagram; a portrait.
6531

圖 像 a picture; a likeness.
圖 寫 to delineate.
圖 工 drawing, etc.
圖 式 a chart; a plan; an illustration; a fashion-plate.
[5]圖 形 a sketch; a plate; the contour; to draw an outline.
圖·書 a private or personal seal; 圖 書 an illustrated book.
　　打 圖·書 to stamp; to affix a seal.
圖 書 公 司 book-publishing house.
圖 書 館 a library. A.w. 圕.
[10]圖 案 drawings; designs; plans, etc.
圖 樣 a plan; a design.
作 工 圖 樣 working drawings or plans.
側 面 圖 樣 elevations.
內 部 圖 樣 internal view.
[15]分 件 圖 樣 detailed plans.
分 段 圖 樣 sectional plans.
剖 面 圖 樣 sectional plans.
大 略 圖 樣 rough sketch or outline.
平 面 圖 樣 a plan.
[20]打 圖 樣 to draw a plan.
機 械 圖 樣 mechanical drawings.
縮 剖 面 圖 樣 vertical section.
縮 長 面 圖 樣 longitudinal section.
詳 細 圖 樣 detailed plan.

25 豎斷面圖樣 vertical section.

配景圖樣 perspective plan.
圖版 plates—as in a book.
圖畫 to draw pictures; pictures, plans, etc.
圖畫放大器 pantagraph.
30 圖畫釘 drawing pins.
圖窮匕首見 when the map was unrolled, a dagger was revealed. See 窮 No. 1247-39.
圖•章 or 印章 a seal.
圖籍 seals and books.
圖繪 to draw a map, plan, design, etc.
35 圖解 an illustration.
圖解地理 an atlas.
圖解佈道 visual evangelism—the use of pictures, etc., to illustrate the preaching.
圖記 a stamp; a seal; a label; a "chop."
圖說 with plates and description—of an illustrated book; a plan of ground leased, with particulars appended.
40 圖面 a plan.
地圖 a map.
天文圖 map of the stars.
截面圖 section-plans.
斷面圖 section-plans.
草圖 a rough sketch-plan.

(a) To scheme. To plan. To desire.

圖免 to seek to evade—payment of duty.
圖吞 to be avaricious.
圖名利 to scheme for fame and wealth.
圖報 to hope to repay—a kindness.
5 圖強 ambitious; emulation.
圖求 to scheme; to plan.
圖益 from interested motives.
圖維 plans; schemes; plots.
圖需 to seek; to desire.
10 圖詐 to seek to injure another.
圖謀 to plot against; to plan.
圖謀惡計 to plot evil.
圖謀抗拒 to plot obstruction.
圖財 to be avaricious.
15 圖賴 to implicate; to accuse falsely; to repudiate; to incriminate.
圖錢 to plan to make money.
圖飽私囊 planning to fill their own pockets.

遠圖 far-reaching schemes.

(b) A sub-division of a 堡 No. 4947, or a 都 No. 6500.

土 3 Earth; land; soil; ground; territory. Opium. Radical 32.
6532 Distinguish 士 No. 5776.

土作 an undertaker; the work of a navvy.
土偶 an image of earth; a block.
土功 labour spent in reclaiming land—from floods.
土化 fertilization of the soil.
5 土囊 a bag for earth; a large earthen cave.
土國 to do the field work in a State.
土地散漫 the territory is undeveloped.
土地測量局 National Survey Bureau.
土地管轄 territorial control.
10 土地部 Ministry of Lands.
土坯 or 土基 unburnt bricks.
土坡 a bank or slope.
土城 or 土臺 or 土堡 an earthen wall; a rampart.
土塊 a clod of earth.
15 土壤 soil; earth.
土壤細流 trifling things may have their uses.
土山 a mound.
土崩 a cataclysm.
土崩瓦解 a collapse—as of a government; utter disorder; insurrection, etc.
20 土工 sextons; undertakers.
土性 the nature of the soil.
土房 an adobe house.
土星 or 煞星 the planet Saturn.
土曜日 Saturday. (Jap.).
25 土木偶人 a blockhead; a dolt.
土木工 building operations.
土木工程 civil engineering.
土業 landed property.
土毛 the produce of the soil, as cereals, etc.
30 土氣 exhalations of the ground; miasma; vulgar; rustic.
土瀝青 asphaltum; bitumen.
土炕 an adobe bed—used in North China.
土牛木馬 clay oxen and wooden horses—useless.
土狗 the mole-cricket.
35 土狼 aard-wolves.
土撥鼠 Cf. 6451.

土田 land (for general crops) and fields (for rice-growing.)
土稅 opium-tax.
土穴 caverns.
土窖 a cellar.
40 土紅 dull, opaque red.
土股 a peninsular.
土脈 the soil, as suitable for crops, etc.
土腰 an isthmus.
土色 pale, ashen hue.
45 土芥 trifles; unimportant things.
土薄 sterile ground; shallow soil.
土蜂 the ground bee.
土角 a cape or promontory.
土質 the nature of the soil.
50 土金屬 earth metals.
土階 steps built of earth.
土饅頭 earthen loaves of bread —a name for graves.
土雞 the partridge.
土雞瓦狗 clay chickens and pottery dogs—toys; useless.
55 后土 Earth—personified.
國土 territory of a country.
歸土 to return to the earth—to die.
水土 climate. See No. 5922-27 ff.
洋土 or 烟土 opium.
灰土 dust.

(a) Local.

土人 natives; aborigines.
土俗 local customs.
土儀 a present of some local productions.
土兵 local soldiers; militia.
5 土匪 local robbers or bandits.
土司 headman among the aborigines.
土地神 or 土地老兒 or 土地菩•薩 local divinities; the local gods of the soil.
土地誕 birthday of the above on the 2nd of the 2nd lunar month.
土娼 local prostitutes.
10 土宜 products of the locality.
土官 officials governing aboriginal tribes in West China.
土寇 local robbers.
土布 native cotton-cloth.
土惡 local rowdies.
15 土戶 villagers.
土棍 local bullies.
土民 natives; aborigines.
土物 local produce.

土 產 products of a country.
[20] 土 神 local deities.
土 絲 Canton silk; fine raw-silk.
土 老 兒 a country rustic.
土 著 aborigines; native peoples.
土 著 之 種 產 民 物 local productions and native peoples.
[25] 土 話 local dialect; patois.
土 豪 劣 紳 local rascals and oppressive gentry.
土 貨 products of a country.
土 賊 local thieves.
土 霸 local ruffians.
[30] 土 音 local pronunciation; brogue.
土 頭 土 腦 rustic; countrified.
土 風 local customs; local folk-songs.

(b) Used for transliterating.

土 耳 其 Turkey.
土 耳 其 斯 坦 Turkestan.

吐 [3,4.] To spit; to vomit. To disclose.
6533

吐 出·來 to vomit food; to disclose.
吐 出 實 情 to come out with the truth.
吐 劑 emetics.
吐 口 水 to spit.
[5] 吐 哺 to eject a mouthful of food—in order to hasten to his visitors on official business, said of 周 公. See below—8.
吐 唾 沫 to spit. (t'u⁴-t'u⁴-·mo)
吐 屬 不 凡 these are no ordinary (verses).
吐 握 from 吐 哺 握 髮 to eject his mouthful of food, (when at his meals,) twist up his half-washed hair, (if in his bath,) and rush to interview his official visitors without delay—said of 周 公. See above—5.
吐 故 納 新 or 吐 納 之 術 exhaling the old and inhaling the new—to avoid sickness and attain to immortality. Taoist breathing exercises.
[10] 吐 根 emetic root, used for ipecacuanha.
吐 棄 to eject from the mouth; to reject.
吐 氣 to give vent to the feelings.
吐 氣 揚 眉 got over his temper and smoothed out his frown.

吐 瀉 or 上 吐 下 瀉 vomiting and purging.
[15] 吐 痰 to cough up phlegm.
吐 盆 a small spittoon.
吐 穗·子 to head out into ears—as grain.
吐 綬 鷄 or 火 鷄 a turkey.
吐 舌 to put out the tongue.
[20] 吐 花 to blossom.
吐 血 to spit blood.
吐 話 or 吐 語 to disclose; to speak openly.
吐 露 心 腹 to tell forth one's mind.
吐 露 眞 情 to come out with the truth.
嘔 吐 retching and vomiting.

(a) Read t'u⁴. Used in transliterating.

吐 火 羅 or 吐 呼 羅 Tochari.
吐 番 (po¹) Tibetans.
吐 谷 (yü⁴·⁵·) 渾 a branch of the 鮮 卑 tribes, (See No. 2716—A.) which migrated west about A.D. 300 and inhabited the country around 青 海 Koko Nor.
吐 魯 番 Turfan.

兔 [4] A hare; a rabbit. Distinguish 免 No. 4492.
6534

兔 死 狐 悲 when the hare dies the fox is sad—sympathy with one of its kind.
兔 穴 a rabbit warren.
兔 缺 hare-lipped.
兔 脫 (to run like) an escaping hare.
[5] 兔 起 鶻 落 as soon as the hare rises the falcon swoops—of rapid action.
兔 穎 or 兔 毫 a rabbit's hair—fine writing-brush.
家 兔·子 rabbits.
山 兔 or 野 兔 hares.
玉 兔 or 兔 兒 爺 a hare which is supposed to dwell in the moon and assist in preparing the elixir of immortality; it is worshipped on the 15th of the 8th lunar month.
跳 兔 the Siberian jerboa.

菟 [4]
6535
Dodder.

菟 絲 or 兔 絲 dodder.
菟 葵 sea-anemone; a kind of mallow.

徒 辻 [2] A follower; a disciple. A crowd. Distinguish 徙 No. 2468; and 從 No. 6919.
6536

徒 伴 pupils and followers.
徒·弟 a disciple; an apprentice.
徒 衆 the people.
匪 徒 bandits; robbers.
[5] 奸 徒 a rogue.
敎 徒 Christian converts; religious disciples.
無 賴 之 徒 a bad scamp; a vagabond rascal.
賭 徒 a gambler.
門 徒 pupils; disciples.

(a) To go on foot; a foot-soldier.

徒 兵 infantry.
徒 卒 infantry.
徒 杠 成 the foot-bridges were finished.
徒 步 to go on foot.
徒 行 to go on foot.
徒 跣 barefooted.

(b) A degree of banishment.

徒 役 penal servitude.
徒 罪 banishment—to another part of the same province for a term not exceeding three years.
問 徒 to condemn to penal servitude.

(c) Only; merely. In vain. Empty; bare.

徒 勞 to labour in vain.
徒 勞 無 功 to labour without success; vain efforts.
徒 勞 無 益 to toil in vain.
徒 取 炫 目 vainly sought to dazzle.
[5] 徒 多 爲 人 所 憎 惡 (wu⁴) 爾 often to make oneself odious for nothing.
徒 手 empty-handed; unarmed.
徒 手 致 富 to become rich without effort.
徒 有 皮 毛 merely on the surface.

徒然 or 徒事 or 徒徒·的 in vain.
¹⁰徒爾 simply; merely.
徒知食 he only thought of his emolument.
徒費 futile; in vain.
徒餔啜 merely for food and drink.
徒首 futile; in vain.
¹⁵非徒無益 ... not merely of no advantage, but....

T'U. (ㄊㄨ)
(T'uh)

禿 ¹·⁵·
6537　Bald; stripped; bare.

禿友 a bald friend, i.e., a worn-out writing-brush.
禿·子 a bald-head.
禿尾騾 a mule with a hairless tail.
禿山 a bare hill.
⁵禿瘡 baldness; scabby head.
禿翁 a bald-headed old man.
禿頭² or 髮禿 bald-headed.
禿鶖 the bald crane—a kind of stork or ibis.
禿鷲 the bald-headed vulture.
¹⁰光禿 bald; stripped bare.
筆禿 a writing-brush worn to a stump—depreciatory term used by writers.

㖦 ¹·⁵·
6538　Tongue-tied; to lisp.

瘌 ¹·⁵·
6539　A scabby bald head.

瘌瘡 a scabby head.

突 ⁴·⁵·　Abruptly; suddenly. To rush out; to run against.
6540　To offend.

突兀 lofty; bold; resolute.
突出 to protrude—as the eyes.
突出物 protuberances.
突告火驚 sudden alarm of fire.
⁵突如其來·的 arrived unexpectedly.
突將 a leader who is skilful in making surprise attacks.
突怒梗道 suddenly protruding and making the path difficult.

突擊 to make a surprise attack.
突收聲 diminuendo.
¹⁰突放聲 crescendo.
突變 mutations.
突然 suddenly.
突破紀錄 to break the record.
突起 protuberances.
¹⁵明亮·的突起 luminous protuberances.
突門 to guard the gates; to rush out of the gates.
突闖 to rush out.
唐突 to give offence; rudeness.
衝·突 to collide; a clash.

(a) Smooth.

突梯 smooth, without corners.

(b) Used in transliterating.

突厥 Turks, a name taken by a branch of the *Hsiung nu* which had been defeated by the *Hsien pi*, 鮮卑, in the 5th century A.D. Their empire was destroyed by the Wigours, 回紇, in the 8th century, after which they were scattered; some were absorbed by the Wigours, others travelled westwards and gradually regained their power.
突厥斯坦 Turkestan.

(c) A chimney.

TUAN. (ㄉㄨㄢ)

端 ¹　A beginning; an extremity. A clue. A reason or pretext.
6541　Principles; doctrines.

端倪 a clue.
端絡 a hint; a clue.
端詳 in minute detail; giving full particulars.
端頭² the cause; the reason of.
⁵一端 a part.
事端 troubles; disturbances.
借端 to make a pretext.
四端 four corners; the four fundamental principles of Confucianism—love, duty, propriety, and wisdom.
執其兩端 took hold of their two extremes.
¹⁰天端 spring; the time of sprouting vegetation.
我叩其兩端而竭焉 I set it forth from one end to the other and exhaust it.

無端 without cause or reason.
異端 heterodoxy.
發端 a point; a beginning.
¹⁵萬端 all kinds of matters.
要端 the important point.
造端 to make a beginning; elementary.
開端 to begin a thing; to make a precedent; the beginning of a thing.

(a) Upright; correct; proper; decent.

端人正士 a correct, high-principled man.
端午 the 5th of the 5th lunar month, the day of the Dragon-boat Festival, a day for settling accounts, etc. *See below*—A. 17.
端嚴 grave and sedate; serious.
端坐 to sit still in a formal manner.
⁵端容 a grave countenance.
端整 proper; in order.
端方 correct; upright; respectable.
端月 the 5th lunar month.
端·正 correct; respectable; proper; upright.
¹⁰端的 indeed; actually; really; truly.
端相·着 gravely; with a sober expression.
端莊 sober; dignified.
端裕 upright and generous.
端視良久 looked steadily at it for a considerable time.
¹⁵端重 grave; sedate.
端門 the south gate of a palace under the *Han* dynasty.
端陽 the 5th of the 5th lunar month. *See above*—A. 2.

(b) To bring; to arrange.

端·上 to set on the table—as food, etc.
端·把椅·子·來 bring a chair.
端盆 to carry a large basin with both hands.
端策拂龜 to arrange the divining straws and prepare the tortoise shell for prognosticating.
端飯 or 端菜 to serve a meal; to bring in the food.

(c) A ceremonial dress of ancient times.

端章甫 (dressed) in the black square robe and the cap of ceremony.

(d) A length of cloth—18 ft. (Chinese).

布 一 端 a piece of cloth.

(e) Name of a place.

端 硯 ink-slabs from 端溪 in Kwangtung Province.

短 ³ Short; deficient.
6542

短·不 了³ it cannot or will not be wanting.

短 中 抽 長 to get good out of a bad business; to make the best of a bad job.

短 人 a dwarf.

短 促 short—of time, or of life; terse.

⁵短 兵 short weapons; a dagger.

短 兵 相 接 to fight at close quarters.

短 刀 or 短 劍 a short sword; a dagger.

短 命 short-lived; to die young.

短 小 精 悍 short in stature and alert.

¹⁰短 少 few; insufficient; not many; to be less than; to fall short of....

短 工 a job; piece-work; day-labourers.

短 情 wanting in proper feelings; indifferent to the rights of others; ungrateful.

短 折 to die young. = 夭折

短 數 short of the proper amount.

¹⁵短 時 間 a short space of time.

短 期 借 欵 short-term loan.

短 期 公 債 short-term public loan.

短 期 學 校 short-term schools.

短 期 期 票 a short-date bill.

²⁰短 期 限 a limited period.

短 欠 to owe to.

短 氣 short of breath; lacking determination or effort; depressed in spirits.

短 波 電 臺 short-wave broadcasting station.

短 波 電 磁 short electro-magnetic waves.

²⁵短 漢 a dwarf.

短 略 succinct; brief; terse.

短 禮 I am deficient in civility; don't think me rude—conventional phrase.

短 篇 小 說 short stories.

短 缺 deficient; a deficiency.

³⁰短 至 winter solstice.

短·處 a defect; a mean act; shortcomings.

短 見 寡 聞 without much experience.

尋 短 見 to attempt suicide.

短 視 眼 睛 short-sighted eyes.

³⁵短 長 short and long; defects and excellencies; right and wrong.

人 各 有 短 everyone has shortcomings.

剪 短 to cut short.

志 短 wanting in energy, determination, etc.

截 短 to cut short.

⁴⁰日 短 short days; the days are short.

簡 短·的 short; brief.

段 ⁴ A section; a division; a piece; a part; a paragraph.
6543 Distinguish 叚 No. 598.

段 落 a paragraph.

一 段 a section; a part; a paragraph.

一 段 故·事 a story.

大 段 for the most part; a paragraph.

手·段 skill; dexterity; a trick or knack; power. See No. 5838-67ff.

煆 鍛 ⁴ To forge metal; from which comes the idea of:-discipline; making perfect, etc.
6544

煆 灰 to calcine.

煆 石 lime; whetstones.

煆 鍊 to work, as metal; wrought; to discipline.

煆 鍊 人 罪 to bring a man in guilty by perverting the law.

煆 鐵 wrought iron.

緞 ⁴ Satin.
6545

緞·子 satin.

緞 布 cotton damasks.

羽 緞 camlets; lastings.

花 緞 brocaded satin.

鍜 ⁴ An infertile egg.
6546

斷 ⁴ To stop. To cut off; to sever; to interrupt.
6547

斷 七 to call in Buddhist or Taoist priests to perform a ritual, 49 days after a death.

斷·了 broken.

斷 交 to break off relations or friendship.

斷 半 to cut in half.

⁵斷 口 fracture. (geol.).

斷 奶 離 懷 weaned.

斷 乳 to wean.

斷 屠 or 斷 宰 to prohibit the slaughter of animals—in times of drought or pestilence, in order to propitiate the gods.

斷 層 fault. (geol.).

¹⁰斷 後 to bring up the rear in a retreat; without posterity.

斷 折 to break off. [radically.

斷 根 without posterity; to cure

斷 機 to break off the shuttle from the loom—as the mother of Mencius did when her son neglected his studies.

斷 止 to stop; to intercept.

¹⁵斷 氣 to cease breathing—to die.

斷 炊 lacking in the necessities of life.

斷 爛 國 聞 記 載 a term of contempt adapted from Wang An-shih 王安石, despising histories, etc.

斷 片 fragments; odds and ends.

斷 癮 to break off the craving—for opium, etc.

²⁰斷 碎 broken to pieces.

斷 絃 to snap the guitar string—to lose one's wife.

斷 絕 broken off; cut off from; to cut off; to cease.

斷 絕 來 往 all intercourse cut off; to cut off communications.

斷 絕 糧 道 supplies cut off; to cut off supplies.

²⁵斷 絕 邦 交 to sever diplomatic relations.

斷 肢 to mutilate.

斷 絕 關 係 to break off relations with.

　交 通 皆 斷 絕 all communications cut off.

斷 編 殘 簡 fragments of literature. A.c. 斷 簡 殘 編

斷 織 to cut the web from the loom and render it useless—to show the necessity for continuance in study. *See above* —13.

[30]斷 腸 heart-broken; pathetic.

斷 路 or 斷 道 to stop the highway—to intercept, as highwaymen.

斷 送 to throw away; to lose that which one has no hope of recovering.

·斷 送 主 權 to throw away their sovereign rights.

斷 酒 to break off alcoholic liquors.

[35]斷 開 to break in two; to sever.

斷 除 to exterminate; to cut off.

斷 頭[2] 將 軍 a leader who prefers death to surrender.

斷 頭[2] 臺 the guillotine.

斷 飲 食 to be without food and drink; to be unable to eat or drink.

[40]斷 髮 文 身 to cut the hair and tattoo the body—describing savages.

往 來 不 斷 uninterrupted intercourse.

打 斷 to break asunder.

(a) To decide; to give judgement.

斷·不 出 來 cannot come to a decision.

斷 事 to decide a matter; to judge.

斷 令 to settle a case and make an order of Court.

斷 償 to sentence a person to pay.

[5]斷 其 疑 惑 cleared up all his doubts.

斷 定 decided; to decide; to settle.

斷 就 to know what the end will be; to have foretold the result.

斷 才 judicial faculty.

斷 押 to sentence to imprisonment.

[10]斷 斷 decidedly honest and sincere.

斷 明 decided; to settle; to decide.

斷 案 to settle a case at law.

斷 爭 to settle a dispute.

斷 獄 to decide criminal cases.

[15]斷 疑 to solve doubts.

斷 禍 福 to divine one's fortune.

斷 結 to settle; to decide; decided.

斷 繳 to sentence a man to pay.

斷 罰 to inflict a fine.

[20]公 斷 a just sentence or decision.

判 斷 a verdict or judgement.

堂 斷 a verdict.

批 斷 to decide and comment on.

枉 斷 an unfair decision.

[25]決 斷 to sentence; to decide.

獨 斷 independent judgement.

遽 斷 summary decision.

(b) An emphatic particle. Certainly, decidedly.

斷 不 承 認 given an emphatic denial or refusal; determined not to acknowledge.

斷 不 是 certainly not.

斷 不 能 impossible; cannot be on any account; under no circumstances.

斷 乎 decidedly; positively; certainly.

[5]斷 乎 不 certainly not....

斷 乎 不 能 on no consideration; under no circumstances.

斷 斷 不 可 it may not be; on no account; perfectly inadmissible.

斷 斷 不 敢 I cannot presume; on no account would I venture.

斷 無 此 理 absolutely nothing of the kind.

[10]斷 然 decidedly; positively; certainly.

斷 難 相 允 it is really impossible to grant—your request.

籪[4] A weir of bamboo to catch fish or crabs.
6548

T'UAN. (ㄊㄨㄢ)

團[2] A mass; a lump; a sphere. To coil; to surround. Vol-
6549 unteers; home guards. A suffix indicating—party, etc.

團 丁 militiamen.

團 副 second in command of a regiment.

團 匪 the *Boxers*.

團 合 huddled together.

[5]團·圓 a perfect circle; rounded out; full—as the moon; together; united—as husband and wife.

團 圓 媳·婦 a girl who, for reasons of poverty, is brought up in the home of her fiancé.

團 圓 節 the Mid-Autumn Festival: 15th of the 8th lunar month.

團 團 conglomerated.

團 團 圍·住 hemmed in on all sides; sitting round in any order.

[10]團 團 然 round.

團 團 的 轉·著 whirled round and round—as dust.

團 團 轉[4] turn round and round.

團 坐 to sit in a circle.

團 契 fellowship.

[15]團 扇 a circular fan.

團 拜 to salute in a body, as when saluting the flag, etc.

團 集 to group; to collect together.

團 欒 (or 圓) circular; round—as the full moon; to gather together.

團 瓢 mat-sheds.

[20]團 積 to accumulate; to collect together.

團 紳 gentry connected with the home guards.

團 結 to include in; to dwell together; to cohere; to collect together; an alliance; affiliation.

團 結 力 cohesive force; united strength.

團 練 militia; home guards.

[25]團 總 captain in a home guard.

團 聚 to collect together; to include in; to accumulate; to dwell together.

團 臍 the shell of a female crab.

團 茶 a name for the finest tea.

團 蒲 round cushions made of rushes.

[30]團 樵 mat-sheds.

團 長 commanding officer of a regiment.

團 體 united body; a group; an organization.

團 體 名 義 name of the organization.

團 體 精·神 *esprit de corps*.

[35]團 魚 a turtle.

團 鳳 a name for the finest tea; an ornament for the person.

團 龍 a coiled-up dragon, such as is seen on flowered crapes; a fine sort of tea. ＝龍 團.

一團和氣 a lump of good-nature—a person with a pleasant face and genial manner.

一團絲 a ball of silk.

⁴⁰一團麵 a lump of dough.

學生團 the student body.

政團 political bloc.

星團 star-clusters.

歌詩團 a choir.

⁴⁵疑團 suspicions; doubts.

縮作一團 coiled up into a lump —like a snake.

傳² Grieved.
6550

摶² To roll round with the hand. To model.
6551 Distinguish 摶 No. 5323.

摶合 to roll together.

摶沙 balls of sand—lacking cohesion.

(a) Read *chuan⁴*. To lead.

摶三國之兵 to lead the troops of three States.

(b) u.f. 專 Only.

漙² Heavy dew.
6552

糐²
糰 Dumplings; doughnuts.
6553

糰子 small cakes made of rice flour.

湯糰 stuffed dumplings of rice flour.

湍¹ Rushing of water; a torrent.
6554

湍水 swirling waters.

湍瀉 erosion of the banks of a river.

疃³
畽 A hamlet. The land outside a city.
6555

彖⁴ A hog running. A hedge-hog; a porcupine.
6556 The definitions of the *Book of Changes*.

彖辭 the summing up of the application of the *Diagrams*.

TUI.   (ㄉㄨㄟ)

堆¹ To heap up; to pile. A heap; a pile; a mass; a crowd.
6557

堆下 to pile up.

堆卡 a small barrier for collecting customs dues.

堆梁 to pile up in order; mensuration.

堆塞 to block up—as a crowd of people.

⁵堆壘 a heap; a pile.

堆房 or 堆棧 a warehouse.

堆積 to store up; piled up.

堆積如山 piled up like a mountain.

堆紅 to put red lacquer on the raised flowers of lacquer-ware.

¹⁰堆絹 to make padded flowers etc., from pieces of silk or satin.

堆花 to make padded flowers. etc., from pieces of silk or satin.

堆藏 to store; to amass.

堆貨人 a stevedore.

堆起來 to heap up.

¹⁵堆金積玉 to accumulate wealth.

土堆 a dust-heap; a mound of earth.

灰堆 a dust-heap.

糞堆 manure-heap.

碓⁴ A pestle, worked with the foot, used to hull rice. To
6558 pound in a mortar.

碓房 an establishment for hulling grain.

碓搗 to pound.

碓架 or 碓牀 the frame by which the pestle is supported.

碓臼 a pestle and mortar.

碓頭 a pestle.

水碓 a water-mill for hulling grain.

鎚¹ Steamed dumplings.
6559

兌⁴ To exchange; to barter; to weigh.
6560

兌交 to pay to.

兌換 to exchange coin or jewelry.

兌換券 draft; bill of exchange.

兌換所 the Exchange.

⁵兌換紙幣 convertible notes.

不兌換紙幣 non-convertible notes.

兌換銀錢 to change silver.

兌支 to advance money.

兌收 to weigh in—as a bank receiving bullion.

¹⁰兌現 to exchange for ready money.

兌稅 to pay duty.

兌給 to pay to; to weigh out.

兌銀子 to weigh silver.

兌錢糧 to pay the land-tax.

¹⁵發兌 to sell wholesale.

(a) To open up, as roads. Straight. The 58th *Diagram*:— to permeate.

松柏斯兌 paths were made through the firs and cypresses.

行道兌矣 and roads for travelling were opened.

(b) Read *yüeh⁵*. u.f. 悅 No. 7702. To gratify.

隊⁴ A file or company of soldiers; an army; a regiment.
6561

隊伍 rank and file; the ranks.

隊伍不齊 uneven ranks.

隊球 volley-ball.

隊長 (*chang³*) a commanding officer.

⁵一隊人 a crowd.

先鋒隊 pioneer corps.

出隊 to go out to battle.

列隊 to marshal the ranks.

前隊 the vanguard.

¹⁰大隊 a battalion.

守備隊 garrison.

小艦隊 naval squadron.

小 隊 a company of soldiers.
工 程 隊 engineering corps.
¹⁵後 隊 the rearguard.
擺 隊 to marshal the ranks.
支 隊 a detachment.
收 隊 to retreat.
步 隊 infantry.
²⁰游 緝 隊 a patrol.-擊- guerrillas.
準 備 軍 隊 territorial army.
礮 隊 artillery corps.│Fifth Column.
縱 隊 a column.   第五縱隊 the
聯 隊 a regiment.
²⁵脂 粉 隊 the rouge and powder
corps—ladies.
艦 隊 fleet.
衛 生 隊 ambulance corps.
衛 隊 body-guard.
軍 隊 an army; troops.
³⁰輜 重 隊 army service corps.
電 信 隊 telegraph corps.
音 樂 隊 the band—as of a regiment. 陸 戰 隊 marines.
馬 隊 cavalry.

(a) Read *chui*⁴. To fall. u.f. 墜
No. 1471.

對
对
6562

⁴ Opposite to; to oppose.
To face. To make a pair.
To compare. To suit;
agreeing with.

對·一·對 to compare; to check—
as accounts, original and copy,
etc.
對·不·住 or 對·不·起 unable to
face a person owing to some
fault, etc.—a form of apology.
對·不·對 does it agree or correspond? is it so?
對 人 信·用 credit granted on the
good faith of a person.
⁵對 人 擔 保 security against the
person.
對 人 權   right in personam
Cf. 61. *(legal.)*   [with.
對·付 to agree; to match; to deal
對·付 之 法 attitude towards.
對 代 物 a substituted article.
¹⁰對 偶 a couple; to·match; to pair.
對 光 to adjust the strength — of
spectacles.
對 內 internal.
對 內 交 涉 internal arbitration.
對 勁ₙ to agree; to match; to "hit
it off",as friends.
¹⁵對 口 the back of the neck; to
verify a statement by reference

to a third party.
對 口 疽 a carbuncle on the back
of the neck—reckoned very
dangerous.
對 句 antithesis.
對 合 in partnership.
對 合·的 利 100 per cent profit.
²⁰對 外 external.
對 外 關 係 foreign relations.
對·子 scrolls; parallel sentences
written on scrolls.
對 審 to confront in court; to
stand trial.
對 局 to play *wei-ch'i* 圍 棋 with
a person. *See* No. 7082-24.
²⁵對 岸 the opposite bank of a river.
對 岸 觀 火 to watch a fire from
the opposite bank—only a
casual interest; unable to help.
對 崎 confronting heights; standing opposite to each other.
對 平 a balance.
對 待 to deal with; attitude towards.
³⁰對·待 方 法 method of dealing
with.
對·得 住 人 or 對·得 過 able to
face others—having nothing to
be ashamed of.
對 戰 to join battle; to fight.
對 手 a match for; one's equal.
對 打 fight with.
³⁵對 抗 to set one demand against
another—as i n negotiations
between two nations.
對 換 to barter; to exchange.
對 敵 to fight; to oppose; an
opponent.
對 數⁴ to check or audit accounts;
logarithms.
對 數 假³數⁴ mantissa of a logarithm.
⁴⁰對 數⁴根 base of a logarithm.
對 數⁴表 table of logarithms.
代 數⁴對 數⁴ a l g e b r a i c logarithms.
常 用 對 數⁴ c o m m o n log-
arithms.
普 通 對 數⁴ g e n e r a l logarithms.
⁴⁵算 術 對 數⁴ arithmetical logarithms.
納 氏 對 數⁴ or 自 然 對 數⁴
Napierian logarithms.
餘 對 數⁴ complement of a logarithm.
對 方 the other side; the opposite
party.

對 方 之 同 意 the consent of the
opposite party.
⁵⁰對·於 as to...; in relation to...;
attitude towards.
對 景 傷 情 facing the scene, my
grief increases.
對 服 to pacify; to be on good
terms with.
對 比 contrast.
對 江 the opposite side of a river.
⁵⁵對 汛 guard-posts on opposite
sides of a frontier.
對 消 to cancel, as in arithmetic,
etc.
對 照 to compare; to contrast.
對 照 表 a balance-sheet; a synopsis.
對 牛 彈 琴 to play a lute before
an ox—to attempt to explain
deep truths to a dull person;
used on notices:—if you do not
heed this warning, it is as
though I played my lute before
an ox—it is all in vain.
⁶⁰對 物 信 用 credit on security of
goods.
對 物 擔 保 security a g a i n s t
goods. * 對 物 權 right in rem.
對 狀 to stand trial; to answer to
the charge.
對 生 葉 leaves which grow opposite to each other.
對 症 發 藥 to suit the remedy to
the disease—used fig.│cross-eyed.
⁶⁵對 眼 pleasing to the eye; 對眼(兒)
對 稱 symmetry. (-*ch'ên*⁴)
對 稿 to correct proofs.
對 立 antithesis; opposites; standing opposite to each other.
對 等 of the same quality, rank,
class, etc.
⁷⁰對 等 條 約 equal treaties.
對 策 attitude.
對 縫 fitting closely at the edges.
對 耦 man and wife; a couple.
對 聯 scrolls; parallel sentences
written on scrolls.
⁷⁵對 胃·口 palatable.
對 襟 single-breasted; garments
that fasten down the front.
對 親·家 to form a marriage
alliance. (-*ch'in*⁴-, or -*ch'ing*⁴-)
對 角 線 diagonal line.
對 設 to place opposite to each
other.
⁸⁰對 調 to exchange officers.
對·證 eye-witness in a lawsuit;
personal evidence.

對 象 the opposite party; opponent; object under consideration.

對·質 to confront—as witnesses.

對 賽 to compete.

85對 過 opposite to; over the way; across the street.

對 鄰 opposite neighbours.

對 量 equivalent.

對 門 the opposite door; over the way; across the street.

對 開 to divide equally between two; half a dollar.

90對 除 外 尙 存 balance in hand.

對 除 外 尙 欠 balance of account due.

對 陣 opposing armies.

對 面 face to face; opposite.

對 面 看·來 looked at from the opposite point of view; on the other hand.

95對 面 笑 to laugh in the face of.

對·頭 an opponent; an enemy; hostile; in an opposite direction.

對 飮 to drink two together.

一 副 對·子 a pair of scrolls.

一 對 a pair—as of vases; a brace.

100不 對 not in agreement, not right; wrong.

反 對 to oppose. *See* No. 1781-42ff.

相 對 relative. *See* No. 2562-45ff.

絕 對 absolute. *See* No. 1703—A.12ff.

(a) To reply to; to respond.

對·他 說 said to him.

對 曰 replied, saying.

對 答 如 流 swift replies.

對 話 or 對 談 conversation.

5對 話 法 Socratic methods.

對 說 to reply.

對 語 篇 dialogue.

無 以 爲 對 nothing to answer.

(b) To add to, as fluids.

對 水 add water, for dilution, etc.

懟 懟 譈

6563

To dislike; to abhor; to hate.
Also read *chui*[4].

以 懟 父 母 incurring the resentment of his parents.

彊 禦 多 懟 "violent oppressors who cause many dissatisfactions."

怨 懟 resentment and hatred.

T'UI.   (ㄊ)

推 [1] To push; to expel. To shirk; to decline. To yield.

6564

推 三 阻 四 to make lame excuses.

推·不 上 來 cannot push it up—as a barrow up a hill.

推·不 出 unable to decline.

推 不 知 to pretend ignorance.

5推·不 開 unable to get out of; unable to shirk.

推 以 有 客 excused himself on the ground of having visitors.

推 來 推 去 each refusing to accept—the presents.

推 倒 to upset; to overthrow.

推·出 去 to push out.

10推 刃 to thrust with a weapon.

推 前 擦 後 to shirk.

推 却 to refuse; to decline.

推 卸 to shift on to somebody else.

推·子 a hair-clipper.

15推 拒 to dismiss; to push away.

推 拏 massage.

推 擁 to hustle.

推 放 to force to or into.

推 故 to shirk; to back out.

20推 敲 to consider words when making poetry, from a story of 賈 島 who was puzzled whether to use the words *push* a door or *knock* at a door.

推 班 postponement of the Court functions; inferior in quality(*Wu-dial.*)

推 磨 to grind; to turn a mill.

推 約 to withdraw from a contract or agreement.

推 翻 to push over; to overthrow.

25推 翻 政 府 to overthrow the government.

推 耳 聾 to pretend deafness.

推 脫 to get out of doing anything.

推 舟 to row a boat.

推 落 to throw over; to speak ill of a person.

30推 託 to make excuses; to shirk.

推 諉 to back out; to make excuses.

推 讓 to yield; to decline—honours, etc.

推 貨 to return purchased goods.

推 賴 to repudiate; to throw the blame on another.

35推 車 to push a wheelbarrow.

推 辭 to shirk; to decline; to refuse; to make excuses.

推·過·來 to push a thing across.

推 進 to push forward; to propel.

推 進 機 a propeller.

40推 進 軸 propeller-shaft.

螺 旋 推 進 機 screw-propeller.

(也)鉋·子 a carpenter's plane.

推 銷 to push sales.

推·開 to have nothing to do with; to evade; to put aside; to change the topic; to push open; to show the application of.

45推·開 天 窗 說 亮 話 push open the skylight and speak clearly—have no secrets; open and above-board.

推 陳 出 新 to find something new in the old.

(a) To extend. To enlarge.

推 以 及 人 to extend to others.

推 廣 to extend—as a principle.

推 廣 商 業 to extend trade and commerce.

推 廣 面 積 extend the area.

5推 恩 to extend favours to.

推 情 to extend sympathy to.

推 敬 to respect.

推 而 滿 之 to carry out fully.

推 行 to carry into operation what has already been decided.

10推 行 及 於 一 切 extended to all.

(b) To infer. To investigate; to deduce. To include.

推·事 an assessor; a justice; a judge or magistrate.

推 其 原 to trace the origins; to analyze.

推 其 極 to find out the full meaning.

推 原 其 故 to analyze; to draw deductions; to trace back to a cause.

5推 命 to tell a fortune.

推 問 to examine into; to investigate.

推 定 to draw a conclusion from certain circumstances; deductions.

推 尋 源 流 to investigate the source and history of.

推得²之因 the inferred reason or cause.
¹⁰推念 to think over; to reason it out.
推想 to infer; deduction.
推斷 to draw a conclusion; to deduce; deductions.
推本溯源 to investigate origins; to ascertain the causes.
推本神話 investigation of myths.
¹⁵推步 to cast a horoscope.
推求 to examine; to investigate.
推測 to fathom; to investigate; to deduce.
推測之詞 inferences; deductions.
推爲 to include as; to consider or treat as.
²⁰推理 reasoning.
推理法 deductive methods.
推知 to deduce from certain premises.
推究 to carry out investigations; to examine.
推算 to calculate; to reckon; to cast a horoscope; to express in terms of; to find the equivalents --as the same date in the Lunar and Solar calendars.
²⁵推衍之文 a dissertation.
推言之 gave it another application.
推論 to infer; to follow out a train of argument; conclusions; deductions.
推造 to cast a horoscope.
推鞫 to make investigations.
³⁰推類 or 類推 to put in the same category; to argue by analogy.
餘可類推 the rest may be inferred.
因一推十 to generalize.
自一推萬 to draw deductions from the particular to the general.
舉源推流 to deduce general truth from a particular instance.

(c) To elect. To promote. To recommend. To praise. To esteem.

推其長厚 praise his magnanimity.
推崇 to hold in high esteem; to value highly.
推升 promoted by seniority.
推爲望族 regarded as an ex-

emplary family.
⁵推爲領袖 chosen as leader.
推舉 to recommend for promotion.
推薦 to recommend.
推許 to praise others.
推賢讓能 select the worthy and give place to the able—that they may fill office.
¹⁰推轂 to recommend for promotion.
推選 to elect.
推選賞罰之約 came to a clear understanding as to rewards and punishments.
推重 to hold in high esteem.
推陞 to be promoted.

(d) To give up. To hand over to.

推己及人 to put oneself in the place of another.
推心置腹 to place one's heart in the body of another man— loyal friendship.
推燥居濕 to give the dry place to her child and take the wet place for herself—maternal unselfishness.
推給別人 to hand over to another.
⁵推衣 to give clothes to the poor.
推解 from 推衣解食 to take off one's clothing and give up one's food—as to a friend in need.
推誠 to place confidence in.
推食 to give food—as to a poor person.

(e) Used in transliterating.

推羅 Tyre.

魋² A fabulous animal, like a small bear.
6565

隤²／墤 To fall in ruins; to collapse; to overthrow. Decayed; ruined; lost. Inter. next.
6566

隤名 to blast a reputation.
隤牆 to throw down a wall.
我馬虺隤 my horses are worn out.

(a) Soft; yielding.

隤柔 soft, pliable—in disposition.

頹² To fall; to descend. Ruined.
6567

頹倒 to fall down.
頹唐 decrepit; failing.
頹喪 defeated; ruined; destroyed.
頹圮 collapsed; broken-down; ruined.
⁵頹墮 to ruin; to overthrow.
頹壞 ruined; destroyed.
頹廢 destroyed; ruined; decadent.
頹思而就牀 to lie down and meditate.
頹惰 lazy; inert.
¹⁰頹惰自甘 lazy and self-indulgent.
頹放 careless and remiss; impolite.
頹敗 routed; overthrown.
頹替 to deteriorate.
頹波 collapsing billows; used fig., of sudden collapse, as of an enterprise.
¹⁵頹然 drooping; relaxing.
頹然而下 gradually decaying; decadent.
頹運 misfortune; one's fortunes are declining.
頹風 depraved customs.
頹齡 declining years.

(a) A scorching whirlwind.

維風及頹 the wind is followed by a tornado.

(b) The chin. A bald-pate.

退⁴ To retire; to withdraw; to recede; to decline. To yield; to abate. To send away.
6568

退一步想 retire a step and think over it—fig.,
退下去 get down!
退不了³ no getting out of it.
退任 to give up office.
⁵退伍 to discharge soldiers.
退位 to abdicate.
退光 polished; burnished.
退光漆 highly polished varnish.
退兩步 step back a few paces.
¹⁰退兵 to retreat; to withdraw troops.
退出去 to retire; to go out.
退出黨籍 expelled from the Party.
退化 decadence.
退化世代 a decadent age.

15退化人羣 a decadent people.
退化器官 atrophied organs.
退却 to decline; to refuse; to re-
退去 to retire; <del>to withdraw.</del> [treat;
退回 to retreat; to shut out—as cargo.
20退回去 to refund.
退城 to evacuate a city.
退堂 to leave the court; to retire from the bench.
退士 a recluse.
退套 to get out of doing something.
25退婚 to break off a betrothal engagement.
退學 to give up study; to give up attendance at school.
退席 to withdraw; to retire.
退後 to retire; to backslide.
退手 to stop; to desist from further action.
30退敵 to cause the enemy to retreat.
退書 a deed renouncing a betrothal engagement.
退·步 to step backwards; to backslide; to retire; retrograde. *
退步思量事事難 retire and ponder a matter, and everything will seem difficult.
倒退一·步 take a step backwards.
35退歸林下 to retire from public life.
退毛 to pluck a fowl; to scrape a pig.
退汗 to arrest perspiration.
退潮 the ebb tide.
退無所止 there was no place to retreat to.
40退熱藥 anti-pyretics.
熱退 the fever subsides.
退皮 desquamation.
退省 to retire and consider one's position, etc.(-hsing³)
退租 to throw up a lease.
45退筆 the stump of a writing-brush.
退縮 to shrink; to draw in.
退老 to retire from public life on account of old age.
退職閒居 to resign and go into private life.
退色 to fade—of colours.(-shai³)
50退親 to break off a matrimonial engagement.
退讓 to cede; to yield.
退走 to retreat; to flee.
*   something to fall back upon.

退貨 returned goods; to return goods which one has purchased.
退辦 to throw up the management of.
55退避 to retire and hide; to keep one's distance.
退避三舍 to retreat ninety li. See 舍 No. 5699—A.
退還 to return unaccepted; retrocession.(-huan²)
退開 to resign office and go into retirement.
退關 to "shut out"—Customs.
60退隱 to retire from business; to go into retirement.
退食 to retire from the Court for meals—to rest.
撤退 evacuation.
水退 the water recedes.
身退 to retire from public life.

(a) To exorcise.

退妖怪 to exorcise evil demons.
祛退 to exorcise evil spirits.

(b) To check. To keep back.

由也兼人故退之 Yu has more than his share of energy, therefore I checked him.

腿
骽 **3**
6569
The leg; the thighs.

腿包 or 綁腿·子 gaiters worn by women.
腿·子 the leg.
腿帶·子 garters.
腿快 fleet-footed.
5腿肚·子 the calf of the leg.
腿腕兒 the ankle.
腿跟 the heel.
腿遲 slow gait, as of the feeble.
腿酸·了 legs aching.
10腿骨 the bones of the leg.
前腿 fore-leg.
大腿 the thigh.
小腿 the leg.
後腿 hind-leg.
15火腿 hams.
茶腿 good hams—suitable for serving with tea.
金腿 hams from Kinhwa, 金華, in Chekiang.

煄 **4** To scald the bristles off a pig or the feathers off a bird.
6570
煄毛 to scald off hair or feathers.

TUN.   (ㄊㄨㄣ)

(Tuen)

敦
惇 **1** To regard as important. To esteem. Honest; sincere; generous.
6571

敦促 to urge; to press.
敦倫 to give importance to human relations; sexual intercourse.
敦勉督促 earnestly press forward.
敦匠事 to superintend the workmen—making the coffin for the mother of Mencius.
5敦厚以崇禮 "he exerts an honest, generous earnestness in the esteem and practice of propriety."
敦厚 or 敦大 honest; sincere; staunch.
敦友於誼 be sincere in dealing with friends.
敦品 trustworthy; respectable.
敦孝弟以重人倫 enforce filial duty and subordination to elder brothers, so as to emphasize social obligations.
10敦崇兩國睦誼 cement the friendly relations between the two nations.
敦序 to have due regard for precedence.
敦樂 to take great delight in.(-lê⁴)
敦睦 cordial and friendly.
敦篤 to consolidate.
15敦請 to give a cordial invitation.
敦趣 to urge a person to start.
敦迫 to urge on.
大德敦化 the greater energies are seen in mighty transformations.
薄夫敦 the niggardly become liberal.

(a) Read t'uan². Growing thickly.

敦彼行葦 those patches of springing wayside rushes.

(b) Read *tui*[1]. To have thrown upon one. Solitary. To deal with. To finish up. To be polished.

敦 商 之 旅 he disposed of the forces of *Shang*.

敦 彼 獨 宿 we passed the night quietly and alone.

敦 琢 其 旅 the polished members of his suite.

王 事 敦 我 the affairs of State are thrown upon me.

(c) Read *tui*[4]. Sacrificial vessels. Vessels for grain.

(d) Read *tiao*[1]. Ornamented.

敦 弓 旣 堅 the ornamented bows are strong.

(e) Read *t'un*[2]. Name of a place.

敦 煌 a District in N. W. Kansu, near the extremity of the great wall.(Now usually pron. *tun*[1]-)

墩
墪
6572
A heap; a mound; a beacon-mound. A block of stone or wood.

墩·子 a mound of earth—as at the base of trees.
墩 堡 beacon-mound.
墩 布 a mop.
墩 臺 a beacon-mound.
[5]涼 墩 porcelain or earthenware stools for use in hot weather.
白 墩·子 *Petuntse*—a white earth used for making porcelain.
門 墩 the stone blocks at each side of the steps outside a house-door.

撴
6573
To jolt. To thump.

撴·的 慌 jolting unpleasantly as when riding on a rough road.

橔
6574
A wooden chopping-block.

橔·子 a butcher's block; a small round block for chopping meat on.

(a) Read *tui*[1] or *t'ui*[1]. The wooden cover of a coffin.

燉
6575
[4] To heat; to stew. Also read *t'un*[1].

燉 水 to boil water.
燉 煌 the noise of burning.
燉 熟 to cook thoroughly.(-*shou*[2])
燉 茶 to warm up tea.
[5]燉 酒 to warm spirits.
燉 飯 to steam rice.
燉 鷄 a steamed fowl.

(a) Read *t'un*[4]. Warm, half-heated.

蹲
6576
[1] To squat on the heels. To reside. Also read *ts'un*[2].

蹲·不 住 unable to squat—as from want of practice.
蹲 伏 to squat.
蹲·到 腿 痠 I have squatted until my legs ache.
蹲 踞 to squat down.

(a) Read *tun*[2]. To assemble.

(b) Read *ts'un*[2]. To move in time to music.

柮
6577
[3] Stump of a tree. Also read *ai*[4] or *o*[5].

柮·子 a tree-stump.

盾
6578
[4] A buckler; a shield. Also read *shun*[3].

盾 狀 腺 the thyroid gland.
盾 狀 軟 骨 the thyroid cartilage.
盾 鼻 the boss on a shield.

(a) Read *tun*[4]. Used for guilders, from *gulden*.

(b) Read *tun*[4]. Inter. next. To hide, etc.

盾 步 走 crept away secretly.

遁
6579
[4] To hide; to escape; to conceal oneself; to vanish.

遁 世 無 悶 to leave the world without regret.

遁 人 a suspicious, nervous person.
遁 北 to flee, as routed troops.
遁·去 to withdraw.
[5]遁 形 to become invisible.
遁 法 the art of becoming invisible.
遁 走 to flee; to abscond.
遁 跡 山 林 to retire to the mountains—to give up official life.
遁 逃 to flee; to abscond.
[10]遁 辭 evasive words.
遁 避 to withdraw into hiding.

躉
6580
[3] To store; to warehouse.

躉 售 價 值 wholesale price.
躉 在 門 口 put it in the doorway.
躉 家 one who corners the market.
躉 批 to sell wholesale.
[5]躉 攅 in bulk.
躉 當 (*tang*[4]) sale of unredeemed pledges.
躉 船 hulks; receiving lighters.
躉 貨 to corner the market.
躉 賣 to sell wholesale.
[10]躉 關 stored under bond; bonded.
大 躉 in the lump.

拖
6581
[4] To move; to shake.

拖 掣 to shake.

瞚
6582
[3,4.] To doze. Dimness of sight.

瞚 睡 or 打 瞚 to doze; to nod.
困 瞚 weary and sleepy.

鈍
6583
[4] Blunt. Obtuse; dull-witted.

鈍 兵 blunt weapons; soldiers without courage or energy.
鈍 尖 a blunt point.
鈍 漢 a dull, stupid person.
鈍 角 an obtuse angle.
[5]刀 鈍 the knife is blunt.
遲 鈍 dull; incapable; inefficient.
頑 鈍 dull-witted; foolish.

頓
6584
[4] To bow the head. To stamp the foot.

頓脚 (or 足) to stamp the foot.
頓首拜 I bow the head—written on cards, etc.

(a) To put in order. To prepare.

安·頓 to prepare, as a room for a visitor; to get ready for; to pacify; to keep quiet.
整頓人馬 to prepare troops for war.

(b) A time. A turn. A rest in music. A meal. To pause. To cease.

頓兵 to halt troops.
頓口無言 not a word to say in reply.
頓挫 new paragraph; to make a break.
頓筆 to pause when writing.
⁵頓轡 to drop the reins—to stop the carriage.
頓頓飯 every meal.
一頓飯 a meal.
一頓飯工·夫 during the space of a meal.
停頓 to pause; to stop; wait a while.
¹⁰句頓 a paragraph; cæsural pause.
少頓·下 make a short pause—when reading.
打·他·一·頓 gave him a beating.

(c) To injure. To lose. To discard. Distressed.

頓壞 ruined; destroyed.
頓失 to lose.
頓捨 to discard; to do without.
頓棄 to reject; to discard.
⁵頓萃 distressed.
頓躓 to stumble by the way—distressed, in poverty.
委頓 failing—of energy, vigour, etc.

(d) Suddenly; immediately.

頓廢 suddenly destroyed.
頓悟 to come to a sudden apprehension of; sudden inspiration.
心神頓悟 suddenly recalled to mind—something that one had forgotten.
頓改前非 sudden reformation.
⁵頓時 at once; forthwith.
頓覺 immediately conscious of....

頓進 to make sudden progress—as in literary skill.

(e) An inn or lodging-place.

(f) To store.

(g) Used for ton—See next.

(h) Inter. 鈍 No. 6583. Blunt.

(i) Amber 頓牟.

頓 ⁴   Used for ton.
6585

噸·數 tonnage.
總噸·數 gross tonnage.
註冊噸·數 registered tonnage.
噸稅 tonnage dues.

遯 ⁴ To hide; to go into obscurity; to conceal oneself. To deceive; to impose upon. Original form of 遁 No. 6579.
6586

遯世而不見 to withdraw from the world and be unknown.
遯心 a rebellious disposition.
遯竄 to abscond; to go into hiding.
遯跡 to conceal one's whereabouts.

T'UN.   (ㄊㄨㄣ)
(T'uen)

吞 ¹ To swallow; to bolt. To appropriate.
6587

吞·下·去 to gulp down.
吞·不·下喉 unable to swallow.
吞丸 to swallow a pill.
吞佔 or 吞併 to usurp; to appropriate; to annex—as territory.
⁵吞公肥己 to embezzle and enrich oneself.
吞刀吐火 sword-swallowing and fire-spitting—conjuring tricks.
吞劍伎 sword-swallowing conjurer.
吞吐 to hum and haw; to speak hesitatingly.

吞吃 to swallow.
¹⁰吞噬 to swallow.
吞天下 to seize the empire.
吞奪 to grasp; to swallow.
吞拜 to engross all; to seize the whole.
吞據 to grab; to appropriate.
¹⁵吞氣 to repress one's anger; to swallow the breath. (Taoist)
吞沒公欵 to embezzle public funds.
吞滅 to encroach upon; to absorb—as territory.
吞聲 to remain silent—as under injustice.
吞落 to swallow down.
²⁰吞金 to swallow gold—a euphemism for taking poison.
吞鈎之魚 a fish that has swallowed the hook; a person who has been caught.
吞雲吐霧 swallowing clouds and breathing out mists—magical tricks, also used of smoking opium.
吞食 to swallow food.
吞騙 to overreach; to cheat out of one's fair share.
²⁵半吞半吐 half revealed and half concealed.
狼吞 to swallow greedily.
直吞 to bolt food.

啍 ¹ To move slowly.
6588

大車啍啍 his great carriage drags slowly along.

(a) Read chun¹. To chatter.

噇 ¹ To swallow hastily. To gobble up. Also read tun¹.
6589

暾 ¹ The sun appearing above the horizon. The full glare of the sun.
6590

暾將出分東方 the sun is just appearing in the east.
日暾暾 the full blaze of the sun.
赤暾暾 the red glare of a fire.

涒 ¹ To vomit. The planet Jupiter.
6591 Also read yün¹. Tortuous.

屯[2]
6592　A camp; a village.

屯 兵 military colonists; soldiers quartered out in villages.
屯 戍 soldier's camps.
屯 溪 a mart in the south of Anhwei famous for the tea-trade.
屯 田 land given to military colonists; to till such land.
屯 紮 to encamp.
屯 蟻 a colony of ants.
屯 駐 to be stationed at a post.

(a) To store up. To collect. To assemble.

屯 戶 wholesale dealers.
屯 積 to amass; to store; to prepare.
屯 糧 to hoard up grain.
屯 聚 to assemble.
5 屯 貯 to store.
屯 賣 to sell wholesale.
屯 門 to bank up the city gates in times of flood.
屯 養 工 人 to support workmen —as when on strike.

(b) Read chun[1]. Difficult. Hard and stingy. To sprout.

屯 其 膏 sparing of favours; to intercept favours.
屯 厚 very thick.
屯 難 (nan[4]) in great difficulty.

囤 箟}[2]
6593　A bin for grain. To store up grain. Also read tun[4].

囤 積 to hoard up; to store.
囤 貨 to monopolize an article by buying it up; to corner the market.
米 囤 a rice-bin.

庉[2]
6594　A village. To dwell together.

沌[4]
6595　Confused; chaotic; turbid. Also read tun[4].
Read ch'uan[2]. Name of a place.

沌 口 a place in Hupeh.

窀[1]
6596　To bury. Also read chün[1].

窀 窆 to inter.
窀 窆 之 敬 contribution towards funeral expenses.

迍[2]
6597　Unable to get on.

魨[2]
6598　See 2370.

鮅[2]
6599　The globe-fish, Spheroides vermicularis. It is able to inflate itself; the flesh is esteemed as a delicacy, but there is a great risk of being poisoned. It is also known as 河 豚. See No. 2111-48.

豚 豘}[2]
6600　A sucking pig. To shuffle along without lifting the feet.

豚 兒 my sons—a conventional term.
豚 蹄 pettitoes.

褪[4]
6601　To draw in; to take off; to take out.

褪 了 顏 色 the colour has faded out.
褪 手 to withdraw the hand; to draw back from an enterprise.
褪 毛 to moult; to cast the hair, as animals.
褪 皮 to cast the skin—as a snake.
褪 褲 子 to take off the trousers.
褪 頭 to draw in the head—as a turtle.
褪 頭 縮 腦 to draw down the head—from fear.

臀[2]
6602　The buttocks.

TUNG. (ㄉㄨㄥ)
(Tong)

冬[1]
6603　Winter. The eleventh lunar month.

冬 伏 hibernating.
冬 令 or 隆 冬 the winter; winter time.
冬 儲 store of provisions for the winter.
冬 天 the winter.
5 冬 季 the winter season.
冬 心 lonely and cheerless.
冬 扇 夏 爐 a fan in winter and a stove in summer—out of season; no longer wanted; discarded.
冬 日 可 愛 the sun in winter is much appreciated—said of a kind man.
冬 月 or 仲 冬 the eleventh lunar month.
10 冬 烘 a village schoolmaster—sitting over the stove in winter.
冬 瓜 a large variety of preserving melon, the dark-green skin is covered with a white bloom like frost; vegetable marrow.
冬 眠 hibernation.
冬 眠 鼠 the dormouse.
冬 節 the winter solstice.
15 冬 至 the winter solstice.
冬 至 線 the Tropic of Capricorn. See 回 No. 2309—51.
冬 芽 winter buds.
冬 藏 winter provisions.
冬 衣 winter clothing.
20 冬 青 Ilex pedunculosa.
三 冬 the three months of winter.
客 冬 last winter.

(a) Used in imitation of sounds. See next.

鼕 鼚}[1]
6604　The rattle of drums. Also read t'ung[1].

東[1]
6605　The east. Eastern. Shantung.

東 一 個 西 一 個 one here, another there.
東 一 拳 西 一 脚 hitting and kicking in all directions.
東 三 省 the Three Eastern Provinces, i.e., Manchuria. Heilungkiang or the Amur River 黑 龍 江, Kirin 吉 林, and Liaoning 遼 寧 (formerly Fengtien or Shengking 奉 天 盛 京)

東 不 成 西 不 就 everything out of order; confusion; nothing finished. *See below*—25.

[5]東 亞 Eastern Asia.

東 亞 和 平 the peace of the Far East.

東 交 民 巷 the Legation Quarter —Peking.

東 京 Tongking; Tokyo; Moukden.

東 京 灣 Gulf of Tongking.

[10]東 作 the spring operations—of ploughing, etc.

東 倒 西 歪 out of the perpendicular; sloping; awry.

東 儲 the heir apparent.

東 北 north-east.

東 半 球 the Eastern Hemisphere.

[15]東 南 西 北 east, south, west, and north; everywhere.

東 印 度 公 司 the East India Company.

東 君 the sun—the Lord of the East.

東 土 or 東 域 China.

東 坦 a son-in-law.

[20]東 夏 the east of China.

東 大 陸 the continents of the Eastern Hemisphere.

東 奔 西 跑 to run all over the place; to bustle about; helter-skelter.

東 宮 the heir apparent.

東 帶 南 east by south.

[25]東 成 西 就 everything arranged and concluded; everything in order; prosperous. *See above*—4.

東 拐 西 騙 swindling on all hands.

東 拉 西 扯 to borrow all round; to accuse others when blamed oneself; by hook or by crook; rambling.

東 斗 西 秤 weights and measures vary according to the locality —every man to his own fancy.

東 方 the east.

[30]東 方 文 化 oriental culture.

東 方 病 夫 the Sick Man of the East.

東 方 發 白 (or 亮) day is breaking.

東 施 效 顰 *Tung Shih* knitted her brows, (in imitation of *Hsi Shih* 西 施, a famous beauty who thought that an air of melancholy enhanced her

charms), and made herself look uglier than before—used of copying others and making oneself look foolish.

東 朝 the heir apparent; the Empress Dowager.

[35]東 洋 the Eastern Sea. Japan.

東 洋 參 ginseng grown in Japan.

東 洋 貨 Japanese goods.

(東) 洋 車 a jinrikisha.

東 清 鐵 路 the Chinese Eastern Railway. = 中 東 鐵 路

[40]東 牀 a son-in-law.

東 皇 God of the Spring.

東 胡 ancient name for the Tungusic tribes.

東 藩 之 臣 the minister of *Ch'i* —*Ch'i* being the eastern boundary.

東 西 east and west; 東·西 things; articles; objects.

[45]不 分 東 西 not to distinguish between east and west— dull; stupid.

不 是 東·西 not even a thing —beneath contempt—abusive.

問 東 答 西 to give evasive replies.

東 貿·易 風 east trade-winds.

東 越 the eastern State of *Yüeh*, part of the present Fukien.

[50]東·邊 the east.

東 都 the eastern capital, formerly Loyang in Honan.

東 門 the east gate.

東 關 the eastern suburb of a city; the Chefoo Customs.

東 隅 the place where the sun rises.

[55]東 風 吹 馬 耳 the east wind blows the horse's ears—indifferent; of no concern to him.

東 鱗 西 爪 here a little, there a little; odds and ends.

向 東 towards the east.

山·東 Shantung.

遠 東 the Far East.

(a) The master of the house. A partner. An owner.

東·家 the master; the landlord; the employer.

東 翁 the master, landlord, etc.

東·道 a dinner; a treat; a spread given by the loser of a wager, etc.

東 道 主 the one who stands

treat; a manager; a caterer.

賭·個 東 兒 to make a wager, the loser to stand treat.

房 東 the landlord.

股 東 a shareholder.

財 東 a capitalist.

鋪 東 the proprietor of a shop.

凍 [4] **To freeze; icy; cold. To congeal; jelly.**
6606

凍 僵 benumbed with cold.

凍 冰 or 結 凍 or 凝 凍 or 上 凍 to freeze; to congeal.

凍 冷 icy cold.

凍 嚴·了 frozen hard. 凍 子 jelly.

[5]凍 手 凍 脚 cold hands and feet.

凍·死 frozen to death.

凍 瘡 chilblains.

凍·的 打 戰 shivering with the cold.

凍 破·了 chapped.

[10]凍 結·實 frozen hard.

凍·着·了 to catch a cold. (--chao-)

凍 餒 cold and hungry.

肉 凍·子 jellied meat.

棟 [4] **The ridge-pole; the beams in a roof.**
6607

棟 宇 a house.

棟 折 榱 崩 the beams and rafters are breaking—the State is going to ruin.

棟 橈 (or 橈) a beam that is weak —used fig.

棟 桴 a ridge-pole.

棟 梁 lesser and greater beams— pillars of State.

棟 梁 之 才 great ability—used of able ministers.

棟 隆 a beam curving upwards.

蝀 [4] **The rainbow.**
6608

洞 [4] **A cave; a grotto. A hole. A ravine. Connected.**
6609

洞 仙 elves, fairies, etc.

洞 天 Fairyland; Paradise; connected with heaven; reaching to heaven.

洞 天 福 地 famous grottoes where the fairies dwell; there are 36 "Cave Heavens," and 72 "Blessed abodes."

洞 府 a fairy grotto; one's home.
5 回 洞 府 to return to one's home.
洞 庭 湖 the Tungting Lake in Hunan.
洞 戶 connected houses.
洞 房 the innermost chambers; a nuptial c h a m b e r; to consummate a marriage.
洞 房 花 燭 the gay candles and the nuptial chamber—wedding festivities.
10 洞 洞 乎 How r e v e r e n t and grave!
洞 穴 a cavern; a grotto.
洞 簫 a bamboo flageolet.
仙 洞 a fairy grotto.
空 洞 the great void—the sky.
15 門 洞 the archway through a city gate.
黑 洞 洞 的 profoundly dark.

(a) To see through. To comprehend. To understand.

洞 分 clearly defined.
洞 啓 to open up—as by drawing aside a screen.
洞 察 a thorough investigation.
洞 察 情 勢 thorough investigation of the circumstances.
5 洞 悉 無 遺 to u n d e r s t a n d thoroughly; perfect comprehension.
洞 明 to see through clearly.
洞 曉 to have a clear knowledge of.
洞 澈 to see through.
洞 然 于 心 my mind is clear on that point.
10 洞 燭 to throw light upon; to show up.
洞 燭 其 奸 I see through his villainy.
洞 疑 undecided.
洞 胸 clear-minded.
洞 腹 penetrated the abdomen.
15 洞 若 觀 火 as clear as looking at a fire.
洞 見 to see through; to understand.
洞 見 癥 結 to examine i n t o abstruse, infinitesimal matters.
洞 視 clear vision; insight.
洞 識 I see through it all.
20 洞 貫 penetrated.
洞 達 intelligent; far-seeing.
洞 鑒 a thorough investigation.
洞 開 to open up—as doors, or by removing a screen or curtain.

胴 [4]
6610
The large intestine.

動 [4] To move; to start; to
6611 shake. To excite; to rouse; to take action.

動·不·動 incessantly; a l w a y s; without cause.
動·不·得 it must not be touched; have nothing to do with it.
動 人 to move or excite a person; exciting; thrilling.
動 作 work; action; movement.
5 動 作 如 法 well-executed movements.
動 刀 兵 or 動 干 戈 or 動 刀 to begin war.
動 刑 to apply punishment.
動 力 power; political power; personal influence.
原 動 力 motive power.
10 發 動 力 motive power.
動 力 學 dynamics.
動 力 說 dynamism—accounting for matter and mind as being merely the action of forces.
動 勁 to use force.
動 員 mobilization; preparation for war.
15 動 員 令 order for mobilization.
動 因 exciting cause.
動 土 to stir the ground; to commence digging; to start building.
動 天 下 之 耳 目 attracted the attention of the whole world.
至 誠 動 天 perfect sincerity will move heaven.
20 動 容 to change countenance; to get angry.
動 容 貌 斯 遠 暴 慢 矣 in his deportment he keeps far from fierceness and remissness.
動 工 or 開 工 to begin work.
動 彈 to move; to stir.
動 心 to excite the mind; pathetic.
25 不 動 心 u n m o v e d—as by avarice, etc.
動 念 motive.
動 怒 to lose one's temper; to get angry.
動 情 to excite the emotions; to arouse the passions.
不 動 情 in cold blood.
30 動 慈 心 moved with compassion.
動 愛 情 moved with love.

動 憐 to excite compassion; to draw forth pity.
動 房 事 sexual intercourse.
動 手 to make a start; to begin work; to begin operations.
35 動 搖 to agitate; unsteady; wavering.
動 植 之 倫 the varieties of fauna and flora.
動 機 motive; inducement.
動 氣 to lose the temper; to get angry.
動 水 學 hydraulics.
40 動 淫 念 moved w i t h lustful thoughts.
動 滑 車 movable pulley.
動 火 to be angry; to lose the temper.
動·物 moving creatures; animals, etc.
動·物 之 分 布 geographical distribution of animals.
45 動·物 分 類 學 systematic zoology.
動·物 園 zoological gardens.
旅 行 動 物 園 travelling menagerie.
動·物 地 理 學 zoo-geography.
動·物 學 zoology.
50 動·物 心 理 學 animal psychology.
動·物 界 the animal kingdom.
動·物 本 能 性 animal instincts.
動·物 磁 力 animal magnetism.
動·物 膠 gelatine.
55 動·物 質 animal matter.
動·物 類 animal species.
極 微 動·物 animalculæ.
動 產 moveable effects; personalty.
不 動 產 real estate; realty.
60 動 用 to apply; to employ; to use.
動 疑 to excite suspicion.
動 目 to attract attention.
動 移 to remove; to shift.
動 粗 to resort to violence; to come to blows.
65 動 聽 to excite a desire to hear; eloquent.
動 聲 色 to show b y o n e's manner.
動 脈 arteries.
動 能 力 dynamic energy.
動 衆 to move the masses; popular movements.
70 動 詞 verbs; 自 動 詞 intransitive verbs; 他 動 詞 transitive verbs.
動 議 to move; to propose.
↑動 態 panorama; situation.

動議人 the mover.
動資 moveable property.
動起手脚 to commence action against.
[75]動身 to start; to set out.
動輪 driving-wheel.
動輒 repeatedly.
動關全局 one move will affect the whole situation.
動關節 moveable joints.
[80]動電 dynamic electricity.
動·靜 motion and rest; movement; circumstances; conduct; deportment.
動頭示意 to motion with the head.
動魄 amazing; appalling.
動魯 to resort to violence; to come to blows.
[85]不動 to stand still; firm; motionless.
主動態 or 能動態 active voice.
主動·的 mover.
妄動 rash actions.
感動 influenced by; influence; touched; moved by.
[90]波動 wave-motion.
發動 moved; taken in labour.
舉·動 behaviour; conduct.
行動 behaviour; deportment; manner.
走動 movement of the bowels.
[95]運·動 to exercise; to move, etc. *See* No. 7763.
震·動 shock caused by concussion, earthquake, etc.
顫動器 vibrator.
驚·動 to start; to alarm; to annoy.

働 [4] Motor. Automatic. A Japanese character.
6612

自働 automatic. *See* No. 6960.

懂 [3] To understand; to comprehend.
6613

懂·不到 I cannot understand.
懂·不·懂 do you understand or not?
懂人·情 to understand human nature.
懂人意 to understand the wishes of another.
[5]懂局 an expert.
懂·得 to comprehend.
懂·得·兩·句 I understood a little.

懂·得書 to understand books; to be able to read.
懂情·理 able to take a correct view of things.
[10]懂門·路 an expert; to know the knack of a thing.

董 [3] To lead people in the right way; to correct.
6614

董之用威 correct them with the majesty—of the law.
董·事 managers; directors; trustees.
董·事會 committee meeting; board of directors.
董·事部 board of directors; board of managers.
[5]董勸 to exhort seriously.
董正 to correct; to regulate.
董治 to superintend; to attend to.
董重 to respect.
古·董 antiques; curios.
[10]紳董 the gentry.

T'UNG. (ㄊㄨㄥ)
(T'ong)

同仝 [2] Together. The same as; alike; identical. All. To share in. And; with.
6615

同一 alike; equally; in conformity with; identity; one and the same.
同中 with the middleman.
同事 to act together; to act as a colleague.
同事·的 a colleague.
[5]同井 the same well—a fellow-countryman; fellow-provincial.
同人 people of the same class; fellow-members; colleagues.
同住 to live together.
同伴 a companion; an equal.
同位 apposition. (*grammar*).
[10]同位角 corresponding angles.
同來 to come together.
同僚 fellow-officials.
同其好 (*hao⁴*) 惡 (*wu⁴*) to share their likes and dislikes.
同具人情 of like passions with us.
[15]同列 of the same class or kind.
同前由 to the same effect as the former statements.

同力合作 co-operation.
同功 (or 宮) 繭 cocoons spun by two silkworms; dupions.
同化 amalgamation; assimilation of peoples, culture, etc.
[20]同化作用 assimilation.
同化力 influence.
同吃 to eat together.
同名數 like number.
同命 to die together.
[25]同品 of equal rank.
同因同果 like cause, like effect.
同國 fellow-countrymen.
同在 together with.
同坐 to sit together.
[30]同堂兄弟 descendants through males of the same grandfather.
同夥 an accomplice; confederates.
同契 to agree together with.
同姓不同宗 of the same surname, but not the same ancestors.
同姦 to have illicit intercourse with.
[35]同字 characters having the same meaning but under different radicals.—as 楷 and 階 steps.
同學 a fellow-student; schoolmates.
同學會 Alumni Association.
同宗 having a common ancestor.
同室操戈 quarrels between brothers.
[40]同家 of the same family.
同宿 or 同寢 to lodge together.
同寅 fellow-officials.
同居 to live together; to cohabit.
同居各炊 to dwell together, each having his own kitchen.
[45]同屋 or 同室 living in the same house.
同屬性 homosexuality.
同席 a fellow-guest.
同年 of the same age.
同庚 of the same age.
[50]同式三紙 triplicate copies.
同式製造 standardization of manufactures.
同式·的 homogeneous.
同得 to obtain equally.
同心 of the same mind.
[55]同心努力 united effort.
同心合意 of one mind.
同心結 a love-knot.
同志 like-minded; comrades.
同志會友 associate-members.
[60]同情 in sympathy with; fellow-feeling. A.c. 同情心.
同情罷工 sympathetic strike.
↑同性戀愛 homosexual love.

同 意 to confirm—as a bill brought forward from another house.
同 房 in the same room; sexual intercourse.
同 數 項 like terms. (*math.*)
65 同 文 同 種 of one speech and one race.
同 文 舘 a college in Peking where foreign languages, etc., were taught.
同 方 in the same place; like-minded.
同 族 of the same tribe.
同 時 at the same time.
70 同 時 之 人 contemporaries.
同 時 解 催 a lock-out.
同 杯 to drink together.
同 格 co-ordination.
同 業 of the same calling or occupation.
75 同 業 組 合 a trade-guild.
同 榜 graduates of the same year.
同 樂 to rejoice together.
同 樣 like; equal; of the same kind.
同 此 the same as this; to the same effect.
80 同 歲 of the same age.
同 死 to die together.
同 氣 連 枝 closely united; brethren.
同 流 合 汚 to go with the stream.
同 溝 共 井 neighbouring farmers; neighbours.
85 同 熱 線 isothermal lines.
同 父 異 母 of the same father, but not the same mother.
同 牀 to sleep together.
同 牀 異 夢 sleeping in the one bed, each having his own dreams—apparently one, but differing widely in outlook.
同 犯 accomplice.
90 同 班 class-mate.
同 甘 苦 sharing joys and sorrows.
同 用 equally applicable; having the same use.
同 病 相 憐 fellow-sufferers have mutual sympathy.
同 盟 to make a covenant; to enter into an alliance; confederacy.
95 同 盟 企 業 a trust.
同 盟 國 allied nations; confederated states.
同 盟 抵 制 united boycott.

同 盟 絕 交 boycott.
同 盟 罷 工 a strike.
100 全 體 同 盟 罷 工 general strike.
總 同 盟 罷 工 general strike.
非 買 同 盟 boycott.
同 知 a sub-Prefect.
同 社 fellow-countrymen.
105 同 種 of the same stock or race.
同 窗 or 窗 友 or 窗 兄 弟 a fellow student; class-mates.
同 等 of the same class or kind.
同 等 之 利 權 equal privileges.
同 等 之 利 益 equal advantages.
110 同 約 to agree upon; an agreement.
不 約 而 同 undesigned co-incidence.
同 罪 the same punishment.
同 羣 of the same class or kind.
同 義 of the same meaning.
115 同 義 語 a synonym.
同 考 官 associate examiners.
同 聲 稱 許 carried by acclamation.
同 胞 兄 弟 uterine brothers; compatriots.
同 舟 共 濟 all in the same boat.
120 同 號 like signs. (*math.*)
同 處 to live in the same place.
同 行 · 的 fellow-travellers.
同 行 (*hang²*) of the same trade or business.
同 行 (*hang²*) 必 妒 two of a trade never agree.
125 同 袍 fellow-soldiers; comrades.
同 謀 to plot together.
同 調 of similar aim; like-minded.
同 軌 in the same rut.
同 輩 of the same generation.
130 同 道 the same profession; in the same line.
同 鄉 fellow-countryman; from the same place.
同 鄉 會 Association of Fellow-Provincials.
同 重 of equal weight.
同 門 fellow-disciples.
135 同 音 of the same sound.
同 音 異 義 homonyms—having the same sound but a different meaning.
同 項 like terms. (*math.*)
同 類 of the same class or kind.
同 食 to eat together.

140 一 同 together with.
不 同 different; not identical.
合 同 a contract or agreement.
大 同 小 異 very similar, having but slight differences.
結 果 相 同 the results are about the same.
145 憂 樂 同 享 sharing joys and sorrows. (-*lê⁴*-)

侗² **Ignorant; rude; rustic.**
6616

侗 然 而 來 came in his simplicity.
侗 而 不 愿 ignorant and yet not attentive.

峒² **A territorial division under the Ming dynasty.**
6617

崆 峒 mountains in Kansu and Honan.

(a) Read *tung¹*. **Districts inhabited by aboriginal tribes.**

峒 丁 a stalwart tribesman.
峒 蠻 aboriginal tribes.

恫² **Dissatisfied Moaning with pain.**
6618

呻 恫 moaning and groaning.
哀 恫 Alas!

桐² **A name applied to various trees.**
6619

桐 · 子 樹 or 桐 樹 *Aleurites cordata*.
桐 月 the 3rd lunar month.
桐 杖 a staff carried at the funeral of a mother.
桐 油 wood-oil made from the seeds of *Aleurites cordata*.
5 桐 油 灰 putty.
桐 葉 灰 fine ashes put into censers.
梧 桐 *Sterculia platanifolia*.
泡 桐 *Pawlonia imperialis*, a quick growing tree having a very light timber; it is used for many purposes, and is especially esteemed for lutes.

痌[2] Moaning with pain. Inter. 恫 No. 6618.
6620

痌瘝 in pain or distress.
痌瘝在抱 sympathizing with the distressed.

筒[2] A tube or pipe; a duct. Inter. 筩 No. 6637.
6621

筒·子 a tube or pipe; a chimney.
筒管 a bamboo tube.
筒車 a water-wheel to raise water for irrigation purposes.
信筒 a bamboo tube for conveying letters, etc.
烟·筒 a chimney; a tobacco-pipe.
號筒 a trumpet.

衕[2] See 2175.
6622

銅[2] Brass; copper; bronze.
6623

銅像 bronze statues; brazen images.
銅印 brass seals.
銅·匠 a coppersmith; a brass-finisher.
銅·器 vessels of brass or copper.
[5]銅圓 copper coins.
銅壺 a copper kettle.
銅壺滴漏 a clepsydra or water-clock.
銅帽 gun-caps.
銅幣局 mint for coining coppers.
[10]銅期世代 the bronze-age.
銅板 bar-copper.
銅樂隊 a brass band.
銅燒青 copper enamel.
銅牆鐵壁 walls of brass and iron—impregnable; unyielding.
[15]銅版 plates for printing from; electrotypes.
　照相銅版 photo-process blocks.
　雕刻銅版 engraved printing-plates.
　電鍍銅版 electrotypes.
銅皮鐵骨 a brass and iron constitution—a strong man.
[20]銅盆帽·子 hats like a shallow brass washing-bowl—the ordin-

ary felt hat as worn by foreigners, etc.
銅盔鐵甲 a suit of armour.
銅磚 ingots of copper.
銅箔 brass-foil.
銅絲 copper or brass wire.
[25]銅綠 verdigris.
銅網 brass gratings; brass network.
銅臭 the smell of brass—said in derision of a mean but wealthy man.
銅葉 or 銅片 sheet-copper.
銅金粉 bronze-powder.
[30]銅鉦 a brass gong.
銅錢 copper coins; "cash."
銅青 copperas.
銅頭[2]鐵額 head of brass and brow of iron—describes boldness and courage.
白銅 white-brass.
[35]紅銅 or 赤銅 copper.
純銅 pure copper.
自然銅 copper ore.
青銅 bronze.
響銅 sounding brass used for making gongs.
[40]黃銅 brass.

佟[2] A name.
6624

佟萬 T'ung Wan, a scholar of Liaotung.

彤[2] Red; vermilion. Name of a State.
6625

彤弓 a bow lacquered with vermilion.
彤管 a red tube—presented by a girl to her lover; the meaning is obscure.
彤雲 red clouds.

童[2] A lad; a youth. A virgin. Pure; undefiled.
6626

童便 boy's urine—a medicine.
童僕 a servant-boy.
童叟無欺 neither old nor young cheated—a shop-sign.
童女 a virgin.
[5]童奴 a servant-boy.
童子[3] or 童男 a young lad.
童子[3]癆 consumption.
童子[3]軍 Boy Scouts.
童子[3]雞 a cockerel.

[10]童工 child-labour.
童年 youthful—between ten and twenty years of age.
童心 a childish disposition.
童心未化 he has not got rid of his childish disposition.
童昏 ignorant; stupid.
[15]童羖 a young ram whose horns have not grown.
童牛 a young calf.
童牙 of tender years.
童生 a student eligible to compete at the examination for the former first degree.
童男女 young unmarried persons.
[20]童習未退 has not yet lost his boyish habits.
童蒙 young and ignorant.
童話 stories for children; fables.
童謠 children's songs; ditties.
童貞 a virgin.
[25]童身 youthful; immature; maiden.
童顏 a youthful complexion.
童養·媳·婦 a girl, who for reasons of poverty, is brought up in the home of her fiancé.
童騃 the foolishness of youth.
童齔 the young boys.
[30]成童 to reach the age of eight years, or of fifteen.
書·童 a boy who waits upon a literary man.
神童 a precocious lad; a prodigy.

(a) Bare.

童粱 a grass that does not produce grain—it resembles millet.
山童 a bare hill.
禿株立童童 a stump standing destitute of leaves and branches.
頭童齒豁 with bald head and gaps in the teeth—old age.

(b) Overhanging and green.

桑樹童童 the green shade of the mulberry-trees.

僮[2] A boy; a servant. Inter. preceding.
6627

僮僕 a young slave.

(a) Standing up high and reverently.

被之僮僮 "with head-dress reverently rising aloft."

曈² The sun about to rise.
6628

曈曨 early dawn, the sun just appearing.

朣² The moon just rising.
6629

橦² A tree which grows in Yunnan, from the flowers of which a cloth is made.
6630

橦布 cloth made from the flowers of this tree.

(a) Read ch'uang². A flag-staff.

尋橦 to climb a pole.

潼² A tributary of the Yellow River. Damp. High. Inter. 潼 No. 1510.
6631

潼關 name of a pass in Shensi.
潼潼 lofty.

獞² Name of a variety of dog. Read chuang¹. Wild tribes in South China.
6632

獞丁 a tribesman.

瞳² The pupil of the eye.
6633

瞳人 the reflection of oneself as seen in the eye of another.
瞳人轉背 or 綠水灌瞳人 a cataract.
瞳孔 the pupil of the eye.

捅³ To lead on; to advance. To strike against; to break through.
6634

捅一個窟窿 punch a hole in it.
捅出禍來 to provoke misfortune.
捅破 to break a hole through.
捅鳥巢 to break up a bird's nest.

桶³ A square wooden vessel containing six pints. A bucket; a tub; a cask.
6635

桶底脫 the bottom of the tub has fallen out—to die, of a Buddhist priest.
桶梁 or 桶杷子 the cross-bar at the top of a Chinese bucket.
水桶 a water-bucket.
馬桶 a commode.

痛⁴ Painful; sore. Pain. Extremely; very.
6636

痛不可忍 intolerable pain.
忍痛 to bear pain.
痛切 trenchant.
痛哉 alas!
痛哭 to weep bitterly.
痛定思痛 to recall past pains.
痛得很 very painful. (S. dial.)
痛心 irritated; pained in heart.
痛心切齒 to gnash the teeth with rage.
痛快 satisfying; outspoken; frank; to the point; prompt.
痛快話 words suitable to the occasion; apposite.
痛恨 bitter hatred.
痛愛 passionate love.
痛悔 bitter repentance.
痛憤 deeply moved.
痛打 to give a severe thrashing.
痛改前非 to reform thoroughly.
痛楚 pain; in pain.
痛毆 to beat cruelly.
痛痛哀號 bitter weeping.
痛癢相關 mutual sympathy.
痛罵 to scold severely.
痛苦 bitter suffering.
痛苦事 a bitter experience.
痛飲 to drink deeply.
憐痛 to feel compassion for.
牙痛 toothache.
產痛 pains of parturition.
疼痛 pain; aching.
酸痛 aches and pains.
頭痛 headache.

筩² A tube or pipe. Inter. 筒 No. 6621.
6637

通¹ Through. To go through; to succeed. Thoroughly. To understand; to be in communication; to circulate.
6638

通事 an interpreter.
通交 or 交通 on good terms; to understand one another thoroughly.

通亮 perfectly light or bright; transparent.
通人 a man of the world.
通以電流 connected with the electric current.
通令 to communicate orders.
通例 usages; custom.
通使 an agent; an envoy.
通信 credentials; letters of introduction; to communicate by letter; correspondence in the press as from a regular correspondent.
通信社 press agencies.
通信處 one's address.
通信錄 address-book.
常任通信員 a regular correspondent to the press, "our own correspondent."
特派通信員 a special correspondent to the press.
通俗 common; popular.
通俗化 to popularize.
通俗教育 popular education.
通俗語 colloquial speech.
通價 current value. (legal).
通儒 a scholar of wide attainments; an accomplished man.
通典 encyclopædia dealing with manners and customs, etc. See below—64, 102.
通分母 or 公分母 common denominator. (arith.).
通分法 method of finding the common denominator.
通判 title of a former assistant sub-Prefect.
通刺 interchange of cards among friends.
通則 a general rule.
通力 a common effort; united strength.
通力合作 co-operative work.
通力輪 a balance-wheel.
通功易事 an interchange of productions and labour.
通史 a comprehensive history.
通同 complicity with; to conspire.
通名 to announce a visitor.
通告 to notify; an announcement.
通告書 a notice or circular.
通咨 to send a circular.
通商 commercial intercourse; trade.
通商公所 Chamber of Commerce. Cf. 5673.24.

通 商 口 岸 a Treaty port.
⁴⁰通 商 各 口 the various Treaty ports.
通 商 各 欵 the various clauses of the Treaty referring to foreign trade.
通 商 局 Commercial Bureau.
通 商 港 a Treaty port.
通 商 稅 則 the tariff for foreign trade.
⁴⁵通 商 章·程 trade regulations; the rules appended to the tariff.
通 商 許 可 licences to trade—as between enemy-countries.
通 報 for general information; a public notice; to report to a high authority; T'oung Pao.
通 塞 open and blocked—conditions, etc.
通 士 an experienced and versatile scholar.
⁵⁰通 天 to influence God; known to the Powers above.
通 天·的 本 事 divinely endowed; exceptional ability.
通 套·的 in general use; synonymous; interchangeable.
通 好 on good terms with.
通 學 day-school.
⁵⁵通 學·生 day-scholars.
通 家 family alliance; an old friend; an expert.
通 寶 currency; money; coin of the realm.
通 常 ordinary; average; regular; customary; uninterrupted.
通 常 犯 an offender against the general laws, as contrasted with one who offends against any particular laws, such as military law, etc.
⁶⁰通 常 社 員 active-partner.
通 常 議 會 ordinary general meeting.
通 庚 the exchange of names, dates, etc., as a preliminary to marriage.
通 心 粉 macaroni.
通 志 encyclopædia dealing with geographical and topographical matters. See above—21, and below—102.
⁶⁵通 房 free to any part of the house.
通 才 intelligent and able to manage affairs.
通 文 elegant language; perspicuous style.

通 文 墨 well-educated; acquainted with literature.
通 方 versed in Taoist practices.
⁷⁰通 方 言 conversant with dialects.
通 日 allowing the sunshine to shine through.
通 明 perspicuous; intelligible.
通 曆 a calendar.
通 曉 to make generally known; to be perfectly acquainted with.
⁷⁵通 書 an almanac.
出 港 通 知 書 c l e a r a n c e notice.
通 本 to send in a memorial.
通 權 達 變 to act as occasion requires.
通 欵 to have intercourse with the enemy; to surrender.
⁸⁰通 氣 animated by the same spirit; unity of sentiment; sympathetic; in connection.
通 氣 管 (or 筒) ventilating o r air pipe.
通 流 current.
通 牒 a despatch.
通 玄 having understanding of the mysteries of Taoism.
⁸⁵通 用 in general use; interchangeable; synonymous.
通 白 to make generally known.
通 知 to notify.
通 知 單 a circular notice.
通 知 書 notification.
⁹⁰通 短 絡 (or 路) short-circuit. (elec.).
通 示 to make generally known.
通 神 to move the gods; in communication with the gods; endued with power.
神 通 supernatural power.
通 票 a through ticket.
⁹⁵通 禮 current usages of society.
通 稱 a general designation; a general term for.
通 劄 to issue circular instructions.
通 籍 to be enrolled as an official.
通 糧 道 to keep the communications open. [through.
¹⁰⁰通 紅 to blush; red through and
通 義 a constant rule.
通 考 encyclopædia dealing with biographical notes. See above —21, 64.
通 脫 not bound by petty and rigid rules of conduct.
通 花 figured on both sides, as cloth, etc.

¹⁰⁵通·融 辦 理 to make a temporary arrangement by which each party abates somewhat of its claims; a compromise; an exceptional arrangement.
絕 對 不 可 通 融 no compromise whatever can be made.
通 行 everywhere c u r r e n t ; general.
禁 止 通 行 no thoroughfare.
↓此 路 不 通 no thoroughfare.
¹¹⁰通 行 券 safe-conduct pass.
通 行 原 則 well-accepted principles.
通 行 布 告 to address a circular note.
通 行 支 銀 憑 信 circular letter of credit.
通 行 曉 諭 general notification.
¹¹⁵通 行 權 right of way.
通 行 稅 toll on transit.
通 行 證 券 safe-conduct passes.
通 行 貨 幣 current coin.
通 行 (hang²) conversant with trade secrets, etc.
¹²⁰通 衢 a public highway.
通 表 to forward a statement to a superior.
通 計 a general estimate.
通 訊 員 reporter; press correspondent.
通 訊 社 Associated Press.
¹²⁵通 詳 for general information; a public notice.
通 話 to have conversation with.
通 論 universal, as opposed to particular. (logic).
通 論 各 省 a general order to all the provinces.
通 譜 of the same clan; sworn brothers.
¹³⁰通 譯 to interpret.
通 財 currency.
通 路 a thoroughfare; through circuit. (elec.). [on a railway
通 車 through train; to begin opera
通 連 a good understanding with another party.
¹³⁵通 透 trenchant; incisive.
通 達 thoroughly versed in; to penetrate.
通 達 世 情 versed in the ways of the world.
通 達 時 務 understanding the times.

通達道路 the way of understanding.

140 通達體要 to apprehend the general idea—of the writings in question.

通道 open roads.

通過 passed through; carried, as a motion.

通過稅 tolls; transit dues.

通過議案 a proposal or bill which has been passed.

145 通都 a city open to traffic from every direction.

通鑑綱目 a condensed History of China. *See* 鑑 No. 841-14.

通·開 to open up; to clear out, as a drain.

通關節 secret understanding for illicit purposes.

通電 to send a circular telegram.

150 通電路 a closed circuit. (*elec.*).

通靈 magic; supernatural powers.

通顯 perspicuous.

通風 a through draught; to divulge; to communicate.

通飭 to issue circular instructions.

155 不通 obstructed; constipated; illogical; ungrammatical.

相通 in communication.

穿通 to bore a hole through; to thread—a needle.

貨不流通 no market for the goods.

↑ 交通 communication; intercourse.

(a) All; universal; the whole.

通共 the whole of; all; completely.

通國 the whole nation.

通夜 the whole night.

通宵達旦 throughout the whole night until the dawn.

5 通昔 the whole night.

通是我·的 all are mine.

通盤 all round; completely; the whole affair.

通盤計·畫 to draw up a complete scheme.

通統 the whole of.

10 通身 the whole of; from first to last; the whole body.

通通 the whole of.

通長 the entire length.

通體 the whole of; the whole body.

(b) Illicit intercourse. In collusion with.

通姦 criminal intercourse.

私通 illicit intercourse.

莊公通焉 Duke *Chuang* committed adultery with her.

(c) u.f. next.

通脫木 the rice-paper plant.

蓪[1] *Aralia papyrifera*, the pith of which is cut into what is 6639 known as rice-paper.

蓪·草畫 rice-paper pictures.

蓪·草(紙) rice-paper.

蓪·草花 flowers made from rice-paper.

木蓪 *Akebia quinata*.

慟[4] Grief; sadness. To mourn. Moved; affected. 6640 Also read *tung*[4].

慟哭 crying from sorrow; moved to tears.

哀慟 mourning.

心慟 moved in heart.

統[3] To govern; to rule; to control. 6641

統兵 to lead troops.

統制 to dominate; to control.

統屬文武 in control of both civil and military departments.

統帥 generalissimo.

5 統帶 to be in command of.

統帶官 a commander; a colonel.

統御 to govern the whole country.

統歸 to fall entirely under the control of; to become the sole property of; to unite and fall into (the sea, as rivers).

統治 having the entire management of.

10 統治權 sovereignty; executive authority.

統治階級 the ruling class.

統率 to have the control and direction of; to lead. (-*shuai*[4]).

統綱 the chief bond.

統轄 to have the general direction of; to oversee.

15 統領 a commandant; to lead troops.

(a) All; the whole. To gather into one.

統一 to unify; union; united; centralized; unity; standardized.

統一共和黨 United Republican Party.

統一其理論 unify the discussion.

統一國語 unify the National Language.

t 統一幣制 unification of the currency.

統一行政組織 uniform system of administration.

統一讀音 standard pronunciation.

一統 altogether; fully; under one head.

內政統一 unity of internal administration.

10 地·方統一 unity of territory.

種族統一 unity of race.

財政統一 unity of financial administration.

軍事統一 unification of military administration.

統例 the general principle of.

15 統云 to summarize.

統共 all; the whole of; entirely.

統共數·目 the total amount; the whole number.

統合 to unite all in one; to put together—as several numbers.

統同 to collect together; to bring or place together.

20 統括 summary; recapitulation.

統攝諸德 uniting all the virtues.

統盤·的籌算 to reckon up all the accounts.

統衆 to collect a crowd.

統系 or 系統 a system. *See* No. 2423—A.

25 統系·的概觀 systematic conception.

統統 the whole; total.

統總 all; the whole of; entirely.

統計 statistics.

統計多·少 what is the total?

30 統計學 study of statistics.

統計家 statistician.

統計局所 Bureau of Statistics.

統計年冊 Statistical Year-Book.

統計處 Bureau of Statistics.

35 統計表 statistical forms or charts.

下列統計 the following data.

人命統計 vital statistics.

死亡統計表 vital statistics.

製造統計 statistics of manufactures.

40 精密統計 accurate statistics or data.

大統 a connected whole; the empire.

(b) A clue. The end of the thread on a cocoon. A beginning; a succession.

統冀 or 統希 or 統望 to hope earnestly.

統承 to carry on the succession—of a dynasty.

統緒 a clue; succession in a dynasty.

統開 to come into being.

⁵正統 the true succession.

體統 propriety; the established custom; dignity; what is fitting to one's position.

TSA.　(ㄗㄚ)

(Tsah)

匝匜迊 2,5.

To go round; to make a circuit; to make a revolution; to turn round.

6642

匝月 a whole moon.

週匝 to revolve; to enwrap.

咂咂 1,5.

To suck; to smack the lips.

6643

咂一咂 suck it; taste it with the tongue.

咂咂兒 the nipples; the breasts.

咂嘴 a sound something like that of smacking the lips, used to indicate admiration; to smack the lips.

咂嘴咂舌 smacking the lips and sucking the tongue—speaking without rhyme or reason.

砸 2,5.　To smash; to strike; to knock.

6644

砸壞·了 smashed by a blow.

砸扁·了 smashed flat.

砸爛 smashed to a jelly.

砸碎 smashed to fragments.

砸苦 a severe beating, as with the fists.

砸開 to smash open.

砸開門 burst open the door.

咱 2,5.

6645　　*See below.*

Also read *tsan²*, and inter. 咨 No. 6674. for you and we.

咱們 (inclusive) we, i.e., you and I

咱兩個 or 咱兩兒 or 咱們倆 you and I.

咱家 we; us.

咱的 why? how's that? (*dial.*)

雜襍 2,5.

Mixed; confused; miscellaneous.

6646

雜亂 confused.

雜亂無章 disorderly.

雜事 miscellaneous matters.

雜介 office-boy; errand-boy.

⁵雜俎 miscellanea.

雜劇 plays; theatricals.

雜務 sundry duties.

雜史 private records; records of particular events.

雜在其內 mixed in with.

¹⁰雜家 miscellaneous writers—one of the nine classes of literature. *See* 九 No. 1198-25.

雜居 a resort for all classes of people.

雜廁 without order or sequence.

雜引 to give miscellaneous quotations.

雜心 a confused mind.

¹⁵雜感 various impressions.

雜技 various kinds of amusements.

雜拌 sundry; miscellaneous.

雜料 all sorts of materials.

雜會 to compound.

²⁰雜案 various charges against a person.

雜樣 all sorts.

雜杏 confused; disorderly.

雜流 an official with various duties.

雜混 confused; in disorder; promiscuous.

²⁵雜湊 miscellaneous articles gathered together into one category.

雜然而塵鄙 dusty, dirty slum conditions.

雜牌·子 a medley.

雜物 miscellaneous articles.

雜生動物 hybrid animals.

³⁰雜碎 entrails of animals—used in abusive language; chopsuev.

雜稅 miscellaneous or irregular taxes.

雜種 mixed seed; half-caste; hybrid; illegitimate child.

雜糧 various cereals.

雜紋 irregular stripes or streaks.

³⁵雜拏 a mixed mob.

雜耍 all kinds of amusements—as at fairs, etc.

雜膾 a hash composed of various articles of food.

雜色⁴ variegated; all kinds.

雜著⁴文集 miscellanea.

⁴⁰雜處³ people from all quarters dwell together.

雜記·的 miscellaneous; disconnected.

雜記簿 a note-book.

雜記賬 sundry accounts; sundries—in accounts.

雜評 notes and comments—in the press.

⁴⁵雜說 all sorts of opinions.

雜誌 magazines or periodicals.

雜·貨 sundries; all sorts of goods.

雜貨品 sundries.

雜·貨舖 a general store; a chandler's shop.

⁵⁰雜費 sundry expenses.

雜質 mixed; miscellaneous.

雜軍 troops that hold no allegiance to any party.

雜遝 many; numerous; mixed.

雜錄 miscellaneous.

⁵⁵雜集 miscellanea.

雜項 miscellaneous items in an account.

雜題 miscellaneous problems.

雜·麪 mixed flour, as that of wheat and millet, etc.

人衆口雜 a motley crowd.

⁶⁰打雜的 a man-of-all-work.

屬雜 promiscuous crowding together.

複雜 complex.

閒雜人 loafers.

紮 6647

1.5. **To bind; to tie; to fasten; to make a bundle.**
Also read *chah*[5].

紮帶·子 to tighten the girdle.
紮帳 to hook curtains back.
紮束 to bind on.
紮營 to pitch a camp.
[5]紮緊 to bind up tightly.
紮縛 or 紮綁 to tie up; to bind together.
紮腳[3] to bind the feet or ankles.
紮腳[3]帶·子 bands fastened round the ankles.
紮裹 to dress up; to bind; to repair.

TS'A. (ㄘㄚ)
(Ts'ah)

擦 6648

1.5. **To scour; to clean; to rub in; to wipe.**

擦乾 to wipe dry.
擦乾淨 to rub clean.
擦了黑 almost dark; dusk.
擦亮 rub it till it shines.
[5]擦傷 an abrasion; to graze the skin.
擦去 to rub out.
擦地板 to scrub the floor; to polish the floor.
擦子 an eraser.
橡皮擦·子 rubber eraser.
10 黑板擦·子 blackboard eraser.
擦布 a duster.
擦抹 to rub and wipe; to rub up —furniture, etc.
擦損 abrasion.
擦掌 to rub the hands.
15 擦汗 to wipe off perspiration.
擦油 to, oil; to varnish; to wipe away oil.
擦洗 to wash—as plates and dishes.
擦淚 to wipe away tears.
擦淨 to rub clean.
20 擦燈罩·子 to clean a lamp-glass.
擦牙 to brush the teeth.
擦玻·璃 to clean glass.
擦耗 abrasion.
擦耳 to grate on the ears.
25 擦肥皂 to wash with soap.
擦胭抹粉 to paint and powder.
擦臉 to rub the face—as with a hot cloth after a meal.
擦銅油 brass-polish.

擦銀粉 polishing-powder for silver.
30擦鞋油 shoe-polish.
輕擦 to graze the skin.

擦 6649

1.5. **Inter. preceding. Also read *sah*[5]. u.f. 撒 No. 5406.**

TSAI. (ㄗㄞ)

哉 6650

[1] **A particle expressing surprise, admiration, or grief. An expletive.**

優優大哉 all-complete is its greatness!
哀哉 Alas!
大哉孔子 Great indeed was Confucius!
尚亦有利哉 "and benefits (to the kingdom) also, may well be looked for from him."
[5]強哉矯 How firm is he in his energy!
思服悠哉 Long he thought, O, long and anxiously!
管仲之器小哉 Small indeed was the capacity of *Kuan Chung*.
至矣哉 How admirable!
誠哉是言也 True indeed is this saying!

(a) **An interrogative particle used with 焉、何、乎 and other particles.**

人焉廋哉 How can a man conceal his character?
何足道哉 How is it worth mentioning?
其何以行之哉 How can it be made to go?
吾有知乎哉 Am I indeed possessed of knowledge?
[5]天何言哉 Does Heaven speak?
夫何爲哉 What can he do to me?
夫召我者而豈徒哉 Can it be without reason that he has invited me?
安得不悲哉 How can I not grieve?
彼惡敢當我哉 How dare he withstand me? (*wu*[1])

(b) **To begin.**

三月哉生魄 in the third month when the moon began

---

to wane. *See* 旣 No. 453—A. 10.
四月哉生明 in the fourth month at the first appearance of the moon—the third of the lunar month. *See* 旣 No. 453 —A. 9.
朕哉自毫 our attack began in *Po*.

栽 6651

[1] **To plant; to care for plants. To flourish.**

栽上 to plant.
栽不活 it will not live if you plant it.
栽培 to tend; to care for; to assist.
栽培的 a husbandman.
[5]栽定 to plant firmly.
栽植 to plant.
栽樹 to plant trees.
栽樹日 Arbor Day.
栽秧 to transplant rice.
10栽種 to plant and sow.
栽穩 to plant firmly.
栽者培之 it nourishes those which are prospering.
栽花 to plant flowers.
栽贓 to place stolen goods with a person to implicate him.

(a) **To fall. To tumble.**

栽倒[3] to fall down; to tumble.
栽折了腿 fell and broke his leg. (-*shê*[2]-)
栽觔斗 (*kên*[1]·*tou*) to turn head over heels.
栽躺下 to fall down.

(b) **Saplings; young trees; cuttings for planting.**

柳樹栽·子 willow slips for planting.
花栽 cuttings of plants.

裁災灾 } 6652

[1] **Calamities from Heaven, as floods, famines, pestilence, etc. Misery; suffering; evil.**

災及其身 misfortune happens to him.
災情 famine conditions.

災晦 unlucky; unfortunate.
災民 calamity-stricken masses.
[5]災煞 noxious influences; suffering and sickness—as of children.
災異 portents, such as eclipses, comets, etc.
災病 or 災疫 a pestilence.
災禍 or 災難 or 災害 or 災殃 or 災變 or 災戾 calamities; misery; trouble; evils; dangers; misfortunes; sufferings, etc.
↓賑災會 Famine Relief Committee.
[10]災黎 the calamity-stricken people.

兵災 outrages committed by the military.
天災流行 judgements from Heaven are abroad.
天降[4]災 God is sending down calamities.
招災 to bring disaster upon oneself.
[15]救災 to deliver those who are suffering from calamity.
水災 floods.
火災 fire.
無災無病 quite well and free from troubles.

載[4] To load; to contain; to carry, as a vessel or cart.
6653 To fill up; to be contained.

載·到 to convey to....
載多。少 how much will it hold or carry?—as a vessel or cart, etc.
載客 to carry passengers.
載有 laden with...; having a cargo of....
[5]載滿 fully laden.
滿載而歸 to return fully loaded.
載糧 to transport army rations.
載脚[3] freight.
載貨 to carry goods; to load goods.
[10]載貨憑單 bill of lading.
載質 to carry the gift needed for introduction.
載道 the whole street.
怨聲載道 the murmurs filled the streets.
載運 to transport; to convey.
[15]不是載福之器 he is not a fit vessel to receive great blessings.

不穀載 not enough for a load.
厚德載福 great virtue receives blessings.
天下莫能載焉 nothing in the world could contain it.
所以載物 thus it contains (all) things.
[20]清酒既載 "his clear spirits in the vessel."
過載 to tranship.

(a) To complete. To record. To enter, as on a register.

載于何書 in what book is that contained?
載入 to enter—in a book.
載入總單 to enter on the cargo certificate.
載籍繁衍 a great multitude of records and volumes.
[5]失載 has not been recorded.
束牲載書 bound the victim and placed the writing upon it.
條約載明 it is clearly stated in the treaty.
記載 or 紀載 to record.

(b) Doings. To go to work. To begin from.

載芟載柞 they clear away the grasses and the bushes.
上天之載無聲無臭 "The doings of the Supreme Heaven have neither sound nor smell."
俶載南畝 we commence on the southern acres.
春日載陽 as the spring days lengthen out.
[5]湯始征自葛載 when T'ang began his work of executing justice, he commenced with Ko.
祗載見瞽瞍 "Reverently performing his duties, he waited on Ku Sou."
秋日載嘗 in autumn comes the sacrifice suitable to the season.
朕載自亳 I commenced in Po—refers to the work of destroying Chieh the tyrant.

(c) A particle used like 則, but often untranslatable.

載好其音 give forth their pleasant notes.
載寢載興 when I lie down and when I rise up.

載沉載浮 now sinking, now rising again.
載胥及溺 you will only go with it to ruin.
載飛載止 now flying, now stopping.
載馳載驅 I gallop them, I urge them on.
載驅薄薄 "she urges on her chariot rapidly."

(d) To wear on the head. u.f. 戴 No. 6003.

載弁俅俅 with his cap on his head, looking so respectful.

(e) Read tsai[3]. A year.

一年半載 about a year; a year or so.
千載 a thousand years.
半載 half a year.
文王初載 during the early years of Wên Wang.

儎[4] To load; to carry, etc.
6654 Inter. preceding.

宰𪗉[3] A ruler; the chief minister in a State. A servant; a steward. To govern; to rule.
6655

宰世 to rule the empire.
宰制 to rule; to direct.
宰執 to rule a State as a prime minister.
宰官 or 邑宰 a District Magistrate.
[5]宰物 able to manage affairs.
宰。相 (hsiang[4]) a prime minister.
有宰。相器 having capacity for statesmanship.
宰職 the office of prime minister.
宰衡 a prime minister.
[10]宰輔 a prime minister.
宰輔之量 capacity for ruling as a prime minister.
宰錄 the office of prime minister.
主宰 a ruler; the controlling power. God.
冢宰 a chief minister.
[15]城宰 a District Magistrate.
眞宰 a Mohammedan term for God.
諸宰 all the servants—the stewards and those under them.

(a) To slaughter animals.

宰 割 to cut up—as meat.
宰 夫 or 膳 宰 or 庖 宰 a cook.
宰 殺 to kill; to slaughter.
宰 牛 to kill an ox.
宰 牲 場 (or 所) a slaughter-house.
宰 肉 to cut up meat.

(b) A mound or grave; similar to 冢 No. 1515.

宰 木 or 宰 樹 trees around a grave.

崽 3 A child; a servant. A diminutive. Inter. 仔 No. 6940-A.
6656

下 崽·子 to litter; to bring forth young.
爛 崽 a worthless fellow.
狗 崽·子 puppies—used as an abusive expression.
細 崽 a servant; a "boy."

在 4 At; in; on. To rest with; to consist in. To be present; to be alive. With reference to; in point of; in the case of.
6657
Distinguish 存 No. 6891.

在 一 塊 兒 all together.
在 上 above; on; at.
在°上·頭 (or 邊) above; on the top.
在 下 below; beneath; self-depreciatory term.
⁵在·不·在 is he dead?
在 世 alive.
在°乎 to consist in 在·乎 to care about.
在·乎 各 人 that depends on each individual.
在 事 to do duty; to be on duty.
¹⁰在 事 人 those on duty; the members of a staff.
在 你 or 在 你 身·上 it is your business; the responsibility is yours.
在 你 看 from your viewpoint; how does it seem to you?
在 位 in the power of; power; on the throne.
在 保 on bail.
¹⁵在 假 on leave.
在 先 beforehand; then; that time.
在 內 within; included.

在 其 中 included; in the midst.
在 前 beforehand; that time; then.
²⁰在 劫 難 逃 what is fated cannot be avoided.
在 卽 at once; immediately; near at hand.
在 在 in every case; everywhere.
在 在 可 虞 there is danger in every place—it is unavoidable.
在 在 有 益 always profitable.
²⁵在 在 皆 是 it is the same everywhere.
在 地·下 below.
在 坐 seated; on the bench—as in a court.
在 場 to be present; on the spot; of the party.
在 外 extra; outside; over and above.
³⁰在 外·面 (or·邊 or·頭) outside.
在 夜 間 during the night.
在 夢 中 in a dream.
在 官 言 官 when in office speak as an official—to speak of one side of a matter only.
在 學 to be in school; to have taken the first degree under the former system.
³⁵在 室 in the home—said of an unmarried girl.
在 家 at home; in the house.
在 家 出 家 to worship Buddha quietly in the heart is as good as leaving home to become a priest.
在 底·下 beneath.
在 座 to be present at.
⁴⁰在 後 behind.
在 心 in one's heart.
在 意 to notice; to bear in mind.
在 意 中 within one's intentions; included in one's objective.
在 我 the matter rests with me; as far as I am concerned.
⁴⁵在 我 看 looked at from my point of view.
在 我 身·上 the burden is on my shoulders.
在 所 不 免 it cannot but be; impossible to be avoided.
在 所 不 能 in the category of the impossible.
在 所 必 it cannot be avoided; it must be.
⁵⁰在 手 in the hand of; in hand; in the power of; in stock.
在 押 in custody.
在 握 in one's power.

在 敎 to be in the sect; to be a Mohammedan or a member of the Christian Church.
在 於 得 已 if it can be managed.
⁵⁵在 明 處 openly.
在 昔 formerly.
在 末 尾 at the tail-end.
在 案 on record; as the records show; has been laid before the court.
在 此 here.
⁶⁰在 民 to be a Chinese, as contrasted with the Manchus.
在 理 in reason; reasonable.
在 當 中 in the middle; among; between.
在 皮 毛 superficial.
在 眼 前 or 在 目 前 before the eyes; at the present time.
⁶⁵在 禮 a Total Abstinence Society.
在 空 中 in the air.
在 職 in office.
在 脚 下 beneath the feet.
在 船 中 交 貨 ex ship.
⁷⁰在 苦 in mourning—for one hundred days after the death of father or mother; used on cards when in mourning.
在 行 (hang²) in the trade; versed in; an expert.
在 裏·頭 (or·邊 or·面) inside.
在 計 畫 之 中 in contemplation; under consideration.
在 途 中 in transit; on the way.
⁷⁵在 那 (na³)·裏 (or·邊 or 兒) where?
在 那 (na⁴)·裏 (or·邊 or 兒) there.
在 野 out of office; in obscurity—contrasted with—67 above.
在 門 下 to be brought up under....
在 露 天 地 in the open air.
⁸⁰不 在 not present; dead.
現 在 now; at present.
自·在 at ease; comfortable; having freedom.
不 自·在 out of sorts.

再 4 Again; a second time; repeated. Then; further. Before a negative it adds emphasis.
6658

再 三 repeatedly; over and over again.
再 三 不 肯 emphatic refusal to assent.
再 三 再 四 again and again.

再 不 來 it never comes again.

[5] 再 世 a second state of existence.

再 乘 to multiply a number by itself a second time; to raise a number to the third power.

再 來 to come again.

再 來 年 the year after next.

再 保 險 reinsurance.

[10] 再 兼 furthermore.

再 再 叮 嚀 gave him repeated injunctions.

再 出 to reissue.

再 分 to subdivide.

再 加·上 or 再 搭·上 and in addition; and still more.

[15] 再 去 to go again.

再 合 to reassemble.

再 啟 a postscript—f u r t h e r; again.

再 四 again and again.

再 四 思 維 to give a matter careful thought.

[20] 再 始 to make a fresh start.

再 宿 to stay for two nights.

再 察 to re-examine.

再 審 a retrial.

再 從 兄 弟 second cousins o f the same surname, having the same paternal grand-uncle.

[25] 再 思 to reconsider.

再 拘 留 to remand a prisoner.

再 接 再 厲 to make a determined effort.

再 收 監 recommitted to prison.

再 數 to re-count.

[30] 再 斯 可 矣 twice is quite sufficient.

再 會 we shall meet again—good-bye.

再 有 to recur.

再 歸 殘 像 recurrent vision.

再 沒·有 話·說 there is nothing more to be said.

[35] 再 版 a second edition.

再 犯 to repeat an offence.

再 生 born a second time—as when delivered from death.

再 生 父 母 you are my second parents—an expression o f gratitude for assistance i n great difficulties.

再 病 to have a relapse of sickness.

[40] 再 發 to have a relapse of sickness.

再 租 to re-lease.

再 立 合 同 to renew an agreement.

再 者 furthermore—introduces a new subject; P. S.

再 興 to revive.

[45] 再 行 again; further.

再 行 延 期 to m a k e further delay.

再 行 錯 to relapse into error.[bye.

再 見 we shall meet again; good-

再 解 官 recommitted t o t h e court.

[50] 再 說 to speak again; to defer a matter; and further....

再 說·一·遍 repeat w h a t y o u have said; to repeat what was said.

再 造 to re-create.

再 過 幾 天 in a few day's time.

再 運 心·思 give the matter further consideration.

[55] 再 選 re-election.

再 醮 or 再 嫁 to re-marry—of widows.

再 開 首 作 to begin again.

再 限 an extension of time.

再 集 to gather together again.

[60] 再 顧 to give a second glance—at a beauty.

TS'AI.　　(ㄘㄞ)

猜[1] To guess.　To suspect; to doubt.

6659

⌜(-chao[2])

猜·不 中 (-chung[4]) or 猜·不 着 unable to guess correctly.

猜·不 透 unable to guess.

猜 單 雙 to guess odd or even.

猜 嫌 to suspect and dislike; to be suspicious of.

[5] 猜 害 envious and malicious.

猜 察 to suspect and make investigations.

猜 尋 to conjecture; to guess.

猜 度 (to[4,5]) to guess; to hazard an opinion.

猜 心 機 to guess one's thoughts.

[10] 猜 忍 cruel and suspicious.

猜 忤 suspicious and perverse.

猜 恨 or 猜 忌 to e n v y; t o suspect; to hate; suspicious.

猜 想 to guess; to conjecture.

猜 意 doubts and suspicions.

[15] 猜 憚 suspicious dislike.

猜 懼 suspicious dread.

猜 拳 or 猜 枚 to play mora or "guess-fingers."

猜 決 to decide.

猜 毀 to envy and slander another.

[20] 猜·猜·看 guess; see if you can guess.

猜 畏 in doubt and fear.

猜 疑 to suspect; to be in doubt.

猜 算 to anticipate; to conjecture.

猜 處 to consider the best way to act.

[25] 猜 詳 to guess; to conjecture.

猜 謗 to slander another because of envious suspicion.

猜 謎 to guess riddles.

猜 警 suspicious and alert.

猜 貳 divided in heart; double-minded.

[30] 猜 量 to form an estimate of.

猜 隙 disagreement arising from envy and suspicion.

猜 鷙 cruel and malicious.

無 猜 without any doubts or suspicions.

才[2] Talent; ability; parts. Power; force.

6660 Distinguish 寸 No. 6892.

才 不 勝 任 abilities inadequate for the position.

才 不 才 亦 各 言 其 子 也 whether a son has ability or not, each father calls his son a son.

才 也 養 不 才 let those who have talents train up those who have not.

才 人 a man of parts; inferior Imperial concubines.

[5] 才 儲 八 斗 having great ability; exceedingly talented.

才 德 全 備 perfect a l i k e in virtue and ability.

才 具 ability; talents; p a r t s; capacity.

才 兼 文 武 having both c i v i l and military genius.

才 分 talents; natural gifts.

[10] 才 力 power and ability to manage affairs.

才 名 a reputation for talent.

才 品 a man's talents.

才 器 capacity f o r managing affairs.

才 地 having both talents and standing.

[15] 才 士 an able man.

才 媛 a talented woman.

才 子 a man of talent; a genius—especially used of novelists.

才 學 ability; learning.
才·幹 talents; ability; power; capacity for affairs.
²⁰才 德 talent and virtue.
才 德 出 衆 extraordinary ability and high integrity.
才 思 mental endowments.
才 情 ability; talents; capacity.
才 慧 intelligence.
²⁵才 拙 incompetent.
才 智 wisdom; talents.
才 望 noted ability.
才 氣 高 邁 great ability.
才 略 ability; talents; capacity for affairs.
³⁰才 疎 學 淺 his talents are inferior and his learning superficial.
才 短 lacking in ability; incompetent.
才 童 a talented youth.
才 能 ability; power; parts; capacity. (Also in sense A.)
才 華 出 衆 talents and ability above the average.
³⁵才 藻 literary talents.
才 調 talent; tact.
才 識 discernment and penetration.
才 貌 talents and personality.
才 貌 雙 全 both pretty and talented—of a woman.
⁴⁰才 質 natural gifts.
才 身 a man of parts.
才 郎 an able man; paramour.
才 難 不 其 然 乎 it is difficult to find ability. Is it not so?
一 表 人 才 a man of fine presence.
⁴⁵三 才 the *Three Powers*, i.e., Heaven, Earth, and Man.
不 才 stupid; dull—term of self-depreciation.
中 人 之 才 mediocre ability.
偏 才 perverted talents.
口 才 eloquence.
⁵⁰多 才 versatile.
大 才 小 用 great talents employed in petty affairs.
文 才 literary talents.
無 才 incompetent.
英 才 great abilities; a genius.
⁵⁵高 才 highly gifted; great talents.

(a) Used as an abbreviation of 纔 No. 6672. Only then; just now, etc.

(b) Used for 裁 No. 6664. To plan, etc.

(c) Used for 材 No. 6661. Materials, etc.

材² Materials; stuff. Qualities. Inter. preceding.
6661 Distinguish 村 No. 6895.

材 人 a man of outstanding ability.
材 伎 outstanding ability in craftsmanship.
材 具 科 Department of Supplies.
材 力 strong—of character.
⁵材 吏 able officers.
材 器 ability; genius; capacity.
材·幹 timber; genius; capacity; ability.
材 木 timber.
材 武 a man of military ability.
¹⁰材·料 materials; character.
材 質 abilities; capacity; qualifications; natural ability.
材 雋 noted abilities.
不 成 材 useless.
五 材 the Five Elements, metal 金, wood 木, water 水, fire 火, and earth 土.
¹⁵棺·材 a coffin.
藥·材 drugs; medicines.
身 材 the build of a man.

財² Wealth; property; valuables. Bribes.
6662

財·主 or 財·主 老 a wealthy man; a capitalist.
財 利 wealth; profit; gain.
財 力 financial resources; the power of wealth.
財 勢 wealth and influence.
⁵財 可 通 神 money will move the gods.
財 命 相 連 wealth and life are closely associated—mean, stingy.
財 團 法 人 juridical person of an association.
財 多 累 己 excess of wealth is an embarrassment.
財 富 valuables; precious things.
¹⁰財 寶 wealth.
財 帛 wealth; personal property.
財·政 finances; administration of finance.
財 政 原 理 principles of finance.

財 政 司 Department of Finance.
¹⁵財 政 困 難 financial embarrassment.
財 政 壟 斷 financial monopoly.
財 政 學 finance, as a course of study.
財 政 專 家 financial expert.
財 政 廳 Provincial Department of Finance.
²⁰財 政 方 針 financial policy.
財 政 案 a finance bill.
財 政 整 理 會 Commission for the Readjustment of Finances.
財 政 科 Bureau of Finance.
財 政 表 a financial statement.
²⁵財 政 觀 the financial outlook.
財 政 部 Ministry of Finance. The Exchequer.
財 政 部 公 債 票 treasury bills or notes.
財 政 部 長 Minister of Finance.
財 政 顧 問 financial advisor.
³⁰財 是 英 雄 money makes the man.
財 東 a capitalist.
財 源 resources.
財 物 property; effects.
財 物 沒 收 confiscation of property.
³⁵財 產 estate; property; assets.
  公 有 財 產 public property.
  特 有 財 產 separate property.
  私 有 財 產 private property.
財 產 之 狀 況 the condition of the assets.
⁴⁰財 產 出 資 contributions of property, etc.
財 產 刑 a fine; pecuniary punishment.
財 產 家 the wealthy.
財 產 權 proprietary rights.
財 產 法 laws relating to property.
⁴⁵財 產 目·錄 inventory of the property or estate.
財 產 稅 property tax.
財 產 蕩 盡 the estate is squandered.
財 產 資 格 property qualification.
財 癖 crazy for wealth.
⁵⁰財 祉 wealth and happiness.
財·神 or 財 帛 星 君 the God of Wealth.
財 禮 betrothal presents.
財 能 壯 膽 wealth gives a man courage.
財 貨 property; effects.
⁵⁵財 賄 bribes.

財 迷 infatuated with the pursuit of wealth.

財 運 good fortune.

不 義 之 財 ill-gotten gains.

分 財 distribution of wealth.

60 外 財 wealth accidentally acquired.

母 財 principal; capital.

生 財 to make money; that which produces wealth.

發 財 to make one's fortune.

破 財 to lose wealth.

戈² To wound with weapons.
6663

裁² To cut out; to cut off; to diminish; to reduce, as the number of servants, etc.; to moderate.
6664

裁 人 to cut down the number of persons employed.

裁 併 to abolish and incorporate —as when amalgamating two official posts, etc.

裁 兵 to reduce the number of troops; disarmament.

裁 其 有 餘 to cut off superfluity.

5裁·出 新 聞 newspaper clippings.

裁 剪 to cut out; to arrange.

裁 撤 to abrogate; abolition.

裁 汰 to make a selection; to cleanse and weed out, as superfluous officials.

裁 減·些 cut off a little; reduce it a little.

10裁 減 列 強 海 軍 Naval Disarmament.

裁 減 軍 備 會 議 Disarmament Conference. A.c. 軍縮會議

裁 答 to write a letter in reply.

裁 紙 to cut paper.

裁 紙 刀 a knife for cutting paper.

15裁·縫 a tailor.

裁 衣 to cut out garments.

裁(衣)尺 the tailor's foot-rule— it is longer than that used by carpenters.

裁 製 to cut out and make—clothing, etc.

裁 遣 to dismiss.

20裁 釐 加 稅 abolish likin and increase the tariff.

裁 銷 to do away with; to abrogate; to dissolve.

裁 長 補 短 "to rob Peter to pay Paul." corrup. of 截 長 補 短 to level off irregularities.

裁 革 to abrogate; to do away with.

(a) To regulate. To plan. To decide. To calculate. To settle.

裁 判 to try; to judge; to sentence; judgement.

聽 候 裁 判 waiting for a decision.

裁 判 員 umpire; referee.

裁 判 官 a judge.

5裁 判 所 a court of justice; tribunal.

裁 判 權 jurisdiction. See 領 No. 4058-5.

裁 判 法 jurisprudence. [sanction.

裁 制 to restrict; to apply forceful

裁 可 to give assent to; to authorize.

10 君 主·的 裁 可 royal assent.

裁 奪 to plan; to decide.

裁 奪 示 遵 to decide and notify those concerned.

裁 度 to plan; to decide.

裁 度 事 理 to exercise judgement on matters.

15裁 成 to regulate and bring to completion.

裁 抑 to repress; to restrain.

裁 赦 to pardon.

裁 斷 to judge; to decide.

裁 正 to regulate and put in order.

20裁 決 to decide.

裁 處 to consider how to act.

裁 許 to give assent to; to authorize.

裁 詩 to compose poetry.

裁 酌 to plan; to decide.

25裁 量 to estimate; to measure.

親 裁 to decide for oneself.

自 裁 to decide for oneself; to commit suicide.

(b) Occurs u.f. 總 No. 6672. Only then, etc.

采³ To pluck; to gather, as flowers.
6665 Inter. 採 No. 6668. Distinguish 釆 No. 5238.

采 名 to seek for fame.

采 撫 to gather together; to collect.

采 集 to gather together, as material, etc.

采 用 to make a selection; to select for use.

5采 緝 to twist hemp into thread; an anthology.

采 芹 to pluck cress—to take the former first degree of Hsiu ts'ai.

采 花 釀 蜜 (bees) gather honey from the flowers.

采 薪 之 憂 the sorrow of gathering firewood,–used for a trifling ailment; an excuse for non-appearance. See 負 No. 1956-37.

采 輯 an anthology.

10采 辦 to buy up.

采 采 to gather again and again; numerous.

喝 采 to applaud; to call "bravo!"

(a) Variegated. Bright colours. Inter. 彩 No. 6667.

采 物 variously coloured things used as badges of rank, etc.

采 章 variegated.

采 色 beautifully coloured objects.

采 采 衣·服 gay clothing.

采 鷄 a variety of the golden pheasant.

(b) Affairs. Business.

亮 采 有 邦 "brilliantly conduct the affairs of the State."

服 采 "those who carry out your measures." Those who do the business of their prince.

疇 咨 若 予 采 "who will search out for me a man equal to the exigency of affairs?"

載 采 采 "he does such and such things?"

(c) Read ts'ai⁴. An allotment to a feudal noble.

采 邑 territory once set apart for feudal nobles.

食 采 to enjoy the revenue of such a district.

寀³·⁴ Officials in charge of the allotment to the feudal nobles.
6666

寀 寀 colleagues; fellow-officials.

彩³ Ornamented; brilliant; gay. Variegated colours.
6667 Lucky; a prize.

彩 旗 ornamented banners.

彩 氣 luck; fortune.

彩 球 the corona around the sun during an eclipse.

彩 畫 to adorn; to paint; coloured pictures.

⁵彩 票 a lottery ticket.

彩 綢 silks hung over doors at weddings.

彩 繡 colours and embroidery.

彩 色⁴ variegated; parti-coloured; colour.

彩 色⁴ 照 像 colour-photography.

¹⁰彩 色⁴ 石 印 chromo-lithography.

彩 資 a prize—for a race.

彩 轎 a bridal sedan-chair.

彩·錢 money spent by the winner in standing treat.

彩·頭 luck; fortune.

¹⁵彩 飾 to beautify; to ornament.

中⁴ 彩 to win a prize.

五 彩 the five colours; colours generally; coloured.

光 彩 brilliant; bright and gay.

喝 彩 to applaud. = 6665.12.

²⁰好 彩 a lucky hit.

奪 彩 to gain the prize.

得 彩 to gain the prize.

無 精 打 彩 listless. [lence.

異 彩 unusually beautiful; excel-

²⁵紅 彩 festoon of red cloth hung over a doorway during a wedding.

結 彩 to festoon.

雲·彩 cloud .

探 ³ To pluck; to choose; to gather; to pick; to collect.
6668

探 光 法 method of lighting—as in a school, etc.

探 取 to select; to adopt—as a system or policy.

探 問 to make inquiries.

探 捕 爲 業 to live by capturing —fish, etc.

⁵探 掘 to mine—as coal.

探 掘 權 mining rights.

探 摘 to pick; to pluck.

探 擇 to make a selection; to adopt—as a policy, etc.

探 桑 to gather mulberry leaves.

¹⁰探 珠 to dive for pearls.

探 生 to snatch the souls of living persons.

探 用 to select for use; selective; adoption.

探 用 理 由 reasons for adopting.

探 石 場 a quarry.

¹⁵探 納 to receive (proposal, etc.)

探 花 to pluck flowers; to deflower.

探 茶 葉 to pick tea-leaves.

探 藥 to gather simples.

探 補 者 流 foxes and other uncanny creatures that are supposed to take the vitality of others to supply their own deficiency.

²⁰探 訪 to make inquiries; to get information; to get news, as a reporter.

探 買 to buy up.

探 辦 to buy up.

探 金 to mine for gold.

探 鑛 權 mining concessions.

²⁵探 集 to gather together, as materials.

睬 ³ To notice; to pay attention to; to greet.
6669

不 要 睬·他 pay no attention to him.

綵 ³ Coloured; variegated. Inter. 彩 No. 6667.
6670

綵 女 or 采 女 concubines; ladies of the palace.

綵 結 net profits.

綵 色 many-coloured.

綵 衣 gay garments.

菜 ⁴ Vegetables; greens; edible herbs; food.
6671

菜 刀 a chopper for kitchen use.

菜 單 a bill of fare.

菜 園 a vegetable garden.

菜·子 rape.

⁵菜 市 vegetable market.

菜 郛·子 outside leaves of cabbage.

菜 攤 a stall for the sale of vegetables.

菜 根 cabbage-stalks.

菜 油 oil expressed from rape-seeds; colza oil.

¹⁰菜 種·子 vegetable seeds.

菜 色⁴ cadaverous.

菜 蔬 vegetables.

菜 飯 food generally.

海 菜 edible seaweeds.

¹⁵生 菜 salads; lettuce.

白 菜 cabbage.

素 菜 vegetable diet.

菠 菜 spinach.

青 菜 greens; vegetables.

²⁰醎 菜 pickled cabbage. A.c. 小菜兒

纔 ² Just now; then; in that case. Before. After.
6672

纔 來 just arrived.

纔 來·一·下 arrived a little while ago.

纔 到 just arrived.

纔 剛 or 剛 纔 just now; a moment ago.

⁵纔 去·了 he has just gone.

纔 好 then and only then is it all right.

纔 明·白·了 I then understood it clearly.

纔 是 that is it; very well; then and only then is it right.

纔 給·他·了 have just given it to him.

¹⁰方 纔 just now; a little while ago.

蔡 ⁴ Name of a small State in what is now Honan. Herbs. A species of tortoise.
6673

蔡 國 a small feudal State as above.

蔡 山 a mountain near Yachow in Szechwan.

(a) Read *sa*⁴·⁵. Criminals undergoing the lesser banishment.

二 百 里 蔡 (the next) 200 *li* were occupied by the criminals undergoing the lesser banishment.

TSAN.   (ㄗㄢ)

咱 喒 偺 ² A dual pronoun; I; you and me; we two. See 咱 No. 6645.
6674

喒·們 we, i.e., you and I or you and we.

多·喒 when? [and we.

棧 ³ An instrument of torture for squeezing the fingers of prisoners or witnesses in order to extort evidence or confession.
6675

贊 贊 [4]

6676
To assist; to second.

贊 一 辭 to help by a word.
贊 佐 to assist.
贊 助 to approve; to acquiesce.
贊 同 to join in advocating; to commend.
[5] 贊 周 易 修 春 秋 he collated the *Book of Changes* and put in order the *Spring and Autumn Annals*.
贊 天 地 之 化 育 assist the transforming and nourishing powers of Heaven and Earth.
贊 成 to help to accomplish; to second; to acquiesce; to agree to a proposition;*
贊 成 人 the seconder; a supporter.
贊 成 員 auxiliary member.
[10] 贊 理 to help to manage.
贊 禮 員 a master of ceremonies.
贊 襄 to assist.
贊 襄 大 臣 an honorary title of the highest kind.
* to favor a motion.

(a) To praise. To admire. Inter. 讚 No. 6681.

贊 歎 to admire; to praise.
贊 美 to praise.
稱°贊 to extol; to praise.

(b) To inform.

徧 贊 賓 客 informed all the guests.

(c) To bring to light.

幽 贊 于 神 明 to afford a mysterious revelation of the divine beings.

儹 [3]
6677
To accumulate; to hoard; to store up.

積 儹 財 寶 在 天 to lay up treasures in Heaven.

灒 [4]
6678
To spatter; to splash; to scatter. Cf. 869.

灒·了 一 點 泥 he spattered me with a little mud.
灒·出 火 星 to scatter sparks.
灒 濕·了 to spatter and wet.

簪 [1]
6679
A clasp; a hair-pin. To stick in the hair.

簪·子 or 簪棒 a hair-pin with flat spoon-shaped ends.
簪 環 hair-pins and ear-rings.
簪 筆 to stick the pen in the hair—behind the ear.
簪 纓 世 冑 a family, the successive generations of which have all had representatives in official life.
簪 花 to wear flowers in the hair.
玉 簪 花 the tuberose.
脫 簪 組 taken off the hat-pin and girdle—retired from official life.

臢 [1]
6680
A hare-lip. Dirty. Also read *tsang*[1].

腌 臢 dirty; greasy and filthy.

讚 [4]
6681
To praise; to eulogize; to commend.

讚 嘆 不 已 praising and lamenting him unceasingly.
讚 善 to praise the virtuous.
讚 得 過 laudable.
讚 揚 to praise; to commend.
[5] 讚 文 a eulogy.
讚 美 to praise.
讚 美 詩 hymns.
讚 羨 to sing the praises of.
讚 語 words of praise.
[10] 讚 賞 to commend and reward.
讚 頌 or 稱 讚 to sing the praises of.

趲 [3]
6682
To hasten; to urge; to hurry.

趲·他 走 make him go faster.
趲 步 to quicken one's pace.
趲 程 to travel fast; to hurry on.
趲 行 to travel fast.
趲 路 to hurry on; to travel fast.
趲 遲 to go slowly.

暫 [4]
6683
For a time; shortly; meanwhile. Suddenly. Also read *chan*[4].

暫 且 for the time being; for a short time.
暫 住 to reside for a time; to lodge temporarily.

暫 候 wait a while.
暫 借 a temporary loan.
[5] 暫 准 援 用 temporarily in force.
暫 別 temporary separation.
暫 寄 to lodge temporarily.
暫 局 temporary state of affairs.
暫 居 to reside for a time.
[10] 暫 延 or 暫 擱 to adjourn.
暫 忍 have patience for a little while; put up with it for the time being. [second form.
暫 新 quite new. Also with 158,
暫 歇 rest for a while.
暫 時 for the time being; for a short time.
[15] 暫 時 之 辦 法 a temporary arrangement.
暫 濟 燃 眉 give me help for my singed eyebrows—oblige me with a temporary loan.
暫 爲 for the time being; for a short time.
暫 留 temporary detention, either of persons or things.
暫 緩 gradually; slowly.
[20] 暫 署 acting—temporarily in office.
暫 行 條 例 temporary regulations.
暫 行 法 temporary laws.
暫 行 試 辦 to give a temporary trial—to a new scheme.
暫 遇 or 暫 面 to meet suddenly.

鏨 [4]
6684
A cold chisel. To cut out; to chisel out; to engrave.

鏨 刀 a graving tool.
鏨 子 an iron chisel.
鏨 字 to engrave characters.
鏨 花 to carve flowers.

TS'AN. (ㄘㄢ)

參 參 [1]

6685
To counsel; to consult together. To take part in. To intervene.

參 事 a councillor.
參 事 會 advisory committee.
參 列 to assist at.
參 加 to take part in; to intervene.
[5] 參 加 可 能 the possibility of taking part in.
參 加 萬 國 博 覽 會 to participate in the World's Fair.

↓參加網球比賽 to take part in a tennis match.

參加付欵 payment for honour —of a protested bill by a third party, to save the honour of the drawer.

參加承諾 (or 受) acceptance for honour; acceptance *supra protest;* acceptance of a protested bill by a third person, in order to save the honour of the drawer.

參將+or 參府 former title of a lieutenant-colonel.

¹⁰參戰 to participate in the war.

參政 to participate in the government; suffrage.

參政運動 suffrage movements.

參政院 Political Council.

參知政事 to assist in the government.

¹⁵參°與+to take part in; identified with.

參°與+行禮 took part in the ceremony.

參觀 to inspect; to pay a visit to —as to a school.

參觀人 spectators; visitors.

參詳 to consult in detail.

²⁰參謀 to advise; a State Counsellor.

參謀官 a staff officer.

參謀長³ Chief of Staff.

參議 to counsel; to advise.

參議員 a senator.

²⁵參議院 the Senate.

參贊 to act as advisor to; a Secretary of Legation; an attaché.

　漢文參贊 Chinese Secretary of Legation.

參酌 to consult; to deliberate.

參預 to participate in.

(a) To consider. To collate. To compare.

參定 to decide after due reflection.

參想 to reflect; to consider.

參看 to compare.

參禪 to sit absorbed in contemplation—as Buddhists. (*ch'an²*)

⁵參考 to examine into; compare; to collate.

參考書 books of reference.

參考樣本 pattern for reference.

參訂無訛 to compare with and find no errors.

參較 to collate; to compare.

¹⁰參透 to think out; thoroughly versed in; to see through a thing.

(b) To impeach. To report against.

參劾 to impeach.

參奏 to send in a joint memorial.

參懲 to impeach and punish.

參究 to impeach.

⁵參罪 a punishment inflicted on constables who fail to catch thieves within a certain time.

參處³ to impeach and punish.

參革 to impeach and deprive of rank.

被參 to be impeached.

請參 to ask for punishment—to throw oneself upon the mercy of a superior.

(c) To mix. To blend.

參互 mixed; confused.

參入 to interpolate.

參製 to mix; to compound.

參雜 confused; mixed.

(d) To visit a superior.

參拜 or 參見 or 參謁 to visit a superior.

參禮 the ceremonial at interviews with superiors.

(e) To reach to; to penetrate.

參天 to penetrate the clouds; reaching to Heaven.

(f) To make one of three.

可以與天地參矣 he may rank as one with Heaven and Earth.

(g) Read *ch'ên¹* or *ts'ên¹*. Uneven; irregular.

參差 (*tz'ŭ¹*) unequal; not uniform; confused; irregular.

(h) Read *shên¹*. The 21st zodiacal constellation; some of the stars in Orion.　A.p. *ts'an¹*.

參商 or 參辰 or 參晨 Orion and Lucifer — which never see each other — enemies.

(i) Read *shên¹*. Ginseng, etc.

人參 ginseng.

洋參 foreign ginseng.

海參 bêche-de-mer, the trepang— *Holothuria edulis.*

紅玉人參 clarified ginseng.

(j) Read *san¹*. u.f. 三.

慘³ Sorrowful; grieved; sad; miserable. Grievous. Cruel.
6686

慘切 grieved in heart.

慘刑 cruel punishment; torture.

慘劇 a tragedy—as a stage-play.

慘急刻深 harsh dealing and irregular exactions—by judges.

⁵慘情 or 悽慘 or 悲慘 or 慘惻 or 慘愴 grieved; sad.

慘懍 bitterly cold.

慘變 a cruel fate.

慘極 very pitiable.

慘殺 cruel massacres.

¹⁰慘沮 full of grief; melancholy.

慘澹 dispirited.

慘澹經營 carefully thought-out plans.

慘然 dispirited.

慘狀 wretchedness; distressing circumstances.

¹⁵慘獄 criminal cases with many executions.

慘痛 deeply grieved.

慘綠 dark green.

慘聲 pitiful cries.

慘虐 exceedingly harsh and cruel treatment.

²⁰慘遭橫禍 to meet with cruelty and unlooked-for misfortunes.

慘酷 callous; cruel.

騲¹ The two outside horses of a team of four abreast.
6687

騪乘 the Imperial carriage.

停騪 to stop the horses; to put up at.

黪³ Mottled grey; speckled; black and white. Mildewed.
6688

黪淡 gloomy; dark.

黪白 grey—as hair.

黑黪黪的 blackened; grimy; dirty.

殘² To injure; to spoil; to
6689   destroy. To oppress. Spoilt;
useless. A remnant; residue.

殘 兵 defeated troops.
殘 冬 the end of the year.
殘 刻 cruel and avaricious.
殘 喘 the last breath—of the
    dying.
⁵殘 壞 to injure; to destroy.
殘 夢 an unfinished dream.
殘 客 remaining visitors.
殘 害 to destroy; to injure.
殘 害 人 道 inhuman.
¹⁰殘 山 賸 水 the remaining rem-
    nants of national territory.
殘 席 a table after a meal.
殘 年 failing years.
殘 廢 maimed; c r i p p l e d; de-
    formed.
殘 廢 傢·伙 damaged or second-
    hand goods.
¹⁵殘 忍 cruel; vindictive; barbarous.
殘 息 the last gasp.
殘 戮 ruthless slaughter.
殘 敗 ruined; withered.
殘 日 the declining day.
²⁰殘 春 (or 夏 秋) the end of
    spring, summer or autumn, re-
    spectively.
殘 暑 great heat.
殘 暴 cruel; vindictive.
殘 暴·的 狠 a ravening wolf.
殘 月 如 弓 the waning moon is
    bow-shaped.
²⁵殘 杯 a half-drained goblet.
殘 杯 冷 炙 broken victuals.
殘 橫 cruel and tyrannical.
殘 殺 to massacre.
殘 毀 to destroy; to ruin.
³⁰殘 水 dirty water.
殘 照 the evening glow.
殘 燈 復 明 the reviving flicker
    of an expiring lamp—the last
    flicker of life in the dying.
殘 生 failing years; the remain-
    ing years of one's life.
殘 留 remains; remnants.
³⁵殘 疾 maimed; c r i p p l e d; de-
    formed; physical deformity.
殘 碑 a broken stone-tablet.
殘 紅 fallen flowers.
殘 缺 deficient; broken.
殘 缺 失 次 spoilt and in wrong
    order.
⁴⁰殘 花 a withered flower; a woman
    whose beauty has gone.
殘 花 敗 柳 faded flowers and
    w i t h e r e d willows—fallen

women.
殘 虐 malicious; cruel.
殘 蜩 an expiring cicada.
殘 賊 之 人 a villain.
⁴⁵殘 酷 cruel and vindictive.
殘 釭 an expiring lamp.
殘 陽 the setting sun.
殘 雪 light snows in spring.
殘 食 or 殘 飯 broken victuals.
⁵⁰殘 餘 remnants.

慙
慚²   Ashamed; to feel
6690   mortified.

慚 形 having the appearance of
    being ashamed.
慚 德 conscious of one's defects;
    the sudden slip of a virtuous
    person.
慚 怍 to feel ashamed.
慚 恨 mortified; hurt.
⁵慚 悚 交 幷 mingled shame and
    fear.
慚 悔 shame and remorse.
慚 愧 or 羞 慚 to be ashamed;
    mortified.
慚 色⁴ blushing; the appearance of
    being ashamed.

粲⁴   Materials for a feast.
6691

還 予 授 子³ 之 粲 兮 when we
    return we will send you a feast.

(a) Bright; splendid; clear; ex-
    cellent; beautiful.

粲 粲 衣 服 in brilliant array.
三 英 粲 兮 How bright are its
    three ornaments!
如 此 粲 者 何 that I should see
    a beauty like this!
精 粲 fresh and bright appearance.
角 枕 粲 兮 How beautiful was
    the pillow of horn! (chüeh²-)

(b) Laughing.

粲 然 而 笑 he laughed boister-
    ously.

燦⁴   Resplendent; brilliant;
6692   glittering.
Also read ts'an³.

燦 燦 glittering.
燦 爛 bright; lustrous.

璨⁴   The lustre of gems. Gems.
6693

餐
飡 ¹   To eat. A meal.
6694

餐 室 dining-rooms.
餐 粥 餐 飯 a meal of congee and
    rice—very poor.
餐 雲 臥 月 to feed on the clouds
    and sleep in the moonlight—
    very poor; hardships of travel.
餐 風 宿 露 to feed on the wind
    and sleep on the dew—very
    poor.
⁵一 餐 飯 a meal.
早 餐 晚 餐 the morning a n d
    evening meals, respectively.
聖 餐 the Lord's Supper.
進 餐 to go on with one's meal.

鱤 ¹   A long narrow fish—
6695   Trichiurus armatus.

噆
噆 ³   If; supposing; neverthe-
嚵   less. Inter. next.
6696

慘 ³   To be sorrowful.
6697

慘 怛 distressed in mind.
慘 惻 pained; grieved.
慘 慘 日 瘁 day by day I am full
    of grief and pain.
慘 痛 於 心 extremely distressed
    in mind.
慘 酷 cruel and oppressive.

(a) Already; nevertheless. A par-
    ticle similar to 曾 No. 6771.

憯 不 畏 明 "Who have no fear
    of the clear will (of Heaven)."
憯 不 知 其 故 I cannot ascertain
    the cause of it.
憯 莫 懲 嗟 "And yet you do not
    correct nor bemoan yourself!"

胡憯莫懲 Why does (the king) not stop these things?

蠶 **蚕**]² 6698   The silkworm. Any caterpillars that weave cocoons.

蠶事 sericulture.
蠶女 girls who attend to silkworms.
蠶姑 or 蠶神 Goddess of Silkworms.
蠶子³ or 蠶種³ silkworms' eggs.
⁵蠶室 a room for rearing silkworms; a prison where the punishment of castration was inflicted.
蠶月 the silkworm season; the 4th lunar month.
蠶桑 the silkworm mulberry.
蠶桑事業 the sericulture industry.
蠶桑學校 School of Sericulture.
¹⁰蠶沙 dung from the silkworms.
蠶病 a disease of silkworms.
蠶眠 the sleep of the silkworm before casting its skin.
蠶簇 or 蠶山 a frame on which the silkworms spin.
蠶紐 dried chrysalises of the silkworm, used as food.
¹⁵蠶繭 the cocoon of the silkworm.
蠶花 a name for the silkworm moth.
蠶荳 broad-beans.
蠶薝 grass-mats on which silkworms are reared.
蠶蛾 the silkworm moth.
²⁰蠶蛹 the chrysalis of the silkworm.
蠶蟲乾 dried chrysalises of the silkworm, used as food.
蠶蟻 a name for the newly-hatched silkworms.
蠶連 paper on which the silkworm moth has deposited its eggs.
蠶食 to gnaw—as a silkworm; stealthy encroachment.
²⁵蠶食政策 an aggressive policy; a policy of encroachment.
蠶食瘋瘋 wasting leprosy.
飼蠶 to feed silkworms.
養蠶 to rear silkworms.

TSANG. (ㄗㄤ)

羊¹ 6699   A ewe.

羊牁 a region under the *Han* dynasty comprising part of Kweichow and adjacent provinces. Name of a river which flows into the West River in Kwangtung.
牂牂 dense foliage.

奘³ 6700   Large; powerful; stout; thick.
    Pron. *chuang³*.
奘·的 細·的 both stout and slender.
奘 粗 thick; coarse.

駔³ 6701   A powerful horse.
駔駿 a fine horse.

(a) A broker. Inferior. Coarse.
駔儈 a broker.
駔·子 a rascal.
駔工 an inferior workman.
駔貨 inferior goods.
駔闠 a market-place.

(b) Read *tsu³*. Similar to 組 No. 6817. A cord attached to a badge, etc.
駔琮 a badge of rank worn under the *Chou* dynasty.

葬 **塟**]⁴ 6702   To bury.
葬埋 or 埋葬 to inter; to bury.
葬身魚腹 buried in the maws of the fishes—drowned.
倮葬 to bury without grave-clothes.
厚葬 an elaborate funeral.
⁵合葬 to bury in one grave.
浮葬 to leave a coffin unburied.
火葬 to cremate.
薄葬 a simple funeral.
送葬 to escort a funeral.
遷葬 to remove a body from one grave to another—in order to

secure better geomantic conditions.

臟¹ 6703   Dirty; filthy; greasy.
髒瘡 syphilis.
骯髒 dirty; filthy.
↑髒土 rubbish.

臧¹ 6704   Good; right; generous.
臧厥臧 to approve what is good.
臧否 is it permissible?
于何不臧 "how bad it is!"
何用不臧 "what does he which is not good?"
⁵庶幾有臧 "they begin to feel that things are right."
終然允臧 "thus the issue has been truly good."
與子偕臧 he and I were happy together.
視爾不臧 "I regard you as in the wrong."
謂我臧兮 you said that I was dexterous.

(a) A runaway male slave. Husband of a slave.
臧獲 an abusive term for male and female slaves; children of slave fathers and mothers, respectively; prisoners of war whose lives have been spared.

(b) u.f. next. Bribes, etc.
坐臧 stolen goods placed with innocent persons in order to implicate them.

(c) Read *tsang¹*. u.f. 臟 No. 6706.

(d) Also occurs u.f. 藏 No. 6718.

贓 **賍**]¹ 6705   Booty; plunder; stolen goods. Bribes.
贓官 a corrupt official.
贓物 spoil; plunder; loot.
贓私 bribes; plunder.
作贓 or 坐贓 to place stolen goods with innocent persons in order to implicate them.

分臟 to divide the spoils.
接臟 to receive stolen property.
收買賊臟 to buy stolen goods.
消臟 to dispose of stolen property.
窩臟 to receive stolen goods.
[10]**繳臟** to hand over stolen property.
認臟 to identify stolen property.
貪臟 to covet bribes.
走臟 to recover stolen property.

臟[4] The viscera; the entrails.
6706

五臟 the viscera, i.e., the heart, liver, lungs, stomach and kidneys.
佛臟 valuables placed inside images of Buddha.

TS'ANG.　(ㄘㄤ)

倉[1] A granary; a bin.
6707

倉場 the official granaries at Peking.
倉官 granary officials; the Chinese dwarf hamster.
倉庚 the oriole. *See* No. 6717.
倉庫 granaries and treasuries.
[5]**倉廩** public granaries.
倉廩實而武備脩 the granaries full and the military equipment complete.
倉房 or **穀倉** a storehouse; a granary.
倉箱 bins in a granary.
倉頡 or **倉史** *Ts'ang Chieh*—the reputed inventor of Chinese writing.
[10]**倉頭** officer in charge of granaries.
倉鼠 granary rats.
貨倉 a warehouse.
開倉 to open the granaries—to dispense grain in times of straitness.

(a) Hurried; flurried.

倉卒 or **倉猝** or **倉惶** startled; hurried; on the spur of the moment. (-*ts'u*[4])
倉惶失措 disturbed; unsettled.
倉猝間 in one's hurry and excitement.

傖[1] Confused. Disorderly.
6708

傖囊 confused; disorderly; disarranged.

(a) Read *ts'ēng*[1]. A dissipated fellow. An outcast.

傖楚 a low fellow.
傖父 an old reprobate.
饑傖 hungry outcasts.

凔[1] Cold. Inter. 滄 No. 6711.
6709

愴[4] Sad; sorry.
6710　Also read *ch'uang*[1].

愴悅昏迷 flurried; confused.
愴愴 sorrowful; distressed; disheartened.
愴惻 sorrow; sick at heart; disappointed.

滄[1] Vast. Cold.
6711　Inter. 凔 No. 6709.

滄桑 convulsions of nature; violent changes in nature—*from below*—6.
滄洲 the land of the Immortals—Fairyland.
滄海 the ocean.
滄海一粟 (like) a grain afloat on the ocean—man, as compared with heaven and earth.
[5]**滄海之量** an ocean capacity—a great drinker.
滄海桑田 the wide ocean has changed into a mulberry orchard—great changes have taken place in the course of time. *See above*—1.
滄海橫流 the changes and disorders of the times.
滄海遺珠 a pearl left in the depths of the ocean by the divers—to leave a talented man in retirement.
滄浪之客 a vagabond.
[10]**滄溟** the ocean.
滄茫 a vast expanse—as of the ocean.

瑲[1] The tinkling sound of gems, etc.
6712

艙[1] The hold of a ship. A cabin.
6713

艙位 the carrying capacity of a vessel; a cabin.
艙口 the hatchway.
艙口罩 a ship's manifest.
艙底 at the bottom of the hold.
[5]**艙房** cabins on a ship or boat.
艙板 the deck of a boat; the boards of the deck.
艙面 the deck of a boat.
客艙 cabins for passengers.
官艙 first-class cabins; first-class saloon.
[10]**封艙** to seal the hatches.
房艙 the 'tween decks; second-class saloon and cabins.
清艙 all the cargo is discharged.
火艙 the stoke-hole.
煤艙 coal-bunkers.
[15]**特艙** special first-class saloon— "foreign first-class."
統艙 quarters for steerage passengers.
貨艙 stowage.
開艙 to open hatches; to break bulk.

蒼[1] Green. The azure of the sky. Hoary; old.
6714

蒼天 the blue sky; also used personally as of God.
蒼松 the green pine-trees.
蒼清玉 beryl; aquamarine.
蒼生 the people; living beings.
[5]**蒼白** grey—as hair.
蒼白頭髮 grey hair.
蒼秀獨絕 unsurpassed for beautiful scenery.
蒼穹 the vault of heaven.
蒼翠 verdant green.
[10]**蒼老** a hoary old man.
蒼耳 burweed.
蒼茫 a vast expanse.
蒼蒼 green—as vegetation.
蒼蔚 luxuriant.
[15]**蒼蠅** flies. *See next*, No. 6715.
蒼蠅紙 fly-papers.
蒼頭 veterans; aged servants.
蒼黃 a greenish yellow.
上蒼 Providence; the Powers above.
[20]**黑蒼** a dark, sallow colour.

蒼[1]
6715

The house-fly.

蒼蠅 the common fly.

鯧
鯧[1]
6716

The pomfret.

鶬[1]
6717

A kind of crane.

鶬鶊 the oriole.
鶬鷄 or 鶬鴰 the black crane—the second is also used for a fabulous bird having nine heads and nine tails.

(a) Read *ch'iang*[1]. The tinkling of gems, bells, etc.

八鸞鶬鶬 the eight bells at their horses' bits all tinkling.
有鶬 all glittering.

藏[2] To hide; to conceal. To hoard.
6718

藏·下 conceal it; to conceal.
藏·不住 cannot be hidden.
藏伏 or 隱藏 to conceal; to lie hid; to hide.
藏刀 to hide a dagger—treacherous.
[5]藏匿 or 潛藏 to hide; to lie hid.
藏器待時 store up a thing against the time it is needed.
藏奸 to harbour treachery.
藏形 to become invisible.
藏拙 to hide one's incompetency —by remaining in retirement.
[10]藏書樓 a library. = 圖書館.
藏板 to keep the blocks of a book; to publish.
藏焉修焉 "even in retirement he sought to perfect himself."
藏私 reserve.
藏蓄 to amass; to heap up.
[15]藏·起·來 to secrete; to hide.
藏身 to hide oneself.
藏身之處 a hiding-place.
藏躲 to lie hid; to hide; to conceal oneself.
藏避 to abscond and hide; to be in hiding.

[20]藏·開 to hide a thing away and keep it out of sight.
藏頭露尾 to secrete the head and leave the tail showing—to give a partial account of; to get an inkling of. (-*lou*[4]-)
家藏 family heirlooms.
窩藏賊匪 to harbour thieves and robbers.

(a) Read *tsang*[1]. A storehouse.

藏庫 or 庫藏 an arsenal; a government storehouse.

(b) Read *tsang*[4]. Tibet.

中藏 the part of Tibet adjacent to Szechwan.
前藏 Central Tibet.
後藏 Ulterior Tibet.
西藏 Tibet.

TSAO.   (ㄗㄠ)

糟
醩[1]
6719

Sediment; dregs. Grains from a distillery. Disordered; spoilt.

糟不可言 indescribable mess
糟·出病·來 to bring disease upon oneself.
糟坊 a distillery.
糟塌 to spoil things.
[5]糟朽 rotten.
糟燒 a clear, mild spirit made from rice.
糟粕 dregs.
糟糕 a cake made of dregs— unlucky; too bad; what a mess!
糟糠 distiller's grains; the wife of a poor man.
[10]糟糠之妻不下堂 the wife who shared his poverty must not be put aside in his prosperity.
糟肉 to pickle meat.
糟豆·腐 pickled bean-curd—used as a derisive term for a southerner.
糟蹋 to spoil; to waste or ruin a thing.
糟蹋 to waste or spoil things.
[15]糟透 drenched; saturated.
糟醃 to put into pickle.
糟錢 filthy lucre.

糟霉 mildewed and spoilt.
糟魚 fish put into grains to cure.
[20]糟鼻·子 the red nose of a toper.
亂七八糟 all at sixes and sevens.
酒糟 grains from a distillery.

遭
遭[1]
6720

To meet with—generally used of things evil or distasteful.

遭事 to meet with calamity.
遭劫 to meet with trouble or calamity.
遭口舌 to be slandered.
遭喪·的家 the house of mourning.
[5]遭回祿 or 遭天災 to have a fire on the premises.
遭報 to meet with a just recompense.
遭·塌人 to abuse a person; to take away a person's character.
遭·塌東·西 to waste and misuse things.
遭害 to meet with disaster.
[10]遭家不造 to meet with family misfortune; to lose one's father or mother.
遭殃 to meet with calamity.
遭災 to meet with calamity.
遭累 to involve.
遭盜劫 to be waylaid and robbed.
[15]遭踐人 to ill-treat a person; to slander or abuse a person.
遭連夜雨 to have rain several nights in succession.
遭·遇 or 遭逢 to meet with.
遭·遇不好 to meet misfortune or trouble.
遭·遇不幸 to meet with misfortune.
[20]遭·遇時變 to meet with the changes of the times.
遭·遇相似 their lots in life were very similar.
遭際 one's lot in life.
遭際不好 a hard lot in life; unlucky.

(a) A time. A turn.

遭走錯路 I took the wrong road every time.
周遭 all round; surrounding.

早 **3** Early. In the morning.
Soon; beforehand; previous.
6721 Ago; some time since. Used
in some districts as a morning salutation.
Distinguish 皂 No. 6722.

早·上 morning.
早 三 個 禮拜 three weeks ago.
早 世 a premature death; to die
young.
早·些 回·來 come back soon.
[5]早 交 貨 early delivery of goods.
早 先 a good while ago; some
time previously.
早 兩 天 two days ago; a few
days ago.
早 前 formerly; long ago.
早·半·天 the forenoon.
[10]早 夭 untimely death; the death
of the young.
早 婚 early marriage.
早 宴 a morning party.
早 已 previously; a good while
ago.
早 已·的 話 that is an old story.
[15]早 市 the morning market.
早 年 some years ago.
早 年 爲 .. in early years he
was a....
早 年 間 in early years; some
years ago.
早 慧 precocity.
[20]早 日 previously; some time ago.
早 早·的 very early.
早 春 茶 early spring tea.
早 晚 sooner or later; at some
time or other; from time to
time; when eventually.
多○早○晚 去 when will you
go?
[25]早 晚 不 同 morning and evening
are not the same—of fluctuating market prices.
早 晚 會 回·來 sooner or later he
will return.
早·晨 early morning.
早 曉·得 I knew some time ago.
早 朝 the morning audience held
by the Emperor at dawn.
[30]早 歸 to keep early hours.
早 田 the early crop which is
reaped before the main crop is
planted.
早 知 如 此 .... if I had only
known....
早 知 有 此 I knew some time
ago.
早 秋 early autumn.

[35]早 稻 early ripening rice, a first
crop of rice gathered before
the main crop is planted.
早 經 was long ago . . . -ed.
早 茶 early-morning tea; breakfast.
早 裝 船 early shipment.
早 走 早 到 if you start early
you will arrive early.
[40]早 起 to get up early; 早起
morning.
早 達 to achieve success in early
life.
早 霞 the rosy clouds of sunrise.
早 頭 formerly; long ago.
早 飯 breakfast. 早點(心) breakfast.
[45]早·點 beforehand; earlier; sooner.
早·點 來 come earlier.
一 早 very early in the morning.
來 早 tomorrow morning.
及 早 as soon as possible.
[50]天 不 早 it is getting late.
太 早 too early.
尚 早 or 還 (hai²) 早 still early.
趁 早 avail yourself of the early
hour.

皂 **4** Black. Police runners,
皁 from the black clothes
6722 formerly worn by them.
Distinguish 早 No. 6721.

皂 布 black cloth.
皂 役 lictors; runners.
皂 斗 acorns.
皂 班 or 皂 隸 lictors; runners.
[5]皂 白 不 分 not to distinguish
black from white—indiscrimi-
nating.
皂 礬 sulphate of iron.
皂 衣 black clothes.
皂 角 (or 莢) the pods of the
Gleditschia sinensis.
皂 莢 木 acacia wood.
[10]皂 青 black.
肥 皂 soap.

(a) A manger.

皂 櫪 a stable.

棗 **3** The buckthorn or jujube,
commonly called dates—
6723 *Ziziphus vulgaris.*

棗 仁 kernels of the date.
棗·子 or 棗 兒 dates—given to a
bride because identical in sound
with 早 子³.

棗 核 date-stones. (-hur²)
棗 糖 色 a reddish-brown.
蜜 棗 preserved dates.
海 棗 imported dates—the true
date.

蚤 **3**
蚆
蚤 A flea. To scratch. The
mortices in the hub for the
6724 spokes of the wheel.

虼·蚤 or 跳 蚤 the flea.

(a) u.f. 早 No. 6721. Early.

蚤 有 譽 於 天 下 early to gain
world-wide praise.
蚤 見 而 豫 待 to perceive be-
forehand and await.
蚤·起 ≡ 早起

(b) Read *chao³*. u.f. 爪 No. 240.
Claws or nails.

懆 **4** Sad; anxious.
Also read *ts'ao¹*.
6725

愁 懆 sorrowful.
煩 懆 anxious; worried.

澡 **3**
6726 To bathe the body.

澡 堂 public baths.
澡 瓶 the water-bowl of a Buddhist mendicant.
澡 盆 or 洗 澡 盆 a bath-tub.
澡 身 to take a bath.
澡 身 浴 德 to bathe the body and
reform the heart.
澡 雪 五 臟 internal cleansing.
澡 雪 而 心 to cleanse the heart.

(a) Read *ts'ao¹*.

澡 澡 欲 沸 bubbling up; on the
point of boiling.

藻 **3** Name of several kinds of
aquatic grasses. Elegant, of
6727 style or composition.

藻 采 紛 披 elegant; flowery—a
fine composition.
藻 飾 adornment.
文 藻 literary culture.
海 藻 edible sea-weeds.

璪³ Pendants of pearls around a coronet.
6728

躁﹞⁴
趮﹞ Easily provoked; hasty. Fierce; cruel.
6729

躁動 bustling; noisy.
躁妄 or 躁率 reckless; hasty; light; impetuous.
躁急 hasty; quick-tempered.
躁擾 to trouble; to annoy.
⁵躁暴 cruel; irascible.
躁蹋 to spoil; to abuse.
躁鬧 to raise a row; to bluster.
煩躁 annoyance; irritation.
發躁 to be vexed or annoyed.

造⁴ To create; to make; to build. To prepare. To institute. To begin from.
6730

造作 to make; to fashion.
造具 to prepare; to make out.
造冊·子 to compile a register.
造冊處 Statistical Department.
⁵造冰機·器 ice-making machine.
造化 to make; to create; the Creator; good luck.
造·化主 God. Nature. The Creator.
天地之造化 the creative energies of Heaven and Earth.
好造·化 a lucky chance.
¹⁰造反 to rebel.
造報 to report.
造孽 to commit a crime which involves punishment in a future life upon earth; to suffer for wrongdoing.
造·就 to complete; to accomplish. See below—A. 2. 〔A. 2.
造·就人才 to train talent. Cf.
¹⁵造·就輿論 to create public opinion.
造工 to work.
造幣局 (or 廠) The Mint.
造幣機 coining machine.
造幸福 to get good luck.
²⁰造意 to suggest an idea; to originate; purposely.
造意犯 instigator of crime; ring-leader.
造成 made; finished.

造換 to renew; to repair.
造攻自牧宮 began the attack in the Mu palace.
²⁵造果 causation.
造橋 to build a bridge.
造燭求明 in making a candle one seeks for light.
造物 to create things.
造物者 The Creator.
³⁰造端 to originate; the beginnings of things.
造端託始 to make a beginning.
造罪 to commit a crime which involves punishment in a future life on earth; to suffer for wrongdoing.
造船 to build boats or ships.
造船廠 a dock-yard.
³⁵造行 a course of action.
造言生事 to cause trouble by false stories.
造詣 attainment.
造誣 to fabricate; false.
造謀 to plan or plot.
⁴⁰造謠·言 to spread rumours.
造象 (or 像) statuary.
造飯 to prepare food.
造·點名·譽 to make a name for himself.
人造·的 artificial.
⁴⁵修造 to repair; to rebuild.
僞造 forgery.
兩造 both parties in a suit.
初造 to originate; to begin a thing.
天造·的 natural, not made.
⁵⁰改造 to alter and rebuild.
自造之禍 trouble brought upon oneself.
製·造 to manufacture.

(a) To go to. To advance.

造其域而不能久也 to reach a position but to be unable to stay long in it.
造·就 to train—as a man for an official position. See above—13.
造府拜候 to go to a person's house to pay one's respects.
造次 hurriedly; disorderly; confusion. (ts'ao⁴-)
⁵造次必於是顛沛必於是 he cleaves to virtue in times of danger and confusion. (ts'ao⁴-)
乃造其曹 he had sent to the herds—for a pig.

小子³有造 the young men made (constant) progress.
深造之以道 makes his advances (in what he is learning) with deep earnestness and by the proper course.

竈﹞⁴
灶﹞ A kitchen-range; a furnace.
6731

竈君 the God of the Kitchen.
竈戶 houses; householders.
竈書 a petition regarding the affairs of the family which is sometimes written out and burnt at the shrine of the Kitchen God.
竈火坑 the fire-hole in a kitchen-range.
⁵竈王 the God of the Kitchen.
竈神 the God of the Kitchen.
竈空 the corner by the stove in the kitchen.
竈臺 a cooking-range.
竈陘 a niche near the fireplace where the God of the Kitchen rests.
¹⁰竈馬 the house-cricket.
竈·頭 a cooking-range.
竈鷄 the house-cricket.
倒³竈 the overturned stove—bad luck.
分竈 to run separate kitchens—in the one house.
¹⁵打竈 to build a cooking-range.
接竈 to welcome back the God of the Kitchen on the last day of the year according to the lunar calendar.
掌竈 a cook.
煤氣竈 a gas-stove for cooking.
祭 (or 祀) 竈 to make offerings to the God of the Kitchen.
²⁰老·虎竈 an establishment for the sale of hot water.
行竈 a portable stove used by caterers for preparing a feast in one's house.
辭竈 to say farewell to the God of the Kitchen when he is sent to report to 天老·爺 on the 23rd of the 12th lunar month.
送竈 to send the Kitchen God on his way to report to the powers above the doings of the year.
電竈 electric cooking-stove.

TS'AO.   (ㄘㄠ)

操¹ To grasp; to manage. To restrain.
6732

操之有要 there is an important plan for grasping it.

操事物之權 to have affairs in one's grasp; to have the game in one's own hand.

操作 to do manual labour.

操刀 to grasp a sword.

⁵操切 hasty measures; harsh dealings.

操剌 rash; fearless.

操券而獲 take the document and obtain—as money; used to express certainty of attainment.

操則存舍則亡 "Hold it fast, and it remains with you. Let it go, and you lose it"—said of the mind.

操勞 painstaking.

¹⁰操勝 to have certain success within one's grasp.

操南音 to speak with a southern accent.

操奇計贏 to engross the whole trade and control the markets.

操守 to hold firmly to; unswerving integrity; resolution.

操守可信 resolute and trustworthy.

¹⁵操履 to restrain the footsteps—uprightness of character.

操心 to take pains; careworn; anxious.

其操心也危 "they use deep precautions against calamity."

操必勝之權 to hold certain success within one's grasp.

操持 resolute; to hold to the right; to manage.

²⁰操持井臼 to draw water and hull rice—duties of a wife.

操政權 to take control of the affairs of State.

操業 conduct; fulfilment of duty.

操琴 to grasp the lute ready for playing.

操生死之權 holding the power of life and death within one's grasp.

²⁵操縱 restraint and leniency—able to manage others; to control the market and raise or lower the prices according to one's desire.

免爲一派所操縱 avoid the domination of any one party.

操縱自如 firm or yielding as it pleases him.

操觚 to grasp the tablets—to write.

(a) To exercise. To drill.

操兵 to drill troops.

操場 a drill-ground.

操演 to drill; to engage in sports, etc.

操練 to drill; to practice.

⁵操行 deportment—as in schools.

操點 to drill and muster the men for roll-call.

閱操 to inspect troops at drill; to review the forces.

體操 drill; gymnastic exercises. *See* No. 6246-16ff.

(b) Read *ts'ao⁴* A principle. A purpose. A restraint imposed upon oneself.

不貳其操 did not swerve from his integrity.

節操 moral principles.

蚓而後充其操者也 a man must be an earthworm before he can carry out such principles.

風操 demeanour; mode of life.

曹² An official. A class. A sign of the plural.
6733

曹平銀 common sycee; the market *tael*.

曹操 *Ts'ao Ts'ao*—the famous general who occupied a prominent place during the Wars of the Three Kingdoms; died A.D. 220.

曹魏 the *Wei* dynasty founded by *Ts'ao Ts'ao*, A.D. 220—264.

兒曹 you, my children.

⁵兩曹 both parties to a suit.

六曹 the Six Boards of State.

天曹 officials in the next world.

官曹 officials.

水曹 Board of Works.

¹⁰爾曹 you all.

秋曹 officials of the former Board of Punishments.

金曹 the former Board of Revenue.

陰曹 the officials in the next world.

雷曹 assistant of the God of Thunder.

(a) A cattle-fold.

乃造其曹 he had sent to the herds—to get a pig.

嘈
譜 } ² Noise; din.
6734

嘈嘲 or 嘈鬧 to wrangle.

嘈耳 to deafen.

嘈雜 a confused noise.

勦² Useless; worn-out; old. Inferior.
6735

勦朽 decayed.

勦爛 or 勦壞 or 勦舊 old; spoilt; worn-out.

槽² A trough; a groove. A manger. A distillery.
6736

槽上 in the stable.

槽刨 a rabbet-plane.

槽坊 a distillery.

槽子 a trough; a groove.

⁵槽櫪 a stable for horses.

槽牙 or 板牙 back teeth; molars.

槽線 or 槽縫 a rabbet.

槽道 or 馬槽 a manger.

水槽 a water-trough; a tank.

¹⁰漏槽 spouting under the eaves.

跳槽 to change one's master; to leave one's employment without due notice.

酒槽 a wine-vat.

漕² To transport by water. A watercourse.
6737

漕官 officials employed in the transport of grain.

漕標 troops formerly employed on the grain-transport service.

漕河 the Grand Canal.

漕督 or 運總 or 漕督部堂 former Director-General of the Grain Transport.

漕糧 or 漕米 tribute rice.

漕 船 a junk for carrying tribute rice.

漕 運 to transport tribute rice to Peking by the Grand Canal; to carry grain by water.

競 漕 or 競 船 or 賽 船 boat-racing.

螬[2]　Grubs in fruit.
6738

草[3]
艸
屮　Grass; straw; herbs; weeds. The last two characters are forms of Radical 140.
6739

草 上 之 風 必 偃 the grass will certainly bend before the wind.

草 上 霜 frost on the grass—a name for "unborn lambskin."

草 人 a man of straw; a dummy or scarecrow.

草 包 bag for fodder tied on the back of a cart; a stupid fellow. *See below*—A. 6.

[5]草 卉 herbage; herbs.

草 原 a grassy plain; meadows.

草 叢 a thicket.

草 地 pasture-land; lawn.

草 場 地 pasture-land.

[10]草 夾 竹 桃 the phlox.

草 字 頭 Radical 140—the "Grass-Character Top." 艹

草 寇 a bandit.

草 寢 to sleep in the wilds.

草 履 straw-sandals.

[15]草 市 a straw-market.

草 席 straw-matting.

草 帽·子 a straw hat. or -兒

草 帽 纓 straw-braid for making hats.

草 廬 a thatched hut; a shed.

[20]草 形 蟲 zoophytes.

草 房 a thatched hut; a shed.

草 把 a twisted bunch of grass or straw.

草 料 food for animals; forage.

草 服 clothing made from certain grasses.

[25]草 木 grass and trees—vegetation.

草 木 皆 兵 the grass and the trees were all troops—imaginary fears of a routed army. *See* 風 No. 1890-52.

草 本 herbs; grasses. *See below* —A. 15.

草 果 the ovoid cardamom.

草 梗 grass stalks.

[30]草 棚 a thatched hut or shed.

草 標 a twisted ring of straw attached to an article, indicating that it is for sale.

草 澤 to dwell in the country.

草 田 uncultivated fields.

草 竊 highway robbery.

[35]草 紙 coarse, rough paper.

草 繩·子 a straw rope.

草 舍 a thatched hut or shed.

草 芥 petty, trifling—like grass or bits of straw.

草 花 grass and flowers.

[40]草 花 粉 pollen.

草 莖 grass stalks.

草 莽 jungle.

草 莽 之 中 from among the rustics.

草 萊 grass; weeds.

[45]草 萊 時 代·的 生·活 rough life in the pioneering days.

草 菅 人 命 to treat human life as grass—of no account, used of rapacious officials.

草 薙 to weed.

草 藥 medicinal herbs.

草 蜢 a grasshopper.

[50]草 蟲 insects that live in the grass.

草 衣 grass made into clothing— a recluse.

草 裏 蛇 a snake in the grass.

草 酸 oxalic acid.

草 鞋 straw-sandals.

[55]草 頭 露 dew on the grass— evanescent.

草 食 獸 herbivorous animals.

草 黃 straw-coloured.

一 根 草 a stalk of grass.

坐 草 to sit on the straw—to be in childbed.

[60]打 草 to get fodder for animals.

敗 草 withered grass.

斬 草 to mow grass; to prepare a grave.

花 草 flowering and other plants.

(a) Careless; hasty. Running-hand style of characters in writing. To draft. The beginnings of things. Rough. Mean.

草 一 名 單 make out a list of the names.

草 一 疏 to write a letter to a superior.

草 具 hastily prepare.

草 創 a rough copy; a rough beginning.

[5]草 創 時 期 in the initial stages.

草 包 irascible; coarse; obstinate. *See above*—4.

草 合 同 draft of a contract or agreement.

草 字 my humble style.

草 字 or 草 寫 running-hand.

[10]草 寫 to write rapidly; to scribble.

草 律 to draft a law.

草 擬 一 詳 細 計 畫 書 to draft a comprehensive scheme.

草 昧 之 初 in the early ages of the world.

天 造 草 昧 when God created the world all was dark and confused.

[15]草 本 a roughly bound copy of a book; annual (plants).

草 案 a draft copy.

草 次 precipitately.

草 率 or 潦 草 carelessly.

草 種[3] (from) inferior stock.

[20]草 稿 a rough draft.

草 章 draft of agreement.

草 約 a draft treaty.

草 約 簽 字 to sign the draft treaty.

草 草 了[3]事 to do a thing carelessly; heedless.

[25]草 野 rustic.

起 草 to make a draft.

(b) The female of certain animals, etc. Inter. next.

草 馬 a mare; an unridden colt.

草 雞 a hen.

草 雞 毛 "a chicken-hearted fellow."

騲[3]　The female of certain animals—horses, etc.
6740

騲 驢 a she-ass.

騲 雞 or 母 雞 a hen.

慅[4]　Sincere.
6741

君 子[3]胡 不 慅 慅 爾 Is it not entire sincerity which marks the superior man?

糙) 糙 4 羲)

6742 Rough; coarse; inferior.

糙米 coarse rice—unhulled.

TSÊ. (ㄗㄜ)
(Tseh)

咋 2,5.
6743 To gnaw. A loud noise.

咋咋然 making a great hubbub.
山咋 a great hubbub.

(a) Read *cha*⁴. Hesitatingly; nervously.

咋舌 to put out the tongue in astonishment or regret.

窄 4,5. Narrow; contracted;
mean.
6744 Usually pron. *chai*³.

窄³小 narrow; of small dimensions.
窄³巴巴的 narrow; straitened.
窄³狹 confined; closely hemmed in.
窄³緊 compressed; tight.
⁵窄³胸 mean and stingy; petty.
窄³道 a narrow road.
窄³門 the "strait gate."
窄³隘 a defile; a narrow pass.
寬窄³ broad and narrow—relative breadth.
¹⁰肚量窄³ of limited capacity; illiberal; narrow-minded.
↑狹窄⁴ narrow-minded.

蚱 2,5.
6745 A variety of locust.

蚱蜢 the edible locust.
蚱蟬 a small cicada which comes late in the season.

則 2,5. A rule; a law; a pattern;
a standard. A list.
6746

則例 or 例則 a tariff; rules; laws.
則傚 to imitate.
則古稱先 to imitate the ancients and follow in the steps of one's ancestors.

則天 to follow the ways of Heaven.
⁵則度 regulations; laws.
則而象之 made him their pattern.
其則不遠 the pattern is not far off.
天下則 a pattern for the world.
天則 the divine law.
¹⁰孝思維則 those filial thoughts became an example to after ages.
常則 fixed laws; an invariable law.
惟堯則之 "only *Yao* corresponded (in his greatness) to (Heaven).
有物有則 there are things, and there are laws for them—"the things specially intended are our constitution and its relation to the world of sense and the various circles of relationship."
法則 a pattern; a rule; a law.
¹⁵準則 a pattern or standard; a rule.
稅則 Customs tariff.

(a) A particle indicating consequence or result—wherefore; then; and so; immediately; in that case; consequently; in accordance with.

則不能安其身 then he would not have been able to make them feel at home and remain with him.
則亦已矣 he then had to retire.
則個 in that case it will do.
則其中 the just and middle course.
⁵則可 then it will be all right; in that case it will do.
　如之何則可 what is the best thing to do?
則吾不知也 we do not know about that.
則將 will accordingly...; will then....
則將應之曰 in that case I would have answered him.
¹⁰則茲不悅 I am dissatisfied on account of this.
則必反予 he would certainly have recalled me.
則是 then it will be all right; in that case it will do.

則是干澤也 that shows that he was seeking his own benefit.
一則二則 in the first place, in the second place.
¹⁵不可則止 when he finds that he cannot do so, he retires.
何則 how then?
居則曰不吾知乎 from day to day you are saying, "We are not known."
然則 so then; well then.
雖則如是 although it is so.
²⁰過則勿憚改 if you have faults do not fear to abandon them.
過則順之 when they have errors they persist in them.

(b) Used like 做 to do, etc.

則甚 what are you doing? what did you want?
則聲 to make a sound.
不則聲 Hold your peace!

鰂 2,5. The cuttle-fish.
6747 See 鱡 No. 6753.

責 2,5. To upbraid. To ask
from; to demand. To
6748 punish.
Also read *chai*².

責人斯無難 it is easy to reprove others.
責令 to compel.
責備 to reprimand; to rebuke.
責償 to compel restitution.
⁵責咎 to blame.
責問 to put to the question under torture or by flogging.
責善 to urge to virtuous deeds.
責善則離 reproving admonitions to what is good lead to alienation—between father and son.
責懲 to rebuke; to blame.
¹⁰責打 or 責杖 to punish by flogging.
責斥 to reprimand; to rebuke.
責治 to punish.
責納 to charge a fee.
責罪 to condemn; to reprove.
¹⁵責罰 to fine; to reprove.
責罵 to blame; to reprimand.
責而歸之 rebuke him and cause him to return.
責詰 to blame.
責讓 to rebuke; to reprimand; to blame.

20責負 to collect a debt.
責賂 to ask for a gratuity.
責辦 to inflict penalties.
責銀 to fine.
責難於君 to urge the prince to difficult (achievements).
25不責報 without asking for any return.
受責 to receive punishment or rebuke.
痛責 to castigate.
自責 to reprove oneself.
薄責於己厚責於人 indulgent to one's own failings and severe with those of others.

(a) Duty; responsibility. To lay a charge upon.

責°任 duties; responsibilities.
以專責·任 in order to give each his proper responsibility.
應負責·任·的 responsible for.
道德之責·任 moral responsibility.
5責°任之負擔 the burden of responsibility.
責°任內閣 a responsible cabinet.
責°任心 a sense of responsibility.
責°任解除 to release from responsibility.
責°任重大 a heavy responsibility.
10責務 a moral obligation.
責塞 or 塞責 perfunctory performance of one's duties, to do no more than one is obliged to do.
責成 to impress upon; to lay a charge or responsibility upon.
責成在我 the responsibility is upon me.
責無旁貸 there is no shirking responsibility.
15職責 responsibility of office.
負責 to shoulder responsibility.

(b) Read *chai*^{4}. u.f. 債 No. 118. Debts, etc.

責主 creditor.

嘖 2.5. 6749 **To call out; to make an uproar.**

嘖嘖稱善 cries of approval.
嘖有煩言 there are many complaints.

幘 2.5. 6750 **A turban. A conical cap.**

喪幘 a mourning-cap.

簀 2.5. 6751 **A mat; a bed-mat.**

易簀 to change the mat—to die. *See* No. 2952—C. 12.

賊 2.5. 6752 **A thief; a rebel. To plunder; to injure. A term of abuse. Usually read *tsei*^{2}.**

賊不改性 a thief cannot change his nature—an abusive expression.
賊兵 rebel troops; the enemy's forces.
賊出關門 to lock the door after the thieves have already gone.
賊匪 robbers; brigands.
5賊夫^{2}人之子^{3} he did evil to that man's son.
賊·子 a wicked youngster.
賊害 to cause injury to another.
賊寇 robbers; brigands; rebels.
賊寨 a rebel's stronghold.
10賊巢 a resort of robbers; the enemy's camp.
賊店 an inn to which robbers, etc., resort.
賊性 given to thieving; ungrateful.
賊恩之禍 the evil of not requiting kindness.
賊星 a meteor.
15賊智 the cleverness of a thief.
賊滑 slippery; tricky.
賊犯 robbers.
賊盜 robbers; brigands; rebels.
賊相 (*hsiang*^{4}) the face of a thief—abusive.
20賊眉鼠眼 having an appearance of guilt.
賊眼 sharp-eyed; suspicious.
賊肉 stubborn—of children.
賊船 a pirate boat.
賊賍 stolen goods; pillage.
25賊賢良 to oppress the virtuous.
賊贓 booty; stolen property.
賊頭^{2}兒 a rebel chief; a head among thieves.
賊頭賊腦·的 a villainous-looking fellow.
賊類 robbers; rebels; brigands.
30賊首 a rebel chief; a leader among thieves.
賊黨 rebels; robbers; brigands.
作賊 to be a thief.
失賊 to suffer burglary.
家賊難防 it is difficult to guard against thieves who reside in the house.
35木賊 the Dutch rush—*Equisetum hiemale*, used for finishing fine wood-work, like sand-paper.
毛賊 petty thieves.
海賊 pirates.

鰂 2.5. 6753 **The cuttle-fish. See 鰂 No. 6747.**

仄 4.5. 6754 **Inclined; slanting. The *oblique* tones in Chinese poetical compositions.** *See below*—6.

仄字 a word in an *oblique* tone. *See below*—6.
仄徑 a by-path.
仄慝 the moon in the east on the first day of the lunar month—behindhand.
仄日 the setting sun.
5仄聞 to hear indirectly.
仄聲 or 仄韻 the *oblique* tones as used in poetry, contrasted with the 平聲, or *even* tones—the 上聲, 去聲, 入聲, are *oblique* tones.
仄頭^{2} or 仄腦 to hold the head awry.
平仄不調 (*t'iao*^{2}) the *even* and *oblique* tones are out of their proper places—in composing poetry.

昃 4.5. 6755 **The sun past the meridian; the afternoon. To decline.**

日中則昃 after noon the sun begins to decline.

TS'Ê. (ㄘㄜ)

(Ts'eh)

册 4.5. 6756 **A register; a list; statistical tables. Also read *ch'ai*^{3}.**

册·子 or 册籍 or 册簿 or 卷册 or 書册 registers; records; archives; documents.

冊式 forms for filling up—as for statistics.

人丁冊 the census; statistics of the population.

註冊 to enrol; to register.

黃冊 the *Yellow Register*—the census.

(a) To appoint.

冊命 "By appointment."

冊封 to appoint.

冊王 to appoint as ruler.

側 4.5. The side. Awry. Preju-diced; perverted. Mean. To
6757 incline towards.

側侍 to wait on; to stand by one's side.

側壓力 lateral pressure.

側媚 insinuating looks.

側室 a side-room; a concubine.

⁵側席 to keep a vacant place on one's left for an expected guest.

側微 low; humble.

側房 a side-room; a concubine.

側根 lateral roots.

側歪 awry; on one side.

¹⁰側目 sidelong glances; askance.

側稜 tilted; inclined.

側線 the lateral line on the body of a fish

側置 overturned; lying on its side.

側耳而聽 to incline the ear and listen.

¹⁵側聞 to hear of a matter indirect-ly.

側臉 a profile.

側臥 to lie on one's side.

側言 one-sided statements.

側身 to turn half-round; lopsided; a widow. 側 is sometimes read *chai*¹ here.

²⁰側身挨近 leaning close to.

側道 a sidewalk.

側邊 on one side.

側重一邊 partial; biassed.

側門 a side-door.

²⁵側陋 mean; vile.

側階 by the side of the steps or stairs.

側面剪影 to cut out a silhouette portrait.

側面圖 a side-elevation; a sil-houette.

側首 to half turn the head.

³⁰偏側 leaning to one side; partial.

反側 to turn over and over; rest-less.

放側 to place a thing crookedly.

河側 by the side of the river.

無反無側 without perversity, without partiality.

惻 4.5. To pity; to sympathize with.
6758

惻仁 to compassionate; a humane sympathy.

惻怛 to commiserate.

惻愴 sick at heart; disappointed.

惻隱之心人皆有之 all men have natural sympathies.

痛惻 pained; having intense pity for.

測 4.5. To fathom; to measure. To estimate.
6759

測候 meteorological observation.

測光術 photometry.

測圜器 cyclometer.

測字 to tell fortunes by means of words.

⁵測尺 a scale.

測度 (*to*⁴·⁵.) to calculate.

測度 (*to*⁴·⁵.) 不到 unfathomable.

測揆 to measure.

測日鏡 an instrument for measuring the angular distance between two stars; heliometer.

¹⁰測測 sharp, keen, as a blade.

測竿 levelling-staff.

測繪生 student draughtsmen.

測繪員 surveyors; draughts-men; cartographers.

測角器 an instrument for mea-suring angles.

¹⁵測路器 hodometer or odometer, an instrument for measuring the distance travelled by wheel-ed vehicles.

測遠鏡 range-finder.

測•量 to measure; to survey; mensuration.

測量員 a surveyor.

測量學 (or 術) surveying.

²⁰測量局 Survey Office.

測量艦 coast-survey vessel.

測量路綫 to mark out a road.

測鉛 sounding-lead.

測鎖 or 測鏈 measuring-chain.

²⁵測音器 acoustic siren.

測驗 tests.

個別智力測驗 individual intellectual tests.

四則測驗 arithmetical tests in the four rules.

團體智力測驗 intellectual tests of groups.

³⁰完成測驗 completion test.

定義測驗 definition test.

常識測驗 general knowledge test.

心理測驗 psychological tests.

³⁵教·育測驗 educational tests.

智力測驗 intellectual tests.

理科測驗 scientific know-ledge tests.

知力測驗 knowledge tests.

程序測驗 sequence tests.

觀察測驗 observation tests.

⁴⁰體格測驗 physical tests.

不測 unfathomable; unexpected, as death, etc.

推測 to infer.

防·備一個不測 be on your guard against unforeseen emer-gencies.

策 4.5. A plan; a scheme. A bundle of bamboo slips for writing on. A question.
6760

策令 Presidential appointments—to office, etc.

策勳 to record meritorious ser-vices.

策命 to order.

策問 questions set at the former public examinations.

⁵策士 a counsellor; a clever strategist.

策府 ancient term for the im-perial library.

策應 to relieve—troops, etc.

策源地 military base.

策略 measures; strategy; policy.

¹⁰緊急策略 emergency mea-sures.

策論 questions and themes—given at the former public examinations.

上策 the best plans.

失策 to fail in one's policy.

妙策 clever strategy; a good plan.

¹⁵對策 answers given by candidates at the former examinations.

政策 policy, as of the govern-ment.

書策 writing-tablets.

無策 without plans.

TS'Ě (Ts'eh)

獻 策 to offer a plan or suggestion—to a superior officer.

20 神 策 an excellent scheme or device, etc.

籌 策 to devise a plan.

良 策 clever strategy.

計 策 a plan or stratagem.

(a) A riding-whip. To whip.

策 勉 or 策 勵 to urge on; to impel.

策 馬 to whip a horse.

執 策 to hold the whip—a groom.

(b) Used to imitate sounds.

策 策 sound as of wind or of falling leaves.

(c) Divining-straws. Inter. next.

推 策 to arrange the straws for prognostication.

端 策 拂 龜 to arrange the divining-straws and prepare the tortoise-shell for prognosticating.

筴 6761

筴 4.5. Divining-straws. To divine by means of grass-stalks. Inter. preceding—C.

筮 筴 to divine by means of straws.

(a) Inter. preceding. A plan, etc.

不 用 其 筴 did not make use of his plans.

神 筴 an excellent plan—from Heaven.

(b) Read *chia*1.5. To take under the arm. Chopsticks.

筴 箸 bamboo chopsticks.

火 筴 pieces of metal like chopsticks used as small fire-tongs.

TSEN. (ㄗㄣ)

怎 6762

怎 3 How? Why? What?

怎 奈 but alas!

怎 得 how? in what way?

怎 得 成 功 how is it going to be finished?

怎 敢 how can one dare?

5 怎 樣 how? in what way?

怎 樣 辦 法 what plan do you propose? how shall it be done?

怎 生 結 果 what will be the outcome?

怎 生 行 去 how is it possible to go on—in such weather?

怎·的 how? in what way?

10 怎 能 how possible? i.e., it is impossible.

怎·麼 or 怎·麼 樣 or 怎·麼·着 how? in what way? how about....?

怎·麼 做·法 how is it done?

怎·麼 好·呢 which is the best way? what had best be done?

怎·麼 敢 how can one dare...?

15 怎·麼 沒·有 風 why is there no breeze?

怎·麼 能·彀 how possible? i.e., it is impossible.

怎·麼 說 what do you say? what is meant by...?

怎·麼 辦 how to proceed? what is to be done?

TS'ÊN. *See* 329-30; 6685 G.

TSÊNG. (ㄗㄥ)

增 6763

增 1 To add to; to increase.

增 價 to raise the price; to appreciate in value.

增 光 to glorify; to shed lustre upon.

增 光 前 人 to reflect honour upon one's ancestors.

增 入 to add to; to enter—as an account.

5 增 兵 reinforcements.

增 其 實 exaggerated the facts.

增 刊 a supplement—as to a newspaper.

增 删 to emendate.

增 劇 increase in severity—as an illness.

10 增 加 to increase; to augment; to add to.

增 加 價 值 to increase in value.

增 加 工 作 時 間 increase of working hours.

增 加 幸 福 increase of happiness.

增 加 生 產 increase of production.

15 增 加 閱 歷 increase of experience.

增 多 increased.

增 大 to enlarge; to swell.

增 幅 器 amplifier—as used in wireless, etc.

增 度 rate of increase.

20 增 強 to reinforce.

增 德 to increase in virtue.

增 惡 to increase in evil. (-o⁴)

增 損 profits and losses.

增 改 新 例 revised regulations.

25 增 殖 propagation.

增 添 to augment; to increase; to add to.

增 減 increase and decrease—fluctuation.

增 減 無 定 it may be cheaper or dearer—as a price.

增 率 (*lü*45) rate of increase.

30 增 生 extra candidates admitted to the degree of 秀 才 under the old system.

增 益 to increase; to augment.

增 盛 increasing prosperity.

增 福 to increase happiness.

增 給 to give an additional amount.

35 增 補 to add on; to supplement; revised and enlarged.

增 見·識 increase of experience.

增·起·來 to increase; to add to.

增 輝 to add the brightness of your presence.

增 進 advancement—as in studies, etc.

40 增 進 自 己·的 利 益 to advance one's own interests.

增 長 (*chang*3) to augment; to add to.

增 防 to increase the defences.

增 音 器 amplifier, for sounds.

增 高 to raise; to advance.

45 增 高 自 己·的 人 格 to raise one's personal status.

戶 口 歲 增 the population increases year by year.

日 增 daily increase; daily advance.

米 價 日 增 the price of rice increases daily.

↑增 援 to reinforce; reinforcement.

憎 6764

憎 1 To hate; to detest.

憎 厭 to hate; to detest.

憎 嫉 jealous hatred; envy.

憎 嫌 人 to dislike; to despise; to turn away from.

憎 恨 to hate; to detest.

憎 惡 (*u*[1]) to hate; to dislike.

憎 愛 不 常 capricious, now hating, now loving.

可 憎 hateful; abominable.

甑[4] A boiler for steaming rice. A pot. A cauldron.

6765 Also read *chêng*[4].

甑 中 生 塵 the dust has collected in the cooking-pot—extreme poverty.

飯 甑 a rice-pot.

矰[1] A bolt for a crossbow. An arrow or a dart with a silk

6766 thread fastened to it.

矰 繳 (*cho*[1.5].) an arrow with a string fastened to it.

繒[1] Silken fabrics.

6767

繒 幡 silken banners.

(a) Inter. preceding.

繳 繳 (*cho*[1.5].) an arrow with a string fastened to it.

罾[1] A large square net, lowered and raised from the bank

6768 of the river.

投 罾 to lower the net into the water.

拉 罾 to raise the net.

贈[4] To give a present. To bestow; to confer.

6769

贈 別 to give a present at parting.

贈 品 a present; a memento; a prize.

贈 序 a composition given to a departing friend.

贈 彩 gifts given with purchases.

[5]贈 與[3] to give as a present; a present or gift.

贈 言 to send a word to.

臨 別 贈 言 parting words of advice.

贈 詩 interchange of poems as presents, usually at parting.

贈 賄 罪 bribery. (*legal*).

[10]贈 賻 gifts to assist a friend with funeral expenses.

贈 送 to give a present at parting.

贈 遺 金 a legacy.

(a) Posthumous honours conferred upon ancestors.

封 贈 titles of honour bestowed as above.

誥 贈 patents for titles of all higher ranks.

鄫[1] Name of a small feudal State in what is now 嶧 縣

6770 in Shantung.

TS'ÊNG. (ㄘㄥ)

曾[2] Already; past. Sign of the past.

6771 Distinguish 會 No. 2345.

曾 幾 何 日 not many days ago.

曾 是 不 意 I never expected this.

曾 是 以 爲 孝 乎 how can this be considered filial piety?

曾 有 there were some.

[5]曾 立 章·程 在 先 rules to which effect are already in existence.

曾·經 already.

曾·經 說·過 I have already spoken about it.

不 曾 there is not; it was not; often used as an interrogative.

吃·了 飯·不·曾 have you taken your food?

[10]不 曾 到 has never been.

不 曾 看·見 have never seen it.

不 曾 聽·見 I have not heard of it.

並 不 曾 it was not so.

何 曾 used as an interrogative expecting an answer in the negative.

[15]可 曾 看·見 have you by any chance seen it?

未 曾 have not yet....

(a) Read *tsêng*[1]. To duplicate; to add to, as generations. A surname.

曾 孫 a great-grandson.

曾 祖 a great-grandfather.

曾 祖 母 a great-grandmother.

層[2] A storey; a layer; a degree; an item. A division of

6772 a subject.

層 出 不 窮 layer upon layer without end—used of vast learning, etc.

層 層 疊 疊 piled up; tier upon tier.

層 峯 疊 嶺 or 層 巒 疊 嶂 range upon range; peaks rising one upon another.

層 巒 聳 翠 range upon range of lofty green hills.

[5]層 次 gradations; series; orders.

層 見 疊 出 occurring more and more frequently.

層 雲 cumulus clouds.

一 層 紙 a layer of paper.

三 層 樓 a three-storied house.

[10]千 層 紙 talc.

第 一 層 the first clause.

蹭[4] To dawdle. To miss one's footing. To collide.

6773

蹭 動 to scrape along the side of, as in passing a boat or ship.

蹭 蹬 dilatory; dispirited; baffled.

蹭 蹬 不 前 not to get on; to fail in one's aim.

TSO. (ㄗㄛ)

左[3] The left side. Inferior. Second to. Depraved. The

6774 east.

左·不 過 most probably; likely; on the whole; it is certainly; nothing else than.

左 之 右 之 they turned to the left, they turned to the right.

左 侍 郎 former title of a senior Vice-President of a Board.

左 側 on the left; the left side.

[5]左·傳 (*chuan*[1]) the *Tso Chuan*—a commentary on the 春 秋, *Spring and Autumn Annals*.

左 右 left and right; near to; this and that; about; nearly; in the presence of.

三 日 左 右 in about three days or so.

不 差 左 右 not much difference between them.

盼 咐 左 右 ordered the attendants.

[10]左 右 兩 難 in a dilemma; difficulties on either hand.

左 右 手 left and right hands—assistants.

左 右 翼 left and right wings of an army.

左 右 袒 to stand neutral. *See below*—24.

左 右 逢 源 to have able as-sistance in managing an affair.
[15] 左 岸 the left bank of a river.
左 彊 crotchety; cantankerous.
左 心 室 left ventricle.
左 心 耳 left auricle.
左 性 cantankerous; crotchety.
[20] 左 思 右 想 thinking of this and that.
左 手 the left hand.
左 派 the left wing—as of a party, etc.
左 脾·氣 cantankerous.
左 袒 to take sides; to give im-proper protection to; to screen. *See above*—13; to bare the left shoulder.
[25] 左 計 a useless plan.
左 轉 to degrade.
左 近 neighbouring; adjacent.
左 道 heretical doctrines; heresy.
左 道 旁 門 heretical doctrines.
[30] 左 遷 to degrade—lit., to send to the left; the right hand being the place of honour in ancient times.
左·邊 on the left; the left side.
左 都 御 史, 左 副 都 御 史 former title of the President and senior Vice-President of the Censorate.
左 鄰 右 舍 near neighbours.
左 顧 右 盼 to look to left and right.
[35] 左 黨 the left wing—of a party.
相 左 both going to the left—at variance; to miss on the way.
開 列 於 左 enumerated below; as follows.

(a) Read *tso*[4]. Inter. next. To assist.

左 證 corroborative evidence.
左 驗 to corroborate; to prove.

佐 [4] To assist; to aid. A sub-ordinate official.
6775

佐 君 布 化 to second the ruler in spreading reformation.
佐 器 a useful vessel—an able man.
佐 治 to assist in the administra-tion.
佐 治 員 Assistant Magistrate.
[5] 佐 理 to aid; to assist.
佐 膳 adjuncts to a meal—dainties, appetizers.

佐 證 corroborative evidence.
佐 貳 Assistant Magistrates.
佐 輔 to aid; to assist.
[10] 佐 雜 官 former term for sub-ordinate officials.
佐 領 former military title equi-valent to "Major or Captain," used under the Manchus.
彼 此 相 佐 they help each other.

做 [4] To make. To be. To act as. To do. Used for 作
6776 No. 6780.

做·不 上 來 I cannot do it—as a piece of work, etc.
做·不 了 [3] not able to; cannot be done.
做·不 來 impracticable; impossi-ble to be done; not used to doing.
做·不。做 隨·你 please yourself about doing it.
[5] 做·不·得 must not be done.
做·不 成 unable to accomplish.
做 人 or 爲 [2] 人 to be a man; to act as a man.
做 作 actions; doings. (*tsou*[4]-)
做 勢 to make a show of power or authority.
[10] 做 好 人 to be good; to do good.
做 官 to be in an official position; to be a magistrate.
做 家 to act as the head of a household.
做 小 to become a concubine.
做 工 to work; to get a livelihood.
[15] 做 工·夫 to do work.
做 庄·稼 to do agricultural work; to be a farmer.
做 得 不 壞 not badly done.
做 得 好 it is well done. book.
做 成 功 finished. 做 書 to make a
[20] 做 活 to get a livelihood; to work.
做。法 the method of doing a thing; how the thing is done.
做 甚 [2] 麼 What are you up to?
做 生·意 to do business.
做 菜 to prepare food.
[25] 做 衣·裳 to make garments.
做 親 to make a marriage alliance.
做 詩 to make poetry; to write verses.
做 買·賣 to trade.
做 賊 to be a thief.
[30] 做 賊 人 心 虛 a thief has a guilty conscience.
做 長 做 短 to do the s a m e amount of work—as somebody else.

做 面·子 活 to render eye-service.
做·頭 the method by which a thing is done; the good of doing.
做 飯 or 弄 飯 to cook or prepare food.

阼 [4] The steps leading to the eastern door.
6777 Also read *tsu*[4].

阼 階 the eastern steps.
阼 踐 to ascend the throne.

TSO. TSUO.   (ㄗㄜ)

坐 [4] To sit. A seat. To try a case at law. To travel by.
6778 To be situated. To assign.

坐·下 to sit down.
坐·不 下 unable to seat—so many.
坐·不 住 unable to sit.
坐·不 安 unable to sit comfort-ably.
[5] 坐·不 穩 unable to sit steady; unsteady, as a thing placed on top of something else.
坐 井 觀 天 sitting in a well look-ing at the sky—a very limited outlook.
坐 以 待 旦 to sit and wait for the dawn.
坐 位 a seat; one's position.
坐 催 to sit in a debtor's house and demand the payment of a debt.
[10] 坐 化 to die—of Buddhist priests.
坐 向 aspect—as of a grave or a house.
坐 商 a merchant who opens a shop, as contrasted with an itinerant trader.
坐 困 impoverished; in straits.
坐 地 to frequent in leisure time.
[15] 坐 地 分 贓 to share plunder—as a receiver of stolen goods.
坐 堂 to sit in court; to sit in judgement.
坐 墊 a cushion.
坐 夏 to go into (Buddhist) re-treat for the summer.
坐 失 to lose; to let slip.
[20] 坐 失 時 機 to allow the oppor-tunity to slip past.
坐 婆 a midwife; a woman who procures abortion.
坐 客 a passenger.
坐 家 欺 客 to take advantage of being among friends to insult strangers.

坐 實 to assume a tangible shape.

25坐 小 月·子 to have a miscarriage.

坐 席 to go to a feast; to partake of a feast.

坐 師 to sit at the feet of—as a disciple.

坐 忘 to sit in a state of mental abstraction.

坐 思 to sit in meditation—as a Buddhist.

30坐 月·子 to be confined; the month following a woman's confinement. A.c. 做月·子.

坐 朝 (*ch'ao²*) an Imperial levee.

坐 煩 了 to have sat for a long time and got tired (bored).

坐 牢 to be in prison.

坐 甫 定 just as we were seated.

35坐 監 to be in prison.

坐 禪 to sit in meditation—as a Buddhist.

坐 究 to submit to a penalty.

坐 索 to sit in a person's house demanding payment for a debt.

坐 罪 于 你 you will be punished.

40坐 臘 a Buddhist retreat—for meditation, etc.

坐 臥 sitting and lying.

坐 臥 具 furniture.

坐 致 to acquire without any trouble.

坐 船 to travel by boat.

45坐 草 to sit in the straw—childbed.

坐 莊 an agency; a branch establishment.

坐 落 to remain at; the position of a house, etc.

坐 蓐 to be in childbed.

坐 藥 suppositories.

50坐 號 the number of one's seat.

坐 褥 a cushion.

坐 視 to sit and look on.

坐 觀 成 敗 to sit and watch the results, success or failure.

坐 言 起 行 feasible.

55坐 討 to sit in a person's house and demand the payment of a debt.

坐 贓 to place stolen property with innocent people in order to implicate them.

坐 車 to travel by cart or barrow.

坐 轎 to ride in a sedan-chair.

坐 辦 員 a secretary.

60坐 針 氈 to sit on a mat of needles —very uneasy position.

坐 隱 a name for *Wei-ch'i* 圍 棋. See 圍 No. 7082-24.

坐 食 to eat in idleness.

坐 食 (or 吃) 山 空 to sit at home eating away one's resources.

坐 首 位 to occupy the chief seat.

65坐 馬 a saddle-horse.

坐 馳 to sit still while the thoughts are roaming far afield.

坐 骨 ischium—the part of the hip-bone on which the body rests when sitting.

坐 黨 死 者 數 百 人 several hundreds belonging to that faction were killed.

上 坐 the seat of honour.

70並 坐 to sit in pairs.

便 坐 to sit at one's convenience.

傍 坐 side-seats.

列 坐 to sit in order.

告 坐 to ask leave to sit.

75打 坐 參 禪 to go into retreat for meditation.

正 坐 the chief seat.

獨 坐 to sit alone.

端 坐 to sit upright in a formal manner.

請 坐 please be seated.

80起 坐 to rise from one's seat.

跌 坐 to squat on the ground; to sit with the legs doubled under.

跨 坐 to sit astride.

陪 坐 to keep a guest company.

座 ⁴ A seat. A throne. A base or socket. A stand.
6779

座 位 a throne; a seat.

座 右 銘 to make a note of instructions or cautions on the side of one's seat, as a reminder.

座·子 a base; a plinth; a stand for a vase, etc. = 座兒.

座 骨 the ischium—the part of the thigh-bone on which the body rests when sitting.

5上 座 the seat of honour.

公 座 a seat of authority.

客 座 private room for visitors.

寶 座 a throne.

法 座 the public hall.

10滿 座 the whole company.

陞 座 to enthrone.

(a) A numerary adjunct or classifier.

一 座 城 a city.

一 座 塔 a pagoda.

一 座 山 a mountain or hill.

一 座 橋 a bridge.

一 座 莊 a village.

TSO.   (ㄗㄨㄛ)
(Tsoh)

作 ⁴·⁵· To make; to do; to act. To write; to compose. To rise. Work.
6780

作·下 to get ready—as food or clothing; to leave; to allow to remain.

作·不·得 must not be done; not allowable.

作 主 to take the responsibility; to advise how to act.

作 之 君 作 之 師 set up a prince and a teacher for them.

5作 乾 or 發 乾 to become or to feel dry.

作 亂 to rebel.

作 事 to work; to act; to do business.

作 事 有 肝 膽 bold and courageous in action.

作 人 to exert an influence upon others; to stimulate others to goodness; to act as becomes a man.

10作 人 傀 儡 to be a mere figurehead; to be used as a tool.

作 人 字 看 it has the meaning of the character 人 'man.'

作 人 家 to be economical; frugal.

作 伐 to act as marriage go-between. See No. 1765—B.

作 伴 to be a companion.

15作 保 to go security for.

作 俑 to originate—always used of something bad; from Mencius: 一 始 作 俑 者 其 無 後 乎 was he not without posterity who first made figures for burying with the dead?—thus giving rise to the practice of burying living persons.

作 假 見 證 to bear false witness.

作 別 to bid farewell.

作 到 家 well done—as work; "at home" in doing anything.

20作 勢 to make a show of power or authority; to put on airs.

作 反 to turn rebel; to rebel.

作 品 a man's work, as in art, etc.

自 己·的 作 品 his own work.

作善事 to do good; 'to act benevolently.

²⁵作坊 (or 場) a workshop or factory.

作壽 to celebrate a birthday—of old people.

作夢 to dream; to labour under a delusion.

作姦犯科 to transgress the law; to be a traitor.

作嫁 or 爲⁴人作嫁 to labour in the interests of another in order to make a living—from the idea of a girl working on the bridal finery of another.

³⁰作媒 to act as a marriage go-between.

作孚 to repose confidence in.

作孽 to meet with retribution; unfortunate; to do evil.

作孽錢 ill-gotten gains.

作安靜人 to be quiet and law-abiding.

³⁵作官 to be an official.

作客 to be a stranger.

作家 an essayist; a writer; a capable person.

作家 to be economical; frugal. See above—12.

作對 or 作對頭 to oppose; to be at enmity with.

⁴⁰作工 to labour; to engage in manual labour.

工作 work; labour.

作幕 to act as a private secretary.

作廢 to make void; to nullify.

作·弄 to do; to make.

⁴⁵作弊 to indulge in corrupt practices.

作得很好 done extremely well.

作怪 to behave in an unseemly manner; to be mischievous.

作息 working and resting—activities.

作情 to oblige; to do one a favour.

⁵⁰作惡多端 up to all kinds of evil.

作惡·的 an evil doer.

作意 the plan or scheme of an essay, etc.

作成 to complete; to accomplish; to do a stroke of business.

作成人 to help a person along.

⁵⁵作威 to assume a stern manner; to act the tyrant.

作戰 military operations.

作戰根據地 base of military operations.

作戰目標 objective of the military operations.

作戰計·畫 plan of military operations.

⁶⁰作房頭 or 作房眼兒 a fore-man; a head-workman.

作投擊勢 made a move as if to throw them at him.

作押 to deposit.

作抵 to substitute; to tender in lieu of....

作¹揖 to make a bow in the Chinese fashion.

⁶⁵作撻 to care little for; recklessly to destroy.

作文·章 to write essays.

作²料 materials; ingredients; spices, etc., for preparing dishes.

作新民 to stir the people to amend.　⌈letter.

作書 to write a book; to write a

⁷⁰作朋 to be friends.

作木·匠 to be a carpenter.

作業過重 over-work; over-strain—as in studies.

作樂 to make merry. (-lê⁴)

作樂 (yüeh⁴) to play music.

⁷⁵作止語默 a man's whole conduct.

作歹 to do wickedly; to behave badly.

作死 to seek death; to kill oneself.

作死馬醫 to try to cure a hopelessly grave illness — from the story of one who said to the doctor, "Although my father's illness is hopeless, I still beseech you to try your best efforts. You could treat him as a dead horse."　See 死 No. 5589-56.

作。法³ a plan of working; process.

⁸⁰作法³自斃 to get into troubles through schemes established by oneself.

作活 to work for a living.

作營生 to work for a living.

作燒 to be feverish; to have a temperature. (dial.)

作爲 conduct; behaviour; acts; doings; to make believe it is; to treat as; to act as.

⁸⁵作王 to be king.

作甚·麼 What are you doing?

作·用 activities; function; use; purpose; work; action; process. See 威 No. 3232-30; 官 No. 3552 \. 3; 生 No. 5738-79.

作用及反作·用 action and reaction.

作·用線 a line of action.

⁹⁰不隨意作·用 involuntary action.

動物性作·用 animal actions.

反作·用 reaction.

反應作·用 reflex action.

化學·的作·用 chemical action.

⁹⁵干涉作·用 interference.

推理·的作·用 the function of reasoning.

特種之作·用 special function — as of an organ in the body.

良心·的作·用 the function of conscience.

間隔作·用 action at a distance—as that of magnetism, electricity, etc.

¹⁰⁰電力·的作·用 electric action.

作痛 to be painful.

作癢 to itch.

作短工 to work by the day.

作祟 to commence their antics—said of spirits.

¹⁰⁵作福 to implore blessings.

作福作威 to be severe and lenient by turns.

作竹工 to work in bamboo.

作線 to act as a spy.

作者七人矣 seven men rose up (and hid from the world).

¹¹⁰作聲 to make a noise; to tell.

作興 allowable by the rule.

作興 (hsing⁴) to be in good spirits; merry.

作舍道邊 to build a house by the roadside—difficult.

作色⁴ to change colour.

¹¹⁵作苦 to live austerely.

作苦工 to do hard labour.

作行 can; allowable; the proper thing to do.

作見·證 to bear witness.

作詩 to compose poetry.

¹²⁰作證 to act as a witness; in witness whereof.

作賀 to congratulate.

作買·賣 to trade.

作足 to put on airs.

作踐 to trample; to oppress; to ill-treat.

¹²⁵作過 to have done already; to have made before.

作速 speedily.

作 道理 to take a course of action.

作 陪 to assist in entertaining visitors; guests.

作 難 to be in trouble; to be in straits; to have difficulty.(*dial.*)

[130]作 項 capital as contrasted with interest.

作 頭[2] a foreman or head-work-man.

作 飽 or 發 飽 flatulence; a sense of fulness.

作 鬧 to commence squabbling or fighting.

作 麼 What are you doing? Why? (-*ma*[2]) (*rare*.)

[135]力 作 to work hard.

動·作 activites.

包 作 work done by the job or contract.

合 作 to work together;cooperate

夜 作 night-work.

[140]或 作 或 輟 off and on; irregu-larly.

操 作 to work.

改 作 to amend; to revise.

水 木 兩 作 both bricklaying and carpentering work under-taken—a small builder's sign-board.　洗 衣 作[1] laundry.

油 然 作 雲 dense clouds gather-ed in the sky.

[145]發 作 to develop into; to break out—as a disease or trouble.

聖 王 不 作 sages and wise rulers have ceased to arise.

著[4]作 authorship; literary work.

風 雨 大 作 a great storm of wind and rain.

怍 [4.5.]

6781　To be ashamed.

怍 色 ashamed; disconcerted.

俯 不 怍 於 人 looking down, he has no occasion to blush before men.

其 言 之 不 怍 則 爲 之 也 難 "He who speaks without modesty will find it difficult to make his words good."

昨 [2.5.]

6782　Yesterday. Lately.

昨 兒(個) yesterday.

昨 兒 晚 上 yesterday evening.

昨·天 yesterday.

昨 宵 or 昨 夜 last night.

[5]昨 日 yesterday.

昨 晚 yesterday evening.

昨 者 some days ago; recently.

昨 聞 I recently heard that....

昨 非 the failings of the past—in one's life.

[10]日 昨 recently; some days ago.

柞 [4.5.]

6783　An oak. Also read *cho*[4.5.]

柞 木 *Myroxylon racemosum*, a spinous evergreen tree.

大 葉 柞 *Quercus dentata*, for which 槲 No. 2201 is also used.

(a) Read *tsê*[4.5.]　To clear away trees or bushes.

筰 [4.5.]

6784　Rope made from bam-boo-splints.

酢 [4.5.]

6785　To pledge a host in wine. To recompense. Also read *cho*[4.5.]

或 獻 或 酢 (the guests) are pledged, and they pledge (the host) in return.

萬 壽 攸 酢 "Myriads of years as the fitting reward."

酌 言 酢 之 (his guests) fill the cup and present it to him.

(a) Read *ts'o*[4.]　Vinegar. It is the original form of 醋 No. 6835.

TSO.　TSUO. (卩ㄛ)

(Tsoh)

鑿 [4.5.]

6786　A chisel. To chisel. A.p. ×*tsao*[2.]

鑿 井 to sink a well.

×鑿·個 眼 兒 to chisel out a hole.

鑿 木 to chisel wood.

鑿 木 鳥 the wood-pecker.

[5]鑿 牙 to knock out a man's tooth.

×鑿 破 to cut a hole in—to scuttle.

×鑿 通 to open a way through; to tunnel.

鑿 鑿 可 據 indisputable proof.

×鑿·開 to open out; to cut a way into.

---

[10]鑿 齒 to knock out the front teeth—as some of the tribes do.

TS'O.　　(ㄘㄛ)

嵯 [2]　The irregular outline of a range of hills.

6787　Also read *ts'ü*[1.]

嵯 峨 the outlines of rocky hills.

搓 [1]　To rub between the hands; to twist by rubbing between the hands.

6788

搓 作 一 團 roll it into a ball.

搓 兩 道 油 漆 to rub it over with varnish twice—i.e., to give it two coats.

搓 手 to rub the hands together.

搓 挪 to rub between the hands.

[5]搓 揉 to crumple up in the hand.

搓 熱 to warm by friction.

搓 碎 to crumble between the hands.

搓 磨 to worry; to scold.

搓 紙 條 to roll paper spills—for pipe-lights, etc.

[10]搓 線 to twist thread.

搓 繩·子 to twist a rope by rolling hemp between the hands.

搓 繩 縛 颶 風 to twist a rope to bind the gale—inadequate.

搓 著 rolling between the hands.

搓 衣·裳 to rub garments when washing them.

[15]搓 香 to roll sticks of incense.

瑳 [3]　The brilliant white lustre of a gem. Lustrous.

6789

瑳 兮 瑳 兮 "How rich and splendid!"—describing a robe.

巧 笑 之 瑳 "How shine the white teeth through the artful smiles!"

磋 [1]　To polish. To correct.

6790

磋 切 to correct carefully.

磋 磨 to polish.

(a) Read *ts'o*[4.]

磋 商 to deliberate; to discuss; repeated conferences.

磋 議 手 續 deliberative pro-cedure.

蹉 1.4.
6791

To slip. To pass by.

蹉 跌 to slip and fall; an error; a slip—as in speech; to pass by.

蹉 跎 to stumble; to let slip.

蹉 跎 光 陰 to waste time.

中 坂 蹉 跎 to slip and fall when half-way up a slope —to fail in one's attempt.

命 運 蹉 跎 bad luck; misfortune.

無 得 蹉 跎 do not allow the occasion to slip past.

醝 2
6792

Brine; salt.

醝 任 the office of Salt Commissioner.

醝 使 Salt Commissioner.

醝 務 the salt monopoly.

錯 4
6793

Wrong; mistake; error; a fault. A blunder. To mistake. To be confused. Alternately.

錯·不 了 no mistake about it; no fear of going wrong.

錯 亂 confused; mixed up; disordered; complicated.

精·神 錯 亂 nerves in disorder.

錯·了 in the wrong; wrong.

錯 大·發·了 a great error; very far wrong.

錯 失 or 失 錯 an error; a mistake.

錯 字 an erroneous character.

錯 寫 to make a mistake in writing.

錯 怪 to blame the wrong person.

錯 愕 amazed and confused.

錯 愛 misplaced affection.

錯 瞧 to make a mistake about; to see wrongly.

錯 禮 to offend against etiquette.

錯 簡 wrong tablets—in the wrong place or order, as a quotation, etc.

錯 綜 to complicate.

其 錯 綜 有 經 緯 there is order in its confusion.

錯 縫 a person's weak points—the "seamy" side of his character.

錯 脚 難 返 it is hard to regain the right path; a false step is not easily recovered.

錯 落 errors and omissions; confused; involved.

錯 薪 bundles of faggots.

錯 處 fault; wrong.

錯 行 alternating progress.

錯 覺 illusion; a wrong impression.

錯 角 alternate angles.

錯 解 misinterpretation.

錯 認 mistaken recognition.

錯 誤 wrong; to make a mistake; mistaken.

錯·誤 改 正 "Errata."

錯·誤·的 親 切 mistaken kindness.

錯·誤 過 失 mistakes and errors or faults.

錯·誤 遺 漏 不 在 此 限 "Errors and omissions excepted." [rect.

絕 對 錯·誤 absolutely incorrect.

錯 車 to let another train pass by.

錯 謬 mistaken; greatly in error.

錯 迕 disordered; blowing from all quarters.

錯·過 had it not been for...; except; with the exception of; unless.

錯 過 必 改 the wrong must be corrected.

錯·過·是 ... apart from...; except; unless.

錯·過 時·候 to have passed by the time; to miss the opportunity; the time has passed—too late.

錯·過 機·會 to miss an opportunity.

錯 雜 confused; mixed up; disordered; complicated.

錯 骨 縫 to dislocate a joint; a dislocation.

不 錯 quite right; no mistake.

差 錯 error; deviation. (ch'a¹-)

午 錯·了 past noon.

挑 (or 找) 錯 to pick faults.

數 錯·了 counted wrongly.

認 錯 to acknowledge a fault. See above—26.

說 錯 to make an error in speech; to be impolite in speech.

賠 錯 to apologize.

走 錯 to take the wrong road.

(a) To inlay; ornamented.

錯 刀 a coin, shaped like a knife and inlaid with gold, issued by *Wang Mang* 王 莽 in 2 B.C. See below—C. 1.

錯 臂 to tattoo the arms.

錯 衡 an ornamented yoke.

以 黃 金 錯 其 文 inlaid the inscription with gold.

(b) Respectful.

錯 然 reverent; respectful.

(c) A grindstone. To polish.

錯 刀 a knife used in dressing and polishing jade, etc. See above—A. 1.

他 山 之 石 可 以 爲 錯 the stones of those hills may be made into grindstones.

(d) Read *ts'u⁴.* **u.f.** 措 **No. 6834. To place; to put by.**

錯 諸 地 placed on the ground.

錯 諸 枉 put aside those who are crooked.

錯 諸 直 set aside those who are upright.

TS'O. TS'UO. (ㄘㄛ)

剉 4
6794

To cut. To file. To trim.

剉 光 to file a thing bright; to polish.

剉·子 a file.

剉 屍 to cut the corpse (of a criminal) in pieces.

剉 平 to file smooth.

剉 折 to file in two; to harass; to be unsuccessful in battle; to fail in one's attempt.

剉 磨 to grind; to harass.

剉 角 to file off corners.

挫 4
6795

To push down. To treat harshly. To grind. To oppose.

挫·了 銳 氣 to damp one's ardour; to take away their zeal; to demoralize.

挫 淨 心 思 to exhaust one's mental powers.

挫 後 to be driven back—as a defeated army.

挫 折 to check; to damp one's ardour; to suffer a defeat; to counteract; obstacles.

挫 於 to be maltreated by....

挫 磨 to force; to coerce; to harass.

挫 衄 to suffer a slight defeat; to damp their ardour.

挫 辱 to humiliate; to disgrace.

挫 鍼 治 繲 (*hsieh*[4]) to work as a tailor, and do washing—for a living.

矬[2]　A dwarf.
6796

矬 人 a short person.

矬 價·錢 to lower the price.

矬·子 a dwarf.

矬 小 short in stature.

矬 漢·子 a dwarf.

矬 陋 squat and ugly.

脞[4]　Minced meat.　Trifles.
6796a

莝[4]　To chop straw fine for animals.
6797

莝 斫 刀 a chopping-knife.

莝 草 Mare's-tail—*Equisetum.*

銼[4]　A file.　An iron pan.
6798

一 把 銼 a file.

TS'O, TS'UO. (ㄘㄛ)
(Ts'oh)

厝[4]　A gravestone.　To cut or engrave.
6799

厝 注 to cut an epitaph.

(a) Read *ts'o*[5] or *ts'u*[5]. To place a coffin in a temporary shelter awaiting proper burial. To place.

合 厝 to place in a coffin and bury.

安 厝 to place a coffin in a temporary shelter.

浮 厝 temporary burial until the geomantic conditions are favourable for proper interment.

撮[4,5]　To take up with the fingers.　A pinch.　A measure of 60 grains of millet.　To bring together; to gather.　To scrape up.　Also read *ts'o*[1].
6800

撮 上 轎 to force into a sedan-chair.

撮 借 錢 to raise a sum of money by borrowing from several people. [have -*ü*- as a medial.

撮 口 to screw up the mouth; to

撮 合 to unite; to bring about a reconciliation; to collect; to bring together.

5 從 中 撮 合 to come to an arrangement.

撮 合 山 a marriage go-between.

撮 哄 to tempt; to entice.

撮 土 to shovel earth.

撮 壤 a pinch of earth—a small quantity.

10撮 弄 to incite; to egg on.

撮 影 to take a photograph.

撮 攦 to hustle off; to coax away.

撮 煤 to shovel coal.

撮 牛 奶 to milk a cow.

15撮 箕 a refuse-basket.

撮 糞 土 to shovel dung.

撮 藥 to make up a prescription.

撮 要 to select the most important points; a resume.

撮·起 灰·塵 (the gust) whirls the the dust.

(a) Read *tsui*[1].　A conical cap.

緇 撮 a black cap, worn in ancient times.

TSOU. (ㄗㄡ)
(Tseo)

伹[1]　Dull; slow; unskilful.　Also read *chü*[1].
6801

掫[1]　To beat the night-watches.　To grasp.
6802

緅[1]　A dark, purplish colour.　Silk of a purplish tint.
6803

諏[1]　To plan; to consult.　To choose.　To deliberate.
6804

諏 吉 to choose a lucky day.

諏 訪 to write and make inquiries.

共 諏 to consult together.

陬[1]　A corner.　A nook.　Secluded; retired; distant.
6805

陬 月 a name for the first lunar month.

陬 隅 a nook or corner.

山 陬 海 隅 some distant nook of mountain or sea.

偏 陬 a secluded place.

四 陬 the four corners of anything.

遐 陬 a far-off secluded spot.

鯫[1]　Small fish.　Minnows.　Read *tsou*[3,4].　A low, mean fellow.
6806

鯫 生 a low sort of person—depreciatory term of oneself.

鯫 生 說 我 a low person advised me.

走[3]　To walk.　To travel.　To go.　Radical 156.
6807

走·不 了[3] no getting away from; no escape.

走·不 到 unable to walk so far.

走·不 動 unable to walk.

走·不·得 not available for traffic; not safe to travel by—as a road that is flooded; must not quit and leave one's responsibilities behind.

5走·不 慣 unaccustomed to walking.

走·不 脫 unable to get away—as a suspected person, etc.

走·不 過 去 no getting past; the road is impassable through robbers, floods, etc.

走·不 開 unable to pass; cannot get out of the way; can't leave the work. [See below—31.

路 窄 汽 車 走·不 開 the road is narrow, motor-cars cannot pass.

10走 乏·了 fatigued with walking.

走·了 一·個·字 a word has been omitted.

走·了 水·了 there is a fire—i.e., premises on fire.

走·了 風 it has leaked out—as a secret.　*See below*—78.

走 作 to transgress certain rules of conduct.

15走 來 走 去 to wander to and fro.

走 倦·了 fatigued through walking.

走 入 to enter.

走·出 to run out; to go out.

走·動 to move; to begin to walk;

(1000)

to have a movement of the bowels.

20 走·動·走·動 to go for a stroll; to take a constitutional.

走 卒 messengers; move the pawn.

走。去 to run off.

走 堂 to serve as a waiter.

走 場·的 stage-waiters.

25 走 好 運 to have good luck.

走 岔·了 to go astray; to take the wrong road.

走 廊 a verandah; a corridor.

走·得 快 to walk fast.

走·得 慢 to go slowly.

30 走·得 稀 seldom visited.

走·得 開 able to pass one another on the road. See above—8.

四 輛 車 並 行 也 走 得 開 four carts can travel abreast—the road is so wide.

走 投 沒 路 there is no escape; no getting out of it.

走 攏·了 to draw near to; to assemble together.

35 走 時·的 人 an up-to-date man; fortunate and flourishing.

不 走 時 behind the times; unlucky.

走 更·的 a night-watchman.

走 樣 unlike the pattern.

走 氣 to escape—as steam, spirits, etc.

40 走 江 湖 to wander from place to place; to travel.

走 海 to travel by sea.

走 漏 消·息 to let out a secret; to leak out as news. See above —13, below—78.

走 漏 風 聲 the secret is out; the thing is noised abroad.

走 無 常 to fall into a trance.

45 走 狗 a sporting-dog—a servile dependant, a term of abuse.

走 獸 beasts; quadrupeds.

走 百 病 ancient custom of women walking out on the night of the first full moon of the lunar year, in order to ward off all kinds of sickness during the coming year.

走 石 飛 沙 flying pebbles and sand—a great dust-storm.

走 禽 類 cursores—a class of birds that cannot fly, as the ostrich or emu.

50 走 私 to smuggle.

走 筆 to take up the pen to write.

走 籌 watchmen.

走 紅 運 to have good luck.

走 索 to walk the tight rope.

55 走 累·了 tired after walking.

走·着 on foot; walking.

走 肚·子 to have diarrhoea.

走 背 運 to have bad luck.

走 讀 學 校 a day-school.

60 走 讀 生 day-pupils.

走 脫 to slip off; to abscond.

走·走 to take an airing; to stroll.

走 路 to walk; to travel.

走 路 幫 to travel in company.

65 走 輈 輈 to walk back and forth; to go for a constitutional.

走 迷·了 路 to go astray.

走 進 to enter.

走 進 城·去 went into the city.

走 道 兒 to travel; to walk.

70 走·過 一 遭 I have been there once.

走·過 幾 省 he has travelled over several provinces.

走 遍 to travel everywhere.

走 遞 夫 letter-carrier.

走 錯·了 路 has taken the wrong road.

75 走。開 get out of the way!—as to a crowd stopping the road.

走 陣 to advance in regular order.

走 頭 無 路 there is no getting out of it.

走 風 to let out a secret; to leak out, as news. See above—13, 42.

走 馬 a riding-horse; an ambling horse.

80 走 馬 燈 a lantern with a circle of paper horses mounted so that the ascending hot air from the candle causes them to revolve.

走 馬 看 花 to look at the flowers while passing on horseback—to give a hurried glance.

走 馬 觀 碑 to read an inscription while passing on horseback—extraordinary ability.

走 魚 是 大·的 the fish that gets away is always the largest—used of exaggerations.

走 黑·的 a burglar; a thief.

奏⁴ To report to the throne; to memorialize the emperor.
6808 Distinguish 秦 No. 1112.

奏 上 to memorialize the emperor.

奏 事 to represent matters to the throne.

奏 他 一 本 to impeach him in a memorial.

奏 任 to recommend for office.

5 奏 假 (kê²·⁵) to present an offering.

奏 淮 to memorialize, requesting the imperial sanction.

奏 功 to have the intended effect; to take effect.

奏 劾 or 奏 叄 to memorialize the throne impeaching another official.

奏 報 to report to the throne.

10 奏 奉 諭 旨 to memorialize and receive an imperial reply.

奏 委 to memorialize requesting the appointment of....

奏 定 在 案 the memorial and decision are on record.

奏 對 replies made to the emperor at an audience.

奏 懇 to petition the emperor that....

15 奏 摺 a memorial to the throne.

奏 擬 to memorialize, proposing that....

奏 效 to have a beneficial result.

奏 明 to memorialize the emperor.

奏 書 a memorial to the throne.

20 奏 本 a memorial to the throne.

奏 爲 to petition with regard to....

奏 疏 a memorial.

奏 皇 上 or 陳 奏 to memorialize the emperor.

奏 稿 a draft memorial.

25 奏 稱 to memorialize the emperor.

奏 章 a memorial to the throne.

奏 聞 to report for the imperial information.

奏 薦 書 a letter of commendation.

奏 請 to petition the emperor that....

30 准 奏 to assent to a memorial.

面 奏 to make a personal report to the throne.

(a) To play music; To celebrate.

奏 凱 to sing a song of triumph.

奏 樂 (yüeh⁴) to play music.

奏 琴 to play the ch'in.

奏 鼓 to beat a drum.

和 奏 to play in harmony.

節 奏 to beat time.

(b) To go forward. To advance. To display.

奏 其 勇 displayed his valour.

奏 庶 to show to the people.

TS'OU. (支)
(Ts'eo)

**湊
湊**[4]
6809　To collect. To amass.
To come together.

湊·上·來 came forward.

湊·不·出 unable to raise the amount.

湊·個 熱·鬧 to join in the fun.

湊·個 趣 兒 to be merry; to make a joke.

[5]湊 借 to contribute as a loan.

湊·出 捐項 to take up a subscription.

湊 分[4]·子 to make a contribution towards.

湊·合 to collect; to assemble; to amass; to converge.

湊 合 兩 國 to bring about amicable relations between the two nations.

[10]湊 在 一 塊 兒 gather them all together—as books, etc.

湊 在 一 處 crowded together into one place.

湊 弄 to assemble; to amass; to collect.

湊 殼 數 enough for the occasion; to make up the proper number.

湊。成 to make in all.

[15]湊。成 整 數 to make up an even amount.

湊 攏 to assemble together.

湊 數 to make up the proper number.

湊 會 to assemble; to collect.

湊 繳 to raise, as money.

[20]湊 聚 to assemble; to collect.

湊 趣 to force oneself to comply.

湊 辦 to gather; to raise money.

湊·過·來 to join in.

湊 集 to assemble; to amass; to collect.

(a) To run into. To happen by chance. To occur.

湊 巧 just as luck would have it; a fortunate coincidence.

事 在 湊 巧 as luck would have it.

湊 手 convenient to the hand; ready to hand.

湊 空 to take advantage of leisure —to do something.

時 來 福 湊 a stroke of luck.

(b) u.f. next. Between the skin and the flesh.

湊 理 between the skin and the flesh.

腠[4]
6810　Between the skin and the flesh.

腠 理 閉 the pores are closed—by the cold.

疾 在 腠 理 the disease is between the skin and the flesh— it is trifling.

輳[4]
6811　The hub of a wheel.

四 方 輻 輳 the centre of things —"the hub of the universe."

TSU. (ㄗㄨ)

俎[3]
6812　A stand for meat at feasts or sacrifices. A dish for food.

俎 上 肉 meat on the stand or platter:—describes the masses under oppressive government.

俎 豆 之 事 affairs of the dish and platter—worship, sacrifices.

梡 俎 a small four-legged wooden stand, used in sacrifices.

為 俎 孔 碩 "they prepare the trays which are very large."

越 俎 代 庖 to step over the vessels in order to assist the cook at the sacrifices—to exceed one's functions, to interfere.

鼎 俎 tripods and stands—for sacrifices, etc.

徂[3]
6813　To advance; to go to. What is past.
A.p. *ts'u[2]*.

徂 征 to reduce refractory States.

徂 旅 invading forces.

徂 齎 孝 孫 "he goes to the filial descendant to convey—the will of the gods."

孝 孫 徂 位 "the filial descendant goes to his place."

我 徂 組 求 定 henceforth we will seek only the settlement— of the kingdom.

自 西 徂 東 from the west to the east.

(a) u.f. next. To die.

殂 落 to die.

殂[3]
6814　To die, generally used of an eminent person such as a ruler.
Also read *ch'u[3]*.

殂 落 to die; to perish.

草 容 殂 謝 the beauty of the flower perishes.

祖[3]
6815　An ancestor; a grandfather. A founder or originator. Origin. Beginning. A prototype.

祖·上 ancestors.

祖 伯 父 a paternal grand-uncle.

祖 傳 handed down from of old; hereditary.

祖 傳 之 病 hereditary maladies.

[5]祖 先 or 妣 祖 ancestors.

祖 先 堂 an ancestral temple or shrine.

祖 國 one's mother country.

祖 基 ancestral lands.

祖 墳 an ancestral grave.

[10]祖 奠 sacrifice offered on the night before a funeral.

祖 妣 male and female ancestors.

祖 姑 a paternal grand-aunt.

祖 娘 a grandmother.

祖·宗 ancestors.

[15]祖 宗 遺 產 ancestral estate.

祖 居 the ancestral home; a family seat.

祖 師 a patron saint; the founder of a sect, used of Buddha and Laotzǔ: the originator of a craft or trade.

祖 廟 an ancestral temple.

祖 德 the virtues of one's ancestors.

[20]祖 業 ancestral inheritance; ancestor's meritorious achievements.

祖 母 a paternal grandmother.

祖 父 a paternal grandfather.

祖 爹 a grandfather.

祖 籍 the ancestral home; the family seat.

[25]祖 考 ancestors; the spirits of ancestors.

祖 識 地 德 he had long known the quality of the land.

祖 述 堯 舜 to hand down the doctrines of *Yao* and *Shun*

as though they had been his ancestors.

祖 遺 inherited.

祖 陵 an ancestral grave.

30 祖 龍 a name given to *Ch'in Shih-huang* 秦始皇.

太 祖 the first emperor of a dynasty.

始 祖 or 世 祖 or 鼻 祖 the first ancestor or founder of a family.

拜 祖 to worship the ancestors.

曾 祖 a great-grandfather.

35 烈 祖 illustrious ancestors.

高 祖 a great-great-grandfather.

鼻 祖 耳 孫 ancestors and posterity, the earliest and the latest members of the family.

(a) To sacrifice to the Spirit of the Roads before starting on a journey or an expedition.

祖 神 the Spirit of the Roads.

祖 道 to sacrifice to the Spirit of the Roads; to prepare a farewell feast.

祖 餞 a farewell feast.

仲 山 甫 出 祖 *Chung Shan-fu* went forth, having sacrificed to the Spirit of the Roads.

租 ¹ To rent; to lease. To tax. Rent.
6816

租 丁 a tenant farmer.

租 借 to let; to lease; to take on lease.

租 借 地 leased territory.

租 價 rent.

⁵租 出 to let.

租 出 去 了 rented.

租 到 to rent.

租 地 to let or rent land.

租 地 批 a deed of lease or rental.

10 租 契 a deed of lease or rental.

租 子 rent.

租 徭 taxes and compulsory service.

租 息 the tax paid for rent of buildings erected on reclaimed foreshore.

租 戶 a tenant.

15 租 房 子 to rent or let a house.

租 雇 to charter; to hire.

租 批 a deed of lease or rental.

租 摺 子 a book for recording the receipt of rents.

租 業 leasehold property.

20 租 界 leased lands—a term used for the "Concessions" at the various Treaty Ports.

租 用 to rent.

租 稅 rent; taxes; excise.

租 薄 a rent receipt-book.

租 米 rice paid as rent by tenant farmers.

25 租 約 a deed of rental or lease.

租 給 to rent or lease to.

租 與 to rent or lease to.

租 賃 to rent or lease.

租 銀 or 租 錢 rent.

30 乾 租 rent—in money.

交 租 to pay the rent.

保 租 to be responsible for the rent.

催 租 to press for payment of rent.

割 租 to reduce the rent.

35 加 租 to raise the rent.

召 租 or 招 租 **"TO LET"**.

房 租 house-rent.

收 租 to receive the rent.

活 租 a provisional lease.

40 減 租 to reduce the rent.

濕 租 rent—in kind.

立 租 契 to draw up a lease.

納 租 to pay the rent.

轉 租 to sub-let.

45 領 租 to take a lease of.

組 ³ A silk band. A silk cord. A girdle. Fringe. Tissue.
6817 Group, section, department.

組 合 organized; to consolidate; to unite; combinations (*math.*); association.

組 合 的 composite.

組 成 to accomplish; to achieve; to convene; to organize; constituted; established.

組 成 體 an organism.

⁵組 立 to establish.

組 織 to weave—thus:—to organize; to establish; to found; to build up; to form; to systematize; composed of; texture; tissue; formation; the structure of anything.

組 織 上 的 organically.

組 織 商 店 的 方 法 method of organizing business houses.

組 織 學 histology.

10 組 織 家 organizers.

組 織 成 就 successful organization.

組 織 才 organizing ability.

組 織 方 法 method of organization.

組 織 服 務 團 organize a band of voluntary helpers.

15 組 織 法 the constitution, texture or natural structure of anything.

組 織 的 原 理 the principles of organization.

組 織 的 問 題 the problem of organization.

組 織 的 意 義 the purpose of the organization.

組 織 的 社 會 organized society.

20 組 織 的 統 一 organic unity.

組 織 的 能 力 power of organization.

組 織 神 學 systematic theology.

組 織 體 an organization.

一 致 的 組 織 a unified system.

25 上 皮 組 織 epithelium.

商 會 之 組 織 organization of the Chamber of Commerce.

工 廠 的 大 組 織 the organization of great factories.

形 態 組 織 form and construction—of an organ of the body.

文 章 的 組 織 the construction of a literary composition.

30 未 組 織 體 an unorganized body.

生 產 的 組 織 the organization of production.

皮 下 組 織 sub-cutaneous tissue.

皮 膜 組 織 epithelium.

眞 理 的 組 織 the fabric of truth.

35 社 會 組 織 the organization of society.

神 經 組 織 nervous tissue.

筋 肉 組 織 muscular tissue.

簡 單 的 組 織 simple organization.

細 胞 組 織 cellular tissues.

40 結 締 組 織 or 結 組 織 connective tissue.

纖 維 組 織 fibrous tissues.

着 手 組 織 to take in hand the organization of. (*cho*¹-)

脂 肪 組 織 fatty tissue.

農 廠 組 織 agricultural organization.

45 這種組·織 this kind of an organization.

部落組·織 the organization of the aboriginal tribes.

組纓 an ornamental cap-string.

組閣 to form a cabinet.

解組歸田 to loosen the official girdle and return home—to retire from public life.

重 (ch'ung²) 組 to reorganize.

詛 ³ To curse; to imprecate.

6818

詛盟 to swear an alliance.

詛盡嘴 to take a dreadful oath; lips filled with curses.

詛祝 to invoke curses upon an enemy.

詛罵 cursing and railing; to curse and revile.

詛誓 to take an oath.

詛逐 to anathematize.

阻 ³ To hinder; to obstruct; to oppose.

6819

阻·不住 unable to hinder.

阻事·情 to hinder business—as an untimely visitor.

阻力 resistance. (physics).

生阻力 producing difficulties; finding hindrances.

5 磨阻力 frictional resistance.

空氣阻力 atmospheric resistance.

阻却 to put off; to avoid.

阻命 to obstruct or disobey orders.

阻塞 to obstruct; to block up.

10 阻害 to encumber—a person's actions.

阻峻 steep.

阻擋 or 攔阻 or 阻擾 or 阻撓 to hinder; to obstruct; to hamper; to impede; to get in the way.

阻攔 or 擋阻 to stand in the way of; to oppose; to block.

阻於風雨 hindered by the weather.

15 阻欠 to fall into arrears.

阻止 to obstruct; to hinder; to impede; to hamper.

阻沮 doubt; suspicion.

阻滯 to get in the way; to impede; to hinder; to obstruct.

阻礙 an encumbrance; to hinder; to impede; to obstruct.

20 阻饟 to check; to put a stop to.

阻路 to bar the way.

阻遏 to hinder; to stop.

阻難 hardships; straits.

多方阻難 (putting) all sorts of difficulties in the way.

25 阻風 a head-wind.

阻駁 to oppose.

阻電器 interrupter. (electric).

(a) A dangerous pass. A defile. Difficult and dangerous.

寀入其阻 boldly he entered its dangerous passes.

道阻且躋 the way is difficult and steep.

道阻且長 the way is difficult and long.

險阻 a hazardous pass—dangerous.

(b) To suffer.

黎民阻饑 the black-haired people are suffering the distress of hunger.

(c) To disdain. To reject.

既阻我德 you disdain my virtues.

(d) To be separated. To separate.

阻隔 a separation; a hindrance; to cut off; to separate.

山川阻深 widely separated by the hills and streams.

自治伊阻 he has brought upon us this separation.

(e) u.f. 沮 No. 1575. To stop, etc.

氣阻志奪 flagging energy and damped ardour.

(f) To rely on.

阻兵 to rely on military power.

(g) Read chu³. To stumble.

馬阻蹄 the horse stumbled.

齟 ³ Unevenly-fitting teeth. Irregular. To gnaw.

6820 Also read chu³.

齟齬 like teeth that do not meet properly; locked tightly—a difference of opinion.

菹 ¹ Pickled fruit or vegetables. Also read chü¹.

6821

菹菜 salted vegetables.

(a) Read chieh¹. A morass.

祚 ⁴ To bless. Honour. Dignity and happiness. The throne. Pron. tso⁴.

6822

祚永 long happiness.

祚胤 posterity—bringing honour.

天祚明德 God blesses illustrious virtue.

帝祚 the imperial throne.

王祚 the dignity of the throne.

踐祚 to ascend the throne.

胙 ⁴ Flesh offered to ancestors; sacrifices. To worship ancestors. Pron. tso⁴.

6823

胙肉 sacrificial flesh.

復胙 a further offering of the sacrifices.

食胙 to eat the sacrifices.

(a) To confer upon.

胙之土 he rewards them with territory.

(b) Happiness.

TSU. (ㄗㄨ)

(Tsuh)

足 2.5. The foot. Radical 157. In some places also read chü².

6824

足下 you; "sir."

足不出戶 without stepping outside the house.

足不履影 he would not tread on the shadow.

足儿 a foot-stool.

5 足容重 a grave and sedate walk.

足塞傷心 if the feet are cold the heart suffers.

足指 the toes.

足球 football.

足痛 gout.

10 足 衣 socks.

足 跡 footprints; traces.

足 蹈 to dance—for joy.

足 踵 the heel.

足 蹛 蹛 如 有 循 he dragged his feet along as if they were held to the ground.

15 足 躩 如 也 his feet had the appearance of moving with difficulty.

足 音 the sound of footsteps.

足 骨 the bones of the foot.

天 足 natural, unbound feet.

失 足 to stumble; to make a slip.

20 手 足 hands and feet—brothers. *See* No. 5838—127ff.

自 首 至 足 from head to foot.

赤 足 barefooted.

(a) Enough. Satisfied. Complete. Pure—as silver.

足 以 quite sufficient to....

足 以 有 臨 也 competent to rule.

足 以 治 其 國 fit to govern the kingdom.

足 備 fully prepared.

5 足 價 the full price.

足 取 信 worthy of credence.

足 可 以 行 it can easily be done; it will do very well.

足 壯 strong; robust; healthy.

足 穀 用 there is abundance for use.

10 足 意 satisfied; content.

足 敷 sufficient to.

足 昭 can well demonstrate.

足 智 多 謀 wise and full of stratagems.

足 有 一 年 quite a full year.

15 足 法 to come up to the correct standard; a perfect example.

足 用 an adequate supply.

足 用 有 餘 overflowing abundance.

足 紋 standard purity—of silver.

足 能 well able to.

20 足 色 紋 銀 silver of standard purity.

足 見 can well perceive.

足 言 足 容 to be careful of one's words and actions.

足 論 worth discussing.

足 足 兩 年 two full years.

25 足 足 找·你 半 天 I have been looking for you all day.

足 足 有 一 百 兩 there is the full amount of $100.

足 足(的)amply sufficient; fully.

足 顯 sufficient to demonstrate.

足 食 足 兵 民 信 之 矣 let there be plenty of food, plenty of military material, and let the people trust their ruler.

30 不 一 而 足 there is not only this one—there are others.

不 知 足 discontented; dissatisfied.

不 足 以 當 大 事 not fit to undertake important matters.

不 足 掛 齒 not worth worrying about.

不 足 道 not worth mentioning.

35 人 心 不 足 the heart of man is never satisfied.

何 足 怪 what is there wonderful in that?

十 足 complete.

心 滿 意 足 perfectly satisfied.

滿 足 full; complete.

40 知 足 content.

豐 足 abundant.

(b) Read *chü*[4]. **Excessive.**

足 恭 excessive respect.

呿 **2.5. To cajole.**
6825

呿 訾 to cajole; to flatter.

喊 **1.5. To be grieved. Ashamed. Used to imitate sounds.**
6826

喊 喊 sound of whispering.

卒 **2.5. A servant; an underling. A pawn in chess.**
6827

卒 伍 soldiers; troops.

兵 卒 soldiers.

士 卒 officers and men.

小 卒 a private.

禁 卒 a gaoler.

(a) To die. To finish. Finally. Completely.

卒 事 to finish.

卒 于 任 內 he died at his post.

卒 業 to finish a course of study.

卒 業 文 憑 a diploma of graduation.

病 卒 died of disease.

終 卒 died.

(b) Read *ts'u*[4.5]. **Unexpectedly. Suddenly. Urgent.**

卒 中 a sudden stroke or seizure.

卒 卒 urgently; hurriedly.

卒 急 in a great hurry; urgent.

卒 然 suddenly; unexpectedly.

卒 至 to arrive suddenly.

捽 [4.5]. **To seize. To grasp. To pull up. To run against.**
6828

捽·住 頭·髮 grasped him by the hair.

捽 擲 to throw down; to dash to the ground.

捽 胡 to seize by the throat.

捽 草 to pull up grass or weeds.

捽 頸 to seize by the throat.

椊 [1.5]. **To fit a handle into a socket. A plug or cork. The top of a pillar where it projects above the cross-beam.**
6829

族 [2.5]. **A clan; a tribe. A class. A family. To collect together. Also read** *ts'u*[2.5].
6830

族 人 clansmen.

族 伯 or 族 叔 older and younger fellow-clansmen of the same generation as one's father.

族 兄·弟 paternal male third cousins.

族 女 daughter of paternal male third cousins.

5 族 姊·妹 paternal female third cousins.

族 姪 sons of paternal third cousins.

族 子 son of paternal male third cousins.

族 孫 grandson of paternal male third cousins.

族 居 to dwell together.

10 族 望 a family of high standing.

族 正 the head of a clan.

族 母 wife of father's cousin.

族 父 father's male third cousin of the same surname.

族 老 an elder of a clan.

15 族 葬 buried with the other members of the clan.

族 誅 to execute the families of a criminal's father, mother and wife.

族 譜 a clan register; a genea-logical table.

族 隣 clansmen.

族 長 (chang³) an elder of a clan.

20 族 類 a tribe; a class; a clan.

三 族 father, son, and grandson; the families of the father, mother and wife.

九 族 the nine generations of a family from the great-great-grandfather downwards.

出 族 to turn a person out of the clan; to expunge the name from the family register.

同 族 of the same clan or class.

25 宗 族 a clan or family.

水 族 aquatic animals.

百 族 all living creatures.

舉 族 去 to go in a swarm.

(a) To destroy the whole family.

罪 人 以 族 along with the crimi-nals he executed a l l t h e i r relatives.

鏃 4.5. The barb of an arrow. The head of a javelin.
6831   Also read ts'u⁴.⁵.

TS'U.   (ㄗㄨ)

怚 ¹ Dull; stupid; suspicious.
6832

秦 王 怚 而 不 信 人 the Prince of Ch'in was suspicious and did not place confidence in others.

(a) Read chü⁴. Proud.

粗
麤
麄
觕
6833   Coarse. Rough. Rude; vulgar. Bulky.

粗 人 a rough, boorish fellow.

粗 俗 coarse, vulgar.

文 理 粗 俗 the style of the composition is very harsh.

粗 壯 robust; strong.

5 粗 大 coarse; bulky.

粗 裝 bulky; unwieldy; thick, as a rope.

粗 婦 a rough, coarse woman.

粗 完 to finish roughly—as when in a hurry.

粗 工 rough w o r k; unskilled labour.

10 粗 心 浮 氣 careless and giddy; unstable in character.

粗 手 笨 脚 awkward and clumsy.

手 粗 rough, heavy-handed; lacking delicacy of touch.

粗 拉 coarse and rude.

粗 斜 紋 布 drills.

15 粗 暴 boorish; churlish and rude.

粗 枝 大 葉 coarse branches and large leaves, i.e., roughly finished.

粗 比 a vulgar comparison.

粗 活 rough w o r k; unskilled labour.

粗 淡 rough and coarse—of home-ly fare. See below—35.

20 粗 率 rough; brusque.

粗 疏 heedless; careless; inatten-tive; rough and coarse.

粗 知 to have a rough idea of.

粗 磁 器 coarse china.

粗 米 coarse rice.

25 粗 粗·的 coarsely; roughly; care-lessly.

粗 糙 coarse and rude.

粗 糙 寒 蹇·的 樣 a coarse, pover-ty-stricken appearance.

粗 紋·的 coarse-grained.

粗 紙 rough, coarse paper.

30 粗 細 coarse and fine; coarseness; texture.

粗 聲 a harsh, rough tone of voice.

粗 肥 coarse and fat; gross.

粗 脖·子 a goitre.

粗 能 ordinary abilities.

35 粗 茶 淡 飯 coarse, homely fare —conventional apology of a host.

粗 莽 brusque; coarse.

粗 蠢 rough, boorish and clumsy.

粗 製 品 roughly manufactured goods; common, cheap wares.

粗 話 obscene language; coarse talk.

40 粗 豪 a rough and ready blusterer.

粗 躁 careless in manner; hasty; impetuous.

粗 重 coarse, rough, heavy and clumsy.

粗 野 vulgar; rustic.

粗 陋 coarse-looking.

---

45 粗 風 暴 雨 a sudden rain-storm; boisterous weather.

粗 食 粗 肥 coarse food makes coarse fat.

粗 香 small, rough sticks of in-cense.

粗 鹵 (or 魯) boorish; rude.

粗 麥 oats.

50 粗 麻 布 coarse linen.

動 粗 to use force; to take rough measures.

精 粗 delicate and coarse.

措 ⁴ To place. To employ. To collect. To arrange. To
6834   manage.
     Also read ts'o⁴.

措 大 a scholar in poor circum-stances.

措 意 to reflect on; to think of; to consider; arrangement of ideas.

措 手 to set the hand to; ready; at hand.

措 手 不 及 not in time with one's hand—as to save something from falling.

5   手 足 無 措 at a loss what to do; cannot move hand or foot.

民 無 所 措 手 足 the people do not know how to move hand or foot—are at a loss, not knowing what to do.

措 理 to arrange; to adjust.

措 緻 to find security for; to raise funds for certain payments.

措 置 to devise ways and means; to place; to arrange.

10 措 置 失 當 out of place; mis-managed.

無 所 措 置 ill at ease—as if he did not know what to do with his hands and feet.

措 辦 to arrange; to collect to-gether; to furnish; to put into operation; to raise—as funds.

措 辭 wording; to couch phrases.

不 知 所 措 in a dilemma; at a loss what to do.

15 故 時 措 之 宜 也 t h e r e f o r e, whenever he (the entirely sincere man) employs them, their action will be right.

無 措 without means.

設 措 to establish; to set up.

(a) To intermit.

學 之 弗 能 弗 措 也 while, in what he has studied, there is anything he cannot understand, he will not intermit his labours.

(b) To publish.

措 施 to publish; to give forth; to distribute; to manifest.

醋 [4] Vinegar.
6835

醋 勁 jealous.
醋 大 a scholar in poor circumstances. (a variant of 6834.1)
醋 心 an envious, jealous disposition.
醋 意 jealousy.
[5] 醋 拌 to serve or dress food in vinegar.
醋 海 生 波 complications caused by jealousy.
醋 炒 to fry with vinegar.
醋 罐·子 a vinegar jar—a jealous woman.
醋 螺·子 a kind of marine polypus from which vinegar is made.
[10] 醋 酸 acetic acid; acetates.
醋 酸 鉛 acetate of lead.
吃 醋 to drink vinegar—to be jealous, said of a woman.
陳 醋 old vinegar.
高 醋 the best vinegar.

TS'U.　　(ㄘ)
(Ts'uh)

崒 崒 [4.5.] Rocky peaks. Lofty and dangerous.
6836

猝 [4.5.] Abrupt; hurried. Inter. 卒 No. 6827—B.
6837

猝 不 及 防 put off one's guard.
猝 然 suddenly; abruptly; unexpectedly.
倉 猝 hurriedly; suddenly; impetuous.

促 [4.5.] To urge. Hurried.
6838

促 之 太 甚 to over-persuade.
促 急 to urge; to stimulate.
促 狹 rude, boorish; slovenly.
促 病 a sudden and violent disease.
[5] 促 織 the house-cricket—lit., to urge to the spinning, alluding to the chirping of the cricket, which sounds like the whirr of the spinning-wheel.
促 裝 to pack one's luggage, etc., in a hurry.
促 迫 to urge; to stimulate.
促 進 to press forward; to promote; to expedite.
促 進 衛 生 to improve hygienic conditions.
促 進 和 協 to promote harmony.

(a) Close; crowded.

促 坐 to sit close together.
促 膝 談 心 to cross the knees and talk over matters—as friends.

猎 猩 [4.5.] Name of a famous dog. Also read ch'io[5].
6839

簇 [4.5.] Small bamboos; a framework on which silkworms spin. A crowd. Crowded. Also read tsü[4.5.].
6840

簇 擁 前 來 to press on in a crowd.
簇 簇 piled up; gathered up; crowded.
簇 簇 新 brand-new; fine; clean.
簇 聚 to crowd together.

(a) Inter. 鏃 No. 6831. Arrowheads.

中[4] 石 沒 簇 to strike a stone and bury the head of the arrow in it.

(b) Read ts'ou[1]. To bud. To burst forth.

太 簇 the third of the standard pitch-pipes. See 律 No. 4297—B.
萬 物 簇 生 all things burst into life—as in the spring.

蔟 [4.5.] A frame on which silkworms spin. See No. 6840. A nest. To collect.
6841

蹴 蹵 [4.5.] To tread on. To kick. Inter. next.
6842

蹴 損 to trample under foot.
蹴 然 uneasy in manner.
蹴 爾 而 與 之 to trample upon (food) and then offer it.
蹴 踘 to kick a football—an ancient game played with a ball of leather stuffed with hair.
蹴 踢 to trample on.

蹙 [4.5.] Wrinkled; contracted. Also read tsu[4.5.].
6843

蹙 蹙 cramped; hampered; distressed; wrinkled.
蹙 頞 to knit the brow—with pain.
蹙 額 or 頻 蹙 to knit the brows.

(a) To be urgent; to coerce.

蹙 剝 a term used under the Sung dynasty for illegal extortions by tax-collectors.
蹙 然 urgent; suddenly; imminently.
促 蹙 to urge; to coerce.
近 蹙 to press closely.

(b) Inter. 蹴 No. 6842. To kick.

蹙 鞠 to kick a football—an ancient game played with a ball of leather stuffed with hair.

顣 [4.5.] To frown. Also read tsu[4.5.]. Inter. preceding.
6844

顣 頞 to knit the brows.

TSUAN.　　(ㄇㄨㄢ)

攢 [1.4.] To collect. To hold in the hand. To bring together. Also read ts'uan[2].
6845

攢 列 to arrange in order.
攢 動 surging—as a mob.
攢 毆 to gather together and beat a person.

攢湊 to gather; to collect.
⁵攢珠 a string of pearls.
攢盒 a box with partitions, used for sweetmeats.
攢眉 to wrinkle the brows.
攢簇 to crowd together.
攢羅列聚 to collect and arrange in order; to pile—as arms.
¹⁰攢聚 to gather; to collect.
攢花 to arrange flowers in a bouquet.
攢賬 to reckon the total of accounts.
攢遶成營 to range (carts) round in a ring and form a camp.
攢錢 to subscribe money. *See below*—B.

(a) **To lay a coffin under a shed.**

攢基 a brick tomb, standing above the ground.
攢宮 an imperial mausoleum.

(b) **Read *tsan³*. To hoard.**

攢錢 to hoard money. *See above* —14.

(c) **Read *tsuan¹*. Occurs u.f. 鑽 No. 6848. To bore.**

攢看其蟲孔 to drill out the holes made by insects in pears, etc.

纘³ **To carry on; to continue. To imitate.**
6846

纘大 (*t'ai⁴*) 王之緒 to continue the work of King *T'ai*.
纘女 the lady who succeeded—as empress.
纘禹舊服 to take up the old mantle of *Yü*—to imitate his virtues.
纘繼 to continue the hereditary succession.

躦² **To jump. Also read *ts'uan¹*.**
6847

鑽鑚¹ **To bore; to pierce; to drill; to worm into; to penetrate. To enter deeply into.**
6848 **Also read *tsan¹*.**

鑽·不動 cannot bore a hole in it.

鑽之彌堅 the deeper I penetrated, the firmer they seemed to be—of the doctrines of Confucius.
鑽井 to bore a well.
鑽人 to swindle a person.
⁵鑽入 to bore or creep into; to enter deeply into.
鑽孔 to puncture; to perforate; to make a hole.
鑽孔機器 drilling machine.
鑽幹 to intrigue.
鑽弄 to plan; to intrigue.
¹⁰鑽心透骨 penetrating the heart and piercing the bone—as a shock.
鑽故紙 to study the writings of the ancients.
鑽木取火 to bore wood and get fire—by friction.
鑽李 to bore a hole through the stone of his plums, as a certain man did, in order to prevent others from using them as seed.
鑽灼 to bore and burn—tortoise-shell for divination.
¹⁵鑽灼經典 to make a diligent study of the classics.
鑽營 to intrigue to get a position.
鑽燧 to bore wood and get fire—by friction.
鑽燧改火 in getting fire by friction we have changed the various woods (during the year).
鑽眼 to bore a hole.
²⁰鑽穴 to bore a hole.
鑽窟窿 to bore a hole.
鑽着心 to do a thing heartily; to persevere.
鑽謀 to intrigue through, head first.
鑽過去 to bore through; to go
²⁵鑽頭 to worm one's way in. *See below*—A. 3, 4.

(a) **Read *tsuan⁴*. A drill; an auger; an awl, etc.**

鑽·子 an awl or drill, etc.
鑽石 or 金剛鑽 a diamond

鑽頭 the point of an awl; a bit or drill.
鑽頭覓縫 the point of the awl finds the openings—to use every effort to secure advantage for oneself; to poke one's way in everywhere.

---

⁵制簧·子鑽 a ratchet-brace.
手鑽 a gimlet; a hand-drill.
扶鑽 a brace.
曲鑽 a twist drill.
板鑽 a ratchet-brace.
¹⁰瓶塞鑽 a corkscrew.
繩鑽 a drill worked by a cord twisted around a shaft; a fiddle-drill.
胸鑽 a breast-drill.
螺·絲鑽 an auger.
開石鑽 a rock-drill.

³   Fat; rich. A stew of fish.
6849

纂³ **To collect materials. To compile; to edit. A compendium.**
6850   Distinguish 篡 No. 1449.

纂修 to prepare materials for publication; to compile.
纂出 or 自纂 to originate; to invent.
纂定 to frame—as laws.
纂訂 to revise and prepare for publication.
⁵纂輯 to prepare materials for publication; to compile.
纂述 to edit; to publish.
纂集 to make a collection of articles, etc., for printing.
新纂 a new edition.
硬纂 to tell yarns; untrue; false.
瞎纂 or 胡纂 to suggest wild schemes.

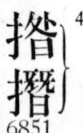⁴   **To hold in the hand; to grasp. To wring.**
6851

搢·不住 unable to grasp tight.
搢乾·了 to wring dry.
搢拳·頭 to close the fists.
搢籌 to carry a tally, as in loading or unloading a ship.
搢着不撒·手 hold tight, don't let go!
搢着筆據 to hold documentary evidence.

(a) **Also read *tsan³*. u.f. 攢 No. 6845.**

TS'UAN. (ㄘㄨㄢ)

竄[4] To sneak away; to skulk. To escape. To expel. Furtive.
6852

竄匿他方 to skulk away and hide in another place.
竄竊 to pilfer; to steal.
竄逸 or 逃竄 to escape.
竄逐 to flee into exile.
亂竄 to flee in disorder.
鼠竄 to run like rats to their holes.

(a) To change; to revise.

竄入 to interpolate.
竄定 to edit and prepare for the press.
竄改 to revise; to change; to correct.

(b) To fumigate.

卽竄以藥旋下病巳 he was made to inhale the smoke of a drug and the disease was cured.

(c) Penetrating.

香竄 a penetrating fragrance.

攛[1] To stir up to evil; to urge. Also read chuan[1].
6853 Distinguish 攛 No. 3762.

攛掇 to incite to evil.

(a) To throw away.

攛梭引線 to throw the shuttle and pass the thread.

驙[4] To leap; to jump. To
躥 spurt out. To eject.
6854

驙不過去 he cannot jump over it.

爨[4] A cooking-stove. A mess. To cook.
6855

爨婢 a kitchen-maid.
爨室 a kitchen.
爨飯 to cook food.
分爨 to mess separately.
同爨 to mess together.
搭爨 to board with another.
炊爨 to blow up the fire—to cook.

TSUI. (ㄗㄨㄟ)

觜[1] The 21st Chinese zodiacal constellation, see appendix. Also read tsŭ[1].
6856 Read tsuï[3]. u.f. next.

嘴[3] The mouth. The bill of a bird. A mouthpiece. A nozzle or spout.
6857

嘴·上咬定 gripped firmly in the mouth.
嘴不好 foul-mouthed.
嘴倈 contradictory; unreasonable talk.
嘴傷人 the mouth wounds others.
⁵嘴唇 the lips.
嘴唇油滑 oily, slippery speech.
嘴喫慣·了 accustomed to good food.
嘴大福大 a large mouth indicates great happiness.
嘴套 a muzzle.
¹⁰嘴·子 a mouth; a spout; a mouthpiece; a jutting point of land.
嘴尖 sharp-beak—said of one who is fond of discussing the failings, etc., of others; also used of a lantern-jawed person.
嘴巧舌能 clever and plausible in speech.
嘴巴[4]子 the cheeks; a smack on the face.
打嘴巴[4] to smack a person on the mouth.
¹⁵賣嘴巴[4]子 to live by one's wits, as story-tellers, etc.
嘴·巴骨 the jaw-bone.
嘴強 firm in speech; obstinate in argument.
嘴快心直 plain-spoken and straightforward.
嘴損 to slander; to malign.
²⁰嘴是無底坑 the mouth is a bottomless pit.
嘴甜心苦 hypocritical; deceitful.
嘴直 straight speaking; blunt and fearless in speech.
嘴硬 obstinate in argument; firm in speech.
嘴碎 or 碎嘴 loquacious; garrulous.
²⁵嘴臉 a face—generally used of ugliness.
嘴臊 bad breath; foul-mouthed; abusive and obscene.

嘴臭 bad. breath; foul-mouthed.
嘴舌 or 唇舌 talk; speech.
嘴·裏 in the mouth or beak.
³⁰嘴說容·易 it is easy enough to talk.
嘴饞 gluttonous.
一嘴兩舌·頭 double-tongued.
不答嘴 not to reply; to take no notice of what is said.
七嘴八舌 conflicting opinions.
³⁵利嘴 sharp-tongued.
努嘴 to pout; to make signs with the lips.
回嘴 to retort.
多嘴 talkative.
張·不開嘴 cannot open the mouth.
⁴⁰拙嘴笨舌 dull and unable to express oneself properly; blundering in speech.
抿嘴 to purse up the lips.
接嘴 to butt in; to take part in a dispute; to interrupt.
插嘴 to interrupt; to interfere in a discussion.
搬嘴 to carry tales; to wrangle.
⁴⁵撇嘴 wry-mouthed; having a crooked spout.
歪嘴 a distorted mouth; wry-mouthed.
油嘴 glib-tongued; oily-mouthed.
滿嘴·裏·的之乎者也 one whose mouth is full of wên-li particles—a pedant.
煙筒嘴 a mouthpiece for a tobacco-pipe.
⁵⁰茶壺嘴 spout of a teapot.
親嘴 to kiss; by one's own mouth.
講嘴 to argue; wordy disputes.
辯嘴 to wrangle.

最[4] Very; exceedingly; most. Superior.
6858

最上 the utmost; the best; the greatest; crowning.
最上成功 the greatest achievement.
最上級 the highest class; superlative degree.
最不中 (chung[1]) 用 not of the least use.
⁵最低寒暖表 (or 計) minimum thermometer.
最低熱度 minimum temperature.
最低額 minimum.
最低限 the minimum limit.

最 佳 the very best.
[10]最 便·當 the most convenient; the handiest.
最 優 之 例 the most favoured-nation clause.
最 先 in the front; the first of all.
最 初 in the very beginning.
最 劣 the worst.
[15]最 更 an official of superior merit in administration.
最 善 very excellent.
最 多 the most.
最 大 greatest; maximum.
最 大 壓 力 maximum pressure.
[20]最 大 密 度 maximum density.
最 大 張 力 maximum tension.
最 大 數 maximum number.
最 大 限 maximum limit.
最 好·的 the very best.
[25]最 小 t h e smallest; minimum. *See above*—7.
最 小 公 倍 數 lowest common multiple.
最 後 一 滴 the last drop.
最 後 問 題 the final question.
最 後 子³ 口 the last barrier; the barrier nearest to a Treaty Port.
[30]最 後 提 議 the final proposition; ultimatum.
最 後·的 final; the last.
最 後·的) 勝 利 final victory.
最 後·的 奮 鬬 final struggle.
最 後·的 手·段 the last resort.
[35]最 後·的 機 會 the last chance; the final opportunity.
最 後·的 目 的⁴ the ultimate objective.
最 後·的 談 判 final negotiations.
最 後 要 求 final demands; ultimatum.
最 後 通 牒 ultimatum.
[40]最 惠 國 the most-favoured nation.
最 惠 國 約 欵 the most favoured-nation clause. [most.(wu⁴)
最 惡 the most evil. (-o⁴); to hate
最 投 the most suitable.
最 新 式 newest form.
[45]最 時 式 ultra-fashionable.
最 時 樣 the latest fashion; ultra-fashionable.
最 時 髦·的 行 動 the most up-to-date movement.
最 殿 superior and inferior merits of officials.
最 為 above all; more than all.
[50]最 為 重 要 of the utmost importance.

以 此 為 最 consider this as the best.
最 短 線 the shortest line. (*geometry*).
最 終·的 final; ultimate.
最 美 the most handsome; the most beautiful.
[55]最 要 緊 the most important.
最 近 the most recent; the nearest.
最 近 發 明·的 the most recently invented.
最 關 緊 要 of the greatest importance.
最 難 very difficult; the most difficult.
[60]最 高 the highest.
最 高 價 maximum price.
最 高 寒 暖 表 (or 計) maximum thermometer.
最 高 機 關 the highest authorities.
最 高 熱 度 maximum temperature.
[65]最 高 裁 判 所 the highest court.
最 高 點 maximum point.

(a) To assemble. To collect.

最 凡 a general summary of a book.
最 目 index; summary of contents —of a book.
投 最 to collect; to assemble.

嶵 [4]
6859
To assemble.

嶵 芮 to collect; to assemble.

(a) Also read *tso⁵*. Petty; contemptible.

嶵 爾 小 國 a petty State.

罪 辠 [4]
6860
Sin, crime, wrong. Suffering; retribution. To blame.

罪·上 加 罪 repeated offences; added punishment.
罪 不 加 衆 punishment cannot be inflicted on a crowd.
罪 不 容 誅 or 罪 不 容 死 an unpardonable offence, for which even death is insufficient.
罪 不 重 (*ch'ung²*) 科 a crime may not be punished twice.

[5]罪 人 a criminal; an offender; a sinner.
罪 人 不 孥 the wives and children of offenders were not involved in their crime.
罪 合 萬 死 s u c h deserves a myriad deaths.
罪·名 sentence; penalty; guilt; crime; charge against.
罪·名 不 小 his crime is no small matter.
[10]罪·名 難 逃 it is difficult to escape punishment.
罪 咎 a crime; an offence.
罪 因 the reason for the crime.
罪 孽 retribution; the evil consequences of a sin.
罪 惡 evil; sin; wickedness. (-o⁴)
[15]罪 惡 滔 天 his offences mount to heaven (-o⁴)
罪 惡 滿 盈 the measure of iniquity is full.
罪 愆 sins; wrong.
罪 戾 crime.
罪 所 應 得² a well-deserved punishment.
[20]罪 案 a criminal case.
罪 梯 the cause of a crime; the steps which led up to a crime.
罪 業 retribution for past sins. *See above*—13.
罪 犯 a criminal; an offender.
犯 罪 to commit a crime; to sin.
[25]故 犯·的 罪 wilful offences.
誤 犯·的 罪 unintentional offences.
罪 狀 criminal charge; the circumstances of the crime.
罪 疑 維 輕 if there is doubt let the punishment be light.
罪 衣 prison clothes.
[30]罪 言 words giving offence to another.
罪 譴 faults; sins.
罪 責 to charge with a fault.
罪 跟 人 punishment will overtake the guilty.
罪·過 transgressions; sins.
[35]罪 障 sin and retribution.
罪 魁 the chief offender; the ringleader.
來 請 罪 to come and apologize.
受 罪 to be punished; to suffer discomfort, pain, distress, etc.
告 罪 to own to a fault; to apologize.
[40]問 罪 to condemn.

定 罪 to fix the punishment.

得·罪 to offend; "I beg pardon."

悔 罪 to repent.

有 罪 guilty.

45死 罪 capital crimes; capital punishment.

消 罪 to cancel guilt; to absolve.

無 罪 innocent.

知 罪 to acknowledge one's fault.

重 罪 heinous crime.

睟[4] A year of a person's life. Also read *sui*[4].
6861

睟 盤 之 期 the test of a child made on the completion of the first year of his life. *See* 周 No. 1293—A. 5.

醉[4] Drunk. Intoxicated.
6862

醉 人·的 狀 態 a fascinating manner.

醉 以 酒 to make drunk with wine.

醉 倒[3] to fall down from drunkenness.

醉 吟 to drink and recite poetry.

5醉 墨 drawing or writings done under the influence of liquor.

醉 夢 a drunken sleep.

醉 客 a drunken man.

醉·得 神 昏 顚 倒[3] fuddled with drink.

醉 心 infatuated.

10醉 心 名 譽 intoxicated with fame.

醉 心 新 文 明 intoxicated with the new culture.

醉 意 a drunken fancy.

醉 朋 a toper; a drunkard.

醉 歌 drunken songs.

15醉 死 dead drunk.

醉·漢 a drunkard; a sot.

醉 狂 mad with drink.

醉 生 夢 死 to lead a befuddled life, as if drunk or in a dream.

醉 眼 sleepy from drink; the appearance of the eyes of an intoxicated man.

20醉 聖 a notable drinker.

醉 臥 to lie in a drunken stupor.

醉 薰 薰 reeking with drink—very drunk.

醉 蟹 crabs steeped in liquor.

醉 言 stupid, drunken talk.

25醉 酒 drunk with wine.

醉 醒 to awake from a drunken sleep; to sober up.

醉 鬼 a drunkard; a sot.

醉 魄 to intoxicate the senses—as with music.

檇[1.4.] A wooden pestle or rammer.
6863

檇 李 ancient name for Kashing in Chekiang; a kind of fruit.

TS'UI.   (ㄘㄨㄟ)

崔[2] A high mountain.
嶵 Precipitous.
6864

崔 嵬 rocky summits; peaks.

(a) Read *ts'ui*[1]. (first only) A surname.

催[1] To urge; to press. To hasten.
6865

催 令 to insist on.

催 促 to press; to expedite; to urge.

催 傳 to press for the appearance of a person in court.

催 告 to urge.

5催 命 符 a death-warrant.

催 差 an underling who collects taxes. (-*ch'ai*[1])

催 提 to press for the appearance of a person in court.

催 歸 the cry of the nightjar or goat-sucker, from which the bird gets one of the names by which it is known.

催 生 midwifery; a present from the mother of the bride when a birth is imminent.

10催 生 娘·娘 the goddess of parturition.

催 生 符 a charm for hastening the birth of a child.

催 眼 歌 a lullaby.

催 眠 藥 sleeping-draughts.

催 眠 術 hypnotism.

15催 稟 a petition urging action in a case at law.

催 科 to press for taxes.

催 租 to press for rent.

催 繳 to press for payment; to dun.

催 討 to dun; to press for payment.

20催 請 to repeat an invitation; to urge the guest to come.

催 賬 to press for payment of an account.

催 趲 to urge forward.

催 辦 to urge that action be taken.

催 迫 or 催 逼 to press; to urge; to expedite.

25催 追 to demand; to press for payment.

催 馬 to urge forward a horse.

摧[1] To destroy; to break down. To cause to cease. To repress.
6866

Distinguish 推 No. 1713.

摧 倒[3] to push over.

摧 剛 爲 柔 to compel the obstinate to become yielding.

摧 堅 to break down the strong centre of an opposing army.

摧 壞 to destroy; to throw down.

5摧 折 to break off; to snap.

摧 抑 to restrain; to repress; to wrench.

摧 拔 to uproot.

摧 枯 拉 朽 to break down a decayed stump—easily accomplished.

勢 若 摧 枯 it was like breaking rotten wood—of an army that was easily defeated.

10摧 殘 to overthrow and destroy.

摧 毀 to destroy; to bring to shame; to bring scorn upon.

摧 燒 to break down and burn.

摧 辱 to humiliate; to bring to disgrace.

摧 陷 to overthrow and destroy.

15先 祖 于 摧 (the sacrifices to) my ancestors would be extinguished.

家 人 交 徧 摧 我 "the members of my family all emulously thrust at me."

梁 柱 其 摧 乎 the strong beam must break—said by Confucius before his death. *See* 泰 No. 6023-6.

(a) To be sad.

(b) Read *tso*[4]. To chop straw for animals. To feed with forage.

濣[1] Having the appearance of depth.
6867

有 濣 者 淵 "deep looks the pool."

璀[1] The lustre of gems. Glittering.
6868

榱[1] The small rafters which project from the eaves and support the tiles.
6869

榱 題 the rafters as above.

縗[1] A piece of sackcloth worn on the breast in mourning. The frayed edges of mourning garments.
6870

See 衰 No. 5908—A.

縗 経 coarse hempen mourning garments.
粗 縗 斬 unhemmed mourning garments of coarse sackcloth.

倅[4] A deputy. Added after the surname of a former sub-Prefect or Prefect.
6871

倅 貳 assistant magistrates.
倅 車 a second carriage.
郡 倅 a former sub-Prefect or assistant sub-Prefect.

(a) Read *tsu*[2.5]. Inter 卒 No. 6827. A company of one hundred soldiers.

啐[4] To taste; to sip. To spit. The sound of sipping.
6872

啐 唾·沫 to spit. (*-t'u*[4]·*mo*)
啐 嘗 to get the flavour of.
啐 醴 to sip wine.
啐 飮 to sip the wine at the close of a sacrifice in ancient times.
吥 啐 to spit at.

(a) Read *ch'ai*[4]. Abusive words. To alarm.

(b) Read *ts'u*[4.5]. Noise, hubbub, clamour.

悴[4] Sad; downcast; distressed.
6873

悴 族 a humble family.
悴 薄 in humble circumstances.
悴 賤 weak and humble.
衰 悴 downcast; grieved.
憔 悴 容 顔 a melancholy expression of countenance.

淬[4] To dip into water. To temper, also used fig. A fire-extinguisher. Inter. next.
6874

淬 勉 to urge; to constrain; to strive.
淬 布 to dye cloth.
淬 水 to plunge into water and temper.
淬 硫 to dip slips of wood into sulphur for use as matches.
淬 礪 to temper and grind—as an edged weapon.
淬 鋼 to temper steel; tempered steel.

(a) To come in contact with. To violate.

(b) Read *tsu*[2.5]. To dive. To flow.

焠[4] To temper, as steel. To burn. Inter. preceding.
6875

焠 其 鋒 tempered the point—of the spear.
焠 鋼 tempered steel.
焠 鐵 to harden iron.

瘁[4] Care-worn. To be distressed. Inter. 悴 No. 6873.
6876

日 瘁 distressed daily.
殄 瘁 torn with distress.
生 我 勞 瘁 "with what toil and suffering ye gave me birth."
盡 瘁 以 仕 worn out in government service.

睟[4] A clear bright eye. Also read *tsui*[4].
6877

睟 然 見 (*hsien*[3]) 於 面 a mild harmony appeared in his countenance.
睟 面 盎 背 "a mild harmony in the countenance, a rich fullness in the back"—of a superior man permeated by the fundamental doctrines of Confucianism.

粹[4] Pure grain. Single. Complete. Unadulterated. Also read *sui*[4].
6878

粹 器 perfect talent.
粹 液 clear liquid without sediment.
粹 然 unadulterated.
粹 白 pure white.
[5]粹 美 pure and handsome.
粹 言 pure words.
國 粹 the special excellencies of literature, art, etc., peculiar to a nation.
精 粹 pure; unadulterated.
純 粹 pure; unadulterated; unmixed.

(a) Read *sui*[4]. u.f. 碎 No. 5528.

粹 折 broken in pieces.

翠[4] The kingfisher; a humming-bird.
6879

翠 微 the blue-green of hills; halfway up a hill—from the blue-green tints of the hillside.
翠 毛 the feathers of the kingfisher.
翠 波 green waves.
翠 玉 a variety of jade.
[5]翠 眉 eyebrows pencilled to make them curved.
翠 碧 鳥 the kingfisher.
翠 空 the azure vault.
翠 竹 the emerald bamboo.
翠 羽 the blue feathers of the kingfisher.
[10]翠 翹 ancient head-dress of feathers, worn by women.
翠 舘 a brothel.
翠 色 a purplish blue; the blue of the kingfisher.
翠 花 flowers worked with kingfisher's feathers.
翠 苔 blue-green mosses.
[15]翠 華 an imperial banner ornamented with kingfisher's feathers, used in ancient times when the emperor was on circuit.
翠 葉 green leaves.
翠 蓋 a name for lotus-leaves.
翠 雀 a kind of kingfisher.
翠 雀 花 the larkspur.
[20]翠 藍 kingfisher-blue.
翠 雲 草 a cryptogamous plant—*Selaginella involvens.*

翠翹 a head-dress adorned with kingfisher's feathers.
點翠 ornamented with kingfisher's feathers.

(a) The rump of a bird.

翠肉 the flesh on the rump of a bird.

萃 4 Thick; close-set; dense. A collection. To collect together.
6880

萃於一堂 brought together into one hall.
萃森 dense; thick-set.
萃錦 collections of elegant extracts.
萃集 collected together.
萃蔡 the rustling of a garment.

膵 4 The pancreas.
6881

膵液 pancreatic juice.
膵液素 pancreatin.

脆 4 Crisp; brittle; short, as
脃 pastry. Trifling and flippant. Fragile.
6882

脆弱 brittle and friable.
脆快 prompt.
脆怯 weak and timid—useless as a soldier.
脆生生的 crisp; quite tender.
脆薄 thin and brittle.
脆輭 friable.
脆骨 cartilage; gristle.

(a) Clear-toned—of voices.

清脆 clear and sharp—of voices.

毳 4 The fine hair on animals; the down on birds. Downy, soft.
6883

毳冕 a plush cap worn in ancient times.
毳布 cloth with a nap on it; plush.
毳幕 a felt tent.
毳毛 down on birds.

(a) u.f. preceding. Crisp; delicate, etc.

得甘毳以養親 get sweet dainties to nourish their parents.

TSUN. (ㄗㄨㄣ)
(Tsuen)

尊 1 Honourable. To honour. To venerate. N.A.
6884

尊上 to venerate one's superiors.
尊仰 to look up to with respect.
尊位 an eminent position.
尊侯 your father.
5 尊兄 you; sir; yourself.
尊內 your wife.
尊公 your father.
尊其瞻視 he throws a dignity into his looks.
尊前 oneself; I—conventional term used in letters, etc.
10 尊卑上下 relative rank or status.
尊卑失序 lacking due regard for precedence.
尊古法製 compounded according to the ancients—of drugs.
尊名 your personal name?
尊君 to respect the sovereign; your father.
15 尊命 your esteemed commands—conventional.
尊嚴 dignity; solemnity.
尊堂 your mother.
尊壽 how old are you? your age?
尊大 worthy; great.
20 尊大人 or 令尊 your father.
尊夫人 your wife.
尊奉 to respect.
尊姓 your surname?
尊尙 to honour.
25 尊崇 to worship; to reverence; to respect; to adore.
尊師重傅 honoured teachers.
尊府 where is your honourable residence?
尊德樂道 to honour virtue and delight in the truth.
尊恙 your complaint or illness.
30 尊意 your esteemed opinion.
尊敎 your valued words; your esteemed teaching or instructions.
尊敬 to reverence; to respect; to esteem; to adore.

尊書 your esteemed favour—your letter.
尊榮 honour; of high standing.
35 尊無二上 peerless.
尊生 to value life.
尊甫 your father.
尊稱 a title of respect.
尊者 the venerable one—a title given to every Buddha.
40 尊處 your honourable abode.
尊處都好麼 Is your honoured family well?
尊親 to honour one's parents.
尊貴 honourable; noble.
尊賤兩宥 excuse mention of my name or yours—a phrase used at the end of a letter where secrecy is desirable.
45 尊賬 your account.
尊賢而容衆 to honour the worthy and be tolerant to all.
尊軀 your honourable person.
尊重 to reverence; to respect; to honour.
尊重公權 respect public rights.
50 尊長 (chang[3]) an elder; a title of respect.
目無尊長 (chang[3]) he has no respect for his superiors.
尊門 your honourable home.
尊顯 honourable.
尊駕 you; sir; yourself; your honour.
55 尊齒 what is your honourable age?
一尊砲 a cannon.
一尊菩薩 an idol.
至尊 the most venerable; the emperor.

(a) u.f. 罇 No. 6886. A bottle; a wine-vessel used in sacrifices. A goblet.

噂 3 To talk together. Conversation.
6884a

噂沓 a multitude of words.
噂議 a babble of discussion.

撙 3 To adjust; to regulate, as expenditure. To restrain.
6885

撙省 to be economical.
撙節 to economize.
撙節開支 economy in expenses.

樽罇墫 [1]
6886

A goblet. A bottle; a wine-jar.
Inter. 罇 No. 6884—A.

遵 [1]
6887

To honour; to obey; to comply. To follow.

遵令 to obey a command.
遵依 to obey; to act in accordance with.
遵命 to obey a command.
遵奉 to reverence; to accord with; to fall in with.
[5]遵奉之日 days appointed to be kept for some special purpose.
遵守 to observe; to keep; to guard carefully.
遵守約章 to observe the treaties.
遵從 to obey; to act in accordance with; to follow.
遵循 to comply with.
[10]遵按 to obey; to comply with.
遵敕 obedient; submissive.
遵斷 to obey a legal decree.
遵旨 to carry out an imperial mandate.
遵札 in accordance with instructions.
[15]遵法 to obey the laws.
遵照 to act in accordance with; to obey.
遵王之路 to walk in the way of the ancient kings.
遵繳 to comply with orders and hand over or pay up.
遵着 to comply with; to accord with; to act in accordance with.
[20]遵義 to follow after righteousness—i.e., the way of the ancient kings; a *hsien* in N. Kweichow.
遵行 to carry out obediently.
遵行儒教 to follow the regulations of Confucianism.
遵路 to take a journey.
遵辦 to obey; to act in accordance with; to follow.
[25]遵陸 to travel by road.
遵養時晦 to dwell in retirement awaiting opportunity for advancement.

鐏 [1]
6888

The butt-end of a spear. The ferule at the end of a sword-handle.

僎 [4]
6889

The governor or master at a village feast.

僎爵 or 僎席 to preside over a feast.

(a) Read *chuan*[4]. Inter. 撰 No. 1434. To collect, etc.

TS'UN. (ㄘㄨㄣ)
(Ts'uen)

皴 [1]
6890

Chapped; cracked.

皴裂 cracked skin.
皴皮 rough, cracked skin; a name for the *lichee* fruit.
凍皴·了 chapped with the cold.

(a) Rules for painting or drawing landscapes. The style of a painting.

皴法 the rules or art of drawing.
皴紋 lines made in drawing.
小斧斫皴 method of depicting the jagged outlines of rocks, etc.
披麻皴 method of depicting the veins, etc., of rocks.
點皴 to finish a drawing by shading, etc.

存 [2]
6891

To keep; to secrete; to retain; to file; to lay by. To preserve. To be in existence. Distinguish 在 No. 6657.

存·下 to lay aside; to keep.
存·不住 unable to retain.
存乎人者 that which is contained in a man's—body.
存了食 undigested; indigestible.
[5]存亡 alive or dead; to preserve or to ruin—as a dynasty; to continue or to destroy; saved or lost.
存仁 to act in a kindly manner.
存備 to keep in store.
存儲所 a depot—as for military stores.
存儲物品 reserve stores.
[10]存儲現金 cash reserves.
存到世世 to continue through the ages.
存厚·道 to maintain cordial relations with; to uphold good

principles of conduct; to be liberal-minded.
存在 being in existence; to continue; to survive.
存多少 how much is still to my credit?
[15]存天良 to have a good conscience—to be grateful; to avoid maliciousness.
存客 a traveller in an inn.
不存客 "we do not accommodate lodgers."—an inn-sign.
存庫 to keep in the treasury; to pay into the treasury.
存心 to have the mind set on; state of mind; to entertain feelings of....
[20]存心不良 to cherish an evil heart.
存成見 to cherish prejudice.
存我·的天性 the natural desire to live.
存摺 a bank pass-book.
存據 to retain as evidence.
[25]存收 to secrete; to store up.
存放 to deposit in....
存有.... in hand; in stock.
存案 to keep as evidence; to retain as proof; to file for reference.
存根 the counterfoil—as of a cheque, etc.
[30]存棧 to store in a warehouse or godown.
存款 a deposit in a bank; balance of deposit.
存款單(or 證書) certificate of deposit.
存款賬 a deposit account.
存款收據 deposit receipt.
[35]存款收條 deposit receipt.
存款票 deposit slip.
存款簿 a bank pass-book.
存款計算 deposit account.
定期存款 fixed deposit.
[40]活期存款 current account.
活期存款支票 deposit slip.
特別存款 special deposit.
存歿 alive or dead. (-*mo*[4])
存水 it holds water; water collects (here).
[45]存沒 alive or dead; to destroy or keep alive; to continue or to fail; saved or lost. (-*mo*[4])
存注 to be remembered; to bear in mind.

存 活 to maintain life.

存 照 to retain as evidence or proof; to file for reference.

存 留 to detain; to lay by; to keep in charge.

[50]存 眷 to think fondly of.

存 神 to retain one's presence of mind.

存 票 a Customs drawback.

存 立 不 住 cannot continue.

存 立 期 間 duration of existence.

[55]存 稿 to retain the draft of a document.

存 積 to store; to lay up; to gather.

存 良 ·心 to have a good conscience; to act conscientiously.

存 ·著 to reserve; to· retain.

存 蓄 to store up; to cherish; to maintain.

[60]存 藏 to keep in store; to store.

存 記 to keep on record; to bear in mind.

存 貨 goods in stock or in storage.

存 貨 單 a warehouse receipt.

存 貨 費 storage charges.

[65]存 財 savings; to save money.

存 貯 to store up; to cherish; to maintain.

存 身 to take care of oneself; to keep out of danger.

存 錢 savings; to save.

存 錄 to keep a record of.

[70]左 關 filed at the Customs; to keep at the Customs.

存 電 瓶 storage battery.

存 項 balance in hand; deposit in a bank.

存 養 to keep and bring up—as foundlings.

保 存 to preserve.

[75]寄 存 ·的 物 件 things deposited.

尙 存 still in existence; still alive —as one's parents.

無 存 none left; nothing left.

(a) To inquire after.

存 候 to inquire after the health of.

存 勞 to pay a visit of condolence —as when a person has been unfortunate or has suffered losses.

存 問 or 告 存 to inquire after the health of.

存 孤 to visit and condole one who has lost his father.

[5]存 恤 to inquire after and relieve.

存 慰 to visit and condole.

存 視 to pay a visit of condolence.

寸 [4] An inch. The tenth of a Chinese foot or 尺. A little.
6892 Radical 41.

寸 函 a short note.

寸 功 未 立 I have performed no public service at all; not the slightest merit.

寸 口 the pulse at the wrist.

寸 土 之 地 a very small piece of land.

[5]寸 字 a short note.

寸 心 or 方 寸 the heart.

寸 心 不 忘 bear it in mind.

寸 晷 an inch of shadow on the dial—time.

寸 楮 a short note.

[10]寸 步 不 離 not to move a step from; not to let out of one's sight.

寸 步 難 行 it is difficult to move a step.

寸 田 the heart—as capable of cultivation.

寸 白 蟲 or 寸 食 蟲 tapeworms.

寸 祿 a small salary.

[15]寸 絲 不 掛 not a stitch of clothing on—stark naked; having no entanglements or anxiety.

寸 縷 an inch of thread; very little.

寸 脉 the pulse at the wrist.

寸 草 不 生 not even a blade of grass grows there—utterly barren.

寸 草 弗 留 not even so much as a blade of grass left.

[20]寸 草 春 暉 a blade of grass (to repay) the spring brightness— one's best efforts to repay the early kindness of one's parents are but poor in comparison.

寸 衷 the heart.

寸 進 a little advance, slight success.

寸 金 地 land worth an inch of gold per inch.

寸 金 難 買 寸 光 陰 an inch of gold cannot buy an inch of time.

[25]寸 鐵 a dagger; a sword—used to illustrate the smallness of the weapon needed in the hands of a clever general.

寸 長 small ability.

寸 隙 a little space—a little leisure.

寸 陰 an inch of shadow on the sundial—time.

寸 陰 自 惜 be careful of your time.

[30]尺 璧 非 寶 寸 陰 是 競 a foot of jade has no real worth, but every inch of time must be contested.

一 寸 ·一 ·寸 ·的 inch by inch.

三 寸 見 方 three inches square.

尺 寸 feet and inches—measurement; dimensions.

方 寸 a square inch. *See above*— 6.

[35]立 方 寸 a cubic inch.

吋 [4] Used for an inch—English measure.
6893

忖 [3] To consider; to reflect.
6894

忖 度 to gauge—what is in the minds of others—by reflection.

忖 思 or 忖 想 to ponder on; to reflect; to think.

忖 量 to suppose.

自 忖 無 能 I consider that I have no ability.

村 郇 [1] A village; a hamlet.
6895

村 俗 rustic; unpolished.

村 堡 a village.

村 墟 a village market.

村 夫 a villager; a countryman.

[5]村 夫 子 the village scholar.

村 ·子 or 鄉 村 a village; country hamlets.

村 學 究 a rustic pedant.

村 戶 a countryman; a rustic.

村 書 old name for elementary school-books such as the Book of Surnames, the Thousand Character Classic, etc.

[10]村 校 village schools under the old system.

村 ·氣 rustic airs and manners.

村 甿 farmers.

村 童 young lads of the villages.

村 舍 a country-village home.

[15]村 莊 a village; a farmstead.

村 落 a village; country places.

村落共產 village communism.
村言 or 村話 rustic talk.
村辱 or 撒村 to abuse; to blackguard; to swear.
20村農 a countryman; a village
farmer.
村里 a village or hamlet.
村野 rustic; countrified.

TSUNG.   (ㄗㄨㄥ)

(Tsong)

宗[1] Ancestral. Clans descend-
6896 ed from a common ancestor.
Kindred. A class; a kind;
a school, as of art, teaching,
etc., a sect.

宗主權 suzerainty.
宗人 one of the same clan;
officers in attendance on the
Minister of Religion in ancient
times.
宗人府 the Court of the Im-
perial Clan which regulated all
matters relating to the Imperial
kindred.
宗伯掌邦禮 the Minister of
Religion who presides over the
ceremonies of the empire—an
ancient office.
5宗兄宗弟 distant clansmen of
the same generation.
宗公 the former dukes of the
ancestral temple, i.e., the
ancestors of Wên Wang 文王.
宗原 origin; source.
宗器 vessels for use in the ancestral temple—sacrificial vessels and musical instruments,
etc.
宗圖 a genealogical tree.
10宗女 a daughter of the Imperial
family.
宗姓 the Imperial family; the
surname of the ruling family.
宗子[3] those of the same surname
as the sovereign.
宗學 schools for the members of
the Imperial family.
宗宗件件 each sort; every kind.
15宗室 the Imperial house; descendants in the male line from
the founder of the dynasty.
宗家 kindred; ancestry.
宗師 a name for the former
Literary Chancellor or 學台.
宗廟 the ancestral temple of the
ruling family.

宗支 of the same clan or surname.
20宗教[4] religion.
宗教上 religious pertaining to
religion.
宗教區別 religious distinctions.
宗教家 theologians.
宗教寬容 religious toleration.
25宗教心 a religious sense.
宗教思想 religious interests.
宗教的意識 a religious con-
sciousness.
宗教戰爭 religious war.
宗教改革 reformation of re-
ligion.
30宗教文明 religious culture.
宗教是人民的鴉片 religion
is the opiate of the masses.
宗教界 the religious world.
宗教的 religious; pertaining to
religion.
宗教聖戰 a Holy War.
35宗教聯合會 Society of the
United Religions.
宗教自由 religious liberty.
宗教觀念 the religious idea;
religious conceptions.
宗教革命 the Reformation.
天啟宗教 revealed religion.
40 比較的宗教 comparative
religions.
眞理的宗教 true religion.
自然宗教 natural religions.
宗族 kindred; ancestry; clan.
宗旨 requirements; standard;
aim; purpose; contents; principle; general scope; platform of
principles.
45宗枝 descendants in the male line
from the founder of a dynasty.
宗樣 a kind or class.
宗法 the classification of the various branches of a clan.
宗派 the branches of a family or
clan; a sect.
宗生 clustered thickly together.
50宗社 ancestral temples and altars
to the spirits of the land.
宗社黨 a royalist party.
宗祀 the ancestral sacrifice; the
line of a family.
宗祊 the ancestral sacrifices.
宗祠 an ancestral temple.
55宗緒 the line of descent.
宗老 the head of a clan.
宗英 a heroic member of a clan.
宗親 kindred; ancestry.
宗譜 a family register.

60宗門 family; clan; kindred.
宗門裁判 or 宗教裁判 the
Inquisition.
宗類 a class; a tribe; a kind or
sort.
上宗 the Minister of Religion in
ancient times.
不一宗 not all of the same stock
or class.
65南北宗 Southern and Northern
Schools of Buddhism, Taoism,
art, painting, etc.
同宗 clansmen; of the same
stock.
地宗 rivers, lakes, seas and
mountains.
大宗 a great family; the elder
branches of a family; goods in
bulk. See No. 5943—82, 83.
大宗郵件 mail matter in bulk.
70天宗 the heavenly bodies.
太宗 the Minister of Religion in
ancient times; a posthumous title
祖宗 ancestors, of several emperors.

(a) The most distinguished. To
honour; to follow. The capital of
Chou, see below—A-I.

宗周 the honoured capital of
Chow.
周宗 the honoured capital of
Chou.
宗國 the State which we
honoured.
宗禮 ceremonies to be honoured
(by general observance).
5亦可宗也 he can make them
his guides and masters.
六宗 the six honoured ones—the
seasons, cold and heat, the sun,
the moon, the stars, and
drought.
公尸來燕來宗 the person-
ators of your ancestors feast
and are honoured.
靡神不宗 "there is no spirit
whom I have not honoured."
君之宗之 acknowledged by
them as ruler, and honoured.
10記功宗 let those distinguished
by merit be recorded.

(b) The appearance of the feudal
princes at court in the summer.

朝宗于海 (the flowing waters
of the Yangtze) hasten to the
court of the sea.

棕 櫚 1
6897

The coir palm tree.

棕 樹 the palm tree.
棕 櫚 the coir palm of Central China—*Trachycarpus excelsa.*
棕 毯 coir matting.
棕 種 the Brown Races.
⁵棕 竹 a variety of black bamboo, the roots of which furnish canes.
棕 筍 clusters of the flower buds of palms—used for food.
棕 箱 a coir trunk.
棕 簑 coir rain-coats.
棕 簟 coir matting.
¹⁰棕 繩 coir rope.
棕·色 brown, the colour of palm fibre.

猔 4
6898

Name of an ancient tribe.

古 猔 a tribe, the remnants of which remain in Yunnan; said to be a branch of the 吐 蕃.

(a) A bitch having one pup at a litter.

瑽 1.2.
6899

An octagonal badge denoting rank; it was made of jade and varied in size according to rank.
Also read *ts'ung*¹·².

粽 糭 4
6900

The dumplings made by wrapping glutinous rice or millet in broad bamboo leaves and boiling them.
A.p. *chung*⁴.

粽·子 or 三 角³ 粽 three-cornered dumplings made as above; these are more specially eaten at the festival on the fifth of the fifth lunar month, usually known as the Dragon-Boat Festival or 端 陽 節.
火 腿 粽·子 dumplings made as above, containing ham.
裹 粽 to wrap glutinous rice, etc., in bamboo leaves in preparation for making these dumplings.
豆 沙 粽·子 dumplings as above, containing sweetened puree of beans.

鹹 肉 粽·子 dumplings, as above, containing salted pork.

綜 4
6901

To arrange the threads for weaving; thus:—to arrange; to gather up; to take count of; to sum up. To inquire into.

綜 合 to gather together; to unite.
綜 合 哲 學 synthetic philosophy.
綜 合 比 較 a general comparison.
綜 合 法 synthetic methods.
⁵綜 合·的 synthetic.
綜 括 to bring together; to generalize; comprehensive.
綜 括 一 句 to sum up in a word.
綜 析 synthesis and analysis.
綜 核 to make a general investigation.
¹⁰綜 核 名 實 to compare the reputation with the facts.
綜 理 to have the general superintendence of.
綜 管 to have the general oversight or superintendence of.
綜 算 to make up the total; to strike a balance.
綜 紛 緒 to arrange in order; to arrange the confused threads.
¹⁵綜 覈 to make a general investigation.
綜 觀 a comprehensive survey.
綜 達 to understand thoroughly.

猔 猻 1
6902

A litter of pigs; a little pig.

賨 1
6903

Tribute paid in cloth by the tribes in Szechwan and Yunnan under the *Han* dynasty.

踪 蹤 1
6904

A footprint; a trace. To follow; to imitate.

蹤 兆 a vestige; a clue.
蹤 尋 to follow up and investigate.
蹤 影 a vestige or trace; a clue.
無 蹤 無 影 not a trace to be seen.
⁵蹤 緒 a clue; a sign; a trace.
蹤 跡 traces; vestiges; to follow up a clue.

蹤 跡 可 疑 suspicious; questionable.
蹤 跡 未 明 uncertain.
不 留 蹤 跡 did not leave a trace.
失 蹤 lost trace of.
追 蹤 to follow up a clue.

鬃 騌 1
6905

A horse's mane. Bristles.

騌 刷 a brush made of bristles.
猪 騌 毛 pig's bristles.

鬘 1
6906

A horse's mane. The back-hair of a lady's head-dress. Inter. preceding.

假 鬘 false hair; a wig.

嵏 1
6907

A mountain in Shensi.

鏉 1
6908

A headstall; ornament on a bridle.

瘲 4
6909

Spasms or convulsions in young children, caused by indigestion.

縱 4
6910

To loose; to allow; to relax; to let go; to let fly; to be indulgent.

縱 囚 to release a prisoner.
縱 子³ 行 兇 to allow one's son to act wickedly.
縱 容 to connive at; to tolerate; to permit.
縱 延 remiss; dilatory.
⁵縱 性 or 縱 意 to follow one's inclinations.
縱 恣 unrestrained indulgence; to give rein to the passions.
縱 情 to give rein to the passions.
縱 情 淫 亂 to give way to lust.
縱 慣 over-indulgence; accustomed to be allowed to do as one pleases.
¹⁰縱 放 to tolerate; to let go; to allow.
縱 敗 禮 "by my self-indulgence I was violating all the rules of propriety."

縱 樂 to give oneself up to pleasure and dissipation. (-lê⁴)

縱 欲 to give rein to the passions.

縱 步 to take long strides.

15 縱 淫 to give oneself over to sensuality.

縱 火 or 縱 燒 to set fire to.

縱 眺 to gaze into the distance.

縱 縱 urgent; to give importance to a matter through urgency.

縱 脫 unrestrained.

20 縱 虎 入 室 to allow a tiger into the house.

縱 觀 or 縱 覽 to take a wide survey.

縱 談 to talk freely.

縱 輕 lightly esteemed.

縱 送 to give the reins to; to discharge, as an arrow or a dart.

25 縱 逸 to indulge in idleness.

縱 酒 given to wine.

縱 釋 to release; to tolerate; to allow.

縱 飲 a drinking bout, a carousal.

縱 養 to bring up a child without restraint; to spoil a child.

30 縱 馬 to give a horse his head.

無 縱 詭 隨 "let us give no indulgence to the wily and the obsequious."

(a) Although; even if; granted that.

縱 不 知 情 although they were not aware of the facts.

縱 使 seeing that; even if; though, etc.

縱 其 否 也 and even if not....

縱 或 though, even if; seeing that, etc.

5 縱 有 although there is....

縱 然 allowing it to be; supposing; admitted that....

縱 遇 if it should happen....

(b) Read *tsung*¹. Perpendicular; vertical.

縱 剖 面 vertical section.

縱 斷 面 vertical section.

縱 擺 動 oscillation.

縱 橫 perpendicular and horizontal; rival political theories, 合 縱 being a confederacy of six States against *Ch'in*, 秦; and 連 橫 being a federation of the States under 秦. Also written 合 從 連 橫. *See* 從 No. 6919 —E. 1.—also used for perverse and unreasonable.

5 縱 縱 橫 橫 criss-cross; placed crosswise in both directions.

縱 橫 家 writers on political subjects.

縱 橫 密 布 close net-work.

縱 橫 寰 宇 travelled the length and breadth of the empire.

縱 橫 面 co-ordinate plane.

10 縱 波 a longitudinal wave.

縱 谷 a longitudinal valley.

縱 長² lengthwise; longitudinally.

縱 隊 a column of troops.

↑縱 標 ordinate.

傯 ⁴
6911
Worn out, having no leisure.

總 ³
摠
捴
6912
All; general. To summarize. The chief. To manage.

總 主 筆 editor-in-chief. = 67.

總 之 finally; in the end; in a word; to sum up; to put it briefly.

總 事 a chairman—as of a council, etc.

總 代 理 general agent.

5 總 代 表 chief delegate.

總 例 a general rule.

總 共 the whole; all; one and all.

總 兵 former title of a Brigade-General.

總 冊 a general table; a statistical summary.

10 總 則 a general rule.

總 務 科 head office.

總 務 處 Bureau of General Affairs.

總 匯 to collect together—as population.

總 卡 a head customs barrier.

15 總 參 謀 長 General Chief of Staff.

總 口 a central Customs station.

總 台 former title of a Brigade-General.

總 司 to take a general oversight of; to superintend.

總 司 令 Commander-in-chief.

20 總 名 a general term for.

總 售 出 額 gross proceeds of sales.

總 單 a cargo certificate.

總 因 the general cause.

總 局 head-office.

25 總 工 會 General Labour Union.

總 工 程 師 chief-engineer of works, etc.

總 帶 in command.

總 帳 an account as recorded in a ledger.

總 帳 簿 a ledger.

30 總 帳 頁 數 ledger-folio.

總 戎 former title of a Brigade-General.

總 批 a critical summary.

總 批 發 wholesale agency.

總 括 a summing up; a recapitulation.

35 總 攝 己 職 all managed their own duties.

總 攬 統 治 權 to hold the power of central authority.

總 攻 擊 a general assault.

總 數 the sum; total amount.

總 是 說 the sum of these remarks is...; always says...

40 總 會 general office. General Assembly—of the Presbyterian Church, etc.

總 會 議 general conference.

總 束 to tie together in bundles.

總 概 total; wholesale.

總 機 關 head-quarters; general organ.

45 總 檢 察 廳 Court of the Procurator-General.

總 檢 察 廳 檢 察 長³ Procurator-General.

總 決 算 general summary of accounts.

總 理 to superintend; to take the general oversight of; a Prime Minister.

總 理 委 員 a deputy in general charge of affairs.

50 總 理 遺 囑 Dr. Sun Yat-sen's will.

總 甲 the head tithing.

總 發 行 所 head warehouse; main office or depot.

總 監 Commissioner—as of the police.

總 目 table of contents; general index.

55 總 督 former title of a Viceroy or Governor-General.

總 稅 務 司 Inspector-General of Chinese Maritime Customs.

總 稽 查 General-Inspector.

總管 a manager; to have the management of.

總算 to sum up; total; all reckoned up.

[60]總簿 a ledger. *See above—29.*

總統 a general summary; the President of a Republic.

總統制 the system of making Presidential appointments to the Cabinet.

總統府 the residence of the President.

總結 summary; the summing up.

[65]總經理 general manager; general agent.

總綱 the chief point or principle; the fundamental principles of.

總編輯 editor-in-chief.

總署 a head-office; the former *Tsung-li yamen.*

總罷工 a general strike.

[70]總而言之 finally; in a word; to sum up; to put it briefly.

總腦 the whole; all included.

總董其事 to take the general direction of affairs.

總行 (*hang*[2]) head-office or depot.

總裁 a director-general; the governor of a bank, etc.

[75]中國銀行總裁 Governor of the Bank of China.

總角 the tufts of hair left on the head of a Chinese child, after shaving.

總角之交 friends from child-hood.

總計 the sum total....; in all.

總論 an introduction; a general summary.

[80]總預算 general budget.

總賣 to sell wholesale.

總贏利額 gross profits.

總起 the general theme; a general introduction.

總辦 a manager; to have the management of.

[85]總選舉 a general election.

總重量額 gross weight.

總鎮 former title of a Brigade-General.

總長[3] a cabinet minister; chief of a department; *now called* 部長[3].

總領事(官) a consul-general.

[90]總頭 or 管總·的 or 亞總 a foreman.

總題 the general theme or sub-ject.

總額 gross amount or number.

總髻 the hair done up in a knob.

(a) An emphatic particle. Always. Probably.

總不肯 without doubt (he is) unwilling; never willing.

總不能應[4]日·子 he could not possibly come on the day which he promised.

總不行 it has never been suc-cessful; it won't do at all.| (-*otei*[3])

總得 to have to somehow; must.

[5]總是·的 or 總是 it is always (so).

總有 there is certainly....; there are at least....; without doubt there are..; there always is ...

總期有成 in the full hope of accomplishing.

總然 although; nevertheless.

總要 must; indispensable.

[10]總要去 you must certainly go.

總該有·的 it is so no doubt; very likely it is there; there should be some.

總須 indispensable; must; neces-sarily.

TS'UNG.　　　　(ㄘㄨㄥ)

(Ts'ong)

濴凘 [2]

[6913] A place where small streams flow into a larger one.

鳧鷖在濴 the wild duck and the widgeon are where the waters meet.

囪 [1]

[6914] A chimney; a flue. Also read *ch'uang*[1].

怱匆悤 [1]

[6915] Excited; hurried.

怱忙 hurriedly; precipitately.

怱怱不及 too hurried to attend to—the business.

怱猝 in a great hurry.

怱遽 to be in haste; pressed for time.

聰聰 [1]

[6916] The hearing; to listen. Astute. Clever. Quick of apprehension.

聰慧 intelligent; quick of ap-prehension.

聰敏 clever; wise; intelligent.

聰·明 clever; intelligent; wise.

聰·明正直 wise and upright.

[5]聰聰祖考之彝訓 hearkening diligently to the constant lessons of their father.

天聰 natural quickness of in-tellect.

尙寐無聰 "I would that I might sleep and hear nothing more."

聖聰 the ear of the emperor.

耳聰 the hearing is good.

[10]聽德惟聰 have your ears ever open and listen to virtue.

聽曰聰 (the virtue of) hearing is in distinctness.

達四聰 to hear with the ears of all—as the emperor should, through his ministers.

葱 [1]

[6917] Onions; leeks; scallions.

葱嶺 the Onion Range—the Belaturgh mountains in Turke-stan.

葱心 the heart of an onion.

葱白 the heart of an onion.

葱綠 a light green.

[5]葱花 chopped onions.

葱蘢 luxuriant growth of vegeta-tion.

葱靈 a kind of ancient baggage waggon.

葱頭 onions.

葱鬚 the rootlets of onions.

[10]洋葱 foreign onions—the com-mon round onion.

胡葱 shallots.

驄驄 [1]

[6918] A piebald horse.

從从 [2] To follow; to comply with; to obey. Distinguish 徒 No. 6536, and 徙 No. 2468.

[6919]

從 一 而 終 to die faithful to one husband—and not remarry.

從 世 俗 according to the course of this world.

從 中 among others; as a mediator; from among them.

從 事 to devote oneself entirely to an object; to discharge one's business.

⁵從 事 破 壞 always destructive.

從 事 職 業 to attend to one's duties.

從 事 革 命 to devote one's life to promoting the revolution.

好 從 事 anxious to be engaged in public employment.

嘗 從 事 於 斯 矣 once I engaged myself in this.

¹⁰ 聖 人 不 從 事 "the true sage does nothing—yet all is accomplished."

從 人 to follow a person. *See below*—C. 1.

從 人 願 to follow the desires of mankind.

舍 己 從 人 to give up one's own opinion to follow that of others.

從 便 at convenience; conveniently.

¹⁵從 俗 to conform to custom.

從 價 稅 *ad valorem* duties.

從 優 liberally; exceptionally.

從 公 to act fairly; to discharge one's duties.

從 其 所 好 according to his own taste.

²⁰從 其 言 took his advice.

從 命 to obey a command; at command; at one's request.

從 善 to follow what is good—to reform.

從 善 如 流 to follow what is right as water flows downward.

從 善 如 登 to follow what is right is like ascending a hill.

²⁵從 嚴 with severity; severely.

從 實 truthfully; with truth.

從 實 地 上 in truth.

從 寬 懲 治 to punish leniently.

從 己 之 欲 to follow one's own desires.

³⁰從 徑 道 亡 to slip away by a short cut.

從 心 at will; at discretion.

從 心 所 欲 to follow the desires of the mind.

從 意 適 便 to follow one's own convenience.

從 政 to be engaged in government service, generally in a subordinate capacity.

³⁵ 可 使 從 政 也 與 Is he fit to be employed as an officer of the government?

從 新 anew; to begin afresh. 重 新

從 新 主 義 modernism—the craze for new things. ╞重²⋯

從 新 再 弄 do it all over again.

從 於 子 放 之 齊 followed in the train of *Tzŭ Ao* to *Ch'i*.

⁴⁰從 時 to make the best of circumstances.

從 權 to comply with circumstances; to act as the exigency requires; to adapt oneself; opportunism. *See* No. 1663—B. 25.

從 欲 以 治 "to follow after and obtain what I desire in my government."

從 正 道 to follow what is right—the right Way.

從 死 sacrifices at the death of an emperor.

⁴⁵從 爲 之 辭 they follow on and make excuses for them.

從 衆 to do as others do.

從 衆 爲 定 the majority decides.

從 緩 to postpone.

從 着 following—a person; obedient; to follow.

⁵⁰從 而 刑 之 follow them up and punish them.

從 而 征 之 they therefore proceeded to tax his wares.

從 而 招 之 they proceed to tie it up by the leg.

從 耳 目 所 欲 following the desires of the eyes and ears.

從 良 to reform—as a prostitute may do by marrying.

⁵⁵從 豐 liberally; plenteously; handsomely.

從 軍 to enlist; to join the ranks.

從 輕 減 罰 to fine on a reduced scale.

從 輿 論 to follow public opinion; to go with the popular trend.

從 逆 凶 the following of evil is bad.

⁶⁰從 遊 to follow a person on his travels.

從 重⁴ 治 罪 to punish severely; to go to the extreme—as when ordering a fine to be paid.

從 量 稅 specific duty.⌐best course.

從 長 計 議│to deliberate on the

五 典 克 從 the five cardinal duties came to be universally observed.

⁶⁵任 從·你 as you please.

依 從 to agree to; to follow certain suggestions.

天 迪 從 子³保 Heaven guided his mind, allowed his descendants to succeed him, and protected him.

曲 從 to comply under compulsion or against one's inclination.

月 之 從 星 則 可 以 風 雨 the course of the moon among the stars gives the wind and the rain.

⁷⁰毋 以 從 前 "let him not therewith follow those who are before him." *See below*—A. 9.

漆 沮 旣 從 the waters of the *Ts'i* and the *Ch'ü* were made to flow—into the *Wei*.

言 曰 從 (the virtue of) speech is accordance (with reason).

面 從 心 違 outward compliance while the heart is opposed.

順 從 to fall in with.

(a) From; by; since; whence; through.

從 上 到 下 from top to bottom.

從 不 never so; it was not so at all.

從 井 救 人 to go down a well to save a man—useless; to injure oneself and not benefit the other man. *See Analects Book* vi. 24.

從 今 以 後 henceforth.

⁵從 何 而 來 where does it come from?

從 來 from the beginning; heretofore; at any time.

從 來 沒 有 there has never been.

從 先 in the past; formerly; the past.

從 前 formerly; from of old. *See above*—70.

¹⁰從 反 面 言 之 speaking from the opposite side.

從 古 以 來 from of old.

從 天 而 下 to come down from heaven—sudden unexpected arrival.

從 天 降 雨 to send down rain from heaven.

從 小 from childhood.

[15]從廣義講 in the broad sense.
從旁觀之 looking at it as a bystander.
從早到晚 from early till late.
從未 never so; it has never been so; it never was...
從未注意到 I have never given heed to it; I have never noticed it.
[20]從根 from the inception; radical.
從此 from this; henceforth; forthwith.
從此以後 henceforth.
從此看來 from which it is evident.
從死復活 to rise from the dead.
[25]從沒見·過 I have never seen it before.
從狹義講 speaking from a narrow viewpoint.
從由 from; proceeding from.
從自 from this—place or time.
從舊 formerly; from of old.
[30]從那 (na³) 兒來·的 where did it come from?
從頭兒再起 commence again from the beginning.
從頭至尾 from head to tail—from beginning to end.
無從入手 there is no place from whence to make a start.

(b) Read *ts'ung*[1]. **Lax; yielding.**

從容 easy; dignified; unembarrassed; leisurely; naturally.
從容不迫 an easy manner.
從容中道聖人也 he who naturally and easily embodies the right Way is a sage.
從容以和 promote harmony by the display of an easy forbearance.
從容穿·了衣·服 leisurely put on his clothes.
從容辦理 to put a matter through without any fuss.

(c) Read *tsung*[4]. **A follower; a second; secondary; accessory.**

從人 followers; attendants. *See above*—11.
從刑 accessory punishment.
從參加人 accessory intervention. (*legal*).
從吏 subordinate officers.
[5]從契約 accessory contract. (*legal*).
從我者 my followers.

從物 an accessory article.
從權利 accessory rights. (*legal*).
從犯 an accessory criminal.
[10]事前從犯者 accessory before the fact. (*legal*).
事後從犯者 accessory after the fact. (*legal*).
從祀 accessory sacrifices.
從者 followers; attendants.
隨從 followers; attendants.
[15]首從 principal and accessory.

(d) Read *tsung*[4]. **A clan or family.**

從兄·弟 paternal first cousins of the same surname.
從堂兄·弟 paternal first cousins of the same surname.
從女 a niece.
從子 a nephew.
從母 maternal aunts; mother's sisters.
從父 father's brothers.

(e) Read *tsung*[1]. **Perpendicular. To plough from north to south. Inter. 縱 No. 6910-B.**

從衡 lengthwise and crosswise; in every direction; rival theories of government, confederation and union under one head, respectively; politics. *See* 縱 No. 6910—B. 4.
衡從其畝 the acres must be ploughed lengthwise and crosswise.
從說 and 衡說 the rival theories of politics during the 列國, or the *Period of the Warring States*; the former advocating a federation of six States in an alliance against *Ch'in,* 秦, and the latter a union of all the States under *Ch'in,* 秦, as the head.

瑽[1]　Tinkling of jade pendants.
6920

叢[2]　A clump of trees. Crowded together; thickset.
6921

叢密 rank—as vegetation.
叢帖 reprinted collection of specimens from famous calligraphists.

叢書 a collection of reprinted works.
叢林 a dense wood—a Buddhist monastery.
[5]叢棘 a place of detention.
叢灌 shrubbery.
叢生 growing in luxuriance.
叢祠 a deserted ancestral hall.
叢箐 dense groves of bamboo.
[10]叢脞 vexatious; a general collection of trifling matters.
叢莽 jungle.
叢萬惡於一身 every kind of evil concentrated in one person.
叢薄 dense undergrowth; jungle.
叢談 collection of biographical notes, etc.
[15]叢集 crowding around.
叢雜 a confused collection of many things.
花叢 flowery groves—brothels.

TZŬ.　　(ㄗ)
(Tsï.)

吱[1]　Used in transliterating. Also read *chih*[1].
6922
〔= 嗶嘰．〕
嗶吱 beige, a kind of cloth.
嘎吱嘎吱·的響 the sound of creaking.

咨諮資[1]
6923
To consult about; to plan. To report in writing to an equal. A despatch.

咨催 to urge.
咨准 to receive from—in reply to a communication.
咨呈 to forward for the consideration of—used by equals.
咨問 to write making inquiries.
[5]咨報 an official report.
咨文 an official despatch between equals.
咨會 or 移咨 to send a communication—between equals.
咨明 to explain to; to notify.
咨籍 to state; saying....
[10]咨行 to send a communication—of equals.
咨覆 to reply to.
咨解 to send, accompanied by a despatch.

咨 訪 to write inquiring about.
咨 詢 to inquire about; to consult; a counsellor.
15 咨 調 to request the production—of a man, etc.
咨 請 to write and request.
咨 謀 to plot; to plan.
咨 送 to send to.
咨 開 a despatch stating that....
20 諮 議 工 程 師 or 顧 問 技 師 a consulting engineer.
諮 議 局 a Provincial Assembly—at the close of the Manchu dynasty.
諮 議 委 員 會 advisory committee.

(a) An interjection. Alas! Ah! Also read *tzŭ*⁴.

咨 嗟 to sigh.
咨 爾 舜 天 之 歷 數 在 爾 躬 Ah you *Shun*! The heaven-appointed succession now rests in you.
帝 曰 咨 禹 ... the emperor said, "Alas! O *Yü*...."

姿 ¹ Manner; air; carriage. Beauty. Disposition; temperament.
6924

姿 勢 carriage; deportment; bearing.
姿 容 beauty—especially female.
姿 態 carriage; deportment.
姿 色 beauty, as of a woman.
姿 貌 beauty.
天 姿 natural disposition or beauty.
性 姿 temperament.

恣 1.4. To throw off restraint. Licentious. Lust.
6925

恣 情 to give rein to the passions.
恣 意 to do as one likes.
恣 意 任 性 unrestrained behaviour.
恣 意 怒 視 to gaze at with anger.
5 恣 欲 to give rein to lust.
恣 睢 to stare at in anger.
恣 肆 licentious.
恣 行 無 忌 to care for nobody; to act recklessly.
放 恣 (or 縱) to give rein to one's passions.

黍 ¹ Common millet.
6926

黍 盛 (*ch'êng*²) vessels of millet—used in sacrifices.

資 ¹ Property; wealth. Subscriptions. Valuables. Fees.
6927 Inter. 貲 No. 6957.

資 主 the owner; capitalist.
資 俸 salary.
資 儲 savings; to hoard.
資 攢 economical; saving.
5 資 料 supplies; munitions, etc.
資 斧 expenses—as in travelling, etc.
資 斧 自 備 paying one's own expenses.
資 本 capital in trade.
資 本 主 義 capitalism.
10 資 本 之 壟 斷 monopoly of capital.
資 本 充 足 amply supplied with funds.
資 本 制 度 the capitalistic system.
資 本 團 a financial syndicate.
資 本 家 capitalists.
15 資 本 帝 國 主 義 the imperialism of capital.
資 本 金 capital in cash.
實 收 資 本 金 paid-up capital.
認 定 資 本 金 subscribed capital.
固 定 資 本 fixed capital.
20 專 注 資 本 specialized capital.
循 環 資 本 circulating capital.
招 集 資 本 to raise capital.
流 動 資 本 floating capital.
預 算 資 本 estimated capital.
25 資 本 階 級 the capitalist class.
資 業 goods; valuables; wealth; property.
資 產 movable and immovable property—assets.
資 產 階 級 the propertied class.
資 益 gain; profits.
30 資 約 economical; frugal.
資 裝 a bridal outfit.
資 財 wealth; property; valuables, etc.
資 貨 goods; stock.
資 金 capital.
35 信 資 or 郵 資 postage.

借 資 to borrow money.
家 資 resources; ways and means.
投 資 to subscribe capital.
筆 資 writer's fees.
40 酒 資 or 茶 資 tips; gratuities.
香 資 money for incense—fees paid to priests for masses, etc.

(a) To aid; to assist. To depend on. To rely on. To protect. Means of a living.

資 之 三 年 sought the assistance of others for three years.
資 兵 to despatch troops.
資 助 to assist; to subscribe towards; financial help.
資 政 院 a nominated Advisory Council or Senate established during the close of the Manchu dynasty.
5 資 治 通 鑑 title of a book—a synopsis of history from the *Chou* dynasty onwards.
資 給 to assist—as a destitute person.
資 送 回 籍 to assist in sending—a distressed person—to his home.
資 遣 to assist—a person with money to return home.
以 資 保 護 to rely on for protection.
10 以 資 熟 手 to avail oneself of an experienced hand.
以 資 補 救 as a means of relief.

(b) One's disposition; natural gifts.

資 分 qualifications; character; standing or seniority.
資 序 standing or seniority.
資 望 reputation.
資 格 qualifications; requisites; character; standing; seniority.
5 資 格 差 遠 far apart in official standing. (*-ch'a*⁴-)
資 格 賦 與 qualifications.
剝 奪 資 格 to disqualify.
有 教 授 的 資 格 he has qualifications for teaching.
有 資 格 的 qualified.
10 無 資 格 not qualified.
特 別 資 格 special qualifications.
被 選 資 格 qualifications for election.
軍 人 資 格 qualifications for military service.

選主資·格 qualifications for member of parliament.

15 選舉資·格 qualifications for the franchise.

資 稟 natural gifts; idiosyncrasies.

資 考 standing; reputation; seniority.

資·質 natural disposition.

資·質 庸 下 ordinary ability.

趑 [1] Hesitating, unable to advance. Also read *ts'ŭ*[1].
6928

趑 趄 to hobble along; hesitating whether to go forward or not.

厜 [1] A mountain peak.
6929

淄 [1] Name of a river in Shantung.
6930

緇 [1] Black silk; a dark, drab colour. Used for Buddhists, from the dark colour of their robes.
6931

緇 塵 dark and dusty (garments)—from travel.

緇 帷 之 林 a dark forest.

緇 撮 a small black cap worn in ancient times.

緇 泥 black mud.

緇 流 Buddhist priests—from the colour of their robes.

緇 衣 羔 裘 he wore a black robe over his garment of lambskin.

緇 黃 Buddhist and Taoist priests—from the dark robe of the one and the yellow cap of the other.

菑 [1] Ground that has been under cultivation for one year. Also read *tsai*[1], and u.f. 災 No. 6652. Evil; calamity, etc.
6932

菑 人 者 必 反 菑 之 he who speaks evil of others will be evil spoken of.

無 菑 無 害 no injury, no hurt—when 后 稷 was born.

輜 [1] Baggage wagons; baggage. The ends of an axle-tree.
6933

輜 重 baggage; impedimenta.

輜 重 隊 Army Service Corps.

錙 [1] An ancient weight; it is defined as equal to six 銖, No. 1354.
6934

錙 介 trifles.

錙 銖 計 較 to look after small, trifling amounts.

茲 [1] This; here; thus; therefore; now.
玆
6935

茲 因 now because of....

茲 定 it is now determined.

茲 有 there is now...

茲 查 it appears; since....

5茲 者 or 今 茲 now; at present; at this time.

茲 間 at the present moment.

如 茲 thus; in this way; now.

(a) A year; a season.

今 茲 來 茲 this year; next year.

(b) A coarse mat.

(c) u.f. 滋 No. 6937. Rich, fertile. Muddy; turbid; black.

(d) Read *ts'ŭ*[2]. Name of a place.

龜 (*chiu*[1]) 茲 Kuchah, a country in Central Asia.

孳 [1.4.] To bear. To grow slowly.
6936

孳 乳 to bring forth abundantly.

孳 尾 to breed, as birds and beasts.

孳 息 to reproduce the species.

孳 生 to multiply; to increase.

孳 茂 to flourish; to produce in abundance.

孳 萌 to bud; to sprout.

孳 蔓 to multiply and spread abroad—as locusts, etc.

(a) Read *tsŭ*[1]. Diligent; untiring. Inter. 孜 No. 6943.

孳 孳 with diligence.

嵫 [1] A hill in 嵫陽縣, Shantung.
6936a

滋 [1] To nourish. To stir up; to excite. Inter. 兹 No. 6935.
滋
6937

滋 亂 to stir up rebellion; to make a disturbance.

滋 事 to make trouble; to get up a disturbance.

滋 味 flavour; taste; a sense of satisfaction.

滋 擾 to disturb the peace; to excite.

5滋 殖 to bring forth in abundance.

滋 深 severely; very deeply.

滋 潤 to fertilize; to mollify; rich.

滋 生 to sprout; to multiply.

滋 茂 flourishing; to increase.

10滋 蔓 a sprouting tendril; to put forth tendrils.

滋 蕃 to increase.

滋 補 to strengthen; to supply what is wanted.

滋 長 to grow larger.

滋 險 full of danger.

15滋 養 to nourish.

滋 養 分 nutrient constituents.

滋 養 品 nourishment; nutritious articles.

滋 養 灌 腸 nutrient enemata.

滋 養 物 (or 料) nutriment.

20滋 養 率 (*lü*[4.5.]) proportion of nutriment in a prescribed diet, etc.

滋 養 的 nutritious.

滋 鬧 to make a disturbance.

(a) Thick; muddy.

何 故 使 我 水 滋 why have you made our water dirty?

(b) Used in the names of several rivers.

鎡 [1] A hoe or mattock.
6938

鎡 基 agricultural implements.

子 [3] A son; a child; posterity. A bride; a wife. To treat as one's own children. Radical 39.
6939
Distinguish 孑 No. 784, 孓 No. 7601.

子 來 to come like children.

子 嗣 posterity.

子 壻 I, your daughter's husband

—term of address used to the parents of one's wife.

子 女 sons and daughters; children.

⁵子 姓 posterity.

子 姪 sons and brother's sons.

子 婦 a son and his wife; a son's wife.

子 子³孫 孫 descendants; posterity.

子。孫 sons and grandsons; descendants; posterity.

¹⁰子 孫 娘·娘 a goddess who is supposed to bestow children.

子 宮 the womb.

子 庶 民 to treat the masses as one's own children.

子。弟 children; juniors.

子 弟 多 賴 most of the young people are good(or lazy).

¹⁵子 息 posterity.

子 惠 困 窮 treat the poor and destitute as if they were your children.

子 戶 a branch of the family.

子 民 citizens; the people.

子 父 責 善 the son urging his father to goodness.

²⁰子 系 posterity.

子 職 the duties of sons and daughters—filial devotion to parents.

子 道 the way of sons and daughters—to serve their parents with filial devotion.

之 子³于 歸 this girl is going to her husband's home.

以 其 子³妻 之 he gave him his own daughter to wife.

²⁵別 子³sons of concubines.

天 子³the emperor.

太 子³the heir-apparent.

宗 子³the eldest son.

小 子³my pupils; my son; young men.

³⁰少 子³the youngest son.

庶 子³sons of concubines.

浪 子³a prodigal son.

猶 子³sons of one's brothers.

獨 生 子³an only son.

³⁵義 子³an adopted son.

赤 子³a baby.

遺 腹 子³a posthumous son.

長 子³the eldest son.

(a) The young of animals, birds and insects. Seeds, eggs. Bullets or shot.

子 房 ovary. (*bot.*).

子 彈 bullets; shot.

子 母 彈 shrapnel.

子 粒 a grain.

⁵子 葉 cotyledons.

子 規 the goatsucker.

子 麻 the female hemp.

下 子³ㄦ to lay eggs—of insects.

犂 牛 之 子³the calf of a brindled cow.

¹⁰花 子 兒³flower seeds.

魚 子³fish-roe.

鷄 子³hen's eggs.

(b) Young; tender.

子 嫩 young and tender.

子 薑 young ginger.

(c) Subordinate places or things. Interest, as on loans, etc.

子 卡 an out-barrier of the Customs.

子 口 an inland Customs station or barrier; a small post affiliated with a larger one.

子 口 稅 transit dues.

子 口 稅 收 據 receipt for transit dues.

⁵子 口 稅 繳 納 證 transit-dues memo.

子 城 a small city within a larger one.

子 數 the numerator of fractions.

子 母 interest and principal; parts and the whole.

子 母 錢 interest and principal.

¹⁰子 母 相 權 equivalence of a unit and the sum of its fractional parts; the interest paid equals the principal.

子 目 an index. ↑子火 a smaller *

子·細 or 仔·細 careful of details.

子 金 interest, as on capital invested.

子 音 consonants. = 輔音.

* opening in a kitchen range.

(d) An enclitic, often interchanged with 兒 No. 1759.

刀·子 a knife.

椅·子 a chair.

箱·子 a box.

舖·子 a shop.

驢·子 a donkey.

鷄(·子)a fowl.

(e) An officer; a gentleman. Complimentary designation of men, sometimes used of women. A philosopher. Used in direct

address for, "You, Sir." The fourth grade of nobility.

子 不 語 怪 力 亂 神 the Sage did not discuss marvels, feats of strength, rebellions and spiritual beings.

子 之 迂 也 you are wide of the mark.

子 其 言 乎 What have you to say?

子 其 釋 之 Can you explain this?

⁵子 帥 以 正 if you lead them with uprightness.

子 曰 the Master said....

子 奚 不 爲 政 Why are you not in the government?

子 程 子³曰 the p h i l o s o p h e r *Ch'êng* said....

子 聞 之 曰 the Master heard the remark and said....

¹⁰子 虛 子³name of an imaginary person used in fiction.

子 集 a collection of the writings of miscellaneous authors.

二 三 子³my friends; my disciples —in addressing them.

告 夫 三 子³inform the chiefs of the three families about it.

孔(·夫)子³the Master *K'ung,* latinized into Confucius.

¹⁵孟 子³the philosopher *Mêng,* latinized into Mencius.

微 子³去 之 箕 子³爲 之 奴 the Viscount of *Wei* withdrew (from the Court,) the Viscount of *Chi* became a slave (to *Chou.*)

我 明 語 子³I will explain the matter clearly.

諸 子³百 家 title of a collection of the writings of various authors, chiefly philosophical.

(f) The first of the *Earthly Branches,* 地 支; it relates to water; its symbol is the rat. 11 p.m. to 1 a.m. The third watch.

子 午 midnight and noon.

子 午 儀 a transit instrument.

子 午 砲 a gun fired at midnight and at noon.

子 午 線 the meridian. *See* 磁 No. 6966-22.

子 時 11 p.m. to 1 a.m.

仔³ To undertake. To bear. Careful.

6940

仔·細 careful; attentive.
仔 肩 重 任 to fill an important post.

(a) Read *tsai*. A diminutive. Inter. 崽 No. 6656.(*Cantonese*)

仔 蟲 larvæ.

孖¹
6941
Twins; a pair.

字⁴
6942
A letter; a written character; a word.

字 位 lettered seats for candidates at the examinations.
字 傍 the radical at the side of a Chinese character.
字 兒 a character; a memorandum or note; the obverse of a coin.
寫 一 個 字 兒 to write a memo, notice, etc.
⁵字 兒·上 (written) in the contract or deed, etc.
字 典 a dictionary.
字 勢 the boldness and vigour of penmanship.
字 句 a phrase.
字 字 有 意 every word has a meaning.
¹⁰字 學 etymology; the study of written charcters.
字 帖 a copy-slip; a rubbing from a stone tablet, used for this purpose.
字 式 a copy-slip.
字 彙 a dictionary; vocabulary.
字 形 the form of a character in writing.
¹⁵字 指 the purpose of a phrase or word.
字 據 a deed; an agreement; a bond; a receipt; documents.
字 文 script; despatches.
字 書 books on etymology, etc.
字 本 a copy-book.
²⁰字 條 a note or memorandum.
字 格 black lines placed under writing-paper as a guide to keep the columns straight.
字 樣 an expression; the form of a written character.
字 母 the "initials" in the Chinese system of spelling. *See* 切 No. 811-28; alphabet.
字 母 拼 音 phonetic spelling.

²⁵字 法 the construction of a written character, its order of strokes, etc.
字 派 a set of characters arranged in a certain order, used to distinguish the different generations of a clan. Each individual male member of a certain generation has tne same character in his name, so that his position in the genealogical tree can be immediately determined.
字 理 phraseology.
字 畫 the *strokes* in a character as written or printed.
字 疑 衍 文 the character is probably a gloss.
³⁰字 盤 a case of type.
字 眼 a phrase; an expression.
別 字 眼 to wrangle.
想·不 起 相 當·的 字 眼 could not think of a suitable word––to express his feelings.
虛 字 眼 a grammatical particle.
³⁵字 眼 淺 his knowledge of characters is shallow; he cannot readily understand the meaning.
字 碼 figures.
字 系 classification of written styles; alphabets, etc.
漢 字 系 Chinese written characters.
羅 馬 字 系 Roman letters.
⁴⁰字 紙 paper having written or printed characters upon it, the Chinese regard this as sacred.
敬 惜 字 紙 "Respect written paper."
字 紙 簍·子 or 字紙簍兒 waste-paper basket.

字 義 the meaning of a word.
字 脚 the radical at the base of a character; a character in Chinese writing.
⁴⁵字·號 a sign; a mark; a designation; a shop-sign in Chinese characters; a firm; a concern.
字 語 literary style.
字 跡 handwriting.
字 部 the radicals of Chinese characters.

字 面 language; phraseology; meaning.
⁵⁰字 面·上 literally.
字 音 the sound or pronunciation of a character or word.
字 韻 the "finals" in the Chinese system of spelling. *See above* —23.
字 頭 the radical of a Chinese character when it is at the top.
竹 字 頭 the "bamboo-character top"—i.e., the character is to be found under the radical for bamboo.
⁵⁵字 體 the style of a written or printed character.
冠 首 字 a prefix.
唇 音 字 labials.
喉 音 字 gutturals.
單 音 字 monosyllables.
⁶⁰多 音 字 polysyllables.
宋 字 the style of printed characters as used in this book.
接 尾 字 a suffix.
正 字 the formal orthodox style of writing Chinese.
活 字 or 鉛 字 movable types.
⁶⁵白 字 characters wrongly written for others of the same sound.
立 字 to execute a deed or agreement, etc.
篆 字 the style of engraving used on seals, etc.
花 字 a monogram.
草 字 the running style of Chinese writing.
⁷⁰雙 音 字 disyllables.
齒 音 字 dentals.

(a) A name or style taken at the age of twenty.

尊 字 What is your honourable style?
表 字 a fancy name; a style.

(b) To betroth a girl.

字 人 to be betrothed to a man.
未 字 not yet given in betrothal.

(c) To nourish. To suckle. To bring forth. To love. To care for.

字 之 dealt kindly with.
字 乳 to bring forth and suckle.
字 孕 to bring forth and nourish —their young.

字 小 to be kind to the young or to the weak.

[5]字 民 to love and care for the masses.

字 爾 幼 孩 nourish your young children.

字 牝 female animals.

于 父 不 能 字 厥 子³ .... and the father who can no longer love his son....

牛 羊 字 於 其 中 the cattle and sheep breed there.

[10]牛 羊 腓 字 之 the sheep and oxen protected him with loving care.

孜 [1]
6943　Unwearied effort.

孜 孜 爲 善 diligently do good.
惟 日 孜 孜 diligent from day to day.

牸 [4]
6944　The female of certain animals. To bring forth young —of animals.

牸 牛 a cow.
牸 馬 a mare.

籽 [3]
6945　The seeds of various kinds of grain. Seeds generally. u.f. 子 No. 6939—A.

籽 粒 seeds of grain.
籽 花 cotton-seed.

耔 [1]
6946　To hoe up the earth around plants.

㞢 [3]
6947　To stop.

姊]
姉] [3]
6948　An elder sister. A. p. chieh³.

姊 丈 an elder sister's husband.
姊 壻 elder sister's husband.
姊 夫 elder sister's husband.
姊·妹 sisters.
姊 妹 花 prostitutes who occupy the same house.
姊 弟 sister and brother.

秭 [3]
6949　One thousand millions; sometimes used for one hundred millions.

萬 億 及 秭 "with myriads, hundreds of thousands, and millions"—of the measures of grain in their granaries.

胏 [3]
6950　Dried meat with bone in it. Broken victuals.

梓 [3]
6951　A stately tree, called the "king of trees;" the wood was used for printing-blocks— Catalpa Kaempferi. Also called 楸 No. 1229.

梓 宮 a coffin containing the body of an emperor.
梓 里 one's native village or country,—from the trees planted around the villages.

(a) A worker in wood.

梓 匠 a wood-engraver.
梓 匠 輪 輿 carpenters and wheelwrights.

滓 [3]
6952　Sediment; dregs.

塵 滓 the vanities of this world.
消 滓 to clear a liquid by allowing it to settle.
渣 滓 sediment; dregs.

眥]
眦] [3.4]
6953　The canthus or corner of the eye.

內 眥 外 眥 the inner and the outer corners of the eye, respectively.

(a) Read ch'ai⁴. To stare in anger.

睚 眥 to stare with anger; angry looks.

紫 [3]
6954　Purple.

紫 塞 the Great Wall.
紫 外 光 線 ultra-violet rays.
紫 宸 the Court; the palace.

紫 府 heaven; the palace of the genii.
[5]紫 梗 渣 shellac.
紫 檀 red sandal-wood.
紫 毫 a fine writing-brush made of rabbit's hair.
紫 水·晶 purple crystal—amethyst; crystalline quartz.
紫 泥 a purple seal on a document or letter, etc.
[10]紫 泥 封 the imperial letter which announced the success of a Hanlin graduate or 狀 元
紫 石 英 fluor-spar.
紫·禁 城 the Forbidden City in Peking. (Peiping).
紫 竹 a variety of bamboo— Bambusa nana.
紫 羅 蘭 the violet.
[15]紫 臉 a swarthy complexion.
紫 色 purple.
紫 花 布 nankeen, a cloth made from a naturally whitey-brown variety of cotton.
紫 茉·莉 jalap—Mirabilis jalapa.
紫 草 a plant yielding a purple dye. (See 茈 No. 6978.)— Lithospermum officinale.
[20]紫°菜 laver, an edible marine algae.
紫 葳 Tecoma grandiflora.
紫 薇 the name of a star, a god invoked when building; the crape-myrtle—Lagerstroemia indica.
紫 薇 星 拱 照 May the Tzŭ Wei illumine—this house!
紫 薇 色 a deep rose colour.
[25]紫 藤 wistaria.
紫 蘇 Perilla nankinensis.
紫 衣 a purple moss.
紫 貝 a valuable cowrie with purple stripes.
紫 金 red gold.
[30]紫 黑 black and blue—of bruises.

骴]
胔] [4]
6955　A putrid carcase.

訾 [3]
6956　To backbite. To dislike.

訾 毀 to backbite; to revile.
訾 病 shame; mortification.

訾 短 to discuss the failings of others.
訾 議 to give unfavourable criticism.
訾 食 fastidious as to food.

(a) Read *tsŭ*[1]. To restrain. To consider. To estimate.

訾 程 to act according to prescribed rules; a limit.
不 訾 而 得 to obtain without planning for it.

(b) u.f. next. Wealth.

(c) A defect. A disease.

禮 之 訾 也 a blemish in the ritual.

貲[1] A fine paid to escape
6957 punishment. Riches; property. Inter. 資 No. 6927.

貲 產 property.
貲 簿 account books.
貲 財 valuables; wealth.
貲 贖 to ransom; to redeem by a money payment.
家 貲 family property.
工 貲 wages.

髭[1] The moustaches.
6958 Inter. 姿 No. 6924.

蠀[1] A species of tortoise called 蠀 蠞 found near the
6959 mouth of the Yellow River. Also read *tsui*[1].

齜[1] Projecting teeth.
6959a

齜 牙·子 a person with projecting teeth.

自[4] Self; private; personal. Natural. Radical 132.
6960

自 主 independent.
自 主 之 權 free-will; sovereign rights; right to independence.
自 主 占 有 personal possession. (*legal*).
自 主 國 an independent State.
[5]自 乘 to square—a number.

自 了[3] to accomplish something without aid; selfish, having no regard for others.
自 了[3] 漢 an independent person.
自 以 爲 然 oneself regarding it as right.
自 以 爲 義 self-righteous.
[10]自 任 to accept a responsibility.
自 作 孽 calamities brought upon oneself.
自 作 聰·明 pretending to be wise.
自 作 自 受 to receive the penalty for one's own sins.
自 作 自 爲 on one's own responsibility.
[15]自 來 水 筆 a fountain-pen.
自 來 水 water laid on to the house; water supply system.
自 來 水 龍 頭 a water-tap.
自 來 火 matches; gas.
自 便 as one pleases; at one's own convenience.
[20]自 信 to flatter oneself; to think it likely; conviction.
自 信 不 準 diffident.
自 信 之 氣 a self-confident air or manner.
自 信 力 self-confidence.
自 信·的 confidently. [from school.
[25]自 修 self-culture; home-work
自 修 室 a room for private study.
自 倡 巨 貲 he led with a large contribution.
自 做 I did it.
自 備 to make provision for oneself; to keep oneself; to provide one's own support, as at school, etc.
[30]自 備 生 self-supporting pupils.
自 光 體 a self-luminous body.
自 出 機 杼 to strike out in an original line—as in literature.
自 分 to accept a position; to be content with one's lot.
自 刎 to cut one's throat.
[35]自 利 selfish.
自 制 self-restraint.
自 力 to accomplish anything by one's own strength.
自 力 救 濟 self-preservation.
自 助 self-dependence.
[40]自 劾 to exert one's powers to accomplish anything.
自 動 self-moving; automatic.
自 動 作 用 automatic functions; automatic action.
自 動 力 automatic power; automatic force.

自 動 放 棄 voluntary relinquishment.
[45]自 動·的 動 作 automatic action; automatic movements.
自 動 玩 具 an automaton.
自 動·的 automatic.
自 動·的 事 automatic employment.
自 動·的 登 記 to register automatically; self-registering.
[50]自 動 詞 intransitive verbs.
自 動 販 賣 器 automatic machines for selling goods.
自 動 鑄 字 機 monotype machine.
自 動 電 話 automatic telephone.
自 動 體 量 器 automatic weighing machine.
[55]自 勝 to conquer self.
自 卑 自 賤 self-abasement.
自 反 常 直 in self-examination constantly upright.
自 反 而 不 縮 if, on self-examination, I find that I am not upright....
自 取 to take on one's own account.
[60]自 取 敗 壞 destruction brought upon oneself.
自 各 兒[3] oneself 他 自 各 兒 he himself.
自 告 奮 勇 to offer to take the responsibility upon oneself.
自 命.... to speak of oneself as....
自 命 不 凡 to pride oneself on being out of the ordinary.
[65]自 問 self-examination.
自 喜 其 力 rejoicing in his own strength.
自 鳴 得 意 singing one's own praises.
自 鳴 鐘 a striking-clock.
自 在 self-existent; free and easy; 自在 comfortable; quiet (as a child).
[70]有 些 不 自 在 a little out of sorts.
逍 遙 自 在[4] easy-going; happy-go-lucky; comfortable; free from trammels.
自 在 畫 freehand drawing.
自 多 self-conceited.
自 失 之 悔 to regret one's mistakes.
[75]自 奉 one's personal expenditure.
自 奉 養 self-support.
自 如 as before.
自 好[4] a good opinion of oneself.
自 娛 to amuse oneself.

[80] 自 媒 to seek a husband without the formalities of a go-between.

自 存 to maintain one's existence; self-existent.

自 守 self-control.

自 宜 it is naturally fitting.

自 容 量 self-contained; compact.

[85] 自·家 self; oneself.

自 寬 to be lenient to oneself; to comfort oneself.

自 封 rigid self-control.

自 尋 苦 惱 to bring trouble upon oneself.

自 專 自 主 to act on one's own responsibility.

[90] 自 己 self; oneself.

自 己 主 張 self-assertion.

自 己 保 存 self-preservation.

自 己 傳 染 auto-infection.

自 己 催 眠 auto-hypnotism.

[95] 自 己 感 應 self-induced.

自 意·識 self-consciousness.

自 己 敎·育 self-education.

自 己 暗 示 auto-suggestion.

自 己 犧 牲 self-sacrifice.

[100] 自 己·的 one's own.

自 己 知·覺 self-consciousness.

自 幸 to congratulate oneself.

自 序 a personal narrative; author's own preface.

自 強 self-reliant; resolute.

[105] 自 律 autonomy.

自 得 contented; satisfied.

自 必 will certainly; will not fail to.

自 怨 自 艾 was contrite and reformed himself.

自 性 the essential nature of a thing.

[110] 自 恨 self-abhorrence.

自 悟 前 失 to see the mistakes which one has made.

自 意·的 voluntarily.

自 愛 self-esteem.

自 慊 self-pleased.

[115] 自 應 捐 釋 should naturally be explained and done away with.

自 成 一 家 to strike out in a new line for oneself—independence.

自 戒 to restrain oneself; temperance; self-control.

自 我 the subjective ego.

自 我 中 心·的 self-centred; ego-centric. 自我主義 egoism.

[120] 自 我 作 古 not bound by conventionality.

自 我 實 現 self-realization.

自我批評 self-criticism.

自 我·的 發 展 the expression of the subjective ego.

自 我·的 知·識 subjective consciousness.

自 我 經 驗 subjective experience.

[125] 自 我 表 現 self-expression.

自 戕 to injure oneself.

自 找 愁 煩 always brooding over one's troubles.

自 投 網 羅 to fall into a snare through one's own fault.

自 招 to bring upon oneself.

[130] 自 招 負 債 taking a burden upon yourself.

自 持 self-control.

自 括·的 self-contained.

自 揣 they themselves estimate ....

自 捲·的 self-winding.

[135] 自 掩 其 功 he concealed his own merits.

自 摧 棄 之 she had ruined herself.

自 料 to manage for oneself; to calculate.

自 斟 自 酌 to have one's own opinion.

自 新 self-renewal; reformation.

[140] 自 新 所 a reformatory.

自 明 self-evident.

自 明 眞 理 self-evident truth.

自 是 self-confident; self-satisfied; conceited; presumptuous.

自 是 之 風 a conceited manner.

[145] 自 暴 自 棄 reckless; to throw oneself away; blind to one's own interests; unambitious.

自 有 自 權 autocratic power.

自 殺 to commit suicide.

自 殺 政 策 a suicidal policy.

自 汗 the weakening perspiration of a sick man.

[150] 自 決 self-determined; self-determination. See 民 No. 4508—56.

自 決 心 self-determination.

自 治 self-government; self-control.

自 治 不 勇 cowardly in self-control.

自 治 之 主 體 subject of self-government. (legal).

[155] 自 治 之 權 autonomy.

自 治 制 度 self-government system; local government system.

自 治 區 self-governing subdivisions or districts.

自 治 團 體 self-governing bodies.

自 治 屬 地 self-governing colonies.

[160] 自 治 局 local government office.

自 治 會 self-governing association, as clubs, etc., in schools.

自 治 權 rights of autonomy.

自 治 職 員 local government officials.

自 治 行 政 the administration of self-government.

[165] 自 治 負 擔 the responsibility of self-government.

地·方 自 治 local self-government.

自 滿 self-satisfied; presumptuous; conceited.

自 炫 心 self-display.

自·然 or 自 然 而 然·的 certainly; of course; naturally; natural; spontaneous; self-existent.

[170] 自 然 不 去 of course you will not go.

自 然 之 理 an axiom.

自 然 人 a natural person. (legal)

自 然 分 類 a natural classification.

自 然 力 the natural forces, as of wind, evaporation, etc.

[175] 自 然 國 境 natural boundaries of a State.

自 然 哲 學 natural philosophy.

自 然 大 natural size.

自 然 存 在 self-existence.

自 然 律 natural law.

[180] 自 然 法 則 natural laws; laws of nature.

自 然 派 the naturalistic school.

自 然 派 詩 人 the school of nature poets.

自 然 淘 汰 natural selection.

自 然 演 化 natural evolution.

[185] 自 然 演 進 natural evolution.

自 然 燃 燒 spontaneous combustion.

自 然 狀 態 the natural aspect; the natural state.

自 然 生 命 natural life; physical life.

自 然 界 the natural world.

[190] 自 然 療 法 natural methods of healing, apart from the use of drugs, etc., using fresh air, bathing, massage, etc.

自 然 發 生 spontaneous generation.

↓自 解 to excuse oneself.

自然·的正義 natural justice.
自然·的現象 natural phenomena.
自然神學 natural theology.
[195]自然科學 natural science.
自然著¹色⁺法 the autochrome process. (-*cho*¹-)
自然銅 native copper.
自然鐵 native iron.
自照行·李 look after your own luggage.
[200]自燃 spontaneous combustion.
自營生計 to support oneself.
自為 I did it.
自為乳兒 when I was a child.
自為風氣 are a law unto themselves.
[205]自甘奴·隸 voluntary slavery.
自生·的 spontaneous.
自生植·物 self-sown plants.
自用 independent, unwilling to heed the exhortations of others; self-satisfied.
自由 liberty; freedom.
[210]自由主義 freedom; the principle of liberty.
自由刑 punishment by curtailing the personal liberty
自由國 a free State.
自由市府 free cities.
自由平等同胞之主義 Liberty, Equality, and Fraternity.
[215]自由幸福 the blessings of freedom.
自由心證 freedom of convictions.
自由思想 free thought.
自由意志 free-will.
自由戀愛 free love.
[220]自由放任主義 the principle of *laissez faire*.
自由政策 an easy-going policy.
自由敎·育 liberal education.
自由民 free peoples.
自由港 a free port.
[225]自由稅率 (*lü*⁴·⁵·) tariff autonomy.
自由競爭 the struggle for liberty; free competition·
自由結婚 freedom of choice in marriage.
自由聯想法 the law of free association.
自由自在 comfortable; contented; in a state of bliss.
[230]自由藝術 the liberal arts.
↓自行 done at one's own initiative; automatically. *See above* 41.

自由行動 freedom of action.
自由言論 freedom of speech.
↓自由詩 vers libre.
自由設立主義 the principle of free establishment.
自由貿易 free trade.
[235]自由運動 free movement; a movement for liberty.
自由鄉 the land of freedom.
自由鐘 the bell of liberty.
自由離婚 freedom of divorce.
自由黨 The Liberal Party.
[240]自發 spontaneous; automatic.
自發·的反應⁴ automatic reaction.
自發運動 automatic movements.
自白 a personal statement.
自白錄 autobiography; personal notes.
[245]自盡 to commit suicide.
自盡其力 to exert all one's energies.
自省 self-examination. (-*hsing*³)
自相分爭 to wrangle; mutual strife.
自相擊殺 to slaughter one another.
[250]自相¹矛盾 self-contradictory.
自相¹衝突 to come to a clash; to be at loggerheads.
自瞞自欺 self-delusion.
自知 self-conscious.
自知錯誤 conscious of one's faults.
[255]自禁 self-restraint.
自私 to seek private or personal advantage; selfish.
自稱¹ to style oneself....
自立 independency.
自立敎會 an independent church.
[260]自立自養 independence and self-support—of churches.
自立門戶 to set up a home for oneself.
自笑 to ridicule oneself.
自節 self-control.
自給 self-feeding; self-supplying.
[265]不足自給 unable to support himself.
自絕 self-destruction.
自經 to commit suicide.
自縊 to strangle oneself.
自縱 self-indulgence.
[270]自習室 a room for private study.

自肥 to enrich oneself.
自若 as before; without change; self-possessed.
談笑自若 went on talking and smiling as before.
自花受精 self-fertilizing flowers.
↑[275]自傳⁴ autobiography.
自處 to accept as one's position.
自衛手段 measures for self-defence.
自衛權 the right of self-defence.
自製 made on the premises; our own manufacture.
[280]自覺 self-conscious.
自覺心 self-consciousness.
自言自語 to soliloquize.
自記寒暑表 self-recording thermometer.
自記風雨表 self-recording barometer.
[285]自記·的 or 自誌·的 self-registering; self-recording.
自訴怨恨 to set forth one's grievances.
自訟 self-accusation.
自認 confession.
自誇 to boast.
[290]自謙 modest; modesty.
自證己錯 self-convicted.
自負 self-important.
自責 self-rebuke; to judge oneself.
自貶 to censure oneself.
[295]自費生 self-supporting pupils.
自賣本身 to sell one's own person.
自贊 self-recommendation.
自足 self-satisfaction; contentment; conceited; self-sufficient.
自身 itself.
[300]主義·的自身無危險 there is no danger in the principle itself.
自輕 to lack self-respect.
自轉 revolving on its own axis —as the planets; 公轉 is the term for the revolution of the planets around the sun.
自轉車 a free-wheel bicycle.
自辦 to manage it oneself; one who imports the goods himself, etc.
[305]自辱 to disgrace oneself.
自逞 boastful; self-assertion.
自逞智慧 to boast of one's wisdom; self-asserted wisdom.
↑自行車ㄦ bicycle. Cf. 1177.24.

自 造 made on the premises; our own manufacture.

自 適·的 姿 態 a self-satisfied air.

[310]自 重ʰ self-respect.

自 陳 a personal statement.

自 靖 to purify oneself.

自 願 voluntarily.

自 顧 自 only looking out for one's own interests; selfish.

[315]自 食 其 力 to live by one's own exertions; to help oneself.

自 食 其 肉 eating their own flesh.

自 餒 lacking self-confidence.

自 首 (shou⁴) to give oneself up to the authorities; voluntary surrender.

自 首 減 等 abatement of the punishment because of voluntary surrender to the authorities.

[320]自 高 conceited; self-exalted; proud.

(a) From.

自 今 以 後 henceforth.

自 今·年 起 beginning with this year.

自 古 以 來 from of old.

自 古 及 今 from of old until now.

[5]自 外 from without; over and above.

自 天 子 達 於 庶 人 from the emperor to the masses of the people.

自 天 申 之 (these favours) came from heaven again and again.

自 幼 from childhood.

自 後 henceforth.

[10]自·從 from....; ever since....

自·從 去·年 since last year.

自 我 意·見 from my point of view.

自 打 from....; ever since....

自 易 及 難 from the easy to the difficult.

[15]自 此 from this place; henceforth.

自 此 爲 止 to cease from this time forth.

自 淺 入 深 proceeding from the shallow to the deep—of progressive studies.

自 經 界 始 begin with the boundaries.

自 蚤 歲 from early years; from youth.

---

[20]自 行 束 脩 以 上 from those who bring a bundle of dried flesh and upwards....

何 自 where do they come from?

來 自 何 處ʰ where have you come from?

問 其 所 自 asked where it came from.

(b) The nose, said to be the original form of 鼻 No. 5100.

刺⁴ To stab; to stick on. To erect.
6961

漬⁴ To soak; to steep. Sodden.
6962

水 漬 saturated with water.

浸 漬 saturated; thoroughly soaked.

漏 漬 to macerate.

鹽 漬 soaked in brine.

胾⁴ To cut meat into pieces; minced meat. A cutlet.
6963

鼒¹ A tripod with a small opening on the top.
6964

TZ'Ŭ.   (ㄘ)
(Ts'ï)

慈慈² Compassion; mercy. Compassionate; kind. An epithet for mothers.
6965

慈 命 the commands of a mother.

慈 和 on friendly terms.

慈 善 merciful and benevolent; kindly disposed; charitable.

慈 善 事 業 charitable causes; philanthropic works.

[5]慈 善 基 金 charitable endowments.

慈 善 家 philanthropists.

慈 善 會 any organization for the purposes of charity.

慈 善 院 a charitable institution.

慈 姑 a kind mother-in-law—said by the daughter-in-law. *See below*—A.

---

[10]慈 寵 favour.

慈 幃 the loving screen—a mother.

慈 幼 to be kind to the young.

慈 從 聽 婉 kind, while condescending, and winning, while obedient—said of mother-in-law and daughter-in-law respectively.

慈 心 a kind heart; tender-hearted.

[15]慈 恩 the kindness of a mother.

慈 恕 merciful and forgiving.

慈 恃 one's mother.

慈 恃 下 my mother is alive.

慈 恤 kind and sympathetic.

[20]慈 惠 以 敎 to teach (his sons) with kindness—the duty of a father.

慈·悲 compassionate; forbearing.

慈 悲 大 士 a term for the goddess *Kuanyin* 觀 音.

慈 愉 kind and cheerful.

慈 愍 sympathetic.

[25]慈 愛 or 仁 慈 love; compassion.

慈 憐 love and compassion.

慈 撫 to show kindness towards and support—the masses.

慈 母 my mother; a kind mother.

慈 母 敗 子 a kind mother spoils her son.

[30]慈 氏 the compassionate—Buddha.

慈 淚 tears of compassion.

慈 鳥 a young crow.

慈 父 見 背 my compassionate father died.

慈 眉 善 目·的 having a benevolent countenance.

[35]慈 睦 kindly disposed; friendly relationship.

慈 祥 merciful and propitious.

慈 禧 太 后 the Empress Dowager who wielded great power at the close of the Manchu dynasty.

慈 竹 a bamboo with many suckers.

慈 篤 kind and generous.

[40]慈 膝 the knees of one's parents.

慈 航 the Barge of Compassion—that of *Kuan yin* 觀 音, which ferries departed spirits from this world of care to the realms of bliss.

慈 親 my mother; a mother.

慈 訓 (or 誨) the teachings of one's mother.

慈 躬 my mother's body.

[45]慈 雲 the merciful cloud which

shades—Buddha; used also as an expression of gratitude.

慈 顏 your kindly face—term of respectful address to elders or parents.

    拜 別 慈 顏 take leave of your kindly face.

令 慈 your mother.

家 慈 my mother.

(a) Inter. 茨 No. 6982. A water-plant. *Caladium.*

慈·姑 or 慈·菇 a water-plant; the bulbs of which are used as food—*Sagittaria sagittifolia.*

(b) Inter. next. A loadstone.

慈 石 a loadstone.

磁
瓷]²   Crockery; porcelain. A loadstone. Magnetic (first form only).
6966

磁 力 magnetic force.
磁 力 線 lines of magnetic force.
磁 動 力 magneto-motive force.
磁 區 變 態 disturbance of the magnetic field.
⁵磁 周 a magnetic circuit.
磁 器 porcelain; china.
   彩 花 磁 器 coloured porcelain.
磁 器 棺 材 a porcelain coffin—a hard-hearted man.
磁 土 kaolin.
¹⁰磁 場 the magnetic field.
磁 學 magnetism, as a study.
磁 性 magnetic properties; of a magnetic nature.
磁 感 magnetic influences.
   得·着 磁 感 magnetized. (-·*chao*)
¹⁵磁 條 a bar magnet.
磁 極 or 吸 磁 極 點 the magnetic pole.
磁 橋 the armature of a magnet.
磁·氣 magnetism.
   動 物 磁 氣 animal magnetism.
²⁰   地 磁 氣 terrestrial magnetism.
磁 氣 修 正 板 magnetic compensator.
磁 氣 子³午 線 magnetic meridian. *See* 子 No. 6939—F.
磁 氣 感 應 magnetic induction.
磁 氣 暴 變 magnetic storm.

²⁵磁 氣 赤 道 the magnetic equator.
磁 氣 體 a magnetic body.
磁 油 glaze on porcelain.
磁 瓶 a porcelain vase.
磁 界 the magnetic field.
³⁰磁 發 電 機 a magneto.
磁 石 a loadstone.
   天 然 磁 石 a natural magnet.
磁 石 棍 a bar magnet.
磁 質 magnetic substances.
³⁵磁 軸 the magnetic axis.
磁 針 the magnetic needle.
磁 針 俯 角 (or 側 度) the magnetic dip.   [(-*ch'a*¹)
磁 針 偏 差 magnetic declination.
磁 針 方 位 magnetic bearings.
⁴⁰磁 鋼 a permanent magnet.
磁 鐵 magnetic iron; a magnet.
   圓 條 磁 鐵 a cylindrical magnet.
   恒 磁 鐵 a permanent magnet.
   馬 蹄 磁 鐵 a horseshoe magnet.
⁴⁵磁 電 electro-magnetism.
傳 磁 to magnetize.
哥 窰 磁·器 crackle-ware.
洋 磁 foreign porcelain or china.
細 磁 fine porcelain.

蟟
蚝]⁴   Hairy and poisonous caterpillars.
6967

鷀]¹·²·   The fishing cormorant.
6968

伺]⁴   To wait upon. Also read *szŭ*⁴.
6969

伺 候 to wait upon—of servants.
   難 伺 候 he is difficult to serve.
伺 候 不 過 來 not to have time to wait upon.
伺 應 to wait upon—of servants.
服 伺 to serve a person.

(a) To examine. To spy.

伺 刦 to waylay and rob.
伺 察 to spy upon.
伺 探 to spy.
伺 查 to examine into.
伺 隙 to wait in secret for an opportunity.

祠]²   To worship ancestors. An ancestral hall or temple. To sacrifice.
6970

祠 堂 an ancestral hall.
祠 祀 to offer sacrifices.
祠 竈 to sacrifice to the kitchen god; to practise alchemy.
生 祠 a shrine erected while the person is still living.

詞]²   An expression. Words; phrases; a part of speech. Tales; stories. A form of poetry.
6971

詞 不 達 意 the sentence does not fully convey the idea.
詞 人 a man of literary ability.
詞 典 or 辭 典 a book of phrases.
詞 句 wording; text.
⁵詞 垣 the *Hanlin Academy.*
詞 宗 a man who is skilful in literary composition.
詞 客 a man of letters.
詞 律 rules of metrical composition.
詞 意 the meaning of a phrase; the purport; the drift.
¹⁰詞 致 style of composition.
詞 林 the *Hanlin Academy.*
詞 氣 the form of an expression.
詞 窮 理 拙 poor in expression and perverted in sense.
詞 章 polished phraseology; a fancy style; ornamental phrases.
¹⁵詞 苑 a collection of literature; literary department.
詞 華 flowery composition; ornate terms.
詞 藻 flowery language.
詞 話 criticism of poetry.
詞 鋒 incisive writings.
²⁰詞 韻 rhythm, expression, etc.
冠 詞 an article—(*grammar*).
冠 頭 詞 a prefix.
副 詞 an adverb.
   否 定 副 詞 a negative adverb.
²⁵   地 位 副 詞 an adverb of place.
   數 量⁴ 副 詞 an adverb of quantity.
   時 間 副 詞 an adverb of time.
   程 度 副 詞 an adverb of degree.
前 置 詞 a preposition. A.c. 介 詞.
³⁰動 詞 a verb. *See* No. 6611-/0.
名 詞 a noun. *See* No. 4524-57 ff.

公 認 名 詞 conventional terms.

否 詞 negatives.

形 容 詞 adjectives.

35 性 質 形 容 詞 an adjective of quality.

指 示 形 容 詞 a demonstrative adjective.

數 量 形 容 詞 an adjective of quantity.

感 歎 詞 an interjection.

接 尾 詞 a suffix. A.c. 詞尾

40 接 續 詞 a conjunction. A.c. 連詞

數 詞 numerals.

文 詞 composition; language.

疑 問 詞 interrogatives.

言 詞 words; language.

45 關。係 詞 relative clauses.

(a) A legal plaint

詞 訟 litigation.

作 詞 to draw up a plaint for another.

口 詞 utterance; e v i d e n c e ; depositions.

對 詞 (or 質) the evidence on both sides.

狀 詞 an accusation; a plaint.

(b) Read *szŭ*⁴. u.f. 飼 No. 5587.

此 ³ This. Here.
6972

此 人 this man.

此 係 this is....

此 刻 at the present time.

此 卽 this is....

5 此 君 the bamboo,—from the line 何 可 一 日 無 此 君.

此 地 this place, here.

此 外 beyond this; additional.

此 布 this for your information.

此 後 hereafter; henceforth.

10 此 復 this in reply.

此 有 己 見 之 存 this has a selfish outlook.

此 次 this occasion.

此 照 according to this; this is the arrangement to be followed.

此 渺 this for your information.

15 此 生 this life.

此 端 this matter.

此 等 such as these.

此 致 順 頌 升 祺 while communicating the above to you, allow me to express my best wishes.

此 處 this place.

---

20 此 請 台 安 with best wishes.

此 達 this for your information.

此 項 this classification; this item.

此 頌 升 祺 with best wishes.

專 此 this is specially to....— closing a letter.

25 彼 此 that and this. *See* No. 5093-7ff.

特 此 卽 請 expressly to wish you....

佌 ³ Small; petty.
6973

佌 佌 之 物 a mere trifle.

佌 佌 彼 有 屋 民 今 之 無 祿 abject creatures, they have their houses, but the masses now have no maintenance— speaking of royal favourites.

泚 ³ Clear; fresh.
6974

新 臺 有 泚 fresh and bright is the new tower.

(a) To perspire.

其 顙 有 泚 perspiration started out on their foreheads.

非 爲 人 泚 it was not on account of others that the perspiration flowed.

玼 ¹ A flaw in a gem. Inter. 疵 No. 6976.
6975

瑕 玼 a flaw in a gem.

(a) Read *tz'ŭ*³. Fresh and bright. Inter. 泚 No. 6974.

玼 兮 玼 兮 How rich! How splendid!—of a robe.

鮮 玼 fresh and bright.

疵 ¹,² A blemish; a flaw; a fault. A mole.
6976

疵 病 or 疵 瑕 b a d h a b i t s ; defects; blemishes.

吹 毛 求 疵 to blow aside the fur, looking for defects.

小 疵 a trifling defect.

跐 ³ To trample; to step; to walk on the ball of the foot.
6977 Usually pron. *ts'ai*³.

跐 不·下 no standing room.

跐 穩 to step firmly and carefully.

跐 蹈 to step; to tread.

茈 ³ A plant yielding a red dye. See 紫 No. 6954-19.
6978

茈 草 a plant yielding a red dye— *Lithospermum officinale*.

雌 ¹,² The female of birds, and sometimes of animals.
6979

雌 性 female.

雌 老 虎 a female tiger—a virago.

雌 蕊 a pistil.

雌 雄 female and male.

5 雌 雄 同 體 花 or 雌 雄 兩 全 花 hermaphrodite. (*bot.*). 分 雌 雄 see who's master!

雌 鷄 啼 鳴 the hen crowing— the wife ruling.

雌 黃 yellow ochre. (*See* No. 3434-3.) Used for blotting out passages in making corrections on the ancient yellow paper—thus:—to criticise; to correct.

次 ⁴ The next in order; secondary. Inferior; lower.
6980

次 之 secondary; inferior; to follow in order.

次 便 a lower seat than the seat of honour.

次 其 先 後 arrange them in their order.

次 子 ³ the second son.

5 次 年 the following year.

次 於 next in order to....

次 日 the next day.

次 早 early the next morning.

次 玉 inferior jade.

10 次·的 second class or quality.

次 等 or 次 一 等 second quality or grade.

次 等 國 a secondary power.

次 等 權 利 secondary rights.

次 級·的 secondary.

15 次 要 secondary; subordinate.

次 長 ³ vice-minister, the second in control of a ministry.

(a) A time. A series. An interval.

次·序 in succession; i n order; sequence.

次第 sequence; in order.
一次 once.
不次 out of order.
[5]依次 in succession.
其次 the next in order.
歷次 on several occasions.
更次 a watch; the time of a watch.
此次 on this occasion.
[10]頭次 the first time.

(b) A place. A halting-place. By; in the midst. To reach. To arrive at. To camp.

次骨 penetrated to the bones—of hatred or severe punishment.
位次 a place or position; a seat.
官次 an official post.
客次 an inn.
[5]席次 at the table.
旅次 an inn.
水次 by the side of the stream.
王次于河朔 the king halted on the north of the river.
畔官離次 they have violated the duties of their office and left their posts.
[10]胸次 in the mind; in the bosom of.
途次一晤 to meet on the road.

(c) The position of the sun and moon in the zodiac.

日窮于次 the sun has gone through all the zodiac.
躔次 the orbits of the planets.

(d) To braid in false hair.

(e) Read tsŭ[1]. u.f. 趑 No. 6928.

次且 (tsu[1]) or 趑趄 to hesitate; to halt, unwilling to enter.

伙[4] To help. Nimble; active.
6981

茨[2] Caltrops—*Tribulus terrestris.*
6982

茨菇 or 慈姑 a water-plant, the roots of which are used as food—*Sagittaria sagittifolia.*
牆有茨不可襄也 the tribulus grows on the wall, but it cannot be removed—as it would ruin the wall to uproot it.

(a) Thatch for roofing.

惟其塗墍茨 then it has to be plastered and thatched.
茅茨 a thatched cottage.

(b) To accumulate.

福祿如茨 (in whom) all happiness and dignity are concentrated.

飺[2] Fried cakes of cooked rice.
6983

辭舜辤[2] Words; speech. A sentence, an expression or phrase. A message; instructions; statements. A form of poetical composition. Inter. 詞 No. 6971.
6984

辭令 to deliver up a command; depositions.
辭典 a cyclopœdia; a book of phrases.
辭吐 one's conversation; what one has said.
辭命 speeches; messages.
[5]辭宗 a master of phrases.
辭曰聞戒 the message (with the present) was, "I hear you are preparing to protect yourself."
辭章 ornate literary efforts.
辭致 one's speech and deportment.
辭色 his speech and the expression of his countenance.
[10]辭若有憾 the words seem as if there were anger in them.
辭藻 elegant, ornate style of literature.
辭說分明 speaking clearly and to the point.
辭費 useless waste of words.
辭賦 irregular style of metrical composition.
[15]辭趣 the thought of a composition.
辭達而已矣 in language it is simply required that it convey the meaning.
不以文害辭不以辭害志 "do not insist on one term so as to do violence to a sentence, nor on a sentence so as to do violence to the general scope."

出辭氣斯遠鄙倍矣 "that in his words and tones he keeps far from lowness and impropriety."
淫辭 extravagant expressions; licentious expressions.
[20]無以辭郤之 when one does not in so many express words refuse the gift....
詖辭 one-sided statements.
說辭 negotiations.
遁辭 evasive statements.
邪辭 depraved expressions.

(a) To resign. To decline or shirk. To take leave. To make excuses (not interchangeable with 6971.)
辭·不下來 he cannot get out of it.
辭以病 to decline on the ground of illness.
辭位 to abdicate; to retire.
辭出 to take leave.
[5]辭別 to take leave of; to bid farewell.
辭前挨後 to shirk.
辭却 to resign; to decline; to dismiss.
辭官 to resign office.
辭富居貧 to decline riches and prefer poverty.
[10]辭尊居卑 to decline an honourable station and occupy a humble one.
辭工 to leave work; to come off duty.
辭帖 a card sent when leaving; a card declining an invitation.
辭歇 to dismiss from employment.
辭朝[2] or 陛辭 to have a parting audience with the emperor.
[15]辭職 to resign office.
辭脫 to resign; to get out of.
辭行 or 告辭 to take leave of; to bid farewell.
辭行帖[3] a card sent when leaving; P.P.C.
辭謝 to decline with thanks; to be excused.
[20]辭讓 to abdicate; to yield the place to.
辭賬 to give up business; to throw up a situation.
辭路 to give up a line of life; to die.
辭退 to give up a position; to refuse; to discharge.

不辭勞苦 not shirking any trouble or inconvenience.

²⁵不辭小官 he did not think it beneath him to be an inferior officer.

不辭而行 to go away without taking formal leave.

又從爲之辭 they go on to apologize for them likewise.

固辭 to decline with firmness.

推辭 to decline; to make excuses.

請辭 I beg leave to decline the office.

刺 ⁴ A thorn. A tentacle. To stab; to pierce; to brand;
6985 from which comes:—to lampoon; to criticize. Inter. next. Distinguish 刾 No. 3757.

刺世譏俗之言 satires; critical essays, etc.

刺傷 to wound by stabbing.

刺入 to pierce.

刺入剖開 to pierce and lay open.

⁵刺刀 a dagger.

鎗上刺刀 a bayonet.

刺刺不休 unceasing chatter.

刺史 the governor of a province under the *Han* dynasty.

刺地 to dig the ground.

¹⁰刺字 to write with a stylus; to brand a criminal by tattooing.

刺。客 an assassin, especially said of one who acts from motives of patriotism.

刺心 to pierce to the heart—with biting words.

刺戟·的 stimulating; irritating; biting.

刺戟藥 stimulant drugs.

¹⁵刺探 to pry into and criticize.

刺撓 uneasy; irritable—as the skin; bruised.

刺時 to satirize the times.

刺棍 a goad.

刺殺 or 行刺 to assassinate.

²⁰刺激 stimulus; to incite; provocation.

刺激性 of a stimulating nature.

刺牙 to pick the teeth.

刺眼 irritating to the eyes.

刺絡 to bleed a person—surgically.

²⁵刺耳·的話 words that irritate the ear.

刺股 to prick the thigh with an awl as 蘇秦 did, in order to

---

prevent himself from falling asleep over his studies—used for diligence in study.

刺臉 to brand the face.

刺船 to pole a boat.

刺花紋 to tattoo.

³⁰刺草 nettles.

刺·蝟 or 毛刺 the hedgehog.

刺衝·的 stimulating; irritating; provoking.

刺訊 to interrogate.

刺譏 to lampoon; to satirize.

³⁵刺責 or 譏刺 or 諷刺 to blame; to ridicule; to scold.

刺配 to brand and banish.

刺透 to stab through; to pierce through.

刺面 to brand the face.

刺馬輪 or 踢馬刺 a spur.

⁴⁰刺骨 penetrating to the bones, as severe cold, or deep, intense hatred.

刺魚 a stickleback.

蜂刺 the sting of a bee or wasp.

魚刺 the small bones and dorsal spines of fish.

(a) A tablet; a card.

投刺 to send in one's card.

(b) Read *ch'i* or *ts'i⁵*. To penetrate.

刺繡 to embroider.

莿 ⁴ A thorn. Inter. preceding. Distinguish 束 No. 5891.
6986

莿兒 thorns.

莿撓 itchy; irritating.

莿松 the juniper.

莿梨 wild roses.

⁵莿玫 wild roses.

莿芳·子 thorns.

莿花 wild roses.

莿菓兒 a prickly fruit—a disagreeable person.

廁 ⁴ A privy; a night-stool. Also read *szŭ⁴*.
6987

          (··*szŭ*)

廁所 or 廁坑 or 茅·廁 or 東廁 a privy.

上廁 or 如廁 to go to stool.

(a) Order; series.

廁之賓客之中 placed among the guests.

(b) The side of a bed.

上常踞廁視之 the emperor leaned upon the side of the bed and received him.

(c) Read *ts'ê⁵*. u.f. 側 No. 6757. By the side of.

廁足 to cover with the foot.

賜 ⁴ To bestow; to confer upon an inferior.
6988 Also read *szŭ⁴*.

賜光 to honour with your presence.

賜卹 to grant special rewards.

賜告 to grant a statesman leave of absence.

賜命 to give orders.

⁵賜姓 to give the right to a family name.

賜宴 to bestow a banquet.

賜帛 to bestow silk—for an official to strangle himself with.

賜恩 to give grace; to bestow favours.

賜惠 to confer a favour.

¹⁰賜教 to condescend to teach; to give an opinion.

賜死 to be allowed to commit suicide.

賜爵 to confer nobility.

賜田 to confer fields upon.

賜示 to be kind enough to inform.

¹⁵賜祭 to honour the spirit of some deceased person.

賜福給他 to bestow grace upon him.

賜給 to bestow.

賜胙 to make a present of flesh from the sacrifices.

賜與 to confer upon; to grant to.

²⁰賜覆 to favour with a reply.

賜見 to grant an audience.

賜覽 to condescend to examine.

賜諭 to grant an edict.

賜辦 to be good enough to deal with.

²⁵賜頂戴 to permit to wear the former official button on the hat; to reward without giving office.

賜 顧 to patronize—as a customer patronizes a shop.

賜 飯 to detain for a meal.

受 賜 to receive a bounty.

天 賜 才 能 Heaven bestows talents upon men.

³⁰賞 賜 a reward; to reward; to confer upon.

WA.   (ㄨㄚ)
(Ua)

哇¹
6989
To vomit.

哇 一 聲 to make the noise of vomiting.

哇 吐 to vomit; to spit out.

出 而 哇 之 he went out and vomited it.

(a) Lascivious music.

哇 俚 lewd or vulgar expressions.

哇 咬 lewd songs.

多 哇 則 鄭 the most lascivious (songs) were those of *Chêng.*

(b) The crying of infants. The attempts of a child to speak.

有 童 哇 哇 there is a child learning to talk.

娃²
6990
A baby. A beautiful woman.

娃·娃 臉 baby-faced.

娃·子 or 小 娃 or 姓·娃 a child. (central, *dial.*)

洼¹
6991
Name of a river. A winding ditch. Inter. next.

窪¹
6992
A swamp. A puddle.

窪 凹 a hollow where the rain collects.

窪 地 marsh land.

窪·子 the lapwing; also the heron.

白 窪·子 the egret.

窪 田 marsh land.

蛙
黽
1
6993
The edible water-frog.

蛙 市 the frog's market—said of the noise of frogs in the evenings.

井 底 蛙 a frog at the bottom of a well—very limited outlook.

(a) Inter. 哇 No. 6989—A. Wanton sounds.

蛙 聲 a wanton voice.

窊¹
6994
A cavity; a depression; a puddle; a hoof-print. Inter. 窪 No. 6992.

窊 地 墊 高 to fill up a hollow; to raise land by filling in.

草 窊 a grassy plain—the grass lands of Mongolia.

喴
呱
4
6995
To wail; to sob, as a child. Also read *ku¹.*

呱 呱·的 哭 a long-continued wail.

呱·的 一 聲 哭·了 burst out into a loud cry.

搲
3.1.
6996
To seize; to grasp.

媧¹
6997
The sister of *Fu Hsi* 伏羲. Also read *kua¹.*

女 媧 the mythical sister and successor of *Fu Hsi;* the legends vary and are extremely fantastic. *See* Mayers' *Chinese Reader's Manual, art.* 521.

瓦
3
6998
A tile. Earthenware; pottery. To roof; to tile. Radical 98.

瓦 上 之 霜 the frost on the tiles —soon gone, illustrative of old age or the brevity of life. *See* 風 No. 1890-41.

瓦 全 to keep the tile whole—to preserve life, etc., when it would be more honourable to die. *See* 寧 No. 4725-9.

瓦·匠 or 泥 水 匠 a mason; a bricklayer.

瓦 口 the ends of a tiled roof.

⁵瓦 合 loosely associated without proper order, like a heap of tiles—no cohesion.

瓦·器 an earthen vessel; earthenware.

瓦 屋 or 瓦 房 a tiled house.

瓦 松 roof-pines.

瓦 桁 the concave channels of a tiled roof.

¹⁰瓦 棺 an earthenware coffin, said to have been used in the days of *Yao* and *Shun.*

瓦 溝 the channels between the rows of tiles on a roof.

瓦 片ₙ broken tiles.

瓦 盤 a glazed earthenware dish.

瓦 硯 inkslabs made from ancient tiles.

¹⁵瓦 磚 tiles and brick.

瓦 礫 potsherds; broken pottery and tiling.

瓦 窯 a kiln where tiles are made.

瓦 稜·子 ribbed shells.

瓦 缶 earthenware in general.

²⁰瓦 罐·子 an earthen jar. or -兒

瓦 背 a tiled roof.

瓦 苔 moss on the tiles.

瓦 裂 broken like a tile.

瓦 解 棋 分 collapse and dismemberment—like loosened tiles, and like players dividing the chessmen between them.

²⁵瓦 解 冰 消 the tiles are broken and the ice is melted— the glory is departed.

勢 必 瓦 解 there will surely be a collapse.

土 崩 瓦 解 disturbances of the earth and collapse of the tiles—a collapse without resistance; upheaval of the masses and factions of the classes.

瓦 釜 雷 鳴 an earthen pot sounding like thunder—an unworthy man in a high position.

瓦 隴 the concave channels of a tiled roof.

³⁰瓦 面 a roof.

瓦 頂 a tiled roof.

瓦 鱗 overlapping tiles, like scales.

車 瓦 a tire.

WA. (ㄨㄚ)

(Uah)

挖 1.5. To scoop out; to dig out; to gouge.
6999

挖 井 to dig a well.
挖·出·來 to scoop out.
挖·刻 人 語 sarcastic ridicule.

挖 刻 to dig out; to excavate.
⁵挖 塜 to rifle tombs.
挖 塾 (carved) in relief.
挖 心 兒·的 concave; hollow in the middle.
挖 斷 路 to break up and destroy the road—as a retreating army.
挖 河 機·器 a dredging apparatus.
¹⁰挖 洞 to dig a hole; to dig through.
挖 煤 to mine for coal.
挖 眼·睛 to gouge out the eyes.
挖·苦 人 (or 窩 or 酷)to ridicule, often sarcastically or in disguise.
挖 窟·窿 to make a hole; to dig out a hole.
¹⁵挖·耳 to pick the ears; an earpick.
挖·補 to cut out a word and paste a new piece of paper over the erasure.
挖 金 砂 to dig gold dust.
挖 門·子 or 買 門 路 to take a bribe; to bribe.

襪
襪 4.5.
韈
韤
7000
} Stockings; socks.

襪 作 or 製 襪 廠 a factory where stockings are made.
襪·子 stockings or socks.
襪·子 筒 the leg of a stocking, often used as a pocket.
襪 帶 garters.
⁵一 雙 襪·子 a pair of stockings or socks.
夾²襪·子 lined socks.
布 襪·子 calico socks.
棉 襪·子 wadded socks.
絲 襪·子 silk stockings.

WAI. (ㄨㄞ)

(Uai)

外 4 Outside; beyond. Foreign; barbarous. Extraordinary.
7001

外 丹 a pill of immortality.
外 交 foreign relations or intercourse.
外 交 事 務 員 a diplomatic agent.
外 交 事 宜 foreign affairs.
⁵外 交 團 the diplomatic corps.
外 交 家 diplomats.
外 交 手 腕 diplomacy; diplomatic procedure.
外 交 手 續 diplomatic procedure.
外 交 政 策 foreign policy.
¹⁰外 交 方 法 diplomatic methods.
外 交 機 關 diplomatic organ.
外 交 界 diplomatic circles.
外 交 緊 急 urgent state of foreign affairs.
外 交 部 Ministry of Foreign Affairs.　　Affairs.
¹⁵外 交 部 長 Minister of Foreign
外·人 an outsider; an alien; people of a different clan.
外 人 干 涉 foreign interference.
外 任 a provincial appointment.
外 來 物 體 foreign bodies, as in the ear or eye, etc.
²⁰外 侮 foreign aggression.
外 傳 biographical records not included in the histories.
外 債 foreign loans.
外 債 條 例 conditions relating to foreign loans.
外 僑 foreign settlers; aliens.
²⁵外 兄 弟 cousins; sons of one's father's sisters.
外 出·息 tips; perquisites.
外 分 to divide externally. (geometry).
外 切 to touch externally. (geometry).
外 力 external force.
³⁰外 務 outside affairs; foreign affairs and relations; misdoings.
外 務 大·臣 former title of the Secretary of State for Foreign Affairs.
外 務 署 a Foreign Office.
外 務 部 the Foreign Office.
外 勤 outdoor service, as in the Customs.

³⁵外 匯 兌 foreign exchange.
外 匯 票 foreign bill of exchange.
外 口 an outport.
外 史 romances; histories with a more or less fictitious basis; a pseudonym often used by writers.
外·國 a foreign country; foreign countries. 外·國 人 foreigners.
⁴⁰外·國 公 使 a Foreign Minister.
外·國 化·的 foreignized.
外·國 法 人 a foreign juridical person. (legal).
外·國 義 勇 隊 the Foreign Legion.
外·國 話 a foreign language; foreign languages.
⁴⁵外 城 the outer or Chinese city of Peking, under the Manchus.
外 埠 an outport.
外 報 the foreign press.
外 境 environs; precincts.
外 大 父 maternal grandfather.
⁵⁰外 套 an overcoat.
外 姑 wife's mother.
外 姓 of a different surname.
外 委 former term for a sergeant or corporal.
外 姪 a wife's nephew.
⁵⁵外 婆 one's mother's mother.
外 婦 a kept mistress.
外 姻 connections by marriage.
外 子³a term once used by a woman for her husband; an illegitimate son.
外·孫 a daughter's son.
⁶⁰外·孫 女 a daughter's daughter.
外 客 a traveller; a stranger.
外 家 the mother's family; a separate establishment for a kept mistress.
外 寇 foreign bandits; the enemy; foreign aggression.
外 導 劑 injections; enemata.
⁶⁵外 平 分 to bisect externally. (geometry).
外 府 former term for a Prefecture other than that situated at the Provincial capital.
外 強 中 乾 outwardly flourishing, inwardly dried up—outward show.
外 待 人 to treat as an outsider.
外 征 a punitive expedition to foreign countries.
⁷⁰外 後 日 three days hence.
外 心 unfaithfulness; inconstancy; estrangement.

外快 extras; perquisites.

外患 trouble coming from without, as a foreign invasion, etc.

外感 external influences; a cold; catarrh.

75 外戚 the families of the mother or the wife of the sovereign.

外戶 a door which opens from the outside.

外披羊皮內藏狼心 a wolf in sheep's clothing.

外抵抗 external resistance.

外援 foreign aid; reinforcements from without or from abroad.

80 外揚 to divulge; to spread a matter abroad.

外攻內效 counter-irritation.

外教 a religion which is foreign to the Chinese; not versed in; unskilled.

外教人 people outside the church; men of the *world*.

外敷藥 fomentations; external applications.

85 專爲外敷 for external application only.

外方 remote places; foreign parts.

外服 foreign dress.

外此爲彼 to abandon one cause for another.

外氏 the mother's family.

90 外氣 ceremony; ceremonious language; unfriendly manner.

外水 extras; perquisites.

外江人 people from beyond the river; a stranger; used by Cantonese for those from other provinces.

外洋 the ocean; the open sea; foreign parts; abroad.

外父 an adopted father.

95 外物 a foreign body, as in the ear or the eye.

外甥 a sister's son.

外甥女 a niece of a different surname.

外用 for external application.

外界 environment; external relations.

100 外界物 external objects.

外界觀察 external observation.

外痔 external piles.

外症 external diseases; unusual complaints.

外省 another province; belonging to another province.

---

105 外祖爹娘 or 外祖父母 grandparents on the mother's side.

外科 surgery.

外科器具 surgical instruments.

外科醫生 a surgeon.

外籍囚人 foreign prisoners in the gaols—Shanghai.

110 外緣 external causes; external influences.

外翁 mother's father.

外耳 the external ear.

外腎 the testicles.

外臣 term used by a statesman of himself in addressing those of another State—in the feudal period.

115 外舅 father of one's wife.

外舵 starboard the helm.

外艱 the death of one's father or grandfather.

外蒙古 Outer Mongolia.

外虛 the penumbra.

120 外號 a nickname.

外行 (*hang*[2]) a raw hand; unskilled; an outsider; one outside the trade.

外行星 the outer planets.

外表 the surface; manifestation; superficial.

外表上 superficial; externally; on the outside.

125 外表兄 a cousin of a different surname.

外褂 an outer coat.

外觀 the external aspects of a thing.

外角[3] external angles. (*geometry*).

外註 marginal notes or comments.

130 外話 slang.

外證 external evidence.

外貌 the external appearance; the exterior aspect.

外財 illegitimate gain; adventitious wealth; a windfall.

外貨之攘奪 the encroachment of foreign goods.

135 外路人 an outsider.

外遇 to live as man and wife in illicit connection; a paramour.

外道 ceremony; ceremoniousness; unfriendly manner.

外邊 outside; the outer surface.

外邦 foreign nations, as compared with China; the heathen nations—as Gentiles compared with the Jews, in translations.

---

140 外邪 all noxious influences from without the body, which are calculated to do injury to a man.

外鄉 a different district; a person belonging to a different district.

外野 the country; uninhabited places.

外長[3] abbrev. for 外交部長[3].

外面 the outer surface; outside.

145 外項 extreme ratio. (*arith.*).

外頭 outside; the outer surface.

外馬 a courier.

外體 a foreign body; a foreign element or substance.

中外 Chinese and foreign.

150 以外 except; apart from; save, etc.

內外 internal and external; domestic and foreign.

出外 to go abroad, or outside.

對外政策 foreign policy.

山外 ultramontane.

155 意外 beyond expectations; accidents.

方外 Buddhistic or Taoistic priests.

格外 extra; beyond measure; extraordinary; specially.

此外 besides this; apart from this.

海外領土 foreign possessions.

160 置之度外 leave it out of the calculation.

門外 out of doors.

歪[1] Aslant; askew; awry; from which comes the meaning:— 7002 depraved.

歪嘴 a wry mouth.

歪心 a heart not upright.

歪念頭 depraved thoughts.

歪戴帽子 to wear the hat awry.

5 歪扭 crooked; awry.

歪纏 illicit entanglements.

歪着 awry; slanting.

歪脖子 a crooked neck; a drunken person.

歪話 preposterous talk.

10 歪頭 a wry neck.

晌午歪了 the shadow on the dial is past noon. (*shang*[3]·*huo*-)

東倒[3]西歪 tumbling about like a drunken man; all awry; in disorder.

巍[1] Mountainous; precipitous.
7003

WAN. (ㄨㄢ)
(Uan)

丸 ² A pill; a pellet; a small ball; a bullet.
7004 Distinguish 凡 No. 1771.

丸藥 pills.
吞丸 to swallow a pill.
和丸 to compound pills. (*huo⁴-*)
弄丸 to juggle with balls.
彈丸之地 a very small piece of land.
搓丸 to roll into pills.
藥丸 medicinal pills.

汍 ² To shed tears.
7005

汍瀾 copious weeping.

紈 ² White silk. White. Also read *huan²*.
7006

紈扇 silk fans or screens.
紈素 fine, thin white silk.
紈袴子弟 fellows with white silken breeches—fops.
冰紈 silk of close, smooth texture.

刓 ² To round off; to trim.
7007

刓角 to round off the corners.

完 ² To finish; to complete; completed. Whole; unbroken.
7008

完·了 done; ended; finished.
完事 to bring a matter to an end.
完人 a complete man—perfect in all respects.
完·備 complete; all ready; fully prepared.
⁵完備·的 elaborately; completely.
完·全 perfect; entire; complete.
完全主權 complete sovereignty.
完全平方 a perfect square. (*math.*)
完全建設 perfect reconstruction.
¹⁰完全數 a whole number. (*arith.*)
完全變態 a complete metamorphosis—as of an insect.

完全獨立 complete autonomy.
完全發達 completely developed.
完全科 a complete course.
¹⁵完全解決 brought to a satisfactory settlement.
完全負責 to undertake full responsibility.
完全花 a perfect flower.
完具 complete; whole.
完卵 unbroken eggs—by analogy, things difficult to preserve intact.
²⁰完善 excellent; efficient.
完固 well-made and strong.
完好 excellent.
完好無損 in good order and condition.
完婚 or 完娶 or 完姻 or 完姻 to consummate a marriage.
²⁵完工 to finish work; to complete a job.
完成 finished; completed.
完整全備 all perfectly arranged.
完案 to bring a case to a conclusion.
完滿 to culminate; to end.
³⁰完璧歸趙 return the unbroken jewel to *Chao*—used of returning things to the owner; to repay debts in full, etc.
完畢 to finish up; completed.
完竣 finished.
完節 to maintain one's integrity.
完結 finished; completed.
³⁵完美 exquisite; perfect.
完美司法 the perfection of justice.
完美結果 perfect results.
完聚 to reassemble—as a family; to bring together—those who are parted.
完計 a perfect plan or stratagem.
⁴⁰完訖 finished; completed.

(a) To settle. To pay, as taxes.

完數 to settle an account.
完清 all squared.
完稅 to pay taxes or duty.
完糧 to pay the land-tax.
⁵完納 to pay, as taxes.
完足 paid in full.
完過 payment has been made.
完餉 to pay taxes or duty.

(b) To repair.

使舜完廩 set *Shun* to repair the granary.

玩 ² To amuse oneself with. To find pleasure in. To play with. To play. Toys; trinkets. To trifle with. To dawdle.
7009

玩世 to despise things in general.
玩之無盡 the enjoyment is unending.
玩人喪德 by trifling with men he loses his virtue. *See below* —20.
玩兒 to play about, as a child.
⁵不是玩兒·的 it is no child's play.
玩具 toys.
玩器 toys; things that are prized.
玩好 to enjoy a thing; to play with.
玩延 to delay.
¹⁰玩弄 to toy with; to romp.
玩意兒 toys; playthings.
玩愒 to neglect one's duty for pleasure; to fritter away one's time.
玩日 to fritter away the time.
玩景 to enjoy the scenery.
¹⁵玩月 to enjoy the moonlight.
玩杠·子 to perform on the horizontal bar.
玩泄 to dawdle.
玩法 to trifle with the law.
玩物 toys; things to be prized.
²⁰玩物喪志 by trifling with curios. etc., he wastes his energies. *See above*—3.
玩狎 to toy with; dalliance, as with a woman.
玩生 to become careless in one's business.
玩笑 to joke; to jest.
玩耍 to dally with; to trifle; to tempt; to play.
²⁵玩藝 toys; playthings.
玩戲 to toy with; to romp.
玩話 jesting; to joke.
玩賞 to find pleasure in; to enjoy, as flowers, pictures, etc.
玩·頭 amusements; entertainments.
古玩 curios; antiques.

(a) To examine. To test.

玩味 to test the flavour of; to get the taste of—as a fine piece of literature.
玩索 to turn over and over in one's mind; to ponder, as abstruse doctrines.

玩索而有得焉 has explored it with delight till he has apprehended it—the teachings of the *Doctrine of the Mean* 中庸.
細玩 to examine with care.

頑[2] Obstinate; wayward; stupid. Corrupt; greedy; covetous. Bigoted.
7010

頑健 I am in good health—conventional term.
頑兒[2] a stupid son; my stupid son.
頑劣 good for nothing.
頑·固 obstinate; reactionary; cantankerous.
[5]**頑·固家** reactionaries.
頑·固黨 the Reactionary Party.
頑夫廉懦夫有立志 the corrupt became pure, the weak acquired determination.
頑悍 overbearing.
頑戶 an obstinate person; a rogue.
[10]**頑抗** perverse; obstinate; cantankerous.
頑昧 dull; stupid.
頑梗 obstinate; perverse.
頑民 the stupid people—the masses.
頑疲 perverse; obstinate; mischievous, as a child.
[15]**頑癬** a kind of ringworm.
頑皮 perverse and obstinate; mischievous, as a child.
頑石 a mere block of stone.
頑石點頭[2] even the stones nodded their heads—when *Shêng Kung,* 生公, preached.
頑福 fortune in spite of incapacity.
[20]**頑軀** my clumsy person—conventional reply to inquiries about one's health. *See above* —1.
頑鄙 dull and vulgar.
頑童 a stupid, obstinate youth.
頑鈍 stupid and dull; obtuse.
頑頓 stupid and dull; obtuse.

(a) u.f. 玩 No. 7009. To play, etc.

頑耍 to sport with; to romp.
頑戲 to play; to dally, as with a woman.

翫[4] To play with.
Inter. 玩 No. 7009.
7011

翫愒 to trifle away one's time.

婉[3] Complaisant; agreeable.
7012

婉婉聽從 obligingly consenting.
婉順 accommodating; kind.

(a) Read *mien*[3] or *wên*[4]. To give birth to a child. *See* 兔 No. 4492—B. and 娩 No. 4496.

婉息 to bring forth and care for children.
分婉 parturition.

挽[3] To draw back; to restore. To pull; to seize.
7013

挽以上車之索 a rope for pulling a person up into a cart.
挽住 to hold back.
挽回 to bring back—as a past state of affairs.
挽回不得 cannot be restored—to what it was before.
[5]**挽回主權** to recover sovereign rights.
挽回利權 to recover lost privileges; to restore economic rights.
挽回大局 to restore the general conditions.
挽回天意 to bring back the favour of Heaven.
挽回惡俗 to reform degenerate customs.
[10]**挽對** scrolls written and sent to a funeral in memory of a friend, etc. Usually with 7015.
挽強 to pull with force—as a bow.
挽手同行 to walk hand in hand.
挽扶 to support; to lead to.
挽救 to save from disaster; to rescue.
[15]**挽柩** to bear a coffin; to act as a pall-bearer.
挽歌 funeral dirges.
挽留 to detain; to hold back; to keep—as a friend.
挽聯 scrolls written in memory of a friend and sent to his funeral. Usually with 7015.
挽舟逆水 to pull a boat against the stream.
[20]**挽袖** to roll up the sleeves.
挽詞 elegies written in memory of a friend.

挽邀 to persuade; to induce.
挽頸 to throw the arms around a person's neck.
挽頹風 to reform degenerate manners.
[25]**挽髻** to do the hair up into a knot; to dress the hair.

晚[3] Evening; late; from which comes:—late in life; a junior.
7014

晚·上 the evening.
晚世 modern times.
晚·了 it is late; behindhand.
晚來一天 came a day late.
[5]**晚去一時** to delay departure for a moment.
晚吹 the evening breeze.
晚夕 the evening.
晚婚 to marry late in life—as a widow re-marrying.
晚學 to be fond of study in old age; to commence one's studies comparatively late; your pupil.
[10]**晚宴** an evening banquet.
晚年 old; late in life.
晚弟 a junior; your pupil or servant—a term for "I."
晚影拖長 the evening shadows lengthen.
晚成 to achieve success comparatively late in life.
[15]**晚暮** late; behind the times.
晚歲 old age; a late harvest.
晚燒晴 a promising evening for a fair day.
晚生 a junior; your pupil or servant—a term for "I."
晚福 happiness in one's closing years.
[20]**晚禾** a late crop; a second crop.
晚節 old age; to maintain one's integrity in later life.
晚翠 plants which keep green until late in the year.
晚蠶 late silkworms.
晚艷 a name for the chrysanthemum.
[25]**晚起** to get up late.
晚輩 a younger generation.
晚近 lately; recently.
晚造 late crops.
晚進 a recent arrival; one who has lately come forward.
[30]**晚運** good fortune in later life.
晚達 to reach official position late in one's life.
晚間 the evening.

晚食當肉 to eat late—when hungry—is as good as having delicacies.

晚飯 the evening meal, supper.

35 晚餐 the evening meal; the Lord's Supper.

晚香玉 Polianthus tuberosa.

下晚 evening.

不晚 it is not late; there is yet time.

今晚 this evening.

40 來的晚 came late.

傍 (pang¹) 晚 towards evening.

悔之晚矣 it is too late to repent.

明晚 tomorrow evening.

昨晚 yesterday evening

輓 ³ **To draw a hearse; to pull a wheel-chair.**
7015

輓祝 or 輓聯 or 祭輓 scrolls sent on the occasion of the funeral of a friend or relative.

輓詩 a funeral ode; an elegy.

推輓其舟而過 pushed and pulled his boat across.

宛 ³ **To yield. Courteous; obliging.**
7016 Also read yüan³.

宛其死矣 "you will drop off in death."

宛在水中央 And lo! he is right in the midst of the water.

宛如 apparently; seemingly; as it were.

宛妙 soft and pleasing—as a voice; insinuating and graceful; plausible.

5 宛宛 graceful—as bamboos or hanging clusters of blossoms; bent; crooked; winding.

宛延 winding; crooked.

宛然 as a matter of course; as if; the same as; according to; still.

宛然左辟 he politely stands aside to the left.

宛若 as if; very like;- still; according to; wives of brothers.

10 宛虹 a dragon; a winding river.

宛轉 yielding; plausible; specious; persuasive; at length.

宛轉如循環 to come to the same point again, as if moving in a circle.

宛邱 ancient name for part of 淮陽縣 in Honan.

(a) Read yüan¹. Small.

宛彼鳴鳩 small is that cooing dove

(b) Read yüan¹. See below.

大宛國 the kingdom of Ferghana—the modern Khokand.

宛馬 horses from the above place —it was famous for its horses.

剜 ¹ **To cut; to cut out; to pick out; to scoop out.**
7017

剜·出·來 pluck it out.

剜削 to pare.

剜割 to cut out.

剜地 to dig; to hoe.

5 剜心待人 to treat people as if one was willing to pluck open one's heart for them.

剜眼 to gouge out the eyes.

剜眼剜皮·的 savagely; brutally.

剜肉補瘡 to cut out a piece of flesh in order to patch up a sore on another part of the body—a foolish proceeding; a makeshift which does not deal with the real trouble.

剜補 to cut out and patch in a piece, as in altering manuscript, etc.

10 剜菜 to cut up vegetables by the root.

剜骨上的肉 to cut away the flesh from the bones.

彫剜 to carve or engrave.

肉上剜瘡 to wound oneself; to give oneself useless trouble.

婉 ³ **Pleasant; agreeable; genial; kindly disposed.**
7018 Inter. 婉 No. 7012.

婉勸 to exhort; to try and make peace.

婉女 a complaisant, yielding woman.

婉婉聽從 pleasant and submissive in speech and manner—said of a wife.

婉婉 flattering; complaisant; the appearance of a flying dragon.

5 婉容 a pleasant countenance.

婉愉 genial and happy.

婉求 entreaties.

婉淑 winning and virtuous; lovable.

婉示 your kind, condescending instructions.

10 婉約 insinuating and plausible, yet clear and perspicuous—said of speech.

婉縟 elegance of style—in writing.

婉言 entreaties.

婉轉 plausible; specious; persuasive; to be agreeable and accommodating; embarrassments.

婉順 to condescend to; agreeable; obliging and accommodating.

(a) Read yüan³. Beautiful; lovely.

婉孌 young and delicate.

清揚婉兮 "Lovely, with clear eyes and fine forehead."

帵 ¹ **Remnants; tailor's cuttings.**
7019

惋 ⁴ **Alarmed; startled; surprised; disappointed.**
7020 Also read yüan⁴.

惋傷 alarmed and distressed.

惋恨 to be angry at.

惋惜 grieved; disappointed; lamentable.

惋悽 sad; pathetic.

惋歎 grieved and sighing.

捥 ³·⁴· **To bend the wrist. Inter. 腕 No. 7023.**
7021

碗 ³
盌
椀 **A bowl; a basin; a cup; a dish.**
7022

碗口 the mouth of a basin or cup.

碗口大·的 as large as the mouth of a bowl.

碗·子青 acorn-black.

碗盞杯盆 crockery-ware.

5 一碗飯 a bowl of rice.

中碗 a medium-sized bowl.

大碗 a large bowl.

海碗 a large bowl such as is used for serving soup, etc.

湯碗 a bowl for soup, etc.

10 火碗 a bowl with a heater to keep the food hot.

破碗 to break a bowl—a form of oath.

金碗 a golden bowl.

鋸碗 to mend a bowl, etc., by rivetting and clamping.

飯碗 a rice-bowl. *See* No. 1787-4, 5.

腕
臂 7023 [4] The wrist. A flexible joint.

腕力 strength of wrist—vigour of penmanship; capacity, ability.

腕子 or 手腕儿 the wrist.

腕筋 the muscles of the forearm.

腕闌 ancient form of bracelet.

腕骨 the bones of the wrist.

扼腕 to clasp the hands.

菀 7024 [3] Luxuriance of growth. Also read *yüan*[4], *yü*[4].

菀彼柳斯 luxuriant grow those willows.

菀結 firm; strong.

有菀者柳 there is a luxuriant willow-tree.

蜿 7025 [1] To creep—as plants. The wriggling movements of a snake. The stealthy approach of an animal. Also read *yüan*[1].

蜿蜿 the undulatory motion of a dragon.

蜿蜒 tortuous; the wriggling motion of a snake; undulating, as hills; to wind around and climb, as a parasitic plant.

蜿壇 a name for the earthworm.

蜿蟬 coiling around.

豌 7026 [1] The garden pea.

綰 7027 [3.4.] To string together; to bind up, as the hair.

綰攝 to unite and assist.

綰結印綬 to attach the cord to the official seal—to take office.

綰臂雙金環 placed two golden bracelets on the arms.

(a) To seize.

綰去舟 seized his departing boat.

(b) To hate. Crimson.

彎 7028 [1] To bend. Bent; curved.

彎不過來 cannot bend it—as a finger, etc.

彎尺 a carpenter's square.

彎屈 curved; crooked.

彎弓 to bend a bow.

彎曲曲的 winding; serpentine; tortuous.

彎脚規 calipers.

彎腰 to stoop.

彎蛾 arched eyebrows.

拐彎儿 to turn a corner; indirectly.

轉彎 to turn a corner; indirectly.

灣 7029 [1] A bay; a cove; a curved shore; a bend, as in a river. Inter. preceding.

灣子 a bend, as in a river; a cove.

灣曲 winding; tortuous.

灣泊 to anchor.

灣船 to anchor; to make fast by the bank.

萬
万 7030 [4] Ten thousand. Large numbers. All.

萬一 in case; 10,000 to 1; if by any chance.

萬一他死了 if he should die.

萬世一系 an unbroken line for many generations.

萬世不易 has never changed through the ages; unchanging.

萬世萬代 for all generations; throughout all ages.

萬主之主 Lord of Lords.

萬乘之公相 "the many charioted territory of a duke." *Giles.*

萬事休 all things are ceased—at death.

萬人塚 the graves on a battle-field.

萬倍 ten thousand-fold.

萬全 perfect; complete.

萬全之計 a perfect scheme; a safe plan.

萬分 in the greatest degree.

萬分之一 10,000 to 1; a very small percentage.

萬千 myriads; a vast number.

萬古 antiquity.

萬古之先 before all things; from eternity. 〔=國際

萬國 all nations; international.

萬國九洲 all countries; the world.

萬國公法 International Law.

萬國公海 the high seas.

萬國共通的 internationally.

萬國勞動會 International Working Men's Association.

萬國史 universal history.

萬國改良會 International Reform Association.

萬國標準時 International Standard Time.

萬國權度通制 International Standard Weights and Measures—The Metric System.

萬國職工協會 International Working Men's Association.

萬國船舶信號 International Code of Signals.

萬國著作權 International Copyright.

萬國郵政同盟 International Postal Congress.

萬國郵會 International Postal Union.

萬國體育協會 World Athletic Association.

萬壽 the emperor's birthday.

萬夫有罪在余一人 "if the people are guilty, I alone am to blame."

萬姓 everybody; the community.

萬安 perfectly safe; perfect peace.

萬幸 a myriad felicities—very fortunate.

萬年青 a small evergreen plant of the lily family which produces a cluster of red berries—*Rhodea japonica.*

萬幾 (or 機) a myriad hidden causes of action—the rule of the emperor.

萬惡之萬能藥 a panacea for all ills.

萬惡滔天 a myriad evils mount to heaven—outrageously wicked.

萬 變 a myriad mutations.

萬 方 all places; everywhere; in every way; by every means.

45 萬 有 all creation; universal.

萬 有 之 上 above all things.

萬 有 之 主 Lord over all.

萬 有 之 首 Head of all creation.

萬 有 在 神 論 pantheism.

50 萬 有 引 力 universal gravitation.

萬 望 anxiously expecting; to long for.

萬 歲 "Long-live...." *Banzai*.

萬 歲 爺 or 萬 萬 歲 the emperor.

萬 歲 牌 the imperial tablet.

55 萬 死 一 生 only one chance in ten thousand of preserving the life.

萬 殊 一 本 all things are different, but they have a common origin.

萬 民 all people; the masses.

萬 民 傘 an umbrella given by the people to a popular official, or to some public benefactor.

萬 民 衣 the clothing given by the people to a popular official when he leaves the district.

60 萬 物 all things; all creation.

萬 物 之 母 the mother of all things.

萬 牲 園 zoological gardens.

萬 狀 a myriad shapes; all sorts of....

萬 王 之 王 King of Kings.

65 萬 目 一 的 all have one object in view.

萬 衆 一 心 all of one heart.

萬 福 every blessing; a woman's bow.

萬 籟 俱 寂 all sounds are hushed.

萬 能 all-powerful.

70 萬 般 all kinds; miscellaneous.

萬 化 筒 a kaleidoscope.

萬 萬 ten thousand times ten thousand; innumerable.

萬 邦 all nations.

萬 里 a great distance—the Great Wall.

75 萬 里 長 城 The Great Wall.

萬 金 買 鄰 it takes ten thousand taels of gold to purchase a (good) neighbour.

萬 靈 all spirits.

百 萬 a million.

千 萬 ten million; by all means.

(a) Used before negatives as an intensive particle.

萬 不 及 — unequalled; unsurpassed.

萬 不 可 must not on any account; under no circumstances.

萬 不 得 巳 if you absolutely can not help it.

萬 不 肯 positively unwilling.

5 萬 不 能 utterly unable.

萬 勿 復 言 on no account return answer.

萬 勿 推 辭 on no account refuse.

萬 無 一 失 or 萬 不 失 一 not the least mistake; absolutely certain.

萬 無 此 理 there is no such principle.

(b) A term used for certain ancient dances with shield and battle-axe.

萬 舞 洋 洋 the various dances all complete.

萑[2] A grass used for making mats. Also read *huan*[2].
7031

萑 葦 reeds; rushes.

(a) Name of a place famous for robbers.

萑 苻 風 戢 *Huan-p'u* (i.e., robbers) has been exterminated.

卍[4] A mystic Buddhist emblem, the Swastika. Used
7032 for 萬 No. 7030; said to have been given the sound of *wan* because all good fortune and virtue was embodied in it; turned in the opposite direction to the Nazi swastika.

卍 字 不 到 頭 a name for an ornamental pattern formed on the basis of this character.

卍 字 欄·杆 a balustrade with lattice worked into this pattern.

卍 字 菓 a name for the *Hovenia dulcis*.

卍 字 錦 ornamentation on silk goods, etc., in the form of this character.

如 來 從 胸 卍 字 涌 出 寶 光 from the swastika symbol on the breast of *Ju lai* (Buddha) issued a precious ray of light.

WANG. (ㄨㄤ)

(Uang)

尢 尣[1]
7033

Lame. The first form is Radical 43, also used as the National Phonetic final for *-ang* Distinguish No. 7511.

亡 込[2]
7034

To die; to perish; to be lost; to go away; absent or escaped.

亡 不 可 復 見 gone, never to be seen again—dead.

亡 人 a fugitive; an exile.

亡 人 得 土 如 得 金 earth is to the dead what gold is to the living—referring to burial.

未 亡 人 I, who have not died —i.e., I, the widow.

5 亡 兄 亡 弟 my deceased elder and younger brothers, respectively.

亡 友 a deceased friend.

亡 命 to abscond; to change one's name and flee from justice; to put forth every effort.

亡 命 之 徒 a ruffian; a desperado.

亡 國 奴 a person without a country.

10 亡 國 敗 家 destruction of the State and ruin of families.

亡 夫 a deceased husband.

亡 失 lost; gone.

亡 妹 my deceased sister.

亡 戟 得 矛 to lose a halberd and gain a lance—the gain equals the loss.

15 亡 故 dead; perished.

亡 沒 or 死 亡 dead; perished.

亡 種 race extinction.

亡 羊 a lost or stray sheep.

亡 羊 得 牛 to lose a sheep and get an ox—the gain is greater than the loss.

20 亡 羊 補 牢 未 爲 遲 也 it is not too late to repair the fold after the sheep has strayed— it is never too late to mend.

亡 過 died.

亡 靈 deserted—as a dwelling.

亡 魂 a disembodied spirit.

不 知 其 亡 也 they are gone and you do not know it.

²⁵出亡 to become a fugitive.

孔子³時其亡也 Confucius chose a time when he was not at home—to go and pay his respects.

流亡 fugitive.

父母雙亡 both parents are dead.

逆天者亡 they who rebel against Heaven perish.

³⁰陣亡 to die in battle; killed in action.

(a) u.f. 忘 No. 7036. To forget.

曷維其亡 How can—the sorrow of my heart—be forgotten?

有所遺亡 there is something I have forgotten.

(b) Read *wu²*. Not; without. Used like 無 No. 7180.

亡何 in a little while.

亡奈 there is no alternative.

亡幾 in a little while.

亡慮 or 無慮 a general scheme in which details are ignored; the general scope of the affair may be known without consideration; about.

⁵亡慮萬二千人 about 12,000 men.

亡是公 Mr. Nobody—a term for an imaginary person in fiction.

亡狀 lacking in propriety.

亡而爲有 to have nothing while professing to have plenty.

亡親戚君臣上下 to disown parents and relatives, and the relations of sovereign and minister, superiors and inferiors.

(Mencius).

妄 ⁴ False; absurd. Foolish; wild; incoherent. Reckless; disorderly.
7035

妄事推測 to make predictions recklessly.

妄人 an abandoned, incorrigible person.

妄作妄爲 unseemly behaviour.

妄作見證 to bear false witness.

⁵妄冒 falsely to assume the name of.

妄動 to rush headlong; to act without due consideration.

妄取 to misappropriate; to squeeze.

妄告 to make a false accusation.

妄對 to answer at random.

¹⁰妄想 vain hopes; fantasy; illusion; to indulge in vain hopes.

妄控 to accuse falsely.

妄斷 to come to a wrong decision; to jump to conclusions.

妄歸其因 foolishly traces its source to....

妄殺 to give no quarter.

¹⁵妄測 to jump to a conclusion.

妄爲 unseemly behaviour.

妄用 to abuse; to misuse.

妄自尊大 self-opinionated; to boast oneself.

妄自賭咒 to make a reckless vow.

²⁰妄言 a lie; to lie.

妄評 rash criticisms.

妄語 wild statements; deliberate lies.

妄語虛詞 false and hollow statements.

妄論 reckless reasoning; illogical reasoning.

²⁵妄談 vain and foolish talk.

妄誕 wild, fabulous stories.

妄證 false witness; perjury.

妄議 reckless proposals.

妄費 waste; unregulated expenditure.

³⁰妄追 a wrongful claim.

忘 ⁴,² To forget; to be unmindful of; to neglect.
7036

忘·不下 I shall not forget it.

忘·不了³ impossible to forget; certain.

忘·了 forgotten.

忘²·八 a term of abuse, i.e., one who forgets the eight cardinal virtues of filial piety, brotherly submission, loyalty, sincerity, propriety, righteousness, modesty and a sense of shame 孝弟忠信禮義廉恥—an utter reprobate.

⁵忘²·八蛋 or 忘²·八羔·子 *from the above*; understood as "spawn of a turtle," i.e., misbegotten; the Chinese believe that the turtle or tortoise does not beget its own offspring—it is a term of vulgar abuse.

忘其所以 he forgets himself—in his elation.

忘勞 to forget one's toil in the interest of one's pursuits.

忘却 to forget.

忘君事讎 to forget one's prince and serve his enemies.

¹⁰忘·失 to forget. (*S. dial.*)

忘年 a friendship in which the difference in years is forgotten.

忘形 to forget one's own form.

忘形交 a friendship in which the physical existence can be forgotten, or in which all outward ceremony of physical existence can be ignored.

忘恩負義 ungrateful; reprobate.

¹⁵忘情 to forget old kindnesses, past affection, old times, etc.

忘憂 to forget care and sorrow—a name for alcoholic drinks.

忘懷 forgetful; having a bad memory.

忘本 to forget the source of good; to forget one's parents; to be ungrateful.

忘機 at peace with the world, without any schemes or plans in the mind.

²⁰忘沒 to consign to oblivion.

忘神 absent-minded.

忘·記 to forget; forgotten.

忘食 to forget to eat—from preoccupation.

健忘 a poor memory.

²⁵坐忘 to sit in abstraction.

遺忘 fallen into oblivion.

王 ² A prince or king. A ruler. Royal.
7037

王事 affairs of State—under a monarchy.

王事適我 the business of the king comes upon me.

王位 the throne or rank of a king.

王佐 a minister of State.

⁵王侯 princes and earls—nobility.

王·八 a term of abuse—misbegotten. *See* 忘 No. 7036-4.

王公 princes and dukes—nobility.

王制 royal regulations.

王化 the civilizing influences—as of government.

¹⁰王化所不及 beyond the reach of civilization.

王命 royal authority—power of life and death.

王 國 a kingdom.

王 城 the capital of a tributary State.

王 妃 the concubine of a prince.

15 王 子 a prince.

王 孫 descendants of a prince; a kind of ape.

王 孫 公 子 the nobility; the aristocracy.

王 宮 the royal palace.

王 室 the royal family; the State under a monarch.

20 王 府 a royal palace.

王 度 the bearing and virtue of a king.

王 族 the royal line.

王 春 the first month of the lunar year.

王 杖 a sceptre.

25 王 業 royal rule or sway.

王 母 a term of respect for one's grandmother.

王 水 *aqua regia*.

王 法 the law of the land—as a monarchy.

王 法 無 親 the law is no respecter of persons.

30 沒 有 王 法 lawless.

王 父 term of respect for one's grandfather.

王·爺 title of a river-god; prince.

王·瓜 = 黃·瓜 the cucumber.

王 章 royal regulations.

35 王 考 my deceased grandfather or father.

王 者 香 fragrance fit for a king —a name for the 蘭 花 or *Epidendrum*.

王 聖 轉 論 a Buddhist term for a universal and holy monarch.

王 蛇 the king of serpents—a boa-constrictor or python.

王 言 the word of a king.

40 王 道 the royal road; the perfect way of the ancient kings; the way of right as opposed to the way of might; a regard for the general welfare of all.

王 陵 or 皇 陵 imperial tombs.

先 王 the ancient kings.

明 王 a wise sovereign.

番 王 Mongol princes.

45 議 政 王 a Prince Regent.

(a) Read *wang⁴*. **To rule. To govern.**

王 天 下 to rule over the empire.

王 此 大 邦 to rule over this great country.

(b) Read *wang³*. **To go to.**

下 民 之 王 the resort of the masses.

及 爾 出 王 (Heaven) is with you in all your goings.

尫
尩 }¹ **Weak. A rickety person. Emaciated.**
7038

尫 羸 out of condition—as a horse.

尫 纖 弱 懦 puny and weak.

天 久 不 雨 吾 欲 暴 (*p'u³*) 尫 Heaven has not sent down rain for a long time; I wish to expose an emaciated person in the sun—to move Heaven to pity.

旺 ⁴ **To prosper; to increase. Prosperous; brilliant; bright.**
7039

旺 地 a prosperous place.

旺 旺 的 bright; shining; flourishing.

旺 相 (*hsiang⁴*) to have a stroke of good fortune.

旺 相 (*hsiang⁴*) 堂 the shrine of the God of Wealth.

5 旺 運 good fortune; lucky.

健 旺 in vigorous health.

火 旺 the blazing up of a fire.

發 旺 to flourish; to prosper; to do well in business; to show signs of vigour; to brighten up, as a fire.

興 旺 to increase; to prosper; prosperity.

枉 ³ **Useless. In vain.**
7040

枉 居 人 世 to be of no use in the world of men.

枉 廢 心 機 to have had all one's pains for nothing.

枉 然 useless; in vain.

枉 空 to spend one's strength in vain.

5 枉 臨 you waste time in coming to visit me—conventional phrase.

枉 費 to spend to no purpose.

枉 顧 you waste time in coming to visit me—conventional phrase.

枉 駕 you waste time in coming to see me—used conventionally.

(a) **Crooked. To do or suffer wrong. Oppression.**

枉 尺 而 直 尋 by bending only one cubit you make eight cubits straight—to do something a little out of the straight course, in order to accomplish a great good.

枉 己 徇 人 to bend one's principles for the sake of others.

枉 己 而 正 人 to bend oneself and at the same time seek to rectify others.

枉 死 城 the abode of the spirits of those who have died through injustice.

5 枉 死 鬼 the spirits of those who have died through injustice.

枉 法 to bend the law to suit his private interests—of an unjust magistrate.

枉 法 贓 bribes received by an unjust magistrate.

枉 矢 a crooked arrow.

枉 誓 願 to force another to make a vow.

10 枉 道 crooked ways; toadying to curry favour.

呼 枉 to shout one's grievances in public.

冤·枉 an injustice.

矯 枉 to right wrongs. *See* No. 692—B. 2.

矯枉過正 overcorrection.

汪 ¹·⁴· **An expanse of water. A pool.**
7041

汪 注 broad and deep—of water.

淚 汪 汪 的 tearfully.

汪 洋 or 汪 洋 大 海 the open sea.

汪 浪 or 汪 漾 used figuratively of a flood of tears.

汪 然 broad and deep—as an expanse of water.

汪 沰 an expanse of water.

迋 ⁴ **To travel. To go to. To scare. To deceive.**
7042

人 實 迋 女 they are deceiving you. (-*ju³*)

子 無 我 迋 do not frighten me.

望
堅
7043 | ⁴ To expect; to hope. To look towards. To gaze at. To face.

望·不見 or 望·不到 unable to see—usually said of distant objects.

望之不似人君 "when I looked at him from a distance, he did not appear like a sovereign"

望乞 to beg; to request.

望候 to pay a call.

⁵望六 nearly sixty years old; in sight of sixty.

望切 expectantly; earnestly hoping.

望包荒 I pray that you will pardon my lack of culture.

望國 a great nation.

望地 reputation and standing.

¹⁰望塵不及 to see the dust raised by a person but be unable to overtake him—hopelessly behindhand.

望塵欸附 to see the dust of the advancing army and make terms with them.

望天 to look up to heaven.

望子 a shop-sign; u.f. 幌 No. 2278—A.

望山跑·死馬 like a man who, seeing a mountain and thinking it near, rides his horse to death—reckless.

¹⁵望影而逃 he runs from a shadow.

望想 to long for.

望慕 to long for.

望族 people who are respected in a neighbourhood.

望日蓮 a name for the sunflower.

²⁰望望然去 left him with a haughty air.

望望焉 an air of disappointment.

望柱 stone pillars placed at the graves of notable persons.

望梅止渴畫餅充饑 to gaze at plums to quench one's thirst, to sketch a cake to satisfy one's hunger—vain hopes.

望樓 a look-out; a signal station.

²⁵望歲 to expect a good harvest.

望氣 to look at the mists—for portents.

望求 to entreat.

望汲引 I hope that you will give me an introduction.

望洋 to look over the ocean. See 若 No. 3126—F.

³⁰望看 or 探望 to look at; to go to visit; to go and see.

望示 I look forward to the receipt of your instructions—conventional in letters.

望空 to look into space—vain hopes.

望穿雙眼 to bore through with both eyes by gazing—of a long-expectant attitude.

望羊 (or 洋) to gaze into the distance; to have a vacant expression, as when startled.

³⁵望聞問切 the four important methods of diagnosis, i.e., to look carefully, to listen, to question, and to feel the pulse.

望臺 a look-out; a signal station; the bridge of a ship.

望色 to take note of the colour of a man's face in diagnosis.

望花甲 within sight of sixty years of age.

望·著 looking towards.

⁴⁰望衡對宇 dwelling in close quarters—houses opposite each other.

望·見 gazing; to look at; to see.

望視 to gaze; to look out for—as from an elevation.

望親 to visit relatives.

望達 ambitious.

⁴⁵望遠 to look into the distance; to look into the future.
遠望 to see it in the distance.

望遠鏡 a telescope.

望邦 a desirable country.

望重 highly distinguished.

⁵⁰望長久遠 to think of the future; foresighted.

望長處想 foresighted; to think of the future.

望開茅塞 I pray that you will enlighten my mind. See 開 No. 3204-145.

望雨 to look for rain.

望雲 to gaze at the clouds as they pass—thinking of absent friends or relatives who dwell beneath them.

⁵⁵望風 looking for fame or reputation; ambitious.

望風倒 unable to maintain one's determination; easily abashed

—it falls at the thought of the wind.

望風懷想 anxiously watching for your return; thinking of.

望風捕影 gazing at the wind and grasping the shadows—said of false rumours, etc.

一線希望 one ray of hope.

⁶⁰不及所望 to fall short of expectations.

久望 long hoped-for.

企望 on the tiptoe of expectation.

仰望 to look up to.

喜出望外 overjoyed.

⁶⁵失望 without hope; to lose hope.

奢望 ambitious.

引領而望之 (the people) would all look to him with outstretched necks.

怨望 to have a grudge against.

日望之 daily hoping for this.

⁷⁰有望 hopeful.

期望 to have hopes of.

民之望之 the longing of the people for him.

民望之 the people had confidence in him.

渴望 ardent longing for, as a thirsty man longs for water.

⁷⁵無所望 without hope; nothing to hope for.

熱望 earnest longings for; ardently desiring.

盼望 to hope; to look forward to.

絕望 hopeless; all hope cut off.

舉首而望之 raise their heads and look for him—as their ruler.

⁸⁰虛望 vain hopes.

(a) The full moon. See 既 No. 453—8.

望月 or 望日 the 15th day of the lunar month—the full moon.

望舒 the driver of the chariot of the moon.

朔望 the 1st and 15th of the lunar month, new moon and full moon respectively.

(b) Name of a sacrifice offered by the emperor to the mountains and streams,—so called because the offerer looked at them from a distance. See 柴 No. 121—A.2.

望于山川 sacrificed to the mountains and streams.

望 祀 the sacrifice offered to the mountains and streams.
望 秩 山 川 offered the sacrifices to the mountains and streams.

冂 网 ³ A net; net-like. Radical 122.

7044

罔 ³ A net. See 網 No. 7047. Distinguish 罔 No. 3269.

7045

罔 市 利 to net the gains of the whole market.
罔 民 to entrap the people.
天 之 降 罔 Heaven (God) is sending down His net—i.e., calamities upon mankind.

(a) A negative. In vain. Not; without. Similar to 無.

罔 不 在 厥 初 生 it all depends on (the training of) his early life.
罔 不 譈 there are none that do not detest him.
罔 之 生 也 幸 而 免 if a man loses (his uprightness) and yet lives, his escape (from death) is sheer luck.
罔 大 罔 小 no matter whether small or great.
⁵罔 有 攸 赦 there can be no forgiveness for him.
罔 極 without any bounds; to transgress.
　士 也 罔 極 it is you, Sir, who transgress the right.
　昊 天 罔 極 it is like Great Heaven, illimitable—of the kindness of one's parents.
　視 人 罔 極 (standing opposite another) he can see through and through him.
¹⁰　謂 我 士 也 罔 極 "they say I am an officer going to the verge of license."
　譖 人 罔 極 the slanderers go to all lengths.
罔 水 行 舟 to sail a boat without water.
罔 然 irresolute and undecided.
罔 見 to see nothing.
學 而 不 思 則 罔 learning without thought is labour lost.

(b) To deceive. To befool.

罔 上 to deceive one's superiors.
勿 罔 君 子 ³ he should not deal deceitfully with superior men.
君 子 ³ 不 可 罔 也 the superior man cannot be befooled.
欺 天 罔 人 to deceive God and man.

(c) See below.

罔 兩 問 景 曰 .. the penumbra said to the umbra .. (景 = 影).
罔 兩 影 外 微 陰 也 wang-liang is the penumbra.
罔 象 an imaginary monster of the waters.

惘 ³ To lose one's self-possession.

7046

惘 懨 disconcerted.
惘 然 irresolute; undecided.

網 ³ A net; a web. Network. Distinguish 網 No. 3271.

7047

網 利 to net in the profits.
網 梭 a shuttle for netting.
網 油 or 油 網 the net-like fat that covers the inwards of a bullock.
網 球 tennis.
⁵網 眼 the meshes of a net.
網 索 netting.
網 絡 network; to include.
網 羅 nets; traps.
網 膜 the retina of the eye.
¹⁰網 衫 a network jacket.
網 魚 to net fish.
塵 網 the entanglements of this life.
天 網 恢 恢 疎 而 不 漏 the net of God is vast and its meshes great, but no one escapes.
布 網 to set a net.
¹⁵撒 網 to cast nets.
漏 網 to escape the net—of justice.
結 網 to make nets.
脫 了 網 羅 escaped from the net.
蛛 網 spiders' webs.
²⁰補 網 to mend a net.
設 網 to set a net.
鐵 絲 網 wire-netting.

輞 ³ The felloe of a wheel; a tire.

7048

魍 ³ An elf. A sprite. An animal which is said to eat the brains of the dead under ground.

7049

魍 魎 sprites; the spirits of the waters.
魍 魎 魑 魅 spirits of the rivers and the hills.

往 彺 ³ To go towards; to depart. ×u. ᶠ 望 wang⁴.

7050

×往 上 冒 to go upward—as smoke.
×往 下 拉 pull it downwards.
往 來 intercourse. See No. 3768-25ff.
往 來 寒 熱 cold and heat alternating.
⁵往 來 無 間 to ply at regular intervals.
往 來 無 阻 freedom of intercourse; coming and going without hindrance.
×往 前 走 to go forward; to advance; to make progress.
往 反 to go and return.
往 回 there and back.
¹⁰×往 好 裏 學 direct your studies to that which is good.
往 復 to go to and fro.
往 晤 to have an interview with.
往 轉 to go and return.
往 返 to go to and fro; to go and return; there and back.
¹⁵往 返 曲 折 zigzag.
×往 那 裏 去 where are you going?
不 知 所 往 do not know where he has gone.
何 往 where are you going?
前 往 蘇 州 to proceed to Soochow.
²⁰向 往 one's bent or intention.

(a) Formerly; past; gone.

往 下 henceforth.
往 世 in past days.
往 事 休 題 let bygones be bygones.
往 古 in the past.
⁵往 古 來 今 from of old until now.
往 常 constantly; usually; heretofore.
往 年 in the past; bygone years.

往 往 often so; frequently; occasionally.

往 往 如 此 it is often thus.

¹⁰往 後 hereafter; in the future.

往 日 in bygone days.

往 昔 in the past; in ancient times.

往 時 in past days; formerly.

往 時 遺 風 antiquated notions.

¹⁵往 罪 past offences.

往 者 不 追 let bygones be bygones.

往 鑒 the example of past days.

旣 往 不 咎 what is past do not blame—let bygones be bygones.

WEI.　　(ㄨㄟ)
(Uei)

威 ¹ Severe; stern; majestic; imposing; awful. Awe; pomp. To overawe.
7051

威 之 to overawe; to terrify.

威 侮 五 行 to waste and misuse the five elements.

威 信 having power to maintain one's own authority—not making a mere demonstration.

威 儀 dignity of demeanour; majesty; a sense of decorum.

⁵威 儀 中 適 a correct dignity of demeanour.

威 力 intimidation.

威 勢 power; authority; influence.

威 名 prestige.

威 嚇 to intimidate; to terrify.

¹⁰威 嚇 主 義 a policy of intimidation.

威 嚴 majestic; stern.

威 壓 to overawe; to oppress; to intimidate.

威 夷 hazardous passes; dangerous points.

威 姑 a husband's mother.

¹⁵威 威 顯 民 he was terrible to those who deserved it, thus getting distinction among the people.

威 宣 his august name is widely known.

威 德 majesty and virtue.

威 怒 fierce rage; severity.

威 服 to overawe.

²⁰威 望 acknowledged authority—prestige.

威 權 power; authority; influence.

威 武 stern; terrible; dignified; martial-looking.

威 氣 majesty; stern demeanour.

威 烈 majestic; stern.

²⁵威 猛 fierce; ferocious.

威 目 to make an awe-inspiring display.

威 福 the august happiness—of the emperor.

擅 作 威 福 to usurp the powers of those in authority—to take the law into one's own hands.

威 而 不 猛 imposing and yet not fierce.

³⁰威 聲 prestige.

威 能 power.

威 脅 to treat cruelly; to coerce; to intimidate.

威 虐 oppressive; tyrannical.

威 逼 to coerce; to treat cruelly; to intimidate.

³⁵威 重 sedate; majestic; august.

威 鎮 海 內 to awe the whole land—into peace.

威 震 to bring terror to.

威 風 an awe-inspiring reputation.

威 風 凜 凜 awe-inspiring fame.

⁴⁰威 風 掃 地 his reputation is dragged in the dust∫showing off.

下 馬 威 prompt severity; the first

作 威 to terrify; to show a stern demeanour towards; to make a demonstration of intimidation.

張 威 to ride the high horse.

旻 天 疾 威 compassionate Heaven arrayed in terrors.

⁴⁵死 喪 之 威 the dreaded occasions of death.

殺 威 a threatening manner.

疾 威 上 帝 How arrayed in terrors is the Supreme!

發 威 to show a stern front.

示 威 舉 動 to make a demonstration, as a procession. *See* 示 No. 5788-6ff.

(a) Used in transliterating.

威 廉 William.

威 林 敦 Wellington.

威 爾 斯 Wales.

威 士 忌 whiskey.

葳 ¹ Luxuriant; flourishing. Used for various plants as below.
7052

葳 蕤 or 萎 蕤 *Polygonatum officinale.*

紫 葳 *Tecoma grandiflora.*

蝛 ¹ The sow-bug; wood-louse.
7053

口 ² An enclosure. Radical 31. Used to indicate lacunæ in ancient texts. Also read *huei*². Ancient form of 國 and 圍.
7054

鮰 ² A small kind of sturgeon, found in the Yangtze.
7055

危 ² Dangerous; perilous. Lofty.
7056

危 乎 其 危 how perilous it is!

危 亡 in great danger, as from rebellion, disorder, etc.

危 在 旦 夕 the danger lies between morning and evening—death is imminent.

危 坐 to sit in a dignified attitude.

⁵危 塞 a strategic point.

危 如 累 卵 as dangerous as a pile of eggs—extremely risky.

危 崖 lofty and precipitous.

危 心 fearful in heart.

危 急 hazardous.

¹⁰危 懼 fearful; agitated.

危 期 a crisis.

危 橋 a perilous bridge.

危 樓 a lofty building; a high tower.

危 機 a crisis of danger; a critical point.

¹⁵危 機 一 髮 hanging by just a thread—in imminent peril.

危 殆 hazardous.

危 病 or 危 疾 a dangerous illness.

危 而 不 持 not to support him when he is in peril.

危 處 a perilous place.

²⁰危 衰 decaying; decadent.

危 言 危 行 lofty and bold in word and action.

危 詞 苦 語 misleading and injurious statements.

危 身 to place oneself in danger—not afraid of peril.

危 迫 dangerous and pressing; in peril; critical.

²⁵危 途 a dangerous road; dangerous ways.

危 邦 不 入 he will not enter a State which is in danger.

危 險 hazardous.
危 險 物 dangerous goods; a menace or danger.
危 險 行 爲 dangerous actions.
³⁰危 難 in danger; dangerous.
危 難 之 間 in times of peril; in the midst of dangers.
危 驚 or 危 篤 very dangerous—as an illness.
安 不 忘 危 in times of peace do not forget danger.
死 危 deadly peril.
³⁵臨 危 at the point of death; in grave danger.

桅²
7057　The mast of a vessel.

桅 夾·子 the socket or supports of a mast or flagstaff.
桅 夾 艙 the hold where the mast is stepped.
桅 尾 the mast-head.
桅 帽 the truck or cap at the top of a mast.
⁵桅 斗 the truck or cap at the top of a mast.
桅 梢 the mast-head.
桅 檣 繩 練 the rigging.
桅 盤 the truck or cap at the top of a mast.
桅·竿 a mast.
¹⁰桅·竿 頂·上 a mast-head.
桅 身 the housing or part of the mast which is below the deck.
桅 頭² 旗 a pennant.
三 頂 桅 the topgallant mast.
二 頂 桅 a topmast.
¹⁵四 頂 桅 the royal mast.
大 桅 or 中 桅 the mainmast.
尾 桅 the mizzen mast.
船 頭 斜 桅 the bowsprit.
落 桅 to lower the mast. (lao⁴-)
²⁰豎 桅 to step a mast.
頭 冲 桅 the bowsprit.

鮠²
7058　A kind of shad with a head like a sturgeon. Sometimes used for 鮰 No. 7055.

爲²
7059　To be; to do; to make; to practise; to act out; to cause. See 以 No. 2932—D.

爲 主 to take responsibility; to decide.
爲 人 to be a man, to act as a man; a class of man; a man's character.

爲 人 在 世 to be a man among men; to perform the duties of life.
爲 人 善 良 he is a good, kind-hearted man.
⁵爲 人 子³ as a son. one's efforts.
爲 力 to use force; to contribute
爲 君 難 it is difficult to be a ruler.
爲 善 to practise virtue; to do good.
爲 大 to be great.
¹⁰爲 大 人 物 he is an important personage.
爲 學 to study.
爲 官 to act as an officer; to be an official.
爲 寃 結 仇 to be enemies.
爲 川 者 those who control the streams.
¹⁵爲 從 to aid and abet.
爲 念 to give attention to; to make one's chief aim.
爲 憑 as evidence or proof.
爲 據 as proof; as evidence.
爲 政 to govern.
²⁰爲 是 to be right or correct.
以 此 爲 是 regard this as right.
爲 時 to last; to endure.
爲 替 money exchange. (Jap.).
爲 望 is what I hope; is what I expect.
²⁵爲 期 as a limit of time.
爲 業 as a business or means of livelihood.
爲 止 as far as to....
爲 法 自 弊 less common form of 6780.80.
爲 滿 for a period of....
³⁰爲 照 as proof or evidence.
爲 理 to arrange; to settle.
爲 用 use.
爲 盜 to rob.
爲 禁 is prohibited.
³⁵爲 禮 to do an act of courtesy.
爲 臣 不 易 it is not easy to be a statesman.
爲 要 to be important.
爲 計 to have a plan or means.
爲 詩 to compose poetry.
⁴⁰爲 證 as proof or evidence; as a witness.
爲 質 to be a pledge or hostage.
爲 道 to be a guide; to study the truth.
爲 間⁴ an interval.
爲 限 as a limit of time.

⁴⁵爲 難 to be in a difficulty; in a dilemma; to obstruct.
爲 非 作 歹 to do evil.
爲 頥 (preceded by other words) was glad to learn that....
爲 頭² to be the head or leader.
爲 首 to be the head or leader.
⁵⁰爲 鬼 爲 域 to be a demon or a yü—to injure others in secret.
不 以 爲 可 to regard as impracticable or improper.
不 以 爲 然 to disapprove; to regard as wrong.
不 叫 爲 也 it cannot be cured, managed, handled, etc.
以 金 爲 之 made of gold.
⁵⁵何 爲 what is this? what are you doing?
所 爲 acts; deeds; what is done.
任 其 所 爲 let him do as he pleases.
無 所 不 爲 there is nothing that he will not do—generally spoken of doing evil.
有 作 有 爲 energetic—of a man of action.
⁶⁰無 爲 to do nothing; the doctrine of inaction or quietism.

(a) Read wei⁴. For; because of; on account of. Wherefore. By; to.

爲 之 聲 announced that, on his behalf....
爲 之 致 死 would die for him.
爲 人 作 嫁 to work on behalf of another. See 作 No. 6780-29.
爲 人 爲 to do for others.
⁵爲 何 why? wherefore?
爲 公 爲 私 in public and private.
爲 利 for gain.
爲 咨 覆 事 in the matter of a reply to your despatch.
爲 國 致 命 to risk life for one's country.
¹⁰爲 己 for oneself.
爲 我 for myself; selfishness; the system of Yang Chu 楊 朱·
爲 此 on this account.
爲 此 而 生 born for this.
爲 照 會 事 I, therefore send this despatch.
¹⁵爲 照 覆 事 in the matter of a reply to your despatch.
爲 王 誦 之 he told his words to the prince.
爲 甚·麼² why?

爲·的·是 because; for the cause; on account of...; with a view to....

爲·着 on account of.

²⁰爲·着何故 for what reason?

爲舊君有服 to wear mourning for a prince whose service one has left

爲·著 on account of. ≡ 19.

爲虎作倀 to act as a helper to an evil person. See 倀 No. 214-2.

爲虎傅翼 to give wings to a tiger—to increase the power of a tyrant to do evil.

²⁵爲這個 on this account.

爲酒困 overcome by intoxicants.

爲顧人 to take interest in the welfare of others.

僞⁴

僞⁴ False; simulated; counterfeit. Sometimes read wei³.
7060

僞充 to pretend to be.

僞作不知 pretended not to know.

作僞 to act hypocritically; forged, as books, etc.

僞做 to fabricate; to counterfeit.

⁵僞名 a pseudonym.

僞君子³ a hypocrite.

僞善 hypocritical. 僞國 puppet state.

僞學 a pretender to scholarship.

僞念 false-hearted.

¹⁰僞政府 the puppet government—a usurping government.

僞洋 counterfeit dollars.

使用僞洋者 one who passes counterfeit dollars.

僞爲 to pretend to.

僞神 a false god.

¹⁵僞稱 a pseudonym.

僞經 apocrypha.

僞義 false principles. 僞裝 camouflage.

僞許 to feign compliance.

僞詐 pretentious.

²⁰僞證 perjury.

僞造·的 counterfeit; fabricated; artificially produced.

僞造·的書 forged books.

僞鈔票 forged bank-notes.

僞錢 counterfeit money.

²⁵得其僞失其實 we have the counterfeit, but we have lost the true.

至誠無僞 perfectly sincere and without guile.

微²,¹

微²,¹ Small; minute; trifling. Subtle; obscure. Mean; humble—used as a depreciative for, "I, my."
7061
Distinguish 徵 No. 358.

微傷 a slight injury.

微分¹子³ corpuscles.

極微分¹子³ or 原子³ atoms —See No. 7725.

微分(學) differential calculus.

⁵微利 small profits.

微動·物 animalculæ.

微塵 fine dust; insignificant.

微妙 minute; subtle.

微妙無窮 extremely mysterious.

¹⁰微妙醉心 subtle; intoxicating.

微子³ a corpuscle.

微小 minute; small.

微弱 sickly; feeble.

微微·的 a very little; in a slight degree.

¹⁵微忱 a slight token of.

微恙 a slight indisposition.

微情 a trifle indicating my regard —conventional.

微故 slight grounds for.

微旨 a deep, abstruse meaning.

²⁰微明 a faint light; dawnings of understanding.

微時 before he came to the front; when he was in a humble position.

微晶質 crystalline.

微末 unimportant; trifling.

微次 or 微微次·些 slightly inferior.

²⁵微毫 trifling; unimportant.

微氣 the ether. = 以太.

微然 a very little; in a slight degree.

微物 trifling; of no value—said of a present.

微生物 microbes, for which 細菌 is also used. [f. 2467.47.

³⁰微生物學 micro-biology. Also u.

微眄 a slight glance.

微睡 a doze.

微積分¹ the calculus. (math.)

微粒·子 corpuscles; particles; a disease of silkworms.

³⁵ 固體·的微粒 a solid particle.

微笑 a smile.

微細 very small and fine; trifling.

微細之事 trifling details; unimportant matters.

微臣 a petty official—depreciatory.

---

⁴⁰微茫 obscure and indistinct.

微菌 germs; bacteria.

微薄 thin; trifling; mean.

微蟲 microbes; bacteria.

微血管 capillaries.

⁴⁵微行 a small path. See below— A. 4.

微視 a slight glance.

微言 subtle and profound language; parabolic.

微詞 a slighting expression.

微賤 or 輕微 vulgar; inferior.

⁵⁰微辭 an ambiguous expression.

微雨 slight rain.

微音器 or 顯微音器 a microphone.

微風 a light breeze.

微點 a point; a dot.

⁵⁵測微器 (or 尺) micrometer.

·至微 the most minute; infinitesimal.

顯微鏡 microscope.

(a) Secret. Invisible. To conceal. To spy.

微察 to spy; to examine secretly.

微指 secretly indicated.

微服 mufti; to go in disguise.

微行 to go in disguise; to go in mufti. See above—45.

隱微 secret; occult.

(b) Used like 無 No. 7180. Not; but for; if not.

微君之故 if it were not for your sake, O prince....

微汝 but for you....

微我無酒 it is not because I have no wine.

微特 not only....

⁵微獨 not only....

微禹吾其魚乎 if it had not been for Yü (the Great) we should all have been fishes— referring to his work of draining the swamps.

微適不來微我弗顧 it is better that (something) should keep them from coming, than that I should have disregarded them.

(c) Ulcerated legs.

既微且尰 with legs ulcerated and swollen.

薇²

薇² Name of a fern—Osmunda regalis. A leguminous plant.
7062 Used with other characters for various plants, as below.

紫薇 t h e crape-myrtle—*Lagerstrœmia indica.*

薔薇 a red rose. *See* No. 677.

朵薇 let us gather the thornferns.

巍² A lofty peak.
7063

唯³ To answer promptly.
7064

唯唯 a prompt, respectful answer.

唯而起 he answered and rose.

唯諾 to answer in assent.

(a) Read *wei*². **Only. Inter. 惟 No. 7066, 維 No. 7067.**

唯一 unique; the only.

唯一之例 a solitary instance.

唯一地位 a unique position.

唯一神主敎 Unitarianism.

⁵唯一論 Monism.

唯何甚 why be so hard?

唯其疾之憂 (parents) a r e anxious lest their children should be ill.

唯其言而莫予違也 only in this that my words (as prince) are not disobeyed.

唯堯則之 only *Yao* matched it.

¹⁰唯心派 idealists.

唯心論 idealism.

唯恐有聞 only feared lest he should hear more.

唯我論 egoistic theories.

唯末之圖 to care only about the outcome and give no thought to the source.

¹⁵唯物派 materialists.

唯物觀念 materialistic c o n - ceptions.

唯物論 materialism.

唯理論 rationalism.

唯酒食是議 they will only have to deliberate about wine and food.

²⁰唯靈論 spiritualism.

帷² A curtain; a screen.
7065

帷堂 a kind of screen or canopy used in funeral rites.

帷帳 or 帷幔 curtains.

帷幄 a tent; a pavilion.

帷幕 a cloth partition or tent.

⁵帷房 a bedchamber; women's apartments.

帷薄 a curtain to a door.

帷薄不修 the door curtain is not repaired, i.e., the men's and women's apartments are not kept strictly apart—used for lewdness.

帷裳 a skirt or apron.

惟² Only; and; with; is. An initial particle, often un-translatable. Used to connect subject and predicate. Inter. 唯 No. 7064.
7066

惟一 unique; the only.

惟予數數也 why do you continue to trouble me only?(-*shuo*⁴·⁵·)

惟他是問 he will be solely responsible.

惟其不遇 but he met with no other—like-minded.

⁵惟利是視 to care only for profits.

惟命是從 to accept one's destiny; to be guided entirely by the orders of.

惟命是聽 to accept one's destiny; to be guided solely by the orders of.

惟堅凝之難 it is consolidation that is difficult.

惟堯則之 *Yao* alone corresponded to it—Heaven.

¹⁰惟孝友于兄弟 you are filial, you are brotherly to your elder and younger brothers.

惟心論 idealism.

惟恐 lest; fearing....

惟我論 egoism.

惟日孜孜 diligent from day to day.

¹⁵惟是 only that....

惟是不去 under the circumstances he will not go.

惟有一人 there is only one person.

惟查前案 however, on examining into previous cases....

惟汝是問 only you are responsible.

²⁰惟然 and this being the case....

惟煩 I am compelled to request ....

惟物論 materialism.

惟獨 only; but.

惟當如此 it can only be so.

²⁵惟願 the only thing I can desire is....; may it be....!

不惟 not only....

(a) To think solemnly. To care for. To consider.

載謀載惟 we consult, we consider the solemn rites.

維² To tie; to hold together; to hold fast.
7067

維持 to aid; to uphold; to regulate; to maintain; to consolidate. *See* 門 No. 4418-57.

以資維持 so as to assist in the regulation of....

設法維持 to devise means to help in the matter.

維持世·界和平 t o maintain world peace.

⁵維持主義 conservatism. Cf. 4946.8

維持人道 to uphold the principles of humanity.

維持公安 to preserve public order.

維持國貨 to encourage native products.

維持市面 to r e g u l a t e the market.

¹⁰維持政體 to uphold the existing form of government.

維持治安 to m a i n t a i n the peace.

維持現狀 to m a i n t a i n the *status quo.*

維持秩序 to maintain order.

維持自治 to encourage self-government.

¹⁵維挽 to haul on—a rope.

維斗 the Polar Star.

維繫 to fasten together; to connect with.

維舟 to moor a boat.

以維風化 in order to care for the public well-being.

²⁰君子³是維 the superior men are the bonds—of society.

四方是維 he should be keeping together the four quarters—of the kingdom.

四維 the cardinal points; the four cardinal virtues, 禮 propriety, 義 righteousness, 廉 integrity, and 恥 modesty.

繫之維之 tether it by the foot, tie it by the collar—of a colt.

(a) An initial particle. Only; but. A copula connecting subject and predicate. It is often untranslatable. Inter. 唯 No. 7064.

維 今 now; at this time.
維 新 modern; to reform, as a government.
　其 命 維 新 its appointment —as a sovereign State—is new.
維 新 黨 reformers.
[5]維 時 at that time.
維 石 巖 巖 rugged are the rocks.
維 艱 in difficulties.
維 谷 in a dilemma. *See* 進 No. 1091-54.
維 難 in difficulties.

(b) Used in transliterating.

維 也 納 會 議 Vienna Conference.
維 多 利 亞 Victoria.
維 多 利 亞 寶 星 The Victoria Cross.
維 爾 塞 Versailles.
↑維 他 命 vitamin. Cf. 5738.72.

濰
2 Name of a river in Shantung.
7068

畏
4 To dread; to fear. Awe.
7069

畏 光 眼 nyctalopia—in the sense of being unable to see clearly except at night.
畏 刑 則 可 免 刑 to dread punishment is the best means of avoiding it.
畏 勞 to be afraid of the trouble and labour.
畏 友 a friend of stern integrity and high moral character.
[5]畏 夜 眼 nyctalopia—in the sense of night-blindness.
畏 怯 or 心 怯 to dread; apprehensive.
畏 惡 (*wu*[4]) to dread and loathe.
畏 懼 or 畏 怕 or 畏 忌 to fear; fear; dread.
畏 敬 to stand in awe of.
[10]畏 日 the dreaded sun—of summer.
畏 日 眼 day-blindness.
畏 服 to submit from fear.
畏 法 to dread the law.

畏 畏 to dread the dreadful.
[15]畏 疑 to dread and suspect.
畏 縮 hesitating; timid; shrinking; cringing; to cringe.
畏 罪 to be afraid of punishment.
畏 羞 bashful; sensitive.
畏 葸 無 能 useless and cowardly; incapacitated through fear.
[20]畏 途 a dangerous road.
畏 避 to skulk.
畏 難 to dread difficulty.
畏 風 to be afraid of the weather.
畏 首 畏 尾 to fear both the beginning and the end—excessive fear.
[25]三 畏 the three things of which the superior man stands in awe,
　畏 天 命 畏 大 人 畏 聖 人 之 言, the will of God, great men, and the teachings of the sages.
後 生 可 畏 a youth should be feared—you do not know what he will become.
無 畏 fearless—a title given to every Buddha.

(a) Used in transliterating.

畏 語 兒 the Ouigours—a Turkish tribe which settled near Turfan, A.D. 640. They were descendants of the Huns. *See* 紇 No. 2086-1, 2; 回 No. 2309—A. 4; and 胸 No. 2812—A.

偎
1 To hug; to cuddle together; to fondle.
7070

偎 傍 to walk closely together.
偎 臉 to hug up to one's face, as a mother with her child.
偎 貼 to snuggle close to.
偎 近 to cuddle closely together.
相 偎 to cuddle; to dally with.

椳
1 The pivots, at the top and bottom of a Chinese door, on which the door turns.
7071

煨
1 To roast in ashes. To stew slowly.
7072

煨 炭 the brown coal found in the north of Hopei; to burn charcoal.
　蹈 煨 炭 to walk through glowing coals—as Taoist magicians do.

煨 爐 to reduce to ashes.
煨 黃 or 煨 焦 to roast brown.

猥
1.3. Many; plentiful. To collect.
7073

猥 多 many; numerous.
猥 大 numerous and flourishing.
猥 盛 full to overflowing.
猥 積 an accumulation, as of stores for the entertainment of visitors.
賢 者 則 猥 來 就 之 worthy men came hurrying in crowds.

(a) Humble. Rustic.

猥 壻 a rustic son-in-law.
猥 承 獎 譽 I am deeply indebted for your recommendation.
猥 瑣 petty; trifling.
猥 細 petty; trifling.
猥 褻 improper liberties.
猥 鄙 or 卑 猥 rustic; unpolished; coarse.

(b) A particle.

猥 云 德 化 if only you influence them by means of virtue....

(c) Defined as a dog barking, being composed of 犬 a dog, and 畏 to fear. A litter of three pups.

隈 湄
1 A cove; a bay. A bend or nook in the hills. The curve of a bow.
7074

胃
4 The stomach. Distinguish 胃 No. 1296.
7075

胃 加 答 兒 gastritis; gastric catarrh.
胃·口 the pylorus; the appetite.
胃·口 不 清 or 無 胃·口 I have no appetite.
　開 胃·口 to excite the appetite by means of condiments or highly seasoned dishes.
[5]胃 寒 cold in the stomach—supposed to be the cause of loss of appetite, dyspepsia, etc.
胃 弱 dyspepsia.
胃 擴 張 dilated stomach.
胃 氣 疼 colic; gripes.

胃 液 gastric juice.
[10]胃 液 素 pepsin.
胃 潰 瘍 gastric ulcers.
胃 火 heat in the stomach—biliousness, etc.
胃 炎 gastritis.
胃 熱 gastric fever.
[15]胃 痙 cramps in the stomach.
胃 癌 cancer of the stomach.
胃 癰 gastric ulcers.
胃 納 the capacity of the stomach; the appetite.
胃 腺 the glands which secrete the gastric juice, etc.
[20]胃 膈 cancer of the stomach.
胃 酸 gastric juice.
胃 風 emaciation f r o m serious gastritis.
不 對 胃 it does not agree with my stomach.
反 胃 to turn the stomach; nauseous.

惘[4]
7076
Disquieted; anxious.

渭[4]
707.7
A large tributary of the Yellow River in Shensi. The roaring of rapids.

渭 陽 the north of the *Wei*.
渭 陽 之 情 the relationship of uncle and nephew—from the *Odes*:—我 送 舅 氏 曰 至 渭 陽, I escorted my mother's nephew to the north of the *Wei*.

猬
蝟[4]
7078
The hedgehog.

蝟 毛 bristling hair.
蝟 縮 to curl up as a hedgehog—fig., of a person who is fearful.
蝟 起 rising up like (the spines of) a hedgehog—all sorts of affairs.
蝟 集 numerous affairs; very busy. *See below*—5.
[5] 事 如 蝟 集 my accumulated affairs are as numerous as the spines of a hedgehog.
蝟 鼠 or 刺 蝟 the hedgehog.
毛 髮 蝟 立 his hair stood on end like the spines of a hedgehog.

謂[4]
7079
To speak of; to say; to style; to be called.

謂 之 何 哉 what then shall I say?
謂 之 曰 he addressed him saying. . . .
謂 之 有 司 this may be said to be acting as a mere official.
不 謂 unexpectedly; did not think.
[5]何 謂 what is meant by. . . .
勿 謂 do not say. . . .
孰 謂 who will say that. . . . ?
或 謂 someone said. . . .
所 謂 the so-called . . .
[10]是 之 謂 . . . . this is what is called. . . .
此 謂 之 or 此 之 謂 this is called. . . .
無 所 謂 of no significance.

韋[2]
7080
Dressed hides. Leather. A thong. Radical 178.

佩 韋 a leather girdle.

(a) Used in transliterating.

韋 陀 the *Vedas;* the name of an idol who stands at the door of every Buddhist temple, with a drawn sword in his hand.

偉[3]
7081
Admirable; extraordinary; fine-looking; powerful.

偉 丈 夫 a very large, powerfully-framed man.
偉 人 a notable; a person of extraordinary powers.
偉 器 a mighty instrument—the pen.
偉 大 的 魔 力 great powers of fascination.
偉 岸 imposing appearance.
偉 男 子 a brave man.
偉 績 a great achievement.

圍[2]
7082
To surround; to invest; to besiege. Circumference; the space between the out-stretched arms; a span.

圍 以 籬 笆 to enclose by a fence or hedge.
圍 住 to surround.
圍 住 的 surrounded; circumscribed.
把 他 圍 住 了 surrounded him.

[5]圍 嘴 子 a child's bib. (or 兒)
圍 困 to besiege; to environ; enclosed.
圍 子 the cover or top of a cart or sedan-chair; a rampart; a rampart; a sluice.
圍 城 to besiege a city.
圍 塲 a hunting-ground.
[10]圍 墻 an enclosing wall.
圍 壘 a rampart.
圍 尺 or 灘 尺 a flexible measure made of bamboo splints, used for measuring logs, etc.
圍 屏 a folding screen.
圍 帳 a screen; a curtain.
[15]圍 抱 to embrace; to encircle.
圍 捕 or 圍 拿 to surround and capture.
圍 掛 a curtain hung before a table.
圍 搜 to surround and search.
圍 攏 closely crowding around; to hem in.
[20]圍 攏 to hem in; to crowd in on; to press round.
圍 攻 to encircle and attack.
圍 木 trees which may be spanned by the two hands.
圍 桌 a curtain hung before a table.
圍 棋 a game played with pips of black and white on a board of 361 squares, the object of each player being to surround the pieces of the other so that he cannot move; called *go* in Jap.
[25]圍 欄 surrounded; hemmed in.
圍 環 to encircle; to environ; to enclose.
圍 繞 to encircle; to enclose.
圍 腰 板 wainscotting.
圍 裙 a skirt; an apron.
[30]圍 裏 to enclose; to environ.
圍 閘 a sluice.
大 數 十 圍 many spans in circumference.
打 圍 to drive game for hunting.
斬 圍 to break through the besieging lines.
[35]範 圍 a plan for a siege; the sphere of. *See No.* 1780-1, ff.
重 (*ch'ung*[2]) 圍 the surrounding forces of the enemy.
↑圍 巾 or 圍 脖 兒 muffler.

幃[2]
7083
A curtain. Women's apartments.

幃 帳 screen curtains.

慈 幃 a mother—the loving screen.

暐 [3] The bright shining of the sun.
7084

煒 [3] A raging fire. Glowing.
7085

煒 盛 blazing; scorching.
光 煒 a bright light.

瑋 [3] A reddish jade. Rare; precious.
7086

瑋 重 valuable and rare.

緯 [3] The woof of a web. Parallels of latitude. Transverse lines. Fringe; tassels. See 經 No. 1123—D.
7087

緯 世 to rule the empire.
緯 以 長 橋 spanned by long bridges.
緯 度 degrees of latitude.

[5] 緯 帽 the former fringed official summer cap.
緯 綫 silk tassels; parallels of latitude.
緯 道 lines running east and west; parallels of latitude.

(a) An excursus or appendix to the classical books.

緯 書 an appendix to a classical book as, 易 緯 書 the appendixes to the *Book of Changes*.

(b) Read *wei*[3]. To tie up; to bind.

葦 [3] A reed.
7088

葦 塘 or 葦 坑 marshy ground covered with reeds.
葦 子 reeds.
葦 灘 a patch where reeds are grown.
葦 蓆 rush mats.
葦 錐 the sprouts of reeds.

衛 衞 [4] To protect; to guard. A military station. u.f. Tientsin.
7089

衞 千 總 former title of a lieutenant in charge of a grain-station.
衞 戍 a garrison.
衞 星 satellites, as the moons of the planets.
衞 生 to take care of the health; hygiene.
[5] 有 礙 衞 生 unsanitary; dangerous to the health.
衞 生 司 Sanitary Department.
衞 生 問 題 problems relating to hygiene, sanitation, etc.
衞 生 學 the study of hygiene.
衞 生 局 Bureau of Public Health. Health Office.
衞 生 法 規 sanitary regulations.
衞 生 紙 toilet-paper.
衞 生 術 sanitation.
衞 生 部 Ministry of Health.
衞 生 隊 health officers.
[15] 衞 身 to care for one's health.
衞 國 閭 to protect the country.
衞 隊 a body-guard. 衞 兵 sentry.
營 衞 a garrison.
護 衞 to protect.
[20] 防 衞 to guard.

(a) An ancient feudal State which occupied what is now Eastern Honan and Southern Hopei.

衞 國 the State of *Wei*— B.C. 1022-241.

讏 [4] To talk in one's sleep.
7090

讏 [4] To exaggerate. Incredible. Inter. 讏 No. 2358.
7091

讏 言 an incredible statement.
讏 飾 exaggeration.

褘 [2] A scent-pouch. A knee-pad. Beautiful.
7092

侅 其 褘 而 (his virtue) was indeed excellent.

(a) Read *hui*[1] or *wei*[1]. The sacrificial robes of a queen.

違 [2] To disobey; to oppose. To disregard. To abandon a purpose. To offend against. To avoid.
7093

違 令 to disobey orders.

違 却 to repudiate.
違 反 contravention.
違 和 indisposed; out of sorts.
[5] 違 常 規 a breach of custom or usage; to commit such a breach of custom.
違 延 disobedience and delay.
違 式 not according to pattern or sample.
違 心 之 事 actions done despite a bad conscience.
違 心 之 論 utterances or discussions which are contrary to what one knows at heart is wrong.
[10] 違 怨 to cherish resentment against. l.u.f. 30.
違 悖 unfit; unseemly; improper.
違 慢 to act rudely.
違 憲 to violate the constitution.
違 憲 行 為 unconstitutional actions.
[15] 違 拗 obstinate; cantankerous; to disobey.
違 教 許 久 I have long been without your teaching—conventional in letters, etc.
違 棄 to reject; to discard.
違 此 例 to offend against this rule.
違 法 的 illegal.
[20] 違 法 監 禁 unlawful detention.
違 法 逮 捕 案 a case of unlawful arrest.
違 犯 to disobey; to act contrary to.
違 理 against reason; contrary to all principle.
違 礙 條 件 obstructive clauses.
[25] 違 禁 to do what is forbidden; to break a prohibition; to offend against contraband regulations.
違 禁 貨 物 contraband goods.
違 章 to disobey regulations.
違 約 contrary to treaty; to break a contract or agreement.
違 者 充 公 under penalty of confiscation.
[30] 違 背 to disobey; to act in opposition.
違 背 信 任 breach of trust.
違 背 合 同 to commit a breach of contract.
違 背 軍 法 to transgress military law.
違 言 contradictory.
[35] 違 警 律 a breach of police regulations; petty offence.
違 警 罪 petty offences against police regulations.

違 逆 to be perverse; to act contrary to.

違 道 干 譽 to go against what is right in search of fame.

違 避 to abscond.

[40]違 阻 to interfere with; to hinder or oppose.

違 限 to exceed a time-limit; to transgress.

違 難 to take refuge.

違 顏 I have not seen you for a long time—conventional.

不 違 時 punctual.

[45]不 違 農 事 not neglecting the proper season for agricultural operations.

久 違 I have not seen you for a long time—conventional.

相 違 contradictory.

自 違 雅 範 since I last had the pleasure of meeting you—conventional in letters, etc.

(a) Distant from.

違 禽 獸 不 遠 not far removed from the birds and beasts.

違 道 不 遠 not far from the Path.

闈[2]
7094   Doors leading to the women's rooms. Gate or doors of the palace.

闈 墨 the essays of successful candidates in the former examination system.

闈 姓 the names of candidates in the examinations—a kind of lottery on the names of successful candidates in the former examinations.

入 闈 出 闈 the entrance and exit, respectively, of the examiners for the second and third degrees under the former system.

春 闈 the annual examination for the third degree, formerly held in the spring at Peking.

棘 闈 the examination halls—as these had brambles set on the walls to prevent illicit scaling.

秋 闈 the triennial examination for the second degree, formerly held in the provincial capitals.

韙[3]
7095   Right; that which is right.

嵬[2]
7096   Precipitous. Rocky.

嵬 壘 stony; rocky, as a mountain path.

嵬 峨 lofty; eminent.

嵬 嵬 lofty and great, as a mountain.

崔 嵬 rocky heights.

隗[2.4.]
7097   A small feudal State. Lofty; eminent.

委[3]
7098   To depute; to send; to put in charge of; to commission.

委 任 to appoint; to commission.

委 任 狀 a proxy; power of attorney; certificate of appointment; a commission.

委 任 管 地 mandated territory. *See below*—19.

委 任 職 a commission, as that of an officer.

[5]委 備 軍 艦 to commission a naval vessel.

委 員 a deputy; a special commissioner.

委°員 制 the committee system of government.

委°員 會 a committee; a commission of investigation, etc.

  常 務 委°員 會 standing committee.

[10] 常 駐 委°員 會 standing committee.

  調 查 委°員 會 a committee of investigation.

委 查 to depute to make inquiries.

委 權 to delegate authority.

委 求 to solicit another to go to some trouble or pains over a matter.

[15]委 禽 to send betrothal presents.

委 託 to commission; to entrust to.

委 託 任 務 to commission.

委 託 管 理 a mandate, as from the League of Nations.

  被 委 託 管 理 之 區 域 mandated territory. *See above*—3.

[20]委 託 管 理 權 mandated authority.

委 託 貨 物 單 consignment invoice.

委 託 販 賣 sale on consignment.

委 託 貿 易 commission business.

委 質 to send a present.

[25]委 輸 to transport—as goods; to pay—as taxes.

委 辦 to commission; a committee.

  執 行 委 辦 executive committee.

委 辦 所 a commission agency.

委 驗 to appoint a deputy to inspect; to appoint a deputy to hold an inquest.

[30]奉 委 to receive an appointment.

差 委 to delegate; to send. (*ch'ai*[1]-)

(a) To give up. To abandon. To throw away. To bow under a burden.

委·下 to put down—as a burden.

委 命 to give up one's life; to yield to fate.

委 地·下 而 去 threw it down and went away.

委 棄 to discard; to throw away.

[5]委 罪 to throw the blame upon another.

委 而 去 之 given up and abandoned—as a city.

委 蛻 to cast the shell—as an insect.

委 身 to submit; to give oneself to.

委 過 to cast the blame upon another.

[10]委 頓 cast down; wearied; ruined; broken down.

委 靡 disastrously unsuccessful; dispirited.

(b) Really; indeed.

委 係 it is really....

委 實 really; truly.

委 無 really was not.

委·的 really; truly.

(c) Read *wei*[4]. Public stores of grain.

委 吏 keeper of the stores—an office once held by Confucius.

委 積 to accumulate; to store.

(d) Read *wei*[1]. Crooked. Petty. A grievance, a wrong.

委·屈 a wrong; a grievance.

委 巷 a wrong; a grievance.

委·曲 crooked; tortuous; involved; exceptional; indirect.

委·曲之辭 involved expressions.

委·曲求全 to stoop in order to accomplish something; to do the best thing possible under the circumstances.

委瑣 petty; insignificant; bigoted.

(e) Read *wei*[1]. **Easy; self-possessed.**

委委佗佗 stylish; easy; self-possessed.

委婉動聽 a specious manner that moves one to listen.

痿[3] **Paralysis. Impotence.**
7099

痿疾 impotence.

痿痹 want of power in the limbs; paralysis.

萎[1.3.] **To wither, as plants.**
7100　Inter. 葳 No. 7052.

萎仁 the dried kernel of a nut used as medicine.

枯萎 withered and dried up.

諉[3] **To excuse oneself; to decline; to shirk. To lay the**
7101 **blame upon others.**

諉宕 to put off.

諉累 to implicate.

諉託 to shirk; to shift on to someone else.

諉謝 to decline with thanks.

諉過 to put the blame upon others.

推諉 to back out of; to shirk; to make excuses.

逶[1] **To sway in walking; to**
7102 **swagger.**

逶蛇 to swagger.

逶迤 a winding path.

餧[4]
喂　　**To feed animals or children.**
7103

餧孩·子 to feed a child.

餧牲·口 to feed domestic animals.

餧眼 to delight the eye.

餧飽他 feed him to the full.

餧馬 to feed a horse.

(a) **Read** *nui* or *nei*[3]. *See* **No. 4767.** Putrid. Hungry, etc.

魏[4] **High; lofty.**
7104 **Inter. next.**

魏闕 or 象魏 the gate of the imperial palace.

(a) **The name of certain States, as below.**

魏國 a small feudal State which occupied the southern part of the present Shansi and the northern part of Honan from 403-241 B.C.

魏紀 the *Wei* dynasty founded by Ts'ao Ts'ao 曹操 —A.D. 220-264.

北魏紀 the Northern *Wei* dynasty or House of Toba 拓跋 A.D. 386-535. It was also called the 元魏紀.

巍[2] **Lofty; eminent.**
7105

巍巍乎 How imposing!

巍蕩 majestic and great—in virtue.

洧[3] **Name of a small river in**
7106 **Honan.**

痏[3] **A bruise or contusion.**
7107

鮪[3] **The snouted sturgeon.**
7108

尾[3] **A tail. The rear; behind;**
　　the end. An extremity. The
7109 **stern. A promontory. To follow. N.A. for fish, etc. Also read** *i*[3].

尾之而行 to follow.

尾來 to come last.

尾大不掉 the tail is too big to wag—fig., of encumbrances, such as dependencies which become too much for the parent State.

尾姦 or 鷄姦 sodomy.

[5]尾巴 a tail. (A.D. *i*[3]-)

尾巴打拉下來 the tail hangs down. (A p. *i*[3]-)

尾巴·的話 the last word. (A p. *i*[3]-)

尾底 the end; the utmost; the bottom.

尾後 afterwards; subsequently.

[10]尾數 outstanding amounts.

尾末 the end; the bottom.

尾椎 caudal vertebræ.

尾綴 to follow up.

尾羽 tail feathers.

[15]尾銀 unpaid parts of an account; odd bits of lump silver.

尾閭 a rock called, "the eye of the sea," to which all the waters of the ocean converge. The posterior.

尾閭骨 the coccyx.

尾隨 to follow.

尾零 or 數尾 odd amounts over.

[20]尾骨 the coccyx.

夾尾 to put the tail between the legs.

巷尾 the bottom of a lane.

接尾 to append.

擺尾 or 搖尾 or 掉尾 to wag the tail.

[25]有頭無尾 it has a beginning but no ending—it begins well but ends poorly.

船尾 the stern of a boat.

跟尾 to follow.

首尾 head and tail; beginning and ending.

娓[3] **To comply with. Active.**
7110

娓勉 to exert oneself.

娓順 accommodating.

尉[4] **To still; to quiet. A**
　　surname. A military
7111 **official.**

陸軍上中少尉 captain, lieutenant, and second lieutenant, in the army. *See* No. 2014—A. 11, for navy.

(a) Read *yü*⁴⋅⁵. **See below.**

尉遲恭 one of the two guardians painted on the door of every *yamen;* he is depicted with a black face and the fingers of one hand twisted up; originally he was a general who assisted in the establishment of the T'ang dynasty.

慰⁴ **To comfort; to console; to pacify; to soothe.**
7112

慰冥 to quiet the dead—as by burning incense, etc.
慰勞 to console with kind words.
慰唁 to condole with.
慰問 to make inquiries after one's health.
⁵慰悅 to delight; to make happy.
慰愜其心 to refresh one's heart.
慰留 to retain in office.
慰解 to alleviate; to mitigate.
勸慰 to console; to soothe and comfort.
¹⁰受慰 to be comforted.
安慰 to comfort; to soothe; to pacify.
弔慰 to condole with.
撫慰 to encourage and comfort.

蔚⁴ } **Luxuriant; elegant.**
蔚 }
7113

蔚茂 luxuriant growth of vegetation.
蔚薈 luxuriant vegetation; rising clouds.

(a) Obscure; abstruse.

其文蔚也 the text is obscure.

(b) *Artemisia japonica.*

(c) Read *yü*⁴. **Deep.**

蔚藍天 a clear, deep blue sky; also defined as referring to the mysterious profundity of Heaven.

未⁴ **Not yet; not; not being.**
Distinguish 末 **No. 4546.**
7114

未之前聞 such was never heard before; I never heard the like.
未之有也 there has never been; such has never been the case.
未之視也 I have not seen it.
未了³公案 an unsettled law-case. ↓ 未來派 futurism.
⁵未來 not yet arrived; the future.
未來的事 things in the future.
未便 inconvenient; undesirable; inadvisable; not in a position to.
未免 unavoidable; necessarily; cannot be prevented.
未入流 unclassed officials.
¹⁰未冠 not yet capped; not of age.
未列 not yet enumerated.
未協 unsatisfactory.
未卽見之 did not see him immediately.
未及 not yet reached; not yet....
¹⁵未可擅便 it should not be done on your own responsibility.
未可知 or 未必見得 quite uncertain; no knowing.
未同而言 to force oneself to speak to those with whom one is not in special agreement.
未嘗 not yet; never.
未嘗不可 it may be done; there is no objection.
²⁰未嘗不顯 always manifested.
未妥 unsatisfactory.
未完 to be continued—as a serial in a newspaper, etc.
未定 uncertain; not yet settled.
未幾 shortly; in a little while; not a great while.
²⁵未必 uncertain; improbable; not necessarily.
未悉 does not know or understand.
未成 not completed; not accomplished.
未成一簣止吾止也 if only one basketful is needed (to complete the mound) and I stop, the stopping is my own doing.
未成丁 in his minority; not yet come of age.
³⁰未成年 not of age.
未易才 a man of unusual talent.
未曾 has not; not yet.
未曾想到 unthought of.
未有 none; there has never been.
³⁵未有頭緒 there is no clue.
未決之點 the unsettled points.
未然 not so; it cannot be.
未盡事宜 inadequate to the

requirements.
未盡的話 words left unsaid.
⁴⁰未知其詳 unacquainted with the details; not knowing the particulars.
未知數 the unknown quantity. (*math.*)
未知死活 not knowing whether dead or alive.
未知生焉知死 you do not know life, how can you know death?
未窺全豹 he did not see the whole leopard—he only saw a few spots—used of narrow, partial views.
⁴⁵未竟之志 an unfulfilled purpose.
未經 has not yet.
未能 cannot; may not.
未能事人焉能事鬼 you cannot serve men as they should be served, how can you serve the spirits of the dead?
未能或之先也 perhaps there were none who could get ahead of him.
⁵⁰未若 it is not so good as....
未見顏色而言 to speak when (the princely man) is not looking towards me.
未詳 the details are not known.
未詳就是 it is not clear which is right.
未識之神 the unknown god.
⁵⁵未通知 no advice of....
未遂犯 an unaccomplished offence; an abortive attempt at crime.
未達 not to be known—to fame; not to reach to; inferior to; not successful.
未達一間 inferior in one respect.
未達時 before he became famous.
⁶⁰未開化的 uncivilized.
未雨綢繆 to take precautions beforehand. *See* 綢 No. 1318 —B. 3.

(a) The eighth of the *Earthly Branches* 地支.

未時 from 1—3 p.m.
未月 the sixth lunar month.

味⁴ **Flavour; taste; smell.**
7115

味兒 flavour; taste; smell.
味其言 to test the flavour of his words.
味外味 its flavour is inexhaustible.
味如嚼蠟 it is like chewing wax—insipid.
5 味官 the sense of taste.
味料 condiments; spices; seasonings.
味氣 flavour; taste or smell.
有氣·味 it has a bad odour.
味淡 it is insipid.
10 味無味 to relish what is flavourless.
味禪 ascetic.
味精 flavouring essences.
味美 of a fine flavour.
味覺[2] the sense of taste.
15 味覺[2]器 the organs of taste.
味趣 taste; flavour, as of literature, etc.
毫無趣·味 utterly uninteresting and dull.
味·道 taste; flavour or smell.
沒有味道 it is pointless; it is flavourless.
20 一味·的 uniformly; persistently.
入味 to appreciate; to find interest in.
合味 to blend flavours.
海味 marine flavours — things from the sea, as bêche-de-mer.
滋味 the flavour of things, as food, poetry, etc.
25 無味 insipid.
知味 to perceive the flavour or interest.
美味 finely flavoured things; delicacies.
走味 it has lost its flavour, as through exposure, etc.
野味 wild flavours—game, etc.
30 開味 to have an appetite; to enjoy oneself; to like.

位[4] **A seat. A position; a situation. Rank or degree. A particle indicating respect.**
7116

位·分 rank; position; that to which a person is entitled.
位·分大·的 an exalted person.
位卑 in humble station.
位大·的 of high rank.
5 位居 a position; an abode.
位所 one's place or position.
位次 series; sequence; order.
位·置 position; seat.
政治·的位·置 political posts.
10 重要之位·置 an important position.
上位 the upper seat; the place of honour.
三位一體 three Persons in One Body—the Trinity.
失位 to lose the throne, position.
客位 the seat of a guest.
15 座·位 a seat.
有幾位 how many persons are there?
本位 its proper place; a sequence; a standard or unit. *See* No. 5025-9ff.
爵位 a rank of nobility.
牌位 an ancestral tablet.
20 神位 an ancestral tablet.
諸位 Gentlemen! Sirs!—in direct address.
讓位 to abdicate.
起位 to rise in one's seat.

壝[3] **A mound; an embankment. Read** *i*[3]. **The earthen altar to the god of the soil.**
7117

亹[3] **Indefatigable; unwearied. Resolute.**
7118

亹亹不倦 willing and unwearied.
亹亹文王 earnest and energetic was *Wên Wang*.

(a) Read *mên*[2]. **A gorge.**

骫 3.4. **To bend. To be twisted.**
7119

骫天下正法 perverted the just laws of the land.

轊[4] **The end of an axle-tree.**
7120

恚[4] **Rage; anger. Also read** *hui*[4].
7121

恚怒 in a towering passion.
恚恨 to hate; bitter resentment.

磑[4] **A mill; to grind; to break to pieces.**
7122

水磑 a water-mill.
風磑 a windmill.

WÊN. (ㄨㄣ)

(Uen)

𥁕[1] **To feed a prisoner.**
7123

搵[4] **To immerse. To wipe.**
7124

搵淚 to dry one's tears.

(a) Read *ên*[4]. **To press down.**

搵·住 to press down.
搵倒[3] to keep a person on the ground by force.

溫[1] **Warm; mild; genial. Gentle; kindly. To warm up, as food.**
7125

溫克 mild and self-restrained.
溫公 friendly and just.
溫厚 honest; bland.
溫·和 amiable; good-natured; genial; suave.
5 溫°存 to hold in one's embrace; to cherish; genial.
溫室 a hot-house.
溫帶 the Temperate Zones.
溫度 degree of temperature.
溫恤 to show special kindness and compassion; to condole with.
10 溫文 genial and cultured.
溫暾 tepid, not too hot.
溫服 take the medicine when it is warm.
溫°柔 meek; gentle; compliant.
溫柔終益己 the mild and gentle finally benefit themselves.
15 溫柔鄉 the region of the gentle—femininity; a brothel.
溫水 warm water.
溫水浴 a warm bath.
溫°泉 hot springs.
溫淳 strongly flavoured.
20 溫涼 warm and cool—the weather.
溫溫恭人 mild and humble.
溫潤可親 lovable.
溫潤而栗然 mild and pleasant, yet dignified.
溫煦 warm; genial.
25 溫煖 warm.
溫而厲 gentle yet dignified.
溫良 gentle and good; amiable.
溫良恭儉讓以得之 (the Sage) obtains (his informa-

tion) by being gentle, upright, courteous, temperate and yielding.

溫 色⁴ a benign countenance.

³⁰溫 血 動·物 warm-blooded animals.

溫 補 tonics.

溫 語 kind words.

溫 謹 a warm regard for.

溫 開 水 water that has been boiled and allowed to cool.

³⁵溫 順 easy-going; submissive; compliant.

溫 顏 a benign countenance.

溫 風 a warm breeze.

溫 食 warm food.

溫 飽 warm and full; well-fed and clothed.

(a) To revive. To review, as a lesson.

溫 故 而 知 新 to review the old and learn new—in studies.

溫 書 to review a lesson; to refresh one's memory—of books.

溫 習 to repeat again and again; to practise; to review, as a lesson.

溫 舊 情 to renew old associations; to talk over old times.

蘊¹ A water-plant used for feeding goldfish. *Hippuris* or mare's tail.
7126

蘊 藻 the above plant.

瘟¹ Epidemic; pestilence; plague.
7127

瘟 氣 infection.

瘟 災 prevailing epidemics, as plague, etc.

瘟·疫 or 瘟 症 or 瘟 病 plague; epidemics.

瘟 疫 流 行 widespread epidemics.

⁵瘟 疫 發 作 the plague breaks out.

瘟 疹 scarlet fever, measles, etc.

瘟 痘 plague; pestilence.

瘟 痧 cholera; pestilence.

瘟 神 the god of plagues.

¹⁰瘟 鬼 the demon of pestilence or plague.

牛 瘟 cattle plague; rinderpest.

解 瘟 to cause an epidemic to break up.

遭 瘟 to catch the plague; plague take him!

輼¹ A hearse.
7128

輼 輬 a hearse.

文² Literature; literary accomplishments; polite studies.
7129 Elegant; refined. Radical 67.

文 不 加 點 the style cannot be improved.

文 人 a literary man; a man of refinement.

文 以 崇 閎 之 建 築 embellished by lofty and imposing buildings.

文·件 papers; despatches; documents.

⁵文 元 the head of letters—a title formerly given to a 舉·人.

文·具 stationery.

文 典 classics.

文 几 a study table.

文 勝 質 則 吏 when the accomplishments excel the solid qualities, we have the manners of a clerk. 文 化 culture.

¹⁰文 化 運·動 a movement towards culture.

文 化 之 精 華 the best in our literary culture.

文 化 侵 客 the cultural aggression.

文 化 曙 光 the dawning light of civilization.

文 化 發 達 之 國 the nations where civilization and enlightenment flourish.

¹⁵文 化 財 a wealth of literary culture.

文 卷⁺ papers; despatches; documents.

文 告 a proclamation.

文 報 an official despatch.

文 墨 writings.

²⁰ 通 文 墨 familiar with letters; educated.

文 墨 事 literary pursuits.

文 壇 the world of letters.

文 士 a literary man.

文 契 a deed, as of property.

²⁵文 字 characters; writing; literature; phraseology.

文 字 之 交 a literary friendship.

文 字 之 戰 爭 a paper war.

文 孫 your grandson.

文 學 墮 落 the decay of literature.

³⁰文 學 家 a man of letters.

文 學 復 興 時 代 the Renaissance.

文 學 會 a literary society.

文 學 界 the literary world.

文 學 科 department of literature.

³⁵文 宗 a man of literary fame.

文 定 to fix a betrothal.

文 家 a literary man.

文 庫 a library.

文 廟 a Confucian temple.

⁴⁰文 弱 weak in body, only able for literary work.

文 彩 literary in taste; elegant; ornamental.

文 復 a despatch in reply from a superior.

文 德 the refining influence of music and literature, etc.

文 思 大 進 great intellectual progress.

⁴⁵文·憑 a diploma.

文 房 器·具 articles for the study —stationery, etc.

文 才 a talent for literature.

文 料 data.

文 昌 a constellation of six stars, forming part of Ursa Major.

⁵⁰文 昌 帝 君 the God of Literature.

文 明 culture; enlightened; up-to-date; often used in combination for foreign; civilization.

文 明 各 國 all civilized nations.

文 明 國 民 civilized peoples.

文·明·的 civilized; enlightened.

⁵⁵文 明 結 婚 a wedding in foreign style.   ⌠secretary.

文·書 an official despatch; a

文 會 a literary society.

文 望 尊 隆 high and honourable renown in literature.

文 案 先·生 a correspondence secretary in a *yamen*.

⁶⁰文 殊 the God of Wisdom, usually depicted as riding on a lion.

文 法 grammar; rules of composition.

文 獻 (= 賢) 不 足 故 也 because their records and wise men are insufficient.

文 牘 科 secretariat.

文 王 課 to inquire of *Wên Wang*—to divine by tossing up three *cash*.

65 文王鼎 a tripod of the date of *Wên Wang*—a tripod ornamented with the 八卦.

文理 grammar; style.

不通文理句法 not in accordance with proper literary style and construction.

文理密察 accomplished, distinctive, concentrative, and searching—said of the Sage.

文礎 ornamental bases for pillars.

70 文科 the liberal arts; the Humanities.

文移 to inform an equal by despatch.

文稿·子 draft of a despatch.

文·章 an essay; whatever is figured or brilliant; orderly and defined.

政治之文·章 political essays.

75 無文章 without ornament.

皆有文章 all are beautiful and elegant.

文筆 style.

文筆塔 small pagodas built in the form of a Chinese writing-brush, generally erected to improve the *fêng shui*. A.c. -風-

文籍 books; documents.

80 文約 a written contract; an agreement.

文縐縐·的 pedantic.

文美 handsome; graceful and elegant.

文義 the meaning or purport of a phrase.

文翰 expressions; composition.

85 文致 the sense or purport of a document.

文草 draft of a despatch.

文苑 literary department—of a newspaper or magazine.

文華殿大學士 title of a former Senior Grand Secretary.

文藝 literature and art, etc.

90 文藝復興 the Renaissance.

文藝作品 artistic or literary productions.

文藝史 the history of art and literature.

文虎章 a decoration granted for military services.

文行 to write to.

95 文衡 literary standards.

文言 literary language.

文詞 expressions; composition; written language.

文話 classical language; literary talk.

文豪 a literary giant.

100 文質 ornamental and real; shadow and substance.

文質彬彬 elegance and solidity equally combined.

文身 to tattoo the body.

文軒 an ornamented carriage—complimentary form of address.

文辭 diction; phraseology.

105 文運 literary fortunes (of a place).

文選 anthologies.

文開 a despatch, stating....

文集 anthologies; collections of essays, etc.

文·雅 or 斯文 refined; polished.

110 文電 despatches and telegrams.

文風 literary spirit or fame.

文體湮沒 the lettering has disappeared.

上下文 the context.

不文 unpolished; not cultured.

115 作文 to compose; to write.

原文 the original text.

古文 ancient writings; ancient style of composition; ancient form of characters.

惡其文之著也 she disliked the display of the elegance—of her embroidered robe.

投文 to deliver a despatch.

120 明文 orders in writing.

時文 modern style of writing.

正文 the correct text.

白文 the text, as opposed to the commentary.

英文 English; the English text.

125 華文 Chinese; the Chinese text.

行有餘力則以學文 "when he has time and opportunity after the performance of these things, he should employ them in polite studies."

闕文 a blank in the text.

(a) Civil officials, as opposed to military.

↓文官 civil service.

文員 or 文官 a civil official.

文憑印信 the civil official trusts to his seal.

文武百官 all the various civil and military officials.

5 文火 a slow fire, as opposed to 武火, a quick fire.

文職 civil appointments.

(b) Stripes; streaks; lines; veins. See No. 7132.

文石 a veined stone.

文貝 veined shells.

水文 a vein in a piece of crystal or stone.

(c) N.A. for *cash*; coins, etc. The obverse of a coin. See 幕 No. 4559—B.

一文不·值 not worth a *cash*.

一文錢 a *cash*.

分文不要 will not take a *cash*.

(d) Read *wên*[4]. To gloss.

文過 to conceal a fault; to disguise evil conduct.

文飾 to gloss; to impose on; to falsify.

扽[4] To rub off.
7130

扽拭 to brush off; to wipe.

扽摩 to stroke; to rub.

扽淚 to wipe away tears.

汶[4] The name of a river in Shantung.
7131

(a) Read *min*[2]. Used for the 岷江 in Szechwan.

(b) Read *mên*[2]. To defile.

汶濛 defiled; dirty.

受物之汶汶 to be defiled by the dust of things.

紋[2] Stripes; lines; streaks; figures. A crack, as in porcelain.
7132

紋水 the difference from fluctuation in the price of silver.

紋理 or 羅紋 the lines of the hands; stripes.

紋理·的 striped; lined.

紋跡 traces of.

5 紋銀 sycee; pure silver.

橫紋 against the grain; transverse lines.

水波紋 ripples on the water.

花紋 the figures on textile fabrics.

裂紋 a crack, as in porcelain; cracked.

紊 ⁴
7133

Tangled; involved.

紊 亂 confused; in a state of anarchy.

有 條 而 不 紊 all is in order without any confusion.

蚊 ²
蟁
蚉
7134

A mosquito; a gnat.

蚊·子 mosquitoes.

蚊 市 a swarm of mosquitoes.

蚊 帳·子 mosquito curtains.

蚊 烟 香 a kind of incense burnt to drive away mosquitoes.

蚊 艇 隊 the mosquito fleet.

蚊 蜹 gnats.

蚊 雷 the buzz of mosquitoes.

雯 ²
7135

The colouring on the clouds.

素 雯 white—of clouds.

赤 雯 rosy-tinted—of clouds.

鮫 ²
7136

The flying-fish.

鮫 鱝 魚 the flying-fish.

刎 ³
7137

To cut across.

刎 喉 or 自 刎 to cut one's throat.

刎 死 to cut one's throat.

刎 頸 交 a friendship that would lead persons to die for each other.

刎 頸 以 見 (hsien⁴) (I am ready) to cut my throat to show that I am in earnest.

吻 ³
脗
呡
7138

The corners of the mouth; the lips.

吻 合 it tallies.

口 吻 不 合 your lips do not fit your mouth---what you say is contradictory.

接 吻 to kiss.

胳 ³
7139

To join; to fit together. Inter. preceding.

胳 合 to join in marriage; it tallies.

穩 ³
儳
7140

Firm; stable; secure.

穩 住 firm; secure; steady.

穩·健 firm; stable in purpose.

穩 健 基 礎 a solid basis.

穩 健 態·度 a steady, firm attitude.

⁵穩 健 派 moderates.

穩 健 進 行 steady, solid advance.

穩 固 stable; firm.

穩 坐 觀 風 to sit firm and see which way the wind blows—to sit on the fence.

坐 穩 sit firmly; sit tight.

¹⁰穩 妥 stable; secure; steady; firm; reliable.

穩 定 firm; fixed; strong; stable.

穩 當 stable; firm; reliable; secure; steady.

穩 睡 to sleep soundly.

穩 重 grave; reserved in manner; formal; serious.

¹⁵穩 靜 態·度 a calm, steady attitude.

墊 穩 to make firm by placing something under one corner, as of a table or cupboard.

把 穩 to grasp with a sure hand.

拏 不 穩 cannot get a firm grasp of it—also used fig.

站 立·得 穩 to stand firm.

²⁰走·得 穩 it goes smoothly—as a horse; walk carefully; watch your step.

(a) u.f. 媼 No. 51. An old woman.

穩 婆 a midwife.

問 ⁴
7141

To ask; to inquire; to investigate. To send. To hold responsible; to require from.

Distinguish 聞 No. 835.

問·一·問 make inquiries.

問·不 出 來 cannot ascertain by questioning; cannot elicit an answer.

問 乾 to reduce to silence by questioning; to stump by a question.

問 事 to make inquiries about; to take responsibility.

⁵問 事 處 Information Bureau.

問 人 於 他 邦 when sending men to make inquiries in another State.

問·他·一·句 ask him a question.

問·他 要 ask him for it.

問·他 說 ask him about it.

¹⁰問·住 or 問 倒 to reduce to silence by questions.

問 供 to elicit evidence.

問 信 to inquire about; to ask the way.

問 俗 to inquire about the customs of a place.

問·候 to ask after the health of another; to send kind regards.

¹⁵問 價 to ask the price of.

問 其 所 來 asked where he had come from.

問 到 家 to get all the information required.

問 卜 to inquire by divination, etc.

問 卦 to inquire by divination, etc.

²⁰問 及 to ask about.

問 名 to ask names as a preliminary to fixing a betrothal.

問 好 to ask after the health or welfare of another.

問 安 to ask kindly after; to send kind regards.

問 官 the magistrate who tries a case.

²⁵問 對 a dialogue; a conversation.

問 心 to examine oneself; to inquire after.

問 明·白 to ask till one understands.

問 案 to try a case.

問 根 底 to make full inquiries into.

³⁰問 柳 尋 花 to associate with prostitutes.

問 津 to ask the way. See Analects Book xviii Ch. 6.

問 疑 to get abstruse points cleared up; to get light on doubtful points.

問 疾 to inquire after a sick person.

問 知 to ascertain.

35 問 程 to ask the way.

問 窮 to put to silence by questioning.

問 答 catechism; dialogue; conversation.

問 答 欄 inquiry column—in the press.

答 非 所 問 the answer is beyond the question.

40 問 細 底 to make a thorough investigation; to go to the root of the matter.

問 號 the mark of interrogation —?.

問 訊 處 Inquiry Office.

問 詞 a question; an interrogative. (*grammar.*)

問 話 to question.

45 問 說 to ask the way; to seek information.

問 語 a query; a question.

問 路 to ask the way.

問 道 to ask the way; to seek instruction; he asked, saying..

問 道 于 盲 to ask a blind man the way—to seek advice from an ignorant person.

50 問 遺 to inquire about; to send presents.

問 難 to ask about matters of which one is in doubt; to get abstruse points cleared up; to heckle.

問 題 a problem; a question; a difficulty, etc.

一 個 大 問 題 a question of prime importance.

不 成 問 題 not worth discussing.

55 不 過 是 時 間 ·的 問 題 it is merely a question of time.

勞 動 ·的 問 題 the labour problem.

宗 教 底 問 題 the religious question.

工 人 組 合 問 題 the labour-union problem.

敎 育 問 題 educational problems or questions.

60 未 決 ·的 問 題 an undecided question.

根 本 問 題 a fundamental problem.

生 活 問 題 the question of a livelihood.

發 生 問 題 gives rise to questions; gives rise to certain problems.

組 織 ·的 問 題 the problem of organization.

65 自 身 ·的 問 題 personal problems.

衛 生 問 題 problems of hygiene.

這 ·個 問 題 有 ·兩 個 觀 點 this question has two points of view.

難 決 ·的 問 題 a knotty point.

領 袖 ·的 問 題 the problem of leadership.

70 問 鼎 to ask about the sacrificial tripods—to usurp the empire.

下 問 to inquire from those of an inferior station.

不 得 過 問 cannot interfere in the matter.

不 問 no matter whether....

不 問 好 歹 no matter whether good or bad—at random.

75 借 問 permit me to ask; may I make inquiries?

再 問 to question further.

凡 事 問 我 hold me responsible for everything.

學 問 scholarship; learning.

審 問 to try a case.

80 承 問 many thanks for your kind inquiry—conventional reply to the usual inquiries about one's well-being, etc.

查 問 to investigate.

泛 問 a superficial inquiry.

詰 問 to interrogate.

詢 問 to inquire; to investigate.

85 請 問 may I ask? I beg to ask you...; I ask your advice.

顧 問 adviser.

(a) To sentence.

問 充 軍 to banish to the frontiers for compulsory military service.

問 定 to condemn; to sentence.

問 徒 to pass a sentence of banishment to another district.

問 抵 to order damages to be made good.

5 問 死 罪 to sentence to death.

問 流 to banish to a distant province.

問 罪 to condemn; to sentence.

問 賠 to order compensation to be made—for damages.

問 斬 to sentence to decapitation.

聞 2 To hear. To smell. Distinguish 開 No. 2672.

7142

聞 一 知 二 to hear one point and know the sequence—apt; to learn with little instruction.

聞 一 知 十 to infer the whole matter after hearing but one point.

聞 ·不 見 I cannot smell it.

聞 信 to hear news of.

5 聞 其 名 而 未 見 其 物 I have heard of it, but I have not yet seen it.

聞 名 to hear of by reputation.

聞 名 不 如 見 面 to know a man by repute is not as good as meeting him face to face.

聞 問 to hear and ask about—intercourse; to take an interest in.

不 相 聞 問 broken off intercourse.

10 聞 報 to hear it reported; to learn of.

聞 所 未 聞 to hear that which one has never heard before.

聞 斯 行 諸 shall I carry out a matter as soon as I hear it?

聞 耗 heard the news.

聞 知 to ascertain; to hear of.

15 聞 義 不 能 徙 to hear of righteousness but be unable to move towards it.「聞 見 to smell.

聞 見 to hear and see; experience.

聞 訊 to hear of; to ascertain.

聞 道 to hear the *Tao*—to hear the Truth; to hear it said.

聞 香 to smell the fragrance.

20 傳 聞 it is rumoured.

可 聞 within hearing.

多 聞 多 見 having much experience.

新 聞 news; tidings.

聽 聞 to hear.

25 風 聞 a rumour; a report; to hear a rumour.

(a) Read *wên*[4]. **To make known to. To state. Reputation; notoriety.**

聞 也 非 達 也 notoriety but not distinction.

聞 人 a celebrity.

聞 于 四 國 to make known throughout the whole kingdom.

聞 於 王 told it to the king.

5 聞 望 celebrated; a reputation.

聞 達 illustrious..

仁 心 仁 聞 a kindly heart and a reputation for benevolence.

以 孝 義 聞 a reputation for filial piety and public spirit.

奏聞上帝 to lay a statement before the Supreme.

聲聞過情 a reputation beyond its merits.

闅[2] To look at closely. Ancient form of the preceding.
7143

闅鄉縣 a district in Honan.

絻[4] Mourning. The ropes attached to the bier and held by mourners.
7144

絻服 mourning garments.
執絻 to hold the ropes of the bier.

(a) Read *mien*[3]. u.f. 冕 No. 4494. A cap, etc.

璺[4] A crack, as in porcelain.
7145

一道璺 a crack.

WÊNG. (ㄨㄥ)
(Uen or Ong)

翁[1] An old man; a title of respect.
7146 Distinguish 翁 No. 1860.

翁仲 statues of men placed near tombs.
翁姑翁婆 a husband's father and mother.
翁婿 father-in-law and son-in-law.
婦翁 wife's father.
[5]尊翁 your father.
新翁 a bridegroom.
白頭翁 a hoary-headed old man.
老翁 an old gentleman; venerable sir.

嗡[1] The lowing of cattle. The hum of insects.
7147

塕[3] A gust of wind.
7148

滃[3] To float, as the clouds. The rising of the clouds.
7149 The appearance of a watery expanse.

滃染 blurred.
滃㳠 a rising mist.

蝓[1] The solitary wasp or *sphex*. Lice on cattle. A kind of gad-fly.
7150

牛蝓 lice that infect cattle.

甕瓮罋[4] An earthen jar. A jar for the ashes of the dead.
7151

甕牖 a small round window like the mouth of a jar.
甕牖繩樞 a round window and a string door-pivot—great poverty.
甕缸 a water-jar.
古甕 antique jars.

(a) The archway under the gate of a city.

甕圈 the enciente of a city gate at Peking.
甕城 the enciente of a city gate —a kind of courtyard between the inner and outer gates.
甕洞 the archway under the gate of a city.

齆[4] The nose stopped up with a cold.
7152

齆膿 the thick speech of a person suffering from a cold in the head.

WO. (ㄨㄛ)
(O)

倭[1] The land of dwarfs. Poor; mean.
7153

倭奴國 the land of dwarfs— used in ancient times for Japan —Yamato.

(a) Read *wei*[4]. To bend. To yield. Bent, winding. Compliant.

周道倭遲 the road from *Chou* was winding and tedious.

渦[1] A whirlpool.
7154

渦旋 an eddy; a whirlpool.

(a) A dimple.

微渦 a little dimple.

(b) Read *kuo*[1]. A river in Anhwei.

窩[1] A nest; a hole; a haunt; a den. To shelter; to receive secretly. A depression.
7155

窩主 a receiver of stolen goods.
窩價 a reserve fund; something in hand for a rainy day.
窩匪 to harbour brigands or robbers.
窩娼 to harbour prostitutes.
[5]窩子 a nest; a lair; a resort for robbers, etc.
窩家 a receiver of stolen property.
窩棚 a shanty or shed.
窩巢 a nest; a den of thieves.
窩留 to harbour.
[10]窩脚 to trip up; to catch the foot in anything.
窩藏 to harbour.
窩賭 to run a gambling-den.
窩逃 to shelter runaways.
窩鋪 a shanty or shed.
[15]窩集 to harbour; a transliteration of a Manchu term for forests— the name of certain ancient tribes in Manchuria.
窩風 to shelter from the wind.
心窩 the pit of the stomach.
架窩 a mule litter.
胳肢窩 the armpits. (A.p. *ka*[1]-)
[20]蜂窩 the nests of wasps or bees.
酒窩 a dimple on the cheek.
鳥窩 a bird's nest.

萵[1] A term for various plants similar to lettuce.
7156

萵笋 the stems of a variety of lettuce, used as a vegetable.
萵苣 lettuce.

媧[3] Delicate; winning; beautiful. A waiting-maid.
7157 Also read *lo*[3].

臥 [4]
7158   To lie down; to rest.

臥 兔 a fur-lined cap worn in the north.

臥 內 in the bedchamber.

臥 具 pillows, mat, coverlet, etc., bedding.

臥 名 利 to cease from the pursuit of fame and wealth.

[5] 臥 床 a bed or couch; to lie on a bed.

臥 床 不 起 dangerously ill.

臥 息 to lie down and rest.

臥 房 a bedroom.

臥 薪 嘗 膽 to lie on faggots and taste gall—to nurse vengeance. *See* 嘗 No. 229-9.

[10] 臥 月 明 to sleep in the moonlight.

臥 榻 a bed or couch; to lie on a bed.

臥 治 to rule without trouble—lying down to it.

臥 游 to travel lying down—said of a person who desires to travel, but cannot realize his ambition; he therefore delights in reading traveller's tales and looking at pictures of scenery.

臥 虎 a crouching tiger—the awe of officials; daring; courage; rapacious underlings.

[15] 臥 龍 the sleeping dragon—a name given to *Chu-ko Liang.*

坐 臥 不 寧 cannot get ease either sitting or reclining.

高 臥 to sleep high—in peace and safety, retired from the cares of public life.

我 [3]
7158½   *see* 4778.

WO.   (ㄛ)
(Oh)

喔 [4.5]
7159   The cackling of fowls. Also read *wu* [4.5].

喔 咿 嚅 唲 the sound of forced laughter.

幄 [4.5]
7160   A tent. A mosquito-net. Also read *wu* [4.5].

帷 幄 a tent.

幕 幄 a tent.

握 [4.5]
7161   To hold fast; to grasp. Also read *wu* [4.5].

握 內 or 在 握 or 在 掌 握 之 中 in one's grasp; under one's control.

握 別 to grasp the hand in parting.

握 力 計 apparatus for testing the strength of the grip.

握 嘴 to cover the mouth with the hand.

[5] 握 定 to grasp firmly.

握 手 to shake hands; to grasp the hand of a friend.

握 政 權 to hold the reins of government.

握 着 眼 睛 to cover the eyes with the hand.

握 要 to grasp the essential point of a matter.

[10] 堅 握 to grip tightly.

把 握 to take hold of; to control.

渥 [4.5]
7162   To moisten; to irrigate; to enrich. Also read *wu* [4.5].

渥 丹 a deep red; to dye a deep red.

渥 澤 enriched with favours.

渥 澤 旁 敷 great bounty extending on all sides.

渥 蒙 to be deeply grateful for.

渥 霈 copious rains; moistened; favoured.

齷 [4.5]
7163   Small; paltry; mean. Dirty.

齷 齪 narrow-minded; dirty; good-for-nothing.

WU.   (ㄨ)
(U)

巫 [1.2]
7164   A wizard or witch; a medium. Magical arts. Dancing and posturing in order to induce the descent of the spirits.

巫 匠 亦 然 the wizard and the maker of coffins are the same.

巫 咒 to recite incantations.

巫 婆 a sorceress; a witch.

巫 山 a mountain and district in the east of Szechwan.

巫 峽 one of the gorges of the Upper Yangtze.

巫 祝 to recite incantations.

巫 蠱 sorcery practised by witches,—burying effigies in order to injure others. *See* 蠱 No. 3475.

巫 術 sorcery; magical arts.

巫 覡 witches and wizards.

[10] 巫 醫 magicians and doctors; treatment of disease by sorcery.

巫 風 sorcery.

事 鬼 神 曰 巫 the service of spiritual beings is called *wu.*

女 巫 witches.

男 巫 wizards.

[15] 神 巫 mediums.

神 降 而 託 於 巫 也 when spirits descend, they enter the body of the medium.

誣 [1.2]
7165   To make a false accusation. False.

誣 罔 善 人 to accuse an innocent person.

誣 告 to accuse falsely.

誣 告 反 坐 a false accusation brings upon the accuser the same punishment which he sought to inflict upon the accused.

誣 控 to accuse falsely.

[5] 誣 揑 to trump up a charge.

誣 殺 to cause the death of a person by means of false accusations.

誣 民 to oppress the masses.

誣 良 爲 娼 to charge a virtuous woman with unchastity.

誣 良 爲 盜 to charge a good man with robbery.

[10] 誣 讒 to calumniate.

誣 謗 to malign.

誣 證 a false witness; to bear false witness.

誣 賴 to implicate falsely.

誣 輕 爲 重 to charge a trifling offence in such a way as to make it appear serious.

[15] 誣 陷 to implicate falsely.

虛 誣 slanderous charges.

烏 [1]
7166   A crow or rook. Black. Distinguish 鳥 No. 4688.

烏 事 disgusting things. *Prob. a corrup. of* 鳥 事 (*tiao*³-) the damn thing. (*vulg.*)

烏 兎 a term for the sun and moon, respectively.

烏 合 to assemble like crows—a disorderly mob which is easily dispersed.

烏 合 之 衆 a set of roughs; an undisciplined mob.

⁵烏 哺 the grace of feeding (its parents) by disgorging—said of the young crows. See below—16, 40.

烏 土 black earth—opium.

烏 師 a professor who trains singing-girls.

烏 木 ebony.

烏 梅 black plums.

¹⁰烏 棗 black dates.

烏 欖 black olives.

烏 江 a river in North Anhwei connected with the death of Hsiang Yü 項 羽.

烏 烟 black smoke—opium.

烏 焉 成 馬 the characters wu and yen become ma—in careless copying or proof-reading.

¹⁵烏 獨 tubers of aconite. See below—32.

烏 私 念 切 filial duty imposes its bonds upon me—from the idea of the young crow feeding its parents. See above—5, and below—40.

烏 米 opium.

烏 綢 black silk.

烏 臼 樹 or 烏 桕 樹 the tallow tree—Stillingea sebifera.

²⁰烏 芋 Sagittaria sagittifolia; also used for the water-chestnut or 荸 薺.

烏 號 the name of a good bow.

烏 蠋 a variety of large destructive caterpillar.

烏 衣 a name for the swallow.

烏 豆 a large variety of black bean.

²⁵烏 賊 the cuttle-fish.

烏 越 越·的 black and staring—eyes.

烏 輪 a name for the sun.

烏 金 an alloy of copper with a certain percentage of gold.

烏 雀 a name for the swallow.

³⁰烏 雜 an undisciplined mob like a flock of crows. See above—3.

烏 雲 black clouds—the hair over the temples of a woman.

烏 頭 the tubers of aconite. See above—15.

烏 頭 白 white-headed crows—an impossibility.

烏 頭 馬 角 (white-headed) crows and horned horses—things that never happen. See above—33.

³⁵烏 騅 the famous piebald horse of Hsiang Yü 項 羽.

烏 骨 鷄 the silky fowl,—its bones are black; it is very much esteemed as a delicacy for invalids.

烏 鬚 藥 dye to blacken the beard.

烏 鬼 a name once used by the Chinese for the negro.

烏 魚 the black fish.

⁴⁰烏 烏 私 情 filial piety—the young crows are said to disgorge in order to feed their parents. See above—5, 16.

烏 鴉 a crow; a rook.

烏 鴉 不 與 鳳 凰 棲 crows do not roost with phœnixes.

烏 鴉 命 the destiny of a crow—black, i.e., unlucky.

烏 鷄 the silky fowl. See above—36.

⁴⁵烏 麥 a name for buckwheat. See 蕎 No. 748.

烏 黑 jet black.

烏 龍 the black dragon.

烏 龍 茶 Oolung tea.

烏·龜 a black tortoise—a cuckold; a term of abuse.

⁵⁰發 烏 to look dull or dead—of colours.

金 烏 the golden crow—a name for the sun.

(a) A negative. An interrogative particle. How? When? An exclamation—Alas! Inter. next.

烏 乎 Alas! How sad!

烏 可 議 廢 者 we cannot discuss the question of destroying—the temples.

烏 有 there is not—gone.

歸 於 烏 有 to revert to nothing; it will vanish away.

⁵烏 有 此 事 no such thing; such a thing never happened.

烏 用 衆 there is no need to use a great number—of men.

烏 知 do not know.

烏 能 ...How can they....?

(b) Used in transliterating.

烏 喇 name of an ancient tribe in Manchuria; Manchu term for a river, as 吉 林 烏 喇.

烏 孫 a race which was driven westward at the end of the 2nd century B.C. by the Hsiung nu.

烏 托 邦 Utopia.

烏 拉 name of a Manchurian tribe; a kind of moccasin worn in Kirin; the ula or system of compulsory service of men, horses, yaks, etc., for official transport in Tibet, Mongolia, etc.

⁵烏 拉 山 the Ural Mountains.

烏 敢 大 Uganda.

烏 滸 the River Oxus.

烏 護 the Ouigours.

嗚¹ An exclamation of regret. Distinguish 鳴 No. 4535.
7167

嗚 呼 Alas! Alack!

嗚 咽 sobbing.

嗚 嗚 crying and sobbing.

塢
隖⁴ A bank; a low wall; an entrenchment.
7168

山 塢 a valley.

村 塢 a village.

營 塢 an entrenchment.

船 塢 a dock.

摀³ To cover with the hand. To hide.
7169

摀·了 faded; mildewed.

摀·死 to smother to death.

摀·着 耳·朶 to cover the ears.

↑·摀·的 and things; and so forth.

熓³ To bank a fire.
7170

鄔¹·⁴· Name of a place.
7171

鄔 程 a district in Chekiang.

鎢¹·⁴ Tungsten.
7172

无² Without. A negative. Not. Radical 71.
7173

圬 杇 7174

To plaster; to whitewash.

圬 人 a plasterer.
圬 牆 to plaster or whitewash a wall.
圬 鏝 a trowel used by plasterers.

污 汙 洿 7175

Stagnant water. Impure; filthy; vile. Mean. To defile.

污 人 名 譽 to take away a man's good name, to defame.
污 俗 filthy customs.
污 吏 corrupt officials.
污 名 a foul reputation.
污 君 a corrupt prince.
污 垢 filth.
污 塗 to defile.
污 心 a lascivious mind.
污 惡 相 累 polluted by evil associations. (-o⁴-)
[10] 污 染 to pollute; to debauch; to be stained with evil; to contaminate.
污 泥 foul mud; to befoul.
污 淫 to have illicit connection with.
污 濁 filthy.
污 瀆 a foul drain; to pollute; to desecrate.
[15] 污 穢 filthiness; impurity; dirt; to dirty; to make unclean; to contaminate.
污 穢 不 堪 disgustingly filthy.
污 窳 filthy; spoilt.
污 臭 foul; filthy; disgusting.
污 著 to debauch; to be contaminated through evil associations. (-cho²)
[20] 污 蠹 to defile and ruin.
污 衊 to desecrate; to pollute; to calumniate.
洿 衊 聖 神 to profane.
污 賊 者 rebels.
污 辱 to debauch; to insult; to profane; to desecrate.
[25] 污 辱 聖 神 to profane; profane.
污 辱 聖 神 之 言 profanity.
污 辱 聲 名 to calumniate.

污 隆 little and much; failure and success.
污 鬼 a foul spirit or demon.
[30] 污 點 blots; stains; stigma; foul spots; a blemish.
同 流 合 污 used like, "birds of a feather flock together."
染 污 to be defiled; to pollute; to debauch.

(a) Read *wu¹*. To wash.

薄 汙 我 私 I will wash my private garments clean.

(b) Read *wa¹*. Lowlying.

汙 不 至 阿 (o¹) 其 所 好 if they had not been in a low state they would not have flattered the one whom they esteemed.
汙 池 ponds and lakes.
汙 渠 drains.
田 卒 汙 萊 our fields are either marshes or moors.

(c) Read *wa¹*. To hollow out.

汙 尊 to hollow out the ground to receive liquids as in a drinking vessel—from which they drank by scooping up the liquid with both hands.

仵 7176

An opponent; a match; an equal. u.f. 伍 No. 7187a.

仵·作 former term for a coroner—now 檢 驗 吏 is used.

午 7177

The seventh of the *Earthly Branches*. The south. Noon. 11 a.m.—1 p.m. Distinguish 牛 No. 4737; 年 No. 4711.

午 刻 noon; midday.
午 前 or 上 午 the forenoon.
午 堂 the midday session—of a court.
午 夜 midnight.
[5] 午 後 or 下 午 the afternoon.
午 日 a day with 午 as one of its cyclical characters—every twelfth day; the fifth of the fifth lunar month.
午 時 11 a.m.—1 p.m.
午 月 the fifth lunar month; the moon at midnight.

午 正 or 正 午 or 中 午 or 晌 午 noon; midday.
[10] 午 礮 the noon gun.
午 門 the imperial palace—as the throne faces the south.
午 飯 or 中 飯 the noon meal.
交 午 about noon.
初 午 11 a.m.
[15] 端 午 the fifth of the fifth lunar month.

(a) Interlacing. Crosswise.

午 割 cut in both directions.
午 午 rising up irregularly like mountain peaks.
午 達 to bind up the hair in a knot—of girls.
旁 午 crosswise; athwart; in both directions. *See* No. 4926-3, 4.
公 事 旁 午 press of official business.

忤 啎 7178 3.4.

Obstinate; disobedient; intractable. Inter. next.

忤 忤 然 stubborn; irritated.
忤 意 to hold to one's opinions.
忤 耳 it grates on the ear.
忤 觸 unmannerly; rude.
忤 逆 wilful; stubborn; unfilial.
忤 逆 不 孝 an obstinate and undutiful son.

迕 7179 3.4.

Obstinate; perverse. Inter. preceding.

迕 旨 to oppose the imperial will.

無 橆 7180 2

Without; apart from; none. A negative.

無 一 不 曉 nothing he does not know.
無 一 可 用 not one of any use.
無 一 缺 少 not one lacking.
無 上 nothing above; the acme; nonpareil.
[5] 無 上 上 品 the most superior class—of goods, etc.
無 上 權 supremacy.
無 不 周 知 everybody knows all about it.

無 中 生 有 or 將 無 作 有 to make something out of nothing—trumped up; fabricated; imagination.

無 主 ownerless.

[10] 無 主 物 ownerless things.

無 了 無 休 to persist to the utmost.

無 事 at leisure; at peace; no annoyance.

無 事 可 作 no work to do.

無 事 忙 very busy about nothing.

[15] 無 事 生 事 to make trouble out of nothing.

無 二 價 uniform prices.

無 二 無 疑 absolutely without doubt; certain.

無 二 鬼 rascals; vagabonds.

無 人 不 .... there is no one who does not....

[20] 無 人 過 問 no one has anything to do with it.

無 介 紹 friendless; having no one to introduce him.

無 以 則 王 乎 if you will not let me cease, then let our talk be about the royal rule.

無 以 尚 之 to esteem (virtue) unsurpassable.

無 以 易 李 伶 there is no one to take the place of the actor *Li*—in the part of *Yen Hsiang-kuo*.

[25] 無 以 爲 家 unable to nourish his family.

無 他 法 no alternative.

無 他 物 there was nothing else.

無 他 說 there is nothing more to be said.

無 代 價 物 priceless things.

[30] 無 任 exceedingly; inadequate for—*used like* 不 勝 No. 5754—B. 7ff.

無 任 感 佩 I am extremely grateful.

無 似 unlike; incomparable; degenerate—a depreciatory term for oneself, I am not at all like—what I should be.

無 何 shortly afterwards; in a little while.

無 何 有 nothing; emptiness.

[35] 無 何 有 之 鄉 used like our Utopia.

無 位 眞 人 there is within you—an unthroned true teacher. (*Taoist*).

無 信 用 not trustworthy; discredited.

無 俚 listless; dejected.

無 備 unprepared.

[40] 無 僞 的 guileless; sincere.

無 僞 之 信 sincere trust.

無 價 之 寶 a priceless treasure.

無 儔 peerless; matchless.

無 償 契 約 a contract without consideration received. (*legal*).

[45] 無 入 而 不 自 得 there is no position in which he is not at ease and self-possessed.

無 兩 without a peer.

無 冬 無 夏 be it winter or be it summer....

無 出 其 右 nothing superior to it; matchless.

無 分 彼 此 no distinction between mine and thine; to have things in common.

[50] 無 分 無 關 no part nor lot; no concern; no connection with.

無 切 實 的 答 覆 an indefinite reply.

無 刊 登 之 價值 of no value as an item for the press.

無 前 foremost.

無 前 例 there is no precedent for this.

[55] 無 則 言 無 if not, then say not.

無 力 without strength; disability.

無 千 大 萬 immense numbers.

無 匹 peerless.

無 厭 insatiable.

[60] 無 及 unavailing; too late.

無 可 不 可 nothing which he must or must not do.

無 可 具 論 nothing to discuss.

無 可 取 not worth anything; nothing to be got out of it.

無 可 名 狀 的 nondescript.

[65] 無 可 如 何 there is no help for it; hopeless.

無 可 無 不 可 indecisive; uncertain; without any preconceived ideas.

無 可 爭 辯 indisputable.

無 名 小 邑 a small city of no repute. 無 名 小 卒 a nobody.

無 名 指 the fourth finger of the hand; the ring finger.

[70] 無 名 氏 a pseudonym; anonymous.

無 名 稿 anonymous articles—in the press.

無 名 骨 the os innominata.

無 告 helpless, having no one to appeal to.

無 君 之 心 a wish to get rid of the prince.

---

[75] 無 命 之 終 without end of life.

無 咎 無 譽 nothing either to blame nor praise.

無 味 的 耗 費 foolish expenditure.

無 善 狀 nothing good to tell about myself—conventional in letters.

無 因 causeless; without reason.

[80] 無 地 可 容 no place for him—not a leg to stand on.

無 垢 衣 the unsoiled garment—the Buddhist cassock.

無 壽 之 終 a life without end.

無 大 小 neither large nor small—just the size.

無 央 unending. (*Taoist*).

[85] 無 失 其 時 do not neglect their—breeding—seasons.

無 奈 but; alas! unfortunately.

無 妄 unexpectedly; untimely.

無 妄 之 災 an unexpected calamity.

無 如 but; alas; notwithstanding; however.

[90] 無 好 感 no good impressions; no good influence.

無 妨 of no consequence; no harm.

無 始 無 邊 without beginning, without bounds—of the teachings of Buddha.

無 委 任 狀 的 non-commissioned.

無 子 彈 blank cartridges.

[95] 無 孔 不 入 there is no opening into which he does not enter—of one who is skilful in intrigue.

無 定 例 irregular; without precedent.

無 定 式 the infinitive mood. (*gramm.*).

無 定 形 amorphous.

無 定 期 intermittent; without any stated period.

[100] 無 家 可 歸 homeless.

無 己 unselfish.

無 已 cannot end; unavoidable; unsatisfied.

無 已 而 帝 will not stop until he is emperor.

無 常 or 無 常 鬼 a demon regarded as the messenger of death; the first also means, inconstant; irregular.

[105] 無 常 心 inconstant; without perseverance.

無 干 having no part in; not connected with.

↑ 無 射 (-*i*[4·5]) a classical pitch corresponding in function to A-sh...

(as disting from B-flat).

無 幾 not much; not many.

無 底 價 priceless.

無 底 坑 the bottomless pit.

110 無 底 洞 a bottomless cavern—something that can never be filled up; by analogy—a covetous heart.

無 庸 費 心 no need to trouble yourself.

無 彈²力 inelastic.

無 形 資 本 invisible capital—certain rights which are equivalent to capital, such as patent rights or copyright.

無 影 無 形 without form or likeness.

115 無 影 無 踪 not a trace left.

無 後 without posterity.

無 後 顧 之 憂 there are no regrets; no worry in looking back.

無 從 there was no way to; there is no opening.

無 從 致 書 no way to obtain books.

120 無 從 躲 no place in which to hide; no means of concealment.

無 復 置 慮 no further cause for anxiety.

無 復 蹊 蹬 there was no longer any path by which to ascend.

無 微 不 燭 to shine everywhere—to see a case clearly.

無 微 不 至 never came short in the smallest details.

125 無 心 inadvertently; unwittingly; unintentionally.

無 心 之 過 unintentional offence.

無 心·想 without thought; without any interest in.

無 心 是 道 to be without thought is Tao—wisdom.

無 怪 乎 此 it is not to be wondered at.

130 無 性·命 之 憂 not fatal—as in a report of an accident.

無 性 生 殖 asexual propagation.

無 恙 quite well; no sickness or indisposition.

無 恥 之 徒 a shameless rascal.

無 情 obdurate; apathetic.

135 無 意 中 thoughtlessly; inadvertently.

無 意 咮 senseless; uninteresting.

無 意 於 人 世 the world has no charms—Giles.

無 意 淘 汰 unconscious selection.

無 意 犯 unintentional crime.

140 無 意 謂·的 nonsensical.

無 意 識 unconscious.

無 意 識·的 意 念 unconscious thought.

無 慮 about. See 亡 No. 7034—B. 4.

無 慮·的 without anxiety.

145 無 懈 可 擊 flawless.

無 成 unsuccessful; incomplete.

無 我 suppression of self.

無 我 者 an unselfish person.

無 惑 乎 it is no marvel that....

150 無 戰 鬥 力 ineffective—as troops, etc.

無 所 不 備 nothing unprepared; fully prepared; everything complete.

無 所 不 在 omnipresent.

無 所 不 爲 there is nothing which he does not do—in the way of evil.

無 所 不 用 其 極 in everything he does his utmost.

155 無 所 不 能 almighty.

無 所 不 至 to go to all lengths; disorderly.

無 所 事 志 nothing which demands the bending of the mind.

無 所 倚 or 無 所 倚 靠 none to trust to; nothing to depend on.

無 所 取 材 nothing at hand to use; unable to use materials ready to hand; unable to judge matters.

160 無 所 可 否·的 non-committal.

無 所 委 蛇 without any dragging on. (-i²)

無 所 懼 怕 utterly without fear.

無 所 指 望 without hope.

無 所 歸 no one to attend to the burial; nowhere to go.

165 無 所 見 聞 he has no experience.

無 所 適 從 with no definite plan to follow.

無 拘·束 unrestrained; unchecked.

無 抵 抗 主 義 the doctrine of non-resistance.

無 損 於 怨 (to give Ch'in 秦 grain) will do nothing to remove his grievance against us.

170 無 據 destitute of resources.

無 擔 保 背 書 endorsement without security.

無 故 causeless; no visible cause

as of death a coroner's verdict.

未 免 無 故 there seems to be no reason for it.

無 故 延 誤 unreasonable delay.

175 無 政 府 anarchy.

無 政 府 主 義 anarchism; nihilism.

無 政 府 黨 anarchists.

無 效 invalid; of none effect; unsuccessful; lacking results.

無 效·力 ineffective.

180 無 效 契 約 an invalid contract. (legal).

無 效 行·爲 futile action; an invalid act.

無 數 innumerable.

無 敵 not equalled; cannot be matched; without a rival.

仁 者 無 敵 the good man has no enemy.

185 無 敵 艦 dreadnought; battleships.

無 敵 艦 隊 a dreadnought squadron.

無 敵 大 戰 艦 superdreadnoughts.

無 文 illiterate; unpolished.

無 方 without limit; unprecedented.

190 無 日 shortly; very soon.

無 日 不 然 it is always so.

無 易 樹 子³ do not change the appointed heir.

無 明 dull; stupid.

無 明 火 anger.

195 無 是 無 非 to have no reason at all; without rhyme or reason.

無 時 unfortunately; unlucky.

無 暇 without leisure.

無 有 此 事 there is no such thing.

無 服 之 殤 children who die before the age of seven, for whom no mourning is worn.

200 無 期 徒 刑 penal servitude with banishment for life.

無 案 牘 可 稽 no documentary records.

無 根 之 草 a ne'er-do-well.

無 根 無 蒂 without foundation or support.

無 極 without limit—the Illimitable, out of which, according to Chinese philosophy, all things were produced. See 太 No. 6020-28; 二 No. 1751-7.

205 無 條 件 unconditional; without conditions.

無條件交還 unconditional rendition.

無條件債務 unconditional obligations.

無條件條款 unconditional clauses.

無條件·的 unconditionally.

210 無條理·的 illogical.

↑無條件投降 unconditional surrender. (-*hsiang*[2])

無機化合物 inorganic compounds.

無機化學 inorganic chemistry.

無機物 inorganic matter.

215 無機體 inorganic.

無欲則剛 he who is without desire is strong.

無比 incomparable; matchless.

無氣·力 without energy or strength.

無水·的 anhydrous.

220 無水酸 anhydrite.

無法 without plan—no help for it.

無法可治 there is no remedy for it; there is no way to settle the matter.

無法投遞之信札 dead-letters.

無法無天 lawless; reckless.

225 無涯 boundless.

無濟於事 of no help in the matter; useless; inadequate.

無災無病 free from calamity and sickness.

無烟火藥 smokeless powder.

無烟煤 smokeless coal; anthracite.

230 無爲 to do nothing; to remain passive; the doctrine of inaction; quietism; non-interference.

無爲之敎[4] the doctrine of non-interference as taught by Laotzŭ.

無爲無所不爲也 do nothing, and there is nothing which cannot be done.

無爲而天下歸之 without effort on his part, the whole empire reverts to him.

無爲而治 to govern by non-interference; to govern without effort.

235 無爲而無不爲 it does nothing, yet it accomplishes everything.

無物件 no effects. (*commercial*).

無狀 unmannerly.

無狀子[3] I, the unfilial son—conventional.

無理 unreasonable; unprincipled.

240 無理取鬧 unreasonable altercation.

無瑕疵占有 unimpeachable possession. (*legal*.)

無甚價·値 of little value.

無甚於生 nothing is greater than life.

無生之始 eternal; without beginning; uncreated.

245 無生無滅 without birth, without destruction. (*Budd*.).

無生物 inanimate things.

無生理....we should have no chance to live.

無產羣衆 the proletariat.

無產階級 the proletariat.

250 無用 useless.

無用·的人 a useless fellow.

無由得入 no way of entry.

無畏戰艦 a dreadnought battleship. *See above*—185.

無異議 there is no dissenting voice.

255 無疆 boundless.

無病呻吟 groaning when not really in pain—making a fuss about nothing; baseless anxiety.

無病而死 to die peacefully without sickness.

無益 unprofitable.

無益於你 unprofitable to you.

260 無盡無休 endless.

無盡藏 unlimited resources.

無目的[4] aimless; purposeless.

無相宗 a sect of Buddhism that denies the existence of form.

無知妄作 rash, foolish actions.

265 無知覺 unconscious; insensible.

無神派 atheists. -論 atheism.

無禁制 unrestrained; unhampered; untrammelled.

無祿 without emolument; unlucky.

無禮無法 without manners and decency.

270 無租地 land free from taxes.

無稽之談 unfounded statements; nonsense.

無窮 inexhaustible.

無端 without cause or reason; nothing in particular; bottomless.

思無端 random thought.

275 無端生有 making trouble out of nothing.

無算 innumerable.

無米爲炊 to prepare to cook the meal without rice—lacking the necessary materials one cannot accomplish one's intentions.

無精打彩 dispirited; listless; apathetic.

無系統的 unclassified; without system.

280 無約國 non-treaty powers.

無紀律 undisciplined.

無紋筋 involuntary muscles.

無縛何解 while you are not bound why seek release? (*Budd*.).

無線電事宜 radio affairs.

285 無線電傳達機 wireless transmitter.

無線電台 wireless stations.

無線電吸收 radio-absorption.

無線電周波數 radio-frequency.

無線電回生的 radio-generative.

290 無線電圈形天線 wireless loop-aerial.

無線電報 wireless telegrams; radiograms.

無線電報務員 wireless operator.

無線電報室 wireless operator's cabin on a ship.

無線電增幅器 radio-amplifier. =301.

295 無線電局 Radio Bureau.

無線電接收站 wireless receiving-station.

無線電接收裝置 wireless receiving-set.

輕便無線電機 portable radio-set.

無線電播送站 radio sending-station.

300 無線電播音者 radio-broadcaster.

無線電擴大器 radio-amplifier.

無線電收音機 wireless receiver.

無線電變壓器 radio-transformer.

無線電桿 wireless mast.

305 無線電檢波器 radio-detector.

無線電生 wireless operator.

無線電盤 wireless panel.

無線電管理局 Radio Bureau.

無線電羅盤 wireless compass.

[310] 無線電術 wireless telegraphy.

無線電話 wireless telephony.

無緣 to have no affinity for.

無緣無故 without cause or reason.

無美不具 everything luxurious; included.

[315] 無着²無靠·的 nothing to trust to. (-chao²-)

無聊 dejected; purposeless; unhappy; uneasy; silly; ennui.

無以聊生 no means of livelihood; no resources.

無聊之極 extreme depression.

無聊苟且 careless; remiss.

[320] 無聊賴 without resources; dejected; dispirited.

無聲無息 neither sound nor smell—of a person who is unknown to fame and without notoriety.

無能 without ability; unable; lacking power.

無能出其右者 no one could excel him.

無能力 disability.

[325] 無能力者 an incompetent person; one suffering from disability. (legal).

無能爲 nothing to be done.

無脊椎動○物 invertebrates.

無腸公子³ the bowelless gentleman—a name for the crab.

無與倫比 incomparable; none can be compared with him.

[330] 無良 without any goodness; evil.

無色⁴界 the world of invisibility, complete absence of thought and matter. (Budd.).

無花布 plain cloths—drills, etc.

無花果ㄦ the fig—the blossomless fruit.

無萬數 innumerable; vast numbers.

[335] 無藉 without resources or means.

無處不在 omnipresent.

無處避難⁴ no refuge; no place of escape.

無虧 without loss; without blame.

無補 or 無裨 unavailing; inadequate; to no purpose.

[340] 無見 without judgement or discrimination.

無視 not to see—to despise; supercilious.

無親無友 without kin or friends.

無言可答 nothing to say in reply; speechless.

無計可施 without any plans which might be used; utterly without resources.

[345] 無記名 unsigned; unregistered.

無記名公債 stock to bearer.

無記名投票 open ballot.

無記名畫線票 an open crossed cheque.

無記名票 a cheque payable to bearer.

[350] 無記名簽批 endorsement in blank.

無記名股 unregistered shares.

無試驗檢定 to accept without preliminary examination.

無誤 or 無訛 O.K., all correct.

無話可說 nothing to say in reply; speechless.

[355] 無話可駁 unanswerable.

無論 or 不論 no matter....; immaterial.

無謀故 unpremeditated.

無謂 unprofitable; useless.

無謂之神話 foolish and unprofitable myths.

[360] 無議·的 indisputable.

無貨物 no effects. (commercial).

無資力 insolvency. (legal).

無賴 without means of support; a worthless—person.

無賴漢 a worthless fellow.

[365] 無賢不肖 not virtuous; unworthy.

無趣 insipid; dreary; dull.

無軌可循 without any precedent for guidance.

無軌電車 railless electric cars.

無較級 the positive degree. (grammar).

[370] 無辜 blameless.

無辭以對 he was unable to answer.

無迹可見 no trace can be found.

無過 without fault.

無過不及 free from excess and deficiency.

[375] 無道之主 an unprincipled ruler.

無遠弗屆 no place too distant to be reached.

無適也無莫也 does not set (his mind) either for anything, or against anything.

無邊無岸 boundless; illimitable.

無那 alas! Similar to 無奈.

[380] 無量² immeasurable. (Budd.).

無量²數⁴ numberless.

無門無閂 without gates or bars.

無間 (chien⁴) without interval.

無間⁴地獄 a Buddhist hell where the torment is incessant.

[385] 無聞⁴然 without a flaw.

無關緊要 unimportant.

無關輕重 of no great importance.

無限 unlimited.

無限公司 unlimited company—an ordinary partnership.

[390] 無限·制 not limited; without qualifications.

無限大 infinity.

無限小數 unlimited decimals.

無限責任 unlimited liability.

無際 unlimited; boundless.

[395] 無隙可鑽 no crack to get in by—no opening; nothing to take hold of.

無雙 matchless; peerless; unique.

無非 or 莫非 without doubt; beyond question; nothing but.

無非事者 neither was purposeless.

無非·是充數而已 merely to make up the required number.

[400] 無韻之什 blank verse.

無須 need not; not necessarily.

無頭無腦 without any clue; the causes are not apparent.

無風三尺浪 waves three feet high rising without any breeze—baseless slanders.

無風帶 the doldrums.

[405] 無骨 without bone—lacking vigour and firmness—of penmanship.

無鹽 the name of a place in which there lived a woman named 鍾離春; she was very repulsive in appearance and having reached the age of forty without finding favour, she demanded an audience of Prince Hsüan of Ch'i 齊宣王

(B.C. 342), upon whom she made such an impression that she was taken by him to wife —from this incident the term has come to mean—an ugly woman.

無麵餺飥 to try and make cakes without flour—desires cannot be achieved if the necessary things are lacking.

全無 not in the least.

永無 never.

410 絕無 not at all.

嫵 / 娬 ³
7181

To please; to cajole; to fawn; to flatter.

嫵媚·的 seductive; fascinating; attractive.

廡 ³
7182

A covered way. A verandah. A porch.

廊廡 a verandah; passages or corridors.

(a) Read *wu*². Luxuriant. Inter. 蕪 No. 7184.

蕃廡 luxuriance of vegetation.

憮 ³
7183

Disappointed; disconcerted. To soothe; to cherish.

憮然爲閒⁴ he was thoughtful for a moment.

夫子³憮然曰 the Master observed, with a sigh....

(a) Read *hsü*³. Arrogant. To fawn upon.

媚憮 to fawn upon.

(b) Read *hu*¹. Great. Arrogant.

亂如此憮 (that I should suffer) from disorders thus great!

昊天泰憮 (the terrors of) great Heaven are very excessive.

毋憮毋傲 do not be rude, do not be haughty.

蕪 ²
7184

A vigorous growth of weeds; jungle. Waste; neglected, as lands.

蕪俚 coarse and vulgar.

蕪廢 neglected and uncultivated.

蕪昧 mentally dark; intellectually dull.

蕪札 my poor screed—conventional.

⁵蕪沒 overgrown with weeds.

蕪湖 Wuhu—a port on the Yangtze in Anhwei.

蕪穢 full of weeds.

蕪茂 luxuriance of growth.

蕪菁 the rape turnip—*Brassica rapa*.

¹⁰蕪雜 obscure; vague—as style.

蕪雜之詞 vague expressions.

荒蕪 neglected and out of cultivation.

舞 ³
7185

To posture; to dance. To brandish. To fence.

舞刀 or 舞劍 to brandish a sword; sword-play.

舞動 to dance; to prance; to brandish.

舞勺 the title of an ancient ode of the *Chou* dynasty; it was the tune of a dance taught to boys at the age of thirteen, being a civilian dance, as opposed to the military dances. *See below*—17.

舞勺之年 the thirteenth year of a lad's age.

⁵舞女 dancing-girls; cabaret girls.

舞弄 to play a trick; to give exhibitions of....

舞文弄墨 to indulge in fancy writing; to tamper with documents, etc., for fraudulent purposes.

舞文弄法 to draw up or tamper with documents for illegal purposes.

舞手弄脚 to posture; to gesticulate.

¹⁰舞弊 to indulge in malpractices—especially of officials.

舞技勇 to perform feats of strength.

舞文以飾之奸 to cover up malpractices by clever writing of memorials, etc.

舞權 to abuse one's authority.

舞法 to pervert the law.

¹⁵舞臺 a stage; a theatre.

舞袖 to wave the sleeves in posturing.

舞象 the military dance of King *Wu*, taught to lads when full-grown, about fifteen years of age; a dancing elephant.

舞象之年 the fifteenth year of a lad's age. *See above*—3, 4.

舞蹈 to dance; to gesticulate—for joy.

²⁰舞雩 an ancient sacrifice for rain in time of drought,—female mediums danced around an altar, hence the name.

風乎舞雩 enjoy the breeze among the rain-altars.

打舞 to posture when dancing.

歌舞 to sing and dance.

跳舞 dancing.

憮 ³
7186

To skip about; to dance for joy.

五 / 乂 ³
7187

Five. The second is an ancient form of the character.

五一節 May Day.

五世其昌 May you prosper for five generations!

五中 the viscera. *See below*—66.

五九紀念 the anniversary of the signing of the assent to the "Twenty One Demands" made by Japan, on May 9th, 1915.

五五二十五 5 times 5 is 25.

⁸五人之當刑 the five men bore the punishment.

五仙 the five classes of supernatural beings. (*Tao.*). Disembodied spirits, 鬼仙, having no place of rest either among men or among the immortals.

Genii of human kind, 人仙, men who have succeeded in freeing themselves from the infirmities of the flesh.

Genii dwelling upon earth, 地仙, human beings who have attained to immortality in this world.

Deified genii, 神仙, immortals who have left the earth

and live in the blissful realms of the blessed.

Celestial gods, 天仙, those who have attained to purity and have won perpetual life in Heaven.

五代 the five dynasties before the T'ang dynasty.
1. 宋. *Sung.* A.D. 420—478.
2. 齊. *Ch'i.* A.D. 479—501.
3. 梁. *Liang.* A.D. 502—556.
4. 陳. *Ch'ên.* A.D. 557—587.
5. 隋. *Sui.* A.D. 581—618.

The five dynasties after the T'ang dynasty.
1. 梁. *Liang.* A.D. 907—922.
2. 唐. *T'ang.* A.D. 923—935.
3. 晉. *Chin.* A.D. 936—946.
4. 漢. *Han.* A.D. 947—950.
5. 周. *Chou.* A.D. 951—959.

五倫 the five relationships—*See* No. 4247-1.

五光十色 gay with variegated colours.

[10]五內 the five viscera. *See below* —66.

五典 the five relationships. *See above*—8.

五分 one half; fifty per cent.

五分四裂 scattered, broken up.

五分明 just light; the first glimmer of dawn.

[15]五分像 a half-length portrait.

五分鐘 five minutes.

五刑 the five punishments. *See* No. 1198-5 for the more ancient classification. The more modern is:—death 死, banishment for life 無期徒刑, banishment for a limited term 有期徒刑, detention 拘役, and fines 罰金.

五勝 the permutations of the five elements. *See below*—72.

五十 fifty.

[20]五味 the five flavours—sweet 甜, sour 酸, bitter 苦, pungent 辣, and salt 鹹:—corresponding to 土 earth, 木 wood, 火 fire, 金 metal, and 水 water, respectively.

五味子 the seeds of *Schizandra chinensis*—used as a tonic.

五四運動 the hostile demonstrations against the Foreign Office on May 4th, 1918, as a protest against the granting of the "Twenty One Demands" made by Japan.

五口通商 opening of the five trade ports—Shanghai, Canton, Ning-po, Foochow and Amoy in 1842.

五大洲 the five continents.

五大洋 the five oceans.

[25]五季 the later 五代. *See above* —7.

五官 the five senses or regulators of the bodily functions—the ear, the eye, the mouth, the nose, and the heart; or, the two hands, the mouth, the eye, and the ear; or, the ears for hearing, the eyes for seeing, the nose for smelling, the tongue for speaking, and the skin for feeling.

五官不正 his features are irregular.

五官清秀 refined features.

五尺之童 a lad; a servant.

[30]五嶺 the five ranges of mountains which formed the Southern boundary of the empire when the *Ch'in* dynasty took the throne. 221 B.C.

大庾, the range between what is now Kiangsi and Kwangtung.

始安, a continuation of the same range.

臨賀, the range between Hunan and Kwangtung.

桂陽, the range north of Kwangsi.

揭陽, the range between Fukien and Kwangtung.

五嶽 the five sacred mountains of China.
東嶽 or 泰山 in Shantung.
南嶽 or 衡山 in Hunan.
西嶽 or 華山 in Shensi.
北嶽 or 恒山 in Hopei.
中嶽 or 嵩山 in Honan.

五帝 the five emperors—2952—2205 B.C.
太昊 *T'ai Hao.*
炎帝 *Yen Ti.*
黃帝 *Huang Ti.*
少昊 *Shao Hao.*
顓頊 *Chuan Hsü.*
Also the five planetary gods 一青帝, 赤帝, 黃帝, 白帝, 黑帝, corresponding with Jupiter, Mars, Saturn, Venus, and Mercury, respectively.

五帝天 a term for heaven.

五帶 the five zones of the globe.

[35]五常 the five constant virtues—benevolence 仁, righteousness 義, propriety 禮, knowledge 智, and sincerity 信.

五戒 the five precepts of Buddhism—
Slay not, 不殺生.
Steal not, 不偷盜.
Lust not, 不邪淫.
Be not light in conversation, 不妄語.
Drink not intoxicants, 不飲酒, nor eat meat, 不食肉.

五數 the five numbers in a decimal series from one to ten thousand, 一, 十, 百, 千, 萬.

五方 the five directions—north, south, east, west and centre.

五族 the five races of China.
漢 Chinese.
滿 Manchu.
蒙 Mongol.
回 Mohammedan.
藏 Tibetan.

[40]五族一家 the five races united in one nation.

五族共和 the union of the five races in the Chinese Republic.

五日京兆 governor of the capital for five days—to hold office for a brief period; also, to act without foresight.

五星 the five planets—
金星 Venus.
木星 Jupiter.
水星 Mercury.
火星 Mars.
土星 Saturn.

五更天 the fifth watch of the night.

[45]五月五 or 五當五 or 五端五 the 5th of the 5th lunar month —the summer festival, when accounts are reckoned up; the day of the dragon-boat festival.

五服 the five divisions of China under *Yü* the Great; the five degrees of mourning according to kinship. *See* No. 1999-2.

五材 the five primary elements. *See below*—71.

五棓子 (or 倍子) gall-nuts.

五權憲法 the quintuple constitution based on the five principles of administrative authority as outlined by Dr. Sun Yat-Sen. *See* 權 No. 1663-A. 51ff.

[50]五步之內 within five paces—a very short distance.

五 毒 the five poisonous creatures— snakes 蛇, toads 蟾蜍, lizards 蜥蜴, scorpions 蠍, and centipedes 蜈蚣; also five classes of poison; five instruments of cruel torture; and by Taoists, the five flavours.

五 氣 the five atmospheric influences. *See below*—71.
> 雨 rain, which is under the influence of 木 wood.
> 暘 fine weather, which is under the influence of 金 metal.
> 燠 heat, which is under the influence of 火 fire.
> 寒 cold, which is under the influence of 水 water.
> 風 wind, which is under the influence of 土 earth.

五 湖 the five lakes of China. *See No. 2168-7, ff.*

五 湖 四 海 the five lakes and the four seas—everywhere.

⁵⁵五 爪 龍 the five-clawed dragon of Imperial China.

五 衆 the five attributes of human beings. *See below*—85.

五 福 the five blessings—represented in pictures by five bats. *See No. 1978-29.*

五 穀 the five grains; all kinds of cereals—the lists vary :—hemp or flax, millet of two kinds, wheat and barley, and pulse; this is an ancient classification, other lists include rice.

五 穀 豐 登 an abundant harvest of all grains.

⁶⁰五 節 the five primary elements. *See below*—71.

五 絕 a poem of four lines having five words to each line.

五 經 the five classics—*See No. 1123-25.*

五 線 譜 the five lines of the staff notation in music.

五 羊 城 the city of the five rams —Canton, from the story of five immortals who rode into the city on five rams, which were turned into stone.

⁶⁵五 美 the five primary elements. *See below*—71.

五 臟 the five viscera—
> 心, the heart, corresponding to 火 fire.
> 肺, the lungs, corresponding to 金 metal.

肝, the liver, corresponding to 木 wood.

腎, the kidneys, corresponding to 水 water.

脾, the stomach, corresponding to 土 earth.

五 色 the five colours—
> 黑, black, corresponding with 水 water.
> 赤, red, corresponding with 火 fire
> 青, azure, corresponding with 木 wood.
> 白, white, corresponding with 金 metal.
> 黃, yellow, corresponding with 土 earth.

五 色 旗 the five-striped flag of the Chinese Republic in its early days—red, yellow, blue, white, and black, one stripe for each of the five races as enumerated above—39.

五 色 雲 coloured clouds, as at sunset or sunrise.

⁷⁰五 蘊 the attributes of human beings. *See below*—85.

五 行 the primary elements. *See above 20, 43, 52, 66, 67.*
> 金, metal.
> 木, wood.
> 水, water.
> 火, fire.
> 土, earth.

五 行 生 剋 the permutations of the five primary elements as they successively produce and destroy each other.
> 土, earth generates 金 metal.
> 金, metal generates 水 water.
> 水, water generates 木 wood.
> 木, wood generates 火 fire.
> 火, fire generates 土 earth.
> 土, earth destroys 水 water.
> 水, water destroys 火 fire.
> 火, fire destroys 金 metal.
> 金, metal destroys 木 wood.
> 木, wood destroys 土 earth.

五 行 (*hang²*) 八 作 small tradesmen of various kinds.

五 角 形 a pentagon.

⁷⁵五 言 詩 verses having five words to each line.

五 賊 the five thieves—
> joy 喜, anger 怒, pleasure 樂, grief 哀, and lust 欲, (*Tao.*).

五 路 財 神 the five gods of wealth.

五 車 書 five loads of books—a great collection.

五 逆 the five rebellions—against one's superiors, i.e., 天, 地, 君, 親, 師.

⁸⁰五 運 the revolutions of the five primary elements *See above*—72.

五 里 霧 a fog five *li* in extent— very dense.

五 釐 公 債 five per cent loan.

五 金 the five metals—metals generally; gold 金 silver 銀, copper 銅, iron 鐵, and tin or pewter 錫.

五 金 行 a hardware store.

⁸⁵五 陰 the five attributes of a human being—form 色, perception 受, consciousness 想, action 行, and knowledge 識. (*Budd.*).

五 雀 六 燕 five sparrows and six swallows—about the same, six of one and half a dozen of the other.

五 音 the five notes of the ancient Chinese musical scale, 宮, 商, 角, 徵, 羽 corresponding to 土, 金, 木, 火, 水, respectively.

五 音 六 律 the five notes and the six rules of music.

五 顏 六 色 all sorts of colours.

⁹⁰五 體 the head, hands and feet. (*Budd.*).

五 體 投 地 the five members fall prostrate in obeisance—the hands, the knees and the head touching the ground.

五 鼓 the fifth watch of the night.

一 五 一 十 的 說 to tell a story in detail.

伍 ³ A file of five men; a company; a comrade. A group 7187a of five families having mutual responsibility. To associate with.

取 我 田 疇 而 伍 之 "We must count our fields by fives, and own a mutual sway."

失 伍 to break rank.

廬 井 爲 伍 the houses and the wells, i.e., families, were grouped in fives and were responsible for each other.

等 伍 to associate with; an equal rank.

羞 與 爲 伍 ashamed to associate with him.

行 (hang²) 伍 the ranks.

隊 伍 the ranks.

(a) Used for 五 No. 7187, in documents, etc., in order to prevent fraud by alteration of the figures.

吾² I, me.
7188

吾 不 懼 焉 should I not fear?

吾 不 徒 行 I did not go on foot.

吾 不 與⁴ 祭 如 不 祭 if I am not present at the sacrifice, it is as if I did not sacrifice.

吾 不 試 故 藝 I am not employed in office, and so have acquired these arts.

⁵吾 人 we; our.

吾 以 子³ 爲 異 之 問 I thought that you would ask about some remarkable persons.

吾 何 以 休 how can we be helped and made happy?

吾 們 we; us.

吾 儕 we; us.

¹⁰吾 兄 my elder brother—conventional between friends.

吾 友 my friend.

吾 子³ you, Sir; my son.

吾 已 矣 夫 it is all over with me!

吾 曹 we; us.

¹⁵吾 治 已 足 my government is complete.

吾 無 行 而 不 與 二 三 子³ 者 I have nothing which I do not tell you, my disciples.

吾 生 若 I saved your life.

吾 等 or 吾 輩 we; us.

吾 非 某 人 I am not So-and-so.

²⁰吾 黨 our party.

(a) To resist. To impede; to defend.

金 吾 name of a fabulous bird which was said to ward off pestilence or misfortune, etc. When the emperor (Han dynasty) travelled, an official preceded him carrying a red staff, on the ends of which this bird was carved and gilded; a chief of police, from the above.

執 金 吾 to grasp the red staff as above—title of the official,

under the *Han* dynasty, whose duty it was to keep the streets clear and prevent accidents, etc., when the emperor was travelling—something like a chief of police. Also read -ya².

悟⁴ To awake; to become aware of; to apprehend.
7189

悟 主 to open the eyes of the ruler.

悟·性 intelligence; power of apprehension.

悟 性 好 quick of apprehension.

悟 會 to understand; to become aware of; to apprehend.

⁵悟·過·來 to come to an understanding of.

悟 道 to apprehend the *Tao*—truth.

執 迷 不 悟 obstinately adhering to error; blindly superstitious.

悔 悟 to become conscious of sin and repent.

自 悟 to come to one's senses.

¹⁰覺 悟 to apprehend; to become aware of.

醒 悟 to arouse oneself from stupor or sleep; to become aware of.

領 悟 作 用 the faculty of apprehension.

晤⁴ To see face to face. To perceive. Inter. preceding.
7190

晤 別 之 時 since the time we parted.

　把 晤 別 後 since we grasped hands and parted—opening phrase in letters.

晤 叙 to discuss at an interview.

晤 商 to discuss at an interview.

⁵晤 會 or 面 晤 a personal interview.

晤 解 to perceive—as after an explanation.

晤 言 to discuss at an interview.

晤 面 to meet face to face.

如 晤 as if face to face—used in letters.

¹⁰許 久 未 晤 it is long since we met.

梧² The name of a tree.
7191

梧·桐 a tree, *Sterculia platanifolia*; it is sometimes called the national tree of China; the trunk is straight and beautifully green; it is said to be the only tree on which the phœnix will rest.

梧 桐 子³ dryandra seeds.

梧 桐 鳥 a hawfinch.

(a) Read *wu⁴*. Well-built and strong—of a man.

身 量 魁 梧 he is a strong, well-built man.

寤⁴ To awake from sleep.
7192

寤 夢 to see something during the day and dream about it at night.

寤 寐 waking and sleeping—at all times.

寤 寐 反 側 tossing and turning.

寤 寐 求 之 waking and sleeping he sought her.

·寤 生 born (as his mother was) waking from unconsciousness.

驚 寤 startled from sleep.

毋² Not; do not. A negative. Radical 80.
7193 Distinguish 母 No. 4582.

毋 不 敬 do not be irreverent.

毋 以 事 上 do not show it in the service of superiors.

毋 以 使 下 do not display it in treatment of inferiors.

毋 任 違 背 do not presume to disobey.

⁵毋 友 不 如 己 者 have no friends not equal to yourself.

毋 吾 以 也 do not consider me —as your senior.

毋 庸 介 意 let it pass; do not allow it to trouble you.

毋 庸 掛 慮 do not be anxious for me.

毋 庸 詳 述 no need for detail.

¹⁰毋 庸 議 there is no need to discuss this.

毋 得 must not....

毋 意 毋 必 毋 固 毋 我 he had no foregone conclusions, no arbitrary predeterminations, no obstinacy, and no egoism—(the

毋 here, is said to be simply negative, not prohibitive.)

毋 望 之 福 sudden, unexpected happiness. *See* 無 No. 7180—87, 88.

毋 望 之 禍 sudden, unexpected disaster or calamity.

¹⁵毋 爲 小 人 儒 do not be a scholar after the style of the mean man.

毋 自 欺 也 allow no self-deception.

毋 自 辱 焉 do not disgrace yourself.

毋 貽 後 悔 do not hand down any cause for regret.

毋 違 此 示 do not disobey this proclamation!

²⁰毋 違 特 示 Do not disobey! Special Proclamation!

毋 須 there is no occasion to....

(a) Read *mou*¹. A black cloth cap called 毋 追 used in the 夏 *Hsia* dynasty.

侮 侮 ³ To insult; to ridicule. Distinguish 悔 No. 2336.
7194

侮 上 to be arrogant.

侮 弄 to make game of; to humbug.

侮 慢 to insult; to be rude to.

侮 狎 to annoy; to treat with undue familiarity.

侮 辱 to make a fool of; to insult; to disgrace.

自 侮 to demean oneself.

武 ³ Military; warlike; fierce; firm; violent.
7195

武 人 a warrior; a hero; an athlete.

武 人 執 政 the reins of government are held by the military.

武 人 干 政 military interference with the government.

武 人 派 the military party.

⁵武 俠 chivalrous.

武 健 strong and daring; courageous and energetic in affairs.

武 備 armaments.

武 備 學 生 military cadets.

武 備 院 the former imperial armoury.

---

¹⁰武 則 天 or 武 后 the Empress *Wu*—who usurped the throne and held the reins of government during the latter half of the 7th century.

武 力 force of arms.

武 力 主 義 militarism.

武 力 壓 制 to ride roughshod over.

武 力 從 事 to resort to arms.

¹⁵武 力 統 一 to seek unity by force of arms.

武 功 merit won by military service.

武 勇 military ardour.

武 員 military officials.

武 器 military equipment.

²⁰武 場 an arena for military trials.

武 士 executioners.

武 夫 a hero; a warrior; an athlete.

武 學 a graduate of the former 1st military degree.

武 定 禍 亂 to suppress disorders by force.

²⁵武 官 military officials.

武 家 a warrior.

武 將 military officials.

武 帝 or 關 帝 or 武 夫 子 the God of War.

武 庫 an armoury.

³⁰武 庫 兵 仗 a whole arsenal of weapons.

武 廟 the temple to the God of War.

武 弁 military officials.

武 彝 (or 夷) 山 the hills in the north of Fukien which give their name to Bohea tea.

武 政 military government; militarism.

³⁵武 斷 arbitrary decisions.

武 斷 政 治 militarism.

武 斷 鄉 曲 to settle matters by force.

武 林 a name for Chekiang or Hangchow.

武 業 the military profession.

⁴⁰武 毅 resolute.

武 火 a quick fire, as opposed to 文 火 a slow fire.

武 童 cadets; military students.

武 職 military commissions.

武 臣 military officers.

⁴⁵武 藝 military arts; tactics; feats of strength.

武 術 military tactics; strategy.

武 裝 armed.

全 身 武 裝 fully armed; armed to the teeth.

武 裝 中 立 armed neutrality.

⁵⁰武 裝 和 平 an armed peace.

武 裝 專 制 military autocracy.

武 裝 強 盜 armed robbers.

武 裝 解 決 to appeal to arms.

武 裝 起 來 暴 動 to take up arms and make a riot.

⁵⁵武 陵 a name for Hangchow.

↑武 官 military attaché.

尙 武 精 神 militarism; the spirit of militarism.

用 武 to use violence.

(a) The title of an ancient king, first ruler of the *Chou* 周 dynasty.

謂 武 盡 美 矣 未 盡 善 也 (Confucius) said of the (music of) King *Wu*, that it was perfectly beautiful, but not perfectly good.

(b) A footprint.

大 武 a large footprint.

履 帝 武 敏 歆 she trod in the great footprint and conceived —"footprint of God." *Giles.*

(c) To continue, as an ancestral line.

下 武 維 周 "successors tread in the steps *of their predecessors* in our *Chou.*"

(d) The rolled-up brim of a hat.

縞 冠 玄 武 a white silk cap with a turned-up brim.

鵡 ³ A cockatoo.
7196

鸚 鵡 a parrot; a cockatoo.

戊 ⁴ The fifth of the *Heavenly Stems* 天 干. Flourishing. Formerly read *mou*¹.
7197

務 ⁴ To devote attention to; to regard as fundamental. Must. Necessary.
7198

務 以 悅 人 studies to please others.

務 以 自 伐 studies his own case.

務 使 it is essential to be certain that....

務 宜 indispensable; by all means; it is necessary to.

⁵務 實 to strive for reality.

務 希 earnestly to hope that....

務 得 by all means; it is absolutely necessary; must positively.

務 心 to apply the mind to.

務 必 must; indispensable; it is positively necessary to; by all means.

¹⁰務 期 earnestly to hope that....

務 本 to attend to what is fundamental.

務 本 業 to attend to one's proper calling.

務 民 之 義 to devote oneself to duty towards one's neighbour.

務 獲 arrest without fail.

¹⁵務 當 must; by all means; it is necessary to; positively must; indispensable.

務 祈 earnestly to hope that....

務 要 by all means; must positively; it is absolutely necessary.

務 財 用 to make the revenue one's chief care.

務 農 to devote oneself to agriculture.

²⁰務 農 的 a farmer.

務 須 indispensable; must necessarily; positively must; by all means.

(a) Used as a suffix to express business, duty, affairs, etc.

世 務 the affairs of the world. *See* No. 5790—A.12ff.

事 務 business; function; duty. *See* No. 5787-18ff.

債 務 obligations. *See* No. 118-5.

內 務 h o m e affairs; domestic affairs.

⁵公 務 public business or affairs. *See* No. 3701-40, 41.

國 務 national affairs.

外 務 foreign affairs.

學 務 educational matters.

家 務 private or domestic affairs.

¹⁰局 務 departmental affairs.

庶 務 general business matters. *See* No. 5874-3ff.

戰 務 matters relating to the war.

政 務 government affairs. *See* No. 355-8, 9.

敎 務 church matters. *See* No. 719—B. 2, 3.

---

¹⁵服 務 service.

本 務 one's duty.

現 務 present-day matters.

礦 務 mining.

農 務 agriculture.

霧⁴ Fog; mist; vapour.
7199

霧 合 to gather together like the mists.

霧 塞 obscured by dense mists.

霧 散 scattering like the mists.

霧 氣 or 雲 霧 mist; fog.

⁵滿 天 霧 氣 a mist over-spreads the sky.

霧 氣 騰 騰 的 foggy; misty; hazy.

霧 燥 damp and muggy.

霧 罩 罩 的 foggy; muddled.

霧 裏 看 花 to s e e f l o w e r s through a mist—obscurely; indistinctly.

¹⁰霧 露 fog; mist.

霧 鬢 風 鬟 m i s t y tresses—describing a woman's hair.

霧 鳥 the fog-bird or the bird of Paradise.

婺⁴ Name of a star called 婺女.
7200

嫡 婺 a widow.

吳² The province of Kiangsu.
7201

吳 國 the most easterly of the *Three Kingdoms*; (A.D. 229-280.) it comprised Chekiang and extended north and west. Soochow was the capital and still bears the name of 吳 縣.

吳 淞 Woosung, at the mouth of the river on which Shanghai is situated.

吳 紀 the State of Wu, as above —1.

(a) Clamorous. To bawl. Some read it *hwa²*, in this connection.

不 吳 不 揚 without noise or display.

不 吳 不 敖 no noise, no insolence.

悞⁴ To impede; to neglect; to delay.
7202 Inter. 誤 No. 7204.

悞 了 時 刻 to be unpunctual; to let the moment pass.

悞 了 工 夫 to waste time.

悞 事 to fail; to cause failure; to hamper.

悞 信 mistaken confidence.

⁵悞 卯 to miss answering the roll-call.

悞 工 to hinder work—by delay or neglect.

悞 時 to be behind time.

悞 會 to misunderstand.

悞 殺 inadvertent manslaughter.

¹⁰悞 犯 unintentional offences.

失 悞 to miss an opportunity.

尤 悞 to hinder; to delay by negligence.

蜈² The centipede.
7203

蜈 蚣 the centipede.

蜈 蚣 梯 a single rope with rounds fastened at regular intervals for use as a ladder.

蜈 蚣 風 箏 a kite made like a centipede.

誤⁴ To impede; to interfere with. To be mistaken.
7204 Inter. 悞 No. 7202.

誤 事 to hinder business; to spoil an affair.

誤 信 人 misplaced confidence.

誤 假 爲 眞 to take the false for the true.

誤 傳 to misinform; to bring in a wrong report.

⁵誤 入 歧 途 unwittingly to take a side track.

誤 入 險 途 unwittingly to run into danger.

誤 公 to obstruct public business.

誤 印 to misprint.

誤 國 害 民 to obstruct the affairs of State and oppress the people.

¹⁰誤 報 to misinform; to bring in a wrong report.

誤 害 to injure by mistake.

誤 害 好 人 to injure a worthy man wrongly.

誤 寫 日 子 to write the wrong dates.

誤 導 to mislead.
[15] 誤 差 (ch'ai[1]) to hinder one's official business.
誤 心 inadvertently.
誤 惑 to mislead.
誤 斷 to misjudge.
誤 書 wrongly written.
[20] 誤·會 to misunderstand; a misconception; a mistaken idea.
誤 殺 manslaughter; unintentional homicide; to kill in mistake for somebody else.
誤 爲 ... to mistake for....
誤 犯 unintentional crime or offences.
誤 犯·的 罪 sins of ignorance.
[25] 誤 用 to misuse.
誤 疑 to suspect wrongly.
誤 盡 蒼 生 to injure all the people.
誤 筆 a clerical error; a slip of the pen.
誤 筆 作 蠅 to make a blot into a fly—when making a picture.
[30] 誤 筆 畫 to make a picture out of a slip of the pen.
誤 算 miscalculation.
誤 約 to break an agreement or treaty.
誤 罰 to fine wrongly.
誤 見 mistaken notions.
[35] 誤 解 a wrong interpretation.
誤 言 to make a mistake in speech.
誤 記 to remember incorrectly.
誤 認 mistaken recognition.
誤 辦 to mismanage; to blunder.
[40] 誤 點 fallacies; points of error.
失 誤 to neglect; to make a mistake.
錯·誤 mistakes; errors.

WU. (ㄨ)
(Uh)

兀 [4.5.] To cut off the feet.
7205

兀 者 a one-legged man.
兀 趾 to have the feet cut off.

(a) High and level on the top. Determined. Resolute.

兀 兀 以 窮 年 steadfastly and toilingly making the best of the years.

兀 坐 sitting upright in a dignified attitude.
兀 日 an unlucky day.
兀 然 不 動 immoveable and steadfast.
兀 立 standing bolt upright.
突 兀 high and grand—of a pagoda; bold and resolute.

(b) A particle. *See below.*
兀 的 不 a conjectural interrogative (in novels, poetry.)
兀 自 一 人 by herself, alone.

(c) u.f. 㐳 No. 7211. Unsteady.

屼 [4.5.] A bare hill.
7206

杌 [4.5.] The stump of a tree; hence, sterility. A square stool.
7207

杌·子 or 杌 橙·子 a square stool.
邦 之 杌 陧 the decadence of a State.

勿 [4.5.] A negative. Not; do not. Distinguish 匆 No. 6915.
7208

勿 乃 仙 乎 surely you must be an immortal?
勿 事 must not employ....
勿 以 善 小 而 不 爲 do not regard any good action as unimportant and neglect to do it.
勿 以 惡 小 而 爲 之 do not regard any evil as trivial and therefore practise it.
[5] 勿 助 長 (chang[3]) 也 do not assist it to grow—let it grow naturally.
勿 動 do not touch; do not move.
勿 宰 耕 牛 do not slaughter the ox which ploughs the fields.
勿 棄 字 紙 do not throw away written or printed paper.
勿 畏 難 do not fear danger or difficulty.
[10] 勿 藥 to get better without medicine.
勿 論 without penal consequences. *See* 格 No. 3309—C. 2.

勿 謂 do not say....
勿 謂 言 之 不 預 do not say that you have not been forewarned.

(a) When repeated it is used as an interjection of desire.

勿 勿 諸 其 欲 其 饗 之 也 O that they would accept—my sacrifice!

(b) A flag with three streamers used for signalling and calling the people together in haste; thus the character gets the meaning of haste, urgency, etc.; the unauthorized character 匆 No. 6915, which bears this meaning is not strictly correct.

(c) The name of a tribe 勿 吉 which dwelt along the Sungari River; they were the most powerful of the Tungusic peoples; in later days, about the 7th century A.D., they were called 靺 鞨 *Mo Ho* and were divided into seven branches.

物 [4.5.] Matter; substance. All living creatures. Things in general. The affairs of this world. Things or matters outside oneself. Others. Goods.
7209

物 主 the owner.
物 主 格 possessive case.
物 主 權 proprietary rights.
物 之 終 始 the beginning and the end of things.
[5] 物 事 affairs; things; articles.
已 知·的 物 事 things one already knows.
經 貫·的 物 事 things that one is accustomed to.
物 件 articles; things.
物 件 單 inventory.
[10] 物 値 the intrinsic value of a thing.
物 候 the times and seasons for things, the times for the migration, as of birds, etc.
物 傷 其 類 animals grieve for their fellow-creatures.
物 價 the price of commodities.
物 價 低 昂 prices vary, now cheap, now dear.

¹⁵物 則 laws of nature.

有 物 有 則 there are things, there are laws—i.e., "to every faculty and relationship is annexed its law."

物 力 one's resources, as the value of one's property and estate, personal effects, etc.

物 化 death; metempsychosis; change of substance.

物 博 之 國 a country rich in natural products.

²⁰地 大 物 博 its territory is wide and its products abundant.

物 原 論 theory of the origin of matter.

物 各 有 主 everything has its owner.

物 品 articles.

物 外 beyond the region of objective existence; transcendental.

²⁵物 形 the shape of an object.

物 怪 something strange; a monstrosity.

物 性 the property of matter.

能 盡 物 之 性 he can give their full development to the natures of animals and things.

物 我 兼 利 of profit both to myself and others.

³⁰物 我 無 間 outside things have no influence over me.

物 換 星 移 things change and the stars move—the changes in the affairs of the world.

物 故 deceased.

物 料 materials; stuff.

物 有 所 不 足 (the tortoise, in divination,) is not sufficient for this.

³⁵物 望 one looked up to by all.

物 格 to learn the nature of things.

物 極 必 反 when a thing reaches its limit, it begins to return—when things are at their worst, they begin to mend.

物 業 raw material; property.

物 權 real right. (legal).

⁴⁰物 歸 原 主 let the thing be returned to its proper owner.

物 爭 自 存 the struggle for existence.

物 理 nature.

物 理 之 當 然 the eternal fitness of things.

物 理(學)physics.

⁴⁵原 子³物 理 學 atomic physics.

物 理 學 之 定 律 a law of physics.

物 理 家 physicists.

物 理 變 化 physical changes.

物 理 派 materialists.

⁵⁰物 理 現 象 physical phenomena.

物 理 界 the physical or material world.

物 生 而 不 窮 the germination of things never ceases.

物 產 local products; household effects.

物 產 會 exhibition of local produce.

⁵⁵物 界 environment; the material world.

物 神 敎 fetishism.

物 種 species.

物 種 之 變 遷 the mutations of species.

物 種 原 始 the origin of species.

⁶⁰物 種·的 由 來 the origin of species.

物 競 the struggle for existence.

物 競 天 擇 natural selection.

物 累 bound by material things.

物 腐 蟲 生 worms breed in decaying matter.

⁶⁵物 色⁴ substance and colour; to search for.

令 以 物 色⁴ 訪 之 he ordered them to search everywhere for a—worthy man, judging him by his qualifications.

現 在 正·在 物 色⁴ at present the search—for such a man—is being made.

迷 於 物 色⁴ deceived by appearances.

都 來 物 色⁴ all came to search for.

⁷⁰物 華 the essence of things.

物 論 the treatment of subjects from various points of view.

物 議 popular criticism of; popular discussion.

招 物 議 to attract criticism; to cause discussion.

物 象 impressions; objective things.

⁷⁵物 資 the intrinsic value of a thing.

物 質 matter.

物 質 上 material; physically.

物 質 主 義 materialism.

物 質 固 有 之 本 性 the properties inherent in matter.

⁸⁰物 質 存 在 physical existence.

物 質 建 設 material reconstruction.

物 質 文 明 material progress.

物 質 變 動 physical changes.

物 質 方 面 from the material standpoint.

⁸⁵物 質 構 成 the constitution of matter.

物 質 生·活 physical life; material life.

物 質 界 the material world; the physical world or realm.

物 質·的 material; physical.

物 質 進 步 material progress; natural evolution.

⁹⁰物 量⁴ 無 窮 matter is infinite.

物 阜 plenty; abundance.

物 類 classes of things; categories; species.

物 體 a body. (physics).

不 物 irregular; eccentric; strange; uncanny.

⁹⁵人 物 a man of standing; men and things, animals, etc.

凡 物 all things; all creation.

動·物 animals. See No. 6611-43ff.

寄 生 物 parasites. See No. 419-7ff.

是 絕 物 也 ....is to cut oneself off for others.

¹⁰⁰植·物 plants, trees, etc.

正 己 而 物 正 者 也 they rectify themselves and others are rectified.

無 機 物 inorganic matter.

礦 物 minerals.

神 物 spiritual or divine creatures.

¹⁰⁵空 洞 無 物 space; the void of the ether.

萬 物 all things; all creation.

貨 物 merchandise.

金 屬 物 metals.

食 物 eatables.

沃 4.5. To water; to enrich. Fertile; rich. Glossy, as leaves, etc. To wash the hands. Pron. wo⁴

7210

沃 土 (or 壤) fertile loam.

沃 度 a Japanese term for iodine. See 碘 No. 6348.

沃 手 to wash the hands.

沃 民 people who dwell in a fertile region.

⁵沃 沃 rich and glossy, like beautiful leaves.

沃 泉 a flowing spring.

沃 滅 to extinguish a fire with water.

沃 潤 fertile; to enrich.

沃 盥 to wash.

¹⁰沃 然 glossy.

沃 田 rich fields.

沃 瘠 fertile and barren—soil.

沃 盥 to pour water and wash the hands.

沃 素 a Japanese term for iodine. *See above*—2.

¹⁵沃 美 rich and fertile—soil.

沃 朕 心 cleanse my mind.

沃 腴 rich and fertile.

沃 若 glossy in appearance, as mulberry leaves, etc.

沃 衍 rich plains.

²⁰沃 野 fertile lands; the west.

沃 雨 to wet with rain.

沃 面 to wet the face.

沃 饒 rich and sumptuous; fruitful.

如 湯 沃 雪 like hot water on snow—easily melted.

㐲 4.5. Uncomfortable. To limp. To be unsteady.
7211

㐲 齷 tottering; unsteady.

屋 1.5. A house—in southern or central China; a room—in northern China.
7212

屋 主 the landlord.

屋 址 or 屋 基 the site for a house.

屋 契 the leasehold deed of a house.

屋·子 a room.

⁵一 間 屋·子 a room in a house.

屋 宇 a house; a cottage.

屋 客 the tenant.

屋 山 the gable of a house.

屋 山 頂 the ridge of a roof.

¹⁰屋 漏 the courtyard in a Chinese house,—it is surrounded by the buildings; a skylight; the house leaks.

不 欺 屋 漏 do not do things, even in your innermost courtyard, of which you might be ashamed.

屋 烏 abbrev. 愛 屋 及 烏 *See* No. 9-19.

屋 租 house-rent.

屋 稅 house-taxes.

¹⁵屋 簷 the eaves.

屋 舍 a house or cottage. [*dial.*]

屋 裏 in the house—a wife. (*Wu-*在 屋 裏 in the room.

屋 角 the corner of a house.

²⁰屋 除 the porch to a house.

屋 頂 花 園 roof-gardens.

同 屋 in the same house.

房 屋 houses.

書 屋 a study.

²⁵蓋 屋 or 起 屋 to build houses.

YA. (ㄚ)

(Ia)

丫 ¹ A bifurcation.
Distinguish 了 No. 3958.
7213 Written ㄚ Nat. Phon. letter for *a*.

丫 叉 the fork of a tree; the fork of the fingers.

丫 枝 a forked branch.

丫 鬟 or 丫·頭 a slave-girl—from the two tufts in which the hair was dressed.

牙 ² The molars. A tooth; toothed; serrated. Ivory.
7214 Radical 92.

牙 刷(·子)a tooth-brush.

牙 力 strong teeth—convincing; able to convince.

牙 工 a worker in ivory.

牙 床 the jawbone; inlaid bedsteads.

⁵牙 慧 stale or trite expressions copied from others.

牙 扇 an ivory fan.

牙 撥 an ivory plectrum for stringed instruments.

牙 灰 tooth-powder. *See below* 21.

牙 牌 dominoes; slips or tablets.

¹⁰牙 爪 teeth and claws—oppressive retainers or underlings.

資 本 制 度·的 牙 爪 the teeth and talons of capitalism.

牙 疳 a gum-boil.

牙°疼 toothache.

牙 皮 the skin of the teeth.

¹⁵牙 磁 the enamel on the teeth.

牙 祭 the meal of meat which shop-assistants and others are entitled to on the 2nd and 16th of the lunar month.

牙 科 dentistry.

牙 科 醫 生 a dentist.

牙 符 an ivory tally used as a credential by messengers.

²⁰牙 籤 兒 a tooth-pick.

牙 粉 tooth-powder.

牙 縫 兒 the space between the teeth.

牙 肉 the gums. 牙 膏 tooth-paste.

牙 腔 dental cavity.

²⁵牙 色 ivory white.

牙 蟲 the worms which are supposed to cause teeth to decay—women travel around the country professing to be able to remove them.

牙 質 dentine.

牙 距 teeth and spurs—*used like* —10 *above*.

牙 車 the jawbone.

³⁰牙 (酸)倒·了 the teeth set on edge.

牙 閉 tetanus; lockjaw.

牙 關 the jawbone.

牙 關 緊 閉 the teeth set; lockjaw.

牙 風 toothache from decayed teeth.

³⁵牙 音 gutturals or velars, so called *

牙 骨 the jawbone.

牙·齒 the teeth.

牙·齒 打 鼓 the teeth chattering, as from cold, fear, etc.

牙·齒 發 麻 the teeth set on edge.

⁴⁰倒 牙 to set the teeth on edge.

出 牙 to cut the teeth.

凸 牙 projecting teeth.

剔 牙 to pick the teeth.

剔 牙 杖 a tooth-pick.

⁴⁵咬 牙 切 齒 to gnash the teeth—with rage.

奶 牙 milk-teeth.

拔 牙 to extract a tooth.

換 牙 to shed the teeth.

替 牙 to shed the teeth.

⁵⁰板 牙 molars.

槽 牙 molars.

爛 牙 decayed teeth.

犬 牙 canine teeth.

猪 牙 projecting teeth.

⁵⁵生 牙 to cut the teeth.

蛀 牙 decayed teeth.

象 牙 ivory.

貳 牙 canine teeth.

鑲 牙 to insert teeth; artificial teeth.

⁶⁰門 牙 the incisors.

(a) A flag with serrated edges.

牙 城 a city from which the commander directs operations.

* because the place of articulation is between the molars.

牙 將 a petty military officer.
牙 旗 the standard of a military leader.
牙 營 the camp where the standard is set up.
牙 門 the standard before the tent of the leader.
建 牙 to set up his standard.

(b) A broker; brokerage. Originally written 与 a form of 互.

牙 人 or 牙 僧 a broker or middleman.
牙 保 a commission agency.
牙 娘 a procuress.
牙 婆 a female broker.
5牙·子 a broker.
牙 帖 a broker's license.
牙 稅 fees for a broker's license.
牙 行 (hang²) licensed brokers or commission agents for the sale of goods on commission.

(c) Used for the male of certain animals.

牙 狗 a male dog.
牙 貓 a tom-cat.

(d) Used in imitation of sounds.

牙 牙 the sound of a child learning to talk.

呀¹ A final particle. The sound of laughter, etc. To creak.
7215

呀 呀 the sound of laughter.
呀·的 一 聲 gave forth a creaking sound.
啊 呀 an exclamation of surprise.

(a) Read hsia². To open the mouth wide. An opening.

呀 岬 the overwhelming appearance of rolling billows.
呀 赫 terrifying appearance of the clouds.
呀 谿 to open the mouth wide like a cavern.
牙 角 何 呀 呀 How threatening look the teeth and horns—of the azure dragon—referring to an eclipse of the moon.

犽² A child whose milk-teeth are not shed.
7216

枒² The felloe of a wheel. Also read yeh².
7217 Inter. 椰 No. 7309.

枒 杈 interlacing branches; a forked branch.

研⁴ To grind; to calender; to polish. To roll with a stone roller.
7218

研 光 to make smooth and glossy by calendering.
研 坊 a shop where calendering is done.

芽² A sprout; a shoot; a germ.
7219

芽 核 germ nucleus.
芽 生 法 the method of reproduction by budding.
芽 甲 buds on trees, etc.
芽 筍 sprouts; shoots; a tenon.
5芽 胞 a spore.
芽 胞 生 殖 reproduction from spores.
芽 胎 an embryo.
芽 茶 bud-tea—a high-grade quality.
芽 菜 bean-sprouts as a vegetable.
10芽 葉 leaf-buds.
冒 芽 to bud.
月 芽 the new moon.
發 芽 to bud; to put forth shoots.
黃 芽 白 Shantung cabbage, a large white variety; celery cabbage.

訝⁴ To express surprise; to exclaim. Inter. next.
7220

無 訝 無 訾 neither complaining nor abusing.
驚 訝 startled; surprised.

迓⁴ To go to meet; to receive, as a guest. Inter. preceding.
7221

迓 衡 to secure the establishment of order.
迓 迎 to meet; to welcome.
予 迓 續 乃 命 于 天 I am endeavouring to prolong your lease of life from Heaven.
敬 迓 天 威 received with reverence the dread (decree) of Heaven.

雅³ Elegant; polished; refined; polite. Used of the sayings and doings of others, it means— your.
7222

雅 人 a man of refinement and culture.
雅 俗 共 賞·的 話 speech which will give pleasure both to the refined and the vulgar.
雅 儀 courteous manners; dignified.
雅 囑 your injunctions.
5雅 座 a literary man's study; a room set apart for special friends; a private alcove in a *
雅 得 狠 extremely refined and elegant.
雅 愛 your love.
雅 意 your fine thought or idea.
雅 懷 refined and cultured in mind.
10雅 故 an old friend.
雅 敎 your excellent instructions.
雅 望 a reputation for culture.
雅 樂 (yüeh⁴) refined music.
雅 歌 the Song of Solomon.
15雅 正 refined and correct in conduct.
雅 步 graceful and easy steps.
雅 淡 or 閒 雅 retirement; cultured leisure.
[雅 潔 refined and pure.
雅 玩 refined amusements.
20雅 範 you; yourself.
雅 粧 elegant attire.
雅·致 refined; polished.
雅 號 your elegant name is....?
雅 觀 a fine sight.
25雅 誨 your graceful admonitions.
雅 論 polished speech; your refined conversation.
雅 誼 your cultured determination.
雅 辭 elegant diction.
雅 道 refined and genteel.
30雅 韻 elegant rhymes.
雅 馴 polished and refined.
不 雅 inelegant; ill-bred.
佳 雅 elegant and refined.
大 雅 小 雅 the titles of two books of the Odes.
35幽 雅 secluded and retired.
文 雅 cultured.
端 雅 fine and elegant.
風 雅 elegant; an air of culture.

(a) Constantly; frequently.

雅 操 (tsao⁴) constancy.
雅 不 欲 it has never been my wish...
* restaurant.

雅 闊 had often heard that....
子 所 雅 言 the topics usually discussed by the Master—Confucius—were....

(b) Name of a wine-vessel.

雅 量 a great capacity for liquor.

(c) Read _ya¹_. Inter. next. Crows, etc.

鴉¹ The crow; the raven; rooks, etc.
7223
鴉 嘴 筆 a tracing pen.
鴉 嘴 鋤 a sharp-edged hoe, like a crow's bill.
鴉 巢 生 鳳 the crow's nest has produced a phœnix—a man of talents or a handsome person has come from a humble family.
鴉 ·片 (烟) opium.
鴉 知 反 哺 the crow knows to disgorge its food—in order to feed its parents—used to illustrate filial piety.
⁵鴉 聲 不 聞 not even the sound of a crow was heard—a dead silence.
鴉 陣 a flock of crows.
鴉 飛 鵲 辭 flocking together like crows and magpies.
鴉 鵲 無 聲 not even the sound of a crow or a magpie's cawing.
鴉 髻 the dressed hair of a Chinese woman.
¹⁰鴉 鬟 a slave-girl.
寒 鴉 the eastern jackdaw.
慈 鴉 the white-necked or parson crow.
老 鴉 crows.
花 鴉 the black and white crow.

衙² A public office; an official residence.
7224
衙 吏 _yamen_ clerks.
衙 役 _yamen_ runners; policemen.
衙 ·門 or 衙 署 or 公 署 a civil or military court; a _yamen_.
排 衙 to open the court; to hold a ceremony of purification after an inquest.

(a) To have an audience of a superior.

早 晚 衙 集 morning and evening the people gathered for an audience.

(b) A flag; the pavilion of a general where the flag was planted.

(c) Read _yii²_.

衙 衙 busy.

亞⁴ Inferior; secondary. Ugly. A character used in names.
7225
亞 于 inferior to....
不 亞 于 人 not inferior to others.
亞 如 or 亞 似 resembling; like.
亞 旅 subordinate officials.
⁵亞 次 secondary; inferior.
亞 聖 second to the Sage—i.e., Mencius.
亞 飯 the second meal.
亞 魁 the second on the list of candidates for the degree of 舉 人.

(a) To weigh down. To press down.

亞 枝 weighed down the branches.
低 亞 weighed down.

(b) Used to imitate sounds.

亞 亞 the cawing of the crow.
亞 細 亞 Asia. A.c. 亞 洲.

啞³ Dumb. Inter. 瘂 No. 7229.
7226
啞 口 無 言 to be silent; unwilling to speak.
啞 ·吧 or 啞 ·子 a dumb person.
啞 謎 a riddle.
啞 鈴 dumb-bells.

(a) Read _ya¹_. **Noise.**

啞 啞 the cawing of crows, etc.
啞 嘔 the attempts of a child to speak.

(b) Read _ê⁵_. **The sound of laughter; also used for other sounds.**

啞 咽 the whimpering of a child.
啞 爾 laughter.

婭⁴ Term of address used between the sons-in-law of a family.
7227
婭 婿 title given to each other by men whose wives are sisters.

椏¹ The forking branch of a tree.
7228
椏 枝 a forking branch.

瘂³ Dumb. Dull, as certain sounds.
7229
瘂 口 不 言 sulky; unwilling to speak.
瘂 ·吧 a dumb person.
瘂 ·吧 吃 黃 連 like a dumb man eating bitter root—he cannot speak of his bitterness.
瘂 喉 to lose the voice.
⁵瘂 嗓 ·子 a hoarse voice.
瘂 ·子 a dumb person.
瘂 板 a (dollar) with a dull ring when struck.
一 點 瘂 a little hoarse.
吃 瘂 ·吧 虧 to suffer in silence like a dumb man.

錏⁴ Soft steel. Ammonium.
7230

YA. (ㄚ)
(Iah)

壓 1.5. To press; to oppress. To crush; to repress. To keep in order. To urge. Inter. 押 No. 7234.
7231
壓 ·下 to keep down with weights.
壓 ·不 下 去 cannot crush it down; cannot keep it down.
壓 人 to floor a person.
壓 ·住 to suppress; to stop—as a riot; to steady; to weight down.
⁵壓 ·住 運 to counteract bad luck.
壓 倒 to upset; to be oppressed; to excel.
壓 制 to bring into subjection; to be overbearing.
壓 制 人 to bring pressure to bear on a person.
壓 制 報 界 to place restrictions on the press.
¹⁰壓 制 手 ·段 suppressive measures.
壓 力 pressure; oppression; tyranny.
作 用 壓 力 working pressure.
低 壓 力 low pressure; low tension—electricity, etc.
均 等 壓 力 uniform pressure.

15 實效壓力 effective pressure.
旁壓力 lateral pressure.
空氣壓力 atmospheric pressure.
通常壓力 normal pressure.
重壓力 heavy pressure; high pressure.
20 高壓力 high pressure; high tension—electricity, etc.
壓力中心 centre of pressure.
壓力線 line of pressure.
壓力表 pressure gauge.
壓勝 to dominate.
25 壓・在底・下 crushed beneath it.
壓塌・了 collapsed under the weight.
壓壞 spoilt by being crushed.
壓守 to maintain by force; to defend.
壓害百姓 to oppress the masses.
30 壓寨夫・人 the wife of a brigand chief.
壓實 to compress tightly; to make solid by pressure.
壓寶 a gambling swindle—a kind of thimble-rig.
壓平 to level by rolling; to flatten by pressure.
壓慾 to repress the passions.
35 壓扁 to press flat.
壓抑 to curb; to repress; to take down a peg or two.
壓搾 to press; compression.
壓搾器 a press.
壓服 to bring into subjection; to control.
40 壓杠・子 a mode of torture.
壓機 a press.
水壓機 a hydraulic press.
螺絲壓機 a screw press.
壓歲盤 a plate of sweetmeats distributed on New Year's Eve for luck.
45 壓歲錢 cash distributed among the children on New Year's Eve for luck.
壓・死人 to crush a man to death.
壓法 in defiance of the law.
壓派 to insist on.
壓滿 to cram full.
50 壓物器具 a compressor.
壓睡 nightmare.
壓破 to break by crushing.
壓碎 to crush to pieces.
壓紙 to keep paper down with weights; to put a weight on the strip of paper which is placed

on the grave as a sign that the proper worship has been attended to.
55 壓緊 to compress tightly.
壓縮 to condense; to compress; to squeeze.
壓縮性 compressibility.
壓春 to bow the back—in servility.
壓覆 to upset; to overthrow.
60 壓覺 pressure-sensation.
壓載之物 ballast.
壓載噸數 net tonnage.
壓迫 hard pressed; oppression; constraint.
須加壓迫 some pressure must be brought to bear.
65 壓邪 to repress noxious influences.
壓量 to take advantage of; to oppress.
壓除 to repress and get rid of.
壓韻 to make rhymes.
壓驚 to allay one's fears, by taking something to eat.
70 壓點 pressure-spots—on the body.
強壓 to suppress by force.
氣壓 atmospheric pressure.
沉壓 to sink down.
自壓 to humble oneself.
75 血壓 blood-pressure.
鎮壓 or 彈壓 to repress—as a riot.
震壓 to repress by fear.

揠 4.5.
7232
To pull up; to eradicate.

軋 4.5.
7233
To crush.

軋出花衣 to gin cotton.
軋布機器 a mangle; a calendering machine.
軋棉機 a cotton gin.
軋棉花 to gin cotton.
5 軋棉車 a cotton press.
軋澀 stammering.
軋石子機 a stone-crushing machine.
軋碎 crushed to pieces.
軋礦 to hull—millet, etc.
10 軋票機 a machine for dating tickets.
軋票眼鉗 a ticket-punch.
軋輪 a roller
↑軋根兒 in the first place; to start with.

軋轢 to crush; the sound of things being crushed
軋辭 involved expressions.
15 天地軋 the universe is in travail.
磨軋 to be crushed flat.

(a) Also read cha[4.5]. To join; to crowd around. (Shanghai).

軋到 to crowd into—a shop, etc.
軋姘頭 to form an illicit connection; to live as man and wife without a regular marriage.
軋朋友 to form a friendship.
軋賬 to settle an account.

(b) Read cha[4.5]. The sound of creaking.

軋軋聲 the creaking of a barrow, oars, a loom, etc.

(c) Read cha[4.5].

軋盤 boundless expanse.

押 1.5. To press down To stamp; to seal; to sign.
7234 A seal.
Inter. 壓 No. 7231.

押名 to sign one's name.
押字 to sign.
押定 to conclude by signing—as an agreement.
押日子 to affix the date.
5 押封 to seal up; to attach—as property.
押署 to sign.
押註 to endorse; to affix a signature.
押號 a private mark.
押韻 to rhyme.
10 不押韻 it does not rhyme—it is not in accordance with what is proper.
畫押 to affix a signature.
簽押 to affix a signature.
花押 a signature composed of several characters made into one,-a kind of monogram.

(a) To mortgage. To pledge. To deposit. A pawn-shop.

押典 to pawn.
押匯 a bill of exchange.
押契 a mortgage deed; written security for a loan.
押房 to mortgage a house.
5 押批銀 a deposit on a lease.

押 抵 to pawn; to mortgage.

押 櫃 a money-bond—as given in the case of an apprentice.

押 欵 a sum lent on a mortgage; a deposit; earnest-money.

押 歲 錢 money distributed among the children on New Year's Eve for luck.

[10]押 清 to pay off the balance of a debt.

押 當 to pawn.

押 租 a deposit given when renting a house.

押 舖 or 小 押 an unlicensed pawn-shop.

押 貨 to mortgage goods.

[15]押 賠 to be surety for repayment.

押 質 to pawn; to mortgage.

押 賬 to leave something as security for an account or a debt.

押 頭 something given as a pledge.

(b) To detain in custody. To keep. To compel. To force. To delay action on an item.

押·他 作 compel him to do it.

押 令 to compel.

押·住 不 放 to detain in custody.

押 冬 things kept over the winter.

[5]押 坐 to place under arrest.

押 守 to detain in custody.

押 寨 夫·人 the wife of a brigand chief.

押 帶 to take in custody to.

押 所 a place of detention.

[10]押 案 to imprison until payment is made.

押 發 to forward under escort— as a prisoner.

押 票 a warrant for arrest.

押 繳 to imprison until payment is made.

押 船 to commandeer a boat for government service.

[15]押 解 to send in custody to.

押 送 to send in custody to.

押 追 to confine until payment is made.

看 押 or 管 押 to detain in custody.

鴨 [1.5.] **A duck.**
7235

鴨·子 or 水 鴨 ducks.

鴨 苗 ducklings.

鴨 蛋 ducks' eggs.

乳 鴨 ducklings.

[5]板 鴨 or 臘 鴨 dried, salted ducks.

焙 鴨 to hatch ducks by artificial heat.

熏 鴨 smoked ducks.

野 鴨 wild ducks.

雛 鴨 ducklings.

YAI. (一牙)
(Iai)

厓 崖 [2] **A precipice; a cliff. Also read** *ai; ngai.* **Inter. next.**
7236

崖 岸 a steep bank; a proud and inaccessible person.

崖 畧 a summary; an abridgement.

崖 石 or 山 崖 a cliff; a rock.

崖 茶 cliff tea—a superior kind.

[5]崖 蜜 cliff honey.

崖 谷 a precipice beneath an overhanging cliff.

崖 際 the edge of a cliff.

乖 崖 perverse; unbending; out of harmony with things in general.

懸 崖 an overhanging cliff.

飛 崖 inaccessible cliffs.

涯 [2] **A shore; a bank. A limit Usually pron.** *ya*[2].
7237 Inter. preceding.

涯 分 one's duty.

涯 涘 a shore; a limit.

涯 際 a shore; a boundary; a limit.

天 涯 the uttermost ends of the earth; the horizon.

水 涯 a shore; a bank.

無 涯 boundless.

生 涯 means of a livelihood; a profession.

睚 [2] **The corner or canthus of the eye. To stare.**
7238

睚 目 to look with a fixed gaze.

睚 眥 (*ch'ai*[4]) to give an angry look.

YANG. (尢)
(Iang)

央 [1] **The centre. To finish. To conclude.**
7239 Distinguish 夬 No. 3535.

中 央 the centre; central.
　　See No 1504.14 ff.

夜 未 央 night is not yet advanced.

時 未 央 time is not yet up.

(a) To beg; to entreat.

央 中 to invite a middleman.

央中 說合 to invite a middleman to negotiate.

央 媒 to engage a go-between.

央 及 to intercede for; to solicit.

央 告 to entreat; to solicit; to appeal.

央 求 to beg; to beseech.

央 浼 to beseech; to solicit.

央 請 to entreat; to beg; to beseech.

(b) When repeated it indicates the tinkling of bells, etc.; also fresh and bright.

和 鈴 央 央 with the tinkling bells on their banners and on the frontboards of their carriages.

旐 旐 央 央 how splendid his various flags; his banners fluttered gaily.

白 旆 央 央 their white streamers fluttered brightly.

映 [1] **An echo; a sound. Inter. preceding.**
7240 Read *yang*[4]. To vomit, as an infant.

怏 [4.3.] **Discontented.**
7241

深 怏 怏 very dispirited.

殃 祅 [1] **Misfortune; calamity; retribution. A departed spirit.**
7242

殃 及 于 身 evil has come upon me.

殃 及 池 魚 the disaster extends even to the fish in the moat— when the city caught fire:— used to illustrate innocent people being involved in trouble.

殃 咎 or 災 殃 calamities.

殃 害 to injure.
⁵殃 榜 notice of death affixed to the front of a coffin; a license for carrying a coffin out of the gates of Peking.
殃 盡 必 昌 when judgement has done its work, prosperity will come.
殃 禍 calamities.
遭 殃 to meet with misfortune or calamity.
降 之 百 殃 all sorts of evil will come upon—those who do wrong.

泱 ¹ Agitated, as the clouds. Impetuous, as a stream.
7243 Violent, as a gale. Broad and deep, as a river.

泱 泱 乎 大 風 how violent is the gale!
維 水 泱 泱 its waters are wide and deep.
雲 山 泱 泱 the clouds w h i r l round the hills.

(a) Read yang². Wide; boundless.

泱 莽 a broad expanse, as of water.

秧 ¹ Young plants, especially rice. Grain in the blade.
7244

秧 ·子 shoots; sprouts; y o u n g plants or seedlings for transplanting.
秧 歌 songs sung when transplanting rice.
秧 田 seed-beds where rice is sown for transplanting.
秧 種⁴ to plant.
ᵇ秧 苗 sprouting grain.
松 秧 seedling pines.
桑 秧 seedling mulberry-trees.
禾 秧 or 稻 秧 rice-plants f o r transplanting.
魚 秧 the fry of fishes.

鞅 ³ A martingale; a halter. Inter. 怏 No. 7241.
7245 Discontented.

鞅 罔 entangled; hard-up.
鞅 掌 perplexed; harassed.

鴦 ¹ The female of the mandarin duck.
7246 See 鴛 No. 7717.

羊 ² A sheep; a goat.
Radical 123.
7247

羊 入 狼 羣 a sheep entering a pack of wolves—perilous.
羊 卜 to divine by burning the bones of sheep—a Tibetan and Mongolian practice.
羊 叫 the bleating of sheep or goats.
羊 圈 a sheep-fold.
⁵羊 城 a name for Canton. See 五 No. 7187-64.
羊 左 abbrev. 羊 角 哀 and 左 佰 桃, the names of two great friends of ancient times; they shared food and clothing and perished together on a journey —used like our David and Jonathan, etc.
羊 排 骨 mutton chops.
羊 撞 籬 笆 a ram caught in a hedge—unable either to advance or retreat.
羊 有 跪 乳 之 恩 the lamb has the grace to kneel when sucking —illustrates filial piety.
¹⁰羊 棗 sheep-dates, a small black variety.
羊 欄 a sheep-fold.
羊 毛 sheep's wool.
羊 毛 包 a woolpack.
羊 毛 囊 the woolsack.
¹⁵羊 毛 脂 lanolin; wool-fat.
羊 毫 a writing-brush made of wool.
羊 癇 瘋 epilepsy.
羊 皮 sheepskin.
羊 皮 紙 parchment.
²⁰羊 絨 fine wool.
羊 羔 a lamb; a kid; name of a wine produced in Shansi.
羊 羔 跪 乳 the lamb kneels to suck—nature herself teaches us filial piety.
羊 羣 flocks of sheep or goats.
一 羣 羊 a flock of sheep or goats.
²⁵羊 肉 mutton.
羊 胛 熟 a short space of time— if the mutton is put on to cook at sunset, it will be dawn by the time it is ready—speaking of the northern regions where the nights are short.
羊 脂 suet.
羊 脂 玉 sheep's-suet jade—t h e whitest variety.

羊 腸 sheep's intestines—used to illustrate a narrow, winding path, tortuous.
³⁰羊 腸 小 道 a narrow, winding path.
羊 腿 a leg of mutton.
羊 膜 the amnion.
羊 落 虎 口 a sheep fallen into the tiger's mouth—hopeless peril.
羊 角 ram's horns; a name for the date—Zizyphus vulgaris.
³⁵羊 角 燈 horn lanterns.
羊 角 瘋 epilepsy.
羊 角 風 a whirlwind.
羊 質 虎 皮 a sheep dressed in a tiger's skin—all outside show.
羊 蹄 草 the dock.
⁴⁰羊 躑 躅 the rhododendron—it is said to cause sheep to stagger and die, hence the name.
羊 酒 a sheep and a jar of wine— anciently given as a present.
羊 駝 the alpaca.
羊 駝 呢 alpaca cloth.
羊 駝 毛 the wool of the alpaca.
⁴⁵羊 鹿 the spotted deer.
羊 齒 植 物 ferns; bracken
公 羊 a ram or he-goat; a double surname.
山 羊 a goat.
棉 羊 a sheep.
⁵⁰母 羊 a ewe or she-goat.
盤 羊 the argali.
羚 羊 the antelope, c h a m o i s, gazelle, etc.
羯 羊 a castrated ram.
駝 羊 the humped goat.

(a) Read hsiang². u.f. 祥 Lucky, etc.

佯 ² To pretend; to simulate; to dissemble. False; feigning.
7248

佯 佯 不 睬 to pretend not to know a person; to treat superciliously.
佯 北 不 勝 to feign defeat.
佯 北 勿 從 do not pursue an enemy who feigns defeat.
佯 向 a vacant stare.
⁵佯 善 hypocritical.
佯 愚 to feign stupidity.
佯 擬 to simulate.
佯 死 to feign death.
佯 爲 to dissemble; to pretend.
¹⁰佯 爲 不 知 to affect lack of knowledge; to connive at.

佯爲熱心 to pretend zeal.
佯狂 to feign madness.
佯病 to feign illness—as an excuse.
佯盲 to feign blindness.
[15] 佯笑 to pretend to laugh.
佯言 to speak falsely.
佯醉 to feign drunkenness.

佯[2]
7249
To stray; to roam.

彷徉 unsettled; hesitating.

恙[4]
7250
A worm which gnaws the heart; thus:—illness; indisposition.
Distinguish 羔 No. 3282.

別來無恙 have you been quite well since we parted?—used in letters.
貴恙痊瘳否 have you fully recovered from your indisposition?
賤恙 my illness.

氧[3]
7251
Oxygen.

洋[2]
7252
The ocean; hence:—things from overseas; foreign.

洋人 foreigners.
洋傘 a foreign umbrella.
洋務 matters which concern foreigners.
洋化·的 foreignized.
[5] 洋商 foreign merchants; a foreign business house.
洋外 overseas.
外洋 foreign parts.
洋布 calico; shirtings; piece goods.
洋廣雜貨 foreign and Cantonese goods—a general term for miscellaneous imported goods.
[10] 洋式 foreign style.
洋文 foreign languages.
洋服 foreign dress.
洋樓 a foreign-style building of more than one storey.
洋油 kerosene or petroleum.
[15] 洋涇浜章程 the Yang King Pang regulations—from the

name of the creek which formerly flowed between the French and the International Settlements in Shanghai.
洋海 the ocean; the sea.
洋海陸地 land and sea.
洋火 matches.
洋灰 or 水門汀 cement—other transliterations are also used.
[20] 洋烟 opium.
洋燭 foreign candles.
洋琴 the butterfly harp; a piano.
洋界 foreign settlements—as in Shanghai, etc.
洋紅 aniline red; foreign red dyes—words for other colours may be substituted.
[25] 洋紗 foreign yarn; muslins.
洋臺 a verandah or balcony.
洋菜 agar-agar.
洋莊 packed for export.
洋葱 foreign onions.
[30] 洋藥 foreign drugs—opium.
洋號 a bugle; a cornet.
洋蚨 dollars; foreign coinage.
洋蠟 foreign candles.
洋行 (hang[2]) a foreign business house; a hong. [book-binding.
[35] 洋裝 foreign style of dress or
洋貨 foreign goods.
洋錢 or 洋銀 silver dollars.
洋鎗 foreign guns or rifles.
洋鐵 tinned iron; galvanized iron.
[40] 洋關 the Maritime Customs.
洋靛 foreign indigo.
洋面 or 汪洋 the open sea; the ocean.
洋面保險單 a marine insurance policy.
洋鬼·子 foreign devil—term of abuse applied to foreigners.
[45] 五洋 the five oceans, as below.
　大西洋 Atlantic Ocean.
　太·平洋 Pacific Ocean.
　北冰洋 Arctic Ocean.
　南冰洋 Antarctic Ocean.
[50] 　印·度洋 Indian Ocean.
出洋 to go abroad.
放洋 to go to sea.
東·洋 the Eastern Sea—Japan.

(a) Wide; vast; extensive.

洋洋乎 overflowing; swelling, as the sound of music.
洋洋自得 elated; self-satisfied.
河水洋洋 the waters of the (Yellow) river, wide and deep.
洋溢 widespread; overspreading.

洋溢乎中國 (his fame) spread all over China.

蚌[3]
7253
A weevil found in rice, etc. Also read mi[3]. It is also known as 米牛, 米象.

養[3]
7254
To nourish; to rear; to bring up; to care for. To bear children. To support; to maintain. Oxygen.

養·不成 unable to rear.
養不敎 to feed without educating.
養·不活 or 養·不住 unable to support—as a family.
養·不過來 unable to support—one's family.
[5] 養之有素 he has nourished it for a long time.
養他·的老 to support him in his old age.
養·個兒[2]子 to give birth to a son.
養傷 to care for injuries received.
養兒女 to bring up children; to bear children.
[10] 養兒防老 children are reared that they might be a support in old age.
養兵 to support or maintain an army.
養其情慾 feeding his passions.
養化 oxidization.
養化劑 oxidizing agents.
[15] 養化物 oxidized articles.
養化鋅 zinc oxide.
養命 to sustain life.
養地 lands, from the produce of which one is supported.
養壯 to restore to health and strength by careful nurture.
[20] 養娘 a foster-mother.
養·媳婦 a daughter-in-law brought up in the home of her future husband. See 圓 No. 6549-6; 童 No. 6626-27.
養子[3] to bear or bring up a son; an adopted son.
未有學養子[3]而后嫁者也 there has never been a girl who learned to bring up a child in order that she might afterwards marry.
養家費 allowance for the family.
[25] 養寇 to foster brigands.
養廉(銀) money formerly paid to officials as a grant in order that

they might have no excuse for extortions.

養 形 to care for the body, as opposed to the spirit. *See below*—64.

養 心 to cultivate the heart; to nurture the inner man; to edify; to cultivate the mental faculties.

養 志 to cherish one's ideals; to carry out the desires of one's parents.

30養 性 self-culture.

養 成 to rear.

養 拙 to act the fool; to pretend to be simple.

養 料 nutriment.

養 晦 to dwell in retirement, awaiting one's opportunity.

35養 望 to foster one's reputation.

養 樹 to care to. trees.

養 正 to cultivate uprightness.

養 母 a foster-mother.

養 氣 oxygen; to control one's temper.

40養 治 to nurture and rule—the people—the duties of a prince.

養·活 to rear; to keep alive; to support—as one's family.

養·活·不 起 cannot afford to bring up—so many.

養 漢 老·婆 a woman who supports her husband by prostitution.

養 熟 to tame, as animals or birds.

45養 父 a foster-father.

養 牧 to care for the welfare of the people.

養 牲 to keep cattle, etc.

養 猫 to keep a cat.

養 生 to beget; to bring up; to earn a living.

50不 會 養 生 cannot make a living.

生 養 to give birth to; to bring up; to rear.

養 生 主 nourishment of the soul —title of a chapter in Chuang-tzŭ.

養 生 學 hygiene. Cf. 7089.8.

養 生 要 素 the necessaries of life.

55養 生 送 死 births and funerals —the affairs of life.

養 晷 to curtail the necessary food and clothing.

養 病 to seek a cure for an illness.

養 病 所 a sanatorium or hospital.

養 瘦 馬 to keep a thin horse— training girls as prostitutes.

60養 癰 to have an abcess.

養 目 to give pleasure to the eye.

養 眞 to nurture the divine element within one; self-culture.

養 眼 神 to rest the eyes by closing them.

養·神 to conserve the energies— by rest; to nurture the soul or spirit, as opposed to the body. *See above*—27.

65養 禍 to bring about calamities or disasters.

養 精·神 to nourish the mental energies.

養 精 蓄 銳 to strengthen the vital forces.

養 素 to nurture one's original constitution.

養 羞 to accumulate food-stuffs.

70養 老 to care for parents in their old age; to pension the aged.

養 老 費 or 年 金 a pension.

扶 養 費 a pension.

養 老 金 a pension.

養 耳 to gratify the ear.

75養 育 to nourish; to rear.

養 育 嬰 孩 to bring up a child.

養 花 天 weather which is fine for the flowers.

養 虎 傷 生 to nourish a tiger and receive injury oneself—to be injured by one to whom nothing but kindness has been shown.

養 虎 自 遺 患 to keep a tiger will only bring trouble upon yourself.

80養 虎 貽 患 rearing a tiger to cause trouble in the future.

養 蜂 to keep bees.

養 蠶 to tend silkworms.

養 視 如 子 brought him up as his son.

養 贍 to provide for—a family.

85養 身 to care for the health.

養 身 工·夫 certain gymnastic exercises as prescribed by the Taoists.

養 靜 to live in retirement.

養 高 to cherish high ideals.

養 鷄 to keep fowls.

90唯 女 子 與 小 人 爲 難 養 也 of all people, girls and servants are the most difficult to deal with.

頤 養 to nurture; to build up one's strength.

(a) Read *yang*[4]. **To support, as scholars, superiors, etc. To care for, as one's parents.**

以 養 其 父 母 in order to support their parents.

今 之 孝 者 是 謂 能 養 the filial piety of today means (merely) the support of one's parents.

同 養 公 田 cultivate in common the public fields.

無 野 人 莫 養 君 子 if there were not the country people, there would be none to support those of superior ranks.

犬 馬 皆 能 有 養 but dogs and horses are able to do something in the way of support....

(b) Read *yang*[3]. **Distressed.**

心 中 養 養 distressed in mind.

(c) Read *yang*[3]. **To itch. Inter. next.**

癢 痒 [3]　　**To itch.**

7255

癢 酥 酥·的 ticklish; itching.

不 知 痛 癢 not sensitive to pain or irritation—numb; callous.

搔 癢 to scratch an itchy place.

觸 癢 ticklish; irritable.

癢·癢 to itch.

(a) Read *yang*[2]. **To be ill.** (*second form only*).

樣 [4] **A kind; a manner; a style; a sort. A pattern or sample. An example.**

7256

樣 制 style; form.

樣·子 a pattern; a model; a plan; a style. or 兒

花 樣·子 cut-out paper patterns of flowers, ornaments, etc., for embroidery work.

不 是 樣·子 it is not the correct thing; quite unsuitable or unseemly.

5樣·子 間 a sample-room.

樣 幣 specimen coins.

樣 式 a pattern; a model; a style.
樣 態 a pose.
樣 本 a specimen copy; a sample.
10樣 本 賣·買 sale by samples.
樣 樣·的 事 all sorts of affairs.
樣 樣 都 有 there are all sorts.
圖 樣 a design.
怎 樣 in what way? how?
15模 樣 a model; a pattern.
裝 模 作 樣 to put on airs.
貨 樣 a pattern or sample.
走 樣兒 to deviate from the pattern.
都·是 一 樣 they are all alike.

漾 瀁
7257

Waves; ripples; rapids.

漾·出·來 to overflow, as a stream.
漾 波 ripples and waves.
漾 馳 而 已 they simply flow faster—as they near the sea.
搖 漾 to stir the ripples.
輕 漾 ripples.

昜² To open out; to expand. Bright; glorious.
7258 Distinguish 易 No. 2952.

揚² To scatter; to spread. To winnow. To publish abroad.
7259 To praise.

揚 名 to become celebrated.
揚 善 to make known the person's good characteristics.
揚 塲 a winnowing-floor.
揚 稻 to winnow rice.
⁵揚 聲 to spread a report; to cry out.
揚 聲 吶 喊 the noise of many persons shouting.
揚 聲 禱 告 to raise the voice in prayer and supplication.
揚 麥·子 to winnow wheat(-mai⁴-)
傳 揚 to publish abroad; to preach; to proclaim.
10宣 揚 to preach; to proclaim; to make known everywhere.
張 揚 to proclaim; to make known; to preach.
發 揚 to expand.
讚 揚 or 頌 揚 to praise.

(a) To raise. To display. To flourish.

揚·不 起 來 cannot lift up—one's arms.

揚 塵 to raise the dust.
揚 帆 to hoist the sails.
揚 手 to raise the hand.
⁵揚 揚 得²意 self-satisfied; conceited; elated.
揚 旗 to hold up a banner.
揚 氣 to be in high spirits; conceited.
揚 目 to open the eyes wide.
揚 眉 to raise the eyebrows—in astonishment.
10揚 眉 吐 氣 to emerge suddenly from a humble station into an honourable position.
揚·起 塵 土 to raise the dust.
揚·起 篷·來 to hoist the sail.
揚 鑣 to raise the bridle; to jerk the reins.
揚 長 而 去 to stride away with the head in the air.
15揚 鞭 to flourish the whip.
一 抑 一 揚 now low, now high —of music.
飛 揚 to soar, as a bird.

(b) A battle-axe.

戚 揚 battle-axes of various sizes.

(c) A high forehead.

揚 且 之 晳 也 her high forehead, so white.
清 揚 婉 兮 clear eyes, a fine forehead, and lovely face.

(d) Waters flowing over rapids.

揚 之 水 rippling waters.

(e) Lofty branches.

以 伐 遠 揚 to lop off the distant branches.

(f) A division of ancient China.

揚。州 one of the nine divisions into which China was divided by Yü the Great. See 九 No. 1198-15. It comprised the territory lying south of the Huai and the Yangtze rivers, and along the sea to Foochow, most of modern Kiangsi, Chekiang, and Fukien; the name of a town in Kiangsu.
揚 子³江 the Yangtze River.

暘²
7260

The rising sun. Sunshine.

暘 谷 the Valley of Sunshine, where under the Emperor Yao an official was stationed to verify the accuracy of the calendar; it is supposed to be a place somewhere in Corea.
時 暘 若 "emblemed by seasonable sunshine."

楊²
7261

The willow; the poplar or aspen.

楊 柳 the willow.
楊 柳 腰 a willowy waist.
楊 桃 the carambola.
楊 梅 the arbutus.
⁵楊 梅 瘡 syphilitic sores.
楊 梅 結 毒 infected with syphilis.
白 楊 the aspen; the white poplar.
赤 楊 the alder.
黃 楊 木 boxwood.

煬 烊²
7262

To roast; to scorch; to warm at the fire.

煬 火 to put before the fire.
煬 炙 to toast; to roast.

(a) Read yang². To fuse; to smelt.

烊 和 to blend together.
烊 暴 impetuous; zealous.
烊 金 to smelt metals.

瘍²
7263

Ulcers; sores.

禓²
7264

To drive out demons, etc., as was done at the new-year. Also read shang¹.

陽 氜 阳²
7265

Clear; bright. The sun. Heat. Pertaining to this world. Superior. Upper. Front. The north of a river; the south of a hill.

陽 世 this world of sense; this life.
陽 中 the spring.
陽 人 陰 鬼 living persons and disembodied spirits, respectively.

陽 光 the light of the sun.

⁵陽 報 a present recompense.

陽 壽 long life.

陽 奉 陰 違 pretended observance [of laws, rules, etc.

陽 字 characters cut in relief.

陽 宅 dwelling places; houses.

¹⁰陽 宗 the sun, as the chief *yang* element.

陽 德 the sun, as the virtue of *yang*.

陽 文 characters cut in relief.

陽 明 sunlight; the sun.

陽 春 the spring.

¹⁵ 小 陽 春 the little spring—the 10th lunar month; Indian summer.

陽·曆 the solar calendar.

陽 月 the 10th lunar month.

陽 溝 an open drain.

陽 溝 塘 翻 船 to overturn a boat in a mere drain—to come to grief in an unexpected place.

²⁰陽 烏 another name for the sun.

陽 燧 a speculum used in ancient times, to produce fire from the sun's rays.

陽 算 the years of life.

陽 臺 a verandah; lovers' rendez-[vous.

陽 識 an inscription in raised characters.

²⁵陽 道 the path of the sun; that which is external. *See below* —A.12.

陽·間 this life; the upper world of light and life as contrasted with the under world of dark-ness and death.

陽 間 地 獄 a hell in this life.

陽 面 the upper surface; the front.

陽 鳥 the wild goose and other migratory birds which follow the sun.

³⁰南 山 之 陽 the southern side of the Southern Hills.

夕 陽 the evening glow; the western slope of hills.

太·陽 the sun.

孔 陽 very brilliant—colours.

朝¹陽 the morning light. 朝ʸ陽 the eastern slopes of hills.

³⁵正 陽 due south.

當 陽 to face south.

端 陽 節 the 5th of the 5th lunar month. *See* 端 No. 6541—A. 2.

老 陽 the sun.

辭 陽 to bid farewell to this life.

↑正 陽 門 the main gate of Peiping.

---

⁴⁰重 (*ch'ung²*)·陽 (節)the 9th of the 9th lunar month.

(a) The male or positive element in nature, as contrasted with the *yin*. (陰 No. 7444.) the female or negative element. The principle of light and life.

陽 事 sexual intercourse.

陽 充 電 a positive charge of electricity.

陽 剛 vigorous and bold.

陽 極 the positive pole.

⁵陽 氣 the male element in nature, which, by its interaction with the female element, produces all things. *See* 二 No. 1751-7.

陽 物 the virile member.

陽 痿 impotence.

陽 精 the essential male element in nature, exemplified in the sun.

陽 線 positive rays.

¹⁰陽 莖 the virile member.

陽 螺 旋 a male screw or thread.

陽 道 virility; the virile member. *See above*—25.

陽 電 positive electricity.

陽 電 性 positive, as opposed to negative electricity.

¹⁵壯 陽 to strengthen the virile powers.

(b) To pretend, etc. u.f. 佯 No. 7248.

陽 尊 pretending to honour.

陽 狂 to feign madness.

陽 言 falsehood.

颺² Tossed by the wind or the waves. To soar; to fly.

7266

颺 場 a winnowing-floor.

飛 颺 to soar, as a bird.

仰³ To look up to. To look up. Face upwards. To swallow, as medicine, from the act of throwing back the head in swallowing. A command; in official papers it is a form of the imperative; to transmit orders to an inferior. Also read *liang³*.

7267

仰 不 愧 於 天 looking up, his conscience is void of shame before Heaven.

仰 之 彌 高 鑽 之 彌 堅 I look-ed (at the doctrine of the Sage) and it seemed to become higher, I penetrated into it and it seemed to become harder.

仰 事 俯 畜 abbreviation of a passage from Mencius which reads:—looking up, they have sufficient wherewith to serve their parents; looking down, they have sufficient wherewith to·support their wives and children—able to support the family.

仰 倚 he leaned back and looked up.

⁵仰 俯 looking up and looking down, respectively.

俯 仰 之 間 between stooping down and looking up—in a moment.

仰 取 俯 拾 in one way or an-other—gained a competency.

仰 天 to look up to heaven.

仰 屋 looking up at the bare house —utterly without resources, destitute.

¹⁰仰 屋 而 居 living in poverty or idleness.

仰 屋 興 嗟 to look up at the house and sigh—without re-sources.

仰 念 to raise one's thoughts; to expect.

仰 慕 to expect; to desire; to look up to with admiration.

仰 懇 to implore.

¹⁵仰 成 raise the head and it is done —very easily.

仰 望 to look; to expect; to look up to.

仰 板 or 仰 棚 a ceiling.

仰 止 the utmost respect and ad-miration for.

仰 毒 to swallow poison.

²⁰仰 求 to implore.

仰 沐 to be the recipient of—kind-ness.

仰 祈 to beseech; to implore.

仰 給 to depend upon others for support; let it be given to....

仰 而 思 之 puzzled; in a brown study.

²⁵仰 臉 to raise the face.

仰 臥 to lie on the back.

仰 蒙 to be indebted to.

仰 藥 to swallow poison.

仰 見 to look up to with respect.
30 仰 視 to look up to; to respect.
仰 視 不 極 on looking up one could not see the summit.
仰 觀 to look up.
仰 角 the angle of elevation.
仰 託 to rely upon.
35 仰 起 臉 來 to turn the face upwards.
仰 跌 to fall face uppermost.
仰 邀 respectfully to invite.
仰 遵 to obey.
仰 面 the front of the body.
40 仰 頭 to raise the head; to look up.
仰 體 to have regard for; to respect.
久 仰 I have long desired to know you—conventional.
信 仰 自 由 religious tolerance.
右 仰 知 悉 let that which is on the right be fully understood, i.e., the text of the above proclamation.

(a) Read *yang*³, also read *yang*⁴ or *liang*⁴. To trust to; to rely on.

仰 人 鼻 息 to rely on others for a living, having to watch their every expression and desire.
仰 仗 to rely on.
仰 息 to toady to. *See above—A. 1.*
仰 賴 to rely on; to trust to.
仰 食 to sponge on others.

(b) Used in transliterating.

仰 光 Rangoon.

YAO.　　　(幺)

(Iao)

凹¹ An indentation; a hollow; concave.
7268 Also read *ao*², *wa*¹.

凹 下 concave; hollowed out.
凹 凸 concave and convex; hollows and projections—the effect of perspective in drawing.
凹 凸 透 鏡 concavo-convex lens.
凹 地 a hollow.
5 凹 坑 a pit.
凹 字 intaglio characters.
凹 處 a hollow; a depression.
凹 面 a concave surface.

凹 面 透 鏡 a concave lens.
10 半 凹 透 鏡 plano-concave lens.
雙 凹 透 鏡 double concave lens.
凹 面 鏡 a concave mirror.
山 凹 a hollow among the hills.
脚 凹 the hollow of the foot.

姚² Handsome; elegant.
7269

姚 冶 fascinating.

珧² Mother-of-pearl.
7270

江 珧 (or 瑤) or 玉 珧 scallops, found in abundance in the China Sea; the shells contain mother-of-pearl, and the compressor muscle or ligament is dried and imported into China as *compoy* (干 貝); also called 江 瑤 柱; it is highly esteemed as an article of food, both in China and Japan.

坳¹ A hollow in the ground; a cavity. Undulating.
均 Also read *ao*¹.
7271

坳 堂 之 上 .... into a depression on the mud-floor....
坳 塘 a small hollow; a small pond.

拗³ To pull; to drag. To break off. To pluck, as a flower.
7272 Also read *ao*⁴.

拗 怒 suppressed anger.
拗 折 to break; to twist off.
拗 斷 to break off.
拗 碎 to snap into shivers.
拗 花 to break off a flower.
拗 轉 說 to bandy words; to speak in a roundabout manner.
拗 辯 to contradict.

(a) Read *ao*⁴ or *niu*⁴. Perverse; obstinate.

拗 執 perverse; mulish; obstinate.
拗 子 a pig-headed person.
拗 強 perverse; obstinate; pig-headed.

拗 性 obstinate; stubborn.
5 拗 煞 perverse.
拗 頸 stiff-necked; perverse; mulish.
拗 體 詩 irregular poetry which does not conform to the rules regarding the even and deflected tones.
一 不 拗 衆 one cannot prevail against the majority.

眑³ Sunken eyes. Deep; abstruse.
7273 Inter. 窅 No. 7296.

窈³ Obscure; secluded. Refined. Also read *miao*³.
7274

窈 冥 昏 默 to meditate in deep seclusion.
窈 窕 retiring; modest; secluded; attractive.
窈 窕 淑 女 the modest, retiring young lady.

靿⁴ The leg of a boot.
7275

邀¹ To invite; to request. To engage. To meet. To intercept.
7276

邀 他 來 invite him to come.
邀 令 to desire one to.
邀 功 eye-service; work done with an eye to reward; to take the merit for service done by another.
邀 功 生 事 to make trouble through vain-glorious desires.
5 邀 喝 runners who go before an official and shout to clear the way.
邀 賓 or 邀 客 to invite guests.
邀 我 去 逛 he invited me to go for a stroll.
邀 截 to intercept.
邀 接 to invite and go to meet.
10 邀 會 to invite others to co-operate.
邀 游 to invite to an excursion.
邀 福 to induce blessings—as by worshipping the gods.
邀 約 to request to; to invite.
邀 請 to invite.
15 邀 買 人 心 to court popularity.

邀集 to call together; to invite to meet together.
相邀 to invite.

夭[1] **Young; fresh-looking; tender.**
7277 **Distinguish 天 No. 6361.**

夭冶之容 a fascinating face—of a woman.
夭之沃沃 with the glossiness of its tender beauty—describing a tree.
夭夭如也 in a pleased manner.
桃之夭夭 the peach-tree is young and beautiful.
棘心夭夭 till the heart of the jujube tree looks tender and beautiful.

(a) **Calamity.**

天夭之椓 "Heaven is pounding us with calamities."
舒夭紹兮 "O to have the chains of my mind relaxed!"

(b) **Read** *yao*[3]. **To die young. Inter. 殀 No. 7280.**

夭亡 to die young.
夭壽 an early death.
夭折 an early death.

仸[4] **Bent; distorted; crooked. Feeble.**
7278

仸僑 bent; distorted; crooked.

妖[1] **Strange; weird; unaccountable; supernatural. A**
7279 **phantom; a goblin.**

妖人 a wizard.
妖孽 omens of misfortune; supernatural appearances.
妖巧 odd; uncanny; weird.
妖·怪 a spook; supernatural appearance; apparition.
[5]妖變 portents.
妖書 magical books.
妖氣 or 妖氛 apparitions; ghosts; evil portents or influences.
妖法 incantations; magic.
妖異 supernatural appearances; something uncanny or weird.
[10]妖·精 a metamorphosis; a fairy fox; an apparition.
妖術 magical arts; sorcery.
妖言 magic spells; strange legends.
妖魔 a bogy; an evil spirit.
妖魔鬼怪 evil spirits of all kinds.
[15]降 (*chiang*[4]) 妖 the spirits have descended—into the medium.
降 (*hsiang*[2]) 妖 to overcome demons.

(a) **Fascinating; bewitching; seductive—of a woman.**

妖冶 fascinating.
妖姬 a seductive woman.
妖媚 meretricious allurements.
妖嬈 seductive; fascinating.

殀[3] **To die young; an untimely end.**
7280 **Inter. 夭 No. 7277—B.**

殀亡 to die young, under thirty.
殀命 an untimely death.
殀壽不貳 when neither premature death nor long life causes double-mindedness....
殀折 to die prematurely, under thirty.

祅[1] **Calamities caused by disturbances of terrestrial**
7281 **things, contrasted with 災, calamities sent from above. Distinguish 祆 No. 2657.**

祅孽伏息 supernatural manifestations ceased.
祅變 portents.

幺
么[1] **Small; tender. One—on dice. Radical 52.**
7282 **Written ㄠ Nat. Phon. letter for** *ao*.

幺二三 one, two, three—in throwing dice.
幺小 diminutive; puny; minute.
幺豚 the last pig of a litter.
幺麼 diminutive; minute.
幺麼小醜 a petty, low blackguard.

吆[1] **To cry goods, as a hawker. To bawl.**
7283

吆二喝三 to cry out repeatedly.
吆喚 to cry goods, as a hawker.
吆喝 to scold; to talk harshly; to vociferate; to shout one's grievances.

䍃[2] **A vase. A pitcher.**
7284

徭
傜[2] **Compulsory service; vassalage; forced labour.**
7285

徭役 forced labour on government service.
徭糧 food supplied to those on this forced service.

愮[2] **Distressed; agitated.**
7285a

愮亂 flurried.

搖[2] **To shake; to agitate; to toss. To scull; to row. To**
7286 **wave. To sway.**

搖來搖去 swinging to and fro.
搖·動 to shake; to be disturbed; oscillating.
地位搖動 the position is insecure.
搖尾 to wag the tail—to humble oneself.
[5]搖尾乞憐 to wag the tail and seek pity—servile humility, like a dog wagging his tail to attract notice; to cringe; cringing.
搖幌 to wave the signals—in ancient warfare the troops watched for the flag signal to advance.
搖惑 irresolute; perturbed.
搖·晃 jolting; shaking.
搖手 to wave the hand.
[10]搖·掉葉·子 to shake down the leaves.
搖挎 to shake down.
搖搖 vacillating; 搖·搖 just shake once.
搖搖幌幌 reeling and staggering.
搖搖擺擺 swaggering; proud bearing.
[15]搖搖欲墜 shaking as if about to fall.
搖搖欲跌 tottering.
搖撼 to disturb; to excite.

搖·撼戰抖 shaking and trembling.

搖攤 a gambling game with dice.

20 搖散 to scatter.

搖旗 to wave a flag.

搖旗吶喊 to wave flags and shout—encouragement given by bystanders.

搖曳 slightly shaking.

搖椅 a rocking-chair.

25 搖櫓 to scull from the stern of a boat.

搖牛奶 to churn milk.

搖漿 to scull; to row; to wave in the wind.

搖筐 or 搖籃 a child's cradle.

搖籤 to shake the divination tallies in a temple.

30 搖脣鼓舌 to shake the lips and drum with the tongue—gossiping.

搖船 to row; to scull a boat with one oar.

搖蕩 to move; to disturb.

搖身一變 with one shake of the body was changed—into another form.

搖鈴 to ring a hand-bell.

35 搖頭 to wag the head.

搖頭幌腦 nodding and rolling the head about—like an idiot.

搖頭擺尾 shaking the head and waving the tail—well content, pleased.

搖首 to shake the head.

搖鼓兒 to shake a pedlar's drum —a hawker.

猺² A jackal. Name of a tribe in Kwangsi, Hunan, etc.
7287

猺民 a tribe which inhabits Kwangsi, Kwangtung, Hunan, etc.; the people are also called 猺公 or 猺戶; the books describe them as being very wild; they are said to have a short tail, and the skin on the soles of their feet is spoken of as being more than one inch in thickness.

瑤² A precious jade; also defined as a precious kind of
7288 stone, inferior to jade. A kind of green jasper. Clear and pure. Precious.

瑤光 the seventh star of the *Dipper—Benetnach*.

瑤函 your esteemed favour—a letter.

瑤句 your precious note.

瑤圃 the home of the immortals —a place in Fairyland.

5 瑤札 your valued favour—your letter.

瑤池 a pool in Fairyland—the country of 西王母; a name for Peking.

瑤琴 a lute with jasper mountings.

瑤笙 a mouth-organ with jasper mountings.

瑤箋 your precious letter—your esteemed favour.

10 瑤臺 a beautiful terrace; your wife.

瑤英 the finest jade.

瑤華 the beauty of fine stone or jade, etc.

瑤輦 a carriage with jade mountings.

(a) Inter. 珧 No. 7270.

窰
窯} ² A kiln; a pottery. A brothel.
7289

窰匠 a potter; a worker in the kilns.

窰印 the furnace stamp on pottery.

窰子 a brothel.

窰工 potter's work.

窰貨 earthenware; pottery.

官窰 a government porcelain kiln.

燒窰 a furnace or kiln.

謠² To sing. A ballad.
7290 Rumour; slander; a false report.

謠傳 unfounded stories; false reports.

謠歌 folk songs.

謠言 rumours; unfounded reports.

謠言惑衆 wild rumours to mislead the masses.

造謠言 to fabricate and spread rumours.

謠諑 (*chuo* or *cho²·⁵.*) slander.

童謠 rustic songs; children's songs.

遙² Distant; remote. Long.
7291

遙制 to control from a distance without taking up residence in the place.

遙夜 a long night.

遙度 to form a wrong estimate; to miscalculate.

遙影盲從 blindly following a distant shadow.

5 遙望 to look into the distance.

遙臨 approaching from afar.

遙遙無期 at some future time —indefinite.

遙遙相對 having a distant resemblance; somewhat similar.

遙遠 very remote; distant; long.

10 遙青 the colour, as of the distant hills.

遙領 an appointment in which the official does not go to the place himself.

路遙知馬力 by the long road we test the strength of a horse.

飇² Floating in the air. Drifting with the wind.
7292

飇颺 blown about by the wind.

飄飄飇飇 blown about; floating about; hither and thither; wandering at random.

鰩² The flying-fish. See 鮫 No. 7136.
7293

鰩魚 the ray. *See* No. 7294. Also called 魟 (*kung¹*).

文鰩魚 the flying-fish.

鷂⁴ A general term for the sparrow-hawk, kite, harrier
7294 and similar birds. A paper kite.

鷂子 a sparrow-hawk; a paper kite.

放鷂子 to fly a kite.

鷂魚 or 海鷂魚 the ray.

鷂鷹 a kite.

(a) Read *yao²*. A crested francolin.

堯² High; eminent. A celebrated emperor who is said
7295 to reigned 2357—2255 B.C.

堯傳之舜 *Yao* handed down—the empire—to *Shun*.

堯天舜日 the days of *Yao* and *Shun*—the golden age of Chinese history.

堯舜其猶病諸 *Yao* and *Shun* were still troubled about this.

堯舜禹湯 *Yao, Shun, Yü,* and *T'ang,* four ancient rulers, during the golden age of Chinese history.

窅 3.4.   Sunken eyes. Deep.
7296

窅一目 blind of one eye.
窅眇寂寥 secluded and solitary.
窅窅 mysterious; sombre.
窅篠 deep; profound; secluded.

杳 3   Obscure; dark; mysterious; vague; sombre. Far off. Also read *miao*[3].
7297 Distinguish 查 No. 103.

杳冥 dark; cloudy; obscure.
杳杳無踪 gone without leaving a trace.
杳無音信 no news of him for a long time.
杳遠 distant and obscure.
日方杳矣 the sun had just set.

咬 3   To bite; to gnaw.
齩   Also read *ngao*[3].
7298

咬一口 to bite a mouthful.
咬·不動 unable to bite into it—too hard.
咬·不眞 cannot enunciate properly.
咬人 to bite a person; to accuse another in giving evidence.
5 狗咬人 the dog bites.
咬·住牙 to set the teeth.
咬傷 to be injured by a bite—as from a dog.
咬唇 to bite the lips.
咬嚼 to masticate.
10咬定牙齒 to set the teeth firmly; determined.
咬文嚼字 to chew phrases and gnaw books—pedantic; skilled in literary phrases, but out of touch with affairs.

咬斷·了 bitten off.
咬牙切齒 to gnash the teeth.
咬破 to bite through; to bite to pieces.
15咬穿 to bite through.
咬緊牙關 to set the teeth firmly—determined.
咬·着舌 to bite the tongue; to clip the words when talking.
咬柔根 to gnaw cabbage stumps—to suffer hardship and poverty in patience.
咬金嚼鐵 to gnaw metals—to stick to what one says.
20咬·開 to bite in two.
一口咬定 to make a bite and hold on—to stick to what one has said.
供證咬實 the evidence quite convicts him.

(a) Read *chiao*[1]. (*first form only*) The twittering of birds.

咬咬 twittering of birds.

舀 3   To bale out water; to dip.
扰   Usually pron. *wai*[3].
7299 Distinguish 舀 No. 2693.

舀一大碗 ladle out a large bowlful.
舀·不乾 cannot bale it dry.
舀·出·來 to bale out.
舀酒 to ladle out spirits.

要 4   Important; necessary; must. To summarize.
7300 Distinguish 要 No. 5904.

要之 to sum up.
要事 a matter of urgency or importance.
要人 a person of importance.
要件 an important item; an important condition.
5要信 an urgent letter; an important letter.
要務 important business; important matters.
要區 an important position or place.
要口 an important Customs barrier.
要因 a factor; an essential cause.
10要圖 an important scheme.
要地 important ground.

要·在 the main point is...
要塞 a strategic point. (-*sai*[4])
要妙 important and abstruse.
15要害之地 an important position.
要故 a sound reason.
要政 an important administrative measure.
要旨 the essentials.
要概 a summary of the important points.
20要津 an important place.
要港 important ports.
要犯 an important criminal; a ringleader.
要略 a summary of the important points.
要目 important items; important factors.
25要眇 wonderfully beautiful.
要端 important details or items.
要素 essential elements; factors; a *sine qua non.*
國富之要素 the elements of national wealth.
幸福之一要素 one of the essential elements of happiness.
30幸福之要素 the essence of happiness.
成功之要素 factors in—his—success.
新聞的要素 the essential news element.
時間以爲要素 time is an important factor.
經濟思想之要素 the essential factors of economic thought.
35要緊 important. 緊要 urgent.
不要緊 unimportant; it doesn't matter.
要義 the essential meaning; the main thought.
要聞 important news.
要衝 an important pass or barrier.
40要言 an important saying.
要言不繁 spoken short and to the point.
要證 important evidence.
要路 an important road—also used fig.
要道 a highway; essential doctrines; fundamentals.
45此之謂要道 this is termed an important rule of conduct.
要鍵 the key—to a situation.
要電 important telegrams.

要 點 essential points; items of importance.

條 約 之 要 點 the principal points of a treaty.

⁵⁰主 要 the vital points; the essentials. [sist on.

定 要 indispensable. 定·要 to in-

必 要 indispensable; must necessarily.

握 要 to maintain the important points.

撮 要 the essentials of; a summary of.

⁵⁵擇 要 to select the essential features or items.

最 要 of the utmost importance.

至 要 most important.

需 要 must; necessarily. *See* No. 2844-6ff.

(a) To want. To wish. To need. To require.

要·不·得 should not want it; undesirable; it is utterly bad.

要·不·要 do you want it or not? Occasionally.

要·不 起 I cannot afford it.

要 主 a purchaser.

⁵要 價 the price asked.

要 命 to want the life—dangerous; deadly.

   不 要 命 reckless of one's life.

   疼 得 要 命 it pains beyond endurance.

要 多 少 how much do you want?

¹⁰要 式 契 約 a formal contract. (*legal*).

要 式 行 爲 a formal legal act.

要·得 desirable. (*S.W. mand.*)

要·是 要‥ I would like it, but‥‥

要 甚²麼 what do you want? what is your business?

¹⁵要 賬 to collect accounts or debts.

要 錢 to want money—greed; avarice; to collect accounts.

要 面 子 desirous of not losing face.

要 飯 to want food—to beg.

要 飯ₙ的 a beggar.

²⁰不 要 臉 no regard for face— shameless; disreputable.

(b) To be about to—a sign of the future.

要 來 about to come.

要·到 上 海 去 I am going to

Shanghai; getting near to Shanghai.

要 死 at the point of death.

要 活 it will live; most likely to live.

要 賠 本ₙ will lose capital—on the transaction.

要 走 about to go.

天 要 晴 the sky is clearing—it will be fine.

(c) If. (*Probably* < 若 *pron. as* *jao.)

∘要·不·是 supposing it is not...; but for ...

∘要·是 if.

要 知 ... if you would know....

(d) Read *yao*¹. **To make an agreement. To seek for. To meet. To force. To demand.**

要 之 以 禮 to compel them by courtesy.

要 勒 to demand with threats.

要 君 to coerce the ruler.

要 挾 to demand; to extort.

⁵ 利 用 借 欵 的 要 挾 take advantage of the loan to force matters.

要 會 to meet together.

要 服 the territory set apart for banished offenders under *Yü* the Great.

要·求 a demand; claims; to demand; to be importunate.

不 敢 要 求 they d a r e not make any demands.

¹⁰ 工 廠 要 求 the demands of the factories.

急 切·的 要 求 urgent demands.

無 理·的 要 求 unreasonable demands.

無 要 求 之 理 has no claims upon.

將 來·的 要 求 future demands.

¹⁵要 求 同 意 to seek agreement.

要 求 損 害 賠 償 a claim for damages.

要 求 條 件 conditions of claim.

要 求 權 right of claim.

要 求 賠 償 claim for compensation.

²⁰要 盟 an extorted agreement.

要 譽 於 鄉 黨 to seek the praise of one's neighbours.

(e) Read *yao*¹. **u.f.** 腰 **No. 7302. The waist. Now pron.** *yao*⁴ **and taken in the first meaning.**

要 領 the neck and loins—the essentials; the crux of a matter.

不 得 要 領 could not come to any agreement; could not bring the matter to a head.

腰¹ **The chirping of grasshoppers, etc. The buzz of mosquitoes.**
7301

喓 喓 草 蟲 the chirping of the grasshoppers.

喓 喝 the buzz of mosquitoes.

腰¹ **The waist; the loins. The middle.**
7302

腰 刀 a short sword; a dagger.

腰 包 the purse of a Chinese, carried at the waist.

腰 包 硬 his purse is hard—he has ready money.

腰 圓 stout around the waist.

⁵腰·子 the kidneys of animals; a band or hoop which goes around the middle of anything.

腰 巾 a waist-band.

腰·帶 a girdle; a pouch, it is often a part of the girdle; the pelvic girdle.

ₗ腰 店·子 intermediate inns on the road.

腰 截 to chop in two at the middle.

¹⁰腰 房 the best room in the middle of an inn-yard.

腰 斬 to cut in twain—of criminals.

腰 椎 the lumbar vertebræ.

腰·疼 lumbago; backache.

腰 眼 the small of the back.

¹⁵腰 站 an intermediate stage.

腰 筋 the muscles of the loins.

腰 纏 pendants hanging from the waist.

腰 扇 a folding fan.

腰 肢 the loins.

²⁰腰 背 the lower part of the back.

腰·袋 a waist-band; a girdle.

腰·裏 沒 錢 no money on the person; indigent.

腰 跨 豐 隆 stout; corpulent. [garme

腰·身 the loins. 腰·身 waist size of a

²⁵腰 部 the loins, as a division of the body.

腰 領 *See* 要 No. 7300—E.

腰 骨 the waist.

山 腰 half-way up a mountain.

半 中 腰 half-way; in the middle.

30彎 着 腰 to stoop; to bend the back.

折 腰 to bow in obeisance.

扭 腰 to strain the muscles of the back.

柳 腰 a willowy waist.

細 腰 a slender waist.

褸¹
7303   A pleat; a fold.

壓 褸 to make a fold or pleat.

騕³
7304   Name of a fabulous horse which could travel 10,000 li a day.

曜⁴
7305   Glorious, as the sun. To dazzle. Also read yüeh⁴.

曜 眼 to dazzle the eyes.

七 曜 the seven sources of brightness—the sun, moon and the five planets.

照 曜 dazzling; brilliant.

耀⁴
7306   Glory; brightness; splendour; honour. Inter. preceding.

耀 眼 to dazzle the eyes.

光 耀 brilliance.

榮 耀 glory; honour; splendour.

YEH.   (ㄧㄝ)
(Ie)

耶²
7307   A final interrogative particle. u.f. 耶 No. 2625—A.

何 耶 What does it mean?

其 信 然 耶 Is this true?

是 耶 非 耶 Is it so or not?

(a) u.f. 爺 No. 7309. A father.

耶 孃 father and mother.

(b) Used in transliterating. (yeh¹⁻²)

耶 和 華 Jehovah.

耶 穌 Jesus.

耶 穌 敎 Christianity—the religion of Jesus; in popular

speech—Protestant Christianity as distinct from Roman Catholicism.

耶¹ 穌 會 The Society of Jesus; Jesuits.

耶 路 撒 冷 Jerusalem.

耶 魯 大 學 Yale University.

揶²
揶
7308   To gesticulate; to play antics; to posture.

揶 揄 to mimic; to ridicule.

椰²
椰
7309   The cocoa-nut palm.

椰 子 the cocoa-nut, also called 人 頭 菓 or 越 王 頭 from a legend that it was transformed from the head of a King of Annam.

椰 子 瓢 a ladle made from a cocoa-nut shell.

椰 殼 the shell of the cocoa-nut.

椰 肉 the flesh of the cocoa nut.

椰 花 酒 toddy; arrack.

椰 荣 a Savoy cabbage.

椰 衣 簑 a coir rain-cloak.

爺²
7310   A father. A term of respect; a gentleman.

爺 們 or 爺 們 兒 men, as contrasted with women; servants.

爺 兒 a husband.

爺 兒 倆 father and son or daughter.

爺 娘 father and mother.

爺 婆 father-in-law and mother-in-law.

爺 爺 a grandfather.

老 爺 a term of respect; an old gentleman; also applied to officials. See No. 3833-12, 45.

琊²
7311   Name of a part of eastern Shantung.

也³
7312   A particle. And; even; also; besides; still.

也 不 彀 still not enough.

也 不 說 也 不 寫 he would neither speak nor write.

也 可 以 very well; that will do.

也 好 will also do; very well.

⁵也 就 .   and then....

也 是 這 樣 also thus.

也 有 there are still....

也 有 道 理 still there is reason in what you say.

也 曾 來 過 (they) have been here too.

10也 未 可 定 it is still uncertain; it cannot yet be decided.

也 未 可 知 who knows but that . . . ; undecided; uncertain.

也 罷 了 very well; that's satisfactory. (-liao³ or -le.)

也 行 all right; that will do too.

也 許 perhaps; also; probably.

15你 不 去 也 不 要 緊 even if you do not go, it does not matter.

(a) A final particle, sometimes coupled with other particles which intensify it; see below.

未 之 有 也 there has never been —such a thing.

是 人 之 所 欲 也 .... are what men desire.

可 謂 好 學 也 已 he may be said indeed to love to learn.

斯 害 也 已 is injurious indeed.

可 謂 至 德 也 已 矣 it may be said that in this case, virtue has reached the highest point indeed.

吾 未 如 之 何 也 已 矣 I can indeed do nothing with him.

(b) It occurs in the middle of a sentence and at the end of correlated clauses, where it often indicates a pause which brings out the meaning better. It also occurs after individual words, giving special emphasis to them. = coll. 阿 -a.

其 爲 人 也 發 憤 忘 食 ... he is a man, who in the pursuit of knowledge forgets his food.

是 可 忍 也 孰 不 可 忍 也 if he can bear to do this, what may he not bear to do?

德 者 本 也 財 者 末 也 virtue is the root, wealth is the result.

仁 也 者 人 也 jên is man

賜 也 始 可 與 言 詩 已 矣 with one like Tz'ŭ, I can begin to talk about the Odes.

冶³ 7313 — To fuse metals; to smelt.

冶坊 a foundry.
冶城 an old name for Nanking.
冶金學 metallurgy.
鎔冶 to smelt; to fuse.

(a) To seduce; to fascinate.

冶冶 or 妖冶 bewitching.
冶容 a fascinating countenance.
冶容誨淫 seductive looks invite lewdness.
冶艷 fascinating; bewitching.
冶遊郎 one who frequents brothels.

野埜³ 7314 — Wild; uncultivated; a wilderness. Rustic. Savage.

野乘 fiction; romances.
野人 an uncouth person; a rustic.
野史 fictitious historical romances; fiction.
野合 an illicit connection.
⁵野味 game; savoury dishes.
野地 waste ground.
野外 desert; open country.
野子 an illegitimate child.
野宴 a picnic; a country excursion.
¹⁰野客 country people; rustics.
野宿 to camp out.
野心 savage disposition; mad ambition.
狼子野心 a savage, wolfish disposition.
野性 restive; a wild nature.
¹⁵野戰 a battle in the open; irregular skirmishing; irregular style of composition.
野戰病院 a field hospital.
野戰砲 field guns.
野服 rustic garments.
野火 or 野燒 a prairie fire; will-o'-the-wisp.
²⁰野熊 the wild bear.
野牛 the wild ox; the bison.
野獸 wild beasts.
野球 baseball.
野瓜 the wild gourd.
²⁵野生 growing spontaneously.
野祭 the worship at the graves during Ts'ing ming.
野種 an illegitimate child.

野羊 the wild sheep or goat.
野老 an aged rustic.
³⁰野花 wild flowers; a prostitute.
野草 (or 薹) jungle; wild growth of vegetation.
野蜜 wild honey.
野蠶絲 silk from wild silk-worms.
野蠻 uncivilized; barbarous; savage.
³⁵野蠻手段 barbarous methods.
野蠻自由 wild license.
野豬 the wild boar.
野貓 a wild cat; a fox; a hare—in some places.
野趣 rustic pleasures.
⁴⁰野錄 fictitious historical romances.
野頭²野腦 wild, boisterous, unruly.
野馬 a wild horse; clouds of dust; a mirage.
野鴨 the wild duck.
野鶴 a wild crane or stork—a recluse.
⁴⁵野鷄 a pheasant; something irregular; not in the regular lines, as a steamer; low-class prostitutes.
打野鷄 to shoot pheasants; to visit low-class brothels.

野鷄船 irregular steamers outside the ring, or those run by a company which has only one or two ships.
野鹿 the wild deer.
四野 the cardinal points.
⁵⁰村野 rustic; countrified.
粗野 coarse and unrefined; uncouth.

夜⁴ 7315 — Night; dark; darkness.

夜上 at night.
夜不收步 not halting at night.
夜中 during the night.
夜來之事 the events of the previous night.
⁵夜來香 the tuberose.
夜光 luminous insects; the moon.
夜分 midnight.
夜半 midnight; late at night.
夜叉 from the Sanskrit—Yaksha. Demons that fly like meteors, messengers from hell.
¹⁰夜合資 prostitute's fees.
夜壺 a chamber-pot.

夜學 night-schools.
夜客 a night-visitor—a burglar.
夜室 the dark house—the grave.
¹⁵夜市 night markets.
夜怖 night terrors—as of children.
夜晚 late at night.
夜景 night-scenes.
夜更 the night-watches.
²⁰夜會 an evening party.
夜禮服 evening dress.
夜校 night-schools.
夜深 late at night.
夜漏 night-time, from the use of the clepsydra in ancient times.
²⁵夜猫·子 the screech-owl.
夜盜 night-robbers.
夜盲症 night-blindness.
夜票 permit to work a vessel at night.
夜禁 prohibitions against being out late at night.
³⁰終夜 the whole night.
↓夜臺 the dark terrace—the grave.
夜航船 night-boats.
夜行 a thief; to travel by night.
夜行軍 a night-march.
³⁵夜裝 evening dress.
夜·裏 at night; night-time.
夜視 night-vision.
夜郎 an aboriginal tribe which occupied the territory to the west of Kweichow during the Han dynasty.
夜郎自大 the self-importance of Yeh-lang—an envoy from the Han dynasty came to that place and was asked by the local chieftain which State was the larger, Yeh-lang or that of Han.
⁴⁰夜間 during the night.
夜間動·物 nocturnal animals.
夜間攻·擊 a night-attack.=夜襲.
夜開花 night-blooming flowers.
夜闌 late at night.
⁴⁵夜露 night-dews.
夜靜 the stillness of the night.
夜飯 supper.
夜鳥 nocturnal birds.
夜鶯 the nightingale.
⁵⁰夜鷹 night-hawks.
夜黑 a dark night.
一夜 all night.
半夜 midnight; late at night.
坐夜 to sit up all night.
⁵⁵打夜工 to do night-work.
放夜 to keep the city gates open all night.

昨 夜 last night.
晝 夜 day and night.
月 夜 a moonlight night.
60 查 夜 night patrols.
熬 夜 to sit up all night, as when working, gambling, etc.
白 天 黑 夜 day and night.
巡 夜 night patrols.
長 夜 the long night—death.

YEH. (ㄧㄝ)
(Ieh)

頁 4.5. A leaf; the page of a
7316 book. A leaf of a door. A lobe of the lungs or liver. The head. Radical 181.

頁·數 folio number.
書 頁 the pages of a book.
百 頁 窗 Venetian blinds.

枼 4.5. A tablet; flat pieces of
7317 wood; a slip; a leaf.

碟 4.5. Half-sitting, half-reclin-
7318 ing.

葉 4.5. A leaf; a petal. A slip;
7319 a card; a plate. A page; u.f. 頁 No. 7316. A hinge. Diminutive—a mere leaf.

葉·子 戲 playing cards.
葉·子 煙 (or 菸) leaf tobacco.
樹 葉·子 leaves of trees.
葉 拱 to place the hands on the bosom and bow.
5 葉 捲 蟲 caterpillars that curl up the leaves.
葉 柄 the stem of a leaf.
葉 片 a leaf.
葉 筋 the midrib of a leaf.
葉 肉 the inner tissues of leaves—mesophyll.
10 葉 脈 the veins, etc., of a leaf.
葉·腦 蓋·子 the forehead.
葉 芽 leaf-buds.
葉 落 歸 根 the leaves fall and return to the root—everything reverts to its original source.
葉 落 知 秋 when the leaves fall we know that autumn is here.
15 葉 針 a botanical term for thorns which are aborted leaves.

秋 葉 autumn leaves.
荷 葉 a lotus-leaf; a door-hinge.
輪 葉 the blade of a propeller.

(a) An age; a generation; a period.

昔 在 中 葉 formerly in the Middle Period....
末 葉 the period at the close of a dynasty, etc.
自 明 中 葉 from the middle of the Ming dynasty.
萬 葉 a myriad generations.

(b) Read shê 4.5. Used in names of places.

葉 公 the Duke of Shê.
葉 縣 a district in Honan.

鍱 4.5.
7320 Thin plates of metal.

業 4.5. Possessions; property. A
7321 profession; a trade; a calling. Instruction. Business. Also read nieh 4.5.

業 主 the owner of property.
業 務 business matters.
業 師 a tutor; an instructor in a profession.
業 歸 原 主 the property to revert to the original owner.
5 業 戶 the owner of property.
業 等 we, the tradesmen—used in petitions.
事 業 occupation; affairs.
停 業 to give up a business.
傳 業 to transmit a calling.
10 功 業 services.
勸 業 to encourage industry; to foster industries.
受 業 to receive instruction—your pupil, conventional.
商 業 commerce.
大 業 the great business—to rule; an emperor.
15 失 業 to be out of employment.
學 業 to learn a business, trade or profession.
家 業 the family estate.
實 業 industries.
實 業 銀 行 The Industrial Bank.
20 專 門 業 the professions.
工 業 industries.

操 業 to engage in a calling.
本 業 one's original calling or profession.
林 業 forestry.
25 正 業 an honest calling; one's proper calling.
海 運 業 the shipping business.
漁 業 fisheries.
無 業 游 民 vagabonds; tramps; the unemployed.
產 業 property; estate, etc.
30 畢 業 to complete a course, as of study; to graduate.
職 業 occupation; profession; calling.
職 業·的 分 類 to classify according to occupations.
藝 業 an art; a handicraft.
航 業 the shipping business.
35 製 造 業 the manufacturing industries.
設 業 to set up a business or industry, etc.
農 業 agriculture.

(a) Already.

業 已 past; already.
業 已 去·了 he had already gone.
業 經 already; past.
業 經 宣 布 it has already been published or propagated.
業 經 組·織 it has already been organized.

(b) Partly finished.

業 屨 partly finished sandals.

(c) To feel in peril.

兢 兢 業 業 wary and fearful.
有 震 且 業 there was a time of shaking and peril.

(d) To be strong.

四 牡 業 業 the four steeds are strong.
赫 赫 業 業 full of grandeur and strength.

(e) The toothed face-board of a stand for bells.

(f) A Buddhist term for evil, retribution, etc.

業 因 karma; destiny.

業 報 retribution for sins.

業 海 overwhelming retribution, like a sea.

業 火 the fire of retribution.

業 緣 a cause which produces effects in another state of existence—*nidâna*.

業 障 retribution in this life for the sins of a previous existence.

三 業 the three instruments by which *karma* operates, i.e., the mouth, the body, and the mind.

鄴 7322 4.5. Name of a small principality in the north of what is now Honan. Also read *nieh*[4.5].

鄴 架 a library—from the title of a man named 李 泌 who lived in the T'ang dynasty,—he received the title of 鄴 侯, and was famous for his vast library which had 30,000 shelves of books.

暍 7323 4.5. Sunstroke. Read *ho*[4.5]. Hot, feverish.

暍 人 a feverish person.

謁 7324 4.5. To visit a superior; visits in general.

謁 刺 a visiting-card.

謁 舍 a reception-room.

謁 見 to visit a superior; to have an audience.

謁 選 to present oneself as a candidate.

拜 謁 to pay a call.

嶭 7325 4.5. Elevated; lofty.

饁 7326 4.5. To carry food to labourers in the field.

夫 耕 妻 饁 the husband ploughs and his wife brings his food.

擪 7327 1.5. To tuck in; to put the finger into; to put in; to stow away. See 捓 No. 3032—B.

擪 在 懷 中 put it into the bosom.

擪·起·來 to tuck in; to put away.

把 舖·蓋 擪 (or 捓)·上 tuck in the quilt.

厴 7328 4.5. The jaws; the cheeks. Read *yen*[3]. A mole or spot on the face.

燁 7329 4.5. A blaze of fire. Splendid. Glorious.

YEN. (ㄧㄢ)
(Ien)

焉 7330 1 An interrogative particle. How? Why? Where?

焉 可 誣 也 how can it fool anybody?

焉 得 富 貴 how can one be rich and honourable?

焉 有 此 理 is there such a principle?

焉 用 殺 why use killing at all?

[5]焉 知 how should I know....?

焉 知 來 者 之 不 如 今 也 how can you know that his future will not be equal to our present?

焉 能 how can it be done? impossible.

焉 能 從 之 how can he follow him?

焉 能 為 有 焉 能 為 亡 what difference can it make if he exists or not? (-*wu*[2])

[10]未 知 生 焉 知 死 you do not know life, what can you know about death?

牛 羊 何 擇 焉 what is there to choose between an ox and a sheep?

(a) Read *yen*[2]. There, in it, at it, in that situation. Cf. Fr. *v*. See *JAOS*, 60, 1–22, 193–207 (1940).1

丘 未 能 一 焉 I have not yet attained to one of these—fulfilments of duty.

人 之 其 所 愛 而 辟 焉 men are partial where they feel affection and love.

君 子 疾 沒 世 而 名 不 稱 焉 the superior man hates the idea of leaving the world with his name unmentioned there.

善 為 我 辭 焉 kindly decline the offer for me.

[5]如 日 月 之 食 焉 like the eclipses of the sun and moon.

天 地 位 焉 萬 物 育 焉 a happy order will prevail throughout the universe, and all things will be nourished and flourish there.

就 有 道 而 正 焉 he consorts with men of principle in order to have himself rectified by them.

心 不 在 焉 .. when the mind is not there: absent-minded.

心 焉 忉 忉 "my heart is full of sorrow."

心 焉 惕 惕 "my heart is full of trouble."

心 焉 數[3] 之 "can be discriminated by the mind."

惄 焉 如 擣 "I think till I am as if pounded—all over."

於 焉 嘉 客 "be here, an admired guest!"

於 焉 逍 遙 "spends his time here at his ease."

有 人 焉 there is a man here.

無 入 而 不 自 得 焉 "he can find himself in no situation in which he is not himself."

王 宝 惠 焉 the king bestowed favours on him.

衆 惡 之 必 察 焉 when all hate a man it is necessary to look into the matter."

嫣 7331 1 Charming; fascinating; captivating.

嫣 然 一 笑 the captivating smile of a woman—ruined a State.

嫣 紅 柔 綠 rich crimson and tender green.

蔫 7332 1 Fading plants. To decay.

蔫 臭 rotten.

蔫 舊 old and faded.

鄢[1] **Name of a district in Honan, 鄢陵縣.**
7333

言[2] **Words; speech. To talk; to speak; to express; to mean. Radical 149.**
7334

言不及行 (*hsing*²) theory is not equal to practice.
言不必信 does not aim at sincerity in his speech.
言不相符 the words are contradictory.
言之不怍 to speak without modesty.
5 言之可恥 it is shameful to speak of it.
言乎 to speak of; to refer to.
言傳 to express in words; to state.
言其 to say that it . . . ..
言出卽行 no sooner said than done.
10 言及於此 when he had got to this point.
言同意不同 to agree in word only; the word agrees but the intent is different.
言和意順 conversation and thoughts in sympathy—of friends.
言和而色彝 his speech was quiet and his countenance normal.
言外之意 an implied meaning—something beyond the literal words.
15 言外求之 seek for the meaning between the lines.
言多必失 much talk leads to error.
言定 to settle; to decide—as an agreement.
言官 or 敢言 a Censor.
言差語錯 bickering.(-*ch'a*¹-)
20 言已盡于今日 I have declared everything today.
言明 to state clearly.
言未及之而言 to speak when it is not the place to speak.
言浮於行 to boast above one's ability.
言盡於此 I have no more to say.
25 一言難盡 mere words cannot fully express it—my gratitude; it is a long story.
言簡意賅 the language is simple and terse but the thought is uncommon.
言者行之表 words are the outer covering of actions.
言而有信 to be as good as one's word.
言行 (*hsing*⁴) words and actions.
30 言行 (*hsing*⁴) 相顧 words corresponding with actions.
言行錄 a biography.
言訂 to settle; to decide—as an agreement.
言詞 words; expressions; language.
言說 to say.
35 言語 speech; conversation. Pron. *yüan*²·*i* to speak, to speak up.
三言兩語 in a few words.
言三語四 to grumble; to find fault.
言語呢喃 jabbering.
言語學 or 語言學 linguistics.
40 言語急燥 hasty in speech.
言語科 department of languages—in a college.=語言系.
言語粗俗 coarse and vulgar in speech.
言論 a discussion; an oration.
言論家 talkers; critics; orators.
45 言論時代 the period of propaganda or discussion—before putting a thing into practice.
言論機關 the organ for discussion, i.e., the press.
言論自由 freedom of speech.
言談 to converse; conversation.
言責 the responsibility of speaking.
50 言辭 language; words; expressions.
言辭辯論 oral disputes.
言過其實 exaggerations; to exaggerate.
言道 to say....
言重 weighty words.
55 言離本題 to digress.
不待言 it goes without saying.
勸言 words of exhortation.
反言 to go back on one's word.
善言 helpful words; good words.
60 多言 loquacity.
大言 boasting; hyperbole.
失言 a slip of the tongue.
宣言 a statement; to announce.
寓言 allegory; parable, etc.
65 巧言 smooth talk; specious talk.
忘言 unspeakable.
敷言 padding; mere words to fill up with.
格言 wise sayings; maxims, proverbs, etc.
泛言 vague expressions.
70 流言 current expressions; rumours.
片言 a few words—in a note.
痛言 sharp speech.
發言權 right of taking part in a discussion.
直言 straightforward speech; a straight talk.
75 箴言 proverbs; maxims, etc.
能言 voluble.
花言 flowery speech; exaggerations.
虛言 empty words; mere talk.
謠言 rumours; false reports.
80 豫言 prophecy.
踐言 to keep one's promise.
食言 to eat one's words; to break a promise; to go back on one's word.
↑語言 language.

(a) An initial particle, not translatable,—some define it as the pronoun, *I*.

言告師氏 I have told the matron.
言秣其馬 I would feed their horses.
靜言思之 silently thinking of my case.
願言則懷 I think of him and my breast is full of pain.

(b) Used like 然, adverbially.

睠言顧之 when I look back and think of it.
興言出宿 I rise and pass the night outside.

(c) High; lofty.

崇墉言言 against the walls of *Ts'ung*, high and great.

炎[2] **A flame. To flame; to blaze. Inflammation. Brilliant.**
7335
Sometimes read *yen*⁴, and used for 餤 No. 7394.

炎上 to flare up; a fire.
炎天 hot weather.
炎帝 *Yen Ti*—the dynastic title of *Shên Nung* 神農, 2838 B.C.
炎徼 the distant southern frontiers.

[5]炎 方 the south.

炎 暑 the summer; hot—of weather.

世 態 炎 涼 the changing aspects of the times—of fickle friends, now hot, now cold.

炎 炎 赫 赫 glowing hot; fierce—as a fire.

炎 熱 very hot.

[10]炎 爔 to flare up.

炎 症 inflammatory diseases.

炎 精 the essence of heat—a name for the sun.

炎 腫 inflammation and swelling.

炎 附 寒 棄 to cleave to in the heat and discard in the cold—fickleness of friends, etc.

[15]炎 陽 the great heat of summer.

炎 風 the north-east wind; a hot wind.

(a) Read *tan*[1] or *t'an*[2]. Skilful in argument.

大 言 炎 炎 小 言 詹 詹 great speech is universal, small speech is particular,—i.e., the former "covers the whole ground in question, leaving no room for positive and negative to appear in antagonism."—*Giles,* note in translation of Chuang Tzŭ.

剡 [3] Sharp; sharp-pointed. To sharpen.
7336

剡 剡 bright; discerning; sharp; alert.

剡 剡 起 屨 he rose up at once.

剡 木 爲 矢 he sharpened the stick for a dart.

剡 銳 sharp-pointed.

(a) Brilliance.

(b) Used in transliterating.

剡 浮 洲 the island of *Jambadvipa*—used by Buddhists for India; also used for the countries of the east. *See* 閻 No. 7395.

扊 [3] An upright bar for fastening a door.
7337

扊 扅 (*i*[2]) the upright bar for fastening a door.

燚 [4] Flames. Same as 燄 No. 7394.
7338

琰 [3]
埈   A gem. The glitter of gems.
7339

琰 圭 a sharp-pointed sceptre—expressing sharp severity against evil.

妍 [2] Beautiful; elegant; handsome; accomplished.
7340

妍 媸 beauty and ugliness.

妍 美 pretty; handsome.

鮮 妍 fresh and beautiful.

研 [2]
礸   To grind; to rub fine; to powder. To calender.
7341

研 墨 to rub ink on the ink-slab for writing.

研 末 to rub to fine powder.

研 碎 to grind to pieces.

研 細 to rub fine.

研 船 a narrow iron mortar, in which drugs are powdered.

(a) To investigate thoroughly—from the above idea of grinding to powder.

研 求 to examine into.

研 審 to make an official investigation.

研·究 to search into; to investigate thoroughly; research.

研 訊 to make an official investigation. ⌈graduate school.

↑研·究 院 research institute;

(b) Read *yen*[1]. u.f. 硯 No. 7401. An ink-slab.

研 室 a case for an ink-slab.

延 [2] To delay; to lengthen; to protract.
7342 Distinguish 廷 No. 6404.

延 不 繳 銀 to delay payment.

延 久 for a long time; to delay.

延 佇 to stand for a long time.

延 及 to involve; to implicate.

---

[5]延 及 他 人 to involve others; to compromise another.

延 壽 to prolong life; advanced age.

延 壽 客 or 延 齡 客 a fancy name for the chrysanthemum.

延 宕 to procrastinate; to delay.

延 宕 手·段 procrastinating methods.

[10]延 年 益 壽 May you prolong your days!

延 捱 to procrastinate.

延 擱 to neglect; to procrastinate; to be dilatory.

延 擱 卸 載 demurrage.

延 擱 貿 易 to hinder business.

[15]延 期 to postpone; to defer; deferment; to extend a time-limit.

延 滯 to delay; to hinder.

開 船 延 滯 demurrage.

延 燒 a fire which involves other buildings.

延 眺 to crane the neck and gaze.

[20]延 祺 to prolong one's happiness.

延 緩 to procrastinate; to delay; to neglect; dilatory; behindhand.

延 纏 dragging on; delayed; hampered; protracted.

延 腦 the *medulla oblongata*—to lengthen life.

延 衺 數 十 里 stretching north and south for many *li*.

[25]延 譽 May your fame extend!

延 遲 slow; dilatory; to dawdle.

不 可 延 遲 let there be no delay!

延 長 for a long time; delay.

延 長 性 or 延 性 ductility.

[30]延 長 戰 線 to extend the fighting line.

延 長 線 extension-line—as of a railway.

延 項 舉 踵 to crane the neck and stand on tiptoe.

延 首 遠 望 to stretch forward the head and gaze into the distance.

延 駐 to reside for some time—in a place.

[35]延 髓 the *medulla oblongata,* the hindmost segment of the brain.

勿 延 without delay; do not delay.

推 延 to procrastinate.

蔓 延 to spread—as creeping plants, used figuratively of evils.

遷 延 歲 月 to delay for months and years.

(a) To invite; to engage. To receive.

延入內庭 to invite into the inner apartments.
延賓 to invite guests.
延師 to engage a teacher.
延祥納福 May every blessing and happiness be yours!
延納 to take in; to receive.
延聘 to engage.
延請 to extend an invitation to.

埏²
7343
A boundary; a limit.

八埏 the eight principal points of the compass.
垓埏 the farthest limits; the bounds of the earth.
遐埏 the horizon.

筵²
7344
A bamboo mat spread on the ground for sitting on. A feast; a banquet. A hall.

筵席 or 筵宴 or 酒筵 a feast; a banquet.
擺筵 to spread a feast.
設筵 to prepare a feast or banquet.

莚²
7345
Creeping or climbing plants.

蜒²
7346
A millipede.

蚰蜒 the millipede.

癌²
7346a
A tumour or cancer.

癌腫 a cancerous swelling.
癌腫性·的 cancerous.
乳癌 cancer of the breast.
唇癌 cancer of the lips.
子宮癌 cancer of the womb.
胃癌 cancer of the stomach.
腸癌 cancer of the bowels.
舌癌 cancer of the tongue.

嚴²
7347
Stern; strict. Majestic; dignified. Private. Very; extremely.

嚴令 peremptory orders.
嚴冷 a cold, severe demeanour.
嚴冬 the depth of winter.
嚴切 strict; rigorous.
⁵嚴切執行 rigorous enforcement.
嚴刑 severe punishment; to punish severely.
嚴剋 harsh; severe.
嚴加管束 to control with rigour.
嚴勒 to coerce.
¹⁰嚴厲 severely strict; stern; rigorous.
嚴厲苛求 rigorous exactions.
嚴君 your father.
嚴命 strict orders; peremptory orders.
嚴嚴·的 severely; straitly.
¹⁵嚴妝 dressed in strict style.
嚴守中立 strict observance of neutrality.
嚴守秘密 to preserve strict secrecy; strictly confidential.
嚴密 secret; close; confidential.
嚴密偵查 confidential inquiry; strict investigation.
²⁰嚴密科學研究 a strict, scientific investigation.
嚴密·的隱遁 in strict seclusion.
嚴寒 excessively cold.
嚴察 to make a close examination.
嚴師 a severe teacher.
²⁵嚴恃下 my father is alive.
嚴慈 father and mother. See below—44.
嚴憚 to dread greatly.
嚴拿 peremptory arrest.
嚴敬 respectful.
³⁰嚴整 strict discipline.
嚴明 positive; peremptory.
嚴束 to restrain with rigour.
嚴格 strict; narrow.
嚴格意義上 in the strict sense of the word.
³⁵嚴格派 the narrow school.
嚴格·的制限 strict limits.
嚴格言之 strictly speaking....
嚴正 severe; grave; stern.
嚴正中立 strict neutrality.
⁴⁰嚴正宗派 the strictly orthodox school.
嚴正秘·密 strictly confidential.
嚴氣正性 strictly proper and unbending.
嚴法 strict laws.
嚴父慈母 stern father and compassionate mother.

⁴⁵家嚴 my father.
尊嚴 your father.
嚴牆 a high wall.
嚴督 strict oversight.
嚴禁 stringent prohibitions; strictly prohibited.
⁵⁰嚴究 to make strict inquiries into.
嚴緊 strict; rigorously; tight.
嚴而泰 dignified yet not constrained.
嚴聲厲色 with stern tones and severe countenance.
嚴肅 or 威嚴 dignified; sedate; grave demeanour.
⁵⁵嚴行 stringent actions.
嚴行封禁 a strict blockade.
嚴親 my father.
嚴詞拒絕 a stern repudiation.
嚴諭 strict orders.
⁶⁰嚴責 severely reprimand.
嚴辦 to deal with severely.
嚴追 to follow up with rigour.
嚴酷 tyrannical; cruel; severe.
嚴重 momentous.
⁶⁵嚴重抗議 a strenuous protest.
嚴重監視 to keep a strict watch.
嚴重之 respected him highly.
嚴重防備 strict precautions.
嚴關 an important barrier or pass.
⁷⁰嚴防 to take strict precautions.
嚴防偷漏 strict precautions against smuggling.
嚴防扒手 beware of pickpockets.
嚴限 a strict limit—as of time.
嚴霜 severe frosts.
⁷⁵嚴飭 to charge strictly.
嚴麗 stately; elegant.
夜嚴 the night watches. [alert.
戒嚴 stringent measures; on the
戒嚴令 martial law.
⁸⁰解嚴 to relax precautions; to suspend martial law; the "all clear" in an air raid alarm.

儼³
7348
Majestic; stern. Like; as.

儼恪 stern and respectful.
儼恭 very precise and formal; particular as to etiquette.
儼然 dignified; stern.
望之儼然 looked at from a distance, he appears stern.
⁵儼然一色 just the same colour.
儼然人望而畏之 thus dignified, he is looked at with awe.

儼 然 可 畏 dignified and awe-inspiring.
儼 若 like as; similar; resembling.

巖 岩 [2]
A cliff; a precipice; a large open cave; a grotto. Dangerous.
7349

巖 徼 a place of strategic importance on the frontier.
巖 洞 an open mountain cave.
巖 牆 a high and dangerous wall.
巖 穴 a cave; a grotto.
[5]巖 穴 之 士 a scholarly recluse.
巖 茶 cliff tea—highly esteemed.
巖 谷 a gorge or defile.
巖 邑 a city of strategic importance.
巖 野 mountain wilds; the retreat of a recluse.

釅 [4] Strong, as a liquid; rich, as gravies, etc.
7350

簷 檐 橧 [2]
The eaves of a house.
7351

簷 下 under the eaves.
簷 口 or 房 簷儿 the eaves.
簷 牙 the projecting tiles on the eaves.
簷 鐵 馬 bells and metal ornaments hung from the eaves to tinkle in the wind.
[5]簷 雨 drippings from the eaves.
簷 頭 the eaves.
簷 馬 bells hung from the eaves. *See above*—4.
帽 簷 the brim of a hat.
雕 簷 carved eaves.

鹽 塩 [2]
Salt; brine.
7352

鹽 井 salt-wells.
鹽 務 the salt gabelle; the administration of the salt monopoly.
鹽 務 稽 核 所 Head Office of the Salt Gabelle.

鹽 商 salt-merchants.
[5]鹽 地 nitrous soil.
鹽 店 a salt-depôt.
鹽 廠 a salt-yard.
鹽 政 the administration of the salt monopoly.
鹽 法 the regulations governing the salt monopoly.
[10]鹽 泉 a brine-spring.
鹽 海 the Dead Sea.
鹽 灘 salt-pans.
鹽 田 nitrous soil.
鹽 礦 salt-mines.
[15]鹽 稅 the salt-tax.
鹽 素 chlorine.
鹽 菜 salted vegetables.
鹽 課 the salt-tax.
鹽 運 使 司 the Salt Commissioner.
[20]鹽 馬 a salt-stack.
鹽 魚 salted fish.
鹽 鹵 natural salt.
官 鹽 salt which has paid duty.
瀉 鹽 Epsom salts.
[25]熟 鹽 salt obtained by evaporation.
生 鹽 natural salt; natural brine.
白 鹽 table-salt.
石 鹽 rock-salt.
私 鹽 smuggled salt.
[30]食 鹽 table-salt.
黑 鹽 dark, impure salt.

台 [3] A marsh at the foot of the hills.
7353

沿 沿 造 [2]
To follow a course; to go along; to coast. To hand down; to continue; to conserve. Along or by, as a road or a coast.
7354

沿 歷 to carry on.
沿 城 following the line of the city-wall.
沿 岸 along the coast.
沿 才 授 職 use men according to their abilities.
[5]沿 改 conservatism and reform—successive changes.
沿 河 or 沿 江 by the riverside; to follow the course of a stream.
河 沿 the riverside.
沿 波 討 源 follow up the waves and seek the source—of a river —to make a thorough investigation of a thing.

沿 海 by the sea-shore; to coast.
[10]沿 海 一 帶 地 方 the whole coastal region.
沿 用 此 制 going back to old methods.
沿 線 land on each side of a railway.
沿 習 to follow old customs.
沿 着 following a course.
[15]沿 襲 handed down; to carry on without change.
沿 路 the whole way; along the road.
沿 近 adjoining; contiguous.
沿 途 the whole way; along the road.
沿 途 情 形 things that happened by the way—the entries in a log-book.
[20]沿 邊 a border or edge.
沿 門 托 鉢 to go from house to house begging—from the custom of Buddhist priests.
沿 革 conservatism and reform—the successive changes, as of dynasties, etc.
歷 代 沿 革 the successive changes of various dynasties.
沿 革 變 遷 successive changes.
[25]相 沿 handed down.

兗 [3] One of the Nine Divisions of the Empire under *Yü* the Great. *See* 九 No. 1198-15. It was the smallest of these divisions, and included the district of 東 昌 *Tung Ch'ang,* the northern portion of *Tsinan,* and the western portion of *Yenchow* in Shantung, with the district of *Taming* in Chihli. To establish.
7355

匽 [3] To hide; to secrete; to repress. To bend. Inter. next.
7356

匽 廁 a privy.
匽 薄 stunted.
興 文 匽 武 encourage the civil and suppress the military—officials.

[3]
To cease; to desist from.
7357

偃 却 disappointed.
偃 息 武 備 cease from military preparations.
偃 旗 息 鼓 put away the flags and silence the drums—on a secret expedition.
偃 武 修 文 to leave military pursuits and promote culture.
偃 蹇 undecided; frustrated; irresolute; obstinate; arrogant.
中 歲 偃 蹇 stranded in middle life.

(a) To sleep; to lie down; to recline.

偃 仆 to fall down flat.
偃 仰 to lie on the back and look up.
偃 臥 to lie down.

(b) To bend.

偃 伏 to bow before.
偃 月 the crescent moon; crescentic.
草 上 之 風 必 偃 the grass must bend when the wind blows —the inferior man must bow to the influences of the superior man.

(c) u.f. next. An embankment.

偃 豬 (or 瀦) a drainage pool.

(d) u.f. 貜 No. 7362. The tapir.

偃 鼠 飲 河 不 過 滿 腹 the tapir drinks from the river, but only enough to quench its thirst.

堰 3.4. A bank of earth; an embankment; a dike. To dam up.
7358

古 堰 an old dike.
石 堰 a bund.

蝘 3 A gecko, called 蝘 蜓. A chameleon. A crested cicada.
7359

郾 3.4. A district in Honan.
7360

鰋 3 The mud-fish.
7361

貜 3 The mole—this character was originally defined as the Malacca tapir, for which 貘 No. 4384, is now used in modern books.
7362

貜 鼠 the tapir; the mole.
貜 鼠 丘 a mole-cast.

晏 4 A clear sky. Bright. Quiet; peaceful.
7363

晏 安 quiet and peaceful.
晏 晏 peaceful; quiet; harmoniously.
晏 閒 leisure.
晏 駕 the death of an emperor.
天 清 日 晏 a cloudless sky.
河 清 海 晏 clear rivers and quiet seas—times of peace.

(a) Late.

晏 起 to get up late.
晏 食 the time of the evening meal.
何 晏 也 why so late?
早 晏 early and late.

宴 } 4 A feast. A banquet. To feast; to entertain.
讌 }
7364

宴 娛 amusements.
宴 宮 a banquet hall.
宴 會 to invite guests; to meet at a feast.
宴 樂 嘉 賓 to entertain distinguished guests.(-lê⁴-)
⁵宴 歌 feasting and singing.
宴 賀 a congratulatory feast.
宴 集 a convivial gathering.
宴 飲 to entertain at a feast.
宴 饗 a feast given to his ministers by the ruler.
¹⁰設 宴 to give a feast.
請 宴 to invite to a feast or banquet.
赴 宴 to attend a feast.
賜 宴 to grant a banquet—as the emperor did to distinguished persons.
↑宴 樂 (yüeh⁴) festival music.
(a) Rest; quiet; repose.

宴 坐 to sit quietly.
宴 安 rest; repose.
宴 安 酖 毒 living at ease is like drinking poisoned wine.

宴 居 to live at ease.
宴 息 to reside at.

鷃 } 4 A small brown speckled bird like the quail.
鶠 }
7365

噞 1.3. The movement of a fish's mouth at the surface of the water.
7366

驗 } 4 To verify; to fulfil. To examine; to hold an inquest.
驗 }
7367

驗 估 核 稅 to charge duty ad valorem.
驗 傷 to examine injuries.
驗 其 前 便 知 其 後 study the past and you will know the future.
驗 勘 to investigate.
⁵驗 問 to examine into.
驗 單 a permit—issued after examination of goods.
驗 夢 the fulfilment of a dream.
驗 契 稅 tax for the examination of deeds.
驗 屍 to hold an inquest.
¹⁰驗 屍 所 the place of an inquest; a morgue.
驗 左 corroborative evidence.
驗 收 to examine and receive.
驗 放 to allow goods to pass after examination.
驗 效 effect; result.
¹⁵驗 明 to examine clearly; to verify.
驗 明 斤 兩 to verify the weights.
驗 查 to examine into.
驗 河 the river of verification— the Indus.
驗 潮 器 tide-gauge.
²⁰驗 疫 quarantine inspection.
驗 看 to examine; to inspect.
驗 稅 duties; examination dues.
驗 筭 斗 to verify finger-prints.
驗 脈 器 a sphymograph.
²⁵驗 船 to examine a vessel.
驗 覆 a second inquest.
驗 視 to inspect; to examine.
驗 訖 Examined.—a label attached to things that have been inspected.

驗試事由 the details of an investigation.

³⁰驗貨 to examine goods—at the Customs.

驗貨手 (or 員) a Customs examiner.

驗金 assaying.

驗電器 electroscope.

驗風俗之盛衰 shows the rise and decay of customs.

³⁵驗風器 anemometer.

應驗 to fulfil; to come true.

相⁴驗 or 檢驗 to hold an inquest.

經°驗 experience. *See* No. 1123-A.11ff.

試·驗 to test; to try; to experiment. *See* No. 5798-40ff.

巘³ 7368　The top of a mountain.

甗³ 7369　An earthenware vessel in two parts,—the bottom of the upper part is perforated for steaming, the bottom part is used for boiling.
Also read *hsien*³.

甗陳 the appearance of a mountain, as if two pots had been placed one above the other.

讞⁴ 7370　To decide judicially.
Also read *yeh*⁴,⁵.

讞典 statutes relating to a criminal case.

讞局 a secondary court to relieve the pressure on the regular courts.

讞牘 archives of the courts.

讞獄 to sentence to imprisonment.

讞語 to sentence a criminal case.

讞讞 an honest expression.

成讞 a precedent—an already existing sentence.

秋讞 the former autumn assizes.

广³ 7371　A covering; a roof. Radical 53.

彥⁴ 7372　Elegant; handsome; accomplished.

彥士 an accomplished scholar.

俊彥 elegant; refined.

美彥 elegant; handsome.

唁
喭⁴ 7373　To condole with.

唁勞 to condole with.

唁失國者 to mourn with one who has lost his kingdom.

唁弔 to condole with.

(a) Read *ngan*⁴. (2nd form only) Coarse; rude.

由也喭 *Yu* is coarse and rude.

諺⁴ 7374　A proverb; a maxim or common saying.

諺云 or 諺有之曰 as says the proverb....

諺語 or 俗諺 common sayings.

諺文 the Korean script.

顏² 7375　Colour. To dye.

顏料 colours for paints; painting materials.

顏·色 colour. (--*sê* or --*shai*)

顏·色幕 a colour-filter.

帶顏·色的 coloured.

走顏·色 to fade.

(a) The face; the countenance. The space between the eyebrows and the eyes. The complexion.

顏厚 thick-skinned; impudent; brazen-faced.

顏容 the expression of the face.

顏貌 the expression of the face.

顏面 the face; the countenance.

⁵和顏悅色 a pleasant expression on the face.

忿顏 an angry countenance.

朱顏 a rosy face.

無顏相見 I have no face to meet him.

紅顏 a rosy countenance—the bloom of youth.

芝顏 your face.

(b) To write an inscription for a tablet.

嶘³ 7376　The appearance of a mountain, as if two pots were standing one upon the other. The steep bank of a stream. A rough mountain path.
Also read *hsien*³.
See also 甗 No. 7369.

弇³ 7377　To cover over; to hide.

弇日 to obscure the sun.

弇蓋 to put a cover over.

(a) The narrow neck of a vase.

弇中 in a narrow defile.

奄¹ 7378　Ere long. To remain; to tarry. Inter. 淹 No. 7381-A.

奄受北國 forthwith to hold the States of the north.

奄忽 suddenly; rapidly.

奄忽長逝 ere long passed away.

奄有下國 anon he was invested with an inferior State.

⁵奄留 to stay for a long time.

奄觀銍艾 (*i*) anon we shall see the sickles at work.

奄遲 to linger; to delay.

氣息奄奄 gasping for breath.

(a) Read *yen*³. Fully; grandly.

奄有九有 grandly possessed the nine regions—of the kingdom.

奄有四方 grandly held all within the four quarters—of the kingdom.

(b) Read *yen*¹. To castrate.
See 閹 No. 7385.

奄人 a eunuch.

崦¹·³ 7379　A mountain in Kansu, where there is a cave into which the sun is said to sink at night.

掩³ 7380　To cover over; to conceal; to shut.

掩·上了 covered it up.

掩·不住 it will not close.

掩 人 善 to hide the goodness of others.

掩 人 耳 目 to deceive others.

⁵掩 其 不 善 to hide his evil.

掩 卷 to close a book.

掩 口 to cover the mouth with the hand.

掩 埋 to cover up; to bury.

掩 惡 to act hypocritically; to cover up evil. (-o⁴˙⁵)

¹⁰掩 戶 closed the door.

掩 旋 the hidden spirals.

掩 映 to screen from the glare.

掩 淚 to hide one's tears.

掩 目 捕 雀 to close the eyes to catch a bird—self-deception.

¹⁵掩 罩 ˙著 covered over.

掩 耳 不 聞 to close the ears to.

掩 耳 盜 鈴 to cover the ears and steal a bell—to befool oneself.

掩 ˙著 耳 朵 to cover the ears; to close the ears. =7169.3.

掩 蓋 or 掩 藏 to conceal; to cover over.

²⁰掩 藏 to secrete; to hide away.

掩 護 射 擊 a protective barrage.

掩 袂 or 掩 袖 to screen the face with the sleeves.

掩 跡 to hide one's tracks.

掩 遮 to conceal.

²⁵掩 醜 to conceal evil; to cover up shame.

掩 門 to shut a door.

掩 面 to hide the face.

掩 飾 to gloss over.

掩 鼻 to stop the nose.

³⁰半 掩 half-shut.

虛 掩 ajar.

(a) To surprise. To seize.

掩 入 to enter stealthily.

掩 取 to take by surprise.

掩 執 to seize.

掩 捕 to arrest.

掩 殺 to fall upon and slay.

淹
渰
7381

To drown; to overflow. Submerged. Also read *ngan*¹.

淹 博 deep and wide—scholarship.

淹 壞 ruined—as by an inundation.

淹 敗 damaged by water.

淹 ˙死 or 淹 斃 drowned; to drown.

---

⁵淹 沒 or 淹 溺 to drown.

淹 消 dissolved.

淹 滅 to hide under; to cover.

淹 濕 soaked.

淹 該 deep and all-embracing—studies.

¹⁰淹 識 well-informed.

淹 貫 to permeate; to have a thorough understanding of.

淹 跡 to lose trace of.

淹 通 thoroughly familiar with.

淹 雅 deeply cultured and refined.

(a) To delay. To tarry. Inter. 奄 No. 7378.

淹 久 long delayed.

淹 恤 to avoid danger.

淹 懈 dilatory; slothful.

淹 旬 to detain for ten days.

⁵淹 晷 to hinder; to procrastinate.

淹 月 to stay for a month.

淹 淹 一 息 at the last gasp.

淹 滯 hindered; hampered.

淹 留 to tarry long.

¹⁰淹 纏 chronic—as an illness.

淹 塞 to tarry; to delay.

淹 遲 to delay; to tarry; to be behindhand.

罨¹
7382

A fishing net.

腌¹ To salt; to pickle. Also read *yeh*¹˙⁵.
7383 Read *a* or *ang*¹. Dirty.

腌 臢 filthy; dirty.

醃¹
7384

To salt; to pickle.

醃 漬 to cover with salt.

醃 肉 to salt meat; salt meat.

醃 腿 to salt hams; smoked hams.

醃 菜 salted vegetables.

醃 製 to salt; to pickle.

醃 魚 salt fish; to salt fish.

閹¹
劁
7385

To castrate.

閹 人 a eunuch; a doorkeeper in the harem.

閹 割 to castrate.

閹 宦 or 內 閹 eunuchs; door-keepers in the harem.

閹 豬 to castrate a boar.

閹 鷄 or 犗 鷄 a capon.

天 閹 a man who is born a eunuch.

黤³
7386

Blue-black.

黤 慘 an intense black; very dark.

厭⁴ To dislike; to detest; to hate; to reject; to be wearied with; to be repugnant. Satiated; bored.
7387

厭 世 sick of the world.

厭 世 主 義 pessimism; cynicism.

厭 世 家 pessimists; cynics.

厭 世 觀 pessimistic views. *See* 悲 No. 4992-23.

⁵厭 事 disinclined for business.

厭 倦 fatigued; weary.

厭 嫌 bothersome; fussy.

厭 恨 to loathe; to detest.

厭 悶 to trouble; to vex; bored with.

¹⁰厭 惡 (*wu*⁴) to abominate; to detest.

厭 故 喜 新 to dislike the old and take a delight in the new.

厭 棄 to reject; to loathe; to detest.

厭 ˙氣 objectionable; distasteful.

厭 煩 to trouble; to vex.

¹⁵厭 物 a bore.

厭 疲 bored; wearied with; to loathe.

厭 聞 tired of hearing.

厭 膩 satiated; to dislike.

厭 見 to dislike to see.

²⁰厭 足 to have had enough.

不 知 厭 足 not to know when one has had enough; insatiable.

厭 食 dislike for food.

何 厭 之 有 how can he ever be satisfied?

可 厭 hateful; repugnant; disagreeable; disgusting; detestable.

²⁵天 厭 之 May God reject me!

學 而 無 厭 to study without satiety.

憎 厭 to hate; to loathe.

惹 厭 to arouse dislike.

有 厭 to be satisfied.

³⁰討 人 厭 to incur odium; to arouse dislike.

(a) Read *yen¹*. To be satisfied.

從獸無厭 to follow the chase without satiety.

樂酒無厭 delighting in wine without satiety. (*lê⁴-*)

(b) Read *yen¹*. Tranquil; serene.

厭厭夜飲不醉無歸 Happily and long into the night we drink; Till all are drunk, there is no retiring.

厭厭良人 tranquil and serene is the good man.

(c) Read *yen³*. To cover; to conceal.

厭目 to shade the eyes.

見君子而后厭然 but when he sees a man of virtue, he instantly tries to conceal himself.

(d) Read *yen⁴* or *yeh⁴·⁵*.

厭浥行露 wet lay the dew on the path.

(e) Read *yeh⁴·⁵*. To repress.

厭勝 to keep in order; to maintain discipline.

將以厭衆 to quiet the minds of the multitude.

(f) Read *yen⁴*. A sacrifice.

有陰厭有陽厭 there is the offering of satisfaction in the dark chamber, and that made in the brighter place.

懕 7388 Satiated. Contented.

檿 7389 The wild mulberry-tree.

禕 7390 To pray to the gods.

禕禳 to pray for blessings.

饜 7391 To eat to repletion; satiated.

饜口 palatable.
饜腹 agreeable to the taste.

饜酒肉 filled himself with wine and meat.

饜飽 or 饜飫 eaten to the full; satiated.

不奪不饜 they will not be satisfied without snatching all.

無饜 insatiable.

魘 7392 Nightmare. Bad dreams.

魘鬼 the nightmare demon.
夢魘 or 睡魘 a nightmare.

黶 7393 Black spots on the body; scars; moles.

黶口 black-mouthed—of animals.
黶班 dark spots.
黶痕 a dark scar.

燄焰 7394 A flame; glowing; blazing; brilliant.

燄光 the glare of a fire.
燄口 to give food in charity—to sacrifice to the orphan spirits.
　放燄口 to celebrate Mass (Budd.) for the dead; Mass for the souls of those who have not had a proper burial, said on the 7th of the 7th lunar month.
燄燄 blazing.
⁵火燄 the blaze of a fire; flames.
烈燄 a roaring blaze.
遠燄 a wide-spread reputation.
青燄 a blue flame.

閻閭 7395 The gate to a village. A hamlet. Also read *nien²*.

里閻 a village or hamlet.

(a) Used in transliterating.

閻扶 or 閻浮樹 a fabulous tree, said to have triangular leaves. Sanskrit:—*jambu*.

閻浮提 or 南贍部洲 the land where the above tree grows—primarily refers to India, but it is also used for the nations of the east. Sanskrit:—*Jambu-dvîpa*.

閻羅王 or 閻君 or 閻摩羅社 the king of Hell; the Chinese Pluto, the *Yama* of the Hindus.

見閻王 to see *Yen Wang*—to die.

(b) Read *yen⁴*. u.f. 豔 No. 7406. Beautiful, etc.

閻妻 the beautiful wife.

咽嚥 7396 To swallow; to gulp.

咽一大口 to swallow a great mouthful.
咽不下去 unable to swallow.
咽氣 to give up the ghost; to expire.
咽泣 to sob.

(a) Read *yen¹*. The throat.

咽喉 the throat; a channel; a narrow pass.
咽喉之地 important strategical places.
咽頭 the pharynx.
咽頭檢診器 pharyngoscope.
咽頭炎 pharyngitis.

(b) Read *yen¹*. The roll of drums.

鼓咽咽 the drums give forth their sound.

(c) Read *yeh⁴*. To swallow. To block up; to stop. Inter. 噎 No. 3066.

咽塞 difficulty in breathing; choking; gasping.
咽食 unable to swallow food.
咽食病 stricture of the œsophagus.
哽咽 to choke.
幽咽 obstructed.

烟煙 7397 Mist; vapour; smoke, hence:—tobacco; opium, etc.

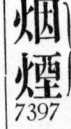

烟包兒 a tobacco-pouch.
烟商 a tobacconist.
烟嘴 a cigarette holder.
烟囱 a chimney.

⁵烟 土 or **洋 烟** or **大 烟** opium.
烟 塵 smoke and dust—the smoke of battle; rebellion.
烟 墩 or **烽 火 墩** a small furnace used to make smoke for signals in case of invasion, etc.
烟 戶 the population.
烟 戶 冊 a register of the population; a census.
¹⁰烟 捲 兒 cigarettes.[smoking pipes.
烟 斗 the bowl of an opium pipe;
烟 景 scenery with light clouds and mists.
烟 槍 an opium pipe.
烟 氣 smoke; mist; the complexion of an opium smoker.
¹⁵烟 氣 上 騰 the smoke went up.
烟 氣 冲 天 smoke rising to the sky.
烟 水 晶 smoky quartz.
烟 波 mists and ripples—mountain and river scenery.
烟 海 a sea of mist.
²⁰烟 火 daily expenses; smoke.
烟·火 fireworks.
　放 烟·火 to let off fireworks.
烟 牀 an opium couch.
烟 煤 bituminous coal.
烟 瘴 地·方 a malarious district.
²⁵烟 癖 甚 深 the opium evil is deep-seated.
烟 癮 the opium habit; a craving for opium.
烟 盤 the pipe-tray used by opium smokers.
烟 禁 opium prohibitions.
烟 突 a chimney.
³⁰烟·筒 a pipe; a chimney; a stove-pipe.
烟 篷 the awning on a steam-launch, beneath which the passengers sit.
烟 絲 cut tobacco prepared for the pipe.
烟 膏 prepared opium paste.
烟·臺 Chefoo—the name Chefoo strictly belongs to another village, but *Yen t'ai* is the Chinese name of the place known as Chefoo by foreigners.
³⁵烟 館 an opium den.
烟 花 prostitution; scenes, circumstances.
烟 苗 poppy-plants for opium.
　鏟除 烟苗 root out the opium poppies.
烟 草 tobacco; the tobacco-plant.

⁴⁰烟 葉 leaf-tobacco; the tobacco plant.　**烟 葉·子** tobacco-leaf.
烟 袋 a tobacco-pipe. A.c. **烟 管儿**.
烟 酒 專 賣 wine and tobacco monopoly. *See* 於 No. 7397a.
烟 酒 稅 tax on wine and tobacco.
烟 銷 火 滅 dissipated in fire and smoke—as when an affair has been settled.
⁴⁵烟 霧 or **濕 烟** fogs and mists.
烟 霞 癖 fondness for mountain and river scenery amounting to a craze—used in derision of an opium smoker.
烟 霧 迷 離 misty; beclouded—used fig.
烟 霧 鎖 重 (*ch'ung²*) **洋** a dense fog enveloped the ocean.
烟 霧 騰 天 the mists reach the skies—used also figuratively of muddling in affairs, etc.
⁵⁰烟 霏 clouds; mists.
烟 頭 a man's daily allowance of opium.
一 溜 烟 a puff of smoke.
人 烟 稠 密 the smoke from human habitations is dense—densely populated.
冒 烟儿 smoking, giving forth smoke.
⁵⁵吃 烟 to smoke, either tobacco or opium. (*Wu-dial.*)
吸 烟 to smoke tobacco.
吸 烟 室 a smoke-room.
呂 宋 烟 Luzon cigars—Manila cigars.
喬 烟 to swallow opium.
⁶⁰小 烟 tobacco as opposed to opium or **大 烟. 抽烟** to smoke.
忌 烟 to give up smoking.
旱 烟 cut tobacco as used in the ordinary pipes. *See below*—64.
暮 烟 smoke from the evening fires—the evening.
水 烟 tobacco cut for the water-pipe.
⁶⁵熟 烟 prepared opium.
聞 烟 to take snuff.
香 烟 or **紙 烟** cigarettes.
鼻 烟 snuff.

於 ¹ Tobacco. Opium. A form of the preceding. **Read** *yü³*.
7397a To fade.

於 酒 公 賣 official sale of wine and tobacco.

於 酒 公 賣 局 licensed depot for the sale of wines and tobacco.
於 酒 稅 wine and tobacco tax.

胭 臙 ¹ Cosmetic; rouge; face-powder.
7398

胭 粉 rouge and powder; cosmetics.
胭·脂 rouge; make-up; cosmetics.
點 胭·脂 to apply rouge, etc.

(a) The throat. Inter. 咽 No. 7396.
咽 喉 the throat; a narrow channel; an important strategic place or pass.

燕 ⁴ The swallow or martin.
7399

燕 剪 a swallow's tail.
燕·子 a swallow.
燕 尾 服 a swallow-tail coat.
燕 巢 於 幕 a swallow's nest in a tent—precarious.
⁵燕 燕 于 飛 the swallows flying around,— a farewell song.
燕 窩 swallow's nests—as used for soup.
　官 燕 or **白 燕** the finest quality of bird's nests.
　常 燕 ordinary quality bird's nests.
　毛 燕 inferior dirty bird's nests.
¹⁰燕 舞 graceful posturing like the flight of a swallow.
燕 語 the twittering of swallows; the chatter of women.
燕 雀 the mountain finch.
燕 麥 wild oats.
土 燕 or **沙 燕** the sand-martin.
¹⁵夜 燕 a name for the bat.
石 燕 the crag-martin.
踢 燕 to kick the shuttlecock.
野 燕 the swift.
金 絲 燕 the esculent swiit—which produces the edible nests.
雨 燕 the swift.

(a) To soothe. To please. To give rest to.
燕 好 (*hao¹*) very fond of.
燕 婉 pleasant and genial.
燕 安 peaceful; at rest.

燕 居 to live at ease.

燕 居 獨 處 to dwell in ease and alone.

燕 昵 harmonious affection.

(b) To give a feast.　To be feasted.

燕 毛 the order of precedence at a feast was determined by the colour of the hair—i.e., by the ages as indicated by the hair.

燕 笑 語 兮 as we feast we laugh and talk.

燕 饗 a banquet.

(c) Read *yen*[1].　Name of certain feudal States.

燕 京 or 燕 都 a name for Peking.

燕 人 a native of Peking.

以 燕 伐 燕 to smite one State of *Yen* by means of another *Yen*; i.e., a State as tyrannical as *Yen* itself, viz., *Ts'i* 齊. *See Mencius* Bk. ii pt. 2. Ch. viii. 2.

眼 [3]
7400　　The eye.

眼 下 beneath the eyes; at the moment.

眼 不 觀 邪 he does not look at obscene things.

眼 中 人 one greatly desired and esteemed.

眼 中 刺 a thorn in the eye—an eyesore, something one detests.

[5]眼 中 無 人 supercilious; despising others. ＝目中無人.

眼 中 釘 a nail in the eye—a person who is a thorn in the flesh.

眼 亮 clear-sighted.

眼 光 eyesight; vision; outlook.

眼 光 散 [3] astigmatism.

[10]眼 光 遠 大 far-sighted.

眼 前 before the eyes; the present moment; now.

只 顧 眼 前 不 思 日 後 only thinks of the present, giving no heed to the future.

眼 前 光 eye-service.

眼 前 歡 the pleasures of the moment.

[15]眼 力 power of vision; perception; shrewdness.

眼 力 不 到 the vision is not equal to that.

眼 力 好 his sight is good.

眼 力 高 he has good judgement.

眼 口 相 引 the eyes leading the mouth—of a vivid narrative.

[20]眼 同 of similar views; to view a thing together.

眼 同 閱 看 to make a joint inspection.

眼 大 心 肥 proud and arrogant.

眼 孔 the vision.

眼 孔 淺 shallow outlook; limited experience.

[25]眼 尖 手 快 or 眼 明 手 快 sharp eyes and quick hands.

眼 巴 巴·的 earnestly; expectantly.

眼 弦 the eyelids.

眼 拙 dull and clumsy.

眼 斜 cross-eyed; squinting.

[30]眼 明 intelligent; bright-eyed.

眼 時 下 beneath the eyes—at the moment; now.

眼 時 間 at the present moment.

眼 暈 dizziness.

眼 毒 keen-sighted.

[35]眼 毛 the eyelashes.

眼 波 bright-eyed—like the ripples on a stream.

眼 淚 tears.

眼 淚 汪 汪 the tears flowed like a flood.

眼 熟 to know by sight.

[40]眼 熱 hot-eyed—envious; covetous.

眼 珠 the pupil of the eye.

有 眼 無 珠 having eyes but seeing not.

眼 球 the eyeball.

眼 界 the field of vision; mental view; outlook.

[45]放·開 眼 界 broaden the vision.

眼 界 大 a wide outlook on things; a liberal view of things.

眼 痛 pain in the eyes.

眼 發 亂 the eyes strained or confused by looking at a number of things.

眼 白(睛) the white of the eyes.

[50]眼 白 瞳 cataract of the eye.

翻 白 眼ㄦ to turn up the whites of the eyes.

眼 皮 the eyelids.

眼 皮 合 閉 to close the eyes.

眼 皮·子 薄 (or 淺) desirous of everything one sees; greedy.

[55]眼 目 the eyes.

眼 目 失 明 the eyes becoming blind.

眼 目 發 直 staring eyes.

眼 看 着 as one is looking; presently; on the point of.

另 眼 看 待 to treat a person differently from the way others treat him—to favour him.

[60]正 眼 看 a straightforward look.

白 眼 看 to look at a person with the whites of the eyes —in disdain. *See* No. 4975-39.

眼 看 手 勿 動 look, but do not touch—the exhibits.

眼 眉 the eyebrows.

眼 眶 the socket of the eye.

[65]眼 眥 the canthus or corner of the eye.

眼 睛 the eyes.

眼 睛 冒 火 eyes flashing fire.

眼 睛 昏 迷 the eyes are dull; the vision is blurred.

眼 睛 迷·糊 blurred vision.

[70]眼 睜 睜·的 before the eyes; plainly visible.

眼 睫 毛 eyelashes.

眼 瞳 the pupil of the eye.

眼 神 the eyes indicate what is in the mind.

眼 福 a delight to the eye.

[75]眼 科 ophthalmology.

眼 空 四 海 supercilious; a profound contempt for everybody and everything.

眼 穿 the eyes boring through— intense desire.

眼 窩 the socket of the eye.

眼 豎 目 橫 to look fierce and determined.

[80]眼 簾 the curtain of the iris.

眼 紅 red-eyed—envious; also red from weeping.

紅·了 眼·睛 became envious of.

眼 線 an informer; a detective; pus in the corner of the eye.

眼 罩 兒 blinkers for a horse.

[85]眼 胞 the eyelids.

眼·色 [4] discrimination; a wink or hint given with the eyes.

眼·色 [4] 好 excellent discrimination; good judgement.

眼 花 eyesight blurred; dim-sighted.

眼 花 撩 亂 the eyes confused by looking at a number of things, etc.

⁹⁰眼 花 耳 熱 eyes blurred and ears hot—the after effects of drunkenness.

眼 衣 eye-shields for dust, etc.

眼 裏 沒 人 supercilious; everybody is beneath his consideration.

不 在 眼·裏 of no account; beneath one's notice.

眼 見 to see with one's eyes; on the point of.

⁹⁵眼 見·得 seen with one's own eyes.

眼 見 目 睹 to see with one's own eyes.

眼 角 the corner of the eye; the canthus.

眼 語 to give hints with the eyes.

眼 跳 twitching of the eye.

¹⁰⁰眼 跳 心 驚 nervous apprehension.

眼 轉 如 電 a glance of his eye is like a flash of lightning.

眼 近·視 short-sighted.

近·視 眼 short-sighted eyes.

眼 錯 不 見 lost sight of; to take one's eyes off an object.

¹⁰⁵眼 鏡 spectacles.

眼 鏡 套 a spectacle-case.

眼 間 beneath the eyes; at the present moment; now.

轉 眼 之 間 in the turning of the eye—immediately.

眼 酸 sore eyes.

¹¹⁰眼 頭 裏 in sight of.

眼 饞 greedy; a greedy look.

眼 高 心 傲 haughty looks and a proud heart.

眼 高 手 低 having a poor conception of the achievements of others and yet unable to equal them oneself.

眼 黑 睛 the iris.

¹¹⁵一 隻 眼 one eye.

勢·力 眼 having an eye on the main chance.

四 眼·的 人 a pregnant woman.

大 眼 large, intelligent-looking eyes.

害 眼 to have sore eyes.

¹²⁰火 眼 bloodshot eyes.

礙 眼 to obstruct the view.

笑 眼 laughing eyes.

虎 眼 tiger-eyed—fierce.

開 眼 to open the eyes; to broaden the vision.

---

¹²⁵青 眼 to look at kindly. *See* No. 1168-29.

鼠 眼 rat-eyed—crafty and cunning like a rat.

(a) A hole; an eyelet. The finger-holes of a flute. A space. N. A. for wells, etc.

眼·子 a person who is easily cheated.

一 眼 井 a well.

雙 眼 井 a well with two openings.

一 眼 鍼 a needle.　[seology.

⁵字 眼 an expression; a word; phra-

心 眼 the holes in the heart; the understanding. *See* No. 2735-126, 127.

打 個 眼 to bore a hole.

窗 戶 眼 a hole in a paper window.

轍 眼 cart-ruts.

¹⁰道 眼 the channels in the road caused by heavy rains.

釘 眼 a hole made by a nail.

鍼 眼 the eye of a needle.

錢 眼 the hole of a *cash*.

硯 ⁴ **The smooth stone on which Chinese ink is rubbed.**
7401

硯 兄 a fellow-student.

硯 水 盒 a fancy vessel to hold water for use on the ink-slab.

硯 池 the depression for water on an ink-slab.

硯 臺 an ink-slab.

同 硯 a fellow-student—lit., using the same ink-slab.

耕 硯 田 to plough the fields of the ink-slab—to get one's living by literature.

衍 ³.⁴. **To overflow; to spread out; to amplify; to gloss.**
7402 **Superfluous. Abundant. Numerous. Extraordinary. Inter. next.**

衍 字 a superfluous letter; a gloss.

衍 文 a gloss; a corruption of the text.

衍 沃 rich, fertile lands—high and low respectively.

衍 溢 overflowing.

⁵衍 盈 abundance.

衍 繹 to deduce; deductive.

衍 義 to elaborate the meaning of.

衍 聖 公 the Holy Duke—a title conferred upon the lineal descendant of Confucius A.D. 1055.

衍 進 evolution; progress.

¹⁰敷·衍 to gloss; to interpolate; verbiage.

繁 衍 numerous; prolific.

演 ³ **Extended; wide; extensive. To practise; to perform; to exercise; to drill. Inter. preceding.**
7403

演 兵 to drill troops.

演 劇 the drama; to act plays.

演 劇 主 任 stage-manager.

演 劇 化 to dramatize.

⁵演 化 論 theories of evolution.

演 員 a speaker, lecturer, etc.

演 唱 musical entertainments.

演 壇 a lecture platform.

演 奏 to perform or practise music.

¹⁰演 戲 to act plays.

演 拳 棒 to practise boxing and fencing.

演 變 progressive changes.

演 文 to repeat the same idea in different language.

演 武 to drill; to practise military exercises.

¹⁵演 武 場 a parade ground.

演 稿 notes of an address or lecture.

演 算 mathematical exercises.

演 繹 deductive; deduction; to deduce.

演 繹 推 理 to deduce.

²⁰演 繹 法 deductive methods.

演 義 to expand the text in a popular version.

演 習 to learn; to practise.

演 藝 館 a place of entertainment.

演 試 to rehearse.

²⁵演 說 to give an address; to lecture; a lecture.

演 說 團 lecture bureau.

演 說 塲 lecture hall.

演 說 家 lecturers; orators.

演 說 會 a public meeting; a debating society.

³⁰演 說 留 聲 話 盤 phonographic record of an address.

演 說 者 speaker or lecturer.

演 說 術 elocution.

演 講 to expound a subject in a lecture; to speak or lecture.

演講法 elocution.
³⁵演進 evolution; progressive change.
演隊 or 操演 to practise military exercises.
天演論 the theory of natural evolution.

雁鴈 ⁴

The wild goose.

7404

雁來 a term for the 9th lunar month.
雁來紅 *Amarantus gangetica*; also *Vinca rosea*.
雁塔題名 to have one's name inscribed on the Pagoda of the Wild Goose—near Sianfu—to have attained the degree of 進士.
雁奴 the sentinel birds which watch when the flocks of wild geese feed at night.
⁵雁帛 a letter. *See below*—15.
雁序 the order of geese in their flight—used figuratively for brothers.
　無雁序之情 without brotherly affection.
雁影分飛 separation—of brothers. *See below*—14.
雁戶 strangers in a district.
¹⁰雁排 in a column, like geese on the wing—used of soldiers.
雁皮 a mountain shrub which bears a close head of small yellow flowers at the end of the stalk; the bark is used for making paper.
雁臣 hostages from the *Hsiung Nu*, because they were allowed to return home during the hot weather.
雁行 to walk like geese—one behind the other.
雁行折翼 a break in the column of geese—separation of brothers.
¹⁵雁足 the foot of the wild goose—a letter,—referring to a letter which *Su Wu* 蘇武, who was a captive among the *Hsiung Nu*, sent from Tartary by a wild goose to whose foot he had tied the letter. (2nd cent. B.C.)

雁陣 wild geese in their column of flight.
雁鵝 or 水雁 a wild goose.
雁齒 order, sequence; from the flight of the wild goose.
天雁 a wild goose.
²⁰孤雁單飛 a solitary flying goose —a widow.
家雁 a domestic goose.
鴻雁 wild geese.

贗贗僞 ⁴

False; counterfeit; spurious.

7405

贗僞 false; spurious.
贗天子³ a pretender to the throne.
贗手 the hand of the forger—as seen in interpolations, glosses, etc.
贗本 a spurious copy; a forgery, as of a book or a picture.
⁵贗製 to counterfeit.
贗鼎 a spurious tripod—the State of *Ts'i*, 齊, defeated that of *Lu*, 魯, and demanded from them the 讒鼎 a famous historical relic; the State of *Lu* sent them a spurious imitation —used in the sense of to forge, to counterfeit, etc.
眞贗莫辨 unable to distinguish true from false.

豔豔艷豔 ⁴

Beautiful; captivating; plump; voluptuous.

7406

豔口爲禍 a ready tongue is an evil.
豔女 a beautiful woman.
豔妻 a beautiful wife.
豔婢 pretty maidservants.
⁵豔射 dazzling beauty.
豔慕 or 艷羨 to admire; to desire.
豔曲 love-songs.
豔歌 love-songs.
豔粧 handsomely dressed.
¹⁰豔色⁴動人 beauty excites men.
豔詩 love-poems.

豔陽 fine, bright weather.
豔魄 the soul of a woman.
豔麗 beautiful; glorious.
¹⁵光豔 gorgeous; brilliant.
嬌豔 fascinating; captivating.
鬭豔 to vie in loveliness.

YIN.　(ㄧㄣ)

(In)

因 ¹ Because; in consequence of. A reason; a cause.
7407 Therefore; then; for this reason:(last group marked "x")

因之 inferring from this; availing myself of this; on this account; in consequence of.
因事故 because of certain affairs.
×因以自勞 I labour because of this.
×因代承之 he therefore took the blame upon himself.
⁵因何 or 何因 why? wherefore?
因何緣由 for what reason?
因何起見 for what cause?
因公 because of public business.
因其 because of....
¹⁰因其所同推以度 (to⁴˙⁵) 物 measures others by what he has in common with them.
因別故 for other reasons.
因原 a cause or reason; origin.
×因問 and then inquired....
因噎廢食 because a man fears choking he refuses food—to lose a great advantage because one fears a little trouble.
¹⁵因子³ factors. *See below*—20.
因小失大 to lose the greater for the less.
因往推來 to judge of the future from the past.
因心則友 because his heart led him to act in a friendly way.
×因思 I infer from the above; to conclude from; as an initial phrase—owing to; in consequence of.
²⁰因數 factors (*math.*)
　二項因數 binomial factors.
　公約因數 common factors.
　消根因數 rationalizing factors.
因明 a system of Hindu logic something like a syllogism.
²⁵因是 because of this.

因 果 cause and effect; conduct in a previous life producing its effect in this. (*Budd.*).

倒⁴果 爲 因 to put cause for effect.

因 果 不 昧 the consequences are manifest.

因 果 之 相 關 the relation between cause and effect.

³⁰因 果 倒⁴置 confusing cause and effect.

因 果 律 the law of cause and effect; causality.

因 果 關·係 the relation between cause and effect.

因 此 on this account; therefore.

因 此 而 識 彼 to know that by means of this.

³⁵因 此 識 彼 to infer one thing from another.

因·爲⁴ because.

因 由 a cause or reason; origin.

因 病 because of sickness.

因 禍 得 福 to get good out of misfortune.

⁴⁰因 緣 the cause which produces effects in a future life. (*Budd.*).

千 里 因 緣 一 線 牽 those destined to be married to each other, though a thousand and *li* apart, are drawn together by a single thread.

除 時 因 緣 unless for some urgent reason.

因 緣 而 起 arising from certain causes.

因·着 because.

⁴⁵因 而 and because of...; on which account...; thus; and hence; and so; thereby.

×因 致 so as to cause.

因 言 以 宣 made known by words.

因 ···· 起 見 on account of....

因 頭 an excuse; a pretext. (*dial.*)

⁵⁰主 因 principal factor; the chief reason.

前 世 因 the life in a previous existence which has led to certain consequences in this.

有 他 因 there are other reasons.

有 因 there is a reason.

未 必 無 因 there surely must be a reason; there must be some grounds for it.

⁵⁵無 因 no excuse or reason; no means.

要 因 essential factors.

近 因 the immediate cause.

遠 因 the remote cause.

(a) To follow. To rely on. To accord with. *See* 般 No. 7423—B.2.

因 之 以 饑 饉 follow this up with a famine of grain and vegetables....

因 不 失 其 親 亦 可 宗 也 if a man relies only upon those with whom it is proper to be intimate, then he can follow them as guides and teachers.

因 人 成 事 to create a job for the benefit of particular persons.

因 以 其 伯 and to preside over them as their chief.

⁵因 仍 to continue as before.

因 仍 苟 且 to continue to be remiss or neglectful.

因 依 to rely on; to trust to.

因 其 事 而 製 禮 he ordained the rites in accordance with the conditions.

因 其 材 而 篤 焉 adapted to their ability.

¹⁰因 其 自 然 let things take their natural course.

因 勢 利 導 to be guided by circumstances.

因 勢 象 形 a lifelike resemblance.

因 地 因 時 according to the time and the place.

因 嬖 人 奏 之 he sent it to the emperor by means of a favourite.

¹⁵因 循·下 來 to agree with; to fall in with; to let matters drift.

因 循 了³事 to be perfunctory.

因 循 怠 緩 heedlessly to follow a routine without regard to exigencies.

因 應⁴ according to the opportunity.

因 才 施 敎 suit the teaching to the ability of the pupil.

²⁰因 時 制 宜 do what is suitable to the occasion; be guided by circumstances.

因 時 損 益 to diminish or increase in accordance with the times.

因 時 百 蠻 to preside over all the wild tribes—of that region.

因 流 溯 源 to trace a stream to its source—*a posteriori*.

×因 無 恆 心 it follows that they will not have a fixed heart.

²⁵因 病 下 藥 suit the medicine to the disease.

因 緣 爲 利 getting advantages through one's marriage connections—such as official positions, etc.

因 襲 to conform to what is handed down.

因 陋 就 簡 to take the easy, slovenly way.

因 風 縱 火 to take advantage of the wind and raise a fire—to use the favourable opportunity to injure another.

³⁰明 置 淸 因 之 it was established by the *Ming* dynasty, and the *Ts'ing* dynasty followed suit.

相 因 in connexion; in sequence.

誰 因 on whom can I rely?

(b) Used in transliterating.

因 制 an inch.

因 陀 羅 Indra.

姻   媟 ¹ Marriage connections; a bride.

7408

姻 兄 (or 弟) a term applied to the male relatives of a married couple.

姻 家 the elders of the families of a husband and wife.

姻 戚 marriage connections.

姻 睦 love.

⁵姻 緣 the fate or influence which brings lovers together.

好 姻 緣 a good match.

姻 親 a wife's relatives.

嘉 姻 a happy marriage.

氤 ¹ The generative forces of heaven and earth, by means of which all things are constantly reproduced.

7409

氤 氳 the generative forces, as above; enshrouding mists.

絪 ¹ A form of the above, No. 7409.

7410

茵 ¹ A cushion.

7411

細草如茵 soft, fine grass like a cushion.

苫茵 a cushion of moss.

(a) A bitter herb.

茵蔯 wormwood.

裀
7412
A mat. Underclothing.

駰
7413
Iron-grey, as a horse.

亜
堙
陻
7414
To restrain. To dam a stream and change its direction. A mound.

堙窒 to dam, as a stream.

湮
7415
To fall into water. To stain; to soak; to spread, as water on paper.

湮沉 to fall—as one's countenance.

湮沒 to be drowned; lost.

湮沒不彰 lost among the crowd; in obscurity.

湮沒無聞 hid in obscurity.

⁵湮淪 perished; lost in water.

湮滅 disappeared; destroyed.

湮濕 saturated; wet.

湮透·了 soaked through.

墨湮 ink stains.

¹⁰墨湮·了 the ink has spread.

禋
7416
A sacrifice. To offer a sacrifice with purity and reverence.

禋于六宗 he sacrificed to the six honoured ones—the seasons, cold and heat, the sun, the moon, the stars, and drought.

來方禋祀 they will come and offer pure sacrifices to the spirits of the four quarters.

克禋克祀 she had presented a pure offering and sacrificed.

蟫
7417
The insect, commonly known as the silver-fish, which destroys books and clothing, etc.

音
7418
A sound; a tone; pronunciation. The initial sound in the Chinese system of pronunciation. A musical note. Radical 180.

音位 phoneme.

音信 news; tidings.

音勢 force—in singing.

音叉 a tuning-fork.

音吐 the sound of speech.

⁵音問 news; tidings.

音塵 news; tidings.

音學 acoustics.＝聲學 phonology.

音容 voice and countenance.

音尾 a drawl in speaking.

¹⁰音度 pitch—as of a voice.

音律 musical pitch according to the standard of the ancient pitch-pipes.｢標 Intern.Phon.Alph.

音標 the pitch of a sound 國際音

音標字 symbols for notes in music.

音樂 (yüeh⁴) music.

¹⁵音樂家 musicians.

音樂專門學校 a school for teaching music only; a conservatoire.

音樂師 a(performing)musician.

音樂會 concerts.

(音)樂隊 a band; an orchestra.

²⁰音母 the letters of an alphabet.

音波 (or 浪) sound-waves.

音程 an interval in music.

音符 notes in music.

音素 sound-elements.

²⁵音義 sounds and explanations—of characters.

音耗 tidings; news.

音聞 report; rumour.

音聲 sound; noise.

音色⁴ timbre.

³⁰音號 a note in music; a phonetic sign.

音訊 news; tidings.

音訓 pronunciation and meaning, as of a character.

音語 language.

音調 a tune.

³⁵音階 a musical scale: ｢phonology.

音韻 a rhyme; pronunciation,

音韻不調² discord.

音響 echo; news.

主音 a keynote.

⁴⁰主音 vowels. Cf. 4582.24

低音 or 次中音 tenor. See below 51, 52, 62. ｢news.

佳音 sweet sounds; your good

八音 the eight sounds used in

music, produced from silk, bamboo, metal, stone, wood, earthenware, leather, and the gourd.

八音班 a band.

⁴⁵口音 pronunciation; accent.

回音 an answer; an echo.｢＝輔音

子音 or 僕音 consonants.

字音 initial sounds of Chinese characters; pronunciation of a word.

土音 local accent.

⁵⁰失音 to be speechless.

最低音 bass. See above—41, below—52, 62.

最高音 soprano. See above—41, 51, below—62.

正音 the correct pronunciation.

氣音字 aspirates.＝送氣字 ｢voiced.

⁵⁵濁音 a note in a low octave: sonant,

牙音 velar ｣sounds. See 7214.35.

發音器 a loud-speaker.

知音 a connoisseur in music; a close friend.

銳音 a sharp note.

⁶⁰領音 the leading tone.

餘音 the dying sounds—as of music.

高音 or 中音 alto. See above 41 51, 52.

↑清音 clear crisp sound · notes in a high octave; surd. voiceless.

喑
7419 7421
To be dumb. The sobbing of infants. Inter. 瘖 No.

喑不能言 dumb, from paralysis.

喑瘂 dumb.

(a) Read yeh⁴.

喑噁 (wu³) 叱咤 bellowing with rage.

愔
7420
Peaceful; solemn. Also read an⁴.

瘖
7421
Dumb. Inter. 喑 No. 7419.

瘖聾 deaf and dumb.

窨
7422
A cellar; a store-room.

窨室 a dark room where silk-worms are kept.

井窨 a dry well for storing vegetables, etc.

殷¹ Abundant; flourishing; great; many. The highest degree of.
7423

殷其盈矣 appearing in crowds.
殷·勤 diligent; attentive.
殷富 wealthy.
殷實 well-off; having property.
⁵殷戶 a wealthy person.
殷拳照拂 cordial hospitality.
殷渥 very kind and gracious.
殷然 heartily.
殷盛 affluent; abundant; prospering.
¹⁰憂心殷殷 my heart is full of sorrow.
繁殷 very numerous.

(a) To determine exactly; to regulate; to be regulated.

九江孔殷 the nine rivers were properly regulated.
以殷中春 you may thus exactly determine mid-spring.

(b) The name of a dynasty.

殷人 the founder of the Yin dynasty.
殷因於夏禮 the Yin dynasty followed the rules of the Hsia.
殷·朝² the Yin dynasty; a name given to the latter part of the Shang dynasty 商·朝², from 1401 to 1137 B.C.
殷當盛世 in the flourishing times of the Yin dynasty.
殷鑒不遠 the warning of Yin is not distant.

(c) Read yen¹. A dark red.

朱殷 a dark red.
血殷 the colour of dried blood.

(d) Read yin³. The roll of thunder.

殷其雷 grandly rolls the thunder.

慇¹ Careful; anxious.
7424

慇心 anxious; to feel for.
慇慇勤勤 very careful of; attentive.
慇勤 attentive; diligent; particular about.

吟² To hum; to intone. To moan. To sigh. To stutter.
7425

吟口 in everybody's mouth—as popular verses, etc.
     口吟 stammering; indistinct utterance.
吟吟 giggling.
吟嘯 moans and sighs.
⁵吟壇 the leader of the 吟社 see —6.
吟社 an association or club formed by a few congenial poets.
吟秋 the autumn songs—of the birds and insects.
吟詠 to recite; to chant.
吟詩 to hum poetry.
¹⁰吟風弄月 to sing in the breezes and enjoy the moon—poetical enthusiasm.
蟬吟 the hum of the cicada.

唫² To hum; to intone, etc. Inter. preceding.
7425a Also read chin³. To close; to shut.

寅² To reverence. Reverently; respectfully. Respect.
7426

寅亮天地 they with reverence diffuse brightly—the powers of —heaven and earth.
寅兄 a colleague in the same department.
寅客 the tiger.
寅賓 to treat a guest with respect.
⁵寅賓出日 respectfully receive as a guest the rising sun.
寅念 to consider with reverence.
寅恭 to show great regard for.
寅承 to receive with respect.
寅獸 the tiger.
¹⁰寅畏 to regard with awe; to dread.
寅誼 respect and friendship between colleagues.
寅餞納日 respectfully to convoy the setting sun.
·同寅 a common reverence for; a colleague in the same department or office.
夙夜惟寅 morning and night you must be respectful.

(a) The third of the Earthly Branches, 地支.

寅刻 (or 時) 3 to 5 a.m.
寅月 the first month of the lunar year.

夤² A distant place. To be leagued with. A girdle. To respect. To advance.
7427

夤夜 late at night.
夤緣 to creep, as a plant; to climb; intrigue; bribery; to rely on others for advancement.
八夤 the regions beyond the 九州, or bounds of ancient China.

繸³ To stitch; to quilt; to baste.
7428

引³ To lead; to guide. To entice. To introduce. To draw out; to stretch. To induce. To conduct. [(-chao²)]
7429

引不著² the fire will not kindle.
引人為²善 to lead men to good ways.
引人笑 to cause laughter.
引伸 to amplify; to infer.
⁵引其君以當道 to lead his prince in the right way.
引力 gravitation; attraction.
     毛管引力 capillary attraction.
引動 to influence; to lead.
引動人心 to allure; to attract; to tempt; to influence.
¹⁰引受 acceptance; to take delivery of.
引受拒絕 non-acceptance.
引咎 to lay the blame on oneself.
引商刻羽 the music began on the note shang and ended with yü.
引壞·了 seduced.
¹⁵引嫌 to lead to ill feeling.
引·子 the starting point; dried yeast; a bait.
引導 to lead; to instruct.
引就 to introduce to.
引布 strips of white cloth or paper attached to the front of a bier.
²⁰引弓 to draw a bow.
引惑 to entice.
引拏 to lead to the arrest of.

引 時間 to extend the time.
引 替 to exchange coin for notes.
25 引 枕 a pillow.
引 柩 to escort a coffin to the grave.
引 水 to lead water—as in irrigation; to pilot.
引 水 人 a pilot. Cf. 4058.19.
引 水 船 a pilot-boat.
30 引 水 費 pilot's fees.
引 決 suicide.
引 河 a canal; an irrigation channel.
引 流 管 drainage tubes.
引 港 •的 a pilot.
35 引 渡 extradition. (Jap.)
引 渡 狀 warrant for extradition.
引 滿 stretched to the full—as a bow; to fill a bumper and drain it dry.
引 火 to kindle a fire; to light.
引 火 奴 tinder. [=燒夷彈燃燒彈.
40 引 火 炸 彈 incendiary bombs.
引 火 門 a touch-hole.
引 火 點 flashing-point; the point at which vapour, etc., from oil will ignite.
引 狼 入 室 to bring a wolf into the house—to bring disaster upon oneself.
引 獲 to lead to the apprehension of.
45 引 用 to bring forward for use.
引 盜 入 室 to lead robbers into the house.
引 線 a needle; a spy; a guide; a go-between; a fuse; to furnish a clue.
引 繼 to continue.
引 至 to introduce to.
50 引 致 to conduce.
引 致 結 果 leading to definite results.
引 藥 excipients.
藥 引 •子 ingredients added to a prescription in order to lead the principal drug to the seat of the disease.
引 行 to lead the way.
55 引 見 presentation, as at court.
引 誘 to lead astray; to seduce; to tempt.
引 誘 爲 非 to seduce to evil.
引 起 注 意 to attract attention.
引 起 順 應 to lead to adjustments.
60 引 路 to show the way; to guide; a finger-post.

引 路 龍 a blind man's staff.
引 近 to bring near.
引 逗 to entice; to encourage to come.
引 進 to bring into notice; to bring forward.
65 引 道 to show the way.
引 酵 dried yeast.
引 重 to move heavy goods; mutual admiration.
引 錯 to mislead.
引 長² to lengthen; to stretch.
70 引 長² 性 elasticity.
引 電 to conduct electricity.
引 領 to stretch out the neck; to look forward to.
　領 引 to bring forward; to lead in.
引 領 望 見 to stretch out the neck and look.
75 引 頸 to crane the neck.
引 頭² a leader; one who heads a subscription.
引 鬼 入 室 to lead demons into a house; to court trouble.
引 魂 旛 streamers borne by a priest to lead the soul of the deceased.
勾 引 to induce; to entice.
80 吸 引 to attract; attraction.
指 引 to point out; to elucidate.
牽 引 to involve; to drag in.
薦 引 to recommend; to introduce —a person.

(a) To decline. To retire. To withdraw.

引 年 to retire on account of age.
引 疾 to retire on account of illness.
引 退 to retire from public life; to withdraw, as troops.
引 避 to avoid; to yield one's place to another.
引 還 to withdraw, as troops.

(b) To quote. An introduction to a book.

引 例 to give an example; to quote a precedent.
引 典 故 to make an historical allusion.
引 •子 the gist or purport.
引 書 to quote books.
5 引 書 爲 證 to make a quotation as proof.
引 用 to quote.

引 經 據 典 to quote from the classics.
引 而 不 發 to quote without enlarging.
引 證 to bring in as evidence; to quote as proof.
10 小 引 an introduction.

(c) A measure of 100 feet, Chinese. A weight of two *catties*. A load of 8 bags of salt, weighing 6¾ *piculs* net.

引 商 salt merchants.
引 地 districts where the certificate for the sale of certain salt held good.
引 票 certificate for the transport of salt.
引 稅 the salt-tax.
引 餉 the salt-tax.
引 鹽 a certificate for a certain quantity of salt.

(d) Used in transliterating.

引 擎 engine.
↑引 得 index.
(e) Read *yin*'. A drag-rope for a hearse.

執 引 or 發 引 to escort a coffin to the grave.

蚓 蟢 }³　　The earthworm.
7430

蚓 而 後 可 者 也 if one becomes an earthworm then he can do this.

垠² 　A bank; a boundary.
7431

垠 岸 a shore; a beach.

銀² Silver. Riches; money; wealth; treasure.
7432

銀 元 silver dollars.
銀 元 局 a mint for coining silver.
銀 兔 the silver hare—a name for the moon.
銀 兩 silver; money.
5 銀 刀 a silver knife—a name for a fish.

銀包 a packet of silver.
銀·匠 a silversmith.
銀單 or 匯 銀單 a money-order; a draft; a cheque.
銀·器 silverware.
[10]銀圓 dollars; silver coins.
銀團 the Consortium.
銀·子 silver; money.
銀定·子 small ingots of silver.
銀師 a shroff.
[15]銀幣局 a mint for coining silver.
銀庫 a treasury.
銀數 a sum of money.
銀星 a silver star; a star god.
銀 本位 a silver standard.
[20]銀杏 the ginko or 白果.
銀根 currency; the money market.
銀樸 silver ore.
銀樓 a shop for the sale of silverware, ornaments, etc.
銀樹開花 a silver tree bursts into blossom—impossible.
[25]銀櫃·子 a chest for silver.
銀款 a sum of money.
銀水 discount; difference in value between various qualities of silver.
銀河 the Milky Way.
銀洋 taels and dollars.
[30]銀海 the silver sea—a dazzling expanse; the eye.
銀漢 the Milky Way. [or -shai³]
銀灰色 a silver-grey colour.(-sê⁴)
銀爐 a silversmith's furnace.
銀牀 a bed ornamented with silver.
[35]銀牌 a silver medal.
銀盤 the market value of silver; exchange.
銀硃 vermilion.
銀礦 a silver mine.
銀票 a draft or cheque; a money-order.
[40]銀穴 a silver mine.
銀竹 silver bamboos—poetical for rain.
銀箔 silver-leaf.
銀箱 a safe.
銀粟 silver grain—snow; the light of fireflies; the flower of the tea-plant.
[45]銀糧 the land-tax.
銀紅色⁴ rose colour.
銀線 (or 絲) silver wire; silver thread.
銀色⁴ the *touch* or quality of silver.
銀花 silver flowers—lamps hung in trees; snow; honeysuckle.

[50]銀號 a bank.
銀行 (hang²) a bank.
銀行休假⁴日 bank-holidays.
銀行來往帳 bank-account.
銀行公會 Bankers' Association.
[55]銀行分行長³ a bank-agent.
銀行利率 (lü⁴·⁵·) bank-rate.
銀行團 the Consortium.
銀行存摺 a bank-book.
銀行存款 bank-account.
[60]銀行學 banking, as a course of study.
銀行家 bankers.
銀行擠兌 a run on the bank.
銀行業 banking business.
銀行監督 director of a bank.
[65]銀行紙幣 bank-notes.
銀貨幣 silver currency.
銀釭 a lamp.
銀鈎 a silver hook—the new moon.
銀錢 money.
[70]銀錢不走空路 wealth does not walk the road in vain—it usually gets what it wants.
銀錁 small ingots of silver.
銀鑛 silver ore.
銀鞘 hollowed logs for transporting bullion.
銀項 an amount.
[75]銀魚 a silver-fish; the silver-fish decoration : granted under the *T'ang* dynasty.
銀鴨 an incense burner.
銀黃 silver and gold.
銀鼠 the ermine; the white squirrel.
水銀 mercury.
[80]鍍 銀·的 silver-plated.

婬² Lewd; obscene. To debauch. Inter. next.
7433

淫² Lewd; immoral; obscene; bad; licentious. To be dissolute. To debauch.
7434

淫亂 licentious; profligate; lewd.
淫人妻女 to violate men's wives and daughters.
淫佚 lewd and indolent.
淫博 debauchery.
[5]淫哇 obscene songs.
淫夫 the father of an illegitimate child.
淫奔 to elope; to become man and wife clandestinely.

淫女 a dissolute woman.
淫姊 a dissolute woman; an adulteress.
[10]淫媒 a procuress.
淫徑 depraved courses.
淫心 lewdness; lustful desire.
淫念 impure thoughts.
淫惠 illicit affection.
[15]淫情 lustful affection.
淫意 lewd thoughts; lascivious intentions.
淫慾 lustful desires.
淫慾過度 lustful excesses.
淫戲 immoral, obscene plays.
[20]淫放 to give rein to the passions.
淫書小說 obscene publications.
淫朋 a lawless confederacy.
淫業 prostitution.
淫樂 lustful pleasures. (-lê⁴)
[25]淫污 impure; unclean.
淫·浪 lewdness; profligacy, especially in a woman.
淫濫 exceedingly obscene and indecent.
淫猥 indelicate; indecent.
淫畫 obscene pictures.
[30]淫瘡 venereal sores.
淫目 lascivious looks.
淫穢 filthy; indecent; obscene.
淫網 entangled by lusts.
淫縱女子³ a licentious woman.
[35]淫色⁴ lust; debauchery.
淫蕩 licentious; profligate; debauched.
淫行 immoral conduct. (-hsing⁴)
淫詞 lewd expressions.
淫談 obscene conversation.
[40]淫謔 obscene jesting.
淫豔 wanton; lewd; lascivious.
淫辭 licentious expressions; extravagant speech.
淫辱 to debauch.
淫近殺 lust is akin to murder.
[45]淫逸 luxurious ease.
淫邪 lascivious and depraved.
淫風 wanton customs; lascivious habits; dissipation.
淫鬼 the demon of lust.
好 (hao⁴) 淫 given to lust.
[50]姦淫 adultery.
富貴不能淫 cannot be debauched by riches and honours.
毋淫視 do not look at obscene things.
烝淫 incest.
私淫 secret fornication.
[55]縱⁴淫 to give oneself over to sensual debauchery.

萬 惡 淫 爲 首 of all vices, lewd-ness is chief.

(a) To go to excess. To overflow. Excessive. Great. Very. For a long time. ×Also in preceding sense.

淫 刑 excessive punishments.

淫 巧 exceedingly skilful; specious; tricky; assumed.

淫 威 great dignity.

×淫 水 floods.

×淫 液 a long drawn-out sound in music, like a sigh.

淫 溢 flooded; exaggerated; excessive.

淫 潦 disastrous floods.

淫 祀 無 福 to offer sacrifices where one has no right to offer them brings no blessing.

×淫 詩 pornographic verse.

10淫 酒 excesses in drinking.

淫 隈 a deep place in a cove or bay.

淫 雨 excessive rains.

滛 淫 to linger for some time.

霪 2
7435
Heavy rain.

霪 雨 連 線 heavy rains falling in continuous streams like cords.

狺 2
7436
The snarling of dogs.

誾 2
7437
To speak gently. Agree-able. Respectful.

誾 誾 如 也 so gentle and courte-ous.

崟 2
7438
High ridges of cliffs.

尹 3
7439
To govern; to rule; to direct; to oversee. A direc-tor or overseer. Earnest, sincere.

尹 爾 多 方 to rule over your many regions.

尹 茲 東 夏 to rule over the eastern portion of this our great land.

令 尹 former title of a district magistrate or hsien.

府 尹 former title of the governor of Shuntienfu or Moukden.

道 尹 a Taoyin or intendant of a circuit.

尢 2
7440
To move on. Read yu². Doubtful.

夂 3
7441
To move on. Radical 54.

鄞 2
7442
The district in which the town of Ningpo is situated.

嚚 2
7443
Insincere; stupid.

陰陰陰氤 1
7444
Shady; secret; dark. Mys-terious. Cold. The nega-tive or female principle in nature; it is the opposite of yang 陽 No. 7265—A. The south of a river. The north of a hill.

陰 下 in the shade; shady.

陰 世 Hades; the dark region; the place of the departed.

陰 中 the autumn.

陰 事 secret matters; matters re-lating to the imperial harem.

5陰 井 a well within the courtyard; a well in a shady place.

陰 伺 to observe secretly.

陰 兔 a name for the moon.

陰 內 to hide; to conceal.

陰 刑 castration, as a punishment.

10陰 功 secret merit.

陰 助 secret assistance.

陰 囊 the scrotum.

陰 地 places that are not reached by the sun's rays.

陰 報 a secret recompense.

15陰 天 dull, cloudy weather.

陰 天 樂 happy on dull days—term for an albino.(-lê⁴)

陰 宅 the tomb.

陰 官 the officials in Hades; the officials in the female apart-ments.

陰 室 private apartments.

20陰 寒 internal chills; dull and cold, of the weather.

陰 府 Hades; the place of the departed.

陰 影 shade.

陰 德 unostentatious virtue; kind acts done in secret.

陰 惡 secret evil. (-o⁴)

25陰 慶 to remember the birthdays of deceased parents.

陰 戶 the female organ.

陰 房 a dark room.

陰 拆 to reprimand in secret.

陰 敎 instruction suitable for women.

30陰 文 incised inscriptions.

陰 暗 or 陰 晦 shady; dark; gloomy; dismal.

陰 曹 the judge in Hades.

陰 果 secret retribution.

陰 極 the negative pole; cathode.

35陰 極 線 cathode rays.

陰 曆 the lunar calendar.

陰 毒 to injure a person secretly.

陰 氣 the female or negative ele-ment in nature, which in inter-action with the male or positive element, produces all things. See 二 No. 1751-7.

陰 沉 木 hard wood which has been long buried.

40陰 涼 cool; shady.

陰 溝 a covered drain.

陰 火 phosphorescence on the sea.

陰 物 the generative organs—male or female.

陰 痿 impotence.

45陰 禮 female propriety.

陰 符 a secret charm against evils.

陰 約 a secret agreement.

陰 翳 covered; shaded; dark.

陰 莖 the male organ.

50陰 螺 絲 a female thread.

陰 蟲 a term for shrimps; also, crickets.

陰 行 其 詐 to act the hypocrite; to play false.

陰 計 secret schemes.

陰 謀 家 conspirators.

55陰 謀 詭 計 dark and crafty schemes.

陰 識 (chih⁴) an inscription in in-taglio.

陰 譴 punishment in Hades.

陰 賊 良 善 to work secret injury to good men.

陰 部 the private parts.

60陰 錯 陽 差 the yin and the yang are both wrong—an unlucky day.(-ch'a¹)

陰 門 the female organ.

陰·間 Hades; the place of the departed.
陰 陰·的 very dark and gloomy.
陰 陽 the dual principle of Chinese philosophy.
65 陰 陽 家 magicians; geomancers.
陰 陽 術 數 4 magical arts.
陰 陽 風·水 geomancy.
陰 險 secret dangers; designing.
陰 雨 fertilizing rains; rainy weather.
70 陰 雲 dark clouds.
陰 電 negative electricity.
陰 霖 long-continued rains.
陰 靈 a disembodied spirit; spirits of the departed.
陰 騭 secret acts; unostentatious benevolence; the blessings that follow such deeds.
75 光·陰 light and shade—time.
向 陰 facing the north.
太 陰 the moon.
會 陰 the perineum.

(a) Read yin⁴. To overshadow. To do good to.

(b) Read yung³. An ice-house.

(c) Read an¹. A hut for meditation near the tombs of the emperors.

癮 4　A disease of the heart. Inter. 癮 No. 7450.
7445

蔭
蔭 4　Shady; shade. To shelter; to protect.
7446

蔭 室 a sheltered house.
蔭 庇 to protect; protection.
蔭 涼 shady; shade.
蔭·生 a holder of hereditary rank conferred for suffering in the public service. (old.)
蔭·生 員 外 a second-class Secretary to a Board, an appointment formerly granted as a recognition of the services of a deceased relative. (old.)
蔭 翳 to cover; to hide; secluded.
蔭 蔚 umbrageous.
蔭 鬱 the dense foliage of trees.

嚚 3　Careful; compassionate. To take an interest in.
7447

隱 3　Hidden; mysterious; secret. To conceal. Small; minute.
7448

隱 伏 to lie concealed.
隱 僻 之 理 obscure and erroneous principles.
隱 刺 insinuations.
隱 力 latent energy.
5 隱 匿 to secrete; to hide.
隱 去 concealed.
隱 名 to conceal one's name.
隱 名·的 anonymous.
隱 地 secluded places; lands which have not been registered in the official books.
10 隱 墨 水 invisible ink.
隱 士 a retired scholar.
隱 姓 埋 名 to conceal one's real name.
隱 害 to work secret injury to another.
隱 密 secret; hidden.
15 隱 居 to dwell in seclusion.
隱 微 obscure; abstruse; infinitesimal.
隱 忍 to bear suffering in patience.
隱 忍·的 態·度 an attitude of patient suffering.
隱 惜 to keep to oneself.
20 隱 情 secret feelings; hidden matters.
隱 意 a hidden intention.
隱 惡 而 揚 善 to conceal the evil and make known the good.
隱 慝 hidden evil.
隱 憂 secret sorrow.
25 隱 掩 to secrete; to cover up; to hide away.
隱 晦 secret; dark.
隱 求 滿 足 seeking secret satisfaction.
隱 沒 unknown to fame.
隱 淪 living in seclusion and lost to public notice.
30 隱 淪 之 術 the black art.
隱 漏 to conceal things in order to evade payment of duty
隱 疾 some defect which is hidden beneath the garments.
隱 瞞 to deceive; to cover up; to conceal from.
隱 示 a hint.
35 隱 祕 secret.
隱 禍 unexpected calamity.
隱 秘 secret; hidden.
隱 約 obscure; indistinct; ambig-

uous; abstruse.
隱 約 其 詞 to speak ambiguously.
40 隱 者 a recluse.
隱 而 不 露 的 態 度 an inscrutable manner.
隱 而 未 顯 concealed.
隱 花 植 物 cryptogamia—ferns, mosses, etc.
隱 蔽 concealment; to conceal; to cover.
45 隱 藏 to secrete; to hide.
隱 處 a hiding-place.
隱 言 意 義 implied meanings.
隱 語 an elliptical sentence; a riddle.
隱 諱 to avoid the mention of names, etc., which are taboo.
50 隱 身 to render oneself invisible. (Taoist).
隱 退 degeneration; recession.
隱 逸 or 隱 遁 or 隱 避 to hide; to abscond.
隱 逸 之 士 retired scholars.
隱 鼠 a name for the mole.

(a) Painful; sore. Grieved.

隱 其 無 罪 而 就 死 地 felt pained by its being led without guilt to the place of death.
隱 心 a melancholy heart.
隱 民 suffering people.
惻 隱 之 心 a feeling of distress; a feeling of commiseration.

(b) Read yin⁴. To lean on.

隱 几 而 臥 he reclined on the bench and slept.

檃 3　A bevel. To bend wood by heat.
7449

檃 栝 a bevel used by carpenters in making the framework of walls, etc.

癮 3　A rash.
7450

癮 疹 an eruption on the body.

(a) A craving, as for opium or drink.

上·了 癮 to become addicted (to smoking, drinking, etc.)

戒癮 to break off the habit.

發癮 to have the craving come upon one.

過癮 to satisfy the craving for the time being.

印 4 To print; to stamp. An official seal; a stamp; a mark.

7451

Distinguish 卯 No. 4369.

↓印兒 a mark; an imprint.

印信 a seal; credentials.

印刷 to print.

印刷品 printed matter.

印刷所 printing-works.

⁵印刷機 printing-machine.

印刷油墨 printing-ink.

印刷物 printed matter.

印刷用紙 printing-paper.

印刷發行 to print and publish.

¹⁰印刷術 the art of printing.

印刷費 printing expenses.

印刷電報機 telegraph printing-machine.

印券 stamped official documents.

印印 to stamp with a seal; to seal.

¹⁵印可 to sanction.

印名 to print a name.

印堂 the space between the eyebrows.

印契 a stamped deed.

印子 a seal-mark; a small loan for a short period at exorbitant interest.

²⁰印字 to print.

印字格 a copy-slip.

印官 an official holding a seal.

印把子 the handle of a seal.

印收 to stamp a receipt.

²⁵印書 to print books.

印書館 a printing and publishing house.

印本 printed books, as contrasted with written copies.

印材 the material on which a seal is engraved.

印板 block for printing purposes.

³⁰印檢 the place where a letter is sealed.

印泥 the ink which is used for stamping with seals, it is usually red.

印照 a stamped pass or certificate.

印璽 general term for seals.

印發 to seal and issue—a document.

³⁵印盒 a small box for holding a seal.

印章 a seal; a badge; a token; an emblem; a sign; a stamp.

印箱 a box in which a seal is kept.

印結 a stamped certificate.

印綬 the ribbon for an official seal.

⁴⁰印色 the ink used for seals, generally red. (→shai)

印色盒 a small vessel for holding the ink for the seals.

印花 the impression of a seal or stamp.

    貼用印花 to affix revenue stamps.

印花布 printed cottons.

⁴⁵印花票 revenue-stamps.

印花稅 the stamp-tax.

印花縐布 printed crêpes.

印花羽緞 printed sateens.

印記 a stamp; a sign or mark.

⁵⁰印證 a sign; a mark in evidence.

印象 an impression; a mental impression; a mental image.

印象主義 impressionism.

印象派 the impressionist school.

印跡 the impression of a seal.

⁵⁵印送 to print and distribute books —for merit.

印鑄局 Bureau of Printing and Engraving.

印開 to spread, as ink on paper.

印顆 a seal.

加印 to seal.

⁶⁰卸印 to hand over the seals of office.

封印 to close the seals—to suspend business in the *yamen* over the new-year holidays.

打印 to stamp or seal.

指印 finger-prints.

接印 to take over the seals of office.

⁶⁵曬印 to print by exposure to the sun—as photographs.

火印 a brand—for animals.

烙印 to brand.

石印 lithography.

脚印 footprints. (*chiao³-yêr⁴*)

⁷⁰蓋印 to seal; to stamp.

開印 to resume public business after the new-year holidays.

(a) Used in transliterating.

印度 India.

印度洋 The Indian Ocean.

胤 4 The succession in a family; posterity; heirs. To inherit; to follow after.

7452

Inter. 允 No. 7759.

天胤 a divinely-appointed heir.

承胤 to continue the succession.

祚胤 posterity.

齗 2 The gums.

7453

齗齗 quarrelling and wrangling.

飲 3 To drink; to swallow.

7454

飲不自節 intemperate drinking.

飲到半酣 to drink till half drunk.

飲和 to treat a man with kindness.

飲品 beverages.

⁵飲啄 to drink and to peck—to feed.

飲器 a wine-vessel; a slop-bucket for dregs of wine.

飲宴 to feast.

飲徒 a toper.

飲恨 to dislike; to hate.

¹⁰飲料 beverages.

飲料水 drinking-water, such as has been boiled or filtered.

飲新娘酒 to attend the wedding feast.

飲杯 to drink a glass.

飲水思源 when drinking the water, give a thought to the fountain.

¹⁵飲泣 to swallow one's tears—dry sobbing.

飲湯 to take soup.

飲灰洗胃 to drink lime and cleanse the stomach—indicating an intense desire to reform.

飲片 medicines prepared in slices.

飲福 to drink the wine after the sacrifice—to give a toast.

²⁰飲羽 to be struck by an arrow so that the shaft and feathers are buried in the flesh.

飲至 to drink in the ancestral hall on return from a victorious campaign.

飲興 (*hsing⁴*) the exhilaration of wine.

飲茶 to drink tea.

飲酒 to drink wine or spirits.

YIN (In) (ㄧㄣ)

25 飲醉 to drink oneself drunk.
飲量⁴ capacity for liquor.
飲○食 food and drink—food.
飲○食有度 temperance in eating and drinking.
飲○食無味 distaste for food.
30 飲饌 to feast.
一飲而盡 emptied it at one draught.
暢飲 to carouse.
濫飲 deep drinking.
狂飲 intemperate drinking; wild carousals.
35 痛飲 to drink deeply.
節飲 to be temperate in drinking.
縱⁴飲 intemperance in drinking.
請飲 to invite to a banquet.

(a) Read *yin*⁴. **To give to drink. To water, as animals.**

飲人 to give—wine—to men.
飲馬投錢 he watered his horse and threw some cash into the river—to pay for it.

(b) Read *yin*³. u.f. 隱 **To conceal.**

飲章 anonymous writings.

懃⁴ **To inquire. To ask respectfully. Moreover.**
7455

不懃遺一老 moreover (Compassionate Heaven) has not left me the aged man, (Confucius) —to support me, said by Duke *Ai* 哀 on the death of Confucius.

(a) **To force oneself to do a thing.**

不懃遺一老 could not bring himself to give up a single minister—from the *Odes*.

(b) **Deficient; broken.**

兩軍之士皆未懃也 the soldiers of our two armies are not yet satisfied—i.e., there has been no decisive fighting.

(c) **But.**

懃使吾君聞勝之死也 but let my master hear of the death of *Shêng*—and it will be a satisfaction to him.

YING. (ㄧㄥ)
(Ing)

賏¹ Pearls or shells strung together.
7456

嬰 攖¹ A baby, especially a girl; an infant.
7457

嬰兒² 生死率 (*lü*⁴·⁵.) infant mortality.
嬰孩 or 嬰兒² babies; infants.
嬰病 children's diseases.
育嬰堂 a foundling institution.

(a) **To run against. To surround. To enclose; to entangle. Hampered and restrained.** *See* 攖 **No. 7459.**

嬰城 to close a city for defence.
嬰疾 to be hampered by illness.
嬰薄 closely invested.
嬰身 to entangle the body—in the net of worldly affairs.
嬰鱗 to rub the scales—of the dragon—the wrong way—to offend the emperor when remonstrating with him.

(b) **To attend to.**

不以職務自嬰 did not pay proper attention to his official duties.

(c) **To add to.**

嬰變 a term in music for sharps and flats, respectively.

嚶¹ The melody of birds; birds calling.
7458

嚶其鳴矣求其友聲 "While *ying* is its cry, seeking with its voice its companion."
嚶鳴 to seek one's friend—from the above.

攖¹ To run counter to; to oppose. To attack.
7459

攖人心 to run counter to the dispositions of others.

攖其鋒 to run upon the spears.
攖鱗 to rub the scales the wrong way—to ruffle a person. *See* 嬰 No. 7457—A. 5.

櫻¹ The cherry. Also read *eng*¹.
7460

櫻口 cherry lips.
櫻·桃 cherries.
櫻唇 cherry lips.

瓔¹ A gem.
7461

癭³ A goitre; a swelling on the neck; a knob on a tree. Also read *ying*¹.
7462

癭瘤 a tumour on the neck.
癭袋 a goitre.
氣癭 swelling of the neck caused by anger.

纓¹ A throat-band to hold the hat. A tassel; a fringe.
7463

纓帽 an official hat.
纓絡 fringes.
纓鎗 tasselled spears.
馬纓 tassels on a bridle.

鸚¹ A parrot; a macaw; a cockatoo.
7464

鸚·鵡 or 鸚鵡 a parrot.
鸚鵡鼻 a Roman nose.
白鸚鵡 a cockatoo.

熒² Bright.
7465

塋² A grave; a family tomb.
7466

塋地 a cemetery.
塋墳 a grave.
塋穴 or 塋窟 a grave.

營² An encampment; a camp; barracks.
7467

營中 in barracks.
營伍 or 營兵 the army.

營 副 second in command of a *ying* or battalion.
營 務 military matters.
⁵營 哨 a patrol.
營 壘 a defenced camp.
營 房 a cantonment; a garrison; a depôt of troops.
營 寨 barracks; a military post.
營 牀 a camp-bed.
¹⁰營 汛 gendarmerie districts; an outpost; a guard-house.
營 盤 an encampment; a barracks.
營 纛 下 under the flag.
營 衞 a garrison.
營 長³ the commander of a *ying* or battalion; a major
集 中 營 concentration camp.

(a) To regulate. To manage. To found. To plan. To build. To define.

營 亂 to regulate disorder.
營 備 to provide; to furnish.
營 利 profit-making.
營 名 營 利 to struggle for fame and wealth.
⁵營 國 built the city.
營 室 to build a house.
營 建 to build.
營 救 to devise ways and means for assisting.
營 業 business; trade; a calling or occupation.
¹⁰自 營 商 業 to do business on one's own account.
營 業 不 正 carrying on an improper business.
營 業 前 途 the future of trade.
營 業 名 片 business cards.
營 業 報 告 business reports.
¹⁵營 業 年 度 the business year.
營 業 性 質 business instincts.
營 業 所 place of business.
營 業 手 段 business methods.
營 業 時 間 hours of business.
²⁰營 業 科 business department.
營 業 稅 tax on businesses.
營 業 費 business expenses.
營 業 錄 business directory.
營 求 prayers; to make an appeal.
²⁵營 營 going to and fro; restless.
營 生 business; occupation or calling.
營 田 fields given to distressed people for cultivation in the public interests.
營 疾 to care for the sick; to nurse.
營 福 to seek happiness.

³⁰營 私 to get private advantages from public funds; to smuggle; to plan or scheme in one's own interests.
營 聚 to make preparations for a feast.
營 葬 to manage a funeral.
營 謀 to scheme; to plan.
營 造 to construct; to build.
³⁵營 造 司 the former Office of Works.
營 造 尺 the standard foot—as introduced by the Board of Works.
營 造 尺 庫 平 制 the standard weights and measures—as regulated by the Board of Works.
營 造 師 an architect or civil engineer.
營 養 to nourish; nutrition.
⁴⁰營 養 作 用 alimentation.
營 養 官 the alimentary canal.
營 養 物 質 nutriment; aliment.
營 養 統 系 the alimentary system.
經 營 to manage; to carry a thing through to completion.

熒² Lights shining; sparkling; twinkling; shimmering.
7468 Also read *yiin²*, *yung* or *jung²*.

熒 惑 星 the planet Mars.
熒 然 brightly.
熒 熒 鬼 火 the glimmering will-o'-the-wisps.
熒 臺 a volcano.

瑩² The lustre of gems. A bright pebble used to make ear-plugs. Bright; lustrous.
7469 Also read *yung* or *jung²*.

瑩 潤 bright, glossy, lustrous.
瑩 潔 pure—as crystal.

罌¹ An earthenware jar with a small mouth and two or four ears. A pot; a pitcher.
7470

罌 粟 or 罌 子 粟 the o p i u m poppy, so called from the shape of the capsules.
水 罌 a water-jar.

螢² A glow-worm; a firefly; luminous insects of any
7471 kind.
Also read *yung²*, *yiin²*.

螢 光 fluorescence.
螢 光 鏡 a fluoroscope.
螢 囊 or 螢 案 to bag fireflies in order to get light for study, as 車 胤 of the 晉 *Chin* dynasty did.
螢 曜 a feeble light.
⁵螢 火 蟲 a firefly.
螢 燭 to use the light from a firefly as a candle—its light is but feeble, used of limited experience.
螢 餤 fluorescence.
螢 石 fluor-spar.
螢 窗 a firefly-window—to study by the light of the fireflies.
螢 蛆 a glow-worm.

鸎¹ The mango-bird. The Chinese oriole.
7472

鸎 歌 the songs of a courtesan.
鸎 花 fashionable prostitutes.
鸎 燕 orioles a n d swallows—fashionable prostitutes.
黄 鸎 the golden oriole.

迎² To meet; to welcome; to receive.
7473

迎 上 來 went up to him.
迎 候 to await a visitor.
迎 刃 而 解 it splits as it meets the edge of the knife—like splitting bamboo, easily done.
迎 合 上 意 to fall in with the wishes of one's superiors.
⁵迎 報 to announce.
迎 娶 to be betrothed; to meet a bride.
迎 客 to receive visitors.
迎 將 to receive, as a guest; meeting and parting.
迎 尸 to receive the personator of the dead—at sacrifices.
¹⁰迎 年 to welcome the new-year.
迎 引 to receive.
迎 接 to receive; to welcome.
迎 接 上 憲 to receive a superior officer.

迎 擊 to attack an advancing foe
[15] 迎 新 送 舊 welcome the coming, speed the parting—official.
迎 旨 to meet one's wishes.
迎 春 to welcome the spring.
迎 春 花 the yellow jasmine.
迎 晨 the early dawn.
[20] 迎 會 a procession in which idols are carried.
迎 歲 to welcome the new-year.
迎 歸 to welcome a bride to her new home.
迎 敵 to encounter the enemy.
迎 神 賽 會 processions in which the idols are carried.
[25] 迎 祥 May you have good luck!
迎·着 頭 來 to come directly towards, as one person meeting another.
迎 裝 to receive the trousseau.
迎 見 to meet; to receive.
迎 親 to go to meet the bride.
[30] 迎 請 to welcome a guest.
迎 謁 to receive; to welcome.
迎 轎 the bridal-chair in which the bride is carried to her new home.
迎 逤 to meet unexpectedly.
迎 阿 to receive and toady to.(-o¹)
[35] 迎 面 to meet coming towards one.
迎 面₂而 來 coming to meet him.
迎 頭²痛 擊 to strike back at a frontal assault.
迎 風 待 月 dalliance with women.
迎 風 流 淚 facing the wind causes the eyes to water.
[40] 迎 風 而 去 to go on against a head-wind.
迎 養 to care for one's parents.
失 迎 to fail to meet— "I am sorry I was out!"
歡 迎 to welcome with pleasure.

(a) To calculate, as lucky days.
迎 日 推 策 calculated the periods.

(b) Read *ying*¹. To go in person to meet.
親 迎 于 渭 in person he met her on the *Wei*.

盈²
7474
Full; overflowing; surplus. To fill.

盈 爵 a full cup.
盈 尺 over a foot—in length.

盈 把 a handful.
盈 歉 之 殊 the difference between fulness and deficiency.
[5] 盈 溢 excessive.
盈 滿 filled full; self-satisfied; conceited.
盈 盈 immeasurable—of distances; shallow and clear—of water; delicate and gracious—as a woman.
盈 盈 樓 上 女 that attractive woman up at the window.
盈 盈 獨 立 standing alone—peerless.
[10] 盈 科 to complete the various grades.
盈 缺 to increase and to decrease; sufficient and insufficient.
盈 縮 or 盈 絀 waxing and waning; increase and decrease.
盈 虛 waxing and waning; sufficient and insufficient; profit and loss.
盈 虧 waxing and waning; profit and loss.
[15] 月 有 盈 虧 the moon waxes and wanes.
盈 血 congestion.
肝 盈 血 congestion of the liver.
盈 豐 or 豐 盈 abundant; full.
盈 餘 an overplus.
[20] 盈 餘 價 值 surplus value.
器 小 易 盈 a small vessel is easily filled—used figuratively.
輕 盈 dainty and elegant; delicate and graceful.

楹²
7475
A column; a pillar.

蠅²
7476
Flies.

蠅 刷 子 a chowry or fly-brush.
蠅 卵 eggs deposited by a fly; fly-blow.
蠅 套 a fly-trap.
蠅·子 or 蒼 蠅 or 烏 蠅 house-flies.
[5] 蠅 屎 點 fly-specks.
蠅 拍 a fly-swatter 蒼 蠅 拍(*p'ai*¹)·子
蠅 拂 a chowry or fly-brush.
蠅 糞 班 fly-specks.
蠅 虎 a fly-eating spider.
[10] 蠅 蚋 gnats.
蠅 蚋 姑 嘬 之 the flies and gnats were biting the corpse.

蠅 豹 a fly-eating spider.
蠅 頭²小 字 writing done in characters as small as the head of a fly.
蠅 頭²微 利 petty profits.
[15] 捕 蠅 器 a fly-trap.
捕 蠅 草 Venus' fly-trap.
青 蠅 the blue-bottle fly.
馬 蠅 horse-flies.

應¹
7477
Ought; should; must; suitable; right; proper; fitting; necessary.

應 仍 ought still; it is necessary to continue to.
應 作·的 that which should be done.
應 值 liable to be valued at....
應 分 (*fen*⁴) fitting; proper; right.
[5] 應 免 duty-free.
應 即 therefore proceed to...; should at once....
應 即 照 會 it is therefore my duty immediately to send a despatch to....
應 取 that which should be taken; necessary.
應 取·的 態 度 the proper attitude to take.
[10] 應 否 should it be so or not?
應 完 dutiable.
應 宜 should; ought; must; it is proper; fitting.
應 役 the service that should be rendered.
應 征 dutiable.
[15] 應 得 or 應 受 what is due to; due; to deserve.
應 得 其 位 has earned his position.
應 得·的 報·應 a merited recompense; deserts.
應 有 盡 有 we have everything you require—used in advertisements.
應 歸 should be referred to....
[20] 應 毋 庸 議 there should be no necessity for discussion.
應 用 品 necessities. *See below*—Λ. 48ff.
應 用 各 物 the various things required; necessaries.
應 當¹ought; should; must; it is right to.
應 當·應 分⁴·的 it is only right to.
[25] 應 稅 dutiable.
應 納 dutiable.
應 給 liable to be paid; due to.

應 行 ought to do; ought to go.
應 行 免 稅 duty free.
30 應 行 (*hang*²) to attend to one's proper business.
應 該 ought; should; must; it is due; it is proper.
應 還 ought to repay.(-*huan*²)
應 需 necessary.
應 辦 ought to be done.
35 一 應 the lot; all.
一 應 俱 全 everything necessary is supplied complete.
不 應 should not; ought not to.
相¹ 應 it is fitting and proper (used in official letters).
(a) Read *ying*'. To reply; to respond; to echo. To correspond to; to fulfil; to be fulfilled.

應 世 present styles.
應 丸 而 落 one—bird—fell for every bullet.
應 之 速 而 無 疑 者 也 responded without the slightest hesitation.
應 事 to fulfil one's duties.
5 以 應 事 勢 之 要 求 in order to conform to the demands of the new order of things.
應 人 要 求 to comply with men's demands.
應 付 to meet, as a situation; to honour, as a draft; to adopt; to respond.
拿 相 當 的 手 段 應 付 meet it with suitable methods.
無 法 應 付 unable to meet it; without resources.
10 預 備 應 付 prepare to meet....
應 付 事 變 to adapt oneself to circumstances.
應 付 所 及 meet the emergency.
應 付 爲² 難 it is difficult to respond to such a call.
應 允 to assent to; to accord.
15 彼 此 應 允 agreed upon.
應 准 to sanction.
應 准 照 行 to sanction the adoption of.
應 制 to compose verses, etc., at the command of the emperor.
應 務 to meet the emergency.
20 應 務 有 餘 abundant ability for every emergency.
應 募 to recruit.
應 募 者 a recruit.
應 化 說 the theory of adaptation.
應 卯 to answer the roll-call.

25 應 合 to respond.
應 命 to answer to a call; to obey.
應 天 順 人 to obey the will of Heaven and be in harmony with men.
應 如 此 之 愚 a response so foolish as this!
應 對 to reply; to answer; to consent.
30 應 對 如 流 his replies flowed like a stream.
應 局 to do their business.[(*ch'ai*¹)
應 差 to attend; to wait upon.
應 弦 而 倒 a man fell for every release of the bow-string.
應 急 sufficient for an emergency; enough for one's wants.
35 應 急 抒 困 to meet an emergency; to relieve a crisis, as by public loans, etc.
應 手 to hand; ready; suitable.
應 承 to accord with; to accept.
應 接 不 暇 have no time to attend to it.
應 援 to render assistance.
40 應 敵 to meet the foe.
應 變 to adapt oneself to circumstances.
應 時 fashionable; seasonable.
應 時 對 景 fashionable.
應 時 自 鳴 (the clocks) struck at the proper times.
45 應 期 不 爽 they come at the proper times without fail—speaking of the tides.
應 期 有 信 at the proper seasons (the wind wafts) the news, i.e., the scent of the flowers.
應 機 to adapt oneself to circumstances; versatility.
應 用 application—as of a lesson; practice, as opposed to theory.
可 應 用 applicable.
50 實 地 應 用 practical application.
適 應 的 practicable; applicable.
應 用 化 學 applied chemistry.
應 用 心 理 學 applied psychology.
應 用 科 學 the applied sciences.
55 應 用 算 學 applied mathematics.
應 用 計 學 practical economics.
應 答 不 錯 to reply correctly.
答 應 to consent; to reply.
應 節 而 生 produced at their proper seasons.
60 應 義 務 之 命 respond to the call of duty.

應 聲 an echo; to answer; to consent.
應 聲 反 響 echo.
應 聲 責 備 answered in reproof.
應 舉 to compete in the examination for the former degree of *Chü jên*.
65 應 萬 事 to be in correspondence with all things.
應 襲 hereditary.
應 許 to promise.
應 詔 to write verses, etc., at the command of the emperor.
應 試 見 遺 to sit for an examination and fail.
70 應 話 it is as it was said to be.
應 請 to request.
應 諾 to assent to.
應 負 to be responsible for.
應 負 賠 償 之 責 to be held responsible for damages.
75 應 身 to adapt oneself.
應 進 士 舉 to compete for the former degree of 進 士.
應 運 而 生 the man for the hour is born at the right moment.
應 選 to accept a post when selected for it.
應 酬 to entertain; to receive, as guests; social intercourse.
80 應 門 to answer the door; a gatekeeper; the chief gate of the ancient imperial palace.
應 響 echo.
應 如 響 it responds like an echo—of an efficacious medicine.
響 應 to respond to.
應 驗 fulfilled; verified.
85 應 驗 在 耶 穌 的 身 上 fulfilled in the person of Jesus.
應 驗 良 方 a specific; a good prescription.
應 龍 a dragon with wings.
口 不 應 心 to profess one thing and mean another.
呼 應 to respond to a call; to echo.
90 反 應 to respond—as to a stimulus, etc.
支 應 法 laws of supply and demand.
有 求 必 應 ask and you shall receive.
照 應 to look after; to oversee and take care of.
相 應 to act in response to. (Cf. first 38)

(b) Read *ying*⁴. A small drum.
應 鐘 a classical pitch corresponding in function to B.

膺[1] The breast. Ornaments on the breast of a horse. To bear; to sustain. To receive; to undertake. To oppose. Inter. preceding.
7478

膺 受 to undertake; to receive.
膺 塞 to block up.
膺 天 命 to receive the appointment of Heaven.
膺 胸 the breast.
膺 親 to give personal attention to.
撫 膺 to beat the breast.
服 膺 to wear on the bosom.

(a) To strike; to smite.

周 公 方 且 膺 之 Chou Kung would be sure to smite them—the tribes of the west and north.
戎 狄 是 膺 he smote the barbarians of the west and north.

鷹[1] An eagle; a falcon; a kite or hawk.
7479

鷹 把 式 a falconer.
鷹 揚 a hawk on the wing—a rapacious official of the government.
鷹 洋 Mexican dollars.
鷹 爪 the talons of a hawk—rapacious underlings.
[5]鷹 犬 falcons and dogs—hired ruffians.
鷹 眼 猴 手 the eye of an eagle and the hand of a monkey—sharp and clever.
放 鷹 to fly a falcon—to palm off a wife as a sister or other relative and sell her into the home of another family, from which she runs away, taking with her as much as she can lay her hands on—the phrase is also used for other similar swindles.
神 鷹 the golden eagle.
貓 頭[2]鷹 the common owl.
魚 鷹 the fish-hawk.

嬴[2] Full; an overplus. To ... out; to produce.
7480 ... 盈 No. 7474.
... up.

瀛[2] The ocean.
7481

瀛 寰 the world.
瀛 洲 the islands of the fairies; a name for Peking.
瀛 海 the ocean.
瀛 眷 respectful term of inquiry after the wife of a friend—your fairy helpmate.

籯[2] A tube to hold chopsticks.
7482

贏[2] An overplus; gain; profit; abundance.
7483

贏 利 profit; gain.
贏 熟 over-ripe.
贏 餘 abundance; surplus.
贏 餘 積 項 a reserve fund.

(a) To win; to excel.

贏·了 won; gained the day—as in a law-suit, battle, etc.
贏 東·道 to win a bet in which the loser has to stand treat.
贏 錢 to win money by gambling.
輸 贏 losses and gains; losing and winning—gambling.

影[3] A shadow; an image; a shadowy form; a reflection.
7484

影 事 shadowy, unreal affairs.
影 像 a likeness; a resemblance; an image.
影 兒 a shadow; a trace; a clue.
影 印 本 a photolithographic edition.
[5]影 印 片 a photogravure.
影 印 石 版 術 photolithography.
影 印 鋅 版 a photo-zinc block.
影 璧 a wall to screen a door from the street; a partition-wall.
影 射 商 標 to counterfeit trade-marks.
[10]影 射 朦 混 to delude; to make false statements; to humbug.
影 射 綽 綽 vague outlines; shadowy; indistinct.
影 戲 to counterfeit a trade-mark.
影 戲 a shadow-graph, now used for motion-pictures.
原 色 活 動 影 戲 moving pictures in natural colours.

[15] 活 動 影 戲 moving-picture show.
活 動 電 影 moving pictures; cinemas.
影 戲 劇 cinema plays.
影 格 or 影 本 a copy-slip for tracing over.
影 片 a photograph; a cinema film.
[20]影 畫 magic-lantern pictures.
影 門 to screen the light from a door.
影 隨 形 the shadow follows the substance.
影·響 shadow and echo—rumour; traces; after-effects; influence.
出 口 業 大 受 影 響 the export trade was greatly affected.
[25] 地 震 有 影 響 於 天 氣 earthquakes affect the weather.
有 影 響 世 界 之 力 would have an effect on the whole world.
馬 克 斯 主 義 之 影 響 the influence of Marxism.
影 響 之 談 mere rumours.
影 響 到 全 國 人 民 affects the whole nation.
[30]影 響 所 及 the effects produced.
倒 影 an inverted image.
小 影 a portrait.
射 影 to cast a shadow.
投 影 to cast a shadow.
[35]捉 影 to catch at shadows.
攝 影 to take a photograph.
日 影 shadows thrown by the sun.
沒 影 兒 not a trace to be seen.

穎
穎[3] A full head of grain, bent over by its own weight. A sharp point. A writing-brush.
7485

穎 悟 or 穎 慧 or 聰 穎 versatile; quick; clever.
毛 穎 a writing-brush.

郢[3] Name of the ancient capital of the State of Ch'u 楚.
7486

郢 州 an old name for Wuchang, the capital of Hupeh.

硬[4] Hard; stiff; firm; obstinate.
7487

硬 剌 剌·的 tough—like leather.
硬 壯 muscular; vigorous.
硬 如 鐵 as hard as iron.
硬 度 degree of hardness.
⁵硬 強 forcibly.
硬 绷 绷·的 firm; stiff.
硬 心 hard-hearted; callous.
硬 性 a perverse, obstinate disposition.
硬 挺 to hold firmly to.
¹⁰硬 掙 positive; firm.
硬 搶 去 to snatch away.
硬 木 hard wood.
硬 札 severe; fierce; stiff.
硬 橡 皮 ebonite.
¹⁵硬 氣 peremptory; positive.
硬 水 hard water.
硬 漢 a firm, determined person.
硬 煤 hard coal; anthracite.
硬 留 to insist on retaining.
²⁰硬 偭 mulish; wilful; straightforward.
硬 紙 板 cardboard.
硬 綁 綁·的 firm; solid; vigorous.
硬 膏 adhesive plasters.
硬 要 determined to have; to make forcible demands.
²⁵硬 話 determined speech.
硬 貨 hard cash; coin.
硬 軟 hard and soft; powerful and feeble.
硬 逼 to coerce.
硬 郎 vigorous and hearty.
³⁰硬 雨 hail.
硬 頸 stiff-necked.
堅 硬 inflexible; hard.
手 硬 hard-fisted.
牌·子 很 硬 that brand is trustworthy.

映
暎
7488
⁴ The sun beginning to decline. Shining; bright. A glare.

映 奪 to dazzle.
映 山 黃 (or 紅) yellow or red azaleas.
映 帶 左 右 shedding lustre on all sides.
映 徹 九 原 their glory penetrated to the next world.
⁵映 日 bright sunlight.
映 日 果 a name for the fig.
映 水 reflected from the water.
映 照 bright and shining.
映 發 to portray.
¹⁰映 眼 dazzling; glaring.

映 紅 the ruby.
映 耀 glory.
映 雪 the glare of snow.
映 雪 讀 書 to reflect the glare from the snow and study by its light.

英
7489
¹ Brave; heroic. Eminent; talented.

英 主 a chief among heroes.
英 偉 great; powerful.
英 勇 martial; brave.
英 年 the days of youthful vigour.
⁵英 威 dignified; majestic.
英 才 superior talents.
英 明 talented; shrewd; clever.
英 武 a military hero.
英 氣 a noble spirit; bravery.
¹⁰英 物 a person of promise—used in praise of the son of another.
英 生 英 子³ heroes beget heroes.
英 畏 a fortunate person—used in praise of the son of another.
英 皇 the daughters of the emperor *Yao* who were married to *Shun*.
英 豪 a hero.
¹⁵英 銳 talented; clever; shrewd.
英 雄 豪 傑 a hero; a leader.

(a) A flower. Beauty.

英 英 白 雲 the beauty of the fleecy clouds.
英 華 發 外 beauty and adornment are displayed on the exterior.
掇 英 to pluck a flower.
玉 英 the beauty of jade.
落 英 fallen flowers.

(b) Used in names of places and for transliterating.

英 國 England; also loosely u.f. Great ⁵ Britain and the British Empire.
英 哥 倫 比 亞 British Columbia.
英 尺 a foot according to the standard English measure of length.
英 屬 British.
⁵英 屬 印 度 British India.
英 文 the English language (written or spoken)
英 格 蘭 England.
英 民 British subjects.
英 法 England and France; British and French.

¹⁰英 石 a blue limestone from 英 德 縣 near Canton.
英 租 界 the British Concession —popularly but wrongly used for the International Settlement in Shanghai.
英 美 會 the Canadian Methodist Mission.
英 華 English and Chinese.
英 語 界 the English-speaking world.
¹⁵英 里 a mile.

瑛
7490
¹ A crystal. Lustrous, used of gems.

紫 石 瑛 rose-quartz.

霙
7491
¹ Sleet; rain and snow falling together.

媵
7492
⁴ A maid who accompanies a bride to her new home. To escort. A concubine.

媵 姜 a concubine.
媵 婢 a maid who accompanies a bride.

YÜEH. YO. (ㄩㄛ)
(Ioh)

約
7493
1.5. A covenant; an agreement. To agree with. To form alliances. To bind; to restrain. A treaty.

約 之 以 禮 to restrain oneself by the rules of propriety.
約 信 a promise; an engagement.
約 合 to come to terms of peace.
約 同 to act with; to agree to go with.
不 約 而 同 to agree without any previous arrangement.
約 同 出 去 to make an appointment to go out with others.
約 單 an agreement; a compact; a contract.
約 外 not in the treaty or agreement.
約 字 a written agreement.
¹⁰約 定 to agree to.
約 定·他 來 settle the time that he should come.
約 定 期 間 within an appointed time.

約定過訪 to promise to pay a call.

約我同·他去 he arranged that I should go with him.

15 約指 a finger-ring.

約據 an agreement or contract.

約書 a written agreement.

約會 to make an appointment to meet.

約期 to fix upon a date; a date agreed upon.

20 約束 to bind; to discipline; to restrain.

約束扣留 to detain in custody.

約束資本 to regulate capital.

約櫃 the Ark of the Covenant.

約欵 the clauses of a treaty.

25 約正 or 鄉約 a village headman.

約法 provisional constitution.

約盟 a sworn compact.

約章 treaty stipulations.

約與 to agree to act with; to agree to go with.

30 約規 treaty regulations or stipulations..

約請 to invite.

約車治裝 engaged the cart and got his baggage ready.

和約 a treaty of peace.

失約 to break an engagement or appointment.

35 條約 a treaty.

爽約 to break an appointment.

私約 a secret agreement; an intrigue.

立約 to make an agreement; to draw up a treaty, deed or contract.

背約 to violate a treaty, agreement; or contract.

40 訂約 to make a treaty.

赴約 to go to keep an appointment.

退約 to withdraw from a treaty or agreement.

非戰公約 general treaty of the renunciation of war.

(a) To be sparing. Economical; frugal; in straitened circumstances. Concise.

約儉 frugal.

約而備 concise yet complete.

約而為泰 straitened and yet making a show of ease.

約而盡 terse and yet exhaustive.

5 約言 an epitome; an abstract.

君子約言 the superior man is sparing of his words.

約言之 to sum up; in a word; briefly.

約食 scanty diet.

省約 frugal; to save—trouble.

處 (ch'u³) 約 to be in straitened circumstances.

(b) About. Nearly. Approximate. To estimate.

約價 to estimate the price.

約摸 about; nearly; to estimate; to guess; to surmise.

約有正午 about noon.

約數 about so many; a number which will divide equally into another number.

約略 or 大約 for the most part; about; probably.

約約⁴分·量 estimate the weight.

約麽 about. *See above*—B. 2.

(c) Used in transliterating.

約但 Jordan.

約翰 John.

↑約瑟 Joseph.

嗍 1.5.
7494
An exclamation.

岳 4.5.
7495
A mountain peak. Inter. 嶽 No. 7502. A wife's parents.

岳母 or 外母 a wife's mother.
岳父 or 岳丈 a wife's father.

龠 4.5.
7496
A flute. A tube. Ancient measure of 1200 grains of millet. Radical 214.

瀹 4.5.
7497
To boil. To wash; to cleanse; to soak.

禴 4.5.
7498
Spring sacrifice in the ancestral temple of the imperial family during the *Hsia* and *Yin* dynasties.

籥 4.5.
7499
An ancient kind of flute; there were two kinds, one with three holes and one with six; the latter was used by dancers. Inter. next. A key.

啟籥見書 he took a key, opened and looked at the oracular explanations.

鑰 4.5.
7500
A key; a lock. Also read *yao⁴*.

鑰·匙 a key.
鑰匙眼 a keyhole.
鑰孔 a keyhole.
鑰牡 a key.
鑰環 a key-ring.
投鑰 to insert a key in the lock.

藥 4.5.
藥
7501
Drugs; medicines; healing herbs. To administer drugs. Usually pron. *yao⁴*

藥不瞑眩厥疾不瘳 if the medicine does not upset the patient, his disease cannot be cured.

藥中甘草 the liquorice in the medicine—of a man who has no great ability and yet is indispensable.

藥丸 pills.
糖衣藥丸子 sugar-coated pills.

5 藥劑師 a pharmacist; apothecary.
藥力 the power of a drug.
藥品 classes of medicines.
藥單 a prescription.
藥局 a druggist's shop.

10 藥師 a physician.
藥店 a druggist's shop.
藥引·子 a disguise, something given with a dose of medicine to conceal its real character; an ingredient in a prescription that will lead to the seat of the disease.

藥性 the nature of a drug.
藥性有君臣 medicines are divided into principal and subordinate.

15 藥房 a druggist's shop; a dispensary. (*new style*)
藥散 medicinal powders.
藥敬 a doctor's fees.
藥料 drugs.
藥方 a prescription. (or 一·子)

20 開藥方 to write a prescription.

藥書 medical works.
藥末 medicinal powders.
藥·材 medicines; drugs. 藥材舖 an old style drugstore.
藥死 to poison.
25 藥水 liquid medicines; lotions.

藥 水 針 a hypodermic needle.
藥 汁 tinctures.
藥 油 ointments.
藥 渣 the refuse left after preparing a decoction.
³⁰藥 物 drugs.
藥 物 學 materia medica.
藥 王 廟 a temple to the Chinese God of Medicine.
藥 珀 散 a powder sprinkled on ulcers.
藥 珠 seed-pearls—used in making pearl powder for ulcers.
³⁵藥 用 medicinal.
藥 石 medicine and acupuncture. See 砭 No. 5326.
　　多 蒙 藥 石 I have had good advice from you.
藥 石 成 仇 good advice makes enemies.
藥 石 無 靈 all remedies are of no avail.
⁴⁰藥 粉 medicinal powders.
藥 線 a fuse.
藥 緣 the affinity of certain persons with certain drugs.
藥 老 鼠 to poison rats.
藥 舖 a chemist's shop. (old style)
⁴⁵藥 草 medicinal herbs.
　　草 藥 simples; local drugs from herbs.
藥 言 good advice; admonitions.
藥 資 expenses for medicines.
藥 酒 medicated wine or spirits.
⁵⁰藥 餌 medicated cakes.
藥 餅 medicine in tablet form.
藥 鼎 an alchemist's furnace used by Taoists.
一 服 藥 a dose of medicine.
不 可 救 藥 medicines are of no avail—used figuratively.
⁵⁵和 藥 mild drugs.
山·藥 Chinese yams.
悶 藥 anæsthetics.
打 藥 cathartics; to buy medicines.
·抓 藥 to make up prescriptions.
⁶⁰服 藥 to take medicine.
毒 藥 poisons.
沒 藥 myrrh.
洋 藥 opium.
瀉 藥 purgatives.
⁶⁵火 藥 gunpowder.
炸 藥 explosives. (cha⁴-)
煎 藥 to make a decoction.
熟 藥 prepared opium. (shou²-)
猛 藥 drastic medicines.
⁷⁰生 藥 raw opium.
膏·藥 plasters.

良 藥 efficacious remedies.
補 藥 tonics.
製 藥 to compound drugs.
⁷⁵配 藥 to make up a prescription.
釺 藥 a flux for soldering.

嶽 4.5.　A high mountain peak.
7502

五 嶽 the five sacred mountains of China. See No. 7187-31.

鸑 4.5.　A young phœnix. A water-fowl like a duck, with red eyes.
鷟 7503

躍 躍 躍 4.5.　To skip; to frisk; to dance. To kick, as a ball.
7504

躍 然 plainly.
躍 馬 to jump on a horse.
一 躍 千 里 a thousand li in one jump—rapid advance.
一 躍 而 爲 巨 富 者 became very wealthy all at once.
超 躍 to surpass.

(a) Repeated and read ti⁴·⁵. Swiftly; merrily.

YU.
(Iu)

幽 1　Dark; gloomy; secret; retired; lonely; subtle.
7505

幽 人 a recluse.
幽 僻 lonely; secluded; a place for retirement.
幽 冥 Hades.
幽 囚 or 幽 困 to imprison; to confine.
⁵幽 居 to live a retired life.
幽 居 守 節 dwelt in seclusion and maintained her chastity.
幽 微 subtle; fine; abstruse; delicate.
幽 思 deep contemplation.
幽 怪 uncanny things; spooks; demons.
¹⁰幽 情 elegant; tasteful.

幽 憂 melancholy.
幽 繫 to imprison.
幽 明 the dead and the living.
幽 暗 dark; gloomy; obscure.
¹⁵幽 曠 a desolate place.
幽 期 an assignation.
幽 深 remote; dismal; dark; deep.
幽 燕 an ancient name for Peking.
幽 猥 dark dealings.
²⁰幽 谷 a dark gorge; a lonely valley.
幽 邃 remote; afar off.
幽 門 the gate of Hades; the pylorus.
幽 閉 secluded; to confine.
幽 閒 lady-like reserve and maidenly quiet.
²⁵幽 隱 to live in seclusion and retirement.
幽 雅 elegant retirement; retired and tasteful.
幽 靈 the spirits of the departed.
幽 靜 lonely; retired.
幽 鬼 ghosts, etc.
³⁰幽 魂 the soul.
祭 幽 to sacrifice to the spirits in Hades.
↑幽 默 humor; humorous.

麀 1　A female deer.
7506

牖 3　A window; a lattice window. To enlighten; to teach.
7507

牖 下 beneath the windows.
牖 戶 windows and doors.
天 之 牖 民 God enlightens the people.
自 牖 執 其 手 grasped his hand through the window.

憂 1　Grief; melancholy; mournful; sad. In mourning for
7508　parents.

憂 傷 mournful; sad; grieved; distressed.
憂 勞 to be concerned about; anxiety.
憂 危 anxiety and dread.
憂 哀 grieved; sorrowful.
⁵憂 形 於 色 grief manifested on the countenance.
憂 心 grieved; distressed.
憂 忿 indignant; sad and angry.

憂 思 to be anxious about.
憂 急 sad and anxious.
10 憂 急 成 病 ill with anxiety and grief.
憂 恤 to show sympathy.
憂 悲 sadness; grief.
憂 愁 or 憂 患 or 憂 悶 mournful; melancholy; distressed; grieved; sad.
憂 慮 care; anxiety; to be anxious.
15 憂 懼 fears; misgivings.
憂 戚 sorrowful; sympathetic.
憂 民 之 憂 者，民 亦 憂 其 憂 if a ruler grieves over the sorrows of his people, they will also grieve over his sorrows.
憂 苦 bitter grief.
憂 鬱 depressed and melancholy; dismal; hypochondria.
20 不 知 憂 free from anxiety.
勸 憂 to exhort; to console.
居 憂 in mourning for parents.
消 憂 to dissipate sorrow.
解 憂 to console; to relieve the grief of another.

優 ¹ Abundant; plenty; enough. Excellent.
7509

優 假 to treat with liberality.
優 優 有 餘 excessive.
優 先 precedence.
優 先 公 債 票 preference bonds.
5 優 先 權 right of precedence; preferential rights; priority.
優 先 紅 利 preferential dividend.
優 先 股 preference shares.
優 免 privileged exemption.
優 加 extraordinarily (kind, etc.).
10 優 劣 good and bad; fit and unfit quality.
優 劣 宜 分 fitness and unfitness should be distinguished.
優 勝 precedence.
優 勝 劣 敗 survival of the fittest.
優 勝 地 位 a position of advantage.
15 優 勢 superiority.
優 卹 compensation awarded to the relatives of soldiers who have died.
優 厚 liberal.
優 獎 a liberal reward.
優 容 a gentle, kindly, forgiving spirit.
20 優 尚 excellent.
優 待 to treat with unusual politeness.

優 待 券 a complimentary ticket.
優 待 室 a reception room.
優 柔 peaceable; easy-going; forbearing.
25 優 游 to stroll; hesitating.
優 游 涵 泳 to be permeated thoroughly.
優 游 自 在 free and easy.
優 渥 great kindness.
優 爲 more than able to.
30 優 生 學 eugenics.
優 異 exceptional—treatment.
優 禮 相 待 to treat with unusual politeness.
優 等 the best class.
優 等 品 位 highest grade.
35 優 級 highest class or grade.
優 給 a present; something exceptional.
優 缺 a lucrative official post.
優 美 excellent; excellence.
優 美 之 情 love of the beautiful.
40 優 裕 liberal; wealthy.
優 越 superlative; excellent.
優 貢 生 a former Senior Licentiate.
優 長 advantage; excellence.
優 點 points of excellence or advantage.
45 優 點 弱 點 points of advantage and disadvantage, respectively.

(a) An actor.

優 人 or 優 伶 or 俳 優 or 娼 優 actors; players.
優 伶 學 校 school of dramatic art.
優 孟 衣 冠 the garments of the actor *Mêng*, (an ancient performer)—to dress up.

櫌 ¹ A harrow; a rake for drawing earth over newly-sown grain.
7510

櫌 而 不 輟 he kept on breaking the clods without stopping.

尤 ² More; very; still more; furthermore; particularly.
7511 Distinguish 犬 No. 1650, 尢 No. 7033.

尤 佳 better still.
尤 其 要 緊 still more important.
尤 加 vastly more.
尤 可 怪 still more surprising.

⁵尤 深 more profound; much deeper.
尤 爲 不 美 still worse.
尤 爲 非 計 this is quite beyond consideration.
尤 物 a rare and beautiful thing; a beautiful woman.
尤 甚 vastly more.
10 尤 異 singular; unlike.
尤 重 to set a high value on.
尤 非 particularly not.

(a) To blame. To bear a grudge. To murmur. An evil; a fault; a calamity.

尤 人 to hate others; to bear a grudge against others.
尤 而 效 之 imitate them in their wrong doings.
尤 違 murmuring and disobedient.
不 尤 人 do not blame others; do not murmur against men.
則 寡 尤 then you will have few occasions for blame.
莫 知 其 尤 I do not know whose fault it is.

疣 肬 ² A swelling; a tumour.
7512

疣·子 a tumour. *See* 贅 No. 1472 —A. 5.

由 ² Cause; means; instrument; source; motive.
7513 Distinguish 田 No. 6362.

由 來 or 來 由 source; cause; means; derivation.
一 個 由 來 one origin.
人 類 之 由 來 the descent of man.
怎·麼 來 由 what was the source of that....
⁵ 沒·有 來 由 there was no cause for it.
物 種·的 由 來 the origin of species.
由 來 已 久 it has been so for some time.
由 天 不 由 人 it depends on Heaven not on man.
由 於 arising from....
10 由 頭 or 所 由 cause; source; means.

不 知 其 由 I do not know the cause.

事 有 因 由 things have their cause.

事 非 無 由 things cannot be without a cause.

充 分 之 理 由 sufficient cause.

15情 由 the circumstances of a case.

成 事 之 由 the ultimate motive.

案 由 the chief points of a case.

根 由 cause; reason; object; motive.

生 由 the cause or origin of.

20理 由 reason.

等 由 .... and such reasons—at the end of a quotation in despatches.

觀 其 所 由 mark a man's motives.

道 無 由 no means; no way.

(a) From; by; by way of; through; because of; according to.

由 乎 中 而 應 乎 外 it springs from within and is carried into practice without.

由 京 而 來 I came from the capital.

由 何 人 from what person?

由 何 而 起 whence did it arise?

5由 儉 入 奢 易 to go from frugality to extravagance is easy. *See below—9.*

由 南 麓 發 we began our ascent from the southern foot of the mountain.

由 衷 from the heart; sincerely; cordially.

由 天 而 降 came down from heaven.

由 奢 入 儉 難 to go from extravagance to frugality is difficult. *See above—5.*

10由 學 而 至 to reach it by study.

由 徑 to take a short cut.

由 微 之 著 from abstruse to obvious. (*-chu*4)

由 是 hence; therefore.

由 此 from this; hence.

15由 此 而 來 henceforth; arising out of this....

由 此 而 出 exit this way.

由 此 觀 之 it is evident from this that....; looking at the matter from this viewpoint.

由 此 門 進 enter by this door.

由 水 道 而 來 came by water.

20由 淺 入 深 from shallow to profound—of progressive studies.

由 百 世 之 後 after the lapse of a hundred years.

由 私 而 公 from private to public.

由 簡 而 繁 from the simple to the complex.

由 蘗 shoots from a fallen tree.

25由 近 而 遠 from near to distant.

由 門 而 入 enter by the door.

由 陸 路 to go by road.

不 由 人 算 not within the calculations of man.

不 由 其 道 by an improper way.

30不 由 正 道 not following the right way.

何 由 知 吾 可 也 How do you know that I am competent for that?

末 由 而 已 I find no way to do so.

經 由 by way of.

(b) To follow. To permit. To allow.

由 不 得 cannot help it; involuntarily.

由 不 得 人 it does not depend on man; it is beyond his power.

由 他 去 作 let him go and do it.

由 他 罷 let him have his way.

5由 你 as you please.

由 你 收 take as many as you want.

由 得 我 it rests with me.

由 我 自 便 let me do as I like.

事 不 由 我 it is beyond my control.

10那 事 由 我 that is my affair.

由 着 性 as one likes.

由 自 取 brought it upon oneself.

由 著 自 己 to go one's own way.

不 由 己 involuntarily.

15可 使 由 之 may be made to follow it.

小 大 由 之 in things small and great we follow them.

自 由 free; independent; of one's own initiative; freedom; liberty.

(c) At ease; self-possessed.

由 由 然 self-possessed.

由 由 自 得 self-satisfied; delighted with.

(d) u.f. 猶 No. 7528. As, still, etc.

由 反 手 也 (as easy as) turning the hand.

由 古 之 樂 (yo4.5.) like the music of antiquity.

由 水 之 就 下 as water flows downward.

(e) Used in transliterating.

由 旬 or 由 延 an Indian measure of distance; it varies,—the longest is a day's journey, about 80 *li.* Sanskrit:—*yôjana.*

柚
欀 }4
7514

The pumelo.

柚 子 the pumelo.

(a) The first form is also read *chu*4.5. The cylinder which carries the threads of the warp.

油 2
7515

Oil; fat; grease; paint; varnish. To varnish.

油 井 an oil-well.

油 作 a painter's trade or shop.

油 傘 an oiled-paper umbrella.

油 光 glossy; varnished.

5油 刺 blackheads.

油 味 a greasy taste.

油 商 an oil merchant.

油 嘴 glib; suave; persuasive.

油 嘴 滑 舌 talkative.

10油 坊 an oil store.

油 布 oiled cloth.

油 條 fritters of twisted dough.

油 榨 an oil-press.

油 氣 oil-gas; greasiness.

15油 氣 味 a greasy taste.

油 水 the moisture or glossiness on the surface of things—small profits out of the ordinary way of business; perquisites.

刮 削 一 些 油 水 you'll get something out of this for yourself.

油 汪 汪 的 swimming with grease—as a bowl of soup.

油 泥 grease; dandruff; greasy filth.

20油 油 glossy—as leaves; dense—as clouds.

油·滑 oily; slippery; sly.
油漆 oil paints; varnish.
油漆匠 a painter.
油潤 moist; soft; glossy.
25 油灰 putty.
油炸檜 fritters of twisted dough.
油炸餅 fritters.
油然 plentifully; amply.
油然作雲 a dense gathering of clouds.
30 油然而生 glibly; smoothly.
油煎 to fry in oil.
油煙 soot; lamp-black.
油畫 oil-paintings.
油簍 an oil-basket.
35 油素 (or 質) olein.
油紙 oiled-paper.
油絲絹 silk gauze for paintings.
油綢 a very shiny kind of silk goods.
油腳 the dregs of oil.
40 油腔滑調 glib, plausible speech.
油·膩 greasy; oily; fatty; dirty.
油菜 rape.
油葫·蘆 a kind of cricket.
油蒙·了心 "the heart is waxed gross."
45 油蓋 an oiled-paper umbrella.
油蟲 cockroaches.
油衣 oilskins.
油跡 oil stains; grease spots.
油鍋 the cauldron of oil—one of the punishments of the Chinese hell.
50 油靴 oiled boots for wet weather.
油頭 to grease the hair.
油頭光棍 a slippery black-guard.
油頭粉面 to oil the hair and rouge the face.
油風 a skin disease characterized by falling hair and redness of the skin accompanied with itching.
55 油鹽醬醋 oil, salt, soy and vinegar—condiments.
油麻 linseed.
上油 to varnish; to paint.
加油 to varnish; to paint; "step
桐油 wood-oil.　　　[or it!"
60 清油 clear oil for varnishing.
火油 or 煤油 petroleum.
豬油 lard.
生油 peanut oil. =花生油.
石油 petroleum.
65 精油 essential oils.
老油·子 an oily-tongued fellow.
茶油 an oil expressed from the

seeds of a kind of camellia.
豆油 oil expressed from beans.
青油 oil expressed from the seeds of the tallow-tree.
70 香油 sweet oil—expressed from sesamum seed.

蚰 2
7516　A millipede; or 蚰蜒.

釉 4
7517　The glaze on porcelain.

釉水 liquid glaze.
釉灰 certain kinds of powdered stone, etc., used to produce glaze.
釉藥 various ingredients used for producing glaze on porcelain.
上釉(子) to glaze

鼬 4　The Siberian weasel; the
7518　North-China polecat.

攸 2　A place. What; that
卣　　which; whereby; who. An
7519　expletive. It is used like 所.

攸介攸止 in a spacious resting place.
攸好德 what one desires is virtue.
攸宜 as was fitting.
攸攝 assisting—at the sacrifice.
5 攸歸 a place in which they feel at home.
攸然而逝 it swam away joyfully—of a fish.
攸爾 cheerfully.
攸行 from which it proceeds.
利有攸往 by which means profits will accrue.
10 名譽攸關 affecting one's reputation.
君子攸行 that which the superior man does.
四方攸同 there were collected together those from the four quarters.
有攸不爲臣 there were some who would not become subjects —of Chou.
相攸 select a home for.
15 福祿攸歸 May blessing and emolument come to this place!

福祿攸降 the place where happiness and dignity descend.
萬壽攸酢 myriads of years as the fitting reward.
萬福攸同 May every happiness come upon them! Around whom all the blessings collect.
風雨攸除 impervious to wind and rain.
20 鳥鼠攸去 offering no cranny to bird or rat.

(a) Distant. Inter. next.

攸攸外寓 living so far from home.

悠 1
7520　Far-reaching; distant.

悠久 for a long time.
悠忽 to fritter away the time.
悠悠之論 common talk.
悠悠我里 far off is my village.
5 悠悠揚揚 soft and loud—of music.
悠悠蒼天 O thou distant and azure heaven!
悠謬 silly; far-fetched.
悠遠 a long stretch; distant.
驕馬悠悠 I would have urged my horses all the long way.

(a) Anxious thought.

悠哉悠哉 long he thought, long and anxiously.
悠悠我心 prolonged is the anxiety of my heart.
悠悠我思 long, long do I think of him.
悠緬 anxiously thinking of those far away.

旒 2　The scallops along the
7521　lower edge of a flag.

游 2　To swim; to float. To
7522　roam; to travel.
Inter. 遊 No. 7524.

游人 a wanderer; a sight-seer.
游供 evasive evidence.
游侶 a travelling companion.
游俠 a roaming knight-errant.
5 游偵 a spy.
游塵 floating dust in the air— mere trifles.

游 女 a wandering woman—a woman of loose character.

游 子³ a wanderer; a son away from home.

游 學 to travel for information; to go abroad for the purpose of study.

¹⁰游 客 指 南 a guide-book.

游 客 雲 集 a great influx of tourists.

游 宦 to travel in search of official employment.

游 履 to travel; to go sight-seeing.

游 廊 a verandah.

¹⁵游 息 之 所 a recreation ground.

游 惰·的 tramps; vagrants.

游·戲 games; recreations; amusements or entertainments.

游 戲 塲 a place of amusement; a recreation ground.

游 戲 文 章 burlesques.

²⁰游 戲 體 操 physical exercises as contrasted with military drill.

游 手 an idler; a loafer.

游 手 好⁴ 閒 the idle love to waste their time; loafing.

游 揚 to praise.

游 牧 nomads.

²⁵游 方 僧 an itinerant Buddhist priest.

游 於 藝 find your relaxation in the arts.

游·歷 to travel for pleasure.

游 民 wanderers; homeless people; vagrants.

游 水 to swim; to play about in the water. [to swim.

³⁰游 泳 to dart to and fro—as fish;

游 波 to traverse the waves—a name for the petrel.

游 湖 to go for an excursion on the lake.

游·玩 to go for an excursion.

游 田 to go hunting.

³⁵游 移 to vary; to depart from; to hesitate.

游 移 不 定 hesitating; uncertain —as to a course of action.

游 移 兩 可 between two opinions.

游 約 to delay; irresolute.

游 絲 floating gossamer threads.

⁴⁰游 翔 to soar; to fly hither and thither.

游 興 (hsing⁴) the exhilaration of travelling.

游 舊 a former companion.

游 蕩 dissipated; vicious; wandering; roving.

㳺 泳 池 swimming pool.

游·藝 會 an exhibition of students' work.

⁴⁵游 行 to travel; to roam; to go from place to place.

游 行 演 說 to go from place to place lecturing; to hold street meetings.

游 覽 to go sight-seeing.

游 言 rumours.

游 說 to travel around as a political agent or propagandist.

⁵⁰游 賞 to go for a stroll around.

游 辭 an unfounded statement.

游 遍 to travel all over a district.

游 邏 to patrol.

游 魂 a wandering soul.

⁵⁵游 龍 speedy; changeable.

上 游 the upper reaches of a stream—superiors.

下 游 the lower reaches of a stream—inferiors.

出 游 to go for a walk; to go out; to travel.

蝣² Ephemera.
7523

遊² To roam; to travel; to saunter.
7524 Inter. 游 No. 7522 q.v.

遊 刃 有 餘 room for the blade and some to spare—of a butcher who was skilful in the use of his knife in separating the joints—used to illustrate the ease with which a task is accomplished when one is skilled in the use of the proper means.

遊 子³ 思 親 the absent son remembers his parents.

遊 必 有 方 when away (from his home), (a son) must have a fixed abode.

遊 擊 or 遊 府 former term for a major in the Chinese army.

⁵遊 星 the planets. = 行 星.

遊 街 to hold a procession.

遊 街 示 威 to hold a procession as a demonstration.

遊 遊 蕩 蕩 lounging; dissipated.

交 遊 a companion or friend.

¹⁰閒 遊 to saunter.

遊 擊 戰 guerrilla warfare.

郵² A post-house where couriers on government service
7525 changed horses. A lodge in the fields.

郵 亭 a lodge for couriers; a

---

lodge for an official who in ancient times superintended agriculture.

郵 件 mail-matter.

國 外 郵 件 international mail-matter.

掛 號 郵 件 registered mail-matter; registered post.

改 寄 郵 件 redirected correspondence.

留 局 候 領 郵 件 poste-restante correspondence.

郵 件 收 發 日 mail-day.

郵 傳 部 the former Board of Posts and Communications.

郵 力 money given to one who brings a letter.

¹⁰郵 務 postal business.

郵 務 便 利 postal facilities.

郵 務 信 櫃 a post-box.

郵 務 分 局 a branch post-office.

郵 務 司 a postmaster.

¹⁵郵 務 工 會 Postal Employees' Union.

郵 務 火 車 a mail-train.

郵 務 總 局 the general post-office.

郵 務 總 辦 Postmaster General.

郵 務 航 空 事 業 air-mail services.

²⁰郵 匯 to remit by a postal money-order.

郵 呈 to address a superior by letter.

郵 寄 to send by post.

郵 寄 代 辦 所 a postal agency.

郵 局 匯 票 postal money-order.

²⁵郵 局 存 信 處 poste restante.

郵 局 通 告 post-office notifications.

郵 局 長³ a postmaster. [(-ch'ai¹)

郵 差 letter-carriers; couriers.

郵 戳 postmark.

³⁰郵 政 postal administration.

郵 政 信 箱 letter-box.

郵 政 儲 蓄 銀 行 Post-office Savings Bank.

郵 政 儲 金 post-office savings deposits.

郵 政 出 版 物 post-office publications.

³⁵郵 政 局 a post-office.

郵 政 明 信 片 postal cards.

郵 政 條 例 postal regulations.

郵 政 章·程 postal guide.

郵 會 Postal Union.

⁴⁰ 萬 國 聯 郵 會 International Postal Union.

郵 會 條 例 Postal Union tariff regulations.

郵 期 mail-day; date of closing the mail.

郵 片 a postal card. = 36.

郵 界 a postal district.

⁴⁵郵 票 postage stamps.

　　欠 資 郵 票 postage-due stamps.

　　汚 損 之 郵 票 soiled or damaged postage stamps.

郵 稅 postage.

郵 筒 a pillar-box.

⁵⁰郵 船 a mail-boat.

郵 袋 mail-bags.

郵 記 postpaid.

郵 費 postage.

　　免 納 郵 費 postage free; exempt from postage.

⁵⁵郵 費 不 足 insufficient postage.

郵 費 已 納·的 postpaid.

郵 資 postage.

郵 路 postal routes.

郵 車 postal vans.

⁶⁰郵 轉 電 報 telegrams forwarded by mail from the nearest telegraph office.

郵 遞 (or 送) to send by mail.

郵 電 post and telegraph.

郵 館 an inn; a lodging-place.

郵 驛 courier stations; posting-houses.

⁶⁵付 郵 to post—a letter, etc.

交 郵 to post—a letter, etc.

(a) Still more. To err. u.f. 尤 No. 7511.

郵 罰 麗 于 事 inadvertent and redeemable offences were determined by—the circumstances of —each particular case.

不 知 其 郵 they became insensible of their errors—when intoxicated.

況 魯 之 君 子 迷 之 郵 者 how much more then may not the Sage of *Lu* be beclouded with error—referring to Confucius.

(b) Superior. Much. u.f. 最 No. 6858.

殿 郵 inferior and superior; last and first, respectively.

酉 ³ Spirits made from newly-ripe millet in the eighth
75.26　month. The tenth of the

Earthly Branches 地 支.
Radical 164.
Distinguish 西 No. 2460, 酋 No. 1235.

酉 時 from 5 to 7 p.m.

栖 櫙 ²·³·
7527　　A soft wood. To lay in stores of firewood.

猶 ²　Like; similar to; as if; as.
7528　Yet; still; even; especially; While still. Undecided.

猶 且 still further; more.

猶 不 足 still insufficient.

猶 之 generally speaking; uniformly; and similarly....

猶 以 尸 諫 as it were rebuked him by means of his corpse.

⁵猶 可 probably; likely; it will do.

猶 可 說 也 there is still something that might be said....

猶 女 like a daughter—a niece.

猶 如 as if.

猶 子 ³ like a son—a nephew.

¹⁰猶 存 there are still...; an overplus; still retained.

猶 己 事 ... as one's own affairs.

猶 復 to still continue to....

猶 日 念 母 daily thinking of her mother.

猶 有 still more; there are still....

¹⁵猶 未 定 still undecided.

猶 求 as though seeking for....

猶 然 just like; just as if....

猶 若 as if....

猶 見 也 ... is again to the front.

²⁰猶 言 it may be said; as though one had said....

猶 質 其 首 they still held the head in pawn—as a means of further extortion.

視 予 猶 父 he regarded me as a father.

(a) The name of a timid suspicious animal.

猶 豫 the name of a very timid, suspicious wild animal which runs up the trees on hearing footsteps—some define it as being two animals suspicious of each other.

猶 與 or 猶 疑 variants of the above.

猶 疑 不 定 undecided.

猶 豫 未 決 lacking in decision; irresolute.

作 事 猶 豫 irresolute; undecided; doubtful.

(b) u.f 猷 No. 7430. To scheme; to plan.

不 我 告 猶 will not tell us anything about the plans.

克 壯 其 猶 but full of vigour were his plans.

我 視 謀 猶 when I look at such counsels and plans.

無 相 猶 矣 and have no schemings against each other.

謀 猶 回 遹 his counsels and plans are crooked and bad.

(c) Used in transliterating.

猶 大 Judah.

猶 太 Judea; Jews; Jewish.

猶 太 國 the land of Judea.

猶 太 殖 民 主 義 Zionism.

蕕 ²　A water-plant with a foul
7529　smell.

薰 蕕 fragrant and stinking.

猷 ²　A scheme; a plan. To
7530　plot; to plan; to consult with. An exclamation. A wise course of action.

猷 訓 wise counsels.

君 子 ³ 有 徽 猷 if the sovereign has good ways....

有 猷 having wise counsels to give.

秩 秩 大 猷 wisely arranged are the great plans.

輶 ²·⁴·　A light carriage.
7531　Light; trifling.

輶 儀 a trifling present.

輶 軒 a light carriage.

羑 ³　To lead.
7532　u.f. 誘 No. 7538.

羑 里 the name of the place where *Wên Wang* was imprisoned, near the present 湯 陰 縣 in Honan.

有[3] To have. To exist; to be. There is; there are; there were.
7533

有 一 利 必 有 一 弊 if there is an advantage, there will surely be something to the contrary—nothing is perfect.

有 一 天 there was a day—once upon a time.

有 一 部 ·分 there is one section; partially.

有 不 是 to be in the wrong; in error.

[5]有 之 I have it; there are some.

有 ·了 I have; enough; there is; here it is; I got it.

有 ·了 嗎 have you any or not? is it here?

有 事 to be engaged; to be in difficulties.

有 ·些 some.

[10]有 ·些 人 there were some persons.

有 人 someone.

有 仇 having enmity.

有 何 what is there?

有 何 妨 what does it matter?

[15]有 何 強 ·處 what advantage has it?

有 作 爲[2] having energy.

有 你 是 問 you are responsible.

有 來 有 去 there is some coming and going in the matter.

有 來 ·歷 has antecedents—he is respectable.

[20]有 偏 a conventional reply—"I have eaten."

有 備 無 患 when there is preparedness there is no disaster.

有 價 値 ·的 valuable.

有 價 約 報 valuable consideration. (legal).

有 價 證 券 valuable documents or securities.

[25]有 價 行 爲 an act of consideration. (legal).

有 僭 I am usurping a place of honour—conventional.

有 其 父 必 有 其 子[3] like father, like son.

有 出 入 uneven, not uniform, — as of prices, etc.

有 分[4]ㄦ having a share in.

[30]有 利 無 害 wholly profitable.

有 則 言 有 if it is so, then say so; if you have it, then say so.

有 力 之 powerful.

有 勁ㄦ putting some interest into it; with force.

有 勢 ·力 influential.

[35]有 口 無 心 he can speak, but his heart is not in it; able to speak but unable to carry it out in practice.

有 口 皆 碑 where there are mouths—to praise him—there are his memorial tablets.

有 司 civil authorities—those who have office.

有 名 無 實 merely nominal; empty profession.

有 名 ·的 noted; celebrated.

[40]有 呢 (yes) there is!

有 味 palatable; intriguing.

有 坐 I have a seat—conventional reply when asked to be seated.

有 多 ·麽 重 how heavy is it?

有 天 下 而 不 與[4] 焉 having possession of the empire and yet seeming as if it were not of importance to him.

[45]有 天 沒[2] 日 ·頭 a sky but no sun—terrible, awful—used of unreasonable language.

有 如 as if; something like.

有 始 有 終 completed, having a beginning and an end.

有 始 無 終 to have a beginning but no end.

有 子[3] 而 好[4] 之 於 紂 he had a daughter whom he loved, whom he gave to Chou.

[50]有 孕 pregnant.

有 定 例 regular.

有 室 married.

有 寃 無 處 訴 to have a grievance and no means of redress.

有 害 無 益 wholly injurious.

[55]有 就 證 如 if it is so, say so.

有 尺 度 having measure; what is done by rule; methodically.

有 己 無 人 utterly selfish.

有 常 識 having common sense.

有 年 a good harvest.

[60]有 年 ·了 long ago.

有 幹 才 having ability to manage affairs; competent.

有 形 visible; concrete.

有 ·得 你 it rests with you.

有 心 人 a man who takes an interest in national affairs, and studies the general well-being of the community.

[65]有 心 哉 擊 磬 乎 his heart is full who thus strikes the musical stones.

有 心 病 uneasy in heart, on account of disagreement with another, etc.

有 心 ·的 intentionally.

有 志 者 事 竟 成 where there's a will there's a way.

有 恒 心 having a persevering disposition; persevering.

[70]有 恥 且 格 they will have a sense of shame and correct themselves.

有 惑 志 is being deceived.

有 情 sentimental.

有 情 有 理 reasonable.

有 情 有 義 ·的 人 a person of a kindly disposition.

[75]有 意 intentionally.

有 意 動 作 intentional actions.

有 意 思 quite interesting; amusing, etc.

有 意 義 ·的 having some purpose or intention; significant.

有 憑 有 據 there is abundant evidence.

[80]有 我 在 此 I am here, what more do you want?

有 所 啟 there is a reason.

有 所 幸 he had a favourite.

有 所 思 I was just considering the matter; preoccupied.

有 所 恃 having something to rely on.

[85]有 才 having ability.

有 把 握 has a grip on it—can manage it; dependable.

有 效 valid; in force; effective.

有 效 力 validity.

有 效 距 離 effective range—of a gun.

[90]有 敎 無 類 in teaching make no class distinctions.

有 數[4] limited in number; not many; can be counted.

有 日 there is a day fixed; some day; one day...; near.

有 時 there are times...; sometimes....

有 是 因 而 後 有 是 果 there must first be a cause and then there will be the effect.

[95]有 期 徒 刑 definite term of penal servitude.

有 朝[1] 一 日 some day—perhaps.

有 案 it is on record; there is such a case.

有 根 有 基 well-established.

有 根 有 梢 both root and branch.

[100]有 條 有 理 in order.

有 條 不 紊 everything in order and well arranged.

有 條 件·的 conditional.
有 機 organic.
有 機 化 學 organic chemistry.
¹⁰⁵有 權 有 位 having authority.
有 毒 poisonous.
有 氣 to have breath—angry; living.
有 求 必 應⁴ ask and you will receive.
有·沒·有 have you any or not? is it here? (--mei-)
¹¹⁰有 注 意 之 價 值 it is worth noticing.
有 滋 有 味 very interesting; well-flavoured.
有 無 不 均 their possessions are not equal.
有 無 相 通 all in common.
有 爲 者 亦 若 是 he who presses on, will also become like this.
¹¹⁵有 物 有 則 there are the various affairs and there are the laws pertaining to them.
有 理 reasonable; in the right.
有 理 性 rational.
有 生 以 來 from birth.
有 產(的)階 級 the propertied class.
¹²⁰有 用·處 useful.
有 病 ill; not well.
有·的 I have; some; there are some. 有·的○是 there are plenty.
有·的 說 some say....
有 益 於 己 of advantage to oneself.
¹²⁵有 益 無 損 wholly advantageous.
有 益·的 profitable.
有 眼 無 珠 unable to discriminate.
有 眼 而 瞎 having eyes, but seeing not.
有 礙 衛 生 insanitary; detrimental to health.
¹³⁰有 福 之 人 不 在 忙 lucky people need not be in a hurry.
有 福·的 happy; blessed.
有 禮 polite.
有 秋 had a good harvest.
有 系 統·的 systematic.
¹³⁵有 約 I have an appointment.
有 素 for quite a while.
有 緣 there is a destiny—when something happens unexpectedly. See 因 No. 7407-41.
有 罪 I am in the wrong; I apologize; guilty.
↓有 聲 電 影 talking movie.

有 聲 有 色⁴ lively (description).
¹⁴⁰有 肚·子 pregnant.
有 脚³書 廚 a walking book-case—a walking encyclopaedia.
有 脚³陽 春 a walking spring—a man of far-reaching benevolence.
有 腿 告 示 a walking proclamation—a gossip, a tale-bearer.
有 臉 having face—respectable.
¹⁴⁵有 膽 courageous; bold.
有 要 沒²緊 of no great importance either way.
有 親·的 consanguineous.
有 話 請 說 if you have anything to say, please say it.
有 請 there is someone asking for you.
¹⁵⁰有 諸 己 而 后 求 諸 人 first take possession yourself, and then you may require others to possess it.
有 講·究 this matter needs—to be undertaken with care.
有 彐 there is some solution to it.
有 趣·的 interesting; having a fine flavour.
有 身 pregnant.
¹⁵⁵有 連 手 having some influence with officials. /respect in a letter.
有 道 having virtue—a term of
¹⁵⁶有 道·理 there is something in it.
有 重 於 社 稷 is of great use to the country.
有 錢 使·得 鬼 推 磨 if you have money you can do anything.
有 限 limited.
¹⁶⁰有 限 公 司 a limited-liability company.
有 限 責 任 limited responsibility.
有 頃 in a little while.
有 馀 there is a surplus; there is some over.
有 頭²有 尾 it has a beginning and an end.
¹⁶⁵有 頭²無 尾 it has a beginning but no end—a thing given up before it is finished.
有 願 在 身 having a vow to perform.
有 顯 者 people of distinction.
有 體 a solid body.
少 有 there were few.
¹⁷⁰沒²有 have not; it is not; there are none.

(a) Read yu¹.　And; also; in addition.

吾 十 有 五 at fifteen years of age, I....

朞 三 百 有 六 旬 有 六 日 a round year consists of three hundred, sixty, and six days.

長 身 有 半 half as long again as his body.

侑⁴ To urge to eat. To entertain guests with music. To stimulate.
7534

侑 卮 an ancient vessel for wine which capsized when too full.
侑 酒 to urge a guest to take wine.
侑 食 to press a person to eat.

囿⁴ A park; an aviary; a menagerie. To enclose; to limit.
7535

囿 于 風 俗 constrained by custom.
囿 苑 or 園 囿 a park or garden.
淺 囿 shallow and limited—in learning and accomplishments.

宥⁴ To be lenient towards; to be indulgent; to forgive.
7536

宥 免 to remit an offence.
宥 罪 to forgive.
宥 過 無 大 刑 故 無 小 pardon inadvertent transgressions, however great; punish wilful faults, however small.
原 宥 to be lenient to; to pardon.
法 所 難 宥 that which the law cannot pardon.

(a) Far-reaching; profound.

夙 夜 基 命 宥 密 day and night he enlarged its foundations by his deep and silent virtue.

莠⁵ Weeds; tares; darnel. Vicious.
7537

莠 民 disloyal subjects.
莠 言 自 口 their offensive words are merely from the mouth.
良 莠 不 齊 good and bad are not in uniform proportions—they are "growing together."

誘 諉
7538

3 To induce; to entice; to mislead; to lead on. Distinguish 誘 No. 7101. Also read *yu*[4].

誘 人 爲 惡 to seduce others to evil. (-*o*[4·5])
誘 以 利 to allure by hope of gain.
誘 入 圈 套 to lure into a snare.
誘 供 to entrap a person into a confession.
[5]誘 兵 troops that pretend to flee in order to lead the enemy into an ambush.
誘 匿 to make off with; to kidnap.
誘 姦 to entice into adultery.
誘 導 to lead; to guide.
誘 惑 to beguile; to tempt to sin.
[10]誘 拐 to entice away; to kidnap.
誘 掖 獎 勸 to help on and encourage.
誘 敵 to draw out the enemy.
誘 物 a decoy; bait; an inducement.
誘 獲 to inveigle.
[15]誘 陷 to beguile; to decoy; to inveigle.
誘 餌 a bait—figuratively.
煝 誘 to lead into error; to delude.
引 誘 to tempt; to seduce.

又
7539

4 And; also; again; in addition to; moreover; further, etc. Radical 29.

又 一 天 still another day.
又 來 了 (he) has come again.
又 便 (*p'ien*[2]) ·宜 又 好 both cheap and good.
又 其 次 也 or 又 次 an inferior sort; something inferior.
[5]又 兼 or 且 又 or 況 又 further; moreover.
又 冷 又 下 雨 it is both cold and rainy.
又 加 ·上 and in addition; and besides.
又 及 phrases used at the end of a postscriptum.
又 名 also called....
[10]又 問 to ask again.
又 因 and further because of....
又 子[3] younger sons.
又 寫 錯 了 written wrongly again. (-*tei*[3]-)
又 ·得[3] 花 錢 still more expense!
[15]又 復 審 訊 I have held a further investigation.

又 打 又 罵 both beating and cursing.
又 換 一 個 生 手 we have changed him for another raw hand.
又 搭 上 and in addition; and besides.
又 ·是 一 個 still another one.
[20]又 ·是 如 此 it is the same as it was before.
又 更 more than ever.
又 有 still there are...; there is still....
又 要 下 雨 it will rain again.
又 要 出 門 he wishes to go on another journey.
[25]又 說 and again....
又 說 又 笑 chatting and smiling.
又 飢 又 渴 both hungry and thirsty.

友
7540

3 A friend; a companion; an associate. Friendly. To make friends of. A group of two. Brotherly regard.

友 之 to be friendly with.
友 于 a (younger) brother—from 友于兄弟 kind to (a younger) brothers.
友 于 肫 篤 given to earnest perseverance—as in studies.
友 人 or 朋 ·友 a friend.
[5]友 其 士 之 仁 者 make friends of the virtuous among the scholars.
友 善 to be friends with the good.
友 悌 brotherly affection.
友 愛 friendliness; to shew affection for.
友 生 a friend.
[10]友 誼 friendly feeling or relationship; friendship.
友 誼 會 a friendly society.
友 道 the way of friendship; rules for the maintenance of friendship; comity. 友 軍 friendly troops.
友 邦 a friendly State.
交 友 to form a friendship.
[15]僚 友 a colleague.
德 友 a virtuous friend.
忘 年 友 friends who do not consider the disparity of their ages.
損 友 a friend that is harmful.
敎[4] 友 a church member.
[20]會 友 member of a society.
益 友 a profitable friend.
窗 友 fellow-students.
老 友 an old friend.
校 (*hsiao*[4]) 友 alumnus.

良 友 a good friend.
[25]親 友 relatives and friends.
賭 友 gambling companions.
酒 友 boon companions.

右
7541

4 The right hand side; that which is on the right. The foregoing. The title of the junior of two officials. Distinguish 古 No. 3447.

右 仰 知 悉 fully acquaint yourself with the foregoing.
右 侍 郎 the former junior Vice-President of a Board.
右 側 on the right hand.
右 僧 a Buddhist nun.
[5]右 列 former term for military officials generally—as subordinate to civil officials.
右 契 the right-hand portion of an agreement, held by the debtor.
右 手 the right hand.
右 派 the right wing—of a political party.
右 派 分[4] 子[3] a right-wing member.
右 文 the phonetic in a character.
[10]右 照 會 the above despatch.
右 眼 the right eye.
右 翼 the right wing—of an army.
右 耳 the right ear.
右 螺 旋 a right-hand thread or screw.
[15]右 貨 the above-mentioned goods.
右 ·邊 or 右 首 the right hand side.

(a) To honour. To esteem—before the Ming dynasty the right hand was the place of honour.

右 文 to esteem polite learning.
右 族 an honourable family.
右 職 high office.
守 成 尙 文 遭 遇 右 武 when things are going well, the civil officials rank first, in times of trouble, the place of honour is given to the military.
無 右 peerless.

(b) Indicates the west.

江 右 Kiangsi.
山 右 west of the hills—Shansi, it being west of the 太 行 山. (-*hang*[2]-)

(c) To assist; to protect. Inter. next.

保 ·右 to protect and help.

佑 [4]
7542　To protect; to help.

佑啓我後人 for the help and instruction of us who come after.

佑賢輔德 assist the worthy and support the virtuous.

祐 [4]
7543　To protect; to shield; to defend. Inter. preceding.

天祐 the protection of Heaven.

庇祐 to protect.

神恩默祐 May the grace of the gods secretly protect you!

幼 [4]
7544　Young; immature; weak; delicate.

幼丁 a person under twenty years of age.

幼不學老何爲 if you do not learn when young, what will you do when you are grown up?

幼主 a youthful monarch.

幼女 a daughter; a little girl.

[5] 幼婦 a young wife.

幼嫩 tender; delicate.

幼子 my little boy.

幼孩 children.

幼學 young pupils; boys' studies; name of a book of miscellaneous elementary studies.

[10] 幼小 or 幼少 (shao[4]) young.

幼年 young; juvenile.

年幼無知 young and inexperienced.

幼弟 a young brother.

幼弱 young and delicate.

[15] 幼稚 young; juvenile; immature.

幼稚園 a kindergarten school.

幼稚時代 the age of the childhood of the race.

幼細 delicate; fine—as lace; pretty.

幼蟲 the larvæ of insects.

[20] 幼視 to look upon as juvenile; supercilious.

幼童 a lad; a boy.

呦 [1]
7545　The bleating of the deer.

泑 [3]
7546　The vitreous glaze on china, porcelain, etc. See 釉 No. 7517.

黝 [3]
7547　Black; dark green.

黝堊 to blacken a wall.

黝牲 black bullocks—fit for sacrifice.

黝糾 dense, as a forest.

黝青 a blue-black.

黝黝 gloomy and dark.

繇 [2]
7548　Cause; means, etc. Inter. 由 No. 7513, 猶 No. 7528. Read yao[2]. u.f. 徭 No. 7285. Forced labour.

繇役 forced labour on government works; serfdom.

(a) Read yao[2]. u.f. 謠 No. 7290. Songs, etc.

繇俗 folk-songs and rustic customs.

(b) Read chou[4], or yu[4]. The interpretations of the *diagrams* or 八卦. The oracular responses of diviners.

繇辭 the interpretation of the *diagrams*.

YUNG.　　(ㄩㄥ)
(Iong)

肜 [1]
7549　To sacrifice on two successive days.

廱 [1]
7550　The Hall of Learning. Inter. next and 雍 No. 7554.

辟廱 the Hall of Learning—the imperial schoolroom.

雝 [1]
7551　A marsh; a poo

于彼西雝 on that western marsh.

(a) Inter. 雍 No. 7554. Harmonious.

雝雝 harmonious, as the songs of the birds; tinkling, as bells; shrill.

(b) Read yung[3]. To obscure.

維塵雝兮 the dust will only becloud you.

灉 [1]
7552　Name of a river in Shantung. A sluice.

癰 [1]
7553　An ulcer; an abscess; a carbuncle; sometimes used for a cancer. See 癌 No. 7346a.

癰疽 an ulcer.

癰瘡 an abcess.

生癰 to have a carbuncle.

雍邕 [1]
7554　Harmony; union. To be harmonious. Concord.

雍和 harmony and peace; to appease.

雍容 peaceful and mild.

雍容揖讓 to show a mild expression and bow complaisantly.

雍熙 harmony and peace.

雍睦 a pleasant manner.

雍雍 affable; courteous; easy with.

(a) Read yung[1]. One of the Nine Divisions of ancient China under Yü the Great. See 九 No. 1198-15.

雍州 the largest of the ancient divisions as above,—it comprised the territory lying west of the Yellow River and north of the River *Wei*.

壅 [1,3]
7555　To stop up; to obstruct.

壅上 or 壅于上聞 to keep from the knowledge of superiors.

壅培 to bank up the roots of plants and trees.

壅塞 to obstruct; to block up; to stop; to dam.

壅滯 obstructed, as the circulation, etc.

壅蔽 to conceal.

擁 [3]
7556　To squeeze; to press; to crowd.

擁上來 to crowd forward; to crowd; to throng.

擁 **上** 前 to crowd forward.

擁 **倒** pushed over—by the crowd.

擁 **入** to push into.

擁 **塞** to block up.

擁 **彗** to use the broom—to sweep the place clean and welcome visitors.

擁 **抱** to embrace; to hug.

擁 **擠** to crowd; to throng.

擁 **擠 不 開** an impassable crowd.

擁 **書** to have numerous books for one's use.

擁 **護** to protect; to escort; to uphold.

擁 **護 中 央** support the central authorities.

擁 **護 共 和** to uphold the republic.

擁 **護 憲 法** to maintain the constitution.

一 **擁** with one rush.

蜂 **擁 而 起** arose in swarms— like hornets.

(a) To conceal.

擁 **被** to wrap oneself up in the bedclothes.

擁 **面** to cover the face.

癕 Loss of the sense of smell. Inter. 癃 No. 7553.
7557

蕹 Ipomoea aquatica—used as a vegetable.
7558

饔 Breakfast, the first meal. Dressed food.
7559

饔 **人** officer in charge of the cooking, etc.

饔 **餼** presents of slaughtered and living animals, respectively— made by a prince to an envoy.

尸 **饔** to supervise the cooking with all its attendant labours of gathering fuel, drawing water, etc.

容 Appearance; manner; bearing.
7560 Pron. jung².

容 **光** appearance; manner.

容 **態** one's appearance and bearing.

容 **止** carriage; demeanour.

容 **步** deportment.

容 **色** looks; expression of the countenance; complexion.

不 見 **容 色** did not show his feelings.

容 **色 自 若** to keep an easy countenance.

容 **華** features and complexion.

容 **表** the expression of one's feelings; air; bearing.

容 **象** a portrait.

容 **貌** appearance; looks; demeanour; expression of the countenance.

容 **質** appearance and disposition.

容 **輝** the light of a person's countenance.

容 **顏** appearance; looks; demeanour; expression of the countenance.

容 **體** carriage; demeanour; bearing.

修 **容** to improve the appearance; to make up the face.

儀 **容** deportment; bearing.

取 **容** to curry favour.

失 **容** to blush; to be disconcerted.

春 **容** the glory of spring; a youthful face.

整 **容** to attend to one's appearance —to visit the barber.

歡 **容** a pleasant expression.

正 **容** to compose the features.

笑 **容** a smiling face.

(a) To allow. To permit. To bear; to endure. To forgive. To contain. To admit. Capacity.

容 **不 下** unable to contain; not large enough to hold it; can't put up with it.

容 **事** with a capacity for business.

容 **人 之 過** be lenient towards the transgressions of others.

容 **他 去** let him go.

容 **光 必 照 焉** admit the light and it cannot but illuminate.

容 **受** to put up with; to make allowances for.

容 **忍** to bear with; to endure.

容 **恕** to pardon.

容 **我 幾 天** give me a few days grace.

容 **日 再 來** I'll come another day.

容 **物** tolerant; liberal-minded.

容 **留** to harbour; to allow to remain.

容 **積** capacity, as of a ship, etc., bulk.

容 **納** to contain; contents; to tolerate; to be kind to.

容 **納 性** capacity.

容 **縱** to indulge; to allow a person to have his own way.

容 **膝** just big enough to get the knees in—cramped quarters.

容 **與** easy in mind, without care or worry.

容 **許** to suffer; to allow; possibly.

容 **諒** to allow; to forgive.

容 **讓** to yield; complaisance.

容 **足 地** a mere footing; a foothold.

容 **身** to stand up in.

容 **量** v o l u m e ; capacity—of things; tolerance—of persons.

容 **隱** to conceal the faults of another.

內 **容** the contents of.

無 **以 自 容** nowhere to hide himself—for shame.

難 **容** unendurable; difficult to bear.

(b) Easy.

容 **易** (i¹) easy.

好 **容 易** how easy!—i.e., not at all easy; after much effort.

榕 The bastard banian, worshipped for long life.
7561 Also read jung².

榕 **城** a name for Foochow—from the trees which are plentiful there.

榕 **樹 公** or 榕 **鬚** t h e pendent rootlets of the banian.

榕 **談** the Foochow dialect.

溶 Water flowing full and gently between its banks.
7562 Also read jung².

溶 **盛** abundant; full.

蓉 The Hibiscus mutabilis or 芙 蓉 花.
7563 Also read jung².

熔
鎔 A mould; a die. To smelt; to fuse metals. To influence.
Also read jung².
7564

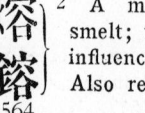

熔 化 to smelt; to influence.
熔 巖 lava.
熔 度 fusing point.
熔 解 to smelt; to fuse.
⁵熔 解 線 fuse-wire.
熔 金 就 範 molten metals take the form of the mould.
熔 銷 to smelt.
熔 鑄 to pour metal into a mould; to cast.
熱 氣 熔 爐 a blast-furnace.

喁² The mouth of a fish at the surface of the water; gasp-
7565　ing for breath.
Read yü². An answering sound.

融² Steam issuing forth. To melt; to fuse metals. In-
7566　terchanged with 熔 No. 7564.

融 化 to destroy; to melt.
融 合 to blend; to mix together; to amalgamate; amalgamation.
融 和 mild; genial—as the weather.
融 散 to dissipate.
⁵融 暢 perspicuous.
融 會 貫 通 to bring together and understand thoroughly.
融 洽 to blend with; mutual understanding.
融 液 to bring into a liquid state.
融 結 to combine.
¹⁰融 解 to fuse; to melt by heat; fusion.
融 解 熱 heat of fusion.
融 解 點 point of fusion.
融 通 permeated.
通 融 辦 理 to arrange a matter by compromise.
¹⁵融 風 genial spring breezes.
交 融 blended.
金 融 the money market; currency. *See No. 1057-54.*

(a) Long.

融 畬 a loud and long-drawn-out sound.
融 畯 stately.

(b) The fullness of intelligence.

昭 明 有 融 May your bright in-telligence become perfect.

用⁴ To use; to employ. To consume. To apply; to put
7567　into practice. Practical, as opposed to theoretical, 體. Radical 101.

用·不 了³ more than can be used.
用·不 完 there is a surplus; more than can be used.
用·不 得 unfit for use; don't use it.
用·不 愁 no anxiety about ex-penses.
⁵用·不 慣 unaccustomed to the use of.
用·不 盡 more than can be used.
用·不 着² useless; need not.(-chao²)
用 世 of some use in the world.
用 之 則 行 舍³ 之 則 藏 when used as an official, perform your duties; when dismissed, remain in retirement.
¹⁰用 事 to have authority; to per-form sacrifices.
用 人 servants; to employ others.
用 人 失 當⁴ to employ a person wrongly.
用 具 appliances.
用 功 to study diligently; to work hard; to give application to.
¹⁵用 功 不 到 lacking in diligence.
用 勁 to make an effort.
用 印 to seal; to stamp.
用 命 to obey an order.
用 品 tools; articles for use.
²⁰用 器 畫 mechanical drawing.
用 工 to work hard; to study, etc., with diligence.
用·度 expenditure.
用 心 to give heed to; to-give attention to; application of the mind.
用 心 過 度 excessive care, anxie-ty, worry, etc.
²⁵用 意 to give heed to; to devote much attention to; intention.
是 他 人 的 用 意 it is an-other person's idea.
用 意 甚 善 the idea is excellent.
用 手 打·他 strike it with the hand.
用 手 托·着 bear it on the palms of the hands.
³⁰用 手 捧·着 to scoop up with both hands.
用·掉 to use up; to expend; to consume.
用 極 端 辦 法 to use extreme measures.

用 武 to resort to violence.
用 法 directions for use; the way to use anything.
³⁵用 盡·了 used up; exhausted.
用 盡 心 機 to exhaust one's devices—at one's wit's end.
用 盡 手·段 used every means available.
用 盡 方 法 used every available method—went to all lengths.
用 眼 傳 神 to convey an idea by a look.
⁴⁰用 罪 用 德 criminals and well-doers, respectively.
用·處 the use of; usefulness.
用 計 to contrive; to use tricks.
用 訊 to declare the truth.
用·途 usage; appropriation—as of funds; the use to which any-thing is put.
⁴⁵用 違 其 才 to employ a person to do something in which he is unskilful.
用 金 middleman's fees; com-mission.
用 錢 to use money; expenditure; commission; middleman's fees.
用 非 所 長 to employ a person to do that which he is not ac-customed to do, or that which he is not skilled in.
用 項 expenditure.
⁵⁰用·頭 of use; the use of.
用 飯 to take a meal.
不 勝¹ 用 more than can be used.
不 彀 用 insufficient for use.
不 敷 用 insufficient for use.
⁵⁵不 適 用 inapplicable.
使 用 use; to use; expenditure; outlay.
信·用 credit; confidence.
儉 用 frugal; thrifty.
利·用 to exploit. *See No. 3867-24.*
⁶⁰受·用 to keep for one's own use; useful; comfortable.
善 用 to put to a good use.
器 用 vessels for use.
妄 用 the improper use of; to misuse.
實 用 practical use.
⁶⁵施 用 use; to use; expenditure or outlay.
日 用 daily use; for every day.
正 用 the lawful or proper use of.
無 用 useless; in vain; worthless.
誤 用 improper use of; misuse.
⁷⁰試 用 to make a trial of.

費用 expenditure or outlay.
領 用 to receive and make use of.

(a) To; so as to. With; by; thereby; therefore. Similar in use to 以.

用 昭 明 于 天 下 thus they became gloriously illustrious throughout the empire.
用 是 wherefore; for this reason....
用 特 I therefore specially....
用 自 絕 thereby cutting yourself off.
[5]用 臻 and thus attain to....
用 資 so that provision may be made for....
用 降 我 凶 德 thereby he removed our evils.
何 用 不 監 how is it that you do not consider the state of affairs?
是 用 作 歌 therefore I make this song.
[10]是 用 大 諫 I therefore strongly admonish you.
是 用 孝 享 and filially present them—the offerings.
茲 用 wherefore.

甬 [3] A measure of ten 斗.
7568 Bursting forth. A raised path. The name of the river at Ningpo.

甬 東 Ningpo.
甬 路 or 甬 道 a raised path.

俑 [3] Wooden figures of men and
7569 women buried with the dead; they had springs in them by means of which they could move about.

作 俑 to originate—things that are evil; from the above, see below—2.
始 作 俑 者 其 無 後 乎 was he not without posterity who first made wooden images to bury with the dead—said by Confucius, as he thought that this invention gave rise to the practice of burying living persons.
為 俑 者 不 仁 it is not in accordance with humanity to make wooden figures to bury with the dead.

埇 [3] A raised path.
7570

勇 [3] Brave; daring; courage.
7571 Irregular troops.

勇 丁 former term for police.
勇 不 可 當 of indomitable courage.
勇 剛 heroism.
勇 力 great strength.
[5]勇 士 or 勇 人 a valiant man.
勇 夫 a brave officer.
勇 往 resolute; intrepid.
勇 敢 intrepid; daring.
勇 武 warlike.
[10]勇 氣 bravery; pluck; courage.
勇 烈 bold.
勇 營 irregulars; braves.
勇 猛 resolutely; fearlessly.
勇 號 a diploma awarded for bravery.
[15]勇 退 to retire when in high office.
小 勇 petty valour—bullying.
血 氣 之 勇 animal courage.

湧 涌 [3] To bubble up. To flow
7572 rapidly.

湧 上 來 to bubble up.
湧 出 to gush forth.
湧 泉 a bubbling spring.
湧 激 the strength of a current.
湧 至 to burst in upon.
湧 進 to come in like a flood.
潮 湧 the tide is flowing.

 [3] To urge; to incite.
7573

慂 客 to urge a guest—to eat.
慫 慂 to egg on; to incite.

蛹 [3] A chrysalis.
7574

蛹 臥 to live in seclusion, like a chrysalis in its cocoon.
被 蛹 a pupa that is enclosed in a cocoon.
裸 蛹 a naked pupa, those which are not enclosed in cocoons.

踴 踊 [3] To leap; to jump. To
7575 have one's toes cut off as a punishment.

踴 貴 to rise in price.
屨 賤 踴 貴 ordinary shoes were cheap, while those for toeless people were dear—there was such a demand for the latter owing to the cruelty of Duke Ching 景 of Ch'i 齊—ironical.
踴 躍 to skip; to jump about for joy; enthusiastic.

庸 [1,2] To employ; to use. To
7576 manifest. Inter. next.
u.f. 用 No. 7567.

庸 作 to receive hire.
庸 保 employees.
庸 命 to carry out an order.
庸 庸 to employ those who are fit.
[5]吁 靜 言 庸 違 Alas! when unemployed, he can talk, but when employed, his actions turn out differently.
弗 克 庸 帝 could not use the warning given him by the Supreme.
弗 詢 之 謀 勿 庸 do not follow undeliberated plans.
毋 庸 遠 慮 do not worry about the distant future.
舜 生 三 十 徵 庸 in the 30th year of his life Shun was called to employment.
[10]若 時 登 庸 one who is in accordance with the times and may be promoted to employment—by the emperor.

(a) Usage. Common; usual; ordinary. Simple. Unchanging.

庸 人 simple, ordinary persons.
庸 俗 commonplace; vulgar.
庸 儒 a mean, worthless scholar.
庸 劣 common, ordinary; without ability.
[5]庸 夫 a simple person.
庸 常 or 平 庸 ordinary; common; inferior.
庸 庸 多 後 福 simple persons have the most happiness.
庸 德 之 行 the practice of ordinary virtues.
庸 惡 陋 劣 mean; vulgar; worthless and degraded. (-o⁴)

[10] 庸 愚 simple and stupid—the masses.

庸 態 the attitude of the common crowd.

庸 才 ordinary ability; mediocre talents.

庸 民 the common people.

庸 狗 an ill-bred dog—term of abuse.

[15] 庸 衆 the masses.

庸 碌 ordinary; inferior; without ability.

庸 碌 之 相[4] commonplace features.

庸 碌 之 輩 a commonplace person.

庸 耳 俗 目 uncultured; not refined.

[20] 庸 行 regular course of action.

庸 言 commonplace talk.

庸 豎 a useless person.

庸 醫 a quack doctor.

(b) Merit; service.

有 能 奮 庸 is there anyone who can vigorously display his merits....

自 庸 to seek one's merit in....

車 服 以 庸 they received chariots and robes according to their merit.

(c) How?

庸 何 or 安 庸 how? in what way?

庸 非 貳 乎 did they not have different intentions?

汝 庸 知 how do you know?

(d) Harmony. That which is constant, admitting of no change.

庸 者 天 下 之 定 理 by yung is denoted the fixed principle regulating all under heaven.

不 易 之 謂 庸 that which admits of no change is called yung.

中 庸 without inclination to either side and admitting of no change —the title of one of the *Four Books--The Doctrine of the Mean.*

傭 [1,2] To hire; to engage, as a labourer.
7577

傭 人 workmen; labourers.

傭 保 employees.

傭 值 殊 儉 the wages were very low.

傭 婦 a woman-servant.

[5] 傭 工 to hire labourers; servants.

傭 役 hired attendants.

傭 書 to be engaged as a writer.

傭 率 (*lü*[4,5].) the rate of wages.

傭 賃 to be hired out.

[10] 傭 資 wages.

(a) Impartial.

昊 天 不 傭 Great Heaven is unjust.

墉 [1,2] A fortified wall. A wall.
7578

墉 塹 the city wall and moat.

慵 [1,2] Indolent; easy-going; careless.
7579 Also read *jung*[2].

慵 妝 untidy appearance; dishevelled.

慵 懦 自 安 to seek one's ease; idle.

慵 惰 lazy; indolent.

慵 懶 or 疎 慵 heedless and indolent.

慵 而 陋 slovenly and dirty.

鏞 [1,2] A large bell, a bell tolled in the Confucian temples.
7580

鱅 [2] A kind of tench.
7581

榮 [2] Glory; splendour; lustrous; honour. Flourishing; prosperous—as vegetation. Beautiful. Used conventionally for "your."
7582 Pron. *jung*[2].

榮 任 何 處 where is your official post?

榮 光 brightness; splendour; glory.

榮 喜 May you have glorious joy!

榮 增 May your happiness increase!

[5] 榮 威 brightness; splendour.

榮 宗 耀 祖 to shed glory on one's ancestors.

榮 旋 to return home with honour —as a retiring statesman.

榮 歸 to return home with honours.

榮 程 your glorious journey.

[10] 榮 美 glorious and beautiful; splendid.

榮 耀 glory; splendour; brightness.

榮 花 beautiful; splendour.

榮 茂 flourishing; glorious.

榮 華 富 貴 splendour, wealth and honour.

[15] 榮 行 your glorious journey.

榮 補 your appointment.

榮 調 your appointment.

榮 貴 prosperous.

榮 and 辱 or 枯 are opposites— flourishing and fading; honoured and disgraced; prosperity and adversity.

(a) Blood.

榮 衛 不 行 五 藏 不 通 when the blood and the vital essences do not circulate freely, the five viscera do not perform their proper functions.

嶸 [2] Lofty; prominent; majestic.
7583 Also read *jung*[2].

崢 嶸 majestic; dignified.

濚 [2] A stream. To eddy; an eddy.
7584 Also read *jung*[2].
Inter. 瀅 No. 7588.

蠑 [2] A kind of lizard found in damp places.
7585

滎 [2] The dashing of waves. Streams of water; brooks.
7586 Read *ying*[2]. Name of an ancient marsh.

滎 澤 an ancient marsh; name of a city and district in Honan.

滎 陽 name of a city and district in Honan.

縈 [2] To wind around; to reel; to entwine; to coil.
7587 Also read *jung*[2], *yün*[2].

縈 回 to go round and round.

縈 懷 entwined around the heart.

縈 繞 to bind round; to encompass.

澯[2] To revolve. To curl in eddies, as rushing water.
.7588 Also read *jung*[2]; *yün*[2].

澯洄 whirling, eddying waters.

永[3] Perpetual; eternal; long; far-reaching.
7589

Distinguish 水 No. 5922; 氷 No. 5283.

永不 never.
永不分離 inseparable; never to be separated.
永不敍用 never to be employed again—of a disgraced official.
永世 endless ages.
[5]永世無竟 for ages and ages without end.
永世無盡 for endless ages.
永久 perpetually; eternally.
永久和平 a permanent or lasting peace.
永久長存 to abide for ever.
[10]永久齒 the permanent teeth.
永代借地 land in perpetual leasehold.
永佃權 right of perpetual lease.
永別 eternal separation—death.
永古 long ages ago.
[15]永古不壞 it will never wear out; it will never spoil.
永命 long life.
永固 permanently fixed.
永壽 long life.
永在 eternally existent.
[20]永夜 the whole night.
永存不廢 in perpetuity.
永存性 permanency; continuance.
永字八法 the character *yung* is supposed to embody the eight different strokes used in writing Chinese:— 側 the dot at the top, 勒 the small horizontal stroke at the top of the upright central stroke, 努 the upright stroke minus the hook, 趯 the hook at the foot of the upright, 策 and 掠 the two strokes at the left side, 啄 and 磔 the two strokes at the right side—the names are different from those in common use.
永安 lasting peace.
[25]永定 permanently fixed.
永常 constantly.
永念 constantly thinking of; to

think of things that are far-distant.

永日 a long day—as of summer.
永晝 a long day—as of summer.
[30]以消永晝 to help pass away the long days—of summer.
永止 to cease for ever.
永歸無有 perish for evermore.
永永 for ever; eternally.
永爲定式 to be fixed as a permanent standard.
[35]永生 eternal life.
永福 everlasting bliss.
永續運動 perpetual motion.
永行弗替 in perpetuity.
永言配命 try always to agree with the commands of Heaven.
[40]永訣 separated for ever—death.
永誓 a perpetual oath that one will see the thing through.
永逝 the long journey—death.
永遠 perpetually; eternally; for ever.
永遠不死 shall never die.
[45]永遠有效 lasting effects.
永遠監禁 life imprisonment.
永遠租借 perpetual leasehold.

泳[3] To dive.
7590 Also read *yung*[3]; *yün*[4].

泳氣鐘 a diving-bell.
游泳 to swim and dive.

詠咏[3] To sing; to hum; to chant.
7591 Also read *yün*[1].

詠嘆 to sigh and chant.
詠歎淫洪 to con over till one is overflowing—quite familiar with it.
詠歸 to return home with singing.
詠詩 to read over verses in a sing-song voice.
唱詠 to sing.

YÜ. (ㄩ)
(Ü)

于[2] To proceed.
7592 Distinguish 干 No. 3211.

于歸 to go as a bride to the house of the bridegroom.

(a) Inter. 於 No. 7643. On; to; with; from, etc.

圩[2] A dike; an embankment. Used in Shanghai for a *lot* of land.
7593

圩岸 a dike; an embankment.
圩田 fields protected by dikes.
圩長 (*chang*[3]) an overseer of dikes.

宇[3] The canopy of heaven; space. To cover; to shelter.
7594

宇下 or 宇內 under heaven; within the universe.
宇內知名 their names were well-known in the world.
宇宙 the universe; cosmos.
宇宙創造說 creationism.
[5]宇宙律 the laws of the universe.
宇宙神敎 universalism—that all will be saved.
宇宙觀 the cosmological view.
土宇 territory.
託人宇下 under the protection of.

(a) The part of a house sheltered by the eaves.

屋宇 houses.
廟宇 temples.
眉宇 the face, i.e., under the eaves of the eyebrows.

盂 盂[2] A basin; a large cup.
7595

盂方則水方 if the bowl be square, the water in it will also be square—denoting the great influence of the prince in moulding the people.
盂鉢 basins and bowls.
吐盂 a spittoon.
痰盂 a spittoon.
盤盂 plates, bowls, etc.
鎗盂·子 cartridges for small arms.

(a) Used in transliterating.

盂蘭盆會 the festival held on the 15th of the 7th lunar month for the deliverance of hungry ghosts—often spoken of as the

Feast of All Souls—from the Sanskrit :-*ullambhana,* deliverance.

竽² A musical instrument consisting of thirty-six reed pipes.
7596
　　See 濫 No. 3800-15,16.

紆¹ To twist; to distort. A cord.
7597
紆 廻 circuitous; indirect.
紆 徐 to walk slowly.
紆 曲 vague; indistinct; distorted.
紆 傺 vague—as speech.

(a) Melancholy; fretting.

紆 軫 discontented; fretting and murmuring against one's lot.
紆 鬱 melancholy and fretting.

芋⁴ The taro and other edible tubers.
7598
芋 葉 the leaves of the taro.
芋·頭 the taro.
芋 子³ the small tubers of the taro.
洋 芋 the potato.

迂¹ Vague; wide of the mark; distant. To pervert; to distort.
7599
迂 久 a long time.
迂 儒 a scholar that is behind the times.
迂·夫 子³ an out-of-date scholar.
迂 廻 winding—as a river.
⁵迂 拘 precise; too particular.
迂 曲 crooked; perverted; distorted.
迂 濘 dull; stupid.
迂 緩 slow; dilatory.
迂 腐 inapt; doltish.
¹⁰迂 見 a distorted view; prejudice.
迂 言 words that are not to the point—inapplicable.
迂 誕 absurd.
迂 道 a roundabout road; a detour.
迂 遠 而 闊 于 事 情 impracticable and inapplicable to affairs —said of the teaching of Mencius.
¹⁵迂 闊 impracticable; wide of the mark; bigoted.
子 之 迂 也 you are wide of the mark, sir.

恐 人 迂 乃 心 I am afraid that men will pervert your minds.

釪² An alms bowl. A small bell.
7600

予² I; me. Inter. 余 No. 7605. Distinguish 矛 No. 4570; 子 No. 6939.
7601
予 不 屑 之 敎 誨 也 者 I refuse, as inconsistent with my character, to teach a man.
予 死 於 道 路 乎 shall I die on the road?

(a) Read *yü³.* Inter. 與 No. 7615. To grant; to confer.

何 以 予 之 what will he give them—for this?
雖 無 予 之 although I have none to give them.

伃 好 ² Handsome and fair. Distinguish 好 No. 2062.
7602

豫 預 ⁴ Beforehand. To prepare; to make ready.
7603
豫 付 to pay in advance.
豫 付 薪 水 to give an advance of salary.
豫 估 to estimate; to forecast.
豫 借 to borrow or draw money in advance.
⁵豫 修 to prepare.
豫 候 to be waiting beforehand.
豫 備 to prepare; to make ready.
豫 備 學 校 a preparatory school.
豫 備 試 驗 preparatory examinations.
¹⁰豫 備 軍 reserve forces.
豫 備 金 appropriations; reserve funds.
豫 像 an antitype; something prefigured.
豫 儲 to provide; to procure; to save up.
豫 先 beforehand.
¹⁵豫 先 備 辦 to keep ready—for use or issue.
豫 先 必 要 的 prerequisite.

豫 先 注 定 predestined; foredoomed.
豫 先 約 定 to provide for.
豫 先 計 畫 to plan beforehand; to forecast.
²⁰豫 先 警 告·的 premonitory.
豫 先 通 告 a preliminary announcement.
豫 兆 a presage; a portent.
豫 卜 to divine beforehand.
豫 向 predisposition.
²⁵豫 告 a preliminary notice.
豫 命 foreordination.
豫 報 to forecast.
天 氣 豫 報 weather forecast.
豫 妥 quite ready.
³⁰豫 定 to decide beforehand; to bespeak; to order or subscribe for—as a newspaper or a new book about to be published.
豫 定 日 期 to fix a time or date.
豫 定·的 結 局 a foregone conclusion.
豫 定 說 the theory of predestination.
豫 審 a preliminary investigation.
³⁵豫 思 premeditation.
豫 想 to presuppose.
豫 戒 to caution; to warn.
豫 支 to take an advance—of wages.
豫 料 to estimate; to forecast.
⁴⁰豫 斷 to judge beforehand.
豫 於 次 before one's turn.
豫 早 beforehand.
豫 期 to do something in anticipation; to do with a view to.
豫 期 必 勝 to anticipate a victory.
⁴⁵豫 杜 to anticipate objections.
豫 查 preliminary investigations.
豫 機 務 to deliberate on State affairs.
豫 決 to predetermine.
豫 泅 to write beforehand.
⁵⁰豫 測 to anticipate; to make plans for.
豫 爲 言 明 to declare clearly beforehand.
豫 留 座 reserved seats.
豫 知 foreknowledge.
豫 示 戰 爭 it forebodes war.
⁵⁵豫 禁 to forbid beforehand.
豫 科 a preparatory course.
豫 算 to estimate; to calculate beforehand; budget.
歲 費 豫 算 annual budget or estimates.

豫 算 委 員 會 Budget Committee.
60 **豫 算 表** a budget statement.
豫 籌 to plan beforehand.
豫 約 a preliminary agreement; to subscribe for a book that is about to be published.
豫 約 券 a coupon for a subscription—as for a book about to be published.
豫 習 preparation—of lessons.
65 **豫 聞** preliminary news or announcements.
豫 行 知 會 to give official notice.
豫 表 to prefigure; presage.
豫 表 凶 事 forbodings of evil.
豫 覺 prescience.
70 **豫 言** prophecy; to predict.
豫 記 to antedate.
豫 謀 forethought.
豫 謀 殺 人 to kill a person by malice prepense.
豫 識 foreknowledge.
75 **豫 證** to bear witness to beforehand.
豫 辦 preliminary preparations.
豫 選 to pre-elect—as by a caucus.
豫 防 to be prepared against.
豫 防 策 precautionary measures.
80 **豫 防 藥** prophylactic medicines.

(a) To be at ease. Pleased; satisfied; comfortable. Indulgent. An excursion. To travel.

不 豫 discontented; dissatisfied.
弗 豫 uncomfortable; not well; ill at ease.
悅 豫 happy; pleased.
戲 豫 dissipation.
暇 豫 pleasurable excursions.
秋 豫 an autumn excursion.
逸 豫 to enjoy oneself; to have pleasure in.

(b) One of the Nine Divisions of ancient China under *Yü* the Great. *See* 九 No. 1198-15. Honan.

豫 州 the central division of ancient China; it comprised the districts of Kaifeng, Kweiteh, Nanyang and Juning in the present Honan, a small portion of Hopei, part of Shantung, the districts of Yingchow and Pochow in Anhwei, and the district of Hsiangyang in Hupeh.
豫 章 a name for Kiangsi.

澦 4 Name of a tributary of the Yangtze River in Szechwan.
7604

余 2 I; me.   Inter. 予 No. 7601.
7605 Distinguish 佘 No. 5694.
余 一 人 or **余 小 子** I, the emperor.
其 如 余 何 what harm can they do me?

畬 2 Fields in the third year of cultivation.
7606

艅 2 A despatch boat.
7607
艅 艎 a fast-sailing boat; a ferry-boat.

餘 2 Overplus; excess; a remainder; a balance. To put by a surplus. The last. Complement of a number, etc.
7608
餘 下 的 the surplus; the balance.
餘 不 到 or **餘 不 起 來** unable to put by—as money.
餘 像 the after-image.
5 **反 餘 像** negative after-image.
正 餘 像 positive after-image.
餘 光 surplus light—that by which others profit without expense to oneself. *See* 分 No. 1851-56.
餘 切 cotangent. (*math*.).
餘 利 profit; earnings; surplus income.
餘 剩 a balance; what is left over.
10 **餘 割** cosecant. (*math*.).
餘 力 surplus energy or strength.
餘 勇 可 賈 I will sell my surplus valour—used to illustrate a person who perseveres until he accomplishes his task.
餘 可 類 推 the rest may be inferred by analogy.
餘 喘 the last gasp of the dying.
15 **餘 地** spare ground; an allowance; a loophole.
餘 外 above and beyond.
餘 多 or **多 餘 的** what is over; the surplus.
餘 夫 extra labourers; youngest sons of feudal retainers who were left to till the land while

their brothers went to fight; also called **餘 子**.
餘 年 the declining years of a man's life.
20 **餘 慶** a surplus of luck—such as comes to virtuous families.
餘 數 the balance; the remainder in division; complement of a number.
餘 暇 leisure; spare time.
餘 暉 the rays of the setting sun.
餘 款 the balance; surplus money.
25 **餘 步** an allowance; a loophole. *See above*—13.
餘 波 the swell after a storm—the trouble is not quite over.
餘 瀝 the last drops—of the rain; of wine, etc.
餘 燼 the remaining ashes—defeated troops.
餘 甘 after sweetness—a name for the olive.
30 **餘 生** the declining years of one's life.
虎 口 餘 生 barely escaping from the tiger's mouth with one's life—used for a narrow escape.
餘 福 abundant blessing.
餘 絃 cosine. (*math*.).
餘 羨 or **富 餘** an abundance of; having abundance.
35 **餘 者** the rest; a balance.
餘 興 (*hsing*4) an extra entertainment at the close of the play.
餘 色 complementary colours.
餘 蓄 savings.
餘 裕 wealthy; having abundance.
40 **餘 角** complementary angle.
餘 言 不 盡 I have not been able to say all that I would like—conventional at the close of a letter.
餘 詳 further details.
餘 財 savings; surplus money.
餘 起 來 to put by—as a surplus; to save—as money.
45 **餘 醒** not yet recovered from a drunken stupor.
餘 醜 the rest of the scoundrels.
餘 錢 or **餘 銀** savings; surplus money.
餘 閒 leisure; spare time.
餘 震 after shocks—of an earthquake.
50 **餘 音 繞 梁** the lingering sounds of the music winds around the beams.

餘 額 the balance; a remainder.
餘 額 移 前 balance carried forward.
餘 額 結 前 balance brought forward.
餘 額 轉 下 balance brought down.
⁵⁵餘 額 過 後 balance carried forward.
餘 風 未 殄 there are still lingering remnants of these customs.
餘 鹽 refuse salt.
餘 黨 the rest of the bandits.
其 餘 the rest; the balance.
⁶⁰有 餘 there is a surplus or balance.
無 餘 刑 非 殺 various punishments, only short of death—lit., no end of punishments.
盈 餘 over and above; extra.
農 有 餘 粟 女 有 餘 布 the farmers will have surplus grain, and the women will have surplus cloth—because of the lack of communications whereby these things could be distributed to other places.

臾²
7609
A moment; a little while.

不 可 須 臾 離 也 (the path) may not be left for an instant.

(a) Read k'uei⁴. u.f. 蕢 No. 3667. A basket.

(b) Read yung³. u.f. 慂 No. 7573. To excite, etc.

縱 臾 to urge; to egg on.

庾 庾 斞³
7610
A stack of grain. A measure of 16 斗. Distinguish 廋 No. 5471; 瘦 No. 5848. Also read yü⁴.

瘐³
7611
To die in prison from cold and hunger. To treat with cruelty. Distinguish 瘦 No. 5848.

瘐 死 獄 中 starved to death in the prison.
瘐 斃 水 手 人 they maltreated the sailors so that they died.

瘐 瘐 而 未 起 weak and unable to get up.

腴²
7612
The fat on the belly of animals. Rich, as good soil.

腴 濃 之 味 a rich, luscious taste.
膏 腴 rich and fertile.
華 腴 luxurious extravagance.

諛²
7613
To flatter.

諛 慕 flattering epitaphs.
諛 色 a simpering, toadying expression.
諛 言 flattery.
面 諛 to flatter to one's face.

舁 2.4.
7614
To raise up; to lift up; to carry. Distinguish 舁 No. 5096.

舁 夫 a porter; a coolie.
舁 扛 to carry on a pole.
舁 拱 or 舁 舉 to raise up; to offer up.
舁 牀 a stretcher.

與 与³
7615
With; by; to; or; and. Distinguish 與 No. 2753.

與 人 不 同 unlike others.
與 他 不 同 different from him.
與 他 何 干 what concern is it of his?
與 他 同 年 the same age as he is.
⁵與 你 玩 笑 joking with you.
與 你 走 I'll go with you.
與 其 .... 不 如 (or 寧) rather than...it is better to....; as compared with...; there is nothing equal to....
與 其 不 孫 也 寧 固 it is better to be mean than insubordinate.
與 其 史 也 寧 野 be rustic rather than pedantic.
¹⁰與 其 奢 也 寧 儉 it is better to be sparing than extravagant.
與 其 媚 於 奧 寧 媚 於 竈 better flatter the furnace than the south-west corner—i.e., flatter the spirits that inhabit these places by sacrificing to them.

與 其 易 也 寧 戚 it is better that there be a deep sorrow rather than a minute observance of ritual—in mourning.
與 匪 類 相 交 to associate with profligates.
與 原 議 不 符 not in accordance with the original agreement.
¹⁵與 及 as also; together with.
與 國 交 in communication with his subjects.
與 天 地 並 立 爲 三 he stands as one of three on an equality with Heaven and Earth—referring to the Sage.
與 天 象 昭 然 clear, like the signs of heaven.
與 我 無 干 no concern of mine.
²⁰與 朋 友 交 in intercourse with friends.
與 朋 友 共 to share with friends.
與⁴ 權 to weigh matters together—to see how they stand in regard to true principles.
與 民 由 之 to carry out his principles in connection with the people—for their benefit.
與 理 不 合 not conformable to reason.
²⁵與⁴ 立 to stand together in court.
義 之 與 比 the according with and keeping near to righteousness.

(a) To give to. To grant. To concede to. To allow.

與 之 gave it to him.
與 人 物 to give a person something.
與 其 潔 也 不 保 其 往 也 I allow his present purity, I do not guarantee his past life.
與 其 進 也 不 與 其 退 也 I take notice of his entrance, not of what he does when he has left.
⁵與 料 or 與 物 data.
吾 與 女 弗 如 也 I grant you, you are not equal to him.
吾 與 點 也 I give my approval to Tien.
天 與 之 God gave it to him.
苟 亦 無 與 do not readily approve....

(b) To wait for.

歲 不 我 與 the years do not wait for us.

(c) Read *yü*². A particle used to express doubt or surprise; it is also used interrogatively, generally implying an answer in the affirmative. Inter. next.

其 此 之 謂 與 Is not this what is said—in the Odes?

其 爲 仁 之 本 與 Are they not the root of all benevolent actions?—referring to filial piety and brotherly submission.

可 得 聞 與 May I hear it?

於 予 與 何 誅 This Yü! What is the use of reproving him?

求 之 與 抑 與 之 與 Does he ask his information, or is it given to him?

舜 其 大 知 與 There was *Shun*: — he indeed was greatly wise!

道 之 將 行 也 與 if my principles are to advance, it is so ordered.

(d) Read *yü*¹. The appearance of dignity; self-satisfaction.

與 與 如 也 grave but self-possessed.

(e) Read *yü*⁴. To share in. To be present at. To be concerned about.

與 人 事 to take part in human affairs.

不 得 與 cannot interfere in.

可 以 與 知 焉 "may intermeddle with the knowledge of it."

吾 不 與 祭 如 不 祭 I consider my not being present at the sacrifice as if I did not sacrifice.

吾 其 與 聞 之 I should have been consulted about it.

而 不 與 焉 as if it were nothing to him.

歟² A final particle indicative of admiration, doubt, surprise, etc.; also used interrogatively. Inter. preceding —C.
7616

也 歟 it is so!

嗟 歟 Alas!

猗 歟 How admirable!

誰 歟 知 Who knows?

譽² To eulogize; to praise; to flatter.
7617

譽 之 不 喜 he is not pleased with flattery.

譽 善 to commend goodness.

揚 譽 to praise.

面 譽 to praise to one's face.

(a) Read *yü*⁴. Fame; praise.

譽 望 a good reputation.

譽 處 fame and prosperity.

名 譽 fame and praise; reputation.

廣 譽 a far-reaching reputation.

清 譽 a clean reputation.

輿 轝² The bottom of a carriage. A carriage or chariot; a sedan-chair.
7618

輿 丁 carriers for sedan-chairs.

輿 人 a carriage-builder; a crowd.

輿 梁 成 the bridges for cart traffic were finished.

輿 皂 a menial.

⁵輿 臺 menials.

輿 薪 a cartload of firing.

輿 車 a small carriage.

輿 馬 carriages and horses.

肩 輿 a sedan-chair for two bearers.

(a) To contain; to hold—from whence comes:—the earth, the people, public, etc.
See 堪 No. 3254—B.

輿 圖 a map of the world.

輿 地 or 地 輿 geography.

輿 地 學 the study of geography; geography as a study.

輿 宅 the grave.

⁵輿 情 popular feeling.

俯 順 輿 情 to yield to popular opinions.

輿 論 public opinion.

輿 論 攻 擊 popular opposition.

輿 論 沸 騰 popular opinion is very disturbed.

舉²
7618a The eastern jackdaw.

旟² A banner emblazoned with falcons, displayed by high officials in feudal times. Naturally wavy hair.
7619

禹³ The name of the reputed founder of the *Hsia* 夏 dynasty, 2205 B.C.
7620

禹 惡 (*wu*⁴) 旨 酒 *Yü* detested the best wine.

禹 穴 name of a defile in the *Wu* mountains, one of the Yangtze gorges.

禹 餘 糧 the remnant of *Yü's* rations—supposed to have been thrown into the water and to have produced a waterplant known as 麥 門 冬.

禺² A monkey. To begin.
7621

禺 中 from 9 to 11 a.m.

禺 淵 the place where the sun sets.

禺 谷 the valley where the sun sets.

端 禺 the beginnings; inception; origin.

寓⁴ To lodge in; to sojourn; to dwell. Metaphor.
7622

寓 兵 于 民 to quarter troops on the people.

寓 居 or 寄 寓 or 僑 寓 to reside at.

寓 意 to entertain a thought.

寓 懷 in one's mind or thoughts.

⁵寓 戒 the hidden moral—of a story.

寓 所 a lodging; a residence.

寓 書 to send a letter to.

寓 次 a dwelling; a lodging.

寓 目 to have a view to.

¹⁰寓 處 a dwelling; a lodging; a residence.

寓 言 metaphor; allegory; fable.

借 寓 to borrow a lodging.

安 寓 客 商 comfortable lodgings for travelling merchants—an inn-sign.

客 寓 an inn.

¹⁵小 寓 to reside temporarily.

旅 寓 an inn; a lodging-place.

流 寓 a residence when one is living away from home.

留 寓 to take in as a lodger.

嵎²
7623 A mountain range.

嵎 夷 the eastern extremity of the ancient Chinese empire under *Yao*.

愚 [2] Stupid; doltish; rude; simple.

7624

愚 下 conventional phrase—I, your humble servant, etc.

愚 人 a fool; a blockhead.

愚 商 unlettered tradesmen.

愚 問 a foolish question.

[5]愚 夫 a foolish fellow.

愚 妄 ignorant and senseless.

愚 弄 to make sport of; to deceive.

愚 弟 your humble servant; I, etc. —conventional phrase.

愚 弱 feeble-minded.

[10]愚 忠 simple but loyal.

愚 忠 愚 孝 simple but loyal and filial.

愚 懦 stupid and feeble.

愚 拙 foolish; stupid.

愚 昧 dark in mind; foolish.

[15]愚 民 the masses; the common people.

愚 濁 muddled; dull and foolish.

愚 狂 conceited and foolish; braggadocio.

愚 直 (my words are) blunt and not to the point—a conventional phrase.

愚 笨 stupid; loutish.

[20]愚 者 your humble servant; I, etc. —a conventional phrase.

愚 者 不 及 也 the stupid do not come up to it—the right Way.

愚 者 豈 無 一 得 has a stupid person not even one accomplishment?

愚 聞 之 師 曰 I have heard my master say....

愚 蒙 simple; stupid.

[25]愚 蠢 blunt-witted.

愚 見 my humble opinion.

愚 見 所 及 as far as my humble opinion goes....

愚 謂 in my humble opinion; I should say....

愚 鈍 obtuse; dull in mind.

[30]愚 陋 stupid and vulgar; rustic.

愚 頑 obstinate; irrational; folly.

愚 駿 stupid.

愚 魯 ignorant and stupid.

夫 婦 之 愚 common people, however ignorant....

[35]雖 愚 必 明 although dull, he will surely become intelligent.

遇 [4] To meet; to happen; to occur. To entertain; to receive.

7625

遇·不 着 to miss meeting.(-*chao*[2])

遇 事 when something happens.

遇 事 則 迷 in an emergency he gets muddled—he lacks presence of mind.

遇 事 生 風 to make mischief.

[5]遇 人 to meet a person.

遇 合 難 期 it is hard to say when we shall meet again.

遇·得 見 met; able to meet.

遇 急 to meet with difficulties; to meet a crisis.

遇 敵 to encounter the foe.

[10]遇 時 to meet the opportune time; to be lucky.

生 不 遇 時 born in a wrong age—unlucky.

遇 有 should there be...; in the event of there being....

遇 有 事 in the event of anything happening.

遇 緣 to meet with one's affinity; to get a chance of good luck.

[15]遇 着 to meet with. (--*chao*)

遇·見 to meet with.

遇 諸 途 met on the road.

遇 豐 年 to meet with a good harvest; to have a prosperous year.

遇 買 主 to meet with a purchaser.

[20]遇 險 in danger; to meet with danger.

遇 險 信 號 signals of distress.

遇 難 to meet with misfortune or difficulty.

遇 難 者 a victim.

遇 雨 caught in the rain.

[25]遇 霧 信 號 fog-signals.

不 約 而 遇 an accidental meeting.

殊 遇 to meet kind treatment.

每 遇 whenever....

相 [1]遇 in agreement.

[30]隆 遇 to meet with kindness at the hands of....

隅 [2] A corner; a nook; a cove; an angle.

7626

隅 反 to infer—from the next:—

舉 一 隅 不 以 三 隅 反 之 if I explain one corner of a subject and he cannot infer the other three from that—I do not continue to

teach him—said by Confucius.

隅 坐 to sit in the corner.

城 隅 the corner of the city wall.

角 隅 an angle; a corner.

髃 腢 [2]

7627

The collar-bone.

俞 兪 [2]

7628

To answer in the affirmative.

兪 允 to accede to a request.

上 竟 兪 其 議 the emperor then adopted his suggestion.

(a) Read *yü*[1]. Quiet.

兪 兪 a quiet and respectful bearing.

喻 俞 [4] A parable. To illustrate; to instruct. To understand. Is acquainted with; knows. Also read *yü*[2]. Inter. 諭 No. 7641.

7629

喻 以 利 害 he explained its advantages and disadvantages.

喻 其 意 he perceived her thoughts.

喻 於 利 is conversant with gain —self-interest.

喻 於 義 is familiar with what is right—public interest and welfare as opposed to self-interest.

[5]喻 言 metaphor.

不 可 喻 indescribable.

不 言 而 喻 it goes without saying.

借 喻 to use as an illustration.

勸 喻 to warn; to admonish.

[10]善 喻 skilled in imparting instruction.

比 喻 for instance; by way of illustration.

譬 喻 an illustration; by way of illustration; for instance.

媮 [2] To slight. To enjoy. Inter. next.

7630

Read *t'ou*[1]. Inter. 偷 No. 6488. Improper; irregular.

媮居幸生 fortunately getting off with one's life—when it would have been more honourable to die.

媮惰 to take one's ease; to shirk work.

媮生 to escape with one's life. *See above*—1.

媮食 caring only about their food.

愉 [2] Contented; happy; to be happy. To please.
7631

愉快 well-contented; comfortable.
愉悦 joyful; glad.
愉愉如也 very pleased.
愉樂 joyful.(-*lê*[4])
愉色 a pleased look.
愉逸 at ease and happy.

愈 [4] To surpass; to excel; more; further.
7632

愈久愈好 the longer the better.
愈加 much more; still; further.
愈己 superior to himself.
愈於已乎 is better than doing away with it altogether.
[5]愈添 much more; further.
愈甚 still; further; much more.
愈疏 to increase the estrangement —between father and child.
憂心愈愈 the sorrow of my heart increases.

(a) Healed. Inter. 瘉 No. 7637.

愈愚 to cure stupidity.
愈飢 to satisfy hunger.
今日愈 I am better today.
今病小愈 today he was a little better.

揄 [2] To show the merits of; to praise.
7633

揄揚 to extol; to recommend.
揄然 laughing and clapping.

(a) To draw out.

揄長袂 with long sleeves flapping.

(b) Read *yu*[2]. To scoop out— grain from a mortar.

或舂或揄 some hull (the grain), some take it from the mortar.

榆 [2] The elm.
7634

榆皮 elm-bark—a tonic medicine.
榆莢 or 榆·錢ん elm-seeds—used as food.

渝 [2] To change. Name of a river near the end of the Great Wall.
7635

渝州 an old name for Chungking in Szechwan.
渝變 to retract—as a promise.
渝盟肆峙 the revocation of a compact and beginning of hostilities.

瑜 [2] The lustre of gems. Excellence; virtues.
7636

瑕不掩瑜 his defects do not hide his excellencies.
瑕瑜互見 had good and bad qualities alternating.

瘉 [3] To be healed; convalescent. To be in trouble.
7637 Also read *yü*[4]. Inter. 愈 No. 7632—A.

痊瘉 cured; quite well again.

(a) Read *yü*[2]. Worthy.

孰爲瘉 who among them is worthy?

窬 [2] A small door or window. A hole in the wall.
7638 Read *t'ou*[4]. To cut through a wall.

窬牆 or 穿窬 to make a hole through a wall.

蝓 [2] A snail.
7638a

褕 [2] A loose garment or cloak.
7639

襍褕 a loose garment or cloak.

(a) Read *yao*[2]. Clothing trimmed with feathers. Fine; beautiful.

褕狄 (or 翟) or 褕狄 a feather-trimmed garment worn by the wives of the highest officials in ancient times.

褕衣 fine clothes.

覦 [2] To long for.
7640

覦心 covetous; desirous.
覬覦 ardently longing for.

(a) To spy upon.

窺覦 to reconnoitre.

諭 [4] To proclaim; to order. An official notice; an edict.
7641

諭仰 to order.
諭令 to order.
諭單 a manifesto; a paper of instructions.
諭委 to delegate; to depute.
[5]諭導 to announce for the guidance of; to order obedience to to a decree.
諭帖 a paper of instructions.
諭旨 an imperial edict.
諭止 to issue orders for the stoppage of.
諭知 to inform by proclamation.
[10]諭示 to notify by proclamation.
諭禁 to prohibit publicly.
諭阻 to issue orders to prevent.
諭飭 to order.
諭飭遵辦 to issue orders for the guidance—of those concerned.
[15]上諭 an imperial edict.
來諭 or 手諭 your commands— conventional in reply to a letter.
曉諭 publicly to notify.
劄諭 orders from a superior.
聖諭 the name of a book—the *Sacred Edict*.
[20]譬諭 an illustration; for instance.
面諭 verbal orders.

逾 [2] To pass over; to exceed. To transgress. Distant.
蹭
7642

逾于 to cross over to; to exceed.
逾分 (*fên*[4]) to exceed one's duties or functions; to trespass in social position.
逾城 to get over the city wall.
逾於五年 to exceed five years.

⁵逾日 to pass a day.
逾時 to pass the time.
不逾時 before long.
逾月 at the expiration of a month.
逾期 to exceed the time-limit.
¹⁰逾格 to go beyond what is proper.
逾牆 to leap a wall.
逾矩 to transgress what is right.
逾節 to go beyond the bounds of propriety; to celebrate a festival.
逾越權限 to exceed one's authority.
¹⁵逾越界限 to go beyond the limits; to go out of bounds.
逾越節 the Passover.
逾過 to exceed; to pass beyond.
逾遠 far distant; to travel far.
逾邁 to pass away—as the years.
逾限 to exceed the limit; to go beyond bounds.

於扲亏 |² In; on; at; by; from. Than. With reference to. Compared with. Inter. 于 No. 7592.
7643

於三年之內 within three years.
於人有益 beneficial to man.
於今 at present; now.
於以見 whereby it appears.
⁵於其所德者 in that by which he was benefited.
於左 on the left—below, in reading.
於後 afterwards; as follows.
於心何忍 where is your patience?
於意云何 what is the meaning?
¹⁰於我如浮雲 they are to me as a floating cloud.
於我殯 let the burial rest with me.
於斯 here; in this place.
於斯為盛 more flourishing than this.
於是 then; thereupon.
¹⁵於是乎 thereupon; with regard to this....
於是日 on that day.
於此 here; in this place.
於民也仁之 he treats the people with kindness.
於滇 in Yunnan.
²⁰於無形中 imperceptibly.

於理甚當 it is quite justifiable.
於該處 in the said place.
於那時 at that time.
於邑 depressed; melancholy.
²⁵問於我 he learned it from me.
易於消化 easy of digestion.
貴於黃金 more precious than gold.

(a) Read wu¹ An interjection.

於乎 Alas! Oh!
於嗟乎 Ah! Oh!
於戲 (hu¹) Alas!—exclamation of regret.
於變時雍 immediately became harmonious.
於穆不已 Ah! profound without end!
於緝熙敬止 how continuous and bright was his reverence for the resting-places!
於菟 a tiger—an expression anciently used in the State of Ts'u.

椇 |⁴ A tray for carrying sacrificial meats.
7644

淤 |¹.⁴ To silt up, as a stream. Mud; sediment.
7645

淤塞不通 the channel is blocked.
淤沙 silt.
淤泥 filthy mud.
淤溉 to irrigate fields with muddy water.
⁵淤漲 to silt up.
淤濁 turbid; muddy.
淤積 to silt up.
淤血 extravasated blood.
淤關 blocked up—as with silt.
¹⁰淤阻 silting up.

瘀 |⁴ Extravasated blood. A contusion.
7646

瘀傷 a bruise; a contusion.
瘀肉 proud-flesh; gangrenous flesh.
瘀血 extravasated blood.

娛 |² To give pleasure to; to amuse; to rejoice. Pleasure.
7647

娛悅 to please; to give pleasure to.

娛樂之場所 places of amusement. (-lê⁴)
娛親 to amuse one's parents.
娛遣 to amuse; to give pleasure to.
娛順 to take pleasure in obliging others.
歡娛 to be pleased.
自娛 to amuse oneself.

虞騪 |² To estimate; to provide against. To think about. Mishap; accident. To be anxious about.
7648

儆戒無虞 admonish yourself to caution, when there seems to be no reason for anxiety.
出入自爾師虞 going out and coming in, seek the judgement of your people about them.
四方無虞 through the four quarters of the empire there is no reason for anxiety.
昊天上帝則不我虞 God in the great heaven does not give a thought to me.
⁵有不虞之譽 there are cases of unexpected praise.
有虞殷自天 and consider (the fate of) Yin as coming from Heaven.
無貳無虞上帝臨女 have no doubts, no anxieties, God is with you.
用戒不虞 be prepared for unforeseen dangers.
防虞 taking precautions against dangers.

(a) Similar to 娛 No. 7647. Happy.

驣虞如 joyful and pleasant.

(b) A sacrifice of repose offered on the day of the funeral when the mourners returned home.

豈若速反而虞乎 would it not have been better, if he had come back hastily to present the sacrifice of repose?

(c) The name of a State.

虞人 a forester.
虞淵 the place where the sun sets.
虞舜 or 有虞氏 or 帝舜 the emperor Shun.

(d) A fabulous beast called the 騶虞; it is known as a righteous beast and is described as a white tiger with black spots; it did not kill living things and only made its appearance when the State was ruled in sincerity and benevolence. Used in the *Odes* as a type of *Wên Wang*.

圄 [3] To imprison. Also read *wu*[3].
7649

敔 [3] An ancient musical instrument which was used to give the signal to cease playing.
7650

語 [3] To talk with. Words; conversation; discourse; phrases; language. A set phrase; a proverb. Soft speech. To give a hint.
7651

語 云 the proverb says....

語 其 理 由 spoke of the cause or reason.

語 冰 to speak of ice—abbreviation of a line from *Chuang tzŭ*—you cannot speak about ice to the summer insects. *See* 夏 No. 2521-21.

語 助 辭 an interjection or particle; an auxiliary word.

[5]語 句 a phrase.

語 句 分 析 analysis of sentences.

語 意 the meaning of a phrase.

語 次 while speaking.

語 氣 wording; expression.

[10]語 法 wording; grammar.

語 源 學 etymology.

語 畫 word-painting.

語 病 speech defect; words with *

語 管 a speaking-trumpet or megaphone.

[15]語 聲 the sound of a voice.

語 言 an expression; a phrase; language. 語言學 linguistics.

語 言 粗 俗 vulgar expressions; patois.　⌈speech intonation.

語 調 the tone of the voice;

語 辭 a word; a particle which usually need not be translated.

[20]語 離 本 題 discursive speech.

語 音 enunciation 語音學 phonetics.

語 體 文 writings in the spoken style; vernacular literature.

＊ possible unintended meanings.

語 鬧 the chattering of birds.

俗 語 a proverb; a common saying.

[25]傳 語 to convey a message.

創 造 新 語 to coin new words.

土 語 dialects.

多 語 的 wordiness.

成 語 ready-made phrases; proverb

[30]手 語 to indicate one's ideas with the hands; sign language.

目 語 to give a hint with the eyes.

短 語 a phrase.

耳 語 to whisper.

英 語 English.

[35]隱 語 mysterious, abstruse sayings; insinuations.

雙 關 語 words having a double meaning; pun.

食 不 語 when eating he did not converse—of Confucius.

(a) Read *yü*[4]. To tell to.

語 之 以 此 spoke to him thus.

語 之 而 不 惰 I tell him something and he is never remiss.

語 人 to tell a person.

居 吾 語 女 sit down, and I will tell them to you.

鋙 [2] A hoe.
7652

鋤 鋙 a hoe; unsuitable; irregular; not well-matched.

(a) Read *yü*[3]. A musical instrument.

(b) Read *wu*[2]. Name of a hill from which a fine kind of steel was brought.

齬 [3] Irregular teeth.
7653

齟 齬 irregular; uneven; friction.

傴 [3] Hunchbacked.
7654

傴 僂 hunchbacked; an attitude of reverence.

嫗 [4] An old woman.
7655

巫 嫗 a witch.

(a) Read *yü*[3]. To brood over; to care for; to protect.

煦 嫗 覆 育 萬 有 to warm and nurse, to cover and produce all things—as Heaven and Earth, respectively.

飫 **嫗** [4] To eat too much; surfeited. To confer.
7656

飫 目 to satisfy the eye.

飫 聞 stale news.

飫 賜 to confer on; to bestow.

嘆 [3.4.] To moan with pain or grief.
7657

羽 [3] Feathers; wings; plumes. A banner of feathers. The fifth note or *la* in the Chinese musical scale. Radical 124.
7658

羽 人 an immortal.

羽 儀 imposing; grand.

羽 化 to become an immortal.

羽 化 而 登 仙 became an immortal and took flight to the regions of immortality—the death of a Taoist priest.

[5]羽 士 or 羽 客 a Taoist priest.

羽 布 bunting; alpaca.

羽 扇 feather fans.

羽 族 the feathered tribes—birds.

羽 旄 plumes and banners.

[10]羽 書 a despatch—from the ancient custom of attaching a feather to the cover as an indication of the need for speed.

羽 林 天 軍 a group of 35 stars in Aquarius.

羽 林 軍 the imperial body-guard.

羽 毛 feathers; plumes.

羽 毛 紗 English camlets.

[15]羽 毛 緞 camlets; lastings.

羽 流 Taoist priests.

羽 紗 English camlets.

羽 綢 imitation camlets; bombazine.

羽 綾 woollen lastings; satinette.

[20]羽 縐 crape lastings.

羽 翼 wings—assistants; helpers.

羽 蟲 birds generally.

羽 衣 garments made of feathers.

羽 類 the feathered tribes—birds.

[25]捌 羽 to preen the feathers.

黨 羽 accomplices; assistants.

圉 [3]
7659　The border; the frontier.

圉守 or 守圉 to guard the frontiers.
疆圉 the frontiers.

(a) A stable. A groom.

圉人 ancient name for an officer in charge of the stables; a groom.
馬圉 a groom.

(b) u.f. 敔 No. 7650.

(c) u.f. 圄 No. 7649.

(d) Read *yü*[4]. To coerce; to restrain. Inter. 禦 No. 7665.

其來也不可圉 you cannot prevent its approach.

(e) Read *yü*[3]. Embarrassed.

圉圉焉 it appeared embarrassed.

齵 [3]　Dirty; useless; weak;
7660　powerless. Cracked; a flaw.

齵惰 weak and indolent.
齵敗 worthless; corrupt.

熨
尉 [4]　To iron. An iron for
7661　smoothing garments.
　　　Also read *yün*[4]. Cf. 6102 A.

熨斗 a flat-iron. (*yün*[4]-)
熨衣服 to iron out clothes.(*yün*[4]-)
熨貼 ironed smooth—used fig., smooth, of compositions; reconciled, etc. (*yü*[4]-)

雨
霝 [3]　Rain. Radical 173.
7662　Distinguish 兩 No. 3953.

雨不破塊 rain which does not break the clods—the gentle rain of the Golden Age.
雨中操場 a covered drill-ground in a school.
雨二指 two fingers' depth of rain.
雨候 the rainy season.
[5]雨傘 an umbrella.

雨具 things for wet weather, umbrellas, rain-garments, etc.
雨前 before the rains—the name given to tea picked before the Grain Rains—a fine quality.
雨布 waterproof cloth.
雨師 the Rain God; one who professes to be able to cause the rain to fall.
[10]雨意 it is about to rain.
雨搭 a shade projecting over a door or window to protect it from the rain.
雨收雲散 the rain stops and the clouds disperse.
雨星 a raindrop.
雨晴 the rain ceases.
[15]雨暘時若 timely rains and sunshine.
雨水 Rain Water—one of the Solar Terms, about February 19—March 4.
雨注 to pour with rain.
雨泣 or 雨淚 tears like rain.
雨淋日炙 wet by the rain and burnt by the sun—the hardships of outdoor toil.
[20]雨淋頭 to be unaware of calamity until it comes upon one.
雨漏 the rain is leaking in.
雨脚 hanging clouds which indicate rain.
雨蛙 a small green frog.
雨蟲 the earthworm.
[25]雨衣 rain-coats; waterproofs.
雨過天青 the blue sky after rain.
雨遮子 a paper umbrella.
雨量[4] the rainfall.
量[2]雨器 a rain-gauge.
[30]雨量計 a rain-gauge.
雨降如注 it is pouring (with rain)
雨集 gathering together as numerous as raindrops.
雨雪交加 rain and snow together.
雨雲 a rain-cloud.
[35]雨霖 continuous rains.
雨露之恩 the bounty of rain and dew—the favour of the emperor.
雨靴 oiled boots for wet weather.
雨點 a raindrop.
雨點一般 like drops of rain—said of falling tears.
[40]一陣雨 a shower of rain.
下雨 it is raining; to rain.

冒雨 to brave the rain.
密雨 fine rain.
微雨 fine, drizzling rain.
[45]時雨 timely, seasonable rains.
暴雨 heavy rains.
未雨綢繆 to prepare for a rainy day.
求雨 to pray for rain.
甘雨 timely rains.
[50]疾雨 heavy rains.
祈 (or 禱) 雨 to pray for rain.
紅雨 red rain—falling peach-blossoms.
苦雨 violent, destructive rains.
落雨 to rain. (*S. dial.*)
[55]過雲雨 a passing shower.

(a) Read *yü*[4]. To rain.

雨粟 it rained grain—when writing was invented.
雨金三日 it rained gold for three days—in the reign of *Fu Hsi*.
雨雪紛紛 a great fall of snow.
矢石雨下 darts and stones fell like rain.

雩 [2]　The summer sacrifice for
7663　rain.

雩雨 to pray for rain.

御
馭 [4]
7664　　　To drive a chariot.

御藝 the art of driving.
御車 to drive a chariot.
御馬 to manage horses; to break in a horse.

(a) To manage. To superintend.

御世 to rule.
御事 to manage affairs.
御眾以寬 to rule the masses with leniency.
御駛 to sail a boat.
統御 to exercise universal authority.

(b) To wait on; to set before, as food; to offer or present to. An attendant.

御侍 or 侍御 an attendant; to wait on; to serve.

御 食 to set food before a person.
傅 御 a principal officer.

(c) Imperial; connected with the emperor.

御 前 in the imperial presence.
御 前 大臣 a Grand Chamberlain.
御 史 a censor,–his duty was to keep the emperor informed on all matters of importance.
御 史 臺 the Censorate.
⁵御 名 an emperor's personal name.
御 園 an imperial garden; a name for Peking.
御 妻 the empress.
御 批 an imperial rescript.
御 書 the imperial autograph.
¹⁰御 服 imperial robes.
御 棍 the imperial sceptre.
御 極 to ascend the throne.
御 河 the grand Canal.
御 營 the imperial guard.
¹⁵御 筆 the imperial autograph.
御 纂 an imperial edition or compilation.
御 街 Peking.
御 衣 imperial robes.
御 覽 for the emperor's inspection.
²⁰御 賜 to bestow imperially.
御 醫 an imperial physician.
御 門 辦 事 to attend at the gate of the palace—to act as a Minister of State.
御 駕 the imperial carriage; the emperor.

(d) Read ya⁴. To invoke; to meet.

以 御 田 祖 we will invoke the Father of Husbandry.
百 兩 御 之 a hundred carriages are meeting her.

禦 ⁴ To withstand; to resist. An opponent. To hinder.
7665 Also read yü³. Inter. preceding.

禦 人 to waylay and rob people.
禦 人 以 口 給 屢 憎 於 人 if you answer others with smartness of speech, you are frequently hated by them.
禦 侮 to resist insult.
禦 外 侮 to resist foreign aggression.
⁵禦 寇 to oppose rebels.
禦 敵 to oppose an enemy.

禦 止 to stop; to hinder.
禦 難 to withstand difficulties.
禦 饑 to ward off hunger.
¹⁰以 禦 寒 氣 in order to keep out the cold.
以 禦 風 寒 in order to keep out the wind and the cold.
抵 禦 to hinder; to oppose.
防 禦 to oppose.
防 禦 線 defense lines.

飫 ⁴ To serve a guest with wine and food.
7665a

玉 玉 ⁴ A gem; a precious stone—particularly refers to jade. Valuable. Used conventionally for "your."
7666 Radical 96.
Also read yü⁵.

玉 不 琢 不 成 器 if jade is not cut and polished, it cannot be made into anything.
玉 京 the city of 玉帝. (Taoist.)
玉 人 a lovely girl; a beautiful woman; a lapidary.
玉 佩 jade pendants to a girdle.
⁵玉 兔 a white hare; the moon, from the hare which is supposed to be there.
玉 器 jade ornaments; a box made of precious stone.
玉 堂 members of the Hanlin Academy.
玉 塵 a name for snow.
玉 女 your daughter.
¹⁰玉 妃 an imperial concubine.
玉 宇 fine buildings; heaven.
玉 容 a beautiful face.
玉 尖 the fingers of a beautiful woman.
玉 屑 a name for snow.
¹⁵玉 山 the jade hill—describing a person's beauty; a hs. in Chekiang.
玉 山 頹 the jade hill is tottering—dead drunk.
玉 工 a lapidary.
玉 帶 a jade girdle.
玉 心 a pure heart.
²⁰玉 成 其 事 to assist a person to complete an affair.
玉 戲 a name for snow.
玉 手 a white hand.
玉 搔 頭 a jade hairpin.
玉 昆 worthy brothers.
²⁵玉 杯 象 箸 jade cups and ivory chopsticks—luxurious extravagance.

玉 桂 cinnamon.
玉 樹 a tree of jade—a handsome or talented young man.
玉 樓 the shoulders; the next world.
玉 液 pearly secretion; dew.
³⁰玉 照 your portrait.
玉 燭 the harmony of the seasons.
玉 版 bamboo shoots; a name for the peony.
玉 版 紙 a fine, pure white paper from Ningkuo in Anhwei.
玉 版 魚 the sturgeon.
³⁵玉 環 a jade bracelet—the moon.
玉 璽 the imperial seal.
玉 皇 大帝 the Supreme Deity of Taoism; he was raised to this position in the Sung dynasty. See 上 No. 5669—A.21.
玉 盒 a box made of jade.
玉 盤 the full moon.
⁴⁰玉 石 jade and stone.
玉 石 不 分 no distinction between jade and stone—indiscriminate slaughter.
玉 石 俱 焚 jade and stone burned together—indiscriminate destruction of good and bad alike.
玉 立 standing like jade—pure, chaste and handsome.
玉 筍 the hand of a beautiful woman.
⁴⁵玉 筋 jade chopsticks; tears.
玉 簪 jade hairpins.
玉 簪 花 the tuberose; also Hosta sieboidiana.
玉 米 maize. A.c. 老玉米.
玉 粒 pearly grains—rice.
⁵⁰玉 色 a bluish green.
玉 蘭 the Magnolia yulan.
玉 蜀 黍 maize.
玉 蟾 a name for the moon.
玉 貌 a beautiful face—your face.
⁵⁵玉 趾 your footsteps.
不 吝 玉 趾 do not refuse to come.
玉 輪 the wheel of jade—the moon.
玉 鏡 the full moon.
玉 雪 pure white.
⁶⁰玉 露 pearly dew—the dew of autumn.
玉 面 a lovely face.
玉 面 狐 狸 a white-faced fox—a pretty woman of loose morals.
玉 顏 a white face.

玉 食 provisions for the emperor; the revenues of the empire; delicacies.

[65] 玉 骨 jade bones—a man of lofty and pure aims.

玉 體 yourself; your person.

玉 髓 chalcedony.

玉 鬢 white hair.

望 賜 玉 音 kindly let me have an answer.

[70] 水 玉 quartz crystal.

碧 玉 green jade.

白 玉 white jade.

裕 [4] Wealthy; abundant; in good circumstances. Generous.
7667

裕 國 便 民 to enrich the State and accommodate the masses.

裕 足 sufficient; ample.

富 裕 wealthy.

寬 裕 liberal; generous.

有 裕 having abundance.

豐 裕 abundance—of crops.

魚 [2] Fish. Radical 195.
7668

魚 之 失 水 a fish out of water.

魚 函 a letter—from various legends that letters have been found in the bellies of fishes.

魚 刺 fish bones.

魚 口 a fish's mouth; a venereal ulcer.

[5] 魚 子 the spawn of fish; the roe of fish.

魚 尾 a fish's tail; the stock of a gun; the fold of a page in a Chinese-bound book.

魚 市 a fish market.

魚 戶 fishermen.

魚 書 a letter—see above—2.

[10] 魚 服 a seal-skin quiver; a disguise.

魚 杈 a fish-spear.

魚 欄 a trap for fish.

魚 毒 a poison made from the boiled flowers of the *Daphne genkwa* 芫草; it is thrown into the water and is said to stupefy the fish.

魚 水 like a fish in water—congenial; amicable relations between ruler and minister or between husband and wife.

[15] 魚 水 和 諧 agreeing like fishes and water—a happy marriage.

魚 池 a fish-pond.

魚 游 釜 中 the fish swimming in the pot—its pleasure is of short duration.

魚 漂 a float for fishing.

魚 爛 之 禍 internal disorders in the State—the bowels of a fish are the first to show signs of decay.

[20] 魚 片 fillets of fish.

魚 狗 a species of kingfisher.

魚 生 粥 minced raw fish with rice gruel. (*Cantonese*)

魚 皮 fish-skins.

魚 皮 韃·子 fish-skin Tartars or Ghiliaks.

[25] 魚 目 混 珠 to mix up fish-eyes and pearls—to confound things that differ **but look alike.**

魚 眼 fishes' eyes; warts; the bubbling of boiling water.

魚 眼 釘 a flat-headed nail.

魚 秧 small fry; minnows.

魚 稅 a tax paid by fishermen.

[30] 魚 竿 a fishing-rod.

魚 笱 a trap for fish.

魚 米 之 鄉 well-watered places where fish and rice are abundant—as in Kiangsi or Hunan.

魚 素 a letter. *See above—*2.

魚 網 a fishing-net.

[35] 魚 線 a fishing-line.

魚 缸 a fish-globe.

魚 翅 the fins of a fish, especially used for the edible shark's fins.

魚 肉 the flesh of fish; fish and flesh.

視 爲 魚 肉 to regard them as fish and flesh—to oppress the people.

[40] 魚 肉 小 民 to make fish and flesh of the people.

魚 肚 (or 胞) fish-maws.

魚 肝 油 cod-liver oil.

魚 肥 fish used as a fertilizer.

魚 膠 isinglass; fish-glue.

[45] 魚 舍 a place where the fish gather together.

魚 苗 small fry; minnows.

魚 虎 the *Diodon holocanthus.*

魚 貫 而 進 coming in succession, one after the other, like fishes.

魚 質 龍 文 the outward marks of a dragon with the disposition of a mere fish—all outward show.

[50] 魚 軒 a carriage ornamented with seal-skin, used in ancient times by a great officer.

魚 還 得² 水 like fishes returning to the water—illustrative of great pleasure, as when old friends meet.

魚 鈎 a fish-hook.

魚 雁 往 來 epistolary correspondence to and fro—from the legends of letters being found in the bellies of fish, and the story of a letter attached to the leg of a goose by *Su Wu* who was a prisoner in Tartary. *See No.* 7404-15.

魚 雷 a torpedo.

[55] 魚 雷 發 射 管 torpedo-tubes.

魚 雷 礮 艦 torpedo-boats.

魚 雷 艇 torpedo-boats.

魚 雷 驅 逐 艦 torpedo-boat destroyers.

魚 食 bait for fishes; to oppress. *See above*—40.

[60] 魚 鰾 the swimming-bladder of fishes.

魚 鱗 the scales of fish—numerous.

魚 鱗 圖 冊 a register of houses, fields, etc. 魚鷹 the cormorant.

魚 鷹·子 the common tern.

魚 鹽 之 鄉 places along the coast which produce fish and salt.

[65] 一 條 魚 or 一 尾 魚 or 一 頭 魚 a fish.

捕 魚 to take fish in a net.

脚 魚 the turtle. ＝ 甲魚.

衣 魚 or 蠹 魚 the silver-fish, an insect that spoils books, clothing, etc.

鈎 魚 to take fish on the hook.

漁 **戫** [2] To fish. To seize.
7669

漁 人 a fisherman.

漁 其 利 he seeks his own gain.

漁 取 to seize on.

漁 夫 a fisherman.

[5] 漁 奪 百 姓 to plunder the people as a fisherman catches fish.

漁 婆 a fishwife.

漁 子 a fisherman.

漁 戶 fishermen.

漁 業 the fishing industry.

[10] 遠 洋 漁 業 deep-sea fisheries.

漁樵耕讀 fishermen, foresters, farmers, and scholars.
漁父 an aged fisherman.
漁翁得利 the fisherman gets the profit. *See* 鷸 No. 7690.
漁船 a fishing-boat.
[15]漁色 inordinate lust, like a fisherman who takes all that comes to his net.

YÜ. (ㄩ)
(Iuh or Ǔ)

峪 [4.5.]
7670　A ravine; a valley.

欲 [4.5.]
7671　To desire; to long for; to wish. On the point of; about to. Inter. next.

欲不可縱 desires must not be gratified.
欲不欲 to desire the absence of desire. (*Taoist*).
欲人勿知莫若勿爲 if you do not wish others to know it, there is nothing better than not doing it.
欲人勿聞莫若勿言 if you wish to prevent others from hearing about it, there is nothing like keeping silence.
[5]欲其稱 (*ch'ên*[4]) 也 wished to be a match for him.
欲前不前 wishing to advance and yet not doing so.
欲圖 to intend.
欲往欲來 undecided as to going.
欲待 to be half inclined to.
[10]欲得 desirous of obtaining; to want.
欲惡 (*wu*[4]) likes and dislikes.
欲望 aspirations; desires; expectations; wishes.
欲止不內 wished to hinder him from entering.
欲求 to desire.
[15]欲海 the sea of desire.
欲炊無米 desirous of cooking the food when he has no rice—impossible.
欲生 to desire life.
欲絕 to the utmost.
欲罷不能 wishing to stop but unable to do so.

[20]欲要 should I want to...; to want to; about to.
欲速不達 undue haste prevents thoroughness.
天欲雨 it is about to rain.
將欲去 about to go.
己所勿欲勿施於人 do not do to others that which you do not wish done to you.
[25]私欲 selfish desires or aims.
隨心所欲 to follow one's own desires.

慾 [4.5.]
7672　Desire; lust; passion; covetous. Inter. preceding.

慾事 passion; lust.
慾壑難塡 the ditch of desire is difficult to fill.
慾情 or 慾心 passion; lust.
慾想 lascivious desires.
[5]慾望 desires; expectations.
慾海 the sea of passion.
慾火焚身 the fire of lust consumes the body.
情慾 lascivious desires; passions; carnal desires.
私慾 the passions; lascivious desires.
[10]節慾 or 戒慾 to restrain the passions.
絕慾 to suppress the passions.
色慾 lascivious desires; carnal passions.

浴 [4.5.]
7673　To wash; to bathe.

浴佛誕 the festival of the bathing of Buddha on the 8th day of the 4th lunar month.
浴堂 or 浴室 a bathing house.
浴尸 to bathe a corpse.
浴德 to bathe oneself in virtue; to cleanse one's moral nature.
[5]浴池 a bathing-pool; a bathing house where all use the same water.
浴潔其身 to wash the body thoroughly clean.
浴盆 a bath-tub.
浴蠶 to wash silkworms in salt water in order to weed out the weaklings.
浴血 as if bathed in blood.
[10]汗浴 a bath of perspiration; a Turkish bath.

沐浴 to bathe.
汽浴 a vapour-bath.
灌水浴 a shower-bath.
補天浴日 to repair the heavens and bathe the sun—a great and meritorious achievement.

(a) To fly up and down like birds.

浴日 the dancing light of the sun on the water in the early morning.

鎔 [4.5.]
7674　A poker. Brass filings. To file.

鵒 [4.5.]
7675　The mynah.

域 [4.5.]
域
7676　A frontier; a boundary; a region; a country. To keep within bounds.

域中 within the bounds of the land. 域外 outlandish; foreign.
異域 a foreign land.
絕域 far-distant lands.
自域 to limit oneself.
西域 Western Regions.

彧 [4.5.]
7677　Elegant; accomplished.

棫 [4.5.]
7678　Thorny shrub bearing a red fruit. A kind of oak.

罭 [4.5.]
7679　A drag-net.

蜮 [4.5.]
7680　A fabulous creature like a turtle; it is said to lie concealed at the bottom of a stream, and when the shadow of a person is cast on the water it casts sand out of its mouth at it, after which the person is sure to die. It is also called 射工. A toad. A worm which injures growing rice.

鬼蜮之人 a treacherous and malicious person.

閾 7681 4.5.
A door-sill or threshold.

行 不 履 閾 he did not step on the threshold—said of Confucius when he went in and out of the palace.

踰 閾 to go beyond the threshold.

昱 7682 4.5.
Bright light.

昱 嶺 a mountain between Hwei-chow in South Anhwei and Ch'ang Hwa in Chekiang.

日 昱 月 昱 the light of the sun and of the moon, respectively.

煜 7683 4.5.
The blaze of fire; glorious shining. Abundant.

煜 耀 glorious.

聿 7684 4.5.
A pencil. To narrate. Thereupon; suddenly. Radical 129.

聿 來 胥 宇 they came and together chose their dwelling-place.

聿 至 suddenly arrived.

歲 聿 其 莫 the year is drawing to its close.

獄 7685 4.5.
A prison. A trial at law. Litigation.

獄 中 in prison.
獄 吏 or 獄 卒 a gaoler.
獄 官 the keeper of a prison.
獄 牢 a prison.
⁵地 獄 the Buddhist purgatory or hell; the Christian hell.
坐 獄 to be in prison.
折 獄 to decide a case.
收 獄 to put in prison.
斷 獄 to decide a case.
¹⁰煉 獄 a term for Purgatory.
訟 獄 litigation.
越 獄 to break prison.

郁 7686 4.5.
Elegant; adorned; refined.

郁 郁 乎 文 哉 how courteous and elegant are the regulations —of the *Chou* dynasty.

郁 郁 紛 紛 brilliant and beautiful—as clouds.

育 毓 7687 4.5.
To give birth to. To nourish; to bring up.

育 嬰 堂 a foundling hospital.
育 子 to rear a child.
育 德 to nourish one's virtue.
育 成 to raise; to bring to completion.
⁵育 才 to foster talent.
育 蠶 to rear silkworms.
育 養 to bring up.
德 育 moral culture.
教 育 education.
¹⁰智 育 intellectual culture.
生 育 to breed; to give birth to a child.
靈 育 spiritual culture.
體 育 physical culture; physical education.

燠 7688 4.5.
A hot sun. Warmth. Also read *ao*³.

燠 熱 extremely hot.
寒 燠 cold and heat.

矞 7689 4.5.
To bore through with an awl. Agitated. Overflowing. Clouds of three colours.

矞 矞 皇 皇 nature bursting into life.
矞 雲 propitious clouds of three colours.
捧 讀 矞 雲 I have respectfully received and read your esteemed favour.
鳳 以 爲 畜 故 鳥 不 矞 with the phœnix to protect them, the birds are not afraid.

鷸 7690 4.5.
The snipe. The turquoise kingfisher.

鷸 蚌 相 持 漁 翁 得 利 when the snipe and the mussel grip each other, the fisherman gets the profit—the bird's beak was caught by the mussel and neither would yield.
北 鷸 Swinhoe's snipe.
山 鷸 the woodcock.
彩 鷸 the painted snipe.

⁵澤 鷸 the marsh sandpiper.
磯 鷸 the common sandpiper.
翠 鷸 the turquoise kingfisher.
麻 鷸 the common curlew.

鬻 7691 4.5.
To sell; to buy. To nourish. Also read *chu*⁴·⁵.

鬻 女 to sell one's daughters.
自 鬻 to sell oneself.

(a) Read *chu*¹·⁵. Inter. No. 1384. Rice-gruel.

欝 鬱 鬰 7692 4.5.
Anxious; grieved; depressed.

鬱 悠 anxiously.
鬱 悶 depressed; melancholy.
鬱 氣 repressed, pent-up feeling.
氣 鬱 症 hysterics.
⁵鬱 結 sullen; depressed.
鬱 邑 grieved; melancholy.
鬱 陶 harassed; anxiously.
鬱 鬱 不 樂 melancholy; churlish.
鬱 鬱 成 病 ill with grief.
¹⁰鬱 鬱 而 亡 died of grief.
憂 鬱 病 hypochondria.
肝 鬱 不 舒 sluggish liver.

(a) Bushy; growing thickly together.

鬱 蔥 flourishing; dense growth.

(b) A fragrant herb.

鬱 金 *Curcoma longa*.
鬱 郁 fragrant.

(c) *Prunus japonica*.

(d) The name of a door-god.

鬱 壘 the second of the two figures painted or pasted on doors as guardian door-gods. *See* 荼 No. 6526—D.

籲 籥 7693 4.
To implore; to beseech; to invoke. To select. (Also read *yo*⁴·⁵.)

籲 天 to cry to God.
籲 懇 to pray earnestly.
籲 求 to implore.
籲 禱 to pray to.
呼 籲 to cry out to.

YÜEH. (ㄩㄝ)
(See also p. 1122 ff.)
(Üeh)

曰 **7694** 1.5. To speak; it is said.
Radical 73.

曰 修身 也 ...namely, the cultivation of their own characters.

曰 君臣 也 ...namely, those between prince and minister....

不 曰 ... if a man does not say....

子 曰 the Master said....

⁵對 曰 said in reply—to a superior.

故 曰 ...hence it is said....

無 曰 not to speak of....

蓋 曰 天之所以爲天 也 t h e meaning is, that it is thus that Heaven is Heaven.

詩 曰 it is said in the Odes....

(a) Used as an expletive.

曰 旣醉 止 but when they have drunk too much.

曰 歸 曰 歸 When shall we return? When shall we return?

借 曰 未 知 still, perhaps you do not know.

其 湛 曰 樂 they are happy and delighted.

⁵旣 曰 告 止 since such an announcement was made.

旣 曰 歸 止 since she went to her husband's home.

昊 天 曰 明 Great Heaven is intelligent.

是 曰 thus.

見 睍 曰 流 but when it feels the sun's heat, it flows away.

汩 **7695** 4.5. To flow fast, as a stream.
Distinguish 汩 No. 3482.

汩 流 rushing, as a torrent.
奔 汩 rushing, as a torrent.
拂 汩 the bubbling of a spring.

(a) Bright.

越 汩 lustrous; bright.

(b) To go through, as a stream.

(c) Read *ku*³ u.f. 汩 No. 3482.

月 **7696** 4.5. The moon; a month.
Radical 74.

月 下 beneath the moon; at night.
月 下 香 the tuberose.
月 事 the menses.
月·亮 the moon; moonlight.
⁵半·個 月·亮 a half-moon.
月 令 the seasons.
月 例 monthly allowances to dependants.
月 信 the menses.
月 俸 (or 奉) monthly salary or allowance.
¹⁰月 光 moonlight.
月·分 牌 a date-block; a calendar.
月 刊 a monthly publication.
半 月 刊 a fortnightly publication.
月 初 the beginning of the month.
¹⁵月 初 生 時 at the time of the new moon.
月 半 the 15th of the lunar month.
半·個 月 a fortnight; half a month.
月 吉 the first day of the month.
月 圓 the full moon.
²⁰月 城 a sort of courtyard within the outer gate of a city having gates leading into the city itself.
月 夕 a moonlight night; the Mid-Autumn Festival on the 15th of the 8th lunar month.
月 大 a month of thirty days in the lunar calendar.
月 娥 the fairy who is supposed to dwell in the moon.
月·子 the month following a woman's confinement; a bull's-eye.
²⁵坐 月·子 the time of a woman's confinement.
小 月·子 a miscarriage.
月·季 the monthly rose.
月 官 the officers for the month—formerly appointed at the monthly drawings of the Board of Civil Office.
月 宮 or 月 府 the palace of the moon.
³⁰月 小 a month of twenty-nine days in the lunar calendar.
月 尾 the end of the month.
月 山 the Mountains of the Moon.
月 底 the end of the month.
月 弦 the quarters of the moon.
³⁵月 旦 the first day of the lunar month.
月 旦 評 a criticism—a m a n named 許 劭 *Hsü Shao* of the *Han* dynasty devoted the first of the month to w r i t i n g

criticisms of things in general.
月 明 moonlight.
月 明 星 稀 when the moon is bright, the stars are few—used figuratively.
月 晦 之 日 the last day of the lunar month.
⁴⁰月 暈 a halo round the moon.
月 暈 爲 風 a halo round the moon indicates wind—anticipation of future events.
月 曜 日 used by some for Monday. (*Jap.*).
月 月 or 每 月 monthly.
月 月 紅 the monthly rose.
⁴⁵月 望 the full moon.
月 朔 the new moon; the first of the lunar month.
月 期 票 a monthly ticket.
月 桂 the laurel.
月 桂 冠 a laurel wreath.
⁵⁰月 水 the menses.
月 淡 星 稀 as the moon grows pale and the stars dwindle—at dawn.
月 滿 the full moon.
做 滿 月 to celebrate the completion of the first month of a child's life.
滿 月 at the end of a month; the full moon; the end of the first month after childbirth.
⁵⁵月 牙ₙ or 蛾 眉 月 the new moon.
月 牙 圈 crescentic; semi-circular.
月 牙 棹·子 a half-round table.
月 牙 鍬 a half-round spade—*Buddhist.*
月 琴 a moon-shaped guitar.
⁶⁰月 當 頭 the full moon of the 11th lunar month.
月 白 a very pale blue.
月 盈 the full moon.
月 盡 頭 the end of a month.
月 石 moonstone.
⁶⁵月 終 the end of the month.
月 給 monthly allowance.(-*chi*³)
月 經 the menses.
月 老 or 月 下 老 人 a god,—the old man of the moon,—he is supposed to unite by an invisible thread those persons destined to be married.
月 脚 the rays of moonlight.
⁷⁰月 臺 a platform, as of a railway station or of a car.
月 臺 票 a platform ticket.
月 色 moonlight.

月 菊 the China aster.

月 華 a lunar corona.

[75] 月 薪 the monthly salary, as of a teacher.

月 角 the right temple.

月 計 monthly accounts.

月 課 a monthly trial for composing essays.

月 貌 a full, round face.

[80] 月 輪 the disc of the moon.

月 錢 monthly allowance of money.

月 闌 a halo round the moon.

月 難 to die in childbed.

月 蝕 or 月 食 a lunar eclipse.

[85] 月·餅 moon cakes, eaten at the Mid-Autumn Festival on the 15th of the 8th lunar month.

月 魄 the part of the moon which is not illuminated.

月 魚 the moonfish.

月 黑 天 a moonless night.

上·月 last month.

[90] 下·月 next month.

四 個 月 four months.

四·月 the fourth month.

帶 月 by moonlight.

按 月 by the month.

[95] 新 月 the new moon.

步 月 to stroll in the moonlight.

水 月 the reflection of the moon in water.

論 月 reckoning by the month.

賞 月 to enjoy the moonlight.

[100] 閏 月 an intercalary month.

(a) Used in transliterating.

月 氏 (*chih*[1]) the name of a nomadic people. *See No. 5785—A.*

刖 4.5.   To cut off the feet as a punishment.
7697

捌 4.5.   To bend.
7698   [(-shê[2]-)

捌 折·了 to snap in bending.

捌·過·來 to bend a thing over.

越 4.5.   To overpass; to exceed; to transgress; to encroach.
7699   Sign of the comparative, more. Thereupon.

越 久 越 惡 the longer they continue the worse they become(-*o*[4])

越 以 and then; thereupon.

越 俎 to exceed one's duty and meddle in the affairs of another. *See No. 6812-5.*

越 分 (*fên*[4]) to overstep the bounds; to overstep one's duty.

[5] 越 哉 Alas! too much!

越 境 to encroach.

越 多 越 好 the more the better.

越 宿 to pass the night.

越 宿 不 候 I will not wait for you beyond tonight.

[10] 越 年 after a year.

越 席 to leave one's place at table and take a higher seat.

越 快 越 好 the faster the better.

越 性 gratuitously.

越 日 the next day; after a day.

[15] 越 早 越 好 the earlier the better.

越 月 after a month.

越 次 out of sequence.

越 法 to transgress the laws of propriety.

越 牆 to get over a wall.

[20] 越 獄 to break prison.

越 理 quite unreasonable.

越 界 to encroach on the territory of another.

越·發 much more.

越·發 好 still better.

[25] 越 禮 to overstep propriety; to be rude.

越 禮 犯 分 to go beyond one's position in life.

越 等 to overstep one's proper rank.

越 級 to skip a grade—as in promotion, etc.

越 若 來 thereupon.

[30] 越 訴 to appeal to a higher court in an irregular manner.

越 蹈 to trespass on.

越 軌 out of the usual rut.

越 過 to transgress; to cross over; to go beyond.

越 過 重·量 overweight.

[35] 越 限 to transgress the limit.

越 階 to overstep one's proper rank.

亦 越 and moreover.

(a) Name of a feudal State. Used for Kuangtung; Annam.

越 南 Annam.

越 國 the ancient State which occupied the present Fukien and Chekiang.

越 王 鳥 the royal bird of Annam —the hornbill.

越 瓜 a kind of melon which first came from the south.

[5] 越 雉 a partridge.

越 鳥 a name for the peacock—the bird from the south.

南 越 an old kingdom which occupied the territory of the present Kuangtung, Kuangsi, and Tongking.

吳 越 the names of two rival feudal States. Kiangsu and Chekiang.

樾 4.5.   The shade of trees.
7700

鉞 戉 4.5.   A battle-axe; a halberd.
7701

鉞 斧 halberds and battle-axes.

悅 4.5.   Pleased; contented; glad; happy. To acquiesce; to give pleasure to.
7702

悅 口 to please the taste.

悅 從 to acquiesce in; to assent.

悅 心·的 acceptable; pleasing.

悅 意 pleasure; pleasantness.

[5] 悅 服 to acquiesce in; to assent.

悅 目 to please the eye.

悅 納 to accept; to delight in.

悅 耳 to please the ear.

悅 豫 pleased; delighted.

[10] 不 悅 displeased.

喜 悅 delighted; joyful.

難 以 取 悅 hard to please.

閱 4.5.   To examine; to inspect; to review. To look over; to read carefully. To pass through.
7703

閱 人 多 矣 having had much experience of men.

閱 兵 to review troops. [papers.

閱 卷 to examine an essay; to mark [examination

閱 報 to read the newspaper.

[5] 閱 報室 reading-room.

閱 實 其 罪 ascertained the facts about his crimes.

閱 悉 to make oneself thoroughly acquainted with.

閱 核 to examine; to peruse.

閱 歷 to experience; experienced; versed in.

[10]閱 演 to inspect.

閱 看 to examine; to view; to survey.

閱 簡 to superintend.

閱 視 to view; to examine.

閱 射 to review archers.

[15]閱 遍 to make a provincial tour—as a Viceroy.

閱 邊 to inspect the frontier.

閱 驗 to examine; to peruse.

評 閱 to examine critically.

粵 4.5. The provinces of Kwangtung and Kwangsi, in which sense it is inter. 越 No. 7699.
7704
Distinguish 與 No. 46.

粵 東 Kwangtung.

粵 海 關 the Canton Customs.

粵 海 關 部 the Customs Superintendent at Canton.

粵 漢 鐵 路 the Canton-Hankow Railway.

粵 省 the province of Kwangtung.

粵 西 Kwangsi.

兩 粵 the two provinces of Kwangtung and Kwangsi.

(a) An initial particle for which 曰 was sometimes used. See No. 7694—A.

粵 若 稽 古 examining into antiquity we find....

軏 4.5. The cross-bar at the end of the pole of a carriage.
7705

小 車 無 軏 其 何 以 行 How can a small carriage be made to go without the arrangement for yoking the horses?

噦 1.5. To belch; to vomit.
7706

乾 噦 to retch without vomiting.

(a) Read *hui*[1]. Wide and deep; spacious. Tinkling, as of bells.

YÜAN.   (ㄩㄢ)
(Üen)

元 [2] The first; the head; the chief. The eldest; the
7707 principal. A head. The *Book of Changes.*

元 亨 利 貞 the opening phrase of the *Book of Changes,* used to denote 1, 2, 3, 4; or 1st, 2nd, 3rd, 4th.

元 位 standard.

元 來 original; primal.

元 元 本 本 from the very beginning.

[5]元 化 the transforming influence of the virtue of a ruler; the beginning of creation.

元 后 the sovereign; the emperor.

元 君 Taoist term for a female immortal.

元 因 the first cause.

元 夕 or 元 夜 the first full moon of the lunar year.

[10]元 始 the beginning; the first cause.

元 始 天 尊 The Primal Celestial Excellency—a Taoist deity.

元 子[3] an atom; the eldest son. *See* 原 No. 7725-42.

元 字 algebraical symbols, as a, b, c, x, y, z, etc.

元 孫 a grandson's grandson.

[15]元 宵 the 15th of the 1st lunar month.

[15½]元·宵 the small round dumplings of rice-flour eaten on that day; percussion music played on that day.

元 帥 a leader; a generalissimo.

元 年 the first year of a reign.

元 形 the original form.

元 戎 a chariot; a general in charge.

[20]元 旦 or 元 日 New Year's Day.

元 月 the first month of a year.

元 服 a cap.

加 元 服 to be crowned.

元 朔 the first new moon of the year—New Year's Day.

[25]元 本 principal or capital as opposed to interest.

元 機 the scheme of creation.

元 正 the first day of the new year.

元 氣 primeval influences—the protoplasm of Chinese theories of evolution; a man's constitution.

大 傷 元 氣 greatly injured his constitution.

[30] 精·神 元 氣 one's vitality and constitution.

元 氣 不 足 his constitution is not sound.

元 物 natural fruit. (*legal*).

元 祖 the first ancestor; the founder of.

元 神 the soul; the constitution; the primeval influences of creation.

[35]元 票 the original warrant.

元 精 a man's original constitution. (*Taoist*).

元 素 original elements.

元 色 the original colour.

元 號 the first. No. 1.

[40]元 質 elementary substances; elements.

元 辰 the first day of the lunar year—a lucky day.

元 配 a man's first wife.

元 金 principal as opposed to interest. 元 音 vowel.

元 首 the head; the leader; the chief executive.

[45]元 首 明 哉 how intelligent is our monarch!

元 魁 first on the list of sucessful candidates for the former second and third degrees.

元 點 a molecule. Cf. 1851 B.6.

上 元 the 15th of the 2nd lunar month.

下 元 the 15th of the 10th lunar month.

[50]中 元 the 15th of the 7th lunar month.

勇 士 不 忘 喪[4] 其 元 the valiant officer does not forget that he may lose his head.

復 元 to recover one's health.

改 元 to change the year-title of a reigning monarch.

還 元 resolved into its elements.

(a) The Mongol dynasty.

元·寶 large ingots of silver weighing about 50 ozs., first made under the Yüan dynasty, hence the name; the same term is used for the mock ingots of tinfoil paper used in idolatry.

元·朝 the Yüan or Mongol dynasty.

元 鍱 small ingots of silver weighing about 10 ozs.

(b) Good; large; great.

元 元 or 黎 元 the masses.

子 惠 元 元 to treat the people as if they were one's children.

元 勳 great distinction.

元 吉 great joy.

[5]元 命 the great appointment—the throne.

元 老 very old.

元 良 greatly good.

元 龜 a large tortoise.

允 元 trust the good.

(c) A dollar. u.f. 圓 No. 7722.

(d) u.f. 玄 No. 2881. Black.

元 駒 a black colt—ants.

元 鳥 the black bird—a swallow.

沅 [2] A long and narrow river in the west of Hunan, flow-
7708 ing into the Tungting Lake.

芫 [2] A plant, the *Daphne yen-*
kwa. See 魚 No. 7668-13.
7709

芫 荽 coriander.

芫 青 a beetle—dried and used as a medicine.

阮 [3] The name of a mountain. The name of a small feudal
7710 State. A surname. Pron. *juan*[3].

黿 [2] The sea turtle, called 黿 鼉
7711

院 [4] A courtyard. A hall; a college; a public building.
7712

院·子 or 院 落 a courtyard, a compound.

院 宅 or 院 宇 premises; residences.

院 宇 深 大 extensive premises.

院 試 or 院 考 the third examination before the Literary Chancellor for the 1st degree under the old system.

[5]博 物 院 a museum.

參 政 院 Advisory Council. Council of State.

司 法 院 Judicial Yüan.

國 務 院 the cabinet.

大 理 院 the former Supreme Court.

[10]孤 兒[2] 院 an orphanage.

學 院 a school or college; the former Literary Chancellor.

審 計 部 the Audit Department.

寺 院 Buddhist monasteries.

平 政 院 the Administrative Court.

[15]書 院 a library; a college.

療 養 醫 院 a sanatorium.

省 務 院 a Provincial Administrative Council.

衆 議 院 the House of Commons.

立 法 院 the Legislative Yüan.

[20]考 試 院 the Examination Yüan.

行 政 院 the Administrative Yüan.

蒙 藏 院 the Bureau of Tibetan and Mongolian Affairs.

議 院 a parliament; congress.

貴 族 院 the House of Lords.

[25]醫 院 a hospital.

養 老 院 an asylum for the aged poor.

高 級 法 院 the Supreme Court.

夗 [3] To turn over when asleep.
7713

怨 [4] To find fault with; to repine; to murmur against;
7714 to harbour resentment. Hatred.
See 宿 No. 5498—A.7.

怨·不·得 他 去 you can't blame him for going; no wonder he went.

怨 乎 did they repent of this?

怨 (*yüan*[1]) 仇 an enemy.

怨 入 骨 髓 the hatred has entered into his very marrow.

[5]怨 命 to murmur at one's lot in life.

怨 天 to murmur against Heaven—complaining of one's lot in life.

怨 女 a woman with a grievance—a spinster.

怨 (*yüan*[1]) 家 an enemy.

怨 尤 to find fault.

[10]怨 府 a place for harbouring animosity—figurative.

怨·得·他 哭 呢 no wonder he is crying!

怨 忿 a grudge; ill-will on account of wrongs.

怨 思 cherished grievances.

怨·恨 hatred; to hate; to bear a grudge against; animosity.

[15]怨 情 resentment; spite; dissatisfaction.

怨 慕 dissatisfied and desirous—of evil.

怨 懟 to dislike; to hate.

怨 是 用 希 few resentments were shewn them.

怨 望 to have a grievance against one's superiors.

[20]懷 怨 望 to cherish a grievance.

怨 毒 deep, malicious hatred.

怨 氣 resentment; spite; dissatisfaction, ill-will.

怨 耦 an unhappy couple.

怨 聲 murmuring; an expression of discontent.

[25]怨·色[4] an expression of hatred.

怨 言 spiteful words; grumbling; repining.

怨 誰 whose fault is it?

怨 謗 or 怨 讟 to hate and malign.

怨 貧 to repine at poverty.

[30]怨 隙 a cause of hatred.

埋·怨 to brood over a grievance; to nurse one's wrath; to murmur against. (*man*[2]-, or *mai*[2]-)

報 怨 to requite an injury.

多 怨 much odium.

招 怨 to cause others to dislike one; to incur odium.

[35]結 怨 to contract a hatred for.

眢 [1] Eyes without brightness.
7715

眢 目 dull, lack-lustre eyes.

(a) A dry well. Empty.

眢 井 a dry well.

苑 [4] A pasture; a park. A term applied to a collec-
7716 tion of extracts from various authors.

苑 風 a typhoon or tornado.

古 文 苑 a collection of extracts from ancient and later writers.

鴛 [1] The drake of the mandarin duck.
7717

鴛 偶 a faithful spouse.

鴛·鴦 the mandarin duck, male and female, used as an emblem of conjugal fidelity, happiness.

鴛 鴦 劍 a pair of swords in a sheath.

鴛 鴦 枕 a double pillow used by a newly-married couple.

窓[1] To bear a grudge against. Inter. 冤 No. 7719.

7718

窓 屈 a wrong; a grievance.

冤 [1] Oppression; injustice. A grievance; a wrong. To

寃 oppress. To spend reck-

7719 lessly. The second form though commonly used, is not strictly correct.

冤 仇 an enemy; enmity.

冤 哉 枉 也 crying and moaning over one's grievances.

冤 單 a statement of one's grievances.

冤 大 頭 the victim of a racket.

[5]冤 孽 (or 業) retribution for evil deeds committed in a previous existence—used for a married couple who cannot agree.

冤 孽 病 retributive illness.

冤 家 an opponent; an enemy; lovers. See 凤 No. 5502—A. 1.

冤 家 路 窄 the road of enemies is narrow—they will be sure to meet.

冤 屈 a grievance; a wrong; a false charge.

[10]冤 屈 得 伸 to have a wrong redressed.

冤 情 the details of a wrong.

冤 抑 to oppress; grievances.

冤 枉 a grievance; a wrong; an injustice; a false charge.

冤 桶 a bucket of grievances—one who brings trouble on himself.

[15]冤 聲 the cry of the wronged.

冤 苦 to grieve over a wrong.

冤 血 innocent blood.

冤 魂 the ghost of one who has suffered a wrong which has not been righted.

不 白 之 冤 a wrong which has not been righted.

[20]伸 冤 to redress a grievance.

含 冤 to have a grievance.

報 冤 to avenge a wrong.

結 冤 to become enemies.

訴 冤 to state one's wrongs.

[25]雪 冤 to wipe out a grievance.

肙 [1] A small worm. To twist. To surround. Empty.

7720

員 [2] An official.

7721

員 外 郎 a former second-class secretary to a Board.

員 弁 officers—civil and military.

委 員 a deputy. See No. 7098-6ff.

官 員 officials.

復 員 demobilization.

能 員 an able officer.

隨 員 an attaché. See No. 5523-17.

(a) An outer border.

員 柵 a palisade.

幅 員 the area of a country.

(b) Inter. next.

圓 [2] Round; circular:—thus, a dollar.

7722

圓 光 to act as a medium.

圓 光 兒 a nimbus.

圓 全 to complete; complete.

圓 分 a segment of a circle.

[5]圓 半 徑 the radius of a circle.

圓 周 the circumference of a circle.

圓 圈 a ring; a circle.

圓 坐 to sit around in a circle.

圓 妙 to have a full understanding of. (Budd.).

[10]圓 寂 the death of a Buddhist priest.

圓 密 or 機 圓 法 密 well planned and executed.

圓 就 to come to terms about.

圓 形 circular; round in shape.

圓 形 的 circular.

[15]圓 徑 the diameter of a circle.

圓 心 the centre of a circle; the heart—of timber.

圓 扁 round and flat.

圓 柱 體 a cylinder.

圓 柱 體 的 cylindrical.

[20]圓 活 accommodating; not bound by prejudice.

圓 滿 finished; rounded out; complete; satisfactory.

圓 球 a sphere.

圓 盤 a disc.

圓 眼 or 柱 圓 longans.

[25]圓 石 a boulder.

圓 筒 a cylinder.

圓 臺 the frustum of a cone.

圓 蟲 the round-worm.

圓 規 compasses.

[30]圓 足 rounded off; complete.

圓 轉 to arrange for a person; accommodating; not bound by prejudice.

圓 通 accommodating; tactful; not bound by one's own ideas; to adapt oneself to circumstances.

圓 運 動 circular motion.

圓 錐 形 conical.

[35]圓 錐 曲 線 conic sections.

圓 頂 a ball-shaped top—to anything.

圓 頭 釘 a round-headed nail.

圓 顱 方 趾 round skull and square feet—man.

尖 圓 體 a cone.

[40]五 圓 five dollars.

月 圓 the full moon.

平 圓 面 a disc.

長 圓 an oval; an ellipse.

長 圓 體 a cylinder.

↑圓 桌 會 議 round-table conference.

(a) To explain; to tell.

圓 夢 to explain a dream.

圓 謊 to tell lies.

自 圓 其 說 he gave an explanation of it; to justify one's views.

淵 [1] A gulf; an abyss. To be deep.

7723

淵 乎 profound!

淵 儒 a deeply-learned man.

淵 博 profound and extensive—of learning.

淵 叢 depths, as a refuge for fish; thickets, as a refuge for birds —figuratively, a refuge or harbour.

[5]淵 圖 deep, far-reaching schemes.

淵 塞 profound, far-reaching and sincere consideration—

淵 客 one who gets his living on the deep, as a fisherman, etc.

淵 富 profound and numerous— of a man's writings.

淵 微 profound and subtle; abstruse.

[10]淵 意 a profound meaning.

淵 盧 deep consideration.

淵 旨 a profound, subtle meaning.

淵 水 a deep river.
淵 沖 profound and intelligent.
15 淵 沼 a deep pool.
淵 泓 deep and vast.
淵 泉 a very deep spring.
淵 洽 profound and extensive.
淵 洞 a deep grotto.
20 淵 海 the ocean; deep and vast—as the ocean.
淵 深 profound, as thought, etc.
淵 淑 very pure and virtuous.
淵 淵 the boom of drums; deep and still.
淵 源 source; origin.
25 道 德 之 淵 源 the fountain of moral virtue.
淵 澄 deep and clear—of water.
淵 潛 hidden in the depths.
淵 然 而 靜 deep and still—as a pool.
淵 玄 profound, mysterious and abstruse.
30 淵 藪 an asylum; a place of refuge. See above—4.
淵 謀 deep schemes.
淵 遠 very far distant.
淵 靜 profound stillness.
淵 默 profound silence.
35 天 淵 之 別 as far apart as sky and sea.

垣² A wall. The space enclosed by a constellation.
7724

垣 衣 moss.
城 垣 a city wall.
塞 垣 the Great Wall.
女 垣 battlements.
省 垣 a provincial capital.
蘇 垣 Soochow.

原² A source; an origin. A beginning; a cause or reason. Original; natural, as a matter of course. Derivation.
7725
Inter. 元 No. 7707.

原 不 想 I really did not think ....
原 不 想 作 I had not intended to do it.
原 不 相¹ 配 truly not at all suited to each other.
原 不 該 作 by rights it should not be done.
5 原 中 middlemen.

原 主 the original or rightful owner.
原 人 the original person; primitive man.
原 任 the late incumbent.
原 件 the original article or document.
10 原 件 鈔 送 the original documents have been copied and sent.
原 來 originally; as a matter of fact; in the nature of the case.
原 來·頭 causes; circumstances; particulars.
原 來 如 此 it has always been so. Oh, is that so?
原 保 the original guarantor.
15 原 係 as before; as a matter of fact; it is ....
原 價 the prime cost.
原 價 及 水 脚 cost and freight.
原 先 primarily; at first.
原 判 the original judgement.
20 原 則 a fundamental principle—of action; a principle.
原 動 the prime mover; the motive power; the moving force.
原 動 力 motive force; originating force.
原 包 the original package, as unopened.
原 原 本 本 的 都 說 了 he told the whole story.
25 原 告 the prosecutor; the plaintiff.
原 單 位 fundamental unit.
原 因 cause.
原 因 他 故 it was, as a matter of fact, for other reasons.
原 因 何 在 for what cause?
30 原 因 結 果 cause and effect.
原 型 prototype.
原 基 radical. (chem.).
原 報 the original report.
原 始 in the beginning; primeval.
35 原 始 人 類 primitive man.
原 始 材·料 original material; data.
原 始 民 族 primitive races.
原 始 狀 態 its primitive state.
原 始 社 會 primitive society.
40 原 始 罪 孽 original sin.
原 委 the beginning and end; circumstances; details.
原 子³ atoms.
原 子³ 價 atomic values; valence.
原 子³ 容 atomic volume.
45 原 子³ 核 atomic nucleus. (-ho²)
原 子³ 浪 wave atoms.

原 子³ 熱 atomic heat.
原 子³ 號·數 atomic numbers.
原 子³ 說 the atomic theory.
50 原 子³ 量⁴ atomic weight.
原 審 the original trial or decision.
原 差 an official underling. (-ch'ai¹)
原 已 previously; already.
原 布 shirtings; plain cotton goods.
55 原 底·子 the original draft or text.
原 形 質 protoplasm.
原 性 of a primary character; its original character.
原 情 the original state of the case.
原 意 the primary meaning—of a word; primary intention or motive.
60 原 所 以 the primary reason; the original motive.
原 摺 the original draft.
原·故 cause; reason. ≡7341.5.
原 文 the original text.
原 料 raw materials; original matter.
65 原 斜 紋 布 twills.
原 早 prior to this; some time ago.
原 是 as a matter of course; in the nature of the case; true indeed; in fact ....
原 有·的 originally.
原 本 origin; root; principal, as opposed to interest; source; an original copy.
70 原 案 the original case.
原 氣 vitality; a man's constitution.
原 泉 a spring of water.
原 源 derivation; source.
原 無 是 理 there is no such principle—it is utterly unreasonable.
75 原 照 the original certificate.
原 爲 as a matter of course it was ....
原 物 the original goods.
原 狀 its original or normal aspect.
原 理 the actual facts; theory; first principles. See below—101.
80 原 生 動 物 primary forms of animal life.
原 生 林 primeval forest.
原 生 物 a germ.
原 由 causes; circumstances; particulars; facts.
原 稿 the original draft.
85 原 籍 the place where a person is

registered; one's original domicile; the old home of the family.

原 粗 布 sheetings.

原 素 elements, as of chemistry.

放 射 性 原 素 radio-active elements.

原 級 positive degree.

[90] 原 罪 original sin.

原 職 one's former post.

原 舊 as before; as of old; original.

原 色 primary colours; the original colour.

原 色 布 unbleached cotton goods; grey shirtings.

[95] 原 處 the original place.

原 被 告 parties in a lawsuit.

原 訂 originally fixed upon.

原 該 如 此 strictly speaking, it should be thus.

原 議 案 the original motion.

[100] 原 貨 憑 單 certificate of origin.

原 質 elements, = 87 above.

原 質 能 不 滅·的 原 理 the theory of the indestructibility of matter.

原 質 記 號 the initial letter, used as a symbol of the elements in chemistry.

原 贓 the stolen property.

[105] 原 起 origins.

原 配 the first wife.

原 重 atomic weight.

原 野 wild. See below A.

原 非 originally it was not .. ; as a matter of fact it was not ...

[110] 原 音 primary sounds or vowels.

推 原 to infer from premises.

本 原 origin.

追 原 the investigation of origins.

還 原 or 復 原 to be restored to health.

(a) A plateau; a plain. A high level.

原 隰 plains and marshes; level heights and low ground.

中 原 Honan, also used for China.

中 原 有 菽 in the midst of the plain there is pulse.

九 原 a cemetery; Hades; the nether world.

南 方 之 原 the plain in the south.

↑原 野 wilderness.

(b) To forgive.

原·諒 or 原 恕 or 原 宥 or 原 鑒 to be lenient; to excuse.

得 原 to obtain pardon.

情 有 可 原 there are extenuating circumstances; excusable.

(c) To repeat.

命 膳 宰 曰 未 有 原 he gave orders to the cook that none of the dishes were to go up again.

嫄² The name of the Princess Consort of the Emperor 嚳, 2256 B.C.; her full name was 姜 嫄.
7726

愿⁴ Sincere; honest. Inter. 願 No. 7729.
7727

愿 而 恭 bluntness combined with respectfulness.

侗 而 不 愿 simple and yet not sincere.

源² A spring; a source. Inter. 原 No. 7725.
7728

源 委 the beginning and end—the details of the whole story.

源 流 the source and history of.

源 清 流 清 the clear stream flows from a clear source.

源 源 接 濟 to continue to supply.

[5] 源 源 而 來 incessantly coming—of a stream of people.

源 究 to make a thorough investigation.

源 遠 流 長 the source is distant and the stream is long—it is well-established or of long continuance.

源 頭 a spring; a source.

來 源 the source; the origin of.

[10] 同 源 異 流 they spring from the same source but take different channels.

正 本 清 源 deal with the root and cleanse the source—of radical reform.

泉 源 a spring.

財 源 a source of wealth.

起 源 a beginning.

[15] 飲 水 思 源 when you drink of the water think of the spring—be grateful for the means by which you have profited.

願⁴ To be willing; to be desirous of. To desire. A vow.
7729

願 乞 終 養 I beg that I may be permitted to care for her to the end.

願 你 平 安 Peace be with you!

願 力 will power. (Budd.).

願 安 承 敎 I wish quickly to receive your teachings.

[5] 願 從 to be willing to comply.

願 得 would that....

願·意 willing.

不 願·意 unwilling.

願 望 to hope for; to look for; to aspire to.

[10] 願 書 a pledge.

願 欲 a strong desire for; to wish.

願 海 a boundless desire, like the sea.

願 王 萬 歲 O king live for ever!

願 者 上 鈎 those that were willing went on to his (barbless) hook—when Chiang T'ai kung went fishing—to do a thing of one's own free will; a voluntary act.

[15] 了 願 to fulfil a vow.

如 願 as one would wish.

心 願 one's heart's desires.

志·願 determination; will.

情·願 perfectly willing; voluntarily.

[20] 自 願 of one's own free will.

許 願 to promise; to make a vow.

遂 願 as one wishes; to do as one wishes; one's wishes fulfilled.

還 願 to fulfil a vow.

袁² A robe.
7730

園² A garden; an orchard. A term applied to tea-houses, theatres, etc.
7731

園 丁 or 園 工 or 園 夫 a gardener.

園 亭 garden and summer house; places of recreation.

園 圃 a park; a garden.

園·子 a garden.

[5] 園 藝 gardening.

園 陵 or 寢 園 or 交 園 an imperial mausoleum.

動 物 園 a zoological garden.

樂 園 a term for Paradise. (lê⁴)

花 園 a flower garden.

[10] 菜 園 a vegetable garden.

猿 猨 蝯 [2]
7732

An ape.

猿 猴 apes and monkeys.
猿 臂 long-armed, like an ape.
類 人 猿 anthropoid apes.

轅 [2]
7733

The shafts of a cart or carriage. A *yamen*.

轅 下 in the shafts—in or under the jurisdiction of a *yamen*.
轅 下 駒 a colt in the shafts—under restraint.
轅 木 shafts.
轅 門 the gates leading through the palisade before a *yamen*.
轅 門 報 the provincial Gazette.

遠 [3]
7734

Distant, in time or place. Remote. Far-reaching. To regard as distant.

遠 人 strangers; persons from a distance.
遠 來 to come from afar.
遠 光 far-sighted—of spectacles.
遠 別 to be separated by a long distance.
[5]遠 及 兒 孫 may it reach to your children and grand-children!
遠 因 the remote cause.
遠 地 點 apogee.
遠 大 vast.
不 大 遠 not very far away.
[10]遠 大 之 器 of far-reaching talents; of lofty aspirations.
遠 大 的 話 far-reaching words.
遠 孫 distant descendants.
遠 客 persons from afar; strangers.
遠 射 砲 long-range guns.
[15]遠 年 many years ago; of long standing.
遠 征 隊 a military expedition.
遠 心 力 centrifugal force.
遠 志 far-reaching ambition.
遠 念 thoughts during separation.
[20]遠 慮 to take thought for the future.
遠 方 a remote place.
遠 族 distant connections.
遠 日 點 aphelion.

遠 望 弗 及 looking from afar but unable to reach it.
[25]遠 望 標 緲 seen in the distance, hazy and indistinct.
遠 東 the Far East.
遠 步 to travel far.
遠 涉 重 洋 to have come from a distance across many seas.
遠 祖 distant ancestors.
[30]遠 處 a distant place.
遠 行 to take a long journey.
遠 見 to see from afar; far-sightedness.
遠 親 distant relatives.
遠 謀 far-sighted plans.
[35]遠 走 to go to a distance.
遠 足 會 a touring party.
遠 路 at or from a distance.
遠 近 far and near—distance; perspective.
遠 近 不 同 the distance is not the same.
[40]遠 近 都 知 known to all, far and near. (-*tou*[1]-)
遠 遊 to travel far.
遠 道 at or from a distance.
遠 遠 的 far-off; remote.
遠 遠 跟 隨 to follow afar off.
[45]遠 遙 or 遙 遠 distant.
遠 鏡 a telescope. =望遠鏡
遠 門 的 distantly related; a distant relative.
  出 遠 門 to go on a long journey.
遠 離 separated by distance; far away from.
[50]疎 遠 distant—of relationship.
差 得 遠 very far removed from; very different. (*ch'a*[4]-)
老 遠 very far off.

(a) Read *yüan*[4]. To keep away from; to send away. To keep at a distance.

遠 之 則 怨 if you maintain a reserve towards them, they are offended.
遠 佞 人 keep far from specious talkers.
遠 其 子 [3] maintained a distant reserve towards his son.
遠 怨 to keep himself from being the object of resentment.
[5]遠 恥 辱 也 to keep oneself from shame and disgrace.
遠 暴 慢 to keep from violence and heedlessness.

遠 色 [4] kept himself from the seductions of beauty.
遠 避 to keep away from.
遠 鄙 倍 to keep from vulgarity and impropriety.
[10]敬 鬼 神 而 遠 之 respect spiritual beings but keep aloof from them. (popularly pron. *yuan*[3] *chih*[1].)

爰 [2]
7735

To lead on to. Therefore; on this account; thereupon—it is often untranslatable.

爰 及 我 朝 (*ch'ao*[2]) down to the present dynasty.
爰 飫 and thereupon.
爰 居 爰 處 here we stay and here we stop.
爰 整 其 旅 he arranged his forces.
[5]爰 方 啟 行 he then commenced his march.
爰 於 日 前 and accordingly I have already....
爰 書 the record of a serious criminal case.
爰 爰 to be slow and cautious.

媛 [4]
7736

A beauty. Beautiful.

令 媛 your daughter.
名 媛 a famous beauty.
英 媛 talented and beautiful.

援 [2]
7737

To lead; to take hold of. To pull up; to rescue; to assist. To adduce as authority or illustration.

援 之 以 手 to pull out with the hand. *See* 嫂 No. 5434-3.
援 以 為 例 to quote (an instance) as a precedent.
援 例 to quote a precedent.
援 免 to bring forward reasons for exemption—to claim exemption from payment of duty.
[5]援 兵 reinforcements.
援 助 to assist; to relieve; to aid.
援 引 to lead on; to guide; to quote; to make a precedent of.
援 引 經 典 to quote from the classics.
援 手 to assist; to lend a hand.
[10]援 拔 to pull out.
援 救 to relieve; to assist.

援 案 to bring forward a case; to quote—as a precedent.

援 梯 a scaling-ladder.

援 溺 to rescue from drowning.

[15]援 照 成 案 according to precedent.

援 爲 to bring forward as...; to quote...as.

援 筆 to take up the pen and write.

援 結 to unite; to draw people together.

援 繫 to assist in arranging a marriage.

[20]援 而 止 之 to press a person to remain.

援 能 promote the men of ability.

援 解 to save; to relieve.

內 援 inside influence—as with the authorities; Fifth Columnist.

↑援 軍 or 援 兵 reinforcements; relief troops.

瑗[4] A large ring of fine jade, used at Court.
7738

鶢[2] A bird which frequents the sea-shore, called a 鶢鶋.
7739

掾[4] A general designation of officials. It is wrongly used for the next.
7740
Also read yüan[2].

緣[2] Destiny; affinity; connexion. A cause; a reason.
7741 Distinguish 緣 No. 4197.

緣 何 why?

緣·分 (fên[4]) affinity; the fate by which persons are brought together. See 因 No. 7407-40ff.

緣 分 (fên[4]) 淺 their affinity was shallow.

緣 因 a cause or reason. ≡7752.27.

[5]緣 故 a cause or reason.

緣 此 for this reason.

緣 法 an affinity. (Budd.).

緣 物 to drag a thing along.

緣 由 the reasons whereby; causes; details; measures, etc.

[10]緣 簿 a subscription list.

緣 起 origin.

前 世 有 緣 今 世 結 destinies arranged in a previous existence are united in this. (Budd.).

前 緣 predestined in a previous existence to meet in this.

天 緣 湊 巧 a lucky coincidence.

[15]宿 緣 predestined to meet or to marry.

後 緣 fated to meet in the next life.

有 緣 having an affinity; bound to meet; in sympathy with.

夙 緣 having an affinity; fated to meet or to marry.

無 緣 without affinity.

[20]良 緣 a happy marriage; a desirable match.

親 緣 related; having affinity.

(a) **To follow. To climb.** See 夤 No. 7427.

緣 城 to climb a city wall.

緣 木 to climb a tree,—from the next—

猶 緣 木 而 求 魚 it is like climbing a tree to seek a fish—only a waste of time.

(b) **The hem or selvedge of a garment.**

緣 袖 口 the hem of a sleeve.

緣 邊 a hem; a border.

緣 飾 以 儒 術 to make a hypocritical parade of learning pretensions to scholarship.

櫞[2] A name given to several species of trees.
7742

香 櫞 an acid variety of orange or citron—Citrus medica.

蝝[2] The young of locusts before the wings appear.
7743

冬 蝝 生 in winter the larvæ of the locusts were produced.

鳶[1] A kite.
7744

鳶 飛 戾 天 the hawk flies up to heaven.

烏 鳶 the kite.

紙 鳶 a paper kite.

風 鳶 a paper kite.

YÜN.   (ㄩㄣ)
(Üin)

云[2] To speak; to say. An expletive.
7745

云 云 all the rest; "etc."

如 此 云 云 etc., etc.

云 何 吁 炎 () how great is my sorrow!

云 然 as they say; as it is said.

[5]云 爲 words and actions.

云 爾 in this way; thus; simply; only; if you please.

不 行 王 政 云 爾 (Sung) is not practising true royal government, and so forth.

徐 徐 云 爾 gently, gently, if you please.

事 之 云 乎 豈 曰 友 之 云 乎 (the scholar) should be served; how should they have merely said that he should be made a friend of?

[10]入 云 則 坐 云 則 坐 食 云 則 食 when he told him to come into his house, he came; when he told him to be seated, he sat; when he told him to eat, he ate.

有 云 it is stated that...; there is a saying that....

沄[2] The rushing of a torrent. Inter. next.
7746

紜[2] Ravelled; confused. Perplexing; numerous.
7747

牛 馬 走 紜 紜 numerous cattle and horses passing to and fro.

紛 紜 in confusion; ravelled.

耘
耘[2] To weed.
7748

耘 田 to weed the rice fields when the young plants are established.

耘 耘 numerous; confused.

耘 耙 a rake for weeding.

耘 草 to root up weeds.

芸[2] Rue.
7749

芸 局 or 芸 閣 a library—because rue was used to keep insects from the books.

芸 帙 a satchel for books.

芸編 books. *See above*—1.
芸臺 or 芸廚 a study. *See above*—1.
芸芝 fragrant flowers.
芸°香 rue.

(a) Numerous.

芸生 the people.
夫物芸芸 all things.

(b) Deep and rich in colour.

芸其黃矣 deep is the yellow of the flowers.
芸黃 deep yellow—fading leaves and flowers.

(c) Inter. preceding. To weed.

芸夫 a farmer.

雲² Clouds; cloudy. Numerous. To gather.
7750

雲中白鶴 a white crane in the clouds—describing the high moral integrity of a man.
雲來霧去 comes in the clouds and departs in the mists—said of exaggerated yarns.
雲出無心 clouds arise without intention—an inadvertent act.
雲°南 the province of Yunnan.
⁵雲收雨止 when the clouds depart, the rain ceases.
雲合霧集 piled together like clouds in vast numbers.
雲外 beyond the clouds.
雲·子 ornamental p a t t e r n s on shoes, etc.
雲屯鳥散 gathering like t h e clouds and scattering like crows —of unstable associations.
¹⁰雲山霧罩 like mountains seen through the mists—vague and mysterious.
雲師 the spirit of the clouds.
雲帶 cloud belts—the ring of Saturn.
雲幕 a tent or canopy.
雲形定規 an instrument f o r drawing curves.
¹⁵雲·彩 clouds.
雲從龍 clouds come with the dragon, i.e., with the positive element in nature.
雲房 a Buddhist priest's room.

雲掩月 the clouds obscure the moon.
雲擾 disturbed and confused like the clouds.
²⁰雲散 the clouds disperse. *See* 風 No. 1890-35.
雲板 boards beaten to announce the progress of officials.
雲柱 the Pillar of Cloud.
雲根 stones or rocks—from the idea that clouds are formed by striking against the rocks.
雲梯 a scaling-ladder; also used figuratively of great heights.
²⁵雲樓 a lofty building.
雲樹 tall trees.
雲母 mica. *See below*—39, 44.
雲母殼 mother of pearl.
雲母車 a carriage ornamented with mica, used only by the highest ranks—ancient.
³⁰雲氣 mist; fog.
雲泥 clouds (in the skies) and mud (on the ground)—used in illustration of the difference in status.
雲消霧散 the clouds melt and the mists disperse—the troubles have been cleared up.
雲海 a sea of clouds.
雲游僧 a wandering Buddhist priest.
³⁵雲液 a name for wine.
雲滿天 the sky is overspread with clouds.
雲漢 the Milky Way.
雲烟 mist; fog.
雲珠 a name for mica. *See above* —27.
⁴⁰雲石 marble from *Tali* in Yunnan.
雲端 above the clouds.
雲端·裏 up in the clouds—used figuratively.
雲箋 a letter.
雲精 the essence of the clouds, a name for mica. *See above*— 27.
⁴⁵雲翳 overshadowed by the clouds.
雲聚 gathering like clouds.
雲肩 a scarf or cape worn by women.
雲腿 hams from Yunnan.
雲英 a name for mica. *See above* —27.
⁵⁰雲蒸霞蔚 greatly advancing in influence.
雲衣 a priest's robes.

雲表 beyond the clouds.
雲輜蔽路 the vast number of baggage-carts blocked the way.
雲開見日 when the clouds part, the sun is seen.
⁵⁵雲雁 the wild goose.
雲集 to assemble in crowds.
雲雨 clouds and rain—grace and favour; s e x u a l intercourse, from the legend of a prince who visited 巫山 and being tired, fell asleep, whereupon a beautiful woman appeared to him and said that she was the lady of Mount *Wu*; she shared his couch and as she took her departure she said, "At dawn I marshal the morning clouds, at night I summon the rain."
雲霄 fleecy clouds; the clouds.
雲霓 clouds and the rainbow.
⁶⁰雲霞 red clouds.
雲霧 mists; fogs.
雲頭 a cloud.
一朵雲彩 a cloud.
卷雲 cirrus clouds.
⁶⁵卿雲 auspicious clouds.
層雲 stratus clouds.
彩雲 rosy clouds.
星雲 nebulæ.
朝¹雲 morning clouds. (*chao*¹-)
⁷⁰浮雲 a passing cloud.
烏雲滿面 black clouds over-spread his countenance.
煙雲 a cloud of smoke.
疊雲 cumulus clouds.
祥雲 auspicious clouds.
⁷⁵雨雲 nimbus clouds.

勻² Equal; in equal parts; even. Distinguish 勾 No. 5829.
7751

勻·不開 cannot divide equally; cannot spare or be spared.
勻之 to divide.
勻出 to portion off; to divide out.
勻分 to divide equally.
⁵勻和 equal; even.
勻期限還 to be paid by regular instalments.
勻·淨 uniform; even.
勻溜 flowing evenly; fluid.
調勻 to mix evenly; to stir thoroughly.

畇² Reclaimed land.
7752

筠[2]
7753
The skin of the bamboo.

筠 冲 a name for Arabia.
筠 籃 bamboo-splint baskets.

慍[2]
7754
To be grieved; sad.

懷 慍 to be filled with grief.

殞[3,4]
7755
To perish; to die. Inter. next.

殞 命 to die; to perish.
殞 滅 perished.

隕[3,4]
磒
7756
To fall from or into.

隕 于 深 淵 to fall into a deep abyss.
隕 墜 falling—as meteorites.
隕 墮 to fall into ruins; to collapse.
隕 星 meteorites.
星 隕 如 雨 meteors fell like rain.
隕 泗 or 隕 涕 to weep; falling tears.
隕 潰 defeated and scattered.
隕 石 a meteorite.
隕 穫 dejected; distressed on account of poverty.
隕 落 to fall—as a meteorite.
隕 越 to fall into; to lapse; to commit error.
隕 越 遺 羞 to commit an error and leave cause for shame.
隕 霜 a fall of frost.
隕 顚 to fall; to fail.

(a) Read yüan[2]. An outer border.

幅 隕 the area of a country.

韻[4]
韵
7757
Rhyme; harmony; expression. A final in the Chinese system of spelling. See 字 No. 6942-23.

韻 事 tasteful things.
韻 士 a poet.
韻 宇 manner and bearing.

韻 度 bearing; manner; deportment.
韻 文 rhyming compositions;poetry
韻 書 a rhyming dictionary.
韻 母 the final of a Chinese syllable;Nat.phon. letters for finals.
韻 脚 a rhyme.
韻 語 rhyming compositions; irregular verse.
不 合 韻 not in rhyme.
倒 (tao[3]) 韻 a false rhyme, one which is in the wrong tone.
官 韻 a word selected for the rhyme on which verses are to be made.
押 韻 to rhyme verses upon a given character; to rhyme.
神 韻 very expressive.
風 韻 之 人 a man of taste and culture.

贇[1]
7758
A good-looking appearance.

允[3]
7759
To grant; to allow; to permit; to consent; to sanction; to assent. To confide in. Sincere; loyal.

允 元 give your confidence to the good.
允 准 to grant; to authorize; to approve.
允 協 to co-operate.
允 受 委 託 to accept a commission.
允 可 to assent; to sanction.
允 和 suitable; satisfactory.
允 執 厥 中 sincerely to hold fast the golden mean.
允 塞 entirely sincere.
允 定 to authorize.
允 宜 to approve as suitable.
允 從 to agree to; to assent.
允 恭 sincerely courteous.
允 書 the reply of a girl's parents to an offer of marriage.
允 服 or 應 允 to assent; to grant.
允 洽 suitable; fit; justly; satisfactorily.
允 當 suitable; satisfactory; fit.
允 納 to respond to; to assent to.
允 肯 to assent; to grant.
允 若 sincere and complaisant.
允 行 to grant; to authorize.
允 諾 or 允 許 to assent; to grant.

公 同 允 許 by common consent.
允 誠 true; sincere; good.
不 允 would not consent.

犾[3]
7760
A tribe of Scythian nomads.

惲[3]
7761
To deliberate; to consult.

惲 謀 to consult upon.
惲 議 to make plans and schemes.

暈[1,4]
7762
A halo; vapours; a mist. To be giddy; dizzy.

暈 忽 or 頭 暈 to feel dizzy; vertigo.
暈 死 復 甦 to faint away and revive.
暈 氣 fog; mist; vapour.
暈 海 or 暈 浪 to be sea-sick.
暈 船 to be sea-sick.
暈 車 to be train-sick, car-sick, etc.
暈 過 去 to faint away.
暈 頭 half-witted.
月 暈 a lunar halo.

運[4]
7763
To transport, as goods; to convey.

運 丁 government grain-junk men.
運 入 to import.
運 出 to export.
運 判 sub-Assistant Salt Comptroller.
運 到 地 土 imported into the locality.
運 務 the Grain Transport Administration.
運 司 a salt comptroller.
運 回 to convey back.
運 帶 to convey; to transport.
運 往 to carry to...; to transport to....
運 復 出 口 to re-export.
運 柩 to transport a coffin containing a corpse.
運 河 the Grand Canal.
運 照 a transport certificate.
運 米 執 照 special certificate for the transport of rice.

運 糧 transport of grain.
運 脚 freight; cost of transport.
運 臺 a salt-comptroller.
運 費 freight.
20 運 費 表 table of freight charges.
運 赴 to convey to....
運 輸 transportation.
運 輸 不 靈 poor means of transportation.
運 輸 交 通 之 開 發 development of transport and communications. [transport planes.
25 運 送 to convey to....運 輸 機
運 送 代 理 人 a forwarding agent.
運 送 佣 金 forwarding agent's commission.
運 送 單 a waybill.
運 送 掮 客 a freight broker.
30 運 送 業 the carrying trade.
運 送 船 a transport—for troops.
挑 運 porterage.
海 運 transportation by sea.
車 運 cartage.
35 轉 運 transportation.
陸 運 transportation by land.

(a) To revolve; to turn round. A revolution or turn of fate. Luck. A circuit or period of time.

運 不 佳 unlucky; unfortunate.
運·動 to move; to be in motion; to influence; to exercise; physical exercise; field sports; to stir up; to work for private ends; to set influences at work; agitation; propaganda movements.
　勞 動 運·動 the Labour Movement.
　動 物 運·動 animal movements.
6 　改 正 運·動 corrective movements.
　文 化 運·動 cultural propaganda.
　機 械·底 運·動 mechanical movements.
　生 命·底 運·動 vital movements.
　私 自 運·動 wire-pulling.
10 　科 學 運·動 propaganda of scientific ideas.
　自 由 運·動 free movements.
　革 命 運·動 revolutionary propaganda.

↓運·動 力 學 kinetics.
運·動 作 用 propaganda work.
運·動 場 the arena; a playground; athletic fields.
15 運·動 家 an athlete; an agitator.
運·動 律 the laws of motion.
運·動 會 an athletic meeting; a sports meeting.
運·動·的 成 敗 the success or failure of the movement.
運·動·的 範 圍 the range of the movement or propaganda.
20 運·動 者 a canvasser; an agitator.
運·動 衫·子 a sports-singlet.
運·動 選 舉 an electioneering campaign; canvassing for votes.
運·動 量 momentum.
運 化 to transform.
25 運 命 已 定 one's fate is settled.
命·運 luck; destiny.
運 命 論 fatalism.
運 數 luck; fortune.
運 晦 unlucky; bad fortune.
30 運·氣 luck; fortune; lucky.
運 用 to carry out; to use; to put to use; to apply.
運 用 法 method of use.
運 用 電 話 機 to operate the telephone.
運 籌 幃 幄 to prepare schemes in the tent—to make plans beforehand.
35 運 行 to revolve; to move to and fro.
　日 月 運 行 the sun and the moon move in their orbits.
運 轉 to revolve; to turn round.
　在 運 轉 中 in motion or operation, as a machine.
運 隆 great prosperity.
40 五 運 the interaction of the *five elements.*
交 運 a turning point in one's fortunes.
倒 3 運 bad luck.
地 運 the luck of a site, as for a grave.
官 運 promotion; official good luck.
45 家 運 the family fortunes.
應 運 to take advantage of a turn of good luck.
時 運 fortune; luck.
走 背 運 a run of bad luck.
↑運·動 學 kinematics.

郞 4 Name of an ancient city in the State of *Lu* 魯, now 7764 郞 城 縣 in Shantung.

孕 4 Pregnant. Also read *jên* 4.
7765
孕 十 月 ten months' gestation.
孕 婦 a pregnant woman.
孕 字 之 時 breeding time.
孕 珠 to conceive.
5 孕 胎 a pregnant womb.
孕 育 to be with young; to give birth to.
受 孕 to conceive.
懷 孕 to be with child.

慍 4 Indignant. To feel hurt. Also read *wên* 4.
7766
慍 於 羣 小 I am hated by the herd of mean creatures.
慍 怒 or 慍 色 irritated; angry.
人 不 知 而 不 慍 not to feel hurt because men do not know me.

氳 1 The life-giving influences of nature.
7767 See 氣 No. 7409; 氛 No. 1856—A.

熨 4 To iron; to smooth out. Inter. 熨 No. 7661.
7768
熨 斗 a smoothing iron.
熨 衣 服 to iron clothes.
熨 黃·了 you have scorched—the clothes—in ironing.

縕 4 Ravelled silk. Quilted with hemp.
7769
縕 袍 a garment quilted with hemp.

(a) Read *yün* 1. Vague; confused; misty.

絪 縕 u.f. 氤 氳 the generative influences of heaven and earth, by which all things are constantly reproduced.
紛 縕 confused; misty; numerous.

(b) Read *wên* 1. An orange colour.

蘊 4 To collect; to bring together. Inter. preceding. 7770 Also read *wên* 4.

蘊 利 hoarded wealth.
蘊 奧 mysterious.
蘊 寶 to collect gems.
蘊 積 如 堆 brought together in-
　to a heap.
[5] 蘊 結 uneasy; oppressed; sad.
蘊 蓄 or 含 蘊 collected; con-
　tained within.
蘊 藉 cultivated and refined.
蘊 藏 to hoard; to collect.

蘊 隆 蟲 蟲 the weather is extremely hot and muggy.

醖 [4] Fermented liquor; spirits;
7771　wine.

醖 藉 reserved in manner.
醖 酒 or 醖 釀 to brew liquor by
　fermentation.

韞 [4]　An orange colour. To
7772　contain.

韞 匵 而 藏 to enclose in a case.
韞 祕 to keep close; to secrete.

蕴 [1.4.]　Hippuris or mare's tail.
7773　See No. 7126.

APPENDIX A. TABLES.

I.—SUMMARY OF CHINESE DYNASTIES WITH THEIR DYNASTIC TITLES.

(*From Mayers' Chinese Reader's Manual.*)

THE LEGENDARY PERIOD. 1.—五帝紀 THE AGE OF THE FIVE RULERS. 647 YEARS.			2.—夏紀 THE HSIA DYNASTY. 439 YEARS.		
DYNASTIC APPELLATION.	ACCESSION.	PERSONAL APPELLATION.	DYNASTIC TITLE.	ACCESSION.	
	B. C.			B. C.	
1. 太昊	2852	伏庖 羲羲 ⎰	大 禹	2205	
			啓	2197	
2. 炎帝	2737	神烈 農山 ⎰	太 康	2188	
			仲 康	2159	
3. 黃帝	2697	有軒 熊轅 ⎰	相	2146	
4. 少昊	2597	金 天	Interregnum of forty years commencing	2118	
5. 顓頊	2513	高 陽	少 康	2079	
帝嚳	2435	高 辛	杼	2057	
帝摯	2365		槐	2040	
唐帝堯	2356	陶 唐	芒	2014	
虞帝舜	2255	有 虞	泄	1996	
			不 降	1980	
			扃	1921	
			廑	1900	
			孔 甲	1879	
			皋	1848	
			發	1837	
			桀 癸	1818	

3.—商 紀 [卽 殷 紀] THE SHANG DYNASTY.
(Also called the Yin Dynasty.)
644 YEARS.

DYNASTIC TITLE.	ACCESSION.	
	B. C.	
成 湯	1766	
太 甲	1753	
沃 丁	1720	
太 庚	1691	
小 甲	1666	
雍 己	1649	
太 戊	1637	
仲 丁	1562	
外 壬	1549	
河 亶	1534	
祖 乙	1525	
祖 辛	1506	
沃 甲	1490	
祖 丁	1465	
南 庚	1433	
陽 甲	1408	
盤 庚	1401	Changed the dynastic title Shang to Yin.
小 辛	1373	
小 乙	1352	
武 丁	1324	
祖 庚	1265	
祖 甲	1258	
廩 辛	1225	
庚 丁	1219	
武 乙	1198	
太 丁	1194	
帝 乙	1191	
紂 辛	1154	

4.—周 紀 THE CHOU DYNASTY.
867 YEARS

DYNASTIC TITLE.	ACCESSION.	
武 王	1122	
成 王	1115	
康 王	1078	
昭 王	1052	
穆 王	1001	
共 王	946	
懿 王	934	

4 —THE CHOU DYNASTY (Continued).

DYNASTIC TITLE.	ACCESSION.	
	B. C.	
孝 王	909	
夷 王	894	
厲 王	878	
宣 王	827	
幽 王	781	
平 王	770	
桓 王	719	
莊 王	696	
僖 王	681	
惠 王	676	
襄 王	651	
頃 王	618	
匡 王	612	
定 王	606	
簡 王	585	
靈 王	571	
景 王	544	
敬 王	519	
元 王	475	
貞 定 王	468	
孝 王	440	
威 烈 王	425	
安 王	401	
烈 王	375	
顯 王	368	
愼 靚 王	320	
赧 王	314	Reigned 59 years. In B.C. 256 surrendered his dominions to the ruler of Chin.
東 周 君	255	Nominally reigned until B.C. 249.

5.—秦 紀 THE CH'IN DYNASTY.
49 YEARS.

DYNASTIC TITLE.	ACCESSION.	
昭 襄 王	255	The 52nd year of his reign as ruler of the State of Chin.
孝 文 王	250	Reigned only three days.
莊 襄 王	249	
王 政	246	
始 皇 帝	221	The title assumed by Prince Chêng on declaring himself, "The first universal Emperor," in the 26th year of his reign.
二 世 皇 帝	209	

6.—漢紀 THE HAN DYNASTY.
(Also styled 前漢 or Former Han, and 西漢 or Western Han.)
231 YEARS

DYNASTIC TITLE OR 廟號.	ACCESSION.	TITLE OF REIGN OR 年號.	ADOPTION OF NIEN HAO.
	B. C.		B. C.
高帝 高祖	206		
惠帝	194		
高后 呂氏	187		
文帝	179	後元	163
景帝	156	中元	149
		後元	143
武帝	140	建元	140
		元光	134
		元朔	128
		元狩	122
		元鼎	116
		元封	110
		太初	104
		天漢	100
		太始	96
		征和	92
		後元	88
昭帝	86	始元	86
		元鳳	80
		元平	74
宣帝	73	本始	73
		地節	69
		元康	65
		神爵	61
		五鳳	57
		甘露	53
		黃龍	49
元帝	48	初元	48
		永光	43
		建昭	38
		竟寧	33
成帝	32	建始	32
		河平	28
		陽朔	24
		鴻嘉	20
		永始	16
		元延	12
		綏和	8

THE HAN DYNASTY (Continued).

DYNASTIC TITLE OR 廟號.	ACCESSION.	TITLE OF REIGN OR 年號.	ADOPTION OF NIEN HAO.
	B. C.		B. C.
哀帝	6	建平	6
		元壽	2
	A. D.		A. D.
平帝	1	元始	1
孺子嬰	6	居攝	6
		初始	8
偽新, 王莽 usurper	9	始建國	9
		天鳳	14
		地皇	20
淮陽王 帝玄	23	更始	23

7.—後漢紀 THE LATER HAN DYNASTY.
(Also styled 東漢 or Eastern Han.)
196 YEARS.

DYNASTIC TITLE OR 廟號.	ACCESSION.	TITLE OF REIGN OR 年號.	ADOPTION OF NIEN HAO.
光武帝	25	建武	25
		中元	56
明帝	58	永平	58
章帝	76	建初	76
		元和	84
		章和	87
和帝	89	永元	89
		元興	105
殤帝	106	延平	106
安帝	107	永初	107
		元初	114
		永寧	120
		建光	121
		延光	122
順帝	126	永建	126
		陽嘉	132
		永和	136
		漢安	142
		建康	144
沖帝	145	永嘉	145
質帝	146	本初	146
桓帝	147	建和	147
		和平	150
		元嘉	151
		永興	153
		永壽	155
		延熹	158
		永康	167

THE LATER HAN DYNASTY (Continued)

DYNASTIC TITLE. OR 廟號	ACCESSION A.D.	TITLE OF REIGN OR 年號	ADOPTION OF NIEN HAO. A.D.
靈帝	168	建寧	168
		熹平	172
		光和	178
		中平	184
少帝	189	光熹 昭寧	189
獻帝 or 愍帝	189	永漢 中平	189
		初平	190
		興平	194
		建安	196
		延康	220

8.—EPOCH OF THE THREE KINGDOMS.

I. 蜀漢紀 The Minor Han Dynasty,
(Established in Szechwan).
44 YEARS.

昭烈帝	221	章武	221
後主	223	建興	223
		延熙	238
		景耀	258
		炎興	263

II. 魏紀 The Wei Dynasty.
45 YEARS.

文帝	220	黃初	220
明帝	227	太和	227
		青龍	233
		景初	237
廢帝 齊王芳	240	正始	240
deposed	254	嘉平	249
少帝 高貴鄉公	254	正元	254
		甘露	256
元帝	260	景元	260
		咸熙	264

EPOCH OF THE THREE KINGDOMS (Continued)
III. 吳紀 The Wu Dynasty.
36 YEARS

DYNASTIC TITLE. OR 廟號	ACCESSION A.D.	TITLE OF REIGN OR 年號	ADOPTION OF NIEN HAO A.D.
大帝	222	黃武	222
		黃龍	229
		嘉禾	232
		赤烏	238
		太元	251
		神鳳	252
廢帝 會稽王	252	建興	252
		五鳳	254
		太平	256
景帝	258	永安	258
末帝 歸命侯	264	元興	264
		甘露	265
		寶鼎	266
		建衡	269
		鳳凰	272
		天冊	275
		天璽	276
		天紀	277

9.—西晉紀 THE WESTERN TSIN DYNASTY.
52 YEARS.

武帝	265	泰始	265
		咸寧	275
		泰康	280
		泰熙	290
惠帝	290	永熙	290
		永平	291
		元康	291
		永康	300
		永寧	301
		太安	302
		永興 永安 建武 永安	304
		光熙	306
懷帝	307	永嘉	307
愍帝	313	建興	313

APPENDIX A. TABLES. (Continued).

10.—東晉紀 THE EASTERN TSIN DYNASTY.
103 YEARS.

DYNASTIC TITLE OR 廟號.	ACCESSION.	TITLE OF REIGN OR 年號.	ADOPTION OF NIEN HAO.
	A. D.		A. D.
元帝	317	建武	317
		太興	318
		永昌	322
明帝	323	太寧	323
成帝	326	咸和	326
		咸康	335
康帝	343	建元	343
穆帝	345	永和	345
		升平	357
哀帝	362	隆和	362
		興寧	363
帝奕 海西公 }	366	太和	366
簡文帝	371	咸安	371
孝武帝	373	寧康	373
		太元	376
安帝	397	隆安	397
		元興	402
		隆安	402
		大亨	402
		元興	403
		義熙	405
恭帝	419	元熙	419

EPOCH OF DIVISION BETWEEN NORTH AND SOUTH.·—南北朝.
169 YEARS.

11.—劉宋紀 THE SUNG DYNASTY.
(House of Liu).
59 YEARS.

武帝	420	永初	420
少帝 營陽王 }	423	景平	423
文帝	424	元嘉	424
孝武帝	454	孝建	454
		大明	457
廢帝	465	永光	465
明帝	465	景和	465
		泰始	465
		泰豫	472
蒼梧王	473	元徽	473
主昱 }			
順帝 }	477	昇明	477

北魏紀 THE NORTHERN WEI DYNASTY.
(拓跋氏 House of Toba).
149 YEARS.

DYNASTIC TITLE OR 廟號.	ACCESSION.	TITLE OF REIGN OR 年號.	ADOPTION OF NIEN HAO.
	A. D.		A. D.
道武帝	386	登國	386
		皇始	396
		天興	398
		天賜	404
明元帝	409	永興	409
In A.D. 420 the Northern Wei commences to be grouped with the Northern and Southern dynastic group.		神瑞	414
		泰常	416

EPOCH OF DIVISION BETWEEN NORTH AND SOUTH 南北朝. (Continued).

12.—齊紀 THE CH'I DYNASTY.
23 YEARS.

DYNASTIC TITLE OR 廟號.	ACCESSION. A.D.	TITLE OF REIGN OR 年號.	ADOPTION OF NIEN HAO. A.D.
高帝	479	建元	479
武帝	483	永明	483
鬱林王	494	隆昌	494
海陵王	494	延興	494
明帝	494	建武	494
		永泰	498
東昏侯	499	永元	499
和帝	501	中興	501

13.—梁紀 THE LIANG DYNASTY.
55 YEARS.

DYNASTIC TITLE OR 廟號.	ACCESSION. A.D.	TITLE OF REIGN OR 年號.	ADOPTION OF NIEN HAO. A.D.
武帝	502	天監	502
		普通	520
		大通	527
		中大通	529
		大同	535
		中大同	546
		太清	547
簡文帝	550	大寶	550
豫章王	551	天正	551
元帝	552	承聖	552
貞陽侯	555	天成	555
敬帝	555	紹泰	555
		太平	556

14.—陳紀 THE CH'ÊN DYNASTY.
32 YEARS.

DYNASTIC TITLE OR 廟號.	ACCESSION. A.D.	TITLE OF REIGN OR 年號.	ADOPTION OF NIEN HAO. A.D.
武帝	557	永定	557
文帝	560	天嘉	560
		天康	566
臨海	567	光大	567
宣帝	569	大建	569
後主	583	至德	583
		禎明	587

THE NORTHERN WEI DYNASTY. (Continued).

DYNASTIC TITLE OR 廟號.	ACCESSION. A.D.	TITLE OF REIGN OR 年號.	ADOPTION OF NIEN HAO. A.D.
太武帝	424	始光	424
		神䴥	428
		延和	432
		太延	435
		太平眞君	440
		正平	452
南安王	452	承平	452
文成帝	452	興安	452
		興光	454
		太安	455
		和平	460
獻文帝	466	天安	466
		皇興	467
孝文帝	471	延興	471
		承明	476
		太和	477
宣武帝	500	景明	500
		正始	504
		永平	508
		延昌	512
孝明帝	516	熙平	516
		神龜	517
		正光	519
		孝昌	525
臨洮王	528	武泰	528
孝莊帝	528	建義	528
		永安	528
		更興	529
東海王	530	建明	530
節閔帝	531	普泰	531
安定王	531	中興	531
孝武帝	532	太昌	532
		永興	532
		永熙	532

西魏紀 THE WESTERN WEI DYNASTY.
22 YEARS.

DYNASTIC TITLE OR 廟號.	ACCESSION. A.D.	TITLE OF REIGN OR 年號.	ADOPTION OF NIEN HAO. A.D.
文帝	535	大統	535
帝欽	552		
恭帝	554		

EPOCH OF DIVISION BETWEEN NORTH AND SOUTH.—南北朝 (Continued.)

東魏紀 THE EASTERN WEI DYNASTY.
16 YEARS.

DYNASTIC TITLE OR 廟 號.	ACCESSION.	TITLE OF REIGN OR 年 號.	ADOPTION OF NIEN HAO.
	A. D.		A. D.
孝靜帝	534	天 平	534
		元 象	538
		興 和	539
		武 定	543

北齊紀 THE NORTHERN CH'I DYNASTY.
39 YEARS.

文 宣 帝	550	天 保	550
廢 帝	560	乾 明	560
孝 昭 帝	560	皇 建	560
武 成 帝	561	太 寧	561
		河 清	562
溫 公	565	天 統	565
[後主]		武 平	570
		隆 化	576
安 德 王	576	德 昌	576
幼 主	577	承 光	577

北周紀 THE NORTHERN CHOU DYNASTY.
32 YEARS.

孝 愍 帝	557	—	—
明 帝	557	武 成	558
武 帝	561	保 定	561
		天 和	566
		建 德	572
宣 帝	578	宣 政	578
		大 成	579
靜 帝	580	大 象	580
		大 定	581

15.—隋紀 THE SUI DYNASTY.
29 YEARS.

DYNASTIC TITLE OR 廟 號.	ACCESSION.	TITLE OF REIGN OR 年 號.	ADOPTION OF NIEN HAO.
	A. D.		A. D.
文 帝	589	開 皇	581
		仁 壽	601

15.—隋紀 THE SUI DYNASTY. (Continued).

煬 帝	605	大 業	605
恭 帝 侑	617	義 寧	617
恭 帝 侗	618	皇 泰	618

DYNASTIC TITLE OR 廟 號.	ACCESSION.	TITLE OF REIGN OR 年 號.	ADOPTION OF NIEN HAO.	DYNASTIC TITLE OR 廟 號.	ACCESSION.	TITLE OF REIGN OR 年 號.	ADOPTION OF NIEN HAO.
	A. D.		A. D.		A. D.		A. D.
高祖	618	武 德	618	玄宗	713	開 元	713
太宗	627	貞 觀	627			天 寶	742
高宗	650	永 徽	650	肅宗	756	至 德	756
		顯 慶	656			乾 元	758
		龍 朔	661			上 元	760
		麟 德	664			寶 應	762
		乾 封	666	代宗	763	廣 德	763
		總 章	668			永 泰	765
		咸 亨	670			大 曆	766
		上 元	674	德宗	780	建 中	780
		儀 鳳	676			興 元	784
		調 露	679			貞 元	785
		永 隆	680	順宗	805	永 貞	805
		開 耀	681	憲宗	806	元 和	806
		永 淳	682	穆宗	821	長 慶	821
		弘 道	683	敬宗	825	寶 曆	825
中宗	684	嗣 聖	684	文宗	827	永 和	827
睿宗	684	文 明	684			開 成	836
武后	684	光 宅	684	武宗	841	會 昌	841
[The Empress Wu, who set aside the rightful sovereign and usurped the Throne for twenty years].		垂 拱	685	宣宗	847	太 中	847
		永 昌	689	懿宗	860	咸 通	860
Adopted the dynastic title of 周 Chou in lieu of 唐 T'ang from this date.		載 初	689	僖宗	874	乾 符	874
		天 授	690			廣 明	880
		如 意	692			中 和	881
		長 壽	692			光 啓	885
		延 載	694			文 德	888
		證 聖	695	昭宗	889	龍 紀	889
		天冊萬歲	695			大 順	890
		萬歲通天	696			景 福	892
		神 功	697			乾 寧	894
		聖 曆	698			光 化	898
		久 視	700			天 復	901
		大 足	701			天 祐	904
		長 安	701	昭宣帝 [哀宗]	905	天 祐	905
中宗 [resumed the Throne]		神 龍	705				
		景 龍	707				
睿宗	710	景 雲	710				
		太 極	712				
		延 和	712				

APPENDIX A. TABLES. (Continued).

EPOCH OF THE FIVE DYNASTIES 五代. 53 YEARS.

I.
17.—後梁紀 THE POSTERIOR LIANG DYNASTY. 16 YEARS.

DYNASTIC TITLE OR 廟號.	ACCESSION. A.D.	TITLE OF REIGN OR 年號.	ADOPTION OF NIEN HAO. A.D.
太祖	907	開平	907
		乾化	911
末帝	915	貞明	915
[均王]		龍德	921

II.
18.—後唐紀 THE POSTERIOR T'ANG DYNASTY. 13 YEARS.

DYNASTIC TITLE OR 廟號.	ACCESSION.	TITLE OF REIGN OR 年號.	ADOPTION OF NIEN HAO.
莊宗	923	同光	923
明宗	926	天成	926
		長興	930
閔帝	934	應順	934
廢帝	934	清泰	934
[潞王]			

III.
19.—後晉紀 THE POSTERIOR TSIN DYNASTY. 11 YEARS.

DYNASTIC TITLE OR 廟號.	ACCESSION.	TITLE OF REIGN OR 年號.	ADOPTION OF NIEN HAO.
高祖	936	天福	936
齊王	943	開運	944

IV.
20.—後漢紀 THE POSTERIOR HAN DYNASTY. 4 YEARS.

DYNASTIC TITLE OR 廟號.	ACCESSION.	TITLE OF REIGN OR 年號.	ADOPTION OF NIEN HAO.
高祖	947	天福	936
		乾祐	948
隱帝	948	乾祐	948

V.
21.—後周紀 THE POSTERIOR CHOU DYNASTY. 9 YEARS.

DYNASTIC TITLE OR 廟號.	ACCESSION.	TITLE OF REIGN OR 年號.	ADOPTION OF NIEN HAO.
太祖	951	廣順	951
世宗	944	顯德	954
恭帝	660	顯德	960

THE TARTAR DYNASTIES.

22—遼紀 THE LIAO DYNASTY. (契丹 Khitan Tartars). 218 YEARS.

DYNASTIC TITLE OR 廟號.	ACCESSION. A.D.	TITLE OF REIGN OR 年號.	ADOPTION OF NIEN HAO. A.D.
太祖	907	神冊	916
		天贊	922
		天顯	925
太宗	927	天顯	925
		會同	937
		大同	946
世宗	947	天祿	947
穆宗	951	應歷	951
景宗	968	保寧	968
		乾亨	978
聖宗	983	統和	983
		開泰	1012
		太平	1020
興宗	1031	景福	1031
		重熙	1032
道宗	1055	清寧	1055
		咸雍	1066
		大康	1074
		大安	1083
		壽隆	1092
天祚	1101	乾統	1101
		天慶	1110
		保大	1119

23.—西遼紀 THE WESTERN LIAO DYNASTY. 43 YEARS.

DYNASTIC TITLE OR 廟號.	ACCESSION.	TITLE OF REIGN OR 年號.	ADOPTION OF NIEN HAO.
德宗	1125	延慶	1125
		康國	1126
感天后	1136	咸清	1136
仁宗	1142	紹興	1142
承天	1154	崇福	1154
		皇德	—
		重德	—
末主	1168	天禧	1168

THE TARTAR DYNASTIES (Continued).
24.—金紀 THE KIN DYNASTY.
(女眞 Nü-chên Tartars).
145 YEARS.

DYNASTIC TITLE OR 廟號	ACCESSION A.D.	TITLE OF REIGN OR 年號	ADOPTION OF NIEN HAO A.D.
太祖	1115	收國	1115
		天輔	1118
太宗	1123	天會	1123
熙宗	1135	天會	1135
		天眷	1138
		皇統	1141
海陵王	1149	天德	1149
		貞元	1153
		正隆	1156
世宗	1161	大定	1161
章宗	1190	明昌	1190
		承安	1196
		泰和	1201
衛紹王	1209	大安	1209
		崇慶	1212
		至寧	1213
宣宗	1213	貞祐	1213
		興定	1217
		元光	1222
哀宗	1224	正大	1224
		天興	1232
		開興	1233
末帝	1234	盛昌	1234

25.—宋紀 THE SUNG DYNASTY.
167 YEARS.

DYNASTIC TITLE OR 廟號	ACCESSION	TITLE OF REIGN OR 年號	ADOPTION OF NIEN HAO
太祖	960	建隆	960
		乾德	963
		開寶	968
太宗	976	太平興國	976
		雍熙	984
		端拱	988
		淳化	990
		至道	995

25.—THE SUNG DYNASTY (Continued).

DYNASTIC TITLE OR 廟號	ACCESSION A.D.	TITLE OF REIGN OR 年號	ADOPTION OF NIEN HAO A.D.
眞宗	998	咸平	993
		景德	1004
		大中祥符	1008
		天禧	1017
		乾興	1022
仁宗	1023	天聖	1023
		明道	1032
		景祐	1034
		寶元	1038
		康定	1040
		慶曆	1041
		皇祐	1049
		至和	1054
		嘉祐	1056
英宗	1064	治平	1064
神宗	1068	熙寧	1068
		元豐	1078
哲宗	1086	元祐	1086
		紹聖	1094
		元符	1098
徽宗	1101	建中靖國	1101
		崇寧	1102
		大觀	1107
		政和	1111
		重和	1118
		宣和	1119
欽宗	1126	靖康	1126

26.—南宋紀 THE SOUTHERN SUNG DYNASTY.
153 YEARS.

DYNASTIC TITLE OR 廟號	ACCESSION	TITLE OF REIGN OR 年號	ADOPTION OF NIEN HAO
高宗	1127	建炎	1127
		紹興	1131
孝宗	1163	隆興	1163
		乾道	1165
		淳熙	1174
光宗	1190	紹熙	1190
寧宗	1195	慶元	1195
		嘉泰	1201
		開禧	1205
		嘉定	1208

THE SOUTHERN SUNG DYNASTY (Continued).

DYNASTIC TITLE OR 廟號.	ACCESSION. A.D.	TITLE OF REIGN OR 年號.	ADOPTION OF NIEN HAO. A.D.
理宗	1225	寶慶	1225
		紹定	1228
		端平	1234
		嘉熙	1237
		淳祐	1241
		寶祐	1253
		開慶	1259
		景定	1260
度宗	1265	咸淳	1265
恭帝	1275	德祐	1275
端宗	1276	景炎	1276
帝昺	1278	祥興	1278

27.—元紀 THE YÜAN DYNASTY.
(Mongols).
88 YEARS.

太祖	1206	Named Gengis	
太宗	1229		
定宗	1246		
憲宗	1251		
世祖	1260	中統	1260
[Kublai-actually seated on the throne of China from A.D. 1280.		至元	1264
成宗	1295	元貞	1295
		大德	1297
武宗	1308	至大	1308
仁宗	1312	皇慶	1312
		延祐	1314
英宗	1321	至治	1321
泰定	1324	泰定	1324
		致和	1328
明宗	1329	天曆	1329
文帝	1330	天曆	1330
		至順	1330
順帝	1333	元統	1333
		至元	1335
		至正	1341

28.—明紀 THE MING DYNASTY.
276 YEARS.

DYNASTIC TITLE OR 廟號.	ACCESSION. A.D.	TITLE OF REIGN OR 年號.	ADOPTION OF NIEN HAO. A.D.
太祖	1368	洪武	1368
惠帝	1399	建文	1399
成祖	1403	永樂	1403
仁宗	1425	洪熙	1425
宣宗	1426	宣德	1426
英宗	1436	正統	1436
代宗) 景帝)	1450	景泰	1450
英宗	1457	天順	1457
[resumed government]			
憲宗	1465	成化	1465
孝宗	1488	弘治	1488
武宗	1506	正德	1506
世宗	1522	嘉靖	1522
穆宗	1567	隆慶	1567
神宗	1573	萬曆	1573
光宗	1620	泰昌	1620
熹宗	1621	天啟	1621
莊烈帝	1628	崇禎	1628

29.— 清紀 THE CH'ING DYNATSY.
(Manchu).
268 YEARS.

世祖章皇帝	1644	順治	1644
聖祖仁皇帝	1662	康熙	1662
世宗憲皇帝	1723	雍正	1723
高宗純皇帝	1736	乾隆	1736
仁宗睿皇帝	1796	嘉慶	1796
宣宗成皇帝	1821	道光	1821
文宗顯皇帝	1851	咸豐	1851
穆宗毅皇帝	1862	同治	1862
德宗景皇帝	1875	光緒	1875
	1908	宣統	1908

The Republic of China   1912

II. ORDINARY AND LITERARY NAMES FOR THE MONTHS.

1	正月	春王	元月	青陽	三陽	孟陽
2	二月	中和	杏月		如	花朝
3	三月	桃月	上巳		寒食	
4	四月	清和	麥秋	槐月	滿	
5	五月	榴月, 蒲月	天中			端月
6	六月	荷月, 伏月	天貺			
7	七月	桐月	巧月	中元	蘭月	
8	八月	桂月	中秋			
9	九月	菊秋	中菊		重陽	
10	十月	陽春	小春, 陽春		梅月	
11	十一月	霞月, 冬月	仲冬		長至	
12	十二月	臘月	嘉平		清祀	

The literary names follow those used colloquially, which are given in the second column.

III. NAMES AND AFFINITIES OF THE TEN CELESTIAL STEMS 天干.

STEMS.	ASTROLOGICAL NAMES.	DUAL COMBINATION.	CORRESPONDING ELEMENTS.	BINARY EXHIBITION. 陽	陰	PLANETS.
1 甲	閼逢	甲 乙	木	Fir.	Bamboo.	木星 Jupiter.
2 乙	旃蒙					
3 丙	柔兆	丙 丁	火	Burning wood.	Lamp flame.	火星 Mars.
4 丁	彊圉					
5 戊	著雍	戊 己	土	Hill.	Plain.	土星 Saturn.
6 己	屠維					
7 庚	上章	庚 辛	金	Weapons.	Kettle.	金星 Venus.
8 辛	重光					
9 壬	玄黓	壬 癸	水	Waves.	Brooks.	水星 Mercury.
10 癸	昭陽					

IV.—THE TWELVE BRANCHES OR HORARY CHARACTERS. 十二地支.

BRANCHES.	SYMBOLICAL ANIMALS.	ZODIACAL SIGNS.	POETICAL NAMES	CORRESPONDING HOURS		POINTS OF THE COMPASS.
1 子	鼠 Rat.	Aries.	困敦	11—1 A.M.	三更	NORTH.
2 丑	牛 Ox.	Taurus.	赤奮若	1—3	四更	NNE ¾ E.
3 寅	虎 Tiger.	Gemini.	攝提格	3—5	五更	ENE ¾ N.
4 卯	兔 Hare.	Cancer.	單閼, 亶安	5—7		EAST.
5 辰	龍 Dragon.	Leo.	執徐	7—9		ESE ¾ S.
6 巳	蛇 Snake.	Virgo.	大荒落, 大芒落	9—11	上午	SSE ¾ E.
7 午	馬 Horse.	Libra.	敦牂	11—1 P.M.	正午	SOUTH.
8 未	羊 Sheep.	Scorpio.	協洽, 汁洽	1—3	下午	SSW ¾ W.
9 申	猴 Monkey.	Sagittarius.	涒灘, 芮漢	3—5		WSW ¾ S.
10 酉	雞 Cock.	Capricornus.	作噩, 作鄂	5—7		WEST.
11 戌	犬 Dog.	Aquarius.	閹茂, 淹茂	7—9	初更	WNW ¾ N.
12 亥	猪 Boar.	Pisces.	大淵獻	9—11	二更	NNW ¾ W.

V.—The Chinese Zodiacal Constellations, with their Corresponding Elements and Animals, the Longitude of their Determinant Stars in A. D. 1800, and their Approximate Constellations. 二十八宿（宮）.

SIGNS.		ELEMENT.	ANIMAL.	LONGITUDE.			CONSTELLATION.
1	角	木	蛟	201	3	0	Spica; ζ, θ, ι Virgo.
2	亢	金	龍	211	42	1	ι, κ, λ, ρ Virgo.
3	氐	土	貉	222	17	35	a, β, γ, ι Libra.
4	房	日	兔	240	8	48	β, δ, π, ν Scorpio.
5	心	月	狐	245	0	25	Antares; σ, τ Scorpio.
6	尾	火	虎	253	27	15	ε, μ, ζ, η, θ, ι, κ, λ, ν Scorpio.
7	箕	水	豹	268	28	15	γ, δ, ε, β Sagittarius.
8	斗	木	獬	277	23	6	μ, λ, ρ, σ, τ, ζ Sagittarius.
9	牛	金	牛	301	15	11	a, β, π Aries; ω, A, B Sagittarius.
10	女	土	蝠	308	55	54	ε, μ, ν, 9 Aquarius.
11	虛	日	鼠	320	36	16	β, Aquarius; a Equuleus.
12	危	月	燕	330	33	45	a Aquarius; ε, θ Pegasus.
13	室	火	猪	350	41	59	a (Markab), β (Scheat) Pegasus.
14	壁	水	貐	6	22	9	γ (Algenib) Pegasus; a Andromeda.
15	奎	木	狼	17	48	12	{ β (Mirach) δ, ε, ζ, η, μ, ν, π Andromeda σ (2), τ, ν, φ, χ, ψ Pisces.
16	婁	金	狗	31	10	39	a, β, γ Aries.
17	胃	土	雉	44	8	47	Musca Borealis.
18	昴	日	雞	57	12	1	Pleiades.
19	畢	月	烏	65	39	58	Hyades; μ, ν Taurus.
20	觜	火	猴	80	54	47	λ, φ (2) Orion.
21	參	水	猿	79	34	6	a, β, γ, δ, ε, ζ, η, κ Orion.
22	井	木	犴	92	30	21	Gemini.
23	鬼	金	羊	122	56	24	γ, δ, η, θ Cancer.
24	柳	土	獐	127	31	4	δ, ε, ζ, η, θ, ρ, σ, ω Hydra.
25	星	日	馬	144	29	44	a, ι, τ (2), κ, ν (2) Hydra.
26	張	月	鹿	152	54	37	κ, λ, μ, ν, φ Hydra.
27	翼	火	蛇	170	56	9	22 stars in Crater and Hydra.
28	軫	水	蚓	187	56	52	β, γ, δ, ε Corvus.

VI.—Combinations of Chinese Cyclical Characters for the Years 1899-2008 inclusive.

A glance at this Table will show that it is formed by combining the Stems and Branches (天干, 地支) in regular order, beginning with the first of each. This gives the same combination every sixty years. Chinese chronology is computed by the cycles thus formed. A list of these cycles from B. C. 2637 to A. D. 1923 may be found in Mayer's Chinese Reader's Manual. The present cycle began in 1924.

己亥	1899–1959	庚子	1900—1960	辛丑	1901—1961	壬寅	1902—1962
甲辰	1904—1964	乙巳	1905—1965	丙午	1906—1966	丁未	1907—1967
己酉	1909—1969	庚戌	1910—1970	辛亥	1911—1971	壬子	1912—1972
甲寅	1914—1974	乙卯	1915—1975	丙辰	1916—1976	丁巳	1917—1977
己未	1919—1979	庚申	1920—1980	辛酉	1921—1981	壬戌	1922—1982
甲子	1924—1984	乙丑	1925—1985	丙寅	1926—1986	丁卯	1927—1987
己巳	1929—1989	庚午	1930—1990	辛未	1931–1991	壬申	1932—1992
甲戌	1934–1994	乙亥	1935—1995	丙子	1936—1996	丁丑	1937—1997
己卯	1939—1999	庚辰	1940—2000	辛巳	1941–2001	壬午	1942—2002
甲申	1944—2004	乙酉	1945—2005	丙戌	1946—2006	丁亥	1947—2007

癸卯	1903—1963
戊申	1908—1968
癸丑	1913—1973
戊午	1918—1978
癸亥	1923—1983
戊辰	1928–1988
癸酉	1933—1993
戊寅	1938 1998
癸未	1943—2003
戊子	1948—2008

VII.—The Twenty-four Solar Terms 二十四節氣.

APPROXIMATE DATES.		THE SOLAR TERMS.		ZODIACAL POSITION OF THE SUN.
Feb.	5	立 春	Spring begins.	Aquarius.
,,	19	雨 水	Rain water.	Pisces.
Mar.	5	驚 蟄	Excited insects.	,,
,,	20	春 分	Vernal equinox.	Aries.
Apr.	5	清 明	Clear and bright.	,,
,,	20	穀 雨	Grain rains.	Taurus.
May	5	立 夏	Summer begins.	,,
,,	21	小 滿	Grain fills.	Gemini.
June	6	芒 種	Grain in ear.	,,
,,	21	夏 至	Summer solstice.	Cancer.
July	7	小 暑	Slight heat.	,,
,,	23	大 暑	Great heat.	Leo.
Aug.	7	立 秋	Autumn begins.	,,
,,	23	處 暑	Limit of heat.	Virgo.
Sep.	8	白 露	White dew.	,,
,,	23	秋 分	Autumnal equinox.	Libra.
Oct.	8	寒 露	Cold dew.	,,
,,	23	霜 降	Hoar frost descends.	Scorpio.
Nov.	7	立 冬	Winter begins.	,,
,,	22	小 雪	Little snow.	Sagittarius.
Dec.	7	大 雪	Heavy snow.	,,
,,	21	冬 至	Winter solstice.	Capricorn.
Jan.	6	小 寒	Little cold.	,,
,,	21	大 寒	Severe cold.	Aquarius.

VIII.—The Chinese Numerals.

	Ordinary style.	Large style to avoid fraud.	碼字		Ordinary style.	Large style to avoid fraud.	Examples.
1.	一	壹	丨	10.	十	拾	13, 丨三
2.	二	貳	丨丨	100.	百	佰	22, 丨丨二
3.	三	叁	丨丨丨	1,000.	千	仟	24, 丨丨乂
4.	四	肆	乂	10,000.	萬	万 abbr.	102, 丨〇二
5.	五	伍	𠄌	100,000.	億		115, 丨一𠄌
6.	六	陸	亠	1,000,000.	兆		1360, 丨三亠〇
7.	七	柒	亠				1335, 丨三三𠄌
8.	八	捌	二				4642, 乂亠乂二
9.	九	玖	文				

The 碼字 are commonly used on accounts where no need exists for special caution, they are used as in the above examples.

THE 214 RADICALS.

N.B.—The numbers in the Dictionary under which the Radicals occur may be ascertained from the Radical Index. The more common Radicals are printed in large type. Such abbreviated forms as, e. g., Nos. 9, 18, etc., do not usually stand alone, but are found in combination only.

Strokes						
1	23 亡	46 山	68 斗	92 牙	115 禾
1 一	24 十	47 巛 川 巜	69 斤	93 牛 牜	116 穴
2 丨	25 卜	48 工	70 方	94 犬 犭	117 立
3 丶	26 卩	49 己	71 无 旡	**5**	**6**
4 丿	27 厂	50 巾	72 日	95 玄	118 竹 ⺮
5 乙	28 厶	51 干	73 曰	96 玉 王 王	119 米
6 亅	29 又	52 幺	74 月	97 瓜	120 糸 糹
2	**3**	53 广	75 木	98 瓦	121 缶
7 二	30 口	54 廴	76 欠	99 甘	122 网 皿
8 亠	31 囗	55 廾	77 止	100 生	123 羊
9 人 亻	32 土	56 弋	78 歹	101 用	124 羽
10 儿	33 士	57 弓	79 殳	102 田	125 老
11 入	34 夂	58 彐 彑	80 毋	103 疋	126 而
12 八	35 夊	59 彡	81 比	104 疒	127 耒
13 冂	36 夕	60 彳	82 毛	105 癶	128 耳
14 冖	37 大	**4**	83 氏	106 白	129 聿
15 冫	38 女	61 心 忄 忄	84 气	107 皮	130 肉 月
16 几	39 子	62 戈	85 水 氵	108 皿	131 臣
17 凵	40 宀	63 戶	86 火 灬	109 目 罒	132 自
18 刀 刂	41 寸	64 手 扌	87 爪 爫	110 矛	133 至
19 力	42 小	65 支	88 父	111 矢	134 白
20 勹	43 尢 尣 尤	66 支 攵	89 爻	112 石	135 舌
21 匕	44 尸	67 文	90 爿	113 示 礻	136 舛
22 匸	45 屮		91 片	114	137 舟

138 艮	152 豕	**8**	181 頁	**11**	207 鼓
139 色	153 豸	167 金	182 風	195 魚	208 鼠
140 艸 廿	154 貝	168 長 長	183 飛	196 鳥	**14**
141 虍	155 赤	169 門	184 食	197 鹵	209 鼻
142 虫	156 走	170 阜 阝	185 首	198 鹿	210 齊
143 血	157 足	171 隶	186 香	199 麥	**15**
144 行	158 身	172 隹		200 麻	211 齒
145 衣 衤	159 車	173 雨	**10**	**12**	**16**
146 西	160 辛	174 青	187 馬	201 黃	212 龍
7	161 辰	175 非	188 骨	202 黍	213 龜
147 見	162 辵 辶	**9**	189 高	203 黑	**17**
148 角	163 邑 阝	176 面	190 髟	204 黹	214 龠
149 言	164 酉	177 革	191 鬥	**13**	
150 谷	165 釆	178 韋	192 鬯	205 黽	
151 豆	166 里	179 韭	193 鬲	206 鼎	
		180 音	194 鬼		

Some radicals in addition to their ordinary sounds, have the following colloquial designations:—

1	一橫	27,53	披厦	85	三點水火旁	122	扁四
2	一豎 or 一直	32	剔土旁 or 挑土	86	四點	130	肉字旁 or 月肉旁
3	一點	40	寶蓋頭	93	剔牛	140	草字頭
4	一撇	45	艸山	94	反犬 犭 獸側	146	西字部
7	兩橫	58	半橫	96	斜玉 王字旁	157	足字路
9	單立人 儿	59	三撇	104	病	162	走之 之
14	禿蓋	60	雙立人 儿	115	禾木字旁	163,170	耳 左耳 or 右耳
15	兩點 水	61	豎心旁	116	穴字頭	173	雨字頭
18	立刀	64	剔手旁	118	竹字頭		
26	小耳	6	反文	120	絞絲旁		

RADICAL INDEX

In this index the characters are arranged under their respective radicals according to the number of strokes used in writing them. The large figures underlined give the number of the radical, the smaller ones over the characters the number of strokes exclusive of the radical, and those at the sides the number under which the character may be found in the body of the dictionary.

Under the figure indicating the number of strokes the characters are arranged in the order of the radicals of their respective phonetics, thus facilitating reference, e.g., if one wishes to find 掃, he would turn up Radical No. 64, 手, and look in the column of characters having 8 strokes exclusive of the radical; the radical of the phonetic being 巾, No. 50, the character would be found in its proper place between characters 据 and 拼, the phonetics of these characters being Nos. 44 and 51, respectively. By this method a person who is familiar with the order of the radicals will be saved much searching up and down a long list of characters, and much uncertainty as to whether he may have overlooked the one for which he is searching.

<u>1</u> 一 3016	世 5790 丙 5284 且 803 丘 1213	中 1504 丰 1876 目 2932 丱 3562 串 1445	久 1188	九 1198 也 4481	于 7592 丁 1408	充 4078 享 2552	仉 204 仿 3839	伍 6188 会 2345	<u>1</u> 一 <u>2</u> 丨
<u>1</u> 七 579 丁 6381 万 742	<u>5</u> 乒 5302 兵 4925 两 3953 丢 6415 丞 385	<u>3</u> 、 1335	<u>3</u> 之 935	乞 564 也 7312 亙 2946 乱 406 乱 4220 乳 3144 龜 3621 乾 3233 亂 4220	亏 7643 云 7745 互 2152 井 1143 五 7187 亙 3344 亘 2889 些 2623 況 3603 亞 7225 亟 483	京 1127 亮 3949 亭 6399 毫 5336 亶 6048 亹 7118	什 5808 仆 1953 仄 6754	伍 7187a 伉 3274 价 630 佽 1498 份 1852 仵 7176 仰 7267 伋 469 任 3101 伕 7278 伊 2936 佖 5727 伐 1765 伎 438 仿 1808 休 2786 企 545 佌 5149 伙 2396 件 862 伏 1964	<u>3</u> 、 <u>4</u> ノ <u>5</u> 乙 <u>6</u> 亅 <u>7</u> 二 <u>8</u> 亠 <u>9</u> 人
<u>2</u> 三 5415 丈 200 上 5669 下 2520 万 7030	<u>6—10</u> 两 3953 並 5292 坙 6487	丸 7004 丹 6026 主 1336	<u>4</u> 乍 80 乏 1761 乎 2154 乑 6947			<u>9</u> 人 3097 1 入 508	<u>3</u> 仗 201 令 4043 以 2932 仡 565 他 5961 伢 3111 仟 907 仕 5777 仔 6940 付 1917 仙 2707 全 6615 代 5996 參 300		
<u>3</u> 不 5379 丕 3883 丑 1330 与 7615 丐 4489 丏 3194	<u>2</u> 刂 3671 丨 1194 个 3366 丫 7213	<u>4</u> ノ 5215 丿 乂 2934 乄 7187 乃 4612 <u>2</u> 乑 921 毛 6459	<u>5</u> 乑 1517 辰 4872 乨 6557 <u>7—10</u> 乖 3532 乘 398 乘 1478 <u>5</u> 乙 3017 亅 7448	<u>6</u> 亅 3408 了 3958 予 7601 爭 365 事 5787 <u>7</u> 二 1751	<u>8</u> 亠 6486 亡 7034 亢 3273 亥 2004 交 702 亦 3021 亨 2099	<u>2</u> 今 1053 仃 6382 仍 3121 介 629 仇 1332 仁 3099 从 6919	<u>4</u> 仲 1505 仔 7602		
<u>4</u> 丕 5137									

(1181)

9 人

5	低 6188	侂 6461	便 5224	倚 2953	側 6757	傑 774	僚 3969	**14**
佀 6801	佽 2881	侚 2920	俤 7194	俺 30	假 7357	備 4997	僦 1211	儔 1321
住 1337	佃 6349	侑 7534	俫 1218	倭 7153	健 854	偈 7285	僎 6889	儜 4726
作 6780	㳠 1296	侏 1347	俑 7569	倘 6106	傄 7405	傌 4317	僝 5575	儇 7140
余 7605	伸 5713	依 6981	傳 5311	倌 3553	偲 5581	傀 3653	僔 879	儘 1083
伶 4044	伯 4977	俾 4567	候 2135	倨 1536	偏 5246		僧 5453	儓 6017
价 4649	佘 5694	佰 4976	俟 5595	倔 1693	做 6776	**11**	憮 7186	儛 7186
你 4649	位 7116	侎 4448	係 2424	倖 2765	偺 6674	偏 7654	僬 722	償 5260
似 5593		佯 7248	俏 759	併 5293	傷 775	傘 914	僞 7060	
修 6624	**6**	俚 1745	信 2748	俯 1929	假 599	傷 6612	僮 6627	儒 3145
伽 581	侖 4246	㑢 2238	俗 5497	修 2794	俪 383	僅 1066	僕 5401	儕 120
伴 4876	侅 3192	侄 991	促 6838	倣 1808	偎 7070	傻 5614	像 2569	
佔 126	佼 703	㑏 2400	俚 3858	倡 207	偏 5134	僂 4137	償 1867	**15**
何 2109	來 3768	俏 1292		借 765	偕 621	傳 1446	價 2673	儳 1726
佋 5689	侁 5721	依 2990	**8**	倮 4108	偟 2284	催 6865	僱 3477	優 7509
估 3448	侇 6281		倈 3769	倏 5885	偶 4801	傭 7577		儱 4958
侗 6969	佺 1667	**7**	倫 4247	條 4997	偭 1570	偬 6911	**13**	儡 4227
佑 7542	份 3024	俎 6812	倪 4662	俗 975	偢 1228	傲 55	儉 848	償 230
佚 3025	供 3710	俛 4493	倆 3954	值 2136	偵 347	傷 5666	儓 5602	
佽 4723	例 3890	俐 3868	俱 1557	候 3723	價 4498	僚 1040	億 3042	**16**
㑊 4754	侲 7038	俞 7628	倒 6134	倀 214	偉 7081	僄 5193	儌 684	儭 342
佇 1365	侊 3622	侵 1108	倝 3234			僤 183	儈 1139	儲 1399
佗 6439	侃 3250	偕 3502	俾 5069	**10**		僇 4208	儳 3546	儱 4259
倪 4655	使 5770	侶 4281	倬 1261	傖 6708		傯 2707	僷 1394	
佐 6775	侗 6616	保 4946	倅 6871	傘 5420		債 118	僵 639	**17**
佈 5365	佳 593	俊 1727	倦 1641	傁 5470		傾 1161	儇 2876	儷 156
伡 5037	侔 649	俠 2631	俶 5882	傭 6118			儀 3003	儸 1982
佛 1982	侈 1038	俘 1937	倜 6266	傻 2426	**12**	儋 6042		
佀 6038	使 2983	偏 1585	倍 5000	傅 1948	傳 2435	價 603		**19**
体 6246	㑶 107	俓 1120	倉 6707	傲 2600	僑 745	儆 6654		儺 4100
低 6973	侍 5778	俦 4279	個 3366	傍 4927	僥 695	僻 5173		儹 6677
侮 7194	佩 5015	俄 4779	倖 1885		僖 170	儂 4769		儽 3915

									2
20	**7—8**	冀 443	**3**	凓 3926	**18**	刷 3505	剝 5143	**12**	人 9
儺 7348	堯 7355		冬 6603		刀 6124	利 3867	剟 6435		儿 10
儻 6106	黨 6094	**13**		**13**	刁 6268	剧 5143	剖 5358	劂 1681	入 11
21—22	**10—12**	冂 1238	**4**	凜 6430		初 1390	剮 6273	劃 2223	八 12
儽 4232	兜 6469	冄 3067	冲 1523	澤 4036	**1—3**	**6**	剒 7385	**13**	冂 13
儾 4628	兢 1132	冉	冴 2153	凛 1078	刃 3110	刻 3322	剜 418	劍 849	冖 14
		冊 6756	冰 5283	**14—15**	刄 id.1462	剌 2703	剛 7017	劊 3639	冫 15
10	**11**	冋 1238	決 1697	凝 4732	分 1851	刮 771	剝 3268	劌 3640	几 16
儿 3098	入 3152	回 2309	**5**	瀆 6515	刈 2935	剂 3642	剕 5337	劇 1593	凵 17
1	亼 7031	冎 6658	冶 7313		切 811	券 3495	剗 164	劈 5174	刀 18
兀 7205	內 4766	再 4373	冷 3844	**16**	刊 3242	制 1652	剟 6262	劉 4093	力 19
2	全 1666	冒 1297	**6**	几 104	刋	刺 986	剟 7336	**14**	
元 7707	㒰 5227	冑 3425	冽 3985	凡 1771	**4**	刹 5905		劍 849	
允 7759	㒰 6662	冕 1494	冼 4409	处 1407	刔 7007	剎 110	**9**	劌 90	
3	兪 1666	**14**	**8**	凭 5309	刎 7137	刾 6985	剪 876	劊 2410	
充 1520	㒰 3953	冖 4462	涼 3946	凰 2285	刑 5605	剕 6420	剮 3508	劇 3013	
兄 2807	兪 7628	冗 3180	凋 6270	凱 3205	划 2213	耵 1746	剭 5247	劑 457	
4		冘 7440	凌 4062	凳 6177	列 3984	到 6133	副 1951	**21**	
光 3583	**12**	冞 4447	凄 556	憑 5310	刖 5635	刮 3518	**10**	劖 3895	
兆 247	八 4845	冠 3564	淞 5553		刐 7697	**7**	剸 1263		
兇 2809	分 2414	冤 7719	凍 6606	**17**	**5**	剋 3321	剶 5750	**19**	
先 2702	六 4189	冥 4528	淨 1153	凵 3241	删 5628	到 6794	創 1162	力 3920	
5—6	公 3701	冢 1515	准 1486	凶 2808	刨 4942	剃 1118	割 3380	**2**	
兌 6560	共 3709	寫 2627	清 1169	凸 6305	判 4893	前 6247	剺 3013	劝 1662	
克 3320	兵 5282	籠 1534	**9**	凹 7268	刦 771	剌 919	剽 3197	**3**	
免 4492	其 525	羃 4467	減 828	出 1409	別 5208	削 2785	**11**	加 580	
兔 4492	具 1556		凌 6869	函 2049	刪 4509	則 6746	劂 3440	功 3698	
菟 6534	典 6347	**15**	淲 5310			**8**	劂 4138		
兒 1759		冫 5283	**10**			剞 6961	剿 164		
兜 5603	兼 830		滄 6709				劋 5194		
							劘 731		

4	動 6611	**1**	噐 4638		卜 5219	脆 7211	厥 1201	双 5915

| 19 力 |
| 20 勹 |
| 21 匕 |
| 22 匚 |
| 23 匸 |
| 24 十 |
| 25 卜 |
| 26 卩 |
| 27 厂 |
| 28 厶 |
| 29 又 |
| 30 口 |

4	動 6611	**1**	噐 4638		卜 5219	脆 7211	厥 1201
劣 4302	勔 4199	勹 5829	匙 5796		占 125	卹 495	
劧 3615	勒 3841			**24**	卡 616	卿 1155	**12**
劦 1060		**2**		十 5807	㕚 247		厰 226
	10	勿 7208	**22**		卦 3514		厮 5575
5	勘 2907	匀 7751	匚 1801	**1**	勴 2335	**27**	厭 7387
助 1370	勝 5754	欠 4939		千 906	卤 7519	厂 2016	**3—4**
劫 id.771	勞 3826	勾 3409	匝 2942	廿 1710			友 爰 1968
劬 1604			匜 6642			**2—6**	叐 3131
劭 5687	**11**	**3**	匠 3275	**2**	**26**	厄 1739	
努 1755	勢 5799	勼 3194	匡 3593	卅 5404	卩 798	底 id.951	**6**
	勤 732	匃	匣 7177	升 5745		厓 7236	変 5245
6	勰 4209	包 4937	匥 662	午			叔 5881
効 2597	勦 1097	㚛 6915	匦 2525		**2—4**	**7**	叚 5905
劾 2088	募 4585		匧 804	**3—4**	卬	厚 2147	受 5810
勋 3594	勔 499	**4—5**	匪 1820	卉 2326	卯 44	厙 5697	取 1615
		匈 2812	匰 7610	半 1875	卭 4369	厘 3883	
7	**12**	匃 5048	匱 3632	卍 7032	印 7451		**7—8**
勉 4195	勱 1682		匯 2353		危 7056	**8**	叚 598
勃 1983	勵 2951	**6**	匵 3638	**6**		厜 6929	叛 4897
勁 1119		匊 6156	匲 6516	卒 6827	**5**	原 7725	叙 2842
勅 1050	**13**	匃 1587		協 2639	卵 4219	厝 6799	変 5470
勇 1517	勵 6019			卓 1260	却 1183		叟 5470
勇 7571	勮 id.2640	**7—9**	**23**	卑 1993	卲 5688	**9**	
	勯 1324	匍 5388	匸 2413	單 6030		厠 6987	**11—16**
8		匏 4967			**6**	厫 3879	叠 6325
勍 1128	**14—18**	匐 1976	匹 5170	**7**	卺 1076		叡 3176
勑 1050 3769	勳 2907		西 4150	南 1620	卷 1640	**10**	叢 6921
	勴 3907	**21**	医 2978		卸 2626	厦 2522	
9	勸 3076	匕 5076	匽 7356	**10—11**	卹 2862	厨 1400	**30**
勘 3253	勸 1662		匾 5229	博 5322		厥 1680	口 3434
勗 2858		化 2211	匭 4678	準 1488	**7—10**	厤 3930	
	20	㐄 4952	區 1599		卻 1183		**2**
務 7198	勹 4937	北 4974		**25**		**11**	号 2064
				卜 5378		厘 1068	可 3381
							司 5585

叮 6383	名 ·1524	叫 700	呦 7545	哆 6417	唐 6116	唵 31	唧 496	嗌 7301	
叫 700	时 6893	听 6402	咈 1983	咵 3527	哦 4780	唛 815	喎 3544	喑 7419	
史 5769	吊 6276	吹 1476	呔 5036	咦 2984	哲 268	啼 5438	喊 2045		
右 7541		呀 7215	味 7115	咤 75	哽 3347	唿 2195	喜 2434	**10**	**30**
只 946	**4**	吽 2376	呧 6189	思 947	唻 5892	唔 7178	喬 744	嗆 678	口
叺 4825	否 1902	吠 1837	呡 7138	咸 2666	哺 5367	唳 3855	喪 5429	嗇 5447	
谷 7353	吾 7188	呈 372	咏 7591	哉 6650	唉 4	啓 4	單 6030	嗛 883	
召 234	吭 2055		呱 6995	咪 1304	睍 6538	啟 542	喚 2249	嗣 5588	
另 3506	含 2017	**5**	呷 2526	咨 6923	哨 5676	唱 208	喫 1047	嘻 2534	
叨 6141	吟 7425	呸 5138	呻 5711	哞 4482	唔 3950	睎 78	喧 2869	嗟 763	
叼 6269	吮 5929	呾 1573	和 2115	咾 3834	唁 7373	唽 2489	喀 3325	嗙 4928	
另 4073	呐 4609	咋 6743		昱 570	員 7721	啖 6052	喔 7159	嗦 5425	
句 1541	吩 1853	呼 2155	音 6492	咱 6645	唄 1865	啌 663	嘗 1041	嗥 5138	
叱 1016	吻 7138	呋 1948		咥 2456	唣 6825	啍 3335	啼 6242	嗚 7167	
叵 5349	呱 id.5138	命 4537	**6**	哎 20	啶 1491	睯 6052	喙 2348	嗥 2073	
叶 2633	呃 1740	周 1293	咺 2866	哀 3	哪 1605	嗉 4193	膽 7373	嗑 2120	
古 3447	吸 2471	咒 1303	咳 3323	哂 5728	唈 3038	唬 2163/2582	喝 2123	嗌 3053	
叩 3435	呂 4280	咀 6432	咬 7298		唖 3859	啄 1266	嗒 6674	嗔 325	
台 6008	告 3287	咖 582	咻 2787	**7**		唫 7425a	喳 68	嗌 6995	
	吞 6587	呴 1963	哈 2003	哼 2100	**8**	問 7141	喋 6316	嗉 5491	
3	吳 7201	呷 6643	眸 2937	啪 4978	唷 7226	啊 2	煦 2833	嗡 7147	
吏 3853	吼 2148	咕 1595	咷 6152	唎 3869	啍 6588	售 5843	喂 7103	嗜 5800	
后 2141	吵 251	呵 2110	咲 2615	唰 4846	啇 5673	唯 7064	嗜 622	嗅 2792	
吒 75	君 1715	咍 2013	哄 2387	哲 3361	商 6219	啡 1821	喤 2286	嗜 id.6052	
吃 1047	呎 2937	呫 6327	㗊 3507	嗳 1109	啘 1760		喝 7565	嗒 5977	
吁 2818	吧 4827	咕 3449	咧 3986	哈 2018	啕 6152	**9**	啾 1206	嗞 6923	
合 2117	呫 6643	胸 2828	响 2559	哥 3363	啐 6872	嘵 3950	喁 7494	嗁 6242	
向 2549	吆 7283	昳 2063	咯 4120	哭 3500	啤 5161	喉 2137	善 5657	嗤 1019	
同 6615	呬 5728	咎 1192	号 4790	唆 5462	啜 1277	喻 7629	喘 1443	置 4746	
吐 6533	吣 1109	映 7240	品 5281	哮 2602	啁 248	喇 3758	喟 3646	嗎 4311	
吉 476	吱 6922	呶 4634	咽 7396	哔 3825	唾 6458	喃 4621	喵 4471	嗝 2134	
各 3368	吝 4040	呢 4656	哇 6989	嗁 2417	唪 1886	卿 2682	嗒 3093/4747	嗋 3316	

11	嘽 6071	噈 685	嚦 5276	四 5598	圈 1655	**4**	坻 1029
嘔 4815	嘵 2593	噲 3537	嚨 4260		圉 7659	坏 5008	坩 3243
煆 3468	嘷 6884a	噦 7706		**3**	國 3738	坍 6056	坡 5343
嘉 592	嘹 3970	噤 1079	**17**	回 2309		坛 6059	垃 3755
嘲 3739	嘱 1386	噬 5764	嚴 7347	囟 2752	**9—10**	坑 3354	
嘍 400	嘽 5551	噶 3367	嚶 7458	因 7407	圍 7082	坐 6778	**6**
嘍 4139	嘰 410	噥 4174	嚳 3502	囝 4618	園 7731	坋 5033	垣 7724
嘛 259	噁 609 (see 7419-A)	噴 5036	嚷 3077	囤 823	圓 7722	坌 1724	垓 3188
嘷 2332	嚘 6052	嚙 4182			圖 6531.9	坂 1782	型 2756
喊 6826	噉 6589	嚷 4770	**18**	**4**	**11**	圾 470	塊 3623
嗽 56	嘶 5576	嚵 5957	嚚 2596	囮 4788	圖 6531	坳 7271	垢 3421
嗽 5482	嘬 1427	噸 6585	嚥 157	园 7007	團 6549	坟 1868	城 380
嗹 5484	嘲 249		嚼 1180	囦 2191	圖 4788	坼 539	垛 6421
嘅 3209	噍 723	**14**	囁 4706	囷 2309		坊 1803	垤 6312
嘗 229	嗾 5572	嚀 4727	囀 1432	囹 6914	**13—19**	坎 3245	垠 7431
嘈 6734	噷 2471	嚔 6258		囿 6593	圜 2255	址 940	垩 7414
嗽 5482	嘯 2618	嚡 2082	**19**	困 3688	圞 4212	坒 5078	
嘽 5121	嘷 2073	嘆 2205	囊 4627				**7**
嘐 2592	嘩 2218	嚎 2073	囅 154	**5**	**32**	**5**	埕 373
嘆 6081	嘴 6857	嚇 2092	囉 4101	囱 4045	土 6532	坵 1213	埋 1692
嘘 2822	噎 3066	嚐 2682	囈 3015	固 3450		坯 5008	埖 5053
嘩 2157	嘟 6501	嚅 3146		囷 1719	**2**	坴 4190	埭 4133
嘖 6749			**20—22**		圣 3499/5753	坰 1238	埂 3348
嗹 4010		**15**	囌 5489	**6—7**		坷 3382	埏 7343
嘛 4304	**13**	囂 7443	囑 4704	圃 7535	**3**	坫 6339	埔 5369
	嚥 7366	噜 4177	囑 1386	圉 7649	在 6657	坭 4660	埵 7570
12	器 549		囔 4629	圂 2049	地 6198	坪 5304	埃 1707
嚕 1101	噩 4799	**16**		圇 5368	圬 7174	坳 7271	埇 4843
嘮 3827	噪 5438	嚥 3932	**31**	圀 2373	圩 7593	坼 289	垻 4319
嘁 1683	嚊 7657	嚥 7396	囗 7054		圭 3609	坦 6057	
嘻 2436	噫 2961	嚥 id.2822		**8**	圮 2931	坤 3684	**8**
嚚 549	嗳 10	嚮 2561	**2** 囚 1234	圖 4248	圯 5141		執 996

執 3014
塱 4808
基 399
塒 1558
埠 5162
埠 5377
培 5011
堂 6107
塌 3264
塚 5436
域 7676
塹 3684
場 3035
埜 7314
堅 825
堊 3245
菫 1065
堥 5994
堆 6557
9
塋 4947
埃 2138
堰 7358
報 4955
塙 3729
塄 4791
塍 7414
堯 7295
塔 387
塓 3160
場 218

30 口
31 口
32 土

堤 6231	城 576	壞 3784	壬 3100	妃 7713	奇 514	奭 5327	妝 1451	娠 3422	32 土
堞 6317	堅 454	壆 2779	壯 1453	夙 5502	佹 7378	奮 1874		姻 7408	33 士
堪 3254	場 218	壟 3337	殼 3406	多 6416	奈 4615		5	娃 6990	34 夊
堵 625	堰 4331	壁 5113	声 5748	夜 7315		38	姐 766	婍 3528	35 夊
埠 9295	境 1136	壙 5537	垂 1478	够 3419	6	女 4776	姊 6948	姦 817	36 夕
堵 6497	墓 4586	甕 7555	壺 2187	夠	奧 2248		姒 5594	姨 2985	37 大
	堇 1067		壻 2836	夢 4433	奕 3022	2	姍 5416	妍 7340	38 女
10	塹 926	14	壹 3016	夤 2397	契 551	奶 4613	妻 555	娥 5560	
塚 1516	墅 5876	壓 7231	壼 3687	夥 7427	奔 5028	奴 4753	姑 3453	威 7051	
塡 2908	塵 328	壑 2128	壽 5846		奎 3643		姰 2829	姝 5850	
塘 6117		壽 6127		37	奓 74	3	始 5772	姿 6924	
寒 5446	12	壞 2908	34	大 5943	奏 6808	她 5961	妳 4613	姜 637	
塍 387	塈 5647	壥 2469	夊 962			妄 7035	妮 4657	姥 4583	
根 6572	墧 738	壧 2068		1	7	妁 5830	妹 4410	姪 992	
塗 6525	墫 6886		35	夫 1908	套 6160	如 3137	妺 4547		
塋 7466	塸 669	15	夊	夫 3535	奘 2425	姜 704	姊 6948	7	
塢 7168	墩 6572	壙 3605	夆 654	天 6361	奚 6700	好 2062	姐 5946	娩 7012	
塡 6373	增 6763	壘 4228	夆 1877	太 6020		妃 1838	姆 4583	娯 7647	
壞 5492	播 1791			夭 7277	8	奸 818	姓 2770	娌 7110	
塑	墟 2823	16	35		奡 53		妯 1377	娣 6202	
塥 7148	壜 6069	壜 6069	夊 5517	2	奲 3643	4	妬 6503	媳 433	
塌 5967	墳 1868	壚 4157		失 5806		妞 4738	委 7098	娥 4781	
塔 5978	墽 6566	壤 2232	炎 1736	央 7239	9	好 7602	妾 814	娑 5455	
輂 6702	墜 1471	壝 7117	复 1991		奢 5696	姶 1054		娟 1628	
塊 3550	墮 6427	壟 4261	夏 2521	3—4	奠 6357	妊 3102	6	娉 5312	
	墨 4386	壥 2816	夐 2816	夸 3526		妖 7279	姮 2106a	娘 4683	
11		壤 3662	夔 3662	奇 2982	10—11	妙 4474	姣 704	娠 312	
塾 3255	13	17—21		夷 611	奥 46	妒 6503	姘 3102	嫂 4745	
墊 6359	壇 6059	壞 3078	36		奩 3997	妓 439	姚 5720	娌 3860	
壞 4140	墻 674	壩 4843	夕 2485	5	奪 6433	妨 1804	姬 7269		
塾 5894	墝 387		33	奉 1884	12—13	妣 5082	姫 408	8	
壙 7578		士 5776	外 7001		奬 5102	妥 6454	始 3624	嫗 7227	
								姑 477	

38 女 39 子 40 宀 41 寸 42 小									
娓 4662a	娜 3821	**12**	**19**	**7**	安 26	宵 2607	審 4956	**5—6**	
婢 4994	**10**	嬉 2437	孿 4298	孫 4496	守 5844	容 7560	**11**	尅 5349	
娶 1616	嫌 2669	嬌 690	~~~	孫 5541	**4**	家 594	寰 3517	封 23	
婉 7018	媾 3426	嬋 5648	**39**	**8—10**	宋 2993	宰 6655	寠 1571	封 1887	
婦 1963	嫄 7726	嬈 3086	子 6939	孰 5893	完 7008	宸 337	寧 4725	**7**	
姸 5297	嫂 5434	嫵 7181	子 784	孱 169	宏 2377	**8**	寨 116	尅 3321	
娼 209	媲 5159	嫣 3619	孑 3708	孳 6936	宋 5565	寧 4725	寢 1110	專 1950	
婚 2360	嫁 596	嫻 2674	**1—2**	孵 1938	**5**	寃 7719	寤 7192	射 5703	
媒 7157	嫋 4687	**13**	孔 3720	**13—14**	宜 2993	寄 3552	察 111	**8**	
娎 3780	媳 2496	嬗 5652	孕 7765	學 2780	官 7016	密 7016	寥 3963	專 1428	
斌 7181	嫐 4417	嬙 675	**3**	孺 3147	宛 4463	寇 4464	寬 4558	尉 7111	
婆 5347	嫉 493	嬡 11	存 6891	孻 3775	宓 4956	寀 3444	實 5821	將 656	
娃 7433	媪 51	嬡 2877	孖 6941	**16—19**	宝 1298	寅 6666	**12**	**9**	
媚 7408	媵 7492	嬴 7480	字 6942	孽 4701	宙 6393	寅 7426	寮 3971	尋 2744	
婁 4136	嬰 4901	孿 5106	**4**	孽	定 6100	**9**	寫 2627	尊 6884	
媖 5189	媸 1020	**14**	孛 5023	孾 7457	宕 6896	寧 4724	審 5729	**11—13**	
婕 788	媽 4312	嬭 4613	孝 2601	孿 4213	**6**	寒 2048	寬 3578	對 6562	
娴 4804	媿 3654	嬲 4691	孜 6943	~~~	宣 2890	寔 5821	**13—16**	導 6137	
婧 1145	**11**	嬪 5261	孚 2780	**40**	客 3324	寐 4416	寰 2256	~~~	
9	嫗 7655	**15—16**	孿 7457	宀 4488	宋 505	富 1952	寶 4956	**42**	
婷 6401	嫠 3880	嬌 5730	**5**	**2**	宥 7536	寍 4725	寵 1534	小 2605	
婾 7630	嫡 6220	嬾 3786	孥 4756	宁 1364	宦 2238	寓 7622	~~~	少 5675	
媢 4374	嫦 222	**17**	孤 3470	宄 3630	室 5820	**10**	**41**	尔 1754	
媧 6997	嫵 2972	孅 2720	孟 4428	宂 3180	**7**	寮 4724	寸 6892	尖 5881	
媞 6232	嫩 4765	孃 4684	季 435	它 6439	害 2015	寢 1093	**2—4**	尗 865	
媟 2648	嫚 4332	孀 5920	**6**	**3**	宮 3705	寘 976	对 6562	尚 5670	
媒 4397	嫛 2972		孩 2005	宅 275	寇 3444	寮 5459	寺 5597	尝 2481	
媛 7736	嫣 7331			宇 7594	宴 7364		导		
媚 4392	嫖 5195								
娑 7200	嬲 4222								
婿 2836	嫪 3837								

(col 9)	(col 8)	(col 7)	(col 6)	(col 5)	(col 4)	(col 3)	(col 2)	(col 1)
寮 3968	尾 7109	屍 2449	**5**	崒 6836	嵯 6787	巉 158	巨 1544	帗 1010
鬱 6735	尿 4686	**12**	岨 1574	崿	嵊 509	巗 2453	巫 7164	袼 6123
~	**5**	履 3893	岳 7495	崖 7236	歲 5538	歸 3670	差 105	帚 1299
43	屌 5896	層 6772	岱 5997	崚 3846	嵩 5554	**18**	~	帕 4855
尣 7033	屈 6259	**14—21**	岡 3269	崦 7379	嵬 7096	巍 7105	**49**	帛 4979
尣	屆 636	履 1572	岸 40	崎 515	**11**	**19**	己 429	帔 5144
尤 7511	屈 1621	屬 5896	岩 6291	崇 1528	嶇 1600	巒 4214	己 2930	帘 3998
尨 4353	居 1535	屭 2459	岵 2164	崛 1694	嶁 4141	嶺 6338	巳 5590	**6**
尲 3187	屍	~	岣 3410	崗 3269	嶎 7113	**20**	巴 4826	帥 5909
尲 7038	屎 5075	**45**	岷 4510	崑 3679	嶃 158	巖 7349	厄 930	帝 6204
就 1210	**6**	屮 283	岫 2800	崩 5038	嶂 184	巘 7368	巷 2553	帟 1646
尵 1512	屍 5759	屯 6592	岩 7349	崧 5554	**12**	~	巽 5550	帨 5818
尶 831	屎 5757	屰 4676	**6**	崢 366	嶠 746	**47**	~	**7**
尷	屋 7212		峒 6617	崆 3724	嶓 5319	川巛 1439	**50**	師 5760
~	**7**	**46**	峙 954	峥 2585	嶝 6171	州 1289	巾 1056	帨 5926
44	展 139	山 5630	峋 2916	崋 2216	嶙 4029	巟 2270	**1**	帬 1738
尸 5756	屐 488	**2—3**	**7**	崟 7438	嶚 1600	巡 2927	市 6642	席 2502
	屑 1219	屵 5538	峻 1728	崔 6864	**13**	巠 1117	**2**	帮 4914
1	屑 2652	屹 566	峯 1878	**9**	嶧 3060	巡 2927	布 5364	**8**
尺 1045	**8**	岘 7206	峽 2531	崴 6907	嶓 7325	巢 253	市 5792	帶 6005
尹 7439	屏 5298	岜 546	峨 4782	崴 7003	嶇 5540	巤 3992	**3—4**	幀 7019
2—3	屌 4805	**4**	峩 760	崶 6656	**14**	~	帆 1772	常 221
尻 3298	**9**	岑 329	峭 2683	崵 1675	巇 794	**48**	帋 953	帡 5299
尼 4654	屜 6259	岎 109	峴 7670	嵌 3249	巉 7583	工 3697	希 2416	帩 5963
尽 1082	屏 5896	岽 471	峪 6131	嵋 4393	嶽 7502	左 6774	**5**	帳 197
4	屠 6529	岐 522	島	崳 7623	嶷 4671	巧 743	帖 5999	帷 7065
局 1584		岐 5538	**8**	嶽 426	嶾 2853		帖 6328	**9**
屁 488	**11**		嶂 3745	嶷 6936a	嶺 4059			帽 4375
屏 5150	屨 4288		嶷 4249	嵐 3783	**17**			幫 4914
			嶙 5258	**10**				
				嶙 364				

3

'50	巾
51	干
52	幺
53	广
54	廴
55	廾
56	弋
57	弓
58	彐
59	彡
60	彳

幄 7160　**幅** 1977　**幍** 752　**幀** 348　**幃** 7083

10　**幌** 2278

11　**幗** 3740　**幔** 4333　**幕**　**幖** 4559　**幘** 6750

12　**幟** 977　**幣** 5103　**幡** 1792　**幬** 2224　**幢** 1464

13　**㠍** 4005　**幭** 1401　**幨** 166　**幩** 1869

14　**幫** 4914　**幬** 6128　**幪** 4438

16—17　**幰** 2698　**纖** 888

51　**干** 3211

10　**平** 5303　**年** 4711　**幵** 819　**并 / 幷** 5292　**幸** 2764　**幹** 3235　**棄** 820

52　**幺** 7282

幻 2235　**幼** 7544　**茲** 6935　**幽** 7505　**絲** 3563　**幾** 409

53　**广** 7371

2　**庀** 5148

3　**広** 4540　**庄** 1450

4　**序** 2851　**庝** 6594　**庋** 440　**床** 1459　**庇** 5083

5　**府** 1928　**庚** 3339　**庖** 4964　**店** 6341　**底** 6190　**庙** 4473

6　**麻** 2788　**度** 6504　**庬** 1052　**庠** 2576

7　**座** 6779　**庭** 6405　**庑** 4352　**庫** 3496

8　**庫** 5070

庵 33　**庿** 6464　**康** 3278　**庶** 5874　**庸** 7576

9　**廁** 6987　**廈** *id.5471*　**廟** 2563　**庚** 7610

10　**廉** 4003　**廋** 5471　**廈** 2522　**廚** 1400　**廌** 1043　**庮** 7550　**廊** 3822　**廘** 2324

11　**厰** 57　**廐** 1201　**廖** 3964　**廑** 1068　**廓** 3753　**廕** 7446

12　**廛** 177　**廠** 226

廝 5575　**廟** 4473　**廡** 7182　**廢** 1848　**廥** 2731　**廣** 3590　**廚** 1400

13　**廧** 674　**廩** 5914　**廪** 4037

16—22　**廬** 4158　**廳** 6403

弁 5223　**弄** 4278　**弇** 7377　**弈** 3023　**弊** 5102

56　**弋** 3018　**式** 3016　**弌** 1751　**弒** 5817　**弑** 5797

57　**弓** 3703

1　**弔** 6276　**引** 7429

2—3　**弗** 1981　**弘** 2380　**弛** 5767

4　**弟** 6201　**弝** 4828

5　**弩** 4757　**弢** 6145　**弦** 6191

弦 2661　**弧** 2184

6　**弮** 1653　**弭** 4457

7　**弱** 3128　**弰** 5677

8　**弶** 670　**弲** 5043　**弸** 5039　**強** 668　**張** 195

9　**弼** 5127　**彀** 3420　**彊** 668

11—19　**彄** 3441　**彈** 6072　**彊** 668　**彌** 4459　**彍** 3751　**彎** 7028

归 3617　**彔** 4192　**彖** 6556　**彗** 2331　**彘** 963　**彙** 2349　**彝** 3001

59　**彡** 5625

形 2759　**彤** 6625　**彧** 7677　**彥** 7372　**彬** 5257　**彪** 5181　**彫** 6273　**彩** 6667　**彭** 5060　**彰** 185　**影** 7484

60　**彳** 1044

4　**彴** 1498　**彷** 1805　**役** 3028

5

祖 681　**往 / 徃** 7050　**彿** 1984　**征** 352　**彼** 5093

6　**徊** 2310　**後** 2143　**待** 6002　**徇** 2917　**徉** 7249　**律** 4297　**很** 2094

7　**徐** 2841　**徑** 1120　**徒** 6536

8　**徠** 3769　**從** 6919　**御** 7664　**徜** 223　**得** 6161　**徙** 2468　**徘** 4869

9　**復** 1992　**徧** 5230

徨 2287	忑 6164	怍 6781	恬 3103	**7**	愩 6377	**9**	意 2960	懸 6166
循 2926	忙 4344	怜 3995	恰 617	患 2240	怒 4653	愉 7631	**10**	懽 4679
10	忘 7036	悅 2276	恍 2276	您 4722	悼 6135	愈 7632	愴 6710	慘 6686
徯 2427	忍 3112	忽 6915	恭 3711	悠 7520	悴 6873	惻 6758	慊 806	慳 826
微 7061	忉 971	怨 7714	恣 6925	悅 7702	倦 1656	愜 805	愿 7727	憂 7508
徬 4929	志 6894	怴 810	恝 605	悟 4040	惠 2339	感 3232	惷 7754	博 6550
徭 7285	忖 432	怙 2165	恊 2640	悟 7189	惙 1278	愕 4792	愲 2374	慰 7112
12	忌 3212	怡 2964	恫 2810	惧 7202	惆 1316	愛 5129	愬 5322	慵 7579
德 6162	忒 6163	怗 6329	恂 2918	惺 374	悽 557	愎 5129	愦 2279	慷 3279
徹 285	**4**	怠 5989	恇 3595	悃 3689	悸 436	愯 3161	愻 5494	慶 1167
徵 358	怀 2233	怪 3536	恉 3625	悛 1676	惋 7020	惇 1249	愯 3927	慧 2333
13	忸 4739	快 7241	恢 2307	恩 6915	窓 7718	惱 4635	憝 1182	慈 5563
徽 686	忠 1506	怒 4758	恪 4040	悖 5003	惝 227	愾 6428	慹 7424	慼 577
徻 2234	忡 1522	怩 4658	恪 3400	慈 6965	悻 2766	愍 4521	愽 2454	慙 6690
14—17	念 4716	怖 5366	恫 6618	悟 4279	惦 6342	慍 7766	慁 7573	慨 3210
徽 2354	忪 1499	怦 5049	恦 2311	悌 6248	惚 2196	愒 807	慦 7447	慢 4334
儴 2572	忧 331	怫 1985	恩 1743	悊 268	懲 384	惺 2361	愻 5734	慾 7672
~~	忿 1854	急 480	恓 3536	悍 2024	惑 2403	惶 2288	愫 5493	憧 186
61	忽 2194	怛 5947	恚 7121	悚 5561	惜 2361	想 2564	慅 7285a	憎 2500
心 忄 小	忴 7178	怵 1411	恈 650	悔 2336	惕 6263	惜 2773	態 6024	慘 3965
2735	忤 5220	恍 5026	恕 5875	惄 6263	惝 3782	愚 7624	慆 6142	蠢 1526
1—2	忳 6021	性 2771	恃 5779	悉 7573	悤 6162	愁 1325	慈 6965	憩 536
必 5109	快 3547	怞 1313	恐 3721	悤 6162	悾 3725	愀 753	慌 2272	慕 4587
忉 6125	忞 6368	思 5580	恐	惆 3725	惘 7046	惴 1473	憋 5430	懂 1099
3	忮 441	怕 4856	恉 958	悄 761	悵 215	惽 7076	愷 3206	慮 4292
志 6074	忻 2727	**6**	恤 2862	悄 3039	悶 4420	惰 6425	愧 3654	慅 6741
	5	恆 2107	息 7250	悝 3645	悶 7066	惹 3094	**11**	**12**
	怚 6832	恒	羞 1036	**8**	惟 1170	慂 889	慴 4500	憭 3828
	怎 6762	恔 2598	恥 6365	惡 4809	悱 1822	惲 7761	慵 7420	憙 2438
		恋 2006	恬 2095	惇 6571	悲 4992	**11**		
		戀 4299	恨 2461	惧 1560		慟 6640 慪 4816		

60 彳 / 61 心

4

| 61 心 | 62 戈 | 63 戶 | 64 手 |

61 心 (cont.)

憚 6031
憲 2697
憭 3972
憖 2053
懊 227
懍 5209
憨 6563
懆 1130
憕 6764
憸 6697
憔 756
憮 7183
慭 7455
憍 1702
憧 1529
憐 3996
憩 536
憤 1870
慣 3567
憒 3637
憫 2675
憫 4521
憑 5310

13
憶 2688
憷 4998
憨 1098
懆 6725
懊 47
憶 3043

憨 2046
戀 4575
懌 3061
懁 2878
懁 4038
懂 6613
懈 2539
憺 6043
憿 1562
懯 3338
懕 7477

14
懕 7388
懤 6129
懞 4436
懟 6563
懣 4420
憼 965
憻 5987
懦 4750

15
懰 4094
懲 384
憒 965

16
懵 4436
懸 2887
懗 7090
懷 2233
懶 3787

17
懷 180

18
懿 2999
懼 1560
懾 272
懽 2265
懾 5561

19—24
戀 4299
孌 4626
戄 2784
戁 1458

62 戈

戈 3358

1
戉 7197
戊 7701

2
成 379
戎 3181
成 5873
戍 2861
戓 6663

3
戒 627
我 4778

4
或 2402
戕 673
戔 866

7
戚 575
戛 6315

8
戞 608
戟 487

9
戡 506
戥 6315
戤 6179
戮 3256
戮 3657
戮 3198
戠 988

10
戯 1462
截 793

11—13
戳 4210
戰 147
戲 2452

14
戴 6003

63 戶 (64 above)

戳 1283

63
戶 2180

1
戹 1739

4
扅 2181
所 5465
房 1806
戾 3854

5
扁 1239
扁 5228

6
扁 5674a see 7337
扆 5642
扇 2054
扊 2991

7
扈 2182

8
扉 7337
扉 1823

64 手

手 / 扌 5838
才 6660

1
扎 86

2
打 5945
扔 3122
抓 4853
扑 5402

3
抖 5837
托 6460
扦 910
扠 97
扣 3436
扛 3261
扞 2027

4
扭 4740
抔 5357
承 386
抒 5854
抗 3276
扵 7643
抝 7299
扮 4878

抛 4962
拘 3411
抹 5221
抑 3031
扭 4810
扳 4899
扱 2472
扶 1909
抉 1696
抄 6581
拖 4829
把 6277
扫 242
找 7130
技 442

5
拄 1338
拖 6440
拊 1919
拾 4046
拙 1273
抱 4938

抾 3762
拜 4860
拌 4894
招 235
拘 1542
拐 3533
拈 4712
抬 6018
挾 1051
挐 6440
拏 4603
拒 1545
抨 5050
拗 7272
挤 4898
拂 1986
祕 5110
拢 4810
拆 290
担 6039
抹 4548
拇 4584
抿 4514
抵 6192
拔 4848
拑 897
抽 1314
押 7234
拍 4986
披 5145
拓 1001/6460
拉 3756

6
拯 360
挍 705
挨 3189
挑 2085
拼 6282
拴 5912
拱 3712
挈 808
拮 780
拿 4603
拾 5809
捐 4639
挂 3515
拳 1654
挐 4603
按 27
挓 76
持 1035
拭 5818
指 959
拽 1419/3008
挖 6999
拷 3300
括 3519
捃 897
拫 2096

7
挽 7013
捌 4847
捐 1630
捊 3040

4

4

攀 4899	攩 6088	攷 6343	**11**	斝竽 602	斿旆 7521 / 5022	旛 7619	昊 2072	晉晋 1088
攔 4229	**21—22**	政 355	毆 1602	料 3959	**6**	**71**	旹 5780	id.233
攞 4864	攬 3805	啟 4513	敵 6221	斛 2200	旅 4286	无 7173	旻 4519	晃 2277
攦 4721	攘 4630	敇 4571	數 5865	斜 2624	旁 4926	既 453	昕 2726	晌 2550
攕 6267	攞 6326	**6**	敷 1950	斝 7610	旄 133		昉 1809	晏 7363
擲 1012		效 2599	整 356	斞 319	旂 5022	**72**	昌 206	時 5780
擷 2636	**65**	**7**	斂 3961	斡 3570	旃 535	日 3124	明 4534	晒 5623
	支 937	敘 2842			旆 4363		昆 3678	
16	鼓 516	敆 7650	**13**	**69**		**1**	昏 2359	**7**
攔 3759		教 719	斂 3999	斤 1059	**7**	旦 6037	旺 7039	晚 7014
攜 2406	**66**	敖 54	斀 3062		旋 4661	旧 1205		晷 5665
攏 4262	攴 攵 5399	敕 1050		斥 1052	旒 4079	**2**	**5**	晤 7190
	2	敏 4517	**14—16**	斧 1934	旌 1142	旭 2855	昨 6782	晧 2076
17	攷 3299	救 1193	斃 5105	斫 1254	旔 1950	旬 2915	昜 5285	晞 2418
攖 7459	收 5837	敗 4866	斅 1533	斬 142	旋 2894	旨 957	昂 7258	晟 5751
攙 159	**3**	**8**	斆 2604	斯 1255	族 6830	旪 2639	昭 4370	晦 2337
攘 3079	攸 7519	敃 420		斲 5574		早 6721	昀 236	晡 5371
攔 3790	攻 3699	敏 225	**67**	新 2737	**9—10**		昝 2830	晝 1302
	改 3196	敢 5101	文 7129	斵 1263	旒 4079	**3**	春 6674	晨 338
18	**4**	敢 3229	齊 560	斷 6547	旛 5686	旱 2023	映 1493	
攜 2443	攽 3244	敔 887	齋 115		旗 535	旰 3213	昳 7488	**8**
攛 6853	放 1807	斁 7437	斐 1824	**70**	旖 2959	旸 7265	昵 6307	普 5384
攝 5710	**5**	散 5421	斌 5257	方 1802			昚 4680	景 1129
	變 3346	**9**	斑 4890		**12**	**4**	昇 5220	晾 3945
19	攺 3383	敫 478	斒 2251	**2—4**	旛 977	昔 2493	昧 4411	晬 6861
攣 4300		敬 1138	煥 4888	斺 7357	旚 2282	昇 2952	昏 2359	晷 3629
攞 4102		**10**	斕 3791	於 7643		昂 5746	昶 231	晣 5213
攢 6845		敲 735			**13—15**		昰 2772	晶 1141
攤 6082				**5**	旜 134	昃 45.	星 5794	晳 2490
20				施 5768	旛 1793	昄 6755	是 7682	晰
攞 1705	攺 3455		斗 6472		旝 3543		昱	智 933
攬 69							**6** 晅 2867	

64 手
65 支
66 攴
67 文
68 斗
69 斤
70 方
71 无
72 日

4

| 72 日 73 日 74 月 75 木 |

72 日

桔 781
格 3309
桐 6619
桂 3610
築 773
案 28
栽 6651
梅 2919
桌 1262
株 1348
栢 4980
栩 2826
栲 3835
栲 3301
桱 993
柏 1203
栝 3520
根 3328
桁 2102
栗 3925
栖 2462

7
梳 5860
梲 1279
梣 5263
梨 3870
棓 3484
梧 7191
梠 4282
梛 3691
楏 5079

枏 6462
查 103
柴 121
柢 6193
染 3071
柒 579
柑 3224
某 4577
柙 2527
柚 7514
柏 4980
柔 3133
柘 266
标 4039
柰 4615
柰 291
柬 845
柳 4097

6
租 2236
核 2089
梭 706
栓 5913
栮 1766
桄 3584
桃 6148
栱 3713
栵 3913
框 3596
桅 7057
桑 5424

枕 2658
枳 5849
枇 5152
杰 774
枒 7217
枉 7040
果 3732

5
柄 5286
柴 7317
栍 2949
桂 1339
柞 6783
棁 1379
栅 93
枷 584
架 583
枸 3412
枹 1962
柩 1191
枳 948
棖 2590
柯 3384
枯 3492
栦 3534
柂 2464
柁 6441
柅 4659
柜 1546
柿 5793

杠 3262
杷 547
杆 3214
杙 3019
杉 5626
材 6661

4
杯 4996
枏 4622
杼 1369
杭 2056
枘 3167
松 5552
枕 308
枌 1855
杵 1389
板 4885
杪 4475
杶 1495
杷 4830
柿 1842
枝 938
枚 4389
料 6474
析 2488
枋 1810
杲 3284
杳 6605
杏 7297
林 4022

75 木

1
末 4546
本 5025
未 7114
朮 5886
札 87

2
朽 2791
杆 6396
朱 1346
朵 6419
杁 4830
束 6986
机 411
朴 5354

3
杖 202
杇 7174
宋 4345
杌 7207
杓 5831
杈 98
杏 2763
呆 5986
束 5891
杜 6495
林 6199
李 3852
村 6895

木 4593
不 6577

阴 7444

4
服 1999
朋 5054

5
朒 1841

6
朓 6283
朓 316
朔 5940

7
望 7043
朢 4534
朗 3808

8
期 526
朞 401
朝 233

10—16
朦 7043
朣 6629
朧 4440
朧 4264

73 日

日 7694

2
曳 3008
曲 1623

3—6
更 3346
曷 2122
書 5857

7
曼 4330
曹 6733

8
曾 6771
最 6858
替 6257
暜 6696

9—12
會 2345
曑 4330
朁 6696

74 月

月 7696

2—3
有 7533

曉 2594
暾 2996
曒 3974
曒 6590
暨 455
睥 2074
曈 6628
暹 2712
曇 6068

13
曖 12
曩 2557

14
曙 5868
曛 2909
曜 7305
曚 4439

15
曠 3606
曝 5403

16
疊 6325
曦 2432
曨 4263

17—19
曩 4633
曬 5623

晴 1170a

9
暇 2514
暄 2870
啓 4513
昺 4330
暘 7260
暍 7323
暖 4763
暌 3659
暑 5866
暎 7488
暉 2319
暈 7762
暐 7084
暗 36

10
暝 4529
暴 2691
暢 219
暠 2080

11
暱 4680
暫 6683
暴 4957
暮 4589
暵 2038

12
曆 3930

4

75 木
76 欠

梭 5463	榿 7228	森 5722	楹 7475	椽 1448	椿 1457	横 2106	櫟 3937	欄 4838
梜 612	極 484	棍 3672	楣 4394	槓 3716	槿 1070	**13**	櫛 796	**22—24**
桴 1939	棄 550	植 1007	楯 5934	槌 1484	模 4590	檀 6060	纀 7742	欝 7692
梡 3582	樽 3747	樣 5286	楸 1229	椰 3823	檟 72	檢 851	櫝 6516	欞 4072
楞 6675	棋 527	梨 3870	榟 3216	樺椎 5549	槲 3747	檣 676	欄 4285	～～～
柂 931	棊	椓 1267	楮 1396	馮 4313	樗 5863	檥 799	櫓 4178	**76**
梃 6407	棼 1865	椻 396	業 7321	榾 3487	櫨 4206	橔 2484		欠 904
梯 6249	棹 1262	椎 1484	椰 7309	槁 3291	**12**	檜 3538	**16**	**2—4**
械 2538	梓 6829	棣 6200	楨 349	槐 2230	檗 1685	檔 6089	櫬 160	次 6980
條 6300	棬 1657	棐 1825	楎 2320		橋 747	檩 4039	櫪 3933	欣 2727
桿 3219	綴 1279	桃 4870a	楓 1891	**11**	橈 3087	椑 see 4097-12	櫚 341	欨 2832
梗 3349	椒 729			樞 5859	樹 5879	櫝 4178	櫧 1363	
梵 1774	棓 5360	**9**	**10**	槠 4178	樽 6886	檐 7351	欁 4702	**6**
梅 4402	棱 3847	楡 7634	槍 680	樓 4143	機 411	檟 604	欐 5277	欬 3323
梁 3951	椅 2954	楠 4622	構 3428	權 1176	橄 3230	橋 6863	櫳 4265	欷 1678
桫 5457	棒 4923	楫 799	榧 1825	榮 658	橙 6574			**7**
棻 5607	椄 801	椷 827	榦 3237	樂 4129	舞 7180	**17**		欵 2419
黍 578	棲 2462	椶 6897	榎 604	槹 2334	橇 737	櫻 7460		欶 3579
桷 1175	棺 3554	楔 2651	檬 583	槲 2201	樵 757	欛 5914		欵 7
桶 6635	棕 6897	楗 856	榕 7561	椠 927	檸 392	欑 7514		欲 7671
梢 5679	椀 7022	櫁 2948	樹 2629	概 3201	橙 388	欅 1568		**8**
槙 3809	棠 6111	楞 3845	槎 106	槽 6736	橘 1592	欄 3792		欺 528
梘 861	棉 4505	椿 1494	榜 4915	樊 1775	橐 6465	隲 7449		欵 1277
棋 5006	械 7678	楊 7261	榥 2280	樗 3951	檉 6630			欹 2956
梓 6951	棧 148	楝 4017a	槃 5942	槷 2973	樸 5354	**18—19**		欻 2857
梛 4912	棯 7644	楂 106	榮 7582	榛 578	檊 3286	權 1663		款 3579
梛 7309	棚 5055	楥 2871	榴 4084	樣 7256	樺 2219	欒 4215		歃 3248
栖 7527	梀 1775	楳 320	榛 291	標 5180	橡 2570	欋 4103		
梩 3861	棘 486	根 7071	榨 83	樟 187	樲 1753	**20—21**		
梟 2589	棗 6723	楚 1393	楊 5969	櫢 2501	樾 7700	欛 6089		
8	棟 6607	楷 623	槳 4902		橘 6457	欖 3806		
	棵 3391		襄 6369			櫊 7510		

9	4	8	79	蚩 5086	罷 1609	求 1217	湖 812	洞 1240	4
歇 2642	歪 7002	殢 485	殳 5849	毘 | 5158	83	炎 4652	汾 1857	泡 4965	76
歌 5618	武 7195	殣 3046	段 6543	毘 | 155	氏 5785	汁 999	沐 5222	泮 4895	欠
歈 2729	歧 523	殘 6689	殷 3406			汜 1777	汲 472	洏 4371	77
10	9—14	殤 2362	殷 7423	82	氏 6187	3	汰 6022	法 1762	止
歔 884	歲/歳 5538	殖 1008	殺 5615	毛 4357	民 4508	汎 7005	決 1697	泼 1969	78
歌 3364	歷 3931	9	毆 4818		氓 4424	池 1032	沃 7210	沼 237	歹
11	歸 3617	殨 4636	殻 3406	毡 135		汚 7175	沙 5606	沾 127	79
歐 4817		殜 7318	殼 2586	毧 4939	84	汗	沌 6595	治 1021	殳
歕 6081	78	10	殿 6354	毬 3182	气 552	汎 1773	沛 5020	河 2111	80
12	歹/歺 5988	殠 7755	毀 2327	毯 1588	氛 1856	汛 2749	沁 1114	沽 3456	毋
歙 2476	2	11	毄 6655	毫 2066	氜 7265	汋 5832	汶 7131	沿/沿 7354	81
歔 2824	死 5589	殤 5667	毆 4818	毳 5612	氝 7444	汊 99	沂 2941	泗 2799	比
歔 2618	4	殣 1071	毅 3010	毽 1220	氣 554	汏 2486	汩 3482	泅 5600	82
歔 5036	殁 4554	12	毈 6546	毹 6075	氤 7409	汝 3142	汨 7695	泱 7243	毛
13—18	殀 7280	殫 6032	殽 3407	毿 6883	氧 7251	汕 5631	沓 5962	泰 6023	83
歔 2052	5	殬 2997	毊 2305	氆 857	氯 4197½	氶 2382	沐 4594	洙 3026	氏
歔 7616	殂 6814	殰 2342		氈 4376	氳 7767	江 638	次 2714	沱 6442	84
歔 1277	殄 6375	13	80	氊 6455		汜 5591	汏 941	泥 4660	气
歔 2266	殆 5990	殮 4001	毋 7193	氄 5970	85	汗 2028	沒 4555	泐 7546	85
77	殃 7242	殭 640	母 4582	氀 3881	水/氵 5922	4	汽 553	沸 1845	水
止 939	6—7	14—17	每 4401	氅 228	1	沔 4490	汪 7041	泓 2381	
1—3	殉 2920	殯 5264	毒 6509	氈 5385	永 5283	沖 1523	5	泌 5087	
正 351	殊 5851	殯 6517	毓 7687	氍 6168	永 7589	洹 2153	泄 2950	沶 5496	
此 6972	殍 5191	殰 864		氎 3186	2	沄 7746	沮 1575	泚 5887	
步 5363			81	氌 135	汀 6397	沆 2057	注 1340	沫 4412	
			比 5077	氐 5439		沕 7708	洹 6442	沬 4549	
				氈 4179		沏 3168	泛 1773	泚 6974	
						沈 332	沴 6376 3889	泯 4511	
							洔 1920	泳 7590	
							況 3603	泫 2882	

85 水

泔 3225	洶 2921	涷 5503	淹 7381	渲 5932	湦 7074	溼 5823	漦 3781	漬 2188
油 7515	洩 2649	涉 5707	淒 556	涓 4377	湟 2289	溪 510	演 7403	潃 6962
泉 1674	洙 5852	海 2014	淀 6352	渝 7635	溢 5035	滓 6952	溥 6552	漣 4012
泊 4987	洫 2856	涌 7572	淙 1460	測 6759	溫 7125	溶 7562	漏 4152	滬 2183
波 5314	洋 7252	浦 5390	淌 6112	渤 4985	湄 4395	溥 5391	潡 5059	漁 7669
泪 4243	洱 1747	涘 5596	涬 2767	湧 7572	渺 4477	溺 4652	漼 6867	滷 4155
沲 6434	津 1081	消 2607a	淅 5300	港 3267	湘 2565	滂 4930	滯 974	瀝 4204
泣 563	洧 7106	浪 3810	滌 4194	漱 2843	湝 2199	溯 5495	漲 196	
泐 3843	洎 446	浴 7673	添 6370	渦 7154	湫 1230	漂 3928	潀 6913	**12**
	活 2401	涊 1286	淺 920	減 828	漢 4407	滅 4483	灃 2241	澇 3830
6	洒 5624	浥 3041	淯 2181	湮 7415	渚 1355	滎 7586	漸 878	潭 6083
洎 6557		浬 3862	淚 4243	渙 2252	湍 6554	溜 4085	漩 2895	澆 696
派 4873	**7**		淤 7645	湊 6809	湖 2168	溢 3054	溉 3202	潠 171
狋 1965	流 4080	**8**	混 2371	渲 2892	湒 7077	滏 3403	漫 4335	澍 5880
洸 3585	泣 3912	涼 3946	溂 5308	渥 7162	湏 2837	溫 7125	漕 6737	潯 2745
洗 2465	涂 6524	淳 5932	淋 4023	渧 6205	湼 4694	滇 6334	滌 6229	潦 3836
洮 6149	涴 4409	淪 4251	深 5719	渡 6505	湳 3362	溱 292	漱 5483	澎 5061
洤 1674	浜 5042	涑 3770	淛 2491	游 5495	渾 2366	漐 5971	漆 578	澈 287
洪 2388	浸 1092	淇 529	淞 5555	涂 7381	湮 1510	溶 7149	漾 7257	潵 5217
洌 3987	涃 6591	淟 6378	淡 6053	滋 6937	湎 4501	滕 6181	漿 659	潹 3231
洵 2811	浩 2077	涵 2050	淨 1153	澂 2477	酒 2847	滔 6144	漪 2957	澌 5578
洽 2529	涓 1631	涮 5906	淫 7434	湃 4874		滋 6937	漂 5196	潒 4335
洛 4121	浚 1729	淘 6153	淵 7723	游 7522	**10**	潯 3155	漓 3897	潛 918
洞 6609	浹 787	淬 6874	淄 6930	渴 3401	滄 6711	滁 1392	漳 188	潮 250
洄 2312	涥 4984	淖 4645	淝 1840	湣 4515	溝 3429	滑 2227	潔 5984	濇 5448
洼 6991	浮 1906	淮 7237	淯 2587	湯 6101	溟 4530		滑 1492	濄 3620
洊 651	浣 2244	淑 5883	淥 1268	涷 4018	滙 2353	**11**	潏 2796	澾 4859
洟 2986	涔 330	涪 1961	淦 3238	渣 69	準 1488	漚 4819	滿 4326	潘 4907
洿 7175	涇 1121	涸 2133	淮 2229	渠 1603	源 7728	漦 5773	漢 2039	澄 389
洳 3138	涎 2714	淶 4063	清 1171	漦 6318	溲 5473	滲 5735	漠 4561	潑 5356
洊 880	涕 6250	液 3033		湛 146	溏 6119	滾 3676	漸 4355	潠 6913
洲 1290	浙 269		**9**	湢 5132	溷 2375	滴 6222	潒 2158	

85
水
86
火

4

湔 5681	濃 4771	瀉 2628	瓚 6678	**4**	威 4483	煆 6544	熅 7768	燔 1794
潼 6631	澾 5980	濾 4293	灘 6083	炕 3277	裁 6652	煙 7397	熊 2815	燈 6169
津 5131	涵 7604	瀑 4959	灑 5624	炙 1000	烨 7465	煥 2253	熙 2451	熰 1209
潔 772	澠 4507	瀑 4130		炒 256	烊 7262	煞 5617	燊 4028	燐 4028
濬 2477		瀆 6518	**21**	炉 4160	烤 3302	照 238	熜 6570	爔 1259
湝 5629	**14**	濺 869	灞 4844	炊 1477	烛 1385	煦 2831	熇 3305	爐 2478
潟 2510	濮 5383	瀁 7257	灝 2079	炎 7335		煬 7262		餤 7394
潭 6063	澨 926				**7**	煜 7683	**11**	燀 7329
潰 2343	濤 6159	**16**	**22—24**	**5**	焉 7330		熰 4820	燖 6064
漬 1845	濘 4730	瀝 3934	灣 7029	炳 5287	烹 5052	**11**	熱 3095	燗 4421
潤 3178	濕 5823	瀛 7481	灤 4631	炷 1341	焖 1241	煉 4019	熱	
澗 836	濼 7584	瀘 4159	灤 4216	炸 89	焄 2905	煤 4398	熟 5895	**13**
潢 2298	濊 2350	瀚 2043	灤 3240	炯 1241	烽 1879	煠 89		營 7467
	淡 7588	瀟 2622		炮 4966		煢 1250	**13**	燥 5440
13	濔 4650	瀨 3777	**86**	炰 6009	**8**	煖 4763	熨 7661	爕 2655
澶 5654	濾 1084	瀦 1358	火灬 2395	炱 238	無 7180	煏 5133	熬 59	爌 7688
澡 6726	濫 3800	瀢 5524		炤 6346	焬 5603	煨 7072	熯 7527	爐 2328
澔 5448	濬 1729	瀯 2544	**1**	点 6085	焠 6875	煌 2290	熠 3049	爛 3785
澳 48	濰 7068	瀕 5265	灺 89	炭 1547	焙 5002	煣 754	熳 2040	爤 6692
澣 2244	濯 1265	瀧 4266		炬 554	尉 7661	煮 1356	熲 3719	爥 1385
濂 4004	濩 2411		**2**	炳 2883	焗 3270	煳 2169		爧 5531
激 479	濛 4442	**17**	灯 6169		焜 2372	煇 2321	**12**	燋 6849
澮 3539	濠 2070	瀰 4460	灰 2306	**6**	焚 1866	煒 7085	熹 2439	
澉 6355	濱 5265	瀲 6172		炰 361	焮 2730	煩 1789	燀 5649	**14**
澤 277	濵 3080	瀼 3080	**3**	烏 7166	焱 7338		燕 7399	爍 3305
濚 5765	濵 3750	瀾 3793	灺 2646	烜 2867	然 3072	**10**	燒 5692	燻 2906
濁 1271	濡 3149	瀏 7497	灼 1256	然 2581	焰 7394	熏 2906	燔 2746	爐 1085
澥 2540	濟 459		灶 6731	烘 2389	焦 721	� 6120	燎 3975	爚 5693
澹 6045		**18**	炙 1189	烈 3988		熔 7564	燼 978	爨 2719
澧 3885	**15**	灌 3573	災 6652	烙 4123	**9**	熄 2497	燉 6575	
潞 4183	瀏 4095	灃 1898	灾	烟 7397	保 4948	煽 5644	燙 6102	**15**
澼 5175	瀋 5731	灘 7552	灯 2389	烟 7397	煎 874	熸 2281	燋 724	爛 5834
		19			熙 2451	熒 7468	燋 2169	
						鴬 7170	燃 3073	

	爆 4960			拳 1647	2	狷 1632	貓 4366	獯 2910	王 7037
	熱 3096	89	92	牸 6944	犯 1779	狼 3811	猶 7528	獲 2412	2—3
		爻 2583	牙 7214	特 6165	3	猖 7436	獣 7530	獴 5266	玎 6384
	16	爽 5917	牚 7216	7	犴 2029	狠 5007			玖 1198
86 火	爐 4160	爾 1754		牽 881	犮 122	狉 6839	10	15	玗 3215
87 爪			93	犂犁 3871	4	狸 3863	孫 5543	獸 5847	
88 爻	17—25	90	牛牜 4737	牼 3355	狙 4741		獅 5761	獵 3993	4
89 爻	爛 3794	爿 672		犉 6833	犿 7760	8	猿 7732	獷 3591	玠 631
90 爿	爤 3573a		2		狃 2149	猊 4663	猶 7287		玦 1698
91 片	爨 6855	2	牝 5280	8	狄 6215	猝 6837	獃 5986	16	玩 1910
92 牙		牀 656	牟 4566	犄 2955	狀 1452	猗 2956	猾 2228	獾 4161	玟 4390
93 牛	87	牀 1459		犀 2463	狂 3601	猓 6898		獻 2699	玩 7009
94 犬		牁 3359	3	犇 5028		猎 6839	11	獺 5985	
95 玄	爪爫叉 240	牂 6699	牠 5961		5	猖 210	獒 60		5
96 玉	爬 4857	牆 682	牣 3114	9	狙 1576	猙 367	獐 189	17—20	玲 4047
	爭 365	牆 674	牤 3437	犎 1888	狗 3413	猋 5183	獄 367	獼 4461	玳 5998
	爰 7735	牆 7351	牡 4576	犍 858	狐 2185	猛 4429	獄 7685	玃 2267	珍 301
	爲 3557		牢 3824		狎 2528	猇 2582		玃 1706	珠 5417
	爵 7059	91		10		猜 6659	12		珊 3385
	爵 1179	片 5256	4	犖 4131	6		獗 1686	95	珂 6344
		版 4886	物 7209	犗 3306	狡 707	9	獠 3976	玄玄 2881	玷 5111
	88	牌 4871	牧 4599	犛 3882	狩 5845	猴 2139	獞 6632	玅 4474	珌 6975
	父 1933	牋 867	牦 4358		狷 2920	献 2699		率 5910	玼 4512
	爸 4831	牒 95		15—16	狠 2097	猻 4759	13	玆 6935	珀 5348
	爹 6304	牓 6319	5	犢 6519		猱 4642	獧 3540		玻 5316
	爺 7310	牕 4916	牯 3457	犧 1334	7	猨 7732	獬 1632	96	
		牖 1461	牴 6194	犧 2433	狲 3872	猩 2774	獸 3062	玉王 7666	6
		牘 7507	牲 5739		狴 5080	猲 2643	獨 6512		珧 7270
		牘 6520		94	狻 5512	猪 1357	獮 2541		珓 7339
			6	犬犭 1650	狹 2532	猾 7078	獷 4643		珞 4124
			牷 1668		狯 4353	猢 2170			
			牿 3437				14 獺 4731 獻 2792		

珪 3609	琢 1269	璏 5467	瓏 4268	鬵 5047	102	留 4083	疇 1322	**5**	
珮 5016	琲 5017	璁 6920	瓔 7461	甗 6765	田 6362	畔 4896	疆 643	病 5288	
珠 1349	**9**	璇 2896	瓖 2573	甑 5116	甲 610	畜 5032	疊 6325	疳 1577	
班 4889	瑜 7636	璧 2974		甕 7151	申 5712	畬 4579		痄 81	
珥 1748	瑂 4378	璃 3898	**97**	甗 7470	由 7513	畚 1412	**103**	疹 303	5
珩 2103	瑕 2515	璋 190	瓜 3504	甎 4269			疋 5169	疼 6180	
	瑄 2893	瑾 1072	瓟 4967	甗 7369	**2**	**6**	疏 5861	痂 585	96 玉
7	瑞 5924	璉 4013	瓞 6308		町 6398	異 3009	疏 964	疱 4968	97 瓜
玲 2019	瑙 4637		瓠 2186	**99**	男 4619	畢 5120	疑 2940	疳 4806	98 瓦
琉 4081	瑟 5451	**12**	瓢 5198	甘 3223	甸 6350	畧 4075		痁 3451	99 甘
斑 6408	瑚 2171	璟 1131	瓣 4892	甚 5724		略 2442	**104**	痞 6345	100 生
球 1221	瑇 5998	璣 413	瓤 4162	甜 6366	**3**		疒 4675	疵 6443	101 用
琇 2804	瑗 7738	璞 5355	瓥 3081		畎 4424	**7**		痹 1846	102 田
環 3812	瑛 3163	璜 2299		**100**	畫 2222	畱 4083	**2**	疸 6040	103 疋
現 2684	瑛 7490		**98**	生 5738	畀 4993	畬 7606	疔 6385	症 353	104 疒
珋 7311	琿 2367	**13**	瓦 6998	甡 5740	畍 1651	畯 1730	疕 701	疵 6976	
理 3864	瑋 7086	璪 6728	瓮 7151	產 163	畐 6932	畫 2222		痰 2662	
		璐 6090	瓴 4048	甥 3175	畝 5096	番 1790	**3**	痔 3226	
8	**10**	環 2258	瓶 5301	甦 5743			疢 1190	疲 5146	
琴 1103	瑱 681/6712	璨 6693	瓷 6966	甦 5487	**4**	**8**	疙 3311	疾 492	
琪 530	瑣 5466	璐 1612	瓿 2020		畏 7069	畸 422	疝 5632		
瑚 6271	瑳 6789	璐 4184	甄 6340	**101**	畊 3343	當 6087		**6**	
琦 517	瑩 7469	璧 5115	瓻 5361	用 7567	界 632	畯 7676	**4**	痊 1669	
瑄 3555	瑠 4081	璲 5532	甄 295	甩 5047½	畛 7752	畺 643	疥 633	痾 6620	
琮 6899	瑶 7288		甍 1305	甫 5907	畟 4579		疢 1783	痿 2987	
琨 3680	瑯 3812	**14**	甓 4821	甬 1942	畐 1975	**9—10**	疣 7512	痔 955	
琳 4024	瑪 4314	璽 2469	甌 6223	甯 7568	畝 6363	睡 6555	疤 4832	痟 7107	
瑶 1763	瑰 3635	璿 2896	甕 4434	*id.1724*	畝 1651	畿 412	疫 3029	痒 7255	
琰 7339		璺 7145	甑 1429			畾 4226	343	痕 2098	
琶 4858	**11**				**5**				
琵 5157	璀 6868	**15—17**			畯 302	**12—17**		**7**	
琥 2162		瓊 1245				疃 6555		痢 3873	

104 广								
痞 5140	癒 7637	癥 5482	癩 797	**2**	嚼 733	盄 2011	溫 6097	眙 2965
瘓 5513	瘌 3760	瘵 117	癢 7255	兒皂阜 4368		盘 7123		眹 6309
瘁 2603	瘕 600	瘭 5199			**107**	盌 7022	**109**	眳 7273
瘈 1122	瘓 2254	瘴 191	**16**			盎 42	**目** 4596	眛 4413
瘙 2733	瘍 7263	瘰 4223	癎 3935	**3**	**皮** 5142			眥 6953
痣 972	瘝 3560	瘳 1328	癲 3778	的 6213		**6**	**3**	眠 4504
痗 4403	瘩 6530	癏 1710	癯 2407		皰 5153	盒 2118	直 1006	眩 2884
瘵 5608	瘦 7611	瘼 4562		**4**	皰 4968	盗 6138	眞 2819	眚 5741
痛 6636	瘖 7421	癃 7445	**17**	飯 3616	皴 6890	盛 5752	肝 4346	䀹 1608
瘍 6539	瘋 1892		癭 7462	皆 620	皸 3479	盃 3647	盲	䀹 5937
痘 6479		**12**	癮 7450	皇 2283	皺 1723	盖 3199		眣 5789
8	**10**	癆 3831	癬 2717		皺 6742		**4**	眸 2900
瘟 7229	瘡 1463	癉 6033		**5**	皺 1306	**7**	眄 4491	
瘁 6876	瘦 5848	療 3977	**18**	皋 3285	皻 73	盗 6138	看 3251	**6**
痼 3451	瘥 3012	癌 7346a	癯 1610	皕 708		盡 1943	眉 4391	眽 4556
痿 7099	瘞 123	癍 5210	癱 7553		**108**	盡 3199	眄 2415	眾 1517
瘠 437	癮 2498	癈 1849		**108**	**皿** 4536		眈 6029	眺 6284
瘖 3556	癮 1679	瘭 2677	**19**	皎 708		**8**	盼 4906	睚 3597
瘀 7646	瘤 4086	癏 4256	癱 6084	皖 2245	**3**	塩 7352	眢 2192	睇 1039
癎 5040	瘟 7127	癀 2300	癲 6335	皓 2078	盂 7595	盞 149	盾 6578	睒 317
痳 4025	瘨 6335				盅	盟 4426	眇 4476	睠 1648
痰 6076	瘠 490	**13**	**105**	**6—7**			眊 6582	睟 4568
痺 5097	瘝 4883	癥 6356	**癶** 5321	皎 708	**4**	**9**	眐 5744	睞 4449
瘭 5097	瘩 5954	癘 3908	癸 3628	皖 2245	盃 4996	盡 1082	省 1811	眼 7400
痴 1025	瘩 4735	癖 5176	登 6167	皓 2078	盅 1507	盥 839	防 2562	
瘃 1382	瘻 3292	癱 7557	發 1768		盆 5034		相 4359	**7**
痕 198				**10—11**	盈 7474	**10**	眊	眾 1517
痾 4806	**14**	**14**		眺 2078	盇 2119	盤 4903		睛 1633
排 1826	癥 1025	癡 1025	**106**	皞 2075			**5**	睏 3692
癟 4305		癟 5214	**白** 4975	皚 24	**5**	**11—12**	眨 92	睞 790
9	**11**			皜 2080	盦 3052	盫 3569	眞 297	睆 2246
猴 2140	瘻 4289	**15**	**1**	皣 2075	盍 2119	盫 3469	睿 7715	
	瘺 6006	癥 359	**百** 4976	皦 687		盧 4156		
	癰 6909							

晞 2420	瞅 *id.1326*	瞶 3663	知 932	砢 4113	碇 6394	碼 4315	礫 3938	**5**
睇 6251	睖 5474	瞷 2678	矧 5732	砮 4760	碗 7022		礦 3909	祖 6815
睅 2237	睹 6498	瞷 3179	矩 1548	砣 6444	碍 23	**11**	礦 3607	祚 6822
睨 2685	瞄 4473a		短 6542	砰 5051	碌 4195	磲 3255	礪 4230	祔 1921
		13	矬 6796	砦 116	硼 5056	磣 334		祝 1380
8	**10**	矓 1326	矮 8	砥 951	碓 6558	磤 3356	**16—18**	祟 5539
睐 3771	瞑 4531	瞿 1608	矯 692	砷 5715		磧 1181	礮 4969	祛 1596
睍 4664	瞍 5474	瞻 151	矰 6766	破 5344	**9**	磚 1429	礱 4269	祓 1970
睥 5163	瞎 2535	瞽 3481			碰 5064	磽 6864	礴 5326a	祜 2166
睟 6877	瞌 3404		**112**	**6**	磁 6966	磨 4543	礵 5921	祠 6970
睠 1643	瞋 326	**14—21**	石 5813	硐 2757	碯 4637	磬 1164	礸 3574	祐 7543
睡 7238		矇 4443		硅 3611	碬 777	礄 4225		祋 7242
督 6508	**11**	矉 5279	**3**	砵 2061	碨 4512	磧 573	**113**	祕 5088
睘 1248	瞘 3443	矑 1704	矶 3498	研 7341	碭 6099		示礻⺬	祗 952
睦 4600	瞤 4681	矔 4163	矸 3263	硃 1350	碟 6320	**12**	祀 5788	祇 5716
睡 5925	瞠 6170	矗 1415	矸 2030	硍 3331	碡 6510	磽 738		祐 5814
睖 3848	瞖 2975	矚 3260			碧 5128	磻 414	**1—2**	
晻 32	瞟 5200	矙 1387	**4**	**7**	碪 321	礁 5064	礼 3886	**6**
睪 3059	瞕 192		砌 559	硤 2533	碩 6444	磻 725	礽 3123	祫 2530
睯 2363	瞒 4327		砂 5610	硜 3356	碩 5815	磴 4908		祧 6285
睒 5640	瞢 4435	**110**	砍 4512	硫 4082		磷 6171	**3**	祭 465
睜 368	瞥 4306	矛 4570	砍 3247	硬 7487	**10**	磺 4074	祁 7498	祥 2577
睫 790			砒 5154	硝 2608	碵 7756	磞 836	社 5701	票 5192
睬 6669	**12**	矜 1115	研 7218	硭 4349	碾 4719	磺 2301	祀 5592	
睢 5518	瞭 3978	矞 7689		硯 7401	磋 6790		祁 537	**7**
睛 1147	瞰 5407		**5**		磅 4917	**13—14**		祲 1094
	瞰 3260		砠 1574	**8**	磊 5427	礎 1395	**4**	
9	瞥 5218	**111**	砭 5236	碁 527	磑 5154	礓 6046	祆 2657	**8**
睿 3176	瞧 741	矢 5784	砲 4969	碘 6348	磋 3405	礌 23	祅 7281	禀 5272
睾 3285	瞪 6170		砥 6644	碑 4995	磊 4225	礐 4969	祈 540	祺 531
瞀 4572	瞳 6633	**2—12**	砙 1764	碎 5528	磐 4904		祇 942	禂 6130
睽 3660	瞬 4030	矣 2938	砧 321	碉 6272	磴 7122	**15**	祇 538	禠 79
	瞬 5937			硾 1474		礜 1776		

右側：5

109 目
110 矛
111 矢
112 石
113 示

| 113 示 | | 114 内 | 115 禾 | | | | | 116 穴 | | 117 立 | 118 竹 |

5

113 示
114 内
115 禾
116 穴
117 立
118 竹

Col. 1 (示)

禁 1077
裸 3565
祿 4196
9
禍 2399
禋 7416
禩 2457
禘 6206
褐 7264
褆 6234
褋 4399
福 1978
禛 350
禪 2971
10—11
禰 4316
禦 7665
12
禧 2440
禫 5650
禫 6065
13
禮 5655
禮 3886
14
禶 4651
禧 6130
襺 7390

Col. 2

16—17
襀 3050
襀 3082
襴 7498
~
114
内 3132
禹 7620
禺 7621
离 3896
禽 1100
~
115
禾 2114
2
秀 2803
禿 6537
私 5569
3
秒 3014
秋 3867
秈 2708
秆 3220
秉 5291
4
种 1524
秏 7748

Col. 3

秫 3350
秒 4479
科 3389
秕 5084
秏 2065
秋 1227
5
租 6816
秤 5009
秭 6949
秩 1011
秦 1112
秧 7244
秬 1549
秤 382
秘 5088
秣 4550
秫 5888
6
秸 624
移 2980
稓 6252
秹 820
秼 6422
7
稊 6494
稅 5927
程 375
稍 1634
稠 3693

Col. 4

稀 2421
稇 6252
稈 3220
稉 3350
稍 5680
稂 3813
5
稟 5273
稘 401
稗 4862
稠 1317
稜 3849
稔 3120
稞 3392
稚 969
9
稱 383
稭 624
稷 4751
種 1511
10
稼 597
稑 969
稽 427
穀 3490
稷 504
稻 6139
稾 3293

Col. 5

11
穬 3280
穆 4601
稱 466
穌 1209
積 500
穎 7486
穌 5487
12
穗 5526
13
穚 5449
穢 2351
穧 4772
穣 5533
14
穠 383
穫 2207
穩 7140
16—17
穤 1227
穰 3083
~
116
穴 2899
2
究 1199

Col. 6

3
穸 2487
空 3722
穹 1246
4
穽 1144
窈 813
窀 6596
穿 1442
突 6540
5
窆 5236a
窄 6744
穻 718
窅 7274
穼 6994
窅 7296
6
窊 6286
窗 1461
窒 994
7
窖 718
窘 1716
窔 1461
8
窣 5501
窟 3503

Col. 7

窠 3393
9
窬 7638
窳 7155
窪 6992
窨 7422
10
窯 5150
窰 7289
窳 7660
竀 6373
窬 7289
窮 1247
11
窶 1571
窺 3648
窵 6280
12
窾 3580
竁 4257
13
竅 751
竄 5534
竊 6852
14—17
竇 1247
竈 6485

Col. 8

籠 4270
篭 6731
竊 813
~
117
立 3921
4
竒 514
5
站 128
竚 1365
竝 5292
6
竢 2007
竟 1135
章 182
7
竣 1731
竦 5562
竢 5595
童 6626
8—10
竪 5877
竭 778
端 6541
競 1133
~

Col. 9 (竹)

118
竹 ⺮ 1373
2
竺 1374
3
竿 7596
竿 3216
4
笘 2058
笏 2193
笈 473
笑 2615
笌 5547
笹 6593
笵 4833
笓 5090
笔 5130
笊 241
5
符 1922
笝 586
筦 5350
笒 1022
笱 3414
筍 5586
笤 6292
笅 4761

第 6203	箷 5763	箭 875	簇 6840	籧 6226	籹 4448	糉 6900	糯 3910	紜 7747	
筥 5948	筵 7344	箧 804	簿 4870a	籍 507	粃 5084	糅 4744		給 1055	
笨 5026	筹 5516	節 795	筆 5122			糒 2838	**16—18**	納 4607	
筐 5742	筷 3548	篋 310	簋 3633	**15**	**5**	糊 2172	糶 6227	紛 1859	**118**
笛 6217	範 4839	箒 5248	簣 3899	籐 6182	粗 6833		糵 4703	索 5459	竹
笠 3922	筸 3221	箧 2291	簥 6751	籟 3779	粘 129	**10**	糷 6303	紘 2378	**119**
	筲 6637	箱 2566	篷 5067		粗 1550	糖 6121		級 474	米
6	筦 5682	箸 1360	籧 4205	**16**	粕 5353	糒 2782		紗 5611	**120**
筬 1766	筸 3814	篆 3127		籛 7482	粒 3923	糓 3490	**120**	純 5930	糸
筌 1670		篆 1438	**12**	籌 6466		糕 3283	糸 5570	絅 335	
筅 2704	**8**	筵 791	簂 2919	籙 4201	**6**	糖 5098		紋 7132	
筐 3598	箕 402	範 1780	筆 6034	籠 4271	粵 7704	糒 1225	**1**	紊 7133	
笞 5951	筲 85		箭 5621		粂 6926		糸 2423	紡 1812	
筒 6621	筘 246	**10**	簪 6679	**17**	粒 1451	**11**	糺 1195	紐 5155	
等 6178	筛 3366	篠 2616	筦 6173	籩 7499	粥 1384	糝 5419		紙 953	
筑 1375	筶 1480	筐 1827	簦 1943	籛 917	粦 4028	糞 6553	**3**		
筭 407	管 3471	篩 5621	簋 2619	簿 5244	粟 5500	糠 3280	紃 7006	**5**	
筍 5547	箒 3557	翁 3129	簫 6360			糟 6719	紀 2086	繼 2647	
笛 1624	算 1299	篥 3929	簣 3664	**18—27**	**7**	糞 1875	紓 7597	組 6817	
筴 6760	筬 5516	篘 1376	籠 837	籲 6548	粲 6691	糨 655	紉 3115	絅 1242	
筶 3303	箱 867	篁 5090	簧 2302	籬 3903	粳 3350	糢 4308	約 7493	終 1500	
筆 5130	箍 898	篡 1449		籮 4104	粉 5609	糜 6742	紐 3438	紬 1274	
筋 1058	箔 3474	篦 1027	**13**	籯 7693	粱 3952	糜 4453	約 1300	絆 4877	
筇 1252	箏 5335	簇 6514	簾 4005		粮 3944		紅 2383	絨 1971	
	筽 369	篩 3294	簽 915	**119**		**12**	紀 430	紹 5689	
7	箎 3727		簿 5375	米 4446	**8**	糧 655		結 5991	
筰 6784	箺 1027	**11**	籔 5318		粹 6878	糧 3944	**4**	絎 1366	
筱 2616	箎 923	箎 6471	籫 7351	**3**	粺 4863			緋 1987	
筋 1360		簞 4144		籹 3143			1903	絳 304	
9	篌 5225	箷 5621	**14**	籽 6941		4742	5717	
筴 7753	篌 2141	篌 4484	簠 3664	籼		5490	紫 6647	
笓 id.3557	箭 2619	箎 5507	簿 1323	**4**		5855	紫 6954	
			籃 3801	粉 1853				

120 糸
121 缶
122 网

絃 2663
紺 3227
紬 1315
細 2467
累 4221

6

絙 3345
絞 709
統 6641
絍 3104
絥 5099
絖 3608
絜 2634
結 782
給 482
絡 4125
絪 7410
絓 3512
絳 652
絝 3497
絮 2849
絣 5044
絨 3183
絇 2888
絁 2650
絲 5571
絰 6313
絕 1703

7

絛 6146
綄 7144
絹 1635
綑 3694
綍 2001
綏 5520
經 1123
絺 1015
綈 6253
綆 3351
綀 5485
綉 2805
綃 2609
綌 2473
綁 4913

8

綸 4252
綦 532
綯 6154
綽 1284
綣 1658
綬 5842
綳 6803
綴 1475
綢 1318
綹 4098
綾 4064
綺 518
[illegible]
綻 [illegible]
綜 [illegible]
綰 [illegible]
綱 3271
綿 4506
緋 5044
綠 4197
綜 4717
綫 2723
緊 543
緄 3673
綳 5041
綝 324
緇 6931
網 7047
緊 1064
緣 6670
維 7067
緋 1828

9

緱 3424
緶 5226
緥 4950
緘 829
緝 571
縇 2872
緜 4506
締 6243
緣 7741
[illegible]
練 4020
緞 6545
線 2723
緩 2242
緲 4478
緗 2567
緒 2850
緹 792
緬 4502
緯 7087

10

縑 832
縓 1665
縛 1901
縐 1307
縉 1090
縠 2203
縈 7587
縕 3055
縕 7769
縝 298
縣 2700
縩 5459
縢 6183
緻 985
縚 6146
[illegible] 6870
[illegible]
縷 4290
縯 7428
縮 5897
縳 1430
繃 5041
繅 5441
繻 6005
繈 647
縱 6910
縰 5774
總 6912
繁 1788
縵 4336
繄 2976
繇 7548
繂 882
縹 5201
縭 3900
縲 4224
繆 4538
績 501
縫 1882
縻 4454

12

繕 5658
繞 3088
繚 3979
[illegible] 5527
[illegible] 989
[illegible] 5420
繪 6767
繙 1795
繣 2225
繡 2805
繢 3665

13

繳 688
繪 2346
繰 5441
繫 2458
繮 641
繯 2259
繹 3063
繲 6795-9
繴 5117
繾 5958
繸 5535
繭 844
繩 5749

14

繼 452
纁 2911
纂 6850
繽 } 5267
繽 }
辮 5241
纀 902
繻 2845

15

纏 178
纆 4387
纊 3608
纍 4231
續 2865
纈 2637
纇 4245

16—17

纑 4164
纖 2721
纔 6672
纓 7463

18—21

纛 6511
纘 6846
纚 5775
纜 3807

121

缶 } 1905
缻 }

3

缸 3264

4

缺 1708
缶 7284

8—10

缾 5301
䍉 3264
罎 104
罃 7470

11

罄 1165
罅 2523

12

罈 6069
罇 6886

13—18

罋 7151
罌 7470
罍 4234
罏 4165
罐 3574

122

网 }
罒 } 7044
⺳ }

3—4

罕 2031
罔 7045
罘 1904

5

罡 3266
罟 3458
罛 3472

6—7

罣 3511
罥 1636

8

罩 246
罨 7382
罭 7679
置 976
罪 6860

9

罱 3788
罳 5583
署 5867
罰 1769

10

罷 4841
罵 4317

11—12

羅 3892
罽 448
罾 6768

14

羆 5166
羅 4099
羃 4467

17—19

羈 424

花 2212
芥 634
苓 1104
芫 7709
芮 3170
芬 1861
芻 1405
苃 475
芙 1911
芭 4836
蒂 1844
芯 2736
芹 1096
芳 1815
芡 905
芷 943
苿 5635
芼 4361
芽 7219

5
苢 2933
苯 3068
茐 5289
苴 1578
苓 4053
茁 4597
苽 2933
茵 1275
茄 802
苞 4941
茀 4372

138
艮 3327
良 3941
艱 834

139
色 5445
艴 1988
艶 7406

140
艸 艹 6739

2
艾 19
芍 6293

3
芋 7598
芒 4347
芃 5065
芍 5833
芉 908
芔 2326

4
芝 936
芌 2852
芸 7749

8—9
艋 4430
艒 4717
艑 5250
艎 2292

10
艙 6713
艘 5435
艜 4918
艛 3056

11—1
艟 6025
艣 658
艢 1530

13
艤 676
艥 799
艦 5067
艧 3004

14
艨 840
艩 4444

15—18
艪 4178
艫 4167
艭 5916

136
舛 1441
舞 5936
7185

137
舟 1291

3
舢 5633
舡 2548

4
航 2059
服 1999
舫 1814
般 4881

5
舲 4052
船 1447
舸 3360
舵 6418
舷 2664
舶 4981

6—7
舺 1530
艅 7607
艇 6410
艄 5683

134
臼 1202
臾 2693
臿 7609
舁 4692
舀 112
舂 7614
舄 7299
舅 1525
2509
與 1204
興 7615
舉 2753
舊 1567
1205

17—19
臝 4117
臟 6706
臢 6680
臠 4301

135
舌 5705
舍 5699
舐 5786
舓 6371
舔 5394
舖 3559
舘 6367

131
臣 327
臥 7158
臧 6704
臨 4027

132
自 6960
臬 4697
臭 1331
臯 3285
臰 4700

133
至 982
致 984
臺 6016
臻 293

膲 3980
臁 646
膨 5062
膰 1797
臌 6881
臗 4673

13
臉 4006
臊 4002
臇 5442
臍 7478
臆 3044
膾 3541
臀 6602
膽 3763
臂 6047
臃 5107
膿 4773
臕 6849
臓 3480

膄 4400
腺 2724
膈 6086
膙 7627
腴 7612
腰 7302
腫 1512

10
膏 3296
膊 5324
膂 4287
膀 4931
膝 3980
膟 5491
膣 5442
腿 6569
膈 3318

11
膛 2798
膜 6108
膧 1424
膝 2508
膘 5202
膠 697
膛 2798
膜 4563
膚 1958

14
膩 5268
膡 4647
臍 561

15
膰 3763
膣 5185

16
臈 7398

脡 6409
脯 1944
脛 6480
脣 1491
脚 1177

8
脥 3034
腆 6379
脾 5164
腌 7383
腊 3558
腕 7023
胼 5254
腐 1930
腑 1931
腊 3763
腔 665
腎 5736
脹 198
胖 1830

9
腳 1177
腭 4793
羸 4116
腹 1994
膝 6810
腦 4638
腮 5412
腥 2775
腸 220

130 肉
131 臣
132 自
133 至
134 白
135 舌
136 舛
137 舟
138 艮
139 色
140 艸

菱 5330	荃 1671	荚 768	萃 6880	菁 1150	葦 7088	菅 3488	蕧 1162	蘵 2085
苛 3386	荆 1116	莫 4557	菽 5884	菲 1831		蒿 2081	蔦 4689	薦 872
若 3126	苅 3989	荽 5521	菩 5387		**10**	蒐 5469	蘇 4307	薇 7062
苟 3416	茘 3913	荸 5135	菌 1720	**9**	舊 925			蕙 2962
苦 3493	茗 4525	荸 1940	菱 4065	葆 4949	蒼 6714	**11**	**12**	薪 2738
苣 5641	苔 5952	莞 2247	菴 33	葡 5389	蓓 5001	蒝 5331	蔾 3832	薈 2347
苔 6011	苗 2313	莛 2761	菇 3454	葭 601	蒙 4437	蓺 3014	滕 5755	薙 2645
茗 6293	茵 7411	莚 6411	萎 7100	葺 572	蕒 4532	蔓 4146	蕨 1687	薆 5723
苑 7716	黃 6245	莚 7345	萋 558	蒿 7156	蒯 3551	蔻 3445	蕎 748	薄 5326
英 7489	茹 3139	莪 4783	菅 816	萼 4794	蕐 2217	蓿 5499	蕘 3089	蘊 7126
苧 1367	荇 928	莜 6301	菀 7024	恭 6372	蔌 5544	蔞 5931	蕛 6070	薑 642
苴 1551	荒 2271	莓 4404	萉 4354	葳 7052	蓉 7563	蔚 7113	蕙 2340	薐 3850
苹 5305	茲 6935	莎 5458	菉 4198	姜 642	蓐 3157	蔕 6007	蕊 3172	蘿 969
茀 1989	茇 748	荻 6216	菢 4939	萱 2873	蕭 2503	蕃 261	蕨 5104	薨 2393
苾 5112	荀 2922	莆 5393	荽 7397a	葑 1889	蒻 3130	蓰 2450	蕞 6859	薛 2653
茂 4580	草 6739	莠 7537	菖 211	蒂 6207	蒲 5398	蔟 6841	蕋 3172	薖 3399
茉 4551	茱 5853	莨 3815	萌 4427	葬 6702	蒔 5781	蔓 4337	蕩 6098	蓬 5959
苺 4404	茶 101	莧 2686	菔 2000	蒽 2466	蒐 5071	蓧 6301	蕉 726	薩 5410
苝 6978	茨 6982	荳 6481	菓 1864	葱 6917	蒞 3912	蔌 5508	蕪 7184	薤 7558
范 1778	茫 4348	莘 2740	菻 5556	葛 3377	蒲 362	蔫 7332	蕕 7529	蕾 6256
苷 3228	茸 3185	辰 4768	蒜 5307 *lin²*	葉 7319	蒸 4119	蒋 660	蕃 1798	蕾 4238
苗 4470	茜 929		萍 5315	落 4122	蒴 2860	蓳 5123	蕭 2620	
首 7597		**8**	菠 6821	蓤 2873	蓄 494	蔬 5862	蕣 5938	**14**
茅 4364	**7**	華 2217	萢 6077	葚 5725	蓋 3199	蔡 6673	蕬 1720	藁 3297
苙 3924	荷 2113	菫 1065	菑 6932	葵 3661	蒜 5515	蔑 4485	蕊 3175	藻 5197
	茷 3912	萊 3772	菧 5071	葩 4840	蒺 294	蔘 3966	蕡 1872	薰 2912
6	茶 6526	菀 6535	萏 6671	萬 7030	蒫 5931	蓇 2202	蕢 3667	甄 296
菱 710	莉 3874	萁 403	蒖 216	蒟 7501	蒢 5801	蓮 4014	藏 176	藍 3802
荄 3190	莒 1569	萴 6986	茮 1925	著 1361	蓑 1405	蓬 5068		薑 1086
茯 1966	莟 1717	菊 1589	崔 7031	葫 2173	萫 5464	蓮 6639	**13**	蘿 5235
荞 2085	堊 6797	萄 6155		菫 2368	舊 2409	蔭 7446	薎 3307	薯 5869
茌 3105	莊 1454	萆 5071		董 6614		陳 340	薊 447	藉 767
							薔 677	

140
艸

140 艸 141 虍 142 虫								
藏 6718	龍 4273	虒 5579	蚩 4425	蛇 5698	蜉 1907	蜻 1151	螟 4533	蟊 4365
薑 6019	**17**	虖 894	虺 2316	蛰 88	蜓 6412	蜚 1832	螄 5475	螺 5203
藐 4480	蘞 4000	**5**	虹 2384	蚯 7134	蜒 7346	**9**	螳 6122	蟆 4111
薐 4320	蘗 4702	處 1407	**4**	蚳 1030	蜑 6050	蝨 4425	蟋 5762	蟆 4309
薺 460	蘘 3084	虜	蚌 4924	蛉 2665	蛾 4784	蝓 7638a	螃 4932	蠦 1619
15	蘧 1613	虖 2156	蚧 635	蚖 3460	蜥 270	蝠 5452	蠢 6507	
藝 3014	蘭 3795	**6**	蚋 3169	蛐 7516		蝘 7359	螢 7471	**12**
蘑 4542	蘇 2718	虛 2821	蚶 3069	蛋 6050	蜩 6351	蝻 4623	螭 1016	蠡 1688
蘆 4294	**18**	虜 4175	蚣 3702	**6**	蛹 7574	蝴 497	蟊 1113	蟢 2441
藪 5481	蘴 1899	**7**	蚤 6724	蛟 711	蜀 5901	蝦 2516	蟓 7150	蟬 5651
藥 7501	**19**	號 2064	蚨 1912	蛤 3373	蛸 5684	蝸 3509	螣 6184	蟮 5660
藤 6182	蘸 145	虜 7648	蚕 6698	蛔 2314	蜋 3816	蝮 1995	螫 4884	蟯 3090
藩 1800	蘁 642	**9**	蚘 2314	蛙 6993	蜺 2687	蠍 7053	螯 6724	蟣 415
蘦 4235	蘿 4105	虩 3744	蚩 1018	蛭 1253	蜚 5737	蝝 7743	螟 3717	蟛 5063
藕 4803	蘺 3904	虪 4957	蚓 7430	蛐 1625	**8**	螆 6967	螂 3816	蟪 2341
蘧 261	蘼 463	**11—12**	蚊 7134	蛛 1351	蜷 1659	蝙 5232	螞 4318	蟠 4909
蘃 3877	**21—25**	虤 3650	蚪 6475	蜂 4569	蝃 6211	蝣 7523	融 7566	蟠 2621
16	虀 4233	虩 2480	蚍 5085	蜣 7253	蝎 6297	蝎 2124	**11**	蟒 4356
櫱 6467	蘽 4423		蚝 6967	蛭 994a	蜜 4465	蝶 6321	螽 1501	蟲 1519
蘄 541		**142**	蚜 6724	蛞 3749	蜿 7025	蝯 7732	蟈 3742	蟫 7417
蘗 3173	**141**	虫 1518	**5**	蚰 3681	蜮 7680	蝠 1979	蟄 998	蟥 6959
藻 6727	虍 2160	**1—2**	蚯 1214	**7**	蛾 3764	蝗 2293	螳 6109	蟥 2303
蘊 7770	**2—3**	虬 1216	蛆 1619	蜈 5872	蜫 3681	蝟 4365	蟥 4147	**13**
蘆 4168	虎 2161	虱 5452	蛙 1342	蜕 5928	蜴 3036	蝌 3390	蟥 7430	蠱 5660
蘅 2105	虐 4734	**3**	蚱 6745	蜊 3875	螺 3734	蝴 2174	蟠 6212	蠍 2644
蘜 15	**4**	虼 3312	蛤 4054	蜋 7203	蜥 2492	蝟 7078	蟀 2507	蟶 394
諸 5869	虓 2582		蚪 3069	蜎 1637	蜣 6608	蛚 6321	螫 5826	蟊 2879
蘭 4041			蚌 4924	蜂 1880	蝱 4431	蜡 5811	蝕 61	蟻 3005
藿 2408			蛄 3460	蛺 769	蜘 934	**10**	蟥 6738	蠃 4118
蘋 5278			蛄 3070		蜺 667	蒼 6715	蟲 7134	蠆 124
蘇 5488					蟒 3169		蟀 5836	蠋 5902

蟹 2542	蠻 6698	**9**	衽 3106	裔 2992	褓 4950	褸 4291	襲 2512	**5**	**6**
蟾 5663	蠻 4343	衚 2175	袂 4456	裙 1738	褕 7639	褵 647	襱 4274	覘 130	142 虫
蠻 2558	~~~	衛 1532	袒 4670	裀 3695	複 1996	褽 4951		視 5789	143 血
蠅 7476	**143**	衛衛 7089	**5**	裝 1455	褊 5233	褶 6324	**17—19**	**6—7**	144 行
	血 2901		袗 305	裌 606	褐 2125	褳 4015	襴 3796	覝 6290	145 衣
14	盂 2275	**10—18**	袋 5999	裘 1222	褒 2802	**12**	襪 6004	覜 2483	146 而
蟒 7585	衄 4777	衝衝 2104	袈 588	裟 5612	褙 1397	禪 6035	襪 273	**8**	147 見
蟟 2208	衃 2734	衢 1611	袍 4970	補 5372	褙 4990	褋 6646	襻 4900	覺 3804	**7**
蟓 4445	衆 1517	~~~	袚 1972	裕 7667	褄 7303	褫 5340	~~~	覥 6380	
蠔 2071	衁 1749	**145**	袤 3675	裋 5878	褌 3686	襆 5380	**146**	**9**	
蠙 5269	衊 4382	衣衤 2989	袤 1010	裡 3865	褘 7092	**13**	而 2524	覦 7640	
蠙 3164	衇 4487	**2**	袒 6058	裏	**10**	襢 6058	西 2460	親 1107	
蟛 562	~~~	衪 2992	袜 4552	裊 4690	褙 891	襖 49	要 7300	覬 6498	
	144	衩 6827	袖 2801	**8**	褲 764	襠 6091	覂 1896	**10**	
15	行 2754	**3**	被 4999	裲 3955	褵 3497	襟 1080	覃 2709	覯 449	
蠣 3911	**3**	衫 100	裒 4574	製 987	襄 5616	襠 167	覆 6061	覲 3430	
蠢 3894	衍 3252	表 5187	袪 3765	裨 5072	褞 2231	襞 5118	覆 1993	**11**	
蠟 3764	衒 7402	衫 5627	**6**	褂 3516	褦 5972	襪 5536	覈 2093	覷 1073	
蠢 1496	**5**	**4**	袱 1967	綴 6438	褥 1242	**14**	覊 425	覶 1620	
蟻 4486	術 5889	衰 5908	衵 3106	褐 1319	褫 4617	襤 3803	~~~	**12**	
	街 2885	衷 1508	裂 3990	綻 144	褯 5955	襦 3150	**147**	覸 4115	
16	**6**	衿 1080	裕 606	裳 5671	褥 1028	**15**	見 860	覷 1620	
蠹 6507	衙 2554	衾 1105	袷 7412	裙 1538	褥 3158	襪 5828	**2**	覹 838	
蟮 5872	衖 6622	衲 4608	裆 3497	裼 2504	**11**	襯 3765	覎 3575	**13—18**	
17	衙 619	**7**	袴 3140	裹 3735	褸 4822	襬 5341	**4**	覺 1178	
蠋 1649		衜 7224	裀 6664	裸 4109	褢 2571	襭 7000	覓 1178	觀 4114	
蠱 3475		袅 3675	裁 5362	裞 3332	褻 2654	襦 2638	規 3618		
蠥 1880		袁 7730	袞 3332	襟 5190		**16**	覔 4469		
18—19			**7**	裝 5018		襯 342			
蠟 2444			裎 376	**9**					
				襄 4951					

148 角
149 言
150 谷

覽 3804
覿 6230
觀 3575

148

角 1174

2—4

觔 1059
觖 1699

5

觜 6856
觝 6194
觚 3473

6

觥 3587
解 } 626
觧 }

7—18

觫 5504
觭 423
觱 5136
觳 2204
觴 5668
觶 970
觵 3587
觸 1416
觿 2445

149

言 7334

2

訂 6386
訇 2391
計 456
訃 1954

3

託 6461
訑 2943
訖 567
訏 2820
訊 2750
訒 3117
討 6157
訕 5634
訓 2914
訌 2385
記 431
訐 786

4

訛 4789
訥 4609
訟 5558
訦 5726
訩 2813
許 2825
訣 1700
訬 257
訠 5732
訝 7220
訢 2728
訪 1816
設 5711

5

詛 6818
註 1343
詐 82
詅 4055
診 306
詋 1303
詗 2817
詘 1622
詔 239
訽 3423
訶 2112
詒 2966
詁 3461
詞 6971
詀 131
詎 1552
評 5306
訴 5494
訹 2864
証 357
訾 6956
詆 6196
詠 7591
詖 5147
詈 3891

6

詵 2273
該 3191
詮 1672
詾 2813
詢 2923
誆 3599
詭 3626
詹 150
詬 3423
詰 783
詿 3513
誇 3530
詫 108
詩 5783
試 5798
詣 3011
誅 1352
詼 2308
詧 111
詳 2579
詡 2827
誄 4242
話 2215
詪 3329

7

說 5939
諙 2215
語 7651
誤 7204
誥 3288
誖 5004
誣 7165
誕 6051
誌 973
認 3113
誠 381
誡 628
誓 5803
誨 2338
誑 3602
誦 5567
誘 7538
誚 762
誩 1133

8

諒 3947
諄 1490
論 4253
諊 1591
誶 5529
諏 6804
調 6298
諉 7101
誼 2994
誹 2108
誔 6051
諗 5733
課 3394
談 6078
諍 370
諂 174
諕 2163
誾 7437
誰 5923
請 1172
誹 1833

9

諭 7641
諵 4621
諤 4795
諴 2667
諮 6923
諠 2874
諦 6208
諺 7374
諞 5251
諟 5795
謁 7324
諫 847
諜 6322
謀 4578
諼 2875
諶 5726
諧 2546
諡 5802
諝 7538
諸 1362
諳 2839
謂 7079
諛 7613
諻 2329
諾 4747
諢 2369
諱 2357
諳 37
諷 1893

10

謙 885
講 645
[illegible] 5476
謌 3364
謑 2428
謇 842
謝 2630
謆 5645
謗 4919
謖 5900
謐 4468
謚 5802
謠 7290
謄 6185
謅 1308
謊 2273
謔 4736
謎 4451

11

謳 4823
謫 279
謪 5674
謷 62
謾 4338
譖 6734
謦 1166
謬 4539
謹 1074
謨 4591
謼 2159

12

譊 4640
譔 1435
譏 416
識 5825
譈 6563
譜 323
譙 758
譌 4789
證 357
譎 1702
䜌 4211
譁 2218
譚 6066

13

譟 5443
警 1139
譆 5386
譭 2329
譯 3064
議 3006
譫 152
譬 5167

14

譽 7617
護 2190
譴 903

15

讄 877
讀 6521
讁 279

16

讈 4795
讌 7364
變 5245
讐 7091
讎 } 1333
讐 }

17

讖 181
讒 161
讓 3085
讕 3797

18—22

讙 2268
讚 6681
讞 7370
讜 6096
讟 6522

150

谷 3483
谺 2513

(Radical index — columns read right-to-left; entries given as character + reference number.)

谷 2021 豁 2404 豀 511

151 豆 6478
豇 653, 豈 544, 豉 5805, 豎 653, 豐 3884, 豎 5877, 豌 7026, 豏 2670, 豔 1076, 豐 1897, 豔 7406

152 豕 5766
1—5: 豗 1381, 豖 2317, 豚 6600, 豘, 象 2568
6: 豪 2243
犴 821, 豦 1561
7: 豪 2067, 豨 2422
8—12: 豩 6902, 豬 1357, 豫 7603, 豳 5258, 豵 6902, 豶 1873

153 豸 1043
3: 豹 4954, 豺 2029, 豻 122
5: 貂 6275
6: 貊 2868, 貅 2789, 貉 2127, 貃 4380
7—18: 貍 3863
貌 4368, 貓 4366, 貔 5160, 貘 4384, 貕 3976, 貛 2267

154 貝 5005
2: 貞 346, 貟 1956
3: 貤 2944, 貢 3715, 財 6662
4: 責 6748, 貭 1009, 貨 2398, 貪 6055, 貧 5274, 販 1784, 貫 3566
5: 貰 5791, 貶 5237, 貸 6000, 貽 3604
貿 4581, 賀 2116, 賍 2967, 貴 3636, 貼 6330, 貰 5027, 貳 1752, 貯 1368, 費 6957, 貴 1847, 買 4322
6: 賅 3192, 賃 3107, 賂 4180, 賍 6705, 賊 6752, 賄 2330, 資 6927, 賅 5706, 賒 2863, 賈 3476
7: 賕 5695, 賓 5259, 賦 7456, 賑 314
8: 賚 3773
賣 5673, 賫 464, 賙 1294, 賠 5012, 賣 4323, 賛 6676, 賓 6903, 賞 5672, 賡 3340, 質 1009, 賤 868, 賜 6988, 賦 1957, 賢 2671, 賬 199
9: 販 1784, 賣 1087, 賭 6499, 賴 3776
10: 賺 1437, 購 3431, 賾 274, 賽 5414, 賻 1949, 膡 5750
11: 贅 980
聽 1437, 贅 1472
12: 贊 6676, 贋 7405, 贗 7758, 贈 6769
13: 賺 1437, 贏 7483, 贍 5664
14: 賣 2671, 贓 6705, 贔 5168, 贐 1087
15—17: 贖 5903, 贗 7405, 贛 3239

155 赤 1048
赦 5702, 赧 4624, 赫 2091, 赭 264

156 走 6807
2: 赴 1196, 赳 1955
3: 起 548, 赶 3222
5: 趄 1579, 趖 1618, 趁 345, 趗 251, 超 7698
6: 趔 6287, 赵 6928, 趟 3991
7: 趧 3222, 趙 244
8: 趣 1617, 趨 6113
趨 4718
䞋 397
9: 遏 6104
10: 趨 6336, 趨 1618
12: 趨 1689, 趨 749
13—19: 趫 6729, 趨 7504, 趲 6682

157 足 6824
2: 趴 4854
3: 跂 3313, 趵 5332
4: 跗 5408, 趼 1913, 趾 524, 跖 944
5: 跙 1579, 跗 1923, 蹁 5418, 跀 589, 跑 4971, 跕 6306, 跎 6012, 趼 6310, 跎 6445, 距 1553, 跟 6463, 蹠 6977, 跋 4849, 跋 5317, 跻 1003
6: 踒 712, 跡 502, 跆 785, 踐 2705, 跳 6287, 跪 3627, 路 4181, 踓 3644, 跨 3531, 踦 822, 踁 1420, 踝 6423, 跟 3330

151 豆
152 豕
153 豸
154 貝
155 赤
156 走
157 足

踒 id.1423

157 足
158 身
159 車
160 辛
161 辰
162 辵

7
踳 5046
跤 1732
踸 1586
踞 434
踴 7575
跟 3942

8
踔 1285
踡 1660
踙 6228
踣 2002
踧 3851
踦 519
踒 4807
踪 6904
踘 224
踞 1539
踐 870
踢 6264
踖 569
踝 2214
踏 5964
跗 1026

9
踰 7642
蹄 6244
蹀 6429
蹁 5252

踢 6105
踶 6236
蹀 6323
踏 70
踩 3135
踹 1423
踵 1513
踽 1570

10
蹌 682
蹊 2429
蹇 843
蹺 6244
蹉 6791
蹋 5973
蹈 6140
蹙 4905

11
蹧 5898
蹝 1002
蹤 2449
蹠 6904
蹩 6843
蹖 6720
蹭 5124
蹰 4328
蹟 502

12
蹶 1690

蹻 750
蹲 6576
蹴 6842
蹵 5211
蹺 6773
蹸 1799
蹬 6174
蹯 1502
蹮 5973
蹴 5381

13
躁 6729
躇 1398
躂 6580
躅 1388
躃 5119
躄 5981

14
躊 1324
躍 7504
躋 461

15
躑 3994
躓 1402
躕 179
躔 3939
躐 2358
躝 966

躚 2710
躜 1013

16—18
躦 4275
蠆 2653a
躞 2656
躟 3798
躠 6854
躡 4707

19
躦 6847
躧 2449

20—21
躪 1714
躩 4042
身 1388

~~~

158
身 5718

1
躬 3704
軏 6029
躰 6288
躱 6424
躲 3704
躳 3817
躺 8
躶 4109
躬 6114

軀 1601
軃 3281
軄 990

~~~

159
車 280

1
軋 7233

2
軌 3631
軍 1722

3
軏 7705
軐 3118
軒 2660

~~~

4
軜 4610
軝 1741
軟 3165

5
軨 307
軩 4991
軪 3387
軫 950
軬 3462
軭 3027
軮 1378

6
較 713
輅 4188
軾 5819
載 6653
輀 1421
輊 1757
輕 983a

7
輓 7015
輏 1156
輔 1945
輖 284

8
輗 3948
輪 4254
輝 2323
輗 4665
輞 3956
輟 1280
輠 284
輡 4066
輦 4720
輣 6115
輥 3674
輤 3736
輧 6933
輨 7048
輩 924
輪 4991

9
輸 5864
輯 503
輶 1997
輮 3165
輳 6811
輮 3136
輰 3379
輱 1980
輯 7531

10
輷 2536
轀 141
轂 3491
轃 7128
輿 7168
轅 7733

11
轉 1431
轇 7120
轈 698
轉 4206

12
轎 693
轍 288
轔 4031

轗 3257
轘 6092
轙 2260
轚 4674
轛 3379

14
轝 7168
轟 2394

15—16
轡 5024
轢 3940
轣 4169

160
辛 2739
辜 3463
辟 5172
辠 6860
辞 6984
辨 5239
辦 3761
辣 693
辨 288
辦 5240
辯 5242

161
辰 336
辱 3154
農 4768

~~~

162
辵 1282

2
边 5243

3
迄 568
迆 2945
迅 7599
迁 2751
迂 911
辻 6536
过 3730
迋 265

4
还 2261
迎 7179
迎 7473
返 1785
迓 7042
迍 6597
迒 6642

162	辵
163	邑
164	酉

6
酪 4526
酩 4126
酬 } 1320
酲 }

7
酴 6528
醒 378
酷 3501
酵 4135
酸 5514
酵 720
醅 5395

8
醇 5933
醉 6862
醊 1281
醋 5013
醃 7384
醋 6835

9
醒 2776
醍 6237
醢 6086
醐 2176
醋 2840

10
醮 2012
醴 7771

鄰 7322

14—24
酆 1311
酈 3592
酃 4070
酆 1900
酈 2446
酈 3917
酈 4070

164
酉 7526

2
酊 6387
酘 1235

3
酌 1257
配 5019
酒 1208

4
酖 5933
酚 309
酖 2834

5
酢 6785
酤 3464
酡 6446
酤 2037
酥 5486

9
甌 7360
鄂 4796
鄄 7525
鄘 4396
都 6500
鄆 7764

10
鄉 2556
鄔 7171
鄒 1309
鄙 2083

11
鄘 5095
鄴 7333
鄣 193
鄞 7442
鄂 2189

12
鄯 5661
鄲 6036
鄭 363
鄂 2928
鄧 6770
鄱 5352
鄧 6175
鄰 4033

13
鄲 3542

邶 5156
邵 5690
郁 6013
郃 6197
邯 2036

6
郊 714
郤 2474
郇 2146
邦 3612
郇 2925
郴 1353
郁 7686
郅 995

7
郜 3289
郡 1718
郢 7486
郲 613
郯 1941
郄 1014
郎 3820
郤 2474
郏 2129

8
郭 3746
聊 1311
部 5376
鄃 6079

邇 4564

15
邐 3766
邊 5243

19
邏 4106
邐 3916

163
邑 阝 } 3037

3
邙 4351
邕 7554
邪 2032
邢 1251

4
邦 4910
那 4604
邠 5258
邶 6895
邢 2760
邪 2625

5
邯 5290
邱 1215
邳 5139

遙 7291
遏 5974
遞 6209
遠 7734

11
適 5822
遲 1024
遭 6261
遮 260
遨 63
遭 6720
遨 6586

12
遷 3088
遶 6887
遼 3981
選 2898
遴 4032
遵 911
遺 2995

13
邀 7276
還 2261
邁 4325
邂 2543
邊 1565
邅 5108

14
邇 1755

進 5045
逵 4199
遏 6265
逮 5992
進 1091

9
逾 7642
退 2517
過 3730
遍 5230
遊 7524
遏 4812
逼 5134
遒 2294
道 6136
遁 6579
遇 7625
達 5956
遄 1444
遂 5530
運 7763
遒 1236
違 7093

10
遣 901
遘 3432
遜 5545
遡 5496
遛 4087
遷 5983

退 6568
逎 4612

7
途 6527
逞 377
造 6730
逢 1881
逡 1733
逑 1125
逖 6209
逝 5804
速 5505
逮 1224
逐 3589
逍 6265
逋 5373
通 6638
透 6493
逍 2610
這 265
逗 6482
逐 1383
退 4866
連 4009

8
逸 3045
週 1295
逵 3651
逴 5030
透 7102
逎 2239

这 265
近 1061
迊 7221

5
迣 445
迤 2947
迴 1243
迦 590
迢 6294
迯 7354
迫 5992
迸 6150
迭 6311
迷 1755
述 5890
迪 6218
迫 4982

6
追 1469
迹 502
逃 6150
逅 2145
迴 2315
逡 2980
逢 5566
逢 4934
逆 4677
迸 5045
迴 2924
迷 4450
适 3522

	醨 3901	釋 5824	鉛 900	銃 1521	鋧 2880	**9**	鎵 5091	**12**	鑛 2209

Radical numbers (left column):
164 酉
165 釆
166 里
167 金

酉 (164):
醨 3901 · 醡 83 · 醜 1327
11 — 醪 3838 · 醨 6719 · 醫 2978 · 醬 661
12 — 醮 727 · 醯 2448 · 醱 5382 · 醲 6067
13 — 醴 3887 · 醸 1566 · 醹 4774
14—20 — 醺 2913 · 釀 4685 · 釁 2734 · 醽 734 · 釅 7350

釆 (165):
釆 · 采 6665 · 釉 7517
165 — 釆 5238

里 (166):
釋 5824
166 — 里 3857 · 重 1509 · 野 7314 · 量 3943 · 釐 3883

金 (167):
167 — 金 1057
2 — 釘 6388 · 針 311
3 — 釺 7600 · 釣 6279 · 釵 119 · 釦 3439 · 釱 5944 · 釧 1440 · 釭 3700 · 釬 2026
4 — 釷 3195 · 釙 4743 · 釜 1935 · 鈴 895 · 鈉 4611

鉛 900 · 鈎 3417 · 鈞 1725 · 鈇 1914 · 鈥 1701 · 鈔 258 · 鈍 6583 · 鈀 4835 · 鉥 6476 · 欽 1095
5 — 鉏 1403 · 鈴 4056 · 鉋 4942 · 鉤 3417 · 鈷 3465 · 鉛 900 · 鐵 6332 · 鉈 6444 · 鉅 1554 · 鈹 7701 · 鉢 5333 · 鉦 354 · 鈸 4850 · 鉉 2886 · 鉗 899 · 鈿 6364 · 鉑 5334 · 鉬 4598
6 — 鉸 715

銃 1521 · 銑 3588 · 銑 2706 · 銚 6289 · 銓 1673 · 鉶 2758 · 銘 4527 · 銅 6623 · 鉿 607 · 銥 6332 · 鉤 1725 · 銖 1354 · 鍔 3304 · 銛 2711 · 銀 7432 · 銜 2681
7 — 銳 3174 · 鋤 1403 · 鋟 913 · 鋁 4283 · 鋙 7652 · 銼 6798 · 鋒 1883 · 鋄 863 · 鋏 770 · 鋌 6413 · 鋪 6254 · 鋦 2026 · 鋪 5396 · 銹 2806

鋧 2880 · 銷 2611 · 銀 3818 · 鋩 4350 · 鉻 7674 · 鋅 2741
8 — 錏 7230 · 鋼 3272 · 錒 2051 · 錂 1644 · 錮 3452 · 錘 1482 · 錡 520 · 錯 5031 · 錳 5965 · 錳 4432 · 錠 6395 · 鋸 1540 · 錦 1063 · 餅 5295 · 錄 4200 · 錢 921 · 錫 2505 · 錯 6793 · 鍊 3395 · 錚 371 · 錙 6934 · 鍊 1270 · 銀 217 · 錐 1467

9 — 鍘 91 · 鍼 311 · 鍋 3731 · 鍐 6908 · 鋏 809 · 鍍 6506 · 鍵 859 · 鍉 5796 · 鍊 4021 · 鍱 7320 · 鍛 6544 · 鎒 2262 · 鏊 4573 · 鏊 755 · 鎂 4408 · 鎇 114 · 鍿 4367 · 鍾 1514
10 — 鎗 683 · 鎌 4007 · 鎁 165 · 鎐 5477 · 鎔 2536 · 鎛 7564 · 鏀 5325 · 鎖 5468 · 鑊 4920 · 鎳 4698

鎵 5091 · 鎢 7172 · 鎰 3057 · 鎮 299 · 鏒 5461 · 鏃 6938 · 鏓 175 · 鎧 3207 · 鎛 4752 · 鎚 1485 · 鎬 2084
11 — 鏑 6224 · 鏗 3357 · 鏜 6110 · 鏤 4148 · 鏑 2806 · 鏞 7580 · 鏐 4096 · 鏢 2262 · 鑿 64 · 鑒 6684 · 鏇 6831 · 鏇 2897 · 鏘 671 · 鏉 165 · 鏢 5204 · 鏡 1137 · 鏈 4016 · 鏖 52

12 — 鐘 1503 · 鐮 1691 · 鐃 4641 · 鐏 6888 · 鐩 3982 · 鐲 648 · 鐵 5422 · 鐶 3581 · 鐋 6103 · 鐙 6176 · 鐳 2806 · 鐘 2220 · 鐔 2742 · 鐍 3638
13 — 鐮 4007 · 鐵 6332 · 鐮 689 · 鐺 6093 · 鐶 2262 · 鐸 6431 · 鐮 1564 · 鐲 1272 · 鐲 4185 · 鑊 863 · 鐳 4239
14 — 鑄 1372 · 鑑 841

鑛 2209 · 鑕 / 鑔 5270 · 鑞 2846
15 — 鑤 3767 · 鑛 3607 · 鑪 4295 · 鑠 5835 · 鑕 6848 · 鋼 4295 · 鑪 5186
16 — 鑠 90 · 鑪 4170 · 鑫 2732
17 — 鑰 7500 · 鑱 162 · 鑲 2574
18 — 鑾 863 · 鑷 4708 · 鑺 3576
19 — 鑼 4107 · 鑾 4217 · 鑿 6786

鑽	6848
20	
鑼	3748
168	
長	213
169	
門	4418
1—2	
閂	5914
閃	5638
3	
閏	7395
閉	2033
閇	5092
4	
閎	2379
開	3204
閔	4520
間	835
閑	2679
閏	3177
開	2672
5	
閘	4646
閟	5089

開	94
6	
閣	17
閡	1767
閨	2390
閤	3600
閣	3369
閣	3374
閨	3613
閡	3571
閬	2054
閩	4522
7	
閱	7703
閫	4284
閣	2696
閬	3819
8	
閻	7143
闍	7385
闌	7681
闊	4814
闈	2364
闃	212
闇	7395
9	
闊	3789
闋	3750
闈	1711

閿	1627
	6502
闄	7094
	38
10	
闐	4699
闢	1712
闐	3571
闈	2121
闔	6374
闌	5975
闒	3208
闋	1465
11	
關	3571
闕	3649
12	
闡	153
闥	3259
闤	2479
闤	3668
13	
闤	2263
闥	5177
闤	5982
170	
阜阝	1960

3	
阤	1033
阡	909
4	
阱	1144
阮	3354
阮	7710
阤	4811
阪	1786
阬	6477
阯	1817
阯	945
5	
阻	6819
阼	6777
陁	6447
附	1924
陔	1598
阿	1
陀	6447
阮	4811
陕	322
陂	5345
6	
陋	4151
陕	3193
降	654
陌	4381
限	2696

7	
除	1391
陛	5081
陞	5747
陝	5637
院	7712
陘	2762
陟	1004
陔	760
陛	6477
陣	322
8	
陰	7444
陶	6156
陣	5165
阪	6805
陪	5014
陸	4191
陲	1481
陵	4067
陳	339
陷	2694
9	
陰	7444
陸	7414
陞	6210
陽	7265
隆	4255
限	7074
隍	2295

隅	7626
隊	730
階	1355
隋	5522
隊	6561
階	625
陛	4695
10	
陳	7376
隕	7756
隙	2481
隖	7168
隘	18
隔	3319
隗	7097
11	
際	467
障	194
隤	2523
12	
隣	4033
隤	6566
13	
險	2689
隩	50
隨	5523
隊	5537
14	
隱	7448

隰	2511
隮	461
15—16	
隴	2355
隴	4276
171	
隶	5993
隸	5599
隸	3905
隸	id.3905
172	
隹	1466
2	
隻	1677
隼	1487
隻	967
难	4625
3	
崔	2130
雀	1185
4	
雁	7404
雄	2814
雇	3477
集	508

雅	7222
5	
雋	1677
雍	7554
雌	3418
雉	6979
雄	1580
雊	968
6—9	
雛	4128
雕	6273
雛	5519
10	
雗	2044
雞	428
巂	2447
雞	7551
雜	6646
雛	1406
雘	2210
雚	3572
雙	5915
11	
離	3902
難	4625
173	
雨䨙	7662

3	
雪	2903
雰	7663
4	
雲	7750
雯	7135
5	
零	4057
電	5338
雷	4236
電	6358
6	
需	2844
7	
霆	6414
霉	4405
霓	333
霈	5021
霄	2612
霑	2725
震	315
8	
霈	4666
霎	5620
霖	4026
霜	132
霍	2405
霖	4595

173 雨
174 靑
175 非
176 面
177 革
178 韋
179 韭
180 音
181 頁
182 風
183 飛
184 食

霏 1834

9
霞 2518
霝 4069
霜 5919
霡 4383
霙 7491

10
霤 4088
霢 4383

11
霧 7199
霪 7435

12
霰 2725
露 4186

13
霹 5178
霸 4842

14
霿 4442
霾 4321
霽 462

16
靂 3936
靈 4071
靄 16

靆 5995

17
靉 13

174
靑 1168
靖 1148
靚 1152
靛 6353
靜 1154
靝 6361

175
非 1819
靠 3308
靡 4455

176
面 4497
靦 6380
靧 2344
靨 7328

177
革 3314

2
靪 6389

3
靭 3119
靮 6214

4
靴 2902
靸 5409
靶 4837
靳 1062

5
鞄 4972
鞊 168
鞀 6151
鞅 7245
靿 7275
靼 5949
靺 4553

6
鞉 6151
鞋 2545
鞍 29
鞏 3718

7
鞔 4342
鞙 1638
鞘 2613

8
鞟 3754
鞠 1590
鞝 205
鞚 3728

9
鞭 5227
鞦 1231
鞫 1591

10—12
韝 3433
鞵 2545
鞹 3754
鞾 2902

13
韄 4921
韁 641
鞴 5099
韂 168
韃 5960

15
韈 7000
韆 912

16—21
[illegible] 4277
韉 873
韊 3799

178
韋 7080
韌 3119
韍 1973
韜 6145
韓 2041
韙 7095
韘 5709
韝 3433
韞 7772
韤 7000
韠 5125

179
韭 1197
韮 1197
韱 916

180
音 7418
韵 7757
韶 5691
[illegible] 665
韻 7757
響 2559

181
頁 7316

2
頂 6390
頃 1160

3
順 5935
項 2555
頇 2034
須 2847

4
預 7603
頑 7060
頌 5559
頒 4879
頏 7010
頋 3478
頓 6584
頊 2859

5
領 4058
頗 5346

6
頦 2008
頜 3375
頫 1929 6290
頤 2969
頡 2635
頟 1742
頣 2752

頞 4813

7
頷 2022
頰 614
頸 1126
頨 3074
頼 3776
頻 5275
頮 2344
頴 7485
穎 7485
頹 6567
頭 6489

8
顆 3396

9
顎 4797
類 4244
額 1742
顏 7375
顒 5412
題 6238
顓 1433

10
願 7729
顖 2752
顯 2692
顙 5428

類 4244
顛 6337
顗 2970

11
顣 6844
顢 4329

12
顧 3478
顥 2078
顦 756

13—18
顫 136
顭 3200
顯 2692
顬 3151
顰 5276
顱 4171
顳 4709
顴 1664

182
風 1890

4
颫 1915

5—6
颮 5183
颯 5405
颳 3523

8
颶 1559
[illegible] 2198

9
颸 5584
颺 7266

10
飀 4089
颼 } 5478
颼 }
颻 7292
颾 5432

11—12
飄 5205
飂 3967
飆 5183

183
飛 1850
飜 1359

184
食 5810

2
飣 6391
飤 5587
飡 6694
飢 417

攵 7665a

3
釬 137

4
飭 1049
飯 1787
飪 3108
飫 7656
飩 6598
飲 7454
殞 5546

5
飴 2968
飼 5587
飽 4943
飾 5812

6
餃 716
餈 6983
餉 2551
餅 5296
餌 1750
養 7254
餂 6371
餃 21

7
餘 7608
餕 1734
餖 4767

餳 5328
餚 5812
餓 4785
餗 5506
餐 6694
餔 5374
餖 6483

8
餞 1645
餟 1281
餧 4767 / 7103
館 3559
餅 5296
餞 871
餚 2588
餳 2778
餛 2370
餜 3737
餤 6080
餡 2695

9
餿 2142
饁 4764
餳 2778
餶 14
餮 6331
餬 2177
餫 2370

10
餿 5479

饈 6121
餼 2455
饁 3283
餾 4090
饀 7326
饅 1226
饀 6559
饁 3656

11
饂 7656
饅 4340
饈 2798
饉 1075
饛 4544

12
饍 5659
饒 3091
饌 1436
饑 417
饐 5423
饙 393
饚 2998
饋 3669

13
饐 137
饗 7559
饕 6147
饔 2560

14—17
饕 7391
饜 1436
饞 4544
饟 157

185
首 5839

馗 3652
艏 6390
馘 3743

186
香 2547

馩 1862
馡 1835
馥 1998
馨 2769
馫 1862

187
馬 4310

2
馮 1895
馭 7664

3
馳 1034

馱 id.6452
馴 2929
馭 1371

4
駃 3549
駅 4296
駉 3125
駁 5342
馱 6452

5
駔 6701
駐 1344
駙 1926
駒 1244
駕 591
駒 1543
駛 5771
駘 6014
駟 5601
駑 4762
駝 6448
駓 1555

6
駰 5721
駭 2009
駮 5342
駱 4127
駥 5771
駉 7413
駕 6186

7
駿 1111
駿 1735
駿 22
騁 395
駤 2777
騊 1005

8
騏 533
騎 521
騍 6905
駢 5255
駿 4202
駘 7367
騠 3397
騅 1468
騑 1836

9
騧 3510
騠 6905
騌 7304
騌 6918
騙 5253
騧 6239

10
騫 892
騸 5646
騮 4091

騰 6186
騶 6740
騙 1310
騷 5433
騭 1005

11
驅 1602
驂 6687
驄 6918
驁 65
驛 5126
驃 5206
驟 4112
驚 4385

12
驕 694
驍 2595
驢 5510
驊 2221

13
驘 4112
驗 7367
驚 1140
驛 3065
驥 7648

14—16
驟 1312
驥 444

驪 4296

17—21
驤 2575
驢 2269
驩 6854
驪 3918
驪 173

188
骨 3486

3
骯 3310
骳 7119
骭 3218

4
骱 41
骴 4838
骰 6491

5
骷 3494
骶 1709
骹 3298
骺 6955

6
骸 2010
骼 3371

7
骾 6569

髁 3352

8
髀 5073
髂 3398

9
髎 615
髏 7627

10—12
髈 4922
髇 4149
髑 1692

13
髒 6703
髓 6513
體 6246
髖 5525

14—16
髕 5268
髏 4171

189
高 3290
髜 5444

190
髟 5182

184 食
185 首
186 香
187 馬
188 骨
189 高
190 髟

190 髟	2—3	鬆 5557	鬱 7692	厭 7392	鰲 2580	鰉 2296	13	鳩 1583	鵝 7196
191 鬥	髟 3685	9—10			鮡 6240	鰍 1232	鱠 3541	鴃 1582	鵑 7675
192 鬯	髡 6260	鬎 2178	193	195	鮪 7108	鰌	鱟 2151	鴉 7223	鵝 1582
193 鬲	4	鬏 6426	鬲 3315	魚 7668	鮮 2716	鯽 498	鱧 3888		8
194 鬼	髦 6086a	鬐 300					鱭 6753	5	鵯 1497
195 魚	髣 1805	鬑 513	鬴 1946	2—3	7	10		鴒 1606	鵰 4787
196 鳥	髦 4362	11—12	鬵 2743	魛 6126	鯁 3352	鰌 6716	14—22	鴞 2591	鶃 6274
	5	鬚 574	鬻 7691	魟 see 7293-1	鯊 6695	鰍 7669	鱮 2854	鴣 3466	鶂 34
	髫 3075	鬟 5454			鯊 5613	鰰 5782	鱷 4800	鴦 4060	鷗 1607
	髯 6295	鬛 2848	194	4	鯆 5397	鰥 3561	鱸 4172	鴛 7717	鶊 3341
	髲 1990	13—15	鬼 3634	魬 4887	鯷 3677	鰡 7293	鱺 2716	鴦 7246	鶉 3683
	髭 6958	鬢 2264		魦 5613	鯉 3866	鰥 5976		鴕 6450	鵲 1184
	髮 1770	鬍 5271	4	魨 6599			196	鴟 6041	鵬 5058
	髮 5094	鬣 3992	魂 2365	魩 7136	8	11	鳥 4688	鴝 1031	鶬 887
			魁 3655	魯 1818	鯨 1158	鰷 6302		鴨 7235	鶩 1134
	6			魯 4176	鯟 3774	鰳 3842	2		
	髻 451	191	5		鯢 4667	鰵 7581	鳳 1894	6	9
	髹 1758	鬥 6484	魅 4414	5	鯜 6806	鰲 66	鳧 1200	鴷 3109	鶯 4798
	髺 3524		魃 4851	鮓 84	鯛 6299	鰾 4518	鳧 1959	鵂 2790	鶿 6241
			魄 4988	鮒 1927	鯪 4068	鰻 4341		鴿 3376	鷀 2126
	7	鬧 4646		鮑 4944	鯧 6716	鰭 5207	3	鵝 6255	鷄 7739
	髮 5271	鬩 2390	7	鮎 4713	鯤 3682	鱄 4017	鳴 4535	鴛 3141	鷙 4602
	髻 451	鬪 2482	魋 2614	鮐 6015	鯗 2580	鱈 2904	鳴 5758	鵒 7365	鷟 1233
	髻 77	鬮 1186	8	鮀 6449	鯖 1173		鳶 7744	鴻 2386	鷦 2179
	髻 6247	鬪 6484	魍 3957	鮏 5662		12		鵠 3525	
	髻 5685	鬭 6484	魏 7104	鮍 4852	9	鱖 3641	4		10
		鬮 1186	魑 7049		鯛 6747	鱓	鳩 309	7	鷯 6717
	8		魑 6565	6	鰛 7361	鱔 5662	鴉 4880	鵑 1639	鷲 833
	髮 1661	192		鮫 717	鰕 2519	鱗 2747	鷗 5171	鵲 3485	鷸 1487
	鬃 6906	鬯 232	10—14	鮬 7058	鰐 4800	鱟 5212	鴇 4953	鵠 5329	鸚 3365
	鬍 5057		魑 1017	鮦 7055	鰓 5413	鱠 4034	鳯 7404	鵝 6255	
			魔 4545	鮭 3614	鰄 5234	鱣 2296		鵞 4786	

鷄 428	鷹 7479	麞 6833	麵 1626	3—4	**204**	鼗 6151	**211**	醒 7163	196
鷟 2701	鸇 2963	麚 5184	麳 4566	黙 3020	黹 956	鼛 5074	齒 1037	**212**	鳥
鶴 2131	鶼 3007	**5**	麴 1626	黯 896				龍 4258	197
鶲 6968	鸄 2781	麈 1345	麷 3737	黝 4388	黼 1974	**208**	2—4	龐 4935	卤
鷄 7365	鷥 4187	麃 4973	麵 4503	**5**	黼 1947	鼠 5871	齔 344	龔 3258	198
穀 3446		麇 1721	麵 2782	黛 6001		鼢 1863	齗 2087	龔 3714	鹿
鶯 7472	14—19	6—7	麷 2304	黜 1410	**205**	鼧 6451	斷 7453	龕 4277	199
鷗 4092	鸞 7503	麇 4452	麷 1614	點 6346	黽 4523	鼩 5816			麥
鶵 3058	鸒 7618a	麐 4035	麵 4565	黝 7547		鼬 7518	**5**		200
鷄 7294	鷥 7472				黿 7711	鼷 2430	齟 6820	**213**	麻
鶴 491	鸕 4173	**8**	**200**	**6**	黿 252	鼩 7362	齡 4061	龜 3621	201
鷄 1406	鸚 7464	麗 3914	麻 4303	黔 2537	黿 1351		齙 4945		黃
鷃 3489	鸛 3577	麚 4668	麼 4540	黲 2981	鼇 6993	**209**	齣 1414	**214**	202
	鸘 1606	麒 534	麼 2325		鼇 66	鼻 5100	齢 3388	龠 7496	黍
11	鸝 3919	麞 1721		**8**	鼇 5212	鼽 2035	齧 6296		203
鷗 4824	鷥 4218	麓 4207	**201**	黥 1159	鼊 6453	鼩 2150	齜 6959a	龢 1476	黑
鷟 981			黃 2297	黨 6095		鼽 6250		龤 2115	204
鷄 5918	197	9—24	黌 2392	黷 7386	**206**	鼽 2793	**6**	龢 208	黹
鷓 262	卤 4153	麞 4458		黲 3878	鼎 6392	鼢 7152	齦 7298	龢 2546	205
鷙 2979		麝 5704				鼺 4775	齧 4704	顜 7693	黽
		麞 189	**202**	**9**	鼐 4614	鼺 6258	齦 3333		206
	鹹 2668	麟 4035	黍 5870	黯 39	鼏 4466	鼺 4632			鼎
12	鹼 852	麤 6833			鼒 6964		**7**		207
鷞 3983	鹾 6792	麤 4049	**11**	**11**		**210**	齷 7653		鼓
鷟 1237	鹺 852		黎 3876	黮 6688		齊 560	齰 1287		208
鶴 728	鹽 7352	**198**	黐	黴 4415	**207**	齊 115			鼠
鷸 7690		麥 4379	黐 4682		鼓 3479	齋 464	**8**		209
鷥 5573	**198**		黏 4714	13—15			齶 4669		鼻
鷦 5511	鹿 4203	**199**		黯 740	鼓 3479		齲 2958		210
鷳 2680		麵 4503	**203**	黶 7393	鼖 6604				齊
	2—4	麩 1916	黑 2090	黷 6523			**9**		211
13	麀 7506						齾 4793		齒
鸇 138									212
									龍
									213
									龜
									214
									龠

LIST OF CHARACTERS

THE RADICALS OF WHICH ARE NOT VERY APPARENT, OR WHICH ARE WRITTEN IN ABBREVIATED OR UNAUTHORIZED FORMS.

N. B.— The figures immediately following the characters give the number of the Radical; those in the second column the number under which the character may be found in the body of the Dictionary.

STROKES

2

万	1— 742
七	1— 579
乂	4—7187
乄	4—2934
乃	4—4612
九	5—1198
了	6—3958
刀	18—6268

3

万	1—7030
丈	1— 200
上	1—5669
下	1—2520
个	2—3366
丫	2—7213
丸	3—7004
乇	4—6459
久	4—1188
乞	5— 564
也	5—7312
于	7—7592
亍	7—1408
亏	7—7643

亡	8—7034
亾	11—7034
凡	16—1771
千	24— 906
么	28—7282
叉	29— 96
子	39— 784
已	49—2930
巳	49— 429
才	64—6660

4

兀	1—3883
不	1—5379
与	1—7615
丏	1—3194
丐	1—4489
丑	1—1330
丰	2—1876
丹	3—6026
之	4— 935
予	6—7601
云	7—7745
互	7—2152
五	7—7187
井	7—1143
从	9—6919
今	9—1053

介	9— 629
允	10—7759
元	10—7707
内	11—4766
公	12—3701
六	12—4189
兮	12—2414
尢	14—7440
凶	17—2808
办	18—1462
切	18— 811
分	18—1851
勿	20—7208
勾	20—3409
化	21—2211
匹	23—5170
升	24—5745
午	24—7177
卅	24—5404
卞	25—5219
卬	26— 44
厄	27—1739
厷	28—3706
及	29— 468
收	29—5837
友	29—7540
反	29—1781
壬	33—3100
夭	37—7277

夬	37—3535
孔	39—3720
少	42—5675
尹	44—7439
尺	44—1045
屯	45—6592
巴	49—4826
廿	55—4710
弔	57—6276
不	75—6577
王	96—7037

5

且	1— 803
世	1—5790
丘	1—1213
丙	1—5284
卯	2—3562
目	2—2932
主	3—1336
弗	4—6947
乍	4— 80
乎	4—2154
乊	4—1761
乬	5—2946
全	9—6615
令	9—4043
以	9—2932

参	9— 300
兄	10—2807
充	10—1520
全	11—1666
冉	13—3067
册	13—6756
冏	13—2309
冬	15—6603
処	16—1407
凸	17—6305
凹	17—7268
出	17—1409
夅	20—6915
匃	20—3194
北	21—4974
半	24—4875
占	25— 125
卡	25— 616
卯	26—4369
去	28—1594
只	30— 946
史	30—5769
右	30—7541
司	30—5585
夗	36—7713
央	37—7239
失	37—5806
孕	39—7765
对	41—6562

尔	42—1754
丱	46—5538
左	48—6774
巨	48—1544
市	50—5792
平	51—5303
弁	55—5223
弗	57—1981
归	58—3617
必	61—5109
戈	62—7701
戊	62—7197
旧	72—1205
未	75—7114
末	75—4546
本	75—5025
尤	75—5886
正	77— 351
母	80—4582
民	83—4508
氺	85—5283
永	85—7589
甩	101—5907
由	102—7513
甲	102— 610
申	102—5712

6

| 壬 | 1—6415 |

両	1—3953
丞	1— 385
乑	4—1517
自	4—6557
辰	4—4872
乱	5— 406
争	6— 365
亘	7—2889
亙	7—3344
交	8— 702
亥	8—2004
亦	8—3021
企	9— 545
兆	10— 247
兒	10—2809
先	10—2702
光	10—3583
全	11—1666
合	11—6662
共	12—3709
再	13—6658
劣	19—4302
酉	23—4150
卍	24—7032
卉	24—2326
危	26—7056
吊	30—6276
合	30—2117
吏	30—3853

囟 31—2752	西 146—2460	尨 43—4353	系 120—2423	卷 26—1640	昏 72—2359	胃 13—1297
在 32—6657	~~~~~	局 44—1584	罕 122—2031	沓 26—1076	易 72—2952	冒 13—4373
夆 34— 654		岁 46—5538	冐 130—7720	卹 26—2862	昔 72—2493	冠 14—3564
夙 36—5502	**7**	巠 47—1117	肖 130—2606	叄 28—5415	服 74—1999	函 17—2049
多 36—6416	串 2—1445	巫 48—7164	良 138—3941	取 29—1615	東 75—6605	前 18— 919
夷 37—2982	些 7—2623	厄 49— 930	~~~~~	叔 29—5881	果 75—3732	南 24—4620
夅 39—6942	況 7—3603	弄 55—4278		受 29—5840	武 77—7195	卽 26— 495
存 39—6891	亨 8—2099	弟 57—6201	**8**	周 30—1293	狀 94—1452	危 26—7211
寺 41—5597	充 8—4078	我 62—4778	兩 1—3953	命 30—4537	画 102—2222	叛 29—4897
尖 42— 865	佘 9—5694	攸 66—7519	乖 4—3532	奎 32—4190	畀 102—5096	叚 29— 598
尽 44—1082	克 10—3320	攻 66—3699	乳 5—3144	垂 33—1478	直 109—1006	咫 30— 947
崩 45—4676	兑 10—6560	辛 67—1567	事 6—5787	夜 36—7315	秉 115—5291	咸 30—2666
州 47—1289	免 10—4492	更 73—3346	亞 7—7225	奇 37— 514	罔 122—7045	哀 30—— 3
巟 47—2270	兔 10—6534	呆 75—5986	亟 7— 483	奈 37—4615	羌 123— 666	哉 30—6650
年 51—4711	兵 12—5282	来 75—3768	享 8—2552	奉 37—1884	肩 130— 824	契 37— 551
戋 62—6663	初 18—1390	束 75—5891	京 8—1127	妻 38— 555	肯 130—3334	叅 37——74
戉 62—2861	卵 26—4219	李 75—3852	侖 9—4246	妾 38— 814	育 130—7687	奕 37—3022
戎 62—3181	君 30—1715	步 77—5363	來 9—3768	季 39— 435	肴 130—2584	奏 37—6808
成 62—5873	含 30—2017	每 80—4401	兒 10—1759	尙 42—5670	臽 134—2693	奔 37—5028
成 62— 379	吳 30—7201	永 85—2382	兔 10—6534	廷 43—7038	臾 134—7609	奐 37—2248
曲 73—1623	告 30—3287	求 85—1217	咒 10—5603	岡 46—3269	舍 135—5699	姜 38— 637
臾 73—3008	坐 32—6778	災 86—6652	其 12— 525	岸 46— 40	表 145—5187	威 38—7051
冇 74—7533	壳 33—3406	灾 86—6652	典 12—6347	幸 51—2764	豕 152—1381	巷 49—2553
未 75—1346	壯 33—1453	灵 86—6652	具 12—1556	拜 51—5292	采 165—5238	帝 50—6204
束 75—6986	声 33—5748	牢 93—3824	函 17—2049	氶 58—4192	~~~~~	幽 52—7505
此 77—6972	癹 35—1736	甫 101—1942	刜 18— 771	或 62—2402		兹 52—6935
死 78—5589	夾 37— 611	甬 101—7568	券 18—1652	所 63—5465	**9**	拜 64—4860
求 85—1217	妥 38—6454	男 102—4619	卑 24—4993	承 64— 386	亨 8—6399	祗 72—____
灰 86—2306	孚 39—1936	卓 106—6722	單 24—6030	斧 69—1934	亮 8—3949	春 72—____
牢 93—4566	孛 39—5023	兒 106—4368	卒 24—6827	昂 72— 45	俎 9—6812	易 72—7258
百 106—4976	孝 39—2601	矣 111—2938	卓 24—1260	昌 72— 206	竞 10—7355	是 72—5794
孛 125—3299	孛 41—4132	秀 115—2803	卸 26—2626	明 72—4534	俞 11—7628	曷 73—2122

柔 75—3133	耑 140—2326	差 48— 105	芻 140—1405	啓 30— 542	率 95—5910
奈 75—4615	覘 147—3575	席 50—2502	荆 140—1116	執 32— 996	畢 102—5120
某 75—4577	軍 159—1722	師 50—5760	虒 141—5579	堂 32—6107	異 102—3009
枲 75—7317	酋 164—1235	弱 57—3128	虖 141—2582	夠 36—3419	眾 109—1517
柬 75— 845	重 166—1509	彖 58—6556	袞 145—3675	婁 38—4136	离 114—3896
歪 77—7002	～～～	恭 61—3711	衷 145—1508	執 39—5893	章 117— 182
惢 81—5086		拳 64—1654	袁 145—7730	寇 40—3444	羞 123—2797
泉 85—1674	**10**	挐 68— 602	豈 151— 544	將 41— 656	翏 124—3962
点 86—6346	乘 4— 398	晉 }72—1088	邕 163—7554	幽 46—5258	耆 125—3415
爰 87—7735	亀 5—3621	晉 73—5857	釜 167—1935	巢 47— 253	屑 130—1491
甚 99—5724	亳 8—5336	書 75—6300	难 172—4625	常 50— 221	脩 130—2795
訧 102—4579	倉 9—6707	條 75—6300	崔 172—2130	帶 50—6005	春 134—1525
畏 102—7069	党 10—6094	毒 80—6509	～～～	絲 52—3563	袞 145—3675
盇 108—2119	兼 12— 830	泰 85—6023		彗 58—2331	裘 145—1010
盾 109—6578	轟 13—3425	烏 86—7166	**11**	彪 59—5181	覓 147—4469
柏 109—2562	冢 14—1515	班 96—4889	曼 1—6487	戚 62— 575	雀 172—1185
省 109—5744	冥 14—4528	畜 102—1412	桼 4—1478	教 66— 719	滄 184—6694
眉 109—4391	務 19—7198	奋 102—5032	乾 5—3233	夢 70—1950	～～～
看 109—3251	鹵 25—7519	眾 109—1517	兜 10—6469	既 71— 453	
禹 114—7620	叟 29—5470	看 109—3251	冕 13—4494	晝 72—1302	**12**
禺 114—7621	哥 30—3363	真 }109—297	凰 16—2285	曹 73—6733	傘 9—5420
幸 117— 514	智 30—3361	眞	勖 }19—2858	望 74—7043	凱 16—3205
委 123—4406	哭 30—3500	崇 113—5539	勗	枭 75— 578	勞 19—3826
委 123—7532	員 30—7721	秦 115—1112	匏 20—4967	梁 75—3951	喜 30—2434
耆 125— 263	唐 30—6116	素 120—5490	匘 21—4638	枭 75—2589	善 30—5657
胃 130—7075	南 31—2049	索 120—5459	匙 21—5796	梵 75—1774	煦 30—2833
背 130—4989	夏 35—2521	羔 123—3282	卿 26—1155	毫 82—2066	喪 30—5429
胡 130—2167	套 37—6160	羞 123— 666	參 28—6685	焉 86—7330	單 30—6030
胤 130—7452	奚 37—2425	智 130—2812	商 30—5673	晉 87—3557	喬 30— 744
胥 130—2835	專 41—1950	能 130—4648	商 30—6219	爽 89—5917	堯 32—7295
舌 134— 112	射 41—5703	臭 132—1331	售 30—5843	牽 93— 881	報 32—4955
异 134—7614	島 46—6131	臽 134—7299	唔 30—7178	犀 93—2463	壺 33—2187

壹 33—3016
揳 33—2836
暴 37— 53
奠 37—6357
屏 39— 169
寮 42—3968
就 43—1210
巽 49—5550
幾 52— 409
弑 56—5797
甇 58— 963
微 60—7061
戠 62— 988
斑 67—4890
弾 68— 602
普 72—5384
景 72—1129
替 73—6257
曾 73—6771
最 73—6858
朝 74— 233
棄 75— 550
棘 75— 486
棗 75—6723
欽 76—3579
渠 85—1603
無 86—7180
焉 86—5603
爲 87—7059
甦 100—5487
甯 101—4724
畫 102—2222

LIST OF CHARACTERS HAVING OBSCURE RADICALS.

疏 } 103—5861
疎 }
發 105—1768
登 105—6167
矞 110—7689
童 117—6626
粦 119—4028
粵 119—7704
羨 123—2715
着 123—1258
耋 125—6314
舒 135—5856
舜 136—5936
菫 140—1065
裒 145—5362
覃 146—6061
象 152—2568
辜 160—3463
量 166—3943
集 172—508
須 181—2847

13

亶 8—6048
僉 9—914
匯 22—2353
疊 29—6325
嗣 30—5588
嗇 30—5447
塍 32—387
塞 32—5446
塟 32—6702
奧 37—46
媵 38—7492
幹 51—3235
[illegible] 51—820
彀 57—3420
彙 58—2349
愛 61—9
暈 72—7762
會 73—2345
楚 75—1393
業 75—7321
歲 77—5538
毓 80—7687
滙 85—2353
準 85—1488
爺 88—7310
献 94—2699
甞 99—229
畺 102—643
睘 109—1248
睪 109—3059
瞢 109—4435
禀 113—5272
禽 114—1100
稟 115—5273
羨 123—2715
義 123—3002
聖 128—5753
肆 129—2939
[illegible] 130—4116
葬 140—6702
號 141—2064
虜 141—4175
蜀 142—5901
詧 149—111
豊 151—3884
辞 160—6984
農 161—4768
雍 172—7554
飧 184—5546

14

兢 10—1132
凳 16—6177
凴 16—5310
嘉 30—592
嘏 30—3468
嘗 30—229
壽 33—5846
夐 35—2816
夢 36—4433
夥 36—2397
夤 36—7427
奩 37—3997
暢 72—219
㬎 72—2691
朢 74—7043
榮 75—7582
疐 103—964
疑 103—2940
睿 109—3176
聚 128—1581
肅 129—5509
肇 129—245
膏 130—3296
臧 131—6704
臺 133—6016
與 134—7615
舞 136—7185
蒙 140—4437
裹 145—3735
養 184—7254

15

勰 19—2640
墫 32—6886
奭 37—5827
尠 42—6735
慕 61—4587
慶 61—1167
憂 61—7508
暴 72—4957
樊 75—1775
滕 85—6181
熨 86—7527
爾 89—1754
皝 106—2078
緜 120—4506
羹 123—3342
翫 124—7011
膚 130—1958
興 134—2753
舖 135—5394
虢 141—3744
賚 154—3340
輝 159—2323
辤 160—6984
靠 175—3308
魯 195—4176
黎 223—3876

16

冀 12—443
噩 30—4799
奮 37—1874
嬴 38—7480
學 39—2780
嶲 46—5540
憲 61—2697
整 66—356
暹 72—2712
曁 72—455
朣 74—6629
橐 75—6465
燕 86—7399
禦 113—7665
穎 115—7486
縣 120—2700
縢 120—6183
羲 123—2431
臲 132—4700
舘 135—3559
豋 151—1076
豫 152—7603
販 154—1784
賴 154—3776

17

徽 60—2354
應 61—7477
戴 62—6003
毚 81—155
營 86—7467
糞 119—1875
糜 119—4453
舉 134—1567
虧 141—3650
襄 145—2571
謄 149—6185
豳 152—5258
賸 154—5750
輿 159—7168 (7618)
隸 171—3905
韱 179—916
鴻 196—2386

18

叢 29—6921
彝 58—3001
斃 66—5105
歸 77—3617
瞿 109—1608
舊 134—1205
醫 164—2978
隳 170—2355
雚 172—3572
巂 172—2447
雘 172—2210

19

嚴 30—7347
嚮 30—2561
繭 120—844
羸 123—4240

20

嚳 30—3502
競 117—1133
辮 120—5241
耀 124—7306
躉 157—6580

21

亹 8—7118
囂 30—2596
曩 72—4633
[illegible] 195—7669

22

囊 30—4627
懿 61—2999
糴 119—6227

聽 128—6402	**23**	贏 187—4112	鹽 197—7352	矗 120—6511	豑 75—7692	鬱 192—7692
贏 130—4117	虁 35—3662			爨 164—2734	爨 86—6855	
巒 159—5024	鐲 142—1649	**24**	**25**		豔 151—7406	
	變 149—5245	贛 154—3239	糶 119—6303	**26—28**	鑿 167—6786